County Name Origins
of the United States

To Carol Haynes Beatty,
my wife and my best friend

County Name Origins
of the United States

MICHAEL A. BEATTY

McFarland & Company, Inc., Publishers
Jefferson, North Carolina, and London

Library of Congress Cataloguing-in-Publication Data

Beatty, Michael A., 1935–
County name origins of the United States / Michael A. Beatty.
p.   cm.
Includes bibliographical references (p.) and index.
ISBN 0-7864-1025-6 (library binding : 50# alkaline paper) ∞
1. Names, Geographical— United States.
2. United States— History, Local.
I. Title.
E155.B33   2001   917.3'01'4 — dc21   2001018034

British Library cataloguing data are available

Manufactured in the United States of America

*McFarland & Company, Inc., Publishers
Box 611, Jefferson, North Carolina 28640
www.mcfarlandpub.com*

Contents

Preface

It was on perhaps my 37th visit to the interlibrary loan desk of the San Jose public library that the employee who customarily handled my interlibrary loans wrinkled her brow and asked: "I mean, like, is there anybody *making* you do this ... like for a degree or anything?" I answered "no" and she left the counter area. Another employee, with a twinkle in her eye, then got up from her desk and asked "Well, why are you doing it?" Until then I hadn't given the matter much thought. An obsessive compulsive personality such as mine really needs no reason for pursuing a quixotic venture such as this, but I gave her an off the cuff answer, which probably hit rather close to the mark. A mountain climber would have answered "because it is there" but I replied that "I rather think of this as carving my own gravestone." Her eyes told me before her mouth did that she understood: "Yes! Immortality!"

The earliest English settlers in colonial America brought the concept of counties (or shires) with them. In feudal England the lord of the manor controlled an area called a shire and employed a strongman to keep order for him. Our word "sheriff" derives from this usage. All of the states in our nation (except Alaska) have counties although in Louisiana the word "parish" is now substituted for "county." In the paragraph dealing with Orleans Parish, Louisiana, a bit of explanation is provided for Louisiana's preference for the term "parish." But by whatever name, just what is a county? The only safe answer that can be universally applied is "lines on the map embracing a geographic subdivision." In a number of states the counties are extremely important governmental units. In others, particularly in some of the New England states, counties serve little governmental purpose (virtually none in Rhode Island). There, smaller political subdivisions, such as townships and municipalities, provide most local government.

Nor do our counties embrace all of the land on our nation's map. First there is our largest state, Alaska, with no counties at all, and then a sprinkling of "independent cities" from Carson City in western Nevada (formerly Ormsby County), to Saint Louis, Missouri, no portion of which lies within the adjacent Saint Louis County, Missouri. A similar situation prevails in Maryland where the city of Baltimore is independent of and located outside Baltimore County. The state of Virginia is our nation's champion owner of independent cities. It has almost 40 of them and as recently as the 1970's Virginia created a new one, the independent city of Suffolk, which absorbed the former county named Nansemond County.

County names, of course, present an interesting study quite apart from the degree of government provided by the county. Often a state's county names reflect the people and events that were important during that state's formative years. Thus in addition to its encyclopedic reference thrust, the work represents an early history of many of the states as told in their county names.

Now retired and living in Florida, my 40 year career with General Electric Company primarily involved tax accounting. By carefully planning nation-wide business travel and coordinating it with vacation time, I was able to visit the libraries of some 55 universities and historical societies and spend about 274 delightful man-days fishing for the facts found in this book. Armed with these resources, I left relatively few stones unturned in my search for our nation's county namesakes but the reader will note that there still are many where the namesake is "Uncertain." There are a few cases, like Archuleta County, Colorado, where it may even have been unclear just whom the namesake was at the very moment that the legislators coined the county's name. However, these cases are unusual. For most "Uncertain" counties there are answers. Perhaps younger generations armed with this book as a weapon will be able to find some of them.

I find in my files letters from history professors and others dated in 1979 and I submitted my manuscript for publication in 2000 so I have been at this just over two decades.

Michael A. Beatty
Ft. Myers, Florida
December, 2000

1

Alabama

(67 counties)

1 *Autauga County*

Autauga Creek—Autauga is an Indian word which is said to mean "land of plenty." The name was first applied to an Indian village (in the form *Atagi*) and to the Autauga Creek in this area. The county was later named for the creek. This county was created on November 21, 1818, by Alabama territory.

2 *Baldwin County*

Abraham Baldwin (1754–1807)— Baldwin was a licensed minister, a chaplain in the Revolutionary War and, later, a lawyer. He served in the Georgia legislature and was active in establishing the University of Georgia. He represented Georgia in the convention which framed the U.S. Constitution and in both houses of the U.S. Congress. He identified himself with the interests of the South; e.g., his proslavery position. This county was formed in 1809, shortly after Baldwin's death.

3 *Barbour County*

James Barbour (1775–1842)— Barbour served in the Virginia legislature, as governor of Virginia and represented Virginia in the U.S. Senate. He served as secretary of war and minister to Great Britain. This county was formed in 1832, shortly after Barbour's retirement from public life. While not a fanatic on the slavery issue, Barbour's consistent support of states rights served to win affection for him in the South.

4 *Bibb County*

William W. Bibb (1781–1820)— Bibb was born in Virginia and practiced medicine before entering politics. He was a member of both the house and senate of the Geor-

gia legislature and represented Georgia as both a congressman and as a senator in the U.S. Congress. He was appointed by President Monroe in 1817 as governor of the newly formed territory of Alabama. When this territory was admitted to the Union as a state, Bibb was endorsed by popular vote and he continued in office as the first governor of the state of Alabama. He rendered valuable service to Alabama in its political infancy; e.g., his contributions in the formation of the state constitution. This county was originally named Cahaba. The name was changed to Bibb in 1820.

5 *Blount County*

Willie G. Blount (1768–1835)— Blount was a native of North Carolina. His early career was as a lawyer in Tennessee territory and later as a judge in the newly admitted state of Tennessee. He served one term in the state legislature and three successive terms (the constitutional maximum) as governor of Tennessee. As governor, Blount gave energetic support to the U.S. cause in the War of 1812 and in the war with the Creek Indians. This county was formed in 1818, three years after Blount's retirement from the office of governor. The name was chosen in appreciation for Blount's aid in 1813, as governor, in sending troops against the Creek Indians.

6 *Bullock County*

Edward C. Bullock (1825–1861)— Bullock served four years in the Alabama senate. He volunteered for service in the Confederate army and was appointed to the rank of colonel. At the age of 36, while on duty with the army at Mobile, Alabama, he contracted typhoid fever and died. In 1866, shortly after the end of the

Civil War, this county was formed and named to honor Colonel Bullock.

7 *Butler County*

William Butler (–1818)— Butler was a native of Virginia and a resident of Georgia where he served in the state legislature. He moved to Alabama and was one of the first settlers of the Butler County area. He served as a captain and company commander in the army and was killed by Indians in 1818. The name chosen for this county in the original bill was Fairfield but the name was changed to Butler prior to final passage in 1819.

8 *Calhoun County*

John C. Calhoun (1782 1850) Calhoun represented South Carolina in both houses of the U.S. Congress. He served as secretary of war, secretary of state and as vice-president. He was a forceful advocate of slavery, states rights and limited powers for the federal government. He resigned the vice-presidency to enter the U.S. Senate where he could better represent the views of South Carolina and the South. This county was originally named Benton. The name was changed to Calhoun in 1858, shortly before the start of the Civil War.

9 *Chambers County*

Henry H. Chambers (1790–1826)— Chambers was a member of the convention which framed the Alabama constitution. He served in the lower house of the Alabama legislature and was twice an unsuccessful candidate for governor of Alabama. He was elected to represent Alabama in the U.S. Senate and served briefly in that body until his death. This county was formed in 1832, six years after Chambers' death.

3

10 *Cherokee County*

Cherokee Indians— The Cherokee Indians were a large tribe who lived in Alabama and several other southeastern states at the time of European contact. By the early 1800's they had adopted many features of civilization. By 1840, most Cherokees had been forced from their lands and removed to Indian territory (now Oklahoma) by court decisions, a fraudulent treaty and military force. The name Cherokee is said to be derived from the Cherokee word for "fire," *chera.* This county was formed in 1836.

11 *Chilton County*

William P. Chilton (1810–1871)— Prior to the Civil War Chilton served in both houses of the Alabama legislature and as a judge of the supreme court of Alabama. He was chief justice of that body from 1852 to 1856. Judge Chilton did not consider secession from the United States to be wise, but when that step was taken by Alabama, he served as an influential member of the Confederate government. He was elected to the provisional Confederate congress and later served as a member of both regular congresses of the Confederate States. This county was originally named Baker. The name was changed to Chilton during the decade after the Civil War.

12 *Choctaw County*

Choctaw Indians— The Choctaw Indians were a large and relatively peaceful tribe who lived in the southern portions of Mississippi and Alabama including the area embraced by this county. By the 1830's they had ceded their lands to the United States government and the majority of them had moved to Indian territory (now Oklahoma).

13 *Clarke County*

Uncertain— This county was formed in 1812. It probably was named for either Elijah Clarke or for his son, John Clark. (John Clark dropped the "e" in the spelling of the family name.)

Elijah Clarke (1733–1799)— Elijah Clarke was a native of South Carolina who moved to Georgia in 1774. He served as a general in the Revolutionary War. After the war, he was involved in an intrigue against Florida and other adventures which were contrary to the policy of the federal government but he remained popular with the people of Georgia.

John Clark (1766–1832)— John Clark, a native of North Carolina, moved to Georgia in his youth. He served as an officer in the Revolutionary War while still in his teens and, later, as a general in the War of 1812. He was a member of both branches of the Georgia legislature and governor of Georgia.

14 *Clay County*

Henry Clay (1777–1852)— Clay represented Kentucky in both branches of the U.S. Congress. For many years he was one of the more prominent figures in American politics but his several bids for the presidency were unsuccessful. He was influential in effecting important compromises between northern and southern interests during the years that secession and civil war were imminent. This county was formed in 1866, shortly after the end of the Civil War.

15 *Cleburne County*

Patrick R. Cleburne (1828–1864)— Cleburne died in combat in the Civil War while representing Arkansas as a general in the Confederate army. This county was formed in 1866, shortly after his death.

16 *Coffee County*

John Coffee (1772–1833)— Born in Prince Edward County, Virginia, on June 2, 1772, Coffee immigrated to Tennessee and in April 1798 he settled on the Cumberland River near what is today the village of Madison, Tennessee. There he became a merchant in partnership with Andrew Jackson and Coffee and Jackson established a friendship which continued throughout Coffee's life. Coffee served in the Tennessee militia and became colonel of a cavalry of some 600 volunteers. He served under General Andrew Jackson in the Natchez expedition of 1812 and fought under him against the British in the battle of New Orleans during the War of 1812. Coffee served with distinction and was promoted to brigadier-general and, later, to major-general. He spent much of his remaining life in survey work in the South and he settled in Florence, Alabama, where he died on July 7, 1833. This Alabama county was formed in 1841.

There are three Coffee Counties in the United States, in Alabama, Georgia and Tennessee. The Georgia county was named for John Coffee (1782–1836), while the Coffee Counties in Alabama and Tennessee honor John Coffee (1772– 1833). These men are easily confused with each other. They were first cousins with identical names who moved south from their native state of Virginia. Both became generals and they died within a few years of one another. Both were associated with Andrew Jackson. The older Coffee (1772–1833) served under Jackson in the 1813–1814 war against the Creek Indians and later at the battle of New Orleans. The General John Coffee for whom Georgia's Coffee County was named did not serve with Jackson during his military campaigns but became a personal friend of his in later years. The younger John Coffee (1782–1836) served in the U.S. House of Representatives, while the John Coffee for whom the Tennessee and Alabama counties were named, was never a member of Congress.

17 *Colbert County*

George Colbert (-) & Levi Colbert (-)— George Colbert and Levi Colbert were brothers and Chickasaw Indian chiefs who lived in the Colbert County area in about the late 1700s. Levi was regarded as the active chief of the tribe but George was also influential.

18 *Conecuh County*

Conecuh River— The county was named for the river which now forms a small portion of the southern boundary of Conecuh County. The origin of the name of the river is uncertain. Possible origins include:

1. Named by settlers from South Carolina for a creek of that name in their native state.

2. Muskogee Indian word meaning "crooked."

3. Corruption from the Creek Indian word *econneka* meaning "land of cane" for the numerous thickets of cane which lined this river and nearby lowlands.

19 *Coosa County*

Coosa River— The county was named for the river which forms its western boundary. The river was named for an Indian town, Coosa or Cosa, which De Soto is said to have visited. The location of this town is not known but perhaps it was a Cherokee Indian town on the upper Coosa River in Alabama.

20 *Covington County*

Leonard W. Covington (1773–1813)— Covington was a native of Maryland who represented that state in the U.S. House of Representatives. He was a general in the War of 1812 and was killed in combat in that war. This county was formed in 1821 but renamed Jones in 1868. Later in 1868 the name was changed to the original and current name.

21 Crenshaw County

Anderson Crenshaw (1786–1847)— Crenshaw practiced law in his native South Carolina and served in the state legislature there. Shortly after moving to Alabama, he was elected judge on the supreme court. Judge Crenshaw later served on the circuit court and as chancellor. This county was formed in 1866.

22 Cullman County

John G. Cullman (–)—Cullman was the founder of the town of Cullman and he is credited with having played an important role in developing the section of Alabama which is now Cullman County.

23 Dale County

Samuel Dale (1772–1841)— Dale spent much of his life on America's southwestern frontier, moving west as the frontier border moved west. While in Alabama he gained fame as an Indian fighter and was appointed by the Alabama legislature as brigadier-general of the militia. In addition to his exploits as scout, trader, guide and Indian fighter, Dale served in the state legislatures of Alabama and, later, Mississippi. This county was formed in 1824 before Dale moved from Alabama to Mississippi.

24 Dallas County

Alexander J. Dallas (1759–1817)— Dallas was born on the island of Jamaica and immigrated to Pennsylvania where he served as secretary of the commonwealth and U.S. district attorney. He later served with distinction as secretary of the treasury during the financially troubled period following the War of 1812. He also served briefly as acting secretary of war.

25 De Kalb County

Johann Kalb, Baron de Kalb (1721– 1780)— Kalb was born in the province of Alsace, which at that time belonged to France. He was a general in the French army and resigned that commission to come to America to assist the colonies in the Revolutionary War. He served as a general in the American revolutionary army and died in combat here.

26 Elmore County

John A. Elmore (1762–1834)— Elmore was a native of Virginia. In 1819 he moved to Alabama and he was one of the first settlers of the Elmore County area. He was a member of the Alabama legislature.

27 Escambia County

Escambia River— Escambia County, Alabama, is bordered on the south by Escambia County, Florida. Both counties were named for the river which flows through them. However, the river is named Conecuh in Alabama and Escambia in Florida. The origin of the name Escambia for the river is uncertain. It may have derived from the Spanish verb *cambiar*, "to exchange or to barter," perhaps applied because the Spanish bartered along this river with Indians. It is at least equally likely that the name is of Indian origin, possibly derived in part from the Indian *abi* meaning "killer." *Abi* was a popular suffix in Indian war titles.

28 Etowah County

Uncertain— The name is of Cherokee Indian origin but the meaning is not known. This county was originally named Baine County. It was abolished and then, in 1868, reestablished with its present name.

29 Fayette County

Marie Joseph Paul Yves Roch Gilbert du Motier, Marquis de Lafayette (1757– 1834)— Lafayette was a French aristocrat who served briefly in the French army. He came to America in 1777 to assist the American revolutionary army. He was granted an honorary commission as major-general by the Continental Congress and served with distinction in a number of battles in the Revolutionary War. This county was formed in 1824 while Lafayette was visiting the United States as an honored guest of the federal government.

30 Franklin County

Benjamin Franklin (1706–1790)— Franklin was a native of Massachusetts who moved to Pennsylvania in his teens. Poverty denied him a formal education but he became the leading printer and editor in North America. Franklin gained fame for his discoveries and inventions in the physical sciences and he distinguished himself as author, philosopher and diplomat. Franklin was a signer of the Declaration of Independence and an important member of the convention which framed the U.S. Constitution. This county was formed in 1818.

31 Geneva County

Town of Geneva, Alabama— This county was named for the town of Geneva, the county seat. The town had been named for Geneva, Switzerland. That Swiss city is believed to have been named by Celtic tribes before the advent of the Romans. The name apparently came from the word *genava*, meaning "mouth" which is similar to the Welsh word *gen* meaning "jaw." At Geneva, Switzerland, an island divides the current flowing from Geneva Lake which gives a jaw-like appearance.

32 Greene County

Nathanael Greene (1742–1786)— Greene was born in Rhode Island and served briefly in the Rhode Island legislature. He gained fame as one of the ablest American generals in the Revolutionary War. After the war he moved to Georgia. This county was formed in 1819.

33 Hale County

Stephen F. Hale (1816–1862)— Hale was a native of Kentucky who moved to Alabama in 1837 or 1838 where he practiced law and served in the Alabama legislature. He was elected to represent his district in the provisional congress of the Confederate States of America. Hale served as an officer in the Confederate army and he died in combat in the Civil War. This county was formed in 1867, shortly after the end of the Civil War.

34 Henry County

Patrick Henry (1736–1799)— Henry was a native of Virginia and a lawyer. He served in the Virginia legislature, as governor of Virginia and as a delegate to the first and second Continental Congresses. Henry was one of America's key revolutionary leaders. He was a great orator and he is remembered for his call to arms against the British "Give me liberty or give me death." Henry opposed Virginia's ratification of the federal constitution and his views played a role in the later adoption of the Bill of Rights.

35 Houston County

George S. Houston (1811–1879)— Houston moved to Alabama in his youth and served in the state legislature there. He represented Alabama in both branches of the U.S. Congress and was governor of Alabama. In 1850 Houston campaigned for congress on an anti-secession platform and was elected. When Alabama seceded from the Union, Houston refused to serve in the Confederate army but he also refused to take the oath of allegiance to the government of the United States. His independence apparently did not alienate the people of Alabama for he was subsequently elected governor and U.S. senator.

36 Jackson County

Andrew Jackson (1767–1845)— Jackson was born on the border of North Carolina and South Carolina. He represented Tennessee in both branches of the U.S. Congress. He gained fame and popularity for his military exploits in wars with the Indians and in the War of 1812. He was provisional military governor of Florida and from 1829 to 1837 General Jackson was president of the United States. His presidency reflected the frontier spirit of America. This county was formed in December 13, 1819, while Jackson was visiting Alabama.

37 Jefferson County

Thomas Jefferson (1743–1826)— Jefferson was a native of Virginia and a member of the Virginia legislature. He served Virginia as governor and he was a delegate to the second Continental Congress. Jefferson was the author of the Declaration of Independence and one of its signers. He was minister to France, secretary of state, vice-president and president of the United States. As president, he accomplished the Louisiana Purchase, and he arranged the Lewis and Clark Expedition to the Pacific Northwest. Jefferson was a true intellectual, thoroughly knowledgeable in the arts and sciences. His political theories were pivotal in the formation of our infant republic. This county was formed in 1819.

38 Lamar County

Lucius Q. C. Lamar (1825–1893)— Lamar, a native of Georgia, served in the state's legislature. He moved to Mississippi and represented that state in both houses of the U.S. Congress. He was an officer in the Confederate army. After the Civil War, he was a spokesman for sectional reconciliation for which he was admired in both the North and the South. He served in the U.S. cabinet as secretary

of the interior and was an associate justice on the U.S. Supreme Court. This county was originally named Jones and, later, Sanford. The current name was adopted in 1877.

39 Lauderdale County

James Lauderdale (–1814)— Lauderdale was a native of Virginia who moved to western Tennessee. He was an officer in the army and was wounded while serving under General Andrew Jackson against the Creek Indians in the Battle of Talladega, Alabama. He later served in the War of 1812 and he died in combat in that war. This county was formed in 1818.

40 Lawrence County

James Lawrence (1781–1813)— Lawrence was an officer in the United States Navy who established a reputation for bravery in the war against Tripoli and in the War of 1812. He died in combat while commanding the Chesapeake against the British near Boston. He is said to have uttered the famous phrase "Don't give up the ship" while he lay mortally wounded in that battle. This county was formed in 1818.

41 Lee County

Robert E. Lee (1807–1870)— Lee was a native of Virginia and, for over 30 years, an officer in the United States army. When Virginia seceded from the Union, Lee refused an offer to command all federal forces and resigned from the U.S. army to accept a commission in the Confederate army. He served with distinction in that army and become general-in-chief of it. This county was formed in 1866, the year following Lee's surrender to Grant which marked the end of the Civil War.

42 Limestone County

Limestone Creek—This county was named for the creek which runs through it. The creek received its name for its bed of hard lime rock.

43 Lowndes County

William J. Lowndes (1782–1822)— Lowndes was a native of South Carolina and he served in the legislature of that state. He represented South Carolina for 12 years in the U.S. House of Representatives including three years as chairman of the ways and means committee. This county was formed in 1830.

44 Macon County

Nathaniel Macon (1758–1837)— Macon was a native of North Carolina and a soldier in the Revolutionary War. He served in the North Carolina senate and was elected to the Continental Congress but declined to serve. He represented North Carolina for 37 years in both branches of the U.S. Congress where he was speaker of the House and president pro tempore of the Senate. He believed strongly in economy of the public money and he was a defender of slavery. This county was formed in 1832, four years after Macon's retirement from the U.S. Senate.

45 Madison County

James Madison (1751–1836)— Madison was born in Virginia, served in the Virginia legislature and in the Continental Congress. He was a member of the convention which framed the U.S. Constitution and he collaborated with Hamilton and Jay in writing a series of papers under the title The Federalist, which explained the new constitution and advocated its adoption. Madison represented Virginia in the U.S. House of Representatives, served for eight years as secretary of state and for eight years as president of the United States. This county was formed in 1808 while Madison was secretary of state in Jefferson's cabinet.

46 Marengo County

Marengo, Italy— Marengo was the site, in 1800, of one of France's great military victories. By defeating the Austrians there, Napoleon set the stage for the end of hostilities and a brief period of continental peace. Marengo was chosen as the name for this county to honor the first white settlers of this area of Alabama who were expatriates from France. This county was formed in 1818.

47 Marion County

Francis Marion (–1795)— Marion is believed to have been born in South Carolina. He served in the army in battles against the Cherokee Indians and was elected to the provisional congress of 1775. He served, with distinction, as an officer in the Revolutionary War and rose to the rank of general in that war. Marion was also a member of the South Carolina senate. This county was created in 1818.

48 Marshall County

John Marshall (1755–1835)— Marshall,

a native of Virginia, served as an officer in the Revolutionary War, in the Virginia legislature and in the U.S. House of Representatives. He briefly served as secretary of state and then, for over 30 years, was chief justice of the U.S. Supreme Court. Marshall's interpretations of the Constitution during America's political infancy left an unmatched impact on the laws and government of this country. Under Marshall, the supreme court shifted power in American government from the states to the central government and to the federal judiciary at the expense of the executive and legislative branches. This county was formed in 1836, about six months after Marshall's death.

49 *Mobile County*

Mobile Bay, Mobile River & Town of Mobile— The Spanish name is cited variously as *maubila, mobila, mauvila* and *mauvilla*. The French name was *mobile*. These names derived from names applied to local Indians, the Maubila Indians, called Mobilians by the French. The origin of these names is uncertain. One possibility is that they were derived from a Choctaw Indian word which meant "paddling," referring to the inability of these Indians to swim.

50 *Monroe County*

James Monroe (1758–1831)— Monroe, a native of Virginia, served in the Revolutionary War. Prior to his election as president of the United States, Monroe served in a wide variety of government posts. He served Virginia in the state legislature and as governor. He was a member of the Confederation Congress and the U.S. Senate. He was minister to France and to Britain and he held two cabinet posts. As president, Monroe stressed limited government and strict construction of the Constitution. He acquired Florida for the U.S. from Spain and he was the author of a policy declaration (later known as the Monroe Doctrine) which proscribed outside interference in North and South America. This county was formed in 1815, shortly before Monroe's election to the presidency.

51 *Montgomery County*

Lemuel P. Montgomery (1786–1814)— Montgomery was a native of Virginia who moved into Tennessee as a youth. He served as an officer in the War of 1812 and died in combat against the Creek Indians at Horseshoe Bend Alabama. This county was formed in 1816.

52 *Morgan County*

Daniel Morgan (1736–1802)— Morgan was a native of the Northeast who moved to Virginia in his youth. He served as a general in the Revolutionary War and was regarded as a hero for important victories scored by his troops. After the war he served one term in congress. This county was originally named Cotaco but was renamed to honor Morgan in 1821.

53 *Perry County*

Oliver H. Perry (1785–1819)— Perry was a native of Rhode Island and an officer in the U.S. navy. During the War of 1812 his squadron defeated the British in a key battle on Lake Erie of which Perry said "We have met the enemy and they are ours." This county was formed in 1819, a few months after Perry died of yellow fever.

54 *Pickens County*

Andrew Pickens (1739–1817)— Pickens was a native of Pennsylvania who moved to South Carolina in his youth. He served as a general in the Revolutionary War. Pickens later served in South Carolina's house of representatives and, briefly, in the U.S. House of Representatives as a representative from South Carolina. This county was formed in 1820.

55 *Pike County*

Zebulon M. Pike (1779–1813)— Pike was a native of New Jersey who served as an army officer on America's frontier following the Revolution. He led an exploratory army expedition to the Rocky Mountains which Pike's Peak in the Colorado Rockies commemorates. Pike served as a general in the War of 1812 and was killed in that war.

56 *Randolph County*

John Randolph (1773–1833)— Randolph was a native of Virginia and he represented that state in both houses of the U.S. Congress for many years. He was an advocate of states rights and strict construction of the federal constitution. He owned slaves and he represented the interests of the South in congress. Randolph also served, very briefly, as minister to Russia. This county was created in 1832, shortly before Randolph's death.

57 *Russell County*

Gilbert C. Russell (1782–1855)— Russell was a native of Virginia. He served in the army as an officer in the South and Southwest and attained the rank of colonel. Shortly after leaving the army (about 1815) he settled in Alabama. This county was formed in 1832.

58 *Saint Clair County*

Arthur St. Clair (1736–1818)— St. Clair was a native of Scotland who moved to Pennsylvania in his twenties. He served, rather ineffectively, as a general in the army in both the Revolutionary War and in later actions against the Indians. He was a Pennsylvania delegate to the Continental Congress and he served as governor of the Northwest territory but President Jefferson was dissatisfied with his conduct and removed him from that post. This county was formed in 1818, a few months after St. Clair's death.

59 *Shelby County*

Isaac Shelby (1750–1826)— Shelby was a delegate to the Virginia legislature and, later, to the North Carolina legislature. He served as a soldier in the Revolutionary War and then moved to Kentucky County, Virginia, where he was active in the movement to separate Kentucky from Virginia. Shelby was inaugurated as Kentucky's first governor on the same day that Kentucky became a state. Shelby also fought in the War of 1812. This county was created in 1818, shortly after Shelby's second term as governor of Kentucky.

60 *Sumter County*

Thomas Sumter (1734–1832)— Sumter, a native of Virginia, fought in the French and Indian Wars and settled in South Carolina. He served as an officer in the Revolutionary War and represented South Carolina in both houses of the U.S. Congress. This county was formed in 1832, about six months after Sumter's death.

61 *Talladega County*

Battle of Talladega— The Battle of Talladega was important in the early settlement of this area. The battle was named for the Indian town named Talatigi, where it was fought. Talatigi was derived from the Muskogee Indian words for "border" (*atigi* or *teka*) and for "town" (*talwa* or *talla*). The Indian town was so named because it was near a tribal boundary line.

62 *Tallapoosa County*

Tallapoosa River— This county was named for the river which flows through it. The name was applied to the river by the Creek Indians and it meant "cat town" in their language.

63 *Tuscaloosa County*

Indian words meaning "black warrior"
The name is from the Choctaw Indian words meaning "black warrior." The Black Warrior River flows through this county.

64 *Walker County*

John Walker (1783–1823) — Walker was a native of Virginia and one of the early settlers of Huntsville, Alabama. He served in the territorial legislatures of Mississippi and Alabama and presided over the convention which framed the constitution of Alabama. Walker was elected as Alabama's first United States senator but he had served in that body only three years when poor health forced him to resign. This county was created shortly after Walker's death.

65 *Washington County*

George Washington (1732–1799) — Washington was a native of Virginia. He served in Virginia's house of burgesses and became one of the colonies' leaders in opposition to British policies in America. He was a member of the first and second Continental Congresses and commander of all Continental armies in the Revolutionary War. Following victory in that war, Washington was elected to be the first president of the United States. This county was formed in 1800, shortly after Washington's death.

66 *Wilcox County*

Joseph M. Wilcox (1791–1814) — Wilcox was a native of Connecticut. He served as an army lieutenant in the Creek War and, in combat along the Alabama River, he

was captured and scalped by the Indians. This county was created in 1819.

67 *Winston County*

John A. Winston (1812–1871) — Winston served in both houses of the Alabama legislature and he became the first native of Alabama to hold the office of governor of Alabama. During the Civil War he served as an officer in the Confederate army. After the close of the war, he was elected U.S. senator from Alabama but he refused to take the oath of allegiance and was denied his seat in the U.S. Senate. This county was originally named Hancock. The name was changed to Winston in 1858, shortly after the end of Winston's second term as governor.

REFERENCES

Alabama Official & Statistical Register: 1967. Montgomery, Skinner Printing Co., 1967.

Alabama Official & Statistical Register: 1979. State of Alabama Department of Archives & History.

Berney, Saffold. *Handbook of Alabama*. Mobile, Mobile Register, 1878.

Brewer, W. *Alabama: Her History, Resources, War Record & Public Men*. Montgomery, Barrett & Brown, 1872.

De Land, T.A., & Smith, A.D. *Northern Alabama Historical & Biographical*. Birmingham, Smith & De Land, 1888.

DeWitt, John H. "Letters of General John Coffee to His Wife, 1813–1815." *Tennessee Historical Magazine*, Vol. 2. Nashville: 1916.

DuBose, Joel Campbell. *Alabama History*. Atlanta, B.F. Johnson Publishing Co., 1908.

The Encyclopedia Americana. New York, Americana Corporation, 1977.

Foscue, Virginia O. *Place Names in Alabama*. Tuscaloosa, University of Alabama Press, 1989.

Halbert, Henry S. "Choctaw Indian Names in Alabama & Mississippi." *Transactions of the Alabama Historical Society*, Vol. 3. Tuscaloosa: 1899.

Hamilton, Peter J. *Colonial Mobile*. Cambridge, Riverside Press, 1910.

Hodge, Frederick W. *Handbook of American Indians North of Mexico*. Totowa, New Jersey, Rowman & Littlefield, 1975.

Marks, Henry S. *Who Was Who in Alabama*. Huntsville, Strode Publishers, 1972.

Morris, Allen. *The Florida Handbook: 1947–1948*. Tallahassee, Florida, Peninsular Publishing Co., 1946.

Northen, William J. *Men of Mark in Georgia*. Atlanta, A. B. Caldwell, 1910.

Owen, Thomas McAdory. *History of Alabama & Dictionary of Alabama Biography*. Chicago, S. J. Clarke Publishing Co., 1921.

Owen, Thomas McAdory, & Pickett, Albert James. *History of Alabama & Annals of Alabama*. Birmingham, Webb Book Co., 1900.

Phelps, Dawson A., & Edward H. Ross. "Place Names Along the Natchez Trace." *Journal of Mississippi History*, Vol. 14, No. 4. Jackson: October, 1952.

Richardson, Jesse M. *Alabama Encyclopedia*. Northport, Alabama, American Southern Publishing Co., 1965.

Riley, B. F. *History of Conecuh County, Alabama*. Columbus, Georgia, Thos. Gilbert, 1881.

Urquhart, Jane McKelway, & von Engeln, O. D. *The Story Key to Geographic Names*. New York, D. Appleton & Co., 1924.

Work Projects Administration. *Inventory of the County Archives of Alabama-Talladega County*. Birmingham, 1940.

Arizona

(14 counties)

68 *Apache County*

Apache Indians — Apache is a generic term for several tribes of Indians. When first encountered by white men, they lived in a vast area of the southwestern United

States including this county. Warfare was very important in the Apache lifestyle and they were extremely able warriors. They were feared by white men and by other Indians. The origin of the name Apache is uncertain. Two explanations are given:

1. The word Apache is derived from the Yuma Indians' words *apa*, meaning "man," *ahwa*, meaning "war," "fight" or "battle" and *tche* which pluralizes the combination.

2. The word Apache is derived from

apachu, a Zuni name meaning "enemy" by which the Zunis called the Navajo Indians. (The Navajos were designated Apaches de Nabaju by early Spanish explorers.)

69 *Cochise County*

Cochise (–1874)— Cochise was a great chief of the militant Chiricahua Apache Indians of southwestern America and northern Mexico. Cochise and his warriors successfully resisted Mexican domination for many years. The American army was unable to subdue him until 1871 when he finally surrendered. This county was created in 1881. The original spelling of the name of this county was Cachise. Proper rendering of the name as spoken by the Indians is *Cheis*, an Apache word meaning "wood."

70 *Coconino County*

Havasupai Indians & Yavapai Indians— Before this county was officially formed, the area was known as Frisco County and the first name suggested for this county in the legislature was Frisco. However, when created in 1891, the name suggested by Dan M. Riordan was adopted. *Coconino* is a corruption of the Hopi Indians' term for their neighbors, the Havasupai Indians and the Yavapai Indians. The Havasupai Indians were a small tribe of Yuman stock who lived primarily in the Coconino County area. The Yavapai Indians were also a Yuman tribe who lived in central and northwestern Arizona including the Yavapai County area. There are numerous purported translations for the name *Coconino* including: (1) "dirty fellows," (2) "uneducated" or "child-like" (in a religious sense), (3) "little water," (4) "people of the green water" and (5) "willow people."

71 *Gila County*

Gila River— The county was named for the river which forms a portion of its southern boundary. The origin of the name of the river is uncertain. Possibilities include:

1. A word of Moorish origin which crossed the Mediterranean Sea and became a part of the Spanish language; then applied by Spanish explorers to the river.

2. A name applied to the river by the Yuma Indians which means flowing water that is salt.

3. An Indian word meaning spider.

4. A corruption of some Indian tribal name.

72 *Graham County*

Graham Mountain— This county was formed in 1881 and named for Graham Mountain which is in the southern portion of Graham County and is the highest mountain in the area. This was the first break in the tradition of naming Arizona counties for local Indians. The origin of the name of the mountain is uncertain. Possibilities include:

1. Lt. Col. James D. Graham of the Topographical Corps of the U.S. Army who was a member of a boundary survey party which visited this area in 1851.

2. Major Lawrence P. Graham who led a squadron of dragoons through this area of Arizona in 1848.

3. Colonel John D. Graham of the Aztec Mining Syndicate.

Some authorities claim that reference to the mountain by the name Graham had been made as early as 1846. If true, this would discount the likelihood that the mountain was named for either James Graham or Lawrence Graham. Nevertheless, most authorities state that the mountain was probably named for Lt. Col. James D. Graham.

James D. Graham (1799–1865)— James D. Graham was a native of Virginia and a graduate of West Point who attained the rank of lieutenant-colonel in the U.S. Army. He participated in border surveys along the U.S.-Canada border as well as in surveys in the West and Southwest. He is credited with early investigation of lunar tides on the Great Lakes.

73 *Greenlee County*

Mason Greenlee (1835–1903)— Greenlee, known by the nickname Mace, came from Virginia and was one of the first prospectors in this section of Arizona. He was an early settler in what is now Greenlee County. Greenlee was a United States mineral surveyor. He first went to this area in 1874 but was forced to leave by Apache Indians. He returned in 1879 and remained until his death. The first name proposed for this county was Lincoln but that name was never adopted.

74 *Maricopa County*

Maricopa Indians— The Maricopa Indians were a Yuman tribe who lived along the Gulf of California and, later, in southern Arizona. They lived with the Pima Indians for purposes of mutual defense. The Maricopa were friendly to whites. The Maricopas' own name for themselves was *pipatsje*. The name Maricopa was applied to them by the Pimas and probably also by Spanish explorers. It is said that the Spanish were reminded of butterflies by the vivid colors which the Maricopa painted on their faces and hair. (*Maricopa* is similar to the Spanish word for "butterfly" which is *mariposa*.)

75 *Mohave County*

Mojave Indians— The Mojave Indians were a large and warlike tribe, related to the Yuma Indians, who lived along the Colorado River in the southwestern portion of this country. Most Arizona sources explain that the name *Mojave* means "three mountains," derived from *hamol* or *hamok* meaning "three" and *avi* meaning "mountain." This term referred to the center of tribal activities near the needle-like formations at The Needles in this county. However, Erwin G. Gudde's scholarly work entitled *California Place Names* disagrees. The name of the Indian tribe is sometimes rendered Mohave. However, the intended spelling for the county name was Mojave. Due to a clerical error, the name Mohave was adopted and this version of the name is still in use.

76 *Navajo County*

Navajo Indians— This county was named for one of the Indian tribes which lives in this county, the Navajos. The Navajos' own name for themselves is *dine* which means the people. The name Navajo was applied to this tribe as early as 1630 when missionary Alonso Benavides referred to them as Apache de Navajo. The origin of the name Navajo is uncertain. Possibilities which have been suggested for the origin of this name include:

1. The name was derived from the Spanish *nava* meaning "field" and *ajo*, a Spanish suffix meaning "small" or, in this context, "somewhat worthless."

2. *Navajo* was based on a term *nabahu* meaning "of the cultivated fields."

3. This tribe may have been named for a pueblo of the Tewa Indians in northwest New Mexico named navahu. It is speculated that Navajos invaded this pueblo and acquired a variant of the name as a result of their invasion.

4. Navajo may have derived from the Spanish word *navaja* meaning "knife" or "razor" because these Indians were keen in their trades with the Spanish.

The name Colorado had been proposed for this county. However, the author of the legislation to create this county, state representative Will C. Barnes, was successful in having the county named for this local Indian tribe.

77 *Pima County*

Pima Indians This county was named in honor of the friendly Indians who lived in the Pima County area. The Pimas often assisted whites in troubles with the Apache Indians. The name Pima is based on a misunderstanding. When Spanish explorers first visited northern Sonora, Mexico and southern Arizona, they asked the local Indians their name. The Indians did not understand the question and replied in the negative, pim, pia or pimatc. The Spaniards took this for their name and applied a variation of that name, Pima, to them. This county had been unofficially called Ewell County on early maps of the area but the name Pima was adopted when this county was officially created in 1864.

78 *Pinal County*

Uncertain— The origin of the county name is uncertain. It probably was derived either from a local band of Indians, the Pinal Apaches, or from the Pinal Mountains on the northeastern edge of this county. The Pinal Apaches ranged over much of Arizona but their organization base was the Pinal Mountains in this area. The word *pinal* may have originated with a Spanish word meaning "of the pine" or with an Apache Indian word for deer. Both pine trees and deer were numerous on the mountains where the Pinal Apaches lived.

79 *Santa Cruz County*

Santa Cruz River— The county was named for the river which flows through it. *Santa Cruz* means "holy cross" in Span-

ish. Padre Kino gave the river its name. Other names which were proposed for this county, but never adopted, included: (1) Grant and (2) Papago.

80 *Yavapai County*

Yavapai Indians— The Yavapai were a Yuman tribe, also known as the Apache-Mohave Indians, who lived in Arizona. The origin of their name is uncertain but these theories have been advanced:

1. Derived from their own name for themselves, sun people. *Enyaeva* meaning "sun" and *pai* meaning "people."
2. Derived from a combination of Apache and Spanish words meaning "people of the hill country." *Yava*— Apache word meaning "the hill" and *pais*— Spanish word meaning "country."
3. Derived from *ya mouth pai* meaning "all mouth" or "talking people."
4. Derived from *nya va pi* meaning "east" (or "sun") "people."

81 *Yuma County*

Yuma Indians— The Yuman family was one of the major branches of North American Indians consisting of several tribes, one of which was the Yuma tribe. The origin of their name is uncertain but possibilities include:

1. Derived from *yahmayo* meaning "son of the captain" or "son of the chief." It is believed that this name was applied to these Indians through a misunderstanding by early Spanish explorers.
2. Derived from the Spanish word for "smoke," *humo*, because of large, smoky fires which these Indians built, presumably to summon rain.

Prior to the creation of this county, the name Castle Dome County had been proposed for it but it was never adopted.

REFERENCES

Barnes, Will C. *Arizona Place Names.* Tucson, University of Arizona Press, 1960.

Bufkin, Don, & Henry P. Walker. *Historical Atlas of Arizona.* Norman, Oklahoma, University of Oklahoma Press, 1979.

Cline, Platt. *They Came to the Mountain.* Flagstaff, Northland Press, 1976.

Doucette, Forrest E. *The Arizona Year Book: 1930–1931.* Phoenix, Manufacturing Stationers, Inc., 1930.

Dreyfuss, John J. *A History of Arizona's Counties & Courthouses.* Tucson, Arizona Historical Society, 1972.

The Encyclopedia Americana. New York, Americana Corporation, 1977.

Goff, John S., & Myles E. Hill. *Arizona Past & Present.* Cave Creek, Arizona, Black Mountain Press, 1970.

Granger, Byrd H. *Arizona Place Names.* Tucson, University of Arizona Press, 1960.

Granger, Byrd H. *Arizona's Names.* Tucson, Falconer Publishing Co., 1983.

Gudde, Erwin G. *California Place Names.* Berkeley, University of California Press, 1965.

Gudde, Erwin G. "Mohave & Mojave." *Western Folklore,* Vol. 7, No. 2. Berkeley: April, 1948.

Hodge Frederick W. *Handbook of American Indians North of Mexico.* Totowa, New Jersey, Rowman & Littlefield, 1975.

Kroeber, A. L. "California Place Names of Indian Origin." *University of California Publications in American Archaeology & Ethnology,* Vol. 12, No. 2. Berkeley: June 15, 1916.

Malach, Roman. *Mohave County: Sketches of Early Days.* New York, Graphicopy, 1974.

Wachholtz, Florence. *Arizona: The Grand Canyon State.* Westminster, Colorado, Western States Historical Publishers, Inc., 1975.

Yates, Charity, & Richard Yates. *1981-82 Arizona Yearbook.* Yuma, Information Press, 1981.

Arkansas

(75 counties)

82 *Arkansas County*

Quapaw Indians— The name *Arkansas* is the surviving version of numerous corruptions by French explorers of the name

by which the Quapaw Indians were known. Quapaw was also rendered as Ugakhpa in some early documents. In either case, the name means "downstream people" and was used to distinguish the tribe of Siouan

Indians who migrated down the Mississippi River while other Siouan Indians moved up the Missouri River. At the time of European contact there were about 5,000 Quapaws living in villages on both the western (Arkansas) and eastern (Mississippi) sides of the Mississippi River. They were mound builders with pleasant dispositions. By the early twentieth century their number had dwindled to about 200 and most of them were on Indian reservations in Oklahoma. This county was established in 1813 by the territorial legislature of Missouri.

83 *Ashley County*

Chester Ashley (1790–1848)— Ashley was a native of Massachusetts who moved to Arkansas when he was about 30 years old. He represented Arkansas in the U.S. Senate where he served as chairman of the judiciary committee. This county was created in 1848, a few months after Ashley's death.

84 *Baxter County*

Elisha Baxter (1827–1899)— Baxter was a native of North Carolina who moved to Arkansas where he served in the state senate. During the Civil War Baxter was a Unionist. He was imprisoned for treason by the Confederates but escaped to serve in the Union army. He later served briefly as chief justice of the Arkansas supreme court. He was elected to the U.S. Senate but was refused his seat in that body. He served as judge of the third circuit under the Reconstruction government and later as governor of Arkansas. This county was formed in 1873 while Baxter was serving as governor.

85 *Benton County*

Thomas H. Benton (1782–1858)— Benton was a native of North Carolina who served in the Tennessee senate and as a soldier in the War of 1812. Following the war he moved to Missouri and he represented that state for thirty years in the U.S. Senate. In that body he championed many interests of the West including free 160 acre homesteads, pony express, telegraph and railroads. Benton was a moderate on the volatile slavery issue. He opposed both abolition of slavery and extension of it. His primary concerns were peace and the preservation of the Union. These moderate positions proved unpopular. Some states which had named counties in Benton's honor renamed them and, in 1850, Missouri failed to return Benton to the senate. Following his ouster from the senate, Benton served briefly in the U.S. House of Representatives. This county was created in 1836 while Benton was still popular in the West.

86 *Boone County*

Uncertain— Two theories are given for the origin of this county's name:

1. The name Boon was intended for this county since creation of it would be a boon to some residents of Carroll County who felt that their current county seat was too far removed from them. (Boone County was created out of land taken from Carroll County and Madison County.)

2. The county was named in honor of Daniel Boone.

Daniel Boone (1734–1820)— A native of Pennsylvania, Boone penetrated Kentucky when it was wilderness country and settled there with his family in 1775. He gained fame on America's rugged western frontier as explorer, Indian fighter and surveyor.

87 *Bradley County*

Hugh Bradley (–)— Bradley was a captain in the army who served under General Andrew Jackson at New Orleans. In the last territorial legislature he represented Union County, from which Bradley County was formed. Hugh Bradley's home served as the first Bradley County courthouse.

88 *Calhoun County*

John C. Calhoun (1782–1850)— Calhoun represented South Carolina in both houses of the U.S. Congress. He served as secretary of war, secretary of state and as vice-president. He was a forceful advocate of slavery, states rights and limited powers for the federal government. He resigned the vice-presidency to enter the U.S. Senate where he could better represent the views of South Carolina and the South. This county was created in 1850, a few months after Calhoun's death.

89 *Carroll County*

Charles Carroll (1737–1832)— Carroll was a native of Maryland and he represented that state in the Continental Congress. He was one of the signers of the Declaration of Independence and he later represented Maryland as a U.S. senator in the first congress of the United States. Carroll lived to be the last surviving signer of the Declaration of Independence and several states recognized that distinction by naming counties for him. This county was created in 1823.

90 *Chicot County*

Point Chicot— This county borders on the Mississippi River and it was named for Point Chicot on the Mississippi. The origin of the name of Point Chicot is uncertain. Possibilities include: (1) Derived from the French word *chicot* meaning "stump" and (2) Derived from Chiska, the name of an Indian village on the eastern bank of the Mississippi which was visited by Hernando De Soto, the explorer.

91 *Clark County*

William Clark (1770–1838)— Clark was a native of Virginia who served in the army in battles with Indians on America's western frontier. Together with Captain Meriwether Lewis, Clark led the Lewis and Clark Expedition (1804–1806) to the Pacific Northwest. The Lewis & Clark party were the first white men, south of Canada, to travel on land to the Pacific Northwest Coast and back. Following the expedition Clark served as superintendent of Indian affairs for Louisiana territory and as governor of Missouri territory. This county was formed in 1818 while Clark was governor of Missouri territory.

92 *Clay County*

Uncertain. Either John M. Clayton (–) or Henry Clay (1777–1852)— This county was created in 1873. It was originally named Clayton in honor of John M. Clayton. In 1875 the name was shortened to Clay. It is not clear whether the shortened version was still intended to honor Mr. Clayton or whether the intent was to honor Henry Clay of Kentucky.

John M. Clayton (–)— Clayton was a member of the Arkansas senate at the time that this county was originally created.

Henry Clay (1777–1852)— Clay represented Kentucky in both branches of the U.S. Congress. For many years he was one of the more prominent figures in American politics but his several bids for the presidency were unsuccessful. He was influential in effecting important compromises between northern and southern interests during the years that secession and civil war were imminent.

93 *Cleburne County*

Patrick R. Cleburne (1828–1864)— Cleburne was a native of Ireland who immigrated to this country in 1849. He settled in Arkansas where he practiced law from 1855 until the outbreak of the Civil War. He was among the first men from

Arkansas to enlist in the Confederate army and he served with distinction in that army, rising to the rank of major-general. He was killed in combat in the Civil War.

94 Cleveland County

Stephen Grover Cleveland (1837–1908)— Grover Cleveland was a native of New Jersey who rose from mayor of Buffalo, New York, in 1881 to governor of New York in 1883 to president of the United States in 1885. He lost his bid for reelection to the presidency to Benjamin Harrison but he later ran and was then elected to a second term as president. Cleveland supported civil service reform and lower tariffs. He sent troops to intervene against Pullman strikers in Chicago. This county was created in 1873 and it was originally named Dorsey in honor of Stephen W. Dorsey who was then one of the U.S. senators from Arkansas. Dorsey became unpopular with the people of Arkansas and the name of the county was changed to Cleveland in 1885 to honor the recently elected president.

95 Columbia County

Columbia, Goddess of America— The term Columbia is derived from Christopher Columbus' name and it has been given various patriotic meanings. As used in the name District of Columbia, it means United States of America. As used in the name of this county, it signifies Goddess of America and/or Goddess of Liberty. The word *Columbus* is a Latin noun meaning a "male dove" or a "male pigeon."

96 Conway County

Henry W. Conway (1793–1827)— Conway was a native of Tennessee who served as an officer in the navy in the War of 1812. He moved to Arkansas territory in 1820 and was elected as a delegate to the U.S. Congress from Arkansas territory. This county was formed in 1825 while Conway was serving as a delegate to congress.

97 Craighead County

Thomas B. Craighead (–)— Craighead was a native of Tennessee who moved to Arkansas in 1838. He was a slave owner and he practiced law in Arkansas and in neighboring counties in Tennessee. Craighead was serving in the Arkansas senate at the time that creation of this new county was proposed and he vigorously opposed the idea. Meanwhile, another state senator, William A. Jones, was championing

the proposed new county. Jones managed to push the bill through to passage at a time when Craighead was absent from the legislative chamber. Upon returning to the chamber, Craighead learned that not only had the new county been created, but it had been named for him.

98 Crawford County

William H. Crawford (1772–1834)— Crawford served in the Georgia legislature and as a U.S. senator from Georgia. He was elected president pro tempore of the senate and he later served as minister to France, secretary of war and secretary of the treasury. Crawford was a serious candidate for the presidency in both 1816 and 1824. This county was created in 1820. At that time it contained a large part of the present state of Oklahoma.

99 Crittenden County

Robert Crittenden (1797–1834)— Crittenden was a native of Kentucky who moved to Missouri territory, settling in the area which became Arkansas territory. He assisted in the formation of a provisional government for Arkansas territory and was appointed by President Monroe to be the first secretary of Arkansas territory. This county was formed in 1825 while Crittenden was serving as territorial secretary.

100 Cross County

Uncertain. Either David C. Cross (–) or Edward Cross (1798–1887)— This county was named either for David C. Cross or for Edward Cross.
David C. Cross (–)— David C. Cross was a colonel in the Confederate army who resided in the area which became Cross County. He owned extensive land there.
Edward Cross (1798–1887)— Edward Cross was a native of Virginia who migrated to Arkansas territory in 1826. He practiced law here and was appointed by President Jackson as judge of the supreme court of the territory. Following Arkansas' admission to statehood, he was elected as Arkansas' one representative in the U.S. Congress. He later served as a special judge of the Arkansas supreme court. During the Civil War, Edward Cross performed some important banking duties for the Confederacy.
This county was created in 1862. Proponents of the view that the county was named for David C. Cross cite as evidence the gravestone of David C. Cross and an

historical marker on the lawn of the Cross County courthouse. Both state that the county was named for David C. Cross.

101 Dallas County

George M. Dallas (1792–1864)— Dallas was a native of Philadelphia, Pennsylvania, and he served as mayor of that city. He was later a U.S. senator, attorney general of Pennsylvania and minister to Russia. In 1844 he was elected vice-president on the Democratic ticket with James K. Polk. He later served as minister to England. This county was formed in 1845, shortly after Dallas was elected vice-president.

102 Desha County

Benjamin Desha (–1835)— Desha served as a captain in the War of 1812 and he was appointed receiver of public monies by President Monroe. He moved from Kentucky to Arkansas in 1822. This county was formed in 1838, three years after Desha's death.

103 Drew County

Thomas S. Drew (1802–1879)— Drew was a native of Tennessee who moved to Arkansas in his youth. He owned several slaves and was a prosperous farmer. He was a member of the Arkansas constitutional convention of 1836 and governor of Arkansas from 1844 to 1849. This county was formed in 1846 while Drew was governor of Arkansas.

104 Faulkner County

Sanford C. Faulkner (1803–1874)— Faulkner was a native of Kentucky who moved to Arkansas in 1829. He served as an officer in the Confederate army. Faulkner is credited with having brought into prominence *The Arkansas Traveler*, a humorous story which is accompanied by a tune on the fiddle. This county was created in 1873.

105 Franklin County

Benjamin Franklin (1706–1790)— Franklin was a native of Massachusetts who moved to Pennsylvania in his teens. Poverty denied him a formal education but he became the leading printer and editor in North America. He gained fame for his discoveries and inventions in the physical sciences and he distinguished himself as author, philosopher and diplomat. Franklin was a signer of the Declaration of Independence and an important member of the convention which framed the U.S. Constitution.

106 *Fulton County*

William S. Fulton (1795–1844)— Fulton was a native of Maryland who served in the army and as private secretary to a close friend of his family, General Andrew Jackson. In 1829, after Jackson had become president, he appointed Fulton to be secretary of Arkansas territory. Fulton later served as the last territorial governor of Arkansas and as a U.S. senator from the newly admitted state of Arkansas. This county was created in 1842, while Fulton was serving in the U.S. Senate.

107 *Garland County*

Augustus H. Garland (1832–1899)— Garland was a delegate to the Arkansas secession convention, a delegate to the provisional congress of the Confederate States and a member of the Confederate House of Representatives. After the Civil War, Garland was elected to the U.S. Senate but he was not allowed to take his seat. He served as governor of Arkansas until he was again elected to the U.S. Senate. He served in that body from 1877 to 1885 when he was appointed attorney general by President Cleveland. This county was formed in 1873, just prior to Garland's election as governor of Arkansas.

108 *Grant County*

Ulysses S. Grant (1822–1885)— Grant was a native of Ohio who graduated from the U.S. military academy at West Point. He served with distinction in the Mexican War and in the Civil War he rose to become commander of all Union forces. After the Civil War Grant served briefly as acting secretary of war and then two terms as president of the United States. He proved to be a rather mediocre president. This county was created in 1869 by the first Reconstruction government of Arkansas. The name was chosen to honor the victorious Union general who had just been elected president.

109 *Greene County*

Nathanael Greene (1742–1786)— Greene was born in Rhode Island and served briefly in the Rhode Island legislature. He gained fame as one of the ablest American generals in the Revolutionary War. After the war he moved to Georgia. This county was formed in 1833. The law creating this county left off the final "e" and named it

Green, in error. That error has never been corrected by the legislature but it has been corrected by common usage.

110 *Hempstead County*

Edward Hempstead (1780–1817)— Hempstead was a native of Connecticut. In 1805 he moved to Saint Louis, which was then in the district of Louisiana. He served as attorney general of the territory of Upper Louisiana and was a member and speaker of the third territorial general assembly. He then represented Missouri territory as the first delegate to the U.S. Congress from that territory. This county was created in 1818 by the legislature of Missouri territory before Arkansas territory was created.

111 *Hot Spring County*

The Hot Springs— This county was formed in 1829 and named for the famous hot springs which were then within its boundaries. When Garland County was later formed, the land that it took from Hot Spring County included the springs. The county name remains as a vestige.

112 *Howard County*

James Howard (–)— This county was formed in 1873 from portions of four bordering counties. Howard was serving in the Arkansas senate at that time representing two of the counties from which Howard County was taken.

113 *Independence County*

Declaration of Independence— The Declaration of Independence was the formal proclamation of separation from Great Britain by the thirteen American colonies. The declaration was drafted by Thomas Jefferson. It was based an a political philosophy of "natural rights" and it listed certain despotic abuses by the king which were judged to be intolerable. The declaration was adopted by the Continental Congress on July 4, 1776, the date generally regarded as America's birthday. This county was formed in 1820.

114 *Izard County*

George Izard (1776–1828)— Izard's family lived in South Carolina although he was born in England where his father had taken the family in 1772. In 1783 he returned to South Carolina with his mother and later served as an officer in the War of 1812, rising to the rank of major-general.

On March 4, 1825, President John Quincy Adams appointed Izard as territorial governor of Arkansas. This county was created in October of that year. As governor, Izard was unable to achieve even minimal harmony with the territorial legislature. The disharmony ended when Governor Izard died in office in Little Rock on November 22, 1828.

115 *Jackson County*

Andrew Jackson (1767–1845)— Jackson was born on the border of North Carolina and South Carolina. He represented Tennessee in both branches of the U.S. Congress. He gained fame and popularity for his military exploits in wars with the Indians and in the War of 1812. He was provisional military governor of Florida and from 1829 to 1837 General Jackson was president of the United States. His presidency reflected the frontier spirit of America. This county was created in 1829 while Jackson was president.

116 *Jefferson County*

Thomas Jefferson (1743–1826)— Jefferson was a native of Virginia and a member of the Virginia legislature. He served Virginia as governor and he was a delegate to the second Continental Congress. Jefferson was the author of the Declaration of Independence and one of its signers. He was minister to France, secretary of state, vice-president and president of the United States. As president, he accomplished the Louisiana Purchase and he arranged the Lewis and Clark Expedition to the Pacific Northwest. Jefferson was a true intellectual, thoroughly knowledgeable in the arts and sciences. His political theories were pivotal in the formation of our infant republic. This county was formed in 1829, shortly after Jefferson's death.

117 *Johnson County*

Benjamin Johnson (1784–1849)— Johnson was a native of Kentucky where he practiced law until he was appointed by President Monroe to be one of Arkansas' territorial judges. His appointment was renewed by successive administrations until 1836 when Arkansas was admitted to statehood. He was then appointed judge of the federal court for the district of Arkansas by President Jackson. He served in that post until his death in 1849. This county was created in 1833, while Johnson was an Arkansas territorial judge.

118 *Lafayette County*

Marie Joseph Paul Yves Roch Gilbert du Motier, Marquis de Lafayette (1757–1834) — Lafayette was a French aristocrat who served briefly in the French army. He came to America in 1777 to assist the American revolutionary army. He was granted an honorary commission as major-general by the Continental Congress and served with distinction in a number of battles in the Revolutionary War. This county was formed in 1827.

119 *Lawrence County*

James Lawrence (1781–1813) — Lawrence was an officer in the United States navy who established a reputation for bravery in the war against Tripoli and in the War of 1812. He died in combat while commanding the *Chesapeake* against the British near Boston. He is said to have uttered the famous phrase "Don't give up the ship" while he lay mortally wounded in that battle. This county was created by the Missouri legislature in 1815, shortly after Lawrence's death. It then included more than half of the present state of Arkansas.

120 *Lee County*

Robert E. Lee (1807–1870) — Lee was a native of Virginia and, for over 30 years, an officer in the United States army. When Virginia seceded from the Union, Lee refused an offer to command all federal forces and resigned from the U.S. army to accept a commission in the Confederate army. He served with distinction in that army and became general-in-chief of it. This county was formed in 1873, shortly after Lee's death.

121 *Lincoln County*

Abraham Lincoln (1809–1865) — Lincoln was a native of Kentucky who moved to Illinois where he was a member of the state legislature. He represented Illinois in the U.S. House of Representatives and later was elected president of the United States. Lincoln's presidency coincided almost exactly with the Civil War. He guided the United States ably through that uniquely turbulent period. As president, he issued the Emancipation Proclamation which declared the freedom of slaves in all states in rebellion. Lincoln was assassinated in 1865, a few days after the Union victory in the Civil War. In 1871 this county was created and named by a Reconstruction government.

122 *Little River County*

Little River — This county was created in 1867 and named for the Little River, a stream which is the northern boundary of the county.

123 *Logan County*

James Logan (–1859) — Logan was a native of Kentucky. About 1829 he moved to what is now western Arkansas as one of the first settlers of that area. He was a member of the first Arkansas legislature. This county was originally named Sarber but the name was changed to Logan in 1875.

124 *Lonoke County*

An oak tree — This county was created in 1873. It was named for a single oak tree at the county seat which was used as a landmark by an early surveyor, George P. C. Rumbough.

125 *Madison County*

Madison County, Alabama — Among the early settlers of this county were immigrants from Alabama and this county was named for Madison County in their home state. Madison County, Alabama, had been named for James Madison.

James Madison (1751–1836) — Madison was born in Virginia, served in the Virginia legislature and in the Continental Congress. He was a member of the convention which framed the U.S. Constitution and he collaborated with Hamilton and Jay in writing a series of papers under the title *The Federalist* which explained the new constitution and advocated its adoption. Madison represented Virginia in the U.S. House of Representatives, served for eight years as secretary of state and for eight years as president of the United States.

Madison County, Arkansas, was created on September 30, 1836, three months after James Madison's death.

126 *Marion County*

Francis Marion (–1795) — Marion is believed to have been born in South Carolina. He served in the army in battles against the Cherokee Indians and was elected to the Provisional congress of 1775. He served, with distinction, as an officer in the Revolutionary War and rose to the rank of general in that war. Marion was also a member of the South Carolina senate. This county was formed in 1835 and named Searcy in honor of Richard Searcy.

Less than a year later, the name was changed to honor this Revolutionary War general. Another Arkansas county was later formed and named to honor Richard Searcy; see Searcy County, below.

127 *Miller County*

James Miller (1776–1851) — Miller was a native of New Hampshire. He served with distinction as an army officer in the War of 1812 for which he was rewarded by congress with promotion to the rank of brevet brigadier-general. He was appointed by President Monroe to be the first governor of Arkansas territory, a post which he held from 1819 to 1825. In 1824 Miller was elected to the U.S. House of Representatives by his native state of New Hampshire but he declined the opportunity to take his seat in that body. This county was formed in 1820, while Miller was serving as territorial governor.

128 *Mississippi County*

Mississippi River — This county was named for the Mississippi River which forms its eastern border. The Mississippi is the longest river in the United States and, counting its various tributaries, one of the world's major river systems. The river was named by the Ojibway Indians of Wisconsin. In their language *missi sipi* meant "great river."

129 *Monroe County*

James Monroe (1758–1831) — Monroe, a native of Virginia, served in the Revolutionary War. Prior to his election as president of the United States, Monroe served in a wide variety of government posts. He served Virginia in the state legislature and as governor. He was a member of the Confederation congress and the U.S. Senate. He was minister to France and to Britain and he held two cabinet posts. As president, Monroe stressed limited government and strict construction of the constitution. He acquired Florida for the U.S. from Spain and he was the author of a policy declaration (later known as the Monroe Doctrine) which proscribed outside interference in North and South America. This county was formed in 1829 and named for the man who had been president when Arkansas territory was created.

130 *Montgomery County*

Richard Montgomery (1738–1775) — Montgomery was born in Ireland and served with the British in the French and

Indian War. He settled in New York state where he was elected to the New York Provisional congress. He served as a general in the American Revolutionary army and he was killed in combat in the Revolutionary War.

131 Nevada County

State of Nevada— This county was formed in 1871 and named for the state of Nevada because the shape of the new county was thought to resemble the shape of that state. The state of Nevada had been named for the beautiful Sierra Nevada mountains in the western part of that state. *Sierra Nevada* is a Spanish name borrowed from the name of a mountain range in Spain. *Sierra* means "mountain" or "mountain range" and *nevada* means "covered with snow" or "white as snow."

132 Newton County

Thomas W. Newton (1804–1853)— Newton, a native of Virginia, served in the Arkansas senate and represented Arkansas, very briefly, in the U.S. House of Representatives.

133 Ouachita County

Ouachita River— This county was formed in 1842 and named for the river which flows through it. The river's name is of Indian origin. A former clan of Indians, probably of the Caddoan family, who were known as the Ouachitas, lived along the river in northern Louisiana. At the time of European contact, this clan numbered less than 200 and soon afterwards their separate identity was lost. The meaning of the word *ouachita* is uncertain. A wide variety of translations have been advanced including "black" and "silver water."

134 Perry County

Oliver H. Perry (1785–1819)— Perry was a native of Rhode Island and an officer in the U.S. navy. During the War of 1812 his squadron defeated the British in a key battle on Lake Erie of which Perry said "We have met the enemy and they are ours."

135 Phillips County

Sylvanus Phillips (1766–1831)— Phillips was one of the pioneers of this section of Arkansas. He built a log cabin and settled near the mouth of the St. Francis River in 1797. He represented this area in the first territorial legislature elected by the people in 1820, the year that this county was formed.

136 Pike County

Zebulon M. Pike (1779–1813)— Pike was a native of New Jersey who served as an army officer on America's frontier following the Revolution. He led an exploratory army expedition to the Rocky Mountains which Pike's Peak in the Colorado Rockies commemorates. Pike served as a general in the War of 1812 and was killed in that war.

137 Poinsett County

Joel R. Poinsett (1779–1851)— Poinsett, a native of South Carolina, served in the South Carolina legislature and in the U.S. Congress. He was minister to Mexico and secretary of war. He had a keen interest in flowers and he developed the poinsettia flower from a Mexican flower and introduced its cultivation in the United States. This county was formed in 1838, while Poinsett was secretary of war.

138 Polk County

James K. Polk (1795–1849)— Polk was a native of North Carolina who moved with his family to the Tennessee frontier in 1806. He served in the lower house of the Tennessee legislature and he represented Tennessee for 14 years in the U.S. House of Representatives where he was speaker. He served one term as governor of Tennessee. Polk became president of the United States as a dark horse candidate of the Democratic Party but he became an unusually strong and effective president. His primary accomplishments involved westward extension of the United States; in the Northwest by settling a territorial dispute with Britain and in California and the Southwest by provoking and winning the Mexican War. This county was formed in 1844, a few weeks after Polk had been elected president.

139 Pope County

John Pope (1770–1845)— Pope was a native of Virginia who moved to Kentucky where he practiced law. He represented Kentucky in the U.S. Senate and, in 1829, President Jackson appointed him governor of Arkansas territory. Upon completion of his terms as territorial governor, he returned to Kentucky and represented that state in the U.S. House of Representatives.

140 Prairie County

Grand Prairie— This county was established in 1846 and named for the Grand Prairie on which it is located. No portion of this county is more than 250 feet above sea level.

141 Pulaski County

Casimir Pulaski (1748–1779)— Pulaski was born in Lithuania and served in the Polish army. He came to America to assist the colonies as an officer in the Revolutionary War. He died in combat in that war during the siege of Savannah, Georgia. This county was created in 1818 by the Missouri territorial legislature.

142 Randolph County

John Randolph (1773–1833)— Randolph was a native of Virginia and he represented that state in both houses of the U.S. Congress for many years. He was an advocate of states rights and strict construction of the federal constitution. He owned slaves and he represented the interests of the South in congress. Randolph also served, very briefly, as minister to Russia. This county was created by the last Arkansas territorial legislature in 1835, shortly after Randolph's death.

143 Saint Francis County

Saint Francis River— This county was created in 1827 and named for the Saint Francis River which flows through it. The Saint Francis River flows through both Arkansas and Missouri and Missouri sources offer information concerning the origin of the river's name. Some sources on the history and geography of Missouri state that the river was named for Saint Francis of Assisi (1181–1226), while others indicate that the river was probably named for that saint.

Saint Francis River— A tributary of the Mississippi River, the Saint Francis rises in southeastern Missouri, flows south to the Missouri-Arkansas border and crosses that border to enter northeastern Arkansas. It continues its journey of some 425 miles flowing in a southern direction through eastern Arkansas and empties its waters into the Mississippi near Marianna, Arkansas.

Saint Francis (1181–1226)— Born in Assisi, Italy, Saint Francis was christened John but called Francesco. His father was a prosperous merchant and as a youth, Francesco devoted himself to pleasure-seeking extravagance. While in his mid twenties, he had a vision which caused him to abandon the pleasures of the flesh and devote his life to God. After a pilgrimage to Rome in 1206, he began a life of poverty. He worked on the repair of ruined churches and cared for the poor and sick, Francesco was never ordained but as he began preaching he attracted followers whom he organized as the Friars Minor (now titled the Franciscan Order). He drew up a rule which was given papal approval in 1210. He attempted on several occasions to convert the Mohammedans in northern Africa but each of these efforts failed. Meanwhile, the order he founded had grown dramatically. Saint Francis lacked the administrative skills needed by the larger order and two of his friars were pressing for less emphasis on simplicity, humility and poverty. Saint Francis resigned as head of the order in 1220. In 1224 he received a stigmata in religious ecstasy. The scars of these wounds remained on his body until his death in 1226.

144 *Saline County*

Local salt works—This county was formed in 1835 and named for salt works which had been established there about 1827 by Allen M. Oakley and William E. Woodruff. Salt was one of the pioneers' critical necessities and this county's salt works supplied most of the salt needs of Arkansas territory and portions of adjoining states.

145 *Scott County*

Andrew Scott (1788–1851)— Scott was a native of Virginia moved to Missouri territory when he was about 20 years old. He practiced law there and was appointed to be one of the first superior court judges for the newly organized territory of Arkansas. He also served as a delegate to the Arkansas constitutional convention of 1836. Judge Scott was a small man physically, weighing less than 135 pounds, but he was courageous. He killed one man in a duel. On another occasion, in 1828, he became involved in an argument with a man, named Edmund Hogan, who had defeated Scott for the legislature in 1827. Hogan, a powerful man who weighed over 200 pounds, knocked Scott to the ground. Scott leapt to his feet and pulled a sword from a cane he was carrying. He stabbed Hogan several times but was acquitted by the court on grounds of self defense. This county was created in 1833.

146 *Searcy County*

Richard Searcy (–1832)— Searcy was a native of Tennessee who moved to Arkansas territory about 1820. In 1823 he was appointed to be one of the judges of that territory. Searcy ran twice for election to be territorial delegate to the U.S. Congress but lost both times to Ambrose H. Sevier by small margins. Another Arkansas county had earlier been named for Richard Searcy but that county's name is now Marion.

147 *Sebastian County*

William K. Sebastian (–1865)— Sebastian was a native of Tennessee who settled in Arkansas territory in 1835. He was one of the first circuit judges of the state of Arkansas. He was an associate justice on the Arkansas supreme court and he served in the Arkansas senate. He was president of that body in 1846 and 1847. Prior to the Civil War, he represented Arkansas for several years in the U.S. Senate. When Arkansas seceded from the Union, Sebastian did not resign his seat in the U.S. Senate as most senators from Confederate states did. The senate, however, was suspicious of his loyalty and expelled him from their body. After Sebastian's death, the U.S. Senate revoked its resolution of expulsion and paid the full amount of his lost senate compensation to his children. This county was formed in 1851 while Sebastian was serving in the U.S. Senate.

148 *Sevier County*

Ambrose H. Sevier (1801–1848)— Sevier was a native of Tennessee who moved to Little Rock, Arkansas in 1821. He was a member of the Arkansas territorial House of Representatives and speaker of that body in 1827. He served as a territorial delegate to the U.S. Congress and, when Arkansas was admitted to the Union, he became one of the first U.S. senators from the state of Arkansas. He later served as minister to Mexico. This county was formed in 1828 while Sevier was serving as a delegate to congress.

149 *Sharp County*

Ephraim Sharp (–)— This county was formed in 1868 and named for Sharp who was serving at that time as a representative in the lower house of the Arkansas legislature. He represented a district which included Sharp County.

150 *Stone County*

Geological structure of the area—This county was formed in 1873. The name Stone was chosen as descriptive of the composition of the numerous hills and mountains which are found in this county.

151 *Union County*

The United States of America—This county was formed in 1829 and named for the union of states which comprise the United States of America.

152 *Van Buren County*

Martin Van Buren (1782–1862)—Van Buren was a native of New York and he served that state as state senator, attorney general and governor. He represented New York in the U.S. Senate and was secretary of state in President Jackson's cabinet. He served one term as vice-president of the United States and one term as president. Van Buren organized an effective political machine in New York state which was one of the first political machines in this country. On the national level, he was one of the early users of the spoils system of filling government jobs. This county was formed in 1833 while Van Buren was vice-president.

153 *Washington County*

George Washington (1732–1799)—Washington was a native of Virginia. He served in Virginia's house of burgesses and became one of the colonies' leaders in opposition to British policies in America. He was a member of the first and second Continental Congresses and commander of all Continental armies in the Revolutionary War. Following victory in that war, Washington was elected to be the first president of the United States.

154 *White County*

Uncertain—This county was created in 1835. It was named either for Hugh L. White or for the White River.

Hugh L. White (1773–1840)—White served in the Tennessee senate and as a judge on Tennessee's highest courts. When Andrew Jackson resigned from the U.S. Senate, White was elected to complete his unexpired senate term. White was a presidential candidate in 1836 and he was quite popular at that time with the people of Arkansas. This county was created while White was campaigning for the presidency.

White River— This river is a tributary of the Mississippi. Rising in northwestern Arkansas, it flows about 700 miles before emptying into the Mississippi. Henry R. Schoolcraft, writing in 1819, remarked that "Its waters, unlike most of the western rivers, are beautifully clear and transparent, being wholly made up of springs which gush from the flinty hills that are found for more than half of its length...." The White River forms most of the eastern boundary of White County.

155 *Woodruff County*

William E. Woodruff (1795–1885)— Woodruff was a native of New York who moved to Arkansas territory in 1819 where he published the territory's first newspaper, the *Arkansas Gazette*. Woodruff was active in the newspaper field in Arkansas for more than 30 years and he was an influential force in Arkansas politics. This county was formed in 1862, about ten years after Woodruff retired from the newspaper business.

156 *Yell County*

Archibald Yell (1797–1847)— Yell was a native of North Carolina who moved to Tennessee where he served in the state legislature. In 1830 he moved to Arkansas territory and he was appointed territorial judge there by President Andrew Jackson. He represented Arkansas in the U.S. Congress and served Arkansas as governor. Yell served as a general in the Mexican War and was killed in combat in that war.

This county was created in 1840, a few weeks after Yell had been inaugurated as governor.

REFERENCES

Branner, John C. *Some Old French Place Names in the State of Arkansas.* Baltimore, 1899.

Calhoun, James. *Louisiana Almanac: 1979–1980.* Gretna, Pelican Publishing Co., 1979.

The Encyclopedia Americana. New York, Americana Corporation, 1977.

Etheridge, Y. W. *History of Ashley County, Arkansas.* Van Buren, Arkansas, Press-Argus, 1959.

Hanks, Bill. *Logan County, Arkansas Marriage Records: 1877–1884.* Hubbard & McLane, 1978.

Hansbrough, Vivian. *History of Greene County, Arkansas.* Little Rock, Democrat Printing & Lithographing Co., 1946.

Harper, Lawrence. *Arkansas Almanac: 1964.* Little Rock, Pioneer Press, 1964.

Harris, Mary Sue, & Bobby McLane. *Independence County, Arkansas Marriage Records: 1826–1877.* Hot Springs National Park, Arkansas, 1970.

Hempstead, Fay. *A Pictorial History of Arkansas.* St. Louis, N. D. Thompson Publishing Co., 1890.

Hennepin, Louis. "Account of the Discovery of the River Mississippi and the Adjacent Country." *Historical Collections of Louisiana.* New York, Wiley & Putnam, 1846.

Herndon, Dallas T. *Centennial History of Arkansas.* Chicago, S.J. Clarke Publishing Co., 1922.

Hodge, Frederick W. *Handbook of American Indians North of Mexico.* Totowa, New Jersey, Rowman & Littlefield, 1975.

Lackey, Walter F. *History of Newton County, Arkansas.* Independence, Missouri, Zion's Printing & Publishing Co., 1950.

Laney, Rex. *Do You Know Louisiana?* Baton Rouge, State of Louisiana Department of Commerce & Industry, 1938.

Read, William A. "Louisiana Place-Names of Indian Origin." *University Bulletin — Louisiana State University & Agricultural & Mechanical College*, 47. 1927.

A Reminiscent History of the Ozark Region. Cape Girardeau, Missouri, Ramfre Press, 1956.

Schoolcraft, Henry R. *A View of the Lead Mines of Missouri.* New York, Charles Wiley & Co., 1819.

Shankle, George Earlie. *State Names, Flags, Seals, Songs, Birds, Flowers & Other Symbols.* New York, H. W. Wilson Co., 1941.

Stuck, Charles A. *The Story of Craighead County.* Jonesboro, Arkansas, Hurley Co., 1960.

Thomas, David Y. *Arkansas & Its People.* New York, American Historical Society, Inc., 1930.

Williams, Harry Lee. *History of Craighead County, Arkansas.* Little Rock, Parke-Harper Co., 1930.

Work Projects Administration. *Inventory of the County Archives of Arkansas — Hot Spring, Polk, Saline & Searcy Counties.* Little Rock, 1940–1942.

California

(58 counties)

157 *Alameda County*

Alameda Creek— This county was named for the principal stream which flows through it. The stream had been named by early Spanish explorers who noted the numerous shade trees along its banks. In the Spanish language *alameda* means "a walk" (or "avenue") "shaded by trees" or "a grove of poplar trees."

158 *Alpine County*

Its mountainous terrain— This county is on the crest of the beautiful Sierra Nevada mountain range and the name was chosen as descriptive of the alpine character of its terrain.

159 *Amador County*

Josef M. Amador (1794–1883)— Amador was a native of San Francisco, a soldier, Indian fighter and majordomo of Mission San Jose. He was a successful miner in the Amador County area during California's gold rush. This county was created in 1854. The name originally proposed in the legislature for this county was Washing-

ton but the name Amador was substituted in the assembly and the senate concurred.

160 *Butte County*

Sutter Buttes— When this county was created in 1850, the Sutter Buttes, also known as the Marysville Buttes, were within its borders. These high hills, an impressive landmark in the Sacramento Valley, are now within Sutter County. The French word *butte* was introduced in northern California about 1829 by Michael Laframboise, a French-Canadian trapper. The French meaning of the word was "small, isolated elevation, knoll" or "mound." As used in California, the term *butte* refers to mountains or peaks and is not limited to hills. Indeed, some of California's buttes soar more than 10,000 feet above sea level.

161 *Calaveras County*

Calaveras River—*Calaveras* is the Spanish word for "skulls" and it was frequently applied by early Spanish soldiers and explorers to places where human skeletons were found as the remains of Indian battles. This is why the Calaveras River was so named and the county, created in 1850, was named for the river which flows through it.

162 *Colusa County*

Colus Indians—This county was named for a subgroup of the Copehan Indians who lived in the Colusa County area on the west side of the Sacramento River. Called Colus by White men, their own name for themselves is rendered variously including Coru and Korusi. The meaning of this tribe's name is uncertain but one explanation is that it meant "scratch" or "scratcher." It was customary for Colus Indian brides, on their wedding nights, to scratch the faces of their new husbands. Whether the scratches were inflicted out of anger, passion or merely custom is not known but the scratches became a hallmark of this tribe and possibly the basis of its name. In the law of 1850 which created this county, the name was spelled Colusi. Since 1854, Colusa has been the accepted spelling of the county name.

163 *Contra Costa County*

The northeastern shore of San Francisco Bay—Early Spanish explorers called the lands across the bay from San Francisco *contra costa* meaning "opposite coast." The term was adopted as the county name when Contra Costa County was created as one of California's original counties. Later, when Alameda County was formed, the name lost much of its significance since Contra Costa gave up to the new county, the coastal lands directly facing San Francisco. The name Mount Diablo County had originally been proposed instead of Contra Costa but that name was never adopted.

164 *Del Norte County*

The northern location of this county—*Del norte* means "of the north" in Spanish and it was chosen for the name of this county as descriptive of its location at the northwestern end of the state. Other names that had been proposed in 1857 when this county was created were Buchanan (for the newly elected U.S. president), Alta, Altissima, Rincon and Del Merritt

165 *El Dorado County*

Gold deposits in the area—*El dorado* is a Spanish term meaning "the golden one," said to have derived from the name of a mythical gilded king. Legend had it that this king received a coat of gold dust every morning which he washed off every evening in a lake, making the lake bottom a treasure chest. During the period of Spanish exploration and conquest in the Americas, the term came to mean "a land containing vast amounts of gold." These promised riches were rarely real. Often, "the el dorados" were invented by terrorized American Indians in their anxiety to speed their Spanish oppressors on their way. In the case of El Dorado County, California, however, the name was appropriate. This county is in the heart of California's gold rush country and it was here, in January, 1848, that gold was discovered by James W. Marshall at Sutter's Mill in Coloma. This county was created in 1850 as one of California's original 27 counties. The name Coloma had been proposed for it but that name was not adopted.

166 *Fresno County*

Local ash trees—*Fresno* is the Spanish word for "ash tree." Early Spanish explorers used this word to describe the region because of the abundant ash trees (genus *Fraxinus*) found here. The name was chosen for the county when it was created in 1856.

167 *Glenn County*

Hugh J. Glenn (1824–1882)—Glenn, a veteran of the Mexican War, graduated from medical school as a dentist. He decided against a dental career and emigrated from Missouri to California in 1849 in search of gold. In the 1860's and 1870's he purchased some 55,000 acres of California farmland and became so successful that he was the state's most important wheat grower and was known as the "wheat king." Glenn was prominent in California politics and commerce. He was an unsuccessful candidate for governor and later he was a powerful figure on the state board of agriculture. This county was created in 1891. Dr. Glenn's estate gave financial backing to the creation and naming of this county.

168 *Humboldt County*

Humboldt Bay—Humboldt County was created in 1853 and it was named for Humboldt Bay on its Pacific Ocean border. The bay had been given various names by early explorers. The surviving name was applied by Hans Buhne and Douglas Ottinger of the ship *Laura Virginia* in 1850 in honor of Baron Alexander von Humboldt, a German scientist who was then prominent.

Friedrich Wilhelm Heinrich Alexander von Humboldt (1769–1859)—Baron von Humboldt was one of the foremost scientists of his time. He participated in expeditions to Latin America and to Asia which gathered valuable scientific data for a number of disciplines including biology, geology and astronomy. His contributions to the physical sciences covered topics ranging from climate and polar magnetism to geology. In 1804 he visited America and met with Thomas Jefferson and other prominent intellectuals. His scientific books enjoyed popularity in America and a Pacific Ocean current which he studied is named in his honor.

169 *Imperial County*

Imperial Valley region—The California Development Company coined the name Imperial for this desert area and for a land company, the Imperial Land Company, which they organized to develop the region. They hoped that this name would attract more settlers than a name emphasizing the desert character of the area. At that time, the Imperial Valley area was in San Diego County. When this region became a separate county in 1907, it was named for the region which comprised it.

170 *Inyo County*

Inyo Mountains—This county had originally been called Coso County but Coso County was never organized and, when the county was officially created in 1866, it was named for the Inyo Mountains. *Inyo* was a name given by local Indians to a group of mountains in this area. The term meant "dwelling place of a great spirit."

171 *Kern County*

Kern River—General John C. Frémont led an expedition through this area in the 1840's and he named the river, in derision, for Edward M. Kern, a member of his party who nearly drowned while attempting to cross this river.

Edward M. Kern (1823–1863)— Kern, a native of Pennsylvania, was an army officer and explorer who served as topographer and artist for Fremont's expedition through Kern County in the 1840's. Kern participated in several military actions which are significant in California history including the Bear Flag Revolt, relief of the Donner party and actions against Indians in the Sacramento Valley.

When Kern County was formed in 1866, it was named for the river which flows through it. This county had originally been authorized by the legislature as Buena Vista County but that county was never officially organized.

172 *Kings County*

Kings River— The Kings River, in this county, had been named in 1805 by a group of Spanish explorers. Their name for the river was *Rio de los Santos Reyes* or, in English, "River of the Holy Kings." The name was chosen to honor the three kings, or wise men, who tradition tells us paid homage to the infant Jesus. It was probably on January 6, the feast day of the three magi, that the explorers first saw the river. When the county was created in 1893, it was named for the river whose name by then had been shortened to Kings.

173 *Lake County*

Clear Lake— This county was formed in 1861 and named for Clear Lake, which is within the county and is its principal feature. While the county is aptly named, the lake is not. Clear Lake is now a rather murky body of water. Large and pretty it is, but clear, it is not.

174 *Lassen County*

Mount Lassen— Much of the Lassen County area was at one time claimed by both Nevada territory and California. Nevada territory organized it as Roop County while California considered it a part of Plumas County. When California prevailed, the disputed area was set apart from Plumas and included in a new county named for Mount Lassen. The mountain had been named earlier for Peter Lassen.

Peter Lassen (1800–1859)— Lassen, a native of Denmark, immigrated to North America and arrived in Mexican California in 1840. He worked in northern California as a blacksmith, saw mill operator and trading post operator. A man of many trades, he was also a prospector, hunter and guide. In 1844 he was naturalized as a Mexican citizen and given a 26,000 acre land grant in California. Lassen was one of the early pioneers of northeastern California, where Mount Lassen is located. He was murdered in 1859 while prospecting for silver north of Pyramid Lake in what is now the state of Nevada.

175 *Los Angeles County*

Los Angeles River— On August 2, 1769, an expedition headed by Gaspar de Portola camped on the banks of the Los Angeles River, which they named in honor of Saint Mary, the virgin mother of Jesus in Roman Catholic theology. Their name for the river was *El Rio Nuestra Senora la Reina de los Angeles de Porciuncula* or "The River of Our Lady, the Queen of the Angels of Porciuncula." The appendage *de porciuncula* was attached in reference to the chapel-shrine at Portiuncula in the basilica of Our Lady of the Angels near Assisi, Italy. The river's name was subsequently applied to the pueblo at Los Angeles and, in the shortened form we now know, to both the city and county of Los Angeles.

Saint Mary (–)— It is a matter of dogma of the Roman Catholic Church that Saint Mary was the virgin mother of the second person of the Trinity, Jesus Christ. Because she had been selected to be the human mother of God, is was axiomatic that her soul be spotless, free of all sin from the moment of her conception. As the mother of Jesus, Mary is considered preeminent among all saints but the veneration and adoration bestowed on her are on a lower plane than those reserved for God in three persons, Father, Son and Holy Spirit.

176 *Madera County*

Town of Madera, California— Lumbering began in this area in the 1870's and a settlement at the place of lumber shipment, where the flume ended, was called *Madera*, the Spanish word for "timber" or "lumber." When the county was organized in 1893, Madera was chosen as its county seat and the county was named for that town.

177 *Marin County*

Local bay, islands and peninsula— This county was created in 1850 and named for local islands, bay and peninsula to which the name Marin had been applied much earlier. The origin of that name is not certain. Three alternatives are mentioned:

1. Name derived from a name applied in 1775 by Juan Manuel de Ayala to honor Saint Mary, the patron Saint of his vessel, the *San Carlos*. It is said that the name he applied to a large inlet on the northwestern arm of San Francisco Bay between San Pedro and San Quentin was Bahia de Nuestra Senora del Rosario la Marinera.

2. Named for a local Indian, a boatman and ferryman, who lived at Mission San Rafael in what is now Marin County. He was baptized by the Spanish padres and given the name Marin or Marinero because of his knowledge of San Francisco Bay. *Marinero* in Spanish means "mariner," "seaman" or "sailor."

3. Named for Marin, a chief of the Licatiut Indian tribe which inhabited this region and fought against the Spanish here. Some accounts say that this Chief Marin was baptized as a Christian by the Spanish padres.

178 *Mariposa County*

Mariposa Creek— This county was created in 1850 and named for Mariposa Creek. The creek had been named earlier by Spanish explorers who were either impressed by butterflies or by colorful wildflowers that reminded them of butterflies. *Mariposa* is the Spanish word for "butterfly." During migrations, butterflies often accumulate in startling profusion at stops along their route.

179 *Mendocino County*

Cape Mendocino— This county was created in 1850 and named for the cape to the north in Humboldt County. (The cape has never been within Mendocino County.) The origin of the name is uncertain but it apparently was named by early Spanish explorers for a viceroy of New Spain (Mexico) named Mendoza; Antonio de Mendoza or Lorenzo Suarez de Mendoza.

Antonio de Mendoza (1490–1552)— Mendoza, a native of Spain, served as Spain's ambassador to Hungary and as the first viceroy of New Spain. He assumed that post in 1535 and skillfully exploited agricultural and mining interests there for Spain. He was, however, rather ruthless in his treatment of the native Mexicans. Keenly interested in exploration, in 1542 he dispatched an expedition to explore the Pacific. If Cape Mendocino was named in his honor, it was this 1542 expedition led by Juan Rodriguez Cabrillo that so named it. After 15 years as viceroy of New Spain, Mendoza was sent to Peru to consolidate Spanish authority there. He accomplished little in Peru prior to his death in 1552.

Lorenzo Suarez de Mendoza (–)— Lorenzo Suarez de Mendoza was viceroy of New Spain from 1580 to 1583.

180 *Merced County*

Merced River— This county was created in 1855 and named for the river which flows through it. The river was originally named *Rio de Nuestra Senora de la Merced* meaning "River of Our Lady of Mercy." The name was given to the river by an expedition of soldiers headed by Gabriel Moraga. They discovered and named the river on September 29, 1806, shortly after the feast day of Our Lady of Mercy, Saint Mary. The name was chosen in gratitude for this badly needed drinking water found after a long, hot and very dry trek from the Livermore Valley.

Saint Mary (–)— It is a matter of dogma of the Roman Catholic Church that Saint Mary was the virgin mother of the second person of the Trinity, Jesus Christ. Because she had been selected to be the human mother of God, it was axiomatic that her soul. be spotless, free of all sin from the moment of her conception. As the mother of Jesus, Mary is considered preeminent among all saints but the veneration and adoration bestowed on her are on a lower plane than those reserved for God in three persons, Father, Son and Holy Spirit.

181 *Modoc County*

Modoc Indians— This county was created in 1874 and named for the Indian tribe which had been subdued about two years earlier in the Modoc War. The Modocs lived in southern Oregon and northern California and they numbered about 1,000 at the time of contact with the Whites. They engaged in frequent conflicts with White settlers and were among the last American Indians to resist conquest. In the Modoc War of 1872–1873, a relatively small band of Modoc warriors repeatedly held off much larger forces of American soldiers. In the end, the Whites prevailed and the surviving Modocs were separated and dispatched to Indian reservations in Oregon and Oklahoma. The Modocs called themselves *Maklak* meaning "the people." The origin of the name *Modoc* is uncertain but it may have derived from a name coined by the Klamath Indians to mean "south." (south of the nearby Klamaths.) Other explanations that have been offered include: (1) The name derived from Modokus, a former chief of the Modocs and (2) The name meant "head of the river" referring to the Pitt River near which the Modocs lived.

182 *Mono County*

Mono Indians— The Mono Indians, a branch of the Shoshoneans, lived on the slopes of the Sierra Nevada Mountains including the Mono Lake area. *Mono* is a Spanish word for "monkey" and is considered by some to be the origin of these Indians' name. This is doubtful. The Monos' western neighbors, the Yokuts, called them Monachi. *Monachi* meant "fly people" and the Monos acquired this name because they used fly pupae as one of their main foods and bartering commodities. These flies were found in abundance in the extraordinarily saline and alkaline waters of Mono Lake. The name Mono probably evolved from the original Monachi. Esmeralda had originally been proposed in the legislature for the name of this county but that name was never officially adopted.

183 *Monterey County*

Monterey Bay, the town of Monterey, California, and the hills and trees east of Monterey Bay— The bay was named by the naval explorer, Sebastian Vizcaino in 1602. He named it in honor of his friend and patron, Gaspar de Zuniga, Count of Monterey (–1606) the then-current viceroy of New Spain (Mexico). The town of Monterey which developed along the bay became the military and social capital of Alta, California during the period of Spanish and Mexican rule. In 1850, when California's original 27 counties were created, the charm of the apt Spanish phrase *monte rey* ("royal forest" or "mountain") as well as the historic names of the bay and town influenced the selection of this county's name.

184 *Napa County*

Uncertain— The name is of Indian origin but its meaning is unknown. The descendants of the Indians who coined the term were stricken with smallpox in 1838. There were few survivors then and the tribe is now extinct. To compound the problem, it must be recognized that although *Napa* is of Indian origin, it is quite possible that *Napa* is a rendering in Spanish of the original Indian term. (The Spaniards used Napa as the tribal name for the Indians of the Napa Valley.) Since speculations tend to flourish in the absence of facts, we are favored with a rich list of speculations about the meaning of the word *napa*: "Homeland, abundant, fish, village, grizzly bear, house (or houses), near mother, near home, motherland, tribe and harpoon point."

185 *Nevada County*

Town of Nevada City, California— The beautiful Sierra Nevada mountains in eastern California and western Nevada were named in 1776 by the Spanish explorer, Pedro Font, who borrowed the name of a mountain range in Spain. *Sierra* means "mountain" or "mountain range" and *nevada* means "covered with snow" or "white as snow." When the City of Nevada (now known as Nevada City), California was incorporated in March, 1851, it was named for these perpetually snow-capped mountains. Just one month later, in April, 1851, Nevada County was created and named for the city, its county seat.

186 *Orange County*

Local orange groves— This county was created in 1889 and named for the local orange groves which supported a flourishing industry there. Oranges are tropical and subtropical trees and shrubs which belong to the genus *Citrus*. Their fruits, and juices from their fruits, enjoy great popularity. Oranges originated in the tropical regions of Asia, spread around the Mediterranean Sea and were introduced in the western hemisphere by Columbus in 1493. Their culture was introduced in California, near Orange County, in 1769. Prior to the creation of this county, the names Anaheim and Santa Ana were proposed for it but neither was ever adopted.

187 *Placer County*

Surface gold deposits in the area— This county was created and named in 1851 during the California gold rush. The placers in this region were among the richest in the state. The term *placer* is of Spanish origin. Its Spanish meaning is "place near riverbank where gold dust and gold nuggets are found." In America, the word refers to surface gold deposits left exposed or contained in loose gravel or sand. Panning for placer gold was the most popular form of mining during the California gold rush. Gold production is no longer significant in the Placer County area.

188 *Plumas County*

Feather River— The Spanish word *plumas* means "feathers" and both the Spanish and English versions of this river's name have signified feather. The origin of the river's name is not certain but it is probable that Captain Luis A. Arguello named this stream Rio de las Plumas (River of the Feathers) when he explored it in 1820 because of the profusion of bright feathers from water fowl that he saw floating on it. By 1854, when the county was created, the river's name had become Feather River but the Spanish version was revived for the name of the county. All of the many branches of the Feather River have their origins in the mountains of Plumas County.

189 *Riverside County*

City of Riverside, California— The Santa Ana River is an intermittent stream which rises in the San Bernardino Mountains, flows through Riverside County and empties in the Pacific Ocean near Newport Beach. In September, 1870, work began on building an upper canal of the Santa Ana River. A settlement acquired the name Riverside when this canal reached it in June, 1871. When the county was created in 1893, it was named for the city, its county seat.

190 *Sacramento County*

Sacramento River— The name Sacramento was first given to the river, then to a town, which is now California's capital city, and finally to the county when it was created in 1850.

Sacramento River— The Sacramento River rises in Siskiyou County in the Klamath mountain range, flows south through Sacramento County and joins the San Joaquin River before emptying into Suisun Bay some 400 miles from its origin. The name Sacramento was first applied in 1808 to a stream that is now known as the Feather River, a tributary of the Sacramento River, by the soldier-explorer, Gabriel Moraga. The Spanish word sacramento refers to one of Christianity's Holy Sacraments. The Holy Sacrament honored by Moraga was the Eucharist in the Roman Catholic Mass. In time, the main river, the Sacramento, became known by the name that Moraga originally bestowed on the Feather River.

191 *San Benito County*

San Juan Creek— On March 21, 1772, one of Saint Benedict's feast days, Father Crespi gave the name San Benito to the creek which is now known as the San Juan Creek. (Benito is a diminutive form of the Spanish Benedicto.) When the county was created in 1874 it was named for the creek.

Saint Benedict (–)— Saint Benedict, founder of the Benedictine monastic order who lived from about A.D. 480 to about 550, was born in Norcia, Italy, and educated in Rome. His studies of the Byzantine monastic centers made a strong impression on him. The vice he observed in the schools and streets of Rome repelled him and he withdrew becoming a hermit in a cave for about three years. During this period shepherds and others paid visits to him to listen to his wisdom. He then directed a monastic community at Vicovers but was forced to leave as a result of rebellion against his strict discipline. He then established 13 monasteries, the last being at Monte Cassino where he wrote a rule for monastic life calling for prayer, reading, manual labor, humility, obedience, zeal, and moderate asceticism. For several centuries after his death his rule greatly influenced the conduct of occidental monasteries and the Benedictine Order survives today in the form of individually governed monasteries united in common adherence to the rule authored by Saint Benedict.

192 *San Bernardino County*

San Bernardino Mountains— The name San Bernardino has been generously scattered in this area of southern California including a valley, mountains, mountain peak, land grant, rancho, city, national forest and county. Apparently the naming chain began on May 20, 1810, Saint Bernard's feast day, when Padre Dumetz applied the name to a temporary chapel. San Bernardino County was created in 1853. The town of San Bernardino, its county seat, was incorporated in 1854. The name San Bernardino as applied to the mountains is now restricted to the chain between the Cajon and San Gorgonio passes.

Saint Bernard (1380–1444)— Saint Bernard or Saint Bernardino of Siena, Italy became a Franciscan preacher in 1402. During his career he walked through most of Italy preaching as he went, often delivering several lively and emotional sermons on the same day. He was extremely popular, moving his audiences to both laughter and tears and the crowds that he drew often were so large that he had to use a pulpit in the open air. His sermons praised penance and voluntary poverty while denouncing gambling, usury, witchcraft, superstition and the power politics of Italy's city — states. He established two schools of theology and was offered three bishoprics which he declined. In the last years of his life he returned to his favorite vocation, traveling preacher.

193 *San Diego County*

San Diego Bay— On November 12, 1602, the feast day of Saint Didacus, priests who had accompanied the explorer Sebastian Vizcaino built a hut to use as a chapel and conducted a Mass on the shores of San Diego Bay. This may have been the first Catholic service conducted on California soil. Vizcaino's flagship was named in honor of Saint Didacus. Vizcaino or the priests named the bay in honor of both the saint and Vizcaino's flagship. (The name San Miguel had originally been given to this huge bay by the Portuguese navigator, Juan Rodriguez Cabrillo when he visited it in 1542.) When Father Junipero Serra founded the first mission in Alta California in 1769, he dedicated it to Saint Didacus and called it *La Mision de San Diego de Alcala*.

Saint Didacus (–1463)— A native of Spain, Saint Didacus or San Diego de Alcala de Henares, was a lay brother in the Order of Friars. In 1445 he was chosen as guardian of the Franciscan community on the Canary Island of Fortaventura. It was unusual for a lay brother to serve as a superior but he performed well and remained superior at Fortaventura until 1449. He next fulfilled the humble role of infirmarian at a convent in Rome. Many patients are said to have been miraculously cured while under his care there. Didacus spent the remainder of his life in Alcala, Spain, in penance, solitude and contemplation.

194 *San Francisco County*

City of San Francisco, California— The city of San Francisco was originally named Yerba Buena. Its name was changed in 1847 to San Francisco, a shortened version of names given earlier to the bay, mission and presidio. All of these names honor Saint Francis of Assisi, the founder of the Franciscan Order that administered all of the California missions. In 1595 the bay's name was conferred by the explorer Rodriguez Cermeno and christened by a member of the Franciscan Order. This name was given to the body of water now known as Drakes Bay. In time, the name shifted from Drakes Bay to the present San Francisco Bay. The San Francisco presidio was dedicated and formally named on the "day of the wounds of Saint Francis," September 17, 1776. The San Francisco mission (*La Mision de Nuestro Serafico Padre San Francisco de Asis a la Laguna de los Dolores*) was also founded and dedicated in 1776. The village of San Francisco (Yerba Buena) grew to absorb the villages at both the presidio and mission. The county was established as one of California's original 27 counties in 1850 and it was named for the city. Since 1856, when San Mateo County was carved from San Francisco County, the city and county of San Francisco have been coterminous.

Saint Francis (1181–1226)— Born in Assisi, Italy, Saint Francis was christened John but called Francesco. His father was a prosperous merchant and as a youth Francesco devoted himself to pleasure-seeking and extravagance. While in his mid twenties he had a vision which caused him to abandon the pleasures of the flesh and devote his life to God. After a pilgrimage to Rome in 1206, he began a life of poverty. He worked on the repair of ruined churches and cared for the poor and the sick. Francesco was never ordained but as he began preaching he attracted followers whom he organized as the Friars Minor (now titled the Franciscan Order). He drew up a rule which was given papal approval in 1210. He attempted on several occasions to convert the Mohammedans in northern Africa but each of these efforts failed. Meanwhile, the order he founded had grown dramatically. Saint Francis lacked the administrative skills needed by the larger order and two of his friars were pressing for less emphasis on simplicity, humility and poverty. Saint Francis resigned as head of the order in 1220. In 1224 he received a stigmata in religious ecstasy. The scars of these wounds remained on his body until his death in 1226.

195 *San Joaquin County*

San Joaquin River— In the early 1800's when California was still under Spanish rule, the noted soldier and explorer Gabriel Moraga named the San Joaquin River or a rivulet which flows into it. He chose the name San Joaquin in honor of Saint Joachim, whom tradition honors as the father of the Virgin Mary. When the county was created in 1850 as one of California's original 27 counties, it was named for this river which flows through it.

Saint Joachim (–)— Joachim is the name traditionally given to the father of the Virgin Mary although he has been known by other names including Heli, Cleopas, Eliacim, Jonachir and Sadoc. Saint Joachim is not mentioned in the Bible but according to legend in the apocryphal Gospel of St. James, he was born in Nazareth and although he wed at an early age, he remained childless for some time. He is said to have gone to the desert to pray and fast for 40 days. There, an angel

appeared and comforted him. In time, the long awaited child was born and this child, the Virgin Mary, was the mother of Jesus.

196 *San Luis Obispo County*

Mision San Luis Obispo de Tolosa— In 1772 Fathers Junipero Serra and Jose Cavaller founded and named this mission. The settlement at this mission grew to become the city of San Luis Obispo and the county was also named for it. The name honors Saint Louis, Bishop of Toulouse, France.

Saint Louis (1274–1297)— Saint Louis was a son of the king of Naples and Sicily and a great-nephew of another saint, the king of France, Louis IX. He is believed to have been born in Nocera. He grew up in Provence and, as a youth, he endured seven years as hostage for his father. He was ordained, joined the Friars Minor and, while still in his early twenties, became bishop of Toulouse, France. He had served in that post but six months when death claimed him.

197 *San Mateo County*

Arroyo de San Matheo— This stream, now called San Mateo Creek, which flows into San Francisco Bay was named in 1776 by the Anza expedition in honor of Saint Matthew. Both the city of San Mateo and the county were named for this creek.

Saint Matthew (–)— An evangelist and one of the apostles of Jesus Christ, Matthew was the author of the first of the four gospels in the Bible. In this work, which he wrote for his fellow Jews in Palestine, he recorded facts about Christ's life, miracles and death. Matthew's early vocation was tax collector for the Romans and the careful arrangement of his gospel into formal divisions reflects his early fondness for numbers and order. Legend holds that he died a martyr.

198 *Santa Barbara County*

Santa Barbara Channel and Mision Santa Barbara, Virgen y Martir— In the early 1600's on December 4th, the feast day of Saint Barbara, Sebastian Vizcaino named this ocean channel and an adjoining island in her honor. The Santa Barbara Presidio (named by Father Junipero Serra) and later mission (built by Father Fermin Francisco de Lasuen and consecrated in 1786) also honored this legendary saint. When the county was created in 1850 it was named for the channel and the mission.

Saint Barbara (–)— It is not known whether Saint Barbara was a real person or merely legendary. She was allegedly born in Asia Minor about the beginning of the third century and was the only child of a rich Roman official, Dioscorum whose duties included persecution and execution of Christians. When Barbara learned of Christianity, she was baptized and determined to follow the gospels as the rule of her life. She considered chastity a sublime virtue and was a life-long virgin. Barbara abhorred her father's pagan idols and he her Christianity. When she refused to forsake her religion, Dioscorus obtained a judicial decree that she be executed and carried it out himself by beheading her.

199 *Santa Clara County*

Mision de Santa Clara de Asis— This mission was founded on January 12, 1777, with Father Tomas de la Pena officiating. The mission was named in accordance with instructions from Mexico in honor of Saint Clare of Assisi, Italy. In 1850 the county was created and named for the mission within its borders. By that time, the name Santa Clara had also been applied to a mountain, the lower portion of San Francisco Bay and to a land grant. About the time that the county was formed, the entire valley area came to be known as the Santa Clara Valley.

Saint Clare (1194–1253)— Famed as the founder or an order of nuns, Clare was born at Assisi, Italy, and was a friend and follower of Saint Francis of Assisi. After listening to Saint Francis preach in 1212, she ran away from home and entered the Benedictine convent of St. Paul near Bastia. Later, at the convent of San Damiano, which she governed as abbess for almost 40 years, she founded the order of nuns known as the Poor Clares. She lived a very austere life and required her community to subsist on day-to-day contributions. Distinguished as one of the great medieval contemplatives, Clare's influence was great and popes, cardinals and bishops frequently came to San Damiano to consult her.

200 *Santa Cruz County*

Mision la Exaltacion de la Santa Cruz— In 1769, a stream was named Santa Cruz by an expedition led by Father Junipero Serra and Gaspar de Portola. *Santa Cruz* which is Spanish for "Holy Cross" refers to the cross on which Jesus died and also to the emblem carried by many of the devout explorers of California. In 1791 a site for a mission on the banks of that creek was consecrated by Father Fermin Francisco de Lasuen, who said Mass and raised a cross there. In January 1797 the viceroy of New Spain (Mexico), the Marques de Branciforte, ordered the establishment of a pueblo near the mission. In July, 1797, the pueblo was founded and named Villa de Branciforte, in honor of the viceroy. When the county was created on February 18, 1850, as one of California's original 27 counties, it was named Branciforte but the name was changed to Santa Cruz on April 5, 1850.

201 *Shasta County*

Mount Shasta— Mount Shasta was originally within Shasta County but the county's size diminished as other counties were carved from it and Mount Shasta now lies just north of the Shasta County line. One explanation given for the origin of the mountain peak's name is that Shasta derived from a corruption of the French word *chaste* meaning essentially the same as the English word chaste. According to this theory, the name was chosen because the beautiful whiteness of the snow-capped peak reminded the explorers of chastity. A similar theory exists for the derivation of this name from the Russian word *tchastal* meaning "white." A different explanation is considered by most authorities to be more likely and it certainly is better documented. This more likely explanation holds that Shasta is the surviving version of a name given to a mountain peak in 1827 by Peter Skene Ogden in honor of a local Indian tribe. There is no doubt that Ogden named a mountain peak in this general area Mount Sastise and he wrote in his journal under the date February 14, 1827 that he chose this name on account of a local tribe of Indians. These Indians have been called by a variety of names including Sastise, Shastika and Shasta. It is possible that the mountain peak now known as Mount McLoughlin is the one that Ogden named Sastise and that today's Mount Shasta got its name second hand from Mount McLoughlin.

Shastika Indians— This tribe of Hokan stock, lived at the base of Mount Shasta and elsewhere in northern California and southern Oregon. They were sometimes called Saiwash on account of their relations with Oregon Indians of that name. The territory of the Shastika included the Klamath River from Bogus Creek down to the Scott River, the Shasta, Little Shasta, Yreka Creek, Upper Salmon and the upper part of the Rogue River. Before their tribal organization was broken up by whites, they

had one chief whose dominion, at least in times of war, was this entire territory. The chief's headquarters were in Scott Valley. The Shastikas built dams to trap fish and trained dogs for hunting. In aboriginal times these Indians numbered about 2,000 but as warfare claimed the abler fighting men, the tribe diminished in numbers. By the middle of the 20th century, only a handful of these Indians (mostly women) remained.

202 *Sierra County*

Sierra Nevada Mountains— This county straddles the northern portion of the beautiful Sierra Nevada mountain range. When the county was created in 1852, it was named for these perpetually snow-capped mountains. The mountains were named in 1776 by the Spanish explorer, Pedro Font, who borrowed the name of a mountain range in Spain. *Sierra* means "mountain" or "mountain range" and *nevada* means "covered with snow" or "white as snow."

203 *Siskiyou County*

Siskiyou Mountains— The Siskiyou mountain range runs along the border between Siskiyou County, California, and Oregon. The origin of the mountain range's name is uncertain. According to some, it was the name of local Indians. Other sources merely say that it is an Indian word whose meaning is unknown. However, two rather specific theories exist:

1. *Siskiyou* is both a Cree Indian and a Chinook Indian word meaning "a bob-tailed horse." In 1828, Archibald R. McLeod, a chief factor of the Hudson's Bay Company, lost many of his animals, including a noted bob-tailed race-horse due to a snowstorm he encountered while crossing these mountains in a pack train. His Canadian followers named the place Siskiyou by which name the entire mountain range came to be known.

2. California State Senator Jacob R. Snyder of San Francisco had been instrumental in creating Siskiyou County when it was formed on March 22, 1852. In a speech which he delivered in the state senate on April 14, 1852, Snyder took the trouble to explain the derivation of the name. According to Snyder, in 1832 Michael La Framboise and his French trappers crossed a stream in these mountains using six rocks in the stream to walk on. They named their ford *six cailloux*, which is French for "six small stones" and

a corrupted version of that name came to be applied to the mountains.

Legislatures rarely trouble to specify origins for the names of the counties they create. While we may be grateful for Senator Snyder's effort to leave tracks concerning this county's name, there really is no evidence that his explanation is more accurate than the alternatives.

204 *Solano County*

Francisco Solano (–)— An early task of the first American state legislature of California was to divide the new state into counties. General Mariano G. Vallejo was selected to be chairman of a special committee formed to accomplish this task and it was at Vallejo's personal request that Solano County was named to honor his friend, Indian Chief Francisco Solano. He was chief of the Suisun and Soscol Indians in the mid 1800's and he ruled most of the area and tribes between Petaluma Creek and the Sacramento River. Chief Solano, six feet, seven inches in height, whose long black hair hung to his waist, was originally named Sem Yeto. He became a friend of the Whites and was converted to Christianity. He was given the name Solano when he was baptized by Padre Altimira at Mision San Francisco Solano, a mission that had been founded by Padre Altimira. (The mission had been named for Saint Francis Solano, a noted 16th century missionary in Peru, South America.) Chief Solano was instrumental in preventing an Indian attack on this mission. In 1835 General Vallejo defeated Solano's forces in a battle but a friendship subsequently developed between the two men and Solano was a frequent guest at Vallejo's home in Sonoma, California.

205 *Sonoma County*

Town of Sonoma, California and Sonoma Mission— Sonoma County was created in 1850 as one of California's original 27 counties. It was named for the town of Sonoma, which Mariano G. Vallejo founded in 1835, and for the name commonly used for the mission. Sonoma derived from the name given by the Spaniards to a local Indian tribe and one of its chiefs, who was baptized and named Sonoma in 1824 by Padre Jose Actimira. Theories concerning the origin of the name of these Indians include:

1. *Sonoma* is an Indian word meaning "valley of the moon." The name was applied because the shape of the Sonoma Valley reminded the Indians of the moon. Jack London, who had a ranch in the

valley, wrote about it in *The Valley of the Moon* (1913).

2. The name *Sonoma* derived from the Indian word *sono* meaning "nose."

3. *Tsonoma* derives from the Indian word *tso* for "earth" or "ground" and *noma* meaning "village." Many nearby Indian villages had names ending in tsonoma.

206 *Stanislaus County*

Stanislaus River— The Stanislaus River rises in the Sierra Nevada Mountains in three branches that join about 60 miles northeast of Modesto, California. Thirteen miles west of that city the river joins the San Joaquin River. In 1829 General Mariano G. Vallejo led an expedition which quelled renegade Indians led by Estanislao. The Indians were defeated along the banks of the *Rio de los Laquisimes* and that river came to be known by the name of the Indian leader who fought so bravely there. When the county was created in 1854 it was named for the river which forms part of its dividing line from San Joaquin County. The name Merced was originally proposed for this county but that name was not adopted for this county, although it was later used for a county created in 1855.

Estanislao (–)— The Indian, Estanislao, was one of Father Narciso Duran's talented musicians whose Christian name probably honored one of the two Polish saints, Stanislas Kostka or Stanislas Cracow. He was educated at Mision San Jose but ran away from there in 1827 or 1828 probably as a result of anti-religious sentiment repeatedly expressed to the mission Indians by Governor Echeandia and other Mexican civil authorities. Estanislao became a leader of other escaped neophyte Indians. These bandits harassed the inhabitants of settlements and missions, stealing cattle, looting and killing. It was feared that they were planning a general uprising against the mission system and military expeditions were launched against them including two led by General Mariano G. Vallejo in 1829. Vallejo's first expedition accomplished nothing but in the second one he defeated the Indians in a battle fought at the Rio de los Laquisimes. Many Indians were killed, women as well as warriors, but Estanislao escaped the slaughter and surrendered to Father Duran at Mision San Jose.

207 *Sutter County*

John A. Sutter (1803–1880)— A native of Baden, Sutter's name was originally rendered as Johann A. Suter. He moved as a youth to Switzerland and served in the Swiss army. He immigrated to the United States in 1834 and settled in California in 1839 where he became a Mexican citizen. Governor Juan Bautista Alvarado gave him an enormous land grant covering more than 48,000 acres at what is now the city of Sacramento. Sutter established a kind of barony there which he named Nueva Helvetia. Sutter, who now called himself general, rendered military aid to competing Mexican politicians but later supported the Americans in their conquest of California. Sutter formed a partnership with James W. Marshall to build a sawmill on Sutter's American River land. Marshall's discovery of gold there in January, 1848, marked the beginning of the California gold rush and the financial ruin of Sutter whose workers deserted him to search for gold. Sutter was a delegate to the 1849 convention that wrote the constitution of the state of California. He died in poverty in Pennsylvania in 1880. Sutter County was created in 1850 as one of California's original counties.

208 *Tehama County*

Town of Tehama, California— The town of Tehama was settled between 1845 and 1849. When the county was created in 1856, it was named for the town which at that time was its county seat. By one account, the town of Tehama was first named by Whites who derived the name from the Mexican word for "shingles" (*tejamanil* or *tajamanil*) on account of the shingled roofs on many of the early houses at Tehama. This Mexican word was derived from the Aztec Indian words for "cleft thing" or "split thing." However, most authorities believe that *tehama* was a California Indian place name for a village or meeting place which probably stood on the west side of the Sacramento River at or near the present town of Tehama. The meaning of this Indian word is uncertain but there are some plausible theories, some of which may not be contradictory:

1. "High water" or "low land." In either case, a location subject to flooding.

2. "Salmon" and also a place where the Indians went to catch salmon.

3. The Indians' word for the specific shallow place where they forded the river.

4. "Plains" or "prairie."

Less plausible explanations have been mentioned, including (1) A word of Hawaiian origin and (2) a word of Arabian origin.

209 *Trinity County*

Trinity River— When this county was created in 1850 as one of California's original 27 counties, it was named for the Trinity River. The Trinity River branches from the Klamath River about 25 miles east of the Pacific Ocean and about 25 miles north of Eureka, California. From there, it runs east about 75 miles to feed Lewiston Lake and Clair Engle Lake, near the Trinity County town of Lewiston. The Trinity River was named in 1845 by Pierson B. Reading in the mistaken belief that it flowed into Trinidad Bay. ("Trinity" in Spanish is *trinidad*.) The bay had been named much earlier, on Trinity Sunday in 1775, by the Spanish explorer, Juan Francisco de la Bodega y Cuadra. It was after the first great Pentecost that the Christian doctrine of the Trinity was proclaimed to the world and Trinity Sunday is celebrated on the first Sunday after Pentecost. The dogma of the Trinity is a central doctrine of orthodox Christian faith. It asserts that God is one in essence but three in persons; i.e., Father, Son (Jesus Christ) and Holy Spirit.

210 *Tulare County*

Tule marshlands of the region— The word "tule" refers to a form of plant life and a place where these plants grow is known as a "tular" or "tulare." These words are Mexican in origin. The type of vegetation to which they refer is not uniform on the North American continent. These words, which derive from the Aztec Indian *tullin* or *tollin*, are found frequently in California place names. In California, they refer to the cattail, bulrush or any similar reed. Before its reclamation, much of the San Joaquin Valley was reedy marshland. When Commandante Fages saw the area in 1772, he described it as "a labyrinth of lakes and tulares." Numerous Spanish soldiers and explorers who followed Fages mentioned the tules and tulares in reference to the region. By the time the county was created in 1852, the term tulare was generally restricted to the lower portion of the San Joaquin Valley in and around Tulare County.

211 *Tuolumne County*

Tuolumne Indians— *Tuolumne* is a collective name for several Indian tribes who lived along California's Stanislaus and Tuolumne Rivers. In 1806 Padre Pedro Munoz accompanied Gabriel Moraga in an expedition through that region. In his diary, Munoz commented that a village of these Indians was built on steep precipices, inaccessible on account of their rough rocks and that the Indians lived in cellars or caves. The Indian suffix *umne* means "people" or "tribe" while *tuol* is the surviving version of the Indians' word for "a village of stone caves." Tuolumne County was created in 1850 as one of California's original 27 counties. The name originally proposed for this county was Oro. The name Tuolumne was adopted at the suggestion of Benjamin S. Lippincott, one of the members of the state senate's committee on county boundaries.

212 *Ventura County*

City of Ventura, California and Mision San Buenaventura— The county was created in 1872. The name chosen for the county was a shortened version of the name of both the mission and the city, its county seat. Mision San Buenaventura was founded by Padre Junipero Serra. He dedicated the mission in 1782 and named it for Saint Bonaventure in accordance with instructions from Inspector General Jose de Galvez, who authorized the mission's founding. The town which grew up around the mission also took the name San Buenaventura and that was still the name used for the town (now Ventura) at the time that the county was created. It was not until 1891 that, in response to petitions from residents, the U.S. post office department changed the name of the post office to Ventura and the Southern Pacific didn't change the name of its station there to the shortened version until 1900.

Saint Bonaventure (1221–1274)— Bonaventure was born in Bagnorea, Italy, clothed in the order of the Friars Minor (now titled the Franciscan Order) and studied at the University of Paris where he later taught theology. He was a recognized scholar in theology and philosophy and authored numerous respected works in those fields. In 1257 Saint Bonaventure and Saint Thomas Aquinas received the degree of doctor of theology together. In that same year Bonaventure was chosen to be minister general of the Friars Minor. In 1260 he produced a set of constitutions on rule which had a permanent effect on Franciscan life. He governed his order for 17 years and is sometimes called its second founder. Bonaventure preferred the humble life to power and prestige. In 1265 Pope Clement IV nominated Bonaventure to be archbishop of York but Bonaventure declined. In 1273 he was offered the post of cardinal-bishop of Albano in terms that made clear that refusal was not an option.

Bonaventure accepted this promotion. In the final weeks of his life, Bonaventure served as a central figure in important meetings held to accomplish reunion with the Greek Church. After Bonaventure's conferences with the Greek delegates, reunion with Rome was agreed upon. In celebration, the pope sang Mass and the Epistle, Gospel and Creed were sung first in Latin and then in Greek. Saint Bonaventure then preached. In the midst of this seeming triumph, Bonaventure died and shortly afterward the Greeks repudiated the reconciliation.

213 *Yolo County*

Yolo Indians— The Yolo Indians were a Patwin tribe who lived in marshy areas of this region, west of the Sacramento River. By the late 1800's there were only about 45 of these Indians living in Yolo County. Yolo is believed to be a corruption of an Indian word *yoloy* or *yodoi* which meant "a place abounding with rushes." Another theory is that the name derived from that of an Indian chief whose name was first applied to a village and then to the Indians who lived there. Fremont was originally proposed as the name for this county but that name was never adopted. The name that was officially adopted on February 18, 1850, was Yola County but the name has since been spelled Yolo.

214 *Yuba County*

Yuba River— The confluence of the Yuba River and the Feather River is about 25 miles east of Yuba City, California. The river itself consists of numerous branches. Since 1950 the three main streams have been officially designated as the North, Middle and South Yuba Rivers. The name Yubu was given to the Yuba River about 1842 by John A. Sutter for some 180 Maidu Indians and their village which was located near the confluence of the Yuba and Feather Rivers. *Yuba* is the surviving version of the name that these Indians gave to themselves and to their village. Early White settlers first spelled the name yubu, as Sutter did, and also yupu and jubu. When the county was created in 1850 it was named for the river which bisects it.

REFERENCES

Aiton, Arthur Scott. *Antonio de Mendoza: First Viceroy of New Spain*. Durham, North Carolina, Duke University Press, 1927.

Bancroft, Hubert Howe. *History of California*. San Francisco, History Company, 1890.

Benedict, John D. *Muskogee & Northeastern Oklahoma*. Chicago, S. J. Clarke Publishing Co., 1922.

Benedictine Monks of St. Augustine's Abbey, Ramsgate. *The Book of Saints*. New York, Thomas Y. Crowell Company, 1966.

Bowman, J. N. "The Meaning of the Name 'Sonoma.'" *California Folklore*, Vol. 5, No. 3. Berkeley: July, 1946.

Bowman, J. N. *Western Folklore*, Vol. 6, No. 1. Berkeley: January, 1947.

California Blue Book or State Register: 1909. Sacramento, State Printing Office, 1909.

California Yearbook: Bicentennial Edition. La Verne, California, California Almanac Co., 1975.

The Catholic Encyclopedia. New York, Robert Appleton Company, 1908.

Corning, Howard McKinley. *Dictionary of Oregon History*. Portland, Binfords & Mort, 1956.

Coy, Owen C. *California County Boundaries*. Fresno, California, Valley Publishers, 1973.

Coy, Owen C. *The Genesis of California Counties*. Berkeley, California Historical Survey Commission, 1923.

Davis, Win J. *An Illustrated History of Sacramento County, California*. Chicago, Lewis Publishing Co., 1890.

Delaney, John J., & James Edward Tobin. *Dictionary of Catholic Biography*. Garden City, New York, Doubleday & Company, Inc., 1961.

Du Gard, Rene C., & Dominique C. Western. *The Handbook of French Place Names in the U.S.A.* Editions des Deux Mondes, 1977.

Eckblom, Frank R. *Mother Lode Action Guide*. Valley Springs, California, 1979.

Eldredge, Zoeth Skinner. *History of California*. New York, Century History Company, 1915.

Elias, Sol P. *Stories of Stanislaus*. Modesto, California, 1924.

Farmer, David Hugh. *The Oxford Dictionary of Saints*. Oxford, England, Clarendon Press, 1978.

Farquhar, Francis P. "Naming America's Mountains: The Cascades." *American Alpine Journal*, Vol. 12, No. 34. New York: 1960.

Fink, Augusta. *Monterey County: The Dramatic Story of Its Past*. Fresno, Valley Publishers, 1978.

Goodwin, Cardinal. *The Establishment of State Government in California*. New York, Macmillan Co., 1914.

Gudde, Erwin G. "The Buttes of California." *Western Folklore*, Vol. 6, No. 3. Berkeley: July, 1947.

Gudde, Erwin G. *California Place Names.* Berkeley, University of California Press, 1965.

Gudde, Erwin G. "Place Names in the San Francisco Bay Counties." *State of California, Department of Natural Resources, Division of Mines Bulletin*, Bulletin No. 154. San Francisco: December, 1951.

Gudde, Erwin G. *Sutter's Own Story.* New York, G. P. Putnam's Sons, 1936.

Hart, James D. *A Companion to California.* New York, Oxford University Press, 1978.

Hisken, Clara & Dorothy H. Huggins. "Tehama: Indian or Aztec?" *Western Folklore*, Vol. 8, No. 1. Berkeley: January, 1949.

Hodge, Frederick W. *Handbook of American Indians North of Mexico.* Totowa, New Jersey, Rowman & Littlefield, 1975.

Huggins, Dorothy M. "The Pursuit of an Indian Chief." *California Folklore Quarterly*, Vol. 4, No 2. Berkeley: April, 1945.

Hunt, Rockwell D. *California & Californians.* Chicago, Lewis Publishing Company, 1932.

Karpenstein, Katherine. "Names & Places: Mono Lake." *California Folklore Quarterly*, Vol. 4, No 1. Berkeley: January, 1945.

Kroeber, A. L. "California Place Names of Indian Origin." *University of California Publications in American Archeology & Ethnology*, Vol. 12, No. 2. Berkeley: June 15, 1916.

Kroeber, A. L. *Handbook of the Indians of California.* Berkeley, California Book Co., Ltd., 1953.

Leland, J. A. C. "Some Eastern Indian Place Names in California." *California Folklore Quarterly*, Vol. 4, No 4. Berkeley: October, 1945.

McArthur, Lewis A. *Oregon Geographic Names.* Binfords & Mort, 1944.

McGroarty, John S. *California: Its History & Romance.* Los Angeles, Grafton Publishing Co., 1911.

McNary, Laura Kelly. *California Spanish & Indian Place Names.* Los Angeles, Wetzel Publishing Co., Inc., 1931.

Marinacci, Barbara & Rudy Marinacci. *California's Spanish Place-Names.* San Rafael, California, Presidio Press, 1980.

Mason, Jesse D. *History of Amador County, California.* Oakland, Thompson & West, 1881.

Mason, Jesse D. *History of Santa Barbara County, California.* Oakland, Thompson & West, 1883.

Merritt, Frank Clinton. *History of Alameda County, California.* Chicago, S. J. Clarke Publishing Co., 1928.

Mills, James. "San Diego: Where California Began." *San Diego Historical Society Quarterly*, Vol. 6, No. 1. San Diego: January, 1960.

Moreno, H. M. *Moreno's Dictionary of Spanish-Named California Cities & Towns.* San Luis Obispo, California, 1916.

National Society of Colonial Dames of America. *Counties & Courthouses of California.* 1964.

New Catholic Encyclopedia. New York, McGraw-Hill Book Company, 1967.

Northrop, Marie E. *Spanish-Mexican Families of Early California: 1769–1850.* New Orleans, Polyanthos, Inc., 1976.

Official Earth Science Student Participation Booklet of the Indians of California. Detroit, Michigan, Hearne Brothers.

Palmer, Lyman L. *History of Mendocino County, California.* San Francisco, Alley Bowen & Co., 1880.

Palmer, Lyman L. *History of Napa & Lake Counties, California.* San Francisco, Slocum, Bowen & Co., 1881.

Powers, Laura Bride. *Old Monterey.* San Francisco, San Carlos Press, 1934.

Powers, Stephen. *Tribes of California.* Berkeley, University of California Press, 1976.

Rockwell, D. Hunt, & Nellie Van de Grift Sanchez. *A Short History of California.* New York, Thomas Y. Crowell Company, 1929.

Rogers, Justus H. *Colusa County: Its History & Resources.* Orland, California, 1891.

Sanchez, Nellie Van de Grift. *Spanish & Indian Place Names of California.* San Francisco, A. M. Robertson, 1914.

Sioli, Paolo. *Historical Souvenir of El Dorado County, California.* Oakland, California, 1883.

Southworth, John R. *Santa Barbara & Montecito.* Santa Barbara, Orena Studios, 1920.

Stone, Adolf. *California Almanac & State Fact Book: 1955–1956.* Maywood, California, California Almanac Company, 1955.

Taylor, Paul S. "Foundations of California Rural Society." *California Historical Society Quarterly*, Vol. 24, No. 3. San Francisco: September, 1945.

Teiser, Ruth. *Historic Spots in California.* Stanford, California, Stanford University Press, 1948.

Thrapp, Dan L. *Encyclopedia of Frontier Biography.* Lincoln, University of Nebraska Press, 1988.

Thurston, Herbert S. J., & Donald Attwater. *Butler's Lives of the Saints.* New York, P. J. Kenedy Sons, 1956.

Torchiana, H. A. van Coenen. *Story of the Mission Santa Cruz.* San Francisco, Paul Elder & Company, 1933.

Vogel, Virgil J. *Indian Place Names in Illinois.* Illinois State Historical Society, 1963.

Wagner, Henry R. "Spanish Voyages to the Northwest Coast in the Sixteenth Century." *California Historical Society Quarterly*, Vol. 8., No. 1. San Francisco: March, 1929.

Waldman, Harry, et al. *Dictionary of Indians of North America.* St. Clair Shores, Michigan, Scholarly Press, Inc., 1978.

Watkins, Rolin C. *History of Monterey & Santa Cruz Counties, California.* Chicago, S. J. Clarke Publishing Co., 1925.

Colorado

(63 counties)

215 *Adams County*

Alva Adams (1850–1922) — Adams was a native of Wisconsin who moved to Colorado with his family in 1871. A Democrat, Adams was elected to the first legislature of the state of Colorado and served two terms as governor. He left office shortly before this county was created in 1902. In 1904 he again ran for governor and was elected but an election dispute was decided against him by an overwhelmingly Republican legislature. He was removed from office after serving only two months. He later served as a member of the Democratic national committee.

216 *Alamosa County*

Alamosa Creek and the town of Alamosa, Colorado—Alamosa is a Spanish word meaning "shaded with cottonwoods." Early Spanish pioneers gave this name to the creek here whose banks held numerous cottonwoods. The name was later applied to the town which is the county seat of Alamosa County. The name was chosen for the town because the original town site was laid out along Alamosa Creek about 15 miles south of its present location. However, flooding of Alamosa Creek prompted a decision to build the town away from the creek. The name of the creek and town were given to the county when it was formed in 1913.

217 *Arapahoe County*

Arapaho Indians—The Arapaho Indians were an important buffalo-hunting, plains tribe of the Algonquian family who were closely associated with the Cheyenne Indians and had a permanent alliance with them. The origin of the name *Arapaho* is uncertain. Possibly it derived from the Pawnee Indians' term for "trader," *tirapihu* or *larapihu*. By the treaty of Medicine Lodge in 1867, the southern Arapaho, together with the southern Cheyenne, were placed on an Indian reservation in Oklahoma. When that reservation was opened to White settlement in 1892, the Indians were granted the rights of American citizenship. Arapahoe County was originally part of Kansas territory. At that time the county covered much of eastern Colorado, an area inhabited by the Arapaho.

218 *Archuleta County*

Uncertain—This county was named for Antonio D. Archuleta or for his father, Jose M. Archuleta, or for both of them.

Antonio D. Archuleta (1855–)—Antonio D. Archuleta was a member of the first legislature of the newly admitted state of Colorado. He later served in the state senate and was a member of that body in 1885 when Conejos County was divided to form Archuleta County. He was a prominent rancher, farmer and merchant in Archuleta County.

Jose M. Archuleta (–)—Jose M. Archuleta was head of one of the oldest and wealthiest Spanish families in this area.

Antonio D. Archuleta introduced the bill in the legislature to create this new county. It was his intention to name the new county Pagosa but his friends in the senate objected and urged adoption of Archuleta as the county name. Whether this was in compliment to the senator, his father, or both of them is not now known and may even have been unclear at the time the county was born.

219 *Baca County*

The Baca family—This county was established in 1889 and named in honor of the Baca family of Trinidad, Colorado. The name was suggested by State Senator Casimero Barela of Trinidad to honor the pioneer Spanish family of this region. Felipe Baca, a pioneer rancher and freighter, provided land for the town site of Trinidad. The Baca house in Trinidad was taken over in 1960 by the State Historical Society of Colorado to be operated as a regional museum.

220 *Bent County*

Bent's Forts and the Bent brothers—This county was named for the four Bent Brothers and for the forts that these mountain men built in southeastern Colorado between 1826 and 1853. While four Bent brothers were involved, Charles and William played the key roles and only William survived to see the last fort.

Bent's Forts—Each of the three forts that the Bent brothers built in southeastern Colorado was erected as a trading post capable of withstanding attack. The first fort was at the foot of the Rocky Mountains while the second, also known as Old Fort, was at the mouth of the Purgatoire River. The last Bent's Fort was built in 1853 on the north bank of the Arkansas River near Las Animas, Colorado. This last fort was more elaborate than the others and was able to shelter a large number of trappers, hunters and scouts.

Charles Bent (1799–1847)—A native of Charleston, Virginia (now West Virginia), Charles was involved in fur trading with his brother, William, along the Missouri River and in the Rocky Mountains. In 1830 Charles formed, with Ceran St. Vrain, the fur trading firm of Bent, St. Vrain and Company. The firm was very successful and Bent's Fort was built to handle the Indian trade. During the 1830's Charles moved to New Mexico. General Stephen W. Kearney appointed Charles as the first American civilian governor of New Mexico. During the Taos rebellion of 1847 Charles was killed and scalped.

George Bent (1814–1847)—A native of St. Louis, George was a partner in the Bent-St. Vrain venture. He headed construction of Fort St. Vrain on the South Platte River. In 1847 he died of fever at Bent's Fort.

Robert Bent (1816–1841)—Robert was born in St. Louis, spent the years from 1832 until his death in the West, and, on some occasions, was placed in charge of Bent's Fort. He was killed by Indians.

William Bent (1809–1869)—William, also a native of St. Louis, played the leading role at the Bent's Forts as fur trader, merchant and Indian agent. He was friendly with the Indians and had at least two Indian wives. When both Charles Bent and Ceran St. Vrain moved to New Mexico, William assumed management of the fort and its extensive trading operations. In 1852 he negotiated to sell Bent's Fort (Old Fort) to the federal government. Infuriated by the low price they offered, Bent personally dynamited the fort in disgust. He then built and managed the final Bent's Fort. He died a wealthy man.

221 *Boulder County*

City of Boulder, Colorado, and Boulder Creek—Boulder Creek and the unincorporated town of Boulder City, Colorado, were named for the numerous rocks and boulders here at the foot of the Red Rocks. When the county was formed in 1861, it was named for the creek and for Boulder City, which is now the city of Boulder, Colorado, its county seat.

222 *Chaffee County*

Jerome B. Chaffee (1825–1886)—A native of New York, Chaffee moved to the gold region of Colorado in 1860. His mining investments were enormously successful and by 1865 he was a wealthy man. He served in the lower house of Colorado's territorial legislature and became speaker of that body in 1864. Later, as territorial delegate to the U.S. Congress, he played a key role in securing Colorado's admission to statehood. The Colorado legislature elected Chaffee as one of the new state's first United States senators. This county was created out of the southern portion of Lake County in 1879, the year that Chaffee retired from the U.S. Senate. At first, the northern portion of the old Lake County was named Carbonate County with the southern portion retaining the name Lake County. The northern people objected, wanting to retain the Lake County name so two days later the legislature renamed the north Lake County and the south Chaffee County.

223 *Cheyenne County*

Cheyenne Indians— The Cheyenne Indians were an important nomadic, hunting tribe who were closely associated with the Arapaho Indians and had a permanent alliance with them. At the time of early contact with Whites, the southern Cheyenne lived in southern Colorado. The origin of their name in uncertain. Possibilities include:

1. A word of the Dakota (Sioux) Indians' meaning "people of alien speech" or "aliens."

2. "Scarred arms" on account of a practice of male Cheyennes of scarring their left arms.

The Cheyenne were engaged in almost constant warfare with neighboring tribes and with Whites. Following slaughter of their women and children by the U.S. army at Ash Hollow and Sand Creek, the northern Cheyenne participated in the rout of General George Custer's forces at Little Big Horn. But the Whites eventually subdued the Cheyenne and both northern and southern branches were resettled in Indian territory (Oklahoma). By the 1960's there were about 3,000 Cheyenne Indians living on reservations in the United States.

224 *Clear Creek County*

Clear Creek— Clear Creek County was named for the stream which crosses it. With a width that varies from a few hundred feet to more than one half mile, this tributary of the South Platte River forms a valley that is one of the most important features of the county. This creek was originally called Vasquez Fork in honor of Louis Vasquez, but by the time this county was formed in 1861, the creek was known as Clear Creek. The waters of this creek were said to be almost transparent then. However, the creek is no longer clear.

225 *Conejos County*

Conejos River and the town of Conejos, Colorado— This county was one of the original 17 counties of Colorado territory that were created effective November 1, 1861. Under that law, this county's name was Guadaloupe County. However, Representative Garcia introduced a bill to change the name to Conejos County and that bill was adopted and signed into law by the governor on November 6, 1861. Conejos had long been the name of the principal river in this county and it was also the name of the town which became the county seat of Conejos County. *Conejos* is the Spanish word for "rabbits" or "hares" which were abundant in the Conejos River area when it was named by Spanish explorers.

226 *Costilla County*

Costilla River and the town of Costilla, New Mexico— The Costilla River here was named by early Spanish explorers and the town of Costilla was named for the river. When the county was formed in 1861, it was named for the river and the town. The town of Costilla is on the Colorado–New Mexico border. The town, formerly in Costilla County, Colorado, is now in Taos County, New Mexico, the present boundary line having been fixed by the United States supreme court on January 26, 1925. *Costilla* is a Spanish word meaning "rib." The Spaniards who named the river may have thought it resembled a long, curved rib.

227 *Crowley County*

John H. Crowley (1849–)— A native of Kentucky, Crowley resided in several states working primarily in the railroad industry. Crowley first moved to Colorado in 1878, lived briefly in Nebraska and Missouri and then settled in Colorado where he became one of the state's leading fruit growers. In 1892 he was elected to the state house of representatives. He served in that body 1893-1894 and again 1897-1898. He was appointed by the governor in 1899 to a six year term on the state board of horticulture. John H. Crowley represented Otero County in the state senate in 1911 when Crowley County was created out of the northern portion of Otero County.

228 *Custer County*

George A. Custer (1839–1876)— This county was created in 1877 and named for the army officer who had perished in his famous "last stand" less than 12 months earlier. Custer was born in Ohio and educated at West Point. As a Union officer in the Civil War his successes led to promotion to the rank of general before his 24th birthday. Following that war, he served in the U.S. cavalry fighting Indians in the West. The flamboyance which had served Custer so well in the Civil War led to his downfall at Little Big Horn. In that battle Custer attacked Indians who greatly outnumbered his forces. Custer and all of his men were slain.

229 *Delta County*

City of Delta, Colorado— This county was created in 1883 and named for the city of Delta, which is its county seat. The city had been named for its location on the delta at the junction of the Gunnison and Uncompahgre Rivers. *Delta* is the fourth letter of the Greek alphabet. The triangular shape of this Greek character accounts for our English word delta being used to describe triangular alluvial deposits at the mouths of the rivers.

230 *Denver County*

City of Denver, Colorado— When the city of Denver was created it was located within Kansas territory and the city was named for James W. Denver, who had recently been governor of Kansas territory.

James W. Denver (1817–1892)— A native of Virginia, Denver served as a captain in the Mexican War. In 1850 he moved to California where he was a state senator. He then served as California's secretary of state and represented California for one term in the U.S. Congress before being appointed commissioner of Indian affairs by President Buchanan. A few months later, he was appointed by the president as secretary of strife-torn Kansas territory. Early in 1858 Buchanan promoted Denver to be governor of Kansas territory. During the Civil War, Denver served as a brigadier-general in the Union army.

231 *Dolores County*

Dolores River— The Dolores River, some 250 miles long, rises in the La Plata mountains of Colorado, traverses the western portion of Dolores County and empties into the Colorado River in Utah. *Dolores* is the Spanish word for "sorrow" or "grief." The original Spanish name for this river was *Rio de Nuestra Senora de los Dolores* meaning "River of Our Lady of Sorrows." In 1776 an exploring party led by Franciscan priests, Francisco A. Dominguez and Silvestre Velez de Escalante lost one of their members, a Black man, who drowned in the river here. Escalante's diary explains that the river was named on account of the sorrow of this man's death.

232 *Douglas County*

Stephen A. Douglas (1813–1861)— Barely five feet tall, the "Little Giant" is most remembered as a political opponent of Abraham Lincoln. Douglas was born in Vermont and moved to Illinois where he enjoyed rapid political success. He served on the state supreme court, in the state legislature and as secretary of state. Following two terms in the U.S. House of

Representatives, Douglas was elected to the U.S. Senate. In that body Douglas took courageous positions on the slavery issue which first outraged abolitionist sentiment and later infuriated the South. In 1858 Douglas ran for reelection to the U.S. Senate against Abraham Lincoln. Following the famous Lincoln-Douglas debates, the Republicans won the popular election but the state legislature reelected Douglas to the senate. Lincoln and Douglas were rivals again in 1860 for the presidency. Following Lincoln's election and the start of the Civil War, Douglas gave the president his active support. Douglas County was created in November, 1861, and named for this American statesman who died five months earlier.

233 *Eagle County*

Eagle River— The Eagle River is a tributary of the Colorado River. The Eagle rises in the mountains north of Leadville, Colorado, traverses Eagle County from east to west and then joins the Colorado in the western part of the county. The origin of the river's name is uncertain. These theories have been mentioned:

1. Derived from the name of a Ute Indian chief.

2. Named for the powerful birds of prey that nested in the mountains here. The golden or rocky mountain eagles were more numerous in this area than were bald eagles.

3. So named because the Eagle River was thought to have as many tributaries as there are feathers in an eagle's tail.

234 *El Paso County*

Ute Pass— El Paso is Spanish for "the pass." The term referred to Ute Pass, north of Pike's Peak and west of Colorado Springs in Teller County. The Ute Indians used this pass to get from South Park to the plains and at the time the county was named, this pass was the only route through the mountains here. At the time that this county was created and named, an attempt was made to name it Scudder County in honor of Representative Edwin Scudder of Colorado's territorial house of representatives. Representative Scudder voted against this proposal to honor him and the proposed amendment was defeated.

235 *Elbert County*

Samuel H. Elbert (1833–1899)— Elbert, a native of Ohio, was a delegate from Nebraska to the Republican national convention which, in 1860, nominated Abraham Lincoln for president. Elbert took an active part in that presidential campaign and in 1862 President Lincoln appointed him secretary of Colorado territory. He later served in Colorado's territorial legislature and was appointed governor of the territory in 1873 by President Grant. After Colorado's admission to statehood, Elbert served on the state supreme court and was, for a time, chief justice. This county was created in 1874 while Elbert was governor of Colorado territory.

236 *Fremont County*

John C. Frémont (1813–1890)— Born in Georgia, Frémont engaged in survey work in wilderness areas of the South and then assisted Joseph N. Nicollet in explorations of Iowa, Dakota and Minnesota. Frémont then performed his greatest service by leading five explorations to the far West. Portions of this vast domain had previously been explored. However, it was Frémont who carefully mapped the areas traveled and prepared notes of his observations. Frémont played a role in winning California from Mexico, served very briefly as a U.S. senator and, in 1856, ran as the Republican party's first presidential candidate. He later served as a Union general in the Civil War and as governor of Arizona territory. He was ineffective in both of these positions. Frémont's travels to the West took him through portions of Colorado several times.

237 *Garfield County*

James A. Garfield (1831–1881)— A native of Ohio, Garfield served in the Ohio senate before becoming a Union officer in the Civil War. He performed ably and rapidly rose to the rank of general. In 1863 Garfield resigned his commission to enter the U.S. House of Representatives where he served until 1880. During Reconstruction Garfield favored harsh treatment of the defeated South. In January, 1880, he was elected to the U.S. Senate but never served in that body. Instead, he was nominated and elected president of the United States, his nomination by the Republican party coming as a compromise on the 36th ballot. Garfield was fatally wounded by an assassin's bullet just four months after beginning his term as president. Garfield County was created in 1883, less than two years after the martyred president died.

238 *Gilpin County*

William Gilpin (1815–1894)— Gilpin attended West Point but left without completing his studies. Nevertheless, much of his career was in the military. He participated in the Seminole Indian Wars in Florida, was a member of John C. Frémont's 1843 expedition to the far West and served in the Mexican War. He next helped protect the Santa Fe trail from Indians, serving with the rank of lieutenant-colonel. Gilpin served as a bodyguard to President-elect Abraham Lincoln, who rewarded Gilpin by appointing him the first governor of Colorado territory. Lincoln became unhappy with Gilpin's performance and dismissed him after less than one year in office. Gilpin County was created in 1861 while Gilpin was serving this brief term as territorial governor.

239 *Grand County*

Grand Lake and Colorado River— The Colorado River, one of North America's greatest rivers, was originally called the Grand River on account of its size. The U.S. Congress changed the name to Colorado in 1921. The river rises in Grand County, Colorado and flows some 1,400 miles toward the Gulf of California through mountains, prairies and deserts carving some of the most beautiful scenes in the world including Arizona's majestic, red Grand Canyon. *Colorado* is one of the Spanish words for "red." Grand Lake is located in Grand County, Colorado.

240 *Gunnison County*

The "Gunnison country"— In 1853 Captain John W. Gunnison of the topographical engineers of the U.S. army led an expedition through this area in search of a route for a continental railroad. The expedition's report disclosed potential mineral wealth here and the area became known as "Gunnison country." Gunnison County contains a river, river valley, national forest and town all named for Captain Gunnison.

John W. Gunnison (1812–1853)— Gunnison was a native of New Hampshire and a graduate of West Point. After early assignments against Indians in the South, he surveyed the boundary line between Michigan and Wisconsin and he surveyed Lake Michigan. Next, Lieutenant Gunnison accompanied Captain Howard Stansbury on an expedition to Utah. Promoted to captain in 1853, Gunnison led the western expedition which triggered Colorado's Gunnison place names and which resulted in the death of Gunnison and some of his men at the hands of Indians in Utah.

241 *Hinsdale County*

George A. Hinsdale (1826–1874)— A native of Vermont and the son of a U.S. Congressman from Vermont, Hinsdale came to Colorado from Nebraska where he had served in the territorial legislature. Troubled by asthma, Hinsdale, his wife and an infant son trekked to Colorado territory by ox team and wagon in search of better health. In this they were not disappointed. The Hinsdales were among the earliest residents of Pueblo, Colorado, where Hinsdale practiced law and held local political offices. In 1865 George A. Hinsdale was elected lieutenant-governor of Colorado territory and in 1868 he was elected to the territorial council. Two years later he was chosen president of that body. Hinsdale County was created and named in 1874, less than one month after George Hinsdale's death.

242 *Huerfano County*

Huerfano River— The Huerfano River is a 90 mile long tributary of the Arkansas River. The Huerfano was named for a single volcanic, cone-shaped butte on the south-bank of the river, about ten miles north of Walsenburg. *Huerfano* is the Spanish word for "orphan." Spanish explorers named the river for this impressive rock formation which stands over 200 feet tall, alone, and strangely out of place, in a gently wooded meadow. U.S. Senator Thomas H. Benton described this butte with flowery eloquence in a speech urging construction of a transcontinental railroad.

243 *Jackson County*

Andrew Jackson (1767–1845)— Jackson was born on the border of North Carolina and South Carolina. He represented Tennessee in both branches of the U.S. Congress. He gained fame and popularity for his military exploits in wars with the Indians and in the War of 1812. He was provisional military governor of Florida and from 1829 to 1837 General Jackson was president of the United States. His presidency reflected the frontier spirit of America.

244 *Jefferson County*

"Jefferson territory"— An original name for Colorado was "Jefferson territory." The residents used this name for their provisional government from late 1858 until February 28, 1861, when Colorado territory was created. "Jefferson territory," named for President Thomas Jefferson, was a creation of the residents, not of congress, and it never had any legal existence. Jefferson County was created in 1861 as one of the original 17 counties of Colorado territory.

245 *Kiowa County*

Kiowa Indians— The Kiowa Indians were nomadic, tepee-dwelling buffalo hunters who, in the mid-19th century, lived in western Kansas, southeastern Colorado and western Oklahoma. *Kiowa* in their language means "principal people." They were among the most warlike Indians of the southern plains. Although devastated by cholera in 1849 and smallpox in 1861-1862 and officially assigned to a reservation in Indian territory in 1868, portions of the tribe remained hostile for a decade. Most remaining Kiowa now live in Oklahoma.

246 *Kit Carson County*

Christopher Carson (1809–1868)— This famous frontiersman, scout and trailbreaker was born in Kentucky but moved with his parents at an early age to Missouri. For a decade, Kit Carson was a mountain man in the Rocky Mountains and then he served as a hunter for Bent's Fort in Colorado. During the early 1840's Carson was a key guide on John C. Frémont's expeditions to the West. Carson served in the Mexican War and in the Civil War. His final military rank was brevet brigadier-general.

247 *La Plata County*

La Plata River and La Plata Mountains— In 1765 and again in 1775 the Spanish explorer Rivera and his associates explored this region of Colorado and northern New Mexico in search of gold and silver. They named the La Plata River and the La Plata Mountains. *Plata* is the Spanish word for "silver" and rich silver mines here have produced great wealth. When the county was created in 1874 it was named for the river and the mountains.

248 *Lake County*

Twin Lakes— The Twin Lakes are well known features near the southern border of this county. When the county was created in 1861 as one of Colorado territory's original 17 counties, it was named for these lakes. These two small lakes now form a reservoir and resort. In 1879 this county's name was changed to Carbonate County but just two days later that name was discarded. See Chaffee County, Colorado, above.

249 *Larimer County*

William Larimer (1809–1875)— Larimer, a founder of Denver and prominent pioneer of Colorado, was born in Pennsylvania where he became prominent in business, banking and railroad affairs. Following the panic of 1857, he moved west living briefly in Nebraska and Kansas before settling in Colorado territory in 1858. He served as treasurer of the town company of Denver. At the outbreak of the Civil War Larimer was appointed colonel and he was active in securing Colorado men for the Union army. He was rewarded with the rank of general but he never saw combat. This county, one of the original 17 counties of Colorado territory, was created in 1861. The name for this county that was originally proposed and almost adopted was Laporte. By amendment, just before passage, the name Larimer was adopted. Laporte was the name of this county's first county seat.

250 *Las Animas County*

Purgatoire River— Boasting one of our nation's more colorful county names, Las Animas County was named for the Purgatoire River, which flows through it. The original Spanish name for this river was *El Rio de las Animas Perdidas en Purgatorio* meaning "The River of the Souls Lost in Purgatory." *Animas* is the Spanish word for "souls." The circumstances surrounding the naming of this river cannot be verified but a plausible case has been made for the following: Sometime during the years 1594–1596, Captain Francisco Leiva Bonilla and Juan de Humana led an expedition which explored beyond the northern limits specified by the governor. The priests refused to continue on the expedition after it violated authority. Before or after the priests departed, Bonilla and Humana quarreled and Bonilla was slain. The expedition continued under Humana but never returned. Some years later another expedition of Spanish explorers found upon the banks of the Purgatoire River, rusted arms of a large force of Spanish soldiers who had apparently been killed by Indians. Because there had been no priests with these slain men, the victims were presumed to have died without receiving the last rites of the church and their souls therefore languishing in purgatory. French trappers operating in the 1800's were responsible for the river's current name.

251 *Lincoln County*

Abraham Lincoln (1809–1865)—Lincoln was a native of Kentucky who moved to Illinois where he was a member of the state legislature. He represented Illinois in the U.S. House of Representatives and later was elected president of the United States. Lincoln's presidency coincided almost exactly with the Civil War. He guided the United States ably through that uniquely turbulent period. As president, he issued the Emancipation Proclamation which declared the freedom of slaves in all states in rebellion. He was assassinated in 1865, a few days after the Union victory in the Civil War.

252 *Logan County*

John A. Logan (1826–1886)— A native of Illinois, Logan served in the Illinois legislature and represented that state in the U.S. Congress in both the house and senate. Having served in the Mexican War as a lieutenant, Logan entered the Civil War as a colonel in the Union army and rose to the rank of major-general. In 1884 he ran for vice-president on the Republican ticket headed by James G. Blaine. Logan long associated himself with matters of veterans' relief and he conceived the idea of Memorial Day which he inaugurated on May 30, 1868. This county was created and named in 1887, shortly after Logan's death.

253 *Mesa County*

Local tablelands particularly the Grand Mesa— Our language is indebted to the Spanish for the word mesa, which we use to describe hills with large, flat tops. In Spanish, *mesa* means both "table" and "mesa" as we use it to describe an elevated plateau. These land formations are very common in the western United States but Mesa County, Colorado, is the only county in our nation named Mesa County. This Colorado county was named for the tablelands common in the area and, particularly, for the Grand Mesa, which is a national forest.

254 *Mineral County*

The mineral resources of the area— The county owes both its name and its existence to its abundant mineral resources. The county was created in 1893 soon after rich silver ores were discovered here by Nicholas C. Creede. The county seat of Mineral County was named in honor of Creede.

255 *Moffat County*

David H. Moffat (1839–1910)—Moffat, an outstanding Colorado pioneer and railroad builder, was a native of New York. He moved to Denver in 1860 where he became a successful merchant, banker and railroad builder. He also served as treasurer of Colorado territory. Moffat owned numerous mines and promoted and financed a number of railroads that played a key role in connecting Colorado and its vast mineral resources with points west of the Rocky Mountains. This county was created in 1911, one year after Moffat's death.

256 *Montezuma County*

Montezuma II (1466–1520)—Born before Columbus discovered the new world, and dead in 1520 as a result of Spanish invasion, Montezuma was the emperor of the Aztecs when the Spaniards under Hernan Cortes invaded. Montezuma II ruled an empire of more than five million inhabitants in central and southern Mexico. He waged incessant wars to conquer territory and to obtain prisoners for human sacrifice. There is no real connection between Montezuma II and his empire and this part of southwestern Colorado but the homes of ancient cliff dwellers and cave dwellers found here were mistakenly thought to be of Aztec origin. Montezuma County is only one of several local place names borrowed from the time and place of Montezuma II at Mexico City. Others include Montezuma Valley, Aztec Divide, Aztec Springs Creek, Aztec Valley and the town of Cortez, the county seat of Montezuma County.

257 *Montrose County*

City of Montrose, Colorado— This county was created in 1883 and named for the city of Montrose, its county seat. The city had been named about one year earlier by one of its two founders, Joseph Selig, for *A Legend of Montrose* (1819), a novel by the Scottish novelist, poet and historian, Sir Walter Scott. Selig was an admirer of Sir Walter Scott.

258 *Morgan County*

Fort Morgan— This county was created in 1889 and named for Fort Morgan. The fort had been established to guard the overland stage route and protect isolated ranchers from Indians. It was named in 1866 in honor of Colonel Christopher A. Morgan. Earlier names for the fort had been Junction, Camp Tyler and Camp Wardwell.

Christopher A. Morgan (–1866)—Morgan enlisted in the Union army as a private in the 39th Ohio volunteers. Displaying courage and sound judgment in combat, he rose to the rank of colonel on the staff of General Pope. Colonel Morgan served as inspector general at Saint Louis, Missouri.

The fort was renamed Fort Morgan on June 23, 1866, in honor of Colonel Morgan who died five months earlier.

259 *Otero County*

Miguel A. Otero (1829–1882) Otero was born in the village of Valencia, New Mexico when it was still part of Mexico. At the age of 24 he was elected to the New Mexico territorial legislature. He later served as delegate to the U.S. Congress from New Mexico territory and President Lincoln appointed him secretary of New Mexico territory. Otero only served in that capacity from April to September, 1861 because congress refused to confirm his appointment on account of his sympathies with the South. Following the Civil War, Otero moved to Kansas where he lived about four years before migrating to Colorado where he was instrumental in establishing commerce in new towns of eastern Colorado. He was one of the founders of La Junta, Colorado, the county seat of Otero County. Otero was chosen as the name for this county at the suggestion of State Senator Barela of Las Animas County.

260 *Ouray County*

Ouray (–1880)— Probably born about 1833 near the Colorado–New Mexico border, Ouray was chief of the Uncompahgre Ute Indian tribe and head of the confederated band of Utes. He grew up among Mexican ranchers and spoke Spanish, English and several Indian dialects. In 1862 the U.S. government appointed him interpreter at the Los Pinos reservation in Colorado. He was perhaps too friendly and cooperative with Whites and signed several treaties with them. His name appears in various forms on these treaties including Uray, Ure and Ouray. The United States reneged on many of their promises in these treaties. Ouray helped thwart actions of rebellious Utes. In appreciation for his help and friendship over the years, the U.S. granted him amnesty. The first Ouray County, Colorado, had its name changed to San Miguel County. The present Ouray County was originally, and very briefly, named Uncompahgre County but three days after passage of that law the name was changed to Ouray County and the name of the former Ouray County was changed to San Miguel County.

261 *Park County*

South Park— Park County was named for South Park which is within Park County. This vast park-like tableland area, some 10,000 feet above sea level, contains the source of the South Platte River. South Park, together with North Park, Middle Park and San Luis Park, forms a giant north-south chain of grassy plateaus enclosed by snow-capped mountains.

262 *Phillips County*

Rufus O. Phillips (1859–)— A native of Illinois Phillips moved with his father at the age of 12 to the West. Here, in both Kansas and Colorado, he engaged in ranching and teaching school. He then held a number of jobs in Las Animas, Colorado and La Junta, Colorado including clerk, postmaster and proprietor of a drug store. He then held the position of cashier in a series of banking jobs in La Junta. Mr. Phillips served as secretary of the Lincoln Land Company, a railroad subsidiary which organized a number of towns in eastern Colorado. Eastern Colorado experienced remarkable growth during the late 1880's due to favorable weather for farming, improved irrigation and the development of new railroads. The railroads' influence was in mind when this eastern Colorado county was created and named in 1889.

263 *Pitkin County*

Frederick W. Pitkin (1837–1886)— Pitkin was a native of Connecticut who practiced law in Milwaukee, Wisconsin until 1872, when he left his practice on account of poor health. He soon moved to southwestern Colorado in the hope that its high altitude and dry climate would benefit his health. Pitkin served as governor of Colorado from 1879 to 1883. As governor he successfully dealt with an uprising by Ute Indians, a strike by silver miners at Leadville and strife between two major railroads. This county was created in 1881 while Pitkin was governor.

264 *Prowers County*

John W. Prowers (1838–1884)— A native of Missouri, Prowers migrated to Colorado at the age of 18 and worked at Bent's Fort for seven years. From 1865 to 1870 he freighted government supplies from Leavenworth, Kansas to Fort Union. Prowers held political office as county commissioner, territorial legislator and state legislator but he gained his fame as a pioneer of the Arkansas Valley and one of the most successful cattlemen of that valley. His activities extended from innovative cattle breeding methods to ranching, slaughtering and shipping meat to eastern markets. He became quite wealthy. This county was established in 1889, five years after Prowers' death.

265 *Pueblo County*

City of Pueblo, Colorado— The Spanish word *pueblo* originally meant "people" but it later came to be applied to the town — dwelling Indian tribes of New Spain (Mexico). Our English word pueblo, taken from this Spanish word, means "town" or "village" of the type found in the southwestern United States and in Latin America. A cluster of adobe houses and a small circular fort were built at the site of the present city of Pueblo, Colorado in the early 1840's for trading with the Indians. This little settlement became known as Pueblo. In the winter of 1859–1860, settlers from Independence, Missouri at first called their town here Independence but the name didn't stick and Pueblo soon replaced Independence. When Pueblo County was created in 1861, it was named for the city of Pueblo, its county seat.

266 *Rio Blanco County*

White River— In 1776 an expedition by Father Francisco Escalante and his party sought to find a route from Santa Fe to California. On this journey, the first by White men through this area, these Spanish explorers discovered the White River here and named it the San Clemente River. That name did not survive and the river is now called the White River. When the county was created in 1889, it was named for the river which traverses its vast width. *Rio Blanco* is Spanish for "White River."

267 *Rio Grande County*

Rio Grande River— The Rio Grande is one of our country's important rivers, forming a large portion of the border between the United States and Mexico. The river rises just a few miles west of Rio Grande County, Colorado, in the San Juan Mountains, flows some 1885 miles through Colorado and New Mexico and along the Texas-Mexico border from El Paso until it empties into the Gulf of Mexico near Brownsville at the southern tip of Texas. *Rio* is Spanish for "river" while *grande* means "large, big, great or grand." In the United States the river is known as Rio Grande. The original Spanish name had been *Rio Grande del Norte*, *del norte* meaning "of the north." In Mexico the river is called *Rio Bravo* or *Rio Bravo del Norte*.

268 *Routt County*

John L. Routt (1826–1907)— Routt, a native of Kentucky, served as an officer in the Civil War including personal service for General Ulysses S. Grant. Following the war Routt held some political positions and in 1875 President Grant appointed Routt to be governor of Colorado territory. He was the last governor of Colorado territory and, when Colorado was admitted to the Union in 1876, he was elected to be its first state governor. This county was created in 1877 while Routt was serving as Colorado's first governor. He later served as mayor of Denver followed by a second term as governor of Colorado.

269 *Saguache County*

Saguache Creek, Saguache Lake, Saguach (Sawatch) Mountains & Saguach Pass— The name *Saguache* derives from a Ute Indian word meaning "blue earth" or "water at the blue earth." The Utes used this term to describe a large spring in which blue clay was found about 20 miles above the present town of Saguache, near Saguache Creek. An approximate rendering of the Indians' word is *saguaguachipa* but White men stumbled with that and it became saguache. The spring's name was applied to Saguache Creek (a major river in this county), Saguache Lake, the Saguach (Sawatch) Mountains and to a pass in the San Juan range. Saguache County and the town of Saguache, its county seat, were named at about the same time in the mid-1860's.

270 *San Juan County*

San Juan River, San Juan Mountains & San Juan region— *San Juan* is Spanish for "Saint John" and early Spanish explorers were responsible for this name being applied to the river, to the mountain range and to the entire vast region known as the San Juan region. The San Juan region covers an enormous area of some 10,000 square miles which extends from Colorado into Utah and New Mexico. The greater portion of this region is in New Mexico. The San Juan River is a 360 mile-long tributary of the Colorado River, that rises in Archuleta County in southwestern Colorado, in the San Juan Mountains. The San Juan flows into San Juan County, New Mexico, in that state's northwestern corner. When it reaches Farmington, in San Juan County, New Mexico, the river bends to the west and later to the northwest. The San Juan River comes very close to touching the "Four Corners," where four of our country's southwestern states meet at one point. There the river again touches Colorado, this time with just a glancing blow, before heading west into San Juan County, Utah. In San Juan County, Utah, the San Juan River has carved a deep box canyon and it is in San Juan County, Utah, that the San Juan River finally empties its waters into those of the Colorado River. T. M. Pearce has written extensively on the origin of place names in New Mexico and Pearce tells us that the river was probably named for Saint John the Baptist. Angelico Chavez wrote an article entitled "Saints' Names in New Mexico Geography," which appeared in the November, 1949 issue of *El Palacio*. In that article Chavez agrees that "the northwest county and its river,... is very likely derived from this same saint." (St. John the Baptist.) Robert Julyan is an expert on New Mexico's geographic names. Julyan is also cautious in his write-up on this subject in *The Place Names of New Mexico*, published in 1996. In that work Julyan tells us that San Juan Pueblo, a settlement in northwestern New Mexico, in Rio Arriba County (which borders on San Juan County, New Mexico) was named on July 12, 1598, by the Spanish explorer and official, Don Juan de Onate, for his personal patron saint, St. John the Baptist. However in his paragraph devoted to the nearby San Juan River, Julyan avoids stating which saint the river's name honors. Robert Julyan's research was extensive and careful. Since our experts on this subject, T. M. Pearce, Angelico Chavez and Robert Julyan are unwilling to state, without reservation, which saint the river was named for, it seems appropriate to conclude that the river was named for a saint of the Roman Catholic church, probably, but not definitely, Saint John the Baptist. There are at least 16 saints whose name starts with John the Baptist. Many of them can be ruled out because they did not become saints until after the San Juan River was named and the others are extremely obscure compared to Saint John the Baptist, who baptized Jesus. That Saint John the Baptist has long been one of the most popular saints of the Roman Catholic Church.

Saint John the Baptist (–)—John lived an austere life in the desert of Judea, southwest of Jerusalem. Clothed in garments of camel's hair and living on a diet of locusts and wild honey, John ministered to men, from Jerusalem and neighboring towns, who flocked to visit him. He demanded two rites of those who came to him: an open confession of their sins and physical baptism. Jesus Christ was among those baptized by John and John apparently came to believe, on that occasion, that Jesus was the Messiah. King Herod Antipas feared John's popularity and power and resented John's criticism of his sex life. The king imprisoned John and had him beheaded.

271 *San Miguel County*

San Miguel River & San Miguel Mountains—San Miguel is Spanish for "Saint Michael." San Miguel County was originally named Ouray County. The name was changed to San Miguel County when the present Ouray County was created in 1883. San Miguel County was named for the San Miguel River and the San Miguel Mountains here. The San Miguel River is the county's principal stream. One branch of the San Miguel River rises in the San Juan Mountains in Marshall, Ingram and Bridal Veil Basins above Telluride, the county seat. The south fork of the river rises in the San Miguel Mountains and the two branches unite about eight miles from their sources. The river then flows some 50 or 60 miles before emptying into the Dolores River. The origin of this geographic name, San Miguel, is unknown. It is likely that the name was conferred by early Spanish explorers and it is possible that they intended to honor Saint Michael, the Archangel, or one of the other many saints named Michael but the facts on this are not known.

272 *Sedgwick County*

Fort Sedgwick—Fort Sedgwick was located near the South Platte River in what is now Sedgwick County. It was established in September, 1864, as a United States army post called Camp Rankin and Post Julesburg. The name was changed in November, 1865, to honor General John Sedgwick who was killed in combat in the Civil War in May, 1864. Fort Sedgwick protected the stage line and emigrants from Indian attack until it was abandoned in May, 1871.

John Sedgwick (1813–1864)—Sedgwick, a native of Connecticut and a graduate of West Point, engaged in actions against In-

dians in the decade preceding the Mexican War. Following the Mexican War, in which he served, Sedgwick held various posts including a command in 1859–1860 at Fort Wise, Colorado. He also engaged in actions against Indians in Colorado in 1857 and 1860. Sedgwick served with distinction in the Civil War suffering wounds in combat on more than one occasion. He had risen to the rank of major-general at the time of his death at Spotsylvania.

273 *Summit County*

Its mountainous terrain—Summit County was one of the original 17 counties of Colorado territory. Originally it was a large county in the northwest corner of Colorado and the eastern boundary of the original Summit County was thought to follow the summit of the snow range. Over the years the county has given up most of its land to new counties and it is now a relatively small county west of Denver. The county's name was chosen to reflect the mountainous character of its territory and in that sense the name is still accurate for this small county perched on the Rocky Mountains.

274 *Teller County*

Henry M. Teller (1830–1914)—Teller, a native of New York, came to Colorado in 1861 and served as a major-general in the territory's militia during Indian troubles in the early 1860's. When Colorado was admitted to the Union, Teller became one of the state's first United States senators. He served in President Chester A. Arthur's cabinet as secretary of the interior for three years. Returning to the senate in 1885, he represented Colorado in that body for nearly 30 years. Teller forcefully advocated free coinage of silver. This county was created and named in 1899 while Teller was serving in the senate. A Colorado town had been established in 1879 which was also named for him but it was abandoned and became a ghost town.

275 *Washington County*

George Washington (1732–1799)—Washington was a native of Virginia. He served in Virginia's house of burgesses and became one of the colonies' leaders in opposition to British policies in America. He was a member of the first and second Continental Congresses and commander of all Continental armies in the Revolutionary War. Following victory in that war, Washington was elected to be the first president of the United States.

276 Weld County

Lewis L. Weld (1833–1865)— Weld, a native of Connecticut and a fervent abolitionist, moved to Kansas territory in the late 1850's to practice law and promote the antislavery cause. In 1860 he came to the extralegal "territory" of Jefferson and when Colorado territory was created in 1861, Weld was appointed by President Abraham Lincoln to be the secretary of the new territory. Weld had journeyed to Washington, D.C., to actively campaign for this appointment. Weld County was created and named in 1861 while Lewis L. Weld was serving as territorial secretary. He subsequently served in the Union army in the Civil War, first as captain in the seventh regiment of the United States Colored Troops. He later was promoted to major of the 41st Colored Infantry. Weld served in combat and rose to the rank of lieutenant-colonel. On the field of battle in late 1864 Weld suffered a head cold that grew steadily worse with exposure. He was removed from the field and taken to a hospital where he died on January 10, 1865. The original name of this county under the provisional "territory" of Jefferson had been St. Vrain County.

277 Yuma County

Town of Yuma, Colorado— The town of Yuma was incorporated in 1887 and named for the Yuma Switch, a nearby siding and switch of the Burlington Railroad. When the county was created in 1889, it was named for this town inside its western border. The railroad tracks were laid here in the 1880's and a number of Yuma Indians, not native to Colorado, were employed as laborers. One of these laborers died at the location of this switch and was buried there, without ceremony, at the side of the road-bed. On account of this, the switch became known as the Yuma Switch.

Yuma Indians— The Yuma family was one of the major branches of North American Indians consisting of several tribes, one of which was the Yuma tribe. The origin of their name is uncertain but possibilities include:

1. Derived from yahmayo, meaning "son of the captain" or "son of the chief." It is believed that this name was applied to these Indians through a misunderstanding by early Spanish explorers.

2. Derived from the Spanish word for "smoke," humo, because of large, smoky fires which these Indians built, presumably to summon rain.

REFERENCES

Abbott, Carl. Colorado: A History of the Centennial State. Boulder, Colorado Associated University Press, 1976.

Bancroft, Hubert Howe. History of the Pacific States of North America: Nevada, Colorado & Wyoming. San Francisco, History Company, 1890.

Black, Robert C. Island in the Rockies: The History of Grand County, Colorado to 1930. Boulder, Pruett Publishing Co., 1969.

Bright, William. Colorado Place Names. Boulder, Johnson Books, 1993.

Brothers, Mary H. "Place Names of the San Juan Basin, New Mexico." Western Folklore, Vol. 10, No. 2. Berkeley: April, 1951.

Chavez, Angelico. "Saints' Names in New Mexico Geography." El Palacio, Vol. 56, No. 11. Santa Fe: November, 1949.

Collins, George W. "Colorado's Territorial Secretaries." Colorado Magazine, Vol. 43, No. 3. Denver: Summer, 1966.

Colorado Writers' Project & State Historical Society's W.P.A. Project. "Colorado Place Names." Colorado Magazine, Vol. 17, No. 4. Denver: July, 1940.

Colorado Writers' Project & State Historical Society's W.P.A. Project. "The Names of Colorado Towns." Colorado Magazine, Vol. 17, No. 1. Denver: January, 1940.

Colorado Writers' Project & State Historical Society's W.P.A. Project. "Place Names in Colorado." Colorado Magazine, Denver:

   Vol. 17, No. 3. May, 1940.
   Vol. 17, No. 5. September, 1940.
   Vol. 17, No. 6. November, 1940.
   Vol. 18, No. 2. March, 1941.
   Vol. 18, No. 4, July, 1941.
   Vol. 18, No. 5. September, 1941.
   Vol. 18, No. 6. November, 1941.
   Vol. 19, No. 1. January, 1942.
   Vol. 19, No. 3. May, 1942.
   Vol. 19, No. 4. July, 1942.
   Vol. 19, No. 6. November, 1942.
   Vol. 20, No. 1. January, 1943.
   Vol. 20, No. 3. May, 1943.

Davidson, Levette J. "Colorado Cartography." Colorado Magazine, Denver:
   Vol. 32, No. 3. July, 1955.
   Vol. 32, No. 4, October, 1955.

Davidson, Levette J., & Olga H. Koehler. "The Naming of Colorado's Towns and Cities." American Speech, Vol. 7, No. 3. Baltimore, Maryland: February, 1932.

Dawson, J. Frank. Place Names in Colorado. Lakewood, Colorado, Jefferson Record, 1954.

Dunning, Harold M. Over Hill & Vale. Boulder, Colorado, Johnson Publishing Co., 1956.

Eichler, George R. Colorado Place Names. Boulder, Colorado, Johnson Publishing Co., 1977.

Ferril, Will C. Sketches of Colorado. Denver, Western Press Bureau Co., 1911.

Geffs, Mary L. Under Ten Flags: A History of Weld County, Colorado. Greeley, Colorado, McVey Printery, 1938.

Hafen, LeRoy R. "Colorado Cities: Their Founding and the Origin of Their Names." Colorado Magazine, Vol. 9, No. 5. Denver: September, 1932.

Hafen, LeRoy R. Colorado & Its People. New York, Lewis Historical Publishing Co., Inc., 1948.

Hafen, LeRoy R. "The Counties of Colorado: A History of Their Creation and the Origin of Their Names." Colorado Magazine, Vol. 8, No. 2. Denver: March, 1931.

Hafen, LeRoy R. "When Was Bent's Fort Built?" Colorado Magazine, Vol. 31, No. 2. Denver: April, 1954.

Hall, Frank. History of the State of Colorado. Chicago, Blakely Printing Co., 1895.

History of the Arkansas Valley, Colorado. Chicago, O.L. Baskin & Co., 1881.

Hodge, Frederick W. Handbook of American Indians North of Mexico. Totowa, New Jersey, Rowman & Littlefield, 1975.

Illustrated History of New Mexico. Chicago, Lewis Publishing Co., 1895.

Julyan, Robert. The Place Names of New Mexico. Albuquerque, University of New Mexico Press, 1996.

Krakel, Dean F. South Platte Country: A History of Old Weld County, Colorado: 1739–1900. Laramie, Wyoming, Powder River Publishers, 1954.

Lamar, Howard R. The Reader's Encyclopedia of the American West. New York, Thomas Y. Crowell Co., 1977.

Lavender, David. Bent's Fort. Garden City, New York, Doubleday Co., Inc., 1954.

Legislative, Historical & Biographical Compendium of Colorado. Denver, C.F. Coleman's Publishing House, 1887.

Leigh, Rufus W. Five Hundred Utah Place Names: Their Origin & Significance. Salt Lake City, Deseret News Press, 1961.

McHendrie. A. W. "Origin of the Name of the Purgatoire River." Colorado Magazine, Vol. 5, No. 1. Denver: February, 1928.

McLoughlin, Denis. Wild & Woolly: An Encyclopedia of the Old West. Garden City, New York, Doubleday & Co., Inc., 1975.

Macy, Guy E. "Organization & Early Development of Pueblo County." Colorado Magazine, Vol. 16, No. 2. Denver: March, 1939.

Matthews, Ruth E. "A Study of Colorado Place Names." M.A. Thesis, Cecil

H. Green Library, Stanford University, Stanford, California, 1940.

"Meaning of Place Names." *Wyoming Annals*, Vol. 10, No. 4. Cheyenne, Wyoming: October, 1938.

Mumey, Nolie. "John Williams Gunnison: Centenary of His Survey & Tragic Death (1853–1953)." *Colorado Magazine*, Vol. 31, No. 1. Denver: January, 1954.

Parsons, Eugene. *A Guidebook to Colorado*. Boston, Little Brown & Co., 1911.

Pearce, T. M. *New Mexico Place Names*. Albuquerque, University of New Mexico Press, 1965.

Pearce, T. M. "Religious Place Names in New Mexico." *Names: Journal of the American Name Society*, Vol. 9, No. 1. Youngstown, Ohio: March, 1961.

Pearce, T. M. "Spanish Place Name Patterns in the Southwest." *Names: Journal of the American Name Society*, Vol. 3, No. 4. Berkeley: December, 1955.

Perrigo, Lynn I. "A Condensed History of Boulder, Colorado." *Colorado Magazine*, Vol. 26, No. 1. Denver: January, 1949.

Portrait & Biographical Record of the State of Colorado. Chicago, Chapman Publishing Co., 1899.

The Resources, Wealth & Industrial Development of Colorado. Agricultural Department, Colorado Exhibit at the World's Columbian Exposition, June 1, 1893.

The Rocky Mountain Directory and Colorado Gazetteer for 1871. Denver, S. S. Wallihan & Co.

Shaw, Dorothy P. & Janet Shaw Le Compte. "Huerfano Butte." *Colorado Magazine*, Vol. 27, No. 2. Denver: April, 1950.

Smiley, Jerome C. *History of Denver*. Denver, Times-Sun Publishing Co., 1901.

Smith, Phyllis. *A Look at Boulder: From Settlement to City*. Boulder, Pruett Publishing Co., 1981.

Sprague, Marshall. *Colorado: A Bicentennial History*. New York, W. W. Norton & Co., Inc., 1976.

Stacher, S. F. "Ouray and the Utes." *Colorado Magazine*, Vol. 27, No. 2. Denver: April, 1950.

Stone, Wilbur F. "Early Pueblo and the Men. Who Made It." *Colorado Magazine*, Vol. 6, No. 6. Denver: November, 1929.

Stone, Wilbur F. *History of Colorado*. Chicago, S. J. Clarke Publishing Co., 1918.

"Tales Told with Markers." *Colorado Magazine*, Vol. 47, No. 3. Denver: Summer, 1970.

Taylor, Morris F. "Trinidad Legends."

Colorado Magazine, Vol. 41, No. 2. Denver: Spring, 1964.

Taylor, Ralph C. *Colorado: South of the Border*. Denver, Sage Books, 1963.

Thatcher, Harold F. & Mary H. Brothers. "Fabulous La Plata River." *Western Folklore*, Vol. 10, No. 2. Berkeley: April, 1951.

Thompson, Enid. "Life in an Adobe Castle, 1833–1849." *Colorado Magazine*, Vol. 54, No. 4. Denver: Fall, 1977.

Vogel, Virgil J. *Iowa Place Names of Indian Origin*. Iowa City, University of Iowa Press, 1983.

Wallace, Betty. *Gunnison Country*. Denver, Sage Books, 1960.

Watrous, Ansel. *History of Larimer County, Colorado*. Fort Collins, Colorado, Courier Printing & Publishing Co., 1911.

Wiegel, C. W. "The Re-burial of Chief Ouray." *Colorado Magazine*, Vol. 5, No. 5. Denver: October, 1928.

Work Projects Administration. *Inventory of the County Archives of Colorado-Hinsdale, Morgan & San Miguel Counties*. Denver, 1939–1941.

Works Progress Administration. *Inventory of the County Archives of Colorado-Bent County*. Denver, 1938.

Connecticut

(8 counties)

278 *Fairfield County*

City of Fairfield, Connecticut — Several sources mention the possibility that the city of Fairfield, Connecticut was named for one of the two communities in England by that name. It is true that many Connecticut localities were named for places in England but the evidence indicates that this particular name was not so chosen. In 1639, Roger Ludlow moved from Windsor, Connecticut, with eight to ten families and began a settlement at a place which the Indians called Uncoway or Unquowa. The area had charmed Ludlow when he visited it about two years earlier and he called it Fairfield on account of its beautiful fields. When Fairfield County was created in 1666, it was named for this community within its borders.

279 *Hartford County*

City of Hartford, Connecticut — In 1635

or 1636 Thomas Hooker and Samuel Stone, together with members of their congregations moved from New Towne, Massachusetts, to Connecticut. Their new settlement was first called New Towne for their mother town in Massachusetts but the name was soon changed to Harteford Towne. Reverend Samuel Stone was born at Hertford, England, about 20 miles north of London, and the Connecticut town was named for the English community in honor of Reverend Stone. When the county was created and named in 1666, it was named for this community within its borders.

280 *Litchfield County*

Town of Litchfield, Connecticut — Litchfield County was created in 1751 and named for its town of Litchfield. In 1719 this attractive town had been named in honor of Lichfield, about 15 miles northeast of Birmingham in Staffordshire, England. There is also in England a village named Litchfield. Although this north Hampshire community's name is spelled the same as the Connecticut town, it was not the source of its name.

281 *Middlesex County*

Uncertain — The origin of this county's name is uncertain. Possibilities include:

1. The former county of Middlesex in England which, since 1965, has been a part of greater London. The English county's name derived from a tribal name of the Middle Saxons which later was used for their territory.

2. The town of Middletown within this Connecticut county. That town's location between Saybrook and the upper river towns may have prompted its name.

282 *New Haven County*

New Haven Colony & City of New Haven, Connecticut — Originally   Connecticut consisted of two colonies, one named Connecticut Colony and the other named New Haven Colony. In 1662, King Charles II granted Connecticut Colony a legal charter which gave Connecticut Colony a large amount of self-government and empowered it to absorb New Haven Colony. The name New Haven reflected the enthusiastic optimism with which the colonists viewed their new home here. In 1639 the captain of the first ship to arrive directly from England was so well pleased with the harbor here that he called it Fayre Haven. The plantation was generally called by its Indian name, Quinnipiac, until 1640 when the name New Haven was adopted. Unlike many other Connecticut place names, New Haven was not taken from any geographic name in the British Isles. There was a very small fishing village named Newhaven on the southern coast of Sussex, England, but none of the New Haven settlers came from there or even from Sussex. Connecticut's New Haven was not named for this English Newhaven nor was it named for a Newhaven in Scotland near Edinburgh. New Haven County was created by Connecticut Colony in 1666.

283 *New London County*

City of New London, Connecticut — From 1649 to 1658 the Connecticut plantation here was alternately referred to as Fair Haven and London. The name Fair Haven was suggested for the official name but in 1658 the legislature, at the urging of the settlers, adopted the official name New London in honor of London, England. The act explained that although many localities in New England had been named for English cities and towns. London had not yet been so honored. Although the legislature specified that the name was New London, in the early years it was sometimes recorded as just London. The English city of London is today the capital of the United Kingdom, the political center of the Commonwealth of Nations and one of the most important cities in the world. When the Romans established it and used it as a trading center, they called it Londinium. New London County, Connecticut, was created and named in 1666 and it was named for the plantation of New London, within its borders.

284 *Tolland County*

Town of Tolland, Connecticut — Tolland County was created in 1785 and named for its township of Tolland, which had been incorporated and named in 1715. The township's name was taken from Tolland, a hamlet in Somersetshire, England, which was the early home of Henry Wolcott. Henry Wolcott came to America in 1630 and, almost a century later, his grandson, Governor Roger Wolcott, was chief patentee of Tolland township.

285 *Windham County*

Town of Windham, Connecticut — The town of Windham, Connecticut, was established in 1692 and named for a community in England. Whether that English community was Windham in Sussex or Wymondham, pronounced Windham, in Norfolk, is not known although Wymondham is considered to be more likely on account of circumstantial evidence relating to the Ripley family. Franklin B. Dexter cited this in his article on Connecticut town names which appeared in 1885 in the Proceedings of the American Antiquarian Society:

"…the Ripley family was among a company of emigrants from Hingham, in Norfolk, who originally settled the town of Hingham, in Massachusetts Bay, and when descendants bearing the same family name pushed out into the Connecticut wilderness and founded a new town, naturally they chose for it the name of Windham, dear to their fathers' ears as the customary pronunciation of Wymondham, the largest place in the immediate vicinity of Old Hingham, on the eastern coast of England."

When Windham County, Connecticut was created in 1726, it was named for the town of Windham and that town was made its county seat.

REFERENCES

Bayles, Richard M. *History of Windham County, Connecticut*. New York, W. W. Preston & Co., 1889.

Caulkins, Frances M. *History of New London, Connecticut*. New London, H. D. Utley, 1895.

Clements, John. *Connecticut Facts: Rhode Island Facts*. Dallas, Texas, Clements Research II, Inc., 1990.

Crofut, Florence S. Marcy. *Guide to the History and the Historic Sites of Connecticut*. New Haven, Yale University Press, 1937.

Dexter, Franklin B. "The History of Connecticut as Illustrated by the Names of Her Towns." *Proceedings of the American Antiquarian Society, New Series*, Vol. 3, Part 4. Worcester: 1885.

The Encyclopedia Americana. New York, Americana Corporation, 1977.

Eno, Joel N. "Connecticut Congregations, Courts, & Counties." *The Magazine of History*, Vol. 26, Nos. 3–4. Tarrytown, New York: January–April, 1922.

Eno, Joel N. "The Nomenclature of Connecticut Towns." *Connecticut Magazine*, Vol. 8, No. 2. Hartford: December, 1903.

French, Mary L. *Chronology & Documentary Handbook of the State of Connecticut*. Dobbs Ferry, New York , Oceana Publications, Inc., 1973.

Heermance, Edgar L. *The Connecticut Guide*, Hartford Emergency Relief Commission, 1935.

Hughes, Arthur H. & Morse S. Allen. *Connecticut Place Names*. Connecticut Historical Society, 1976.

Morgan, Forrest. *Connecticut as a Colony and as a State, or One of the Original Thirteen*. Hartford, Publishing Society of Connecticut, 1904.

Rockey, J. L. *History of New Haven County, Connecticut*. New York, W. W. Preston & Co., 1892.

Sellers, Helen E. *Connecticut Town Origins*. Stonington, Connecticut, Pequot Press, Inc., 1964.

Sellers, Helen E. "Origins of the Names of the Connecticut Towns." *State of Connecticut Register & Manual: 1942*. Hartford: 1942.

Sperry, Kip. *Connecticut Sources for Family Historians & Genealogists*. Logan, Utah, Everton Publishers, Inc., 1980.

Van Dusen, Albert E., Professor of History, University of Connecticut, Storrs, Connecticut. Letter to the author dated September 26, 1980.

White, Alain C. *The Bi-Centennial Celebration of the Settlement of Litchfield, Connecticut: August 1–4, 1920*. Litchfield, Enquirer Print, 1920.

White, Alain C. *The History of the Town of Litchfield, Connecticut: 1720–1920*. Litchfield, Enquirer Print, 1920.

Delaware

(3 counties)

286 *Kent County*

Kent County, England — When Delaware was under Dutch control, this county was part of Hoornkill District Court. In 1664, England conquered all of New Netherland and Delaware became part of the Duke of York's province of New York. In 1680 Hoornkill was divided into two counties, St. Jones County and Deal County. In 1682 the Duke of York granted the Delaware counties to William Penn and, in that same year, Penn changed this county's name from St. Jones to Kent, in honor of Kent County, England. The English county's name probably derived from the Celt's *canto*, meaning "rim, border, border land" or "district."

287 *New Castle County*

Town of New Castle, Delaware — This county was formed in 1673 when courts were established at New Castle and the county was named for the town of New Castle. The town had been named New Amstel under the Dutch. In 1664 England, under Colonel Richard Nicolls, conquered all of New Netherland and Delaware became part of the Duke of York's province of New York. Although it cannot be documented, it is believed that, in April, 1665, Colonel Nicolls coined the name New Castle for the Delaware town. Why he chose the name is uncertain but there are two plausible theories:

Town of Newcastle, England — Newcastle, England, was so named because it was the site of a new castle built in 1080 to replace one destroyed by William the Conqueror.

William Cavendish (1592–1676) — Cavendish, a knight and a peer, was further elevated when he was made earl of Newcastle on March 7, 1628. In 1638 he was appointed governor of the young Prince of Wales, who later became King Charles II. During the rebellion against King Charles I, Cavendish was loyal to the crown, raising troops and leading them into battle for the king. As a result of his loyalty to Charles I, who was beheaded in 1649, Cavendish lost his offices. When crown was restored to power and Charles II took the throne, he rewarded Cavendish for his sufferings and services, making him duke of Newcastle on March 16, 1665.

March 16, 1665, was just 38 days before Colonel Nicolls' first known use of New Castle as a Delaware place name. Nicolls would have known that it would please the duke of York to have this recently conquered Dutch settlement named for the man who had supported his father, King Charles I. There was sufficient time (with favorable winds) for the news to reach Nicolls that the Newcastle title had been restored to Cavendish or Nicolls may have known of this in advance.

288 *Sussex County*

Sussex County, England — When Delaware was under Dutch control, this county was part of Hoornkill District Court. In 1664, England conquered all of New Netherland and Delaware became part of the Duke of York's province of New York. In 1680 Hoornkill was divided into two counties, St. Jones County and Deal County. In 1682 the Duke of York granted the Delaware counties to William Penn and in that same year Penn changed this county's name from Deal to Sussex in honor of his own county in England. The Sussex County name in England derived from the name of the South Saxons who lived there. The English geographic names Essex, Middlesex and Sussex referred to the tribes of people who lived there, the East Saxons, Middle Saxons and South Saxons, respectively. These names were then used for the kingdoms that these people established and they survive as English geographic names.

REFERENCES

Delaware Tercentenary Commission. *Delaware Tercentenary Almanack & Historical Repository.* 1938.

deValinger, Leon Jr. *Delaware: The Diamond State.* Dover, Delaware, State Board of Agriculture, 1948.

Ekwall, Eilert. *The Concise Oxford Dictionary of English Place-Names.* Oxford, Clarendon Press, 1960.

Heck, L. W., et al. "Delaware Place Names." *Geological Survey, U.S. Department of the Interior and the Coast and Geodetic Survey, U.S. Department of Commerce Geological Survey,* Bulletin No. 1245. Washington: 1966.

Higgins, Anthony. *New Castle on the Delaware.* Newark, Delaware, New Castle Historical Society, 1973.

Reaney, P. H. *The Origin of English Place-Names.* London, Routledge and Kegan Paul, 1960.

Reed, H. Clay. *The Delaware Colony.* New York, Crowell-Collier Press, 1970.

Scharf, J. Thomas. *History of Delaware: 1609–1888.* Philadelphia, L. J. Richards & Co., 1888.

Urquhart, Jane McKelway & O. D. von Engeln. *The Story Key to Geographic Names.* New York, D. Appleton & Co., 1924.

Weslager, C. A. "New Castle, Delaware and its Former Names." *Names: Journal of the American Name Society,* Vol. 24, No. 2. Potsdam, New York: June, 1976.

Florida

(67 counties)

289 *Alachua County*

Town of Alachua, Florida — When the county was created in 1824, it was named for the settlement of Alachua which occupies part of the area, in Alachua County, of an early Indian settlement named Alachua. By 1680 the Indian place name was used for a Spanish ranch in this vicinity. The meaning of the Indian word *allachua* is uncertain but these possibilities have been suggested:

1. "The great dark moon tree of the little water." ("Dark moon" referring to the moon in its shaded phases, "tree" referring to an oak tree and "little water" meaning, simply, rain.)
2. "Grassy."
3. "Marshy."
4. Derived from *la*, the Spanish word for "the" together with *chua*, an Indian word for "sink" referring to the many sink holes in the vicinity.
5. Derived from *luchuwa*, an Indian word for "jug" or "a place where water sinks low as into a jug," referring to a large chasm in the earth about two and one half miles southeast of the present city of Gainesville in Alachua County.

290 *Baker County*

James M. Baker (1822–1892) — Two years after graduation from college, this North Carolina native moved to Florida where he served as solicitor of the eastern judicial circuit court and later as judge of the Suwannee judicial circuit court. In 1856 Baker ran unsuccessfully for a seat in the U.S. House of Representatives. During the Civil War, Baker represented Florida in the senate of the Confederate States of America. After the war, he was an associate justice of Florida's supreme court but, because of restrictions on office holding by ex–Confederates, he left the supreme court in 1869. After Reconstruction Baker was a judge of the fourth judicial circuit court.

291 *Bay County*

St. Andrew's Bay — This county's border with the Gulf of Mexico includes several bays, one of which is beautiful St. Andrew's Bay, for which the county was named. G. M. West's history of the St. Andrews, Florida, area published in 1922 speculates that the bay was probably named for a saint of the Roman Catholic Church by early Spanish explorers and then lists as possibilities Saint Andrew Corsini, Saint Andrew Avellino and an otherwise undifferentiated Saint Andrew whose feast day West cites as November 30.

292 *Bradford County*

Richard Bradford (–1861) — Captain Bradford was the first Florida officer in the Confederate army to die in combat in the Civil War. He fell in the battle of Santa Rosa Island in western Florida on the night of October 8, 1861, when Confederate troops unsuccessfully attempted to occupy federally held land adjacent to Fort Pickens on the island. This county was originally named New River County. The name was changed to Bradford County just two months after Bradford's death. At that time the Civil War was in its early stages and hopes of victory by the South were still high.

293 *Brevard County*

Theodore W. Brevard (1804–1877) — Brevard was a native of North Carolina and a member of one of the distinguished families there named Brevard. This relationship has contributed to one misunderstanding concerning the source of this county's name. Theodore W. Brevard moved in 1833 to Alabama where he practiced law and served as county judge of Macon County. In 1847 he moved to Pensacola, Florida. During most of the time from 1855 to 1861 he was comptroller of the state of Florida. Brevard County, Florida, was named for this Theodore W. Brevard (1804–1877) but some confusion on this matter exists. Some writers mistakenly state that the county may have been named for a famous relative, Dr. Ephraim Brevard, who lived from about 1750 to about 1783 and was a North Carolina patriot. Dr. Ephraim Brevard practiced medicine in Charlotte, North Carolina and was secretary of the famous Mecklenburg convention in 1775. He was the author of the Mecklenburg Declaration of Independence. Other writers mistakenly confuse Theodore W. Brevard's son, whose name was the same, with the man for whom this county was named. The son served with distinction as an officer in the Confederate army during the Civil War but this county was not named for him. He died in 1881. Brevard County was originally named Saint Lucie County. The name was changed to Brevard County on January 6, 1855. Saint Lucie County's name was restored to the Florida map in 1905 when a new county named Saint Lucie was created.

294 *Broward County*

Napoleon B. Broward (1857–1910) — This colorful native of Florida grew up under hardships during Reconstruction years. He was a steamboat captain on the Saint Johns River and later he constructed and operated a small steamer which he commanded in eluding both U.S. and Spanish authorities to supply war materials and men to Cuban revolutionists. Broward was sheriff of Duval County and in 1900 he was elected to the state house of representatives. In 1904 he was elected governor of Florida. As governor, Broward played a leading role in draining the Everglades. This draining, an engineering triumph but an ecological disaster, began in what is now Broward County. In 1910 Broward was nominated for the U.S. Senate. His nomination as the Democratic candidate was virtually equivalent to election but he died before the vote was taken. This county was created five years after Broward's death.

295 *Calhoun County*

John C. Calhoun (1782–1850) — Calhoun represented South Carolina in both houses of the U.S. Congress. He served as secretary of war, secretary of state and as vice-president. He was a forceful advocate of slavery, states' rights and limited powers for the federal government. He resigned the vice-presidency to enter the U.S. Senate where he could better represent the views of South Carolina and the South. This county was created in 1838 while Calhoun was at the height of his popularity.

296 *Charlotte County*

Charlotte Harbor — Charlotte County was created in 1921 and named for Charlotte Harbor (which earlier was named Charlotte Bay), on which it borders. Since the time that the English gained control of Florida, Charlotte Harbor's name has honored the wife of King George III of England who was Queen Charlotte Sophia of Mecklenburg-Strelitz.

Queen Charlotte Sophia of Mecklenburg-Strelitz (1744–1818) — As the wife of King George III, Charlotte was queen of England at the time of the American Revolution, but prior to the Revolution her name was applied to some American places such as the city of Charlotte and the county of Mecklenburg in North Carolina as well as Charlotte Harbor, Florida. Charlotte's marriage to George III was arranged and she did not meet him until their wedding day. At that time, in 1761, Charlotte was described as "… not tall nor a beauty. Pale and very thin but looks sensible and genteel." Charlotte's life as queen was entirely domestic and she was happy with it. She had neither interest nor influence in political matters. The king was devoted to her and she was faithful to him. Apparently her only vice was stinginess in money matters. Charlotte became responsible for the royal household and for the care of the king during his lengthy physical and mental illnesses.

Before the English took control of Florida from Spain, the Spanish called Charlotte Harbor Bahia de Carlos in honor of Charles I, king of Spain from 1516 to 1556. *Carlos* is Spanish for "Charles."

King Charles I of Spain (1500–1558) — King Charles I of Spain was also Charles V, Holy Roman Emperor from 1519 to 1556. Defense of his vast empire resulted in constant conflict with the French, Turks, Protestant princes in Germany and others. As a boy, Charles' religious teacher was Adrian of Utrecht, who later became Pope Adrian VI. Many of the wars of Charles' reign were fought to defend the prerogatives of Catholicism and to promote its universality. By the Edict of Worms (May 26, 1521), Charles attempted to banish Protestants from the empire. Charles' reign was marked by chronic and severe economic problems. By 1554 he was tired and depressed and he soon relinquished his possessions and authority. He entered a monastery where he died in 1558.

This Spanish name, *Carlos*, for Charlotte Harbor, evolved from an earlier name, *Calos*, which had been applied to it on account of the Calusa Indians who lived in and controlled much of south Florida including Charlotte County.

Calusa Indians — This important and powerful tribe held dominion over most of southwest Florida, south of Tampa Bay and portions of central Florida extending to Lake Okeechobee and Cape Canaveral. They were fierce fighters and they successfully resisted Spanish arms after other Florida Indians had been subdued. They practiced human sacrifices on captives on a wholesale basis and probably cannibalism. In the 18th century they were driven from the Florida mainland to the Florida Keys by Creek Indians and other Indian allies of the English. By the time of the American Revolution, few Calusa Indians were living and many of them had migrated to Cuba. However, some Calusa remained in Florida to the close of the Second Seminole War. The meaning of the tribe's name, Calusa, is not known.

297 *Citrus County*

Citrus fruit — Citrus fruits are cultivated throughout the world, primarily in subtropical areas. The United States produces more citrus fruit than any other nation, and Florida, with its warm climate and abundant water supplies, leads the nation in citrus output. The genus *Citrus* consists of many species including various types of orange, grapefruit, lemon and lime. The Spanish introduced citrus fruits to Florida in the 1500's for domestic consumption rather than commerce. It was not until Spain ceded Florida to England in 1763 that these delicious and nutritious fruits were shipped north in large quantities.

298 *Clay County*

Henry Clay (1777–1852) — Clay represented Kentucky in both branches of the U.S. Congress. For many years he was one of the most prominent figures in American politics but his several bids for the presidency were unsuccessful. He was influential in effecting important compromises between northern and southern interests during the years that secession and civil war were imminent. It is surprising that the Florida legislature named one of its counties for this foe of Florida's hero, Andrew Jackson, but at the time that this county was created in 1858 there was still hope that Clay's slavery compromise of 1850 would prevent civil war.

299 *Collier County*

Barron G. Collier (1873–1939) — Collier was born in Tennessee and became one of America's first great advertising tycoons. From streetcar advertising and other business ventures he amassed a fortune. Collier used his great wealth to acquire more than one million acres of land, much of it swamp land, in southwest Florida and he believed that a new county should be created there. Collier constructed a major highway, the Tamiami Trail, through his property and used his influence to have the road extended. The new county that he wanted was created in 1923 and named for him. Collier had great plans for the development of southwest Florida. He founded towns, created hotels, banks, newspapers and telephone service. He announced plans to provide drainage and transportation and open additional land to settlement but the Great Depression of the 1930's drained his fortune before many of his plans could be realized.

300 *Columbia County*

Cristoforo Colombo (1451–1506) — Colombo, whose name we render as Christopher Columbus, was a native of Italy who believed the theory that the earth is round and that Asia could be reached by sailing west from Europe. He persuaded Ferdinand and Isabella of Spain to equip an expedition for him to test this theory. Sailing from Europe August 3, 1492, he first sighted land in the Americas in the Bahama Islands on October 12, 1492. On this voyage he left a colony of 40 men on the Hatian coast. Columbus returned several times to the New World before his death in 1506. Popularly known as the discoverer of America, Columbus was certainly not the first European to reach the Western Hemisphere. Leif Ericsson had accomplished this about the year 1000. But it was Columbus' expedition that triggered rapid exploration, conquest and settlement of the Americas by Europeans.

301 *Dade County*

Francis L. Dade (–1835) — A native of Virginia, Dade was appointed a commissioned officer in the U.S. army without having been trained at West Point. His original commission was as third lieutenant. He served under General Jackson at Pensacola where he met and married a local girl. By 1828 he had risen to the rank of brevet major. Stationed at Fort Brooke on Tampa Bay in 1835, Dade was ordered to put down unrest among some Seminole Indians. On December 28, 1835, near the present town of Bushnell, Florida, a party of Seminole Indians and Blacks ambushed and massacred Dade and all but about three of his force of some 110 men. When news of this massacre, which marked the start of the Second Seminole War, reached the territorial legislature at Tallahassee, Dade's name was inserted in a bill that was pending to create this new county. The name originally planned for this county was Pinkney, in honor of U.S. Senator William Pinkney from Maryland who had championed the cause of slave-holding states during debates on the Missouri Compromise.

302 *De Soto County*

Hernando De Soto (1500–1542) — De Soto, the famous Spanish conquistador, was one of Europe's early explorers of the Americas and the discoverer of the Mississippi River. Following successful campaigns in Central America, De Soto was prominent in the conquest of the Inca empire in Peru. In 1539 De Soto landed in Florida at Charlotte Harbor and, in a futile search for riches, he and his men explored Florida and a large area of the southeastern United States, torturing and slaughtering Indians as they went. It was this expedition that discovered the Mississippi River. Florida has a second county, Hernando County, that is also named for this man.

303 *Dixie County*

Nickname of the South — This county was given the name of the popular term used to denote the South, particularly those states which formed the Confederate States of America. This nickname became well known as a result of the popularity of the song "Dixie," written and set to stirring music in 1859 by Daniel Decatur Emmett. This song was played at the inauguration of Confederate President Jefferson Davis on February 18, 1861, and it came to be regarded as the Confederate national anthem. The term at first denoted only New Orleans, later Louisiana, and finally the entire South. Its origin is unknown but three possibilities are mentioned:

1. The term is somehow connected with the Mason and Dixon line.

2. Dixie was the name of a New York slave owner who was kind to his slaves.

3. The term evolved from the French word *dix*, meaning "ten", which, before 1860, the Citizens Bank of New Orleans printed on its ten dollar notes as a convenience for its French-speaking customers. In those days this was an impressive sum of money and salesmen traveling on the Mississippi spoke of their hopes to pick up some dixies in the South.

304 *Duval County*

William P. DuVal (1784–1854) — DuVal, who styled his name with a capital V, was a native of Virginia who lived most of his life on America's frontier. He moved to Kentucky about 1799 when he was still in his early teens, to Florida in 1822 just before it became a territory and to the infant state of Texas in 1849. DuVal represented Kentucky in the U.S. Congress from 1813 to 1815. In 1821 President Monroe appointed DuVal to be a judge in East Florida but he held that post only one month when Florida became a territory, and President Monroe promoted him to be Florida's first territorial governor. He was re-appointed to that post by Presidents John Quincy Adams and Andrew Jackson and he served as territorial governor from 1822 to 1834. This county was created on August 12, 1822, shortly after DuVal became Florida's first civil governor.

305 *Escambia County*

Escambia River — Escambia County, Florida is bordered on the north by Escambia County, Alabama. Both counties were named for the river which flows through them. However, the river is named Conecuh in Alabama and Escambia in Florida. The origin of the name Escambia for the river is uncertain. It may have derived from the Spanish verb *cambiar*, "to exchange" or "to barter," perhaps applied because the Spanish bartered along this river with Indians. It is at least equally likely that the name is of Indian origin, possibly derived in part from the Indian *abi* meaning "killer." *Abi* was a popular suffix in Indian war titles.

306 *Flagler County*

Henry M. Flagler (1830–1913) — Brought up in poverty in New York state, Flagler amassed an enormous fortune as a grim, shrewd and ruthless business associate of John D. Rockefeller in the Standard Oil Company. Flagler first visited Florida in 1883 and decided to personally develop Florida's east coast. He soon built a string of palatial hotels from St. Augustine to Miami and a railroad system spanning the entire east coast of the Florida peninsula and beyond, to Key West. Through his railroad venture, Flagler acquired enormous amounts of state land. He encouraged settlement on this land, making concessions including free seed and reduced freight rates. Flagler also built many schools, churches and hospitals. This county was created in 1917, four years after Flagler's death.

307 *Franklin County*

Benjamin Franklin (1706–1790) — Franklin was a native of Massachusetts who moved to Pennsylvania in his teens. Poverty denied him a formal education but he became the leading printer and editor in North America. Franklin gained fame for his discoveries and inventions in the physical sciences and he distinguished himself as author, philosopher and diplomat. Franklin was a signer of the Declaration of Independence and an important member of the convention which framed the U.S. Constitution.

308 *Gadsden County*

James Gadsden (1788–1858) — Gadsden was born in South Carolina and served as General Andrew Jackson's aide-de-camp in the War of 1812. In 1818 he took part in a campaign in Florida against the Seminole Indians. President James Monroe appointed Gadsden in 1823 to be U.S. commissioner for the removal of the Seminole Indians to reservations. Later, as President Franklin Pierce's minister to Mexico, he gained national fame by negotiating the Gadsden Purchase from Mexico which added an enormous area of land to the United States in southern Arizona and southwestern New Mexico. This county was created in 1823 in recognition of Gadsden's services against the Seminole Indians, before James Gadsden negotiated any treaties with them and before he gained national prominence as an American diplomat.

309 *Gilchrist County*

Albert W. Gilchrist (1858–1926) — Gilchrist was the son of Floridians but was born in South Carolina during his mother's visit to that state. Educated at West Point, he served in the Spanish American War. Following the war, he lived in Punta Gorda, Florida where he was a civil engineer and orange grower. He also engaged in real estate. Gilchrist served in Florida's house of representatives and was speaker of that body in 1905. In November, 1908, he was elected governor of Florida and he held that office from 1909 to 1913. The name that was planned for this new county was Melon. At the last minute the legislature changed the proposed new county's name to Gilchrist when they learned that the former governor was dying in a New York hospital. Gilchrist rallied and death did not claim him until five months later, in May, 1926.

310 *Glades County*

Florida's Everglades — Situated at the edge of the tropics, Florida's Everglades are a wilderness region of usually flooded swamps and prairies covered with tall grasses. It extends over some 4,000 square miles from Lake Okeechobee to the Gulf of Mexico. Teeming with alligators and other animals and plants, some of which are found nowhere else on earth, much of the Everglades is included in Everglades National Park. This "River of Grass" consists of a series of vast swamps, lagoons, marshes and saw-grass prairies, interspersed with stands of cypress, pine and palmetto. The name Everglades was invented in Florida to describe a phenomenon that exists nowhere else in the world. Although the derivation of the term is uncertain, it is speculated that the *ever* portion developed in pattern of evergreen, signifying interminable. *Glade* is an old English — word which earlier meant "shining" or "bright" and now refers to an open, grassy place in the forest or to a moist, swampy area.

311 *Gulf County*

Gulf of Mexico — On a straight-line basis, Florida has approximately 1,800 miles of coastline and well over half of it adjoins the Gulf of Mexico. Gulf County's southern shore is washed by it. The gulf is an enormous arm of the Atlantic Ocean which is almost surrounded by the United States and Mexico. From east to west it measures about 1,000 miles and from north to south about 775 miles. Its warm waters provide a living for commercial fishermen and are a year-round delight to water sports enthusiasts.

312 *Hamilton County*

Alexander Hamilton (–1804) — A native of the West Indies, Hamilton moved to New York and served as an officer in America's Revolutionary army. One of his assignments during the war was aide-de-camp to General George Washington. After the war Hamilton was a member of the convention which framed the U.S. Constitution. He collaborated with Madison and Jay in writing a series of papers entitled *The Federalist* which explained the new constitution and advocated its adoption. A conservative and an advocate of a strong central government, he served as the United States' first secretary of the treasury. In 1804 he engaged in a duel with Aaron Burr and Hamilton died of wounds he suffered in that duel.

313 *Hardee County*

Cary A. Hardee (1876–1957) — Hardee was a native of Florida who taught school before beginning a legal practice in 1900. He served in Florida's house of representatives, was speaker of that body and later was elected governor of the state of Florida. This county was created in 1921 while Hardee was serving as governor. Agitation in favor of dividing De Soto County had been going on since the early 20th century. It was earlier intended that the portion of De Soto which now forms Hardee should be called Seminole County. However, in 1913, long before the De Soto division controversy was resolved, a different Florida county was created and the name Seminole was given to it. Several other names were now suggested for this county including the Indian name, Cherokee, Goolsby for a pioneer resident and Wauchula, the name of the town that became the county seat. Promoters of the proposed new county settled on the name Hardee to insure the governor's support.

314 *Hendry County*

Francis A. Hendry (1833–1917) — Hendry was born in Georgia and moved to Florida in 1851. Here he became an important cattleman, pioneering the improvement of Florida cattle, buying purebreds and importing grass to improve pastures and herds. At one time he owned about 50,000 head of cattle and was known as the cattle king of south Florida. Prior to the Civil War, Hendry served in both houses of the Florida legislature. He voted against secession but, when overruled by the majority, he accepted a captain's commission in the Confederate cavalry. After the war he was a pioneer in local town and county politics in the Ft. Myers area and he served at length in the state legislature. This county was created in 1923, six years after Hendry's death.

315 *Hernando County*

Hernando De Soto (1500–1542) — Hernando De Soto, the famous Spanish conquistador, was one of Europe's early explorers of the Americas and the discoverer of the Mississippi River. Following successful campaigns in Central America, De Soto was prominent in the conquest of the Inca empire in Peru. In 1539 De Soto landed in Florida at Charlotte Harbor and, in a futile search for riches, he and his men explored Florida and a large area of the southeastern United States, torturing and slaughtering Indians as they went. It was this expedition that discovered the Mississippi River. This county was established as Hernando County on February 24, 1843. On March 6, 1844, its name was changed by the territorial legislature to Benton County in honor of Senator Thomas H. Benton of Missouri. However, Benton's moderation on the slavery issue proved unpopular and several states, including Florida, which had named counties in honor of Senator Benton renamed them. This county's name was changed from Benton back to Hernando on December 24, 1850. Florida has a second county, De Soto County, that is also named for Hernando De Soto.

316 *Highlands County*

The pleasant hilly nature of the area — Florida boasts many marvelous features but really high land is not among them. All things being relative, in this flat state this county's approximate elevation of 145 to 160 feet is rather high, or so the legislators thought when they created and named this county in 1921. Actually, the state's highest point is not here but far to the north in Walton County where an elevation of 345 feet is found and several Florida counties have higher average elevations than Highlands County.

317 *Hillsborough County*

Hillsborough Bay — Hillsborough Bay lies at the northern end of Tampa Bay and the waters of both of these bays wash Hillsborough County's shores. Hillsborough Bay was named during the period of English occupation of Florida for Wills Hill, Earl of Hillsborough.

Wills Hill, Earl of Hillsborough (1718–1793) — A native of England, Hill took a seat in the Irish house of peers in 1743 and in the privy council in 1754. He later served as first commissioner of trade and plantations and postmaster general and he was principal secretary of state for the American department during the American Revolution. Hill received a large grant of land in Florida during the period of English occupation and, although he never visited Florida himself, he was very interested in it. Hill sent Bernard Romans, a surveyor and naturalist, to explore Florida and it was on a 1774 map of Romans' that Hill's name first appeared for Hillsborough Bay.

318 *Holmes County*

Holmes Creek—This county was created in 1848 and named for the creek which forms its eastern boundary. The creek had been named earlier for Holmes Valley. The origin of the valley's name is uncertain. Three possibilities are mentioned:

1. An Indian chieftain who had been given the English name of Holmes.

2. Thomas J. Holmes, who came from North Carolina and settled in the Holmes Valley vicinity near the Choctawhatchee River approximately 1830 to 1834.

3. A half-breed Indian known as Holmes who lived in this area and was killed in 1818 by a raiding party sent by Andrew Jackson to sweep the Choctawhatchee River.

319 *Indian River County*

Indian River—This county was created in 1925 and named for the Indian River, a coastal lagoon which is some 165 miles long and passes this county's edge. A long, narrow barrier of land protects and separates the Indian River from the Atlantic Ocean. The river had been named earlier for the Indians who lived in the area, the Ays or Ais Indians. At first the river was known as the Ays River but by the time that Florida came under American control, the river was simply called the Indian River.

Ais Indians—The Ais lived in the area traversed by the Indian River from about the southern end of Cape Canaveral to the Saint Lucie River. Unlike Indians of northern Florida, the Ais were not agricultural. They lived on an ample supply of fish and, when in season, palm berries, coco plums and sea grapes. They engaged in elaborate Indian religious ceremonies and these were continued even after their chief was made a Christian at St. Augustine. They held their chief in great esteem but elder members of the tribe were not treated respectfully. From 1700 to 1750 the Ais Indians were decimated by slave raids, disease and alcoholic drinking. By 1760 there were no Ais left in this region.

320 *Jackson County*

Andrew Jackson (1767–1845)—Jackson was born on the border of North Carolina and South Carolina. He represented Tennessee in both branches of the U.S. Congress. He gained fame and popularity for his military exploits in wars with the Indians and in the War of 1812. He was provisional military governor of Florida and from 1829 to 1837 General Jackson was president of the United States. His presidency reflected the frontier spirit of America. This county was created on August 12, 1822, shortly after Jackson's term as provisional military governor of Florida ended.

321 *Jefferson County*

Thomas Jefferson (1743–1826)—Jefferson was a native of Virginia and a member of the Virginia legislature. He served Virginia as governor and he was a delegate to the second Continental Congress. Jefferson was the author of the Declaration of Independence and one of its signers. He was minister to France, secretary of state, vice-president and president of the United States. As president, he accomplished the Louisiana Purchase and he arranged the Lewis and Clark Expedition to the Pacific Northwest. Jefferson was a true intellectual, thoroughly knowledgeable in the arts and sciences. His political theories were pivotal in the formation of our infant republic. This county was created in January, 1827, seven months after Jefferson's death.

322 *Lafayette County*

Marie Joseph Paul Yves Roch Gilbert du Motier, Marquis de Lafayette (1757–1834)—Lafayette was a French aristocrat who served briefly in the French army. He came to America in 1777 to assist the American Revolutionary army. He was granted an honorary commission as major-general by the Continental Congress and served with distinction in a number of battles in the Revolutionary War. In December, 1824, the U.S. Congress granted to Lafayette a township of land in Florida territory, just east of Tallahassee, as a token of gratitude for his services. Lafayette was in the United States at that time as an honored guest of the federal government and President Monroe hoped that Lafayette might decide to become a resident of Florida. That never happened and, in fact, Lafayette never visited Florida. but he took an interest in his Florida land and arranged a number of agricultural experiments on it.

323 *Lake County*

Numerous lakes within its borders—In 1887 Lake County was created and named for the many lakes within it. This county boasts more than 500 lakes, the largest of which is Lake Griffin which has a surface area of 16,505 acres.

324 *Lee County*

Robert E. Lee (1807–1870)—Lee was a native of Virginia and, for over 30 years, an officer in the United States army. When Virginia seceded from the union, Lee refused an offer to command all federal forces and resigned from the U.S. army to accept a commission in the Confederate army. He served with distinction in that army and became general-in-chief of it. The name Lee was selected for this new county in 1887 by Francis A. Hendry. Years later, in 1923 when Lee County was divided to form two additional counties, one of these new counties was named for Francis A. Hendry.

325 *Leon County*

Juan Ponce de Leon (1460–1521)—Ponce was a native of Spain who served in the Moorish wars and then accompanied Columbus on his second voyage to the New World in 1493. From 1508 to 1509 he explored and settled Puerto Rico. During Easter season in 1513 Ponce was searching for new lands, gold and a legendary fountain of youth when he sighted and landed on Florida, named it and claimed it for the king of Spain. He later campaigned against the Carib Indians and occupied Trinidad. In 1521 he led another expedition to Florida and landed near Charlotte Harbor. Wounded by Indians, Ponce died soon afterward in Cuba. *de Leon* is a distinguishing phrase added to Juan Ponce's family name to indicate his family's place of origin or residence in the province of Leon in Spain.

326 *Levy County*

David Levy Yulee (1810–1886)—David Levy, whose name was changed in 1846 to David Levy Yulee, was born on St. Thomas in the Virgin Islands. When David was nine, he was sent to school in Virginia and his parents moved to Florida. Levy was a delegate to the first constitutional convention of Florida territory. From 1841 to 1845 he served as the territory's delegate to the U.S. Congress and, when Florida was admitted to statehood in 1845, he became one of the state's first two U.S. senators. He withdrew from the U.S. Senate in 1861 to enter the political service of the Confederate States of America and he served in both Confederate congresses. On March 10, 1845, Levy County was created and named. On January 12, 1846, at the request of David Levy, the Florida legislature legally changed his name to David Levy Yulee, but left the county's name unchanged.

327 *Liberty County*

The American ideal of freedom of choice— Liberty County was created and named in 1855, just ten years after Florida was admitted to statehood. The name was chosen as an expression of pride in the great objective of the people who founded and built the United States.

328 *Madison County*

James Madison (1751–1836)— Madison was born in Virginia, served in the Virginia legislature and in the Continental Congress. He was a member of the convention which framed the U.S. Constitution and he collaborated with Hamilton and Jay in writing a series of papers under the title *The Federalist* which explained the new constitution and advocated its adoption. Madison represented Virginia in the U.S. House of Representatives, served for eight years as secretary of state and for eight years as president of the United States. This county was formed in 1827, ten years after Madison retired from the presidency.

329 *Manatee County*

Manatees or sea cows— Manatees are large, aquatic mammals that constitute the family, Trichechidae. In the United States, they are rarely found outside Florida. These slow—moving creatures feed on marine vegetation in shallow coastal waters such as those along the shore of Manatee County. A typical adult manatee is ten feet long and weighs 1,000 pounds. Both friendly and harmless, Florida's manatees are an endangered species. Because of their low reproduction rate, they have been unable to cope with man. Although they are no longer hunted, loss of their feeding areas continues. Many deaths and injuries to the manatees are caused by reckless use of propellers on motorboats. During the last decade of the 20th century manatee deaths were continuing to increase. The English word "manatee" derives from the Spanish *manati* meaning "sea cow." The Spanish word came from a Carib Indian word designating the female breast, a prominent characteristic of manatees.

330 *Marion County*

Francis Marion (–1795)— Marion is believed to have been born in South Carolina. He served in the army in battles against the Cherokee Indians and was elected to the Provisional congress of 1775. He served, with distinction, as an officer in the Revolutionary War and rose to the rank of general in that war. Marion was also a member of the South Carolina senate. Marion County, Florida, drew many of its first settlers from South Carolina.

331 *Martin County*

John W. Martin (1884–1958)— Martin was a native Floridian who served three terms as mayor of Jacksonville from 1917 to 1924. He then served as governor of Florida during the four years that the state went from boom to bust in the early phase of the Great Depression. Early in Martin's term as governor, a campaign was waged by some residents of Palm Beach County to create a new county out of the northern portion of Palm Beach County. Their desire for a new county made little headway until Governor Martin learned of the proposed new county and the plan to name it in his honor. The governor encouraged leaders in the legislature to proceed with the creation of this new county and this was done effective May 30, 1925.

332 *Monroe County*

James Monroe (1758–1831)— Monroe, a native of Virginia, served in the Revolutionary War. Prior to his election as president of the United States, Monroe served in a wide variety of government posts. He served Virginia in the state legislature and as governor. He was a member of the Confederation congress and the U.S. Senate. He was minister to France and to Britain and he held two cabinet posts. As president, Monroe stressed limited government and strict construction of the constitution. He acquired Florida for the U.S. from Spain and he was the author of a policy declaration (later known as the Monroe Doctrine) which proscribed outside interference in North and South America. This county was created in 1823 while Monroe was serving as president.

333 *Nassau County*

Nassau River— The Nassau River forms part of the boundary between Nassau County and Duval County, Florida. When the English occupied Florida, they named the river in honor of Nassau, the capital town of the Bahama Islands. Many of the settlers of this section of Florida had come from the Bahamas. When Nassau in the Bahamas was founded it was named Charles Towne in honor of King Charles II of England. Its name was changed to Nassau when William III came to the throne of England. Nassau, the family name of William III, derived from the name of a former duchy in Germany. The House of Nassau was named for the town of Nassau on the Lahn River, an eastern tributary of the Rhine, near which the family's ancestral castle stood. In Old High German *naz* meant "damp, marshy" and *augia* meant "land."

334 *Okaloosa County*

Uncertain— The name is of Indian origin but its meaning is uncertain. Some sources indicate that okaloosa meant "pleasant place." The more likely derivation given by other authorities is that the name came from the Choctaw Indian words *oka* meaning "water" and *lusa* meaning "black" and referred to what is now the Blackwater River, which flows through Okaloosa County. Two other names for this county had been proposed, Yellow River and Wilson, but neither of those names was ever officially adopted.

335 *Okeechobee County*

Lake Okeechobee— This shallow, saucer-shaped lake touches the southern end of Okeechobee County where the Everglades begin. The Indians' name for Lake Okeechobee meant "big water." The name was formed from two Hitchiti words, *oki* for "water" and *chubi* or *chobi* which meant "big." The name was well chosen. This lake covers more than 700 square miles and is, by far, the largest lake in Florida. In fact, Lake Okeechobee is the third largest fresh water lake that is completely within the United States (after Lake Michigan and Iliamna Lake, Alaska).

336 *Orange County*

Local orange groves— Oranges are tropical and subtropical trees and shrubs which belong to the genus *Citrus*. Their fruits and juices from their fruits enjoy great popularity. Oranges originated in the tropical regions of Asia, spread around the Mediterranean Sea and were introduced in the Western Hemisphere by Columbus in 1493. The Spanish introduced oranges to Florida in the 1500's for domestic consumption rather than commerce. It was not until Spain ceded Florida to England in 1763 that these delicious and nutritious fruits were shipped north in large quantities. This county was originally named Mosquito County. That ridiculous name lasted until 1845 when the name was changed to Orange County in honor of the abundant orange groves here.

337 *Osceola County*

Osceola (–1838)— Osceola, the leader of Florida's Seminole Indians during the Second Seminole War, was born in Alabama or Georgia about 1804 and moved with his mother to Florida territory. In 1835, when the United States government attempted to move the Seminoles from Florida to Indian territory (now Oklahoma) Osceola led the opposition which the Seminoles conducted, guerrilla style, from the Everglades. In October, 1837, Osceola and several other Indians went to St. Augustine under a flag of truce for a parley with General Thomas S. Jesup. Osceola was captured and kidnapped by the unscrupulous Jesup and placed in prison at Ft. Moultrie, South Carolina. Weakened by chronic malaria and quinsy, he lost the will to live in captivity and he died on January 30, 1838. Osceola's name derived from the Creek Indians' *assiyahola* which meant "singer at the black drink." This referred to a customary cry uttered by the serving attendant during distribution of a ceremonial black drink made from the caffeine-rich leaves of the yaupon. State Senator J. Milton Bryan was responsible for this county's name. He proposed it to the legislature in 1887 when they created and named this county.

338 *Palm Beach County*

Town of Palm Beach, Florida— The county was created in 1909 and named for its town of Palm Beach. The town was first named Palm City. In 1887 it was given its current name which honors its lovely Atlantic Ocean beaches and their numerous palm trees. The town of Palm Beach, a fashionable island community, was Florida's first luxury wintering spot for northern tourists and many rich and famous international personages still maintain winter homes here. Palm trees are numerous in Florida and sand beaches account for approximately 1,016 miles of Florida's coast. To many, both palm trees and ocean beaches are symbolic of the state.

339 *Pasco County*

Samuel Pasco (1834–1917)— Pasco was born in England and immigrated to the United States. In 1859 he moved to Florida. During the Civil War, he served in the Confederate infantry, was wounded in combat and taken prisoner. Pasco later served as president of Florida's constitutional convention, and in the Florida legislature as speaker of the house of repre-sentatives. For 12 years he represented Florida in the United States senate. This county was created and named on June 2, 1887, just two weeks after Pasco had been elected by the legislature to the U.S. Senate. The name that was originally proposed for this county was Banner County but that name was never adopted.

340 *Pinellas County*

Pinellas Peninsula and Point Pinellas, Florida— Pinellas County, which was created in 1911, consists primarily of a peninsula which, for centuries, has been known as Pinellas Peninsula. The tip of this peninsula was known as Point Pinellas. The origin of this unique name is uncertain. Most published speculations on this subject indicate that the name was derived from the Spanish *punta pinal* or *pinta pinal* meaning "point of pines" or "pine grove point." It seems likely that punta pinal is correct. The pine is a common tree in Florida, *punta* is the Spanish word for "point" or "tip" and *pinal* is an obsolete form of the modern Spanish word *pinar* which means "pine grove."

341 *Polk County*

James K. Polk (1795–1849)— Polk was a native of North Carolina who moved with his family to the Tennessee frontier in 1806. He served in the lower house of the Tennessee legislature and he represented Tennessee for 14 years in the U.S. House of Representatives where he was speaker. He served one term as governor of Tennessee. Polk became president of the United States as a dark horse candidate of the Democratic Party but he became an unusually strong and effective president. His primary accomplishments involved westward extension of the United States; in the Northwest by settling a territorial dispute with Britain and in California and the Southwest by provoking and winning the Mexican War.

342 *Putnam County*

Uncertain— This county was created on January 13, 1849. Some authorities state that the county was named for Benjamin A. Putnam while others indicate that the man honored was Israel Putnam.

Benjamin A. Putnam (1801–1869)— A native of Georgia, Putnam served as an officer in the Second Seminole War in Florida and later served in both houses of Florida's legislature. Putnam was serving as speaker of the house in Florida's general assembly in 1849 when Putnam County was created. President Zachary Taylor appointed Putnam to be surveyor-general of Florida and he held that post from May, 1849 to 1854.

Israel Putnam (1718–1790)— Putnam was born in Massachusetts and moved, when he was about 21, to Connecticut. He served as an officer in the French and Indian Wars and later was a member of the Connecticut legislature. At the beginning of the Revolutionary War, news of the battle at Lexington, Massachusetts reached Putnam while he was farming. In a dramatic gesture which became famous, Putnam left his plow and, without bothering to change clothes, hurried to Lexington. He was appointed major-general in the Continental army. Although he enjoyed great popularity, he lacked the ability for high command. In 1779 a paralytic stroke ended his military career.

343 *Saint Johns County*

Saint Johns River— The Saint Johns is a slow moving river, so wide at points that it resembles a series of lakes. It flows in northern Florida for over two hundred miles and empties with a violent clash into the Atlantic Ocean at Jacksonville. It forms much of the western boundary of Saint Johns County. The river was named for a Spanish mission, San Juan del Puerto, which had been established on Fort George Island at the mouth of the river, and named for Saint John the Baptist.

Saint John the Baptist (–)— John lived an austere life in the desert of Judea southwest of Jerusalem. Clothed in garments of camels' hair and living on a diet of locusts and wild honey, John ministered to men from Jerusalem and neighboring towns who flocked to visit him. He demanded two rites of those who came to him: an open confession of their sins and physical baptism. Jesus Christ was among those baptized by John and John apparently came to believe on that occasion that Jesus was the Messiah. King Herod Antipas feared John's popularity and power and resented John's criticism of his sex life. The king imprisoned John and had him beheaded.

344 *Saint Lucie County*

Several natural features— This county was named for several natural features whose names derived from an ancient fort, named Santa Lucia, that the Spanish built near Cape Canaveral in 1565. The fort was named in honor of Saint Lucy of Syracuse. Florida's first Saint Lucie County was established in 1844 but that county's name was changed to Brevard eleven years later. The present Saint Lucie County was created in 1905.

Saint Lucy (–)—It is known that Saint Lucy was born in Syracuse on the island of Sicily and died about A.D. 304 but other information about this virgin martyr is legendary. Legend tells us that her parents were wealthy nobles. Lucy was brought up as a Christian and she made a secret vow of virginity in her youth. On one occasion, Lucy persuaded her mother to visit the tomb of St. Agatha to pray for a medical miracle. Lucy accompanied her mother on this pilgrimage and her mother was miraculously cured. When Lucy announced her vow of virginity, a rejected suitor reported her for being a Christian to Roman authorities who were then vigorously persecuting Christians. She was executed by thrusting a sword down her throat. Possibly because her name is suggestive of light, Saint Lucy has been associated with festivals of light and prayers against blindness.

345 *Santa Rosa County*

Santa Rosa Island—Santa Rosa County was formed in 1842 and named for Santa Rosa Island which lies in the Gulf of Mexico off this county's mainland, near the end of the Florida panhandle. The island had been named much earlier by the Spanish in honor of Saint Rose of Viterbo, Italy.

Saint Rose (1234–1252)—This virgin saint was born in poverty in Viterbo, Italy. Much of the following information about Saint Rose is based on legend: When she was only about twelve years old she began preaching in the streets of Viterbo. For about two years she denounced Emperor Frederick II who had been harassing the pope. Some of the emperor's supporters demanded her death but the authorities merely banished her and her parents from the city of Viterbo. Marvels were attributed to this spirited girl and she was much revered by the people but the convent of the Poor Clares refused to admit her into its community for want of a dowry. After her death, however, her body was laid to rest in that convent by order of the pope. Rose was canonized in 1457.

346 *Sarasota County*

Uncertain—This county was established and named in 1921. It is not known whether the county was named for the city of Sarasota, its county seat, or for its Sarasota Bay nor is the origin of the name *Sarasota* known. In the absence of facts, specula-

tions abound and all of the following possibilities have been mentioned:

1. Derived from Hernando De Soto's last name. It has been fairly well established that De Soto set foot on Sarasota soil but the name connection is merely a guess.

2. Derived from a legend about Hernando De Soto's beautiful daughter, said to be named Sara Sota.

3. Derived from an Indian word applied to a prominent feature of the shoreline known as Point of Rocks which extends into the Gulf of Mexico near Crescent Beach. *Sarasecota* is said to be an Indian word meaning "a landfall easily observed."

4. Derived from a corruption of the Spanish expressions *sarao* and *sota* meaning "a place of dancing." The idea is that this referred to the celebrations held by the Indians on or near the shore of the bay here. However, no words in modern Spanish give this meaning to the name.

5. Derived from the Spanish *soto* for "grove" or "thicket" on account of numerous palm trees here.

6. Derived from the Spanish *zarzosa* meaning "brambly."

7. Derived from the Spanish word *sarro* meaning "crust" or "encrustation on boats." The thought here is that De Soto or other Spanish explorers may have used the Sarasota area to scrape and clean their boats. The name De Soto might have been linked to *sarro* to denote a boat cleaning place of De Soto's.

8. Derived from the Sahara Desert because of the appearance of the white sand here when viewed from a distance. A suffix *zota* is said to be an Indian word meaning "clear, blue, limpid, beautiful."

9. Derived from the Spanish *cara* meaning "taking the initiative against the enemy" which was linked with Soto because De Soto landed here despite the opposition of hostile Indians.

10. Derived from Indian words *sua* for "sun," *ha* for "water" and *zota* for "shadow." Indian fancy suggested that clouds were white shadows cast by the sun itself. Thus interpreted the name means "water of the white sun shadow."

347 *Seminole County*

Seminole Indians—The Seminole, a Muskogean-speaking people, evolved as a distinct tribe in Florida at about the time of the American Revolution. The Seminole consisted of a nucleus of Oconee Indians, a subdivision of the Creeks of Alabama and Georgia, who migrated to Florida in the mid-1700's. The Oconee combined with Yamasee Indians who had

been driven from South Carolina and with remnant groups of Florida Indians and runaway Black slaves to form the tribe known as Seminole. The Seminole are noted for their fierce resistance to attempts by Whites to drive them from their homeland in Florida. During Florida's Seminole Wars, many of the Seminole were driven to Indian territory (now Oklahoma) but some eluded the American troops in the Everglades and more than 1,000 surviving Seminole still live in central and southern Florida. The origin of the name Seminole is uncertain but these possibilities have been suggested:

1. The Creek Indian word *simanole* or *siminole* which means "runaways" or "those who separate."

2. The Creek Indian words *ishti semoli* which mean "wild men."

3. The Spanish word *cimarron* meaning "wild," "unruly" or "runaway slave."

348 *Sumter County*

Thomas Sumter (1734–1832)—Sumter, a native of Virginia, fought in the French and Indian Wars and settled in South Carolina. He served as an officer in the Revolutionary War and represented South Carolina in both houses of the U.S. Congress. This section of Florida was largely settled by immigrants from South Carolina and the county was created in 1853, two decades after Sumter's death.

349 *Suwannee County*

Suwannee River—The Suwannee River rises in Georgia, west of the Okefenokee Swamp, flows into northern Florida where it soon forms the western boundary of Suwannee County and travels a total of about 240 miles before emptying into the Gulf of Mexico southwest of Gainesville. The Suwannee River is famous because Stephen Foster used a shortened version of its name in his famous song "Old Folks at Home." Legend has it that Foster never saw the river; that he merely needed the name of a southern river with two syllables. When he spotted the Suwannee on a map, he shortened this three syllable name to "Swanee" for his song. The origin of the Suwannee River's name is uncertain. These theories are known:

1. Derived from the Indian word *suwani, sawani* or *sawni* meaning "echo."

2. Derived from a corruption of the Spanish *San Juan* meaning "Saint John." During the 17th century a Franciscan mission called San Juan de Guacara was situated on a bank of the Suwannee River.

3. Derived from an Indian word meaning "water beloved of the Sun God."

4. Derived from an Indian word or words meaning "winding river" or "long, crooked river."

5. Derived from the name of an early female chief of the Seminole Indians.

350 Taylor County

Zachary Taylor (1784–1850)— Taylor was born in Virginia but moved as an infant to Kentucky where he grew to manhood on a farm near Louisville. A career soldier, Taylor served as an officer in the War of 1812, the Black Hawk War and the Second Seminole War in Florida territory. Because of his troops' victory in the important battle of Okeechobee, he was promoted to brigadier-general and given command of all troops in Florida territory. Taylor's service in the Mexican War made him a national hero and resulted in his election as president of the United States. Although he was a slave-owner, he opposed the extension of slavery beyond the 15 states where the institution was already legal. Taylor had served only 16 months as president when he died in office on July 9, 1850. This county was created in 1856, six years after Taylor's death.

351 Union County

The united opinion that the new county should be created— Union County was carved out of the western section of Bradford County on May 20, 1921. The name was chosen to reflect the union of opinion within Bradford County that the county should be split into two counties. Originally the name for the new county was to have been New River County. The sponsor of the amendment to change the name to Union County was quoted in the *Florida Times-Union* of May 6, 1921, as stating that the eastern and western sections of Bradford County "were united this time in asking for the divorce though the two parts of the (Bradford) county have never before been able to get together on this proposition."

352 Volusia County

The former settlement of Volusia Landing, Florida— Volusia County was created in 1854 and named for a post called Volusia Landing. This settlement was within Volusia County on the Saint Johns River, near Lake George. The origin of Volusia Landing's name is uncertain but the following possibilities have been mentioned:

1. Derived from the name of an early English settler, named Volus.

2. Derived from the name of a Frenchman or Belgian named Veluche, who owned a trading post at the landing.

3. Derived from the name of a plantation in this vicinity which a Mr. George Woodruff purchased in the early 1820s which he named Volusia.

353 Wakulla County

Wakulla Springs and/or Wakulla River— This county was created in 1843 and named for the Wakulla Springs and/or the Wakulla River here. The Wakulla Springs are one of Florida's major springs with a discharge of up to 1,870 cubic feet of wonderfully clear water per second. They spring from a limestone foundation in the heart of a dense cypress swamp and measure some 400 feet in diameter. The Wakulla River is fed by the Wakulla Springs and is but ten miles in length. It unites with Saint Marks River and falls into the Gulf of Mexico's Apalachee Bay. The name *Wakulla* is a corruption by the Indians of the Spanish *Guacara*. That Spanish *Guacara* was a phonetic spelling of an aboriginal Indian name whose meaning is uncertain. The popular belief that wakulla meant "mystery" is only a guess. Other unsubstantiated guesses include "loon" and "misting."

354 Walton County

George Walton (–)— Walton served as a colonel and aide to General Andrew Jackson and, in 1821, he became secretary of West Florida under Jackson who was military governor. When Jackson left Florida and returned to Tennessee in 1821, Walton governed West Florida until the expiration of Jackson's nominal term in June, 1822. From 1822 to 1826 Walton served as secretary of the entire Florida territory. It was during this period, in 1824, that Walton County was created. Walton's father, also named George Walton, was one of the signers of the Declaration of Independence and later served as governor of Georgia.

355 Washington County

George Washington (1732–1799)— Washington was a native of Virginia. He served in Virginia's house of burgesses and became one of the colonies' leaders in opposition to British policies in America. He was a member of the first and second Continental Congresses and commander of all Continental armies in the Revolutionary War. Following victory in that war, Washington was elected to be the first president of the United States.

REFERENCES

Beer, William. "The Dixie Bill." *The Magazine of History*, Vol. 20, No. 1. Poughkeepsie, New York: January, 1915.

Bloodworth, Bertha E. "Florida Place-Names." Ph.D. Thesis, University of Florida, Gainesville, Florida, 1959.

Bloodworth, Bertha E., & Alton C. Morris. *Places in the Sun*. Gainesville, University Presses of Florida, 1978.

Boyd, Mark F. "The Seminole War: Its Background & Onset." *Florida Historical Quarterly*, Vol. 30, No. 1. Gainesville, Florida: July, 1951.

Bullen, Adelaide K. *Florida Indians of Past & Present*. Delray Beach, Florida, Southern Publishing Co., 1965.

Cabell, Branch & A. J. Hanna. *The St. Johns: A Parade of Diversities*. New York, Farrar & Rinehart, Inc., 1943.

Cash, W. T. *The Story of Florida*. New York, American Historical Society, Inc., 1938.

Corse, Herbert M. "Names of the St. Johns River." *Florida Historical Quarterly*, Vol. 21, No. 2. St. Augustine, Florida: October, 1942.

Coulson, John. *The Saints: A Concise Biographical Dictionary*. New York, Hawthorn Books, Inc., 1958.

Covington, James W. *The Story of Southwestern Florida*. New York, Lewis Historical Publishing Co., Inc., 1957.

Dau, Frederick W. *Florida Old & New*. New York, G. P. Putnam's Sons, 1934.

Delaney, John J., & James Edward Tobin. *Dictionary of Catholic Biography*. Garden City, New York, Doubleday & Co., Inc., 1961.

Douglas, Marjory S. *The Everglades: River of Grass*. New York, Rinehart & Co., Inc., 1947.

Drew, Frank. "Florida Place-Names of Indian Origin." *Quarterly Periodical of the Florida Historical Society*, Vol. 6, No. 4. Gainesville, Florida: April, 1928.

Drew, Shelley. "Place Names in Ten Northeastern Counties of Florida." *American Speech*, Vol. 37, No. 4. New York: December, 1962.

The Encyclopedia Americana. New York, Americana Corporation, 1977.

Florida: Historic, Dramatic, Contemporary. New York, Lewis Historical Publishing Co., Inc., 1952.

Frech, Mary L. *Chronology & Documentary Handbook of the State of Florida*.

Dobbs Ferry, New York, Oceana Publications, Inc., 1973.

Gold, Pleasant D. *History of Volusia County, Florida.* De Land, Florida, E. O. Painter Printing Co., 1927.

Goodwin, Hal, & Libby Goodwin. *The Indian River: An American Lagoon.* Arlington, Virginia, Compass Publications, Inc., 1976.

Grismer, Karl H. *History of St. Petersburg.* St. Petersburg, Tourist News Publishing Co., 1924.

Grismer, Karl H. *The Story of Sarasota.* Tampa, Florida Grower Press, 1946.

Hanna, Alfred J., & Kathryn A. Hanna. *Lake Okeechobee.* Indianapolis, Bobbs-Merrill Co., 1948.

Hebel, Ianthe B. *Centennial History of Volusia County, Florida.* Daytona Beach, Florida, College Publishing Co., 1955.

Heliier, Walter R. *Indian River: Florida's Treasure Coast.* Coconut Grove, Florida, Hurricane House Publishers, Inc., 1965.

Hine, C. Vickerstaff. *On the Indian River.* Chicago. Charles H. Sergel & Co., 1891.

Hodge, Frederick W. *Handbook of American Indians North of Mexico.* Totowa, New Jersey, Rowman & Littlefield, 1975.

Hutchinson, Janet. *History of Martin County.* Hutchinson Island, Florida, Gilbert's Bar Press, 1975.

Jahoda, Gloria. *Florida: A History.* New York, W. W. Norton & Co., 1976.

McKay, D. B. *Pioneer Florida.* Tampa, Florida, Southern Publishing Co. 1959.

McMullen, Edwin W. *English Topographic Terms in Florida.* Gainesville, University of Florida Press, 1953.

McMullen, E. Wallace. "The Origin of the Term Everglades." *American Speech,* Vol. 28, No. 1. February, 1953.

Marks, Henry S. *Who Was Who in Florida.* Huntsville, Alabama, Strode Publishers, 1973.

Marth, Del, & Martha J. Marth. *The Florida Almanac: 1983-84.* Gretna, Louisiana, Pelican Publishing Co., 1983.

Marth, Del, & Martha J. Marth. *The Florida Almanac: 1986-87.* Gretna, Louisiana, Pelican Publishing Co., 1985.

Matschat, Cecile H. *Suwannee River: Strange Green Land.* Athens, University of Georgia Press, 1938.

Mayo, Nathan. *The Fifth Census of the State of Florida: Taken in the Year 1925.* Tallahassee, T. J. Appleyard, Inc.

Mayo, Nathan. *Know Florida.* Tallahassee, State of Florida Department of Agriculture, 1950.

Mayo, Nathan. *North & Northwest Florida.* Tallahassee, Department of Agriculture.

Michaels, Brian E. "Leon County Voters in the First Statewide Election: May 26, 1845." *Florida Armchair Researcher,* Vol. 1, No. 1. Hampton, Georgia: Winter, 1984.

Morris, Allen. *The Florida Handbook: 1947-1948.* Tallahassee, Peninsular Publishing Co, 1946.

Morris, Allen. *The Florida Handbook: 1983-1984.* Tallahassee, Peninsular Publishing Co., 1983.

Morris, Allen. *Florida Place Names.* Coral Gables, Florida, University of Miami Press, 1974.

New Catholic Encyclopedia. New York, McGraw-Hill Book Company, 1967.

Read, William A. *Florida Place-Names of Indian Origin & Seminole Personal Names.* Baton Rouge, Louisiana State University Press, 1934.

Rigg, J. Linton. *Bahama Islands.* New York, D. Van Nostrand Co., Inc., 1951.

Roberts, Albert H. "The Dade Massacre." *Quarterly Periodical of the Florida Historical Society,* Vol. 5, No. 3. Gainesville, Florida: January, 1927.

Room, Adrian. *Place-Names of the World.* Plymouth, England, Latimer Trend & Co., Ltd., 1974.

Simpson, J. Clarence. "Middle Florida Place Names." *Apalachee: The Publication of the Tallahassee Historical Society,* Tallahassee: 1946.

Tebeau, Charlton W. *Florida's Last Frontier: The History of Collier County.* University of Miami Press, 1966.

Thurston, Herbert S. J. & Donald Attwater. *Butler's Lives of the Saints.* New York, P. J. Kenedy & Sons, 1956.

Utley, George B. "Florida County Names." *The Magazine of History,* Vol. 8, No. 2. New York: August, 1908.

Utley, George B. "Origin of the County Names in Florida." *Publications of the Florida Historical Society,* Vol. 1, No. 3. Jacksonville: October, 1908.

Verrill, A. Hyatt. *Romantic & Historic Florida.* New York, Dodd, Mead & Co., 1935.

Vogel, Virgil J. *Indian Names in Michigan.* Ann Arbor, University of Michigan Press, 1986.

Wentworth, Harold, & Stuart B. Flexner. *Dictionary of American Slang.* New York, Thomas Y. Crowell Co., 1975.

West, G. M. *St. Andrews, Florida: Historical Notes Upon St. Andrews and St. Andrews Bay.* St. Andrews, Florida, Panama City Publishing Co., 1922.

Work Projects Administration. *Inventory of the County Archives of Florida-Wakulla County.* Jacksonville, Florida, 1942.

Works Progress Administration. *Inventory of the County Archives of Florida-Charlotte, Okaloosa & Sarasota Counties.* Jacksonville, Florida, 1938-1939.

Georgia

(159 counties)

356 *Appling County*

Daniel Appling (1787–)—Appling was a native of Georgia whose family had long been prominent in the Columbia County area. He was educated in private schools in Georgia and, in 1805, at the age of 18, he enlisted in the army and was commissioned lieutenant. Appling participated in actions against the Indians and then became a hero in the War of 1812, first as a major, in the battle of Sandy Creek at Lake Erie and later, as a lieutenant-colonel, at Plattsburg, New York. At the close of the war Appling returned to Georgia but he died soon after, in either 1817 or 1818. Appling County was created on December 15, 1818.

357 *Atkinson County*

William Y. Atkinson (1854–1899)—Following graduation from the University of Georgia, this Georgia native practiced law in Newnan and served as solicitor of Coweta County. Elected to the Georgia legislature in 1886, he served four consecutive terms in that body. During his final term he was speaker of the House of Representatives. Atkinson was elected governor of Georgia in 1894 and reelected once in 1896. As governor he tried, unsuccessfully, to eliminate lynching in Georgia.

358 Bacon County

Augustus O. Bacon (1839–1914) — This Georgia native joined the Confederate army soon after he graduated from the University of Georgia with a law degree. Bacon attained the rank of captain. Soon after the war he entered politics, serving first in Georgia's house of representatives where he became speaker pro tempore for two years and later speaker of the house for eight years. Bacon was then elected by the Georgia legislature to the U.S. Senate and he served in that body for about 19 years. He died while still in office in February, 1914, and the Georgia legislature created and named this county in his honor later that year.

359 Baker County

John Baker (–1792) — A native of Georgia and a prosperous farmer, Baker served the colony of Georgia as a lieutenant in the British army. He also served as a member of colonial Georgia's provincial congress and later as an American hero in the Revolutionary War. After the Revolution, Colonel Baker fought against the Indians under General James Jackson.

360 Baldwin County

Abraham Baldwin (1754–1807) — Baldwin was a licensed minister, a chaplain in the Revolutionary War and, later, a lawyer. He served in the Georgia legislature and was active in establishing the University of Georgia. He represented Georgia in the convention which framed the U.S. Constitution and in both houses of the U.S. Congress. Baldwin identified himself with the interests of the South; e.g., his proslavery position. This county was created in 1803 while Baldwin was still alive.

361 Banks County

Richard E. Banks (1784–1850) — Born in Elbert County, Georgia, Banks graduated from the University of Georgia and received his medical degree from the University of Pennsylvania in 1820. After a year in hospital work he returned to Elbert County, Georgia. His medical and surgical practice embraced an area of about 100 square miles in rural upper Georgia and western South Carolina, which he visited

on horse back. He was particularly successful in the removal of cataracts and other operations on the eye. In 1832 Dr. Banks moved to Gainesville, Georgia where he lived the rest of his life within a few miles of the Cherokee Indians and the federal government frequently employed him to attend to the Cherokee Indians. When this new county was created in 1858 within the area that the popular doctor had traveled, it was named in his honor.

362 Barrow County

David C. Barrow (1852–1929) — Dr. Barrow was a native of Georgia and a graduate of the University of Georgia who spent his life as an educator and executive at that university. After graduation from the university, Barrow participated in the geological survey of Georgia. He began his teaching career at the university as instructor of mathematics. In 1883 he was promoted to professor of civil engineering and six years later he was selected as head of the department of mathematics. Barrow was serving as dean of the university's Franklin College when the chancellor of the University of Georgia died in 1906. Dr. Barrow was selected as the new chancellor and he served in that position until 1925. This county was created in 1914 while Barrow was serving as chancellor.

363 Bartow County

Francis S. Bartow (1816–1861) — Bartow was born in Savannah, Georgia, and became a prominent lawyer in that city. He served in both houses of the Georgia legislature and later, in 1857, he ran unsuccessfully for a seat in the U.S. House of Representatives. He was an influential figure in the early days of the Confederate States of America. He vigorously supported secession at the Georgia convention. Later, as chairman of the military affairs committee of the provisional and first Confederate congresses, Bartow was responsible for selecting the gray uniform of the Confederate army. He left the Confederate congress in 1861 to join the Confederate army as an officer. Soon after, on July 21, 1861, at the battle of First Manassas, Brigadier-general Bartow was killed in combat while personally leading a charge against a Union canon. This county was originally named Cass County in honor of Lewis Cass. When Cass took an antisouthern stand, indignant Georgians decided to rename the county. The name was changed in December, 1861, to honor General Bartow who died a hero five months earlier.

364 Ben Hill County

Benjamin H. Hill (1823–1882) — Hill was born in Georgia and served in both houses of the Georgia legislature. He was elected to the provisional congress of the Confederate States of America in 1861 and soon after to the senate of that body where he served throughout the Civil War. Following the war he was imprisoned for a few months for his Confederate activities. During the years following the Civil War, Hill became an important political leader who vigorously opposed the infamous Reconstruction measures that were imposed on the South. He was elected to the U.S. Congress in 1875 and he later served in the U.S. Senate.

365 Berrien County

John M. Berrien (1781–1856) — A native of New Jersey and a lawyer, Berrien served as solicitor of the eastern district of Georgia and later as judge of the same district. He then served briefly in the state senate until he was elected by the Georgia legislature to the U.S. Senate. In 1829 President Jackson appointed Berrien to serve in his cabinet as attorney general. Berrien later represented Georgia again in the U.S. Senate, serving from 1841 to 1852. He died on January 1, 1856, and the Georgia legislature created and named this county in his honor just two months later.

366 Bibb County

William W. Bibb (1781–1820) — Bibb was born in Virginia and practiced medicine before entering politics. He was a member of both the house and senate of the Georgia legislature and represented Georgia in both houses of the U.S. Congress. Bibb was appointed by President Monroe in 1817 as governor of the newly formed territory of Alabama. When that territory was admitted to the Union as a state, Bibb was endorsed by popular vote and he continued in office as the first governor of the state of Alabama. This county was created in 1822.

367 Bleckley County

Logan E. Bleckley (1827–1907) — A native of Georgia, Bleckley was admitted to the bar at the age of 18 and served as solicitor general (prosecuting attorney) in the Atlanta area. He joined the Confederate army as a private but his service in the field was brief on account of poor health. In 1875 he was appointed an associate justice of the Georgia supreme court and he later served for seven years as chief justice of that court. This county was created by constitutional amendment which was ratified by a popular election held on October 2, 1912.

368 *Brantley County*

Uncertain—There are conflicting versions of the origin of this county's name. The two possibilities are Benjamin. D. Brantley and William G. Brantley.

Benjamin D. Brantley (1832–1891)—Benjamin D. Brantley, who was born in Georgia, was named Joseph at birth but his name was changed to Benjamin three weeks later in honor of his father who was then dying. The younger Benjamin Brantley served in the Confederate army as a private and later represented Pierce County for one term in Georgia's house of representatives. Benjamin D. Brantley spent most of his adult life as a commercial entrepreneur and he also served for about 18 years as county treasurer of Pierce County. An article in the *Savannah Morning News* dated August 15, 1920, states that Brantley County was named for this man and that those who became Brantley County's first citizens when it was created in 1920 selected its name.

William G. Brantley (1860–1934)—William G. Brantley of Brunswick, Georgia was a lawyer who served in both houses of the Georgia legislature. He also was solicitor-general of Pierce County, Georgia.

369 *Brooks County*

Preston S. Brooks (1819–1857)—A native of South Carolina, Brooks served in the South Carolina legislature and later served as a captain in the Mexican War. He was elected to represent South Carolina in the U.S. House of Representatives in 1853 and he served in that body until his death, just four years later at the age of 38. He was intensely southern in sentiment and a zealous defender of southern rights. He became famous in May, 1856, when he caned U.S. Senator Charles Sumner of Massachusetts because of a speech Sumner had made that day which was offensive to the South. This county was created in 1858, about one year after Brooks' sudden death.

370 *Bryan County*

Jonathan Bryan (1708–1788)—A native of South Carolina, Bryan came with James E. Oglethorpe to Savannah to help establish the colony of Georgia. He served on His Majesty's council for Georgia and as a justice of the general court. During the years that preceded the American Revolution, Bryan became an early and very active opponent of the British. On December 9, 1769, King George III suspended him from his seat on the council "and removed from any office he might hold in Georgia." He represented the town and district of Savannah in the provincial congress which met at Savannah in 1775 and was a member of the council of safety. During the Revolutionary War, Bryan was captured by the British and held prisoner on Long Island, New York, for about two years. This county was created in 1793, five years after Bryan's death.

371 *Bulloch County*

Archibald Bulloch (–1777)—This South Carolina native moved with his parents to Georgia where he practiced law and was elected to the Georgia legislature. Bulloch became president of Georgia's provincial congress and one of Georgia's delegates to the Continental Congress. In 1776, when the British royal governor fled, Bulloch became "president and commander-in-chief of Georgia." He personally led a party of militia and Creek Indians that destroyed a British and Tory base on Tybee Island in March, 1776.

372 *Burke County*

Edmund Burke (1729–1797)—Burke was born in Dublin, Ireland and pursued a literary career. He entered the British parliament where he became a ranking Whig, noted orator and statesman. In parliament and in his political writings Burke was a champion of liberty for the American colonies and an advocate of human rights. His speech in 1774 entitled *American Taxation* and another on *Conciliation with America* in 1775 were examples of his efforts on our behalf. This county was originally laid out as the parish of St. George. It received its present name on February 5, 1777, in the Georgia constitution.

373 *Butts County*

Samuel Butts (1777–1814)—A native of Virginia, Butts moved to Georgia with his family when he was a young man and engaged in mercantile pursuits here. During the War of 1812, Butts joined the Georgia troops, under General John Floyd, as a private and was soon promoted to captain. Butts served on the frontier in upper western Georgia and eastern Alabama against hostile Indians. His company performed ably in a number of actions against the Indians before Butts was killed in combat on January 27, 1814, in what is now the state of Alabama. Butts County was created in 1825.

374 *Calhoun County*

John C. Calhoun (1782–1850)—Calhoun represented South Carolina in both houses of the U.S. Congress. He served as secretary of war, secretary of state and as vice-president. He was a forceful advocate of slavery, states' rights and limited powers for the federal government. He resigned the vice-presidency to enter the U.S. Senate where he could better represent the views of South Carolina and the South. This county was created in 1854.

375 *Camden County*

Charles Pratt, Earl of Camden (1714–1794)—Pratt, who was born in London, England, served as attorney general and was a member of parliament. In 1761 he became chief justice of the court of common pleas and a decision that he rendered in the trial of John Wilkes concerning freedom of speech and freedom of the press made him one of the most popular men in England. A bit later, now titled Baron Camden, he became lord chancellor. He opposed England's treatment of the American colonies which earned him wide popularity here and was the reason that this county was named for him when it was created on February 5, 1777, in the Georgia constitution. In 1786 Baron Camden was made first earl of Camden and viscount Bayham. He served more than ten years as president of the council.

376 *Candler County*

Allen D. Candler (1834–1910)—A native of Georgia, Candler served in the Confederate army and later was a member of the Georgia general assembly. Candler then served in the U.S. House of Representatives, after which he was Georgia's secretary of state. He was elected governor of Georgia and served two very conservative terms as governor from 1898 to 1902. From 1903 until his death he was Georgia's state historian. Candler County was created in 1914.

377 *Carroll County*

Charles Carroll (1737–1832)—Carroll was a native of Maryland and he represented that state in the Continental Congress. He was one of the signers of the Declaration of Independence and he later represented Maryland as a U.S. senator in the first congress of the United States. Carroll lived to be the last surviving signer of the Declaration of Independence and several states recognized that distinction by naming counties for him.

378 *Catoosa County*

Catoosa Springs, Georgia—This county was created in 1853 and named for the springs here, four miles east of Ringgold, the Catoosa county seat. These springs attracted health seekers since 1840, or even earlier. Their name probably derived from the Cherokee Indian word *gatusi* signifying "hill, small mountain, high place," or even "mound." Presumably this name was applied on account of a series of ridges and small mountains that slope across the area near Catoosa Springs from the northeast to the southwest. Other, less likely explanations that have been suggested:

1. Named for an Indian, supposed to be a chief.
2. Named for an Indian tribe.

From the Cherokee words *gatu gitse* meaning "new settlement place."

4. From the Cherokee term *catoose* which was said to mean "wind." This is unlikely since the usual Cherokee term for wind is *unauli*, also rendered by the Whites as *unawle* or *unawleh*.

5. From a Cherokee word *gituzi* meaning "people of light."

379 *Charlton County*

Uncertain—Charlton County was created on February 18, 1854, one month to the day after the death of Robert M. Charlton and the county was probably named for him. However, there is an element of doubt on this. A second possibility for this county's namesake is his father, Thomas U. P. Charlton. It is also possible that the death of the younger Charlton triggered the naming of this county in the joint honor of both father and son.

Robert M. Charlton (1807–1854)—After serving in the lower house of the Georgia legislature, this Georgia native served as U.S. attorney for the district of Georgia. Before his 30th birthday he became judge of the eastern judicial circuit and he then served three terms as mayor of Savannah. He was elected by the Georgia legislature to the U.S. Senate but had served in that body little more than a year when he died on January 18, 1854. Charlton County was created on February 18, 1854.

Thomas U. P. Charlton (1779–1835)—Thomas Charlton was born in South Carolina but moved to Georgia as a boy. At the age of 21 he entered the Georgia legislature and later served as attorney general of Georgia. While still in his 20's, he became judge on the eastern circuit bench. He served six terms as mayor of Savannah, which at that time was Georgia's leading city. During the War of 1812 he was chairman of the committee of public safety.

380 *Chatham County*

William Pitt, Earl of Chatham (1708–1778)—Pitt, an Englishman and the first earl of Chatham, was one of England's greatest and most famous statesmen. He was a member of parliament and held the positions of vice treasurer of Ireland and paymaster general of the forces. He became secretary of state and virtually prime minister in 1756 but in 1760 King George III took the throne and Pitt was forced to resign. In 1766 he formed a new ministry but served for only 15 months. Chatham County was created in the Georgia constitution in 1777. The earl of Chatham had become very popular on this side of the Atlantic for his opposition to the alleged right of the English parliament to tax the American colonies without their consent. On the eve of the American Revolution he urged reconciliation and after the war started he favored any peace settlement that would keep the American colonies in the British empire. Several of our country's counties are named for him.

381 *Chattahoochee County*

Chattahoochee River—This county's name is not spelled uniformly but Chattahoochee is the version currently used by the board of county commissioners and the name of the river for which the county was named is customarily spelled Chattahoochee as well. The Chattahoochee is one of the South's major rivers, forming a large section of the Georgia—Alabama border, and it is an important source of drinking water for Atlanta, Columbus and several other communities. It rises in the Blue Ridge mountains and travels more than 400 miles, uniting with the Flint River in Georgia's southwestern corner and then emptying into the Gulf of Mexico southwest of Tallahassee, Florida. In Florida, where some swamps are found along the river, the combined Flint and Chattahoochee Rivers are known as the Apalachicola River. *Chattahoochee* is the surviving version of the Indians' *chatto hoche* meaning "stone marked" or "flowered." Painted rocks, stained red and pink by nature, are found in the upper reaches of the Chattahoochee River. This county was created in 1854 and named for the river which borders it on the west.

382 *Chattooga County*

Chattooga River—There are three rivers in Georgia containing the name Chattooga; i.e., two Chattooga Rivers and one West Chattooga River. This county was created in 1838 and named for the river that rises in Walker County in northwestern Georgia, flows through the middle of Chattooga County and continues until it reaches Alabama where it joins Little River and thence on to the Coosa River. *Chattooga* is an Indian name that is common in the southern United States but its meaning is not known. One suggestion concerning the origin of this particular Chattooga River's name is offered:

This Chattooga may have initially derived from the name by which an early Cherokee town was known. That town stood on the South Carolina side of Georgia's other Chattooga River at Georgia's northeastern corner. Apparently the Cherokee abandoned this town by 1760. This town's name may have been *Tsatu gi*, *Chato-algi* or *Chato-agi*, If so, the Cherokee probably borrowed it from some other tribe such as the Creek and it may have meant "full of rocks."

383 *Cherokee County*

Cherokee Indians—The Cherokee Indians were a large tribe who lived in Georgia and several other southeastern states at the time of European contact. By the early 1800's they had adopted many of the features of civilization. By 1840, most Cherokees had been forced from their lands and removed to Indian territory (now Oklahoma) by court decisions, a fraudulent treaty and military force. The removal of some 17,000 Cherokee Indians from their ancient tribal lands in northwestern Georgia was a dark chapter in Georgia's history. Their journey to Indian territory was marked by indescribable suffering from which some 4,000 Cherokees died. The name Cherokee is said to be derived from the Cherokee word for "fire," *chera*.

384 *Clarke County*

Elijah Clarke (1733–1799)—Clarke was a native of South Carolina who moved to Georgia in 1774. He served as a general in the Revolutionary War. After the war, he was involved in an intrigue against Florida and other adventures which were contrary to the policy of the federal government but he remained popular with the people of Georgia. This county was created in December, 1801, less than three years after Clarke's death.

385 *Clay County*

Henry Clay (1777–1852)—Clay represented Kentucky in both branches of the U.S. Congress. For many years he was one of the more prominent figures in American politics but his several bids for the presidency were unsuccessful. He was influential in effecting important compromises between northern and southern interests during the years that secession and civil war were imminent. This county was created in 1854.

386 *Clayton County*

Augustin S. Clayton (1783–1839)—About one year after Clayton's birth in Virginia, his family moved to Georgia and he lived most of his life in Athens, Georgia. He served in both branches of the Georgia legislature and then was elected judge of the western superior circuit court. Clayton became a member of the U.S. House of Representatives in 1831 where he served two terms as a champion of states' rights. This county was created in 1858, about two years before the Civil War began.

387 *Clinch County*

Duncan L. Clinch (1787–1849)—This North Carolina native was a career officer in the United States army who served in the War of 1812 and in the Seminole Indian Wars in Florida. In 1829 he was promoted to brigadier-general. He resigned from the army in 1836 and engaged in planting in Camden County, Georgia. Eight years later he entered the U.S. Congress as a representative from Georgia and served one term. This county was created in February, 1850, just a few months after General Clinch's death.

388 *Cobb County*

Thomas W. Cobb (1784–1830)—A native of Georgia, Cobb was a lawyer who represented Georgia in both branches of the U.S. Congress where he gained a reputation as an eloquent debater. While serving in the House of Representatives, he took a prominent part in the debates on the Missouri Compromise. Cobb resigned from the U.S. Senate in 1828 and he spent the final months of his life as a superior court judge. This county was created and named in Judge Cobb's honor in 1832.

389 *Coffee County*

John Coffee (1782–1836)—Coffee, who was born in Virginia moved to Georgia in 1800 and served as a general in the Georgia militia during the Creek Indian war. He supervised the construction of a road through Georgia, called the Coffee Road, which was cut through the state to carry munitions of war to Florida during wars with the Indians there. Coffee served several terms in the Georgia legislature and he later served in the U.S. Congress representing Georgia in the House of Representatives from 1833 until his death.

There are three Coffee Counties in the United States, one in Georgia named for John Coffee (1782–1836) and the other two in Alabama and Tennessee which were named for John Coffee (1772–1833). These men are easily confused with each other. They were first cousins with identical names who moved south from their native state of Virginia. Both became generals and they died within a few years of one another. Both were associated with Andrew Jackson. The older Coffee (1772–1833) served under Jackson in the 1813–1814 war against the Creek Indians and later at the battle of New Orleans. Georgia's Coffee (1782–1836) did not serve with Jackson during his military campaigns but became a personal friend of his in later years. Georgia's John Coffee (1782–1836) served in the U.S. House of Representatives while the older Coffee (1772–1833) did not.

390 *Colquitt County*

Walter T. Colquitt (1799–1855)—Colquitt was born in Virginia but moved to Georgia when he was still a small boy. A Methodist preacher as well as a lawyer, this versatile man continued to attend to Methodist preaching duties while practicing law and engaging in politics. Colquitt became a Chattahoochee superior court judge at the age of 27. After serving in the Georgia senate, Colquitt was a member of both houses of the U.S. Congress. He resigned his seat in the U.S. Senate in 1848 for reasons that are now unknown. Colquitt was a champion of the rights of the South and he also advocated Georgia's secession from the Union. This county was created on February 25, 1856, less than a year after Colquitt's death.

391 *Columbia County*

Cristoforo Colombo (1451–1506)—Colombo, whose name we render as Christopher Columbus, was a native of Italy who believed the theory that the earth is round and that Asia could be reached by sailing west from Europe. He persuaded Ferdinand and Isabella of Spain to equip an expedition for him to test this theory. Sailing from Europe August 3, 1492, he first sighted land in the Americas in the Bahama Islands on October 12, 1492. On this voyage he left a colony of 40 men on the Hatian coast. Columbus returned several times to the New World before his death in 1506. Popularly known as the discoverer of America, Columbus was certainly not the first European to reach the Western Hemisphere. Leif Ericsson had accomplished this about the year 1000. But it was Columbus' expedition that triggered rapid exploration, conquest and settlement of the Americas by Europeans. Columbia County, Georgia, was created on December 10, 1790.

392 *Cook County*

Philip Cook (1817–1894)—A native of Georgia, Cook was practicing law and serving in the Georgia senate at the outbreak of the Civil War. He enlisted in the Confederate army as a private in 1861, was wounded several times in combat and rose rapidly to the rank of brigadier-general. Cook was a member of the state constitutional convention of 1865 and he served in the U.S. Congress from 1873 to 1883. In 1890 General Cook was elected Georgia's secretary of state, in which office he served until his death.

393 *Coweta County*

Lower Creek Indians—Coweta County, Georgia was named for the Coweta, or Lower Creek, Indians. It was formed from some of the land acquired under treaty with the Indians and the name was chosen as a compliment to the chief of the Cowetas, General William McIntosh, in gratitude for the part Chief McIntosh had taken in ceding these Indian lands to the Whites. This treaty so infuriated some of McIntosh's fellow Indians that they murdered him in retribution. Two of the towns of the Lower Creek Indians contained the word *kawita* in their name. These towns were about 2-1/2 miles away from each other on the Chattahoochee River. One of them was called Upper Kawita and the other Kawita Talahasi, or Old Kawita. The term Coweta derived from the names of these two towns. The meaning of the term *kawita* is not known but it might have referred to falls on the Chattahoochee River.

Lower Creek Indians—The Creek Indians were a large and powerful confederacy of agricultural tribes. Their 18th century population numbered perhaps 20,000, living in a large area of the southeastern United States including most of Georgia and Alabama. Until the 1813-1814 Creek War with the Whites, in military actions they were usually successful. They frequently executed their prisoners of war by burning them at the stake. By 1840 most of the Creeks had been removed to Indian territory (now Oklahoma) where about 20,000 still live.

The Lower Creeks were part of the Creek confederacy who lived near the lower Chattahoochee River and its tributaries. In the early 18th century there were about 2,400 Lower Creek Indians. The names Coweta (Kawita), Apalachula (Apalachicola) and Ucheesee or Ochesee (Ochisi) were often used to designate the Lower Creek Indians.

394 *Crawford County*

William H. Crawford (1772–1834) — Crawford served in the Georgia legislature and as U.S. senator from Georgia. He was elected president pro tempore of the senate and he later served as minister to France, secretary of war and secretary of the treasury. Crawford was a serious candidate for the presidency in both 1816 and 1824. This county was created in December, 1822, while he was in the presidential limelight.

395 *Crisp County*

Charles F. Crisp (1845–1896) — Crisp was born in England to parents who were American citizens, visiting the British Isles and he grew up in Savannah and Macon, Georgia. He served in the Confederate army for three years, rising to lieutenant before being captured and taken prisoner of war. In 1872 Crisp was appointed solicitor-general of Georgia's southwestern circuit and he later served five years as a judge of the superior court of that circuit. In 1883 he entered the U.S. House of Representatives and he served in that body, including four years as speaker of the house, until his death. Crisp County, Georgia, was created in 1905.

396 *Dade County*

Francis L. Dade (–1835) — A native of Virginia, Dade was appointed a commissioned officer in the U.S. army without having been trained at West Point. His original commission was as third lieutenant. He served under General Jackson at Pensacola, Florida, where he met and

married a local girl. By 1828 he had risen to the rank of brevet major. Stationed at Fort Brooke on Tampa Bay in 1835, Dade was ordered to put down unrest among some Seminole Indians. On December 28, 1835 near the present town of Bushnell, Florida, a party of Seminole Indians and Blacks ambushed and massacred Dade and all but about three of his force of some 110 men. This massacre marked the start of the Second Seminole War in Florida. Dade County, Georgia, was created effective Christmas Day in 1837.

397 *Dawson County*

William C. Dawson (1798–1856) — Dawson was born on the extreme western frontier of Georgia and he served in both branches of the Georgia legislature. In 1836 he was elected to the U.S. House of Representatives where he represented Georgia for three years before returning to Georgia to practice law. Dawson was judge of the Ocmulgee judicial circuit for less than one year and later was elected by the Georgia legislature to the U.S. Senate where he served one term from 1849 to 1855. This county was created in December, 1857.

398 *De Kalb County*

Johann Kalb, Baron de Kalb (1721–1780) — Kalb was born in the province of Alsace, which at that time belonged to France. He was a general in the French army and resigned that commission to come to America to assist the colonies in the Revolutionary War. He served as a general in the American Revolutionary army and died in combat here.

399 *Decatur County*

Stephen Decatur (1779–1820) — Decatur, who was born in Maryland, was an officer in the U.S. navy who served in the Mediterranean Sea from 1801 to 1805 in the Tripolitan War. His bravery and successes in that war made him a popular hero in America and earned him promotion to captain. During the War of 1812, Decatur reinforced his reputation as a naval hero. Following that war Decatur, now a commodore, again served in the Mediterranean where he captured the Algerian flagship *Mashuda*. His display of naval force exacted peace terms from Algeria and indemnities for un-neutral acts from Tunis and Tripoli. This brought an end to the plundering of American shipping by the Barbary powers. Decatur's life ended in a duel fought in March, 1820, and

Decatur County was created in December, 1823.

400 *Dodge County*

William E. Dodge (1805–1883) — Dodge was a native of Connecticut who represented New York for one term in the U.S. House of Representatives. He was a wealthy financier who purchased extensive tracts of pine land in Canada and in several states in our country. He purchased an estate on St. Simons Island, Georgia, and established a sawmill here. His purchases included an enormous estate of pine land in Georgia that included much of the present counties of Dodge, Laurens, Pulaski, Telfair and Montgomery. In congress, Dodge was a friend in need to the South who urged moderation in Reconstruction measures following the Civil War. From 1865 until his death he was president of the National Temperance Society. This county was created in 1870. Mr. Dodge expressed his appreciation for that honor by having a handsome county courthouse built for Dodge County at his expense.

401 *Dooly County*

John Dooly (1740–1780) — Born in North Carolina, Dooly was a very spirited man who moved to Georgia in 1762 with his wife, three sons and three orphan nephews. These pioneers settled near the South Carolina border in the Lincoln County-Wilkes County area and Dooly became an Indian fighter. In the Revolution, he was a colonel in the militia and his troops participated in an important victory over a Loyalist brigade at Kettle Creek on February 14, 1779. Dooly also served in 1779 as the state's attorney in the first court held in Wilkes County and some nine Tories were sentenced to hang as a result of Dooly's efforts. This earned Dooly the hatred of the Tories and in 1780 a band of them, headed by Captain Corker, forced entry into Dooly's home and murdered him in front of his wife and children. Three of these Tories were caught and hanged but about six of them continued on to visit the Revolutionary heroine, Nancy Hart, who captured them. (See Hart County, Georgia, below.)

402 *Dougherty County*

Charles Dougherty (–1853) — Charles Dougherty was born in Oglethorpe County, Georgia about the beginning of the 19th century. He practiced law in Athens, Georgia, and was elected by the Georgia legislature to be judge of the western judicial circuit. For many years he was a leader of the Whig party in Georgia and was identified with the wing of that party which took strong stands in favor of states' rights and the rights of the South. On December 15, 1853, the Georgia legislature passed the bill to create this new county. They considered naming it Fannin County but that name was never officially adopted. Instead, the name Dougherty was chosen to honor Judge Dougherty who had died in Athens a few days earlier.

403 *Douglas County*

Stephen A. Douglas (1813–1861) — Barely five feet tall, the "Little Giant" is most remembered as a political opponent of Abraham Lincoln. Douglas was born in Vermont and moved to Illinois where he enjoyed rapid political success. He served on the state supreme court, in the state legislature and as secretary of state. Following two terms in the U.S. House of Representatives, Douglas was elected to the U.S. Senate. In that body Douglas took courageous positions on the slavery issue which first outraged abolitionist sentiment and later infuriated the South. In 1858 Douglas ran for reelection to the U.S. Senate against Abraham Lincoln. Following the famous Lincoln-Douglas debates, the Republicans won the popular election but the state legislature reelected Douglas to the senate. Lincoln and Douglas were rivals again in 1860 for the presidency. Following Lincoln's election and the start of the Civil War, Douglas gave the president his active support. This county was created on October 17, 1870, during Reconstruction.

404 *Early County*

Peter Early (1773–1817) — A native of Virginia, Early's parents moved to Georgia while he was attending law school. Upon completion of his studies, Early settled in Georgia and began the practice of law. He was a member of the board of trustees of the University of Georgia, serving from 1797 to 1808 and again from 1811 until his death. Early represented Georgia in the U.S. House of Representatives where he consistently opposed proposed abolition legislation. He next became judge of Georgia's Ocmulgee judicial circuit and he held that post until his election, in 1813, as governor of Georgia. Early's veto of a proposed law concerning the rights of debtors and creditors was overridden and this unpopular veto led to his defeat when he ran for reelection. However, the voters of his home county of Greene still liked him and

they elected Early to the Georgia senate in 1816. His first term as state senator had not yet expired at the time of his death and Early County was created one year later.

405 *Echols County*

Robert M. Echols (–1847) — Echols was born in Wilkes County, Georgia, about 1800 and spent much of his life as a citizen of Walton County, Georgia. He represented that county for more than 20 years in both houses of the Georgia legislature. Echols served several terms as president of the Georgia senate. He was once a candidate for the U.S. House of Representatives but lost that election by a narrow margin. In the Mexican War Echols served as a colonel in the U.S. army and he was soon promoted to brigadier-general. During a dress parade at Natural Bridge, Mexico, he was thrown from his horse. The injuries sustained in this fall caused his death.

406 *Effingham County*

Thomas Howard, Earl of Effingham (1746–1791) — Howard was the third earl of Effingham and also held the titles of ninth Baron Howard and deputy earl-marshal. He was a member of the house of lords and an officer in the English army at the time that the American colonies declared their independence from England. When his regiment was ordered to bear arms against the American colonists and assist in putting down the American Revolution, Effingham refused to do so and he resigned his commission in the English army rather than comply. He stated that although it had been his life's ambition to serve England as a military officer "…a resignation which appeared to me the only method of avoiding the guilt of enslaving my country and embruing my hands in the blood of her sons." The citizens of Georgia were so impressed by this gesture that they chose to honor Effingham in the name of one of the eight counties that they created in 1777 in the Georgia constitution.

407 *Elbert County*

Samuel Elbert (–1788) — Elbert was born in South Carolina about 1740 and moved to Savannah, Georgia, where he engaged in mercantile pursuits and served in the Georgia commons house of assembly from 1769 to 1771. In June, 1775, Elbert was a member of Georgia's first council of safety. He was a delegate to the provincial

congress in Savannah in 1775 and served with distinction in the American Revolutionary army rising to the rank of major-general. He declined election to the Continental Congress in 1784 but became governor of Georgia in 1785 and served from January 14, 1785, to January 9, 1786. This county was created in 1790.

408 *Emanuel County*

David Emanuel (–1808) — One of Georgia's more obscure chief executives, Emanuel was born in Pennsylvania about 1744 and settled, when still a young man, in the area of Georgia that was soon to become Burke County. He served as an officer in the Georgia militia during the Revolution and later represented Burke County for many years in both branches of the Georgia legislature. Emanuel was serving as president of Georgia's senate when the governor of Georgia, James Jackson, resigned. As president of the senate, Emanuel assumed the governorship of Georgia and served from March 3, 1801, until Josiah Tattnall was inaugurated as governor on November 7, 1801. Emanuel then continued his duties as president of the Georgia senate until his death in 1808. Emanuel County was created in 1812.

409 *Evans County*

Clement A. Evans (1833–1911) — Evans, the son of a prosperous plantation owner, was born in Stewart County, Georgia, where he practiced law and was a county judge. In 1859 he was elected to the Georgia senate. In 1861 he enlisted in the Confederate army where he enjoyed rapid promotions and rose, in May, 1863 to the rank of brigadier-general. Most of Evans' Civil War duty was in the Army of Northern Virginia and he was wounded in combat on several occasions. In late 1864 he was promoted to acting major-general. After the war, Evans entered the clergy as a Southern Methodist minister and he was also active in the overthrow of the odious Reconstruction measures. He participated for many years in the leadership of the United Confederate Veterans' Association and was for a time commander-in-chief of that organization. This county was created in 1914.

410 *Fannin County*

James W. Fannin (1804–1836) — Fannin, a native of Georgia, moved to Texas in 1834 where he engaged in slave trading and agitating for Texas independence from Mexico. Early in the Texas Revolution, in

1835, he participated in the battle of Gonzales and in the battle of Concepcion. In March, 1836, Fannin, now a colonel, and his men were surrounded and forced to surrender at the battle of Coleto. Imprisoned by the Mexicans at Goliad, most of Fannin's men were massacred by order of Santa Anna on March 27, 1836. Because Fannin was wounded, he was executed separately, but on the same day. In 1837 a Fannin County was created in Texas to honor this man and Georgia honored her native son when it created its Fannin County in 1854.

411 *Fayette County*

Marie Joseph Paul Yves Roch Gilbert du Motier, Marquis de Lafayette (1757–1834)— Lafayette was a French aristocrat who served briefly in the French army. He came to America in 1777 to assist the American Revolutionary army. He was granted an honorary commission as major-general by the Continental Congress and served with distinction in a number of battles in the Revolutionary War. Fayette County, Georgia was created in 1821.

412 *Floyd County*

John Floyd (1769–1839)— Floyd, a native of South Carolina, moved to Camden County, Georgia, in 1791 and served as a brigadier-general in the War of 1812. His success against the Indian allies of the British made possible the relatively peaceful settlement by Whites of northwest Georgia including the Floyd County, Georgia, area. General Floyd served in the Georgia House of Representatives from 1820 to 1827 and he then represented Georgia in the U.S. House of Representatives for one term from 1827 to 1829. This northwestern Georgia county was created in 1832, seven years before Floyd died on his plantation in Camden County, Georgia.

413 *Forsyth County*

John Forsyth (1780–1841)— This illustrious orator was born in Virginia but moved to Georgia when he was a boy of four. His political career began as attorney general of the state of Georgia after which he served in the U.S. House of Representatives and, very briefly, as a U.S. senator. He resigned his seat in the senate in February, 1819, to accept an appointment as minister to Spain. As minister, he secured ratification by the king of Spain to the treaty that ceded Florida to the United States. Forsyth then returned to the national House of Representatives where he served four years before becoming governor of Georgia. He was Georgia's chief executive for just one two year term after which he returned to the U.S. Senate. This county was created in 1832 while Forsyth was serving this term in the senate. In 1834 he was appointed U.S. secretary of state and he held that position under presidents Andrew Jackson and Martin Van Buren.

414 *Franklin County*

Benjamin Franklin (1706–1790)— Franklin was a native of Massachusetts who moved to Pennsylvania in his teens. Poverty denied him a formal education but he became the leading printer and editor in North America. Franklin gained fame for his discoveries and inventions in the physical sciences and he distinguished himself as author, philosopher and diplomat. He was a signer of the Declaration of Independence and an important member of the convention which framed the U.S. Constitution. Franklin County, Georgia, was created in 1784.

415 *Fulton County*

Uncertain— This county was created on December 20, 1853. There are conflicting theories concerning the origin of this county's name from two standpoints: There is uncertainty about whom the county's name was intended to honor and there is also doubt concerning the identity of the person who decided upon the name Fulton for this Georgia county. Some sources state that the name was suggested by Georgia's State Senator John Collier of neighboring De Kalb County, Georgia. Others say that the idea for the county's name was first suggested by Dr. Needom L. Angier, who had come to Georgia from New Hampshire. There is no doubt that Senator Collier made the motion on December 7, 1853, that inserted the name Fulton in the pending bill in place of the blank that had been left where the new county's name was to go. But we do not know whether the idea was Senator Collier's or Dr. Angier's or even whether the idea originated with someone else. Most sources state that Georgia's premier county was named for Robert Fulton but a case is also made in support of the possibility that Dr. Angier had Hamilton Fulton in mind when he coined this name.

Hamilton Fulton (–)— Hamilton Fulton was a native of Scotland and he received his education there. A civil engineer, Fulton worked for a number of years in England before migrating to the United States. He became chief engineer of the state of Georgia. While in that post, he suggested a proposed railroad through what is now Fulton County, Georgia. He urged its construction and surveyed a proposed route for this railroad.

Robert Fulton (1765–1815)— A native of Pennsylvania, as a young man Fulton supported himself as an artist. He later gained fame for his inventions dealing with marine vessels. He invented a submarine which he successfully demonstrated in the year 1800. He invented mines to be used in naval warfare and was one of the inventors of the steamboat. The steamboat became a commercial success for Fulton and made him famous. This invention contributed greatly to the development of America.

The central argument against the idea that it was Robert Fulton whom the county's name was intended to honor mentions that an inventor, William Longstreet of Augusta, operated a steam powered vessel on the Savannah River in November, 1808, and that "There had never been a steamboat within 70 miles of Fulton County as there were no navigable rivers nearer than that and the people here then had no interest in river navigation." This argument presumes the parochial view that the people of the Fulton County area and/or the Georgia legislators were indifferent to the invention that played a central role in the development of the huge agricultural country that was the United States.

But we are not yet done with uncertainties concerning names associated with Fulton County. On January 1, 1932, three Georgia counties, Campbell County, Fulton County and Milton County were merged into one county. The surviving county carried the name Fulton and Campbell and Milton were abolished. Campbell County had been named for Duncan G. Campbell (1787–1828), a lawyer, member of the Georgia legislature and advocate of higher education for women. But it is not certain for whom the former Milton County was named. Some sources state that the name honored John Milton, an early secretary of state of the state of Georgia, while other sources indicate that it was Homer V. Milton who was so honored.

416 *Gilmer County*

George R. Gilmer (1790–1859)— This Georgia native served as an infantry officer in the 1813 to 1815 campaign against the Creek Indians. He later served in the houses of representatives of both Georgia and the

United States and was Georgia's governor. Gilmer was first elected governor of Georgia in 1829 and he served from November of that year until November, 1831. Gilmer County was created and named in his honor in December, 1832. Five years later, Gilmer again ran for governor and was elected as the states' rights candidate. Again be served just one term as governor.

417 *Glascock County*

Thomas Glascock (1790–1841)— A native of Georgia, Glascock was a delegate to the constitutional convention of 1798. He served as a captain in the War of 1812 and later was a brigadier-general during the Seminole War in 1817. On several occasions Glascock served in Georgia's house of representatives and he was speaker of that body in 1833 and 1834. In 1835 he was elected to represent Georgia in the U.S. House of Representatives. Reelected in 1837, Glascock served until 1839 when he returned to Georgia to resume his legal practice. This county was created in 1857.

418 *Glynn County*

John Glynn (1722–1779)— Glynn County was created on February 5, 1777, in Georgia's constitution and named for John Glynn, an English nobleman who was a friend of the American colonies during their struggles for justice and independence from England. He was legal adviser to the city of London, England, in which capacity he held the title sergeant of London. Glynn acted as legal counsel to John Wilkes and he served in the English parliament where he was an ally of the American colonies.

419 *Gordon County*

William W. Gordon (1796–1842)— A native of Georgia, Gordon attended schools in New Jersey and Rhode Island and then entered the U.S. military academy at West Point from which he graduated in 1815. During his military service Gordon served as aide to General Gaines. He resigned his commission in the army and moved to Savannah, to study law under James M. Wayne and he practiced law until 1836 when he became the first president of the Central Railroad and Banking Company of Georgia. Gordon was an advocate of internal improvements and railroads in Georgia and he supervised the planning and construction of railroads in Georgia from 1836 until his early death in 1842. This county was created in 1850.

420 *Grady County*

Henry W. Grady (1850–1889)— A native Georgian and a graduate of the University of Georgia, Grady began his career in journalism on newspapers in Rome, Georgia. A man of means, Grady acquired ownership interests in the newspapers with which he was associated, first in Rome and later in Atlanta, where he became managing editor of the *Atlanta Constitution*. He became nationally known as an eloquent orator as well as a journalist and was considered an important spokesman for the entire Reconstruction South or, to use the term that Grady coined, the "New South." He decried the evils of Reconstruction and succeeded in softening the hearts of many northerners toward their defeated brethren in the South. He urged the need for reconciliation and economic recovery. Mentioned as a possible running mate for Grover Cleveland in 1888, Grady died in his prime at the age of 39 of pneumonia. This county was created in 1905.

421 *Greene County*

Nathanael Greene (1742–1786)— Greene was born in Rhode Island and served briefly in the Rhode Island legislature. He gained fame as one of the ablest American generals in the Revolutionary War. After the war Greene retired to a plantation near Savannah, which was given to him by the state of Georgia, and he was living there when this county was created on February 3, 1786.

422 *Gwinnett County*

Button Gwinnett (–1777)— Born in England about 1732, Gwinnett immigrated to America and lived in Savannah, Georgia. He bought the 21 square mile St. Catherines Island in the Atlantic Ocean near Savannah. In 1776 Gwinnett was elected as a delegate from Georgia to the Continental Congress and he was one of the signers of the Declaration of Independence. He was a member of the assembly which wrote Georgia's first constitution and was the author of major portions of that document. Gwinnett was one of Georgia's early governors, his official title being president of the council and commander in chief of the army. He served in that post only two months from March to May, 1777. This county was created in 1818.

423 *Habersham County*

Joseph Habersham (1751–1815)— Habersham was born in Savannah, Georgia, and served as an officer in the Revolutionary War, rising to the rank of colonel. He served in the Continental Congress and was a member of the convention which ratified the constitution of the United States. President George Washington appointed Habersham to serve in his cabinet as postmaster-general and he continued in that post under President John Adams. Habersham County was created on December 15, 1818, three years after his death.

424 *Hall County*

Lyman Hall (1724–1790)— A native of Connecticut and a graduate of Yale College, Hall was a minister in the Congregational church and later became a medical doctor. At about the age of 34, Hall settled in St. John's Parish, Georgia, and was a planter as well as a physician. Hall served as a delegate to the Continental Congress, first as a non-voting delegate of St. John's Parish and later as a part of Georgia's voting delegation. Hall also was a signer of the Declaration of Independence. His properties were largely destroyed and confiscated by the British army during the war. St. John's Parish sent him to the Georgia legislature and he was chosen by that body to be governor of Georgia. This county was created in 1818.

425 *Hancock County*

John Hancock (1737–1793)— A native of Massachusetts and a graduate of Harvard, Hancock served in the Massachusetts legislature and was president of the Massachusetts provincial congress. He was elected to the Second Continental Congress and became its president. As president of the Continental Congress when the Declaration of Independence was signed, he was, on July 4, 1776, the first signer of that document. He signed it with such a flourish that the name John Hancock became a synonym for "signature." He later commanded the Massachusetts militia, served as governor of that state for many years and presided over the Massachusetts convention that ratified the U.S. Constitution. The state of Georgia honored John Hancock by creating and naming this county for him on December 17, 1793, just two months after his death.

426 *Haralson County*

Hugh A. Haralson (1805–1854)— A native of Georgia and a graduate of Franklin College at Athens (now the University of

Georgia), Haralson served in both houses of the Georgia legislature and as an officer in the Georgia militia during troubles with the Indians. He attained the rank of major-general in the militia. Elected to represent Georgia in the U.S. House of Representatives, Haralson was reelected three times and served continuously from March, 1843, to March, 1851. He was a strong states' rights advocate. This county was created in January, 1856, less than two years after Haralson's death.

427 *Harris County*

Charles Harris (1772–1827)—Harris, a member of a prominent English family, was born in that country, obtained his early education in France and immigrated to Savannah, Georgia, in 1788 at the age of 16. He studied law in the office of Samuel Stirk, a prominent Savannah lawyer, and became a prominent lawyer in that city himself. Harris served for more than 20 years in the positions of mayor and alderman in Savannah. The death of his wife in 1815 and his own poor health prompted Harris' early retirement from public life. At least twice, he declined appointments to judgeships in eastern Georgia and on one occasion he refused an offer by powerful Georgia political leaders that he represent the state in the U.S. Senate. Harris died in March, 1827, and this county was created and named in his honor in December of that year.

428 *Hart County*

Nancy Morgan Hart (–)—Nancy Morgan married, while still in her teens, to Benjamin Hart. She and her husband settled, before the American Revolution, in northeastern Georgia, a few miles above a ford on the Broad River, which was known as Fishdam Ford. Six feet tall, muscular and rather unattractive, Nancy Morgan Hart had both a violent temper and unusual depths of courage which she combined with her talent for sharp shooting during Revolutionary days. This heroine's home was a retreat for her fellow patriots and she hated Tories with a vengeance that knew no compassion. On one occasion, in a fort with only children and other women, she successfully defended the fort from several attacks by Tories and Indians. On several other occasions she acted as a spy and otherwise displayed her courage and patriotism. But her most celebrated exploit concerned her bold and single-handed capture of about six Tories who came upon her in her home. The visitors

had just come from murdering John Dooly (see Dooly County, Georgia, above) and they demanded food. Hart at first lulled them into thinking that they were dealing with a helpless woman. She got the drop on them, killed one of the band who tried to resist, and held the others captive until her husband and some other men arrived to assist her. All of these Tories were immediately hung on the spot until dead. After her husband's death, Hart remarried and moved to Kentucky where she is buried in Henderson County. Hart County, Georgia was created in 1853 in the section of Georgia where Nancy Hart performed her exploits. It is the only county in Georgia that is named for a woman and one of the very few in the United States whose name honors a woman.

429 *Heard County*

Stephen Heard (1740–)—A native of Virginia, Heard fought in the French and Indian War before migrating to northeastern Georgia where he was a pioneer and fought against the Tories during the American Revolution. Elected to Georgia's executive council, Heard became president of that body and as president of the council he was Georgia's chief executive officer or de facto governor. During the Revolution, Augusta, Georgia fell into the hands of the enemy and Heard transferred the seat of Georgia's government to Heard's Fort where it remained until Augusta was retaken for Georgia. The year of his death is variously placed at 1810, 1813 and 1815. Heard's tombstone gives the date of his death as November 15, 1815, "in the 75th year of his age."

430 *Henry County*

Patrick Henry (1736–1799)—Henry was a native of Virginia and a lawyer. He served in the Virginia legislature, as governor of Virginia and as a delegate to the first and second Continental Congresses. Henry was one of America's key revolutionary leaders. He was a great orator and he is remembered for his call to arms against the British "Give me liberty or give me death." Henry opposed Virginia's ratification of the federal constitution and his views played a role in the later adoption of the Bill of Rights.

431 *Houston County*

John Houstoun (1744–1796)—This native of Georgia played a key role in instigating Georgia's revolt from England. Houstoun participated in efforts which resulted in the creation of the council of

safety and he was a Georgia delegate to the Continental Congress. He served as governor of Georgia and as commander-in-chief of the Georgia militia during the Revolution from January 8, 1778, to December 29, 1778. Houstoun served another one year term as Georgia's governor from January 9, 1784, to January 14, 1785. He later was Georgia's chief justice, justice for Chatham County, mayor of Savannah and judge of the superior court of the eastern circuit. Houston County, Georgia's name is rendered omitting the final "u" in John Houstoun's name.

432 *Irwin County*

Jared Irwin (–1818)—Irwin, whose first name is spelled "Jarried" in an Irwin County history, copyright 1942, was born in North Carolina about 1751 and moved with his parents to Georgia when he was still a boy. He served as on officer in the Revolution and was a member of conventions in 1789 and 1798 which revised Georgia's constitution, serving as president of the 1798 convention. Irwin was president of the Georgia senate several times and he was governor of Georgia twice. He first served as governor from January, 1796, to January, 1798. Irwin again became the state's chief executive on September 23, 1806, because he was president of the senate when Governor John Milledge resigned. Irwin served in this capacity until his own election as governor and continued this second term as governor until November 9, 1809. He died on March 1, 1818, and Irwin County was created on December 15 of that year.

433 *Jackson County*

James Jackson (1757–1806)—Jackson was born in England and immigrated to Georgia while still in his teens. He served as a member of Georgia's first constitutional convention and was an army officer during the Revolution. After the Revolution, Jackson was appointed colonel in the Chatham County, Georgia militia and in 1786 he was made a brigadier-general. He served in both houses of the U.S. Congress and in the Georgia legislature where he led the fight for repeal of the Yazoo act. Jackson became governor of Georgia on January 12, 1798, and he held that office until March 3, 1801, when he resigned to return to the U.S. Senate. This county was created in 1796.

434 *Jasper County*

William Jasper (–1779)—This Revolutionary War hero was born in South Carolina about 1750 but moved to Georgia where he grew up on a farm. He first became a hero in a dramatic event at the battle of Fort Moultrie when he courageously exposed himself to enemy fire to recover a flag which had been shot down. For this heroism Sergeant Jasper was awarded a sword and offered a promotion to lieutenant but he declined the promotion. Later employed as a scout, Jasper made several trips behind enemy lines in Georgia while operating from the swamps there. In a dramatic exploit near Savannah, Georgia, he and his close friend, John Newton (for whom Newton County, Georgia was named), rescued several Americans who were prisoners and took their guards as prisoners of war. Jasper was shot and killed during the siege of Savannah while recovering the flag which had been shot down. This county was originally named Randolph County, in honor of John Randolph of Virginia. Randolph became unpopular when he opposed the War of 1812 and the county's name was changed to Jasper County on December 10, 1812. However, in 1828 the Georgia legislature created a second Randolph County which also honors John Randolph. Geographic names in several of our states link the names of the two heroic sergeants, Jasper and Newton. In some, as in Georgia, two counties are named for them. In others, a county is named for one and its county seat is named for the other.

435 *Jeff Davis County*

Jefferson Davis (1808–1889)—A native of Kentucky, Davis moved with his family to Mississippi when he was a small boy. He graduated from the U.S. military academy at West Point and served as an officer in the Black Hawk and Mexican Wars. He represented Mississippi in both houses of the United States congress where he was a spokesman for the South, states' rights and strict construction of the constitution. President Franklin Pierce appointed Davis to his cabinet as secretary of war and he served in that position from 1853 to 1857. In February, 1861 Jefferson Davis was inaugurated as president of the Confederate States of America. He was the first and only president that the Confederacy had and he served in that post until the end of the Civil War in 1865. This county was created in 1905.

436 *Jefferson County*

Thomas Jefferson (1743–1826)—Jefferson was a native of Virginia and a member of the Virginia legislature. He served

Virginia as governor and he was a delegate to the second Continental Congress. Jefferson was the author of the Declaration of Independence and one of its signers. He was minister to France, secretary of state, vice-president and president of the United States. As president, he accomplished the Louisiana Purchase and he arranged the Lewis and Clark Expedition to the Pacific Northwest. Jefferson was a true intellectual, thoroughly knowledgeable in the arts and sciences. His political theories were pivotal in the formation of our infant republic. This county was created in 1796, the year before Jefferson became vice-president.

437 *Jenkins County*

Charles J. Jenkins (1805–1883)—A native of South Carolina, Jenkins moved to Georgia in his youth. He was a member of both branches of the Georgia legislature and served several terms as speaker of the state's house of representatives. Jenkins also served as Georgia's attorney general and was a member of Georgia's supreme court before becoming governor of Georgia in December, 1865, eight months after the Civil War ended. During Reconstruction, Georgia was occupied by the military forces of the federal government. Jenkins was removed from the office of governor by General George Meade, who commanded the military district of which Georgia was a part. In a dramatic gesture, Jenkins took Georgia's executive seal with him when he left Georgia and safeguarded it from the federal military. Jenkins County was created in 1905. The name that was originally proposed for this county was Dixie, the popular term used to denote the South, particularly those states which formed the Confederate States of America. That name was never officially adopted for any Georgia county.

438 *Johnson County*

Herschel V. Johnson (1812–1880)—A native of Georgia and a graduate of Franklin College at Athens (now the University of Georgia), Johnson represented Georgia briefly in the United States senate and later served two terms as Georgia's governor. In 1860, when Stephen A. Douglas ran for president of the United States against Abraham Lincoln, Herschel Johnson ran with Douglas as the vice-presidential candidate. Johnson was a delegate to Georgia's secession convention in 1861 and he was a member of the senate of the Confederate States of America from 1862 to 1865. He was president of Georgia's con-

stitutional convention in 1865 and the following year he was elected to the U.S. Senate but he was not permitted to serve. At the time of his death, Johnson was judge of the middle circuit of Georgia. This county was created on December 11, 1858, shortly before Johnson ran for the vice-presidency.

439 *Jones County*

James Jones (–1801)—Jones was born in Maryland but moved to Georgia in his youth and attended school in Augusta, Georgia. He was admitted to the bar and practiced law in Savannah. In 1790 Jones was a first lieutenant in the Chatham County militia and he later represented Chatham County in the state legislature serving from 1796 to 1798. In May, 1798 he was a member of Georgia's constitutional convention and he represented Georgia in the U.S. House of Representatives from March 4, 1799, until his death on January 11, 1801. This county was created in 1807.

440 *Lamar County*

Lucius Q. C. Lamar (1825–1893)—Lamar, a native of Georgia, served in the Georgia legislature before moving to Mississippi and representing that state in both houses of the U.S. Congress. He was an officer in the Confederate army. After the Civil War, he was a spokesman for sectional reconciliation for which he was admired in both the North and the South. He served in the U.S. cabinet as secretary of the interior and was an associate justice on the U.S. Supreme Court. Lamar County, Georgia, was created in 1920.

441 *Lanier County*

Sidney C. Lanier (1842–1881)—This noted American poet was born in Macon, Georgia, and served as a private in the Confederate army. During the Civil War he was captured and imprisoned at Point Lookout, Maryland, where he contracted the lung disease which plagued him the rest of his life. Following release from prison, Lanier worked at various jobs including hotel clerk, teacher and legal clerk while beginning his career as a writer. In 1873 he moved to Baltimore, Maryland, where he joined the Peabody Symphony Orchestra as a flute player. Lanier was a member of that orchestra for seven years. Famous as a poet, much of Lanier's work reflected his love of Georgia and the rest of the South and his concern for its welfare. He also wrote prose, essays and scholarly treatises. He died of tuberculosis at the age of 39.

442 *Laurens County*

John Laurens (1754–1782)—A native of South Carolina, Laurens attended school in Europe and was married there. Wanting to take part in the American Revolution, he returned to America in 1777 and became an aide to General George Washington. Soon commissioned as lieutenant-colonel, he participated in combat, was wounded at Germantown and later taken prisoner of war. Laurens was released as part of a prisoner exchange and commissioned by congress as an envoy extraordinary to France where he succeeded in persuading the French to supply money and military supplies to America. He returned home in time to fight at Yorktown and, in 1782, he was killed in combat in South Carolina during irregular warfare that still persisted there.

443 *Lee County*

Richard H. Lee (1732–1794)—This native of Virginia was one of the key figures in the decision of the American colonies to revolt from England. On June 7, 1776, he introduced a resolution in the Continental Congress calling for independence of the colonies from England and he was one of Virginia's signers of the Declaration of Independence. After the Revolution Lee again was a member of the Continental Congress and was president of that body for the 1784-1785 session. He later represented Virginia in the U.S. Senate. Suggestions that this county may have been named for General Henry Lee (1756–1818) are unsupported and a sign in front of the Lee County, Georgia, courthouse states that this county was named for Richard H. Lee (1732–1794).

444 *Liberty County*

Leading role of the colonists here in asserting independence for America from England—This county was created on February 5, 1777, in the Georgia constitution. Its name honors the early role that the colonists here, at Midway and Sunbury, took in gaining independence for America from England. Before the rest of Georgia decided to participate in the Continental Congress at Philadelphia, the citizens here took it upon themselves to send their own delegate, Dr. Lyman Hall, to represent them in that body. Dr. Hall was permitted to sit as a non-voting delegate. He later became part of Georgia's official voting delegation and a signer of the Declaration of Independence.

445 *Lincoln County*

Benjamin Lincoln (1733–1810)—Lincoln, a native of Massachusetts, was a member of the Massachusetts legislature and of the provincial congress. He served as an officer in the Revolutionary War and rose to the rank of major-general. In 1779, as commander of the southern department of the Continental army, he attempted, unsuccessfully to rescue Savannah, Georgia, from the British. In 1781 General George Washington gave Lincoln the honor of accepting Cornwallis' sword when the British surrendered at Yorktown. Later in 1781 Lincoln was made secretary of war and he held that post for two years. He died on May 9, 1810, in Hingham, Massachusetts, in the same house in which he was born. This county was created in 1796.

446 *Long County*

Crawford W. Long (1815–1878)—Long was a native of Georgia and a graduate of Franklin College at Athens (now the University of Georgia) and of the medical department of the University of Pennsylvania. He was the first physician to administer ether as a surgical anesthetic in a practical application. The use of anesthesia has reduced human suffering enormously and it has permitted many life-saving surgical procedures that were impossible without it. Long first administered ether in a practical application at Jefferson, Georgia on March 30, 1842, but did not publish his experiences until 1849. The delay resulted in controversy concerning priority in anesthesia.

447 *Lowndes County*

William J. Lowndes (1782–1822)—Lowndes was a native of South Carolina and he served in the legislature of that state. He represented South Carolina for 12 years in the U.S. House of Representatives including three years as chairman of the ways and means committee. Lowndes County, Georgia was created in 1825.

448 *Lumpkin County*

Wilson Lumpkin (1783–1870)—Lumpkin was born in Virginia but moved with his parents to Georgia when he was a baby. He served several terms in the Georgia legislature and then became a member of the U.S. House of Representatives. Lumpkin later served again in the Georgia legislature and again in the U.S. House of Representatives, was governor of Georgia from 1831 to 1835 and a member of the United States senate from 1837 to 1841. As governor of Georgia, Lumpkin's main concern was the removal of the Cherokee Indians from their ancient tribal lands in northwestern Georgia to Indian territory. (Now Oklahoma.) Their removal was marked by indescribable suffering from which some 4,000 of the Cherokee Indians died. This county was created in 1832 while Lumpkin was governor of Georgia.

449 *McDuffie County*

George McDuffie (1790–1851)—McDuffie was born in Georgia near Thomson, in what is now McDuffie County, Georgia, but he moved to South Carolina in his youth and it was in that state that he made his reputation as an orator and statesman. His political career began in the lower house of the South Carolina legislature and he then represented South Carolina for about 13 years in the U.S. House of Representatives. In 1832 McDuffie was a delegate to South Carolina's Nullification convention. In 1834 he was elected governor of South Carolina and he served one two-year term in that office. He later held the office of United States district judge and his final public service was in the U.S. Senate as a senator from South Carolina. This county was created in 1870 and an historical marker here stands at Senator McDuffie's birthplace.

450 *McIntosh County*

Uncertain—This county was created in 1793. Most authorities state that the county was named for the McIntosh family but there are views from reputable authorities that the county was not named for the McIntosh family. One of these sources says that it was just one member of the McIntosh family, Lachlan McIntosh, whom the county's name was intended to honor while another says that it was the chief of the Lower Creek Indians, William McIntosh, who was so honored.

McIntosh family—The McIntosh family originated in the highlands of Scotland and they were among Georgia's earliest settlers. They settled in Georgia in 1735 or early 1736. Members of this McIntosh family were military and political leaders in Georgia from the time of their arrival until the creation of this county in 1793 and for years afterward.

John Mohr McIntosh (1701–)—John Mohr McIntosh was born in Scotland and he led a group of some 170 Scottish Highlanders to settle in Georgia. He and his group settled in Georgia at a point they named New Inverness about 1736. This location is now named Darien, Georgia. His eldest son was named William McIntosh and his second son was named Lachlan McIntosh. Some references to John Mohr McIntosh refer to him as Captain and some references render his name John McIntosh Mohr.

Lachlan McIntosh (1727–1806)—Lachlan McIntosh was born in Scotland and immigrated with his father, John Mohr McIntosh, to Georgia when he was a boy. As an officer in the Continental army during the Revolution, Lachlan McIntosh served in Georgia and later became the most famous member of the McIntosh family, rising to the rank of brigadier-general on General George Washington's staff. He received the most prestigious appointment of his career in May, 1778, when he was given command of the Western department with headquarters at Ft. Pitt. McIntosh was able to establish two outposts, Ft. McIntosh and Ft. Laurens, which helped America's claims to the western frontier after the Revolutionary War ended. As punishment for killing Button Gwinnett in a duel, Lachlan McIntosh was suspended from service but later vindicated by congress and further honored with a promotion to major-general.

John McIntosh (–1826)—This Georgia native was one of the early members of the family of Georgia McIntoshes. He was a grandson of the founder, John Mohr McIntosh, and he became an heroic figure during the American Revolution when the British had Ft. Morris at Sunbury, Georgia under siege, in November, 1778, British Colonel L. V. Fuser sent a note to John McIntosh, who had command of the fort, demanding its surrender. McIntosh refused and replied "Come and take it." Fuser failed to accomplish this. John McIntosh held the rank of colonel in the army and he had a long and distinguished career throughout the Revolution and the War of 1812. Colonel McIntosh had a plantation at Fairhope, about 13 miles north of Darien, Georgia. He was a nephew of Lachlan McIntosh.

William McIntosh (–1825)—William McIntosh was born in Georgia about 1775, the son of a Scottish captain in the British army who was stationed in Georgia and a Creek Indian woman. He received a good education and he became a tribal leader in Georgia during the period that the Whites were anxiously pushing the Indians out of Georgia. William McIntosh recognized that the Indians would ulti-mately lose their lands with or without compensation and he urged the Indians to strike the best deals that they could make. Many of his fellow Creek Indians were unhappy at losing their homes and they sided with the British during the War of 1812 but William McIntosh persuaded his fellow Lower Creeks, or Cowetas, to side with the Americans and he was commissioned a general in the U.S. army. After the War of 1812 he continued on friendly terms with the White Americans and he signed many treaties with them although he often spoke for less than ten percent of the Indians affected. McIntosh's signing of a treaty with the Whites at Indian Springs, Georgia proved to be the final straw to his fellow Indians and they murdered him on May 1, 1825. While it is certain that Coweta County, Georgia received its name in compliment to this William McIntosh, it is unlikely that McIntosh County, Georgia's name was chosen to honor him. The birth year of William McIntosh is not known but he was probably still in his teens in 1793 when McIntosh County was created and named and in 1793 he had not yet endeared himself to the White American namers of county names.

451 *Macon County*

Nathaniel Macon (1758–1837)—Macon was a native of North Carolina and a soldier in the Revolutionary War. He served in the North Carolina senate and was elected to the Continental Congress but declined to serve. He represented North Carolina for 37 years in both branches of the U.S. Congress where he was speaker of the house and president pro tempore of the senate. He believed strongly in economy of the public money and he was a defender of slavery. This county was created in December, 1837, six months after Macon's death.

452 *Madison County*

James Madison (1751–1836)—Madison was born in Virginia, served in the Virginia legislature and in the Continental Congress. He was a member of the convention which framed the U.S. Constitution and he collaborated with Hamilton and Jay in writing a series of papers under the title *The Federalist* which explained the new constitution and advocated its adoption. Madison represented Virginia in the U.S. House of Representatives, served for eight years as secretary of state and for eight years as president of the United States. This county was created in 1811 while Madison was president.

453 *Marion County*

Francis Marion (–1795)—Marion is believed to have been born in South Carolina. He served in the army in battles against the Cherokee Indians and was elected to the provisional congress of 1775. He served, with distinction, as an officer in the Revolutionary War and rose to the rank of general in that war. Marion was also a member of the South Carolina senate. This county was created in 1827.

454 *Meriwether County*

David Meriwether (1755–1822)—Meriwether was a member of a wealthy family who served as an officer during the American Revolution. He was taken prisoner at the siege of Savannah and then paroled. While on parole he married a lady from Wilkes County, Georgia, and he settled there. After the war he was commissioned a brigadier-general in the Georgia militia and he served in the Georgia legislature where he was speaker of the house. Meriwether later represented Georgia in the U.S. House of Representatives and he effectively represented the government on several occasions in dealings with the Indians. Meriwether County, Georgia, was created in 1827.

455 *Miller County*

Andrew J. Miller (1806–1856)—This Georgia native attended the U.S. military academy at West Point one term before leaving to pursue a legal career in Georgia. In 1836 Miller was elected to Georgia's general assembly. This marked the beginning of 20 years of continuous service in the Georgia legislature. After his initial term in the lower house, the remainder of Miller's legislative career was in the Georgia senate. He was twice president of that body and he long championed legislation to give married women separate property rights. Miller died before his 50th birthday on February 3, 1856, and his colleagues in the Georgia legislature created and named this county in his honor just 23 days later, on February 26, 1856.

456 *Mitchell County*

Henry Mitchell (1760–1837)—Mitchell was born in Sussex County, Virginia, but migrated to Georgia after the Revolution and lived here for some 50 years in Hancock County and the adjoining county of

Warren. At about age 17 he joined the Continental army and while holding the rank of ensign Mitchell was wounded at Hanging Rock, South Carolina. He fought again near Petersburg, Virginia. After the Revolution Mitchell held the rank of brigadier-general of Georgia troops, served several terms in the Georgia legislature and was president of Georgia's senate. Mitchell was also a member of the electoral college in 1812, 1816 and 1820. Mitchell County was created in 1857 and most sources state that it was named for Georgia's Governor David B. Mitchell. However, the Georgia laws of 1857 as shown in the senate journal for that year specify that this county was named in honor of General Henry Mitchell. The name was chosen at the suggestion of D. W. Lewis, representative in the Georgia legislature from General Mitchell's county of Hancock.

457 *Monroe County*

James Monroe (1758–1831) — Monroe, a native of Virginia, served in the Revolutionary War. Prior to his election as president of the United States, Monroe served in a wide variety of government posts. He served Virginia in the state legislature and as governor. He was a member of the Confederation congress and the U.S. Senate. He was minister to France and to Britain and he held two cabinet posts. As president, Monroe stressed limited government and strict construction of the constitution. He acquired Florida for the U.S. from Spain and he was the author of a policy declaration (later known as the Monroe Doctrine) which proscribed outside interference in North and South America. This county was created in 1821 while Monroe was serving his second term as president.

458 *Montgomery County*

Richard Montgomery (1738–1775) — Montgomery was born in Ireland and served with the British in the French and Indian War. He settled in New York where he was elected to the New York provisional congress. He served as a general in the American revolutionary army and he was killed in combat in the Revolutionary War. Montgomery County, Georgia, was created in 1793.

459 *Morgan County*

Daniel Morgan (1736–1802) — Morgan was a native of the Northeast who moved to Virginia in his youth. He served as a general in the Revolutionary War and was regarded as a hero for important victories scored by his troops. After the war he served one term in congress. Morgan County was created in 1807.

460 *Murray County*

Thomas W. Murray (1790–1832) — Murray was born in Georgia, received his early education in Abbeville district, South Carolina, and studied law in Elberton, Georgia. He practiced law for several years and entered the Georgia legislature in 1818. Murray represented Lincoln County in Georgia's house of representatives several terms and became speaker of the house in 1825. In 1832 the legislature created and named Murray County in his honor. Murray was unopposed as a candidate for the U.S. Congress but he died before the election.

461 *Muscogee County*

Creek Indians — The name Muscogee, or Muskogee, embraces the Creek Indians and several others including the Choctaw, Chickasaw, Seminole and other tribes, but it was the Creek Indians that the Georgia legislature had in mind when it selected the name for this county. The Creek were a large and powerful confederacy of North American tribes who occupied an enormous area of the southeastern United States including most of Georgia and Alabama. They were an agricultural people but hunting and fishing were important supplements to their farming. In military actions against other Indians the Creek were very capable warriors. They were known to burn captives of war at the stake. In the 18th century their population was estimated to be about 20,000. The Creek Indians revolted against the Americans in the Creek War of 1813-1814 and they were badly defeated. By 1841 most Creek had been moved from the southeastern United States to Indian territory (now Oklahoma) where large numbers of Creek Indians still live.

462 *Newton County*

John Newton (–1780) — Newton was born in Charleston, South Carolina, about 1752 and was the son of a pastor of a Baptist church. In 1775, early in the armed resistance to Great Britain, Newton enlisted in South Carolina's Revolutionary army. He served as piper and corporal in Captain Dunbar's company before being promoted to sergeant. In a dramatic exploit near Savannah, Georgia, Newton and his close friend, William Jasper (for whom Jasper County, Georgia, is named), rescued several Americans who were prisoners and took their guards as prisoners of war. Newton was more fortunate than his friend, Jasper, in that he survived the siege of Savannah. However, when Charleston fell to the British in 1780, Newton was taken prisoner and he died of smallpox shortly afterward. Geographic names in several of our states link the names of the two heroic sergeants, Jasper and Newton. In some, as in Georgia, two counties are named for them. In others, a county is named for one of them and its county seat is named for the other.

463 *Oconee County*

Oconee River — This county was created in 1875 and named for the Oconee River which forms its eastern boundary. The Oconee River, which rises near Lula in Hall County in northern Georgia, is about 250 miles long and is an affluent of the Altamaha River. The Oconee River derived its name from a former Oconee Indian settlement called Oconee Old Town, which was about four miles south of Milledgeville, Georgia, just below the Rock Landing. The Indians abandoned Oconee Old Town about 1715 and moved to the Chattahoochee River.

464 *Oglethorpe County*

James E. Oglethorpe (1696–1785) — Oglethorpe was the founder of Georgia and its first colonial governor. He was born in England, served as an officer in the English army and was a member of parliament. He and some 20 other trustees were granted a charter to establish the colony of Georgia in America. With about 150 settlers he sailed for America late in 1732 and in early 1733 established a settlement which is now the city of Savannah, Georgia. Oglethorpe became Georgia's governor under the trustees on July 15, 1732. In 1743 he went back to England and he never returned to Georgia although he continued as Georgia's governor until June 9, 1752, when the trustees resigned their charter. In England he became involved in military affairs and was given the rank of general.

465 *Paulding County*

John Paulding (–1818) — During the American Revolution, the adjutant general of the British army, Major John Andre, secretly met behind American lines with General Benedict Arnold of the Continental army. Benedict Arnold was one of our highest officers, the hero of the battle of Saratoga and the current commander of our critical fort at West Point, New York. Arnold was partially successful in committing his planned treason against America in that he escaped and joined the British army. However, Major Andre was captured by three obscure New York militiamen, John Paulding, Isaac Van Wart and David Williams. In commemoration of this dramatic capture, the state of Ohio named three of its counties for these three captors of Major Andre and Georgia created and named Paulding County in John Paulding's honor. The first county seat of Paulding County, Georgia, was named for Isaac Van Wart. Paulding was born in 1758 or 1759. He was a poor farm lad in Westchester County, New York, who entered New York's militia during the Revolution. He had been a British prisoner of war but escaped from prison shortly before the capture of Major Andre. On the day of the capture, Paulding and seven companions were on duty near Tarrytown, New York, south of West Point fort, attempting to waylay any Tory cattle rustlers they might find operating in the area. The party of eight divided, five stationing themselves on a nearby hill and Paulding, Van Wart and Williams taking positions at a bridge. It was there that they captured Major Andre, rather by accident. Paulding was a big, square man and the leader of the three. He was the only literate member of the trio and it was he who read the documents hidden in Andre's boots and suspected their importance. New York state honored John Paulding for his part in this dramatic and strategically important capture by giving him a farm, near Cortland, New York. Congress granted each of the three captors an annuity for life and a silver medal which was personally presented by George Washington.

466 *Peach County*

Georgia's peaches—Peaches are one of Georgia's leading agricultural products and one of the state's unofficial nicknames is the Peach State. Peach County, Georgia, was so named because of its location in one of the richest peach growing regions of Georgia. At the time that the county was created in 1924, peaches had become its leading agricultural product although cotton was also important. Peaches are a delicious and nutritious fruit which grow on small trees, about 20 feet in height, whose botanical name is *Prunus persica*. Probably of Chinese origin, peaches were first introduced in the Americas by the Spanish in the 16th century in Florida. They are now grown widely in the United States and Canada.

467 *Pickens County*

Andrew Pickens (1739–1817)—Pickens was a native of Pennsylvania who moved to South Carolina in his youth. He served as a general in the Revolutionary War. By a successful expedition against the Cherokee Indians in 1782, he gained from them a large strip of territory which later became part of the state of Georgia. He later served in South Carolina's House of Representatives and, briefly, in the U.S. House of Representatives as a representative from South Carolina.

468 *Pierce County*

Franklin Pierce (1804–1869)—Pierce was born in New Hampshire and served in the lower house of that state's legislature. He represented New Hampshire in both houses of the U.S. Congress and served as an officer in the Mexican War rising to the rank of brigadier-general. In 1852 Pierce was nominated for president by the Democratic party on the 49th ballot as a compromise candidate who was not objectionable to the South. He was elected to that office and served one term. As president, he viewed the slavery issue in a legalistic way and was unable to accept the North's moral objections to slavery. Pierce failed to secure his party's nomination for a second term and his presidency ended on March 3, 1857. This county was created in December of that year.

469 *Pike County*

Zebulon M. Pike (1779–1813)—Pike was a native of New Jersey who served as an army officer on America's frontier following the Revolution. He led an exploratory army expedition to the Rocky Mountains which Pike's Peak in the Colorado Rockies commemorates. Pike served as a general in the War of 1812 and was killed in that war.

470 *Polk County*

James K. Polk (1795–1849)—Polk was a native of North Carolina who moved with his family to the Tennessee frontier in 1806. He served in the lower house of the Tennessee legislature and he represented Tennessee for 14 years in the U.S. House of Representatives where he was speaker. He served one term as governor of Tennessee. Polk became president of the United States as a dark horse candidate of the Democratic party but he became an unusually strong and effective president. His primary accomplishments involved westward extension of the United States; in the Northwest by settling a territorial dispute with Britain and in California and the Southwest by provoking and winning the Mexican War. Polk County, Georgia, was created in 1851.

471 *Pulaski County*

Casimir Pulaski (1748–1779)—Pulaski was born in Lithuania and served in the Polish army. He came to America to assist the colonies as an officer in the Revolutionary War. He died in combat in that war during the siege of Savannah, Georgia. Pulaski County, Georgia, was created and named in 1808 and a statue, the Pulaski monument, was placed in Savannah in 1855.

472 *Putnam County*

Israel Putnam (1718–1790)—Putnam was born in Massachusetts and moved, when he was about 21, to Connecticut. He served as an officer in the French and Indian Wars and later was a member of the Connecticut legislature. At the beginning of the Revolutionary War, news of the battle at Lexington, Massachusetts reached Putnam while he was farming. In a dramatic gesture which became famous, Putnam left his plow and, without bothering to change clothes, hurried to Lexington. He was appointed major-general in the Continental army. Although he enjoyed great popularity, he lacked the ability for high command. In 1779 a paralytic stroke ended his military career. This county was created in 1807.

473 *Quitman County*

John A. Quitman (1798–1858)—Quitman was born in New York state but spent his adult life and political career as a resident of Mississippi. He was a member of both houses of the Mississippi legislature and he was chancellor of that state. Quitman served as a general officer during the Mexican War, rising to the rank of major-general. After the war he was elected governor of Mississippi and he later represented that state in the U.S. House of Representatives. This strong advocate of states' rights died in July, 1858. In December of that year the Georgia legislature created and named this county in his honor.

474 *Rabun County*

William Rabun (1771–1819)—Rabun was born in North Carolina but moved to Georgia with his family as a young boy. Largely self-educated, with little formal schooling, he became a justice of the inferior court of Hancock County. Rabun was a member of both houses of the Georgia legislature and was president of the senate for several years. When Governor David B. Mitchell resigned in March, 1817, Rabun was made ex-officio governor of Georgia. Later that year he was formally elected governor by the general assembly. He died in office in October, 1819, and Rabun County was created and named in his honor two months later

475 *Randolph County*

John Randolph (1773–1833)—Randolph was a native of Virginia and he represented that state in both houses of the U.S. Congress for many years. He was an advocate of states' rights and strict construction of the federal constitution. He owned slaves and he represented the interests of the South in congress. Randolph also served, very briefly, as minister to Russia. In 1807 Georgia created a county in the central part of the state named Randolph in honor of this Virginia statesman. Randolph's opposition to the War of 1812 and his positions on other issues were unpopular in Georgia and the state changed that county's name to Jasper County on December 10, 1812. By 1828, Randolph was again in good odor in Georgia on account of his forceful defense of the constitutional rights of slave-holders and this county in southwestern Georgia was created and named in his honor.

476 *Richmond County*

Charles Lennox, Duke of Richmond (1735–1806)—This county was created in February, 1777, early in the American Revolution, and named for Charles Lennox, the third duke of Richmond, a member of the English parliament and a supporter of the American cause. In one of his speeches he declared that the resistance of the colonies was "neither treason nor rebellion but is perfectly justifiable in every possible political and moral sense." He favored independence for the American colonies and in 1778 Richmond proposed the withdrawal of English troops from America. He had served as an officer in the English army himself and had risen to the rank of general. In addition to his military service and membership in the house of lords, Richmond's career included the posts of ambassador extraordinary and minister plenipotentiary to Paris, secretary of state for the southern department and master-general of the ordnance with a seat in the cabinet. In 1782 he was elected and invested as a knight of the garter.

477 *Rockdale County*

Rockdale Church—This county was created in 1870 and named for the Rockdale Church here. The church had been named after the immense subterranean vein of granite rock which lies under this region of north-central Georgia.

478 *Schley County*

William Schley (1786–1858)—Schley was born in Maryland but moved while still in his youth to Georgia. Admitted to the Georgia bar in 1812, Schley practiced law in Augusta and became judge of the superior court of the middle circuit. He later served in the lower house of the state legislature and represented Georgia in the U.S. House of Representatives. In 1835 he was elected governor of Georgia and he served one term before losing in a bid for reelection. Schley was still living in December, 1857, when this county was created and named in his honor.

479 *Screven County*

James Screven (–1778)—Screven, who was born about 1744 in South Carolina, moved to Georgia and settled in the vicinity of Midway Church. Before most of Georgia decided to participate in the Continental Congress at Philadelphia, colonists at Midway and Sunbury, Georgia, took it upon themselves to send their own delegate, Dr. Lyman Hall, to Philadelphia. James Screven was among those who signed the credentials that Dr. Hall presented to congress. In July, 1775, Screven was a delegate to Georgia's provincial congress and he was a member of the council of safety. In January, 1776, he was commissioned a captain in a company of volunteers from Midway and he rose to the rank of brigadier-general during the Revolution. In 1778, he was wounded in combat near Midway Church, Georgia, and he died a few days later from those wounds. This county's name was misspelled as Scriven in the 1793 act that created it and it is believed that this error has never been officially corrected by the Georgia legislature.

480 *Seminole County*

Seminole Indians—The Seminole, a Muskogean-speaking people, evolved as a distinct tribe in Florida at about the time of the American Revolution. The Seminole consisted of a nucleus of Oconee Indians, a subdivision of the Creeks of Alabama and Georgia, who migrated to Florida in the mid-1700's. The Oconee combined with Yamasee Indians who had been driven from South Carolina and with remnant groups of Florida Indians and runaway Black slaves to form the tribe known as Seminole. The Seminole are noted for their fierce resistance to attempts by Whites to drive them from their homeland in Florida. During Florida's Seminole Wars, many of the Seminole were driven to Indian territory (now Oklahoma) but some eluded the American troops in the Everglades and more than 1,000 surviving Seminole still live in central and southern Florida. The origin of the name Seminole is uncertain but these possibilities have been suggested:

1. The Creek Indian word *simanole* or *siminole* which means "runaways" or "those who separate."
2. The Creek Indian words *ishti semoli* which mean "wild men."
3. The Spanish word *cimarron* meaning "wild," "unruly" or "runaway slave."

481 *Spalding County*

Thomas Spalding (1774–1851)—This Georgia native was a wealthy and prominent planter, a slave-holder and one of the earliest cotton planters in Georgia. He served in both houses of the Georgia legislature and was a member of Georgia's constitutional convention of 1798. Spalding also served very briefly in the U.S. House of Representatives. He died in January, 1851, and Spalding County, was created and named in his honor in December of that year.

482 *Stephens County*

Alexander H. Stephens (1812–1883)—After serving in both houses of the Georgia legislature this native of Georgia was elected to the U.S. House of Representatives. He was a member of that body for 16 years from 1843 to 1859. Although Stephens was a reluctant secessionist, he was elected as the first and only vice-president of the Confederate States of America. When the Civil War ended, he was arrested by federal officials and imprisoned for five months. In 1866 he was elected to the U.S. Senate but he was denied his seat.

Stephens again served in the U.S. House of Representatives from 1873 until 1882, when he was elected governor of Georgia.

483 *Stewart County*

Daniel Stewart (1759–1829)—A native of Georgia, Stewart entered the army at the age of 15 and was wounded in combat during the American Revolution. By the end of the war, he had risen to the rank of general. He later served in the Indian wars from the Savannah River to Florida and was breveted for bravery. During the War of 1812 Stewart again saw service as a brigadier-general of cavalry. This county was created in 1830.

484 *Sumter County*

Thomas Sumter (1734–1832)—Sumter, a native of Virginia, fought in the French and Indian Wars and settled in South Carolina. He served as an officer in the Revolutionary War and represented South Carolina in both houses of the U.S. Congress. Sumter County, Georgia, was created in 1831.

485 *Talbot County*

Matthew Talbot (–1827)—Talbot was born in Virginia and moved to Georgia with his family in 1783. He served in the lower house of the Georgia legislature for about 30 years, was a member of the 1798 convention which framed Georgia's constitution and was president of the Georgia senate from 1818 to 1823. Upon the death of Governor William Rabun in October, 1819, Talbot served as interim governor of Georgia for a few weeks until John Clark became governor. Talbot died in September, 1827, and this county was created in December of that year.

486 *Taliaferro County*

Benjamin Taliaferro (1750–1821)—Taliaferro was born in Virginia and served as an officer in the Continental army during the Revolution. After the war he settled in Georgia where he was a member of the state senate and was, for a time, president of that body. He was a delegate to the 1798 convention that framed Georgia's constitution and he represented Georgia in the U.S. House of Representatives, serving in that body from 1799 to 1802. Taliaferro County was created in 1825.

487 *Tattnall County*

Josiah Tattnall (1764–1803)—This Georgia native served as an officer in the Georgia militia during the American Revolution and in actions against the Creek Indians in Georgia. He later served in the Georgia legislature and from 1796 to 1799 he represented Georgia in the U.S. Senate. Tattnall was inaugurated as governor of Georgia on November 7, 1801, and he had the honor of signing the act that created Tattnall County one month later. At that time, the governor's health was failing and the Georgia legislature named this county in his honor as a delicate compliment to him. He resigned on account of his health in November, 1802, and died in June, 1803.

488 *Taylor County*

Zachary Taylor (1784–1850)—Taylor was born in Virginia but moved as an infant to Kentucky where he grew to manhood on a farm near Louisville. A career soldier, Taylor served as an officer in the War of 1812, the Black Hawk War, the Second Seminole War in Florida territory and the Mexican War. Taylor's service in the Mexican War made him a national hero and resulted in his election as president of the United States. Although he was a slave owner, he opposed the extension of slavery beyond the 15 states where the institution was already legal. Taylor had served only 16 months as president when he died in office on July 9, 1850. Taylor County, Georgia was created 18 months later, in January, 1852.

489 *Telfair County*

Edward Telfair (–1807)—Telfair was born in Scotland about 1735 and came to America where he lived in Virginia and North Carolina before settling, in 1766, in Savannah, Georgia. A patriot and a staunch supporter of the American cause in the Revolution, Telfair was a member of the council of safety, a delegate to the provincial congress in Savannah in 1776, a signer of the Articles of Confederation and one of Georgia's delegates to the Continental Congress. Telfair served twice as Georgia's governor and was a delegate to the state convention which unanimously ratified the constitution of the United States. He died in September, 1807, and Telfair County was created and named in his honor three months later, in December of that year.

490 *Terrell County*

William Terrell (1778–1855)—A native of Virginia, Terrell moved with his parents to Georgia. He pursued classical studies and graduated as a doctor from medical college in Pennsylvania. Dr. Terrell practiced his profession in Sparta, Georgia, and became interested in politics. He was elected to the lower house of the Georgia legislature and later represented Georgia in the U.S. House of Representatives. He donated $20,000 to the University of Georgia to establish a chair of agriculture to which his name was attached. Dr. Terrell died in July, 1855 and Terrell County was created in February of the following year.

491 *Thomas County*

Jett Thomas (1776–1817)—A native of Virginia, Thomas moved to Georgia with his parents at the close of the Revolution. He became a contractor and he built the state house at Milledgeville, Georgia. Thomas also built the original structure in which Franklin College (now the University of Georgia) was housed. During the War of 1812 he served as an artillery officer under General John Floyd and saw action against the Creek Indians. The Georgia legislature honored him with a jeweled sword and he was made a major-general in the state militia. The act to create Thomas County was introduced in the Georgia legislature by Thomas J. Johnson in 1825. Johnson's brother-in-law was a relative of General Jett Thomas.

492 *Tift County*

Nelson Tift (1810–1891)—Tift County was officially named for Nelson Tift who was born in Connecticut and lived in Florida and South Carolina before settling in Georgia about 1835. He served in Georgia's house of representatives and was the founder and editor of the *Albany Patriot*. During the Civil War Tift held the rank of captain in the navy of the Confederate States of America, serving in the navy's supply department. After the war he briefly represented Georgia in the U.S. House of Representatives and was later a delegate to Georgia's constitutional convention in 1877.

Tift County, Georgia, which was created in August, 1905, was officially named for Nelson Tift, but to understand the source of the name we must look to its county seat, Tifton, and Tifton's founder, Henry H. Tift.

Henry H. Tift (1841–)—Henry H. Tift was born in Mystic, Connecticut, studied marine engineering and spent several years at sea before moving to Albany, Georgia to operate a lumber business for two of his uncles. After working for his uncles, Nelson Tift and A. F. Tift, for two years,

Henry H. Tift purchased 4,000 acres of virgin timber land and sawmill machinery, built a shack and began his sawmill. Around that shack the settlement of Tifton grew. Lena was one of Tifton's early names in honor of Henry H. Tift's sweetheart in Connecticut. The settlement also was known as Slab Town because the sawmill laborers built shacks out of slabs from the mill. But George Badger, an employee at the sawmill, decided to honor the founder of the village and he placed a sign saying Tifton on a pine tree here. The name stuck and Tifton was incorporated as a city in 1890. When Tift County was created in 1905, Tifton became its county seat. The sawmill prospered and by 1887 Henry H. Tift had accumulated 100,000 acres of land. He was joined by his two brothers, William O. Tift and Edmund H. Tift, who helped him with his expanding business ventures. The business grew to include farming and canning operations, a dry goods business, a cotton mill and ownership of two railroads.

When creation of a new county here was under consideration, it was suggested that it be called Tift County in honor of Henry H. Tift. However, a committee of the Georgia legislature had recently decided that no new county should be named for a living man. To name this proposed new county for Henry H. Tift would have violated that rule so it was decided that this county was officially named for Nelson Tift, the distinguished uncle of Henry H. Tift.

493 *Toombs County*

Robert A. Toombs (1810–1885) — This Georgia native was an army officer in the Creek War in 1836 after which he served several terms in the lower house of the Georgia legislature. Toombs represented Georgia in the U.S. House of Representatives for eight years and later served in the U.S. Senate. Soon after Abraham Lincoln was elected president, Toombs resigned from the senate. He became secretary of state of the Confederate States of America in Jefferson Davis' cabinet and later served as a brigadier-general in the Confederate army. Bitterly opposed to Reconstruction, Toombs never took the oath of allegiance after the Civil War ended.

494 *Towns County*

George W. B. Towns (1801–1854) — A native of Georgia, Towns served in both branches of the Georgia legislature and represented Georgia in the U.S. House of Representatives for several years. In 1847

Towns was elected governor of Georgia. Reelected in 1849, he served a total of four years as governor. Towns County was created and named for him in March, 1856, less than two years after his death.

495 *Treutlen County*

John A. Treutlen (1726–1782) — A native of Austria, Treutlen immigrated to America to live in Georgia where he was a member of the Georgia commons house of assembly in the early 1770's but decided to support the patriot cause in the Revolution. He was a member of Georgia's provincial congress of 1775. Elected governor over the popular patriot, Button Gwinnett, Treutlen served as Georgia's first governor under the state constitution of 1777. The circumstances of his death are not known but there is a tradition that he was murdered by Tories in South Carolina.

496 *Troup County*

George M. Troup (1780–1856) — Troup was born in 1780 on land that was then part of Georgia but is now within the state of Alabama. In 1801 he was elected as a representative from Chatham County to Georgia's general assembly and he was twice reelected to two-year terms. He later served in both branches of the U.S. Congress and was governor of Georgia from 1823 to 1827 when he took strong states' rights positions in clashes with President John Quincy Adams. Troup County was created and named in his honor while he was serving as governor. Troup again represented Georgia in the U.S. Senate from 1829 to 1833.

497 *Turner County*

Henry G. Turner (1839–1904) — A native of North Carolina, Turner moved to Georgia in 1859. He enlisted as a private in the Confederate army, served throughout the Civil War and rose to the rank of captain. At the battle of Gettysburg he was severely wounded. In the 1870's Turner served in the lower house of the Georgia legislature and he represented Georgia in the U.S. House of Representatives for 16 years from 1881 to 1897. Turner was appointed associate justice of the supreme court of Georgia in 1903. This county was created in 1905, fourteen months after Turner's death.

498 *Twiggs County*

John Twiggs (1750–1816) — Twiggs was born in Maryland but moved to Georgia

in his youth. During the American Revolution, he served with distinction and rose to the rank of brigadier-general. In 1783 Twiggs was appointed as an Indian commissioner and he assisted in concluding treaties with the Creeks. He held the rank of major-general in the Georgia militia and served in action against the Creeks and in preparations for the War of 1812. This county was created in 1809.

499 *Union County*

America's union of states — In 1832 when this county was created, Andrew Jackson was president and the tariff issue was creating conflicts between sectional interests and union loyalty. Nullification, which threatened disunion, was a popular doctrine in the South. The county's name was chosen as a reflection of the unionist sentiment held by the residents here while a secession voice was heard in other parts of the South. John Thomas, who represented this region in the Georgia legislature, was the one who suggested the new county's name. He is reported to have said "Name it Union, for none but Union men reside in it."

500 *Upson County*

Stephen Upson (–1824) — Upson was born in Connecticut about 1785 and graduated from Yale College there. Forced to move to the South for his health, he became a successful attorney in Lexington, Georgia. Upson was a trustee of the University of Georgia and, from 1820 to 1824, he represented Oglethorpe County in the Georgia legislature. He died in August, 1824, and Upson County was created and named in his honor in December of that year.

501 *Walker County*

Freeman Walker (1780–1827) — A native of Virginia, Walker moved to Georgia while in his teens. He became a prominent attorney, served in Georgia's house of representatives and was mayor of Augusta in 1818 and 1819. Walker represented Georgia in the U.S. Senate for two years and later served again as mayor of Augusta. Walker County was created in 1833.

502 *Walton County*

George Walton (–1804) — Born in Virginia sometime in the 1740's, Walton moved to Savannah, Georgia, in 1769 where he rapidly rose to prominence. He was secretary of Georgia's provincial congress and president of the council of safety. Walton was one of Georgia's three signers of the Declaration of Independence and a delegate to the Continental Congress. During the Revolution he served as a colonel in Georgia's militia and was wounded and taken prisoner at the battle of Savannah, Georgia. On two occasions Walton served as governor of Georgia and he sat as chief justice of Georgia's superior court. He later represented Georgia in the U.S. Senate. Georgia's first Walton County was created and named in honor of George Walton in the early 1800's while he was still living. By 1818 it had been determined that Walton County was inside the state of North Carolina so Georgia's first Walton County ceased to exist. The present Walton County, also named for George Walton, was created December 15, 1818, prudently located many miles south of the North Carolina border.

503 *Ware County*

Nicholas Ware (–1824)— Ware was born in Virginia about the time of the American Revolution. He studied law in Litchfield, Connecticut and became an attorney in Augusta, Georgia. He served several terms in the lower house of the Georgia legislature and was mayor of Augusta. Ware entered the U.S. Senate in 1821, having been appointed to fill the unexpired term of Georgia's Senator Freeman Walker who had resigned. Ware was elected to a full six-year term but died in September, 1824 before completing that term in the U.S. Senate. Ware County, Georgia was created and named in his honor three months later, in December, 1824.

504 *Warren County*

Joseph Warren (1741–1775)— This county was created in 1793 and named in honor of the American Revolutionary War hero, Joseph Warren. A native of Massachusetts and a graduate of Harvard College, Warren practiced medicine in the Boston area, was a member of the committee of safety and president pro tempore of the Massachusetts provincial congress. In June, 1775 he was commissioned a major-general and he died in combat a few days later at the battle of Bunker Hill.

505 *Washington County*

George Washington (1732–1799)—Washington was a native of Virginia. He served in Virginia's house of burgesses and became one of the colonies' leaders in opposition to British policies in America. He was a member of the first and second Continental Congresses and commander of all Continental armies in the Revolutionary War. Following victory in that war, Washington was elected to be the first president of the United States. This county was created in 1784, before Washington became president.

506 *Wayne County*

Anthony Wayne (1745–1796)—A native of Pennsylvania, Wayne was a successful brigadier-general in the Revolutionary War and became a hero for his daring exploits. During the bitter winter of 1777-1778 at Valley Forge, Pennsylvania, Wayne shared the sufferings of his men although his comfortable estate was only five miles away. He played an important role in the final overthrow of the British forces in Georgia. After the war, in 1785, Wayne moved to Georgia and he represented Georgia for about six months in the U.S. House of Representatives. In 1792 President Washington recalled Wayne to serve as a major-general against the Indians in the Northwest territory. Once again his military efforts were successful. This county was created in 1803.

507 *Webster County*

Daniel Webster (1782–1852)—Webster was born in New Hampshire and represented that state in the U.S. House of Representatives. He later represented Massachusetts in both houses of the U.S. Congress and served as secretary of state under three presidents. Webster felt that slavery was evil but not as evil as disunion of the United States. This view was relatively moderate for a powerful northern politician and it won Webster favor in the South. When this county was created in 1853, it was named Kinchafoonee County, after a neighboring stream the Kinchafoonee Creek. The word is a corruption of the Muskogee Indians' words for "mortar bone" (in which to pound materials with a pestle). The name became a source of amusement so the county's name was changed to Webster in 1856 to end the teasing.

508 *Wheeler County*

Joseph Wheeler (1836–1906)—A native of Georgia and a graduate of the U.S. military academy at West Point, Wheeler resigned from the U.S. army in 1861 to serve in the Confederate army during the Civil War. Almost constantly in battle and wounded three times, Wheeler became a hero and rose to become one of the South's highest generals with the three star rank of lieutenant-general. After the war he moved to Louisiana and then settled in Alabama. Wheeler represented Alabama for a number of years in the U.S. House of Representatives where he worked for reconciliation between the North and the South. At an advanced age, he served as a major-general of cavalry in the U.S. army during the Spanish-American War. This county was created in 1912.

509 *White County*

Uncertain—This county was created on December 22, 1857. It is not certain for whom it was named but there are just two possibilities:

David T. White (1812–1871)—David T. White was born in Davidson, North Carolina. He moved to Georgia and represented Newton County in the lower house of the Georgia legislature. Those who believe that White County was named for David T. White claim that the bill to create this county was introduced in the Georgia legislature by Representative William Shelton. By this account, after Shelton's bill was defeated, Representative David T. White moved that the house reconsider. This was done and the bill passed. In gratitude, Representative Shelton named the new county for Representative White.

John White (–)—John White was born in England sometime prior to the American Revolution and served as a surgeon in the British navy. On leaving the naval service, he moved to America and lived in Philadelphia. In the Revolutionary War he entered our colonial army as a captain and rose to the rank of colonel. During the siege of Savannah, Georgia, John White accomplished a dramatic capture, by bluff, which made him a hero. With a small body of men he convinced a British force that they were surrounded. They surrendered and more than 100 British and their five armed naval vessels were captured. John White later died in Virginia from lung disease brought on by exposure and fatigue.

510 *Whitfield County*

George Whitefield (1714–1770)—This county, created in 1851, was named for George Whitefield, although the county's official letterhead now omits the "e" and uses Whitfield as the county's name. George Whitefield was born in England, educated at Oxford and ordained in the Church of England. He arrived in America as a missionary about 1738. Viewed as a controversial figure by church leaders but a gifted orator and popular with the masses in the British Isles as well as in America, Reverend Whitefield established an orphanage, the Bethesda Orphanage, near Savannah, Georgia. This orphanage emphasized spiritual matters and rigid, even brutal, discipline was administered there. Whitefield's home remained in England but he visited America at least six times and died here, in Massachusetts, in 1770.

511 *Wilcox County*

Uncertain—This county was created on December 22, 1857. It is not certain whether the county was named for John Wilcox or for his son, Mark Wilcox.

John Wilcox (–)—John Wilcox was a captain in the army who fought in battles against the Indians in Georgia. He was one of the earliest settlers in the wilderness of south-central Georgia about where Telfair County is now located. He was a well-to-do man and the father of Major-general Mark Wilcox.

Mark Wilcox (–1850)—Mark Wilcox was born in Georgia about 1800. He held the office of high sheriff in Telfair County, Georgia, for a number of years and represented that county for several sessions in the state legislature. At about the same time that he was serving in the legislature, he also entered the Georgia militia and rose to the rank of major-general. Mark Wilcox was the son of Captain John Wilcox.

512 *Wilkes County*

John Wilkes (1727–1797)—Wilkes County was created in Georgia's constitution of 1777 and named for John Wilkes, a member of the English parliament who strenuously opposed the harsh and unjust measures toward the American colonies which finally resulted in the Revolution. He was born in England and was a writer as well as a member of parliament. Wilkes was persecuted and imprisoned for his writings which included satires and lampoons of important English personages.

513 *Wilkinson County*

James Wilkinson (1757–1825)—A native of Maryland, Wilkinson served as an officer in the colonial army during the American Revolution and rose to the rank of brevet brigadier-general. He later served in actions against the Indians in the Northwest territory where he became general-in-chief. In 1802 the state of Georgia acquired a large body of land from the Creek Indians. General Wilkinson was one of the U.S. commissioners who negotiated this treaty with the Indians and Wilkinson County, one of the three counties that Georgia created from this land in 1803, was named in his honor. In 1805 President Thomas Jefferson appointed Wilkinson to be the civil and military governor of the recently acquired Louisiana territory. He later was commissioned major-general in the War of 1812 but performed poorly in Canada and was relieved of his command.

514 *Worth County*

William J. Worth (1794–1849)—A native of New York, Worth enlisted in the army as a private in the War of 1812 and rose to the rank of major. At the close of the war Worth became commandant of the U.S. military academy at West Point. He later served as a brigadier-general against the Seminole Indians in Florida and became a national hero as a successful major-general in the Mexican War. One of the men who served under Worth in Mexico was William A. Harris. In 1853, when this part of Georgia became Worth County, Harris was living here and he is the person who chose the new county's name in honor of his former commander.

REFERENCES

Averitt, Jack N. *Georgia's Coastal Plain*. New York, Lewis Historical Publishing Co. Inc., 1964.

Baker, Pearl. *A Handbook of History: McDuffie County, Georgia 1870-1970*. Progress-News Publishing Co.

Barfield Louise C. *History of Harris County, Georgia*. Columbus, Georgia, Columbus Office Supply Co., 1961.

Battey, George M. *A History of Rome & Floyd County*. Atlanta, Webb & Vary Co., 1922.

Biographical Souvenir of the States of Georgia & Florida. Chicago, F. A. Battey & Co., 1889.

Bonner, James C. *A Short History of Heard County*. Milledgeville, Georgia, The Woman's College of Georgia, 1962.

Bowen, Eliza A. *The Story of Wilkes County, Georgia*. Marietta, Continental Book Co., 1950.

"Brantley County: A Sketch of the Life of the Late Benjamin Daniel Brantley for Whom the Proposed County is Named." *Savannah Morning News*, August 15, 1920.

Brinkley, Hal E. *How Georgia Got Her Names*. Lakemont, Georgia, CSA Printing & Bindery, Inc., 1967.

Butler, John C. *Historical Record of Macon & Central Georgia*. Macon, J. W. Burke Co., 1960.

Campbell, N. L. *1964 In Georgia Directory*. Atlanta, Dixie Publishing Co.

Clements, J. B. *History of Irwin County*. Atlanta, Foote & Davies Co., 1942.

Coastal Plain Area Planning & Development Commission. *Remembered Places & Leftover Pieces....* Valdosta, Georgia, 1976.

Cobb, Mrs. Wilton P. *History of Dodge County*. Spartanburg, South Carolina, Reprint Co., 1979.

Coleman, Kenneth & Charles S. Gurr. *Dictionary of Georgia Biography*. Athens, University of Georgia Press, 1983.

Cook, Anna M. G. *History of Baldwin County, Georgia*. Anderson, South Carolina, Keys-Hearn Printing Co., 1925.

Cooper, Walter G. *Official History of Fulton County*. Atlanta, W. W. Brown, 1934.

Coulter, Ellis M., et al. *History of Georgia*. New York, American Book Co., 1954.

Covington, W. A. *History of Colquitt County*. Atlanta, Foote & Davies Co., 1937.

Crutchfield, James A. *The Georgia Almanac*. Nashville, Tennessee, Rutledge Hill Press, 1986.

Cunyus, Lucy J. *History of Bartow County, Georgia: Formerly Cass*. Easley, South Carolina, Southern Historical Press, Inc., 1983.

Davidson, Victor. *History of Wilkinson County*. Macon, Georgia, J. W. Burke Co., 1930.

Davis, Nellie C. *The History of Miller County, Georgia: 1856–1980*. Colquitt, Georgia, Citizens Bank, 1980.

Department of Agriculture. *Georgia: Historical & Industrial*. Atlanta, Franklin Printing & Publishing Co., 1901.

DeWitt, John H. "Letters of General John Coffee to His Wife, 1813–1815." *Tennessee Historical Magazine*, Vol. 2. Nashville: 1916.

Dockstader, Frederick J. *Great North American Indians: Profiles in Life & Leadership*. New York, Van Nostrand Reinhold Co., 1977.

Dorsey, James E. *Footprints Along the Hooppee: A History of Emanuel County, 1812–1900*. Spartanburg, South Carolina, Reprint Co., 1978.

Dupuy, Trevor N. & Gay M. Hammerman. *People & Events of the American Revolution*. New York, R. R. Bowker Co., 1974.

The Encyclopedia Americana. New York, Americana Corporation, 1977.

Evans, Lawton B. *First Lessons in Georgia History*. New York, American Book Co., 1922.

Evans, Lawton B. *A History of Georgia: For Use in Schools.* New York, American Book Co., 1898.

Faulk, J. L. O., & Billy W. Jones. *History of Twiggs County, Georgia.* Columbus, Georgia, Columbus Office Supply Co., 1960.

Flanigan, James C. *History of Gwinnett County, Georgia.* Hapeville, Georgia, Tyler &, Co., 1943.

Foster, W. A., & Thomas A. Scott. *Paulding County: Its People & Places.* Roswell, Georgia, W. H. Wolfe Associates, 1983.

French, Allen. *The First Year of the American Revolution.* New York, Octagon Books, Inc., 1968.

Goff, John H. *Placenames of Georgia.* Athens, University of Georgia Press, 1975.

Goff, John H. "Short Studies of Georgia Place Names." *Georgia Mineral Newsletter*, Atlanta: Vol. 9, No. 1. Spring, 1956; Vol. 11, No. 2. Summer, 1958.

Goolsby, Iva P., et al. *Randolph County, Georgia: A Compilation of Facts, Recollections & Family Histories.* 1977.

Governor Treutlen Chapter Daughters of the American Revolution. *History of Peach County, Georgia.* Atlanta, Cherokee Publishing Co., 1972.

Grubbs, Lillie M. *History of Worth County, Georgia.* Macon, Georgia, J. W. Burke Co., 1934.

Hatch, Robert M. *Major John Andre: A Gallant in Spy's Clothing.* Boston, Houghton Mifflin Co., 1986.

Hatcher, George. *Georgia Rivers.* Athens, University of Georgia Press, 1962.

Heitman, Francis B. *Historical Register of Officers of the Continental Army During the War of the Revolution.* Washington, D.C., Rare Book Shop Publishing Co., Inc., 1914.

"The Historical Work of the Daughters of the American Revolution." *The Magazine of History*, Vol. 4, No. 4. New York: October, 1906.

Hodge, Frederick W. *Handbook of American Indians North of Mexico.* Totowa, New Jersey, Rowman & Littlefield, 1975.

Holmes, Marian B. *State of Georgia: Georgia Official & Statistical Register: 1977-1978.* Atlanta, Perry Communications, Inc.

Howell, Clark. *History of Georgia.* Chicago, S. J. Clarke Publishing Co., 1926.

Hunt, Elmer M. *New Hampshire Town Names.* Peterborough, New Hampshire, William L. Baughan, 1970.

Huxford, Folks. *The History of Brooks County, Georgia.* Quitman, Georgia, Hannah Clarke Chapter Daughters of the American Revolution, 1948.

Jasper County Historical Foundation, Inc. *History of Jasper County, Georgia.* Roswell, Georgia, W. H. Wolfe Associates, 1976.

Jones, Mary G., & Lily Reynolds. *Coweta County Chronicles for One Hundred Years.* Atlanta, Stein Printing Co., 1928.

Jordan, Robert H. *There Was a Land: A History of Talbot County Georgia & Its People.* Columbus, Georgia, Columbus Office Supply Co., 1971.

Jordan, Robert H., & J. Gregg Puster. *Courthouses in Georgia: 1825-1983.* Norcross, Georgia, Harrison Co., 1984.

Knight, Lucian L. *Georgia's Bi-centennial Memoirs & Memories.* 1933.

Knight, Lucian L. *Georgia's Landmarks, Memorials & Legends.* Atlanta, Byrd Printing Co., 1913.

Knight, Lucian L. *A Standard History of Georgia & Georgians.* Chicago, Lewis Publishing Co., 1917.

Krakow, Kenneth K. *Georgia Place-Names.* Macon, Winship Press, 1975.

Lee County Historical Society. *Lee County, Georgia: A History.* Atlanta, W. H. Wolfe Associates, 1983.

McCall, Mrs. Howard H. *Roster of Revolutionary Soldiers in Georgia.* Atlanta, Georgia Society Daughters of the American Revolution, 1941.

McCall, Hugh. *The History of Georgia.* Atlanta, Cherokee Publishing Co., 1969.

McDaniel, Susie B. *Official History of Catoosa County, Georgia.* Dalton, Georgia, Gregory Printing & Office Supply, 1953.

McDonald, Mary Lou L., & Samuel J. Lawson. *The Passing of the Pines: A History of Wilcox County, Georgia.* Roswell, Georgia, W. H. Wolfe Associates, 1984.

McQueen, Alex S. *History of Charlton County.* Atlanta, Stein Printing Co., 1932.

Mann, Floris P. *History of Telfair County: From 1812 to 1949.* Macon, Georgia, J. W.. Burke Co., 1949.

Melton, Ella C., & Augusta G. Raines. *History of Terrell County, Georgia.* Roswell, Georgia, W. H. Wolfe Associates, 1980.

Montague-Smith, Patrick. *Debrett's Peerage & Baronetage.* London, England, Debrett's Peerage, Ltd.

Murray County History Committee. *Murray County Heritage.* Roswell, Georgia, W . H. Wolfe Associates, 1987.

"Names of the Governors of Georgia: From the First Settlement of the State in 1732 to 1840." *Collections of the Georgia Historical Society*, Vol. 1. Savannah: 1840.

Northen, William J. *Men of Mark in Georgia.* Atlanta, A. B. Caldwell, 1910.

Nottingham, Carolyn W., & Evelyn

Hannah. *History of Upson County, Georgia.* J. W. Burke Co., 1930.

Pate, John B. *History of Turner County.* Atlanta, Stein Printing Co., 1933.

Perryman, Clinton J. *History of Lincoln County, Georgia.* 1933.

Pugh, Jesse F. *Three Hundred Years Along the Pasquotank: A Biographical History of Camden County.* Durham, North Carolina, Seeman Printery, Inc., 1957.

Rand, Clayton. *Sons of the South.* New York, Holt, Rinehart & Winston, 1961.

Read, William A. "Indian Stream-Names in Georgia II." *International Journal of American Linguistics*, Vol. 16, No. 4. Baltimore, Maryland: October, 1950 .

Roberts, Albert H. "The Dade Massacre." *Quarterly Periodical of the Florida Historical Society*, Vol. 5, No. 3. Gainesville, Florida: January, 1927.

Rogers, William W. *Antebellum Thomas County: 1825–1861.* Tallahassee, Florida State University, 1963.

Rowland, A. R. *Historical Markers of Richmond County, Georgia.* Augusta, Georgia, Richmond County Historical Society, 1966.

Rutherford, Mildred L. *Georgia: The Thirteenth Colony.* Athens, Georgia, McGregor Co., 1926.

Sams, Anita B. *Wayfarers in Walton.* Monroe, Georgia, General Charitable Foundation of Monroe, Georgia, Inc., 1967.

Scruggs, Carroll P. *Georgia Historical Markers.* Helen, Georgia, Bay Tree Grove, 1973.

Sell, Edward S. *Geography of Georgia.* Oklahoma City, Harlow Publishing Corporation, 1950.

Shirk, George H. *Oklahoma Place Names.* Norman, University of Oklahoma Press, 1974.

Smith, Charles H. *A School History of Georgia.* Boston, Ginn & Company, 1893.

Smith, George G. *The Story of Georgia and the Georgia People: 1732 to 1860.* Atlanta, Franklin Printing & Publishing Co., 1900.

Spence, Margaret, & Anna M. Fleming. *History of Mitchell County: 1857-1976.*

Stevens, William B. *A History of Georgia.* Savannah, Beehive Press, 1972.

The Story of Georgia: A School History of Our State. Atlanta, Science Research Associates, 1942.

Suarez, Annette M. *A Source Book on the Early History of Cuthbert & Randolph County, Georgia.* Atlanta, Cherokee Publishing Co., 1982.

Tate, Luke E. *History of Pickens County.* Atlanta, Walter W. Brown Publishing Co., 1935.

Telfair, Nancy. *A History of Columbus, Georgia: 1828–1928*. Columbus, Georgia, Historical Publishing Co., 1929.

Temple, Sarah B. G. *The First Hundred Years: A Short History of Cobb County in Georgia*. Atlanta, Walter W. Brown Publishing Co., 1935.

Terrill, Helen E. *History of Stewart County, Georgia*. Columbus, Georgia, Columbus Office Supply Co., 1958.

Townend, Peter. *Burke's Genealogical & Heraldic History of the Peerage, Baronetage & Knightage*. London, England, Burke's Peerage, Ltd., 1967.

Trogdon, Kathryn C. *The History of Stephens County, Georgia*. Toccoa, Georgia, Toccoa Womans Club, Inc., 1973.

Vogel, Virgil J. *Indian Names in Michigan*. Ann Arbor, University of Michigan Press, 1986.

Walker, Laura S. *History of Ware County, Georgia*. Macon, Georgia, J. W. Burke Co., 1934.

Webb, Walter P., et al. *The Handbook of Texas*. Austin, Texas State Historical Association, 1952.

Weston Woman's Club. *History of Webster County, Georgia*. Roswell, Georgia, W. H. Wolfe Associates, 1980.

White County History Book Committee. *A History of White County: 1857–1980*.

White, Dabney, & T. C. Richardson. *East Texas: Its History and Its Makers*. New York, Lewis Historical Publishing Co., 1940.

White, George. *Historical Collections of Georgia*. New York, Pudney & Russell, 1855.

Whitfield County History Commission. *Official History of Whitfield County, Georgia*. Dalton, Georgia, A. J. Showalter Co., 1936.

Willard, Margaret W. *Letters on the American Revolution: 1774–1776*. Boston, Houghton Mifflin Co., 1925.

Williams, Carolyn W. *History of Jones County, Georgia*. Macon, Georgia, J. W. Burke Co., 1957.

Williams, Ida B. *History of Tift County*. Macon, Georgia, J. W. Burke Co., 1948.

Work Projects Administration. *Henderson: A Guide to Audubon's Home Town in Kentucky*. Northport, New York, Bacon, Percy & Daggett, 1941.

Work Projects Administration. *Inventory of the County & Town Archives of Georgia-Cook, Dougherty & Lee Counties*. Atlanta, 1941-1942.

Hawaii

(5 counties)

515 *Hawaii County*

Island of Hawaii—Hawaii County consists of the island of Hawaii. The entire Hawaiian archipelago was named for Hawaii, the largest island of the group and Hawaii County was named for that island also. The island of Hawaii measures about 4,000 square miles and contains about two thirds of all the land in the archipelago. Tourism and sugarcane production are important industries here. The island has four volcanic mountains and it has been suggested that Hawaii's name translates as "little Java" or "burning Java" on account of these volcanoes. Hawaiian linguists find this etymology unlikely. The origin of Hawaii's name is lost in pre-history but surviving legends offer three explanations:

1. Name of the original home of the Hawaiian people named Hawaiki or Havaiki. Its location is unknown but in several accounts this ancestral homeland is said to be a small island near Tahiti.

2. Name of the legendary Polynesian fisherman and navigator, Hawaii-Loa, who discovered or rediscovered the Hawaiian islands. In one version of the legend his name is given as Hawaii-Nui.

3. A mythical land after death or "beyond the doors of death."

In support of the first theory, it has been noted that there are other islands in the Pacific Ocean with very similar names including Avaiki, Havaii, Havaiki, Hawaiki and Savaii.

516 *Honolulu County*

City of Honolulu, Hawaii—On August 31, 1850, the king of Hawaii made Honolulu a city and the capital of the kingdom. Later, when Hawaii's counties were created in the early 1900's, Honolulu County was named for the city with which it is coterminous and which became its county seat. Honolulu is the state's most populous city, the commercial and industrial center of the state and the state's capital. In practice, the city consists of some 80 square miles on the island of Oahu although legally the city and county include all of Oahu and most of the northwestern islands and reefs in the Hawaiian archipelago from Nihoa Island to Kure Island some 1,300 miles away. Most authorities state or imply that the city of Honolulu was named for its harbor but others believe that the city was named for a small, ancient district which is now part of the city. The translation of the name is also disputed. Most translations refer to a protected or sheltered bay, harbor or cove or to a fair haven but a number of other translations have also been suggested. The possibilities include:

— Protected bay
— Sheltered bay
— Protected harbor
— Sheltered harbor
— Calm harbor
— Quiet harbor
— Protected cove
— Sheltered cove
— Sheltered port
— Fair haven
— Quiet haven
— Abundance of calm or peace
— A wind-sheltered place in the flats between two mountain ranges
— A flat space joining the hills that is sheltered from the wind
— A pleasant slope of restful land
— A sheltered hollow or valley with a bay in front of it
— Where the back of the neck is sheltered from the wind

517 *Kalawao County*

A land division on Molokai Island—Kalawao County is an administrative unit under the jurisdiction of the state department of health for the Kalaupapa leprosy settlement on Molokai Island. Here the heroic Father Damien devoted his life to the lepers and finally contracted the disease himself and died of it. The name *Kalawao* derived from the name of an ancient ahupuaas, or land division, here. The meaning of the name is lost in antiquity but "announce mountain area" and "mountain-side wild woods" have been suggested and these translations would accurately describe this flat seven mile, triangular peninsula in that it backs up to steep cliffs, convenient for isolating the lepers.

518 *Kauai County*

Island of Kauai — Kauai County consists of two major islands, Kauai and Niihau, as well as some smaller islands. When Hawaii's counties were established in the early 1900's, Kauai County was named for its largest island. With some 550 square miles, Kauai Island is fourth largest in the state and by far the largest in Kauai County. Sugarcane production is an important industry on this volcanic island. Kauai has more untamed land than Hawaii's other islands and numerous small rivers and streams are found here. Kauai's name was coined in pre-history and its meaning is now unknown. Translations which have been suggested include:

— Drying out place
— Things that are dried out (such as driftwood)
— To place out to dry
— Food season
— Fountainhead of many waters from on high and bubbling up from below
— Abundance of good

It is not certain that the correct translation is among them.

519 *Maui County*

Island of Maui — Maui County consists of the island of Maui, for which it was named, and several smaller islands. This volcanic island, second largest in the Hawaiian archipelago, had been named in prehistory for the popular Polynesian demigod, Maui.

Maui — Legends concerning this demigod are found throughout Polynesia. The Hawaiians had major gods and countless minor gods but Maui was not one of them. He was a demigod, part god and part man. The complex stories about him have several versions. Maui was abandoned as a child and raised by ocean gods. He then returned to land where his numerous exploits included fishing the land out of the sea and raising the sky to separate it from the earth. In order to provide more hours of sunlight for fishing, getting food and drying tapa cloths, Maui captured the sun and made it promise to go more slowly across the sky. He is also credited with bringing fire to man, making birds visible to man and inventing both the spear and the barbed fishhooks.

According to Hawaiian mythology, when Maui born he was scrawny and deformed and his mother didn't like him. She cut off a lock from her hair, tied it around him and threw him in the ocean. This is said to explain a long version of his name meaning "Maui formed in the topknot."

REFERENCES

All About Hawaii: Standard Tourist Guide. Honolulu Star-Bulletin, 1928.

Anderson, Isabel. *The Spell of the Hawaiian Islands and the Philippines.* Boston, Page Co., 1916.

Andrews, Lorrin, & Henry H. Parker. *A Dictionary of the Hawaiian Language.* Honolulu, Board of Commissioners of Public Archives of the Territory of Hawaii, 1922.

Armstrong, Louise B. *Facts & Figures of Hawaii.* New York, Henry M. Snyder, 1933.

Beckwith, Martha W. *Kepelino's Traditions of Hawaii.* Honolulu, Bernice P. Bishop Museum, 1932.

Castle, William R. *Hawaii Past & Present.* New York, Dodd, Mead & Co., 1920.

Clark, Sydney. *All the Best in Hawaii.* New York, Dodd, Mead & Co., 1959.

Cotterell, Arthur. *A Dictionary of World Mythology.* New York, G. P. Putnam's Sons, 1979.

Coulter, John W. *A Gazetteer of the Territory of Hawaii.* Honolulu, University of Hawaii, 1935.

Davenport, William W., et al. *Hawaii 1961.* New York, David McKay Co., Inc., 1961.

The Encyclopedia Americana. New York, Americana Corporation, 1977.

Fergusson, Erna. *Our Hawaii.* New York, Alfred A. Knopf, 1942.

Fujii, Jocelyn K. *The Best of Hawaii.* New York, Crown Publishers, Inc., 1988.

Gessler, Clifford. *Tropic Landfall: The Port of Honolulu.* Garden City, New York, Doubleday, Doran & Co., Inc., 1942.

Hazard, Patrick D. *The Dolphin Guide to Hawaii.* Garden City, New York, Dolphin Books, 1965.

Jennings, Helen. *Chronology & Documentary Handbook of the State of Hawaii.* Dobbs Ferry, New York, Oceana Publications, Inc., 1978.

Joesting, Edward. *Kauai: The Separate Kingdom.* University of Hawaii Press and Kauai Museum Association, Ltd., 1984.

Judd, Gerrit P. *Hawaii: An Informal History.* New York, Collier Books, 1961.

Judd, Laura F. *Honolulu.* Chicago, R. R. Donnelley & Sons Co., 1966.

Kanahele, George H. S. *Ku Kanaka Stand Tall: A Search for Hawaiian Values.* University of Hawaii Press & Waiaha Foundation, 1986.

Krauss, Bob. *Here's Hawaii.* New York, Coward-McCann, Inc., 1960.

Kuykendall, Ralph S., & A. Grove Day. *Hawaii: A History.* New York, Prentice-Hall, Inc., 1948.

Kyselka, Will, & Ray Lanterman. *Maui: How It Came to Be.* Honolulu, University Press of Hawaii, 1980.

Lyons, C. J. "The Meaning of Some Hawaiian Place-Names." *The Hawaiian Annual.* Honolulu: 1901.

Michener, James A. *Hawaii.* New York, Bantam Books, Inc., 1959.

Nellist, George F. *The Story of Hawaii & Its Builders.* Honolulu, Honolulu Star-Bulletin Ltd., 1925.

Nergal, Ory M. *The Encyclopedia of American Cities.* New York, E. P. Dutton, 1980.

The New Encyclopaedia Britannica. Chicago, Encyclopaedia Britannica, Inc., 1984.

Porteus, Stanley D. *Calabashes & Kings: An Introduction to Hawaii.* Palo Alto, California, Pacific Books, 1945.

Pratt, Helen G. *The Hawaiians: An Island People.* Rutland, Vermont, Charles E. Tuttle Co., 1963.

Pukui, Mary K., & Samuel H. Elbert. *Hawaiian Dictionary.* Honolulu, University Press of Hawaii, 1971.

Pukui, Mary K., & Samuel H. Elbert. *Place Names of Hawaii.* University of Hawaii Press, 1966.

Pukui, Mary K., et al. *Place Names of Hawaii.* Honolulu, University Press of Hawaii, 1974.

Republican State Central Committee of Hawaii. *Republican Party of Hawaii Almanac.* Honolulu, 1973.

Smith, Bradford. *The Islands of Hawaii.* Philadelphia, J. B. Lippincott Co., 1957.

Stewart, George R. *Names on the Land.* Boston, Houghton Mifflin Co., 1967.

Thrum, Thomas G. *Hawaiian Folk Tales.* Chicago, A. C. McClurg & Co., 1917.

Weaver, Samuel P. *Hawaii, U.S.A.* New York, Pageant Press, Inc., 1959.

Wenkam, Robert. *Hawaii.* Chicago, Rand McNally & Co., 1972.

Westervelt, W. D. *Hawaiian Historical Legends.* New York, Fleming H. Revell Co., 1923.

Westervelt, W. D. *Hawaiian Legends of Volcanoes*. Rutland, Vermont, Charles E. Tuttle Co., 1963.

Westervelt, W. D. *Legends of Old Honolulu*. Boston, George H. Ellis Co., 1915.

Wolk, Allan. *The Naming of America*. Nashville, Thomas Nelson, Inc., 1977.

Idaho

(44 counties)

520 *Ada County*

Ada C. Riggs (1863–)— Ada County was created by the legislature of Idaho territory in December, 1864, and named for Ada C. Riggs, the first White child born in Boise City. She was the oldest daughter of H. C. Riggs, who was a member of the House of Representatives of Idaho's territorial legislature at the time that Ada County was created. H. C. Riggs had come to Idaho from Missouri and he was one of the founders of Boise City.

521 *Adams County*

John Adams (1735–1826)— Adams, a native of Massachusetts, was a delegate to the first Continental Congress and a signer of the Declaration of Independence. He participated in Paris with Benjamin Franklin and John Jay in negotiating peace with England and, after the war, he was our country's first minister to England. Adams became the first vice-president of the United States under George Washington and when Washington retired, Adams was elected to be our nation's second president. Adams County, Idaho, was created in 1911. All of its land was carved from Washington County and thus the county named for the second president came from the county named for the first president.

522 *Bannock County*

Bannack Indians— The Bannack, a branch of the Shoshonean Indians, lived in Bannock County, Idaho, and other areas of the plains and plateaus of southeastern Idaho and western Wyoming. They were a semi-nomadic tribe and they made buffalo hunting excursions to the Great Plains although buffalo never became a staple of their diet. The Bannack Indians were not numerous. Their population probably never exceeded 2,000. They were generally tall, straight and athletic people, more courageous than many other Indians and often hostile to Whites. In the late 1860's a reservation was established for the Bannack at Ft. Hall, Idaho. Their name derives from two Indian words *bamp*, which means "hair" and *nack* or *neck*, meaning "backward motion." The name referred to the manner in which Bannack Indians wore tufts of hair thrown back from their foreheads. The tribe's name is also rendered as Bannock and it was this version that was used when the county's name was selected. The Scottish word *bannock* means a kind of pancake, much used in the American West by early traders and settlers.

523 *Bear Lake County*

Bear Lake— This county was created in 1875 and named for Bear Lake, half of which is located in the southern part of the county. The other half of this 125 square mile lake extends into Utah. Bear Lake is almost 20 miles long and has an average width of over six miles. Oval shaped with flattened ends, it has an average depth of about 50 feet. Nestled in the mountains almost 6,000 feet above sea level, Bear Lake with its morning glory blue waters is one of the most beautiful lakes in the world. It is now used as a storage reservoir for excess water from Bear River to be used for irrigation. The lake was originally named Miller Lake during the winter of 1811–1812 by the first party of White men known to visit it. The name honored Joseph Miller, their leader and guide. It was later named Black Bear Lake by Donald McKenzie, the leader of the Hudson Bay Company's Snake River expedition, when he visited this area in 1818 and observed numerous black bears here.

524 *Benewah County*

Benewah (–)— The Coeur d' Alene Indians were one of the principal tribes in Idaho. Although no Idaho county has been named directly for them, since 1915 when Benewah County was created in Idaho's panhandle, the tribe has been honored indirectly. Benewah was a former chief of the Coeur d' Alene Indians.

525 *Bingham County*

Henry H. Bingham (1841–1912)— Bingham, a native of Pennsylvania, served as an officer in the Union army during the Civil War and rose to the rank of brigadier-general. After the war he was Philadelphia's postmaster. Bingham later represented Pennsylvania in the U.S. House of Representatives from 1879 until his death in 1912. Henry Bingham never had any connection with Idaho but he was a friend of Idaho's territorial governor, William Bunn, who named the new county in honor of his friend. Governor Bunn was strongly anti–Mormon and Bingham County was purposely created in 1885 as part of an anti–Mormon program. Although the Church of Jesus Christ of Latter-Day Saints (Mormon) has been the leading religion in Idaho for more than a century, Mormons are still the minority in Idaho and from time to time they have been targets for hostility. Bingham County was purposely created as part of an anti–Mormon movement, to add one new county with a non–Mormon majority to elect anti–Mormon legislators.

526 *Blaine County*

James G. Blaine (1830–1893)— Blaine, a native of Pennsylvania, moved to Maine where he served three terms in the state legislature. He then represented Maine in both houses of the U.S. Congress and, for a number of years, was speaker of the House of Representatives. In 1881 Blaine became secretary of state under President James A. Garfield and he was the Republican Party's candidate for president of the United States in 1884, losing to Grover Cleveland. When Benjamin Harrison became president in 1889, he appointed Blaine to be his secretary of state. Blaine County, Idaho was created in 1895, two years after Blaine's death.

527 *Boise County*

Boise River— The Boise River, a tributary of the Snake River, rises in the mountains northeast of the city of Boise, flows west at first through rugged mountains and lava canyons, then through a beautiful, wide valley with rolling farmland rich in trees and loam. The Boise flows through the city of Boise and empties into the Snake River at the Oregon border just west of Parma, Idaho. *Bois* is a French word for "woods" or "forest" and the river received its name on account of the great number and variety of trees growing along its banks. Legend has it that a party of French-Canadians, led by the American, Captain B. L. E. Bonneville, exclaimed "Les Bois! Les Bois!" when they came upon the river in the summer of 1834. They had traveled through many miles of hot, dry, dusty and treeless plains and the sight of the Boise River and its trees delighted them.

528 *Bonner County*

Edwin L. Bonner (–)— Bonner was a businessman from Walla Walla in Washington territory who was one of Northern Idaho's early settlers. In 1863 or 1864 he bought the rights to cross the Kootenai River here from the Indians and he built the first ferry where the town of Bonners Ferry, Idaho is now located. Soon after, Bonner secured an exclusive five-year franchise from Idaho's territorial legislature to operate the ferry. This was a key crossing for prospectors in search of the newly discovered gold in British Columbia. He charged $1.50 for loaded pack animals and 50 cents per person on foot. By the mid-1870s the mining boom had subsided and Bonner sold or leased the ferry rights to Richard A. Fry, a native of Illinois. Edwin L. Bonner also lived for a number of years in western Montana.

529 *Bonneville County*

Benjamin Louis Eulalie de Bonneville (1793–1878)— One of Idaho's earliest explorers, B. L. E. Bonneville was born in France and immigrated to America about the time of the French Revolution. His family had friends among the rich and famous in America and Bonneville had no trouble securing an appointment to the U.S. military academy at West Point. After graduation Bonneville served some 15 years in light artillery, infantry and construction posts and rose to the rank of captain. In the early 1830's Captain Bonneville secured a leave of absence from the army to develop a fur-trading venture in the far West. His hopes for wealth as a fur trader were unsuccessful but the explorations of Bonneville and his parties during the early 1830's from the Rocky Mountains to California became famous when Bonneville's journal was amplified and published in a book by Washington Irving entitled *Adventures of Captain Bonneville*. Also, Captain Bonneville drew valuable maps of the country he explored which were later published by congress. Bonneville's western travels took him throughout the Snake River area probably including what is now Bonneville County. Bonneville later served in the U.S. army in the Mexican War and during the Civil War he rose to the rank of brevet brigadier-general. Bonneville County was created in 1911. The bill to create this new county was drawn up and introduced in the Idaho legislature by Senator Clency St. Clair of Bingham County. The name originally suggested for the new county was Snake River County but that name was not adopted.

530 *Boundary County*

Uncertain— Boundary County is located in the extreme northern portion of Idaho's panhandle giving it boundaries with one Idaho county, two other states and one foreign country. Specifically, it borders Bonner County, Idaho, on the south and west, Montana on the east, the state of Washington on the west and the Canadian province of British Columbia on the north. It is uncertain whether the county's name was chosen on account of its border with Canada or because of its unusual configuration of borders with other states as well as Canada. The location of our country's northwestern border with Canada here had earlier been an emotional issue in America with calls for "54-40 or fight." But we didn't get 54-40 and we didn't fight. Instead we got 49-0. In June, 1846, President James K. Polk signed a treaty with Great Britain that set America's northwestern boundary here much further south than 54-40, at the 49th parallel. This once important and emotional issue had long since been forgotten when Boundary County, Idaho, was created and named in 1915 and no authority suggests that the name was chosen on account of the earlier boundary dispute with Great Britain.

531 *Butte County*

Uncertain— The source of this county's name is uncertain because reliable authorities offer three different, although closely related, explanations:

1. The buttes that are characteristic of the area.
2. *Trois Buttes* or "Three Buttes."
3. Big Butte.

Big Butte is a prominent, detached butte of volcanic origin elevated some 2,350 feet from the surrounding plain. It is the largest of the broad, dome-shaped Three Buttes here, about 23 miles southeast of Arco, the Butte County seat. The other two buttes are East Butte, which is 700 feet high and Middle Butte, which rises only about 400 feet above its desert surroundings. These two smaller buttes are also known as Twin Buttes. Because of their isolation, the Three Buttes served as conspicuous landmarks to early emigrants over the Oregon Trail.

532 *Camas County*

Big Camas Prairie— Camas County was named for the Big Camas Prairie within its borders in the valley of the Malad River and Camas Creek. Big Camas Prairie's name refers to the camas plant whose roots were an important item in the Indians' diet. Camas were common in Idaho and elsewhere in the Northwest and they once covered Big Camas Prairie. *Camas* is derived from *kamass* in Chinook jargon meaning "sweet" but its original source was *chamas* which also signified "sweet" in the Nootka language of Vancouver. Camas roots have a sweetish taste when eaten fresh although they are more palatable when baked. They resemble onions. The term *camas* includes any species of plant in the genus *Camassia*. In Camas County their blue, hyacinth-like flowers bloom in late May or early June. Large groups of Indians once traveled hundreds of miles to harvest these plants. They were jealous of their rights to this important food and they fought the White settlers when those rights were violated.

533 *Canyon County*

Uncertain— Canyon County is located in southwestern Idaho with the Snake River as its western and southern border. It was named either for the narrow canyon of the Boise River at the Canyon County seat of Caldwell or for the Snake River Canyon which forms a natural boundary for the county. Reliable authorities differ on which of the two canyons the county's name honors.

534 *Caribou County*

Caribou Mountains or Caribou Mountain in Idaho— Caribou County was created in

1919 and named for the mountains which start near its northern border and extend for about 50 miles across the southeastern portion of Bonneville County from the southeast to the northwest. The Caribou Mountains are one of the larger ranges in the Idaho-Wyoming chain and they run to a width of some 15 miles. Caribou Mountain is in this range and some authorities indicate that it is this one mountain that the county's name honors. Caribou Mountain, with an elevation of some 9,800 feet, is two miles west of the ghost town of Caribou City. These mountains were named for a prospector, nicknamed Cariboo, who came to Idaho after taking part in the 1860 gold rush in the Cariboo region of British Columbia. The Cariboo Mountains there are part of the Canadian Rocky Mountains in the great bend of the Fraser River. The Canadian name derived from the name for the member of the deer family which was called *cariboeuf* or *cerf-boeuf* by French-Canadians. This term may have been a corruption of the Algonquian Indian name for these animals which was *xalibu* meaning "the pawer" or "the scratcher." Caribou are found only in the northern part of North America and are unique among deer in that both sexes generally carry antlers. It was from the Cariboo region in Canada that our hero got his nickname. Most authorities say that his name was Cariboo Fairchild but some use Fairchilds and Jesse Fairbanks is also given. By whatever name, he came to the Caribou Mountains in Idaho after his participation in the British Columbia gold rush and discovered gold here. The mining town which grew up near his discovery, Caribou City, is now a ghost town. Cariboo discovered his gold in company with a man named George Chapin. They discovered gold on Caribou Mountain and staked out claims for both placer and lode discoveries. It is said that Cariboo Fairchild also participated in silver mining in northern Idaho.

535 *Cassia County*

Cassia Creek — Cassia County was created in 1879 and named for a creek which is within its borders. Cassia Creek is a small tributary of the Raft River, which in turn is a tributary of the mighty Snake. Cassia Creek rises on Albion Mountain and flows about 20 miles in a northeast direction before entering Raft River just north of the town of Malta. Most authorities state that the creek was named by Hudson's Bay Company trappers for the cassia plants which they found along it. *Cassia*, also known as "wild senna," are long stemmed plants with pinnately arranged leaves, each with 8 to 20 leaflets. The flowers of the cassia plant are yellow. Three other possibilities have been suggested as the origin of Cassia Creek's name:

1. Derived from *cajeaux*, a peasant French word meaning "raft."

2. Named for James J. Cazier, who was a member of the LDS church, the Mormon battalion and a captain of an emigrant train; the creek's name evolved to Cassier and finally to Cassia.

3. Named for a Frenchman named De Cassia, who is said to have led an early expedition across this area.

536 *Clark County*

Sam K. Clark (–) — Clark, a pioneer cattleman of southwestern Montana and northeastern Idaho, was an early settler in this area. In addition to cattle, Clark also raised sheep and he represented Frémont County in the Idaho legislature. When Clark County was created from Fremont County and named for him in 1919, Clark became the new county's first state senator. This was the second time that Idaho had used the name Clark for one of its counties. In 1905 Kootenai County was abolished to form two new counties named Lewis County and Clark County in honor of the leaders of the Lewis and Clark Expedition. The creation of these counties was declared unconstitutional and Kootenai County was re-established with new boundaries.

537 *Clearwater County*

Clearwater River — Clearwater County was created in 1911 and named for its largest river, a tributary of the Snake. Clearwater River rises at an altitude of some 6,000 feet in the mountainous plateaus just west of the serrated Bitterfoot Mountain range. It flows to the northwest through rugged, timbered mountains and rolling prairies until it joins the Snake River. The Clearwater's confluence with the Snake is at Idaho's border with Washington at Lewiston where the altitude is only 700 feet. The Indians' name for the river meant "clear water" on account of its brilliantly clear transparency. That Indian name is rendered as *Koos-koos-kia* and several similar variations. The Clearwater got its present name in 1805 from William Clark, one of the leaders of the Lewis and Clark Expedition. Clark translated the river's Indian name into our language but kept its apt meaning. This is Idaho's second Clearwater County. In March, 1901, a county named Clearwater was created from parts of Shoshone and Nez Perce Counties but this earlier Clearwater County was never organized and it was declared void.

538 *Custer County*

General Custer Mine — Custer County was created in 1881 by Idaho's territorial legislature and named for the General Custer Mine, which at that time was one of the more prominent gold mines in the area. The mine had been named for General George A. Custer.

George A. Custer (1839–1876) — Custer was born in Ohio and educated at West Point. As a Union officer in the Civil War, his successes led to promotion to the rank of general before his 24th birthday. Following that war he served in the U.S. cavalry fighting Indians in the West. The flamboyance which had served Custer so well in the Civil War led to his downfall at Little Bighorn. In that battle, famous as "Custer's last stand," he attacked Indians who greatly outnumbered his forces. Custer and all of his men were slain.

Consideration had been given to naming this new county Lincoln, in honor of Abraham Lincoln who was president in 1863 when Idaho territory was established, but the name Custer prevailed and Idaho did not create a Lincoln County until 1895.

539 *Elmore County*

Ida Elmore Mine — Elmore County was created in 1889 by the last legislature of Idaho territory and named for the Ida Elmore Mine. The Elmore County area was a leading producer of both gold and silver in the early mining history of Idaho and the Ida Elmore quartz mine near Rocky Bar was one of the best gold-producing mines. In 1863 prospectors had discovered rich ore here at the South Fork of the Boise River and several mines, including the Ida Elmore, were opened.

540 *Franklin County*

Town of Franklin, Idaho — Franklin County was created in 1913 and named for the historic town just inside its southern border. The town of Franklin, which is one mile north of the state of Utah, was the first permanent agricultural settlement by Whites in Idaho. It was founded in 1860 by Mormon settlers who didn't realize that they had traveled just beyond the northern border of their Utah territory into Idaho territory. They named the town Franklin, in honor of their leader, Franklin D. Richards.

Franklin D. Richards (1821–1899)— This Mormon leader and close confidant of Brigham Young was a native of Massachusetts. At the age of 17 Richards affiliated himself with the Church of Jesus Christ of Latter-Day Saints and became involved in missionary work in America and the British Isles. In 1848 he acted as the captain of a train of more than 50 wagons across the plains to the Great Salt Lake. In 1849 Richards became a member of the Council of Twelve Apostles and he continued in that capacity for some 50 years. In the 1850's and again in the 1860's Apostle Richards served the church in England and on the European continent and he was president of the European mission. In business life Richards was a pioneer in Utah's iron industry and he had interests in agriculture and mill building. He served in the legislature of Utah territory and was a civil judge of Weber County, Utah. In 1898 Richards became president of the Twelve Apostles and he occupied that position until his death.

541 *Fremont County*

John C. Frémont (1813–1890)— Born in Georgia, Frémont engaged in survey work in wilderness areas of the South and then assisted Joseph N. Nicollet in explorations of Iowa, Dakota and Minnesota. Frémont then performed his greatest service by leading five explorations to the far West. Portions of this vast domain had previously been explored. However, it was Frémont who carefully mapped the areas traveled and prepared notes of his observations. Frémont played a role in winning California from Mexico, served very briefly as a U.S. senator and, in 1856, ran as the Republican party's first presidential candidate. He later served as a Union general in the Civil War and as governor of Arizona territory. He was ineffective in both of these positions. Frémont's travels to the West took him across southern Idaho in 1843.

542 *Gem County*

Uncertain— The state of Idaho's nickname is "Gem State" and Gem County, which was created in 1915, has a shape that resembles Idaho with left and right sides reversed. Although it is uncertain why this county was named Gem, it has been suggested that it may have been named for the nickname of the state which it resembles. The most frequently suggested source of this county's name is merely "Idaho: Gem of the Mountains." In any event, the county's name is appropriate on account

of its own gems. Fire opals and light blue agates are found here.

543 *Gooding County*

Frank R. Gooding (1859–1929)— Gooding, a native of England, immigrated with his parents to America when he was a boy and moved to Idaho in 1881 where he became a pioneer sheep rancher. He gradually extended his land ownership and his sheep operations were the largest in Idaho by the time of his death. He was the founder and first mayor of the town of Gooding, which later became the Gooding County seat. In 1898 Gooding was elected to Idaho's senate and in 1900 he served as president *pro tempore* of that body. He then served two terms as governor of Idaho. Gooding County was created and named in his honor in 1913, five years after his second term as governor ended. Gooding later represented Idaho in the U.S. Senate.

544 *Idaho County*

Uncertain— Since Idaho County was created by the legislature of Washington territory before Idaho territory existed, it is certain that Idaho County was not named for the state of Idaho or for Idaho territory. Beyond that, there is little certainty concerning this county's name. A number of authorities state that Idaho County was named for the steamboat *Idaho* or *Idahoe* which plied the Northwest in the early 1860's. Most authorities say that this steamboat traveled on the Columbia River but the Snake River and the Fraser River are also mentioned. The steamer served miners during the gold rush and it is said that the areas that these miners worked became known as the Idaho mines. This vessel was built by the Yale Steamboat Company and its name was changed from *Idaho* to *Fort Yale*. Operated by the Oregon Steam Navigation Company, it blew up when its boiler exploded.

Prior to the steamboat, the name Idaho was known to exist in what is now the state of Colorado. A locality there was named Idaho Springs. Later, the name Idaho was seriously considered for the territory itself, which was instead named Colorado territory. Some sources indicate that Idaho is of Indian origin while others insist that it is a coined word. Most suggested translations of the word center around (1) gem of the mountains or (2) sunrise or morning. Comments about possible origins and meanings of the word include:

1. Gem of the mountains. This meaning from the lustrous rim of light shining

from the mountain crown or diadem at sunrise.

2. The Indian word *ee-dah-how* or *e-dah-hoe* consisting of three parts: The first conveys the idea of "coming down" as in "snow coming down." The second syllable, *dah*, signifies both "sun" and "mountain." The syllable *how*, or *hoe* denotes an exclamation mark. The Indian thought thus conveyed was "Behold! The sun coming down the mountain." or "It is sunup." or "It is morning."

3. Light on the mountain

4. The greeting, "Good morning."

5. Get up. It is morning.

6. Salmon tribe or salmon eaters.

7. The name used by the Kiowa-Apache Indians for the Comanche Indians, which was *Idahi*.

545 *Jefferson County*

Thomas Jefferson (1743–1826)— Jefferson was a native of Virginia and a member of the Virginia legislature. He served Virginia as governor and he was a delegate to the second Continental Congress. Jefferson was the author of the Declaration of Independence and one of its signers. He was minister to France, secretary of state, vice-president and president of the United States. As president, he accomplished the Louisiana Purchase and he arranged the Lewis and Clark Expedition to the Pacific Northwest. Jefferson was a true intellectual, thoroughly knowledgeable in the arts and sciences. His political theories were pivotal in the formation of our infant republic.

546 *Jerome County*

Uncertain— The village of Jerome. is the county seat of Jerome County, Idaho, and it was named for Jerome Kuhn. The county's name also honors Jerome Kuhn but it is uncertain whether the county was named directly for Kuhn for the village. Since the village was laid out and named about twelve years before the county was created, it seems probable that the county was named for the village.

Village of Jerome, Idaho— This village in southern Idaho was laid out in 1907 in advance of settlement. It was the creation of promoters of the Twin Falls North Side Irrigation Project. It was irrigation of land by this project that sparked the settlement and development of the village of Jerome and Jerome County. Among the promoters of this project were W. S. Kuhn and his brother, both of Pittsburgh, and Jerome C. Hill. The village was named in 1907 for Jerome Kuhn, the young son of W. S.

Kuhn. It was incorporated in 1909 and when Jerome County was created in 1919, it became the county seat of the new county.

Jerome Kuhn (–) —The June 21, 1907, issue or the *Twin Falls News* contained the following.

"…the naming of Jerome … is a compliment to the young son of Mr. W.S. Kuhn of Pittsburgh, president of the TFNSL&W Co. The boy thus honored is the grandson of Jerome Hill, Sr., and the nephew of Jerome Hill, Jr., consequently the name is very appropriate as well as euphonic."

547 *Kootenai County*

Kutenai Indians —Kootenai County was named for the remote tribe of Indians who once were buffalo hunters on the plains and then migrated to northern Idaho, western Montana and southern Canada. The Kutenai, who were river and lake Indians, consisted of the Upper Kutenai in Canada and the more primitive Lower Kutenai who lived primarily in the Boundary County area of northern Idaho. The Lower Kutenai lived mostly on fish and small forest animals. These Indians were skilled in sign language. Most Kutenai were clean, neat, handsome and relatively tall. They were also described as intelligent and hospitable but rather melancholy. Many of them were addicted to gambling. Their artistic skills were employed in decorations on their bark canoes and on their baskets and beaded costumes. Never numerous, the Kutenai population was about 1,000 in the United States and Canada in 1970. Although the meaning of the name *Kutenai* is not certain, most authorities indicate that it means "water people." Other translations that have been suggested include "deer robes" and "bow" as in "bow and arrow."

548 *Latah County*

Latah Creek —Latah County was named for a creek which drains its northwest corner. The creek's name derived from two Nez Perce Indian words meaning "place of pine" and "pestle." The Nez Perce frequently came here to harvest camas roots which were an important staple in their diet. *La-kah* in their language meant "pine trees" or "place of pine trees" while *Tah-ol* meant "pestle." The name Latah evolved for the area and for the Latah Creek on account of the profusion of white pine trees here and the stone pestles which the Indians ground the camas roots into a kind of flour. This county was originally created by Idaho's territorial legislature in 1864 as Lah-toh, Lah-Toh or Lah Toh County. Because of controversy over location of the county seat, Lah-toh County was never organized and the act creating it was repealed on January 9, 1867. But those who wanted a county with its seat at Moscow, Idaho were not to be denied. They next took their case to the U.S. Congress where they enlisted the support of Idaho's territorial delegate to congress, Fred T. Dubois. Since Idaho was still a territory, it was under the jurisdiction of the federal government. Dubois persuaded Senator John H. Mitchell from Oregon to get congress to create the new county. The bill passed congress in 1888 and the present Latah County was born.

549 *Lemhi County*

Fort Lemhi —In 1855 a colony of Mormon missionaries from Utah territory established the Salmon River Mission here on the bank of the Lemhi River near the mouth of Pattee Creek. To protect from Indian attacks, they fortified it and they named the fort Limhi, which soon transposed to Lemhi. The mission was constructed of mud walls which were three feet wide at their base and some nine feet high. Adjoining the wall on the north was a stockade containing log cabins. In 1857, when the population had grown to about 100 persons, a second fort was built about two miles south to better protect those farming there. It was a theory of the leader, Brigham Young, that it was cheaper to feed the Indians than to fight them and the colony of Mormons at Fort Lemhi pursued that program for three years but they were driven out in 1858 by Indian hostility. The Mormons abandoned the mission and forts and returned to Utah territory. They had named Fort Limhi in honor of King Limhi, a personage in the *Book of Mormon*.

King Limhi (–) —According to the *Book of Mormon*, King Limhi was king of the Nephites, a son of King Noah and a grandson of Zeniff. However, Limhi's reign was little more than nominal for his people were under bondage to the Lamanites. The Nephites were obliged to pay the Lamanites one half of all they owned and one half of the produce from their toil. Under the guidance of King Limhi together with Ammon and Gideon, the Nephites escaped from the cruel Lamanites and reached the land of Zarahemla in safety.

The Mormons regarded the American Indians as descendants of the Lamanites and the Mormon mission at Fort Lemhi was established to lead these Lamanites back to righteous Nephite traditions.

550 *Lewis County*

Meriwether Lewis (1774–1809) —A native of Virginia and a neighbor and friend of Thomas Jefferson, Lewis served as an officer in the army and then, in 1801, President Jefferson selected him to be his aide. From 1804 to 1806 Meriwether Lewis and William Clark led the Lewis and Clark Expedition which President Jefferson sent to explore the Northwest to the Pacific Ocean and the members of that expedition were the first known White men to visit Idaho. Lewis served as governor of Louisiana territory from 1807 until his death in 1809. Lewis County was created in 1911. This was the second time that Idaho had a Lewis County named for Meriwether Lewis. In 1905 Kootenai County was abolished to form two new counties named Lewis County and Clark County in honor of the leaders of the Lewis and Clark Expedition. The creation of these counties was declared unconstitutional and Kootenai County was re-established.

551 *Lincoln County*

Abraham Lincoln (1809–1865) —Lincoln was a native of Kentucky who moved to Illinois where he was a member of the state legislature. He represented Illinois in the U.S. House of Representatives and later was elected president of the United States. Lincoln's presidency coincided almost exactly with the Civil War. He guided the United States ably through that uniquely turbulent period. As president, he issued the Emancipation Proclamation which declared the freedom of slaves in all states in rebellion. Lincoln was assassinated in 1865, a few days after the Union victory in the Civil War. It was under the administration of Abraham Lincoln that Idaho territory was created and Idaho came close to naming a county for him several times. In 1879 the name Lincoln was proposed for the county which was instead named for George Washington. The legislators decided that no other president should be so honored before the first. The name was again considered in 1881 but lost to Custer, whose Last Stand at Little Big Horn was fresh in the minds of Idaho settlers. In 1891 a Lincoln County was finally created but that law was declared unconstitutional. The present Lincoln County was not created until 1895.

552 *Madison County*

James Madison (1751–1836)— Madison was born in Virginia, served in the Virginia legislature and in the Continental Congress. He was a member of the convention which framed the U.S. Constitution and he collaborated with Hamilton and Jay in writing a series of papers under the title *The Federalist* which explained the new constitution and advocated its adoption. Madison represented Virginia in the U.S. House of Representatives, served for eight years as secretary of state and for eight years as president of the United States.

553 *Minidoka County*

Uncertain— Minidoka County was established in 1913 and named either for its first permanent settlement, the town of Minidoka, or for the Minidoka Reclamation Project. Construction of the reclamation project began in 1904 and was essentially completed by 1909. The heart of the project was Minidoka Dam. Gravity irrigation served some farms while the project's hydroelectric powered generators ran pumps that supplied water to others. The town of Minidoka was first established as a siding by the Union Pacific Railroad in the early 1880's. The Union Pacific made it a practice to name sidings and stations with Indian words to avoid duplication. Almost all sources say that *minidoka* is a Shoshoni word meaning "broad expanse" which is appropriate because the broadest expanse of the Snake River plain lies here. "Well spring" is also mentioned as a possible translation.

554 *Nez Perce County*

Nez Perce Indians— This county was created by the legislature of Washington territory in 1861 and named for the Nez Perce Indians who lived in the Snake River area of northeastern Oregon, eastern Washington and northern Idaho including Nez Perce County, Idaho. The Nez Perce possessed a high level of culture, were courageous, trustworthy, hospitable and generally friendly to Whites. Their primary sources of food were salmon, camas roots and berries. They also hunted buffalo on annual visits to the Great Plains. They used teepees for their homes. In the Nez Perce War of 1877, these Indians fought the Whites, lost and were confined to reservations. At the time of first contact with Whites in the early 1800's there were some 6,000 Nez Perce Indians. By 1960 their population had declined to about

2,000. *Nez Perce* is French meaning "pierced nose" and the name was given to these Indians by French-Canadian trappers. Authorities differ on the accuracy of this name for the Nez Perce Indians. Some sources state that these Indians made a practice of piercing their noses in order to wear decorative shells there. Others contend that these Indians did not practice nose piercing and that the French *nez presse* meaning "pressed, squeezed" or "flattened nose" was intended on account of the flattened appearance of their noses. Perhaps *nez presse* referred to the name of this tribe in Indian sign language which was a gesture involving the nose and referred to their compressed noses.

555 *Oneida County*

City Oneida, New York and/or Oneida Lake, New York— A number of early settlers of this area of southeastern Idaho had come from the Oneida, New York, area and when this Idaho county was created in 1864, it was named for their New York home. Oneida, New York, was founded in 1829 and is about five miles southeast of Oneida Lake in central New York. The lake has an area of some 80 square miles and is a popular summer resort for swimming, fishing and boating. Both the city of Oneida, New York, and Oneida Lake carry the name of the Oneida Indians.

Oneida Indians— The Oneida were the least populous tribe of the Iroquois confederacy in central New York. At the time of their first contact with Whites in the 1600's their population was less than 1,000. They possessed Oneida Lake and the territory surrounding the lake. About the year 1720 the Oneida Indians were joined by a group of Tuscarora Indians who had migrated from North Carolina. Most Oneida Indians sided with the American colonists during the American Revolution. By the 1990's there were still 1,000 Onedia Indians living in New York state. Their name has been variously translated as "standing stone," "granite people" or "stone people" and it refers to a large stone at one of their early villages which was a monument and became their tribal emblem.

556 *Owyhee County*

Owyhee River— The Owyhee River, a tributary of the Snake River, is formed by the junction of forks in Owyhee County, Idaho, and then flows in a westerly direction into Oregon. It is about 300 miles long and most of it is in Oregon. The river's name derives from an early name

for the distant Hawaiian islands. In 1819 or 1820, two or three Hawaiians, who were in the service of the Hudson's Bay Company, perished here and the river and the area came to be known as Owyhee. The Hawaiians had been sent into the area to trap for beaver and to trade with Indians. According to some accounts, these Hawaiians were murdered by Indians while other versions merely indicate that they disappeared and it was presumed that Indians killed them.

557 *Payette County*

Payette River— This county in southwestern Idaho was created in 1917 and named for the Payette River which flows through it. The Payette, a 55 mile long tributary of the Snake River, was named for Francois Payette.

Francois Payette (–)— Payette was born near Montreal, Canada about 1793. As a sailor, fur trapper and explorer, he traveled widely visiting South America and Hawaii. Payette spent most of his working years in the Pacific Northwest. He came to southwestern Idaho in 1818 and about 1820 he brought the first cattle to Boise Valley. It was during this period, prior to 1822, that the Payette River was named for him. Later, in 1835, Hudson's Bay Company put him in charge of the first Fort Boise as postmaster. When business exceeded expectations, Payette built a second Fort Boise on the eastern bank of the Snake River. At Fort Boise, Payette became well known as a genial fat man to many emigrants traveling over the Oregon Trail. In 1844 he retired and returned to Montreal where he drew a substantial sum in accumulated wages.

558 *Power County*

Hydroelectric power at American Falls— The American Falls on the Snake River in Power County were an early scenic attraction. At the falls, the river narrowed to less than one thousand feet and dropped about 45 feet over a series of beautiful cascades. Beginning in 1901, three power plants were built along the American Falls. In 1913 Power County was created and named for the hydroelectric power at the falls. In 1916 Idaho Power Company was established from the merger of several smaller companies and it acquired the power plants here. Then, in the 1920's, a huge dam was constructed slightly upstream from the power plants, thereby obliterating the American Falls.

559 *Shoshone County*

Shoshoni Indians—Shoshone County was created by the legislature of Washington territory before Idaho territory was established and was named for the Shoshoni Indians, the most northerly of the Shoshonean tribes. They once ranged the plains on their ponies over vast portions of Colorado, Wyoming, Utah, Nevada and Idaho but were driven into the mountains and robbed of their ponies by the Blackfeet and other tribes who had obtained firearms. The stronghold of the Shoshoni was the Snake River area in Idaho. Staples of their diet included camas roots which they gathered on seasonal migrations and salmon. They were also adept at loosely organized group hunting. In the early 19th century the Shoshoni population was almost 20,000. By 1970 it had been cut in half to about 10,000, most on reservations in territory they once held. Most authorities indicate that the name Shoshoni derived from two Indian words, *shawnt* meaning "abundance," and *shaw-nip* meaning "grass," because they originally camped where there was plenty of grass from which to weave their homes. However, other translations have been mentioned including "valley dwellers."

560 *Teton County*

Teton Mountains—Teton County, in eastern Idaho on the Wyoming border, was created in 1915 and named for the three Teton Mountains which lie just to the east in Wyoming and overlook the county. French-Canadian trappers found a resemblance between these peaks and female breasts and named them *Les Trois Tetons*, meaning "The Three Breasts." The Tetons, part of the Rocky Mountain range, rise almost perpendicularly more than a mile above the valleys below them. Viewed from their Idaho side, these three peaks have long been beacons to travelers giving definite means of orientation. The peaks are called Grand, South and Middle Teton. Grand Teton, with a height of 13,747 feet above sea level, is the tallest of the three and is considered by some to be the most beautiful mountain in all of the Rockies.

561 *Twin Falls County*

Twin Falls in the Snake River—This county was created in 1907 and named for the picturesque waterfalls here in the Snake River, near the northeast corner of the county. A huge rock formation divides the river into two channels and splits the falls into two parts. The Twin Falls are now partially blocked by a hydroelectric dam of Idaho Power Company and the falls are no longer twins but just one.

562 *Valley County*

Long Valley—Valley County was created in 1917 and named for Long Valley, which lies within its borders. Named for its length, Long Valley extends north some 50 miles starting near Cascade, which is the county seat of Valley County, and ending at Upper Payette Lake. The valley is traversed by the North Fork of the Payette River. Another name that is used for the valley is Payette Valley, whose name honors Francois Payette. (See Payette County, Idaho, above, for a biographical sketch of Francois Payette.)

563 *Washington County*

George Washington (1732–1799)—Washington was a native of Virginia. He served in Virginia's house of burgesses and became one of the colonies' leaders in opposition to British policies in America. He was a member of the first and second Continental Congresses and commander of all Continental armies in the Revolutionary War. Following victory in that war, Washington was elected to be the first president of the United States. The name Lincoln, in honor of Abraham Lincoln, had been proposed in 1879 when this county was created but that name was not adopted. The Idaho territorial legislators decided that no other president should be so honored before the first. However, Idaho did create a Lincoln County later, in 1895.

REFERENCES

Adams, Mildretta. *Historic Silver City: The Story of the Owyhees*. Homedale, Idaho, Owyhee Chronicle, 1960.

Akrigg, G. P. V., & Helen B. Akrigg. *1001 British Columbia Place Names*. Vancouver, Discovery Press, 1970.

Beal, M. D. *A History of Southeastern Idaho*. Caldwell, Idaho, Caxton Printers, Ltd., 1942.

Beal, Merrill D., & Merle W. Wells. *History of Idaho*. New York, Lewis Historical Publishing Co., Inc., 1959.

Boone, Lalia. *Idaho Place Names: A Geographical Dictionary*. Moscow, Idaho, University of Idaho Press, 1988.

Boone, Lalia P. "Names of Idaho Counties." *Names: Journal of the American Name Society*, Vol. 16, No. 1. Potsdam, New York: March, 1968.

Bridger, Clyde A. "The Counties of Idaho." *Pacific Northwest Quarterly*, Vol. 31, No. 2. Seattle, Washington: April, 1940.

Chittenden, Hiram M. & Alfred T. Richardson. *Life, Letters & Travels of Father Pierre-Jean De Smet, S. J.: 1801–1873*. New York, Francis P. Harper, 1904.

Conley, Cort. *Idaho for the Curious*. Cambridge Idaho, Backeddy Books, 1982.

Defenbach, Byron. *Idaho: The Place & Its People*. Chicago, American Historical Society, Inc., 1933.

Donaldson, Thomas. *Idaho of Yesterday*. Caldwell, Idaho, Caxton Printers, Ltd., 1941.

Elsensohn, M. Alfreda. *Pioneer Days in Idaho County*. Caldwell, Idaho, Caxton Printers, Ltd., 1951.

The Encyclopedia Americana. New York, Americana Corporation, 1977.

Etulain, Richard W. & Bert W. Marley. *The Idaho Heritage*. Idaho State University Press, 1974.

French, Hiram T. *History of Idaho*. Chicago, Lewis Publishing Co., 1914.

Fryxell, Fritiof. *The Teton Peaks & Their Ascents*. Grand Teton National Park, Wyoming, Crandall Studios, 1932.

Gibbs, Grenville H. "Mormonism in Idaho Politics, 1880–1890." *The Idaho Heritage*. Idaho State University Press, 1974.

Groefsema, Olive. *Elmore County: Its Historical Gleanings*. Caldwell, Idaho, Caxton Printers, Ltd., 1949.

Hafen, LeRoy R. *The Mountain Men and the Fur Trade of the Far West*. Glendale, California, Arthur H. Clark Co., 1968.

Hailey, John. *The History of Idaho*. Boise, Syms-York Co., Inc., 1910.

Hawley, James H. *History of Idaho*. Chicago, S. J. Clarke Publishing Co., 1920.

History of the Development of Southeastern Idaho. Daughters of the Pioneers, 1930.

Hobson, George C. *Gems of Thought & History of Shoshone County*. Kellogg Evening News Press, 1940.

Hodge, Frederick W. *Handbook of American Indians North of Mexico*. Totowa, New Jersey, Rowman & Littlefield, 1975.

Holmes, Kenneth L. "Francois Payette." *The Mountain Men and the Fur Trade of the Far West*, Vol. 6. Glendale, California: 1968.

Hylander, Clarence J. *The World of Plant Life*. London, Collier-MacMillan, Ltd., 1956.

Idaho Members of Poets' & Writers' Guild. *The Idaho Story*. Iona, Idaho, Ipas Publishing Co., 1967.

Idaho Yesterday & Today: Souvenir

Handbook: 1834–1934. Pocatello, Idaho, Graves & Potter, Inc., 1934.

Jaeger, Edmund C. *The North American Deserts.* Stanford, California, Stanford University Press, 1957.

Jenson, Andrew. *Latter-Day Saint Biographical Encyclopedia.* Salt Lake City, Utah, Andrew Jenson History Co., 1901.

Josephy, Alvin M. *The Nez Perce Indians and the Opening of the Northwest.* New Haven, Yale University Press, 1965.

Koch, Elers. "Geographic Names of Western Montana, Northern Idaho." *Oregon Historical Quarterly*, Vol. 49, No. 1. Portland, Oregon: March, 1948.

Kramer, Fritz L. "Idaho Place Name Records." *Western Folklore*, Vol. 12, No. 4. Berkeley: October, 1953.

Kramer, Fritz L. "Idaho Town Names." M.A. Thesis, Main Library, University of California, Berkeley, California, 1953.

Kramer, Fritz L. "Idaho Town Names." *Twenty-Third Biennial Report of the Idaho State Historical Department: 1951–1952.*

Kramer, Fritz L. "More on Idaho." *Western Folklore*, Vol. 12, No. 3. Berkeley: July, 1953.

Leland, J. A. C. "Eastern Tribal Names in California." *California Folklore Quarterly*, Vol. 5, No. 4. Berkeley: October, 1946.

Liljeblad, Sven. "The Indians of Idaho." *The Idaho Heritage.* Idaho State University Press, 1974.

Limbaugh, Ronald H. *Rocky Mountain Carpetbaggers: Idaho's Territorial Governors: 1863–1890.* Moscow, University Press of Idaho, 1982.

Lovell, Edith H. *Captain Bonneville's County.* Idaho Falls, Idaho, Eastern Idaho Farmer, 1963.

McConnell, W. J. *Early History of Idaho.* Caldwell, Idaho, Caxton Printers, 1913.

McLeod, George A. *History of Alturas & Blaine Counties, Idaho.* Hailey, Idaho, Hailey Times, 1938.

McLoughlin, Denis. *Wild & Wooly: An Encyclopedia of the Old West.* Garden City, New York, Doubleday & Co., Inc., 1975.

Mumey, Nolie. *The Teton Mountains: Their History & Tradition.* Denver, Colorado, Artcraft Press, 1947.

"The Name Idaho." *Twenty-Sixth Biennial Report of the Secretary of State of Idaho: 1941–1942.*

The New Encyclopaedia Britannica. Chicago, Encyclopaedia Britannica, Inc., 1984.

Otness, Lillian W. *A Great Good Country: A Guide to Historic Moscow & Latah County, Idaho.* Moscow, Idaho, Latah County Historical Society, 1983.

Peterson, F. Ross. *Idaho: A Bicentennial History.* New York, W. W. Norton & Co., Inc., 1976.

Powers, Alfred. "Foreward: Bonneville & Irving." In: Irving, Washington. *Adventures of Captain Bonneville.* Portland, Oregon, Binfords & Mort, 1954.

Rawlins, Jennie B. *Exploring Idaho's Past.* Salt Lake City, Utah, Deseret Book Co., 1963.

Rees, John E. *Idaho: Chronology, Nomenclature Bibliography.* Chicago, W.B. Conkey Co., 1918.

Reynolds, George. *A Dictionary of the Book of Mormon.* Salt Lake City, Utah, J. H. Parry, 1891.

Ricketts, Virginia. Retired County Clerk, Jerome County, Idaho. Letter to the author dated May 4, 1990.

"Rivers of Idaho." *Twenty-Fourth Bien-*

nial Report of the Idaho State Historical Department: 1953–1954.

Shankle, George Earlie. *State Names, Flags, Seals, Songs, Birds, Flowers & Other Symbols.* New York, H. W. Wilson Co., 1941.

Spinden, Herbert J. "The Nez Perce Indians." *Memoirs of the American Anthropological Association*, Vol. 2, No. 9. Lancaster, Pennsylvania.

Stevensville Historical Society. *Montana Genesis.* Missoula, Montana, Mountain Press Publishing Co., 1971.

Stewart, George R. *Names on the Land.* New York, Random House, 1945.

Talbert, Ernest W. "Some Non-English Place Names in Idaho." *American Speech*, Vol. 13, No. 3. October, 1938.

Twin Falls News. June 21, 1907.

Vogel, Virgil J. *Indian Names in Michigan.* Ann Arbor, University of Michigan Press, 1986.

Walgamott, Charles S. *Six Decades Back.* Caldwell, Idaho, Caxton Printers, Ltd., 1936.

Wells, Merle W. "Origins of the Name 'Idaho' and How Idaho Became a Territory in 1863." *The Idaho Heritage*, Idaho State University Press, 1974.

Williams, Thomas H. *Miracle of the Desert.* Kaysville, Utah, Inland Printing Co., 1957.

Wolk, Allan. *The Naming of America.* Nashville, Thomas Nelson, Inc., 1977.

Works Progress Administration. *The Idaho Encyclopedia.* Caldwell, Idaho, Caxton Printers, Ltd., 1938.

Works Progress Administration. *Idaho: A Guide in Word & Picture.* New York, Oxford University Press, 1937.

Illinois

(102 counties)

564 *Adams County*

Uncertain— Most sources state that this county was named for the sixth president of the United States, John Quincy Adams, but a case is also made for his father, the second president of the United States, John Adams.

John Adams (1735–1826)— Adams, a native of Massachusetts, was a delegate to the first Continental Congress and a signer of the Declaration of Independence. He participated in Paris with Benjamin Franklin and John Jay in negotiating peace with England and, after the war, he was our country's first minister to England. Adams became the first vice-president of the United States under George Washington and when Washington retired, Adams was elected to be our nation's second president.

John Q. Adams (1767–1848)— John Quincy Adams was the son of the second president of the United States, John Adams, and like his father, he was a native of Massachusetts. John Quincy Adams served in the U.S. Senate and as minister to several European countries. He was a very able secretary of state under President James Monroe, for whom he helped formulate the Monroe Doctrine. He became our sixth president in 1825, defeating Andrew Jackson and two other candidates but when he ran for reelection in 1828, Jackson defeated him. Adams then entered the U.S. House of Representatives where he represented Massachusetts and opposed states' rights and slavery for 17 years until his death in 1848.

According to William D. Barge, writing in the May, 1909, issue of *The Magazine of History,* "... we have the testimony of those participating in the organization of Adams that it was named for President John Quincy Adams." *The History of Adams County, Illinois,* published in 1879 by Murray, Williamson and Phelps supports Mr. Barge and explains that the county was named for John Quincy Adams because voters there had given John Quincy Adams their majority in the recent presidential election. But William R. Sandham makes a plausible case for the older Adams, John Adams, in the April–July, 1932, issue of the *Journal of the Illinois State Historical Society.* Mr. Sandham tells us that a large majority of the Illinois general assembly, which created and named Adams County, "were intensely pro Andrew Jackson and equally intensely anti John Quincy Adams and would not, on any consideration, vote to name a county after John Quincy Adams."

The county seat of Adams County, Illinois was and is Quincy, seemingly strong evidence that the county was named for John Quincy Adams. Mr. Sandham again at least raises doubt when he explains that the county seat's name was chosen because Quincy, Massachusetts was the birthplace and historic home of John Adams.

565 *Alexander County*

William M. Alexander (–)—Alexander County was created on March 4, 1819, and named for Dr. William M. Alexander, a physician, who was one of the early settlers of this section of southernmost Illinois. While practicing his profession as physician, he also acted as agent of the proprietors of the town of America here. America became the first county seat of Alexander County. Not long after Alexander County was created, Dr. Alexander entered the general assembly of the Illinois legislature where he served from 1820 to 1824. He first represented Pope County in the second legislature of the newly created state of Illinois. He then represented Alexander County and became speaker of the house during Illinois' third state legislature. After serving in the Illinois legislature, Alexander moved to Kaskaskia, Illinois. He finally moved south where he died. In the *History of Alexander, Union & Pulaski Counties, Illinois,* edited by William Perrin and published in 1883, it is suggested that the Illinois legislature gave Dr. Alexander the authority to select the name of the new county and that he chose to name it for himself.

566 *Bond County*

Shadrach Bond (1773–1832)—A native of Maryland, Bond moved to Illinois in 1794 where he engaged in farming and held a variety of military and civilian positions. From 1812 to 1814 he was a delegate from Illinois territory to the U.S. Congress and in 1818 when Illinois was admitted to the Union as a state, Bond became the state's first governor. He served as governor from 1818 to 1822. Bond County was created on January 4, 1817, before Shadrach Bond became governor.

567 *Boone County*

Daniel Boone (1734–1820)—A native of Pennsylvania, Boone penetrated Kentucky when it was wilderness country and settled there with his family in 1775. He gained fame on America's rugged western frontier as explorer, Indian fighter and surveyor.

568 *Brown County*

Jacob J. Brown (1775–1828)—A native of Pennsylvania with little military experience, Brown found himself in command of a section of the frontier at the start of the War of 1812. His successful defense of the important American base, Sackett's Harbor on Lake Ontario resulted in his appointment in July, 1813, as brigadier-general in the army and six months later he was made major-general. Brown later served with distinction in other important battles of the War of 1812. After the war, in 1821, he was assigned the command of the United States army which he held until his death. Brown County, in the western portion of central Illinois, was created in 1839. Earlier, in the 1828-1829 session, the Illinois legislature had considered creating a Brown County in northeastern Illinois, near Chicago, but that effort failed.

569 *Bureau County*

Bureau Creek—Bureau County was created in 1837 and named for Bureau Creek. The creek had been named for Pierre de Beuro, who established the first post in this area for trading with the Indians about 1818. His trading post was located near Bureau Creek's mouth on the Illinois River. Some accounts say that Beuro was French and one indicates that he was a "half-breed." The spelling of his last name is in doubt. The choices are Beuro, Buero and Bureo.

570 *Calhoun County*

John C. Calhoun (1782–1850)—Calhoun represented South Carolina in both houses of the U.S. Congress. He served as secretary of war, secretary of state and as vice-president. He was a forceful advocate of slavery, states' rights and limited powers for the federal government. He resigned the vice-presidency to enter the U.S. Senate where he could better represent the views of South Carolina and the South. This county was created on January 10, 1825, when Calhoun was vice-president-elect of the United States.

571 *Carroll County*

Charles Carroll (1737–1832)—Carroll was a native of Maryland and he represented that state in the Continental Congress. He was one of the signers of the Declaration of Independence and he later represented Maryland as a U.S. senator in the first congress of the United States. Carroll lived to be the last surviving signer of the Declaration of Independence and several states recognized that distinction by naming counties for him. This county was created in 1839. The name Carroll had been proposed for an Illinois county, much earlier, in 1821, but it was named Greene, instead.

572 *Cass County*

Lewis Cass (1782–1866)—A native of New Hampshire, Cass served in the army in the War of 1812 and rose to the rank of brigadier-general. Following that war Cass held a variety of important political positions and was the candidate of the Democratic party in 1848 for president of the United States. He lost to Zachary Taylor. Cass served as governor of Michigan territory, secretary of war under Andrew Jackson, minister to France, U.S. senator from Michigan and secretary of state under James Buchanan. Cass County, Illinois was created in 1837 while Cass was minister to France. Two other names had been considered by the legislature for this new county but they were rejected. Richard B. Servant had proposed the name Marshall and Benjamin Bond had proposed the name Moredock, in honor of the late Colonel John Moredock of Monroe County.

573 *Champaign County*

Champaign County, Ohio— Champaign County, Illinois was surveyed by John W. Vance. He agreed to waive the $900.00 fee that had been agreed upon for his services if he were permitted to select the name of the new county and its county seat. This was agreed and when Vance was elected to the state legislature which met in December, 1832, he introduced a bill to create and name both Champaign County and its county seat, Urbana. The bill became law and Champaign County, Illinois, was created on February 20, 1833. Vance named them in honor of Champaign County, Ohio, and its county seat, named Urbana. Vance's sentimental attachments to the Ohio county and town were deep for he had courted his first wife, Margaret Rutherford, there and when she died he buried her on a hillside near Urbana, Ohio, before moving west.

Champaign County, Ohio— Champaign County, Ohio, was created in 1805. Its name derived from the French word, *champagne*, for "open, level country." The name was chosen as descriptive of the county's surface, about half of which is level or only slightly undulating.

By coincidence, the name chosen to describe the Ohio county's surface is also descriptive of Illinois' Champaign County which consists largely of flat land.

574 *Christian County*

Christian County, Kentucky— This county was originally created as Dane County, Illinois on February 15, 1839. The name had been suggested by William S. Frink, a prominent politician at that time who took an active part in forming the county, and it honored Nathan Dane (1752–1835) of Massachusetts, who was the author of the article in the Ordinance of 1787 which excluded slavery from the Northwest territory. However, Nathan Dane was politically distasteful to the inhabitants of the county and, led by Daniel C. Goode, an old settler and a Jackson Democrat, they circulated petitions to have the county's name changed. A mass meeting of the citizens was also held on the open prairie where Thomas P. Bond made a motion, which was approved, to change the county's name from Dane to Christian. The name Christian was selected because many of the inhabitants of the county were from Christian County, Kentucky. The Illinois legislature complied with this local sentiment and on February 1, 1840, the county's name was officially changed. Christian County, Kentucky had been named for William Christian.

William Christian (–1786)—A native of Virginia and a brother-in-law of Patrick Henry, Christian served as an army officer in the French and Indian Wars prior to the American Revolution. By 1774 he was a colonel of militia and the following year he was a member of Virginia's general state convention. During the Revolution, Christian served first as colonel in the Virginia line of the regular army and later in command of the militia in his area of Virginia. After the war Christian served for several years in the Virginia legislature and in 1785 he moved to Kentucky. The following year he was killed by Indians.

575 *Clark County*

George R. Clark (1752–1818)— A native of Virginia, George Rogers Clark was a frontiersman and military hero. During the American Revolution he secured a commission as lieutenant-colonel to attack the British, Indians and Loyalists in Indiana and Illinois. He successfully captured Vincennes, Cahokia and Kaskaskia and, after the British retook Kaskaskia, Clark won it a second time. These military victories together with skillful negotiating by Benjamin Franklin enabled the United States to acquire the Northwest territory during the peace negotiations with the British at the end of the Revolution.

576 *Clay County*

Henry Clay (1777–1852)— Clay represented Kentucky in both branches of the U.S. Congress. For many years he was one of the more prominent figures in American politics but his several bids for the presidency were unsuccessful. He was influential in effecting important compromises between northern and southern interests during the years that secession and civil war were imminent. This county was created in December, 1824, while Clay was a candidate for president.

577 *Clinton County*

De Witt Clinton (1769–1828)— This New York state native held many important political offices of that state. Clinton served in both houses of the state legislature and as mayor of New York City. He represented New York in the U.S. Senate and in 1812 he was the Federalist candidate for president, running against President James Madison. In 1817 Clinton was elected as New York's governor. As governor, he was the principal promoter of the Erie Canal which was instrumental in linking the vast agricultural lands in our country's West with eastern markets. The canal spurred our nation's growth. Clinton County, Illinois was created in late December, 1824, shortly before the Erie Canal formally opened in October, 1825. In 1839 the state of Illinois created and named a second county in De Witt Clinton's honor named De Witt County.

578 *Coles County*

Edward Coles (1786–1868)— Coles was a native of Virginia and a wealthy slave owner. In 1809 he became the private secretary of James Madison, who was then president, and he served in that capacity until 1815. Coles moved to Illinois in 1818 and brought his slaves with him. Upon reaching Illinois, he set all of them free and gave 160 acres of land to each family head. Coles served as register of the land office in Illinois and then, in 1822, he became the second state governor of Illinois. He successfully led the fight against making Illinois a slave state. This county was created in 1830, four years after Coles left the governor's office.

579 *Cook County*

Daniel P. Cook (1794–1827)— Cook died of consumption in the same Kentucky county that he had been born in, just 32 years earlier, but he crowded a number of important positions into that short lifetime. In 1815 Cook moved to Edwardsville, Illinois territory, and soon after he became auditor of public accounts. He later served as judge of the western circuit and when Illinois became a state in 1818, he became the state's first attorney general. Cook entered the U.S. Congress in 1819 and he served four terms in that body as the only representative from the state of Illinois. Cook County, Illinois, was created in January, 1831, less than four years after Cook's death.

580 *Crawford County*

William H. Crawford (1772–1834)— Crawford served in the Georgia legislature and as a U.S. senator from Georgia. He was elected president *pro tempore* of the senate and he later served as minister to France, secretary of war and secretary of the treasury. Crawford was a serious candidate for the presidency in both 1816 and 1824. This county was created in December, 1816, shortly after Crawford's unsuccessful bid for the presidency.

581 *Cumberland County*

Cumberland Road— Prior to the advent of canals and railroads, the vast agricultural lands to the west of the Allegheny Mountains and east of the Mississippi River were rather isolated from commerce with the eastern United States. The Cumberland Road was an early national paved highway which linked the East with the West all the way from Cumberland, Maryland, to Vandalia, Illinois, just a few miles west of Cumberland County, Illinois. The Cumberland Road was built during the first half of the 19th century. The last important federal appropriation of funds for it came in 1838. Cumberland County, Illinois, was created in 1843.

582 *De Kalb County*

Johann Kalb, Baron de Kalb (1721–1780)— Kalb was born in the province of Alsace, which at that time belonged to France. He was a general in the French army and resigned that commission to come to America to assist the colonies in the Revolutionary War. He served as a general in the American Revolution and died in combat here. Dr. Henry Madden was the Illinois legislator who procured the passage of a bill to create De Kalb County in 1837. The legislature had rejected two other proposed names for this new county: Benton and Marshall.

583 *De Witt County*

De Witt Clinton (1769–1828)— This New York state native held many important political offices of that state. Clinton served in both houses of the state legislature and as mayor of New York City. He represented New York in the U.S. Senate and in 1812 he was the Federalist candidate for president, running against President James Madison. In 1817 Clinton was elected as New York's governor. As governor he was the principal promoter of the Erie Canal which was instrumental in linking the vast agricultural lands in our country's West with eastern markets. The canal spurred our nation's growth. Governor Clinton's given name, De Witt, was selected because it was the maiden name of his mother, Mary De Witt, who was of Dutch ancestry. De Witt County, Illinois was created in March, 1839. This was the second Illinois county to be named for De Witt Clinton. Clinton County, Illinois had been created in late December, 1824, shortly before the Erie Canal formally opened in October, 1825.

584 *Douglas County*

Stephen A. Douglas (1813–1861)— Barely five feet tall, the "Little Giant" is most remembered as a political opponent of Abraham Lincoln. Douglas was born in Vermont and moved to Illinois where he enjoyed rapid political success. He served on the state supreme court, in the state legislature and as secretary of state. Following two terms in the U.S. House of Representatives, Douglas was elected to the U.S. Senate. In that body Douglas took courageous positions on the slavery issue which first outraged abolitionist sentiment and later infuriated the South. In 1858 Douglas ran for reelection to the U.S. Senate against Abraham Lincoln. Following the famous Lincoln-Douglas debates, the Republicans won the popular election but the state legislature reelected Douglas to the senate. Lincoln and Douglas were rivals again in 1860 for the presidency. Following Lincoln's election and the start of the Civil War, Douglas gave the president his active support. The selection of county names seldom involves much controversy and even less passion but Douglas County, Illinois, was created in February, 1859, when the "Little Giant's" name was highly controversial throughout the country and in the Illinois legislature, as well. State Senator W. D. Watson, a Republican, initially proposed that the new county be named Richman, in honor of its first White inhabitant. The name Watson was also suggested. When Stephen Douglas' name was offered, a strong resistance developed which was not relaxed until it became obvious that the new county would be created as Douglas County, or not at all. A promise was even given that the county's name would be changed but that never happened.

585 *Du Page County*

Du Page River— More of a stream than a river, the Du Page is relatively short and it has never been navigable. Two branches of this stream rise near the northern boundary of Du Page County and travel south through the county until they meet just below the county's southern border with Will County, Illinois. The Du Page River then travels south and west until it meets the Des Plaines River near Channahon, Illinois. In early days the Du Page River was a treasure on the open prairie where great flocks of ducks and geese stopped on their annual migrations and wild game came to drink its waters. A French-Indian trader and trapper established a trading post on or near the banks of the Du Page River before 1800. During the 1820's, settlers here at Walker's Grove named the river for him and, in 1839 when the county was created, it was named for the river which flows through it in two branches.

586 *Edgar County*

John Edgar (–1832)— Edgar was born in Ireland and served as an officer in the British navy during the American Revolution. He married an American woman who persuaded him to desert the British and join the American army. Edgar served for awhile in the American Revolutionary army but then sought greater safety and moved west to Kaskaskia where he became a very successful businessman and miller of flour. He acquired ownership of some 50,000 acres of land in southern Illinois. Edgar served as judge of the common pleas court, represented Saint Clair County in the legislature of the Northwest territory and was appointed major-general of the militia. Edgar County was created in 1823.

587 *Edwards County*

Ninian Edwards (1775–1833)— A native of Maryland and a lawyer, Edwards moved to Kentucky in 1795 and was soon elected to the state legislature there. He also served as judge and became chief justice of Kentucky's court of appeals. In 1809 President James Madison appointed Edwards to be the first governor of Illinois territory and he served in that position until 1818 when Illinois became a state. He then represented Illinois in the U.S. Senate as one of the state's first two U.S. senators. Edwards later served as governor of the state of Illinois. This county was created in 1814 while Edwards was serving as territorial governor.

588 *Effingham County*

Uncertain— Effingham County was created in 1831. The bill to incorporate the county was the work of three men, General W. L. D. Ewing, William Linn and Joseph Duncan. It was General Ewing who suggested the name but it is not known whom he intended to honor. Two possibilities are mentioned, Edward Effingham and Thomas Howard, who was the third earl of Effingham.

Edward Effingham (–)— Edward Effingham was said to be an Englishman by birth and he was the United States surveyor who laid out Effingham County, Illinois. Most accounts refer to him as General Edward Effingham.

Thomas Howard, Earl of Effingham (1746–1791) — Thomas Howard, third earl of Effingham, also held the titles of ninth Baron Howard and deputy earl-marshal. He was a member of the house of lords and an officer in the English army at the time that the American colonies declared their independence from England. When his regiment was ordered to bear arms against the American colonists and assist in putting down the American Revolution, Effingham refused to do so and he resigned his commission in the English army rather than comply. He stated that although it had been his life's ambition to serve England as a military officer, "…a resignation which appeared to me the only method of avoiding the guilt of enslaving my country and imbruing my hands in the blood of her sons."

589 *Fayette County*

Marie Joseph Paul Yves Roch Gilbert du Motier, Marquis de Lafayette (1757–1834) — Lafayette was a French aristocrat who served briefly in the French army. He came to America in 1777 to assist the American Revolutionary army. He was granted an honorary commission as major-general by the Continental Congress and served with distinction in a number of battles in the Revolutionary War. Fayette County, Illinois, was created in 1821.

590 *Ford County*

Thomas Ford (1800–1850) — A native of Pennsylvania, Ford moved to Illinois as a youth with his family. He studied law and became state's attorney for the fifth judicial district. After serving in the army during the Black Hawk War, Ford served as judge on several courts including the Illinois supreme court. Elected as governor of Illinois in 1842, Ford served as governor from December, 1842, to December, 1846. This county was created in 1859.

591 *Franklin County*

Benjamin Franklin (1706–1790) — Franklin was a native of Massachusetts who moved to Pennsylvania in his teens. Poverty denied him a formal education but he became the leading printer and editor in North America. Franklin gained fame for his discoveries and inventions in the physical sciences and he distinguished himself as author, philosopher and diplomat. He was a signer of the Declaration of Independence and an important member of the convention which framed the U.S. Constitution. Franklin County was created in 1818 by the legislature of Illinois territory.

592 *Fulton County*

Robert Fulton (1765–1815) — A native of Pennsylvania, as a young man Fulton supported himself as an artist. He later gained fame for his inventions dealing with marine vessels. He invented a submarine which he successfully demonstrated in the year 1800. He invented mines to be used in naval warfare and was one of the inventors of the steamboat. The steamboat became a commercial success for Fulton and made him famous. This invention contributed greatly to the development of America. Fulton County, Illinois, was created in 1823.

593 *Gallatin County*

Abraham Alfonse Albert Gallatin (1761–1849) — Albert Gallatin was born in Europe to an aristocratic family of the city of Geneva. He moved to America during the American Revolution and settled in Pennsylvania. During the winter of 1789-1790 he was a member of the convention which revised the Pennsylvania constitution. Gallatin later represented Pennsylvania in the U.S. House of Representatives and when Thomas Jefferson became president in 1801, he selected Gallatin to be his secretary of the treasury. Gallatin served as secretary of the treasury under Presidents Jefferson and Madison until 1814 and was in that position when Gallatin County was created in 1812 by the Illinois territorial legislature. Albert Gallatin also represented the United States as a diplomat in Europe for some ten years.

594 *Greene County*

Nathanael Greene (1742–1786) — Greene was born in Rhode Island and served briefly in the Rhode Island legislature. He gained fame as one of the ablest American generals in the Revolutionary War. Greene County, Illinois was created in 1821. It had originally been proposed that this new county would be named Carroll but the name was changed to Greene in the state senate as a result of a motion made by Senator Leonard White.

595 *Grundy County*

Felix Grundy (1777–1840) — A native of Virginia, Grundy moved to Kentucky with his family in his youth. There he became a member of the state's constitutional convention and served in the state legislature. In 1806 Grundy was appointed to Kentucky's supreme court and in 1807 he was made its chief justice. Finding the salary inadequate, Grundy resigned and moved to Tennessee where he again became active in politics and gained national notice. He served in the Tennessee legislature and represented that state in both houses of the U.S. Congress. In 1838 President Martin Van Buren appointed Grundy to serve in his cabinet as attorney general. This county was created in February, 1841, just two months after Grundy's death. Its name was suggested to the legislature by William E. Armstrong of Ottawa, Illinois, who had successfully lobbied for creation of the new county.

596 *Hamilton County*

Alexander Hamilton (–1804) — A native of the West Indies, Hamilton moved to New York and served as an officer in America's Revolutionary army. One of his assignments during the war was aide-de-camp to General George Washington. After the war Hamilton was a member of the convention which framed the U.S. Constitution. He collaborated with Madison and Jay in writing a series of papers entitled *The Federalist* which explained the new constitution and advocated its adoption. A conservative and an advocate of a strong central government, he served as the United State's first secretary of the treasury. In 1804 he engaged in a duel with Aaron Burr and Hamilton died of wounds he suffered in that duel.

597 *Hancock County*

John Hancock (1737–1793) — A native of Massachusetts and a graduate of Harvard, Hancock served in the Massachusetts legislature and was president of the Massachusetts provincial congress. Elected to the second Continental Congress, he became its president. As president of the congress when the Declaration of Independence was signed, he was, on July 4, 1776, the first signer of that document. He signed it with such a flourish that the name John Hancock became a synonym for "signature." He later commanded the Massachusetts militia, served as governor of that state for many years and presided over the Massachusetts convention that ratified the U.S. Constitution.

598 *Hardin County*

Hardin County, Kentucky — This county was created in March, 1839, and named for the Kentucky county where many of the county's early settlers had originated. Kentucky's Hardin County had been created in December, 1792, and named for the recently murdered John Hardin.

John Hardin (1753–1792) — This military man was born in Virginia and served as an ensign in Lord Dunmore's 1774 war against the Indians. He later served as a lieutenant in the American Revolution and in 1786 he settled in Kentucky. Hardin then served in military actions against the Indians rising to the rank of colonel. He also briefly held the rank of brigadier-general in the Kentucky militia. In 1792 Hardin was murdered by Indians while he was engaged in peace negotiations with them.

599 *Henderson County*

Uncertain — Henderson County, Illinois was created in January, 1841. It is not certain whether the county was named for the Henderson River, a tributary of the Mississippi which flows through it, or for Henderson County, Kentucky, where many of this Illinois county's settlers originated. Both the river and the county in Kentucky had been named for Richard Henderson.

Richard Henderson (1735–1785) — A native of Virginia, Henderson moved as a youth with his family to North Carolina where he studied law and was appointed by Governor Tryon to be one of North Carolina's associate justices. Henderson later formed a company which purchased from the Indians an enormous tract of land comprising about half of what is now the state of Kentucky. This country was given the name Transylvania, laws were enacted to govern it and Henderson was made its president. Both Virginia and North Carolina declared Transylvania to be illegal but Henderson and his associates were given extensive tracts of land to compensate them for opening up this wilderness country. Richard Henderson was often known as "Colonel Henderson."

600 *Henry County*

Patrick Henry (1736–1799) — Henry was a native of Virginia and a lawyer. He served in the Virginia legislature, as governor of Virginia and as a delegate to the first and second Continental Congresses. Henry was one of America's key revolutionary leaders. He was a great orator and he is remembered for his call to arms against the British "Give me liberty or give me death." Henry opposed Virginia's ratification of the federal Constitution and his views played a role in the later adoption of the Bill of Rights.

601 *Iroquois County*

Iroquois River — Iroquois County, Illinois was created on February 26, 1833, and named for the river which flows through it. The Iroquois River is about 120 miles long. It rises in adjacent northwestern Indiana and flows west into Iroquois County, Illinois, and then north to enter the Kankakee River about five miles southeast of the city of Kankakee. The river was named for the Iroquois Indians because of an ancient battle which legend tells us was fought on its banks between Iroquois and Illinois Indians. We do not know when the river received its name but by 1721 at the time of Father Pierre Charlevoix's visit, it was known as the Iroquois River.

Iroquois Indians — The Iroquois were a loose confederacy of five tribes (later six) whose center of activities was upstate New York. They made occasional forays into Illinois and were partly responsible for the decimation of the Illinois Indians. The original five Iroquois tribes were the Cayuga, Mohawk, Oneida, Onondaga and Seneca. A sixth tribe, the Tuscarora joined the Iroquois confederacy later, in the early 1700's. The Iroquois subsisted on primitive agriculture and hunting. Their military power was great and they practiced both the taking of scalps and occasional cannibalism. There are still substantial numbers of Iroquois Indians living on reservations, mainly in New York, Wisconsin and Canada. The meaning of the name Iroquois is disputed. Possibilities which have been suggested include:
— Real adders (snakes)
— Tobacco people
— To smoke
— Bear
— The word *hiro* or *hero* with which these Indians closed their address meaning "I have said" combined with *koue*, which is a cry, sometimes of joy, sometimes of sadness.

602 *Jackson County*

Andrew Jackson (1767–1845) — Jackson was born on the border of North Carolina and South Carolina. He represented Tennessee in both branches of the U.S. Congress and gained fame and popularity for his military exploits in wars with the Indians and in the War of 1812. He was provisional military governor of Florida and from 1829 to 1837 General Jackson was president of the United States. His presidency reflected the frontier spirit of America. This county was created in January, 1816, just twelve months after Jackson de-

feated the British in the battle of New Orleans during the War of 1812.

603 *Jasper County*

William Jasper (–1779) — This Revolutionary War hero was born in South Carolina about 1750 but moved to Georgia where he grew up on a farm. He first became a hero in a dramatic event at the battle of Fort Moultrie when he courageously exposed himself to enemy fire to recover a flag which had been shot down. For this heroism Sergeant Jasper was awarded a sword and offered a promotion to lieutenant but he declined the promotion. Later employed as a scout, Jasper made several trips behind enemy lines in Georgia while operating from the swamps there. In a dramatic exploit near Savannah, Georgia, he and his close friend, John Newton, rescued several Americans who were prisoners and took their guards as prisoners of war. Jasper was shot and killed during the siege of Savannah while recovering the flag which had been shot down. Geographic names in several of our states link the names of the two heroic sergeants, Jasper and Newton. In some, as in Illinois, a county is named for one and its county seat is named for the other. In others, two counties are named for them.

604 *Jefferson County*

Thomas Jefferson (1743–1826) — Jefferson was a native of Virginia and a member of the Virginia legislature. He served Virginia as governor and was a delegate to the second Continental Congress. Jefferson was the author of the Declaration of Independence and one of its signers. He was minister to France, secretary of state, vice-president and president of the United States. As president, he accomplished the Louisiana Purchase and he arranged the Lewis and Clark Expedition to the Pacific Northwest. Jefferson was a true intellectual, thoroughly knowledgeable in the arts and sciences. His political theories were pivotal in the formation of our infant republic. This county was created in 1819, ten years after Jefferson retired from his presidency.

605 *Jersey County*

Town of Jerseyville, Illinois — In 1827 the town of Hickory Grove, Illinois, was founded but in 1834, when a post office was established there, the town's name was changed to Jerseyville since many of its settlers had come from the state of New Jersey. Later, in 1839 when Jersey County was created, it was named for the town of Jerseyville, which became its county seat. New Jersey was so named in 1664 in the grant from the Duke of York to its proprietors, one of whom was Sir George Carteret. Its name honored the island of Jersey where Carteret was born. The island of Jersey is one of the Channel Islands in the English Channel. Its name derived from *jer*, a contraction of "Caesar" and *ey*, meaning an "island" and thus it meant "Caesar's Island." When the bill to create this new county was being considered in the lower house of the Illinois legislature, three possible names were proposed: Jersey, Benton and Allen. The name Jersey prevailed.

606 *Jo Daviess County*

Joseph H. Daveiss (1774–1811)— Daveiss was born in Virginia but moved with his parents to the wilderness of Kentucky when he was still a young boy. There he studied law and became a successful attorney. In 1807 Daveiss, as attorney for the United States, prosecuted Aaron Burr for treason. Burr was acquitted. In the fall of 1811 Daveiss joined General William Henry Harrison's army to fight the Indians. Colonel Daveiss died in the battle of Tippecanoe in Indiana territory in November, 1811, leading a charge of his men against the Indians. Daviess County, Illinois was created in 1827. The name that was originally suggested for this county was Ludlow but the lower house of the Illinois legislature decided to honor Colonel Daveiss, instead. In doing so they misspelled the colonel's last name. The Illinois house also added Jo to the proposed county's name because one of their members was named Daviess and they wanted to make it clear that it was the slain hero from Kentucky rather than the Illinois legislator that the county's name would honor. According to one account, the incorporation of Jo in the county's name was done in jest with the expectation that it would be removed in the senate. However, the Illinois senate passed the bill without amendment.

607 *Johnson County*

Richard M. Johnson (1780–1850)— Johnson County lies in southern Illinois, not far from the Kentucky border, and it was created in 1812 when Illinois was still a territory. The county was named for Richard M. Johnson who was then representing Kentucky in the U.S. House of Representatives and was a friend of Ninian Edwards, the current governor of Illinois territory. Johnson was a native of Kentucky who had served in the Kentucky legislature prior to his election to the U.S. Congress. He later became a hero as a colonel in the War of 1812, represented Kentucky in the U.S. Senate and was vice-president of the United States under President Martin Van Buren.

608 *Kane County*

Elias K. Kane (1794–1835)— In some accounts Kane's name is rendered as Elisha, possibly due to confusion with the arctic explorer, Elisha K. Kane (1820–1857) who had the same middle name, Kent. Kane County's namesake was born in New York City, graduated from Yale College and, in 1814, moved to Illinois territory. Here he served as a judge and was a delegate to the first constitutional convention of the state of Illinois in 1818. He later served as secretary of state of Illinois and in the lower house of the Illinois legislature. In 1825 he became a U.S. senator from Illinois and he died in that office while still a young man in December, 1835. Kane County was created and named in his honor in January, 1836, the month following Senator Kane's death.

609 *Kankakee County*

Kankakee River— The Kankakee River rises in northern Indiana near the city of South Bend and flows some 135 miles south and west through English Lakes and then west into Illinois. In Kankakee County, Illinois the river unites with the Iroquois River from the south. It then flows north and west until the Des Plaines River from the north joins it to form the Illinois River. The Kankakee was once a sluggish stream which flowed through flat and marshy lands in Indiana but civilization has claimed the marshlands and the Kankakee now moves swiftly. The name *Kankakee* is a corruption by Whites of an Indian name but the origin and meaning of it are uncertain and disputed. One suggestion is "low land" or "swampy country." Other possible translations which have been mentioned include "among the meadows," "raven," "wolf" or "wolf country" and "the river of the beautiful land."

610 *Kendall County*

Amos Kendall (1789–1869)— A native of Massachusetts and a graduate of Dartmouth College, Kendall moved to Kentucky where he became a journalist and a supporter of Andrew Jackson. This led to his membership in Jackson's influential group of advisors known as the "Kitchen Cabinet" and to his selection as postmaster general. Kendall later was a very successful business associate of Samuel F. B. Morse. He assisted Morse in developing his telegraph business. Kendall County, Illinois was created in 1841. Its proposed name in the original act was Orange but Ebenezer Peck of Will County moved to change the name to Kendall and the motion carried. Joseph Gillespie of Madison County had voted against naming the new county for this Jackson man. Gillespie then moved to change the county's name again to "Honest Amos Kendall County." That motion was placed on the table where it still lies.

611 *Knox County*

Henry Knox (1750–1806)— This Massachusetts native participated in many of the important military engagements of the American Revolution and rose to the rank of major-general. After the war, Knox commanded West Point and he conceived and organized the Society of Cincinnati, an elite group of former Revolutionary officers. In 1785 he was appointed secretary of war under the Articles of Confederation and he retained that position in the first United States cabinet under President George Washington.

612 *La Salle County*

Rene Robert Cavelier, Sieur de la Salle (1643–1687)— A native of Rouen, France, La Salle came to North America about 1667 and engaged in fur trading in Canada and in the Illinois country. In 1682, in company with Henri de Tonty and others, La Salle led an expedition which sailed down the Mississippi River and was the first to trace the Mississippi to its mouth at the Gulf of Mexico. La Salle named this vast area Louisiana and he claimed it for France. He also erected a number of trading posts and forts in North America and one of these forts, erected in 1682, was in La Salle County, Illinois. La Salle was the name of an estate near Rouen, France, which belonged to the Cavelier family.

613 *Lake County*

Uncertain— Lake County's entire eastern border ends at the shore of Lake Michigan and many sources state that the county was named for that lake. However, a number of other sources, some quite reliable, indicate that the county was named for the large number of small lakes within its borders. In his 1877 *History of Lake County*, E. M Haines tells us that the county's name derived both from its location on Lake Michigan and its great number of small lakes.

Lake Michigan — This lake is one of the five Great Lakes and, until Alaska was admitted to statehood, Lake Michigan's 22,400 square miles made it the largest fresh water lake that was completely inside the United States. The St. Lawrence Seaway provides Lake Michigan with access to world ports. *Michigan* is a corruption of an Indian name meaning "big, vast" or "monstrous lake."

614 *Lawrence County*

James Lawrence (1781–1813) — Lawrence was an officer in the United States navy who established a reputation for bravery in the war against Tripoli and in the War of 1812. He died in combat while commanding the *Chesapeake* against the British near Boston. He is said to have uttered the famous phrase "Don't give up the ship" while he lay mortally wounded in that battle. This county was created in 1821.

615 *Lee County*

Uncertain— Lee County, Illinois, was created in 1839. The origin of the county's name is uncertain and at least four possibilities have been mentioned: Henry Lee (1756–1818), Richard H. Lee (1732–1794), Robert E. Lee (1807–1870) and the village of Lee Centre. It is easy to rule out two of these suggestions. Robert E. Lee was an unknown officer in the United States army in 1839 when this county was created and Lee Centre, a village and township in Lee County, was not yet known by that name in 1839. The remaining two possibilities are:

Henry Lee (1756–1818)— Lee was born in Virginia and served with distinction as an officer during the American Revolution. He was known as "Light Horse Harry Lee." He represented Virginia in the Continental Congress, served three consecutive terms as governor of the state of Virginia and commanded troops ordered to suppress the "Whiskey Rebellion" in western Pennsylvania. Lee was appointed a major-general in 1798 and also served one term in the U.S. House of Representatives.

Richard H. Lee (1732–1794)— This native of Virginia was one of the key figures in the decision of the American colonies to revolt from England. On June 7, 1776, he introduced a resolution in the Continental Congress calling for independence of the colonies from England and he was one of Virginia's signers of the Declaration

of Independence. After the Revolution Lee again was a member of the Continental Congress and was president of that body for the 1784-1785 session. He later represented Virginia in the U.S. Senate.

In his 1918 history of early Lee County, William D. Barge states that a man named Dutcher claimed the credit of selecting the county's name and that "when he chose it, he had in mind General Henry Lee (Light Horse Harry) of the Revolutionary Army." Other sources consulted are about equally divided between Henry Lee (1756–1818) and Richard H. Lee (1732–1794).

616 *Livingston County*

Edward Livingston (1764–1836)— Livingston was born in New York, represented that state in the U.S. House of Representatives and served as mayor of New York City. Because of personal problems, Livingston moved to Louisiana to start a new life in 1804. There he served as Andrew Jackson's aide in the battle of New Orleans and was elected to the Louisiana legislature. He later represented Louisiana in both houses of the U.S. Congress and was President Andrew Jackson's secretary of state. Livingston drafted President Jackson's Proclamation to the People of South Carolina which asserted the supremacy of the federal government in response to South Carolina's 1832 Ordinance of Nullification. His last post was minister to France. Edward Livingston died in May, 1836 and this county was created and named in his honor less than one year later, in February, 1837. The county's name was suggested by Jesse W. Fell and it was chosen due to Livingston's popularity as author of the Proclamation to the People of South Carolina.

617 *Logan County*

John Logan (1788–1852)— Logan came to this country from Ireland early in the 19th century and settled in Missouri. He subsequently moved to Illinois where he was a pioneer physician. Logan also served very briefly as a corporal in the Black Hawk War. Dr. Logan served in the general assembly of the state of Illinois where he met Abraham Lincoln. Lincoln was chairman of the legislature's committee on counties in February, 1839. Despite the fact that Dr. Logan was a Democrat and Lincoln was then a Whig, Lincoln and Logan became friends and it was Abraham Lincoln who suggested that this county be named for the doctor. Logan was serving in the general assembly when this county was created and named in his

honor on February 15, 1839. Dr. Logan was the father of Major-General John A. Logan (1826–1886) of Civil War fame.

Most sources agree that Logan County, Illinois was named for Dr. John Logan but a few mention other possibilities. Stephen T. Logan (1800–1880) is one. He was also a member of the Illinois general assembly and was a partner of Abraham Lincoln. Other possibilities mentioned are Indian Chief Logan, Logan County, Kentucky and even General John A. Logan, who was only 13 years old when this county was created. However, Lawrence B. Stringer's *History of Logan County, Illinois* published in 1911 documents facts to demonstrate that this county was named for Dr. John Logan. Stringer mentioned that the *Sangamo Journal* of Springfield, Illinois carried an article in its February 16, 1839 issue, the day after Logan County was created, which said that "Logan County is named in honor of Dr. John Logan, the present representative from Jackson County in this state and an old resident of Illinois."

618 *McDonough County*

Thomas Macdonough (1783–1825)— A native of Delaware, Macdonough entered the U.S. navy in 1800 as a midshipman and served in the war with Tripoli. During the War of 1812 Macdonough commanded our fleet on Lake Champlain and defeated the British in the decisive battle of Plattsburg in September, 1814. That victory gave the United States undisputed control of Lake Champlain and forced General George Prevost's army to retreat to Canada. Macdonough died at sea in November, 1825, and this county was created just two months later, in January, 1826. Naming this county in honor of a hero of the War of 1812 was appropriate for much of the land here was part of a military tract that the U.S. Congress had set aside to provide 160 acres of land for soldiers and sailors who served in that war. Although he styled his name Macdonough, the county's name is rendered as McDonough. By coincidence McDonough was the version that Macdonough's parents used for the name.

619 *McHenry County*

William McHenry (–1835)— McHenry came to Illinois territory from Kentucky in 1809 and settled in White County. Soon after this he served as a soldier in the War of 1812. Much later, in 1832, McHenry was an army officer during the Black Hawk War and he participated in the battle of

Bad Axe. He was a member of the first general assembly of the new state of Illinois and subsequently served a number of terms in both houses of the Illinois legislature. McHenry died in 1835 while serving in the Illinois general assembly and this county was created and named in his honor by his fellow legislators in January of the following year.

620 *McLean County*

John McLean (1791–1830) — A native of North Carolina and later a resident of Kentucky, McLean came to Illinois territory in 1815 and practiced law in Gallatin County. When Illinois was admitted to the Union in December, 1818, McLean was elected to be the new state's first representative in the U.S. Congress. He served only a few months and then was defeated by Daniel P. Cook when he ran for reelection. McLean next served several terms in the Illinois House of Representatives and was once speaker of that body. He also represented Illinois in the U.S. Senate and was serving there when he died. About the time of McLean's death in October, 1830, there was agitation for the creation of a new Illinois county with its county seat at or near Blooming Grove. At that time the speaker of the Illinois house was William Lee D. Ewing. Mr. Ewing agreed that the new county would be created provided its name honored his friend, John McLean, and the new county was born effective Christmas Day, 1830, just two months after McLean's death.

621 *Macon County*

Nathaniel Macon (1758–1837) — Macon was a native of North Carolina and a soldier in the Revolutionary War. He served in the North Carolina senate and was elected to the Continental Congress but declined to serve. He represented North Carolina for 37 years in both branches of the U.S. Congress where he was speaker of the house and, later, president pro tempore of the senate. He believed strongly in economy of the public money and he was a defender of slavery. This county was created in 1829, the year following Macon's retirement from the U.S. Senate.

622 *Macoupin County*

Macoupin Creek — Macoupin County was created in 1829 and named for its principal stream, the Macoupin Creek. The Macoupin is a tributary of the Illinois River in western Illinois. It flows through Macoupin County and touches the north-ern edge of Jersey County. The Macoupin then continues its westward journey through Greene County where it unites with the Illinois River. Its name is of Indian origin and means "white potato" or "white yam." Pierre de Liette mentioned this root in his 1702 account and said that of all the roots gathered by the women of the Illinois tribes, "the one which they like the best is the macopine." These large roots were once found in abundance along Macoupin Creek. Pierre Charlevoix also left an account which mentioned "the river of the Macopines" and stated that these large roots were poisonous when eaten raw but when roasted for at least five hours on a slow fire, they became safe to eat.

623 *Madison County*

James Madison (1751–1836) — Madison was born in Virginia, served in the Virginia legislature and in the Continental Congress. He was a member of the convention which framed the U.S. Constitution and he collaborated with Hamilton and Jay in writing a series of papers under the title *The Federalist* which explained the new constitution and advocated its adoption. Madison represented Virginia in the U.S. House of Representatives, served for eight years as secretary of state and for eight years as president of the United States. Madison County was created in 1812, when Illinois was still a territory and Madison was serving his first term as president.

624 *Marion County*

Francis Marion (–1795) — Marion is believed to have been born in South Carolina. He served in the army in battles against the Cherokee Indians and was elected to the provisional congress of 1775. He served, with distinction, as an officer in the Revolutionary War and rose to the rank of general in that war. Marion was also a member of the South Carolina senate. This county was created in 1823.

625 *Marshall County*

John Marshall (1755–1835) — Marshall, a native of Virginia, served as an officer in the Revolutionary War, in the Virginia legislature and in the U.S. House of Representatives. He briefly served as secretary of state and then, for over 30 years, was chief justice of the U.S. Supreme Court. Marshall's interpretations of the constitution during America's political infancy left an unmatched impact on the laws and government of this country. Under Marshall, the supreme court shifted power in American government from the states to the central government and to the federal judiciary at the expense of the executive and legislative branches. This county was formed in 1839, less than four years after Marshall's death.

626 *Mason County*

Mason County, Kentucky — John Ritter suggested the name for this county which was created in 1841 and named for Mason County, Kentucky. A number of its early settlers had come from Kentucky. Mason County, Kentucky, was created in 1788 by the Virginia legislature and named for George Mason, who had participated in the 1787 convention which wrote the U.S. Constitution. (In 1792 Kentucky separated from Virginia and was admitted to the Union as a separate state.)

George Mason (–1792) — Mason, who was born in Virginia in 1725 or 1726, was prominent in the agitations which led to the American Revolution. He was a confidant of George Washington and Thomas Jefferson, a member of Virginia's house of burgesses and served on the committee of safety. Mason wrote a major portion of Virginia's constitution, served in Virginia's assembly and participated in our country's birth at the 1787 constitutional convention. Although Mason was a southerner, he opposed slavery.

627 *Massac County*

Fort Massac — Massac County, Illinois, was created in 1843 and named for the old French fort within its borders. The French first established a trading post here on the Ohio River in 1702. Later, to assist them in their battles against the British, the French converted the trading post to a fort on orders from Paris signed by the Marquis de Massiac. This was about 1758. Some seven years later the British took possession of the fort but they didn't maintain it. After the American Revolution, in 1794, Fort Massac was rebuilt on orders from President George Washington. The fort was abandoned after the War of 1812 and it was allowed to disintegrate until 1908 when Fort Massac was made a state park. The origin of the fort's name is uncertain and disputed. Some sources indicate that it was named for a young subaltern and engineer named Marsiac or Massaiac who, they say, supervised the fort's construction. The second possibility mentioned is that the fort was named for its first commander, named Marsiac, Massiac or Massac. The most frequently mentioned theory is that the fort's name was chosen because the Marquis de Massiac signed the orders to convert it from a trading post to a fort. The marquis was minister of marine and colonies back in Paris, France.

Claude Louis, Marquis de Massiac (1686–1770)— Massiac was an officer in the French naval service and he rose to the rank of lieutenant-general. He was a protege of the mistress of King Louis XV of France, Antoinette Poisson, Marquise de Pompadour, and on June 1, 1758, Massiac was appointed minister of marine and colonies. However, he soon declined in favor and was destitute by the time of his death in Paris on August 15, 1770. Massiac was the name of a small town in the department of Cantal in south central France from which the marquis' family had come.

A fourth possibility for the origin of Fort Massac's name which is mentioned by several sources is that the name is a corruption of the French word *massacre* which came from an alleged slaughter here of some French soldiers by Indians The legendary account of this battle is complete down to bearskin disguises worn by the Indians to dupe the French soldiers but there is no certainty that this battle and massacre actually occurred. The word *massacre* has the same meaning in French that it has in English.

When the bill to create this new county was being considered in the lower house of the Illinois legislature, six possible names were suggested: Wilcox, Massac, Benton, Harrison, Ohio and Van Buren. The name Massac, which had been proposed by Andrew J. Kuykendall of Johnson County, was selected.

628 *Menard County*

Pierre Menard (1766–1844)— A native of Canada, Menard moved to Indiana about 1787. There he was a fur trader and served in the militia in which he achieved the rank of lieutenant-colonel. Menard then moved west to Kaskaskia, Illinois, and was a member of the territorial council of the legislature of Indiana territory. (At that time Illinois was part of Indiana territory.) After the creation of Illinois territory, Menard was elected to its first legislative council and he was the first president of that body. He was also, for several years, a government agent assigned to negotiate with the Indians. In December, 1818 Illinois joined the Union as a state and Menard became its first lieutenant-governor. He was so popular that the state's first constitutional convention changed the constitution's eligibility requirements concern-

ing citizenship and residency for the office of lieutenant-governor so that Menard would be eligible for the office. At that time Menard had been naturalized for only one or two years. This county was created in 1839, some 17 years after Menard retired from political office and while he was still alive.

629 *Mercer County*

Hugh Mercer (–1777)— Mercer was born about 1725 in Scotland and educated as a physician. He immigrated to America about 1747 and served in the army here as an officer during the French and Indian War. At the outbreak of the American Revolution, Mercer entered the Continental army and attained the rank of brigadier-general. He served with distinction under General George Washington in the surprise attack on the British at Trenton, New Jersey, in late December, 1776. One week later, at the battle of Princeton, New Jersey, Mercer was severely wounded and he died from those wounds on January 12, 1777.

630 *Monroe County*

James Monroe (1758–1831)— Monroe, a native of Virginia, served in the Revolutionary War. Prior to his election as president of the United States, Monroe served in a wide variety of government posts. He served Virginia in the state legislature and as governor. He was a member of the confederation congress and the U.S. Senate. He was minister to France and to Britain and he held two cabinet posts. As president, Monroe stressed limited government and strict construction of the constitution. He acquired Florida for the U.S. from Spain and he was the author of a policy declaration (later known as the Monroe Doctrine) which proscribed outside interference in North and South America. This county was created in January, 1816. At that time Illinois was a territory and Monroe was serving as secretary of state. He became president one year later.

631 *Montgomery County*

Richard Montgomery (1738–1775)— Montgomery was born in Ireland and served with the British in the French and Indian War. He settled in New York state where he was elected to the New York provisional congress. Montgomery served as a general in the American Revolutionary army and he was killed in combat in the Revolutionary War.

632 *Morgan County*

Daniel Morgan (1736–1802)— Morgan was a native of the Northeast who moved to Virginia in his youth. He served as a general in the Revolutionary War and was regarded as a hero for important victories scored by his troops. After the war he served one term in congress. Morgan County was created in 1823.

633 *Moultrie County*

William Moultrie (1730–1805)— A native of South Carolina, Moultrie served as an officer in South Carolina's provincial regiment during the Cherokee War. He later served with distinction in the Continental army during the American Revolution and rose to the rank of major-general. Moultrie served in the provincial congress of South Carolina and in both houses of the legislature of the state of South Carolina. He was also lieutenant-governor and governor of the state of South Carolina. The name that had originally been proposed for this Illinois county was Fleming. However, Senator William Williamson was responsible for the selection of the final name, Moultrie.

634 *Ogle County*

Joseph Ogle (1741–1821)— Ogle was born in Virginia and came to Illinois as an early pioneer in 1785. He first settled in what would later be Monroe County, Illinois, and then moved to Saint Clair County near the town of O'Fallon. Ogle served as an officer in the territorial militia in actions against the Indians and held the ranks of lieutenant and captain. Legend has it that Joseph Ogle was the earliest convert to Methodism in Illinois. It was Thomas Ford who suggested the name for this county when it was created in 1836.

635 *Peoria County*

Peoria Indians— This county was created in 1825 and named for the tribe of Indians who once inhabited this part of Illinois. They were the largest of the six tribes that made up the Illinois confederacy. At one time they lived near the mouth of the Wisconsin River and later moved south to the mouth of the Des Moines River. By 1688 they were located on the Upper Iowa River. Following annihilation of the Illinois Indians by northern tribes, the Peoria scattered. The main body, numbering no more than a few score, remained here on the Illinois River. Later they were consigned to Indian territory (now Oklahoma) and there are no longer any full blooded Peoria Indians alive although remnants of Illinois tribes are called by this name. The meaning of the name *Peoria* is a mystery. Most sources confidently translate it as a French form of an Indian word, *piwarea*, meaning "he comes carrying a pack on his back" or the shortened versions "carriers" and "packers." However, Virgil J. Vogel, who is an authority on Indian names, states in his *Indian Place Names in Illinois* that these translations are implausible.

636 *Perry County*

Oliver H. Perry (1785–1819) — Perry was a native of Rhode Island and an officer in the U.S. navy. During the War of 1812 his squadron defeated the British in a key battle on Lake Erie of which Perry said 'We have met the enemy and they are ours." This county was created in 1827, some eight years after Commodore Perry's death.

637 *Piatt County*

Uncertain — The origin of this county's name cannot be given with certainty. It was created in January, 1841, and named for either the Piatt family, Benjamin Piatt or James A. Piatt. Emma C. Piatt's 1883 *History of Piatt County* states with no ambiguity that the county was named for James A. Piatt and she presents a rather convincing case to support that view.

The Piatt family — The Piatt family were very early residents of the area that became Piatt County. Among its members were James A. Piatt (1789–1838) and his two wives, Jemima Ford Piatt and Mahala Oxley Piatt, and their children. The children, in order of their birth, were William H., John, James A., Richard F., Anna Belle, Noah N., Jacob and Mary J. Jemima was the mother of the first seven children. She died in March, 1836, and James A. Piatt remarried in December, 1837, to Mahala. Mary J. Piatt was the only child of this second marriage.

Benjamin Piatt (–) — Benjamin Piatt was an attorney general of Illinois territory. He held that office from 1810 to 1813.

James A. Piatt (1789–1838) — The Piatt family moved from New Jersey to Pennsylvania about the time of James A. Piatt's birth. He was born on April 21, 1789, probably in Pennsylvania. Although Piatt spent only about six months in school, he managed to acquire a fair education and he even taught one term of school in Pennsylvania. Before settling in Illinois, Piatt also lived in Oxford, Ohio, and in several Indiana communities including Brook-

ville and Indianapolis. He moved to what is now Monticello, Illinois, the county seat of Piatt County, in the spring of 1829 and for a number of years he was the leading citizen of the new settlement.

When creation of the new county was under consideration, George A. Patterson was appointed to lobby the legislature for its creation. Patterson called a meeting at the house of Abraham Marquiss to discuss what the new county's name should be. William Barnes proposed the name Piatt while Isaac Demorest suggested the name Webster. There was also talk of using the name Grundy for this county but this was opposed as "party political" and Grundy County was not placed on the Illinois map until about three weeks after Piatt County's birth.

638 *Pike County*

Zebulon M. Pike (1779–1813) — Pike was a native of New Jersey who served as an army officer on America's frontier following the Revolution. He led an exploratory army expedition to the Rocky Mountains which Pike's Peak in the Colorado Rockies commemorates. Pike served as a general in the War of 1812 and was killed in that war. Pike County, Illinois, was created in January, 1821.

639 *Pope County*

Nathaniel Pope (1784–1850) — Pope was born in Kentucky and graduated from Transylvania University there. He lived briefly in both Louisiana and Missouri before settling in Kaskaskia, Illinois, in 1808. The following year he was appointed as the first secretary of the newly created Illinois territory. Pope later served as a delegate from Illinois territory to the U.S. Congress and was instrumental in securing statehood for Illinois in 1818. He then was appointed U.S. district judge and he held that office for more than 30 years until his death in 1850. Pope County was created and named in his honor in 1816.

640 *Pulaski County*

Casimir Pulaski (1748–1779) — Pulaski was born in Lithuania and served in the Polish army. He came to America to assist the colonies as an officer in the Revolutionary War and died in combat in that war during the siege of Savannah, Georgia. Pulaski County, Illinois, was created in 1843.

641 *Putnam County*

Israel Putnam (1718–1790) — Putnam was

born in Massachusetts and moved when he was about 21, to Connecticut. He served as an officer in the French and Indian Wars and later was a member of the Connecticut legislature. At the beginning of the Revolutionary War, news of the battle at Lexington, Massachusetts, reached Putnam while he was farming. In a dramatic gesture which became famous, Putnam left his plow and, without bothering to change clothes, hurried to Lexington. He was appointed major-general in the Continental army. Although he enjoyed great popularity, he lacked the ability for high command. In 1779 a paralytic stroke ended his military career.

642 *Randolph County*

Uncertain — Tradition has it that this general area in southern Illinois was informally named Randolph County by George Rogers Clark when he claimed it for Virginia and that he meant to honor Edmund Randolph of Virginia. This is uncertain but it is known that later, in 1795, when Illinois was part of Northwest territory, Governor Arthur St. Clair created Randolph County by proclamation. It is not clear whether St. Clair intended to honor Edmund Randolph or Beverly Randolph, who also was a Virginian.

Beverly Randolph (1754–1797) — Beverly Randolph was a native of Virginia and a graduate of the College of William and Mary there. During the American Revolution he commanded a regiment and he also served in Virginia's house of delegates. Beverly Randolph later served three consecutive one year terms as governor of Virginia from December 1, 1788, to December 1, 1791.

Edmund Randolph (1753–1813) — Edmund Randolph was also a native of Virginia and a student at the College of William and Mary. He served as attorney general of Virginia, was a Virginia delegate to the Continental Congress and to our country's 1787 constitutional convention in Philadelphia. Like Beverly Randolph, Edmund Randolph served as governor of Virginia. President George Washington appointed Edmund Randolph to be our nation's first attorney general and Randolph later served as secretary of state in Washington's cabinet.

643 *Richland County*

Richland County, Ohio — Richland County, Illinois was created in February, 1841. A man who was prominent in the agitation for creation of this new county was a Methodist minister, Reverend Joseph H. Reed, who had come to Illinois from Richland County, Ohio. In recognition of Reverend Reed's efforts and success in obtaining the new county, it was named for his former home county in Ohio. That county had been created some three decades earlier and named for the rich character of its soil. The soil covering much of Richland County, Ohio, rests on clays and takes its general character from them. The soil there also contains a relatively large quantity of lime, derived mainly from limestone fragments. This character of the soil combined with a decently high elevation and thorough surface drainage provides rich land in most of the county which is hospitable to a variety of agricultural products. The Ohio county's name is indeed appropriate.

644 *Rock Island County*

Rock Island— Rock Island County was created in 1831 and named for the large island at its western edge in the Mississippi River. The island is some three miles long with a width that varies from about one-half mile to about three-quarters of a mile. It lies opposite the city of Rock Island, Illinois. The island is about three miles above the confluence of the Rock River with the Mississippi. Its base is solid rock although it has a covering of fertile soil. The island has been used by the U.S. government for military purposes for more than a century and a half. During the Black Hawk War it was the sight of Fort Armstrong and it later was used to confine Confederate prisoners of war. More recently it has been the site of an armory and a large arsenal.

645 *Saint Clair County*

Arthur St. Clair (1736–1818)— St. Clair was a native of Scotland who moved to Pennsylvania in his twenties. He served, rather ineffectively, as a general in the army in both the Revolutionary War and in later actions against the Indians. He was a Pennsylvania delegate to the Continental Congress and he served as governor of the Northwest territory but President Jefferson was dissatisfied with his conduct and removed him from that post. On April 27, 1790, during his first visit to the Illinois country, Arthur St. Clair created this county by proclamation and named it for himself. At that time he was governor of Northwest territory and Illinois was part of that territory.

646 *Saline County*

Uncertain— Saline County, Illinois was created on February 25, 1847. *Saline* is an adjective which refers to salt and this county was named either directly or indirectly for its salt. Salt was one of the pioneers' critical necessities and six of our nation's county names honor it. Three possible sources for the name of Saline County, Illinois, are mentioned:

1. Saline Creek
2. Numerous salt springs in the area
3. Numerous salt springs or salt deposits in the area

647 *Sangamon County*

Sangamon River— The Sangamon River, which is some 225 miles long, is an important tributary of the Illinois River. The Sangamon's North Fork and South Fork rise to the north and east of Sangamon County and flow to the southwest. Near Springfield, the county seat of Sangamon County, the Sangamon's two forks join. The Sangamon flows through Sangamon County and then travels first north and then west until it meets the Illinois River near Browning, Illinois. It broadens as it approaches the Illinois River but the Sangamon's average width is perhaps 150 feet. An earlier form of the river's name was Sangamo. *Sangamo* or *Sangamon* derives from an Indian word or words but its meaning is uncertain. In the absence of certainty, speculations abound and we are favored with a long list of guesses for this name including:

— "Chief"
— "The country where there is plenty to eat"
— "Good earth"
— "Good hunting ground"
— "River of the Sauks"
— "Loon-lake river"
—Name of a Kickapoo Indian chief
— "Place of the outlet" or "river mouth"
— "He pours out"

Another theory is that the river's name is not Indian but came from an early surveyor in the area whose name was transcribed as St. Gamoin. Dr. Virgil J. Vogel, who is an authority on Indian names, admits in his *Indian Place Names in Illinois* that even he is uncertain about the meaning of this name. However, he supplies references that predate the St. Gamoin entry and thus refutes that theory. Vogel goes on to give reasons why most of the translations mentioned above are unlikely and he concludes that the meaning is probably "place of the outlet" or, literally, "river

mouth" and doubtless also is related to the Indian word for "he pours out."

648 *Schuyler County*

Philip J. Schuyler (1733–1804)— A native of New York, Schuyler served as an officer in the French and Indian War and was a delegate from New York to the Continental Congress. During the American Revolution, he held the rank of major-general in the Continental army. Schuyler later served New York in its senate and he became one of New York state's first two United States senators.

649 *Scott County*

Scott County, Kentucky— Many of this county's early settlers had come from Kentucky and when this new Illinois county was created in 1839, it was named for Scott County in their home state. Scott County, Kentucky had been created in 1792 and named for Charles Scott.

Charles Scott (1739–1813)— A native of Virginia, Scott served in the Continental army during the American Revolution and rose to the rank of brevet major-general. After the Revolution he moved to Kentucky and commanded Kentucky troops in campaigns against the Indians. Scott also served in the Virginia assembly while Kentucky was still part of Virginia. In 1808 Scott was elected governor of Kentucky and he served in that position until 1812.

650 *Shelby County*

Uncertain— This county was named either directly or indirectly for Isaac Shelby (1750–1826). Most sources state that Shelby County, Illinois, was named directly for him but some say that it was named for Shelby County, Kentucky. That Kentucky county had been created in 1792 and named for Isaac Shelby.

Isaac Shelby (1750-1826)— Shelby was a delegate to the Virginia legislature and, later, to the North Carolina legislature. He served as a soldier in the Revolutionary War and then moved to Kentucky County, Virginia, where he was active in the movement to separate Kentucky from Virginia. Shelby was inaugurated as Kentucky's first governor on the same day that Kentucky became a state. Isaac Shelby also fought in the War of 1812.

Shelby County, Illinois, was created in January 1827, shortly after Shelby's death.

651 *Stark County*

John Stark (1728–1822)— A native of

New Hampshire, Stark served as an officer during the French and Indian War. He later became a hero during the American Revolution winning fame at Breed's Hill, Fort Edward, Trenton, Princeton and Bennington and he rose to the rank of brevet major-general. Stark County was created in March, 1839. Two years earlier, a new county had been proposed for this general area with the name Coffee County, but it never became a reality because it failed to receive the required approval of voters in Knox County and Henry County, Illinois.

652 *Stephenson County*

Benjamin Stephenson (–1822)—A native of Kentucky, Stephenson moved to Illinois territory in 1809 and he was a colonel of Illinois militia in the War of 1812. He also served as adjutant general of Illinois territory and represented Illinois territory for one term in the U.S. Congress as a territorial delegate. Later, Stephenson was a member of the 1818 convention which framed the first constitution of the new state of Illinois.

653 *Tazewell County*

Littleton W. Tazewell (1774–1860)—A native of Virginia and a graduate of the College of William and Mary, Tazewell served in Virginia's house of delegates and he represented Virginia in both houses of the U.S. Congress. He was a member of Virginia's constitutional convention of 1829-1830 and served on the committee appointed to draft the new Virginia constitution. Tazewell served two years as governor of Virginia from March, 1834, to March, 1836. Tazewell County, Illinois, was created in 1827 while Littleton W. Tazewell was a U.S. senator from Virginia.

654 *Union County*

A religious union revival meeting held here—About 1816 or 1817 a revival meeting was held in what is now southeastern Union County, Illinois that featured two pioneer Christian preachers of rival denominations. That meeting was called the "union meeting." One of the men was a Baptist preacher named Jones and the other was a Dunker (German Baptist) preacher named George Wolf. Jones had been holding a series of meetings described as "remarkable" when he and Wolf met, shook hands and agreed to hold or continue the meeting with both men sharing the preaching. This was done and that meeting was called the "union meeting." When Union

County was created soon after, on January 2, 1818, it was named for that union revival meeting. Later, in 1850, the Union County commissioners adopted a seal that illustrated this historic event and showed the two preachers standing and shaking hands. One is shown in what was then conventional ministerial dress while the other is pictured in a shad-bellied coat and vest, broad brimmed hat and long hair.

655 *Vermilion County*

Vermilion River—There are two main rivers in Illinois named Vermilion, neither of which is very long. One is a tributary of the Illinois River, some 50 miles in length, which is formed by the junction of two forks in Livingston County, Illinois. Vermilion County, Illinois, was named for the other Vermilion River, the main stream of which is but 28 miles long. It is formed by the union of three forks, the North, Middle and South Forks, all of which rise in Illinois and come together near Danville, the county seat of Vermilion County, Illinois. It then flows to the southeast into Vermillion County, Indiana, where it enters the Wabash River. There is also a Little Vermilion River which enters the Wabash about seven or eight miles below our Vermilion River and ours is sometimes called the Big Vermilion to distinguish between the two. *Vermilion* is an English word derived from the French language which denotes a variety of shades of bright red color averaging a vivid reddish orange. The Vermilion River was so named on account of the fine red earth which colors its waters. Its earlier French name was Vermillion Jaune. Both Vermilion County, Illinois (one l), and Vermillion County, Indiana, (two l's) were named for the same river.

656 *Wabash County*

Wabash River—This county was created in 1824 and named for the major river which forms its eastern boundary. The Wabash rises in western Ohio and flows some 475 miles through mostly rich farm land before emptying into the Ohio River at the tri-state junction where Kentucky, Indiana and Illinois meet. In its journey it crosses Indiana and forms the southern portion of the border between Indiana and Illinois. The origin of the river's name is uncertain but it was rendered by the French as *Ouabachei* or *Ouabachi* which are believed to derive from an Indian name *Wahbahshikki* or perhaps *Wabaciki* or *Wapaciki* meaning "pure white" or "white stone river." The Indians bestowed this

name on the Wabash on account of the river's white limestone bed in its upper part. However, there is another theory: that the name derived from *Wabashkisibi* which meant "bog river." The Indians here also called the lower Ohio River their name for the Wabash, believing it to be just a part of their river.

657 *Warren County*

Joseph Warren (1741–1775)—This county was created in 1825 and named in honor of the American Revolutionary War hero, Joseph Warren. A native of Massachusetts and a graduate of Harvard College, Warren practiced medicine in the Boston area. He was a member of the committee of safety and president *pro tempore* of the Massachusetts provincial congress. In June, 1775 he was commissioned a major-general and he died in combat a few days later at the battle of Bunker Hill.

658 *Washington County*

George Washington (1732–1799)—Washington was a native of Virginia. He served in Virginia's house of burgesses and became one of the colonies' leaders in opposition to British policies in America. He was a member of the first and second Continental Congresses and commander of all Continental armies in the Revolutionary War. Following victory in that war, Washington was elected to be the first president of the United States.

659 *Wayne County*

Anthony Wayne (1745–1796)—A native of Pennsylvania, Wayne was a successful brigadier-general in the Revolutionary War and became a hero for his daring exploits. During the bitter winter of 1777-1778 at Valley Forge, Pennsylvania, Wayne shared the sufferings of his men although his comfortable estate was only five miles away. He played an important role in the final overthrow of the British forces in Georgia. After the war, in 1785, Wayne moved to Georgia and he represented Georgia for about six months in the U.S. House of Representatives. In 1792 President Washington recalled Wayne to serve as a major-general against the Indians in the Northwest territory. Once again his military efforts were successful.

660 *White County*

Uncertain—White County, Illinois, was created on December 9, 1815, and it was named for either Isaac White or Leonard

White. Although Isaac White's prominence had already been achieved by December, 1815 and Leonard White's principal fame came just a bit later, it is uncertain whether the county's name honors Isaac White or Leonard White.

Isaac White (1811) This hero of the battle of Tippecanoe was born in Virginia about 1776 and lived there until approximately 1800 when he moved with his brother, Thomas to Vincennes in what is now Indiana. By 1805 he had moved to what is now Illinois and was placed in charge of the salt works at Saline Creek as agent for the United States by Territorial Governor William Henry Harrison. These salt works were contiguous to the village of Equality in what is now Gallatin County, Illinois. White County, Illinois, was taken from Gallatin County and those two counties share a common border in southeastern Illinois. Although slavery was generally illegal here in the Northwest territory, Isaac White owned some slaves. About 1806 he was appointed a captain in the militia and by February, 1809, he had risen to the rank of colonel. In November, 1811, Isaac White was killed in combat by Indians in the battle of Tippecanoe.

Leonard White (–)—Leonard White was a pioneer settler of Gallatin County, Illinois, which was the county from which White County was created. He was prominently connected with the salt industry in southeastern Illinois and he served as a captain under Colonel Isaac White in the militia. By 1811 Leonard White had become a colonel in the Illinois militia. Leonard White was a member of the 1818 convention which wrote the constitution of the new state of Illinois. In the balloting to select the first two U.S. senators from the state of Illinois, Ninian Edwards and Jesse B. Thomas were elected. Edwards won on the first ballot while Thomas won with 21 votes on the third ballot defeating Leonard White who had 18. When Jesse B. Thomas later was a candidate for reelection to the U.S. Senate, Leonard White was again one of the candidates whom Thomas defeated. Leonard White represented White County, Illinois in the Illinois senate in the early 1820's and he was secretary of the Illinois senate from December, 1834, to January, 1836.

661 *Whiteside County*

Samuel Whiteside (–)—A native of North Carolina, Whiteside moved to western Indiana territory (now Illinois) about 1806 and became a captain in the militia. Whiteside participated in a number of actions against the Indians in this area from about 1812 through the Black Hawk War in 1832 and rose to the rank of brigadier-general. He also served in the first general assembly when Illinois achieved statehood in 1818. One source gives the year of Whiteside's death as 1861 while another shows 1866. Whiteside County was created in January 1836, less than four years after the Indians had been beaten back from the upper Mississippi River during the Black Hawk War. The legislature had considered and rejected two other proposed names for this new county: Chippewa and Dunn.

662 *Will County*

Conrad Will (–1835)—Conrad Will was born in Pennsylvania in either 1778 or 1779. A physician by profession, he moved to Brownsville in the southwestern portion of Illinois territory in 1815 and there he practiced medicine and engaged in the manufacture of salt. Will also became active in local politics at this time and he was a member of the 1818 convention which framed the constitution of the new state of Illinois. He was elected to the state legislature in 1818 and he served continuously in the Illinois legislature until his death on June 11, 1835; first as a senator for one term, then as a representative for four terms and again as a senator for four terms. Will County was created and named in his honor by his colleagues in the Illinois legislature on January 12, 1836, just seven months after his death.

663 *Williamson County*

Williamson County, Tennessee—Williamson County, Illinois was created in 1839 and named for the county in Tennessee from which many of the early settlers had come. The Tennessee county had been created just before the turn of the century, in 1799, and named for Dr. Hugh Williamson.

Hugh Williamson (1735–1819)—Williamson was born in Pennsylvania and graduated from the University of Pennsylvania. This versatile man studied theology and was licensed to preach and he worked as a professor of mathematics, astronomer and physician. He settled in North Carolina about 1776 and was surgeon general of North Carolina's troops during the American Revolution. Dr. Williamson also served in North Carolina's house of commons and was a delegate from North Carolina to the Continental Congress. He was one of North Carolina's five delegates to the 1787 convention which framed the U.S. Constitution and he represented the state of North Carolina in the U.S. House of Representatives during the first two congresses of our country. Williamson was a friend of Abram Maury, on whose land in Franklin, the county seat of Williamson County, Tennessee, was built.

664 *Winnebago County*

Winnebago Indians—At the time of early contact with Whites, the Winnebago tribe lived in central Wisconsin from Green Bay and Lake Winnebago to the Mississippi River and along the Rock River in southern Wisconsin and here in extreme northern Illinois. Winnebago County was named for this Indian tribe because the Rock River, which flows through it, was the boundary between lands of the Winnebago Indians and the Potawatomi Indians. In their material culture, the Winnebago were distinctly timber people. They sided with the British during both the American Revolution and the War of 1812. In the early and mid 1800's, the Winnebago were forced from their lands here and in Wisconsin by the Whites using both treaties and military force. First they were moved to northern Iowa, then to Minnesota, next to South Dakota and then to a reservation in northeastern Nebraska. However, many Winnebago in Nebraska made their own way back to Wisconsin. Although never huge in numbers, their population was estimated at about 5,000 in the first half of the 19th century. These Indians called themselves "big fish people" but it is the Algonquian name for them, Winnebago, that has stuck. Its precise meaning is uncertain but translations for it relate to "stinking" and "water" and include "stinking water," "dirty water people" and "stinking water people." Both Father Marquette and Cadillac were careful to record that the Winnebago's name did not signify any unclean habits of these Indians but pertained to water. It is likely that the name Winnebago referred to their earlier northern home, perhaps in Canada, and originally meant "people of the sea."

665 *Woodford County*

Woodford County, Kentucky—Woodford County, Illinois was created in 1841. The person most responsible for its birth was Thomas Bullock, who had come here from Kentucky. Bullock was allowed to select the new county's name and he chose the name of his home county in Kentucky. That county had been created in 1788 and named for William Woodford.

William Woodford (–1780)— This military man was born in Virginia in 1734 or 1735 and distinguished himself in the French and Indian War and in the American Revolution. In 1775 he was commissioned a colonel in the Virginia militia and in December of that year, at Great Bridge, his forces fought and defeated Loyalist troops recruited by the royal governor of Virginia, Lord Dunmore. Appointed brigadier-general by the Continental Congress, Woodford participated in actions at Brandywine Creek, Germantown, Monmouth and Charleston. It was at Charleston, in 1780, that Woodford was taken prisoner by the British and he died later that year.

REFERENCES

Ackerman, William K. *Early Illinois Railroads.* Chicago, Fergus Printing Co., 1884.

Adams, James N., & William E. Keller. *Illinois Place Names.* Springfield, Illinois State Historical Society, 1968.

Alexander, W. E. *History of Winneshiek & Allamakee Counties, Iowa.* Sioux City, Iowa, Western Publishing Co., 1882.

Allen, John W. *Legends & Lore of Southern Illinois.* Carbondale, Southern Illinois University, 1963.

Barge, William D. *Early Lee County.* Chicago, 1918.

Barge, William D. "Illinois County Names." *The Magazine of History*, Vol. 9, No. 5. New York: May, 1909.

Barge, William D. "The Rejected Illinois County Names." *Transactions of the Illinois State Historical Society*, Publication No. 11. Springfield: 1906.

Barge, William D., & Norman W. Caldwell. "Illinois Place-Names." *Journal of the Illinois State Historical Society*, Vol. 29, No. 3. Springfield: October, 1936.

Bastian, Wayne. *Whiteside County, Illinois Sesquicentennial Edition.* Morrison, Illinois, Whiteside County Board of Supervisors, 1968.

Bateman, Newton, & Paul Selby. *Historical Encyclopedia of Illinois.* Chicago, Munsell Publishing Co., 1900.

Beckwith, H. W. *History of Iroquois County.* Chicago, H. H. Hill & Co., 1880.

Bent, Charles. *History of Whiteside County, Illinois.* Clinton, Iowa, L. P. Allen, 1877.

Boies, Henry L. *History of De Kalb County, Illinois.* Chicago, O. P. Bassett, 1868.

Carpenter, Richard V. "The Illinois Constitutional Convention of 1818." *Journal of the Illinois State Historical Society*, Vol. 6, No. 3. Springfield, Illinois: October, 1913.

Chapman, Mrs. P. T. *A History of Johnson County, Illinois.* Press of the Herrin News, 1925.

Church, Charles A. *Past & Present of the City of Rockford & Winnebago County, Illinois.* Chicago, S. J. Clarke Publishing Co., 1905.

Clayton, John. *The Illinois Fact Book & Historical Almanac: 1673–1968.* Carbondale, Southern Illinois University Press, 1970.

Clements, John. *Illinois Facts.* Dallas, Texas, Clements Research II, Inc., 1989.

Cochrane, Joseph. *Centennial History of Mason County.* Springfield, Illinois, Rokker's Steam Printing House, 1876.

Collins, Lewis. *History of Kentucky.* Louisville, Kentucky, 1877.

Counties of Cumberland, Jasper & Richland, Illinois: Historical & Biographical. Chicago, F. A. Battey & Co., 1884.

County of Douglas, Illinois: Historical & Biographical. Chicago, F. A. Battey & Co., 1884.

Crutchfield, James A. *The Tennessee Almanac: And Book of Facts.* Nashville, Tennessee, Rutledge Hill Press, 1986.

Davidson, Alexander, & Bernard Stuve. *A Complete History of Illinois from 1673 to 1873.* Springfield, Illinois Journal Co., 1876.

Davis, William W. *History of Whiteside County, Illinois.* Chicago, Pioneer Publishing Co., 1908.

Dictionary of American History. New York, Charles Scribner's Sons, 1976.

Dunn, Jacob P. "Indian Names." *Teaching Indiana History*, Vol. 1, No. 5. February & March, 1963.

Dunn, Jacob P. "Indiana Geographical Nomenclature." *Indiana Quarterly Magazine of History*, Vol. 8, No. 3. Indianapolis: September, 1912.

Dunn, Jacob P. *True Indian Stories with Glossary of Indiana Indian Names.* Indianapolis, Sentinel Printing Co., 1908.

The Encyclopedia Americana. New York, Americana Corporation, 1977.

Ford, Henry A. *The History of Putnam & Marshall Counties.* Lacon, Illinois, 1860.

French, Allen. *The First Year of the American Revolution.* New York, Octagon Books, Inc., 1968.

Gemmill, William N. *Romantic America.* Chicago, Jordan Publishing Co., 1926.

Graham, A. A. *History of Richland County, Ohio.* Mansfield, Ohio, A. A. Graham & Co.

Haines, E. M. *The Past & Present of Lake County, Illinois.* Chicago, William Le Baron & Co., 1877.

Hallwas, John E. *McDonough County Heritage.* Macomb, Illinois, Illinois Heritage Press, 1984.

Harper, Herbert L. "The Antebellum Courthouses of Tennessee." *Tennessee Historical Quarterly*, Vol. 30, No. 1. Nashville, Tennessee: Spring, 1971.

Harrington, George B. *Past & Present of Bureau County, Illinois.* Chicago, Pioneer Publishing Co., 1906.

Heitman, Francis B. *Historical Register & Dictionary of the United States Army.* Washington, Government Printing Office, 1903.

Hicks, E. W. *History of Kendall County, Illinois.* Aurora, Illinois, Knickerbocker & Hodder, 1877.

The History of Adams County, Illinois. Chicago, Murray, Williamson & Phelps, 1879.

History of Christian County, Illinois. Philadelphia, Brink, McDonough & Co., 1880.

The History of Coles County, Illinois. Chicago, William Le Baron, Jr. & Co., 1879.

The History of Edgar County, Illinois. Chicago, William Le Baron, Jr. & Co., 1879.

History of Grundy County, Illinois. Chicago, O. L. Baskin Co., 1882.

The History of Jo Daviess County, Illinois. Chicago, H. F. Kett & Co., 1878.

The History of Livingston County, Illinois. Chicago, William Le Baron, Jr., & Co., 1878.

History of Logan County, Illinois. Chicago, Interstate Publishing Co., 1886.

History of McHenry County, Illinois. Chicago, Interstate Publishing Co., 1885.

The History of Menard & Mason Counties, Illinois. Chicago, O. L. Baskin & Co., 1879.

The History of Peoria County, Illinois. Chicago, Johnson & Co., 1880.

History of Sangamon County, Illinois. Chicago, Interstate Publishing Co., 1881.

History of Stephenson County: 1970. Freeport, Illinois, County of Stephenson, 1972.

History of White County, Illinois. Chicago, Interstate Publishing Co., 1883.

Hodge, Frederick W. *Handbook of American Indians North of Mexico.* Totowa, New Jersey, Rowman & Littlefield, 1975.

Howlett, Michael J. *Handbook of Illinois Government.* State of Illinois, 1974.

Hughes, Edward J. *Blue Book of the State of Illinois: 1935–1936.*

Illinois Sesquicentennial Commission. *Illinois Guide & Gazetteer.* Chicago, Rand McNally & Co., 1969.

Jasper County Historical Foundation, Inc. *History of Jasper County, Georgia.*

Roswell, Georgia, W. H. Wolfe Associates, 1976.

Lansden, John M. *A History of the City of Cairo, Illinois.* Chicago, R. R. Donnelley & Sons Co., 1910.

Lawler, Lucille. *Gallatin County: Gateway to Illinois.* East St. Louis, Illinois, Saunders Printing Service, Inc., 1968.

Le Jeune, R. P. L. *Dictionnaire General … du Canada.* Universite D'Ottawa, Canada, 1931.

Leland, J. A. C. "Indian Names in Missouri." *Names: Journal of the American Name Society,* Vol. 1, No. 4. Berkeley: December, 1953.

Lobmann, Karl B. *Cities & Towns of Illinois: A Handbook of Community Facts.* Urbana, University of Illinois Press, 1951.

McCall, Hugh. *The History of Georgia.* Atlanta, Cherokee Publishing Co., 1969.

Masters, Edgar L. *The Sangamon.* New York, Farrar & Rinehart, Inc., 1942.

May, George W. *History of Massac County, Illinois.* Galesburg, Illinois, Wagoner Printing Co., 1955.

Montague, E. J. *History of Randolph County, Illinois.* Sparta, Illinois, 1948.

Montague-Smith, Patrick. *Debrett's Peerage & Baronetage.* London, England, Debrett's Peerage, Ltd.

Moore, Roy L. *History of Woodford County.* Eureka, Illinois, Woodford County Republican, 1910.

Moses, John. *Illinois, Historical & Statistical.* Chicago, Fergus Printing Co., 1889.

"Names of Indiana Counties: White County…" *Indianapolis News,* March 19, 1919.

Nichols, Fay F. *The Kankakee.* Brooklyn, New York, Theo. Gaus' Sons, Inc., 1965.

Nothstein, Ira O. "Rock Island and the Rock Island Arsenal." *Journal of the Illinois State Historical Society,* Vol. 4, No. 4. Springfield, Illinois: January, 1912.

Page, O. J. *History of Massac County, Illinois.* Metropolis, Illinois, 1900.

Parrish, Randall. *Historic Illinois: The Romance of the Earlier Days.* Chicago, A. C. McClurg & Co., 1906.

The Past & Present of Rock Island County, Illinois. Chicago, H. F. Kett & Co., 1877.

The Past & Present of Woodford County, Illinois. Chicago, William Le Baron, Jr., & Co., 1878.

Perrin, William H. *History of Alexander, Union & Pulaski Counties, Illinois.* Chicago, O. L. Baskin & Co., 1883.

Perrin, William H. *History of Crawford & Clark Counties, Illinois.* Chicago, O. L. Baskin & Co., 1883.

Perrin, William H. *History of Effingham County, Illinois.* Chicago, O. L. Baskin & Co., 1883.

Piatt, Emma C. *History of Piatt County.* Chicago, Shepard & Johnston, 1883.

Portrait & Biographical Album of Whiteside County, Illinois. Chicago, Chapman Brothers, 1883.

Reynolds, John. *The Pioneer History of Illinois.* Chicago, Fergus Printing Co., 1887.

Richmond, Mabel E. *Centennial History of Decatur & Macon County.* Decatur, Decatur Review, 1930.

Rose, James A. *Blue Book of the State of Illinois.* Springfield, Illinois, Phillips Bros., 1903.

Sandham, William R. "Historical Notes." *Journal of the Illinois State Historical Society,* Vol. 25, Nos. 1–2. Springfield, Illinois: April–July, 1932.

Shallenberger, Mrs. E. H. *Stark County and Its Pioneers.* Cambridge, Illinois, B. W. Seaton, 1876.

Shankle, George Earlie. *State Names, Flags, Seals, Songs, Birds, Flowers & Other Symbols.* New York, H. W. Wilson Co., 1941.

Smith, George W. *History of Illinois & Her People.* Chicago, American Historical Society, Inc., 1927.

Smith, George W. *A History of Southern Illinois.* Chicago, Lewis Publishing Co., 1912.

Smith, George W. "The Salines of Southern Illinois." *Transactions of the Illinois State Historical Society,* Publication No. 9. Springfield: 1904.

Snyder, J. F. "The Armament of Fort Chartres." *Transactions of the Illinois State Historical Society,* Publication No. 11. Springfield: 1906.

Snyder, J. F. "Forgotten Statesmen of Illinois." *Transactions of the Illinois State Historical Society,* Publication No. 9. Springfield, Illinois: 1904.

Snyder, John F. "Forgotten Statesmen of Illinois: Hon. Conrad Will." *Transactions of the Illinois State Historical Society,* Publication No. 10. Springfield: 1906.

Stennett, William H. *A History of the Origin of the Place Names Connected with the Chicago & North Western & Chicago, St. Paul, Minneapolis & Omaha Railways.* Chicago, 1908.

Stevens, William B. *A History of Georgia.* Savannah, Georgia, Beehive Press, 1972.

Stringer, Lawrence B. *History of Logan County, Illinois.* Chicago, Pioneer Publishing Co., 1911.

Tate, H. Clay. *The Way It Was in McLean County.* Bloomington, Illinois, Pantagraph Printing & Stationery Co., 1972.

Tilton, Clint C. "The Genesis of Old Vermilion." *Journal of the Illinois State Historical Society,* Vol. 20, No. 1. Springfield, Illinois: April, 1927.

Townend, Peter. *Burke's Genealogical & Heraldic History of the Peerage, Baronetage & Knightage.* London, England, Burke's Peerage, Ltd., 1967.

Vexler, Robert I. *Chronology & Documentary Handbook of the State of Illinois.* Dobbs Ferry, New York, Oceana Publications, Inc., 1978.

Vogel, Virgil J. *Indian Names in Michigan.* Ann Arbor, University of Michigan Press, 1986.

Vogel, Virgil J. "Indian Place Names in Illinois." *Journal of the Illinois State Historical Society,* Vol. 55. 1962.

Vogel, Virgil J. *Iowa Place Names of Indian Origin.* Iowa City, University of Iowa Press, 1983.

Walker, Charles A. *History of Macoupin County, Illinois.* Chicago, S. J. Clarke Publishing Co., 1911.

Walker, Charles L. "History to the Title to Lands in Rock Island County, Illinois." *Journal of the Illinois State Historical Society,* Vol. 4, No. 4. Springfield: January, 1912.

Walton, Ivan H. "Origin of Names on the Great Lakes." *Names: Journal of the American Name Society,* Vol. 3, No. 4. Berkeley: December, 1955.

White, Dabney & T. C. Richardson. *East Texas: Its History and Its Makers.* New York, Lewis Historical Publishing Co., 1940.

Wilcox, David F. & Lyman McCarl. *Quincy & Adams County.* Chicago, Lewis Publishing Co., 1919.

Willard, Margaret W. *Letters to the American Revolution: 1774–1776.* Boston, Houghton Mifflin Co., 1925.

Wilson, L. A. *Wilson's History & Directory for Southeast Missouri & Southern Illinois.* Cape Girardeau, Missouri, 1875–1876.

Wilson, William E. *The Wabash.* New York, Farrar & Rinehart, Inc., 1940.

Work Projects Administration. *Du Page County: A Descriptive & Historical Guide: 1831–1939.* Edwards Brothers, Inc., 1948.

Work Projects Administration. *Illinois: A Descriptive & Historical Guide.* Chicago, A. C. McClurg & Co., 1939.

Work Projects Administration. *Inventory of the County Archives of Illinois-Ogle & Piatt Counties.* Chicago, 1940.

Works Progress Administration. *Inventory of the County Archives of Illinois-Champaign, Logan & Sangamon Counties.* Chicago, 1938-1939.

Indiana

(92 counties)

666 *Adams County*

John Q. Adams (1767–1848)— John Quincy Adam was the son of second president of the United States, John Adams, and a native of Massachusetts. John Quincy Adams served in the U.S. Senate and as minister to several European countries. He was secretary of state to President James Monroe, for whom he helped formulate the Monroe Doctrine. He became our sixth president in 1825, defeating Andrew Jackson and two other candidates but when he ran for reelection in 1828, Jackson defeated him. Adams then entered the U.S. House of Representatives where he represented Massachusetts and opposed states' rights and slavery for 17 years until his death in 1848.

667 *Allen County*

John Allen (–1813)— Allen was born in Virginia in 1771 or 1772 and moved to Kentucky with his parents when he was still a boy. The Allen's first Kentucky home was near Danville but they later settled on a farm near Bardstown, Kentucky. Allen studied law in his native Virginia and then returned to Kentucky in 1795 to practice law in Shelby County. He became active in politics and served in both houses of the Kentucky legislature. In 1808 Allen was a candidate for governor of Kentucky but lost to Charles Scott. Early in the War of 1812 Allen raised a regiment of riflemen to serve in the campaign under William Henry Harrison in the Northwest. On June 5, 1812, he received a commission as lieutenant-colonel. Allen died in combat at the battle of the River Raisin in Michigan in 1813. Allen County, Indiana, was created and named in his honor ten years later, in 1823. The county's name was suggested by John Tipton.

668 *Bartholomew County*

Joseph Bartholomew (1766–1840)— A native of New Jersey, Bartholomew moved to Indiana in 1799 when it was still part of Northwest territory. As an officer in the local militia, he participated in a number of actions against the Indians. He served as a lieutenant-colonel at the battle of Tippecanoe in 1811 and was severely wounded early in that battle. Bartholomew later served in the War of 1812 and rose to the rank of major-general. About 1818 or 1819 he became a member of the lower house of the Indiana legislature and he later served in the state senate. In 1831 he moved to Illinois where he died. This county was created in 1821 while Bartholomew was serving in Indiana's senate. The county's name was suggested by Samuel Merrill and the motion to name the county Bartholomew was made by John Tipton, who was a friend of Bartholomew.

669 *Benton County*

Thomas H. Benton (1782–1858)— Benton was a native of North Carolina, who served in the Tennessee senate and as a soldier in the War of 1812. Following the war he moved to Missouri and he represented that state for thirty years in the U.S. Senate. In that body he championed many interests of the West including free 160 acre homesteads, pony express, telegraph and railroads. Benton was a moderate on the volatile slavery issue. He opposed both abolition of slavery and extension of it. His primary concerns were peace and preservation of the union. These moderate positions proved unpopular. Some states which had named counties in Benton's honor renamed them and, in 1850, Missouri failed to return Benton to the senate. Following his ouster from the senate, Benton served briefly in the U.S. House of Representatives. This county was created in 1840 while Benton was still popular in the West. It was originally proposed that this county be named Tipton but Benton was selected instead and it was not until 1844 that a Tipton County was placed on Indiana's map.

670 *Blackford County*

Isaac N. Blackford (1786–1859)— A native of New Jersey and a graduate of the College of New Jersey (now Princeton University), Blackford came to Indiana territory about 1812, practiced law and edited a newspaper. He served briefly as judge of the first judicial circuit and as a member of the lower house of Indiana's first state legislature. In 1817 Governor Jonathan Jennings appointed Blackford to Indiana's supreme court where he served some 35 years from 1817 to 1853. Judge Blackford wrote eight important law volumes known as "Blackford's Reports." From 1855 until his death in 1859 Blackford served on the U.S. court of claims in Washington, D.C.

671 *Boone County*

Daniel Boone (1734–1820)— A native of Pennsylvania, Boone penetrated Kentucky when it was wilderness country and settled there with his family in 1775. He gained fame on America's rugged western frontier as explorer, Indian fighter and surveyor. This county was created in 1830. After considering the names Ray and Mercer, the legislators decided to name the county in honor of Daniel Boone.

672 *Brown County*

Jacob J. Brown (1775–1828)— A native of Pennsylvania with little military experience, Brown found himself in command of a section of the frontier at the start of the War of 1812. His successful defense of the important American base, Sackett's Harbor, on Lake Ontario, resulted in his appointment in July, 1813, as brigadier-general in the army and six months later he was made major-general. Brown later served with distinction in other important battles of the War of 1812. After the war, in 1821, he was assigned the command of the United States army which he held until his death. Brown County, Indiana, was created in 1836.

673 *Carroll County*

Charles Carroll (1737–1832)— Carroll was a native of Maryland and he represented that state in the Continental Congress. He was one of the signers of the Declaration of Independence and he later represented Maryland as a U.S. senator in the first congress of the United States. Carroll lived to be the last surviving signer of the Declaration of Independence and several states recognized that distinction by naming counties for him. This county was created in 1828. The law which created it specified that the county's name honored Charles Carroll and that he was then "the only surviving signer of the Declaration of Independence."

674 *Cass County*

Lewis Cass (1782–1866)—A native of New Hampshire, Cass served in the army in the War of 1812 and rose to the rank of brigadier-general. Following that war Cass held a variety of important political positions and was the candidate of the Democratic party in 1848 for president of the United States. He lost to Zachary Taylor. Cass served as governor of Michigan territory, secretary of war under Andrew Jackson, minister to France, U.S. senator from Michigan and secretary of state under James Buchanan. Cass at one time had been a United States commissioner and he was involved in treaties with the Indians which gave the United States ownership of the land which comprises Cass County, Indiana. This county was created in 1828.

675 *Clark County*

George R. Clark (1752–1818)—A native of Virginia, George Rogers Clark was a frontiersman and military hero. During the American Revolution he secured a commission as lieutenant-colonel to attack the British, Indians and Loyalists in Indiana and Illinois. He successfully captured Vincennes, Cahokia and Kaskaskia and, after the British retook Kaskaskia, Clark won it a second time. These military victories together with skillful negotiating by Benjamin Franklin enabled the United States to acquire the Northwest territory during the peace negotiations with the British at the end of the Revolution. In 1784 the state of Virginia awarded Clark large tracts of land in the areas he had captured. Some of that land is in Clark County, Indiana, which was created in 1801 when Indiana was a territory.

676 *Clay County*

Henry Clay (1777–1852)—Clay represented Kentucky in both branches of the U.S. Congress. For many years he was one of the more prominent figures in American politics but his several bids for the presidency were unsuccessful. He was influential in effecting important compromises between northern and southern interests during the years that secession and civil war were imminent. This county was created in 1825 shortly after Clay lost in a bid for the presidency to John Quincy Adams. The county's name was chosen by Daniel Harris, a Whig, who was a member of the Indiana general assembly from Owen County.

677 *Clinton County*

De Witt Clinton (1769–1828)—This New York state native held many of the important political offices in that state. Clinton served in both houses of the state legislature and as mayor of New York City. He represented New York in the U.S. Senate and in 1812 he was the Federalist candidate for president, running against President James Madison. In 1817 Clinton was elected as New York's governor. As governor, he was the principal promoter of the Erie Canal which was instrumental in linking the vast agricultural lands in our country's West with eastern markets. The canal spurred our nation's growth. This county was created in 1830.

678 *Crawford County*

Uncertain—Crawford County, Indiana, was created in 1818 and named for a William Crawford but it is uncertain whether it was Colonel William Crawford (1732–1782) or William H. Crawford (1772–1834) who was so honored.

William Crawford (1732–1782)—A native of Virginia, Crawford was a farmer, surveyor and soldier. Before the American Revolution he fought in the French and Indian War, the Pontiac War and Lord Dunmore's War. During the Revolution, Crawford took part in battles at Long Island, Trenton, Princeton, Brandywine and Germantown and rose to the rank of colonel. About 1778 he moved to the West where he engaged in defense of the frontier and in actions against the Indians. In 1782 he was captured by Delaware Indians, tortured and burned at the stake near Upper Sandusky, Ohio.

William H. Crawford (1772–1834)—Crawford served in the Georgia legislature and as a U.S. senator from Georgia. He was elected president pro tempore of the senate and he later served as minister to France, secretary of war and secretary of the treasury. Crawford was a serious candidate for the presidency in both 1816 and 1824.

679 *Daviess County*

Joseph H. Daviess (1774–1811)—Daviess was born in Virginia but moved with his parents to the wilderness of Kentucky when he was still a young boy. There he studied law and became a successful attorney. In 1807 Daviess, as attorney for the United States, prosecuted Aaron Burr for treason. Burr was acquitted. In the fall of 1811 Daviess joined General William Henry Harrison's army to fight the Indians. Colonel Daviess died in the battle of Tippecanoe in Indiana territory in November, 1811, leading a charge of his men against the Indians. Daviess County, Indiana was created on December 24, 1816, in an act that became effective on February 15, 1817. Colonel Daviess' name was misspelled in the act that created this county.

680 *De Kalb County*

Johann Kalb, Baron de Kalb (1721–1780)—Kalb was born in the province of Alsace, which at that time belonged to France. He was a general in the French army and resigned that commission to come to America to assist the colonies in the Revolutionary War. He served as a general in the American Revolution and died in combat here.

681 *Dearborn County*

Henry Dearborn (1751–1829)—A native of New Hampshire and a physician, Dearborn served with distinction as an officer in the Revolutionary War. After the war he became a brigadier-general and later a major-general of the militia in Maine when it was still part of Massachusetts and he represented Massachusetts in the U.S. Congress for two terms. In 1801, when Thomas Jefferson became president, he appointed Dearborn to his cabinet as secretary of war and Dearborn served in that position throughout Jefferson's eight years as president. Dearborn later served as a senior major-general in the War of 1812 and as minister to Portugal. This county was created in 1803 while Dearborn was serving as secretary of war.

682 *Decatur County*

Stephen Decatur (1779–1820)—Decatur, who was born in Maryland, was an officer in the U.S. navy who served in the Mediterranean Sea from 1801 to 1805 in the Tripolitan War. His bravery and successes in that war made him a popular hero in America and earned him promotion to captain. During the War of 1812, Decatur reinforced his reputation as a naval hero. Following that war Decatur, now a commodore, again served in the Mediterranean where he captured the Algerian flagship *Mashuda*. His display of naval force exacted peace terms from Algeria and indemnities for un-neutral acts from Tunis and Tripoli. This brought an end to the plundering of American shipping by the Barbary powers. Decatur's life ended in a duel fought in March, 1820, and Decatur County was created in December, 1821, effective March, 1822.

683 *Delaware County*

Delaware Indians— When the Europeans first encountered the Delaware Indians, they were living along the Delaware River basin in large areas of present day Delaware and New Jersey as well as eastern Pennsylvania. They were an agricultural people who cleared the land of trees and undergrowth by burning. Because this burning limited the length of time that the land was fertile, the Delaware Indians moved their villages frequently. Farming was done by women, their most important crop being corn. The Delaware began to move westward as early as 1720 and Delaware County, Indiana was one of the areas where they established villages. They lived here from about 1770 to 1818. Delaware County, Indiana was created in 1827. Today the Delaware are scattered with many living in Canada and Oklahoma. *Delaware* is the name by which the Whites called these Indians. That name derived from the Delaware River, the river having derived from Delaware Bay. The bay was named for Thomas West, Lord De La Warr (1577–1618) who was a British governor of colonial Virginia.

684 *Dubois County*

Toussaint Dubois (–1816)— Dubois was a native of France who emigrated to lower Canada and later settled in Vincennes where he became a successful and wealthy merchant and fur trader. About 1809 he purchased land in what later became Dubois County, Indiana. Dubois volunteered his services to assist with the vexing Indian problems of the day and General William Henry Harrison employed him as a messenger to various Indian tribes. Harrison appointed Dubois captain in charge of spies and guides in the militia and Dubois participated in the 1811 battle of Tippecanoe. In September, 1812, he was commissioned a commandant of spies. Dubois County, Indiana, was created by the legislature in December, 1817, in a law that became effective in February, 1818. The signature on Toussaint Dubois' last will and testament shows that he used the style Dubois for his surname rather than Du Bois.

685 *Elkhart County*

Uncertain— The origin of this county's name cannot be given with certainty but the evidence strongly suggests that it was named directly or indirectly for the Elkhart River. Many sources state that the county was named directly for the river while others indicate that it was named for some Indians who lived along the river. According to one legend, there was an Indian chief named Chief Elkhart whose daughter was the beautiful Princess Mishawaka. The Elkhart River, which flows through both Noble and Elkhart Counties, is about 38 miles long. It is a tributary of the Saint Joseph River, which it joins at the city of Elkhart. The Indians named this river for an island at its mouth which they thought resembled the heart of an elk. The later French and English versions of the river's name were literal translations of the Indians' name for it. The English names for this river have been Elk Heart, Elksheart, Elkheart and now Elkhart.

686 *Fayette County*

Marie Joseph Paul Yves Roch Gilbert du Motier, Marquis de Lafayette (1757–1834)— Lafayette was a French aristocrat who served briefly in the French army. He came to America in 1777 to assist the American Revolutionary army. He was granted an honorary commission as major-general by the Continental Congress and served with distinction in a number of battles in the Revolutionary War. Fayette County was created and named in 1818.

687 *Floyd County*

Uncertain— Floyd County, Indiana was created in 1819. Although it is uncertain whom the county's name honors, there are only two viable possibilities: Davis Floyd and John Floyd.

Davis Floyd (1772–)— A native of Virginia and a lawyer, Floyd moved to Kentucky in 1799 and then to Indiana territory in 1801. He was sheriff of Indiana territory's Clark County from 1803 to 1806 and a member of the territorial house of representatives from 1805 to 1806. Floyd was an associate of Aaron Burr in the illegal expedition against Spanish territory and, according to one account, he was indicted for this and sentenced to serve one half hour in jail. Floyd was prominent in the government of Indiana territory serving as its auditor and later as its treasurer and he was a member of Indiana's constitutional convention of 1816. From 1817 to 1823 Floyd was a judge here in southeastern Indiana and he was one of the men who successfully lobbied for the new county which was created and named Floyd County in 1819. In 1823 Davis Floyd moved to Florida territory where he served as one of three U.S. commissioners to settle land claims. The date of Judge Floyd's death is not known but it was prior to July 9, 1834.

John Floyd (–1783)— Colonel John Floyd was born in Virginia about 1750 and was a public surveyor prior to the American Revolution. In this capacity he performed numerous surveys of Virginia's land in what is now the state of Kentucky and he briefly served as the principal surveyor for Richard Henderson's short-lived country named Transylvania. During the American Revolution Floyd was involved in naval warfare against the British and was successful in destroying some British vessels. He was captured and held for about one year in England before he escaped and returned to America. Here he established his reputation as an Indian fighter in Kentucky and it was at the hands of Indians that he met his death. In April, 1783, Colonel Floyd was mortally wounded by Indians on the Kentucky side of the Ohio River directly opposite from the present site of New Albany, Indiana, which is the county seat of Floyd County.

688 *Fountain County*

James Fountain (–1790)— James Fountain was a major from Kentucky who was killed at the head of the mounted militia during battle on the Maumee River near Fort Wayne in 1790. The spelling of his surname is uncertain. A number of sources indicate Fountain but about an equal number list Fontaine and one source renders his name as Fountaine. This county was created in December, 1825. A name that had been suggested for it was Fairfield but that name was never officially adopted. The name Fountain was suggested by a Judge Watts.

689 *Franklin County*

Benjamin Franklin (1706–1790)— Franklin was a native of Massachusetts who moved to Pennsylvania in his teens. Poverty denied him a formal education but he became the leading printer and editor in North America. Franklin gained fame for his discoveries and inventions in the physical sciences and he distinguished himself as author, philosopher and diplomat. He was a signer of the Declaration of Independence and an important member of the convention which framed the U.S. Constitution.

690 *Fulton County*

Robert Fulton (1765–1815)— A native of Pennsylvania, as a young man Fulton supported himself as an artist. He later gained fame for his inventions dealing with marine vessels. He invented a submarine which he successfully demonstrated in the year 1800. He invented mines to be used in naval warfare and was one of the inventors of the steamboat. The steamboat became a commercial success for Fulton and made him famous. This invention contributed greatly to the development of America.

691 *Gibson County*

John Gibson (1740–1822)— A native of Pennsylvania and a frontier soldier and fur trader, Gibson was captured by Indians and spent about one year living with them as a captive. He later served as an officer during the American Revolution and rose to the rank of colonel. After the Revolution, Gibson lived in Pennsylvania where he was a judge, major-general of the militia and served as a member of Pennsylvania's constitutional convention. In 1800 he was appointed as secretary of the new Indiana territory and he held that post from 1800 until 1816. Gibson County was created in 1813 while John Gibson was serving as territorial secretary. Gibson also served, at least twice, as acting governor of Indiana territory.

692 *Grant County*

Samuel Grant (–1789) & Moses Grant (–1789)— Little is known about namesakes of this county beyond the information contained in the 1831 act which created it: "... shall form and constitute the county of Grant, in memory of Capt. Samuel Grant and Moses Grant of Kentucky who fell in the battle with the Indians in the year 1789, in that part of the state now known as Switzerland County ..." It is known that Samuel Grant and Moses Grant were brothers and that they were killed near a creek later named for them, Grant or Grants Creek. This creek is a small stream in northeastern Switzerland County, Indiana. A tiny tributary of the Ohio River, this creek joins the Ohio about four miles below the town of Rising Sun, Indiana. But deaths at the hands of Indians were certainly not rare in the late 1700's so why this seemingly obscure event in 1789 captured the imagination of the Indiana legislators some 42 years later is a mystery. Two other names were suggested for this county, Logan and Fulton, but the legislature rejected them and settled on Grant.

693 *Greene County*

Nathanael Greene (1742–1786)— Greene was born in Rhode Island and served briefly in the Rhode Island legislature. He gained fame as one of the ablest American generals in the Revolutionary War. Greene County, Indiana was created in 1821.

694 *Hamilton County*

Alexander Hamilton (–1804)— A native of the West Indies, Hamilton moved to New York and served as an officer in America's Revolutionary army. One of his assignments during the war was aide-de-camp to General George Washington. After the war Hamilton was a member of the convention which framed the U.S. Constitution. He collaborated with Madison and Jay in writing a series of papers entitled *The Federalist* which explained the new constitution and advocated its adoption. A conservative and an advocate of a strong central government, he served as the United States' first secretary of the treasury. In 1804 he engaged in a duel with Aaron Burr and Hamilton died of wounds he suffered in that duel.

695 *Hancock County*

John Hancock (1737–1793)— A native of Massachusetts and a graduate of Harvard, Hancock served in the Massachusetts legislature and was president of the Massachusetts provincial congress. He was elected to the second Continental Congress and became its president. As president of the Continental Congress when the Declaration of Independence was signed, he was, on July 4, 1776, the first signer of that document. He signed it with such a flourish that the name John Hancock became a synonym for "signature." He later commanded the Massachusetts militia, served as governor of that state for many years and presided over the Massachusetts convention that ratified the U.S. Constitution. The name Tecumseh was also considered for this county by the Indiana legislature when they created it in 1827 but that name was never adopted.

696 *Harrison County*

William H. Harrison (1773–1841)— William Henry Harrison was a native of Virginia whose early career was in the army, serving as an officer in actions against the Indians. In 1798 President John Adams appointed Harrison to be secretary of Northwest territory and the following year he became that territory's delegate to the U.S. Congress. In 1800 Indiana territory was created and President John Adams appointed Harrison to be the new territory's first governor. He served in that post until 1812 and was territorial governor when this county was created in 1808. Harrison commanded the army in the battle of Tippecanoe and he served in the War of 1812 rising to the rank of major-general. He later served in the Ohio state legislature and represented Ohio in both houses of the U.S. Congress. In December, 1839 Harrison became the Whig party's candidate for president of the United States with John Tyler as his vice-presidential running mate. Their famous campaign slogan was "Tippecanoe and Tyler too." Harrison was elected president but he served only one month before dying.

697 *Hendricks County*

William Hendricks (1782–1850)— A native of Pennsylvania, Hendricks moved to Indiana territory in 1812 where he practiced law and published a newspaper. He served in the territory's house of representatives and was secretary of Indiana's 1816 constitutional convention. When Indiana was admitted to statehood Hendricks became the new state's first representative in the U.S. Congress. He served three terms there before being elected governor of Indiana in 1822. William Hendricks was serving as Indiana's governor in December, 1823 when this county was created and named in his honor. He later represented Indiana in the U.S. Senate from 1825 to 1837.

698 *Henry County*

Patrick Henry (1736–1799)— Henry was a native of Virginia and a lawyer. He served in the Virginia legislature, as governor of Virginia and as a delegate to the first and second Continental Congresses. Henry was one of America's key revolutionary leaders. He was a great orator and he is remembered for his call to arms against the British "Give me liberty or give me death." Henry opposed Virginia's ratification of the federal constitution and his views played a role in the later adoption of the Bill of Rights.

699 *Howard County*

Tilghman A. Howard (1797–1844)— Howard was born in South Carolina and studied law in Tennessee. There he was admitted to the bar, practiced law and served in the Tennessee senate. In 1830 Howard came to Indiana where he was appointed U.S. district attorney for Indiana. He represented Indiana briefly in the U.S. House of Representatives before resigning to run, unsuccessfully, for the Indiana governor's office. In June, 1844 Howard was appointed charge d'affaires to the independent republic of Texas. Soon after his arrival in Texas he contracted yellow fever and he died there in August, 1844. This county had been created in 1844 and named Richardville County in honor of a Miami Indian chief named Jean Baptiste Richardville. Its name was changed to Howard County in 1846 by Tilghman A. Howard's friends in the Indiana legislature.

700 *Huntington County*

Samuel Huntington (1731–1796) — A native of Connecticut and a lawyer, Huntington was a member of Connecticut's colonial assembly. He later served as king's attorney for Connecticut and was a judge of Connecticut's superior court. Influential in the events surrounding our nation's birth, Samuel Huntington was one of the signers of the Declaration of Independence and he was also one of the signers of the Articles of Confederation. He represented Connecticut in the Continental Congress and, for a time, was president of that body. He later served as chief justice of the superior court of Connecticut and was Connecticut's lieutenant-governor. Huntington was elected governor of Connecticut in 1786. Reelected annually, he was Connecticut's governor when it entered the Union as a state in 1788 and he continued in office as governor until his death on January 5, 1796. Huntington County, Indiana was created in 1832. Its name was suggested by Elias Murray, who was a member of the Indiana legislature at the time.

701 *Jackson County*

Andrew Jackson (1767–1845) — Jackson was born on the border of North Carolina and South Carolina. He represented Tennessee in both branches of the U.S. Congress and gained fame and popularity for his military exploits in wars with the Indians and in the War of 1812. He was provisional military governor of Florida and from 1829 to 1837 General Jackson was president of the United States. His presidency reflected the frontier spirit of America. This county was created in December, 1815, just eleven months after Jackson defeated the British in the battle of New Orleans during the War of 1812.

702 *Jasper County*

William Jasper (–1779) — This Revolutionary War hero was born in South Carolina about 1750 but moved to Georgia where he grew up on a farm. He first became a hero in a dramatic event at the battle of Fort Moultrie when he courageously exposed himself to enemy fire to recover a flag which had been shot down. For this heroism Sergeant Jasper was awarded a sword and offered a promotion to lieutenant but he declined the promotion. Later employed as a scout, Jasper made several trips behind enemy lines in Georgia while operating from the swamps there. In a dramatic exploit near Savannah, Georgia, he and his close friend, John Newton, rescued several Americans who were prisoners and took their guards as prisoners of war. Jasper was shot and killed during the siege of Savannah while recovering the flag which had been shot down. Geographic names in several of our states link the names of the two heroic sergeants, Jasper and Newton. In some states, two counties are named for them and this is true in Indiana where Jasper County and Newton County are side by side in the northwestern part of the state. In other states, a county is named for one of the men and its county seat is named for the other.

703 *Jay County*

John Jay (1745–1829) — A native of New York City and a graduate of King's College (later Columbia University), Jay was a lawyer who represented New York in the Continental Congress and served briefly as president of that body. During the American Revolution Jay was our minister plenipotentiary to Spain and he later served with Benjamin Franklin in Paris negotiating terms of peace with Britain. Jay collaborated with Hamilton and Madison in writing a series of papers under the title *The Federalist*, which explained the new constitution and advocated its adoption. Upon formation of our new national government, President George Washington appointed Jay to be the first chief justice of the U.S. Supreme Court. As chief justice, Jay sought to extend federal powers to promote a strong central government. He later served as minister to England and governor of New York. Jay County, Indiana, was created in 1835.

704 *Jefferson County*

Thomas Jefferson (1743–1826) — Jefferson was a native of Virginia and a member of the Virginia legislature. He served Virginia as governor and he was a delegate to the second Continental Congress. Jefferson was the author of the Declaration of Independence and one of its signers. He was minister to France, secretary of state, vice president and president of the United States. As president, he accomplished the Louisiana Purchase and he arranged the Lewis and Clark Expedition to the Pacific Northwest. Jefferson was a true intellectual, thoroughly knowledgeable in the arts and sciences. His political theories were pivotal in the formation of our infant republic. Thomas Jefferson retired from his presidency in 1809 and this county was created by the legislature of Indiana territory in 1810. This county's name was suggested by John Paul.

705 *Jennings County*

Jonathan Jennings (1787–1834) — The place of Jennings' birth is not known but it is thought to have been New Jersey. He grew up in western Pennsylvania and moved to Indiana territory in 1806 where he was admitted to the bar and became active in politics. In 1809 Jennings ran as an antislavery candidate to be the territory's delegate to the U.S. Congress and he was elected. He was reelected to congress several times and it was Jennings who presented to the U.S. Congress the petition from the territorial legislature requesting statehood for Indiana. Jennings next served as a member and president of Indiana's 1816 constitutional convention and when Indiana was admitted to the Union as a state on December 11, 1816, Jennings became the new state's first governor. Jennings County was created on December 27, 1816. Jonathan Jennings served two terms as governor and later represented Indiana in the U.S. House of Representatives.

706 *Johnson County*

John Johnson (–1817) — The date and place of John Johnson's birth are uncertain although one account lists the year of his birth as 1776. He arrived in Indiana before it became a territory, studied law and practiced in the early courts of Indiana territory. Johnson served several terms in the territorial general assembly and in 1809 he was an unsuccessful candidate for delegate to the U.S. Congress. In 1816 Johnson was a member of Indiana's constitutional convention and when Indiana entered the Union as a state in December, 1816, he was appointed to be one of the judges on the state's first supreme court. He died less than one year later. Johnson County was created in 1822. Its name was proposed by Oliver H. Smith, who was a member of the legislature.

707 *Knox County*

Henry Knox (1750–1806)— This Massachusetts native participated in many of the important military engagements of the American Revolution and rose to the rank of major-general. After the war, Knox commanded West Point and he conceived and organized the Society of Cincinnati, an elite group of former Revolutionary officers. In 1785 he was appointed secretary of war under the Articles of Confederation and he retained that position in the first United States cabinet under President George Washington. This county was created in 1790 while Knox was serving as secretary of war and Indiana was still part of the Northwest territory. It was an enormous county then, extending from the Ohio River to Canada and west far into what is now the state of Illinois.

708 *Kosciusko County*

Tadeusz Andrzej Bonawentura Kosciuszko (1746–1817)— Kosciuszko was born in the Palatinate of Breesc, which was then part of the Grand Duchy of Lithuania and later part of Poland. Known in America as Thaddeus Kosciuszko or Kosciusko, he came here to fight in our army during the American Revolution. He served with distinction and rose to the rank of brigadier-general. At the conclusion of our war he returned to Poland where he led unsuccessful efforts to gain Poland's independence from Russia.

709 *La Grange County*

A home of the Marquis de Lafayette (1757–1834)— On December 28, 1818, the state of Indiana created and named Fayette County in honor of America's French friend, the Marquis de Lafayette. Later, in 1832, when this county was being created, the legislature considered several names for it: La Grange, Warsaw, De Kalb, Ray and Tecumseh. The legislators selected the name La Grange to honor Lafayette a second time. La Grange was the name of the country estate, about 40 miles from Paris, France, which the Marquis de Lafayette owned. De Kalb was later used as the name for one of Indiana's counties but Warsaw, Ray and Tecumseh were never used as county names in Indiana.

710 *La Porte County*

French words for "the door" for a natural opening in the forest here— The French were the first White residents of this region and La Porte County's name is a direct heritage from them. *La Porte* means "the door" and here it referred to a natural opening or corridor through the forest which connected two prairies. The present Door Village in La Porte County was the site of such a natural opening in the forest. This county was created in 1832. Legend has it that during discussion of the proposed name for the new county, one of the legislators argued that if "door" was the meaning "Why not call it Door County at once and let these high-flown, aristocratic French names alone?" But the curmudgeon's advice was not taken and Indiana's place name roster is the richer for it.

711 *Lake County*

Lake Michigan— Lake County was named for Lake Michigan, which borders the county on the north. This lake is one of the five Great Lakes and, until Alaska was admitted to statehood, Lake Michigan's 22,400 square miles made it the largest freshwater lake that was completely inside the United States. The St. Lawrence Seaway provides Lake Michigan with access to world ports. The lake's name is a corruption of an Indian name meaning "big, vast" or "monstrous lake."

712 *Lawrence County*

James Lawrence (1781–1813)— Lawrence was an officer in the United States navy who established a reputation for bravery in the war against Tripoli and in the War of 1812. He died in combat while commanding the *Chesapeake* against the British near Boston. He is said to have uttered the famous phrase "Don't give up the ship" while he lay mortally wounded in that battle. This county was created in 1818.

713 *Madison County*

James Madison (1751–1836)— Madison was born in Virginia, served in the Virginia legislature and in the Continental Congress. He was a member of the convention which framed the U.S. Constitution and he collaborated with Hamilton and Jay in writing a series of papers under the title *The Federalist* which explained the new constitution and advocated its adoption. Madison represented Virginia in the U.S. House of Representatives, served for eight years as secretary of state and for eight years as president of the United States. Madison County was created in 1823.

714 *Marion County*

Francis Marion (–1795)— Marion is believed to have been born in South Carolina. He served in the army in battles against the Cherokee Indians and was elected to the provisional congress of 1775. He served, with distinction, as an officer in the Revolutionary War and rose to the rank of general in that war. Marion was also a member of the South Carolina senate. This county was created in 1821. It was originally proposed that its name be Centre County on account of its location at the geographic center of the state. However, the name was changed to Marion County by amendment in the state senate.

715 *Marshall County*

John Marshall (1755–1835)— Marshall, a native of Virginia, served as an officer in the Revolutionary War, in the Virginia legislature and in the U.S. House of Representatives. He briefly served as secretary of state and then, for over 30 years, was chief justice of the U.S. Supreme Court. Marshall's interpretations of the constitution during America's political infancy left an unmatched impact on the laws and government of this country. Under Marshall, the supreme court shifted power in American government from the states to the central government and to the federal judiciary at the expense of the executive and legislative branches.

716 *Martin County*

Uncertain— It is not known who Martin County, Indiana's name honors. The two most frequently mentioned possibilities are John P. Martin of Kentucky and Thomas Martin, also of Kentucky.

John P. Martin (1811–1862)— A native of Virginia, John P. Martin moved to Harlan County, Kentucky, in 1828. About seven years later he settled in Floyd County, Kentucky, which thereafter was his home. He served in both houses of the Kentucky legislature and represented Kentucky in the U.S. House of Representatives. Most accounts refer to him as a "colonel." It is certain that Martin County, Kentucky, was named for him but it is not very likely that Martin County, Indiana, was because it was created in January, 1820, when John P. Martin was still a young boy.

Thomas Martin (–1819)— Thomas Martin, of Newport, Kentucky, fought in the American Revolution and attained the rank of major. He died in January, 1819.

Other possibilities that have been mentioned include:

Jeremiah Martin, a Kentucky volunteer in the War of 1812, from Maysville, Kentucky. He fought in the battle of the Thames.

Thomas E. Martin, one of Martin County, Indiana's first road supervisors and a resident of the county at the time that it was created.

Asa Martin, who is buried in a family cemetery near the old town of Hindostan, Indiana (now spelled Hindustan) in Monroe County.

There is no solid reason to believe that the correct namesake is any one of the five possibilities mentioned here.

717 Miami County

Miami Indians— This county was created in 1832 and named for the Miami Indians, a major tribe who lived in Wisconsin and, rather briefly, in Michigan. They later inhabited northern Illinois, this area of northern Indiana and a portion of northwestern Ohio. By 1840 most Miami Indians had been forced to move west by the encroaching Whites. Most of the Miami were first moved to Kansas. They were later resettled from Kansas to reservations in Oklahoma and California. The origin and meaning of the name Miami is uncertain and disputed. Possibilities which have been mentioned by authorities on Indian names include:

— People of the peninsula
— Pigeon
— Derived from rendering by the French of the name by which the Delaware Indians called the Miami, which was *Wemiamik*. This literally meant "all beavers" or "all beaver children" but figuratively it meant "all friends" which accurately described the relationship between the Miami and Delaware Indians.

The name Miami in Florida is not related to this Indian tribe's name.

718 Monroe County

James Monroe (1758–1831)— Monroe, a native of Virginia, served in the Revolutionary War. Prior to his election as president of the United States, Monroe served in a wide variety of government posts. He served Virginia in the state legislature and as governor. He was a member of the Confederation congress and the U.S. Senate. He was minister to France and to Britain and he held two cabinet posts. As president, Monroe stressed limited government and strict construction of the constitution. He acquired Florida for the U.S. from Spain and he was the author of a policy

declaration (later known as the Monroe Doctrine) which proscribed outside interference in North and South America.

719 Montgomery County

Richard Montgomery (1738–1775)— Montgomery was born in Ireland and served with the British in the French and Indian War. He settled in New York state where he was elected to the New York provisional congress. He served as a general in the American Revolutionary army and he was killed in combat in the Revolutionary War.

720 Morgan County

Daniel Morgan (1736–1802)— Morgan was a native of the Northeast who moved to Virginia in his youth. He served as a general in the Revolutionary War and was regarded as a hero for important victories scored by his troops. After the war he served one term in congress. Morgan County was created in 1821.

721 Newton County

John Newton (–1780)— Newton was born in Charleston, South Carolina about 1752 and was the son of a pastor of a Baptist church. In 1775, early in the armed resistance to Great Britain, Newton enlisted in South Carolina's Revolutionary army. He served as piper and corporal in Captain Dunbar's company before being promoted to sergeant. In a dramatic exploit near Savannah, Georgia, Newton and his close friend, William Jasper, for whom Jasper County, Indiana, is named, rescued several Americans who were prisoners and took their guards as prisoners of war. Newton was more fortunate than his friend, Jasper, in that he survived the siege of Savannah. However, when Charleston fell to the British in 1780, Newton was taken prisoner and he died of smallpox shortly afterward. Geographic names in several of our states link the names of the two heroic sergeants, Jasper and Newton. In some states two counties are named for them and this is true in Indiana where Newton County and Jasper County are side by side in the northwestern part of the state. In other states, a county is named for one of the men and its county seat is named for the other. It had been suggested that this county be named Beaver County but that name was never officially adopted.

722 Noble County

Uncertain— This county was created on

February 7, 1835, and organized in 1836. It was named for either James Noble, a U.S. senator from Indiana or for his brother, Noah Noble, who was serving as governor of Indiana at the time that the county was created.

James Noble (1785–1831)— A native of Virginia, James Noble moved to Brookville when Indiana was still a territory. Here he practiced law and served as a judge. He also served in the territorial house of representatives and later was a member of the 1816 constitutional convention. When Indiana was admitted to statehood in 1816 James Noble became a member of the state's first legislature. That body elected him to be one of Indiana's first two U.S. senators and he represented Indiana in the U.S. Senate until his death in 1831.

Noah Noble (1794–1844)— A native of Virginia, Noah Noble moved to Brookville, Indiana where he engaged in a number of business enterprises and was sheriff of Franklin County. In 1824 he was elected to the lower house of the Indiana legislature and he later served as receiver of public monies for the Indianapolis land office. In 1831 Noah Noble was elected governor of Indiana. Reelected in 1834, Noah Noble served as the state's governor until 1837 and thus was governor when this county was created in 1835.

The two dozen sources consulted which express opinions on the origin of this county's name are about equally divided between James Noble and Noah Noble. Interestingly, none of these sources suggest that the county's name was chosen to honor both of these men.

723 Ohio County

Ohio River— Created in 1844, this county in southeastern Indiana was named for the Ohio River which forms its eastern border with the state of Kentucky. The Ohio River is one of the most important commercial rivers in the United States and it is a tributary of the Mississippi River. Formed at Pittsburgh, Pennsylvania, by the confluence of the Allegheny River and the Monongahela River, the Ohio flows generally southwestward some 981 miles before joining the Mississippi at Cairo, Illinois. The Ohio contributes more water to the Mississippi than any of its other tributaries. There is uncertainty about the origin and meaning of the river's name but many authorities believe that the name derived from an Iroquois word, *Oheo*, *Oyo*, *Ohion-hiio* or *Oyoneri* which meant "beautiful." In 1680 the French explorer, La Salle, wrote of this river "The Iroquois call it Ohio…" Other suggested meanings of the Ohio River's name include "Great river," "The river red with blood" and "White with froth."

724 *Orange County*

Orange County, North Carolina—Orange County, Indiana, was created in December, 1815, and named for the county in North Carolina from which a number of its early settlers had come. The origin of Orange County, North Carolina's name is not as easily given. It is known that Orange County, North Carolina, was created in 1752, when North Carolina was still a British colony and that its name was intended as a compliment to the English throne. But it is not known whether Orange referred directly to William of Orange, who had been King William III of England or to one of his collateral descendants.

King William III (1650–1702)—William, Prince of Orange, was born in the Netherlands. He was the grandson of King Charles I of England and in 1677 he married his cousin, Mary, who was then the presumptive heir to the English throne. In 1688 William invaded England, supported by both Dutch and English troops and on April 11, 1689 William and his wife were crowned king and queen of England. They ruled as joint sovereigns, titled King William III and Queen Mary II until Mary's death in 1694. William continued on the English throne until his death in 1702.

The title, Orange, belonged to William's family, the Nassaus, on account of a tiny pocket of independent territory within southern France, near the Rhone River, named Orange, which had earlier been an ancient Roman town. It is now merely a small city in France, 17 miles north of Avignon, France.

Most sources simply state that Orange County, North Carolina, was named for King William III (1650–1702), William of Orange. However, two authorities on North Carolina's county names, William S. Powell and Kemp P. Battle, suggest the possibility that Orange County, North Carolina, was named for a mere collateral descendant of King William III. In *The North Carolina Gazetteer*, Professor Powell reminds us that Orange County, North Carolina, was created in 1752, half a century after the death of King William III and he speculates that the county may have been named for the infant William V of Orange (1748–1806), a grandson of King George II of England. George II was king of England in 1752 when Orange County, North Carolina, was created.

William V (1748–1806)—Anne (1709–1759) was a daughter of King George II of England who married William IV (1711–1751), Prince of Orange. William V (1748–1806) was their son and thus was a grandson of King George II of England. William V (1748–1806) of Orange was not a direct descendant of King William III (1650–1702) because King William III and Queen Mary II had no children.

725 *Owen County*

Abraham Owen (1769–1811)—A native of Virginia, Owen moved to Kentucky in 1785 and served in military actions against the Indians under General James Wilkinson and General Arthur St. Clair. In 1796 Owen was a surveyor in Shelby County, Kentucky and he later served as a magistrate and in both houses of the Kentucky legislature. In 1799 he was chosen as a member of Kentucky's constitutional convention. Owen was a colonel in the Kentucky militia and he served as aide-de-camp to General William Henry Harrison at the battle of Tippecanoe, Indiana territory where he was killed in November, 1811. Tradition has it that the Indians had earlier seen General Harrison riding a white horse and when they saw Colonel Owen riding a white horse, they mistook him for the general and made him their early target. While this is conjecture, it is known that Colonel Owen was killed very early in the battle. Owen County, Indiana, was created and named in Colonel Owen's honor in 1818.

726 *Parke County*

Benjamin Parke (1777–1835)—A native of New Jersey and a lawyer, Parke served as attorney general of Indiana territory, was a member of Indiana's territorial house of representatives and was a delegate to the U.S. Congress from Indiana territory. He also served as an officer in the militia and fought at the battle of Tippecanoe. Parke was a territorial judge and a member of Indiana's state constitutional convention of 1816. Following Indiana's admission to statehood, Parke served as judge of the U.S. district court for Indiana from 1817 until his death in 1835. Parke County was created and named in his honor in 1821 while he was serving as U.S. district court judge.

727 *Perry County*

Oliver H. Perry (1785–1819)—Perry was a native of Rhode Island and an officer in the U.S. navy. During the War of 1812 his squadron defeated the British in September, 1813, in a key battle on Lake Erie of which Perry said "We have met the enemy and they are ours." This county was created one year later, in September, 1814.

728 *Pike County*

Zebulon M. Pike (1779–1813)—Pike was a native of New Jersey who served as an army officer on America's frontier following the Revolution. He led an exploratory army expedition to the Rocky Mountains which Pike's Peak in the Colorado Rockies commemorates. Pike served as a general in the War of 1812 and was killed in that war. Pike County, Indiana, was created in 1816. Some accounts of Indiana's battle of Tippecanoe list Zebulon M. Pike as a participant. That is an error. Although Pike's military unit participated in the battle of Tippecanoe, Pike, himself, did not because he was detained on duties in the Southwest in November, 1811 when that battle was fought.

729 *Porter County*

David Porter (1780–1843)—A native of Massachusetts, Porter was an officer in the U.S. navy whose successful command of the frigate *Essex* early in the War of 1812 made him a naval hero. In 1813 the British defeated Porter in the Pacific near Valparaiso, Chile. The county seat of Porter County, Indiana, was originally named Portersville but the name was changed to Valparaiso to commemorate Porter's naval battle there. Porter later served the U.S. navy in the Caribbean Sea, suppressing piracy but he resigned from the U.S. navy to serve briefly as commander-in-chief of the Mexican navy. The last years of Porter's life were spent serving the U.S. government as a diplomat in the Middle East and he died near Constantinople in 1843.

730 *Posey County*

Thomas Posey (1750–1818)—A native of Virginia and a soldier, Posey fought in the French and Indian Wars and was an officer during the American Revolution. He then served in the Northwest in actions against the Indians and was given the rank of brigadier-general in 1793. Posey moved to Kentucky in 1794 where he served in the state senate and was lieutenant-governor of Kentucky. He next moved to Louisiana and upon the resignation of one of Louisiana's U.S. senators, Posey was appointed to fill the vacancy and he briefly served in the U.S. Senate from October, 1812, until February, 1813. One month later President

James Madison appointed Thomas Posey to be governor of Indiana territory and Posey was serving in that position in September, 1814, when this county was created.

731 *Pulaski County*

Casimir Pulaski (1748–1779)— Pulaski was born in Lithuania and served in the Polish army. He came to America to assist the colonies as an officer in the Revolutionary War and died in combat in that war during the siege of Savannah, Georgia. Pulaski County, Indiana, was created in 1835.

732 *Putnam County*

Israel Putnam (1718–1790)— Putnam was born in Massachusetts and moved, when he was about 21, to Connecticut. He served as an officer in the French and Indian Wars and later was a member of the Connecticut legislature. At the beginning of the Revolutionary War, news of the battle at Lexington, Massachusetts reached Putnam while he was farming. In a dramatic gesture which became famous, Putnam left his plow and, without bothering to change clothes, hurried to Lexington. He was appointed major-general in the Continental army. Although he enjoyed great popularity, he lacked the ability for high command. In 1779 a paralytic stroke ended his military career.

733 *Randolph County*

Uncertain— Randolph County, Indiana, was created on January 10, 1818. Some sources indicate that it was named for Randolph County, North Carolina, from which some of its early settlers had come, while other sources state that the county's name honors Thomas Randolph, who was killed at the battle of Tippecanoe. One source, *The Muncie Star*, dated May 19, 1968, lists both of these possibilities and then adds a third in an article entitled "Origin of Randolph County's Name Still Not Certain 150 Years After Its Creation." The third possibility mentioned is that one of the members of the Indiana legislature at the time that Randolph County, Indiana, was created was Robert Hill, a native of Randolph County, North Dakota, and the Indiana county's name may have been chosen to honor Randolph County, North Dakota. This third possibility is easily refuted. There is no Randolph County in North Dakota now and in 1818, when Randolph County, Indiana, was created, North Dakota was an unsettled area which had no counties at all.

Randolph County, North Carolina— Randolph County, North Carolina was created while the American Revolution was in progress and it was named for Peyton Randolph.

Peyton Randolph (–1775)— Peyton Randolph was born in Virginia about 1721 and educated at the College of William and Mary there. He studied law in England and served as the king's attorney for Virginia. Peyton Randolph was a member of colonial Virginia's house of burgesses for some 25 years and he played a leading role in the events which led to our Declaration of Independence. Randolph represented Virginia in the Continental Congress and was the first president of that body.

Thomas Randolph (–1811)— Thomas Randolph, a cousin of Thomas Jefferson, served in the Virginia legislature and later moved to Indiana territory. Soon after his arrival he was appointed attorney general of Indiana territory. He was an unsuccessful candidate for delegate to the U.S. Congress from Indiana territory. Thomas Randolph later served as a private in the Indiana militia and was killed at the battle of Tippecanoe in November, 1811.

734 *Ripley County*

Eleazar W. Ripley (1782–1839)— A native of New Hampshire and a graduate of Dartmouth College there, Ripley was a lawyer who became active in politics in Massachusetts where he served in both houses of the state legislature. Ripley entered the army as an officer when the War of 1812 began and received rapid promotions for distinguished service in that war. In July, 1814 he was made brevet major-general and later that year he was severely wounded in combat. When he resigned from the army in 1820, Ripley settled in Louisiana where he again became active in politics, serving in the state senate and representing Louisiana in the U.S. House of Representatives. Ripley County, Indiana, was created and named in his honor in December, 1816.

735 *Rush County*

Benjamin Rush (1745–1813)— A native of Pennsylvania and a graduate of the College of New Jersey (now Princeton University), Rush was a medical doctor. An agitator for both the abolition of slavery and independence of the American colonies from England, Dr. Rush represented Pennsylvania in the Continental Congress and was one of the signers of our Declaration of Independence. During the Revolution, Rush served briefly as surgeon-general of the armies of the middle department. After the war, Dr. Rush was a member of the Pennsylvania convention which ratified the proposed constitution of the United States. Rush County, Indiana, was created in December, 1821. Its name was suggested by Dr. William B. Laughlin, a leading citizen of the area and a former pupil of Dr. Benjamin Rush. Dr. Laughlin was a member of the Indiana legislature in December, 1821, and he was responsible for the legislative act which named this new county for Dr. Rush.

736 *Saint Joseph County*

Saint Joseph River— Saint Joseph County, Indiana was created in 1830 and named for the Saint Joseph River which flows through it. This Saint Joseph River is some 210 miles long. It rises in Hillsdale County in southern Michigan, flows in a southwestern direction across Michigan and into Indiana. In Indiana the Saint Joseph makes an abrupt turn at the city of South Bend, Indiana, which is the county seat of Saint Joseph County, and then flows due north for about six miles to reenter the state of Michigan. From there it flows in a northwestern direction across Michigan finally ending at Lake Michigan. There are three Saint Joseph Rivers in this general region. Saint Joseph County, Indiana, was named for the one that has the sharp bend at the city of South Bend, Indiana. This Saint Joseph River's name derived from the name of a French fort that was built on a high bluff near the banks of the Saint Joseph River where the city of Niles, Michigan is now located. This fort, named Fort Saint Joseph or Fort Saint Joseph's, had been named for the Mission of Saint Joseph which had been built here by Father Allouez somewhat earlier. Together the mission and the fort comprised an important French post for commerce and for missionary activity among the Indians. It is not known for whom the mission was named. Some accounts speculate that the name honored the Saint Joseph who in Catholic theology was the husband of Saint Mary, the virgin mother of Jesus. Other sources indicate that a Roman Catholic priest named Father Joseph was an early settler in the area and a leader in French missionary work here. These sources imply that the mission was named for him and that "Saint Joseph" was merely a euphemism that referred to Father Joseph.

737 *Scott County*

Charles Scott (1739–1813)— A native of Virginia, Scott served in the Continental army during the American Revolution and rose to the rank of brevet major-general. After the Revolution he moved to Kentucky and commanded Kentucky troops in campaigns against the Indians. Scott also served in the Virginia assembly while Kentucky was still part of Virginia. In 1808 Scott was elected governor of Kentucky and he served in that position until 1812. Scott County, Indiana, was created in 1820.

738 *Shelby County*

Isaac Shelby (1750–1826)— Shelby was a delegate to the Virginia legislature and, later, to the North Carolina legislature. He served as a soldier in the Revolutionary War and then moved to Kentucky County, Virginia where he was active in the movement to separate Kentucky from Virginia. Shelby was inaugurated as Kentucky's first governor on the same day that Kentucky became a state. He also fought in the War of 1812.

739 *Spencer County*

Spear Spencer (–1811)— This native of Kentucky came to Vincennes, Indiana territory about 1809. He subsequently moved to Corydon, Indiana territory where he became the first sheriff of Harrison County. He also ran a tavern in Corydon, the Oak Street Tavern. Spencer served as a captain in Indiana's 1811 battle of Tippecanoe. Because the company which he had organized had yellow trimmed uniforms, they were called "Spencer's Yellow Jackets." Captain Spencer displayed unusual heroism at the battle of Tippecanoe and he died in combat there. In General William Henry Harrison's official report of this battle, he told that Captain Spencer was first wounded in the head and then in both thighs but continued to exhort his mounted riflemen to fight valiantly until a final shot through his body ended his life. Spencer County, Indiana, was created in January, 1818, less than seven years after the battle of Tippecanoe. Daniel Grass was a member of the Indiana legislature at that time and he had been Spencer's friend. Grass played a leading role in the selection of Spencer County's name. President Abraham Lincoln lived in Spencer County, Indiana, when he was a boy and in the late 1950's a movement was organized to change the county's name from Spencer County to Lincoln County in connection with the sesquicentennial celebration of Abraham Lincoln's birth. That movement failed and Indiana still has no county named in honor of Abraham Lincoln.

740 *Starke County*

John Stark (1728–1822)— A native of New Hampshire, Stark served as an officer during the French and Indian War. He later became a hero during the American Revolution winning fame at Breed's Hill, Fort Edward, Trenton, Princeton and Bennington and he rose to the rank of brevet major-general. Starke County was created in 1835. The county's name ends with an "e" which John Stark did not use in rendering his name.

741 *Steuben County*

Friedrich Wilhelm August Heinrich Ferdinand von Steuben (1730–1794)— Known in America as Baron von Steuben or Baron de Steuben, this military man was born in Prussia, entered the Prussian army at the age of 17 and served in it throughout the Seven Years' War. He rose to the position of general staff officer and aide-de-camp to King Frederick the Great at royal headquarters. In 1777 Baron von Steuben came to America to serve in our Continental army. As inspector general, he introduced badly needed Prussian methods of military efficiency and discipline to our ragtag troops and trained them in the skills required for effective combat. As the war progressed, his prestige rose and General George Washington consulted him on a variety of questions of strategic and administrative policy. At the end of the war Baron von Steuben became an American citizen and he was a resident of New York at the time of his death in 1794.

742 *Sullivan County*

Uncertain— Sullivan County, Indiana was created on December 30, 1816. Most sources state that the county was named for Daniel Sullivan, who was killed by Indians in 1790 but a few sources say that the county's name honors the American Revolutionary General John Sullivan. If there had been early records in the Sullivan County courthouse to resolve this conflict, they no longer exist for all of those records were destroyed when the county courthouse burned on February 7, 1850.

Daniel Sullivan (–1790)— Daniel Sullivan came to Vincennes in what is now southwestern Indiana in 1785 and in the following year he settled Sullivan's Station on the Patoka River. Sullivan had a violent disposition as well as a dubious character and he conducted raids against local Indians. The French and Indians here hated him. He was killed by Indians in 1790 while carrying public papers between Vincennes

and Louisville. There was another Daniel Sullivan living in what is now southwestern Indiana at about the same time who served as sheriff of Knox County. This man may have been a son of our Daniel Sullivan but he was certainly not the same man for he served as sheriff of Knox County in the early 1800's and our hero was killed by the Indians in 1790.

John Sullivan (1740–1795)— The location of John Sullivan's birth is given variously as Berwick, Maine and Somersworth, New Hampshire. The two towns are adjacent. He practiced law in New Hampshire and represented New Hampshire in the Continental Congress. During the American Revolution he served as a brigadier-general and later was promoted to major-general. John Sullivan served with distinction in a number of the important engagements of the Revolution until late 1779 when he resigned. He then represented New Hampshire again in the Continental Congress. Sullivan later served as attorney general of New Hampshire, president (or governor) of New Hampshire and he was a member of the New Hampshire convention that ratified the proposed federal constitution. He also was speaker of New Hampshire's house of representatives. In 1789 President George Washington appointed John Sullivan as judge of the U.S. district court of New Hampshire and Sullivan held that position until his death in 1795.

743 *Switzerland County*

The European country, Switzerland— In 1796, John James Dufour, who was a native of Switzerland, selected land in this area, suitable for the cultivation of grapes. Under his leadership a group of 17 colonists came here from Switzerland arriving about 1801 or 1802. Several of the 17 were also named Dufour and one of those was John Francis Dufour. They called their new communal home here in southeastern Indiana territory New Switzerland. Later, in 1814, when this county was created, the territorial legislators gave John Francis Dufour the privilege of selecting the new county's name. He chose Switzerland in honor of the colonists' home country in Europe. Switzerland is a small country, noted for its mountains, the Alps, its tradition of neutrality in Europe's many wars and its economic prosperity. Most of the Swiss people speak German but both French and Italian are also used. This country derived its name from the small forest canton called Schwyz, which was one of three cantons from which the country was built. The origin and meaning of the word, *Schwyz* is uncertain but two possibilities that have been mentioned are:

1. An old high German word *suedan* which meant "to burn," possibly given on account of a memorable forest fire here.

2. The old German word for "sweat" which contains an old German "s" superimposed on an old German "c" following *schwei*. This name may have been given because of the numerous springs at the bases of the mountains.

744 *Tippecanoe County*

Uncertain—Although several Indiana counties were named in honor of heroes of the battle of Tippecanoe and although that battle was fought within Tippecanoe County less than 15 years before this county was created in 1826, it is not clear that Tippecanoe County was named for that battle. The battle of Tippecanoe, which was named for the Tippecanoe River, was fought here near the junction of the Tippecanoe River with the Wabash River on November 7, 1811. However, few sources state that the county was named for the battle. Rather, the origin of Tippecanoe County's name is given by various sources as:

Tippecanoe River or Tippecanoe battleground

— Tippecanoe River and Tippecanoe battleground

— Tippecanoe River

— Tippecanoe battleground

— Tippecanoe River and the battle of Tippecanoe

Battle of Tippecanoe & Tippecanoe battleground—During the summer of 1811, Indian raids had created fear among White frontier settlers which induced General William Henry Harrison, Indiana's territorial governor, to take the initiative against the Indians and the battle of Tippecanoe was that initiative. Although Harrison's troops suffered heavy losses, they finally beat back the Indians and razed the Indians' nearby village. This battle was considered a victory for the American forces and although it failed to end the Indian threat along the frontier here, it strengthened American morale and helped make Harrison a national hero. Later, in December, 1839, Harrison became the Whig party's candidate for president with John Tyler as his vice-presidential running mate. Their famous campaign slogan was "Tippecanoe and Tyler too." The battleground has been preserved as a state memorial about seven miles northeast of Lafayette, Indiana.

Tippecanoe River—A tributary of the Wabash River, the Tippecanoe rises in Tippecanoe Lake north of Warsaw, Indiana. It then flows west and south on a crooked course some 200 miles before entering the Wabash in Tippecanoe County near the Tippecanoe battleground. The river's name is of Indian origin but its meaning is uncertain. "Tippecanoe" may be a corruption of the Potawatomi Indians' *ketapekonnong*, which meant "town" or "place" and was the name of an Indian town below the mouth of the river. The Miami Indians' name for the river was *ketapkwon*, meaning "buffalo fish" which were common in the Tippecanoe River.

745 *Tipton County*

John Tipton (1786–1839)—Tipton was born in 1786 on land that is now within the state of Tennessee and he moved to Indiana territory in 1807. He entered the militia as a private and less than one month before the battle of Tippecanoe he attained the rank of ensign. Tipton served in Captain Spear Spencer's company in the battle of Tippecanoe and was promoted to the rank of captain during the battle. When John Tipton later became powerful in Indiana politics, he influenced the legislature to name several Indiana counties for heroes of the battle of Tippecanoe. Tipton subsequently attained the rank of major-general in the militia. He served in the lower house of the Indiana legislature and he represented Indiana in the U.S. Senate from 1831 until his death in 1839. Tipton County was created and named in Senator Tipton's honor in 1844.

746 *Union County*

Uncertain—Sources differ on the origin of this county's name. Possibilities mentioned include:

— The union of states which comprise the United States of America.

— A general gesture of patriotism and harmony.

— Symbolical of union of interests.

— Named for an early town in this area, named Union, that had been established before 1810 on the east bank of Hanna's Creek.

— Name suggested by the method in which Union County was formed with land taken to form it from three adjacent counties, Franklin, Wayne and Fayette.

— Named in recognition (or hope) that creation of this new county would settle conflicting territorial and other claims among the three counties which had land taken from them to form Union County.

— Name selected to harmonize and discourage county seat fights which had taken place in nearby Wayne and Fayette Counties. This possibility, which is cited by a number of sources, has the ring of plausibility to it. Normally, when a new county and its county seat are created, the selection of the new county's name stirs little interest but bitter disputes often attend the selection of the county seat for it is there that the seat of justice will reside generating jobs and money. Union County, Indiana was created on January 5, 1821. It is bordered on the north by Wayne County, created about ten years earlier and on the west by Fayette County, which was created just two years before Union County's birth. The memory of bitter county seat fights in these counties certainly could have prompted the selection of Union for the new county's name. The town of Brownsville, Indiana, was selected as the original county seat of Union County. Ironically, agitation started almost immediately and the county seat of Union County was moved to the town of Liberty, Indiana, in 1823.

747 *Vanderburgh County*

Henry Vanderburgh (1760–1812)—A native of Troy, New York, Vanderburgh served as an officer during the American Revolution and rose to the rank of captain. Soon after the war ended he moved to Vincennes. In 1791 Arthur St. Clair, who was governor of the Northwest territory, appointed Vanderburgh justice of the peace and judge of the probate court of Knox County, which at that time was enormous. He later served on the legislative council of Northwest territory and was president of that council. Indiana territory was created in 1800 and Judge Vanderburgh was selected as one of the first judges over the new territory. He served as a territorial judge until his death in 1812. This county was created and named in his honor in 1818. "Vanderburg" is given as the spelling of both Henry Vanderburgh's name and the county's name by some sources. The Indiana Board on Geographic Names ruled on June 15, 1962, that "Vanderburgh" is the official spelling of the county's name and the county officials' current letterhead spells the name that way.

748 *Vermillion County*

Vermilion River—There are two main rivers in Illinois named Vermilion, neither of which is very long. One is a tributary of the Illinois River, some 50 miles in length, which is formed by the junction of two forks in Livingston County, Illinois. Vermillion County, Indiana, was named for the other Vermilion River, the main stream of which is but 28 miles long. It is formed by the union of three forks, the North, Middle and South Forks, all of which rise in Illinois and come together near Danville, the county seat of Vermilion County, Illinois. It then flows to the southeast into Vermillion County, Indiana, where it enters the Wabash River. There is also a Little Vermilion River which enters the Wabash about seven or eight miles below our Vermilion River and ours is sometimes called the Big Vermilion to distinguish between the two. *Vermilion* is an English word derived from the French language which denotes a variety of shades of bright red color averaging a vivid reddish orange. The Vermilion River was so named on account of the fine red earth which colors its waters. Its earlier French name was Vermillion Jaune. Both Vermillion County, Indiana (two l's) and Vermilion County, Illinois (one l's) were named for the same river. At least one source claims that the Indiana county was named for the Illinois county. That is incorrect since the Indiana county was created two years before the Illinois county was created.

749 *Vigo County*

Joseph Maria Francesco Vigo (1747–1836)— Vigo was born on the island of Sardinia in the Mediterranean Sea, west of the Italian peninsula. Known in this country as Colonel Francis Vigo, he came to America as a private in the Spanish army but quit the army in 1772 to engage in fur trading at Saint Louis. He acquired some wealth from these activities and during the American Revolution Vigo provided extensive supplies to the destitute American army of George Rogers Clark. He also served as a spy for Clark and assisted Clark in the capture of Vincennes. Vigo County, Indiana, was created and named in his honor in 1818 while Francis Vigo was still alive. In gratitude for this honor, Vigo set aside $500.00 in his will for the purchase of a bell to be hung in the Vigo County courthouse at Terre Haute.

750 *Wabash County*

Wabash River— This county was named for the major river which flows through it. The Wabash rises in western Ohio and flows some 475 miles through mostly rich farm land before emptying into the Ohio River at the tri-state junction where Kentucky, Indiana and Illinois meet. In its journey it crosses Indiana and forms the southern portion of the border between Indiana and Illinois. The origin of the river's name is uncertain but it was rendered by the French as *Ouabachei* or *Ouabachi* which are believed to derive from an Indian name *Wahbuhshikki* or perhaps *Wabaciki* or *Wapaciki* meaning "pure white" or "white stone river." The Indians bestowed this name on the Wabash on account of the river's white limestone bed in its upper part. However, there is another theory: that the name derived from *Wabashkisibi* which meant "bog river."

751 *Warren County*

Joseph Warren (1741–1775)— This county was created in 1827 and named in honor of the American Revolutionary War hero, Joseph Warren. A native of Massachusetts and a graduate of Harvard College, Warren practiced medicine in the Boston area. He was a member of the committee of safety and president *pro tempore* of the Massachusetts provincial congress. In June, 1775 he was commissioned a major-general and he died in combat a few days later at the battle of Bunker Hill.

752 *Warrick County*

Jacob Warrick (–1811)— Warrick came to Indiana territory from Kentucky and was associated with Ratliff Boon in attempting to bring civilization to the country here just north of the Ohio River. He later served as a captain in the battle of Tippecanoe and died in combat there. In General William Henry Harrison's official report of the battle of Tippecanoe he reported that "Warwick [sic] was shot through the body; being taken to the surgeon to be dressed, as soon as it was over, (being a man of great bodily vigor and still able to walk) he insisted upon going back to head his company although it was evident that he had but a few hours to live." Captain Warrick died in November, 1811, and this county was created and named in his honor just 16 months later, in March, 1813.

753 *Washington County*

George Washington (1732–1799)— Washington was a native of Virginia. He served in Virginia's house of burgesses and became one of the colonies' leaders in opposition to British policies in America. He was a member of the first and second Continental Congresses and commander of all Continental armies in the Revolutionary War. Following victory in that war, Washington was elected to be the first president of the United States.

754 *Wayne County*

Anthony Wayne (1745–1796)— A native of Pennsylvania, Wayne was a successful brigadier-general in the Revolutionary War and became a hero for his daring exploits. During the bitter winter of 1777-1778 at Valley Forge, Pennsylvania, Wayne shared the sufferings of his men although his comfortable estate was only five miles away. He played an important role in the final overthrow of the British forces in Georgia. After the war, in 1785, Wayne moved to Georgia and he represented Georgia for about six months in the U.S. House of Representatives. In 1792 President Washington recalled Wayne to serve as a major-general against the Indians in the Northwest territory. Once again his military efforts were successful.

755 *Wells County*

William Wells (–1812)— In 1774, when William Wells was a boy of about eight years of age and living in what is now the state of Kentucky, he was kidnapped by a band of Miami Indians who raised him as one of their own. Wells adopted the Indians' ways and became a favorite of the influential Chief Little Turtle and married into the chief's family. Wells fought with the Indians against the Americans and acted as the Indians' interpreter in treaty negotiations with the Whites. However, he eventually left the Indians and joined his own people serving the Americans as an Indian agent and as a captain in the American army. Ironically, Wells lost his life at the hands of Indians in 1812 during an attempt to evacuate Fort Dearborn at the beginning of the War of 1812.

756 *White County*

Isaac White (–1811)— This hero of the battle of Tippecanoe was born in Virginia about 1776 and lived there until approximately 1800 when he moved with his brother, Thomas to Vincennes in what is now Indiana. By 1805 he had moved to what is now Illinois and was placed in charge of the salt works at Saline Creek as agent for the United States by Territorial Governor William Henry Harrison. These salt works were contiguous to the village of Equality in what is now Gallatin County, Illinois. Although slavery was generally illegal here in the Northwest territory, Isaac White owned some slaves. About 1806 he was appointed a captain in the militia and by February, 1809, he had risen to the rank of colonel. In November, 1811, Isaac White was killed in combat by Indians in the battle of Tippecanoe in Indiana territory.

757 *Whitley County*

William Whitley (1749–1813) — A native of Virginia, Whitley decided as a young man to seek his fortune in the wilderness country which is now the state of Kentucky. He first explored Kentucky between 1775 and 1780 and shortly afterward he moved his family from Virginia proper to the Kentucky country. In Kentucky he engaged in seemingly endless actions against the Indians and accounts of these various Indian actions refer to Whitley as captain, major and colonel. By the time the War of 1812 began, William Whitley had reached the age of about 63. Nevertheless, he volunteered to serve as a private in the Kentucky militia in the War of 1812 and he died in combat in October, 1813, during the American victory over the British and Indians in the battle of the River Thames in Canada.

REFERENCES

Ade, John. *Newton County.* Indianapolis, Bobbs-Merrill Co., 1911.

Alexander, Mary M. & Capitola G. Dill. *Sketches of Rush County, Indiana.* Rushville, Indiana, Jacksonian Publishing Co., 1915.

Anderson, Emil V. *Taproots of Elkhart History.* Elkhart Indiana Daily Truth, 1949.

Atlas of Union County, Indiana: 1884. Chicago, J. H. Beers & Co., 1884.

Baird, Lewis C. *Baird's History of Clark County, Indiana.* Indianapolis, B.F. Bowen & Co., 1909.

Baker, Ronald L. "County Names in Indiana." *Indiana Names*, Vol. 2, No. 2. Terre Haute, Indiana: Fall, 1971.

Baker, Ronald L., & Marvin Carmony. *Indiana Place Names.* Bloomington, Indiana University Press, 1975.

Bald, F. Clever. "Colonel John Francis Hamtramck." *Indiana Magazine of History*, Vol. 44, No. 4. Bloomington, Indiana: December, 1948.

Ball, T. H. *Northwestern Indiana: From 1800 to 1900.* 1900.

Banta, D.D. *A Historical Sketch of Johnson County, Indiana.* Chicago, J. H. Beers & Co., 1881.

Barger, Harry D. *Teaching Indiana History: A Handbook.* 1983.

Barnhart, John D. "A New Letter About the Massacre at Fort Dearborn." *Indiana Magazine of History*, Vol. 41, No. 2. Bloomington, Indiana: June 1945.

Barnhart, John D., & Dorothy L. Riker. *Indiana to 1816: The Colonial Period.* Indianapolis, Indiana Historical Bureau & Indiana Historical Society, 1971.

Barr, Arvil S. "Warrick County Prior to 1818." *Indiana Magazine of History*, Vol. 14, No. 4. Bloomington, Indiana: December, 1918.

Bartholomew, H. S. *Stories & Sketches of Elkhart County.* Nappanee, Indiana, E. V. Publishing House, 1936.

Bartholomew, Henry S. *Pioneer History of Elkhart County, Indiana.* Goshen, Indiana, Goshen Printery, 1930.

Battle, Kemp P. "Glimpses of History in the Names of Our Counties." *The North Carolina Booklet*, Vol. 6. July, 1906.

Battle, Kemp P. "North Carolina County Names." *The Magazine of History*, Vol. 7, No. 4. New York: April, 1908.

Beard, Reed. *The Battle of Tippecanoe.* Lafayette, Indiana, 1889.

Beckwith, H. W. *History of Vigo & Parke Counties.* Chicago, H. H. Hill & N. Iddings, 1880.

The Biographical Encyclopaedia of Kentucky. Cincinnati, J. M Armstrong & Co., 1878.

Biographical & Historical Souvenir for the Counties of Clark, Crawford, Harrison, Floyd, Jefferson, Jennings, Scott & Washington, Indiana. Chicago, John M. Gresham & Co., 1889.

Biographical Record of Bartholomew & Jackson Counties, Indiana. B. F. Bowen, 1904.

Blanchard, Charles. *Counties of Clay & Owen, Indiana.* Chicago, F. A. Battey & Co, 1884.

Branigan, Elba L. *History of Johnson County, Indiana.* Indianapolis, B.F. Bowen & Co., 1913.

Brice, Wallace A. *History of Fort Wayne.* Fort Wayne, Indiana, D. W. Jones & Son, Steam Book & Job Printers, 1868.

Brolley, Thomas W. *State of Indiana Bureau of Statistics: Fourteenth Biennial Report for 1911 & 1912.* Indianapolis, William B. Burford, 1913.

Cauthorn, Henry S. *A History of the City of Vincennes, Indiana from 1702 to 1901.* Terre Haute, Indiana, Moore & Langen Printing Co., 1902.

Chamberlain, E. *The Indiana Gazetteer.* Indianapolis, 1849.

Cheney, John L. *North Carolina Manual: 1977.* Raleigh.

Clements, John. *Indiana Facts.* Dallas, Texas, Clements Research, Inc., 1987.

Clift, G. Glenn. *Remember the Raisin!* Frankfort, Kentucky, Kentucky Historical Society, 1961.

Cline, George. *An Educational History of Tipton County, Indiana.* Tipton, Indiana, 1962.

Cockrum, William M. *Pioneer History of Indiana.* Oakland City, Indiana, Press of Oakland City Journal, 1907.

Collins, Lewis. *History of Kentucky.* Louisville, Kentucky, 1877.

Conard, Howard L. *Encyclopedia of the History of Missouri.* New York, Southern History Co., 1901.

Conklin, Julia S. *The Young People's History of Indiana.* Young People's Indiana History Co., 1900.

Corbitt, David L. *The Formation of the North Carolina Counties: 1663–1943.* Raleigh, State Department of Archives & History, 1950.

Counties of Warren, Benton, Jasper & Newton, Indiana: Historical & Biographical. Chicago, F. A. Battey & Co., 1883.

Crittenden, Charles C. & Dan Lacy. *The Historical Records of North Carolina.* Raleigh, North Carolina Historical Commission, 1938.

Danglade, Annette. "Early Days in Switzerland County." *Indiana Magazine of History*, Vol. 13, No. 2. Bloomington: June, 1917.

DeHart, R. P. *Past & Present of Tippecanoe County, Indiana.* Indianapolis, B.F. Bowen & Co., 1909.

Donehoo, George P. *A History of the Indian Villages & Place Names in Pennsylvania.* Harrisburg, Pennsylvania, Telegraph Press, 1928.

Dufour, Perret. *The Swiss Settlement of Switzerland County, Indiana.* Indianapolis, Indiana Historical Commission, 1925.

Dunn, Jacob P. "Indiana Geographical Nomenclature." *Indiana Magazine of History*, Vol. 8, No. 3. Indianapolis: September, 1912.

Dunn, Jacob P. *Indiana & Indianans.* Chicago, American Historical Society, 1919.

Dunn, Jacob P. *True Indian Stories with Glossary of Indiana Indian Names.* Indianapolis, Sentinel Printing Co., 1908.

Eastby, Allen G. "The Baron." *American History Illustrated*, Vol. 25, No. 5. Harrisburg, Pennsylvania: November-December, 1990.

"Editorial & Miscellaneous: Local History Contributions." *Indiana Magazine of History*, Vol. 2, No. 1. Indianapolis: March, 1906.

Elliott, Joseph P. *A History of Evansville & Vanderburgh County, Indiana.* Evansville, Indiana, Keller Printing Co., 1897.

"Empire Builders Memorialized in Katterjohn Work." *The Evansville Courier*, March 13, 1938.

The Encyclopedia Americana. New York, Americana Corporation, 1977.

Esarey, Logan. *History of Indiana*. New York, Harcourt, Brace & Co., 1922.

Esarey, Logan. *History of Indiana from Its Exploration to 1922: Also a History of Tippecanoe County & the Wabash Valley*. Dayton, Ohio, National Historical Association, Inc., 1928.

Feeger, Luther M. "Boundaries of Wayne County & Its Townships." *Indiana Magazine of History*, Vol. 24, No. 1. Bloomington: March, 1928.

Feightner, Harold C. "Indiana County Government." *Indiana History Bulletin*, Vol. 9, No. 6. Indianapolis: March, 1932.

Ferris, Robert G. *Founders & Frontiersmen*. Washington, D.C., United States Department of the Interior, National Park Service, 1967.

Findings of the Indiana Board on Geographic Names: May, 1961 Through June, 1962. Indianapolis, Indiana Board on Geographic Names, 1963.

Ford, Ira, et al. *History of Northeast Indiana*. Chicago, Lewis Publishing Co., 1920.

"Forgotten Hoosiers, No. 8: Isaac Blackford, Pioneer Jurist." *Teaching Indiana History*, Vol. 2. No. 1. Indiana Historical Society, September & October, 1963.

Fortune, Will. *Warrick & Its Prominent People*. 1881.

Fox, George R. "Place Names of Berrien County." *Michigan History Magazine*, Vol. 8, No. 1. Lansing: January, 1924.

Fulkerson, A. O. *History of Daviess County, Indiana*. Indianapolis, B.F. Bowen & Co., Inc., 1915.

Gary, A. L., & E. B. Thomas. *Centennial History of Rush County, Indiana*. Indianapolis, Historical Publishing Co., 1921.

Goodrich, DeWitt C., & Charles R. Tuttle. *An Illustrated History of the State of Indiana*. Indianapolis, Richard S. Peale & Co., 1875.

Gookins, S. B. *1880 History of Vigo County, Indiana*. Chicago, H. H. Hill & N. Iddings, 1880.

Greene, George E. *History of Old Vincennes & Knox County, Indiana*. Chicago, S. J. Clarke Publishing Co., 1911.

Griswold, B. J. *The Pictorial History of Fort Wayne, Indiana*. Chicago, Robert O. Law Co., 1917.

Guthrie, James M. *A Selection of Newspaper Articles Entitled Sesquicentennial Scrapbook*. Indiana Sesquicentennial Commission, 1966.

Guthrie, Wayne. "Inside Hoosierland: Floyd County's Name Puzzles Historians." *Indianapolis News*, August 15, 1961.

Guthrie, Wayne. "Ringside in Hoosierland: Lagrange Worth Extended Visit." *Indianapolis News*, September 13, 1967.

Guthrie, Wayne. "Ringside Hoosier-land: Martin County's Naming Is Puzzle." *Indianapolis News*, May 20, 1974.

"Harrison's Report on the Battle of Tippecanoe." *Teaching Indiana History*, Vol. 2, No. 1. Indiana Historical Society, September & October, 1963.

Haymond, W. S. *An Illustrated History of the State of Indiana*. Indianapolis, S. L. Marrow & Co., 1879.

Helderman, L. C. "The Northwest Expedition of George Rogers Clark, 1786-1787." *Mississippi Valley Historical Review*, Vol. 25, No. 3. December, 1938.

Helderman, Leonard C. "Danger on Wabash: Vincennes Letters of 1786." *Indiana Magazine of History*, Vol. 34, No. 4. Bloomington: December, 1938.

Helm, Thomas B. *History of Cass County, Indiana*. Chicago, Brant & Fuller, 1886.

Here Is Your Indiana Government. Indianapolis, Indiana Chamber of Commerce, 1989.

Historic Background of South Bend & St. Joseph County in Northern Indiana. South Bend, Indiana, Schuyler Colfax Chapter Daughters of the American Revolution, 1927.

History of Allen County, Indiana. Chicago, Kingman Brothers, 1880.

History of Bartholomew County, Indiana: 1888. Columbus, Indiana, Bartholomew County, Historical Society, 1976.

History of Gibson County, Indiana. Edwardsville, Illinois, Jas. T. Tart & Co., 1884.

History of Grant County, Indiana. Chicago, Brant & Fuller, 1886.

History of the Ohio Falls Cities & Their Counties. Cleveland, L. A. Williams & Co., 1882.

History of Pike & Dubois Counties, Indiana. Chicago, Goodspeed Bros. & Co., 1885.

"History of Sullivan County, Indiana." *Sullivan County Historical Society Newsletter*, Vol. 7, No. 5. Sullivan, Indiana: September, 1980.

History of Vanderburgh County, Indiana. Brant & Fuller, 1889.

History of Warrick & Its Prominent People. Boonville, Indiana, Crescent Publication Co., 1909.

History of Warrick, Spencer & Perry Counties, Indiana. Chicago, Goodspeed Bros. & Co., 1885.

Hixson, Jerome C. "Some Approaches to Indiana Place Names." *Indiana Names*, Vol. 1, No. 1. Terre Haute, Indiana: Spring, 1970.

Holt, Harry Q. *History of Martin County, Indiana*. Paoli, Indiana, Stout's Print Shop, 1953.

Howard, Timothy E. *A History of St. Joseph County, Indiana*. Chicago, Lewis Publishing Co., 1907.

Howe, Daniel W. "A Descriptive Catalogue of the Official Publications of the Territory & State of Indiana: From 1800 to 1890." *Indiana Historical Society Publications*, Vol. 2, No. 5. Indianapolis: 1890.

Hubbard, Kin, et al. *A Book of Indiana*. Indiana Biographical Association, 1929.

Hulbert, Archer B. *The Ohio River*. New York, G. P. Putnam's Sons, 1906.

Hunt, Thomas J. "History Lessons from Indiana Names." *Indiana History Bulletin*, Vol. 3, Extra No. 2. Indianapolis: March, 1926.

Hyman, Max R. "A Survey of the State by Counties." *Centennial History & Handbook of Indiana*. Indianapolis, 1915.

"Indiana County Names." *The Magazine of History*, Vol. 2, No. 6. New York: December, 1905.

"Indiana Geographical Nomenclature." *Indiana Magazine of History*, Vol. 8, No. 2. Indianapolis: June, 1912.

Indiana Historic Sites & Structures Inventory: Elkhart County: Interim Report. 1978.

Jasper County Historical Foundation, Inc. *History of Jasper County, Georgia*. Roswell, Georgia, W. H. Wolfe Associates, 1976.

"Jaycees Back Spencer County Name Change to Honor Lincoln." *Indianapolis Star*, October 16, 1958.

Lawlis, Chelsea L. "Migration to the Whitewater Valley, 1820–1830." *Indiana Magazine of History*, Vol. 43, No. 3. Bloomington: September, 1947.

Leary, Edward A. *Indiana Almanac & Fact Book*. Indianapolis, Ed Leary & Associates, 1967.

Lockridge, Ross F. "History on the Mississinewa." *Indiana Magazine of History*, Vol. 30, No. 1. Bloomington: March, 1934.

McCarty, C. Walter. *Indiana Today*. New Orleans, Louisiana, James O. Jones Co., 1942.

McCormick, Chester A. *McCormick's Guide to Starke County*. 1902.

McKesson, Jon. "Most Counties Named to Honor Men Who Helped Make History." *Indianapolis Star*, April 17, 1966.

Monks, Leander J., et al. *Courts & Lawyers of Indiana*. Indianapolis, Federal Publishing Co., Inc., 1916.

Morrow, Jackson. *History of Howard County, Indiana*. Indianapolis B. F. Bowen & Co., 1870.

"Names of Indiana Counties: White County…" *Indianapolis News*, March 19, 1919.

Osterhus, Grace B. "Names of Northern Indiana Counties Reflect Pioneer Thinking." *1943 Yearbook of the Society of Indiana Pioneers*.

Packard, Jasper. *History of La Porte County, Indiana*. La Porte, S. E. Taylor & Co., 1876.

Pence, George. "General Joseph Bartholomew." *Indiana Magazine of History*, Vol. 14, No. 4. Bloomington: December, 1918.

Pence, George, & Nellie C. Armstrong. "Indiana Boundaries: Territory, State, & County." *Indiana Historical Collections*, Vol. 19. Indianapolis: 1933.

Pirtle, Alfred. *The Battle of Tippecanoe*. Louisville, Kentucky, John P. Morton & Co., 1900.

Pleasant, Hazen H. *A History of Crawford County, Indiana*. Glendale, California, Arthur H. Clark Co., 1926.

A Popular History of Indiana. Indianapolis, Indianapolis Sentinel Co., 1891.

Powell, William S. *The North Carolina Gazetteer*. Chapel Hill, University of North Carolina Press, 1968.

Quinlan, James E. *History of Sullivan County*. Liberty, New York, W. T. Morgans & Co., 1873.

Quisenberry, Anderson C. *Kentucky in the War of 1812*. Frankfort, Kentucky, Kentucky State Historical Society, 1915.

"Review of Books: A History of Sullivan County." *Indiana Magazine of History*, Vol. 6, No. 2. Bloomington: June, 1910.

Robbins, D. P. *The Advantages & Surroundings of New Albany, Indiana, Floyd County*. New Albany, Indiana, Ledger Co., 1892.

Roll, Charles. *Indiana: One Hundred & Fifty Years of American Development*. Chicago, Lewis Publishing Co., 1931.

Rose, Dorothy, & Joyce Buckner. *History of Wells County, Indiana: 1776–1976*. Bluffton, Indiana, 1975.

Sesquicentennial Historical Record Commemorating the 150th Anniversary of Union County, Indiana: 1821–1971.

Shankle, George Earlie. *State Names, Flags, Seals, Songs, Birds, Flowers & Other Symbols*. New York, H. W. Wilson Co., 1941.

Shepherd, Rebecca A., et al. *A Biographical Directory of the Indiana General Assembly*. Indianapolis, Select Committee on the Centennial History of the Indiana General Assembly in Cooperation with the Indiana Historical Bureau, 1980.

Shockley, Ernest V. "County Seats & County Seat Wars in Indiana." *Indiana Magazine of History*, Vol. 10, No. 1. Bloomington: March, 1914.

Simmons, Virgil M., et al. *Indiana Review: Pictorial, Political, Historical*. Indianapolis, 1938.

Somes, Joseph H. V. *Old Vincennes*. New York, Graphic Books, 1962.

Souvenir History: New Albany Centennial Celebration: October 12 to 16, 1913. New Albany, Indiana, 1913.

Sparks, Jared. "Lives of Count Rumford, Zebulon Montgomery Pike & Samuel Gorton." *Library of American Biography*, Vol. 5. Boston: 1855.

"Spencer County." *Kokomo Tribune*, September 11, 1929.

Stewart, James H. *Recollections of the Early Settlement of Carroll County, Indiana*. Cincinnati, Hitchcock & Walden, 1872.

Stiles Ruby H. "A County in the Making." *Shoals News*, December 30, 1949.

Strassweg, Elsa. *A Brief History of New Albany & Floyd County, Indiana*. New Albany, Indiana, Floyd County Historical Society, 1951.

Talbert, Charles G. "William Whitley: 1749–1813." *Filson Club History Quarterly*, Vol. 25, No. 2. Louisville, Kentucky: April, 1951.

Taylor, Charles W. *Biographical Sketches & Review of the Bench & Bar of Indiana*. Indianapolis, Bench & Bar Publishing Co., 1895.

Thomas, Lucille. "Origin of Randolph County's Name Still Not Certain 150 Years After Its Creation." *Muncie Star*, May 19, 1968.

Thornbrough, Gayle, & Dorothy Riker. "Journals of the General Assembly of Indiana Territory: 1805–1815." *Indiana Historical Collections*, Vol. 32. Indianapolis: 1950.

Trease, Geoffrey. *Seven Kings of England*. New York, Vanguard Press, 1955.

Trease, Geoffrey. *The Seven Queens of England*. New York, Vanguard Press, 1953.

Urquhart, Jane McKelway & O. D. von Engeln. *The Story Key to Geographic Names*. New York, D. Appleton & Co., 1924.

Vexler, Robert I. *Chronology & Documentary Handbook of the State of Indiana*. Dobbs Ferry, New York, Oceana Publications, Inc., 1978.

Voegelin, Erminie W. "Indians of Indiana." *Teaching Indiana History*, Vol. 2, No. 2. Indiana Historical Society, November & December, 1963.

Vogel, Virgil J. *Indian Names in Michigan*. Ann Arbor, University of Michigan Press, 1986.

Walsh, Justin E. *The Centennial History of the Indiana General Assembly: 1816–1978*. Indianapolis, Select Committee on the Centennial History of the Indiana General Assembly, 1987.

Webb, Walter P., et al. *The Handbook of Texas*. Austin, Texas State Historical Association, 1952.

White, Dabney, & T. C. Richardson. *East Texas: Its History & Its Makers*. New York, Lewis Historical Publishing Co., 1940.

Whitson, Rolland L., et al. *Centennial History of Grant County, Indiana*. Chicago, Lewis Publishing Co., 1914.

Wilson, George R. *History & Art Souvenir of Dubois County*. Jasper, Indiana, 1896.

Wilson, George R. *History of Dubois County from Its Primitive Days to 1910*. Indianapolis, Jos. Ratti, 1910.

Wilson, William E. *The Wabash*. New York, Farrar & Rinehart, Inc., 1940.

Woollen, William W. *Biographical & Historical Sketches of Early Indiana*. Indianapolis, Hammond & Co., 1883.

Work Projects Administration. *Indiana: A Guide to the Hoosier State*. New York, Oxford University Press, 1941.

Work Projects Administration. *Inventory of the County Archives of Indiana-Warrick County*. Indianapolis, 1940.

Works Progress Administration. *Inventory of the County Archives of Indiana-Boone County*. Indianapolis, 1937.

Young, Bennett H. *The Battle of the Thames*. Louisville, Kentucky, John P. Morton & Co., 1903.

Iowa

(99 counties)

758 *Adair County*

John Adair (1757–1840) — This South Carolina native served in the Revolutionary War and spent part of it as a prisoner of war. In 1786 he moved to Kentucky where he engaged in military actions against the Indians and became active in politics. Adair served nine terms as a member of Kentucky's house of representatives and was, for a time, speaker of that body. He briefly represented Kentucky in the U.S. Senate and later served as an officer and hero in the War of 1812. Adair was given the rank of brevet brigadier-general of the Kentucky militia and in 1020 he became governor of the state of Kentucky. He later represented Kentucky in the U.S. House of Representatives. Adair County, Iowa, was created in 1851.

759 *Adams County*

John Adams (1735–1826)— Adams, a native of Massachusetts, was a delegate to the first Continental Congress and a signer of the Declaration of Independence. He participated in Paris, with Benjamin Franklin and John Jay in negotiating peace with England and, after the war, he was our country's first minister to England. Adams became the first vice-president of the United States under George Washington and when Washington retired, Adams was elected to be our nation's second president.

760 *Allamakee County*

Uncertain— Some sources speculate that this county's name is of Indian origin, perhaps derived from *anameekee*, a Sauk-Fox Indian word for "thunder." In support of this theory it is pointed out that the present county seat of Allamakee County is named Waukon and *waukon* is a Winnebago Indian word with several meanings, one of which is also "thunder." However, most sources indicate that the county was named for Allan Makee, a trapper who traded with the Indians here along the upper Mississippi River. His name is given variously in different accounts as Allan Makee, Allen Makee, Allen Magee and Allen McKee. Another source attributes the county's name to a different Indian trader named Alexander McKee. There was a British agent among the Indians of Pennsylvania and Ohio during the 1700's named Alexander McKee but it is doubtful that this trader ever got to Iowa.

761 *Appanoose County*

Appanoose (–1845)— Appanoose was a chief of the allied Sauk and Fox Indian tribes whose band lived for several years along the Des Moines River where the city of Ottumwa, Iowa, is now located. His name appears on treaties with various spellings including Appenioce, Appinuis, Apanoose, Appanozeokemar and Appa-

noose. His name means "a little child" or "a chief when a child." Chief Appanoose belonged to the peace faction of the Sauk-Fox alliance at the time of the Black Hawk War in 1832. In 1837 he was one of the prominent Indians who visited several eastern cities including Washington, D.C. From 1842 until his death in 1845 Chief Appanoose lived on a farm in Wapello County, Iowa. Appanoose County was created and named in his honor in 1843.

762 *Audubon County*

John J. Audubon (1785–1851)— This famous ornithologist and artist was born on the island of Santo Domingo (now Hispaniola) in the Caribbean Sea but moved to France in his early childhood. To escape Napoleon's draft, he came to the United States in 1803. Audubon devoted most of his life to art, specializing in painting birds but also drawing some pictures of animals. He traveled extensively in America to find new specimens to paint and in 1843 he visited Iowa to paint pictures of birds for his great book entitled *The Birds of America*. Soon after this trip his eyesight failed and then his mental facilities declined. This county was created on January 15, 1851, just 12 days before his death. The act which created it misspelled the name as Audibon but the correct spelling of Audubon's name is used as the spelling of the county's name.

763 *Benton County*

Thomas H. Benton (1782–1858)— Benton was a native of North Carolina who served in the Tennessee senate and as a soldier in the War of 1812. Following the war he moved to Missouri and he represented that state for thirty years in the U.S. Senate. In that body he championed many interests of the West including free 160 acre homesteads, pony express, telegraph and railroads. Benton was a moderate on the volatile slavery issue. He opposed both abolition of slavery and the extension of it. His primary concerns were peace and preservation of the Union. These moderate positions proved unpopular. Some states which had named counties in Benton's honor renamed them and, in 1850, Missouri failed to return Benton to the senate. Following his ouster from the senate, Benton served briefly in the U.S. House of Representatives. This county was created in 1837 by the legislature of Wisconsin territory when Iowa was a part of Wisconsin territory. Benton had been influential in persuading congress to create Wisconsin territory in 1836.

764 *Black Hawk County*

Black Hawk (1767–1838)— This famous chief of the Sauk Indians and of the Sauk-Fox alliance was born in Illinois in 1767. During the War of 1812, Black Hawk took the side of the British against the Americans and was present with his warriors on the British side in actions at River Raisin, Fort Meigs, Fort Stephenson and Moraviantown. In April, 1832, Chief Black Hawk led the dissident portion of his tribe from Iowa back to Illinois in an attempt to reoccupy lands from which they had recently been expelled. Federal troops fired on them near Stillman Valley, Illinois. Black Hawk led his people, numbering some nine hundred including women and children in a retreat to Wisconsin but federal troops pursued them and decimated the Indians near the mouth of Bad Axe River on August 2, 1832. Chief Black Hawk was captured and held prisoner for several months. These actions from April to August, 1832, are known as the Black Hawk War. Chief Black Hawk was taken to Washington, D.C., where he met President Andrew Jackson. After touring several other eastern cities, Black Hawk returned to Iowa where he lived peacefully until his death near the Des Moines River in 1838. Black Hawk County, Iowa, was created by the legislature of Iowa territory in February, 1843.

765 *Boone County*

Nathan Boone (1780–)— Nathan Boone, who was born in Kentucky, was the youngest son of Daniel Boone, the famous explorer and Indian fighter. About 1798 Nathan moved with his father from Kentucky to Missouri where he soon married and engaged in farming and trapping along the Missouri River. In 1803 the United States acquired Missouri as part of the Louisiana Purchase and Nathan Boone was employed by the federal government to survey portions of this largely unknown area. In 1807 Nathan entered the salt manufacturing business in partnership with his brother, Daniel. This salt business was soon commanding handsome profits but by 1808, because of escalating hostilities between the Indians and encroaching Whites, Nathan enlisted in the territorial militia as a captain. By 1815 Boone had risen to the rank of major and was mustered out of the military. He next engaged in farming and was a delegate to Missouri's constitutional convention. The federal government again employed Nathan Boone to survey lands acquired in the Louisiana Purchase, this time in Iowa. In 1832 when the Black Hawk War began, he enlisted in the military as a captain. Congress soon reorganized the unit in which Boone was serving and named it the First Dragoon regiment under the command of General Henry Dodge. Nathan Boone spent most of his remaining life in the military and during this period he again led explorations in Iowa. By 1853 when he retired to his home in Missouri, Boone had risen to the rank of lieutenant-colonel. Nathan Boone died in Missouri in 1856 or 1857. Boone County, Iowa, was created by Iowa territory in 1846.

766 Bremer County

Frederika Bremer (1801 1865)— Frederika Bremer was a Swedish author, traveler and early feminist. Bremer County, Iowa was created in 1851. Its name was suggested by General A. K. Eaton, who was an active member of the committee on counties in the Iowa legislature. Bremer's writings were popular at that time and General Eaton was an admirer of them.

767 Buchanan County

James Buchanan (1791–1868)— A native of Pennsylvania, Buchanan served in a variety of political posts for more than 40 years. After brief duty in the military during the War of 1812, Buchanan began his political career in the Pennsylvania assembly and then he represented Pennsylvania for ten years in the U.S. House of Representatives. Following an assignment as minister to Russia, Buchanan was elected to represent Pennsylvania in the U.S. Senate where he served from 1834 to 1845. When James K. Polk became president, Buchanan joined his cabinet as secretary of state. Buchanan subsequently was our minister to Great Britain. Four years before the start of the Civil War, Buchanan was elected as a Democrat to be president of the United States. During his presidency the nation moved rapidly toward Civil War and Buchanan was unable to avert it. Buchanan County, Iowa was created on December 21, 1837, by the legislature of Wisconsin territory when Iowa was part of that territory. At that time Buchanan was a U.S. senator from Pennsylvania and he had materially aided in securing passage of the bill that created Wisconsin territory. The county's name was suggested by S. P. Stoughton, who, like Buchanan, was a Democrat. Stoughton was a prominent resident of the area that became Buchanan County.

768 Buena Vista County

Battle of Buena Vista— Buena Vista County, Iowa was created in January, 1851, three years after the United States defeated Mexico in the Mexican War. At the time that many of Iowa's counties were being created and named, patriotic war fervor was high and several of Iowa's counties were named for battles and heroes of the Mexican War. The Battle of Buena Vista was an important American victory in that war. It was fought in February, 1847, near the Mexican hacienda of Buena Vista in northeastern Mexico, a few miles from Saltillo, Mexico. There, American troops commanded by Major-General Zachary Taylor decisively defeated a much larger force led by Mexico's commanding officer himself, Antonio Lopez de Santa Anna. Santa Anna then retreated 660 miles south to Mexico City so our victory at the Battle of Buena Vista marked the end of the war in northern Mexico. *Buena Vista* is Spanish for "beautiful view" or "good view." The act which created this Iowa county misspelled the name as Buna Vista County but the correct spelling is now used as the spelling of the county's name.

769 Butler County

William O. Butler (1791–1880)— Butler was born in what is now Kentucky one year before it became a state. When war with Great Britain was declared in 1812, Butler volunteered to serve as a private. He served with distinction in the War of 1812 and rose to the rank of brevet major. In 1817 Butler resigned from the army and was soon elected to the Kentucky legislature. He later represented Kentucky in the U.S. House of Representatives. When war was declared against Mexico in 1846, President James K. Polk appointed Butler to be a major-general and Butler served with distinction in the Mexican War. He was wounded at Monterrey, Mexico and was present when Mexico City was captured. Shortly before the 1848 treaty of peace was signed with Mexico, Butler was given command of U.S. forces in Mexico. Later, in 1848, he ran unsuccessfully for vice-president of the United States on the Democratic ticket headed by Lewis Cass. Butler County, Iowa was created less than three years later in January, 1851.

770 Calhoun County

John C. Calhoun (1782–1850)— Calhoun represented South Carolina in both houses of the U.S. Congress. He served as secretary of war, secretary of state and as vice-president. He was a forceful advocate of slavery, states' rights and limited powers for the federal government. He resigned the vice-presidency to enter the U.S. Senate where he could better represent the views of South Carolina and the South. This county was originally created in January, 1851 and named Fox County in honor of the Fox Indians. During the January, 1853, session of the legislature it was proposed that Fox County's name be changed to Calhoun. This suggestion met some resistance but was finally agreed to on condition that Calhoun County's neighboring county on the east also be renamed as Webster County, in honor of Daniel Webster, a political foe of Calhoun. This was done and the new names were adopted for both counties during January, 1853.

771 Carroll County

Charles Carroll (1737–1832)— Carroll was a native of Maryland and he represented that state in the Continental Congress. He was one of the signers of the Declaration of Independence and he later represented Maryland as a U.S. senator in the first congress of the United States. Carroll lived to be the last surviving signer of the Declaration of Independence and several states recognized that distinction by naming counties for him. This county was created in 1851.

772 Cass County

Lewis Cass (1782–1866)— A native of New Hampshire, Cass served in the army in the War of 1812 and rose to the rank of brigadier-general. Following that war Cass held a variety of important political positions and was the candidate of the Democratic party in 1848 for president of the United States. He lost to Zachary Taylor. Cass served as governor of Michigan territory, secretary of war under Andrew Jackson, minister to France, U.S. senator from Michigan and secretary of state under James Buchanan. Cass County, Iowa, was created in January, 1851, less than three years after his unsuccessful 1848 bid for the presidency.

773 Cedar County

Cedar River— Cedar County, Iowa was created in December, 1837, by the legislature of Wisconsin territory when Iowa was a part of that territory. It was named for the Cedar River, a major tributary of the Iowa River. The Cedar River rises about 1,300 feet above sea level in southern

Minnesota. There, and in northern Iowa as well, it is called the Red Cedar River. In central, southern and eastern Iowa it is called the Cedar River. About 330 miles long, the Cedar River crosses the southwestern corner of Cedar County, Iowa, and then flows south to join the Iowa River southwest of Muscatine, Iowa. The Cedar (or Red Cedar) River had been named by the Sauk-Fox Indians *Moskwahwakwah* meaning "red cedar" on account of the presence of red cedar trees along its banks. The later English names for this river are merely translations of the Indians' name. Red cedar trees are technically junipers of the cyprus family. They range in shape from narrow to cone-like and can grow to 100 feet.

774 *Cerro Gordo County*

Battle of Cerro Gordo— This county was created in January, 1851, three years after the United States defeated Mexico in the Mexican War. At the time that many of Iowa's counties were being created and named, patriotic war fervor was high and several of Iowa's counties were named for battles and heroes of the Mexican War. The Battle of Cerro Gordo was an important American victory in that war. It was fought on April 17 and April 18, 1847, at Cerro Gordo, Mexico, a mountain pass in eastern Mexico between Veracruz and Jalapa. There, American forces commanded by General Winfield Scott routed a larger force of Mexicans led by Mexico's commanding officer himself, Antonio Lopez de Santa Anna. The battle witnessed a good deal of hand-to-hand combat. More than 1,000 Mexicans were killed or wounded and some 3,000 of their officers and men were captured as prisoners of war. American losses were about 400 killed or wounded. In the original act which created this Iowa county, the name was erroneously spelled as Cerro Gorda. The correct version, *Cerro Gordo* is Spanish meaning "large, important hill."

775 *Cherokee County*

Cherokee Indians— The Cherokee Indians were a large tribe who lived in several southeastern states at the time of European contact. By the early 1800's they had adopted many features of civilization. By 1840, most Cherokees had been forced from their lands and removed to Indian territory (now Oklahoma) by court decisions, a fraudulent treaty and military force. The name Cherokee is said to be derived from the Cherokee word for "fire," *chera*. This county was formed in 1851. It is not known

why this tribe's name was chosen for the name of one of Iowa's counties, since the Cherokee tribe had no historic connection with Iowa.

776 *Chickasaw County*

Chickasaw Indians The Chickasaw Indians were an important warlike tribe whose main home was in northern Mississippi and western Tennessee along the Yazoo, Tombigbee, Tallahatchie and Mississippi Rivers. Their principal landing place on the Mississippi was where the city of Memphis, Tennessee, is now located. An outlying colony of Chickasaw Indians had earlier lived on the Savannah River near what is now the city of Augusta, Georgia, but trouble with the Creeks drove them westward again. Beginning in the 1830's, the Chickasaw were removed to Indian territory (now Oklahoma). Although they belong to the Muskhogean linguistic family whose other members are the Creek, Choctaw and Seminole Indians, they were hostile to neighboring Muskhogean tribes. The Chickasaw Indians were also extremely hostile to French settlers. The meaning of the name *Chickasaw* is uncertain and it is also unknown why the Iowa legislature chose to name a county for this southern tribe when they created Chickasaw County in 1851, since the Chickasaw tribe had no historic connection with Iowa.

777 *Clarke County*

James Clarke (1812–1850)— A native of Pennsylvania, Clarke learned the printing trade before migrating west. In Saint Louis he obtained employment on the *Missouri Republican* and when congress created Wisconsin territory in 1836, Clarke moved there and established the *Belmont Gazette*. He soon became Wisconsin's official territorial printer. At this time Iowa was part of Wisconsin territory and when the territorial legislators moved to Burlington, Iowa, Clarke moved there with them. In Burlington he established another newspaper and he also served as official librarian for Wisconsin territory. In June, 1838, Iowa territory was created and in 1839 the Democratic president, Martin Van Buren, appointed Clarke, also a Democrat, to be secretary of Iowa territory. When the Whigs took the presidency in 1841, Clarke was removed as secretary. He returned to Burlington where he ran a newspaper and served as the city's mayor. In 1845, James K. Polk, another Democrat, became president and he appointed Clarke to be governor of Iowa territory. Clarke later served as vice chairman of the Democratic

national convention. Clarke County, Iowa, was created in January, 1846 by Iowa's territorial legislature while James Clarke was serving as territorial governor.

778 *Clay County*

Henry Clay, Jr. (–1847)— Clay County, Iowa was created in January, 1851, three years after the United States had defeated Mexico in the Mexican War. At the time that many of Iowa's counties were being created and named, patriotic war fervor was high and several of Iowa's counties were named for battles and heroes of the Mexican War. One of those heroes was Henry Clay, Jr., a son of the famous Kentucky politician and statesman, Henry Clay (1777–1852). Henry Clay, Jr., was born in Kentucky about 1811 and he graduated from both Transylvania University and the U.S. military academy. He practiced law and served in the Kentucky legislature. During the Mexican War Clay served as lieutenant-colonel of the second regiment of Kentucky volunteers. In February, 1847 he died in combat at the Battle of Buena Vista, in Mexico. That battle was an important American victory in the Mexican War.

779 *Clayton County*

John M. Clayton (1796–1856)— A native of Delaware and a graduate of Yale, Clayton practiced law in Delaware with great success. In 1828 he was elected to represent Delaware in the U.S. Senate and in 1834 he was reelected. After sitting two and one half years as chief justice of the state of Delaware, Clayton left public life to pursue private interests but in 1845 he again accepted election as a U.S. senator from Delaware. When Zachary Taylor became president he selected John M. Clayton to be his secretary of state. Clayton later represented Delaware a final time in the U.S. Senate before his death in 1856. Clayton County, Iowa was created on December 21, 1837, by the legislature of Wisconsin territory while Iowa was part of that territory. In the U.S. Senate, John M. Clayton had assisted in securing passage of the bill which created Wisconsin territory.

780 *Clinton County*

De Witt Clinton (1769–1828)— This New York state native held many of the important political offices in that state. Clinton served in both houses of the state legislature and as mayor of New York City. He represented New York in the U.S. Senate and in 1812 he was the Federalist candidate for president, running against President James Madison. In 1817 Clinton was elected as New York's governor. As governor, he was the principal promoter of the Erie Canal which was instrumental in linking the vast agricultural lands in our country's West with eastern markets. The canal spurred our nation's growth. Clinton County, Iowa was created by the Wisconsin territorial legislature in December, 1837, while Iowa was part of Wisconsin territory.

781 *Crawford County*

William H. Crawford (1772–1834)—Crawford served in the Georgia legislature and as a U.S. senator from Georgia. He was elected president pro tempore of the senate and he later served as minister to France, secretary of war and secretary of the treasury. Crawford was a serious candidate for the presidency in both 1816 and 1824.

782 *Dallas County*

George M. Dallas (1792–1864)—Dallas was a native of Philadelphia, Pennsylvania and he served as mayor of that city. He was later a U.S. senator, attorney general of Pennsylvania and minister to Russia. In 1844 he was elected vice-president on the Democratic ticket with James K. Polk. He later served as minister to England. Dallas County, Iowa, was created by the legislature of Iowa territory in January, 1846, while Dallas was vice-president.

783 *Davis County*

Garret Davis (1801–1872)—A native of Kentucky and a lawyer, Davis was elected to the Kentucky legislature in 1833 and served three terms in that body. He later represented Kentucky in the U.S. House of Representatives from 1839 to 1847. Although Kentucky was a slave state, it did not secede from the Union and join the Confederate side in the Civil War and Garret Davis did much to keep Kentucky on the Union side. As a reward, he was elected to represent Kentucky in the U.S. Senate. Davis County, Iowa, was created in February, 1843, by the legislature of Iowa territory while Garret Davis was serving in the U.S. House of Representatives. Other names that were considered for this county were Massaaskuc, Musquakee and Seponoma but none of them were ever officially adopted.

784 *Decatur County*

Stephen Decatur (1779–1820)—Decatur, who was born in Maryland, was an officer in the U.S. navy who served in the Mediterranean Sea from 1801 to 1805 in the Tripolitan War. His bravery and successes in that war made him a popular hero in America and earned him promotion to captain. During the War of 1812, Decatur reinforced his reputation as a naval hero. Following that war Decatur, now a commodore, again served in the Mediterranean where he captured the Algerian flagship *Mashuda*. His display of naval force exacted peace terms from Algeria and indemnities for un-neutral acts from Tunis and Tripoli. This brought an end to the plundering of American shipping by the Barbary powers. Decatur's life ended in a duel fought in March, 1820. Decatur County was created in January, 1846, by the legislature of Iowa territory.

785 *Delaware County*

Uncertain— This county was created on December 21, 1837, by the legislature of Wisconsin territory while Iowa was part of that territory. Most sources state that the county was named for the state of Delaware as an indirect tribute to U.S. Senator John M. Clayton (1796–1856) of Delaware, who had assisted in securing passage of the bill which created Wisconsin territory. Also on the same day, December 21, 1837, the Wisconsin territorial legislators had directly honored Senator Clayton when they created and named Clayton County in his honor. Both Clayton County and Delaware County of Wisconsin territory are now part of the state of Iowa. However, there are a few sources which indicate a different origin for Delaware County's name. According to them, the name was chosen by Thomas McCraney of Dubuque, who was a member of the Wisconsin territorial legislature and McCraney chose the name in honor of Delaware County in New York state from which he had come.

State of Delaware— Delaware, the first colony to ratify the proposed U.S. Constitution, thereby gained the distinction of being the first state to enter the Union. The state of Delaware's name derived from the Delaware River, the river's name having derived from Delaware Bay. The bay was named for Thomas West, Lord De La Warr (1577–1618), who was a British governor of colonial Virginia.

Delaware County, New York— Delaware County, New York, in the western Catskill Mountain region, was created on March 10, 1797, and named for the Delaware River which is formed within its borders by the junction of the East Branch and West Branch Rivers. The Delaware River then flows south to form the southwestern border of Delaware County, New York, and there it is also the boundary between New York state and Pennsylvania. The Delaware is 280 miles long and carries extensive commercial traffic. It empties into Delaware Bay on the Atlantic Ocean. As mentioned above, the Delaware River was named for Delaware Bay and the bay was named for Thomas West, Lord De La Warr (1577–1618), who was a British governor of colonial Virginia.

786 *Des Moines County*

Des Moines River— The Des Moines River, a tributary of the Mississippi, is formed by the junction of its East Fork and West Fork in the northern portion of central Iowa. The longest river in Iowa, the Des Moines then flows some 330 miles in a southeastern direction, cutting a diagonal across Iowa before emptying into the Mississippi at the city of Keokuk, Iowa, in the southeastern corner of the state. Des Moines County, Iowa, was created in 1834 by the legislature of Michigan territory when Iowa was part of that territory. This county was one of the first counties to be created in what is now the state of Iowa and it was named for the river which then ran through it. Since 1834 this county has been greatly reduced in size. As a result, although the Des Moines River still flows near Des Moines County, it no longer flows through it. The original spelling of the county's name in the bill which created it was Demoine County. The Des Moines River's name derived from the name of a now-vanished branch of the Illinois Indian confederacy who lived, at least briefly, in Iowa. They were called variously by French explorers as Moingwena, Moingouena, Moingina or Moingona. An expert on names of Indian origin, Professor Virgil J. Vogel, speculates in his *Iowa Place Names of Indian Origin* that the Indian name may have referred to the loon, "taken from its totemic bird or one of its clan totems." There have been sporadic attempts over the decades to associate the current version of the river's name with the French language resulting in spurious translations such as "River of Monks, River of Mines, River of Means" and "River of Mounds."

787 *Dickinson County*

Daniel S. Dickinson (1800–1866)— A native of Connecticut, Dickinson moved with his parents to New York state when he was a young boy. There he practiced law, became prominent in the Democratic party and was elected president of the city of Binghamton. He later served in the New York senate and was the state's lieutenant-governor. Upon the resignation of New York's U.S. Senator N. P. Tallmadge, the governor appointed Dickinson to fill the remainder of his term. The New York legislature then elected him to serve in the U.S. Senate for the ensuing full term, 1845-1851. Dickinson was soon recognized as one of the leading Democrats in the senate and he rendered important service on behalf of compromise measures enacted in 1850 that were intended to avert secession and civil war. After leaving the senate, Dickinson held a variety of political posts and he was a strong contender to be Abraham Lincoln's vice-presidential running mate on the National Union ticket of 1864. This county was created in 1851, shortly after Daniel S. Dickinson's important service in the U.S. Senate for the compromise measures of 1850.

788 *Dubuque County*

Julien Dubuque (1762–1810) — Dubuque was born of Norman ancestry in New France (now Canada) in 1762 at St. Pierre-les-Becquets about 50 miles north of the city of Quebec. When he was 23 years of age he moved to where Prairie du Chien now stands in southwestern Wisconsin on the Mississippi River, some 30 miles above the present city of Dubuque, Iowa. There, on the eastern side of the Mississippi River, from Prairie du Chien to the vicinity of what is now Galena, Illinois, he engaged in trading with the Indians and learned from them of lead mines on the western side of the Mississippi. On the basis of a lease, written in French, which Dubuque persuaded his Fox Indian friends to sign, he moved to the western side of the Mississippi in 1788 and became the first permanent White settler in what is now the state of Iowa. There Dubuque engaged in fur trading with the Indians and mining lead and he also established a settlement for lead miners. Julien Dubuque's trading house and dwelling were located at the mouth of Catfish Creek, about ten miles below the present city of Dubuque, Iowa. Dubuque called his lead mines the Mines of Spain because he had also gotten Spain to endorse his grant to these mines. Iowa was a part of what later became the Louisiana Purchase and Spain had not yet ceded this vast territory to France. Dubuque remained at his lead mines until his death in 1810. Dubuque County, Iowa, was created in 1834 by the legislature of Michigan territory when what is now Iowa was part of Michigan territory.

789 *Emmet County*

Robert Emmet (1778–1803) — Emmet was born in Dublin, Ireland, to a prominent Anglo-Irish Protestant family in 1778. He studied at Trinity College in Dublin where he excelled in his studies and won a reputation as a fiery orator. There he joined the radical group known as the Society of United Irishmen. This society, inspired by recent revolutions in the United States and France, had as its goal, freedom for Ireland from England. In 1798 Emmet left Trinity College due to an inquisition into students' political views. During the next five years of his brief life Emmet lived in both France and Ireland and engaged in continuous revolutionary activities. On July 23, 1803, Emmet issued a proclamation establishing a provisional government for an Irish republic but this rebellion was promptly crushed by British soldiers. The following month Emmet was captured by the British and in September, 1803, he was executed by hanging. Although Emmet's revolutionary activities met little success, Thomas Moore wrote poems about him and Emmet became a celebrated martyr for Irish nationalism. Irish immigrants in the United States were particularly loyal to his memory and Emmet County, Iowa, was created and named in his honor in 1851. The law which created this county misspelled the Irish patriot's name as Emmett but by about 1868 the correct spelling was being used for the county's name.

790 *Fayette County*

Marie Joseph Paul Yves Roch Gilbert du Motier, Marquis de Lafayette (1757–1834) — Lafayette was a French aristocrat who served briefly in the French army. He came to America in 1777 to assist the American Revolutionary army. He was granted an honorary commission as major-general by the Continental Congress and served with distinction in a number of battles in the Revolutionary War. Fayette County, Iowa, was created by the legislature of Wisconsin territory on December 21, 1837, when Iowa was part of that territory.

791 *Floyd County*

Uncertain — This county was created on January 15, 1851. It is believed to have been named for either Charles Floyd, a member of the Lewis and Clark Expedition, or for William Floyd, a signer of the Declaration of Independence from New York. A third possibility also exists: that the county was named for a topographical engineer who died near Sioux City about the time his labors as surveyor were completed. A fourth possibility which is mentioned is John B. Floyd, a governor of Virginia and a Confederate general. This fourth possibility is known to be false.

Charles Floyd (–1804) — Charles Floyd, a member of the Lewis and Clark Expedition, was probably born in Jefferson County, Kentucky between 1780 and 1785. He joined the Lewis and Clark Expedition at Louisville during October, 1803, as it headed west on the Ohio River but it was not until March 31, 1804, that he and 24 others were formally enlisted by Captains Lewis and Clark as members of the expedition. On the following day, April 1, 1804, three of these men were appointed sergeants and one of these new sergeants was Charles Floyd. Sergeant Floyd was one of the men on the Lewis and Clark Expedition who kept a journal. By mid July, 1804, the expedition reached Iowa country. From August 13 through August 19 the expedition camped on a sand bar on the Nebraska side of the Missouri River near the present Sioux City, Iowa. There Charles Floyd contracted an illness which Captain William Clark described in his journal as "Bilose Chorlick," a violent colic. The expedition left the sand bar on August 20, 1804 to continue its journey and Sergeant Floyd died that day. He was buried on the Iowa side of the Missouri River within the corporation limits of the present Sioux City. He thus became the first White man known to have been buried in Iowa.

William Floyd (1734–1821) — William Floyd was born on Long Island, New York, and he represented his district in the New York senate during the American Revolution. He also represented New York in the Continental Congress, serving in that body from about 1774 to 1777 and again from 1778 to 1783. Floyd was also one of the signers of the Declaration of Independence, the first New York delegate to sign it. He also held the rank of major-general in New York's militia. William Floyd later was a member of the U.S. House of Representatives, serving one term in the first congress of the United States. He then moved upstate to the Oneida County, New York area, and represented that area in the New York senate.

During the Civil War, the Iowa legislature considered changing Floyd County's name because some of the members thought that it had been named for John B. Floyd (1806–1863), a former governor of Virginia and a major-general in the

Confederate army. Indeed, an article in the January, 1888 issue of the *Iowa Historical Record* perpetuates this misconception. Senator Redfield introduced a bill to change the county's name to Baker and Senator Ainsworth moved to amend that bill to change the name to Lyon. But Senator John F. Duncombe of Fort Dodge, Iowa preserved the county's name by assuring the legislature that Floyd County had been named for Sergeant Charles Floyd of the Lewis and Clark expedition. While it is certain that the county was not named for John B. Floyd (1806–1863), it is not certain that it was named for Charles Floyd (–1804). Some sources point to the name of the county seat, which is Charles City, as evidence that the county was named for Charles Floyd. This is another error. The county seat was named for Kelly St. Charles, a son of Joseph Kelly, the first White settler in the county and the founder of the town of The Ford. In fact, the county seat of Floyd County was originally named St. Charles but its name was changed to Charles City in 1869.

792 *Franklin County*

Uncertain— Franklin County, Iowa, was created on January 15, 1851, and most sources state that it was named for Benjamin Franklin. However, a degree of uncertainty is expressed by some sources because another Franklin was famous in 1851. He was Sir John Franklin (1786–1847).

Benjamin Franklin (1706–1790)— Franklin was a native of Massachusetts who moved to Pennsylvania in his teens. Poverty denied him a formal education but he became the leading printer and editor in North America. He gained fame for his discoveries and inventions in the physical sciences and distinguished himself as author, philosopher and diplomat. He was a signer of the Declaration of Independence and an important member of the convention which framed the U.S. Constitution.

John Franklin (1786–1847)— A native of England and a career officer in the English navy, Franklin served in several battles around the world including action against the United States in the War of 1812. In 1818 he commanded a brig in an unsuccessful attempt to reach the north pole. Franklin later commanded an expedition to explore and map the vast wilderness of northern North America. In 1825 he sailed again to explore the Arctic but this venture encountered difficulties and was forced to turn back in the fall of 1826. In 1836 he was appointed lieutenant-governor of Van

Diemen's Land (now the Australian island state of Tasmania) and he remained in that post nearly seven years. On a later Arctic expedition Franklin and his party disappeared in northern Canada in the winter of 1846–1847. Both British and American search parties and relief expeditions were sent out from 1847 until about 1857 looking for the lost expedition. There was world-wide anxiety about the fate of Sir John Franklin and his party throughout this period. In 1859 relics of the lost Franklin expedition were found together with a paper which fixed the date of Sir Franklin's death as June 11, 1847.

793 *Fremont County*

John C. Frémont (1813–1890)— Born in Georgia, Frémont engaged in survey work in wilderness areas of the South and then assisted Joseph N. Nicollet in explorations of Iowa, Dakota and Minnesota. Frémont then performed his greatest service by leading five explorations of the far West. Portions of this vast domain had previously been explored. However, it was Frémont who carefully mapped the areas traveled and prepared notes of his observations. Frémont played a leading role in winning California from Mexico, served very briefly as a U.S. senator and, in 1856, ran as the Republican party's first presidential candidate. He later served as a Union general in the Civil War and as governor of Arizona territory. He was ineffective in both of these positions. During the spring and summer of 1841 Frémont had led an exploration of the Des Moines River Valley and drawn maps of large sections of Iowa territory. Frémont County, Iowa was created and named in his honor six years later, in February, 1847.

794 *Greene County*

Nathanael Greene (1742–1786)— Greene was born in Rhode Island and served briefly in the Rhode Island legislature. He gained fame as one of the ablest American generals in the Revolutionary War. Greene County was created in 1851.

795 *Grundy County*

Felix Grundy (1777–1840)— A native of Virginia, Grundy moved to Kentucky with his family in his youth. There he became a member of the state's constitutional convention and served in the state legislature. In 1806 Grundy was appointed to Kentucky's supreme court and in 1807 he was made its chief justice. Finding the salary

inadequate, Grundy resigned and moved to Tennessee where he again became active in politics and gained national notice. He served in the Tennessee legislature and represented that state in both houses of the U.S. Congress. In 1838 President Martin Van Buren appointed Grundy to serve in his cabinet as attorney general.

796 *Guthrie County*

Edwin Guthrie (1806–1847)— Guthrie was born at Smyrna, New York, on December 11, 1806. He was a manufacturer of chemicals and a distiller at Sackets Harbor, New York, and he moved to Iowa territory about 1840. In Iowa he was employed as warden of the penitentiary at Fort Madison. In the spring of 1847 a call was received to organize a company of Iowa volunteers for service in the Mexican War. In response, Frederick Mills and Edwin Guthrie promptly organized Company K of the 15th United States infantry regiment. Mills served as a major in the regiment and Edwin Guthrie was made a captain and company commander of Company K. His company was actively engaged in combat in the Mexican War from the time it landed at Vera Cruz until the end of the war but Captain Guthrie's service with his company was brief. On June 20, 1847, he was mortally wounded during a skirmish at Lahoya Pass, Mexico, between Vera Cruz and Perote. Captain Guthrie died from those wounds at Perote exactly one month later. Guthrie County, Iowa, was created and named in January, 1851, less than four years after Guthrie's death. The county's name was suggested by his friend, Theophilus Bryan, who was appointed organizing sheriff of this new county.

797 *Hamilton County*

William W. Hamilton (–)— A native of England, Hamilton settled in Iowa territory at Dubuque upon his arrival in America in 1845. Here he practiced law and served as probate judge of Dubuque County from 1849 to 1852. By this time Iowa had been admitted to statehood and in 1854 Judge Hamilton was elected to Iowa's state senate. When the state's sixth general assembly convened a joint session of its house and senate, Democrats were a minority and Judge Hamilton, who was a Whig, was elected president of the Iowa senate. He was serving as the presiding officer of the Iowa senate when this county was created and named in his honor on December 22, 1856.

798 *Hancock County*

John Hancock (1737–1793)— A native of Massachusetts and a graduate of Harvard, Hancock served in the Massachusetts legislature and was president of the Massachusetts provincial congress. He was elected to the second Continental Congress and became its president. As president of the Continental Congress when the Declaration of Independence was signed, he was, on July 4, 1776, the first signer of that document. He signed it with such a flourish that the name John Hancock became a synonym for "signature." He later commanded the Massachusetts militia, served as governor of that state for many years and presided over the Massachusetts convention that ratified the U.S. Constitution.

799 *Hardin County*

John J. Hardin (1810–1847)— John J. Hardin was born in Frankfort, Kentucky, and moved to Illinois, settling in Jacksonville, Illinois about 1831. He practiced law and engaged in politics and was twice a rival of Abraham Lincoln's: First in the Illinois legislature and later for election to the U.S. House of Representatives. Hardin served in the army during the Black Hawk War and was a colonel in the Mexican War. He was killed in combat while leading his troops at the Battle of Buena Vista in northeastern Mexico in February, 1847. Hardin County, Iowa was created and named in his honor on January 15, 1851, three years after the United States defeat of Mexico in the Mexican War. Buena Vista County, Iowa was created on the same day. At the time that many of Iowa's counties were being created and named, patriotic fervor was high and several Iowa counties were named for battles and heroes of the Mexican War.

800 *Harrison County*

William H. Harrison (1773–1841)— William Henry Harrison was a native of Virginia whose early career was in the army, serving as an officer in actions against the Indians. In 1798 President John Adams appointed Harrison to be secretary of Northwest territory and the following year he became that territory's delegate to the U.S. Congress. In 1800 Indiana territory was created and President John Adams appointed Harrison to be the new territory's first governor. Harrison commanded the army in the battle of Tippecanoe and he served in the War of 1812 rising to the rank of major-general. He later served in the Ohio state legislature and represented Ohio in both houses of the U.S. Congress. In December, 1839 Harrison became the Whig party's candidate for president of the United States with John Tyler as his vice-presidential running mate. Their famous campaign slogan was "Tippecanoe and Tyler too." Harrison was elected president but he served only one month before dying.

801 *Henry County*

Henry Dodge (1782–1867)— Dodge was born in Vincennes in what is now the state of Indiana in 1782. He served with distinction as an officer in the War of 1812 and rose to the rank of lieutenant-colonel. In 1827 he moved to the wilderness of what is now Wisconsin and served in actions against the Indians. By now a full colonel, in 1835 Dodge led an expedition to the Rocky Mountains. In 1836 President Andrew Jackson appointed Henry Dodge to be governor of Wisconsin territory and superintendent of Indian affairs. Dodge later represented Wisconsin territory in the U.S. Congress as a delegate and the state of Wisconsin as a U.S. senator. Henry County, Iowa, was created on December 7, 1836, by the Wisconsin territorial legislature. At that time Iowa was part of Wisconsin territory and Henry Dodge was governor of the territory.

802 *Howard County*

Tilghman A. Howard (1797–1844)— Howard was born in South Carolina and studied law in Tennessee. There he was admitted to the bar, practiced law and served in the Tennessee senate. In 1830 Howard moved to Indiana where he was appointed U.S. district attorney for Indiana. He represented Indiana briefly in the U.S. House of Representatives before resigning to run, unsuccessfully, for the Indiana governor's office. In June, 1844, Howard was appointed charge d'affaires to the independent republic of Texas. Soon after his arrival in Texas he contracted yellow fever and he died there in August, 1844.

803 *Humboldt County*

Friedrich Wilhelm Heinrich Alexander von Humboldt (1769–1859)— Baron von Humboldt was a German and one of the foremost scientists of his time. He participated in expeditions to Latin America and to Asia which gathered valuable scientific data for a number of disciplines including biology, geology and astronomy. His contributions to the physical sciences covered topics ranging from climate and polar magnetism to geology. In 1804 he visited America and met with Thomas Jefferson and other prominent intellectuals. His scientific books enjoyed popularity in America and a Pacific Ocean current which he studied is named in his honor. Humboldt County, Iowa was originally created and named for Baron von Humboldt on January 15, 1851, but it was never organized and became extinct in 1855 when its territory was taken to form other counties. On February 26, 1857, the current Humboldt County was created and it was also named for Baron von Humboldt.

804 *Ida County*

Mount Ida on the Greek island of Crete— Mount Ida on the Greek island of Crete rises to 8,058 feet above sea level making it the highest mountain on Crete. On Mount Ida are found a classical shrine and the cave in which, mythology tells us, the Greek God Zeus was reared. Zeus was called the king of Gods by the ancient Greeks. Other English renderings of Mount Ida's name are Idi, Idhi and Idha. Ida County, Iowa was created in 1851 and there are two versions of the origin of its name, which are not necessarily contradictory. According to most sources, the county's name was suggested by Eliphalet Price. Other sources tell us that the county's name was suggested by one or more early surveyors who saw Indian fires on the hill overlooking the present town of Ida Grove, which is the county seat of Ida County. The fires were said to remind the surveyor(s) of the sacred fires on Mount Ida which could be seen by true believers in the Gods of antiquity.

805 *Iowa County*

Iowa River— The Iowa River, a tributary of the Mississippi, is formed by the confluence of branches in north-central Iowa. It flows some 300 miles from Crystal Lake in a southeastern direction until it enters the Mississippi about 15 miles below the city of Muscatine, Iowa. Through most of its course, the Iowa moves slowly through broad valleys. Prior to the arrival of railroads, the Iowa River was a boon to Iowa's commerce with the rest of the country and a number of steamboats plied the lower portion of the river between Iowa City and the Mississippi. But the Iowa River was mostly shallow with numerous sandbars so navigation was difficult. Iowa County, Iowa, was created in February, 1843 by the legislature of Iowa territory and it was named for the Iowa River which crosses the county. The river had been named for the Iowa (or Ioway) Indian tribe. At one time this tribe occupied all of what is now the state of Iowa except the northwestern portion. By 1838 they had given up all of their Iowa lands and were removed to a reservation at the junction of the Nemaha and Missouri Rivers. Numerous meanings have been offered for this Indian tribe's name but none have been substantiated. In 1843 when the territorial legislators were deciding upon a name for this new county, the name Tecumseh was considered. However, that name was never officially adopted.

806 *Jackson County*

Andrew Jackson (1767–1845)— Jackson was born on the border of North Carolina and South Carolina. He represented Tennessee in both branches of the U.S. Congress. He gained fame and popularity for his military exploits in wars with the Indians and in the War of 1812. He was provisional military governor of Florida and from 1829 to 1837 General Jackson was president of the United States. His presidency reflected the frontier spirit of America. This county was created in December, 1837 by the legislature of Wisconsin territory when Iowa was a part of that territory. Jackson's second term as president had ended earlier that year.

807 *Jasper County*

William Jasper (–1779)— This Revolutionary War hero was born in South Carolina about 1750 but moved to Georgia where he grew up on a farm. He first became a hero in a dramatic event at the battle of Fort Moultrie when he courageously exposed himself to enemy fire to recover a flag which had been shot down. For this heroism Sergeant Jasper was awarded a sword and offered promotion to lieutenant but he declined the promotion. Later employed as a scout, Jasper made several trips behind enemy lines in Georgia while operating from the swamps there. In a dramatic exploit near Savannah, Georgia, he and his close friend, John Newton, rescued several Americans who were prisoners and took their guards as prisoners of war. Jasper was shot and killed during the siege of Savannah while recovering the flag which had been shot down. Geographic names in several of our states link the names of the two heroic sergeants, Jasper and Newton. In some, as in Iowa, a county is named for one of them and its county seat is named for the other. In others, two counties are named for them.

808 *Jefferson County*

Thomas Jefferson (1743–1826)— Jefferson was a native of Virginia and a member of the Virginia legislature. He served Virginia as governor and he was a delegate to the second Continental Congress. Jefferson was the author of the Declaration of Independence and one of its signers. He was minister to France, secretary of state, vice-president and president of the United States. As president, he accomplished the Louisiana Purchase and he arranged the Lewis and Clark Expedition to the Pacific Northwest. Jefferson was a true intellectual, thoroughly knowledgeable in the arts and sciences. His political theories were pivotal in the formation of our infant republic. This county was created in 1839 by the legislature of Iowa territory.

809 *Johnson County*

Richard M. Johnson (1780–1850)— Johnson, a native of Kentucky, served in the Kentucky legislature prior to his election to the U.S. House of Representatives. He later became a hero as a colonel in the War of 1812, represented Kentucky in the U.S. Senate and was vice-president of the United States under President Martin Van Buren. This county was created in December, 1837 by the legislature of Wisconsin territory. At that time Iowa was part of Wisconsin territory and Johnson was serving as vice-president.

810 *Jones County*

George W. Jones (1804–1896)— A native of Vincennes, Indiana territory, Jones moved in 1827 to Michigan territory and settled about seven miles from Dubuque. He later served in the army during the Black Hawk War. In 1833 he was appointed judge of the U.S. district court and in 1835 Jones was elected to be Michigan territory's delegate to the U.S. Congress. In that capacity he was instrumental in securing passage of the bill that created Wisconsin territory effective April 20, 1836, and he then became the first delegate to the U.S. Congress from Wisconsin territory. He soon became active in congress with an effort to create a separate Iowa territory. That effort also met with success effective June 12, 1838. Jones later served as surveyor-general of Iowa and Wisconsin. In 1845 he moved to Dubuque. In December of the following year Iowa was admitted to statehood and Jones soon became one of Iowa's first United States senators. He represented Iowa in the senate for some 12 years and later was President Buchanan's minister to New Granada (now Colombia). Jones County was created in December, 1837, by the legislature of Wisconsin territory when Iowa was part of Wisconsin territory.

811 *Keokuk County*

Keokuk (1780–1848)— Keokuk, a chief of the Sauk Indian tribe, was born in what is now Illinois near the Rock River. When Chief Black Hawk supported the British in the War of 1812 Keokuk assisted the Americans. Partly of French descent, Keokuk was not a chief by birth but he was appointed chief of the Sauk tribe by the American General Winfield Scott in 1832 in violation of Sauk tribal traditions and without the consent of the Indians. Although the Indians acknowledged Keokuk as their leader, he never won their devotion. After the Black Hawk War, Keokuk and his followers moved from Illinois to the Iowa side of the Mississippi River. They spent just a few years in Iowa before being forced to move to Kansas. Chief Keokuk twice visited Washington, D.C. He died at the Sac (i.e., Sauk) Agency in Kansas in 1848. Keokuk signed some ten treaties with the United States government including one which gave the Whites title to the land now occupied by Keokuk County, Iowa. His name is spelled variously on these treaties and depending on the spelling, his name could be translated as either "the watchful fox" or "he who has been everywhere." Other possible translations of Chief Keokuk's name which have been mentioned include "running fox" and "one who moves about alert." Iowa's first Keokuk County was created by the Wisconsin territorial legislature on December 21, 1837, when Iowa was part of Wisconsin territory. That Keokuk County was abolished on July 30, 1840. By 1843 Iowa territory had been established and the legislators of Iowa territory were considering names for several new counties that they were creating. The name Keokuk was proposed for one of these counties but the legislators also considered both Dodge and Iowa as alternatives. The controversy was resolved by using Keokuk as the name of the new county directly south of the new Iowa County. However, in the February 17, 1843, act which created this county, the name was spelled as Keokuck. At that time this was the common American spelling of this Indian chief's name.

812 *Kossuth County*

Louis Kossuth (1802–1894)— Louis (or Lajos) Kossuth, the foremost leader of the

Hungarian revolution of 1848-1849, was born at Monok in northern Hungary in 1802. After practicing law he became a member of the Hungarian diet where he vigorously pressed for freedom for Hungary from its subordination to Austria. What Kossuth wanted was freedom for a Magyar Hungary. He was intolerant toward other ethnic groups in Hungary. Kossuth was imprisoned for his political views from 1837 to 1840 by the Austrians. Upon his release from prison, Kossuth continued to press his extremist views, first in a paper that he founded and later in the Hungarian diet. In 1848, when Hungary's moderate government fell, Kossuth gained dictatorial control of the revolution as chairman of the committee of national defense. However, Russia soon intervened and Kossuth fled to Turkey to escape Austrian and Russian troops. He later visited England and the United States to gain support for Hungarian independence. Kossuth County, Iowa was created on January 15, 1851, about the time of Kossuth's seven month tour of the United States.

813 *Lee County*

Uncertain— Lee County, Iowa was created in December, 1836, by the legislature of Wisconsin territory when Iowa was part of Wisconsin territory. The origin of the county's name is uncertain and disputed. Three possibilities are mentioned: (1) Albert M. Lea, an early explorer of Iowa, (2) Robert E. Lee, who was later general-in-chief of all Confederate armies during the Civil War, and (3) William E. Lee, who was a member of a New York land speculation company which owned extensive lands in the Lee County area.

Albert M. Lea (1808–)— A native of Tennessee and an 1831 graduate of the U.S. military academy at West Point, Lea participated in an 1835 expedition which crossed portions of frontier Iowa investigating sites for a possible fort. Although he was only a young lieutenant on this mission commanded by Lieutenant-Colonel Stephen W. Kearny, Albert Lea wrote a booklet about this exploration in which he used the name Iowa District for the area. His booklet, entitled *Notes on the Wisconsin Territory*, was published by Henry Tanner of Philadelphia in 1836. This little publication was significant for it established Iowa as a geographic name in America's vocabulary. Lea resigned his U.S. army commission in 1836 and the following year he became chief engineer for Tennessee. He later was a U.S. com-

missioner to mark the boundary line between Missouri and Iowa and he served briefly as acting secretary of war under President Millard Fillmore. During the Civil War Lea served on the Confederate side as an engineer in the Confederate army. After the war he settled in Texas where he died in 1891 or 1892.

Robert E. Lee (1807–1870)— Lee was a native of Virginia and, for over 30 years, an officer in the United States army. When Virginia seceded from the Union, Lee refused an offer to command all federal forces and resigned from the U.S. army to accept a commission in the Confederate army. He served with distinction in that army and became general-in-chief of it.

William E. Lee (–)— William E. Lee was a member of a New York land speculation firm which owned extensive lands in Iowa's "half-breed tract" here. (His name is incorrectly given as Charles Lee in some sources.) The partners of this Albany, New York, firm are named in the 1915 issue of the *Iowa Journal of History and Politics* as Samuel Marsh, William E. Lee and Edward C. Delavan. The name of their partnership, which owned all or most of the "half-breed tract" was New York Land Company.

Lee County was created and named in December, 1836, the year that Albert M. Lea published his book establishing the name Iowa in America's geographic name vocabulary and Albert M. Lea, himself later claimed that Lee County, Iowa had been named for him. Lea stated that the county's name was originally spelled Lea but was transcribed as Lee by clerical error. This circumstantial evidence is compelling but historians have not yet reached a consensus that it is conclusive. Meanwhile, there is no doubt that a city just north of Iowa in southern Minnesota was named for Albert M. Lea because the city's name is not just Lea, it is Albert Lea.

It is unlikely that Lee County, Iowa was named for the illustrious Confederate general, Robert E. Lee. At the time that Lee County was created, Robert E. Lee was an obscure lieutenant in the U.S. army whose activities in Iowa (survey of the Des Moines Rapids for improvement of navigation on the Mississippi) began after 1837, which was after Lee County had been created and named. During the Civil War the pro–Union Iowa legislature would certainly have renamed Lee County had they known or thought that an Iowa county was named for this Confederate leader. But this is not a conclusive argument because Iowa's Civil War era legislators likely knew less about this subject than you and

I do. Moreover, Albert M. Lea also served in the Confederate army, albeit much less conspicuously.

According to T. J. Fitzpatrick's article in the July, 1929 issue of *Annals of Iowa*, a man named Isaac Galland claimed that it had originally been proposed that this county be named for him (Galland) but that he declined the honor and suggested that the county be named for William E. Lee of the New York Land Company, instead.

As stated several hundred words earlier, the origin of Lee County, Iowa's name is uncertain.

814 *Linn County*

Lewis F. Linn (1795–1843)— Lewis F. Linn, who was born near Louisville, Kentucky, in 1795, decided to make medicine his career. Although he had not yet completed his medical training, he served in the War of 1812 as a surgeon. After the war he completed his medical training and settled on our country's frontier in Missouri where he practiced medicine and became an authority on Asiatic cholera. During the late 1820's Dr. Linn served one term in Missouri's state senate. In 1833, when U.S. Senator Alexander Buckner died, Linn was appointed by Missouri's governor to fill Buckner's seat. Dr. Linn was twice reelected to the U.S. Senate and he was serving in that body at the time of his death in 1843. Linn County, Iowa, was created in December, 1837, by the legislature of Wisconsin territory when Iowa was part of that territory. The U.S. Congress had created Wisconsin territory effective April 20, 1836, and Senator Linn had been an active supporter of the bill to create Wisconsin territory.

815 *Louisa County*

Louisa Massey (–)— Louisa County was created on December 7, 1836, by the legislature of Wisconsin territory when Iowa was a part of that territory. The county was named for Louisa Massey of Dubuque, who was a daughter of Dr. Isaiah Massey and Sarah Coffeen Massey. Louisa had become a frontier heroine a few months prior to the creation of this county by shooting a ruffian named Smith who had participated in the murder of one of her brothers because of a land claim dispute. According to some sources Smith also threatened the life of another of Louisa Massey's brothers and was believed to be seeking an opportunity to carry out the threat when she shot him.

816 *Lucas County*

Robert Lucas (1781–1853)— A native of Shepherdstown, Virginia, in what is now West Virginia, Lucas moved with his parents to the Scioto River Valley of the Northwest territory, part of which soon became the state of Ohio. There he served in the lower house of the state legislature and was an officer in the militia in which he reached the rank of major-general. After duty as a detached officer in the War of 1812, Lucas served in both houses of the Ohio legislature and he was elected governor of Ohio in 1832. That same year he was chairman of the Democratic party's first national convention. In 1834 Lucas was reelected to another term as governor of Ohio. President Martin Van Buren appointed Lucas in 1838 to be the first governor of the newly created Iowa territory and he also served as superintendent of Indian affairs in Iowa territory. This county was created and named in Robert Lucas' honor in January, 1846.

817 *Lyon County*

Nathaniel Lyon (1818–1861)— A native of Connecticut and an 1841 graduate of the U.S. military academy at West Point, Lyon participated in actions against the Seminole Indians in Florida and later in the Mexican War. Very early in the Civil War, in May, 1861, President Lincoln promoted him to brigadier-general and he was given command of Union forces in Saint Louis. In August, 1861, General Lyon commanded an attack on Confederate troops at Wilson's Creek, Missouri, which was the first Civil War battle in which Iowa troops participated. In the battle of Wilson's Creek, the Confederate army scored a victory and General Lyon was killed in combat. This Iowa county had originally been named Buncombe, in honor of Buncombe County, North Carolina. General Lyon's death at the head of his troops early in the Civil War made him a national hero and a martyr, and Iowa changed the name of this county to Lyon in 1862.

818 *Madison County*

James Madison (1751–1836)— Madison was born in Virginia, served in the Virginia legislature and in the Continental Congress. He was a member of the convention which framed the U.S. Constitution and he collaborated with Hamilton and Jay in writing a series of papers under the title *The Federalist* which explained the new constitution and advocated its adoption. Madison represented Virginia in the U.S. House of Representatives, served for eight years as secretary of state and for eight years as president of the United States. Iowa's first Madison County was created and named for James Madison in February, 1844, but that county was never organized. The present Madison County, Iowa, also named for James Madison, was created in January, 1846.

819 *Mahaska County*

Mahaska (1784–1834)— Mahaska was probably born near the mouth of the Iowa River. He was the son of a chief of the Iowa Indians named Mauhawgaw or "Wounding Arrow" and became a great chief of the Iowas himself. He led a number of war parties against the Sioux and Osage Indians. Chief Mahaska had seven wives. In 1824 he visited Washington, D.C., to take part in a treaty conference. Later, in 1833, Superintendent William Clark asked Mahaska to turn over one of his warriors to be tried for raiding the Omaha Indians. Chief Mahaska complied and in 1834 that warrior escaped from prison and shot and killed his chief in revenge. Chief Mahaska signed treaties in 1824, 1825 and 1830. In these treaties his name is rendered variously as Mohasca and Mahoska. The name means "White Cloud." In February, 1843, when the legislators of Iowa territory were considering names for this new county, the name Lucas was first proposed for it but they decided upon Mahaska and Lucas was not adopted as a name for an Iowa county until 1846. When Chief Mahaska died in 1834 his son, also named Mahaska, succeeded him as chief. Mahaska County, Iowa was named for the elder Chief Mahaska.

820 *Marion County*

Francis Marion (–1795)— Marion is believed to have been born in South Carolina. He served in the army in battles against the Cherokee Indians and was elected to the provisional congress of 1775. He served, with distinction, as an officer in the Revolutionary War and rose to the rank of general in that war. Marion was also a member of the South Carolina senate. This county was created by Iowa territory on June 10, 1845. Other names that had been proposed for this county were Nebraska, Pulaski and Center. It was Mr. Bainbridge who suggested the name Marion and his motion was seconded and adopted by unanimous vote.

821 *Marshall County*

John Marshall (1755–1835)— Marshall, a native of Virginia, served as an officer in the Revolutionary War, in the Virginia legislature and in the U.S. House of Representatives. He briefly served as secretary of state and then, for over 30 years, was chief justice of the U.S. Supreme Court. Marshall's interpretations of the constitution during America's political infancy left an unmatched impact on the laws and government of this country. Under Marshall, the supreme court shifted power in American government from the states to the central government and to the federal judiciary at the expense of the executive and legislative branches.

822 *Mills County*

Frederick D. Mills (–1847)— An 1840 graduate of Yale College, Mills moved to Iowa territory in 1841 and settled in Burlington where he practiced law. He became active in local politics and in 1845 he participated in successful opposition to a plan for statehood for Iowa. Although the plan was backed by the Democrats and although Mills was a Democrat, he opposed it because it would have resulted in a much smaller Iowa than we now have. At the beginning of the Mexican War, Mills received a commission as a major in the army. In the spring of 1847 a call was received to organize a company of Iowa volunteers for service in the Mexican War. In response, Frederick Mills and Edwin Guthrie promptly organized K Company of the 15th United States infantry regiment. Mills served as a major in that regiment. During August, 1847, American forces were advancing on the Mexican capital, Mexico City, and Mills participated in an important battle in that advance, the battle of Churubusco. Although our troops scored an important victory in this battle, Major Mills died in it on August 20, 1847. Mills County, Iowa was created in January, 1851, less than four years after Mills' death and Major Mills' name was inscribed on a mural tablet in the chapel at the U.S. military academy at West Point in honor of his heroism at the battle of Churubusco.

823 *Mitchell County*

John Mitchell (1815–1875)— This patriot and champion of nationalism for Ireland was born in County Londonderry, Ireland, in November, 1815. Educated at Trinity College in Dublin, Mitchell's early occupations were bank clerk and solicitor. In 1845 he entered the field of journalism and for the next few years he worked for a variety of publications championing nationalism for Ireland. In February, 1848, Mitchell began publishing his own weekly newspaper in Dublin, *The United Irishman*, in which he openly incited his fellow countrymen to rebellion. Just a few weeks later he was arrested for sedition. Although not convicted on that charge, he was again arrested in May, 1848, under the new treason felony act. This time he was convicted and sentenced to 14 years. In 1853 he escaped from confinement on Van Diemen's Land (now Tasmania, an island state of Australia) and made his way to America where he received an enthusiastic welcome. Here he engaged in journalism and his articles opposed abolition of slavery and generally took the southern side before, during and after the American Civil War. Following our Civil War, Mitchell lived in France, America and Ireland. In Ireland his supporters twice elected him to political office although they were of little consequence. He died in Ireland in March, 1875. Mitchell County, Iowa, was created in January, 1851 and this was none too soon. At that time Mitchell was still popular in most of our country as an Irish patriot. Just two years later Mitchell arrived in America and began publishing his anti-abolition and pro-southern articles which were offensive to the majority of Iowa's pro-Union legislators.

824 *Monona County*

Uncertain— Monona County, Iowa was created on January 15, 1851. Most sources simply state that its source is of Indian origin but that its meaning is unknown. Some accounts indicate that Monona was an Indian maiden who killed herself by jumping from a high rock into the Mississippi River because she believed that her tribesmen had killed her White lover. Virgil J. Vogel, who is an authority on Indian names, speculates in his *Iowa Place Names of Indian Origin* that Monona is not a true Indian name but an invented name and that the Monona legend is a transplanted variation of the legend of the Indian maiden Winona, for whom the city and county of Winona, Minnesota, were named. Even though Winona County, Minnesota, was created in February, 1854, three years after Monona County, Iowa, was created, it is quite plausible that the Winona legend was the source of the Monona County, Iowa geographic name. This is because the Winona legend was told as early as 1823 by William Keating and subsequently retold, with embellishments, by Mary Eastman in her 1849 *Life & Legends of the Sioux*. In the Winona legend, the Indian maiden's lover was not a White but an Indian whom she had been forbidden to marry but in their other major features, suicide by drowning on account of romantic disappointment, the legends are very similar.

825 *Monroe County*

James Monroe (1758–1831)— Monroe, a native of Virginia, served in the Revolutionary War. Prior to his election as president of the United States, Monroe served in a wide variety of government posts. He served Virginia in the state legislature and as governor. He was a member of the confederation congress and the U.S. Senate. He was minister to France and to Britain and he held two cabinet posts. As president, Monroe stressed limited government and strict construction of the constitution. He acquired Florida for the U.S. from Spain and he was the author of a policy declaration (later known as the Monroe Doctrine) which proscribed outside interference in North and South America. When this county was originally created in 1843 it was named Kishkekosh in honor of a minor chief of the allied Sauk and Fox Indian tribes. Its name was changed in 1846 to honor President Monroe.

826 *Montgomery County*

Richard Montgomery (1738–1775)— Montgomery was born in Ireland and served with the British in the French and Indian War. He settled in New York state where he was elected to the New York provisional congress. He served as a general in the American Revolutionary army and he was killed in combat in the Revolutionary War. Montgomery County, Iowa, was created in 1851.

827 *Muscatine County*

Muscatine Island, Iowa— This county was created on December 7, 1836, by Wisconsin territory when Iowa was part of that territory. In the original act creating this county, its name was spelled as Musquitine. The county was named for a spacious, sandy, prairie island in the Mississippi River, just south of the city of Muscatine, Iowa, the present county seat of Muscatine County. Due to the partial filling in of the Muscatine Slough, Muscatine Island is no longer a true island. Many sources indicate that the island was named for an Indian tribe or sub-tribe, the Mascoutens, who were known to have lived in Michigan, Wisconsin and Illinois. If the Mascoutens ever were a truly independent tribe, they were absorbed by the Sauk, Fox and Kickapoo tribes and there is no evidence that the Mascoutens ever lived on or near Muscatine Island. The island's name probably did not derive from the Mascouten Indians' name. It is more likely that it came from the Fox Indians' word for "prairie," an apt description of Muscatine Island.

828 *O'Brien County*

William S. O'Brien (1803–1864)— A native of County Clare, Ireland, and a graduate of Trinity College at Cambridge, O'Brien served in Great Britain's house of commons for about 15 years where he was a champion of legislation to assist the poor in Ireland and to promote elementary public education in Ireland. In 1843 he became one of the leaders of the Repeal Association, which advocated independence for Ireland from Great Britain. By 1848 O'Brien's efforts on behalf of independence for Ireland had escalated and he openly led an aborted insurrection in the south of Ireland for which he was arrested and tried for high treason. On October 9, 1848, he was sentenced to be hanged, drawn and quartered. This sentence was soon commuted to life imprisonment "in transportation" and he was taken to Van Diemen's Land (now Tasmania, an island state of Australia). In 1854 he received a restricted pardon and two years later O'Brien was fully pardoned and allowed to return to Ireland. O'Brien County, Iowa, was created and named in January, 1851, while William O'Brien was a martyr for Irish independence confined on Van Diemen's Land.

829 *Osceola County*

Osceola (–1838)— Osceola, the leader of Florida's Seminole Indians during the second Seminole War, was born in Alabama or Georgia about 1804 and moved with his mother to Florida territory. In 1835, when the United States government attempted to move the Seminoles from Florida to Indian territory (now Oklahoma), Osceola led the opposition which the Seminoles conducted guerrilla style from the Everglades. In October, 1837, Osceola and several other Indians went to St. Augustine under a flag of truce for a parley with General Thomas S. Jesup. He was captured and kidnapped by the unscrupulous Jesup and placed in prison at Ft. Moultrie, South Carolina. Weakened by chronic malaria and quinsy, he lost the will to live in captivity and he died on January 30, 1838. Osceola's name derived from the Creek Indians' *assiyahola* which meant "singer at the black drink." This referred to a customary cry uttered by the serving attendant during distribution of a ceremonial black drink made from the caffeine-rich leaves of the yaupon.

830 *Page County*

John Page (–1846) — Page County, Iowa, was created on February 24, 1847. At the time that many of Iowa's counties were being created and named, patriotic Mexican War fervor was high and several of Iowa's counties were named for battles and heroes of the Mexican War. One of those heroes was John Page, a captain in the Fourth U.S. Infantry. The battle of Palo Alto was the first battle of the Mexican War and it was fought on May 8, 1846, near the water hole of Palo Alto, twelve miles northeast of Brownsville, Texas. Although our troops were significantly outnumbered, they won the battle. It was in this initial engagement of the Mexican War that Captain John Page was mortally wounded. This county was created and named in Captain Page's honor less than one year after his death.

831 *Palo Alto County*

Battle of Palo Alto — Palo Alto County, Iowa was created in January, 1851, three years after the United States had defeated Mexico in the Mexican War. At the time that many of Iowa's counties were being created and named, patriotic war fervor was high and several of Iowa's counties were named for battles and heroes of the Mexican War. The battle of Palo Alto was the first battle in that war. In fact, it took place five days before the United States officially declared war on Mexico. The battle was fought on May 8, 1846, near the water hole of Palo Alto, twelve miles northeast of Brownsville, Texas. America's troops under the command of General Zachary Taylor numbered less than 2,500 but they defeated a Mexican force more than double their number. The Mexican troops were commanded by General Mariano Arista. Only nine U.S. soldiers were killed while the Mexicans lost several hundred men.

832 *Plymouth County*

Plymouth Colony in New England — Plymouth County, Iowa, was created on January 15, 1851, and named in honor of Plymouth Colony in New England where the Pilgrims landed in 1620 and founded the first permanent settlement of Europeans in New England. The Pilgrims were a small band of Puritans who were separatists from the Church of England. They traveled first to the Netherlands and then sailed from Plymouth, England across the Atlantic Ocean to North America in search of freedom from religious persecution. Plymouth, New England was an English colony and it included parts of what are now southeastern Massachusetts and eastern Rhode Island. Plymouth Colony was absorbed into another English colony, Massachusetts Bay Colony, in 1691. The Pilgrims apparently named their landing place in New England for two reasons:

1. The name Plymouth had already been inserted in this general vicinity on a map of New England by Prince Charles (who later became King Charles I of England) when he chose a number of English names to replace Indian names here.

2. The Pilgrims left the Netherlands to sail to North America on two ships, the *Speedwell* and the *Mayflower* but when the *Speedwell* proved unseaworthy it was abandoned at Plymouth, England in Devonshire. There the Pilgrims were treated with kindness by some Christians before they all crowded on the tiny *Mayflower* to continue their voyage to North America.

Plymouth, England is located in what is now called Devon County, England between the Plym and Tamar estuaries and its name came from the Plym River there. Its name means "place at the mouth of the river Plym." The river's name came from a mother settlement there, Plympton whose name meant "plum tree village." (In the late 1990's plums were still being grown here.)

833 *Pocahontas County*

Pocahontas (–1617) — Pocahontas was an American Indian girl who was born about 1596. Her father, Powhatan, was chief of a loose alliance of eastern tribes in tidewater Virginia when English colonists founded the settlement of Jamestown in 1607 on the Indians' land. The colonists' leader, Captain John Smith, was captured by the Indians and legend tells us that Pocahontas interceded to save Smith's life. Whether Smith's life was actually in danger on this occasion is uncertain but it is known that Pocahontas became friendly with the English colonists at Jamestown and was an important emissary between them and her father, Chief Powhatan. In 1614 Pocahontas married one of the colonists, John Rolfe, and that marriage resulted in a period of peace between the White settlers and the Indians. In 1616 Pocahontas and her husband paid a visit to England where she died in 1617. Pocahontas, of course, never had the slightest connection with Iowa. The idea to name an Iowa county in her honor belonged to Iowa Senator John Howell. Howell suggested this to Senator Phineas M. Casady. Senator Casady was a member of the senate's committee on new counties and it was through his efforts that Pocahontas was chosen as the name for this new county when it was created in January, 1851.

834 *Polk County*

James K. Polk (1795–1849) — Polk was a native of North Carolina who moved with his family to the Tennessee frontier in 1806. He served in the lower house of the Tennessee legislature and he represented Tennessee for 14 years in the U.S. House of Representatives, where he was speaker. He served one term as governor of Tennessee. Polk became president of the United States as a dark horse candidate of the Democratic party but he became an unusually strong and effective president. His primary accomplishments involved westward extension of the United States; in the Northwest by settling a territorial dispute with Britain and in California and the Southwest by provoking and winning the Mexican War. Polk County was created in January, 1846, by the legislature of Iowa territory while Polk was serving as president. Later that year President Polk signed the law that admitted Iowa to the Union as a state.

835 *Pottawattamie County*

Potawatomi Indians — Apparently the three tribes that we now know as Potawatomi, Chippewa and Ottawa were once one people. According to tradition, the Potawatomi migrated from somewhere northeast of Michigan. When they were first encountered by the French, they were living in the region around Green Bay, Wisconsin and on or near the shores of Lake Michigan. There they served as middlemen in the French fur trade. The women of this Algonquian tribe made pottery and the men made fine birch-bark canoes. Tattooing was common among the men and both men and women used body paint. The Potawatomi were relentlessly driven south and west by both Indians and Whites. For a time they lived in southern Michigan and northern Illinois and in the late 1700's they participated in the struggle for control of the Ohio River Valley. By 1800 they were scattered in some 100 villages spread over Wisconsin, Illinois, Michigan and Indiana. By the 1830's the Potawatomi had ceded most of those lands and had been pushed west. By treaties made on June 5, 1846, and June 17, 1846, the Potawatomi Chippewa and Ottawa Indians ceded to the United States all lands in Iowa to which they had any claims. This area extended all the way westward to the Missouri River and included the land which was soon to become Pottawattamie County, Iowa. There was a Potawatomi Indian reservation here from 1835 to 1848. Many of the Potawatomi were pushed further west to Kansas and Oklahoma. Numerous spellings for the tribal name are encountered. *Potawatomi* is the version approved by the former Bureau of American Ethnology. Various translations of the name are also mentioned but there is little doubt that the name refers to "fire."

836 *Poweshiek County*

Poweshiek (1797–)—Poweshiek was a chief of the Fox Indian tribe at the time that the Fox Indians were allied with the Sauk Indians. He is said to have been a daring warrior but wise and temperate in his dealings with Whites. Poweshiek and his Fox Indians were among the first Indians to leave Illinois and cross the Mississippi River to live in Iowa. This move reduced the fighting forces available to Chief Black Hawk in his resistance to White domination. Chief Poweshiek signed treaties with the Whites ceding Indian lands to them in 1832, 1836, 1837 and 1842. When the Whites began to push Poweshiek to leave Iowa and move still further west, he resisted for a time using a variety of ruses to postpone the day of removal. However, Chief Poweshiek and a band of his Fox Indians were expelled to Kansas in 1846 and he died there a few years later. This county was created on February 17, 1843, by the legislature of Iowa territory. Its name in the original bill was Wapello County but Poweshiek was the name finally selected for this county. Wapello was, however, used for the name of another new county that was created on the same day.

837 *Ringgold County*

Samuel Ringgold (1800–1846)—A native of Maryland and a graduate of the U.S. military academy at West Point, Ringgold entered the U.S. army as a lieutenant of artillery in 1818 and served for a time as an aide to General Winfield Scott. By 1834 Ringgold had been promoted to the rank of captain. He served with distinction in actions against the Indians in Florida and was promoted to brevet major. Ringgold's entire military career was in the artillery and he invented several improvements to artillery equipment. At the outbreak of the Mexican War, Ringgold organized a unit known as a "flying artillery" and this unit participated in the battle of Palo Alto, the first battle of the Mexican War. Although our troops were badly outnumbered, they won this battle. It was in this initial engagement of the Mexican War that Major Ringgold was mortally wounded by a cannon ball and he died three days later. Ringgold County, Iowa, was created on February 24, 1847, less than one year after Major Ringgold's death. At the time that many of Iowa's counties were being created and named, patriotic war fervor was high and several of Iowa's counties were named for battles and heroes of the Mexican War.

838 *Sac County*

Sauk Indians—The Sauk Indians' name is rendered by some as Sac and it was this version that the Iowa legislature chose when it created and named this county in 1851. At one time the Sauk Indians lived in eastern Michigan. Other Indians forced them from that area and they next settled in the vicinity of Green Bay, Wisconsin. During this period the Sauk were woodland dwellers who lived in bark lodges, cultivated vegetables and traded furs to the French. The Sauk tribe allied themselves with the Fox Indians and these united tribes moved to Missouri and later to Illinois. When they were driven from Illinois by the U.S. army and other Indians, the allied Sauk and Fox tribes took control of Iowa from the Dakota Indians. At one time the allied Sauk and Fox Indians possessed nearly the entire state of Iowa. The Whites later forced the Sauk out of Iowa to Kansas and finally from Kansas to Indian territory (now Oklahoma). The name *Sauk* derived from a name which meant "yellow earth," referring to the clay from which their supreme deity was said to have created them.

839 *Scott County*

Winfield Scott (1786–1866)—A native of Virginia, Scott joined the U.S. army in 1808. His heroic service in the War of 1812 resulted in rapid promotions to brevet major-general. He later played important military roles during the 1832 nullification crisis in South Carolina, against the Indians in Florida and as general-in-chief of the United States army during the Mexican War. Scott was the Whig party's candidate for president in 1852 but he lost to Franklin Pierce. When the Civil War began, Scott remained loyal to the Union side despite his southern roots but he retired from the U.S. army in October, 1861 on account of age and ill health. Scott County, Iowa, was created on December 21, 1837, by Wisconsin territory, when Iowa was part of that territory. In 1832 General Scott had negotiated the first purchase of lands from the Indians in what is now Iowa. The treaty that accomplished that was made in what later became Scott County, Iowa.

840 *Shelby County*

Isaac Shelby (1750–1826)—Shelby was a delegate to the Virginia legislature and, later, to the North Carolina legislature. He served as a soldier in the Revolutionary War and the moved to Kentucky County, Virginia, where he was active in the movement to separate Kentucky from Virginia. Shelby was inaugurated as Kentucky's first governor on the same day that Kentucky became a state. Shelby also fought in the War of 1812.

841 *Sioux County*

Dakota Indians—This county was created in January, 1851, and named for the Dakota, a vast alliance of American Indians, who are more commonly known as the Sioux Indians. The name *Sioux* was the terminal portion of a derogatory Ojibwa-(Chippewa) French name for the Dakotas, *Nadouaissioux*, which literally meant "like unto adders" or "like unto snakes" with the implied meaning "our enemies." The Dakotas consist of three general dialect and culture groups: the Santee, Wiciyela and Teton. At one time the Dakota possessed a large portion of northwestern Iowa. When the Whites first encountered the Dakotas, about 1640, they found them living in southern Minnesota and adjacent areas subsisting by hunting, fishing, gathering lake and forest products and growing corn. They were forced west by other Indians who had been armed by the French and by the mid-1700's some Dakotas had crossed the Missouri River and reached the Black Hills. There they changed their lifestyle to that of nomadic tepee-dwelling buffalo hunters. The Dakota, or Sioux, are well known American Indians, probably because they were among the last to engage in dramatic armed conflict with the United States army highlighted by the famous battles of Little Bighorn and Wounded Knee in the late 1800's. By the late 1970's there were about 40,000 Dakota Indians, most of whom were living on reservations in North Dakota and South Dakota.

842 *Story County*

Joseph Story (1779–1845)— A native of Massachusetts, graduate of Harvard and lawyer, Story served in the lower house of the Massachusetts legislature and was, for a time, its speaker. He also represented Massachusetts briefly in the U.S. House of Representatives. In 1811 President James Madison appointed Story to be an associate justice of the U.S. Supreme Court and he remained on the U.S. Supreme Court from 1811 until his death on September 10, 1845. Story County, Iowa, was created and named just four months later, on January 13, 1846, by Iowa territory. The county's name was suggested by a member of the territorial general assembly from Des Moines whose name is given in some accounts as P. M. Casady and in others as P. M. Cassady.

843 *Tama County*

Tama (–)—Tama, a chief of the Fox Indians, was born about 1780. During the late 1820's and early 1830's he and his people lived near the present site of Burlington, Iowa. In 1824 Chief Tama visited Washington, D.C., to negotiate a treaty with the Whites. He is also known to have signed two other treaties with the Whites, one at Prairie du Chien in what is now Wisconsin on August 19, 1825, and another at Fort Armstrong on September 21, 1832. Tama signed these treaties with an "X." His name was inscribed on the treaties by the Whites. On these treaties his name appears variously as Faimah, Tiamah and Tayweemau. It is believed that Tama's name meant "sudden crash" (of thunder) and Chief Tama was a member of the thunder clan. He died about 1833. Some sources indicate that Tama County, Iowa, was named for a wife of the Fox Indian chief Poweshiek. This is simply incorrect. However, the county's name was not selected easily. It was during February, 1843, that Iowa's territorial legislature created and named this county. In the original bill its name was to be Tecumseh but an amendment proposed that the name Winani be used instead. The name Tama was finally selected and it became the county's name when it was created on February 17, 1843.

844 *Taylor County*

Zachary Taylor (1784–1850)— Taylor was born in Virginia but moved as an infant to Kentucky where he grew to manhood on a farm near Louisville. A career soldier, Taylor served as an officer in the War of 1812, the Black Hawk War, the second Seminole War in Florida territory and the Mexican War. Taylor's service in the Mexican War made him a national hero and resulted in his election as president of the United States. Although he was a slave owner, he opposed the extension of slavery beyond the 15 states where the institution was already legal. Taylor had served only 16 months as president when he died in office on July 9, 1850. Taylor County, Iowa, was created and named on February 24, 1847, while General Taylor was gaining fame and popularity in the Mexican War. At the time that many of Iowa's counties were being created and named, patriotic war fervor was high and several of Iowa's counties were named for battles and heroes of the Mexican War. Taylor became president of the United States two years after this county was created.

845 *Union County*

Preservation of America's union of states— Union County, Iowa was created on January 15, 1851. In the original bill to create this county its proposed name was Mason, in honor of Judge Charles Mason, a former chief justice of the supreme court of the territory and currently the principal code commissioner. However, upon a motion by Senator Morton from Henry County, the name was changed to Union County for two reasons: One reason for the change was to avoid injustice to other men occupying prominent positions in the state by selecting Judge Mason for this honor; but the more important reason involved the fervent hope that preservation of America's union of states was now possible. For several decades tension had been building between the North and the South over the slavery issue and preservation of the union began to seem precarious. But in September, 1850, the tide seemed to turn when the U.S. Congress enacted five compromise measures which were later given the collective term "Compromise of 1850." Hopes were still high then, four months later on January 15, 1851, when the Iowa legislators chose the name Union County, that the union of states could be preserved and secession and civil war averted. They were, of course, wrong. Just ten years later secession and Civil War became a reality.

846 *Van Buren County*

Martin Van Buren (1782–1862)— Van Buren was a native of New York and he served that state as state senator, attorney general and governor. He represented New York in the U.S. Senate and was secretary of state in President Jackson's cabinet. He served one term as vice-president of the United States and one term as president. Van Buren organized an effective political machine in New York state which was one of the first political machines in this country. On the national level, he was one of the early users of the spoils system of filling government jobs. Van Buren County was created on December 7, 1836, by the legislature of Wisconsin territory when Iowa was part of that territory and named for the president-elect, Martin Van Buren. At that time Van Buren was vice-president of the United States. His term as president began on March 4, 1837.

847 *Wapello County*

Wapello (1787–1842)— Wapello, a chief of the Fox Indians, was born in 1787 where Prairie du Chien, Wisconsin, now stands. Later his principal village was on the east side of the Mississippi River where the city of Rock Island, Illinois, was subsequently laid out. In 1829 he moved his village across the Mississippi to Iowa near Muscatine Island and he subsequently moved his people several times to other locations in Iowa. Wapello did not participate in the Black Hawk War and although he was opposed to the forced removal of Indians from their lands by the Whites, his opposition was peaceful and essentially ineffective. Between 1822 and 1837 Chief Wapello signed five treaties with the Whites. He was one of the Indian chiefs who accompanied Chief Black Hawk and Chief Keokuk to Washington, D.C., in 1837. His favorite hunting grounds were along the Skunk River but he finally moved his village to the banks of the Des Moines River where Ottumwa, Iowa, now stands. Chief Wapello died on March 15, 1842, and less than one year later, on February 17, 1843, the legislators of Iowa territory created and named this county in his honor. Wapello County embraces both Chief Wapello's former home at Ottumwa and his grave which is located near Agency, Iowa.

848 *Warren County*

Joseph Warren (1741–1775)— This county was created in January, 1846, by the legislature of Iowa territory and named in honor of the American Revolutionary War hero, Joseph Warren. A native of Massachusetts and a graduate of Harvard College, Warren practiced medicine in the Boston area. He was a member of the committee of safety and president *pro tempore* of the Massachusetts provincial congress. In June, 1775, he was commissioned a major-general and he died in combat a few days later at the battle of Bunker Hill.

849 *Washington County*

George Washington (1732–1799) — Washington was a native of Virginia. He served in Virginia's house of burgesses and became one of the colonies' leaders in opposition to British policies in America. He was a member of the first and second Continental Congresses and commander of all continental armies in the Revolutionary War. Following victory in that war, Washington was elected to be the first president of the United States. This county was originally created as Slaughter County in 1837 by Wisconsin territory when Iowa was part of that territory. Its name honored William B. Slaughter, a secretary of Wisconsin territory. In January, 1839, the county's name was changed to Washington by the legislature of Iowa territory.

850 *Wayne County*

Anthony Wayne (1745–1796) — A native of Pennsylvania, Wayne was a successful brigadier-general in the Revolutionary War and became a hero for his daring exploits. During the bitter winter of 1777-1778 at Valley Forge, Pennsylvania, Wayne shared the sufferings of his men although his comfortable estate was only five miles away. He played an important role in the final overthrow of the British forces in Georgia. After the war, in 1785, Wayne moved to Georgia and he represented Georgia for about six months in the U.S. House of Representatives. In 1792 President Washington recalled Wayne to serve as a major-general against the Indians in the Northwest territory. Once again his military efforts were successful.

851 *Webster County*

Daniel Webster (1782–1852) — Webster was born in New Hampshire and represented that state in the U.S. House of Representatives. He later represented Massachusetts in both houses of the U.S. Congress and served as secretary of state under three presidents. Webster felt that slavery was evil but not as evil as disunion of the United States. He played a key role in the passage of the five laws in the U.S. Congress which are known as the "Compromise of 1850" which were intended to avert secession and civil war between the North and

the South over the slavery issue. Daniel Webster died on October 24, 1852, and Webster County was named in his honor just three months later, in January, 1853. This was part of a compromise in which Calhoun County, Iowa, was named for South Carolina's fiery Senator John C. Calhoun provided a county was also named for Calhoun's political foe, Daniel Webster. Webster County was formed by uniting two existing counties, Risley County and Yell County, which had been named for heroes of the Mexican War.

852 *Winnebago County*

Winnebago Indians — At the time of early contact with Whites, the Winnebago tribe lived in central Wisconsin from Green Bay and Lake Winnebago to the Mississippi River and along the Rock River in southern Wisconsin and extreme northern Illinois. In their material culture, the Winnebago were distinctly timber people. They sided with the British during both the American Revolution and the War of 1812. In the early and mid 1800's, the Winnebago were forced from their lands in northern Illinois and in Wisconsin by the Whites using both treaties and military force. First they were moved to northern Iowa, then to Minnesota, next to South Dakota and then to a reservation in northeastern Nebraska. However, many Winnebago in Nebraska made their own way back to Wisconsin. Although never huge in numbers, their population was estimated at about 5,000 in the first half of the 19th century. These Indians called themselves "big fish people" but it is the Algonquian name for them, Winnebago, that has stuck. Its precise meaning is uncertain but translations for it relate to "stinking" and "water" and include "stinking water" and "dirty water people" and "stinking water people." Both Father Marquette and Cadillac were careful to record that the Winnebago's name did not signify any unclean habits of these Indians but pertained to water. It is likely that the name Winnebago referred to their earlier northern home, perhaps in Canada, and originally meant "people of the sea."

853 *Winneshiek County*

Winneshiek (1812–) — Winneshiek was a chief of the Winnebago Indians but there were at least three prominent Winnebago chiefs named Winneshiek. Winneshiek County, Iowa, was named for the one who was born in 1812 at Portage, Wisconsin. During the Black Hawk War in 1832, he supported the Sauk chief, Black

Hawk, in his war with the U.S. army. In 1840 Winneshiek accompanied his people when they were removed from Wisconsin and forced to move to Iowa. By 1845 the U.S. government decided that Winneshiek had become cooperative enough to be appointed by them as head chief of the Winnebagos. However, in 1859 when he and his people had been forced from Iowa and moved to the Mankato, Minnesota area, Winneshiek refused to sign away more Indian lands to the Whites and he was promptly deposed for insubordination. Winneshiek and his people were next removed to South Dakota and then to a reservation in northeastern Nebraska. He died about 1872. Winneshiek County, Iowa, was created and named in his honor in 1847 while he was still cooperating with White authority.

854 *Woodbury County*

Levi Woodbury (1789–1851) — A native of New Hampshire and a graduate of Dartmouth College there, Woodbury was a lawyer. He served in his native state on the state supreme court, as governor and as a member of the state legislature. In 1825 Woodbury entered the United States senate where he represented New Hampshire until 1831. In May, 1831, President Andrew Jackson appointed him to serve in the cabinet as secretary of the navy. He later served in Jackson's cabinet as secretary of the treasury and he remained in that position when Martin Van Buren assumed the presidency in 1837. After serving ten consecutive years as a cabinet officer, Woodbury was returned to the U.S. Senate. In September, 1845, President James K. Polk appointed Woodbury to be an associate justice on the U.S. Supreme Court. He remained on the court until his death on September 4, 1851. Wahkaw County, Iowa had been created in January, 1851. Its name was changed to honor Judge Woodbury in January, 1853. (In the legislature's journal of the act changing the county's name, the original name is spelled Wahkah.)

855 *Worth County*

William J. Worth (1794–1849) — A native of New York, Worth enlisted in the army as a private in the War of 1812 and rose to the rank of major. At the close of the war Worth became commandant of the U.S. military academy at West Point. He later served as a brigadier-general against the Seminole Indians in Florida and became a national hero as a successful major-general in the Mexican War.

General Worth died on May 7, 1849, and this county was created and named in his honor less than two years later, on January 15, 1851. At the time that many of Iowa's counties were being created and named, patriotic war fervor was high and several of Iowa's counties were named for battles and heroes of the Mexican War.

856 *Wright County*

Joseph A. Wright (1810–1867) & Silas Wright (1795–1847)— This county was created on January 15, 1851, and its name was selected before it was agreed among the legislators precisely whom the county's name was intended to honor. The legislators final consensus was that the county would be named Wright County and that its name would honor both Joseph A. Wright, the current governor of the state of Indiana, and Silas Wright, a prominent New York statesman.

Joseph A. Wright (1810–1867)— A native of Pennsylvania, Joseph Wright moved with his parents to Indiana when he was still a boy. There he graduated from Indiana University, studied law and began a practice in Rockville, Indiana. Joseph Wright was elected to the state's house of representatives and he later served in the Indiana senate before being elected to represent Indiana in the U.S. House of Representatives. He next was elected governor of Indiana and served in that office from 1849 to 1857. For the next four years he was our country's minister to Prussia. On February 5, 1862, during the Civil War, Indiana's U.S. Senator Jesse D. Bright was expelled from the senate for sending a complementary letter to Jefferson Davis, who was then president of the Confederate States of America. Joseph A. Wright, a Unionist, was chosen to take Bright's seat in the senate. However, in the election in the fall of 1862, Indiana's voters sent a Democratic majority to their general assembly. The new Indiana legislature promptly elected Democrats to represent Indiana in the senate, thus ending Joseph Wright's brief term as a U.S. senator. He was then sent once again as our country's minister to Prussia.

Silas Wright (1795–1847)— A native of Massachusetts and a lawyer, Silas Wright served in the New York senate and, in 1827, he was appointed brigadier-general of the New York state militia. He later represented New York in both houses of the U.S. Congress, serving eleven years in the United States senate. In 1844, Silas Wright, a Democrat, was nominated to run as James K. Polk's vice-presidential running mate but he declined the nomination. He then served one term as governor of New York state.

REFERENCES

Abernethy, Alonzo. "Early Iowa Indian Treaties & Boundaries." *Annals of Iowa*, Vol. 11, No. 4. Des Moines: January, 1914.

Ackerman, William K. *Early Illinois Railroads*. Chicago, Fergus Printing Co., 1884.

Alexander, W. E. *History of Winneshiek & Allamakee Counties, Iowa*. Sioux City, Iowa, Western Publishing Co., 1882.

Andrews, H. F. *History of Audubon County, Iowa*. Indianapolis, Indiana, B. F. Bowen & Co., Inc., 1915.

Baylies, Francis. *An Historical Memoir of the Colony of New Plymouth*. Boston, Wiggin & Lunt, 1866.

Biographical & Historical Memoirs of Story County, Iowa. Chicago, Goodspeed Publishing Co., 1890.

Biographical & Historical Record of Ringgold & Decatur Counties, Iowa. Chicago, Lewis Publishing Co., 1887.

Biographical & Historical Record of Wayne & Appanoose Counties, Iowa. Chicago, Interstate Publishing Co., 1886.

Blanchard, Charles. "Religion in Iowa: The Catholics." *Annals of Iowa*, Vol. 3, No. 1. Des Moines: April, 1897.

Brewer, Guy S. *The Iowa Official Register: For the Years 1909–1910*. Des Moines, Emory H. English, State Printer, 1909.

Briggs, John E. "New Counties in 1843." *The Palimpsest*, Vol. 24, No. 12. Iowa City: December, 1943.

Brown Don D. *Iowa: The Land Across the River*. Des Moines, Wallace-Homestead Co., 1963.

Calhoun County History. Rockwell City, Iowa, Calhoun County Historical Society, 1982.

Casady, P. M. "The Naming of Iowa Counties." *Annals of Iowa*, Vol. 2, No. 1. Des Moines: April, 1895.

Chidsey, Donald B. *The War with Mexico*. New York, Crown Publishers, Inc., 1968.

Childs, Chandler C. *Dubuque: Frontier River City*. Dubuque, Iowa, Research Center for Dubuque Area History, 1984.

Childs, C. C. "Names of Iowa Counties." *Iowa Historical Record*, Vol. 4, No. 1. January, 1888.

Clements, John. *Iowa Facts*. Dallas, Texas, Clements Research, Inc., 1988.

Clift, G. Glenn. *Remember the Raisin!* Frankfort, Kentucky, Kentucky Historical Society, 1961.

Cole, Cyrenus. *Iowa Through the Years*.

Iowa City, State Historical Society of Iowa, 1940.

Crawford, Lewis F. *History of North Dakota*. Chicago, American Historical Society, Inc., 1931.

Curtiss-Wedge, Franklyn. *History of Freeborn County, Minnesota*. Chicago, H. C. Cooper, Jr. & Co., 1911.

Davis, William T. *History of the Town of Plymouth*. Philadelphia, J. W. Lewis & Co., 1885.

Dictionary of Indians of North America. St. Clair Shores, Michigan, Scholarly Press, Inc., 1978.

Donehoo, George P. *A History of the Indian Villages & Place Names in Pennsylvania*. Harrisburg, Pennsylvania, Telegraph Press, 1928.

Donnel, William M. *Pioneers of Marion County*. Des Moines, Republican Steam Printing House, 1872.

"Dubuque's Grave." *Annals of Iowa*, Vol. 1, No. 1. Des Moines: April, 1893.

Dwelle, Jessie M. *Iowa Beautiful Land: A History of Iowa*. Mason City, Iowa, Klipto Loose Leaf Co., 1954.

Field, Homer H., & Joseph R. Reed. *History of Pottawattamie County, Iowa*. Chicago, S. J. Clarke Publishing Co., 1907.

Field, John. *Place-Names of Great Britain & Ireland*. Totowa, New Jersey, Barnes & Noble Books, 1980.

"The First Hundred Years: A Brief History of Iowa." *Iowa Journal of History & Politics*, Vol. 31. Iowa City: 1933.

Fitzpatrick, T. J. "The Place-Names of Appanoose County, Iowa." *American Speech*, Vol. 3, No. 1. Baltimore: October, 1927.

Fitzpatrick, T. J. "The Place-Names of Des Moines County, Iowa." *Annals of Iowa*, Vol. 21, No. 1. Des Moines: July, 1937.

Fitzpatrick, T. J. "The Place-Names of Lee County, Iowa." *Annals of Iowa*, Vol. 17, No. 1. Des Moines: July, 1929.

Fitzpatrick, T. J. "The Place-Names of Van Buren County, Iowa." *Annals of Iowa*, Vol. 18, No. 1. Des Moines: July, 1931.

Fleming, William H. "Floyd County Named for William Floyd." *Annals of Iowa*, Vol. 12, No. 8. Des Moines: April, 1921.

Freeman, Douglas S. *R. E. Lee: A Biography*. New York, Charles Scribner's Sons, 1934.

Frost, J. *The Mexican War & Its Warriors*. New Haven, H. Mansfield, 1850.

Gallaher, Ruth A. "Albert Miller Lea." *Iowa Journal of History & Politics*, Vol. 33. Iowa City: July, 1935.

Gallaher, Ruth A. "Albert Miller Lea." *The Palimpsest*, Vol. 16, No. 3. Iowa City: March, 1935.

Garver, Frank H. "History of the Establishment of Counties in Iowa." *Iowa*

Journal of History & Politics, Vol. 6. Iowa City: 1908.

Garver, Frank H. "The Story of Sergeant Charles Floyd." *Proceedings of the Mississippi Valley Historical Association for the Year 1908–1909*, Vol. 2. Cedar Rapids, Iowa: 1910.

Gemmill, William N. *Romantic America*. Chicago, Jordan Publishing Co., 1926.

Gilliam, Charles E. "Pocahontas-Matoaka." *Names: Journal of the American Name Society*, Vol. 2, No. 3. Berkeley: September, 1954.

Gover, J. E. B., et al. *The Place-Names of Devon*. Cambridge, University Press, 1931.

Gue, Benjamin F. *History of Iowa*. New York, Century History Co., 1903.

Hake, Herbert V. *Iowa Inside Out*. Ames, Iowa, Iowa State University Press, 1968.

Harlan, Edgar R. *A Narrative History of the People of Iowa*. Chicago, American Historical Society, Inc., 1931.

Hastie Eugene N. *High Points of Iowa History*. Perry, Iowa, 1966.

Herriott, F. I. "Whence Came the Pioneers of Iowa?" *Annals of Iowa*, Vol. 7, No. 1. Des Moines: April, 1905.

Hickenlooper, Frank. *An Illustrated History of Monroe County, Iowa*. Albia, Iowa, 1896.

Hills, Leon C. *History & Legends of Place Names in Iowa: The Meaning of Our Map*. Omaha, Nebraska, Omaha School Supply Co., 1938.

The History of Boone County, Iowa. Des Moines, Union Historical Co., 1880.

History of the Counties of Woodbury & Plymouth, Iowa. Chicago, A. Warner & Co., 1890–1891.

History of Elkhart County, Indiana. Chicago, Chas. C. Chapman & Co., 1881.

History of Floyd County, Iowa. Chicago, Interstate Publishing Co., 1882.

History of Guthrie & Adair Counties, Iowa. Springfield, Illinois, Continental Historical Co., 1884.

History of Johnson County, Iowa. Iowa City, 1883.

The History of Keokuk County, Iowa. Des Moines, Union Historical Co., 1880.

The History of Lee County, Iowa. Chicago, Western Historical Co., 1879.

The History of Mahaska County, Iowa. Des Moines, Union Historical Co., 1878.

The History of Muscatine County, Iowa. Chicago, Western Historical Co., 1879.

The History of Polk County, Iowa. Des Moines, Union Historical Co., 1880.

History of Scott County, Iowa. Chicago, Interstate Publishing Co., 1882.

History of Tama County, Iowa. Springfield, Illinois, Illinois Union Publishing Co., 1883.

The History of Wapello County, Iowa. Chicago, Western Historical Co., 1878.

Hodge, Frederick W. *Handbook of American Indians North of Mexico*. Totowa, New Jersey, Rowman & Littlefield, 1975.

Hoffmann, M. M. *Antique Dubuque: 1673–1833*. Dubuque, Telegraph-Herald Press, 1930.

Hull, John A. T. *Census of Iowa for 1880*. Des Moines, F. M. Mills & Geo. E. Roberts, State Printers, 1883.

Hurd, D. Hamilton. *History of Plymouth County, Massachusetts*. Philadelphia, J. W. Lewis & Co., 1884.

Ide, George A. *History of Union County, Iowa*. Chicago, S. J. Clarke Publishing Co., 1908.

Jackson, Alfred A. "Abraham Lincoln in the Black Hawk War." *Collections of the State Historical Society of Wisconsin*, Vol. 14. Madison: 1898.

Jackson, Ronald V., et al. *Iowa 1836 Territorial Census Index*. Bountiful, Utah, Accelerated Indexing Systems, Inc., 1976.

Jasper County Historical Foundation, Inc. *History of Jasper County, Georgia*. Roswell, Georgia, W. H. Wolfe Associates, 1976.

Keyes, Charles R. "Spanish Mines: An Episode in Primitive American Lead-Mining." *Annals of Iowa*, Vol. 10, No. 1. Des Moines: April, 1911.

Lathrop, H. W. "The Naming of Lee County." *Iowa Historical Record*, Iowa City: July, 1893.

Lea, Albert M. "Albert Miller Lea." *Iowa Historical Record*, Iowa City: January, 1892.

Lea, Albert M. "Iowa District of Wisconsin Territory: General Description." *Annals of Iowa*, Vol. 3, No. 1. Des Moines: April, 1897.

Leitch, Barbara A. *A Concise Dictionary of Indian Tribes of North America*. Algonac, Michigan, Reference Publications, Inc., 1979.

Leonard, Arthur G. "History of Lead & Zinc Mining in Iowa." *Annals of Iowa*, Vol. 36, No. 1. Des Moines: Summer, 1961.

Lutz, Jule. *Iowa Official Register: 1979–1980*.

McKenney, Thomas L. & James Hall. *The Indian Tribes of North America*, Edinburgh, John Grant, 1933.

Mason, Emily V. *Popular Life of Gen. Robert Edward Lee*. Baltimore, John Murphy & Co., 1872.

Merryman, Robert M. *A Hero Nonetheless: Albert Miller Lea, 1808–1891*. Lake Mills, Iowa, Graphic Publishing Co., Inc., 1983.

Moir, William J. *Past & Present of Hardin County, Iowa*. Indianapolis, B. F. Bowen & Co., 1911.

Montzheimer, O. H. "Judicial Districts in Northwestern Iowa." *Annals of Iowa*, Vol. 20, No. 7. Des Moines: January, 1937.

"Naming of Iowa Counties." *Annals of Iowa*, Vol. 3, No. 1. Des Moines: April, 1897.

"Naming of Iowa Counties." *Annals of Iowa*, Vol. 36, No. 5. Des Moines: Summer, 1962.

Needham, Sherman W. *Iowa Official Register: 1957–1958*.

Nelson, H. L. *A Geography of Iowa*. Lincoln, University of Nebraska Press, 1967.

"The Oldest Land Titles in Iowa." *Iowa Journal of History & Politics*, Vol. 13. Iowa City: 1915.

Oldt, Franklin T. *History of Dubuque County, Iowa*. Chicago, Goodspeed Historical Association.

Parvin, T. S. "A Bundle of Errors." *Iowa Historical Record*, Iowa City: April, 1893.

Parvin, T. S. "General Robert Lucas." *Annals of Iowa*, Vol. 2, No. 6. Des Moines: July, 1896.

Peck, J. L. E., et al. *Past & Present of O'Brien & Osceola Counties, Iowa*. Indianapolis, B. F. Bowen & Co., Inc., 1914.

Perkins, D. A. W. *History of O'Brien County, Iowa*. Sioux Falls, South Dakota, Brown & Saenger, 1897.

Petersen, William J. *Iowa: The Rivers of Her Valleys*. Iowa City, State Historical Society of Iowa, 1941.

Petersen, William J. *The Story of Iowa: The Progress of an American State*. New York, Lewis Historical Publishing Co., Inc., 1952.

Phillips, Semira A. *Proud Mahaska*. Oskaloosa, Iowa, Herald Print, 1900.

Polk, Harry H. "Old Fort Des Moines." *Annals of Iowa*, Vol. 3, No. 1. Des Moines: April, 1897.

Porter, Will. *Annals of Polk County, Iowa & City of Des Moines*. Des Moines, George A. Miller Printing Co., 1898.

Portrait & Biographical Album of Lee County, Iowa. Chicago, Chapman Brothers, 1887.

Posten, Margaret L. *This Is the Place: Iowa*. Ames, Iowa, Iowa State University Press, 1965.

Powell., Clifford. "The Contributions of Albert Miller Lea to the Literature of Iowa History." *Iowa Journal of History & Politics*, Vol. 9, Iowa City: 1911.

Powell, Henry F. *Tercentenary History of Maryland*. Chicago, S. J. Clarke Publishing Co., 1925.

Pratt, LeRoy G. *The Counties & Courthouses of Iowa*. Mason City, Iowa, Klipto Printing & Office Supply Co., 1977.

Reed, Benjamin F. *History of Kossuth County, Iowa.* Chicago, S. J. Clarke Publishing Co., 1913.

Robarts, William H. *Mexican War Veterans: A Complete Roster of the Regular & Volunteer Troops in the War Between the United States & Mexico from 1846 to 1848.* Washington, D.C., A. S. Witherbee & Co., 1887.

Roberts, Nelson C., & S. W. Moorhead. *Story of Lee County, Iowa.* Chicago, S. J. Clarke Publishing Co., 1914.

Sabin, Henry, & Edwin L. Sabin. *The Making of Iowa.* Chicago, A. Flanagan Co., 1900.

Sage, Leland. *A History of Iowa.* Ames, Iowa State University Press, 1974.

Salter, William. *Iowa: The First Free State in the Louisiana Purchase.* Chicago, A. C. McClurg & Co., 1905.

Semi-Centennial Souvenir Edition of the Muscatine Journal. Muscatine, Iowa, January, 1891.

Shambaugh, Benjamin F. "The Origin of the Name Iowa." *Annals of Iowa,* Vol. 36, No. 1. Des Moines: Summer, 1961.

Shankle, George Earlie. *State Names, Flags, Seals, Songs, Birds, Flowers & Other Symbols.* New York, H. W. Wilson Co., 1941.

Shiras, Oliver P. "The Mines of Spain." *Annals of Iowa,* Vol. 5, No. 5. Des Moines: April, 1902.

Smith, William. *A New Classical Dictionary of Greek & Roman Biography, Mythology & Geography.* New York, Harper & Brothers, 1871.

Stennett, William H. *A History of the Origin of the Place Names Connected with the Chicago & North Western & Chicago, St. Paul, Minneapolis & Omaha Railways.* Chicago, 1908.

Sterling, Dorothy. Letter to the Editor of the *New York Times,* November 11, 1989.

Stiles, Edward H. "Prominent Men of Early Iowa." *Annals of Iowa,* Vol. 10, No. 1. Des Moines: April, 1911.

Stiles, Edward H. *Recollections & Sketches of Notable Lawyers & Public Men of Early Iowa.* Des Moines, Homestead Publishing Co., 1916.

Stout, Joseph A. *Frontier Adventurers: American Exploration in Oklahoma.* Oklahoma City, Oklahoma Historical Society, 1976.

Stoutenburgh, John. *Dictionary of the American Indians.* New York, Bonanza Books, 1960.

Swisher, Jacob A. *Iowa in Times of War.* Iowa City, State Historical Society of Iowa, 1943.

"Tesson's Apple Orchard." *The Palimpsest,* Vol. 4. Iowa City: 1923.

"Three Forts Des Moines." *Annals of Iowa,* Vol. 25, No. 1. Des Moines: July, 1943.

Thrift, William H. *Roster & Record of Iowa Soldiers in Miscellaneous Organizations of the Mexican War, Indian Campaigns, War of the Rebellion & the Spanish-American & Philippine Wars.* Des Moines, Emory H. English, State Printer, 1911.

Tregillis, Helen C. *The Indians of Illinois.* Decorah, Iowa, Anundsen Publishing Co., 1983.

Upham, Cyril B. "The Mexican War." *Iowa & War,* No. 12. Iowa City: June, 1918.

Upham, Warren & Rose B. Dunlap. "Minnesota Biographies: 1655–1912." *Collections of the Minnesota Historical Society,* Vol. 14. St. Paul, Minnesota: June, 1912.

Urquhart, Jane McKelway, & O. D. von Engeln. *The Story Key to Geographic Names.* New York, D. Appleton & Co., 1924.

Vexler, Robert I. *Chronology & Documentary Handbook of the State of Iowa.* Dobbs Ferry, New York, Oceana Publications, Inc., 1978.

Vogel, Virgil J. *Indian Names in Michigan.* Ann Arbor, University of Michigan Press, 1986.

Vogel, Virgil J. *Iowa Place Names of Indian Origin.* Iowa City, University of Iowa Press, 1983.

Wakefield, George W. "Sergeant Charles Floyd." *Annals of Iowa,* Vol. 2, No. 1. Des Moines: April, 1895.

Webb, Walter P., et al. *The Handbook of Texas.* Austin, Texas State Historical Association, 1952.

White, Dabney, & T. C. Richardson. *East Texas: Its History & Its Makers.* New York, Lewis Historical Publishing Co., 1940.

Whitmore, William H. "On the Origin of the Names of Towns in Massachusetts." *Proceedings of the Massachusetts Historical Society,* Vol. 12. Boston: 1871–1873.

Williams, William. *The History of Early Fort Dodge & Webster County, Iowa.* Fort Dodge, Iowa, Walterick Printing Co., 1950.

Wilson, William E. *Indiana: A History.* Bloomington, Indiana University Press, 1966.

Woodbury County Genealogical Society. *The History of Woodbury County, Iowa.* Dallas, Texas, National ShareGraphics, Inc., 1984.

Work Projects Administration. *Lee County History.* Lee County Superintendent of Schools, 1942.

Work Projects Administration. *The Origin of Massachusetts Place Names.* New York, Harian Publications, 1941.

Works Progress Administration. *Inventory of the County Archives of Iowa-Ida County.* Des Moines, 1938.

Kansas

(105 counties)

857 *Allen County*

William Allen (1803–1879)—A native of North Carolina, Allen made his way to Ohio at an early age. There he studied law, was admitted to the bar and became prominent in politics. In 1832 he defeated his future father-in-law for a seat in the U.S. House of Representatives and he later represented Ohio for more than ten years in the U.S. Senate. He left the senate in 1848. Much later, during the 1870's, Allen served one term as governor of Ohio. Allen County was created in 1855 by Kansas' first territorial legislature. At that time William Allen favored perpetuation of slavery and opposed the free-soil point of view. He was anti-civil war and anti–Abraham Lincoln. These views were popular with the majority of the members of Kansas' first territorial legislature.

858 *Anderson County*

Joseph C. Anderson (–)—Anderson was a young attorney whose home was in Lexington, Missouri. He was elected to

Kansas' first territorial legislature by other Missouri residents who invaded Kansas territory merely to vote in the election and then returned to their homes in Missouri. This legislature is known as the "bogus legislature." Anderson served as speaker *pro-tempore* of the territorial house of representatives. Anderson County was created in 1855 by Kansas' first territorial legislature while Joseph C. Anderson was a member of that body. He was a pro-slavery advocate and that view was popular with the majority of the members of the first territorial legislature.

859 *Atchison County*

David R. Atchison (1807–1886)— A native of Kentucky and a lawyer, Atchison moved to Missouri in 1830. There he became a member of the lower house of the state legislature and served as an officer in the state militia. In 1838 he was promoted to the rank of major-general. In 1843 Atchison entered the U.S. Senate and he represented Missouri in that body until 1855. He became a powerful figure in the senate and on 16 occasions he was chosen as president *pro-tempore* of the senate. Atchison played an active pro-slavery role in the senate in securing passage in 1854 of the Kansas-Nebraska bill which created both Kansas territory and Nebraska territory and permitted slavery in these new territories. After leaving the senate, Atchison was active in the pro-slavery cause in Kansas territory and he supported the Confederate side during the Civil War. Atchison County was created in 1855 by Kansas' first territorial legislature. David Atchison's pro-slavery views were popular with the majority of the members of the first territorial legislature. At least one source indicates that Atchison County was named for David R. Atchison indirectly; that the town of Atchison, Kansas territory was created in the spring of 1855 and named for Senator Atchison and that Atchison County was created later that year and named for the town.

860 *Barber County*

Thomas W. Barber (–1855)— A native of Pennsylvania, Barber moved to Richmond, Indiana in the early 1830's where he was involved in the operation of a woolen mill in partnership with his brother, Oliver. Soon after passage of the Kansas-Nebraska bill in 1854, Barber moved to Kansas territory and settled on a land claim in Douglas County about seven miles southwest of Lawrence. At that time the slavery question was the subject of vigor-

ous debate in Kansas territory and the debates often flared into armed conflict. In early December, 1855, Barber journeyed to Lawrence to assist in its defense from pro-slavery forces. On the morning of December 6, 1855, Thomas W. Barber left Lawrence to return home in company with his brother Robert Barber and Thomas M. Pierson. On the way home, about four miles from Lawrence, Barber and his companions encountered a party of some 14 pro-slavery men who killed Thomas W. Barber with gunfire. Friends who attended Barber's funeral feared for their own safety and some men dressed as women, in long dresses and large bonnets, to disguise themselves. The 1867 law which created and named this county in honor of Thomas W. Barber misspelled the county's name as Barbour. That error was corrected by a special act of the legislature in 1883.

861 *Barton County*

Clara H. Barton (1821–1912)— A native of Massachusetts, Barton taught school and later worked in the U.S. patent office in Washington, D.C. Early in the Civil War she learned of the lack of supplies and comforts available to wounded Union soldiers. Without any official appointment, title, rank or organization, Clara Barton served as a nurse in the field during the Civil War. Eventually she was given the rank of superintendent of nurses in the army. She also gathered records to permit identification of thousands of dead Union soldiers. In 1867, two years after the Civil War ended, Barton County, Kansas, was created and named in her honor. Clara Barton later came in contact with the International Red Cross in Europe and she was largely responsible for the founding of the American Red Cross in 1881. She served as the first president of the American Red Cross until 1904.

862 *Bourbon County*

Bourbon County, Kentucky— Bourbon County was created in 1855 by Kansas' first territorial legislature and named for Bourbon County, Kentucky.

Bourbon County, Kentucky— Bourbon County, Kentucky was created in the mid-1780's by the legislature of the state of Virginia before Kentucky became a separate state. It was named in honor of the royal Bourbon dynasty of France. The Bourbons had rendered valuable aid in the form of both money and fighting men to the American colonies in their struggle for independence from Britain. The duchy of Bourbon had been created in France during the

tenth century and the house of Bourbon was one of the most powerful royal houses in Europe for centuries. At various times they ruled Spain, Naples, Sicily and Tuscany as well as France.

This Kansas county's name was suggested by Samuel A. Williams, who was a member of Kansas' territorial house of representatives. Williams had formerly lived in Bourbon County, Kentucky. At least one source indicates that William Barbee, also from Kentucky, participated with Williams in selecting this Kansas county's name.

863 *Brown County*

Uncertain— This county was created on August 30, 1855, by Kansas' first territorial legislature and named Browne County. It is not certain for whom the county was named, but only two possibilities are mentioned. They are Albert G. Brown and Orville H. Browne. Although the county's name was spelled Browne in the original law that created it, the "e" was left off the county's seal, apparently by accident. Subsequent references to the county's name consistently spell it as Brown rather than Browne.

Albert G. Brown (1813–1880)— A native of South Carolina, Brown attended college in Mississippi and studied law there. He was admitted to the Mississippi bar and became active in local politics. Prior to the Civil War, Brown was a member of the lower house of the Mississippi legislature and he subsequently represented Mississippi in both houses of the U.S. Congress. He was a member of the U.S. Senate when Kansas territory was created. Brown also served two antebellum terms as governor of Mississippi. During the Civil War Brown was a member of the senate of the Confederate States of America and he was a captain in the Confederate army.

Orville H. Browne (–)— Browne was a member of the house of representatives of Kansas' first territorial legislature when Browne County was created by that body on August 30, 1855. He represented what was then the third district and resided in Douglas County, which also was created in August, 1855. Orville H. Browne was said to have been a brilliant but very eccentric man.

Uncertainty about the origin of this county's name is not of recent vintage. In the 1883 *History of the State of Kansas* published by A. T. Andreas, extensive evidence in support of both of the possibilities is presented together with a tentative conclusion that Orville H. Browne was probably the county's namesake. Since Albert G. Brown of Mississippi was well known and popular with the pro-slavery majority of Kansas' first territorial legislature, the Andreas work suggests that those legislators knew how to spell his name and if they had intended to honor him, they would have spelled the new county as Brown rather than Browne.

864 *Butler County*

Andrew P. Butler (1796–1857)— A native of Edgefield district in South Carolina and an 1817 graduate of South Carolina College, Butler studied law, was admitted to the bar and established a law practice in Columbia. He served in both hoses of South Carolina's legislature and later sat as a judge high in the state court system. Butler represented South Carolina in the United States senate for a decade and was serving in the senate at the time of his death in 1857. There he was a zealous advocate of slavery, the fugitive slave law and the right of the South to introduce slavery into Kansas territory. This county was created in August, 1855, by Kansas' first territorial legislature. The majority of the members of that legislature favored slavery and admired Butler, who was serving in the U.S. Senate at that time.

865 *Chase County*

Salmon P. Chase (1808–1873)— A native of New Hampshire and a graduate of Dartmouth College there, Chase moved to Ohio in 1830 and became active in the anti-slavery movement. He represented Ohio in the U.S. Senate and served as governor of the state of Ohio. In both 1856 and 1860 Chase was an avowed candidate for the presidency. In 1860 Chase was again elected to represent Ohio in the U.S. Senate but he soon resigned to accept President Abraham Lincoln's offer to join his cabinet as secretary of the treasury. In October, 1864, President Lincoln appointed Chase to be chief justice of the U.S. Supreme Court. This county was created in February, 1859, while Kansas was still a territory and while Salmon P. Chase was governor of Ohio. The territorial legislator who suggested that the new county be named for Chase was Samuel Wood, who had come to Kansas territory from Ohio and was an admirer of Governor Chase. Kansas is the only state to have a county named for Salmon P. Chase but he has another honor. If you look in your wallet and examine your $10,000 bills, you will find Salmon P. Chase's portrait on all of them.

866 *Chautauqua County*

Chautauqua County, New York— In 1875 the Kansas legislature divided Howard County into two new counties and named these counties Chautauqua County and Elk County. Chautauqua's name was suggested by Edward Jaquins (or Jacquins), a member of the Kansas legislature from Howard County who had formerly lived in Chautauqua County, New York. He introduced the bill to divide Howard County into two counties. Tom E. Thompson objected to the name Chautauqua, stating that there would be mighty few people in the county who could either spell or pronounce this name. Thompson was probably correct because the Chautauqua circuit did not become well known until the late 19th and early 20th centuries.

Chautauqua County, New York— Chautauqua County, New York, was created in 1808 and named for Chautauqua Lake within its borders. At that time the spelling was rendered Chautauque. This lake lies in the extreme southwestern corner of New York, some 700 feet above its huge near neighbor, Lake Erie. Chautauqua Lake is about 18 miles long. Its width varies but most of it is from one to three miles wide. Resort communities abound here and here also the Chautauqua institution was established in 1874. The original intent of the institution was to educate Methodist Sunday school teachers but its content gradually broadened to emphasize popular education, cultural pursuits and entertainment. These activities were generally held outdoors or under a tent. The success of the Chautauqua institution here led to the founding of several hundred local chautauquas throughout the United States during the late 19th and early 20th centuries.

Chautauqua is a name of Indian origin which has been given countless spellings by Whites. The meaning of the Indians' original word has been lost but possible translations include:
— "A moccasin," referring to the shape of the lake
— "A bag (or pack) tied in the middle," also a description of the lake's shape
— "Something raised up." (Chautauqua Lake is elevated some 700 feet above Lake Erie.)
— "Where fish were taken out."
— "Foggy place."
— "Two moccasins fastened together."
— "The place of easy death" or "the place where one was lost" or "the place where one disappears and is seen no more." These translations are associated with a

legend about a young Indian squaw who, after eating a root which created a tormenting thirst, took a drink from the lake's water and disappeared in its depths.
— "Place where a child was swept away by waves."

The creation in 1875 of Chautauqua and Elk Counties, Kansas, out of Howard County was the latest in a long series of county name changes for this area.

Howard County had been created and named in 1867 in honor of Oliver O. Howard (1830–1909), who served as a general in the Union army during the Civil War and worked for integration of former slaves after the Civil War ended. He was also instrumental in founding Howard University for Blacks in Washington, D.C. But Howard County's original name was Godfrey County. That name honored Bill Godfrey, a trader among the Osage Indians. Godfrey County's name was changed to Seward County in honor of William H. Seward (1801–1872), the secretary of state who is remembered for negotiating the purchase of Alaska. Although Seward County's name was changed to Howard County in 1867, Kansas later created and named another Seward County in honor of William H. Seward.

867 *Cherokee County*

Cherokee Indians— The Cherokee Indians were a large tribe who lived in several southeastern states at the time of European contact. By the early 1800's they had adopted many features of civilization. By 1840, most Cherokees had been forced from their lands and removed to Indian territory (now Oklahoma) by court decisions, a fraudulent treaty and military force. The name Cherokee is said to be derived from the Cherokee word for "fire," *chera*. This county was originally created and named McGee County in 1855 by Kansas' first territorial legislature. That name honored Mobillon W. McGee, a pro-slavery member of that first territorial legislature, which was known as the "bogus legislature." McGee was from Missouri and remained a Missouri resident while he served in the Kansas territorial legislature. The county's name was changed in the 1860's to honor the Cherokee Indians because the county's borders included a large portion of a Cherokee Indian reservation.

868 *Cheyenne County*

Cheyenne Indians— The Cheyenne Indians were an important nomadic, hunting tribe who were closely associated with the Arapaho Indians and had a permanent alliance with them. At the time of early contact with Whites, the southern Cheyenne lived in southern Colorado. The origin of their name is uncertain. Possibilities include:

1. A word of the Sioux Indians meaning "people of alien speech" or "aliens."

2. "Scarred arms" on account of a practice of male Cheyennes of scarring their left arms.

The Cheyenne were engaged in almost constant warfare with neighboring tribes and with Whites. Following slaughter of their women and children by the U.S. army at Ash Hollow and Sand Creek, the northern Cheyenne participated in the rout of General George Custer's forces at Little Bighorn. But Whites eventually subdued the Cheyenne and both northern and southern branches were resettled in Indian territory (now Oklahoma). By the 1960's there were about 3,000 Cheyenne living on reservations in the United States. Cheyenne County, Kansas was created in March, 1873. It consists of high plains country in the extreme northwestern corner of Kansas. The Cheyenne Indians lived and hunted in this area for a number of years.

869 *Clark County*

Charles F. Clarke (–1862) — Charles F. Clarke, of Junction City, Kansas, served as a captain in the Union army during the Civil War in the Sixth Kansas cavalry. On June 12, 1862, he was commissioned assistant adjutant-general. He died at Memphis, Tennessee on December 10, 1862. In the original law that created this county, its name was spelled correctly as Clarke. However, in later bills and legislation affecting this county the final "e" has been dropped.

870 *Clay County*

Henry Clay (1777–1852) — Clay represented Kentucky in both branches of the U.S. Congress. For many years he was one of the more prominent figures in American politics but his several bids for the presidency were unsuccessful. He was influential in effecting important compromises between northern and southern interests during the years that secession and civil war were imminent. This county was created in 1857, five years after Clay's death, by the legislature of Kansas territory.

871 *Cloud County*

William F. Cloud (1825–1905) — A native of Ohio, Cloud enlisted in the army in 1846 and served in the Mexican War. During that war he was promoted to first sergeant and at the close of the Mexican War, Cloud was promoted to captain in the Ohio volunteer militia. In 1859 Cloud moved from Ohio to Michigan where he resided briefly before coming to Kansas territory. After a short residence at Lawrence, he moved to Emporia. At the outbreak of the Civil War, Cloud enlisted in the Union army and he participated in two of the early battles in the Civil War, the battle of Wilson's Creek, Missouri, and the battle of Cane Hill, Arkansas. At the expiration of his first enlistment, Cloud assisted in organizing the Second Kansas cavalry and he was commissioned a colonel of the regiment by Governor Charles Robinson. Later Colonel Cloud was transferred to the 15th Kansas cavalry and he served in campaigns against the Indians in western Kansas and Indian territory (now Oklahoma). When this county was originally created on February 27, 1860, by the legislature of Kansas territory, it was named Shirley County. Its name was changed to Cloud County in February, 1867. There are two conflicting versions of the origin of the original name, Shirley:

1. The name Shirley was chosen in jest by the spirited territorial legislators for it honored a well known prostitute named Jane Shirley, of Lawrence, Kansas territory.

2. The original name Shirley was chosen to honor the governor of colonial Massachusetts, William Shirley (1694–1771), who served as governor from 1741 to 1757. (D. L. Chandler, one of Kansas' territorial legislators, claimed that he had chosen the county's name to honor this obscure governor from Chandler's home state of Massachusetts.)

Although neither these possible origins of the name Shirley has been completely ruled out, one has the feeling that it was the prostitute whose name was honored and that the colonial governor of Massachusetts version was contrived because children might be listening. The 1867 name change from Shirley to Cloud was proposed to the legislature by John B. Rupe, who was then representing the county in the legislature. Legend has it that Rupe asked his fellow legislators to change the name to rid the county of "the stigma and burlesque attached to the county's name."

872 *Coffey County*

Asbury M. Coffey (1804–1879) — Coffey was a native of Kentucky. His name appears on an 1851 "Official Kansas Roster" as a U.S. Indian agent. Coffey's agency was the Osage River Agency. He was a member of the first legislature of Kansas territory and on August 30, 1855, his fellow members of that legislature created and named this county in his honor. Although Coffey was in favor of slavery, while serving in the legislature, he supported preservation of the Union. In addition to serving in the legislature, Coffey held the rank of major-general in Kansas' territorial militia. In the Civil War, Coffey served as a colonel in the Confederate army in Indian territory (now Oklahoma).

873 *Comanche County*

Comanche Indians — The Comanche Indians' language and traditions closely resemble those of the Shoshoni Indians. It is probable that the Comanche were a part of the Shoshoni when they lived in the Rocky Mountains of Wyoming. As the Comanche migrated south, they acquired horses and began to pursue a nomadic, teepee-dwelling life style and to subsist largely by hunting buffalo. These plains Indians were fierce warriors and by the 18th century, Spanish explorers reported that the Comanche were replacing the Apache Indians in eastern Colorado and eastern New Mexico. During this period the Comanche also hunted in western Kansas. The Comanche acquired enormous wealth in firearms and horses. (One Comanche Indian was reported to have owned more than one thousand horses.) They were recognized as the finest horsemen in the West. This ability, coupled with their warlike disposition made them formidable foes to both Whites and other Indians. Comanche raiding parties usually spared their female captives, often raping them and then either selling them or keeping them as slaves. The Comanche continued to drift south and in 1795 they formed a close confederation with the Kiowa Indians. The confederation's center of activity shifted to Oklahoma and Texas where they terrorized the White settlers. It was not until 1875 that the American army was able to finally subdue the Comanche and get them to agree to live on an Indian reservation. In the late 18th century, the Comanche population was estimated at more that 20,000 but an epidemic reduced that figure to about 9,000 in 1816. By 1960 there were estimated to be just 3,000 remaining Comanche Indians, most of whom were living on a reservation in Oklahoma. The name *Comanche* has been translated as meaning "enemies" in the Ute Indians' language. Comanche County, Kansas, is in the western half of Kansas on the Oklahoma border. It was created in 1867 and named for the Indians who once hunted buffalo here.

874 *Cowley County*

Matthew Cowley (–1864)— Cowley served in the Union army during the Civil War. He was first lieutenant of Company I in the Ninth Kansas cavalry. He died at Little Rock, Arkansas, near the end of the Civil War, in 1864. Most accounts spell his given name as Matthew but several render it as Mathew. When this county was originally created in 1855, it was much larger and it was named Hunter. That name honored Robert M. T. Hunter, who represented Virginia in both houses of the U.S. Congress. He was serving as a U.S. senator from Virginia when the county was created and named for him by Kansas pro-South and pro-slavery first territorial legislature. During the Civil War Hunter served as president *pro tempore* of the senate of the Confederate States of America. After the Civil War, the Kansas legislature reduced the county's size and renamed it Cowley in honor of the Union soldier who died in 1864.

875 *Crawford County*

Samuel J. Crawford (1835–1913)— This native of Indiana moved to Kansas territory in 1859 where he practiced law and became active in local politics. When Kansas was admitted to the Union in 1861, Crawford was elected to the lower house of the state's first legislature. Just a few weeks later the Civil War began and Crawford left the legislature to serve as an officer in the Union army. He served with distinction and rose to the rank of colonel commanding a Colored infantry regiment. His final promotion was to brevet brigadier-general. While still in the army, Crawford was elected governor and he was just 29 years old when he became the third governor of the state of Kansas. He was reelected to a second term but resigned in November, 1868, before completing that term to lead a military campaign against the Indians. Crawford County was created and named in his honor in 1867 while he was serving as governor.

876 *Decatur County*

Stephen Decatur (1779–1820)— Decatur, who was born in Maryland, was an officer in the U.S. navy who served in the Mediterranean Sea from 1801 to 1805 in the Tripolitan War. His bravery and successes

in that war made him a popular hero in America and earned promotion to captain. During the War of 1812, Decatur reinforced his reputation as a naval hero. Following that war Decatur, now a commodore, again served in the Mediterranean where he captured the Algerian flagship *Mashuda*. His display of naval force extracted peace terms from Algeria and indemnities for un-neutral acts from Tunis and Tripoli. This brought an end to the plundering of American shipping by the Barbary powers. Decatur's life ended in a duel fought in March, 1820.

877 *Dickinson County*

Daniel S. Dickinson (1800–1866)— A native of Connecticut, Dickinson moved with his parents to New York state when he was a young boy. There he practiced law, became prominent in the Democratic party and was elected president of the city of Binghamton. He later served in the New York senate and was the state's lieutenant-governor. Upon the resignation of New York's U.S. Senator N. P. Tallmadge, the governor appointed Dickinson to fill the remainder of his term. The New York legislature then elected him to serve in the U.S. Senate for the ensuing full term, 1845–1851. Dickinson was soon recognized as one of the leading Democrats in the senate and he rendered important service on behalf of compromise measures enacted in 1850 that were intended to avert secession and civil war. After leaving the senate, Dickinson held a variety of political posts and he was a strong contender to be Abraham Lincoln's vice-presidential running mate on the National Union ticket of 1864. He lost to Andrew Johnson.

878 *Doniphan County*

Alexander W. Doniphan (1808–1887)— A native of Kentucky and a lawyer, Doniphan settled in Missouri in 1830 where he became a prominent criminal lawyer and served in the lower house of the state legislature. Doniphan also held the rank of brigadier-general in the state's militia. During the Mexican War, Doniphan took a prominent part in the conquest of New Mexico. He then led his troops on a march into Mexico that took them through 3,000 miles of mountain and desert country. His troops scored important victories during that march, which became known as Doniphan's Expedition. Following the Mexican War, Doniphan returned to Missouri where he served in the state legislature. At that time he was in favor of extending the institution of slavery into Kansas territory.

This view was very popular with the majority of the members of Kansas' first territorial legislature and it was that legislature that created and named this county in Doniphan's honor in August, 1855.

879 *Douglas County*

Stephen A. Douglas (1813–1861)— Barely five feet tall, the "Little Giant" is most remembered as a political opponent of Abraham Lincoln. Douglas was born in Vermont and moved to Illinois where he enjoyed rapid political success. He served on the state supreme court, in the state legislature and as secretary of state. Following two terms in the U.S. House of Representatives, Douglas was elected to the U.S. Senate. In that body Douglas took courageous positions on the slavery issue which first outraged abolitionist sentiment and later infuriated the South. In 1858 Douglas ran for reelection to the U.S. Senate against Abraham Lincoln. Following the famous Lincoln-Douglas debates, the Republicans won the popular election but the state legislature reelected Douglas to the senate. Lincoln and Douglas were rivals again in 1860 for the presidency. Following Lincoln's election and the start of the Civil War, Douglas gave the president his active support. During 1854 it had been Senator Douglas, chairman of the committee on territories, who introduced the bill which resulted in the creation of Kansas and Nebraska territories. Kansas territory was allowed to be either slave or free, thus repealing the Missouri Compromise. Douglas County was created the following year, in August, 1855, by Kansas' first territorial legislature, the majority of whose members held pro–South and pro-slavery views.

880 *Edwards County*

Uncertain— Edwards County, Kansas was created on March 7, 1874. Most sources state that the county was named for William C. Edwards and it probably was, but a degree of uncertainty exists because these other possibilities are mentioned: (1) William C. Edwards and his brother, R. E. Edwards, distinguished pioneers. (According to the *History of the State of Kansas* published by A. T. Andreas in 1883, R. E. Edwards did not move to Kansas until 1874, the year that Edwards County was created.) and (2) John H. Edwards, of Ellis, a colonel and a state senator. He later moved from Kansas to New Mexico. It is most likely that the county was named for William C. Edwards.

William C. Edwards (1846–)—William Corydon Edwards was never famous but he did become wealthy and he did have the desire to have a Kansas county named in his honor. Apparently that goal was realized. He was born at Virgil, New York, in August, 1846. He soon moved to Cortland, New York, where he lived until he moved to Chicago, Illinois, at the age of twelve, where he found employment as a shipping clerk on a lumber dock. Edwards next moved to Grand Haven, Michigan, where he was superintendent of sawing and shipping from four saw mills. He also ran a large saw mill operation for J. P. Hart & Company. In the summer of 1869, Edwards opened his own lumber yard in New Windsor, Illinois, but in the fall of that same year he sold that business. Edwards came to Kansas in the spring of 1870 and became active in the lumber business in several communities including Solomon City, Cottonwood Falls, Cedar Grove, Newton, Hutchinson and Sterling. Edwards and his family owned extensive lands south of Kinsley. At the time that Henry Flick was planning a trip to the state capitol in Topeka to promote creation of this new county, Flick asked William C. Edwards what it would be worth to him to have a county named in his honor. Edwards paid Flick's expenses to Topeka which apparently sufficed, because when the new county was created on March 7, 1874, it was named Edwards. At Kinsley, Kansas, the county seat of Edwards County, William C. Edwards erected several buildings including the first brick building in Kinsley. It was used for several years as the county's courthouse. In 1874 William's brother, R. E. Edwards, moved to Kansas and joined him in his business ventures. These included lumber yards in various Kansas communities, hardware stores in Kinsley and Spearville, a bank in Kinsley and dry goods and grocery stores in Kinsley. As William C. Edwards' wealth grew, he acquired a large cattle ranch in Comanche County, extensive land holdings and numerous lumber yards and hardware stores. In 1895 William C. Edwards served as Kansas' secretary of state.

881 *Elk County*

Elk River—On March 3, 1875, the Kansas legislature divided Howard County into two new counties and named these counties Chautauqua County and Elk County. (For comments on the origin of Howard County's name and earlier county names for the area which is now Elk County, see Chautauqua County, Kansas,

above.) Elk County was named for the Elk River which traverses the county diagonally from the northwest to the southeast. At the time that Elk County was created, the Elk River's tributaries included the Rock, Paw Paw, Hitchin, Painterhood and Wild Cat Creeks and the Fall River. It was the Indians who named the Elk River for the species of deer found along its banks. The river's current name is the English translation of the Indians' name. At one time, elks roamed over Kansas in great herds, primarily here in eastern Kansas where they could find safety and water among the trees and brush along streams and rivers. In North America the name "elk" refers to the large deer whose genus and species are *Cervus canadensis*. (In Europe, the term "elk" refers to a different species, the European moose.) A typical male elk stands five feet high at the shoulders and can weigh from 500 to 1,100 pounds. Male elks often pose displaying their beautiful antlers which spread some five feet. Female elks are smaller than the males and they have no antlers. Elks were once found over much of the United States and southern Canada but their numbers have been greatly reduced by hunters. Most remaining elks live west of the Rocky Mountains.

882 *Ellis County*

George Ellis (–1864)— Ellis was an Irishman from Pennsylvania who migrated to Olathe Kansas. He enlisted in the Union army and rose to the rank of first lieutenant in Company I of the Twelfth Kansas infantry. Ellis was staying in the Eldridge House in Lawrence. Kansas on August 19, 1863, when William Quantrill and his guerrilla gang of about 300 outlaws raided Lawrence, burning, looting and killing like savages. Although the Eldridge House was burned, Ellis managed to escape. During the Civil War Ellis served under General Frederick Steele. Ellis was ill and poorly equipped when he was killed in combat at Jenkins' Ferry, Arkansas, on April 30, 1864, during General Steele's retreat to Little Rock. Ellis County was created and named in his honor less than three years later, on February 26, 1867.

883 *Ellsworth County*

Fort Ellsworth, Kansas— Ellsworth County was created on February 26, 1867, and named for an army fort which had, for a time, been quite well known. The fort's name was Fort Ellsworth.

Fort Ellsworth — Fort Ellsworth was established (but not yet named) by the Union

army during the Civil War in June, 1864, to protect remote frontier settlements, and the construction area of the Kansas Pacific Railroad, from Indian attacks. Construction of this fort was supervised by Lieutenant Allen Ellsworth. He and his troops, about 40 in number, built this block house fort at Page's deserted ranch on the north bank of the Smoky Hill River. Being on bottom land, Fort Ellsworth was soon ravaged by floods. It was moved to higher ground near Kanopolis in 1866 and its name was changed to Fort Harker. The new fort was located just three-fourths of a mile northeast from the original Fort Ellsworth. It is very likely that Fort Ellsworth was named for Lieutenant Allen Ellsworth, who supervised its construction, but there is a trace of doubt on this because a few sources mention the possibility that the fort may have been named for Colonel Ephraim E. Ellsworth, also a member of the Union army during the Civil War.

Allen Ellsworth (–)—Allen Ellsworth was from Iowa and he was mustered into the Union army during the Civil War at Davenport, Iowa as a second lieutenant on July 13, 1863. He was a member of Company H of the Seventh Iowa cavalry. In 1864 he supervised construction of an army fort on the Smoky Hill River in Kansas which was soon after named Fort Ellsworth.

Ephraim E. Ellsworth (–1861)—The Civil War had just begun when Ephraim Elmer Ellsworth (called in some accounts Elmer Ellsworth) became the first Union fatality of the Civil War. He was shot and killed on May 24, 1861, while attempting to remove a Confederate flag from a hotel roof in Alexandria, Virginia, just across the Potomac River from the Union capitol, Washington, D.C. At the time of his death Ellsworth was just 24 years old and was a colonel leading the Eleventh New York regiment. Ellsworth was shot by a hotel keeper named James Jackson. The Union army had its first martyr.

Although the circumstances surrounding the death of Ephraim E. Ellsworth were dramatic and memorable, surviving circumstantial evidence strongly indicates that Fort Ellsworth was not named for him but for the obscure Lieutenant Allen Ellsworth from Iowa. This fort was established in June, 1864, under the supervision of Lieutenant Ellsworth and during the following month, July, 1864, the fort was given its name by General Samuel R. Curtis, who was commander of the Department of Kansas, and thus in charge of Fort Ellsworth. While Allen Ellsworth and his men were on dress parade for the general at Fort Larned, they heard the general read a name for the new fort and that name was Fort Ellsworth.

884 *Finney County*

David W. Finney (1839–)— A native of Indiana, Finney was raised on a farm in that state. During the Civil War Finney enlisted as a private in the Union army and participated in some 35 Civil War engagements. He was also captured as a prisoner of war but was held in prison only one month before being released in an exchange of prisoners. Finney participated in the infamous raid through Georgia led by Union General William T. Sherman. At the time of his discharge from the army, Finney held the rank of orderly sergeant. He came to Kansas in 1866 and was a merchant. He became active in local politics, serving in both houses of the Kansas legislature. In the state senate, Finney rose to be president of that body. He was elected lieutenant-governor of Kansas in the fall of 1880. Reelected in the fall of 1882, Finney served as the state's lieutenant governor from, January, 1881, to January, 1885. This county was originally created in 1873 and named Sequoyah County in honor of the American Indian who invented an alphabet for the Cherokee language to enable his people to read and write. The county's name was changed to Finney in 1883 while David W. Finney was the state's lieutenant-governor. In 1887 the eastern portion of Finney County was taken to form a new county named Garfield, in honor of President James A. Garfield. However, Garfield County did not contain enough land area to comply with statutory requirements so it was dissolved and again made a part of Finney County.

885 *Ford County*

James H. Ford (–1867)— James Hobart Ford was an officer in the Union army during the Civil War. He rose from captain of a Colorado infantry company to colonel of the Second Colorado cavalry. As a captain he participated in an important battle against Confederate forces in New Mexico territory at La Glorietta Pass in March, 1862. As a colonel, in October, 1864, Ford participated in the battles of Little Blue River, Westport and Newtonia against Confederate forces who were commanded by General Sterling Price. At the conclusion of these battles the Confederate army was forced to abandon their attempted conquest of Missouri and Kansas. Ford's final promotion came late in the Civil War on December 10, 1864, when he was appointed brevet brigadier-general. In this capacity he served with the U.S. volunteers in the forces of the Department of Kansas and participated in campaigns against the plains Indians. It was James H. Ford who built Fort Dodge, near the present Dodge City, Kansas, within the county that is now named for him and he served as the first commander of Fort Dodge. Ford County was created in February, 1867.

886 *Franklin County*

Benjamin Franklin (1706–1790)— Franklin was a native of Massachusetts who moved to Pennsylvania in his teens. Poverty denied him a formal education but he became the leading printer and editor in North America. Franklin gained fame for his discoveries and inventions in the physical sciences and he distinguished himself as author, philosopher and diplomat. He was a signer of the Declaration of Independence and an important member of the convention which framed the U.S. Constitution.

887 *Geary County*

John W. Geary (1819–1873) A native of Pennsylvania, Geary served as an army officer during the Mexican War and rose to the rank of colonel. In 1856 President Franklin Pierce appointed him to be governor of Kansas territory. At that time conditions in Kansas were turbulent and dangerous as a result of conflict between pro-slavery and anti-slavery activists. After less than a year in office, Geary's life was threatened and his private secretary was beaten. Geary resigned as territorial governor on March 4, 1857, and returned to Pennsylvania. During the Civil War he served as an officer in the Union army and rose to the rank of brevet major-general. He later served two terms as governor of Pennsylvania. This county was originally created and named Davis County on August 30, 1855, by Kansas' first territorial legislature. That body was pro–South and pro-slavery and they named the county in honor of Jefferson Davis (1808–1889) who was then serving as secretary of war in U.S. President Franklin Pierce's cabinet but later became president of the Confederate States of America. It was not until 1889 that this county's name was changed from Davis to Geary.

888 *Gove County*

Grenville L. Gove (–1864)— Gove was born about 1841 and was living in Riley County, Kansas at the outbreak of the Civil War. In August, 1861, he entered the Union army as a private in Company F of the Sixth Kansas Volunteer cavalry regiment. Gove served in several engagements while he was a member of this unit. In August, 1862, he was promoted from the ranks of enlisted men to become an officer in the Union army with the rank of second lieutenant and he was assigned to be a recruiting officer. In that capacity he raised Company G of the Eleventh Kansas volunteers. He was promoted to first lieutenant in that unit and participated in the Arkansas battles of Cane Hill and Prairie Grove. When the Eleventh Kansas volunteers was later reorganized as a cavalry regiment, Grenville L. Gove was promoted to captain of the regiment's G Company. When the Union general, Samuel R. Curtis, was given command of the Department of Kansas, Gove's company was chosen to be the general's escort. Gove served in actions against the Indians and in the successful campaign to protect Missouri and Kansas from Confederate forces led by General Sterling Price. By this time Gove's health had begun to fail but that didn't prevent him from participating in the battles of Little Blue River and Westport against General Price's troops. A short time later, on November 7, 1864, Captain Gove died at Olathe, Kansas. This county was created and named in his honor in March, 1868.

889 *Graham County*

John L. Graham (1832–1863)— John Livingston Graham was born in Richford, New York on May 27, 1832. In 1857 he came to Kansas and settled in Nemaha County, where he served for a time as a township clerk. In 1861, when the Civil War began, Graham entered the Union army and was assigned to D Company of the Eighth Kansas volunteer infantry regiment. That regiment remained in Kansas until January, 1863, when it was ordered to go south. Graham served as an officer in Company D, holding the ranks of second lieutenant, first lieutenant and, finally, captain. On September 19th and 20th, 1863, the important and bloody battle of Chickamauga was fought northeast of Chattanooga, Tennessee along the banks of the Chickamauga Creek. Both Union and Confederate forces suffered staggering losses in this battle and Captain Graham was among them, losing his life in combat on September 19th. Graham County, Kansas, was created and named in his honor on February 26, 1867.

890 *Grant County*

Ulysses S. Grant (1822–1885)— Grant was a native of Ohio who graduated from the U.S. military academy at West Point. He served with distinction in the Mexican War and in the Civil War he rose to become commander of all Union forces. After the Civil War Grant served briefly as acting secretary of war and then two terms as president of the United States. He proved to be a rather mediocre president. Grant County was created on March 6, 1873, at the beginning of Grant's second term as president.

891 *Gray County*

Alfred Gray (1830–1880)— Alfred Gray was born in Erie County, New York, on December 5, 1830. During his youth he worked on farms in western New York and spent three summers as a merchant sailor on Lake Erie where he rose to the rank of first mate. Gray graduated from law school in 1855 and practiced law in Buffalo, New York for two years before coming to Kansas territory in 1857. Here he resumed his law practice, purchased a large farm and became active in local politics. He served as chief clerk of Kansas' last territorial house of representatives and when Kansas was admitted to statehood in 1861, Gray became a member of the new state's first house of representatives. During the Civil War he served as a quartermaster in the Union army from April, 1862, to March, 1864, but was obliged to resign on account of ill health. In 1866 Gray was elected a director of the state agricultural society and in 1872 he was elected to be the first secretary of Kansas' state board of agriculture. He served in that post until his death on January 23, 1880. Gray County was originally named Foote County, in honor of Admiral Andrew H. Foote (1806–1863) who served in the Union navy during the Civil War.

892 *Greeley County*

Horace Greeley (1811–1872)— A native of New Hampshire and a lifelong newspaperman, Greeley served his journalistic apprenticeship in Vermont before settling in New York City in 1831. He engaged in a series of journalistic ventures which had varying degrees of success before founding the newspaper which was to become world famous, the *New York Tribune*. As editor of that paper, Greeley gained a reputation as an editorial genius. He expressed his strong views on a wide variety of political issues. A vigorous foe of slavery, Greeley denounced the Kansas Nebraska bill of 1854 because it permitted admission of those two territories with or without slavery. He is credited with coining the phrase "Go west young man" and he personally visited Kansas twice; first in 1859 when Kansas was still a territory and a second time in 1870. In 1872 Greeley ran for president against the incumbent President Ulysses S. Grant. Greeley received 2,834,000 popular votes but lost to Grant who got 3,597,000. Broken by the unsuccessful presidential campaign and by both business and personal problems, Greeley died on November 29, 1872, just a few weeks after his defeat in the election. Greeley County, Kansas, was created and named in his honor on March 6, 1873, less than four months after his death.

893 *Greenwood County*

Alfred B. Greenwood (1811–1889)— A native of Georgia and a graduate of Franklin College at Athens, Georgia, Greenwood settled in Bentonville, Arkansas, where he practiced law and was elected to the lower house of the Arkansas legislature. He later represented Arkansas in the U.S. House of Representatives, serving from March 4, 1853, to March 3, 1859. He was then named to be a U.S. commissioner of Indian affairs and in that capacity he came to Kansas territory and swindled the Indians out of extensive land holdings. During the Civil War Greenwood served in the Confederate legislature. Greenwood County was created in August, 1855, by Kansas' first territorial legislature while Alfred B. Greenwood was representing Arkansas in the U.S. Congress. The majority of the members of Kansas' first territorial legislature were pro-slavery and pro–South and Greenwood County was one of several counties that they named in honor of prominent southerners.

894 *Hamilton County*

Alexander Hamilton (–1804)— A native of the West Indies, Hamilton moved to New York and served as an officer in America's Revolutionary army. One of his assignments during the war was aide-de-camp to General George Washington. After the war Hamilton was a member of the convention which framed the U.S. Constitution. He collaborated with Madison and Jay in writing a series of papers entitled *The Federalist* which explained the new constitution and advocated its adoption. A conservative and an advocate of a strong central government, he served as the United States' first secretary of the treasury. In 1804 he engaged in a duel with Aaron Burr and Hamilton died of wounds he suffered in that duel.

895 *Harper County*

Marion Harper (–1863)— Harper enlisted as a private in the Union army early in the Civil War, on November 25, 1861. He rose to the rank of first sergeant in Company E of the Second Kansas cavalry regiment. On December 1, 1863, that regiment was moved to Waldron, Arkansas, assigned to scouting and picket duty in hostile country. The soldiers' duties at Waldron were laborious, disagreeable and dangerous. The weather had become quite cold, the ground was covered with snow and the soldiers had only short rations. On December 29, 1863, Marion Harper was mortally wounded at Waldron, Arkansas and he died the following day. His comrades said that he took his impending death with pluck. When brought in wounded he proposed a wager that he would be dead within a certain number of hours. Harper won the bet and this county was created and named in his honor some three years later on February 26, 1867.

896 *Harvey County*

James M. Harvey (1833–1894)— Harvey was born in 1833 near Salt Sulphur Springs in what was then the state of Virginia but is now a part of West Virginia. In 1859 he settled in Kansas territory as a farmer and rancher. During the Civil War Harvey served as an officer in the Union army. He later served in both houses of the Kansas legislature and from January, 1869, to January, 1873, Harvey was governor of Kansas. In 1874 he was elected by the state legislature to fill an unexpired term in the U.S. Senate which had been created by the resignation of Senator Alexander Caldwell. James M. Harvey represented Kansas in the U.S. Senate from 1874 to 1877. This county was created in 1872 while Harvey was governor of Kansas.

897 *Haskell County*

Dudley C. Haskell (1842–1883)— A native of Vermont, Haskell moved in his youth to Lawrence, Kansas territory, with his parents. He later participated in the gold rush near Pike's Peak and served in the Union army during the Civil War. Haskell served in the lower house of the Kansas legislature and he was speaker of the house in 1876. In 1877 he became a member of the U.S. House of Representatives and he represented Kansas in that body until his death on December 16, 1883. Haskell County was created and named in his honor less than four years later, in March, 1887.

898 *Hodgeman County*

Amos Hodgman (–1863)—Hodgman came to Kansas from Massachusetts and worked as a carpenter in Leavenworth. Shortly after enlisting in the Union army during the Civil War, Hodgman met and married a Leavenworth lady named Kitty. She joined her husband at Corinth, Mississippi, where he was serving as a captain in the Seventh Kansas cavalry regiment. On October 10, 1863, Hodgman was mortally wounded in combat at Wyatt, Mississippi, and he died six days later on October 16, 1863, near Oxford, Mississippi. There is some dispute concerning the correct spelling of Amos Hodgman's surname. The official spelling of the county's name is Hodgeman but most sources state that this official spelling is incorrect because Amos Hodgman's name was spelled without any "e."

899 *Jackson County*

Andrew Jackson (1767–1845)—Jackson was born on the border of North Carolina and South Carolina. He represented Tennessee in both branches of the U.S. Congress and gained fame and popularity for his military exploits in wars with the Indians and in the War of 1812. He was provisional military governor of Florida and from 1829 to 1837 General Jackson was president of the United States. His presidency reflected the frontier spirit of America. This county was originally created and named Calhoun County on August 30, 1855. The body that created it was Kansas' first territorial legislature, the majority of whose members were pro–South and pro–slavery. They named the county in honor of a pro-slavery advocate named John Calhoun. However, there are conflicting reports concerning which pro-slavery John Calhoun the county's original name honored. Most sources indicate that it was for the famous John C. Calhoun (1782–1850) of South Carolina, who resigned as vice-president of the United States in order to better represent the views of the. South in the U.S. Senate. But other sources, including Helen G. Gill's article in volume 8 of the *Transactions of the Kansas State Historical Society*, state that the John Calhoun was a Kansas surveyor general. In either case the name was repugnant to the members of Kansas' 1859 territorial legislature, which was dominated by free-state legislators, and they changed the county's name to Jackson County on February 11, 1859.

900 *Jefferson County*

Thomas Jefferson (1743–1826)—Jefferson was a native of Virginia and a member of the Virginia legislature. He served Virginia as governor and he was a delegate to the second Continental Congress. Jefferson was the author of the Declaration of Independence and one of its signers. He was minister to France, secretary of state, vice-president and president of the United States. As president, he accomplished the Louisiana Purchase which included most of what is now the state of Kansas, and he arranged the Lewis and Clark Expedition to the Pacific Northwest. Jefferson was a true intellectual, thoroughly knowledgeable in the arts and sciences. His political theories were pivotal in the formation of our infant republic. This county was created in 1855. One of the legislators, Dr. William H. Tebbs, proposed that the county's name should be Sauterelle, which is French for "grasshopper" or "locust" but that name was never adopted.

901 *Jewell County*

Lewis R. Jewell (1822–1862)— This Civil War hero was born on August 16, 1822, at Marlborough, Massachusetts. He spent a good portion of his youth living with his uncle in Ohio. It was in Ohio that Jewell met and married Susan Hutchinson and it was there that he worked for several years as a salesman for a large manufacturing company. For a short time Jewell owned and operated a steamboat which plied both the Ohio River and the Mississippi River. A few years after creation of Kansas territory, Jewell moved here and settled on a farm in the southeastern portion of the territory near the present town of Arcadia. When troubles on the border began, Jewell joined an army unit called the Home Guards and he served as a captain in that unit. In the fall of 1861 the Home Guards were disbanded and merged into the Union army's new Sixth Kansas cavalry regiment. Jewell was promoted to lieutenant-colonel in that organization. On November 28, 1862, Colonel Jewell was mortally wounded in combat at Cane Hill, Arkansas, and he died on November 30, 1862. This county was created on February 26, 1867.

902 *Johnson County*

Thomas Johnson (1802–1865)— Reverend Thomas Johnson was born in Virginia on July 11, 1802. When he was still a relatively young man he moved to Missouri where he prepared himself for the ministry in the Methodist Episcopal Church. In 1829 or 1830 Johnson was selected as a missionary to the Shawnee Indians, living just west of the Missouri border in what is now Kansas. There he established a mission of the Methodist Episcopal Church and later a rather large manual training school for the Shawnee Indians and Indians of other tribes who wished to participate. The mission and school were located about one mile from Missouri and some eight miles from Kansas City within what is now Johnson County, Kansas. About eleven years after Johnson had established the mission and manual training school, his health began to fail and he was compelled to resign and move east. By the fall of 1847, his health had recovered sufficiently to permit him to resume as superintendent of the mission and school and he held that post until 1858 when he retired from mission work and returned to Missouri. Johnson was a southerner by birth and sympathetic to the South in the years preceding the Civil War but he opposed secession. When secession and Civil War became a reality, Johnson was loyal to the Union side. His pro–Union views were unpopular in Missouri and they cost him his life on January 2, 1865, when bushwhackers sacked his house and murdered him. In 1854 Kansas territory was created and Johnson served as president of the territorial council. He was also one of the leaders of Kansas' first territorial legislature. It was that legislature which created and named this county in Reverend Johnson's honor in August, 1855.

903 *Kearny County*

Philip Kearny (–1862)— Kearny was born in New York City in 1814 or 1815 to a family of great wealth. He graduated from Columbia University there in 1833 and about four years later he was commissioned as a second lieutenant in the U.S. army. Both Philip Kearny and his more famous uncle, General Stephen W. Kearny, served in the Mexican War. At the battle of Churubusco, Mexico, Philip Kearny's left arm was shattered and it was amputated. For his gallant conduct, Philip Kearny was promoted to brevet major. After resigning from the U.S. army, Kearny served briefly in the French army of Napoleon III. In 1861 when the Civil

War broke out, he was commissioned a brigadier-general in the Union army and in 1862 he was promoted to major-general. Kearny was killed in combat at the battle of Chantilly (Ox Hill), Virginia, on September 1, 1862. This county was created on March 6, 1873, but its name was spelled as Kearney. It was not until 1889 that the Kansas legislature corrected the spelling of the county's name.

904 *Kingman County*

Samuel A. Kingman (1818–1904)—Samuel Austin Kingman was born in Worthington, Massachusetts on June 26, 1818. When he was about 20 years old he moved to Kentucky where he taught school, studied law and was admitted to the bar. Kingman practiced law in Kentucky and became active in local politics. He was county clerk of Livingston County, Kentucky, district attorney and a member of Kentucky's state legislature. He took part in framing a new constitution for the state. In the spring of 1856 Kingman moved to Iowa and in the spring of the following year he settled in Kansas territory. Here he practiced law and in 1859 he was prominent and influential as a delegate to the Wyandotte constitutional convention. Kansas was admitted to statehood in 1861 and Samuel Kingman became an associate justice on the new state's first supreme court. He held that post until 1864. In 1866 he was elected chief justice and he served in that position about ten years until he retired on account of ill health. This county was created in February, 1872, while Kingman was serving as chief justice of the Kansas supreme court.

905 *Kiowa County*

Kiowa Indians—The Kiowa Indians were a nomadic, tepee-dwelling tribe of buffalo hunters who, in the mid-19th century lived in western Kansas and southeastern Colorado and in western Oklahoma. *Kiowa* in their language means "principal people." They were among the most warlike Indians of the southern plains. Although devastated by cholera in 1849 and smallpox in 1861–1862 and officially assigned to a reservation in Indian territory in 1868, portions of the tribe remained hostile for a decade. Most remaining Kiowa now live in Oklahoma. Kansas originally created a Kiowa County in 1867 but abolished it in 1875. The present Kiowa County was created on February 10, 1886.

906 *Labette County*

Labette River—This county was officially created on February 7, 1867, by the state of Kansas and named for the Labette River, which is a tributary of the Neosho River. The Labette River is the second largest stream in the county, the Neosho River being the largest. Unofficially the county was created and named earlier by the residents of the area who elected a full set of county officers and a representative to the state legislature, Charles H. Bent. These actions had no legal validity but when Charles H. Bent reported to the state legislature with a petition signed by 225 citizens, the legislature accepted the petition, created Labette County and gave Mr. Bent a seat in the legislature. The source of the Labette River's name is uncertain and disputed. Several authorities indicate that the stream was named for Pierre Labette, an early French Canadian fur trader, hunter and guide, who resided in the area near the mouth of the Labette River. His name is rendered variously as Labette, Labaete, La Baete, Le Bete, Billette and Beatte. He served as a guide for the author, Washington Irving (1783–1859). Irving rendered his guide's name as Beatte. However, other sources indicate that the name of the stream was originally rendered *La Bette*, which in French means "the beet" but probably was a misspelled version of the French word for "the beast" which is *la bete*. *La bete* is also a derivation of a French Canadian word for "the skunk." An 1836 map called the stream La Bete Creek. According to one legend, some French trappers pitched camp near this stream, a few miles above its confluence with the Neosho River. During their brief absence from camp to pursue a deer, a "beast" (skunk) visited their camp and left enough odor to force the trappers to break camp and depart at once. One French Canadian name for "skunk" is *bete puante*. Originally Labette County had been part of a now extinct county named Dorn County. Several sources indicate that Dorn County was named for Earl Van Dorn (1820–1863), an officer in the U.S. army who later served as a major-general in the Confederate army during the Civil War. However, other sources indicate that Dorn County's name honored Andrew J. Dorn, who became a U.S. Indian agent at the Neosho Indian agency in Kansas territory in the mid-1850's.

907 *Lane County*

James H. Lane (1814–1866)—Lane was born on June 22, 1814. His place of birth is uncertain but thought to be Indiana. He studied law, was admitted to the bar and, in 1846 when the Mexican War began, he enlisted in the army as a private. Lane served with distinction in that war and rose to the rank of colonel. After the war he returned home to Indiana where he was elected lieutenant-governor. He later represented Indiana in the U.S. House of Representatives. In 1855 Lane came to Kansas territory and was active in the movement to secure statehood for Kansas. He also recruited immigrants to come to Kansas territory to attack the pro-slavery forces there. It is said that the depredations of Lane's anti-slavery men were as atrocious as those of the pro-slavery ruffians. Upon admission of Kansas to statehood in 1861, Lane became one of the new state's first U.S. senators. Almost immediately, the Civil War erupted and Lane entered the Union army where he attained the rank of brigadier-general. He was later reelected to the U.S. Senate where he represented Kansas until his death in 1866. This county was created in 1873.

908 *Leavenworth County*

Fort Leavenworth—Leavenworth County was created on August 30, 1855, by Kansas' first territorial legislature and named for the military fort within its borders, Fort Leavenworth. This fort was the first permanent abode of White men in Kansas. The fort's site, on the west side of the Missouri River, was selected in 1827 by Colonel Henry Leavenworth. Its original purposes were to protect caravans on the Santa Fe Trail and to be among the chain of forts along the Indian frontier that ranged from Fort Snelling, Minnesota, in the north to Fort Jesup, Louisiana, in the south. The fort was first called Cantonment Leavenworth, in honor of its founder, Colonel Henry Leavenworth, but on February 8, 1832, the U.S. secretary of war issued a directive that all cantonments be called forts. As a result, this cantonment was renamed Fort Leavenworth. By whatever name, in 1827, Fort Leavenworth was the westernmost military outpost of our nation. This tiny frontier post consisted of huts built of logs and bark. Later a stone wall with loopholes for rifles was built south of the fort for protection against Indian attacks. In later years Fort Leavenworth grew to become a U.S. army installation of major importance.

Henry Leavenworth (1783–1834)—A native of Connecticut who became a lawyer in New York state, Leavenworth entered the U.S. army as an infantry captain, served with distinction in the War of 1812 and rose to the rank of brevet colonel. On a brief leave of absence from the military, Leavenworth served one term in the New York legislature. Back in the army, Leavenworth was active in our nation's West, fighting Indians and building cantonments, which were later named forts. In what is now Minnesota, he established Fort Snelling and in 1827 he built Fort Leavenworth in what is now Kansas. That fort was named in his honor. On July 25, 1824, Henry Leavenworth was appointed brevet brigadier-general but his official rank was colonel at the time he built Fort Leavenworth in 1827. Early in 1834 Leavenworth was given command of the entire southwestern frontier but he died of fever in July of that year.

909 *Lincoln County*

Abraham Lincoln (1809–1865)— Lincoln was a native of Kentucky who moved to Illinois where he was a member of the state legislature. He represented Illinois in the U.S. House of Representatives and later was elected president of the United States. Lincoln's presidency coincided almost exactly with the Civil War. He guided the United States ably through that uniquely turbulent period. As president, he issued the Emancipation Proclamation which declared the freedom of slaves in all states in rebellion. Lincoln was assassinated in April, 1865, a few days after the Union's victory in the Civil War. This county was created less than two years later, in February, 1867.

910 *Linn County*

Lewis F. Linn (1795–1843)— Lewis F. Linn, who was born near Louisville, Kentucky, decided to make medicine his career. Although he had not yet completed his medical training, he served in the War of 1812 as a surgeon. After the war he completed his medical training and settled on our country's frontier in Missouri where he practiced medicine and became an authority on Asiatic cholera. During the late 1820's Dr. Linn served one term in Missouri's state senate. In 1833, when U.S. Senator Alexander Buckner died, Linn was appointed by Missouri's governor to fill Buckner's seat. Dr. Linn was twice reelected to the U.S. Senate and he served in that body until his death. Linn County was created on August 30, 1855, by Kansas' first territorial legislature. Many of the legislators in that body, the so-called "bogus legislature," were from Missouri.

911 *Logan County*

John A. Logan (1826–1886)— A native of Illinois, Logan served in the Illinois legislature and represented that state in the U.S. Congress in both the house and senate. Having served in the Mexican War as a lieutenant, Logan entered the Civil War as a colonel in the Union army and rose to the rank of major-general. In 1884 he ran for vice-president on the Republican ticket headed by James G. Blaine. Logan long associated himself with matters of veterans' relief and he conceived the idea of Memorial Day which he inaugurated on May 30, 1868. When this county was originally created in 1881 it was named St. John County, in honor of John P. St. John (1833–1916), who was then governor of Kansas. He served as governor from January, 1879 to January, 1883. However, his presidential ambitions and his activities on behalf of prohibition of alcohol made him unpopular with many members of the Kansas legislature. General John A. Logan died on December 26, 1886, and just two months later, on February 24, 1887, the legislature changed this county's name from St. John to Logan.

912 *Lyon County*

Nathaniel Lyon (1818–1861)— A native of Connecticut and an 1841 graduate of the U.S. military academy at West Point, Lyon participated in actions against the Seminole Indians in Florida and later in the Mexican War. Very early in the Civil War, in May, 1861, President Abraham Lincoln promoted him to brigadier-general and he was given command of Union forces in Saint Louis. In August, 1861, General Lyon commanded an attack on Confederate troops at Wilson's Creek, Missouri. In that battle the Confederate army scored a victory and General Lyon was killed in combat. When this county was originally created in February, 1857, by the legislature of Kansas territory, it was named Breckinridge County, in honor of Vice-president-elect John C. Breckinridge (1821–1875). He served as vice-president under President James Buchanan during the four years immediately preceding the Civil War. Breckinridge was from Kentucky and he was an advocate of slavery. The composition of the Kansas legislature had dramatically changed by 1862 and pro-slavery views were no longer popular. The Kansas legislature changed this county's name from Breckinridge to Lyon on February 5, 1862.

913 *McPherson County*

James B. McPherson (1828–1864)— A native of Ohio, McPherson attended the U.S. military academy at West Point, where he graduated in 1853 at the head of his class. In the years preceding the Civil War, he taught practical engineering at West Point and then was involved in river harbor improvement and seacoast fortification duties. McPherson served with distinction in the Union army during the Civil War and rose from the rank of mere first lieutenant in August, 1861, to brigadier-general of volunteers on May 15, 1862. Later that year he was promoted to major-general of volunteers. His final promotion occurred effective August 1, 1863, when he was made brigadier-general of the regular army. In March, 1864, McPherson was given command of the army of the Tennessee, which he led in the campaign in north Georgia. McPherson was killed on July 22, 1864, during the battle of Atlanta, Georgia. This county was created and named in his honor less that three years later, on February 26, 1867.

914 *Marion County*

Marion County, Ohio— The first Marion County in Kansas territory was created in August, 1855, by Kansas' first territorial legislature and named for a hero of the American Revolution, General Francis Marion (–1795). This first Marion County was only a narrow strip, a hundred miles long, which reached the Oklahoma border. It disappeared in 1857. Later, in 1860, a member of Kansas' territorial legislature named Samuel N. Wood, who had been born in Ohio, introduced a bill in the legislature to create the present Marion County, Kansas, but the name was intended to honor Marion County in Samuel N. Wood's home state of Ohio. Wood specifically stated that Marion County "… was named in honor of my native county, Marion, in Ohio." This brings us full circle because Marion County, Ohio, had been created in 1820 and named for the same General Francis Marion (–1795).

Francis Marion (–1795)— Marion is believed to have been born in South Carolina. He served in the army in battles against the Cherokee Indians and was elected to the provisional congress of 1775. He served, with distinction, as an officer in the Revolutionary War and rose to the rank of general in that war. Marion was also a member of the South Carolina senate.

915 *Marshall County*

Francis J. Marshall (1816–1895)— Francis J. Marshall, whose name is rendered as

Frank in many accounts, was born in Virginia on April 3, 1816, and educated at the College of William and Mary there. When still a young man, Marshall moved to Missouri. In 1849, following the discovery of gold in California, Marshall came from Missouri to what is now Kansas and established a ferry to cross the Big Blue River for the use of travelers bound for California. He established his first ferry at Independence Crossing but in the spring of 1851 he moved his crossing point about nine miles upstream to where Marysville now stands. Here he built several rude log cabins, a blacksmith shop and a combination saloon and general store. Marshall engaged in trade with immigrants to California and with the Indians. On May 30, 1854, Kansas territory was created and the following year the new territory held the first session of its territorial legislature. Marshall was a member of the lower house of that legislature. He was a southerner by birth and by sentiment and his pro-slavery views were popular with the majority of his fellow members of this so-called bogus legislature. In August, 1855, Kansas' first territorial legislature created and named Marshall County in honor of Francis J. Marshall. The county seat of Marshall County was named Marysville, in honor of Marshall's wife, Mary. In 1857 Marshall was a pro-slavery candidate for governor but he lost the election by an extremely narrow margin to the free state candidate, George W. Smith. When gold was discovered in the late 1850's in the northwestern portion of Kansas territory (which is now in Colorado), Marshall moved there. A number of accounts refer to Marshall as "General Marshall." He never served in any military unit and the title of general was purely nominal.

916 Meade County

George G. Meade (1815–1872)— A native of Cadiz, Spain, Meade graduated from the U.S. military academy at West Point in 1835. He served as an officer in the U.S. army in the Second Seminole Indian War in Florida and later was cited for gallant conduct during the Mexican War. Shortly after the Civil War began in 1861, Meade was promoted to brigadier-general in the Union army. He served with distinction in the Civil War and attained the rank of major-general and command of the army of the Potomac. Meade's most famous Civil War achievement was his victory in the battle of Gettysburg over Confederate General Robert E. Lee's forces. Meade County, Kansas was first created in 1873

but was later abolished. It was recreated on March 7, 1885.

917 Miami County

Miami Indians— The Miami Indians were a major tribe who lived in Wisconsin and, rather briefly, in Michigan. They later inhabited northern Illinois, northern Indiana and a portion of northwestern Ohio. By 1840 most Miami Indians had been forced to move west by the encroaching Whites. Most of the Miami were first moved here to Kansas. They were later resettled from Kansas to reservations in Oklahoma and California. The origin and meaning of the name Miami is uncertain and disputed. Possibilities which have been mentioned by authorities on Indian names include:

— People of the peninsula
— Pigeon
— Derived from rendering by the French of the name by which the Delaware Indians called the Miami, which was *Wemiamik*. This literally meant "all beavers" or "all beaver children" but figuratively it meant "all friends" which accurately described the relationship between the Miami and Delaware Indians.

The name Miami in Florida is not related to this Indian tribe's name.

This county was originally created and named Lykins County in August, 1855, by Kansas' first territorial legislature. Its name honored David Lykins, a physician and one of the first White settlers within what is now Miami County. He came here in 1844. In 1853 Lykins was connected with a Baptist Indian mission for the Potawatomi Indians. In 1855 he was a member of Kansas' first territorial council and also superintendent of an Indian mission for the Wea, Piankashaw, Peoria and Kaskaskia Indians. Lykins also acted as a missionary to the Miami Indians and the county's name was changed to honor that tribe on June 3, 1861. The bill to change the county's name to Miami was introduced by Colonel Colton, of Lykins County.

918 Mitchell County

William D. Mitchell (–1865)— Mitchell came from Massachusetts with his parents in 1855 and settled in Kansas territory on Seven Mile Creek, near Ogden. Early in the Civil War, during the spring of 1861, Mitchell enlisted in the Union army at Junction City as a private in the Second Kansas cavalry. He served with distinction in the Civil War and was transferred to a Kentucky cavalry unit with the rank of first lieutenant. His final promotion

was to the rank of captain. Mitchell was killed in combat in a skirmish at Monroe's Cross Roads, South Carolina on March 10, 1865, just one month before the end of the Civil War. At the time of his death William D. Mitchell was just 24 years old. This county was created just two years later, on February 26, 1867.

919 Montgomery County

Richard Montgomery (1738–1775)— Montgomery was born in Ireland and served with the British in the French and Indian War. He settled in New York state where he was elected to the New York provisional congress. He served as a general in the American Revolutionary army and he was killed in combat in the Revolutionary War. Montgomery County, Kansas, was created in 1867.

920 Morris County

Thomas Morris (1776–1844)— A native of Pennsylvania and the child of an abolitionist mother and father, Morris grew up in a portion of Virginia which is now in West Virginia. In 1795 he settled on our country's frontier in the Northwest territory. There Morris studied law and became active in local politics. Soon after Ohio's admission to statehood in 1803, he was elected to the Ohio legislature. Morris served numerous terms in both houses of the Ohio legislature and he later represented Ohio in the U.S. Senate. He believed slavery was a moral evil and our greatest national sin. After leaving the U.S. Senate Morris continued his fight against slavery and in the election of 1844 he was the nominee of the Liberty Party for vice-president of the United States. When this county was originally created on August 30, 1855, by Kansas' first territorial legislature, it was named Wise County in honor of Virginia's Governor-elect Henry A. Wise (1806–1876), a native of Virginia and an advocate of slavery. The majority of the members of Kansas' first territorial legislature were pro–South and pro-slavery. However, by early 1859 the composition and sentiments of Kansas' territorial legislature had changed. S. N. Wood, who was Wise County's representative in the legislature, introduced a bill to change the county's name from Wise to Morris and it passed and became law effective February 11, 1859.

921 Morton County

Oliver H. P. T. Morton (1823–1877)— There is some confusion regarding the rendering of Morton's surname. Originally the family name was Throckmorton but Oliver's father shortened the name to Morton. Oliver H. P. T. Morton resumed the use of Throck, but only as a fourth given name. Oliver Morton was a native of Indiana who attended Miami University in Oxford, Ohio, studied law and was elected a circuit court judge. In 1860 Morton ran for lieutenant-governor of Indiana on the Republican ticket headed by Abraham Lincoln with Henry S. Lane as the party's candidate for governor. Lincoln, Lane and Morton were all victorious but just two days after Lane and Morton were sworn into their new offices, Lane was elected to the U.S. Senate by the Indiana legislature and Morton became Indiana's governor. Morton was reelected as governor in 1864 and thus served as Indiana's governor throughout the Civil War. In 1867 he was elected to the U.S. Senate where he represented Indiana until his death in 1877. This county was created and named in Morton's honor in 1886. Early in Morton's political career he had refused to support the Kansas-Nebraska bill. He remained on the free soil side in subsequent debates about Kansas. He was popular in Kansas for these reasons and for his full financial support, while governor of Indiana, of the Union's military efforts in the Civil War.

922 *Nemaha County*

Nemaha River— Nemaha County was created in August, 1855, by Kansas' first territorial legislature and named for a river which lies primarily in Nebraska. One of the Nemaha River's branches drains the northern half of Nemaha County, Kansas, and is the county's principal stream. The Nemaha, a tributary of the Missouri River, is about 150 miles long. It rises in Lancaster County, in southeastern Nebraska and flows into the Missouri River near the tri-state junction of Kansas, Nebraska and Missouri. The Nemaha River is also called the Big Nemaha River or Great Nemaha River to distinguish it from the Little Nemaha River, which is also in Nebraska, north of our Nemaha River. The river's name is of Sioux Indian origin but its meaning is unknown. Translations which have been offered include:
— "River of the Mahas"
— "Stream of the Omaha's"
— "River of cultivation"
— "No papoose"
— "Miry water river"

923 *Neosho County*

Neosho River— The Neosho River, a tributary of the Arkansas River, is the principal river in southeastern Kansas. It rises in Morris County in east-central Kansas, flows in a southerly direction and crosses Neosho County, Kansas, from the northwestern corner of the county to its southeastern corner. (Most of Neosho County lies within the valley of the Neosho River.) The Neosho then continues its journey through southeastern Kansas and into Oklahoma. In Oklahoma the Neosho is called the Grand River. The Neosho finally recognizes its obligation to the Arkansas River when it completes its 460 mile journey in Muskogee County in eastern Oklahoma and flows into the Arkansas River. Neosho is the surviving version of several French and English renderings of the name given to the river by the Indians. There is little agreement on the meaning of the name *Neosho*. Translations which have been offered include:
— "Clear water"
— "Dirty" or "muddy water"
— "Clear, cold water"
— "Stream with water in it" (The legendary explanation of this seemingly redundant translation involves a party of thirsty Indians who first came to a dried up stream but proceeded on until they came to the Neosho and were delighted to find it filled with water.)
— "River with pot-holes" or "water hole" or "water pocket"
— "Stream having deep places or bowls" or "sudden deep places shaped like bowls"
— "A river full of deep places"
— "Water like the skin of a summer cow Wapiti" (i.e., cow elk.)
Originally Neosho County had been part of a now extinct county named Dorn County. Several sources indicate that Dorn County was named for Earl Van Dorn (1820–1863), an officer in the U.S. army who later served as a major-general in the Confederate army during the Civil War. However, other sources indicate that Dorn County's name honored Andrew J. Dorn, who became a U.S. Indian agent at the Neosho Indian agency in Kansas territory in the mid-1850's. During the Civil War Andrew J. Dorn served as a quartermaster in the Confederate army. On June 3, 1861, the Kansas legislature abolished Dorn County and created Neosho County.

924 *Ness County*

Noah V. Ness (–1864)— In 1867 when the Kansas Pacific (Union Pacific) Railroad was building westward toward Denver, the Kansas legislature created some 30 new counties and about two-thirds of them were named for Civil War heroes. Ness County, created February 26, 1867, was one of them. It was named in honor of Corporal Noah V. Ness of the Union army. *The History of the State of Kansas*, published in 1883 by A. T. Andreas shows Humboldt, Kansas as Corporal Ness' place of residence. Ness served in Company G of the Seventh Kansas cavalry regiment and was mortally wounded in combat at Abbeyville, Mississippi in August, 1864, He died a few days later, on August 22, 1864.

925 *Norton County*

Orloff Norton (1837–1864)— Norton was born in Delaware County, Ohio, and came to Kansas territory in 1860. Here he settled in the valley of the Neosho River. During the Civil War, Norton enlisted as a private in the Union army and served in the 12th Kansas Volunteer infantry regiment. In the fall of 1863, Norton was promoted from enlisted man to officer when he was commissioned as a second lieutenant in the 15th Kansas Volunteer cavalry regiment. He served with distinction during the Civil War and participated in battles at Lexington, Little Blue, Byrom's Ford, Big Blue, State Line, Westport and Newtonia. He was promoted to captain in the 15th Kansas Volunteer cavalry regiment and was serving as captain of Company L in that regiment at the time of his death. Norton is presumed to have been killed by Confederate guerrillas (bushwhackers) in November, 1864, near Cane Hill, Arkansas, while he and his regiment were on their homeward march from the Arkansas River. Norton was in charge of foraging parties near Cane Hill on November 12, 1864, when last heard from. Since Norton and his men were being closely pursued by a larger force of Confederate guerrillas, it is presumed that he met his death at their hands on or about November 12, 1864. At the time of his death. Norton was just 27 years old. Less than three years later, on February 26, 1867, Norton County, Kansas, was named in his honor. Norton County's new name was suggested by Preston B. Plumb, who was then speaker of the Kansas house of representatives. Previously, since the late 1850's, the county had been named Oro on account of the gold which the gold rushers hoped to find in Colorado's gold country. After the change from Oro to Norton, the county's name remained unchanged until March 6, 1873, when its name was changed to Billings

County. The name Billings referred to one N. H. Billings, a member of the legislature whose district included Norton County. The name change to Billings was done in jest and to please the vanity of Mr. Billings. The reaction to the name change was both rapid and hostile. The legislature changed the county's name back to Norton during their next session, on February 19, 1874.

926 *Osage County*

Marais des Cygnes River— The river for which this county was named was at one time called the Osage River. That river is now known as the *Marais des Cygnes River*, a French name meaning "marsh of the swans," an excellent translation of the name that the Osage Indians had given to this river. It rises in eastern Kansas in Wabaunsee County and flows in an eastern direction through Osage County, Kansas. Headwaters of the Marais des Cygnes River drain most of Osage County, Kansas. The Marais des Cygnes River ends its 150 mile journey in Missouri where it flows into Missouri's Osage River, a 500 mile-long tributary of the Missouri River. Both the present Osage River in Missouri and the former Osage River in Kansas were named for the Osage Indians, an important western division of the Sioux Indians. When first encountered by Whites, the Osage Indians lived in Kansas, Missouri, Arkansas and Illinois. In Kansas the Osage Indians controlled the valleys of the Neosho River and the Marais des Cygnes River. They were prairie Indians who subsisted by hunting buffalo together with some village agriculture. The Osage Indians were ultimately resettled to Indian territory (now Oklahoma) through a series of treaties with the Whites. The name *Osage* is our current rendering of a name given to these Indians by Algonquian Indians, which was Ouasash. When Father Jacques Marquette first heard the name in 1673 he recorded it two ways: Ouchage and Outrechaha. Later French traders spelled the name in a variety of ways including Ouazhaghi, and Ousage. According to some sources the meaning of the original name given to this tribe by the Algonquians was "bone men" but this is a speculation. This county was originally named Weller County when it was created on August 30, 1855, by Kansas' first territorial legislature. That name honored John B. Weller (1812–1875), who represented Ohio in the U.S. House of Representatives and represented California in the U.S. Senate. Weller also served California as governor and was our nation's minister to Mexico. On February 11, 1859, Kansas' territorial legislators changed the county's name to Osage County.

927 *Osborne County*

Vincent B. Osborne (1839–1879)— A native of Massachusetts, Osborne immigrated to Kansas and served in the Union army during the Civil War. On July 10, 1861, he enlisted as a private in Company E of the Second Kansas Volunteer infantry regiment. Just one month later, early on the morning of August 10, 1861, at the battle of Wilson's Creek, Missouri, Osborne was severely wounded in the thigh of his left leg. He continued to fight after receiving this wound until the battle was won by the Confederate forces in the afternoon. When the battle ended, Osborne used his gun as a crutch. He was hospitalized at Saint Louis, Missouri where the bullet was removed from his leg. Osborne was discharged from the army on October 31, 1861, but on February 19, 1862, he re-enlisted in Company A of the Second Kansas Volunteer cavalry regiment. In that regiment, Osborne held the rank of sergeant. During January, 1865, his regiment was ordered to report to regimental headquarters at Clarksville, Arkansas, and then proceed to Little Rock, Arkansas. On January 17, 1865, during the regiment's passage down the Arkansas River on the steamer *Anna* (or *Annie*) *Jacobs*, they were fired upon by Confederate artillery forces. Osborne was severely wounded by an artillery shell resulting in amputation of his good leg, the right one. After the Civil War, Osborne was appointed by Secretary of War Edwin M. Stanton to be sutler (provisioner) at Fort Harker. Osborne County, Kansas was created and named in his honor on February 26, 1867. When Osborne's service at Fort Harker ended, he settled in Ellsworth, Kansas, in July, 1867, where he helped to organize Ellsworth County. In 1871 he was elected to the Kansas legislature and he served in that body during the session of 1872. In 1875 he was admitted to the bar and he practiced law in Ellsworth, Kansas. At the time of his death in Ellsworth on December 1, 1879, Vincent B. Osborne was just 40 years old.

928 *Ottawa County*

Ottawa Indians— When first encountered by Whites, the Ottawa Indians were living in what is now the province of Ontario, Canada. Initially the name Ottawa was used by the French to denote all tribes living on the shores of Lake Huron in upper Michigan and west along Lake Superior. Since then, the name has generally been confined to Indians of the Algonquian linguistic family who lived in Ohio, Indiana, Michigan and Wisconsin. During the French and Indian War, the Ottawa Indians sided with the French against the British. The Ottawa Indians were pushed steadily westward, first by the Iroquois Indians and later by the Whites. They resisted efforts to push them out of eastern lands into less desirable western areas but these efforts failed. By December, 1836, some Ottawas were resettled to a part of the old Indian territory that is now in Kansas. However, other Ottawas remained in Michigan and Ontario, Canada. Dispirited by this forced relocation and in poor health, nearly half of the Ottawa Indians who had been moved to Kansas were dead within five years. The Ottawas in Kansas were again moved in 1870 to the Indian territory that is now Oklahoma. The name *Ottawa* derives from an Indian name meaning "trader" or "barterer." The Ottawa Indians were adept at trading and even served as middle-men facilitating trades between Whites and other Indians and among several Indian tribes. Ottawa County, Kansas, was created and named on February 27, 1860, while Kansas was still a territory and while the Ottawa Indians were still living in Kansas. Ottawa County is located some 100 miles northwest of the section of Kansas where the Ottawas lived. The name that was first proposed for this new county was Wade County, in honor of Benjamin F. Wade (1800–1878), a then-famous anti-slavery senator from Ohio, but that name was rejected by the legislators and Ottawa was chosen, instead.

929 *Pawnee County*

Pawnee River— The Pawnee River is a Kansas tributary of the Arkansas River. Its source is in southwestern Kansas, in Gray County. It flows some 110 miles north and east until it joins the Arkansas River at Larned, Kansas in Pawnee County in central Kansas. The Pawnee River was named for the Pawnee Indians, a tribe of the Caddoan linguistic family. They once lived in the valley of the lower Mississippi River and along the Red River. They migrated to the lower Arkansas River and the lower Missouri River. By the time the Pawnees had a large population, they lived and hunted further west. in Nebraska, Kansas and areas south to Texas. The Pawnee subsisted primarily by village agriculture, supplemented by buffalo hunting. They traveled vast distances on foot to steal horses and eventually acquired sufficient numbers of them to become skilled horsemen. The Pawnee were in constant warfare with most neighboring tribes and captured Pawnee Indians were often sold as slaves. However, The Pawnee Indians were usually friendly toward Whites. During the mid-1870's they were moved to Indian territory (now Oklahoma). The origin and meaning of the name *Pawnee* is uncertain. Many sources indicate that the name means "horn" and refers to a unique method of dressing hair scalp-locks, standing them erect and curved backward like a horn. Other sources indicate that the name means "a braid," "a twist," "to curve," "to bend up," (all referring to hair) while another source suggests that the name derives from "hunter." A more likely explanation relates to the Indian term for "slave" and its application to the Pawnee Indians on account of the large numbers of Pawnees who were taken as slaves by the Apache Indians, the Illinois Indians and other tribes. Pawnee County, Kansas, was created in 1867 before the Pawnee tribe had been resettled in Indian territory. Pawnee County had been within the hunting grounds of the Pawnee Indians.

930 *Phillips County*

William Phillips (–1856)—Kansas became a territory of the United States on May 30, 1854. The burning issue at that time was whether or not slavery should be permitted in Kansas. Passions ran high and controversy about this issue was not confined to polite debate. Rather, a series of violent incidents surrounded this issue and Kansas territory became known as "Bleeding Kansas." William Phillips was a lawyer and a resident of Leavenworth who opposed slavery. He was to die a martyr to that cause. The first major indignity that Phillips suffered for his views on the slavery question occurred in the spring of 1855. Phillips had been ordered to leave Kansas by pro-slavery thugs but he refused to comply. In punishment he was captured by a group of vigilantes and taken to nearby Weston, Missouri where one side of his head was shaved and he was stripped to the waist, tarred and feathered. He was then forced to ride a rail for about one and one-half miles. Next, a mock auction was conducted as if Phillips were a slave being sold. All of this took place on May 17, 1855. The final indignity to Phillips occurred on September 1, 1856, when a band of pro-slavery ruffians, most of whom were from western Missouri, took it upon themselves to terrorize Leavenworth in Kansas terri-

tory. This band, led by Frederick Emory, entered houses and stores of persons thought to oppose slavery, abused and robbed them and drove them into the streets without regard to their age, sex or condition of health. When these vigilantes reached Phillips' house he was ready for them and he managed to kill two of the bullies before being shot to death himself in front of his wife. Phillips County, Kansas, was created and named in his honor on February 26, 1867, soon after the Civil War had ended and the slavery question had finally been settled.

931 *Pottawatomie County*

Potawatomi Indians—Apparently the tribes that we now know as Potawatomi Chippewa and Ottawa were once one people. According to tradition, the Potawatomi migrated from somewhere northeast of Michigan. When they were first encountered by the French, they were living in the region around Green Bay, Wisconsin, and on or near the shores of Lake Michigan. There they served as middlemen in the French fur trade. The women of this Algonquian tribe made pottery and the men made fine birch-bark canoes. Tattooing was common among the men and both men and women used body paint. The Potawatomi were relentlessly driven south and west by both Indians and Whites. For a time they lived in southern Michigan and northern Illinois and in the late 1700's they participated in the struggle for control of the Ohio River Valley. By 1800 they were scattered in some 100 villages spread over Wisconsin, Illinois, Michigan and Indiana. By the 1830's the Potawatomi had ceded most of those lands and been pushed west. By treaties made on June 5, 1846, and June 17, 1846, the Potawatomi, Chippewa and Ottawa Indians ceded to the United States all lands in Iowa to which they had any claims. Pottawatomie County was created on February 20, 1857, when Kansas was still a territory. At one time the Potawatomi Indians had a reservation that extended into a large portion of what is now Pottawatomie County, Kansas. Numerous spellings for the tribal name are encountered. *Potawatomi* is the version approved by the former Bureau of American Ethnology. Various translations of the name are also mentioned but there is little doubt that the name refers to "fire."

932 *Pratt County*

Caleb S. Pratt (–1861)—Pratt came to Kansas from Boston, Massachusetts, where

he had been a merchant, and settled in the city of Lawrence. Here he became active in local politics when Kansas was still a territory. Pratt held the position of auditor of Douglas County and was a commissioner of the penitentiary. He also served as both county clerk of Douglas County and city clerk of Lawrence. He established a ferry on the Kansas River and was active in the local real estate market. Early in 1861 Pratt entered the Union army as a second lieutenant. On August 10, 1861, Caleb S. Pratt was killed in combat during the bloody battle of Wilson's Creek, Missouri, which was won by the Confederate army. Pratt was just 29 years old at the time of his death. This county was created on February 26, 1867, not long after the end of the Civil War.

933 *Rawlins County*

John A. Rawlins (1831–1869)—Rawlins was a native of Illinois and a lawyer. Early in the Civil War, when Ulysses S. Grant was still a brigadier-general, Grant asked Rawlins to be his aide-de-camp. During the Civil War, as General Grant rose in rank and responsibility to be supreme commander of all Union armies, John A. Rawlins remained Grant's principal staff officer and most intimate and influential adviser and he received promotions parallel to Grant's. On April 9, 1865, Confederate General Robert E. Lee surrendered to Union General Ulysses S. Grant at Appomattox Courthouse, Virginia, thus ending the Civil War. On that same day John A Rawlins was promoted to his highest army rank which was major-general in the regular army. Grant became president of the United States on March 4, 1869, and just one week later Rawlins joined Grant's cabinet as secretary of war. He died in that office six months later. Rawlins County, Kansas, was created and named in his honor in March, 1873.

934 *Reno County*

Jesse L. Reno (1823–1862)—Reno, whose surname was originally Renault, was born at Wheeling, in what was then Virginia but is now a part of West Virginia. An 1846 graduate of the U.S. military academy at West Point, Reno served as an officer in the Mexican War and was honored by the army for gallantry in that war. In the years between the Mexican War and the Civil War, Reno remained in the army with various duties including command of the arsenal at Fort Leavenworth, Kansas. He served with distinction in the Union army during the Civil War and rose to the rank of major-general of volunteers. During the campaign in Maryland, Reno was mortally wounded in the battle of South Mountain on September 14, 1862. Reno County, Kansas was created and named in his honor on February 26, 1867, shortly after the Civil War ended. Some of the soldiers who had served under General Reno settled in Kansas after the war and a few of them were members of the Kansas legislature when this county was created.

935 *Republic County*

Republican River—The Republican River rises in eastern Colorado and enters Kansas briefly at Cheyenne County but then continues north into Nebraska. Its journey of some 420 miles takes it along southern Nebraska and then back into Kansas where the borders of Republic County, Kansas, and Jewell County, Kansas, meet Nebraska. The Republican then flows through Republic County, Kansas, from its northern border to its southern end. It continues flowing south to Junction City, Kansas, where it unites with the Smoky Hill River to form the Kansas River. The Republican River was named for the Republican Pawnee Indians. The *Kitkehahki*, called "Republican" by Whites, is one of the four confederated bands of the Pawnee Indians. When the Kitkehahkis set up their own tribal village, independent of the other Pawnees, the French were so impressed that they called them the Pahni Republicaine and their organization the Pahni Republique. At one time the Republican band of the Pawnees lived along the Republican River in north-central Kansas and an important village of theirs was located three miles southwest of what later became the town of Republic in Republic County. During the mid-1870's the Republican Pawnees and the other Pawnee bands were resettled to Indian territory (now Oklahoma). Republic County was created by Kansas territory on February 27, 1860, before the Republican Pawnee Indians had been resettled to Indian territory.

936 *Rice County*

Samuel A. Rice (1828–1864)—A native of New York and a graduate of Union College in that state, Rice also studied law at Union College. He then moved to Iowa where, in 1851, he established a law practice at Oskaloosa. He was elected county attorney in 1853 and just three years later he was elected attorney general of the state of Iowa. During the Civil War, Rice served, with distinction, as an officer in the Union army and was promoted to the rank of brigadier-general of volunteers. At the battle of Jenkins Ferry, Arkansas, on April 30, 1864, General Rice was wounded in combat. He was taken back to his home town of Oskaloosa, Iowa, where he died from those wounds on July 6, 1864. This county was created on February 26, 1867.

937 *Riley County*

Fort Riley—Fort Riley was established in Kansas by the United States army in 1852 on the Kansas River, about one half mile from the confluence of the Smoky Hill River and the Republican River, near what is now Junction City, Kansas. It was originally called Camp Center on account of its location near the geographic center of the United States. Temporary buildings were erected during 1853 and 1854 but in December, 1854, the U.S. Congress appropriated funds for more permanent structures. The new buildings were made of white limestone, erected in the shape of a square. Camp Center was more of a post for quartering soldiers and horses than a fort. It had no cannons. Barrack accommodations were provided for twelve companies of soldiers with adjacent stables to house 600 horses. Both the barracks and a parade ground were enclosed by an attractive fence. On June 9, 1853, a retired army officer named Bennet Riley died and, in an order dated June 27, 1853, issued under the authority of Secretary of War Jefferson Davis, this military post's name was changed to Fort Riley, in honor of Bennet Riley.

Bennet Riley (1787–1853)—According to some sources this career army officer was born in Alexandria, Virginia. Other authorities give his place of birth as St. Marys County, Maryland. But there is general agreement that Bennet Riley entered the U.S. army in January, 1813, as an ensign, and that he served on the New York border during the War of 1812. At the conclusion of that war Riley remained in the army protecting our nation's frontier and serving in various military actions against the Indians. One of his assignments during this period was the command of Fort Leavenworth. By the time the Mexican War began, Riley had risen to the rank of brevet colonel. He served with distinction during the Mexican War and was promoted to brevet major-general. Late in 1848 Riley was made commander of the department of the Pacific, which made him military governor of California.

Riley County was created in August, 1855, by Kansas' first territorial legislature.

938 *Rooks County*

John C. Rooks (1835–1862)—John Calvin Rooks was born in Potter County, in north-central Pennsylvania. Rooks and his parents as well as several brothers and sisters migrated to Kansas territory in 1858 and settled in what was then Weller County but was soon renamed Osage County. Here he preempted more than one quarter section of rich farmland near Burlingame. Our subject was known by his middle name, Calvin, perhaps to distinguish him from his father, John L. Rooks. Calvin Rooks enlisted in the Union army as a private on September 1, 1862, and served in the Civil War in Company I of the Eleventh Kansas Volunteer cavalry regiment. Rooks participated in the battle of Cane Hill, Arkansas, on November 28, 1862. Less than two weeks later, during the battle of Prairie Grove, Arkansas, on December 7, 1862, Rooks was mortally wounded. Taken to Fayetteville, Arkansas, he died on December 11, 1862. Rooks County, Kansas, was created and named in his honor on February 26, 1867, less than two years after the end of the Civil War. Rooks County is the only Kansas County that was named for a Civil War private.

939 *Rush County*

Alexander Rush (–1864)—Rush served as an officer in the Union army during the Civil War. He was a White man who was captain of Company H of the Second Kansas Colored Volunteer infantry regiment. At the battle of Jenkins Ferry, Arkansas, on April 30, 1864, Captain Rush was killed in combat. At that time, Colonel Samuel J. Crawford (1835–1913) was Captain Rush's commanding officer. Crawford became governor of Kansas in January, 1865, shortly before the Civil War ended. This county was created and named in honor of Alexander Rush on February 26, 1867, while Crawford was serving as Kansas' governor.

940 *Russell County*

Avra P. Russell (1833–1862)—Russell was born in Wayne County, New York, on April 7, 1833. As a young man he taught school in upstate New York and later worked as a traveling salesman. This work took him as far away as Illinois where he met and fell in love with a Lockport, Illinois girl. Apparently they planned to marry but fate had other plans in store for Avra P. Russell. At the age of 25 he came to Kansas and established an express line from

Leavenworth to Pike's Peak. Russell served as an officer in the Union army during the Civil War and participated in various early Civil War actions, including the battle of Wilson's Creek, Missouri, on August 10, 1861. On April 5, 1862, he received a promotion to captain of Company K in the Second Kansas Volunteer cavalry regiment. Russell's youngest brother, Oscar Russell, lived in the South and when the Civil War began he enlisted in the Confederate army and became an aide to Confederate General Thomas C. Hindman. The two brothers lived in dread that they would some day face each other in battle and this very nearly happened at the battle of Prairie Grove, Arkansas, on December 7, 1862. Fortunately Confederate General Hindman knew that his aide had a brother who would be fighting in the Union army in that battle and General Hindman arranged for Oscar Russell to be assigned other duties on that fateful day. But Avra P. Russell had no other duties assigned to him and he fought in the battle of Prairie Grove, Arkansas, on December 7, 1862, and was mortally wounded in that battle. He died a few days later, on December 12, 1862, at a nearby field hospital. Russell County, Kansas was created and named in his honor on February 26, 1867, about two years after the end of the Civil War.

941 Saline County

Saline River—The Saline River is a tributary of the Smoky Hill River. The Saline rises in Thomas County, in northwestern Kansas, and flows in a southeastern direction some 200 miles until it enters the Smoky Hill River near the city of Salina, in Saline County, in central Kansas. The river's name refers to its salt content. The Indians called it Ne Miskua meaning "Salt River" and the French merely translated the Indians' name into their language. In both French and English saline refers to things consisting of or containing salt. This county was created on February 15, 1860, by Kansas territory and named for the river whose waters drain a large area of the county.

942 Scott County

Winfield Scott (1786–1866)—A native of Virginia, Scott joined the U.S. army in 1808. His heroic service in the War of 1812 resulted in rapid promotions to brevet major-general. He later played an important military role during the 1832 nullification crisis in South Carolina and in actions against the Indians in Florida. He was general-in-chief of the United States army during the Mexican War. In 1852 Scott was the Whig party's candidate for president but he lost to Franklin Pierce. When the Civil War broke out, Scott remained loyal to the Union side despite his southern roots but he retired from the army in October, 1861, on account of age and ill health. This county was created in March, 1873.

943 Sedgwick County

John Sedgwick (1813–1864)—Sedgwick, a native of Connecticut and a graduate of West Point, engaged in actions against the Indians in the decade preceding the Mexican War. Following the Mexican War, in which he served, Sedgwick held various posts including actions against the Indians in Colorado in 1857 and 1860. During that period, most of the present state of Colorado was part of Kansas territory. Sedgwick served with distinction in the Union army during the Civil War, suffering wounds in combat on more than one occasion. He had risen to the rank of major-general at the time of his death at Spotsylvania in May, 1864. Sedgwick County, Kansas, was created in February, 1867, just three years after General Sedgwick's death in combat in the Civil War.

944 Seward County

William H. Seward (1801–1872)—A native of New York and a graduate of Union College in that state, Seward served in the New York senate and later was the state's governor. In 1849 he was elected to represent New York in the United States senate. In that body Seward advocated the exclusion of slavery from all new states and he gave an eloquent speech in the senate opposing the admission of Kansas as a slave state. He later enthusiastically supported the proposal to admit Kansas to statehood as a free state. In 1861 President Abraham Lincoln appointed him to his cabinet as secretary of state and Seward continued in that office when Andrew Johnson succeeded Lincoln as president. In 1867 Seward negotiated the purchase of Alaska from Russia at a price of $7,200,000, which was an enormous cost in those days. The purchase of Alaska was known as "Seward's folly." The present Seward County is Kansas' second Seward County. The first one made its appearance on June 3, 1861, when what was formerly Godfrey (or Godfroy) County was renamed Seward County. This Seward County existed from 1861 to 1867 when its name was changed to Howard County in honor of Oliver O. Howard (1830–1909). Howard had served as a general in the Union army during the Civil War and had worked for integration of former slaves when the Civil War ended. Seward County was restored to Kansas' county map, this time in southwestern Kansas, in March, 1873.

945 Shawnee County

Shawnee Indians—The Shawnee Indians are one of the imortant tribes of the Algonquian linguistic family and are closely related to the Delaware Indians. During prehistoric times the Shawnee lived along the Ohio River but they were forced to move southeast by the Iroquois Indians. When first encountered by Europeans, most Shawnee Indians were living in South Carolina and Georgia with some as far south as Florida. During the late 1700's and early 1800's the Shawnee migrated north and then west and by about 1750 many Shawnee were living near the lands of their ancestors in the Ohio River valley. The Shawnee sided with the French against the British in the French and Indian War and when the United States became a nation, the Shawnee were openly hostile to it. There is little reason to believe that their destiny would have been merrier even if they had been friendly to the White Americans. As the territory of the United States expanded to the west, the Shawnee Indians were driven from their lands to make room for Whites. During the first half of the 19th century the Shawnee were allowed to possess some rich farmland in Kansas but they were forced to give up essentially all rights to this land in an 1854 treaty. Most Shawnee were resettled to Indian territory (now Oklahoma). Shawnee County was created in August, 1855, by Kansas' first territorial legislature out of land which had recently belonged to the Shawnee Indians. There was some dispute among the territorial legislators concerning the name for this new county. However, General H. J. Strickler, a member of the territorial council and a member of the joint committee on counties, felt that the county's name should be Shawnee and his view prevailed. The source and meaning of the name Shawnee has not been proven but many authorities believe that it derived from words which meant "south" or southerners" and that the Shawnee acquired this name as a result of their early residence in South Carolina, Georgia and Florida.

946 Sheridan County

Philip H. Sheridan (1831–1888)—Sheridan was born in 1831 but his place of birth is in doubt. He graduated from the U.S. military academy at West Point and became a career officer in the United States army. When the Civil War began, Sheridan had almost a decade of military service behind him but he was still only a lieutenant. During the Civil War Sheridan served with distinction in the Union army and rocketed from obscurity to high rank and responsibility. By the closing weeks of the Civil War he had been promoted to major-general. After the Civil War ended, Sheridan remained in the army enforcing the odious Reconstruction Acts in Louisiana and Texas. He later served at Fort Leavenworth in Kansas. Sheridan ultimately became commanding general of the entire U.S. army and attained the rank of full general. This county was created in March, 1873.

947 *Sherman County*

William T. Sherman (1820–1891) — A native of Ohio and an 1840 graduate of the U.S. military academy at West Point, Sherman served as a junior officer in actions against the Indians and in the Mexican War. During the Mexican War Sherman was not assigned any combat duties. By 1853 he had become bored with military life and resigned from the army to pursue civilian occupations in California, Kansas territory and Louisiana. At the outbreak of the Civil War in 1861, Sherman accepted a commission in the Union army as a colonel and by 1862 he had risen to the rank of major-general. In 1864, When Ulysses S. Grant was promoted to commander of all Union armies, Sherman was given command in the South. Starting at Atlanta, Georgia in November, 1864, Sherman led his infamous "March to the Sea," burning a swath across the heart of Georgia some 40 to 60 miles wide and 300 miles long. Factories, cotton gins and warehouses were burned. Bridges and public buildings were destroyed. With Sherman's approval, his troops engaged in wild looting of civilian property. Sherman then marched north, wreaking even greater destruction in South Carolina. These and other depredations earned Sherman the hatred of several generations of White southerners. After the war Sherman remained in the military and ultimately became general-in-chief of the army. He was periodically considered as a presidential candidate. His succinct refusal to the Republicans in 1884 has become a classic: "I will not accept if nominated and will not serve if elected." This county was created in March, 1873.

948 *Smith County*

James N. Smith (1837–1864) — James Nelson Smith was born in January, 1837, at Beaver Dam in Erie County, Pennsylvania, and he graduated from Meadville College in that state. Smith is known to have resided in Kansas territory, in the town of Elwood in Doniphan County, in 1859. He subsequently moved to the mountains of Colorado. In 1861, when the Civil War started, Smith enlisted in the Union army in a regiment described as the First Colorado. When the Third Regiment of Colorado Volunteers was later organized, Smith was commissioned as a major in that regiment. This regiment was later consolidated with the Second Regiment of Colorado Volunteer cavalry under the command of Colonel James Ford and it was while serving with the Second Colorado that Major Smith met his death. Smith participated in combat at Cabin Creek, Honey Springs and Perryville and was subsequently a member of the force that occupied Fort Smith, Arkansas. He was later stationed on the western border of Missouri in the Second Regiment of Colorado Volunteer cavalry. During this period Smith and his men saw action at Camden Point, Missouri and Liberty, Missouri. In mid–October, 1864, Smith's troops occupied Independence, Missouri. Just a few days later, on the morning of October 21, 1864, Smith was killed in combat at the battle of the Little Blue in Missouri, between Independence, Missouri, and the Little Blue River. This county was created on February 26, 1867, less than three years after his death in combat. In a number of accounts Major Smith's name is incorrectly given as Nathan.

949 *Stafford County*

Lewis Stafford (–1863) — Stafford was an early settler in the town of Holton in Kansas territory and one of the first to build a home there. At Holton he served as clerk of the probate court of Calhoun County and also was clerk of the board of supervisors. (In 1859 Calhoun County's name was changed to Jackson County.) In 1861, soon after the Civil War began, Stafford joined the Union army as a first lieutenant of Company E of the First Kansas Volunteer infantry regiment. He eventually was promoted to captain in that organization. In August, 1861, Stafford participated in the battle of Wilson's Creek, Missouri. He was a prisoner of war for a time at the terrible Confederate prison in Andersonville, Georgia. On January 31, 1863, Captain Stafford was accidentally killed at Young's Point, Louisiana. This county was created on February 26, 1867, less than two years after the Civil War ended.

950 *Stanton County*

Edwin M. Stanton (1814–1869) — A native of Ohio and a lawyer, Stanton moved to Pennsylvania in 1847 where he gained a reputation as one of our country's outstanding attorneys. In 1856 Stanton moved to Washington, D.C., to better enable him to handle cases before the U.S. Supreme Court. In 1860 President James Buchanan appointed Stanton to his cabinet as attorney general. When Abraham Lincoln succeeded Buchanan as president, Stanton returned to private life but in January, 1862, in the midst of the Civil War. President Lincoln appointed Stanton to serve in his cabinet as secretary of war. Stanton remained in that critical position until the Civil War ended in victory for the Union and continued as secretary of war when Andrew Johnson succeeded Lincoln as president. In 1868 Johnson removed him from that post. Stanton died in December, 1869 and this county was created and named in his honor in March, 1873.

951 *Stevens County*

Thaddeus Stevens (1792–1868) — A native of Vermont and a graduate of Dartmouth College, Stevens settled in Pennsylvania in 1814. There he studied law, was admitted to the bar and became active in local politics. He served several terms in Pennsylvania's house of representatives and was a delegate to Pennsylvania's constitutional convention in 1838. Stevens later represented Pennsylvania in the U.S. House of Representatives for many years and was a violent opponent of slavery. He opposed President Abraham Lincoln's plan of reconstruction in the South in favor of harsh measures. When the Civil War ended and Lincoln was assassinated, Stevens became the leader of the radical Republicans in congress who succeeded in imposing harsh military Reconstruction on the South. He also played a key role in the early stages of the impeachment proceedings against President Andrew Johnson. This county was created in March, 1873.

952 *Sumner County*

Charles Sumner (1811–1874) — A native of Massachusetts, a graduate of Harvard and a lawyer, Sumner was elected in 1851 to represent Massachusetts in the U.S.

Senate. He was a member of that body from 1851 until his death in 1874 and became very powerful and prominent. Sumner was a fierce opponent of slavery and he opposed the extension of slavery into Kansas. In May, 1856, he delivered an eloquent speech on that subject entitled "The Crime Against Kansas." Sumner's speech was inflammatory and it enraged Preston S. Brooks (1819–1857), a member of the house from South Carolina. On account of this speech, Brooks physically assaulted Senator Sumner with a cane and the injuries Sumner sustained caused him to be absent from the senate for some three years. When it was proposed in the Kansas legislature in 1867 that this county be created and named in Sumner's honor, a curious objection was raised. The protest was that it was inappropriate to name such an unimportant "treeless and trackless portion of the great American desert" for such a great statesman. The protest failed and Sumner County, Kansas was created on February 26, 1867.

953 Thomas County

George H. Thomas (1816–1870) — A native of Virginia and an 1840 graduate of the U.S. military academy at West Point, Thomas was a career officer in the United States army. He participated in actions against the Seminole Indians and in the Mexican War. After the Mexican War he had a variety of assignments including brief service as an instructor at West Point and duty on the Indian frontier in Texas. Despite his southern roots, Thomas remained loyal to the U.S. army when the Civil War began and he served as an officer in the Union army throughout the Civil War and rose to the rank of major-general. After the Civil War, Thomas remained in the army until his death on March 28, 1870. This county was created three years later in March, 1873.

954 Trego County

Edgar P. Trego (–1863) — Trego, of Preemption, Illinois, served as an officer in the Union army during the Civil War. Early in the war he held the rank of second lieutenant in a unit which had been raised for service in New Mexico. In February, 1862, Trego's unit was consolidated with the Eighth Kansas Volunteer infantry regiment and Trego was promoted to captain of Company H in that regiment. Trego's regiment participated in several engagements against the Confederate army including the bloody battle of Chickamauga in Tennessee, northeast of Chat-

tanooga. This battle was fought along the Chickamauga Creek on September 19 and September 20, 1863. Captain Trego was killed during this battle on September 19. This county was created and named in his honor on February 27, 1867, less than two years after the end of the Civil War.

955 Wabaunsee County

Waubansee (–) — Born in Indiana, Waubansee's year of birth is cited in some sources as 1760 and in one as "about 1780." He became the principal warrior chief of the Potawatomi tribe when they resided on the Kankakee River in Illinois. In a famous incident in October, 1811, Waubansee jumped on board one of Governor William Henry Harrison's supply boats on the Wabash River and killed one of Harrison's men. He later was one of the leaders in the Indians' massacre of the American troops at Fort Dearborn on August 15, 1812, but he stayed to protect the White Kinzie family after the battle. Waubansee was neutral during the Winnebago Indian troubles in 1827 and he fought on the side of the Illinois militia in the Black Hawk War of 1832. In gratitude for his changed attitude toward the Americans, Chief Waubansee was granted five sections of land on the Fox River in Illinois in the treaty of Prairie du Chien. In the late 1820's and early 1830's Waubansee and his people lived in a village near Aurora, Illinois. The Potawatomi were later moved west of the Mississippi River and he lived for a time near Council Bluffs in western Iowa. The translation of Chief Waubansee's name is uncertain. A frequently cited translation is "dawn of day," with an accompanying explanation that Chief Waubansee claimed that when he killed his enemies a paleness came over them that resembled the first light of day. Another translation that is mentioned is "foggy." The story behind this one (that two of Chief Waubansee's daring attacks occurred on foggy mornings) is known to be true although its link to the chief's name is not certain. A third theory also claims that the name means "dawn of day" and was given to Waubansee because, while he was still a youth, he performed a successful solo expedition into an Osage Indian encampment to avenge the death of a friend. During this exploit the daring Waubansee was said to have tomahawked at least one, and possibly several, Osage Indians and then escaped from their camp just as day was dawning. Other translations have also been mentioned for the chief's name. The year of Chief Wau-

bansee's death is also uncertain. One authority lists the year as 1845 but another shows 1848. This county was originally created as Richardson County by Kansas' first territorial legislature and named for William P. Richardson, a member of the upper house (council) of the first legislature of the territory. He was a local leader on the Democratic side in the debate concerning the Kansas-Nebraska bill when it was under consideration in the U.S. Congress. Richardson was born in Kentucky about 1802, moved to Illinois and later to Kansas. From 1842 to 1846 Richardson was a sub-agent for several Indian tribes. On August 30, 1855, the legislature of Kansas territory created and named Richardson County in his honor and on the following day he was commissioned as a major-general in the northern division of the militia of Kansas territory. Richardson was prominent in the pro-slavery faction in the early days of Kansas territory when those views were popular with the territorial legislature. He died in 1857. By 1859 the composition of Kansas' territorial legislature had changed and pro-slavery sympathizers were no longer held in esteem. Richardson County's name was changed to Wabaunsee County in February, 1859.

956 Wallace County

William H. L. Wallace (1821–1862) — Wallace was born in Ohio but while still a young boy he moved, with his father, to Illinois. There he studied law and was admitted to the bar. In 1847 Wallace enlisted in the army as a private to fight in the Mexican War. He served with distinction in that war and was promoted to the rank of first lieutenant by the war's end. During the Civil War, Wallace joined the Union army as a colonel and he was promoted to the rank of brigadier-general on March 21, 1862. Just two weeks later, during the battle of Shiloh, Tennessee, Wallace was mortally wounded and he died a few days later, on April 10, 1862. This county was created on March 2, 1868, three years after the end of the Civil War. At that time there was a military post in Wallace County whose name had been changed to Camp Wallace in 1866 to honor General William H. L. Wallace. Thus it is possible that the county was named indirectly for General Wallace, by being named for the camp, but all sources consulted indicate that the county was named directly for him rather than indirectly via Camp Wallace (which later became Fort Wallace).

957 *Washington County*

George Washington (1732–1799)— Washington was a native of Virginia. He served in Virginia's house of burgesses and became one of the colonies' leaders in opposition to British policies in America. He was a member of the first and second Continental Congresses and commander of all Continental armies in the Revolutionary War. Following victory in that war, Washington was elected to be the first president of the United States.

958 *Wichita County*

Wichita Indians— The Wichita Indians were a confederacy of tribes of the Caddoan linguistic family who occupied a large area of America's southern and central plains from northern Texas into Oklahoma and Kansas. When the earliest European explorers visited Kansas in the 16th century, they found Wichita Indians living here. The Spanish explorer, Francisco Vasquez de Coronado, encountered Wichita Indians living in Kansas in 1541. Some of the Wichita were teepee-dwelling buffalo hunters while others were farmers who depended less on buffalo meat for their subsistence. Although the Wichita sometimes practiced cannibalism on enemies killed in battle, they were generally friendly to the Whites. In 1801 a smallpox epidemic killed large numbers of those Wichita Indians who were then living in Texas and their numbers continued to diminish rapidly over the next few decades as a result of encroaching Americans and raids on them by the Osage Indians. By the time of the American Civil War, most Wichita had moved to Indian territory (now Oklahoma). During the Civil War many Wichita moved briefly to Kansas but they returned to Indian territory when the Civil War ended. The meaning of the name *Wichita* is not known. possible translations which have been mentioned include: "Painted faces," "Scattered lodges," "Raccoon eyed," "Men of the north" and "Big arbor." It was a custom of the Wichitas to paint and tattoo their faces which could explain either "painted faces" or "raccoon eyed" but the meaning of the Wichita Indians' name is uncertain.

959 *Wilson County*

Hiero T. Wilson (1806–)— This early Kansas pioneer was born near Russellville, Kentucky, in September, 1806. In 1834 he moved to Fort Gibson in Indian territory (now Oklahoma) where he became a clerk for his brother, Thomas E. Wilson, who was the sutler (provisioner) at Fort Gibson and an Indian trader. In 1842 the U.S. army built a military post named Fort Scott in what is now Kansas and in September, 1843 Hiero T. Wilson moved there. The town of Fort Scott, Kansas grew up around the military post. Hiero T. Wilson became the sutler for the army at Fort Scott and he was the first White settler in the town of Fort Scott. Here he established a business as a merchant and Indian trader. Wilson spoke three Indian languages: Osage, Cherokee and Creek. The army troops were withdrawn from Fort Scott in 1853 and Wilson purchased one of the military buildings for his residence. When the town company for the town of Fort Scott was created, Wilson became its treasurer and acting secretary. He eventually disposed of his mercantile business and engaged in a real estate and insurance venture. Wilson also served as Fort Scott's postmaster for several years, and was a delegate to the Lecompton constitutional convention and a member of the first legislature of Kansas territory. It was that legislature which created and named this county in Wilson's honor in August, 1855.

960 *Woodson County*

Daniel Woodson (1824–1894)— Woodson was born in Albemarle County, Virginia, in May, 1824. Orphaned at an early age, he became an apprentice printer while still a young boy. In subsequent years he developed skill as a writer and an interest in political matters. He became coeditor and publisher of the *Lynchburg Republican* and also edited the *Republican Advocate* in Richmond, Virginia. In spite of their names, both of these newspapers were Democratic in their political sympathies, as was Daniel Woodson. Kansas territory was created on May 30, 1854, and in June of that year President Franklin Pierce, a Democrat, appointed Woodson to be the first secretary of Kansas territory. Woodson arrived in Kansas territory in October, 1854, and he served as secretary of the territory until 1857. During this period Woodson served as acting governor of the territory on several occasions when territorial governors resigned, were dismissed from office or were absent from the territory. Woodson spent the remainder of his life in Kansas where his occupations included farming and newspaper activities. He also served as city clerk of Coffeyville, Kansas for some twelve years. It is clear that this county was named for Daniel Woodson. Dozens of sources were consulted and all but one of them agree that this county was named for him. One source says that this county was named for Missouri's governor, Silas Woodson (1819–1896). Woodson County was created and named in August, 1855, by Kansas' first territorial legislature which was dominated by pro-slavery advocates, many of whom actually lived in Missouri. So the suggestion that this county might have been named for a Missouri governor is plausible. However, it has been refuted. In his work entitled *Kansas Place-Names*, John Rydjord attributes the following statement to John Martin: "The county was named in honor of the Honorable Daniel Woodson ... Governor Silas Woodson was not even thought of in connection with the naming of the county." John Martin had been an assistant clerk in the territorial house of representatives at the time that Woodson County was created. The full text of John Martin's letter on this subject can be found in volume 13 of the *Collections of the Kansas State Historical Society* in an article entitled "Woodson County Courthouse" by Leander Stillwell. Silas Woodson did not become governor of Missouri until 1873, almost two decades after the creation of this county. In 1855, when Woodson County was created and named, Silas Woodson was an obscure attorney in Missouri, whereas Daniel Woodson was serving as secretary of Kansas territory and his pro-slavery views were no secret. At that time, pro-slavery views were very popular with the legislators of Kansas territory who were the namers of the county names here.

961 *Wyandotte County*

Wyandot Indians— The early French explorer, Jacques Cartier (1491–1557) encountered the Wyandot in Canada near Montreal and Quebec. At that time they were one of the four tribes that comprised the Huron alliance. Although the Huron belong to the Iroquoian linguistic family, it was Iroquois Indians who forced most Huron Indians to move west. Sometime after 1650 they settled near Detroit, Michigan, and on Sandusky Bay in Ohio. They eventually claimed most of Ohio and part of Indiana. These Huron Indians called themselves Wendat and over time that name evolved to Wyandot. Beginning in 1795 the Wyandot Indians ceded all of their lands to the United States in various treaties. In 1842 or 1843 those Wyandot Indians who had been living in Ohio moved to Kansas. Here they purchased land from the Delaware Indians and settled in what is now Wyandotte County, Kansas. In 1867

the Whites forced the Wyandots to move on, this time to Indian territory (now Oklahoma). Wyandotte County, Kansas, was created in 1859 while Kansas was still a territory and while the Wyandot Indians were still living in Kansas territory. The meaning of the name *Wendat* and its various other forms is uncertain. Translations which have been suggested include:
— "Islanders"
— "Dwellers on the peninsula"
— "People dwelling in the vicinity of bays and inlets of a large body of water"
— "People of one speech"
— "Calf of the leg"

REFERENCES

Adams, Donna S. *Ford County, Kansas Marriages.* Dodge City, Kansas, Kansas Genealogical Society, 1970.

Adjutant General's Office. *Official Army Register of the Volunteer Force of the United States for the Years 1861, '62, '63, '64, '65: Part 7: Missouri, Wisconsin, Iowa, Minnesota, California, Kansas, Oregon, Nevada.* Washington, D.C., 1867.

Admire, W. W. *Admire's Political & Legislative Hand-Book for Kansas.* Topeka, George W. Crane & Co., 1891.

Arnold, Anna E. *A History of Kansas.* Topeka, Kansas State Printing Plant, 1914.

Ashton, William E. "Names of Counties & County Seats." *Names: Journal of the American Name Society,* Vol. 2, No. 1. Berkeley: March, 1954.

Atchison, Theodore C. "David R. Atchison." *Missouri Historical Review,* Vol. 24, No. 4. Columbia, Missouri: July, 1930.

Austin, Edwin A. "The Supreme Court of the State of Kansas." *Collections of the Kansas State Historical Society,* Vol. 13. Topeka: 1915.

Barber County History Committee. *Chosen Land: A History of Barber County, Kansas.* Dallas, Texas, Taylor Publishing Co., 1980.

Beauchamp, William M. "Aboriginal Place Names of New York." *New York State Museum Bulletin,* Bulletin 108, Archaeology 12. Albany: May, 1907.

"Biographies of the Members of the Free-State Legislature of 1857-'58." *Transactions of the Kansas State Historical Society,* Vol. 10. Topeka: 1908.

"Biographies of Members of the Legislature of 1861." *Transactions of the Kansas State Historical Society,* Vol. 10. Topeka: 1908.

Blackburn, Anona S., & Myrtle S. Cardwell. *History of Republic County: 1868–1964.* Belleville, Kansas, Belleville Telescope, 1964.

Blackmar, Frank W. *Kansas.* Chicago, Standard Publishing Co., 1912.

Blanchard, Leola H. *Conquest of Southwest Kansas.* Wichita Eagle Press, 1931.

Boatner, Mark M. *The Civil War Dictionary.* New York, David McKay & Co., Inc., 1959.

Bowers, D. N. *Seventy Years in Norton County, Kansas: 1872–1942.* Norton, Kansas, Norton County Champion, 1942.

Bowman, John S. *The Civil War Almanac.* New York, World Almanac Publications, 1983.

Bright, John D. *Kansas: The First Century.* New York, Lewis Historical Publishing Co., Inc., 1956.

Bullard, Cora W. "Horticulture in Kansas." *Transactions of the Kansas State Historical Society,* Vol. 7. Topeka: 1902.

Business Directory & History of Wabaunsee County. Topeka, Kansas Directory Co., 1907.

Caldwell, Martha B. "When Horace Greeley Visited Kansas in 1859." *Kansas Historical Quarterly,* Vol. 9, No. 2. Topeka: May, 1940.

"Captain John Livingston Graham." One page biographical sketch in the in files of the Kansas State Historical Society, Memorial Building, Topeka, Kansas.

Case, Nelson. *History of Labette County, Kansas.* Topeka, Crane & Co., 1893.

Chitwood, Oliver P., et al. *The United States from Colony to World Power.* New York, D. Van Nostrand Co., Inc., 1949.

Clark County Chapter of the Kansas State Historical Society. *Notes on Early Clark County, Kansas.* Ashland, Kansas, 1939–1940.

Clements, John. *Kansas Facts.* Dallas, Texas, Clements Research II, Inc., 1990.

Collins, Lewis. *History of Kentucky.* Louisville, Kentucky, 1877.

Committee on Geographic Names. "Origin of Names of New York State Counties." *University of the State of New York Bulletin to the Schools,* Vol. 10. January–May, 1924.

Connelley, William E. *A Standard History of Kansas & Kansans.* Chicago, Lewis Publishing Co., 1919.

Cooper, Frank A. *It Happened in Kansas.* Lyons, Kansas, Velma C. Cooper, 1969.

Corley, Wayne E. *County & Community Names in Kansas.* Denver, Colorado, 1962.

Cory, C. E. "The Osage Ceded Lands." *Transactions of the Kansas State Historical Society,* Vol. 8. Topeka: 1904.

Cory, Charles E. *Place Names of Bourbon County, Kansas.*

Cory, Charles E. "The Sixth Kansas Cavalry & Its Commander." *Collections of the Kansas State Historical Society,* Vol. 11. Topeka: 1910.

Cover, Anniejane H. "Some Place Names of Kansas." *Heritage of Kansas,* Vol. 4. No. 4. Emporia, Kansas: November, 1960.

Crawford, Samuel J. *Kansas in the Sixties.* Chicago, A. C. McClurg & Co., 1911.

Curran, Thomas J. *Manual for the Use of the Legislature of the State of New York: 1951.* Albany, Williams Press, Inc., 1951.

Dabney, Virginius. *Virginia: The New Dominion.* Charlottesville, University Press of Virginia, 1971.

Deatherage, Charles P. *Early History of Greater Kansas City, Missouri & Kansas.* Kansas City, Missouri, Interstate Publishing Co., 1927.

Denison, W. W. "Battle of Prairie Grove." *Collections of the Kansas State Historical Society,* Vol. 16. Topeka: 1925.

Downs, John P., & Fenwick Y. Hedley. *History of Chautauqua County, New York & Its People.* Boston, American Historical Society, Inc., 1921.

Duncan, L. Wallace, & Charles F. Scott. *History of Allen & Woodson Counties, Kansas.* Iola, Kansas, Iola Register, 1901.

The Encyclopedia Americana. New York, Americana Corporation, 1977.

Endacott, John. "Addresses at the Dedication of the Monument at Turner to Mark the Site of the First Methodist Mission to the Shawnee Indians in Kansas." *Collections of the Kansas State Historical Society,* Vol. 14. Topeka: 1918.

Farlow, Joyce, & Louise Barry. "Vincent B. Osborne's Civil War Experiences." *Kansas Historical Quarterly,* Vol. 20. Topeka: 1952.

Fensten, Joe. "Indian Removal." *Chronicles of Oklahoma,* Vol. 11, No. 4. Oklahoma City: December, 1933.

Ferris, Robert G. *Founders & Frontiersmen.* Washington, D.C., United States Department of the Interior, 1967.

Forter, Emma E. *History of Marshall County, Kansas.* Indianapolis, B. F. Bowen & Co., Inc., 1917.

Fox, S. M. *Report of the Adjutant General of the State of Kansas: 1861–'65.* Topeka, Kansas State Printing Co., 1896.

Gihon, John H. *Gihon's History of Kansas.*

Gill, Helen G. "The Establishment of Counties in Kansas." *Transactions of the Kansas State Historical Society,* Vol. 8. Topeka: 1904.

Graves, W. W. *History of Neosho County.* St. Paul, Kansas, Journal Press, 1949.

Gray, J. Rufus. *Pioneer Saints & Sinners: Pratt County from Its Beginnings to 1900.* Pratt, Kansas, Printing Press, 1977.

Harrington, W. P. *History of Gove County, Kansas.* Scott City, Kansas, News Chronicle Printing Co., Inc., 1973.

Hemphill, William E., et al. *Cavalier Commonwealth: History & Government of Virginia*. New York, McGraw-Hill Book Co., Inc., 1957.

Hickman, Russell K. "The Reeder Administration Inaugurated." *Kansas Historical Quarterly*, Vol. 36, No. 3. Topeka: Autumn, 1970.

Hinton, Richard J. *Rebel Invasion of Missouri & Kansas & the Campaign of the Army of the Border Against General Sterling Price in October & November, 1864*. Chicago, Church & Goodman, 1865.

History of the State of Kansas. Chicago, A. T. Andreas, 1883.

History of Woodson County, Kansas. Dallas, Texas, Curtis Media Corp., 1987.

Hodge, Frederick W. *Handbook of American Indians North of Mexico*. Totowa, New Jersey, Rowman & Littlefield, 1975.

Howes, Cecil. "How Counties Got Their Names." *Kansas Teacher*, Vol. 58. April, 1950.

Hunt, Elvid, & Walter E. Lorence. *History of Fort Leavenworth: 1827–1937*. Fort Leavenworth, Kansas, Command & General Staff School Press, 1937.

Ingalls, Sheffield. *History of Atchison County, Kansas*. Lawrence, Standard Publishing Co., 1916.

Isely, Bliss, & W. M. Richards. *Four Centuries in Kansas*. Wichita, McCormick-Mathers Co., 1936.

Jelinek, George. *Ellsworth, Kansas: 1867–1947*. Ellsworth, Kansas, Consolidated-Salina.

Johnson, Harry. *A History of Anderson County, Kansas*. Garnett, Kansas, Garnett Review Co., 1936.

Johnson W. A. *The History of Anderson County, Kansas*. Garnett, Kansas, Kauffman & Iler, Garnett Plaindealer, 1877.

Johnson, William, et al. "Letters from the Indian Missions in Kansas." *Collections of the Kansas State Historical Society*, Vol. 16. Topeka: 1925.

Jones, Howel. "Judge Samuel A. Kingman." *Transactions of the Kansas State Historical Society*, Vol. 9. Topeka: 1906.

"Kansas County Names." *The Magazine of History*, Vol. 7, No. 6. New York: June, 1908.

Kansas Facts: Volume 4. Topeka, Kansas Facts Publishing Co., 1933.

Kansas State Adjutant General's Report: 1861–1865. Topeka, 1896.

Kansas Year Book: 1937–1938. Topeka, Kansas State Chamber of Commerce.

Kersey, Ralph T. *History of Finney County, Kansas*. Finney County Historical Society, 1950.

Kessinger, Ed L. *Historic Fort Riley: 1853–1953*. Junction City Republic, 1953.

King, Joseph B. "The Ottawa Indians in Kansas & Oklahoma." *Collections of the Kansas State Historical Society*, Vol. 13. Topeka: 1915.

Kingman, Samuel A. "Reminiscences." *Transactions of the Kansas State Historical Society*, Vol. 7. Topeka: 1902.

Langsdorf, Edgar. "The Letters of Joseph H. Trego, 1857–1864, Linn County Pioneer." *Kansas Historical Quarterly*, Vol. 19, No. 3. Topeka: August, 1951.

Laune, Seigniora R. "Avra P. Russell." *Collections of the Kansas State Historical Society*, Vol. 14. Topeka: 1918.

Leitch, Barbara A. *A Concise Dictionary of the Indian Tribes of North America*. Algonac, Michigan, Reference Publications, Inc., 1979.

Linton, Calvin D. *The Bicentennial Almanac*. Nashville, Tennessee, Thomas Nelson, Inc., 1975.

List of Fargo Division Stations Showing Origins of the Station Names. Office Division Superintendent, Fargo Division, Northern Pacific Railway Company, 1944.

McCoy, Sondra V. M. & Jan Hults. *1001 Kansas Place Names*. Lawrence, University Press of Kansas, 1989.

McGonigle James A. "First Kansas Infantry in the Battle of Wilson's Creek." *Collections of the Kansas State Historical Society*, Vol. 12. Topeka: 1912.

McKenney, Thomas L. & James Hall. *The Indian Tribes of North America*. Edinburgh, John Grant, 1933.

McLoughlin, Denis. *Wild & Woolly: An Encyclopedia of the Old West*. Garden City, New York, Doubleday & Co., Inc., 1975.

McMahon, Helen G. *Chautauqua County: A History*. Buffalo, Henry Stewart, Inc., 1958.

Malin, James C. "J. A. Walker's Early History of Edwards County." *Kansas Historical Quarterly*, Vol. 9, No. 3. Topeka: August, 1940.

Manning, Edwin C. "A Kansas Soldier." *Transactions of the Kansas State Historical Society*, Vol. 10. Topeka: 1908.

Mead, James R. "The Pawnees as I Knew Them." *Transactions of the Kansas State Historical Society*, Vol. 10. Topeka: 1908.

Mead, James R. "The Wichita Indians in Kansas." *Transactions of the Kansas State Historical Society*, Vol. 8. Topeka: 1904.

Merrill, Arch. *Southern Tier*. New York, American Book-Stratford Press, Inc., 1954.

Millbrook, Minnie D. *Ness: Western County Kansas*. Detroit, Millbrook Printing Co., 1955.

Monaghan, Jay. *Civil War on the Western Border: 1854–1865*. Boston, Little, Brown & Co., 1955.

Morgan, Perl W. *History of Wyandotte County, Kansas & Its People*. Chicago, Lewis Publishing Co., 1911.

Morrall, Albert. "Dr. Albert Morrall: Pro-Slavery Soldier in Kansas in 1856." *Collections of the Kansas State Historical Society*, Vol. 14. Topeka: 1918.

Newcomb, W. W. *The Indians of Texas*. Austin, University of Texas Press, 1961.

"Official Kansas Roster." *Collections of the Kansas State Historical Society*, Vol. 16. Topeka: 1925.

"Origin of City Names." *Transactions of the Kansas State Historical Society*, Vol. 7. Topeka: 1902.

"Origin of County Names." *Transactions of the Kansas State Historical Society*, Vol. 7. Topeka: 1902.

Prentis, Noble L. *A History of Kansas*. Topeka, 1909.

Pride, W. F. *The History of Fort Riley*. 1926.

Raser, Margaret H., & Ina Rumford. *A History of Hodgeman County*. Jetmore Printing Co., 1961.

Rath, Ida E. *Early Ford County*. North Newton, Kansas, Mennonite Press, 1964.

Rayburn, J. A. "Geographical Names of Amerindian Origin in Canada." *Names: Journal of the American Name Society*, Vol. 15, No. 3. Potsdam, New York: September, 1967.

Redmond, John. *First Hand Historical Episodes of Early Coffey County*.

Rennick, Robert M. *Kentucky Place Names*. University Press of Kentucky, 1984.

Richardson, Myrtle H. *Oft' Told Tales: A History of Edwards County, Kansas to 1900*. Lewis, Kansas, Lewis Press, Inc., 1976.

Rinehart, Mrs. Bennett, et al. *Blaze Marks on the Border: The Story of Arkansas City, Kansas Founded 1870–1871*. North Newton, Kansas, Mennonite Press, 1970.

Robinson, Sinclair, & Donald Smith. *NTC's Dictionary of Canadian French*. Lincolnwood, Illinois, National Textbook Co., 1991.

Robley, T. F. *History of Bourbon County, Kansas*. Fort Scott, Kansas, Monitor Book & Printing Co., 1894.

Rooks County Historical Society. *Lest We Forget*. Osborne, Kansas, Osborne County Farmer, 1981.

Rush County Book Committee. *Rush County, Kansas: A Century in Story & Pictures*. Rush County Historical Society, 1976.

Rydjord, John. *Indian Place-Names*. Norman, University of Oklahoma Press, 1968.

Rydjord, John. *Kansas Place-Names*. Norman University of Oklahoma Press, 1972.

Savage, I. O. *A History of Republic County, Kansas*. Beloit, Kansas, Jones & Chubbic, 1901.

Scheffer, Theo. H. "Geographical Names in Ottawa County." *Kansas Historical Quarterly*, Vol. 3, No. 3. Topeka: August, 1934.

Schoewe, Walter H. "The Geography of Kansas." *Transactions of the Kansas Academy of Science*, Vol. 51, No. 3. Lawrence, Kansas: September, 1948.

Schruben, Francis W. *The Naming of Rooks County*.

Shively, S. J. "The Pottawatomie Massacre." *Transactions of the Kansas State Historical Society*, Vol. 8. Topeka: 1904.

"Sketches of Early Days in Kearny County." *Kansas Historical Quarterly*, Vol. 7, No. 1. Topcka: February, 1938.

Slagg, Winifred N. *Riley County, Kansas*. Brooklyn, New York, Theo. Gaus' Sons Inc., 1968.

Socolofsky, Homer E. *Kansas Governors*. Lawrence, University Press of Kansas, 1990.

Socolofsky, Homer E., & Huber Self. *Historical Atlas of Kansas*. Norman, University of Oklahoma Press, 1972.

Speer, John. "Accuracy in History." *Transactions of the Kansas State Historical Society*, Vol. 6. Topeka: 1900.

Spencer, Joab. "The Shawnee Indians: Their Customs, Traditions & Folklore." *Transactions of the Kansas State Historical Society*, Vol. 10. Topeka: 1908.

Stillwell, Leander. "Woodson County Courthouse." *Collections of the Kansas State Historical Society*, Vol. 13. Topeka: 1915.

Stratford, Jessie P. *Butler County's Eighty Years*. 1934.

Suderow, Bryce A. Letter to the author dated March 17, 1984.

Tennal, Ralph. *History of Nemaha County, Kansas*. Lawrence, Kansas, Standard Publishing Co., 1916.

Tregillis, Helen C. *The Indians of Illinois*. Decorah, Iowa, Anundsen Publishing Co., 1983.

Tuttle, Charles R. *A New Centennial History of the State of Kansas*. Madison, Wisconsin, Interstate Book Company, 1876.

A Twentieth Century History & Biographical Record of Crawford County, Kansas. Chicago, Lewis Publishing Co., 1905.

The United States Biographical Dictionary: Kansas Volume. Chicago, S. Lewis & Co., 1879.

Verwyst, Chrysostom. "Geographical Names in Wisconsin, Minnesota & Michigan Having a Chippewa Origin." *Collections of the State Historical Society of Wisconsin*, Vol. 12. Madison, Wisconsin: 1892.

Vexler, Robert I. *Chronology & Documentary Handbook of the State of Kansas*. Dobbs Ferry, New York, Oceana Publications, Inc., 1978.

Vexler, Robert I. *Chronology & Documentary Handbook of the State of Ohio*. Dobbs Ferry, New York, Oceana Publications, Inc., 1978.

Vogel, Virgil J. *Indian Names in Michigan*. Ann Arbor, University of Michigan Press, 1986.

Vogel, Virgil J. "Indian Place Names in Illinois." *Journal of the Illinois State Historical Society*, Vol. 55. 1962.

Vogel, Virgil J. *Iowa Place Names of Indian Origin*. Iowa City, University of Iowa Press, 1983.

Waters, Joseph G. "Samuel A. Kingman." *Transactions of the Kansas State Historical Society*, Vol. 9. Topeka: 1906.

Webb, Walter P., et al. *The Handbook of Texas*. Austin, Texas State Historical Association, 1952.

White, Mrs. S. B. "My First Days in Kansas." *Collections of the Kansas State Historical Society*, Vol. 11. Topeka: 1910.

Wilder, D. W. *The Annals of Kansas*. Topeka, T. Dwight Thacher, Kansas Publishing House, 1886.

Wilson, Francis L. *A History of Ellsworth County, Kansas*. Ellsworth County Historical Society, 1979.

Wilson, William E. *Indiana: A History*. Bloomington, Indiana University Press, 1966.

Windrow, Martin, & Francis K. Mason. *A Concise Dictionary of Military Biography*. New York, John Wiley & Sons, Inc., 1991.

Work Projects Administration. *A Guide to Leavenworth, Kansas*. Leavenworth, Kansas, Leavenworth Chronicle, 1940.

Work Projects Administration. *Inventory of the County Archives of Kansas—Gove & Gray Counties*. Topeka, 1939–1941.

Wright, Muriel H. *A Guide to the Indian Tribes of Oklahoma*. Norman, University of Oklahoma Press, 1951.

Kentucky

(120 counties)

962 *Adair County*

John Adair (1757–1840)— This South Carolina native served in the Revolutionary War and spent part of it as a prisoner of war. In 1786 he moved to Kentucky where he engaged in military actions against the Indians and became active in politics. Adair served nine terms as a member of Kentucky's house of representatives and was, for a time, speaker of that body. He briefly represented Kentucky in the U.S. Senate and later served as an officer and hero in the War of 1812. Adair was given the rank of brevet brigadier-general of the Kentucky militia and in 1820 he became governor of Kentucky. He later represented Kentucky in the U.S. House of Representatives.

963 *Allen County*

John Allen (–1813)— Allen was born in Virginia in 1771 or 1772 and moved to Kentucky with his parents when he was still a boy. The Allens' first Kentucky home was near Danville but they later settled on a farm near Bardstown. Allen studied law in his native Virginia and then returned to Kentucky in 1795 to practice law in Shelby County. He became active in politics and served in both houses of the Kentucky legislature. In 1808 Allen was a candidate for governor of Kentucky but lost to Charles Scott. Early in the War of 1812 Allen raised a regiment of riflemen to serve in the campaign under William Henry Harrison in the Northwest. On June 5, 1812, he received a commission as lieutenant-colonel. Allen died in combat at the battle of the River Raisin in Michigan on January 22, 1813. This county was created just two years later, in January, 1815.

964 *Anderson County*

Richard C. Anderson, Jr. (1788–1826)— A native of Kentucky when it was still a part of Virginia, and a graduate of William & Mary College in Virginia proper, Richard Clough Anderson, Jr., studied law in Virginia before returning to Louisville, Kentucky, to begin his law practice. He served several terms in the lower house of the Kentucky legislature and represented Kentucky in the U.S. House of Representatives. Anderson subsequently served again in Kentucky's house of representatives and was chosen speaker of that body in 1822. He was chosen by President James Monroe to be minister plenipotentiary to Colombia. In 1826 he was confirmed as one of our country's two delegates to the congress of nations to be held in Panama but he died in Panama of yellow fever enroute to the congress on July 24, 1826. This county was created in January, 1827.

965 *Ballard County*

Bland W. Ballard (1761–1853)— A native of Virginia, Ballard moved with his father to Kentucky in 1779. Here he joined the militia and defended the frontier from Indian attacks. In 1788 a party of Delaware Indians murdered several members of Ballard's family. He subsequently avenged their deaths and he claimed to have killed more than 30 Indians in battle. Ballard served as a guide to the troops of General Winfield Scott and General James Wilkinson during their incursions in country controlled by Indians. He also served under General Anthony Wayne in the American victory over the Indians in the battle of Fallen Timbers in Northwest territory (now northwestern Ohio). Ballard served several terms in the lower house of the Kentucky legislature. He also served as a major in the War of 1812 and led an advance in the disastrous battle of the River Raisin, where he was wounded and taken as a prisoner of war. This county was created in February, 1842.

966 *Barren County*

The Kentucky barrens— The Kentucky barrens are a large area of prairie grassland which are relatively barren of trees. The barrens cover the northern third of Barren County, the eastern portion of Warren County, the northern end of Metcalfe County and the southern portion of Hart County, Kentucky. The barrens were named by early explorers who presumed that this land lacked fertility and would be poor farmland. That judgment was false and the land later proved to be quite fertile, but the name stuck. Barren County, Kentucky, was created in 1798 and named for this large prairie area in Kentucky, a portion of which is within its borders.

967 *Bath County*

Medicinal bathing springs within the county— Within the borders of Bath County, Kentucky there are numerous medicinal mineral springs used for bathing. Most of these springs are in the eastern and southeastern sections of the county. Bath County was created on January 15, 1811, and named for these bathing springs. An account book dating back to about the time of the county's creation has been found in Olympia Springs. These springs were one of Kentucky's most popular resorts in the 19th century. The account book shows charges for the use of the bath and the bathhouse there.

968 *Bell County*

Joshua F. Bell (1811–1870)— A native of Kentucky and a graduate of Centre College in this state, Bell studied law at Transylvania University in Lexington, Kentucky and established a law practice in Danville, Kentucky. He represented Kentucky in the U.S. House of Representatives for one term from March, 1845, to March, 1847. In February, 1861, Bell served as a commissioner to a peace convention in Washington, D.C. That convention was unsuccessful in its last gasp attempt to avert civil war. Bell later served in the lower house of the Kentucky legislature and was active in the legislature in efforts to create this new county. When it was created in 1867 it was named Josh Bell County. It was in 1872 or 1873 that the Kentucky legislature officially changed the county's name to the more traditional form, Bell County.

969 *Boone County*

Daniel Boone (1734–1820)— A native of Pennsylvania, Boone penetrated Kentucky when it was wilderness country and settled there with his family in 1775. He gained fame on America's rugged western frontier as explorer, Indian fighter and surveyor. During much of this period, Kentucky was part of Virginia. In 1792 Kentucky was admitted to the Union as a separate state. Some six years later, in December 1798, Boone County, Kentucky was created and named in Daniel Boone's honor. To many of us, much of Kentucky still seems quite rural at the second millennium year 2000 but to Daniel Boone, Kentucky was already becoming too crowded for his taste by 1799. In September, 1799, accompanied by some members of his family, Boone immigrated to what is now the state of Missouri

970 *Bourbon County*

Royal Bourbon dynasty of France— Bourbon County, Kentucky, was created in the mid-1780's by the legislature of the state of Virginia before Kentucky became a separate state. It was named in honor of the royal Bourbon dynasty of France. The Bourbons had rendered valuable aid in the form of both money and fighting men to the American colonies in their struggle for independence from Britain. The duchy of Bourbon had been created in France during the tenth century and the house of Bourbon was one of the most powerful royal houses in Europe for centuries. At various times they ruled Spain, Naples, Sicily and Tuscany as well as France.

971 *Boyd County*

Linn Boyd (1800–1859)— Boyd was a native of Tennessee, who moved to Kentucky in 1826. His given name is rendered in some accounts as Lynn. In 1827 Boyd was elected to Kentucky's house of representatives and he served several terms in that body. He later represented Kentucky for some 18 years in the lower house of the U.S. Congress. From 1851 to 1855 Boyd was speaker of the U.S. House of Representatives. In 1859 he was elected lieutenant-governor of Kentucky but when the Kentucky senate convened, he was too ill to preside over its deliberations. Boyd died on December 17, 1859, and this county was created and named in his honor just two months later, on February 16, 1860.

972 *Boyle County*

John Boyle (1774–)— Boyle was born near Tazewell, Virginia and moved with his family to the Kentucky wilderness when he was still a young boy. A lawyer by profession, Boyle served in the lower house of the Kentucky legislature. In 1803 he was elected to represent Kentucky in the U.S. House of Representatives. He served three consecutive terms in that body. Almost immediately after leaving congress, Boyle was appointed as associate justice of Kentucky's court of appeals. In 1810 he became chief justice of that body. Boyle served as chief justice until 1826 when he was appointed by President John Quincy Adams to be U.S. district judge for the district of

Kentucky. Judge Boyle served in that position until his death. The date of John Boyle's death is not clear. It is shown by one reliable source as January 28, 1834, but other sources known for accuracy show other dates. One gives February 28, 1834, while two other sources list January 28, 1835.

973 Bracken County

Uncertain— It is known that Bracken County was named either directly for William Bracken or for two creeks, Big Bracken Creek and Little Bracken Creek, which had been named for him.

William Bracken (–)— This county's namesake was one of Kentucky's early pioneers, coming to Kentucky in 1773. Bracken was with the early survey parties of Kentucky headed by Robert McAfee (1745–1795) and Thomas Bullitt (1730–1778). He accompanied the McAfee party along the Salt River in Mercer County, Kentucky and down the Kentucky River in a survey of central and north-central Kentucky. The areas surveyed included present day Harrodsburg and Frankfort. His survey activities with Thomas Bullitt were at the Falls of the Ohio River at Louisville. William Bracken was one of Bracken County's first settlers. He lived near the Ohio River along either Big Bracken Creek or Little Bracken Creek, where he was a trapper and Indian fighter. Bracken was killed by Indians.

Big Bracken Creek and Little Bracken Creek— Both of these creeks were named for William Bracken. They converge and empty into the Ohio River between Covington, Kentucky, and Maysville, Kentucky.

974 Breathitt County

John Breathitt (1786–1834)— A native of Virginia, Breathitt moved to Kentucky with his family when he was still a boy. Breathitt entered the legal profession in 1810 when he was admitted to the Kentucky bar. He served in the lower house of the Kentucky legislature and was the state's lieutenant-governor from 1828 to 1832. In September, 1832, he became Kentucky's governor but less than 18 months later he died of tuberculosis. While governor of antebellum Kentucky, Breathitt urged pro–Union and anti-secession sentiment in the state. This county was created in 1839.

975 Breckinridge County

John Breckinridge (1760–1806)— A native of Virginia, Breckinridge was elected to Virginia's house of burgesses while he was still a student at the College of William and Mary. In 1792 or 1793 Breckinridge moved to the wilderness of Kentucky where he practiced law, managed his huge farm, owned some 65 slaves and was a wealthy man. A grandson of his, John C. Breckinridge (1821–1875), was one of three major opponents of Abraham Lincoln in the 1860 presidential election. Our subject, the namesake of Breckinridge County, served as attorney general of Kentucky and in the lower house of the Kentucky legislature where he rose to become speaker of the house. He represented Kentucky in the U.S. Senate from 1801 to 1805 when he resigned to accept President Thomas Jefferson's appointment as attorney general of the United States. This county was created in 1799, before Breckinridge left Kentucky to serve in the federal government.

976 Bullitt County

Alexander S. Bullitt (–1816)— Bullitt was born in 1761 or 1762 in Dumfries, Virginia, and in 1782 he was elected to the Virginia legislature. He crossed the mountains to settle in the Kentucky wilderness in 1783 or 1784. At that time Kentucky was still part of Virginia. Bullitt was a member of the Kentucky statehood convention which met at Danville in 1788 and he served as a delegate, in April, 1792, to the convention which drafted the first constitution for the new state of Kentucky. He was elected to the first senate of the state and he served as speaker of that body for some eight years starting in 1792. In 1800 Bullitt became Kentucky's first lieutenant-governor and he held that post until 1804. He returned to the Kentucky legislature in 1804 and served there until 1808. This county was created in December, 1796 while Bullitt was serving as speaker of the Kentucky senate.

977 Butler County

Richard Butler (–1791)— Butler was born in the 1740's in Ireland. Some sources list his year of birth as 1743 while others indicate that he was born in 1748. He came with his family to America, settled in Pennsylvania and served as an army officer during the American Revolution. He participated in battles at Saratoga, New York, and Stony Point, New York, and spent the latter part of the war in Georgia. After the Revolution, Butler served as a commissioner to negotiate treaties with several Indian tribes and he was made superintendent of Indian affairs for the northern district. He also served briefly in the Pennsylvania senate. In 1791 he was recalled to military duty, given the rank of major-general and made second in command to General Arthur St. Clair, who was then governor of Northwest territory. Butler was killed in combat by Indians on November 4, 1791, near the present site of Ft. Wayne, Indiana, during the Indians' defeat of General St. Clair's forces. This county was created in 1810.

978 Caldwell County

John W. Caldwell (1757–1804)— A native of Prince Edward County, Virginia, Caldwell crossed the mountains to settle in the Kentucky wilderness when it was still a part of Virginia. He settled near what is now Danville, Kentucky, in 1781. Caldwell served in the military in actions against the Indians and rose in rank from common soldier to major-general of the militia. In 1786 George Rogers Clark led a military expedition against the Wabash Indian tribes and John W. Caldwell served under Clark in that campaign. Caldwell was active in the efforts to separate Kentucky from Virginia and secure Kentucky's admission to the Union as a separate state. After Kentucky achieved statehood, he served in the Kentucky senate and in 1804 he was elected lieutenant-governor, but he had served only two months in that office at the time of his death in November, 1804. This county was created on January 31, 1809.

979 Calloway County

Richard Callaway (–1780)— Callaway was born in Virginia about 1722. He served in the army in the French and Indian Wars and rose to the rank of major. In early 1775 Richard Henderson (1735–1785) purchased an enormous tract of land from the Indians. It comprised about half of what is now the state of Kentucky and it was called Transylvania. Richard Callaway and Daniel Boone were among those invited by Henderson to participate in the Transylvania Company's activities and both of them accepted Henderson's invitation. In the spring of 1775 Callaway was among those who constructed a fort at what later became Boonesborough and he was a member of the party that traced the Wilderness Road from the Clinch River to Boonesborough. Callaway served as a representative in the Transylvania Company and he was a justice of the court of Kentucky County, Virginia. He also was elected to sit as a burgess in the Virginia legislature representing Kentucky County, Virginia. Callaway was promoted to the rank of colonel in actions against the Indians. Callaway was granted a franchise to run a ferry across the Kentucky River at Boonesborough but he was killed by Indians on March 8 or March 9, 1780, while building his ferryboat. The Indians scalped both Callaway and one of his helpers. Callaway County, Kentucky, was named for Richard Callaway. The difference in spelling is due to a clerical error.

980 *Campbell County*

John Campbell (–1799)— Campbell was born in Ulster in northern Ireland about 1735 and came to America where he served under British General Edward Braddock in the French and Indian War. Campbell subsequently became a successful fur trader with the Indians on the western frontier and he supported Virginia's claim to dominion over the area that now includes Pittsburgh, Pennsylvania. Virginia rewarded Campbell's support by granting him co-ownership of some 4,000 acres of land at the Falls of the Ohio River, adjacent to what is now the city of Louisville, Kentucky. This land grant made Campbell a very wealthy man. During the American Revolution Campbell was taken prisoner by the British and held at Montreal until late 1782. Upon his return to Kentucky, which was still a part of Virginia, Campbell served as a justice of the Jefferson County, Virginia, court and he represented Jefferson County in the Virginia legislature. He was a delegate to two Kentucky statehood conventions and a member of the April, 1792, convention which wrote Kentucky's first state constitution. Kentucky was admitted to the Union as a state on June 1, 1792, and Campbell entered the new state's legislature soon afterward. He was serving on the floor of the state senate at the time of his sudden death in 1799. This county had been created in 1794.

981 *Carlisle County*

John G. Carlisle (1835–1910)— A native of Kentucky and a lawyer, Carlisle became active in antebellum politics and won a seat in Kentucky's house of representatives. He later served in the Kentucky senate and was the state's lieutenant-governor from 1871 until 1875. In 1877 Carlisle entered the U.S. House of Representatives where he represented Kentucky for a number of years and rose to become speaker of the house. In 1890 he left the house to become a member of the U.S. Senate, filling the unexpired term of the recently deceased James B. Beck (1822–1890). President Grover Cleveland appointed John G. Carlisle to serve in his cabinet as secretary of the treasury and Carlisle resigned from the senate to accept that position. He served as Cleveland's secretary of the treasury from 1893 to the end of Cleveland's term as president in 1897. This county was created in 1886 while Carlisle was speaker of the U.S. House of Representatives.

982 *Carroll County*

Charles Carroll (1737–1832)— Carroll was a native of Maryland and he represented that state in the Continental Congress. He was one of the signers of the Declaration of Independence and he later represented Maryland as a U.S. senator in the first congress of the United States. Carroll lived to be the last surviving signer of the Declaration of Independence and several states recognized that distinction by naming counties for him. This county was created in 1838.

983 *Carter County*

William G. Carter (–1850)— William Grayson Carter entered Kentucky's state senate in 1834 and he was a member of that body in 1838 when this county was created and named in his honor by his fellow legislators. Carter offered to donate the land where the Carter County courthouse would be located if the town of Grayson was selected as the county seat. Grayson was selected and the county courthouse was built on the land donated by Senator Carter. That courthouse stood until 1907 when it was torn down and replaced. Carter owned a large amount of land in the area and he later donated another parcel of land for building a Methodist church. In 1847 Carter moved to Arkansas but he died in Kentucky. He was visiting Lexington, Kentucky, in 1850 when he died of cholera.

984 *Casey County*

William Casey (1754–1816)— A native of Virginia and a veteran of the Revolutionary War, Casey came to Kentucky in the winter of 1779–1780 when it was still part of Virginia. In 1791, with a party of soldier settlers, Casey erected a blockhouse and fort far in the Kentucky wilderness, some 50 miles from the nearest White settlement. In 1792 he was commissioned a lieutenant-colonel of the militia. Casey later served in both houses of the Kentucky state legislature and he was a member of the state's second constitutional convention which was held in 1799. This county was created and named in Colonel Casey's honor in 1806.

985 *Christian County*

William Christian (–1786)— A native of Virginia and a brother-in-law of Patrick Henry, Christian served as an army officer in the French and Indian Wars prior to the American Revolution. By 1774 he was a colonel of the militia and the following year he was a member of Virginia's general state convention. During the Revolution, Christian served first as colonel in the Virginia line of the regular army and later in command of the militia in his area of Virginia. After the war Christian served for several years in the Virginia legislature and in 1785 he moved to Kentucky. The following year he was killed by Indians. This county was created in 1796.

986 *Clark County*

George R. Clark (1752–1818)— A native of Virginia, George Rogers Clark was a frontiersman and military hero. During the American Revolution he secured a commission as lieutenant-colonel to attack the British, Indians and Loyalists in Indiana and Illinois. He successfully captured Vincennes, Cahokia and Kaskaskia and, after the British retook Kaskaskia, Clark won it a second time. These military victories together with skillful negotiating by Benjamin Franklin enabled the United States to acquire the Northwest territory during the peace negotiations with the British at the end of the Revolution.

987 *Clay County*

Green Clay (1757–1826)— Clay was born in Virginia on August 14, 1757, to a family that had been prominent in Virginia since the 1600's. Henry Clay (1777–1852), was a second cousin of his. Green Clay moved to Kentucky about 1780 and worked as a surveyor. He acquired enormous tracts of land as a result of his successful land speculations and became one of the wealthiest men in Kentucky. He owned farms, distilleries, taverns and gristmills and was a slave owner. While Kentucky was still a part of Virginia, Clay served in the Virginia legislature and he was a member of the Virginia convention which ratified the constitution of the United States. After Kentucky became a separate state in 1792, Green Clay served in both houses of the Kentucky legislature. During the War of 1812 Clay held the rank of brigadier-general and he led a troop of some 3,000 Kentucky volunteers. Clay and his troops assisted General William Henry Harrison in defeating the British and their Indian allies at Fort Meigs.

988 *Clinton County*

Uncertain— This county was created in the mid-1830's. Virtually all sources state, without reservation, that the county was named in honor of New York Governor De Witt Clinton (1769–1828) but a few sources disagree and say that it was, or might have been, named for Clinton Winfrey.

De Witt Clinton (1769–1828)— This New York state native held many of the important political offices in that state. He served in both houses of the state legislature and as mayor of New York City. He represented New York in the U.S. Senate and in 1812 he was the Federalist candidate for president, running against President James Madison. In 1817 Clinton was elected as New York's governor. As governor, he was the principal promoter of the Erie Canal which was instrumental in linking the vast agricultural lands in our country's West with eastern markets. The canal spurred our nation's growth.

Clinton Winfrey (–)—At the time that Clinton County, Kentucky was created in the mid 1830's, Clinton Winfrey was a 12 year old son of Francis H. Winfrey, the member of the Kentucky house of representatives who sponsored the act that created this new county.

989 *Crittenden County*

John J. Crittenden (–1863)—Crittenden was born in Kentucky in 1786 or 1787 while it was still a part of Virginia and he graduated from the College of William and Mary at Williamsburg, Virginia. A lawyer by profession, Crittenden was appointed attorney general of Illinois territory and aide de camp to Ninian Edwards (1775–1833), the governor of Illinois territory. In 1811 Crittenden was elected to Kentucky's house of representatives and he served several terms in that body and rose to become its speaker. He also served in the military during the War of 1812. Crittenden later represented Kentucky in both houses of the U.S. Congress, served as attorney general in the cabinets of Presidents William Henry Harrison, John Tyler and Millard Fillmore and was governor of Kentucky.

990 *Cumberland County*

Cumberland River—Cumberland County, Kentucky was created on Decem-

ber 14, 1798, and named for the river which flows through it. The Cumberland is a 700 mile-long navigable tributary of the Ohio River. It rises near Whitesburg, Kentucky, in Letcher County in a ridge of the Cumberland Mountains that forms the boundary between Kentucky and its parent state, Virginia. From there the Cumberland flows principally west and south along a crooked course into Tennessee, where it flows west and then north, making a large loop to reenter Kentucky in the extreme southwestern area of the state. The Cumberland then flows north until enters the Ohio River near Paducah, Kentucky. The Cumberland River was named in 1750 when colonial America was still part of England. Its name was given by the explorer, Dr. Thomas Walker (1715–1794) in honor of England's Duke of Cumberland (1721–1765), a son of King George II. In 1750 when Dr. Walker bestowed this name, George II was king of England. During a trip to England some years earlier, Dr. Walker had the privilege of meeting the duke of Cumberland. The duke's name is shown in most works as William Augustus but in some the form William August is used.

991 *Daviess County*

Joseph H. Daveiss (1774–1811)—Daveiss was born in Virginia but moved with his parents to the wilderness of Kentucky when he was still a young boy. There he studied law and became a successful attorney. In 1807 Daveiss, as attorney for the United States, prosecuted Aaron Burr for treason. Burr was acquitted. In the fall of 1811 Daveiss joined General William Henry Harrison's army to fight the Indians. Colonel Daveiss died in the battle of Tippecanoe in Indiana territory in November, 1811, leading a charge of his men against the Indians. Daviess County, Kentucky, was created on January 14, 1815. The enrolling clerk misspelled the name making the county's name officially Daviess. Later the Kentucky general assembly passed an act making Daveiss the legal name but the original erroneous version has continued in use.

992 *Edmonson County*

John M. Edmonson (–1813)—The spelling of our hero's name is uncertain. Virtually all sources show his name as John Edmonson but G. Glenn Clift renders his name as John Montgomery Edmiston in the scholarly work entitled *Remember the Raisin!* The year of Edmonson's birth is also uncertain. Most sources list 1764 but

in some the year 1757 is given. There is, however, no doubt that he was born in Virginia and that he served as a private in the militia during the American Revolution. On October 7, 1780, Edmonson participated in the battle of King's Mountain on the border between the two Carolinas. Edmonson worked as a clerk of the court in Abingdon, Virginia, and in 1790 he purchased land in the Kentucky wilderness. At that time Kentucky was still part of Virginia. He farmed his land in Kentucky until the War of 1812 when he formed a company of volunteer riflemen. At that time Edmonson was about 50 years old. He was made a captain of the company he had formed but he resigned his commission as an officer and served as a private. Edmonson was killed in combat during the American defeat at the battle of River Raisin in Michigan on January 22, 1813. Nearly 300 Americans lost their lives during this battle and many more were massacred by the Indian allies of the British after they had been taken as prisoners of war. Most of those who lost their lives during and after this battle were from Kentucky and several Kentucky counties have been named for heroes of the battle of River Raisin. When this county was created on January 12, 1825, it was named for one of those heroes, John M. Edmonson (or Edmiston).

993 *Elliott County*

Uncertain— This county was created in 1869. Almost all sources consulted state, without qualification, that it was named for John M. Elliott (1820–1879). However, both *The Kentucky Encyclopedia*, edited by John E. Kleber and Robert M. Rennick's book entitled *Kentucky Place Names* mention the possibility that the county might have been named for John M. Elliott's father, John L. Elliott.

John L. Elliott (–)—John L. Elliott came to Kentucky from Scott County, Virginia about 1830 and settled in Lawrence County, Kentucky. Here he was a farmer and he was elected to Kentucky's house of representatives. He served in that body in 1836 and 1837. Later, from 1851 to 1853, John L. Elliott was a member of the Kentucky senate.

John M. Elliott (1820–1879)—A native of Virginia, John Milton Elliott came to Kentucky about 1830 with his parents, studied law and began a law practice at Prestonsburg, Kentucky in 1843. He soon became active in local politics and was elected to the lower house of the Kentucky legislature. Elliott later represented

Kentucky in the antebellum U.S. House of Representatives from March 4, 1853, to March 3, 1859. John M. Elliott was a slave owner and sympathetic to secession sentiments of the South. Although Kentucky never seceded from the Union and was not a member of the Confederate States of America, representatives living in Kentucky participated in the Confederate government. John M. Elliott was one of them. He served as one of the Kentucky representatives in several terms of the Confederate congress. After the Civil War he sat on the bench as a judge in Kentucky. Judge Elliott was assassinated on March 26, 1879, by an irate litigant.

994 *Estill County*

James Estill (1750–1782) — A native of Augusta County, Virginia, Estill crossed the mountains to settle in the Kentucky wilderness. He arrived at what is now Madison County, Kentucky, in 1775. There, about three miles southeast of present day Richmond, Kentucky, James Estill and his brother, Samuel, founded a fort known as Estill's station. An Indian fighter, Estill held the rank of captain in the military. In 1781 his arm was broken by a rifle shot in a battle with Indians. In March, 1782, while James Estill and about 40 other men were absent from Estill's station, a party of Indians attacked it and killed a girl who lived there. When Captain Estill was informed of this attack, he and most of his party of 40 immediately began to pursue the Indians to retaliate. On March 22, 1782, Captain James Estill and his party made contact with the Indians. Captain Estill was among those killed by the Indians in the battle that ensued. This episode in early Kentucky history has come to be known as Estill's defeat at the battle of Little Mountain. It took place about one and one–half miles south of what is now the city of Mount Sterling, Kentucky. In 1808 the Kentucky legislature created and named this county in honor of Captain James Estill.

995 *Fayette County*

Marie Joseph Paul Yves Roch Gilbert du Motier, Marquis de Lafayette (1757–1834) — Lafayette was a French aristocrat who served briefly in the French army. He came to America in 1777 to assist the American Revolutionary army. He was granted an honorary commission as major-general by the Continental Congress and served with distinction in a number of battles in the Revolutionary War. Fayette County was created in 1780, during the American Rev-

olution, while Kentucky was still part of Virginia. Much later, on May 16, 1825, Lafayette visited this Kentucky county that had been named in his honor, during a tour of the United States as an honored guest of the federal government.

996 *Fleming County*

John Fleming (1735–) — John Fleming was born in Virginia in 1735. His father died when he was just a five year old boy and he was raised by his grandparents. In 1750 Fleming began farming land adjacent to the Potomac River in Virginia. He also ran a ferry there. In 1776 Fleming came down the Ohio River in a canoe and then explored the area where Fleming County, Kentucky, now stands. During this visit Fleming made some improvements and landmarks. In April, 1780, while Kentucky was still part of Virginia, Fleming obtained title to land in the area of his 1776 trip. He subsequently moved to Kentucky and settled near the present city of Winchester, Kentucky. Here Fleming was employed as a surveyor, first as deputy surveyor in Fayette County and later as deputy surveyor of Bourbon County. In 1790 he completed construction of Fleming's station within what is now Fleming County. Most accounts refer to him as Colonel John Fleming without explaining the source of the military title. Since it sometimes seemed difficult to throw a snowball in any direction in Kentucky without hitting a "colonel," the significance of this title in John Fleming's case is uncertain. The year of Fleming's death is also uncertain since it is given in some sources as 1791 and in others as 1794. George P. Stockton was a half brother of John Fleming's and Stockton had been involved with Fleming in several of the adventures cited above. After Fleming died, Stockton offered a portion of his land for the county seat of the new county. His offer was accepted and Fleming County was created in 1798 and named for Stockton's half brother, John Fleming. The county seat, Flemingsburg, was also named in John Fleming's honor.

997 *Floyd County*

John Floyd (–1783) — Colonel John Floyd was born in Virginia about 1750 and was a public surveyor prior to the American Revolution. In this capacity he performed numerous surveys of Virginia's land in what is now the state of Kentucky and he briefly served as the principal surveyor for Richard Henderson's short-lived country named Transylvania. During the American Revolution Floyd was involved

in naval warfare against the British and was successful in destroying some British vessels. He was captured and held for about one year in England before he escaped and returned to America. Here he established his reputation as an Indian fighter in Kentucky and it was at the hands of Indians that he met his death. In April, 1783, Colonel Floyd was mortally wounded by Indians on the Kentucky side of the Ohio River. This county was created in 1799.

998 *Franklin County*

Benjamin Franklin (1706–1790) — Franklin was a native of Massachusetts who moved to Pennsylvania in his teens. Poverty denied him a formal education but he became the leading printer and editor in North America. Franklin gained fame for his discoveries and inventions in the physical sciences and he distinguished himself as author, philosopher and diplomat. He was a signer of the Declaration of Independence and an important member of the convention which framed the U.S. Constitution. Franklin County, Kentucky, was created in 1794.

999 *Fulton County*

Robert Fulton (1765–1815) — A native of Pennsylvania, as a young man Fulton supported himself as an artist. He later gained fame for his inventions dealing with marine vessels. He invented a submarine which he successfully demonstrated in the year 1800. He invented mines to be used in naval warfare and was one of the inventors of the steamboat. The steamboat became a commercial success for Fulton and made him famous. This invention contributed greatly to the development of America. Fulton County, Kentucky, is in the southwestern corner of the state and the Mississippi River forms its western border.

1000 *Gallatin County*

Abraham Alfonse Albert Gallatin (1761–1849) — Albert Gallatin was born in Europe to an aristocratic family of the city of Geneva. He moved to America during the American Revolution and settled in Pennsylvania. During the winter of 1789-1790 he was a member of the convention which revised the Pennsylvania constitution. Gallatin later represented Pennsylvania in the U.S. House of Representatives and when Thomas Jefferson became president in 1801, he selected Gallatin to be his secretary of the treasury. Gallatin served as secretary of the treasury under Presidents

Jefferson and Madison until 1814. Albert Gallatin also represented our nation as a diplomat in Europe for some ten years.

1001 *Garrard County*

James Garrard (1749–1822)— A native of Virginia, Garrard served in Virginia's house of delegates during the American Revolution and he held the rank of colonel in the militia. In 1783 or 1784 he crossed the mountains and settled in Kentucky in what later became Bourbon County. Here he was a Baptist minister and a farmer. Although he was a slave owner, he agitated for the emancipation of slaves. In 1785 Garrard was again elected to Virginia's house of delegates. At that time Kentucky was still a part of Virginia. Garrard later became active in the movement to secure statehood for Kentucky and in 1796 he became the second governor of the young state of Kentucky. He served in that office from 1796 to 1804. This county was created and named in Governor Garrard's honor on December 17, 1796, early in his term as governor.

1002 *Grant County*

Uncertain— Grant County, Kentucky was created on February 12, 1820. Most sources agree that the county was named for one or more brothers of the Grant family but it is uncertain whether the county was named for one, two or three of these brothers. The brothers' names were John, Samuel and Squire.

John Grant (1754–1826)— A native of Rowan County, North Carolina, John Grant first came to Kentucky in 1779 or 1780 and erected a fort near what is now the city of Paris, Kentucky. Fearing trouble with Indians, John Grant returned to North Carolina and he subsequently moved to Virginia. He came back to Kentucky in 1784 and entered into an agreement with Samuel Bryan and Charles Morgan to supply salt to customers in the Bluegrass region, in east-central Kentucky. The salt was obtained at Grant's Lick, in what is now Campbell County. John Grant and his associates were pioneer salt producers in the valley of the Licking River. He subsequently spent some time in Illinois but returned to Kentucky and died here in 1826. In some accounts his name is rendered as Colonel John Grant but it is not clear whether the title was derived from military service or was merely nominal.

Samuel Grant (–)— Samuel Grant was born about 1762. His brother, John Grant, came to Kentucky in 1779 or 1780 and Samuel probably came with him at that time. He worked as a surveyor here and was killed by Indians near the north bank of the Ohio River in Indiana. The year of his death is uncertain since both 1789 and 1794 are mentioned.

Squire Grant (1764–1833)— Squire Grant was a surveyor who became the owner of large amounts of land in the present Campbell County, Kentucky. He served in the Kentucky senate from 1801 to 1806 and later, in 1810, held the office of sheriff. He lived in Kentucky until his death in 1833. His name is given as General Squire Grant in some accounts but it isn't known whether the title was honorary or derived from military service.

An entirely different origin for Grant County's name is also mentioned as a possibility. According to this version, a man named William Littell had repeatedly tried to get the Kentucky legislature to create this new county. These efforts were unsuccessful so when the legislators finally did grant Littell a hearing concerning his proposed bill to create this new county, the word "grant" was used facetiously for the county's name. In Robert M. Rennick's book entitled *Kentucky Place Names*, this version of the origin of the county's name is said to be "An oft-repeated 19th cent [sic] story with no validity whatever."

1003 *Graves County*

Benjamin F. Graves (1771–1813)— Graves was born in Spotsylvania County, Virginia, in 1771. He moved 1791 with his widowed mother and siblings to be a farmer on the Kentucky frontier. At that time Kentucky was still a part of Virginia. After Kentucky was admitted to the Union as a separate state, Graves served as a representative in the lower house of the Kentucky legislature. He later served as an officer in the Kentucky militia during the War of 1812. His commission as a major was dated August 7, 1812. Major Graves participated in the American defeat in the battle of River Raisin in Michigan on January 22, 1813. Nearly 300 Americans lost their lives during this battle and many more were massacred by the Indian allies of the British after they had been taken as prisoners of war. Graves was wounded during the Battle, taken as a prisoner of war and then apparently he was among those murdered by the Indians since he was never seen again. Most of the soldiers who lost their lives during and after this battle were from Kentucky and several Kentucky counties have been named for heroes of the battle of River Raisin.

1004 *Grayson County*

William Grayson (–1790)— Grayson was born in Prince William County, Virginia, about 1736. During the American Revolution he served as an officer and aide-de-camp to General George Washington. Promoted to colonel in January, 1777, he participated in the battles of Long Island, White Plains, Brandywine Creek, Germantown and Monmouth. In 1784 Grayson was elected to Virginia's house of delegates and he later represented Virginia in the Continental Congress. As a member of the Virginia convention to consider adoption of the proposed U.S. Constitution. Grayson opposed its ratification but after it was ratified he became one of Virginia's first two United States senators. This county was created on January 25, 1810.

1005 *Green County*

Nathanael Greene (1742–1786)— Greene was born in Rhode Island and served briefly in the Rhode Island legislature. He gained fame as one of America's ablest generals in the Revolutionary War. Green County, Kentucky, was created on December 20, 1792, just seven months after Kentucky's admission to the Union as a state. The general's name is spelled Greene but the Kentucky county that was named in his honor is spelled Green.

1006 *Greenup County*

Christopher Greenup (–1818)— Greenup was born in the colony of Virginia about 1750 and served as an officer in the American Revolution, rising to the rank of colonel. He moved across the mountains and settled on the Kentucky frontier in the early 1780's. Here he practiced law and became active in local politics. At that time Kentucky was still part of Virginia. Greenup represented his district in the Virginia house of delegates and was later active in the movement to secure statehood for Kentucky. When Kentucky was separated from Virginia and became a separate state in 1792, Christopher Greenup was elected to be one of the new state's first two representatives in the U.S. House of Representatives. He later served in the lower house of the Kentucky legislature and in 1804 Greenup was elected as Kentucky's governor. He served in that office from 1804 to 1808. This county was created in 1803.

1007 *Hancock County*

John Hancock (1737–1793)— A native of

Massachusetts and a graduate of Harvard, Hancock served in the Massachusetts legislature and was president of the Massachusetts provincial congress. He was elected to the Second Continental Congress and became its president. As president of the Continental Congress when the Declaration of Independence was signed, he was, on July 4, 1776, the first signer of that document. He signed it with such a flourish that the name John Hancock became a synonym for "signature." He later commanded the Massachusetts militia, served as governor of that state for many years and presided over the Massachusetts convention that ratified the U.S. Constitution.

1008 *Hardin County*

John Hardin (1753–1792)— This military man was born in Virginia and served as an ensign in Lord Dunmore's 1774 war against the Indians. He later served as a lieutenant in the American Revolution and in 1786 he settled in Kentucky. Here he served in military actions against the Indians and rose to the rank of colonel. He also briefly held the rank of brigadier-general in the Kentucky militia. In 1792 Hardin was murdered by Indians while he was engaged in peace negotiations with them. This county was created and named in John Hardin's honor in December, 1792, just a few months after his death.

1009 *Harlan County*

Silas Harlan (–1782)— Harlan was born in Virginia in 1752 or 1753 in what is now Berkeley County, West Virginia. He moved to Kentucky in 1774, engaged in hunting and served in the militia in which he attained the rank of major. At this time much of Kentucky was owned by the Transylvania Land Company governed by Richard Henderson (1735–1785). Harlan was active in the effort to make Kentucky a part of Virginia and this movement met with success in late 1776 when Kentucky County, Virginia, was created. During the American Revolution, George Rogers Clark led actions against the British, Indians and Loyalists on America's western frontier and Harlan served under Clark in a variety of military activities. In 1777 he assisted in delivering gunpowder to settlers in Kentucky and in 1778, with the help of his brother and his uncle, he built a log stockade, known as Harlan's Station near what is now Danville, Kentucky. Harlan subsequently served under George Rogers Clark in the successful Illinois campaign of 1778–1779 and in a raid on Old Chillicothe in the present state of Ohio in 1779.

He also assisted Clark in establishing Fort Jefferson, five miles below the mouth of the Ohio River in what is now western Kentucky. In April, 1782, the American Revolution began drawing to a close and peace talks were started in Paris, France. However, fighting continued in America. In the summer of 1782 British forces operating from Detroit pushed south into Kentucky. The British and their Indian and Loyalist allies won a victory here on August 19, 1782, at the battle of Blue Licks in north-central Kentucky. It was in that battle that Major Harlan lost his life.

1010 *Harrison County*

Benjamin Harrison (–1808)— The details of Harrison's birth are unclear but it is believed that he was born in Pennsylvania about 1745. He first came to Kentucky in 1776 but returned to Pennsylvania to fight in the American Revolution. During the Revolution, Harrison attained the rank of colonel. About 1783 he came back to Kentucky and settled in what is now the county named in his honor. He lived here about three miles south of the present Cynthiana, Kentucky. At this time Kentucky was still part of Virginia and Colonel Harrison was active in the movement to separate Kentucky from Virginia and secure statehood for Kentucky. In April, 1792, he participated in the convention held at Danville, Kentucky, that drafted the first constitution for the state. He also attained the rank of general in the Kentucky militia. In 1793 Harrison was elected to the Kentucky legislature as a representative in the general assembly and in December, 1793, while he was serving in that body, his fellow legislators created and named this county in his honor. In 1800 Harrison moved to Missouri and he died there in 1808.

1011 *Hart County*

Nathaniel G. S. Hart (–1813)— Hart was born in Hagerstown, Maryland, about 1784. His father, Thomas Hart, was one of the proprietors of the Transylvania Land Company, which owned about half of the present state of Kentucky. The elder Hart moved to Lexington, Kentucky, with his family in 1794. Here Nathaniel G. S. Hart studied law under the guidance of his brother-in-law, Henry Clay (1777–1852). Nathaniel G. S. Hart practiced law and also participated in a hemp rope business with his father and an older brother. Early in the War of 1812, Hart organized a company consisting of some 100 men to fight against the British and their Indian

allies. Hart served as a captain of that company and he later became deputy inspector of the left wing of the northwestern army. Hart participated in the American defeat in the battle of River Raisin in Michigan on January 22, 1813. Nearly 300 Americans lost their lives during the battle and many more were massacred by the Indian allies of the British after they had been taken as prisoners of war. The Indian allies of the British scalped and killed Hart while he was a prisoner. Most of the soldiers who lost their lives during and after this battle were from Kentucky and several Kentucky counties have been named for heroes of the battle of River Raisin. This county was created in January, 1819. In most accounts Hart's name is rendered as Nathaniel G. T. Hart. This is an error. His name is Nathaniel Gray Smith Hart.

1012 *Henderson County*

Richard Henderson (1735–1785)— A native of Virginia, Henderson moved as a youth with his family to North Carolina where he studied law and was appointed by Governor Tryon to be one of North Carolina's associate justices. Henderson later formed a company which purchased from the Indians an enormous tract of land comprising about half of what is now the state of Kentucky. This country was given the name Transylvania, laws were enacted to govern it and Henderson was made its president. Both Virginia and North Carolina declared Transylvania to be illegal but Henderson and his associates were given extensive tracts of land to compensate them for opening up this wilderness country. Richard Henderson was often known as "Colonel Henderson." This county was created on December 21, 1798.

1013 *Henry County*

Patrick Henry (1736–1799)— Henry was a native of Virginia and a lawyer. He served in the Virginia legislature, as governor of Virginia and as a delegate to the first and second Continental Congresses. Henry was one of America's key revolutionary leaders. He was a great orator and he is remembered for his call to arms against the British "Give me liberty or give me death." Henry opposed Virginia's ratification of the Federal constitution and his views played a role in the later adoption of the Bill of Rights. Patrick Henry was governor of Virginia while Kentucky was still a part of Virginia and he owned several thousand acres of land in Kentucky.

Henry County, Kentucky was created on December 14, 1798.

1014 *Hickman County*

Paschal Hickman (–1813) — A native of Virginia, Hickman moved to Kentucky with his family when he was still a boy. The Hickman family came to Kentucky in 1784 when Kentucky was still part of Virginia. As a successful businessman and farmer Paschal Hickman amassed considerable wealth in land, slaves and other property. He also served in military actions against the Indians. On August 20, 1794, Hickman fought under General Anthony Wayne in the victory over Indians at the battle of Fallen Timbers in what is now northwestern Ohio. In 1802 he was an ensign in the Kentucky militia and in 1803 he was promoted to lieutenant. Hickman fought in the War of 1812 against the British and their Indian allies. He had risen to the rank of captain when he participated in the battle of River Raisin in Michigan in January, 1813. The American forces were badly beaten in this battle. Nearly 300 Americans lost their lives during the battle and many more were massacred by the Indian allies of the British after they had been taken as prisoners of war. Hickman was wounded during an initial skirmish at Frenchtown and taken as a prisoner. He was among those prisoners whom the Indians butchered. Most of the soldiers who lost their lives during and after the battle of River Raisin were from Kentucky and several Kentucky counties have been named for heroes of that battle.

1015 *Hopkins County*

Samuel Hopkins (1753–1819) — Hopkins was born in Albemarle County, Virginia, on April 9, 1753. He served as an officer during the American Revolution and rose to the rank of colonel. During the Revolution he served briefly on the staff of General George Washington. He also participated in the battles of Trenton, Princeton, Brandywine Creek, Germantown and Monmouth. Hopkins was wounded at Germantown. He later fought at Charleston, South Carolina, and at the conclusion of that battle he was taken as a prisoner of war. In 1796 or 1797 Hopkins moved across the mountains to Kentucky, studied law, was admitted to the bar and became active in local politics. In 1799 he was appointed as a judge and he served in both houses of the Kentucky legislature. During the War of 1812 Hopkins was given the title of major-general and the responsibility of

commanding the western frontier areas of Indiana territory and Illinois territory. He led expeditions against the Indians there in the latter part of 1812. Hopkins subsequently represented Kentucky for one term in the U.S. House of Representatives. This county was created and named in his honor in 1806 during the general time period that Hopkins was serving in the lower house of the Kentucky legislature.

1016 *Jackson County*

Andrew Jackson (1767–1845) — Jackson was born on the border of North Carolina and South Carolina. He represented Tennessee in both branches of the U.S. Congress. He gained fame and popularity for his military exploits in wars with the Indians and in the War of 1812. He was provisional military governor of Florida and from 1829 to 1837 General Jackson was president of the United States. His presidency reflected the frontier spirit of America. This county was created in 1858.

1017 *Jefferson County*

Thomas Jefferson (1743–1826) — Jefferson was a native of Virginia and a member of the Virginia legislature. He served Virginia as governor and he was a delegate to the second Continental Congress. Jefferson was the author of the Declaration of Independence and one of its signers. He was minister to France, secretary of state, vice president and president of the United States. As president, he accomplished the Louisiana Purchase and he arranged the Lewis and Clark Expedition to the Pacific Northwest. Jefferson was a true intellectual, thoroughly knowledgeable in the arts and sciences. His political theories were pivotal in the formation of our infant republic. This county was created in 1780 while Kentucky was still part of Virginia. When the county was created, Thomas Jefferson was Virginia's governor.

1018 *Jessamine County*

Uncertain — This county was created on December 19, 1798, and its name was chosen by Colonel John Price, a member of the state legislature. A letter written by Colonel Price which is dated November 13, 1820, indicates that the county was simply named for the jessamine flower, which grows on many creeks in Jessamine County. However, numerous sources offer different slants on just how this county's name evolved.

Jessamine Creek — The Jessamine Creek was named by early pioneers either for

Jessamine Douglass (see below) or for the jessamine flower which grew along its banks in profusion. The creek is a tributary of the Kentucky River and a rather large one for a creek. Its length is given as about 20 miles. It flows in a southern direction until it enters the Kentucky River about three miles south of the present Wilmore, Kentucky, in Jessamine County. The 1877 edition of Lewis Collins' *History of Kentucky* describes the Jessamine Creek as rising in the northwestern part of Jessamine County and "... of good size, and as large near its source as at its termination. It rises at two points, about 10 feet apart; at one it boils up from a bed of gravel; at the other, gushes from between two large smooth rocks, and is very deep..."

Jessamine flower — The jessamine is a type of jasmine. The jasmine can be any of numerous shrubs of the genus *Jasminum*, which are members of the olive family. The type of jasmine flower that is called jessamine is yellow with sweet-scented flowers. The jessamine flourishes in this region of Kentucky and they were found in profusion along the banks of Jessamine Creek and other creeks in the county.

Jessamine Creek and jessamine flower — Some sources indicate that Kentucky Representative John Price, who selected the county's name, mentioned that he had chosen the name in honor of both Jessamine Creek and the jessamine flower that grew along its banks.

Jessamine Douglass (–) — Jessamine Douglass was the daughter of a Kentucky pioneer of Scottish ancestry. According to some accounts he was born in Scotland. His name was James Douglass and he was a surveyor during Kentucky's infancy. According to one surviving bit of folklore, Jessamine Douglass was tomahawked by an Indian while she rested at the creek and the creek was then named for her. In Lewis Collins' *History of Kentucky*, the Jessamine Douglass account is given as factual without reservation but Robert M. Rennick's 1984 work entitled *Kentucky Place Names* asserts that "The popular legend that it was named for (her) ... is without foundation." Bennett H. Young's book published in 1898 entitled *A History of Jessamine County, Kentucky* offers evidence that Jessamine Creek was named before Jessamine Douglass came to this section of Kentucky.

Bennett H. Young's book mentioned immediately above quotes a letter dated November 13, 1820, from Colonel John Price which states that the county's name was "... selected from a flower that grows on many creeks in the county." Colonel Price was the member of the Kentucky legislature who had selected this county's name when it was created in 1798.

1019 *Johnson County*

Richard M. Johnson (1780–1850)— Richard Mentor Johnson was born in Kentucky when it was still a part of Virginia. Kentucky was admitted to the Union as a separate state in 1792 and Johnson served in the lower house of the Kentucky legislature from 1804 to 1806. He later represented Kentucky for a decade in the U.S. House of Representatives with an interruption to serve as a colonel in the War of 1812. The Kentucky forces that Colonel Johnson led at the battle of the Thames River, in Canada, scored an important victory which made Johnson a hero but he was severely wounded in that battle. He later represented Kentucky in the U.S. Senate and then returned to the national house of representatives. From March 4, 1837, to March 3, 1841, Richard Mentor Johnson was vice-president of the United States under President Martin Van Buren. Johnson County, Kentucky, was created and named in his honor in 1843.

1020 *Kenton County*

Simon Kenton (1755–1836)— This frontiersman and Indian fighter was born in Virginia in April, 1755. He didn't attend school and remained illiterate all his life. When he was 16 years old, thinking that he had killed a man in a fight, Kenton fled across the Allegheny Mountains and assumed the name Simon Butler. His flight took him to Fort Pitt and also to Kentucky. During Lord Dunmore's War in 1774, Kenton served as a scout. In 1775 he came down the Ohio River to the confluence of the Ohio and Limestone Creek. Within a mile of what is now Washington, Kentucky, Kenton planted an acre of corn. Here in Kentucky he became one of the famous early pioneers and he associated with other noted Kentucky pioneers including Daniel Boone, Robert Patterson and George Rogers Clark. On one occasion, Kenton saved Daniel Boone's life during an Indian attack at Boonesborough. During the American Revolution, Kenton was a spy in defense of the frontier under George Rogers Clark, who was then commander of the frontier militia. In 1778 he served under Clark in the capture of the British base at Kaskaskia. Kenton was later captured by the Indians and taken to Detroit by the British as a prisoner of war.

However, Kenton soon managed to escape and he served as a scout under Clark again in the early 1780's. In 1794 Kenton served as a major under General Anthony Wayne in actions against the Indians in the Northwest territory and by 1805 he had become a brigadier general in the Ohio militia. Kenton later fought in the War of 1812 and he participated in the important victory at the battle of the Thames River in Canada. This county was created in January, 1840, less than four years after Kenton's death.

1021 *Knott County*

J. Proctor Knott (1830–1911)— James Proctor Knott was born in Kentucky but he moved to Missouri in 1850 where he practiced law, served in the Missouri legislature and was attorney general of the state. Early in the Civil War, Knott's sympathies were with the Confederate States of America and he was arrested by Union officials for refusing to take a loyalty oath. Soon after his release he returned to Kentucky where he practiced law. When the Civil War ended, Knott was elected to represent Kentucky in the U.S. House of Representatives and he served in that body for about a dozen years. In 1883 Knott was elected governor of Kentucky and he held that office from 1883 to 1887. This county was created in 1884 while Knott was Kentucky's governor.

1022 *Knox County*

Henry Knox (1750–1806)— This Massachusetts native participated in many of the important military engagements of the American Revolution and rose to the rank of major-general. After the war, Knox commanded West Point and he conceived and organized the Society of Cincinnati, an elite group of former Revolutionary officers. In 1785 he was appointed secretary of war under the Articles of Confederation and he retained that position in the first United States cabinet under President George Washington. This county was created and named for General Knox in 1799. Kentucky's famous Fort Knox was also named for him.

1023 *Larue County*

John P. LaRue (1746–1792)— A native of Virginia, LaRue took part in the American Revolution. In 1779 LaRue and his brother built a cabin on Guist Creek in what is now Shelby County, Kentucky. In 1783 John LaRue married Mary Brooks in Virginia. He returned to the Kentucky wilderness with his wife in 1784. They settled at

the mouth of Beech Fork, about 50 miles from what is now the city of Louisville. At that time Kentucky was still part of Virginia. LaRue acquired enormous tracts of land and became quite wealthy. He eventually owned some 40,000 acres of land in Kentucky. John LaRue and his wife, Mary, had four children, one of whom was Rebecca LaRue (1784–) who became the mother of John LaRue Helm, speaker of the house in the Kentucky legislature and later governor of Kentucky. When this county was created in 1843, its name was selected by John LaRue Helm (1802–1867) in honor of his maternal grandfather, John P. LaRue (1746–1792). (According to a few accounts, Helm chose the county's name to honor John LaRue and the LaRue family. In addition to Rebecca LaRue, John and Mary Brooks LaRue had three other children. They were Squire LaRue [1785–1859], Margaret [Peggy] LaRue [1789–1864] and Phebe LaRue [–]).

1024 *Laurel County*

Uncertain— Laurel County, Kentucky, was created on December 12, 1825, and the vast majority of sources consulted state that the county was named for the Laurel River, which flows through the southern section of the county. These sources indicate that the river was named for the beautiful laurels and/or rhododendrons that grew in abundance along the banks of the Laurel River at the time that the county was formed and named. However, a handful of authorities state that the county was not named for the Laurel River but directly for the laurel shrubs, which grew in profusion along the banks of many of the county's creeks and streams. The true laurel can be any member of the genus *Laurus* of the family *Lauraceae*. However, of the many varieties of shrubs that grow in Kentucky, it is not the true laurel that is common but the mountain laurel, a shrub that resembles the true laurel. The mountain laurel can grow to a height of five or six feet. When in bloom, its funnel-shaped flowers are beautiful but they last for only a few days. The flowers of the mountain. laurel vary in color from pale pink to deep carmine. Some accounts about the source of the Laurel River's name also mention the rhododendron. In Kentucky, the rhododendron blooms about two weeks after the mountain laurel has bloomed. Since both the mountain laurel and the rhododendron require similar soil conditions (acid soil and good root drainage) they are found in similar locations. The type of rhododendron that is most common in

Kentucky is the pink variety, which grows to a height of six to ten feet and has large, leathery leaves.

1025 *Lawrence County*

James Lawrence (1781–1813) — Lawrence was an officer in the United States navy who established a reputation for bravery in the war against Tripoli and in the War of 1812. He died in combat while commanding the *Chesapeake* against the British near Boston. He is said to have uttered the famous phrase "Don't give up the ship" while he lay mortally wounded in that battle. This county was created on December 14, 1821.

1026 *Lee County*

Uncertain — Lee County, Kentucky was created in 1870, just a few years after the end of the Civil War and most sources state, without qualification, that this county was named for Robert E. Lee (1807–1870), the general-in-chief of the Confederate forces during the Civil War. However, a few sources demur on the grounds that pro-Union sentiments were strong in Kentucky. These sources indicate that it is more probable that Lee County, Kentucky, was named for Lee County, Virginia, since a number of citizens of the new Kentucky county had come from Lee County, Virginia. Either theory is possible but outright dismissal of the Robert E. Lee possibility is specious. While it is true that Kentucky did not secede from the Union and never was a member of the Confederate States of America, it is also true that Kentucky was a slave state and part of the South in spirit and outlook on many matters. Large numbers of Kentucky citizens volunteered to serve in both the Confederate and Union armies during the Civil War. Moreover, when this county was created in 1870, the victorious North was enforcing its vicious Reconstruction on the defeated South and the Kentucky legislature may very well have chosen this county's name in honor of Confederate General Robert E. Lee as a gesture of respect and sympathy for the defeated Confederacy.

Robert E. Lee (1807–1870) — Robert E. Lee was a native of Virginia and, for over 30 years, an officer in the United States army. When Virginia seceded from the Union, he refused an offer to command all federal forces and resigned from the U.S. army to accept a commission in the Confederate army. He served with distinction in that army and became general-in-chief of it. When this county was created early in 1870, Robert E. Lee was president of Washington College (now Washington & Lee University) in Lexington, Virginia.

Lee County, Virginia — Lee County, Virginia, was created on October 25, 1792, and named for Henry Lee, who was then governor of Virginia.

Henry Lee (1756–1818) — Henry Lee was born in Virginia on January 29, 1756, and graduated from the College of New Jersey (now Princeton University). He served with distinction as an officer during the American Revolution, rising to the rank of lieutenant-colonel and acquiring the nickname "Light Horse Harry Lee." Congress presented a gold medal to him for bravery. From 1785 to 1788 Henry Lee represented Virginia in the Continental Congress. In 1788 Virginia ratified the proposed constitution of the United States to become the tenth state to join the Union. From December 1, 1791, to December 1, 1794, Henry Lee served as governor of Virginia. He later represented Virginia in the U.S. House of Representatives.

1027 *Leslie County*

Preston H. Leslie (1819–1907) — A native of Kentucky and a lawyer, Leslie served in both houses of the Kentucky legislature and in 1869 he was elected president of the state's senate. When Kentucky's Governor John W. Stevenson resigned in February, 1871 to represent Kentucky in the U.S. Senate, Leslie succeeded him as governor. Later that year Leslie was elected to a full term as governor and he served in that office from 1871 to 1875. President Grover Cleveland appointed Leslie to be governor of Montana territory in 1887. Both President Cleveland and Preston H. Leslie were Democrats. Shortly after Benjamin Harrison, a Republican, became president, he removed Leslie as Montana's territorial governor and replaced him with a Montana Republican, Benjamin F. White (1839–1920). Leslie remained in Montana where he practiced law and became president of the Montana bar association. Leslie County Kentucky was created and named in his honor in 1878.

1028 *Letcher County*

Robert P. Letcher (1788–1861) — Letcher was born on February 10, 1788, in Goochland County, Virginia, and moved with his parents to Kentucky about 1800. Here he practiced law and became active in local politics. Letcher served in the lower house of the Kentucky legislature for several years and then represented Kentucky in the U.S. House of Representatives for more than a decade. After returning to Kentucky, he again served in the state house of representatives and became speaker of the house. In 1840 Letcher was elected governor of Kentucky and he held that office from 1840 to 1844. He then served as a minister to Mexico for three years shortly after the U.S. victory in the Mexican War. This county was created in 1842 while Letcher was governor of Kentucky.

1029 *Lewis County*

Meriwether Lewis (1774–1809) — A native of Virginia and a neighbor and friend of Thomas Jefferson, Lewis served as an officer in the army and then, in 1801, President Jefferson selected him to be his aide. From 1804 to 1806 Meriwether Lewis and William Clark led the Lewis and Clark Expedition which President Jefferson sent to explore the Northwest to the Pacific Ocean. Their successful journey ended in September, 1806 when they returned to civilization at Saint Louis in what is now the state of Missouri. Lewis then served as governor of Louisiana territory from 1807 until his death in 1809. Lewis County, Kentucky, was created on December 2, 1806, less than three months after the Lewis and Clark Expedition ended.

1030 *Lincoln County*

Benjamin Lincoln (1733–1810) — Lincoln, a native of Massachusetts, was a member of the Massachusetts legislature and of the provincial congress. He served as an officer in the Revolutionary War and rose to the rank of major-general. In 1779, as commander of the southern department of the Continental army, he attempted, unsuccessfully to rescue Savannah, Georgia, from the British. In 1781 General George Washington gave Lincoln the honor of accepting Cornwallis' sword when the British surrendered at Yorktown. Later in 1781 Lincoln was made secretary of war and he held that post for two years. He died on May 9, 1810, in Hingham, Massachusetts, in the same house in which he was born. This county was created in 1780, during the American Revolution, while Kentucky was still a part of Virginia.

1031 *Livingston County*

Robert R. Livingston (1746–1813) — Livingston was born in New York City and he represented New York in the Continental Congress. He also assisted in drafting our nation's Declaration of Independence from England. In the Continental Congress

Livingston served as secretary for foreign affairs. In 1801 President Thomas Jefferson appointed him minister to France with instructions to negotiate peaceful rights for Americans on the Mississippi River and at the port of New Orleans. James Monroe was later sent to France to assist Livingston in the negotiations. Their efforts were amply rewarded when France offered to sell the United States all of Louisiana. We accepted the French offer and the resulting Louisiana Purchase doubled the size of our country. Livingston County, Kentucky, was created in 1798, before Robert Livingston was appointed as minister to France.

1032 *Logan County*

Benjamin Logan (–1802)— Logan was born about 1743 in Virginia and he served as an officer in the Virginia militia during Lord Dunmore's War against the Indians in 1774. About 1775 Logan crossed the mountains and became one of the first pioneers to settle in the Kentucky wilderness. During the American Revolution he was a noted and high ranking Indian fighter. Benjamin Logan served in the Virginia legislature during the 1780's while Kentucky was still part of Virginia. He participated in the movement to separate Kentucky from Virginia and was a member of the 1792 convention that drafted Kentucky's first constitution. After Kentucky was admitted to the Union as a state, Logan served in the lower house of the state legislature and he was a general in the Kentucky militia. This county was created and named in his honor in 1792, shortly after Kentucky became our nation's 15th state.

1033 *Lyon County*

Uncertain— Lyon County, Kentucky was created on January 14, 1854. It was named either for Matthew Lyon or for his son Chittenden Lyon. Those sources that have been found to be reliable on other aspects of Kentucky history state that the county was named for Chittenden Lyon.

Chittenden Lyon (–1842)— Chittenden Lyon was born in Vermont about 1787 and he moved with his parents to Kentucky when he was still a teenager. There the Lyon family engaged in extensive farming. Chittenden Lyon served in the lower house of the Kentucky legislature and later was a member of the state's senate. From March 4, 1827, to March 3, 1835, he represented Kentucky in the U.S. House of Representatives.

Matthew Lyon (–1822)— Matthew Lyon was born in Ireland in the mid to late 1740's and came to America as an indentured servant. After earning enough as a farm worker in Connecticut to purchase his freedom, Lyon moved to Vermont. There he served in the American Revolution and became prominent in local politics. He served in the lower house of the Vermont legislature and later represented Vermont in the U.S. House of Representatives. In 1801 Matthew Lyon moved with his family to Kentucky and he was soon sent by that state to represent it in the lower house of the U.S. Congress. He represented Kentucky in that body from 1803 to 1811. Matthew Lyon later was appointed as a U.S. factor to the Cherokee Indian nation in Arkansas territory. He subsequently was elected as a delegate to the U.S. Congress from Arkansas territory but he died before taking his seat.

1034 *McCracken County*

Virgil McCracken (–1813)— Virgil McCracken was the son of Cyrus McCracken, an early Kentucky settler, who built a group of cabins one mile south of Frankfort about 1776. Virgil McCracken represented Woodford County in the lower house of the Kentucky legislature in 1810 and 1811. Early in the War of 1812, he raised a company of Kentucky soldiers and on June 13, 1812, he was commissioned as captain of that company. McCracken's company was assigned to the First rifle regiment and sent north in a vain attempt to aid General William Hull (1753–1825) in his inept military efforts in the Detroit area. McCracken was wounded in the battle of River Raisin in Michigan in January, 1813. The American forces were badly beaten in that battle. Nearly 300 Americans lost their lives during the battle and many more were massacred by the Indian allies of the British after they had been taken as prisoners of war. Captain Virgil McCracken was among those prisoners whom the Indians butchered. Most of the soldiers who lost their lives during and after the battle of River Raisin were from Kentucky and several Kentucky counties have been named for heroes of that battle.

1035 *McCreary County*

James B. McCreary (1838–1918)— A native of Kentucky and a graduate of Centre College at Danville, McCreary served in the Confederate army during the Civil War and rose to the rank of lieutenant-colonel. After the war he returned to Kentucky where he practiced law and became active in local politics. McCreary served in the lower house of the Kentucky legislature and was its speaker from 1871 to 1875. He became Kentucky's governor in 1875 and subsequently represented Kentucky in both houses of the U.S. Congress. In 1911, more than a quarter century after McCreary's first term as governor, he was once again elected as the state's governor. This county was created in 1912, while he was serving as governor.

1036 *McLean County*

Alney McLean (1779–1841)— A native of North Carolina, McLean moved to Kentucky when he was about 20 years old. Here he was employed as a surveyor and later practiced law. He represented Muhlenberg County in the Kentucky legislature in 1812 and 1813 and then served as a captain during the War of 1812. He fought at the battle of New Orleans. McLean later represented Kentucky in the U.S. House of Representatives and he served as a circuit judge for some 20 years from 1821 until his death. This county was created and named in McLean's honor in 1854.

1037 *Madison County*

James Madison (1751–1836)— Madison was born in Virginia, served in the Virginia legislature and in the Continental Congress. He was a member of the convention which framed the U.S. Constitution and he collaborated with Hamilton and Jay in writing a series of papers under the title *The Federalist* which explained the new constitution and advocated its adoption. Madison represented Virginia in the U.S. House of Representatives, served for eight years as secretary of state and for eight years as president of the United States. This county was created in 1785 when Kentucky was still a part of Virginia and before James Madison became our president.

1038 *Magoffin County*

Beriah Magoffin (1815–1885)— Magoffin was born in Harrodsburg, Kentucky, in 1815 and he graduated from Centre College and from Transylvania University's law department. He practiced law briefly in Mississippi but returned to Harrodsburg, Kentucky, in 1839. Here he established a successful law practice and became active in local politics as a Democrat. Magoffin served in Kentucky's senate and in 1859 he defeated Joshua F. Bell (1811–1870) in the gubernatorial election. Magoffin served as governor of Kentucky from

1859 to 1862 and was governor when the Civil War began. He believed in both states' rights and slavery. Although Kentucky is a southern state, it never seceded from the Union nor was it ever a member of the Confederate States of America. Although Magoffin rejected calls to supply troops which he received from both Confederate and Union officials, his pro–Confederate leanings made his position as governor uncomfortable and ineffective. He resigned as governor on August 18, 1862, early in the Civil War. This county was created in February, 1860 while Magoffin was serving as Kentucky's last antebellum governor.

1039 *Marion County*

Francis Marion (–1795)— Marion is believed to have been born in South Carolina. He served in the army in battles against the Cherokee Indians and was elected to the provisional congress of 1775. He served, with distinction, as an officer in the Revolutionary War and rose to the rank of general in that war. Marion was also a member of the South Carolina senate.

1040 *Marshall County*

John Marshall (1755–1835)— Marshall, a native of Virginia, served as an officer in the Revolutionary War, in the Virginia legislature and in the U.S. House of Representatives. He briefly served as secretary of state and then, for over 30 years, was chief justice of the U.S. Supreme Court. Marshall's interpretations of the constitution during America's political infancy left an unmatched impact on the laws and government of this country. Under Marshall, the supreme court shifted power in American government from the states to the central government and to the federal judiciary at the expense of the executive and legislative branches. This county was formed in 1842.

1041 *Martin County*

John P. Martin (1811–1862)— A native of Virginia, John P. Martin moved to Harlan County, Kentucky, in 1828. About seven years later he settled in Floyd County, Kentucky, which thereafter was his home. He served in both houses of the Kentucky legislature and represented Kentucky in the U.S. House of Representatives. Most accounts refer to him as a "colonel." This county was created and named in his honor in 1870.

1042 *Mason County*

George Mason (–1792)— Mason, who was born in Virginia in 1725 or 1726, was prominent in the agitations which led to the American Revolution. He was a confidant of George Washington and Thomas Jefferson, a member of Virginia's house of burgesses and served on the committee of safety. Mason wrote a major portion of Virginia's constitution, served in Virginia's assembly and participated in our country's birth at the 1787 constitutional convention. Although Mason was a southerner, he opposed slavery. This county was created in 1788 while Kentucky was still a part of Virginia.

1043 *Meade County*

James M. Meade (–1813)— Meade was born in Kentucky and he volunteered for military service late in 1811 while he was still quite young. He fought against the Indians under General William Henry Harrison in the battle of Tippecanoe in Indiana territory on November 7, 1811. On account of the bravery and daring which he displayed at Tippecanoe, he was appointed as a captain on March 12, 1812. Meade was an officer in the Seventeenth U.S. infantry when he was sent in a vain attempt to aid General William Hull (1753–1825) in his inept military efforts in the War of 1812 in the Detroit area. Meade was killed in the battle of River Raisin in Michigan early in the action of January 22, 1813. The American forces were badly beaten in that battle. Nearly 300 Americans lost their lives during the battle and many more were massacred by the Indian allies of the British after they had been taken as prisoners of war. Most of the soldiers who lost their lives during and after the battle of River Raisin were from Kentucky and several Kentucky counties were named for heroes of that battle. This county was created and named in honor of Captain Meade on December 17, 1823.

1044 *Menifee County*

Richard H. Menefee (1809–1841)— A native of Kentucky and a graduate of Transylvania University, in Lexington, Kentucky, Menefee was appointed commonwealth's attorney for the 11th judicial district. He later served in the lower house of the Kentucky legislature and then represented Kentucky in the U.S. House of Representatives from March 4, 1837, to March 3, 1839. In 1841 U.S. Senator John J. Crittenden (–1863) resigned his seat in the senate to become attorney general in

the cabinet of President Harrison. Although Richard H. Menefee was dying of tuberculosis when Crittenden announced his intention to resign from the senate, Menefee's fellow Whigs in the Kentucky legislature honored their dying colleague by electing him to fill Crittenden's seat in the U.S. Senate. Menefee died before ever taking his seat in that body. When this county was created in 1869, the name was misspelled as Menifee.

1045 *Mercer County*

Hugh Mercer (–1777)— Mercer was born about 1725 in Scotland and educated as a physician. He came to America about 1747 and served in the army here as an officer during the French and Indian War. At the outbreak of the American Revolution, Mercer entered the Continental army in which he attained the rank of brigadier-general. He served with distinction under General George Washington in the surprise attack on the British at Trenton, New Jersey, in late December, 1776. One week later, at the battle of Princeton, New Jersey, Mercer was severely wounded and he died of those wounds on January 12, 1777. At the time of his death, Mercer's residence was in Virginia. This county was created in 1785, while Kentucky was still a part of Virginia.

1046 *Metcalfe County*

Thomas Metcalfe (1780–1855)— Metcalfe was born in Fauquier County, Virginia, and moved to Kentucky with his parents while he was still a boy. He was a member of the lower house of the Kentucky legislature and served as a captain in the army during the War of 1812. In that war he led a company of volunteers in the battle of Fort Meigs, near Lake Erie. Metcalfe later represented Kentucky for almost a decade in the U.S. House of Representatives and in 1828 he was elected governor of Kentucky. After his four year term as governor, Metcalfe served in the state senate. When John J. Crittenden (–1863) resigned from the U.S. Senate, Thomas Metcalfe was appointed to his seat where he served from the summer of 1848 until March 3, 1849. He died of cholera during an epidemic in 1855 and this county was created and named in his honor in 1860.

1047 *Monroe County*

James Monroe (1758–1831)— Monroe, a native of Virginia, served in the Revolutionary War. Prior to his election as president of the United States, Monroe served in a wide variety of government posts. He served Virginia in the state legislature and as governor. He was a member of the confederation congress and the U.S. Senate. He was minister to France and to Britain and he held two cabinet posts. As president, Monroe stressed limited government and strict construction of the constitution. He acquired Florida for the U.S. from Spain and he was the author of a policy declaration (later known as the Monroe Doctrine) which proscribed outside interference in North and South America. Monroe County, Kentucky was created on January 19, 1820, while James Monroe was president of the United States. Its county seat, Tompkinsville, was named for Monroe's vice-president, Daniel D. Tompkins (1774–1825).

1048 *Montgomery County*

Richard Montgomery (1738–1775) — Montgomery was born in Ireland and served with the British in the French and Indian War. He settled in New York state where he was elected to the New York provisional congress. He served as a general in the American Revolutionary army and was killed in combat in the Revolutionary War. This county was created in 1796.

1049 *Morgan County*

Daniel Morgan (1736–1802) — Morgan was a native of the Northeast who moved to Virginia in his youth. He served as a general in the Revolutionary War and was regarded as a hero for important victories scored by his troops. After the war he served one term in congress. This county was created and named in his honor in 1822.

1050 *Muhlenberg County*

John P. G. Muhlenberg (1746–1807) — John Peter Gabriel Muhlenberg, referred to in a number of accounts as Peter Muhlenberg, was born in Pennsylvania and attended the Academy of Philadelphia (now the University of Pennsylvania) and the University of Halle in Germany. While in Europe he served in a German regiment of dragoons. Upon his return to America, Muhlenberg studied theology and was ordained as a minister. He served in Virginia's house of burgesses before joining the American Revolutionary army as a colonel. He served with distinction during the Revolutionary War and rose to the rank of major-general. After the war Muhlenberg settled in Pennsylvania and was elected vice-president of Pennsylva-

nia. Muhlenberg served under Pennsylvania's president, Benjamin Franklin, and he was reelected as Pennsylvania's vice-president several times. He later represented the infant state of Pennsylvania in both branches of the United States congress. This county was created and named in his honor in 1798. General Muhlenberg had made two trips to Kentucky in 1784, while it was still part of Virginia, and he acquired extensive tracts of land in Kentucky.

1051 *Nelson County*

Thomas Nelson (1738–1789) — Nelson was born in York County, Virginia, and studied at Christ's College in Cambridge, England. He returned to America in 1761 and served in Virginia's house of burgesses for several years. By 1775 Nelson had become an active opponent of England's policies toward her American colonies. He served in several sessions of the Continental Congress and he was one of the signers of our nation's Declaration of Independence. During the American Revolution. Nelson held the rank of brigadier-general and for a few years he commanded Virginia's militia. In June, 1781, he was elected to succeed Thomas Jefferson as governor of Virginia but he was forced to resign in November of that year on account of ill health. This county was created and named in his honor by the Virginia legislature in 1784, just three years after Nelson had been Virginia's governor. In 1784 Kentucky was still a part of Virginia.

1052 *Nicholas County*

George Nicholas (–1799) — Nicholas was born in Virginia about 1743 and graduated from the College of William and Mary there. He served as an officer during the American Revolution and was a member of the Virginia legislature. Nicholas also was a delegate to the Virginia convention in 1788 that ratified the proposed constitution of the United States. Soon afterward Nicholas moved across the mountains to settle in Kentucky, which then was still part of Virginia. He became active in the movement to separate Kentucky from Virginia, played a leading role in drafting Kentucky's first state constitution and served as the first attorney general of the state of Kentucky. He died in July, 1799, and this county was created and named in his honor just five months later, in December, 1799.

1053 *Ohio County*

Ohio River — The Ohio River is one of

the most important commercial rivers in the United States and it is a tributary of the Mississippi. Formed at Pittsburgh, Pennsylvania, by the confluence of the Allegheny River and the Monongahela River, the Ohio flows generally southwestward some 981 miles before joining the Mississippi at the western end of Kentucky, near Cairo, Illinois. The Ohio contributes more water to the Mississippi than any of its other tributaries. There is uncertainty about the origin and meaning of the river's name but many authorities believe that the name derived from an Iroquois word, *Oheo, Oyo, Ohion-hiio* or *Oyoneri* which meant "beautiful." In 1680 the French explorer, La Salle, wrote of this river "The Iroquois call it Ohio..." Other suggested meanings of the Ohio River's name include "Great river," "The river red with blood" and "White with froth."

This county was created in 1798 and at that time the Ohio River formed the county's northern border. Later, Daviess County and Hancock County were created north of Ohio County so Ohio County, Kentucky, no longer touches the river for which it was named.

1054 *Oldham County*

William Oldham (1753–1791) — A native of Virginia, Oldham served as an officer during the American Revolution. He entered the army as an ensign and later was promoted to the rank of captain. In the spring of 1779 he resigned from the army and moved across the mountains to the wilderness of Kentucky County, which was then part of Virginia. Oldham settled in the area where Louisville, Kentucky, now stands. On November 4, 1791, he commanded a regiment of Kentucky militia under General Arthur St. Clair in a battle with Indians on a branch of the Wabash River about 22 miles north of Fort Jefferson. The Indians soundly defeated the largely untrained White militia and William Oldham was one of several hundred of St. Clair's men who lost their lives in this battle. Most accounts refer to Oldham as Colonel Oldham. Apparently that was his rank at the time of his death.

1055 *Owen County*

Abraham Owen (1769–1811) — A native of Virginia, Owen immigrated to Kentucky in 1785 and served in military actions against the Indians under General James Wilkinson and General Arthur St. Clair. In 1796 Owen was a surveyor in Shelby County, Kentucky and he later served as a magistrate and in both houses of the Kentucky legislature. In 1799 he was chosen as a member of Kentucky's constitutional convention. Owen was a colonel in the Kentucky militia and he served as aide-de-camp to General William Henry Harrison at the battle of Tippecanoe, Indiana territory where he was killed in November, 1811. Tradition has it that the Indians had earlier seen General Harrison riding a white horse and when they saw Colonel Owen riding a white horse, they mistook him for the general and made him their early target. While this is conjecture, it is known that Colonel Owen was killed very early in the battle. This county was created in 1819.

1056 Owsley County

William Owsley (1782–1862)— Owsley was born in Virginia on March 24, 1782, and moved to Kentucky with his parents the following year. At that time Kentucky was still a part of Virginia. He served in the lower house of the Kentucky legislature and was justice of the court of appeals from 1813 to 1828. Owsley was reelected to Kentucky's house of representatives in 1831 and he subsequently served in the Kentucky senate. He was secretary of state under Governor James T. Morehead (1797–1854) and from 1844 to 1848 Owsley was governor of Kentucky. This county was created and named in his honor in January, 1843.

1057 Pendleton County

Edmund Pendleton (1721–1803)— A native of Virginia and a lawyer, Pendleton was elected to Virginia's house of burgesses in 1752 and in 1774 he became one of Virginia's representatives in the first Continental Congress. Pendleton became president of Virginia's committee of safety in 1775. Because the British governor of colonial Virginia, John Murray (1732–1809), fled Virginia to return to England, as president of the committee of safety, Pendleton became head of Virginia's temporary government. He later worked with Thomas Jefferson, George Wythe (1726–1806) and others drafting Virginia's first constitution and revising its laws. Pendleton took a conservative stance in these deliberations and he opposed Jefferson's efforts to separate church from state and to abolish primogeniture and entails. Pendleton later served in Virginia's house of delegates and was speaker of that body. In 1779 he became president of Virginia's supreme court of appeals and he held that position until his death in 1803.

1058 Perry County

Oliver H. Perry (1785–1819)— Perry was a native of Rhode Island and officer in the U.S. navy. During the War of 1812 his squadron defeated the British in September, 1813 in a key battle on Lake Erie of which Perry said "We have met the enemy and they are ours." Perry died of yellow fever in August, 1819, and this county was created and named in his honor in November of the following year.

1059 Pike County

Zebulon M. Pike (1779–1813)— Pike was a native of New Jersey who served as an army officer on America's frontier following the Revolution. He led an exploratory army expedition to the Rocky Mountains which Pike's Peak in the Colorado Rockies commemorates. Pike served as a general in the War of 1812 and was killed in that war. Pike County, Kentucky, was created in 1821.

1060 Powell County

Lazarus W. Powell (1812–1867)— A native of Kentucky and a lawyer, Powell was elected to Kentucky's house representatives in 1836 but was defeated in 1838 when he ran for reelection. In 1851 he was elected governor of Kentucky and he held that office from 1851 to 1855. In 1859, while the tension that preceded the Civil War was mounting, Powell was sent to represent Kentucky in the U.S. Senate. He was a slave owner and strongly sympathetic to the South but he also opposed secession. Kentucky never seceded from the Union and never was a member of the Confederate States of America and Powell remained in the U.S. Senate until March 3, 1865, when the Civil War was essentially finished. This county was created in 1852 while he was Kentucky's governor.

1061 Pulaski County

Casimir Pulaski (1748–1779)— Pulaski was born in Lithuania and served in the Polish army. He came to America to assist the colonies as an officer in the Revolutionary War and died in combat in that war during the siege of Savannah, Georgia. This county was created on December 10, 1798. Its name was suggested by Nicholas Jasper.

1062 Robertson County

George Robertson (1790–1874)— Robertson was born in Kentucky when it was still a part of Virginia. From 1817 until 1821 he represented Kentucky in the U.S. House of Representatives. He later served in the lower house of the Kentucky legislature and was speaker of that house for some four years. Robertson then briefly held the office of secretary of state of Kentucky. He then served as both an associate justice and chief justice of Kentucky's court of appeals. From 1834 to 1857 Robertson taught law at Transylvania University in Lexington, Kentucky. During a few of those years he doubled as a member of the lower house of the Kentucky legislature and at times was speaker of the house. In 1864, when he was over 70 years old, Robertson rejoined the court of appeals and sat on the bench of that court until a stroke forced him to resign in 1871. This county was created in 1867 while Robertson was serving on the court of appeals.

1063 Rockcastle County

Rockcastle River— The Rockcastle River is a tributary of the Cumberland River. The Rockcastle is about 75 miles long and it varies in width but much of the river is about 200 to 250 feet wide. Great portions of the bed of the river are lined with rocks, both large and small. It has two principal sources: (1) the Middle Fork, which rises in southern Jackson County, Kentucky at the confluence of Laurel Fork and Indian Creek and (2) the South Fork, which originates just west of Laurel County, Kentucky and forms most of the border between Laurel and Clay Counties. The Middle Fork and South Fork meet to form the Rockcastle River near the confluence of Horse Lick Creek on the Jackson County line. The Rockcastle then flows south and constitutes the southeastern border of Rockcastle County. The Rockcastle River was earlier named the Lawless River by the explorer, Dr. Thomas Walker (1715–1794) and that name honored a member of Dr. Walker's exploration party. In 1767 it was named the Rockcastle River by Isaac Lindsey on account of one or more huge natural rock formations on the river's banks. In those days such huge formations were often referred to as rock castles. Their smaller counterparts were called mere rock houses. The rock castles often had overhangs large enough to provide shelter for a large number of people.

1064 Rowan County

John Rowan (1773–1843)— A native of Pennsylvania, Rowan moved to the wilderness of Kentucky with his family when he was about ten years old. It was here that he was educated, studied law and was admitted to the bar in 1795. Rowan was a member of Kentucky's second state constitutional convention, which was held in 1799. He subsequently served as Kentucky's secretary of state and he represented Kentucky in the U.S. House of Representatives from 1807 to 1809. Rowan then served several terms in the lower house of the Kentucky legislature before becoming a judge of Kentucky's court of appeals. In 1824 he was elected to the United States senate and he represented Kentucky in that body from 1825 to 1831. This county was created in 1856.

1065 *Russell County*

William Russell (1758–1825) — Russell was born in Culpeper County, Virginia, and he served in the army during the American Revolution. During that war he participated in the American victory in the battle of King's Mountain in 1780 and he also fought at the battle of Guilford Courthouse in 1781. In 1783 Russell moved across the mountains to Kentucky, which then was still part of Virginia. During the 1790's he participated in several expeditions against Indians. He served in the Virginia legislature and then, when Kentucky was separated from Virginia in 1792, he served several terms in the lower house of the Kentucky legislature. In 1808 Russell was appointed a colonel in the regular army and in 1811 he fought in Indiana territory against the Indians in the battle of Tippecanoe. When General William Henry Harrison was given command of the Army of the Northwest in September, 1812, William Russell replaced Harrison as commander on the Indiana, Illinois and Missouri frontiers. During the War of 1812 Russell and his men played a key role in breaking the Indians' siege of Fort Harrison on the Wabash River above Vincennes. Russell died on July 3, 1825, and this county was created and named in his honor just five months later, on December 14, 1825.

1066 *Scott County*

Charles Scott (1739–1813) — A native of Virginia, Scott served in the Continental army during the American Revolution and rose to the rank of brevet major-general. After the Revolution he moved to Kentucky and commanded Kentucky troops in campaigns against the Indians. Scott also served in the Virginia assembly while Kentucky was still part of Virginia. In 1808 Scott was elected governor of Kentucky and he served in that position until 1812. This county was created on June 22,

1792, just 21 days after Kentucky was admitted to the Union as our 15th state.

1067 *Shelby County*

Isaac Shelby (1750–1826) — Shelby was a delegate to the Virginia legislature and, later, to the North Carolina legislature. He served as a soldier in the Revolutionary War and then moved to Kentucky County, Virginia, where he was active in the movement to separate Kentucky from Virginia. Shelby was inaugurated as Kentucky's first governor on the same day that Kentucky became a state. This county was created and named in Shelby's honor on June 23, 1792, less than a month after he had been inaugurated as governor. Shelby later fought in the War of 1812.

1068 *Simpson County*

John Simpson (–1813) — Simpson was born in Virginia and moved with his father to Kentucky when he was still a young boy. In 1794 he fought against the Indians at the battle of Fallen Timbers under General Anthony Wayne. Simpson later studied law, was admitted to the bar and became active in Kentucky politics. In 1806 he was elected to Kentucky's house of representatives and he was returned to the Kentucky house in 1808. He served in that body until 1811 and was speaker of it in 1810 and 1811. In 1812 Simpson ran for a seat in the U.S. House of Representatives against the incumbent, Stephen Ormsby (1765–1846). Simpson won the election but he enlisted in the army to serve in the War of 1812 and never took his seat in congress. Simpson was commissioned as a captain and he was killed at the battle of River Raisin in Michigan on January 22, 1813. The American forces were badly beaten in that battle. Nearly 300 Americans lost their lives during the battle and many more were massacred by the Indian allies of the British after they had been taken as prisoners of war. Most of the soldiers who lost their lives during and after the battle of River Raisin were from Kentucky and several Kentucky counties were named for heroes of that battle. This county was created in 1819.

1069 *Spencer County*

Spear Spencer (–1811) — A native of Kentucky, Spencer moved to Vincennes, Indiana territory, about 1809. He subsequently moved to Corydon, Indiana territory, where he became the first sheriff of Harrison County. He also ran a tavern in Corydon, the Oak Street Tavern. Spencer

fought against the Indians as a captain in Indiana's 1811 battle of Tippecanoe. Because the company which he had organized had yellow trimmed uniforms, they were called "Spencer's Yellow Jackets." Captain Spencer displayed unusual heroism at the battle of Tippecanoe and died in combat there. In General William Henry Harrison's official report of this battle, he told that Captain Spencer was first wounded in the head and then in both thighs but continued to exhort his mounted riflemen to fight valiantly until a final shot through his body ended his life.

1070 *Taylor County*

Zachary Taylor (1784–1850) — Taylor was born in Virginia but moved as an infant to Kentucky where he grew to manhood on a farm near Louisville. A career soldier, Taylor served as an officer in the War of 1812, the Black Hawk War, the Second Seminole War in Florida territory and the Mexican War. This county was created in January, 1848, just before the Mexican War ended in victory for America. The Mexican War made Taylor a national hero and he was elected in November, 1848, to be president of the United States. Although he was a slave owner, he opposed the extension of slavery beyond the 15 states where the institution was already legal. Taylor had served only 16 months as president when he died in office on July 9, 1850.

1071 *Todd County*

John Todd (1750–1782) — Todd was born in Pennsylvania on March 27, 1750, but educated in Virginia. He was admitted to the Virginia bar in 1771 and practiced law there. In 1774, during Lord Dunmore's War, Todd served as an aide to General Andrew Lewis (1720–1781) at the battle of Point Pleasant, at the mouth of the Great Kanawha River in what is now West Virginia. Todd moved to the Kentucky wilderness about 1775 and in 1777 he was elected to represent Kentucky County, Virginia, in the Virginia legislature. At that time Kentucky was still part of Virginia. In the Virginia legislature Todd introduced a bill to emancipate slaves. John Todd and two brothers, Levi (1756–1807) and Robert, acquired enormous tracts of land in Kentucky and Tennessee and with this wealth behind them a dynasty of great political influence was founded. After General George Rogers Clark conquered Illinois, John Todd was appointed county lieutenant of Illinois by Virginia's governor, Patrick Henry. The modest title of county lieutenant carried with it considerable power and responsibility. On August 19, 1782, during the American Revolution, Todd was killed in combat at the battle of Blue Licks in Kentucky. Most accounts refer to John Todd as Colonel Todd. This county was created in 1819.

1072 *Trigg County*

Stephen Trigg (1742–1782)— Trigg was born in Virginia and he served as a justice of Botetourt County there. He also served as a member of the Virginia legislature. He first visited Kentucky in the fall of 1779, when it was still part of Virginia, as a member of a court of land commissioners to settle conflicting land claims on Virginia's western frontier. When that body had concluded its mission, Trigg decided to make his home in Kentucky. He represented Kentucky in the Virginia legislature in 1780 and was a trustee of Kentucky's Transylvania University. After acquiring a reputation as an Indian fighter of some note, Trigg was appointed in 1781 as a colonel in the militia. In the following year, during the American Revolution, Trigg was killed on August 17, 1782, in the battle of Blue Licks in Kentucky. This county was created on January 27, 1820.

1073 *Trimble County*

Robert Trimble (–1828)— Trimble was born about 1777 Virginia and moved with his parents to Kentucky while he was still a young boy and while Kentucky was still part of Virginia. He studied law and was admitted to the bar in 1800 in Paris, Kentucky, which was home to Trimble for the rest of his life. He served one term in the lower house of the Kentucky legislature and subsequently served two years as judge of Kentucky's court of appeals. In 1817 President James Madison appointed Trimble as a judge of the U.S. district court of Kentucky. Trimble served on that court until May 9, 1826, when President John Quincy Adams' nomination of Trimble to the U.S. Supreme Court was confirmed by the senate. Trimble served as an associate justice on our nation's highest court little more than two years when his tenure abruptly ended with his death on August 25, 1828.

1074 *Union County*

Uncertain— There is little agreement about the origin of this county's name. Several sources consulted state simply "in doubt" while others hedge their bets (as your author is doing here) with comments like "alleged to have been named for... " Stated possibilities for the origin of this county's name include the following:
— The commonwealth of Kentucky
— The motto on the Kentucky state seal: "Commonwealth of Kentucky: United We Stand. Divided We Fall."
— Sentiment
— The union of states comprising the United States of America
— The desire to preserve the United States of America. Union County was created in 1811. By that time some felt that there might be a need to declare war against Great Britain to preserve our new country. This fear proved to be well founded in June, 1812, when America declared war against Great Britain and the War of 1812 became official. (This war is also known as our country's second war for independence or the second American Revolution.)

Although the origin of Union County's name is uncertain, about half the sources consulted indicate that the county's name derived from the united opinion that it should be created. The details surrounding this possible origin of Union County's name are presented below:

Union County was carved out of a section of Henderson County on January 15, 1811. It was established as a separate county on account of the remoteness of the area that became Union County from the town of Henderson, which was and is the county seat of Henderson County. Bad roads frequently prevented attendance at court sessions and military musters, both of which were held at the county seat of Henderson. At that time, military service was largely compulsory. Union County was named, according to this version, to reflect the united opinion of its residents that the new county should be created with its own county seat much closer to the residents of the new county. Further supporting the "united" desire that this county should be created was the fact that there was no opposition from the residents of Henderson County to losing some of their territory. They recognized the need for a new county. Presley N. O'Bannon was the member of the Kentucky house of representatives who was instrumental in getting the new county created. He did not live within the proposed new county but he possessed some 1,500 acres of land in the portion of Henderson County that became Union County. Other leading citizens who shared the "united" opinion that this new county should be formed included Jeremiah Riddle, Hugh McElroy, Joseph Delaney, Fielding Jones, John Blue, Daniel McKenney, Robert Gilchrist, John Chapman, Joseph Owens, Samuel Givens, Samuel May, John Waggener and Samuel Casey.

1075 *Warren County*

Joseph Warren (1741–1775)— This county was created in 1796 and named in honor of the American Revolutionary War hero, Joseph Warren. A native of Massachusetts and a graduate of Harvard College, Warren practiced medicine in the Boston area. He was a member of the committee of safety and president *pro tempore* of the Massachusetts provincial congress. In June, 1775 he was commissioned a major-general and he died in combat a few days later at the battle of Bunker Hill.

1076 *Washington County*

George Washington (1732–1799)— Washington was a native of Virginia. He served in Virginia's house of burgesses and became one of the colonies' leaders in opposition to British policies in America. He was a member of the first and second Continental Congresses and commander of all Continental armies in the Revolutionary War. Following victory in that war, Washington was elected to be the first president of the United States. Kentucky was admitted to the union as our 15th state on June 1, 1792. This county was created 21 days later, on June 22, 1792, while George Washington was president.

1077 *Wayne County*

Anthony Wayne (1745–1796)— A native of Pennsylvania, Wayne was a successful brigadier-general in the Revolutionary War and became a hero for his daring exploits. During the bitter winter of 1777–1778 at Valley Forge, Pennsylvania, Wayne shared the suffering of his men although his comfortable estate was only five miles away. He played an important role in the final overthrow of the British forces in Georgia. After the war, in 1785, Wayne moved to Georgia and he represented Georgia for about six months in the U.S. House of Representatives. In 1792 President Washington recalled Wayne to serve as a major-general against the Indians in the Northwest territory. Once again his military efforts were successful. General Wayne died on December 15, 1796, and this county was created and named in his honor just four years later, on December 18, 1800.

1078 *Webster County*

Daniel Webster (1782–1852)— Webster was born in New Hampshire and he represented that state in the U.S. House of Representatives. He later represented Massachusetts in both houses of the U.S. Congress and served as secretary of state under three presidents. Webster felt that slavery was evil but not as evil as disunion of the United States. He played a key role in the passage of the five laws in the U.S. Congress which are known as the "Compromise of 1850" which were intended to avert secession and civil war between the North and the South over the slavery issue. Daniel Webster died on October 24, 1852. Webster County, Kentucky, was created and named in his honor on February 29, 1860. At that time the civil war that Webster had labored to avert was becoming very close to reality.

1079 *Whitley County*

William Whitley (1749–1813)— A native of Virginia, Whitley decided as a young man to seek his fortune in the wilderness country which now is the state of Kentucky. He first explored Kentucky between 1775 and 1780 and shortly afterward he moved his family from Virginia proper to the Kentucky country. In Kentucky he engaged in seemingly endless actions against the Indians and accounts of these various Indian actions refer to Whitley as captain, major and colonel. By the time the War of 1812 began, William Whitley had reached the age of about 63. Nevertheless, he volunteered to serve as a private in the Kentucky militia in the War of 1812 and he died in combat in October, 1813, during the American victory over the British and Indians in the battle of the River Thames in Canada. This county was created in January, 1818.

1080 *Wolfe County*

Nathaniel Wolfe (1810–1865)— Wolfe was a native of Richmond, Virginia, and an 1829 graduate of the law department of the University of Virginia. A few years after graduation, he moved across the mountains to Louisville, Kentucky, where he established a law practice which became very successful. In 1839 he became commonwealth's attorney for Jefferson County, Kentucky and he continued in that position until 1852. The following year Wolfe was elected to serve in Kentucky's senate and was a member of the senate for two years. In 1859 he was elected to the lower house of the Kentucky legislature and he was serving in that body on March 5, 1860, when this county was created and named in his honor. In Kentucky's house of representatives Wolfe played a leading role in

the decision of the commonwealth of Kentucky to remain neutral during the Civil War. Although Kentucky was a slave state, it never seceded from the federal Union and it never was a member of the Confederate States of America. Wolfe left the Kentucky legislature in 1863 and died two years later, on July 3, 1865.

1081 *Woodford County*

William Woodford (–1780)— This military man was born in Virginia in 1734 or 1735 and distinguished himself in the French and Indian War and in the American Revolution. In 1775 he was commissioned a colonel in the Virginia militia and in December of that year, at Great Bridge, his forces fought and defeated Loyalist troops recruited by the royal governor of Virginia, Lord Dunmore. Appointed brigadier-general by the Continental Congress, Woodford participated in actions at Brandywine Creek, Germantown, Monmouth and Charleston. It was at Charleston, in 1780, that Woodford was taken prisoner by the British and he died later that year. This county was created and named in General Woodford's honor in 1788, while Kentucky was still part of Virginia.

REFERENCES

Allen, William B. *A History of Kentucky.* Louisville, Bradley & Gilbert, 1872.

Baker, Clauscine R. *First History of Caldwell County, Kentucky.* Madisonville, Kentucky, Commercial Printers, 1936.

Bate, R. Alexander. "Colonel Richard Callaway." *Filson Club History Quarterly*, Vol. 29, No. 2. Louisville: April, 1955.

Battle, J. H. *County of Todd, Kentucky: Historical & Biographical.* Chicago, F. A. Battey Publishing Co., 1884.

Beach, Mrs. James, & James H. Snider. *Franklin & Simpson County: A Picture of Progress.* Tompkinsville, Kentucky, Monroe County Press, 1976.

Beard, Reed. *The Battle of Tippecanoe.* Lafayctte, Indiana, 1889.

The Bell County Story: 1867–1967. Pineville, Kentucky, Sun Publishing Co., 1967.

Best, Edna H. *The Historic Past of Washington, Mason County, Kentucky.* Cynthiana, Kentucky, Hobson Book Press, 1944.

Biggs, Nina M., & Mabel L. Mackoy. *History of Greenup County, Kentucky.* Evansville, Indiana, Unigraphic, Inc., 1975.

Biographical Cyclopedia of the Commonwealth of Kentucky. Chicago, John M. Gresham Co., 1896.

The Biographical Encyclopaedia of Kentucky. Cincinnati, J. M. Armstrong & Co., 1878.

Biographical Sketch of the Hon. Lazarus W. Powell. Frankfort, S. I. M. Major, Public Printer, 1868.

Bladen, Wilford A. *Geography of Kentucky.* Dubuque, Iowa, Kendall Hunt Publishing Co., 1984.

Bryan, Charles W. "Addenda to Biography of Richard Callaway." *Filson Club History Quarterly*, Vol. 9, No. 4. Louisville: October, 1935.

Bryan, Charles W. "Richard Callaway, Kentucky Pioneer." *Filson Club History Quarterly*, Vol. 9, No. 1. Louisville: January, 1935.

Carter County Bicentennial Committee. *Carter County History: 1838–1976.*

Clark, Thomas D. *A History of Kentucky.* New York, Prentice-Hall, Inc., 1937.

Clements, John. *Kentucky Facts.* Dallas, Texas, Clements Research II, Inc., 1990.

Clements, John. *Virginia Facts.* Dallas, Texas, Clements Research II, Inc., 1991.

Clift, G. Glenn. *Governors of Kentucky: 1792–1942.* Cynthiana, Kentucky, Hobson Press, 1942.

Clift, G. Glenn. *Remember the Raisin!* Frankfort, Kentucky Historical Society, 1961.

Cockrum, William M. *Pioneer History of Indiana.* Oakland City, Indiana, Press of Oakland City Journal, 1907.

Collins, Lewis. *History of Kentucky.* Louisville, 1877.

"Counties in Kentucky & Origin of Their Names." *Register of Kentucky State Historical Society*, Vol. 1. Frankfort: 1903.

Cridlin, William B. *A History of Colonial Virginia.* Richmond, Williams Printing Co., 1923.

Darnell, Ermina J. *Filling the Chinks.* Frankfort, Roberts Printing Co., 1966.

Daviess, Mrs. Maria T *History of Mercer & Boyle Counties.* Harrodsburg, Kentucky, Harrodsburg Herald, 1924.

Donehoo, George P. *A History of the Indian Villages & Place Names in Pennsylvania.* Harrisburg, Pennsylvania, Telegraph Press, 1928.

Drake, Mrs. W. Preston, et al. *Kentucky in Retrospect: Noteworthy Personages & Events in Kentucky History: 1792–1967.* Frankfort, Kentucky Historical Society, 1967.

Dunn, C. Frank. "Captain Nathaniel G. S. Hart." *Filson Club History. Quarterly*, Vol. 24, No. 1. Louisville: January, 1950.

Dunn, Jacob P. *True Indian Stories with Glossary of Indiana Indian Names.* Indianapolis, Sentinel Printing Co., 1908.

Dyche, Russell. *Laurel County, Kentucky.* London, Kentucky, Sentinel-Echo, 1954.

Edmonson County Historical Society. *Edmonson County, Kentucky Family Histories: 1825–1989*. Paducah, Kentucky, Turner Publishing Co.

Encyclopedia of Kentucky: A Volume of Encyclopedia of the United States. New York, Somerset Publishers, 1987.

Everman, H. E. *Governor James Garrard*. Cooper's Run Press, 1981.

Faber, Harold. *From Sea to Sea: The Growth of the United States*. New York, Farrar, Straus & Giroux, 1967.

Griswold, B. J. *The Pictorial History of Fort Wayne, Indiana*. Chicago, Robert O. Law Co., 1917.

Hall, Mitchell. *Johnson County, Kentucky: A History of the County & Genealogy of Its People up to the Year 1927*. Louisville, Standard Press, 1928.

Hammack, James W. *Kentucky & the Second American Revolution: The War of 1812*. Lexington, University Press of Kentucky, 1976.

Hardy, Emmett L. "An Introduction to the Study of the Geographic Nomenclature of Kentucky's Counties, Cities & Towns." M. S. Thesis, University of Kentucky, Lexington, Kentucky, 1949.

Harrison, Lowell H. "Attorney General John Breckinridge." *Filson Club History Quarterly*, Vol. 36, No. 4. Louisville: October, 1962.

Harrison, Lowell H. "John Breckinridge of Kentucky." *Filson Club History Quarterly*, Vol. 34, No. 3. Louisville: July, 1960.

Harrison, Lowell H. "John Breckinridge and the Vice Presidency, 1804: A Political Episode." *Filson Club History Quarterly*, Vol. 26, No. 2. Louisville: April, 1952.

Harrison, Lowell H. *Kentucky's Governors: 1792–1985*. Lexington, University Press of Kentucky, 1985.

"Harrison's Report on the Battle of Tippecanoe." *Teaching Indiana History*, Vol. 2, No. 1. Indiana Historical Society, September & October, 1963.

Henderson, Dorothy. *Kentucky Treasure Trails*. Nashville, Favorite Recipe Press, 1978.

Hickman County Historical Society. *Hickman County History*. Dallas, Texas, Taylor Publishing Co., 1983.

Hiden, Martha W. *How Justice Grew: Virginia Counties: An Abstract of their Formation*. Williamsburg, Virginia, Virginia 350th Anniversary Celebration Corp., 1957.

Historical Scrapbook & Program of the Sesquicentennial Celebration of Bath County: 1811–1961. Fostoria, Ohio, John B. Rogers Producing Co.

History of the Ohio Falls Cities & Their Counties. Cleveland, Ohio, L. A. Williams & Co., 1882.

Howe, Henry. *Historical Collections of Virginia*. Charleston, South Carolina, W. R. Babcock, 1849.

Hulbert, Archer B. *The Ohio River*. New York, G. P. Putnam's Sons, 1906.

Johnson, E. Polk. *A History of Kentucky & Kentuckians*. Chicago, Lewis Publishing Co.,1912.

Joyes, Morton V. "Letter by Colonel John Todd, Jr., 1778." *History Quarterly*, Vol. 2, No. 4. Louisville: July, 1928.

Kerr, Charles, et al. *History of Kentucky*. Chicago, American Historical Society, 1922.

Kleber, John E. *The Kentucky Encyclopedia*. Lexington, University Press of Kentucky, 1992.

Lafferty, Maude W. *The Lure of Kentucky: A Historical Guide Book*. Detroit, Singing Tree Press, 1971.

Levin, H. *The Lawyers & Lawmakers of Kentucky*. Chicago, Lewis Publishing Co., 1897.

Lipscomb, A. B. *The Commercial History of the Southern States Covering the Post-Bellum Period: Kentucky*. John P. Morton & Co., 1903.

McAfee, John J. *Kentucky Politicians: Sketches of Representative Corn-Crackers & Other Miscellany*. Louisville, Courier-Journal Job Printing Co., 1886.

McCague, James. *The Cumberland*. New York, Holt, Rinehart & Winston, 1973.

McClure, Daniel E. *Two Centuries in Elizabethtown & Hardin County, Kentucky*. Hardin County Historical Society, 1979.

McKee, Lewis W., & Lydia K. Bond. *A History of Anderson County: 1780–1936*. Frankfort, Roberts Printing Co.

Perrin, W. H., et al. *Kentucky: A History of the State*. Louisville, F. A. Battey Publishing Co., 1885.

Perrin, William H. *Counties of Christian & Trigg, Kentucky*. Louisville, F. A. Battey Publishing Co., 1884.

Pirtle, Alfred. *The Battle of Tippecanoe*. Louisville, John P. Morton & Co., 1900.

Puetz, C. J. *Kentucky County Maps*. Lyndon Station, Wisconsin, County Maps.

Quisenberry, Anderson C. *Kentucky in the War of 1812*. Frankfort, Kentucky State Historical Society, 1915.

Ragan, Allen E. "John J. Crittenden, 1787–1863." *Filson Club History Quarterly*, Vol. 18, No. 1. Louisville: January, 1944.

Ranck, George W. *History of Lexington, Kentucky*. Cincinnati, Robert Clarke & Co., 1872.

Reed, Billy. *Famous Kentuckians*. Louisville, Data Courier, Inc., 1977.

Rennick, Robert M. *Kentucky Place Names*. Lexington, University Press of Kentucky, 1984.

Richards, J. A. *An Illustrated History of Bath County, Kentucky*. Yuma, Arizona, Southwest Printers, 1961.

Robinson, Morgan P. "Virginia Counties: Those Resulting from Virginia Legislation." *Bulletin of the Virginia State Library*, Vol. 9. Richmond: 1916.

Rone, Wendell H. *An Historical Atlas of Kentucky & Her Counties*. Mayfield, Kentucky, Mayfield Printing Co., 1965.

Rothert, Otto A. *A History of Muhlenberg County*. Louisville, Standard Printing Co., 1964.

Salmon, Emily J. *A Hornbook of Virginia History*. Richmond, Virginia State Library, 1983.

Scomp, H. A. "Kentucky County Names." *The Magazine of History*, Vol. 7, No. 3. New York: March, 1908.

Shankle, George Earlie. *State Names, Flags, Seals, Songs, Birds, Flowers & Other Symbols*. New York, H. W. Wilson Co., 1941.

Smith, Z. F. *The History of Kentucky*. Louisville, Courier-Journal Job Printing Co., 1895.

Smith, Z. F. *School History of Kentucky*. Louisville, Courier-Journal Job Printing Co., 1889.

Smith, Z. F. *Youth's History of Kentucky*. Louisville, Courier-Journal Job Printing Co., 1898.

Steger, Samuel W. *Caldwell County History*. Paducah, Kentucky, Turner Publishing Co., 1987.

Talbert, Charles G. "William Whitley: 1749–1813." *Filson Club History Quarterly*, Vol. 25, No. 2. Louisville: April, 1951.

Taylor William S., et al. "Kentucky's Resources: Their Development & Use." *Bulletin of the Bureau of School Service, College of Education, University of Kentucky*, Vol. 18, No. 2. Lexington: December, 1945.

Thompson, Ed P. *A Young People's History of Kentucky*. St. Louis, A. R. Fleming Co., 1897.

Trover, Ellen L. *Chronology & Documentary Handbook of the State of Virginia*. Dobbs Ferry, New York, Oceana Publications, Inc., 1979.

Van Hook, Joseph O. *The Kentucky Story*. Chattanooga, Harlow Publishing Corp., 1959.

Vexler, Robert I. *Chronology & Documentary Handbook of the State of Kentucky*. Dobbs Ferry, New York, Oceana Publications, Inc., 1978.

Wallis, Frederick A., & Hambleton Tapp. *A Sesqui-Centennial History of Kentucky*. Hopkinsville, Kentucky, Historical Record Association, 1945.

Warren, K. S. Sol. *A History of Knox*

County, Kentucky. Barbourville, Kentucky, Daniel Boone Festival, Inc., 1976.

Watkins, W. M. *The Men, Women, Events, Institutions & Lore of Casey County, Kentucky*. Louisville, Standard Printing Co., Inc., 1939.

Wells, Dianne, & Mary Lou S. Madigan, *Update. Guide to Kentucky Historical High-way Markers*. Frankfort, Kentucky Historical Society, 1983.

Wells, J. W. *History of Cumberland County*. Louisville, Standard Printing Co., 1947.

Wilkie, Katharine E., & Elizabeth R.

Moseley. *Kentucky Heritage*. Austin, Texas, Steck-Vaughn Co., 1966.

Williams, Frances M., et al. *The Story of Todd County, Kentucky: 1820–1970*. Nashville, Parthenon Press, 1972.

Wilson, Vincent. *The Book of the States*. Brookeville, Maryland, American History Research Associates, 1979.

Wingfield, Marshall. *A History of Caroline County, Virginia*. Richmond, Trevvet Christian & Co., Inc., 1924.

Wolfe County Woman's Club. *Early & Modern History of Wolfe County*. Campton, Kentucky.

Woods, Robert E. *Heroes of the War of 1812 for Whom Kentucky Counties Are Named*.

Work Projects Administration. *Union County: Past & Present*. Louisville, Schuhmann Printing Co., 1941.

Young, Bennett H. *The Battle of the Thames*. Louisville, John P. Morton & Co., 1903.

Young, Bennett H. *A History of Jessamine County, Kentucky*. Louisville, Courier-Journal Job Printing Co., 1898.

Young, V. B. *An Outline History of Bath County*. Lexington, Transylvania Printing & Publishing Co., 1876.

Louisiana

(64 parishes)

All of the United States except Alaska and Louisiana have counties. In Louisiana, the term "parish" is used instead of "county." A bit of the history and evolution of Louisiana's parishes as civil governmental units is contained in the material on Orleans Parish, Louisiana, below.

1082 *Acadia Parish*

The original Louisiana county named Acadia— In 1803 the United States purchased Louisiana from France. At that time Louisiana was so enormous that the Louisiana Purchase roughly doubled the size of the United States. In 1805 Acadia County was created within what was then Orleans territory. Acadia County was named for the Acadian refugees from Nova Scotia, Canada. In 1886 a bill was introduced in the Louisiana general assembly to create a new parish in southern Louisiana named Nicholls Parish in honor of Louisiana Governor Francis T. Nicholls. In committee, the name of the proposed parish was changed to Acadia, the name of the county created in 1805. The name honored the Acadian refugees from Nova Scotia, Canada. Nova Scotia, in Canada, had been a part of New France, but France ceded Nova Scotia to England in 1713 by the treaty of Utrecht. The Acadians living in Nova Scotia were of French descent and large numbers of them refused to take an oath of loyalty to the British crown. As a result, in 1755, during the French & Indian War, the Acadians were forcibly driven from their homes and farms in Nova Scotia by the British. The Acadians suffered countless hardships in their subsequent attempts to find a new home. They were told that they were not welcome in the En-

glish colonies of Massachusetts, New York, Connecticut, Pennsylvania, Virginia, Maryland, South Carolina and Georgia. They were also refused permission to settle on the island of Santo Domingo (now Hispaniola) in the Caribbean Sea. At one point in their odyssey the Acadians were even shipped back to England but they were soon sent back to North America. The Acadians finally found a place where they would be accepted and that place was southern Louisiana. Here they were welcomed, given assistance in finding homes and farms, by both the French and the Spanish. A few Acadians arrived in southern Louisiana about 1756 but it was not until the 1760's that large numbers of Acadians began to settle here. The name *Acadia* derived from *Acadie*, the ancient French designation of Nova Scotia. The French Canadian word *Acadia* now includes the Canadian provinces of New Brunswick, Prince Edward Island and Nova Scotia together with the state of Louisiana in the United States. The names *Acadien* and *Acadian* are often shortened to "Cajun."

1083 *Allen Parish*

Henry W. Allen (1820–1866)— A native of Virginia, Allen lived in Missouri, Mississippi and Texas during his teens and early manhood before settling in Louisiana in 1852. The following year Allen

was elected to the Louisiana legislature. He then studied law at Harvard, toured Europe and visited Cuba. When Louisiana seceded from the Union, Allen enlisted in the Confederate army as a private but he was soon elected a lieutenant-colonel. He served with distinction and was seriously wounded during the Civil War and he rose to the rank of brigadier-general. In November, 1863, Allen was elected as Louisiana's governor, and from January 25, 1864, to June 2, 1865, he was governor of the portion of Louisiana that was not controlled by the Union army. Michael Hahn (1830–1886) served as governor of the Union-occupied section of Louisiana. Henry W. Allen moved to Mexico City in 1865 to escape the merciless Reconstruction which followed the Civil War. He died in Mexico in 1866.

1084 *Ascension Parish*

Old ecclesiastical district named Ascension— Ascension Parish was given its present name by the legislature of the territory of Orleans in March, 1807. It was named for the old ecclesiastical district named Ascension, whose name commemorated the ascension of Jesus Christ into heaven. The ecclesiastical parish had been named in 1772 by its first priest, Father Angelus de Reullagodos. (His name is variously rendered as Reuillagodos, Reuillogados, Revillagodos as well as Reullagodos.) Some sources indicate that the ecclesiastical district had been named for the feast of ascension rather than directly for the ascension itself, but Father Reullagodos recorded in writing that "This parish is dedicated to the Ascension of Our Lord." It is a matter of dogma of the Roman Catholic Church that Jesus Christ was tortured and killed by crucifixion. The Catholic dogma further holds that Jesus was then miraculously resurrected from the dead and that he then ascended into heaven. It is this ascension by Jesus that is commemorated in Ascension Parish's name. In its widest sense, the doctrine concerning Jesus' ascension includes three moments:

1. The final departure of Jesus from his disciples.

2. His passage into heaven in body and soul.

3. His exaltation at the right hand of God, the Father.

An essential difference between the doctrine concerning the ascension of Jesus and the assumption into heaven of Mary (see Assumption Parish, immediately below) is that Jesus, being God, was able to ascend into heaven by his own power, while Mary was not.

1085 *Assumption Parish*

Roman Catholic Church of the Assumption at Plattenville, Louisiana— The Roman Catholic church at Plattenville, named for the assumption into heaven of the Virgin Mary, is the oldest church in the state. It was founded by Father Bernardo de Deva in 1793 and its construction was completed the same year. At that time the church was small, really little more than a shack. Assumption Parish was created in 1807 by the legislature of Orleans territory. It was named for the historic church in Plattenville. The old church was replaced by a newer structure in 1856. In a November 1, 1950, definition of the assumption of the Virgin Mary into heaven, Pope Pius XII (1876–1958) enunciated the dogma with these words: "The Immaculate Mother of God, the ever–Virgin Mary, having completed the course of her earthly life, was assumed body and soul into heavenly glory." Jesus Christ, being God, had ascended into heaven by his own power. (See Ascension Parish, immediately above.) Since Mary was not God, it was necessary for her to be assumed, or drawn up through the power of God, into heaven.

1086 *Avoyelles Parish*

Avoyel Indians— The Avoyel Indians were early inhabitants of this area of Louisiana, residing along the Red River near its junction with the Mississippi River. They lived in the areas where Alexandria and Marksville now stand, and at Marksville, they built temple mounds. The Avoyel were never a large tribe and they lived primarily by farming. They also raised long horned cattle, engaged in trade for minerals from far away places and were known for the beauty of the pottery that they made. They sold cattle, horses and oxen to French settlers here. The Avoyel lived in villages and were generally peaceful and prosperous. During both the French and Spanish rule of this section of Louisiana, the Avoyel Indians and their fertile lands were protected from encroaching White settlers by soldiers stationed at Avoyelles post. Nevertheless, by the beginning of the 19th century, new diseases and war had rendered the Avoyel extinct. The meaning of the name *Avoyel* is uncertain. Possible translations that have been mentioned include: "Flint people," "Nation of the rocks" and "People of the rocks."

1087 *Beauregard Parish*

Pierre G. T. Beauregard (1818–1893)— A native of Saint Bernard Parish, Louisiana and an 1838 graduate of the U.S. military academy at West Point, Beauregard served with distinction in the Mexican War and was twice honored for bravery. In January, 1861, shortly before the start of the Civil War, Beauregard was assigned to be superintendent of the U.S. military academy but his appointment lasted only a few days because of his known sympathy toward the South. After Louisiana seceded from the Union in late January, 1861, Beauregard resigned his commission in the U.S. army and was appointed brigadier-general of the provisional army of the Confederate States of America. On April 12, 1861, Confederate batteries under the command of General Beauregard opened fire on the U.S. forces at Fort Sumter, South Carolina, and the Civil War was begun. Fort Sumter was surrendered to General Beauregard after 34 hours of intense bombardment. Beauregard later fought at the first battle of Manassas and was promoted to full general in the regular Confederate army. He continued to serve with distinction throughout the Civil War. Beauregard Parish was created in 1912. A group of area women promoted the idea of naming the new parish in honor of General Beauregard.

1088 *Bienville Parish*

Jean Baptiste le Moyne, Sieur de Bienville (1680–)— Bienville was born in Montreal, Canada, in 1680 and baptized in the parish of Ville-Marie in Montreal on February 23 of that year. He entered the French military at an early age and in 1697 he was wounded in a military engagement with the English. He recuperated in France. In 1682 Rene Robert Cavelier, Sieur de la Salle (1643–1687) had named the vast area along the Mississippi River "Louisiana" and he had claimed it for France. In 1698 Bienville was sent by the French government to establish French colonies at the southern end of Louisiana along the Gulf of Mexico. He was largely successful in this effort and on several occasions Bienville served as governor of French Louisiana. His first term as governor began in 1701 and in 1718 he founded the city of New Orleans. During the 1730's and early 1740's Bienville was engaged in rather constant warfare with the Indians. This strain, together with sciatica, exhausted him. In the early 1740's Bienville left Louisiana and retired in Paris, France on a modest government pension. He died there in 1767 or 1768.

1089 *Bossier Parish*

Pierre E. J. B. Bossier (1797–1844)— A native of Louisiana, Bossier was a descendant of a Creole family which was among the first settlers of the French colony of Louisiana. Pierre E. J. B. Bossier was a cotton planter and a member of the Louisiana senate. He served in that body from 1833 to 1843. He also held the title of general in the Louisiana militia. On March 4, 1843, Bossier began a term representing Louisiana in the U.S. House of Representatives. He died in 1844 before completing that term. This parish was created and named in his honor on February 24, 1843, after Bossier had been elected to congress but just before the start of his service in that body.

1090 *Caddo Parish*

Caddo Indians— Hernando de Soto (1500–1542) encountered some tribes of the Caddo Indian confederations during his explorations of the southeastern United States but these Indians did not become well known until the French explorer, Rene Robert Cavelier, Sieur de la Salle (1643–1687) came upon them in the 1680's. When encountered by La Salle, most of the Caddo were gathered in three loose confederations. These were the Hasinai, Wichita and Kadohadacho. The

Kadohadacho, or Caddo proper, were the Indians for whom Caddo Parish was named. The name *Caddo* is merely a contraction of *Kadohadacho*, which means "real chiefs. The Kadohadacho lived along the bend of the Red River in southwestern Arkansas and eastern Texas, with other settlements further south along the Red River in northwestern Louisiana. Here the name Caddo perpetuates their memory in the name of a large lake as well as in the parish name. The Caddo were farmers, hunters and traders. They had acquired horses in their early contacts with the Spanish explorers and they traded these horses as far north as the Illinois River. Europeans who wrote of their contacts with the Caddo Indians were favorably impressed by them. They were said to be industrious, intelligent, courageous and unusually friendly to visitors. In 1835 the Caddo Indians sold their territory to the United States for $80,000. The territory that they sold contained a section of northwestern Louisiana, including all of the present Caddo Parish and the portions of southwestern Arkansas and eastern Texas that were controlled by the Caddo Indians. Caddo Parish, Louisiana was created and named for them on January 18, 1838. The parish's name was selected by Mr. W. H. Spark. After leaving the territory that they sold to the U.S., the Caddo lived a rather perilous existence in Texas where they were persecuted and killed by both Comanche Indians and White settlers. In 1855 the federal government established a tract for the Caddo near the Brazos River in Texas. However, in 1859 it was learned that a group of White settlers had set a date to massacre all Caddo Indians. Under the direction of Indian Agent Robert S. Neighbors (1815–1859), who had been a consistent friend of the Caddo, these Indians were promptly relocated to the banks of the Washita River in what is now Caddo County, Oklahoma. Few pure Caddo Indians remain today. Many of them have mixed White and Caddo ancestry while others are the products of intermarriage among Caddo and other Indian tribes.

1091 *Calcasieu Parish*

Uncertain— Calcasieu Parish was created on March 24, 1840, but the origin of its name is uncertain. Several explanations of the source of the name have been suggested. They include:
— Calcasieu River in southwestern Louisiana. The Calcasieu River is about 200 miles long and it flows through Calcasieu Parish. The river's name may have been

derived from one of the two name origins mentioned below.
— War cry or war title of a chief of the now-extinct Atakapa (or Attakapa) Indian tribe in Louisiana. As he went into battle, this chief is said to have shouted a peculiar noise, which sounded like the cry of an eagle. *Calcasieu* has been translated as "crying eagle." Some sources state that calcasieu was not merely a war cry of this Indian chief but his title during times of war.
— Derived from the colloquial French *quelques chaux* (or *choux*) which has been translated to mean "some cabbages." Early French settlers along the Calcasieu River raised cabbages.

1092 *Caldwell Parish*

Uncertain— It is known that Caldwell Parish was created on March 6, 1838, but the origin of its name is uncertain. The possibilities that are mentioned are:
— The distinguished Caldwell family of this region. Robert Caldwell (1831–) was a member of this family.
— Robert Caldwell (1831–), a parish judge.
— Matthew Caldwell, a noted frontiersman from North Carolina.
If 1831 is correct for the year of Robert Caldwell's birth, the odds are slim that this parish was named for him. He was only seven years old when the parish was created.

1093 *Cameron Parish*

Simon Cameron (1799–1889)— A native of Pennsylvania, Cameron was involved in diverse business ventures and amassed a fortune before his 40th birthday. In 1838 he first became involved in national politics when he was appointed as a commissioner to settle certain claims of the Winnebago Indians. In 1845 Cameron was elected to represent Pennsylvania in the U.S. Senate. He left the senate in 1849 but was returned to that body in 1857. By this time Cameron had become one of the nation's most successful machine politicians and he was a candidate for the presidential nomination at the Republican national convention in 1860. He was defeated for that nomination by Abraham Lincoln, who received the votes of Cameron's Pennsylvania delegates. Cameron's reward for providing Lincoln with these votes was a position in Lincoln's cabinet as secretary of war. Cameron was serving as secretary of war when the Civil War began in 1861 but his administration was inefficient and corrupt and Lincoln appointed Edwin M.

Stanton (1814–1869) to replace him in 1862. In that same year Cameron was sent as minister to Russia but his service in that post was very brief. In 1867 Pennsylvania returned Cameron to the U.S. Senate and he was serving in that body when Cameron Parish, Louisiana was created in 1070. A few sources indicate that Cameron Parish was not named for Simon Cameron but for Robert Alexander Cameron, who was said to have been a soldier in the Confederate army and later commander of the district of Lafourche. It is difficult to take this suggestion seriously. Cameron Parish was created on March 15, 1870. At that time Louisiana was under the vicious rule of Reconstruction, which the victorious Union government had imposed, following the Civil War. Reconstruction had been imposed on Louisiana and other former members of the Confederacy. Grant Parish, named for Ulysses S. Grant (1822–1885), the commander of all Union forces in the Civil War, had been created and named by Louisiana's Reconstruction government just one year earlier, in March, 1869. Lincoln Parish was named for Abraham Lincoln, who was president of the Union states when they defeated the Confederate states in the Civil War. Lincoln Parish was created on February 27, 1873, and it was also named by Louisiana's Reconstruction government. Reconstruction did not end in Louisiana until 1877. There would seem to be little doubt that it was the secretary of war in Abraham Lincoln's Civil War cabinet, Simon Cameron, whom Louisiana's Reconstruction legislature chose to honor when it created Cameron Parish in 1870.

1094 *Catahoula Parish*

Uncertain— Circumstantial evidence indicates that Catahoula Parish was named for Catahoula Lake.
Catahoula Lake— There are two lakes in Louisiana named Catahoula. One is a small lake in south-central Louisiana about nine miles northeast of the city of Saint Martinville. That lake has no connection with the naming of Catahoula Parish. The lake for which Catahoula Parish is believed to have been named is a larger lake, which is essentially an expansion of Little River. Located in La Salle Parish, Louisiana, this Catahoula Lake is about 15 miles long and varies in depth to a maximum of about 15 feet. At the time that Catahoula Parish was created in 1808, Catahoula Lake was entirely within its borders. A century later, in 1908, La Salle Parish was created from the western portion of Catahoula Parish.

As a result, Catahoula Lake now lies within La Salle Parish, rather than Catahoula Parish.

Not all sources agree that Catahoula Parish was named for Catahoula Lake. Other possibilities that have been mentioned are:

1. Catahoula Indians— The Catahoula Indians were a tribe who lived on Catahoula Creek in Catahoula Parish. They may have been a remnant of the Taensa tribe. The Catahoula Indians are now extinct.

2. Name conferred on the area and then on the parish because of the many beautiful, clear creeks that traverse the region.

The origin and meaning of the name catahoula are also uncertain. The following possibilities are known to have been suggested:

— "Beloved lake"

— Distortion of the Indians' name for Little River, which was *etacoulow*, meaning "river of the great spirit"

— "Beautiful white water"

— French corruption of the Indians' words for "lake" and "people"

A scholarly discussion of the merits of the above possibilities is contained in an article written by William A. Read. That article was entitled "Louisiana Place-Names of Indian Origin." It was published in the February, 1927 issue (Vol. 19, No. 2) of the *University Bulletin Louisiana State University & Agricultural & Mechanical College*.

Other suggested translations that have been mentioned are "big, clear lake" and "beautiful, clear water."

1095 *Claiborne Parish*

William C. C. Claiborne (1775–1817)— A native of Virginia and a lawyer, Claiborne moved to Tennessee when it was still a territory. There he practiced law and served in Tennessee's constitutional convention of 1796. When Tennessee was admitted to statehood, Claiborne served briefly on the supreme court of the new state but he was soon elected to represent Tennessee in the U.S. House of Representatives. Thomas Jefferson became president of the United States in March, 1801, and he soon appointed Claiborne governor of Mississippi territory. When the U.S. acquired Louisiana from France in the Louisiana Purchase, President Jefferson appointed Claiborne, along with General James Wilkinson (1757–1825), to represent our country at the ceremonial transfer of Louisiana from France to our country and Claiborne was then appointed governor-general and intendent of the U.S. province of Louisiana. In that capacity he acted, for all practical purposes, as the benign dictator of Louisiana. He subsequently was appointed governor of Orleans territory and served in that position until 1812, when Louisiana was admitted to the Union. Claiborne was elected as the new state's first governor and he held that office until 1816. In January, 1817, he was elected to represent Louisiana in the U.S. Senate but he died before taking his seat in that body. Claiborne Parish was created in 1828.

1096 *Concordia Parish*

Spanish military post named Post of New Concordia, Post of Concordia or Post of Concord— During the period that Spain-ruled Louisiana, a military outpost was established on the western bank of the Mississippi River at what is now Vidalia, the parish seat of Concordia Parish. This post was established about 1768 directly across the river from Natchez, in what is now the state of Mississippi. In some accounts the location of this post is given incorrectly as Natchez, when a more accurate description would have been "near Natchez." The mistake may well have arisen from the fact that, in the early days, the military post had no name of its own. After it was named (New Concordia, Concordia or Concord), the adjacent territory came to be known as Concordia. Two theories for the origin of the military post's name are known:

1. The name was inspired by an amicable agreement (or concord) between the local Spanish and American authorities concerning the mutual surrender and exchange of fugitive slaves.

2. The military post's name came from the name of the magnificent residence of the Spanish governor-general of Louisiana, Manuel Gayoso de Lemos (–1798). This residence, which was named Concord, was located at Natchez. The name of this residence is said to have been inspired in recognition of the friendly relations between the English-speaking settlers in the Natchez district and their Spanish rulers.

1097 *De Soto Parish*

Hernando De Soto (1500–1542)— De Soto, the famous Spanish conquistador, was one of Europe's early explorers of the Americas and the discoverer of the Mississippi River. Following successful campaigns in Central America, De Soto was prominent in the conquest of the Inca empire in Peru. In 1539 De Soto landed in Florida and, in a futile search for riches, he and his men explored Florida and a large area of the southeastern United States, torturing and slaughtering Indians as they went. It was this expedition that discovered the Mississippi River.

1098 *East Baton Rouge Parish*

East Baton Rouge Parish — French words for "reddened Maypole" or, more simply, "red stick"—The French-Canadian naval commander and explorer, Pierre le Moyne, Sieur d' Iberville (1661–1706), was an explorer of the Mississippi River. On a voyage up the Mississippi in 1699, Iberville kept a journal that recorded the details of that exploration. In it he mentioned a "reddened Maypole," on the banks of a tributary of the Mississippi and he said that this pole separated the hunting grounds of two groups of Indians. The Indians' names are given in Iberville's Journal as Bayougoulas (or Bayogoulas) and Houmas (or Oumas). Iberville and others have mentioned that this reddened Maypole may also have been used for religious purposes by the Indians. European settlers in the vicinity of this red stick called their community Baton Rouge and that settlement grew to become the city which is the capital of the state of Louisiana. Two Louisiana parishes were created in this area named East Baton Rouge Parish and West Baton Rouge Parish. The names of these parishes, of course, have their origin in the "reddened Maypole" described by Iberville in 1699. Several other theories have been suggested for the origin of the name Baton Rouge but Professor William O. Scroggs examined them and provided a credible position in support of the "reddened Maypole" origin. Dr. Scroggs' article on this subject appeared in the August, 1917 issue (Vol. 8, No. 8) of the *Proceedings of the Historical Society of East and West Baton Rouge*. The title of the article is "Origin of the Name Baton Rouge."

1099 *East Carroll Parish*

Charles Carroll (1737–1832)— Carroll was a native of Maryland and he represented that state in the Continental Congress. He was one of the signers of the Declaration of Independence and he later represented Maryland as a U.S. senator in the first congress of the United States. Carroll lived to be the last surviving signer of the Declaration of Independence and several states recognized that distinction by naming counties and parishes in his honor. In 1832 Louisiana created and named Carroll Parish for him. Later, in 1877, Carroll Parish was divided into two parishes, East Carroll Parish and West Carroll Parish.

1100 East Feliciana Parish

Spain's Distrito de Feliciana in West Florida— On October 27, 1810, President James Madison issued a proclamation which claimed West Florida for the United States and authorized its military occupation as a part of our country's Orleans territory. At that time Spain claimed ownership of West Florida, which included the Distrito de Feliciana. On December 7, 1810, Territorial Governor William C. C. Claiborne (1775–1817) issued an ordinance creating the county of Feliciana from this newly acquired region. Fifteen days later, on December 22, 1810, Governor Claiborne issued a second proclamation establishing four parishes within the county of Feliciana. One of these four parishes was Feliciana Parish. On February 17, 1824, Feliciana Parish was divided into two parishes, East Feliciana Parish and West Feliciana Parish. The origin of the name *Feliciana* is uncertain and disputed. Most sources indicate that it was a word signifying "happy land" or "land of happiness." It has also been suggested that the name Feliciana was chosen to honor the wife of a Spanish governor of Louisiana, Bernardo de Galvez (1746–1786). The wife of Bernardo de Galvez was Maria Feliciana (or Felicite) de Saint-Maxent. She was a native of New Orleans and a descendant of two distinguished French families, Saint-Maxent and Maroche. She was a widow of Juan Bautista d' Estrehan at the time of her marriage to Don Bernardo de Galvez on December 2, 1777. A third possibility for the source of the original name Feliciana has also been mentioned. According to this version, the Spanish explorer, Juan Ponce de Leon (1460–1521) bestowed the name Nueva Feliciana on the area "in recognition of its salubrity of climate, beautiful variety of forest, its clear waters and fertile soil."

1101 Evangeline Parish

Evangeline, the fictive heroine of Henry W. Longfellow's poem entitled Evangeline: A Tale of Acadie— In 1755, during the French & Indian War, Acadians of French descent, living in Nova Scotia, Canada, were forcibly driven from their homes and farms by the British because they refused to take an oath of loyalty to the British crown. After suffering countless hardships (see Acadia Parish, Louisiana, above) the Acadians were permitted to settle in southern Louisiana. The names Acadien and Acadian are often shortened to "Cajun." Henry W. Longfellow (1807–1882) wrote a poem about these Acadian exiles entitled *Evangeline: A Tale of Acadie*, which was released in 1847. This epic poem tells the story of betrothed lovers, Evangeline and Gabriel, who were separated during the forced exodus of Acadians from Nova Scotia. This tale in hexameters sends Evangeline on an arduous search for her lover. She traces him to southern Louisiana only to learn that he has recently left Louisiana. Evangeline continues her search for Gabriel for many years before abandoning hope of finding him. At this point Longfellow has Evangeline enter a convent and devote her declining years to hospital work in Philadelphia where she finally finds Gabriel, on his death bed. Evangeline Parish is in southern Louisiana where the Acadians settled in the 1750's and 1760's. According to local tradition, Evangeline was a real person. The most popular version of this legend renders her name as Emmeline Labiche and a grave and a statue in the yard of the Saint Martin de Tours Catholic Church in St. Martinville, Louisiana, mark the site where this alleged inspiration for Longfellow's heroine is buried. Carl A. Brasseaux studied the facts and fictions surrounding Evangeline and published his conclusions in 1988 in a scholarly work entitled *In Search of Evangeline: Birth & Evolution of the Evangeline Myth*. Brasseaux makes a strong case that the portion of Longfellow's poem that deals with Evangeline and her fiance is fiction. But we must not be too hard on this confusion of fact with fiction because Evangeline Parish owes its name to a burst of Acadian pride and fervor in the early 20th century. Southern Louisiana Mardi Gras parades featured Evangeline floats, southern Louisiana began to promote itself as the "Land of Evangeline" and, in 1910, Evangeline Parish was created.

1102 Franklin Parish

Benjamin Franklin (1706–1790)— Franklin was a native of Massachusetts who moved to Pennsylvania in his teens. Poverty denied him a formal education but he became the leading printer and editor in North America. Franklin gained fame for his discoveries and inventions in the physical sciences and he distinguished himself as author, philosopher and diplomat. Franklin was a signer of the Declaration of Independence and an important member of the convention which framed the U.S. Constitution.

1103 Grant Parish

Ulysses S. Grant (1822–1885)— Grant was a native of Ohio who graduated from the U.S. military academy at West Point. He served with distinction in the Mexican War and in the Civil War he rose to become commander of all Union forces. After the Civil War, Grant served briefly as acting secretary of war and then two terms as president of the United States. He proved to be a rather mediocre president. This parish was created in March, 1869, the month that Ulysses S. Grant began his term as president. It may seem surprising that Louisiana, which had recently been a member of the Confederacy, would name a parish in honor of the leading general of the Union forces. However, when this parish was created and named, Louisiana was under the harsh military Reconstruction rule imposed by the victorious northern states.

1104 Iberia Parish

City of New Iberia, Louisiana— Iberia Parish is located in southern Louisiana where it borders the Gulf of Mexico. Among the early settlers of this section of Louisiana were Spanish colonists and they named the area after their Iberian Peninsula in southwestern Europe. Spain shares the Iberian Peninsula with Portugal but Spain's share of the land area is more than five times as great as Portugal's. In fact, in ancient times, the name *Iberia* meant "Spain" alone. This name derived from the name of the second longest river in Spain, the Iberus, which is now called the Ebro River. When the city of New Iberia was named, it was given the name that had long been used for this general area of southern Louisiana. Iberia Parish was created in 1868 and it was named for the city of New Iberia, which was chosen to be the seat of justice for Iberia Parish.

1105 Iberville Parish

Pierre le Moyne, Sieur d' Iberville (1661–1706)— A native of Montreal, Canada, and a French naval officer, Iberville first distinguished himself in 1686 during the French campaign to drive the English from Hudson Bay. In 1688 he defeated an English attempt to recapture their Hudson Bay posts. During King William's War (1689–1697), Iberville continued to fight the English and English colonists from Hudson Bay to Schenectady, New York, and Newfoundland. By 1698 Iberville's attentions had shifted to Louisiana. He built a fort near the present city of Biloxi, Mississippi, led several expeditions of colonists to settle Louisiana for France and, in 1699, became the first governor of Louisiana. He died of yellow fever on his flagship in the Caribbean Sea during Queen Anne's War.

1106 *Jackson Parish*

Andrew Jackson (1767–1845)— Jackson was born on the border of North Carolina and South Carolina. He represented Tennessee in both branches of the U.S. Congress. He gained fame and popularity for his military exploits in wars with the Indians and as the defender of New Orleans in the War of 1812. He was provisional military governor of Florida and, from 1829 to 1837, General Jackson was president of the United States. His presidency reflected the frontier spirit of America. This parish was created in February, 1845, just three months before Andrew Jackson died.

1107 *Jefferson Parish*

Thomas Jefferson (1743–1826)— Jefferson was a native of Virginia and a member of the Virginia legislature. He served Virginia as governor and he was a delegate to the second Continental Congress. Jefferson was the author of the Declaration of Independence and one of its signers. He was minister to France, secretary of state, vice-president and president of the United States. As president, he accomplished the Louisiana Purchase and he arranged the Lewis and Clark Expedition to the Pacific Northwest. Jefferson was a true intellectual, thoroughly knowledgeable in the arts and sciences. His political theories were pivotal in the formation of our infant republic. This parish was formed in 1825. The name that was first proposed for this new parish was Tchoupitoulas, in honor of a local sub-tribe of Indians, but that name was never officially adopted. The name Jefferson had earlier been considered for the state's name but Louisiana was chosen instead.

1108 *Jefferson Davis Parish*

Jefferson Davis (1808–1889)— A native of Kentucky, Davis moved with his family to Mississippi when he was a small boy. He graduated from the U.S. military academy at West Point and served as an officer in the Black Hawk and Mexican Wars. He represented Mississippi in both houses of the United States congress where he was a spokesman for the South, states' rights and strict construction of the constitution.

President Franklin Pierce appointed Davis to his cabinet as secretary of war and he served in that position from 1853 to 1857. In February, 1861, Jefferson Davis was inaugurated as president of the Confederate States of America. He was the first and only president of the Confederacy, and he served in that post until the end of the Civil War in 1865. A number of sources show the affectionate nickname Jeff Davis as the name of this parish but the legislative act that created it in 1912 used the full name, Jefferson Davis Parish, and that is the style used by the parish today on its official letterhead.

1109 *La Salle Parish*

Rene Robert Cavelier, Sieur de la Salle (1643–1687)— A native of Rouen, France, La Salle came to North America about 1667 and engaged in fur trading in Canada and in the Illinois country. In 1682, in company with Henri de Tonty and others, La Salle led an expedition which sailed down the Mississippi River and was the first to trace the Mississippi to its mouth at the Gulf of Mexico. La Salle named this vast area Louisiana and he claimed it for France. La Salle was the name of an estate near Rouen, France which belonged to the Cavelier family.

1110 *Lafayette Parish*

Marie Joseph Paul Yves Roch Gilbert du Motier, Marquis de Lafayette (1757–1834)— Lafayette was a French aristocrat who served briefly in the French army. He came to America in 1777 to assist the American Revolutionary army. He was granted an honorary commission as major-general by the Continental Congress and served with distinction in a number of battles in the Revolutionary War. Lafayette returned to France in 1781. In 1803 the United States purchased Louisiana from France and in 1805 President Thomas Jefferson requested Lafayette to be governor of Louisiana but Lafayette declined. This parish was created in January, 1823. According to some sources, Lafayette was visiting the United States as an honored guest of the federal government at the time that Lafayette Parish was created. That chronology is in error. Lafayette did not arrive for his visit until 1824. However, the parish name may have been chosen in anticipation of his visit and Lafayette did visit Louisiana while he was here.

1111 *Lafourche Parish*

Bayou Lafourche— This parish was cre-

ated as a county on April 10, 1805, and as a parish on March 31, 1807. Lafourche was a part of Orleans territory on both of these dates. It was named for Bayou Lafourche, an outlet of the Mississippi River. *La fourche* is French and means "the fork." The bayou's name may have been chosen because of the fork formed at the present site of Donaldsonville, Louisiana. Bayou Lafourche is about 110 miles long and it runs from the Mississippi River at Donaldsonville, in Ascension Parish, through the entire length of Lafourche Parish to the Gulf of Mexico. From Lockport to the Gulf of Mexico, Bayou Lafourche is one of the busiest waterways in southern Louisiana on account of traffic generated by the Inter-coastal canal. The term *bayou* was derived from a Choctaw Indian word. It is used to describe creeks, secondary watercourses and minor rivers as well as marshes swamps and bogs. In his 1942 doctoral dissertation on Louisiana place names, Jack A. Reynolds defined a bayou as "a slow, sleepy waterway of secondary importance." In a later doctoral dissertation (1970) dealing with generic terms in the place names of Louisiana, Randall A. Detro demonstrated that the term *bayou* is used in Louisiana to describe a wide variety of water bodies possessing differing characteristics.

1112 *Lincoln Parish*

Abraham Lincoln (1809–1865)— Lincoln was a native of Kentucky who moved to Illinois where he was a member of the state legislature. He represented Illinois in the house of representatives and later was elected president of the United States. Lincoln's presidency coincided almost exactly with the Civil War. He guided the United States ably through that uniquely turbulent period. As president, he issued the Emancipation Proclamation which declared the freedom of slaves in all states in rebellion. Lincoln was assassinated in 1865, a few days after the Union victory in the Civil War. This parish was created and named in 1873, while Louisiana was under the harsh military Reconstruction rule imposed after the Civil War by the victorious northern states.

1113 *Livingston Parish*

Uncertain— Livingston Parish, Louisiana, was created on February 10, 1832, and named for either Edward Livingston (1764–1836) or his brother, Robert R. Livingston (1746–1813).

Edward Livingston (1764–1836)— Edward Livingston was born in New York, represented that state in the U.S. House of Representatives and served as mayor of New York City. Because of personal problems, he moved to Louisiana to start a new life in 1804. Here he served as Andrew Jackson's aide in the battle of New Orleans and was elected to the Louisiana legislature. He later represented Louisiana in both houses of the U.S. Congress and was President Andrew Jackson's secretary of state. Livingston drafted President Jackson's Proclamation to the People of South Carolina, which asserted the supremacy of the federal government in response to South Carolina's 1832 Ordinance of Nullification. His last post was minister to France.

Robert R. Livingston (1746–1813)— Robert R. Livingston was born in New York City and represented New York in the Continental Congress. He also assisted in drafting our nation's Declaration of Independence. In the Continental Congress Livingston served as secretary of foreign affairs. In 1801 President Thomas Jefferson appointed him as minister to France with instructions to negotiate peaceful rights for Americans on the Mississippi River and at the port of New Orleans. James Monroe was later sent to France to assist Livingston in the negotiations. Their efforts were amply rewarded when France offered to sell the United States all of Louisiana. We accepted the French offer and the resulting Louisiana Purchase doubled the size of our country.

1114 *Madison Parish*

James Madison (1751–1836)— Madison was born in Virginia, served in the Virginia legislature and in the Continental Congress. He was a member of the convention which framed the U.S. Constitution and he collaborated with Hamilton and Jay in writing a series of papers entitled *The Federalist*, which explained the new constitution and advocated its adoption. Madison represented Virginia in the U.S. House of Representatives, served for eight years as secretary of state and for eight years as president of the United States.

1115 *Morehouse Parish*

Abraham Morhouse (–1813)— This parish was created on March 25, 1844, and named for Abraham Morhouse, who had been an early settler and colonizer of Louisiana. Morhouse spent his early life in New York and he claimed to have been a colonel in the New York militia. In 1790 he

married Abigail Young in New York. Colonel Morhouse deserted his wife, without first obtaining a divorce, and lived for a time in the wilderness of Kentucky, where he acquired considerable property. Felipe Enrique Neri, Baron de Bastrop (–1827), who was active in establishing colonies in Louisiana from about 1795 to about 1803, met Abraham Morhouse in Kentucky and induced Morhouse to accompany him to Louisiana to assist in colonizing the area. In addition to his colonizing activities in Louisiana, Morhouse was active in a flour milling business and, in September, 1799, he became a bigamist when he married Eleanor Hook. Although the parish is named Morehouse, it is clear from historical records that the parish's namesake spelled his name Morhouse.

1116 *Natchitoches Parish*

Natchitoches Indians— The Natchitoches Indians were one of the four tribes of the Kadohadacho confederacy of Caddo Indians. The Kadohadacho Indians lived along the bend of the Red River in southwestern Arkansas and eastern Texas, with other settlements further south along the Red River in northwestern Louisiana, in the vicinity of the town of Natchitoches, which is the parish seat of Natchitoches Parish. The Natchitoches subsisted by hunting, fishing, farming and harvesting wild berries and plants. They also manufactured salt and were recognized for their artistic abilities. In 1690 the explorer, Henri de Tonty (–1704), encountered these Indians and made an alliance with them on behalf of France. Somewhat later, but very early in the 18th century, the French Canadian explorer, Louis Juchereau de Saint Denis (1676–1744), reinforced the Natchitoches Indians' alliance with the French. In a 1713 exploration mission, Saint Denis ascended the Red River and found Natchitoches Indians living on an island in the Red River. Presumably that island was the present town of Natchitoches. (The Red River changed its course about 1825 and moved some five miles east of the town of Natchitoches.) Never a large tribe, by 1805 the population of the Natchitoches had been reduced to about 50, primarily as a result of new diseases introduced by the Whites. Soon after 1805 the Natchitoches ceased to exist as a separate tribe and the few survivors were absorbed by other tribes of the Caddo Indians. The meaning of the name *Natchitoches* is uncertain. Suggested translations include "chestnut eaters," "chinquapin eaters," "pawpaw eaters," and "pawpaws."

1117 *Orleans Parish*

Uncertain— Sources consulted differ on whether Orleans Parish was named for the city of Orleans, in France, or for Philippe II, Duke of Orleans (1674–1723).

City of Orleans, France— Orleans, the capital of the department of Loiret, is located on the Loire River in north-central France. This city, with a population of about 100,000, lies some 75 miles southwest of Paris. Orleans produces manufactured goods and is in one of France's agricultural regions. Conquered by the Roman Empire in 52 B.C., Orleans became a major cultural center during the middle ages. The French King Philip VI (1293–1350), made the city a royal duchy and peerage in favor of his son. The city of Orleans, together with the surrounding Orleanais Province was given at times as an appanage to members of the French royal family (dukes of Orleans.)

Philippe II, Duke of Orleans (1674–1723)— This member of the French royal family served with distinction in the military and, in 1701, upon the death of his father, Philippe I, Duke of Orleans (1640–1701), he became duke of Orleans. When the French king, Louis XIV (1638–1715), died, the duke of Orleans, a nephew of the king, became regent of France and de facto ruler of the country. He ruled until the heir to the throne, a five-year old great-grandson of the ancient Louis XIV, reached his majority in 1723. This great-grandson was Louis XV (1710–1774). Thus the duke ruled France as regent from 1715 to 1723. The duke of Orleans guided his young charge, Louis XV, to his majority without compromising royal authority. During the regent's tenure, he offered new initiatives for France at home and abroad and served as a patron of French artistic life. History knows Philippe II, Duke of Orleans, primarily as an immoral, dissolute scoundrel because of his notorious life style. The duke's interest in alchemy serves as another target for derision as does his support of the financial schemes of the banker, John Law (1671–1729). As mentioned below, it was Law who gave the city of New Orleans, in Louisiana, its name. In August, 1723 the duke of Orleans became prime minister of France and he held that office until his death in December of that year.

The city of New Orleans, Louisiana, which is the parish seat of Orleans Parish, was founded in 1717 or 1718 by Jean Baptiste le Moyne, Sieur de Bienville (1680–), but its name was bestowed by the Scottish-born French banker, John Law (1671–1729). Law named the city in honor of his protector, who was regent of France when

New Orleans was founded; i.e., Law named the city of New Orleans in honor of Philippe II, Duke of Orleans (1674–1723). In 1803 the United States purchased Louisiana from France. President Thomas Jefferson only desired to purchase the city of New Orleans and perhaps a small buffer around it. The seaport city of New Orleans was vital to the transportation and commerce of the infant United States. However, it was not just New Orleans that we got but all of Louisiana, an enormous area that roughly doubled the size of our country. In 1804 congress designated the portion of the Louisiana Purchase that was south of the 33rd parallel of north latitude as the territory of Orleans. On April 10, 1805, the "County of Orleans" was created as one of the twelve civil divisions (i.e., counties) of Orleans territory. The second session of the first legislature of Orleans territory divided the territory into 19 parishes on March 31, 1807. These civil parishes were based largely on existing ecclesiastical parishes of the Roman Catholic Church. These new civil parishes were superimposed on the twelve counties but the counties were not abolished. One of the new 19 parishes was designated as "The city of New Orleans with its precincts as they formerly stood …" Although this act did not specifically name the parish containing the city of New Orleans, it is this March 31, 1807, act that is cited as the one that created Orleans Parish. In 1812 Louisiana was admitted to the Union as our 18th state.

The constitution of the new state mentioned both counties and parishes but did not specify county government or parish government. However, the first legislature of the new state divided Louisiana into judicial districts by parishes rather than by counties. From about that time to this day, the term "parish" has supplanted the term "county" in Louisiana. Louisiana's revised constitution of 1845 formally abolished counties in Louisiana by failing to mention them at all and by using the term "parish" exclusively.

Many sources consulted state that Orleans Parish was named for the city of Orleans in France, while roughly an equal number of sources say that the parish's name honors Philippe II, Duke of Orleans (1674–1723). Since the duke's title derived from the name of the French city of Orleans, the apparent conflict may be no conflict at all. Orleans Parish's name may accurately be said to derive from both the city of Orleans, in France, and from Philippe II, Duke of Orleans, depending how far back along the naming chain one wishes to go.

1118 *Ouachita Parish*

Ouachita Indians— The Ouachita were a former clan of Indians, who lived along the Ouachita River in northern Louisiana. At the time of European contact, these Indians, who were probably of the Caddoan family, numbered less than 200 and soon after their separate identity was lost. The meaning of the word *ouachita* is uncertain. A wide variety of translations have been advanced, including "black" and "silver water."

1119 *Plaquemines Parish*

Fruit of the persimmon tree— This parish was created on March 31, 1807, when it was part of Orleans territory. At that time its content was defined to include " … all that part of the country on both sides of the Mississippi below the Parish of St. Bernard as far as the Balize." Its name recognized the persimmon, which is the fruit of the persimmon tree (*Diospyros virginiana*), which is found in much of Louisiana. In Louisiana-French, the persimmon tree is called "plaqueminier," while one of the French-Louisiana names for its fruit is "plaquemine." The fruit of the persimmon tree are edible berries which are usually orange in color and up to two inches in diameter. The French-Louisiana name "plaquemine" derived from a dialect of the Maubila Indians, whom the French called Mobilians. Since the name plaquemine(s) had earlier been applied to a military fort and to a bend in the Mississippi River where the fort, was built, it is possible the parish name came indirectly from one or both of them rather than directly from the fruit of the persimmon tree.

1120 *Pointe Coupee Parish*

Cut point the Mississippi River formed by a change in its course— This parish is located in eastern Louisiana on the Mississippi, River and it is from a cut-off of the Mississippi that the parish got its French name. *Pointe coupee* means "cut point." As used here, it denotes a place where the Mississippi shortened itself to form a cut point of land. Apparently this cut point was already in the process of forming when Pierre le Moyne, Sieur d' Iberville (1661–1706) explored the area in 1699. To avoid navigating a 22 mile long curve in the Mississippi, Iberville had his men transport their boats about four miles across a neck of land here. To ease their portage, they cleared trees and underbrush that obstructed their way. By about 1722, the Mississippi River had carved a channel through this cleared area and adopted it as its main course.

1121 *Rapides Parish*

Former rapids in the Red River— The Red River flows through Rapides Parish in central Louisiana and the parish's name commemorates a former series of low rapids or waterfalls that were found here just above the city of Alexandria. *Rapides* is the French word for "rapids." At times these rapids represented a serious threat to navigation, even for the smallest of water craft. The parish was named almost two centuries ago and the rapids have long been gone. Norman M. Walker wrote an article, published in 1883, on geographic nomenclature in Louisiana in which he commented on these former rapids: "Scarcely a ripple marks their place to-day [sic]."

1122 *Red River Parish*

Red River— This parish was named for the major American river that flows through it. The Red River, a tributary of the Mississippi, was named for its color, acquired from the red clay and sandstone over which it flows. The red color is most noticeable when the river overflows its banks during floods. The Red River rises on the high plains of eastern New Mexico and flows across the Texas panhandle into Arkansas. There it turns south and enters Louisiana near the tri-state junction of Texas, Louisiana and Arkansas. The Red River flows southeast across Louisiana and divides into two branches just west of the Felicianas. One branch enters the Atchafalaya River, while the other joins the Mississippi River thus completing a journey of about 1,000 miles. There are two other significant Red Rivers in our nation; one that flows in Kentucky and Tennessee and another, called the Red River of the North, in the Minnesota-Dakota-Canada area. Both of these other Red Rivers are substantially shorter than ours. Our Red River is sluggish today but it was mighty in earlier days and cut crevices up to 800 feet deep in the Texas panhandle. Prior to the arrival of Europeans, much of the Red River in Louisiana was clogged with a strange mass of logs and river debris, forming logjams interspersed with patches of open water. Geologists have speculated that this "Great Raft," as it was called, dated back to at least the 15th century.

1123 *Richland Parish*

Rich, fertile character of its soil— Richland Parish, in northeastern Louisiana, was named for the fertility of its soil. Agricultural products which this rich soil has produced include cotton, corn, oats, hay, sugar cane, sweet potatoes, Irish potatoes and pecan. Truck vegetables and fruits are also grown in Richland Parish and both beef cattle and dairy cattle are raised here. The rich soil has nurtured large areas of timber, including oak, gum, cypress, hickory and poplar trees. The rich alluvial soil of the delta section of Richland Parish has been compared to the soil found along the productive regions of the Nile River in Africa.

1124 *Sabine Parish*

Sabine River— Sabine Parish lies in west-central Louisiana along the beautiful Sabine River, for which it was named. This navigable river begins in northeastern Texas, then flows southeast to form more than two-thirds of the Louisiana-Texas border. More than 500 miles long, the Sabine ends its journey by emptying into the Gulf of Mexico through Sabine Lake and Sabine Pass, near Port Arthur, Texas. The Sabine River was earlier named by Spanish explorers and one of the Spaniards' names for it was *Rio Sabinas*, which means "River of Cedar Trees." This name was chosen on account of the cedar trees (genus *Juniperus*) growing along its banks. The French later changed the name from Sabinas to Sabine. Numerous sources mention a different and incorrect, origin for the river's name. According to this version, a party of Frenchmen captured a number of attractive Indian women near the Sabine River and raped them. Since this incident resembled a famous gang-rape in Roman mythology, known as "The Rape of the Sabines," the river's name is said by some to derive from that incident in Roman mythology. It is certainly possible that some crude Frenchmen captured and gang-raped Indian women in this area, but even if they did, that incident was not the source of the river's name.

1125 *Saint Bernard Parish*

Old ecclesiastical district named Saint Bernard Parish— Saint Bernard Parish was created and named on March 31, 1807, by the legislature of Orleans territory. It was named for the existing ecclesiastical district of the Roman Catholic Church, named Saint Bernard Parish. The name of the church parish derived from the name of a specific church, named Saint Bernard Church. Saint Bernard Church had been built at the expense of the king of Spain

for the use of Spanish colonists, many of whom came to this area from Spain's Canary Islands in 1783, when Bernardo de Galvez (1746–1786) was serving as Spain's governor of Louisiana. A few sources indicate that the church's name was chosen to honor Governor Bernardo de Galvez directly. However, most sources indicate that the church's name honored Governor Galvez indirectly; i.e., that the church's name was chosen in honor of the patron saint of the governor, and that patron saint was named Saint Bernard. The Roman Catholic Church has several saints named Saint Bernard and sources consulted give scant information on which Saint Bernard was the patron saint of Governor Bernardo de Galvez. However, Robert I. Vexler's *Chronology & Documentary Handbook of the State of Louisiana* states that the particular Saint Bernard is Saint Bernard of Clairvaux. During a telephone conversation with the author on May 14, 1995, Father Donald M. Byrnes, the pastor of the present Saint Bernard Roman Catholic Church in Saint Bernard, Louisiana, confirmed that his church was named for Saint Bernard of Clairvaux.

Bernardo de Galvez (1746–1786)— A native of Spain and an officer in the Spanish army, Galvez served in combat against Portugal and in America fighting the native Indians. Appointed ad interim governor of Louisiana, Galvez served as Louisiana's governor from 1777 to 1785. Very early in his term as governor, he took as his wife Maria Feliciana (or Felicite) de Saint-Maxent. She was a native of New Orleans and this marriage increased the governor's popularity. Galvez provided significant aid to the American colonists in their war for independence from England. He also defeated the British at Baton Rouge, Natchez, Mobile and Pensacola. When his service as governor of Louisiana ended, Galvez was honored by Spain with Castilian titles of nobility and he was appointed captain general of the Floridas and Louisiana. In 1785 Galvez became viceroy of New Spain (Mexico) and he died there in 1786.

Saint Bernard (1090–1153)— The son of a French nobleman, Saint Bernard of Clairvaux was born in the family castle in Burgundy, France. As a young man he lived a charming but dissipated life. In the year 1113, he entered a monastery and in 1115 he was appointed as the abbot of a daughter monastery at Langres, in northeastern France. Under Bernard's leadership this monastery grew dramatically in membership and its name was changed to Clairvaux. Bernard and his monks at Clairvaux

subsequently founded some 70 monasteries. A few of these were in Britain. In the year 1128, Bernard drew up the statutes for the military order of Knights Templars, whose responsibilities included defense of the church. Bernard led a studious, ascetic life, yet it was he who kindled enthusiasm in France for the second crusade against the Turks; a crusade which was far less successful for the Christian warriors than was the first crusade. Bernard was active in church politics but he had his greatest influence as a spiritual teacher through his passionate piety and through his writings. He wrote some 340 sermons and more than 400 other works. Saint Bernard was canonized in the year 1174, little more than 20 years after his death on August 20, 1153.

1126 *Saint Charles Parish*

Old ecclesiastical district named Saint Charles Parish— Saint Charles Parish was created and named on March 31, 1807, by the legislature of Orleans territory. It was named for the existing ecclesiastical district of the Roman Catholic Church, named Saint Charles Parish. The ecclesiastical district had been named for its parish church, which had been erected about 1740. This church burned and was rebuilt in 1806. Its name, the Red Church of Saint Charles Borromeo, honored Saint Charles Borromeo (1538–1584).

Saint Charles (1538–1584)— Saint Carlo (Charles) Borromeo was born to a wealthy and titled Italian family. His father was Count Gilbert Borromeo, his mother was a member of the Medici family and his uncle, Giovanni Angelo de Medici (1499–1565), became pope, titled Pope Pius IV, in 1559. Soon after uncle became pope, Carlo was appointed as secretary of state and administrator of Milan. In an even greater act of nepotism, the pope appointed Carlo a cardinal and archbishop of Milan, even though Carlo had not yet been ordained as a priest. In keeping with his position in society, Carlo Borromeo kept a large household and spent money extravagantly. This extravagance disturbed Carlo and in his later years he did much to atone for it by providing relief to the poor and suffering. Carlo Borromeo provided relief to the poor during the famine of 1570 and assisted those in need during the plague of 1575–1576. He was an avid chess player and possessed excellent organization skills. These talents served to make him an able administrator and he played a significant role in bringing the Council of Trent (1545–1563) to a successful conclusion. In 1563 Carlo

Borromeo was finally ordained and by 1566 he had become active in implementing the reforms which he had advocated at the Council of Trent. During his later years he lived humbly to set an example for others and distributed his wealth to the needy. Saint Carlo Borromeo was canonized in 1610.

1127 *Saint Helena Parish*

Spanish district in West Florida named Distrito de Santa Helena— On October 27, 1810, President James Madison issued a proclamation announcing U.S. possession of West Florida as a part of Orleans territory. The governor of Orleans territory, William C. C. Claiborne (1775–1817), created several parishes out of this territory, also by proclamation. One of these new parishes was the Parish of Saint Helena. All or most of this parish had previously been the Spanish Distrito de Santa Helena, named for the Roman Catholic saint, Saint Helen (–330). The Distrito de Santa Helena had been created Bernardo de Galvez (1746–1786), when he captured this region for Spain from the British.

Saint Helen (–330)— Saint Helen, who was born about the year 255 in Bithynia in Asia Minor, was the mother of the Roman emperor, Constantine the Great (–337). It was not until she was in her 60's that Helen converted to Christianity and was baptized as a Christian. Helen and her son, the emperor, did much to promote the growth of Christianity and Constantine the Great is known as the first Christian emperor. Helen gave financial support to the erection of Christian churches. She loved the poor and it was her practice to dress humbly and modestly. When she was an elderly lady, in her 70's, Helen made a pilgrimage to the Holy Land. One legend has it that Helen discovered the cross on which Jesus Christ had been crucified during this trip.

1128 *Saint James Parish*

Old ecclesiastical district named Saint James Parish— Saint James Parish was created and named on March 31, 1807, by the legislature of Orleans territory. It was named for the existing ecclesiastical district of the Roman Catholic Church, which had derived its name from Saint James Church in the town of Saint James. The church had been named for the patron saint of Jacques Cantrelle (*Jacques* is the French word for "James"), who came from France to Louisiana in 1720. Cantrelle's patron saint was Saint James, an apostle of Jesus Christ. However, Jesus had two apostles named James. In order to minimize confusion, one of these saints is referred to as James the Great, while the other is known as James the Less or James the Younger. It is uncertain which of these two apostles was Jacques Cantrelle's patron saint and hence the original source of this parish's name.

Saint James (–)— James the Great was one of the twelve apostles of Jesus Christ. According to the Bible, James was a brother of John (Saint John the Evangelist), who was also one of Jesus' apostles. At the time that Jesus called James and John to join him as missionaries and teachers, the brothers were mending fishing nets at the Lake of Genesareth, where their father, Zebedee had a fishing boat. James and John remained with Jesus throughout his life and apparently were among his closest friends. James the Great is mentioned in the Gospel accounts about the healing of Peter's mother-in-law and the raising of the daughter of Jairus. Legend has it that James preached in Spain but if so, he returned to Jerusalem by about the year A.D. 42. There he was beheaded on orders from Herod Agrippa, thereby becoming the first apostle to be martyred. In some accounts the year of his death as given as about A.D. 42 but in others circa A.D. 44 is cited.

Saint James (–)— Saint James the Less, or James the Younger, was one of the twelve apostles of Jesus Christ. After Jesus was crucified, James became bishop of Jerusalem and he played a major role in the development of Christianity during its infancy. Legend tells us that he spent so much time on his knees in prayer that their skin hardened and came to resemble the knees of a camel. Although James was popular with the Jewish people and was held in veneration by some of them, about A.D. 62 their doctors of law, or Pharisees, arrested him and he was thrown off a temple roof. He survived the fall but was then stoned and clubbed to death.

1129 *Saint John the Baptist Parish*

Old ecclesiastical district named Saint John the Baptist Parish— This parish was created and named on March 31, 1807, by the legislature of Orleans territory. It was named for the existing ecclesiastical district of the Roman Catholic Church, whose name derived from the old settlement of Saint John. The village of Edgard is the parish seat of Saint John the Baptist Parish and it now stands where the former settlement named Saint John had been located. The Roman Catholic Church has canonized or beatified a large number of men who are referred to as Saint John the Baptist. Since no complete list of Roman Catholic saints exists, there can be no complete list of saints named Saint John the Baptist. Your author has located biographical material on about 16 saints whose name starts with John the Baptist; for example, the French saint, John the Baptist Vianney (1786–1859). However, at least twelve of these 16 saints can be ruled out as possibilities because they did not become saints until after the Louisiana ecclesiastical district had been created and named. Of the remaining four saints whose name contains John the Baptist, three are relatively obscure. As a practical matter, then, it seems likely, but not certain, that the parish's namesake was the famous Saint John the Baptist, who baptized Jesus. He has long been one of the most popular saints of the Roman Catholic Church.

Saint John the Baptist (–)— John lived an austere life in the desert of Judea, southwest of Jerusalem. Clothed in garments of camel's hair and living on a diet of locusts and wild honey, John ministered to men from Jerusalem and neighboring towns who flocked to visit him. He demanded two rites of those who came to him: an open confession of their sins and physical baptism. Jesus Christ was among those baptized by John and John apparently came to believe on that occasion that Jesus was the Messiah. King Herod Antipas feared John's popularity and power and resented John's criticism of his sex life. The king imprisoned John and had him beheaded.

1130 *Saint Landry Parish*

Old ecclesiastical district named Saint Landry Parish— This parish was created and named on March 31, 1807, by the legislature of Orleans territory. It was named for the existing parish of the Roman Catholic Church, whose name derived from a specific church, named Saint Landry, which had been built in 1777. That church had been named for a bishop of Paris, France, named Saint Landry, who is also referred to as Saint Landericus.

Saint Landry (–)— This devout Frenchman loved the poor and the sick. To get money to feed the poor during a famine, Saint Landry pawned his personal possessions as well as some vessels and furniture of the church. He was made bishop of Paris, France in the year 650. In those days there were no hospitals in Paris for the care of the sick, Tradition credits Saint Landry with founding the city's first real hospital. It was dedicated under the name of Saint Christopher. That hospital subsequently developed into a great institution named Hotel Dieu. The year of Saint Landry's death is uncertain. One source says he died about A.D. 656, another says about 661, while a third source says that the year of his death was no earlier than 660.

1131 *Saint Martin Parish*

Old ecclesiastical district named Saint Martin Parish— When the legislature of Orleans territory divided their territory into 19 parishes on March 31, 1807, the following language was contained in the act concerning Saint Martin Parish: "And the Parish of Attacapas [sic], called the Parish of Saint Martin shall form the nineteenth (parish)." On April 17, 1811, the territorial legislature created two parishes within the County of Attakapas (sic) to be known, respectively as the Parish of Saint Martin and the Parish of Saint Mary. (For a discussion of Louisiana's unusual use of both parishes and counties, see the material under Orleans Parish, above.) The name of the civil parish, Saint Martin, derived from the ecclesiastical parish of Saint Martin, whose name derived from the parish church, located in Saint Martinville. The church parish was established in 1765 and that date was inscribed on the cornerstone of the original church of Saint Martin. The church was named for Saint Martin, the patron saint of France.

Saint Martin (–)— Saint Martin of Tours was born in the fourth century, about A.D. 320 in the Roman province of Pannonia in eastern Europe. He was the son of a pagan Roman army officer and he served in the army himself. While in the army, Saint Martin was converted to Christianity and he left the army and returned to Pannonia. He suffered persecution there and was forced to flee, first to Italy, and later to France. In France, Saint Martin became a disciple of Saint Hilary of Poitiers. About the year 360, Saint Martin founded a monastery at Liguge, near Poitiers, France. A decade later he was made bishop of Tours, France. Saint Martin became famous as a reputed worker of miracles and he drew large numbers of visitors. To escape and find a degree of solitude, Saint Martin established the monastery of Marmoutier, near Tours, and he made that monastery his residence. He died about the year 400. He is the patron saint of France.

1132 *Saint Mary Parish*

Ecclesiastical district named Saint Mary Parish— This parish was created and named on April 17, 1811, by the legislature of Orleans territory. It was named for the existing parish of the Roman Catholic Church, whose name had derived from the Church of Saint Mary, located in the village of Franklin. But for which Saint Mary was the church named? Of several dozen sources consulted, only three have been located which address this question. Two of these sources state that the church was named for Saint Mary, the mother of Jesus Christ. However, an article in the *St. Mary & Franklin Banner-Tribune*, dated April 28, 1959, states that the name derived from "the French saint." Since the mother of Jesus was not French, we have a conflict.

There are some 75 saints named Mary, but relatively few of them are French. Moreover, some of the French saints were not beatified or canonized by the Roman Catholic Church until after the Saint Mary Church in Louisiana had been named. Even with these eliminations, there are at least six saints named Mary who might have been the French saint that the writer for the *St. Mary & Franklin Banner-Tribune* had in mind. The six known possibilities are:

— Saint Mary of the Incarnation
— Saint Mary Magdalen of Lidoin
— Saint Mary Ann Piedcourt
— Saint Mary Hanisset
— Saint Mary Tresel
— Saint Mary Dufour

Saint Mary of the Incarnation died in 1618 and was made a saint in 1791. The other five French saints were put to death by guillotine in Paris in 1794, during the French Revolution. The village of Franklin was not laid out until 1808 and that is where the Saint Mary Church was located. Hence it is possible that the church was named for one of these six French saints but it seems far more plausible that the church's namesake (and hence the parish's namesake) was Saint Mary, the mother of Jesus. But how do we dispose of the "French saint" origin cited by our trouble-making friend at the *St. Mary & Franklin Banner-Tribune*? We cannot disprove it but we can offer circumstantial evidence which would explain the error.

Saint Mary Parish was created by the legislature of Orleans territory simultaneously with the creation of Saint Martin Parish, Louisiana. Saint Martin Parish's namesake definitely was a French saint, Saint Martin of Tours. It seems possible, even probable, that the writer for the *Banner-Tribune* glanced hastily at some historical reference that mentioned the creation of Saint Mary Parish in the same sentence, or in the same paragraph, that contained the words "French saint," and mistakenly linked the two.

Thus two available sources state that the parish's name derived from the Virgin Mary, while the only other available source states that it derived from a "French saint." There is reason to doubt the French saint version. On balance, it seems most likely that the name of Saint Mary Parish, Louisiana derived from the mother of Jesus, Saint Mary.

Saint Mary (–)— It is a matter of dogma of the Roman Catholic Church that Saint Mary was the virgin mother of the second person of the Trinity, Jesus Christ. Because she had been selected to be the human mother of God, it was axiomatic that her soul be spotless, free of all sin from the moment of her conception. As the mother of Jesus, Mary is considered preeminent among all saints but the veneration and adoration bestowed on her are on a lower plane than those reserved for God in three persons, Father, Son and Holy Spirit.

1133 *Saint Tammany Parish*

Tamenend (–)— This parish was one of the Florida parishes and was created in 1810 by proclamation of the governor or Orleans territory, William C. C. Claiborne. The name honored a chief of the Delaware Indians, named Chief Tamenend. This chief had become very popular with his own people and with the American colonists in the late 17th century; so popular that almost a century later, in some quarters he was still remembered by the colonists and referred to as the colonists' "patron saint," Saint Tammany. He definitely was not a saint of the Roman Catholic Church. When William Penn (1644–1718) bought a large tract of land from the Delaware Indians in 1683 for his new colony of Pennsylvania, Chief Tamenend represented the Delaware Indians and his name appears on the deed (in the form Tamanen). Chief Tamenend was well remembered and esteemed in New York City in the late 1780's when populist citizens founded Tammany Hall, a political action group. Sadly, Tammany Hall later became synonymous with boss control and corruption in politics and government. The Delaware Indians had no written language so Chief Tamenend's name is found rendered with countless spellings, including Tammany. By whatever spelling, the name meant "the affable." A few sources say that the parish name was chosen because of the large number of Indians who lived there and/or had lived there. They were not Delaware Indians. Neither the Delaware Indians nor Chief Tamenend had any connection with Louisiana or the Florida parishes that are now in the state of Louisiana.

1134 *Tangipahoa Parish*

Tangipahoa Indians— The Tangipahoa Indians lived in the general vicinity of what is now Tangipahoa Parish, Louisiana. They lived along the Tangipahoa River and on both sides of Lake Pontchartrain, just north of New Orleans. The French explorer, Henri de Tonty, mentioned the Tangipahoa Indians and said that they resided, in 1682, on the lower Mississippi River. The Tangipahoa are believed to be extinct and they may have become extinct as a separate entity by the late 17th century. However, one source indicates that some Tangipahoa Indians may have migrated to the town of Philadelphia in the state of Mississippi and that they still lived there in the early 20th century. The meaning of the name *Tangipahoa* is uncertain but essentially all sources indicate that it relates to maize (Indian corn). Translations that have been mentioned include "Parched maize," "White maize," "Corn cob people," "Those who gather maize stalks" and "Those who gather maize cobs."

1135 *Tensas Parish*

Taensa Indians— This parish, in northeastern Louisiana, on the Mississippi River, was created in March, 1843, and named for the Natchez-speaking Indian tribe who formerly lived in this area. In 1682 the French explorer, Rene Robert Cavelier, Sieur de la Salle (1643–1687), descended the Mississippi River to its mouth. In La Salle's account of this expedition, he mentioned a "large and powerful tribe of Indians" on the lower Mississippi River, called the Taensas. The Taensa Indians were a relatively large tribe at that time and they were capable of savage and barbarous conduct. On one occasion the Taensa Indians were granted asylum by another tribe and permitted to live among them. The Taensa expressed their appreciation by overpowering their hosts, killing some of them and expelling the remainder. In another treachery, the Taensa offered hospitality to Chitimacha and Yakne Chitto Indians. The Taensa promptly imprisoned their guests and sold them into slavery. At the time of La Salle's 1682 expedition, the Taensa Indians

lived in the area of Lake Saint Joseph, a cut-off of the Mississippi River, in what is now Tensas Parish, Louisiana. They had seven or eight villages on the western end of this lake and another village a bit to the south, on the Tensas River, near present day Clayton in Concordia Parish. Probably as a result of diseases introduced by Europeans, the Taensa Indian population decreased rapidly very soon after their first contact with White men. By 1700 the Taensa Indians numbered about 700 or 800. During the 1700's the Taensa migrated extensively, living for a time in the Mobile, Alabama area and later along the Red River.

1136 *Terrebonne Parish*

Uncertain— This parish was created in 1822 from a portion of Lafourche Parish. The origin of its name is uncertain but these possibilities have been suggested:

1. A parish in Canada. According to this version, Henry Scheryler Thibodaux selected this name because the Canadian parish was the birthplace of his father-in-law.

2. The French words *terre bonne*, which mean "good land" or "rich land." This would be an appropriate description of the lands of the parish which consist of rich, alluvial soil. Agriculture is important in Terrebonne Parish. The principal crop is sugar cane.

3. A corruption of the name of an early settler named Derbonne or Derbene.

4. Terrebonne (or its variants: Therebonne and Derbonne), which was a titular appendage to the early Bienvenue-Dupre family. This family was prominent here in the 18th century.

5. Named for a prominent bay and/or stream here. The stream is Bayou Terrebonne and it flows through the parish in a southern direction from the parish seat of justice at Houma, Louisiana. It empties into Terrebonne Bay on the eastern shore of Terrebonne Parish.

These possible origins of the parish's name are not necessarily mutually exclusive. For example, the parish may have been named for Terrebonne Bay, whose name may have originated in the title of the Bienvenue-Dupre family.

1137 *Union Parish*

Uncertain— Very little information is available concerning the origin of this parish name. Lengthy newspaper articles that appeared about the time of the centennial celebration of Union Parish are silent about the source of the parish's

name. Most of the sources that comment on the meaning of Union Parish's name seem to do so in an offhand manner, indicating a probable absence of factual basis. For example:

— The spirit of unity in the United States

— The patriotic sentiment which activates the American people

— The sentiment of the time.

However, there is one possibility that is mentioned as the source of the parish's name that is both specific and credible. That source was a phrase contained in a speech delivered by Daniel Webster in the U.S. Senate in January, 1830. Senator Webster concluded this lengthy speech with the inspiring words "…Liberty *and* Union, now and forever, one and inseparable." This speech was said to be one of the most eloquent orations ever delivered in the United States senate. It no doubt was still well remembered nine years later, in March, 1839, when Union Parish was created and named. Louisiana was a slave state and it later seceded from the Union to join the Confederate States of America. However, that secession occurred in 1861, more than 20 years after the creation of Union Parish. When Union Parish was created in 1839, there were large numbers of people in the South who fervently hoped that the Union could somehow be preserved in spite of the tensions that were building between the North and the South over the slavery issue. It is thus plausible, but far from certain, that Union Parish owes its name to the word "Union" in Daniel Webster's inspiring senate speech of 1830.

1138 *Vermilion Parish*

Vermilion River & Vermilion Bay— Vermilion Parish is located in southern Louisiana, on the Gulf of Mexico. The parish was named for the Vermilion River, which flows through the parish from north to south, and for Vermilion Bay, on the Gulf of Mexico, where the Vermilion River ends. Both the Vermilion River and Vermilion Bay were named for their red, or vermilion, color, acquired from the color of the bluff lands along the course of the Vermilion River. The English word *vermilion* derived from the French word *vermillion*. The English spelling of the word, with one l, is the form used for the name of the parish, the river and the bay.

1139 *Vernon Parish*

Uncertain— The origin of Vernon Parish's name is uncertain but four possible explanations have been mentioned:

Mount Vernon—Vernon Parish was created and named in 1871. At that time, Louisiana already had a parish named in honor of George Washington. It was (and is) Washington Parish, in eastern Louisiana, which had been created in 1819. According to the Mount Vernon version of the origin of Vernon Parish's name, admirers of our first president wished to honor him with a second parish name and to do so, they chose the name of his home and estate, Mount Vernon. This estate overlooks the Potomac River, just 15 miles below our nation's capital. The estate originally consisted of some 5,000 acres when it was first acquired by the Washington family some four generations prior to George Washington. The estate was given its present name by George Washington's elder half-brother, Lawrence Washington. It was named in honor of Admiral Edward Vernon (1684–1757), of the British navy, under whom Lawrence Washington had served in the Caribbean Sea.

A popular teacher—According to this version, Vernon Parish was named for a popular teacher to avoid dispute among the parish founders, who were interested in having the parish named in their honor. The name of this teacher is unknown but it is mentioned that he had previously been an officer (one source specifies "lieutenant") in the British navy. It seems probable that some facts have been transposed here on account of the British naval source of Mount Vernon's name.

A race horse—One member of the committee appointed to suggest a name for the new parish was Joseph Moore. According to this explanation of Vernon Parish's name, at Moore's suggestion, the parish was named for his fast race horse in the hope that the parish would grow as fast as his horse could run. Horse racing was a popular sport here in 1871 at the time that Vernon Parish was created.

A mule—The story behind this one is just ridiculous enough to give it a degree of credibility. It seems that a store in Leesville, Louisiana, owned by Mr. I. O. Winfree and Dr. Edmund E. Smart, was frequently used by local men to trade and swap stories. According to this version of the source of the parish's name, it was at this store that the question of a name for the new parish was discussed and resolved. A barrel of liquor was at hand for those who wished to imbibe during their deliberations and by the time the parish's name was chosen, a number of the parish namers were rather intoxicated. Near the end of their discussion, a former slave (this was in 1871, during Reconstruction) came up to the store with his mule. The men asked him the name of his mule and when he replied "Vernon," the name for the new parish was obvious.

1140 *Washington Parish*

George Washington (1732–1799)—Washington was a native of Virginia. He served in Virginia's house of burgesses and became one of the colonies' leaders in opposition to British policies in America. He was a member of the first and second Continental Congresses and commander of all Continental armies in the Revolutionary War. Following victory in that war, Washington was elected to be the first president of the United States. This parish was formed in 1819.

1141 *Webster Parish*

Daniel Webster (1782–1852)—Webster was born in New Hampshire and represented that state in the U.S. House of Representatives. He later represented Massachusetts in both houses of the U.S. Congress and served as secretary of state under three presidents. Webster felt that slavery was evil but not as evil as disunion of the United States. This view was relatively moderate for a powerful northern politician and it won Webster favor in the South prior to the Civil War. This parish was created in 1871, after the Civil War, during Reconstruction.

1142 *West Baton Rouge Parish*

French words for "reddened Maypole" or, more simply, "red stick"—The French-Canadian naval commander and explorer, Pierre le Moyne, Sieur d' Iberville (1661–1706), was an explorer of the Mississippi River. On a voyage up the Mississippi in 1699, Iberville kept a journal that recorded the details of that exploration. In it he mentioned a "reddened Maypole," on the banks of a tributary of the Mississippi and he said that this pole separated the hunting grounds of two groups of Indians. The Indians' names are given in Iberville's Journal as Bayougoulas (or Bayogoulas) and Houmas (or Oumas). Iberville and others have mentioned that this reddened Maypole may also have been used for religious purposes by the Indians. European settlers in the vicinity of this red stick called their community Baton Rouge and that settlement grew to become the city which is the capital of the state of Louisiana. Two Louisiana parishes were created in this area named East Baton Rouge Parish and West Baton Rouge Parish. The names of these parishes, of course, have their origin in the "reddened Maypole" described by Iberville in 1699. Several other theories have been suggested for the origin of the name Baton Rouge but Professor William O. Scroggs examined them and provided a credible position in support of the "reddened Maypole" origin. Dr. Scroggs' article on this subject appeared in the August, 1917 issue (Vol. 8, No. 8) of the *Proceedings of the Historical Society of East and West Baton Rouge*. The title of the article is "Origin of the Name Baton Rouge."

1143 *West Carroll Parish*

Charles Carroll (1737–1832)—Carroll was a native of Maryland and he represented that state in the Continental Congress. He was one of the signers of the Declaration of Independence and he later represented Maryland as a U.S. senator in the first congress of the United States. Carroll lived to be the last surviving signer of the Declaration of Independence and several states recognized that distinction by naming counties and parishes in his honor. In 1832 Louisiana created and named Carroll Parish for him. Later, in 1877, Carroll Parish was divided into two parishes, East Carroll Parish and West Carroll Parish.

1144 *West Feliciana Parish*

Spain's Distrito de Feliciana in West Florida—On October 27, 1810, President James Madison issued a proclamation which claimed West Florida for the United States and authorized its military occupation as a part of our country's Orleans territory. At that time Spain claimed ownership of West Florida, which included the Distrito de Feliciana. On December 7, 1810, Territorial Governor William C. C. Claiborne (1775–1817) issued an ordinance creating the county of Feliciana from this newly acquired region. Fifteen days later, on December 22, 1810, Governor Claiborne issued a second proclamation establishing four parishes within the county of Feliciana. One of these four parishes was Feliciana Parish. On February 17, 1824, Feliciana Parish was divided into two parishes, East Feliciana Parish and West Feliciana Parish. The origin of the name *Feliciana* is uncertain and disputed. Most sources indicate that it was a word signifying "happy land" or "land of happiness." It has also been suggested that the name Feliciana was chosen in honor of the wife of a Spanish governor of Louisiana, Bernardo de Galvez (1746–1786). The wife of Bernardo de Galvez was Maria Feliciana (or Felicite) de Saint-Maxent. She was a native of New Orleans and a descendant of two distinguished French families, Saint-Maxent and Maroche. She was a widow of Juan Bautista d' Estrehan at the time of her marriage to Don Bernardo de Galvez on December 2, 1777. A third possibility for the source of the original name Feliciana has also been mentioned. According to this version, the Spanish explorer, Juan Ponce de Leon (1460–1521) bestowed the name Nueva Feliciana on the area "in recognition of its salubrity of climate, beautiful variety of forest, its clear waters and fertile soil."

1145 *Winn Parish*

Uncertain— Winn Parish was created in 1852. It probably was named for Walter O. Winn but other possibilities have also been mentioned so the origin of the parish's name is uncertain.

Walter O. Winn (–)— Walter O. Winn was a prominent lawyer from Alexandria, Louisiana and he was one of the founders of the Louisiana State Seminary of Learning & Military Academy in Pineville, Louisiana. That institution was the forerunner of Louisiana State University. Winn was a member of the first board of supervisors of the seminary. One of the other members of the board of supervisors was the governor of Louisiana. Walter O. Winn was a member of the state legislature when Winn Parish was created and he was the representative who introduced the bill in the lower house to create Winn Parish. In some accounts he is referred to as Colonel Walter O. Winn, but it is not clear whether this was a military title or merely an honorary reference. He was only 45 years old at the time of his death.

Richard Winn (–)— Richard Winn was a lawyer and had been a candidate to represent Louisiana in the U.S. House of Representatives. He was favored to win this seat in congress but he died shortly before the election was held.

A Methodist preacher— According to this version, Winn Parish was named for a Methodist preacher from Natchitoches, Louisiana. He was said to have been a member of the state legislature when the bill was introduced to create Winn Parish.

A surveyor or engineer— One story has is that both Winn Parish and its parish seat of Winnfield were named for the surveyor or engineer who fixed the bounds of both Winn Parish and Winnfield. A variation on this is that it was the surveyor or engineer who selected the name of the new parish and he chose Winn, in honor of Walter O. Winn (above).

Winfield Scott (1786–1866)— A native of Virginia, Scott joined the U.S. army in 1808. His heroic service in the War of 1812 resulted in rapid promotions to brevet major-general. He later played important military roles during the 1832 nullification crisis in South Carolina, against the Indians in Florida and as general-in-chief of the United States army during the Mexican War. Scott was the Whig party's candidate for president in 1852 but he lost to Franklin Pierce. When the Civil War broke out, Scott remained loyal to the Union side despite his southern roots but he retired from the U.S. army in October, 1861, on account of age and ill health.

The name that had first been proposed for this new parish was Dugdemona Parish and the legislature tentatively adopted that name but changed the name to Winn Parish before the parish was officially created. Dugdemona was the name of a fishing stream that traversed the borders of Winn Parish.

REFERENCES

Alleman, Elise A. "The Legend & History of the Place-Names of Assumption Parish." M.A. Thesis, Hill Memorial Library, Louisiana State University, Baton Rouge, 1936.

Arthur, Stanley C. *Old Families of Louisiana*. New Orleans, Harmanson, 1931.

Attwater, Donald. *Names & Name-Days*. London, Burns Oates & Washbourne, Ltd., 1939.

Barber, Patsy K. *Historic Cotile*. Baptist Message Press, 1967.

Bartlett, John. *Familiar Quotations*. Boston, Little Brown & Co., 1955.

Beauregard Parish Historical Society. *History of Beauregard Parish, Louisiana*. Dallas, Texas, Curtis Media Corp., 1986.

Belisle, John G. *History of Sabine Parish, Louisiana*. Sabine Banner Press, 1912.

Benedictine Monks of St. Augustine's Abbey, Ramsgate. *The Book of Saints*. New York, Thomas Y. Crowell Co., 1966.

Bentley, James. *A Calendar of Saints: The Lives of the Principal Saints of the Christian Year*. New York, Facts on File Publications, 1986.

Bergerie, Maurine. *They Tasted Bayou Water: A Brief History of Iberia Parish*. New Orleans, Pelican Publishing Co., 1962.

Boatner, Mark M. *Encyclopedia of the American Revolution*. Mechanicsburg, Pennsylvania, Stackpole Books, 1994.

Boeta, Jose R. *Bernardo de Galvez*. Madrid, Spain, Publicaciones Espanolas, 1977.

Bourgeois, Lillian C. *Cabanocey: The History, Customs & Folklore of St. James Parish*. New Orleans, Pelican Publishing Co., 1957.

Branner, John C. *Some Old French Place Names in the State of Arkansas*. Baltimore, 1899.

Brasseaux, Carl A. *The Founding of New Acadia*. Baton Rouge, Louisiana State University Press, 1987.

Brasseaux, Carl A. *In Search of Evangeline: Birth & Evolution of the Evangeline Myth*. Thibodaux, Louisiana, Blue Heron Press, 1988.

Brasseaux, Carl A., et al. *The Courthouses of Louisiana*. Lafayette, Louisiana, Center for Louisiana Studies, University of Southwestern Louisiana, 1977.

Briley, Richard. *Briley's Memorial History & Cemetery Directory of Winn Parish, Louisiana*. Montgomery, Louisiana, Mid-South Publishers, 1966.

Brown, Dave H. *A History of Who's Who in Louisiana Politics in 1916*. Louisiana Chronicle Democrat, 1916.

Byrnes, Reverend Donald M., Pastor of Saint Bernard Roman Catholic Church, Saint Bernard, Louisiana. Telephone conversation with the author on May 14, 1995.

Calhoun, James. *Louisiana Almanac: 1979–1980*. Gretna, Louisiana, Pelican Publishing Co., 1979.

Calhoun, Robert D. "A History of Concordia Parish, Louisiana." *Louisiana Historical Quarterly*, Vol. 15, No. 1. New Orleans: January, 1932.

Calhoun, Robert D. "The Origin & Early Development of County-Parish Government in Louisiana: 1805–1845." *Louisiana Historical Quarterly*, Vol. 18, No. 1. New Orleans: January, 1935.

Carleton, Mark T. *Louisiana History*, Vol. 10, No. 3. Summer, 1969.

The Catholic Encyclopedia. New York, Robert Appleton Co., 1908.

Chambers, Henry E. *A History of Louisiana*. Chicago, American Historical Society, Inc., 1925.

Conrad, Glenn R. *A Dictionary of Louisiana Biography*. New Orleans, Louisiana Historical Association, 1988.

Cupit, John T. *A Brief History of Vernon Parish, Louisiana*. Rosepine, Louisiana, 1963.

Current, Richard N. *Encyclopedia of the Confederacy*. New York, Simon & Schuster, 1993.

Davis, Edwin A. *Louisiana: The Pelican State*. Baton Rouge, Louisiana State University Press, 1959.

Davis, Edwin A. *Plantation Life in the Florida Parishes of Louisiana, 1836–1846: As Reflected in the Diary of Bennet H. Barrow*. New York, AMS Press, Inc., 1967.

Davis, Edwin A. *The Rivers & Bayous of*

Louisiana. Baton Rouge, Louisiana Education Research Association, 1968.

Davis, Ellis A. *The Historical Encyclopedia of Louisiana.* Louisiana Historical Bureau.

Dawson, Joseph G. *The Louisiana Governors: From Iberville to Edwards.* Baton Rouge, Louisiana State University Press, 1990.

Department of Commerce & Industry, State of Louisiana. *Louisiana Tourist Bulletin,* Vol. 3, No. 8. Baton Rouge: August 30, 1940.

Detro, Randall A. "Generic Terms in the Place Names of Louisiana: An Index to the Cultural Landscape." Ph.D. Thesis, Hill Memorial Library, Louisiana State University, Baton Rouge, 1970.

Dufour, Charles L. *Ten Flags in the Wind: The Story of Louisiana.* New York, Harper & Row, 1967.

Du Gard, Rene C. & Dominique C. Western. *The Handbook of French Place Names in the U.S.A.* Editions des Deux Mondes, 1977.

Eagles, Ray. "Winn Parish Creation Told by Historian." *Alexandria Daily Town Talk,* February 25, 1968.

Eakin, Sue. *Rapides Parish: An Illustrated History.* Northridge, California, Windsor Publications, Inc., 1987.

Encyclopaedia Britannica. Chicago, Encyclopaedia Britannica, Inc., 1971.

The Encyclopedia Americana. New York, Americana Corporation, 1977.

Englebert, Omer. *The Lives of the Saints.* New York, Barnes & Noble, Inc., 1994.

Eskew, Harry G., & Elizabeth Eskew. *Alexandria 'Way Down in Dixie.* Alexandria, Louisiana, 1950.

Eyraud, Jean M., & Donald J. Millet. *A History of St. John the Baptist Parish.* Marrero, Louisiana, Hope Haven Press, 1939.

Faber, Harold. *From Sea to Sea: The Growth of the United States.* New York, Farrar, Straus & Giroux, 1967.

Faragher, John M. *The Encyclopedia of Colonial & Revolutionary America.* New York, Facts on File, 1990.

Fontenot, Mary, & Paul B. Freeland. *Acadia Parish, Louisiana.* Baton Rouge, Claitor's Publishing Division, 1976.

Fortier, Alcee. *A History of Louisiana.* New York, Manzi, Joyant & Co., 1904.

Fortier, Alcee. *Louisiana: Comprising Sketches of Counties, Towns, Events, Institutions & Persons Arranged in Cyclopedic Form.* Atlanta, Southern Historical Association, 1909.

Fortier, Alcee. *Louisiana: Comprising Sketches of Parishes, Towns, Events, Institutions & Persons Arranged in Cyclopedic Form.* Century Historical Association, 1914.

Fortier, Alcee. *Louisiana Studies: Literature, Customs & Dialects, History & Education.* New Orleans, F. F. Hansell & Bro., 1894.

Foy, Felician A. *Catholic Almanac: 1994.* Huntington, Indiana, Our Sunday Visitor, Inc., 1994.

Frazar, Mrs. Lether E. "Early Annals of Beauregard Parish." M.A. Thesis, Hill Memorial Library, Louisiana State University, Baton Rouge, 1933.

Georgacas, Demetrius J. "From the River Systems in Anatolia: The Names of the Longest River." *Names: Journal of the American Name Society,* Vol. 12, Nos. 3–4. Madison, New Jersey: September–December, 1964.

Gilley, B. H. *North Louisiana.* Ruston, Louisiana, McGinty Trust Fund, 1984.

The Government of Louisiana. Baton Rouge, Louisiana Legislative Council, 1959.

Griffin, Harry L. *The Attakapas Country: A History of Lafayette Parish, Louisiana.* New Orleans, Pelican Publishing Co., 1959.

Hardin, J. Fair. *Northwestern Louisiana: A History of the Watershed of the Red River.* Louisville, Kentucky, Historical Record Association.

Hardon, John A. *Modern Catholic Dictionary.* Garden City, New York, Doubleday & Co., Inc., 1980.

History Book Committee of Edward Livingston Historical Association. *History of Livingston Parish, Louisiana.* Dallas, Texas, Curtis Media Corp., 1986.

The History & Government of Louisiana. Baton Rouge, Louisiana Legislative Council, 1964.

Hodge, Frederick W. *Handbook of, American Indians North of Mexico.* Totowa, New Jersey, Rowman & Littlefield, 1975.

Jones, Alison. *The Wordsworth Dictionary of Saints.* Hertfordshire, England, Wordsworth Editions, Ltd., 1994.

Kelly, Sean, & Rosemary Rogers. *Saints Preserve Us! Everything You Need to Know about Every Saint You'll Ever Need.* New York, Random House, 1993.

Kendall, John S. *History Of New Orleans.* Chicago, Lewis Publishing Co., 1922.

Kirkley, Gene. *A Guide to Texas Rivers & Streams.* Houston, Texas, Lone Star Books, 1983.

Klorer, John D. *The New Louisiana.* New Orleans, Franklin Printing Co., Inc.

Kniffen, Fred B. *The Indians of Louisiana.* Baton Rouge, Louisiana State University & Agricultural & Mechanical College, 1965.

Kniffen, Fred B., et al. *The Historic Indian Tribes of Louisiana.* Baton Rouge, Louisiana State University Press, 1987.

Laney, Rex. *Do You Know Louisiana?* Baton Rouge, State of Louisiana Department of Commerce & Industry, 1938.

Laney, Rex. *This Is Louisiana.* Baton Rouge, Tourist Bureau, State Department of Commerce & Industry, 1940.

Lang, Samuel. "Edward Livingston 1765 1856: Wrote New Deal for Felons 100 Years Ago." *Times Picayune,* July 21, 1935.

Lawrence, Bessie. "Timber & Troops Tell Story." *Alexandria Daily Town Talk,* July 15, 1957.

Leeper, Clare D. *Louisiana Places: A Collection of Columns from the Baton Rouge Sunday Advocate: 1960–1974.* Baton Rouge, Legacy Publishing Co., 1976.

Leeper, Clare D. *Louisiana Places: A Collection of Columns from the Baton Rouge Sunday Advocate: 1975 Supplement.* Baton Rouge, Legacy Publishing Co., 1976.

Lewis, W. H. *The Scandalous Regent: A Life of Philippe, Duc d' Orleans 1674–1723 & of His Family.* New York, Harcourt Brace & World, Inc., 1961.

Looking Backward: Memoirs of the Early Settlement of Morehouse Parish. Press of Mer Rouge Democrat, 1911.

Lorio, Elaine C. "The Place-Names of Pointe Coupee Parish." M.A. Thesis, Hill Memorial Library, Louisiana State University, Baton Rouge, 1932.

Louisiana: Its History, People, Government & Economy. Baton Rouge, Louisiana Legislative Council, 1955.

Love, Dhale & Eugene F. Love. *Looking Back: Winn Parish: 1852–1986.* Bossier City, Louisiana, Everett Companies, 1986.

Marchand, Sidney A. *The Flight of a Century (1800–1900) in Ascension Parish, Louisiana.* Donaldsonville, Louisiana, 1936.

Marchand, Sidney A. *The Story of Ascension Parish, Louisiana.* Donaldsonville, Louisiana, 1931.

Meyer, J. Ben. *Plaquemines: The Empire Parish.* Laborde Printing Co., Inc., 1981.

Michaud, Burris A. *Medical Doctors of Morehouse Parish, Louisiana.* Bastrop, Louisiana, 1982.

Mitchell, Jennie O. & Robert D. Calhoun. "The Marquis de Maison Rouge, the Baron de Bastrop & Colonel Abraham Morhouse: Three Ouachita Valley Soldiers of Fortune." *Louisiana Historical Quarterly,* Vol. 20, No. 2. New Orleans: April, 1937.

Morrison, Betty L. *A Guide to the Highway Historical Markers in Louisiana.* Gretna, Louisiana, Her Publishing Co., Inc., 1977.

Morrison, Betty L. *The Louisiana Parish Courthouses.* Gretna, Louisiana, Her Publishing Co., Inc.

New Catholic Encyclopedia. New York, McGraw-Hill Book Co., 1967.

New Larousse Encyclopedia of Mythology. Hamlyn Publishing Group, Ltd., London, England, 1968.

Notes for a History of St. Martin Parish. 1957.

"Old Seminary Near City Was Forerunner of LSU." *Alexandria Daily Town Talk*, July 15, 1957.

Parkerson, Codman. *Those Strange Louisiana Names*.

Perrin, William H. *Southwest Louisiana: Biographical & Historical*. New Orleans, Gulf Publishing Co., 1891.

Pinkston, George P. D. *A Place to Remember: East Carroll Parish, La: 1832–1976*. Baton Rouge, Claitor's Publishing Division, 1977.

Poole, T. W. *Some Late Words about Louisiana*. New Orleans, Crescent Steam Print, 1891.

Portre-Bobinski, Germaine & Clara M. Smith. *Natchitoches: The Up-to-Date Oldest Town in Louisiana*. New Orleans, Damermon-Pierson Co., Ltd., 1936.

Post, Lauren C. *Cajun Sketches: From the Prairies of Southwest Louisiana*. Louisiana State University Press, 1962.

Pourciau, Betty. *St. Martin Parish History*. Dallas, Texas, Curtis Media Corp., 1985.

Rand, Clayton. *Men of Spine in Mississippi*. Gulfport, Mississippi, Dixie Press, 1940.

Rand, Clayton. *Sons of the South*. New York, Holt, Rinehart & Winston, 1961.

Read, William A. "Istrouma." *Louisiana Historical Quarterly*, Vol. 14. New Orleans: January–October, 1931.

Read, William A. "Louisiana-French." *Louisiana State University Studies*, No. 5. Baton Rouge: 1931.

Read, William A. "Louisiana Place-Names of Indian Origin." *University Bulletin Louisiana State University & Agricultural & Mechanical College*, Vol. 19, No. 2. Baton Rouge: February, 1927.

The Reader's Digest Family Encyclopedia of American History. Pleasantville, New York, Reader's Digest Association, Inc., 1975.

Reed, Thomas B. *Modern Eloquence: Political Oratory*. Philadelphia, John D. Morris & Co., 1901.

Reeves, Miriam G. *The Felicianas of Louisiana*. Baton Rouge, Claitor's Book Store, 1967.

Reeves, Miriam G. *The Governors of Louisiana*. Gretna, Pelican Publishing Co., 1972.

Reynolds, Jack A. "Louisiana Place-Names of Romance Origin." Ph.D. Thesis, Hill Memorial Library, Louisiana State University, Baton Rouge, 1942.

Riffel, Judy. *A History of Pointe Coupee Parish & Its Families*. Baton Rouge, Le Comite des Archives de la Louisiane, 1983.

Riffel, Judy, & Arthur Perkins. *Iberville Parish History*. Dallas, Texas, Curtis Media Corp., 1985.

Robinson, Sinclair, & Donald Smith. *NTC's Dictionary of Canadian French*. Lincolnwood, Illinois, National Textbook Co., 1991.

Rowland, Dunbar. *Official Letter Books of W. C. C. Claiborne: 1801–1816*. Jackson, Mississippi, Mississippi Department of Archives & History, 1917.

St. Mary & Franklin Banner-Tribune. April 28, 1959.

Saucier, Corinne L. *History of Avoyelles Parish, Louisiana*. New Orleans, Pelican Publishing Co., 1943.

Scroggs, William O. "Origin of the Name Baton Rouge." *Proceedings of the Historical Society of East & West Baton Rouge*, Vol. 8, No. 8. Baton Rouge: August, 1917.

Shennan, J. H. *Philippe, Duke of Orleans: Regent of France 1715–1723*. London, England, Thames & Hudson, Ltd., 1979.

Spleth, Jo L. "Big Red Ruddy River of the North." *Texas Highways*, Vol. 38, No. 9. Austin, Texas: September, 1991.

Sternberg, Hilgard O. "The Names 'False River' & 'Pointe Coupee': An Inquiry in Historical Geography." *Louisiana Historical Quarterly*, Vol. 31, No. 3. New Orleans: July, 1948.

Swanson, Betsy. *Historic Jefferson Parish*. Gretna, Louisiana, Pelican Publishing Co., 1975.

Swent, Vivian. *Imperial Calcasieu Records: Antioch Primitive Baptist Church*. San Francisco, California, 1966.

Taft, William H. III. *County Names: An Historical Perspective*. National Association of Counties, 1982.

Taylor, Joe G. *Louisiana: A Bicentennial History*. New York, W. W. Norton & Co., Inc., 1976.

Thurston, Herbert J. & Donald Attwater. *Butler's Lives of the Saints*. New York, P. J. Kenedy & Sons, 1956.

Vexler, Robert I. *Chronology & Documentary Handbook of the State of Louisiana*. Dobbs Ferry, New York, Oceana Publications, Inc., 1978.

Wakelyn, Jon L. *Biographical Dictionary of the Confederacy*. Westport, Connecticut, Greenwood Press, 1977.

Walker, Norman M. "The Geographical Nomenclature of Louisiana." *The Magazine of American History*, Vol. 10. New York: July–December, 1883.

Walsh, Michael. *Butler's Lives of the Saints*. San Francisco, Harper & Row, 1985.

Webb, Walter P., et al. *The Handbook of Texas*. Austin, Texas State Historical Association, 1952.

Westlake, Donald E. *Brothers Keepers*. Greenwich, Connecticut, Fawcett Publications, Inc., 1975.

Whitbread, Leslie G. *Place-Names of Jefferson Parish, Louisiana*. Metairie, Louisiana, Jefferson Parish Historical Commission, 1977.

White, Dick. "Catahoula Parish Got Its Name." *Alexandria Daily Town Talk*, July 22, 1957.

Whittington, G. P. *Rapides Parish, Louisiana: A History*. Baton Rouge, Franklin Press, Inc.

Whittington, G. P. "Rapides Parish, Louisiana: A History." *Louisiana Historical Quarterly*, Vol. 15, No. 4. New Orleans: October, 1932.

Williamson, Frederick W., & George T. Goodman. *Eastern Louisiana*. Louisville, Kentucky, Historical Record Association.

Winn Parish Historical Society. *Winn Parish History*. Dallas, Texas, Taylor Publishing Co., 1985.

Wise, Erbon W. *Tall Pines: The Story of Vernon Parish*. Sulphur, Louisiana, West Calcasieu Printers, 1971.

Wise, L. F., & E. W. Egan. *Kings, Rulers & Statesmen*. New York, Sterling Publishing Co., Inc., 1967.

Work Projects Administration. *County-Parish Boundaries in Louisiana*. 1939.

Work Projects Administration. *Inventory of the Parish Archives of Louisiana-Assumption, Beauregard, Bossier, Lafourche, Ouachita, Plaquemines, Sabine & Terrebonne Parishes*. 1939–1942.

Work Projects Administration. *Louisiana: A Guide to the State*. New York, Hastings House, 1941.

Works Progress Administration. *Inventory of the Parish Archives of Louisiana-Calcasieu, Natchitoches, Saint Bernard & Saint Charles Parishes*. 1937–1938.

Wright, Muriel H. *A Guide to the Indian Tribes of Oklahoma*. Norman, University of Oklahoma Press, 1951.

Yoes, Henry E. *A History of St. Charles Parish to 1973*. Norco, St. Charles Herald Publishers, 1973.

Maine
(16 counties)

1146 *Androscoggin County*

Uncertain— Most sources indicate that this county was named directly for the Arosaguntacook Indians, but some sources state that it was named for the Androscoggin River, which had been named for the Arosaguntacook Indians.

Arosaguntacook Indians— The Arosaguntacook Indians were a tribe of the Abnaki confederacy, who at one time, had their village on the Androscoggin River, probably near what is now the city of Lewiston, in Androscoggin County. The Arosaguntacook lived near the edge of the first English settlements in Maine so they were drawn into numerous wars with the English there. Their village was burned by the English in 1690. Other tribes joined the Arosaguntacook Indians and since the Arosaguntacook were the main tribe, the Abnaki dialect was adopted by the combined tribes and they were called, collectively, the Arosaguntacook. After a defeat in 1725, the combined Arosaguntacook tribe moved to Saint Francis, Canada. The Indians had no written language so it was left to Europeans to render these Indians' name in written form. Numerous versions are found and they are often disparate. In his encyclopedic *Handbook of American Indians North of Mexico*, Frederick W. Hodge uses Arosaguntacook as the primary rendering. The *Dictionary of Indian Tribes of the Americas*, published in 1993, concurs in this rendering of the tribe's name. The meaning of the name, by whatever spelling, seems to relate to fish, and particularly to a place where fish are cured by drying and smoking. The name Androscoggin has been applied in Maine to a river, an island, a lake and the present Androscoggin County. The Andros portion was derived in compliment to Edmund Andros (1637–1714). In June, 1686, Andros had been commissioned as England's royal governor of the Dominion of New England, which included Maine.

Edmund Andros (1637–1714)— Andros was born on the English Channel Island of Guernsey on December 6, 1637. In 1666, with the rank of major in the English army, Andros sailed with an expedition to the West Indies to defend England's possessions there against intrusions by the Dutch. Andros was subsequently appointed

to a wide variety of prestigious positions in England's colonies and possessions in North America. In June, 1686, he was commissioned royal governor of the Dominion of New England. Before returning to England in 1698, Andros had governed and/or ruled the colony of New York, all of British New England, both East Jersey and West Jersey, Virginia and Maryland. Meanwhile, back in England, honors were being heaped upon him. He was knighted about 1681 and was made a gentleman of the privy chamber to King Charles II in 1683. Andros died in London, England, in February, 1714.

Androscoggin River— The Androscoggin rises in Umbagog Lake on the Maine-New Hampshire border and then flows south in New Hampshire. It abruptly turns east to cross the Maine border and flows into the Kennebec River near Bath, Maine. The length of the Androscoggin River has been estimated to be 157 miles.

1147 *Aroostook County*

Aroostook River— The Aroostook River originates in northeastern Piscataquis County in northern Maine and travels northeast through Aroostook County to enter the Canadian province of New Brunswick. There it ends its journey by joining the Saint John River. The Aroostook River is approximately 140 miles long. *Aroostook* in an Indian name. Its meaning is uncertain but translations which have been suggested include "Beautiful river," "Good water," "Smooth water" (for easy passage by boats) and "Shining river."

1148 *Cumberland County*

William Augustus, Duke of Cumberland (1721–1765)— William Augustus was a son of England's King George II (1683–1760). Born on April 15, 1721, William was made a royal duke and given the title duke of Cumberland in July, 1726. Cumberland was educated for the navy but was permitted to follow his preference for the army and was given the rank of major-general in 1742. He was a rather poor general and his troops were defeated in several important actions on the European continent. His only significant military victory was at home in the British Isles,

where he defeated Prince Charles Edward Stuart (1720–1788), the pretender to the thrones of Scotland and England. This victory took place at Culloden, Scotland in 1746. The duke's name is shown in most works as William Augustus, but in some the form William August is used. Cumberland County was created in 1760 when Maine was part of Massachusetts Bay, a British colony. The name was chosen as a compliment to the British throne.

1149 *Franklin County*

Benjamin Franklin (1706–1790)— Franklin was a native of Massachusetts who moved to Pennsylvania in his teens. Poverty denied him a formal education but he became the leading printer and editor in North America. Franklin gained fame for his discoveries and inventions in the physical sciences and he distinguished himself as author, philosopher and diplomat. He was a signer of the Declaration of Independence and an important member of the convention which framed the U.S. Constitution. Franklin County was created in 1838.

1150 *Hancock County*

John Hancock (1737–1793)— A native of Massachusetts and a graduate of Harvard, Hancock served in the Massachusetts legislature and was president of the Massachusetts provincial congress. He was elected to the Second Continental Congress and became its president. As president of the Continental Congress when the Declaration of Independence was signed, he was, on July 4, 1776, the first signer of that document. He signed it with such a flourish that the name John Hancock became a synonym for "signature." He later commanded the Massachusetts militia, served as governor of that state for many years and presided over the Massachusetts convention that ratified the U.S. Constitution. This county was created on June 25, 1789, when Maine was part of the state of Massachusetts. At the time that the county was created, John Hancock was the governor of Massachusetts.

1151 *Kennebec County*

Kennebec River— The Kennebec, one of

Maine's most important rivers, rises in Moosehead Lake in central Maine and flows south to the Atlantic Ocean. During its journey of some 150 miles, the Kennebec traverses the length of Kennebec County. The Kennebec enters the Atlantic Ocean about a dozen miles below the city of Bath, Maine. The Kennebec is navigable for large vessels from the ocean up to Bath, a fact which led to Bath's eminence in the shipbuilding industry. The river was named by the Abnaki Indians. A number of translations have been suggested for the river's name. They include "Long, quiet water," "Long, level river without rapids" and "Long water place." The translations which indicate a slow river without rapids accurately describe only the lower portion of the river. The upper portion of the Kennebec that the Indians knew was swift with numerous rapids, which were dangerous to their canoes. Some sources mention that the river's name resembles the Indians' word for "snake" and suggest the name may have been chosen because some snakes are long. This possible origin of the name is considered to be unlikely. Kennebec County was created in 1799, while Maine was part of the state of Massachusetts.

1152 *Knox County*

Henry Knox (1750–1806)— This Massachusetts native participated in many of the important military engagements of the American Revolution and rose to the rank of major-general. After the war, Knox commanded West Point and he conceived and organized the Society of Cincinnati, an elite group of former Revolutionary officers. In 1785 he was appointed secretary of war under the Articles of Confederation and he retained that position in the first cabinet of the United States under President George Washington.

1153 *Lincoln County*

Town of Lincoln, England— Lincoln County was created on May 28, 1760, while Maine was part of Massachusetts Bay, a royal colony of England. The county's name was chosen in compliment to Thomas Pownall (1722–1805), who was the royal governor of Massachusetts Bay Colony from 1757 to 1760. Pownall was born in Lincoln, England and attended grammar school there.

Lincoln, England— During the years that England was occupied by the Roman Empire, Lincoln was an important town named Lindum Colonia. A castle was built here during the reign of King William I and a magnificent cathedral with three

towers was erected about the beginning of the 13th century. The town of Lincoln, in eastern England, was one of the wealthiest towns in provincial England during the Middle Ages. In the 1300's it ranked 6th in wealth (excluding London and its suburbs) and by the early 1500's it had only slipped to the 15th rank. Its wealth came largely from clothing and other textile manufactures but by 1515, this industry was disappearing from Lincoln, leaving it in decay. The imposition by the town fathers of inward-looking restrictions on craftsmen and capitalists hastened Lincoln's economic decline from its medieval greatness. Lincoln suffered major plagues during the decades of the 1580's and 1590's but lesser plagues were in almost constant attendance in Lincoln for centuries. In spite of all this, Lincoln remained one of England's most populous towns. Its population was estimated to be 4,100 in the year 1676. Railroad trains began to provide service to Lincoln in 1846. The town of Lincoln is the county town of Lincolnshire.

1154 *Oxford County*

Town of Oxford, Massachusetts— Oxford County, Maine was created in 1805, when Maine was still a part of the state of Massachusetts. One of the early settlers of what is now Oxford County, Maine, chose the county's name in honor of the town of his birth in Massachusetts proper; i.e., he chose the name in honor of the town of Oxford, Massachusetts. The name of this early settler is given in some accounts as David Leonard. In others, General Learned is cited. These names are similar enough to prompt the thought that they may refer to the same man. Oxford, Massachusetts, had been named for one or more of the Oxfords in England: Oxford University, in the city of Oxford, which is the county borough of Oxfordshire, England. According to one source, the name *Oxford* originally referred to a "ford used by wagons at a river or stream for crossing with oxen."

Oxford, Massachusetts— The town of Oxford is located in central Massachusetts, in Worcester County, about ten miles south-southwest of the city of Worcester. Historically, Oxford's main products were steel springs and woolens. A town was originally settled here by the French in 1687 but they abandoned it on account of Indian attacks. Settlers from other Massachusetts communities reestablished a community here in 1713 and named it Oxford.

Oxford University— England's famous Oxford University, whose history dates back to the 12th century, consists of some 20 colleges and five halls, all located in Oxford, England. The colleges are very wealthy but the wealth is retained by the Church of England. One of Oxford's most famous colleges is Christ Church, which was founded in the 1500's. Most of the university's buildings were erected during the 15th, 16th and 17th centuries.

Oxford, England— Located in south-central England at the confluence of the Thames and Cherwell Rivers, Oxford is about 50 miles west-northwest of London. The city of Oxford, which is the county borough of Oxfordshire, is dominated by Oxford University. Portions of medieval walls from the 13th century can still be seen here.

Oxfordshire, England— This English county is some 50 miles long and 30 miles wide. It has no factories and little industrial activity so its air is relatively pure. Hunting for game is a popular local sport. Corn and grass are the chief products of Oxfordshire's fertile soil. This county has only one city, its county borough of Oxford, but it also has some 12 towns and 50 villages.

1155 *Penobscot County*

Penobscot River— This county was created in 1816, when Maine was still part of the state of Massachusetts, and named for the important river which flows through it. The river was named for the Penobscot Indian tribe.

Penobscot River— The Penobscot River is formed by the confluence, in north-central Penobscot County, of the East branch and the West branch. It flows some 100 miles south to enter the Atlantic Ocean via Penobscot Bay. The river is navigable for large ships up to Bangor, Maine, the county seat of Penobscot County. The Penobscot, together with its East and West headwaters, is the longest river in Maine and almost all of it lies within Penobscot County. This river was frequently used by both Indians and Whites for travel to and from Canada. The name Penobscot means "the rocky river" or "the rocky place," or "the descending ledge place." The river's name in all of these translations referred to the rapid series of waterfalls between Old Town, Maine and Bangor.

Penobscot Indians— The Penobscot are a tribe of the former Abnaki Indian confederacy and at one time they were among the largest tribes of that confederation. According to their own tradition, they came to Maine from the southwest and it is known that their influence extended at least as far southwest as the Merrimack River in southern New Hampshire. Early in the 16th century, the Penobscot were encountered in Maine along both banks of the Penobscot River by European explorers. The French explorer, Samuel de Champlain, encountered Penobscot Indians in 1604 or 1605. The Penobscot assisted the French in their battles with the English until 1749 when they made a treaty of peace. Unlike other tribes of the Abnaki confederacy, the Penobscot did not migrate to Canada in the 18th century but remained in Maine. According to the U.S. census of 1930, there were 301 Indians living in Penobscot County, Maine. Most of them were Penobscots.

1156 *Piscataquis County*

Piscataquis River— This northern Maine county was created in 1838 and named for its most important river, the Piscataquis. The river flows from west to east and is entirely contained within Piscataquis County. Its name is easily confused with the better-known Piscataqua River, in southernmost Maine, which forms part of the boundary between Maine and New Hampshire. There is even confusion regarding the spelling of the county's name. In its 1979 issue of the *National ZIP Code & Post Office Directory*, the U.S. Postal Service rendered the county's name as *Piscataq*. The letterhead currently in use by the Piscataquis County commissioners confirms that the correct spelling of the county's name is *Piscataquis*. The Piscataquis River is the largest tributary of the Penobscot River and joins the Penobscot at Howland, Maine. The river was named by the Abnaki Indians and various translations of their name for the river have been suggested including "A branch of the river," "At the river branch," "At the little divided stream" and "Little branch stream."

1157 *Sagadahoc County*

The lower section of the Kennebec River— This county was created in 1854, along the lower portion of the Kennebec River. The Abnaki Indians' name for this lower, main channel, of the Kennebec was Sagadahoc and it was also called by that name by early White explorers and settlers. The portion of the Kennebec River that was called Sagadahoc started at the confluence of the Kennebec and Androscoggin Rivers at Merrymeeting Bay and extended to the Atlantic Ocean. The Kennebec is one of

Maine's most important rivers and its lower section is navigable for large vessels from the ocean for about a dozen miles up to the city of Bath, Maine, the county seat of Sagadahoc County. Bath became eminent in the shipbuilding industry as a result of its location on the navigable (Sagadahoc) portion of the Kennebec River. Translations which have been suggested for the Indians' name *Sagadahoc* include: "The mouth of the river," "The mouth or entrance into a river" and "The outflowing of the swift stream as it nears the sea." The name *Sagadahoc* was also an old name for the Androscoggin River.

1158 *Somerset County*

Somersetshire, England— Ferdinando Gorges (–1647) was an English military and naval commander, who was awarded an enormous tract of land in North America including a large section of the present state of Maine. He was made lord proprietary of Maine in 1639. It was Gorges who selected the name New Somersetshire, naming it after Somersetshire, the county in England where his residence was located. This English name was discontinued for a time in Maine but it was called to active duty again in 1809 when our Somerset County was created. In 1809 Maine was still part of the state of Massachusetts.

Somersetshire, England— This county in southwestern England lies on Bristol Channel. The Somersetshire area was conquered by the Roman Empire about A.D. 43 and remains from their period of occupation can still be seen. By A.D. 658 the area was under control of the West Saxons. Subject to periodic incursions by the Danes, Somersetshire later was controlled, almost entirely, by the Norman invaders from France. This county is bounded on three sides by hills and on the fourth side by the sea. Considerable areas of the county are sparsely populated. Below the hills, Somersetshire's climate is mild. The name *Somerset* evolved from various earlier Latin and Old English forms. It originally meant "the Somerset people" and later became the name of the district. "Dwellers at Somerton" and "people dependent on Somerton" were early translations of the names which finally evolved into Somersetshire.

1159 *Waldo County*

Samuel Waldo (1695–1759)— Waldo was a merchant, capitalist and land speculator in Boston at the time that Massachusetts Bay was an English colony. Among his imports were Black slaves from Africa. He

also was an official mast-agent, charged with securing white pines in New England and delivering them to the coast for the British royal navy. Waldo's chief interest, however, was land speculation and he acquired an enormous tract of land in Massachusetts Bay Colony in what is now coastal Maine. He was active in attracting settlers to his land in Maine, which became known as the Waldo patent. During King George's War, Waldo served England as a brigadier-general fighting the French. In the Louisbourg campaign in 1745, Waldo was second in command of Massachusetts forces. He died on May 23, 1759, at Bangor.

1160 *Washington County*

George Washington (1732–1799)— Washington was a native of Virginia. He served in Virginia's house of burgesses and became one of the colonies' leaders in opposition to British policies in America. He was a member of the first and second Continental Congresses and commander of all Continental armies in the Revolutionary War. Following victory in that war, Washington was elected to be the first president of the United States. This county was created on June 25, 1789, just two months after George Washington became our first president. Maine was part of the state of Massachusetts at that time.

1161 *York County*

Uncertain— In the spring of 1652, England permitted its colony in New England, named Massachusetts Bay Colony, to annex a portion of the Province of Maine. Later that same year, on November 20, 1652, York County (rendered in some accounts as Yorkshire) was created by the general court (i.e., the legislature) of Massachusetts Bay Colony. The southern section of York County, including the town of York, Maine, was the first area of Maine to contain civilized communities and from the 1690's until 1760, York County contained all of the present state of Maine. The origin of the county's name is uncertain. Some authorities say that it was named for the town of York in Maine while others say that it was named for the town of York or the county of Yorkshire, in England. These suggestions are plausible and not necessarily mutually exclusive. However, other authorities state that York County owes its name to King James II (1633–1701) of England, who was duke of York and Albany in 1652 when this county was created. The case for the English town or county being the source of

York County, Maine's name (either directly or indirectly via the town of York in Maine) is better demonstrated but the possibility that the county was named for King James II cannot be dismissed. In 1652, when York County was created, James was the brother of the king of England, Charles II (1630–1685).

York, Maine — As early as 1640, the English name of York had been acquired by portions of Ferdinando Gorges' enormous tract of land in Maine. The town of York, in southernmost Maine, is a survivor of that era. York, which lies on the Atlantic Ocean, had been settled in 1624 by the English captain, John Smith (1580–1631), who had explored the area in 1614. The town of York, Maine, owes its name to the town of York (now a major city) and/or the county of Yorkshire, in England. In its early years York, Maine subsisted primarily on farming, fishing, lumbering and fur-trading. By 1742 shipbuilding had also become an important industry here. Volunteers from York rushed to Concord in Massachusetts in April, 1775, immediately after hearing of its attack by British redcoats. In later years York became a summer resort community for wealthy vacationers from Boston and elsewhere. Although the beaches at York now have a gaudy atmosphere, most of York, which is away from the ocean, retains its early New England charm.

York and Yorkshire, England — Lying about mid-way between London and Edinburgh, Scotland, with a population of several million, the city of York and the county of Yorkshire, in England, represent one of England's most important metropolitan areas. Yorkshire borders on the North Sea and extends almost to the Irish Sea. The Roman empire conquered the area and built a strategic fortress here about A.D. 72. Remains of this fortress can still be seen. The Yorkshire plain is fertile for agriculture and the West Riding area is rich in coal deposits. The Danes captured York in A.D. 867 and its present name came from their name *Yorvick*. York was later subjugated by the West Saxons and in 1066 it fell to the Norman invaders from France.

King James II (1633–1701) — James was the second surviving son of England's King Charles I (1600–1649). He was given the title of duke of York and Albany soon after his christening. When James' father died, his elder brother, Charles, succeeded to the throne as King Charles II (1630–1685). In 1664 King Charles II made an enormous grant of land to his brother, the duke of York and Albany, which included York County, Maine. The duke was awarded more power over his domain than any other English proprietor. Although King Charles II had many children, none of them were legitimate so when King Charles II died in 1685, his brother James became king of England as King James II. The first wife of the duke of York and Albany had been Anne Hyde, who died in 1671. In 1673 James remarried to Mary of Modena (1658–1718), a Catholic, and sometime during this period James professed his own Catholicism. This spelled his eventual downfall as king. In 1689 the throne passed to William of Orange (1650–1702), who ruled as joint sovereign with his wife, Queen Mary II (1662–1694). Mary was a daughter of King James II. The former King James II devoted the final years of his life to religious exercises.

REFERENCES

Andrews, Allen. *The Royal Whore: Barbara Villiers, Countess of Castlemaine*. Philadelphia, Chilton Book Co., 1970.

Attwood, Stanley B. *The Length & Breadth of Maine*. Orono, University of Maine, 1973.

Chadbourne, Ava H. *Maine Place Names and the Peopling of Its Towns*. Portland, Bond Wheelwright Co., 1955.

Coe, Harrie B. *Maine: Resources, Attractions and Its People*. New York, Lewis Historical Publishing Co., Inc., 1928.

Dictionary of Indian Tribes of Americas. Newport Beach, California, American Indian Publishers, Inc., 1993.

Douglas-Lithgow, R. A. *Dictionary of American-Indian Place & Proper Names in New England*. Salem, Massachusetts, Salem Press Co., 1909.

Duncan, Roger F. *Coastal Maine: A Maritime History*. New York, W. W. Norton & Co., 1992.

Eckstorm, Fannie H. "Indian Place-Names of the Penobscot Valley & the Maine Coast." *Maine Bulletin*, Vol. 44, No. 4. Orono: November, 1941.

Ekwall, Eilert. *The Concise Oxford Dictionary of English Place-Names*. Oxford, Oxford University Press, 1960.

Encyclopaedia Britannica. Chicago, Encyclopaedia Britannica, Inc., 1971.

Grant, Bruce. *Concise Encyclopedia of the American Indian*. Avenel, New Jersey, Wings Books, 1989.

Hatch, Louis C. *Maine: A History*. New York, American Historical Society, 1919.

Hodge, Frederick W. *Handbook of American Indians North of Mexico*. Totowa, New Jersey, Rowman & Littlefield, 1975.

Hubbard, Lucius L. *Woods & Lakes of Maine*. Somersworth, New Hampshire, New Hampshire Publishing Co., 1971.

Huden, John C. *Indian Place Names of New England*. New York, Museum of the American Indian, Heye Foundation, 1962.

Kenyon, J. P. *Dictionary of British History*. Ware, England, Wordsworth Editions, Ltd., 1992.

Kleber, John E. *The Kentucky Encyclopedia*. Lexington, University Press of Kentucky, 1992.

McCague, James. *The Cumberland*. New York, Holt, Rinehart & Winston, 1973.

Maine Register, State Year-Book & Legislative Manual. Portland, Fred L. Tower Cos., 1954.

Maine Writers Research Club. *Maine: Past & Present*. Boston, D. C. Heath & Co., 1929.

Moule, Thomas. *The County Maps of Old England*. London, Studio Editions, 1990.

National ZIP Code & Post Office Directory. Washington, D.C., U.S. Postal Service, 1979.

Patten, John. *English Towns: 1500–1700*. Kent, England, William Dawson & Sons, Ltd., Cannon House, 1978.

Paullin, Charles O. *Atlas of the Historical Geography of the United States*. Carnegie Institution of Washington and the American Geographical Society of New York, 1932.

Price, Edward T. *Dividing the Land: Early American Beginnings of Our Private Property Mosaic*. Chicago, University of Chicago Press, 1995.

Rutherford, Phillip R. *The Dictionary of Maine Place-Names*. Freeport, Maine, Bond Wheelwright Co., 1970.

Smith, Marion J. *A History of Maine: From Wilderness to Statehood*. Portland, Falmouth Publishing House, 1949.

Stahl, Jasper J. *History of Old Broad Bay & Waldoboro*. Portland, Bond Wheelwright Co., 1956.

Sturtevant, William C. *Handbook of North American Indians*. Washington, D.C., Smithsonian Institution, 1978.

Swanton, John R. *The Indian Tribes of North America*. Washington, D.C., Smithsonian Institution Press, 1952.

Taft, William H. III. *County Names: An Historical Perspective*. National Association of Counties, 1982.

Varney, George J. *A Gazetteer of the State of Maine*. Boston, B. B. Russell, 1882.

Vexler, Robert I. *Chronology & Documentary Handbook of the State of Maine*. Dobbs Ferry, New York, Oceana Publications, Inc., 1978.

Vogel, Virgil J. *Iowa Place Names of Indian Origin*. Iowa City, University of Iowa Press, 1983.

Whitmore, William H. "On the Origin of the Names of Towns in Massachusetts." *Proceedings of the Massachusetts Historical Society*, Vol. 12. Cambridge: 1873.

Whitworth, Rex. *William Augustus,* *Duke of Cumberland: A Life*. London, England, Leo Cooper, 1992.

Williamson, William D. *The History of the State of Maine*. Hallowell, Glazier, Masters & Smith, 1839.

Works Progress Administration. *Maine: A Guide 'Down East'*. Boston, Houghton Mifflin Co., 1937.

Maryland

(23 counties)

1162 *Allegany County*

Potomac River — This county, which was created in 1789, is located in far western Maryland, near the end of the state's panhandle. The Potomac River separates Allegany County, Maryland, from the state of West Virginia. All sources consulted agree that *allegany* is an Indian word and there is a consensus that the name came from the Indian word *oolikhanna*, which meant "beautiful stream." This beautiful stream is the Potomac River, which is formed by the confluence of the North Branch and the South Branch. The Potomac flows some 290 miles from its sources in West Virginia, in a generally eastern course, touching Maryland and Virginia. As the Potomac nears the end of its journey, it crosses through our nation's capital, Washington, D.C., where it abruptly turns south to pass the United States Marine Corps' base at Quantico, Virginia. The river ends its journey by emptying into Chesapeake Bay, southeast of Washington. The Potomac River is navigable for large vessels from Chesapeake Bay north to Washington, D.C.

1163 *Anne Arundel County*

Anne Arundell Calvert (1615–1649) — This county was created in 1650, when Cecil Calvert (1605–1675) was the second lord Baltimore and the lord proprietor of Maryland. (In a number of accounts Cecil Calvert's given name is rendered as Cecilius and one source spells it Caecillius.) Anne Arundel County was named for Cecil Calvert's wife, Anne Arundell Calvert, a daughter of Thomas, Baron Arundell of Wardour (1560–1639). Her mother was Anne Philopson. Cecil Calvert was a Catholic and by marrying Anne Arundell in 1628, Calvert allied himself with one of the greatest Catholic houses in England. Anne's grandfather was Sir Matthew Arundell and her great-grandfather, Sir Thomas Arundell, was beheaded on Tower Hill in 1552. Charles Calvert (1637–1715), who became the third lord Baltimore, was the son of Anne Arundell and Cecil Calvert. Many Maryland history books render Anne's name with one "l" as "Arundel" and that is the style used for the county's name. However, Great Britain's prestigious *Concise Dictionary of National Biography* uses two "l's" (i.e., Arundell), for her father. Anne Arundell Calvert died in 1649 at the age of 34. In 1654, members of the Puritan religious movement revolted against the established Maryland government and took control of it for themselves. Their religion frowned on such ritual trappings as images and vestments, which were plentiful in the Roman Catholic Church. The Puritans found the county name Anne Arundel to be offensive, since it honored a Roman Catholic. In 1654 the Puritans changed the county's name to Providence, the name which had been used for the area until April, 1650, when Anne Arundel County was created. The Puritans' name change was short-lived. In 1656 the name Anne Arundel was restored as the county's name.

1164 *Baltimore County*

Baltimore, Ireland, the Irish barony of the Calverts — In February, 1625, England's King James I (1566–1625) made George Calvert (–1632) a baron with the title lord Baltimore, making him the first lord Baltimore. Calvert later petitioned the English crown for a grant of land in North America, on which to establish a new English colony. In June, 1632, shortly after George Calvert's death, this petition was granted by England's King Charles I (1600–1649). The grant permitted establishment of a colony (Maryland) north of the Potomac River. At the time that this petition was granted, George Calvert's son, named Cecil (1605–1675), had become the second baron of Baltimore and the 1632 grant by the English crown made Cecil Calvert lord proprietor of Maryland. The grant contained the phrase "absolute lord of Maryland and Avalon." Baltimore County, Maryland was created in 1659. Its name honored the Calverts' Irish barony. There are two known places named Baltimore in Ireland, both in southern Ireland in the country which is now officially called the Republic of Ireland. Sources consulted differ on which of the two Irish Baltimores was the source of the title of the baron of Baltimore. Some indicate that it was the fishing village in County Cork, on Baltimore Bay, eight miles southwest of Skibbereen. In the June, 1954, issue of *Maryland Historical Magazine*, Hamill Kenny refuted the County Cork possibility and supplied the correct answer with solid documentation. As Kenny explained it, the source of the barony's name, and hence the source of Baltimore County, Maryland's name, is a portion of Cloonageehir, along the east bank of the Rinn River, in County Longford. In 1942 that section of Cloonageehir in County Longford was still called Baltimore. Perhaps it still is.

1165 *Calvert County*

Uncertain — This county was first created in 1650 with the name Charles County. The county's name was changed to Calvert County in July, 1654. Also in 1654, the Puritans in Maryland began a revolt against the established authorities and their revolt became successful when they took control of Maryland's government. In November, 1654, the Puritans changed the name of Calvert County to Patuxent County. The name was chosen on account of the county's location on both sides of the Patuxent River. The county's name remained Patuxent from 1654 to 1658, when the government of Maryland again became established in the hands of representatives of the Calvert family. In 1658,

Patuxent County was renamed Calvert County. Sources consulted offer varying, but generally similar explanations for the source of Calvert County's name:
— The Calvert family
— The family name of Lord Baltimore
— The family name of the proprietary
— The lords proprietor
— George Calvert, baron of Baltimore
— Cecil Calvert, second lord Baltimore

Calvert was the family name of the several lords Baltimore who founded and, for many years, controlled the English colony of Maryland. In 1654 ,when the name Calvert was first used for this county, only three of Maryland's numerous important Calverts had become prominent enough to be likely sources for this county's name. These three Calverts were:
— Cecil Calvert (1605–1675)
— George Calvert (–1632)
— Leonard Calvert (1606–1647)

Biographical sketches of these three Calverts follow:

Cecil Calvert (1605–1675) — Cecil Calvert was the eldest son of George Calvert (–1632), the first lord Baltimore. Cecil Calvert was born in Kent County, England, on August 8, 1605, and he was named in honor of his father's patron, Sir Robert Cecil (1563–1612), England's principal secretary of state. In a number of accounts Cecil Calvert's given name is rendered as Cecilius and one source spells it Caecillius. Cecil's father, George Calvert, had petitioned the crown for a grant of land in North America, on which to establish an English colony. When George Calvert died in April, 1632, Cecil became the second lord Baltimore. Thus when the crown granted his father's petition, Cecil became lord proprietor of Maryland. The grant contained the phrase "absolute lord of Maryland and Avalon." (The name *Avalon* referred to an unsuccessful attempt by George Calvert [–1632] to establish a colony on the island of Newfoundland.) The power contained in the king's grant to Cecil Calvert was enormous. Maryland now differed from an independent kingdom only in the stipulation that a yearly tribute was required to be paid to the English crown. Although Cecil Calvert never visited Maryland, he was intensely interested in it and he spent more than 40 thousand pounds of his own money during his efforts to establish Maryland as a haven for persecuted Catholics. Cecil appointed his younger brother, Leonard Calvert (1606–1647), to be Maryland's first governor.

George Calvert (–1632) — George Calvert was born about 1580 at Kipling, in Yorkshire, England. In 1606 he became the private secretary of Sir Robert Cecil (1563–1612), England's principal secretary of state. Cecil held great political power and he used a bit of it to advance the career of his young protege. In 1606 George Calvert became clerk of the crown for the province of Connaught, in County Clare, in Ireland. George Calvert became a member of the British parliament in 1609 and during the following decade and a half he held a variety of important posts including temporary secretary of state and, later, secretary of state. In 1625 Calvert professed to be a Roman Catholic. In February of that year, King James I (1566–1625) made Calvert a baron with the title lord Baltimore; i.e., George Calvert became the first lord Baltimore. Calvert later petitioned the crown for a grant of land in North America on which to establish a new English colony. In June, 1632, shortly after George Calvert's death, his petition was granted and his son, Cecil Calvert (1605–1675), established the English colony of Maryland.

Leonard Calvert (1606–1647) — Leonard Calvert was the second son of George Calvert (–1632), the first lord Baltimore. Leonard was born in England in 1606 and he traveled with his father to Newfoundland in 1628 during an unsuccessful attempt to establish a colony there. In November, 1633, Leonard Calvert was appointed by his elder brother, Cecil, the lord proprietor of Maryland, to be Maryland's first governor. Leonard's official title was not "governor" but "lieutenant-general, admiral, chief captain and commander." Although he did not carry the title, he was, in reality, Maryland's first governor. He served in that capacity until his death in June, 1647. Leonard Calvert remained in Maryland throughout the time he was governor, except for a few relatively brief absences and one longer one (from April, 1643, to September, 1644, when Giles Brent served as Maryland's governor).

1166 *Caroline County*

Caroline Calvert Eden — In 1773, two delegates from Dorchester County, named William Richardson and Thomas White, introduced a bill in Maryland's colonial legislature to create a new county on Maryland's eastern shore. The bill passed, and in 1774 Caroline County was created. The new county was named for Lady Caroline Calvert Eden. Caroline was the wife of Robert Eden (1741–1784) and at the time that Caroline County was created, Robert Eden was serving England as governor of its colony of Maryland. Caroline Calvert Eden was a daughter of Charles Calvert (1699–1751) and his wife, Mary Janssen. Charles Calvert was the fifth lord Baltimore and his son, Frederick Calvert (1731–1771), Caroline's brother, was the sixth and last lord Baltimore. Robert Eden met and wooed Caroline Calvert in England and they were married there on April 26, 1765, by Reverend Gregory Sharpe, curate at St. Gregory's, Hanover Square, in London. It is not entirely clear that romantic interest was the sole driving force in Robert Eden's pursuit of Caroline Calvert. By allying himself with the powerful Calvert family, Eden must have guessed that his political fortune would improve. Caroline Calvert Eden and her husband, Robert had three children: (1) Sir Frederick Morton Eden (1766–1808), a distinguished economist, (2) Major-general William Thomas Eden (1768–1851) and (3) Catherine Eden (1770–1835). Robert Eden's alliance with the Calvert family began to bear fruit soon after his marriage to Caroline Calvert. Eden was granted an annuity of 100 pounds, payable semi-annually, in revenues received from Maryland. In 1768, Frederick Calvert appointed his brother-in-law to be governor of Maryland, replacing Horatio Sharpe (1718–1790). Although Eden owed his governorship to nepotism, he proved to be a generally able and popular colonial governor. Soon after his appointment as governor, Eden brought his wife, Caroline, and two children to Maryland. Their third child, Catherine, was born in 1770 in Annapolis, Maryland. Although Eden was a popular governor, he was England's governor of colonial Maryland and when revolution and war with England began to look inevitable, Eden was asked by the citizens of Maryland to leave. Robert Eden and his family sailed for England in the summer of 1776. It is not clear whether Caroline Calvert Eden ever visited Maryland again but her husband did. The purpose of Eden's visit was to claim some property here. He died during this visit, at Annapolis, Maryland, on September 2, 1784.

1167 *Carroll County*

Charles Carroll (1737–1832) — Charles Carroll was a Catholic, whose ancestors had received huge grants of land in Maryland. He was a native of Maryland and represented it in the Continental Congress. He was one of the signers of the Declaration of Independence and later represented Maryland as a U.S. senator in the first congress of the United States. Carroll lived to be the last surviving signer of the

Declaration of Independence and several states recognized that distinction by naming counties in his honor. Sources consulted differ on the year that Carroll County, Maryland, was created for this reason: At the time that creation of this new county was being considered by Maryland's general assembly, it was required that an initiating act be approved by one session of the general assembly followed by a confirming act of the next general assembly. Carroll County, Maryland, resulted from passage of chapter 256 of the session of 1835 and chapter 19 of the session of 1836. This second act was passed on January 19, 1837, four years after Charles Carroll's death on November 14, 1832, at the age of 95. Westminster was originally proposed for the name of this county, in honor of the town of Westminster, which became the county seat of Carroll County. The name Westminster was never officially adopted for this county's name.

1168 *Cecil County*

Cecil Calvert (1605–1675)— Cecil Calvert was the eldest son of George Calvert (– 1632), the first lord Baltimore. Cecil Calvert was born in Kent County, England, on August 8, 1605, and he was named in honor of his father's patron, Sir Robert Cecil (1563–1612), England's principal secretary of state. In a number of accounts Cecil Calvert's given name is rendered as Cecilius and one source spells it Caecillius. Cecil's father, George Calvert, had petitioned the crown for a grant of land in North America, on which to establish an English colony. When George Calvert died in April, 1632, Cecil became the second lord Baltimore. Thus when the crown granted his father's petition, Cecil became lord proprietor of Maryland. The grant contained the phrase "absolute lord of Maryland and Avalon." (The name *Avalon* referred to an unsuccessful attempt by George Calvert [–1632] to establish a colony on the island of Newfoundland.) The power contained in the king's grant to Cecil Calvert was enormous. Maryland now differed from an independent kingdom only in the stipulation that a yearly tribute was required to be paid to the English crown. Although Cecil Calvert never visited Maryland, he was intensely interested in it and he spent more than 40 thousand pounds of his own money during his efforts to establish Maryland as a haven for persecuted Catholics. This county was created by proclamation of the governor, Charles Calvert (1637–1715), on June 6, 1674. Cecil Calvert was the father of Governor Charles Calvert.

1169 *Charles County*

Charles Calvert (1637–1715)— Charles Calvert was a son of Cecil Calvert (1605–1675), the second lord Baltimore, and Cecil's wife Anne Arundell Calvert (1615–1649). When Cecil Calvert died in 1675, Charles Calvert became the third lord Baltimore and proprietor of Maryland. Charles was born in London, England on August 27, 1637. He was commissioned governor of Maryland in 1661 and he moved from England to Maryland that year. Except for two interruptions to visit England, Charles Calvert served as Maryland's governor from 1661 to 1684. Calvert was a Catholic and , while he was governor of Maryland, he had to contend with recurrent conflicts between Maryland's Catholic and Protestant residents. When Calvert's service as governor ended in 1684, he returned to England where he died on February 21, 1715. This county was created in 1658. Maryland had earlier had a county named Charles. That county was created in 1650 but its name was changed to Calvert County in 1654.

1170 *Dorchester County*

Uncertain— All sources agree that this county was created in either 1668 or 1669 and that it was named for the Earl of Dorset, an Englishman, who was a friend of the Calverts and of the English royal family. However, some reliable sources say that the man for whom this county was named was the fourth earl of Dorset, Edward Sackville (1591–1652), while other, equally reliable, sources indicate that the man whom the county's name honors was Richard Sackville (1622–1677), the fifth earl of Dorset.

Edward Sackville, Earl of Dorset (1591–1652)— Edward Sackville, the fourth earl of Dorset, was a distinguished English nobleman during the reigns of King James I (1566–1625) and King Charles I (1600–1649). He was educated at Oxford University's Christ Church. Edward Sackville was a member of the British parliament, ambassador to France, governor of the Bermuda Islands Company and commissioner for planting Virginia. He later was privy councilor and lord chamberlain to Henrietta Maria (1606–1699), the queen consort of King Charles I and the lady for whom Maryland was named. During England's Civil War, Edward Sackville remained loyal to King Charles I.

Richard Sackville, Earl of Dorset (1622–1677)— Richard Sackville, the fifth earl of Dorset, was a son of Edward Sackville, the fourth earl of Dorset. Richard Sackville,

who was something of a poet, served as a member of the British parliament during the years 1640–1643. However, he was imprisoned by parliament in 1642 for his political beliefs. At the coronation of England's King Charles II (1630–1685), Richard Sackville was lord sewer. He was a favorite at the royal court and honors and well-paying offices were heaped upon him. Richard Sackville had inherited the peerage at the time that Dorchester County, Maryland was created. Before his death he was elected a fellow of the select Royal Society.

1171 *Frederick County*

Uncertain— Most sources indicate that this county was named for Frederick Calvert (1731–1771), the sixth and last lord Baltimore. However, a few authorities mention the possibility that the county's name honors England's Frederick Louis (1707–1751), a son of King George II (1683–1760). Both Frederick Louis and King George II were alive in 1748, when this county was created and George II was the reigning king of England at that time. It is certainly possible that the name for this county in the English colony of Maryland was chosen to honor Frederick Louis, in compliment to the English crown.

Frederick Calvert (1731–1771)— A native of England, who never visited Maryland, Frederick Calvert was the eldest son of Charles Calvert (1699–1751), the fifth lord Baltimore. Historians have little good to say about Frederick Calvert. A generic recap of the insults heaped upon him stated that he was "the sixth, the worst and the last, lord Baltimore." On one occasion he was tried for rape in the kingdom of Ireland. Although it was generally believed that he was guilty, he was acquitted. At the time that Frederick County, Maryland, was created in 1748, the fifth lord Baltimore, Charles Calvert, was still alive so Frederick Calvert was not yet lord Baltimore, but he was heir apparent to that title. Frederick married Lady Diana Egerton (1732–1758) in 1753 but they had no children so when Frederick Calvert died in 1771, the title of lord Baltimore died with him. However, Frederick Calvert fathered illegitimate children with Hester Rhelan (– 1812). One of these illegitimate children was Henry Harford (1758–1834). See Harford County, Maryland, below.

Frederick Louis (1707–1751)— Frederick was the eldest son of George August (1683–1760), who later became England's King George II. Frederick was born in Hanover, Germany and he was forced to remain there when his father and the rest of the family moved to London, England, in 1714. In fact, he was not permitted to come to England until some 18 months after his father became king of England. Frederick Louis was created duke of Gloucester in 1717 and duke of Edinburgh in 1727. He was made prince of Wales in 1729 and he held that title and was heir apparent to the English throne when Frederick County, Maryland, was created in 1748. However, Frederick never became king. When he died in 1751, his father, King George II, was still reigning. As a result, when King George II died, it was the eldest son of Frederick Louis who became king. That new king was George III (1738–1820). It was during the reign of King George III that the American colonists successfully revolted from England and founded our new nation.

1172 *Garrett County*

John W. Garrett (1820–1884)—John Work Garrett was born in Baltimore, Maryland, on July 31, 1820. He was the second son of Robert Garrett (1783–1857), who immigrated to the United States from Ireland and became wealthy in commercial activities in Baltimore. John W. Garrett joined his father's firm at the age of 19. Sources consulted describe the firm as a "commission house" and indicate that John W. Garrett's first assignment there was in the "counting room." John W. Garrett became a stockholder in the Baltimore and Ohio Railroad Company and in 1857 he became active in the affairs of the railroad. In October of that year he was elected a member of the railroad's board of directors. Just one year later, in November, 1858, Garrett was elected president of the B. & O. Railroad. Within two years, Garrett succeeded in improving the railroad's perilous financial condition. During the Civil War, Garrett supported the Union, and as president of a railroad running near the border of the Confederacy and the Union, he was able to provide Union officials with early indications of hostile movements by Confederate forces. Under Garrett's direction, the B. & O. Railroad was an important means of transport for troops and supplies to Union forces. In the years following the Civil War, the B. & O. Railroad expanded its operations under the direction of its president, John W. Garrett. This county was created in 1872.

1173 *Harford County*

Henry Harford (1758–1834)—Harford County was created in 1773 and named for Henry Harford, who was the proprietor of Maryland at that time. Harford was born on April 5, 1758, in London, England. He was the illegitimate son of the sixth lord Baltimore, Frederick Calvert (1731–1771) and Hester Rhelan (–1812), who used the alias, "Mrs. Harford." When Frederick Calvert, sixth baron of Baltimore and fifth proprietor of Maryland, died in 1771, he left no legitimate children. Under English law, there was no way that Frederick Calvert could have made his illegitimate son, Henry Harford, legitimate. There were no provisions for adoption that would accomplish this and even by marrying Hester Rhelan (–1812), after the death, in 1758, of his wife, Lady Diana Egerton Calvert, he could not have made Henry Harford legitimate under English law. This prevented Calvert from passing on the title, baron of Baltimore, to his natural son but through his will, Frederick Calvert succeeded in passing on the Maryland proprietorship to him. Thus upon the death of Frederick Calvert in 1771, his son Henry Harford became the sixth and last proprietor of Maryland even though he did not hold the title baron of Baltimore. When Harford became proprietor of Maryland, he was still in his youth. He studied at Eton from 1772 to 1775 and later at Oxford University. Harford took little interest in Maryland apart from the financial income his proprietorship afforded him. At the conclusion of the American Revolution, Harford visited Maryland to press claims on the Maryland legislature for a monetary settlement as reimbursement for relinquishing his lands. The Maryland legislature denied Harford's claims but the British government later granted him a monetary settlement for the loss of his lands in Maryland. In spite of Harford's illegitimate birth, he held a high social standing in London society and was a wealthy man.

1174 *Howard County*

John E. Howard (1752–1827)—John Eager Howard was born in Maryland on June 4, 1752, the son of a wealthy Maryland planter. Howard served as an officer in the Maryland line during the American Revolution and rose to the rank of lieutenant-colonel. (Later, in 1798, during a brief undeclared war with France, Howard was promoted to the rank of brigadier-general.) John E. Howard was one of Maryland's delegates to the Continental Congress and he became governor of Maryland in 1788. He served in that office until 1791. In 1795 President George Washington offered Howard a position in his cabinet as secretary of war but Howard declined that offer. Howard also served in Maryland's senate and in November, 1796, the Maryland legislature elected him to fill the unexpired term of U.S. Senator Richard Potts (1753–1808). Soon afterward, Howard was elected by the Maryland legislature to a full term in the U.S. Senate. In 1816 Howard ran as the Federalist party's nominee for vice-president of the United States with presidential candidate Rufus King (1755–1827). The Federalists were easily defeated in this election by the Democratic Republicans. James Monroe (1758–1831) was elected president and Daniel D. Tompkins (1774–1825) was elected vice-president.

1175 *Kent County*

Kent Island, Maryland—In 1631, William Claiborne, of England's Virginia colony, set up a trading post and farming settlements on Kent Island, in Chesapeake Bay and he named the island in honor of Kent County, England. Several sources state that Kent County, England was William Claiborne's former home. In June, 1632, England's King Charles I (1600–1649) made a grant to lord Baltimore to establish a colony (Maryland) north of the Potomac River. After a brief dispute, Virginia reluctantly gave up its claim to Kent Island (which lies well north of the Potomac River) and allowed it to become a part of Maryland. By 1642, mention is found in Maryland's surviving colonial records of a "sheriff of Kent County." Large sections of Maryland's eastern shore became included in the area variously called "Kent County" and "the Isle of Kent." Some nine Maryland counties were eventually created from this territory and even the island which was the source of the county's name was lost by Kent County. Kent Island first was made a part of Talbot County and it was later given to Queen Anne's County. Kent County, Maryland, is now one of Maryland's smallest counties. By coincidence, the county's eastern border touches Kent County, Delaware, whose name also derived from Kent County, in southeastern England. This section of England was once a separate Anglo-Saxon kingdom. The kingdom converted to Roman Christianity in A.D. 597, making it the first Christian kingdom in England. Kent was absorbed by Wessex in the ninth century. The English county's name probably derived from the Celt's *canto*, meaning "rim, border, border land" or "district."

1176 *Montgomery County*

Richard Montgomery (1738–1775)—Montgomery was born in Ireland and served with the British in the French and Indian War. He settled in New York state where he was elected to the New York provisional congress. He served as a general in the American Revolutionary army and he was killed in combat in the Revolutionary War. This county was created in 1776.

1177 *Prince George's County*

Prince George of Denmark (1653–1708)—This county was created in 1695 by the English colony of Maryland. The name was chosen in compliment to the English throne. At the time that this county was created, Prince George was the husband of England's Princess Anne (1665–1714). She was then next in line for the throne and she did, in fact, later become queen of England and rule it from 1702 to 1714. The explanation of the fact that Princess Anne was next in line for the English throne in 1695 is a bit tricky to follow but the patient reader will see the pattern.

Under a 1689 Declaration of Rights, while King William III (1650–1702) and Queen Mary II (1662–1694) were ruling England as joint sovereigns, it was declared that Princess Anne would be next in line for the throne if King William III and his wife, Queen Mary II, left no legitimate children. Queen Mary II died of smallpox in 1694 without leaving any legitimate children.

Now we know why the English colony of Maryland would want to name a county for Prince George of Denmark so let's learn a bit about him. George was born in April, 1653, while his father, King Frederick III (1609–1670), was king of Denmark. He received some naval training and saw duty under arms. In 1674 efforts were made to place Prince George on the Polish throne but his aversion to Roman Catholicism caused the scheme to abort. In 1681 he visited England as a preliminary to his marriage to England's Princess Anne, which occurred in July, 1683. Prince George was disliked by England's king, William III, and when Princess Anne took the throne as Queen Anne in 1702, Prince George was denied the title of king. He did enjoy other prestigious titles including duke of Cumberland, generalissimo, lord high admiral and fellow of the Royal Society. Prince George had a mild and gentle temper. He loved his wife and they enjoyed a long and happy marriage. Prince George died of a severe asthmatic malady in 1708.

1178 *Queen Anne's County*

Queen Anne (1665–1714)—This county was formed in 1706, when Maryland was a colony of England and while Queen Anne was the reigning monarch of England. Anne was the second daughter of England's King James II (1633–1701) and his first wife, Anne Hyde (–1671). Queen Anne's elder sister, Mary, had also been queen of England, ruling as Queen Mary II (1662–1694), joint sovereign with her husband, King William III (1650–1702). Under a 1689 Declaration of Rights, it was declared that Anne (then Princess Anne) would be next in line for the throne if King William III and Queen Mary II left no legitimate children. Queen Mary II died of smallpox in 1694 without leaving any legitimate children. After the death of Queen Mary II, King William III ruled England alone. When he died in 1702, Princess Anne ascended to the throne. Her reign was brief (just twelve years) but effective. She enjoyed a happy marriage with Prince George of Denmark (1653–1708) but the royal couple failed to produce an heir to succeed Queen Anne. They had a large number of children (15 according to one account; 17 per another) but most of them were stillborn. Only one boy survived. He was Prince William (1689–1700). Medical science at that time was unable to effectively assist one of the most wealthy and powerful couples on planet Earth in their repeated efforts to leave an heir to the throne. This personal tragedy resulted in a practical problem for England as well, since the heir to the throne when Queen Anne died in 1714 was her half-brother, James Francis Edward Stuart (1688–1766); but James Stuart was a Catholic and England wanted no Catholic on its throne. The nation closed ranks against James Stuart and all other Catholic contenders for the crown and reached all the way to Hanover, in Germany, for a successor to Queen Anne. There they found George Lewis (1660–1727), the elector of Hanover, who had a drop or two of royal English blood in his veins and thus some semblance of a claim to the English throne. He became England's King George I. The new king never bothered to learn much of the English language but he did succeed in remaining Protestant throughout his reign.

1179 *Saint Mary's County*

Uncertain—The origin of this county's name is uncertain and the date that it was created is not known. However, it is known that by 1637 reference was made to Saint Mary's County in early Maryland records.

Most sources state that this county was named for Saint Mary, the virgin mother of Jesus, in Catholic theology. However, a few sources indicate the possibility that the county's name honors Henrietta Maria (1606–1669), the queen consort of King Charles I (1600–1649), While it is unlikely, but possible, that this county was named for Henrietta Maria, it is certain that the English colony of Maryland, and hence our present state of Maryland, was named in her honor.

Saint Mary (–)—It is a matter of dogma of the Roman Catholic Church that Saint Mary was the virgin mother of the second person of the Trinity, Jesus Christ. Because she had been selected to be the human mother of God, it was axiomatic that her soul be spotless, free of all sin from the moment of her conception. As the mother of Jesus, Mary is considered preeminent among all saints but the veneration and adoration bestowed upon her are on a lower plane than those reserved for God in three persons, Father, Son and Holy Spirit.

Queen Henrietta Maria (1606–1669)—It was England's King Charles I (1600–1649) who granted the petition which permitted the establishment of the colony of Maryland. He made this grant in June, 1632. At that time, his wife and queen consort was Henrietta Maria, the third daughter of the former French king, Henry IV (1553–1610). Many royal marriages were arranged for political, rather than romantic reasons and there was a political element in the decision that Charles, then prince of Wales and heir apparent to the English throne, should marry Henrietta Maria, even though she was a Catholic. Prince Charles and Henrietta were married by proxy and Henrietta came to England in 1625. She was a beautiful young lady and Charles fell in love with her. On account of this love, she was able to exert considerable influence over the king. In Norah Lofts' work entitled *Queens of England*, Henrietta Maria's influence is captured with these words: "Charles had many bad advisors, but the worst was the wife whom he adored." As a Catholic, Henrietta Maria refused to be crowned with her husband at his Protestant coronation, but she permitted her children to be baptized as Protestants in the Church of England. Two of these children later became kings of England. They were: King Charles II (1630–1685) and King James II (1633–1701).

1180 *Somerset County*

Mary Arundell Somerset—This county

was created in 1666, when Cecil Calvert (1605–1675), was lord Baltimore and lord proprietor of Maryland. Cecil Calvert stated that the county was named "...in honr [sic] to our Deare [sic] Sister the Lady Mary Somersett [sic]." Mary Arundell Somerset was actually Cecil Calvert's sister-in-law, rather than his sister, since she was the sister of Anne Arundell Calvert (1615–1649), who was Cecil Calvert's wife. Apparently, in those days, one referred to a sister-in-law as a "sister." The two sisters, Anne Arundell Calvert and Mary Arundell Somerset, both had Maryland counties named in their honor. These sisters were daughters of Thomas, Baron Arundell of Wardour (1560–1639) and his second wife, Anne Philopson. Mary Arundell became the wife of Sir John Somerset.

1181 *Talbot County*

Uncertain — This county was created about 1661 or 1662, while Cecil Calvert (1605–1675) was lord Baltimore and lord proprietor of Maryland. Most sources state that the county was named for Grace Calvert Talbot (1614–1672), a sister of Cecil Calvert's. However there are two other credible possibilities:

1. Frances Arundell Talbot, a sister-in-law of Cecil Calvert (1605–1675).

2. A sweeping gesture to honor the numerous Talbots with whom Cecil Calvert was connected by blood or marriage.

Dickson J. Preston drives the uncertainty home with this comment in his 1983 book on the history of Talbot County: "According to tradition, the county was named for Lady Grace Talbot, sister of Lord Baltimore and wife of Sir Robert Talbot, an Irish patriot and statesman. There is no recorded confirmation of this belief. It rests merely on the assumption that because she was Lord Baltimore's sister, she must have been the person honored by the name."

Grace Calvert Talbot (1614–1672) — Grace Calvert was a daughter of George Calvert (–1632), the first lord Baltimore and his first wife, Lady Anne Mynne (1579–1622). Grace was one of eleven children of this first marriage of George Calvert's. One of her brothers was Cecil Calvert (1605–1675), who was the second lord Baltimore and lord proprietor of Maryland at the time that Talbot County, Maryland, was created. Another brother, Leonard Calvert (1606–1647), was appointed to be Maryland's first governor in 1633. Grace Calvert married Robert Talbot of County Kildare, Ireland, who was a brother of Richard Talbot, Earl of Tyrconnel. Robert Talbot's father was William Talbot (–1633). Grace Calvert Talbot and her husband, Robert, had at least four children: William Talbot, George Talbot, Mary Talbot and Frances Talbot (–1718), who married her cousin, Richard Talbot (–1703).

Frances Arundell Talbot (–) — Frances Arundell was a sister of Anne Arundell Calvert (1615–1649), whose husband, Cecil Calvert (1605–1675), was the second lord Baltimore and lord proprietor of Maryland at the time that Talbot County, Maryland, was created. We have seen that Cecil Calvert caused one Maryland County to be named in honor of one of his sisters-in-law, Mary Arundell Somerset. (See Somerset County, Maryland, immediately above.) Hence the possibility that Talbot County, Maryland's name may honor a sister-in-law rather than a sister is real. Frances Arundell married John Talbot, the earl of Shrewsbury, as his second wife. Known children of this union were: Thomas Talbot, John Talbot, Bruno Talbot and Anna Maria Talbot.

A sweeping gesture to honor the numerous Talbots with whom Cecil Calvert (1605–1675) was connected by blood or marriage — The list of Talbots contained within the above paragraphs for Grace Calvert Talbot (1614–1672) and Frances Arundell Talbot (–) should give the reader a good start. Other are listed in Mrs. Russel Hastings' article in the December, 1927 issue of the *Maryland Historical Magazine* starting on page number 315. The title of her article is "Calvert & Darnall Gleanings from English Wills."

1182 *Washington County*

George Washington (1732–1799) — Washington was a native of Virginia. He served in Virginia's house of burgesses and became one of the colonies' leaders in opposition to British policies in America. He was a member of the first and second Continental Congresses and commander of all Continental armies in the Revolutionary War. Following victory in that war, Washington was elected to be the first president of the United States. This county was created in September, 1776, when George Washington was commander in chief of the American colonies' revolutionary armies.

1183 *Wicomico County*

Wicomico River — Wicomico County was created in 1867 and named for the Wicomico River. There are at least four rivers and creeks in Maryland and Virginia that are named Wicomico or close approximations of that name. Our Wicomico River is the one which bisects Wicomico County, Maryland. The river was named several centuries ago by the Indians. Captain John Smith (1580–1631), of Pocahontas fame, mentioned the Wicomico River on his map from a 1606 exploration of the Chesapeake Bay region. The Wicomico River begins as a narrow stream in northeastern Maryland, near the Maryland-Delaware border. It flows in a southern course through Salisbury, Maryland, the county seat of Wicomico County and it widens considerably during its journey through the city. After leaving the southern end of Salisbury, the Wicomico flows to the south and to the west and widens still more as it curves through salt marshes before ending its journey by emptying into Monie Bay. The Wicomico River's length is about 33 miles. The river's name came from Indian words and since the Indians had no written language, it was left to Europeans to render the sounds in writing. They did so with abandon and their efforts produced diverse spellings. There is often disagreement about the translation of Indian words and names among etymologists but sources consulted for the meaning of the Indian words that were used to name the Wicomico River are essentially in agreement. Apparently the Indian words referred to a house or building, possibly round in shape, or to a village, on the Wicomico River's banks, which was a pleasant place to live. The Indians who lived in the vicinity of the Wicomico River came to be called by the name of the river. The name of this tribe is rendered as Wicocomoco by Frederick W. Hodge in his definitive study of American Indian tribes entitled *Handbook of American Indians North of Mexico*.

1184 *Worcester County*

Uncertain — In 1669, Cecil Calvert (1605–1675) was lord Baltimore and proprietor of Maryland. At that time, Calvert was concerned about protecting his rights to a section of Maryland that was in dispute. As one step to protect his territory, Calvert ordered that two new counties were to be erected within the disputed area. In 1669 Durham County was created and in 1672 Maryland's first Worcester County was created. Neither of these counties were ever fully organized nor represented in the Maryland legislature. Both of these counties contained land that is now within the state of Delaware and neither Durham County nor this first Worcester County survived. In 1742 Maryland created a Worcester County for the second time.

Although this Worcester County had far different boundaries that the first Worcester County, its boundaries also included a portion of what is now the state of Delaware. In 1767 the boundary line between Maryland and Delaware was adjusted to its present location through negotiation. Virtually all sources consulted state that Worcester County, Maryland, was named for the earl of Worcester although the possibility that the name was taken from Worcester, England, is also mentioned; but *which* Worcester County, Maryland? It would appear that the present Worcester County, Maryland, was considered to be a reincarnation of the first Worcester County, Maryland, which had been created in 1672 and then allowed to die. Thus to find the source of the name of Maryland's county named Worcester, we must determine the source of the name of the earlier Worcester County. Although this earlier Worcester County was probably named for an earl of Worcester, either Edward Somerset (1553–1628), the fourth earl of Worcester or Edward Somerset (1601–1667) the sixth earl of Somerset, we will discuss Worcester, England, as well, because of the possibility that Maryland's original Worcester County was named for Worcester, in England.

Edward Somerset, Earl of Worcester (1553–1628)— This Edward Somerset, who was the fourth earl of Worcester, was a notable Catholic leader and the grandfather of John Somerset; presumably the same John Somerset who was the husband of Mary Arundell Somerset, for whom Somerset County, Maryland, was named. In spite of his Roman Catholicism, Edward Somerset became a favorite of England's Queen Elizabeth I (1533–1603) and he continued in royal favor when James I (1566–1625) succeeded to the throne in 1603. Edward became the earl of Worcester when his father, William Somerset (1526–1589), died. Edward held a variety of prestigious titles. He succeeded Robert Devereaux, the second earl of Essex (1566–1601), as Queen Elizabeth's master of the horse in 1601. Edward Somerset later became lord privy seal and he was great chamberlain at the coronation of England's King Charles I (1600–1649).

Edward Somerset, Earl of Worcester (1601–1667)— This Edward Somerset became the sixth earl of Worcester and the second marquis of Worcester upon the death of his father, Henry Somerset (1577–1646). From 1628 to 1644 Edward Somerset's name was styled Lord Herbert of Ragland. To further complicate the name confusion, he was created earl of Glamorgan in 1644.

Edward Somerset served England's King Charles I (1600–1649) in military actions in South Wales and in Ireland. In April, 1644, he was given a commission as generalissimo of three armies: English, Irish and foreign; and as admiral of a fleet at sea. Edward Somerset was a Roman Catholic and in 1645 he was involved in a secret treaty which granted Roman Catholics possession of all of the churches in Ireland which they had seized since October 23, 1641. Although this treaty was part of a plan to furnish England's King Charles I with needed Irish troops, it was unpopular in Protestant England. Edward Somerset was eventually imprisoned for two years. Following his release from prison in 1654, he devoted the remainder of his life to mechanical experiments and he produced some remarkable mechanical inventions.

Worcester, England— Worcester, or Worcestershire, is a county in west-central England in the West Midlands section of the country. Large sections of Worcester are covered with forests and the Severn River traverses portions of these forests. The Severn also drains low-lying marshlands of the county. Other rivers here are the Avon, Salwarp, Teme and Stour. Worcester is about 35 miles long and some 30 miles wide. When the Roman Empire occupied England, they took little interest in the Worcester area. About A.D. 577, the West Saxons conquered Worcester but control of the area passed to the Mercians. In the year A.D. 825, Egbert (–839), who was king of Wessex, took brief control of Worcester but Mercian influence was reestablished in A.D. 830. In the latter part of the ninth century, the barbaric Danes conquered Worcester and raided and plundered its monasteries and cathedrals. It was not until A.D. 1017 that a period of internal peace began when the Dane, Canute the Great (–1035), became king of England. In 1651 an important battle in English history was fought here when Oliver Cromwell (1599–1658), who was then dictator and lord protector of England, defeated an attempt to restore England to monarchy. Today's Worcester has some industry but it is primarily an agricultural county. Its soil, which is chiefly composed of clay and loam, is very fertile. *Worcester* is the surviving version of a long series of names for this area. Authorities differ on the origin and translation of the earlier names from which *Worcester* evolved. The following possibilities have been mentioned:
— "Dwellers by the winding river"
— "Winding river"
— "Fort of the Huiccii"
— "A grove"
— "Roman town of the Weogora tribe"
— "The forest of the Wigoran"
— "The forest men"

REFERENCES

Allstrom, C. M. *Dictionary of Royal Lineage of Europe & Other Countries*. Chicago, Press of S. Th. Almberg, 1902.

Andrews, Charles M. *The Colonial Period of American History*. New Haven, Yale University Press, 1936.

Andrews, Matthew P. *History of Maryland: Province & State*. Garden City, New York, Doubleday, Doran & Co., Inc., 1929.

"Ann Arrundell, Lady Baltimore." *Anne Arundel County History Notes*, Vol. 20, No. 4. Severna Park, Maryland: July, 1989.

Baer, Elizabeth. *Seventeenth Century Maryland: A Bibliography*. Baltimore, John Work Garrett Library, 1949.

Baltimore: Its History and its People: Biographical. New York, Lewis Historical Publishing Co., 1912.

Bartholomew, John. *The Survey Gazetteer of the British Isles*. Edinburgh, John Bartholomew & Son, Ltd., 1950.

Beirne, Francis F. *The Amiable Baltimoreans*. New York, E. P. Dutton & Co., Inc., 1951.

The Biographical Cyclopedia of Representative Men of Maryland & District of Columbia. Baltimore, National Biographical Publishing Co., 1879.

Bolton, Charles K. *The Founders: Portraits of Persons Born Abroad Who Came to the Colonies in North America Before the Year 1701*. Baltimore, Genealogical Publishing Co., Inc., 1976.

Boyd, Laslo V. *Maryland Government & Politics*. Centreville, Maryland, Tidewater Publishers, 1987.

Bradford, James C. *Anne Arundel County, Maryland: A Bicentennial History*. Annapolis, Anne Arundel County & Annapolis Bicentennial Committee, 1977.

Browne, Wm. Hand. *George Calvert & Cecilius Calvert: Barons Baltimore*. New York, Dodd, Mead & Co., 1890.

Brugger, Robert J. *Maryland: A Middle Temperament: 1634–1980*. Baltimore, Johns Hopkins University Press & Maryland Historical Society, 1988.

Buchholz, Heinrich E. *Governors of Maryland from the Revolution to the Year 1908*. Baltimore, Williams & Wilkins Co., 1908.

Chapelle, Suzanne E., et al. *Maryland: A History of Its People*. Baltimore, Johns Hopkins University Press, 1986.

Clark, Charles B. *The Eastern Shore of*

Maryland & Virginia. New York, Lewis Historical Publishing Co., Inc., 1950.

Clark, Raymond B. *Index to Kent County, Maryland Wills: 1642–1777.* Arlington, Virginia, 1982.

Clark, Raymond B., & Sara S. Clark. *Calvert County, Maryland Wills: 1654–1700.* St. Michaels, Maryland, 1974.

Clark, Raymond B., & Sara S. Clark. *Caroline County, Maryland Marriage Licenses: 1774–1825 and a Short History of Caroline County.* St. Michaels, Maryland, 1969.

Cochrane, Laura C., et al. *History of Caroline County, Maryland.* Federalsburg, Maryland, J. W. Stowell Printing Co., 1920.

Creighton, Mandell. *The Story of Some English Shires.* London, Religious Tract Society.

Earle, Swepson. *The Chesapeake Bay Country.* Baltimore, Thomsen-Ellis Co., 1924.

Earle, Swepson, *Maryland's Colonial Eastern Shore.* New York, Weathervane Books, 1975.

Elsenberg, Gerson G. *Marylanders Who Served the Nation.* Annapolis, Maryland, Maryland State Archives, 1992.

Ekwall, Eilert. *The Concise Oxford Dictionary of English Place-Names.* Oxford, Oxford University Press, 1960.

Emory, Frederic. *Queen Anne's County, Maryland.* Baltimore, Maryland Historical Society, 1950.

Faragher, John M. *The Encyclopedia of Colonial & Revolutionary America.* New York, Facts On File, 1990.

Footner, Hulbert. *Maryland Main and the Eastern Shore.* Hatboro, Pennsylvania, Tradition Press, 1967.

Foster, James W. *George Calvert: The Early Years.* Museum & Library of Maryland History, Maryland Historical Society, 1983.

Foster, Vera A. *Your Maryland.* Lanham, Maryland, Maryland Historical Press, 1965.

Fraser, Antonia. *The Lives of the Kings & Queens of England.* Berkeley, University of California Press, 1995.

Frese Diane P. *Maryland Manual: 1991–1992.* Annapolis, Maryland, State Archives of the State of Maryland, 1991.

Gazetteer of the British Isles. Edinburgh, Scotland, John Bartholomew & Son, Ltd., 1966.

Hall, Clayton C. *The Lords Baltimore and the Maryland Palatinate.* Baltimore, John Murphy Co., 1902.

Hammett, Regina C. *History of St. Mary's County, Maryland.* Ridge, Maryland, 1977.

Hastings, Mrs. Russel. "Calvert & Darnall Gleanings from English Wills." *Mary-land Historical Magazine,* Vol. 21, No. 4. Baltimore: December, 1926.

Hastings, Mrs. Russel. "Calvert & Darnall Gleanings from English Wills." *Maryland Historical Magazine,* Vol. 22, No. 4. Baltimore: December, 1927.

Hattery, Thomas H. *Western Maryland: A Profile.* Mt. Airy, Maryland, Lomond Books, 1980.

Hemphill, William E., et al. *Cavalier Commonwealth: History & Government of Virginia.* New York, McGraw-Hill Book Co., Inc., 1957.

Hodge, Frederick W. *Handbook of American Indians North of Mexico.* Totowa, New Jersey, Rowman & Littlefield, 1975.

Hopkins, G. M. *Atlas of Anne Arundel County, Maryland.* Philadelphia, 1878.

"How Well Are You Up in Easton History?" *Easton Star-Democrat,* February 2, 1945.

Jackson, Elmer M. *Annapolis.* Annapolis, Maryland, Capital-Gazette Press, 1936.

Joelson, Annette. *England's Princes of Wales.* New York, Dorset Press, 1966.

Johnson, James. *Place Names of England & Wales.* London, England, Bracken Books, 1994.

Johnston, George. *History of Cecil County, Maryland.* Baltimore, Regional Publishing Co., 1972.

Kaessmann, Beta, et al. *My Maryland: Her Story for Boys & Girls.* Baltimore, Maryland Historical Society, 1955.

Kaminkow, Marion J. *Maryland A to Z: A Topographical Dictionary.* Baltimore, Magna Carta Book Co., 1985.

Keatley, J. Kenneth. *Place Names of the Eastern Shore of Maryland.* Queenstown, Maryland, Queen Anne Press, 1987.

Kelly, J. Reaney. *Quakers in the Founding of Anne Arundel County, Maryland.* Baltimore, Maryland Historical Society, 1963.

Kenny, Hamill. "Algonquian Names." *Names: Journal of the American Name Society,* Vol. 4, No. 1. Orinda, California: March, 1956.

Kenny, Hamill. "Baltimore: New Light on an Old Name." *Maryland Historical Magazine,* Vol. 49, No. 2. Baltimore: June, 1954.

Kenny, Hamill. *The Origin & Meaning of the Indian Place Names of Maryland.* Baltimore, Waverly Press, 1961.

Kenny, Hamill. "The Origin & Meaning of the Indian Place-Names of Maryland." Ph.D. Thesis, Theodore R. McKeldin Library, University of Maryland, College Park, Maryland, 1950.

Kenny, Hamill. *The Placenames of Maryland: Their Origin & Meaning.* Baltimore,

Museum & Library of Maryland History, Maryland Historical Society, 1984.

Kenyon, J. P. *Dictionary of British History.* Ware, England, Wordsworth Editions, Ltd., 1992.

Kingman, Dan C., Chief of Engineers, United States Army. Letter to the Secretary of War dated January 18, 1915, estimating cost of improvement of Wicomico River, Maryland.

Klapthor, Margaret B. & Paul D. Brown. *The History of Charles County, Maryland.* La Plata, Maryland, Charles County Tercentenary, Inc.

Kummer, Frederic A. *The Free State of Maryland: A History of the State and Its People: 1634–1941.* Baltimore, Historical Record Association.

Land, Aubrey C. *Colonial Maryland: A History.* Millwood, New York, KTO Press, 1981.

Lankford, Wilmer O., Somerset County Historical Society, Princess Anne, Maryland. Letter to the author dated August 6, 1987.

Lantz, Emily E. *The Spirit of Maryland.* Baltimore, Waverly Press, Inc., 1929.

Lofts, Norah. *Queens of England.* Garden City, New York, Doubleday & Co., Inc., 1977.

Luckett, Margie H. *Maryland Women.* Baltimore, King Bros., Inc., 1931.

McCarthy, Justin. *The Reign of Queen Anne.* London, Chatto & Windus, 1902.

McSherry, James. *History of Maryland from Its First Settlement in 1634, to the Year 1848.* Baltimore, John Murphy, 1849.

Map of Wicomico County with Salisbury, Maryland. Cincinnati, Ohio, Merchant Maps Mass Marketing, Inc., 1992.

Maryland Genealogical Society, Inc. *Cecil County, Maryland: 1800 Census.* Baltimore, 1972.

Maryland Genealogies: A Consolidation of Articles from the Maryland Historical Magazine. Baltimore, Genealogical Publishing Co., Inc., 1980.

Maryland State Planning Commission & Department of Geology, Mines & Water Resources. *Gazetteer of Maryland.* Baltimore, Johns Hopkins University, 1941.

Mathews, Edward B. *The Counties of Maryland: Their Origin, Boundaries & Election Districts.* Baltimore, Johns Hopkins Press, 1907.

Merriken, Ellenor. *Commemorating the 200th Anniversary of Caroline County, Maryland: 1774–1974.*

Miller, Mary R. *Place-Names of the Northern Neck of Virginia.* Richmond, Virginia, Virginia State Library, 1983.

Mills, A. D. *A Dictionary of English Place Names.* Oxford, Oxford University Press, 1991.

Morris, Clay L. *You Take the High Road: A Guide to the Place Names of the Colonial Eastern Shore of Maryland*. Easton, Maryland, Easton Publishing Co., 1970.

Morris, John G. *The Lords Baltimore*. Baltimore, 1874.

Moule, Thomas. *The County Maps of Old England*. London, Studio Editions, 1990.

Nicklin, John B. C. "The Calvert Family." *Maryland Historical Magazine*, Vol. 16, No. 1. Baltimore: March, 1921.

Papenfuse, Edward C. *Archives of Maryland: New Series: An Historical List of Public Officials of Maryland*. Annapolis, Maryland, Maryland State Archives, 1990.

Papenfuse, Edward C., et al. *A Biographical Dictionary of the Maryland Legislature: 1635–1789*. Baltimore, Johns Hopkins University Press, 1979.

Parran, Alice N. *Register of Maryland's Heraldic Families-Series II*. Baltimore.

Paullin, Charles O. *Atlas of the Historical Geography of the United States*. Carnegie Institution of Washington and the American Geographical Society of New York, 1932.

Preston, Dickson J. *Talbot County: A History*. Centreville, Maryland, Tidewater Publishers, 1983.

Preston, Walter W. *History of Harford County, Maryland*. Baltimore, Press of Sun Book Office, 1901.

Price, Edward T. *Dividing the Land: Early American Beginnings of Our Private Property Mosaic*. Chicago, University of Chicago Press, 1995.

Radoff, Morris L. *The County Courthouses & Records of Maryland*. Annapolis, State of Maryland Hall of Records Commission, 1960.

Radoff, Morris L., & Frank F. White. *Maryland Manual: 1969–1970*. Annapolis, Maryland Hall of Records Commission, 1970.

Rand, Clayton. *Sons of the South*. New York, Holt, Rinehart & Winston, 1961.

Riley, Elihu S. *History of Annapolis, in Maryland*. Annapolis, Record Printing Office, 1887.

Riley, Elihu S. *A History of Anne Arundel County in Maryland*. Annapolis, Maryland, Charles G. Feldmeyer, 1905.

Rollo, Vera F, *Henry Harford: Last Proprietor of Maryland*. Maryland Bicentennial Commission, Harford County Committee, 1976.

Rollo, Vera F. "Henry Harford, Maryland's Last Proprietor: How He Became Proprietor & Reasons for His Lack of Success in Maryland Following the American Revolution." M.A. Thesis, Theodore R. McKeldin Library, University of Maryland, College Park, Maryland, 1976.

Rollo, Vera F. *The Proprietorship of Maryland*. Lanham, Maryland, Maryland Historical Press, 1989.

Rollo, Vera F. *Your Maryland: A History*. Lanham, Maryland, Maryland Historical Press, 1993.

Room, Adrian. *Dictionary of Place-Names in the British Isles*. London, England, Bloomsbury Publishing, Ltd., 1989.

Scharf, John T. *History of Western Maryland*. Philadelphia, 1882.

Skirven, Percy G. *The First Parishes of the Province of Maryland*. Baltimore, Norman Remington Co., 1923.

Spencer, Richard H. *Genealogical & Memorial Encyclopedia of the State of Maryland*. New York, American Historical Society, Inc., 1919.

Steiner, Bernard C. "The Beginnings of Charles County." *Maryland Historical Magazine*, Vol. 21, No. 3. Baltimore: September, 1926.

Steiner, Bernard C. "Life & Administration of Sir Robert Eden." *Johns Hopkins University Studies in Historical & Political Science*, Series 16, Nos. 7, 8 & 9. Baltimore: July–September, 1898.

Stiverson, Gregory A. *Maryland Manual: 1981–1982*. Annapolis, Maryland,

Archives Division, Hall of Records, Department of General Services.

Stockett, Letitia. *Baltimore: A Not Too Serious History*. Baltimore, Grace Gore Norman, 1936.

Summers, Festus P. *The Baltimore & Ohio in the Civil War*. New York, G. P. Putnam's Sons, 1939.

Taft, William H. III. *County Names: An Historical Perspective*. National Association of Counties, 1982.

Tilghman, Oswald. *History of Talbot County, Maryland: 1661–1861*. Baltimore, Williams & Wilkins Co., 1915.

Torrence, Clayton. *Old Somerset on the Eastern Shore of Maryland*. Richmond, Virginia, Whittet & Shepperson, 1935.

Truitt, Reginald V. & Millard G. Les Callette. *Worcester County: Maryland's Arcadia*. Snow Hill, Maryland, Worcester County Historical Society, 1977.

Vexler, Robert I. *Baltimore: A Chronological & Documentary History*. Dobbs Ferry, New York, Oceana Publications, Inc., 1975.

Vexler, Robert I. *Chronology & Documentary Handbook of the State of Maryland*. Dobbs Ferry, New York, Oceana Publications, Inc., 1978.

Virta, Alan. *Prince George's County: A Pictorial History*. Norfolk, Virginia, Donning Co., 1984.

Warfield, J. D. *The Founders of Anne Arundel & Howard Counties, Maryland*. Baltimore, Kohn & Pollock, 1905.

White, Frank F. *The Governors of Maryland: 1777–1970*. Annapolis, State of Maryland, Hall of Records Commission, 1970.

Williamson, David. *Kings & Queens of Britain*. New York, Dorset Press, 1992.

Wise, L. F. & E. W. Egan. *Kings, Rulers & Statesmen*. New York, Sterling Publishing Co., Inc., 1967.

Work Projects Administration. *Inventory of the County & Town Archives of Maryland-Anne Arundel County*. Baltimore, 1941.

Massachusetts

(14 counties)

1185 *Barnstable County*

Town of Barnstable, Massachusetts — The town of Barnstable, Massachusetts was first settled in the late 1630's by Pilgrims who came to Cape Cod from the Plymouth Colony towns of Plymouth and Duxbury and by settlers from Lynn, in Massachusetts Bay Colony. There, near the center of the Cape Cod peninsula, they established the town of Barnstable as a new settlement for Plymouth Colony. The pioneer settlers may have been attracted by the salt marshes that yielded an abundance of hay for their cattle. A church for Indians was established here. It had a congregation of about 500 by 1674. By the early 1700's, Barnstable had become a trading center. Commodities traded included codfish, rum and molasses. In later years, Barnstable became involved in fur trading. Today Barnstable is one of the many popular summer resorts on Cape Cod. When the settlers named their new community on Cape Cod in the late 1630's, they named it for Barnstaple, a town in Devon County, in southwestern England. Note the difference in the spelling of the English Barnstaple and the Massachusetts Barnstable. Barnstaple, England, is a seaport town located on the Taw River estuary, about 50 miles north of Plymouth, England. It boasts a bridge that dates back to the 13th century and a church that was built in the 14th century. The origin and meaning of Barnstaple, England's name is uncertain. Possibilities that have been mentioned include:

— "Bearded post"; i.e., a post marked with a besom or the like and used as a landmark or seamark.

— "Beaked ships"; i.e., a post to which warships were moored

Our Barnstable County was created on June 2, 1685. Its namesake, the town of Barnstable, was made its original county seat and, three centuries later, Barnstable is still the county seat of Barnstable County. At the time that it was created, Barnstable County was a part of Plymouth Colony.

1186 *Berkshire County*

Berkshire County, England — Berkshire County, Massachusetts was created in the early 1760's as a part of England's Massachusetts Bay Colony. This new county was named for Berkshire County, England. The word *shire* is a British word for "county." Our Berkshire County's namesake in England is referred to in various sources as Berks County, Berks Shire and Berkshire County. This English county is located in southern England, about 50 miles west of London. It lies largely in the basin formed by the Thames River. Its other important streams are the Kennet, Loddon, Auburn and Blackwater Rivers. England's Berkshire County is about 40 miles long and some 25 miles wide. Its soil is underlain by chalk and chalk downs extend through the center of the county. Their name is the Berkshire Downs. The name *Berkshire* is derived from an ancient Celtic name, the meaning of which is uncertain. Possibilities that have been mentioned include "a wood grove," "the forest shire," "shire district," and "hilly place."

1187 *Bristol County*

Town of Bristol, Rhode Island — Bristol County was created on June 2, 1685, as a part of England's Plymouth Colony. The county was named for its first county seat, the town of Bristol, which became part of Rhode Island on May 28, 1746, when a change was made by the British parliament to the boundary line between the colonies of Massachusetts Bay and Rhode Island & Providence Plantations. The town of Bristol, which is now the county seat of Bristol County, Rhode Island, was first settled about 1669 and it was involved in King Philip's War of 1675–1676. Bristol was bombarded by British ships in 1775 and it was invaded, pillaged and burned by the British in 1778, during the American Revolution. At one time the town of Bristol was important in the whale-fishing industry. Today it is a residential community. The town of Bristol in New England was named for the town of Bristol in England, a seaport in Avon County. In the 17th century, when our town of Bristol was named, the city of Bristol, England, was second in importance to London. Bristol, England, is located in southwestern England, about 110 miles west of London, at the confluence of the Avon and Frome Rivers. Its population was estimated to be 400,000 in 1981. During an English Civil War, Bristol was captured in 1643 by royalists, under Prince Rupert (1619–1682) but recaptured by parliamentary forces in 1645. During the 17th and 18th centuries Bristol was active in maritime trade, dealing in Black slaves from West Africa, cocoa, tobacco and sugar. Bristol was repeatedly bombed by the German air force during the second World War. The name *Bristol* derived from a name dating back to about the eleventh century. Several translations have been offered and they are quite similar:

— "Assembly place by" (or "near") the bridge"

— "The shrine near the bridge"

— "The site of the bridge"

— "Bridge-place"

There has been, from time immemorial, a bridge over the Avon River at Bristol. It was apparently near this bridge that the settlement of Bristol grew to become the major city that it is today.

1188 *Dukes County*

King James II (1633–1701) — This county was created by England's colony of New York in 1683. It was named for the duke of York and Albany, who later became England's King James II. When it was established in 1683, Dukes County contained the islands of Nantucket, Martha's Vineyard, Chappaquiddick, No Mans Land and the Elizabeth Islands, some 16 in number. The duke of York and Albany considered these islands a part of his vast New York domain. In 1692 (when James II was no longer king of England) these islands were granted to England's Massachusetts Bay colony. On June 22, 1695, Massachusetts Bay colony established two counties from these islands: Nantucket and Dukes.

King James II (1633–1701) — James was the second surviving son of England's King Charles I (1600–1649). He was given the title duke of York and Albany soon after his christening. When James' father died, his elder brother, Charles, succeeded to the throne as King Charles II (1630–1685). In 1664 King Charles II made an enormous grant of land to his brother, the duke of York and Albany, which included the present Dukes County, Massachusetts. The duke was awarded more power over his domain than any other English proprietor. Although King Charles II had many children, none of them were legitimate so when King Charles II died in 1685, his brother, James, became king of England as King James II. The first wife of the duke of York and Albany had been Anne Hyde, who died in 1671. In 1673 James remarried to Mary of Modena (1658–1718), a Catholic, and some time during this period James professed his own Catholicism. This spelled his eventual downfall as king. In 1689 the throne passed to William of Orange (1650–1702), who ruled as joint sovereign with his wife, Queen Mary II (1662–1694). Mary was a daughter of King James II. The former King James II devoted the final years of his life to religious exercises.

1189 *Essex County*

Essex County, England — A large proportion of the early settlers of what is now the state of Massachusetts, came from the eastern region of Anglia, in southern England. Many of the geographic names that these early settlers used for their towns and counties in the new world were taken directly from town and county names in the east Anglia section of England. Essex County was one of the first counties to be established in the present state of Massachusetts. It was created on May 10, 1643, and named for Essex County in the eastern section of Anglia, in southern England. This seacoast county facing the European continent was an important center when it was occupied by the Roman Empire and it continued to be an important population center, containing the city of London, when the East Saxons invaded it. The name *Essex* means "territory of the East Saxons." Essex was one of the seven Anglo-Saxon kingdoms of Britain known as the Heptarchy. In the seventh century Essex was conquered by Mercia, one of the other kingdoms of the Heptarchy, and later, in the ninth century, Wessex, which had been another member of the Heptarchy, conquered it. The Essex County of today's England no longer contains London. Essex County, England, is about 54 miles long and some 48 miles wide. Its principal rivers are the Thames, Stour, Colne, Blackwater and Lea.

1190 *Franklin County*

Benjamin Franklin (1706–1790) — Franklin was born in Boston, Massachusetts, on January 17, 1706, but he moved to Pennsylvania when he was in his teens. Poverty denied him a formal education but he became the leading printer and editor in North America. Franklin gained fame for his discoveries and inventions in the physical sciences and he distinguished himself as author, philosopher and diplomat. He was a signer of the Declaration of Independence and an important member of the convention which framed the U.S. Constitution. Franklin County was created in 1811.

1191 *Hampden County*

John Hampden (1594–1643) — John Hampden was an Englishman on the side of his first cousin, Oliver Cromwell (1599–1658), in the British Civil War of 1642 to 1649. This Civil War arose from differences between King Charles I (1600–1649) and parliamentary forces, whose members included John Hampden and Oliver Cromwell. The parliamentarians were victorious and King Charles I was beheaded in 1649. John Hampden had died in 1643 as a result of wounds suffered in an engagement at Chalgrove Field so he did not live to see his side win the Civil War. Hampden was born in London in 1594, the son of an old and wealthy English family. He studied at the Magdalen College of Oxford University. From the time that King Charles I was crowned as king in 1625, John Hampden associated with opponents to the king. Hampden served several terms in parliament, the first as a representative from the borough of Grampound from 1621 to 1625. He was imprisoned in 1627 for refusing to pay a forced loan. Hampden is remembered as the most popular member of the so-called Short Parliament (April 13 to May 5, 1640) and he was influential in the early proceedings of the Long Parliament which began in 1640. He died in combat in 1643. Hampden County, Massachusetts, was created in 1812.

1192 *Hampshire County*

Hampshire County, England — Quite a few of the early Puritan settlers of Massachusetts Bay Colony came from Hampshire County, in southern England. Hampshire County, Massachusetts, was established on May 7, 1662, and named for Hampshire County, England, whose important municipalities include Portsmouth, Southampton and Bournemouth. This English county lies on the English Channel near the Isle of Wight, which is considered part of Hampshire County for purposes of civil administration. Excluding the Isle of Wight, Hampshire County is approximately 42 miles long and some 38 miles wide. Hampshire is one of England's most fertile counties. A range of chalk downs runs through a northern portion of the county. Hampshire's principal rivers are the Avon, Test, Itchen and Stour. In the sixth century A.D., Cerdic (–534) and his Saxons invaded and conquered much of southern England, including the present Hampshire County. This was the beginning of Wessex, the kingdom of the West Saxons. Hampshire possesses relatively little in the way of magnificent architecture, but it can boast an ancient cathedral in its city of Winchester. The name *Hampshire* evolved from the earlier *Hamtunscir*. The *scir* portion of the name became *shire*, which is one of the words used in England for our word "county." Possible origins and translations of the *Ham* and *tun* portions of the earlier name include:

Ham— "A home, dwelling or house"
tun— "A garden, field or enclosure"

In his work entitled *A Dictionary of English Place Names*, A. D. Mills stated that *Hampshire* derived from an earlier name *Hamtunscir,* which meant "district based on Hamtun"; i.e., "district based on Southampton."

1193 *Middlesex County*

Middlesex County, England — A large number of the early Puritan settlers of what is now the state of Massachusetts came from what was then England's premier county, Middlesex, which then contained the city of London. Our Middlesex County was created on May 10, 1643 as one of the original counties of Massachusetts Bay Colony. Middlesex County, in southeastern England, was the home of the Middle Saxon tribe. It became a shire (county) in the tenth century A.D. Its name derived from the tribal name of the Middle Saxons. An early version of the county's name was *Middelseaxan,* which meant "territory of the Middle Saxons." The Middlesex County area was occupied by the Roman Empire from A.D. 43 to A.D. 409. From Anglo-Saxon times it grew to be England's center of trade. Middlesex County suffered a severe plague in 1665 and a great fire in London in 1666. During World War II Middlesex County was bombed extensively by the German air force. Middlesex County is relatively small in size, with a length of about 22 miles and a width of only 14 miles. Its principal streams are the Thames, Lea and Colin Rivers. Middlesex County, England ceased to exist as a separate entity in 1965 when it was absorbed as a part of a metropolitan county named Greater London.

1194 *Nantucket County*

Nantucket Island, Massachusetts — Nantucket Island lies in the Atlantic Ocean about 25 miles south of Cape Cod and some 15 miles east of the island named Martha's Vineyard. Nantucket Island is approximately 14 miles long and a bit over 3 miles wide at its broadest point. It is a low island; less than 100 feet above sea level at its loftiest point. This island was inhabited by Indians when English explorers first visited it. The English explorer, Bartholomew Gosnold (–1607) chartered the island in 1602. In 1683, Nantucket Island was made a part of England's colony of New York, included in Dukes County. The duke of York and Albany considered Nantucket Island a part of his vast New York domain. In 1692 Nantucket was given back to Massachusetts Bay Colony and in 1695 Nantucket Island, together with some small adjacent islands, was made a county named Nantucket County. Today Nantucket Island is a popular summer resort. There is little agreement among sources consulted concerning the origin and meaning of the name *Nantucket*. All sources agree that it derived from an Indian name (thus making Nantucket County the only county in Massachusetts with an Indian name). The Indians had no written language so seemingly endless versions of the Indians' name for the island have survived. At least 29 versions are known ranging, alphabetically, from Naiantukq to Neutocket.

Translations of the Indian names that have been mentioned include:

— "In the midst of waters"
— "At the land far away"

— "At the far off (at sea) place"

— "Where it is the sea gets broader"

— "Far off among the waves"

— "Far away island"

— "Point of land in the stream" (or "river")

— "Narrow" (tidal) "river at," referring to the channel between Nantucket Island and a tiny adjacent island

— "At the promontory"

— "Sandy, sterile soil tempted no one"

It is frustrating to have to contend with such a long list of possible translations of Indian names. However, the American Indians were not alone in leaving us with semantic difficulties. Note the following paragraph which is quoted from Franklin B. Hough's work entitled *Papers Relating to the Island of Nantucket*: "On the Succeffion of William and Mary to the Throne of England, a new Charter was granted to New England, in which Nantucket was expreffly declared a part of Maffachufetts."

1195 *Norfolk County*

Norfolk County, England — Massachusetts Bay Colony created a Norfolk County in 1643 and named it for Norfolk County in eastern England. A great proportion of the early Puritan settlers of what is now the state of Massachusetts came from the eastern region of Anglia, in England. Many of the geographic names that these early settlers used for their towns and counties in the new world were taken directly from town and county names in the east Anglia section of England. Norfolk County was one of the first counties to be established in the present state of Massachusetts. It was created on May 10, 1643, and named for Norfolk County, England. On February 4, 1680, Norfolk County in Massachusetts Bay Colony ceased to exist. Most of it had been given to New Hampshire and its remaining territory was absorbed by Massachusetts Bay's Essex County. However, on March 26, 1793, after the British had been defeated in the American Revolution and after the United States of America had been created, including Massachusetts as one of its states, a new Norfolk County was created as a county in the state of Massachusetts. England's Anglian county of Norfolk is in eastern England on the North Sea, facing the European continent. This English county is about 70 miles long and some 40 miles wide. Its principal city is Norwich and its main rivers are the Great Ouse, Nen, Little Ouse, Waveney, Wensum, Yare and Bure. Along Norfolk's coast, winds are frequent, sharp and piercing and at one time windmills were profuse in this area. England's King James I (1566–1625) was said to have been enamored of the county on his first visit to it and he later purchased a house here. Norfolk County's name means "the northern people" (or "folk") or "the territory of the northern people" (or "folk") to distinguish it from Suffolk (now a county immediately south of Norfolk County, in East Anglia).

1196 *Plymouth County*

Town of Plymouth and/or Plymouth Colony — On June 2, 1685, Plymouth Colony created three counties from its territory. They were Barnstable County, Bristol County and Plymouth County. The Pilgrims landed at Plymouth in 1620 and founded the first permanent settlement of Europeans in New England. These Pilgrims were a small band of Puritans who were separatists from the Church of England. They traveled first to the Netherlands and then sailed from Plymouth, England across the Atlantic Ocean to North America in search of freedom from religious persecution. Plymouth, New England, was an English colony and it included parts of what are now southeastern Massachusetts and eastern Rhode Island. Plymouth Colony was absorbed into another English Colony, Massachusetts Bay Colony, in 1691. The Pilgrims apparently named their landing place in New England for two reasons:

1. The name Plymouth had already been inserted in this general vicinity on a map of New England by Prince Charles (who later became King Charles I of England) when he chose a number of English names to replace Indian names here.

2. The Pilgrims left the Netherlands to sail to North America on two ships, the *Speedwell* and the *Mayflower* but when the *Speedwell* proved unseaworthy it was abandoned at Plymouth, England in Devonshire. There the Pilgrims were treated with kindness by some Christians before they all crowded on the tiny *Mayflower* to continue their voyage to North America.

Plymouth, England is located in what is now called Devon County, England, between the Plym and Tamar estuaries and its name came from the Plym River there. Its name means "place at the mouth of the river Plym." The river's name came from a mother settlement there, Plympton, whose name meant "plum tree village." (In the late 1990's plums were still being grown here.)

1197 *Suffolk County*

Suffolk County, England — A large proportion of the early settlers of what is now the state of Massachusetts, came from the eastern region of Anglia, in England. Many of the geographic names that these early settlers used for their towns and counties in the new world were taken directly from town and county names in the east Anglia section of England. Suffolk County was one of the first counties to be established in the present state of Massachusetts. It was created on May 10, 1643, by England's Massachusetts Bay Colony and named for Suffolk County in Anglia in eastern England. Suffolk County, England, is approximately 50 miles long and some 30 miles wide. It lies on the North Sea, where it faces the European continent. Its principal rivers are the Little Ouse, Great Ouse, Waveney, Stour, Breton, Orwell, Deben, Ore and Blyth. King James I (1566–1625) was enamored by Suffolk when he visited it (as he also was by Norfolk County; see above) and he purchased a house here. Suffolk County's name derived from a name which meant "the southern people" (or "folk") or "the territory of the southern people" (or "folk") to distinguish it from Norfolk (now a county, immediately north of Suffolk in East Anglia.)

1198 *Worcester County*

Worcester, England — In 1684, the present city of Worcester, Massachusetts was given its name and in April, 1731, England's Massachusetts Bay Colony created Worcester County. Most of the geographic names that were used by the English settlers of what is now the state of Massachusetts, for naming their towns and counties in the new world were taken directly from town and county names in England. Sources consulted are largely in agreement that Worcester County, Massachusetts was named either directly or indirectly for the English county named Worcester; i.e., Massachusetts Bay Colony's Worcester County was either named directly for the county in England named Worcester or it was named for that English county indirectly; by being named for the town of Worcester in Massachusetts Bay Colony, which had been named in the 17th century for the county of Worcester, in England.

Worcester, England — Worcester, or Worcestershire, is a county in west-central England in the West Midlands section of the country. Large sections of Worcester are covered with forests and the Severn River traverses portions of these forests.

The Severn also drains low-lying marsh-lands of the county. Other rivers here are the Avon, Salwarp, Teme and Stour. Worcester is about 35 miles long and some 30 miles wide. When the Roman Empire occupied England, they took little interest in the Worcester area. About A.D. 577, the West Saxons conquered Worcester but control of the area passed to the Mercians. In the year A.D. 825, Egbert (–839), who was king of Wessex, took brief control of Worcester but Mercian influence was reestablished in A.D. 830. In the latter part of the ninth century, the barbaric Danes conquered Worcester and raided and plundered its monasteries and cathedrals. It was not until A.D. 1017 that a period of internal peace began when the Dane, Canute the Great (–1035), became king of England. In 1651 an important battle in English history was fought here when Oliver Cromwell (1599–1658), who was then dictator and lord protector of England, defeated an attempt to restore England to monarchy. Today's Worcester has some industry but it is primarily an agricultural county. Its soil, which is chiefly composed of clay and loam, is very fertile. Worcester is the surviving version of a long series of names for this area. Authorities differ on the origin and translation of the earlier names from which Worcester evolved. The following possibilities have been mentioned:

— "Dwellers by the winding river"
— "Winding river"
— "Fort of the Huiccii"
— "A grove"
— "Roman town of the Weogora tribe"
— "The forest of the Wigoran"
— "The forest men"

References

Barber, John W. *Historical Collections: Being a General Collection of Interesting Facts, Traditions, Biographical Sketches, Anecdotes &C., Relating to the History & Antiquities of Every Town in Massachusetts.* Worcester, Dorr Howland & Co., 1839.

Barnhart, Clarence L. *The New Century Handbook of English Literature.* New York, Appleton Century Crofts, 1967.

Baylies, Francis. *An Historical Memoir of the Colony of New Plymouth.* Boston, Wiggin & Lunt, 1866.

Bradley, A. G. *The Rivers & Streams of England.* London, Adam & Charles Black, 1909.

Brigham, Albert P. *Cape Cod and the Old Colony.* New York, G. P. Putnam's Sons, 1920.

Brown, Richard D. *Massachusetts: A Bicentennial History.* New York, W. W. Norton & Co., Inc., 1978.

Burroughs, Polly. *Guide to Nantucket.* Chester, Connecticut, Globe Pequot Press, 1984.

Chrisman, Lewis H. "The Origin of Place Names in West Virginia." *West Virginia History,* Vol. 7, No. 2. Charleston, West Virginia: January, 1946.

Clements, John. *Massachusetts Facts.* Dallas, Texas, Clements Research, Inc., 1987.

Cook, Louis A. *History of Norfolk County, Massachusetts: 1622–1918.* New York, S. J. Clarke Publishing Co., 1918.

Creighton, Mandell. *The Story of Some English Shires.* London, Religious Tract Society.

Crosby, Everett U. *Nantucket in Print.* Nantucket Island, Massachusetts, Tetaukimmo Press, 1946.

Cutter, William R. *Historic Homes and Places and Genealogical and Personal Memoirs Relating to the Families of Middlesex County, Massachusetts.* New York, Lewis Historical Publishing Co., 1908.

Darby. H. C. *A New Historical Geography of England.* Cambridge, England, Syndics of the Cambridge University Press, 1973.

Davis, Charlotte P. *Directory of Massachusetts Place Names.* Massachusetts Daughters of the American Revolution, 1987.

Davis, William T. *History of the Town of Plymouth.* Philadelphia, J. W. Lewis & Co., 1885.

Douglas-Lithgow, R. A. *Dictionary of American-Indian Place & Proper Names in New England.* Salem, Massachusetts, Salem Press, 1909.

Douglas-Lithgow, R. A. *Nantucket: A History.* New York, Knickerbocker Press, 1914.

Drake, Samuel A. *Old Landmarks & Historic Fields of Middlesex.* Boston, Roberts Brothers, 1888.

Dutton, Ralph. *Hampshire.* London, England, B. T. Batsford, Ltd., 1970.

Ekwall, Eilert. *The Concise Oxford Dictionary of English Place-Names.* Oxford, Oxford University Press, 1960.

Encyclopedia of Massachusetts. New York, New York. Somerset Publishers, 1984.

"English Sources of Emigration to the New England Colonies in the Seventeenth Century." *Proceedings of the Massachusetts Historical Society,* Vol. 60. Boston: 1927.

Field, John. *Place-Names of Great Britain & Ireland.* Totowa, New Jersey, Barnes & Noble Books, 1980.

Forbes, Allan & Ralph M. Eastman.

Town & City Seals of Massachusetts. Boston, State Street Trust Co., 1950.

Gannett, Henry. *The Origin of Certain Place Names in the United States.* Williamstown, Massachusetts, Corner House Publishers, 1978.

Gazetteer of the British Isles. Edinburgh, Scotland, John Bartholomew & Son, Ltd., 1966.

Gelling, Margaret. *The Place-Names of Berkshire.* Cambridge, Cambridge University Press, 1973.

The General Court of Massachusetts: 1630–1930: Tercentenary Exercises. Boston, Wright & Potter, 1931.

Giambarba, Paul. *Cape Cod and Cape Cod National Seashore.* Barre, Massachusetts, Barre Publishers, 1968.

Gover, J. E. B., et al. *The Place-Names of Devon.* Cambridge University Press, 1931.

Green, Eugene, & William L. Sachse. *Names of the Land: Cape Cod, Nantucket, Martha's Vineyard and the Elizabeth Islands.* Chester, Connecticut, Globe Pequot Press, 1983.

Guba, Emil F. *Nantucket Odyssey: A Journey into the History of Nantucket.* Watertown, Massachusetts, Eaton Press, Inc., 1951.

Guzzi, Paul. *Historical Data Relating to Counties, Cities & Towns in Massachusetts.* Commonwealth of Massachusetts, 1975.

Hart, Albert B. *Commonwealth History of Massachusetts.* New York, States History Co., 1930.

Hawkyard, Alasdair. *The Counties of Britain: A Tudor Atlas by John Speed.* London, England, Pavilion Books, Ltd., 1995.

History of Berkshire County, Massachusetts. New York, J. B. Beers & Co., 1885.

History of the Connecticut Valley in Massachusetts. Philadelphia, Louis H. Everts, 1879.

Hough, Franklin B. *Papers Relating to the Island of Nantucket.* Albany, 1856.

Huden, John C. *Indian Place Names of New England.* New York, Museum of the American Indian Heye Foundation, 1962.

Hurd, D. Hamilton. *History of Bristol County, Massachusetts.* Philadelphia, J. W. Lewis & Co., 1883.

Hurd, D. Hamilton. *History of Essex County, Massachusetts.* Philadelphia, J. W. Lewis & Co., 1888.

Hurd, D. Hamilton. *History of Plymouth County, Massachusetts.* Philadelphia, J. W. Lewis & Co., 1884.

Hurd, D. Hamilton. *History of Worcester County, Massachusetts.* Philadelphia, J. W. Lewis & Co., 1889.

Johnson, James. *Place Names of England & Wales.* London, England, Bracken Books, 1994.

Johnson, Stephanie L. *The Best of the Berkshires*. Chester, Connecticut, Globe Pequot Press, 1979.

Kenyon, J. P. *Dictionary of British History*. Ware, England, Wordsworth Editions, Ltd., 1992.

Kull, Irving S., & Nell M. Kull. *A Short Chronology of American History*. Westport, Connecticut, Greenwood Press, 1952.

Lockwood, John H., et al. *Western Massachusetts: A History: 1636–1925*. New York, Lewis Historical Publishing Co., Inc., 1926.

MacCracken, Henry N. *Old Dutchess Forever!: The Story of an American County*. New York, New York, Hastings House, 1956.

Mills, A. D. *A Dictionary of English Place Names*. Oxford, Oxford University Press, 1991.

Moule, Thomas. *The County Maps of Old England*. London, Studio Editions, 1990.

Nason, Elias. *A Gazetteer of the State of Massachusetts*. Boston, B. B. Russell, 1890.

Nutt, Charles. *History of Worcester and its People*. New York, New York, Lewis Historical Publishing Co., 1919.

Reaney, P. H. *The Origin of English Place-Names*. London, Routledge & Kegan Paul, 1960.

Room Adrian. *Dictionary of Place-Names in the British Isles*. London, England, Bloomsbury Publishing Ltd., 1989.

Seltzer, Leon E. *The Columbia Lippincott Gazetteer of the World*. Morningside Heights, New York, Columbia University Press, 1962.

Shankle, George Earlie. *State Names, Flags, Seals, Songs, Birds, Flowers & Other Symbols*. New York, H. W. Wilson Co., 1941.

Starbuck, Alexander. *The History of Nantucket*. Boston, C. E. Goodspeed & Co., 1924.

Stevens, William O. *Nantucket: The Far-Away Island*. New York, Dodd, Mead & Co., 1936.

Stewart, George R. *American Place-Names*. New York, Oxford University Press, 1970.

Stewart, George R. *Names on the Land*. New York, Random House, 1945.

Taft, William H., III. *County Names: An Historical Perspective*. National Association of Counties, 1982.

Vexler, Robert I. *Chronology & Documentary Handbook of the State of Massachusetts*. Dobbs Ferry, New York, Oceana Publications, Inc., 1978.

Whitmore, William H. "On the Origin of the Names of Towns in Massachusetts." *Proceedings of the Massachusetts Historical Society*, Vol. 12. Boston: 1871–1873.

Work Projects Administration. *The Origin of Massachusetts Place Names*. New York, Harian Publications, 1941.

Works Progress Administration. *Rhode Island: A Guide to the Smallest State*. Boston, Houghton Mifflin Co., 1937.

Worth, Henry B. "Nantucket Lands & Land Owners." *Nantucket Historical Association Bulletin*, Vol. 2, No. 6. 1910.

Wrenn, C. L. "The Name Bristol." *Names: Journal of the American Name Society*, Vol. 5, No. 2. Berkeley, California: June, 1957.

Michigan

(83 counties)

1199 *Alcona County*

A contrived or pseudo–Indian name — This county was originally created on April 1, 1840, and named Negwegon County in honor of an Ottawa Indian chief, named Ningwegon or Newaygo or Negwegon. He had been a friend to the Americans in their conflicts with the British, which culminated in the War of 1812. The county's name was changed to Alcona on March 8, 1843. Alcona is one of the many contrived (half–Indian or pseudo Indian) geographic names which are scattered over Michigan's map. Most of these contrived names were coined by Henry R. Schoolcraft (1793–1864). According to Professor Virgil J. Vogel's scholarly *Indian Names in Michigan* (the definitive work on this subject), the name Alcona was concocted in this manner:

Al — Reportedly from the Arabic *al*

co — Although said to be from an Ojibwa Indian root meaning "plain" or "prairie," this supposed Indian syllable does not have any meaning.

na — Supposedly means "excellence" but according to Father Frederich Baraga (1797–1868)

na — is an Indian interrogatory or used as an interjection. For further information about Father Baraga, see Baraga County, Michigan, below. Professor Vogel's conclusion is that the na in Alcona is just a Latin suffix, as in Indiana.

1200 *Alger County*

Russell A. Alger (1836–1907) — A native of Ohio and a lawyer, Alger came to Michigan about 1860 and began a lumber business. He enlisted as a private in the Union army during the Civil War and distinguished himself in some 66 battles and skirmishes while rising to the rank of brevet major-general of volunteers. At the end of the war he returned to his lumber business in Michigan and in 1884 was elected governor of the state. He served in that office from January 1, 1885, to January 1, 1887. William McKinley was elected president in the election of 1896 and he immediately asked Alger to serve in his cabinet as secretary of war. Alger accepted and he became secretary of war on March 5, 1897. In April, 1898, the U.S. declared war on Spain. Although our navy was well equipped to engage in this conflict and although we ultimately won this Spanish-American War, our ill-equipped army was considered a disgrace when the war started. Alger was a handy scapegoat and he was forced to resign as secretary of war on August 1, 1899. From 1902 until his death, Russell A. Alger represented Michigan in the U.S. Senate. This county was created and named in March, 1885, while Alger was Michigan's governor.

1201 *Allegan County*

Alleghany Indians — This county in southwestern Michigan was created in 1831, when Michigan was still a territory. Its name was suggested in that year by Henry R. Schoolcraft (1793–1864), when he was a member of Michigan's territorial legislative council. Schoolcraft stated that the name *Allegan* was derived from the name of a prehistoric Indian tribe named the Alligewi Indians. Alligewi was one of the versions of the name by which the Alleghany Indians were known. The Alleghany were a tribe who lived in the 18th century near present day Pittsburgh, Pennsylvania, where the Allegheny River joins with the Monongahela River to form the Ohio River. The Alleghany Indians' name derived from the name of the river along which they lived. The river was apparently first named by the Iroquois Indians and later modified by Delaware Indians. The Alleghany Indians were found in a wider area than simply present-day Pittsburgh. In his work entitled *Indian Villages & Place Names in Pennsylvania*, George P. Donehoo states that "The term [Allegheny] applied to all of the Indians living west of the waters of the Susquehanna [River] within the region drained by the Ohio [River]."

1202 *Alpena County*

A contrived or pseudo–Indian name— This county was created on April 1, 1840 and named Anamickee County, in honor of an Indian chief. Its name was changed to Alpena on March 8, 1843. Alpena is one of the many contrived (half Indian or pseudo–Indian) geographic names that dot Michigan's map. Most of these names were coined by Henry R. Schoolcraft (1793–1864). According to Virgil J. Vogel's scholarly *Indian Names in Michigan* (the definitive work on this subject), Henry R. Schoolcraft explained that the name Alpena was created in this manner:

Al—Reportedly contracted from the Arabic *al*

pena—Part of *penaisee*, an Ojibwa Indian word for "bird."But elsewhere Schoolcraft said that the *pena* came from *penai* meaning "partridge." As a result, many sources indicate that the county's name means "partridge," "good partridge country," or variations on the partridge theme.

1203 *Antrim County*

Northern Ireland's County Antrim—This county was created on April 1, 1840, and named Meegisee County (or Meegistee; sources consulted differ on the spelling). Its name was changed to Antrim County on March 8, 1843. The name honors County Antrim in the northeast-most corner of Northern Ireland. (It was originally erroneously printed as Antim in the 1843 Michigan legislative act that created it.) Michigan's legislature of 1843 changed

the names of several other counties on March 8, 1843, to honor persons and places of Irish origin. The Northern Ireland county's name is shown as Antrym on John Speed's map, which was drawn about 1600. Antrim, and most of Northern Ireland, was a part of Gaeldom throughout the 16th century. England was anxious to control the area but the Irish people were resistant to change and divided by local feuds. England's Queen Elizabeth I (1533–1603) tried to gain control of the area but failed. In 1603 King James I (1566–1625) succeeded to the English crown. Also in 1603, the crowns of Scotland and England were united with King James I ruling Scotland as King James VI. At this time Antrim came under control of the British crown and remains so today, in the late 1990's.

1204 *Arenac County*

A contrived or pseudo–Indian name— This county's name is another of Michigan's contrived county names (half Indian or pseudo–Indian). Most of these names were the creations of Henry R. Schoolcraft (1793–1864). Schoolcraft stated that Arenac was concocted from the Latin *arena*, meaning "sand" and an Algonquian Indian word *akee* meaning "land." This county was created in 1831 while Michigan was still a territory and while Henry R. Schoolcraft was a member of Michigan territory's legislative council.

1205 *Baraga County*

Irenaeus Frederich Baraga (1797–1868)— Frederich Baraga was born in Austria to a wealthy family in 1797 and in 1823 he was ordained as a Roman Catholic priest. Shortly after the formation, in Vienna, of the Leopoldine Society for promoting missions in North America, Baraga learned of it and took interest. In 1831 he came to Cincinnati to join the diocese there, which at that time included present-day Michigan. Later that year Father Baraga arrived in Michigan territory and began his missionary work among the Indians. That work lasted until his death in 1868. During his first year, at L'Abre Croche, Baraga established two schools for Ottawa Indians and a church with a congregation of some 700 members of that tribe. Life in those days on our country's northern frontier was tough for everyone but Baraga's hardships were unusually plentiful. On occasion he walked as many as 40 miles in a day on snowshoes to make visitations. He encountered trouble and opposition from Indian medicine men, Protestant

opponents and drunken Indians. His work among the Chippewa Indians at La Pointe lasted many years. During his life with the Indians, Father Baraga wrote a prayer book in the Ottawa Indians' language and both a dictionary and a grammar book in the language of the Chippewa Indians. Starting about 1845, Baraga also began to attend to the spiritual needs of an influx of immigrants from Europe, who were attracted to Michigan's northern peninsula by the newly developing copper mining industry there. Many of these immigrants were Catholic. On November 1, 1853, Father Baraga was consecrated as a bishop and made vicar-apostolic of Upper Michigan. His vicarate was later erected into the diocese of Sault Sainte-Marie and Baraga was appointed as the first bishop of this new see. In 1865 the see was transferred to Marquette and Baraga moved there. Baraga County, on Michigan's northern peninsula, was created in 1875, seven years after Baraga's death.

1206 *Barry County*

*William T. Barry (1784–1835)—*A native of Virginia and a lawyer, Barry moved to Lexington, Kentucky, and was soon elected to the lower house of the Kentucky legislature. He served several terms in that body rising to become speaker of the house. In 1815 Barry entered the U.S. Senate to fill a vacancy caused by a resignation but Barry, himself resigned from the senate the following year. He then held a variety of political positions in Kentucky including judge, state senator, lieutenant-governor, secretary of state and chief justice of the state supreme court. Barry assisted Andrew Jackson in his successful bid for the presidency and, in repayment of that political debt, President Jackson appointed Barry to be his first postmaster general. At that time the postmaster general was a member of the president's cabinet. Barry was serving in Jackson's cabinet as President Jackson's postmaster general when this county was created. He later was appointed minister to Spain but he died while enroute to Madrid. In 1829 Michigan had been a territory since 1805 and by October, 1829, thoughts of potential statehood may have been on the minds of Michigan's territorial legislators. For whatever reason, on October 29, 1829, Michigan territory created counties named for Andrew Jackson, who was then president, John C. Calhoun (1782–1850), who was Jackson's first vice-president, and all members of President Jackson's first cabinet, including William T. Barry.

1207 *Bay County*

Saginaw Bay—Bay County is located on the eastern shore of Michigan's lower peninsula on Lake Huron's Saginaw Bay. The county's name was chosen because of its location along the bay. Saginaw Bay is some 60 miles long and about 25 miles wide at its broadest point. The Saginaw River is one of the major streams which feed water into Saginaw Bay. Several sources indicate that Saginaw Bay was named for the former presence in the area of the Sauk Indians, an Algonquian tribe, who were closely allied to the Fox Indians. Although this origin for Saginaw Bay's name is possible, it is more likely that *Saginaw* was derived from the Ojibwa Indians' word *saging*, meaning "at the mouth." If Sauk Indians ever lived in the area around Saginaw Bay, it was before the arrival of Europeans.

1208 *Benzie County*

Uncertain—Although this county was created in 1863, which makes it one of Michigan's newer counties, the origin of its name is difficult to determine. Many sources state "uncertain" and then list some or all of the alternatives and that is what will be done here:

Betsie River—The Betsie River lies within Benzie County and drains into Lake Michigan on the county's western border. The Betsie River is some 40 miles long and, together with its tributaries, traverses about 73 miles and drains approximately 250 square miles of Michigan. A number of sources incorrectly refer to the Betsy River in their comments about the origin of Benzie County's name. It is true that an early spelling of the Betsie River's name was Betsy but one of the few facts about Benzie County's name that is known with certainty, is that the county was not named for Michigan's present Betsy River. Benzie County is located on the west side of Michigan's lower peninsula, while the Betsy River has its mouth in Chippewa County in Michigan's upper peninsula. Chippewa County's eastern border nestles against the province of Ontario, in Canada. This Betsy River on the upper peninsula is only 19 miles long and is more than 100 miles northeast of both Benzie County and the Betsie River. However, the Betsie River may very well be the source of the county's name. The Betsie River's name was an English language corruption of the name by which it was known by the French, *Riviere Aux Bec Scies*. This French name meant "river with the saw bills," referring to saw-billed ducks which were noted along the river in early days.

Village of Benzonia—Benzonia originated about 1858 when a group of Protestants settled near here with the intent of forming, in the remote northern wilderness, a Christian colony with an institution of higher learning. The proposed Christian colony was intended to be modeled after earlier Congregational settlements in Oberlin, Ohio, and Olivet, Michigan. This goal of a Christian institution of higher learning was accomplished when Grand Traverse College was chartered in 1863 as an integral part of the Benzonia community. The college's name was later changed to Benzonia College. About 1900 its efforts were directed at college preparatory work and the school's name was changed to Benzonia Academy. This educational institution was closed in 1918. According to some sources, the name *Benzonia* came from a combination of Hebrew words meaning "sons of light," or "sons of life," or "sons of toil." Other sources refute this with the comment that a Professor Craig, at the University of Michigan reviewed these translations and found them faulty. He indicated that it was improbable that the word *Benzonia* was derived from the Hebrew language, but if it was, none of these proposed translations would have been correct. Professor Craig went on to state that if the name was given in the belief that it had such a meaning, it is probable that the scholarship was faulty. Indeed, it has recently been suggested to the author that the Hebrew *Benzonia* means "sons of Zion." Another source states that *Benzonia* is not of Hebrew origin and suggests, instead, that it is possibly a Greek-Latin hybrid. From about 1872 to 1895, Benzonia was the county seat of Benzie County. By the early 1980's Benzonia's population was only about 400.

A contrived name—The possibility is mentioned by several sources that the county's name, Benzie, may have been formed by contracting the first part of Benzonia's name and joining it with a modified version of the last syllable of the Betsie River's name. If so, this was an appropriate combination because the Betsie River was an instrumental means of transportation for both settlers and commodities in establishing the new Christian colony in the northern wilderness.

1209 *Berrien County*

John M. Berrien (1781–1856)—A native of New Jersey and a lawyer, Berrien served as solicitor of the eastern district of Georgia and later as judge of the same district. He then served briefly in the Georgia senate until he was elected, by his state senate colleagues, to represent Georgia in the U.S. Senate. In 1829 President Jackson appointed Berrien to serve in his cabinet as attorney general. Berrien later represented Georgia again in the U.S. Senate, serving from 1841 to 1852. In October, 1829, Michigan had been a United States territory since 1805 and thoughts of potential statehood may have been on the minds of Michigan's territorial legislators. For whatever reason, on October 29, 1829, Michigan territory created counties named for Andrew Jackson, who was then president, John C. Calhoun (1782–1850), who was Jackson's first vice-president, and all members of President Jackson's first cabinet, including John M. Berrien.

1210 *Branch County*

John Branch (1782–1863)—A native of North Carolina, Branch served several terms in the North Carolina senate and was its speaker from 1815 to 1817. In December, 1817, he was elected governor of North Carolina and he served in that office for three years. Branch was an active member of the American Colonization Society, which raised funds to return emancipated slaves to Africa. In 1820, while he was governor, Branch refused to grant clemency to a man sentenced to death for murdering a slave. Branch later served in the North Carolina senate again, and subsequently in the U.S. Senate. In 1829, he resigned from the U.S. Senate to accept the offer of the newly elected president, Andrew Jackson, to serve in his cabinet as secretary of the navy. Branch later served in the U.S. House of Representatives, the North Carolina senate (again) and he became the last territorial governor of Florida. This county was created and named in John Branch's honor on October 29, 1829. As mentioned immediately above under Berrien County, Michigan, Michigan's territorial legislators created and named counties for President Andrew Jackson, for his first vice-president and for all members of Jackson's first cabinet on the same day, October 29, 1829. John Branch was serving in President Jackson's first cabinet as secretary of the navy on that date. Presumably Michigan's territorial legislators were coveting statehood and thought that this county-naming gesture would improve their prospects.

1211 *Calhoun County*

John C. Calhoun (1782–1850)—Calhoun

represented South Carolina in both houses of the U.S. Congress. He served as secretary of war, secretary of state and as vice-president. He was a forceful advocate of slavery, states' rights and limited powers for the federal government. He resigned the vice-presidency to enter the U.S. Senate where he could better represent the views of South Carolina and the South. Michigan had been a United States territory since 1805 and by October, 1829, thoughts of potential statehood may have been on the minds of Michigan's territorial legislators. For whatever reason, on October 29, 1829, Michigan territory created counties named for Andrew Jackson, who was then president, John C. Calhoun, who was then serving as Jackson's first vice-president, and all members of President Jackson's first cabinet.

1212 *Cass County*

Lewis Cass (1782–1866)—A native of New Hampshire, Cass served in the army in the War of 1812 and rose to the rank of brigadier-general. Following that war Cass became governor of Michigan territory and he served as the territory's governor for 18 years. He then held a variety of important political positions and was the candidate of the Democratic party in 1848 for president of the United States. He lost to Zachary Taylor. When Cass left the office of governor of Michigan territory, he became secretary of war under President Andrew Jackson. Later he was minister to France, U.S. senator from Michigan and secretary of state under President James Buchanan. This county was created in October, 1829, while Lewis Cass was governor of Michigan territory.

1213 *Charlevoix County*

Pierre F. X. de Charlevoix (1682–1761)— Pierre Francois Xavier de Charlevoix was born at St. Quentin, France, in October, 1682 and was ordained as a Roman Catholic priest in 1704. A Jesuit, Charlevoix came to New France (Canada) in 1705 and taught at a Jesuit college in Quebec for about four years. In 1709 he was recalled to France to teach at the chief French seminary of the Jesuits, College Louis-le-Grand. One of his students there was Voltaire (1694–1778). In 1720 Charlevoix was sent back to New France to determine the boundaries of Acadia and to find a new route to the western sea. His explorations took him through the Great Lakes, present day Mackinac, Michigan, and down the Mississippi River to its mouth. During this trip he visited most, if not all, of the posts

which constituted France's frontier in North America. He took extensive notes during this journey. Charlevoix spent much of the remainder of his life in France, engaged in literary work and he wrote the first general narrative history of New France. It was published in Paris in 1744. Charlevoix died at La Fleche, France, on February 1, 1761. Charlevoix County, Michigan was initially created in 1840 and named Keskkauko (or Keshkauko; or other spellings; sources consulted differ on this). That name honored an Indian chief. The county's name was changed on March 8, 1843, to Charlevoix, in honor of this Jesuit explorer and historian.

1214 *Cheboygan County*

Uncertain—This county lies at the northern end of Michigan's lower peninsula, with the straits of Mackinac forming its northern border. It was created on April 1, 1840, and authorities consulted are in agreement that the name derived from an Indian word or words. However, one finds a wide variety of suggestions for the origin and meaning of the Indian word or words. Possibilities which have been mentioned include:

He portion of the name derived from an Ojibwa Indian word meaning "big" while *boygan* was a variant of the Indian word for "pipe." The resulting translation under this theory would be "big pipe." Even if this were the correct origin of the county's name, its significance is uncertain since we do not know what the Indians meant by "big pipe." Possibly some coastline feature along the straits of Mackinac resembled a big pipe, or the name may commemorate some large stone of the type that the Indians used to carve ceremonial peace pipes. Other origins of the meaning of the Indians' word(s) which have been mentioned: Indian word or words meaning "wild rice fields."

A number of sources indicate that the original Indian name was first applied to a particular body of water. Several possibilities are mentioned for that particular body of water including:

— "A river emptying into the straits of Mackinac from the south." This would be the 40 mile long Cheboygan River. Suggested translations of that river's name are numerous and include one version which mentions "ore" and at least two which mention "pipe."

— "A river that comes out of the ground."

— An "entrance," "portage" or "harbor."

— "A water pass from one lake to an-

other lake." This would have been an apt description of the Cheboygan River.

That is not the end of the list of suggested translations. There are other suggestions which seem less likely including a folk tale originating at Sheboygan, Wisconsin. There, as the story goes, a local Indian chief had a number of daughters but no sons. Hoping that his next child would be a son, when a girl arrived the fable tells us that the chief said "she boy 'gain." Don't believe it.

1215 *Chippewa County*

Chippewa Indians—This county, at the northeastern end of Michigan's upper peninsula, was created in 1826, when Michigan was still a territory. It was named for the Chippewa (also known as Ojibwa) Indians, who had the largest population of any Indian tribe in Michigan. The name *Chippewa* is a corruption of the name *Ojibwa*, which has known dozens of alternative spellings. The Chippewa were one of the largest and most powerful tribes of the Algonquian linguistic family. They were a nomadic, woodland tribe, who controlled much of the Great Lakes area. Their domain extended from the Iroquois Indians' territory in the Northeast to the edge of the Great Plains, which were dominated by the Dakota (also known as Sioux) Indians. The Chippewa lived around the shores of three of the Great Lakes: Huron, Michigan and Superior, and dwelled in what today are the states of Michigan, Wisconsin, Minnesota and North Dakota. The first European explorers to encounter the Chippewa found them near Sault Sainte Marie, which is now the county seat of Chippewa County, Michigan. Many Chippewa lived in birch bark covered wigwams with grass mats. Their birch bark rolls were carried from one campsite to another. They subsisted by hunting, trapping, fishing and collecting wild plant food. A bit of maize (corn) farming was engaged in by those Chippewa who occupied the southern edges of the Chippewa's territory. The Chippewa were noted for their fine craftsmanship in constructing birch bark canoes. As recently as 1986 there was a large Chippewa population in Michigan, living on reservations on both of Michigan's peninsulas. Other Chippewa reservations may be found today in Canada's Ontario province and in our states of Wisconsin, Minnesota, North Dakota and Montana. The Chippewa Indians were parties to most of the important treaties from 1795 to 1842, which ceded Indian lands in Michigan to the United States. Michigan's territorial legislative council asked Henry R. Schoolcraft (1793–1864) to submit suggested names for this new county. Schoolcraft responded with three suggestions: Algonac, Allegan and Chippewa, and the legislative council chose Chippewa. The meaning of the Chippewa (or Ojibwa) tribe's name is uncertain.

1216 *Clare County*

County Clare, Republic of Ireland — This county was created on April 1, 1840, and named Kaykakee County (or Raykakee; sources consulted differ on the spelling but most render the name as Kaykakee.) This original county name honored an Indian chief. The county's name was changed on March 8, 1843, to Clare County, in honor of the county in Ireland. Michigan's legislature changed the names of several other counties on March 8, 1843, to honor persons and places or Irish origin. County Clare is within the Republic of Ireland's Munster province. The county has an area of some 1,200 square miles and, in the early 1980's, this Irish county had a population of approximately 90,000. County Clare is bordered on the west by the Atlantic Ocean and is drained by the Fergus River, the Shannon River, and their tributaries. County Clare boasts a number of ancient structures including abbeys and round towers. The ancient fort of Cahercommaunfort was excavated by archeologists in 1936. Shannon airport, an important international airport, is located in County Clare. The origin of this Irish county's name is uncertain. According to Seward's *Topographical Dictionary of Ireland*, the county was named in honor of a Sir Richard de Clare. It is known that Ireland's Clare had become a place of some importance by the end of the 12th century so perhaps the Richard de Clare mentioned was the Richard de Clare who died in 1176. This Richard de Clare conquered some territory in Ireland which was coveted by England's King Henry II (1133–1189). Military actions took place among troops loyal to the king versus those loyal to de Clare. Richard de Clare was eventually granted Wexford, Waterford and Dublin, but soon afterward, in 1174, he was defeated at Munster. However, a different origin for the name of Ireland's County Clare is deemed more probable in "Letters Containing Information Relative to the Antiquities of the County of Clare Collected During the Progress of the Ordnance Survey in 1839." That origin is said to have been a board or plank, which was placed across the Fergus River for passengers to cross upon. This board or plank was needed until a bridge had been built here.

1217 *Clinton County*

De Witt Clinton (1769–1828) — This New York state native held many of the important political offices in that state. Clinton served in both houses of the state legislature and as mayor of New York City. He represented New York in the U.S. Senate and in 1812 he was the Federalist candidate for president, running against President James Madison. In 1817 Clinton was elected as New York's governor. As governor, he was the principal promoter of the Erie Canal, which was instrumental in linking the vast agricultural and timber lands in our country's West with eastern markets. The canal spurred our nation's growth. In 1825, when the Erie Canal was completed from the Hudson River in New York state to Lake Erie in the West, the remote wilderness of Michigan was, in effect, moved hundreds of miles closer to eastern markets. This county was created in March, 1831, just three years after Clinton's death.

1218 *Crawford County*

Uncertain — The genealogy of Crawford County, Michigan, is a bit complex. In 1818 a Crawford County was created in Michigan territory by proclamation of the territorial governor, Lewis Cass (1782–1866). In 1836 Wisconsin territory was established and in the resulting shifting of boundaries, Michigan territory lost its Crawford County to Wisconsin territory. That Crawford County survives in the state of Wisconsin. Its name honors William H. Crawford (1772–1834).

William H. Crawford (1772–1834) — Crawford served in the Georgia legislature and as a U.S. senator from Georgia. He was elected president pro tempore of the senate and he later served as minister to France, secretary of war and secretary of the treasury. Crawford was a serious candidate for the presidency in both 1816 and 1824.

On April 1, 1840, the state of Michigan created a county named Shawono. Its name honored an Indian chief. On March 8, 1843, Michigan changed that county's name to Crawford County. It is known that the name was suggested by Jonathan Lamb, of Washtenaw County, Michigan, but it is not known if the new Crawford County was intended to be a reincarnation of Michigan territory's earlier Crawford County, named for William H. Crawford (1772–1834). Most sources consulted indicate that the present Crawford County, Michigan, that was named in 1843, was named in honor of Colonel William Crawford (1732–1782).

William Crawford (1732–1782) — A native of Virginia, Crawford was a farmer, surveyor and soldier. Before the American Revolution he fought in the French and Indian war, the Pontiac war and Lord Dunmore's war. During the Revolution, Crawford took part in battles at Long Island, Trenton, Princeton, Brandywine and Germantown and rose to the rank of colonel. About 1778 he moved to the West, where he engaged in defense of the frontier and in actions against the Indians. In 1782 he was captured by Delaware Indians, tortured and burned at the stake near Upper Sandusky, Ohio.

1219 *Delta County*

Original shape of the county similar to the Greek letter, delta — When this county, on Michigan's upper peninsula, was created and named in 1843, it was named for its triangular shape, which resembled the fourth letter in the Greek alphabet, which is *delta*. In his article on the "History & Meaning of the County Names of Michigan," which was published in 1912 by the Michigan Pioneer & Historical Society, William L. Jenks stated that the original boundaries of Delta County gave it the shape of an isosceles triangle. The Greek letter *delta* is an isosceles triangle. The boundaries of Delta County have been changed since 1843 but, with a little imagination, one can discern the rough shape of a triangle in today's Delta County. However, even with a lot of imagination, the county no longer resembles an isosceles triangle.

1220 *Dickinson County*

Donald M. Dickinson (1846–1917) — Dickinson was born in New York state but moved to Michigan with his family when he was still an infant. A graduate of the law school of the University of Michigan, Dickinson practiced law in Detroit and argued a number of cases before the U.S. Supreme Court. He also became the leader of Michigan's Democratic political machine. He was said to be the man in Michigan who had to be seen to secure appointment to a Federal job. When President Grover Cleveland's postmaster general, William F. Vilas (1840–1908), became secretary of Interior in 1888, Donald M. Dickinson took his place in President Cleveland's cabinet. This county, on Michigan's upper peninsula, was created and named in 1891, when the Democratic party controlled the Michigan legislature.

1221 *Eaton County*

John H. Eaton (1790–1856)—A native of North Carolina, Eaton moved to Tennessee in 1808 or 1809. He arrived in Tennessee as a wealthy man and in Tennessee he increased that wealth. His family owned slaves. Although wealthy, Eaton was still relatively unknown until it was announced, in 1816, that Eaton was completing a biography of Tennessee's hero, Andrew Jackson (1767–1845). To increase interest in this biography, a Nashville newspaper mounted a campaign to call favorable attention to the young Eaton. Although the biography proved to be unremarkable, the pre-publication publicity triggered Eaton's career in politics. He represented Tennessee in the U.S. Senate from 1818 to 1829. Later in 1829, he became secretary of war in President Andrew Jackson's first cabinet. He subsequently served as governor of Florida territory and minister to Spain. In October, 1829, Michigan had been a U.S. territory since 1805 and thoughts of statehood may have been on the minds of Michigan's territorial legislators. For whatever reason, on October 29, 1829, Michigan territory created counties named for Andrew Jackson, who was then president, John C. Calhoun, President Jackson's first vice-president, and all members of President Jackson's first cabinet, including Secretary of War John H. Eaton.

1222 *Emmet County*

Robert Emmet (1778–1803)—This county was originally created on April 1, 1840, and named Tonedagana County, in honor of an Indian chief. Its name was changed to Emmet on March 8, 1843, to honor the Irish patriot, Robert Emmet. Michigan's legislature of 1843 changed the names of several other counties on March 8, 1843, to honor persons and places of Irish origin. Emmet was born in Dublin, Ireland, to a prominent Anglo-Irish family, in 1778. He studied at Trinity College in Dublin where he excelled in his studies and won a reputation as a fiery orator. There he joined a radical group, the Society of United Irishmen. This society, inspired by recent revolutions in the United States and France, had as its goal, freedom for Ireland from England. In 1798 Emmet left Trinity College due to an inquisition into students' political views. During the next five years of his brief life Emmet lived in both France and Ireland and engaged in continuous revolutionary activities. On July 23, 1803,

Emmet issued a proclamation establishing a provisional government for an Irish republic but this rebellion was promptly crushed by British soldiers. The following month Emmet was captured by the British and in September, 1803, he was executed by hanging. Although Emmet's revolutionary activities met little success, Thomas Moore wrote poems about him and Emmet became a celebrated martyr for Irish nationalism.

1223 *Genesee County*

Genesee County, New York—Genesee County was created in 1835, when Michigan was still a territory. It was named for Genesee County, in western New York state, because a large number of Michigan settlers had come from that area of New York. Genesee County in New York had been created in 1802 and named for the *valley* through which the Genesee River flows. That river rises in northern Pennsylvania, crosses the New York border near Wellsville, New York, and travels virtually due north across the agricultural region of western New York, until it empties into Lake Ontario, near the city of Rochester, New York. (Rochester had previously been named Genesee Falls.) The Genesee River is some 144 miles long. Its name is of Seneca Indian origin and is generally translated as "beautiful valley."

1224 *Gladwin County*

Henry Gladwin (1729–1791)—This county was created in 1831 and named for the British army officer who had commanded Fort Detroit and successfully defended it against the Indians during Pontiac's rebellion of 1763. Gladwin and his troops resisted this siege, which lasted a number of months, until reinforcements reached Detroit in late July, 1763. Gladwin then attempted an attack on Pontiac's Indians but it was repulsed at the battle of Bloody Ridge. Gladwin, whose name is rendered in several accounts as Gladwyn, was born in England in 1729 and commissioned a lieutenant in the British infantry in 1753. Ordered to America, Gladwin participated in 1755 with Lieutenant-colonel George Washington (1732–1799) and England's General Edward Braddock (1695–1755) in a defeat by the French and Indians near Fort Duquesne. Braddock was mortally wounded in that battle. George Washington led Gladwin and the other British and colonial survivors back to Fort Cumberland. Gladwin participated in military actions at Louisbourg, Fort Carillion, Fort Saint Frederic and Montreal. Now a

major, he became the British commander of the captured French Fort de Levis, near Ogdensburg, New York. In 1761 Gladwin was ordered to Fort Detroit. There he commanded British forces during Pontiac's rebellion, mentioned above. In 1763 he was promoted to lieutenant-colonel, in 1777 to colonel on the retired list and in 1782 to major-general on the half-pay list. According to several accounts, Gladwin served in the British army against the colonists in the American Revolution. That is not true. In 1764 or 1765, well before the American Revolution, Gladwin became weary of life in the wilderness and returned to England. He never came back to America and he died in England in 1791. However, there was a period of time after 1765 when Gladwin was listed as deputy adjutant general of British forces in America.

1225 *Gogebic County*

Lake Gogebic & Gogebic iron district—This county, at the western end of Michigan's upper peninsula, was created in 1887. Some sources say that it was named for Lake Gogebic, one of the largest lakes on the upper peninsula, which is located within both Gogebic County and Ontonagon County. Other sources say that the county was named for the Gogebic iron district here. Both answers are correct. The Gogebic iron district became active in 1884, when the Milwaukee, Lake Shore & Western Railway Company extended its line to the iron district. Iron ore had been discovered here in 1871, or perhaps even earlier. The iron range took its name from the prominent, 12 mile long, lake near the eastern end of the range. The Gogebic iron range extends through three counties in northeastern Wisconsin, Bayfield County, Ashland County and Iron County as well as Gogebic County in Michigan. The name *Gogebic* is of Indian origin. Since the Indians had no written language, it was left to Europeans to render Indian names as best they could and a variety of earlier names for Lake Gogebic are encountered in the literature on this subject. Professor Virgil J. Vogel, a recognized scholar on the subject of Indian names in Michigan, and elsewhere, concluded in his work entitled *Indian Names in Michigan*, that "The meaning of the name cannot, apparently, be determined with any certainty." In 1964 State Senator Charles S. Blondy introduced a resolution in the Michigan legislature to change Gogebic County's name to Van Wagoner County. He encountered opposition and withdrew his resolution.

1226 *Grand Traverse County*

Grand Traverse Bay — French explorers and fur traders who paddled their canoes southward on Lake Michigan from the Straits of Mackinac saw two indentations on the northwestern shore of Michigan's lower peninsula. In crossing these bays from one headland to another, they called the smaller indentation La Petite Traverse and the larger one, some ten miles across, La Grande Traverse. The name for the larger bay, *La Grande Traverse*, meant "the long crossing." The bays behind these indentations are now called Little Traverse Bay and Grand Traverse Bay. This county, which is located at the southern end of Grand Traverse Bay, was originally created on April 1, 1840, and named Omeena County. Its name was changed to Grand Traverse County by the Michigan legislature in 1851. However, the legislative act of 1851 was defective, in that it inadvertently left small portions of the old Omeena County out of the new Grand Traverse County. (The portions inadvertently excluded were townships 28 of ranges nine and ten, west.) These surviving portions of the old Omeena County were made a part of Grand Traverse County by the legislature in 1853. Grand Traverse Bay, in northeastern Lake Michigan, has as its western border, Leelanau Peninsula. The southern end of Grand Traverse Bay is separated by the 18-mile-long Old Mission Peninsula, into a West Arm and an East Arm. Grand Traverse Bay is about ten miles wide and 30 miles long. Several port towns on Grand Traverse Bay were active during logging boom days. Today Grand Traverse Bay is a recreational area.

1227 *Gratiot County*

Uncertain — This county was created in 1831 when Michigan was a territory. It is clear that the name honors the U.S. army officer, Charles Gratiot (1786–1855), but sources consulted differ on whether the county was named directly for him or indirectly, by being named for Fort Gratiot.

Charles Gratiot (1786–1855) — A native of Saint Louis in what is now the state of Missouri, Gratiot won appointment to the U.S. Military Academy at West Point, from which he graduated in 1806. In October of that year, Second-lieutenant Charles Gratiot was assigned to the army's corps of engineers. In 1808 he was promoted to captain and that was still his rank in 1814, when he supervised construction of a fort, in what is now the state of Michigan, at the southern end of Lake Huron. The fort was named Fort Gratiot, in his honor.

Throughout the War of 1812, Gratiot served on our country's western frontier as chief engineer of the forces under General William H. Harrison (1773–1841). During that war, Gratiot participated in actions at Fort Meigs and Fort Mackinac. Following the War of 1812, Gratiot rose in rank in the army and in 1828 he became brevet brigadier-general and chief engineer of the United States army, with his headquarters in Washington, D.C. He held that office for ten years until he was dismissed for allegedly failing to repay the U.S. treasury certain funds which had been placed in his hands. Gratiot died on May 18, 1855.

Fort Gratiot — The French, under the command of Daniel Greysolon, Sieur Du Luth (1639–1710), had fortified a point here at the southern end of Lake Huron in 1686. Only a few years later the French found it necessary to abandon the fort and they burned it so that it couldn't be used against them by the British. This French fort was named Fort St. Joseph. In 1805 Michigan was made a territory of the United States and the U.S. military began to take interest in defending our border along the St. Clair River. During the War of 1812 it was decided that a U.S. fort was needed at the site of the former French Fort St. Joseph. Accordingly, troops under the command of a Major Forsyth, supported by Captains Cobb, Roe and Charles Gratiot (1786–1855) left Detroit on May 11, 1814, to establish an effective defense there. They reached their destination two days later and proceeded to erect a fort on the St. Clair River, where the city of Port Huron, Michigan, is now located. The U.S. army officer in charge of erecting the fort was Captain Charles Gratiot and the fort was named in his honor. According to one account, the cost to erect the fort was $305.25. By 1826, the fort had become badly dilapidated. In 1828 troops were sent to the fort and one year later they had succeeded in rebuilding it. Thereafter the fort was used from time to time for military purposes but it also served as both a school and a church. By 1881 all of the fort's land and buildings had passed from the U.S. government to private hands.

1228 *Hillsdale County*

The county's rolling, diversified surface — At the time that this county was created and named in 1829 by Michigan's territorial legislature, the expression "up hill and down dale" was often used to describe the kind of topography found in Hillsdale County. The county's name is apt in de-

scribing the rolling, diversified surface of the county, but its hills are not very tall. On the other hand, when Hillsdale County was created in 1829, it was located on one of Michigan's highest tables of land; some 615 feet above the surface of Lake Michigan and 600 feet above Lake Erie. At one time a petition was sent to the legislature to change this county's name to Washington but nothing came of it and Michigan still has no county named in honor of our nation's first president.

1229 *Houghton County*

Douglass Houghton (1809–1845) — Houghton was born in New York state and graduated from Rensselaer Polytechnic Institute at Troy, New York. After graduation, Houghton was kept on at Rensselaer as an instructor in chemistry and natural history. In 1830 he was invited to Detroit, in Michigan territory, to deliver a series of lectures on chemistry, geology and general science. Houghton remained in Detroit and in addition to teaching he practiced medicine and dentistry. Houghton proposed to the Michigan legislature that they fund a scientific study of both the upper and lower peninsulas of Michigan. The proposed study was to embrace geology, zoology, botany and topography. The legislature approved his proposal in 1837 and put Houghton in charge of the project as Michigan's first state geologist. His comments in his annual reports to the legislature called the world's attention to the existence of copper and iron deposits on Michigan's upper peninsula. In 1844 he received permission from the U.S. secretary of the interior to launch an extensive scientific study of the western part of our nation but he died in October, 1845, as a result of a boating accident on Lake Superior. In addition to his explorations and scientific activities, Houghton was mayor of the city of Detroit from 1842 to 1844. On March 19, 1845, Houghton County was created near the western end of Michigan's upper peninsula bordering Lake Superior, where Dr. Houghton lost his life just seven months later.

1230 *Huron County*

Uncertain — This county is located on the eastern shore of Michigan's lower peninsula, bordering on Lake Huron. Sources consulted disagree on whether the county was named for the Huron Indians or for Lake Huron (which had been named for the Huron Indians). *The Encyclopedia of Michigan*, published in 1981, states that Huron County, Michigan, was "Named for the Huron Indians and the lake which forms the...borders of the county"; i.e., for both the Huron Indians and for Lake Huron.

Huron Indians — Prior to about 1650 most of the Huron Indians (the surviving portion of these Indians are known as the Wyandot Indians) lived on Georgian Bay, a Canadian inlet of Lake Huron. An early French explorer, Jacques Cartier (1491–1557) encountered the Huron in Canada in 1534. Although the Huron belong to the Iroquoian linguistic family, it was Iroquois Indians who forced most Huron Indians to move west. Sometime after 1650 they settled near Detroit, Michigan and on Sandusky Bay in Ohio. They eventually claimed most of Ohio and part of Indiana. These Huron Indians called themselves Wendat and, over time, that name evolved to Wyandot. But what was the origin and meaning of the name *Huron*? Many sources consulted say (approximately) that the name was given to these Indians by the French, who called them *hures*, a French term for "wild boars" or *huron*, a French term for "an unkempt person, knave, ruffian, lout or wretch." However, Dr. Virgil J. Vogel, a recognized scholar of Indian names in Michigan and elsewhere, argues convincingly in his work entitled *Indian Names in Michigan*, that several less insulting origins of the name Huron exist. The insulting French origins of the name were said to have been inspired by an unusual hair style of the Huron Indians but many other Indian tribes styled their hair in forms that could have been considered wild and primitive by the French. Beginning in 1795, the surviving Huron Indians, now called the Wyandot Indians, ceded all of their lands to the United States in various treaties. In 1842 or 1843 the Wyandot Indians, who by then were living in Ohio, moved to Kansas. There they purchased land from the Delaware Indians and settled in what is now Wyandotte County, Kansas. In 1867, the Whites forced the Wyandots to move on, this time to Indian territory (now Oklahoma).

Lake Huron — Lake Huron is one of North America's Great Lakes and it is the second largest of them. Of the five Great Lakes, only Lake Michigan is wholly within the United States. The others, including Lake Huron, are shared by Canada and our country. The French named the present Lake Huron several times. Earlier names included Mer Douce and Lake Orleans. By the early 18th century French maps began to associate the lake's name with the Huron Indians. Early examples of this were Lac

Huron ou Michigane and L. des Hurons. Lake Huron is some 206 miles long and 183 miles wide, at its broadest point. It connects with Lake Michigan through the Straits of Mackinac and with Lake Superior and Lake Erie via rivers and canals. These connecting waterways among the Great Lakes make them the largest fresh water body in the world. Lake Huron is noted for the natural beauty of its shores and the lake is a popular recreation area in both summer and winter.

1231 *Ingham County*

Samuel D. Ingham (1779–1860) — A native of Pennsylvania, Ingham managed a paper mill and served in the Pennsylvania legislature. He represented Pennsylvania in the U.S. House of Representatives and he served some half-dozen terms in that body. When Andrew Jackson was elected president, he appointed Samuel D. Ingham to serve in his first cabinet as secretary of the treasury. Ingham served in that post from 1829 to 1831. He spent the remainder of his life in coal mining, railroad, canal and banking endeavors. This county was created on October 29, 1829. At that time, Michigan had been a territory since 1805 and thoughts of potential statehood may have been on the minds of Michigan's territorial legislators. For whatever reason, on the same day that Ingham County was created, Michigan territory created and named counties for Andrew Jackson, who was then President, John C. Calhoun, who was President Jackson's first vice-president, and all members of President Jackson's first cabinet. Ingham County is located on Michigan's lower peninsula and it shares a border with Jackson County.

1232 *Ionia County*

The portion of ancient Greece known as Ionia — Ionia was an area of western Asia Minor which was developed during the classical era by Ionian Greeks. This area consisted of a strip of coastal land on the eastern side of the Aegean Sea. Ancient Ionia was relatively small, with a coastal strip some 30 miles long and an inland depth of about 90 miles. Most of Ionia rested within the valleys of three rivers: the Hermus, Cayster and Maeander. Ionia was settled by Greeks from Attica about 1,000 B.C. Serious colonization of the area by Ionian Greeks began in the seventh century B.C. and the early portion of the sixth century B.C. This was part of a larger colonization of much of the Black Sea coast. Under this Grecian influence, Ionia soon prospered from trade and in-

dustry but Ionia is best remembered for the high level of culture achieved here. Ionia was a cradle of Greek epic and elegiac poetry, natural philosophy, history, geography and medicine. The Ionians developed a new style of simple, but majestic architecture which we still call Ionic. About 550 B.C. Ionian cities were conquered and lost their independence. Control of the area passed first from the classical Greeks to the Lydian kingdom and then to Persia. After a return to control by Athenian and other Greek kingdoms, Ionia passed to the Roman Empire about 130 B.C. The area that constituted classical Greek Ionia is now part of Turkey. The principal Turkish city here is Izmir. Ionia County, Michigan was created in 1831, while Michigan was still a territory and while Henry R. Schoolcraft (1793–1864) was a member of the territorial legislature. While serving in that body, Schoolcraft suggested a large number of Michigan's county names and although a smoking gun has not been found to link him with the choice of this county's name, one senses that the inscrutable Schoolcraft was at work here. It has been suggested that this county's name was but one of a number of place-names in Michigan that were of classical origin. In his article entitled "Naming Michigan's Counties," in the September, 1975, issue of *Names: Journal of the American Name Society*, Albert H. Marckwardt stated that Ionia County's name was "...unquestionably a by-product of the classical revival movement which was then sweeping the state [sic]. This was reflected elsewhere in town names (Sparta, Ithica, Romulus)..." This general classical trend is more apparent than real. Both Ithica and Romulus were merely transplanted names which early Michigan settlers brought with them from New York state. Even if Marckwardt had expanded his list to include Parma, Smyrna and Utica, Michigan, the conclusion would be much the same; i.e., most can be traced to a New York state origin. The name Ionia is also found in New York state but that does not prove that our eclectic friend Henry R. Schoolcraft played no role in the selection of this county's name.

1233 *Iosco County*

A fictive American Indian hero — This county was originally created in 1840 and named Kanotin County. On March 8, 1843, the Michigan legislature changed the county's name to Iosco. Henry R. Schoolcraft (1793–1864) suggested many of Michigan's county names and there is no doubt that Iosco County's name can be traced to him. *Iosco* was a favorite name of Schoolcraft's. In 1838 he published a poem, some 14 pages long, entitled "Iosco," or "The Vale of Norma." The following year Schoolcraft published a body of translations and adaptations of Indian tales in a volume entitled *Algic Researches*. A story about a small group of young Indian men, the eldest of whom was named Iosco, was included in *Algic Researches*. The title of this story was "Iosco," or a "Visit to the Sun and Moon." Schoolcraft, himself, made the following statement about the story of Iosco in *Algic Researches*: "The story itself, so far as respects the object, is calculated to remind the reader of *South American* [italics added] history of the alleged descent of Manco Capac and the children of the Sun." Manco Capac was the legendary founder of the Inca dynasty in South America. Our friend, Henry R. Schoolcraft, was indeed eclectic.

1234 *Iron County*

Iron ore in the county—This county is located in the western portion of Michigan's upper peninsula, which contains extensive iron ore deposits. This iron was noted about 1830 but an iron ore industry didn't develop here until half a century later. Dr. Douglass Houghton (1809–1845) explored Michigan's upper peninsula in the early 1830's and noted the presence of copper and iron ore here. Later, as Michigan's first state geologist, Dr. Houghton made annual reports to the state legislature and by the early 1840's his reports to the legislature had called the world's attention to the presence of copper and iron deposits in the western section of Michigan's upper peninsula. In 1851, a United States surveyor, named Harvey Mellen discovered iron ore in what is now Iron County. It was located on the west side of Stambaugh Hill. About 1880, the Todd, Stambaugh Company, of Youngstown, Ohio, acquired the Iron River iron mine here, which later was renamed the Stambaugh mine. In 1882 the first shipments of iron ore left the Iron River mine and the Nanaina mine. Both mining and lumbering came to be important industries here and in 1885, the Michigan legislature created and named Iron County. Since November, 1979, the iron ore industry in Iron County, Michigan has been inactive and tourists now visit the old mine shafts here.

1235 *Isabella County*

Queen Isabella I of Spain (1451–1504)—

Isabella's father was the ruler of the portion of present-day Spain which was called the Kingdom of Castile and Leon United. She married Ferdinand II (1452–1516). She ascended to the throne of Castile and Leon United, and Ferdinand II ascended to the throne of the Kingdom of Aragon United to Catalonia, thereby uniting most of Spain under one monarchy. This was a major event. Control of Spain had shifted back and forth between Christians and Moors for centuries and what is now Spain was divided into various independent kingdoms from time to time. Ferdinand's name was styled Ferdinand V when he ruled Spain jointly with his wife, Queen Isabella I. Thus Queen Isabella and King Ferdinand V had already made their mark in history when they supported the Italian sailor, Christopher Columbus (1451–1506) in his expedition which reached the Americas in 1492. Columbus was certainly not the first European to reach the Western Hemisphere. Leif Ericsson had accomplished that about A.D. 1000. However, it was Columbus' expedition that triggered the rapid exploration, conquest and settlement of America by Europeans. It was Queen Isabella I who financed Columbus' famous expedition. Isabella was intensely religious and she played a leading role in the infamous Inquisition in Spain and the expulsion or execution of most of Spain's Jews. Shifting fast forward more than three centuries, we come to Isabella County, Michigan. This county was created on March 2, 1831, when Michigan was still a territory. It was named for Queen Isabella I (1451–1504), but an alternative origin for the county's name is erroneously cited in a number of reference sources. That erroneous origin can be traced to Henry Gannett's popular work entitled *The Origin of Certain Place Names in the United States*, which states that the county's namesake was "…the daughter of John Hurst, who was the first white child born within its limits." That origin is incorrect. The county was created and named in 1831 and John Hurst and his wife did not move to Isabella County until 1855. At the time that Isabella County was created, Henry R. Schoolcraft (1793–1864) was a member of the Michigan territorial legislature. It was Schoolcraft who suggested this county's name and he named it for the Spanish queen.

1236 *Jackson County*

Andrew Jackson (1767–1845)—Jackson was born on the border of North Carolina and South Carolina. He represented Ten-

nessee in both branches of the U.S. Congress and gained fame and popularity for his military exploits in wars with Indians and in the War of 1812. He was provisional military governor of Florida and from 1829 to 1837 General Jackson was president of the United States. His presidency reflected the frontier spirit of America. By October, 1829, Michigan had been a territory since 1805 and thoughts of statehood may have been on the minds of Michigan's territorial legislators. For whatever reason, on October 29, 1829, Michigan territory created and named counties for Andrew Jackson, who was then president, John C. Calhoun, who was then vice-president, and all members of President Jackson's first cabinet.

1237 *Kalamazoo County*

Kalamazoo River—This county was created in 1829, while Michigan was still a territory, and it was named for the Kalamazoo River, which flows through it. When the legislature created this county it was a wilderness in the southern section of Michigan territory. The Kalamazoo River rises in Hillsdale County, in south-central Michigan and flows north and then west to empty into Lake Michigan at Saugatuck, Michigan. One source estimates the river's length at 160 miles while another, more generous source, uses 200 miles as its estimate of the river's length. In either case, the Kalamazoo, together with its tributaries, clearly forms a major river system, more than 1,000 miles long. *Kalamazoo* is the surviving version of an Indian name for the river. The Indians had no written language and numerous early written spellings of the river's name are found. Countless alleged translations of the river's Indian name are also encountered. Professor Virgil J. Vogel, a recognized scholar of Indian place-names in Michigan and elsewhere, discusses these purported translations in his work entitled *Indian Names in Michigan*. He then dismisses most of them as "etymological absurdity…"

1238 *Kalkaska County*

Uncertain—This county was originally created in 1840 as Wabassee County. Its name was changed on March 8, 1843, to Kalcasca County but the official spelling was changed to its present form, Kalkaska, in 1871. According to several sources, the county's first name, Wabassee, honored an Indian chief. This is possible, but it has not been substantiated. This, then, is an uncertainty, but we have other, more important, uncertainties concerning this county's name with which we must deal. One thing is known: The county was not named for its county seat, the town of Kalkaska; rather, the town was named for the county. But what was the origin of the county's name (either Kalcasca or Kalkaşka will do)? The answer is that this is uncertain. One has to wonder if the intrepid namer of county names, Henry R. Schoolcraft (1793–1864) might have been involved. Schoolcraft was famed for suggesting names for counties but one theory about Kalkaska (or Kalcasca) County's name is that it may have been named *for* both Schoolcraft and Lewis Cass (1782–1866), who had been governor of Michigan territory for 18 years; perhaps Kalcraft for Schoolcraft and Cass for Lewis Cass. (James Calcraft was a great-grandfather of Henry R. Schoolcraft). Far fetched? Of course. We are not dealing with certainties here but wild speculation. Another origin/translation of the county's name that is seen in numerous sources, without explanation or substantiation, is that it came from an Indian term for "burned over."

1239 *Kent County*

James Kent (1763–1847)— A native of New York and a lawyer, Kent was elected to the lower house of the New York legislature three times. He was a professor of law at New York City's Columbia College until 1798 when he was appointed to the state's supreme court. He served as chief justice of that body for ten years. Kent was a legal scholar and during the early years after the United States had separated from England, he did much to define the limitations of English common law in its application in our new country. Judge Kent was appointed chancellor of the state of New York in 1814. He later wrote four volumes, published as *Commentaries on American Law*, which formed a definitive basis for instruction of law students. The last of these four volumes was published in 1830 and in the following year, 1831, Michigan territory created and named this county in his honor. Later, in the 1836–1837 time frame, James Kent was retained by Michigan to assess Michigan's legal rights to territory at its southern border with Ohio. That boundary dispute had earlier sparked the so-called Toledo War between Michigan and Ohio and the dispute was not satisfactorily resolved until the 20th century.

1240 *Keweenaw County*

Keweenaw peninsula, Michigan—The Keweenaw peninsula forms the northernmost tip of Michigan's upper peninsula. Its width is 20 miles at its base and it juts out in a curve some 75 miles long into Lake Superior. Most sources consulted trace the name *Keweenaw* to an Indian word for "portage," signifying a crossing by land, to travel from one body of water to another, or a place where such a portage is made. If that were the correct origin of the peninsula's name, it would apply to a popular portage on Keweenaw peninsula, some 60 miles below the peninsula's point. However, in Virgil J. Vogel's *Indian Names in Michigan*, the author discusses this possible source for the peninsula's name as well as others and concludes that the translation of the original Indian name is uncertain. Vogel indicates that "portage" is quite unlikely and that a more probable translation is "point which we go around in a canoe," "the bend" or "the detour." Keweenaw County was created in 1861 and it now includes both Keweenaw peninsula and the islands which once comprised a separate county named Isle Royale County. These islands lie near the north shore of Lake Superior, much closer to Canada than to Keweenaw peninsula.

1241 *Lake County*

Numerous lakes within its borders— This county was originally created on April 1, 1840, and named Aishcum County, in honor of an Indian chief but its name was changed on March 8, 1843, to Lake County. The new name was chosen on account of the county's many lakes. Although Lake County is relatively near Lake Michigan, it does not border on that Great Lake and never did. This county was not named for Lake Michigan. Sources consulted give wildly differing opinions about the quantity of lakes within this county. One source says that the name is "…peculiarly inappropriate to this county, as it is an inland county, contains but few lakes and none of any size." Another source concurs stating that "…there are very few lakes in Lake County." However, several other sources indicate that the county has numerous lakes and the facts support that view. One source says that Lake County has 156 lakes. On a map of the entire state of Michigan, which gives scant space to Lake County, one can easily see Big Bass Lake, Big Star Lake, Wolf Lake and the Chain o' Lakes.

1242 *Lapeer County*

Flint River—At the time that this county was created in 1822, it contained a signifi-cant portion of the present Genesee County and the Flint River was the principal stream of that earliest version of Lapeer County. The Flint rises in southeastern Michigan, flows through the city of Flint, Michigan and turns northwest and then unites with the Shiawassee River. Together these two rivers form the Saginaw River. The Flint River's name has meant (approximately) "flint" from the time that the Indians named it, to the time that French traders translated it into their language as *La Pierre*, until the Americans named the river Flint and the county Lapeer. *Lapeer* is merely a corruption of the French name for the Flint River. The Indians' name for the river reflected the importance of flint in making arrow and spear heads. Lapeer County was created on September 10, 1822, while Michigan was still a territory. The governor of the territory, Lewis Cass (1782–1866), chose the county's name. On that same day, September 10, 1822, Governor Cass created and named some other counties. Two of these new counties were named for the principal rivers with which the Flint River is associated; i.e., the Shiawassee River and the Saginaw River.

1243 *Leelanau County*

A fictive American Indian maiden— All sources consulted credit this county's name to Henry R. Schoolcraft (1793–1864). These sources say that when the Michigan legislators created this county in 1840, they used the name suggested to them by Schoolcraft. (In 1840 the Michigan legislature also created several other counties using names suggested by Henry R. Schoolcraft.) This county's name had been coined by Schoolcraft earlier in his work entitled *Algic Researches*. There he spelled the Indian maiden's name Leelinau. *Algic Researches* was a body of translations and adaptations of Indian tales. Included in that volume was a story entitled "Leelinau or the Lost Daughter." The story depicts Leelinau as a timid daughter of an Indian hunter, who lived at the shore of Lake Superior and spent much of her time alone in a pine forest. Her parents arranged a marriage for her to the son of a neighboring Indian chief but the shy, reclusive Leelinau opposed the marriage and avoided it by disappearing into her pine forest. Some time later she was seen near the lake shore by an Indian fishing party but she disappeared again into the pines never to be seen again. Although unanimity concerning the origin of a county name is delightful, and we have that unanimity concerning the origin of this county's name (attributing it to Schoolcraft) there is a troubling aspect to this explanation: A major portion of the county consists of Leelanau peninsula. Henry R. Schoolcraft was a champion county-name-giver but he was not known to be an author of names for natural features such as rivers, lakes or peninsulas. It would follow, then, that the county was created and named first and then the peninsula acquired its name from the county; a highly unusual sequence. When counties share names with natural features within them, normally the county acquires its name from the nature feature. Other natural features within Leelanau County are Lake Leelanau and Lower Leelanau Lake. The apparent conflict concerning the peninsula's name has a possible explanation in that the peninsula had an earlier name which was Sleeping Bear peninsula.

1244 *Lenawee County*

Indian word for "people"—Lenawee County lies in southern Michigan, on the Ohio border. This county was created on September 10, 1822, while Michigan was still a territory, by proclamation of Lewis Cass (1782–1866), the territorial governor. The county's name came from an Indian word meaning "man," in the genderless sense or, more properly, "people"; i.e., Indian people.

1245 *Livingston County*

Edward Livingston (1764–1836)—Livingston was born in New York, represented that state in the U.S. House of Representatives and served as mayor of New York City. Because of personal problems, he moved to Louisiana to start a new life in 1804. There he served as Andrew Jackson's aide in the battle of New Orleans and was elected to the Louisiana legislature. He later represented Louisiana in both houses of the U.S. Congress and was President Andrew Jackson's secretary of state. Livingston drafted President Jackson's Proclamation to the People of South Carolina, which asserted the supremacy of the federal government in response to South Carolina's 1832 Ordinance of Nullification. His last post was minister to France. This county was created in March, 1833. At that time Michigan was still a territory and Edward Livingston was secretary of state in President Jackson's cabinet.

1246 *Luce County*

Cyrus G. Luce (1824–1905)—Luce was born in Ohio but when he was about 12 years old, his family moved to Indiana. There he worked in a woolen mill and managed to save enough from his wages to purchase 80 acres of land in Branch County, Michigan. In 1848 or 1849 he moved to Michigan and began clearing his land for farming. Luce served relatively brief terms in both houses of the Michigan legislature and was later nominated by the Republican party to run for governor. Luce won that election in 1886 and on January 1, 1887, became Michigan's governor. This county was created and named in his honor just two months later, on March 1, 1887. In 1888, Luce was re-elected to a second term. As governor, Luce's chief interests were prohibition of alcoholic beverages and conservation. His prohibition efforts met very limited success but on the conservation front, he was able to create the office of state game warden. This was the first time that Michigan had such an office and it was a conservation milestone.

1247 *Mackinac County*

Indian name for "turtle"—This county, on the south shore of Michigan's upper peninsula, was created on October 26, 1818, as Michilimackinac County. On March 9, 1843, the Michigan legislature lopped off the first seven letters of the county's name to form the present version, Mackinac County. In 1715, the French built a fort on the south side of the Straits of Mackinac. These straits form a narrow opening which separates Michigan's upper and lower peninsulas. The original fort here was of great strategic importance during the protracted period when the French, British and Americans were fighting for control of large sections of the North American continent. The fort, named Michilimackinac, was occupied by the French and later by British forces. The British feared an American attack and in 1780 and 1781 they destroyed the old fort at the tip of the lower peninsula and built a new fort on nearby Mackinac Island. This second fort changed hands from British to American to British to American. Rivers of ink have been expended debating the history, meaning, spelling and pronunciation of the two versions of the county's name. (Michigan residents pronounce the present county name *Mackinaw*.) In just one issue of *Michigan History*, the December, 1958, issue, there are seven articles discussing these controversies. Later, in the March, 1965, issue of *Michigan History*, Donald E. Chaput published "A Plea for Moderation in Place-name Controversies." Good point.

Dr. Virgil J. Vogel, a recognized scholar of Indian names in Michigan and elsewhere, has examined the evidence and concluded that the present county name came from an Indian word for "turtle," while the original county name was an Indian word for "great turtle," or "big turtle." (See Vogel's *Indian Names in Michigan*, published in 1986 by the University of Michigan Press.)

1248 *Macomb County*

Alexander Macomb (1782–1841)—This county was created on January 15, 1818, by proclamation of Michigan's territorial governor, Lewis Cass (1782–1866). He named the county in honor of his friend, General Alexander Macomb, who had been born in Detroit when it was still controlled by the British. Macomb devoted his adult life to the army. He was commissioned a cornet of cavalry in 1798 and he was soon promoted to second lieutenant. He was one of the first two students to receive formal training at West Point and complete a course of study there. When our country declared war on Great Britain in 1812, Macomb became a colonel of artillery. After participating in the capture of Fort George, he was promoted to brigadier-general. However, it was at Plattsburg, New York, that Macomb made his biggest mark on U.S. military history. There he skillfully led the defense of our position. Macomb and his troops at Plattsburg were honored by the U.S. Congress and Macomb was promoted to brevet major-general for this victory. He remained in the army after the War of 1812 and was stationed at Detroit in command of our country's northwestern frontier. In 1828 Macomb was promoted to senior major-general and commanding general of the United States army. He held that position until his death in 1841.

1249 *Manistee County*

Manistee River—The Manistee River rises in Crawford County, in the north-central portion of Michigan's lower peninsula, and flows toward Lake Michigan through the counties of Kalkaska, Wexford and Manistee. Its waters reach lake Michigan after first emptying into Manistee Lake at the city of Manistee. Both Manistee Lake and the city of Manistee are located in Manistee County. Estimates of the Manistee River's length vary considerably. The 1988 edition of *Webster's New Geographical Dictionary* shows 150 miles while C. J. D. Brown's work entitled *Michigan Streams*, published in 1944, puts the figure at 223 miles for the Manistee River and 908 miles for the main river and all of its tributaries. The name *Manistee* is an Indian word and various translations have been suggested for it. Differing translations of Indian names are not uncommon when they are examined centuries after their origination. The complications are multiplied, in this case, by some confusion between our Manistee River on the lower peninsula and the Manistique River on Michigan's upper peninsula. For example, both rivers were called *Manistie* on early maps and John T. Blois' *Gazetteer of the State of Michigan*, published in 1838, is said to have used the name *Monetee* for both the Manistee River and the Manistique River. This county was created in 1840. Its name was suggested by Henry R. Schoolcraft (1793–1864).

1250 *Marquette County*

Jacques Marquette (1637–1675)—This Roman Catholic priest, Jesuit missionary and explorer was born in France and he was sent by his superiors to New France (Canada) in 1666. There he became proficient in several Indian languages. Marquette was active at a number of missions, converting Indians to Christianity and attending to their spiritual needs. One of these missions was at Sault Sainte Marie and another was just north of the Straits of Mackinac. In May, 1673, Father Marquette, together with the French Canadian fur trader and explorer Louis Jolliet (1645–1700), left on a journey to find the great river to the west, which had been reported by Indians. Marquette, Jolliet and their party first sighted the Mississippi River in June, 1673. The expedition traveled down the Mississippi to the vicinity of the mouth or the Arkansas River. They turned north there to begin an arduous return trip. By the time they reached a northern mission near present De Pere, Wisconsin, they had traveled some 2,900 miles and Father Marquette's health was broken. Marquette was left at De Pere. During the short remainder of his life, Father Marquette attempted missionary work but during each attempt his health failed him. He died near the present Ludington, Michigan on May 18, 1675.

1251 *Mason County*

Stevens T. Mason (1811–1843)—Stevens Thomson Mason was born in Virginia but moved to Kentucky with his family when he was still an infant. In 1830 President Andrew Jackson appointed Mason's father, John T. Mason, to be secretary of

Michigan territory. John T. Mason resigned as territorial secretary in 1831. However, he somehow persuaded President Jackson to appoint his son, Stevens Thomson Mason, to succeed him as secretary of Michigan territory. The new territorial secretary was only 19 years old. Although the office of territorial secretary commanded little power, whenever the territorial governor was out of the territory (which happened frequently during Stevens T. Mason's tenure as secretary) the territorial secretary became the acting territorial governor. On account of his age, when Stevens T. Mason filled this role he was derisively called "the boy governor." When death took Territorial Governor George B. Porter in July, 1834, the "boy governor" became acting Michigan territorial governor for an extended term. Mason proved to be popular and the voters elected him to be the first governor of the state of Michigan. He was sworn in to this office on November 3, 1835. All of this was a bit premature. Michigan did not become a state until January 26, 1837. However, Mason was reelected in November, 1837, leaving unquestioned his status as the state's first governor. He died on January 4, 1843. Just two months later, on March 8, 1843, Michigan's Notipekago County was renamed Mason County, in his honor.

1252 *Mecosta County*

Mecosta (–)—This county, in the central portion of Michigan's lower peninsula, was created on April 1, 1840. Its name honors an Indian chief of a small tribe of the larger Potawatomi Indian tribe. Chief Mecosta had signed a treaty with the Whites in Indiana just four years before this county was created and named in his honor. That treaty was signed on April 22, 1836. The meaning of Chief Mecosta's name is uncertain but the most probable translations involve the word "bear." Suggested translations include "bear cub," "little bear" and "young bear." "Big bear" has been proposed but rejected as a possible translation but we have one more bear-related possibility to add to our list. That is "bear's head."

1253 *Menominee County*

Menominee River—The Menominee River forms the border between Menominee County, on Michigan's upper peninsula, and the state of Wisconsin. Formed by the confluence of the Michigamme River and the Brule River, the Menominee flows southeast until it empties into Lake

Michigan's Green Bay. The Menominee's length is approximately 125 miles but the main river, together with all of its tributaries, has a length of some 1,500 miles. The Menominee River was named for the Menominee Indians.

Menominee Indians—The Menominee are a tribe of the Algonquian linguistic group that once lived in northern Michigan near Mackinac Island. When first met by Europeans, in the 1630's, they had moved west to the Menominee River area and Green Bay. Some Menominee ranged as far west as the Mississippi River and as far south as the Fox River. There is also a Menominee County in Wisconsin, about 40 miles southwest of Menominee County, Michigan. The Wisconsin county consists entirely of the Menominee Indian "reservation." (The Indians own about 99% of the land there.) The Menominee of today harvest wild rice as their ancestors did centuries ago. The name *Menominee* means "wild rice people." The Menominee Indians won a lawsuit against the U.S. federal government on a charge of mismanagement of tribal affairs. Their $9,500,000 award was placed in trust and the first payments to the Indians were made in 1954.

Menominee County, Michigan, was created in 1861 with the name Bleeker County. Bleeker was the maiden name of the wife of a local legislator, Anson Bangs. The county's name was changed to Menominee in 1863.

1254 *Midland County*

Central location on Michigan's lower peninsula—Midland County was created and named in 1831, when Michigan was still a territory, and it was named for its central location on the lower peninsula. Although Michigan has added many counties and shifted numerous county boundaries since this county was created in 1831, probably by luck, Midland County's name is still accurate concerning the county's central location. In an unpublished 1968 manuscript on Michigan place names, Theodore G. Foster describes the name as "distinctly locative." Although this county is only 15 miles west of Lake Huron, because of Michigan's irregular shape, Midland County is located near the geographic center of the lower peninsula.

1255 *Missaukee County*

Missaukee (–)—Henry R. Schoolcraft (1793–1864) suggested the name for this county to the Michigan legislature and they agreed and created Missaukee County on April 1, 1840. The county's name honors a chief of the Ottawa Indians, who signed treaties with the Whites on August 30, 1831, and February 18, 1833, at Maumee Bay, where Toledo, Ohio, now stands. In both treaties the chief's name is spelled Mesaukee. Father Chrysostom Verwyst believed that the name meant "at the large mouth of a river" and numerous subsequent writers have perpetuated that translation. In his work entitled *Indian Names in Michigan*, Virgil J. Vogel discusses Father Verwyst's translation but concludes that the chief's name derived from the Ottawa Indian words *missi*, meaning "great" and *aukee*, which means the "world," "earth," "land," "country" or "soil." Dr. Vogel is a recognized scholar of Indian names in Michigan and elsewhere.

1256 *Monroe County*

James Monroe (1758–1831) — Monroe, a native of Virginia, served in the Revolutionary War. Prior to his election as president of the United States, Monroe served in a wide variety of government posts. He served Virginia in the state legislature and as governor. He was a member of the confederation congress and the U.S. Senate. He was minister to France and to Britain and he held two cabinet posts. As president, Monroe stressed limited government and strict construction of the constitution. He acquired Florida for the U.S. from Spain and he was the author of a policy declaration (later known as the Monroe Doctrine) which proscribed outside interference in North and South America. Early in his term as president, Monroe made a tour by boat from Buffalo to Detroit, where he arrived in August, 1817. This county was created on July 14, 1817, in anticipation of the president's five day visit to Michigan territory. Monroe was the first American president to venture this far west.

1257 *Montcalm County*

Louis-Joseph, Marquis de Montcalm-Gozon de Saint-Veran (1712–1759) — A native of France, Montcalm was the son of a nobleman whose title he inherited. Montcalm entered the French army as an ensign at the age of 15 and he rose in rank while participating in a variety of military engagements on the European continent. In 1756 he was promoted to major-general and sent to command French troops in New France (Canada), while the French and Indian War was in progress. Montcalm's troops scored a few victories in that war but these French-Canadian troops were

defeated and Montcalm was killed by British forces on Plains of Abraham during the battle of Quebec, in September, 1759. Just one year later, all of Canada passed from the French to the British and British forces took possession of Detroit and other Great Lake posts.

1258 *Montmorency County*

Uncertain — A number of sources consulted identify, with apparent certainty, the person for whom this county was named but sources found to be generally reliable flatly state that the origin of this county's name cannot be determined with any degree of certainty. It is known that this county was created on April 1, 1840, with the name Cheonoquet County. That name honored a Chippewa Indian chief who was a party to peace treaties with the Whites which were signed in 1807, 1815, 1825 and 1837. It is also known that the Michigan legislature changed the county's name to Montmorency on March 8, 1843. However it is uncertain whom the Michigan legislators wished to honor with this new county name. Four possibilities have been identified but that is all they are: possibilities. The history of Michigan was linked with that of Canada for many years during the period that France explored and later controlled Canada, which they named New France. Most of the possible origins of this county's name that have survived involve persons associated with Canada and/or France. The name Montmorency dates back a millennium in French history. As early as A.D. 950, a Lord Montmorency was among the great lords of the feudal kingdom of France. In his biography of Bishop Francois de Laval-Montmorency (1623–1708), A. Leblond de Brumath states that the house of Montmorency "…became allied to several royal houses, and gave to the elder daughter of the Church several cardinals, six constables, twelve marshals, four admirals and a great number of distinguished generals and statesmen." Some of the members of this house of Montmorency are among the possible namesakes of Montmorency County, Michigan.

Francois de Laval-Montmorency (1623–1708) — This first Roman Catholic bishop of Quebec, New France, was born on April 30, 1623, in the department of Eure-et-Loir in France to that country's illustrious Montmorency family. He was educated at Jesuit colleges and ordained as a priest in 1647. Father Laval-Montmorency was trained for missionary work under the Jesuits and he arrived in New France in

1659. In October, 1674, he was named to be the first bishop of Quebec. In New France the bishop organized the parochial system and missionary efforts. In 1659 he had become a member of the Quebec council and thus exercised powerful influence on the secular as well as religious life of New France. He attempted to maintain high moral standards and opposed the sale of liquor to Indians. Bishop Laval-Montmorency died in Quebec city in May, 1708.

Henri, Second Duke de Montmorency (1595–1632) — A son of Henri, Count of Danville and Duke de Montmorency, the second duke of Montmorency was born in France in 1595. In 1619 or 1620 he purchased the lieutenant-generalship of New France (Canada) but sold it a few years later without ever having set foot on the North American continent. One source calls him a viceroy of New France (1619–1624); another refers to him as "governor of Languedoc and admiral of France who served as viceroy of New France (1620–1625)." The 1881 *Report of the Pioneer Society of the State of Michigan* refers to him under the caption "Another List of Michigan Governors" as a member of the viceroyalty and marshal. The index to the 1874–1890 volumes of the *Reports & Collections of the Michigan Pioneer & Historical Society* calls him "governor of Canada (1620)." Canada's Montmorency River and its magnificent waterfall, the Montmorency Falls, were named by the explorer Samuel de Champlain (–1635) in honor of this duke of Montmorency.

Raymond de Montmorency (1806–1889) — A French soldier and officer of the Tenth Hussars, this Lord Montmorency was indicted for libel and sentenced to 12 months imprisonment in 1852.

An otherwise unidentified Count Morenci — This individual is reported to have aided the 13 American colonies in their war for independence from England.

1259 *Muskegon County*

Muskegon River — This county, on the western edge of Michigan's lower peninsula, was created in 1859 and named for the Muskegon River, which flows through it. Houghton Lake in central Michigan is the source of the Muskegon River. From there, the Muskegon flows southwest until it empties into Lake Michigan via Muskegon Lake, at the city of Muskegon, the county seat of Muskegon County. The Muskegon River is some 200 miles long, while the main river, together with all of its tributaries, has a combined length of about 1,300 miles. These rivers drain an estimated area of 2,600 square miles. The river's name came from Chippewa Indian words for "swamp" (or "marsh") and "place." "Swampy place" was an accurate description of the land at the lower end of the Muskegon River when the Chippewa Indians controlled this area.

1260 Newaygo County

Uncertain—Henry R. Schoolcraft (1793–1864) suggested the names for several Michigan counties that were created in 1840. One of them was Newaygo County, which was created on April 1, 1840. Newaygo County's name honors a relatively obscure Indian chief but there is uncertainty concerning which obscure chief it honors. Many sources consulted specify that Newaygo County's namesake was the Indian chief who signed a treaty at Saginaw on September 24, 1819. His name appears as Nuwagon on that treaty. There was an Indian chief who signed a treaty at Detroit on July 31, 1855, whose name was rendered as Naywawgoo. This may have been the same chief who signed the earlier treaty at Saginaw. Professor Virgil J. Vogel is a recognized authority on Indian names in Michigan, and elsewhere. In his 1986 work entitled *Indian Names in Michigan*, Dr. Vogel mentions these possible sources of Newaygo County's name but states that the true origin is uncertain. Vogel speculates that it is more likely that Newaygo County's name was chosen in honor of an Ottawa Indian chief, named Ningwegon, who visited Henry R. Schoolcraft at Mackinac Island on August 19, 1833. At that time Chief Ningwegon was elderly (about 76). On account of his age, poverty and record of friendship with the Americans, this Chief Ningwegon was granted an annuity of one hundred dollars per year in a treaty signed in our nation's capital on March 28, 1836, just four years before this Michigan county was created.

1261 Oakland County

Prevalence of oak trees in the county in 1819—This county, in southeastern Michigan, was created in 1819 by proclamation by Michigan's territorial governor, Lewis Cass (1782–1866). At that time, much of southern Michigan had stretches of open land with scattered clusters of oak trees. These were called "oak openings." These oaks have also been described as "majestic orchards of oaks." The county's name was chosen because of the oak trees that were prevalent here in 1819. By the early 1980's few oaks remained and Oakland County was primarily an industrial sub-

urb of Detroit. Most of the county's surviving oaks were to be found in the northwestern section of the county near high income residential properties and golf courses.

1262 Oceana County

Uncertain—This county, which borders on the eastern shore of Lake Michigan, was originally created and named on March 2, 1831, while Michigan was still a territory. Most authorities consulted agree that the name was chosen because of the county's location on the shore of Lake Michigan. On the surface, this explanation appears credible. Certainly our numerous small inland lakes would have made Lake Michigan and the other Great Lakes seem like oceans. According to some sources, Oceana County's name was chosen because of the county's border on Lake Michigan, which was considered by some to be a virtual fresh water ocean. However, two sources of information on the origin of Michigan county names offer an alternative explanation. These sources suggest the possibility that the name came from the title of a book written by an Englishman, James Harrington (1611–1677). The title of that book was *The Commonwealth of Oceana*. The two sources suggesting this seemingly far-fetched possibility have proven to be relatively unreliable regarding the origins of other county names in Michigan. However, there is a third source which lends credibility to the possibility that the county's name was chosen from the title of James Harrington's 17th century book. That third source is entitled: *Oceana County: Pioneers & Business Men of To-Day*, written by L. M. Hartwick and W. H. Tuller and published in 1890. These authors performed extensive research concerning the origin of Oceana County's name. As a result of their research, one must conclude that although the origin of this county's name is uncertain, there is a genuine possibility that it came from the title of the 17th century book. Hartwick and Tuller assert that when Oceana County was named in 1831, the name applied to territory lying south of today's Oceana County; that territory comprised portions of the present counties of Montcalm, Kent, Newaygo and Muskegon "...but did not include *any* [italics added] of the territory now embraced in Oceana County." Only one of these four counties, Muskegon County, currently borders on Lake Michigan. The July, 1918, issue of *Michigan History Magazine* contained an article by William H.

Hathaway entitled "County Organization in Michigan." In the appendix to that article, Hathaway provided meticulous descriptions of the boundaries of Michigan's counties and he asserted that in 1831, Oceana County was "set off in territory which is now a part of Kent, Montcalm, Newaygo and Muskegon Counties, entirely different from the present location" (i.e., of Oceana County) and that its borders were changed in 1840. Additional support for the case made by Hartwick and Tuller appeared in the *Historical Collections of the Michigan Pioneer & Historical Society's* 1912 issue. That issue contained an article by William L. Jenks concerning the history and meaning of county names in Michigan. In it, Jenks states that "as originally laid out and named, it [i.e., Oceana County] all lay south of Town 13 North of the base line. In 1840 the name was retained but applied to an *almost* [italics added] entirely different territory lying on the shore of Lake Michigan and *mostly* [italics added] north of its former north line, its former territory being absorbed into the counties of Kent, Newaygo and Mecosta." (The present Mecosta County is also an inland county.) While these descriptions of the location of Oceana County when it was first named are not in complete agreement, they do harmonize on the fact that Lake Michigan was not an important "ocean" boundary of the original county and thus an unlikely inspiration for the county's name. The 1890 detective work of Hartwick and Tuller contains a biographical sketch of the English author, James Harrington, and even manages to include a possible connection to North America by connecting Harrington's book with the studies of Jacques Marquette (1637–1675). But even Hartwick and Tuller conclude that the true origin of Oceana County's name is uncertain.

1263 Ogemaw County

Ogemakegato (1794–1840)—This county's name is based on the Ojibwa Indians' name for "chief" or "head speaker," but this county was not named for chiefs in general but for a specific Indian chief, Ogemakegato (1794–1840). Chief Ogemakegato signed treaties with the Whites in 1819, 1837, 1838 and 1839. In a petition to the U.S. Congress dated October 3, 1832, Ogemakegato asked it to honor a treaty commitment to reimburse Indians for improvements to ceded lands. Ogemakegato was a chief of the Saginaw band of Indians and he died in 1840, the year that this county was created and named. The name was suggested to the Michigan legislature by Henry R. Schoolcraft (1793–1864). Chief Ogemakegato was buried at Bay City, Michigan. A bronze plaque there rendered his named as Ogemakegate, but other versions of his name have also been used. Since the Indians had no written language, it was left to Whites to reduce the Indian names to written form and it is common to encounter Indian names with a variety of spellings.

1264 *Ontonagon County*

Ontonagon River — This county, which is near the western end of Michigan's upper peninsula, was created in 1843 and named for the Ontonagon River, which runs through it. The river empties into Lake Superior at the village of Ontonagon, the county seat. The Ontonagon River is some 150 miles long and is popular with canoeists. The Ontonagon and all its tributaries, have a combined length of 1,100 miles and they drain more than 1,300 square miles. The river's name is of Indian origin but the translation of that name is uncertain. Possibilities that have been mentioned include "bowl," "hunting river," "lost dish," "place where game is shot by guess," "fishing place" and others. In May, 1964, a member of Michigan's senate, Charles S. Blondy, introduced a resolution to change the name of this county to honor one of Michigan's then-recent governors. Blondy encountered stiff opposition and withdrew his resolution.

1265 *Osceola County*

Osceola (–1838) — Osceola, the leader of Florida's Seminole Indians during the Second Seminole War, was born in Alabama or Georgia about 1804 and moved with his mother to Florida territory. In 1835, when the United States government attempted to move the Seminoles from Florida to Indian territory (now Oklahoma) Osceola led the opposition which the Seminoles conducted guerrilla style from the Everglades. In October, 1837, Osceola and several other Indians went to St. Augustine under a flag of truce for a parley with General Thomas S. Jesup. He was captured and kidnapped by the unscrupulous Jesup and placed in prison at Ft. Moultrie, South Carolina. Weakened by chronic malaria and quinsy, he lost the will to live in captivity and died on January 30, 1838. Osceola's named derived from the Creek Indians' *assiyahola* which meant "singer at the black drink." This referred to a customary cry uttered by the serving attendant during distribution of a ceremonial black drink made from the caffeine-rich leaves of the yaupon. This Michigan county was originally created and named Unwattin County in 1840. That name honored a local Ottawa Indian chief whose name was referred to in an 1836 treaty. The Michigan legislature changed the name of Unwattin County to Osceola County on March 8, 1843. Osceola and the heroic opposition of his Seminole Indians to their removal from Florida had gained national attention.

1266 *Oscoda County*

A contrived or pseudo–Indian name — Oscoda is one of the many contrived, pseudo–Indian county names on Michigan's map. Most of these were coined by Henry R. Schoolcraft (1793–1864). Oscoda was one of 29 proposed county names that Schoolcraft submitted to the Michigan legislature about 1840. The name was constructed from these Indian words:

Os — Taken from *ossin*, meaning a "pebble" or "stone"

Coda — Taken from *mushcoda* meaning a "prairie" or "meadow"

The Michigan legislature adopted many of Schoolcraft's 29 proposed county names and Oscoda was one of them. It was created on April 1, 1840.

1267 *Otsego County*

Otsego County, New York — This county was originally created on April 1, 1840, and named Okkuddo County. Its name was changed to Otsego on March 8, 1843. The new name honored a county in New York state, the state from which many of Michigan's pioneer settlers had come. Sources consulted that deal with the history and geographic names of Michigan offer suggestions concerning the meaning of the Iroquois Indians' name *Otsego*. Translations offered include "clear water," "welcome water," "place where meetings are held" and "beautiful lake." In his work entitled *Indian Names in Michigan*, Professor Virgil J. Vogel is more cautious. This scholar of Indian names in Michigan and elsewhere merely mentions that the translation is thought by many to be unknown although "place of the rock" has been suggested. Vogel's caution is certainly justified when one notes the small amount of information on the translation of the word *otsego* in works dealing with the history of geographic names in New York state. Indeed, even though beautiful Otsego Lake is the most remarkable feature in Otsego County, New York, sources dealing with New York state's history and geography avoid attributing the New York county's name to the lake. Otsego Lake is about nine miles long and has an average width of one mile. This lake featured prominently in novels written by James Fenimore Cooper (1789–1851) and Cooper died near the southern end of Otsego Lake, New York. In his work entitled *The Deerslayer*, Cooper described Otsego Lake as "a broad sheet of water, so placid and limpid that it resembled a bed of pure mountain atmosphere compressed into a setting of hills and woods." By the late 1990's some of the woods had become farms but little else had changed the accuracy of Cooper's description.

Otsego County, New York, was created on February 16, 1791, from territory formerly embraced by Montgomery County. The town of Otsego, New York, was created within Montgomery County on March 7, 1788, and when Otsego County was created, the town of Otsego included much of the new county. New York state sources tell us that the name *otsego* is of Iroquois Indian origin but most of these New York sources say that the meaning of the name is unknown. A few of these New York state sources mention the possibility that the name may relate to "rock." One of the New York sources is William M. Beauchamp. In his article entitled "Aboriginal Place Names of New York," published by the New York State Education Department in May, 1907, Beauchamp admits that the true translation of the name is uncertain but he builds a plausible case for the possibility that *otsego* might mean "place of the rock." This rock may have been a large rock at the outlet of Otsego Lake, which James Fenimore Cooper mentioned in *The Deerslayer*. It is possible, then, to hypothesize a genealogy for Otsego County, Michigan's name which traces it from Otsego County, New York, to Otsego Lake, New York, to a prominent rock on the shore of Otsego Lake, New York.

1268 *Ottawa County*

Ottawa Indians — When first encountered by Whites, the Ottawa Indians were living at what is now the province of Ontario, in Canada. Initially the name Ottawa was used by the French to denote all tribes living on the shores of Lake Huron in upper Michigan and west along Lake Superior. Since then, the name has generally been confined to Indians of the Algonquian linguistic family, who lived in Ohio, Indiana, Michigan and Wisconsin.

During the French and Indian War, the Ottawa Indians sided with the French against the British. The Ottawa were pushed steadily westward, first by the Iroquois Indians and later by Whites. They resisted efforts to push them out of eastern lands into less desirable western areas but these efforts failed. By December, 1836, some Ottawas were resettled to a part of the old Indian territory that is now in Kansas. However, other Ottawas remained in Michigan and Ontario, Canada. Dispirited by this forced relocation and in poor health, nearly half of the Ottawa Indians who had been moved to Kansas were dead within five years. The Ottawas in Kansas were again moved to the Indian territory that is now Oklahoma in 1870. The name *Ottawa* derives from an Indian name meaning "trader" or "barterer." The Ottawa Indians were adept at trading and even served as middlemen facilitating trades between Whites and other Indians and among several Indian tribes as well. This county was created in 1831, when Michigan was still a territory.

1269 *Presque Isle County*

Presque Isle peninsula — This county borders on Lake Huron at the northeastern corner of Michigan's lower peninsula. Created in 1840, it was named for its narrow peninsula, named Presque Isle, which juts out into Lake Huron. French explorers thought the peninsula resembled an island and called it *presque isle*, meaning "almost an island." In an 1820 work, Henry R. Schoolcraft (1793–1864) mentioned one strip of the peninsula that connected the larger portion to the mainland. Schoolcraft stated that this strip of land was so narrow that by portaging his canoe a mere 200 yards, he was able to reduce his journey by six to eight miles.

1270 *Roscommon County*

Roscommon County, Republic of Ireland — This Michigan county was originally created on April 1, 1840, and named Mikenauk County, in honor of an Ottawa Indian chief. Its name was changed on March 8, 1843, to Roscommon County, in honor of a county in Ireland. Michigan's legislature changed the names of several other counties on March 8, 1843, to honor persons and places of Irish origin. Roscommon County is within Ireland's Connacht province and has an area of some 950 square miles. In the early 1980's, its population was approximately 50,000. This Irish county's capital city, also named Roscommon, is located near both the Shannon River and a tributary of the Shannon, named the Suck River. The county and city of Roscommon have names honoring the founder (and the abbot) of the first monastery located at Roscommon, Ireland. He is referred to in some sources as "Saint Coman" but he was not a saint of the Roman Catholic Church; merely an abbot. The old–Irish prefix *ros* is translated as a "point" or "promontory" or as "wood." This *ros*, linked with the abbot's name, Coman, gave Roscoman, which transposed over time to the present version, Roscommon. One source indicates that "Saint Coman" was a young man in the year A.D. 550 while another puts the year of his death as either A.D. 746 or 747. Since this second source gives his age at the time of his death as 200 years, all of these dates are suspect. However, it is not surprising that the namesake of Roscommon County, Ireland, has been incorrectly presumed by some to have been a saint. In James F. Kenney's 1929 work entitled *The Sources for the Early History of Ireland*, it is pointed out that "…Not having those of martyrs, the Irish monks began to enshrine and display the relics of their first abbots."

1271 *Saginaw County*

Saginaw River — This county was created on September 10, 1822, by proclamation of Michigan's territorial governor, Lewis Cass (1782–1866). Cass personally named the new county for the Saginaw River, a navigable river, and one of the major streams which feed water into Lake Huron's Saginaw Bay. The Saginaw River carries ship traffic to and from numerous Great Lake ports. Several sources indicate that the name *Saginaw* derived from the former presence, in the area, of the Sauk Indians. The Sauk are an Algonquian tribe who were closely allied to the Fox Indians. It is more likely that the name *Saginaw* derived from the Ojibwa Indians' word *saging*, meaning "at the mouth." If Sauk Indians ever lived in the area around the Saginaw River, it was before the arrival of Europeans.

1272 *Saint Clair County*

Saint Clair township, Macomb County, Michigan territory — Sir Walter Scott (1771–1832) observed "Oh, what a tangled web we weave, when first we practise to deceive!" Truth tellers don't always have an easy time, either. Observe, if you will, the genealogy of Saint Clair County, Michigan's name: Saint Clair County was created on March 28, 1820, when Michigan was still a territory. This new county was created from a portion of Macomb County, Michigan territory, and it was named for Macomb County's Saint Clair township. In fact, at the time that Saint Clair County was created, its entire land area consisted of this Saint Clair township. The origin of the township's name is uncertain but only two possibilities are mentioned in the literature on this subject and both are plausible:

Arthur St. Clair (1736–1818) — The township's name may have honored General Arthur St. Clair, the first governor of the Northwest territory. All of the present state of Michigan was a part of the Northwest territory when Arthur St. Clair was its governor and there are indications that the township was named about 1818, when Arthur St. Clair died. St. Clair was a native of Scotland who moved to Pennsylvania in his twenties. He served, rather ineffectively, as a general in the army in both the Revolutionary War and in later actions against the Indians. He was a Pennsylvania delegate to the Continental Congress and he served as governor of the Northwest territory but President Jefferson was dissatisfied with his conduct and removed him from that post.

Lake St. Clair — The township's name may have been taken from the name of the lake on which it bordered. The lake had been named in honor of the Roman Catholic saint, Saint Clare of Assisi (1194–1253), by the French explorer, the Sieur de la Salle (1643–1687), when he discovered the lake on Saint Clare's feast day, August 12, 1679.

Saint Clare (1194–1253) — Famed as the founder of an order of nuns, Clare was born at Assisi, Italy, and was a friend and follower of Saint Francis of Assisi. After listening to Saint Francis preach in 1212, she ran away from home and entered the Benedictine convent of St. Paul, near Bastia. Later, at the convent of San Damiano, which she governed as abbess for almost 40 years, she founded the order of nuns known as the Poor Clares. She lived a very austere life and required her community to subsist on day-to-day contributions. Distinguished as one of the great medieval contemplatives, her influence was great and popes, cardinals and bishops frequently came to San Damiano to consult her.

1273 *Saint Joseph County*

Saint Joseph River — Saint Joseph County, Michigan was created in 1829 and named for the Saint Joseph River, which flows through it. This Saint Joseph River is some

210 miles long. It rises in Hillsdale County, in southern Michigan, flows in a southwestern direction across Michigan and into Indiana. In Indiana, the Saint Joseph makes an abrupt turn at the city of South Bend, Indiana, and then flows due north for about six miles to reenter the state of Michigan. From there it flows in a northwestern direction across Michigan, finally ending at Lake Michigan. There are three Saint Joseph Rivers in this general region. Saint Joseph County, Michigan, was named for the one that has the sharp bend at the city of South Bend, Indiana. This Saint Joseph River's name derived from the name of a French fort that was built on a high bluff near the banks of the Saint Joseph River, where the city of Niles, Michigan, is now located. This fort, named Fort Saint Joseph or Fort Saint Joseph's, had been named for the Mission of Saint Joseph which had been built here by Father Allouez somewhat earlier. Together the mission and the fort comprised an important French post for commerce and missionary activity among the Indians. It is not known for whom the mission was named. Some accounts speculate that the name honored the Saint Joseph who, in Catholic theology, was the husband of Saint Mary, the virgin mother of Jesus. Other sources indicate that a Roman Catholic priest named Father Joseph was an early settler in the area and a leader in French missionary work here. These sources imply that the mission was named for him and that "Saint Joseph" was merely a euphemism that referred to Father Joseph.

1274 *Sanilac County*

Sannilac, a fictive American Indian spirit warrior — This county was created by proclamation by Governor Lewis Cass (1782–1866) on September 10, 1822, as part of Michigan territory. Governor Cass spelled the name Sanilac; i.e., the same as the current spelling of the county's name. This 1822 proclamation was the first known use of the name, and if Henry Whiting had not written a poem entitled "Sannilac" (or "Sannillac," but not "Sanilac"), which was published in Boston by Carter and Babcock in 1831, there would be little evidence of the origin of the name. In 1831 Henry Whiting was a major in the United States army. He was stationed for a number of years at Detroit. In an appendix to his "Sannilac" poem, Whiting included notes made by both Governor Lewis Cass (1782–1866) and Henry R. Schoolcraft (1793–1864). Schoolcraft was a champion namer of Michigan counties. The notes by Cass and Schoolcraft preserved some Indian traditions and the tradition which was preserved in the name Sannilac involved a spirit warrior, who led the Wyandot Indians and won the love of an Indian maiden, named Wona, by defeating the enemy. Numerous reference works dealing with Michigan's history and geography state or imply that Sannilac (by whatever spelling) was a real American Indian. He was not. In the preface to his poem, Henry Whiting stated that his purpose was "…not so much to fill up the outline of history, as to exhibit manners and customs, which are generally characteristic of the sons of the forest."

1275 *Schoolcraft County*

Henry R. Schoolcraft (1793–1864) — Our nation's county names have a fascinating random nature to them; a president here, a territorial governor there and an Indian tribe between them. Military heroes are common with many in Iowa associated with the Mexican War, while just a bit to the west, in Kansas, the military heroes honored are those of the Civil War since that was the prominent war at the time Kansas formed many of her counties. Oklahoma is a special case. Many of its counties were named on one day, July 16, 1907, by members of Oklahoma's constitutional convention and a large number of the county names honor delegates to that convention. Henry Rowe Schoolcraft carved his own niche in this county name panorama. Schoolcraft invented the largest number of artificial county names of any person in our nation's history. Indeed, apart from Schoolcraft's Michigan county names, there are few invented county names in America. To say that Schoolcraft was "eccentric" is certainly accurate, but it is rather like calling Albert Einstein "intelligent." Linguists have criticized Schoolcraft for striving for euphony but missing the mark, at times joining syllables from two or more languages. Michigan legislators have rebelled at Schoolcraft's county names by renaming handfuls of them. But even after these legislative deletions, Schoolcraft-coined county names are still numerous in Michigan. Many of these contrived names are half American Indian or pseudo–Indian.

Henry Rowe Schoolcraft was born in upstate New York an educated at Middlebury College in Vermont and Union College in Schenectady, New York. In 1817, apparently with no prompting, Schoolcraft headed west to study the geography and geology west of the Mississippi River in our present states of Arkansas and Missouri. His work entitled *A View of the Lead Mines of Missouri*, published in 1819, gave an account of his observations. In 1820 he was a member of a party headed by General Lewis Cass (1782–1866) that explored Lake Superior and the upper valley of the Mississippi River. In 1822 Schoolcraft was appointed Indian agent in northern Michigan territory and he married Janet Johnston, a granddaughter of an Ojibwa Indian chief. From 1828 to 1832 he was a member of Michigan's territorial legislature and in 1832 he led a party of explorers who traced the Mississippi River to its source in Minnesota's Itasca Lake. At that time Itasca Lake was within Michigan territory. Schoolcraft subsequently served in treaty negotiations with the Indians which secured 16 million acres of new land for the United States. At the request of the Michigan legislature, Schoolcraft supplied them with a list, in 1840, of some 29 names for new Michigan counties and many of them were used. In 1843 the Michigan legislature created and named Schoolcraft County in his honor. It was at about this time that the Royal Antiquarian society of Denmark honored Schoolcraft by making him an honorary member of their society. From 1845 to 1848 Schoolcraft was engaged in a census of the six powerful nations of the Iroquois Indian confederacy. He devoted the remainder of the active portion of his life to writing about American Indians and his explorations among them. Although Schoolcraft lived until 1864, his active career was truncated some seven years earlier by rheumatic paralysis.

1276 *Shiawassee County*

Shiawassee River — The Shiawassee River, a tributary of the Saginaw River, rises in Oakland County in southeastern Michigan. It winds, in a generally northwestern direction, through Shiawassee County and then turns north to join the Flint River, near Saginaw, Michigan. Together, the Shiawassee River and the Flint River form the Saginaw River. The Shiawassee is about 95 miles long and its length, when combined with its tributaries is estimated at 635 miles. The Shiawassee River system drains a land area of almost 1,000 square miles. Shiawassee County was created in 1822, while Michigan was still a territory, and named for the Shiawassee River. At the time that this county was created, the Shiawassee River divided the county into two nearly equal parts. However, Shiawassee County's size and shape have changed since then because new counties have been created out of its original territory. The Shiawassee River's name is of Indian origin but its meaning is unknown. Countless translations have been attempted including "twisting," "straight," "green" and "beautiful."

1277 *Tuscola County*

A contrived, pseudo–Indian name — At the request of the Michigan legislature, Henry R. Schoolcraft (1793–1864) supplied them, in 1840, with a list of some 29 names for new counties and many of these names were used. The list of 29 proposed county names contained a number of contrived, half Indian or pseudo–Indian names. *Tuscola* was one of the 29 contrived names that Schoolcraft suggested and the legislature used it when they created this county on April 1, 1840. The meaning of the name was not even clear to its inventor. Schoolcraft translated it in one place as "warrior prairie" but elsewhere he stated that it came from *dusinagon*, which he said meant "level," and *cola*, which Schoolcraft translated as "lands."

1278 *Van Buren County*

Martin Van Buren (1782–1862) — Van Buren was a native of New York and he served that state as state senator, attorney general and governor. He represented New York in the U.S. Senate and was secretary of state in President Jackson's cabinet. He served one term as vice-president and one term as president of the U.S. Van Buren organized an effective political machine in New York state which was one of the first political machines in this country and on the national level, he was an early user of the spoils system of filling government jobs. By October, 1829, Michigan had been a territory since 1805 and thoughts of statehood may have been on the minds of Michigan's territorial legislators. For whatever reason, on October 29, 1829, Michigan territory created counties named for Andrew Jackson, who was then president, John C. Calhoun, President Jackson's first vice-president and all members of President Jackson's first cabinet. When this county was created, Martin Van Buren was serving in the cabinet as secretary of state.

1279 *Washtenaw County*

Grand River — *Washtenong* was an Indian name for the Grand River on Michigan's lower peninsula. That river rises in Jackson County (just a bit west of the present Washtenaw County border), flows north through Lansing and then turns west. As the Grand River travels from central Michigan toward Lake Michigan, it widens considerably. The Grand ends its journey at Grand Haven, Michigan, where it empties into Lake Michigan. Sources consulted differ greatly on the length of the Grand River. One source puts its length at 260 miles while another shows 478 miles. Presumably the discrepancy is due to inclusion and exclusion of one or more tributaries in tallying the length of the Grand. The length of the Grand River, combined with all of its tributaries is about 3,350 miles and this river system drains some 5,500 square miles. The Grand River is navigable for approximately 40 miles from its mouth on Lake Michigan. Washtenaw County was created on September 10, 1822, by proclamation of Michigan's territorial governor, Lewis Cass (1782–1866). The new county's name was a slightly altered version of the Indian name *Washtenong*. A variety of explanations of the Indian name are mentioned in literature on the history and geography of Michigan but the true translation is not known.

1280 *Wayne County*

Anthony Wayne (1745–1796) — A native of Pennsylvania, Wayne was a successful brigadier-general in the Revolutionary War and became a hero for his daring exploits. During the bitter winter of 1777-1778 at Valley Forge, Pennsylvania, Wayne shared the sufferings of his men although his comfortable estate was only five miles away. He played an important role in the final overthrow of the British forces in Georgia. After the war, in 1785, Wayne moved to Georgia and he represented Georgia for about six months in the U.S. House of Representatives. In 1792, President Washington recalled Wayne to serve as a major-general against the Indians in the Northwest territory. Once again his military efforts were successful. On August 20, 1794, forces under Wayne's command defeated the Indians in the battle of Fallen Timbers in northwestern Ohio. That battle was decisive in ending Indian hostilities in the region and moving America's frontier further north and west. Before long, British forces also evacuated the northern country and Americans moved in. A treaty, which Anthony Wayne had executed with the Indians in 1795, gave America formal ownership of large tracts of Indian land. A portion of that land was made into Wayne County in Michigan territory on November 21, 1815, by proclamation of the territorial governor, Lewis Cass (1782–1866). However, Governor Cass did not originate the use of the name Wayne County for land within Michigan territory. In August, 1796, Winthrop Sargent (1753–1820), the acting governor of the original Northwest territory, created a Wayne County extending westward from the Cuyahoga River in Ohio to the western side of Indiana and north to the Canadian border. General Wayne was touched by this gesture and on November 14, 1796, he wrote a letter expressing his thanks. This original Wayne County included virtually all of what later became Michigan territory. Starting in 1803, the Northwest territory was broken into component parts and in 1805 Wayne County ceased to exist until Lewis Cass proclaimed the new Wayne County in Michigan territory in 1815.

1281 *Wexford County*

County Wexford, Republic of Ireland — This county was originally created on April 1, 1840, and named Kautawaubet County, in honor of an Indian chief. That name had been suggested by Henry R. Schoolcraft (1793–1864). The county's name was changed to Wexford on March 8, 1843, but the act that changed the county's name incorrectly spelled the name of the original county as Rautawaubet County. Michigan's legislature changed the names of several counties on March 8, 1843, to honor persons or places of Irish origin. Wexford County is in southeastern Ireland, facing Wales across Saint George's Channel. Wexford County, Ireland, is within Leinster Province. The county has an area of approximately 900 square miles and one source lists its population in the late 1960's at 83,000 while another source shows its population as 99,000 in the early 1980's. Four centuries earlier, in the late 1500's, John Speed drafted maps of the British Isles and Alasdair Hawkyard provided commentary on those maps in his 1995 work entitled *The Counties of Britain: A Tudor Atlas by John Speed*. In that work, Hawkyard tells us that Wexford County, Ireland and the other counties of Leinster Province were more favorably disposed toward England than other sections of Ireland and the English returned the favor, forming a mutual admiration society, of sorts. However, Hawkyard points out, in matters religious, the counties of Leinster Province were conservative and resisted the efforts of England's King James I (1566–1625) to replace the Roman Catholic Church with Protestantism.

REFERENCES

Allen, Rolland C. "Dr. Douglass Houghton." *Michigan Historical Collections*, Vol. 39. Lansing: 1915.

Allen, R. C., & Helen M. Martin. "A Brief History of the Geological & Biological Survey of Michigan: 1837 to 1872." *Michigan History Magazine*, Vol. 6, No. 4. Lansing: 1922.

"Another List of Michigan Governors." *Report of the Pioneer Society of the State of Michigan*, Vol. 3. Lansing; 1881.

Anspach, Charles L. *We're Proud of Michigan & Proud to Present Montmorency County.* 1959.

Armitage, B. Phillis. "A Study of Michigan's Place-Names." *Michigan History Magazine*, Vol. 27. Lansing: October–December, 1943.

Atwell, Willis. *Do You Know: An Illustrated History of Michigan.* Booth Newspapers, Inc., 1937.

Bacon, Edwin F. *Otsego County, New York: Geographical & Historical.* Oneonta, New York, Oneonta, Herald, 1902.

Ball, Fanny D. *Bishop Baraga.* Grand Rapids, Michigan, School of Printing, Grand Rapids Junior High School.

Bartholomew, H. S. *Stories & Sketches of Elkhart County.* Nappanee, Indiana, E. V. Publishing House, 1936.

Beauchamp, William M. "Aboriginal Place Names of New York." *New York State Education Department Bulletin*, Bulletin No. 108, Archeology 12. Albany: May, 1907.

Beers, F. W. *Gazetteer & Biographical Record of Genesee County, N. Y.* Syracuse, New York, J. W. Vose & Co., 1890.

Bingham, S. D. *Early History of Michigan with Biographies of State Officers, Members of Congress, Judges & Legislators.* Lansing, Thorp & Godfrey, 1888.

Bradish. "Doctor Douglass Houghton." *Report of the Pioneer Society of the State of Michigan*, Vol. 4. Lansing: 1906.

Brown, C. J. D. *Michigan Streams.* Ann Arbor, Michigan, Michigan Department of Conservation, 1944.

Brown, Charles R. *The Government of Michigan: Its History & Jurisprudence.* Kalamazoo, Michigan, Moore & Quale, 1874.

Burmeister, Charles. "Short History of Benzie County." *Collections & Researches Made by the Michigan Pioneer & Historical Society*, Vol. 18. Lansing: 1892.

Burton, Clarence M., & M. Agnes Burton. *History of Wayne County and the City of Detroit, Michigan.* Chicago, S. J. Clarke Publishing Co., 1930.

Butterfield, George E., & Seventh Grade Teachers, Bay City Public Schools. *Bay County: Past & Present: Centennial Edition.* Bay City, Michigan, Bay City Board of Education, 1918.

Campbell, James V. *Outlines of the Political History of Michigan.* Detroit, Schober & Co., 1876.

The Canadian Encyclopedia. Edmonton, Alberta, Canada, Hurtig Publishers, 1985.

The Canadian Global Almanac: 1992: A Book of Facts. Toronto, Canada, Global Press, 1992.

Carlisle, Fred. *Wayne County Historical & Pioneer Society: Chronology of Notable Events in the History of the Northwest Territory & Wayne County.* Detroit, O. S. Gulley, Bornman & Co., 1890.

Carpenter, Warwick S. *The Summer Paradise in History.* Albany, Delaware & Hudson Co., 1914.

Case, Leonard. *Benzie County: A Bicentennial Reader.* Benzie County Bi-Centennial Commission, 1976.

Case, W. L. "The Founding of Grand Traverse College at Benzonia." *Michigan History Magazine*, Vol. 11, No. 3. Lansing: July, 1927.

Case, William L. "A Bit of Benzie History." *Michigan History Magazine*, Vol. 9. Lansing: 1925.

Case, William L. "On the Trail of a Vision: Benzonia." *Michigan History Magazine*, Vol. 23. Lansing: Winter, 1939.

Catton, Bruce. *Michigan: A Bicentennial History.* New York, W. W. Norton & Co., Inc., 1976.

Catton, Bruce. "Our American Heritage." *Michigan History*, Vol. 48, No. 4. Lansing: December, 1964.

Catton, Bruce. *Waiting for the Morning Train: An American Boyhood.* Garden City, New York, Doubleday & Co., Inc., 1972.

Chaput, Donald E. "A Plea for Moderation in Place-name Controversies." *Michigan History*, Vol. 49, No. 1. Lansing: March, 1965.

Child, Hamilton. *Gazetteer & Business Directory of Otsego County, N. Y. for 1872–3.* Syracuse, 1872.

Clements, John. *Michigan Facts.* Dallas, Texas, Clements Research II, Inc., 1990.

Clements, John. *Wisconsin Facts.* Dallas, Texas, Clements Research II, Inc., 1990.

Committee on Geographic Names. "Origin of Names of New York State Counties." *University of the State of New York Bulletin to the Schools*, Vol. 10. 1924.

The Counties of New York State. New York Telephone Co., 1948.

Cutcheon, Byron M. "Fifty Years of Growth in Michigan." *Collections & Researches Made by the Michigan Pioneer & Historical Society*, Vol. 22. Lansing: 1894.

Davis, Charles M. *Readings in the Geography of Michigan.* Ann Arbor, Michigan, Ann Arbor Publishers, 1964.

De Brumath, A. Leblond. *The Makers of Canada: Bishop Laval.* Toronto, Morang & Co., Ltd., 1906.

Dickinson, Julia T. *The Story of Leelanau.* Omena, Michigan, Solle's Bookshop, 1951.

Dodge, Mrs. Frank P. "Landmarks of Lenawee County." *Collections & Researches Made by the Michigan Pioneer & Historical Society*, Vol. 38. Lansing: 1912.

Donehoo, George P. *Indian Villages & Place Names in Pennsylvania.* Harrisburg, Pennsylvania, Telegraph Press, 1928.

Du Gard, Rene C. & Dominique C. Western. *The Handbook of French Place Names in the U.S.A.* Edition des Deux Mondes, 1977.

Du Mond, Neva. *Adventures in Michigan's Thumb Area: Thumb Diggings.* Lexington, Michigan, 1962.

Dunbar, Willis F. *Michigan Through the Centuries.* New York, Lewis Historical Publishing Co., Inc., 1955.

Dunbar, Willis F., & George S. May. *Michigan: A History of the Wolverine State.* Grand Rapids, Michigan, William B. Eerdmans Publishing Co., 1980.

Dustin, Fred. "Some Indian Place-Names Around Saginaw." *Michigan History Magazine*, Vol. 12, No. 4. Lansing: October, 1928.

Encyclopedia Canadiana. Toronto, Grolier Ltd., 1972.

Encyclopedia of Michigan. St. Clair Shores, Michigan, Somerset Publishers, 1981.

Englebert, Omer. *The Lives of the Saints.* New York, Barnes & Noble, Inc., 1994.

Eno, Joel N. "New York County Names." *The Magazine of History*, Vol. 23, No. 1. Poughkeepsie, New York: July, 1916.

Eno, Joel N. "A Tercentennial History of the Towns & Cities of New York: Their Origin, Dates & Names." *Proceedings of the New York State Historical Association*, Vol. 15. 1916.

Esarey, Logan. *History of Indiana from Its Exploration to 1922: Also a History of Tippecanoe County & the Wabash Valley.* Dayton, Ohio, National Historical Association, Inc., 1928.

Faragher, John M. *The Encyclopedia of Colonial & Revolutionary America.* New York, Facts on File, 1990.

Farmer, Silas. *History of Detroit & Wayne County & Early Michigan.* Silas Farmer & Co., 1890.

Foster, Theodore G. "A Dictionary of Michigan Place Names." Unpublished manuscript dated 1968, Michigan State Library, Lansing, Michigan.

Foster, Theodore G. "More Michigan Place Names." *The Totem Pole*, Vol. 35, No. 5. Algonac, Michigan: February 7, 1955.

Fox, George R. "Place Names of Berrien County." *Michigan History Magazine*, Vol. 8, No. 1. Lansing: January, 1924.

Fox, Truman B. *History of Saginaw County*. East Saginaw, Enterprise Print, 1858.

Fries, Bernice W. R. *Gladwin History: Then & Now*. 1989.

Frost, John. *The American Generals*. Hartford, Case, Tiffany & Co., 1850.

Fuller, George N. *Historic Michigan: Land of the Great Lakes*. Lansing, National Historical Association, Inc., 1924.

Gannett, Henry. *Origin of Certain Place Names in the United States*. Williamstown, Massachusetts, Corner House Publishers, 1978.

Gardner, Washington. *History of Calhoun County, Michigan*. Chicago, Lewis Publishing Co., 1913.

Gellert, W., et al. *The VNR Concise Encyclopedia of Mathematics*. New York, New York, Van Nostrand Reinhold Co., 1975.

"General Charles Gratiot." *South Dakota Historical Collections*, Vol. 1. Aberdeen, South Dakota: 1902.

Gillard, Kathleen I. *Our Michigan Heritage*. New York, New York, Pageant Press, Inc., 1955.

Gille, Frank H., et al. *Encyclopedia of New York*. St. Clair Shores, Michigan, Somerset Publishers, 1982.

Glassman, Michael. *New York State (and New York City) Geography, History, Government*. Great Neck, New York, Barron's Educational Series, Inc., 1964.

Grant, Bruce. *Concise Encyclopedia of the American Indian*. Avenel, New Jersey, Wings Books, 1989.

Greenman, Emerson F. *The Indians of Michigan*. Lansing, Michigan Historical Commission, 1961.

Grimm, Joe, Assistant to the Managing Editor, *Detroit Free Press*. Letter to the author dated June 2, 1987.

Hamilton, Mrs. Charlotte. "Chippewa County Place Names." *Michigan History Magazine*, Vol. 27. Lansing: October–December, 1943.

Hamilton, William B. *The Macmillan Book of Canadian Place Names*. Toronto, Macmillan of Canada, 1978.

Hanna, Roberta. *The Lewiston Story & Montmorency County Notes*.

Hartwick, L. M. & W. H. Tuller. *Oceana County: Pioneers & Business Men of To-Day*. Penwater, Michigan, Penwater News Steam Print, 1890.

Hathaway, William H. "County Organization in Michigan." *Michigan History Magazine*, Vol. 2, No. 3. Lansing: July, 1918.

Hawkyard, Alasdair. *The Counties of Britain: A Tudor Atlas by John Speed*. London, England, Pavilion Books, Ltd., 1995.

Hills, Leon C. *History & Legends of Place Names in Iowa: The Meaning of Our Map*. Omaha, Nebraska, Omaha School Supply Co., 1938.

Historic Background of South Bend & St. Joseph County in Northern Indiana. South Bend, Indiana, Schuyler Colfax Chapter Daughters of the American Revolution, 1927.

"Historical News: Notes & Comment." *Michigan History Magazine*, Vol. 3, No. 2. Lansing: April, 1919.

History of Allegan & Barry Counties, Michigan. Philadelphia, D. W. Ensign & Co., 1880.

"History of Fort Gratiot." *Collections & Researches Made by the Michigan Pioneer & Historical Society*, Reprint Vol. 18. Lansing: 1911.

History of Michigan Counties. Michigan Department of State. 1968.

History of Saginaw County, Michigan. Chicago, Chas. C. Chapman & Co., 1881.

History of the Upper Peninsula of Michigan. Chicago, Western Historical Co., A. T. Andreas, 1883.

Howard, Timothy E. *A History of St. Joseph County, Indiana*. Chicago, Lewis Publishing Co., 1907.

"Indian Names." *Report of the Pioneer Society of the State of Michigan*, Vol. 7. Lansing: 1886.

Indiana Historic Sites & Structures Inventory: Elkhart County: Interim Report. 1978.

The Interpreter's Dictionary of the Bible. New York, Abingdon Press, 1963.

Jacobson, Carol S. *Life in the Forest: The History of Montmorency County, Michigan*. Montmorency County Historical Society, 1981.

Jenks, William L. "History & Meaning of the County Names of Michigan." *Collections & Researches Made by the Michigan Pioneer & Historical Society*, Vol. 38. Lansing: 1912.

Jenks, William L. "History & Meaning of the County Names of Michigan." *Michigan History Magazine*, Vol. 10, No. 4. Lansing: October, 1926.

Jezernik, Maksimilijan. *Frederick Baraga*. New York, Studia Slovenica, 1968.

Kelton, Dwight H. "Ancient Names of Rivers, Lakes, etc." *Collections of the Pioneer Society of the State of Michigan*, Vol. 6. Lansing: 1883.

Kenney, James F. *The Sources for the Early History of Ireland*. New York, Columbia University Press, 1929.

Kenny, Hamill. "The Origin & Meaning of the Indian Place-Names of Maryland." Ph.D. Thesis, Theodore R. McKeldin Library, University of Maryland, College Park, Maryland, 1950.

Ker, Edmund T. *River & Lake Names in the United States*. New York, Woodstock Publishing Co., 1911.

King, Joseph B. "The Ottawa Indians in Kansas & Oklahoma." *Collections of the Kansas State Historical Society*, Vol. 13. Topeka: 1915.

Kirk, Des B. "Little Known Facts about Michigan." *Inside Michigan Magazine*, Vol. 3, No. 2. Ann Arbor, Michigan: February, 1953.

Kirk, Des B. "Little Known Facts about Michigan." *Inside Michigan Magazine*, Vol. 3, No. 4. Ann Arbor, Michigan: April, 1953.

L'Allier, Martha C. *Touring Michigan*. Hillsdale, Michigan, Hillsdale Educational Publishers, 1965.

Lanman, Charles. *The Red Book of Michigan*. Detroit, E. B. Smith & Co., 1871.

Larzelere, Claude S. *Government of Michigan*. Hillsdale, Michigan, Hillsdale School Supply & Publishing Co., 1935.

Le Jeune, Le R. P. L. *Dictionnaire General … du Canada*. University of Ottawa, Canada.

Leland, J. A. C. "Eastern Tribal Names in California." *California Folklore Quarterly*, Vol. 5, No. 4. Berkeley: October, 1946.

Leland, J. A. C. "Indian Names in Missouri." *Names: Journal of the American Name Society*, Vol. 1, No. 4. Berkeley: December, 1953.

Leland, J. A. C. "Some Eastern Indian Place Names in California." *California Folklore Quarterly*, Vol. 4, No. 4. Berkeley: October, 1945.

Letters Containing Information Relative to the Antiquities of the County of Clare Collected During the Progress of the Ordnance Survey in 1839. Bray, 1928.

Letters Containing Information Relative to the Antiquities of the County of Roscommon Collected During the Progress of the Ordnance Survey in 1837. Bray, 1927.

Lossing, Benson J. *The Empire State: A Compendious History of the Commonwealth of New York*. Hartford, Connecticut, American Publishing Co., 1888.

McCarty, Dwight G. *The Territorial Governors of the Old Northwest: A Study in Territorial Administration*. Iowa City, Iowa, State Historical Society of Iowa, 1910.

McCormick, W. R. "A Trip from Detroit to the Saginaw Valley over Fifty Years Ago." *Report of the Pioneer Society of the State of Michigan*, Vol. 7. Lansing: 1886.

McHenry, Robert. *Webster's American Military Biographies*. New York, Dover Publications, Inc., 1984.

Manor, Michael J. *Profiles of the Lewiston Area*.

Marckwardt, Albert H. "Naming Michigan's Counties." *Names: Journal of the American Name Society*, Vol. 23, No. 3. Potsdam, New York: September, 1975.

Michigan Almanac & Buyers Guide. Detroit, Republican State Central Committee of Michigan, 1963.

Michigan Biographies. Lansing, Michigan Historical Commission, 1924.

Michigan History, Vol. 42, No. 4. Lansing: December, 1958.

Michigan Manual: 1973–1974. Department of Administration.

Michigan Pioneer & Historical Society: Index to the Reports & Collections, Vols. 1–15 (1874–1890). Lansing: 1904.

Michigan Pioneer & Historical Society: Index to the Reports & Collections, Vols. 16–30 (1890–1906). Lansing: 1907.

Monette, Clarence J. *Some Copper Country Names & Places*. Lake Linden, Michigan, Welden H. Curtin, 1975.

Moore, Charles. *History of Michigan*. Chicago, Lewis Publishing Co., 1915.

Morison, Samuel E. *Samuel de Champlain: Father of New France*. Boston, Little, Brown & Co., 1972.

Murhead, Russell L. *Ireland*. London, Ernest Benn, Ltd., 1949.

Murray, J. Franklin. "Jesuit Place Names in the United States." *Names: Journal of the American Name Society*, Vol. 16, No. 1. Potsdam, New York: March, 1968.

"News & Comments: Markers." *Michigan History Magazine*, Vol. 27. Lansing: Winter, 1943.

Nutling, Wallace. *Ireland Beautiful*. Framingham, Massachusetts, Old America Co., 1925.

Oliver, David D. *Centennial History of Alpena County, Michigan*. Alpena, Michigan, Argus Printing House, 1903.

"Origin of the Names of New York State Counties." *University of the State of New York Bulletin to the Schools*, Vol. 10. 1924.

Parkman, Francis. *Montcalm & Wolfe*. Boston, Little, Brown & Co., 1894.

Peterson, C. Stewart. *First Governors of the Forty-Eight States*. New York, New York, Hobson Book Press, 1947.

Pound, Arthur. "Michigan, New York's Daughter State." *New York History*, Vol. 23, No. 3. Cooperstown, New York: July, 1942.

Powers, Perry F. *A History of Northern Michigan and Its People*. Chicago, Lewis Publishing Co., 1912.

Quaife, M. M. "Detroit Biographies: Alexander Macomb." *Burton Historical Collection Leaflet*, Vol. 10, No. 1. Detroit: November, 1931.

Quaife, Milo M. *Condensed Historical Sketches for Each of Michigan's Counties*. Detroit, J. L. Hudson Co., 1940.

Rayburn, J. A. "Geographical Names of Amerindian Origin in Canada." *Names: Journal of the American Name Society*, Vol. 15, No. 3. Potsdam, New York: September, 1967.

Reed, George I. *Bench & Bar of Michigan*. Chicago, Century Publishing & Engraving Co., 1897.

"Reports of Counties, Towns & Districts." *Report of the Pioneer Society of the State of Michigan*, Vol. 1. Lansing: 1877.

Reynolds, Elon G. *Compendium of History & Biography of Hillsdale County, Michigan*. Chicago, A. W. Bowen & Co., 1903.

Robison, Mabel O. *Minnesota Pioneers*. Minneapolis, T. S. Denison & Co., 1958.

Romig, Walter. *Michigan Place Names*. Detroit, Wayne State University Press, 1986.

Rosten, Leo. *The Joys of Yiddish*. New York, McGraw-Hill Book Co., 1968.

Rowland-Entwistle, Theodore & Jean Cooke. *Great Rulers of History: A Biographical Dictionary*. New York, Barnes & Noble Books, 1995.

Rydjord, John. *Indian Place-Names*. Norman, University of Oklahoma Press, 1968.

Sawyer, Alvah L. *A History of the Northern Peninsula of Michigan and Its People*. Chicago, Lewis Publishing Co., 1911.

Schenck, John S. *History of Ionia & Montcalm Counties, Michigan*. Philadelphia, D. W. Ensign & Co., 1881.

Schlesinger, Arthur M., Jr. *The Almanac of American History*. New York, G. P. Putnam's Sons, 1983.

Schoolcraft, Henry R. "Geographical Names." Letter to Michigan Governor Stevens T. Mason dated January 12, 1838. Michigan State Library, Lansing, Michigan.

Schultz, Gerard. *The New History of Michigan's Thumb*. 1969.

Scripps, J. E. & R. L. Polk. *Michigan State Gazetteer & Business Directory for 1873*. Detroit, Tribune Book & Job Office, 1873.

A Souvenir of Michigan's Centennial Year Containing Thirty-Six Historical Articles. Detroit, J. L. Hudson Co., 1937.

Sprague, Elvin L. & Mrs. George N. Smith. *Sprague's History of Grand Traverse & Leelanau Counties, Michigan*. B. F. Bowen, 1903.

Stennett, William H. *A History of the Origin of the Place Names Connected with the Chicago & North Western and Chicago,* St. Paul, Minneapolis & Omaha Railways. Chicago, 1908.

Stewart, George R. *American Place-Names*. New York, Oxford University Press, 1970.

Sullivan, James. *History of New York State: 1523–1927*. New York, Lewis Historical Publishing Co., Inc., 1927.

Symon, Charles A. *Alger County: A Centennial History: 1885–1985*. Munising, Michigan, Bayshore Press, 1986.

Taft, William H. III. *County Names: An Historical Perspective*. National Association of Counties, 1982.

This Is New York: The Empire State. Bronxville, New York, Cambridge Book Co., 1962.

Thrapp, Dan L. *Encyclopedia of Frontier Biography*. Lincoln, University of Nebraska Press, 1988.

A Treasury of Michigan Names. Ann Arbor, Michigan, University of Michigan Broadcasting Service.

Trover, Ellen L. *Chronology & Documentary Handbook of the State of New York*. Dobbs Ferry, New York, Oceana Publications, Inc., 1978.

Tucker, Willard D. *Gratiot County, Michigan: Historical, Biographical, Statistical*. Saginaw, Michigan, Seemann & Peters, 1913.

Turrell, Archie M. "Some Place Names of Hillsdale County." *Michigan History Magazine*, Vol. 6, No. 4. Lansing: 1922.

Utley, Henry M., & Byron M. Cutcheon. *Michigan as a Province, Territory & State, the Twenty-Sixth Member of the Federal Union*. New York, New York, Publishing Society of Michigan, 1906.

Verway, David I. *Michigan Statistical Abstract: Twentieth Edition: 1986-7*. Detroit, Bureau of Business Research, Wayne State University School of Business Administration.

Verwyst, Chrysostom. "Geographical Names in Wisconsin, Minnesota & Michigan Having a Chippewa Origin." *Collections of the State Historical Society of Wisconsin*, Vol. 12. Madison, Wisconsin: 1892.

Verwyst, Chrysostom. "Life & Labors of Bishop Baraga: A Short Sketch of the Life & Labors of Bishop Baraga the Great Indian Apostle of the Northwest." *Collections & Researches Made by the Michigan Pioneer & Historical Society*. Vol. 26. Lansing: 1896.

Verwyst, Chrysostomus. *Life & Labors of Rt. Rev. Frederic Baraga*. Milwaukee, Wisconsin, M. H. Wiltzius & Co., 1900.

Vexler, Robert I. *Chronology & Documentary Handbook of the State of Michigan*. Dobbs Ferry, New York, Oceana Publications, Inc., 1978.

Vogel, Virgil J. *Indian Names in Michigan*. Ann Arbor, University of Michigan Press, 1986.

Vogel, Virgil J. "The Missionary as Acculturation Agent: Peter Dougherty and the Indians of Grand Traverse." *Michigan History*, Vol. 51, No. 3. Lansing: Fall, 1967.

Walton, Ivan. "Indian Place Names in Michigan." *Midwest Folklore*, Vol. 5, No. 1. Bloomington, Indiana: Spring, 1955.

Walton, Ivan H. "Origin of Names on the Great Lakes." *Names: Journal of the American Name Society*, Vol. 3, No. 4. Berkeley: December, 1955.

Webster's New Geographical Dictionary. Springfield, Massachusetts, Merriam-Webster, Inc., 1988.

Whiting, Henry. *Sannilac*. Boston, Carter & Rabcock, 1831.

Williams, Ethel W. *The Counties & Townships of Michigan: Past & Present*. 1972.

Williams, Mentor G. "Henry R. Schoolcraft." *Missouri Historical Society Collections*, Vol. 2, No. 2. St. Louis: April, 1903.

Windrow, Martin & Francis K. Mason. *A Concise Dictionary of Military Biography*. New York, John Wiley & Sons, Inc., 1991.

Wise, L. F., & E. W. Egan. *Kings, Rulers & Statesmen*. New York, Sterling Publishing Co., Inc., 1967.

Wood, Edwin O. *Historic Mackinac*. New York, MacMillan Co., 1918.

Wood, Edwin O. *History of Genesee County, Michigan*. Indianapolis, Indiana, Federal Publishing Co., 1916.

Work Projects Administration. *Knowing the Thunder Bay Region: A Guide to Northeastern Michigan*. Alpena County Board of Supervisors, 1941.

Wright, Muriel H. *A Guide to the Indian Tribes of Oklahoma*. Norman, University of Oklahoma Press, 1951.

Yenne, Bill. *The Encyclopedia of North American Indian Tribes*. New York, Crescent Books, 1986.

Minnesota

(87 counties)

1282 *Aitkin County*

William A. Aitkin (1785–1851)— This county was created in 1857, when Minnesota was still a territory. The county's name was originally spelled Aiken but that spelling error was corrected by an 1872 act of the Minnesota legislature. William Alexander Aitkin was born in Scotland and came to America's northwestern frontier about 1802, when he was still a youth. He was employed as a servant by a fur trader named John Drew, but Aitkin married an Indian maiden whose family was influential and Aitkin was soon trading furs with the Indians on his own account. In 1831 the American Fur Company appointed Aitkin as the factor of their Fond du Lac department, with headquarters at Sandy Lake, in what is now Aitkin County, Minnesota.

1283 *Anoka County*

Town of Anoka, Minnesota— The town of Anoka, Minnesota, in Anoka County, was first settled by Whites in the early 1850's. The town's name was chosen by White settlers but it comes from the Dakota Indians' language and means "on both sides." The town's name was chosen on account of its location on both sides of the Rum River in southeastern Minnesota. The town was founded by Orrin W. Rice, Neal D. Shaw and others. Anoka County was created on May 23, 1857, by Minnesota territory. On that same day,

May 23, 1857, Minnesota's territorial legislators created Manomin County. That small county lived only 13 years and was then absorbed as a part of Anoka County. The town of Anoka, Minnesota was made into a city on March 2, 1878, and it is the present county seat of Anoka County.

1284 *Becker County*

George L. Becker (1829–1904)— A native of New York and a lawyer, Becker settled in St. Paul in 1849. Here he became active in local politics and was soon elected to St. Paul's city council and later was elected mayor of St. Paul. In 1857, Minnesota territory made preparations for admission to the Union as a state. Three representatives were elected to represent Minnesota in the U.S. House of Representatives and George Becker was one of them. It was later deemed that Minnesota would be entitled to only two representatives and George Becker became the odd man left out. When Becker County was created on March 18, 1858, and named in his honor, that honor was intended, at least in part, to thank Becker for his gracious acquiescence to being dropped from Minnesota's first U.S. congressional delegation. Becker later was the Democratic party's unsuccessful candidate for governor and he ran for congress in 1872. Although he failed in these efforts, he was elected to the Minnesota senate. He was active in Minnesota's railroad industry and was generally referred to as

General Becker. This was because Governor Henry H. Sibley (1811–1891) had appointed Becker to the rank of brigadier-general on his staff in 1858.

1285 *Beltrami County*

Giacomo C. Beltrami (1779–1855)— A native of Bergamo, Italy, Beltrami was involved in Italian politics and held a number of official positions in Italy. About 1821 he fell out of favor and was exiled from Italy. Beltrami traveled for some time in Europe and then decided to visit America. He arrived in Philadelphia on February 21, 1823. Before the year was over, Beltrami would make his mark on Minnesota's history. From Philadelphia, Beltrami traveled to Pittsburgh, where he met Lawrence Taliaferro (1794–1871), who was the Indian agent at Fort St. Anthony (soon to be renamed Fort Snelling). Beltrami persuaded Taliaferro to allow him to come along on his return trip to Fort St. Anthony. Accordingly, Taliaferro and Beltrami traveled down the Ohio River by steamboat and then up the Mississippi River on the steamboat *Virginia*, the first steamboat to ascend the upper Mississippi River. On May 10, 1823, Taliaferro and Beltrami arrived at Fort St. Anthony, the majestic perch which overlooks the confluence of the Minnesota River with the Mississippi River. From there, Beltrami set out on an extensive and arduous exploration of what is now eastern North Dakota and northern and central Minnesota. During this 1823 trip, Beltrami traveled through this northern Minnesota county, which bears his name. He intended to determine the source of the Mississippi River and when he returned to civilization he announced (incorrectly) that he had done so. During his later life Beltrami published accounts of his exploration of northern Minnesota. He died in Italy in February, 1855.

1286 *Benton County*

Thomas H. Benton (1782–1858)— Benton was a native of North Carolina who served in the Tennessee senate and as a soldier in the War of 1812. Following the war, he moved to Missouri and he represented that state for thirty years in the U.S. Senate. In that body he championed many interests of the West including free 160 acre homesteads, pony express, telegraph and railroads. Benton was a moderate on the volatile slavery issue. He opposed both abolition of slavery and the extension of it. His primary concerns were peace and preservation of the union. These moderate positions proved unpopular. Some states which had named counties in Benton's honor renamed the and, in 1850, Missouri failed to return Benton to the senate. Following his ouster from the senate, Benton served briefly in the U.S. House of Representatives. This county was formed in October, 1849, a few months after Minnesota territory had been created. At that time, Thomas Hart Benton was nearing the end of his service to Missouri in the U.S. Senate.

1287 *Big Stone County*

Big Stone Lake— Big Stone Lake is a relatively small lake, located on the western edge of Big Stone County, Minnesota, and an adjacent portion of the state of South Dakota. Big Stone lake is not a true lake but more of a balloon in the Minnesota River. The lake is crooked and extends about 26 miles from northwest to southeast. Its width varies but for the most part, it falls within a range of one mile to one and one half miles. The lake's name is merely an English translation of the Dakota Indians' name for Big Stone Lake. Most sources consulted state that the Indians' name for the lake was chosen on account of the conspicuous outcrops of granite and gneiss in the valley of the Minnesota River, one half mile to three miles below the foot of the lake. However one source departs from this standard explanation giving the "big stone" specificity and attaching religious significance to it. That source is an article in the March 13, 1870, issue of the *Saint Paul Pioneer*. It states that the Dakota Indians chose their name for Big Stone Lake because of "...a huge boulder near its lower end, worshipped by the Dakotas as sacred."

1288 *Blue Earth County*

Blue Earth River— The Blue Earth River, a tributary of the Minnesota River, has its mouth near the present city of Mankato, Minnesota. Our name for the river is merely an English translation of the Sisseton Indians' name for it. The river's name described the color of the water which came from beds of blue-green clay. The Indians had no written language so it was left to European explorers to render the Indians' names in writing. The Sissetons' name for the Blue Earth River was, approximately, *Mahkahto*. Thus the name of Blue Earth's county seat, Mankato, also preserves the Sisseton Indians' name for the Blue Earth River and the unusual pigment which colors it. The French explorer, Pierre C. Le Sucur (1657–1704), mined a large amount of this blue-green earth in the mistaken belief that it contained a valuable copper ore.

1289 *Brown County*

Joseph R. Brown (1805–1870)— A native of Maryland, Brown came to what is now Minnesota when he was only 14. At that time, he was a drummer boy in the United States army serving with the troops who built Ft. St. Anthony (soon renamed Ft. Snelling). After leaving the army, Brown married a half–Indian woman and ran a grocery and liquor store on the shore of the Mississippi River. With the help of his wife, Brown learned the languages of the Dakota and Chippewa Indians and became successful in trading with them. He was also an able manipulator of the Indians and he assisted in conning them out of their land by negotiating treaties for the U.S. government. In 1836 Wisconsin territory was created. Since the Missouri River was its western border, the new territory included all of the present state of Minnesota. Joseph Renshaw Brown served as a member of Wisconsin's territorial legislature and he was later active in the effort to secure territorial status for Minnesota. When that goal was achieved, he was a leading figure in the early affairs of Minnesota territory. He was chosen as secretary of the upper house (council) of Minnesota's first territorial legislature and he was serving as a member of Minnesota's sixth territorial legislature when this county was created and named in his honor on February 20, 1855. Brown later was active in drafting Minnesota's state constitution and he was an unsuccessful candidate for one of Minnesota's first two seats in the U.S. Senate.

1290 *Carlton County*

Reuben B. Carlton (1812–1863)— Carlton was born in Onondaga County, in upstate New York. About 1847 he moved to Fond du Lac and lived among the Indians as a farmer and blacksmith. He was appointed by the federal government as an Indian agent at Fond du Lac and in that capacity he attempted to teach the Indians the skills needed to succeed as blacksmiths and farmers. Carlton was active in attempting to attract White settlers to the wilderness area of Fond du Lac and environs and he promoted transportation enterprises toward that end including both ship and rail. This county was created by Minnesota territory on May 23, 1857. Carlton was also honored by being elected to serve in the senate of Minnesota's first state legislature.

1291 *Carver County*

Jonathan Carver (1710–1780)— A native of Massachusetts, Carver was raised in Canterbury, in colonial Connecticut. During the French & Indian War, he fought on the British side and was wounded during the battle of Fort William Henry in 1757. By the end of the war, Carver had risen to the rank of captain. Major Robert Rogers (1731–1795), the commander of Fort Michilimackinac, persuaded Carver to explore portions of present day Wisconsin and Minnesota. In 1766 Carver traveled via the Fox and Wisconsin Rivers to the Mississippi River. He then traveled up the Mississippi as far as the present Twin Cities of Minneapolis and St. Paul. He spent the winter of 1766–1767 there. Carver then proceeded to explore the Minnesota River and the upper Mississippi River. His explorations in northern Minnesota took him to the western end of Lake Superior and along its northern shore. By 1768 Carver had returned to Boston, Massachusetts, and the following year he moved to London, England, where he became an author. His works included descriptions of his explorations in Minnesota. Carver County was created and named in his honor in 1855, while Minnesota was still a territory.

1292 *Cass County*

Lewis Cass (1782–1866)—A native of New Hampshire, Cass served in the army in the War of 1812 and rose to the rank of brigadier-general. Following that war Cass held a variety of important political positions and was the candidate of the Democratic party in 1848 for president of the United States. He lost to Zachary Taylor. Cass served as governor of Michigan territory, secretary of war under Andrew Jackson, minister to France, U.S. senator from Michigan and secretary of state under President James Buchanan. This county was created in 1851, while Minnesota was still a territory. Lewis Cass had commanded an 1820 expedition which explored the upper valley of the Mississippi River in what is now Minnesota.

1293 *Chippewa County*

Chippewa River—This county in southwestern Minnesota was created on February 20, 1862, and named for the Chippewa River, which flows through it. The Chippewa River is a tributary of the Minnesota River. It was the Dakota Indians, rather than the Chippewa Indians, who were the principal Indian tribe along the Chippewa River and the area which now comprises Chippewa County. The Dakota Indians named the Chippewa River and they chose the name because their enemies, the Chippewa, used the Chippewa River when raiding the Dakota Indians.

Chippewa Indians—The Chippewa are also known as the Ojibwa Indians. In fact, the name *Chippewa* is a corruption of the name *Ojibwa*, which has known dozens of alternative spellings. The Chippewa were one of the largest and most powerful tribes of the Algonquian linguistic family. They were a nomadic, woodland tribe, who controlled much of the Great Lakes area. Their domain extended from the Iroquois Indians' territory in the Northeast to the edge of the Great Plains, which were dominated by the Dakota (also known as Sioux) Indians. The Chippewa lived around the shores of three of the Great Lakes: Huron, Michigan and Superior, and dwelled in what today are the states of Michigan, Wisconsin, Minnesota and North Dakota. The first European explorers to encounter the Chippewa found them near Sault Sainte Marie, Michigan. Many Chippewa lived in birch bark covered wigwams with grass mats. Their birch bark rolls were carried from one campsite to another. They subsisted by hunting, trapping, fishing and collecting wild plant food. A bit of maize (corn) farming was engaged in by those

Chippewa who occupied the southern edges of the Chippewa's territory. The Chippewa were noted for their fine craftsmanship in constructing birch bark canoes. Chippewa reservations may be found today in Canada's Ontario province and in our states of Michigan, Wisconsin, Minnesota, North Dakota and Montana. The meaning of the Chippewa (or Ojibwa) tribe's name is uncertain.

1294 *Chisago County*

Chisago Lake—This county in eastern Minnesota was created in 1851, when Minnesota was still a territory, and named for Chisago Lake, which was then, and is today, within the borders of Chisago County. In William H. C. Folsom's work entitled *Fifty Years in the Northwest*, published in 1888, Folsom stated that he was the person who proposed this new county's name. He stated that Chisago Lake was the largest and most beautiful lake in what would be the new county. Folsom indicated that the lake's name came from the Chippewa Indians' *kichi*, meaning "large" and *saga*, for "fair" or "lovely." (It should be noted that other translations of the Chippewas' name for this lake have also been mentioned, including "large lake" and translations involving the word "skunk.") In Folsom's 1888 work, he further explained that the Indians' name was modified to *Chisaga* to make it more pleasing to the ear. So Chisaga County was the name that Minnesota's territorial legislators thought they were approving when they passed the legislation to create this new county. However, through clerical error, the last letter of the county's name got changed from an "a" to an "o" and the error has never been corrected.

1295 *Clay County*

Henry Clay (1777–1852)—This county was originally named Breckinridge County when it was created on March 18, 1858. That name honored John C. Breckinridge (1821–1875), who was then the vice-president of the United States. However, by March 1862, the Civil War was well under way and Breckinridge was a brigadier-general in the Confederate army. The Minnesota legislature wanted to rid the state's map of this county name honoring a leading figure in the enemy army. Accordingly, the county's name was changed from Breckinridge to Clay on March 6, 1862. The new name honored Henry Clay, who had represented Kentucky in both branches of the U.S. Congress. For many years he was one of the more prominent

figures in American politics but his several bids for the presidency were unsuccessful. He was influential in effecting important compromises between northern and southern interests during the years that secession and civil war were imminent.

1296 *Clearwater County*

Clearwater River & Clearwater Lake—This county was created in 1902 and named for the Clearwater River and Clearwater Lake, both of which are partially located within the county's borders. This Clearwater River is a tributary of the Red Lake River. The Clearwater flows through the northern portion of Clearwater County and from there to Red Lake River. At one time the lumber industry was very important here in northern Minnesota and this Clearwater River and its tributaries were used extensively to float logs to Clearwater Lake and thence to sawmills at Crookston, Minnesota, via Clearwater River and Red Lake River. Minnesota has another Clearwater River and Clearwater Lake pair with which this county's namesakes might easily be confused. A key to distinguish between them is that our Clearwater River feeds its waters, via Red Lake River, to Crookston, Minnesota, in Polk County, while the other Clearwater River empties its waters into the Mississippi River in Wright County, Minnesota. The names of our Clearwater River and Clearwater Lake are merely English translations of the names given to them by the Chippewa Indians. These names were aptly chosen. The waters of Clearwater River are remarkably clear compared to large, murky rivers like the Missouri, and Mississippi and even compared to other small streams in northern Minnesota.

1297 *Cook County*

Michael Cook (1828–1864)—Michael Cook was born in Morris County, New Jersey, on March 17, 1828. According to one account, he became acquainted with Horace Greeley (1811–1872) of "Go west young man" fame. For whatever reason, Cook did go west and moved to Minnesota territory and settled in Faribault in 1855. There he was a carpenter and was involved in constructing some of Faribault's first frame houses. Cook also served in Minnesota's territorial legislature and, after Minnesota achieved statehood, he was a member of the state senate. In 1862 he enlisted in the Union army as an officer with the rank of captain. Subsequently he was promoted to major and that was the rank that he held when he was mortally wounded during the Civil War battle of Nashville in December, 1864. He died on December 27, 1864. This county was created and named in Michael Cook's honor on March 9, 1874. Some sources state that the county was named for John Cook (–1872) who, with his entire family, was killed by Indians near Audubon, Minnesota, in 1872. However, Charles Graves, the state legislator who introduced the bill to create this county in the Minnesota legislature later confirmed that this county was named for Michael Cook. Graves, who was a state senator from Duluth, stated that it was his original intention that this county be named Verendrye. That named would have honored the French-Canadian explorer of Minnesota's northern boundary, Pierre Gaultier de Varennes et de la Verendrye (1685–1749). However, Graves reported that the legislature chose to name the county Cook, instead, in honor of the Civil War hero, Michael Cook.

1298 *Cottonwood County*

Cottonwood River— This county in southwestern Minnesota was created on May 23, 1857, by Minnesota territory, and named for the Cottonwood River, which touches the northeastern corner of Germantown Township, in Cottonwood County. The Cottonwood is a tributary of the Minnesota River. About 130 miles long, it rises in Lyon County, Minnesota, and flows east to empty into the Minnesota River near New Ulm, Minnesota. The river's name is merely an English translation of the Dakota Indians' name for the river which was *waraju* or *wareju*. The Indians gave that name to the river on account of the abundance of cottonwood trees which grew along its banks. Cottonwood trees are relatively tall trees, and they are rather common in southern Minnesota, particularly at the southern end of the valley of the Red River. Cottonwood trees are fast-growing and they are frequently planted for shade and for shelter from the wind. In the spring these cottonwood trees shed their seeds in tassels resembling cotton.

1299 *Crow Wing County*

Crow Wing River— This county was created in 1857 by Minnesota territory, and named for the Crow Wing River which touches the county. The Crow Wing, a tributary of the Mississippi, is formed by branches in Wadena County, Minnesota, and flows southeast and then east, emptying its waters into the Mississippi at the southwestern corner of this Crow Wing County. The Chippewa Indians were the first to name this river and their name for it would be translated as "Raven's Wing River," or "Raven's Quill River," according to the scientist and explorer Henry R. Schoolcraft (1793–1864). Early French explorers translated the Indians' name with enough accuracy to preserve the correct species of the bird: Raven, species *corax*. The raven was relatively common in Canada, Minnesota, Michigan and Maine but rare in other areas of the eastern U.S. Probably because the early English-speaking explorers of this area were from the eastern U.S., where crows (species *brachyrhynchos*) are common and because crows and ravens are somewhat similar in appearance (both are members of the genus *Corvus*), when the name of this river was translated into English, it was erroneously dubbed the Crow Wing River.

1300 *Dakota County*

Dakota Indians— The Dakota are a vast alliance of American Indians who are more commonly known as the Sioux Indians. These Indians' name for themselves is *Lakota* or *Dakota* meaning "friends" or "allies," while *Sioux* was a derogatory Chippewa-French name for them. The Dakotas consist of three general dialect and culture groups: the Santee, Wiciyela and Teton. When the Whites first encountered the Dakotas, about 1640, they found them living in southern Minnesota and adjacent areas subsisting by hunting, fishing, gathering lake and forest products and growing corn. In 1805 the Dakotas signed their first treaty giving up some of their Minnesota lands and by 1858 they had been pressured into signing treaties giving up almost all of their land in Minnesota. In return, they were to receive food, annuities, education and other necessities. These promises were broken and in 1862 the Dakotas began a final, futile struggle against the Whites in Minnesota, who had systematically robbed and mistreated them. They lost this struggle and 38 of their members were hanged on a mass gallows at Mankato, Minnesota, on December 26, 1862. Remaining Dakota Indians in Minnesota were deported to reservations in Dakota territory (now South Dakota and North Dakota), where live in misery to this day.

1301 *Dodge County*

Uncertain— This county was created on February 20, 1855, while Minnesota was still a territory. Some sources state that the county was named for Henry Dodge (1782–1867) while other sources indicate that the county was named for both Henry Dodge and his son, Augustus C. Dodge.

Henry Dodge (1782–1867)— Henry Dodge was born in Vincennes in what is now the state of Indiana, in 1782. He served with distinction as an officer in the War of 1812 and rose to the rank of lieutenant-colonel. In 1827 he moved to the wilderness of what is now Wisconsin and served in actions against the Indians. By now, a full colonel, in 1835 Henry Dodge led an expedition to the Rocky Mountains. In 1836 President Andrew Jackson appointed him to be governor of Wisconsin territory and superintendent of Indian affairs. Henry Dodge later represented Wisconsin territory in the U.S. Congress as a delegate and the state of Wisconsin as a U.S. senator.

Augustus C. Dodge (1812–1883)— August C. Dodge, a son of Henry Dodge (1782–1867), was born in what is now the state of Missouri on January 2, 1812. On December 8, 1840, Augustus Dodge took a seat in the U.S. Congress as a delegate from Iowa territory. On December 7 of the following year, his father, Henry Dodge, joined Augustus in the U.S. Congress. The elder Dodge represented Wisconsin territory as their congressional delegate. Augustus Dodge continued to represent Iowa territory in the U.S. Congress as its delegate until Iowa achieved statehood. On December 26, 1848, Augustus Dodge began his term as one of Iowa's first two United States senators. He served in the senate until 1855 when he resigned to accept an appointment as minister to Spain.

1302 *Douglas County*

Stephen A. Douglas (1813–1861)— Barely five feet tall, the "Little Giant" is most remembered as a political opponent of Abraham Lincoln. Douglas was born in Vermont and moved to Illinois where he enjoyed rapid political success. He served on the state supreme court, in the state legislature and as secretary of state. Following two terms in the U.S. House of Representatives, Douglas was elected to the U.S. Senate. In that body Douglas took courageous positions on the slavery issue which first outraged abolitionist sentiment and later infuriated the South. In 1858 Douglas ran for reelection to the U.S. Senate against Abraham Lincoln. Following the famous Lincoln-Douglas debates, the Republicans won the popular election but that state legislature reelected Douglas to the senate. Lincoln and Douglas were rivals again in 1860 for the presidency. Following Lincoln's election and the start of the Civil War, Douglas gave the president his active support. This county was created on March 8, 1858, while Stephen Douglas was serving in the United States senate. Douglas had actively supported the successful efforts of Minnesota territory to achieve statehood. Just two months after this county was created Minnesota became a member of the federal union of states. Earlier, in 1849, Senator Douglas had been a key supporter of the creation of Minnesota territory. He maneuvered the Minnesota territory bill through congress on the last day of the session and it was signed into law on March 3, 1849, by President James K. Polk on Polk's final day as president of the United States.

1303 *Faribault County*

Jean B. Faribault (1774–1860) — Jean Baptiste Faribault was born near Quebec, Canada, and was employed for a short time as a clerk in a mercantile establishment. Finding this work tedious and boring, about 1798 Faribault came to what was then America's northwestern frontier to trade among the Dakota Indians. Here he was placed in charge of a trading post on the Kankakee River, near the southern end of Lake Michigan. He soon moved west to the even more remote region of today's central Iowa and continued trading with the Indians. It was not until 1803 that Faribault came to Minnesota, which was then also wilderness. Here he took charge of a trading post at the Little Rapids of the Minnesota River, a few miles above the present sites of Chaska and Carver, Minnesota. During all or most of these trading post assignments, Faribault was acting for the Northwest Fur Company. He subsequently became a trader on his own account at Prairie du Chien in what is now Wisconsin and in 1820, he returned to Minnesota to trade from Pike Island at the confluence of the Minnesota and Mississippi Rivers. About 1826, Faribault moved to higher ground at Mendota and there he built a substantial stone house for his family. Fur trading had been profitable for Jean Baptiste Faribault. He divided his time for some years between his home at Mendota and his trading post at Little Rapids in the present Carver County, Minnesota. This Minnesota pioneer died on August 20, 1860, at the home of his daughter in Faribault, Minnesota. This town had been named in honor of Jean Faribault's eldest son, Alexander Faribault (1806–1882). Although the town was named for

Alexander, Faribault County was named for Jean Baptiste Faribault. This county was created and named on February 20, 1855, when Minnesota was still a territory and while the old pioneer was still alive.

1304 *Fillmore County*

Millard Fillmore (1800–1874) — Fillmore was born to an impoverished family in upstate New York and was apprenticed to a firm of cloth-dressers, from whom he eventually purchased his release. After studying law and being admitted to the New York bar, Fillmore was elected to the lower house of the New York legislature and he later represented New York in the U.S. House of Representatives. In 1848 the Whig party nominated the Mexican War hero, Zachary Taylor, for president with Millard Fillmore on the ticket as the vice-presidential running mate. They won the election and took their offices in 1849 but Zachary Taylor died in 1850 and Millard Fillmore became president. As president during an intense period of North versus South controversy relating to slavery, Fillmore favored the South and states' rights. However, Fillmore also supported the economic development of our nation's frontier, which then included Minnesota territory, and he assisted in arranging the first federal land grants for railroad construction. Fillmore was a candidate for the Whig's presidential nomination in 1852 but he lost to Winfield Scott (1786–1866). This county was created by Minnesota territory on March 5, 1853, and named in honor of Fillmore, whose tenure as president had ended two days earlier, on March 3, 1853.

1305 *Freeborn County*

William Freeborn (1816–) — Freeborn was born in Ohio and came to St. Paul in 1848, before Minnesota became a territory. In 1853 he moved to Red Wing, Minnesota, and was a pioneer in the development of that community. He served briefly as Red Wing's mayor. Freeborn served in the upper house (council) of Minnesota's territorial legislature from 1854 to 1857. In 1864 he headed west, mining for gold in Montana and then moving to Oregon to cultivate fruit. In 1868 he moved to California and was known to be a resident of that state as late as 1899. Freeborn County was created on February 20, 1855, during the sixth session of Minnesota's territorial legislature. On that date, William Freeborn was one of just ten members of the upper house of the territorial

legislature and the legislators named this county for one of their members.

1306 *Goodhue County*

James M. Goodhue (1810–1852) — Minnesota's earliest newspaper publisher was a native of Hebron, New Hampshire and a graduate of Amherst College. He chose the law as his profession and practiced it for a time. In Illinois he earned his living by both farming and practicing law. After moving to Wisconsin, Goodhue, rather by accident, became the editor of a newspaper there, the *Wisconsin Herald*, published in Lancaster. He found newspaper work enjoyable and purchased newspaper equipment and supplies and had them shipped to St. Paul in early 1849. Minnesota territory was created effective March 3, 1849, and just two months later, on April 28, 1849, James M. Goodhue published the first newspaper in Minnesota, the *Minnesota Pioneer*. This was an important step in bringing civilization to the wilderness of Minnesota territory. The newspaper's name was later changed to the *St. Paul Pioneer*. Goodhue died while he was still in his early 40's but the newspaper was continued after his death. He died in 1852, and early in the following year, on March 5, 1853, Minnesota's territorial legislature created this county.

1307 *Grant County*

Ulysses S. Grant (1822–1885) — Grant was a native of Ohio who graduated from the U.S. Military Academy at West Point. He served with distinction in the Mexican War, and in the Civil War he rose to become commander of all Union forces. After the Civil War, Grant briefly served as acting secretary of war and then two terms as president of the United States. He proved to be a rather mediocre president. This county was created on March 6, 1868. Later that year Grant was elected as our nation's president.

1308 *Hennepin County*

Louis Hennepin (1640–1705) — Hennepin was born at Ath in what today is Belgium. He entered the Recollet branch of the Roman Catholic Franciscan order, whose regimen was unusually severe and arduous, and he eventually was ordained as a Roman Catholic priest. Father Hennepin was fascinated with North America and he persuaded his superiors to send him to New France (Canada). He explored the Great Lakes region and the upper Mississippi River and it was Father Hennepin who named the Falls of St. Anthony in the center of Hennepin County's city of Minneapolis. He came upon this scenic waterfall in 1680 and named it for his patron saint, Saint Anthony of Padua (–1231). At one point in his explorations in what is now Minnesota, Hennepin and his companions were captured by a band of Dakota Indians and held in captivity for several months but apparently they were not mistreated. Upon Hennepin's return to Europe, he wrote of his travels and explorations and engaged in significant plagiarism and major exaggeration of facts. These misdeeds served to tarnish Father Hennepin's reputation. This county was created in 1852 by Minnesota territory. The bill to create the county was drafted by John H. Stevens and his suggestion for the county's name was Snelling. In the act that created this county, the name was changed from Snelling to Hennepin at the suggestion of Martin McLeod (1813–1860), who was then serving in the upper house of the territorial legislature.

1309 Houston County

Samuel Houston (1793–1863) — A native of Virginia, Houston moved with his family to Tennessee when he was about 14 years old. After serving in the U.S. army in actions against the Indians, he studied law and became active in local politics. Elected to represent Tennessee in the U.S. House of Representatives, he later served as governor of Tennessee. In 1829 Governor Houston married Eliza Allen, but Mrs. Houston left him to return to her parents before the marriage was four months old. This event was traumatic for Houston and a turning point in his life. He resigned as Tennessee's governor and moved to Indian country, where he lived for half a dozen years. In November, 1835, he was made a major-general of the army of the provisional government of the Republic of Texas. In early March, 1836, when Texas formally seceded from Mexico and officially declared itself an independent republic, Houston was named commander-in-chief of the new republic's army. The Mexican army responded immediately with force and brutality. Not long after the infamous Mexican massacre of Texans at the Alamo, Texas, under Sam Houston's command, turned the tide and defeated the Mexicans at the battle of San Jacinto. Houston was elected president of the Republic of Texas and later, when Texas became a member of the United States, he was one of the new state's first two U.S. senators. He subsequently was elected

governor of the state of Texas but when Texas seceded from the Union, Houston refused to take an oath of loyalty to the Confederacy and he was deposed as Texas' governor. This county was created in 1854 by Minnesota territory while Houston was serving in the U.S. Senate.

1310 Hubbard County

Lucius F. Hubbard (1836–1913) — A native of Troy, in upstate New York, Hubbard came to Minnesota territory in 1857 and was editor of a newspaper named the *Red Wing Republican*, which he established. In December, 1861, Hubbard enlisted as a private in the Union army and he served with distinction throughout the Civil War and rose to the rank of brevet brigadier-general. After the war he was active in grain, flour and railroad businesses in Minnesota and was elected to the Minnesota senate. In 1881 Minnesota's voters elected Hubbard to be their governor and he was serving in that office when this county was created and named in his honor in 1883. Hubbard later held the rank of brigadier-general during the Spanish-American War, although the war ended before Hubbard and his troops were called to active duty.

1311 Isanti County

Santee Indians — *Santee* is the name for a large, now obsolete, division of the Dakota Indians. About 300 years ago, the Santee lived in east-central Minnesota's Mille Lacs area and in the region of the Rum River. The French explorer, Father Louis Hennepin (1640–1705), referred the large lake, which is now called Mille Lacs, as the lake of the Isantis and to the Rum River as the river of the Isantis. Another French explorer, Daniel Greysolon, Sieur Du Luth (1639–1710) also recorded the name for Mille Lacs Lake with a word resembling Isanti. (Duluth's spelling of the lake's name is quoted with more than one version.) Although the origin and meaning of the Santee, or Isanti, Indians' name is not certain, the few sources willing to speculate on this subject propose that the name might have meant "knife Indians." Given that hypothesis, the possibility that the Indians were given that name on account of their living in the vicinity of Minnesota's Knife Lake is offered. According to some, the Santee Indians' knives were made of stone, but other sources indicate that the Santee may have been the first Minnesota Indians to obtain metal knives. Some sources get quite specific about these metal knives and assert that

the Santee Indians obtained them from the pair of French explorers: Medard Chouart, Sieur des Groseilliers and Pierre Radisson. However, there are authorities on Minnesota history who doubt that this pair of explorers ever got as far west as Minnesota.

1312 Itasca County

Itasca Lake — Itasca Lake in northern Minnesota's Clearwater County is the source of the Mississippi River. Its area is about two square miles and it is located 1,475 feet above sea level. In 1832 Henry Rowe Schoolcraft (1793–1864) led a party of explorers who traced the Mississippi River to its source in Itasca Lake and it was Schoolcraft who coined the lake's name. Gallons of ink have been expended explaining and debating the meaning of the name *Itasca*. To understand why the explanation is neither simple nor direct, one needs to know a bit about Schoolcraft and his penchant for coining artificial geographic names. The state of Michigan has numerous artificial county names that came from Schoolcraft's inventive mind. (For further information about him, see Schoolcraft County, Michigan, above.) The origin and meaning of Itasca Lake's name is less than certain because Henry R. Schoolcraft's writings contain confusing and contradictory comments on this subject. Perhaps the most plausible of the many explanations of Itasca's name was published in the June 16, 1872 issue of the *St. Paul Pioneer*. That issue contained valuable information on this question from Rev. William T. Boutwell, who was a member of the 1832 expedition which discovered the source of the Mississippi. As Rev. Boutwell explained it, Schoolcraft, having uppermost in his mind the source of the Mississippi, asked Boutwell for the Greek and Latin expressions for the headwaters or true source of a river. Boutwell could not recall the answer in Greek but he was able to give Schoolcraft the Latin *veritas caput*, meaning "truth head." Boutwell went on to relate that he wrote these Latin words on a slip of paper and gave them to Schoolcraft, who struck out the first three and last three letters of these words and announced to Boutwell "Itasca shall be the name." While some doubt remains that this is the correct origin of the lake's name, there is no doubt about the origin of Itasca County's name. This county was created on October 27, 1849, by Minnesota territory and named for Itasca Lake. The lake then was within the county's borders but when new counties were carved out of Itasca County, it lost the lake, which today is within Clearwater County.

1313 *Jackson County*

Uncertain— This county was created by the legislature of Minnesota territory on May 23, 1857. Most sources consulted state that the county was named for Henry Jackson (1811–1857), a pioneer resident of St. Paul, but this opinion is not unanimous. According to some sources, the county may have been named for President Andrew Jackson. These sources report that William Pitt Murray (1825–1910), who was a member of the territorial legislature that created this county, stated that it was the legislature's intention to honor President Jackson when it created and named this county. Considering this very real conflict of opinion, it may be appropriate to consider the possibility that some of the legislators thought that they were honoring Henry Jackson when they approved this county's name, while others, including William P. Murray, assumed that the honor was intended for our nation's former president.

Andrew Jackson (1767–1845)— Andrew Jackson was born on the border of North Carolina and South Carolina and he represented Tennessee in both branches of the U.S. Congress. He gained fame and popularity for his military exploits in wars with the Indians and in the War of 1812. He was provisional military governor of Florida and, from 1829 to 1837, General Andrew Jackson was president of the United States. His presidency reflected the frontier spirit of America.

Henry Jackson (1811–1857)— Henry Jackson was born in Abingdon, Virginia, on February 1, 1811. He wandered widely in his early manhood, fighting in Texas with the rank of orderly sergeant, marrying in Buffalo, New York, to Angelina Bivins and living for a time in both Green Bay, Wisconsin, and Galena, Illinois. When Henry Jackson's business in Galena failed, he came to St. Paul. This was in 1842, before Minnesota had become a territory. In St. Paul he engaged in fur trade from a cabin with his partner, William Hartshorn. Several accounts refer to Henry Jackson as St. Paul's first merchant. In 1843, St. Paul was within Wisconsin territory and that territory's governor, Henry Dodge (1782–1867), appointed Henry Jackson to be the first justice of the peace in St. Paul. Henry Jackson was also St. Paul's first postmaster. In 1847 and 1848 Jackson was a member of the legislature of Wisconsin territory and he later was a member of the house of representatives of the first legislature of Minnesota territory. In 1853 Henry Jackson moved from St. Paul to Mankato, Minnesota, and he died there on July 31, 1857.

1314 *Kanabec County*

Snake River— The Snake River for which this county was named is a tributary of the St. Croix River. This Snake rises in east-central Minnesota near the southern end of Aitkin County, flows south into Kanabec County and continues its southern course until it nears the southern border of Kanabec County. There it finally recognizes its obligation to the St. Croix and takes an abrupt turn to the east. It empties into the St. Croix River at Pine County, Minnesota's eastern border. The Snake is about 135 miles long. Writing in the early 1900's about Minnesota's geographic names, Warren Upham (1850–1934) mentioned the picturesque Upper Falls and Lower Falls of the Snake River as being "...respectively about two miles and three miles south of the north boundary of this [Kanabec] county." Kanabec County's name is a version of the Chippewa Indians' name for the Snake River. Chrysostom Verwyst described the name *kanabec* as a corruption of the Chippewa Indians' name for the Snake River, *ginebic*. Verwyst's translation can be found in the 1892 issue (volume 12) of the *Collections of the State Historical Society of Wisconsin*. Kanabec County was created on March 13, 1858, while Minnesota was still a territory. The county's name was suggested by William H. C. Folsom.

1315 *Kandiyohi County*

The several Kandiyohi lakes— The present Kandiyohi County resulted from the merger of two counties, Monongalia County and Kandiyohi County. Monongalia County was named for Monongalia County, Virginia. In 1863, the state of West Virginia was formed and Virginia lost a number of its counties to West Virginia, including Monongalia County. Later, in 1870, Monongalia County, Minnesota, was abolished and all of its territory was absorbed by Kandiyohi County. Having postponed as long as decently permissible, discussion of the awkward Dakota Indian name, *kandiyohi*, we shall now address that topic. The original (smaller) Kandiyohi County was created and named on March 20, 1858, when Minnesota was a territory. The Indians had applied the term Kandiyohi to the entire group of lakes which form the sources of the Crow River and the county was named for those lakes. The Indian name *kandiyohi* meant, approximately "where buffalo fish arrive in," or "land of buffalo fish." At the time that the Dakota Indians controlled this area, these so-called buffalo fish and kindred species came up the rivers and small streams every spring to spawn in the Kandiyohi lakes. In Warren Upham's *Minnesota Geographic Names*, the genus and species of three of these fish are given as *Ictiobus cyprinella, Ictiobus urus* and *Ictiobus bubalus*. At times these spawning fish involved enormous numbers of fish and each of the fish was quite large, weighing anywhere from 20 to 40 pounds. By 1856 White men had begun dispensing specific names to the various lakes which the Indians called, collectively, the Kandiyohi lakes. The name Kandiyohi was retained by the Whites for only two of the several Kandiyohi lakes. The two survivors are Big Kandiyohi Lake and Little Kandiyohi Lake. Little Kandiyohi Lake is connected by stream to Big Kandiyohi Lake. Big Kandiyohi Lake covers about 4,200 acres. Both lakes are located within Kandiyohi County.

1316 *Kittson County*

Norman W. Kittson (1814–1888)— Kittson was born near Sorel, Canada, on March 5, 1814. He came to Fort Snelling on the upper Mississippi River in 1834 and engaged in fur trading there. In 1843 or 1844 Kittson established a trading post at Pembina in the northern Dakota country. His superior in trading activities there was Henry H. Sibley (1811–1891). Kittson represented the Pembina district in the upper chamber of the legislature of Minnesota territory in 1852, 1853, 1854 and 1855. He also traded furs at St. Paul and he was one of the early mayors of that city. In 1864 Hudson Bay Company appointed Norman Kittson to be their director of steamboat traffic on the Red River (of the North) and he later was employed by the railroad promoter, James J. Hill (1838–1916) in railroad development in North Dakota. Kittson died in May, 1888. This county is located in Minnesota's northwestern corner. When this county was created on April 24, 1862, it was named Pembina County. (An earlier Pembina County had been one of the nine enormous counties into which Minnesota territory was originally divided on October 27, 1849. That Pembina County extended west to the Missouri River in today's North Dakota.) The later Pembina County's name was changed to Kittson to honor Norman Kittson on March 9, 1878.

1317 *Koochiching County*

The great falls of the Rainy River at International Falls— This county is one of our nation's younger counties. It was created early in the 20th century, on December 19, 1906, and named for the great waterfalls of the Rainy River on the Canadian border at International Falls, Minnesota, and Fort Frances, Ontario, Canada. The name *koochiching* was used by Cree and Chippewa Indians for Rainy River and its great falls and rapids at the present city of International Falls, which is the county seat of Koochiching County. The falls are still called Koochiching Falls. The Cree and Chippewa also called Rainy Lake here by the name Koochiching. Before a dam was built (it was completed in 1908), the falls of the Rainy River nearly always created rainbows when there was sunshine. The Rainy River is about 80 miles long. It flows from Rainy Lake to Lake of the Woods and for this 80 mile stretch, Rainy River represents the international border between our country and Canada. The meaning of the name *Koochiching* is uncertain.

1318 *Lac qui Parle County*

Lac qui Parle (lake)— On February 20, 1862, the Minnesota legislature created a Lac qui Parle County but that act was not ratified by the voters. This first, aborted, Lac qui Parle County had different borders than the present Lac qui Parle County and its territory was entirely on the opposite (north) side of the Minnesota River. On March 6, 1871, the present Lac qui Parle County was created and named for the lake which is on the border between Lac qui Parle County and Chippewa County, Minnesota. This small lake is not a true lake but an expansion of the Minnesota River. All of the territory of the present Lac qui Parle County lies south of the Minnesota River. The Indians were the first to name this lake and they gave it a name which meant, approximately, "speaking lake," probably because of echoes thrown back from bluffs bordering the lake. In the December, 1953, issue of *Names: Journal of the American Name Society*, R. W. Keller reported that the murmuring sounds which the Indians heard at the outlet to the lake were still (1953) audible "...when the water level is about normal." Early French explorers liked the Indians' name and they translated it into their language as *Lac qui Parle*, meaning "lake that talks." Sources consulted are not unanimous that Lac qui Parle owes its name to

echoes. A variety of alternative explanations have been mentioned including:

— Sounds produced by waves breaking on the rocky shore; in one version of this explanation these sounds are a distinct musical note.

— Creaking or groaning noises of ice on the lake in the winter and spring which occur when the water level fluctuates.

— A variant of the creaking ice theory that includes echoes of those creaking noises thrown from adjacent bluffs.

— A constant sound of murmuring or gurgling.

1319 *Lake County*

Lake Superior— This county in northeastern Minnesota was created on March 1, 1856, and named for Lake Superior, which forms the county's southern border. Lake Superior is the largest of the five Great Lakes and is, in fact, the largest body of fresh water in the world. This lake is about 350 miles long and has a surface area of almost 32,000 square miles. The St. Lawrence Seaway provides Lake Superior and the other Great Lakes with access to world ports.

1320 *Lake of the Woods County*

Lake of the Woods— This county was created in 1922 and named for the lake at its northern end, which it shares with Canada. French soldiers called it *Lac des Bois* on their maps, meaning "Lake of Woods," and the present name is merely an English adaptation of the French name. The lake is 72 miles long and varies in width from 10 to 60 miles. Lake of the Woods covers an area of some 1,700 square miles, of which 642 are in the United States. The rest of the lake is shared by the Canadian provinces of Ontario and Manitoba. At the time that the lake was named by the French in the 18th century, it was entirely surrounded by woods, despite the fact that the great prairie region is nearby, on the western side of the lake.

1321 *Le Sueur County*

Pierre C. Le Sueur (1657–1704)— A native of France, Le Sueur came to New France (Canada) and from there he moved on to the upper Mississippi country where he engaged in trade with the Indians. Le Sueur was with Nicolas Perrot (–1717) in 1689 when Perrot formally took possession, for France, of much of the upper valley of the Mississippi River and its tributaries. Le Sueur was the French com-

mandant at Chequamegon Bay, on the southwestern side of Lake Superior and he built forts for France on Madeline Island in Lake Superior and on an island in the Mississippi River near the present site of Red Wing, Minnesota. He visited France and, upon his return to North America, he came to Louisiana where one of his wife's relatives, Pierre le Moyne, Seur d' Iberville (1661–1706), was serving France as governor of Louisiana. Iberville sent Le Sueur back to Dakota country to search for copper. Le Sueur built a fort on the Blue Earth River and he mined a large amount of blue-green earth near the junction of the Blue Earth River with the Minnesota River near today's city of Mankato, Minnesota. Le Sueur's mistaken belief was that this blue-green earth contained valuable copper ore and he shipped a large amount of it to France. This county was created by Minnesota territory in 1853. Today's Le Sueur County is only about ten miles away from Le Sueur's former blue-green earth mines at Mankato.

1322 *Lincoln County*

Abraham Lincoln (1809–1865)— Lincoln was a native of Kentucky who moved to Illinois where he was a member of the state legislature. He represented Illinois in the U.S. House of Representatives and later was elected president of the United States. Lincoln's presidency coincided almost exactly with the Civil War. He guided the United States ably through that uniquely turbulent period. As president, he issued the Emancipation Proclamation which declared the freedom of slaves in all states in rebellion. Lincoln was assassinated in April, 1865, a few days after the Union's victory in the Civil War. This county was created in 1873. There had been three earlier attempts to name a Minnesota county in President Lincoln's honor but they all failed. The first try was in May, 1861, just two month's after President Lincoln's inauguration, when the Minnesota legislature passed a bill to create a Lincoln County, but the voters failed to ratify it. In 1866, one year after Abraham Lincoln's assassination, the legislature voted to change the name of Rock County to Lincoln County but the law was ineffectual, being ignored by the residents of Rock County. On February 12, 1870, the anniversary of Abraham Lincoln's birthday, a third attempt was made to create a Lincoln County but the voters failed to ratify it. Finally, in March, 1873, the present Lincoln County, was created.

1323 *Lyon County*

Nathaniel Lyon (1818–1861) — A native of Connecticut and an 1841 graduate of the U.S. Military Academy at West Point, Lyon participated in actions against the Seminole Indians in Florida and later in the Mexican War. Very early in the Civil War, in May, 1861, President Abraham Lincoln promoted him to brigadier-general and he was given command of Union forces at St. Louis. In August, 1861, General Lyon commanded an attack on Confederate troops at Wilson's Creek, Missouri. The Confederate army scored a victory and General Lyon was killed in combat.

1324 *McLeod County*

Martin McLeod (1813–1860) — McLeod was born in Canada in 1813 and came to Minnesota's Ft. Snelling in 1837 via two extremely arduous trips. The portion of the first of these trips that was on foot took McLeod some 600 miles from northern Lake Superior to the Red River settlement at what is today Winnipeg, Manitoba, Canada. From there, McLeod and a few others left for Ft. Snelling, far to the south at Minnesota's present Twin Cities. This party encountered a blizzard in which two members were killed. McLeod arrived at Ft. Snelling about the first of April, 1837. He soon found himself in charge of fur trading at a post on the St. Croix River and was successively in charge of trading posts at Traverse des Sioux, Big Stone Lake, Lac qui Parle and Yellow Medicine River. When Minnesota territory was created, McLeod became a member of the upper house (council) of the first territorial legislature. He continued to serve on the territory's legislative council from 1849 to 1853 and was president of that body in 1853. He died on his farm in Bloomington, Minnesota, on November 20, 1860. This county was created by the legislature of Minnesota territory in 1856.

1325 *Mahnomen County*

An Indian word for "wild rice" — This county was created in 1906. Its name was taken from the Chippewa Indians' language and signifies "wild rice," an important crop for the Indians here in northwestern Minnesota. The Chippewa Indians developed great skill in making birchbark canoes, which they used to harvest wild rice. In early times wild rice was one of the main articles of food on which the Chippewa subsisted. Wild rice later became a profitable commodity for the Indians

when Whites acquired a taste for it. One source consulted states that the county's name was chosen because the Wild Rice River flows through it. Although the Wild Rice River does flow here, other sources consulted are agreed that the county's name was chosen for the wild rice itself, rather than for the river. In 1857 when Minnesota was still a territory, a very small county was created in the eastern part of Minneapolis. That county was named Manomin County and its name was merely a different spelling of the Indians' name for "wild rice." This earlier Manomin County ceased to exist in 1869.

1326 *Marshall County*

William R. Marshall (1825–1896) — A native of Missouri, Marshall worked in the lead mines of Illinois and Wisconsin before coming to Minnesota's present Twin Cities area about 1849. He was a pioneer merchant, banker and newspaper publisher in St. Paul and he also owned a dairy farm. Marshall was an army officer during the hostilities with the Dakota Indians in 1862 and 1863 and in the Civil War he served with distinction in the Union army and rose to the rank of brevet brigadier-general. William Marshall was active in creating the Republican party in Minnesota and he was elected on the Republican ticket as the state's governor in 1865. Reelected to a second term, Marshall's tenure as governor extended from January 8, 1866, to January 9, 1870. This county was created in 1879.

1327 *Martin County*

Uncertain — Martin County was created on May 23, 1857, when Minnesota was a territory. Sources consulted disagree on the source of the county's name but there are only three possibilities worthy of consideration. They are Henry Martin (1829–1908), Morgan L. Martin (1805–1887) and Martin McLeod (1813–1860).

Henry Martin (1829–1908) — Henry Martin was born in Meriden, Connecticut, on February 14, 1829. He went to California in 1849, attempting to profit from the gold rush boom by engaging in an auction business in San Francisco. In 1851 he returned to Connecticut and was that state's bank commissioner from 1854 to 1856, when he came to Minnesota territory. Sources which state that this county was, or might have been, named for Henry Martin describe him variously including:

— "A Mankato pioneer."
— "A prominent pioneer citizen of Mankato."

— "...in 1856, or thereabouts, dealt largely in Minnesota lands."
— "An early settler."
— "One of the early landholders."

Fortunately, Warren Upham's *Minnesota Geographic Names*, which was first published by the Minnesota Historical Society in 1920 (as volume 17 of the society's *Collections...*) and later republished by that society in 1969, provides far more details on Henry Martin's association with Minnesota. According to this account by Upham, after Henry Martin came to Minnesota in 1856, he purchased some 2,000 acres of lands here for himself and for his eastern associates. He "resided temporarily in Mankato" and adjacent to Martin Lake (which is in Martin County and is named for him) "...he built a house and partly [sic] planned to settle here. Within about one year he returned to Wallingford, Connecticut, where his family had continuously resided and that town was ever after his home." Warren Upham was able to provide these extensive details about Henry Martin because Upham had received a letter and biographical sketch from Henry Martin, himself, in 1905. According to Upham's *Minnesota Geographic Names*, after Henry Martin returned to Connecticut from Minnesota, he was involved in manufacturing and was a deputy sheriff of New Haven County, Connecticut. He died in Wallingford, Connecticut, in 1908.

Morgan L. Martin (1805–1887) — A native of New York state, Morgan Martin moved to Green Bay and was elected as a delegate to the United States congress from Wisconsin territory, succeeding Henry Dodge (1782–1867). Morgan Martin served just a single two year term in congress starting December 1, 1845. He died on December 10, 1887. On December 23, 1846, Morgan Martin had introduced a bill in the U.S. House of Representatives for organization of Minnesota territory out of a portion of Wisconsin territory. On March 3, 1847, this bill was tabled because Minnesota's population was still very sparse. However, this delay was only temporary. Exactly two years later, on March 3, 1849 (after Morgan Martin had departed from congress), Minnesota territory was created. Those who state that this county was or might have been named for Morgan L. Martin point out that Martin's December 23, 1846, bill for the creation of Minnesota territory would likely have made Henry H. Sibley (1811–1891) governor of the new territory. Martin County was created on May 23, 1857, by Minnesota's territorial legislature. Henry H. Sibley had been a member of that body in 1855 and in mid 1857 he would become president of Minnesota's statehood convention. He was a powerful political figure whose recommendation (if he made one) for a new county's name would certainly have been given serious consideration by the territorial legislature of 1857.

Martin McLeod (1813–1860)—It is certain that McLeod County, Minnesota, was named in honor of Martin McLeod. That county was created on March 1, 1856, by Minnesota's territorial legislature. It is possible, but far from certain, that Martin County, Minnesota, was also named for Martin McLeod. It is rare, but not unknown for a state to have two counties named for the same person. For example, Florida has both Hernando County and De Soto County named for the same despicable Spanish conquistador, Hernando De Soto (1500–1542), and Minnesota, itself, *may* have a two county/same man situation with Norman County and Kittson County.

Martin McLeod was born in Canada in 1813 and came to Minnesota's Ft. Snelling in 1837 via two extremely arduous trips. The portion of the first of these trips that was on foot took McLeod some 600 miles from northern Lake Superior to the Red River settlement at what is today Winnipeg, Manitoba, Canada. From there, McLeod and a few others left for Ft. Snelling, far to the south at Minnesota's present Twin Cities. This party encountered a blizzard in which two members were killed. McLeod arrived at Ft. Snelling about the first of April, 1837. He soon found himself in charge of fur trading at a post on the St. Croix River and was successively in charge of trading posts at Traverse des Sioux, Big Stone Lake, Lac qui Parle and Yellow Medicine River. When Minnesota territory was created, McLeod became a member of the upper house (council) of the first territorial legislature. He continued to serve on the territory's legislative council from 1849 to 1853 and was president of that body in 1853. He died on his farm in Bloomington, Minnesota, on November 20, 1860.

In assessing which of these men is the most likely namesake of Martin County, Minnesota, it is important to note that Warren Upham (1850–1934) had a change of opinion on this subject. In his article which appeared in the October, 1908, issue of *The Magazine of History*, entitled "Minnesota County Names," Upham stated that the county might have been named for Martin McLeod (1813–1860) or Morgan L. Martin (1805–1887) with no men-

tion of Henry Martin. This October, 1908, article was issued as the second in a series. The first article, covering Minnesota county names in the first portion of the alphabet, was published in the September, 1908, issue of *The Magazine of History*. However in Upham's "Minnesota Geographic Names," which first appeared in the 1920 volume of the *Collections of the Minnesota Historical Society*, he strongly infers that Martin County was named for Henry Martin (1829–1908). In this 1920 publication, comments about Morgan L. Martin (1805–1887) are limited to the context that the territorial legislators "…may have been partly influenced in favor of this name…" and Martin McLeod (1813–1860) is not even mentioned as a possibility. The opinion of Warren Upham on the origin of this county's name carries great weight. He was secretary and librarian of the Minnesota Historical Society from 1895 to 1914 and devoted enormous amounts of time and effort to the study of Minnesota's place names. We know that by 1905 Upham had obtained biographical material from Henry Martin himself and when Upham's work on "Minnesota Geographic Names" was published by the state historical society in 1920, Upham's studies of the subject led him to say in the first sentence of his chapter about Martin County "…being named, according to the concurrent testimony of its [Martin County's] best informed early citizens yet living, in honor of Henry Martin of Wallingford, Connecticut." Apparently Upham came to this conclusion between the time he received biographical material from Henry Martin in 1905 and the time he wrote the article that was first published in 1920.

1328 *Meeker County*

Bradley B. Meeker (1813–1873)—Meeker was born in Fairfield, Connecticut, on March 13, 1813, and educated at nearby Yale College (now Yale University). Upon leaving Yale, he moved to Kentucky where he taught at a seminary and studied law. After he was admitted to the Kentucky bar, Meeker practiced law there and wrote articles dealing with defects in Kentucky's constitution. In the spring of 1849, President Zachary Taylor selected Meeker to be an associate justice on the supreme court of Minnesota territory. The territory had been created on March 3, 1849, and Meeker's term as an associate justice on the territorial supreme court began on June 1, 1849, and ended in 1853. Meeker also served as a member of the board of

regents of the University of Minnesota. After leaving the supreme court, Meeker was involved in real estate ventures in the Twin Cities area and he was a member of Minnesota's constitutional convention in 1857. This county was created by Minnesota territory on February 26, 1856.

1329 *Mille Lacs County*

Mille Lacs Lake—The Chippewa Indians' name for this lake meant "all sorts," "great" or "everywhere lake." The French modified the Indians' name a bit when translating it into their language as *Mille Lacs*, meaning "thousand lakes" and applied it to the whole Mille Lacs region. Eventually the name Mille Lacs came to be associated with this largest lake in the area, which is on the border of Mille Lacs County and Aitkin County, Minnesota. The lake has an area of about 200 square miles and a diameter of some 16 miles. The county was created in 1857, when Minnesota was a territory.

1330 *Morrison County*

Allan Morrison (1803–1877) & William Morrison (1785–1866)—Allan and William Morrison were brothers, who were born in Canada and engaged in fur trading together in the Minnesota wilderness in the early 1800's. William Morrison holds the distinction of being the first recorded White man to see Itasca Lake, the source of the Mississippi River.

Allan Morrison (1803–1877)—Born at Terrebonne, near Montreal, Canada, on June 3, 1803, Allan Morrison came to Fond du Lac in Wisconsin and then to northern Minnesota, where he engaged in fur trading with his brother, William Morrison. Allan Morrison was placed in charge of trading posts at Sandy Lake, Leech Lake, Red Lake and Mille Lacs. He also traded furs at the junction of the Crow Wing and Mississippi Rivers for a number of years and later farmed there. There was an Allen (sic) Morrison, who was a member of Minnesota's first territorial legislature and most sources state that this territorial legislator was our Allan Morrison. Our Allan Morrison died on the White Earth Indian reservation in Minnesota in 1877.

William Morrison (1785–1866)—This Morrison brother was also born in Canada, at Montreal on March 7, 1785. He came to Minnesota to trade furs at Grand Portage on the north shore of Lake Superior in 1802. William Morrison subsequently traded furs at Leech Lake, at the headwaters of the Crow Wing River and at Rice Lake. In 1804 William Morrison visited

Itasca Lake, the source of the Mississippi River. This was the first recorded visit by a White man to this important lake. Henry R. Schoolcraft's (1793–1864) party discovered and named Itasca Lake in 1832 and it was that party that determined Itasca Lake to be the source of the Mississippi River but their visit came a quarter of a century later than that of William Morrison in 1804. In 1826 William Morrison returned to Canada and lived their until his death in 1866.

During the first 14 years that William Morrison traded furs in Minnesota, he was employed by Sir Alexander MacKenzie (–1820). About the time that Allan Morrison joined his brother in Minnesota, it was John Jacob Astor (1763–1848), and his American Fur Company, who employed the Morrison brothers. In February, 1856, Allan Morrison transmitted a letter written by his brother, William Morrison, which described their fur trading activities and visits to Itasca Lake. Since this county was created by Minnesota territory on February 25, 1856, it is suggested by some sources that this letter may have sparked the territorial legislators' interest in naming this county in honor of the Morrison brothers. (If Allan Morrison was ever a member of Minnesota's territorial legislature, it was not during the session that created and named Morrison County. Allen [sic] Morrison was a member of the first Minnesota territorial legislature, which convened from September 3, 1849, to November 1, 1849.)

1331 *Mower County*

John E. Mower (1815–1879)— A native of Bangor, Maine, Mower moved in 1842 to the St. Croix River valley, in what was then Wisconsin territory. In 1844 he settled at today's Stillwater, Minnesota, and soon afterward moved to the nearby locality of Arcola, on the St. Croix River. His occupation was lumbering. When Minnesota territory was created in 1849, Stillwater and Arcola on the west side of the St. Croix River came under the new territory's dominion. John E. Mower was elected to serve in the upper house (council) of the fifth legislative session of Minnesota territory. He was reelected to serve in the sixth territorial legislature and it was that session of the legislature of Minnesota territory that created and named this county for one of their own members on February 20, 1855. Two decades later Mower served in the legislature of the state of Minnesota. He died on June 11, 1879, at his home in the former village of Arcola, Minnesota, on the St. Croix River.

1332 *Murray County*

William P. Murray (1825–1910)— This Ohio native attended Miami University in southwestern Ohio and took his law degree at Indiana University in 1849. He came to St. Paul, in Minnesota territory that same year and was soon elected to the territorial legislature. He served in both houses of the territorial legislature and was president of the upper house (council) for one of those sessions. In 1857 Murray was a member of Minnesota's state constitutional convention and after Minnesota became a state, he served in both houses of the state legislature. Almost continuously, from 1861 to 1879, Murray was a member of the St. Paul city council. This county was created on May 23, 1857, which was the last day of the last session of the legislature of Minnesota territory. William Pitt Murray was a member of the lower house of that legislature when his fellow legislators created and named this county in his honor.

1333 *Nicollet County*

Joseph N. Nicollet (1786–1843)— Joseph Nicolas Nicollet was born in Europe in the former nation of Savoy, whose territory now belongs to France and Italy. In his childhood and early youth, he was both impoverished and a mathematical prodigy. After a period of residence in Paris as an astronomer and college professor, Nicollet came to New Orleans, arriving in 1832. From there he headed up the Mississippi River, making numerous stops including Minnesota's Fort Snelling. Nicollet continued up the Mississippi River from Fort Snelling, seeking to find the origin of the Mississippi and he succeeded in reaching it, Itasca Lake. He later explored the Minnesota River and the upper reaches of the Red River (of the North) and the upper Missouri River. Nicollet's skills as a mathematician and astronomer proved to be valuable on these explorations, enabling him to draw maps and fix longitudes with accuracy that far surpassed earlier efforts. This county was created and named in his honor by Minnesota territory in 1853.

1334 *Nobles County*

William H. Nobles (1816–1876)— A native of New York state, Nobles headed west when he was about 25 years old. He lived briefly in St. Croix Falls and Hudson, in Wisconsin territory. In 1843 he moved to Stillwater, Minnesota, which then was also within Wisconsin territory. Nobles went to California in 1849, swelling the gold rush a bit. There he discovered a pass through the Sierra Nevada Mountains, which shortened the distance into California's gold country by several hundred miles. This route was the one that the Union Pacific Railroad later used and the pass here is named in William Nobles' honor. Upon his return to Minnesota territory, Nobles served in the territorial legislature and began construction of a wagon road to cross southwestern Minnesota (including Nobles County). His intent was that the road be extended westward to the Rocky Mountains. Nobles served as a lieutenant-colonel in the Union army during the Civil War. This county was created in 1857 by Minnesota territory. Although Nobles had been a member of the territorial legislature, he was not a member when this county was created.

1335 *Norman County*

Uncertain— This county in northwestern Minnesota was created on February 17, 1881. Sources consulted differ on whether this county was named for (1) Norman W. Kittson (1814–1888) or (2) Norwegians, Northmen, Norsemen or Normans on account of the state's (and, more spectacularly, the county's) large Norwegian population. As recently as the 1950's, one could walk along the street of the business district of Tracy, in southwestern Minnesota, and hear only the Norwegian language being spoken. According to Warren Upham's book entitled *Minnesota Geographic Names*, "By the census of 1910, in a total population of 13,446, in Norman County, 2,957 were born in Norway; and both parents of 4,651 others, among those born in America, were Norwegian." Upham also observes that "In Norway, a native is referred to as a Norsk or Norman." Upham studied the question of the origin of Norman County's name in some detail. He learned that a convention was held about 1880 at Ada, Minnesota, in the present Norman County, at which residents proposed that a new county be created and that they (reportedly) selected the name Norman for the proposed new county. Some of those who attended that convention later reported that it was their recollection that the county's name was intended to commemorate the large Norwegian population. Although Norman Kittson was an important figure in the early history of the Red River Valley, which forms the western border of Norman County, he already had a Minnesota county named for him. Just three years prior to the creation of Norman County, the Minnesota legislature changed the name of Pembina County to Kittson County, in his honor. It is rare, but not unknown, for a state to have more than one county named for the same person. For example, Florida has both Hernando County and De Soto County named for the same despicable Spanish conquistador, Hernando De Soto (1500–1542) and Oklahoma's "Alfalfa" Bill Murray (1869–1956) has two counties named for him and could have gotten half a dozen had he chosen to nod his head at Oklahoma's constitutional convention in 1907.

Norman W. Kittson (1814–1888)—Kittson was born near Sorel, Canada, on March 5, 1814. He came to Fort Snelling on the upper Mississippi River in 1834 and engaged in fur trading there. In 1843 or 1844 Kittson established a trading post at Pembina in the northern Dakota country. His superior in trading activities there was Henry H. Sibley (1811–1891). Kittson represented the Pembina district in the upper chamber of the legislature of Minnesota territory in 1852, 1853, 1854 and 1855. He also traded furs at St. Paul and he was one of the early mayors of that city. In 1864 Hudson Bay Company appointed Norman Kittson to be their director of steamboat traffic on the Red River (of the North) and he later was employed by the railroad promoter, James J. Hill (1838–1916) in railroad development in North Dakota. Kittson died in May, 1888.

Norwegians, Northmen, Norsemen or Normans—Early ancestors of the fine Norwegian citizens of today's Minnesota were the Northmen, Norsemen, Norman or Vikings of Scandinavia. These pagan, barbaric sea rovers successfully plundered and terrorized western Europe and one of their members, Leif Ericsson, is known to have preceded Christopher Columbus to North America by 500 years. Early Norman explorers may even have penetrated as far inland as Minnesota. The most spectacular (and controversial) piece of evidence supporting this theory is the Kensington stone. Some seven years after Norman County, Minnesota, was created, one Olaf Ohman found the so-called Kensington stone on his farm. This was in 1898 near the village of Kensington, Minnesota. This 202 pound slab has characters on it which closely resemble Norse runes. Professor O. J. Breda, an expert in Scandinavian languages at the University of Minnesota, declared the Kensington stone to be a hoax. Scholars at Northwestern University supported that view. However, subsequent scholars' studies have indicated that the Kensington stone was quite possibly an authentic relic of a Viking visit

to Minnesota about the year A.D. 1362. Of course the authenticity of the Kensington stone has no bearing on the origin of Norman County's name because it was discovered after the county was created. More to the point, there is no doubt about the large Norwegian population in Minnesota in 1881 when this county was created and the even larger proportion of Norwegians in Norman County (the largest proportion of Norwegians of any Minnesota county according to the 1910 census). Certainly the attendees at the Ada, Minnesota, convention could have carried the vote to name the county in honor of their Norwegian ancestors if they had chosen to do so. The Minnesota legislature had the last word on the choice of this county's name but it seems likely that the legislature would have chosen to honor the wishes of the Norwegian members, who held the majority at the Ada, Minnesota, convention, rather than name a second Minnesota county for Norman W. Kittson just three years after naming Kittson County for him.

1336 *Olmsted County*

Uncertain—This county was created on February 20, 1855, when Minnesota was still a territory, and it was named for a man who served in the upper chamber (council) of Minnesota's territorial legislature. However, sources consulted offer differing views on which territorial legislator was honored as the namesake of this county. The vast majority of sources consulted state that the honor belongs to David Olmsted (1822–1861), who was president of the upper house of Minnesota's first territorial legislature. However, other sources claim that the county was named for S. Baldwin Olmstead (1810–1878), who was a member of the territorial legislature during the session that those legislators created and named this county. Henry A. Castle tells us in his *Minnesota: Its Story & Biography*, that the county's name honors "...one or both of two pioneers of that name, both members of the Territorial Legislature."

David Olmsted (1822–1861)—A native of Fairfax, Vermont, David Olmsted immigrated to the lead mining region of Wisconsin territory in 1838. Two years later, with his brother, Page Olmsted, he moved to Iowa and he was a pioneer settler of Monona, Iowa. David Olmsted was a member of the convention that drafted the original constitution of the state of Iowa in 1846. He came to Minnesota in 1848 and was a pioneer settler here before

Minnesota territory was created. He initially lived at Long Prairie, Minnesota, and had an Indian trading post there. When Minnesota became a separate territory, David Olmsted was chosen as a member of the upper house of the first territorial legislature and he served as president of that body. He also served on the council of Minnesota's second territorial legislature, although not as president. In 1853 he became the owner and editor of the *Minnesota Democrat*, published in St. Paul and he served a one year term as the first mayor of St. Paul. In 1855 David Olmsted ran for election to be Minnesota territory's delegate to the U.S. Congress but he lost that election to Henry M. Rice (1816–1894).

S. Baldwin Olmstead (1810–1878)—S. Baldwin Olmstead was born in Otsego County, New York, and came to Minnesota before it was a state and perhaps even before it was a territory. He was a farmer and contractor at Belle Prairie and at Ft. Ripley and was a member and president of the upper house of Minnesota territory's fifth (1854) legislature. S. Baldwin Olmstead also served as a member of that body during the sixth (1855) legislative session, but not as president; William Pitt Murray (1825–1910) held that honor. It was this 1855 session of the territorial legislature that created and named Olmsted County. S. Baldwin Olmstead moved to Texas when the Civil War ended and he died on his farm there on January 27, 1878. Note that the county's name is spelled Olmsted, while this man's surname is Olmstead. That does not rule out the possibility that Olmsted County was named for him. If this is a spelling error here, it would be one of many in our nation.

1337 *Otter Tail County*

Otter Tail Lake & Otter Tail River—The Chippewa Indians saw a resemblance to the tail of an otter in the present Otter Tail Lake here in Otter Tail County in west-central Minnesota. Our name of the lake is merely an English translation of the Chippewa Indians' name for it. At the time that the Indians named Otter Tail Lake, otters were common animals around the lakes of Minnesota where they subsisted on fish which they caught with their great speed. Otters have been rare in this area for at least a century. The geographic feature that resembled an otter's tail to the Indians was a long, narrow sand bar near the eastern end of the lake. That sand bar was covered with woods, thereby hiding the otter tail, long ago. The Otter Tail River is some 200 miles long and got its name from that of Otter Tail Lake. However Otter Tail is not the only name of this river. It has different names for different sections of it. The Otter Tail River flows from Otter Tail Lake to the west, then south and then west again where it unites with the Bois des Sioux River at Breckenridge, Minnesota, to form the Red River (of the North). The Otter Tail River flows through so many lakes on its journey to the Red River that it might be more correct to call it a waterway of connecting lakes, rather than a river. Warren Upham's book entitled *Minnesota Geographic Names*, gives a description of the sand bar that inspired the unusual name for the lake. The description was based on personal visits to Otter Tail Lake by one J. V. Brower in 1863, 1882 and 1899: "…the height of the bar varies from 10 to 25 feet above the lake; that its length slightly exceeds a mile, while its width, somewhat uniform, is only about 50 to 75 feet…" Another description of our otter-tail-shaped sand bar is contained in John W. Mason's 1916 *History of Otter Tail County, Minnesota*: "At the head of Otter Tail lake is a narrow ridge of land one mile and a half long by two or three rods in width, and curved to the contour of the head of the lake." J. V. Brower speculates that the sand bar was formed by wave and ice action while John W. Mason suggests that the sand bar was probably forced up by ages of expanding ice, year after year and that its length was extended as the inflowing river was forced across its point.

1338 *Pennington County*

Edmund Pennington (1848–1926)— Pennington was born in La Salle, Illinois, on September 16, 1848, and began his career in the railroad industry when he was a young man, about 21 years old. By 1888 he had risen to the management level of the Minneapolis, St. Paul, and Sault Ste. Marie Railway Company. Between 1888 and 1909 he held the positions of superintendent, general manager and vice-president of this railroad company and in 1909 he became its president. This county was created and named in his honor in the following year, on November 23, 1910.

1339 *Pine County*

Uncertain— This county on Minnesota's eastern border with Wisconsin was created on March 1, 1856, when Minnesota was a territory. Its name may have been chosen on account of the magnificent stands of pine forests, which were exten-

sive here at the time that the county was created. The three types of pine trees common to this area of Minnesota are the white pine, the red pine and the jack pine. The jack pine is small and has little value as lumber but it is useful as fuel. Since 1856, large numbers of white pine and red pine have been removed from the county by the lumber industry because the logistics in the county are ideal for that industry. Sawmills were set up on the county's many lakes and streams and the Snake River and the Kettle River were used to get the logs to the St. Croix River and thence to civilization. Both the Minnesota government and private citizens thought the supply of lumber was inexhaustible and little or no thought was given to conservation. The Stillwater Lumber Company and the Rutledge Lumber Company were among the earliest of the logging companies to be located in Pine County. While the pine trees no doubt were involved in the selection of this county's name, it is suggested by some sources that the county's name may have derived not only from its pine forests but from its pine lakes and the Pine River, as well. The pine lakes here would include Big Pine Lake, Upper Pine Lake and Lower Pine Lake. The Pine River is a tributary of the Kettle River.

1340 *Pipestone County*

The sacred Indian pipestone quarry here— Pipestone County and Rock County, Minnesota, are two adjacent counties in the southwestern corner of Minnesota. Both of these counties were first created on May 23, 1857, by the last legislature of Minnesota territory. The pipestone for which Pipestone County was named is found at an Indian quarry where sacred red pipestone (called by some catlinite) has been mined for centuries. When it was discovered that the pipestone mine for which this county was named was actually within Rock County rather than Pipestone County, the Minnesota legislature switched the names of the two counties and the pipestone mine is now within Pipestone County. The corrective legislation became law on February 20, 1862. The March 13, 1870, issue of the *St. Paul Pioneer* described the origin of Pipestone County's name this way: "From the celebrated quarry of red stone used by the Indians for pipes from time immemorial." The soft, red pipestone mined here is used to make the bowls of ceremonial pipes for smoking tobacco. The artist, George Catlin (1796–1872) visited this Indian quarry in 1836.

Some reports incorrectly state that he was the first White man to visit the sacred quarry but he was not. It is known that the fur trader Philander Prescott (1801–1862) visited the quarry before Catlin did but Catlin's visit was better publicized and his name has been preserved in one version of the name for this soft, red clay as catlinite. The term steatite is also used for this clay. This pipestone quarry has been considered sacred ground by Indians and there are rules concerning it. Two of these rules are (1) Indians who had long fought for ownership of this pipestone quarry must henceforth visit it only as friends and never as foes and (2) Whites were forbidden entry to the quarry. This prohibition was backed by formal treaty signed in Washington, D.C., on April 19, 1858. This treaty was soon ignored and it was not until 1937 that a measure of protection was enacted by establishment of Pipestone National Monument. This national monument is open to visitors of all races. In his work entitled *Minnesota and Its People*, published in 1924, Joseph A. A. Burnquist included an interesting recitation of one version of the Indians' legend concerning this sacred pipestone quarry and a visit to it by the Great Spirit. Henry W. Longfellow (1807–1882) also referred to it in his 1855 poem, *The Song of Hiawatha*. The red pipestone found here in a layer almost two feet thick has been quarried by Indians for centuries and the mine now extends about a mile from north to south.

1341 *Polk County*

James K. Polk (1795–1849)— Polk was a native of North Carolina who moved with his family to the Tennessee frontier in 1806. He served in the lower house of the Tennessee legislature and he represented Tennessee for 14 years in the U.S. House of Representatives, where he was speaker. He served one term as governor of Tennessee. Polk became president of the United States as a dark horse candidate of the Democratic party but he became an unusually strong and effective president. His primary accomplishments involved westward extension of the United States: in the Northwest by settling a territorial dispute with Britain and in California and the Southwest by provoking and winning the Mexican War. President Polk signed the legislation to create Minnesota territory on his last day as president, March 3, 1849. This county was created in July, 1858, just two months after Minnesota's admission to the Union as a state.

1342 *Pope County*

John Pope (1822–1892)— A native of Kentucky, Pope was an 1842 graduate of West Point, with the rank of brevet second lieutenant in the topographical engineers. He served in the Mexican War and in 1849 he turned his attention to Minnesota. Here he explored the valley of the Red River (of the North) and reported on the soil, geography, weather and natural resources of this area and of the Pembina region further west. After leaving Minnesota, Pope was involved in the army's explorations in the West, Southwest and Texas. Early in the Civil War John Pope was made a brigadier-general and he played a major role in the Union army's disastrous loss of the Second Battle of Bull Run. President Lincoln then sent him where he could do less damage and he was given command of the department of the Northwest, with headquarters at St. Paul, Minnesota. He arrived here in September, 1862, and was a vigorous participant in the brutality against the Dakota Indians, which culminated in the hanging of 38 of them at a mass gallows at Mankato, Minnesota, in December, 1862. A good portion of Pope's remaining 24 year army career was devoted to Indian suppression but his attitude toward the Indians evolved to a somewhat compassionate one. He retired from the army in 1886 as a major general. This county was created on February 20, 1862, after Pope had established his reputation as an explorer of the Red River region but before his participation in the Second Battle of Bull Run.

1343 *Ramsey County*

Alexander Ramsey (1815–1903)— A native of Pennsylvania, Ramsey studied law and was admitted to the bar of that state in 1839. He represented Pennsylvania in the U.S. House of Representatives and when Minnesota territory was created in 1849, President Zachary Taylor appointed Ramsey to be the new territory's first governor. Minnesota's first territorial legislature divided the large new territory into nine counties on October 27, 1849, and they named one of them for Alexander Ramsey, who was governor at that time and continued as the territory's governor until May 15, 1853. He later served as mayor of St. Paul and was the second governor of the state of Minnesota. Ramsey represented Minnesota in the U.S. Senate from 1863 to 1875. In 1879, President Rutherford B. Hayes appointed Ramsey to be his secretary of war. Ramsey remained in that cabinet post until President Hayes' term as president ended in 1881. Ramsey died in St. Paul, Minnesota, in the county that bears his name, on April 22, 1903.

1344 *Red Lake County*

Red Lake River— This relatively small county in northwestern Minnesota was created in 1896 and named for the Red Lake River, a tributary of the Red River (of the North). Red Lake River passes through Red Lake County on its 196 mile journey from Lower Red Lake to the Red River (of the North) at Grand Forks, North Dakota. The Red Lake River's name was taken from the name of Minnesota's largest lake, Red Lake, which is divided into two huge sections, Upper Red Lake and Lower Red Lake. Warren Upham tells us in his *Minnesota Geographic Names* that Red Lake's name was inspired by its beautiful wine-red hue at sunset on a calm summer evening; not from bloody battles on its shores nor from iron-colored clay or gravel in the area. The Chippewa Indians named Red Lake and Red Lake River and our present names for them are merely English translations of the Indians' names.

1345 *Redwood County*

Redwood River— The Redwood River is a 90 mile long tributary of the Minnesota River. It travels in Lyon County, in southwestern Minnesota, and flows to the northeast and east through Redwood County, where it joins the Minnesota River two to three miles below Redwood Falls, near Morton, Minnesota. The river was named by the Dakota Indians because of either red trees or red bushes near its banks. If it were trees that caught the Indians attention, we have two possibilities for the origin of the Redwood River's name. The first choice is straight forward: red cedar trees. However, the second tree choice involves a tree or trees which the Indians marked with red paint. The paint may have been applied to a number of trees to guide Indian travelers (or warriors) but the Italian explorer Giacomo C. Beltrami (1779–1855) recorded in his writings that the Indians painted a red mark for religious or sacred reasons. However, the Redwood River's name may have nothing to do with any kind of tree; it may have been inspired by bushes. If the Indians named the Redwood River on account of bushes, we know which ones they had in mind. There were the abundant, straight and slender willow-like bushes with red bark, which the Indians sometimes scraped off and smoked, at times mixed with tobacco. The red color of these bushes is found on an inner bark of the two species of these bushes found here: *Cornus sericea*, the silky cornel, and *Cornus stolonifera*, the red-osier dogwood.

1346 *Renville County*

Joseph Renville (–1846)— Renville was born about 1779 on the banks of the Mississippi River near Minnesota's present Twin Cities. His father was French and his mother was a Dakota Indian. Renville was raised among the Dakota Indians until he was about ten years old, when his father took him to Canada. There he was given a few years education by French Roman Catholic priests. After returning to Minnesota, he served as a guide and interpreter for the U.S. army's explorer, Zebulon M. Pike (1779–1813). During the War of 1812, the British gave Renville the rank of captain in their army and Renville led a company composed of Dakota warriors against the U.S. on the northwestern frontier. In 1815 he resigned from the British army and identified himself with American interests thereafter. He erected a trading house at Lac qui Parle and remained there until his death in 1846. Renville's mother was an Indian and he married a Dakota Indian, himself. His knowledge of the Indians' language and customs enabled him to assist the Presbyterian missionary, Thomas S. Williamson (1800–1879), in converting Indians to Christianity. Renville assisted other Christian missionaries as well and he participated in translating large portions of the *Bible* (some accounts say the entire *Bible*) into the language of the Dakota Indians. This county was created by Minnesota territory in 1855.

1347 *Rice County*

Henry M. Rice (1816–1894)— A native of Vermont, Rice moved west while still a young man and lived on America's wilderness frontier residing in Michigan, Iowa, Wisconsin and Minnesota before they were admitted to statehood. In 1839 Rice came to Ft. Snelling; this was ten years before Minnesota became a territory. For many years he was an agent of the Chouteau fur companies and he was in charge of their fur trading posts from Lake Superior to Red Lake and into Canada. He assisted in negotiating treaties with the Indians in which the Indians ceded their lands to the Whites and got little or nothing in return. On March 4, 1853, Rice succeeded Henry H. Sibley (1811–1891) as Minnesota territory's delegate to the U.S. Congress and he remained in that position until 1857. When

Minnesota was admitted to the Union as a state, Rice became one of the new state's first two United States senators. He served in the U.S. Senate from May 12, 1858, to March 3, 1863. This county was created on March 5, 1853, by Minnesota's territorial legislature and named for their new delegate to the U.S. Congress.

1348 *Rock County*

The huge reddish brown mound or rock near Luverne, Minnesota— Rock County and Pipestone County are two adjacent counties in the southwestern corner of Minnesota. Both of these counties were created on May 23, 1857, by the last legislature of Minnesota territory. The rock for which Rock County was named is not a mere rock or boulder, but an enormous outcrop of reddish brown quartzite, which occupies an area of more than three square miles and stands up in stark contrast to the flat prairie land surrounding it, below. A discovery was made that the May 23, 1857, act which created Rock County and Pipestone County was based on faulty geography. The gigantic rock, which is Rock County's namesake, fell within the boundaries of Pipestone County and the Indians' sacred pipestone quarry honored in Pipestone County's name was within Rock County. Since the counties were adjacent, new and sparsely populated, the fix was easy. The Minnesota legislature merely switched the names of the two counties by a law which became effective on February 20, 1862. In 1866 the Minnesota legislators attempted to change again the name of Minnesota's south-western-most county by changing its name from Rock to Lincoln. The residents were weary of these changes and this 1866 legislative attempt was ignored. The rock for which Rock County, Minnesota was named sits today firmly within the borders of Rock County and is located about three miles north of Luverne, Minnesota, on the west side of the Rock River and 175 feet above that river. This huge rock or mound forms a gradually ascending plateau from the west and north but terminates abruptly on its eastern and southern sides. Both the WPA's 1940 *Inventory of the County Archives of Minnesota* for this county and the state's official highway map for 1990 refer to this geological wonder as "Blue Mound(s)." This is because weathering over the ages has caused the reddish gray quartzite to become flecked with blue. In his 1988 work entitled *The Necessity of Empty Spaces*, Paul Gruchow, stated that "they aren't blue, actually; they are red and brown ...

an Indian red ... tending toward purple..."

1349 *Roseau County*

Roseau River & Roseau Lake—Roseau is the French word for "reed." Coarse grass or reeds (*Phragmites communis*) are common along the shallow edges of ponds and lakes and slow streams here in northwestern Minnesota and in Canada's adjacent Manitoba province. Roseau River and Roseau Lake owe their names to these reeds. According to one source, these reeds grow to a height of eight to twelve feet. Hazel H. Wahlberg elaborated in her 1975 work entitled *The North Land: A History of Roseau County*. She stated that "The grass grew to 8 to 10 feet high around the rim of the lake and on the banks of the river." The Roseau River is a tributary of the Red River (of the North). It is formed by its North and South forks which unite at the village of Malung, Minnesota, in Roseau County. The Roseau River's course after leaving Malung is to the northwest and after crossing Roseau County, it touches Kittson County, Minnesota, and then enters Manitoba province, Canada, where it finally flows into the Red River (of the North).

1350 *Saint Louis County*

Saint Louis River— The Saint Louis River is the largest of the rivers and streams that flow into Lake Superior. The Saint Louis River rises near the eastern border of this county, north of Lake Superior, and flows some 160 miles before emptying into Lake Superior at Duluth, Minnesota. The Saint Louis River's watershed is one of the largest in Minnesota, 3,584 square miles, most of which are within Saint Louis County. When this county was first created on February 20, 1855, by Minnesota's territorial legislature, it was named Superior County. On March 3, 1855, the territorial legislature changed the county's name from Superior to Saint Louis and made necessary technical changes on March 1, 1856, to fully implement this name change. Warren Upham reports in his work entitled *Minnesota Geographic Names*, that "The king of France, in 1749, shortly before the death of Verendrye, conferred on him the cross of St. Louis as a recognition of the importance of his discoveries and thence the name of the St. Louis river appears to have come." The Verendrye to whom Upham referred was Pierre Gaultier de Varennes et de la Verendrye (1685–1749), whose explorations took him along Minnesota's northern border and through the

environs of the Saint Louis River. The French king in 1749, who would have conferred this honor upon Verendrye was King Louis XV (1710–1774), but the cross of Saint Louis, which was awarded to Verendrye, honored an earlier French monarch, King Louis IX (1214–1270), who is a saint of the Roman Catholic Church.

Saint Louis (1214–1270)— Louis was a boy of only about 11 or 12 when his father, King Louis VIII (1187–1226), died and he was consecrated as king of France, under the name Louis IX. His mother ruled France as regent while Louis IX was a minor but after Louis IX assumed his role as monarch of France his reign was long and comparatively peaceful although it began with a revolt by certain vassals, aided by the English. Louis IX put down that revolt and soon was off to the Holy Lands on a crusade against the infidels on behalf of Christianity. His troops scored some victories but he was captured. The Christian crusaders had captured Damietta, Egypt and their offer of Damietta as ransom for the king's release was accepted. After his release, Louis visited Christian holy places and repaired shrines in Syria, which were still in Christian hands. Upon his return to France he governed well and was admired for his piety and wisdom. He presided over a period of magnificent Christian architecture including the soaring Sainte-Chapelle in Paris. His second participation in a crusade ended in his death near Tunis, in Africa. He was canonized in 1297.

1351 *Scott County*

Winfield Scott (1786–1866)— A native of Virginia, Scott joined the U.S. army in 1808. His heroic service in the War of 1812 resulted in rapid promotions to brevet major-general. He later played an important military role during the 1832 nullification crisis in South Carolina and in actions against the Indians in Florida. He was general-in-chief of the United States army during the Mexican War. Scott was the Whig party's candidate for president in 1852 but he lost to Franklin Pierce. When the Civil War broke out, Scott remained loyal to the Union side despite his southern roots but he retired from the army in October, 1861, on account of age and ill health. This county was created by Minnesota's territorial legislature on March 5, 1853, shortly after Winfield Scott's unsuccessful bid for the presidency.

1352 *Sherburne County*

Moses Sherburne (1808–1868)— A native

of Maine, Sherburne practiced law in that state and was a member of both houses of Maine's state legislature. In April, 1853, President Franklin Pierce appointed him to serve as an associate justice of the supreme court of Minnesota territory. Sherburne served on that bench from April 7, 1853, to April 13, 1857. This county was created and named in Judge Sherburne's honor on February 25, 1856, while he was an associate justice of the territorial supreme court. Moses Sherburne was a member of Minnesota's constitutional convention in 1857 and he was one of two compilers of the statutes of Minnesota, published in 1859. In 1867 he moved to the community of Orono in Sherburne County, thereby becoming a resident of the county named in his honor.

1353 *Sibley County*

Henry H. Sibley (1811–1891) — Sibley was born on our country's northwestern frontier, in Detroit and he came to Minnesota in 1834 as a fur trading agent of the American Fur Company. When Wisconsin entered the Union as a state in 1848, it left behind the Minnesota portion of the former Wisconsin territory. On January 15, 1849, Henry H. Sibley became the delegate to the U.S. Congress from this surviving slice of Wisconsin territory. (Both the new state of Wisconsin and this version of Wisconsin territory were represented in the 30th U.S. Congress.) When Minnesota territory was created from that residual slice of Wisconsin territory, Sibley became the first delegate to congress from Minnesota territory and he served as the territory's delegate until March 3, 1853. Two days later, on March 5, 1853, the legislature of Minnesota territory created and named this county in his honor. When Minnesota was admitted to the union as a state, Sibley was elected as the new state's first governor. In 1862 the Dakota Indians in Minnesota began their final futile struggle against the Whites who had systematically robbed and mistreated them. Sibley led in the successful suppression of this rebellion and 38 of the Dakota Indians were hanged at a mass gallows at Mankato, Minnesota on December 26, 1862. Remaining Dakota Indians in Minnesota were deported to Indian reservations in Dakota territory (now South Dakota and North Dakota) where they live in misery to this day. During the Civil War Sibley held the rank of brigadier-general of U.S. volunteers and was later promoted to brevet major-general.

1354 *Stearns County*

Charles T. Stearns (1807–1898) — A native of Pittsfield, Massachusetts, Stearns immigrated to Illinois and then came to Minnesota in 1849, about the time that Minnesota territory was created. He served in the upper house (council) of the Minnesota territorial legislature from January 4, 1854, to March 3, 1855. When Stearns first came here he settled at St. Anthony but in 1855 he moved to St. Cloud in Stearns County, thus becoming a resident of the county named for him. At St. Cloud he was the proprietor of a hotel for some 14 years. About 1870 Charles Stearns decided to move to a warmer climate. He first went to Alabama and later to Louisiana where he was described as a "wealthy planter." In 1855 the bill that created this county passed both houses of Minnesota's territorial legislature with the name Stevens County, in honor of Isaac I. Stevens (1818–1862), who was then governor of Washington territory. However, through clerical error, in the final act that created this county effective February 20, 1855, the name had been changed to Stearns. It was decided that the error would not be corrected. Charles T. Stearns was a member of the upper chamber of Minnesota's territorial legislature when this county was created and he was deemed to be worthy of this form of public recognition, albeit in error. Later a county was named for Isaac I. Stevens. In fact, two counties were named for him; one in Minnesota (in 1862) and one in Washington (in 1863).

1355 *Steele County*

Franklin Steele (1813–1880) — This Pennsylvania native realized that with ingenuity and hard work one could make a lot of money on our nation's northwestern frontier and he proceeded to do just that. He erected a crude cabin on the St. Croix River to lay claim to water rights there and he hired a small group of men to cut timber for him. Sensing that more money would be needed to make his lumbering venture boom, Steele went to St. Louis and found backers for a new company. A dam was built on the St. Croix River at the present site of Taylor Falls, Minnesota, and a sawmill was placed in operation there. Steele soon had a similar venture in operation in what is now Minneapolis at the Falls of St. Anthony, where he owned valuable land. Franklin Steele soon began to accumulate wealth and he eventually owned a large portion of the land in Minneapolis. In 1851 he was elected by the legislature of

Minnesota territory to membership on the first board of regents of the University of Minnesota. The territorial legislature created and named this county in his honor in 1855.

1356 *Stevens County*

Isaac I Stevens (1818–1862) — Isaac Ingalls Stevens was born near Andover, Massachusetts, and graduated at the head of his class from the U.S. Military Academy at West Point in 1839. While serving in the Mexican War, he was severely wounded in the assault on Mexico City. Stevens was breveted captain and major for this gallantry. In 1853 he became associated with Minnesota and her history when he organized and commanded the initial phase of a survey for a northern railroad route from St. Paul to Puget Sound, an arm of the Pacific Ocean. While this exploration was in progress, President Franklin Pierce appointed Major Stevens to be the first governor of Washington territory. As governor, Stevens continued to promote development of a northern railroad. He subsequently represented Washington territory as its delegate to the U.S. Congress. In 1860 Stevens was a leading figure in the extreme pro-slavery presidential bid of John C. Breckinridge (1821–1875). Of course Abraham Lincoln won that election and when the Civil War started, despite his previous pro-slavery connections, Stevens entered the Union army as a colonel. He served with distinction and was promoted to the rank of brigadier-general and that was the rank that he held when he was killed in combat on September 1, 1862, at the battle of Chantilly. Stevens was posthumously promoted to major-general, back dated to July 18, 1862. This Minnesota county was created and named in his honor on February 20, 1862, when Stevens was serving in the Civil War as a brigadier-general. The legislature of Minnesota territory had tried, in 1855, to name a county for Isaac Ingalls Stevens but due to clerical error, the county was named Stearns County. That error was allowed to stand and Minnesota still has that Stearns County as well as this Stevens County.

1357 *Swift County*

Henry A. Swift (1823–1869) — A native of Ohio and an 1842 graduate of Western Reserve College in that state, Swift studied law and was admitted to the Ohio bar in 1845. He moved to Minnesota territory in 1853 and soon became active in the efforts to secure statehood for Minnesota.

Swift served in the senate of Minnesota's state legislature and he was elected by his fellow senators to be president of the senate. This made him the legal successor to replace Alexander Ramsey (1815–1903) as governor, when Ramsey resigned in 1863 to enter the U.S. Senate. Swift was Minnesota's third state governor and his term was brief, lasting from July 10, 1863, to January 11, 1864. Swift did not run for another term as governor but he did serve again in Minnesota's senate before his death on February 25, 1869. This county was created and named in Governor Swift's honor on February 18, 1870, just one year after his death.

1358 *Todd County*

John B. S. Todd (1814–1872)— John Blair Smith Todd was a native of Kentucky and an 1837 graduate of the U.S. Military Academy at West Point. He served as an officer in the war against the Seminole Indians in Florida and as a captain in the Mexican War. Todd was transferred to serve on our nation's northwestern frontier, first at Minnesota's Fort Snelling and subsequently as commander of Minnesota's Fort Gaines (later renamed Fort Ripley). He resigned from the army in 1856 and became an Indian trader at Fort Randall in Dakota territory. While at Fort Randall he managed to study enough law to be admitted to the bar. During the Civil War, Todd served in the Union army as a brigadier-general and he represented Dakota territory in the U.S. Congress as that territory's delegate to congress. He later was speaker of the house in the lower chamber of Dakota territory's legislature. This county was created on February 20, 1855, when Minnesota was a territory and shortly before Todd's tenure as commander of Fort Ripley ended. For almost a decade after it was built in 1849, Fort Ripley dominated the countryside in this part of central Minnesota. According to some accounts, John B. S. Todd was governor of Dakota territory from 1869 to 1871. That is incorrect. Todd never served as Dakota territory's governor. John A. Burbank was governor of Dakota territory from 1869 to 1871.

1359 *Traverse County*

Lake Traverse— This county was created on February 20, 1862, and named for the lake on the county's western border with the state of South Dakota. The lake is about 30 miles long, but quite narrow. The Bois de Sioux River at its northern end is an outlet and a headstream of the Red River (of the North). An important tributary of Lake Traverse is the Mustinka River. The material available on the origin of the name of Lake Traverse is not satisfying. It is clear that the name originated with the Dakota Indians and was translated, without change in meaning, first into French as *Lac Travers* and then into English as Lake Traverse. The French word *travers* means "across" or "crosswise" and one of the meanings of the English word *traverse* is the same as the French meaning. We are told that William H. Keating was a geologist and explorer, who visited Lake Traverse in 1823 and that Keating explained that Lake Traverse was so named because it lies "…in a direction nearly traverse to that of Big Stone and Lac qui Parle lakes." Big Stone Lake and Lac qui Parle are in the same general vicinity of western Minnesota as Lake Traverse and all three are on or near Minnesota's western border with South Dakota. Big Stone Lake and Lac qui Parle have similar shapes and it is true that either of them would form something approximating a right angle (90 degree angle) if they were joined to the southern end of Lake Traverse. It is certainly possible that some inventive Indian mind noted this right angle relationship among the lakes and then named Lake Traverse on account of it. However, this explanation seems a bit much to swallow. If this explanation for the Indians' name of the lake is accurate, then the flow from the Indian language to French to English might have been rather automatic. Fortunately, an alternative, and more satisfying explanation of Lake Traverse's name has also been suggested. This second explanation involves a change in the direction of the flow of the water in the Minnesota River at exceptionally high flood stages. The western end of the Minnesota River normally flows out of Big Stone Lake in a southeastern direction. However, at exceptionally high flood stages, at least in the early days of settlement of western Minnesota, the upper Minnesota River flowed backwards (i.e., north), giving canoes a continuous route to traverse from Big Stone Lake to Lake Traverse. Although this second explanation of Lake Traverse's name seems less contrived than the first (right angle) suggestion, we really don't know which, if either, of these is the correct source of Lake Traverse's name.

1360 *Wabasha County*

Town of Wabasha, Minnesota— The present city of Wabasha, Minnesota, just downstream from Lake Pepin on the Mississippi River, was founded as a town and named in 1843. Its name honored the last of a succession of hereditary chiefs of Dakota Indians named Wapashaw. This Chief Wapashaw, became chief of his people in 1836 when his father died. He signed treaties with the Whites in 1836, 1837, 1851 and 1858. The Chief Wapashaw whose name was honored in the name of the town and from there to the name of this county, occupied territory below Minnesota's Lake Pepin, which lies at the northern end of today's Wabasha County. His principal village was on Rolling Stone Creek, near today's Minnesota City, Minnesota. The beautiful prairie southeast of this chief's headquarters at Rolling Stone Creek was at one time called Wapashaw's prairie. That prairie today is the site of Minnesota's lovely city of Winona. This Chief Wapashaw died in Nebraska on April 23, 1876. The title Wapashaw was bestowed by French explorers and fur traders upon the Indian chief who ruled this red leaf country in southeastern Minnesota. The name *Wapashaw* derives from "red leaf." The red leaves that the White explorers found here were on oak trees (*Quercus tinctoria* and *Quercus rubra*) which were unusual because their red foliage remained in view throughout the long winters. Minnesota territory was created on March 3, 1849, and later that year, on October 27, 1849, the new territory was divided into just nine counties. One of these nine counties was Wabashaw County, and its name was taken from the town of Wabasha. The Chief Wapashaw for whom the town of Wabasha was named is described in some sources as the last chief of three consecutive generations of hereditary chiefs titled Wapashaw. However, this hereditary line of Dakota Indian chiefs titled Wapashaw goes back much farther than three generations. This topic is addressed by both Frederick W. Hodge in his encyclopedic *Handbook of American Indians North of Mexico* and by Charles C. Willson in his article entitled "The Successive Chiefs Named Wabasha," in volume number 12 of the *Collections of the Minnesota Historical Society* (1908). Hodge states that this succession of chiefs "…extending through tradition to time immemorial…" Wilson estimates that the Wapashaw hereditary dynasty ruled the southeastern part of Minnesota for nearly two hundred years. The duration of the Wapashaw dynasty is important in defending the translation "red leaf" against an alternative translation which is mentioned involving a red cap. The red cap referred to the cap from an English soldier's uniform which was reportedly given by the English governor of Canada to a Chief Wapashaw sometime after 1763. If the dynasty was only three generations long this might have been the source of the name but since the dynasty (and its name) lasted something on the order of two hundred years, the "red leaf" origin is the only credible suggested origin of the name. The county's name was initially spelled Wabashaw, while the name of the Indian chief being honored is rendered variously but frequently seen as Wapashaw. Both the county and its county seat are now spelled Wabasha.

1361 *Wadena County*

Wadena trading post— This county in north-central Minnesota was created on June 11, 1858, just one month after Minnesota had been admitted the Union as a state. It was named for the Wadena trading post which was then located in the southeastern corner of Wadena County in Thomastown township. To be more specific, this trading post was located on the Crow Wing River, between the mouths of the Leaf River and the Partridge River. A town grew up around this Indian trading post and its name, of course, was Wadena. About 1872, when the Northern Pacific Railroad ran tracks through southern Wadena County, the town of Wadena was moved 15 miles west to be on the railroad line. This newer municipality, named Wadena, is the present county seat of Wadena County. The old Wadena trading post, the county's namesake, had become a ghost town by 1899. The name *Wadena* is from the Chippewa Indian language. Its meaning is uncertain but both "village" and "little round hill" have been mentioned as possible translations. The name Wadena has also been used as a personal name of individual Chippewa Indians who lived in Minnesota.

1362 *Waseca County*

Indian word meaning "fertile"— In 1856, some citizens from Winona, Minnesota, planned a town site in what is now the southwestern part of Woodville township in Waseca County. They named this proposed town Waseca. The name was a word in the Dakota Indians' language which was given by the Indians in response to inquiries by the Whites about the richness of the soil. The Indians answered *waseca*, which they explained meant "fertile" or "rich in provisions." These citizens from Winona then petitioned the Minnesota territorial legislature to split Winona County into two counties and name they new county Waseca County. The territo-

rial legislators were not impressed with this scheme and they turned it down. However, they did like the euphony of the name Waseca and they used it on February 27, 1857, when they split Steele County and gave this new county formed by the split, the name Waseca.

1363 *Washington County*

George Washington (1732–1799)— Washington was a native of Virginia. He served in Virginia's house of burgesses and became one of the colonies' leaders in opposition to British policies in America. He was a member of the first and second Continental Congresses and commander of all Continental armies in the Revolutionary War. Following victory in that war, Washington was elected to be the first president of the United States. On March 3, 1849, Minnesota territory was created and in October of that year, the territory was divided into nine counties, one of which was Washington County.

1364 *Watonwan County*

Watonwan township, Blue Earth County, Minnesota— Blue Earth County was created on March 5, 1853, when Minnesota was still a territory. One of Blue Earth County's townships was named Watonwan township and when the Minnesota state legislature carved a new county out of a portion of Blue Earth County on February 25, 1860, Watonwan township became Watonwan County. The township had been named for the Watonwan River, a tributary of the Blue Earth River. The Watonwan River rises in Cottonwood County, Minnesota, and then flows 90 miles in a generally eastern direction across Watonwan County and into Blue Earth County, where it empties into the Blue Earth River, southwest of Mankato, Minnesota. The river's name is an Anglicized version of an original Indian name and its meaning has been lost. However, sources consulted are willing to offer guesses for the translation of the river's name. Guesses suggested include "fish bait," "where fish abound," "where fish bait abounds," "I see" and "he sees."

1365 *Wilkin County*

Alexander Wilkin (1820–1864)— A native of upstate New York, Wilkin served as a captain in the U.S. army in the Mexican war. He came to St. Paul in 1849, where he practiced law and served as secretary of Minnesota territory from October 23, 1851, to May 15, 1853. The title of territo-

rial secretary sounds rather bland and in fact the office has little power. However, when the territorial governor is absent from the territory, the secretary stands in as acting governor. Alexander Wilkin recruited a company of soldiers to serve in the Union army during the Civil War and he held the rank of colonel when he was killed in combat during the Union army's victory at the battle of Tupelo, Mississippi, in July, 1864.

When this county was first created on March 18, 1858, it was named Toombs County, in honor of Robert Toombs (1810–1885), who represented the state of Georgia in both houses of the U.S. Congress. That name had been suggested by Henry M. Rice (1816–1894), for whom Rice County, Minnesota, is named. When Robert Toombs became a founding father of the Confederate States of America, the state of Minnesota banished his name from its county map and in 1863 the county was renamed Andy Johnson County. The new name honored Andrew Johnson (1808–1875), of Tennessee, the only southern senator who still supported the Union side after 1861. Soon after this county's name had been changed from Toombs County to Andy Johnson County, Andrew Johnson became President Abraham Lincoln's vice president and Johnson succeeded Lincoln as president on April 15, 1865, as a result of President Lincoln's assassination. As president, Johnson was viewed as being too lenient toward the defeated southern states and he soon became unpopular; very unpopular. The U.S. House of Representatives took the unprecedented step of instituting impeachment proceedings against President Johnson. Although Johnson was acquitted when he was tried by the U.S. Senate, the acquittal was only by one vote and Johnson emerged from the impeachment proceedings drained of political support. Minnesota's legislators certainly wanted no county named in his honor but what were they to do? They had twice named this county for men who subsequently infuriated them. It seemed the only safe course would be to rename the county for a dead man to be sure that no subsequent actions of his would displease them. So Andy Johnson County's name was changed to Wilkin on March 6, 1868, in honor of the deceased Colonel Alexander Wilkin.

1366 *Winona County*

Village of Winona, Minnesota— The charming city of Winona, Minnesota, which is the present county seat of Winona

County, was earlier known as Wapashaw's prairie. That name honored Chief Wapashaw, the last in a succession of hereditary chiefs of Dakota Indians who ruled this area of southeastern Minnesota. Wapashaw prairie's name was subsequently changed to Montezuma, honoring a different Indian. The city's present name, Winona, was suggested by Henry Huff, who bought an interest in the town site in 1853. Winona was used as the name of the first post office here and afterward it was adopted as the name of the village, which grew into the present city of Winona. Minnesota's territorial legislature created Winona County on February 23, 1854, and named it for the village of Winona. The Winona geographic names here derived from a particular legendary Dakota Indian maiden. However, *Winona* is a personal name in the language of the Dakota Indians, for a first-born daughter and there were many first-born female Dakota Indian babies born in this area of southeastern Minnesota. We know that the last Chief Wapashaw (for whom Wapashaw's prairie, which later became Winona, was named) had a cousin named Winona and that her name is mentioned in connection with the 1848 removal of the Winnebago Indians from Iowa to Wapashaw's prairie here. However, the legendary Dakota Indian named Winona, was far more romantic and famous than this cousin of Chief Wapashaw. The main outline of the Winona legend is told easily enough: This legendary Indian maiden is said to have committed suicide by leaping from a high rock (known as "the maiden's rock") on the east side of Lake Pepin, about 50 miles up the Mississippi River from Winona. Lake Pepin is not a true lake but a wide bulge in the Mississippi. This legendary Winona took her own life to escape marrying the man chosen for her by her parents because she loved a different young Indian man. This legend was told as early as 1823 by William Keating and subsequently retold, with embellishments, by Mary Eastman in her 1849 *Life & Legends of the Sioux*. A life-size statue and gravestone-style monument are now on display in downtown Winona. The words chosen for the monument capture the legend this way: "We-no-nah, meaning the first born daughter in the Dakota language, is the namesake for our city and county. Legend tells of her love for a simple hunter instead of the warrior chosen by her father, Chief Wahpashaw. Rather than marry a man she didn't love, We-no-nah climbed to the top of a bluff overlooking the river, proclaimed her true love and jumped to

her death." A longer version of the Winona legend may be found in Lafayette H. Bunnell's work entitled *Winona*, which was published in 1897.

1367 *Wright County*

Silas Wright (1795–1847) A native of Massachusetts and a lawyer, Wright served in the New York senate and, in 1827, he was appointed brigadier-general of the New York state militia. He later represented New York in both houses of the U.S. Congress, serving eleven years in the United States senate. In 1844, Silas Wright, a Democrat, was nominated to run as James K. Polk's vice-presidential running mate but he declined the nomination. He then served one term as governor of New York state. This county was created on February 20, 1855, by the legislature of Minnesota territory. Its name was suggested by W. G. McCrory, who was a member of the three man committee who went to St. Paul to petition the legislature to create this new county. McCrory's first choice for the new county's name had been Seward County, in honor of U.S. Senator William H. Seward (1801–1872) of New York. The other two members of the committee, S. T. Creighton and Samuel McManus, rejected the Seward County suggestion but they were willing to accept McCrory's second choice, Silas Wright, as the county's namesake. McCrory was a native of New York state and he claimed to be an acquaintance of Silas Wright.

1368 *Yellow Medicine County*

Yellow Medicine River— This county on Minnesota's western border with South Dakota was created on March 6, 1871, and named for the Yellow Medicine River which flows through the southeastern section of the county. The Yellow Medicine River is a tributary of the Minnesota River. Its two branches rise in far western Minnesota, near the South Dakota border, and join a bit east of Taunton, Minnesota. From that junction, the remainder of the Yellow Medicine's journey is short. It empties its waters into the Minnesota River about eight miles southeast of Granite Falls, Minnesota, which is the county seat of Yellow Medicine County. Dr. Thomas M. Young has supplied some interesting information on the origin and meaning of Yellow Medicine River's name. Dr. Young at one time was in charge of a government school for Indian children at the Sisseton agency in South Dakota. He learned that the Dakota Indians named this river for a long, slender root to the moonseed (*Menispermum*

canadense), which grew abundantly in thickets in the valley of the Yellow Medicine River. This root is yellow in color and quite bitter to taste. The Indians used it as a medicine.

REFERENCES

Ackermann, Gertrude W. "Joseph Renville of Lac qui Parle." *Minnesota History*, Vol. 12, No. 3. St. Paul: September, 1931.

Andrews, C. C. *History of St. Paul, Minnesota*. Syracuse, New York, D. Mason & Co., 1890.

Baker, James H. "Lives of the Governors of Minnesota." *Collections of the Minnesota Historical Society*, Vol. 13. St. Paul: 1908.

Balmer, Frank E. "The Farmer & Minnesota History." *Minnesota History*, Vol. 7, No. 3. St. Paul: September, 1926.

Beatty, Rob. Letter to the author dated September 22, 1997.

Bentley, James. *A Calendar of Saints: The Lives of the Principal Saints of the Christian Year*. New York, Facts on File Publications, 1986.

Bergstrom, Vernon E. & Marilyn McGriff. *Isanti County, Minnesota: An Illustrated History*. Braham, Minnesota, 1985.

Berthel, Mary W. "Names of the Mille Lacs Region." *Minnesota History*, Vol. 21. St. Paul: 1940.

Biographical Sketches of the Justices of the Minnesota Supreme Court from Territorial Days to 1976.

Bjornson, Val. *The History of Minnesota*. West Palm Beach, Florida, Lewis Historical Publishing Co., Inc., 1969.

Blegen, Theodore C. *The Land Lies Open*. Minneapolis, University of Minnesota Press, 1949.

Blegen, Theodore C. *Minnesota: A History of the State*. Minneapolis, University of Minnesota Press, 1975.

Blegen, Theodore C. "That Name 'Itasca.'" *Minnesota History*, Vol. 13, No. 2. St. Paul: June, 1932.

Brower, J. V. *The Mississippi River and Its Source*. Minneapolis, Harrison & Smith 1893.

Brown, John A. *History of Cottonwood & Watonwan Counties*. Indianapolis, Indiana, B. F. Bowen & Co., Inc., 1916.

Bryant, Charles S. *History of the Sioux Massacre*. Minneapolis, North Star Publishing Co., 1882.

Bunnell, Lafayette. H. *Winona*. Winona, Minnesota, Jones & Kroeger, 1897.

Burnquist, Joseph A. A. *Minnesota and Its People*. Chicago, S. J. Clarke Publishing Co., 1924.

"Capt. Jonathan Carver and His Explorations." *Collections of the Minnesota Historical Society*, Vol. 1. St. Paul: 1902.

Carroll, Francis M. *Crossroads in Time: A History of Carlton County, Minnesota.* Cloquet, Minnesota, Carlton County Historical Society, 1987.

Castle, Henry A. *Minnesota: Its Story & Biography.* Chicago, Lewis Publishing Co., 1915.

The Catholic Encyclopedia. New York, Robert Appleton Co., 1908.

The Centennial History of Cottonwood County, Minnesota: 1970. Cottonwood County Historical Society.

Chaput, Donald E. "A Plea for Moderation in Place-name Controversies." *Michigan History*, Vol. 49, No. 1. Lansing, Michigan: March, 1965.

Christianson, Theodore. "The Long & Beltrami Explorations in Minnesota One Hundred Years Ago." *Minnesota History Bulletin*, Vol. 5, No. 4. St. Paul: November, 1923.

Compendium of History & Biography of Central & Northern Minnesota Containing a History of the State of Minnesota. Chicago, Geo. A. Ogle & Co., 1904.

Corbett, William P. "The Red Pipestone Quarry: The Yanktons Defend a Sacred Tradition, 1858–1929." *South Dakota History*, Vol. 8, No. 2. Pierre, South Dakota: Spring, 1978.

Curtiss-Wedge, Franklyn. *History of Dakota & Goodhue Counties*, Minnesota. Chicago, H. C. Cooper, Jr., & Co., 1910.

Curtiss-Wedge, Franklyn. *The History of Redwood County, Minnesota.* Chicago, H. C. Cooper, Jr., & Co., 1916.

Curtiss-Wedge, Franklyn. *The History of Renville County, Minnesota.* Chicago, H. C. Cooper, Jr., & Co., 1916.

Curtiss-Wedge, Franklyn. *History of Rice & Steele Counties, Minnesota.* Chicago, H. C. Cooper, Jr., & Co., 1910.

Curtiss-Wedge, Franklyn. *The History of Winona County, Minnesota.* Chicago, H. C. Cooper, Jr., & Co., 1913.

Curtiss-Wedge, Franklyn. *History of Wright County, Minnesota.* Chicago, H. C. Cooper, Jr., & Co., 1915.

Dickson, R. "The Fur Trade in Wisconsin: 1812–1825." *Collections of the State Historical Society of Wisconsin*, Vol. 20. Madison: 1911.

"Documents: Selections from the Murray Papers." *Minnesota History Bulletin*, Vol. 1, No. 3. St. Paul: August, 1915.

Englebert, Omer. *The Lives of the Saints.* New York, Barnes & Noble, Inc., 1994.

Fairchild, Henry S. "Memorial Address in Honor of William Pitt Murray." *Collections of the Minnesota Historical Society*, Vol. 15. St. Paul: 1915.

Farmer, David H. *The Oxford Dictionary of Saints.* Oxford, England, Clarendon Press, 1978.

Flandrau, Charles E. *Encyclopedia of Biography of Minnesota.* Chicago, Century Publishing & Engraving Co., 1900.

Folsom, W. H. C. *Fifty Years in the Northwest.* Pioneer Press Co., 1888.

Folwell, William W. *A History of Minnesota.* St. Paul, Minnesota Historical Society, 1956.

French, C. A., & Frank B. Lamson. *Condensed History of Wright County: 1851–1935.* Delano, Minnesota, Eagle Printing Co., 1935.

Fritzen, John. *Historic Sites & Place Names of Minnesota's North Shore.* Duluth, Minnesota, St. Louis County Historical Society, 1974.

"Gazetteer of Pioneers & Others in North Dakota Previous to 1862." *Collections of the State Historical Society of North Dakota*, Vol. 1. Bismarck, North Dakota: 1906.

Goodhue County, Minnesota: Past & Present. Red Wing, Minnesota, Red Wing Printing Co., 1893.

Grant, Bruce. *Concise Encyclopedia of the American Indian.* Avenel, New Jersey, Wings Books, 1989.

Gruchow, Paul. *The Necessity of Empty Places.* New York, St. Martin's Press, 1988.

Hart, Irving H. "The Origin & Meaning of the Name 'Itasca.'" *Minnesota History*, Vol. 12, No. 3. St. Paul: September, 1931.

Hauge, Elder L. J. "Did the Norsemen Visit the Dakota Country?" *South Dakota Historical Collections*, Vol. 4. Sioux Falls, South Dakota: 1908.

Heilbron, Bertha L. *The Thirty-Second State: A Pictorial History of Minnesota.* St. Paul, Minnesota Historical Society, 1966.

Heritage of Faribault County, Minnesota. Tuff Publishing, Inc., 1987.

Hiebert, John M. "Historical Names of Minnesota Counties." *Gopher Historian*, Vol. 9, No. 1. St. Paul: Fall, 1954.

Historical Highlights: State of Washington. Olympia, Belle Reeves, Secretary of State, 1941.

History of the Red River Valley. Chicago, C. F. Cooper & Co., 1909.

History of Steele & Waseca Counties, Minnesota. Chicago, Union Publishing Co., 1887.

History of Winona County. Chicago, H. H. Hill & Co., 1883.

Hodge Frederick W. *Handbook of American Indians North of Mexico.* Totowa, New Jersey, Rowman & Littlefield, 1975.

Holcombe, Return I. *Minnesota in Three Centuries.* Mankato, Minnesota, Publishing Society of Minnesota, 1908.

Holcombe, R. I., & William H. Bingham. *Compendium of History & Biography of Carver & Hennepin Counties, Minnesota.* Chicago, Henry Taylor & Co., 1915.

Holmquist, June D., & Jean A. Brookins. *Minnesota's Major Historic Sites: A Guide.* St. Paul, Minnesota Historical Society, 1972.

Hughes, Thomas. *History of Blue Earth County.* Chicago, Middle West Publishing Co., 1909.

Illustrated Album of Biography of the Famous Valley of the Red River of the North and the Park Regions. Chicago, Alden, Ogle & Co., 1889.

Kane, Lucile M. *The Falls of St. Anthony.* St. Paul, Minnesota Historical Society Press, 1987.

Keller, R. W. "Names that Talk." *Names: Journal of the American Name Society*, Vol. 1, No. 4. Berkeley: December, 1953.

Kennedy, Roger G. *Men on the Moving Frontier.* Palo Alto, California, American West Publishing Co., 1969.

Kiester, J. A. *The History of Faribault County, Minnesota.* Minneapolis, Harrison & Smith, 1896.

Kingsbury, George W. *History of Dakota Territory.* Chicago, S. J. Clarke Publishing Co., 1915.

Kirk, T. H. *Illustrated History of Minnesota.* St. Paul, D. D. Merrill, 1887.

Lamar, Howard R. *The Reader's Encyclopedia of the American West.* New York, Thomas Y. Crowell Co., 1977.

Leitch, Barbara A. *A Concise Dictionary of Indian Tribes of North America.* Algonac, Michigan, Reference Publications, Inc., 1979.

Leland, J. A. C. "Names in Brief: Isanti-Kathio." *Names: Journal of the American Name Society*, Vol. 1, No. 1. Berkeley: March, 1953.

Leland, J. A. C. "Some Eastern Indian Place Names in California." *California Folklore Quarterly*, Vol. 4, No. 4. Berkeley: October, 1945.

Leonard, Joseph A. *History of Olmsted County, Minnesota.* Chicago, Goodspeed Historical Association, 1910.

Livingston, John. *Portraits of Eminent Americans Now Living.* New York, Cornish, Lamport & Co., 1853.

Mason, John W. *History of Otter Tail County, Minnesota.* Indianapolis, Indiana, B. F. Bowen & Co., Inc., 1916.

Mason Philip P. *Schoolcraft's Expedition to Lake Itasca.* East Lansing, Michigan, Michigan State University Press, 1958.

"Meaning of 'Itasca.'" *The Sawmill Gazette*, Grand Rapids, Minnesota, Sawmill Inn.

"Memoir of Hon. David Olmsted."

Collections of the Minnesota Historical Society, Vol. 3. St. Paul: 1880.

"Minnesota Historical Society Notes." *Minnesota History Bulletin*, Vol. 2, No. 7. St. Paul: August, 1918.

Mitchell, William B. *History of Stearns County, Minnesota*. Chicago, H. C. Cooper, Jr., & Co., 1915.

Moss, Henry L. "Biographical Notes of Old Settlers." *Collections of the Minnesota Historical Society*, Vol. 9. St. Paul: 1901.

Moyer, L. R., & O. G. Dale. *History of Chippewa & Lac qui Parle Counties, Minnesota*. Indianapolis, Indiana, B. F. Bowen & Co., Inc., 1916.

Murray, William P. "Recollections of Early Territorial Days & Legislation." *Collections of the Minnesota Historical Society*, Vol. 12. St. Paul: 1908.

Neill, E. D. "A Sketch of Joseph Renville." *Collections of the Minnesota Historical Society*, Vol. 1. St. Paul: 1872.

Neill, Edward D. *The History of Minnesota*. Philadelphia, J. B. Lippincott & Co., 1858.

Neill, Edward D. *History of the Minnesota Valley*. Minneapolis, North Star Publishing Co., 1882.

Neill Edward D. *History of Ramsey County and the City of St. Paul, Including the Explorers & Pioneers of Minnesota*. Minneapolis, North Star Publishing Co., 1881.

Neill, Edward D. *History of Washington County and the St. Croix Valley*. Minneapolis, North Star Publishing Co., 1881.

Neufeld, Jean. "Indian Names of Minnesota Counties." *Gopher Historian*, Vol. 8, No. 2. St. Paul, Winter, 1953–1954.

"News & Comment." *Minnesota History*, Vol. 20, No. 3. St. Paul: September, 1939.

Newson, T. M. *Pen Pictures of St. Paul, Minnesota & Biographical Sketches of Old Settlers*. St. Paul, Brown, Treacy & Co., 1886.

Nute, Grace Lee. "The Diary of Martin McLeod." *Minnesota History Bulletin*, Vol. 4, Nos. 7–8. St. Paul: August–November, 1922.

Official Minnesota Highway Map. Minnesota Department of Transportation & Minnesota Office of Tourism. St. Paul, 1990.

Pederson, Kern O. *Makers of Minnesota*. St. Paul, Marric Publishing Co., 1971.

Peterson Roger T. *A Field Guide to the Birds*. Cambridge, Massachusetts, Riverside Press, 1947.

Pinckney, Roger. "Minnesota's Vikings." *American History*, Vol. 30, No. 6. Harrisburg, Pennsylvania: February, 1996.

Pine County Historical Society. *One Hundred Years in Pine County*. Askov, Minnesota, American Publishing Co., 1949.

Poatgieter, A. Hermina, & James T. Dunn. *Gopher Reader: Minnesota's Story in Words & Pictures: Selections from the Gopher Historian*. St. Paul, Minnesota Historical Society & Minnesota Statehood Centennial Commission, 1966.

Ruff, Willis H. *Pioneers in the Wilderness*. Grand Marais, Minnesota, Cook County Historical Society, 1981.

Renville County History Book: 1980. Dallas, Texas, Taylor Publishing Co., 1981.

Rife, Clarence W. "Norman W. Kittson: A Fur-trader at Pembina." *Minnesota History*, Vol. 6, No. 3. St. Paul: September, 1925.

Riggs, Stephen R. "Dakota Portraits." *Minnesota History Bulletin*, Vol. 2, No. 8. St. Paul: November, 1918.

Robinson, De Lorme W. "Editorial Notes on Historical Sketch of North & South Dakota." *South Dakota Historical Collections*, Vol. 1. Aberdeen, South Dakota: 1902.

Robison, Mabel O. *Minnesota Pioneers*. Minneapolis, T. S. Denison & Co., 1958.

Rolfsrud, Erling N. *The Story of North Dakota*. Alexandria, Minnesota, Lantern Books, 1963.

The Romance of Mendota. Sibley House Association, Minnesota Daughters of the American Revolution, 1939.

Rose, Arthur P. *An Illustrated History of the Counties of Rock & Pipestone, Minnesota*. Luverne, Minnesota, Northern History Publishing Co., 1911.

Rose, Arthur P. *An Illustrated History of Jackson County, Minnesota*. Jackson Minnesota, Northern History Publishing Co., 1910.

Rose, Arthur P. *An Illustrated History of Nobles County, Minnesota*. Worthington, Minnesota, Northern History Publishing Co., 1908.

Rose, Arthur P. *An Illustrated History of Yellow Medicine County, Minnesota*. Marshall, Minnesota, Northern History Publishing Co., 1914.

Rosenfelt, W. E. & Henry Hull. *Minnesota: Its People & Culture*. Minneapolis, T. S. Denison & Co., Inc., 1982.

Rottsolk, James E. *Pines, Mines & Lakes: The Story of Itasca County, Minnesota*. Itasca County Historical Society, 1960.

Schell, Herbert S. *South Dakota: Its Beginnings & Growth*. New York, American Book Co., 1942.

Seelhammer, Cynthia & Mary Jo Mosher. *The Growth of Sherburne County: 1875–1975: As Seen Through Newspapers*. Becker, Minnesota, Sherburne County Historical Society.

Shankle, George Earlie. *State Names, Flags, Seals, Songs, Birds, Flowers & Other Symbols*. New York, H. W. Wilson Co., 1941.

Smith, Julie. "Local Names Have Roots in Indian Lore." *Winona Daily News*, September 5, 1997.

Stanchfield, Daniel. "History of Pioneer Lumbering on the Upper Mississippi & Its Tributaries, with Biographical Sketches." *Collections of the Minnesota Historical Society*, Vol. 9. St. Paul: 1901.

Stennett, William H. *A History of the Origin of the Place Names Connected with the Chicago & North Western & Chicago, St. Paul, Minneapolis & Omaha Railways*. Chicago, 1908.

Stevens, John H. "Recollections of James M. Goodhue." *Collections of the Minnesota Historical Society*, Vol. 6. St. Paul: 1894.

Stewart, George R. *The California Trail*. New York, McGraw-Hill Book Co., Inc., 1962.

Swanson, Roy. *The Minnesota Book of Days*. St. Paul, Perkins-Tracy Printing Co., 1949.

Taft, William H. III. *County Names: An Historical Perspective*. National Association of Counties, 1982.

Thrapp, Dan L. *Encyclopedia of Frontier Biography*. Lincoln, University of Nebraska Press, 1988.

Thurn, Karl, & Helen Thurn. *Round Robin of Kandiyohi County*. Raymond, Minnesota, Raymond Press, 1958.

Turrell, Orlando B. "The Early Settlement & History of Redwood County." *Collections of the Minnesota Historical Society*, Vol. 9. St. Paul: 1901.

The United States Biographical Dictionary: Minnesota Volume. New York, American Biographical Publishing Co., 1879.

Upham, Warren. "Memorial Address in Honor of Governor Lucius Frederick Hubbard." *Collections of the Minnesota Historical Society*, Vol. 15. St. Paul: 1915.

Upham, Warren. "Minnesota County Names." *The Magazine of History*, New York: Vol. 8, No. 3. September, 1908; Vol. 8, No. 4. October, 1908; Vol. 8, No. 5. November, 1908.

Upham, Warren. *Minnesota Geographic Names*. St. Paul, Minnesota Historical Society, 1969.

Upham, Warren. "Minnesota Geographic Names." *Collections of the Minnesota Historical Society*, Vol. 17. St. Paul: 1920.

Upham, Warren, & Mrs. Rose Barteau Dunlap. "Minnesota Biographies: 1655–1912." *Collections of the Minnesota Historical Society*, Vol. 14. St. Paul: 1912.

Van Brunt, Walter. *Duluth & St. Louis County, Minnesota*. Chicago, American Historical Society, 1921.

Varney, Herbert C. "The Birth Notices of a State." *Minnesota History Bulletin*, Vol. 3, No. 2. St. Paul: May, 1919.

Verwyst, Chrysostom. "Geographical Names in Wisconsin, Minnesota & Michigan Having a Chippewa Origin." *Collections of the State Historical Society of Wisconsin*, Vol. 12. Madison, Wisconsin: 1892

Vexler, Robert I. *Chronology & Documentary Handbook of the State of Minnesota*. Dobbs Ferry, New York, Oceana Publications, Inc., 1978.

Vogel, Virgil J. *Indian Names in Michigan*. Ann Arbor, University of Michigan Press, 1986.

Vogel, Virgil J. "Indian Place Names in Illinois." *Journal of the Illinois State Historical Society*, Vol. 55. 1962.

Vogel, Virgil J. *Iowa Place Names of Indian Origin*. Iowa City, University of Iowa Press, 1983

Wahlberg, Hazel H. *The North Land: A History of Roseau County*. Roseau County Historical Society, 1975.

Waters, Thomas F. *The Streams & Rivers of Minnesota*. Minneapolis, University of Minnesota Press, 1977.

Webb, Walter P., et al. *The Handbook of Texas*. Austin, Texas State Historical Association, 1952.

Webb, Wayne E., & J. I. Swedberg. *Redwood: The Story of a County*. St. Paul, North Central Publishing Co., 1964.

West, Mrs. Jessie C. *A Pioneer History of Becker County, Minnesota*. St. Paul, Pioneer Press Co., 1907.

Wheelhouse, Mary E. "The History of Central Minnesota: A Survey of Unpublished Sources." *Minnesota History*, Vol. 9, No. 3. St. Paul: September, 1928.

Wilkin County Family History Book: 1977: A History of Wilkin County, Minnesota. Breckenridge, Minnesota, Wilkin County, Historical Society, 1977.

Williams, J. Fletcher. *A History of the City of St. Paul to 1875*. St. Paul, Minnesota Historical Society Press, 1983.

Williams, J. Fletcher. *Outlines of the History of Minnesota*. Minneapolis, North Star Publishing Co., 1881.

Williams, John F. "Our County Names: For What or for Whom Each County in Minnesota Was Named." *Saint Paul Pioneer*, March 13, 1870.

Willson, Charles C. "The Successive Chiefs Named Wabasha." *Collections of the Minnesota Historical Society*, Vol. 12. St. Paul: 1908.

Wise, L. F., & E. W. Egan. *Kings, Rulers & Statesmen*. New York, Sterling Publishing Co., Inc., 1967.

Woodbridge, Dwight E. & John S. Pardee. *History of Duluth & St. Louis County: Past & Present*. Chicago, C. F. Cooper & Co., 1910.

Work Projects Administration. *Guide to Historical Markers Erected by the State Highway Department Cooperating with the Minnesota Historical Society*. St. Paul, 1940.

Work Projects Administration. *Inventory of the County Archives of Minnesota*. St. Paul: 1939–1942.
— Aitkin County
— Anoka County
— Beltrami County
— Big Stone County
— Chippewa County
— Goodhue County
— Jackson County
— Martin County
— Meeker County
— Mille Lacs County
— Morrison County
— Murray County
— Nobles County
— Rock County

Work Projects Administration. *Kittson County: (A School History)*. 1940.

Work Projects Administration. *The Mayors of St. Paul: 1850–1940*. 1940.

Works Progress Administration. *Inventory of the County Archives of Minnesota*. St. Paul: 1938–1939.
— Faribault County
— Nicollet County
— Olmsted County
— Traverse County
— Wabasha County

Yenne, Bill. *The Encyclopedia of North American Indian Tribes*. New York, Crescent Books, 1986.

Mississippi

(82 counties)

1369 *Adams County*

John Adams (1735–1826)— Adams, a native of Massachusetts, was a delegate to the first Continental Congress and a signer of the Declaration of Independence. He participated in Paris, with Benjamin Franklin and John Jay in negotiating peace with England and, after the war, he was our country's first minister to England. Adams became the first vice-president of the United States under George Washington and when Washington retired, Adams was elected to be our nation's second president. This county was created in 1799, while John Adams was president.

1370 *Alcorn County*

James L. Alcorn (1816–1894)— A native of Illinois, Alcorn was raised in Kentucky and served in that state's legislature. While still a young man, he moved to Mississippi where he practiced law and served in both houses of the Mississippi legislature. In 1857 Alcorn ran against Lucius Q. C. Lamar (1825–1893) for a seat in the U.S. house of representatives. At that time the possibility of Mississippi seceding from the Union over the slavery issue was a key political issue and Alcorn's opposition to session contributed to his losing the congressional election to Lamar. Although he had opposed secession, when Mississippi's secession ordinance passed, Alcorn reluctantly signed it. He declined a seat in the Confederate congress to seek a commission as a brigadier-general in the Confederate army. He was permitted little field service on account of his lack of military training. When the Civil War ended, Alcorn was elected to represent Mississippi in the U.S. Senate but he was denied his seat in that body. During Reconstruction Alcorn was installed, with the support of the carpetbagger military governor, Adelbert Ames (1835–1933), as governor of Mississippi. Alcorn had been serving as Mississippi's governor just one month when this county was created and named in his honor on April 15, 1870. He later represented Mississippi in the U.S. Senate.

1371 *Amite County*

Amite River— The Amite River consists of two branches, both of which flow southward across Amite County. These two branches, or forks, merge just south of the Mississippi state border, in Louisiana. From that junction, the Amite River flows south across Louisiana bayou country, and finally empties its waters into Lake Maurepas, near New Orleans. The source of the river's name is uncertain. The vast majority of sources dealing with the history and geography of Mississippi state that the name was given to the river by the French, in commemoration of the friendly manner in which they had been received by the local Indians. The French word *amitie* means "friendship." However, in a 1939 Louisiana State University doctoral thesis on Indian place names in Mississippi, Lea L. Seale suggests the possibility that the name may be of Indian origin. Both Seale and Dr. William A. Read, an authority on Indian names in Louisiana and Mississippi, suggest that the popular notion that *amite* came from the French may merely have been the result of the similar appearance of the river's name to the French word *amitie*, for "friendship."

1372 *Attala County*

Atala, the fictive American Indian heroine— In 1791 the French writer and statesman, Francois Rene, Vicomte de Chateaubriand (1768–1848), visited the brand new United States of America. In 1801 he wrote a romantic tale about Atala, which featured a fictive American Indian heroine of that name. Chateaubriand's inspiration for that work came from his brief (1791–1792) visit to our country. The tale was translated into English in 1818 entitled *The Interesting History of Atala, the Beautiful Indian of the Mississippi, with Explanatory Notes, Exhibiting Singular Customs of the Natives, Forest Scenery &c.* In spite of the long-winded title, the story enjoyed sufficient popularity in America to serve as the namesake for this Mississippi county when it was created in 1833. However, there was a clerical error in transcribing the name. Attala County has two "t's" while the heroine of Chateaubriand's work had only one "t" in her name. That error has never been corrected.

1373 *Benton County*

Samuel Benton (1820–1864)— Benton was a native of Tennessee, and was a school teacher there. He later moved to Mississippi and settled in Holly Springs. Here he became a prominent lawyer and was active in local politics. Benton served in the Mississippi state legislature and was a member of Mississippi's secession convention of 1861. He served as an officer in the Confederate army during the Civil War and rose from the rank of captain to colonel. During the battle of Atlanta, on July 22, 1864, Colonel Benton was mortally wounded in combat. One foot was amputated in a vain attempt to save his life and Benton died six days later. He was granted a posthumous promotion to the rank of brigadier-general, back dated to July 26, 1864. Although this county was created on July 21, 1870, during Reconstruction, its name honors one of the Confederacy's military heroes.

1374 *Bolivar County*

Simon Bolivar (1783–1830)— This South American soldier, revolutionary leader and liberator is called by some the George Washington of South America. He was born in Caracas, Venezuela and his early efforts to overthrow South America's European rulers began in that Spanish colony. He scored some significant victories in Venezuela before he was defeated and forced to flee. After a series of attempts, Bolivar and his supporters finally succeeded in liberating Venezuela and soon defeated the Spanish in Colombia, as well. Simon Bolivar was installed as the president of Colombia. Other South American colonies soon fell to Bolivar and his liberation armies. He freed Peru from Spain, was made president of Peru and a new country was formed, which was named Bolivia, in his honor. This Mississippi county was created and named in Simon Bolivar's honor on February 9, 1836, less than six years after his death.

1375 *Calhoun County*

John C. Calhoun (1782–1850)— Calhoun represented South Carolina in both houses of the U.S. Congress. He served as secretary of war, secretary of state and as vice-president. He was a forceful advocate of slavery, states' rights and limited powers for the federal government. He resigned the vice-presidency to enter the U.S. Senate where he thought he could better represent the views of South Carolina and the South. This county was created and named in his honor on March 8, 1852, just two years after his death.

1376 *Carroll County*

Charles Carroll (1737–1832)— Carroll was a native of Maryland and he represented that state in the Continental Congress. He was one of the signers of the Declaration of Independence and he later represented Maryland as a U.S. senator in the first congress of the United States. Carroll lived to be the last surviving signer of the Declaration of Independence and several states recognized that distinction by naming counties for him. This certainly was Mississippi's motivation. Carroll County, Mississippi was created and named in his honor on December 23, 1833, just 13 months after his death, on November 14, 1832.

1377 *Chickasaw County*

Chickasaw Indians— The Chickasaw Indians were an important warlike tribe whose main home was in northern Mississippi and western Tennessee along the Yazoo, Tombigbee, Tallahatchie and Mississippi Rivers. Their principal landing place on the Mississippi was where the city of Memphis, Tennessee is now located. An outlying colony of Chickasaw Indians had earlier lived on the Savannah River near what is now the city of Augusta, Georgia, but trouble with the Creeks drove them westward again. Beginning in the 1830's, the Chickasaws were removed to Indian territory (now Oklahoma). Although they belong the Muskhogean linguistic family, whose other members are the Creek, Choctaw and Seminole Indians, they were hostile to neighboring Muskhogean tribes. The Chickasaw Indians were also extremely hostile to French settlers. The meaning of the name *Chickasaw* is uncertain. This Mississippi county was created on February 9, 1836 from part of the territory which had been ceded by the Chickasaws to the United States by the treaty of Pontotoc in October, 1832.

1378 *Choctaw County*

Choctaw Indians— The Choctaw Indians were a large and relatively peaceful tribe who lived in the southern portions of Mississippi and Alabama, including the area embraced by this county. Choctaw County, Mississippi was created on December 23, 1833, from a portion of the land ceded by the Choctaws to the United States in the 1830 treaty of Dancing Rabbit Creek. After ceding their lands to the United States in the 1830's, the majority of Choctaw Indians moved to Indian territory (now Oklahoma).

1379 *Claiborne County*

William C. C. Claiborne (1775–1817)— A native of Virginia and a lawyer, Claiborne moved to Tennessee when it was still a territory. There he practiced law and served in Tennessee's constitutional convention of 1796. When Tennessee was admitted to statehood, Claiborne served briefly on the supreme court of the new state but he was soon elected to represent Tennessee in the U.S. House of Representatives. Thomas Jefferson became president of the United States in March, 1801, and a few months later he appointed Claiborne to be governor of Mississippi territory. This county was created by Mississippi territory on January 27, 1802, while Claiborne was serving as the territory's governor. When the United States acquired Louisiana from France in the Louisiana Purchase, President Jefferson appointed Claiborne, along with General James Wilkinson (1757–1825) to represent our country at the ceremonial transfer of Louisiana from France to our country. Claiborne was later appointed governor-general and intendent of the U.S. province of Louisiana. In that capacity he acted, for all practical purposes, as a benign dictator of Louisiana. He subsequently was appointed governor of Orleans territory and he served in that position until 1812, when Louisiana was admitted to the Union as a state. Claiborne was then elected as the new state's first governor and he held that office until 1816. In January, 1817, Claiborne was elected to represent Louisiana in the U.S. Senate but he died before taking his seat in that body.

1380 *Clarke County*

Joshua G. Clarke (–1828)— A native of Pennsylvania, Clarke came to Mississippi prior to its admission to statehood and practiced law here. He represented Claiborne County in Mississippi's territorial legislature and was chosen to be one of Claiborne County's four delegates to Mississippi's 1817 constitutional convention. In 1818 he was elected as one of the judges of Mississippi's state supreme court, succeeding William B. Shields, who resigned to preside over the United States district court. On November 27, 1821, the Mississippi legislature, by a unanimous vote, chose Joshua G. Clarke to be the first chancellor of Mississippi's supreme court of chancery. Clarke held that position until his death at Port Gibson on July 23, 1828. This county was created in 1833, five years after Judge Clarke's death.

1381 *Clay County*

Henry Clay (1777–1852)— Clay represented Kentucky in both branches of the U.S. Congress. For many years he was one of the more prominent figures in American politics but his several bids for the presidency were unsuccessful. He was influential in effecting important compromises between northern and southern interests during the years that secession and civil war were imminent. This county was originally created on May 12, 1871, while Reconstruction ruled Mississippi. It was named Colfax County, in honor for Schuyler Colfax (1823–1885), who was then serving as vice-president under the Union army's hero, President Ulysses S. Grant. By 1876 the carpetbaggers and scalawags no longer controlled Mississippi's government. This county's name was changed from Colfax to Clay on April 10, 1876, to honor a man whose memory was held in esteem in post–Reconstruction Mississippi.

1382 *Coahoma County*

Uncertain— This county in northwestern Mississippi was created on February 9, 1836. The name is of Indian origin and essentially all sources consulted indicate that the name means "red panther." In a 1939 Louisiana State University doctoral thesis on Indian place names in Mississippi, Lea L. Seale states that according to an earlier authority, named Harry Warren, the name meant "red panther" but honored a Choctaw Indian chief who was also known as William McGillivray. In Linton Weeks' 1982 history of Clarksdale and Coahoma County, the suggestion is made that the name Coahoma was taken from that of a beautiful Choctaw Indian princess who was the daughter of a chief named Sheriff. The Sheriff family is said to have lived on Purvis Lake, whose name was subsequently changed to Mackey Lake. We are told that the pioneers referred to this beautiful Indian princess as "Sweet Coahoma." Weeks suggests that the author of the name of this county may have been Mississippi's Governor Alexander G. McNutt. McNutt was a member of the Mississippi senate before he became governor and it was while he was serving in the state senate that this county's name was chosen and adopted. In their 1898 work entitled *A History of Mississippi for Use in Schools*, Robert Lowry and William H. McCardle also state that Alexander G. McNutt was the author of this county's name.

1383 *Copiah County*

Indian words for "screaming panther"— This county was created on January 21, 1823, and given a name from the Choctaw Indians' language. In their tongue, *koi* mean "panther" while *panya* meant "to scream" or "to cry out."

1384 *Covington County*

Leonard W. Covington (1773–1813)— Covington was a native of Maryland who represented that state in the U.S. House of Representatives. He was a general in the War of 1812 and he was killed in combat in that war in the battle of Chrysler's Farm, near Morrisburg, Ontario, Canada. Before Covington's promotion to general and before the War of 1812, he had served in the U.S. army for a period of time in Mississippi territory. This county was created and named in his honor on February 5, 1819.

1385 *De Soto County*

Hernando De Soto (1500–1542)— This county in Mississippi's northwestern corner, bordering on the Mississippi River, was created on February 9, 1836, and named for the famous Spanish conquistador, who was one of Europe's early explorers of the Americas and the discoverer of the Mississippi River. Following successful campaigns in Central America, De Soto was prominent in the conquest of the Inca empire in Peru. In 1539 De Soto landed in Florida and, in a futile search for riches, he and his men explored Florida and a large area of the southeastern United States, torturing and slaughtering Indians as they went. De Soto and his party spent the winter of 1540–1541 in what is now Mississippi and it was while they were in the northwestern corner of the present state of Mississippi that De Soto's expedition discovered the Mississippi River.

1386 *Forrest County*

Nathan B. Forrest (1821–1877)— A native of Tennessee, Forrest became responsible for the support of his family while he was in his mid-teens and he received little formal education. He was, however, an astute businessman and he worked his way up from farm hand to owner of a cotton plantation in northwestern Mississippi. He became a very wealthy man. At the outbreak of the Civil War, Forrest was eager to fight to defend the South's feudal society and he enlisted as a private in the army of the Confederate States of America. In that army he gained rank rapidly in recognition of his brilliance as a military leader. Early in the war, Forrest was promoted to lieutenant-colonel as a reward for raising a cavalry battalion on his own. His subsequent promotions were rapid and all were awarded for his outstanding military leadership. He was promoted to full colonel for his part in the defense of Fort Donelson (February, 1862), to brigadier-general for Shiloh (April, 1862) and to major-general for a wide variety of raids and battles including his role at Chickamauga (September, 1863). Forrest's final promotion, to lieutenant-general resulted largely from his greatest military victory, at Brice's Cross Roads, Mississippi (June, 1864). Some pronounce him one of the finest cavalry officers ever produced in America. Clearly he was an uniquely able military leader but it is also without question that he was a racist. In his early manhood he was a slave trader and on his Mississippi cotton plantation, slave labor produced his wealth. After the Civil War, Forrest was a leading organizer of the Ku Klux Klan and he held the rank of grand wizard in this evil organization. This Mississippi county was created early in the 20th century, on April 19, 1906.

1387 *Franklin County*

Benjamin Franklin (1706–1790) — Franklin was a native of Massachusetts who moved to Pennsylvania in his teens. Poverty denied him a formal education but he became the leading printer and editor in North America. Franklin gained fame for his discoveries and inventions in the physical sciences and he distinguished himself as author, philosopher and diplomat. Franklin was a signer of the Declaration of Independence and an important member of the convention which framed the U.S. Constitution. This county was formed on December 21, 1809, while Mississippi was still a territory.

1388 *George County*

James Z. George (1826–1897) — A native of Georgia, James Zachariah George moved with his family to Mississippi in 1834. He studied law and was admitted to the Mississippi bar when he was only 20 years old. George served as a private in the U.S. army during the Mexican War under Colonel Jefferson Davis (1808–1889). In 1861 George was a delegate to Mississippi's secession convention where he served as one of 15 members who drafted the ordinance providing for the withdrawal of Mississippi from the United States in anticipation of joining with other seceding states to form the Confederate States of America. During the Civil War he served as an officer in the Confederate army but was captured and taken as a prisoner of war. George remained a prisoner of the Union

army until the end of the war between the states. He then resumed his legal practice in Mississippi. In 1875 George became chairman of the state executive committee of the Democratic party and under his leadership, the carpetbagger government which had been installed during Reconstruction, was overthrown in Mississippi. Majority rule ended, and White supremacy and repression of Blacks returned. In 1878 he was appointed to Mississippi's supreme court and that body elected him as their chief justice. Subsequently elected to represent Mississippi in the U.S. Senate, George was serving his third term in that body when he died on August 14, 1897. This county was created and named in his honor on March 16, 1910.

1389 *Greene County*

Nathanael Greene (1742–1786) — Greene was born in Rhode Island and served briefly in the Rhode Island legislature. He gained fame as one of the ablest American generals in the Revolutionary War. After the war he moved to Georgia. This county was created on December 9, 1811, while Mississippi was a territory.

1390 *Grenada County*

City of Grenada, Mississippi — According to one account, the name for the city of Grenada, Mississippi was suggested by John Balfour, an old river ferryman of Spanish ancestry. Another source says that a physician, Dr. Allen Gillespie (1801–1869) suggested the name. Some accounts indicate that Grenada was first used as the name for this Mississippi municipality in 1836, when two rival towns, Pittsburg, Mississippi, and Tullahoma, Mississippi, were united to form the new city of Grenada. However, other sources allege that the name Grenada was already being used as the name for the former town of Tullahoma in 1835, the year before Pittsburg and Tullahoma were united. In any event, on May 9, 1870, when this county was created, it was named for the city of Grenada, Mississippi, which was declared its county seat. All Mississippi sources consulted are agreed that the inspiration for the name came from Spain and its province and city of Granada. Therefore, the spelling of the name of both the city of Grenada, Mississippi, and Grenada County, Mississippi, are in error because the Spanish namesake is spelled Granada. This error is easy to understand if the John Balfour origin of the name is accepted because Balfour is said to have suggested the name orally at a 4th of July picnic in 1836. This oral sug-

gestion could very easily have been transcribed as Grenada for the city's name and then perpetuated in the county's name when it was created in 1870.

Granada, Spain — The city of Granada, Spain lies at the foot of the Sierra Nevada mountains in Granada province, Spain and the province borders on the Mediterranean Sea. The settlement here at one time belonged to the Roman empire but it did not become important until it came under the control of the Moors, from Africa. The city of Granada was the capital of the Moorish kingdom of Granada and Granada later became the Moors' final stronghold in Spain before it fell to Christian forces in 1492. The Moors' palace in Granada, the Alhambra, is one of many important tourist attractions in the ancient city of Granada.

1391 *Hancock County*

John Hancock (1737–1793) — A native of Massachusetts and a graduate of Harvard, Hancock served in the Massachusetts legislature and was president of the Massachusetts provincial congress. He was elected to the Second Continental Congress and became its president. As president of the Continental Congress when the Declaration of Independence was signed, he was, on July 4, 1776, the first signer of that document. He signed it with such a flourish that the name John Hancock became a synonym for "signature." He later commanded the Massachusetts militia, served as governor of that state for many years and presided over the Massachusetts convention that ratified the U.S. Constitution. This county was created on December 18, 1812, by the legislature of Mississippi territory, while America was fighting its second war for independence from England, the War of 1812.

1392 *Harrison County*

William H. Harrison (1773–1841) — William Henry Harrison was a native of Virginia whose early career was in the army, serving as an officer in actions against the Indians. In 1798 President John Adams appointed Harrison to be secretary of Northwest territory and the following year he became that territory's delegate to the U.S. Congress. In 1800 Indiana territory was created and President John Adams appointed Harrison to be the new territory's first governor. Harrison commanded the army in the Battle of Tippecanoe and he served in the War of 1812 rising to the rank of major-general. He later served in the Ohio state legislature and represented

Ohio in both houses of the U.S. Congress. In December, 1839, Harrison became the Whig party's candidate for president of the United States with John Tyler as his vice-presidential running mate. Their famous slogan was "Tippecanoe and Tyler too." Harrison was elected president but he served only one month before dying. This county was created on February 5, 1841, and named in honor of President-elect Harrison, who took office as our nation's president one month later, on March 4, 1841.

1393 *Hinds County*

Thomas Hinds (1780–1840)— Hinds was born in Virginia but moved to Greenville, Mississippi, before serving as a cavalry major in the War of 1812. As a reward for his gallantry at the Battle of New Orleans, he was given the rank of brevet brigadier-general. In late 1820 or early 1821 the Mississippi legislature decided that the state's capitol should be located near the center of the state and a three member commission was appointed to select a suitable site for the capital city of Mississippi. The members of that commission were General Thomas Hinds, William Lattimore and James Patton. They selected the site of the present city of Jackson to be the state's capital city. On February 12, 1821, the Mississippi legislature chose to honor the chairman of that site selection committee by creating and naming Hinds County for the lands surrounding Jackson. (General Hinds had previously assisted General Andrew Jackson in obtaining a huge tract of land in this area for the United States from the Choctaw Indians.) Hinds later represented Mississippi in the U.S. House of Representatives, serving from October 21, 1828, until March 3, 1831.

1394 *Holmes County*

David Holmes (1770–1832)— A native of Pennsylvania, Holmes moved to Virginia in his youth. There he practiced law and became active in local politics. He represented the state of Virginia in the U.S. House of Representatives from 1797 to 1809. President James Madison appointed Holmes to be governor of Mississippi territory and he held that office from March, 1809, until October, 1817. He was Mississippi's last territorial governor. By the time the territory had been admitted to statehood on December 10, 1817, the popular territorial governor had been elected to be Mississippi's first state governor. He later represented Mississippi in the U.S. Senate and subsequently served as Mississippi's

fifth state governor. This term was truncated after just a few months on account of Governor Holmes' failing health. Governor Holmes died on August 20, 1832, and this county was created just six months later, on February 19, 1833.

1395 *Humphreys County*

Benjamin G. Humphreys (1808–1882)— This native of Mississippi territory was admitted to the U.S. Military Academy at West Point, where he was a classmate of Robert E. Lee (1807–1870). However, Humphreys failed to graduate because he and several other students were dismissed for breach of discipline. He served in both houses of the Mississippi legislature and in 1861 he entered the army of the Confederate States of America. He served with distinction throughout the Civil War and rose in rank from captain to brigadier-general. When the war ended, Humphreys was elected as governor of Mississippi. He served as the state's governor until June 15, 1868, when he was physically ejected from his office by an armed force on orders from the military commander of Reconstruction Mississippi. This county is one of our nation's younger counties. It was not created until 1918.

1396 *Issaquena County*

Mississippi's Deer Creek— The name *Issaquena* derived from the Choctaw Indians' words *isi* for "deer" and *okhina*, which meant "stream" or "creek." The Choctaw Indians applied that name to a creek in the central portion of western Mississippi. That creek's name has been anglicized to Deer Creek but when the Mississippi legislature created a new county in this area on January 23, 1844, the Choctaw Indians' version of the name was preserved in the new county's name.

1397 *Itawamba County*

Levi Colbert (–1834)— Colbert was of mixed French and Chickasaw Indian ancestry. The Chickasaw called him Itawamba-Minco, an honorary name which was given when he was a youth of 16. He was given this honorary name for bravery in organizing the Chickasaws to defend themselves against an invasion by a party of Indians from another tribe. Although Colbert was only 16 when this incident occurred, it fell to him to organize the defense because all the Chickasaw warriors were absent on a hunting expedition. Levi Colbert organized the old men, women and children and they successfully with-

stood the attack. During the 1820's Colbert encouraged Presbyterian missionaries to build a mission school for his people in Mississippi to better educate them to deal with the pressures of White expansion into their country. Shortly before his death he was made an unofficial chairman of the Chickasaw's board, or council. Colbert died in 1834 and the Mississippi legislature created and named this county in his honor on February 9, 1836.

1398 *Jackson County*

Andrew Jackson (1767–1845)— Jackson was born on the border of North Carolina and South Carolina. He represented Tennessee in both branches of the U.S. Congress. He gained fame and popularity for his military exploits in wars with the Indians and in the War of 1812. He was provisional military governor of Florida and, from 1829 to 1837, General Jackson was president of the United States. His presidency reflected the frontier spirit of America. This county was created in December, 1812, when Mississippi was still a territory.

1399 *Jasper County*

William Jasper (–1779)— This Revolutionary War hero was born in South Carolina about 1750, but moved to Georgia where he grew up on a farm. He first became a hero in a dramatic event at the battle of Fort Moultrie, when he courageously exposed himself to enemy fire to recover a flag which had been shot down. For this heroism Sergeant Jasper was awarded a sword and offered a promotion to lieutenant but he declined the promotion. Later employed as a scout, Jasper made several trips behind enemy lines in Georgia while operating from the swamps there. In a dramatic exploit near Savannah, Georgia, he and his close friend, John Newton, rescued several Americans who were prisoners and took their guards as prisoners of war. Jasper was shot and killed during the siege of Savannah while recovering the flag which had been shot down. This county was created and named in Sergeant Jasper's honor in 1833.

1400 *Jefferson County*

Thomas Jefferson (1743–1826)— Jefferson was a native of Virginia and a member of the Virginia legislature. He served Virginia as governor and was a delegate to the second Continental Congress. Jefferson was the author of the Declaration of Independence and one of its signers. He was minister to France, secretary of state, vice-president and president of the United States. As president, he accomplished the Louisiana Purchase and he arranged the Lewis and Clark Expedition to the Pacific Northwest. Jefferson was a true intellectual, thoroughly knowledgeable in the arts and sciences. His political theories were pivotal in the formation of our infant republic. This county named in his honor in 1802, while Mississippi was a territory and while Thomas Jefferson was serving as our nation's president.

1401 *Jefferson Davis County*

Jefferson Davis (1808–1889)— A native of Kentucky, Davis moved with his family to Mississippi when he was a small boy. He graduated from the U.S. military academy at West Point and served as an officer in the Black Hawk and Mexican Wars. He represented Mississippi in both houses of the United States congress where he was a spokesman for the South, states' rights and strict construction of the constitution. President Franklin Pierce appointed Davis to his cabinet as secretary of war and he served in that position from 1853 to 1857. In February, 1861 Jefferson Davis was inaugurated as president of the Confederate States of America. He was the first and only president that the Confederacy had, and he served in that post until the end of the Civil War in 1865. This Mississippi county was created and named in his honor in 1906.

1402 *Jones County*

John P. Jones (1747–1792)— A native of Scotland, John Paul Jones immigrated to America when he was a youth of only twelve and he was employed here in a variety of merchant marine activities. By the time the Continental navy was founded for the Revolutionary War, Jones was an experienced seaman. In December, 1775, he was commissioned as a senior lieutenant and assigned to the Continental navy's frigate *Alfred*. In 1778 a vessel under his command captured the English sloop *Drake*. This was the first surrender of a British warship to a Continental vessel. In 1779, during an apparently lost naval engagement against the British frigate *Serapis*, John Paul Jones was asked to surrender. Legend has it that it was on this occasion that he uttered the famous reply "I have not yet begun to fight." In any event, Jones did manage to snatch victory from the jaws of defeat by capturing the *Serapis* with his outmanned and outgunned forces. Jones survived the Revolutionary

War and died in Paris, France on a mission to ransom American captives in the hands of Algiers. This county was created in 1826.

1403 *Kemper County*

Uncertain Sources consulted disagree on whether this county was named for Reuben Kemper (–1827) or for three Kemper brothers, Reuben, Nathan and Samuel Kemper (–1815). There were an additional four brothers in the Kemper family: James, George, Presley and Stephen, but nobody has suggested that this county's name might honor any of them. Most sources state that this county was named for Reuben Kemper alone. Reuben, Nathan and Samuel Kemper were born in Virginia and moved with their father to Ohio in 1800. By 1801 the Kemper brothers, were living in the vicinity of Pinckneyville in Mississippi territory, and they were described as tall, large and nasty. In Dunbar Rowland's *History of Mississippi: The Heart of the South*, Reuben Kemper is described as "…of a somewhat reckless and fiery disposition, but intensely patriotic…" The Kemper brothers' homes were within territory of the United States but just a few miles away from Spain's West Florida and apparently the Kemper brothers made a good deal of trouble along the border between Spanish West Florida and the United States. On August 7, 1804, they invaded Spanish territory but found no residents willing to join with them in proclaiming an independent West Florida. On August 11, 1804, Spain's representative in West Florida sent a letter to Mississippi's territorial governor William C. C. Claiborne (1775–1817) complaining that the Kemper brothers were constantly threatening Spain's peaceful inhabitants along the border with the United States. In reply, Governor Claiborne stated that any insurgents in West Florida had received no encouragement from the United States and that non-intervention in West Florida would continue to be the strictly enforced policy of the United States. On September 3, 1805, armed parties broke into the residences of the three Kemper brothers and carried them across the border into Spanish West Florida. They were eventually rescued by a party of American soldiers and returned to Mississippi territory. Agitation along this troubled border continued and in September, 1810, the West Floridians declared their independence from Spain, and proclaimed the Republic of West Florida. They also requested annexation by the United States. On October 27, 1810, President Madison issued a

proclamation claiming U.S. ownership of the western portion of West Florida, between the Mississippi and Perdido Rivers. The Kemper brothers' armed rebellion against Spanish authority in West Florida hastened the actual annexation of this territory to the U.S. This county was created on December 23, 1833.

1404 *Lafayette County*

Marie Joseph Paul Yves Roch Gilbert du Motier, Marquis de Lafayette (1757–1834)— Lafayette was a French aristocrat who served briefly in the French army. He came to America in 1777 to assist the American Revolutionary army. He was granted an honorary commission as major general by the Continental Congress and served with distinction in a number of battles in the Revolutionary War. This county was formed in 1836.

1405 *Lamar County*

Lucius Q. C. Lamar (1825–1893)— Lamar, a native of Georgia, served in the Georgia legislature before moving to Mississippi and representing this state in both houses of the U.S. Congress. He was an officer in the Confederate army. After the Civil War, he was a spokesman for sectional reconciliation for which he was admired in both the North and the South. He served in the U.S. cabinet as secretary of the interior and was an associate justice on the U.S. Supreme Court. Lamar County, Mississippi was created in 1904.

1406 *Lauderdale County*

James Lauderdale (–1814)— Lauderdale was a native of Virginia who moved to western Tennessee. He was an officer in the army and was wounded while serving under General Andrew Jackson against the Creek Indians in the battle of Talladega, Alabama. He later served in the War of 1812 and he died in combat in that war. This county was created and named in his honor on December 23, 1833.

1407 *Lawrence County*

James Lawrence (1781–1813)— Lawrence was an officer in the United States navy who established a reputation for bravery in the war against Tripoli and in the War of 1812. He died in combat while commanding the *Chesapeake* against the British, near Boston. He is said to have uttered the famous phrase "Don't give up the ship" while he lay mortally wounded in that battle. He died on June 4, 1813, and this county was created on December 22, 1814.

1408 *Leake County*

Walter Leake (1762–1825)— Leake was a native of Virginia and he served in the legislature of that state. President Thomas Jefferson appointed him as a federal judge in Mississippi territory and when Mississippi was admitted to statehood in 1817, Judge Leake became one of the new state's first two United States senators. He resigned from the senate in 1821 to run for the Mississippi governor's office and he was elected to that post on August 6, 1821. He served as Mississippi's third state governor from January 7, 1822, until his death in office on November 17, 1825. This county was created on December 23, 1833.

1409 *Lee County*

Robert E. Lee (1807–1870)— Lee was a native of Virginia and, for over 30 years, an officer in the United States army. When Virginia seceded from the Union, Lee refused an offer to command all federal forces and resigned from the U.S. army to accept a commission in the Confederate army. He served with distinction in that army and became general-in-chief of it. By April, 1865, the Confederacy had lost the war and Robert E. Lee surrendered to the commanding general of the Union forces, Ulysses S. Grant. This county was created on October 26, 1866.

1410 *Leflore County*

Greenwood Leflore (1800–1865)— Leflore's father was a French-Canadian named Louis Le Fleur (rendered in some accounts as La Fleur) and his mother was a Choctaw Indian, whose surname was Cravat. Greenwood changed his surname to Leflore. Said to have been an intelligent child, Leflore received some schooling in Tennessee. This education combined with his native intelligence and some considerable business savvy enabled him to become a very wealthy man. He acquired large amounts of land in Mississippi and a partial interest in an enormous tract of land in Texas. His Mississippi land included a large cotton plantation cultivated by some 400 Black slaves whom Greenwood Leflore owned. Leflore was serving as the chief of the western district of the Choctaw Indian nation during the period that the Whites were planning to move the entire Choctaw nation to Indian territory (now Oklahoma). Leflore recognized that there was no way to avert this removal of his people but he held out for the best terms that he could get. His compromise ideas formed a portion of the 1830 treaty of Dancing Rabbit

Creek. Under the terms of that treaty, the entire Choctaw nation was moved to Indian territory. Although Leflore was one of the three principal Choctaw chiefs who signed the treaty, he did not move with his people to Indian territory. He stayed in Mississippi where he was elected to the state senate. When Mississippi seceded from the federal Union, Leflore's sympathies and actions were with the Union side and he refused to ally himself with the Confederacy. This county was created in 1871. The county seat of Leflore County was named Greenwood, in his honor.

1411 *Lincoln County*

Abraham Lincoln (1809–1865)— Lincoln was a native of Kentucky who moved to Illinois where he was a member of the state legislature. He represented Illinois in the house of representatives and later was elected president of the United States. Lincoln's presidency coincided almost exactly with the Civil War. He guided the United States ably through that uniquely turbulent period. As president, he issued the Emancipation Proclamation which declared the freedom of slaves in all states in rebellion. Lincoln was assassinated in 1865, a few days after the Union victory in the Civil War. This county was created and named in 1870, while Mississippi was under the harsh military Reconstruction rule imposed after the Civil War by the victorious northern states.

1412 *Lowndes County*

William J. Lowndes (1782–1822)— Lowndes was a native of South Carolina and he served in the legislature of that state. He represented South Carolina for 12 years in the U.S. House of Representatives including three years as chairman of the ways and means committee. Lowndes County, Mississippi, was created in 1830.

1413 *Madison County*

James Madison (1751–1836)— Madison was born in Virginia and served in the Virginia legislature and in the Continental Congress. He was a member of the convention which framed the U.S. Constitution and he collaborated with Hamilton and Jay in writing a series of papers under the title *The Federalist*, which explained the new constitution and advocated its adoption. Madison represented Virginia in the U.S. House of Representatives, served for eight years as secretary of state and for eight years as president of the United States. This county was created and named in his

honor on January 29, 1828, after Madison had retired from public life.

1414 *Marion County*

Francis Marion (–1795)— Marion is believed to have been born in South Carolina. He served in the army in battles against the Cherokee Indians and was elected to the provisional congress of 1775. He served, with distinction, as an officer in the Revolutionary War and rose to the rank of general in that war. Marion was also a member of the South Carolina senate. This county was created and named for General Marion in 1811, while Mississippi was still a territory.

1415 *Marshall County*

John Marshall (1755–1835)— Marshall, a native of Virginia, served as an officer in the Revolutionary War, in the Virginia legislature and in the U.S. House of Representatives. He briefly served as secretary of state and then, for over 30 years, was chief justice of the U.S. Supreme Court. Marshall's interpretations of the Constitution during America's political infancy left an unmatched impact on the laws and government of this country. Under Marshall, the supreme court shifted power in American government from the states to the central government and to the federal judiciary at the expense of the executive and legislative branches. Marshall died on July 6, 1835, and this county was created seven months later, on February 9, 1836.

1416 *Monroe County*

James Monroe (1758–1831)— Monroe, a native of Virginia, served in the Revolutionary War. Prior to his election as president of the United States, Monroe served in a wide variety of government posts. He served Virginia in the state legislature and as governor. He was a member of the Confederation congress and the U.S. Senate. He was minister to France and to Britain and he held two cabinet posts. As president, Monroe stressed limited government and strict construction of the constitution. He acquired Florida for the U.S. from Spain and he was the author of a policy declaration (later known as the Monroe Doctrine) which proscribed outside interference in North and South America. This county was created in 1821, while Monroe was serving as our nation's president.

1417 *Montgomery County*

Richard Montgomery (1738–1775)— Montgomery was born in Ireland and served with the British in the French and Indian War. He settled in New York state where he was elected to the New York provisional congress. He served as a general in the American Revolutionary War and he was killed in combat in the Revolutionary War. This county was created in 1871

1418 *Neshoba County*

Indian word for "wolf"— This county in central Mississippi was created on December 23, 1833, from lands recently taken from the Choctaw Indian nation. The county's name is from the Choctaw language and it means "wolf."

1419 *Newton County*

Isaac Newton (1642–1727)— This mathematical genius was born in England and resided there throughout his life. He enrolled at Cambridge University and studied there for a time but it was during an absence from Cambridge, during 1665 and 1666 on account of plague that Newton discovered the binomial theorem, differential calculus and integral calculus. Also during this period Newton conceived the idea of universal gravitation. With these accomplishments behind him, he returned to Cambridge University. His subsequent illustrious career included additional contributions in mathematics, natural philosophy and physics with emphasis on optics, astronomy and celestial mechanics. He was elected as a fellow of the Royal Society and knighted. To call Sir Isaac Newton a genius errs by understating the case. *The World of Mathematics*, published in 1956, contains a brief biography of Newton by E. N. da Costa Andrade. The first sentence of that biography elegantly captures the uniqueness of Isaac Newton's genius: "From time to time in the history of mankind a man arises who is of universal significance, whose work changes the current of human thought or of human experience, so that all that comes after him bears evidence of his spirit. Such a man…was Newton."

1420 *Noxubee County*

Noxubee River— The Noxubee River, a tributary of the Tombigbee River, rises near the northwestern corner of Noxubee County and traverses the county from its northwestern corner to its southeastern corner, which borders on the state of Alabama in east-central Mississippi. The Noxubee is about 140 miles long. This county was created on December 23, 1833, from lands recently taken from the Choctaw Indian nation. The name comes from the Choctaw language and means, approximately, "creek of which the water has the odor of freshly caught fish."

1421 *Oktibbeha County*

Uncertain— There are two streams in Mississippi with the Indian name *Oktibbeha* but the translation of that name is disputed. One translation that has been mentioned is "noisy water" but many alternative translations have been suggested. The two more popular translations are "fighting water" and "ice therein," or "blocks of ice therein." Lea L. Seale's' 1939 doctoral thesis on "Indian Place-Names in Mississippi" states that the correct translation is "ice therein" or "blocks of ice therein."

1422 *Panola County*

Indian word for "cotton"— This county in northwestern Mississippi was created in 1836 from lands ceded in 1832 by the Chickasaw Indian nation but its name comes from the language of the Choctaw Indians and means "cotton." The fertile land here is well suited to cotton farming and cotton has been important to the economy of this area.

1423 *Pearl River County*

Pearl River— The Pearl River rises in central Mississippi and flows southwest and then south to empty its waters into the Gulf of Mexico after a journey of some 490 miles. At the northwestern corner of Pearl River County, the river begins to serve as the boundary line between Mississippi and Louisiana and the Pearl River comprises the entire western border of Pearl River County. Early French explorers of the lower Pearl River named it *Riviere des Perles*. The French hoped to make a fortune from pearls found in mussels here but they found the pearls to be few in number and of little commercial value. However, the Pearl River was anything but worthless. The Pearl was an enormously important transportation route in the early years of our nation and large steamboats regularly plied its waters. By the middle of the 20th century the river's waters had been largely diverted and the once mighty Pearl was mighty no more.

1424 *Perry County*

Oliver H. Perry (1785–1819)— Perry was a native of Rhode Island and an officer in the U.S. navy. During the War of 1812 his squadron defeated the British in a key battle on Lake Erie of which Perry said "We have met the enemy and they are ours." Perry died on August 23, 1819, and this county was created and named in his honor less than six months later, on February 3, 1820.

1425 *Pike County*

Zebulon M. Pike (1779–1813)— A native of New Jersey, Pike served as an army officer on America's frontier following the Revolution. He led an exploratory army expedition to the Rocky Mountains in Colorado which Pike's Peak in the Colorado Rockies commemorates. Pike served as a general in the War of 1812 and was killed in combat in that war on April 27, 1813. This county was created and named in his honor by Mississippi territory on December 9, 1815.

1426 *Pontotoc County*

Town of Pontotoc, Mississippi— The first known White settler of what is now the town of Pontotoc, Mississippi was Henry Love. He is known to have resided here in 1832. Apparently it was Mr. Love who coined the town's name and he rendered it as Pontetok. In his *Handbook of America Indians North of Mexico*, Frederick W. Hodge indicates that this name had been used earlier by Chickasaw Indians for their village here. In any event, Henry Love's town name was later changed from Pontetok to Pontotoc and when Pontotoc County was created on February 9, 1836, the town of Pontotoc was made its county seat. Most sources indicate that the name came from Indian words which meant "weed prairie." However, several other suggestions have been made and the true translation of the name is uncertain. In a 1939 doctoral thesis entitled "Indian Place-Names in Mississippi," Lea L. Seale mentions several possible origins of the name but declines to select any of them as the correct choice.

1427 *Prentiss County*

Sergeant S. Prentiss (1808–1850)— A native of Maine and a lawyer, Prentiss immigrated to Mississippi where he was admitted to the bar in 1829. He practiced law in Vicksburg and served in the lower house of the Mississippi legislature. From May 30, 1838, to March 3, 1839, Prentiss represented Mississippi in the U.S. House of Representatives. He subsequently practiced law in Vicksburg and in New Orleans,

Louisiana. Prentiss' given name is rendered variously as Sergeant, Seargent and Sargent.

1428 Quitman County

John A. Quitman (1798–1858) — Quitman was born in New York state but spent his adult life and political career as a resident of Mississippi. He was a member of both houses of the Mississippi legislature and he was chancellor of this state. Quitman served as a general officer during the Mexican War, rising to the rank of major-general. After the war he was elected governor of Mississippi and he later represented Mississippi in the U.S. House of Representatives where he championed states' rights until his death in 1858.

1429 Rankin County

Christopher Rankin (1788–1826) — A native of Pennsylvania, Rankin immigrated to Mississippi territory where he practiced law and served in the territorial legislature. In preparation for Mississippi's admission to statehood, a constitutional convention was called in 1817 and Christopher Rankin was a prominent member of that convention. He offered himself as a candidate to be one of Mississippi's first United States senators and although Rankin failed in that bid, he was soon elected to represent Mississippi in the U.S. House of Representatives. He served in that body from March 4, 1819, until his death on March 14, 1826. This county was created and named in his honor just two years later, on February 4, 1828.

1430 Scott County

Abram M. Scott (–1833) — Scott was born in South Carolina about 1786. He immigrated to Mississippi when it was still a territory and he represented Wilkinson County in Mississippi's constitutional convention of 1817. After Mississippi's admission to statehood, Scott served in the upper house of the state legislature and from 1828 to 1830 he was the state's lieutenant-governor. Elected as Mississippi's governor in the election of August, 1831, he served the state as governor from January 9, 1832, until his death caused by cholera on June 12, 1833. This county was formed and named in his honor six months later, on December 23, 1833.

1431 Sharkey County

William L. Sharkey (1797–1873) — Sharkey was born in Tennessee and moved with his family to Mississippi territory in 1803. Here he practiced law and after Mississippi's admission to statehood, he served in the lower house of the Mississippi legislature. After serving as a circuit judge, Sharkey was appointed in 1832 as a justice of Mississippi's highest court and soon afterwards he was chosen by his fellow justices as their chief justice. When secession and Civil War were imminent, Sharkey opposed Mississippi's plan to secede from the Union and join the Confederate States of America. Thus when the Civil War ended in defeat for the Confederacy, William Sharkey was one of the few prominent men of Mississippi who were acceptable to the victorious Union government. President Andrew Johnson appointed Sharkey to be provisional Reconstruction governor of Mississippi and he assumed that office on June 13, 1865. His relations with the Union army's occupying military forces were strained. Later in 1865 Mississippi held a constitutional convention which elected Sharkey and James L. Alcorn (1816–1894) to represent Mississippi in the U.S. Senate. However, both Sharkey and Alcorn were denied their seats in that body. William L. Sharkey died in July, 1873, and this county was created and named in his honor on March 29, 1876.

1432 Simpson County

Josiah Simpson (–1817) — A native of Pennsylvania, Simpson attended Princeton College, studied law and began the practice of that profession. In 1812 he was appointed to succeed Judge Oliver Fitts as one of the judges of Mississippi territory. In preparation for Mississippi's admission to statehood, a constitutional convention was called in the summer of 1817 and Judge Simpson was one of Adams County's delegates to that convention. He died on September 21, 1817, soon after the convention ended. This county was created in 1824.

1433 Smith County

David Smith (1753–1835) — David Smith was born in North Carolina on October 9, 1753. During the Revolutionary War he served as a private at the battle of King's Mountain in 1780 and he later saw action during the Revolution at Cowpens and Eutaw Springs, both in 1781. After the Revolution Smith resided in Tennessee, Kentucky and Mississippi territory. He then returned to Kentucky, where he was a resident of Christian County, Kentucky, and held the rank of major in the Kentucky militia. When Smith was almost 60 years old, he once again served in the army, leading a company of mounted volunteers in the Creek War. Although he is referred to as "Major Smith of Hinds County, Mississippi," he served as a captain in the Creek War. The higher rank of major was the one granted to him earlier by Kentucky's Governor James Garrard (1749–1822). When these Indian hostilities concluded, Smith returned to Kentucky. It is known that he owned slaves during this period of residence in Kentucky. It was not until 1822, that Smith moved near the city of Jackson, in Hinds County, Mississippi. No doubt Major Smith was a patriotic soldier and a fine man, but his connection with Mississippi was primarily near the end of his life and this connection was certainly not very dramatic. Why then would Mississippi choose to name one of her counties for this man? One of David Smith's daughters, Aurelia Smith, married Hiram G. Runnels (1796–1857) on April 8, 1823. On November 20, 1833, Runnels became governor of Mississippi and this county was created and named in honor of Governor Runnels' father-in-law, David Smith, just one month later, on December 23, 1833.

1434 Stone County

John M. Stone (1830–1900) — A native of Tennessee, Stone moved south to Mississippi where he was employed as a clerk in a country store and later served as a station agent for the Memphis & Charleston Railroad. In 1861 John Stone entered the army of the Confederate States of America as a captain and he soon was promoted to colonel. After the Civil War, Stone became a member of the Mississippi senate and it was because he was president *pro tempore* of the Mississippi senate at a critical juncture in the state's history that be became Mississippi's governor. A Black gentleman, named Alexander K. Davis was serving as a Reconstruction lieutenant-governor when the carpetbagger Mississippi governor, Adelbert Ames (1835–1933), resigned. To prevent the Black lieutenant-governor, Alexander K. Davis, from becoming governor, the Mississippi legislature impeached Davis. With neither a governor nor a lieutenant-governor on the scene, the president *pro tempore* of the state senate was elevated to governor. Stone served as Mississippi's governor from March 29, 1876, to January 29, 1882, and he later served another six year stint as governor from January 13, 1890, to January 20, 1896. This county was created in 1916.

1435 *Sunflower County*

Sunflower River— This northwestern Mississippi county was created in 1844 and named for the Sunflower River, which meanders sluggishly from the county's northern border to its southern border with Humphreys County. The Sunflower is a tributary of the Yazoo River and its entire 240 mile journey is within the state of Mississippi. The Sunflower rises in Coahoma County, flows south into Sunflower County and continues to flow in a generally southern direction throughout its journey to the Yazoo. The Sunflower joins the Yazoo River on the border between Yazoo County and Sharkey County. The Quiver River is the largest tributary of the Sunflower River.

1436 *Tallahatchie County*

Tallahatchie River— On December 23, 1833, Mississippi created this county in northwestern Mississippi and named it for the important river which flows across the entire length of the county from north to south. The Tallahatchie River rises in Tippah County, Mississippi, and then flows sluggishly in a predominantly southwestern direction toward, and then into, Tallahatchie County. There, the river turns south and, after crossing this county's southern border, the Tallahatchie joins the Yalobusha River in Leflore County, where the two rivers unite to form the Yazoo River. At the time that this county was created, the Tallahatchie River provided an important mode of transportation for the area's cotton production. One source gives the Tallahatchie River's length as 301 miles; another shows 310. Let's be daring and call it 300. About one-third of the Tallahatchie's length is navigable. The river's name came from two words in the Choctaw Indians' language, *tali*, meaning "rock" and *hacha*, which signifies "river."

1437 *Tate County*

Uncertain— This county was created in 1873, primarily from the southern portion of De Soto County, Mississippi. Sources consulted are about equally divided concerning the origin of this county's name. About half state that the county was named for Thomas Simpson Tate, while the remaining sources indicate that the county was named for the prominent Tate family, of which Thomas Simpson Tate was a leading member. A number of sources call Thomas S. Tate "Colonel Tate," while a few refer to him as "Hon. T. S. Tate." De Soto County, Mississippi, is in the extreme northwestern corner of the state, being bounded on the north by the state of Tennessee and on the west by the Mississippi River. It was in De Soto County that Thomas S. Tate and the Tate family first became somewhat prominent. The village of Tatesville, Mississippi, was founded by Thomas Simpson Tate when it was a part of De Soto County. Thomas S. Tate became a merchant of some prominence in Tatesville. Among the business concerns in the village of Tatesville was the firm of Tate and Arnold, general merchants. When the Mississippi & Tennessee Railroad was completed to Senatobia, Mississippi, in the middle of the 19th century, Tatesville was absorbed by the town of Senatobia and Tatesville ceased to exist. In 1867 the crops of De Soto County were poor, prices were low and there was a shortage of farm laborers. Famine was a clear threat and a six delegates from De Soto County were selected to attend a conference at the state capital in Jackson, Mississippi. This conference was called "the Immigration Convention" and it was held on March 31, 1868. Thomas S. Tate was one of De Soto County's six delegates to this important meeting. As one response to this agricultural crisis, a company was organized to deal with it. The company's name was the Free Land & Colonization Company of De Soto County, Mississippi. Thomas S. Tate was chosen as one of the five trustees who managed the affairs of this company. On April 15, 1873, the Mississippi legislature created Tate County, primarily from the southern portion of De Soto County. According to some sources, Thomas S. Tate was more influential than anyone else in securing the creation of Tate County. Thomas S. Tate proposed that the new county be named Bell County but he was overruled by his friends in the legislature and the county was named Tate County. Thomas S. Tate was a member of the new county's first board of supervisors and he represented Tate County in the lower house of the Mississippi legislature. (A few sources state that the first representatives from Tate County in Mississippi's house of representatives were Thomas S. Tate and T. B. Garrett.) During Reconstruction, the sheriff's office of De Soto County was filled by a Black gentleman, named J. J. Evans, who had formerly been a slave. Evans was elected on November 4, 1873, and a bond in the amount of $75,000 was posted on behalf of Sheriff J. J. Evans. Thomas S. Tate was one of the seven bondsmen for Evans' $75,000 bond. The *Biographical & Historical Memoirs of Mississippi*, published in 1891, indicate that Thomas S. Tate was a Republican in politics and that he died about 1881.

1438 *Tippah County*

Uncertain— Several sources who are generally reliable on the origins of Mississippi place names state that this county was named for an Indian princess, the wife of an Indian chief named Pontotoc. However, it is not certain that there ever was an Indian chief named Pontotoc or a Princess Tippah. It seems more probable that the county's name came from the original Indian name of Tippah Creek, whose upper end lies within Tippah County. In a 1939 doctoral thesis entitled "Indian Place-Names in Mississippi," Lea L. Seale pointed out that Tippah Creek has four distinct branches near its head, and that it would be plausible to conclude that the original Indian name of Tippah Creek was *Bok tapa*, meaning "separated creek" in the language of the Choctaw Indians. At the time that Tippah County was created in February, 1836, Tippah Creek flowed across much of the county from east to west before emptying into the Tallahatchie River.

1439 *Tishomingo County*

Tishomingo (–)— This county was created in 1836 from lands ceded to the United States by the Chickasaw Indian nation. Its name honors a great chief of that nation, Tishomingo, the last full-blooded chief of the Chickasaws. Tishomingo was born about 1737 and died about one hundred years later. He directly governed one-fourth of the Chickasaw nation and, as chief advisor and guard to the king of all Chickasaws, for a time, he indirectly held control over the entire nation. Tishomingo was personally acquainted with at least four of our country's early presidents, George Washington, Thomas Jefferson, James Monroe and Andrew Jackson. During much of Tishomingo's life, his principal residence was in the what is now the northeastern portion of the state of Mississippi. In October, 1832, Tishomingo was one of the chiefs of the Chickasaw nation who signed the treaty which ceded all remaining Chickasaw lands east of the Mississippi River to the United States government. When his people were forced by the Whites to emigrate to Indian territory (now Oklahoma), Tishomingo headed west with them. However, the 100 year old chief died on the rigorous journey before reaching Indian territory.

1440 *Tunica County*

Tunica Indians— Tunica County, Mississippi, was created on February 9, 1836. Its county seat is also named Tunica, but this county was not named for its county seat. Earlier county seats of Tunica County had been at Petyton, Commerce and Austin. It was not until 1884 that the town of Tunica was laid out on land owned by Edwin L. Harris and the county seat was moved to Tunica soon after that. In 1887 a substantial courthouse and jail were erected in the town of Tunica. Thus Tunica County was not named for its county seat but for a small tribe of Indians, the Tunica, who were members of the Algonquian linguistic group. The Tunica Indians lived along the valley of the lower Mississippi River and along the southern side of the Yazoo River, not far away from its mouth at the Mississippi River. One source indicates that at one time Tunica Indians lived in the southwestern corner of the present Tunica County, Mississippi. That is certainly possible. The name *Tunica* is Indian and means "the people" but the Tunica Indians preferred the name *Yoron* to *Tunica* when referring to themselves. In the early history of European occupation of the lower Mississippi River valley, the Tunica were allies of the French. Apparently the number of Tunica Indians was never very large. One early French explorer estimated that their population was contained within 260 cabins. The Tunica lived principally on corn. While the men cultivated the crops, the women worked inside making pottery and clothing. One reference states that the Tunica did no hunting but another source mentions them dressing deer skins and buffalo skins. In the year 1706 the Tunica were driven from their villages along the Mississippi and Yazoo Rivers by the Chickasaw and Alibamu Indians. The Tunica then joined the Huma Indians but subsequently killed more than half of their Huma hosts and then occupied the territory of the Humas. During the 1700's the Tunica lived primarily in the present state of Louisiana. By 1930 only one Tunica Indian was known to be still alive.

1441 *Union County*

The United States of America— This county was created on July 7, 1870, after the Confederate States of America had lost the Civil War and while the Mississippi legislature was controlled by a Reconstruction government. It was named for the entire United States of America, including former Confederate and Union states. Although this county was created and named in 1870, during Reconstruction, within five years control of Mississippi's government reverted to the White majority. If there were lingering resentment among Mississippi's White citizens over the choice of this county's name, they have had more than a century to change the county's name and failed to do so. Whether this should be attributed to lethargy or sincerity is speculative. Certainly there were many citizens of Mississippi during Reconstruction, both Black and White, who wished to put the past behind them and let a new era of mutual respect begin.

1442 *Walthall County*

Edward C. Walthall (1831–1898)— A native of Virginia, Walthall moved with his parents to Holly Springs, Mississippi, and attended classical school here at St. Thomas Hall. Later he studied law and after admission to the Mississippi bar in 1852, Walthall entered a law practice at Coffeeville, Mississippi. In 1861, he entered the army of the Confederate States of America as a first-lieutenant. He served with distinction in the Civil War and had been promoted to brigadier-general by December, 1862 and to major-general during the summer of 1864. Two decades later, in 1885, Mississippi's U.S. Senator Lucius Q. C. Lamar (1825–1893) was appointed to President Cleveland's cabinet and the Mississippi legislature elected Walthall to fill Lamar's seat in the senate. Apart from a one year absence owing to ill health, Walthall represented Mississippi in the U.S. Senate from 1885 until his death in 1898. This county was created in 1910.

1443 *Warren County*

Joseph Warren (1741–1775)— A native of Massachusetts and a graduate of Harvard College, Warren practiced medicine in the Boston area. He was a member of the committee of safety and president *pro tempore* of the Massachusetts provincial congress. In June, 1775, he was commissioned a major-general and he died in combat a few days later at the battle of Bunker Hill. Warren County was created and named in honor of this Revolutionary War hero on December 22, 1809, while Mississippi was still a territory.

1444 *Washington County*

George Washington (1732–1799)— Washington was a native of Virginia. He served in Virginia's house of burgesses and became one of the colonies' leaders in opposition to British policies in America. He was a member of the first and second Continental Congresses and commander of all Continental armies in the Revolutionary War. Following victory in that war, Washington was elected to be the first president of the United States. This county was created in 1827.

1445 *Wayne County*

Anthony Wayne (1745–1796)— A native of Pennsylvania, Wayne was a successful brigadier-general in the Revolutionary War and became a hero for his daring exploits. During the bitter winter of 1777–1778 at Valley Forge, Pennsylvania, Wayne shared the sufferings of his men although his comfortable estate was only five miles away. He played an important role in the final overthrow of the British forces in Georgia. After the war, in 1785, Wayne moved to Georgia and he represented Georgia for about six months in the U.S. House of Representatives. In 1792, President Washington recalled Wayne to serve as a major-general against the Indians in the Northwest territory. Once again his military efforts were successful. This county was created and named in Wayne's honor on December 21, 1809, while Mississippi was a territory.

1446 *Webster County*

Daniel Webster (1782–1852)— Webster was born in New Hampshire and represented that state in the U.S. House of Representatives. He later represented Massachusetts in both houses of the U.S. Congress and served as secretary of state under three presidents. Webster felt that slavery was evil but not as evil as disunion of the United States. He played a key role in the passage of five laws in the U.S. Congress which are known as the "Compromise of 1850" which were intended to avert secession and civil war between the North and the South over the slavery issue. This county was originally created on April 6, 1874, when Reconstruction ruled Mississippi following the Civil War. The county's original name was Sumner County. That name honored U.S. Senator Charles Sumner (1811–1874) of Massachusetts, a fierce opponent of slavery. Sumner was an ardent supporter of the harsh military Reconstruction measures which the victorious North imposed on the defeated South after the Civil War. In fact, Sumner felt that these harsh Reconstruction measures were too lenient. It was a Reconstruction era Mississippi legislature that created and named this county in Charles Sumner's honor. Soon after Reconstruction ended in Mississippi, Whites regained control of the legislature and the hated named of Sumner was banished from Mississippi's roster of county names. The legislature changed the name of Sumner County to Webster County on January 30, 1882, to honor one of our country's statesmen from the North who was more palatable to Mississippi's post–Reconstruction White legislators.

1447 *Wilkinson County*

James Wilkinson (1757–1825) — A native of Maryland, Wilkinson served as an officer in the colonial army during the American Revolution and rose to the rank of brevet brigadier-general. He later served in actions against the Indians in the Northwest territory where he became general-in-chief. Wilkinson first appeared in the affairs of Mississippi about 1787 when he journeyed to Natchez and was involved in efforts to sever the portion of the southwestern United States, which was east of the Mississippi River, and form a separate nation allied with Spain. This new nation would have included the present state of Mississippi. His involvement in this intrigue was apparently not fully recognized at high levels of the U.S. government and Wilkinson was subsequently sent to head U.S. troops guarding what was then our nation's southwestern frontier at Fort Adams in the present Wilkinson County, Mississippi. For a brief period in 1798 Wilkinson was military governor of Mississippi territory. Very early in the 19th century, General Wilkinson secured from the Chickasaw and Choctaw Indians the rights to a road through their territory which ran from Tennessee to the regions of Natchez and Fort Stoddard. On January 30, 1802, Mississippi territory created and named Wilkinson County in honor of General James Wilkinson. In 1805 President Jefferson appointed Wilkinson to be civil and military governor of the recently acquired Louisiana territory. He later was commissioned major-general in the War of 1812 but performed poorly in Canada and was relieved of his command.

1448 *Winston County*

Louis Winston (–) — Winston was a scholarly lawyer who came to Mississippi territory from Virginia when he was a young man. When Mississippi territory was preparing for admission to statehood, a constitutional convention was called for July, 1817, and young Louis Winston had

the honor of serving as that historic convention's secretary. In 1821 he was elected to serve as judge of the second circuit court. Dunbar Rowland's history of Mississippi published in 1907 states that Winston's opponent in the election to be judge of the second circuit court was Bela Metcalf. Winston served in that judgeship for four years. Dunbar Rowland's 1907 work also states that Winston "… was afterwards a circuit judge under the constitution of 1832."

1449 *Yalobusha County*

Yalobusha River — When this county was originally created in 1833 primarily from land ceded by the Choctaw Indians, its boundaries included a portion of the Yalobusha River, for which it was named. Since its original formation, Yalobusha County has been reduced in size considerably as a result of giving up land to form new counties. The Yalobusha rises in Chickasaw County in northern Mississippi and flows some 80 miles in a western and southwestern direction before joining the Tallahatchie River in Leflore County, where the two rivers unite to form the Yazoo River. The name *Yalobusha* comes from two words in the language of the Choctaw Indians, *yaloba*, for "tadpoles," and *asha*, meaning "to be there." Thus the river's name means "tadpoles are there," or "tadpole place."

1450 *Yazoo County*

Uncertain — The current county seat of Yazoo County is Yazoo City. Although the origin of this county's name is not certain, we do know that it was not named for its county seat. When Yazoo County was created on January 21, 1823, its county seat was the town of Beattie's Bluff and in 1829 the seat of justice was moved to the town of Benton. Yazoo City did not become the county seat of Yazoo County until 1849. Sources consulted are about equally divided concerning the source of this county's name. About half indicate that it was named for the Yazoo River, which flows through it, while the other half state that the county's name honors a small tribe of Indians, named to Yazoo. Since the Yazoo River was named for the Yazoo Indians we know that the county's name honors that tribe of Indians either directly or indirectly.

Yazoo River — This navigable tributary of the Mississippi River is located in west-central Mississippi. It is formed in Leflore County by the confluence of the Tallahatchie and Yalobusha Rivers. The Yazoo

flows across Yazoo County before emptying its waters into the Mississippi above Vicksburg, Mississippi. The alluvial deposits of the Mississippi River near its junction with the Yazoo, provide farmers of the Yazoo River's basin with extremely fertile soil. The Yazoo River was named for the Yazoo Indians.

Yazoo Indians — This small Indian tribe lived near the mouth of the Yazoo River, where it joins the Mississippi River, in a village or group of villages which they shared with the Tunica, Koroa and Ofo Indians. Most of these Indians shared a resemblance in their speech, using the phonetic sound of the letter "r." Most other Indian tribes in this area did not use the letter "r" in speaking. The Yazoo lived in cabins that were round and shaped like ice-house igloos. In 1729 the Yazoo and some of their Indian associates attacked and destroyed a French fort near the mouth of the Yazoo River. Although the Yazoo did not remain in this area too long after that attack, there were still some 150 Indians of the Yazoo and Koroa tribes living near the mouth of the Yazoo River as late as 1731. The Yazoo were soon driven from the area and by 1740 they and the Koroa Indians had fused with the Chickasaw and Choctaw Indians and the Yazoo became extinct as a separate tribe.

REFERENCES

Allison, John. *Notable Men of Tennessee.* Atlanta, Georgia, Southern Historical Association, 1905.

"And Another Revolutionary Soldier is Gone: Obituary of Major David Smith." *The Mississippian*, Jackson, Mississippi, December 18, 1835.

Andrade, E. N. da Costa. "Isaac Newton." *The World of Mathematics*, New York: 1956.

Arthur Stanley C. *Old Families of Louisiana.* New Orleans, Harmanson, 1931.

Arthur, Stanley C. "The Story of the Kemper Brothers: Three Fighting Sons of a Baptist Preacher Who Fought for Freedom when Louisiana Was Young." *St. Francisville Democrat*, July 8, 1933, July 15, 1933, July 22, 1933 & July 29, 1933.

Bell, Mrs. Helen D. "The History of a County." *Publications of the Mississippi Historical Society*, Vol. 4. Oxford, Mississippi: 1901.

Bettersworth, John K. *Mississippi: Yesterday & Today.* Austin, Texas, Steck-Vaughn Co., 1964.

Biennial Report of the Secretary of State to the Legislature of Mississippi: July 1, 1929 to July 1, 1931.

Biographical & Historical Memoirs of Mississippi. Chicago, Goodspeed Publishing Co., 1891.

Bounds, Beth. "Kemper County: Its Beginnings." *Kemper County Messenger,* Dekalb, Mississippi, August 23, 1990.

Brandfon, Robert L. *Cotton Kingdom of the New South: A History of the Yazoo Mississippi Delta from Reconstruction to the Twentieth Century.* Cambridge, Massachusetts, Harvard University Press, 1967.

Brieger, James F. *Hometown Mississippi.*

Brinegar, Bonnie. "Choctaw Place-Names in Mississippi." *Mississippi Folklore Register,* Vol. 11, No. 2. Hattiesburg, Mississippi: Fall, 1977.

Brinson, Carroll. *Jackson: A Special Kind of Place.* Jackson, City of Jackson, Mississippi, 1977.

Bromme, Traugott. "Mississippi: A Geographic, Statistic, Typographic Sketch for Immigrants & Friends of Geography & Ethnology." *Journal of Mississippi History,* Vol. 4, No. 2. Jackson: April, 1942.

Brown Andrew. *History of Tippah County, Mississippi: The First Century.* Ripley, Mississippi, Tippah County Historical & Genealogical Society, Inc., 1976.

Brown, Dave H. *A History of Who's Who in Louisiana Politics in 1916.* Louisiana Chronicle Democrat, 1916.

Burger, Nash K., & John K. Bettersworth. *South of Appomattox.* New York, Harcourt, Brace & Co., 1959.

Carpenter, Howard. *A History of Tate County.* Senatobia, Mississippi, B. C. Printing Co., 1975.

Carroll, Thomas B., et al. *Historical Sketches of Oktibbeha County (Mississippi).* Gulfport, Mississippi, Dixie Press, 1931.

Claiborne, J. F. H. *Mississippi as a Province, Territory & State with Biographical Notices of Eminent Citizens.* Jackson, Power & Barksdale, 1880.

Cochran, Fan A. *History of Old Tishomingo County, Mississippi Territory.* Oklahoma City, Oklahoma, Barnhart Letter Shop, 1971.

Coleman, James P. *Choctaw County Chronicles: A History of Choctaw County, Mississippi: 1830–1973.* Nashville, Tennessee, Benson Printing Co., 1974.

Conrad, D. H. "David Holmes: First Governor of Mississippi." *Publications of the Mississippi Historical Society,* Vol. 4. Jackson: 1921.

Conrad, Glenn R. *A Dictionary of Louisiana Biography.* New Orleans, Louisiana, Louisiana Historical Association, 1988.

Cowings, Ralph. "Letters." *New York Times Book Review,* April 3, 1994.

Current, Richard N. *Encyclopedia of the Confederacy.* New York, Simon & Schuster, 1993.

Dawson, Joseph G. *The Louisiana Governors: From Iberville to Edwards.* Baton Rouge, Louisiana State University Press, 1990.

DeCell, Harriet & Jo Anne Prichard. *Yazoo: Its Legends & Legacies.* Yazoo Delta Press, 1976.

Deupree, Mrs. N. D. "Greenwood Le Flore." *Publications of the Mississippi Historical Society,* Vol. 7. Oxford, Mississippi: 1903.

Drake, Winbourne M. "Mississippi's First Constitutional Convention." *Journal of Mississippi History,* Vol. 18, No. 2. Jackson: April, 1956.

Faber, Harold. *From Sea to Sea: The Growth of the United States.* New York, Farrar, Straus & Giroux, 1967.

Fant, Mabel B., & John C. Fant. *History of Mississippi: A School Reader.* Mississippi Publishing Co., 1923.

Foner, Eric. *Reconstruction: America's Unfinished Revolution: 1863–1877.* New York, Harper & Row, 1988.

Gannett, Henry. "The Origin of Certain Place Names in the State of Mississippi." *Publications of the Mississippi Historical Society,* Vol. 6. Oxford, Mississippi: 1902.

Garner, James W. "The Senatorial Career of J. Z. George." *Publications of the Mississippi Historical Society,* Vol. 7. Oxford, Mississippi: 1903.

Golden Harold G. *Low-Flow Characteristics: Sunflower River Basin, Mississippi.* United States Geological Survey & Mississippi Board of Water Commissioners, 1960.

Gonzales, John E. *A Mississippi Reader: Selected Articles from the Journal of Mississippi History.* Jackson, Mississippi Historical Society, 1980.

Grant, Bruce. *Concise Encyclopedia of the American Indian.* Avenel, New Jersey, Wings Books, 1989.

Guyton, Pearl V. *The History of Mississippi: From Indian Times to the Present Day.* Syracuse, New York, Iroquois Publishing Co., Inc., 1935.

Guyton, Pearl V. *Our Mississippi.* Austin, Texas, Steck Co., 1952.

Hamilton, William B. "Book Review: Tarnished Warrior: The Story of Major-General James Wilkinson by Major James R. Jacobs." *Journal of Mississippi History,* Vol. 1, No. 4. Jackson: October, 1939.

Harper, Jean C. *Mississippi: Her People, Places & Legends.* Jackson, 1977.

Harthorn, J. C. *A History of Grenada County.*

Headley, Katy M. *Claiborne County,*

Mississippi. Baton Rouge, Louisiana, Moran Industries, Inc., 1976.

Hines, Regina. "History of Clarke County Did Not Go Up in Flames." *Biloxi Sun-Herald,* December 13, 1990.

Historical Booklet Committee. *Simpson County Sesquicentennial Historical Booklet: Honoring the Past: 1824–1974.*

History of Smith County, Mississippi: Bicentennial Edition. Bicentennial History Committee of Smith County.

Hodge, Frederick W. *Handbook of American Indians North of Mexico.* Totowa, New Jersey, Rowman & Littlefield, 1975.

Hudson, Arthur P. "Bethel Lodge & Palmer's Hall in Mississippi: 1849–1869." *Journal of Mississippi History,* Vol. 13, No. 1. Jackson: January, 1951.

Ivy, Pam M. "Our Heritage: De Soto County, Mississippi." *North Mississippi Times.*

Jasper County Historical Foundation, Inc. *History of Jasper County, Georgia.* Roswell, Georgia, W. H. Wolfe Associates, 1976.

Johnston, Frank. "The Public Services of Senator James Z. George." *Publications of the Mississippi Historical Society,* Vol. 8. Oxford, Mississippi: 1904.

Jones, Billy M. *Heroes of Tennessee.* Memphis, Tennessee, Memphis State University Press, 1979.

"Josiah Simpson." Subject file, Mississippi Department of Archives & History, Jackson, Mississippi.

Kemper County Sesquicentennial Celebration: 1833–1983.

Kleber, John E. *The Kentucky Encyclopedia.* Lexington, Kentucky, University Press of Kentucky, 1992.

"Know Your State: Kemper Has Large Area." *Jackson Daily News,* February 27, 1963.

Kosciusko-Attala History. Kosciusko-Attala Historical Society.

Kyle, John W. "Reconstruction in Panola County." *Publications of the Mississippi Historical Society,* Vol. 13. University, Mississippi: 1913.

Ladner, Heber. *Mississippi Official & Statistical Register: 1976–1980.*

Lowry, Robert, & William H. McCardle. *A History of Mississippi: From the Discovery of the Great River by Hernando De Soto including the Earliest Settlements Made by the French Under Iberville, to the Death of Jefferson Davis.* Jackson, Mississippi, R. H. Henry & Co., 1891.

Lowry, Robert, & William H. McCardle. *A History of Mississippi for Use in Schools.* New York, University Publishing Co., 1898.

Lynch, James D. *The Bench & Bar of Mississippi.* New York, E. J. Hale & Son, 1881.

McBee, May W. *The Life & Times of David Smith: Patriot, Pioneer & Indian Fighter*. Kansas City, Missouri, E. L. Mendenhall, Inc., 1959.

McCain, William D. "The Naming of Smith County." Biographical sketch of David Smith dated December 21, 1950 in Smith County subject file, Mississippi Department of Archives & History, Jackson, Mississippi.

McCain, William D. *The Story of Jackson*. Jackson, J. F. Hyer Publishing Co., 1953.

McCraw, Edythe W. "River Transportation on the Mighty Pearl." *The Jacksonian*, January, 1963.

McLemore, Richard A. & Nannie P. McLemore. "The Birth of Mississippi." *Journal of Mississippi History*, Vol. 29, No. 4. Jackson: November, 1967.

Mississippi: America's State of Opportunity. Mississippi State Board of Development, 1944.

Mississippi Statistical Summary of Population: 1800–1980. Economic Research Department, Mississippi Power & Light Co., 1983.

Napier, John H. "Lower Pearl Has Troubled History." *Picayune Item*, November 24, 1985.

Nichols, Irby C. "Reconstruction in De Soto County." *Publications of the Mississippi Historical Society*, Vol. 11. University, Mississippi: 1910.

Owen, Thomas M. "Federal Courts, Judges, Attorneys & Marshals in Mississippi: 1798–1898." *Publications of the Mississippi Historical Society*, Vol. 2. Oxford, Mississippi: 1899.

Panola County Genealogical & Historical Society. *History of Panola County, Mississippi*. Dallas, Texas, Curtis Media Corp., 1987.

Parkerson, Codman. *Those Strange Louisiana Names*.

Pereyra, Lillian A. *James Lusk Alcorn: Persistent Whig*. Louisiana State University Press, 1966.

Phelps, Dawson A. & Edward H. Ross. "Place Names Along the Natchez Trace." *Journal of Mississippi History*, Vol. 14, No. 4. Jackson: October, 1952.

Price, Beulah M. D. "Flooded Pearl River Area Rich in Mississippi History." *Daily Corinthian*, Corinth, Mississippi, May 2, 1979.

Rabinowitz, Howard N. *Southern Black Leaders of the Reconstruction Era*. Urbana, University of Illinois Press, 1982.

Rand, Clayton. *Men of Spine in Mississippi*. Gulfport, Mississippi, Dixie Press, 1940.

Rand, Clayton. *William L. Sharkey*. Mississippi Power & Light Co.

Read, William A. "Louisiana Place-Names of Indian Origin." *University Bulletin Louisiana State University & Agricultural & Mechanical College*, Vol. 19, No. 2. Baton Rouge: February, 1927.

Reed, Forrest F. *Itawamba: A History: Story of a County in Northeast Mississippi*. Nashville, Tennessee, Reed & Co., 1966.

Reeves, Carolyn K. *The Choctaw Before Removal*. Jackson, University Press of Mississippi, 1985.

Reeves, Miriam G. *The Governors of Louisiana*. Gretna, Pelican Publishing Co., 1972.

Riley, Franklin L. *School History of Mississippi*. Richmond, Virginia, B. F. Johnson Publishing Co., 1915.

Rowland, Dunbar. *Courts, Judges & Lawyers of Mississippi: 1798–1935*. Jackson, State Department of Archives & History and Mississippi Historical Society, 1935.

Rowland, Dunbar. *History of Mississippi: The Heart of the South*. Chicago, S. J. Clarke Publishing Co., 1925.

Rowland, Dunbar. *Mississippi: Comprising Sketches of Counties, Towns, Events, Institutions & Persons Arranged in Cyclopedic Form*. Atlanta, Southern Historical Publishing Association, 1907.

Rowland, Dunbar. "Mississippi's First Constitution and Its Makers." *Publications of the Mississippi Historical Society*, Vol. 6. Oxford, Mississippi: 1902.

Rowland, Dunbar. *Official Letter Books of W. C. C. Claiborne: 1801–1816*. Jackson, Mississippi Department of Archives & History, 1917.

Rowland, Dunbar. *The Official & Statistical Register of the State of Mississippi: 1904*. Nashville, Tennessee, Brandon Printing Co., 1904.

Rowland, Dunbar. *The Official & Statistical Register of the State of Mississippi: 1924–1928*. New York, J. J. Little & Ives Co.

Seale, Lea L. "Indian Place-Names in Mississippi." Ph.D. Thesis, Hill Memorial Library, Louisiana State University, Baton Rouge, 1939.

Soil Survey: Sunflower County, Mississippi. United States Department of Agriculture Soil Conservation Service and Mississippi Agricultural Experiment Station, Washington, D.C., 1959.

Spiro, Robert H. "Place Names in Mississippi." *Mississippi Magazine*, Clinton Mississippi: January, 1955.

Stafford, James D. *The Way of the River*.

Stewart, George R. *American Place-Names*. New York, Oxford University Press, 1970.

Stone, James H. "The Economic Development of Holly Springs During the 1840's." *Journal of Mississippi History*, Vol. 32, No. 4. Jackson: November, 1970.

Stoutenburgh, John. *Dictionary of the American Indian*. New York, Bonanza Books, 1960.

Stroupe, Phil. "Once-Gushing Pearl River Dropped to Mere Trickle, Others Sank to New Lows." *Jackson Daily News*, October 5, 1954.

Sullivan, Bob. "Know Your State: Clarke County Formed in '33." *Jackson Daily News*, January 24, 1963.

Sumners, Cecil L. *Chief Tishomingo: A History of the Chickasaw Indians & Some Historical Events of Their Era*. Amory, Mississippi, Amory Advertiser, 1974.

Sumners, Cecil L. *The Governors of Mississippi*. Gretna, Pelican Publishing Co., 1980.

Taft, William H., III. *County Names: An Historical Perspective*. National Association of Counties, 1982.

"Tate County." Subject file, Mississippi Department of Archives & History, Jackson, Mississippi.

Taylor, Walter, N. *Mississippi: A History*. Hopkinsville, Kentucky, Historical Record Association.

Tennessee Old & New: Sesquicentennial Edition: 1796–1946. Nashville, Tennessee, Tennessee Historical Commission and Tennessee Historical Society.

Thrapp, Dan L. *Encyclopedia of Frontier Biography*. Lincoln, University of Nebraska Press, 1988.

Tyson, John A. *Historical Notes of Noxubee County, Mississippi*. Macon, Mississippi, 1928.

Vexler, Robert I. *Chronology & Documentary Handbook of the State of Mississippi*. Dobbs Ferry, New York, Oceana Publications, Inc., 1978.

Vogel, Virgil J. *Indian Names in Michigan*. Ann Arbor, University of Michigan Press, 1986.

Vogel, Virgil J. *Iowa Place Names of Indian Origin*. Iowa City, University of Iowa Press, 1983.

Waldman, Carl. *Who Was Who in Native American History: Indians & Non-Indians from Early Contacts Through 1900*. New York, New York, Facts On File, Inc., 1990.

Webb, Walter P., et al. *The Handbook of Texas*. Austin, Texas Historical Association, 1952.

Weeks, Linton. *Clarksdale & Coahoma County: A History*. Clarksdale, Mississippi, Carnegie Public Library, 1982.

White, Dabney, & T. C. Richardson. *East Texas: Its History and Its Makers*. New York, Lewis Historical Publishing Co., 1940.

"Hon. William L. Sharkey: Provisional Governor of Mississippi." *Frank Leslie's Illustrated Newspaper*, October 7, 1865.

Wills, Brian S. *A Battle from the Start: The Life of Nathan Bedford Forrest.* New York, New York, Harper Collins, 1992.

Winston, E. T. *Story of Pontotoc: Part I–The Chickasaws.* Pontotoc Progress Print, 1931.

Winter, William F. "Journal of the Constitutional Convention of 1817." *Journal of Mississippi History*, Vol. 29, No. 4. Jackson: November, 1967.

Woods, Thomas H. "A Sketch of the Mississippi Secession Convention of 1861: Its Membership & Work." *Publications of the Mississippi Historical Society,* Vol. 6. Oxford, Mississippi: 1902.

Work Projects Administration. *Inventory of the County Archives of Mississippi: Tippah County.* Jackson, 1942.

Wright, Muriel H. *A Guide to the Indian Tribes of Oklahoma.* Norman, University of Oklahoma Press, 1951.

Yenne, Bill. *The Encyclopedia of North American Indian Tribes.* New York, Crescent Books, 1986.

Missouri

(114 counties)

1451 *Adair County*

Adair County, Kentucky — Adair County, in northern Missouri, was created on January 29, 1841, and named for Adair County in Kentucky. Many of the early settlers of this section of Missouri had come from Kentucky and it was their wish that this new county be named for Adair County in their home state. Adair County, Kentucky had been created in 1801 and named for John Adair (1757–1840).

John Adair (1757–1840) — This South Carolina native served in the Revolutionary War and spent part of it as a prisoner of war. In 1786 he moved to Kentucky where he engaged in military actions against the Indians and became active in politics. Adair served nine terms as a member of Kentucky's house of representatives and was, for a time, speaker of that body. He briefly represented Kentucky in the U.S. Senate and later served as an officer and hero in the War of 1812. Adair was given the rank of brevet brigadier-general of the Kentucky militia and in 1820 he became governor of the state of Kentucky. Adair later represented Kentucky in the U.S. House of Representatives.

1452 *Andrew County*

Andrew J. Davis (–) — This county in northwestern Missouri was one of six counties that were carved out of land known as the "Platte Purchase." When Andrew County was created, the name of its county seat was Union. Later, Union's name was changed to Savannah, which is the current county seat of Andrew County. This county's name honors Andrew Jackson Davis, a lawyer, who was said to have been a prominent citizen and a lawyer in both Savannah and Saint Louis.

1453 *Atchison County*

David R. Atchison (1807–1886) — On February 23, 1843, the Missouri legislature created Allen County, Missouri. However, on February 14, 1845, the legislature created Atchison County out of the territory earlier assigned to Allen County. Atchison County was named in honor of David R. Atchison, who was then representing Missouri in the U.S. Senate. It was not until 1847 that the Missouri legislature repealed the law that had established boundaries for an Allen County. David R. Atchison was a native of Kentucky and a lawyer. He moved to Missouri in 1830 and here he became a member of the lower house of the state legislature. He also served as an officer in Missouri's state militia and in 1838 he was promoted to the rank of major-general. In 1843 Atchison entered the U.S. Senate and he represented Missouri in that body until 1855. He became a powerful figure in the senate and on 16 occasions he was chosen as president *pro tempore* of the senate. He played an active pro-slavery role in securing passage, in 1854, of the Kansas-Nebraska bill which created both Kansas territory and Nebraska territory and permitted slavery in these new territories. After leaving the senate, Atchison was active in the pro-slavery cause in Kansas territory and he supported the Confederate side during the Civil War.

1454 *Audrain County*

Uncertain — Sources consulted offer differing opinions concerning the namesake of this county. Audrain County was created on January 12, 1831. Some sources say that its name honors Samuel Audrain "the first actual settler within its limits" while others indicate that the name honors a member of the Missouri legislature who represented Saint Charles County. This legislator's name is rendered variously as James H. Audrain, James S. Audrain and Charles H. Audrain although most accounts agree that his date of death was November 10, 1831. He is referred to as Colonel Charles H. Audrain in a *History of Audrain County, Missouri* published in 1884 by National Historical Company. In an earlier work, published in 1876, William S. Bryan and Robert Rose collaborated in compiling a *History of the Pioneer Families of Missouri.* Some biographical information is given by Bryan and Rose about the Missouri legislator who died on November 10, 1831. They indicate that his name was James H. Audrain:

James H. Audrain (1782–1831) — James H. Audrain, a son of Peter Audrain, was born in Pennsylvania on December 29, 1782. He lived for some time in Fort Wayne, Indiana where he was engaged in merchandising and he later served as a captain in the War of 1812. In 1816 James H. Audrain moved his family to Missouri territory. He was appointed colonel of militia, although it is not clear whether this promotion was made before or after his 1816 move to Missouri territory. Following residence in Saint Louis, Audrain moved to Saint Charles County, where he built a mill and distillery. In 1830 James H. Audrain was elected to the Missouri legislature and he died on November 10, 1831.

In William S. Bryan's and Robert Rose's work, the statement is made that Audrain County, Missouri was named in honor of this James H. Audrain (1782–1831).

1455 *Barry County*

Uncertain — There are numerous sources available to consult concerning the origin of this county's name and none of them are bashful about stating, with apparent certainty, what that origin is, but they are about equally divided between two answers to the question. About half name John Barry (–1803), the naval hero of the American Revolution, while the remainder assert that the county was named for William T. Barry (1784–1835), of President Andrew Jackson's cabinet.

John Barry (–1803)— Barry was born in Ireland about 1745 but immigrated to the American colonies at an early age. By 1760 he was a resident of Philadelphia. He became a successful merchant seaman and early in the American Revolution he was commissioned as a captain in the Continental navy. During the Revolution ships under his command scored both significant victories as well as some losses. He is deemed one of America's heroes of the American Revolution. After the war he saw further military service in our navy.

William T. Barry (1784–1835)— A native of Virginia and a graduate of the College of William & Mary in that state, Barry studied law, was admitted to the bar and then settled in Lexington, Kentucky. He soon found himself elected to the lower house of the Kentucky legislature and he served several terms in that body rising to become speaker of the house. In 1815 Barry entered the U.S. Senate to fill a vacancy caused by a resignation but Barry, himself resigned from the senate the following year. He then held a variety of political positions in Kentucky including judge, state senator, lieutenant-governor, secretary of state and chief justice of the state supreme court. Barry assisted Andrew Jackson in his successful bid for the presidency and, in repayment of that political debt, President Jackson appointed William T. Barry to be his first postmaster general. At that time the position of postmaster general was a member of the president's cabinet. He resigned from the cabinet on April 10, 1835, to accept his appointment as minister to Spain but he died enroute to Madrid on August 30, 1835.

This county was created on January 5, 1835. That date offers little clue concerning the namesake of Barry County. At that time William T. Barry was still serving as postmaster general in Andrew Jackson's cabinet and presumably doing little to call attention to himself. The only other Missouri county created that day, Polk County, offers no clue. It was named for James K. Polk (1795–1849) who eventually became president of our country, but on January 5, 1835, Polk was serving as a Tennessee representative in the U.S. House of Representatives.

1456 *Barton County*

David Barton (1783–1837)— A graduate of Greenville College in Tennessee, Barton studied law in that state. In 1809 he immigrated with his two brothers to Louisiana–Missouri territory and he settled in Saint Charles. After serving in the army during the War of 1812, Barton established a law practice in Saint Louis and became involved in the politics of Missouri territory. He served as attorney general of Missouri territory, as a judge of the Saint Louis circuit court and as a member of the house of representatives of Missouri territory. He was made speaker of the territorial house of representatives. In 1820, in preparation for Missouri's admission to statehood, a constitutional convention was held and David Barton was chosen as president of that convention. Missouri's first state legislature elected Barton to be one of the new state's first two United States senators. He represented Missouri in the U.S. Senate from December 3, 1821, to March 3, 1831. This county was created on December 12, 1855. George E. Ward was instrumental in securing creation of the new county and it was Mr. Ward who suggested that the new county be named in honor of Senator David Barton.

1457 *Bates County*

Uncertain— Sources consulted differ on the origin of this county's name but only two possibilities are mentioned: Edward Bates (1793–1869), who was attorney general in President Abraham Lincoln's cabinet and Frederick Bates (1777–1825), one of Missouri's early governors. Edward and Frederick Bates were brothers.

Edward Bates (1793–1869)— A native of Virginia, Edward Bates served in the army during the War of 1812. In 1814 he moved to Saint Louis, in Missouri territory and studied law. He was admitted to the bar in 1817. In 1820, in preparation for Missouri's admission to statehood, a constitutional convention was held and Edward Bates was a member of that convention. After Missouri was admitted to the Union, Edward Bates served in the lower house of the Missouri legislature and represented Missouri in the U.S. House of Representatives. After losing a bid for reelection to the federal congress, Edward Bates served in both houses of the Missouri legislature. Although Edward Bates owned slaves, he was on the side of the free-soilers and gradually became prominent as an anti-slavery advocate during the years when the slavery issue was becoming increasingly volatile. When Abraham Lincoln became president, he appointed Edward Bates to his cabinet as attorney general and Bates served in that post from March, 1861, to September, 1864.

Frederick Bates (1777–1825)— A native of Virginia and a lawyer, Frederick Bates moved to Michigan territory and was appointed by President Thomas Jefferson to be a judge in Michigan territory. Frederick Bates later served as secretary of Louisiana territory and from time to time he served as acting governor of that territory. From 1812 to 1820 Frederick Bates was secretary of Missouri territory. In August, 1824 he was elected governor of the state of Missouri and he was inaugurated in that office on November 15, 1824. He had served as Missouri's governor less than one year when he died in office on August 4, 1825.

Howard L. Conard's *Encyclopedia of the History of Missouri* published by the Southern History Company in 1901 states that "Some annalists [sic] have asserted that it [Bates County] was named in honor of Edward Bates of St. Louis, afterward attorney general in the cabinet of President Lincoln. This is an error. It was named for the elder brother of Edward Bates, Frederick Bates who was … governor of the state of Missouri." However, Conard offers no evidence to support this statement so we must still conclude that the origin of this county's name in uncertain.

1458 *Benton County*

Thomas H. Benton (1782–1858)— Benton was a native of North Carolina who served in the Tennessee senate and as a soldier in the War of 1812. Following the war, he moved to Missouri and he represented that state for thirty years in the U.S. Senate. In that body he championed many interests of the West including free 160 acre homesteads, pony express, telegraph and railroads. Benton was a moderate on the volatile slavery issue. He opposed both abolition of slavery and the extension of it. His primary concerns were peace and preservation of the union. These moderate positions proved unpopular. Some states which had named counties in Benton's honor renamed the and, in 1850, Missouri failed to return Benton to the senate. Following his ouster from the senate, Benton represented Missouri briefly in the U.S. House of Representatives. This county was formed on January 3, 1835, during Benton's thirty year term in the U.S. Senate.

1459 *Bollinger County*

George F. Bollinger (–1842)— A native of North Carolina and the son of a Revolutionary War soldier who was shot in his home by Tories, George Frederick Bollinger immigrated to the Cape Giradeau district in 1796. At that time this area was controlled by Spain. The Spanish commander of the post at Cape Giradeau promised Bollinger concessions of land if he would find potential settlers for this wilderness area and persuade them to move here. Bollinger returned to North Carolina and induced some twenty families to return with him and settle here. These colonists made the trip from North Carolina in wagons and they crossed the Mississippi River at Sainte Genevieve on January 1, 1800. These colonists were all members of the German Reformed church. They settled on the Whitewater River and, upon orders from the Spanish commander of the district, they formed a militia under the command of Major George F. Bollinger. Major Bollinger built a log mill here about 1801 which he soon replaced with a stone mill. Bollinger was a member of Missouri territory's first legislature and, when Missouri was admitted to the Union as a state, Bollinger served several terms in the state's senate. In 1828 he was president *pro-tempore* of the Missouri senate. This county was created in 1851.

1460 *Boone County*

Daniel Boone (1734–1820)— A native of Pennsylvania, Boone penetrated Kentucky when it was wilderness country and settled there with him family in 1775. He gained fame on America's rugged western frontier as explorer, Indian fighter and surveyor. To many of us, much of Kentucky still seems quite rural at the second millennium year of 2000 but to Daniel Boone, Kentucky was already becoming too crowded for his taste by 1799. In September, 1799, accompanied by some members of his family, Boone immigrated to what is now the state of Missouri. When Boone arrived here Missouri was under the control of Spain. He continued to live a long and hearty life and died in Saint Charles, Missouri on September 26, 1820. The Missouri territorial legislature created and named this county in his honor just two months later, on November 16, 1820.

1461 *Buchanan County*

James Buchanan (1791–1868)— A native of Pennsylvania, Buchanan served in a variety of political posts for more than 40 years. After brief duty in the military during the War of 1812, Buchanan began his political career in the Pennsylvania assembly and then he represented Pennsylvania for ten years in the U.S. House of Representatives. Following an assignment as minister to Russia, Buchanan was elected to represent Pennsylvania in the U.S. Senate where he served from 1834 to 1845. When James K. Polk became president, Buchanan joined his cabinet as secretary of state. Buchanan subsequently was our minister to Great Britain. Four years before the start of the Civil War, Buchanan was a elected as a Democrat to be president of the United States. During his presidency the nation moved rapidly toward Civil War and Buchanan was unable to avert it. Buchanan County, Missouri was created on December 31, 1838, before James Buchanan had become president. At the time that this Missouri county was created James Buchanan was serving Pennsylvania as a U.S. senator. Although it is surprising that Missouri would choose to name one of her counties for this still relatively obscure easterner, it has been verified that this county was named for this James Buchanan. On page number 123 of the house journal for December 13, 1838, it is shown that the house had under consideration a bill to create counties named Platte and De Kalb. Representative John P. Morris of Howard County moved to strike out the word "De Kalb" and substitute "Buchanan, in honor of James Buchanan, of Pennsylvania." Mr. Morris' motion prevailed 46 to 39.

1462 *Butler County*

William O. Butler (1791–1880)— Butler was born in what is now Kentucky one year before it became a state. When war with Great Britain was declared in 1812, Butler volunteered to serve as a private. He served with distinction in the War of 1812 and rose to the rank of brevet major. In 1817 Butler resigned from the army and was soon elected to the Kentucky legislature. He later represented Kentucky in the U.S. House of Representatives. When war was declared against Mexico in 1846, President James K. Polk appointed Butler to be a major-general and Butler served with distinction n the Mexican War. He was wounded at Monterrey, Mexico, and was present when Mexico City was captured. Shortly before the 1848 treaty of peace was signed with Mexico, Butler was given command of U.S. forces in Mexico. Later, in 1848, he ran for vice-president of the United States on the Democratic ticket headed by Lewis Cass. The Cass-Butler ticket won in Missouri but was unsuccessful in carrying the nation. This Missouri County was created and named in William O. Butler's honor on February 27, 1849, just a few months after his defeat at the polls for vice-president.

1463 *Caldwell County*

Uncertain— It is known that this county was created on December 29, 1836, and that the county's name was selected by Alexander W. Doniphan (1808–1887), who served in the Missouri legislature. It is also known that Alexander W. Doniphan intended the new county's name as an honor to a friend of his father's, Joseph Doniphan. However, sources consulted differ on whether that friend was John W. Caldwell (1757–1804) or Mathew Caldwell (–1842).

John W. Caldwell (1757–1804)— A native of Prince Edward County, Virginia, John W. Caldwell moved across the mountains to settle in the Kentucky wilderness when it was still a part of Virginia. He settled near what is now Danville, Kentucky, in 1781. Caldwell served in the military in actions against the Indians and rose in rank from common soldier to major-general of the militia. In 1786 George Rogers Clark (1752–1818) led a military expedition against the Wabash Indian tribes and John W. Caldwell served under Clark in that campaign. John W. Caldwell was active in the efforts to separate Kentucky from Virginia and secure Kentucky's admission to the Union as a separate state. He represented Nelson County in statehood conventions held in 1787 and 1788. After Kentucky achieved statehood in 1792, Caldwell served in the Kentucky senate. In 1804 he was elected lieutenant-governor of Kentucky but he had served only two months in that office at the time of his death in November, 1804.

Mathew Caldwell (–1842)— Mathew Caldwell was born about 1798 in either North Carolina or Kentucky. He immigrated to Missouri, where he conducted a trading business with the Indians. During the early 1830's, Mathew Caldwell moved from Missouri to Texas and he was one of the signers of Texas' 1836 Declaration of Independence. He served as a captain in Texas army defending Goliad and was wounded at the Council House fight with the Comanche Indians. That fight proved to be a major strategic blunder in the White-Texans relations with the Comanche Indians. Caldwell later participated in a more successful engagement against the Comanche in the Plum Creek fight. During Texas' war with Mexico for independence he was captured and held prisoner in Mexico. Upon his release he participated in the victory in the battle of the Salado. He died on December 28, 1842, in Gonzales, Texas, and was buried with military honors.

1464 *Callaway County*

James Callaway (1783–1815)— This Kentucky native was a grandson of the famous Daniel Boone (1734–1820), and like his grandfather, he emigrated from Kentucky to Missouri. However, Callaway returned to Kentucky to attend school and then returned to Missouri in 1805. In 1813 he organized a company of rangers and fought against Indians in the vicinity of Rock Island, Illinois. In 1815 Captain Callaway organized a new company of rangers to protect settlers in Missouri territory from marauding Indians. He lost his life in a battle with Indians about 60 miles west of Saint Louis, near a branch of the Loutre River, in early March, 1815. This county was created on November 25, 1820. At that time Missouri was still a territory.

1465 *Camden County*

Camden County, North Carolina— When this county was created on January 29, 1841, Martin Van Buren was president of our country. The county's original name was Kinderhook County, and that name was chosen in honor of President Van Buren, who was born in Kinderhook, New York. However Van Buren soon fell out of favor in Missouri and on February 23, 1843, Kinderhook County's name was changed to Camden County. The new name was chosen in memory of Camden County, North Carolina, from which a number of early settlers had come. The North Carolina county had been created and named in 1777, in honor of Charles Pratt, Earl of Camden (1714–1794). Van Buren County, Missouri, also had its name changed (to Cass County) although that name change did not take place until 1849.

Charles Pratt, Earl of Camden (1714–1794)— Pratt, who was born in London, England, served as attorney general and was a member of parliament. In 1761 he became chief justice of the court of common pleas and a decision that he rendered in the trial of John Wilkes concerning freedom of speech and freedom of the press made him one of the most popular men in England. A bit later, now titled Baron Camden, he became lord chancellor. He op-

posed England's treatment of the American colonies which earned him popularity here and was the reason that Camden County, North Carolina, was named for him. In 1786 Baron Camden was made First Earl of Camden and Viscount Bayham. He served more than ten years as president of the council.

1466 *Cape Girardeau County*

The Spanish district named Cape Girardeau which had been located here— Cape Girardeau County was created on October 1, 1812, before Missouri territory was officially created. On June 4, 1812, the portion of Louisiana–Missouri territory which was not within the relatively new state of Louisiana, was named Missouri territory. That June 4, 1812, organic act became official on December 7, 1812. In the interim, Cape Girardeau County was created. The name came from the name of the district that had been located here when Spain controlled Cape Girardeau and the Spanish district was named for a promontory, just north of the present city of Cape Girardeau, Missouri. The cape's name originated with the name of an ensign with French troops who at one time was stationed across the Mississippi River and a bit north of Cape Girardeau at Kaskaskia in the present state of Illinois. His name was Jean B. Girardot and he was stationed at Kaskaskia from about 1704 to about 1720. In 1735, after resigning from the French military, Jean B. Girardot established an Indian fur trading post on a high rock bluff which commanded a view of the promontory (Cape Girardeau) and provided protection for boats. His trading post became a common stop for boatmen and missionaries traveling on the Mississippi River. Early maps show various spellings for the cape's name and for the bend in the Mississippi River above the present city of Cape Girardeau These names include "Cape Girardot," "Cap Girardot," "Cape Girardo," and "Cape Girardeau." To be more precise about the naming chain, Cape Girardeau County was named for one of the five administrative districts into which Missouri was divided in 1804 after the United States acquired Missouri from France as part of the Louisiana Purchase. That U.S. administrative district's name merely perpetuated the name of the Spanish district here, which was named for the cape which was named for Ensign Jean B. Girardot. The ensign's name is rendered in some accounts as Slewe Girardah and in others as Sieur de Girardot.

1467 *Carroll County*

Charles Carroll (1737–1832)— Carroll was a native of Maryland and he represented that state in the Continental Congress. He was one of the signers of the Declaration of Independence and he later represented Maryland as a U.S. senator in the first congress of the United States. Carroll lived to be the last surviving signer of the Declaration of Independence and several states recognized that distinction by naming counties for him. This certainly was Missouri's motivation. In the original bill to create this new county, its name was to be Wakenda, which is the name of a stream that flows in this area of Missouri. The bill to create this new county as Wakenda County had passed the first and second readings in the legislature when the Missouri legislators received the news that the last surviving signer of the Declaration of Independence, Charles Carroll, had died on November 14, 1832. The name of the new county was changed to Carroll and the new county was born with that name on January 2, 1833.

1468 *Carter County*

Zimri A. Carter (1794–1870)— A native of the Abbeville district of South Carolina, Zimri A. Carter came to Missouri in 1812 and became the first known White settler of the present Carter County. He made his home a few miles south of the present town of Van Buren, Missouri. Carter was soon joined by the Chilton, Kennard, Snyder and Kelly families, all of whom settled near Zimri A. Carter's residence. Carter at one time was a judge of the county court. This county was created on March 10, 1859.

1469 *Cass County*

Lewis Cass (1782–1866)— A native of New Hampshire, Cass served in the army in the War of 1812 and rose to the rank of brigadier-general. Following that war Cass held a variety of important political positions and was the candidate of the Democratic party in 1848 for president of the United States. He lost to Zachary Taylor. Cass served as governor of Michigan territory, secretary of war under Andrew Jackson, minister to France, U.S. senator from Michigan and secretary of state under President James Buchanan. This county was originally created in 1835 and named Van Buren County for Martin Van Buren, who was then serving as vice-president under President Andrew Jackson. Van Buren was elected as a Democrat in the

1836 election for president and he held that office from 1837 to 1841. However, in the 1848 election, Martin Van Buren ran for president on the Free Soil party, which infuriated large numbers of citizens in the slave state of Missouri and Van Buren contributed to the defeat of the Democratic party's nominee, Lewis Cass. The Democratic party's platform, on which Cass had run, avowed its readiness to tolerate slavery in the territories recently acquired from Mexico. On February 19, 1849, the Missouri legislature banished the name Van Buren from Missouri's map of counties and replaced it with the name Cass, in honor of the presidential nominee whom Van Buren had betrayed in the 1848 presidential election.

1470 *Cedar County*

Cedar Creek— This county in western Missouri lies in the northern section of the Ozark Mountains. It was created on February 14, 1845, and named for one of the streams that flows through it, Cedar Creek. Other significant streams here are Sac River, Little Sac River and Horse Creek. Cedar Creek was named for the cedar trees which were plentiful along the banks of Cedar Creek. *Cedar* is the common name applied to a number of different genera and families of trees. Actually other trees are more plentiful in Cedar County than cedars. These trees include maple, oak, walnut and hickory.

1471 *Chariton County*

Chariton River and/or the town of Chariton, Missouri territory— Chariton County, in north-central Missouri, was created on November 16, 1820, and named for the Chariton River, which flows through it, and/or the town a Chariton, which had been laid out here in 1817 or 1818. At the time that Chariton County was created, it was part of Missouri territory and it stretched north all the way to what is now the southern border of the state of Iowa.

Chariton River— The Chariton, some 280 miles long, is a major tributary of the Missouri River. It rises in southern Iowa, flows east and then south across the Missouri border and continues to head essentially due south as it flows across northern Missouri, and through Chariton County. It ends its journey and spills its waters into the Missouri River near the border between Chariton County, Missouri, and Howard County, Missouri. According to some accounts the Chariton River was named for a fur trader who had a trading camp near the mouth of the Chariton

River. His name is rendered variously as Chariton, Charaton and Chorette. One source indicates that this fur trader was a Frenchman named John Chariton while other sources speculate that the name may have come from that of a French fur trader from Saint Louis, Joseph Chorette (–1795). When the Lewis and Clark Expedition passed through here in 1804, while ascending the Missouri River, they passed the mouths of both the Big Chariton River and the Little Chariton River. These two rivers then had separate mouths on the Missouri River. Erosion and high waters subsequently united these two streams into one Chariton River.

Town of Chariton, Missouri territory— The town of Chariton was laid out in 1817 or 1818 near the mouth(s) of the Chariton River(s), for which it was named. When Chariton County was created in 1820, the town of Chariton was the new county's first seat of justice. It was never large. In 1821, when it was the height of its prosperity there were only about 35 families residing here. At that time it had a courthouse, schoolhouse, steam mill and one store. In 1824 the Missouri River overflowed and did significant damage to the town. Its residents began moving elsewhere and by 1832 it had been completely abandoned. According to one account, the former town of Chariton had become part of a farm and, by 1900, and no evidence remained of the structures which formerly resided here.

1472 *Christian County*

Christian County, Kentucky— This Missouri County was created on March 8, 1859. Its name was suggested by Mrs. Thomas Neaves (or Neeves), who had immigrated to this section of Missouri from Christian County, Kentucky. That Kentucky county had been created in 1796 and named for William Christian (–1786).

William Christian (–1786)— A native of Virginia and a brother-in-law of Patrick Henry, Christian served as an army officer in the French and Indian wars prior to the American Revolution. By 1774 he was a colonel of the militia and during the following year he was a member of Virginia's general state convention. During the Revolution, Christian served first as a colonel in the Virginia line of the regular army and later in command of the militia in his area of Virginia. After the war Christian served for several years in the Virginia legislature and in 1785 he moved to Kentucky. The following year he was killed by Indians.

1473 *Clark County*

William Clark (1770–1838)— Clark was a native of Virginia who served in the army in battles with Indians on America's western frontier. Together with Captain Meriwether Lewis, Clark led the Lewis and Clark Expedition (1804–1806) to the Pacific Northwest. The Lewis & Clark party were the first White men, south of Canada, to travel on land to the Pacific Northwest coast and back. Following the expedition Clark served as superintendent of Indian affairs for Louisiana territory. In the spring of 1813, President James Madison appointed William Clark to be governor of Missouri territory. His appointment became effective on June 16, 1813, and Clark served as Missouri's final territorial governor prior to Missouri's admission to statehood. Clark County, Missouri, was created on December 13, 1836. It lies in the northeastern corner of Missouri adjacent to Lewis County, Missouri, which was named for the other leader of the Lewis and Clark Expedition, Meriwether Lewis (1774–1809).

1474 *Clay County*

Henry Clay (1777–1852)— Clay represented Kentucky in both branches of the U.S. Congress. For many years he was one of the more prominent figures in American politics but his several bids for the presidency were unsuccessful. He was influential in effecting important compromises between northern and southern interests during the years that secession and civil war were imminent. This county created on January 2, 1822.

1475 *Clinton County*

De Witt Clinton (1769–1828)— This New York state native held many of the important political offices in that state. Clinton served in both houses of the state legislature and as mayor of New York City. He represented New York in the U.S. Senate and in 1812 he was the Federalist candidate for president, running against President James Madison. In 1817 Clinton was elected as New York's governor. As governor, he was the principal promoter of the Erie Canal, which was instrumental in linking the vast agricultural and timber lands in our country's West with eastern markets. The canal spurred our nation's growth. In 1825, when the Erie Canal was completed from the Hudson River in New York state to Lake Erie in the West, the remote wilderness of Missouri was, virtually, moved hundreds of miles closer to eastern markets.

This county was created on January 2, 1833, five years after De Witt Clinton's death. A number of sources on the history and geography of Missouri state that this county was named for George Clinton (1739–1812), who served as President Thomas Jefferson's vice-president. However, the language in the law that created this county makes it very clear that it was named for De Witt Clinton, rather than George Clinton. Some of the pertinent language is "…the same is hereby declared to be a separate and distinct county, to be known and called by the name of Clinton, in honor of De Witt Clinton, of New York."

1476 Cole County

Stephen Cole (–1822)— Cole was one of the first pioneers of central Missouri. He settled with a small party at, or near, the present site of Boonville, in the what is now Cooper County, Missouri. He was instrumental in the erection of Cole's Fort at Boonville and both the fort and Stephen Cole were important in the successful defense of the settlement here against Indians during the War of 1812. He is described in James E. Ford's 1938 history of Jefferson City and Cole County as "…a large, strong, uneducated frontiersman, a captain of militia and an Indian fighter." He was a participant in trade along the Santa Fe trail and he was killed by an Indian on the banks of the Rio Grande River in 1822. Cole County was created and named in his honor on November 16, 1820, while Missouri was still a territory.

1477 Cooper County

Uncertain— This county was created on December 17, 1818. At that time, Missouri was still a territory. It is uncertain whom the namesake of this county was. A number of sources consulted indicate that this county was named for Sarshall Cooper, but a few sources state that the name was intended to honor Colonel Benjamin Cooper. Howard L. Conard's 1901 *Encyclopedia of the History of Missouri* admits that it is uncertain whether the county was named for Benjamin Cooper or Sarshall Cooper.

Benjamin Cooper— Colonel Benjamin Cooper, originally of Madison County, Kentucky, came with his family to Missouri before it became Missouri territory. He settled in remote country in what would later be Howard County, Missouri. He was ordered by the territorial governor to move, with his family, to a better protected site and he complied, but in 1810 he re-

turned to the site that he had originally selected and made his permanent home there. Benjamin Cooper served in the Missouri senate in 1820.

Sarshall Cooper (–)— Sarshall Cooper was a member of a Virginia family from Culpeper County, who immigrated to Kentucky. He soon moved still further west, to Missouri, while it was part of Louisiana — Missouri territory. He arrived here in 1810 and he settled in what is now Saint Charles County. There Sarshall Cooper built a fort on the north bank of the Missouri River. The fort was known as Cooper's Fort. During the War of 1812 he was active in protecting Missouri settlers from Indians but was shot by Indians, himself, while inside his cabin within the fort. One account states that Sarshall Cooper died in the spring of 1815, while other sources place the date of his death at various dates in 1814. Most sources indicate that Sarshall Cooper was shot and killed by a lone Indian through a chink in his cabin. These sources indicate that he was holding an infant in his lap at the time that he was shot but that the infant escaped injury.

1478 Crawford County

William H. Crawford (1772–1834)— Crawford served in the Georgia legislature and as a U.S. senator from Georgia. He was elected president *pro tempore* of the senate and he later served as minister to France, secretary of war and secretary of the treasury. Crawford was a serious candidate for the presidency in both 1816 and 1824. This Missouri county was created and named in his honor on January 23, 1829.

1479 Dade County

Francis L. Dade (–1835)— A native of Virginia, Dade was appointed a commissioned officer in the U.S. army without having been trained at West Point. His original commission was as third lieutenant. He served under General Jackson at Pensacola, Florida, where he met and married a local girl. By 1828, he had risen to the rank of brevet major. Stationed at Fort Brooke on Florida's Tampa Bay, in 1835 Dade was ordered to put down unrest among some Seminole Indians. On December 28, 1835, near the present town of Bushnell, Florida, a party of Seminole Indians and Blacks ambushed and massacred Dade and all but about three of his force of some 110 men. This massacre marked the start of the second Seminole war in Florida. Dade County, Missouri,

was created and named in Major Dade's honor in January, 1841.

1480 Dallas County

George M. Dallas (1792–1864)— Dallas was a native of Philadelphia, Pennsylvania, and he served as mayor of that city. He was later a U.S. senator, attorney general of Pennsylvania and minister to Russia. He subsequently served as vice-president of the United States and minister to England. When this county was originally created in 1841, it was named Niangua County. That name honored the Niangua River, which flows through this county. On December 4, 1844, the Democratic ticket of James K. Polk for president and George M. Dallas for vice-president won the popular election. This county's name was changed to Dallas County on December 16, 1844, when George M. Dallas was vice-president-elect.

1481 Daviess County

Joseph H. Daveiss (1774–1811)— Daveiss was born in Virginia but moved with his parents to the wilderness of Kentucky when he was still a young boy. There he studied law and became a successful attorney. In 1807, Daveiss, as attorney for the United States, prosecuted Aaron Burr for treason. Burr was acquitted. In the fall of 1811 Daveiss joined General William Henry Harrison's army to fight the Indians. Colonel Daveiss died in the battle of Tippecanoe in Indiana in November, 1811, leading a charge of his men against the Indians. Daviess County, Missouri, was created on December 29, 1836. In the act that created this county, Joseph H. Daveiss' name is misspelled: "…in honor of Colonel Joseph H. Daviess, who fell at the battle of Tippecanoe."

1482 De Kalb County

Johann Kalb, Baron de Kalb (1721–1780)— Kalb was born in the province of Alsace, which at that time belonged to France. He was a general in the French army and resigned that commission to come to America to assist the colonies in the Revolutionary War. He served as a general in the American revolutionary army and he died in combat here.

1483 Dent County

Lewis Dent (–)— Lewis Dent was a one of a number of emigrants from Tennessee who were the early settlers of this area of Missouri. Lewis Dent came here about 1835 and settled near the site of the present Salem, Missouri. After Dent County had been created and named in his honor on February 10, 1851, Lewis Dent became the new county's first representative in the lower house of the state legislature. Of the dozens of sources consulted to determine the origin of this county's name, all sources but one agree that this county's name honors Lewis Dent. The source with a different opinion is Nathan H. Parker. In his work entitled *Missouri as it is in 1867*, Parker states that this county "...was named in honor of Frederick Dent, an early and respected citizen of the state." Parker offers no evidence to substantiate this claim nor does he give any further information about this Frederick Dent. Most of the sources who claim that the county's name honor Lewis Dent offer a little bit of information about him and Howard L. Conard's *Encyclopedia of the History of Missouri* published in 1901 states that Lewis Dent is the man and provides a bit of information about him.

1484 *Douglas County*

Stephen Douglas (1813–1861) — Barely five feet tall, the "Little Giant" is most remembered as a political opponent of Abraham Lincoln. Douglas was born in Vermont and moved to Illinois where he enjoyed rapid political success. He served on the state supreme court, in the state legislature and as secretary of state. Following two terms in the U.S. House of Representatives, Douglas was elected to the U.S. Senate. In that body Douglas took courageous positions on the slavery issue which first outraged abolitionist sentiment and later infuriated the South. In 1858 Douglas ran for reelection to the U.S. Senate against Abraham Lincoln. Following the famous Lincoln-Douglas debates, the Republicans won the popular election but that state legislature reelected Douglas to the senate. Lincoln and Douglas were rivals again in 1860 for the presidency. Following Lincoln's election and the start of the Civil War, Douglas gave the president his active support. This county was created on October 29, 1857, four years before the start of the Civil War, while Stephen Douglas was serving in the United States senate.

1485 *Dunklin County*

Daniel Dunklin (1790–1844) — A native of the Greenville district of South Carolina and a lawyer, Dunklin came to Missouri territory in 1810, and he served in the territorial militia here. Dunklin was elected to the state of Missouri's house of representatives, where he served in 1822 and 1823. From 1828 to 1832, he was Missouri's lieutenant-governor and on August 6, 1832, he was elected by popular vote to be the state's governor. He served in that office from November 19, 1832, until September 30, 1836. As governor, Dunklin gave priority to improving the common and public schools of Missouri.

1486 *Franklin County*

Benjamin Franklin (1706–1790) — Franklin was a native of Massachusetts who moved to Pennsylvania in his teens. Poverty denied him a formal education but he became the leading printer and editor in North America. Franklin gained fame for his discoveries and inventions in the physical sciences and he distinguished himself as author, philosopher and diplomat. Franklin was a signer of the Declaration of Independence and an important member of the convention which framed the U.S. Constitution. This county was formed on December 11, 1818, while Missouri was still a territory.

1487 *Gasconade County*

Gasconade River — This county was created on November 25, 1820, as part of Missouri territory. It was named for the Gasconade River, a major tributary of the Missouri River, which flows through it. Back in 1820, the Gasconade River traversed the entire length of Gasconade County, from south to north. Since that time Gasconade County has been reduced in size and the Gasconade River now enters Gasconade County on its western border near the present Mt. Sterling, Missouri. However, it is still within Gasconade County and the final portion of the Gasconade River's 265 mile journey, from its source, on Missouri's Ozark plateau, takes place here. The origin of the name *Gasconade* is uncertain but several writers on Missouri's history and geography have commented on it. Floyd C. Shoemaker provides a possible source for the name in his work entitled *Missouri & Missourians*, published in 1943. Shoemaker states that "It probably derived from the French word *gascon* meaning 'boaster, braggart' which may have been applied to the people who lived along the river and who may have been inclined to brag about their exploits..." Walter Williams' 1904 book entitled *The State of Missouri* elaborates on this possible explanation, stating that it was "...so called by the French settlers, after Gascon, inhabitant of Gascony

in France, who was distinguished for bragging and bluster." More on this theme for the origin of the Gasconade River's name is given in David W. Eaton's article on Missouri's place name origins, which appeared in the January, 1917, issue of the *Missouri Historical Review*. Eaton states the Gascon-Gascony-boastfulness theory but infers that it applied, in general, to the people of Gascony, in France rather than to one individual there. Eaton then states that the term "...was applied by the early French to the Indians living on its banks who bragged about their exploits." The English language contains both the words *gascon* and *gasconade*, and both of these words are of French origin and refer "boasting."

1488 *Gentry County*

Richard Gentry (1788–1837) — A native of Kentucky and a lieutenant in the Kentucky militia by the age of twenty, Gentry was soon promoted to captain and then to regimental ensign of Kentucky volunteers. These volunteers assisted General William Henry Harrison in the War of 1812. At the conclusion of that war, Gentry took his family and slaves and moved to Missouri territory. He arrived at Saint Louis in 1816 but moved inland from the Mississippi River and in 1820 he was one of the founders of the town of Columbia in central Missouri territory. He built a hotel here and made Columbia his home. In 1821 Gentry was appointed captain in the Missouri state militia and he was promoted to colonel the following year. In 1826 Richard Gentry was elected to the Missouri senate and he served in that body four years. In 1832, when northern Indians were threatening to raid Missouri, Gentry was promoted to major-general and commander of all Missouri troops. Indians were also causing the United States government problems elsewhere. In Florida territory the Second Seminole Indian War broke out in late 1835 and by 1837 President Martin Van Buren appealed to Missouri for assistance against the Seminoles. Missouri readily accepted this challenge and General Richard Gentry was assigned the rank of colonel when he led some 600 Missouri volunteers into battle against the Seminole Indians. He was killed in combat in Florida territory on Christmas Day, 1837.

1489 *Greene County*

Nathanael Greene (1742–1786) — Greene was born in Rhode Island and served briefly in the Rhode Island legislature. He gained fame as one of the ablest American generals in the Revolutionary War. This Missouri county was created on January 2, 1833, and named in honor of General Nathanael Greene. However the new county's name was misspelled as "Green" in the original act that created this county.

1490 *Grundy County*

Felix Grundy (1777–1840) — A native of Virginia, Grundy moved to Kentucky with his family in his youth. There he became a member of the state's constitutional convention and served in the state legislature. In 1806 Grundy was appointed to Kentucky's supreme court and in 1807 he was made its chief justice. Finding the salary inadequate, Grundy resigned and moved to Tennessee where he again became active in politics and gained national notice. He served in the Tennessee legislature and represented that state in both houses of the U.S. Congress. In 1838 President Martin Van Buren appointed Grundy to serve in his cabinet as attorney general. Felix Grundy died on December 19, 1840, and this county was created on January 29, 1841.

1491 *Harrison County*

Albert G. Harrison (–1839) — A native of Kentucky and a lawyer, Harrison immigrated to Fulton, Missouri. Here he was elected to represent Missouri in the U.S. House of Representatives and he served in that body from December 7, 1835, until March 3, 1839. He died at Fulton, Missouri on September 7, 1839. Sources consulted differ on the date that this county was created but the dates most frequently mentioned are February 22, 1843, and February 14, 1845.

1492 *Henry County*

Patrick Henry (1736–1799) — Henry was a native of Virginia and a lawyer. He served in the Virginia legislature, as governor of Virginia and as a delegate to the first and second Continental Congresses. Henry was one of America's key revolutionary leaders. He was a great orator and he is remembered for his call to arms against the British "Give me liberty or give me death." Henry opposed Virginia's ratification of the federal constitution and his views played a role in the later adoption of the Bill of Rights. This county was originally created on December 13, 1834, and named Rives County, in honor of William C. Rives (1793–1868), who had represented Virginia, as a Democrat, in the United States senate. In the presidential election of 1840, Rives opposed the Democratic President Martin Van Buren's bid for reelection and supported his Whig opponent, William Henry Harrison. On account of this William C. Rives became unpopular in Missouri and a move was initiated to change the name of Rives County, Missouri. The first name suggested was Albemarle County. However, the name which was finally selected when Rives County was renamed in February, 1841, was Henry County, in honor of Patrick Henry.

1493 *Hickory County*

Andrew Jackson (1767–1845) — Hickory trees abound in the upland areas of this county but the county was not named for them. Rather, this is one of two Missouri counties that are named in honor of Andrew Jackson. The first was created in 1826 and named Jackson County. This second Missouri county to be named in his honor derives its name from Andrew Jackson's nickname "Old Hickory." Andrew Jackson was born on the border of North Carolina and South Carolina. He represented Tennessee in both branches of the U.S. Congress and gained fame and popularity for his military exploits in wars with the Indians and in the War of 1812. He was provisional military governor of Florida and, from 1829 to 1837, General Jackson was president of the United States. His presidency reflected the frontier spirit of America. This second Missouri county to be named in Andrew Jackson's honor was created on February 14, 1845, just four months prior to Andrew Jackson's death. The original county seat of Hickory County was in the home of Joel B. Halbert. By December, 1846, the county seat of Hickory County, Missouri, was in the community named Hermitage, Missouri. Andrew Jackson's home is Tennessee is called the Hermitage.

1494 *Holt County*

David R. Holt (1803–1840) — David Rice Holt was born in Greene County, Tennessee, on March 8, 1803. A graduate of Washington College in Virginia, Rice first chose the ministry as his profession and he was licensed by his presbytery. Soon afterward he changed his vocation to medicine. After completion of a course of study in medicine, Dr. Holt practiced medicine for the remainder of his brief life. In 1838 Holt moved to the area of Missouri which became Platte County on December 31, 1838. In 1840 he was elected to represent Platte County in the Missouri legislature and it was during this term of the legislature that Dr. Holt died. He died in Jefferson City in December, 1840, and was buried in that city. This county in northwestern Missouri was originally named Nodaway County when it was created on January 29, 1841. Less than three weeks later, on February 15, 1841, the legislature changed the county's name to Holt in honor of their fellow legislator who had died during the current legislative session. Nodaway County still appears on Missouri's map of counties but this is a different Nodaway County, which was organized in 1845. Nodaway County is also in northwestern Missouri and for a few miles Holt County and Nodaway County share a common border.

1495 *Howard County*

Benjamin Howard (1760–1814) — A native of Virginia, Howard moved with his family to the wilderness of what is now Kentucky in the early 1770's. There he became a lawyer and served in the lower house of the Kentucky legislature. He also represented Kentucky in the U.S. House of Representatives. On April 18, 1810, President James Madison appointed Howard as governor of Louisiana–Missouri territory, which then included the present state of Missouri. On June 4, 1812, while Howard was still the territorial governor, President Madison signed the organic law changing the status of the portion of Louisiana–Missouri territory which was Missouri and designating it (effective December 7, 1812), Missouri territory. This name change was necessary to avoid confusion with the recently created state of Louisiana. Benjamin Howard continued as governor of the nascent Missouri territory while its status changed on December 7, 1812, to that of an official territory of the United States, named Missouri territory, but he resigned as territorial governor on March 12, 1813, to accept an appointment as brigadier-general in the army. Thus Howard was, briefly, the first official governor of Missouri territory. He was on duty with the army at Saint Louis when he died, unexpectedly, on September 18, 1814. Howard County, Missouri territory, was created just 16 months later, on January 23, 1816.

1496 *Howell County*

Uncertain — In the 1830's a Mr. Howell became the first known White settler of this area of southern Missouri. He settled at what is now the community of West Plains, Missouri, which is the present county seat of Howell County. Most accounts render this pioneer settler's name as James Howell but one source refers to him as Josiah Howell. As other settlers arrived to join Mr. Howell in this area, the valley here came to be called Howell Valley. Howell County, Missouri, was created on March 2, 1857, and named either directly for the early settler, James (or Josiah) Howell, or for Howell Valley, which was named for him. Howard L. Conard tells us in his *Encyclopedia of the History of Missouri*, published in 1901, that "It was not until 1832 that any fixed settlement was made. That year James Howell, after whom the county was named, settled on the present site of West Plains, and the valley, a few years later ... was called Howell Valley."

1497 *Iron County*

Iron ore in the county— This county in southeastern Missouri lies in the eastern end of the Ozark Mountains. It was created on February 17, 1857, and named for its extensive iron ore deposits. Pilot Knob here has been a particularly rich source of iron ore.

1498 *Jackson County*

Andrew Jackson (1767–1845)— Jackson was born on the border of North Carolina and South Carolina. He represented Tennessee in both branches of the U.S. Congress and gained fame and popularity for his military exploits in wars with the Indians and in the War of 1812. He was provisional military governor of Florida and, from 1829 to 1837, General Jackson was president of the United States. His presidency reflected the frontier spirit of America. Jackson, who was very popular in Missouri, first ran for the presidency in 1824. He received more popular votes than any other candidate and although he also received more electoral votes than any other candidate, he lacked a majority and the election was decided in the house of representatives. The house selected John Quincy Adams to be our president. Jackson County, Missouri, was created and named in Andrew Jackson's honor after that defeat, on December 15, 1826, before he was elected president. This is one of two Missouri counties that are named in honor of Andrew Jackson. A second Missouri county, named Hickory County, was created and named in his honor on February 14, 1845, just four months prior to Jackson's death. That county derived its name from Andrew Jackson's nickname, "Old Hickory."

1499 *Jasper County*

William Jasper (–1779)— This Revolutionary War hero was born in South Carolina about 1750, but moved to Georgia where he grew up on a farm. He first became a hero in a dramatic event at the battle of Fort Moultrie, when he courageously exposed himself to enemy fire to recover a flag which had been shot down. For this heroism Sergeant Jasper was awarded a sword and offered a promotion to lieutenant but he declined the promotion. Later employed as a scout, Jasper made several trips behind enemy lines in Georgia while operating from the swamps there. In a dramatic exploit near Savannah, Georgia, he and his close friend, John Newton, rescued several Americans who were prisoners and took their guards as prisoners of war. Jasper was shot and killed during the siege of Savannah while recovering the flag which had been shot down. Geographic names in several of our states link the names of the two heroic sergeants, Jasper and Newton. In some a county is named for one of them and its county seat is named for the other. In others, like Missouri, two counties are named for them. Jasper County, Missouri, was created in January, 1841, from the northern portion of Newton County and these two counties are today adjacent to each other in southwestern Missouri.

1500 *Jefferson County*

Thomas Jefferson (1743–1826)— Jefferson was a native of Virginia and a member of the Virginia legislature. He served Virginia as governor and was a delegate to the second Continental Congress. Jefferson was the author of the Declaration of Independence and one of its signers. He was minister to France, secretary of state, vice-president and president of the United States. As president, he accomplished the Louisiana Purchase and he arranged the Lewis and Clark Expedition to the Pacific Northwest. Jefferson was a true intellectual, thoroughly knowledgeable in the arts and sciences. His political theories were pivotal in the formation of our infant republic. This county was created on December 8, 1818, from territory which Thomas Jefferson had acquired for our country from France as part of the Louisiana Purchase. At the time that this county was created, Missouri was still a territory.

1501 *Johnson County*

Richard M. Johnson (1780–1850)— Richard Mentor Johnson was born in Kentucky when it was still a part of Virginia. Kentucky was admitted to the union as a separate state in 1792 and Johnson served in the lower house of the Kentucky legislature from 1804 to 1806. He later represented Kentucky for a decade in the U.S. House of Representatives with an interruption to serve as a colonel in the War of 1812. The Kentucky forces that Colonel Johnson led at the battle of the Thames River, in Canada, scored an important victory, which made Johnson a hero but he was severely wounded in that battle. He later represented Kentucky in the U.S. Senate and then returned to the U.S. House of Representatives. From March 4, 1837, to March 3, 1841, Richard Mentor Johnson was vice-president of the United States under President Martin Van Buren. Johnson County, Missouri was created and named in his honor on December 13, 1834.

1502 *Knox County*

Henry Knox (1750–1806)— This Massachusetts native participated in many of the important military engagements of the American Revolution and rose to the rank of major-general. After the war, Knox commanded West Point and he conceived and organized the Society of Cincinnati, an elite group of former Revolutionary officers. In 1785 he was appointed secretary of war under the Articles of Confederation and he retained that position in the first cabinet of the United States under President George Washington.

1503 *Laclede County*

Pierre Laclede Liguest (–1778)— Pierre Laclede Liguest was born in the Pyrenees Mountains of France about 1724. Known as Pierre Laclede, he immigrated to North America and arrived at New Orleans in 1755. He became a member of the firm of Maxent, Laclede & Company, which traded with the Indians. In August, 1763, Laclede ascended the Mississippi River. In December of that year he selected a site for a trading post on the west bank of the Mississippi River. It was located about ten miles below the confluence of the Mississippi and Missouri Rivers. Starting in February, 1764, building of the trading post commenced. Laclede named his post Saint Louis, and Pierre Laclede is recognized in history as the founder of Saint Louis, Missouri. The Saint Louis area was rugged frontier country at that time and it was considered a major accomplishment when he persuaded about 40 families to settle here. On account of this colony, for about 18 months Pierre Laclede was *de facto* dictator of upper Louisiana. He is, however, remembered as a benevolent dictator. Laclede encountered business difficulties and spent two years in New Orleans trying to improve his situation. In the spring of 1778, he fell seriously ill but he attempted to return to Saint Louis. On that return trip, he fell ill and died.

1504 *Lafayette County*

Marie Joseph Paul Yves Roch Gilbert du Motier, Marquis de Lafayette (1757–1834) — Lafayette was a French aristocrat who served briefly in the French army. He came to America in 1777 to assist the American Revolutionary army. He was granted an honorary commission as major general by the Continental Congress and served with distinction in a number of battles in the Revolutionary War. This county was created on November 16, 1820, and named Lillard County, in honor of a Mr. Lillard, who was the member of the Missouri legislature who introduced the bill to create this new county. Lillard's name is given in some accounts as James Lillard and in others as William Lillard. Lillard had represented Cooper County in the 1820 Missouri constitutional convention and he was a member of Missouri's first state legislature. Lillard had come to Missouri from Tennessee and he returned to that state. This county's name was changed from Lillard County to Lafayette County on February 16, 1825, for two reasons. Lillard suffered ill health while residing in Missouri and was believed to comment disparagingly upon the Missouri climate about the time that he returned to Tennessee. More importantly, the Marquis de Lafayette came to the United States in 1824 as an honored guest of the Federal government. On April 29, 1825, he visited Saint Louis, Missouri, where about half the population assembled to greet him. It was very likely in anticipation of this visit to Missouri by Lafayette (as well as the fact that Mr. Lillard was no longer in good odor here) that the Missouri legislature changed this county's name to honor our nation's beloved French benefactor.

1505 *Lawrence County*

James Lawrence (1781–1813) — Lawrence was an officer in the United States navy who established a reputation for bravery in the war against Tripoli and in the War of 1812. He died in combat while commanding the *Chesapeake* against the British, near Boston. He is said to have uttered the famous phrase "Don't give up the ship"

while he lay mortally wounded in that battle. He died on June 4, 1813.

1506 *Lewis County*

Meriwether Lewis (1774–1809) — A native of Virginia and a neighbor and friend of Thomas Jefferson, Lewis served as an officer in the army and then, in 1801, President Jefferson selected him to be his aide. From 1804 to 1806 Meriwether Lewis and William Clark led the Lewis and Clark Expedition which President Jefferson sent to explore the Northwest to the Pacific Ocean. Their successful journey ended in September, 1806, when they returned to civilization at Saint Louis in what is now the state of Missouri. Lewis then served as governor of Louisiana territory from 1807 until his death in 1809. Lewis County, Missouri was created and named in his honor on January 2, 1833. When Clark County, Missouri was later created on December 13, 1836, Missouri had counties honoring both of the leaders of the Lewis and Clark Expedition. These two counties lie adjacent to each other in the northeastern corner of Missouri.

1507 *Lincoln County*

Lincoln County, Kentucky & Lincoln County, North Carolina — This county was created on December 14, 1818, by the legislature of Missouri territory. Major Christopher Clark was the member of the territorial legislature who selected this new county's name. According to a work entitled *History of Lincoln County, Missouri*, published by Goodspeed Publishing Company in 1888, Christopher Clark was an early resident of the portion of Saint Charles County from which this new county was to be carved. Goodspeed tells us that Major Clark gave the following speech when proposing his choice for the new county's name: "Mr. Speaker, I was the first man to drive a wagon across Big Creek, the boundary of the proposed new county, and the first permanent white settler within its limits. I was born, sir, in Link-horn [sic] County, N.C. I lived for many years in Link-horn [sic] County, in old Kaintuck [sic]. I wish to live, the remainder of my days, and die in Link-horn [sic] County, in Missouri; and I move, therefore,… the name Link-horn [sic]." Both Lincoln County, North Carolina, and Lincoln County, Kentucky, had been named for General Benjamin Lincoln (1733–1810). The clerk of the Missouri territorial legislature revised the spelling of the proposed new county's name from Link-horn to Lincoln, sacrificing a bit of local

color but producing a name for the county that was more correct, both grammatically and historically.

Benjamin Lincoln (1733–1810) — A native of Massachusetts, Lincoln was a member of the Massachusetts legislature and of the provincial congress. He served as an officer in the Revolutionary War and rose to the rank of major-general. In 1779, as commander of the southern department of the Continental army, he attempted, unsuccessfully, to rescue Savannah, Georgia, from the British. In 1781 General George Washington gave Lincoln the honor of accepting Cornwallis' sword when the British surrendered at Yorktown. Later in 1781 Lincoln was made secretary of war and he held that post for two years. He died on May 9, 1810, in Hingham, Massachusetts, in the same house in which he had been born.

1508 *Linn County*

Lewis F. Linn (1795–1843) — Lewis F. Linn, who was born near Louisville, Kentucky, in 1795, decided to make medicine his career. Although he had not yet completed his medical training, he served in the War of 1812 as a surgeon. After the war, he completed his medical training and settled on our country's western frontier in Missouri, where he practiced medicine and became an authority on Asiatic cholera. During the late 1820's Dr. Linn served one term in Missouri's state senate. In 1833, when U.S. Senator Alexander Buckner died, Linn was appointed by Missouri's governor to fill Buckner's seat. Dr. Linn was twice reelected to the U.S. Senate and he was serving in that body at the time of his death in 1843. This county was created and named in his honor on January 6, 1837, while Linn was a member of the U.S. Senate.

1509 *Livingston County*

Edward Livingston (1764–1836) — Livingston was born in New York, represented that state in the U.S. House of Representatives and served as mayor of New York City. Because of personal problems, Livingston moved to Louisiana to start a new life in 1804. There he served as Andrew Jackson's aide in the battle of New Orleans and was elected to the Louisiana legislature. He later represented Louisiana in both houses of the U.S. Congress and was President Andrew Jackson's secretary of state. Livingston drafted President Jackson's Proclamation to the People of South Carolina, which asserted the supremacy of the federal government in response to

South Carolina's 1832 Ordinance of Nullification. His last post was minister to France. Edward Livingston died in May, 1836, and this county was created on January 6, 1837.

1510 *McDonald County*

Alexander McDonald (–)— In the southwestern corner of Missouri there are three counties named for heroes of the American Revolution. All three of these men were sergeants and they all were from South Carolina. They served under another South Carolinian, General Francis Marion (–1795) and were known as "Marion's men." These three Missouri counties sit on top of each other; the northernmost of the three is Jasper County, named for Sergeant William Jasper (–1779) directly south of Jasper County lies Newton County, named for Sergeant John Newton (–1780); finally, below Newton County, in the extreme southwestern corner of Missouri, we find McDonald County, named for Sergeant Alexander McDonald. Alexander McDonald was from South Carolina, served in the American Revolution as a sergeant under General Francis Marion and had red hair. Beyond these known facts, other details about Sergeant McDonald are sketchy. After one engagement in the Revolution, General Francis Marion was deserted by all of the men who were with him at that time with two exceptions. The exceptions were Sergeant McDonald and Sergeant Davis. In Edward McCrady's work entitled *The History of South Carolina in the Revolution*, published in 1901, these two sergeants are said to have "afterwards distinguished themselves in his service." Hugh F. Rankin's 1973 biography of General Francis Marion mentions Sergeant McDonald a few times. From Rankin we learn that Sergeant McDonald fought under Marion in August, 1780 when Marion's troops defeated enemy forces at Nelson's Ferry, South Carolina. Rankin also tells us that Marion was camped at Indian Town, in South Carolina when he sent McDonald to spy on the enemy forces located at Georgetown, South Carolina. A final comment gleaned from Hugh F. Rankin's biography of General Marion tells us that Sergeant McDonald had red hair. This bit of trivia is mentioned in a paragraph that tells of McDonald's sharp shooting a British officer through the knee from a high perch in an oak tree. That British officer's name is Lieutenant George Torriano and this sharpshooting incident took place near the Black River, in South Carolina.

Bobby Gilmer Moss compiled a comprehensive *Roster of South Carolina Patriots in the American Revolution*, which was published in 1983. That roster lists four South Carolina soldiers of the American Revolution named Alexander McDonald:

1. Enlisted in the second regiment on August 1, 1779, as a sergeant under Captain Richard Baker. Re-enlisted November 1, 1779.

2. Served in the first regiment and was charged in 1779 with stealing soap. Found guilty by court-martial and sentenced to receive 75 lashes on his bare back.

3. Born 1750 and died 1844. Enlisted in the second regiment on November 4, 1775, as a sergeant. Promoted to sergeant-major on November 16, 1778. Re-enlisted under Captain Thomas Dunbar on November 1, 1779.

4. Enlisted in the first regiment on November 4, 1775, and re-enlisted during December, 1776. Served under Captain William Jackson in 1780.

Effective January 1, 1847, the Missouri legislature passed an act which was intended to create a new county named Seneca County. However, the creation of Seneca County was never perfected and the creation of this county was abandoned. On March 3, 1849, the Missouri legislature created McDonald County out of the same land which they earlier had intended to name Seneca.

1511 *Macon County*

Nathaniel Macon (1758–1837)— Macon was a native of North Carolina and a soldier in the Revolutionary War. He served in the North Carolina senate and was elected to the Continental Congress but declined to serve. He represented North Carolina for 37 years in both branches of the U.S. Congress, where he was speaker of the house and, later, president *pro tempore* of the senate. He believed strongly in economy of the public money and he was a defender of slavery. This county was created on January 6, 1837, about six months prior to Nathaniel Macon's death on June 29, 1837.

1512 *Madison County*

James Madison (1751–1836)— Madison was born in Virginia and served in the Virginia legislature and in the Continental Congress. He was a member of the convention which framed the U.S. Constitution and he collaborated with Hamilton and Jay in writing a series of papers under the title *The Federalist*, which explained the new constitution and advocated its

adoption. Madison represented Virginia in the U.S. House of Representatives, served for eight years as secretary of state and for eight years as president of the United States. James Madison's term as president ended on March 3, 1817, and this county was created and named in his honor on December 14, 1818, by the legislature of Missouri territory.

1513 *Maries County*

Maries River & Little Maries River— This county in central Missouri was created on March 2, 1855, and named for two rivers which flow through it, the Maries River and the Little Maries River. The Maries is a tributary of the Osage River and the Osage is an important tributary of the Missouri River. The Maries River and the Little Maries River both enter Maries County at the southern boundary of the county. Both of them then flow north through Maries County and unite and become one river just below Maries County's northern border. The combined stream is called the Maries River for the remainder of its brief journey to the Osage River. The confluence of the Maries and Osage Rivers is only about five miles below the confluence of the Osage River with the mighty Missouri River. The origin of the name Maries is uncertain. One suggested source involves the French word *marais*, which means "marsh," or "swamp." From that word may have derived a French name for the river *Le Marais des Cygnes*, which would have meant "marsh of swans." Some sources suggest that the Maries River and Little Maries River may have been named for two French girls but no support is given for this speculation, and even if this were the correct answer it is too vague to be of much help. French Catholics were the early White explorers of Missouri. An article which appeared in the August 2, 1925, issue of the *Saint Louis Globe Democrat* mentions, as a possibility, that these French Catholics may have named the two rivers in honor of Saint Mary. It is a matter of dogma of the Roman Catholic Church that Saint Mary was the virgin mother of Jesus Christ. This article in the *Globe Democrat* explains that the plural Maries may denote two rivers, both named for one saint, Saint Mary.

1514 *Marion County*

Francis Marion (–1795)— Marion is believed to have been born in South Carolina. He served in the army in battles against the Cherokee Indians and was elected to the provisional congress of 1775.

He served, with distinction, as an officer in the Revolutionary War and rose to the rank of general in that war. Marion was also a member of the South Carolina senate. This county was created and named for General Marion on December 14, 1822.

1515 *Mercer County*

Uncertain— This county was created in the 1840's and named for an officer in our nation's Revolutionary army, but sources consulted differ on which officer that was. Only two possibilities are mentioned: Hugh Mercer (–1777) and John F. Mercer (1759–1821). However, sources dealing with the history and geography of Missouri are about equally divided between those two choices.

Hugh Mercer (–1777)— Hugh Mercer was born about 1725 in Scotland and educated as a physician. He immigrated to America about 1747 and served in the army here as an officer during the French and Indian War. At the outbreak of the American Revolution, Hugh Mercer entered the Continental army, in which he attained the rank of brigadier-general. He served with distinction under General George Washington in the surprise attack on the British at Trenton, New Jersey, in late December, 1776. One week later, at the battle of Princeton, New Jersey, Hugh Mercer was severely wounded and he died of those wounds on January 12, 1777.

John F. Mercer (1759–1821)— A native of Virginia and a graduate of the College of William & Mary there, John F. Mercer served as an officer in the American Revolution from January, 1777, to 1779. He returned to Virginia and studied law under Thomas Jefferson. In 1780 he returned to the army. In 1781 John F. Mercer served under General Lafayette (1757–1834) and later raised and commanded a unit of militia grenadiers. He served in the Virginia legislature and as a Virginia delegate to the Continental Congress. In 1785 John F. Mercer moved to Maryland and he represented Maryland in the convention formed to draft a Constitution for a federal union. He was a strong opponent of the proposed constitution and he attacked the idea of allowing the federal supreme court to review decisions of lower courts and rule on their constitutionality. He walked out of this constitutional convention. He later served in the Maryland legislature, represented Maryland in the U.S. House of Representatives and was governor of Maryland.

It seems more probable that this county that this county was named for General Hugh Mercer than John F. Mercer. General Hugh Mercer lost his life from wounds that he suffered in the battle of Princeton, New Jersey. The county seat of Mercer County is named Princeton. David W. Eaton tells us that this was not just a coincidence. In his article dealing with Missouri place names, which appeared in the January, 1917, issue of the *Missouri Historical Review*, Eaton states that the county seat of Mercer County was named Princeton "after the battle in which the Revolutionary General Hugh Mercer lost his life." Howard L. Conard agrees. In Conard's *Encyclopedia of the History of Missouri*, published in 1901, he states that the town of Princeton, the Mercer County seat "was named after the place at which was fought the historic battle in which General Mercer lost his life."

1516 *Miller County*

John Miller (1781–1846)— Miller was born in Berkeley County, Virginia, which now is a part of the state of West Virginia. He moved to Steubenville, Ohio, where he edited and published two newspapers. Miller served as an officer during the War of 1812 and rose to the rank of colonel. We know that by 1818 Miller had moved to Missouri territory for he was registrar at the land office in Franklin, Missouri, in 1818. He held that post until 1825 when he was elected to be Missouri's fourth governor. Miller was re-elected and served as Missouri's governor from 1826 to 1832. He later represented Missouri in the U.S. House of Representatives for three consecutive two-year terms. In 1842 he decided not to run for a fourth term in congress and retired to private life when his term in congress ended in March, 1843. This county was created and named in Governor Miller's honor on February 6, 1837, after Miller's final term as Missouri's governor but before the start of his service in the U.S. House of Representatives.

1517 *Mississippi County*

Mississippi River— This county in southeastern Missouri borders the Mississippi River, for which it was named. In fact, apart from a short 20 mile stretch in northeastern Missouri, the Mississippi River constitutes the entire eastern border of the state of Missouri. The Mississippi River is the longest river in the United States and, counting its various tributaries, one of the world's major river systems. The river was named by the Ojibway Indians of Wisconsin. In their language *missi sipi* meant "great river." Mississippi County, Missouri, was created on February 14, 1845.

1518 *Moniteau County*

Moniteau Creek— This county in central Missouri was created on February 14, 1845 and named for Moniteau Creek, which flows through the western portion of Moniteau County and is a tributary of the Missouri River. A description of the Moniteau Creek's route is contained in an 1889 work published by the Goodspeed Publishing Company. Its title is *History of Cole, Moniteau, Morgan, Benton, Miller, Maries and Osage Counties, Missouri*. The description reads: "The Moniteau rises in Cooper County, receives Little Brush Creek seven miles above its mouth, and Little Moniteau two miles above its confluence with the Missouri." This description is more than one century old and rivers and streams change their courses over time so even if Goodspeed's words were entirely correct when this book was published, portions of it may no longer be accurate. That same 1889 work tells us that Moniteau Creek enters the Missouri River "above the old town of Marion." Moniteau Creek's name is a French corruption of an Indian name for the Deity, Sprit, or God. Most sources state that the Indians named Moniteau Creek for their Great Spirit because of the image of a man on a stone formation near the confluence of the Missouri River and Moniteau Creek. According to some of these sources, this stone formation had a painted figure of a man on it, which the Indians took to resemble the Great Spirit. However in J. E. Ford's book entitled *A History of Moniteau County, Missouri*, published in 1936, the rock wasn't painted but merely resembled the figure of a man when viewed from the correct angle. We won't be able to inspect this stone formation to determine which version is correct. It was blasted to bits during construction of the route for the Missouri Pacific Railroad.

1519 *Monroe County*

James Monroe (1758–1831)— Monroe, a native of Virginia, served in the Revolutionary War. Prior to his election as president of the United States, Monroe served in a wide variety of government posts. He served Virginia in the state legislature and as governor. He was a member of the Confederation congress and the U.S. Senate. He was minister to France and to Britain and he held two cabinet posts. As president, Monroe stressed limited government and strict construction of the constitution.

He acquired Florida for the U.S. from Spain and he was the author of a policy declaration (later known as the Monroe Doctrine) which proscribed outside interference in North and South America. This county was created in 1831.

1520 *Montgomery County*

Uncertain— Montgomery County, Missouri, was created on December 14, 1818, by the legislature of Missouri territory. Most sources dealing with the history and geography of Missouri merely state that this county was named for the American Revolutionary general, Richard Montgomery (1738–1775). All sources are agreed that this Missouri county's named honors General Richard Montgomery but there are a minority of sources who state that this county's name honors General Montgomery indirectly rather than directly. These sources contend that Montgomery County in Missouri territory was named for Montgomery County, Kentucky. That Kentucky county had been created in 1796 and named for General Richard Montgomery (1738–1775). Since no source has been found which states that this county was *not* named for Montgomery County, Kentucky, one is inclined to believe that it was named for that Kentucky county and that the sources which fail to mention this are merely taking a short cut and providing only the name of the hero who is the ultimate namesake of Montgomery County, Missouri.

Richard Montgomery (1738–1775)— Montgomery was born in Ireland and served with the British in the French and Indian War. He settled in New York state where he was elected to the New York provisional congress. He served as a general in the American Revolutionary War and he was killed in combat in that war.

1521 *Morgan County*

Daniel Morgan (1736–1802)— Morgan was a native of the Northeast who moved to Virginia in his youth. He served as a general in the Revolutionary War and was regarded as a hero for important victories scored by his troops. After the war he served one term in congress. This county was created and named in his honor on January 5, 1833.

1522 *New Madrid County*

The Spanish district named New Madrid which had been located here— New Madrid County was created on October 1, 1812, before Missouri territory was officially

created. On June 4, 1812, the portion of Louisiana–Missouri territory which was not within the relatively new state of Louisiana, was named Missouri territory. That June 4, 1812, organic act became official on December 7, 1812. In the interim, New Madrid County was created. The name came from the name of the district that had been located here when Spain controlled this area. New Madrid was colonized by an American land speculator who obtained a grant of land here from Spain. He was George Morgan (1743–1810) and in addition to securing a large land grant, he was given permission to erect a city here. His stated intent was that this city would be a magnificent one. Sources consulted differ on whether it was George Morgan who coined the name New Madrid or if the name was chosen by the Spanish commandant here. That Spanish commandant's name is rendered in one account as Pierie Foucher but in another as Pierre Forcher. (Howard L. Conard's *Encyclopedia of the History of Missouri,* published in 1901 provides enough detail to lead one to conclude that the Spanish commandant did not arrive at New Madrid until after George Morgan had named it.) In any event, the name was chosen in honor of Madrid, the capital city of Spain.

Madrid, Spain— In A.D. 932 this Moorish fortress was captured by Ramiro II of the kingdom of Leon (one of several kingdoms on the Iberian peninsula). Retaken again by the Moors, it was captured about A.D. 1083 by Alfonso VI of the kingdoms of Leon & Castile United. It was not until the year 1561 that Madrid was made the capital city of Spain by King Philip II (1527–1598). Madrid is located in central Spain on the Manzanares River. As one might expect, it is Spain's most populous city although Barcelona's population is not far behind that of Madrid. The current name of *Madrid* derived from earlier names given by the Moors including Majerit and Majrit.

1523 *Newton County*

John Newton (–1780)— Newton was born in Charleston, South Carolina, about 1752 and was the son of a pastor of a Baptist church. In 1775, early in the armed resistance to Great Britain, Newton enlisted in South Carolina's revolutionary army. He served as a piper and corporal in Captain Dunbar's company before being promoted to sergeant. In a dramatic exploit near Savannah, Georgia, Newton and his close friend William Jasper rescued several Americans who were prisoners and

took their guards as prisoners of war. Newton was more fortunate than his friend William Jasper, in that he survived the siege of Savannah. However, when Charleston fell to the British in 1780, Newton was taken prisoner and he died of smallpox shortly afterward. Geographic names in several of our states link the names of the two heroic sergeants, Jasper and Newton. In some states a county is named for one of them and its county seat is named for the other. In others, like Missouri, two counties are named for them. Newton County was created in December, 1838 and Jasper County was created from the northern portion of Newton County in January, 1841. These two counties are adjacent to each other in southwestern Missouri.

1524 *Nodaway County*

Nodaway River— This county in northwestern Missouri was organized in 1845. It was named for the Nodaway River, which flows through it. The Nodaway, a tributary of the Missouri River, rises in southwestern Iowa , flows south across the Iowa–Missouri border into Nodaway County, Missouri. It continues its journey of some 150 miles by traversing the entire length of Nodaway County, from north to south and then into Andrew County, Missouri. In Andrew County its waters join those of the Missouri River at the state of Missouri's western border with Kansas. Earlier, on January 29, 1841, the Missouri legislature had created a different Nodaway County. Less than three weeks later, on February 15, 1841, the legislature changed the name of that Nodaway County to Holt County, in honor of their fellow legislator, David R. Holt (1803–1840), who had died during the current legislative session.

1525 *Oregon County*

Oregon country in America's Pacific Northwest— The first political convention of Americans in Oregon was held in 1843, at a time when the United States and Great Britain were disputing ownership of a vast area of what is now the southwestern portion of Canada and the northwestern portion of our country. The political convention of Americans in Oregon in 1843 consisted of about 100 settlers, who met at Champooick in what is now the state of Oregon. (Champooick's name is now rendered as Champoeg.) The settlers met to form a provisional government and it was not until August 14, 1848, that the United States government officially created Oregon territory. In the interim, on

February 14, 1845, Oregon County, Missouri, was created and named for the Oregon country in the Pacific Northwest. At that time this area was a very hot political topic. The position of the U.S. was that the border between the United States and British territory in our Pacific Northwest should be at the latitude of 54 degrees, 40 minutes, north. The slogan "54–40 or fight!" was on the lips of many Americans. Well, we didn't get a 54–40 border nor did we fight. The border agreed upon by the British and American governments was far south of that (at the 49 degree line) but that border kept the present state of Oregon (as well as Washington) in American hands. Gallons of ink have been expended debating the origin and meaning of the name *Oregon*. It seems fairly clear that the first person to use the term *Oregon*, spelled that way, was the explorer Jonathan Carver (1710–1780). The name was later applied to our country's important trail to the West, the Oregon Trail. Information on the origin and meaning of the name *Oregon* can be found in the following sources:

Oregon Geographic Names by Lewis A. McArthur (1992)

American Place Names by George R. Stewart (1970)

State Names, Flags, Seals, Songs, Birds, Flowers & Other Symbols by George E. Shankle (1941)

Articles in *Names: Journal of the American Name Society*: September, 1967, article by George R. Stewart; March, 1968, article by J. Franklin Murray; June, 1968, article by Virgil J. Vogel.

After reading these works one will likely conclude that the answer is "We don't really know."

1526 *Osage County*

Osage River— This county in central Missouri was created on January 29, 1841, and named for the Osage River, which forms most of Osage County's western border. The Osage River is the Missouri River's largest tributary. Formed by the union of two rivers in western Missouri, near the Kansas border (the Little Osage River and Marais des Cygnes River), the Osage River flows east and northeast for about 500 miles before finally emptying its waters into the Missouri River. The confluence of the Osage with the Missouri River is about ten miles east of Jefferson City, Missouri. The Osage River was named for the Osage Indians, an important western division of the Sioux Indians. When first encountered by Whites, the Osage In-

dians lived in Missouri, Kansas, Arkansas and Illinois. They were prairie Indians who subsisted by hunting buffalo together with some village agriculture. The Osage Indians were ultimately resettled to Indian territory (now Oklahoma) through a series of treaties with the Whites. The name *Osage* is our current rendering of a name given to the Osage Indians by the Algonquian Indians, which was Ouasash. When Father Jacques Marquette first heard the name in 1673 he recorded it two ways: Ouchage and Outrechaha. Later French traders spelled the name in a variety of ways including Ouazhaghi and Ousage. According to some sources the meaning of the original name given to this tribe by the Algonquians was "bone men" but this is speculation.

1527 *Ozark County*

Ozark Mountains— The Missouri legislature struggled to settle on a name for this county. It was originally created on January 29, 1841, and given its present name, Ozark County. However, on February 22, 1843, the Missouri legislature changed this county's name to Decatur County, in honor of the U.S. naval hero, Stephen Decatur (1779–1820). Finally, on March 24, 1845, the county's original name was restored by the legislature. Ozark County, Missouri, lies in south-central Missouri in the Ozark Mountains, for which the county was named. The heavily forested Ozark Mountains extend from south-central Missouri across north-central Arkansas into eastern Oklahoma. These mountains have eroded over eons to their present height, which ranges from 1,500 feet to 2,500 feet above sea level. The Ozarks cover about 50 thousand square miles of our country. The name "Ozark" has derived from the French words *aux arcs*, which meant "with bows." This was one of the terms that the French applied to Indians living in this area. Another surviving corruption of the numerous French names for these Indians is Arkansas.

1528 *Pemiscot County*

The county's principal bayou— This county in extreme southeastern Missouri was created on February 19, 1851, and named for its principal bayou. All sources consulted are agreed that *Pemiscot* derived from an Indian name and all sources but one are agreed that the word means "liquid mud." That certainly would be descriptive of the sluggish nature of most bayous. The dissenter is J. A. C. Leland, who tells us in his article entitled "Indian

Names in Missouri" that the name comes from *hem*, meaning "by" or "along side of" and *eskaw*, for "go" or "run," which could transpose to "a side channel." Leland's article appeared in the December, 1953, issue of *Names: Journal of the American Name Society*.

1529 *Perry County*

Oliver H. Perry (1785–1819)— Perry was a native of Rhode Island and an officer in the U.S. navy. During the War of 1812 his squadron defeated the British in a key battle on Lake Erie of which Perry said "We have met the enemy and they are ours." Perry died on August 23, 1819, and this county was created and named in his honor in the following year, on November 16, 1820. At that time Missouri was still a territory.

1530 *Pettis County*

Spencer Pettis (1802–1831)— A native of Virginia and a lawyer, Pettis came to Missouri about 1821 and established a law practice here. From 1826 to 1828 he served as the secretary of state of the state of Missouri. Pettis was elected to represent Missouri in the U.S. House of Representatives and he served in that body from December 7, 1829, to March 3, 1831. Because Missouri's population was very small at that time, the state had two U.S. senators but Pettis was its only representative in congress. Spencer Pettis was killed in a duel fought in August, 1831. This county was created and named in his memory on January 26, 1833.

1531 *Phelps County*

John S. Phelps (1814–1886)— John Smith Phelps was born on December 22, 1814, in Simsbury, Connecticut. He moved to Missouri about 1837 and settled at Springfield where he practiced law and became active in local politics. He was elected to the lower house of the Missouri legislature and, from 1845 to 1863 Pettis represented Missouri in the U.S. House of Representatives. He also served as a general in the Union army during the Civil War and attained the rank of brigadier-general. In 1862 President Abraham Lincoln appointed Phelps to be the military governor of Arkansas. Phelps resumed his law practice in Missouri in 1864. In 1876 he was elected governor of Missouri and he held that office from January 8, 1877, until January 10, 1881. This county was created on November 13, 1857, while he was representing Missouri in the lower house of the United States congress.

1532 *Pike County*

Zebulon M. Pike (1779–1813)— A native of New Jersey, Pike served as an army officer on America's frontier following the Revolution. He led an exploratory army expedition to the Rocky Mountains in Colorado which Pike's Peak in the Colorado Rockies commemorates. Pike served as a general in the War of 1812 and was killed in combat in that war on April 27, 1813. This county was created and named in his honor by Missouri territory on December 14, 1818.

1533 *Platte County*

Platte purchase— This county in northwestern Missouri was part of the United States government's Platte purchase of extensive lands from the Indians, and for a time the federal government used the area of the Platte purchase to settle Indians who had been removed from their homes further east. The White voters of Missouri considered this to be a waste of valuable land and they lobbied congress to have the Platte purchase land added to the state of Missouri. In June, 1836, the U.S. Congress passed legislation to add the Platte purchase lands to Missouri and in March, 1837 President Martin Van Buren proclaimed this land to be a part of the state of Missouri. Several Missouri counties were carved out of the Platte purchase including Platte County, Missouri, which was created on December 31, 1838, and named for the Platte purchase. The Platte purchase area had been named for the Platte River which flows in Iowa and Missouri. (There is another major river in our country named Platte, which is in Nebraska. Both the Missouri–Iowa Platte River and Nebraska's Platte River are tributaries of the Missouri River.)

Platte River— The Platte River for which the Platte purchase was named is a tributary of the Missouri River, which rises in southern Iowa and flows some 300 miles in a mostly southern direct across northwestern Missouri. It enters the Missouri River in Platte County, Missouri, not far from Kansas City, Missouri. *Platte* is French and one of its meanings is "flat," or "shallow."

1534 *Polk County*

James K. Polk (1795–1849)— Polk was a native of North Carolina who moved with his family to the Tennessee frontier in 1806. He served in the lower house of the Tennessee legislature and he represented Tennessee for 14 years in the U.S. House of Representatives, where he was speaker. He served one term as governor of Tennessee. Polk became president of the United States as a dark horse candidate of the Democratic party but he became an unusually strong and effective president. His primary accomplishments involved westward extension of the United States: in the Northwest by settling a territorial dispute with Britain and in California and the Southwest by provoking and winning the Mexican War. Polk County, Missouri, was created and named in his honor on January 5, 1835, while James K. Polk was serving as a Tennessee representative in the U.S. House of Representatives. David W. Eaton wrote an article which appeared in the April–July, 1917, issue of the *Missouri Historical Review*, which explains why Missouri would choose to name one of her counties for a Tennessee representative in congress. The article's title is "How Missouri Counties, Towns & Streams Were Named" and it explains that John P. Campbell was an early settler in the area of Missouri which would become Polk County and it was Campbell who suggested that the county be named in honor of his second cousin, James K. Polk.

1535 *Pulaski County*

Casimir Pulaski (1748–1779)— Pulaski was born in Lithuania and served in the Polish army. He came to America to assist the colonies as an officer in the Revolutionary War. He died in combat in that war during the siege of Savannah, Georgia. This Missouri county was created and named in his honor on January 19, 1833.

1536 *Putnam County*

Israel Putnam (1718–1790)— Putnam was born in Massachusetts and moved, when he was about 21, to Connecticut. He served as an officer in the French and Indian Wars and later was a member of the Connecticut legislature. At the beginning of the Revolutionary War, news of the battle at Lexington, Massachusetts, reached Putnam while he was farming. In a dramatic gesture which became famous, Putnam left his plow and, without bothering to change clothes, hurried to Lexington. He was appointed a major-general in the Continental army. Although he enjoyed great popularity, he lacked the ability for high command. In 1779 a paralytic stroke ended his military career. This county was created on February 22, 1843.

1537 *Ralls County*

Daniel Ralls (–1820)— A native of Virginia, Ralls moved westward to Kentucky in his youth and lived for a short time in Sharpsburg, Kentucky. He later pushed further west with his family, arriving in Missouri territory in October, 1817. He first settled in Saint Louis County but in 1818 he moved to a farm near New London, Missouri territory. The farm that was his home at the time of his death in 1820, was located four miles west of New London, which today is the county seat of Ralls County. In 1820, as part of the preparation for Missouri's admission to statehood, a state legislature was elected and one of the early duties of that legislature was to elect the first two senators to represent Missouri in the United States senate. Daniel Ralls was a relatively obscure member of this first legislature. He served in the general assembly as one of two representatives from Pike County. At that time Ralls was only about 35 years old. He attended the first few legislative sessions but then became extremely ill. In very early October, the Missouri legislature was scheduled to vote on the election of its first two U.S. senators. One of the candidates, Thomas Hart Benton (1782–1858), was counting on Daniel Ralls' vote. Accordingly, Ralls was carried from his sick bed (in the Missouri Hotel, in the same building where the legislature was meeting) into the legislative hall. Ralls cast his vote for Thomas H. Benton, and Benton became one of Missouri's first two U.S. senators. Benton went on to represent Missouri in the U.S. Senate for 30 years, serving from 1821 to 1851. After casting his vote, Daniel Ralls lingered less than one month before dying on October 30, 1820. Immediately following his death, on November 4, 1820, his colleagues in the lower house of the legislature passed a bill to create a new county out of the western portion of Pike County and name it Ralls County, in honor of Daniel Ralls. On November 7 this bill was sent to the Missouri senate where it was approved on November 14; it was signed into law by the governor on November 16, 1820.

1538 *Randolph County*

John Randolph (1773–1833)— Randolph was a native of Virginia and he represented that state in both houses of the U.S. Congress for many years. He was an advocate of states' rights and strict construction of the federal constitution. He owned slaves and he represented the interests of the South in congress. Randolph also served, very briefly, as minister to Russia. This Missouri county was created on January 22, 1829. The original bill to create this county called it Smith County. That name would have honored Blandermin Smith, one of the leaders of the group who pressed the Missouri legislature to create this new county. However, the name Smith was never officially adopted for this county's name.

1539 *Ray County*

John Ray (–1820)— In 1820, in preparation for Missouri's admission to statehood, a constitutional convention was held and John Ray was a delegate to that convention from Howard County. He later served in the general assembly of the first legislature of the state of Missouri but he was absent from the legislative hall due to illness when the critical vote for the new state's first U.S. senators was held. John Ray died during this legislative session and this county was created and named in his memory by his fellow legislators. The act creating this county became effective on November 16, 1820.

1540 *Reynolds County*

Thomas Reynolds (1796–1844)— A native of Kentucky and a lawyer, Reynolds moved to Illinois where he became a prominent politician. He was the state's attorney general and speaker of the Illinois house of representatives. From 1822 to 1825 Reynolds was chief justice of Illinois' supreme court. About 1829 he moved to Missouri where he again became active in local politics. He was a member of the lower house of the Missouri legislature and became its speaker. In August, 1840, Reynolds was elected governor of Missouri and took office in November, 1840. He committed suicide on February 9, 1844, while serving as governor. This county was created on February 25, 1845, largely as a result of the efforts of his friend, Pate Buford.

1541 *Ripley County*

Eleazar W. Ripley (1782–1839)— A native of New Hampshire and a graduate of Dartmouth College there. Ripley was a lawyer who became active in politics in Massachusetts where he served in both houses of the state legislature. Ripley entered the army as an officer when the War of 1812 began and received rapid promotions for distinguished service in that war. In July, 1814, he was made brevet majorgeneral and later that year he was severely

wounded in combat. When he resigned from the army in 1820, Ripley settled in Louisiana where he served in the state senate and represented Louisiana in the U.S. House of Representatives.

1542 *Saint Charles County*

The Spanish district named Saint Charles which had been located here— Saint Charles County was created on October 1, 1812, before Missouri territory was officially created. On June 4, 1812, the portion of Louisiana–Missouri territory which was not within the relatively new state of Louisiana, was named Missouri territory. That June 4, 1812, organic act became official on December 7, 1812. In the interim, Saint Charles County was created. The name came from the name of the district that had been located here when Spain controlled this area. Sources consulted differ concerning the original namesake of the district which eventually became Saint Charles County, Missouri. The possibilities that are mentioned are:

King Charles IV (1748–1819) of Spain
Saint Charles (1538–1584) of Borromeo
King Charles V (1338–1380) of France

Circumstantial evidence favors King Carlos (i.e., Charles) IV (1748–1819) of Spain. We know that Louis Blanchette (–1793), a Canadian fur trader, established the first pioneer settlement here in 1769 and that he named it *Les Petites Cotes*, meaning "The Little Hills." Blanchette's nickname was *Le Chasseur* meaning "the hunter," and in some accounts Chasseur is said to be his surname. We also know that Blanchette served as civil and military governor of this settlement when it was owned by Spain. It was Blanchette who changed the name of the post to Saint Charles. According to some sources he renamed his settlement in honor of "Don Carlos, the Spanish monarch." Here we encounter a bit of difficulty. If the name was intended to honor a Spanish king named Don Carlos, just which King Carlos would that have been? The Spanish King Carlos III was born in 1716 and died in 1788. He was king of Spain from 1759 to 1788. His son, King Carlos IV, was born in 1748 and did not die until 1819, but he abdicated his throne in 1808 and thus he was the reigning monarch of Spain from 1788 to 1808. Spain acquired "Louisiana" (an enormous land mass which included all of the present state of Missouri) in 1762 by the treaty of Fontainebleu. Apart from a period of some ten months of so-called "independence," the vast territory of Louisiana was owned by Spain from 1762 to

October 1, 1800, when a secret treaty between Spain and France transferred ownership to France. (That treaty was confirmed by a second treaty on March 21, 1801). In a journal kept by one Julius Rodman, the pioneer settlement here was still called (in his words) *Petite Cotes* in 1791. Thus it seems reasonable to conclude that if Louis Blanchette intended to honor his reigning Spanish king, it would have been the King Carlos (i.e., Charles) who was on the throne during the period from 1791 to October 1, 1800. That Spanish monarch was King Charles IV (1748–1819).

In support of the possibility that the Spanish district was not named for a king but for a Roman Catholic saint, it is perhaps noteworthy that the first church here was a Roman Catholic church named the Church of St. Charles Borromeo. Records of that church date back to 1792 and those records disclose that the first baptism performed in a "neat frame building" took place on July 21, 1792. This "neat frame building" for the church was erected under the authority of Louis Blanchette (–1793) and it replaced an earlier humble log house which was the original Church of St. Charles Borromeo here.

Nothing has been found to support of the possibility that the county's original namesake was the ancient French king, King Charles V (1337–1380), who died long before Europeans had knowledge or interest in this part of North America. Out of the dozens of sources consulted, only two could be found which even mentioned King Charles V (1337–1380) in connection with Saint Charles County, Missouri. and neither of them offer any evidence to support this seemingly unlikely possibility.

King Charles IV of Spain (1748–1819)— This very weak monarch succeeded his father, King Charles III (1716–1788), to the throne of Spain in 1788. He cared little for the affairs of state and knew almost nothing about this subject, delegating both large and small decisions to his wife and advisors chosen by her. King Charles IV was the reigning monarch of Spain during the traumatic revolution in nearby France. He opposed France's revolutionary government and this spelled his doom. French troops invaded Spain in 1794 and made it virtually a satellite of France. It was during the reign of King Charles IV that the vast North American land mass called Louisiana was retroceded by Spain to France in 1800. In 1807 Napoleon occupied Spain, which led to the abdication of the Spanish throne by King Charles IV in 1808. He spent the remainder of his life in exile.

Saint Charles (1538–1584) — Saint Carlo (Charles) Borromeo was born to a wealthy and titled Italian family. His father was Count Gilbert Borromeo, his mother was a member of the Medici family and his uncle, Giovanni Angelo de Medici (1499–1565) became pope, titled Pope Pius IV, in 1559. Soon after his uncle became pope, Carlo was appointed as secretary of state and administrator of Milan. In an even greater act of nepotism, the pope appointed Carlo a cardinal and archbishop of Milan, even though Carlo had not yet been ordained as a priest. In keeping with his position in society, Carlo Borromeo kept a large household and spent money extravagantly. This extravagance disturbed Carlo and in his later years he did much to atone for it by providing relief to the poor and suffering. Carlo Borromeo provided relief to the poor during the famine of 1570 and assisted those in need during the plague of 1575–1576. He was an avid chess player and possessed excellent organization skills. These talents served to make him an able administrator and he played a significant role in bringing the Council of Trent (1545–1563) to a successful conclusion. In 1563 Carlo Borromeo was finally ordained and by 1566 he had become active in implementing the reforms which he had advocated at the Council of Trent. During his later years he lived humbly to set an example for others and he distributed his wealth to the needy. Saint Carlo Borromeo was canonized in 1610.

King Charles V of France (1338–1380) — This French king first ruled France as the regent for his father, King John II (1319–1364), who was captured by the English in 1356. An excellent tactician in protecting his right of succession to the French throne, he ascended as king of France in 1364. King Charles V was an intelligent, dedicated and effective ruler. Having implemented a number of significant internal reforms by 1369, he went to war with England. By the time of the death of King Charles V, much of his patrimony, that had earlier been conquered by England, had been restored to France.

1543 *Saint Clair County*

Arthur St. Clair (1736–1818) — St. Clair was a native of Scotland who moved to Pennsylvania in his twenties. He served, rather ineffectively, as a general in the army in both the Revolutionary War and in later actions against the Indians. He was a Pennsylvania delegate to the Continental Congress and he served as governor of the Northwest territory but President Jefferson was dissatisfied with his conduct and removed him from that post.

1544 *Saint Francois County*

Saint Francis River — This county was created on December 19, 1821, and named for the Saint Francis River, which runs through it. Some sources on the history and geography of Missouri state that the river was named for Saint Francis (1181–1226) of Assisi, while others indicate that the river was probably named for that saint. Only one source has been found which indicates that the county was named directly for Saint Francis (1181–1226) and that particular source has proven to be somewhat unreliable concerning the origins of a few other Missouri counties.

Saint Francis River — A tributary of the Mississippi River, the Saint Francis rises in southeastern Missouri, flows south to the Missouri–Arkansas border and crosses that border to enter northeastern Arkansas. It continues its journey of some 425 miles flowing in a southern direction through eastern Arkansas and empties its waters into the Mississippi near Marianna, Arkansas.

Saint Francis (1181–1226) — Born in Assisi, Italy, Saint Francis was christened John but called Francesco. His father was a prosperous merchant and as a youth, Francesco devoted himself to pleasure-seeking extravagance. While in his mid twenties, he had a vision which caused him to abandon the pleasures of the flesh and devote his life to God. After a pilgrimage to Rome in 1206, he began a life of poverty. He worked on the repair of ruined churches and cared for the poor and sick. Francesco was never ordained but as he began preaching he attracted followers whom he organized as the Friars Minor (now titled the Franciscan Order). He drew up a rule which was given papal approval in 1210. He attempted on several occasions to convert the Mohammedans in northern Africa but each of these efforts failed. Meanwhile, the order he founded had grown dramatically. Saint Francis lacked the administrative skills needed by the larger order and two of his friars were pressing for less emphasis on simplicity, humility and poverty. Saint Francis resigned as head of the order in 1220. In 1224 he received a stigmata in religious ecstasy. The scars of these wounds remained on his body until his death in 1226.

1545 *Saint Louis County*

The Spanish district named Saint Louis, which had been located here — The city of Saint Louis, Missouri, is now an independent city, not a part of any county, but at the time that Saint Louis County was created and named on October 1, 1812, the city of Saint Louis was part of that county and it had been part of the Spanish district here named Saint Louis. (It was not until 1876 that the city of Saint Louis became an independent city. It remains an independent city today.) The Spanish district had been named for the city of Saint Louis, which was founded in 1764 by Pierre Laclede Liguest (–1778), who is generally referred to as Pierre Laclede. The settlers wished to name the town in honor of Pierre Laclede but he refused the honor. Laclede had been born in the Pyrenees Mountains of France about 1724 and he insisted that his new community be named in honor of his French king, King Louis XV (1710–1774). King Louis XV was not a saint, but that Roman Catholic king's patron saint was Saint Louis (1214–1270). Admittedly this is confusing. Robert L. Ramsay explained this naming chain for us in his articled which appeared in the December, 1953 issue of *Names: Journal of the American Name Society*: "…we are inclined to say merely that it was so named by its founder Laclede in 1764, in compliment to his royal master Louis XV of France. If the objection is raised that Louis XV would hardly have been called a saint, even by his grossest flatterers, we must go on to explain that the French settlers felt it to be a more delicate compliment to name the place for the king's name-saint than for himself. So we can honestly say, especially before a Catholic audience, that the city was at least ostensibly named for the king's ancestor, Louis IX, who really was a saint."

Saint Louis (1214–1270) — Louis was a boy of only about 11 or 12 when his father, King Louis VIII (1187–1226), died and he was consecrated as king of France, under the name Louis IX. His mother ruled France as regent while Louis IX was a minor but after Louis IX assumed his role as monarch of France his reign was long and comparatively peaceful although it began with a revolt by certain vassals, aided by the English. Louis IX put down that revolt and soon was off to the Holy Lands on a crusade against the infidels on behalf of Christianity. His troops scored some victories but he was captured. The Christian crusaders had captured Damietta, Egypt, and their offer of Damietta as ransom for the king's release was accepted. After his release, Louis visited Christian holy places and repaired shrines in Syria, which were still in Christian hands. Upon his return to France he governed well and was admired for his piety and wisdom. He presided over a period of magnificent Christian architecture including the soaring Sainte-Chapelle in Paris. His second participation in a crusade ended in his death near Tunis, in Africa. He was canonized as Saint Louis in the year 1297.

1546 *Sainte Genevieve County*

The Spanish district named Sainte Genevieve which had been located here— The Spanish district had been named for the town of Sainte Genevieve, which was created and named when France controlled what is now Missouri. (France did not relinquish control of the vast area called Louisiana and turn it over to Spain, until 1762.) The original town of Sainte Genevieve was located on the west bank of the Mississippi River, but flooding resulted in removal of the community to its present site. The feast day of the Roman Catholic saint, Sainte Genevieve, is January 3 and at least one source indicates that this saint's name was applied to the proposed settlement here because it was on January 3 that a party of French Canadians landed here. That supposition has not been substantiated but it is clear that the community's name (and hence this county's name) did derive from the French saint, Sainte Genevieve.

Sainte Genevieve (–)— Born about A.D. 422 in Nanterre, near Paris, France, Genevieve heard a sermon when she was only seven years old, which inspired her to consecrate her life to God. At the age of 15, she was received as a virgin by the bishop of Paris, who gave her the religious veil. About the year A.D. 451, troops commanded by the infamous Attila the Hun approached Paris and Genevieve is given credit for persuading the citizens of Paris to stand fast and not leave the city. Her advice depended upon complete faith in God since the Parisians had only God to defend them. Genevieve's advice proved to be sound. Attila's troops veered away from Paris and besieged Orleans, instead. Renowned for her charitable deeds, Genevieve died about A.D. 500 but there are a number of claims of her subsequent protection of Paris (e.g., deliverance from a pestilence in the year 1129). She is the patron saint of Paris, France, and her feast day is January 3.

1547 *Saline County*

Numerous salt springs in the area— This county was created on November 25, 1820, and named for its many salt springs. Nathan H. Parker's work entitled *Missouri as It Is in 1867*, commented that "Springs, both saline and fresh, are numerous." William B. Napton's history of Saline County, Missouri, published in 1910 elaborated: "This county was named from the character of the water of many of its streams. There were salt works at one or two places in the county ... The opinion was prevalent that the manufacture of salt would be the leading industry of the county."

1548 *Schuyler County*

Philip J. Schuyler (1733–1804)— A native of New York, Schuyler served as an officer in the French and Indian war and was a delegate from New York to the Continental Congress. During the American Revolution, he held the rank of major-general in the Continental army. Schuyler later served New York in its senate and was one of New York state's first two U.S. senators.

1549 *Scotland County*

Scotland on the island of Great Britain— Scotland County, Missouri, was created on January 29, 1841. The new county's name was suggested by Stephen W. B. Carnegy. According to some accounts, Carnegy was born in Scotland. Others sources say that it was the land of Carnegy's ancestors. Today's Scotland is a member of the United Kingdom in the British Isles. The other members of the United Kingdom are England, Wales and Northern Ireland. Scotland lies at the northern part of the island of Great Britain, which it shares with England and Wales. Ironically, the name *Scotland* derived from the Celtic speaking Scots, who came to Scotland from Ireland about A.D. 500. Prior to 1603, Scotland had a long history that was relatively independent of its powerful southern neighbor, England. At the time that today's Scotland was invaded by the Roman Empire about A.D. 80, it was occupied by the Picts. In addition to the Picts and Romans, others who have ruled some or all of Scotland include the Scots, Anglo-Saxons and the Norse. The Scottish ruler, Malcom II (–1034), is credited with forging a version of a united Scottish kingdom. From 1034 to 1603, Scotland was generally independent of its powerful southern neighbor, although there were many periods of conflict between England and Scotland and England ruled potions of Scotland at times. The beginning of today's formal union of Scotland with England occurred in 1603 when Scotland's King James VI (1566–1625) was also installed on the English throne. He ruled Scotland as James VI and England as James I. Scotland is a cold, mountainous country with a relatively sparse population. Its capital city is Edinburgh. In addition to its territory on the island of Great Britain, Scotland includes three important island groups: The Shetland, Orkney and Hebrides Islands.

1550 *Scott County*

John Scott (–1861)— Scott was born in Virginia about 1782 and graduated from Princeton College. He studied law, was admitted to the bar and came to Missouri about 1805 where he established a law practice at Sainte Genevieve. Scott represented Missouri territory as a delegate to the U.S. Congress and he was a key participant in persuading congress to allow Missouri to draft a state constitution. This was a necessary prelude for a territory wishing to be admitted to statehood. When Missouri territory became the state of Missouri, Scott was elected to be the new state's first, and only, representative in congress. Because of Missouri's sparse population, the new state was granted two U.S. senators, but only one representative in the house. Scott served Missouri in the lower house of congress from August 10, 1821, to March 3, 1827. This county was created and named in his honor on December 28, 1821, shortly after the beginning of Scott's first term as a representative in congress.

1551 *Shannon County*

George Shannon (1787–1836)— Meriwether Lewis selected this Pennsylvania native to be a member of the Lewis and Clark Expedition to the Pacific Northwest. That expedition began in 1804, when George Shannon was only a 18 years old. He was assigned the rank of private. Accounts of the Lewis and Clark Expedition indicate that George Shannon served faithfully, but he received a severe wound in one of his legs during a battle with Indians. When the expedition reached Saint Louis, Missouri, on their return trip, Shannon had the bad leg amputated. He procured a wooden leg, shaped at the end like a peg, studied law and opened a practice in Lexington, Kentucky. He was appointed a circuit judge in that state. In 1828 Shannon moved to Missouri, where he practiced law and served briefly in the state senate. He became United States attorney for Missouri and later practiced criminal law. In 1836 George Shannon died suddenly in the courthouse at Palmyra, Missouri, while defending a client who had been indicted for murder. Shannon County, Missouri, was created and named in his memory, on January 29, 1841.

1552 *Shelby County*

Isaac Shelby (1750–1826)— Shelby was a delegate to the Virginia legislature and, later, to the North Carolina legislature. He served as a soldier in the Revolutionary War and then moved to Kentucky County, Virginia, where he was active in the movement to separate Kentucky from Virginia. Shelby was inaugurated as Kentucky's first governor on the same day that Kentucky became a state. He also fought in the War of 1812. This county was formed on January 2, 1835.

1553 *Stoddard County*

Amos Stoddard (1762–1813)— A native of Connecticut, Stoddard first enlisted in the army in 1779. When the American Revolution was successfully behind us, Stoddard studied a bit of law but he returned to the army to assist in suppressing Shay's Rebellion in Massachusetts in late 1786 and early 1787. By 1793 he had completed his study of law and he was admitted to the Massachusetts bar that year. Stoddard represented what is now the State of Maine in the Massachusetts legislature in 1797. In 1798 he returned to the army with the rank of captain. Stoddard was serving in the western part of our country when President Thomas Jefferson purchased Louisiana from France. That acquisition doubled the size of our country and the land mass that we acquired included all of the present state of Missouri. The formal transfer of lower Louisiana from Spain to France and then from France to the United States had taken place in 1803. By the end of February, 1804, a similar formal, ceremonial transfer had not yet occurred for upper Louisiana. In March, 1804, Amos Stoddard was given the opportunity to make a unique mark in history, at Saint Louis. Although Amos Stoddard held only the relatively low rank of captain, in the United States army he was selected *by France* to formally accept upper Louisiana from Spain on behalf of France. The French official who made this unusual request was Pierre Clement Laussat and he selected Amos Stoddard because Stoddard had already been chosen to represent the United States in formally accepting upper Louisiana from France. Stoddard accepted this responsibility and on March 9,

1804, Stoddard, of behalf of France, took formal possession of upper Louisiana from Spain. The flag of Spain was lowered and the French flag took its place. On the following day, March 10, 1804, Captain Stoddard performed the same formal ritual on behalf of both our country and France. The French flag was taken down and the United States flag was raised in its place. Amos Stoddard, on behalf of the United States, had taken formal possession and civil and military authority over upper Louisiana from Amos Stoddard, the French representative. Early in the War of 1812, Stoddard, now a major, was killed in combat during the siege of Fort Meigs. This county was created on January 2, 1835.

1554 *Stone County*

Uncertain— The dozens of sources consulted offer three very different opinions on the origin of this county's name yet none of these sources indicate that there is any uncertainty about their selection:

1. A judge (some sources say of Taney County, Missouri) named William Stone. Taney County borders Stone County and Taney County was created in 1837, before Stone County was created (1851). Therefore, this suggestion is possible. However it is essentially impossible that the William Stone for whom this county was named was the William J. Stone (1848–1918) who was elected governor of Missouri in 1892. Although that man was a lawyer, by profession, he was less than three years old when Stone County, Missouri, was created and named.

2. Early settlers of that name from eastern Tennessee. This possibility is mentioned by more than one source but is otherwise unsubstantiated.

3. Stony character of the county. This suggestion is plausible. Howard L. Conard's *Encyclopedia of the History of Missouri*, published in 1901, comments about the county's beautiful caves, which feature stalactites and gem-like formations on their floors. Even apart from these caves, Conard's description of the county leaves the impression that we have here a stony, hilly county in the Ozark Mountains, much of which is ill-suited to agriculture. Conard tells us that "Along the streams are many rugged bluffs." Also that "…blue limestone and onyx abound…"

1555 *Sullivan County*

Sullivan County, Tennessee— Sullivan County, in northeastern Tennessee, was created in 1779, when it was still a part of North Carolina. As early as 1784 there was

a movement to form a new state, separate from North Carolina, to be named "Franklin," or "the Free State of Franklin" and Sullivan County was one of the counties which would have been part of that new state. The movement to form a new state named Franklin died, and when the state of Tennessee was admitted to the Union in 1796 Sullivan County, North Carolina, became Sullivan County, Tennessee. When it was created in 1779, Sullivan County, North Carolina, had been named for the Revolutionary War hero, Major-General John Sullivan (1740–1795).

JohnSullivan (1740–1795)— The location of John Sullivan's birth is given variously as Berwick, Maine, and Somersworth, New Hampshire. The two towns are adjacent. He practiced law in New Hampshire and represented New Hampshire in the Continental Congress. During the American Revolution Sullivan served as a brigadier-general and later was promoted to major-general. John Sullivan served with distinction in a number of important engagements of the Revolution until late 1779 when he resigned. He then represented New Hampshire again in the Continental Congress. Sullivan later served as attorney general of New Hampshire, president (or governor) of New Hampshire and was a member of the New Hampshire convention that ratified the proposed federal constitution. He also was speaker of New Hampshire's house of representatives. In 1789 President George Washington appointed John Sullivan as judge of the U.S. district court of New Hampshire and Sullivan held that position until his death in 1795.

When this Missouri county was originally created on February 17, 1843, it was named Highland County. In February, 1845, the county was fully organized and its name was changed to Sullivan County at the request of a member of the Missouri legislature, E. C. Morelock, who said that he chose the name in honor of his native county in Tennessee.

A number of sources that deal with the history and geography of Missouri state that Sullivan County, Missouri, was named for General James Sullivan of the American Revolution. These sources are wrong. General John Sullivan (1740–1795) had a younger brother named James Sullivan (1744–1808) and the place of that brother's birth is also given as Berwick, Maine. But this James Sullivan became famous as a politician and was not a general during the American Revolution. There was no American general named James Sullivan, who served during the American Revolution.

1556 *Taney County*

Roger B. Taney (1777–1864)— A native of Maryland and a lawyer, Taney served in the Maryland senate and as that state's attorney general. In 1831 President Andrew Jackson appointed Taney to his cabinet as attorney general and in 1833 Jackson made Roger Taney his secretary of the treasury, another cabinet post. In 1836 Taney was appointed by President Jackson to replace John Marshall (1755–1835) as chief justice of the U.S. Supreme Court. Marshall had used the supreme court to shift power in American government from the states to the central government. Roger Taney pushed in the other direction, empowering state and local governments. Taney believed in strict construction of the constitution and judicial restraint. These views clashed in the mid 1850's when the supreme court was considering the landmark Dred Scott case. Taney was opposed to slavery and he had given freedom to the slaves whom he inherited. However, Chief Justice Taney felt that he was bound to decide cases based on our country's constitution rather than on his personal views. Thus in 1857 when Chief Justice Taney delivered the court's decision in the Dred Scott case, his ruling favored pro-slavery forces on several points. Perhaps the most important point contained in Taney's Dred Scott opinion was the decision that the U.S. Congress had no constitutional authority to bar slavery from territories of the United States. The Dred Scott decision was popular in the slave state of Missouri, but it was not the reason that Taney County was named in Judge Taney's honor. Taney County had been created on January 6, 1837, long before the Dred Scott decision. At the time that Taney County was created, President Jackson, who was very popular in Missouri, had recently appointed Roger Taney to be chief justice of our nation's highest court.

1557 *Texas County*

The republic of Texas— When this county was created on February 17, 1843, it was named Ashley County. It is uncertain whom that name intended to honor although Missouri's U.S. Congressman. William H. Ashley (1778–1838) has been mentioned as a possibility. In any case, the county's name did not remain Ashley very long. It was renamed Texas County on February 14, 1845, in honor of the republic of Texas. That independent republic did not become a state of the United States until ten months later, when it was admitted to statehood on December 29, 1845.

However, at the time that this county was created in February, 1845, Texas was very much in the news and various proposals for annexation were being discussed in both Texas and in the United States. The republic of Texas was very popular in the United States, where its recent struggle for independence from Mexico was admired and supported. In Missouri, Texas' popularity was particularly high in February, 1845, because Texas law permitted slavery and another slave state represented in the U.S. Congress would surely assist the slaves states in their running congressional battles with abolitionist members of congress from the North. George E. Shankle's book dealing with the origins of the names of our states tells us that the name *Texas* had been applied to the Indians of this region, who banded themselves together for mutual protection. The region occupied by these Indians was called Texas, as early as 1689. The Indians used the name *Texia*, while the Mexican form was *Tejas*, meaning "allies," "friends" or "confederates." Since this area was controlled at an early time by both Indians and Mexicans, these origins seem credible. Confirmation of this explanation of the term *Texas* may be found in Z. T. Fulmore's work entitled *The History & Geography of Texas as Told in County Names.* Fulmore tells us that in 1689 there were about a dozen Indian tribes, each with a specific name, who were members of a confederacy, allied for mutual protection and defense, who were designated by the collective term *Texas.*

1558 *Vernon County*

Miles Vernon (1786–1866)— Miles Vernon was born in Charlotte County, Virginia, on March 26, 1786. When he was still a boy, he moved to Tennessee and grew to manhood there. During the War of 1812, he served under his fellow Tennessean, General Andrew Jackson, at the battle of New Orleans. Vernon also served as a member of the Tennessee state legislature. In 1839 he moved to Missouri and settled in what was then Pulaski County. By 1850, Laclede County had been carved from a portion of Pulaski County and although Miles Vernon was illiterate, the voters of Laclede County elected him in 1850 to represent them in the state senate and they returned him to office several times. Vernon County was created and named in Miles Vernon's honor by his fellow legislators on February 27, 1855, while Vernon was serving in the Missouri state senate. By October, 1861, the Confederate States

of America had been formed by the eleven states who seceded from the federal Union. On October 28, 1861, Miles Vernon and his allies tried to add Missouri to the list and make it twelve. Vernon was the presiding officer of the Missouri senate when the Missouri legislature passed a bill to secede from the Union on October 28, 1861. Although Missouri Governor Claiborne F. Jackson (1806–1862) signed the bill, it was defective and never became law. The October 28, 1861, session of the Missouri legislature was held in Neosho, Missouri, and that session of the Missouri legislature has been termed a "rump" session because neither the state senate nor the lower house possessed a quorum. Missouri never became a member of the Confederate States of America; rather, the state divided into opposing armed groups. Miles Vernon allied himself with the Confederacy during the Civil War. He died at Rolla, Missouri, in 1866, shortly after the Civil War ended.

1559 *Warren County*

Joseph Warren (1741–1775)— A native of Massachusetts and a graduate of Harvard College, Warren practiced medicine in the Boston area. He was a member of the committee of safety and president *pro tempore* of the Massachusetts provincial congress. In June, 1775, he was commissioned a major-general and he died in combat a few days later at the battle of Bunker Hill. Warren County was created and named in his honor on January 5, 1833.

1560 *Washington County*

George Washington (1732–1799)— Washington was a native of Virginia. He served in Virginia's house of burgesses and became one of the colonies' leaders in opposition to British policies in America. He was a member of the first and second Continental Congresses and commander of all Continental armies in the Revolutionary War. Following victory in that war, Washington was elected to be the first president of the United States. This county was created on August 21, 1813, by the legislature of Missouri territory.

1561 *Wayne County*

Anthony Wayne (1745–1796)— A native of Pennsylvania, Wayne was a successful brigadier-general in the Revolutionary War and became a hero for his daring exploits. During the bitter winter of 1777–1778 at Valley Forge, Pennsylvania, Wayne shared the sufferings of his men although his comfortable estate was only five miles away. He played an important role in the final overthrow of the British forces in Georgia. After the war, in 1785, Wayne moved to Georgia and he represented Georgia for about six months in the U.S. House of Representatives. In 1792, President Washington recalled Wayne to serve as a major-general against the Indians in the Northwest territory. Once again his military efforts were successful. This county was created on December 11, 1818, while Missouri was still a territory.

1562 *Webster County*

Daniel Webster (1782–1852)— Webster was born in New Hampshire and represented that state in the U.S. House of Representatives. He later represented Massachusetts in both houses of the U.S. Congress and served as secretary of state under three presidents. Webster felt that slavery was evil but not as evil as disunion of the United States. He played a key role in the passage of five laws in the U.S. Congress which are known as the "Compromise of 1850" which were intended to avert secession and civil war between the North and the South over the slavery issue. Daniel Webster died on October 24, 1852, and this county was created on March 3, 1855.

1563 *Worth County*

William J. Worth (1794–1849)— A native of New York, Worth enlisted in the army as a private in the War of 1812 and rose to the rank of major. At the close of the war, Worth became commandant of the U.S. Military Academy at West Point. He later served as a brigadier-general against the Seminole Indians in Florida and became a national hero as a successful major-general in the Mexican War. This county was created on February 8, 1861.

1564 *Wright County*

Silas Wright (1795–1847)— A native of Massachusetts and a lawyer, Wright served in the New York senate and, in 1827, he was appointed brigadier-general of the New York state militia. He later represented New York in both houses of the U.S. Congress, serving eleven years in the United States senate. In 1844, Silas Wright, a Democrat, was nominated to run as James K. Polk's vice-presidential running mate but he declined the nomination. He then served one term as governor of New York state. This county was created on January 29, 1841.

REFERENCES

Ambrose, Stephen E. *Undaunted Courage*. New York, Simon & Schuster, 1996.

Atchison, Theodore C. "David Atchison." *Missouri Historical Review*, Vol. 24, No. 4. Columbia, Missouri: July, 1930.

Bay, W. V. N. *Reminiscences of the Bench & Bar of Missouri*. St. Louis, F. H. Thomas & Co., 1878.

Benedictine Monks of St. Augustine's Abbey, Ramsgate. *The Book of Saints*. New York, Thomas Y. Crowell Co., 1966.

Bentley, James. *A Calendar of Saints: The Lives of the Principal Saints of the Christian Year*. New York, Facts on File Publications, 1986.

Best, Hugh. *Debrett's Texas Peerage*. New York, Coward-McCann, Inc., 1983.

Bradford, M. E. *A Worthy Company: Brief Lives of the Framers of the United States Constitution*. Marlborough, New Hampshire, Plymouth Rock Foundation, 1982.

Bryan, William S., & Robert Rose. *A History of the Pioneer Families of Missouri*. St. Louis, Bryan, Brand & Co., 1876.

Burt, Jesse, et al. *Your Tennessee: Teacher's Edition*. Austin, Texas, Steck-Vaughn Co., 1979.

Calhoun, James. *Louisiana Almanac: 1979–1980*. Gretna, Louisiana, Pelican Publishing Co., 1979.

Campbell, R. A. *Campbell's Gazetteer of Missouri*. St. Louis, 1875.

Chouteau, Auguste. "Journal of the Founding of St. Louis: Original & Translation." *Missouri Historical Society Collections*, Vol. 4, No. 4. St. Louis: 1911.

Christian County: Its First 100 Years. Ozark, Missouri, Christian County Centennial, Inc., 1959.

Clements, John. *Flying the Colors: Texas*. Dallas, Texas, Clements Research, Inc., 1984.

Clements, John. *Missouri Facts*. Dallas, Texas, Clements Research II, Inc., 1991.

Collier, James E. *Missouri Information Pamphlets: Geographic Areas of Missouri*. Parkville, Missouri, Missouri Council for Social Studies, 1959.

Conard, Howard L. *Encyclopedia of the History of Missouri*. New York, Southern History Co., 1901.

Crawford, Lewis F. *History of North Dakota*. Chicago, American Historical Society, Inc., 1931.

Crowell, Gentry. *Tennessee Blue Book: 1985–1986*. Nashville, Tennessee, State of Tennessee, 1985.

Crutchfield, James A. *The North Carolina Almanac & Book of Facts: 1989–1990*. Nashville, Tennessee, Rutledge Hill Press, 1988.

Crutchfield, James A. *The Tennessee Almanac & Book of Facts*. Nashville, Tennessee, Rutledge Hill Press, 1986.

Davis, Walter B., & Daniel S. Durrie. *An Illustrated History of Missouri*. St. Louis, A. J. Hall & Co., 1876.

Dent County Historical Society. *Ozark Heritage: Dent County*. Dallas, Texas, Taylor Publishing Co., 1980.

Douglass, Robert S. *History of Southeast Missouri*. Cape Girardeau, Missouri, Ramfre Press, 1961.

Du Gard, Rene C., & Dominique C. Western. *The Handbook of French Place Names in the U.S.A.* Editions des Deux Mondes, 1977.

Eaton, David W. "How Missouri Counties, Towns & Streams Were Named." *Missouri Historical Review*, Columbia, Missouri: Vol. 10, No. 3, April, 1916; Vol. 10, No. 4, July, 1916; Vol. 11, No. 2, January, 1917; Vol. 11, Nos. 3 & 4, April–July, 1917; Vol. 13, No. 1, October, 1918.

Ellsberry, Elizabeth P. *Adair County, Missouri Marriage Records*, Chillicothe, Missouri, 1961.

Ellsberry, Elizabeth P. *Chariton County, Missouri Wills & Administration*, Chillicothe, Missouri.

Ellsberry, Elizabeth P. *Early Marriage Records (1819–1850) & Will Records (1820–1870) of Cooper County, Missouri*. Chillicothe, Missouri, 1959.

Ellsberry, Elizabeth P. *Early Will Records of North Central Counties of Missouri*. Chillicothe, Missouri.

Ellsberry, Elizabeth P. *Lillard & Lafayette County, Missouri Marriage Records*, Chillicothe, Missouri, 1959.

Ellsberry, Elizabeth P. *Sullivan County, Missouri Marriage Records*, Chillicothe, Missouri, 1961.

Englebert, Omer. *The Lives of the Saints*. New York, Barnes & Noble, Inc., 1994.

Faber, Harold. *From Sea to Sea: The Growth of the United States*. New York, Farrar, Straus & Giroux, 1967.

Faragher, John M. *The Encyclopedia of Colonial & Revolutionary America*. New York, Facts on File, 1990.

Farmer, David H. *The Oxford Dictionary of Saints*. Oxford, England, Oxford University Press, 1992.

Fletcher, Christine. *100 Keys: Names Across the Land*. Nashville, Abingdon Press, 1973.

Foley, William E. *A History of Missouri: Volume 1: 1673 to 1820*. Columbia, Missouri, University of Missouri Press, 1971.

Ford, James E. A *History of Jefferson City, Missouri's State Capital and of Cole County*. Jefferson City, Missouri, New Day Press, 1938.

Ford, J. E. *A History of Moniteau County, Missouri.* California Democrat, 1936.

Foy, Felician A. *Catholic Almanac: 1994.* Huntington, Indiana, Our Sunday Visitor, Inc., 1994.

Fulmore, Z. T. *The History & Geography of Texas as Told in County Names.* Austin, Texas, 1926.

Gammon, William J. *A Belated Census of Earliest Settlers of Cape Girardeau County, Missouri.* Washington, D.C., 1958.

Gannett, Henry. *The Origin of Certain Place Names in the United States.* Williamstown, Massachusetts, Corner House Publishers, 1978.

Glenn, Allen. *History of Cass County, Missouri.* Topeka, Historical Publishing Co., 1917.

Goodspeed's History of Southeast Missouri. Cape Girardeau, Missouri, Ramfre Press, 1955.

Guitar, Sarah, & Floyd C. Shoemaker. "The Missouri Chronicle: 1673–1924." *Missouri Historical Review,* Vol. 19. Columbia, Missouri: 1925.

Hall, Kermit L., et al. *The Oxford Companion to the Supreme Court of the United States.* New York, Oxford University Press, 1992.

Harrington, Betty & Dolly Bottens. *Records of Jasper County, Missouri.* Carthage, Missouri, 1969,

Haswell, A. M. *The Ozark Region: Its History and Its People.* Springfield, Missouri, Interstate Historical Society, 1917.

Hennepin, Louis. "Account of the Discovery of the River Mississippi and the Adjacent Country." *Historical Collections of Louisiana.* New York, Wiley & Putnam, 1846.

Historical, Pictorial & Biographical Record of Chariton County, Missouri. Salisbury, Missouri, Pictorial & Biographical Publishing Co., 1896.

History of Adair, Sullivan, Putnam & Schuyler Counties, Missouri. Chicago, Goodspeed Publishers, 1888.

History of Andrew & Dekalb Counties, Missouri. St. Louis, Goodspeed Publishing Co., 1888.

History of Audrain County, Missouri. St. Louis, National Historical Co., 1884.

A History of Callaway County, Missouri. Fulton, Missouri, Kingdom of Callaway Historical Society, 1983.

The History of Cass & Bates Counties, Missouri. St. Joseph, Missouri, National Historical Co., 1883.

History of Cole, Moniteau, Morgan, Benton, Miller, Maries & Osage Counties, Missouri. Chicago, Goodspeed Publishing Co., 1889.

The History of Daviess County, Missouri. Kansas City, Missouri, Birdsall & Dean, 1882.

History of Franklin, Jefferson, Washington, Crawford & Gasconade Counties, Missouri. Chicago, Goodspeed Publishing Co., 1888.

The History of Gentry & Worth Counties, Missouri. St. Joseph, Missouri, National Historical Co., 1882.

History of Greene County, Missouri. St. Louis, Western Historical Co., 1883.

The History of Henry & St. Clair Counties, Missouri. St. Joseph, Missouri, National Historical Co., 1883.

History of Hickory, Polk, Cedar, Dade & Barton Counties, Missouri. Chicago, Goodspeed Publishing Co., 1889.

History of Holt County, Missouri. St. Joseph, Missouri, Midland Printing Co.

History of Howard & Cooper Counties, Missouri. St. Louis, National Historical Co., 1883.

History of Lincoln County, Missouri. Chicago, Goodspeed Publishing Co., 1888.

The History of Linn County, Missouri. Kansas City, Missouri, Birdsall & Dean, 1882.

The History of Nodaway County, Missouri. St. Joseph, Missouri, National Historical Co., 1882.

The History of Pettis County, Missouri. Kansas City, Missouri, Kansas City Historical Company, 1882.

History of Randolph & Macon Counties, Missouri. St. Louis, National Historical Co., 1884.

History of Ray County, Missouri. St. Louis, Missouri Historical Co., 1881.

History of St. Charles, Montgomery & Warren Counties, Missouri. St. Louis, National Historical Co., 1885.

History of Southeast Missouri. Chicago, Goodspeed Publishing Co., 1888.

History of Vernon County, Missouri. St. Louis, Brown & Co., 1887.

Houck, Louis. *A History of Missouri.* Chicago, R. R. Donnelley & Sons Co., 1908.

Howard, Goldena R. *Ralls County, Missouri.* Marceline, Missouri, Walsworth, 1980.

Jasper County Historical Foundation, Inc. *History of Jasper County, Georgia.* Roswell, Georgia, W. H. Wolfe Associates, 1976.

Jennett, Elizabeth L., et al. *Biographical Directory of the Texan Conventions & Congresses: 1832–1845.* Austin, Texas, 1941.

Johnston, Carrie P., & W. H. S. McGlumphy. *History of Clinton & Caldwell Counties, Missouri.* Topeka, Historical Publishing Co., 1923.

Jones, Alison. *The Wordsworth Dictionary of Saints.* Hertfordshire, England, Wordsworth Editions, Ltd., 1994.

Keisling, Phil. *1991–92 Oregon Blue Book.* Salem, Oregon, Secretary of State of Oregon.

Kelly, Sean, & Rosemary Rogers. *Saints Preserve Us! Everything You Need to Know About Every Saint You'll Ever Need.* New York, Random House, 1993.

Kleber, John E. *The Kentucky Encyclopedia.* Lexington, Kentucky, University Press of Kentucky, 1992.

La Coss, Louis. "A Travelog of Missouri Counties: Maries County." *Saint Louis Globe Democrat,* August 2, 1925.

Leland J. A. C. "Indian Names in Missouri." *Names: Journal of the American Name Society,* Vol. 1, No. 4. Berkeley: December, 1953.

Loughead, George R. *Early History of Butler County, Missouri.* Stinson Press, 1987.

McArthur, Lewis A. *Oregon Geographic Names,* Portland, Oregon, Oregon Historical Society Press, 1992.

McBrien, Richard P. *The Harpercollins Encyclopedia of Catholicism.* New York, Harper Collins, Inc., 1995.

McCandless, Perry. *A History of Missouri: Volume 2: 1820 to 1860.* Columbia, Missouri, University of Missouri Press, 1972.

McCrady, Edward. *The History of South Carolina in the Revolution: 1775–1780.* New York, Macmillan Co., 1901.

McDermott, John F. *The Early Histories of St. Louis.* St. Louis, St. Louis Historical Documents Foundation, 1952.

"Missouriana." *Missouri Historical Review,* Vol. 26, No. 1. Columbia, Missouri: October, 1931.

"Missouriana." *Missouri Historical Review,* Vol. 34, No. 4. Columbia, Missouri: July, 1940.

"Missouriana." *Missouri Historical Review,* Vol. 35, No. 2. Columbia, Missouri: January, 1941.

"Missouriana: Missouri Counties, Past & Present." *Missouri Historical Review,* Vol. 34, No. 4. Columbia, Missouri: July, 1940.

Moss, Bobby G. *Roster of South Carolina Patriots in the American Revolution.* Baltimore, Genealogical Publishing Co., 1983.

Napton, William B. *Past & Present of Saline County, Missouri.* Indianapolis, Indiana, B. F. Bowen & Co., 1910.

New Catholic Encyclopedia. New York, McGraw-Hill Book Co., 1967.

Norton, Nell D. *Early Settlers of Ralls County, Missouri.* Chicago, Illinois, Institute of American Genealogy, 1945.

Old Cape Girardeau. Cape Girardeau, Missouri, Naeter Brothers Publishing Co., 1946.

Parker, Nathan H. *Missouri As It Is in 1867.* Philadelphia, J. B. Lippincott & Co., 1867.

Parrish, William E. *A History of Missouri: Volume 3: 1860 to 1875.* Columbia, Missouri, University of Missouri Press, 1973.

Parrish, William E., et al. *Missouri: The Heart of the Nation.* St. Louis, Missouri, Forum Press, 1980.

Ponder, Jerry. *History of Ripley County, Missouri.* 1987.

Powell, William S. *The North Carolina Gazetteer.* Chapel Hill, University of North Carolina Press, 1968.

Priddy, Bob. *Across Our Wide Missouri.* Independence, Missouri, Independence Press, 1982.

Progressive St. Charles. St. Charles, Missouri, Press of Thomas J. Campbell, 1916.

Rader, Perry S. *The History of Missouri.* Jefferson City, Missouri, Hugh Stephens Co., 1917.

Rafferty, Milton D. *Historical Atlas of Missouri.* Norman, Oklahoma, University of Oklahoma Press, 1982.

Ramsay, Robert L. "Scyldings & Shields." *Names: Journal of the American Name Society,* Vol. 1, No. 4. Berkeley: December, 1953.

Rankin, Hugh F. *Francis Marion: The Swamp Fox.* New York, Thomas Y. Crowell Co., 1973.

A Reminiscent History of the Ozark Region. Cape Girardeau, Missouri, Ramfre Press, 1956.

Robinson, Doane. *Doane Robinson's Encyclopedia of South Dakota.* Pierre, 1925.

Robinson, Doane. "Lewis & Clark in South Dakota." *South Dakota Historical Collections,* Vol. 9. Pierre, South Dakota: 1918.

Rydjord, John. *Indian Place-Names.* Norman, University of Oklahoma Press, 1968.

Ryle, Walter H. "A Study of Early Days in Randolph County: 1818–1860." *Missouri Historical Review,* Vol. 24, No. 2. Columbia, Missouri: January, 1930.

Schaaf, Mrs. Ida M. "The Founding of Ste Genevieve, Missouri." *Missouri Historical Review,* Vol. 27, No. 2. Columbia, Missouri: January, 1933.

Scharf, J. Thomas. *History of Saint Louis City & County.* Philadelphia, Louis H. Everts & Co., 1883.

Sedillot, Rene. *An Outline of French History.* New York, Alfred A. Knopf, 1967.

Shankle, George Earlie. *State Names, Flags, Seals, Songs, Birds, Flowers & Other Symbols.* New York, H. W. Wilson Co., 1941.

Shoemaker, Floyd C. *Missouri & Missourians.* Chicago, Lewis Publishing Co., 1943.

Shoemaker, Floyd C. *Missouri's Hall of Fame: Lives of Eminent Missourians.* Columbia, Missouri, Missouri Book Co., 1918.

Smith, T. Berry, & Pearl S. Gehrig. *History of Chariton & Howard Counties, Missouri.* Topeka, Historical Publishing Co., 1923.

Squires, Monas N. "A New View of the Election of Barton & Benton to the United States Senate in 1820." *Missouri Historical Review,* Vol. 27, No. 1. Columbia, Missouri: October, 1932.

Stevens, Walter B. *Centennial History of Missouri.* St. Louis, S. J. Clarke Publishing Co., 1921.

Stevens, Walter B. *Missouri: The Center State: 1821–1915.* Chicago, S. J. Clarke Publishing Co., 1915.

Stevens, Walter B. *St. Louis: The Fourth City: 1764–1911.* St. Louis, S. J. Clarke Publishing Co., 1911.

Stewart, George R. *American Place-Names.* New York, Oxford University Press, 1970.

Switzler, W. F., et al. *Switzler's Illustrated History of Missouri.* St. Louis, C. R. Barns, 1881.

Thrapp, Dan L. *Encyclopedia of Frontier Biography.* Lincoln, University of Nebraska Press, 1988.

Thurston, Herbert J. & Donald Attwater. *Butler's Lives of the Saints.* New York, P. J. Kenedy & Sons, 1956.

Tucker, Phillip T. "Missouri." *A Nation of Sovereign States: Secession & War in the Confederacy,* Vol. 10. Murfreesboro, Tennessee, 1994.

Vexler, Robert I. *Chronology & Documentary Handbook of the State of Missouri.* Dobbs Ferry, New York, Oceana Publications, Inc., 1978.

Violette, E. M. *History of Adair County.* Kirksville, Missouri, Journal Printing Co., 1911.

Walsh, Michael. *Butler's Lives of the Saints.* San Francisco, Harper & Row Publishers, 1985.

Wanamaker, George W. *History of Harrison County, Missouri.* Topeka, Historical Publishing Co., 1921.

Warner, Ezra J. & W. Buck Yearns. *Biographical Register of the Confederate Congress.* Baton Rouge, Louisiana State University Press, 1975.

Webb, Walter P., et al. *The Handbook of Texas.* Austin, Texas State Historical Association, 1952.

White, Dabney, & T. C. Richardson. *East Texas: Its History and Its Makers.* New York, Lewis Historical Publishing Co., 1940.

Williams, Walter. *A History of Northeast Missouri.* Chicago, Lewis Publishing Co., 1913.

Williams, Walter. *A History of Northwest Missouri.* Chicago, Lewis Publishing Co., 1915.

Williams, Walter. *The State of Missouri: An Autobiography.* Columbia, Missouri, E. W. Stephens, 1904.

Wilson, L. A. *Wilson's History & Directory for Southeast Missouri and Southern Illinois.* Cape Girardeau, Missouri, 1875–1876.

Wise, L. F., & E. W. Egan. *Kings, Rulers & Statesmen.* New York, Sterling Publishing Co., Inc., 1967.

Wolk, Allan. *The Naming of America.* Nashville, Thomas Nelson, Inc., 1977.

Woodruff, Mrs. Howard W. *The Marriage Records of Ralls County, Missouri.* Kansas City, Missouri, 1969.

Work Projects Administration. *Inventory of the County Archives of Missouri-McDonald County.* St. Louis, Missouri, 1942.

Work Projects Administration. *Inventory of the County Archives of Texas-Caldwell County.* 1941.

Yoes, Henry E. *A History of St. Charles Parish to 1973.* Norco, St. Charles Herald Publishers, 1973.

Montana

(56 counties)

1565 *Beaverhead County*

Beaverhead River— Beaverhead County was first created as a part of Idaho territory on January 16, 1864. After Montana territory was formed from the northeastern portion of Idaho territory, Montana's territorial legislature passed an act, effective February 2, 1865, which created Beaverhead County as a part of Montana territory. The county was named for the Beaverhead River, which flows through it. The river's name was given by Indians on account of a particular rock formation along the banks of Beaverhead River, which to them, resembled the head of a beaver. This rock formation consists of a perpendicular wall which is about 300 feet high. It is located about six miles above the mouth of the Ruby River, approximately 12 miles south of the town of Twin Bridges, Montana, and some 18 miles north of Dillon, Montana, which is the county seat of Beaverhead County. The journals of the Lewis and Clark Expedition contain an entry dated August 8, 1805, which mentions that the Indian woman, Sacagawea, pointed this rock formation out to the Lewis & Clark party and explained that its name came from a supposed resemblance to a beaver's head. This rock formation was long known to native American Indians, who used it as a landmark to guide them in their travels.

1566 *Big Horn County*

Big horn sheep— This county is Montana's second county named Big Horn County. The first was originally created a part of Idaho territory on January 16, 1864. After Montana territory was formed from the northeastern portion of Idaho territory, Montana's territorial legislature passed an act, effective February 2, 1865, which created Big Horn County as a part of Montana territory. That Big Horn County's name was changed to Custer County soon after the 1876 battle of the Little Big Horn, in which General George A. Custer (1839–1876) and all of his men were slain. Montana's present Big Horn County was created on January 13, 1913. The name of the county and of the Big Horn River, which flows through it, commemorates the wild big horn sheep, which are relatively nu-merous here. Big horn sheep can be found from British Columbia to North Dakota in the north and as far south as New Mexico. However, their largest concentration lies near the headwaters of the Yellowstone River in Montana and Wyoming. Rocky Mountain big horn sheep are identified by zoologists as members of the genus *Ovis* and the species *canadensis*. Their common name, big horn, refers to the massive horns of the male big horn sheep, which sweep backward in an arc and measure about 40 inches along the outer curve; a "big horn," indeed on a body that is but five feet in length and stands less than 20 inches tall at the shoulder.

1567 *Blaine County*

James G. Blaine (1830–1893)— Blaine, a native of Pennsylvania, moved to Maine where he served three terms in the state legislature. He then represented Maine in both houses of the U.S. Congress and, for a number of years, was speaker of the house of representatives. In 1881 Blaine became secretary of state under President James A. Garfield and he was the Republican party's candidate for president of the United States in 1884, losing to Grover Cleveland. When Benjamin Harrison became president in 1889, he appointed Blaine to be his secretary of state. Starting in 1893, the year of Blaine's death, bills were introduced from time to time in the Montana legislature to create a county named in his honor. However, it was not until 1912 that Blaine County, Montana, was finally created.

1568 *Broadwater County*

Charles A. Broadwater (1840–1892)— Charles Arthur Broadwater was born in Saint Charles, Missouri on September 25, 1840. In 1861 he moved to Colorado and by 1863 he had relocated to Virginia City where he was involved with mining activities. Broadwater acquired some wealth by successfully completing construction of Fort Maginnis, for the government. James J. Hill (1838–1916), the railroad tycoon, selected Charles Broadwater to manage his Montana operations and appointed him as president of the Montana Central Railroad. Under Broadwater's manage-ment, railroad lines were constructed from Butte to Great Falls, via Helena, and the Rimini & Marysville and Neihart branches were also constructed under his leadership. More importantly, Broadwater induced James J. Hill to extend his Great Northern railroad system into Helena and Butte. The railroad was, of course, vital to the development of infant Montana and every extension of Montana's railroads was a significant achievement. Charles A. Broadwater was a resident and commercial developer in Helena and was involved in the affairs of the Montana National Bank and other financial institutions in Montana. He also had interests in mining and cattle operations in Montana and became a very wealthy man.

1569 *Carbon County*

Extensive coal deposits in the county— Carbon County is located in south-central Montana, on the Wyoming border. Coal was first discovered here at the point where Rock Creek Valley narrows into a basin as its approaches the mountains. A crude mining camp here grew to become the prosperous town of Red Lodge, Montana, and coal mining communities developed in other nearby areas. As a result of the development of these settlements, it was decided that a new county should be created to provide legal and other county services reasonably close to the homes of the miners and other settlers. Thus Carbon County was born on March 4, 1895, and named for the extensive coal deposits within its borders. The town of Red Lodge was selected to be the county seat. At the millennium year 2000, coal is still actively mined in Montana.

1570 *Carter County*

Thomas H. Carter (1854–1911)— A native of Ohio and a lawyer, Carter emigrated from the midwest to Montana territory in 1882 and settled in Helena. There he practiced law and in 1888 Carter was elected to represent Montana territory as a delegate to the U.S. Congress. When Montana was admitted to statehood in November, 1889, it was awarded two seats in the U.S. Senate but only one seat in the house of representatives on account of its sparse population. Thomas H. Carter was elected to occupy that first Montana seat in the U.S. House of Representatives. He later represented Montana in the nation's senate. In the U.S. Congress, Carter supported many of Montana's interests but, sadly, he was a vigorous opponent of conservation measures advocated by Presidents Cleveland and Roosevelt. Montana's state Senator John Oliver was largely responsible for the creation of this new county but Senator Oliver wanted the new county to be named Sykes County. However, other members of the Montana legislature preferred to honor Thomas H. Carter. Their view prevailed and Carter County was born on February 22, 1917.

1571 *Cascade County*

Cascading Great Falls in the Missouri River here— This county in central Montana was created in September, 1887, while Montana was still a territory, and named for the cascading waterfalls of the Missouri River in the northern portion of the county. These cascading falls were named the "Great Falls" by the Lewis and Clark Expedition and they were so identified in a June 13, 1805, entry in the journals of the Lewis and Clark Expedition. Meriwether Lewis (1774–1809) called these cascading falls a "sublimely grand spectacle."

1572 *Chouteau County*

Uncertain— Chouteau County was first created as a part of Idaho territory on January 16, 1864. After Montana territory was formed from the northeastern portion of Idaho territory, Montana's territorial legislature passed an act, effective February 2, 1865, which created Chouteau County as a part of Montana territory. Sources consulted differ concerning the person or persons for whom this county was named. Roberta C. Cheney's *Names on the Face of Montana* says that the name honors Auguste Chouteau and Pierre Chouteau and Tom Stout's history of Montana published in 1921 agrees. However Robert I. Vexler's *Chronology & Documentary Handbook of the State of Montana*, published in 1978 gives the honor to Charles P. Chouteau and Helen F. Sanders' *A History of Montana*, published in 1913 agrees that Charles P. Chouteau is our man. The *1959–60 Montana Almanac* says that the county's name honors "the Chouteau family, founders of the Missouri River Fur Company." (The 1957 edition of the *Montana Almanac* agrees but adds the comment that "Pierre Chouteau, Sr., was the founder of the Missouri River Fur Company and his son,

Pierre Jr., was for many years associated with the American Fur Company.") Michael A. Leeson's *History of Montana*, published in 1885 states that the county was named for Pierre Chouteau, Jr. Information about a number of members of the Chouteau family who were engaged directly or indirectly in the family's fur trading activities follows:

Auguste Chouteau (–1829)— Auguste (Rene) Chouteau was born about 1749 in New Orleans. He was little more than 13 years old when he accompanied Pierre Laclede Liguest (–1778), known as Pierre Laclede, in his ascent of the Mississippi River which resulted in the founding of the city of Saint Louis. Under Laclede's direction, Auguste Chouteau supervised a team of workers in clearing the site for the infant city of Saint Louis. When Laclede died in 1778, Auguste Chouteau became the patriarch of Saint Louis. Auguste spent his life primarily in the Saint Louis area but he sent others acting on his behalf, to trade with Indians over a wide area north and west of Saint Louis. His business interests were said to extend up the Missouri River some 600 miles from Saint Louis; about half-way to the present state of Montana.

Auguste P. Chouteau (1786–1838)— Auguste Pierre Chouteau was a son of Pierre Chouteau (1758–1849). Auguste P. Chouteau was born in Saint Louis on May 9, 1786. He attended the U.S. Military Academy at West Point and graduated from that institution in 1806. However, he served only a short period of time in the army before entering into fur trading activities. Auguste's early fur trading efforts encountered a series of obstacles from Indians encountered on several trips up the Missouri River from Saint Louis. Auguste Chouteau became a partner in the St. Louis Missouri Fur Company. He pursued trading opportunities over a vast geographic area and was imprisoned for 48 days in Santa Fe, in what was then Mexico. His business and financial affairs fell apart in 1838 and he died in what is now our state of Oklahoma on Christmas Day, 1838.

Charles B. Chouteau (1808–1884)— Charles B. (not P.) Chouteau was a son of Pierre (Jean) Chouteau (1758–1849) and Pierre's second wife Brigette Saucier (1778–1828). In 1821 Charles Chouteau opened a fur trading post along the banks of the Missouri River and became one of the founders of the present Kansas City, Missouri.

Charles P. Chouteau (1819–1901)— Charles P. Chouteau was born in Saint Louis on December 2, 1819. His father was Pierre (Cadet) Chouteau, Jr. (1789–1865).

Charles joined the family's business in Saint Louis in 1838 and had a long and successful business career in that city but there is no evidence that he had any connection with the Rocky Mountain fur trade. Charles P. Chouteau died at Saint Louis in 1901.

Francois G. Chouteau (1797–1838)— A son of Pierre (Jean) Chouteau (1758–1849), Francois Gesseau Chouteau was born in Saint Louis on February 27, 1797. His career centered in what is now western Missouri and eastern Kansas and he had little, if any, connection with the Rocky Mountain fur trading activities of the Chouteau family.

Gabriel S. Chouteau (1794–1887)— Gabriel Sylvestre Chouteau, a son of Auguste (Rene) Chouteau (–1829), was born at Saint Louis on December 31, 1794. After serving in the army on frontier duty under Nathan Boone (1780–), Gabriel S. Chouteau engaged in fur trading activities until 1829 when his father died. He then returned to Saint Louis where he engaged in business until 1853, when he retired. Gabriel Chouteau's personal fur trading activities were east of the Rocky Mountains but he was certainly a fur trading member of the Chouteau family.

Pierre Chouteau (1758–1849)— Born at New Orleans on October 10, 1758, Pierre (Jean) Chouteau moved to the wilderness of Saint Louis in 1794. Pierre Chouteau engaged in fur trading among the Indians in what is our present state of Missouri. He also built a fort, Fort Carondelet in southwestern Missouri, and served as the fort's commandant for Spain, which then controlled this area of North America. In 1804 President Thomas Jefferson appointed Pierre Chouteau to serve as an Indian agent for the Osage Indians. About five years later, in 1809, Pierre Chouteau joined forces with Manuel Lisa (1772–1820) and others to form the St. Louis Missouri Fur Company. This firm engaged in fur trading activities up the Missouri River. Pierre Chouteau commanded an expedition among the Mandan Indians in 1809. The Mandan inhabited areas east of today's state of Montana, along the Missouri River in central North Dakota. Pierre Chouteau died in Saint Louis on July 10, 1849.

Pierre Chouteau, Jr. (1789–1865)— Pierre (Cadet) Chouteau, Jr., was born at Saint Louis on January 19, 1789. He entered the fur trading business when he was only 15 years old. He prospered and eventually sold furs and goods to the Rocky Mountain Fur Company. By 1827 Pierre Chouteau was surpassing his rivals in the Rocky

Mountain fur trade and he eventually acquired control of John Jacob Astor's (1763–1848) American Fur Company. Pierre Chouteau, Jr., terminated his participation in the Rocky Mountain fur trade about 1839 and turned his attention to other business ventures including mining and railroads. He became a very wealthy man but he went blind in 1859. Pierre (Cadet) Chouteau, Jr., died at Saint Louis on September 6, 1865.

1573 *Custer County*

George A. Custer (1839–1876)— Custer was born in Ohio and educated at West Point. As a Union officer in the Civil War, his successes led to promotion to the rank of general before his 24th birthday. Following that war, he served in the U.S. cavalry fighting Indians in the West. The flamboyance which had served Custer so well in the Civil War led to his downfall at the battle of Little Big Horn in Montana territory on June 25, 1876. In that battle, famous as "Custer's last stand," he attacked Indians who greatly outnumbered his forces. Custer and all of his men were slain. Soon after that battle, this county's name (which was originally Big Horn County) was changed to honor General George A. Custer. This change in the county's name was made effective February 16, 1877. (Montana later created a different county with the name Big Horn County, on January 13, 1913.)

1574 *Daniels County*

Mansfield A. Daniels (1858–1919)— Daniels was born in Addison, Pennsylvania, on April 2, 1858. He moved to Iowa with his parents when he was about ten years old and subsequently was employed in Iowa as a clerk in a general store and as a carpenter. He also earned his living for a time as a traveling salesman. By 1896 Daniels felt that his health was becoming impaired and that it would be improved by a move to Montana. Daniels and his wife arrived by rail at Poplar, Montana in April, 1896. He was employed for a few years in the Poplar area by the federal government; first as a carpenter at the Fort Peck Indian agency and later as a United States land agent at Poplar, Montana. In 1901 Daniels visited the area that is now the town of Scobey, Montana, and decided to move here. The area was essentially empty when Daniels settled here. Tom Stout's history of Montana, published in 1921, states that there were only four prior settlers at what is now Scobey when Daniels and his wife moved here. Daniels became

a pioneer farmer, rancher, and, in time, the proprietor of a general store. Daniels worked long and hard and had managed to acquire 2,260 acres for his ranch by the time of his death on April 15, 1919. It was little more than one year later, in August, 1920, that the Montana legislature created and named this county in honor of Mansfield A. Daniels. Its county seat is located at Scobey, Montana.

1575 *Dawson County*

Andrew Dawson (1817–1871)— Dawson was born in Scotland on April 25, 1817, and immigrated to America in 1843. In 1844 he ascended the Missouri River to engage in fur trading but his first stop was to be at Fort Pierre where he had documents to deliver. This initial part of Dawson's journey became unnecessarily arduous when his companion decided to return to Saint Louis and take the horses with him. For six weeks Dawson traveled alone, subsisting at times on wild berries. After eventually arriving at Fort Pierre, Dawson traveled up to Fort Clark, where he was employed for a number of years by the American Fur Company. He was well liked by the Indians and was promoted by his superiors to be the American Fur Company's chief trader at Fort Clark. He held that post from 1850 to about 1854. Dawson moved briefly to Fort Union and then, for about ten years, he was stationed at Fort Benton. This was an extremely important trading post on account of its location at the head of steamboat navigation on the Missouri River. Andrew Dawson grew wealthy from trading furs at Fort Benton in the north-central section of what is today's state of Montana and he was able to retire comfortably in 1864. Dawson returned to his native land of Scotland and died there on September 16, 1871. This county was created and named in Andrew Dawson's honor on January 15, 1869, by Montana territory.

1576 *Deer Lodge County*

Town of Deer Lodge, Idaho territory— Deer Lodge County was first created as a part of Idaho territory on January 16, 1864, and it was named for the town of Deer Lodge there. After Montana territory was formed from the northeastern portion of Idaho territory, Montana's territorial legislature passed an act, effective February 2, 1865, which created Deer Lodge County as a part of Montana territory. The name of the town of Deer Lodge (first named Deer Lodge Town Company) grew out of an early name for the river valley of the

Clark Fork River, which bisects the present town of Deer Lodge, Montana. The valley was once called "the lodge of the white-tailed deer." These deer visited the valley in droves on account of natural salt licks here. The "Lodge" portion of the county and town name arose because of a mound at or near one of the salt licks which was thought to resemble an Indian lodge, in the morning, with steam coming from it. As a result of the creation of new counties and county boundary changes by Montana territory and the state of Montana, the town of Deer Lodge is now located in Powell County, Montana, just north of Deer Lodge County, Montana. In 1901 the Montana legislature passed a law to change the name of Deer Lodge County to Daly County. However, the Montana supreme court invalidated that law, declaring it to be unconstitutional under Montana's constitution.

1577 *Fallon County*

Benjamin O'Fallon (1793–1842)— A native of Kentucky and a nephew of William Clark (1770–1838), of Lewis & Clark fame, O'Fallon was appointed by his uncle, Clark, in 1816 as special Indian agent. He served in that capacity at Prairie du Chien and later served as an Indian agent for several Missouri River tribes. O'Fallon was a member of the 1819 expedition headed by Henry Atkinson (1782–1842), which established a permanent post at Old Council Bluffs, in what is now Nebraska. O'Fallon later supervised Indian agents on the upper Missouri River and he participated in an 1825 expedition to the Yellowstone River. In 1826 O'Fallon resigned on account of ill health. Benjamin O'Fallon is sometimes confused with the mountain man William O. Fallon (–1848).

1578 *Fergus County*

James Fergus (1813–1902)— Born in Scotland on October 8, 1813, Fergus immigrated to North America when he was about 19 years old. He first went to Canada, where he spent about three years and then to Illinois, where he was a member of the paper manufacturing firm of Wheelock & Fergus at Moline, Illinois. Fergus later engaged in the construction and operation of mills at Savanna, Illinois. He was very adept at constructing and improving mechanical devices and machines. In 1854 Fergus removed to Minnesota territory. While living there, Fergus and one C. A. Tuttle collaborated in erecting a dam across the Mississippi River. Also while living in Minnesota, James Fergus supplied outfits and provisions to an expedition which staked out the town of Fergus Falls, Minnesota. That town, which is now the county seat of Otter Tail County, Minnesota, was named in honor of James Fergus although he never visited it. In 1862 Fergus joined Captain James L. Fisk's (1835–1902) expedition to the West. Fergus' motive was to find gold in Montana and he engaged in mining here at the early mining camp named Bannack. After moving to the area of Helena, Montana territory, Fergus was elected to two terms as a county commissioner and he served in the legislature of Montana territory. He was an initiator of the idea of establishing Yellowstone National Park. Fergus had a friend who represented Minnesota in the U.S. Congress, named Ignatius Donnelly (1831–1901), who pushed the idea of Yellowstone National Park based on the ideas suggested to him by James Fergus. About this time Fergus decided to move toward the center of Montana to find room for an extensive cattle ranch. He prospered in this venture and he also had a patented mine in the Judith Mountains. When statehood was proposed for Montana, James Fergus served as a member of Montana's first constitutional convention. This county was created and named in James Fergus' honor on March 12, 1885, and Fergus automatically became a resident of the county named in his honor. He died near Lewiston, in Fergus County, Montana, on June 25, 1902.

1579 *Flathead County*

Salish Indians — This county was named for the Indians who called themselves *Se 'lic*, meaning "people." The name *Flathead* was mentioned in the journal of the Lewis and Clark Expedition, when the Indians being described were, in fact, the Salish Indians. The term "Flathead" is a misnomer for the Salish Indians. They did not make it a practice to flatten the heads of their children. That practice is said by some to have been common among Indians living further west, near the mouth of the Columbia River. It is possible, but far from certain, that the Lewis & Clark party noticed some flat-headed Indians whom the Salish had captured and were using as slaves. However, in a work entitled *Marcus Whitman, Crusader*, edited by Archer B. Hulbert and Dorothy P. Hulbert, published in 1936, the idea that *any* Indians, in what is now the northwestern portion of our country, had artificially flattened heads is challenged. In that work, the Hulberts quote from a letter dated February 20,

1836, written by H. H. Spalding which was later published in the *Missionary Herald* in October, 1837. In that letter, Spalding says "Permit me in this communication to correct a mistake respecting the appellation Flat Head. In its original appellation [sic] it doubtless was applied in derision to the natural head. All the tribes of the coast, for 200 or 300 miles inland, are in the habit of forming their heads into the shape of a wedge... These tribes called all others who had not their heads pitched before and behind by these artificial means, like the roof of a house, *flat heads*, that is, having their heads in the normal shape, using the term in the way of contempt. The name finally settled down on what is now called the Flat Head tribe, who suffer their heads to remain in their natural shape. The fact ... has lead to the belief that the story about flattening the heads is all without foundation and that there are no unnatural heads in this country..."

The Salish Indians were known to be mild and friendly Indians. Olga W. Johnson heaps lavish praise upon them in her work entitled *Flathead & Kootenay*, published in 1969. She quotes Osborne Russell's *Journal of Trapper* as follows: "...the Salishan Flatheads were a brave, friendly, generous and hospitable tribe, strictly honest, with a mixture of pride which exalts them far above the rude appellation of Savages when contrasted with the tribes around them." The journals of the Lewis and Clark Expedition also confirm that these Indians were fine people referring to them as "...a timid, inoffensive and defenseless people." The Salish lived primarily in today's Idaho and two areas of present day Montana. The first was in southern Montana, near the Three Forks, where the confluence of the Jefferson River, Madison River and Gallatin River forms the Missouri River. The second important area in which the Salish lived was in the Bozeman Pass, also in southern Montana. From these two primary concentrations the Salish Indians ranged east as far as the present city of Billings and beyond to the Big Horn Mountains of southeastern Montana and north central Wyoming. The Salish organized themselves into bands of related families who camped together. Between 1700 and 1730 the Salish began to acquire horses and they moved the main center of their activities to the Bitter Root Valley. Here they harvested the roots of the plant which they called "bitter root." With horses they were able to return from time to time to the Three Forks region to hunt buffalo for meat and also for skins which the Salish used to construct conical,

buffalo-skin teepees for their homes. Smallpox epidemics during the 1760's and wars with Blackfoot Indians decimated the Salish population. By 1891 essentially all Salish Indians had become impoverished and pushed out of the White man's way to Indian reservations. Montana created and named this county in their honor in 1893, after they no longer represented a problem to the White American namers of county names.

1580 *Gallatin County*

Gallatin River — When Thomas Jefferson commissioned the Lewis and Clark Expedition, his instructions included a mandate to trace the Missouri River to its source. Thus it was a significant accomplishment when the expedition found that source in late July, 1805, at Three Forks, where the Jefferson River, Madison River and Gallatin River combine to form the Missouri River. The leaders of the expedition, Captain Meriwether Lewis (1774–1809) and Captain William Clark (1770–1838), agreed to name these three rivers, whose confluence forms the mighty Missouri River, in honor of our country's president, Thomas Jefferson, his secretary of state, James Madison and his secretary of the treasury, Albert Gallatin. It was Meriwether Lewis who recorded the three rivers' new names in the expedition's journal for July 28, 1805, and he only spelled one of the three correctly. Lewis rendered the rivers' names as "Jefferson's River, Maddison's River and Gallitin's River." This latter river is now correctly spelled as the Gallatin River. It is some 125 miles long. The Gallatin River rises in northwestern Wyoming in Yellowstone National Park and flows north into Montana, where it unites with the Jefferson River and the Madison River to form the Missouri River. The Gallatin River was named for President Thomas Jefferson's secretary of the treasury, Abraham Alfonse Albert Gallatin.

Abraham Alfonse Albert Gallatin (1761–1849) — Albert Gallatin was born in Europe to an aristocratic family of the city of Geneva. He moved to America during the American Revolution and settled in Pennsylvania. During the winter of 1789–1790, he was a member of the convention which revised the Pennsylvania constitution. Gallatin later represented Pennsylvania in the U.S. House of Representatives and when Thomas Jefferson became president in 1801, he selected Gallatin to be his secretary of the treasury. Albert Gallatin was serving in that post in 1805 when the

Gallatin River was named in his honor. Gallatin served as secretary of the treasury under Presidents Jefferson and Madison until 1814. He subsequently represented the United States as a diplomat in Europe for some ten years.

Montana territory created Gallatin County on February 2, 1865.

1581 *Garfield County*

James A. Garfield (1831–1881)—A native of Ohio, Garfield served in the Ohio senate before becoming a Union officer in the Civil War. He performed ably and rapidly rose to the rank of general. In 1863 Garfield resigned his commission to enter the U.S. House of Representatives where he served until 1880. During Reconstruction, Garfield favored harsh treatment of the defeated South. In January, 1880 he was elected to the U.S. Senate but never served in that body. Instead, he was nominated and elected president of the United States. His nomination by the Republican party came as a compromise on the 36th ballot. Garfield was fatally wounded by an assassin's bullet just four months after beginning his term as president. This county was created in 1919.

1582 *Glacier County*

Glacier National Park—This county in northwestern Montana was created on February 17, 1919, and named for Glacier National Park, which is located in this area of Montana. A portion of the park area extends into Canada, where it is named Waterton Lakes National Park. Our country's Glacier National Park was created by the U.S. Congress effective May 11, 1910, and named for the many mountain glaciers within its borders. There are some 60 large glaciers here and countless smaller ones. Our country's Glacier National Park together with Canada's Waterton Lakes National Park form the Waterton-Glacier International Peace Park with a combined area in excess of one million acres.

1583 *Golden Valley County*

A promotional name to attract settlers—This county was created on October 4, 1920, and ostensibly named for its rich soil and numerous streams which combine to render about 85 percent of the county suitable for agriculture. However, Golden Valley County's name was really coined in an attempt to attract settlers to this central portion of the state of Montana. Figures taken from the 1990 Federal census indicate that Montana had a population of 799,065 spread over 147,046 square miles, or fewer than six persons per square mile. In Golden Valley County, the population is very sparse numbering but one person per square mile. While these statistics may properly be viewed as paradise by wilderness buffs, the sparse population presents problems in financing important services. Montana's efforts to attract settlers like the 1920 choice in naming this county have met with limited success.

1584 *Granite County*

Granite Mountain Silver Mine—This county in western Montana was created on March 2, 1893, and named for its Granite Mountain Silver Mine. The mountain was named for its granite rock content. The Granite Mountain mine was discovered about 1873 but it was some eight years later that the mine became famous for its precious metals. The pioneer who diligently prospected at Granite Mountain was Charles McClure, who had worked as a foreman of the Hope Mine at nearby Philipsburg. When McClure discovered precious metals here in quantity about 1881 the mining camp named Granite became a boom town. Granite Mountain was mined 24 hours each day and produced between $20 million and $25 million dollars worth of silver and gold. This county was created in 1893, just about the time that the silver and gold boom at Granite Mountain died. Today the mine is inactive and the town of Granite is a ghost town.

1585 *Hill County*

James J. Hill (1838–1916)—A native of Canada, this man who would one day be world-renowned as a railroad financier and tycoon, settled in St. Paul, Minnesota, territory in 1856. His early career was near the bottom of the ladder in the transportation industry. He worked as a clerk for steamboats plying the Mississippi River and as a freight agent for the St. Paul & Pacific Railroad. Early in his railroad career Hill determined that the wood fuel currently in use was inefficient and he became an expert on the methods to acquire and use coal for fueling trains. Hill collaborated with countless other figures in the transportation industry to piece together a railroad empire that became the Great Northern Railroad System. From 1882 to 1907 he was president of the Great Northern empire and from 1907 to 1912 he was chairman of its board of directors. Railroads were, of course, vital to the development of the United States during the years that Hill was at the heart of this industry. The railroad was of particular interest to Montana which needed links to the rest of the country. Hill developed railroads in Montana, and a number of other states, and he also combed Scandinavia for settlers of the vast potential farmlands served by his railroads. The methods employed by James J. Hill to develop his railroads and his personal fortune were, at times, unethical and on at least one occasion they were held to be illegal by the U.S. Supreme Court. Hill was a shrewd and discerning businessman who built his railroad lines where potential traffic justified them and then operated them with cost-conscious efficiency. He also removed or subdued competition at every opportunity. Hill's far flung interests included the rich Mesabi ore range in northern Minnesota. On one occasion, in May, 1890, James J. Hill was able to convert about $50 million of his assets into cash. This county was created on February 28, 1912. Hill died four years later in St. Paul, Minnesota.

1586 *Jefferson County*

Jefferson River—Jefferson County was first created as a part of Idaho territory on January 16, 1864. After Montana territory was formed from the northeastern portion of Idaho territory, Montana's territorial legislature passed an act, effective February 2, 1865, which created Jefferson County as a part of Montana territory. The county was named for the Jefferson River, which today forms a portion of its southern boundary. When Thomas Jefferson commissioned the Lewis and Clark Expedition, his instructions included a mandate to trace the Missouri River to its source. Thus it was a significant accomplishment when the expedition found that source in late July, 1805, at Three Forks, where the Jefferson River, Madison River and Gallatin River combine to form the Missouri River. The leaders of the expedition, Captain Meriwether Lewis (1774–1809) and Captain William Clark (1770–1838), agreed to name these three rivers, whose confluence forms the mighty Missouri River, in honor of our country's president, Thomas Jefferson, his secretary of state, James Madison and his secretary of the treasury, Albert Gallatin. It was Meriwether Lewis who recorded the three rivers' new names in the expedition's journal for July 28, 1805, and he rendered this river's name as "Jefferson's River." The Jefferson is about 200 miles long. It rises in Madison County, Montana, and flows north and east to unite at Three Forks, Montana, with the Madison River and the Gallatin River to form the Missouri River.

Thomas Jefferson (1743–1826)— Jefferson was a native of Virginia and a member of the Virginia legislature. He served Virginia as governor and was a delegate to the second Continental Congress. Jefferson was the author of the Declaration of Independence and one of its signers. He was minister to France, secretary of state, vice–president and president of the United States. As president, he accomplished the Louisiana Purchase and he arranged the Lewis and Clark Expedition to the Pacific Northwest. Jefferson was a true intellectual, thoroughly knowledgeable in the arts and sciences. His political theories were pivotal in the formation of our infant republic

1587 *Judith Basin County*

The basin of the Judith River in Montana— The ultimate namesake of this county is Julia Hancock (1791–1820), of Fincastle, Virginia, who became the first wife of William Clark (1770–1838). Captain William Clark, together with Meriwether Lewis (1774–1809), led the Lewis and Clark Expedition to the Pacific Northwest. However, before getting to Julia Hancock, there are some intermediate namesakes which must be mentioned.

This county was created on December 10, 1920, and named for Judith Basin, which is formed by mountains that largely encircle a basin of the Judith River. The Judith Basin was named for the Judith River, which flows through the basin's rich grazing land and farmland. The Judith River is a 100 mile long tributary of the Missouri River. It rises in central Montana in Judith Basin County and flows northeast and north through both that county and Fergus County, Montana, before emptying its waters into the Missouri River at the Judith Landing Recreation Area, northwest of the town of Winifred, Montana. During the Lewis and Clark Expedition in the early part of the 19th century, the leaders of the expedition, Captains Lewis and Clark, named numerous rivers. Some of those names have been retained while other rivers' names have been changed. The Judith River was named by Captain William Clark (1770–1838) and the name is shown as Judith's River in a May 29, 1805, entry in the journal of the Lewis and Clark Expedition. Clark chose the name Judith's River because he thought that his sweetheart's official given name was Judith, since she used the name Judy.

At that time Clark's future bride was no more than 14 years old.

Julia Hancock (1791–1820)— The Lewis and Clark Expedition ended its successful exploration mission on September 23, 1806, when they returned to Saint Louis, Missouri. Little more than one year later, on January 5, 1808, William Clark married Julia Hancock at Fincastle, Virginia. Julia and William Clark had six children: John Clark, Meriwether Lewis, William Preston, Mary Margaret, George Rogers Hancock and John Julius. Clark had been appointed brigadier-general of militia for Louisiana (later Missouri) territory and superintendent of Indian affairs at Saint Louis. Julia and William Clark made their home in Saint Louis. William Clark was appointed as governor of Missouri territory in the spring of 1813. As the territory's chief executive during the War of 1812, Clark had to deal with defending Missouri territory against the Indians and he personally took part in many of the journeys associated with that effort. Julia Hancock Clark lacked the rugged health required for life on our country's frontier and William Clark usually had to leave his wife during an illness or return to find her sick. In 1820 William Clark was a candidate for governor of what would be the new state of Missouri. By then, his wife, Julia's health had become weak enough that Clark dared not leave her for extensive campaigning and he took her back to Virginia during the final illness of her life. Julia Hancock Clark died in Virginia at her family's estate of Fotheringay on June 27, 1820. Clark's loss to Alexander McNair (1775–1826) in the campaign to become Missouri's first state governor resulted in large part from his being a fine husband to his first wife, Julia Hancock, and attending to her needs to the best of his ability. William Clark later remarried to a widow, named Harriet Kennerly Radford.

1588 *Lake County*

Flathead Lake— This county in northwestern Montana was created on May 11, 1923, and named for Flathead Lake. This lake is about 30 miles long and varies from 12 to 14 miles in width. Flathead Lake's area is about 200 square miles and it occupies much of the northern end of Lake County. The lake was named for the Salish Indians. For a discussion of the term "Flathead" as applied to the Salish Indians, see Flathead County, Montana, above.

1589 *Lewis and Clark County*

Lewis and Clark Expedition— This

county was originally created by Montana's territorial legislature on February 2, 1865, and given the name Edgerton County. That name honored Montana territory's first governor, Sidney Edgerton (1818–1900), who was serving as territorial governor at the time that this county was named in his honor. This county's name was changed to honor the Lewis and Clark Expedition on December 20, 1867. An early proposal called for naming the county Clark and Lewis County. It was subsequently determined that the name of Captain Meriwether Lewis (1774–1809) should come first since that was the order of names adopted for the journals kept by the leaders of the Lewis and Clark Expedition. Having gotten the order of names correct, the territorial legislature misspelled one of the names. The county's new name as adopted by the Montana territorial legislature was Lewis and Clarke County. That spelling error remained uncorrected for almost 40 years. It was not until February 10, 1905, that the legislature of the state of Montana officially corrected the spelling of this county's name.

President Thomas Jefferson never traveled much further west than his estate named Monticello, near Charlottesville, Virginia. As an intellectual, he was, of course curious about what could be found on the western fringes of North America. President Jefferson also had a very practical reason for learning more about the West. While Jefferson was providing Meriwether Lewis with his instructions for the expedition, the president had representatives in France arranging the Louisiana Purchase. When that purchase from France was accomplished, the size of our nation was approximately doubled. But Jefferson's curiosity extended west of the territory acquired from France. The term *Manifest Destiny* had not yet been coined, but it is likely that President Jefferson was thinking ahead to the time when our nation's borders might spread from the Atlantic to the Pacific, and precious little was known about much of the western portion of this vast area. Jefferson's negotiators in Paris accomplished the Louisiana Purchase on May 2, 1803, and the U.S. Senate ratified the purchase treaty in October, 1803. The Lewis and Clark Expedition, under the command of Captain Meriwether Lewis (1774–1809) and Captain William Clark (1770–1838) departed from Saint Louis on May 21, 1804, on the epic journey to the Pacific Ocean and they returned to that city with their mission successfully accomplished on September 23, 1806. The members of the Lewis and Clark

Expedition were the first White men known to visit what is the present state on Montana.

LEADERS OF THE LEWIS AND CLARK EXPEDITION

Meriwether Lewis (1774-1809) A native of Virginia and a neighbor and friend of Thomas Jefferson, Lewis served as an officer in the army and then, in 1801, President Jefferson selected him to be his aide. From 1804 to 1806 Meriwether Lewis and William Clark led the Lewis and Clark Expedition, which President Thomas Jefferson sent to explore the Northwest to the Pacific Ocean. Following the expedition's return to Saint Louis, Lewis served as governor of Louisiana territory. He was appointed to that post by President Jefferson on March 3, 1807, and he served as the territorial governor until his death in 1809.

William Clark (1770–1838) — Clark was a native of Virginia who served in the army in battles with Indians on America's western frontier. Together with Captain Meriwether Lewis, Clark led the Lewis and Clark Expedition (1804–1806) to the Pacific Northwest. Following the expedition, Clark served as brigadier-general of militia for Louisiana (later Missouri) territory, and superintendent of Indian affairs at Saint Louis. In the spring of 1813 President James Madison appointed Clark to be the governor of Missouri territory.

MEMBERS OF THE LEWIS AND CLARK EXPEDITION

John Boyle — Enlisted for the expedition but dropped out.

William Bratton — A blacksmith & gunsmith who served as a private. Later served in War of 1812. Died in Waynetown, Indiana in 1841.

Toussaint Charboneau — Indian guide picked up by the expedition at Mandan Indian villages and was with the expedition on the return trip as far as the Mandan villages. Husband of Sacajawea, the expedition's invaluable Indian "Bird Woman."

John Collins — Private. A man named John Collins was killed in a fight with Arikara Indians June 2, 1823; possibly same man.

John Colter — Private. Praised by Clark for his service and permitted to leave expedition on return trip at Mandan Indian villages. Probably was the discoverer of the area which became Yellowstone National Park. Died in Saint Louis in 1813.

Pierre Cruzatte — Hired as a guide and interpreter. Son of a French father and an Omaha Indian mother. Skilled in sign language and spoke the Omaha language. Lewis swore him into the army as a private. Excellent boatman. Accidentally shot and injured Captain Lewis while they were hunting elk but suffered no disciplinary consequences.

Pierre Dorian — A French frontiersman hired as a guide and interpreter to the Dakota Indians. Said to have been a very old man at the time of the expedition.

George Drouillard — Hired as a guide and interpreter. Son of a French Canadian father and a Shawnee Indian mother. Traded furs with Indians after expedition. Killed by Blackfoot Indians in 1810.

Joseph Fields — Private. He and his brother Reuben Fields, who served on the expedition, were from Kentucky.

Reuben Fields — Private. He and his brother Joseph Fields, who served on the expedition, were from Kentucky

Charles Floyd — Sergeant. During August, 1804, the expedition camped on a sandbar of the Missouri River near today's Sioux City, Iowa. Floyd died near there of a violent colic illness on August 20, 1804.

Robert Frazier — Private. Kept a journal during the expedition. Most of journal was lost but his map of the Northwest is in the Library of Congress.

Patrick Gass — From Pennsylvania. Private who was elected as a sergeant after the death of Sergeant Charles Floyd. Kept of diary of the expedition, which was published. After the expedition, served in the War of 1812. Died in 1870.

George Gibson — Private. Pennsylvania native. Died in Saint Louis in 1809.

Silas Goodrich — Private. Massachusetts native. Best fisherman among the expedition's members. Re-enlisted in the army following the expedition.

Hugh Hall — Private. Settled at Saint Louis after the expedition.

Thomas P. Howard — Raised at Brimfield, Massachusetts. Captain Clark said of Howard "He never drank water." Captain Lewis named a creek in Montana for him.

Francis Labiche — Hired as a guide and interpreter. He spoke several Indian languages. Lewis swore him into the army as a private.

Baptiste Le Page — Private. Enlisted with the expedition at the Mandan Indian villages.

Hugh McNeal — Private. Hired because of his knowledge of Shoshone Indians. Died young, possibly as a result of venereal disease acquired from having sex with Indians during the expedition.

John Newman — Private. Was tried for "mutinous expression," convicted and discharged from the military but kept on as a "camp drudge" until the Mandan Indian villages were reached. He was sent back to Saint Louis in 1805 with river men.

John Ordway — Sergeant and a key man. Usually in charge when Captains Lewis and Clark were absent. New Hampshire native. After expedition, he settled near New Madrid, Missouri territory, and became prosperous land owner and planter. Kept a journal of the expedition which was lost until 1913.

John Potts — Private. Permitted to leave expedition on return trip at Mandan Indian villages. Hired by Manuel Lisa to trade on upper Missouri River for a time. Killed by Blackfoot Indians.

Nathaniel Pryor — Sergeant. Praised by Captains Lewis and Clark for his work. After expedition joined army (at least twice) and rose to the rank of captain under General Andrew Jackson at New Orleans in the War of 1812. Died in 1831.

Moses Reed — Discharged from the army for attempted desertion. Kept on as a laborer until the Mandan Indian villages were reached.

Sacajawea — A Shoshone Indian woman picked up by the expedition at Mandan Indian villages with her husband, Toussaint Charboneau and they both served as guides and interpreters. This invaluable "Bird Woman" turned out to be uniquely valuable to the expedition. On the return trip she left the expedition at Mandan villages with her husband.

George Shannon — "Boy private." Born 1787 in Pennsylvania. Served faithfully but received severe leg wound during battle with Indians. Upon expedition's return to Saint Louis, leg was amputated and replaced by "peg leg." Studied law and served as judge, Missouri state senator and criminal lawyer. Died in 1836. Shannon County, Missouri, was named in his honor.

John Shields — Private. Recruited by William Clark because of his skills as woodsman and hunter. Also reputed to be skilled artistic craftsman.

William Werner — Private. Served throughout the expedition and later was appointed by Missouri's territorial governor, William Clark, as an Indian agent.

Joseph Whitehouse — Private. Kept a journal of the expedition which served as a basis for the eight volumes published by Reuben Gold Thwaites entitled *Original Journals of the Lewis and Clark Expedition.*

Alexander H. Willard — Private. New Hampshire native. Blacksmith and good hunter. After expedition served in War of

1812. Later lived in Wisconsin and California. Died 1865.

York — Captain William Clark brought his Black slave, named York, with him on the expedition. York suffered the many trials of the expedition and upon its successful return to Saint Louis, asked his owner, William Clark, to give him his freedom. Clark refused, thus denying York not only his freedom, but the company of his wife, who belonged to someone else and lived in Louisville, Kentucky. Clark referred to York's subsequent behavior as "insolent and sulky." Little can be added to Stephen E. Ambrose's comment in his work entitled *Undaunted Courage*, published in 1996: "York had helped pole Clark's keelboat, paddled his canoe, hunted for his meat, made his fire, had shown he was prepared to sacrifice his life to save Clark's, crossed the continent and returned with his childhood companion, only to be beaten because he was insolent and sulky and denied not only his freedom but his wife, and we may suppose, children."

Thus ends on a very sad note, the tale of the glorious Lewis and Clark Expedition.

1590 *Liberty County*

Uncertain — This county was created on February 11, 1920. The origin of its name is not certain but it seems likely that it was inspired by our nation's victory in World War I, which had recently ended. At that time, the war was simply called the World War. Nobody knew that there would be a second one very soon. Our participation in the war began on April 6, 1917, when President Woodrow Wilson signed congress' declaration of war. It ended on November 11, 1918, when Germany signed an armistice treaty. For a number of years our country's national holiday on November 11 was named Armistice Day. It is know called Veterans Day, to honor soldiers from all wars. World War I cost our country about 120,000 lives and more than 200,000 wounded. Our European allies in the war had almost four million of their soldiers killed and more than eleven million wounded. President Wilson had declared the need to make the world safe for democracy. The choice of Liberty for this county's name, shortly after World War I ended, may well have reflected that sentiment.

1591 *Lincoln County*

Uncertain — This county was created on March 9, 1909. It may have been named in honor of President Abraham Lincoln on account of his importance to both Mon-

tana and our nation. It was President Lincoln who signed the bill, on May 26, 1864, which created Montana territory. However, authorities on Montana's place names, such as Roberta C. Cheney, avoid stating that this county was named for him. The *1959–60 Montana Almanac* is only willing to say that the county "is believed to have been named for President Abraham Lincoln."

Abraham Lincoln (1809–1865) — Lincoln was a native of Kentucky who moved to Illinois where he was a member of the state legislature. He represented Illinois in the U.S. House of Representatives and later was elected president of the United States. Lincoln's presidency coincided almost exactly with the Civil War. He guided the United States ably through that uniquely turbulent period. As president, he issued the Emancipation Proclamation which declared the freedom of slaves in all states in rebellion. Lincoln was assassinated in April, 1865, a few days after the Union's victory in the Civil War.

1592 *McCone County*

George McCone (1854–) — McCone was born on April 4, 1854, in Livingston County, New York and moved, the following year with his parents to Michigan. In 1877 McCone moved to Indian territory (now Oklahoma), where he carried the mail between Fort Reno and Fort Sill. After only one year in Indian territory, George McCone moved north to Bismarck, in Dakota territory, where he continued as a mail carrier and also served as the U.S. government's agent in charge of hay, grain and wood used by horse teams for postal purposes. In the spring of 1882, McCone came to Montana territory and settled on Burns Creek, about 40 miles from the infant town of Glendive. Here he became a cattle and sheep rancher and was very successful in this business. At one time McCone shipped more cattle, sheep and horses from this section of Montana than anybody else. In 1900 the voters of Dawson County elected McCone to the lower house of the Montana legislature. He later served in Montana's state senate and he was very active in that body in lobbying to have this new county created. In reward for that effort, when the Montana created this county in February, 1919, they named it in his honor.

1593 *Madison County*

Madison River — Madison County, Montana, is named for the Madison River, which flows through it. When Thomas Jefferson

commissioned the Lewis and Clark Expedition, his instructions included a mandate to trace the Missouri River to its source. Thus it was a significant accomplishment when the expedition found that source in late July, 1805, at Three Forks, where the Jefferson River, Madison River and Gallatin River combine to form the Missouri River. The leaders of the expedition, Captain Meriwether Lewis (1774–1809) and Captain William Clark (1770–1838), agreed to name these three rivers, whose confluence forms the mighty Missouri River, in honor of our country's president, Thomas Jefferson, his secretary of state, James Madison, and his secretary of the treasury, Albert Gallatin. It was Meriwether Lewis who recorded the three rivers' new names in the expedition's journal for July 28, 1805, and he only spelled one of the three correctly. Lewis rendered the rivers' names as "Jefferson's River, Maddison's River and Gallitin's River." Madison County was first created as a part of Idaho territory on January 16, 1864. After Montana territory was formed from the northeastern portion of Idaho territory, Montana's territorial legislature passed an act, effective February 2, 1865, which created Madison County as a part of Montana territory. The Madison River is a 180 mile-long tributary of the Missouri River. It rises in southwestern Montana, in Gallatin County, and flows west and north through Madison County until it reaches Three Forks where it unites with the Jefferson River and the Gallatin River to form the Missouri River.

James Madison (1751–1836) — Madison was born in Virginia and served in the Virginia legislature and in the Continental Congress. He was a member of the convention which framed the U.S. Constitution and he collaborated with Hamilton and Jay in writing a series of papers under the title *The Federalist*, which explained the new constitution and advocated its adoption. Madison represented Virginia in the U.S. House of Representatives, served for eight years as secretary of state and for eight years as president of the United States.

1594 *Meagher County*

Thomas F. Meagher (1823–1867) — Thomas Francis Meagher was born in Waterford, Ireland, in August, 1823. He participated in efforts to secure independence for Ireland and was sentenced to death by England for those treasonous activities. That sentence was commuted to lifelong banishment to Tasmania and Meagher arrived there in 1849. About three years later he managed to escape and came to the United States. Meagher was a resident of New York state when the Civil War started. In 1862 President Abraham Lincoln appointed him a brigadier-general of volunteers. In 1865 Meagher resigned from the army and later that same year he was appointed to be secretary of the infant Montana territory. Territorial secretaries generally have little power but Meagher became acting governor of Montana territory almost as soon as he arrived. It seems that Montana's first territorial governor, Sidney Edgerton (1818–1900), became disenchanted with Montana and its politics and left the territory without bothering to resign or take an official leave. Thomas F. Meagher then became acting governor of the territory and he served in that capacity from September, 1865, until October, 1866, when Green C. Smith (1832–1895) arrived to serve as Montana territory's second official governor. On July 1, 1867, Thomas F. Meagher boarded a steamboat on the Missouri River and was never seen again. It is presumed that he fell overboard and drowned.

1595 *Mineral County*

The county's mineral resources in its many mines and prospective mines—This county in western Montana was created in August, 1914, and named for its miles of minerals within the mines and prospective mines here. The county contains several important mountains including the Bitter Root Mountain range on its western border with Idaho and the Coeur d' Alene Mountains at its northern end. The Mineral Mountain range is also found here. Although the county was named for its mineral resources, the only significant mining boom here was the Cedar Creek gold rush from about 1870 to 1873. However the county's mines have also produced quantities of silver, copper and lead.

1596 *Missoula County*

Uncertain—This county is in western Montana, and the city of Missoula, Montana, is its county seat. It is certain that this county was not named for that municipality because the county was created a number of years before the present city of Missoula existed. There was an early Indian village in this vicinity, which was also named Missoula, but none of the sources consulted indicate that Missoula County was named for that Indian village. There is also a Missoula River, which flows through the city of Missoula, Montana,

but again, none of the sources consulted state that the county was named directly for that river. (One of the possible origins detailed below, "river of awe," is said by one source to refer to this Missoula River.) What we do know is that Missoula County was first created by Washington territory on December 14, 1860. That territory's original borders extended eastward embracing what are today northern Idaho and part of northwestern Montana. Idaho territory was created as a separate entity from the eastern end of Washington territory on March 3, 1863. Missoula County was next created as a part of Idaho territory on January 16, 1864. After Montana territory was formed from the northeastern portion of Idaho territory, Montana's territorial legislature passed an act, effective February 2, 1865, which created Missoula County as a part of Montana territory. All sources consulted agree that the name *Missoula* derived from the language of the Salish Indians. However there are differences of opinion about that original Salish name and the translation of it. Some of the possibilities that have been mentioned are:

— Derived from *isul*, meaning "cold," or "chilly," either due to the temperature or from surprise or fear. This derivation and translation was provided by Elers Koch in his article on northwestern place names which appeared in the March, 1948, issue of *Oregon Historical Quarterly*. Koch gives credit to the writings of Father Lawrence B. Palladino for supplying this information.

—*Issoul*, meaning "horrible." This name referred to Hell Gate Canyon near the present city of Missoula. When Salish Indians passed through this canyon on their way to buffalo hunting grounds on the plains, they were attacked often enough by Blackfoot Indians to call the canyon by this name.

—*Imisuleetiku*—Said to be the Salish Indians' name for Hell Gate Canyon and translated as "by or near the place of fear or ambush."

— *Inmissouletka*—A Salish Indian word said to mean "river of awe."

— An unspecified Salish Indian word meaning "sparkling waters."

A thread of similarity may be extracted from these somewhat disparate sources which could result in a translation involving being chilled by fear at the canyon (or stream) where horrible ambushes had occurred. Unfortunately, it is not safe to conclude from this that we have established the true origin of the name *Missoula*.

1597 *Musselshell County*

Musselshell River—This county in central Montana was named for the Musselshell River which runs across the entire county from west to east. The Musselshell is a 300 mile long tributary of the Missouri River. It rises in Meagher County, Montana, and flows east across several Montana counties, including Musselshell County, and then turns north to enter the Missouri River in Garfield County, Montana. In the journals of the Lewis and Clark Expedition there is an entry dated May 20, 1805, which mentions "This stream we take to be that called by the Minnetarees the Muscleshell River…" The journals noted that at the point that the Musselshell River entered the Missouri River, it was 110 yards wide, and "…by no means rapid … being navigable by canoes for a considerable distance." This county was created on February 11, 1911. Much earlier, on April 10, 1866, a "bogus legislature" of Montana territory had created a Muscle-Shell County. In June, 1866, all actions of that "bogus legislature" were declared invalid by Judge Lyman E. Munson, an associate justice of the supreme court of Montana territory.

1598 *Park County*

Yellowstone National Park—This county in southern Montana was created on February 23, 1887, when Montana was still a territory. It was named for Yellowstone National Park, which it borders. This national park was created by an act of the U.S. Congress on March 1, 1872, as the first real indication that our nation's leaders attached some value to preserving our wilderness areas. Prior to 1872, the general approach to dealing with wilderness areas had been to give them away and exploit them. Yellowstone National Park was named for the Yellowstone River, which flows through it. For a bit of information about the Yellowstone River, see Yellowstone County, Montana, below. Most of Yellowstone National Park is in Wyoming but its borders also extend into Idaho and Montana. This park is the oldest of our country's national parks and contains seemingly endless areas of wilderness beauty. The park contains about 200 geysers. For most of the park's millions of visitors, viewing one of these geysers, named "Old Faithful," is a must. Old Faithful is famous and popular for both the height of its eruptions and their regularity. When Old Faithful spews forth every 40 to 80 minutes, its massive eruption shoots hot water more than 100 feet in the air and sometimes approach 200 feet in height.

1599 *Petroleum County*

Petroleum produced at Cat Creek oil fields— Montana's first commercially successful oil strike occurred in 1920 at the Mosby Dome, in the settlement of Cat Creek, in central Montana. During the next two or three years the little settlement of Cat Creek became a booming oil mining camp and Petroleum County was created on November 24, 1924, in recognition of the importance of the oil boom here. The Cat Creek oil fields are located within Petroleum County. The 1920 oil strike here occurred as the infant automobile industry was beginning to accelerate throughout America. The hope was that oil here and automobiles everywhere would result in riches for Montana. The Cat Creek oil fields eventually had about 150 producing oil wells and it was suggested that Montana might eventually be one of the nation's leading oil-producing states. At Cat Creek the boom subsided and by 1975 there were only about 35 oil wells in operation. However, petroleum is still one of Montana's important mineral products.

1600 *Phillips County*

Benjamin D. Phillips (1857–)— This county was created on February 5, 1915. All sources but two state that the county was named for Benjamin D. Phillips. The two sources that disagree are (1) Tom Stout in his *Montana: Its Story & Biography* and (according to Roberta C. Cheney's 1971 edition of her *Names on the Face of Montana*) (2) the *Phillips County Jubilee Booklet*. These two sources state that the county was named for the American orator and abolitionist, Wendell Phillips (1811–1884). It seems safe to dismiss Wendell Phillips as a possibility. The sources which state that this county was named for Benjamin D. Phillips support that claim with credible evidence about the circumstances surrounding this county's creation. Benjamin D. Phillips was a member of the Montana senate. In 1912 he used his influence to have the county seat of Blaine County (which was created in 1912) established at Chinook, Montana, in the hope that he would be repaid by having an additional county created and named in his honor. He succeeded when this county was created in 1915.

Benjamin D. Phillips (1857–)— Born in Brigham City, Utah territory, on May 9, 1857, Phillips moved with his parents several times before they settled in Montana territory by 1865. He received most of his education in Deer Lodge County. About

September, 1878, Phillips settled as a squatter on a claim south of Fort Benton on Willow Creek and began a career in stock raising. In 1881 he decided that his prospects would be better on Wolf Creek. He moved there and took homestead, desert and timber culture claims. During the next decade Phillips' sheep and cattle operations became extensive and he decided to move to the north side of the Missouri River. He made that move in 1890. In 1894 he formed the beginning of what would be a very extensive estate and ranch on Warm Springs Creek about 18 miles from Wagner, Montana and some 25 miles from Malta, Montana. From 1890 to 1894 Phillips resided in Oakland, California, where his mother was living, but he retained his interests in his Montana properties. During his stay in California he engaged in the real estate business but his primary interest was in his Montana ranch. By this time his ranch was primarily devoted to sheep. Phillips returned to Montana about 1894 and in 1896 he was elected to the lower house of the state legislature. In 1898 Phillips was elected to the state senate. By that time his sheep ranches were among the most extensive in Montana. Phillips County was created and named in his honor in 1915.

1601 *Pondera County*

Uncertain— Sources consulted offer two different explanations for the origin of this county's name. One possibility is the Pondera River while the other is the Pend d' Oreille Indians.

Pondera River— The Pondera River runs through Pondera County in the northwestern section of Montana. It also touches Teton County, Montana.

Pend d' Oreille Indians— The Pend d' Oreille Indians, whose name was given to them by the French, lived in the what is now the Canadian province of British Columbia, northern Idaho and northwestern Montana. The name *Pend d' Oreille* meant "hanging ear," and it was bestowed on these Indians because of the large shell ornaments which many of them wore on their ears. The Pend d' Oreille are classified as belonging to the Salishan linguistic group and they share an Indian reservation in Montana with the Salish Indians. The Pend d' Oreille are related to some of the Indians who shared the same geographic area in northwestern America including the Kalispel Indians, the Coeur d' Alene Indians and the Salish Indians. This group of Indians was dominated by the Spokane Indians. The Pend d' Oreille

subsisted primarily on fish and large game. The explanation for the name *Pondera* as a county name to honor the Pend d' Oreille Indians as related in both Roberta C. Cheney's *Names on the Face of Montana* and in the *Montana Almanac* is that the name was changed in Montana to *Pondera*, which is alleged to be a phonetic version of the French name, Pend d' Oreille, to prevent confusion with Pend d' Oreille names for a town and a lake in Idaho.

1602 *Powder River County*

Powder River— The Powder River, a tributary of the Yellowstone River, is formed by the confluence of forks in northeastern Wyoming. It flows north into Powder River County, in southeastern Montana, and then continues its journey in a generally northern direction until its waters empty into the Yellowstone River in Prairie County, Montana. Approximately 375 miles long, the Powder River was named because of the gunpowder-colored sand on its banks. Indians had also called it by the name Powder because the windblown sand made its waters muddy and unfit for drinking. An often quoted description of the river tells us that it is "a mile wide and an inch deep." Struthers Burt assures us in his work entitled *Powder River: Let 'er Buck*, that this description is inaccurate. This county was created on March 7, 1919, and named for the river that traverses it from its southern border to its northern border.

1603 *Powell County*

John W. Powell (1834–1902)— A native of New York, Powell served as an artillery officer in the Union army during the Civil War. He lost his right arm, to the elbow, during the Shiloh campaign of 1862 but continued to serve in the army and reached the rank of major. After the war Powell taught geology at Illinois Wesleyan College in Bloomington, Illinois, and in 1867 and 1868 he took his students on field trips across the plains to the Rocky Mountains. On one of these expeditions, Powell and one of his students climbed Mount Powell in the Colorado Rocky Mountains; quite an accomplishment for a one-armed mountain climber. His student companion left a can with their names in it at the 13,398 foot summit of Mount Powell. In 1869 Powell and some companions explored from Green River, in Wyoming territory, through the Grand Canyon to the lower Colorado River. After other explorations in the West, Powell was appointed as the director of the federal survey of the Rocky Mountain region and, later, the director of both the Bureau of American Ethnology and the U.S. Geological Survey. John Wesley Powell was one of our country's early advocates of conservation. This county was created and named in his honor on January 31, 1901. In March, 1901, the Montana legislature passed a law to change the name of Powell County to Deer Lodge County. However, the Montana supreme court invalidated that law, declaring it to be unconstitutional under Montana's constitution.

1604 *Prairie County*

The topography of the area— This county in the central portion of eastern Montana, was created on February 5, 1915, and named for the topography of this area. The name is accurate for much of the county's 1,700 square miles although there are mountains in Prairie County's northwestern section.

1605 *Ravalli County*

Antonio Ravalli (1811–1884)— This Roman Catholic priest and Jesuit missionary was born in Ferrara, Italy, on May 16, 1811. He taught for some years in Italy and then joined Father Pierre-Jean De Smet (1801–1873) in a trip to North America in 1844. Here he attended to the spiritual needs of the Kalispel Indians at the St. Ignatius mission in what is now Montana. Father Ravalli subsequently was placed in charge of St. Mary's mission, which Father De Smet had established in 1841 to minister to the Salish Indians. The St. Mary's mission was located where the town of Stevensville, Montana, now stands. Ravalli later served as a missionary to the Coeur d' Alene Indians. In 1857 his missionary work took him to the present state of Washington. Ravalli retired in 1860 at Santa Clara College, a Catholic institution in California. He grew restless there and returned to his Indians in Montana in 1863 where he spent the remainder of his life. Father Ravalli became knowledgeable in several Indian languages and he had both medical and mechanical skills which were rare and very useful in his work among Montana's Indians. He died here on October 2, 1884. This county was created on February 16, 1893.

1606 *Richland County*

A promotional name to attract settlers— This county in eastern Montana borders on North Dakota. It is well watered by the Yellowstone River, other streams and irrigation, and most of the county's land is suitable for some form of agricultural pursuit. However, the primary reason that the Montana legislature chose to name this county *Richland*, when they created it in 1914, was to attract settlers to this sparsely populated section of the sparsely populated state of Montana. That effort met with limited success. The county now has a population of about five people per square mile, about the same as the statewide population density (or sparsity) of six persons per square mile. Only about one-fourth of the county's land contains crops but more than three quarters of it consists of farms and ranches, so the county's name is reasonably apt.

1607 *Roosevelt County*

Theodore Roosevelt (1858–1919)— A native of New York City and a graduate of Harvard, Roosevelt bought a cattle ranch in the badlands of North Dakota and lived there two years as a rancher and hunter. Roosevelt County, Montana, borders on North Dakota and Roosevelt visited this section of Montana. During the Spanish-American War, Roosevelt and his "Rough Riders" gained national attention for their military exploits in Cuba. In 1898 he was elected governor of New York and he subsequently served as vice-president under President William McKinley. When President McKinley was assassinated in September, 1901, Theodore Roosevelt became our nation's youngest president, and a very vigorous one. He fought corporate monopoly, regulated railroad rates, and promoted conservation. Under his administration the pure food and drug act and employers' liability laws were enacted. He boldly took Panama away from Colombia, making a desired canal through the Isthmus of Panama possible. In 1908 Roosevelt urged the Republican Party to nominate William H. Taft. Taft was nominated and elected but his performance displeased Roosevelt. In 1912 Theodore Roosevelt bolted the Republican party and ran for president on a third, "Bull Moose" party ticket. This split the potential Republican vote between Taft and Roosevelt and assured victory for the Democratic candidate, Woodrow Wilson. Theodore Roosevelt died on January 6, 1919, and this county was created on February 18, 1919.

1608 *Rosebud County*

Rosebud Creek— This county in east-central Montana was created in 1901 and named for the Rosebud Creek, which flows through it. The Rosebud is a tributary of the Yellowstone River and an important one even though it is called a creek. The Rosebud rises in Big Horn County, Montana, and flows northeast about 100 miles until its waters empty into the Yellowstone River in Rosebud County. The name *Rosebud* was inspired by the wild roses, which grow in profusion along the banks of this creek.

1609 *Sanders County*

Wilbur F. Sanders (1834–1905)— A native of New York and a lawyer, Sanders served as an officer in the Union army during the Civil War. After resigning from the army in 1863, he settled in Bannack in the portion of Idaho territory which would very soon become part of Montana territory. Here he became a pioneer, mine operator, stock raiser and, according to several accounts, a vigilante. He also became active in politics in Montana territory and was several times a member of the lower house of the territory's legislature. When Montana was admitted to the Union as a state in 1889, Wilbur Fiske Sanders became one of the new state's first two U.S. senators. He died on July 7, 1905, five months after this county had been created and named in his honor, on February 7, 1905.

1610 *Sheridan County*

Philip H. Sheridan (1831–1888)— Sheridan was born in 1831 but his place of birth is in doubt. He graduated from the U.S. Military Academy at West Point and became a career officer in the United States army. When the Civil War began, Sheridan had almost a decade of military service behind him but was still only a lieutenant. During the Civil War Sheridan served with distinction in the Union army and rocketed from obscurity to high rank and responsibility. By the closing weeks of the Civil War, he had been promoted to major-general. After the Civil War ended, Sheridan remained in the army enforcing the odious Reconstruction Acts in Louisiana and Texas. Sheridan ultimately became commanding general of the entire U.S. army and attained the rank of full general. This county was created in March, 1913.

1611 *Silver Bow County*

Silver Bow Creek— Silver Bow Creek was named by gold and silver prospectors in the 1860's about the time that Montana territory was created. No credible evidence remains to tell us with certainty what inspired the creek's name. One legend has it that a prospector known as Seven-Up Pete told of the naming of Silver Bow Creek because "…The crick was full of curves and bends and the sun a-glacin' along its waters made these curves, as we looked eastward, to look like so many silver bows." Another legendary explanation for the origin of the creek's name involves the shape of the creek and the existence of silver near its banks. This county was created in February, 1881, while Montana was still a territory, and named for its principal creek, a few miles west of Butte, the county seat of Silver Bow County.

1612 *Stillwater County*

Stillwater River— The Stillwater is a short tributary of the Yellowstone River. The Stillwater rises near the northeast corner of Yellowstone National Park near the Wyoming-Montana border. It flows 70 miles in a generally northeastern direction between the Absaroka and Beartooth Mountain ranges and adds its waters to those of the Yellowstone River at Columbus, Montana, the county seat of Stillwater County. The river's name seems quite inappropriate. In her work entitled *Names on the Face of Montana*, Roberta C. Cheney describes the Stillwater River as "…a stream that rushes along mile after mile … dashing over giant boulders or whirling in arching riffles … with never of a cessation in its mad sprint for the Yellowstone." This county was created in March, 1913.

1613 *Sweet Grass County*

Uncertain— This county in south-central Montana was created on March 5, 1895. Three reputable sources offer three different origins for this county's name:

1. The 1957 edition of the *Montana Almanac* tells us that the county was named for Sweet Grass Hills, which were so named because of the sweet grasses in their vicinity.

2. Tom Stout's work entitled *Montana: Its Story & Biography*, published in 1921 states that the county was named for Sweet Grass Creek, which flows "…from the eastern slope of the Crazy Mountains to the Yellowstone River." Stout tells us that Judge William G. Strong chose this county's name and that Sweet Grass Creek was named for the abundant fragrant grasses which grow in the valley of Sweet Grass Creek. The word "sweet," Stout says was applied because of a sweet odor, like that of vanilla, that comes forth from these sweet grasses. Stout is certainly correct

when he says that Sweet Grass Creek flows through Sweet Grass County.

3. Roberta C. Cheney, in both the 1971 and 1983 editions of her *Names on the Face of Montana*, says that the person who suggested this county's name was Mrs. Paul Van Cleve, Sr., and that she chose the name on account of the abundant sweet grasses on the prairie near her home in Melville, Montana. Melville is located in northern Sweet Grass County on Sweet Grass Creek.

The sweet grasses which directly or indirectly inspired this county's name also were the source of names of a town in Toole County, Montana, very near the Canadian border, and the Sweetgrass Arch, which is a series of oil fields beginning at the municipality of Sunburst, Montana, and extending north of Sunburst. These same sweet grasses also were the source of the names of Sweet Grass Hills and Sweet Grass Creek, in this county.

1614 *Teton County*

Teton River & Teton Peak— This county in northern Montana was created on February 7, 1893, and named for the Teton River and Teton Peak, both of which can be found within the borders of Teton County. The Teton River is a 160 mile long tributary of the Missouri River, which rises in western Teton County and flows east across Teton County and Chouteau County, Montana. The Teton River empties its waters into the Missouri River at Fort Benton, in Chouteau County. Teton Peak in the Rocky Mountains has an altitude of 8,400 feet at its summit. It is located in western Teton County, near the Continental Divide.

1615 *Toole County*

Joseph K. Toole (1851–1929)— A native of Missouri and a lawyer, Joseph Kemp Toole came to Montana territory in 1869 and soon became active in local politics. He was elected to the legislature of Montana territory and subsequently represented Montana territory as its delegate to the U.S. Congress from December 7, 1885, to March 3, 1889. In congress Toole worked to secure Montana's admission to statehood and when that goal was achieved in 1889, Montana's voters elected him to be their first state governor. Toole did not run for reelection in 1892 but in 1900 he again ran successfully to be Montana's governor. Reelected in 1904, Toole retired from the governor's office on April 1, 1908, for health reasons. This county was cre-

ated and named in his honor six years later, on May 7, 1914.

1616 *Treasure County*

A promotional name to attract settlers— This county in the southern portion of central Montana was created on February 7, 1919, and given a name to attract settlers to the area. That effort was not successful. Figures taken from the 1990 Federal census indicate that Montana had a population of 799,065 spread over 147,046 square miles, or fewer than six persons per square mile. In Treasure County, the population is very sparse numbering but one person per square mile. While these statistics may properly be viewed as paradise by wilderness buffs, the sparse population presents problems in financing important services. Montana's efforts to attract settlers like the 1919 choice in naming this county have met with little success.

1617 *Valley County*

Valleys in the county— This county in northern Montana, on the Canadian border, was created on February 6, 1893, and named for its valleys. The central portion of this county lies in the valley of the Milk River and the valley of the Missouri River comprises Valley County's southern border. Apart from the valleys of the Milk and Missouri Rivers, most of this county's area is rolling prairie, much of which is suitable for cultivation.

1618 *Wheatland County*

Rich farmland suitable for cultivation of wheat— This county, near the center of Montana, was created on February 22, 1917, and named for the rich wheat lands within its borders. It was Montana state senator William E. Jones, who introduced the bill to create Wheatland County on January 19, 1917, and that effort resulted in success. Earlier names for a county here had been proposed as early as 1910. Merino County was one suggestion and Musselshell County was another. Montana never used Merino as a county name but it did use the name Musselshell in 1911 when it created a county by that name a bit east of the present Wheatland County. The northern and western sections of Wheatland County are mountainous and not suited to farming, but much of the rest of Wheatland County consists of rich, chocolate loam, on which both winter and spring wheat are grown.

1619 *Wibaux County*

Uncertain— This county was created on August 17, 1914. It was named for Pierre Wibaux, either directly, or indirectly, by being named for the town of Wibaux, Montana, which had been named in honor of Pierre Wibaux.

Town of Wibaux, Montana — In 1895 the post office and town here in what is now Wibaux County, had its name changed to Wibaux, in honor of Pierre Wibaux. This town had originally been named Keith and later Mingusville. Pierre Wibaux brought importance to this community by persuading the Northern Pacific Railroad to build stockyards and related accommodations for cattle here. Pens were also built for sheep and in one year some 1,500,000 sheep were shipped from loading pens at Wibaux.

Pierre Wibaux (1858–)— A native of Roubaix, France and a member of a wealthy family there, Pierre Wibaux served in the French army one year and then toured manufacturing facilities in England for his father's business. Rather than wait to succeed his father at the head of the family's extensive European business operation, Pierre Wibaux came to Montana territory in 1883. Here he inspected the badlands of eastern Montana territory and decided to settle in the area. He completed the formalities necessary to establish himself as a formal settler and went to Iowa and Minnesota to purchase his first herd of cattle. He also visited the stockyards of Chicago to learn, firsthand, the economics of the cattle industry. Wibaux returned to Europe in 1884 and married there. He returned with his new bride to the primitive conditions then extant in the badlands of eastern Montana territory. The newlyweds' first home was a sod house on Beaver Creek. When the herd of cattle owned by Pierre Wibaux grew to substantial numbers, he induced the Northern Pacific Railroad to build stockyards and shipping accommodations at a location convenient to Wibaux's ranch on Beaver Creek. These stockyards were built at a small community called Mingusville. This was the community which soon would be renamed Wibaux, in honor of Pierre Wibaux. He raised enough alfalfa on his ranch to provide feed for his cattle during Montana territory's long, harsh winters. However, the winter of 1886–1887 was particularly severe and an estimated 360,000 head of Montana cattle perished. That number represented 60 percent of the beef production of all of Montana territory and the losses were highest at the eastern end of the territory, where Wibaux's ranch was

located. Many ranchers here went bankrupt and Pierre Wibaux's herd was wiped out. However, Wibaux survived the disaster by returning to France to obtain additional credit. Later, during the hard winter of 1890, Wibaux prospered by purchasing cattle at bargain prices from ranchers who were forced to sell their stock. Wibaux eventually built his W-Bar herd to between 65,000 and 75,000 head of cattle. At one time Wibaux also owned about 200,000 acres of land in Texas and additional land in North Dakota. As his wealth grew, Wibaux extended his business interests, owning a bank in Montana and having investments in California, Mexico, the Klondike region and France. Wibaux also owned a gold mine in the Black Hills.

1620 *Yellowstone County*

Yellowstone River— Yellowstone County, Montana, was created in February, 1883, while Montana was still a territory. The county was named for the Yellowstone River, which flows across it from southwest to northeast. The journals of the Lewis and Clark Expedition tell us that the river had already been named by French trappers before Lewis and Clark got to it. The French name was *Roche Jaune*, meaning "Yellow Rock." According to most sources, the name simply came from the color of the rocks along its banks. However, there is another theory, which is plausible when we consider that the Yellowstone River is 671 miles long. According to this second theory, Crow Indians had given a name to the river in their language which meant "Elk River," which the French misunderstood and translated into their language as *Roche Jaune*. In any event, the Yellowstone River is an important tributary of the Missouri River. It rises in northwestern Wyoming and flows north through Yellowstone National Park. Soon after crossing Montana's southern border, the Yellowstone's course changes to east and then to northeast. The Yellowstone River ends its journey by pouring its waters into the Missouri River, just below Buford, North Dakota, less than five miles east of Montana's border with North Dakota. The Yellowstone is navigable for almost half of its 671 miles, during high water.

REFERENCES

Akrigg, G. P. V., & Helen B. Akrigg. *1001 British Columbia Place Names*. Vancouver, Discovery Press, 1970.

Ambrose, Stephen E. *Undaunted Courage*. New York, Simon & Schuster, 1996.

Arps, Louisa W., & Elinor E. Kingery. *High Country Names: Rocky Mountain National Park*. Estes Park, Colorado, Rocky Mountain Nature Association, 1972.

Bakeless, John. *Lewis & Clark: Partners in Discovery*. New York, William Morrow & Co., 1947.

Bonney, Orrin H., & Lorraine Bonney. *Guide to the Wyoming Mountains & Wilderness Areas*. Denver, Sage Books, 1960.

Burlingame, Merrill G., & K. Ross Toole. *A History of Montana*. New York, Lewis Historical Publishing Co., Inc., 1957.

Burt, Struthers. *Powder River: Let 'er Buck*. New York, Farrar & Rinehart, Inc., 1938.

Carpenter, Allan. *The Encyclopedia of the Central West*. New York, Facts on File, 1990.

Carpenter, Allan. *The Encyclopedia of the Far West*. New York, Facts on File, 1991.

Cheney, Roberta C. "Montana Place Names." *Montana: The Magazine of Western History*, Vol. 20, No. 1. Helena, Montana: January, 1970.

Cheney, Roberta C. *Names on the Face of Montana*. University of Montana, 1971.

Cheney, Roberta C. *Names on the Face of Montana*. Missoula, Mountain Press Publishing Co., 1983.

Conard, Howard L. *Encyclopedia of the History of Missouri*. New York, Southern History Co., 1901.

Contributions to the Historical Society of Montana. Vol. 2. Helena, Montana: 1896.

Coutant, C. G. *The History of Wyoming: From the Earliest Known Discoveries*. Laramie, Wyoming, Chaplin, Spafford & Mathison, 1899.

Crawford, Lewis F. *History of North Dakota*. Chicago, American Historical Society, Inc., 1931.

Dawson, James. "Major Andrew Dawson: 1817–1871." *Contributions to the Historical Society of Montana*, Vol. 7. Helena: 1910.

Defenbach, Byron. *Idaho: The Place & Its People*. Chicago, American Historical Society, Inc., 1933.

"Directory of Officers of the Territory of Montana." *Contributions to the Historical Society of Montana*, Vol. 6. Helena, Montana: 1907.

Du Gard, Rene C., & Dominique C. Western. *The Handbook of French Place Names in the U.S.A.* Editions des Deux Mondes, 1977.

Field, Sharon, Genealogy Department, Laramie County Public Library, Cheyenne, Wyoming. William Clark's family group computer record furnished to the author July 3, 1996.

Fletcher, R. H. *Historical Markers*. State Highway Commission of Montana.

Fletcher, Robert H. *Montana Highway Historical Markers*. Helena, Montana, Naegele Printing Co., 1938.

Foley, William E. *A History of Missouri: Volume 1: 1673 to 1820*. Columbia, Missouri, University of Missouri Press, 1971.

Foley, William E., & C. David Rice. *The First Chouteaus: River Barons of Early St. Louis*. Urbana, University of Illinois Press, 1983.

Gibbs, George. "Tribes of Western Washington & Northwestern Oregon." *Contributions to North American Ethnology*, Vol. 1. Washington, D.C.: 1877.

Grinnell, George B. *Beyond the Old Frontier*. Williamstown, Massachusetts, Corner House Publishers, 1976.

Harlowton Woman's Club, Wheatland County. *Yesteryears & Pioneers*. Harlowton, Montana, Western Printing & Lithography, 1972.

Hart, Herbert M. *Old Forts of the Northwest*. New York, Bonanza Books, 1963.

Hawke, David F. *Those Tremendous Mountains: The Story of the Lewis and Clark Expedition*. New York, W. W. Norton & Co., 1980.

Hayden, Elizabeth W., & Cynthia Nielsen. *Origins: A Guide to the Place Names of Grand Teton National Park and the Surrounding Area*. Moose, Wyoming, Grand Teton Natural History Association, 1988.

Holbrook, Stewart H. *The Story of the American Railroads*. New York, Crown Publishers, 1947.

Holloway, David. *Lewis & Clark and the Crossing of North America*. New York, New York, Saturday Review Press, 1974.

Hulbert, Archer B., & Dorothy P. Hulbert. *Marcus Whitman, Crusader*. Denver, Colorado, Smith-Brooks Press, 1936.

Hyde, William & Howard L. Conard. *Encyclopedia of the History of St. Louis*. New York, Southern History Co., 1899.

Johnson, Olga W. *Flathead & Kootenay: The Rivers, the Tribes and the Region's Traders*. Glendale, California, Arthur H. Clark Co., 1969.

Josephson, Matthew. *The Robber Barons: The Great American Capitalists: 1861–1901*. New York, Harcourt Brace & Co., 1934.

The Journals of Lewis & Clark. New York, New American Library, 1964.

Kane, Joseph N., et al. "Montana." *Facts about the States*. New York, H. W. Wilson Co., 1993.

Kingsbury, George W. *History of Dakota Territory*. Chicago, S. J. Clarke Publishing Co., 1915.

Koch, Elers. "Geographic Names of Western Montana, Northern Idaho." *Oregon Historical Quarterly*, Vol. 49, No. 1. Portland, Oregon: March, 1948.

Leeson, Michael A. *History of Montana: 1739–1885*. Chicago, Warner, Beers & Co., 1885.

Linford, Dee. *Wyoming Stream Names*. Cheyenne, Wyoming, Wyoming Fish & Game Department, 1975.

McCandless, Perry. *A History of Missouri: Volume 2: 1820 to 1960*. Columbia, Missouri, University of Missouri Press, 1972.

McLoughlin, Denis. *Wild & Woolly: An Encyclopedia of the Old West*. Garden City, New York, Doubleday & Co., Inc., 1975.

Malone, Michael P., & Richard B. Roeder. *Montana: A History of Two Centuries*. Seattle, University of Washington Press, 1976.

The Montana Almanac: 1957 Edition. Missoula, Montana, Montana State University Press, 1957.

1959–60 Montana Almanac. Missoula, Montana, Montana State University Press, 1958.

Moulton, Gary E. *The Journals of the Lewis and Clark Expedition: The Journals of John Ordway, May 14, 1804–September 23, 1806 and Charles Floyd, May 14–August 18, 1804*. Lincoln, University of Nebraska Press, 1995.

Mouton, Gary E., & Thomas W. Dunlay. *The Journals of the Lewis and Clark Expedition: Vol. 4, April 7–July 27, 1805*. Lincoln, University of Nebraska Press, 1987.

National Park Service, Department of the Interior. *General Information Regarding Glacier National Park: 1919*. Washington, D.C., Government Printing Office, 1919.

Noyes, Al J. *In the Land of the Chinook: Or the Story of Blaine County*. Helena, Montana, State Publishing Co., 1917.

Owings, Ralph E. *Montana Directory of Public Affairs: 1864–1955*. Ann Arbor, Michigan, Edwards Brothers, Inc., 1956.

Partoll, Albert J. "The Flathead-Salish Indian Name in Montana Nomenclature." *Montana Magazine of History*, Vol. 1, No. 1. Helena, Montana: January, 1951.

Pemberton, W. Y. "Changing the Name of Edgerton County." *Contributions to the Historical Society of Montana*, Vol. 8. Helena: 1917.

Progressive Men of the State of Montana. Chicago, A. W. Bowen & Co.

Raymer, Robert G. *Montana: The Land and the People*. Chicago, Lewis Publishing Co., 1930.

Robinson, Doane. *Doane Robinson's Encyclopedia of South Dakota*. Pierre, 1925.

Robinson, Doane. "Lewis & Clark in South Dakota." *South Dakota Historical Collections*, Vol. 9. Pierre, South Dakota: 1918.

Sanders, Helen F. *A History of Montana*. Chicago, Lewis Publishing Co., 1913.

Shifting Scenes: A History of Carter County, Montana. Ekalaka, Montana, Carter County Geological Society, 1978.

Spence, Clark C. *Montana: A History*. New York, W. W. Norton & Co., Inc., 1978.

Spence, Clark C. *Territorial Politics & Government in Montana: 1864–89*. Urbana, University of Illinois Press, 1975.

Stearns, Harold J. *A History of the Upper Musselshell Valley of Montana*. Harlowton & Ryegate, Montana, Times-Clarion Publishers, 1966.

Steffen, Jerome O. *William Clark: Jeffersonian Man on the Frontier*. Norman, University of Oklahoma Press, 1977.

Stout, Tom. *Montana: Its Story & Biography*. Chicago, American Historical Society, 1921.

Stoutenburgh, John. *Dictionary of the American Indian*. New York, Bonanza Books, 1960.

Taft, William H. III. *County Names: An Historical Perspective*. National Association of Counties, 1982.

Thrapp, Dan L. *Encyclopedia of Frontier Biography*. Lincoln, University of Nebraska Press, 1988.

Triggs, J. H. *History of Cheyenne & Northern Wyoming*. Omaha, Nebraska, Herald Steam Book & Job Printing House, 1876.

Upham, Warren. *Minnesota Geographic Names*. St. Paul, Minnesota Historical Society, 1969.

Vexler, Robert I. *Chronology & Documentary Handbook of the State of Montana*. Dobbs Ferry, New York, Oceana Publications, Inc., 1978.

Whittlesey, Lee H. *Yellowstone Place Names*. Helena, Montana Historical Society Press, 1988.

Yenne, Bill. *The Encyclopedia of North American Indian Tribes*. New York, Crescent Books, 1986.

Nebraska

(93 counties)

1621 *Adams County*

John Adams (1735–1826)— Adams, a native of Massachusetts, was a delegate to the first Continental Congress and a signer of the Declaration of Independence. He participated in Paris, with Benjamin Franklin and John Jay, in negotiating peace with England and, after the war, he was our country's first minister to England. Adams became the first vice-president of the United States under George Washington and when Washington retired, Adams was elected to be our nation's second president. This county was created on February 16, 1867.

1622 *Antelope County*

A particular antelope shot for food here— This county in northeastern Nebraska was created on March 1, 1871. Its name was suggested by a member of the Nebraska legislature named Leander Gerrard (1837–1913) in memory of a particular young antelope. The particular antelope for which this county was named was killed for food by Leander Gerrard and his companions. This event occurred in the summer but the exact year is uncertain. Various sources mention 1867, 1868 and 1870. The precise circumstances surrounding the killing of this antelope also vary among sources consulted. Some of them state that Gerrard and his companions were chasing Indians who had stolen from White settlers. Other sources indicate that it was merely a hunting party that killed this antelope. All accounts agree that Gerrard and his associates were hungry, killed the young antelope for food, and then ate it. Gerrard was inspired to suggest this unusual name for this county because the state legislature had drafted a bill for the creation of a new county, within whose borders the antelope had recently been shot. Pronghorn antelopes such as the one commemorated in this county's name are members of the genus *Antilocapera* and the species *americana*. They were quite common in Nebraska when White settlers began arriving here. These deer-like animals roamed in herds consisting of some 20 to 100 members. These antelopes had two characteristics which led to their demise: They were both curious of people and insufficiently afraid of them, making them easy prey for hunters like Leander Gerrard. Antelopes are now rare.

1623 *Arthur County*

Chester A. Arthur (1830–1886)— A native of Vermont and a graduate of Union College in Schenectady, New York, Arthur became active in New York politics soon after his admission to the bar in 1854. He became an important member of the political machine headed by the Republican, Roscoe Conkling (1829–1888), and Arthur was appointed collector and head of customs at the port of New York. This position gave Chester Arthur the opportunity to practice the spoils system with abandon and he awarded thousands of jobs to Republicans. In June, 1880, the Republican party held its national convention and Chester Arthur was nominated as the party's vice-presidential candidate under presidential nominee James A. Garfield. The Republicans won the election of 1880 and Chester Arthur became vice-president in March, 1881. Later that year he became president when President Garfield died from an assassin's bullet. President Arthur, the former champion of the spoils system, surprised the nation by running an honest administration and by signing into law the Civil Service Act of 1883, which established merit as the basis for federal employment. However, the Republican party failed to nominate Arthur as the party's 1884 presidential candidate and he left office on March 3, 1885. This county was created and named in his honor two years later, On March 31, 1887.

1624 *Banner County*

Expectation that the county would become the state's best county— This county in western Nebraska was created in 1888. Names that were considered for the new county included Wrights County, Frelinghuysen County and Banner County. G. L. Shumway, a former deputy secretary of Nebraska's department of agriculture, was among those who selected the name for this county. According to Shumway, the name selected was chosen by enthusiastic citizens who wished to announce their intention to make Banner County "the brightest star in the constellation of Nebraska counties." Beauty is, of course, in the eye of the beholder so it is impossible to say that this goal was never achieved. However, it does seem a bit of an exaggeration. Banner County consists of fertile land, rolling valleys and prairies and some scenic geological formations. Its land is devoted primarily to ranching and farming and its most populous community is Harrisburg, which has fewer than 5,000 residents.

1625 *Blaine County*

James G. Blaine (1830–1893)— Blaine, a native of Pennsylvania, moved to Maine where he served three terms in the state legislature. He then represented Maine in both houses of the U.S. Congress and, for a number of years, was speaker of the house of representatives. In 1881 Blaine became secretary of state under President James A. Garfield and he was the Republican party's candidate for president of the United States in 1884, losing to Grover Cleveland. When Benjamin Harrison became president in 1889, he appointed Blaine to be his secretary of state. This county's name was suggested by George W. Brewster, who was a wealthy Republican newspaper publisher and a resident of the county. The county was created on March 5, 1885, a few months after Blaine's defeat in the presidential election of 1884.

1626 *Boone County*

Daniel Boone (1734–1820)— A native of Pennsylvania, Boone penetrated Kentucky when it was wilderness country and settled there with his family in 1775. He gained fame on America's rugged western frontier as explorer, Indian fighter and surveyor. To many of us, much of Kentucky still seems quite rural at the second millennium year of 2000 but to Daniel Boone, Kentucky was already becoming too crowded for his taste by 1799. In September, 1799, accompanied by some members of his family, Boone immigrated to what is now the state of Missouri. This county in east-central Nebraska was created on March 1, 1871.

1627 *Box Butte County*

A butte, about six miles north of Alliance, Nebraska— The word *butte* came to us from the French. In that language the word means a "small, isolated elevation, knoll or mound." This county was named for a particular butte, within the county, near its eastern end. This butte is about six miles north of the town of Alliance, Nebraska. The shape of this butte approximates that of a rectangular box; hence the name. French trappers were the first to name this particular butte and the American cattlemen who came later liked the name. They called the whole area contiguous to this butte "the Box Butte Country." Railroad surveyors perpetuated this unusual place name on their maps. Thus when this county was created on November 2, 1886, it was not surprising that it was named for this box-shaped butte.

1628 *Boyd County*

James E. Boyd (1834–1906)— A native of Ireland, Boyd immigrated with his family to Ohio when he was ten years old. He came to Nebraska territory about 1857. In 1866 Boyd was elected to the legislature and he later served as mayor of Omaha. It was about this time that Boyd became prominent in the affairs of the Democratic party. He was a delegate to the Democratic national conventions of 1884, 1888 and 1892. In 1890 he was elected to be Nebraska's governor and he took office in January, 1891. The Nebraska supreme court ruled that since Boyd was not a citizen, he was not eligible to be the state's governor. As a result, Boyd's predecessor, Governor John M. Thayer (1820–1906), again became governor and Thayer served from May 5, 1891, to February 8, 1892. The U.S. Supreme Court ruled that Boyd was eligible to be governor and should be reinstated in the office. Boyd then served the remainder of his fragmented term as governor from February 8, 1892, until his term ended in 1893. He was not nominated for a second term. This county was created on March 20, 1891, while Boyd was governor.

1629 *Brown County*

Uncertain— This county was created on February 19, 1883, and named for one or more members of the Nebraska legislature. Some sources claim that this county was named in honor of Charles Brown, who was a member of the state legislature from Omaha, Nebraska at the time that this county was created. Other sources indicate that the county was named for two members of the legislature who reported the bill for creation of Brown County. This second suggestion appears unlikely. The members of the Nebraska legislature who introduced the bills to create Brown County were Moses P. Kinkaid in the senate and Frank North in the house of representatives. Kinkaid represented the twelfth senatorial district while North represented Nebraska's 23rd district in the house. Since neither of these men were named Brown, it seems unlikely that this county was named for "two members of the legislature who reported the bill for creation of Brown County." However, there is a third possibility for the origin of this county's name that is mentioned by several sources. According to this third theory, there were five members of the Nebraska legislature named Brown at the time that this county was created and the name Brown County was chosen to honor all of them. In John T. Link's Ph.D. thesis entitled "The Toponomy of Nebraska," dated May, 1932, specificity is given to this third choice for the origin of Brown County's name. Link tells us that at the time the bill to create this county was introduced in the legislature, their were five members of the legislature named Brown, four in the senate and one in the house.

1630 *Buffalo County*

Bison herds that roamed Nebraska— This county was created on March 14, 1855, when Nebraska was still a territory and while herds of bison still roamed on the plains of Nebraska. The county was named Buffalo County since that is the common, but incorrect, name given to these bison. These animals were the staff of life to nomadic Indian hunters. For a time they also provided a bit of revenue to White hunters and traders. When Nebraska territory was created on May 30, 1854, bison herds were plentiful here. By the time that Nebraska was admitted to statehood on March 1, 1867, these bison had become relatively rare in Nebraska. The slaughter of these animals was not, of course, limited to Nebraska. In the early 1800's, bison in America numbered in the tens of millions. Today very few remain and most of them are protected on government lands or private preserves.

1631 *Burt County*

Francis Burt (1807–1854)— Francis Burt was born in South Carolina, and he was educated and practiced law there. He served in South Carolina's legislature twelve years and was elected to be the state's treasurer in 1844. From 1847 to 1851 Burt edited the Pendleton, South Carolina *Messenger*. Francis Burt was a Democrat and in 1854 our country's president, Franklin Pierce, was also a Democrat. On August 2, 1854, President Pierce appointed Burt to be the first governor of the recently created territory of Nebraska. Burt's trip from the East to Nebraska took nearly four arduous weeks and Burt was in poor health prior to and during this trip. A physician whom he consulted *en route* in Saint Louis urged him to terminate the trip but Burt pushed on and was inaugurated on October 16, 1854, as the first governor of Nebraska territory. He died two days later, on October 18, 1854. In the following month, November, 1854, the acting territorial governor, Thomas B. Cuming, created and named this county in Burt's honor by proclamation.

1632 *Butler County*

William O. Butler (1791–1880)— Butler was born in what is now Kentucky one year before it became a state. When war with Great Britain was declared in 1812, Butler volunteered to serve as a private. He served with distinction in the War of 1812 and rose to the rank of brevet major. In 1817 Butler resigned from the army and was soon elected to the Kentucky legislature. He later represented Kentucky in the U.S. House of Representatives. When war was declared against Mexico in 1846, President James K. Polk appointed Butler to be a major-general and Butler served with distinction in the Mexican War. He was wounded at Monterrey, Mexico, and was present when Mexico City was captured. Shortly before the 1848 treaty of peace was signed with Mexico, Butler was given command of U.S. forces in Mexico. Later, in 1848, he ran for vice-president of the United States on the Democratic ticket headed by Lewis Cass. The Cass-Butler ticket lost the election and Zachary Taylor became president. In 1854 President Franklin Pierce offered Butler the opportunity to be the first governor of Nebraska territory. Butler declined and Francis Burt (1807–1854) won the appointment. A number of sources state that this county was named for David C. Butler (1829–1891), the first state governor of Nebraska. It is true that David C. Butler was the first state governor of Nebraska but this county was not named for him. As John T. Link explained in his Ph.D. thesis entitled "The Toponomy of Nebraska," dated May, 1932, this county was created on January 26,

1856, while Nebraska was still a territory. David Butler did not immigrate to Nebraska until 1858 and he was not elected governor of Nebraska until 1866. He was not nationally prominent so there would have been no reason to name this county for him in 1856.

1633 *Cass County*

Lewis Cass (1782–1866) — A native of New Hampshire, Cass served in the army in the War of 1812 and rose to the rank of brigadier-general. Following that war Cass held a variety of important political positions and was the candidate of the Democratic party in 1848 for president of the United States. He lost to Zachary Taylor. Cass served as governor of Michigan territory, secretary of war under Andrew Jackson, minister to France, U.S. senator from Michigan and secretary of state under President James Buchanan. This county was created in November, 1854, shortly after Nebraska territory was created.

1634 *Cedar County*

Presence of cedar trees here — This county in northeastern Nebraska was created on February 12, 1857, when Nebraska was still a territory. It was named for the cedar trees within its borders. However, Alfred T. Andreas was not particularly impressed by the cedar trees here. In his *History of the State of Nebraska*, published in 1882, just 25 years after the county was created, Andreas stated that in Cedar County "There are considerable quantities of timber … elm, basswood, box-elder, ash, hickory, soft maple, black walnut, red cedar, willow and the coffee tree are to be found." Similarly, in J. Mike McCoy's *History of Cedar County, Nebraska*, published in 1937, cedar trees are mentioned but they are near the end of a rather long list of trees in the county.

1635 *Chase County*

Champion S. Chase (1820–1898) — A native of New York and a lawyer admitted to practice before the U.S. Supreme Court, Chase served as a paymaster in the Union army during the Civil War. In 1866 he practiced law in Omaha, Nebraska, and from February 21, 1867, to January 11, 1869, he served as the first attorney general of the state of Nebraska. He later served as mayor of Omaha 1874–1875, 1879–1880 and 1883–1884. Champion Chase was also a member of the first board of regents of the University of Nebraska. This county was created and named in his honor on

February 27, 1873, before his first term as mayor of Omaha.

1636 *Cherry County*

Samuel A. Cherry (1850–1881) — This county was created on February 23, 1883, and named for a young army lieutenant, who had been killed less than two years earlier. Samuel A. Cherry was a graduate of the U.S. Military Academy at West Point and at the time of his death he was a lieutenant in the cavalry, stationed at Fort Niobrara, in Dakota territory. He was killed on May 11, 1881, while attempting to apprehend criminals. The tale begins with news reaching Fort Niobrara that there were plans to rob the paymaster, who was the *en route* from Omaha to Fort Niobrara to pay the troops. Lieutenant Cherry was dispatched with some enlisted men to meet the paymaster, Colonel Thaddeus H. Stanton (1835–1900), and escort him safely to Fort Niobrara. This mission was accomplished. However, on the night of May 9, 1881, a Private Johnson from Fort Niobrara and two civilians attempted an armed robbery of a drunken party at a nearby ranch where, presumably, money from the recent payroll disbursement was being freely spent. The culprits stole army horses and although they failed to get the money they came for, they killed one man and wounded at least two others during the attempt. Cherry and a score of assistants were dispatched to catch the desperadoes. It was during this pursuit of the armed robbers that Lieutenant Cherry was killed. However it appears that none of the armed robbers were responsible for his death. It was one of the soldiers serving under Lieutenant Cherry on this mission, Private Thomas W. Locke, who was convicted of manslaughter and sentenced to prison. Although the evidence against Private Locke was persuasive enough to convict him, it was certainly not beyond reasonable doubt, so the identity of the killer of Lieutenant Cherry is still in doubt. Cherry was buried at Fort Niobrara but in March, 1882, the father and fiancee of Lieutenant Cherry removed his body for burial at La Grange, Indiana, his boyhood home.

1637 *Cheyenne County*

Cheyenne Indians — The Cheyenne Indians were an important nomadic, hunting tribe, who were closely associated with the Arapaho Indians and had a permanent alliance with them. At the time that the Lewis & Clark Expedition encountered the Cheyenne Indians, they were living in the Black Hills of South Dakota. The hostile

Dakota Indians subsequently pushed the Cheyenne from the Black Hills and the Cheyenne lived for a time in an area that now includes Cheyenne County, Nebraska. The southern Cheyenne eventually lived in southern Colorado. The origin of their name in uncertain. Possibilities include:

1. A word of the Dakota Indians' meaning "people of alien speech" or "aliens."

2. "Scarred arms" on account of a practice of male Cheyennes of scarring their left arms.

The Cheyenne were engaged in almost constant warfare with neighboring tribes and with Whites. Following slaughter of their women and children by the U.S. army at Ash Hollow and Sand Creek, the northern Cheyenne participated in the rout of General George Custer's forces of Little Bighorn. But Whites eventually subdued the Cheyenne and both northern and southern branches were resettled in Indian territory (now Oklahoma). By the 1960's there were about 3,000 Cheyenne living on reservations in the United States. This county was created on June 22, 1867.

1638 *Clay County*

Henry Clay (1777–1852) — Clay represented Kentucky in both branches of the U.S. Congress. For many years he was one of the more prominent figures in American politics but his several bids for the presidency were unsuccessful. He was influential in effecting important compromises between northern and southern interests during the years that secession and civil war were imminent. This county created by Nebraska territory on March 7, 1855.

1639 *Colfax County*

Schuyler Colfax (1823–1885) — A native of New York, Colfax moved to Indiana where he became the proprietor and editor of the South Bend, Indiana *Register*. He was occupied in that capacity for nearly two decades. Colfax was elected to represent Indiana in the U.S. House of Representatives and he served in that body for some 14 years. In 1863 he was elected speaker of the house. In the election of 1868, Colfax ran for vice-president on the Republican ticket headed by Ulysses S. Grant. The Grant-Colfax ticket won the election and Schuyler Colfax served as our country's vice-president from March 4, 1869, to March 3, 1873. This county was created on February 15, 1869, and named in honor of the vice-president-elect.

1640 *Cuming County*

Thomas B. Cuming (1828–1858)—Thomas Cuming was born in Genesee County, New York, on Christmas Day, 1828. He moved to Michigan while still a boy and graduated from the University of Michigan at Ann Arbor. Upon graduation, Cuming worked as a geologist on an expedition in the area of Lake Superior. During the Mexican War, Cuming served as a lieutenant but apparently was not engaged in combat activities. His next venture was in the newspaper field. At Keokuk, Iowa Cuming was placed in charge of the newspaper named the *Dispatch*. When Cuming was only 25 years of age he secured an appointment from the federal government to be the first secretary of the newly created territory of Nebraska. The office of territorial governor held great power but the position of territorial secretary provided some prestige but little real authority. Circumstances developed which elevated Cuming to the role of acting territorial governor of Nebraska for extended periods. The first territorial governor of Nebraska, Francis Burt (1807–1854), died two days after he was sworn into office. As the territory's secretary, Thomas Cuming became acting governor of Nebraska territory and he served in that capacity from October 18, 1854, until February 20, 1855. Later, when Nebraska's second territorial governor, Mark W. Izard (1799–1866) resigned, Thomas B. Cuming again became the territory's acting governor, serving from October 25, 1857, until January 12, 1858. Throughout this period Thomas B. Cuming continued to serve as the territorial secretary and his tenure in that office ran from August 13, 1854, until his death on March 12, 1858. This county was created and named in his honor on March 16, 1855, following Cuming's first stint as acting governor of the territory.

1641 *Custer County*

George A. Custer (1839–1876)—Custer was born in Ohio and educated at West Point. As a Union officer in the Civil War, his successes led to promotion to the rank of general before his 24th birthday. Following that war, he served in the U.S. cavalry fighting Indians in the West. The flamboyance which had served Custer so well in the Civil War led to his downfall at the battle of Little Big Horn in Montana territory on June 25, 1876. In that battle, famous as "Custer's last stand," he attacked Indians who greatly outnumbered his forces. Custer and all of his men were slain. Less than one year after that battle,

on February 17, 1877, this county was created.

1642 *Dakota County*

Dakota Indians—The Dakota are a vast alliance of American Indians who are more commonly known as the Sioux Indians. These Indians' name for themselves is *Lakota* or *Dakota* meaning "friends" or "allies," while *Sioux* was a derogatory Chippewa-French name for them. The Dakotas consist of three general dialect and culture groups: the Santee, Wiciyela and Teton. When the Whites first encountered the Dakotas, about 1640, they found them living in southern Minnesota and adjacent areas subsisting by hunting, fishing, gathering lake and forest products and growing corn. In 1805 the Dakotas signed their first treaty giving up some of their Minnesota lands and by 1858 they had been pressured into signing treaties giving up almost all of their land in Minnesota. In return, they were to receive food, annuities, education and other necessities. These promises to the Indians were broken and in 1862 the Dakotas began a final, futile struggle against the Whites in Minnesota, who had systematically robbed and mistreated them. The Dakotas lost this struggle and 38 of their members were hanged on a mass gallows at Mankato, Minnesota, on December 26, 1862. Remaining Dakota Indians in Minnesota were deported to Indian reservations in Dakota territory (now South Dakota and North Dakota), where they have lived in misery to this day. This county was created on March 7, 1855, less than one year after Nebraska had been established as a United States territory.

1643 *Dawes County*

James W. Dawes (1844–1918)—A native of Ohio and a lawyer, Dawes came to Nebraska in 1871. He settled in Crete, Nebraska, where he practiced law and became active in politics. Dawes was a member of Nebraska's constitutional convention of 1875 and he served in the Nebraska legislature. In the gubernatorial election of 1882, Dawes was elected by a resounding margin and he easily won reelection to a second term. He served as Nebraska's fifth state governor from 1883 to 1887. He later practiced law in Crete, Nebraska and subsequently served as an officer in the U.S. army. This county was created on February 19, 1885, while Dawes was governor.

1644 *Dawson County*

Jacob Dawson (–)—Dawson was a newspaper publisher in Iowa before he came to Nebraska territory. He came to the town of Wyoming in Nebraska territory in 1856 and became editor of the weekly *Wyoming Telescope*. At Wyoming, Dawson also served as a land agent and surveyor. During the summer of 1863, he moved to Lancaster, Nebraska (now renamed Lincoln, the state capitol), and built a log cabin for his residence. When Dawson was appointed as the postmaster here on September 15, 1864, his log cabin residence became the post office. The first term of the district court was held in November, 1864, in Dawson's log cabin, Judge Elmer S. Dundy presiding. Dawson later erected a stone structure which served as his residence and the post office. Jacob Dawson was elected as the county clerk of Lancaster County in 1865 and he was superintendent of public instruction in 1867 and 1868. He also continued to serve as postmaster here until the fall of 1868. A number of sources refer to Jacob Dawson as the first postmaster of Lincoln (née Lancaster). It appears that there was a previous postmaster in this vicinity in 1863. The post office was named Gregory's Basin, in honor of its postmaster, John S. Gregory. We know this because Gregory bragged that his salary as postmaster was $3.00 per year with an extra $12.00 per year for carrying the mail weekly from Saltillo.

1645 *Deuel County*

Harry P. Deuel (1836–1914)—Harry Porter Deuel was born in Clarkson, New York, on December 11, 1836. He moved with his parents to Illinois while he was a baby and he later attended Lombard University at Galesburg, Illinois. In November, 1859 Deuel moved to Omaha, Nebraska territory, and he operated a large steamboat agency here until the railroads began to supersede river transportation. He then obtained employment as the Omaha agent of the Kansas City & St. Joseph Railroad. During Deuel's career he worked for several railroads including the Chicago, Burlington & Quincy Railroad, the Burlington & Missouri Railroad and the Union Pacific Railroad. In 1896 he became superintendent of the Burlington's Omaha station. Deuel left the railroad industry in 1899 to become auditor of Douglas County, Nebraska. At that time he held the longest continuous service in the railroad industry of any person in Omaha. In 1901 he was elected register of deeds. This county was created as a result of an election held in 1888. The state legislature set the boundaries of this new county in January, 1889. The name Cody had been suggested for this county but that name was rejected in favor of Deuel.

1646 *Dixon County*

Uncertain— This county was created on January 26, 1856, soon after Nebraska territory was established. Sources dealing with the history, geography and place names of Nebraska fail to provide the origin of this county's name. Some of them say that it was named for an early pioneer, while others describe the county's namesake as an early settler of northeastern Nebraska. William Huse's *History of Dixon County, Nebraska*, published in 1896, states that Dixon County was named for the town of Dixon, within its borders. Lilian L. Fitzpatrick disagrees. In her work entitled *Nebraska-Place Names*, Fitzpatrick states that the town of Dixon "...was named after the county in which it is situated."

1647 *Dodge County*

Augustus C. Dodge (1812–1883)— Augustus C. Dodge, a son of Henry Dodge (1782–1867), was born in what is now the state of Missouri on January 2, 1812. On December 8, 1840, Augustus Dodge took a seat in the U.S. Congress as a delegate from Iowa territory. On December 7 of the following year, his father, Henry Dodge, joined Augustus in the U.S. Congress. The elder Dodge represented Wisconsin territory as their congressional delegate. Augustus Dodge continued to represent Iowa territory in the U.S. Congress as its delegate until Iowa achieved statehood. On December 26, 1848, Augustus Dodge began his term as one of Iowa's first two United States senators. He served in the senate until 1855 when he resigned to accept an appointment as minister to Spain. This county was created in November, 1854, about five months after Nebraska territory had been established. Senator Dodge had been an active supporter of the Kansas-Nebraska act, which resulted in the creation of Nebraska territory on May 30, 1854.

1648 *Douglas County*

Stephen A. Douglas (1813–1861)— Barely five feet tall, the "Little Giant" is most remembered as a political opponent of Abraham Lincoln. Douglas was born in Vermont and moved to Illinois where he enjoyed rapid political success. He served on the state supreme court, in the state legislature and as secretary of state. Following two terms in the U.S. House of Representatives, Douglas was elected to the U.S. Senate. In that body Douglas took courageous positions on the slavery issue which first outraged abolitionist sentiment and later infuriated the South. In 1858 Douglas ran for reelection to the U.S. Senate against Abraham Lincoln. Following the famous Lincoln-Douglas debates, the Republicans won the popular election but the Illinois legislature reelected Douglas to the senate. Lincoln and Douglas were rivals again in 1860 for the presidency. Following Lincoln's election and the start of the Civil War, Douglas gave the president his active support. This county was created as part of Nebraska territory in November, 1854. It was Senator Stephen A. Douglas who had introduced the Kansas-Nebraska bill in the U.S. Senate, which resulted in the creation of Nebraska territory on May 30, 1854.

1649 *Dundy County*

Elmer S. Dundy (1830–1896)— Dundy was born in Trumbull County, Ohio on March 5, 1830. He studied law in Pennsylvania and was admitted to the bar in that state. In 1857 Elmer Dundy moved to Nebraska territory and settled in Richardson County. He was elected to the territorial legislature and was a member of the supreme court of Nebraska territory from 1863 to 1867. Following Nebraska's admission to statehood, Judge Dundy served as a U.S. circuit judge for the district of Nebraska for almost 30 years. He died on October 28, 1896. This county had been created and named in his honor 23 years earlier, on February 27, 1873.

1650 *Fillmore County*

Millard Fillmore (1800–1874)— Fillmore was born to an impoverished family in upstate New York and was apprenticed to a firm of cloth-dressers, from whom he eventually purchased his release. After studying law and being admitted to the New York bar, Fillmore was elected to the lower house of the New York legislature and he later represented New York in the U.S. House of Representatives. In 1848 the Whig party nominated the Mexican War hero, Zachary Taylor, for president with Millard Fillmore on the ticket as the vice-presidential running mate. They won the election and took their offices in 1849 but Zachary Taylor died in 1850 and Millard Fillmore became president. As president during an intense period of North versus South controversy relating to slavery, Fillmore favored the South and states' rights. However, Fillmore also supported the economic development of our nation's frontier, which then included the area which would soon be Nebraska territory and he assisted in arranging the first federal land grants for railroad construction. Fillmore's term as president ended on March 3, 1853, and he was not nominated by his party for reelection. This county was created as part of Nebraska territory on January 26, 1856, three years after Millard Fillmore's term as president ended.

1651 *Franklin County*

Benjamin Franklin (1706–1790)— Franklin was a native of Massachusetts who moved to Pennsylvania in his teens. Poverty denied him a formal education but he became the leading printer and editor in North America. Franklin gained fame for his discoveries and inventions in the physical sciences and he distinguished himself as author, philosopher and diplomat. Franklin was a signer of the Declaration of Independence and an important member of the convention which framed the U.S. Constitution. This county was formed on February 16, 1867.

1652 *Frontier County*

Location of the county on Nebraska's frontier at the time it was created— This county in southwestern Nebraska was created on January 17, 1872. It was named Frontier County because, at the time that it was created, its area was located on Nebraska's western frontier, on the border of civilization. The first railroad tracks connecting Frontier County with the rest of Nebraska were not completed until 1886.

1653 *Furnas County*

Robert W. Furnas (1824–1905)— A native of Ohio, Furnas gained experience in the publishing industry in that state and in Kentucky. He came to Nebraska territory in March 1856 and founded the *Nebraska Advertiser* here. He was the owner, publisher and editor of that publication. Furnas served in Nebraska's territorial legislature from January 5, 1857, to January 13, 1860. In that body he vigorously supported an act to bar the holding of slaves in Nebraska territory. Furnas served as an officer in the Union army during the Civil War and as an Indian agent to the Omaha tribe in the mid-1860's. His 1872 campaign to be Nebraska's governor was successful and he served one term in that office. This county was created on February 27, 1873, just one month after Furnas' inauguration as governor on January 13, 1873.

1654 *Gage County*

William D. Gage (1803–1885)— William D. Gage was born in Pennsylvania on December 5, 1803. Orphaned when he was only six years old, the young Gage leaned the trade of shoemaking and was engaged in that trade for perhaps a decade. At the age of 21 Gage joined the Methodist Church and when he was 25 he entered the ministry of that church. Gage served as a Methodist minister in New York, Illinois, Arkansas and Missouri before coming to Nebraska in early 1853. Gage was appointed minister of the Nebraska City Methodist mission in 1854. According to some sources he was the first Methodist minister in Nebraska. Gage was selected to be the chaplain of the first legislative assembly of the newly established territory of Nebraska. The territorial legislators elected Reverend Gage to be their chaplain on January 17, 1855, but it wasn't until February 3 of that year that anybody thought to notify Gage that he was the chaplain. It was this first territorial legislature that created and named Gage County in Reverend Gage's honor. The county was created on March 16, 1855, which was the last day that the first territorial legislature was in session. At about this time Gage ran a store in Cassville, that sold dry goods and patent medicines. He died on November 20, 1885, at Weeping Water, Nebraska, at the residence of one of his daughters, Mrs. Bailey.

1655 *Garden County*

Intent that this would become the "garden spot of the West"— This county was created as the result of an election held on November 2, 1909. Two men who were engaged in real estate business in Oshkosh, Nebraska, selected the county's name as the potential "garden spot of the West," in an attempt to lure settlers and promote business. The two real estate men who were the authors of this county's name were John T. Twiford and William R. Twiford. The community where they had their business headquarters, Oshkosh, Nebraska, was selected as the county seat.

1656 *Garfield County*

James A. Garfield (1831–1881)— A native of Ohio, Garfield served in the Ohio senate before becoming a Union officer in the Civil War. He performed ably and rapidly rose to the rank of general. In 1863 Garfield resigned his commission to enter the U.S. House of Representatives where he served until 1880. During Reconstruction, Garfield favored harsh treatment of the defeated South. In January, 1880, he was elected to the U.S. Senate but never served in that body. Instead, he was nominated and elected president of the United States. His nomination by the Republican party came as a compromise on the 36th ballot. Garfield was fatally wounded by an assassin's bullet just four months after beginning his term as president. He died on September 19, 1881. This county was created as the result of a vote held on November 8, 1881. An injunction delayed the official birth of this county until November 8, 1884.

1657 *Gosper County*

John J. Gosper (–1913)— Gosper served as an officer in the Union army during the Civil War. He settled in Lincoln, Nebraska, in the fall of 1869 and engaged in breeding hogs and horses. He was also active in real estate ventures in Lincoln. In October, 1872 Gosper was elected to be Nebraska's secretary of state. He served in that office from 1873 to 1875 and it was in 1873, while Gosper was secretary of state, that this county was created and named in his honor. As secretary of state, he served as Nebraska's acting governor on several occasions. Gosper was a Republican and in 1877, our nation's Republican president, Rutherford B. Hayes, appointed Gosper to be secretary of Arizona territory. The office of territorial secretary carried little power but in 1878 John C. Frémont (1813–1890) was appointed to be Arizona's territorial governor. Frémont was a rather ineffective territorial governor and he was absent from Arizona territory for lengthy periods on a number of occasions. When that happened, John J. Gosper became the acting territorial governor, a powerful position. Gosper subsequently moved to southern California, where he died on May 4, 1913 at the age of 71.

1658 *Grant County*

Ulysses S. Grant (1822–1885)— Grant was a native of Ohio who graduated from the U.S. Military Academy at West Point. He served with distinction in the Mexican War, and in the Civil War he rose to become commander of all Union forces. After the Civil War, Grant briefly served as acting secretary of war and then two terms as president of the United States. He proved to be a rather mediocre president. This county was created on March 31, 1887.

1659 *Greeley County*

Horace Greeley (1811–1872)— A native of New Hampshire and a lifelong newspaperman, Greeley served his journalistic apprenticeship in Vermont before settling in New York City in 1831. He engaged in a series of journalistic ventures, which had varying degrees of success, before founding the newspaper which was to become world famous, the *New York Tribune*. As editor of that paper, Greeley gained a reputation as an editorial genius. He expressed his strong views on a wide variety of political issues. A vigorous foe of slavery, Greeley denounced the Kansas-Nebraska bill of 1854 because it permitted admission of those two territories, with or without slavery. He is credited with coining the phrase "Go west young man." In 1872 Greeley ran for president against the incumbent President Ulysses S. Grant. Greeley received 2,834,000 popular votes but lost to Grant who got 3,597,000. Broken by the unsuccessful presidential campaign and by both business and personal problems, Greeley died on November 29, 1872, just a few weeks after his defeat in the election. This county was created on March 1, 1871.

1660 *Hall County*

Augustus Hall (1814–1861)— Hall was born in Batavia, New York, on April 29, 1814. He studied law, was admitted to the bar and practiced law for a time in Ohio, where he was prosecuting attorney of Union County from 1840 to 1842. Hall moved to Iowa and 1844 and in 1854 he was elected to represent that state as one of Iowa's two representatives in the U.S. House of Representatives. He was unsuccessful in his bid for reelection and his term in congress ended in 1857. President Buchanan appointed Augustus Hall in 1858 to be chief justice of the supreme court of Nebraska territory. Hall served in that office until his death on February 1, 1861. This county was created on November 4, 1858, while Hall was chief justice of Nebraska territory.

1661 *Hamilton County*

Alexander Hamilton (–1804)— A native of the West Indies, Hamilton moved to New York and served as an officer in America's revolutionary army. One of his assignments during the war was aide-de-camp to General George Washington. After the war Hamilton was a member of the convention which framed the U.S. Constitution. He collaborated with Madison and Jay in writing a series of papers entitled *The Federalist*, which explained the new constitution and advocated its adoption. A conservative and an advocate of a strong central government, he served as the first secretary of the treasury of the U.S. In 1804 he engaged in a duel with Aaron Burr and died of wounds he suffered in that duel. This county was created on February 16, 1867.

1662 *Harlan County*

Uncertain— This county was created on June 3, 1871. Sources consulted differ on who this county's namesake was. Three choices are mentioned and the vote is almost equally spread among those three choices:

James Harlan (1820–1899)— A native of Illinois, James Harlan moved to Iowa where he became president of Iowa Wesleyan University. He was elected to represent Iowa in the U.S. Senate and he served in that body until March, 1865, when President Abraham Lincoln appointed him to his cabinet as secretary of the interior. In the senate Harlan championed causes of great interest on our country's western frontier including homesteads, college land grants and development of railroads. After President Lincoln was assassinated, Harlan continued for a time as secretary of the interior under President Andrew Johnson but he resigned from that position in July 1866. Iowa sent him back to the U.S. Senate and he served there From March 4, 1867, to March 3, 1873.

Thomas Harlan (–)— Thomas Harlan was a pioneer who brought settlers to form a colony to the area of the Republican River in Nebraska from Cheyenne, in Wyoming territory.

An unidentified nephew of Senator James Harlan (1820–1899), of Iowa— This nephew was said to have been a revenue collector who at one time lived near Republican City, Nebraska.

1663 *Hayes County*

Rutherford B. Hayes (1822–1893)— A native of Ohio and a lawyer, Hayes served very effectively as an officer in the Union army during the Civil War and rose the rank of brevet-major general. He was elected to congress while still in the army and he resigned his commission to enter the U.S. House of Representatives. Hayes later served as governor of Ohio and in 1876 he was elected president of the United States. This county was created on February 19, 1877, when Hayes was our nation's president-elect. He was inaugurated as president two weeks later, on March 4, 1877.

1664 *Hitchcock County*

Phineas W. Hitchcock (1831–1881)— A native of New York, Hitchcock graduated from Williams College in Massachusetts, studied law and was admitted to the bar. He came to Omaha and practiced law here. Hitchcock was elected to be Nebraska territory's delegate to the U.S. Congress and he served from March 4, 1865, until March 1, 1867, when Nebraska was admitted to statehood. He later was elected as a U.S. senator from Nebraska and he served in that body from March 4, 1871, to March 3, 1877, and thus was a U.S. senator from Nebraska when this county was created on February 27, 1873.

1665 *Holt County*

Joseph Holt (1807–1894)— A native of Kentucky, Holt practiced law in both Kentucky and Mississippi and became a wealthy man. In 1856 he worked for the election of James Buchanan as president and when Buchanan won the election, he rewarded Holt by appointing him U.S. commissioner of patents. In 1859 President Buchanan elevated him to the cabinet level as postmaster general. On January 1, 1861, Buchanan promoted him again, this time to the cabinet position of secretary of war. The storm clouds of an approaching Civil War were now evident and Holt devoted considerable effort to keeping his home state of Kentucky, which was a slave state, from seceding from the Union. Kentucky declared itself neutral during the Civil War. President Abraham Lincoln appointed Holt as judge-advocate general of the army on September 3, 1862. In that capacity Holt later prosecuted those accused of conspiracy in the assassination of President Lincoln. This county was originally created by Nebraska territory on January 13, 1860, and named West County. Its name was changed by Nebraska territory on January 9, 1862, to honor Joseph Holt.

1666 *Hooker County*

Joseph Hooker (1814–1879)— A native of Massachusetts and an 1837 graduate of the U.S. Military Academy at West Point, Hooker entered the Mexican War as a second lieutenant and because of his courage, gallantry and effectiveness in that war, he was promoted to brevet lieutenant-colonel. In 1853 he resigned from the army but upon the outbreak of the Civil War, Hooker offered his services to the Union army. He was accepted and given the rank of brigadier-general. Hooker served effectively during the Civil War and by the time he retired from the army in 1868, he had risen to the rank of major-general. This county was created on March 29, 1889.

1667 *Howard County*

Oliver O. Howard (1830–1909)— A native of Maine and a graduate of Bowdoin College in that state, Howard also attended the U.S. military academy at West Point and graduated in the academy's class of 1854. His record as a leader of Union troops during the Civil War was mixed, but at one point he held the rank of major-general and he emerged from the war a brigadier-general, missing one arm lost in combat. After the war he worked for the integration of former slaves and was instrumental in founding Howard University for Blacks in Washington, D.C. He was president of that university from 1869 to 1873, held various commands in the army and was superintendent of West Point. He was promoted to major-general in 1886. This county was created in 1871, while Oliver O. Howard was serving as Howard University's president.

1668 *Jefferson County*

Thomas Jefferson (1743–1826)— Jefferson was a native of Virginia and a member of the Virginia legislature. He served Virginia as governor and was a delegate to the second Continental Congress. Jefferson was the author of the Declaration of Independence and one of its signers. He was minister to France, secretary of state, vice-president and president of the United States. As president, he accomplished the Louisiana Purchase and he arranged the Lewis & Clark Expedition to the Pacific Northwest. Jefferson was a true intellectual, thoroughly knowledgeable in the arts and sciences. His political theories were pivotal in the formation of our infant republic. On January 26, 1856, the legislature of Nebraska territory created a Jones County and a Jefferson County. Over the next 15 years boundaries were shifted and names were changed. There no longer is a Jones County but there now is a Thayer County. Today's Jefferson County, Nebraska, is due east of today's Thayer County, Nebraska.

1669 *Johnson County*

Richard M. Johnson (1780–1850)— Richard Mentor Johnson was born in Kentucky when it was still a part of Virginia. Kentucky was admitted to the union as a separate state in 1792 and Johnson served in the lower house of the Kentucky legislature from 1804 to 1806. He later represented Kentucky for a decade in the U.S. House of Representatives with an interruption to serve as a colonel in the War of 1812. The Kentucky forces that Colonel Johnson led at the battle of the Thames River, in Canada, scored an important victory, which made Johnson a hero but he was severely wounded in that battle. He later represented Kentucky in the U.S. Senate and then returned to the U.S. House of Representatives. From March 4, 1837, to March 3, 1841, Richard Mentor Johnson was vice-president of the United States under President Martin Van Buren. This county was created by Nebraska territory on March 2, 1855.

1670 *Kearney County*

Fort Kearny— The Fort Kearny which is commemorated in this county's name was established in 1848, to protect travelers on the Oregon trail. It was located just south of the Platte River in the present Kearney County, Nebraska. The site for the fort was chosen in the fall of 1847 by First Lieutenant Daniel P. Woodbury, of the army's corps of engineers. The fort was constructed under the supervision of Lieutenant-Colonel Ludwell E. Powell and it was first called "Post at Grand Island." This fort was later unofficially known as Fort Childs, in honor of Major Thomas Childs, an army artillery officer. The fort was officially named Fort Kearny on December 30, 1848. It was referred to as New Fort Kearny, to distinguish it from an earlier Fort Kearny, located about 50 miles below Omaha, on the Missouri River. The New Fort Kearny, for which Kearney County, Nebraska, was named, was abandoned in 1871. Both the first Fort Kearny and the second Fort Kearny were named for Stephen Watts Kearny (1794–1848). At the time that Nebraska territory created and named this county on January 10, 1860, most of Fort Kearny (i.e., the "New" or "second" Fort Kearny) was located within its boundaries.

Stephen W. Kearny (1794–1848)— A native of New Jersey, Kearny was commissioned as a first lieutenant in the U.S. army in 1812. During the War of 1812, he was wounded and captured at the battle of Queenston Heights and Kearny was pro-

moted to captain in 1813 for his service in the War of 1812. The majority of Kearny's service in the army was on our nation's western frontier, where he served some 30 years and rose in rank first to major and successively on to brigadier-general. General Kearny served, with distinction, during the Mexican War first in our present states of New Mexico and California and later in Mexico proper. There he served for short periods of time as governor general of Veracruz and later of Mexico City. In September, 1848, Kearny was promoted to major-general but he did not live long to enjoy the honor. He died of a tropical disease on October 31, 1848.

Both Fort Kearny and the general whose name it honors are correctly spelled Kearny, with no "e" in the last syllable. The county's name (as well as a town in adjacent Buffalo County) are incorrectly spelled as Kearney. An explanation for the error is given in Roy C. Bang's work entitled *Heroes Without Medals: A Pioneer History of Kearney County, Nebraska*, published in 1952. Bang quotes Moses Sydenham, who was postmaster at the fort in 1856, when he tells us "...the word was misspelled by someone in the War department or Post Office department giving the name as K-E-A-R-N-E-Y. It has been spelled that way ever since I took charge." By the time Kearney County was created in 1860, the wrong version had been in use (for the name of the town and post office) long enough to lead to its perpetuation in the county's name.

1671 *Keith County*

Morell C. Keith (1824–1899)— Morell Case Keith was born in Silver Creek, New York, in 1824. At the age of 30, he decided to take Horace Greeley's advice and "Go west young man." He married Susan Smith of Hanover, New York and several years later Keith and his wife moved west to Apple Grove, Iowa. Keith and his wife operated a hotel in Apple Grove, which served a stage coach line and the Keiths became acquainted with numerous adventurers heading west. It was while in Iowa that this future member of the Cowboy Hall of Fame in Oklahoma City first tried his hand at running a ranch. He acquired the necessary land, horses and cattle, and wrote glowing letters to his father back in New York, urging him to come west and join in the opportunities in ranching. Morell C. Keith and his wife moved to Topeka, Kansas, in 1861 where Keith engaged in the freight business. Six years later Keith moved to Ogallala, Ne-

braska. From his ranch there he led cattle drives for several years between Texas and Ogallala. By 1873 Keith had moved to North Platte where he operated a railway hotel and, in partnership with Guy Barton, owned more than one thousand head of cattle valued at $93,600. This county was created and named in his honor on February 27, 1873. While living in North Platte, Keith invested in real estate and he was the moving force behind an effort to provide irrigation for the region. Morell C. Keith was a grandfather of a later governor of Nebraska, Keith Neville (1884–) and Morell C. Keith reared Keith Neville, from boyhood. Keith Neville, a Democrat, served as Nebraska's governor from 1917 to 1919. The governor's grandfather Keith was also a Democrat, but was little involved in politics. However, on September 6, 1876, the Democratic state convention elected Keith as one of the party's presidential electors. Morell Case Keith operated his ranch until his death on September 29, 1899. Sometime around 1960 Morell C. Keith was inducted in the Cowboy Hall of Fame, in Oklahoma City.

1672 *Keya Paha County*

Keya Paha River— The Keya Paha River is a 101 mile long tributary of the Niobrara River. The Keya Paha rises in southern South Dakota and flows in a southeastern direction across the state line into Keya Paha County, Nebraska. It continues its southeastern journey, in a virtually straight line aimed at the Niobrara River, crossing northern Keya Paha County and the northwestern corner of Boyd County, Nebraska. The Keya Paha ends its journey, emptying its waters into those of the Niobrara southeast of Naper, Nebraska, in Boyd County. The river was named by the Dakota Indians. In their language *keya* means "turtle," and *paha* means "hill," or "hills." Several Nebraska sources indicate that the Indians chose their name for this river as descriptive of the numerous small, rounded hills in the vicinity of the Keya Paha River.

1673 *Kimball County*

Village of Kimball, Nebraska— The village of Kimball lies in western Nebraska near the state line borders of both Wyoming and Colorado. Originally named Antelopeville, because of the presence of antelope in the area, the village began as a water station for the Union Pacific Railroad. The rails of that company reached Antelopeville on September 23, 1867. The first residences here were adobe shacks for the railroad workers and the village's most important structure contained the water which served as a source of steam for the railroad's locomotives. Because there was another post office elsewhere in Nebraska named Antelope, the village was required to change its name. The name change occurred in 1885 when Antelopeville became Kimball. The name was chosen in honor of Thomas Lord Kimball (1831–1899), a vice-president and general manager of the Union Pacific Railroad. James Lynch was the Union Pacific's section foreman residing in Antelopeville and he and his wife Mary were friends of Thomas L. Kimball. The railroad official frequently visited James and Mary Lynch, sidetracking his personal railroad car on trips through the area. It can be safely assumed that Mr. and Mrs. Lynch were prominent in the selection of the name Kimball to replace Antelopeville as the new name for the village. At the time the village's name was changed, it could boast only about 100 residents. However, Kimball was strategically located for growth. It was, of course on the major transcontinental route connecting the western portion of our country with the East and just a few miles west of Kimball, on the Union Pacific line, were the Wyoming municipalities of Cheyenne and Laramie. The important city of Denver, Colorado, is due south of those Wyoming municipalities. By 1886 Kimball had become something of a trading center and settlers were arriving in numbers to purchase lands offered for sale by the railroad or to select homesteads under the Federal government's Homestead act. An irrigation district was soon centered here and in 1922 Kimball was made a second class city. Kimball County was created by vote on November 6, 1888, and named for the village of Kimball, which became its county seat.

1674 *Knox County*

Henry Knox (1750–1806) — This Massachusetts native participated in many of the important military engagements of the American Revolution and rose to the rank of major-general. After the war, Knox commanded West Point and he conceived and organized the Society of Cincinnati, an elite group of former Revolutionary officers. In 1785 he was appointed secretary of war under the Articles of Confederation and he retained that position in the first cabinet of the United States under President George Washington. This county had two earlier names. It was originally created by Nebraska territory on February 10, 1857, and given the awkward French

name of L' Eau Qui Court County but its name was changed to Emmett County on February 18, 1867. The current name, Knox County, was adopted on February 21, 1873. We are told that a member of the Nebraska legislature named David Quimby requested that this county's name be changed but it is not clear whether Quimby initiated the change from L' Eau Qui Court to Emmett or from Emmett to Knox.

1675 *Lancaster County*

County and city of Lancaster, Pennsylvania — Lancaster County was created by Nebraska territory on March 6, 1855. It was named for Lancaster County, in southeastern Pennsylvania, and for its county seat, the city of Lancaster. The earliest settlers of that part of Pennsylvania came from England and when a new county was established there in 1729, it was named Lancaster, in honor of Lancashire, England. The county seat of Lancaster County, Pennsylvania, the city of Lancaster, also owes its name to Lancashire, England. Although the English settlers of southeastern Pennsylvania did much of the naming of places, it was the German immigrants (known as "Pennsylvania-Dutch") who created the local color of Lancaster and Lancaster County, Pennsylvania. Largely self-sufficient German religious communities such as the Amish and Mennonites developed here. Their adherence to the simple and old-fashioned ways of doing things have enchanted many visitors from the fast-track portions of America.

Lancashire, England — The county named Lancashire, in northwestern England, on the Irish Sea has a name that dates back to the time that the Roman Empire occupied England. An early version of its name, Loncastre, meant "Roman fort (or camp) on the river Lune." A later (14th century) version of the name was Lancastreshire, which derived from Lancaster and the Old English word *scir*, which meant "district." Lancashire, England, is 75 miles long and averages about 30 miles in width. In the northern and eastern portions of the county, mountains can be found which reach altitudes of more than 2,000 feet. Wide moor lands are found between many of these mountains. More land is used for grazing than for planting crops. Iron, coal, slate and other building materials are found in Lancashire. Its city of Liverpool is one of the most important seaports in the United Kingdom and its other principal city, Lancaster, also carries on foreign trade.

1676 *Lincoln County*

Abraham Lincoln (1809–1865) — Lincoln was a native of Kentucky who moved to Illinois where he was a member of the state legislature. He represented Illinois in the U.S. House of Representatives and later was elected president of the United States. Lincoln's presidency coincided almost exactly with the Civil War. He guided the United States ably through that uniquely turbulent period. As president, he issued the Emancipation Proclamation which declared the freedom of slaves in all states in rebellion. Lincoln was assassinated in April, 1865, a few days after the Union's victory in the Civil War. This county was originally created on January 7, 1860, and named Shorter County. Its name was changed to Lincoln in 1866 in honor of our nation's recently assassinated president.

1677 *Logan County*

John A. Logan (1826–1886) — A native of Illinois, Logan served in the Illinois legislature and represented that state in the U.S. Congress in both the house and senate. Having served in the Mexican War as a lieutenant, Logan entered the Civil War as a colonel in the Union army and rose to the rank of major-general. In 1884 he ran for vice president on the Republican ticket headed by James G. Blaine. Logan long associated himself with matters of veterans' relief and he conceived the idea of Memorial Day which he inaugurated on May 30, 1868. This county was created and named in General Logan's honor on February 24, 1885, shortly after his defeat in his 1884 bid for the vice-presidency.

1678 *Loup County*

North Loup River — This county in north-central Nebraska was created on March 6, 1855, when Nebraska was still a territory. Its original name was Taylor County. In 1883, the county's name was changed to Loup County on account of the county's largest river, the North Loup River. The North Loup River is one of three branches of the Loup River system, all of which are in Nebraska and all of which are tributaries of the Platte River. The three branches are the North Loup River, the Middle Loup River and the South Loup River. The only branch which enters Loup County is the North Loup River. The three branches unite into one in Howard County, and their combined waters flow in a generally eastern direction until they enter the Platte River at

Columbus, Nebraska. The name *Loup* was applied by French explorers. It means "wolf."

1679 *McPherson County*

James B. McPherson (1828–1864) — A native Ohioan, McPherson attended the U.S. Military Academy at West Point, New York where he graduated in 1853 at the head of his class. In the years preceding the Civil War, he taught practical engineering at West Point and then was involved in river harbor improvement and seacoast fortification duties. McPherson served with distinction in the Union army during the Civil War and rose from the rank of mere first lieutenant in August, 1861 to brigadier-general of volunteers on May 15, 1862. Later that year he was promoted to major-general of volunteers. His final promotion occurred effective August 1, 1863, when he was made brigadier-general of the regular army. In March, 1864, McPherson was given command of the army of the Tennessee, which he led in the campaign in north Georgia. McPherson was killed on July 22, 1864, during the battle of Atlanta, Georgia. This county was created on March 31, 1887.

1680 *Madison County*

City of Madison, Wisconsin — A number of sources dealing with the history, geography and place names of Nebraska state that this county was named in honor of Madison County, Wisconsin. There never has been a Madison County in Wisconsin so this county was not named for it. However, several sources make a point to specify that this county was not named directly for President James Madison, but indirectly by perpetuating a place name in Wisconsin and on this point they are correct. Madison County in Nebraska was not named for a Madison County in Wisconsin, but for the city of Madison, Wisconsin, which is that state's capitol city. The surveying and platting of the city of Madison were completed by November, 1836. Judge James D. Doty (1799–1865) was in charge of the platting of Madison and he suggested to the Wisconsin territorial legislature that they name the city in honor of President James Madison, who had died just five months earlier, on June 28, 1836. Doty also suggested that it be made the capitol city of Wisconsin territory. The Wisconsin territorial legislators adopted the name Madison for the city on November 28, 1836, and made it the territorial capitol city at a later date.

James Madison (1751–1836) — Madison was born in Virginia and served in the Virginia legislature and in the Continental Congress. He was a member of the convention which framed the U.S. Constitution and he collaborated with Hamilton and Jay in writing a series of papers under the title *The Federalist*, which explained the new constitution and advocated its adoption. Madison represented Virginia in the U.S. House of Representatives, served for eight years as secretary of state and for eight years as president of the United States.

1681 *Merrick County*

Elvira Merrick De Puy (–) — This county was created on November 4, 1858, when Nebraska was still a territory. At that time Henry W. De Puy was a member of the territorial house of representatives. De Puy's fellow legislators honored De Puy by naming this new county Merrick, in honor of De Puy's wife Elvira, whose maiden name was Merrick. Sources consulted are agreed that this is the origin of this county's name although several of these sources state, incorrectly, that De Puy was speaker of the territorial house of representatives when this county was created. H. P. Bennet of Otoe County was speaker when this county was created. Henry W. De Puy did not become speaker of the territorial house until the seventh legislative assembly, which convened on December 3, 1860. Little is known about either Elvira Merrick De Puy or her husband. Page 37 of the 1860 Census of the post office of Fontanelle, in Washington County lists Mrs. De Puy's age as 30, so she was born about 1830. That census shows her husband, Henry W. De Puy's age as 38 and his occupation as farmer. Henry W. De Puy was nominated on August 24, 1859, at a convention of the Republican party of Nebraska territory, to run as the Republican's candidate for auditor.

1682 *Morrill County*

Charles H. Morrill (1843–1928) — Charles Henry Morrill was born in Concord, New Hampshire, in July, 1843. In 1863, at the age of 20, he enlisted as a private in the Union army and he remained in the army until the end of the Civil War. After leaving the army Morrill lived briefly in Rockford, Illinois, and then for a somewhat longer period in Iowa, near the Des Moines River. In 1871 he came to Nebraska and established a homestead near the Big Blue River in what is now the community of Stromsburg, Nebraska. Four years later

Morrill became a co-owner of Stromsburg's first store. In 1879 Charles H. Morrill was the private secretary of Nebraska's governor, Albinus Nance (1848–1911). Probably as a result of acquaintances he established as the governor's private secretary, Morrill's fortunes improved rapidly. He became an officer in three banks and was the president of two of them. He was president of three land development companies and in 1902 he was elected president of the Boston Investment Company. Morrill was honored in 1889 by being elected to the board of regents of the University of Nebraska and in 1892 he was made president of the board. He served in that capacity for ten years. Starting in 1892, Charles H. Morrill financed annual geological expeditions which gathered materials from many parts of Nebraska. The materials collected on these expeditions have been housed in exhibits at various locations including the University of Nebraska, in Lincoln, and in a number of high schools around Nebraska. This county was created in 1908.

1683 *Nance County*

Albinus Nance (1848–1911) — A native of Illinois, Nance served as a private in the Union army during the Civil War. At the close of the war he returned to Illinois, studied law and was admitted to the bar in 1870. The following year Nance moved west and established a homestead in Polk County, Nebraska. He later moved to Osceola, Nebraska, and practiced law there. In 1874 he was elected to Nebraska's house of representatives and he was reelected to that body in 1876 and chosen as speaker of the house. In 1878 Nance was the Republican party's candidate for governor of Nebraska and he won that election. Known as "boy governor," because he was only 30 years old when he won the election, Nance was inaugurated as governor early in 1879. This county was created and named in his honor on February 13, 1879, shortly after his inauguration as governor. Nance served a second term as governor and then retired to private life as a lawyer and as a broker of railroad stocks and bonds.

1684 *Nemaha County*

Nemaha River — This county was originally created in November, 1854, by proclamation of the acting governor of Nebraska territory, Thomas B. Cuming (1828–1858). He named the county Forney County, in honor of James W. Forney (1817–1881), a journalist and government official who was clerk of the U.S. House of Representatives at the time that the county was created and named. Nebraska's territorial legislators changed the county's name in 1855 from Forney to Nemaha. The name change was not made in objection to James W. Forney, but as an expression of resentment toward the man who had named the county, Acting Governor Thomas B. Cuming. The new name was taken from the Nemaha River which flows just west and south of the present borders of Nemaha County, Nebraska.

Nemaha River— The Nemaha River is a 150 mile long tributary of the Missouri River. It rises in Lancaster County, in southeastern Nebraska, and flows in a generally southeastern direction until its waters join those of the Missouri River near the tristate junction of Kansas, Nebraska and Missouri. The Nemaha River is also called the Big Nemaha River or Great Nemaha River to distinguish it from the Little Nemaha River, which is also in Nebraska, located north of the Nemaha River. In fact, the Little Nemaha River flows across Nemaha County, Nebraska, but when the county's name was chosen, county borders were different than they are today. Nemaha County, Nebraska, was named for the Nemaha River, which does not flow through it (today), rather than for the Little Nemaha River which does (today) flow through it. The Nemaha River's name is of Sioux Indian origin but its meaning is unknown. Translations which have been offered include:
— "River of the Mahas"
— "Stream of the Omaha's"
— "River of cultivation"
— "No papoose"
— "Miry water river"

1685 *Nuckolls County*

Uncertain— This county was created on January 13, 1860, when Nebraska was still a territory. Most sources state that the county was named for Stephen F. Nuckolls (1825–1879) but two sources have been found which say that the county's name honors both Stephen F. Nuckolls and his brother, Lafayette Nuckolls.

Stephen F. Nuckolls (1825–1879)— A native of Virginia, Stephen Nuckolls came to Nebraska territory in 1854 and he was the founder of Nebraska City, Nebraska. He was the first southerner to bring slaves into Nebraska territory. Stephen F. Nuckolls was a representative in the lower house of the Nebraska legislature during the session of the legislature which created and named this county. He moved around the country quite a bit after that. From Ne-

braska territory he moved to Colorado territory, then to New York City and back west to Dakota territory in 1867. When Wyoming territory was created in 1868, Stephen F. Nuckolls was elected to be the new territory's first delegate to the U.S. Congress. He later served in Wyoming's territorial legislature. Stephen F. Nuckolls died in Salt Lake City, Utah territory, on February 14, 1879.

Lafayette Nuckolls (–)— A younger brother of Stephen F. Nuckolls, Lafayette was elected to the upper house (council) Nebraska's first territorial legislature when he was only 19 years old.

1686 *Otoe County*

Oto Indians— This county was originally named Pierce County when it was created in November, 1854. Its name was changed to Otoe County in 1855. The original name honored Franklin Pierce (1804–1869), who was then serving as our nation's president. The 1855 name change was not made in objection to President Pierce but as an expression of resentment toward the man who had named the county, Acting Governor Thomas B. Cuming (1828–1858). In fact, Nebraska's territorial legislators created and named a Pierce County in honor of President Pierce a very short time later. The current name was chosen to honor the Oto Indian tribe, who are closely related to the Missouri tribe. In their present home in the state of Oklahoma the combined tribe is referred to as the Oto Indian tribe. (The Missouri Indians lost their separate tribal identity as a result of their relatively small numbers.) According to tribal tradition, the Oto once lived in the vicinity of the Great Lakes. They migrated through present-day Minnesota, Iowa and Nebraska. French explorers found the Oto in the region of the Des Moines River in Iowa about 1690–1700. Edwin A. Curley stated in his 1875 work about Nebraska and its resources that Otoe County, Nebraska, was named after the Indians "who, in the beginning of the century, held all surrounding territory … till finally the white race, in the tidal wave of civilization, crossed the Missouri River westward, and extinguished the Indian title, when the Otoes sank into insignificance on a small reservation…" Sad to say, Edwin A. Curley's colorful account is not very wide of the mark. The Oto and Missouri Indians signed their first treaties with the United States government in 1817. In 1854 they ceded virtually all their Nebraska lands to the Americans and by the middle of the 20th

century they had a combined population of less than 1,000 living in the northeastern part of Noble County, Oklahoma.

1687 *Pawnee County*

Pawnee Indians— This county was created on March 6, 1855, when Nebraska was a territory, and it was named for the Pawnee Indians. The Pawnee are a tribe of the Caddoan linguistic family, who once lived in the valley of the lower Mississippi River and along the Red River. They migrated to the lower Arkansas River and the lower Missouri River. By the time the Pawnees had a large population, they lived and hunted further west, in Nebraska, Kansas and areas south to Texas. The Pawnee subsisted primarily by village agriculture, supplemented by buffalo hunting. They traveled vast distances on foot to steal horses and eventually acquired sufficient numbers of them to become skilled horsemen. The Pawnee were in constant warfare with most neighboring tribes and captured Pawnee Indians were often sold as slaves. However, the Pawnee Indians were usually friendly toward Whites. During the mid-1870's they were moved to Indian territory (now Oklahoma). The origin and meaning of the name *Pawnee* is uncertain. Many sources indicate that the name means "horn" and refers to a unique method of dressing hair scalp-locks, standing them erect and curved backward like a horn. Other sources indicate that the name means "a braid," "a twist," "to curve," "to bend up" (all referring to hair), while another source suggests that the name derives from "hunter." A more likely explanation relates to the Indian name for "slave" and its application to the Pawnee Indians on account of large numbers of Pawnees who were taken as slaves by the Apache Indians, the Illinois Indians and other tribes.

1688 *Perkins County*

Charles E. Perkins (1840–1907)— Charles Elliott Perkins was born in Cincinnati, Ohio, in 1840. He became associated with the railroad industry and developed a personal friendship with the powerful railroad tycoon, James J. Hill (1838–1916). In 1881 Perkins became the second president of the Chicago, Burlington & Quincy Railroad, replacing the railroad's first president, John M. Forbes (1813–1898). Charles Perkins added a number of subsidiary railroad lines to the Chicago, Burlington & Quincy's network and during his tenure as president, from 1881 to 1901 the railroad's financial strength grew. He died in

Westwood, Massachusetts, in 1907. The railroads were, of course, vital in linking the vast agricultural lands in Nebraska and the rest of our nation's western frontier with consumers in the Mid-West and East. The Chicago, Burlington & Quincy Railroad laid rails through what is now Perkins County, Nebraska during the summer of 1887 and the first train entered the town of Grant here on July 4, 1887. Perkins County, Nebraska, was created just four months later, in November 1887. At that time Charles E. Perkins was the president of the Chicago, Burlington & Quincy Railroad.

1689 *Phelps County*

William Phelps (1808–)— A native of New York, Phelps immigrated west and for a number of years was a steamboat captain on the Missouri River or the Mississippi River (or perhaps both). This county was created on February 11, 1873. Its name was suggested by C. J. Dilworth, who later served as Nebraska's attorney general. Dilworth suggested that the county be named Phelps, in honor of his father-in-law, William Phelps, who was then a resident of Lewiston, Illinois. In 1872 C. J. Dilworth had become one of the first homesteaders of the section of Nebraska that became Phelps County in 1873. Material contained in *Heritage of Progress: A History of Phelps County, Nebraska,* copyright 1981, supplies information which helps explain C. J. Dilworth's motivation in suggesting that this county be named for his father-in-law. In that book, a child of C. J. Dilworth's, and hence a grandchild of William Phelps', explains that the county name of Phelps "was the name of my maternal grandfather, who at that time resided in Lewiston, Illinois, and from whom we expected pecuniary aid in building our new home."

1690 *Pierce County*

Franklin Pierce (1804–1869)— Pierce was born in New Hampshire and served in the lower house of that state's legislature. He represented New Hampshire in both houses of the U.S. Congress and served as an officer in the Mexican War, rising to the rank of brigadier-general. In 1852 Pierce was nominated for president by the Democratic party on the 49th ballot as a compromise candidate who was not objectionable to the South. He was elected to that office and served one term, from March 4, 1853, to March 3, 1857. As president, he viewed the slavery issue in a legalistic way and was unable to accept the

North's moral objections to slavery. Pierce failed to secure his party's nomination for a second term. This Pierce County in today's Nebraska was first created with the name Otoe County by Nebraska territory on January 26, 1856. A different county had been created and named for President Pierce in November, 1854, but its name was changed in 1855. Consequently, when this county's name was changed from Otoe County to Pierce County, Nebraska territory did not have two Pierce Counties; just this one.

1691 *Platte County*

Platte River— The Platte River, a tributary of the Missouri River, is Nebraska's most important river. It is formed by the junction of two branches at the city of North Platte, in west-central Nebraska. The two rivers which unite there to form the Platte River are the North Platte River and the South Platte River. The combined waters of the Platte then travel some 310 miles in a generally eastern direction across Nebraska. The Platte River forms a portion of the southern boundary of Platte County, in eastern Nebraska before it empties its waters into the Missouri River below Omaha, Nebraska. The Oregon Trail, across our country's vast plains to Oregon country, followed the course of the Platte River. The river was named by early French explorers. In their language one of it the meanings of *Platte* is "flat," or "shallow." This county was created on January 26, 1856, when Nebraska was still a territory.

1692 *Polk County*

James K. Polk (1795–1849)— Polk was a native of North Carolina who moved with his family to the Tennessee frontier in 1806. He served in the lower house of the Tennessee legislature and he represented Tennessee for 14 years in the U.S. House of Representatives, where he was speaker. He served one term as governor of Tennessee. Polk became president of the United States as a dark horse candidate of the Democratic party but he became an unusually strong and effective president. His primary accomplishments involved westward extension of the United States: in the Northwest by settling a territorial dispute with Britain and in California and the Southwest by provoking and winning the Mexican War. This county was created on January 26, 1856, when Nebraska was a territory.

1693 *Red Willow County*

Red Willow Creek— This county is in south-central Nebraska, and its southern border is the state of Kansas. The county was created on February 27, 1873, and named for Red Willow Creek, which flows in this county. Red Willow Creek is a tributary of the Republican River. It rises in Hayes County, Nebraska, and flows in a southeastern direction in Hayes County and through Red Willow Reservoir, a state recreation area. From there Red Willow Creek continues to flow in a southeastern direction until it enters the Republican River, near the center of Red Willow County. The creek's name resulted from an erroneous translation of the Dakota Indians' name for the it. They called it *Chashasha Wakpala,* which meant "Red Dogwood Creek." Red dogwood trees were abundant along the banks of this creek.

1694 *Richardson County*

William A. Richardson (1811–1875)— This county was named for one of Nebraska's territorial governors, but it was created three years before he was appointed to that post. It was the acting governor of Nebraska territory, Thomas B. Cuming (1828–1858), who created this county by proclamation on November 23, 1854. Cuming chose the name for the very political reason that William A. Richardson was a close friend of the powerful Stephen Douglas (1813–1861). Richardson was born near Lexington, Kentucky, on January 16, 1811. He studied at Centre College and Transylvania University in that state, after which he studied law. Admitted to the bar in 1831, Richardson opened his practice in Illinois. He served in both houses of the Illinois legislature and was speaker of the lower house from 1844 to 1846. He served effectively as an officer in the Mexican War and rose to the rank of lieutenant-colonel. After the war Richardson was elected to represent Illinois in the U.S. House of Representatives, filling a vacancy caused by Stephen A. Douglas' election to the U.S. Senate. Richardson was chairman of the house's committee on territories and his support of the Kansas-Nebraska bill aided Nebraska in being admitted to territorial status on May 30, 1854. On December 10, 1857, President James Buchanan appointed Richardson to be governor of Nebraska territory. Richardson served in that position from January 12, 1858, to December 5, 1858, when he resigned and returned to Illinois. He represented Illinois in the U.S. House of Representatives and when Illinois Senator Stephen A. Douglas died,

Richardson was elected to replace him in the U.S. Senate.

1695 *Rock County*

Rock Creek— There are some 14 Rock Creeks in Nebraska. The one of interest to us rises in Rock County, in north central Nebraska, near the hay flats, about seven miles northwest of Newport, Nebraska. Rock Creek flows northward from its origin and empties its waters into the Niobrara River at Rock County's northern border. Some exceptionally fine building stone is to be found at a rock quarry located about mid-way between the source and mouth of Rock Creek. It is suggested that Rock Creek's name may have been chosen on account of those fine building rocks. A number of sources state that this county was named for the rocky composition of its soil. Pearl H. Davis makes a persuasive case that the county was named for Rock Creek in her article about the naming of this county which appeared in *Those Who Came Before Us: A History of Rock County Compiled During the Bicentennial Year 1976.* John T. Link agrees that this county was named for Rock Creek and he tells us so in his May, 1932 Ph.D. thesis entitled "The Toponomy of Nebraska."

1696 *Saline County*

Belief that significant salt deposits were located here— This county in southeastern Nebraska was created on March 6, 1855, shortly after Nebraska territory was established. The word *saline* relates to salt. This county's name was chosen in the belief that significant salt deposits and/or salt springs were to be found here. That supposition has proven false and this county's name is inappropriate.

1697 *Sarpy County*

Peter A. Sarpy (1805–1865)— Peter Sarpy was born on November 3, 1805. His name at birth was recorded as Pierre Sylvester Gregoire Sarpy, which he shortened to Peter L'Abadie Sarpy. He became an early fur trader in Nebraska, working at first north of the Platte River for the American Fur Company. Sarpy and another fur trader, Henry Fraeb (–1841), formed a partnership and operated from Fort Jackson on the South Platte River but that joint venture lasted only about two years. Peter Sarpy's wife was an Indian woman and she was extremely valuable in connection with fur trading activities. One source speculates that Sarpy's Indian wife may have saved him from death at the hands of Indians on at least one occasion. For more than a quarter of a century, Sarpy operated an American Fur Trading Company post at what is now the town of Bellevue, Nebraska. This location was near the confluence of the Platte River with the Missouri River and just across the Missouri River from Iowa. Sarpy conducted some of his business on the Iowa side of the River. He also published a newspaper at one time called *The Nebraska Palladium.* Sarpy died on January 4, 1865, at Plattsmouth, Nebraska territory, where he had been engaged in a steam ferry business. His Indian widow became the recipient of his pension. In the original act to create this county, it was proposed that the new county's name be Omaha County. That name was never adopted and Sarpy County, Nebraska territory, was created on February 7, 1857.

1698 *Saunders County*

Alvin Saunders (1817–1899)— A native of Kentucky, Saunders moved to Illinois with his family in 1829. He subsequently moved to Iowa, when it was part of Wisconsin territory. Iowa was admitted to statehood in 1846, and a few years later Saunders was elected to the state senate. In 1860 he chaired Iowa's delegation to the Republican national convention, which supported the nomination of Abraham Lincoln for president. Lincoln was, of course, elected and his term as office as president began on March 4, 1861. Just 22 days later, President Lincoln appointed Saunders to be governor of Nebraska territory. Saunders served in that position from May 1, 1861, until February 21, 1867, and thus was Nebraska's last territorial governor. He later was elected to represent the state of Nebraska in the U.S. Senate for one term from March, 1877, to March 1883. This county was originally created on January 26, 1856, and named Calhoun County. That name honored a hero of the antebellum South, John C. Calhoun (1782–1850). Calhoun had been a forceful advocate of slavery, states' rights and limited powers for the federal government. Those views were unpopular in Nebraska territory in 1862, while Nebraska boys were dying in the Civil War. This county's name was changed from Calhoun to Saunders on January 8, 1862, while Alvin Saunders was serving as governor of Nebraska territory.

1699 *Scotts Bluff County*

A geological formation in the county named Scotts Bluff— This county lies at the western end of Nebraska, on the Wyoming border. Its most conspicuous geological feature is a large bluff, named Scotts Bluff, which is now a national monument. This large bluff is very prominent, rising as it does some 800 feet above the treeless plain below it. One can safely assume that its has been a noted travelers' landmark for centuries. We know that it was along the route of the Oregon trail and was noted and mentioned by emigrants on their journey to the far West. This large bluff, which lies near the North Platte River, was named for Hiram Scott, an early fur trader and mountain man, whose death, under unusual circumstances, came to be associated with this 800 foot bluff in Scotts Bluff County, Nebraska.

Hiram Scott (–)— Scott was born about 1805 in what is now Saint Charles County, Missouri. While he was still a teenager, he responded to an advertisement which was placed in the February 13, 1822, edition of the *Missouri Gazette & Public Advertiser.* The advertisement had been placed by William H. Ashley (–1838) and it indicated that Ashley was looking for 100 enterprising young men to engage in the fur collecting business. Hiram Scott and his fellow recruits joined Ashley in his 1822–1823 expedition up the Missouri River. The Ashley party was attacked by Indians at the Arikara villages, but both Ashley and Scott survived this incident. When this expedition ended, Scott decided to make his life in the wilderness and mountains acquiring furs and he did this for several years. He sold many of the furs that he obtained to the Chouteau fur trading family in Saint Louis. Scott died about 1828 and no two of the accounts of his death are the same. Given this caveat, the elements common in most accounts state that just before his death, Scott and some companions were descending a river, traveling in frail bark canoes. The canoes overturned leaving the party in the wilderness, miles from any type of civilization. They were without food and without the means to hunt for food because their gunpowder was wet. It was at about this point in the sequence of events that Hiram Scott fell ill. His companions, now traveling on foot, decided that they were unable to carry Scott with them and they left him to die alone. Some time later, perhaps the following summer, human bones were found near the base of Scotts Bluff. Among the party that discovered the bones was at least one of the travelers who had accompanied Scott on the ill-fated trip. The bones were declared to be those of Hiram Scott. This may be true or false but even if true, we have quite a tangled web to work our way through to discover more about Hiram Scott's death. Some accounts indicate that when he was left to die, Hiram Scott was some 60 miles (others say 40 miles) distant from Scott's Bluff. If so, he managed to limp and crawl 40 to 60 miles in his seriously ill condition. Other accounts say that he was left to die at or near Scotts Bluff, which makes more sense, logistically, but adds nothing to our understanding of the forensic achievement of the identification the skeletal remains. In 1934 the U.S. National Park Service published an excellent work by Donald D. Brand entitled *The History of Scotts Bluff Nebraska*. In that work Dr. Brand recites numerous variations of the accounts surrounding Hiram Scott's death and the purported subsequent discovery of his bones. Another excellent and comprehensive survey of the facts and traditions surrounding the Hiram Scott tale is contained in *Nebraska History* (volume 26, number 3, July–September, 1945). The author is Merrill J. Mattes and the title of the article is "Hiram Scott, Fur Trader."

1700 *Seward County*

William H. Seward (1801–1872)— A native of New York and a graduate of Union College in that state, Seward served in the New York senate and later was the state's governor. In 1849 he was elected to represent New York in the United States senate. In that body, Seward advocated the exclusion of slavery from all new states. In 1861 President Abraham Lincoln appointed him to his cabinet as secretary of state and Seward continued in that office when Andrew Johnson succeeded Lincoln as president. In 1867 Seward negotiated the purchase of Alaska from Russia at a price of $7,200,000, which was an enormous cost in those days. The purchase of Alaska was known as "Seward's folly." This county was originally named Greene County, when it was created by Nebraska territory on March 6, 1855. That name honored U.S. Senator James Stephen Green (1817–1870) of Missouri. This county's name was changed from Greene to Seward in January, 1862, early in the Civil War. Green had left the U.S. Senate on March 3, 1861, and Nebraska's territorial legislators were not pleased with Green's loyalties concerning the Civil War. They changed the county's name to Seward County, while William H. Seward was serving Abraham Lincoln as his Civil War secretary of state.

1701 *Sheridan County*

Philip H. Sheridan (1831–1888)— Sheridan was born in 1831 but his place of birth is in doubt. He graduated from the U.S. Military Academy at West Point and became a career officer in the United States army. When the Civil War began, Sheridan had almost a decade of military service behind him but was still only a lieutenant. During the Civil War Sheridan served with distinction in the Union army and rocketed from obscurity to high rank and responsibility. By the closing weeks of the Civil War, he had been promoted to major-general. After the Civil War ended, Sheridan remained in the army enforcing the odious Reconstruction Acts in Louisiana and Texas. In 1884 Sheridan became commanding general of the entire U.S. army. He was elevated to the rank of full general from June 1, 1888. General Sheridan died on August 5 of that year. This county was created and named in his honor on February 25, 1885.

1702 *Sherman County*

William T. Sherman (1820–1891)— A native of Ohio and an 1840 graduate of the U.S. military academy at West Point, Sherman served as a junior officer in actions against the Indians and in the Mexican War. During the Mexican War Sherman was not assigned any combat duties. By 1853 he had become bored with military life and resigned from the army to pursue civilian occupations in California, Kansas territory and Louisiana. At the outbreak of the Civil War in 1861, Sherman accepted a commission in the Union army as a colonel and by 1862 he had risen to the rank of major-general. In 1864, When Ulysses S. Grant was promoted to commander of all Union armies, Sherman was given command in the South. Starting at Atlanta, Georgia in November, 1864, Sherman led his infamous "March to the Sea," burning a swath across Georgia, some 40 to 60 miles wide and 300 miles long. Factories, cotton gins and warehouses were burned. Bridges and public buildings were destroyed. With Sherman's approval, his troops engaged in wild looting of civilian property. Sherman then marched north, wreaking even greater destruction in South Carolina. These an other depredations earned Sherman the hatred of several generations of White southerners. After the war Sherman remained in the military and ultimately became general-in-chief of the army. He was periodically considered as a presidential candidate. His succinct refusal to the Republicans in 1884 has become a classic: "I will not accept if nominated and will not serve if elected." This county was created on March 1, 1871.

1703 *Sioux County*

Dakota Indians— The Dakota are a vast alliance of American Indians who are more commonly known as the Sioux Indians. These Indians' name for themselves is *Lakota* or *Dakota* meaning "friends" or "allies," while *Sioux* was a derogatory Chippewa-French name for them. The Dakotas consist of three general dialect and culture groups: the Santee, Wiciyela and Teton. When the Whites first encountered the Dakotas, about 1640, they found them living in southern Minnesota and adjacent areas subsisting by hunting, fishing, gathering lake and forest products and growing corn. In 1805 the Dakotas signed their first treaty giving up some of their Minnesota lands and by 1858 they had been pressured into signing treaties giving up almost all of their land in Minnesota. In return, they were to receive food, annuities, education and other necessities. These promises to the Indians were broken and in 1862 the Dakotas began a final, futile struggle against the Whites in Minnesota, who had systematically robbed and mistreated them. The Dakotas lost this struggle and 38 of their members were hanged on a mass gallows at Mankato, Minnesota, on December 26, 1862. Remaining Dakota Indians in Minnesota were deported to Indian reservations in Dakota territory (now South Dakota and North Dakota), where they have lived in misery to this day. This county was created on February 19, 1877. Nebraska territory had earlier created and named Dakota County for this same tribe of Indians. That county was created on March 7, 1855, and it remains today as one of Nebraska's counties, so Nebraska has two counties named for the same tribe: Dakota County and Sioux County.

1704 *Stanton County*

Edwin M. Stanton (1814–1869)— A native of Ohio and a lawyer, Stanton moved to Pennsylvania in 1847, where he gained a reputation as one of our country's outstanding attorneys. In 1856 Stanton moved to Washington, D.C., to better enable him to handle cases before the U.S. Supreme Court. In 1860 President James Buchanan appointed Stanton to his cabinet as attorney general. When Abraham Lincoln succeeded James Buchanan as president, Stanton returned to private life. However, in January, 1862, in the midst of the Civil War, President Lincoln appointed Stanton to serve in his cabinet as secretary of war. Stanton remained in that critical cabinet post until the Civil War ended in victory for the Union. He continued as secretary of war when Andrew Johnson succeeded Lincoln as president but Johnson removed him from that post in 1868. This county was first created on March 6, 1855, when Nebraska was a territory, and named Izard County, in honor of Mark W. Izard (1799–1866), who was then serving as governor of Nebraska territory. Izard resigned as the territory's governor on October 25, 1857, and returned to his home in Arkansas. On January 10, 1862, early in the Civil War, Nebraska's territorial legislature changed this county's name from Izard to Stanton. In his Ph.D. thesis entitled "The Toponomy of Nebraska," dated May, 1932, John T. Link stated that "As a result of intense sentiment aroused as a result of the Civil War, counties bearing the names of Southern men or men whose names were obnoxious to the people, were given different names." Link states that Izard County was one of those that was renamed for this reason. This county's name was changed from Izard to Stanton of January 10, 1862. Just five days later, on January 15, 1862, Edwin M. Stanton became President Lincoln's secretary of war.

1705 *Thayer County*

John M. Thayer (1820–1906) — A native of Massachusetts and a graduate of Brown University, Thayer practiced law in Worcester, Massachusetts, before moving to Nebraska territory in 1854. He was elected to the upper house of Nebraska's territorial legislature shortly before the outbreak of the Civil War. Thayer was an officer in the Union army during the Civil War and served with distinction, rising to the rank of brevet-major-general. After Nebraska was admitted to statehood, Thayer was elected to represent the new state in the U.S. Senate and he served in that body from 1867 to 1871. President Ulysses S. Grant appointed Thayer to be governor of Wyoming territory and he served in that office from March 1, 1875, to May 29, 1878. In 1886 he ran for the office of governor of the state of Nebraska and was elected. Reelected in 1888, Thayer served as the state's governor from January 6, 1887, to January 15, 1891. When the Nebraska supreme court ruled that Thayer's successor was ineligible, he was called back to serve again as Nebraska's governor. This stint lasted from May 5, 1891, to early February, 1892. This county was originally created by Nebraska territory on January 26, 1856, and named Jefferson County. On that same date a Jones County was created. Over the next 15 years boundaries were shifted and names were changed. There no longer is a Jones County. Today's Thayer County is due west of today's Jefferson County.

1706 *Thomas County*

George H. Thomas (1816–1870) A native of Virginia and an 1040 graduate of the U.S. military academy at West Point, New York, Thomas was a career officer in the United States army. He participated in actions against the Seminole Indians and in the Mexican War. After the Mexican War, Thomas had a variety of assignments including brief service as an instructor at West Point and duty on the Indian frontier in Texas. Despite his southern roots, Thomas remained loyal to the U.S. army when the Civil War began and he served as an officer in the Union army throughout the Civil War. Near the end of the Civil War he was promoted to the rank of major-general. After the Civil War, Thomas remained in the army until his death on March 28, 1870. This county was created and named in his honor on March 31, 1887.

1707 *Thurston County*

John M. Thurston (1847–1916) — A native of Vermont, Thurston moved with his parents to Wisconsin where he graduated from college. After he was admitted to the bar, Thurston set up a law practice in Omaha, Nebraska, and he was elected to Nebraska's state legislature. The Union Pacific Railroad appointed him to their legal staff in 1877 and made him general solicitor for the railroad in 1888. Thurston was elected to represent Nebraska in the U.S. Senate and he served in that body from March 4, 1895, to March 3, 1901. In 1896, John M. Thurston was chairman of the Republican party's national convention, which was held in Saint Louis. This county was originally created by Nebraska territory on March 7, 1855, with the name Blackbird County. It was reestablished by the state of Nebraska, on March 28, 1889, as Thurston County.

1708 *Valley County*

Location of much of the county in valley lands — This county in central Nebraska lies largely in valley lands between the higher table land of the North Loup River, in the northeastern section of the county and similar table land of the Middle Loup River in Valley County's southwestern corner. The individual valleys between these table lands vary in width from three to ten miles and are very fertile. In *Johnson's History of Nebraska*, written by Harrison Johnson and published in 1880, the author estimates that about 30 percent of the county's area consists of valley and bottom lands. Thus the name that was chosen for this county, when it was created on March 1, 1871, was and is descriptive of the county's topography.

1709 *Washington County*

George Washington (1732–1799) — Washington was a native of Virginia. He served in Virginia's house of burgesses and became one of the colonies' leaders in opposition to British policies in America. He was a member of the first and second Continental Congresses and commander of all Continental armies in the Revolutionary War. Following victory in that war, Washington was elected to be the first president of the United States. This county was created in November, 1854, shortly after Nebraska territory was established.

1710 *Wayne County*

Anthony Wayne (1745–1796) — A native of Pennsylvania, Wayne was a successful brigadier-general in the Revolutionary War and became a hero for his daring exploits. During the bitter winter of 1777–1778 at Valley Forge, Pennsylvania, Wayne shared the sufferings of his men although his comfortable estate was only five miles away. He played an important role in the final overthrow of the British forces in Georgia. After the war, in 1785, Wayne moved to Georgia and he represented Georgia for about six months in the U.S. House of Representatives. In 1792, President Washington recalled Wayne to serve as a major-general against the Indians in the Northwest territory. Once again his military efforts were successful. This county was created in March, 1871.

1711 *Webster County*

Daniel Webster (1782–1852) — Webster was born in New Hampshire and represented that state in the U.S. House of Representatives. He later represented Massachusetts in both houses of the U.S. Congress and served as secretary of state under three presidents. Webster felt that slavery was evil but not as evil as disunion of the United States. He played a key role in the passage of five laws in the U.S. Congress which are known as the "Compromise of 1850" which were intended to avert secession and civil war between the North and the South over the slavery issue. This county was created on February 16, 1867.

1712 *Wheeler County*

Daniel H. Wheeler (1834–1912)— Wheeler was born in Saint Joseph County, Michigan, on November 26, 1834. He worked on farms in his youth, while attending school, and after completion of his studies, Wheeler was employed by his uncle as a clerk and bookkeeper for a distillery. In 1856 Wheeler headed west and obtained employment from Nuckolls & Company, which had general merchandise stores in Glenwood, Iowa, and Plattsmouth, in Nebraska territory. Wheeler made collections for his employer in both of these communities. In January, 1857, he returned to Michigan to get married. Wheeler and his bride established their residence at Plattsmouth and Wheeler opened his own store in that community selling stoves, tin and hardware. He remained in this business some 20 years. In 1859 Wheeler was elected county clerk of Cass County, Nebraska territory. In 1862 he was elected justice of the peace and in 1864 the Cass County commissioners appointed him to fill a temporary vacancy in the office of county judge. Daniel H. Wheeler served on the bench of Cass County for six months. After Wheeler was elected county clerk he studied law in his spare time and by 1868 he was admitted to the bar of the state of Nebraska. Soon afterward he was elected mayor of Plattsmouth and he served one term in that position. In 1868 Wheeler was elected secretary of Nebraska's state board of agriculture. He held that position continuously until 1881 but was reelected in 1882 and continued as the state's secretary of agriculture one more year. In 1873 Wheeler was elected secretary of the Nebraska senate and he was reelected to that body for two regular sessions and one special session. After moving to Omaha in June, 1885, Wheeler was elected several times to Omaha's city council. He died at his home in Omaha in November, 1912. This county was created on February 17, 1877.

1713 *York County*

Uncertain— This county was created on March 13, 1855, shortly after Nebraska territory was established. Four explanations for the origin of this county's name have been found in the literature concerning Nebraska's history, geography and place names:

England's royal house of York— This royal dynasty descended from Edmund de Langley (1341–1402), who was England's first duke of York. Langley was the fifth son of England's King Edward III (1312–1377) and although Langley never ruled England, his title passed on to members of later generations who became kings of England. The last member of the York dynasty died in 1499 and the York dynasty was replaced by the House of Tudor on the throne of England. However, the title "duke of York" has been given to numerous later members of the English royal family, including King James II (1633–1701). King James II is also mentioned as a possible namesake for York County, Nebraska. See below.

King James II (1633–1701)— James was the second surviving son of England's King Charles I (1600–1649). He was given the title duke of York and Albany soon after his christening. When James' father died, his elder brother, Charles, ascended to the throne as King Charles II (1630–1685). In 1664 King Charles II made an enormous grant of land in North America to his brother, the duke of York and Albany, which initially included much of present-day Pennsylvania. The duke of York was awarded more power over his domain than any other English proprietor. Although King Charles II had many children, none of them were legitimate so when King Charles II died in 1685, his brother, James, became king of England as King James II. About 1673 King James II professed his Catholicism and this spelled his eventual downfall as king. In 1689 the throne passed to William of Orange (1650–1702), who ruled as joint sovereign with his wife, Queen Mary II (1662–1694). Mary was a daughter of King James II. The former King James II devoted the final years of his life to religious exercises.

York and Yorkshire, England— Lying about mid-way between London and Edinburgh, Scotland, with a population of several million, the city of York and the county of Yorkshire, in England, represent one of England's most important metropolitan areas. Yorkshire borders on the North Sea and extends almost to the Irish Sea. The Roman Empire conquered the area and built a strategic fortress here about A.D. 72. Remains of this fortress can still be seen. The Yorkshire plain is fertile for agriculture and the West Riding area is rich in coal deposits. The Danes captured York in A.D. 867 and its present name came from their name *Yorvick*. York was later subjugated by the West Saxons and in 1066 it fell to the Norman invaders from France.

York County, Pennsylvania— Alfred D. Jones (1814–) was apparently involved in selecting names for some of Nebraska territory's early counties. He was born in Philadelphia, Pennsylvania, on January 30, 1814. According to some accounts, it was Alfred D. Jones who suggested the name for this new county in Nebraska territory. As a Pennsylvania native it seems plausible that Jones may have suggested that this county be named for York County, in Pennsylvania. York County, Pennsylvania, was created in the mid 1740's. Sources consulted offer differing opinions on the origin of this Pennsylvania county's name. York and Yorkshire in England are suggested by some authorities while others say that England's King James II (1633–1701) was the namesake. Information on each of these choices is presented immediately above in the material on York County, Nebraska.

REFERENCES

Andreas, Alfred T. *History of the State of Nebraska*. Chicago, Western Historical Co., 1882.

Andrews, Allen. *The Royal Whore: Barbara Villiers, Countess of Castlemaine*. Philadelphia, Chilton Book Co., 1970.

Antelope County Historical Society. *The History of Antelope County, Nebraska: 1868–1985*. Dallas, Texas, Curtis Media Corporation, 1986.

Arbor Lodge: Volume 3, Arbor Day & Tree Planting.

Arnold, W. H. *Complete Directory of Phelps County, Nebraska: 1909*. Holdrege, Nebraska, Progress Printing Co., Inc.

Bang, Roy C. *Heroes Without Medals: A Pioneer History of Kearney County, Nebraska*. Minden, Nebraska, Warp Publishing Co., 1952.

Bangs, S. D. "History of Sarpy County." *Transactions & Reports of the Nebraska State Historical Society*, Vol. 2. Lincoln, Nebraska: 1887.

Banner County and Its People. Harrisburg, Nebraska, Banner County Historical Society, 1982.

A Biographical & Genealogical History of Southeastern Nebraska. Chicago, Lewis Publishing Co., 1904.

"Biographical Notices: William D. Gage." *Transactions & Reports of the Nebraska State Historical Society*, Vol. 2. Lincoln, Nebraska: 1887.

Brand, Donald D. *The History of Scotts Bluff, Nebraska*. Berkeley, California, U.S. National Park Service, 1934.

Buss, William H., & Thomas T. Osterman. *History of Dodge & Washington Counties, Nebraska and Their People*. Chicago, American Historical Society, 1921.

Cassidy, Frederic G. *Dane County Place-Names*. Madison, University of Wisconsin Press, 1968.

Centennial Committee. *City of Alliance & Box Butte County, Nebraska*. Dallas, Texas, Curtis Media Corporation, 1988.

Chase, Harold, et al. *Biographical Dictionary of the Federal Judiciary*. Detroit, Michigan, Gale Research Co., 1976.

Chase County History: Centennial Edition. Chase County Historical Society, Inc., 1965.

Clements, John. *Wisconsin Facts*. Dallas, Texas, Clements Research II, Inc., 1990.

"County Names, Namesakes." *Lincoln Sunday Journal & Star*, May 30, 1954.

Cox, W. W. *History of Seward County, Nebraska*. Lincoln, Nebraska, State Journal Co., 1888.

Creigh, Dorothy W. *Nebraska: A Bicentennial History*. New York, W. W. Norton & Co., Inc., 1977.

Curley, Edwin A. *Nebraska: Its Advantages, Resources & Drawbacks*. New York, American & Foreign Publication Co., 1875.

Dale, Raymond E. "William D. Gage." *Otoe County Pioneers: A Biographical Dictionary*. Unpublished manuscript, Nebraska State Historical Society, Lincoln, Nebraska.

"Daniel H. Wheeler is Dead." *Nebraska State Journal*, November 28, 1912.

Danker, Donald F. & Paul D. Riley. *Out of Old Nebraska*. Lincoln, Nebraska State Historical Society, 1971.

Davis, Pearl H. *Those Who Came Before Us: A History of Rock County Compiled During the Bicentennial Year 1976*.

Day, Barbara & Karlie Koinzan. *Wheeler County History Book*. 1977.

"Death of John J. Gosper." *Lexington Clipper-Citizen*, May 30, 1913.

DeLand, Charles E. "Fort Tecumseh & Fort Pierre Journal & Letter Books." *South Dakota Historical Collections*, Vol. 9. Pierre, South Dakota: 1918.

Denney, James. "Route to the Hall of Fame." *Omaha World-Herald*, March 4, 1962.

Deuel County Historical Society. *Deuel County History*. Des Moines, Iowa, Hansen Printing, Inc., 1984.

Dobbs, Hugh J. *History of Gage County, Nebraska*. Lincoln, Nebraska, Western Publishing & Engraving Co., 1918.

Dundy County History Book Committee. *History of Dundy County, Nebraska: 1880–1987*. Dallas, Texas, Curtis Media Corporation, 1988.

Ekwall, Eilert. *The Concise Oxford Dictionary of English Place-Names*. Oxford, Oxford University Press, 1960.

Encyclopaedia Britannica. Chicago, Encyclopaedia Britannica, Inc., 1971.

Fitzpatrick, Lilian L. *Nebraska Place-Names*. Lincoln, University of Nebraska Press, 1960.

Foght, H. W. *The Trail of the Loup*. 1906.

Frazer, Robert W. *Forts of the West*. Norman, University of Oklahoma Press, 1965.

Frost, J. *The Mexican War and Its Warriors*. New Haven, H. Mansfield, 1850.

Gage County History Book Committee. *Gage County, Nebraska History*. Dallas, Texas, Taylor Publishing Co., 1983.

Gilmore, G. H. "Ghost Towns in Cass County, Nebraska." *Nebraska History Magazine*, Vol. 18, No. 3. Lincoln, Nebraska: July–September, 1937.

Gilmore, Melvin R. "Some Indian Place Names in Nebraska." *Publications of the Nebraska State Historical Society*, Vol. 19. Lincoln: 1919.

Graff, Jane. *Nebraska: Our Towns: Central & North-Central*. Dallas, Texas, Taylor Publishing Co., 1989.

Graff, Jane. *Nebraska: Our Towns: The Panhandle*. Dallas, Texas, Taylor Publishing Co., 1988.

Graff, Jane. *Nebraska: Our Towns: South Central*. Dallas, Texas, Taylor Publishing Co., 1988.

Greater York Area Genealogical Society. *The History of York County, Nebraska*. Dallas, Texas, Curtis Media Corporation, 1988.

Hart, Herbert M. *Old Forts of the Northwest*. New York, Bonanza Books, 1963.

Heritage of Progress: A History of Phelps County, Nebraska. Holdrege, Nebraska, Phelps County Historical Society, 1981.

History of Antelope County: 1883–1973. Service Press, Inc., 1976.

History of Chase County. Chase County Historical Society, 1938.

History of Pottawattamie County, Iowa. Chicago, O. L. Baskin & Co., 1883.

Holbrook, Stewart H. *The Story of the American Railroads*. New York, Crown Publishers, 1947.

Huse, William. *History of Dixon County, Nebraska*. Norfolk, Press of the Daily News, 1896.

"J. J. Gosper." *Nebraska State Journal*, January 5, 1913.

Johnson, Harrison. *Johnson's History of Nebraska*. Omaha, Nebraska, Herald Printing House, 1880.

Jones, Lillian L. *Days of Yore: Early History of Brown County, Nebraska*. Ainsworth, Nebraska, 1937.

Kearney Business & Professional Women's Club. *Where the Buffalo Roamed: Stories of Early Days in Buffalo County, Nebraska*. Shenandoah, Iowa, World Publishing Co.

Kenyon, J. P. *Dictionary of British History*. Ware, England, Wordsworth Editions, Ltd., 1992.

Keya Paha County Centennial Book Committee. *The History of Keya Paha County, Nebraska: 100 Years: 1885–1985*. Freeman, South Dakota, Pine Hill Press, Inc., 1985.

Kleber, John E. *The Kentucky Encyclopedia*. Lexington, University Press of Kentucky, 1992.

Leitch, Barbara A. *A Concise Dictionary of Indian Tribes of North America*. Algonac, Michigan, Reference Publications, Inc., 1979.

"Lieut. Samuel A. Cherry." *Transactions & Reports of the Nebraska State Historical Society*, Vol. 4, Lincoln, Nebraska: 1892.

Link, J. T. *The Origin of the Place-Names of Nebraska*. Lincoln, University of Nebraska Press, 1960.

Link, John T. "The Toponomy of Nebraska." Ph.D. Thesis, University of Nebraska, Lincoln, Nebraska, May, 1932.

Loudon, Betty, Research Associate, Nebraska State Historical Society, Lincoln, Nebraska. Letters to the author dated February 3, 1986, January 3, 1987 & March 3, 1987.

McCoy, J. Mike. *History of Cedar County, Nebraska*. 1937.

McLoughlin, Denis. *Wild & Wooly: An Encyclopedia of the Old West*. Garden City, New York, Doubleday & Co., Inc., 1975.

Magie, John Q. & Carl H. Jones. *A History & Historic Sites Survey of Johnson, Nemaha, Pawnee & Richardson Counties in Southeastern Nebraska*. Lincoln, Nebraska, Nebraska State Historical Society, 1969.

Mattes, Merrill J. "Hiram Scott, Fur Trader." *Nebraska History*, Vol. 26, No. 3. Lincoln, Nebraska: July–September, 1945.

Mead, James R. "The Pawnees as I Knew Them." *Transactions of the Kansas State Historical Society*, Vol. 10. Topeka: 1908.

Merrick County History Book Committee. *History of Merrick County, Nebraska: 1981*. Dallas, Texas, Taylor Publishing Co., 1981.

Mills, A. D. *A Dictionary of English Place Names*. Oxford, Oxford University Press, 1991.

Morton, J. Sterling. *Illustrated History of Nebraska*. Lincoln, Jacob North & Co., 1907.

Morton, J. Sterling, & Albert Watkins. *History of Nebraska from the Earliest Explorations of the Trans-Mississippi Region*. Lincoln, Nebraska, Western Publishing & Engraving Co., 1918.

Moule, Thomas. *The County Maps of*

Old England. London, Studio Editions, 1990.

Nebraska Society of the Daughters of the American Revolution. *Collection of Nebraska Pioneer Reminiscences.* Cedar Rapids, Iowa, Torch Press, 1916.

Nebraskans: 1854–1904. Omaha, Nebraska, Bee Publishing Co., 1904.

Nemaha County Book Committee. *Nemaha County, Nebraska.* Dallas, Texas, Taylor Publishing Co., 1987.

Nimmo, Sylvia, & Mary Cutler. *Nebraska Local History & Genealogy Reference Guide.* Papillion, Nebraska, 1987.

Nuckolls County Centennial, Inc. *The Wonderful Years: A History of Nuckolls County, Nebraska: 1871–1971.* Superior-Express, 1971.

Old Settlers' History of York County. 1913.

"The Oldest Nebraska House." *Nebraska History Magazine.* Vol. 13, No. 2. Lincoln, Nebraska: April–June, 1932.

Paullin, Charles O. *Atlas of the Historical Geography of the United States.* Carnegie Institution of Washington and the American Geographical Society of New York, 1932.

The Pennsylvania Almanac & Buyers' Guide. 1964.

Perkins County: Diamond Jubilee: 1887–1962: Souvenir Album.

Phillips, G. W. *Past & Present of Platte County, Nebraska.* Chicago, S. J. Clarke Publishing Co., 1915.

"Pioneer History of Harlan County." Subject file, Nebraska State Historical Society, Lincoln, Nebraska.

"Place Name Stories." *Nebraska Folklore,* Pamphlet 14, 1938.

Plains Genealogical Society of Kimball County. *Kimball County, Nebraska: 100 Years: 1888–1988.* Dallas, Texas, Curtis Media Corporation, 1988.

Portrait of Progress in Phelps County: Phelps County, Nebraska Centennial: 1873–1973.

Price, Edward T. *Dividing the Land: Early American Beginnings of Our Private Property Mosaic.* Chicago, University of Chicago Press, 1995.

Reece, Charles S. *A History of Cherry County, Nebraska.* Simeon, Nebraska, 1945.

Reece, C. S., Jr. *Murder on the Plains: The Story of Lt. Samuel A. Cherry for Whom Cherry County Was Named.* Cherry County Historical Society, 1974.

Rosenfelt, W. E. *Nebraska: Its People & Culture.* Minneapolis, T. S. Denison & Co., Inc., 1974.

Rydjord, John. *Indian Place-Names.* Norman, University of Oklahoma Press, 1968.

Rydjord, John. *Kansas Place-Names.* Norman, University of Oklahoma Press, 1972.

Saunders County, Nebraska History. Saunders County Historical Society, Dallas, Texas, Taylor Publishing Co., 1983.

Savage, James W., et al. *History of the City of Omaha, Nebraska & South Omaha.* New York, Munsell & Co., 1894.

Schroeder, Betty N. R. *McPherson County.* Callaway, Nebraska, Loup Valley Queen, 1986.

"Scotts Bluff National Monument." *Newsweek,* Vol. 121, No. 17. New York, New York: April 26, 1993.

Sedgwick, T. E. *York County, Nebraska and Its People.* Chicago, S. J. Clarke Publishing Co., 1921.

Shafer, Gladys. *A Proud Heritage.* 1969.

Sheldon, A. E. "The Editor's Table: Nebraska's First White Settler." *Nebraska History,* Vol. 19, No. 2. Lincoln: April–June, 1938.

Sheldon, Addison E. *History & Stories of Nebraska.* Chicago, University Publishing Co., 1913.

Sheldon, Addison E. *The Nebraska Blue Book & Historical Register: 1918.* Lincoln, Nebraska, Nebraska Legislative Reference Bureau, 1918.

Shumway, Grant L. *History of Western Nebraska and Its People.* Lincoln, Nebraska, Western Publishing & Engraving Co., 1921.

Stennett, William H. *A History of the Origin of the Place Names Connected with the Chicago & North Western and Chicago, St. Paul, Minneapolis & Omaha Railways.* Chicago, 1908.

"Stories of Early Nemaha County Settlers." *Nebraska History & Record of Pioneer Days,* Vol. 1, Nos. 3 & 4. Lincoln, Nebraska: April–May, 1918.

Switzer, Colleen. *The Settlement of Loup & Blaine Counties.* Broken Bow, Nebraska, Purcell's Inc., 1977.

Taft, William H., III. *County Names: An Historical Perspective.* National Association of Counties, 1982.

Tennal, Ralph. *History of Nemaha County, Kansas.* Lawrence, Kansas, Standard Publishing Co., 1916.

Thrapp, Dan L. *Encyclopedia of Frontier Biography.* Lincoln, University of Nebraska Press, 1988.

Tipton, Thomas W. *Forty Years of Nebraska: At Home and in Congress.* Lincoln, Nebraska, State Journal Co., 1902.

True, M. B. C. "County Names." *Transactions & Reports of the Nebraska State Historical Society,* Vol. 4. Lincoln, Nebraska: 1892.

Tuttle, Charles R. *A New Centennial History of the State of Kansas.* Madison, Wisconsin, Interstate Book Co., 1876.

United States Census, June, 1860. Post Office of Fontanelle, Washington County, Nebraska territory. Nebraska State Historical Society, Lincoln, Nebraska.

Vexler, Robert I. *Chronology & Documentary Handbook of the State of Nebraska.* Dobbs Ferry, New York, Oceana Publications, Inc., 1978.

Vogel, Virgil J. "Indian Names in Illinois." *Journal of the Illinois State Historical Society,* Vol. 55. 1962.

Vogel, Virgil J. *Iowa Place Names of Indian Origin.* Iowa City, University of Iowa Press, 1983.

Waterman, John H. *General History of Seward County, Nebraska,* Beaver Crossing, Nebraska, 1916.

Watkins, Albert. "Historical Sketch of Cheyenne County, Nebraska." *Collections of the Nebraska State Historical Society,* Vol. 17. Lincoln, Nebraska, 1913.

Weddel, Mrs. T. G. *Keya Paha County Diamond Jubilee Edition: 1885–1960.*

Westbrook, C. H. *The Pennsylvania Manual: 1939.* Harrisburg, Pennsylvania, 1940.

Western Nebraska: Scottsbluff: Gering. Scottsbluff/ Gering United Chamber of Commerce.

White, John B. "Index Guide to the Contents of the Publications & Magazine of the Nebraska State Historical Society." *Nebraska State Historical Society Publications,* Vol. 24. Lincoln, Nebraska: 1958.

Who's Who in Nebraska: Bicentennial Edition of Notable Nebraskans. Omaha, Merit Publishers, Inc., 1976.

Williams, Helen R. "Old Wyoming." *Nebraska History Magazine,* Vol. 17, No. 2. Lincoln, Nebraska: April–June, 1936.

Wilson, D. Ray. *Fort Kearney on the Platte River.* Dundee, Illinois, 1980.

Woolworth, J. M. "Thomas B. Cuming." *Transactions & Reports of the Nebraska State Historical Society,* Vol. 4. Lincoln, Nebraska: 1892.

Work Projects Administration. *Inventory of the County Archives of Nebraska-Loup & Merrick Counties.* Lincoln, Nebraska, 1941 & 1942.

Works Progress Administration. *Inventory of the County Archives of Nebraska-Seward County.* Lincoln, Nebraska, 1939.

Works Progress Administration. *Lincoln City Guide.* Lincoln, Nebraska, Nebraska State Historical Society, 1937.

Works Progress Administration. *Nebraska: A Guide to the Cornhusker State.* New York, Nebraska State Historical Society, 1939.

Works Progress Administration. *Origin of Nebraska Place Names*. Lincoln, Ne braska, Nebraska State Historical Society, 1938.

Wright, Muriel H. *A Guide to the Indian Tribes of Oklahoma*. Norman, University of Oklahoma Press, 1951.

Nevada

(16 counties)

1714 *Churchill County*

Fort Churchill— This county was created on November 25, 1861, just nine months after Nevada territory was established. It was named for Fort Churchill, on the northern bank of the Carson River, approximately 30 miles northeast of Carson City, Nevada. There have been numerous boundary changes and several new Nevada counties have been created since November 25, 1861. Currently, Fort Churchill lies within Lyon County, Nevada, about ten miles west of Churchill County. The fort had been constructed in response to a perceived threat from Indians resulting primarily from the so-called Pyramid Lake Indian War during May, 1860. Captain Joseph Stewart, of the Third U.S. artillery, was sent from California to end the "war" (which he did starting on May 31, 1860), and to construct a fort. The proposed fort was intended as protection from Indian attacks for the overland mail route, pony express and a proposed transcontinental telegraph line. At the time Fort Churchill was erected, it was at the extreme western edge of Utah territory. Nevada territory had not yet been created. A sign erected at the present Nevada state historic park here says, in part "...Following Indian raids on way stations along the Overland Trail... On July 20, 1860, the fort was established as a United States military post under the command of Captain Joseph Stewart. Six days later it was officially named in honor of General Sylvester Churchill, inspector general of the United States Army..." The name was suggested by Captain Stewart and approved by Major W. W. Mackall and the secretary of war. Captain Joseph Stewart had served with General Churchill at the Presidio in San Francisco and was attached to him. The feared Indians attacks failed to materialize but Fort Churchill served during the Civil War as a supply depot and base of operations for Union troops in the Nevada area. In 1869 it was determined that the fort was no longer needed for protection from Indian attacks.

The soldiers abandoned the fort on September 29, 1869 and it was subsequently sold at auction. Fort Churchill is now a state historic park of the state of Nevada. The original adobe walls crumbled badly over the years but have been reconstructed.

Sylvester Churchill (–)— A native of Vermont, Churchill became a commissioned officer in the U.S. army on March 12, 1812, and he participated in the War of 1812. In 1841 he was appointed inspector general. In this capacity he traveled many miles to inspect the army's frontier outposts. Churchill participated in the Mexican War and it was in reward for valor during the battle of Buena Vista in that war that Churchill was promoted to brigadier-general.

1715 *Clark County*

William A. Clark (1839–1925)— A native of Pennsylvania, Clark immigrated to our country's West in stages, first moving with his family to Iowa in 1856, later to Missouri to teach school and then on to present day Colorado about 1860. In Colorado, Clark mined for gold and later, about 1863, he was successful in washing $1,500 in gold from Horse Prairie Creek in today's Montana. This was quite a handsome sum of money but Clark was astute enough to realize that a more reliable flow of earnings could be made by transporting goods to satisfy the miners needs. He started with tobacco and then broadened his stock to include general merchandise. About 1867 Clark was appointed to carry the mails between Missoula and Walla Walla. He prospered from these ventures and invested his profits in banking, mining, smelting and railroad ventures. His railroad venture was of particular interest to Nevada. Clark built the San Pedro, Los Angeles & Salt Lake Railroad. On June 2, 1905, at the tiny community of Jean, Nevada, in what is now Clark County, the final railroad spike was driven on the same day that passengers boarded trains in both Salt Lake City and Los Angeles to cross

the Nevada desert by rail. Clark sold his San Pedro, Los Angeles & Salt Lake Railroad to the Union Pacific. While William A. Clark was becoming wealthy from his business enterprises, he also was active in Montana politics. He presided over Montana's constitutional conventions held in 1884 and 1889 and he later represented the state of Montana in the U.S. Senate. This Nevada county was created and named in William Clark's honor in 1909. In fact, if Clark had not succeeded in building a railroad across this section of Nevada desert, no new county would have been needed here. On June 2, 1905, when the final railroad spike was driven, what is now Clark County, Nevada, consisted of a few small communities scattered in the desert. One of these small communities was Las Vegas, Nevada.

1716 *Douglas County*

Stephen A. Douglas (1813–1861)— Barely five feet tall, the "Little Giant" is most remembered as a political opponent of Abraham Lincoln. Douglas was born in Vermont and moved to Illinois where he enjoyed rapid political success. He served on the state supreme court, in the state legislature and as secretary of state. Following two terms in the U.S. House of Representatives, Douglas was elected to the U.S. Senate. In that body Douglas took courageous positions on the slavery issue which first outraged abolitionist sentiment and later infuriated the South. In 1858 Douglas ran for reelection to the U.S. Senate against Abraham Lincoln. Following the famous Lincoln-Douglas debates, the Republicans won the popular election but the Illinois legislature reelected Douglas to the senate. Lincoln and Douglas were rivals again in 1860 for the presidency. Following Lincoln's election and the start of the Civil War, Douglas gave the president his active support. In the senate Stephen Douglas had been chairman of the committee on territories at the time that Nevada territory was established on

March 2, 1861. Douglas died on June 3, 1861, and this county was created by Nevada territory on November 25, 1861.

1717 *Elko County*

Town of Elko, Nevada— The county of Elko in northeastern Nevada was created on March 5, 1869, and named for the town of Elko, which is the county seat of Elko County. The town site for the town of Elko was selected in December, 1868, and this town of Elko was named for a railroad station stop here. In its early days, the town of Elko was also a way station for wagon trains headed for our nation's westernmost lands. Today the town of Elko, in northeastern Nevada, is the center of Nevada's cattle country. The movie star and singer, Bing Crosby (1904–1977), owned a cattle ranch near the town of Elko and he was a regular visitor to the coffee houses and diners in Elko. The town is located on the high plains, 5,060 feet above sea level. In 1998 the town of Elko had a population of about 15,000. Although it is small, Elko is the urban center for a vast area of northeastern Nevada and northwestern Utah because it has no true nearby urban neighbors. Salt Lake City in 240 miles east, Boise, Idaho, is 235 miles north and Reno is 300 miles west. To the south, there is no city of any size except Las Vegas almost 500 miles away from Elko. The origin and meaning of the original name *Elko* for the railroad station stop is uncertain and debated. This particular name was very popular with railroad officials when they were selecting names for station stops. In our country there are at least seven states which have (or had) a railroad station named Elko and there is an additional railroad station in the Canadian province of British Columbia that is named Elko. In our nation, the use of Elko as a railroad name has been found in Alabama, Colorado, Georgia, Minnesota, Nevada, South Carolina and Virginia. John H. Goff published an article dealing with Georgia place names in the summer, 1957 issue of *Georgia Mineral Newsletter* which mentioned that "Another interesting station name is Elko, on the Southern Railway in lower Houston County. For some reason which the writer has not been able to discover, this tab is a favored name for railroad folk. The *Official Guide of the Railways* lists six "Elkos" in the United States and one in the Canadian province of British Columbia. Another such term is "Arcola…" The name Elko sounds like it may have derived from the animal name, elk. Maybe it did, but maybe it didn't. A rather vast body of literature has developed discussing and vigorously debating the possible origins of this name and several of those works are listed here:

— Allotta, Robert I. *Signposts & Settlers: The History of Place Names West of the Rockies.* 1994.
— Brown, Thomas P. "Names & Places: Elko, Nevada." *Western Folklore*, Vol. 9, No. 4. October, 1950.
— Carlson, Helen S. *Nevada Place Names: A Geographical Dictionary.* 1974.
— "Elko, Nevada." *Western Folklore*, Vol. 8, No. 4. October, 1949.
— Gannet, Henry. *The Origin of Certain Place Names in the United States.* 1978.
— Glass, Mary Ellen, & Al Glass. *Touring Nevada.* 1983.
— Mack, Effie M., & Byrd W. Sawyer. *Our State: Nevada.* 1940.
— Patterson, Edna. *Who Named IT? History of Elko County Place Names.* 1964.
— Patterson, Edna B., et al. *Nevada's Northeast Frontier.* 1969.
— Stewart, George R. *American Place-Names.* 1970.
— Stewart, George R. "Elko, Nevada." *Western Folklore*, Vol. 9, No. 2. April, 1950.
— Work Projects Administration. *Origin of Nevada Place Names.* 1941

1718 *Esmeralda County*

Esmeralda mining district— This county was created on November 25, 1861, when Nevada was a territory, and named for its Esmeralda mining district on the Wassuk Mountain range. That mining district was located some 90 miles southeast of Virginia city and only four miles east of the California border. On August 25, 1860, J. M. Cory, E. R. Hicks and James M. Braly located four claims here, from which the Esmeralda mining district grew. Just five days later, on August 30, 1860, Cory, Hicks and Braly returned with about 20 men to lay out the mining district and work the mines. It was J. M. Cory who suggested the name for the mining district. *Esmeralda* is the Spanish word for "emerald." Presumably Cory thought the name an appropriate symbol for the mineral riches which he and his associates hoped to find here. Some sources speculate that the name came from Esmeralda, the heroine of Victor Hugo's (1802–1885) novel, *Notre Dame de Paris*. The boom town of Aurora soon blossomed and although the important phase of the boom here was relatively short, it was extremely profitable. The mines of the Esmeralda mining district produced more than 29 million dollars worth of ore during their first ten years of operation. Mining continued for decades after that but the riches had been drained during the first ten years. Only about two million dollars worth of ore was obtained from these mines during several decades after the early 1870's. During the boom years there were 18 mills located at Aurora, which was the first county seat of Esmeralda County, Nevada territory. Nearby California claimed that the Esmeralda mining district fell within its borders and in the spring of 1861, the state of California made the mining town of Aurora the county seat of Mono County, California. Nevada ultimately prevailed and the area in dispute now belongs to Nevada. However, Aurora is a ghost town today.

1719 *Eureka County*

Town of Eureka, Nevada— Rich ledges of ore were found in the mountains here in 1864 and the towns of Eureka and Ruby Hill were settled soon afterward. The town of Eureka was named for the Eureka mining district here. There are several versions of the instant when the word "Eureka!" was yelled here and then used for the name of the mining district but all of the versions involve mining and/or smelting of ore found here and they all mean "I have found it!" *Eureka* is a Greek word, which means "I have found it!" The word has an ancient and interesting history. A noted Greek mathematician, physicist and inventor, named Archimedes, lived in the third century B.C. The term Eureka! is associated with Archimedes because of a discovery of a law of physics which he made in response to a request from his king. The king asked Archimedes to determine whether his crown was made of pure gold, or gold mixed with less precious metals. Archimedes was pondering this puzzle while naked in his bath tub. When the answer occurred to him, Archimedes raced from his home, naked, crying "Eureka!" This incident was dramatic and interesting enough to give the word Eureka! a place in our vocabulary to this day. Skipping fast forward some 22 centuries to the town of Eureka, Nevada, we find that the town's heyday was in the 1870's and that the most important metal extracted from the surrounding mines was lead, rather than gold or silver. The mining and smelting of lead was lucrative and the boom it sparked was dramatic enough to attract a population of some 10,000 citizens who had about 100 saloons from which to choose. The town of Eureka today retains none of its former glory and it boasts a population of perhaps 800 citizens. When the Nevada legislature created a new county in this area on March 1, 1873, during the mining boom, they named it for the boom town of Eureka and Eureka is the present seat of justice of Eureka County.

1720 *Humboldt County*

Humboldt River— The Humboldt River rises in Elko County, in northeastern Nevada and flows some 290 miles in a generally western direction until it empties its waters into the Rye Patch reservoir in north-central Nevada. The Humboldt River crosses a relatively small section of southeastern Humboldt County in a crescent-shaped curve. In early days much of the westward migration across Nevada followed the Humboldt River's course and today Interstate highway 80 runs close to the Humboldt River as it crosses northern Nevada. The river was named by John C. Frémont (1813–1890) during his exploration of our nation's West in the mid 1840's. Frémont wrote a letter dated February 29, 1881 which confirmed that the Humboldt River's name was his idea. Frémont named the river in honor of Alexander von Humboldt, who was then prominent.

Friedrich Wilhelm Heinrich Alexander von Humboldt (1769–1859)— Baron von Humboldt was one of the foremost scientists of his time. He participated in expeditions to Latin America and to Asia, which gathered valuable scientific data for a number of disciplines, including biology, geology and astronomy. His contributions to the physical sciences covered topics ranging from climate and polar magnetism to geology. In 1804 he visited America and met Thomas Jefferson and other prominent intellectuals. His scientific books enjoyed popularity in our country and a Pacific Ocean current, which he studied, is named in his honor.

When Nevada was a part of Utah territory, that territory created a Humboldt County within the borders of the present state of Nevada. Nevada territory was created on March 2, 1861, and just nine months later, on November 25, 1861, the territory of Nevada created its own Humboldt County. (The state of Utah currently has no county named Humboldt.)

1721 *Lander County*

Frederick W. Lander (1821–1862)— A native of Massachusetts, Lander studied civil engineering and performed survey work for railroads in the East before moving on to the western frontier. He subsequently participated in the 1853 expedition to chart a railway route from St. Paul, Minnesota territory, to the Puget Sound. Lander was appointed superintendent and chief engineer in charge of charting the major transcontinental overland wagon route for settlers heading west. He participated in five transcontinental expeditions and Lander and his men were attacked by Indians on more than one occasion. Frederick Lander met with Chief Winnemucca of the Northern Paiute Indians and successfully negotiated a cessation in hostilities, albeit brief. Lander served in the Union army during the Civil War and on May 17, 1861, he was promoted to brigadier-general for gallantry in battle. He continued to receive praise for his military efforts as his health began to fail. General Lander died suddenly on March 2, 1862, of natural causes. This county was created by Nevada territory on December 19, 1862.

1722 *Lincoln County*

Abraham Lincoln (1809–1865)— Lincoln was a native of Kentucky who moved to Illinois where he was a member of the state legislature. He represented Illinois in the U.S. House of Representatives and later was elected president of the United States. Lincoln's presidency coincided almost exactly with the Civil War. He guided the United States ably through that uniquely turbulent period. As president, he issued the Emancipation Proclamation which declared the freedom of slaves in all states in rebellion. Lincoln was assassinated in April, 1865, a few days after the Union's victory in the Civil War. This county was created on February 26, 1866. It was initially proposed that this new county be named Stewart, in honor of Nevada's U.S. senator, William M. Stewart (1827–1909), but that proposal was rejected and the county was named for our nation's recently assassinated president. President Lincoln had sponsored Nevada's admission to the Union and he issued the official proclamation which granted statehood to Nevada on October 31, 1864.

1723 *Lyon County*

Uncertain— This county was created on November 25, 1861, when Nevada was a territory. Sources consulted offer two different opinions on the identity of the county's namesake. Some say that the name honors General Nathaniel Lyon while sources indicate that the county was named for Captain Robert Lyon, who participated in the so-called Pyramid Lake Indian War.

Nathaniel Lyon (1818–1861)— A native of Connecticut and an 1841 graduate of the U.S. military academy at West Point, Lyon participated in actions against the Seminole Indians in Florida and later in the Mexican War. Very early in the Civil War, in May, 1861, President Abraham Lincoln promoted him to brigadier general and he was given command of Union forces at St. Louis. In August, 1861, General Lyon commanded an attack on Confederate troops at Wilson's Creek, Missouri. In that battle the Confederate army scored a victory and General Lyon was killed in combat.

Robert Lyon (–)— Captain Robert Lyon, who is referred to as an Indian scout, came to what is now Nevada by wagon train in June, 1850. He participated in the so-called Pyramid Lake Indian War of May, 1860, and, according to one account, he was killed in combat in that engagement. However, Robert Lyon wrote a report of that war, a difficult accomplishment if he had been killed in it. There is an explanation, which would permit both statements to be true, which centers on the fact that the so-called Pyramid Lake Indian War was fought in two separate phases at two locations, both during May, 1860. The first phase was fought on May 12, 1860, just a few miles from Pyramid Lake in northwestern Nevada. An estimated 76 Whites were killed in this encounter. The second, and final phase, began on May 31, 1860, and ended in very early June, 1860. It occurred at the big bend in the Truckee River, near the present site of Wadsworth, Nevada. The Whites outnumbered the Indians in this second battle and it is said that the Indians were "routed." It is possible, that Captain Robert Lyon participated in the May 12 phase of this so-called war, wrote a report about it, and then was killed in the second phase of the war. This explanation appears to be false because Captain Robert Lyon's report refers to the death of Captain Edward F. Storey (1828–1860) and Captain Storey died as a result of wounds which he suffered on June 2, 1860. Thus it is unlikely that Robert Lyon died in combat in the Pyramid Lake Indian War of 1860. An index card in the files of the Nevada Historical Society in Reno, Nevada states that Captain Robert Lyon was a brother-in-law of Chauncey Noteware, that he participated in the Pyramid Lake War and that Lyon County, Nevada was named for him. No author's name appears on this index card.

1724 *Mineral County*

The mineral resources of the county—

This county at the western edge of central Nevada was created on February 10, 1911, and named for its varied and valuable mineral resources. The county contains numerous silver lodes, scheelite and other valuable minerals. *Scheelite* is native calcium tungstate, an ore from which tungsten can be obtained. Since tungsten has the highest melting point of all metals, it is valuable for use as filaments in electric light bulbs and for alloying steel.

1725 *Nye County*

James W. Nye (1814–1876)— James W. Nye, the first, last and only governor of Nevada territory, was born in poverty in New York state. In spite of financial obstacles, Nye studied law, was admitted to the bar and practiced his profession in New York state. During the election of 1860 he supported William H. Seward (1801–1872) for the Republican party's presidential nomination but when the party nominated Abraham Lincoln, Nye gave Lincoln his active support. Following victory in that election, Lincoln was inaugurated as our nation's president on March 4, 1861, and just 18 days later, on March 22, 1861, the president appointed Nye to be governor of the newly created territory of Nevada. During the Civil War Nye raised infantry, cavalry and local militia units to support the Union army. He devoted considerable attention to winning statehood for Nevada, no small challenge given the small population of Nevada territory. With President Lincoln's support, Nevada was admitted to statehood on October 31, 1864. In December of that year, Nevada's state legislature elected Nye and William M. Stewart (1827–1909) to be Nevada's first two United States senators and they took their seats in that body on February 1, 1865. This county was created on February 16, 1864, while Nye was serving as territorial governor of Nevada.

1726 *Pershing County*

John J. Pershing (1860–1948)— A native of Missouri and a graduate of the U.S. Military Academy at West Point, Pershing was a career officer in the U.S. army. He participated in several campaigns against Indians and, from 1891 to 1895 he was an instructor in military tactics at the University of Nebraska, a subject which he subsequently taught at West Point. In the Spanish-American War, Pershing served in Cuba and won a silver star citation for gallantry. In 1901 he was sent to the Philippines to pacify insurgents there. With this distinguished career record behind him, Pershing was still only a captain. That was soon corrected. In 1906 he leap-frogged from captain to brigadier-general. In 1916 the renegade revolutionary forces of Mexico's Pancho Villa (1877–1923) raided our country and killed a number of Americans during their visits. Pershing was sent on a punitive mission against Villa, which was proceeding well until it was aborted for diplomatic reasons. Following our country's entry into World War I, Pershing was promoted to the rank of full general and commander of the American expeditionary forces sent to France. This county was created on March 18, 1919, just five months after our victory in World War I was recognized by the signing of an armistice agreement on November 11, 1918. Pershing later was promoted to general of the armies and was the chief of staff of the U.S. army.

1727 *Storey County*

Edward F. Storey (1828–1860)— Edward Faris Storey was born in Jackson County, Georgia, on July 1, 1828. He moved with his parents to Texas in 1844 and he served in the Mexican War. In 1848 he was made a lieutenant and in the following year he was married. Edward Storey and his wife, Adelia, had one child, a daughter, prior to Mrs. Storey's death in 1852. Following his wife's death, Storey moved, with his daughter, to California, where he engaged in stock raising in Tulare County. Attracted to Nevada by the Washoe (Comstock) mines, Storey immigrated here in 1859. At that time this northwestern section of today's state of Nevada was part of Utah territory. In retaliation for an attack by Paiute Indians, Storey raised a company of riflemen, which participated in an attack on the Paiutes on June 2, 1860. The Indians were defeated but Captain Storey lost his life in this battle and died in June, 1860. The date of his death is given in some accounts as June 2, 1860, and in others as June 7, 1860. This county was created and named in Captain Storey's honor on November 25, 1861, shortly after Nevada territory was established. It is a very small county. Its northern border is formed by the Truckee River at or near the location where Captain Edward F. Storey was mortally wounded on June 2, 1860.

1728 *Washoe County*

Washo Indians— Nearly 30 Indian tribal groups have lived in Nevada but only four of them have been given much attention by historians. These four are the Shoshoni, the Southern Paiute, the Northern Paiute and the Washo Indians. The Washo were the smallest of these four Nevada tribes and the territory which they controlled was much smaller than the territories of the other three. When first encountered by Americans, the Washo occupied most of the 120 mile long valley of the Truckee River, from the present Placer County in eastern California, east into the extreme western end of what is today the state of Nevada, and then north to Pyramid Lake in northwestern Nevada. The Washo tribe also controlled the nearby portions of the Carson River valley and the shores of Lake Tahoe. It was a practice of the Washo Indians to spread their members into tiny communities. Tribe members living near forests used conical-bark slabs for their homes in the winter. During warm months, many Washo simply lived in the great outdoors without benefit of housing structures. Prior to the arrival of Americans in Nevada, the Washo Indians' territory extended further east but they were driven to the western locations described above by the Paiutes. In fact, the Paiutes were a chronic threat to the Washo Indians even after the arrival of Americans in Nevada. When hostilities broke out, the Washo, being so small in number (estimated at 900 members as of 1859), invariably lost. Starting about 1860, while Americans were establishing Nevada as a territory of the United States, the Paiutes forced a series of unreasonable demands on the Washo. The Paiutes forbade the Washo to own horses (and they strictly enforced this edict) and they compressed the territory which they permitted the Washo to occupy into a narrow area of land between Reno and Carson City, Nevada. The United States government never has seen fit to establish an Indian reservation for the Washo, so they subsist as best they can, taking minimum wage jobs, when they are available. However, unlike many Indian tribes, the Washo have managed to survive into the late 20th century. Their population (still located primarily between Reno and Carson City, Nevada) was estimated at about 900 in the 1970's. The names "Washoe" and "Washo" are the White American forms for this tribe's name which was approximately *Washiu*, which means "person." This county was created on November 25, 1861, while Nevada was a territory. Just a few years later, when preparations were being made to admit this new territory to statehood, some suggested that the new state's name should be Washoe.

1729 *White Pine County*

White Pine Mining District— Soon after

the 1865 discovery of silver, copper and lead in the White Pine Mountains here, a mining district was established, which was named for those White Pine Mountains. By 1869 thousands of prospectors had come to the area in search of riches and a new county was established to service that population. Thus White Pine County was created in 1869, named for the White Pine Mining District, which was named for the White Pine Mountains. In all cases, the name was incorrect. The pine trees which are conspicuous on the White Pine Mountains are not white pine trees but bristlecone pine trees (genus *Pinus*; species *aristata*). The bristlecone pines are not only conspicuous here, but they are truly unique botanical specimens. Some of the individual bristlecone pine trees now far surpass the age of redwood and giant sequoia trees, which are famed for their longevity. In fact, some individual bristlecone pine trees on Nevada's White Pine Mountain range, had been alive 1,000 to 2,000 years when Jesus Christ was born and they are still living. These bristlecone pines are the slowest growing and longest-lived organisms on planet Earth. The oldest specimens are found near an elevation of 10,000 feet above sea level, in dry, rocky wilderness areas. These trees grow very slowly, adding but an inch per century to their girth. With so little tissue to nourish, the bristlecone pines can essentially hibernate during lean years. These unusual trees are found only in the United States and only in southwestern regions of our country.

REFERENCES

Abel, James F. "Gen. Fred Lander, Pioneer Nevadan." *Nevada State Journal*, June 5, 1949.

Addenbrooke, Alice B. *The Enchanted Fort*. Sparks, Nevada, Western Printing & Publishing Co., 1968.

Alotta, Robert L. *Signposts & Settlers: The History of Place Names West of the Rockies*. Chicago, Bonus Books, Inc., 1994.

Angel, Myron. *History of Nevada*. Oakland, Thompson & West, 1881.

"Archimedes." *The World of Mathematics*, Vol. 1. New York: 1956.

"Aurora." Subject file, Nevada Historical Society, Reno, Nevada.

Averett, Walter R. *Directory of Southern Nevada Place Names*. 1962.

Bauer, K. Jack. *The Mexican War: 1846–1848*. New York, Macmillan Publishing Co., Inc., 1974.

Bonar, John A. *Pride, Power, Progress: Wyoming's First 100 Years*. Casper, Wyoming, Wyoming Historical Press, 1987.

Braga, Marcia de. *Dig No Graves*. Sparks, Nevada, Western Printing & Publishing Co., 1964.

Bray, Florence L. "The Nomenclature in Lyon County." *Biennial Report of the Nevada Historical Society*, Vol. 3. Carson City, Nevada: 1913.

California Nevada Tour Book. Heathrow, Florida, AAA Publishing, 1997.

Carlson, Helen S. *Nevada Place Names: A Geographical Dictionary*. Reno, Nevada, University of Nevada Press, 1974.

Carpenter, Allan. *The Encyclopedia of the Far West*. New York, Facts on File, 1991.

Cleator, Cora M. "The Nomenclature in Douglas, Ormsby & Storey Counties." *Biennial Report of the Nevada Historical Society*, Vol. 3. Carson City, Nevada: 1913.

Crandall, Jim. "The Battle Born Fort." *Nevada*, Vol. 45, No. 2. Carson City, Nevada: March-April, 1985.

Davis, Sam P. *The History of Nevada*. Reno, Nevada, Elms Publishing Co., 1913.

Downs, James F. *The Two Worlds of the Washo: An Indian Tribe of California & Nevada*. New York, Holt, Rinehart & Winston, 1966.

"Edward F. Storey." Subject file, Nevada Historical Society, Reno, Nevada.

Elliott, Russell R. "The Early History of White Pine County, Nevada: 1865–1887." M.A. Thesis, University of Washington, Seattle, Washington, 1938.

Elliott, Russell R. *History of Nevada*. Lincoln, University of Nebraska Press, 1987.

Emerson, Connie. "Eureka." *Nevada Magazine*, Vol. 44, No. 4. Carson City, Nevada: July-August, 1984.

Eureka and Its Resources: A Complete History of Eureka County, Nevada. Reno, Nevada, University of Nevada Press, 1982.

Fairfield, Asa M. *Fairfield's Pioneer History of Lassen County, California*. San Francisco, H. S. Crocker Co., 1916.

"Fort Churchill." *Nevada Magazine*, Carson City, Nevada: 1979.

Fortey, Richard. "Eureka!" *The American Scholar*, Vol. 67, No. 2. Washington, D.C.: Spring, 1998.

Frazer, Robert W. *Forts of the West*. Norman, University of Oklahoma Press, 1965.

"General John H. Pershing." *Nebraska History & Record of Pioneer Days*, Vol. 1, No. 1. Lincoln, Nebraska: February, 1918.

Glass, Mary Ellen & Al Glass. *Touring Nevada*. Reno, Nevada, University of Nevada Press, 1983.

Goff, Jeff H. "Short Studies of Georgia Place Names." *Georgia Mineral Newsletter*, Vol. 10, No. 2. Atlanta, Georgia: Summer, 1957.

Gudde. Erwin G. *California Place Names*. Berkeley, University of California Press, 1965.

Hasch, Vera Ellen. "The Nomenclature in Churchill County." *Biennial Report of the Nevada Historical Society*, Vol. 3. Carson City, Nevada: 1913.

Hearne Brothers Official Earth Science Polyconic Projection Map of Nevada. Detroit, Michigan, Hearne Brothers.

Hodge, Frederick W. *Handbook of American Indians North of Mexico*. Totowa, New Jersey, Rowman & Littlefield, 1975.

Hulse, James W. "The Afterlife of St. Mary's County: or Utah's Penumbra in Eastern Nevada." *Utah Historical Quarterly*, Vol. 55, No. 3. Salt Lake City, Utah: Summer, 1987.

Hulse, James W. *Lincoln County, Nevada: 1864–1909*. Reno, Nevada, University of Nevada Press, 1971.

Hulse, James W. *The Nevada Adventure*. Reno, Nevada, University of Nevada Press, 1969.

Jones, Florence L., & John F. Cahlan. *Water: A History of Las Vegas*. Las Vegas, Nevada, Las Vegas Valley Water District, 1975.

Koontz, John. *Political History of Nevada*. Carson City, Nevada, 1965.

Leigh, Rufus W. *Nevada Place Names: Their Origin & Significance*. Las Vegas, Southern Nevada Historical Society & Lake Mead Natural History Association, 1964.

"Lyon, Captain Robert." Subject file, Nevada Historical Society, Reno, Nevada.

Mack, Effie M. *Nevada: A History of the State from the Earliest Times through the Civil War*. Glendale, California, Arthur H. Clarke Co., 1936.

Mack, Effie M., & Byrd W. Sawyer. *Our State: Nevada*. Caldwell, Idaho, Caxton Printers, Ltd., 1940.

McLoughlin, Denis. *Wild & Wooly: An Encyclopedia of the Old West*. Garden City, New York, Doubleday & Co., Inc., 1975.

Marsh, Andrew J. *Letters from Nevada Territory: 1861–1862*. State of Nevada, Legislative Council Bureau, 1972.

Morgan, Dale L. *The Humboldt*. New York, Farrar & Rinehart, Inc., 1943.

Morganthau, Tom, et al. "A Basin of Beauty: The Latest National Park off a Lonely Nevada Highway, Boasts the Oldest Living Thing on Earth." *Newsweek*. New York: August 24, 1987.

"Muench's Gallery." *Nevada*, Vol. 43, No. 5. Carson City, Nevada: September-October, 1983.

"Muench's Gallery." *Nevada*, Vol. 45, No. 6. Carson City, Nevada: November-December, 1985.

Nevada: The Silver State. Carson City, Nevada, Western States Historical Publishers, Inc., 1970.

"Of Captain Storey on Memorial Day: Brave Pioneer Was Mortally Wounded on June 2, 1860 at the Memorable Battle of Pyramid Lake." *Virginia Chronicle.*

Paher, Stanley W., & Kathryn Totton, *Fort Churchill: Nevada Military Outpost of the 1860's.* Las Vegas, Nevada, Nevada Publications, 1981.

Patterson, Edna. *Who Named It?* Elko Independent, 1964.

Patterson, Edna B., et al. *Nevada's Northeast Frontier.* Sparks, Nevada, Western Printing & Publishing Co., 1969.

Pershing, John J. *My Experiences in the World War.* Blue Ridge Summit, Pennsylvania, TAB Books, Inc., 1931.

Picker, Marc. "A Look at White Pine County: Welcome to Bristlecone Country." *Ely Daily Times,* June 9, 1983.

Rippetoe, Judith M., Nevada Historical Society, Reno, Nevada. Letter to the author dated November 19, 1979.

Ruhlen, George. "Early Nevada Forts." *Nevada Historical Society Quarterly,* Vol. 7, Nos. 3–4. Reno, Nevada. 1964.

Schulman, Edmund. "Bristlecone Pine: Oldest Known Living Thing." *National Geographic Magazine,* Vol. 113, No. 3. Washington, D.C.: March, 1958.

Soldier & Brave: Indian & Military Affairs in the Trans-Mississippi West: Including a Guide to Historic Sites & Landmarks. New York, Harper & Row, 1963.

Swackhamer, William D. *Political History of Nevada.* Carson City, Nevada, 1974.

Thrapp, Dan L. *Encyclopedia of Frontier Biography.* Lincoln, University of Nebraska Press, 1988.

Thrapp, Dan L. *Encyclopedia of Frontier Biography: Supplemental Volume 4.* Spokane, Washington, Arthur H. Clark Co., 1994.

Totton, Kathryn. "The History of Fort Churchill." Report submitted to Nevada Division of State Parks, April, 1978.

Vexler, Robert I. *Chronology & Documentary Handbook of the State of Nevada.* Dobbs Ferry, New York, Oceana Publications, Inc., 1978.

Work Projects Administration. *Origin of Place Names: Nevada.* Reno, Nevada, Nevada State Department of Highways & Nevada State Department of Education, 1941.

Wren, Thomas. *A History of the State of Nevada.* New York, Lewis Publishing Co., 1904.

New Hampshire

(10 counties)

1730 *Belknap County*

Jeremy Belknap (1744–1798)— Belknap was born in Boston on June 4, 1744, and after graduating from of Harvard, Belknap moved to Dover, New Hampshire, where he was ordained as pastor of the Congregational Church. At that time the Congregational Church was the established church of the colony of New Hampshire and only persons holding exemptions could escape paying tithes to the Congregational Church. Reverend Belknap was one of the four most prominent Congregational ministers in New Hampshire. In 1775 he was appointed chaplain for New Hampshire's Revolutionary troops and although Belknap supported the American colonies' revolt against England, he declined this appointment as military chaplain for health reasons. Essentially all of the Congregational ministers in Colonial New Hampshire supported the Revolution against England. These Congregational clergymen feared that New Hampshire's colonial governor, Sir John Wentworth (1737–1820), would attempt to establish the Episcopal Church (i.e., the Church of England) as the established church of New Hampshire. In 1787 Belknap moved to Boston, where he served as the pastor of the Federal Street Church. Belknap was sympathetic to the problems of Indians and Blacks in colonial America, he spoke out against the evil of slavery and he did what he could to help Indians and Blacks living in his local area. In addition to his duties as a member of the clergy, Belknap was a writer and a historian. He was the founder of an antiquarian society which grew to become the Massachusetts Historical Society and he produced the first history of New Hampshire, and thus was New Hampshire's first historian. On February 17, 1791, the usually parsimonious legislature of the state of New Hampshire generously voted to award Reverend Belknap 50 pounds "…as an encouragement for his laudable undertaking of compiling and perfecting the history of this state." Belknap also wrote on religious and biographical topics. From 1787 until his sudden death on June 20, 1798, Reverend Belknap was the pastor of the Federal Street Church in Boston. This New Hampshire county was created and named in his honor on December 22, 1840.

1731 *Carroll County*

Charles Carroll (1737–1832)— Carroll was a native of Maryland and he represented that state in the Continental Congress. He was one of the signers of the Declaration of Independence and he later represented Maryland as a U.S. senator in the first congress of the United States. Carroll lived to be the last surviving signer of the Declaration of Independence and several states recognized that distinction by naming counties for him. Carroll County, New Hampshire, was created and named in his honor on December 22, 1840.

1732 *Cheshire County*

Cheshire County, England— This county's name was chosen by New Hampshire's colonial governor, Sir John Wentworth (1737–1820), and it was created by the New Hampshire legislature on April 29, 1769. The king of England, King George III (1738–1820), approved the creation of this county and its name on March 19, 1771. Cheshire was one of five original counties in the British colony of New Hampshire. According to some sources on the history of New Hampshire, Governor Wentworth chose all five of New Hampshire's original county names in compliment to his friends among the English nobility. Four of New Hampshire's original five counties were definitely given the title of an English nobleman. However, it is far from clear that this is true of the name Cheshire. According to all but two, out of dozens of sources consulted, Cheshire County, New Hampshire was named for Cheshire County, England. One of the two sources which

disagrees is the 1975 edition of the *Manual for the General Court of the State of New Hampshire*. That manual implies that Cheshire County, New Hampshire was named for Admiral Edward Vernon (1684–1757), or Admiral Edward Vernon (1723–1794), whose home was in Cheshire County, England. The other dissenter is Frank B. Sanborn. In his history of New Hampshire published in 1904, Sanborn states that the county was named for the earl of Cheshire. Since all other sources consulted state that Cheshire County, New Hampshire, was named for Cheshire County, England, it follows that if Governor Wentworth intended to honor either of the two Admiral Edward Vernons or the earl of Cheshire, he did so indirectly, by naming the New Hampshire county for Cheshire County, England.

Cheshire County, England — This county, in western England, has a harsh climate in spite of the moderating influence of the adjacent Irish Sea. The county is about 60 miles long and its width is said to be 30 miles. Cheshire County consists primarily of flat land with hills and uplands confined primarily to the county's borders. At the beginning of the 17th century, the county was still heavily wooded. Extensive cattle grazing has taken place in the county and Cheshire County, England, is known for the high quality of its cheese. Sheep are also grazed in Cheshire County and salt is one of the county's important products. For a period of time Cheshire County's ports had a virtual monopoly on the trade between England and Ireland. By the middle of the middle of the 20th century, Cheshire County's population was slightly over 900,000 persons crowded into just 928 square miles. An earlier name for this county appears in the Domesday Book of A.D. 1086 as *Cesrtre Scire*, which meant "the province of the city of Chester." Chester is the county seat of England's Cheshire County. The abbreviated version of that ancient name was merely *Cestre*, similar to the present Cheshire.

1733 *Coos County*

Uncertain — This county occupies the entire northern end of New Hampshire, filling perhaps one fifth of the state's land area. Coos County was created on December 24, 1803. All sources consulted agree that this is an Indian name (although some of these sources mention, in passing, that there is an unrelated Coos in *The Holy Bible*), and only two possibilities are given for the translation of the county's Indian name: (1) "pine trees" (or "place of pines") and (2) "crooked." The Connecticut River forms almost the entire western boundary of Coos County and the translation "crooked" refers to the configuration of the Connecticut River at some points. One source tells us that *Coos* was the Indians' name for the Connecticut River. Otis G. Hammond wrote an article entitled "New Hampshire County Names," which appeared in the January, 1909, issue of *The Magazine of History*. In that article Hammond stated that this Indian word meant "crooked," and referred to "the winding course of the Connecticut River at Lancaster [which was originally called Upper Cohoes], and at Haverhill [originally Lower Cohoes]." The Haverhill referred to by Otis Hammond is in Grafton County, New Hampshire. Lancaster is in Coos County. A large number of sources agree with Hammond that the name *Coos* derived from an Indian word which meant "crooked." However, about an equally large number of sources translate the Indian name as "pine trees" or "place of pines." Pine trees are certainly common in this portion of New Hampshire. The Indians had no written language so it was left to the Whites to render the Indians' words in writing. Several versions of the original Indian word which we now call Coos have been in circulation. These versions include Cohoes, mentioned by Otis G. Hammond, Cohoss, Cohos and Cowass, There is a second Coos County in our nation. That county is in Oregon but it is of no help in translating this New Hampshire county's name. Coos County, Oregon, also has an Indian name but it is of local origin and refers to an Indian tribe that lived in the area of Coos Bay in the Pacific Northwest.

1734 *Grafton County*

Augustus H. Fitzroy, Duke of Grafton (1735–1811) — This county's name was chosen by New Hampshire's colonial governor, Sir John Wentworth (1737–1820), and it was created by the New Hampshire legislature on April 29, 1769. The king of England, King George III (1738–1820), approved the creation of this county and its name on March 19, 1771. Grafton was one of five original counties in the British colony of New Hampshire. According to some sources on the history of New Hampshire, Governor Wentworth chose all five of New Hampshire's original county names in compliment to members of the English nobility. Although it is not entirely clear that this is true for Cheshire County, it is true for the other four counties, including Grafton County. Augustus Henry Fitzroy was born on October 1, 1735, and was educated at Cambridge. In 1756 he entered parliament and he inherited the title duke of Grafton in 1757. He rose rapidly in English politics and came to wield considerable power. In 1765 he became secretary of state for the northern department. As a result of the continuing illness of William Pitt, Earl of Chatham (1708–1778), Grafton was made first minister in 1768 and served in that capacity until January, 1770, when he resigned. In March, 1782, he joined the second cabinet of Prime Minister Charles Watson-Wentworth, Marquis of Rockingham (1730–1782), as lord privy seal. Prime Minister Rockingham died on July 1, 1782, and Grafton retired from public life at that time. Much earlier, when he had been a student at Cambridge, Augustus Fitzroy made it known that he was less than enthusiastic about the Anglican (Episcopal) Church, the state church of England. In his retirement years he wrote works defending Unitarianism.

1735 *Hillsborough County*

Wills Hill, Earl of Hillsborough (1718–1793) — This county's name was chosen by New Hampshire's colonial governor, Sir John Wentworth (1737–1820), and it was created by the New Hampshire legislature on April 29, 1769. The king of England, King George III (1738–1820), approved the creation of this county and its name on March 19, 1771. Hillsborough was one of five original counties in the British colony of New Hampshire. According to some sources on the history of New Hampshire, Governor Wentworth chose all five of New Hampshire's original county names in compliment to members of the English nobility. Although it is not entirely clear that this is true for Cheshire County, it is true for the other four counties, including Hillsborough County. Hill was born on May 30, 1718, at Fairford, England. In May, 1742, he succeeded his father as viscount Hillsborough, in the peerage of Ireland. He took a seat in the Irish house of peers in 1743, was made an Irish earl in 1751, and took a seat in the privy council in 1754. After King George III took the English throne in 1760, Hill served as president and first commissioner of England's board of trade and plantations and he was principal secretary of state for the American department during the American Revolution. Hill pursued a harsh policy towards America.

1736 *Merrimack County*

Merrimack River— This county in south-central New Hampshire was created on July 1, 1823, and named for the 110 mile-long Merrimack River, which flows through it. A number of New Hampshire streams and rivers provide water for the Merrimack River, but those waters do not acquire the name Merrimack until they reach a point near Franklin, New Hampshire, in Merrimack County. There Pemigewasset and Winnipeasaukee Rivers join to form the river named the Merrimack. From Franklin, New Hampshire, the Merrimack flows south through the state and continues in a southern direction as it crosses the New Hampshire–Massachusetts border at Nashua, New Hampshire. In Massachusetts the Merrimack flows in a southern direction only a few miles before making a dramatic turn to the northeast. It flows in that direction until its waters enters the Atlantic Ocean at Newburyport, Massachusetts. The name *Merrimack* is of Indian origin and its meaning is uncertain. Among the possible translations mentioned are "strong (or swift) river," "profound river," "at the deep place" and "sturgeon."

1737 *Rockingham County*

Charles Watson-Wentworth, Marquis of Rockingham (1730–1782)— This county's name was chosen by New Hampshire's colonial governor, Sir John Wentworth (1737–1820) and it was created by the New Hampshire legislature on April 29, 1769. The king of England, King George III (1738–1820), approved the creation of this county and its name on March 19, 1771. Rockingham was one of five original counties in the British colony of New Hampshire. According to some sources on the history of New Hampshire, Governor Wentworth chose all five of New Hampshire's original county names in compliment to members of the English nobility. Although it is not entirely clear that this is true for Cheshire County, it is true for the other four counties, including Rockingham County. Later, in 1773, Rockingham successfully intervened on behalf of New Hampshire's colonial Governor John Wentworth in a serious legal dispute. Charles Watson-Wentworth was born on May 13, 1730, at Wentworth Park, in England. He attended Westminster school and served in the English army against Scottish insurgents. Young Watson-Wentworth came from a family with good political connections and shortly after his 30th birthday he was given the highest

honor of the English court, the Garter. In 1765 he became England's prime minister, while King George III was on the throne. As prime minister, he infuriated the king by securing the repeal of the Stamp act and softening the American colonies' grievances on matters of commerce. This term as prime minister lasted only from 1765 to 1766. However, sixteen years later, Rockingham returned as prime minister. His goals throughout much of this period from 1765 until his death on July 1, 1782, were rather extreme. These goals included resolution of the grievances of the American colonies, even if that meant the end of British sovereignty over of those colonies, sharply reduced power for the English monarch and, at all cost, avoidance of armed warfare with the American colonies. It seems safe to speculate that news of Rockingham's death in 1782 caused no grief to King George III.

1738 *Strafford County*

Thomas Wentworth, Earl of Strafford (1593–1641)— This county's name was chosen by New Hampshire's colonial governor, Sir John Wentworth (1737–1820) and it was created by the New Hampshire legislature on April 29, 1769. The king of England, King George III (1738–1820), approved the creation of this county and its name on March 19, 1771. Strafford was one of five original counties in the British colony of New Hampshire. According to some sources on the history of New Hampshire, Governor Wentworth chose all five of New Hampshire's original county names in compliment to members of the English nobility. Although it is not entirely clear that this is true for Cheshire County, it is true for the other four counties, including Strafford County. Thomas Wentworth, Earl of Strafford, had been a relative of New Hampshire's colonial governor, John Wentworth. Thomas Wentworth, was born in England on April 13, 1593, educated at Cambridge and first entered England's parliament in 1614. He opposed war with Spain and showed hostility toward Puritanism. By the late 1620's Wentworth had become the virtual leader of the house of commons. King Charles I (1600–1649) soon made Wentworth a court favorite and honors were heaped upon him. Wentworth urged force in England's dealings with Ireland and Scotland. In May, 1639, he became the informal chief advisor to the king and in 1640 he was made baron Raby and earl of Strafford (the first earl of Strafford). C. V. Wedgwood's biography of Strafford, published in 1962, tells us

that Strafford was a ruthless servant of King Charles I, who came to be the most powerful and most hated man in the British Isles. That may overstate the case a bit but it is true that Strafford was impeached by the house of commons and sent to the Tower of London for execution in 1640. That impeachment was abandoned but in the spring of 1641 a bill of attainder was passed against him by both houses of parliament. King Charles I sought to save Strafford's life but the king's plea was ignored by parliament and Strafford was executed on Tower Hill in May, 1641.

1739 *Sullivan County*

John Sullivan (1740–1795)— The location of John Sullivan's birth is given variously as Berwick, Maine, and Somersworth, New Hampshire. The two towns are adjacent. He practiced law in New Hampshire and represented New Hampshire in the Continental Congress. During the American Revolution Sullivan served as a brigadier-general and later was promoted to major-general. John Sullivan served with distinction in a number of important engagements of the Revolution until late 1779 when he resigned. He then represented New Hampshire again in the Continental Congress. Sullivan later served as attorney general of New Hampshire, president (or governor) of New Hampshire and was a member of the New Hampshire convention that ratified the proposed federal constitution. He also was speaker of New Hampshire's house of representatives. In 1789 President George Washington appointed John Sullivan as judge of the U.S. district court of New Hampshire and Sullivan held that position until his death in 1795. This county was created and named in General Sullivan's honor on July 5, 1827.

REFERENCES

Birkenhead, Earl of. *Strafford*. London, Hutchison & Co., 1938.

Bouton, Nathaniel. *Documents & Records Relating to the Province of New Hampshire: 1764–1776*. Nashua, Orren C. Moore, State Printer, 1873.

Child, Hamilton. *Gazetteer of Grafton County, New Hampshire*. Syracuse, New York, Syracuse Journal Co., 1886.

Clements, John. *New Hampshire Facts*. Dallas, Texas. Clements Research, Inc., 1987.

Colby, Fred M. "The Nomenclature of Some New Hampshire Towns." *The Magazine of History*, Vol. 11, No. 3. New York: March, 1910.

Coolidge, A. J., & J. B. Mansfield. *History & Description of New England.* Boston, Austin J. Coolidge, 1860.

Corning, Howard M. *Dictionary of Oregon History.* Portland, Oregon, Binford & Mort, 1989.

Currie, Andrew M. *Dictionary of British Place Names.* London, Tiger Books International, 1994.

Daniell, Jere R., Chairman-Department of History, Dartmouth College, Hanover, New Hampshire. Letter to the author dated August 18, 1980.

Daniell, Jere R. *Colonial New Hampshire.* Millwood, New York, KTO Press, 1981.

Douglas-Lithgow, R. A. *Dictionary of American-Indian Place & Proper Names in New England.* Salem, Massachusetts, Salem Press, 1909.

Falkus, Christopher. *The Life & Times of Charles II.* Garden City, New York, Doubleday & Co., 1972.

Farmer, J., & J. B. Moore. *Collections: Topographical, Historical & Biographical, Relating Principally to New Hampshire.* Concord, Hill & Moore, 1822.

Fogg, Alonzo J. *The Statistics & Gazetteer of New Hampshire.* Concord, New Hampshire, D. L. Guernsey, 1874.

Gardner, William M. *State of New Hampshire Manual for the General Court: 1977.* Concord, New Hampshire, 1977.

Goodwin, Del, & Dorcas Chaffee. *Perspectives '76: Being a Compendium of Useful Knowledge about Old-Time Vermont & New Hampshire.* Hanover, New Hampshire, Regional Center for Education & Training, 1975.

Hall, Benjamin H. *History of Eastern Vermont.* New York, D. Appleton & Co., 1858.

Hammond, Otis G. "New Hampshire County Names." *The Magazine of History,* Vol. 9, No. 1. New York: January, 1909.

Hawkyard, Alasdair. *The Counties of Britain: A Tudor Atlas by John Speed.* London, England, Pavillion Books, Ltd., 1995.

Hayward, John. *Gazetteer of New Hampshire.* Boston, John P. Jewett, 1849.

Hazlett, Charles A. *History of Rock-ingham County, New Hampshire.* Chicago, Richmond-Arnold Publishing Co., 1915.

Hoffman, Ross J. S. *The Marquis: A Study of Lord Rockingham, 1730–1782.* New York, Fordham University Press, 1973.

Holden, Raymond P. *The Merrimack.* New York, Rinehart & Co., Inc., 1958.

Huden, John C. *Indian Place Names of New England.* New York, Museum of the American Indian, Heye Foundation, 1962.

Hunt, Elmer M. *New Hampshire Town Names & Whence They Came.* Peterborough, New Hampshire, William L. Bauhan, 1970.

Hurd, D. Hamilton. *History of Cheshire & Sullivan Counties, New Hampshire.* Philadelphia, J. W. Lewis & Co., 1886.

Hurd, D. Hamilton. *History of Rockingham & Strafford Counties, New Hampshire.* Philadelphia, J. W. Lewis & Co., 1882.

Kirsch, George B. "Jeremy Belknap and the Coming of the Revolution." *Historical New Hampshire,* Vol. 29, No. 3. Concord, New Hampshire: Fall, 1974.

Kirsch, George B. "Jeremy Belknap and the Problem of Blacks & Indians in Early America." *Historical New Hampshire,* Vol. 34, Nos. 3 & 4. Concord, New Hampshire: Fall & Winter, 1979.

McFarland, Asa. "Names of Counties & Towns in New Hampshire." *Granite Monthly,* Vol. 1. Dover, New Hampshire: 1877–1878.

Miller, Lillian B. *The Dye is Now Cast: The Road to American Independence, 1774–1776.* Washington, D.C., Smithsonian Institution Press, 1975.

Mills, A. D. *A Dictionary of English Place Names.* Oxford, Oxford University Press, 1991.

Morison, Elizabeth F., & Elting E. Morison. *New Hampshire: A Bicentennial History.* New York, W. W. Norton & Co., Inc., 1976.

Moule, Thomas. *The County Maps of Old England.* London, Studio Editions, 1990.

New Hampshire Register & Legislative Manual: 1980. Portland, Maine, Tower Publishing Co., 1980.

Powers, Grant. *Historical Sketches of the Discovery, Settlement & Progress of Events in the Coos Country and Vicinity.* Haverhill, New Hampshire, J. F. C. Hayes, 1841.

Purcell, L. Edward. *Who Was Who in the American Revolution.* New York, Facts on File Inc., 1993.

Quinlan, James E. *History of Sullivan County.* Liberty, New York, W. T. Morgans & Co., 1873.

Sanborn, Edwin D. *History of New Hampshire.* Manchester, New Hampshire, John B. Clarke, 1875.

Sanborn, Frank B. *New Hampshire: An Epitome of Popular Government.* Boston, Houghton Mifflin & Co., 1904.

Scales, John. *History of Strafford County, New Hampshire.* Chicago, Richmond-Arnold Publishing Co., 1914.

Stark, Robert L. *State of New Hampshire Manual for the General Court: 1975.* Concord, New Hampshire, 1975.

Swift, Esther M. *Vermont Place-Names.* Brattleboro, Vermont, Stephen Greene Press, 1977.

Upton, Richard F. *Revolutionary New Hampshire.* Hanover, New Hampshire, Dartmouth College Publications, 1936.

Vexler, Robert I. *Chronology & Documentary Handbook of the State of New Hampshire.* Dobbs Ferry, New York, Oceana Publications, Inc., 1978.

Wedgwood, C. V. *Thomas Wentworth: First Earl of Strafford: 1593–1641: A Revaluation.* New York, Macmillan Co., 1962.

Wiley, Benjamin G. *Incidents in White Mountain History.* Boston, Nathaniel Noyes, 1856.

Wise, L. F., & E. W. Egan. *Kings, Rulers & Statesmen.* New York, Sterling Publishing Co., Inc., 1967.

Work Projects Administration. *Inventory of the County Archives of New Hampshire-Coos County.* Manchester, New Hampshire, 1940.

Works Progress Administration. *New Hampshire: A Guide to the Granite State.* Boston, Houghton Mifflin Co., 1938.

New Jersey

(21 counties)

1740 Atlantic County

Atlantic Ocean— This county in southeastern New Jersey borders on the Atlantic Ocean and it was named for that enormous body of water, when the county was created on February 7, 1837. The Atlantic Ocean separates the continents of Europe and Africa in the east from the continents of North and South America in the west. Of the earth's oceans, the Atlantic is second in size to the Pacific. Its area, excluding dependent seas, is about 32 million square miles and with the dependent seas included, its area is 41 million square miles. Although the Atlantic Ocean is not the world's largest ocean, because of the slope of the land of the four continents which feed water to it, the Atlantic Ocean has by far the greatest drainage area of any ocean. Its drainage area is about four times that of the Pacific Ocean. The ocean's name, *Atlantic*, derived from Greek mythology and means "the sea of Atlas," a Greek God. New Jersey has a second county named for the Atlantic Ocean. That county is Ocean County, created on February 15, 1850.

1741 *Bergen County*

Village of Bergen, New Jersey— The Dutch came to trade in what is now the state of New Jersey as early as 1618. In 1658 a patent was granted by Peter Stuyvesant (1592–1672), the Dutch administrator in America, permitting certain Dutch patentees to establish a tract in northeastern New Jersey and in 1660 these Dutch patentees exercised that patent by founding the village of Bergen. This was the first permanent settlement by Europeans in what is now the state of New Jersey. Bergen was laid out as an 800 square-foot fortified community, bounded by a wooden palisade. Land outside the enclosure was farmed and cattle grazed there although the cattle were brought within the wooden protective walls at night. This ancient village of Bergen is now part of the territory of the municipality of Jersey City, New Jersey, which is the county seat of the present Hudson County, New Jersey. Jersey City lies just across the Hudson River from New York City's Manhattan Island. The original square, which comprised the village of Bergen, is preserved in the present Jersey City, New Jersey. Logic tells us that the Dutch would have chosen a name from their homeland, the Netherlands, when they named this first permanent settlement in New Jersey (rather, for example, than naming it for a Scandinavian city). Most authorities on the history, geography and place names of New Jersey agree that this is precisely what these ancient Dutch men did; i.e., the Dutch named their settlement Bergen for the city of Bergen op Zoom in the southern part of the Netherlands, in Europe. It must be noted that there is a minority opinion which holds that the original settlement of Bergen here was named for Bergen, a seaport city in Norway rather than for Bergen op Zoom in the Netherlands. Those holding that view offer no compelling evidence but

merely mention that perhaps this was done because of the presence of some Swedes and Norwegians in the group that settled here. This county was created on March 1, 1683, just 23 years after the village was established.

1742 *Burlington County*

Town of Burlington, New Jersey— Burlington County was created on May 17, 1694, and named for the town of Burlington, within its borders. That town, on the Delaware River, just east of Philadelphia, Pennsylvania, is still within Burlington County, New Jersey, and now has a population of about 10,000. The town, which was laid out in 1677, was settled by Quakers, from England and it had two earlier names before its present name, Burlington, was fixed. The earlier names were New Beverly and, later, Bridlington. The name Bridlington was chosen in honor of the town of Bridlington in Yorkshire, England. (Most of the Quaker settlers had come from two sections of England: London and Yorkshire.) A map drawn in 1682 shows this New Jersey town's name as Bridlington. When the New Jersey town's name was changed from Bridlington to Burlington, the new name still honored Bridlington, England, but its spelling was changed to conform more closely with the oral pronunciation of the name. The town of Burlington in New Jersey was a very important one in our nation's early history. In 1681 the assembly of the province of West Jersey selected the town of Burlington as the capital city of their colony.

1743 *Camden County*

Village of Camden, New Jersey— Camden County was created on March 13, 1844, and named for the village of Camden, New Jersey. That village had been founded as a ferry landing about 1772, and initially its name was Cooper's Creek. At that time it was in Newton township. In 1828 the village of Cooper's Creek was separated from Newton township and its name was changed to Camden. That name honored Charles Pratt, Earl of Camden (1714–1794), who had been one of the American colonies' friends in England in the era of the American Revolution. The village of Camden, just across the Delaware River from the southern end of Philadelphia, Pennsylvania, has grown to be the industrial and transportation center of southern New Jersey. Now a city with a population of about 90,000, Camden is the county seat of Camden County.

Charles Pratt, Earl of Camden (1714–

1794)— Pratt, who was born in London, England, served as attorney general and was a member of parliament. In 1761 he became chief justice of the court of common pleas and a decision that he rendered in the trial of John Wilkes concerning freedom of speech and freedom of the press made him one of the most popular men in England. A bit later, now titled Baron Camden, he became lord chancellor. He opposed England's treatment of the American colonies which earned him popularity here and was the reason that Camden, New Jersey, was later named for him. In 1786 Baron Camden was made First Earl of Camden and Viscount Bayham. He served more than ten years as president of the council.

1744 *Cape May County*

Cape May promontory, New Jersey— At New Jersey's southernmost end, at the entrance to Delaware Bay, lies a promontory, named Cape May. This cape is formed by Delaware Bay on its west and the Atlantic Ocean to the south and east. The assembly of the province of West Jersey created Cape May County on November 12, 1692, and named the county for this promontory at the southern end of the county. The cape had been named by and for the sea captain, Cornelius J. Mey, who explored this area from 1614 to the 1620's. He named the cape in his own honor in 1620 when he visited it as captain of his own vessel, the *Glad Tidings*. Some sources say that Captain Mey named everything that he discovered for himself; an exaggeration, of course, but it contains more than a little truth. The Cape May promontory is one of the oldest seacoast resorts in our nation, and during the first half of the 19th century Cape May rivaled Newport, Rhode Island, as a playground for the wealthy.

Cornelius J. Mey (–)— Cornelius Jacobsen Mey, from Doorn, in the central Netherlands, sailed in 1614 to North America. There were three to five ships in this convoy. Mey served aboard one of them, a ship named the *Fortune*. According to several accounts Mey was this ship's captain; other sources list him as navigator of the *Fortune*. Also in 1614 Mey was a member of an expedition that came around Cape May to explore the Delaware River. (Later, in 1623, Mey established the first European settlement on the east bank of the Delaware River. Twenty-four colonists were left there, at Ft. Nassau, near today's Gloucester.) In 1620, Mey returned as captain of his own ship, the

Glad Tidings, and named Cape May in his own honor and claimed the area for the Netherlands. Captain Mey named the bay of New York "Port Mey," Delaware Bay "New Port Mey," the north cape of Cape May "Cape Mey" and the south cape of Cape May "Cape Cornelius." The only name to survive, was Cape May, altered in form from "Cape Mey." Mey gave New Jersey the ultimate Dutch compliment when he pronounced the climate of New Jersey to be "like Holland." Under the terms of the organization of the Dutch West India Company, the chief power throughout all New Netherlands territory in North America was vested in a director. The first person to exercise that power as director of the Dutch West India Company (and therefore of New Netherlands) was Cornelius J. Mey, and his title was director general. In 1623 Cornelius Mey and Joriz Tienpont sailed from Europe to New Netherlands in the ship named the *New Netherlands*, carrying Protestant fugitives from the Catholic Belgian provinces. Prior to that time, the Dutch intent in acquiring territory in North America had been solely to acquire the profits to be made in trade. This 1623 colonization effort was apparently motivated primarily to discourage encroachment on New Netherlands' territory by the English in Virginia and New England. Mey held the post of director general of the Dutch West India Company for about a year in 1624 and 1625, and was succeeded in the spring of 1625 by William Verhulst.

1745 *Cumberland County*

William Augustus, Duke of Cumberland (1721–1765) — William Augustus was a son of England's King George II (1683–1760). Born on April 15, 1721, William was made a royal duke and given the tittle Duke of Cumberland in July, 1726. Cumberland was educated for the navy but was permitted to follow his preference for the army and was given the rank of major-general in 1742. He was a rather poor general and his troops were defeated in several important actions on the European continent. His only significant victory was at home, in the British Isles, where he defeated Prince Charles Edward Stuart (1720–1788), the pretender to the thrones of Scotland and England. This victory took place at Culloden, Scotland, in 1746. The duke's name is shown in most works as William Augustus, but in some the form William August is used. Cumberland County was created on January 19, 1748. Its name was chosen by England's colo-

nial governor of New Jersey, Jonathan Belcher (1682–1757). Belcher had good reason to try to curry favor in England by naming this county in honor of the son of King George II, who was England's reigning king at the time this New Jersey county was created. Jonathan Belcher had been dismissed as the colonial governor of Massachusetts and New Hampshire and was, in 1748, trying to regain his status with the crown as the colonial governor of New Jersey.

1746 *Essex County*

Essex County, England — Sources consulted are virtually unanimous in their opinion that this county was named for Essex County, England. However, there is one dissenting opinion, that of Cornelius C. Vermeule, whose article on early New Jersey place names appeared in the April, 1926, issue of the *Proceedings of the New Jersey Historical Society*. In that article, Vermeule tells us that this county was named for an English Earl of Essex, who committed suicide in prison in 1683. That Earl of Essex was Arthur Capel (1631–1683), who was made Earl of Essex in April 1661. All other sources tell us that this county, which was created by the assembly of the province of East Jersey on March 1, 1683, was named for Essex County, England.

Essex County, England — Essex County is in the eastern section of Anglia, in southern England. This seacoast county facing the European continent was an important center when it was occupied by the Roman Empire and it continued to be an important population center, containing the city of London, when the East Saxons invaded it. The name *Essex* means "territory of the East Saxons." Essex was one of the seven Anglo-Saxon kingdoms of Britain known as the Heptarchy. In the seventh century Essex was conquered by Mercia, one of the other kingdoms of the Heptarchy, and later, in the ninth century, Wessex, which had been another member of the Heptarchy, conquered it. The Essex County of today's England no longer contains London. It is about 54 miles long and some 48 miles wide. Its principal rivers are the Thames, Stour, Colne, Blackwater and Lea.

1747 *Gloucester County*

Gloucester, England and/or Gloucestershire, England — The creation of this county is unique in the annals of New Jersey history. At the time that it was created on May 28, 1686, New Jersey was divided into

two provinces, East Jersey and West Jersey. Gloucester County was not the creation of the assembly of either of those provinces but a creation by the people of the Third and Fourth Tenths, of West Jersey, who conceived their new county to be a separate governing body from either of the two Jersey provinces. They met on May 26, 1686, at Arwanus and organized their county government. The proceedings of that body were formally entered into the public records of Gloucester dated May 28, 1686. The county was named for the city of Gloucester and or the county (shire) of Gloucester (Gloucestershire), England. As was the case with Essex County, New Jersey, we again have a dissenting opinion on the origin of this county's name from the same Cornelius C. Vermeule. That opinion was expressed in his article on early New Jersey place names, which appeared in the April, 1926, issue of the *Proceedings of the New Jersey Historical Society*. In that article, Vermeule tells us that this county was named for William, Duke of Gloucester (1689–1700). This Duke of Gloucester was a son of England's Queen Anne (1665–1714) and the only child of hers who did not die at birth or in very early infancy. Queen Anne had 17 children so infant mortality was a constant issue for her. Unlike Cornelius C. Vermeule's dissenting opinion regarding the origin of Essex County, New Jersey's name, we may safely disregard his opinion concerning the origin of Gloucester County, New Jersey's name. This is because Gloucester County, New Jersey, was created in 1686 but William, Duke of Gloucester, was not born until July 24, 1689, so the county could not have been named for him.

Gloucester, England and/or Gloucestershire, England — The name derived from the Anglo-Saxon *Glou Ceaster*, meaning "A Roman camp on the site of the ancient Celtic city of Glou." This town became important to the Romans after they founded it about A.D. 97. At a later time Gloucester was the capital of Mercia, one of the seven Anglo-Saxon kingdoms of Britain known as the Heptarchy. Gloucester is the county seat of Gloucestershire, England. The county's length is 60 miles and its width is no more than 26 miles. Gloucestershire has an area of 1055.2 square miles and its population in the early 1980's was just over half a million. Its agricultural products include cider, perry, bacon, grain and dairy products. Fishing and manufacturing activities are also found in Gloucestershire. The county lies in western England on the Bristol Channel. Its rivers include the Severn, Avon and

Wye. The Severn carries tidal waves which periodically rush up Gloucester with waves up to nine feet high. Special embankments have been erected below Gloucester to protect the city from these tidal waves of the Severn. Gloucester boasts an ancient and magnificent cathedral.

1748 *Hudson County*

Hudson River and/or Henry Hudson (–)—This county, which borders on the Hudson River, was created on February 22, 1840. Sources consulted are about equally divided concerning the origin of this county's name between two possibilities: (1) the Hudson River and (2) Henry Hudson, the early naval explorer for whom the Hudson River was named.

Hudson River—The lower end of the Hudson River separates New Jersey from the state of New York but for most of its 306 mile length, the Hudson's waters are confined to New York state. The Hudson River rises in the Adirondack Mountains in eastern New York and flows almost due south for the majority of its journey to Upper New York Bay, an inlet of the Atlantic Ocean, which borders on Hudson County, New Jersey, and on New York City. The Hudson River is navigable as far north as Troy, New York. The largest tributary of the Hudson River is the Mohawk River. The Mohawk flows generally from west to east and enters the Hudson River at Cohoes, New York, just above Troy, New York. This configuration of rivers, with the Hudson River on the Atlantic Ocean and the Mohawk River, its principal tributary, with waters extending some 150 miles west of the Hudson, was the cornerstone of the Erie Canal. That canal formed a transportation network which permitted shipment of goods from the agricultural regions of our country near the Great Lakes all the way to the Atlantic Ocean. The Erie Canal was vital to the development of our young nation. The Hudson River was discovered by Henry Hudson, by accident, in 1609 while he was trying to discover a water route from the Atlantic Ocean to the East Indies. Although the Hudson River was discovered by an employee of the Dutch, that employee was an Englishman. The Dutch refrained from naming the river in Hudson's honor. They had several names for the Hudson River but it was not until the English gained control of this area that it was renamed "Hudson's Riv r"(sic).

Henry Hudson (–)—Little is known of this English sea captain's early life and we have only approximate knowledge of the time and place of his death. In May, 1607 he set sail on the *Hopewell* on behalf of the English Muscovy Company to discover a northeast passage to the Orient. That voyage failed. It reached only Greenland and the Spitsbergen archipelago of Norway on the Arctic Ocean. He returned to England in 1607. In 1608 Hudson made a second unsuccessful voyage on the *Hopewell* but because he was blocked by ice everywhere he returned and ended this mission in August, 1608. Undaunted by these two failures, Hudson secured employment from the Dutch East India Company, again trying to find a water route from the Atlantic Ocean to the East Indies. It was on this 1609 journey that he discovered the Hudson River. This trip took him to the shores of northern Norway and to North America's Virginia coast, up the Delaware River, and then north along the Atlantic Ocean shore of New Jersey. Further north he discovered the harbor of New York City and continued up the Hudson River and anchored near today's Albany, New York. When he returned to England, the British government forbade him to undertake further explorations for foreigners. In 1610 he began a fourth and final journey, financed by English money, which discovered Hudson Bay. After being iced in for the winter followed by a few weeks of exploration, Hudson's crew mutinied, and in 1611 he was set adrift by them, without provisions, and Hudson was never seen again.

1749 *Hunterdon County*

Robert Hunter (–1734)—Hunter was born in Scotland at Hunterson in the shire of Ayr. The date of his birth is unknown. He served in the British army and fought in the War of Spanish Succession, participating in the British victory at the 1704 battle of Blenheim. By the time Hunter left the British army he had been promoted to the rank of lieutenant-colonel. Named lieutenant-governor of England's North American colony of Virginia, Hunter was captured at sea in 1707 by a privateer. By the time he returned to England, his Virginia commission had expired. In October, 1709, England made Hunter captain general and governor-in-chief of her colonies of New York and New Jersey. He arrived here to discharge his new duties in June, 1710. Hunter served as England's colonial governor of both New Jersey and New York from 1710 to 1719. As governor he successfully dismantled corrupt practices installed by his predecessors and, at least in New Jersey, he was a popular gov-

ernor. In July, 1719, Hunter returned to England. He served there as comptroller general of customs. From 1727 until his death, Hunter was the British governor of colonial Jamaica. This county was created on March 13, 1714, while Robert Hunter was serving as the colonial governor of both New Jersey and New York.

1750 *Mercer County*

Hugh Mercer (–1777)—Mercer was born about 1725 in Scotland and educated as a physician. He immigrated to America about 1747 and served in the army here as an officer during the French and Indian War. At the outbreak of the American Revolution, Mercer entered the Continental army, in which he attained the rank of brigadier-general. He served with distinction under General George Washington in the surprise attack on the British at Trenton, New Jersey, in late December, 1776. One week later, at the battle of Princeton, New Jersey, on January 3, 1777, Hugh Mercer was severely wounded and he died of those wounds on January 12, 1777. This county was created and named in General Mercer's honor on February 22, 1838.

1751 *Middlesex County*

Middlesex County, England—This county was created by the English province of East Jersey on March 1, 1683, and named for what was then England's premier county, Middlesex, which then contained the city of London. Middlesex County, in southeastern England, was the home of the Middle Saxon tribe. It became a shire (county) in the tenth century A.D. Its name derived from the tribal name of the Middle Saxons. An early version of the county's name was *Middelseaxan*, which meant "territory of the Middle Saxons." The Middlesex County area was occupied by the Roman Empire from A.D. 43 to A.D. 409. From Anglo-Saxon times it grew to be England's center of trade. Middlesex County suffered a severe plague in 1665 and a great fire in London in 1666. During World War II Middlesex County was bombed extensively by the German air force. Middlesex County is relatively small in size, with a length of about 22 miles and a width of only 14 miles. Its principal streams are the Thames, Lea and Colin Rivers. Middlesex County, England, ceased to exist as a separate entity in 1965 when it was absorbed as a part of a metropolitan county named Greater London.

1752 *Monmouth County*

Uncertain— This county was created on March 1, 1683, by England's province of East Jersey. Sources consulted mention three conflicting possibilities for this county's namesake:

James Scott, Duke of Monmouth & Buccleuch (1649–1685)— At the time that England's province of East Jersey created Monmouth County, King Charles II (1630–1685) was the reigning monarch of England. King Charles II had no legitimate children; that is the reason that his brother, King James II (1633–1701), became king upon the death of King Charles II. Although Charles II had no legitimate children, he had an active sex life with several mistresses and had numerous illegitimate children. James Scott was the eldest of these illegitimate children and, according to some sources, he was the favorite of King Charles II. Monmouth's mother was Lucy Walter (–1658). The Duke of Monmouth & Buccleuch served at or near the head of the English army in actions against the Dutch and the French and in quelling an insurrection in Scotland. He claimed a legal right to the throne of England, a position much demand in 1685. Others disagreed with his claim to the throne and Monmouth was executed in the Tower of London on July 15, 1685. Cornelius C. Vermeule, whose article on early New Jersey place names appeared in the April, 1926, issue of the *Proceedings of the New Jersey Historical Society* tells us that this county was named for this duke of Monmouth. Vermeule has, however, proven to be fallible; see Gloucester County, New Jersey, above.

Rhode Island's Monmouth Society settlers— During the Great Depression of the 1930's, America's federal government sponsored a great deal of research and writing concerning place name origins in our country. Under the umbrella of that financial support, the Work Projects Administration compiled a comprehensive manual entitled *The Origin of New Jersey Place Names,* which was reissued by the New Jersey Public Library Commission in 1945. In that manual the WPA writer(s) assert that Monmouth County was named for "Rhode Island Monmouth Society, settlers." An early name for what later came to be the Monmouth patent here in East Jersey was Navesink and its settlers included 80 members from Rhode Island and Massachusetts. If this county's name were Navesink rather than Monmouth, the namesake given by the WPA would be more credible.

Monmouthshire County, Wales— Lewis Morris, Sr. (–1691) was a member of a group of land speculators from Barbados, who purchased more than 15,000 acres of land in colonial New Jersey. Some of these land speculators, including Lewis Morris, Sr., moved to New Jersey and brought slaves with them. The 1964-65 edition of the *New Jersey Almanac* tells us that Colonel Lewis Morris bought 3,540 acres of land along the Shrewsbury River and that when Monmouth County was being created, Lewis Morris, Sr. "had it named Monmouth, after his native Monmouthshire in Wales." John T. Cunningham's work entitled *This Is New Jersey,* published in 1953 agrees that Lewis Morris, Sr., caused this county to be named Monmouth in memory of his native county in Wales. In Franklin Ellis' *History of Monmouth County, New Jersey,* published in 1885, the author agrees that the county was named at the request of Colonel Lewis Morris, "…the most powerful and influential citizen then residing within her boundaries," and that his Monmouth County estate was inherited by his nephew, Lewis Morris (1671–1746), who served, several times, as governor of England's province of New Jersey. Edwin Salter's 1890 history of Monmouth & Ocean Counties shares that view as does *History of Monmouth County, New Jersey: 1664–1920,* published in 1922 by the Lewis Historical Publishing Co., Inc.

1753 *Morris County*

Lewis Morris (1671–1746)— Morris was born in what is now New York City on October 15, 1671. His parents died suddenly in 1672 and young Lewis Morris was raised by an elderly and wealthy uncle, also named Lewis Morris (–1691), who lived in the East Jersey portion of what is now the state of New Jersey. When the elder Lewis Morris died in 1691, his nephew, Lewis Morris, inherited his considerable estate. The younger Lewis Morris served in a variety of political positions in England's provinces of New York and New Jersey and he served either as governor or acting governor of colonial New Jersey on four occasions: 1703, 1719–1720, 1731–1732 and 1738–1746. This county was created and named in his honor on March 15, 1739, during Lewis Morris' last term as New Jersey's colonial governor. Early in his political career Morris assisted in New Jersey's struggle to free itself from the influence of New York's royal governors. Those royal governors exercised control over New Jersey as well as New York from 1703 to 1738. When Lewis Morris was commissioned governor-in-chief and captain general of New Jersey in March, 1738, he became an English governor of New Jersey who was not concurrently governor of the English province of New York.

1754 *Ocean County*

Atlantic Ocean— This county in eastern New Jersey borders on the Atlantic Ocean and it was named for that enormous body of water, when the county was created on February 15, 1850. The Atlantic Ocean separates the continents of Europe and Africa in the east from the continents of North and South America in the west. Of the earth's oceans, the Atlantic is second in size to the Pacific. Its area, excluding dependent seas, is about 32 million square miles and with the dependent seas included, its area is 41 million square miles. Although the Atlantic Ocean is not the world's largest ocean, because of the slope of the land of the four continents which feed water to it, the Atlantic Ocean has by far the greatest drainage area of any ocean. Its drainage area is about four times that of the Pacific Ocean. The ocean's name, *Atlantic,* derived from Greek mythology and means "the sea of Atlas," a Greek God. New Jersey has a second county named for the Atlantic Ocean. That county, Atlantic County, was created on February 7, 1837.

1755 *Passaic County*

Passaic River— The Passaic River is a relatively short stream, about 80 miles in length. Its waters are confined to the state of New Jersey. The Passaic rises in a large swamp in Morris County, in northeastern New Jersey and then takes a very crooked course before crossing into Passaic County. In downtown Paterson, New Jersey, the county seat of Passaic County, the Great Falls of the Passaic River are found. These falls are about 70 feet high. From Paterson the Passaic flows northeast and combines its waters with those of the Hackensack River. These combined waters empty into the Newark Bay of the Atlantic Ocean. The Passaic is a navigable river for just a bit over ten miles. Tributaries of the Passaic include the Pequannock, Rockaway and Wanaque Rivers. Passaic County was created on February 7, 1837, and named for the Passaic River. Passaic County is the only New Jersey county with a name of American Indian origin. The translation of the Indians' name for this river is disputed. Possible translations which have been mentioned include "peace," "black, silty earth," "valley," "place where land splits," "place where river splits," and "to split or divide." William M. Beauchamp's article on "Aboriginal Place Names of New York" included comments on Indian names in New Jersey. In that article Beauchamp states that the Passaic River's name means "a valley." This article by Beauchamp was published by the New York state education department in 1907. Another authority on American Indian names, E. M. Ruttenber, agrees with Beauchamp's translation. Ruttenber stated that the name means "vale," or "valley," in his article on "Indian Geographical Names…" published in 1906, in volume 6 of the *Proceedings of the New York State Historical Association*. J. A. C. Leland's article on Indian names in the December, 1953, issue of *Names: Journal of the American Name Society*, also translates the name as "valley."

1756 *Salem County*

Village of New Salem in England's Province of West Jersey— This area was first successfully settled in 1675 by English Quakers led by John Fenwick (1618–1683). These Quakers wanted their new home to be a place of peace and they named their village on the Delaware River here, New Salem. The name "Salem" comes from the *Holy Bible* and the Hebrew version of the word is *shalom*, meaning "peace." The Quakers, whose formal designation is the Religious Society of Friends, place great emphasis on peace and many of their members have resisted going to war as conscientious objectors. When England's province of West Jersey created a new county here on May 17, 1694, they named it for the main village within its borders. The village of New Salem, now known as Salem, was incorporated as a city in 1858. The port at Salem, at the confluence of the Salem River with the Delaware River, had strategic importance during the American Revolution and the British occupied Salem during that war. The city of Salem is the county seat of Salem County and in the late 1990's this city had a population of 6,900.

1757 *Somerset County*

Uncertain— This county was created by England's province of East Jersey in May, 1688. Sources consulted are virtually unanimous in their opinion that the county was named for Somersetshire, England. However, there is one dissenting opinion, that of Cornelius C. Vermeule, whose article on early New Jersey place names appeared in the April, 1926 issue of the *Proceedings of the New Jersey Historical Society*. In that article, Vermeule tells us that this county was named for the English-

man, Charles Seymour, Duke of Somerset (1662–1748). In support of that contention, Vermeule states that "…he had borne arms for William, Prince of Orange, who, in 1688, when Somerset County was named, had become William III of England." This statement is in error. It is true that Somerset County was created in 1688, but Prince William of Orange did not become king of England, as King William III, until April 11, 1689, eleven months after Somerset County, East Jersey, was created.

Somersetshire, England— This county, in southwestern England, lies on Bristol Channel. The Somersetshire area was conquered by the Roman Empire about A.D. 43 and remains from their period of occupation can still be seen. By A.D. 658 the area was under the control of the West Saxons. Subject to periodic incursions by the Danes, Somersetshire later was controlled, almost entirely, by the Norman invaders from France. This county is bounded on three sides by hills and on the fourth side by the sea. Considerable areas of the county are sparsely populated. Below the hills, Somersetshire's climate is mild. The name *Somerset* evolved from various earlier Latin and old English forms. It originally meant "the Somerset people" and later became the name of the district. "Dwellers at Somerton" and "people dependent on Somerton" were early translations.

Charles Seymour, Duke of Somerset (1662–1748)— Educated at Cambridge University's Trinity College, Charles Seymour succeeded his brother, Francis, when he became the sixth duke of Somerset in 1678. He married well in 1682 to Lady Elizabeth Percy (1667–1722), the sole heiress of Josceline Percy, Earl of Northumberland. During the reign of King Charles II (1630–1685), Somerset was made gentleman of the bedchamber. He later was colonel of the queen's dragoons (now styled as the third Hussars). In 1687, while King James II (1633–1701) was on the English throne, Somerset took up arms for Prince William of Orange (1650–1702), who soon (on April 11, 1689) became joint sovereign of England with his wife, Queen Mary II (1662–1694). In 1689 the Duke of Somerset became chancellor of Cambridge University and later was speaker of England's house of Lords. Under England's Queen Anne (1665–1714) and, later, King George I (1660–1727), Somerset was in royal favor, and then out; then back in royal favor, then out. When he was dismissed by King George I in 1716 he retired and lived on his estates.

1758 *Sussex County*

Sussex County, England— Sussex County, in southeastern England lies on the English Channel and at one time was one of the seven Anglo-Saxon kingdoms of Britain known as the Heptarchy. Because of its location, Sussex was a frequent landing area for French and other armies invading England. In 1066 the Normans started their successful invasion at Hastings, in Sussex County, and over the next 500 years Sussex was subject to periodic invasions. These incidents resulted in Sussex dividing itself into six "rapes," each with its own stretch of coastline and its own castle. Later, when the Anglican Church became the state church of England, the citizens of Sussex avoided total capitulation and both Roman Catholicism and Puritanism claimed fair numbers of adherents in Sussex. The name *Sussex* derived from the name of the South Saxons, who lived there. The English names Essex, Middlesex and Sussex referred to the tribes of people who lived there, the East Saxons, Middle Saxons and South Saxons, respectively. These names were then used for the kingdoms that these people established and they have survived as English geographic names. This county was created in May, 1688, by what was then England's province of East Jersey.

1759 *Union County*

Uncertain— This county was created on March 19, 1857, from the southern portion of Essex County. Very little information is available on the origin of this county's name and what little information is available is conflicting.

Town of Union (or Connecticut Farms)— Joel N. Eno wrote an article which appeared in the September–October, 1917, issue of *The Magazine of History*, entitled "New Jersey County Names." In that article Eno states that the county was named for "…the town of Union, or 'Connecticut Farms' settled from Connecticut in 1667." No other source has been located which confirms that view. However very few sources exist which offer any opinion on the origin of Union County's name. During the American Revolution a battle was fought at Connecticut Farms on June 7 and June 8, 1780. The town which had formerly been known as Connecticut Farms is now named Union.

Preservation of America's union of states— At the time that this county was created, in 1857, tension had been building for several decades between the North and South over the slavery issue. Preservation of the

Union of states forming the United States of America seemed precarious in 1857 and a few sources suggest that this county's name was chosen to express the patriotic hope that the Union could be preserved. That hope was short-lived. By 1861 a number of southern states had seceded from the Union and the Civil War had begun.

Union of several communities in the new county — For a number of years the residents of the rural areas south of Newark had chafed for freedom from domination by the heavily populated northern portions of Essex County. They wanted their own county and on March 19, 1857, they got it. One Moses M. Crane deserves much of the credit for accomplishing the creation of this new county, which was destined to become that last county created in New Jersey. To facilitate the creation of the new county, both political parties, as well as those in favor of a new county and those opposed, agreed to make equal division of the county offices which would be created when the new county was born.

Three choices are given above for the origin of this county's name. It is quite possible that the true answer is not among them.

1760 *Warren County*

Joseph Warren (1741–1775) — A native of Massachusetts and a graduate of Harvard College, Warren practiced medicine in the Boston area. He was a member of the committee of safety and president *pro tempore* of the Massachusetts provincial congress. In June, 1775, he was commissioned a major-general and he died in combat a few days later at the battle of Bunker Hill. Warren County was created on November 20, 1824.

REFERENCES

Allstrom, C. M. *Dictionary of Royal Lineage of Europe and Other Countries*. Chicago, Press of S. Th., Almberg, 1902.

Alotta, Robert I. *Signposts & Settlers: The History of the Place Names in the Middle Atlantic States*. Chicago, Bonus Books, Inc., 1992.

Andrews, Allen. *The Royal Whore: Barbara Villiers, Countess of Castlemaine*. Philadelphia, Chilton Book Co., 1970.

Armor, William C. *Lives of the Governors of Pennsylvania*. Philadelphia, James K. Simon, 1872.

Barber, John W,. & Henry Howe. *Historical Collections of the State of New Jersey*. New York, New York, S. Tuttle, 1844.

Beauchamp, William M. "Aboriginal Place Names of New York." Albany, New York State Education Department, 1907.

Becker, Donald W. *Indian Place-Names in New Jersey*. Cedar Grove, New Jersey, Phillips-Campbell Publishing Co., Inc., 1964.

Bishop, Gordon. *Gems of New Jersey*. Englewood Cliffs, New Jersey, Prentice-Hall, Inc., 1985.

Bradley, A. G. *The Rivers & Streams of England*. London, Adam & Charles Black, 1909.

Cawley, James, & Margaret Cawley. *Exploring the Little Rivers of New Jersey*. New Brunswick, New Jersey, Rutgers University Press, 1942.

Clements, John. *New Jersey Facts*. Dallas, Texas, Clements Research II, Inc., 1988.

Cunningham, John T. *New Jersey: America's Main Road*. Garden City, New York, Doubleday & Co., Inc., 1966.

Cunningham, John T. *The New Jersey Shore*. New Brunswick, New Jersey, Rutgers University Press, 1958.

Cunningham, John T. *This Is New Jersey*. New Brunswick, New Jersey, Rutgers University Press, 1953.

Cutter, William R. *Historic Homes and Places and Genealogical and Personal Memoirs Relating to the Families of Middlesex County, Massachusetts*. New York, Lewis Historical Publishing Co., 1908.

Drake, Samuel A. *Old Landmarks & Historic Fields of Middlesex*. Boston, Roberts Brothers, 1888.

Ekwall, Eilert. *The Concise Oxford Dictionary of English Place-Names*. Oxford, Oxford University Press, 1960.

Ellis, Franklin. *History of Monmouth County, New Jersey*. Philadelphia, R. T. Peck & Co., 1885.

Elmer, Lucius Q. C. *History of the Early Settlement & Progress of Cumberland County, New Jersey*. Bridgeton, New Jersey, George F. Nixon, 1869.

Encyclopaedia Britannica. Chicago, Encyclopaedia Britannica, Inc., 1971.

Eno, Joel N. "New Jersey County Names." *The Magazine of History*, Vol. 25, Nos. 3–4. Poughkeepsie, New York: September-October, 1917.

Faragher, John M. *The Encyclopedia of Colonial & Revolutionary America*. New York, Facts on File, 1990.

Fisher, George J. B. "The Southern Outpost of New Netherlands: Cape May: 1609–1664." *Cape May County, New Jersey Magazine of History & Genealogy*, Vol. 3, No. 3. June, 1949.

Gannett, Henry. *The Origin of Certain Place Names in the United States*. Williamstown, Massachusetts, Corner House Publishers, 1978.

Godfrey, Carlos E. "Origin of the Counties in New Jersey." *Proceedings of the New Jersey Historical Society*, Vol. 9, No. 4. Newark, New Jersey: October, 1924.

Gordon, Thomas F. *A Gazetteer of the State of New Jersey*. Trenton, Daniel Fenton, 1834.

Harvey, Cornelius B. *Genealogical History of Hudson & Bergen Counties, New Jersey*. New York, New Jersey Genealogical Publishing Co., 1900.

Hawkyard, Alasdair. *The Counties of Britain: A Tudor Atlas by John Speed*. London, England, Pavilion Books, Ltd., 1995.

Hazard, Samuel. *Annals of Pennsylvania from the Discovery of the Delaware: 1609–1682*. Philadelphia, Hazard & Mitchell, 1850.

Historic Roadsides in New Jersey. Plainfield, New Jersey, Society of Colonial Wars in the State of New Jersey, 1928.

History of Monmouth County, New Jersey: 1664–1920. New York, Lewis Historical Publishing Co., 1922.

Honeyman, A. Van Doren. *History of Union County, New Jersey: 1664–1923*. New York, Lewis Historical Publishing Co., Inc., 1923.

Kennedy, Steele M., et al. *The New Jersey Almanac: 1964–1965*. Upper Montclair, New Jersey, New Jersey Almanac, Inc., 1963.

Kenyon, J. P. *Dictionary of British History*. Ware, England, Wordsworth Editions, Ltd., 1992.

Kleber, John E. *The Kentucky Encyclopedia*. Lexington, University Press of Kentucky, 1992.

Lee, Francis B. *New Jersey as a Colony and as a State*. New York, Publishing Society of New Jersey, 1903.

Leland, J. A. C. "Indian Names in Missouri." *Names: Journal of the American Name Society*, Vol. 1, No. 4. Berkeley: December, 1953.

McCague, James. *The Cumberland*. New York, Holt, Rinehart & Winston, 1973.

McMahon, William. *South Jersey Towns: History & Legend*. New Brunswick, New Jersey, Rutgers University Press, 1973.

Manual of the Legislature of New Jersey: 1984. Trenton, New Jersey, Edward J. Mullin, 1984.

Miller, Richmond P. "What is a Quaker?" *A Guide to the Religions of America*, New York, Simon & Schuster, 1955.

Mills, A. D. *A Dictionary of English Place Names*. Oxford, Oxford University Press, 1991.

Moule, Thomas. *The County Maps of Old England*. London, Studio Editions, 1990.

Myers, William S. *The Story of New Jer-*

sey. New York, Lewis Historical Publishing Co., Inc., 1945.

Nelson, William. "The History of the Counties of New Jersey." *Proceedings of the New Jersey Historical Society*, Vol. 52, No. 197. Newark, New Jersey: April, 1934.

Nelson, William & Charles A. Shriner. *History of Paterson and Its Environs*. New York, Lewis Historical Publishing Co., 1920.

New Jersey Pennsylvania Tour Book. Heathrow, Florida, AAA Publishing, 1998.

Pomfret, John E. *Colonial New Jersey: A History*. New York, Charles Scribner's Sons, 1973.

Price, Edward T. *Dividing the Land: Early American Beginnings of Our Private Property Mosaic*. Chicago, University of Chicago Press, 1995.

Radko, Thomas R. *Discovering New Jersey*. New Brunswick, New Jersey, Rutgers University Press, 1982.

Raum, John O. *The History of New Jersey*. Philadelphia, John E. Potter & Co., 1877.

Reaney, P. H. *The Origin of English Place-Names*. London, Routledge & Kegan Paul, 1960.

Rosten, Leo. *The Joys of Yiddish*. New York, McGraw-Hill Book Co., 1968.

Ruttenber, E. M. "Indian Geographical Names in the Valley of Hudson's River, the Valley of the Mohawk and on the Delaware." *Proceedings of the New York State Historical Association*, Vol. 6. 1906.

Salter, Edwin. *A History of Monmouth & Ocean Counties*. Bayonne, New Jersey, E. Gardner & Son, 1890.

Sheridan, Eugene R. *Lewis Morris: 1671–1746*. Syracuse, New York, Syracuse University Press, 1981.

Smith, Samuel. *The History of the Colony of Nova-Caesaria, or New Jersey*. Burlington, New Jersey, James Parker, 1765.

Stansfield, Charles A. *New Jersey: A Geography*. Boulder, Colorado, Westview Press, 1983.

Stellhorn, Paul A. & Michael J. Birkner. *The Governors of New Jersey: 1664–1974: Biographical Essays*. Trenton, New Jersey Historical Commission, 1982.

Stevens, Lewis T. *The History of Cape May County, New Jersey*. Cape May, New Jersey, 1897.

Stewart, George R. *American Place-Names*. New York, Oxford University Press, 1970.

Stewart, George R. *Names on the Land*. New York, Random House, 1945.

"The Story Behind County Names." *Weston's Record*. Dalton, Massachusetts, Byron Weston Company.

Taft, William H. III. *County Names: An Historical Perspective*. National Association of Counties, 1982.

Thayer, Theodore. *Colonial & Revolutionary Morris County*. Morristown, Compton Press, Inc., 1975.

Tracy, Frank B. *The Tercentenary History of Canada*. Toronto, P. F. Collier & Son, 1908.

Van Winkle, Daniel. *Old Bergen*. Jersey City, John W. Harrison, 1902.

Vermeule, Cornelius C. "Some Early New Jersey Place-Names." *Proceedings of the New Jersey Historical Society*, Vol. 10, No. 3. Newark: July, 1925.

Vermeule, Cornelius C. "Some Early New Jersey Place-Names." *Proceedings of the New Jersey Historical Society*, Vol. 11, No. 2. Newark: April, 1926.

Vexler, Robert I. *Chronology & Documentary Handbook of the State of New Jersey*. Dobbs Ferry, New York, Oceana Publications, Inc., 1978.

Westergaard, Barbara. *New Jersey: A Guide to the State*. New Brunswick, Rutgers University Press, 1987.

Westervelt, Frances A. *History of Bergen County, New Jersey: 1630–1923*. New York, Lewis Historical Publishing Co., Inc., 1923.

Whitehead, William A. *East Jersey Under the Proprietary Governments*. Newark, New Jersey, Martin R. Dennis, 1875.

Whitworth, Rex. *William Augustus, Duke of Cumberland: A Life*. London, England, Leo Cooper, 1992.

Who Was Who in America: Historical Volume: 1607–1896. Chicago, Illinois, A. N. Marquis Co., 1967.

Winfield, Charles H. *History of the County of Hudson, New Jersey*. New York, Kennard & Hay, 1874.

Work Projects Administration. *Bergen County Panorama*. Hackensack, New Jersey, 1941.

Work Projects Administration. *Inventory of the County Archives of New Jersey–Bergen & Ocean Counties*. 1939 & 1940.

Works Projects Administration. *The Origin of New Jersey Place Names*. Trenton, New Jersey, New Jersey Public Library Commission, 1945.

New Mexico

(32 counties)

1761 *Bernalillo County*

Town of Bernalillo, New Mexico territory— When the United States took control of New Mexico in 1846, eight counties already existed, as survivals of the old Mexican scheme. Bernalillo was one of these eight counties which the United States inherited from Mexico, having been set up by the Republic of Mexico in 1844. Bernalillo County was officially created as a county of America's New Mexico territory on January 9, 1852, just 16 months after New Mexico territory had been established. Albuquerque is the present county seat of Bernalillo County. Bernalillo County, New Mexico territory, was named for the town of Bernalillo, although Ranchos de Albuquerque was its first county seat. However, this county's seat of justice has been changed many times over the years and, and on at least two occasions (1849 and 1878), the county seat was the county's namesake, the town of Bernalillo, As a result of the shifting of county boundaries over the years, the municipality of Bernalillo is now located in Sandoval County, New Mexico, just north of the Bernalillo County line, about 17 miles north of Albuquerque. The present town of Bernalillo, in Sandoval County, was named soon after the 1692 Reconquest of New Mexico by the Spanish governor, Don Diego de Vargas (–1704). Some confusion in nomenclature exists because of changes in the official designation of this municipality shortly after its founding. In 1696 it is mentioned as the Real de Bernalillo, the Spanish word *real*, in this case, being the legal term for a mining town. Bernalillo never developed into much of a mining town and that term was soon dropped. Father Juan Alvarez called the town the Villa de Bernalillo in 1706. Under Spanish law, a villa had specific rights conferred upon it by the crown of Spain and there is doubt that Bernalillo ever enjoyed those rights. Perhaps Father Alvarez erred. In documents from the early 18th century, Bernalillo is usually called a *puesto*, meaning "a place." *Bernalillo* is the diminutive form of the name *Bernal* and it means "Little Bernal." However, it is uncertain how the town derived its name. Suggestions which have been mentioned include:

Gonzales-Bernal family — The Gonzales-Bernal family lived in the area before and after the 1692 Reconquest of New Mexico by Governor Don Diego de Vargas (–1704) and his troops. T. M. Pearce's work entitled *New Mexico Place Names*, published in 1965, suggests the possibility that perhaps Bernalillo was named for a member of the Gonzales-Bernal family who was of small stature; or, perhaps a "Junior," who was "thus distinguished from the 'Senior' of the same name." Robert Julyan tells us in his 1996 work entitled *The Place Names of New Mexico*, that "among the (Spanish) families who established estates here were the Bernals; Pascuala Bernal had accompanied her husband Juan Griego on the Onate expedition of 1598 and while some of her sons took the Griego name, at least one son and several daughters chose Bernal." Juan Griego's wife's name is shown as Catalina Bernal in Fray Angelico Chavez's *Origins of New Mexico Families in the Spanish Colonial Period*. That work also lists two sons from the Griego-Bernal marriage: Juan Griego and Francisco Bernal and comments "Why Francisco took his mother's name while Juan took his father's, is not known, unless they were half-brothers." Chavez tells us that "The Bernal individuals living at the time of the 1680 Indian Rebellion were descendants either of Francisco Bernal or of the Bernal sisters."

Francisco Bernal — This son of Juan Griego and Pascuala (or Catalina) Bernal either came to New Mexico as a boy in 1598, or was born at San Gabriel at a later date. Francisco Bernal married Bernardina Moran, said to be 20 years old in 1631.

Francisco Bernal — A second Francisco Bernal is mentioned in the records of this period of New Mexico's history. He was described as 22 years old, with a family of eight: mother, brothers, sisters, nephews and nieces. Said to be a native of New Mexico, he was probably a child from the marriage of Francisco Bernal and Bernardina Moran.

Isabel Bernal — Isabel was another child of the Griego-Bernal marriage. She married Sebastian Gonzales and Isabel and her husband were progenitors of the vast clan known as Gonzales-Bernal.

Juan Bernal — A Juan Bernal is listed as a soldier escort of 1608, according to Fray Angelico Chavez's *Origins of New Mexico Families in the Spanish Colonial Period*. However, Chavez speculates that he "very likely was the younger Juan Griego."

Juan Bernal (–1680) — T. M. Pearce's work entitled *New Mexico Place Names*, published in 1965 mentions the possibility that the town of Bernalillo may have been named by Don Fernando de Chavez, the leading citizen of this area, after his friend Fray Juan Bernal (–1680), who was martyred in 1680.

Francisco Bernal (–) — Bernal was a soldier at El Paso (the present Juarez, Mexico), who was 60 years old in 1691. This Francisco Bernal may have been the soldier who was described about 11 years earlier as "Francisco Bernal passed muster on foot and without arms of any kind; he is extremely poor, a bachelor with a family of eight persons-mother, brothers, and nephews. He did not sign because he did not know how." The possibility that this Bernal was the original in the Bernalillo naming chain is mentioned by F. Stanley in his 1964 work, *The Bernalillo, New Mexico, Story*. Stanley speculates that this Bernal may have asked for discharge from the army and his pension and that it may have been granted with the stipulation that a garrison be maintained on Bernal's parcel of land to guard against further Indian uprisings.

Bernal Diaz del Castillo (–1581) — There is no reason to believe that the original town of Bernalillo was named for Bernal Diaz del Castillo. However, several sources on the history, geography and place names of New Mexico mention him as the possible namesake of the town of Bernalillo. It is very likely that these sources mention his name only because he was very famous in the early history of the exploration and conquest of New Spain (Mexico), and his name contains an element of the word *Bernalillo*. Bernal Diaz del Castillo, the son of a magistrate in Spain named Francisco Diaz del Castillo, was a Spanish soldier and historian who served with Hernando Cortes (1485–1547) in conquering Mexico. Earlier he had served in the New World in Cuba and on the Yucatan peninsula in Central America. Bernal Diaz del Castillo was a member of the party of Spanish conquistadors under Cortes, who conquered Mexico for Spain

during the period 1519 to 1521. He was also the author of a comprehensive work dealing with that conquest. The work's title (in English) was *The True History of the Conquest of New Spain* (i.e., Mexico). This work was republished in English in 1956 by Farrar Straus and Cudahy entitled *The Discovery & Conquest of Mexico: 1517–1521*.

1762 *Catron County*

Thomas B. Catron (1840–1921) — A native of Missouri and an 1860 graduate of the University of Missouri, Catron served in the Confederate army during the Civil War and participated in numerous battles, major and minor, in that war. After a brief return to his native state of Missouri, Catron immigrated across the Great Plains to the vast and beautiful territory of New Mexico. Here he practiced law and soon became active in politics. Catron also acquired enormous wealth here in the form of 1.5 million acres of former Spanish land grants. Catron was a member of New Mexico's territorial legislature and from 1895 to 1897 he was New Mexico territory's delegate to the U.S. Congress. When New Mexico was admitted to statehood in 1912, Catron was elected to be one of the new state's first two U.S. senators. His term in the U.S. Senate ran from March 27, 1912, to March 3, 1917. This county was created on February 25, 1921, shortly before Catron's death on May 15, 1821.

1763 *Chaves County*

Jose F. Chaves (1833–1904) — Chaves was born in the community of Padillas, Mexico, which subsequently became part of New Mexico territory. He studied medicine at New York College of Physicians and Surgeons but he then engaged in agricultural and commercial pursuits in New Mexico territory. Chaves served several terms in New Mexico's territorial legislature. In that body he became president of the territorial council. He served as an officer in the Union army during the Civil War and was promoted to the rank of lieutenant-colonel. Chaves was elected as the delegate to the U.S. Congress from the territory of New Mexico and he served three terms in that body. This county was created on February 25, 1889. The name that was originally proposed for it was Llano County. The name was changed to Chaves County, in honor of Jose F. Chaves at the suggestion of Joseph C. Lea (1841–1904), a close friend of Chaves and the man for whom Lea County, New Mexico was named. Jose F. Chaves was murdered in 1904.

1764 *Colfax County*

Schuyler Colfax (1823–1885)— A native of New York, Colfax moved to Indiana where he became the proprietor and editor of the South Bend, Indiana *Register*. He was occupied in that capacity for nearly two decades. Colfax was elected to represent Indiana in the U.S. House of Representatives and he served in that body for some 14 years. In 1863 he was elected speaker of the house. In the election of 1868, Colfax ran for vice-president on the Republican ticket headed by Ulysses S. Grant. The Grant-Colfax ticket won the election and Schuyler Colfax served as our country's vice-president from March 4, 1869, to March 3, 1873. This county was created on January 25, 1869, and named in honor of the vice-president-elect.

1765 *Curry County*

George Curry (–1947)— The year of Curry's birth is listed by various sources as 1861, 1862 and 1863. We know that he was born in Louisiana and that he moved with his widowed mother to Dodge City, Kansas, when he was about 12 years old. He came to Lincoln County in New Mexico territory shortly after his mother's death in 1879. Curry was elected to several positions by the voters of Lincoln County including county clerk, county assessor and sheriff. He subsequently was elected to the senate of New Mexico territory. During the Spanish-American War, Curry served as an officer in Theodore Roosevelt's Rough Riders but he was not allowed to participate in the action in Cuba. Instead he remained on the mainland expediting the flow of supplies to the Rough Riders in Cuba. However Curry did see combat action in the Philippine Islands. Also in the Philippines, during the early years of the 20th century Curry served as governor of three Philippine provinces. On April 1, 1907, President Theodore Roosevelt appointed his fellow Rough Rider, George Curry, to be governor of New Mexico territory. Curry assumed the duties of territorial governor on August 8, 1907. This county was created on February 25, 1909, while Curry was serving as New Mexico's territorial governor. The county was named in his honor at the suggestion of Charles A. Scheurich, a grandson of the first American civilian governor of New Mexico, Charles Bent (1799–1847). When New Mexico was admitted to statehood in 1912, George Curry was elected to be the new state's first representative in the U.S. House of Representatives. He died on November 24, 1947, in Albuquerque.

1766 *De Baca County*

Ezequiel C. de Baca (1864–1917)— Ezequiel Cabeza de Baca was born November 1, 1864, at Las Vegas, New Mexico territory. He held some minor posts in San Miguel County government and in 1900 was a delegate to the Democratic party's national convention. De Baca served as the first lieutenant governor of the new state of New Mexico from 1912 to December 31, 1916. Elected in November, 1916, to be the second governor of the state of New Mexico, de Baca took office on January 1, 1917, but died in office during the following month, on February 18, 1917. This county was created on February 28, 1917, just ten days after Governor De Baca's death. The legislature had been considering the name Sumner for this county but in light of the governor's recent death, they named it De Baca, instead, in his honor.

1767 *Dona Ana County*

Village of Dona Ana, New Mexico territory— This county was created on January 9, 1852, just 16 months after New Mexico territory was established. Its name was taken from the village which was its first county seat. That village, a farming settlement, five miles north of Las Cruces, New Mexico, is now so small that it no longer is shown on some maps of New Mexico. However this village has its own U.S. Postal Service zip code: 88032. The settlement of Dona Ana had been named perhaps two centuries before this American county was created. We know this because Governor Otermin mentioned the village in his 1682 report of an attempt to recapture Santa Fe. New Mexico sources mention several possible namesakes of the village of Dona Ana but most of them admit that the origin of the village's name not certain.

Senorita Ana— Several sources mention the legend that the name Dona Ana came from the capture by Indians, of a daughter of a colonel in the Mexican (or Spanish) army, Colonel Ana. It is said that, after her capture, Colonel Ana's daughter was never seen again. A version of this legend which contains more details appears in the *History of Mew Mexico*, which was published by Pacific States Publishing Company in 1907. In that account, of the legend, the young lady was "engaged in playing hand-ball or some other solitary game, in a secluded place in the Gila river region" when she was abducted. According to this version of the legend the girl was very beautiful or her father was a man of considerable standing.

Dona Ana Robledo— Several sources mention a Dona Ana, who was reputed to have lived here in the 17th century. She was said to be famous for her charity and good deeds. Some reports tell us that she was an 80 year old widow and the granddaughter of Pedro Robledo. According to this version Ana Robledo died here and the place of her burial was given her name.

Dona Ana Maria, Nina de Cordoba— This lady owned a sheep ranch in this vicinity according to a 1693 letter from a Spanish officer, Don Gabriel del Castillo, to the viceroy of New Spain.

El Ancon de Dona Ana— In 1839 the governor of Chihuahua, Mexico issued a grant known as *El Ancon de Dona Ana*, translated variously as "The Dona Ana bend colony" or "The Dona Ana cove, or bend," to Jose Maria Costales and 116 colonists. The present New Mexican communities of Dona Ana, Las Cruces and Tortugas are located on land that had constituted this colony.

1768 *Eddy County*

Charles B. Eddy (1857–)— A native of Milford, New York, Eddy immigrated west to Colorado and then, about 1881 he came to New Mexico territory and settled in the region below Seven Rivers, where seven arroyos lead into the Pecos River. Here Eddy entered the cattle business. Eddy had a brother, John Arthur Eddy, who participated with Charles B. Eddy in some of his ventures in New Mexico territory but this county was named for Charles B. Eddy; not for his brother. Charles B. Eddy was one of the leaders in forming an irrigation company here to tame the waters of the Pecos River. The Pecos is a major, 500-mile-long river, which rises in northeastern New Mexico and flows south across the state, and through Eddy County to the county's southern border with Texas. Charles B. Eddy and his associates were successful in turning thousands of acres of formerly arid land into fertile agricultural land. From 1889 to 1894 Charles B. Eddy was the manager of this irrigation company, which has enjoyed several names including the Carlsbad irrigation project. Charles B Eddy was also a leading figure of a railroad subsidiary of the New Mexico Railway & Coal Company. This county was created by the legislature of New Mexico territory on February 25, 1889, and all sources consulted indicate that it was named directly for Charles B. Eddy; not indirectly by being named for the town of Eddy, which previously had been named in his honor.

1769 Grant County

Ulysses S. Grant (1822–1885) — Grant was a native of Ohio who graduated from the U.S. Military Academy at West Point. He served with distinction in the Mexican War, and in the Civil War he rose to become commander of all Union forces. After the Civil war, Grant briefly served as acting secretary of war and then two terms as president of the United States. He proved to be a rather mediocre president. This county was created on January 30, 1868, by New Mexico's territorial legislature. Later that year, Ulysses S. Grant was elected president.

1770 Guadalupe County

Saint Mary (–) — This county was created on February 26, 1891, and named for the patron saint of Mexico, Our Lady of Guadalupe, the sainted Virgin Mary. There have been numerous reported visions of the Virgin Mary, around the world, but it was the famous vision near Mexico City, New Spain (Mexico), in December, 1531, which inspired the name Guadalupe to be used for the Virgin Mary in Mexico. The name *Guadalupe* is the European rendering of the name which the Virgin Mary called herself in 1531 during her reported appearance near Mexico City. The audience of this vision was a 51 year old Aztec Indian peasant , named Juan Diego. Diego and his wife had recently been converted to Christianity, when Juan Diego reportedly saw Mary appear on a hillside, near the Aztec religious shrine of Tepeyac. When Juan Diego reported his vision to the Spanish conquistadors, the Aztec phonetics were rendered as *Guadalupe*. Our Lady of Guadalupe was the name of a city and shrine in the Estremadura region in west-central Spain, with which the conquistadors were very familiar. That shrine is, of course, Roman Catholic, but the word *Guadalupe* as used in Spain actually has a Moorish origin. This Arabic name would be translated as "the river of black gravel," and it refers to the river named Guadalopillo in Spain, which passes through coal country. In any event, the 1531 apparition was instrumental in converting Mexicans to Roman Catholicism, and that religion is still predominant in Mexico.

Saint Mary — It is a matter of dogma of the Roman Catholic Church that Saint Mary was the virgin mother of the second person of the Trinity, Jesus Christ. Because she had been selected to be the human mother of God, it was axiomatic that her soul be spotless, free of all sin from the moment of her conception. As the mother of Jesus, Mary is considered preeminent among all saints but the veneration and adoration bestowed upon her are on a lower plane than those reserved for God in three persons, Father, Son and Holy Spirit.

The original act to create this county in 1891 was not signed by the governor so a supplementary act was passed in 1893 to correct this defect. Then, in 1903, the New Mexico territorial legislature changed Guadalupe County's name to honor General Leonard Wood (1860–1927), who was Theodore Roosevelt's superior officer in Cuba during the Spanish-American War. This change in the county's name proved to be very unpopular with the citizens of New Mexico territory and in 1905 the legislature changed the county's name back to Guadalupe County.

1771 Harding County

Warren G. Harding (1865–1923) — A native of Ohio, Harding edited a newspaper before entering politics and being elected to the Ohio senate. He served as Ohio's lieutenant governor but was defeated in a 1910 election to be governor of the state. Elected to the U.S. Senate in 1914, Harding supported conservative positions in that body. During the Republican national convention in 1920, the delegates had difficulty agreeing on a candidate for the presidency and Warren G. Harding was nominated as a compromise candidate on the tenth ballot. Harding easily won the national election and was inaugurated as our nation's president on March 4, 1921. Harding County, New Mexico, was created on that same day. As president Harding continued to favor conservative and pro-business measures. However his administration is primarily remembered for several scandals, including the infamous Teapot Dome. These scandals involved improper actions by men Harding had appointed to powerful positions but Harding's personal life, while he was president, also became a source of scandal and damaged his reputation. He died in office on August 2, 1923.

1772 Hidalgo County

Uncertain — Sources dealing with the history, geography and place names of New Mexico offer two different opinions on the origin of this county's name: (1) The treaty of Guadalupe Hidalgo, which was signed at the town of Guadalupe-Hidalgo, Mexico, in 1848 and (2) Miguel Hidalgo y Costilla (1753–1811), the priest who was a leader in Mexico's Revolution which resulted in Mexican independence from Spain.

Treaty of Guadalupe Hidalgo signed at the town of Guadalupe-Hidalgo, Mexico in 1848 — The treaty of Guadalupe Hidalgo ended the Mexican War and gave to the United States an enormous land mass stretching from the middle of New Mexico and north to western Colorado; then westward to embrace the entire states of Utah, Nevada and California as well as most of Arizona. Hidalgo County, New Mexico, was created on February 25, 1919, and some of the land taken to create Hidalgo County was ceded to the United States by the treaty of Guadalupe Hidalgo. (New Mexico's present borders do not form a rectangle. There is a small panhandle in the extreme southwestern corner of New Mexico which violates the shape of a rectangle. That panhandle is also part of Hidalgo County but it was not acquired by the treaty of 1848; rather, it was purchased from Mexico in the Gadsden Purchase of 1853.) Since Our Lady of Guadalupe is the patron saint of Mexico (see Guadalupe County, New Mexico, above), some sources speculate that Mexico chose the town of Guadalupe-Hidalgo for the peace treaty ending their war with the U.S. in the hope that the Blessed Lady of Guadalupe would bring favor to the Mexican side.

Miguel Hidalgo y Costilla (1753–1811) — Born near Guanajuato, Mexico on May 8, 1753, Hidalgo was educated to be a Roman Catholic priest and he was ordained in 1779. As a priest, Padre Hidalgo attended to the spiritual needs of his Mexican parishioners in the village of Dolores and introduced them to a various forms of industry. Meanwhile Padre Hidalgo was avidly reading accounts of the French Revolution and was suspected by Spanish authorities of having revolutionary thoughts for Mexico. They were right. By 1808, events on the European continent had removed King Carlos IV (1748–1819) from the throne of Spain and made France's Joseph Bonaparte (1768–1844) the ruler of Spain. Various Latin American colonies declared themselves unwilling to accept a French ruler. Mexico was among this group and Mexicans such as Padre Hidalgo engaged in activities which were the prelude to a bid for independence from all European domination. Hidalgo led several hundred of his parishioners in the September 16, 1810, seizure of a prison at Dolores, Mexico, which began what was, in fact, the revolution against Spanish and Creole rule of Mexico. Hidalgo's forces ranged as far west as Guadalajara, Mexico, and then returned to capture Mexico City. That capital was ill-defended and had Hidalgo attacked, his forces might have taken it; however, instead of advancing on Mexico City, Hidalgo turned north when he reached a mountain road overlooking the city. In March, 1811, Hidalgo was captured by trickery, degraded from the priesthood and executed. The date on which he was shot and killed was either July 31 or August 1, 1811. Hidalgo had set in motion forces which would continue to propel Mexico to independence which was achieved a decade after Hidalgo's death, on September 27, 1821.

1773 *Lea County*

Joseph C. Lea (1841–1904)— Lea County occupies the southeastern corner of New Mexico. In 1912 Robert F. Love proposed that a county be created here named Heard County, in honor of Allen C. Heard, one of the founders of the High Lonesome ranch. That proposal was defeated. In 1917 a bill was introduced before the New Mexico legislature by Representative Eaves to create a county here named Llano County. That name was inspired by the *Llano Estacado*, or "Staked Plain," the 35,000 square mile plateau, which extends from southeastern New Mexico to northwestern Oklahoma and western Texas. In committee, William H. H. Llewellyn, the speaker of New Mexico's house of representatives, denigrated this suggestion, commenting that "nobody would be able to pronounce the name,… much less spell it correctly." The matter was resolved by creating and naming the new county Lea County on March 7, 1917, in honor of Joseph C. Lea (1841–1904). Lea was born in Cleveland, Tennessee on November 8, 1841, and moved during his boyhood with his family to Missouri. When he was about 19 years old he got in trouble with the law and decided that the best way to avoid arrest would be to join the Confederate army. In that army he served with distinction during the Civil War and was promoted to the rank of colonel after less than three years service. Possibly his most notable accomplishments occurred when he held the rank of captain. Much of the literature about New Mexico's history refers to him as Captain Lea. It is also possible that this title refers

to the rank of captain that Lea held, until his death, in a Confederate veterans' association in New Mexico territory. At the end of the Civil War Colonel Lea lived for a time in Georgia and then in Louisiana and Mississippi. In 1876 he came to New Mexico territory. In 1877 Lea settled in New Mexico's Pecos River Valley, where he raised cattle and engaged in mercantile pursuits. He also accumulated vast amounts of New Mexican land and became a wealthy man. When Roswell, New Mexico territory was incorporated as a city, Joseph C. Lea was elected to be the city's first mayor. He died on February 4, 1904, from a sudden attack of pneumonia.

1774 *Lincoln County*

Abraham Lincoln (1809–1865)— Lincoln was a native of Kentucky who moved to Illinois where he was a member of the state legislature. He represented Illinois in the U.S. House of Representatives and later was elected president of the United States. Lincoln's presidency coincided almost exactly with the Civil War. He guided the United States ably through that uniquely turbulent period. As president, he issued the Emancipation Proclamation which declared the freedom of slaves in all states in rebellion. Lincoln was assassinated in April, 1865, a few days after the Union's victory in the Civil War. This county was created on January 16, 1869. Some sources indicate that this county was named for President Lincoln indirectly, by being named for the town of Lincoln. T. M. Pearce's work entitled *New Mexico Place Names* demurs, stating that the town of Lincoln was first named Las Placitas and then Bonito. Pearce goes on to explain that it was after Lincoln County was created that the town's name was changed to Lincoln as well.

1775 *Los Alamos County*

City of Los Alamos, New Mexico— The Spanish name *Los Alamos* came from the presence of "the cottonwood trees" in this area. The name *Los Alamos* is used widely in New Mexico for ranches, hamlets at least one mountain and at least one creek. Our city of Los Alamos is located in north-central New Mexico and it is the county seat of Los Alamos County. Today's Los Alamos is a creature of the Atomic Age. As recently as 1880 the community of Los Alamos consisted of but seven adobe houses. After the turn of the century, a Los Alamos Ranch School for Boys was started here. In 1942, not long after America entered World War II, the federal gov-

ernment took over the area for the top secret work of developing atomic weapons by the Manhattan project. The atomic bombs which ended World War II were built here. However, the first successful atomic explosion took place in southern New Mexico, at Alamogordo on July 16, 1945. Just three weeks later, the U.S. army air corps dropped an atomic bomb on Hiroshima, Japan; the first time in the history of our planet that an atomic weapon was used in anger. Today Los Alamos National Laboratory here is a major research institution and the city of Los Alamos' population has grown to about 20,000. Los Alamos County was created on March 16, 1949.

1776 *Luna County*

Solomon Luna (1858–1912)— Born at Los Lunas, New Mexico territory, on October 18, 1858, Luna attended college in Saint Louis, Missouri. After college, Luna returned to New Mexico territory and continued his family's long history of involvement in stock-raising. Solomon Luna was a sheep man, and eventually was one of the leading sheep owners of the entire Southwest. In 1904 Luna was named president of the Bank of Commerce in Albuquerque, New Mexico territory. Solomon Luna was also president of the New Mexico Sheep Growers Association. In 1908 New Mexico's territorial governor, George Curry, appointed Luna to a Territorial conservation commission. In 1910 New Mexico territory prepared for admission to statehood and a convention was held to draft the constitution for the new state. According to Thomas J. Mabry's account in an article in the April, 1944 issue of *New Mexico Historical Review*, Luna had a major influence on the constitution of New Mexico. Mabry tells us that "Luna never made a speech in the convention, but it is said that he needed only to lift a finger or his eyebrows, to stop any proposal which he… (opposed)." Luna served as treasurer and tax collector of Valencia County when New Mexico was a territory and he held those posts after New Mexico became a state. For a quarter of a century he was the leading Republican in the territory and the state of New Mexico. Between 1881 and 1901 bills had been introduced in New Mexico's territorial legislature to create a new county out of the south-eastern portion of Grant County. Proposed names for this new county included Logan County and Florida County. However, it was not until March 16, 1901, that New Mexico's territorial legislature made this new county a reality by creating a new county from an eastern portion of Grant County and the western side of Dona Ana County. At that time Solomon Luna was the territorial leader of the Republican party here.

1777 *McKinley County*

William McKinley (1843–1901)— A native of Ohio, McKinley enlisted in the Union army during the Civil War. He served with distinction and rose to the rank of brevet-major. At the end of the war he practiced law in Canton, Ohio and became active in politics. He represented Ohio in the U.S. House of Representatives and was governor of Ohio. In 1896 he ran for president on the Republican ticket against William Jennings Bryan (1860–1925). McKinley won the election and was our president during the Spanish-American War. Elected to a second term, McKinley was assassinated in September, 1901, at Buffalo, New York. McKinley County lies on New Mexico's western border near the northwest corner of New Mexico. The citizens of the new county had been agitating to have a new county created here for about a decade. Those citizens had suggested that the new county's name should be Summit County. However, when the county was finally created by the legislature of New Mexico territory, on February 23, 1899, William McKinley was serving as president and the new county was named in his honor.

1778 *Mora County*

Town of Mora, New Mexico territory— The town of Mora is located at the western end of Mora County, on the Mora River, in north-eastern New Mexico and it is the county seat of Mora County. This county was created on February 1, 1860, by the legislature of New Mexico territory and it was named for the new county's principal town. The town of Mora took its name from that of an entire region of New Mexico which was well traveled by both Indians and Europeans. Early documents refer to the present town of Mora as *Demora*, the Spanish word for a "camp" or "stop over," which derived from the Spanish *demora*, meaning a "delay." The town of Mora was also known as *Lo de Mora*, meaning "a stopping place." In an decree dated September 28, 1835, Governor Albino Perez gave strips of land in this area to 76 settlers. The settlers founded the town of San Antonio de lo de Mora (now Cleveland, New Mexico) at the upper end of the valley and Santa Gertrudis de lo de Mora (our present town of Mora, New Mexico) at the lower end of the valley. Governor Perez was flexing the muscle of Mexico when he granted this land the colonists and his motive apparently had to do with concern about the large number of Americans who were infiltrating this (New Mexican) portion of Mexico. Thus we are able to explain the origin of the county's name with certainty, and we are able to explain the origin of the name of the town of Mora with a degree of certainty. However, there is greater difficulty in pinpointing the derivation of the name *Mora* for this entire region of New Mexico. Some sources indicate that the region, and hence the town, owes its name to the Mora River but that explanation fails to pinpoint the original derivation of the name. Three explanations are encountered in the literature on this subject: (1) *moras*, meaning "mulberry trees," (a suspect explanation because there are few mulberry trees in this region today), (2) a family surname of Mora (this choice is certainly plausible. Several individuals of that name came to this area after the 1692 Reconquest of New Mexico by the Spanish governor, Don Diego de Vargas) and (3) a choice which involves a trapper of French extraction, named Ceran St. Vrain (1802–1870) who allegedly found a dead man on the banks of the Rio de la Casa and named the area *L' Eau de Mort*, which is French for "the water of the dead." Ceran St. Vrain certainly could have discovered a dead man in this area. His travels carried him widely and he was known to have visited Taos as early as 1825. Later, in 1844, St. Vrain became part owner of a huge land grant in New Mexico. (At least two other legends are offered in support of a French name for this region; both of them involve death.)

1779 *Otero County*

Miguel A. Otero II (1859–1944)— Born at Saint Louis, Missouri, on October 17, 1859, Otero's parents took him to their home in New Mexico territory when he was still a baby. Educated at St. Louis University in Missouri and the University of Notre Dame, at South Bend, Indiana, Otero held positions in accounting and finance and first entered government service as the treasurer of the city of Las Vegas, New Mexico. He subsequently served as probate clerk of San Miguel County and as clerk of the fourth judicial district. This certainly does not sound like the resume of a man whom President William McKinley would appoint to be governor of New Mexico territory but that is exactly what happened on June 2, 1897. The appointment resulted from the political power held by Otero's, father Miguel A. Otero (1829–1882), who had been New Mexico's territorial delegate to congress and was appointed by President Abraham Lincoln to be secretary of New Mexico territory. The elder Otero also owned one million acres of New Mexican land in association with his brother. While the entrance of the younger Miguel A. Otero may have been a product of nepotism, the young governor developed to be quite a political power himself. As a Hispanic, Governor Otero enjoyed a measure of popularity simply because he was the 15th American governor of New Mexico territory but the first one of Hispanic ancestry. Under his administration a mining industry emerged and, aided by irrigation, large-scale agricultural ventures emerged in New Mexico. Despite his Hispanic roots, Governor Otero supported the Spanish-American War. He served as the territorial governor from July 14, 1897, to January 22, 1906. This county was created and named in his honor on January 30, 1899, while he was governor of New Mexico territory. It had first been proposed that this new county's name should be Sacramento County, in honor of the dominant mountain range in the area, but, to help secure the governor's support in creating a new county here, it was named in his honor.

1780 *Quay County*

Matthew S. Quay (1833–1904)— A native of Pennsylvania and a lawyer, Quay served as an officer in the Union army during the Civil War. After the war he served in the lower house of the Pennsylvania legislature, owned and edited a newspaper and was treasurer of the state of Pennsylvania. In 1887 Quay was elected to represent Pennsylvania in the U.S. Senate and he was serving in that body when New Mexico territory created and named this county in his honor on February 28, 1903. In the U.S. Senate, Quay forcefully advocated the admission of New Mexico to statehood and his efforts on behalf of New Mexico were recognized when this county was created. Senator Quay was serving in the U.S. Senate when he died in 1904. There is a town named Quay in Quay County but the county was not named for it. The county was created in 1903 but the town was not named until 1904.

1781 *Rio Arriba County*

Area of New Mexico in the region of the

upper Rio Grande River— When the United States took control of New Mexico in 1846, eight counties already existed, as survivals of the old Mexican scheme. Rio Arriba was one of these eight counties, which the United States inherited from Mexico, and it was recreated as part of America's New Mexico territory on January 9, 1852, just 16 months after New Mexico territory had been established. The present Rio Arriba county lies in northern New Mexico, less than 20 few miles west of the point where the Rio Grande River flows south from its origin in southern Colorado into New Mexico. The Rio Grande River also cuts across a small portion of southeastern Rio Arriba County. *Rio* is the Spanish word for "river," and *arriba* means "upper," or "upstream." At first the Hispanic authorities roughly divided New Mexico into an upper (*arriba*) section and a downstream (*abajo*) section. About 1610 a middle section was also recognized. Thus for about two centuries, when New Mexico was under Spanish and Mexican control, all of New Mexico was divided into three general regions, which referred to sections of the Rio Grande River. The names of these regions, translated into English, were the upper, middle and lower sections of the Rio Grande, as that river marched from north to south across New Mexico. Thus the name of Rio Arriba County preserves an ancient name for the upper portion of the Rio Grande River.

1782 *Roosevelt County*

Theodore Roosevelt (1858–1919)— A native of New York City and a graduate of Harvard, Roosevelt bought a cattle ranch in the badlands of North Dakota and lived there two years as a rancher and hunter. During the Spanish-American War, Roosevelt and his "Rough Riders" gained national attention for their military exploits in Cuba. New Mexico territory sent some 340 volunteers, who served as "Rough Riders." with Roosevelt. In 1898 he was elected governor of New York and he subsequently served as vice-president under President William McKinley. When President McKinley was assassinated in September, 1901, Theodore Roosevelt became our nation's youngest president, and a very vigorous one. He fought corporate monopoly, regulated railroad rates, and promoted conservation. Under his administration the pure food and drug act and employers' liability laws were enacted. He boldly took Panama away from Colombia, making a desired canal through the Isthmus of Panama possible. In 1908 Roose-velt urged the Republican Party to nominate William H. Taft. Taft was nominated and elected but his performance displeased Roosevelt. In 1912 Theodore Roosevelt bolted the Republican party and ran for president on a third, "Bull Moose" party ticket. This split the potential Republican vote between Taft and Roosevelt and assured victory for the Democratic candidate, Woodrow Wilson. This county was created on February 28, 1903, while Roosevelt was our nation's president.

1783 *San Juan County*

San Juan River—San Juan is Spanish for "Saint John." The San Juan, a 360 mile-long tributary of the Colorado River, rises in Archuleta County in southwestern Colorado, in the San Juan Mountains. The San Juan flows into San Juan County, in the northwestern corner of New Mexico. When it reaches Farmington, in San Juan County, New Mexico, the river bends to the west and later to the northwest. The San Juan River comes very close to touching the "Four Corners," where four of our country's southwestern states meet at one point. There the river again touches Colorado, this time with just a glancing blow, before heading west into San Juan County, Utah. In San Juan County, Utah, the San Juan River has carved a deep box canyon and it is in San Juan County, Utah, that the San Juan River finally empties its waters into those of the Colorado River. T. M. Pearce has written extensively on the origin of place names in New Mexico and Pearce tells us that the river was probably named for Saint John the Baptist. Angelico Chavez wrote an article entitled "Saints' Names in New Mexico Geography," which appeared in the November, 1949 issue of *El Palacio*. In that article Chavez agrees that "the northwest county and its river, ... is very likely derived from this same saint." (St. John the Baptist.) Robert Julyan is an expert on New Mexico's geographic names. Julyan is also cautious in his write-up on this subject in *The Place Names of New Mexico*, published in 1996. In that work Julyan tells us that San Juan Pueblo, a settlement in northwestern New Mexico, in Rio Arriba County (which borders on San Juan County, New Mexico) was named on July 12, 1598, by the Spanish explorer and official, Don Juan de Onate, for his personal patron saint, St. John the Baptist. However in his paragraph devoted to the nearby San Juan River, Julyan avoids stating which saint the river's name honors. Robert Julyan's research was extensive and careful. Since our experts on this subject, T. M. Pearce, Angelico Chavez and Robert Julyan are unwilling to state, without reservation, which saint the river was named for, it seems appropriate to conclude that the river was named for a saint of the Roman Catholic church, probably, but not definitely, Saint John the Baptist. There are at least 16 saints whose name starts with John the Baptist. Many of them can be ruled out because they did not become saints until after the San Juan River was named and the others are extremely obscure compared to Saint John the Baptist, who baptized Jesus. That Saint John the Baptist has long been one of the most popular saints of the Roman Catholic Church.

Saint John the Baptist (–)—John lived an austere life in the desert of Judea, southwest of Jerusalem. Clothed in garments of camel's hair and living on a diet of locusts and wild honey, John ministered to men, from Jerusalem and neighboring towns, who flocked to visit him. He demanded two rites of those who came to him: an open confession of their sins and physical baptism. Jesus Christ was among those baptized by John and John apparently came to believe, on that occasion, that Jesus was the Messiah. King Herod Antipas feared John's popularity and power and resented John's criticism of his sex life. The king imprisoned John and had him beheaded.

San Juan County, New Mexico, was created in February 1887, when New Mexico was a territory of the United States.

1784 *San Miguel County*

Town of San Miguel del Bado, New Mexico territory— When the United States took control of New Mexico in 1846, eight counties already existed, as survivals of the old Mexican scheme. San Miguel County had been created by the Republic of Mexico in 1844 and was thus one of the eight counties, which the United States inherited from Mexico. This county was recreated as part of America's New Mexico territory on January 9, 1852, just 16 months after New Mexico territory had been established. The town of San Miguel del Bado is today just a small settlement on the Pecos River in western San Miguel County, New Mexico. The town was founded about 1794 by Indians, who had been ostracized by their tribes because they had been converted to the Roman Catholic faith. This is one of New Mexico's oldest towns. It was built on a land grant given to these Indians by Governor Fernando Chacon. This town was the first county seat of San Miguel County under American administration. The county's seat of justice was moved to the town of Las Vegas, New Mexico in 1864 and that city is still the county seat. The Indians built a stone church here, at the settlement of San Miguel del Bado, in 1805 or 1806. It still stands with walls three feet thick and twenty feet high. While still a part of Mexico, in 1827 the census listed 2,893 inhabitants at San Miguel del Bado. When railroad tracks reached Las Vegas in 1879, San Miguel del Bado's the population dwindled greatly and the town it is no longer shown on all maps. Those maps that still show it render its name variously as San Miguel del Bado, San Miguel del Vado, or simply San Miguel. The Spanish word *bado* means "ford," and the name of the settlement came from the fact that there was a ford across the Pecos River here that was important on the Santa Fe Trail. San Miguel del Bado lies less than 40 miles away from Santa Fe, New Mexico. The *San Miguel* or "Saint Michael" in the town's name honors the Roman Catholic archangel, Saint Michael.

Saint Michael — One of the more popular saints of the Roman Catholic Church, Saint Michael as well as Saint Gabriel and Saint Raphael is mentioned as an archangel in the *Holy Bible*. From the early years of the Christian Church, Saint Michael has been looked upon as a protector of souls from snares of the devil and a defender of Christians from their enemies. This saint is also revered as a provider of consolation to Christians experiencing difficulties and hardships. Given this reputation, Saint Michael became popular to the faithful within the Church and he replaced several gods and demigods who preceded Christianity. Near Hierapolis, in the early history of the Church in Asia Minor, Saint Michael took the place of the god of thermal waters. In Gaul he replaced Mercury and in Germany Saint Michael was sometimes substituted for Wotan. A church was built and dedicated to Saint Michael near Constantinople about the fourth century A.D. An apparition of Saint Michael was reported in southern Italy in A.D. 492 and the site became a favorite destination for pilgrimages to this area. The Lombards chose Saint Michael as their patron saint, and struck coins bearing his likeness. A well-known church in Rome's Salerian Way was built in his honor. The cult of Saint Michael the Archangel is closely linked with Christianity's early Jewish heritage.

1785 *Sandoval County*

Sandoval family of north-central New Mexico territory— This county was created on March 10, 1903, while New Mexico was still a territory, and named for the Sandoval family which settled this region of north-central New Mexico. The first Sandoval known to have been in New Mexico was Sebastian de Sandoval, who was mentioned as being in Santa Fe in 1640. The records show him to have been an abusive individual, who was murdered in Santa Fe in 1640 because of his slanders against local men and women. He had earlier been excommunicated from the Roman Catholic Church so the question of where to bury him became a problem. He was not a native of New Mexico and if he had any children they were not related to the Sandoval family which became prominent in north-central New Mexico. The Sandoval family for whom this county was named are descended from Juan de Dios Sandoval Martinez (–1735). He was born in Mexico City and came to New Mexico with the Spanish governor, Don Diego de Vargas (–1704) during the 1692 Reconquest of New Mexico. Juan de Dios Sandoval Martinez had two wives. His first wife was named Juana Hernandez, (or Medina). When Juan and his wife, Juana came to New Mexico in the 1690's their 18 year old son, Miguel accompanied them. Juana Hernandez (or Medina) died in 1695, and Juan de Dios Sandoval Martinez remarried. His second wife's name was Gertrudis de Herrera, a widow of Jose Nunez. A son named Antonio Sandoval was born from this second marriage. An Antonio Sandoval is mentioned in Betty Woods' work entitled *101 Men & Women of New Mexico*. Ms. Woods tells us that one Antonio Sandoval was active in New Mexico in the 1850's, as a slave trader who raided Navajo and other Indian communities and sold his captives as slaves. This Antonio Sandoval could not reasonably have been a son of Juan de Dios Sandoval Martinez because he was active more than a century after Juan died. Whether or not he was a later member of the family honored in this county's name is uncertain. The Sandoval family for whom this county was named are descended from Juan de Dios Sandoval Martinez. The children of Juan de Dios de Martinez dropped the Martinez portion of the family name. The subsequent Sandoval husbands and wives were good Catholics and prolific. Extensive details (beyond the scope of this narrative) about the progeny of Juan de Dios Sandoval Martinez and his two wives may be found in Angelico Chavez's work enti-

tled *Origins of New Mexico Families in the Spanish Colonial Period*. Later prominent New Mexicans with the Sandoval surname include Alejandro Sandoval (1845–), a rancher and a member of New Mexico's territorial legislature and Jose Pablo Sandoval (1850–), another rancher who also served in the territorial legislature. Jose Pablo Sandoval represented San Miguel County and later Guadalupe County in the territorial legislature. Both of these counties are relatively near Sandoval County, geographically. One Julian Sandoval is mentioned as a prosperous merchant in this general section of New Mexico. His mercantile operations were in San Miguel County. Julian Sandoval also owned a ranch near Doretta. He died in 1913 at the age of 83. Another Sandoval surname belongs to Francisco D. Sandoval, who was a leading rancher in the Sandoval County area. The town of Sandoval in Sandoval County was named for this Francisco D. Sandoval. Still another Sandoval prominent in north-central New Mexico was Lorenzo J. Sandoval (1885–). He was treasurer of Santa Fe County. Lorenzo's grandfather was Felippe Sandoval, of Spanish ancestry, who settled on land which is now part of Sandoval County, New Mexico. Felippe Sandoval had a son named Ramon Sandoval, a cattleman at Cerrillos, New Mexico territory. (This Ramon Sandoval was the father of Lorenzo J. Sandoval, mentioned above.) Robert Julyan tells us in his 1996 work entitled *The Place Names of New Mexico*, that members of the Sandoval family still live in Sandoval County, New Mexico.

1786 *Santa Fe County*

City of Santa Fe, New Mexico territory— When the United States took control of New Mexico in 1846, eight counties already existed, as survivals of the old Mexican scheme. Santa Fe County had been created by the Republic of Mexico in 1844 and was thus one of the eight counties, which the United States inherited from Mexico. This county was recreated as part of America's New Mexico territory of on January 9, 1852. The city of Santa Fe and its name are ancient. It was established in 1609–1610 by the Spanish governor, Don Pedro de Peralta as the capital of the Spanish province of New Mexico. This event occurred a decade before the Mayflower colonists arrived to settle in New England. Peralta named this New Mexican city *La Villa Real de Santa Fe*. The English translation of this name is "The Royal Town of the Holy Faith." The town was named for a town in Spain, near the city of Granada, which Queen Isabella I (1451–1504) and King Ferdinand V (1452–1516) had established and named in honor of the Holy Faith of the Roman Catholic Church. Queen Isabella and King Ferdinand established the town of Santa Fe in Spain to celebrate their victory over the Moors in 1492. In its early years the entire settlement of Santa Fe in New Mexico was a fortification having no windows and only one door, protected by trenches and towers. Today Santa Fe, New Mexico, is the oldest city in New Mexico and it is the state's capital city. In 1997 the population of the city of Santa Fe was about 56,000. Many sources, both old and new, would have us believe that Santa Fe's first official name was *La Villa Real de Santa Fe de San Francisco de Assisi*. If that had been the city's first name, it would have honored Saint Francis of Assisi (1181–1226), the founder of the Friars Minor (now titled the Franciscan Order). This is incorrect. The city's first name was *La Villa Real de Santa Fe*. The longer name came into use a century after the city was founded in 1609–1610. It was not until 1714 when a patronal church was built here and dedicated to Saint Francis of Assisi, that the city's name was informally lengthened to the longer version. T. M. Pearce explains this in his article entitled "Spanish Place Name Patterns in the Southwest," which appeared in the December, 1955, issue of *Names: The Journal of The American Name Society*. Since the erroneous version has circulated widely (e.g., *The Encyclopedia Americana*, and the 1997 edition of *AAA Arizona New Mexico Tour Book*), it is appropriate to authenticate T. M. Pearce's view. To accomplish this we refer to Fray Angelico Chavez, the New Mexican poet and historian. Fray Angelico Chavez tells us: "In no document, even among the oldest, have I ever seen it referred to as 'La Villa Real de la Santa Fe de San Francisco,' although, as a Franciscan, I wish I could find such a reference. I'm afraid the title is post–1693…" This quotation was taken from the *New Mexico Place-Name Dictionary (First Collection-Committee Report May 14, 1949)*. Fray Angelico Chavez also discusses this, with a bit less detail, in his article entitled "New Mexico Religious Place-names Other than Those of Saints," which appeared in the January, 1950 issue of *El Palacio*.

1787 *Sierra County*

Uncertain— This county was created on April 3, 1884, by the legislature of New Mexico territory. The Spanish word *sierra* means "mountain" or "mountain range." The *Official New Mexico Blue Book* for 1979–1980 speculates that the county's name may honor the Sierra de los Caballos range of mountains in the county. The 1975 edition of *The New Mexico Almanac* agrees, saying that the county was "presumably" named for that mountain range within the county. T. M. Pearce's 1965 work entitled *New Mexico Place Names* indicates that in Spain, the term *sierra* refers to "high, saw-tooth mountains." Pearce indicates that this would be an apt description of the Sierra de los Caballos range of mountains. Robert Julyan's more recent work on New Mexico place names, published in 1996 speculates that the county's name likely honors the Black Mountain range, along the border between Sierra County and Grant County, in southwestern New Mexico. Julyan tells us that formation of Sierra County was spearheaded by Nicholas Galles, a lawyer and legislator who also had mining interests. The Black Mountains were the focus of mining activity at the time that this county was created and named. There are additional mountains and ranges in Sierra County, New Mexico, which might have inspired Sierra County's name. These would include the San Andres, Mimbres, Fra Cristobal and the southern end of the San Mateo Mountains in the Cibola national forest. Charles F. Coan's work entitled *A History of New Mexico* implies a broad namesake for this county when he tells us that the county was "…so named on account of the mountainous country included within its limits." In his work dealing with Spanish place names in New Mexico, Rene Coulet du Gard admits that the county might have been named for a mountain range but offers an additional possibility, Nicolas de la Sierra, "who lived at Guadalupe del Paso in 1758." T. M. Pearce's 1965 work also mentions this individual and states that he was a native of Spain and that he moved to Santa Fe about 1766.

1788 *Socorro County*

Town of Socorro, New Mexico territory— When the United States took control of New Mexico in 1846, eight counties already existed, as survivals of the old Mexican scheme. Socorro County had been created by the Republic of Mexico in 1844 and was thus one of the eight counties, which the United States inherited from Mexico. This county was recreated as part of America's New Mexico territory of in July, 1850. *Socorrer* is a Spanish verb meaning "to assist, aid, help, succor." The name dates back to June, 1598, when the Spanish conquistador, Don Juan de Onate and his hungry colonists, both men and women, were in desperate need of food. The Indians here gave them aid and succor, in the form of "much corn." Because of this kindness, Onate gave the name Socorro to the Indian pueblo here, named Teypana, just seven miles north of the present city of Socorro, New Mexico. The name was transplanted to the present city of Socorro, on the west bank of the Rio Grande River, between 1626 and 1628 when a Franciscan mission was established here. By the mid-1860's, Socorro had become rather destitute. A British visitor described it in late 1861 as "…a small, wretched place … every countenance seemed marked by vice and debauchery…" By about 1880 Socorro had become a booming mining town but most of the ore to be mined here was soon depleted. Socorro is the present seat of justice for Socorro County and in 1997 the city had a population of about 8,000.

1789 *Taos County*

Settlement of Taos, New Mexico territory— When the United States took control of New Mexico in 1846, eight counties already existed, as survivals of the old Mexican scheme. Taos County had been created by the Republic of Mexico in 1844 and named for its principal settlement here. Thus this county was one of the eight counties, which the United States inherited from Mexico. This county was recreated as part of America's New Mexico territory on January 9, 1852. The name was originally given to the settlement by its Indian occupants and "Taos" is merely the Spanish approximation of the sound of the Indians' name, which was, approximately, *Towi, Towih, Tuota* or *Tuatah*. This village, or pueblo, nearly 7,000 feet above sea level, consisted of two large communal dwellings, five and six stories high, made of adobe. This pueblo had been known to the Spanish conquistadors from the time of Juan Vasquez de Coronado (–1565), when members of his army were here. It was first mentioned under its present name by Juan de Onate, who visited it in 1598. Early Taos was an important trading center for both Taos Pueblo and Plains Indians. Taos was not settled by Europeans until about 1617 when Fray Pedro de Miranda built a mission here. French traders visited Taos in the 18th century and Anglo-American fur traders began to visit Taos early in the 19th century. From about the middle of the 19th century artists were attracted to settle in Taos because of its dramatic setting, 7,000 feet above sea level, on a sage-dotted plain between the Rio Grande River and the Sangre de Cristo range of the Rocky Mountains. From then until today many artists and writers have made their homes in Taos. The present city of Taos, New Mexico, is located three miles southwest of the original Taos Pueblo and had a 1997 population of about 4,000.

1790 *Torrance County*

Francis J. Torrance (–)— This county was created on March 16, 1903, when New Mexico was still a territory, and it was named for a railroad developer, Francis J. Torrance, from Pennsylvania. About 1900 he and William H. Andrews, also from Pennsylvania, and their associates, established the railroad that came to be the New Mexico Central Railroad. In 1902 grading for the railroad was underway and about that time the town of Torrance, also named for Francis J. Torrance, was established as the terminus of the New Mexico Central Railroad. This railroad link to civilization was vital to the commercial life of this region. At one time as many as 1,500 people lived in the town of Torrance, in Torrance County, but they have all left and the community no longer exists. The New Mexico Central Railroad was later taken over by the Southern Pacific. At least two works dealing with the history of New Mexico contain errors, which result in confusion regarding the origin of this county's name. In Robert W. Larson's 1968 work entitled *New Mexico's Quest for Statehood: 1846–1912*, the author refers to "W. H. Torrance, the head of a group of Pennsylvania capitalists…" who were involved in building the railroad here. The W. H. portion of the name is in error and probably came from William H. Andrews, the Pennsylvania associate of Francis J. Torrance. That same "W. H. Torrance" error is also contained in Robert W. Larson's article entitled "Statehood for New Mexico: 1888–1912," which appeared in the July, 1962, issue of *New Mexico Historical Review*.

1791 *Union County*

The united opinion that the new county should be created uniting portions of three former counties in one county— Union County lies in New Mexico's northeastern corner. Before it was created out of land taken from the eastern ends of three older counties, Colfax, Mora and San Miguel, the citizens of the eastern portions of those counties complained of the great distances which they had to travel (prior to the advent of motor vehicles) to attend to legal matters and conduct other business at their respective county seats. Meetings were held of representatives of the eastern portions of these three counties. While there was not early agreement on the location of the new county seat, there was a union of sentiment that a new county should be formed out of the eastern portions of Colfax, Mora and San Miguel Counties. After a number of preliminary meetings of the promoters of the new county, a definitive meeting was held in late 1889 or early 1890 at the ranch of Don Jose Manuel Gonzales. Selection of a county name apparently was deferred at this time. Rarely does a county's name have financial impact. However, agreement on the location of the new county seat was difficult to achieve. Wherever the county seat would be, new jobs and commercial opportunities would arise. These difficulties were ironed out at the meeting at Gonzales' ranch and it was agreed that Clayton would be the new county seat. The spokesmen for the new county took their proposal to the territorial legislature in 1889 and the idea was rejected. Colfax County was being asked to cede the most land but Mora and San Miguel Counties' areas would also diminish significantly. In the 1890–1891 session of the territorial legislature the idea of a new county here was again rejected but a name for the new county was born in the debates of 1890–1891. It would be Union County, signifying the united opinion that the new county should be created, uniting portions of three former counties in one county. In 1892 a stronger and more determined delegation went to the territorial capitol to lobby for the new county. They had some money with them and they apparently used some of it effectively. Union County was finally created on February 23, 1893.

1792 *Valencia County*

The village of Valencia, New Mexico territory— When the United States took control of New Mexico in 1846, eight counties already existed, as survivals of the old Mexican scheme. Valencia County had been created by the Republic of Mexico in 1844 and named for its principal settlement here, about two miles east of Los Lunas. Thus this county was one of the eight counties, which the United States inherited from Mexico. Valencia County was recreated as part of America's New Mexico territory on January 9, 1852. Sources consulted differ on the identity of the namesake of the village of Valencia. Several sources, including the *Roadside History of New Mexico*, by Francis L. Fugate and Roberta B. Fugate, indicate that its name derived from Francisco de Valencia, a lieutenant-general for Spain's Rio Abajo in the middle of the 16th century. General Francisco Valencia had a hacienda here. Other sources, including T. M. Pearce's *New Mexico Place Names*, state that the name came from the hacienda of Juan de Valencia. That hacienda was established in this area in the 17th century. Juan de Valencia was a grandson of Blas de Valencia, who came to New Mexico in 1598 with Don Juan de Onate. Information contained in Angelico Chavez's work entitled *Origins of New Mexico Families in the Spanish Colonial Period* mentions persons named Valencia with given names of Francisco, Juan and Blas. That information with respect to Blas de Valencia confirms that he came as a soldier with Onate's forces, when he was 20 years old. Chavez tells us that he later was an escort of Governor Zevallo and that "He was most likely the father of Francisco de Valencia of the next generation." It is with respect to General Francisco de Valencia that we have a conflict. Angelico Chavez's work states that "About the years 1661 to 1664 he declared himself to be fifty to fifty-four years of age…" Chavez states that this General Francisco de Valencia and his wife, Maria Lopez Millan lived on the site of the present town of Valencia and that he was a lieutenant general for the Rio Abajo area. There is only one conflict concerning Francisco de Valencia, and that is dates. The Fugates put General Francisco de Valencia as living in the middle of the 16th century, while Fray Chavez places him a century later. There is no comparable conflict concerning Juan de Valencia. Chavez tells us that Juan de Valencia was a captain in 1660 and that he escaped the Pueblo massacre of 1680 with his widowed mother and other family members. Chavez specifies that this widowed mother was the widow of Francisco de Valencia.

REFERENCES

Alvis, Berry N. "History of Union County, New Mexico." *New Mexico Historical Review*, Vol. 22, No. 3. Albuquerque: July, 1947.

Anderson, George B. *History of New Mexico: Its Resources & People*. Los Angeles, Pacific States Publishing Co., 1907.

Arizona New Mexico Tour Book. Heathrow, Florida, AAA Publishing, 1997.

Armstrong, Ruth W. *New Mexico: From Arrowhead to Atom.* New York, A. S. Barnes & Co., 1969.

Beck, Warren A., & Ynez, D. Haase. *Historical Atlas of New Mexico.* Norman, University of Oklahoma Press, 1969.

Blawis, Patricia B. *Tijerina and the Land Grants.* New York, International Publishers, 1971.

Bonney, Cecil. *Looking Over My Shoulder: Seventy-five Years in the Pecos Valley.* Roswell, New Mexico, Hall-Poorbaugh Press, Inc., 1971.

Boyd, E. "A New Mexican Retablo and Its Mexican Prototype." *El Palacio*, Vol. 56, No. 12. Santa Fe: December, 1949.

Briggs, Donald C., & Marvin Alisky. *Historical Dictionary of Mexico.* Metuchen, New Jersey, Scarecrow Press, Inc., 1981.

Brothers, Mary H. "Place Names of the San Juan Basin, New Mexico." *Western Folklore*, Vol. 10, No. 2. Berkeley: April, 1951.

Brown, Frances R. "How They Were Named." *New Mexico: The State Magazine of National Interest*, Vol. 13, No. 8, August, 1935; Vol. 13, No. 9. September, 1935; Vol. 13, No. 10. October, 1935.

Cassidy, Ina S. "Names & Places: Taos, New Mexico." *Western Folklore*, Vol. 8, No. 1. Berkeley: January, 1949.

Cassidy, Ina S. "New Mexico Place Name Studies." *Western Folklore*, Vol. 14, No. 2. Berkeley: April, 1955.

Cassidy, Ina S. "New Mexico Place Names: Taos." *El Palacio*, Vol. 61, No. 9. Santa Fe: September, 1954.

Castillo, Bernal Diaz de. *The Discovery & Conquest of Mexico: 1517–1521.* Farrar, Straus & Cudahy, 1956.

Chavez, Angelico. "New Mexico Religious Place-Names Other Than Those of Saints." *El Palacio*, Vol. 57, No. 1. Santa Fe: January, 1950.

Chavez, Angelico. *Origins of New Mexico Families in the Spanish Colonial Period.* Santa Fe, William Gannon, 1975.

Chavez, Angelico. "Saints' Names in New Mexico Geography." *El Palacio*, Vol. 56, No. 11. Santa Fe: November, 1949.

Coan, Charles F. *A History of New Mexico.* Chicago, American Historical Society, Inc., 1925.

Dargan, Marion. "New Mexico's Fight for Statehood.: 1895–1912." *New Mexico Historical Review*, Vol. 14, No. 1. Albuquerque: January, 1939.

Dillon, M. L. "Captain Jason W. James: Frontier Anti-Democrat." *New Mexico Historical Review*, Vol. 31, No. 2. Albuquerque: April, 1956.

Do You Remember Luna: 100 Years of Pioneer History: 1883–1983. Albuquerque, Adobe Press, 1983.

Du Gard, Rene C. *Dictionary of Spanish Place Names: New Mexico.* Editions des Deux Mondes.

The Encyclopedia Americana. New York, Americana Corporation, 1977.

Englebert, Omer. *The Lives of the Saints.* New York, Barnes & Noble, Inc., 1994.

Faber, Harold. *From Sea to Sea: The Growth of the United States.* New York, Farrar, Straus & Giroux, 1967.

Fergusson, Erma. *New Mexico: A Pageant of Three Peoples.* New York, Alfred A. Knopf, 1964.

Fleming, Elvis E., & Minor S. Huffman. *Roundup on the Pecos.* Roswell, New Mexico, Chaves County Historical Society, 1978.

Fletcher, Christine. *100 Keys: Names Across the Land.* Nashville, Abingdon Press, 1973.

Fodor's New Mexico: Santa Fe, Taos & Albuquerque. New York, Fodor's Travel Guides, 1985.

Frazer, Robert W. *Forts of the West.* Norman, University of Oklahoma Press, 1965.

Frost, Max. *New Mexico: Its Resources, Climate, Geography & Geological Condition.* Santa Fe, New Mexican Printing Co., 1890.

Frost, Max, & Paul A. F. Walter. *Santa Fe County.* Bureau of Immigration of New Mexico, 1906.

Fugate, Francis L., & Roberta Fugate. *Roadside History of New Mexico.* Missoula, Montana, Mountain Press Publishing Co., 1989.

Fulton, Maurice G., & Paul Horgan. *New Mexico's Own Chronicle.* Dallas, Banks Upshaw & Co., 1937.

Galbraith, Den. *Turbulent Taos.* Santa Fe, Sunstone Press, 1983.

Hanosh, Eugene J. "A History of Mora: 1835–1887." M.A. Thesis, New Mexico Highlands University, Las Vegas, New Mexico, 1967.

Hardon, John A. *Modern Catholic Dictionary.* Garden City, New York, Doubleday & Co., Inc., 1980.

Heflin, Reuben W. "New Mexico Constitutional Convention." *New Mexico Historical Review*, Vol. 21, No. 1. Albuquerque: January, 1946.

Hening, H. B. *George Curry: 1861–1947: An Autobiography.* Albuquerque, University of New Mexico Press, 1958.

Herring, Hubert. *A History of Latin America.* New York, Alfred A. Knopf, 1968.

Hinshaw, Gil. *Lea: New Mexico's Last Frontier.* Hobbs, New Mexico, Hobbs Daily News-Sun, 1977.

The History of Luna County. Deming, New Mexico, Luna County Historical Society, Inc., 1978.

History of New Mexico: Its Resources & People. Los Angeles, Pacific States Publishing Co., 1907.

History of Sierra County, New Mexico. Truth or Consequences, New Mexico, Sierra County Historical Society, Inc., 1979.

History of Torrance County, New Mexico. Estancia, New Mexico, 1959.

A History of Union County: 1803–1980. Dallas, Texas, Taylor Publishing Co., 1980.

Hodge, Frederick W. *Handbook of American Indians North of Mexico.* Totowa, New Jersey, Rowman & Littlefield, 1975.

Hodge, Frederick W., & Charles F. Lummis. *The Memorial of Fray Alonso de Benavides: 1630.* Chicago, 1916.

Horgan, Paul. *The Centuries of Santa Fe.* New York, E. P. Dutton & Co., Inc., 1956.

Hundertmark, C. A. "Reclamation in Chaves & Eddy Counties: 1887–1912." *New Mexico Historical Review*, Vol. 47, No. 4. Albuquerque: October, 1972.

Illustrated History of New Mexico. Chicago, Lewis Publishing Co., 1895.

Jones, Alison. *The Wordsworth Dictionary of Saints.* Hertfordshire, England, Wordsworth Editions, Ltd., 1994.

Julyan, Robert. *The Place Names of New Mexico.* Albuquerque, University of New Mexico Press, 1996.

Larson, Robert W. *New Mexico's Quest for Statehood: 1846–1912.* Albuquerque, University of New Mexico Press, 1968.

Larson, Robert W. "Statehood for New Mexico: 1888–1912." *New Mexico Historical Review*, Vol. 37, No. 3. Albuquerque: July, 1962.

Leigh, Rufus W. *Five Hundred Utah Place Names.* Salt Lake City, Utah, Desert News Press, 1961.

Lovell, Emily K. *A Personalized History of Otero County, New Mexico.* Alamogordo, New Mexico, Star Publishing Co., Inc., 1963.

Mabry, Thomas J. "New Mexico's Constitution in the Making: Reminiscences of 1910." *New Mexico Historical Review*, Vol. 19, No. 2. Albuquerque: April, 1944.

McAlavy, Don, & Harold Kilmer. *Curry County, New Mexico.* Dallas, Texas, Taylor Publishing Co., 1978.

McAlavy, Don, & Harold Kilmer. *High Plains History: 1879–1979.* High Plains Historical Press, 1980.

McLoughlin, Denis. *Wild & Woolly: An Encyclopedia of the Old West.* Garden City, New York, Doubleday & Co., Inc., 1975.

McWilliams, Carey. *North from Mexico.* Philadelphia, J. B. Lippincott Co., 1949.

Mann, E. B., & Fred E. Harvey. *New Mexico: Land of Enchantment.* East Lansing, Michigan State University Press, 1955.

Mathews, Henry. *New Mexico Blue Book:* 1975–1976.

Meier, Matt S. *Mexican American Biographies: A Historical Dictionary: 1836–1987.* Westport, Connecticut, Greenwood Press, 1988.

Meier, Matt S., & Feliciano Rivera. *Dictionary of Mexican American History.* Westport, Connecticut, Greenwood Press, 1981.

Motto, Sytha. *More than Conquerors: Makers of History: 1528–1978.* Albuquerque, Adobe Press, 1980.

"Necrology: Miguel Antonio Otero II." *New Mexico Historical Review,* Vol. 19, No. 4. Albuquerque: October, 1944.

New Mexico Folklore Society. *New Mexico Place-Name Dictionary (First Collection-Committee Report May 14, 1949).* Place-Name Committee of the New Mexico Folklore Society, 1949.

New Mexico: Mythology, Tradition, History. Washington, D.C. United States Government Printing Office, 1930.

Old Santa Fe & Vicinity. El Palacio Press, 1930.

Otero, Miguel A. *My Nine Years as Governor of the Territory of New Mexico: 1897–1906.* Albuquerque, University of New Mexico Press, 1940.

Pearce, T. M. "The Lure of Names." *New Mexico Quarterly,* Vol. 32, Nos. 3 & 4. Albuquerque: Autumn & Winter, 1962–1963.

Pearce, T. M. "Names on the Land." *Western Folklore,* Vol. 9, No. 4. Berkeley: October, 1950.

Pearce, T. M. *New Mexico Place Names.* Albuquerque, University of New Mexico Press, 1965.

Pearce, T. M. "Religious Place Names in New Mexico." *Names: Journal of the American Name Society,* Vol. 9, No. 1. Youngstown, Ohio: March, 1961.

Pearce, T. M. "Some Indian Place Names of New Mexico." *Western Folklore,* Vol. 10, No. 3. Berkeley: July, 1951.

Pearce, T. M. "Spanish Place Name Patterns in the Southwest." *Names: Journal of the American Name Society,* Vol. 3, No. 4. Berkeley: December, 1955.

Peterson, C. S. *Representative New Mexicans.* Denver, Colorado, 1912.

Powers, Marcella. *New Mexico Blue Book: 1977–1978.*

Powers, Marcella. *Official New Mexico Blue Book: 1979–1980.* Valliant Printing Co.

Prince, L. Bradford. *A Concise History of New Mexico.* Cedar Rapids, Iowa, Torch Press, 1914.

Read, Benjamin M. *Illustrated History of New Mexico.* 1912.

Reeve, Frank D. *History of New Mexico.* New York, Lewis Historical Publishing Co., Inc., 1961.

Richardson, Elmo R. "George Curry and the Politics of Forest Conservation in New Mexico." *New Mexico Historical Review,* Vol. 33, No. 4. Albuquerque: October, 1958.

Rivera, Lloyd D. *Grito de Aztlan.* Llano del Coyote, New Mexico, 1979.

Roberts, Calvin A., & Susan A. Roberts. *New Mexico.* Albuquerque, University of New Mexico Press, 1988.

Roberts, Frank H. H., & Ralph E. Twitchell. *History & Civics of New Mexico.* Albuquerque, Charles Ilfeld Co., 1914.

Romero, Alicia. *New Mexico Blue Book: 1947–48.* Santa Fe, Southwestern Publishing Co.

Simmons, Marc. *Albuquerque: A Narrative History.* Albuquerque, University of New Mexico Press, 1982.

Simmons, Marc. *New Mexico: A History.* New York, W. W. Norton & Co., Inc., 1977.

Spencer, J. R. *The New Mexico Almanac: 1975.* Clovis, New Mexico, 1975.

Spencer, J. R. *The New Mexico Digest: 1976.* Clovis, New Mexico, 1976.

Spencer, J. R. *The New Mexico Digest: 1977.* Clovis, New Mexico, 1977.

Stanley, F. *The Bernalillo, New Mexico, Story.* Pep, Texas, 1964.

Stanley, F. *The Los Alamos, New Mexico, Story.* Pantex, Texas, 1961.

Stanley, F. *The Mora, New Mexico, Story.* Pep, Texas, 1963.

Stanley, F. *Socorro: The Oasis.* Denver, Colorado, World Press, 1950.

Stoudemire, Sterling A. "Santiago, Guadalupe, Pilar: Spanish Shrines/Spanish Names." *Names: Journal of the American Name Society,* Vol. 26. Potsdam, New York: 1978.

Thrapp, Dan L. *Encyclopedia of Frontier Biography.* Lincoln, University of Nebraska Press, 1988.

Tibon, Gutierre. "The Name of Guadalupe." *Names: Journal of the American Name Society,* Vol. 1, No. 2. Berkeley: June, 1953.

Tittman, Edward D. "New Mexico Constitutional Convention: Recollections." *New Mexico Historical Review,* Vol. 27, No. 3. Albuquerque: July, 1952.

Twitchell, Ralph E. *The Leading Facts of New Mexican History.* Albuquerque, Horn & Wallace, 1963.

Twitchell, Ralph E. *Old Santa Fe.* Santa Fe, New Mexican Publishing Corporation, 1925.

Vexler, Robert I. *Chronology & Documentary Handbook of the State of New Mexico.* Dobbs Ferry, New York, Oceana Publications, Inc., 1978.

Watson, Julee F. *My Land.* Lubbock, Texas, Craftsman Printers, Inc.

Webb, Walter P., et al. *The Handbook of Texas.* Austin, Texas State Historical Association, 1952.

Whisenhunt, Donald W. *New Mexico Courthouses.* El Paso, Texas Western Press, 1979.

White, Marjorie B. "What's in a Name?" *New Mexico Magazine,* Vol. 38, No. 7. Santa Fe: July, 1960.

Wise, L. F., & E. W. Egan. *Kings, Rulers & Statesmen.* New York, Sterling Publishing Co., Inc., 1967.

Wolk, Allan. *The Naming of America.* Nashville, Thomas Nelson, Inc., 1977.

Woods, Betty. *101 Men & Women of New Mexico.* Santa Fe, Sunstone Press, 1976.

Work Projects Administration. *Inventory of the County Archives of New Mexico-Dona Ana, Hidalgo & Sierra Counties.* Albuquerque, 1940–1942.

Work Projects Administration. *New Mexico: A Guide to the Colorful State.* New York, Hastings House, 1953.

Works Progress Administration. *Inventory of the County Archives of New Mexico-Eddy County.* Albuquerque, 1939.

New York

(62 counties)

1793 *Albany County*

King James II (1633–1701)— James was the second surviving son of England's King Charles I (1600–1649). He was given the title duke of York and Albany soon after his christening. When James' father died, his elder brother, Charles succeeded to the throne as King Charles II (1630–1685). In 1664 King Charles II made an enormous grant of North American land to his brother, the duke of York and Albany. The duke was awarded more power over his domain that any other English proprietor. Although King Charles II had many children, none of them were legitimate so when King Charles II died in 1685, his brother, James became king of England as King James II. The first wife of the duke of York and Albany had been Anne Hyde, who died in 1671. In 1673 James remarried to Mary of Modena (1658–1718), a Catholic, and some time during this period James professed his own Catholicism. This spelled his eventual downfall as king. In 1689 the throne passed to William of Orange (1650–1702), who ruled as joint sovereign with his wife, Queen Mary II (1662–1694). Mary was a daughter of King James II. The former King James II devoted the final years of his life to religious exercises. When the English province of New York was divided into counties on November 1, 1683, Albany County was created as one of the original counties. At that time James had not yet been crowned king of England. The title "Albany" derived from James' Scottish title. That name, *Albany* or *Albainn*, was an ancient name of the highlands of Scotland.

1794 *Allegany County*

A trail which followed the Allegheny River— This county in southwestern New York was created on April 7, 1806. Some sources indicate that the name honors the Allegheny River of southwestern New York and northwestern Pennsylvania. Other sources are more specific, indicating that the county was named for a trail which followed the Allegheny River. Both the river and the trail that followed it share their names with the Alleghany Indians. The Allegheny River rises in northwestern Pennsylvania, flows in a northwestern direction into the southwestern section of New York, and then returns to Pennsylvania. The Allegheny is a 325 mile-long tributary of the Ohio River and for some 200 of those miles, it is a navigable stream. The Allegheny River completes its journey at Pittsburgh, Pennsylvania, where it unites with the Monongahela River to form the Ohio River.

Alleghany Indians— The Alleghany were a tribe who lived in the 18th century near present-day Pittsburgh, Pennsylvania, where the Allegheny River joins with the Monongahela River to form the Ohio River. The Alleghany Indians' name derived from the name of the river along which they lived. The river was apparently first named by the Iroquois Indians and later modified by Delaware Indians. The Alleghany Indians were found in a wider area than simply present-day Pittsburgh. In his work entitled *Indian Villages & Place Names in Pennsylvania*, George P. Donehoo states that "The term (Allegheny) applied to all of the Indians living west of the waters of the Susquehanna (River) within the region drained by the Ohio (River)."

1795 *Bronx County*

Bronx Borough, New York City— Effective January 1, 1898, the land around the harbor of New York was consolidated into one city and the Bronx was designated as one of the New York City's five boroughs. The borough of the Bronx was named for the Bronx River, a short stream which rises in Westchester County, just north of New York City, and flows south through the center of Bronx Borough into the East River Strait. In the first half of the 17th century, when the Netherlands controlled this area, a Scandinavian man, named Jonas Bronck (–1643), became the first European to settle north of Manhattan Island. Here Bronck had a 500, acre farm, and a river adjacent to his farm came to be known as Bronck's River. We know that river today as the Bronx River. In *The Encyclopedia of New York City*, edited by Kenneth T. Jackson, the location of this farm is pinpointed at the corner of 132nd Street and Lincoln Avenue. There is controversy about the nationality of Jonas Bronck in the literature dealing with this subject. Apparently he sailed to New Amsterdam in North America from Hoorn, Holland, in 1639, under protection of the Dutch flag. Some sources have assumed from this that Bronck was Dutch. That is incorrect. Jonas Bronck was Scandinavian, although it is not clear whether he was Danish or Swedish. Here he crossed the Harlem River and settled north of it in 1641 and erected a stone dwelling, several tobacco houses, a barn and two barracks for his farm hands and servants. He died in April, 1643. Although the borough of the Bronx was created late in the 19th century, it was not until the second decade of the 20th century that Bronx County was established. Prior to that Bronx Borough had been included in New York County.

1796 *Broome County*

John Broome (1738–1810)— John Broome was a merchant in New York City and a leader in New York's participation in the American Revolution. In 1777 he was a member of New York's constitutional convention. He was a member of the Committee of 51 with John Jay (1745–1829), and belonged to the Committee of 100 with James Duane (1733–1797). With Philip Livingston (1716–1778), Broome was a member of the Committee of Observation. After the Revolution he was a candidate for a seat in the U.S. House of Representatives but he was defeated by John Lawrence (1750–1810). Defeated for office at the federal level, Broome became one of the organizers of state government in New York. He served in the new state's senate and was subsequently elected as lieutenant-governor of New York. Broome died in 1810 while he was serving as lieutenant-governor under New York's Governor Daniel D. Tompkins (1774–1825). This county was created on March 28, 1806, while Broome was New York's lieutenant-governor. In appreciation of that honor John Broome designed a handsome silver seal which he presented to the authorities of the new Broome County.

1797 *Cattaraugus County*

Cattaraugus Creek— This county in southwestern New York was created on March 11, 1808, and named for the creek which today forms the county's northern border. Cattaraugus Creek is about 70 miles long. Its tributaries include streams named Buttermilk and Connoirtoirauley. The waters of Cattaraugus Creek flow in a western direction and empty into Lake Erie at Irving, New York, within the Cattaraugus Indian Reservation. *Cattaraugus* is an Indian name and was intended by them to be derogatory. Sources consulted differ on the translation of this derogatory name. Some say the Indian name meant "bad-smelling banks," while others translate the name as "where ooze mud falls." Presumably the object of the Indians' derision was the odor of natural gas and/or petroleum, which proved to be valuable commodities to later White entrepreneurs. Natural gas is the more likely suspect since the county's petroleum deposits are primarily at the southern end of the county, away from Cattaraugus Creek.

1798 *Cayuga County*

Cayuga Indians— The Cayuga were a tribe of the powerful Iroquois Indian confederation. They lived in the valley of New York's Mohawk River and points west as far as the shores of Cayuga Lake, in western New York. In 1660 their population was estimated at 1,500 but by the time of the American Revolution their numbers had decreased almost by one-third to about 1,100. At the beginning of the American Revolution many Cayuga Indians moved to Canada but two centuries later, in 1985, there were 413 Cayuga Indians counted who were living on Indian reservations in New York. The Iroquois tribes subsisted on primitive agriculture and hunting. Their military power was great and they practiced both the taking of scalps and occasional cannibalism. The translation of the Indian name *Cayuga* is uncertain. The Indians had no written language so it was left to Europeans to record Indian words in writing. William M. Beauchamp wrote an article entitled "Aboriginal Place Names of New York," which was published by the New York State Education Department in 1907. In that article Beauchamp offers both "where they haul boats out," and "from the water to the shore" as possible translations of the name. If either of these translations is correct, one might suspect that the Cayuga Indians' name was first applied to Cayuga Lake and subsequently to the tribe of Indians who lived on its shores. Support for this theory is found in a *History of Cayuga County, New York*, published in 1908. That work refers to the Cayuga Indians in this fashion: "The wan-

dering band entered Cayuga Lake from the Seneca River and settled upon the eastern bank. They were a nameless offshoot from the parent tribe at Oswego, until they settled, when they became known as the Cayugas or 'People at the Mucky Land.'" Cayuga County, New York, was created and named on March 8, 1799.

1799 *Chautauqua County*

Chautauqua Lake, New York— This county was created on March 11, 1808, and named for the lake within its borders. At that time the spelling was rendered Chautauque. This lake lies in the extreme southwestern corner of New York state, some 700 feet above its huge near neighbor, Lake Erie. Chautauqua Lake is about 18 miles long. Its width varies but most of the lake is from one to three miles wide. Resort communities abound here and the Chautauqua institution was established here in 1874. The original intent of that institution was to educate Methodist Sunday school teachers but its content gradually broadened to emphasize popular education, cultural pursuits and entertainment. These activities were generally held outside under a tent and their success led to the founding of hundreds of local chautauquas throughout the United States during the late 19th and early 20th centuries. *Chautauqua* is a name of Indian origin which has been given countless spellings by Whites. The meaning of the Indians' original word has been lost but possible translations abound including:
— "A moccasin," referring to the shape of the lake.
— "A bag (or pack) tied in the middle," also a description of the lake's shape.
— "Something raised up." (Chautauqua Lake is elevated some 700 feet above Lake Erie.)
— "Where fish were taken out."
— "Foggy place."
— "Two moccasins fastened together."
— "The place of easy death" or "the place where one was lost" or "the place where one disappears and is seen no more." These translations are associated with a legend about a young Indian squaw who, after eating a root which created a tormenting thirst, took a drink from the lake's water and disappeared in its depths.
— "Place where child was swept away by waves."

1800 *Chemung County*

Chemung River— The Chemung River is a tributary of the Susquehanna River. The Chemung is formed in southern New

York by the confluence of the Tioga River and the Cohocton River near the city of Corning. The Chemung flows east from the Corning area into Chemung County to Elmira and turns southeast after leaving Elmira and crosses the Pennsylvania border where it soon reaches the Susquehanna River. The Chemung River's name is of Indian origin and like many other Indian names, its translation is uncertain. However the translations encountered most frequently are "a horn," "big horn," or "antlers" and the "big horn" possibility has a very interesting background. Several sources indicate that the name of the Chemung River, and that of an Indian village on its banks, can be traced to a large horn or tusk which was found in the Chemung River. Chemung County, New York, was created in 1836, long after the river had been named by the Indians. However, about 1855 another tusk was found in the Chemung River and an English scientist who examined it identified it a tusk of an elephant or similar animal probably now (1855) extinct. These references to the horn or tusk are contained in William M. Beauchamp's article entitled "Aboriginal Place Names of New York," which was published by the New York State Education Department in 1907. George P. Donehoo's 1928 work dealing with Indian place names in Pennsylvania indicates that the tusk theory may be valid and says that the tusks were "probably of the mammoth…," which, of course, have long been extinct in North America. However Donehoo also offers a menu of less colorful explanations for the river's name including "antlers," (of a deer or elk) and even terms of rank such as "chief," or "superior." Arch Merrill's work entitled *Southern Tier*, published in 1954 endorses the mammoth theory for the origin of the river's name. He tells us that "In prehistoric time, the mammoth, a fearsome creature with tusks seven to nine feet long…" wandered along the shores of the Chemung River. The possibility that the Chemung River owes its name to ancient mammoth tusks is mentioned in a variety of New York sources. One of them gets quite specific, telling us that "In volume 4, page 42 of the 'American Museum,' published in Philadelphia, 1788 by Matthew Carey, appears the 'description of a horn or bone, lately found in the river Chemung or Tyoga, a western branch of the Susquehanna, about twelve miles above Tioga Point.' It was 6 feet 9 inches long, 21 inches in circumference at the larger, and 15 at the smaller, end … incurvated like the arc of an extended circle. Two or three feet from each end of the tusk seemed to have perished, or broken off; the entire length presumed to have been ten or twelve feet."

1801 *Chenango County*

Uncertain— Sources consulted are in essentially unanimous agreement that the name *Chenango* is of Indian origin and that it means "bull thistle(s)," or "large bull thistle(s)." However it seems very unlikely that the New York legislature would have decided to name a new county for an Indian word meaning "bull thistle(s)," whether large or not. Rather, the legislators undoubtedly named this county for something that already had been given the name *Chenango*. There at least four possibilities including (1) Chenango River, a 100 mile-long tributary of the Susquehanna; the Chenango River traverses the entire length of Chenango County from north to south, (2) Chenango Lake, (3) the Chenango Canal and (4) an Indian village named Chenango which was located on the Chenango River. The Indians kept their captives and vassals in this village on the Chenango River. They apparently occupied the village for only about six years from 1748 to 1754. It is unlikely that Chenango County was named for the Chenango Canal. The county was created on March 15, 1798, and the canal was not completed from Utica to Binghamton until about 1833. However it does seem likely that the county was named for the Chenango River, Chenango Lake or the Indian village named Chenango; we just don't know which one.

1802 *Clinton County*

George Clinton (1739–1812)— Born on July 26, 1739, at Little Britain, New York, Clinton served in the legislature of England's New York colony. He became one of America's leaders in opposition to England's treatment of her colonial citizens and he was a New York delegate to the second Continental Congress. Clinton also was a brigadier-general in our Revolutionary army. On July 30, 1777, George Clinton became New York's first elected governor and when New York was admitted to the new federal Union of states, Clinton became the first governor of the state of New York. During the period that the original 13 colonies were debating the formation of a central, federal government, Clinton was an outspoken critic of certain aspects of the proposed federal Constitution. Nevertheless, he served our nation at the federal level, as vice-president under Presidents Thomas Jefferson and James Madison. This county was created on March 7, 1788, while Clinton was New York's governor.

1803 *Columbia County*

A patriotic name derived from the name of Christopher Columbus— The term *Columbia* was derived from Christopher Columbus' name and it has been given various patriotic meanings. Used in the name of the District of Columbia, it means the United States of America. The word *Columbus* is a Latin noun and means a "male dove" or "male pigeon." This New York county was created on April 4, 1786, while the 13 former English colonies were taking tentative steps toward formation of a central federal government. According to at least one source, the name *Columbia* was then being considered as a possible name for the new nation.

Cristoforo Colombo (1451–1506)— Colombo, whose name we render as Christopher Columbus, was a native of Italy who believed the theory that the earth is round and that Asia could be reached by sailing west from Europe. He persuaded Ferdinand and Isabella of Spain to equip an expedition for him to test this theory. Sailing from Europe August 3, 1492, he first sighted land in the Americas in the Bahama Islands on October 12, 1492. On this voyage he left a colony of 40 men on the Hatian coast. Columbus returned several times to the New World before his death in 1506. Popularly known as the discoverer of America, Columbus was certainly not the first European to reach the Western Hemisphere. Leif Ericsson accomplished that about the year A.D. 1000. But it was Columbus' expedition that triggered rapid exploration, conquest and settlement of the Americas by Europeans.

1804 *Cortland County*

Pierre van Cortlandt (1721–1814)— This county's namesake descended from an important and wealthy Dutch family that owned enormous amounts of land in New Netherland. When England seized control of New York, the former Dutch owners' property and inheritance rights were permitted to continue. Pierre van Cortlandt was born on January 10, 1721. He served in the provincial militia during the French and Indian Wars and was a member of the legislature of England's province of New York. He was a member of the provincial convention, and was president of the council of safety. During the American Revolution van Cortlandt entertained Washington, Franklin and Lafayette at his manor house. In 1777, Pierre van Cortlandt became the first elected lieutenant-governor of New York. He held that office for 18 years and thus when New York was admitted to the new federal Union of states, van Cortlandt became the first lieutenant-governor of the state of New York. Van Cortlandt also presided over the convention which framed New York's first state constitution. Our Pierre van Cortlandt is sometimes confused with his son, Pierre van Cortlandt II (1762–1848), who represented New York in the U.S. House of Representatives. This county was created on April 8, 1808. At that time, the van Cortlandt family still owned extensive land in New York.

1805 *Delaware County*

Delaware River— This county in the western Catskill Mountain region was created on March 10, 1797, and named for the Delaware River which is formed within its borders by the junction of the East Branch and West Branch Rivers. The Delaware River then flows south to form the southwestern border of Delaware County, New York and there it is also the boundary between New York and Pennsylvania. The Delaware is some 280 miles long and carries extensive commercial traffic. It empties into Delaware Bay on the Atlantic Ocean. The Delaware River was named for this Delaware Bay and that bay was named for Thomas West, Lord De La Warr (1577–1618), who was a British governor of colonial Virginia.

1806 *Dutchess County*

Mary Beatrice of Modena, Duchess of York & Albany (1658–1718)— Mary Beatrice of Modena was the second wife of James, the duke of York and Albany (1633–1701) and her title (as spelled in those days) was dutchess of York and Albany. James was the second surviving son of England's King Charles I (1600–1649). He was given the title duke of York and Albany soon after his christening. When James' father died, his elder brother, Charles succeeded to the throne as King Charles II (1630–1685). In 1664 King Charles II made an enormous grant of North American land to his brother, the duke of York and Albany. The duke was awarded more power over his domain that any other English proprietor. Although King Charles II had many children, none of them were legitimate so when King Charles II died in 1685, his brother, James became king of England as King James II.

The first wife of the duke of York and Albany had been Anne Hyde, who died in 1671. In 1673 James remarried to Mary Beatrice of Modena (1658–1718), a Catholic, and some time during this period James professed his own Catholicism. This spelled his eventual downfall as king. In 1689 the throne passed to William of Orange (1650–1702), who ruled as joint sovereign with his wife, Queen Mary II (1662–1694). Mary was a daughter of King James II, from his first marriage to Anne Hyde.

Mary Beatrice of Modena, Duchess of York & Albany (1658–1718)— The only daughter of the Italian Alfonso IV, duke of Modena, Mary's education in northern Italy was religious in nature and by the age of 14 Mary Beatrice had decided to become a nun of the Salesian Order of the Roman Catholic Church. Her marriage to England's duke of York and Albany was arranged through the influence of the French king, Louis XIV (1638–1715). She had been persuaded that she could accomplish more for the Roman Catholic faith by marrying the duke of York and Albany (who already was showing pro–Catholic symptoms) than through the vocation of a nun. In September, 1673 Mary Beatrice was married, by proxy to the 40 year-old duke of York and Albany. At that time May was only 15 years of age. Upon her arrival in England she was received with great honors by the English court. Mary became fond of her husband's two children from his first marriage to Anne Hyde, and she came to sincerely love her husband in spite of his habitual adultery with mistresses. Sadly, all of the five children whom Mary Beatrice conceived with her husband, James, died very young. When her husband was crowned king of England on February 6, 1685, Mary Beatrice became queen consort of England. As Mary had hoped, King James II professed his Catholicism but rather than promoting that faith in England, it resulted in his downfall as king of England, and the king and his queen consort, Mary Beatrice, fled to France.

When the English province of New York was divided into counties on November 1, 1683, Dutchess County was created as one of the original counties. At that time James had not yet been crowned king of England, and Mary Beatrice of Modena had not yet become queen consort.

1807 *Erie County*

Erie Indians— This county in western New York borders on Lake Erie. It was cre-ated in April, 1821, while the Erie Canal was under construction. De Witt Clinton (1769–1828) broke ground with a ceremonial first spade of earth for the construction of the Erie Canal just four years before Erie County was created. The Erie Canal, of course, was destined to become instrumental in building our nation by linking the vast agricultural lands in our West, to eastern markets. However, sources dealing with the history, geography and place names on New York refrain from crediting either Lake Erie or the Erie Canal as the namesake of this county. Rather, these sources state that the county was named for the Erie Indians, a tribe that disappeared from history almost two centuries before this county was created. Henry Gannett's work entitled *The Origin of Certain Place Names in the United States*, states that Lake Erie was named for the Erie Indians and then Erie County, New York was named for the lake. This certainly seems to be the most rational explanation, but Gannett appears to be the only vote for that choice (and his work is known to contain factual errors concerning the origins of some county names in other states) so we will accept the majority view that this county was named for the Erie Indians.

Erie Indians— Frederick W. Hodge's *Handbook of American Indians North of Mexico*, tells us that the Erie were a populous sedentary tribe, who resided, in the 17th century, from Lake Erie, probably south as far as the Ohio River and east along the watershed of the Allegheny River. The Erie subsisted primarily on maize. Although they were an Iroquois-speaking tribe, the Erie never were a member of the Iroquois Nation. In fact, by 1656, most Erie Indians had been slain by the Iroquois and any survivors were adopted by the Iroquois or other tribes, thus removing the Erie tribe as a separate entity, a full century before the American Revolution.

1808 *Essex County*

Uncertain— Most sources dealing with the history, geography and place names of New York tell us that Essex County, New York, was named for Essex County, England. This New York county was created on March 1, 1799, little more than a decade after the American colonists had won their freedom from England in the bloody American Revolution. It seems very doubtful that New York would name one of her new counties directly for a county in England, when memories of that war were still very fresh. Joel N. Eno provides an explanation for this seemingly bizarre county name in his article entitled "New York County Names," which appeared in the April, 1916, issue of *The Magazine of History*. As Eno explains it in that article, Essex County, New York, was created in 1799 and named for the town of Essex within its borders and that town had been named for Essex County, Massachusetts. Since that county had been created long before the American Revolution and named for Essex County, England, Eno's explanation makes sense.

Essex County, Massachusetts & Essex County England— A large proportion of the early settlers of what is now the state of Massachusetts, came from the eastern region of Anglia, in southern England. Many of the geographic names that these early settlers used for their towns and counties in the new world were taken directly from town and county names in the east Anglia section of England. Essex County, Massachusetts, was one of the first counties to be established in the present state of Massachusetts. It was created on May 10, 1643, and named for Essex County in the eastern section of Anglia, in southern England. This seacoast county facing the European continent was an important center when it was occupied by the Roman Empire and it continued to be an important population center, containing London, when the East Saxons invaded it. The name *Essex* means "territory of the East Saxons." Essex was one of the seven Anglo-Saxon kingdoms of Britain known as the Heptarchy. In the seventh century Essex was conquered by Mercia, one of the other kingdoms of the Heptarchy, and later, in the ninth century, Wessex, which had been another member of the Heptarchy, conquered it. The Essex County of today's England no longer contains London. Essex County, England, is about 54 miles long and some 48 miles wide. Its principal river is the Thames.

Two facts need to be established to validate Joel Eno's explanation in the April, 1916, issue of *The Magazine of History*: (1) There must be (or have been) a town or village in Essex County, New York, named Essex. This need is satisfied. There is a community named Essex (zip code 12936) in Essex County, New York. (2) That town or village must have been named prior to March 1, 1799, when Essex County, New York was created. On this point we encounter difficulty and the conflict is provided to us by the same authority on New York place names, Joel N. Eno. An article entitled "A Tercentennial History of the Towns & Cities of New York:

Their Origin, Dates and Names" was included in volume 15 of the *Proceedings of the New York State Historical Association*, dated 1916. In that article Eno states that that the town or village of Essex in Essex County, New York, was not established until April 4, 1805. It is this conflict in the naming chronology which results in our classifying the origin of Essex County, New York's name as "Uncertain."

1809 *Franklin County*

Benjamin Franklin (1706–1790)—Franklin was a native of Massachusetts who moved to Pennsylvania in his teens. Poverty denied him a formal education but he became the leading printer and editor in North America. Franklin gained fame for his discoveries and inventions in the physical sciences and he distinguished himself as author, philosopher and diplomat. Franklin was a signer of the Declaration of Independence and an important member of the convention which framed the U.S. Constitution. In 1808 the New York legislature was petitioned to create a new county here and the proposed name of that new county was Norfolk. The legislature created the new county on March 11, 1808, but named it Franklin rather than Norfolk.

1810 *Fulton County*

Robert Fulton (1765–1815)—A native of Pennsylvania, Fulton supported himself while a young man as an artist. He later gained fame for his inventions dealing with marine vessels. He invented a submarine which he successfully demonstrated in the year 1800. He invented mines to be used in naval warfare and was one of the inventors of the steamboat. The steamboat became a commercial success, made Fulton famous and created greatly in the development of America. Fulton County, New York, was created on April 18, 1838.

1811 *Genesee County*

Valley of New York's Genesee River— Genesee County was created on March 30, 1802 and named for the *valley* through which the Genesee River flows. That river rises in northern Pennsylvania, crosses the New York border near Wellsville, New York, and travels virtually due north across the agricultural region of western New York, until it empties into Lake Ontario, near the city of Rochester, New York. (Rochester had previously been named Genesee Falls.) The Genesee River is some 144 miles long. Its name is of Seneca Indian

origin and is generally translated as "beautiful valley."

1812 *Greene County*

Nathanael Greene (1742–1786)— Greene was born in Rhode Island and served briefly in the Rhode Island legislature. He gained fame as one of the ablest American generals in the Revolutionary War. This New York county was created on March 25, 1800, and named in honor of General Nathanael Greene. However the new county's name was misspelled as "Green" in the original act that created this county.

1813 *Hamilton County*

Alexander Hamilton (–1804)— A native of the West Indies, Hamilton moved to New York and served as an officer in America's revolutionary army. One of his assignments during the war was aide-de-camp to General George Washington. After the war Hamilton was a member of the convention which framed the U.S. Constitution. He collaborated with Madison and Jay in writing a series of papers entitled *The Federalist*, which explained the new constitution and advocated its adoption. Hamilton was New York's only signer of the U.S. Constitution. A conservative and an advocate of a strong central government, he served as the United States' first secretary of the treasury. In 1804 he engaged in a duel with Aaron Burr and Hamilton died of wounds he suffered in that duel. This county was created in 1816.

1814 *Herkimer County*

Nicholas Herkimer (1728–1777)— Herkimer was the son of German immigrants who settled in the valley of New York's Mohawk River near what is today the city of Herkimer, the county seat of Herkimer County. Nicholas Herkimer served the English crown as a lieutenant in the Schenectady battalion of the militia during the French and Indian Wars. His surname was rendered as Herchkeimer on the commission which made him a lieutenant in this militia. During the years leading up to the American Revolution, Herkimer was a critic of British policies toward her North American colonies and he was head of his county's committee of safety. In 1776 he was commissioned a brigadier-general in the New York militia of our Revolutionary armies. His assignment was to protect New York from attacks by Indians and Tories. On August 6, 1777, Herkimer and his troops were attacked by Indians and Tories at Oriskany, New York,

and General Herkimer was mortally wounded. His leg was amputated in an unsuccessful attempt to save his life and Herkimer died ten days later, on August 16, 1777. All sources consulted agree that this county was created on February 16, 1791, and that the county's name honored the German-American Revolutionary general who died on August 16, 1777. However, there are various opinions concerning the spelling of both the county's original name and the general's surname. Spellings encountered for General Herkimer's surname include Erghemar, Herchkeimer, Herkheimer, Hareniger, Harkemeir, Herchamer, Harchamer and Harkemar. A work published in Philadelphia 1879 by Everts & Ensign entitled *History of Tioga, Chemung, Tompkins and Schuyler Counties, New York*, tells us that when Herkimer County was originally created in 1791, its name was spelled Erghemer. Benson J. Lossing's 1888 work entitled *The Empire State: A Compendious History of the Commonwealth of New York* says that the original spelling of Herkimer County's name was Erghemar. J. H. French's *Gazetteer of the State of New York*, published in 1860, agrees that Erghemar was the first version of this county's name.

1815 *Jefferson County*

Thomas Jefferson (1743–1826)— Jefferson was a native of Virginia and a member of the Virginia legislature. He served Virginia as governor and was a delegate to the second Continental Congress. Jefferson was the author of the Declaration of Independence and one of its signers. He was minister to France, secretary of state, vice-president and president of the United States. As president, he accomplished the Louisiana Purchase and he arranged the Lewis & Clark Expedition to the Pacific Northwest. Jefferson was a true intellectual, thoroughly knowledgeable in the arts and sciences. His political theories were pivotal in the formation of our infant republic. This county was created on March 28, 1805, while Jefferson was president.

1816 *Kings County*

King Charles II (1630–1685)— In 1664 King Charles II made an enormous grant of North American land to his brother, the duke of York and Albany. The duke was awarded more power over his domain that any other English proprietor. On November 1, 1683, the duke's North American province of New York was divided into twelve counties, and one of them,

King's County, was named for the reigning monarch of England, King Charles II.

King Charles II (1630–1685) — In 1649 King Charles I (1600–1649) lost the throne of England to revolutionary forces headed by Oliver Cromwell (1599–1658) and the king was beheaded. Cromwell and his associates ruled England until the monarchy was restored in 1660 when Charles II became king of England. At that time, Charles II was the eldest surviving son of King Charles I and Queen Henrietta Maria (1609–1669). As England's king under the restored monarchy, Charles II found it necessary to become an artful politician and appease various factions to preserve the monarchy. In many ways Charles II skillfully accomplished the required Machiavellian gamesmanship. In light of this it seems difficult to understand the king's reckless disregard of public opinion concerning two subjects: Religion and marital fidelity. Regarding religion, King Charles II rather openly flirted with Roman Catholicism, which he could hardly have failed to notice was unpopular in England. With respect to marital fidelity, King Charles II had little or none. On May 21, 1662, he married Catherine of Braganza (1638–1705). In the years that followed he had several mistresses. (One whole book is devoted to them: *The Mistresses of Charles II* by Brian Masters.) Although King Charles II had many children, none of them were legitimate so when King Charles II died in 1685, his brother, James (1633–1701) became king of England.

1817 *Lewis County*

Morgan Lewis (1754–1844) — A native of New York City and a graduate of the College of New Jersey (now Princeton), Lewis was studying law when the American Revolution interrupted those studies. He served in the Revolutionary army and rose to the rank of colonel as chief of staff for General Horatio Gates (1728–1806). At the end of the war, Lewis completed his legal studies, established a practice in New York City and was elected to the New York legislature. In 1791 he became the state's attorney general and the following year was made a justice on New York's supreme court. In 1801 he became its chief justice. In 1804 Lewis was elected governor of New York and he served one four-year term. Defeated in a bid for reelection by Daniel D. Tompkins (1774–1825), Lewis later served in the New York senate. When the War of 1812 began, President James Madison offered Morgan Lewis a seat in his cabinet as secretary of war. Lewis declined that appointment but agreed to serve instead, as a 58-year-old quartermaster general. He was promoted to the rank of major-general in 1813 and he commanded troops first on the Niagara frontier and later around New York City. This county was created on March 28, 1805, while Lewis was governor of New York.

1818 *Livingston County*

Robert R. Livingston (1746–1813) — Livingston was born in New York City and represented New York in the Continental Congress, where he served as secretary for foreign affairs. He also assisted in drafting our nation's Declaration of Independence. In 1801 President Thomas Jefferson appointed Livingston as minister to France with instructions to negotiate peaceful rights for Americans on the Mississippi River to the port of New Orleans. James Monroe was later sent to France to assist Livingston in the negotiations. Their efforts were amply rewarded when France offered to sell to the United States all of Louisiana. We accepted, and the resulting Louisiana Purchase doubled the size of our country. Livingston County, New York, was created on February 23, 1821. On that same date, the New York legislature created and named Monroe County, to honor the other member of the team which accomplished the Louisiana purchase.

1819 *Madison County*

James Madison (1751–1836) — Madison was born in Virginia and served in the Virginia legislature and in the Continental Congress. He was a member of the convention which framed the U.S. Constitution and he collaborated with Hamilton and Jay in writing a series of papers under the title *The Federalist*, which explained the new constitution and advocated its adoption. Madison represented Virginia in the U.S. House of Representatives, served for eight years as secretary of state and for eight years as president of the United States. This county was created on March 21, 1806, while Madison was serving in President Thomas Jefferson's cabinet as secretary of state.

1820 *Monroe County*

James Monroe (1758–1831) — Monroe, a native of Virginia, served in the Revolutionary War. Prior to his election as president of the United States, Monroe served in a wide variety of government posts. He served Virginia in the state legislature and as governor. He was a member of the Con-federation congress and the U.S. Senate. He was minister to France and to Britain and he held two cabinet posts. As president, Monroe stressed limited government and strict construction of the constitution. He acquired Florida for the U.S. from Spain and he was the author of a policy declaration (later known as the Monroe Doctrine) which proscribed outside interference in North and South America. This county was created on February 23, 1821, while Monroe was our nation's president.

1821 *Montgomery County*

Richard Montgomery (1738–1775) — Montgomery was born in Ireland and served with the British in the French and Indian War. He settled in New York state where he was elected to the New York provisional congress. He served as an American general in the Revolutionary War and he was killed in combat in that war. This county was originally created on March 12, 1772, and named Tryon County in honor of William Tryon (1729–1788), England's governor of her province of New York. After the Revolution, the odious name was banished from New York's county map and replaced with the name of the Revolutionary War hero, Richard Montgomery. New York also had a Charlotte County, named on March 12, 1772, for a member of the English royal family. Sources consulted differ on whether Charlotte County's name honored the queen consort of King George III (1738–1820), Queen Charlotte Sophia of Mecklenburg-Strelitz (1744–1818) or the eldest daughter of King George III, Charlotte Auguste Mathilda (1766–1828), the princess royal. England's province of North Carolina had a similar place name situation with Wake County honoring Margaret Wake, the wife of England's governor, William Tryon (who governed North Carolina before coming to New York) and both a city (Charlotte) and a county (Mecklenburg), named for the queen consort of King George III, Queen Charlotte Sophia of Mecklenburg-Strelitz (1744–1818). Intuition might lead us to suspect that the Southerners of North Carolina would be more chivalrous than the Yankees of New York about changing place names after the American Revolution. In this case intuition provides the correct answer. On April 2, 1784, New York banished both of the odious English names from her map substituting Montgomery for Tryon and Washington for Charlotte. The chivalrous North Carolinians allowed Margaret Wake's name to remain on her map, as Wake County, where

North Carolina's capital is located. North Carolina also allowed both of the names honoring the queen consort of our foremost British antagonist, King George III to remain; i.e., the important commercial city of Charlotte and the county which surrounds it (Mecklenburg County).

1822 *Nassau County*

King William III (1650–1702) — This county on New York's Long Island was not created until April 27, 1898, more than a century after the American Revolution had removed English control of our country. However, the county's name had been coined (as a name for all of Long Island) in 1693, while King William III was ruling England as joint sovereign with his wife, Queen Mary II (1662–1694). Nassau was the family name of King William III, derived from the name of a former duchy in Germany. The House of Nassau was named for the town of Nassau on the Lahn River, an eastern tributary of the Rhine, near which the family's ancestral castle stood. In Old High German *naz* meant "damp, marshy" and *augia* meant "land." Skipping fast forward two centuries from 1693 to 1898, we learn that the citizens of three municipalities on Long Island desired to have the affairs of their municipalities "…free from any entangling alliances with the great city of New York." These municipalities were Oyster Bay, Hempstead and North Hempstead. They were then part of Queens County, which was part of New York City. When Nassau County was created April 27, 1898, these municipalities were removed from Queens County and hence from New York City. A committee of the group desiring that a new county be created was formed to select a name for the proposed new county here. That committee was headed by P. Halstead Scudder of Oyster Bay, New York and it chose the name Nassau for the new county. This committee, like the elephant, never forgets. They recalled that on April 10, 1693, when King William III was ruling England, the present Long Island had been designated as Nassau Island by New York's provincial assembly, in honor of the reigning monarch of England. The name had been dormant for 205 years until this committee revived it.

King William III (1650–1702) — William, Prince of Orange, was born in the Netherlands. He was the grandson of England's King Charles I (1600–1649) and in 1677 William married his cousin, Mary (1662–1694), who was then the presumptive heir to the English throne, occupied by her father, King James II (1633–1701). In 1688 William invaded England, supported by both Dutch and English troops and on April 11, 1689, William and his wife were crowned king and queen of England. They ruled as joint sovereigns, titled King William III and Queen Mary II until Mary's death in 1694. William continued on the English throne until his death in 1702.

1823 *New York County*

King James II (1633–1701) — James was the second surviving son of England's King Charles I (1600–1649). He was given the title duke of York and Albany soon after his christening. When James' father died, his elder brother, Charles succeeded to the throne as King Charles II (1630–1685). In 1664 King Charles II made an enormous grant of North American land to his brother, the duke of York and Albany. The duke was awarded more power over his domain that any other English proprietor. On November 1, 1683, the duke's North American province of New York was divided into twelve counties, and one of them, New York County, was named for the duke of York and Albany. King Charles II had many children, but none of them were legitimate so when he died in 1685, his brother James became king of England as King James II. The first wife of the duke of York and Albany had been Anne Hyde, who died in 1671. In 1673 James remarried to Mary of Modena (1658–1718), a Catholic, and some time during this period James professed his own Catholicism. This spelled his eventual downfall as king. In 1689 the throne passed to William of Orange (1650–1702), who ruled as joint sovereign with his wife, Queen Mary II (1662–1694). The former King James II devoted the final years of his life to religious exercises.

1824 *Niagara County*

Niagara River — This county was created on March 11, 1808, and named for its Niagara River in western New York. The Niagara is a very short strait, which connects two of the Great Lakes, Lake Erie and Lake Ontario. The boundary line between the U.S. and Canada passes through the center of the 36 mile-long Niagara River. The river was named by the Indians and since they had no written language it was left to Europeans to render their name in writing. Several New York sources claim that the origin and meaning of the name *Niagara* are lost in antiquity. However several other sources indicate that the meaning is not lost and that the translation is "bisected bottom-lands." William M. Beauchamp's article entitled "Aboriginal Place Names of New York," which was published by the New York State Education Department in 1907 provides an alternative translation, "the neck." Beauchamp says that this neck connected the two Great Lakes, much as the neck of the human body connects the head with the torso below. The French were the first Europeans to explore this section of North America and they recognized its strategic importance by building a fort, Fort Niagara, here. The British captured that fort and refused to evacuate it at the end of the American Revolution. It was not until 1796 that the British turned Fort Niagara over to America. To several generations of honeymooning newlyweds, the scenic and majestic Niagara Falls have been more famous than either the river or its fort. However, today's Niagara Falls have lost much of their former splendor. More than half of the water which previously fed Niagara Falls is diverted into tunnels and canals for hydroelectric power.

1825 *Oneida County*

Oneida Indians — The Oneida were the least populous tribe of the Iroquois confederacy in central New York. At the time of their first contact with Whites, in the 1600's, their population was less than 1,000. They possessed Oneida Lake, the eastern portion of which is located in today's Oneida County, New York. The Oneidas also controlled the territory surrounding Oneida Lake. About the year 1720, the Oneida Indians were joined by a group of Tuscarora Indians, who had migrated from North Carolina. Most Oneidas sided with the American colonists during the American Revolution. By the 1990's there were still 1,000 Oneida Indians living in New York state. *Oneida* has been variously translated as "standing stone," "granite people," or "stone people" and it refers to a large stone at one of their early villages which was a monument and became their tribal emblem. This county was created on March 15, 1798.

1826 *Onondaga County*

Onondaga Indians — The Onondaga were members of the Iroquois confederation, which consisted of five tribes (later six), whose center of activities was upstate New York. The Onondaga's territory extended from the Thousand Islands in the Saint Lawrence River on the New York–Canada border, south to the Susquehanna River in central New York. In the middle of the 17th century Jesuit missionaries of the Roman Catholic church established a mission for the Onondaga Indians at the eastern boundary of today's Onondaga County, near Manlius, New York. Most translations of the tribal name *Onondaga* indicate that the name relates to "hill" or "mountain top," and some say that the hill referred to was here, near Manlius, New York. The Onondaga tribe were keepers of the fire for the entire Iroquois nation, which meant that their main village was the capital of the Iroquois confederacy. Surviving Onondagas make their home right here in Onondaga County on a reservation south of Syracuse. A census of the tribe taken in 1985 counted 669 Onondaga Indians living here. This county was created on March 5, 1794.

1827 *Ontario County*

Lake Ontario — This county in western New York was created on January 27, 1789, and at that time Lake Ontario was the county's northern border. As a result of the creation of new counties and changed county boundaries, Ontario County no longer borders the lake for which it was named. However its northern border is only about 25 miles south of its namesake. The lake was named by Iroquois. Other Indians deferred to the powerful Iroquois confederation, and called the lake "the Lake of the Iroquois." However, the Iroquois' own name for the lake, *Ontario*, survives today. There is virtually unanimous agreement that the Indians' name, *Ontario*, means "beautiful lake," or a very close approximation of that. Lake Ontario is the easternmost and smallest of North America's five Great Lakes. It borders the United States on its eastern and southern shore, while Canada borders the lake on the north and at its western end. In the U.S., Lake Ontario borders only New York state and in Canada its shores are limited to the province of Ontario. Although it is the smallest of the Great Lakes, Lake Ontario is not small. It has an area of 7,600 square miles. The Saint Lawrence Seaway provides Lake Ontario with access to world ports.

1828 *Orange County*

King William III (1650–1702) — When the English province of New York was divided into counties on November 1, 1683, Orange County was created as one of the original counties. At that time William had not yet been crowned king of England and he was titled Prince of Orange. When Orange County in England's province of New York was created, William was a nephew of the reigning king of England, King Charles II (1630–1685).

King William III (1650–1702) — William, Prince of Orange, was born in the Netherlands. He was the grandson of England's King Charles I (1600–1649) and in 1677 William married his cousin, Mary (1662–1694), who was then the presumptive heir to the English throne, occupied by her father, King James II (1633–1701). In 1688 William invaded England, supported by both Dutch and English troops and on April 11, 1689, William and his wife were crowned king and queen of England. They ruled as joint sovereigns, titled King William III and Queen Mary II until Mary's death in 1694. William continued on the English throne until his death in 1702. King William's title, Orange, belonged to William's family, the Nassaus, on account of a tiny pocket of independent territory within southern France, near the Rhone River, named Orange, which had earlier been an ancient Roman town. It is now merely a small city in France, 17 miles north of Avignon, France.

1829 *Orleans County*

Uncertain — When the New York legislature was preparing to create this new county in 1824, two names were proposed for it: Adams and Jackson. John Quincy Adams defeated Andrew Jackson in the 1824 presidential election and it seems reasonably safe to assume that the proposed county names of Adams and Jackson referred to these two men. When the legislators could not agree on either of these names for the new county, they chose to name it Orleans. New York sources are not agreed on the origin of the county's name. Some say that it honored the royal French house of Orleans, while others say that it honors the French city of Orleans.

Royal French House of Orleans — Orleans is the name of the cadet branch of Valois and Bourbon houses. Four distinct royal French houses have been known by the name Orleans. The first three of these houses ranged from the 14th century to the mid 17th century and are unlikely candidates for the American state of New York to honor with a county name. However, France aided the American colonies in their successful revolution from England and memory of that aid was still fresh in the minds of the New York legislature when it created this county in November, 1824. One member of the fourth house of Orleans, who might well have been remembered favorably by the New York legislators in 1824 for having advocated the cause of the American colonies during the American Revolution was Louis Philippe Joseph (1747–1793), who was made duke of Orleans in 1785. He is referred to in some sources as Philippe-Egalite.

City of Orleans, France — Orleans, the capital of the department of Loiret, is located on the Loire River in north–central France. This city, with a population of about 100,000, lies some 75 miles southwest of Paris. Orleans produces manufactured goods and is in one of France's agricultural regions. Conquered by the Roman Empire in 52 B.C., Orleans became a major cultural center during the middle ages. The French King Philip VI (1293–1350), made the city a royal duchy and peerage in favor of his son. The city of Orleans, together with the surrounding Orleanais Province was given at times as an appanage to members of the French royal family (dukes of Orleans).

1830 *Oswego County*

Oswego River — This county in central New York was created on March 1, 1816, and named for the 23 mile-long river which flows through it. The Oswego River is formed in Onondaga County, New York by the junction of the Seneca and Oneida Rivers. From there the Oswego River flows almost due north through Oswego County, where it empties its waters into Lake Ontario. The Oswego River was named by the Indians and their name for it referred to the mouth of the Oswego River where it flows into Lake Ontario. William M. Beauchamp wrote an article entitled "Aboriginal Place Names of New York," which was published by the New York State Education Department in 1907. In that article Beauchamp provides two alternative translations of the Indian name *Oswego*: "Flowing out," and "small water flowing into that which is large."

1831 *Otsego County*

Uncertain — This county was created on February 16, 1791, but exactly what it was named for cannot be stated with certainty. We have strong circumstantial evidence that the county was named for Otsego Lake, New York, and that Otsego Lake was named for a prominent rock on the shore of the lake. In the works dealing with the history, geography and place names of New York a few works suggest that "place of the rock," was the origin of this county's name. It seems very unlikely that the New York legislators would have directly named a county for an Indian word meaning "place of the rock." Even though beautiful Otsego Lake is the most remarkable feature in Otsego County, New York, sources dealing with the origins of New York state's county names avoid attributing the New York county's name to the lake. Otsego Lake is about nine miles long and has an average width of one mile. This lake featured prominently in novels written by James Fenimore Cooper (1789–1851) and Cooper died near the southern end of Otsego Lake, New York. In his work entitled *The Deerslayer*, Cooper described Otsego Lake as "a broad sheet of water, so placid and limpid that it resembled a bed of pure mountain atmosphere compressed into a setting of hills and woods." By the late 1990's some of the woods had become farms but little else had changed the accuracy of Cooper's description.

When Otsego County, New York was created on February 16, 1791, its territory came from land formerly embraced by Montgomery County. The town of Otsego, New York, was created within Montgomery County on March 7, 1788, and when Otsego County was created, the town of Otsego included much of the new county. New York state sources tell us that the name *otsego* is of Iroquois Indian origin but most of these New York sources say that the meaning of the name is unknown. One source is William M. Beauchamp. In his article entitled "Aboriginal Place Names of New York," published by the New York State Education Department in 1907, Beauchamp admits that the true translation of the name is uncertain but he builds a plausible case for the possibility that *otsego* might mean "place of the rock." This rock may have been a large rock at the outlet of Otsego Lake, which James Fenimore Cooper mentioned in *The Deerslayer*. It is possible, then, to hypothesize a genealogy for Otsego County, New York, from Otsego Lake, New York to a prominent rock on the shore of Otsego Lake, New York. However, there are weak links in this chain and it is, at best, conjecture.

1832 *Putnam County*

Israel Putnam (1718–1790)— Putnam was born in Massachusetts and moved, when he was about 21, to Connecticut. He served as an officer in the French and Indian wars and later was a member of the Connecticut legislature. At the beginning of the Revolutionary War, news of the battle at Lexington, Massachusetts reached Putnam while he was farming. In a dramatic gesture which became famous, Putnam left his plow and, without bothering to change clothes, hurried to Lexington. He was appointed a major-general in the Continental army. Although he enjoyed great popularity, he lacked the ability for high command. In 1779 a paralytic stroke ended his military career. This county was created on June 12, 1812.

1833 *Queens County*

Queen Catherine of Braganza (1638–1705)— In 1664 King Charles II made an enormous grant of North American land to his brother, the duke of York and Albany. The duke was awarded more power over his domain that any other English proprietor. On November 1, 1683, the duke's North American province of New York was divided into twelve counties, and one of them, Queens County, was named for the queen consort of the current reigning monarch of England, King Charles II (1630–1685). Catherine was a daughter of the duke of Braganza (1604–1656), who was crowned king of Portugal in 1640. Her marriage to Charles was arranged as a political expedient. Catherine of Braganza, a Catholic, sailed to Portsmouth, England, where she and the king were wed on May 21, 1662, first, secretly under the auspices of the Roman Catholic Church and subsequently in a public Anglican ceremony. This marriage produced miscarriages but no children. However, the king enjoyed an enthusiastic sex life and had several mistresses. (One whole book is devoted to them: *The Mistresses of Charles II* by Brian Masters.) King Charles II had many children with these mistresses and Queen Catherine submissively accepted his infidelities. In fact, Catherine showed kindness toward the king's several illegitimate children. Since none of the king's children were legitimate when King Charles II died in 1685, his brother, James (1633–1701) became king of England as King James II. History tells us that Queen Catherine of Braganza persuaded her husband, King Charles II, to profess Catholicism as his faith on his death bed. After the death of her husband, his widow, Catherine, lived for a time in England. She had enjoyed popularity there but after the very Protestant King William III (1650–1702) and his wife, Queen Mary II (1662–1694) took the English throne in 1689, life in England became uncomfortable and Catherine moved to Lisbon, Portugal. There she lived there from 1692 until her death in December, 1705.

1834 *Rensselaer County*

The van Rensselaer family and their enormous patroonship here— When the Dutch controlled New York, and called it New Netherland, it was managed by the Dutch West India Company. That company was concerned with trade, rather than colonization but in 1629 the company became involved in colonization when it established the status of patroon, for stockholders in the company, meeting certain criteria for settlement of their patroonships. A patroonship was equivalent to a large manor in England and in the English colonies. The Dutch patroons in New York were granted essentially feudal power over their tenants. When England seized control of New York, the former Dutch owners' property and inheritance rights were permitted to continue. This county was created on February 7, 1791. Its name descended from an important and wealthy Dutch family that owned enormous amounts of land in New Netherland, named Rensselaerswyck. Kiliaen van Rensselaer (1580–1643) was a stockholder in the Dutch West India Company and he was the original patroon of Rensselaerswyck. His patroonship contained much of the present New York counties of Rensselaer, Albany and Columbia, along the Hudson River. In 1791, when Rensselaer County was created, the van Rensselaer family still owned enormous amounts of land here. Descendants of Kiliaen van Rensselaer (1580–1643), who have been associated with the family's lands in New York include Jan Baptist van Rensselaer, Jeremias van Rensselaer (1632–1674), Nicolaes van Rensselaer (–1678) and another Kiliaen van Rensselaer. This Kiliaen was the grandson of the original patroon, and he succeeded to the patroonship of his grandfather. In 1704 England's Queen Anne (1665–1714) confirmed this Kiliaen van Rensselaer's rights to his New York estate. This made him the first lord of the manor of Rensselaerswyck, of which he was also the fourth patroon. From this Kiliaen van Rensselaer and his brother, Hendrik, all subsequent New York van Rensselaers have descended. Kiliaen, the fourth patroon, married his cousin Maria van Cortlandt. Their eldest son, Jeremias was the fifth patroon. Because Jeremias never married, the second son of Kiliaen, the fourth patroon, named Steven van Rensselaer, became the sixth patroon. His son Steven II became the seventh patroon, and we now know that we are approaching the birth of the new nation of the United States, because this seventh patroon married Catherine Livingston, a daughter of Philip Livingston (1716–1778), a New York signer of the Declaration of Independence.

1835 *Richmond County*

Charles Lennox, Duke of Richmond (1672–1723)— In 1664 England's King Charles II (1630–1685) made an enormous grant of North American land to his brother, James, the duke of York and Albany (1633–1701). The duke was awarded more power over his domain that any other English proprietor. Although King Charles II had many children, none of them were legitimate. One of the children of King Charles II was Charles Lennox (1672–1723), who was given the title duke of Richmond (and also duke of Lennox, in the peerage of Scotland.) On November 1, 1683, the English province of New York was divided into twelve counties, and one of them, Richmond County was named for Charles Lennox, the first duke of Richmond, one of the illegitimate sons of the reigning monarch of England, King Charles II. Richmond's mother was Louise Renee de Keroualle (1649–1734). She took him to France in 1685 and he was received with great honor there by the French king, Louis XIV (1638–1715), who persuaded Richmond's mother to have Richmond join the Roman Catholic Church. Richmond's mother, whose title was the Duchess of Portsmouth, agreed, Charles Lennox was given instruction in the Catholic religion and became a Catholic in 1685. The French king gave Charles Lennox important assignments in the French army and he served ably in that army. Charles Lennox left France to assist William of Orange (1650–1702) and Charles Lennox married Anne Bellasis. The couple had three children. In 1681 he was made governor of Dumbarton castle. Richmond renounced Catholicism and was converted to the Anglican Church on May 15, 1692. From 1693 to 1702 he was aide-de-camp in Flanders and later was lord of the bedchamber of King George I.

1836 *Rockland County*

Rocky land of this region— This county lies on the western bank of the Hudson River, just above New York City. Early settlers commented on its rocky nature and a portion of this rock structure is quite visible to an observer standing on the eastern shore of the Hudson River, at the northern end of New York City, looking across the Hudson River to its western bank. The great outcroppings that are seen here are called the Palisades. Although the Palisades pale in comparison to geological formations in our nation's West, there is nothing to match them in New York City's metropolitan area. The Palisades line the western bank of the Hudson River for about 15 miles and they are shared by Rockland County, New York, with its southern neighbor, the state of New Jersey. *Webster's New Geographical Dictionary* calls the Palisades "A line of high cliffs of traprock..." The quarries of Rockland County supplied large amounts of the stone from which New York City was constructed. Within Rockland County one can see parallel lines, cut deeply into the rock surface, which are thought to be the work of glaciers pushing hard particles of rock for miles to etch their image on the softer rock below. Quartz and brick have been products of this county. It was created on February 23, 1798.

1837 *Saint Lawrence County*

Saint Lawrence River— This county in northern New York was created on March 3, 1802. Its northern and western border for about 50 miles is the Saint Lawrence River. From the northeastern corner of Saint Lawrence County, New York, the Saint Lawrence River forms the international boundary between the U.S. and Canada and Saint Lawrence County faces on about 50 miles of that border. The Saint Lawrence River is a 760 mile-long navigable river, which flows out of Lake Ontario. Most of its 760 mile length is within Canada. The Saint Lawrence flows in a northeastern direction into the deep Gulf of Saint Lawrence of the Atlantic Ocean between the Island of Newfoundland and the Canadian mainland. The waterway provided by the entire Saint Lawrence Seaway, which links the Great Lakes to the Atlantic Ocean is 2,000 miles long. It is vital in linking the Mid-west of Canada and the U.S. with eastern North America and with the entire world for exports and imports. The river took its name from Saint Lawrence Bay, which the French explorer, Jacques Cartier entered and named on August 10, 1535. This is a small bay, opposite Anticosti Island. Cartier selected the bay's name because August 10 is the feast day of the Roman Catholic saint, Saint Lawrence. The name spread from the bay to the Gulf of Saint Lawrence and to the main river which feeds that gulf, our Saint Lawrence River.

Saint Lawrence (–)— Born in Spain, Lawrence was an archdeacon and treasurer of the Roman Catholic Church, in Rome. He was stationed in Rome about A.D. 257. Under the unholy reign of the Roman Emperor Valerian, Lawrence was instructed to gather all of the church's wealth and surrender it to the governing authorities. He asked for and was given several days to complete this task. On the final day he assembled at the prefect's palace a cast of thousands of lepers, orphans, those who were blind and those who were lame. Lawrence also included in this assemblage a number of widows and virgins. On presenting them to the prefect, Lawrence announced "Here is all the Church's treasure." This of course enraged the prefect and he caused Lawrence to be subjected to a series of ghastly tortures. He was stretched on the rack, scourged, branded, clubbed and roasted alive on a gridiron. Pope Sixtus II was also martyred and put to death during this heinous episode. The pope died on August 7 and Lawrence died three days later. This chronology served to fix the feast day of Saint Lawrence as August 10. Although there is room to doubt the historic accuracy of all of these details, enough of them have been accepted to cause Saint Lawrence to be venerated as the most celebrated of the many martyrs to the Roman civil government.

According to some sources on the history of upstate New York and New France (Canada), Saint Lawrence was chosen as the patron saint of New France (Canada). That is incorrect. Saint Anne and Saint George are the patron saints of Canada although two Saint Lawrences (Saint Lawrence and Saint Lawrence O'Toole) are patrons of villages and/or districts within Canada.

1838 *Saratoga County*

Uncertain—*Saratoga* is an Indian name and it was used as early as 1684 for the name of an Indian hunting ground on both sides of the Hudson River, east of Saratoga Lake. N. B. Sylvester tells us in his 1876 work concerning Saratoga that the Indian name *Saratoga* meant "hillside country of the great river." Saratoga County was created on February 7, 1791, shortly after our nation was born from the successful American Revolution. By the time the county was created, the name *Saratoga* had been used for a variety of subjects, which the New York legislature might have been thinking of when they named this county. A band of Mohawk Indians had a village at Saratoga, and Saratoga Springs was beginning to acquire a reputation for the medicinal powers of its waters. The relatively small, but beautiful Saratoga Lake was within the borders of the new county of Saratoga and that lake could have been the county's namesake. However, it seems far more likely that the New York legislators were recalling a dramatic event during the American Revolution, when they named this county. In October, 1777, General John Burgoyne (1722–1792) was captured at Saratoga, New York. At that time, Burgoyne had supreme command of English forces in Canada. Captured at Saratoga, along with Burgoyne were 5,700 of his troops. They were marched to Boston and shipped to England after pledging to never again serve in the war against the American colonists. The translation of the original Indian name *Saratoga* has been lost but two of the possibilities that have been mentioned (as possibilities) are "beaver place," and "hillside of the great river." William M. Beauchamp admits, in his article entitled "Aboriginal Place Names of New York," published by the New York State Education Department in 1907, that the true translation of the name is uncertain. The original Saratoga, New York, was later named Schuylerville, New York.

1839 *Schenectady County*

City of Schenectady, New York— This county was created on March 7, 1809, and named for the city which the Dutch had begun to settle almost two centuries earlier. The city of Schenectady, the county seat of Schenectady County, lies near the eastern end of the Mohawk River, on its south side, about 15 miles west of the Mohawk's confluence with the Hudson River. The Dutch established an Indian trading post here in 1620 and in 1661 Dutch pioneers led by Arendt van Curler (1620–1667) built the first community of Schenectady. Van Curler is considered to be the founder of Schenectady. On February 9, 1690, during King William's War, Schenectady was captured in a surprise night attack by Indians and French, who burned the settlement to the ground. The Indians massacred many of the survivors and took the remainder as captives. When the city was rebuilt, Dutch influence continued in the architecture and can be seen today in the oldest section of the city, the Stockade district. Schenectady was patented with certain municipal rights on November 4, 1684, and chartered as a borough on October 23, 1765. On March 26, 1798, Schenectady was made a city. Schenectady became the headquarters of the General Electric Company, which was incorporated in 1892. That company was built on

the genius of Thomas A. Edison (1847–1931) and others. The G. E. factory grew to employ more than 30,000 workers and the American Locomotive Company also established a large factory here. American Locomotive closed its doors in the 1960's and the G.E. factory here today is a small shadow of its former self. As a result, the population of Schenectady was only about 65,000 in the 1990's. The name *Schenectady* is the surviving version of scores of similar Dutch and Indian names. The 1661 deed from the Mohawk Indians to the Dutch uses the term *Skonowe*, the Dutch word for "great flat." A Dutch map from 1656 calls this *Schoon Vlaack Land*, the Dutch meaning of which was "fine flat land." When Arendt van Curler and his Dutch colleagues took possession of this land in 1661 they called it *Schaenechstede*, which would be the orthographic pronunciation of the Dutch *Schoonehetstede*, meaning "the beautiful town." The origin of Schenectady's name could be debated endlessly with no certainty of reaching the true answer. Your author resided here for ten years and can testify that the term "flat land," if not the historic source of the name, is at least an accurate description.

1840 *Schoharie County*

Town of Schoharie, New York— One of the early towns of upstate New York, Schoharie was settled by Germans about 1711 or 1712. They named the community Brunnen Dorf, but this name was later changed to Schoharie, the name of a creek here. The settlement of Schoharie was made a district on March 24, 1772, and a town on March 7, 1788. In the late 1990's the town of Schoharie had a population of about 1,000. Schoharie Creek was named by the Indians. Since they had no written language, it was left to Europeans to render the Indians' names in writing. Essentially all sources consulted agree that the name *Schoharie* derived from the Indians' word for "driftwood," and that the Indians gave that name to Schoharie Creek because driftwood accumulated on it. After this we encounter some disagreement about the details. Some sources indicate that driftwood regularly accumulated here because of the configuration of the creek's water flow. Other sources are inclined to attribute the naming of the creek to one or two dramatic accumulations of driftwood on the surface of the creek. When this county was created on April 6, 1795, it was named for the town of Schoharie, the county seat of Schoharie County.

1841 *Schuyler County*

Philip J. Schuyler (1733–1804)— A native of New York, Schuyler served as an officer in the French and Indian War and was a delegate from New York to the Continental Congress. During the American Revolution, he held the rank of major-general in the Continental army. Schuyler later served New York in its senate and he became one of New York state's first two United States senators.

1842 *Seneca County*

Seneca Indians— This county in western New York was created in March, 1804, and named for the Seneca Indians, the largest tribe of the Iroquois confederation, which consisted of five tribes (later six), whose center of activities was upstate New York. The land in what is now Seneca County had been a hunting ground of the Seneca Indians and also of the Cayuga Indians, another tribe of the Iroquois confederation. Some sources indicate that the Seneca were the most warlike of the Iroquois tribes. E. W. Vanderhoof raises the ante in his *Historical Sketches of Western New York*, published in 1907. Vanderhoof tells us that the Seneca were "The most intelligent, numerous and powerful of the six tribes which … formed the League of the Iroquois." The name *Seneca* has been translated variously but a number of authorities agree that the name relates to "stone." In his work on *Indian Names in Michigan*, Dr. Virgil J. Vogel translates the New York tribe's name as "place of the stone," or "stony earth." Muriel H. Wright also supports a stone-related translation. In her work entitled *A Guide to the Indian Tribes of Oklahoma*, she tells us that the tribal name derived from "people of the standing or projecting rock or stone." In 1985 there were still 5,548 Seneca Indians living on reservations in western New York state. Indians known as the Senecas also now live in Oklahoma. Apparently the Senecas in Oklahoma are relatives of the New York Seneca Indians rather than members of the identical tribe.

1843 *Steuben County*

Friedrich Wilhelm August Heinrich Ferdinand von Steuben (1730–1794)— Known in America as Baron von Steuben or Baron de Steuben, this military man was born in Prussia, entered the Prussian army at the age of 17 and served in it throughout the Seven Years' War. He rose to the position of general staff officer and aide-de-camp to King Frederick the Great, at royal headquarters. In 1777 Baron von Steuben came to America to serve in our Continental army. As inspector general, he introduced badly needed Prussian methods of military efficiency and discipline to our ragtag troops and trained them in the skills required for effective combat. As the war progressed, his prestige rose and General George Washington consulted him on a variety of questions of strategic and administrative policy. At the end of the war Baron von Steuben became an American citizen and a resident of New York state. New York granted von Steuben a farm in Remsen, New York and he died at that farm on November 28, 1794. Some 16 months later, on March 18, 1796, Steuben County, New York was created and named in his honor.

1844 *Suffolk County*

Suffolk County, England— In 1664 King Charles II made an enormous grant of North American land to his brother, the duke of York and Albany. The duke was awarded more power over his domain that any other English proprietor. On November 1, 1683, the duke's North American province of New York was divided into twelve counties, and one of them, Suffolk County, was named for Suffolk County in Anglia in eastern England. Suffolk County, England is approximately 50 miles long and some 30 miles wide. It lies on the North Sea, where it faces the European continent. Its principal rivers are the Little Ouse, Great Ouse, Waveney, Stour, Breton, Orwell, Deben, Ore and Blyth. King James I (1566–1625) was enamored by Suffolk when he visited it and he purchased a house here. Suffolk County's name derived from a name which meant "the southern people" (or "folk") or "the territory of the southern people" (or "folk") to distinguish it from Norfolk (now a county, immediately north of Suffolk in East Anglia).

1845 *Sullivan County*

John Sullivan (1740–1795)— The location of John Sullivan's birth is given variously as Berwick, Maine and Somersworth, New Hampshire. The two towns are adjacent. He practiced law in New Hampshire and represented New Hampshire in the Continental Congress. During the American Revolution Sullivan served as a brigadier-general and later was promoted to major-general. John Sullivan served with distinction in a number of important engagements of the Revolution including action against the Indians near present-day Elmira, New York. Soon after that 1779 campaign, he fell ill and resigned from the army. He then represented New Hampshire again in the Continental Congress. Sullivan later served as attorney general of New Hampshire, president (or governor) of New Hampshire and was a member of the New Hampshire convention that ratified the proposed federal constitution. He also was speaker of New Hampshire's house of representatives. In 1789 President George Washington appointed John Sullivan as judge of the U.S. district court of New Hampshire and Sullivan held that position until his death in 1795. This county was created and named in General Sullivan's honor on March 27, 1809.

1846 *Tioga County*

Tioga River— The Tioga River rises in northern Pennsylvania, near the town of Tioga, in Pennsylvania's Tioga County and flows essentially due north across the New York state border. The Tioga continues to flow north until its waters unite with those of the Cohocton River, near Corning, New York to form the Chemung River. The Tioga is a short river, just 40 miles long. Tioga County, New York, was created on February 16, 1791. At that time, the Tioga River flowed through New York's Tioga County but as New York created new counties (Steuben in 1796 and Chemung in 1836), the western border of Tioga County, New York was pushed eastward. As a result, the river for which the county was named no longer flows through Tioga County, New York. The name *Tioga* is an Indian name and it was first applied by them to a point at the junction of the Susquehanna River with the Chemung River, below the town of Athens, Pennsylvania. Sources consulted differ on the translation of this Indian name but a meaning of "at the forks," is cited by enough authorities to lend it credibility. That name relates to the junction of the Susquehanna River with the Chemung River, which was a well known meeting place for the Indians. In attempting to describe the location of this famous Indian meeting point, confusion arises because some references call the Tioga River (or portions of it) the Chemung River. The point for which the Tioga River was named lies just three or four miles south of the present southwestern border of Tioga County, New York. At one time there was an Indian village here at Tioga Point.

1847 *Tompkins County*

Daniel D. Tompkins (1774–1825)— A native of New York and a lawyer, Tompkins practiced law in New York City. He soon became active in local politics and was a delegate to the state's constitutional convention of 1801. Soon afterward he was elected to the lower house of the New York legislature. In 1804 Tompkins was elected to represent New York in the U.S. House of Representatives but he resigned before taking his seat in that body in order to accept his appointment as a judge on the New York supreme court. In 1807 Tompkins defeated New York's Governor Morgan Lewis (1754–1844) in his bid for reelection. Tompkins was twice reelected as the state's governor. In 1816 Tompkins was the vice-presidential candidate on the Democrat Republican ticket headed by James Monroe. Monroe and Tompkins were elected and later reelected to second terms and they both served eight years heading our national government. This county was created in April, 1817, just one month after New York's Daniel D. Tompkins began his eight year stint as vice president of the United States.

1848 *Ulster County*

King James II (1633–1701)— James was the second surviving son of England's King Charles I (1600–1649). He was given the title duke of York and Albany soon after his christening and was made earl of Ulster on May 10, 1672. When James' father died, his elder brother Charles succeeded to the throne as King Charles II (1630–1685). In 1664 King Charles II made an enormous grant of North American land to his brother, James (1633–1701), the duke of York and Albany. The duke was awarded more power over his domain that any other English proprietor. Although King Charles II had many children, none of them were legitimate so when King Charles II died in 1685, his brother James became king of England as King James II. The first wife of the duke of York and Albany had been Anne Hyde, who died in 1671. In 1673 James remarried to Mary of Modena (1658–1718), a Catholic, and some time during this period James professed his own Catholicism. This spelled his eventual downfall as king. In 1689 the throne passed to William of Orange (1650–1702), who ruled as joint sovereign with his wife, Queen Mary II (1662–1694). Mary was a daughter of King James II. The former King James II devoted the final years of his life to religious exercises. When the English province of New York was divided into counties on November 1, 1683, Ulster County was created as one of the original counties. At that time James had not yet been crowned king of England. The title "Ulster" derived from James' Irish earldom. James was made earl of Ulster on May 10, 1672.

1849 *Warren County*

Joseph Warren (1741–1775) — A native of Massachusetts and a graduate of Harvard College, Warren practiced medicine in the Boston area. He was a member of the committee of safety and president *pro tempore* of the Massachusetts provincial congress. In June, 1775, he was commissioned a major-general and he died in combat a few days later at the battle of Bunker Hill. Warren County was created on March 12, 1813.

1850 *Washington County*

George Washington (1732–1799) — Washington was a native of Virginia. He served in Virginia's house of burgesses and became one of the colonies' leaders in opposition to British policies in America. He was a member of the first and second Continental Congresses and commander of all Continental armies in the Revolutionary War. Following victory in that war, Washington was elected to be the first president of the United States. This county was originally created on March 12, 1772, with the name Charlotte County. That name honored a member of the English royal family, although sources consulted differ on whether Charlotte County's name honored the queen consort of King George III (1738–1820), Queen Charlotte Sophia of Mecklenburg-Strelitz (1744–1818), or the eldest daughter of King George III, Charlotte Auguste Mathilda (1766–1828), the princess royal. England's province of North Carolina had a similar place name situation with both a city (Charlotte) and a county (Mecklenburg), named for the queen consort of King George III, Queen Charlotte Sophia of Mecklenburg-Strelitz (1744–1818). Intuition might lead us to suspect that the Southerners of North Carolina would be more chivalrous than the Yankees of New York about changing place names after the American Revolution. In this case intuition provides the correct answer. On April 2, 1784, New York changed Charlotte County's name to Washington County. However, the chivalrous North Carolinians allowed both names honoring the queen consort of our British antagonist, King George III, to remain; i.e.,

the important commercial city of Charlotte and the county which surrounds it (Mecklenburg County).

1851 *Wayne County*

Anthony Wayne (1745–1796) — A native of Pennsylvania, Wayne was a successful brigadier-general in the Revolutionary War and became a hero for his daring exploits. During the bitter winter of 1777–1778 at Valley Forge, Pennsylvania, Wayne shared the sufferings of his men although his comfortable estate was only five miles away. He played an important role in the final overthrow of the British forces in Georgia. After the war, in 1785, Wayne moved to Georgia and he represented Georgia for about six months in the U.S. House of Representatives. In 1792, President Washington recalled Wayne to serve as a major-general against the Indians in the Northwest territory. Once again his military efforts were successful. This county was created on April 11, 1823.

1852 *Westchester County*

The former township of Westchester, south of White Plains, New York — In 1664 King Charles II made an enormous grant of North American land to his brother, the duke of York and Albany. The duke was awarded more power over his domain that any other English proprietor. On November 1, 1683, the duke's North American province of New York was divided into twelve counties, and one of them, Westchester County, was named for the existing township of Westchester. In the early history of New York City, there were two nearby communities, named the township of East Chester and the township of Westchester. The township of Westchester is described in a history of Westchester County by Robert Bolton, which was published in 1881 as "…sixteen miles south of the village of White Plains, distant twelve miles from New York, … bounded on the north by Eastchester, east, by the Eastchester Bay or Long Island Sound, south by the East River and west by the Bronx." Since the city of White Plains is the county seat of today's Westchester County, New York, the county can no longer be 16 miles south of White Plains. It is apparent that the boundaries of the former township of Westchester and the present Westchester County differ somewhat. Richard M. Lederer's 1978 work entitled *The Place-Names of Westchester County, New York*, fixes the location of the early township of Westchester a bit differently: "…in the area

where Co-Op City in the Bronx is now … called it West Chester or westernmost camp of the New Haven Colony … West Chester was south of Eastchester, and Westchester Square in the Bronx marks the spot." It could well be that both descriptions are accurate for the point in time being described because boundaries in the New York City area were shifting rapidly in the last half of the 17th century. In any case, New York's townships of East Chester and Westchester were both named in honor of Chester, in England. Harry Hansen provides a description of the contents of New York's original (1683) Westchester County in his work entitled *North of Manhattan: Persons & Places of Old Westchester*: "…the County should comprise West Chester, East Chester, Bronx Land, Forhan, Anne Hook's Neck, Delancey's Neck, Minford's Island and 'all land on the Maine east of Manhattan Island and the Yoncker's Land and north as far as the Highlands.'"

Chester, England — This city in western England, is the administrative center of Cheshire County. Its climate is harsh in spite of the moderating influence of the nearby Irish Sea. Conquered, named and occupied by the Roman Empire in the first century A.D., the Roman's name for Chester was *Cestre*, similar to the present Cheshire. The Romans were long gone when William I the Conqueror (1027–1087) invaded England and was crowned its king. He made it his business to send troops north soon after his arrival, to quell rebels here in Chester and in Wales. For a period of time Cheshire County's ports had a virtual monopoly on the trade between England and Ireland but by 1600 the port of Chester was no longer viable on account of silting. Chester was granted a royal charter in 1506. Little more than a century later, the city was badly battered during the decade-long English Civil Wars, which began in 1642. By the middle of the 18th century, Chester was a prosperous and quiet country town. The population of all of Cheshire County in 1981 was slightly more than 900,000 persons crowded into just 928 square miles.

1853 *Wyoming County*

An Indian word meaning "on the broad plain" — This county in western New York was created in May, 1841, and given an Indian name that poorly describes the hilly topography of this county. In the early 1700's the Delaware Indians had a village at the present site of Wilkes-Barre, in the valley of the Susquehanna River, in eastern Pennsylvania. The Indians called both the valley there, and their village within it *M'chewomink*, which meant "on the broad plain," or "upon the great plains." The Indians had no written language so it was left to Whites to render the name in writing and the name took several forms, one of which approximated the word *Wyoming*. During the last half of the 18th century the Wyoming Valley became well known because of battles between Indians and Whites here. Also, the name *Wyoming* was used in the title of a poem by Thomas Campbell, entitled "Gertrude of Wyoming," which was published in 1809. That poem enjoyed some popularity and helped perpetuate the name. This county in western New York is not even remotely near the Indian village of Wyoming. The New York county lies more than 200 miles northwest of the old Indian village in Pennsylvania, named Wyoming. The New York county was created in 1841. The state of Pennsylvania created a Wyoming County the following year. That county is located on both sides of the Susquehanna River Valley, just north of the present Wilkes-Barre; i.e., very close to the original Indian village of Wyoming.

1854 *Yates County*

Joseph C. Yates (1768–1837) — A native of Schenectady, New York, Joseph Christopher Yates practiced law there. On March 26, 1798, Schenectady was made a city and Yates became the new city's first mayor. In 1805 he was elected to the state senate and in 1808 he was appointed as a justice on New York state's supreme court. Yates served on that court for 14 years and was also a regent of the University of New York. In 1822 Joseph C. Yates was overwhelmingly elected as New York's governor, receiving 120,493 votes, compared to his opponent's 2,910 votes. He assumed office on January 1, 1823, and this county was created one month later, on February 5, 1823. Governor Yates signed the act which created this new county, which was named in his honor. Yates' popularity soon evaporated and he retired from politics at the end of one term as governor. He lived the remainder of his life in Schenectady, where he is buried.

REFERENCES

Alexander, DeAlva S. *A Political History of the State of New York*. New York, Henry Holt & Co., 1906.

Allstrom, C. M. *Dictionary of Royal Lineage of Europe and Other Countries*. Chicago, Press of S. Th. Almberg, 1902.

Anderson, George B. *Landmarks of Rensselaer County, New York*. Syracuse, New York, D. Mason & Co., 1897.

Andrews, Allen. *The Royal Whore: Barbara Villiers, Countess of Castlemaine*. Philadelphia, Chilton Book Co., 1970.

Bacon, Edwin F. *Otsego County, New York: Geographical & Historical*. Oneonta, New York, Oneonta Herald, 1902.

Battle, Kemp P. "Glimpses of History in the Names of Our Counties." *The North Carolina Booklet*, Vol. 6. July, 1906.

Battle, Kemp P. "North Carolina County Names." *The Magazine of History*, Vol. 7, No. 4. New York: April, 1908.

Beauchamp, William M. "Aboriginal Place Names of New York." *New York State Museum Bulletin*, Bulletin 108, Archeology 12. Albany: May, 1907.

Bedell, Cornelia F. *Now and Then and Long Ago in Rockland County, New York*. Suffern, New York, Rampo Valley Independent, 1941.

Beers, F. W. *Gazetteer & Biographical Record of Genesee County, New York*. Syracuse, New York, J. W. Vose & Co., 1890.

Benedictine Monks of St. Augustine's Abbey, Ramsgate. *The Book of Saints*. New York, Thomas Y. Crowell Co., 1966.

Benton, Nathaniel S. *A History of Herkimer County: Including the Upper Mohawk Valley*. Albany, J. Munsell, 1856.

Berton, Pierre. *Niagara*. New York, Kodansha International, 1997.

Blake, William J. *The History of Putnam County, N. Y.* New York, Baker & Scribner, 1849.

Blodgett, Bertha. *Stories of Cortland County*. Cortland, New York, Cortland County Historical Society, 1952.

Bolton, Robert. *The History of the Several Towns, Manors & Patents of the County of Westchester*. New York, Chas. F. Roper, 1881.

Brodhead, John R. *History of the State of New York*. New York, Harper & Brothers, 1872.

Bryant, Margaret M. "Some Indian & Dutch Names Reflecting the Early History of Brooklyn." *Names: Journal of the American Name Society*, Vol. 20, No. 2. Potsdam, New York: June, 1972.

Byrne, Thomas E. *Chemung County: 1890–1975*. Elmira, New York, Chemung County Historical Society, Inc.

Cannon, John. *The Oxford Companion to British History*. Oxford, Oxford University Press, 1997.

Carpenter, Warwick S. *The Summer Paradise in History*. Albany, Delaware & Hudson Co., 1914.

The Catholic Encyclopedia. New York, Robert Appleton Co., 1908.

Chapman, Isaac A. *The History of Wyoming*. Cottonport, Louisiana, Polyanthos, Inc., 1971.

Cheney, John L. *The North Carolina Manual: 1977*. Raleigh.

Child, Hamilton. *Gazetteer & Business Directory of Cattaraugus County, N. Y. for 1874–5*. Syracuse, Journal Office, 1874.

Child, Hamilton. *Gazetteer & Business Directory of Otsego County, N. Y. for 1872–3*. Syracuse, Journal Office, 1872.

Child, Hamilton. *Gazetteer & Directory of Franklin & Clinton Counties with an Almanac for 1862–3*. Ogdensburg, Advance Office, 1862.

Clark, Joshua V. H. *Onondaga: Or Reminiscences of Earlier & Later Times*. Syracuse, Stoddard & Babcock, 1849.

Clayton, W. W. *History of Steuben County, New York*. Philadelphia, Lewis Peck & Co., 1879.

Clements, John. *New York Facts*. Dallas, Texas, Clements Research, Inc., 1986.

Committee on Geographic Names. "Origin of Names of New York State Counties." *University of the State of New York Bulletin to the Schools*, Vol. 10. 1924.

Cook, Harry T. *The Borough of the Bronx: 1639–1913*. New York, 1913.

Cook, Petronelle. *Queen Consorts of England: The Power Behind the Throne*. New York, Facts on File, Inc., 1993.

Cookinham, Henry J. *History of Oneida County, New York*. Chicago, S. J. Clarke Publishing Co., 1912.

Corbitt, David L. *The Formation of North Carolina Counties: 1663–1943*. Raleigh, State Department of Archives & History, 1950.

The Counties of New York State. New York Telephone Co., 1948.

Crittenden, Charles C., & Dan Lacy. *The Historical Records of North Carolina*. Raleigh, North Carolina Historical Commission, 1938.

Crutchfield, James A. *The North Carolina Almanac & Book of Facts: 1989–1990*. Nashville, Tennessee, Rutledge Hill Press, 1988.

Curran, Thomas J. *Manual for the Use of the Legislature of the State of New York: 1951*. Albany, Williams Press, Inc., 1951.

Darlington, Oscar G. *Glimpses of Nassau County's History*. Mineola, New York. Nassau County Trust Co., 1949.

Donehoo, George P. *A History of the Indian Village & Place Names in Pennsylvania*. Harrisburg, Pennsylvania, Telegraph Press, 1928.

Doty, Lockwood R. *History of the Genesee Country*. Chicago, S. J. Clarke Publishing Co., 1925.

Downs, John P. & Fenwick Y. Hedley. *History of Chautauqua County, New York*

& Its People. Boston, American Historical Society, Inc., 1921.

Dutchess County. William Penn Associates of Philadelphia, 1937.

Eastby, Allen G. "The Baron." *American History Illustrated*, Vol. 25, No. 5. Harrisburg, Pennsylvania: November–December, 1990.

Ekwall, Eilert. *The Concise Oxford Dictionary of English Place-Names.* Oxford, Oxford University Press, 1960.

Ellis, Edward R. *The Epic of New York City.* New York, Coward-McCann, Inc., 1966.

Encyclopaedia Britannica. Chicago, Encyclopaedia Britannica, Inc., 1971.

The Encyclopedia Americana. New York, Americana Corporation, 1977.

Eno, Joel N. "New York County Names." *The Magazine of History*: Vol. 22, No. 3, March, 1916; Vol. 22, No. 4, April, 1916; Vol. 22, No. 5, May, 1916; Vol. 23, No. 1, July, 1916.

Eno, Joel N. "A Tercentennial History of the Towns & Cities of New York: Their Origin, Dates & Names." *Proceedings of the New York State Historical Association*, Vol. 15. 1916.

Faber, Harold. *From Sea to Sea: The Growth of the United States.* New York, Farrar, Straus & Giroux, 1967.

Faragher, John M. *The Encyclopedia of Colonial & Revolutionary America.* New York, Facts on File, 1990.

Flick, Alexander C. "New York Place Names." *History of the State of New York*, Vol. 9. New York: 1937.

Foster, Joseph. *The Peerage, Baronetage & Knightage of the British Empire for 1880.* Westminster, Nichols & Sons.

French, J. H. *Gazetteer of the State of New York.* Syracuse, New York, R. Pearsall Smith, 1860.

Fried, Marc B. *The Early History of Kingston & Ulster County, N. Y.* Kingston, New York, Ulster County Historical Society, 1975.

Gannett, Henry. *The Origin of Certain Place Names in the United States.* Williamstown, Massachusetts, Corner House Publishers, 1978.

Gille, Frank H., et al. *Encyclopedia of New York.* St. Clair Shores, Michigan, Somerset Publishers, 1982.

Glassman, Michael. *New York State (and New York City) Geography, History, Government.* Great Neck, New York, Barron's Educational Series, Inc., 1964.

Gordon, Thomas F. *Gazetteer of the State of New York.* Philadelphia, T. K. & P. G. Collins, 1836.

Greene, Nelson. *History of the Valley of the Hudson.* Chicago, S. J. Clarke Publishing Co., 1931.

Halsey, Francis W. *The Old New York Frontier: Its Wars with Indians & Tories: Its Missionary Schools, Pioneers & Land Titles: 1614–1800.* Port Washington, New York, Ira J. Friedman, Inc., 1901.

Hamm, Margherita A. *Famous Families of New York.* New York, G. P. Putnam's Sons, 1901.

Hansen, Harry. *North of Manhattan: Persons & Places of Old Westchester.* New York, Hastings House Publishers, 1950.

Hawkyard, Alasdair. *The Counties of Britain: A Tudor Atlas by John Speed.* London, England, Pavilion Books, Ltd., 1995.

Healy, Diana D. *America's Vice-Presidents.* New York, Atheneum, 1984.

History of Cayuga County, New York. Auburn, New York, 1908.

History of Clinton & Franklin Counties, New York. Philadelphia, J. W. Lewis & Co., 1880.

History of Clinton & Franklin Counties, New York. Plattsburgh, New York, Clinton County American Revolution Bicentennial Commission, 1978.

History of Greene County, New York. New York, J. B. Beers & Co., 1884.

History of Tioga, Chemung, Tompkins & Schuyler Counties, New York. Philadelphia, Everts & Ensign, 1879.

Hodge, Frederick W. *Handbook of American Indians North of Mexico.* Totowa, New Jersey, Rowman & Littlefield, 1975.

Holley, Orville L. *A Gazetteer of the State of New York.* Albany, J. Disturnell, 1842.

Homberger, Eric. *The Historical Atlas of New York City.* New York, Henry Holt & Co., 1994.

Hough, Franklin B. *Gazetteer of the State of New York.* Albany, Andrew Boyd, 1872.

Hough, Franklin B. *A History of Lewis County in the State of New York.* Albany, Munsell & Rowland, 1860.

Hough, Franklin B. *A History of St. Lawrence & Franklin Counties, New York.* Albany, Little & Co., 1853.

Hufeland, Otto. *Westchester County During the American Revolution.* White Plains, New York, Westchester County Historical Society, 1926.

Hull, Raymona. "Names on the Land in St. Lawrence County."*North Country Life*, Vol. 6, No. 1. Ogdensburg, New York: Winter, 1952.

Jackson, Kenneth T. *The Encyclopedia of New York City.* New Haven, Yale University Press, 1995.

Jenkins, John S. *Lives of the Governors of the State of New York.* Auburn, Derby & Miller, 1852.

Johnson & Crisfield. *Centennial History of Erie County, New York.* Buffalo, New York, Matthews & Warren, 1876.

Kammen, Michael. *Colonial New York: A History.* New York, Charles Scribner's Sons, 1975.

Kelly, Sean, & Rosemary Rogers. *Saints Preserve Us! Everything You Need to Know about Every Saint You'll Ever Need.* New York, Random House, Inc., 1993.

Kenny, Hamill. "The Origin & Meaning of the Indian-Place Names of Maryland." Ph.D. Thesis, Theodore R. McKeldin Library, University of Maryland, College Park, Maryland, 1950.

Kenyon, J. P. *Dictionary of British History.* Ware, England, Wordsworth Editions, Ltd., 1992.

Kouwenhoven, John A. *The Columbia Historical Portrait of New York.* Garden City, New York, Doubleday & Co., Inc., 1953.

Lauber, Almon W. "The Valleys of the Susquehanna and the Delaware." *History of the State of New York*, Vol. 4. 1934.

Lederer, Richard M. *The Place-Names of Westchester County, New York.* Harrison, New York, Harbor Hill Books, 1978.

Leland, J. A. C. "Eastern Tribal Names in California." *California Folklore Quarterly*, Vol. 5, No. 4. Berkeley: October, 1946.

Leland, J. A. C. "Indian Names in Missouri." *Names: Journal of the American Name Society*, Vol. 1, No. 4. Berkeley: December, 1953.

Leland, J. A. C. "Some Eastern Indian Place Names in California." *California Folklore Quarterly*, Vol. 4, No. 4. Berkeley: October, 1945.

Lossing, Benson, J. *The Empire State: A Compendious History of the Commonwealth of New York.* Hartford, Connecticut, American Publishing Co., 1888.

MacCracken, Henry N. *Old Dutchess Forever!* New York, Hastings House Publishers, 1956.

McGee, Dorothy H. *Framers of the Constitution.* New York, Dodd Mead & Co., 1968.

Mack, Arthur C. *The Palisades of the Hudson.* Edgewater, New Jersey, Palisade Press, 1909.

McKnight, W. J. *A Pioneer Outline History of Northwestern Pennsylvania.* Philadelphia, J. B. Lippincott Co., 1905.

McMahon, Helen G. *Chautauqua County: A History.* Buffalo, Henry Stewart, Inc., 1958.

McNamara, John. *History in Asphalt: The Origin of Bronx Street & Place Names.* Harrison, New York, Harbor Hill Books, !978.

Mahon, John K. *The War of 1812.* Gainesville, Florida, University Presses of Florida, 1972.

Marshall, Orasmus H. *The Niagara Frontier: Embracing Sketches of Its Early History*. 1865.

Masters, Brian. *The Mistresses of Charles II*. London, Blond & Briggs, Ltd., 1979.

Merrill, Arch. *Southern Tier*. New York, American Book-Stratford Press, Inc., 1954.

Mills, A. D, *A Dictionary of English Place Names*. Oxford, Oxford University Press, 1991.

Morison, Samuel E. *Samuel de Champlain: Father of New France*. Boston, Little Brown & Co., 1972.

Moule, Thomas. *The County Maps of Old England*. London, Studio Editions, 1990.

Murray, Louis W. *A History of Old Tioga Point & Early Athens, Pennsylvania*. Athens, Pennsylvania, Raeder Press, 1908.

Nelson, Paul D. *William Tryon and the Course of Empire*. Chapel Hill, University of North Carolina Press, 1990.

New York State Vacationlands. Albany, Travel Bureau, State of New York Department of Commerce.

New York Tour Book. Heathrow, Florida, AAA Publishing, 1998.

"Notes & Queries: Indian Local Names with Their Interpretations." *Pennsylvania Magazine of History & Biography*, Vol. 9, No. 3. Philadelphia: 1885.

Noyes, Marion F. *A History of Schoharie County*. Richmondville Phoenix, 1964.

Oakley, Amy. *Our Pennsylvania*. Indianapolis, Bobbs-Merrill Co., Inc., 1950.

O'Callaghan, E. B. *Documents Relative to the Colonial History of the State of New York Procured in Holland, England & France by John Romeyn Brodhead, Esq*. Albany, Weed Parsons & Co., 1857.

O'Callaghan, E. B. *General Index to the Documents Relative to the Colonial History of the State of New York*. Albany, Weed Parsons & Co., 1861.

Parkman, Francis. *The Jesuits in North America in the Seventeenth Century: France & England in North America*. Williamstown, Massachusetts, Corner House Publishers, 1980.

Paterson, Basil A. *Manual for the Use of the Legislature of the State of New York: 1980–81*. Albany, New York Department of State.

Paullin, Charles O. *Atlas of the Historical Geography of the United States*. Carnegie Institution of Washington and the American Geographical Society of New York, 1932.

Pearson, Jonathan. *A History of the Schenectady Patent in the Dutch & English Times*. Albany, New York, 1883.

The Pennsylvania Almanac & Buyers' Guide. 1964.

Peterson, C. Stewart. *First Governors of the Forty-Eight States*. New York, Hobson Book Press, 1947.

Pound, Arthur. *Lake Ontario*. Indianapolis, Bobbs-Merrill Co., 1945.

Powell, Lyman P. *Historic Towns of the Middle States*. New York, G. P. Putnam's Sons, 1906.

Powell, William S. *The North Carolina Gazetteer*. Chapel Hill, University of North Carolina Press, 1968.

Price, Edward T. *Dividing the Land: Early American Beginnings of Our Private Property Mosaic*. Chicago, University of Chicago Press, 1995.

Quinlan, James E. *History of Sullivan County*, Liberty, New York, W. T. Morgans & Co., 1873.

Reaney, P. H. *The Origin of English Place-Names*. London, Routledge & Kegan-Paul, 1960.

Roberts, George S. *Old Schenectady*. Schenectady, New York, Robson & Adee.

Rockland County Data Book. New York, Rockland County Planning Board, 1968.

Ruttenber, E. M. "Indian Geographical Names." *Proceedings of the New York State Historical Association*, Vol. 6. 1906.

Sanders, Bob. "Onondaga Relics Returned to Home." *Syracuse Post-Standard*, October 14, 1989.

Seaver, Frederick J. *Historical Sketches of Franklin County and Its Several Towns*. Albany, J. B. Lyon Co., 1918.

Shankle, George Earlie. *State Names, Flags, Seals, Songs, Birds, Flowers & Other Symbols*. New York, H. W. Wilson Co., 1941.

Shonnard, Frederic, & W. W. Spooner. *History of Westchester County, New York*. New York, New York History Co., 1900.

Signor, Isaac S. *Landmarks of Orleans County, New York*. Syracuse, New York, D. Mason & Co., 1894.

Simms, Jeptha R. *History of Schoharie County & Border Wars of New York*. Albany, Munsell & Tanner, 1845.

Smith, H. P. *History of Broome County*. Syracuse, New York, D. Mason & Co., 1885.

Smith, Ray B. *History of the State of New York: Political & Governmental*. Syracuse, New York, Syracuse Press, Inc., 1922.

Smits, Edward J. *Nassau: Suburbia U.S.A : The First Seventy-five Years of Nassau County, New York*. Garden City, New York, Doubleday & Co., Inc., 1974.

Sousa, Manuel A. E. *Catherine of Braganza: Princess of Portugal: Wife to Charles II*. Lisbon, Marconi Global Communications, 1994.

Souvenir Book: Cortland County Sesquicentennial Celebration: July 20–26, 1958.

Spafford, Horatio G. *A Gazetteer of the State of New York*. Albany, B. D. Packard, 1824.

Spafford, Horatio G. *A Gazetteer of the State of New York*. Albany, H. C. Southwick, 1813.

Stewart, George R. *American Place-Names*. New York, Oxford University Press, 1970.

Stewart, George R. *Names on the Land*. New York, Random House, 1945.

Stokes, I. N. Phelps. *New York: Past & Present: 1524–1939*. New York, 1939.

Stone, William L. *The Poetry & History of Wyoming: Containing Campbell's Gertrude, and the History of Wyoming from Its Discovery to the Beginning of the Present Century*. Wilkes-Barre, C. E. Butler, 1869.

Sullivan, James. *History of New York State: 1523–1927*. New York, Lewis Historical Publishing Co., Inc., 1927.

Sylvester, N. B. *Saratoga & Kay-Ad-Ros-Se-Ra*. Troy, New York, William H. Young, 1876.

Taft, William H., III. *County Names: An Historical Perspective*. National Association of Counties, 1982.

Talman, Wilfred B. *How Things Began in Rockland County: And Places Nearby*. New York, Historical Society of Rockland County, 1977.

Tenney, Howell. *Bi-Centennial History of Albany: History of the County of Albany, N. Y. from 1609 to 1886*. New York, W. W. Munsell & Co., 1886.

This Is New York: The Empire State. Bronxville, New York, Cambridge Book Co., 1962.

Thurston, Herbert J. & Donald Attwater. *Butler's Lives of the Saints: Complete Edition*. Westminster, Maryland, Christian Classics, 1987.

Tracy, Frank B. *The Tercentenary History of Canada*. New York, P. F. Collier & Son, 1908.

Trease, Geoffrey. *Seven Kings of England*. New York, Vanguard Press, 1955.

Trover, Ellen L. *Chronology & Documentary Handbook of the State of New York*. Dobbs Ferry, New York, Oceana Publications, Inc., 1978.

Turner, O. *Pioneer History of the Holland Purchase of Western New York*. Buffalo, Jewett, Thomas & Co., 1849.

Vanderhoof, E. W. *Historical Sketches of Western New York*. Buffalo, New York, Matthews-Northrup Works, 1907.

van der Zee, Henri & Barbara van der Zee. *A Sweet & Alien Land: The Story of Dutch New York*. New York, Viking Press, 1978.

Vogel, Virgil J. *Indian Names in Michigan*. Ann Arbor, University of Michigan Press, 1986.

Vogel, Virgil J. "Indian Place Names in Illinois." *Journal of the Illinois State Historical Society*, Vol. 55. 1962.

Vogel, Virgil J. *Iowa Place Names of Indian Origin.* Iowa City, University of Iowa Press, 1983.

Wallace, W. Stewart. *The Encyclopedia of Canada.* Toronto, University Associates of Canada, 1948.

Walton, Ivan H. "Origin of Names on the Great Lakes." *Names: Journal of the American Name Society*, Vol. 3, No. 4. Berkeley: December, 1955.

Weise, A. J. *History of the Seventeen Towns of Rensselaer County from the Colonization of the Manor of Rensselaerwyck to the Present Time.* Troy, New York, J. M. Francis, & Tucker, 1880.

Weise, Arthur J. *The History of the City of Albany, New York.* Albany, E. H. Bender, 1884.

White, Truman. *Our County and Its People: A Descriptive Work on Erie County, New York.* Boston History Co., 1898.

Wise, L. F., & E. W. Egan. *Kings, Rulers & Statesmen.* New York, Sterling Publishing Co., Inc., 1967.

Wolcott, Walter. *The Military History of Yates County, N. Y.* Penn Yan, New York, Express Book & Job Printing House, 1895.

Wolk, Allan. *The Naming of America.* Nashville, Thomas Nelson, Inc., 1977.

Work Projects Administration. *Inventory of the County Archives of New York City-Bronx County.* New York, 1940.

Work Projects Administration. *New York: A Guide to the Empire State.* New York, Oxford University Press, 1940.

Work Projects Administration. *A Souvenir of the Founding of Rensselaer County.* Troy, New York, Rensselaer County Board of Supervisors.

Wright, Carol van P. *New York Blue Guide.* New York, W. W. Norton & Co., Inc., 1983.

Wright, Muriel H. *A Guide to the Indian Tribes of Oklahoma.* Norman, University of Oklahoma Press, 1951.

Yenne, Bill. *Encyclopedia of North American Indian Tribes.* New York, Crescent Books, 1986.

Zimm, Louise H., et al. *Southeastern New York.* New York, Lewis Historical Publishing Co., Inc.,1946.

North Carolina

(100 counties)

1855 *Alamance County*

Battle of Alamance— Almost a decade before the American Revolution, the Regulators, back country men of western North Carolina, were operating as an organized group, protesting treatment by the crown of England. Their complaints included lack of representation for their mountain areas in the North Carolina legislature, embezzlement of funds by public officials, and other grievances by the crown's North Carolina officials. The aggrieved men, led by Herman Husbands (1724–1795), formed themselves into a group "to assemble ourselves for conference for regulating public grievances and abuses of power...." which became known as the Regulators. Husbands and his men took up arms in 1768 and as the movement gained popular support, the Regulators became increasingly disorderly in taking the law into their own hands. In January, 1771, England's colony of North Carolina passed a law which deemed rioters guilty of treason. The royal governor of North Carolina, William Tryon (1729–1788), sent two groups of militia to force the Regulators into submission. General Hugh Waddell (–1773) led one and Governor Tryon personally led the other group. Waddell was intercepted by a band of Regulators and failed to participate in the May 16, 1771, battle of Alamance. However, Governor Tryon participated very effectively in the battle of Alamance, routing a force of some 2,000 Regulators in only two hours. Since the battle was fought near the banks of Alamance Creek, it was named the battle of Alamance. The state has established a 40 acre state historic sight and museum for the Alamance battlegound in what is now Alamance County. This county was created on January 29, 1849. The *Centennial History of Alamance County*, published in 1949, states that Giles Mebane was the North Carolina legislator who introduced the bill to create this new county and that the name had been suggested to him by his wife "in memory of the battle of Alamance."

1856 *Alexander County*

Uncertain— This county was created on January 15, 1847. Sources dealing with the history, geography and place names of North Carolina offer differing opinions concerning this county's namesake and some of them admit that the answer is uncertain. Possibilities mentioned are Abraham Alexander (1717–1786), Nathaniel Alexander (1756–1808) and William J. Alexander (1797–1857).

Abraham Alexander (1717–1786)— A justice of the peace of Mecklenburg County and a member of the North Carolina assembly from that county, Abraham Alexander also was a member of Mecklenburg County's committee of safety. Lile Pittard's 1958 history of Alexander County entitled *Prologue: A History of Alexander County, North Carolina*, states that Abram (sic) Alexander was the chairman of the May, 1775 convention in Charlotte which produced the so-called Mecklenburg Declaration of Independence. William E. White's 1926 history of this county also states that Abram (sic) Alexander was the chairman of that convention. Kemp P. Battle's *Names of the Counties of North Carolina* confirms this and provides the correct spelling of the chairman's given name; i.e., Abraham.

Nathaniel Alexander (1756–1808)— Born on March 5, 1756, near Concord, North Carolina, Nathaniel Alexander studied medicine and surgery and served as a surgeon during the American Revolution. He practiced medicine in Santee, South Carolina, and in Charlotte, North Carolina. He served in both houses of the North Carolina legislature and represented North Carolina in the U.S. House of Representatives from 1803 until 1805, when he resigned to become governor of North Carolina, serving as the state's governor from 1805 to 1807. He died on March 8, 1808, at Salisbury, North Carolina.

William J. Alexander (1797–1857)— William Julius Alexander of Mecklenburg County was a member of the general assembly of the North Carolina legislature and a member of North Carolina's house of commons. In 1828 he was speaker of that body and subsequently was solicitor of the western district.

Kemp P. Battle was a leading authority on the origins of North Carolina county names and Battle tells us that Alexander County's name honors William J. Alexander. About 90% of the several dozen sources consulted agree that this county was named for William J. Alexander.

1857 *Alleghany County*

Uncertain — This county in northwestern North Carolina was created in 1859. Sources consulted differ on the origin of the county's name but essentially all sources on the history, geography and place names of North Carolina state that this county was named for an Indian tribe (which would be the Alleghany Indians) or for a corruption of the Delaware Indians' name for the Allegheny and Ohio Rivers. The Alleghany were a tribe who lived in the 18th century near present-day Pittsburgh, Pennsylvania where the Allegheny River joins with the Monongahela River to form the Ohio River. The Alleghany Indians' name derived from the name of the river along which they lived. The river was apparently first named by the Iroquois Indians and later modified by Delaware Indians. The Alleghany Indians were found in a wider area than simply present-day Pittsburgh. In his work entitled *Indian Villages & Place Names in Pennsylvania*, George P. Donehoo states that "The term [Allegheny] applied to all of the Indians living west of the waters of the Susquehanna [River] within the region drained by the Ohio [River]."

1858 *Anson County*

George Anson (1697–1762) — This county was created in 1749, while North Carolina was an English colony. It was named for the British naval officer, George Anson, who had recently (1748) been elevated to the peerage of England. He entered the navy in 1712, served with distinction, and by 1723 attained the rank of captain. From 1724 to 1731 Anson commanded English naval forces defending the Carolina coast against pirate attacks and Spanish raids. In 1744 he completed a successful circumnavigation of the globe and he returned to England as a hero. Soon promoted to high rank in the English navy, Anson was raised to the English peerage in 1748. Although he served on the admiralty board (and was made first lord of the admiralty in 1751), Lord Anson continued to participate in selected naval combat missions.

1859 *Ashe County*

Samuel Ashe (1725–1813) — A native of North Carolina and a lawyer, Ashe was appointed assistant attorney for the crown of the Wilmington, North Carolina, district. He became one of North Carolina's early leaders in opposition to England's treatment of her American colonies. He participated in North Carolina's first revolutionary convention, served as a member of the provincial congress and on North Carolina's council of safety. Ashe was made president of that body in 1776. He was a member of the convention which framed North Carolina's first constitution and served in the North Carolina legislature, where he became speaker of the senate. Ashe also served for a time as an officer in our Revolutionary army. In 1777 he became presiding judge of North Carolina's revolutionary superior court and he remained North Carolina's chief justice for some 18 years. At the age of 70, Ashe was elected to be North Carolina's governor and he served in that office from 1795 to 1798. Ashe County, North Carolina, was created and named in his honor in 1799.

1860 *Avery County*

Waightstill Avery (1741–1821) — A native of Connecticut and a lawyer, Avery moved to England's colony of North Carolina in 1769. Here he practiced law and was elected as a member of the provincial assembly. In 1772 Avery was appointed as North Carolina's attorney general for the crown of England. He was a member of the May, 1775, convention in Charlotte which produced the so-called Mecklenburg Declaration of Independence and he was one of the signers of that historic document. As one of North Carolina's leaders in opposition to England's treatment of her American colonies, he was a delegate to the provincial congress and a member of the provincial council of 13. On May 10, 1776, he resigned from his position as the crown's attorney general and in November of that year he was a member of the congress at Halifax. Avery personally drafted a large portion of North Carolina's first constitution for this 1776 congress at Halifax. North Carolina did not become a state until 1789 but nascent state government was being established in 1776 and Avery served in its first general assembly and was its first attorney general. Avery also served for a time as a colonel in North Carolina's Revolutionary army. After leaving the Revolutionary army Colonel Avery served in both houses of the North Carolina legislature. Waightstill Avery was a slave owner. He was challenged to a duel by Andrew Jackson, who later became our nation's president. Avery accepted the challenge and the duel was held but neither participant was hurt. When Avery County was created on February 23, 1911, it became the 100th and youngest county in North Carolina.

1861 *Beaufort County*

Henry Somerset, Duke of Beaufort (1684–1714) — On December 3, 1705, the province of Carolina created the Pamptecough Precinct. About 1712 that name was changed to Beaufort County, to honor one of the proprietors of Carolina, Henry Somerset, the second duke of Beaufort (1684–1714). In 1663 England's King Charles II (1630–1685) had granted proprietorships in Carolina to eight Englishmen. These proprietary interests in Carolina passed from generation to generation as proprietors died. In some cases these proprietary interests were sold. By 1729, when the Carolina charter was surrendered to the English crown, nearly 50 different individuals had served as proprietors of Carolina or had been entitled to do so. Henry Somerset, Duke of Beaufort, was one of the later proprietors. He inherited his Carolina proprietorship in 1707, from his mother, Lady Rebecca Granville. Henry Somerset was born at Monmouth castle in 1684 and by 1702 became acquainted with Queen Anne (1665–1714). In 1705 he became a member of England's house of lords. A pillar of the Tory party, Somerset subsequently was made lord lieutenant of the English counties of Hampshire and Gloucestershire and of the cities of Bristol and Gloucester. In 1712 he was made a knight of the garter.

1862 *Bertie County*

James Bertie (1673–1735) or both James & Henry Bertie (1675–1735) — This county was created as Bertie Precinct in 1722 and named for either the lord proprietor, James Bertie or for both James Bertie and his brother, Henry Bertie, who also was a Carolina proprietor. In 1663 England's King Charles II (1630–1685) had granted proprietorships in Carolina to eight Englishmen. These proprietary interests in Carolina passed from generation to generation as proprietors died. In some cases these proprietary interests were sold. By

1729, when the Carolina charter was surrendered to the English crown, nearly 50 different individuals had served as proprietors of Carolina or had been entitled to do so. James Bertie (1673–1735) and Henry Bertie (1675–1735) acquired a trust interest in a share of the Carolina proprietorship of Seth Sothel (–1694) when Sothel's heirs in England sold Sothel's proprietary share to Hugh Watson in trust for James and Henry Bertie. That share was later assigned to James Bertie alone. Hugh Watson also acquired a second proprietary share in 1725 from Mary and John Danson, also held in trust for James and Henry Bertie. That share was later allotted to Henry Bertie alone. Henry Bertie held his share until 1729 when he sold it to the English crown. James Bertie's share of the Carolina proprietorship was conveyed to his son, Edward Bertie and other men. James Bertie represented England's county of Middlesex in the English parliament for a number of years. The brothers James and Henry Bertie were sons of James Bertie, the first earl of Abingdon.

1863 *Bladen County*

Martin Bladen (1680–1746)— This English soldier and politician was educated at Westminster. He served in the English army in the Low Countries, Spain, and in Portugal, where he was a colonel in command of a regiment of foot soldiers. Martin Bladen served as a member of the British parliament from 1715 to 1746 and he was made comptroller of the mint in 1714. His connection with North Carolina began in 1717, when he became commissioner of trade and plantations, which supervised colonial affairs. He served in that post from 1717 to 1746 and this county was created in 1734 while Bladen was supervising England's colonies, including North Carolina.

1864 *Brunswick County*

The former town of Brunswick, North Carolina— This county was created in 1764 and named for a town in England's colony of North Carolina named Brunswick. The county was not named for the present town of Brunswick in Columbus County, North Carolina, which was founded in 1771. Rather its name honors the former town in England's colony of North Carolina, on the Cape Fear River. That former town is located in what is now Brunswick County, North Carolina, and is now a state historic sight. Settled about 1725, while King George I (1660–

1727) was the reigning monarch of England, the town was named in honor of the king, who was duke of Brunswick-Luneburg. Brunswick was the name of a ruling family, duchy and state in north-central Germany. King George I was a member of this family. In 1569 the Brunswick-Luneburg line was founded and it later took the name Hanover. Skipping fast forward to the early 18th century in North Carolina, we find that Maurice Moore was the founder the first town of Brunswick. He chose the sight for his town on a low bluff on the west bank of the Cape Fear River, where the river was about one and a half miles wide and an excellent harbor for large transoceanic vessels. The town consisted of 360 acres, which was part of a 1,500 acre grant that Maurice Moore had received on June 3, 1725. A portion of the 360 acres was set aside for common use and the remainder was divided into 336 half-acre lots. This earlier town of Brunswick, which was Brunswick County's namesake, was incorporated in 1745. It was abandoned about 1776, but a few families returned after the American Revolution. By 1830, this town of Brunswick had been completely ruined.

King George I (1660–1727) Born in Osnabruck, Hanover, in what is now Germany, and named at birth George Lewis (also styled Georg Ludwig in some accounts), George was an important military leader in Europe. In 1698 he succeeded his father, Ernst August (1622–1698), as elector of Hanover and duke of Brunswick-Luneburg. He was the first English monarch of the house of Brunswick (later styled Hanover, now Windsor), and that royal house still rules Great Britain. King George I, and his successors, owe their hold on the throne of Great Britain to two factors: (1) deep-seated religious animosity in England against Roman Catholicism and (2) the inability of England's Queen Anne (1665–1714) to produce an heir to the throne. Queen Anne had a large number of children (15 according to one account; 17 per another) but most of them were stillborn. Only one boy survived. He was Prince William (1689–1700). Medical science at that time was unable to effectively assist the queen of England in repeated efforts to leave an heir to the throne. This personal tragedy resulted in a practical problem for England as well, since the heir to the throne when Queen Anne died in 1714 was her half-brother, James Francis Edward Stuart (1688–1766); but James Stuart was a Catholic, and England wanted no Catholic on its throne. The na-

tion closed ranks against James Stuart and all other Catholic contenders for the crown and reached all the way to Hanover, in Germany, for a successor to Queen Anne. There they found George Lewis (1660–1727), the elector of Hanover, who had a drop or two of royal English blood in his veins and thus some semblance of a claim to the English throne. He became England's King George I. The new king never bothered to learn much of the English language but he did succeed in remaining Protestant throughout his reign from 1714 until his death in 1727.

1865 *Buncombe County*

Edward Buncombe (1742–1778)— Buncombe was born to English parents on the island of Saint Kitts, in the West Indies and was educated in England. About 1768 he inherited from his uncle, a large estate located in England's colony of North Carolina, and he moved here. The estate was located in what was then Tyrrell County. Edward Buncombe constructed a rather impressive mansion on his estate and called it Buncombe Hall. In 1771 Buncombe became a justice for Tyrrell County's court of pleas and quarter sessions and about this time he was made a colonel of the provincial troops in Tyrrell County. Early in the American Revolution, Colonel Buncombe fought at the battles of Brandywine and Germantown, in Pennsylvania. At Germantown he was seriously wounded and taken as a prisoner of war. By the spring of 1778, Buncombe's battle wounds were healing but he fell while sleep-walking opening one of his battle wounds, and he bled to death. This county was created and named in honor of Colonel Edward Buncombe in the legislative session that began December 5, 1791. In a 1923 work entitled *Buncombe County: Economic & Social*, the date of the county's creation is given as January 17, 1792.

1866 *Burke County*

Uncertain— Burke County was created on April 8, 1777, in an act which was to become effective on June 1, 1777. Sources dealing with the history, geography and place names of North Carolina are not unanimous concerning this county's namesake. A strong majority of these sources state that this county was named for Thomas Burke (–1783) but several sources disagree and claim that the county's name honors the English statesman, Edmund Burke (1729–1797).

Edmund Burke (1729–1797)— A native of Ireland and a member of the British parliament, Edmund Burke became a ranking Whig, noted orator and statesmen. In parliament and in his political writings, Burke was a champion of liberty for the American colonies and an advocate of human rights. His speech in 1774 entitled American Taxation and another on Conciliation with America in 1775 were examples of his efforts on our behalf.

Thomas Burke (–1783) — Born in Ireland about 1747, Thomas Burke moved to colonial Virginia about 1759 and to North Carolina about 1771. Here he practiced law, and served in North Carolina's provincial congresses from 1774 to 1776 and was one of North Carolina's representatives to the Continental Congress from 1777 to 1781. Burke had objections to many of the provisions which had been presented for the proposed Articles of Confederation. He is given credit for personally and successfully advocating an amendment "to reserve to the states all powers not specifically granted to the central government." He was a controversial figure in the Continental Congress and left it in June, 1781 when he was chosen as governor of North Carolina, while the American Revolution was in process. Governor Burke and his council were captured by Tories in September, 1781 and he was taken as a prisoner of war but escaped in January, 1782, and returned to North Carolina to complete his term as governor.

Abram Nash (–1786), who was governor of North Carolina from 1780 to 1781 had been speaker of North Carolina's house of commons in April, 1777, when this county's name was chosen and it is very likely that he knew who the new county's name was intended to honor. Governor Nash has stated in writing that the county's name was chosen to honor Thomas Burke.

1867 *Cabarrus County*

Stephen Cabarrus (1754–1808) — This native of France moved to North Carolina in 1776, in the midst of the American Revolution. Here he married Jeanne Henriette Damery Bodley, a wealthy widow, who was about 17 years his senior. That astute move enabled Cabarrus to accumulate, by 1777, an estate consisting of 1,980 acres of North Carolina land and 60 slaves. He was elected to the North Carolina house of commons in 1784 and served in the North Carolina legislature until he retired from politics in 1805. On several occasions he served as speaker in the legislature. Cabarrus took an interest in education and was chosen to be a mem-

ber of the first board of trustees of the University of North Carolina in 1789. This county was created in 1792, while Cabarrus was serving in the legislature. In a history of Cabarrus County prepared during the 1930's by the sixth grade pupils of Corbin Street School, it is stated that Stephen Cabarrus cast the deciding vote in the legislature that created Cabarrus County. Just one year earlier, in 1791, the North Carolina legislature had abolished Dobbs County and established two new counties to occupy Dobbs County's land. The name Cabarrus was proposed at that time for one of those two counties but it was not adopted and it was not until the following year that Stephen Cabarrus was honored as the namesake of a North Carolina County.

1868 *Caldwell County*

Joseph Caldwell (1773–1835) — Caldwell was born on April 21, 1773, in Lamington, New Jersey, and graduated from the College of New Jersey (now Princeton University) in 1791. He became a tutor of mathematics at his alma mater and later was a professor of mathematics at the University of North Carolina. He also served as president of the University of North Carolina at Chapel Hill. Although his occupations were in the field of education, Caldwell was also an ordained minister of the Presbyterian Church. Elisha P. Miller was a member of the North Carolina legislature, who attempted to have a new county created during the legislative session of 1838–1839. That effort failed, but in late 1840 Miller again introduced a bill to have a new county created. This second try was successful and Caldwell County was created on January 11, 1841. Nancy Alexander's history of Caldwell County entitled *Here Will I Dwell: The Story of Caldwell County*, tells a bit about the selection of the new county's name. According to Alexander's work, it was Charles Manley, the clerk of the house, who suggested that the new county be named Caldwell, in honor of the former president of the state's university. Since Elisha P. Miller's wife was a Caldwell, and since Elisha P. Miller really didn't care very much what they named the new county, the name Caldwell was selected and Caldwell County was created and named in honor of Dr. (honorary doctor of laws degrees) Joseph Caldwell.

1869 *Camden County*

Charles Pratt, Earl of Camden (1714–1794) — Pratt, who was born in London,

England, served as attorney general and was a member of parliament. In 1761 he became chief justice of the court of common pleas and a decision that he rendered in the trial of John Wilkes concerning freedom of speech and freedom of the press made him one of the most popular men in England. A bit later, now titled Baron Camden, he became lord chancellor. He opposed England's treatment of the American colonies which earned him popularity here and was the reason that this county was named for him when it was created in 1777. In 1786 Baron Camden was made first earl of Camden and viscount Bayham. He served more than ten years as president of the council.

1870 *Carteret County*

John Carteret, Earl of Granville (1690–1763) — In 1722, England's colony of North Carolina created Carteret County and named it for one of the later lords proprietors, John Carteret (1690–1763). In 1663 England's King Charles II (1630–1685) had granted proprietorships in Carolina to eight Englishmen and one of these men was Sir George Carteret (–1680). These proprietary interests in Carolina passed from generation to generation as proprietors died. In some cases these proprietary interests were sold. By 1729, when the Carolina charter was surrendered to the English crown, nearly 50 different individuals had served as proprietors of Carolina or had been entitled to do so. John Carteret (1690–1763) was one of the later proprietors. He inherited his Carolina proprietorship in 1695, upon the death of his father, George Carteret, first Baron Carteret (1667–1695). The proprietor for whom Carteret County, North Carolina, was named, John Carteret, was educated at Oxford and took a seat in the British house of lords in 1711. There he was a champion of Protestant succession to the throne of England which became an extremely important consideration when Queen Anne (1665–1714) died and left no heirs. Queen Anne was succeeded as England's monarch by the German Protestant, King George I (1660–1727), and Carteret became a favorite of the new king because he spoke German and the king never gained much fluency in the English language. Carteret served as secretary of state from 1721–1724 When John Carteret's mother died in 1744, he succeeded to the title of earl of Granville. Carteret was the only one of the lords proprietors who was unwilling to sell his share to the crown in 1729. The portion of Carolina that Carteret retained was known as the Granville District or Granville Grant.

1871 *Caswell County*

Richard Caswell (1729–1789) — This Maryland native came to North Carolina when he was 17 years old. He brought with him a letter of introduction from Maryland's royal governor to Gabriel Johnston (1699–1752), the royal governor of North Carolina. Caswell was appointed deputy surveyor for the province. He also served several terms in the lower house of the legislature of England's colony of North Carolina and was speaker of that body from 1770 to 1771. Caswell subsequently represented North Carolina in the first and second Continental Congresses from 1774 to 1776. North Carolina did not become a state until 1789 but nascent state government was being established in 1776 and Richard Caswell became its first governor on an interim basis in December, 1776. He served as interim governor until the general assembly met in April, 1777, and officially elected him governor. The state legislature reelected Caswell as governor several times. There was an interval between his first and second periods as governor and Caswell served in the Revolutionary War as a major-general of the state militia during this interval. This county was created on April 8, 1777, effective June 1, 1777. Caswell had begun serving as governor for the first time just four months earlier, in December, 1776.

1872 *Catawba County*

Uncertain — This North Carolina county was created on December 12, 1842. Most North Carolina sources consulted indicate that the county was named for the Catawba Indians but a few of these sources indicate that the county was named for the Catawba River, which forms much of Catawba County's northern border. The difference is more apparent that real because the Catawba River was named for the Catawba Indians.

Catawba River — The Catawba River is a tributary of South Carolina's Santee River. The Catawba rises in western North Carolina in the Blue Ridge Mountains. From its origin in southwestern McDowell County, North Carolina the Catawba flows northeast through McDowell County before turning east and soon forms much of the northern border of Catawba County. That county's northern border is created by Lake Hickory, the Catawba River and Lake Norman. From Catawba County,

North Carolina, the Catawba River flows south through North Carolina into South Carolina, where it is given a new name, the Wateree River. In South Carolina the Wateree River joins the Congaree River to form the Santee River. The combined length of the Catawba-Wateree Rivers is 395 miles.

Catawba Indians — The Catawba Indians were a prominent Siouan-speaking tribe who lived in what is now western and southern South Carolina, when first encountered by Europeans about the middle of the 16th century. The Catawba's own traditional history holds that they migrated to South Carolina from the northwest, where they had lived as farmers and hunters. In South Carolina the Catawba lived in rectangular barrel-roofed houses and subsisted largely on maize. They engaged in periodic warfare with Shawnee and Iroquois Indians, but were generally friendly to Whites and sided with the American colonists against the British during the American Revolution. Their population in 1822 was estimated to be 450. In 1840 the Catawba signed a treaty ceding more than one hundred thousand fertile acres to the state of South Carolina for a few thousand dollars. After signing this treaty, the Catawba migrated to North Carolina shortly before Catawba County, North Carolina was created, but North Carolina failed to provide a place for the Catawbas to live and most of them returned to the region of their old homes in South Carolina. Most Catawba Indians remained in South Carolina although a smaller number moved to Indian territory (now Oklahoma). In 1944 the South Carolina legislature passed legislation granting Catawba Indians all the rights and privileges of South Carolina citizens. At that time there were about 300 Catawbas, predominantly of mixed Indian and White blood, living in South Carolina.

1873 *Chatham County*

William Pitt, Earl of Chatham (1708–1778) — Pitt, an Englishman and the first earl of Chatham, was one of England's greatest and most famous statesmen. He was a member of parliament and held the positions of vice treasurer of Ireland and paymaster general of the forces. He became secretary of state and virtually prime minister in 1756, but in 1760 King George III took the throne and Pitt was forced to resign. In 1766 he formed a new ministry but served for only 15 months. Chatham County, North Carolina was created by the legislative session that began on De-

cember 5, 1770. The act creating this county was ratified on January 26, 1771, and became effective April 1, 1771. During 1770 and 1771 the Earl of Chatham had become very popular on this side of the Atlantic for his opposition to the alleged right of the English parliament to tax American colonies without their consent. Later, after this county had been created, Pitt urged reconciliation between Britain and her American colonies. After the American Revolution began he favored any peace settlement that would keep the American colonies in the British empire. This was the second North Carolina county whose name honored William Pitt, Earl of Chatham (1708–1778). Earlier, in an act passed in 1760 to become effective January 1, 1761, North Carolina had named Pitt County in his honor.

1874 *Cherokee County*

Cherokee Indians — The Cherokee Indians were a large and powerful tribe who lived in North Carolina, Georgia and Tennessee at the time of their first contact with Europeans. They were the most powerful Indian tribe in North Carolina. By the early 1800's they had adopted many of the features of civilization. By 1840, most Cherokees had been forced from their lands and removed to Indian territory (now Oklahoma) by court decisions, a fraudulent treaty and military force. The removal of some 17,000 Cherokee Indians from their ancient tribal lands in western North Carolina, northwestern Georgia and eastern Tennessee was a dark chapter in our nation's history. Their journey to Indian territory was marked by indescribable suffering from which some 4,000 Cherokees died. A few Cherokee Indians refused to join the forced march to Indian territory and other Cherokees have returned from Oklahoma. Virtually all of these eastern Cherokee Indians now live on the Qualla Indian reservation in western North Carolina. Cherokee County, North Carolina, is North Carolina's westernmost county and part of the Qualla reservation is within its borders. Cherokee County was created on January 4, 1839, while the Cherokee Indians were being herded to Indian territory during the winter of 1838–1839. The name Cherokee is said to be derived from the Cherokee word for "fire," *chera*.

1875 *Chowan County*

Uncertain — About 1668 the Shaftesbury Precinct was created within Carolina's Albemarle County. About a dozen years later, in the 1680's the precinct's name was changed to Chowan Precinct. The precinct's area embraced many of the present North Carolina counties which surround Albemarle Sound on the Atlantic Ocean and those that border the Chowan River, but the precinct's area excluded the areas now in far northeastern North Carolina. Twenty four sources were consulted concerning the origin of the name of Chowan Precinct (now Chowan County). Four sources merely said that it was an Indian name while 18 stated that the name honored an Indian tribe (whose name they rendered variously as Chowan, Chowanoc, Chowanoke and Chowanor. Frederick W. Hodge uses the form Chowanoc in his *Handbook of American Indians North of Mexico*). Only one source states that the county's name honors the Chowan River, but that source is William S. Powell's *The North Carolina Gazetteer*. Professor Powell was for many years a history professor and expert on North Carolina history at the University of North Carolina in Chapel Hill. He was also the Librarian of the North Carolina collection of that university's library. Thus William S. Powell's opinion on this subject should not be taken lightly. The 24th source was George R. Stewart's *American Place Names*, published in 1970. Professor Stewart was the Berkeley Fellow at the University of California and taught there for many years. Stewart tells us that the name Chowan "...from a name recorded as that of 'a great town called Chawanook' by Amadas and Barlowe in 1584. It was probably also the name of a tribe, and has been doubtfully translated as Algonquian 'southern people.'"

Chowan River—The Chowan River is formed in North Carolina by the confluence of the Blackwater and Nottoway Rivers, just south of the Virginia state line. Only only about 50 miles long, the Chowan's waters enter the Atlantic Ocean via Albemarle Sound. The river's name honors the tribe of Indians who lived in this section of Carolina, when Europeans first explored it.

Chowanoc Indians—The Chowanoc Indians lived along the Chowan River in northeastern North Carolina, near the Meherrin River and Nottoway River and inland from these rivers for several miles. When first encountered by Europeans about 1585, the Chowanoc Indians were the principal tribe in northeastern Carolina. They had about four villages in this area and in one of them alone, Ohanoak, there were about 700 warriors. By 1701 their population had decreased greatly and

they occupied only one village on Bennetts Creek. In 1711 and 1712 the Chowanoc joined with other Indians to war on the Whites and when these hostilities ended, the Chowanoc population had dwindled to about 240. Frederick W. Hodge's *Handbook of American Indians North of Mexico* reports that by 1820 the Chowanoc Indians were extinct.

1876 *Clay County*

Henry Clay (1777–1852)—Clay represented Kentucky in both branches of the U.S. Congress. For many years he was one of the more prominent figures in American politics but his several bids for the presidency were unsuccessful. He was influential in effecting important compromises between northern and southern interests during the years that secession and civil war were imminent. This county created on February 20, 1861, perhaps in sadness that all compromise measures to avert civil war were failing. Just three months later, on May 20, 1861, North Carolina seceded from the Union and joined the Confederate States of America.

1877 *Cleveland County*

Benjamin Cleaveland (1738–1806)—A native of Virginia, Cleaveland moved with relatives to the western frontier of North Carolina when he was about 21 years old. In 1775 he was appointed an ensign in the North Carolina line and, after serving in combat against Indians in 1776, was promoted to captain. In August, 1777, he was made a colonel of the militia. Cleaveland was also chairman of Surry County's committee of safety and was elected to both houses of North Carolina's legislature. In 1780 he became a Revolutionary War hero for his participation in the battle of Kings Mountain on the border between North and South Carolina. In that battle, our Revolutionary forces killed or captured the entire enemy force of some 1,100, while suffering only 90 casualties. The American forces were led by backwoodsmen, including Colonel Cleaveland. In 1781 he was captured by Tory forces but was soon rescued. After the Revolution, he moved to South Carolina and died there. This North Carolina County was created on January 11, 1841, and its name was spelled correctly, as Cleaveland County. The present, incorrect, spelling of the county's name was adopted by the North Carolina legislature in 1887. Grover Cleveland first became president of the United States on March 4, 1885, and the correct spelling of

the president's name was soon well known. Lee B. Weathers' 1956 history of Cleveland County, North Carolina, indicates that the spelling of the president's name contributed to the faulty change in the spelling of this county's name.

1878 *Columbus County*

Cristoforo Colombo (1451–1506)—Colombo, whose name we render as Christopher Columbus, was a native of Italy who believed the theory that the earth is round and that Asia could be reached by sailing west from Europe. He persuaded Ferdinand and Isabella of Spain to equip an expedition for him to test this theory. Sailing from Europe August 3, 1492, he first sighted land in the Americas in the Bahama Islands on October 12, 1492. On this voyage he left a colony of 40 men on the Hatian coast. Columbus returned several times to the New World before his death in 1506. Popularly known as the discoverer of America, Columbus was certainly not the first European to reach the Western Hemisphere. Leif Ericsson had accomplished that about the year A.D. 1000. But it was Columbus' expedition that triggered rapid exploration, conquest and settlement of the Americas by Europeans. This county was created on December 15, 1808.

1879 *Craven County*

Uncertain—Craven County's genealogy is a bit complicated. On December 3, 1705, Bath County in the province of Carolina, was divided into three precincts, one of which was named Archdale Precinct. In either 1711 or 1712, Archdale Precinct's name was changed to Craven Precinct. We now know it as Craven County. Craven Precinct's name honored one of the Carolina proprietors. In 1663 England's King Charles II (1630–1685) had granted proprietorships in Carolina to eight Englishmen and one of these men was William Craven, Earl of Craven (1606–1697). These proprietary interests in Carolina passed from generation to generation as proprietors died. In some cases these proprietary interests were sold. By 1729, when the Carolina charter was surrendered to the English crown, nearly 50 different individuals had served as proprietors of Carolina or had been entitled to do so. In the January, 1945, issue of the *North Carolina Historical Review*, Alonzo T. Dill states that Craven Precinct was "...obviously named for William Lord Craven, who became Lord Palatine in 1708 and died October 9, 1711 ... not to be confused with

William, Earl of Craven (1608[sic]–1697), the earlier Proprietor…" However Zae H. Gwynn tells us, in a work entitled *The 1850 Census of Craven County, North Carolina*, that this precinct was named for, the original Carolina proprietor, William Craven, Earl of Craven (1606–1697). Another opinion on the origin of this county's name comes to us from William S. Powell, an authority on both North Carolina place names and on the proprietors of Carolina. In Powell's work entitled *The North Carolina Gazetteer*, he expresses the view that Craven Precinct was probably not named for the original proprietor, William Craven, Earl of Craven (1606–1697). Powell tells us that it more likely was named for his relative, William, Lord Craven (1668–1711). However Powell admits the possibility that we have yet a third contender for the honor of this precinct's namesake, and that would be William, Lord Craven (1700–1739).

William Craven, Earl of Craven (1606–1697)—A prominent English military officer, Craven was knighted for his services in 1627. He aided King Charles I (1600–1649) during the English Civil War and was deprived of all of his lands when Charles I lost his throne to the forces of Oliver Cromwell (1599–1658). When the monarchy was restored, Craven recovered all or most of his estates. In 1663 he was made one of Carolina's original eight proprietors and he was made Earl of Craven in 1664.

William, Lord Craven (1668–1711)— When the first Carolina proprietor of the Craven line died unmarried on April 9, 1697, his Carolina proprietorship passed to his relative, William, Lord Craven (1668–1711). Some accounts refer to him as a grand nephew of the first lord Craven, while others call him a distant cousin. This Carolina proprietor was the second Lord Craven. He took a seat in the English house of lords in 1697 and in 1702 he was made lord lieutenant of Berkshire.

William, Lord Craven (1700–1739)—One of three sons of William, Lord Craven (1668–1711), this proprietor became the third lord Craven and a Carolina proprietor upon the death of his father in 1711. During his youth, a gentleman named Fulwar Skipwith, a relative on his mother's side, signed official Carolina documents on behalf of the young proprietor. This third lord Craven was educated at Rugby and Cambridge. He held his Carolina proprietorship until 1729 when all Carolina proprietorships, except those in the Carteret line, were sold to the crown.

1880 *Cumberland County*

William Augustus, Duke of Cumberland (1721–1765)—In 1754, when this county was created, North Carolina was an English colony and King George II (1683–1760) was the reigning monarch of Britain. England's American colonies used various devices to curry favor from the crown and one employed by several of the colonies was to name counties in honor of the monarch or members of the monarch's family. William Augustus was a son of England's King George II. Born on April 15, 1721, William was made a royal duke and given the tittle duke of Cumberland in July, 1726. He was educated for the navy but was permitted to follow his preference for the army and given the rank of major-general in 1742. A rather poor general, his troops were defeated in several important actions on the European continent. Cumberland's only significant victory was at home, in the British Isles, where he defeated Prince Charles Edward Stuart (1720–1788), the pretender to the thrones of Scotland and England. That victory took place at Culloden, Scotland in 1746. The duke's name is shown in most works as William Augustus, but in some the form William August is used. In the spring of 1784, after the American colonies had defeated Britain in the Revolutionary War, the North Carolina legislature changed this county's name from Cumberland County to the more patriotic name of Fayette County. The next session of the legislature met in November, 1784, and changed this county's name back to Cumberland County.

1881 *Currituck County*

Uncertain—This county in extreme northeastern North Carolina contains part of the state's Outer Banks on the Atlantic Ocean. Most North Carolina sources indicate that the name honors a former Indian tribe that lived here and some of those sources specify that this tribe was a small Algonquian tribe. Other reliable sources agree that the name is of Indian origin, but indicate that it was merely an Indian word and not a tribal name. Several sources say that the traditional translation of this Indian word is "wild geese." This county was first created in the late 17th century, in England's colony of Carolina, as Currituck Precinct of Albemarle County. If this precinct was not named for an Indian tribe, there are several geographical features in this area named Currituck, from which Currituck Precinct's name might have been taken; e.g., the large Currituck

Sound, which separates the eastern and western portions of Currituck County, Currituck Banks, Currituck Inlet and Currituck Creek. Currituck Sound is approximately 30 miles long and has a width of about four miles at its widest point.

1882 *Dare County*

Virginia Dare (1587–)—Virginia Dare was born on Roanoke Island in what was then England's nascent colony of Virginia. Roanoke Island now belongs to Dare County, North Carolina. In 1584 Sir Walter Ralegh (–1618) had been granted a patent by Queen Elizabeth I (1533–1603), to take possession of unknown lands in America in the queen's name. The nascent English colony was to be centered on Roanoke Island and a party of colonists sailed from England on April 26, 1587. They landed on Roanoke Island in July and on August 18, 1587, the first child of English parents was born on American soil here on Roanoke Island. The child's father was Ananias Dare, and her mother was Eleanor White Dare. (Her given name is rendered variously as Eleanor, Elenor and Ellinor.) The child was a girl, and she was named Virginia, in honor of the English colony-to-be. Virginia Dare was baptized, according to the rites of the Anglican Church, on the Sunday following her birth and nothing more is known about her. The main party returned to England for supplies nine days after Virginia Dare's birth but nobody returned from England to join the colonists on Roanoke Island until 1591. When they returned, no trace could be found of either Virginia Dare or the other settlers. Because of this, these colonists came to be known as the "lost colonists." Dare County, North Carolina, was created on February 3, 1870.

1883 *Davidson County*

William L. Davidson (–1781)—Davidson was born about 1746 in Pennsylvania but moved with his family to North Carolina when he was still a small child. As the Revolutionary War approached, Davidson was appointed a member of the committee of safety of Rowan County and in 1775 he was commissioned as an officer in our Continental army. He served with distinction at the battle of Germantown and was promoted from major to lieutenant-colonel. He later was commissioned as a brigadier-general of the North Carolina militia and participated in several battles in North Carolina. In January, 1781, he was ordered to hold the Catawba River against attack from forces under the British general, Charles Cornwallis (1738–1805). On February 1, 1781, the British attacked at Cowan's ford on the Catawba, General Davidson was killed and his rag tag militiamen scattered. North Carolina first created a county to honor General Davidson in 1783 but when Tennessee was separated from North Carolina, they took that Davidson County with them. That defect was remedied on December 9, 1822, when North Carolina created a Davidson County for the second time, named in honor of General William L. Davidson. No other state has seized this second Davidson County and taken it from North Carolina ... yet.

1884 Davie County

William R. Davie (1756–1820)— Davie was born in England and came with his family to America about 1763. He graduated from the College of New Jersey (now Princeton University) in 1776 and served with distinction as an officer in our Revolutionary army, but soon after being promoted to the rank of major Davie was wounded in the battle of Stono, South Carolina, and he retired from the army to complete his study of the law. Called back to military service again in about 1780, Davie rose to the rank of commissary general. He served in the North Carolina legislature and was one of North Carolina's delegates to the 1787 federal constitutional convention in Philadelphia. He was appointed as a major-general of the North Carolina militia in 1794 and in 1798 President John Adams appointed him a brigadier-general in the U.S. army. On December 4, 1798, Davie was elected to be North Carolina's governor but he served in that position very briefly, resigning on September 10, 1799, to accept an appointment by President John Adams as a peace commissioner in France. This county was created on December 20, 1836.

1885 Duplin County

Thomas Hay, Viscount Dupplin (1710–1787)— This county was created in England's colony of North Carolina in 1750 and named for the English Viscount of Dupplin. The name of the North Carolina county is misspelled, with just one "p." The name Donegal had also been considered as a name for this county but that name was never officially adopted. Presumably the proponents of the name Donegal had in mind the name of the county in Ireland. Thomas Hay was the eldest son of George Hay (–1758), the seventh earl of Kinnoull. Thomas Hay served as a member of the house of commons in the British parliament from 1741 to 1758 and he also had been made a member of the board of trade and plantations, which supervised colonial affairs, shortly before this county in colonial North Carolina was created and named in his honor. Other positions and titles held by this English statesman were commissioner of Irish revenue, lord of trade, lord of the treasury, joint paymaster, chancellor of the duchy of Lancaster, privy councillor and ambassador-extraordinary to Portugal. Upon the death of his father in 1758, Thomas Hay succeeded him and became the eighth Earl of Kinnoull.

1886 Durham County

City of Durham, North Carolina— This county was created on February 28, 1881, and named for the city of Durham, its county seat. Today's Durham has a population of about 140,000 and is home to Duke University. It is part of the educational triangle formed by the proximity of three of the state's important institutions of higher learning, Duke in Durham, the University of North Carolina in Chapel Hill and North Carolina State University at Raleigh. Durham was first called Durhamville station, in honor of Dr. Bartlett Durham (1822–1858), who had donated four acres of land for a railroad station here. The community's name was changed to Durham's and eventually the present Durham. The small gift of four acres led to Durham having a railroad station and eventually to its prominence in the commerce and trade of eastern Orange County, North Carolina. Durham was incorporated in 1866 as the town of Durham in Orange County, North Carolina. When Durham County was carved from Orange County in 1881, the municipality of Durham became the county seat of the new county.

1887 Edgecombe County

Richard Edgcumbe, Baron Edgcumbe (1680–1758)— This English nobleman was educated at Cambridge in Trinity College and became a member of the house of commons of the English parliament in 1701. In 1716 he was made lord of the treasury and later was vice-treasurer, receiver-general, treasurer of war and paymaster general of the crown's revenues in Ireland. He was elevated to the peerage in 1742 as the first Baron Edgcumbe. On May 16, 1732, the residents on the south side of the Roanoke River had petitioned North Carolina's colonial governor, George Burrington (–1759) to erect a new precinct here. Governor Burrington, with the consent of his council, complied and ordered the establishment of Edgecombe Precinct. A dispute developed concerning the power of the governor and council to create new precincts without the consent of the legislature, which represented the citizens of the colony. In July, 1733, North Carolina's colonial general assembly refused to seat the representatives from Edgecombe Precinct. In 1734 a bill to erect Edgecombe Precinct passed two readings in the general assembly but was not enacted into law. Another attempt in the legislature in 1735 also failed. It was not until April 4, 1741, that the law officially creating Edgecombe (as a county, not a precinct) was enacted into law and the county was officially born. Even then, the legislature failed to spell the name correctly. Edgecombe County's name honors Richard Edgcumbe.

1888 Forsyth County

Benjamin Forsyth (–1814)— Forsyth was born in the early 1760's in Virginia or North Carolina. He was a resident of Stokes County, North Carolina, when he served in the state legislature in 1807 and 1808. By 1810 Forsyth had accumulated some wealth in the form of 3,000 acres of land in Stokes County and seven slaves. He was commissioned as a second-lieutenant in the U.S. army in 1800, but was honorably discharged two months later. About four years before the War of 1812, Forsyth was made a captain in the army. He served with distinction prior to and during the War of 1812 and was promoted to the rank of brevet lieutenant-colonel. Forsyth was killed in combat during the War of 1812 near the Saint Lawrence River on the border between Canada and upstate New York. This county was created and named in his honor on January 16, 1849.

1889 Franklin County

Benjamin Franklin (1706–1790)— Franklin was a native of Massachusetts who moved to Pennsylvania in his teens. Poverty denied him a formal education but he became the leading printer and editor in North America. He gained fame for his discoveries and inventions in the physical sciences and he distinguished himself as author, philosopher and diplomat. Franklin was a signer of the Declaration of Independence and an important member of the convention which framed the U.S. Constitution. This county was created in 1779.

1890 *Gaston County*

William J. Gaston (1778–1844)—A native of North Carolina and a lawyer, Gaston served in both houses of the North Carolina legislature and was speaker of the house of commons in 1808. He was elected to represent North Carolina in the U.S. House of Representatives and he served two terms in that body from May, 1813, until March, 1817. He left congress to resume his law practice, but by 1818 he was back in politics, serving in the North Carolina senate. He served from time to time in the North Carolina legislature during the 1820's and early 1830's. In November, 1833 he was elected him as a justice on the state's supreme court. Although Gaston owned slaves, his opinions, while serving on the state supreme court were consistently in favor of the rights of slaves. Justice Gaston died in January, 1844, and this county was created and named in his honor less than three years later, on December 21, 1846. There had been suggestions that this new county should be named Carroll or Alexander but neither of those names was adopted. North Carolina still has no Carroll County, although an Alexander County was created less than four weeks later, January 15, 1847.

1891 *Gates County*

Horatio Gates (–1806)—Born in England about 1728, the son of a duke's housekeeper, Gates entered the British army at an early age and served as a lieutenant in North America, in Nova Scotia, in 1749 and 1750. In 1754 he was promoted to captain in the British army, initially stationed in New York, and he served the crown in America during most of the French & Indian War. After a very successful mission in Martinique, Gates retired from the army and returned to England. However, Gates' experiences in America had made him sympathetic to our grievances with England. In August 1772, Gates and his family sailed from England for America and they settled on a plantation in what is now the state of West Virginia. In 1775 he was commissioned as a brigadier-general in our Continental army and he soon rose to major-general and supreme commander of our northern army. In September and October, 1777, near Saratoga, New York, General Gates' troops won major battles of the American Revolution. There,

troops under Gates' command faced forces under General John Burgoyne (1722–1792), defeated that large British force, captured them and sent them back to England. In 1800 Gates became a member of New York's legislature. This county was created in 1779, during the American Revolution, while General Gates' victory over Burgoyne at Saratoga was a recent memory.

1892 *Graham County*

William A. Graham (1804–1875)—A native of North Carolina and a lawyer, Graham served in the state's house of commons and was speaker of that body. He subsequently represented North Carolina in the U.S. Senate and was governor of the state from 1845 to 1849. From 1850 to 1852 Graham served in the cabinet of President Millard Fillmore, as secretary of the navy. He resigned from the cabinet in 1852 to run for vice president of the United States on the Whig party's ticket, headed by General Winfield Scott (1786–1866). After the Whig's loss in that election, Graham served in the North Carolina senate. During the years preceding the Civil War, Graham urged moderation and preservation of the Union. However, with the outbreak of the Civil War, Graham allied himself on the Confederate side and five of his sons became officers in the Confederate army. Graham was elected to the senate of the Confederate States of America but by early 1865 he had become a leader of the peace movement within that body. Following the Civil War, Graham was elected to represent North Carolina in the U.S. Senate but was not allowed to take his seat. Reconstruction ended in North Carolina by 1871 and on January 30, 1872, this county was created and named in Graham's honor.

1893 *Granville County*

John Carteret, Earl of Granville (1690–1763)—In 1746, England's colony of North Carolina created Granville County and named it for one of the later lords proprietors, John Carteret, Earl of Granville (1690–1763). In 1663 England's King Charles II (1630–1685) had granted proprietorships in Carolina to eight Englishmen and one of these men was Sir George Carteret (–1680). These proprietary interests in Carolina passed from generation to generation as proprietors died. In some cases these proprietary interests were sold. By 1729, when the Carolina charter was surrendered to the English crown,

nearly 50 different individuals had served as proprietors of Carolina or had been entitled to do so. John Carteret (1690–1763) was one of the later proprietors. He inherited his Carolina proprietorship in 1695, upon the death of his father, George Carteret, first Baron Carteret (1667–1695). The proprietor for whom Granville County, North Carolina, was named, John Carteret, was educated at Oxford and took a seat in the British house of lords in 1711. There he was a champion of Protestant succession to the throne of England which became an extremely important consideration when Queen Anne (1665–1714) died and left no heirs. Queen Anne was succeeded as England's monarch by the German Protestant, King George 1 (1660–1727), and Carteret became a favorite of the new king because he spoke German and the king never learned much English. Carteret served as secretary of state from 1721–1724. When John Carteret's mother died in 1744, he succeeded to the title of earl of Granville. Carteret was the only one of the lords proprietor who was unwilling to sell his share to the crown in 1729. The portion of Carolina that Carteret retained was known as the Granville District or Granville Grant. It was set off in 1744 as a sixty mile wide, strip in what is now the northern portion of North Carolina, running from the Atlantic Ocean to Bath, North Carolina.

1894 *Greene County*

Nathanael Greene (1742–1786)—Greene was born in Rhode Island and served briefly in the Rhode Island legislature. He gained fame as one of the ablest American generals in the Revolutionary War. This county was originally created in 1791 and named Glasgow County, in honor of James Glasgow, who had been North Carolina's secretary of state from 1777 to 1798. Its name was changed to honor Nathanael Greene in 1799. North Carolina first created a county to honor General Greene in 1783 but when Tennessee was separated from North Carolina, they took that Greene County with them. That defect was remedied in 1799 when North Carolina created this Greene County. General Greene had rendered extremely effective service in our Revolutionary War both in northern areas and in the South, where he saved the Carolinas from the British.

1895 *Guilford County*

Francis North, Earl of Guilford (1704–1790)—This Englishman was elected in

1727 to the house of commons of the British parliament. In 1729 he succeeded his father as the third baron Guilford, and he took his seat in the house of lords on January 13, 1730. In 1750 Francis North was appointed governor of the two royal princes, Edward August (1739–1767) and George William Frederick (1738–1820). It was George William Frederick who came to the throne as King George III in 1760. As a result of this early relationship with the king-to-be, Francis North became a personal friend of both King George III (1738–1820) and his queen consort, Queen Charlotte Sophia of Mecklenburg-Strelitz (1744–1818). Francis North was made Earl of Guilford in 1752 or 1753 and treasurer of Queen Charlotte in 1773. This county in Britain's colony of North Carolina was created by the legislative session of December 5, 1770. Some sources state that the county was created by that legislature in 1770, while others fix the date in 1771. In either case, we have a date that was just prior to the American Revolution, while there was, perhaps, still hope of placating King George III and avoiding armed rebellion.

1896 *Halifax County*

George Montagu Dunk, Earl of Halifax (1716–1771)— Educated at Eton and at Trinity College in Cambridge, Dunk, attained the rank of colonel in 1745. In 1748 he was made president of the board of trade and plantations, which had control of commerce and trade in the colonies. He served as president of that board from 1748 to 1761 and has been called "father of the colonies," for his success in extending American commerce. In 1749 he was made a privy councillor. Dunk aided in founding the colony of Nova Scotia, and the capital of that colony was named Halifax in his honor. In 1759 he was made a lieutenant-general and he subsequently held the positions of lord-lieutenant of Ireland, first lord of the admiralty, secretary of state and lord privy seal. In late 1757, North Carolina's royal governor, Arthur Dobbs (1689–1765), and his council heard a petition from residents requesting the creation of this new county. A committee of those petitioners and the North Carolina assembly asked Governor Dobbs to select a name for the new county. Dobbs agreed, and he selected the name Halifax in honor of George Montagu Dunk, who was then the president of the British board of trade and plantations. This county was created in 1758, but the act did not become effective until January, 1759.

1897 *Harnett County*

Cornelius Harnett (1723–1781)— Born in a rural area of North Carolina on April 20, 1723, Harnett inherited a rather large estate and became a merchant in Wilmington. He represented Wilmington in North Carolina's colonial general assembly from 1754 until royal government here was dissolved in 1775. In the years just preceding the American Revolution, Harnett was a leading spokesman in opposition to British policies. Harnett was a member of four of North Carolina's provincial congresses and was president of the provincial congress which met from 1775 to 1776. He also was president of the provincial council of safety. Harnett sponsored the motion in the provincial congress which instructed North Carolina to vote for independence from England in the Continental Congress. From 1777 to 1780, Harnett was one of North Carolina's delegates to the Continental Congress and one of the three North Carolina signers of the Articles of Confederation. Because Harnett had moved North Carolina to prepare for war, he was named an outlaw by England. In 1781 he was captured by the British and his health declined rapidly in prison. He was paroled but died on April 28, 1781, at Wilmington, North Carolina, while still on parole as a prisoner of the British. This county was created on February 7, 1855.

1898 *Haywood County*

John Haywood (1755–1827)— Haywood was born in Edgecombe County, North Carolina, on February 23, 1755. In 1781 he was elected as a clerk of North Carolina's senate and he served in that position until December 30, 1786, when he was elected to be North Carolina's treasurer. He served as the state's treasurer for 40 years, from 1787 until his death on November 18, 1827. Haywood was also one of the original trustees of the University of North Carolina at Chapel Hill and he remained on the university's board of trustees from 1789 until his death. Haywood was a slave owner. After John Haywood died in 1827, an examination of his accounts disclosed an alleged shortage of $68,906.80. Haywood, being dead, was unable to defend himself against this accusation and the shortage, except his widow's dower rights, was claimed as a debt of Haywood's estate. In an article dealing with North Carolina newspapers from 1815 to 1835, which appeared in the July, 1953 issue of the *North Carolina Historical Review*, Daniel M. McFarland stated that Haywood was found innocent of the charges. This county was created and named in John Haywood's honor on December 15, 1808, while he was still alive and serving as the popular treasurer of North Carolina.

1899 *Henderson County*

Leonard Henderson (1772–1833)— Henderson was born in Granville County, North Carolina, on October 6, 1772. He studied law at Williamsboro, under Judge John Williams (1732–1799) and after admission to the bar he served for a time as clerk of the district court at Hillsborough, North Carolina. In 1807 Henderson was appointed as a commissioner of the town of Williamsboro and in 1808, the North Carolina general assembly elected him to the superior court bench. He resigned that position in 1816 to resume his law practice, but while serving on the superior court, Judge Henderson opened a law school in his home in Williamsboro and he continued to teach at this law school after 1816. This school is said to be the forerunner of the law schools of Richmond Hill and the University of North Carolina. In 1818 Leonard Henderson became an associate justice of North Carolina's supreme court and after the death of Chief Justice John L. Taylor in 1829, Henderson became the chief justice. He served in that capacity until his death on August 13, 1833. This county was created five years later, on December 15, 1838.

1900 *Hertford County*

Francis Seymour Conway, Earl of Hertford (1719–1794)— This county in England's colony of North Carolina was created in the 1750's and named for this English nobleman who had been made Earl of Hertford in 1750. Conway succeeded his father as second baron Conway in 1732 and on August 3, 1750, he was created both viscount Beauchamp and earl of Hertford. He held numerous prestigious positions and titles including lord of the bedchamber, knight of the garter, and privy councillor. The earl of Hertford was ambassador extraordinary to France, lord-lieutenant of Ireland and lord chamberlain. On July 3, 1793, he was made earl of Yarmouth and marquis of Hertford. He also was lord-lieutenant of Warwickshire from 1757 until his death on June 14, 1794. There is nothing in this resume to suggest any accomplishment of importance to North Carolina and the peacock-like strutting of all of these titles makes one thankful that our nation's founding fathers prohibited the granting of titles of nobility, when they drafted our Articles on Confederation and federal constitution.

1901 *Hoke County*

Robert F. Hoke (1837–1912) — Born in Lincolnton, North Carolina, Hoke graduated from the Kentucky Military Institute in 1854. He entered the army of the Confederate States of America as a second-lieutenant in 1861 and soon was in combat at the engagement of Big Bethel, in Virginia. He served with distinction from the Seven Days campaign in Virginia, in 1862 to the campaign of Chancellorsville, Virginia, in 1863, in which he was severely wounded. In reward for his meritorious service, Hoke was promoted rapidly, and became brigadier-general effective from January 17, 1863. He was promoted to major-general effective from April 20, 1864, and served effectively as a Confederate general until the end of the Civil War. This county was created on February 17, 1911, when General Hoke was 73 years old. He died in Raleigh, North Carolina, on July 3rd of the following year.

1902 *Hyde County*

Edward Hyde (–1712) — Born in England about 1650, Hyde arrived in America in August, 1710, to become deputy governor of the northern part of the English colony of Carolina. He was to receive his commission as deputy governor from Edward Tynte (–1710) but Tynte died suddenly on June 26, 1710, and when Hyde arrived in August of that year, he had no official status. However, he was soon selected as a compromise candidate for president of the northern Carolina council. The compromise involved a struggle for dominance of the colony, between Anglicans and Quakers. Edward Hyde was an Anglican. As president of the council of northern Carolina, Hyde also was the acting governor of the portion of Carolina "north and east of the Cape Fear River," from 1711 to May, 1712. On May 9, 1712, he officially became governor of England's colony of North Carolina. (On January 24, 1712, the English crown had recognized the separate Carolinas, North Carolina and South Carolina.) Since Hyde died in September, 1712, of yellow fever, he had little time to accomplish much as the first governor of the separate colony of North Carolina and what little he did accomplish after arriving in America in 1710 was often incorrect or ineffective. This county was first created on December 3, 1705, as the Wickham Precinct of Bath County. That precinct's name was changed to Hyde County, about 1712, in honor of Edward Hyde.

1903 *Iredell County*

James Iredell (1751–1799) — Born in Lewes, England on October 5, 1751, Iredell immigrated to the American colonies at the age of 17. Through influential relatives named McCulloh, Iredell gained a position collecting customs for the crown at the port of Roanoke, in the town of Edenton, North Carolina. He continued as a customs collector from 1768 to 1776. Iredell had become licensed to practice law in 1771, and after ending his customs work, he became active in revolutionary activities and served as a North Carolina superior court judge. He subsequently was North Carolina's attorney general. In August, 1788, North Carolina had rejected the proposed federal constitution at the first ratifying convention but Iredell had supported ratification at that convention and he became an influential leader in gaining support for the proposed federal Constitution and North Carolina ratified it in November, 1789. In February, 1790, President George Washington appointed Iredell to be an associate justice on the supreme court of the United States. He was President Washington's second choice to become the sixth justice on the supreme court. The president had first nominated, and the senate had confirmed, Robert H. Harrison (1745–1790), but Harrison declined the position and Iredell was nominated in his place. James Iredell served on our nation's supreme court from 1790 to 1799 and President Washington was so pleased with Judge Iredell that he considered him for chief justice in 1795 when Associate Justice William Cushing (1732–1810) declined to accept the promotion to chief justice. This county was created in 1788 before James Iredell joined the U.S. Supreme Court.

1904 *Jackson County*

Andrew Jackson (1767–1845) — Jackson was born on the border of North Carolina and South Carolina. He represented Tennessee in both branches of the U.S. Congress, and gained fame and popularity for his military exploits in wars with the Indians and in the War of 1812. He was provisional military governor of Florida and, from 1829 to 1837, General Jackson was president of the United States. His presidency reflected the frontier spirit of America. This county was created on January 29, 1851.

1905 *Johnston County*

Gabriel Johnston (–1752) — Born about 1698 in the lowlands of Scotland, Gabriel Johnston moved to London, England, when he was a young man, and began writing for a weekly literary and political publication, *The Craftsman*, about 1730. As a result of his association with *The Craftsman*, Johnston became acquainted with Spencer Compton, Earl of Wilmington (–1743), a powerful politician, and he was a boarder in the Compton household for several years. It is likely that this link to political power was the factor which resulted in Johnston's appointment in 1733 or 1734 to be the crown's royal governor of the colony of North Carolina. He was inaugurated as the colony's royal governor in November, 1734, and served in that position until his death in July, 1752. His 18 year tenure as North Carolina's chief executive was longer than that of any other North Carolina governor, including those before and after the American Revolution. During Johnston's administration, North Carolina progressed economically and its population grew. Governor Johnston personally encouraged Scots to immigrate to the colony. Although there were instances of political turmoil which were not addressed effectively, some of them were caused by policies of the crown, which Johnston lacked the power to change. During his administration printing and newspapers were begun in North Carolina and the laws of the colony were collected and printed. Governor Johnston's administration was generally successful. This county was created in 1746, while Johnston was serving as royal governor.

1906 *Jones County*

Willie Jones (1741–1801) — Jones was born to wealthy parents in Surry County, Virginia, on May 25, 1741. In the early 1750's, Jones moved with his family to the present Northampton County, North Carolina, near Halifax. He was sent to England to attend his father's alma mater, Eton, but left that institution in 1758 to tour the European continent. When he returned to North Carolina he lived in splendor. In just one district of Halifax County, Jones owned about 10,000 acres of land and 120 slaves. Until March, 1774, he was a contented citizen of England's colony of North Carolina, and he became an aide-de-camp to the crown's royal governor, William Tryon (1729–1788). On March 9, 1774, Jones was appointed to his majesty's council of the province of North Carolina, and this date gives us an approximate fix on the date that Willie Jones joined the patriot cause in North Carolina because he refused to accept this position on account of his now-radical views. He was elected to five provincial congresses and in the fifth congress, he served on the committee to draft a state constitution for North Carolina. As a leader of the radical movement in North Carolina, Jones was elected to represent the Halifax area in the house of commons from 1777 to 1780 and he subsequently served in North Carolina's senate. From 1780 to 1781 he was one of North Carolina's delegates to the Continental Congress. This county was created in either 1778 or 1779, after Willie Jones had converted from loyalist to radical revolutionary. In August, 1788, North Carolina rejected the proposed federal constitution at the first ratifying convention. Willie Jones played a major role in defeating this first attempt by North Carolina to join the proposed federal union. He did not run to be a delegate to North Carolina's second convention dealing with the proposed federal constitution and that convention ratified it in November, 1789. During the last decade of his life, Jones stayed out of politics, but he did serve on the original board of trustees of the University of North Carolina.

1907 *Lee County*

Robert E. Lee (1807–1870)— Lee was a native of Virginia and, for over 30 years, an officer in the United States army. When Virginia seceded from the Union, Lee refused an offer to command all federal forces and resigned from the U.S. army to accept a commission in the Confederate army. He served with distinction in that army and became general-in-chief of it. By April, 1865, the Confederacy had lost the war and Robert E. Lee surrendered to the commanding general of the Union forces, Ulysses S. Grant. This county was created on March 6, 1907.

1908 *Lenoir County*

William Lenoir (1751–1839)— A native of Virginia, Lenoir moved with his family to North Carolina when he was about eight years old. He joined the American Revolutionary army as an orderly sergeant and served in several engagements. He had risen to captain In 1780, when he served under Colonel Benjamin Cleaveland (1738–1806) in the battle of Kings Mountain on the border between North and South Carolina. In that battle, our Revolutionary force of backwoodsmen

killed or captured the entire enemy force of some 1,100, while suffering only 90 casualties. William Lenoir was one of the casualties, suffering wounds in both the arm and the side. After the war he served in the North Carolina militia for a number of years and held the rank of major-general in it. He served in both houses of the North Carolina legislature and was speaker of the North Carolina senate. In 1791, when this county was created, William Lenoir was speaker of the state's senate. In December of that year, a bill was introduced to abolish Dobbs County, North Carolina, which had been created prior to the American Revolution and named for one of the crown's royal governors, Arthur Dobbs (1689–1765). The plan was to create two new counties from the territory of Dobbs County. The first draft of the legislation to accomplish this, used Lenoir and Glasgow as the names for the new counties. In a second draft, the name Lenoir was changed to Cabarrus, but in the final law, which was ratified on December 21, 1791, the names Lenoir and Glasgow were used. Although Cabarrus County did not become a reality in 1791, it did so very soon. In 1792, Cabarrus County was created, honoring Stephen Cabarrus (1754–1808), who was a member of the legislature at that time.

1909 *Lincoln County*

Benjamin Lincoln (1733–1810)— Lincoln, a native of Massachusetts, was a member of the Massachusetts legislature and of the provincial congress. He served as an officer in the Revolutionary War and rose to the rank of major-general. In 1779, as commander of the southern department of the Continental army, he attempted, unsuccessfully, to rescue Savannah, Georgia, from the British. In 1781, General George Washington gave Lincoln the honor of accepting Cornwallis' sword when the British surrendered at Yorktown. Later in 1781, Lincoln was made secretary of war and he held that post for two years. He died on May 9, 1810, in Hingham, Massachusetts, in the same house in which he was born. This North Carolina county was named in his honor during the American Revolution, in 1779. Prior to the Revolution, a Tryon County had been created in North Carolina and named for one of the crown's royal governors, William Tryon (1729–1788). During the Revolution, that odious name was banished from North Carolina's map of counties and replaced with two counties named in honor of the Revolutionary War heroes, Benjamin Lincoln

and Griffith Rutherford (–1800). Prior to the Revolution, North Carolina also had created a county, honoring Governor Tryon's wife, Margaret Wake. Although the name Tryon was removed from North Carolina's map of counties during the American Revolution, the chivalrous Southerners of allowed Margaret Wake's name to remain on her map, as Wake County, where the state's capital is located.

1910 *McDowell County*

Joseph McDowell (1756–1801)— This native of Virginia moved with his family to North Carolina, where they settled at Quaker Meadows. In North Carolina McDowell became active as an Indian fighter and as a soldier in the American Revolution. In 1780 Joseph McDowell became a Revolutionary War hero for his participation in the battle of Kings Mountain on the border between North and South Carolina. In that battle, our Revolutionary forces killed or captured the entire enemy force of some 1,100, while suffering only 90 casualties themselves. The American forces were led by backwoodsmen, such as Major Joseph McDowell (1756–1801). Since there is a good deal of confusion concerning which McDowell participated in the 1780 battle of Kings Mountain, a quotation from Mark M. Boatner's work entitled *Landmarks of the American Revolution* is useful here. Boatner states that "…The leader of the 160 Burke County militia at Kings Mountain therefore was Maj. Joseph McDowell of Quaker Meadows and not, as some have argued, the Joseph McDowell of Pleasant Gardens." Boatner also explains that Charles McDowell, was another McDowell who was not in action at Kings Mountain. After Kings Mountain, Joseph McDowell participated in the Revolutionary War battle of Cowpens, South Carolina, and in military actions against the Indians. He later served in both branches of the North Carolina legislature. He opposed North Carolina's ratification of the proposed federal constitution, but after it was ratified and North Carolina became one of the 13 states of the United States of America, Joseph McDowell represented North Carolina on two occasions in the U.S. House of Representatives. Numerous sources on North Carolina history refer to Joseph McDowell as Colonel Joseph McDowell. When he participated in the 1780 battle of Kings Mountain, Joseph McDowell (1756–1801) was still a major and as late as January 17, 1781, at the battle of Cowpens this Joseph McDowell (1756–1801) was still a major.

Following the battle of Cowpens, our Joseph McDowell saw military combat against the Cherokee Indians and may have been promoted. This county was created on December 19, 1842.

1911 *Macon County*

Nathaniel Macon (1758–1837) — This North Carolina native rose to national prominence. Born on December 17, 1758, in what is now Warren County, North Carolina, Macon served as a private in the North Carolina militia during the Revolutionary War. He subsequently was a member of the North Carolina senate and although he was elected to the Continental Congress, he declined to serve. He represented North Carolina for 37 years in both branches of the U.S. Congress, where he was speaker of the house and, later, president *pro tempore* of the senate. Macon believed strongly in economy of the public money and he was a defender of slavery. This county was created in 1828, the year that he resigned from the U.S. Senate.

1912 *Madison County*

James Madison (1751–1836) — Madison was born in Virginia and served in the Virginia legislature and in the Continental Congress. He was a member of the convention which framed the U.S. Constitution and he collaborated with Hamilton and Jay in writing a series of papers under the title *The Federalist*, which explained the new constitution and advocated its adoption. Madison represented Virginia in the U.S. House of Representatives, served for eight years as secretary of state and for eight years as president of the United States. This county was created on January 27, 1851.

1913 *Martin County*

Josiah Martin (1737–1786) — Martin was born in Ireland in April, 1737 and served as an officer in the British army from 1757 to 1769, when he was forced to sell his rank of lieutenant-colonel on account of ill health. He came to America and was living in the colony of New York in 1771, when King George III (1738–1820) appointed him to be royal governor of North Carolina. Because of hostilities toward England preceding the American Revolution, Josiah Martin was the last royal governor of North Carolina. He was inaugurated as North Carolina's royal governor on August 12, 1771, and soon became embroiled in disputes with the North Carolina legislature and other citizens of the

colony over a variety of issues. These included an attempt to establish courts of Oyer and Terminer, designed to operate without legislative approval. By early 1774 North Carolina's courts had essentially collapsed. Meanwhile, events associated with the American Revolution were moving at a brisk pace and Martin was forced to flee from office in July, 1775, aboard a British ship in the Cape Fear River. Over the next few years Martin served with British forces attempting to quell the American Revolution. Two of his early military efforts, at Charleston, South Carolina, and Moore's Bridge, North Carolina, met with failure but the former royal governor participated in other British campaigns which were more successful and he served under the British general, Charles Cornwallis (1738–1805) in the capture of Charleston in 1780. This North Carolina county was created on March 2, 1774, and named in honor of Josiah Martin, who was then serving as North Carolina's royal governor. The colony of North Carolina had previously created and named counties in honor of other British royal governors, Arthur Dobbs (1689–1765) and William Tryon (1729–1788), which were later renamed. Why, one wonders, did North Carolina allow the county named in honor of Britain's Royal Governor Josiah Martin to remain on its map of counties? In their works dealing with the place names of North Carolina, both David L. Corbitt and William S. Powell offer the same plausible explanation. Corbitt and Powell speculate that Martin County's name might have been changed along with the names of Dobbs County and Tryon County were it not for the popularity of Alexander Martin (1740–1807), who served as North Carolina's governor from 1782 to 1785 and from 1789 to 1792. Alexander Martin subsequently represented the state in the U.S. Senate. Although Martin County was not named for him, the popular Alexander Martin might have been offended if Martin County's name had been changed.

1914 *Mecklenburg County*

Queen Charlotte Sophia of Mecklenburg-Strelitz (1744–1818) — This county in England's royal colony of North Carolina was created in 1762, while King George III (1738–1820) ruled England and North Carolina. It was named for the bride whom the king had married in 1761 and made his queen consort. Charlotte's marriage to George was arranged and she did not meet him until her wedding day. In 1761 she was described as "…not tall nor a beauty. Pale

and very thin but looks sensible and genteel." Charlotte's life as queen was entirely domestic and she was happy with it. She had neither interest nor influence in political matters. The king was devoted to her and she was faithful to him. Apparently her only vice was stinginess in money matters. Charlotte became responsible for the royal household and for the care of the king during his lengthy physical and mental illnesses. Charlotte bore her husband 15 children, two of whom later came to the throne as kings of England. These two kings were August Frederick, who came to the throne in 1820 as King George IV (1762–1830) and Edward Frederick, who reigned as King William IV (1765–1837). As the wife of King George III, Charlotte was queen of England during and after the American Revolution. Prior to the Revolution, the queen's names had been given to the county of Mecklenburg in North Carolina and its county seat, the important commercial city of Charlotte. The colony of New York also named one of her counties Charlotte in honor of a member of the royal family of King George III (1738–1820); i.e., either his wife and queen consort, or his eldest daughter. The colonies of New York and North Carolina had also both named counties for William Tryon (1729–1788), who had governed both colonies and North Carolina had named a county for Governor Tryon's wife, Margaret Wake. When King George III and his associates came to be roundly hated on this side of the Atlantic, both North Carolina and New York were confronted with the question of whether or not to rename counties associated with King George III and the crown's governors. Intuition might lead us to suspect that the Southerners of North Carolina would have been more chivalrous than the Yankees of New York about changing place names after the American Revolution. In this case intuition provides the correct answer. On April 2, 1784, New York banished both of the odious English names from her map substituting Montgomery for Tryon and Washington for Charlotte. The chivalrous North Carolinians also banished William Tryon's name from its map of counties but allowed both of the names honoring the queen consort of our foremost British antagonist, King George III, to remain; i.e., both the city of Charlotte and Mecklenburg County were and are named in honor of Queen Charlotte Sophia of Mecklenburg-Strelitz (1744–1818). North Carolina also allowed the name of Governor Tryon's wife to remain as Wake County, even though it had banished the name honoring Margaret Wake's husband, Governor Tryon.

1915 Mitchell County

Elisha Mitchell (1793–1857)— A native of Connecticut, Mitchell attended Yale in that state, and earned both bachelor's and master's degrees there. (Two decades later, he was awarded an honorary doctor's degree and is often referred to as Dr. Mitchell.) He arrived at Chapel Hill in 1818 to teach at the University of North Carolina, and to serve as a minister of the Presbyterian Church. At the university, Mitchell taught primarily mathematics and science courses and his name came to be applied to a mountain in western North Carolina as a result of his interest in geology, mineralogy and mountain climbing. In 1825 Mitchell took charge of North Carolina's geological survey and, starting about 1827, he climbed many of the state's mountains, particularly those in the Black Mountain range of western North Carolina. It was while climbing the highest peak in the Black Mountain range that Dr. Mitchell fell and lost his life on June 27, 1857. Mitchell did not know it, but that peak is the highest point in the United States, east of the Mississippi River. This peak was named Mount Mitchell in honor of Dr. Mitchell and, on February 16, 1861, Mitchell County in western North Carolina was named in his honor. Several accounts indicate that Dr. Mitchell was buried at the top of Mount Mitchell. A history of these mountains was prepared by S. Kent Schwarzkopf and published in 1985. That work contains a rather comprehensive biography of Dr. Elisha Mitchell and it states that his remains were buried in a graveyard next to the Presbyterian church in Asheville, North Carolina, where Dr. Mitchell's funeral was held.

1916 Montgomery County

Richard Montgomery (1738–1775)— Montgomery was born in Ireland and served with the British in North America in the French and Indian War. He settled in New York where he was elected to the New York provisional congress. Montgomery served as a general in the American Revolutionary army and he was killed in combat in Quebec, Canada, on December 31, 1775. This county was created in 1779.

1917 Moore County

Alfred Moore (1755–1810)— A native of North Carolina and a lawyer, Moore was elected a captain in North Carolina's Revolutionary army. He served with that rank in combat at Moore's Creek, North Carolina, and in the defense of Charleston, South Carolina. Moore resigned his commission in March, 1777, and returned home, although he continued to be active in combat in North Carolina's militia and held the rank of colonel of militia. In 1782 he entered North Carolina's senate and he served as North Carolina's attorney general for more than eight years. The American Revolution had greatly depleted Moore's fortune but in 1790 he still owned 48 slaves. He later served as a judge on North Carolina's superior court and in December, 1799, President John Adams appointed Moore to serve as an associate justice on our young nation's supreme court. He was forced to resign from the supreme court in 1804 because of poor health. This county was created in 1784, after Moore's military service in the American Revolution and during his term as North Carolina's attorney general. Alfred Moore did not become a member of our nation's highest court until 15 years after this county was created and named in his honor.

1918 Nash County

Francis Nash (–1777)— Nash was born in Virginia about 1742 and came to North Carolina some 21 years later, settling at Childsburgh (now called Hillsborough). Here he earned his living as a merchant, lawyer and justice of the peace. He also served several terms in the legislature of England's colony of North Carolina. Nash served as a captain in the colony's militia, and he fought against the Regulators in the May 16, 1771, battle of Alamance. He later joined North Carolina's efforts to rebel against England, and he served in the second and third provincial congresses. In the Revolutionary army Nash was elected a lieutenant-colonel. He served with distinction in the Revolution and was promoted, first to colonel, and then to brigadier-general. At the battle of Germantown, Pennsylvania, Nash commanded all North Carolina troops, and he was mortally wounded in combat during that battle. He died on October 7, 1777, and this county was created and named in his honor just one month later, on November 15, 1777.

1919 New Hanover County

English royal house of Hanover— This county was initially created as a precinct, in England's colony of North Carolina on November 27, 1729. In that year seven of the eight proprietorships in Carolina had been sold the crown and North Carolina had become a royal colony. In 1729 King George II (1683–1760) was the reigning monarch of England, having succeeded to the throne in 1727 upon the death of his father, King George I (1660–1727). Technically, the house of Hanover had its initial roots in Italy, but in both England and America, the house of Hanover is considered to be thoroughly German. King George I was the first member of the house of Hanover to rule England and the present English monarch, Queen Elizabeth II (1926–), is a member of that same royal house although its name was changed from Hanover to Windsor on July 17, 1917, as a result of the anti–German hysteria associated with World War I. At the time that this county was created (as a precinct) in 1729, only two members of the German house of Hanover had been ruling monarchs of England (and thus of North Carolina). They were King George I (1660–1727) and his son, King George II (1683–1760). In 1698 the future English monarch King George I (1660–1727) had succeeded his father, Ernst August (1622–1698), as elector of Hanover. The German, King George I, and his successors, owe their hold on the throne of Great Britain to two factors: (1) deep–seated religious animosity in England against Roman Catholicism and (2) the inability of England's Queen Anne (1665–1714) to produce an heir to the throne. Queen Anne had a large number of children (15 according to one account; 17 per another) but most of them were stillborn. Only one boy survived. He was Prince William (1689–1700). Medical science at that time was unable to effectively assist the queen of England in her repeated efforts to leave an heir to the throne. This personal tragedy resulted in a practical problem for England as well, since the heir to the throne when Queen Anne died in 1714 was her half-brother, James Francis Edward Stuart (1688–1766); but James Stuart was a Catholic and England wanted no Catholic on its throne. The nation closed ranks against James Stuart and all other Catholic contenders for the crown and reached all the way to Hanover, in Germany, for a successor to Queen Anne. There they found George Lewis (1660–1727), the elector of Hanover, who had a drop or two of royal English blood in his veins and thus some semblance of a claim to the English throne. He became England's King George I.

1920 *Northampton County*

James Compton, Earl of Northampton (1687–1754)— This county was created in 1741 in England's colony of North Carolina and named for James Compton, Earl of Northampton (1687–1754). Some sources state that James Compton was the father of Spencer Compton, Earl of Wilmington, who was England's prime minister in 1742 and 1743. This cannot be true because Spencer Compton was born in 1673, more than a decade before the birth of James Compton, Earl of Northampton. Spencer Compton, the English prime minister, was born in 1673 and died in 1743.

1921 *Onslow County*

Arthur Onslow (1691–1768)— This county was created, as a precinct, in 1734, while North Carolina was a colony of England. Many counties on and near the eastern seacoast of our nation were named for important English personages while England ruled the American colonies, and this county was one of them. Arthur Onslow, an English statesman, was born on October 1, 1691, at Chelsea England. He was a lawyer in Oxford for a time and entered the house of commons, of the British parliament in 1720. He served in that body some 40 years, from 1720 to 1761. He was unanimously elected speaker of the house of commons on January 23, 1728, and he held that important position more than 30 years, until March, 1761. Onslow was the recipient of other honors. He was made privy councillor in 1728 and the following year he became chancellor to Queen Caroline of Anspach (1683–1737), the queen consort of King George II (1683–1760). During the period 1734 to 1742, Onslow was also treasurer of the navy.

1922 *Orange County*

Uncertain— This county was created in 1752, while North Carolina was still a British colony and its name was intended as a compliment to the English throne. But it is not known whether Orange referred directly to William of Orange, who had been King William III of England or to one of his collateral descendants.

King William III (1650–1702)— William, Prince of Orange, was born in the Netherlands. He was the grandson of England's King Charles I (1600–1649) and in 1677 he married his cousin, Mary (1662–1694), who was then the presumptive heir to the English throne. In 1688 William invaded England, supported by both Dutch and English troops, and on April 11, 1689, William and his wife were crowned king and queen of England. They ruled as joint sovereigns, titled King William III and Queen Mary II, until Mary's death in 1694. William continued on the throne until his death in 1702.

The title, Orange, belonged to William's family, the Nassaus, on account of a tiny pocket of independent territory within southern France, near the Rhone River, named Orange, which had earlier been an ancient Roman town. It is now merely a small city in France, 17 miles north of Avignon, France.

Most sources simply state that Orange County, North Carolina was named for King William III (1650–1702), William of Orange. However, two authorities on North Carolina's county names, William S. Powell and Kemp P. Battle, suggest the possibility that Orange County, North Carolina, was named for a mere collateral descendant of King William III. In *The North Carolina Gazetteer*, Professor Powell reminds us that Orange County, North Carolina was created in 1752, half a century after the death of King William III and he speculates that the county may have been named for the infant William V of Orange (1748–1806), a grandson of King George II (1683–1760) of England. King George II was king of England in 1752 when Orange County was created and he was the grandfather of William V (1748–1806).

William V (1748–1806)— Anne (1709–1759) was a daughter of King George II of England, who married William IV (1711–1751), Prince of Orange. William V (1748–1806) was their son, and thus a grandson of King George II of England. William V (1748–1806) of Orange was not a direct descendent of King William III (1650–1702). King William III and Queen Mary II (1662–1694) had no children.

1923 *Pamlico County*

Pamlico Sound, North Carolina— This county at the eastern end of central North Carolina was created on February 8, 1872, and named for the Pamlico Sound of the Atlantic Ocean, on which it borders. Pamlico Sound is separated from the Atlantic Ocean by a portion of North Carolina's Outer Banks, a string of rather small islands which extend more than 175 miles south from the Virginia state line to below Cape Lookout, North Carolina. Pamlico Sound is a generally shallow body of water, particularly at its northern end. It is about 80 miles long and varies in width from eight to 30 miles. Pamlico Sound was named for a tribe of Indians, who formerly lived in this area. They were an Algonquian tribe, whose name is rendered variously but is spelled Pamlico by Frederick W. Hodge in his *Handbook of American Indians North of Mexico*. Hodge tells us that at one time they lived along the Pamlico River in what is now Beaufort County, North Carolina. The Pamlico River's mouth is on Pamlico Sound, and Beaufort County, North Carolina, is just north of Pamlico County. The Pamlico Indians were nearly wiped out by a smallpox epidemic in 1696. About 75 Pamlico Indians survived that epidemic and settled in a single village. Hodge tells us that at the close of the 1711 Tuscarora War, "...the Tuscarora under treaty with the English, agreed to exterminate them." Any surviving Pamlico Indians probably were made Tuscarora slaves.

1924 *Pasquotank County*

Pasquotank Indians— In 1663 England's King Charles II (1630–1685) had granted proprietorships in Carolina to eight Englishmen and the proprietors soon established Albemarle County as a "county palatine" of Carolina. By 1681 (and perhaps as early as 1670; authorities consulted differ on the year), Pasquotank had been created as a precinct of Albemarle County. The name of the precinct (today a county) honors an Algonquian tribe, or band, of Indians who were living on the north shore of Albemarle Sound in North Carolina when encountered by Europeans. Pasquotank County, North Carolina, is in the northeastern area of the state and it borders on Albemarle Sound.

1925 *Pender County*

William D. Pender (1834–1863)— A native of North Carolina and an 1854 graduate of the U.S. Military Academy at West Point, Pender served with the U.S. army's dragoons in New Mexico, California, Oregon and Washington. He was distressed by the prospect of Civil War but on March 21, 1861 he resigned his first lieutenant's commission in the U.S. army to serve in the army of the Confederate States of America. He entered that army as a captain of artillery and had risen in rank to colonel by July, 1861, when he fought at the battle of First Manassas, Virginia. Pender later participated in a number of important battles and rose in rank to major-general. On the first day of the battle of Gettysburg, Pennsylvania, Pender was a hero but the following day he was wounded in the leg. While traveling south, an infection set in and on July 18, 1863 General Pender died following amputation of the wounded leg. This county was created on February 16, 1875. Dr. Elisha Porter, a Confederate veteran, then living in Rocky Mount, North Carolina, was given the honor of selecting this county's name and he chose to name it for General William Dorsey Pender, under whom he had served during the Civil War.

1926 *Perquimans County*

Perquiman Indians— In 1663 England's King Charles II (1630–1685) had granted proprietorships in Carolina to eight Englishmen and the proprietors soon established Albemarle County as a "county palatine" of Carolina. By 1679 (and perhaps as early as 1670; authorities consulted differ on the year), Perquimans had been created as a precinct of Albemarle County. The name of the precinct (today a county) honors an Algonquian tribe, or band, of Indians who were living on the north side of Albemarle Sound in North Carolina when encountered by Europeans. It is on the north side of Albemarle Sound that today's Perquimans County is located.

1927 *Person County*

Thomas Person (1733–1800)— A native of Virginia, Person moved with his family to North Carolina about 1740. He became a wealthy plantation owner in North Carolina and served in the North Carolina legislature, when it was still an arm of the English colonial system. However, he took up the Revolutionary cause early and represented the Granville District in all of North Carolina's patriotic provisional assemblies starting in 1774. Person also served on the council of safety and was a member of the committee which drafted a state constitution for North Carolina. From 1777 to 1797 Person served in both houses of the North Carolina legislature. During the American Revolution he held the rank of brigadier-general of North Carolina militia. In 1784 he was elected as a delegate to the Continental Congress but failed to take his seat in that body. During the debates concerning a possible federal union of the 13 colonies which had won independence from England, Person opposed North Carolina's entry into the federal union and even had harsh words to say about General George Washington at North Carolina's first convention dealing with ratification of the proposed federal constitution. Person was a trustee of the University of North Carolina and made a

substantial financial contribution to that institution. This county was created in 1791 in an act to become effective February 1, 1792.

1928 *Pitt County*

William Pitt, Earl of Chatham (1708–1778)— Pitt, an Englishman and the first earl of Chatham, was one of England's greatest and most famous statesmen. He was a member of parliament and held the positions of vice treasurer of Ireland and paymaster general of the forces. He became secretary of state and virtually prime minister in 1756, but in 1760 King George III took the throne and Pitt was forced to resign. In 1766 he formed a new ministry but served for only 15 months. Pitt County, North Carolina was created in 1760 in an act to become effective January 1, 1761. Later, during 1770 and 1771, the Earl of Chatham became very popular on this side of the Atlantic for his opposition to the alleged right of the English parliament to tax American colonies without their consent. When Chatham County, North Carolina, was created effective April 1, 1771, it became the second North Carolina County named in his honor. Pitt urged reconciliation between Britain and her American colonies. After the American Revolution began he favored any peace settlement that would keep the American colonies in the British empire.

1929 *Polk County*

William Polk (1758–1834)— Polk was born near Charlotte, North Carolina, on July 9, 1758. In April, 1775 he entered our Revolutionary army as a second lieutenant attached to the Fourth South Carolina regiment of mounted infantry. (Charlotte, North Carolina, is on the South Carolina border.) He was soon severely wounded at the battle of Canebrake, South Carolina, in December, 1775. In November of the following year North Carolina called Polk to a higher command, electing him a major in a regiment of North Carolina troops in the Continental line. He served with distinction during the American Revolution and was wounded in combat at Brandywine Creek, Pennsylvania, Germantown, Pennsylvania and Eutaw Springs, South Carolina. By 1782 he had again been assigned to South Carolina's military and was a lieutenant-colonel in the Fourth South Carolina cavalry. He served in the North Carolina legislature during most of its terms from 1785 through 1790 and was supervisor of internal revenue for North

Carolina from 1791 to 1808. Authorities consulted offer differing opinions on the date that this county was created, and with good reason. It was created twice. It was first created in January, 1847, and the act creating it specified that the county was named in honor of the late Lieutenant-colonel William Polk. This act was repealed in 1848. On January 20, 1855, an act was ratified which recreated Polk County.

1930 *Randolph County*

Peyton Randolph (–1775)— Randolph was born in Virginia about 1721 and he was educated at the College of William and Mary there. He studied law in England and served as the king's attorney for Virginia. Peyton Randolph was a member of colonial Virginia's house of burgesses for some 25 years and he played a leading role in the events which led to our Declaration of Independence. Randolph represented Virginia in the Continental Congress and was the first president of that body. This North Carolina county was created and named in his honor in 1779.

1931 *Richmond County*

Charles Lennox, Duke of Richmond (1735–1806)— This county was created in 1779, during the American Revolution, and named for Charles Lennox, the third duke of Richmond, a member of the English parliament and a supporter of the American colonists' cause. In one of his speeches he declared that the resistance of the colonies was "neither treason nor rebellion but is perfectly justifiable in every possible political and moral sense." He favored independence for the American colonies and in 1778 Richmond proposed the withdrawal of English troops from America. He had served as an officer in the English army himself and had risen to the rank of general. In addition to his military service and membership in the house of lords, Richmond's career included the posts of ambassador extraordinary and minister plenipotentiary to Paris, secretary of state for the southern department and master-general of the ordnance with a seat in the cabinet. In 1782 he was elected and invested as a knight of the garter.

1932 *Robeson County*

Thomas Robeson, Jr. (1740–1785)— This county was created in 1787 and named for Thomas Robeson, Jr. He is confused in some accounts with his father, Thomas Robeson, Sr., who was born in England's North American colony of West Jersey.

Thomas Robeson, Jr., was born on January 11, 1740, at Walnut Grove, in Bladen County, in England's colony of North Carolina. Thomas Robeson, Jr., was a member of the provincial convention at Hillsboro (now spelled Hillsborough) in August, 1775, which made preparations for armed rebellion against England. Robeson also was a member of the North Carolina provincial congress which met in Halifax in April, 1776, and authorized North Carolina's delegates to the Continental Congress to join the colonies' movement in declaring independence from England. He served as an officer during the American Revolution and fought at the battles of Moore's Creek and Elizabethtown in North Carolina. At Elizabethtown our forces scored a key victory over the Tories. Thomas Robeson, Jr., was a colonel in our Revolutionary army and it is easy to confuse him with his brother, Captain Peter Robeson, who fought with Colonel Thomas Robeson, Jr., at the battle of Moore's Creek. There was an attempt to create Robeson County in 1785 but that motion was defeated in North Carolina's house of commons. On December 17, 1786, a second attempt was made to create a Robeson County here, when Senator Thomas Browne introduced a bill to create this new county. That act was passed on January 6, 1787. Thomas Robeson, Jr., had represented Bladen County in the North Carolina legislature both before and after the American Revolution and when the idea was first proposed of carving a new county from Bladen County, he resisted it. To gain the support of this key political leader, the name Robeson was chosen as the name of the proposed new county and that gesture accomplished its intent. While this incident may reflect unfavorably on Thomas Robeson, Jr., it should be noted that he had a complex personality and was also capable of unusual generosity. For example, the troops who served at the battle of Elizabethtown, North Carolina, were paid with Colonel Robeson's own personal funds.

1933 *Rockingham County*

Charles Watson-Wentworth, Marquis of Rockingham (1730–1782)— Charles Watson-Wentworth was born on May 13, 1730, at Wentworth Park, in England. He attended Westminster school and served in the English army against Scottish insurgents. Young Watson-Wentworth came from a family with good political connections and shortly after his 30th birthday he was given the highest honor of the En-

glish court, the garter. In 1765 he became England's prime minister, while King George III was on the throne. As prime minister, he infuriated the king by securing the repeal of the Stamp Act and softening the American colonies' grievances on matters of commerce. This term as prime minister lasted only from 1765 to 1766. However, sixteen years later, Rockingham returned as prime minister. His goals throughout much of this period from 1765 until his death on July 1, 1782, were rather extreme. These goals included resolution of the grievances of the American colonies, even if that meant the end of British sovereignty over of those colonies, sharply reduced power for the English monarch and, at all cost, avoidance of armed warfare with the American colonies. This county was created in 1785.

1934 *Rowan County*

Matthew Rowan (–1760)— Rowan was born in Ireland and immigrated to England's colony of Carolina. Neither the year of his birth nor the year of his arrival in Carolina are known, but he was well established in Bath, North Carolina, by 1729. Here he became a prominent planter and owned more than 9,000 acres of land and 26 slaves. His fellow citizens elected him to serve in the colonial legislature. Rowan was also a member of North Carolina's council from 1734 to 1760. In 1752 Nathaniel Rice was the president of that council at the time of the death of England's royal governor, Gabriel Johnston (–1752), and Rice became the acting royal governor of North Carolina. However Rice soon died (on January 29, 1753), and Matthew Rowan, who had succeeded Rice as president of the council, now succeeded him as acting royal governor. Rowan served as the crown's acting governor of North Carolina from January, 1753, until October 31, 1754, when Arthur Dobbs (1689–1765) and was sworn into office. After he was relieved of his duties as acting royal governor, Rowan continued to serve on the governor's council until his death in 1760. Rowan County was initially established as an act of North Carolina's general assembly in 1753. However, England's King George II (1683–1760) revoked that act in 1754. A work published in 1890, entitled *Western North Carolina*, tells us that "the next year having been better informed of the reasons for establishing this county, he allowed its re-establishment, which was accordingly sanctioned by an act of the assembly in 1756."

1935 *Rutherford County*

Griffith Rutherford (–1805)— Rutherford was born in Ireland about 1731, came to America in 1739 and settled in the vicinity of Salisbury, North Carolina. In 1775 he was elected to North Carolina's provincial congress and in June, 1776, he was appointed a brigadier-general in the North Carolina militia. It was in 1776 that Rutherford and his troops crushed the Cherokee Indians in western North Carolina. Rutherford participated in the battle of Camden, South Carolina, in 1780 and shortly after that defeat, Rutherford was captured as a prisoner of war at the battle of Sanders Creek. He was released in an exchange of prisoners. After the American Revolution Rutherford served in the North Carolina legislature and later moved west to what is now Tennessee. When the present state of Tennessee was the territory South of the River Ohio, President George Washington appointed Rutherford to the legislative council of that territory, and Rutherford was chairman of that council. This North Carolina county was named in his honor during the American Revolution, in 1779. Prior to the Revolution, a Tryon County had been created in North Carolina and named for one of the crown's royal governors, William Tryon (1729–1788). During the Revolution, that odious name was banished from North Carolina's map of counties and replaced with two counties named in honor of the Revolutionary War heroes, Benjamin Lincoln (1733–1810) and Griffith Rutherford (–1805). Prior to the Revolution, North Carolina also had created a county, honoring Governor Tryon's wife, Margaret Wake. Although the name Tryon was removed from North Carolina's map of counties during the American Revolution, the chivalrous Southerners allowed Margaret Wake's name to remain on her map, as Wake County, where the state's capital is located.

1936 *Sampson County*

John Sampson (–1784)— A native of Ireland, Sampson immigrated to North Carolina about 1734. By 1740 he held grants to 940 acres of land in New Hanover County and he was elected sheriff of that county in 1742. An uncle of John Sampson's, in Ireland, named George Vaughn, had received a land grant, or barony, of 12,500 acres of land in England's colony of North Carolina. John Sampson settled on this land about 1761 and his plantation became one of the wealthiest in southeastern North Carolina. He owned approximately

12,000 acres of land in the vicinity of the settlement of Clinton, which is now within Sampson County. John Sampson also owned numerous slaves. Sampson engaged in lumber, sawmill, tar and turpentine enterprises. He served on the governor's council of three of North Carolina's royal governors, Arthur Dobbs (1689–1765), William Tryon (1729–1788) and Josiah Martin (1737–1786). John Sampson is referred to in most works as Colonel John Sampson. In 1748 he had commanded the militia during an alarm of Spanish attack on Wilmington. Perhaps he was awarded the rank of colonel (or lieutenant-colonel) then. Oscar M. Bizzell's 1983 work entitled *The Heritage of Sampson County, North Carolina* tells us that when the Regulators took up arms in 1768 in the so-called War of the Regulation, "Beginning on September 22, 1768, John Sampson was commissioned as a lieutenant-general." This very likely is a typographical error. A lieutenant-general is a three star general, a very high rank, held by few. If the word "general," should have been "colonel," this would make the statement credible and explain the references to "Colonel John Sampson." (It would be both grammatically and militarily correct to refer to Lieutenant-colonel Sampson as Colonel Sampson.) During the American Revolution, Sampson was a patriot and was appointed to the board of war by Governor Richard Caswell (1729–1789). This county was created in 1784.

1937 *Scotland County*

Scotland on the island of Great Britain— This county was created in 1899 and named for Scotland on the island of Great Britain. It lies at the southern edge of the central part of the state. Most North Carolina sources indicate that this county's name was chosen because many of the early settlers of this region had come from Scotland. Other sources phrase it a bit differently, mentioning Scottish Highlanders as ancestors of many of the citizens of the area when this county was created in 1899. Today's Scotland is a member of the United Kingdom in the British Isles. The other members of the United Kingdom are England, Wales and Northern Ireland. Scotland lies at the northern part of the island of Great Britain, which it shares with England and Wales. The name *Scotland* derived from the Celtic speaking Scots, who came to Scotland from Ireland about A.D. 500. Prior to 1603, Scotland had a long history that was relatively independent of its powerful southern neigh-

bor, England. At the time that today's Scotland was invaded by the Roman Empire about A.D. 80, it was occupied by the Picts. In addition to the Picts and Romans, others who have ruled some or all of Scotland include the Scots, Anglo-Saxons and the Norse. The Scottish ruler, Malcom II (–1034) is credited with forging a version of a united Scottish kingdom. From 1034 to 1603, Scotland was generally independent of its powerful southern neighbor, although England ruled potions of Scotland at times. The beginning of today's formal union of Scotland with England occurred in 1603 when Scotland's King James VI (1566–1625) was also installed on the English throne. He ruled Scotland as James VI and England as James I. Scotland is a cold, mountainous country with a relatively sparse population. Its capital city is Edinburgh. In addition to its territory on the island of Great Britain, it includes three important island groups: The Shetland, Orkney and Herbrides Islands.

1938 *Stanly County*

John Stanly (1774–1834)— This North Carolina native was born on April 9, 1774, at New Bern. John Stanly studied law and was admitted to the North Carolina bar in 1799. He was a member of North Carolina's state legislature in 1798 and 1799 before being elected to represent North Carolina in the U.S. House of Representatives. He served two terms in that body, the first from 1801 to 1803 and the second from 1809 to 1811. Stanly subsequently served several terms in the North Carolina legislature and was speaker of its house of commons. This county was created and named in his honor on January 11, 1841.

1939 *Stokes County*

John Stokes (1756–1790)— A native of Virginia, Stokes served as an officer during the American Revolution. He is referred to in a number of works as Colonel Stokes, but it is not clear that he ever attained that rank (or that of lieutenant-colonel). The last combat that Stokes participated in took place on May 29, 1780, at the settlements of the Waxhaws, near the border between North and South Carolina, and he was a captain at that time. Stokes was badly wounded in that action and taken captive by Tories. After his capture, Stokes' arm was savagely destroyed by his Tory captors and was amputated. Stokes subsequently served in both houses of the North Carolina legislature. In 1790 he was appointed by President George

Washington to be a U.S. district court judge but Stokes died on the way to attend his first court session. This county had been created and named in his honor in 1789, while he was serving in the state legislature.

1940 *Surry County*

Uncertain— This county was created effective April 1, 1771, in England's colony of North Carolina, while William Tryon (1729–1788) was the royal governor of North Carolina and Governor Tryon was involved in the selection of this county's name. Twenty six North Carolina sources offer an opinion on the origin of this county's name. According to 19 of them, the county was named to honor an English statesman, a lord (some say earl) of Surry (or Surrey). None of these 19 sources which claim that the county's name honors an English nobleman, provide the year of birth, death or other distinguishing characteristic for this English nobleman titled Surry (or Surrey) although several of them say that he was a member of parliament who opposed English taxation of the American colonies. Six of the 26 works offering an opinion on the origin of this county's name say that it was named for the English county of Surrey, since that was where Governor Tryon was born. (It is true that North Carolina's royal governor, William Tryon was born on his family's estate, named Norbury Park in 1729. That estate was in Surrey County, England, and Governor Tryon grew up on this family estate. He sold it when he came to North Carolina). Only one of the 26 sources admits that there is uncertainty about the origin of this county's name. That source is John M. Mullen's *Facts to Know North Carolina*, published in 1937. Mullen states that "Opinion as to origin of name is divided between the County of Surry [sic], in the south of England, and Lord Surry, foe of heavy taxation of the American Colonists." The fact that 19 of our sources favor the English nobleman versus only six votes for Surrey County, England, really means little. Many of the 19 were copying from each other, as, no doubt, were at least some of the six sources who chose Surrey County, England. What we need is a citation of a reason for the choice and these are in short supply. Kemp P. Battle shares the reason for his opinion that this county was named for an English nobleman. Battle states in his article entitled "North Carolina County Names," which appeared in the April, 1908, issue of *The Magazine of History*, that "...Governor

Tryon procured the incorporation of four new counties, and wishing to please all parties he called one after the Earldom of Guilford, of which Lord North was heir apparent, another Surry, in honor of Lord Surry, afterwards Duke of Norfolk, a follower of Chatham; a third Chatham, after the great opponent of Lord North, with its county-seat at Pittsborough, and the fourth Wake, after the maiden name of his wife." Although Kemp P. Battle does not provide years of birth or death for his Lord Surry, ironically, one of the sources which supports the Surrey County, England, origin, mentions precisely which English nobleman it was that this county was *not* named for. That source is Professor William S. Powell, who tells us in his *North Carolina Gazetteer*, that it was Edward Howard, Duke of Norfolk (1686–1777) and that Howard used his ranking title of Norfolk rather than the Surrey title, which he also held. Although your curiosity about the origin of this county's name must be pretty well satisfied by now, a word or ten about Surrey County, England is in order. It lies in southeastern England, just south and mostly west, of London. Sussex County lies below it on the English Channel and Kent County, to its east, denies it salt-water access on that side. Its name was Suthrige in A.D. 722, and evolved to Sudrie by A.D. 1086. "Southerly district" is the translation of these versions of the name and they refer to the geographic relation to Middlesex. The Thames River on Surrey County's northern border separates it from England's Middlesex County, so the translation is plausible.

1941 *Swain County*

David L. Swain (1801–1868) — This North Carolina native attended the University of North Carolina at Chapel Hill for just a few months before moving to Raleigh to study law. Admitted to the bar in 1823, Swain soon became active in politics and represented Buncombe County in North Carolina's house of commons from 1824 to 1830. While serving as a judge of the state's superior court in 1832, David Lowry Swain was elected governor of North Carolina on December 1, 1832, and was inaugurated just five days later. He served as governor for the constitutional limit of three years, from 1832 to 1835. The trustees of the University of North Carolina made him president of that institution and he served in that position from 1835 to 1868. During the Civil War years Swain had kept the university open to delay conscription of its students, but by 1868 it had

fallen into financial ruin and was forced to close. In 1863 David Swain declined the offer by North Carolina's Confederate governor, Zebulon B. Vance (1830–1894), that Swain serve in the Confederate senate. This county was created in February, 1871.

1942 *Transylvania County*

Latin words, trans and sylva — This county was created on February 15, 1861. Mary Jane McCrary's history of this county, published in 1984, indicates that the county's name was probably chosen by a member of the North Carolina legislature named Joseph P. Jordan. McCrary bases that statement on comments contained in a memoir written by Cathleen Erwin. The county's name was formed from a combination of two Latin words, *trans*, meaning "across," and *sylva* which is translated as "woods," or "forest." This county lies on North Carolina's southwestern border, within the beautiful Blue Ridge Mountains and its location and physical setting presumably inspired its unusual name. North Carolina is the only state which has a county named Transylvania. However, about a century before this North Carolina county was created, Richard Henderson (1735–1785) formed a company which purchased an enormous tract of land from the Indians comprising about half of what is now the state of Kentucky. Henderson gave this land the name Transylvania, enacted laws to govern it and made himself its president. Both Virginia and North Carolina declared that Transylvania to be illegal. However, Henderson and his associates were given extensive tracts of land, within what is today's Henderson County, Kentucky, to compensate them for opening up this wilderness country. Henderson County, Kentucky, is about 150 miles away from Transylvania County, North Carolina. None of the North Carolina sources consulted suggest that Richard Henderson's aborted Transylvania inspired the name of this North Carolina county.

1943 *Tyrrell County*

John Tyrrell (1685–1729) — This county in England's colony of North Carolina was created in 1729 and named for Sir John Tyrrell, one of the later proprietors of Carolina. In 1663 England's King Charles II (1630–1685) had granted proprietorships in Carolina to eight Englishmen. These proprietary interests in Carolina passed from generation to generation as proprietors died. In some cases these proprietary

interests were sold. By 1729, when the Carolina charter was surrendered to the English crown, nearly 50 different individuals had served as proprietors of Carolina or had been entitled to do so. Sir John Tyrrell was one of the later proprietors. Sometime prior to May 28, 1725, Tyrrell purchased his proprietorship. The proprietorship which he purchased had originally been granted by King Charles II to Anthony Ashley Cooper, Earl of Shaftesbury (1621–1683). That proprietorship had passed from the original proprietor to his son, Anthony (1652–1699), who, in turn passed it on to his son, Anthony (1671–1713). The proprietorship remained in the family when it was passed to a Maurice Ashley (1675–1726) but it left the family when he sold it to Sir John Tyrrell, the namesake of this county. Tyrrell was educated at St. Catherine's College at Cambridge University. In 1715, John Tyrrell's father, Sir Charles Tyrrell, died and John inherited his estate.

1944 *Union County*

Uncertain — Sources dealing with the history, geography and place names of North Carolina present two different versions of the origin of this county's name:

The American, federal Union — This county was created on December 19, 1842, when tension between the North and South were building over the slavery issue and civil war was becoming a distinct possibility. A decade earlier, John C. Calhoun (1782–1850) had resigned as our nation's vice-president to better represent the views of South Carolina and the South in the U.S. Senate and Calhoun had expounded the Doctrine of Nullification, allowing individual states in the Union to declare acts of the federal congress unconstitutional and unenforceable within the state's borders. President Andrew Jackson nullified that Nullification theory but civil war storm clouds kept brewing as a steady flow of petitions reached the federal congress calling for the abolition of slavery. The sources which state that this county was named for the American union or the federal union of states have in mind this historic setting when they say that the county was named in honor the American federal union of states. One source, Kemp P. Battle, in his article entitled "North Carolina County Names," which appeared in the April, 1908 issue of *The Magazine of History*, specifically cites Calhoun's theory of Nullification as the inspiration for this county's name.

Compromise name selected instead of

Clay or Jackson—At the time that this county was created on December 19, 1842, Henry Clay (1777–1852) was the leading figure of the Whig party in America while the former president, Andrew Jackson (1767–1845) was an idol of the Democrats. One of the theories that is advanced by several sources as the origin of Union County's name involves a compromise name chosen after agreement could not be reached between proponents of the name Clay County and those who favored calling the new county Jackson. According to this version, since land was being taken from two counties (Anson and Mecklenburg) to create this county, it would be called Union County. That was in 1842. North Carolina later honored both Henry Clay and Andrew Jackson by naming counties for them; Jackson on January 29, 1851, and Clay on February 20, 1861.

1945 *Vance County*

Zebulon B. Vance (1830–1894)—A native of North Carolina and a lawyer, Vance was elected as a Whig to the North Carolina legislature but later ran for congress as the nominee of the American Party and was elected. He served in the U.S. House of Representatives from 1858 to 1861, while events leading to our nation's Civil War were escalating. When the Civil War began, Vance entered the army of the Confederacy as a captain, saw combat duty and was soon promoted to colonel. When North Carolina's next gubernatorial election was held in 1862, North Carolina was a member of the Confederate States of America. Zebulon B. Vance won that election and was inaugurated as North Carolina's Confederate governor on September 8, 1862. He was reelected in 1864 but on April 9, 1865 the Civil War ended and Governor Vance was arrested by presidential order on May 13, 1865. In 1870 he was elected to represent North Carolina in the U.S. Senate but was denied a seat in that body. In 1876 Vance was a candidate for the North Carolina governor's office. He won that election and became, for the first time, governor of North Carolina as a member of the United States of America. He was later elected to the U.S. Senate and this time was allowed a seat in that body and served there from 1879 until his death in 1894. This county was created on March 5, 1881, while Vance was serving in the U.S. Senate. The name Vance had not been the first choice for this new county's name. In 1879 a bill was drafted, which would have named this county Gilliam County, in honor of Judge Robert B. Gilliam of Oxford. In a

second attempt the county's name was to be Dortch County and that bill passed its first and second readings but was not enacted. In 1881 the speaker of the North Carolina house, C. M. Cook of Franklin County, stated that he would support the creation of a new county (by now the proposed name was to be Vance) if the new county would take over all of the Tar River, thus saving the taxpayers of Franklin County the expense of building bridges over the Tar River. It was on that basis that agreement was reached to create the new county, named Vance County. However, the Tar River does flow through today's Franklin County and does not flow through today's Vance County. A change in borders was enacted in 1909, which changed both counties' borders with respect to the Tar River.

1946 *Wake County*

Margaret Wake Tryon (1733–1819)—This county was created effective in 1771, in England's colony of North Carolina, while William Tryon (1729–1788) was the royal governor of North Carolina, and Governor Tryon selected the name in honor of the maiden name of his wife, Margaret Wake. She was a wealthy heiress, of fashionable Hanover Street in London. William Tryon and Margaret Wake were married in England, in 1757. Margaret brought a dowry of 30,000 pounds to this marriage. She was related to the rising Wills Hill, Earl of Hillsborough (1718–1793), who soon became president and first commissioner of England's board of trade and plantations. The Tryons had two children, Margaret Tryon (–1791) and a son, who was born in North Carolina but died a few months after his birth. When William Tryon was appointed to be lieutenant-governor of England's royal colony of North Carolina, Margaret came with her husband to America. Lieutenant-governor Tryon, Margaret Wake Tryon and their four-year-old daughter arrived in North Carolina at Brunswick on October 10, 1764. There were others in the party including Fountain Elwin, a cousin of Margaret Wake Tryon's. Esther Wake, a sister of Margaret Wake, joined the Tryons in North Carolina. While living in colonial North Carolina, the Tryon family established at least four residences. One at Wilmington, another at New Bern, a villa three miles outside New Bern and a so-called "castle," within sight of a sea inlet at Brunswick. In April, 1765, Tryon succeeded Arthur Dobbs (1689–1765) as North Carolina's royal governor and was officially commis-

sioned in that post in July, 1765. Tryon served as royal governor until July, 1771, when Tryon and his wife, Margaret Wake Tryon, sailed from North Carolina for England's colony of New York, where Tryon was to be the king's governor. Thus Margaret Wake's period of residence in colonial North Carolina was from 1764 to 1771. On the night of December 29, 1773, the Tryons' house in Manhattan, New York, burned to the ground and virtually all of the family's personal possessions were destroyed, but no lives were lost. During the American Revolution Tryon remained in America to fight for England. Presumably Margaret Wake Tryon returned to England early in the war. If not, she surely did so by 1780 when her husband returned to England because of his ill health. Margaret's husband died in London in 1788 and she died in February, 1819. Prior to the American Revolution a county had also been created in North Carolina that was named in honor of the husband of Margaret Wake, Governor William Tryon. Although the odious name Tryon was removed from North Carolina's map during the Revolution, the chivalrous Southerners of North Carolina allowed Margaret Wake's name to remain on the map, as Wake County, where the state's capital is located. In 1805 an attempt was made to change Wake County's name to Raleigh County but several hundred people petitioned to oppose that name change. The petitioners charged that the proposed change "…was based upon uninformed charges against the character of the Lady by whose maiden Name the county was called." In the North Carolina legislature the bill to change the name of Wake County to Raleigh County was referred to committees in both the house and senate and neither the house nor the senate ever reported them out of committee. North Carolina has proven its chivalry even more dramatically by retaining names honoring the queen consort of the hated king of England, King George III (1738–1820). She was Queen Charlotte Sophia of Mecklenburg-Strelitz (1744–1818) and the names of both the county of Mecklenburg and that county's seat, the important commercial city of Charlotte, still honor her.

1947 *Warren County*

Joseph Warren (1741–1775)—A native of Massachusetts and a graduate of Harvard College, Warren practiced medicine in the Boston area. He was a member of the committee of safety and president *pro tempore* of the Massachusetts provincial congress.

In June, 1775, he was commissioned a major-general and he died in combat a few days later at the battle of Bunker Hill. Warren County, North Carolina, was created and named in honor of this Revolutionary War hero in 1779.

1948 *Washington County*

George Washington (1732–1799)— Washington was a native of Virginia. He served in Virginia's house of burgesses and became one of the colonies' leaders in opposition to British policies in America. He was a member of the first and second Continental Congresses and commander of all Continental armies in the Revolutionary War. Following victory in that war, Washington was elected to be the first president of the United States. This county was created in 1799. North Carolina had earlier created a county to honor George Washington. That earlier county was first established as Washington District of North Carolina in 1776 and that district was made a county in 1777. However, when Tennessee was separated from North Carolina, they took that Washington County with them. The absence of a Washington County on North Carolina's map was remedied in 1799 when this county was created.

1949 *Watauga County*

Watauga River— This county in northwestern North Carolina was created in January, 1849, and named for the Watauga River, which rises in this county, near Grandfather Mountain. The Watauga flows northwest across Watauga County into Tennessee, where its waters join those of the south fork of the Holston River, near Kingsport, Tennessee. The Watauga is only about 60 miles long. In 1772, settlers in the valley of the Watauga River found themselves southwest of any organized government, with no courts and no militia. These settlers founded their own self-government, and called it the Watauga Association. They established courts and administered swift justice. The land of the Watauga Association was then in western North Carolina but is in what is now the state of Tennessee. The name *Watauga* is of Indian origin and several sources indicate that it was the name of a tribe that lived in this area. That is doubtful, but it is known that there was an early Indian village on the Watauga River which was named Watauga. That village was near what is now Elizabethton, in Carter County, Tennessee.

1950 *Wayne County*

Anthony Wayne (1745–1796)— A native of Pennsylvania, Wayne was a successful brigadier-general in the Revolutionary War and became a hero for his daring exploits. During the bitter winter of 1777–1778 at Valley Forge, Pennsylvania, Wayne shared the sufferings of his men although his comfortable estate was only five miles away. He played an important role in the final overthrow of the British forces in Georgia. After the war, in 1785, Wayne moved to Georgia and he represented Georgia for about six months in the U.S. House of Representatives. In 1792, President Washington recalled Wayne to serve as a major-general against the Indians in the Northwest territory. Once again his military efforts were successful. This North Carolina county was created in 1779, during the American Revolution.

1951 *Wilkes County*

John Wilkes (1727–1797)— This county was created in 1777, during the American Revolution, in an act to become effective February 15, 1778. The county's name honors John Wilkes, a member of the English parliament who strenuously opposed the harsh and unjust measures toward the American colonies which finally resulted in the Revolution. He was born in England and was a writer as well as a member of parliament. Wilkes was persecuted and imprisoned for his writings which included satires and lampoons of important English personages.

1952 *Wilson County*

Louis D. Wilson (1789–1847)— This North Carolina native served, almost without interruption, from 1815 to 1846, in one branch of the North Carolina legislature, or the other. When the Mexican War was in its early stages, he delivered an impassioned speech in the North Carolina senate, urging North Carolina to support the war. At that time Louis Wilson was about 57 years old. A younger senator rose to taunt Wilson saying "It's all very well for the honorable gentleman from Edgecombe to be so enthusiastic about this contemptible war since he knows that he is too old to be expected to go." Wilson responded immediately by resigning from the senate and raising a company of soldiers to serve in the Mexican War and he served in the war himself, first as a captain, and later as a colonel. He died on August 12, 1847, during the war, at Veracruz, Mexico. The cause of his death was fever. Wilson was a wealthy man at the time of his death, with an estate which included both land and slaves. This county was created and named in his honor on February 13, 1855. Sources on the history, geography and place names of North Carolina consistently render Wilson's given name as Louis. In K. Jack Bauer's work entitled *The Mexican War: 1846–1848*, the name is rendered as Colonel Lewis D. Wilson.

1953 *Yadkin County*

Yadkin River— The 202 mile-long Yadkin River of central North Carolina rises in Watauga County, flows in an eastern direction to Yadkin County and forms Yadkin County's northern border. Just northeast of East Bend, North Carolina, the Yadkin makes a 90 degree turn to the south and then forms much of the eastern border of Yadkin County. The river continues to flow south until it joins the Uwharrie River to form the Pee Dee River. The Yadkin River's name is of Indian origin and uncertain meaning. It is known that the Indians traditionally treated the valley of the Yadkin River as a neutral zone. Before going to war, Indians of one or more tribes could deposit their women, children and old men in this valley and be assured of their safety. This county was created on December 28, 1850.

1954 *Yancey County*

Bartlett Yancey (1785–1828)— A native of North Carolina, a lawyer and an excellent orator, Yancey was elected to represent North Carolina in the U.S. House of Representatives. He served in that body from 1813 to 1817 but declined to run for an additional term because the pay was inadequate to support his growing family. Yancey returned to North Carolina to practice law and he entered the North Carolina senate. He served for a decade in that body from 1817 to 1827, was its speaker and presiding officer, and was an early advocate of a public school system for the state. In 1826 President John Quincy Adams offered Yancey an appointment as minister to Peru but he declined that nomination. His death in August, 1828 came after a brief illness. This county was created and named in his honor in 1833.

REFERENCES

Abraham, Henry J. *Justices & Presidents: A Political History of Appointments to the Supreme Court.* New York, Oxford University Press, 1992.

Absher, Mrs. W. O. *The Heritage of Wilkes County*. Winston-Salem, North Carolina, Wilkes Genealogical Society, Inc., 1982.

The Ahoskie Era of Hertford County. Ahoskie, North Carolina, Parker Brothers, Inc., 1939.

Alexander, Nancy. *Here Will I Dwell: The Story of Caldwell County*. 1956.

Alleghany Historical-Genealogical Society, Inc. *Alleghany County Heritage*. Winston-Salem, North Carolina, Hunter Publishing Co., 1983.

Allen, W. C. *History of Halifax County*. Boston, Cornhill Co., 1918.

Allen, W. C., & Clarence W. Griffin. *The Story of Our State: North Carolina*. Raleigh, Dixie Press, 1942.

Allstrom, C. M. *Dictionary of Royal Lineage of Europe and Other Countries*. Chicago, Press of S. Th. Almberg, 1902.

Amis, Moses N. *Historical Raleigh*, Raleigh, Commercial Printing Co., 1913.

Arthur, John P. *Western North Carolina: A History*. Raleigh, Edwards & Broughton Printing Co., 1914.

Ashe, Samuel A. *History of North Carolina*. Greensboro, North Carolina, Charles L. Van Noppen, 1908.

Ashe, Samuel A., et al. *Biographical History of North Carolina*. Greensboro, North Carolina, Charles L. Van Noppen, 1905–1917.

Battle, Kemp P. *The Early History of Raleigh*. Raleigh, Edwards & Broughton, 1893.

Battle, Kemp P. "Glimpses of History in the Names of Our Counties." *North Carolina Booklet*, Vol. 6. July, 1906.

Battle, Kemp P. *The Names of the Counties of North Carolina and the History Involved in Them*. Winston, North Carolina, William A. Blair, 1888.

Battle, Kemp P. "North Carolina County Names." *The Magazine of History*, Vol. 7, No. 4. New York: April, 1908.

Bauer, K. Jack. *The Mexican War: 1846–1848*. New York, Macmillan Publishing Co., Inc., 1974.

Belvin, Lynne, & Harriette Riggs. *The Heritage of Wake County, North Carolina*. Winston-Salem, North Carolina, Wake County Genealogical Society, 1983.

Bizzell, Oscar M. *The Heritage of Sampson County, North Carolina*. Winston-Salem, North Carolina, Sampson County, Historical Society, 1983.

Blackburn, George T. *The Heritage of Vance County, North Carolina*. Winston-Salem, North Carolina, Vance County Historical Society, 1984.

Bloodworth, Mattie. *History of Pender County, North Carolina*. Richmond, Virginia, Dietz Printing Co., 1947.

Boatner, Mark M. *Encyclopedia of the American Revolution*. Mechanicsburg, Pennsylvania, Stackpole Books, 1994.

Boatner, Mark M. *Landmarks of the American Revolution*. Harrisburg, Pennsylvania, Stackpole Books, 1973.

Bowman School Eighth Grade. *Mitchell County Then & Now*. Bakersville, North Carolina, 1950.

Boyd, William K. *The Story of Durham: City of the New South*. Durham, North Carolina, Duke University Press, 1925.

Brown, Joseph P. *The Commonwealth of Onslow: A History*. New Bern, North Carolina, Owen G. Dunn Co., 1960.

Burgess, Fred. *Randolph County: Economic & Social*. Ramseur, North Carolina, 1924.

Butchko, Tom. *An Inventory of Historic Architecture: Sampson County, North Carolina*. Raleigh, Contemporary Litho.

Casstevens, Frances H. *The Heritage of Yadkin County*. Yadkinville, North Carolina, Yadkin County Historical Society, 1981.

Chamberlain, Hope S. *History of Wake County, North Carolina*. Raleigh, Edwards & Broughton Printing Co., 1922.

Cheney, John L. *North Carolina Manual: 1977*. Raleigh.

Cheshire, Joseph B. *Nonnulla: Memories, Stories, Traditions, More or Less Authentic*. Chapel Hill, University of North Carolina Press, 1930.

Cisco, Jay G. *Historic Sumner County, Tennessee*. Nashville, Tennessee, Folk-Keelin Printing Co., 1909.

Clements, John. *North Carolina Facts*. Dallas, Texas, Clements Research, Inc., 1988.

Connor, R. D. W. *Antebellum Builders of North Carolina*. Greensboro, North Carolina, North Carolina College for Women, 1930.

Connor, R. D. W. *Makers of North Carolina History*. Raleigh, Thompson Publishing Co., 1911.

Connor, R. D. W. *Revolutionary Leaders of North Carolina*. Greensboro, North Carolina, North Carolina College for Women, 1930.

Cook, Petronelle. *Queen Consorts of England: The Power Behind the Throne*. New York, Facts on File, Inc., 1993.

Cooper, Edwin B., et al. *The Heritage of Lenoir County*. Winston-Salem, North Carolina, Hunter Publishing Co., 1981.

Cooper, Francis H. "Some Colonial History of Beaufort County, North Carolina." *James Sprunt Historical Publications*, Vol. 14, No. 2. Chapel Hill: 1916.

Cope, Robert F., & Manly W. Wellman. *The County of Gaston: Two Centuries of a North Carolina Region*. Charlotte, Heritage Printers, Inc., 1961.

Copeland, Elizabeth H. *Chronicles of Pitt County, North Carolina*. Winston-Salem, North Carolina, Pitt County Historical Society, Inc., 1982.

Corbin Street School Sixth Grade Pupils. *A Short History of Cabarrus County & Concord*. Concord, North Carolina, Snyder Printing Co., 1932.

Corbitt, D. L. "Judicial Districts of North Carolina: 1746–1934." *North Carolina Historical Review*, Vol. 12, No. 1. Raleigh: January, 1935.

Corbitt, David L. *The Formation of the North Carolina Counties: 1663–1943*. Raleigh, State Department of Archives & History, 1950.

Crabtree, Beth G. *North Carolina Governors: 1585–1974*. Raleigh, Division of Archives & History, 1974.

Crittenden, Charles C., & Dan Lacy. *The Historical Records of North Carolina*. Raleigh, North Carolina Historical Commission, 1938.

Crutchfield, James A. *The North Carolina Almanac & Book of Facts*. Nashville, Tennessee, Rutledge Hill Press, 1986.

Crutchfield, James A. *The North Carolina Almanac & Book of Facts: 1989–1990*. Nashville, Tennessee, Rutledge Hill Press, 1988.

Cumming, William P. "Naming Carolina." *North Carolina Historical Review*, Vol. 22, No. 1. Raleigh: January, 1945.

Daves, Graham. "Virginia Dare." *North Carolina Booklet*, Vol. 1, No. 1. Raleigh: 1901.

Davis, David E. *History of Tyrrell County*. Norfolk, Virginia, James Christopher Printing, 1963.

Davis, Pat D., & Kathleen H. Hamilton. *The Heritage of Carteret County, North Carolina*. Beaufort, North Carolina, Carteret Historical Research Association, 1982.

Dill, Alonzo T. "Eighteenth Century New Bern: A History of the Town & Craven County: 1700–1800." *North Carolina Historical Review*, Vol. 22, No. 1. Raleigh: January, 1945.

Dill, Alonzo T. *Governor Tryon and His Palace*. Chapel Hill, University of North Carolina Press, 1955.

Donehoo, George P. *A History of the Indian Villages & Place Names in Pennsylvania*. Harrisburg, Pennsylvania, Telegraph Press, 1928.

Dupuy, Trevor N., et al. *The Harper Encyclopedia of Military Biography*. Edison, New Jersey, Castle Books, 1995.

Dykeman, Wilma. *Tennessee: A Bicentennial History*. New York, W. W. Norton & Co., Inc., 1975.

Eaker, Madeline H. *The Heritage of Person County*. Winston-Salem, North Carolina, Person County Historical Society, 1981.

Ehringhaus, J. C. B., & Mrs. Carl Goerch. *North Carolina Almanac & State Industrial Guide: 1954–1955*. Raleigh, Almanac Publishing Co., 1953.

Evans, Virginia P. *Iredell County Landmarks: A Pictorial History of Iredell County*. Iredell County American Revolution Bicentennial Commission, 1976.

Faragher, John M. *The Encyclopedia of Colonial & Revolutionary America*. New York, Facts on File, 1990.

Fletcher, Arthur L. *Ashe County: A History*. Jefferson, North Carolina, Ashe County Research Association, Inc., 1963.

Foglia, Virginia S. *Albemarle, Stanly County Centennial: May 11–18, 1957*. 1957.

Foote, William H. *Sketches of North Carolina: Historical & Biographical*. New York, Robert Carter, 1846.

Footprints in Northampton: 1741–1776–1976. Northampton County Bicentennial Committee, 1976.

Fossett, Mildred B. *History of McDowell County*. Marion, North Carolina, McDowell County American Revolution Bicentennial Commission, 1976.

Freeman, Ozell K. *History of North Carolina for Youth: "The Goodliest Land."* Charlotte, Delmar Companies, 1980.

Gaillard, Frye, & Dot Jackson. *The Catawba River*. Boiling Springs, Gardner-Webb College Press, 1983.

Georgia, North Carolina, South Carolina Tour Book. Heathrow, Florida, AAA Publishing, 1997.

Griffin, Clarence W. *History of Old Tryon & Rutherford Counties, North Carolina: 1730–1936*. Asheville, North Carolina, Miller Printing Co., 1937.

Gwynn, Zae H. *The 1850 Census of Craven County, North Carolina*. Kingsport, Tennessee, Kingsport Press, Inc., 1961.

Hadley, Wade, et al. *Chatham County: 1771–1971*.

Hardy, Marion W. *A Glimpse of Pamlico County*. Charlotte, Herb Eaton, Inc.

Harriett, Julia P. *The History & Genealogy of Jones County, North Carolina*. New Bern, North Carolina, Owen G. Dunn Co., 1987.

Hastings, Charlotte I. *Our North Carolina Heritage*. Charlotte, School Printing Service, 1956.

Haywood, Marshall D. *Governor William Tryon and His Administration in the Province of North Carolina*. Raleigh, E. M. Uzzell, 1903.

The Heritage of Onslow County. Winston-Salem, North Carolina, Onslow County Historical Society, 1983.

Higgins, Jody. *Common Times: Written & Pictorial of Yancey County*. Burnsville, North Carolina, Yancey Graphics, 1982.

Historic Vance County and "Happy, Healthy, Hustling Henderson."

Hodge, Frederick W. *Handbook of American Indians North of Mexico*. Totowa, New Jersey, Rowman & Littlefield, 1975.

Hoffman, Ross J. S. *The Marquis: A Study of Lord Rockingham, 1730–1782*. New York, Fordham University Press, 1973.

Hollingsworth, J. G. *History of Surry County*. Mount Airy, North Carolina, 1935.

Jackson, Hester B. *The Heritage of Surry County, North Carolina*. Winston-Salem, North Carolina, Surry County Genealogical Association, 1983.

Johnson, F. Roy. *Legends & Myths of North Carolina's Roanoke-Chowan Area*. Murfreesboro, North Carolina, Johnson Publishing Co., 1966.

Joiner, Harry M. *Tennessee Then & Now*. Athens, Alabama, Southern Textbook Publishers, Inc., 1983.

Julyan, Robert H. *Mountain Names*. Seattle, The Mountaineers, 1984.

Keever, Homer M. *Iredell: Piedmont County*. Iredell County Bicentennial Commission, 1976.

Kenny, Hamill. "The Origin & Meaning of the Indian-Place Names of Maryland." Ph.D. Thesis, Theodore R. McKeldin Library, University of Maryland, College Park, Maryland, 1950.

Kleber, John E. *The Kentucky Encyclopedia*. Lexington, Kentucky. University Press of Kentucky, 1992.

Langguth, A. J. *Patriots: The Men Who Started the American Revolution*. New York, Simon & Schuster, 1988.

Lawrence, Robert C. *The State of Robeson*. New York, J. J. Little & Ives Co., 1939.

Lee, Lawrence. *The History of Brunswick County, North Carolina*. 1978.

Lefler, Hugh T. *North Carolina History Told by Contemporaries*. Chapel Hill, University of North Carolina Press, 1965.

Lefler, Hugh T., & Albert R. Newsome. *The History of a Southern State: North Carolina*. Chapel Hill, University of North Carolina Press, 1973.

Lewis, Samuel. *Topographical Dictionary of England*. London, S. Lewis & Co., 1842.

McCague, James. *The Cumberland*. New York, Holt, Rinehart & Winston, 1973.

McCrary, Mary J. *Transylvania Beginnings: A History*. Easley, South Carolina, Southern Historical Press, Inc., 1984.

McFarland, Daniel M. "North Carolina Newspapers, Editors & Journalistic Politics: 1815–1835." *North Carolina Historical Review*, Vol. 30, No. 3. Raleigh: July, 1953.

McGehee, Montford. *Life & Character of the Hon. William A. Graham*. Raleigh, News Job Office & Book Bindery, 1877.

Manning, Francis M., & W. H. Booker. *Martin County History*. Williamston, North Carolina, Enterprise Publishing Co., 1977.

Medley, Mary L. *History of Anson County, North Carolina*. Wadesboro, North Carolina, Anson County Historical Society, 1976.

Miller, E. H. *Statesville & Iredell County Directory: 1907–1908*. Asheville, North Carolina, Press of Hackney & Moale Co., 1907.

Miller, Lillian B. *The Dye Is Now Cast*. Washington, D.C., Smithsonian Institution Press, 1975.

Mills, A.D. *A Dictionary of English Place Names*. Oxford, Oxford University Press, 1991.

Mitchell, Memory F. *North Carolina's Signers: Brief Sketches of the Men Who Signed the Declaration of Independence and the Constitution*. Raleigh, State Department of Archives & History, 1964.

Moore, John W. *History of North Carolina*. Raleigh, Alfred Williams & Co., 1880.

Moser, A. M., et al. *Buncombe County: Economic & Social*. Asheville, North Carolina, Inland Press, 1923.

Moule, Thomas. *The County Maps of Old England*. London, Studio Editions, 1990.

Mullen, John M. *Facts to Know North Carolina*. Lincolnton, North Carolina, Mullen Feature Syndicate, 1937.

Murray, Elizabeth R. *Wake: Capital County of North Carolina*. Raleigh, Capital County Publishing Co., 1983.

Nash, Francis. "Presentation of Portrait of Governor Alexander Martin in the State of North Carolina in the Hall of the House of Representatives at Raleigh, November 16, 1908, by the North Carolina Sons of the Revolution."

Nelson, Paul D. *William Tryon and the Course of Empire*. Chapel Hill, University of North Carolina Press, 1990.

Neuffer, C. H. "The Lord Proprietors and Their Influence on South Carolina Place Names." *Names in South Carolina*, Vol. 17. Columbia, South Carolina: Winter, 1970.

Newsome, Albert R., & Hugh T. Lefler. *The Growth of North Carolina*. Yonkers on Hudson, New York, World Book Co., 1940.

The North Carolina Information & Fact Book: The Tar Heel Almanac. Greenville, North Carolina, C. R. Cannon, 1979.

North Carolina: Its Past and Its Future. North Carolina Republican Executive Committee, 1966.

North Carolina: The Land of Opportunity. Raleigh, State Board of Agriculture, 1923.

Olds, Fred A. *Story of the Counties of North Carolina.* Raleigh, Press of Oxford Orphanage.

Parramore, Thomas C. *Cradle of the Colony: The History of Chowan County & Edenton, North Carolina.* Edenton Chamber of Commerce, 1967.

Patton, Sadie S. *Sketches of Polk County History.* Asheville, North Carolina, Miller Printing Co., 1950.

Patton, Sadie S. *The Story of Henderson County.* Asheville, North Carolina, Miller Printing Co., 1947.

Pearson, Bruce L. "On the Indian Place-Names of South Carolina." *Names: Journal of the American Name Society,* Vol. 26, No. 1. Potsdam, New York: March, 1978.

Peele, J. W. *Lives of Distinguished North Carolinians.* Raleigh, 1898.

Phifer, Edward W. *Burke: The History of a North Carolina County: 1777–1920.* Morganton, North Carolina, 1977.

Pittard, Lile. *Prologue: A History of Alexander County, North Carolina.* Taylorsville, North Carolina, 1958.

Powell, William S. *Annals of Progress: The Story of Lenoir County & Kinston, North Carolina.* Raleigh, State Department of Archives & History, 1963.

Powell, William S. *The Carolina Charter of 1663.* Raleigh, State Department of Archives & History, 1954.

Powell, William S. *Dictionary of North Carolina Biography.* Chapel Hill, University of North Carolina Press, 1979–1988.

Powell, William S. *North Carolina: A Bicentennial History.* New York, W. W. Norton & Co., Inc., 1977.

Powell, William S. *The North Carolina Gazetteer.* Chapel Hill, University of North Carolina Press, 1968.

Powell, William S. *Paradise Preserved.* Chapel Hill, University of North Carolina Press, 1965.

Powell, William S. *The Proprietors of Carolina.* Raleigh, Carolina Charter Tercentenary Commission, 1963.

Powell, William S. *When the Past Refused to Die: A History of Caswell County, North Carolina: 1777–1977.* Durham, North Carolina, Moore Publishing Co., 1977.

Powell, William S. *Ye Countie of Albemarle in Carolina.* Raleigh, State Department of Archives & History, 1958.

Preslar, Charles J. *A History of Catawba County.* Salisbury, North Carolina, Rowan Printing Co., 1954.

Price, Edward T. *Dividing the Land: Early American Beginnings of Our Private Property Mosaic.* Chicago, University of Chicago Press, 1995.

Puetz, C. J. *North Carolina County Maps.* Lyndon Station, Wisconsin, County Maps.

Ray, Lenoir. *Postmarks: A History of Henderson County, North Carolina.* Chicago, Adams Press, 1970.

Redwine, John M. *Union County, North Carolina: 1842–1953.*

Robinson, Blackwell P. *The Five Royal Governors of North Carolina: 1729–1775.* Raleigh, Carolina Charter Tercentenary Commission, 1963.

Robinson, Blackwell P. *A History of Moore County, North Carolina.* Southern Pines, North Carolina, Moore County Historical Association, 1956.

Robinson, Blackwell P. *The North Carolina Guide.* Chapel Hill, University of North Carolina Press, 1955.

Robinson, Blackwell P., & Alexander R. Stoesen. *The History of Guilford County, North Carolina, U.S.A.* Guilford County American Revolution Bicentennial Commission, 1976.

Rockingham County Club. *Rockingham County: Economic & Social.* Raleigh, Edwards & Broughton Printing Co., 1918.

Rowley, Barbara. "The Parks Less Traveled." *The Walking Magazine,* Vol. 7, No. 4. Boston, Massachusetts: August, 1992.

Rumple, Jethro. *A History of Rowan County, North Carolina.* Salisbury, North Carolina, J. J. Bruner, 1881.

Sanders, W. M., & G. Y. Ragsdale. *Johnston County: Economic & Social.* Smithfield, North Carolina, Smithfield Observer, 1922.

Schwarzkopf, S. Kent. *A History of Mt. Mitchell and the Black Mountains.* Raleigh, Division of Parks & Recreation, North Carolina Department of Natural Resources & Community Development, 1985.

Sharpe, Bill. *A New Geography of North Carolina.* Raleigh, Sharpe Publishing Co., 1954–1965.

Sharpe, Bill. "Robust Robeson." *The State: Weekly Survey of North Carolina,* Vol. 20, No. 26. Raleigh: November 29, 1952.

Sharpe, Ivey L. *Stanly County, U.S.A: The Story of an Era and an Area.* Greensboro, North Carolina, Piedmont Press, 1972.

Sherrill, William L. *Annals of Lincoln County, North Carolina.* Baltimore, Regional Publishing Co., 1972.

Shrader, Charles R. *Reference Guide to United States Military History: 1607–1815.* New York, Facts on File, 1991.

Siewers, Charles N. *Forsyth County: Economic & Social.* 1924.

Sikes, Leon H. *Duplin County Places: Past & Present.* Wallace, North Carolina, Wallace Enterprise, 1984.

Sims, Carlton C. *A History of Rutherford County.* Murfreesboro, Tennessee, 1947.

Spencer, Cornelia P. *First Steps in North Carolina History.* New York, American Book Co., 1888.

Stewart, George R. *American Place-Names.* New York, Oxford University Press, 1970.

Stick, David. *The Outer Banks of North Carolina: 1584–1958.* Chapel Hill, University of North Carolina Press, 1958.

The Story of Robeson County, North Carolina. Lumberton, North Carolina, Lumberton Chamber of Commerce & Agriculture.

Stroup, Carolyn M. *A Pictorial Walk Through Lincoln County.* Lincolnton, North Carolina.

The Supreme Court of the United States: Its Beginnings and Its Justices: 1790–1991. Commission on the Bicentennial of the United States Constitution, 1992.

Thomas, Maud. *Away Down Home: A History of Robeson County, North Carolina.* 1982.

Thomson, George M. *The Prime Ministers: From Robert Walpole to Margaret Thatcher.* New York, William Morrow & Co., Inc., 1981.

Tompkins, D. A. *History of Mecklenburg County and the City of Charlotte from 1740 to 1903.* Charlotte, Observer Printing House, 1903.

Trease, Geoffrey. *Seven Kings of England.* New York, Vanguard Press, 1955.

Turner, J. Kelly, & J. L. Bridgers. *History of Edgecombe County, North Carolina.* Raleigh, Edwards & Broughton Printing Co., 1920.

Vexler Robert I. *Chronology & Documentary Handbook of the State of North Carolina.* Dobbs Ferry, New York, Oceana Publications, Inc., 1978.

Waddell, Alfred M. *A History of New Hanover and the Lower Cape Fear Region.* Wilmington, 1909.

Waggoner, Sara M. *North Carolina: The Tar Heel State.* Bryn Mawr, Pennsylvania, Dorrance & Co., Inc., 1988.

Wake County: Economic & Social. Wake County Club, University of North Carolina, 1918.

Walden, H. Nelson. *History of Union County.* Charlotte, Heritage Printers, Inc., 1964.

Walker, Alexander M. *New Hanover County Court Minutes: 1738–1769.* Bethesda, Maryland, 1958.

Walser, Richard, & Julia M. Street. *North Carolina Parade.* Chapel Hill, University of North Carolina Press, 1966.

Warner, Ezra J., & W. Buck Yearns. *Biographical Register of the Confederate Con-*

gress. Baton Rouge, Louisiana State University Press, 1975.

Watson, Alan D. *Bertie County: A Brief History*. Raleigh, Department of Cultural Resources, Division of Archives & History, 1982.

Watson, Joseph W. *Abstracts of Early Records of Nash County, North Carolina: 1777–1859*. Rocky Mount, North Carolina, Dixie Letter Service, 1963.

Weathers, Lee B. *The Living Past of Cleveland County: A History*. Shelby, North Carolina, Star Publishing Co., 1956.

Western North Carolina. Charlotte, A.D. Smith & Co., 1890.

Wheeler, John H. *Historical Sketches of North Carolina from 1584 to 1851*. Philadelphia, Lippincott Grambo & Co., 1851.

Wheeler, John H. *Reminiscences & Memoirs of North Carolina & Eminent North Carolinians*. Columbus, Ohio, Columbus Printing Works, 1884.

Whitaker, Walter. *Centennial History of Alamance County*. Burlington, North Carolina, Burlington Chamber of Commerce, 1949.

White, William E. *A History of Alexander County, North Carolina*. Taylorsville, North Carolina, Taylorsville Times, 1926.

Whitworth, Rex. *William Augustus, Duke of Cumberland: A Life*. London, England, Leo Cooper, 1992.

Williamson, David. *Kings & Queens of Britain*. New York, Dorset Press, 1992.

Winslow, Raymond A. *Perquimans County History*. Hertford, North Carolina, 1984.

Winston, Robert W. "Leonard Henderson: Address Presenting the Portrait of Chief Justice Henderson to the Supreme Court of North Carolina."

Wise, L. F., & E. W. Egan. *Kings, Rulers & Statesmen*. New York, Sterling Publishing Co., Inc., 1967.

Woodward, John R. *The Heritage of Stokes County, North Carolina*. German-ton, North Carolina, Stokes County Historical Society, 1981.

Work Projects Administration. *Charlotte: A Guide to the Queen City of North Carolina*. News Printing House, 1939.

Work Projects Administration. *How They Began: The Story of North Carolina County, Town and Other Place Names*. New York, Harian Publications, 1941.

Work Projects Administration. *Raleigh: Capital of North Carolina*. New Bern, North Carolina, Owen G. Dunn Co., 1942.

Wright, Marilyn. *Sketch Book of Scotland County*.

Wright, Muriel H. *A Guide to the Indian Tribes of Oklahoma*. Norman, University of Oklahoma Press, 1951.

Wright, Stuart T. *Historical Sketch of Person County*. Danville, Womack Press, 1974.

Yenne, Bill. *The Encyclopedia of North American Indian Tribes*. New York, Crescent Books, 1986.

North Dakota

(53 counties)

1955 *Adams County*

John Q. Adams (1848–1919)— This county lies in the southwestern section of North Dakota, where the Chicago, Milwaukee & St. Paul Railroad extended its main line toward the Pacific coast during 1906 and 1907. Railroads were, of course, vital to the development of North Dakota in linking its potentially vast agricultural output with distant markets. In addition to agricultural products, the area that is now Adams County, North Dakota, had extensive coal available to be mined once railroad transportation was provided to the area. This county was created in April, 1907 and its name reflects the importance of railroads to North Dakota. John Quincy Adams (1848–1919) had come to North Dakota from Spencer, Iowa, and he was general land and town site agent for the Chicago, Milwaukee & St. Paul Railroad. This county was named in his honor in recognition of the importance of the railroad here. Adams County's growth and prosperity began when the Chicago, Milwaukee & St. Paul Railroad decided to run its Puget Sound extension through the southwestern area of North Dakota.

1956 *Barnes County*

Alanson H. Barnes (1818–1890)— In works dealing with the history, geography and place names of North Dakota and Dakota territory, A. H. Barnes' given name is rendered in some accounts as Alanson and in others as Alphonso. Most sources duck the issue by presenting his name as A. H. Barnes. By whatever name, our hero was an important figure in the history of Dakota territory and this county's name (now Barnes, previously Burbank) has an interesting story behind it. Barnes was one of the justices of the supreme court of Dakota territory. In that capacity, he was a representative of the federal government and Judge Barnes served the federal government as an associate justice of the supreme court of Dakota territory from 1873 to 1881. When this county was created, it was named Burbank County, in honor of John A. Burbank (1827–1905), who was then the governor of Dakota territory. During much of Burbank's term as governor, political fighting was unusually bitter as were sectional brawls, which often originated within the ranks of the governor's own political party. The matter which triggered this county's name to be changed involved railroads and the scheme to finance one. It seems that Governor Burbank planned to have a railroad built which was to be funded, in part, by taxing each county through which the new railroad would pass. Governor Burbank asked Judge A. H. Barnes to approve this scheme and Judge Barnes refused to do so. Governor Burbank threatened to banish Judge Barnes to Pembina at the Canadian border. Ignoring this threat, Judge Barnes rode by horseback to the nearest train station and thence by railroad to our nation's capitol to inform the president of Governor Burbank's plan. Governor Burbank was removed from office and this county's name was changed from Burbank County to Barnes County by the legislature of Dakota territory. The literature on this subject specifically states that the county's name was changed "to punish" Governor Burbank and to honor the "incorruptible" Judge Barnes. Apparently Governor Burbank had the last laugh from all of this. He was a wealthy man when returned to Richmond, Indiana. The wealth had come primarily from railroad and town site selection schemes in which he had been involved.

1957 *Benson County*

Bertil W. Benson (–)— Benson was a Scandinavian who came to Dakota territory from Rushford, Minnesota. Benson's primary association with Dakota territory was as a land agent for the Northern Pacific Railroad. However, he also was a merchant in Valley City and served in the Dakota territorial legislature. Benson was a member of that body in 1883, which is the year that Benson County was created and named in his honor. One source states that he was a banker in Valley City. It is known that Benson was a resident of Valley City, North Dakota, at the time that he moved west to settle in Washington about 1890. Bertil W. Benson was a resident of the community of Bellingham, in the state of Washington, in August, 1907.

1958 *Billings County*

Frederick Billings (1823–1890)— A native of Vermont, Billings graduated from the University of Vermont in 1844, moved to California in 1849 and made a fortune during the gold rush era. Billings gained his entree by opening a law office in San Francisco, which grew to be the leading San Francisco law firm of the time. Billings was one of the original partners of the Northern Pacific Railroad and his fortune grew as his participated in the enormous profits of the railroad industry during the last half of the 19th century. At the Northern Pacific, Billings organized the railroad's land department. He became president of the Northern Pacific in 1879 and secured financing which permitted the railroad to extend its tracks from Dakota territory to the Columbia River on the Pacific coast. The state railway commissioner of Minnesota estimated that Billings was responsible for doubling the acreage devoted to wheat production. Billings established a system of grain elevators from Duluth, in northeastern Minnesota to points west. Although he was largely responsible for the successful completion of the Northern Pacific's tracks from the Great Lakes to the West Coast in 1883, he was not present to see the final ceremonial spike driven because he had lost control of the railroad in a hostile takeover. This county was created and named in Frederick Billings' honor on February 10, 1879, by the legislature of Dakota territory. At that time the Northern Pacific Railroad owned extensive lands in Dakota territory and Billings' activities had led to the growth of Dakota territory's population, wheat production, and prosperity.

1959 *Bottineau County*

Pierre Bottineau (–1895)— In works dealing with the history, geography and place names of North Dakota and Dakota territory, Bottineau's place of birth is given by some as within what is now North Dakota and by others as Minnesota. The year of his birth is also uncertain and the range of possibilities is wide. Some sources list 1810, others 1814 and still others 1817. Pierre Bottineau's father was French while his mother was a Chippewa Indian. Pierre Bottineau became a scout, guide, translator and fur trader, with headquarters initially in Canada. In the winter of 1836 or 1837, Bottineau and three companions undertook a 26 day journey to Fort Snelling. Much of the journey was by snowshoe and two of Bottineau's fellow-travelers died on the trip. Bottineau settled in what today is St. Paul, Minnesota. There Bottineau acquired land by squatter's right and entered the real estate business. His success with real estate made him a prosperous and influential man. In the mid-1850's Bottineau was operating near the present Fargo, North Dakota. Although Bottineau was half Indian, and had a wife of French-Indian ancestry, From the 1850's through the 1860's Bottineau allied himself with Americans in various confrontations with Indians. He helped arrange Indian treaties, accompanied an expedition to arrest some Chippewa Indians accused of murder, and acted as a guide in assisting the U.S. army in finding sites for their military establishments. In 1863 he assisted the U.S. army in military actions against the Sioux Indians. These activities, of course, endeared Bottineau to the White American givers of county names and the legislature of Dakota territory created and named this county in his honor on January 4, 1873. The county seat of Bottineau County is also named Bottineau but Bottineau County was named for Pierre Bottineau and not for the community that is its county seat. We know this because Bottineau County was created in 1873 and the community of Bottineau did not receive its present name until 1884. Prior to that this community was named Oak Creek. In 1869 Pierre Bottineau guided a survey party on a long and arduous search for a railroad route. In 1876 he retired to a farm outside Red Lake Falls, Minnesota. Pierre Bottineau died on July 26, 1895.

1960 *Bowman County*

Edward M. Bowman (–)— Bowman was an attorney in Saint Louis, Missouri, who immigrated to Dakota territory in the early 1880's. Here he was active in promoting the town site of Minnesela, in what is now South Dakota. Minnesela became the first county seat of Butte County, in what is now South Dakota, but when the county seat was moved to Belle Fourche, the town of Minnesela folded. This county was created on March 8, 1883, by the legislature of Dakota territory. At that time Edward M. Bowman was a member of Dakota territory's legislature. The 1927 edition of the *South Dakota Legislative Manual* lists Bowman as a member of the lower house of the legislature of Dakota territory from Minnesela. When the town of Minnesela folded. Bowman left the area and is presumed to have returned to Saint Louis to resume his law practice. The county seat of Bowman County is also named Bowman but Bowman County was named directly for Edward M. Bowman and not for the community that is its county seat. We know this because Bowman County was created in 1883 and the community now named Bowman was first called Twin Buttes and later renamed Lowden. Its third name was Eden. Finally, on January 1, 1908, the community was given its present name, Bowman.

1961 *Burke County*

John Burke (1859–1937)— A native of Iowa and a graduate of the University of Iowa, Burke moved to North Dakota about the time that Dakota territory was divided into two states, North and South Dakota. Burke served in both houses of North Dakota's state legislature. He was a member of the Democratic party and when he won the 1906 gubernatorial election, he became the young state's first Democratic governor. John Burke was re-elected as North Dakota's governor in 1908 and 1910 and he served as the state's governor from January 9, 1907, to January 8, 1913. President Woodrow Wilson appointed John Burke to be treasurer of the United States and he later was elected to North Dakota's supreme court. John Burke served on that court as both an associate justice and as chief justice. He was serving as an associate justice at the time of his death on May 14, 1937. There was an earlier governor of the state of North Dakota named Burke, whose name was Andrew H. Burke. He served as the state's second governor from 1891 to 1892. However, all sources consulted are agreed that John Burke (1859–1937) was this county's namesake. The county was created in July, 1910, while John Burke was serving as governor.

1962 *Burleigh County*

Walter A. Burleigh (1820–1896)— Walter Atwood Burleigh was born in Waterville, Maine on October 25, 1820. He studied medicine and practiced that profession for a time in both Maine and Pennsylvania. During this period of his life Dr. Burleigh also studied law. He accepted an appointment by the federal government to become an Indian agent of the Yankton Sioux Indians and came to Greenwood in Dakota territory. He was there in 1863 when Indian-American hostilities threatened to overrun the territory. From 1865 to 1869 Dr. Burleigh was Dakota territory's delegate to the U.S. Congress. He subsequently served in the legislature of Dakota territory and engaged in railroad contracting work for the Northern Pacific Railroad here. In 1879 Burleigh moved west to Montana territory, where he practiced law and engaged in politics. In 1893 he returned to the Dakotas, this time settling in South Dakota, and he was a member of South Dakota's state senate. This county was created on January 4, 1873, while Dakota was still a territory. Walter A. Burleigh was not a member of the territorial legislature during the legislative session that created this county but he was president of the upper house of the 12th session of the legislature, which convened on January 12, 1877.

1963 *Cass County*

George W. Cass (1810–1888)— A native of Ohio and an 1832 graduate of the U.S. Military Academy at West Point, Cass served as an engineer with the army's topographical engineers. During the period from 1832 to 1836, he assisted in building the Cumberland Road, the early national paved highway which linked the country from the East, at Cumberland, Maryland, to the West, at Vandalia, Illinois. Cass resigned his army commission to enter business and one of his early ventures was a steamboat line on the Monongahela River. He later was the founder and president of the Adams Express Company and was president of two railroads. One of these railroads was the Northern Pacific and it was because of his association with that railroad that this county was created and named in his honor by the legislature of Dakota territory. Railroads were, of course, vital to the development of Dakota territory in linking its potentially vast agricultural output with distant markets. In 1872 the Northern Pacific line was completed into Dakota territory and on January 4, 1873, this county in Dakota territory was created and named in honor of George W. Cass. By the fall of 1873 the Northern Pacific line extended from Duluth, Minnesota, to Bismarck, Dakota territory.

1964 *Cavalier County*

Charles T. Cavileer (1818–1902)— Charles T. Cavileer was born in Springfield, Ohio, on March 6, 1818. There is confusion concerning the correct spelling of his surname. Virtually all sources on the history, geography and place names of North Dakota spell it Cavalier, the same as the spelling of the county's name. However, a biographical sketch of this county's namesake which appeared in volume 12 of *North Dakota History*, published by the State Historical Society of North Dakota in 1945, renders his name as "Charles Turner Cavileer." Cavileer lived for a time in Illinois and then moved on to Saint Louis where he ascended the Mississippi River, by steamboat, to what is now St. Paul, Minnesota. He arrived in St. Paul in May, 1841. The following year he explored further north, and traversed the Minnesota wilderness to the vicinity of today's city of Duluth. After returning to St. Paul, Cavileer opened that community's first harness shop. (During his residence in Illinois, Cavileer had learned the saddler's trade.) He later operated a drug store at St. Paul and in 1849 Cavileer was appointed by Minnesota's territorial governor, Alexander Ramsey (1815–1903) to be the territorial librarian. President Millard Fillmore appointed Cavileer collector of customs for the district of Minnesota and inspector of revenue for the post at Pembina. Cavileer arrived at Pembina in 1851 and in addition to performing his customs chores, he established an agricultural colony here. Cavileer assessed customs duties on furs entering the United States from Canada. Since these furs were in competition with furs traded by Norman W. Kittson (1814–1888), the customs duties gave Kittson a competitive advantage and Cavileer and Kittson were soon in business together, trading furs, at Pembina. Charles T. Cavileer crossed the Red River on August 16, 1851, and remained in the Red River Valley of what is now North Dakota until his death, half a century later, on July 27, 1902. He performed customs work at Pembina from 1851 to 1855 and then operated stores at Walhalla and Fort Garry. In 1864 he was appointed postmaster at Pembina and he was postmaster there for some 20 years. He also served as Pembina's mayor for several terms. Many sources say that Cavileer was the first, or one of the first, permanent White settlers of what is now the state of North Dakota. W. B. Hennessy's *History of North Dakota*, published in 1910, states that Cavalier (sic) "was believed to have been the first white settler to take up a permanent residence in what is now known as North Dakota." This county was created and named in his honor by the legislature of Dakota territory on January 4, 1873.

1965 *Dickey County*

George H. Dickey (1858–1923)— George H. Dickey was an attorney in Valley City, Dakota territory. He represented Barnes County in the lower house of Dakota's territorial legislature in the session which convened on January 11, 1881. It was during that legislative session that Dakota's territorial legislators created and named this county for one of their members, George H. Dickey (1858–1923). Many, if not most, of the sources consulted, which deal with the history, geography and place names of North Dakota, incorrectly attribute this county's name to Alfred Dickey, of Jamestown. A letter to the author dated August 29, 1988, from Frank E. Vyzralek of Great Plains Research in Bismarck, North Dakota supplied interesting background on the origin of this county's name. Vyzralek spent at least 25 years collecting information on North Dakota place names and he furnished the following remarks concerning Dickey County: "Dickey County was not, repeat, not named for Alfred Dickey of Jamestown who in 1881 was a relatively obscure land dealer. The latter attribution appeared after the Jamestown Dickey served as the state's first elected Lieutenant Governor and continued, perhaps due to misplaced sympathy, after he died prematurely in 1899."

1966 *Divide County*

The vote to divide Williams County into two counties— At the general election in November, 1910, the voters of Williams County, North Dakota approved a proposal to divide that county into two counties. At that time Williams County was in the northwestern corner of the state. Thus Divide County's name derived from the voters' decision to divide one county into two. Divide County was officially separated from Williams County in December, 1910, with Divide County taking the northern portion of the former Williams County and Williams County retaining the southern portion. It is now Divide County that occupies North Dakota's northwestern corner. Some sources suggest that the county was named because of mountains which divide the county. There is no truth to this. There are no mountains in Divide County. Other sources suggest that the county was named for the Continental Divide but that contention is also false. The Continental Divide lies some 300 miles west of North Dakota.

1967 *Dunn County*

John P. Dunn (1839–1917)— John Piatt Dunn established a homestead within the present town site of Bismarck, North Dakota, about 1872. He opened a drug store in Bismarck, Dakota territory, which was the first drug store in what is now North Dakota. Dunn operated that store for a number of years and also served as mayor of Bismarck. This county was created on March 9, 1883, while Dakota was still a territory. The new county's name was suggested by Erastus A. Williams (1850–1930), a powerful figure in Dakota politics, who was speaker of the house in the territorial legislature which convened on January 9, 1883. Williams represented Bismarck and Burleigh County in that legislature. This county was named for John P. Dunn (1839–1917), and not for either Dunn or Dunn Center. Dunn Center is a municipality within Dunn County, but it was established after Dunn County was created and, in fact, was named for the county. Dunn was a post office located near the Dunn-Mercer County line. This post office was also born after Dunn County was created. It was established June 2, 1909, and discontinued on January 15, 1914.

1968 *Eddy County*

Ezra B. Eddy (1829–1885)— Ezra B. Eddy was born in Ohio on December 14, 1829. He moved to the northwestern frontier area of Minnesota territory in 1855 and erected a building on government land, at what is now Plainview, in southeastern Minnesota, and operated a farm there. At the outbreak of the Civil War, Eddy enlisted as a first lieutenant in a Minnesota volunteer infantry company. After about two years of military service he was forced to resign because of failing health. Eddy resumed farming in Minnesota but in 1865 he lost a hand in a threshing machine accident and the resulting disability forced him to change his vocation. In the Plainview, Minnesota, area Eddy engaged in hardware, insurance and banking businesses and founded the Plainview Bank, the first bank in Wabasha County, Minnesota. In 1878 Eddy founded the First National Bank of Fargo in Dakota territory and in 1879 he disposed of his interests in Minnesota and moved to Fargo. Here Eddy was president of Fargo's First National Bank until his death in 1885 and he was active in developing the portion of the Red River Valley near Fargo. Ezra B. Eddy and one of his three sons, Ernest C. Eddy (1856–), founded the Fargo Loan Agency, with a firm name of E. B. Eddy & Son. In 1879 Ezra B. Eddy also platted an addition to the city of Fargo known as the Eddy & Fu'ler outlots. Some of Eddy's business enterprises were unsuccessful, and some of the loans he made turned sour but his endeavors served to build the city of Fargo into one of the thriving cities on our country's northwestern frontier. The 16th legislature of Dakota territory convened in Bismarck on January 13, 1885. It was during this session of the legislature that Eddy County was created and named in honor of Ezra B. Eddy, who had recently died.

1969 *Emmons County*

James A. Emmons (1845–1919)— Emmons was a steamboat operator and an early Bismarck pioneer, merchant and entrepreneur. At one time he was the post trader at Camp Hancock, at Bismarck. W. B. Hennessy's *History of North Dakota*, published in 1910, states that Emmons "…afterwards moved to Oklahoma territory, where he took a leading part in the early development of that country." This county was created on February 10, 1879, by the legislature of Dakota territory.

1970 *Foster County*

James S. Foster (1828–1890)— A native of Salisbury, Connecticut, Foster moved with his parents to New York state. There he taught school for several years before emigrating to Dakota territory in the spring of 1864. Foster lead a party consisting of about one hundred families in this 1864 emigration to Dakota. Upon their arrival here, he was the head of the colony that they established. Foster became Dakota territory's first superintendent of public instruction. Later, for a period of about ten years, he was the commissioner of immigration for Dakota territory. Through his efforts several colonies were planted here, one of which was a Mennonite colony. Foster's activities in Dakota territory were within what is today the state of South Dakota, and particularly in the southeastern section of South Dakota, at Yankton and Mitchell. He entered into newspaper work in Yankton and was editor and proprietor of the *Yankton Union* and *Dakotian*. In 1880 he moved to Mitchell and engaged in real estate business there. On September 30, 1890, Foster was accidentally killed by the discharge from a gun, which he was removing from a buggy. By then Dakota territory had been split into two states, which were admitted to the Union in 1889. However, this county was created and named in Foster's honor on January 4, 1873, while Dakota was still a territory. Several sources on the history, geography and place names of North Dakota, South Dakota and Dakota territory state that James S. Foster was a territorial legislator. This appears to be an incorrect statement for two reasons: (1) the rather complete biographical sketch of James S. Foster (1828–1890) which appeared in the 1902 issue (volume 1) of *South Dakota Historical Collections*, mentions no legislative involvement for James S. Foster and (2) the alphabetical listing of all members of the legislature of Dakota territory contained in the 1950 (volume 25) issue of *South Dakota Historical Collections* lists just one Foster and his name is Everett W. Foster. Everett W. Foster was a member of the upper house (council) of the Dakota territorial legislature which convened on January 11, 1887. He represented Spink County.

1971 *Golden Valley County*

Golden Valley Land & Cattle Company of St. Paul, Minnesota— This county in far western North Dakota was created by the state legislature on November 19, 1912. Its name was taken from the name of a St. Paul, Minnesota, firm, whose Golden Valley Land & Cattle Company was a major land owner here. In 1941, the federal government's Work Projects Administration published an *Inventory of the County Archives of North Dakota* for Golden Valley County. That publication explains how the St. Paul firm decided upon the name for their land company here in western North Dakota: "In the autumn of 1902 a group of men were inspecting … with a view to organizing a land company. While on their tour of inspection, they drove [sic] to the top of a small butte from which they obtained an excellent view of the valley. They were so impressed with the golden hue of the sun-cured grasses that they called the area 'Golden Valley.'" There is also a municipality named Goldenvalley (one word) in Mercer County, North Dakota. This community is about 75 miles east of Golden Valley County and is separated from it by both Dunn County and Billings County. Hence there appears to be no relationship between that community's name and this county's name. The community of Goldenvalley acquired its name from George V. Bratzell's store and post office in Mercer County. George V. Bratzell's store was in a locality named Olanta, North Dakota. When he established a post office at his store on May 11, 1909, he named it Goldenvalley (one word). Bratzell moved his store and post office to a town site with railroad service in 1914. The townspeople there adopted the name of Bratzell's post office for their town. This town of Goldenvalley is very likely the same town as the one where the Northern Pacific Railroad has a station named Golden Valley. The Golden Valley railroad station was on the Oberon branch of the Fargo division of the Northern Pacific Railroad. A 1944 list of Fargo division stations issued by the Northern Pacific Railway Company mentions this Golden Valley station and states that its "…name was suggested by the rich valley lands, so well adapted to the growth of golden grain." Thus it appears that the initial inspiration (golden grains and grasses) for the name of Golden Valley County may have been similar to the inspiration for the Northern Pacific's station in Mercer County, North Dakota, but the county was named for the St. Paul, Minnesota, land company and not for Mercer County, North Dakota's community or railroad station.

1972 *Grand Forks County*

The village of Grand Forks, Dakota territory— The settlement here at the Grand Forks, where the waters of two rivers unite, had been known for centuries to the Indians and then to French explorers and fur traders. The French called it *Grandes Fourches*, or the singular *Grand Fourche* and used the location as a depot or outpost for about a century before American settlers started arriving in the mid 1860's. The present English (and plural) version of the name was suggested to the U.S. Post Office department by Sanford C. Cady, who became its first postmaster on June 15, 1870. At that time the village had only 30 inhabitants. The settlement, and later village, here were named for the forks formed by the junction of the Red Lake River with the Red River. The forks produced when the Red Lake River empties its waters into the Red River is so impressive (or grand) that it was well known by its French name long before the arrival of Americans. Warren Upham supplied a translation of the

Indians' name for these forks in his work entitled *Minnesota Geographic Names*. Upham stated that the Indians called it "the big forks, that is, where the rivers are so large in either fork that you don't know which to go into." The village of Grand Forks, about 75 miles north of Fargo, faces Minnesota on the other side of the Red River. With a population, in the late 1990's of 49,000, Grand Forks serves as an agricultural processing center for wheat, potatoes and sugar beets. The state's oldest and largest institution of higher learning, the University of North Dakota, is located here. Grand Forks County was created on January 4, 1873, by the legislature of Dakota territory and named for the village of Grand Forks, which became its county seat.

1973 *Grant County*

Ulysses S. Grant (1822–1885)— Grant was a native of Ohio who graduated from the U.S. Military Academy at West Point. He served with distinction in the Mexican War, and in the Civil War he rose to become commander of all Union forces. After the Civil War, Grant briefly served as acting secretary of war and then two terms as president of the United States. He proved to be a rather mediocre president. This county was created in November, 1916. A large number of the counties in both North Dakota and South Dakota were created while Dakota was still a territory. One result of this chronology is that North Dakota and South Dakota have just one county, Grant County, that uses the same name. South Dakota's Grant County was also named for Ulysses S. Grant (1822–1885).

1974 *Griggs County*

Alexander Griggs (1838–1903)— Griggs was born in Marietta, Ohio, in October, 1838, and moved with his parents to St. Paul, in Minnesota territory when he was still a boy. There the Mississippi River was nearby and he learned how to operate steamboats on the mighty Mississippi. By the age of 20, Griggs was given command of a steamboat. He continued his steamboat activities on the Mississippi River until 1870 when he immigrated to the Red River on the western border of Minnesota and the eastern border of Dakota territory. In that year the transportation tycoon James J. Hill (1838–1916) commissioned Griggs to build the steamboat, *Selkirk*, from timber to be cut at Otter Tail River, the headwaters of the Red River.

The *Selkirk* venture was a success. Griggs entered into a partnership with James J. Hill and Norman W. Kittson (1814–1888) and for a decade their firm enjoyed a near monopoly of the steamboat traffic on the Red River. During this period Alexander Griggs was captain of one or more of the firm's steamboats. Griggs became a founder of the present city of Grand Forks, North Dakota, and eventually came to own a nice, two story, frame residence in Grand Forks. Alexander Griggs continued to ply the Red River by steamboat between Grand Forks, Dakota territory, and Winnipeg, Canada, until 1890. In the Grand Forks area Griggs became active in banking, a gas works and a roller mill firm. He was a member of the North Dakota constitutional convention held in Bismarck, in the summer of 1889 and after North Dakota's admission to statehood, Griggs served as the state's railroad commissioner. He served Grand Forks as both its mayor and postmaster. In December, 1892 Griggs left North Dakota on account of failing health and moved west, settling on the upper Columbia River. There he established boat service for both freight and passenger traffic. He died on January 25, 1903. This county was created and named in Alexander Griggs' honor by the legislature of Dakota territory on February 18, 1881.

1975 *Hettinger County*

Mathias Hettinger (1810–1890)— Mathias Hettinger came to America from Alsace, in Europe and worked his way from our eastern states to Stephenson County, Illinois. He settled there in 1842 and soon was forced to put a local bully in his place. The bully was William "Tutty" Baker (1793–1855) and Hettinger bested him in a potential knife fight. The moral victory over this bully made Mathias Hettinger a hero to the area's German immigrants. Hettinger started the first wagon shop in Stephenson County, Illinois, and it was located in Freeport. He also started the Yellow Creek Brewery in 1845 on the road between Freeport and Rockford, Illinois, in partnership with John Hettinger, presumably a relative of Mathias Hettinger's. Mathias Hettinger also became active in banking and insurance in Freeport, Illinois. Although his bank initially had a more formal name, which included the name Hettinger, it was universally referred to as "the German bank." In 1894, after Hettinger's death, the bank was reincorporated as an Illinois state bank, and was actually named the German Bank. This North Dakota county was created on

March 9, 1883, while Dakota was still a territory. The new county's name was suggested by Erastus A. Williams (1850–1930), a powerful figure in Dakota politics, who was speaker of the house in the territorial legislature, which convened on January 9, 1883. On February 19, 1882, Erastus A. Williams had married Jennie E. Hettinger (–1894), a daughter of Mathias Hettinger. In a romantic gesture, Erastus A. Williams used his political power as speaker of Dakota's territorial legislature, to cause one of the territory's counties to be named for his bride's father. Mr. and Mrs. Williams were united in marriage at Freeport, Illinois, and they were the parents of five children. Of course, all five of these children were grandchildren of the man for whom this North Dakota county was named.

1976 *Kidder County*

Jefferson P. Kidder (–1883)—Sources consulted differ on the year of Kidder's birth. Possibilities mentioned are 1815, 1816 and 1818. Jefferson Parrish Kidder was born in Vermont, studied law and was admitted to Vermont's bar. He held a number of important political positions in Vermont before emigrating to our nation's western frontier. In Vermont Kidder was a member of the state's constitutional convention, state's attorney, state senator and lieutenant-governor. In 1857 he moved to St. Paul, in Minnesota territory. Kidder remained at St. Paul until 1865 and was three times elected to Minnesota's legislature. In February, 1865, President Abraham Lincoln appointed Kidder to be an associate justice on the supreme court of Dakota territory and he sat on that bench from 1865 to 1875. In 1874 Kidder was elected to represent Dakota territory as a delegate to the U.S. Congress. Reelected in 1876, he represented the territory as a congressional delegate from March 4, 1875, until March 3, 1879. In 1879 Kidder was once again appointed an associate justice of Dakota territory and he served on that court until his death in 1883. This county was created and named in honor of Jefferson P. Kidder on January 4, 1873, while he was a member of the supreme court of Dakota territory.

1977 *La Moure County*

Judson La Moure (1839–1918)—La Moure was born on March 27, 1839, in Canada, in what is now the province of Quebec. At the age of 20 he immigrated to the western frontier of the United States and ar-

rived at Davenport, Iowa, in 1859. Soon after his arrival at Davenport, La Moure participated in the Pike's Peak gold rush. He came to what would soon be Dakota territory in the fall of 1860, and thus was already a settler here when Dakota territory was created on March 2, 1861. For a number of years after his arrival here he was engaged in the transportation activities of H. D. Booge (or Vooge) & Company. In 1865 La Moure was appointed as a sub-agent to the Indians in what is now northwestern North Dakota at the junction of the White Earth River with the Missouri River. Clement A. Lounsberry's *Early History of North Dakota*, published in 1919, states that La Moure was elected to the legislature of Dakota territory in 1866 but refused to take his seat. In 1870 La Moure ended his involvement with the Indians and began farming in Pembina County, Dakota territory. Starting in 1872, Judson La Moure served four terms in Dakota's territorial legislature. He served in the lower house in the sessions which began in 1872 and 1881 and in the upper house (council) in the sessions which began in 1877 and 1885. It was during the first of these four legislative sessions, which convened on December 2, 1872, that La Moure County, Dakota territory was created and named in his honor by his fellow territorial legislators. The date given for this county's creation is January 4, 1873. In 1878 La Moure went into the mercantile business in Pembina and continued to earn his living as a merchant in Pembina, North Dakota while serving in the state senate. La Moure served continuously as a state senator from the time that North Dakota was admitted to statehood until his retirement from politics at the close of the 12th state legislature. He died in Florida on March 16, 1918. This county was named directly for Judson La Moure, and not for the municipality of La Moure, which is the county seat of La Moure County. The municipality was named for the county. It was platted and named in October, 1882.

1978 *Logan County*

John A. Logan (1826–1886)—A native of Illinois, Logan served in the Illinois legislature and represented that state in the U.S. Congress in both the house and senate. Having served in the Mexican War as a lieutenant, Logan entered the Civil War as a colonel in the Union army and rose to the rank of major-general. In 1884 he ran for vice president on the Republican ticket headed by James G. Blaine. Logan long associated himself with matters of

veterans' relief and he conceived the idea of Memorial Day which he inaugurated on May 30, 1868. This county was created by the legislature of Dakota territory on January 4, 1873.

1979 *McHenry County*

James McHenry (–)—McHenry was an early resident of Vermillion in the present state of South Dakota. He established Vermillion's first store, and in his house Dr. Caulkins taught the first school held in a civilian settlement in what is now South Dakota; an appropriate milestone for Vermillion since the state's leading educational institution, the University of South Dakota, is now located here. McHenry represented Vermillion and Clay County in the lower house of Dakota's territorial legislature which convened in December, 1865, and he was the postmaster at Vermillion from 1867 to 1869. This county was created by Dakota territory on January 4, 1873.

1980 *McIntosh County*

Edward H. McIntosh (–1901)—Edward H. McIntosh was born in 1822 or 1823. Most biographical sketches issued during his lifetime use 1823 but his tombstone shows a birth year of 1822. McIntosh was one of 12 members of the upper house (council) of Dakota's territorial legislature just once, and that was during the session that convened on January 9, 1883. It was during that session of the legislature that McIntosh County, Dakota territory was created and named in his honor. The date given for this county's creation is March 9, 1883. Edward H. McIntosh died in Iowa in 1901. There is an interesting tale behind the selection of this county's name. During this 1883 session of the territorial legislature, Erastus A. Williams (1850–1930) was speaker of the lower house. Williams had introduced bills to create a number of new counties and his bills had passed in the house but were tied up in the council. When Erastus A. Williams asked a member of the council, John R. Jackson, of Valley Springs, about the delay, Jackson explained to Speaker Williams that "I don't want you to say anything, but McIntosh, chairman of the committee on counties, feels that there should be a county named for him." Speaker Williams asked "Is that all?" and when Jackson replied that this was the only roadblock, Speaker Williams said "That will be all right. Divide Logan County in the middle and name the south half for McIntosh. Nice old man, McIntosh, probably from Aurora County." This bit of colorful history was captured for us by Nina F. Wishek in her work entitled *Along the Trails of Yesterday: A Story of McIntosh County*, published in 1941. Wishek indicated that Erastus A. Williams (1850–1930) furnished this history to the state historical library on his last visit to the capital, just two weeks before his death.

1981 *McKenzie County*

Alexander McKenzie (1851–1922)— McKenzie came to Dakota territory in 1867, while still a youth, and served as leader of a construction gang for the Northern Pacific Railroad. In 1872 he was in charge of laying tracks west from Fargo, Dakota territory, and when the tracks reached Bismarck in 1873, McKenzie left the railroad and settled in Bismarck. Here he engaged in the manufacture and sale of carbonated beverages and became a popular local figure. Following the death of Burleigh County's sheriff, McKenzie was appointed to take over the vacancy. He was officially elected in 1876 as the county sheriff and reelected several times, serving as the county sheriff at Bismarck, Dakota territory, for about a decade. While serving as sheriff he also held the position of deputy U.S. marshal. West of Bismarck there was no civilization and Alexander McKenzie was the kind of county sheriff featured in motion pictures about the Wild West. He also was a powerful force in the politics of Dakota territory. The capital of the territory was initially established at Yankton, in what is now southern South Dakota. Alexander McKenzie desired that the territorial capital should be moved to his town of Bismarck. Having survived rough encounters with both Indians and outlaws, McKenzie thought nothing of taking on the establishment to get the territorial capital moved. A commission of nine men was authorized to select a new city to be Dakota territory's capital. This commission was to meet in Yankton but Yankton citizens announced that no commission that intended to take away her capital would get into Yankton to convene. To Alexander McKenzie, who was a member of the commission, this sentiment was only a minor inconvenience. McKenzie arranged with the Milwaukee Railroad to have a special train prepared to meet the commission's needs. The commission members boarded at Sioux City, traveled to Yankton and then held their meeting on the railroad car but within Yankton, as required by their charter. The commission subsequently visited several cities before

adopting Alexander McKenzie's choice, Bismarck as the new capital of Dakota territory. Clement A. Lounsberry's *Early History of North Dakota*, published in 1919 stated that McKenzie was "the most prominent and influential citizen of North Dakota in the construction period of its existence." Merle Potter's article entitled "The North Dakota Capital Fight," in the October, 1932, issue of *North Dakota Historical Quarterly*, implies that McKenzie's motive in moving the territorial capital to Bismarck was profit for himself, in real estate. Since McKenzie owned real estate in Bismarck, it would seem logical that he would profit by a relocation of the territorial capitol to his city. However, Clement A. Lounsberry's work, cited above, states "Whatever may be said of him, it must be said that he has never used his political powers for his own advantage either financially or politically." He was political boss of northern Dakota territory during the last decade of its existence and continued in that role for a year after North Dakota became a state. McKenzie later moved to Alaska. This county was originally created by Dakota territory in 1883. It was abolished in 1891 due to lack of settlement but recreated by the state in 1905.

1982 *McLean County*

John A. McLean (1849–1916)— A native of Canada, John A. McLean came to the United States when he was still a young man. He became a contractor supplying railroad ties and other material to the Northern Pacific Railroad west from Duluth, Minnesota. In Bismarck, Dakota territory, he was a merchant in the firm of McLean and Macnider, general merchants and contractors. A prominent citizen of Bismarck during territorial days, McLean served as one of that city's early mayors. In 1874 Colonel George A. Custer (1839–1876), reported the discovery of gold on land in the Black Hills of western Dakota territory. The gold was located on land previously (1868) reserved by treaty for the Indians. The Indians had been assigned this land on the assumption that is was worthless. Since that assumption was now known to be false, White Americans demanded that the Indians be prevented from interfering with their gold rush to the Black Hills. John A. McLean was a member of the party that visited President Ulysses S. Grant in Washington, D.C., and convinced the president to order a halt to interference with miners then in the Black Hills or en route there. McLean was involved in establishing the Northwestern

Stage & Transportation Company, which established a daily line of stage coaches and other transportation from Bismarck to the Black Hills. In her work entitled *Pioneer Days of Washburn, North Dakota & Vicinity*, Mary Ann Barnes Williams states that this county's name honors John A. McLean and Ms. Williams supplies a rather detailed version of how the county's name was chosen. According to Ms. Williams, a gentleman named Erastus A. Williams (1850–1930) was serving as speaker of the house of Dakota's territorial legislature when he received a letter from John Satterlund, in which Satterlund "expressed his wish that the county be named McLean, in honor of Honorable or Sir John A. McLean, then a very prominent and influential Scotsman, of Burleigh County, but who had large land holdings near Hancock. Mr. Satterlund, ever the politician, wanted his support from that portion of the territory." According to Ms. Mary Ann Barnes Williams, this letter to Speaker Erastus A. Williams was accompanied by a check for $250.00. Erastus A. Williams, expressed the view that the county should really be named for Mr. Satterlund, but that if he wanted it named for John A. McLean, it would be so named. This county was created by the legislature of Dakota territory on March 8, 1883, while John A. McLean was mayor of Bismarck and while Erastus A. Williams (1850–1930) was serving as speaker of the house of Dakota's territorial legislature. In fairness to Erastus A. Williams (1850–1930), it should be pointed out that the speaker of the territorial house no doubt felt that the choice of a name for a county in Dakota territory was merely an administrative detail. Erastus A. Williams personally chose the names of several of Dakota territory's counties.

1983 *Mercer County*

William H. H. Mercer (1844–1901)— A native of Pennsylvania, William Henry Harrison Mercer was a Civil War veteran when he settled at Painted Woods, on the Missouri River in 1869. During that year he built the first residence in what is now Burleigh County, North Dakota. It was constructed from logs. Mercer was a farmer and rancher in the present Burleigh County. During the 1880's he lived for a time on his Coteax ranch near the present site of the municipality of Mercer. William H. H. Mercer was a member of the first board of county commissioners of Burleigh County. Mercer County was created and named in honor of William H. H. Mercer by the legislature of Dakota territory on January 14, 1875. The county was named directly for Mr. Mercer. The county was not named for any of the several Mercer and Mercer City localities (municipalities, township, post offices and railroad station) in this vicinity. All of these were named after Mercer County had been created. Mary Ann Barnes Williams' work entitled *Origins of North Dakota Place Names* states that William H. H. Mercer was a close friend of Erastus A. Williams (1850–1930), a territorial legislator "who named Mercer County in his honor." During the session of the Dakota territorial legislature which created this county, Erastus A. Williams (1850–1930) was a member of the upper house (council) representing Burleigh County. William H. H. Mercer was of German ancestry and his surname was Musser, until it was changed to Mercer. Mr. Mercer died in August, 1901.

1984 *Morton County*

Oliver H. P. T. Morton (1823–1877)— There is some confusion regarding the rendering of Morton's surname. Originally the family name was Throckmorton but Oliver's father shortened the name to Morton. Oliver H. P. T. Morton resumed the use of Throck, but only as a fourth given name. Oliver Morton was a native of Indiana who attended Miami University in Oxford, Ohio, studied law and was elected a circuit court judge. In 1860 Morton ran for lieutenant-governor of Indiana on the Republican ticket headed by Abraham Lincoln with Henry S. Lane as the party's candidate for governor. Lincoln, Lane and Morton were all victorious but just two days after Lane and Morton were sworn into their new offices, Lane was elected to the U.S. Senate by the Indiana legislature and Morton became Indiana's governor. Morton was reelected governor in 1864 and thus served as Indiana's governor throughout the Civil War. In 1867 he was elected to the U.S. Senate where he represented Indiana until his death in 1877. This county was created by Dakota territory on January 8, 1873, while Morton was serving in the U.S. Senate.

1985 *Mountrail County*

Uncertain— This county was created on January 4, 1873, by the legislature of Dakota territory. According to Lutie T. Breeling's work entitled *When the Trail Was New in Mountraille*, published in 1956, this county's name was chosen by Enos Stutsman (1826–1874) and Morgan T. Rich

(1832–1898). Breeling's work states that "In 1873 ... several of the counties were named. The naming is credited to Enos Stutsman and Morgan T. Rich. Enos Stutsman was a representative from Pembina and on his way to Yankton, spent a night at the home of Morgan T. Rich of Wahpeton and at this time they selected upon the principal names, Mountraille being one of them." F. G. Callan's work entitled *A History of Richland County, North Dakota* confirms Breeling's account although it does not specifically mention either Mountrail or Mountraille County. Enos Stutsman was a member of the upper house (council) of the territorial legislature during the session that this county was created. At that time, there were only a handful of people living in the northern portion of Dakota territory, but the Northern Pacific Railroad wanted to issue promotional maps portraying Dakota territory as more settled than it actually was. The territorial legislature assisted the railroad in bruiting this fiction, by creating counties in largely unsettled areas, and this particular county was created as part of that effort. Since there were several individuals living in northern Dakota territory whom the territorial legislators may have chosen to honor, it is uncertain who this county's namesake really is. The potential namesakes were all descended from marriages between French-Canadian fur traders and Indian women. Their surnames were spelled Mountraille or Montreille. The county that was created by Dakota territory in 1873 was spelled Mountraille County but that county was abolished by the North Dakota legislature in 1891. Today's Mountrail County, North Dakota, was created, with its current (erroneous) spelling, in 1909 as a result of a vote at the general election in November, 1908. Sources dealing with the history, geography and place names of Dakota territory and North Dakota either refrain from offering information on the origin of this county's name or state that it was named for Joseph Mountraille, or descendants of Joseph Mountraille. Although this gives us a degree of unanimity, albeit imprecise, we cannot, with certainty, say that it is the correct answer.

Joseph Mountraille (–)— The *North Dakota Blue Book—1981* refers to him as "a metis voyageur of some prominence." In another work his name is rendered as Joseph Montreille and he is describes as a "Halfbreed mail carrier employed by Kittson, 1856." The article which provided that thumbnail sketch was entitled "A Gazetteer of Pioneers & Others in North

Dakota Previous to 1862." That article appeared in the 1906 issue (volume 1) of the *Collections of the State Historical Society of North Dakota*. Lutie T. Breeling's work entitled *When the Trail Was New in Mountraille* published in 1956 states that the county was named "...for a prominent half-blood family, descendants of Joseph Mountraille, an early voyageur. The name was French." Breeling then quotes C. A. Lounsberry in telling us that Joseph Mountraille was a mail carrier from the Pembina post office which had been established in 1851. The mail was carried to Crow Wing, the headquarters of the Northwest Fur Company, and from Crow Wing it was carried to St. Paul. Quoting Lounsberry (a historian, who was quoting someone else), Lutie T. Breeling passes on the following: "Our carriers were all half breeds and the most reliable men to be had. Our best man was 'Savage' (Joseph) Mountraille. He had the endurance of a blood hound. Tough as an oak knot, fearless and faithful..." In recounting one of Joseph Mountraille's exploits in carrying mail under arduous conditions, Lounsberry, via Lutie T. Breeling, mentions a brother named Alex.

1986 *Nelson County*

Nelson E. Nelson (1830–1913)— Nelson was an early settler at Pembina, in what is now the state of North Dakota. One source indicates that he entered the first homestead of record in what is now North Dakota, while another source states that Nelson's homestead was the second here. In either case, he certainly was a pioneer homesteader in North Dakota. For a number of years he was a collector of customs at Pembina. Most sources specify that he was a deputy collector of customs there but Clement A. Lounsberry's *Early History of North Dakota*, published in 1919, refers to Nelson as "Collector of customs at Pembina." Nelson was a member of the lower house of the Dakota territorial legislature during the 1883 session which created this county on March 9, 1883. Many sources incorrectly state that he was a member of the 1885 legislature rather than that of 1883. We know that the reference to the 1885 session is incorrect for two reasons: (1) the alphabetical listing of all members of the legislature of Dakota territory contained in the 1950 (volume 25) issue of *South Dakota Historical Collections* lists N. E. Nelson just once, as a member of the territorial house, in the 1883 session. That listing shows our N. E. Nelson as a representative from Pembina,

Pembina County. The only other Nelson listed is Torger Nelson from Yankton, who served in the 1867 legislature. (No entries are found for "Nelsen.") (2) W. B. Hennessy's *History of North Dakota*, published in 1910, lists all members of the legislature of Dakota territory, session by session, from the first territorial legislative session, which convened on March 17, 1862, until statehood. This comprehensive listing confirms that Nelson served in the 1883 legislature, which created and named this county in his honor, but not in the 1885 session. Nelson E. Nelson later served at Lisbon as postmaster.

1987 *Oliver County*

Harry S. Oliver (1855–1909) — Oliver was born in Chautauqua County, New York, on July 27, 1855. His father died in 1859 and his mother passed away in 1866, leaving eleven children, of which Harry S. Oliver was the youngest. He worked at Jamestown, New York, in a wholesale firm and, for a short time, he operated a hardware store in the community of Friendship, New York. In 1880 Oliver came to Lisbon, Dakota territory. In December, 1880 he purchased a farm about 12 miles from Lisbon, which grew to become a large wheat farm of about 1,000 acres. He served as the county assessor here in 1882 and 1884, and, in 1885, he was a member of the lower house of the legislature of Dakota territory. It was during that session of the legislature that this county was created, on March 12, 1885. Since Harry S. Oliver was chairman of that legislature's committee on county boundaries, it seems safe to assume that he had a hand in deciding that this county should be named in his honor. Soon after North Dakota achieved statehood, Oliver was elected to the state legislature. During the 1891–1893 session he was chairman of the house's committees on both banks and banking and grain grading and warehousing. By the early 1890's Oliver had moved with his family to the city of Lisbon, with a tenant farmer in charge of his wheat farm, 12 miles away. Several sources indicate that Oliver's given name was Henry. They are wrong. It was Harry.

1988 *Pembina County*

Pembina, the earliest European trading post in Dakota territory — This county lies in the northeastern corner of North Dakota. It was very large when it was created on January 9, 1867, by the legislature of Dakota territory. Since that time it has been greatly reduced in size. It borders Canada, to its north and the state of Minnesota to the east. The use of the name *Pembina* by Europeans, predates the American Revolution, and Pembina had been used as a county name twice before it was adopted in 1867 as a name for a county in Dakota territory. The first Pembina County had been one of the nine enormous counties into which Minnesota territory was originally divided on October 27, 1849. That Pembina County extended west from Minnesota's Lake of the Woods to the Missouri River and it embraced perhaps half of today's North Dakota. The second Pembina County in this region was created on April 24, 1862, by the state of Minnesota. That second Pembina County's name was later (March 9, 1878) changed to Kittson County and it is Kittson County, Minnesota that borders Pembina County, North Dakota today. The earliest European trading post in what would later become Dakota territory, was made at Pembina in 1797 by the North West Company. Although that post was short-lived, the North West Company erected a fort near the confluence of the Pembina River and the Red River here in 1801. Until about 1812 this wilderness area was occupied only by Indians and fur traders. In the winter of 1812–1813, Thomas Douglas, Earl of Selkirk (1771–1820), led the first White settlers to establish a colony here. They had been members Selkirk's colony of Scottish and Swiss emigrants, near Winnipeg, Canada. Except for a few years between 1823 and 1840, Pembina has been occupied by Whites continuously from 1801 to the present time. Pembina was considered to belong to England until 1818, when the boundary between Canada and the United States was set. The U.S. military did not establish their Fort Pembina here until, 1870, three years after this county in Dakota territory had been created and named. Although the community of Pembina has a colorful history, it has few residents today. In the late 1990's its population was only about 600. Some variation of the present name *Pembina* was originally applied by Indians here because of the presence of "high bush cranberries" (genus *Viburnum*, species *opulus*). The Indians' name was mangled and then reduced to written form by European explorers before the American Revolution.

1989 *Pierce County*

Gilbert A. Pierce (1839–1901) — A native of New York, Pierce moved to Indiana, studied law at the University of Chicago for two years and then entered the Union army early in the Civil War. He served with distinction in that war and rose from second-lieutenant to colonel. Upon returning to Indiana, Pierce practiced law and served in the lower house of the Indiana legislature. In 1872 he moved to Chicago and during more than a decade of newspaper work, he became a prominent newspaperman there. His newspaper editorials had supported Chester A. Arthur (1829–1886) during the period when President Hayes was removing Arthur as collector of customs in New York. Chester A. Arthur became president in 1881, and in 1884 he appointed Pierce to be governor of Dakota territory. As the territory's governor, Pierce advocated, but failed to secure, the admission of Dakota to the Union as two states. He also vetoed a bill which would have granted suffrage to women within the territory. On November 15, 1886, Pierce resigned as Dakota's governor. He remained here as a newspaper reporter in Bismarck. When North and South Dakota were admitted to the Union as two states in 1889, he was elected to be one of North Dakota's first two United States senators. After losing a bid for reelection in 1891, Pierce moved to Minneapolis, Minnesota, and purchased a half-ownership of the *Minneapolis Tribune*. He was later appointed minister to Portugal but failing health forced him to resign just three months after his appointment. That was in early 1893. Pierce devoted the next eight years of his life seeking a geographical cure for his failing health. He lived briefly in Florida, Colorado, California, Washington and British Columbia. He died on February 15, 1901, at age 62.

1990 *Ramsey County*

Alexander Ramsey (1815–1903) — A native of Pennsylvania, Ramsey studied law and was admitted to the bar of that state in 1839. He represented Pennsylvania in the U.S. House of Representatives and when Minnesota territory was created in 1849, President Zachary Taylor appointed Ramsey to be the new territory's first governor. Minnesota's first territorial legislature divided the large new territory into nine counties on October 27, 1849, and they named one of them for Alexander Ramsey, who was governor at that time and continued as the territory's governor until May 15, 1853. He later served as mayor of St. Paul and was the second governor of the state of Minnesota. Ramsey represented Minnesota in the U.S. Senate from 1863 to 1875. During his term as a U.S. senator, Ramsey advocated annexation by the United States of a large amount of sparsely settled Canadian plateau country. This scheme, of course, aborted before it got very far but apparently the impetus in Senator Ramsey's mind was the relationship between the settlement at Pembina, Dakota territory and the Selkirk colony near Winnipeg, Canada. In 1879, President Rutherford B. Hayes appointed Ramsey to be his secretary of war. Ramsey remained in that cabinet post until President Hayes' term as president ended in 1881. Ramsey died in St. Paul, Minnesota, on April 22, 1903, in the Minnesota county that bears his name. The only other Ramsey County in our nation is in North Dakota. It was created by Dakota territory on January 4, 1873, while Alexander Ramsey was serving in the U.S. Senate from the state of Minnesota.

1991 *Ransom County*

Fort Ransom, Dakota territory— This county in southeastern North Dakota was created on January 4, 1873, when Dakota was still a territory. It was named for the U.S. army's Fort Ransom, which was located in what is now the northwestern section of Ransom County, North Dakota. The fort was established on June 18, 1867. Its sight was chosen by General Alfred H. Terry (1827–1890), on the Sheyenne River, about 75 miles above that river's mouth on the Red River. More specifically, the fort was located at a hill whose name is rendered variously as Bear Den Hill, Bear's Den Hillock and Grizzly Bear Hill. The fort was erected under the direction of Captain George H. Crossman. This fort was located here to protect settlers in the area and travelers emigrating from Minnesota to Montana territory from Indian attacks. A prairie fire on October 10, 1867, almost wiped out the new fort when it was barely four months old. Fort Ransom survived that fire and was actively used as a U.S. military post from 1867 to 1872. It was abandoned on July 31, 1872, and is now an 887 acre state park. Fort Ransom was named in honor of General Thomas E. G. Ransom (1834–1864).

Thomas E. G. Ransom (1834–1864)— A native of Vermont Thomas Edward Greenfield Ransom graduated from Norwich University in that state in 1851. He was employed as an engineer in Illinois when the Civil War began. Ransom served as an officer in the Union army during the Civil War and was wounded in combat several times, and cited for gallantry by his supe-

riors. By April 15, 1863, he had been promoted to brigadier-general of volunteers, back dated to November 29, 1862. Ransom participated in the Vicksburg campaign, the Red River (of the South) campaign and was placed in charge of Union forces pursuing retreating Confederate soldiers through North Georgia into Alabama. General Ransom died in northwestern Georgia, near Rome, Georgia, on October 29, 1864, from illness and aggravation of his incompletely healed combat wounds. He was breveted major-general effective September 1, 1864.

1992 *Renville County*

Uncertain— This county was first created on January 4, 1873, by the legislature of Dakota territory. It was dissolved in 1891 by the state of North Dakota but then recreated by the state in 1910. The county's name was chosen by Enos Stutsman (1826–1874) and Morgan T. Rich (1832–1898). Enos Stutsman was a representative in the Dakota territorial legislature from Pembina, and on his way to Yankton, he spent a night at the home of Morgan T. Rich of Wahpeton. At this time they selected a number of names for new counties, Renville being one of them. Enos Stutsman was a member of the upper house (council) of the territorial legislature during the session that this county was created. At that time, there were only a handful of people living in the northern portion of Dakota territory, but the Northern Pacific Railroad wanted to issue promotional maps portraying Dakota territory as more settled than it actually was. The territorial legislature assisted the railroad in bruiting this fiction, by creating counties in largely unsettled areas, and this particular county was created as part of that effort. Sources dealing with the history, geography and place names of Dakota territory and North Dakota are not unanimous concerning the namesake of this county but only two possibilities are mentioned: Gabriel Renville and Joseph Renville. Gabriel Renville (–1892) was a nephew of Joseph Renville (–1846).

Gabriel Renville (–1892)— Gabriel Renville was born in 1824 or 1825 at Sweet Corn's village, on the west shore of Big Stone Lake, in what is today's state of Minnesota. That lake lies on Minnesota's western border, not far from the junction of the present states of North and South Dakota. He was the son of Victor Renville (–1834) and Winona Crawford, both of whom descended from marriages between French-Canadians and Indians. In 1862 the Dakota Indians began their final futile

struggle against the Whites in Minnesota, who had systematically robbed and mistreated them. They were successfully suppressed and 38 of their members were hanged at a mass gallows at Mankato, Minnesota, on December 26, 1862. At that time Gabriel Renville owned a farm in Graceville, Minnesota, and he remained on good terms with the Whites. After the Dakotas in Minnesota had been suppressed, surviving Dakotas in Minnesota were deported to Indian reservations in Dakota territory (now South Dakota and North Dakota) where they live in misery to this day. After the U.S. military removed Gabriel Renville's band of Dakota Indians to a reservation in the northeastern portion of today's state of South Dakota, General Henry H. Sibley (1811–1891) appointed him to be chief of scouts, defending the frontier. Later, supported by the U.S. army, Gabriel Renville became a chief of the Sisseton and Wahpeton bands of Dakota Indians. He died at Brown's Valley, within ten miles of his birthplace on August 26, 1892.

Joseph Renville (–1846)— Joseph Renville was born about 1779 on the banks of the Mississippi River near Minnesota's present Twin Cities. His father was French and his mother was a Dakota Indian. Renville was raised among the Dakota Indians until he was about ten years old, when his father took him to Canada. There he was given a few years education by French Roman Catholic priests. After returning to Minnesota, he served as a guide and interpreter for the U.S. army's explorer, Zebulon M. Pike (1779–1813). During the War of 1812, the British gave Renville the rank of captain in their army and Renville led a company composed of Dakota warriors against the U.S. on the northwestern frontier. In 1815 he resigned from the British army and identified himself with American interests thereafter. He erected a trading house at Lac qui Parle and remained there until his death in 1846. Renville's mother was an Indian and he married a Dakota Indian himself. His knowledge of the Indians' language and customs enabled him to assist the Presbyterian missionary, Thomas S. Williamson (1800–1879), in converting Indians to Christianity. Renville assisted other Christian missionaries as well and he participated in translating large portions of the Bible (some accounts say the entire Bible) into the language of the Dakota Indians.

1993 *Richland County*

Morgan T. Rich (1832–1898)— Morgan T. Rich first visited Dakota territory in

1864 with General Alfred Sully's (1821–1879) expedition but Rich continued on to gold fields west of the Missouri River. Lewis F. Crawford's *History of North Dakota* refers to him as "Captain Morgan T. Rich." In 1868 he returned to Dakota territory and operated a ferry over the Bois de Sioux River at what is now the municipality of Wahpeton, Richland County, North Dakota. In 1869 Rich became a settler on the site of the present Wahpeton, which eventually became the county seat of the county named in his honor. His homestead was granted here in 1869. Morgan T. Rich is considered to be the founder of the municipality of Wahpeton. (That community's was first named Richville, but when the county was named for M. T. Rich, the municipality's name was changed to Wahpeton, to avoid overkill.) This county was created on January 4, 1873, by the legislature of Dakota territory. The county's name was chosen by Enos Stutsman (1826–1874) and Morgan T. Rich (1832–1898). Enos Stutsman was a representative in the Dakota territorial legislature from Pembina, and on his way to Yankton, he spent a night at the home of Morgan T. Rich of Wahpeton. At this time they selected a number of names for new counties, Richland being one of them. Enos Stutsman was a member of the upper house (council) of the territorial legislature during the session that this county was created. Morgan T. Rich was one of the first three county commissioners of the new Richland County.

1994 *Rolette County*

Joseph Rolette (1820–1871)— Rolette was born on October 23, 1820, at Prairie du Chien, Wisconsin, when it was part of Michigan territory. He received some education in New York City, and during his stay there he was conspicuous walking down the street in his buckskin suit, with a rifle over his shoulder. In 1841 Henry H. Sibley (1811–1891) of the American Fur Company dispatched Rolette to operate the firm's trading post at Pembina. Rolette used ox carts, commercially, at Pembina, in the early 1840's. He established a route from the Red River to St. Paul and thus became a significant competitor of Hudson's Bay Company. In 1853 Rolette became a representative of Pembina County in Minnesota's territorial legislature. He was a member of the lower house of that legislature during the 1853–1855 session and he served in that legislature's upper house (council) during the 1856–1857 session. He also served as a customs official

at Pembina and was the first person to file for a homestead on land at Pembina. Joseph Rolette died at Pembina on May, 16, 1871, and this county was created and named in his honor by the legislature of Dakota territory two years later, on January 4, 1873.

1995 *Sargent County*

Homer E. Sargent (1822–)— Sargent was general manager of the Northern Pacific Railroad from October 1879 to April 1881 and it was because of his association with that railroad that this county was created and named in his honor by the legislature of Dakota territory. Railroads were, of course, vital to the development of Dakota territory in linking its potentially vast agricultural output with distant markets. In 1883 the Northern Pacific's tracks were completed from the Great Lakes to the West Coast. Homer E. Sargent invested in considerable land in northern Dakota territory and was a well-known figure here in 1883. This county was created on March 3, 1883. The year of Sargent's death is uncertain although it was probably 1901. Sargent left a will and the probate process was started for that will during July, 1901.

1996 *Sheridan County*

Philip H. Sheridan (1831–1888)— Sheridan was born in 1831 but his place of birth is in doubt. He graduated from the U.S. Military Academy at West Point and became a career officer in the United States army. When the Civil War began, Sheridan had almost a decade of military service behind him but was still only a lieutenant. During the Civil War Sheridan served with distinction in the Union army and rocketed from obscurity to high rank and responsibility. By the closing weeks of the Civil War, he had been promoted to major-general. After the Civil War ended, Sheridan remained in the army enforcing the odious Reconstruction Acts in Louisiana and Texas. In 1884 Sheridan became commanding general of the entire U.S. army. He was elevated to the rank of full general from June 1, 1888. General Sheridan died on August 5 of that year. This county was first created and named in his honor by Dakota territory on January 4, 1873. At that time, there were only a handful of people living in the northern portion of Dakota territory, but the Northern Pacific Railroad wanted to issue promotional maps portraying Dakota territory as more settled than it actually was. The

territorial legislature assisted the railroad in bruiting this fiction, by creating counties in largely unsettled areas, and this particular county was created as part of that effort. It was subsequently abolished and its territory was absorbed by the county on its western border, McLean County, but then recreated as a result of a general election held in November, 1908.

1997 *Sioux County*

Dakota Indians— The Dakota are a vast alliance of American Indians who are more commonly known as the Sioux Indians. These Indians' name for themselves is *Lakota* or *Dakota* meaning "friends" or "allies," while *Sioux* was a derogatory Chippewa-French name for them. The Dakotas consist of three general dialect and culture groups: the Santee, Wiciyela and Teton. When the Whites first encountered the Dakotas, about 1640, they found them living in southern Minnesota and adjacent areas subsisting by hunting, fishing, gathering lake and forest products and growing corn. In 1805 the Dakotas signed their first treaty giving up some of their Minnesota lands and by 1858 they had been pressured into signing treaties giving up almost all of their land in Minnesota. In return, they were to receive food, annuities, education and other necessities. These promises to the Indians were broken and in 1862 the Dakotas began a final, futile struggle against the Whites in Minnesota, who had systematically robbed and mistreated them. The Dakotas lost this struggle and 38 of their members were hanged on a mass gallows at Mankato, Minnesota, on December 26, 1862. Remaining Dakota Indians in Minnesota were deported to Indian reservations in Dakota territory (now South Dakota and North Dakota), where they have lived in misery to this day. This North Dakota county was created in 1914 but it appears that its name was chosen merely because the Standing Rock Indian reservation is located here and not because of any newfound affection by the Whites for the Indians.

1998 *Slope County*

The Missouri Slope— This county lies in southwestern North Dakota. It was named for the Missouri Slope, referring to the slope of the land west of the Missouri River. The term "Missouri Slope" is said to be a common designation for the area of North Dakota west of the Missouri River. Slope County, and 13 other North Dakota counties, in the southwestern portion of

North Dakota, lie west of the Missouri River. This county was created as a result of a vote at the general election held on November 3, 1914. Sources consulted differ on the date that this county was officially created; some say December 31, 1914, while others put the date two weeks later, on January 14, 1915.

1999 *Stark County*

George Stark (–)— George Stark was associated with the Northern Pacific Railroad and it was his association with that railroad that prompted the legislators of Dakota territory to name this county in his honor when they created it on February 10, 1879. Railroads were, of course, vital to the development of Dakota territory in linking its potentially vast agricultural output with distant markets. The Northern Pacific Railroad had gone bankrupt in 1873 and George Stark was a member of the committee which helped reorganize the railroad during the summer of 1875. He then served as vice president of the Northern Pacific Railroad from September, 1875, to September, 1879. Many works that deal with the history, geography and place names of Dakota territory and North Dakota state that George Stark was a general manager of the Northern Pacific Railroad. That is incorrect. A letter to the author dated August 29, 1988, from Frank E. Vyzralek of Great Plains Research in Bismarck, North Dakota, who spent at least 25 years collecting information on North Dakota place names, points out that George Stark was a vice president of the railroad, but never its general manager. During the 1880's George Stark owned an experimental agricultural farm near Bismarck, named the Stark farm, which was opened to promote settlement along the Northern Pacific's route by demonstrating the fertility of the land in Dakota territory and its adaptability to general farming. Stark's activities with the Northern Pacific Railroad had a significant impact on Dakota territory but he also was active in other ventures of interest to the railroad including a line to link coal discovered in the foothills of the Cascade Mountains in the Pacific Northwest, with navigable waters near the Pacific Ocean.

2000 *Steele County*

Uncertain— This county was created by the legislature of Dakota territory on March 8, 1883. Most sources dealing with the history, geography and place names of Dakota territory and North Dakota state

that this county was named for Franklin Steele (1813–1880) of Minneapolis, who, they claim, was associated with the Red River Land Company. These sources indicate that the Red River Land Company owned extensive acreage in the vicinity of Steele County and that this firm played a role in causing this county to be created. However, a letter to the author dated August 29, 1988, from Frank E. Vyzralek of Great Plains Research in Bismarck, North Dakota, who spent at least 25 years collecting information on North Dakota place names, states that this county was named for Edward H. Steele (1846–1899). Vyzralek's research led him to the conclusion that Franklin Steele had no connection with either Steele County in Dakota territory or the Red River Land Company. Frank E. Vyzralek is not the only authority who claims that this county was named for Edward H. Steele (1846–1899), but that view is the minority opinion.

Edward H. Steele (1846–1899)— Edward H. Steele had headquarters in Minneapolis and was secretary of the Red River Land Company, which owned some 50,000 acres of land in the vicinity of what would be Steele County, Dakota territory. The land company played an active role in lobbying the Dakota territorial legislature to create Steele County and their efforts met with success on March 8, 1883, when this county was created. Finley, North Dakota is the present county seat of Steele county but the county had two earlier seats of justice. The first was at Hope, and the second was at Sherbrooke. The first county seat, Hope, was named for Edward H. Steele's wife according to Frank E. Vyzralek of Great Plains Research in Bismarck, North Dakota.

Franklin Steele (1813–1880)— This Pennsylvania native realized that with ingenuity and hard work one could make a lot of money on our nation's northwestern frontier and he proceeded to do just that. He erected a crude cabin on the St. Croix River to lay claim to water rights there and he hired a small group of men to cut timber for him. Sensing that more money would be needed to make his lumbering venture boom, Steele went to St. Louis and found backers for a new company. A dam was built on the St. Croix River at the present site of Taylor Falls, Minnesota, and a sawmill was placed in operation there. Steele soon had a similar venture in operation in what is now Minneapolis at the Falls of St. Anthony, where he owned valuable land. Franklin Steele soon began to accumulate wealth and he eventually owned a large portion of the land in Minneapolis. In

1851 he was elected by the legislature of Minnesota territory to membership on the first board of regents of the University of Minnesota. Although it is uncertain whether or not Steele County in Dakota territory was named for Franklin Steele (1813–1880) there is no doubt that Minnesota territory created and named the present Steele County, Minnesota for him in 1855.

2001 *Stutsman County*

Enos Stutsman (1826–1874)— Enos Stutsman was born in Indiana on February 14, 1826. He moved with his family to Illinois, while still in his youth and there he taught school and studied law. He was admitted to the bar in 1851 in Illinois and held some minor political offices in that state. In 1855 he moved west across the Mississippi River into Iowa and lived in both Des Moines and Sioux City. At Sioux City, Iowa he engaged in real estate ventures which failed to meet his expectations. Stutsman next moved about 50 miles northwest to Yankton, in southeastern Dakota. At that time Dakota territory had not yet been formed, and was merely unorganized territory, lying west of the states of Iowa and Minnesota. In 1860 Enos Stutsman was the secretary of the Yankton Townsite Company. Dakota territory was created on March 2, 1861, and Stutsman was involved in the government and politics of the territory from that time until his death. He was elected to represent Yankton in the upper house (council) of the first legislature of Dakota territory and soon became a leader in the legislature. When the second territorial legislature convened in 1862, Stutsman was president of the upper house. He subsequently served numerous terms in both houses of Dakota's territorial legislature representing Yankton in some sessions and Pembina in others. Stutsman resigned his seat in the legislature in 1866 to accept an appointment from the federal government as a customs agent. After leaving that position he represented Pembina in the territorial legislature. On December 19, 1868, Stutsman introduced a bill calling for full suffrage for women in the territory, but he was premature. (Several later efforts in Dakota territory and the state of North Dakota also either failed, or granted women only limited suffrage. North Dakota women had to wait until 1920 to obtain the full right to vote.) While living at Pembina, Stutsman held the office of receiver at the U.S. land office there. This county was created on January 4, 1873, by the legislature of

Dakota territory. The county's name was chosen by Enos Stutsman (1826–1874) and Morgan T. Rich (1832–1898). At the time this county's name was chosen, Enos Stutsman was a representative in the Dakota territorial legislature from Pembina, and on his way to Yankton, he spent a night at the home of Morgan T. Rich of Wahpeton. At this time they selected a number of names for new counties, Stutsman County being one of them. Enos Stutsman was a member of the upper house (council) of the territorial legislature during the session that this county was created. Stutsman died of a lung malady at Pembina, just one year later, on January 24, 1874, while Dakota was still a territory.

2002 *Towner County*

Oscar M. Towner (1842–1897)— There is contradictory information concerning Towner's early life. Mary Ann Barnes Williams says this about him in her *Origins of North Dakota Place Names*: "Col. Oscar M. Towner, a Civil War Confederate Soldier, a promoter and land speculator, and one of the earliest ranchers in the county," (McHenry County, Dakota territory). Several other sources refer to Oscar M. Towner as Colonel Towner, which would indicate that he attained the rank of either lieutenant-colonel or colonel in some army. A letter from Virginia George dated September 24, 1960, to the Missouri Historical Society quotes the *Grand Forks Herald* newspaper dated June 13, 1897: "O. M. Towner was a graduate of West Point, served through the war as Chief of Staff for Gen. Price of the Confederate Army." However, Dorothy A. Brockhoff, Reference Librarian of the Missouri Historical Society wrote a letter to Virginia George on September 16, 1960, in which she stated that she had performed extensive research and concluded that Oscar M. Towner did not graduate from West Point. (This, of course, does not rule out the possibility that he attended West Point.) Ms. Brockhoff goes on to say "With regard to his reported service with General Sterling Price, we have many books dealing with Price and his Civil War activities, and I cannot find Oscar Towner listed in any of them. Other chiefs of staff are listed, but not Towner … there is no indication in the *Official War Record of the Rebellion* records (some 100 volumes) that Towner participated in the Civil War as an officer of the Confederacy. If he were a non-commissioned officer, his name might not appear…" Since a person with the title of "colonel" is a commissioned (not non-commissioned) officer, the caveat offered by Ms. Brockhoff fails to resolve the discrepancy. We do know that Oscar M. Towner was the founder of the Elk Valley farm in Grand Forks County and that he raised cattle in the vicinity of the municipality of Towner, which today is the county seat of McHenry County. Both McHenry and Towner Counties are in northern North Dakota, but not adjacent. Towner County, Dakota territory, was created in March 1883. It was named in honor of Oscar M. Towner (1842–1897) because he was a member of the lower house of the territorial legislature during the session that created this county.

2003 *Traill County*

Walter J. S. Traill (1847–1933)— Walter John Strickland Traill was born in 1847 in what is today, the Canadian province of Ontario. In 1866 he secured a five year contract as a junior clerk for Hudson's Bay Company to be stationed on the western frontier of civilization. His first assignment was at Fort Garry, near the junction of the Red River with the Assiniboine River, near Winnipeg, Canada. After completing his training there he served Hudson's Bay Company in their Swan Lake district, west of Lake Manitoba, and at Fort Pelly, Fort Ellice, Riding Mountain and Qu' Appelle. His duties were varied and, at times, conditions were brutal. He kept clerical records of business transactions with the hunters and trappers, including sales of supplies to them and, for furs purchased from them, Traill inspected and appraised the furs and recorded the transactions. He was obliged to visit outposts by saddle horse, snow shoes or dog teams and check the trappers. Traill's letters mention frequent heavy snow, blizzards, 40 degree-below-zero temperatures and, when his food supply ran out, eating boiled dog meat. In 1869 the Metis, (i.e., "mixed blood"), under Louis D. Riel (1844–1885), captured Fort Gary during the Red River Rebellion. The Hudson's Bay Company placed Walter J. S. Traill in charge of a brigade of escapees with orders to retreat from Canada into Dakota territory. This mission was successfully accomplished when Traill and his companions reached the Hudson's Bay post at Georgetown, and Traill was then placed in charge of the company's operations there. Traill soon visited the prisoners in Canada but he was expelled from Canada by Riel as "an undesirable citizen who had exported a valuable amount of furs without Riel's consent." The Hudson's Bay Company put Traill in charge of all of their posts in the Red River Valley. About 1871 Traill took out naturalization papers to become as U.S. citizen and in 1871 he established a new trading post at Caledonia, which was then called Goose River. Hudson's Bay Company was forced to close its posts in the United States in 1875 and Traill supervised the liquidation. He subsequently engaged in buying and selling grain at St. Paul, Minnesota, but after the death of an only son, he moved to a farm, which he owned, at Pembina, Dakota territory. He later lived two decades at Kalispell, Montana and finally moved to orchard country in British Columbia, where he died at the age of 85. This county was created by Dakota territory on January 12, 1875.

2004 *Walsh County*

George H. Walsh (1845–1913)— Born in Canada on November 24, 1845, Walsh immigrated with his parents to Minnesota territory at the age of ten. He served in the Union army during the Civil War from 1862 to 1865. When Walsh moved to Grand Forks, in northern Dakota territory he became the publisher of one of North Dakota's earlier newspapers. He also studied law and became very active in politics, serving as a member of the upper house (council) of Dakota territory's legislature almost continuously from 1879 until North Dakota was admitted to statehood in 1889. He then was a member of the house of representatives of North Dakota's first state legislature and was speaker of the house during the state's third legislative session in 1893. In 1899 Walsh settled at Cass Lake, Minnesota. This county was created by Dakota territory's territorial legislature on February 18, 1881. George H. Walsh was president of the upper house of the territorial legislature during the session of the legislature that created and named this county.

2005 *Ward County*

Mark Ward (1844–1902)— This county was created by the legislature of Dakota territory on April 14, 1885, and named for one of their members. During that legislative session there were two members of the legislature named Ward, both of whom represented areas now within the state of South Dakota. They were James P. Ward (1834–1916) and Mark Ward (1844–1902). Most sources on the history, geography and place names of Dakota territory and North Dakota incorrectly state that this county's namesake was James P. Ward (1834–1916), of Canistoa. This county was named for the other Ward in this session of the legislature, Mark Ward (1844–1902), of Kimball, in Brule County. Mark Ward was the chairman of the house committee on counties during the 1885 session of Dakota's territorial legislature, which created this county

2006 *Wells County*

Edward P. Wells (1847–1936)— This county was originally created by Dakota territory on January 4, 1873, and named Gingras County, in honor of Antoine Blanc Gingras (1821–1877), an early fur trader who amassed a fortune of $60,000, and was said to be the wealthiest man in northern Dakota. Gingras was a Metis, (i.e., "mixed blood"), and he served in the legislature of Minnesota territory, representing the Pembina district. During the 1881 session of Dakota's territorial legislature, Edward Payson Wells (1847–1936) was a member of the lower house of the legislature and his fellow legislators changed Gingras County's name to Wells County, in his honor on February 26, 1881. Wells was born in Troy, Wisconsin, on November 9, 1847. He engaged in the produce commission and life insurance business in Milwaukee, Wisconsin and Minneapolis, Minnesota during the period from about 1864 to 1878. In 1878 he moved to Jamestown, in what is now the east-central portion of the state of North Dakota. On November 10, 1880, Wells was an invited guest of the Northern Pacific Railroad for the ceremonial driving of a silver spike on the railroad's line at the Dakota-Montana territorial line Also in 1880, the voters of the Jamestown district elected him to represent them in Dakota's territorial legislature and he served in that body's house of representatives during just one session, the 1881 session that changed Gingras County's name to Wells County, in his honor. In Jamestown, Wells was a banker, financier and early promoter of the James River Valley. Wells was chairman of Dakota territory's Republican party in 1883–1884 and he founded the James River National Bank in 1881 and was its president for two decades. In 1901 he moved from Jamestown to Minneapolis, Minnesota and before his death in 1936, he accumulated wealth valued at one million dollars.

2007 *Williams County*

Erastus A. Williams (1850–1930)— Williams was born at Mystic, Connecticut, on October 14, 1850. In 1859 he moved, with his family to Wisconsin and ten years later Williams graduated from the law department of the University of Michigan. While he was in law school, his family had moved to Freeport, Illinois. Upon graduation from law school Erastus Williams also moved to Freeport and lived with his parents long enough to be admitted to the Illinois bar and to meet and his future bride, Jennie E. Hettinger (–1894), a daughter of Mathias Hettinger. (Later, in a romantic gesture, Erastus A. Williams used his political power as speaker of Dakota's territorial legislature to cause one of the territory's counties to be named for his bride's father. For details see Hettinger County, North Dakota, above.) In 1871 Williams immigrated to Dakota territory. He settled first at Yankton, in southeastern Dakota. Here he was appointed assistant U.S. district attorney at the age of 21. Williams' attention was soon directed to the plans of the Northern Pacific Railroad to stretch their tracks from St. Paul, Minnesota to the Pacific coast and he moved to what is now Bismarck, and there was involved in the effort to construct the first 50 miles of the rail line, east from the Missouri River. He also became the first lawyer of Bismarck. His first membership in the territorial legislature was during the session of 1872–1873. Will G. Robinson's alphabetical listing of all members of the legislature of Dakota territory, which appeared in the 1950 (volume 25) issue of *South Dakota Historical Collections & Report*, indicates that Williams was a representative of Edwinton, Buffalo County, in the 1872–1873 territorial legislature. That same source shows that in all of the many subsequent sessions of the territorial legislature in which Williams served, he represented Bismarck and Burleigh County. He became a powerful figure in Dakota politics, and was speaker of the house in the territorial legislature of 1883. Williams County was created and named in his honor by his fellow legislators in the territory's legislature on January 8, 1873, during Williams' first term as a member of the territorial legislature. When statehood was on the horizon for both North and South Dakota, Williams was a member of the North Dakota constitutional convention, which convened on July 4, 1889. He entered a motion for passage of a constitution, which clearly favored railroad interests. That version of the constitution for the new state was not adopted. Williams later served in the legislature of the state of North Dakota and counting both sessions of the Dakota territorial legislature

and the North Dakota state legislature, he served about ten terms. In 1897 he was speaker of the state's house of representatives. President Benjamin Harrison had appointed Williams to be surveyor general for North Dakota, soon after the new state was born. He served in that position until 1907, when he resigned, the tasks assigned to him having largely been completed. In 1910 he was elected president of Bismarck's city commission. Erastus Williams retired from active life in 1925 and died on March 26, 1930.

REFERENCES

Ackermann, Gertrude W. "Joseph Renville of Lac qui Parle." *Minnesota History*, Vol. 12, No. 3. St. Paul: September, 1931.

Armstrong, M. K. "History and Resources of Dakota, Montana & Idaho." *South Dakota Historical Collections*, Vol. 14. Pierre, South Dakota: 1928.

Ashley Diamond Jubilee Historical Book Committee. *Ashley Diamond Jubilee: Ashley, North Dakota: 1888–1963*. 1963.

Bailey, Dana R. *History of Minnehaha County, South Dakota*. Sioux Falls, Brown & Saenger, 1899.

Baker, James H. "Lives of the Governors of Minnesota." *Collections of the Minnesota Historical Society*, Vol. 13. St. Paul: 1908.

Balmer, Frank E. "The Farmer & Minnesota History." *Minnesota History*, Vol. 7, No. 3. St. Paul: September, 1926.

Barnes County Historical Society, Inc. *Barnes County History*. Dallas, Texas, Taylor Publishing Co., 1976.

Barrett, Mrs. John W. *History of Stephenson County: 1970*. Freeport, Illinois, County of Stephenson, 1972.

Beal, Leonard, et al. *Yesteryears in Traill: Traill County, North Dakota*. Dallas, Texas, Taylor Publishing Co., 1976.

Bern, Enid. *Our Hettinger County Heritage*.

Bill, Fred. "Steamboating on the Red River." *North Dakota Historical Quarterly*, Vol. 2, No. 3. Bismarck: April, 1928.

Black, R. M. *A History of Dickey County, North Dakota*. Ellendale, North Dakota, Dickey County Historical Society, 1930.

Breeling, Lutie T. *When the Trail Was New in Mountraille*. Ross, North Dakota, 1956.

Brockhoff, Dorothy A., Reference Librarian, Missouri Historical Society, St. Louis, Missouri. Letter to Virginia George dated September 16, 1960. Archives, Missouri Historical Society, St. Louis, Missouri.

Burdick, Usher L. *Great Judges & Lawyers of Early North Dakota.* Williston, North Dakota, Williston Plains Reporter, 1956.

Callan, F. G. *A History of Richland County and the City of Wahpeton, North Dakota.*

Carpenter, Allan. *North Dakota.* Chicago, Childrens Press, 1968.

Cavileer, Charles. "The Red River Valley in 1851." *North Dakota History*, Vol. 12, No. 4. Bismarck: October, 1945.

"The Census of 1860." *South Dakota Historical Collections*, Vol. 10. Pierre, South Dakota: 1920.

Compendium of History & Biography of North Dakota. Chicago, George A. Ogle & Co., 1900.

Cotroneo, Ross R. "The History of the Northern Pacific Land Grant: 1900–1952." Ph.D. Thesis, University of Idaho, Moscow, Idaho, 1966.

Crawford, Lewis F. *History of North Dakota.* Chicago, American Historical Society, Inc., 1931.

Curtiss-Wedge, Franklyn. *The History of Renville County, Minnesota.* Chicago, H. C. Cooper Jr. & Co., 1916.

Dayton, Edson C. *Dakota Days: May, 1886–August, 1898.* Hartford, Connecticut, Case, Lockwood & Brainard Co., 1937.

Dickerson, Inga H. "Dakota Territorial Governors." Unpublished manuscript.

Dickson, R. "The Fur Trade in Wisconsin." *Collections of the State Historical Society of Wisconsin,* Vol. 20. Madison: 1911.

Elliott, Thomas P., President, Barnes County Historical Society, Inc. Letter to the author dated July 12, 1987.

Faber, Harold. *From Sea to Sea: The Growth of the United States.* New York, Farrar, Straus & Giroux, 1967.

Folwell, William W. *A History of Minnesota.* St. Paul, Minnesota Historical Society, 1956.

Frazer, Robert W. *Forts of the West.* Norman, University of Oklahoma Press, 1965.

"Gazetteer of Pioneers and Others in North Dakota Previous to 1862." *Collections of the State Historical Society of North Dakota,* Vol. 1. Bismarck: 1906.

George, Virginia. Letter to Dorothy A. Brockhoff, Reference Librarian, Missouri Historical Society, St. Louis, Missouri, dated September 24, 1960. Archives, Missouri Historical Society, St. Louis, Missouri.

"Gifts to the State Historical Museum." *North Dakota Historical Quarterly*, Vol. 2, No. 2. Bismarck: January, 1928.

Grand Forks Herald, June 13, 1897.

Hart, Herbert M. *Old Forts of the Northwest.* New York, Bonanza Books, 1963.

Hedges, James B. *Henry Villard and the Railways of the Northwest.* New Haven, Yale University Press, 1930.

Heinemeyer, C. B., & Mrs. Ben Janssen. *History of Mercer County, North Dakota: 1882 to 1960.* Hazen Star.

Hennessy, W. B. *History of North Dakota.* Bismarck, Bismarck Tribune Co., 1910.

Historical Atlas of Dakota. Chicago, A. T. Andreas, 1884.

History of the Red River Valley. Chicago, C. F. Cooper & Co., 1909.

A History of Richland County: Richland County, North Dakota. Dallas, Texas, Taylor Publishing Co., 1977.

History of Southeastern Dakota: Its Settlement & Growth. Sioux City, Iowa, Western Publishing Co., 1881.

Holcombe, Return I. *Minnesota in Three Centuries.* Mankato, Minnesota, Publishing Society of Minnesota, 1908.

Hubbard, Walter, et al. "The Memoirs." *South Dakota Historical Collections,* Vol. 3. Aberdeen, South Dakota: 1906.

Jennewein, J. Leonard, & Jane Boorman. *Dakota Panorama.* Mitchell, South Dakota, Dakota Territory Centennial Commission, 1961.

Kingsbury, George W. "Enos Stutsman." *Collections of the State Historical Society of North Dakota,* Vol. 1. Bismarck: 1906.

Kingsbury, George W. *History of Dakota Territory.* Chicago, S. J. Clarke Publishing Co., 1915.

Kuhn, Bertha M. "The History of Traill County, North Dakota." M.A. Thesis, University of North Dakota, Grand Forks, North Dakota, 1917.

Lamar, Howard R. *Dakota Territory: 1861–1889: A Study of Frontier Politics.* New Haven, Yale University Press, 1956.

Lamar, Howard R. *The Reader's Encyclopedia of the American West.* New York, Thomas Y. Crowell Co., 1977.

Law, Laura T. *History of Rolette County, North Dakota & Yarns of the Pioneers.* Minneapolis, Minnesota, Lund Press, Inc., 1953.

Lee, Mrs. Gilmore. *History of Grand Forks County, North Dakota.* Arvilla, North Dakota, Kempton Homemakers Club, 1964.

Leitch, Barbara A. *A Concise Dictionary of Indian Tribes of North America.* Algonac, Michigan, Reference Publications, Inc., 1979.

List of Fargo Division Stations Showing Origins of the Station Names. Northern Pacific Railway Company, Office Division Superintendent, Fargo Division, 1944.

Lounsberry, C. A. "Early Development of North Dakota." *Collections of the State Historical Society of North Dakota*, Vol. 1. Bismarck: 1906.

Lounsberry, Clement A. *Early History of North Dakota.* Duluth, F. H. Lounsberry & Co., 1913.

Lounsberry, Clement A. *Early History of North Dakota: Essential Outlines of American History.* Washington, D.C., Liberty Press, 1919.

Lounsberry, Clement A. *North Dakota History & People: Outlines of American History.* Chicago, S. J. Clarke Publishing Co., 1917.

"Name Origins of North Dakota Cities, Towns & Counties." *North Dakota History,* Vol. 13, No. 3. Bismarck: July, 1946.

Neill, E. D. "A Sketch of Joseph Renville." *Collections of the Minnesota Historical Society,* Vol. 1. St. Paul: 1872.

North Central Tour Book. Heathrow, Florida, AAA Publishing, 1998.

North Dakota Blue Book: 1942. Bismarck Printing Co., 1942.

North Dakota Blue Book: 1961. Bismarck Tribune, 1961.

North Dakota Blue Book: 1981. N.p.

Oyos, Lynwood E., et al. *Over a Century of Leadership: South Dakota Territorial & State Governors.* Sioux Falls, South Dakota, Center for Western Studies, 1987.

Pfaller, Louis. *Stark County Heritage & Destiny.* Bismarck, Taylor Publishing Co., 1978.

Pielder, Mrs. John A. "Correspondence." *South Dakota Historical Collections,* Vol. 2. Aberdeen, South Dakota: 1904.

Piper, Marion J. *Dakota Portraits.* Mohall, North Dakota, 1964.

Potter, Merle. "The North Dakota Capital Fight." *North Dakota Historical Quarterly,* Vol. 7, No. 1. Bismarck: October, 1932.

Qualey, Carlton C. "Pioneer Norwegian Settlement in North Dakota." *North Dakota Historical Quarterly,* Vol. 5, No. 1. Bismarck: October, 1930.

Ransom, Frank L. *The Sunshine State: A History of South Dakota.* Mitchell, South Dakota, Educator School Supply Co., 1917.

Red Lake County Historical Society, Inc. & Red Lake County Bicentennial Committee. *A History of Red Lake County: Red Lake County, Minnesota.* Dallas, Texas, Taylor Publishing Co., 1976.

Riggs, Stephen R. "Dakota Portraits." *Minnesota History Bulletin,* Vol. 2, No. 8. St. Paul: November, 1918.

Robinson De Lorme W. "Editorial Notes on Historical Sketch of North & South Dakota." *South Dakota Historical Collections,* Vol. 1. Aberdeen, South Dakota: 1902.

Robinson, Doane. *Doane Robinson's Encyclopedia of South Dakota*. Pierre, 1925.

Robinson, Doane. *History of South Dakota: Together with Personal Mention of Citizens of South Dakota*. B. F. Bowen & Co., 1904.

Robinson, Doane. *South Dakota Sui Generis*. Chicago, American Historical Society, Inc., 1930.

Robinson, Elwyn B. *History of North Dakota*. Lincoln, University of Nebraska Press, 1966.

Robinson, Will G. "Members of the Territorial Legislature of Dakota." *South Dakota Historical Collections & Report*, Vol. 25. Pierre, South Dakota: 1950.

Robison, Mabel O. *Minnesota Pioneers*. Minneapolis, T. S. Denison & Co., 1958.

Rolfsrud, Erling N. *The Story of North Dakota*. Alexandria, Minnesota, Lantern Books, 1963.

Ruth, Kent. *Landmarks of the West: A Guide to Historic Sights*. Lincoln, University of Nebraska Press, 1986.

Sandborn, Ruth E. "The United States and the British in the Northwest: 1865–1870." *North Dakota Historical Quarterly*, Vol. 6, No. 1. Bismarck: October, 1931.

Sanderson, Laura B. *In the Valley of the Jim*. Bismarck Tribune.

Schell, Herbert S. *South Dakota: Its Beginnings & Growth*. New York, American Book Co., 1942.

Schell, James P. "History of the Early Presbyterian Church of North Dakota." *Collections of the State Historical Society of North Dakota*, Vol. 4. Fargo, North Dakota: 1913.

Smith, George M. *South Dakota: Its History and Its People*. Chicago, S. J. Clarke Publishing Co., 1915.

South Dakota Legislative Manual. Pierre, State Publishing Co., 1927.

Spokesfield, Walter E. *The History of Wells County, North Dakota and Its Pioneers: With a Sketch of North Dakota History and the Oregin (sic) of the Place Names*. Jamestown, North Dakota, 1929.

State of North Dakota: 1907 Legislative Manual. Bismarck, Tribune Printers & Binders, 1907.

State of North Dakota: 1919 Legislative Manual. Bismarck, Bismarck Tribune Co., 1919.

State Parks & Historic Sights in North Dakota. Bismarck, State Parks Committee, State Historical Society, 1950.

Stennett, William H. *A History of the Origin of the Place Names Connected with the Chicago & North Western & Chicago, St. Paul, Minneapolis & Omaha Railways*. Chicago, 1908.

Sullivan, Helen J. *Know Your North Dakota: A Handbook of Information for the Schools of North Dakota*. Fargo, North Dakota, Department of Public Instruction, 1929.

Thompson, George, Publisher, *Adams County Record*, Hettinger, North Dakota. 1987 letter to Mrs. DeLores M. Tollefson, Secretary-treasurer, Hettinger County Historical Society, Regent, North Dakota.

Thrapp, Dan L. *Encyclopedia of Frontier Biography*. Lincoln, University of Nebraska Press, 1988.

Tofsrud, O. T. *A History of Pierce County*. Rugby, North Dakota, 1936.

Tollefson, Mrs. DeLores M., Secretary-treasurer, Hettinger County Historical Society, Regent, North Dakota. Letter dated July 10, 1987 to the *Adams County Record* Editor, Hettinger, South Dakota.

Tollefson, Mrs. DeLores M., Secretary-treasurer, Hettinger County Historical Society, Regent, North Dakota. 1987 letter to the author.

Tweto, Alma. "History of Abercrombie Township, Richland County." *Collections of the State Historical Society of North Dakota*, Vol. 3. Bismarck: 1910.

Tweton, D. Jerome, & Theodore B. Jeliff. *North Dakota: The Heritage of a People*.

Fargo, North Dakota Institute for Regional Studies, 1976.

Upham, Warren. *Minnesota Geographic Names*. St. Paul, Minnesota Historical Society, 1969.

Upham, Warren, & Mrs. Rose Barteau Dunlap. "Minnesota Biographies: 1655–1912." *Collections of the Minnesota Historical Society*, Vol. 14. St. Paul: 1912.

Vexler, Robert I. *Chronology & Documentary Handbook of the State of North Dakota*. Dobbs Ferry, New York, Oceana Publications, Inc., 1978.

Vogel, Virgil J. *Iowa Place Names of Indian Origin*. Iowa City, University of Iowa Press, 1983.

Vyzralek, Frank E., Great Plains Research. Letter to the author dated August 29, 1988.

White, Hugh L. *Who's Who for North Dakota: A Biographical Directory*. Bismarck, North Dakota State Historical Society, 1954.

Williams, Mary Ann Barnes. *Origins of North Dakota Place Names*. Bismarck, Bismarck Tribune, 1966.

Williams, Mary Ann Barnes. *Pioneer Days of Washburn, North Dakota & Vicinity*. Washburn, North Dakota, Washburn Leader, 1936.

Wills, Brent L. *North Dakota Geography & Early History*. Grand Forks, North Dakota, University of North Dakota, 1967.

Wilson, William E. *Indiana: A History*. Bloomington, Indiana University Press, 1966.

Winks, Robin W. *Frederick Billings: A Life*. New York, Oxford University Press, 1991.

Wishek, Nina F. *Along the Trails of Yesterday: A Story of McIntosh County*. Ashley Tribune, 1941.

Work Projects Administration. *Inventory of the County Archives of North Dakota-Golden Valley & Mercer Counties*, 1941.

Work Projects Administration. *The Mayors of St. Paul: 1850–1940*. 1940.

Ohio

(88 counties)

2008 *Adams County*

John Adams (1735–1826)— Adams, a native of Massachusetts, was a delegate to the first Continental Congress and a signer of the Declaration of Independence. He participated in Paris, with Benjamin Franklin and John Jay in negotiating peace with England and, after the war, he was our country's first minister to England. Adams became the first vice-president of the United States under George Washington and when Washington retired, Adams was elected to be our nation's second president. This county was created on July 10, 1797, when Ohio was still the Northwest territory, and when John Adams had recently begun serving as president. The county's name was chosen and proclaimed by the territory's governor, Arthur St. Clair (1736–1818)

2009 *Allen County*

Ethan Allen (1738–1789)— Born in Litchfield, Connecticut in January, 1738, Allen served in the French & Indian War and then settled in what is today's state of Vermont. There he led Vermont residents in opposition to rule by England's colony of New York and became a colonel in the Green Mountain Boys, Vermont's militia formed to oppose the colony of New York. When the American Revolution began, the Green Mountain Boys united with troops of the Continental army in attacking British forts at Ticonderoga and Crown Point, New York. Ethan Allen led the Green Mountain Boys in their role in these successful missions, which gave our Revolutionary forces control of lower Lake Champlain. Allen petitioned the Continental Congress to have the Green Mountain Boys absorbed in the Continental army and congress granted the request but took away much of Allen's command role. Captured by the British as a prisoner of war but released in a prisoner exchange, Allen was commissioned a brevet-colonel in the Continental army before he returned to Vermont. There, he attempted to have Vermont recognized as an independent entity but died in 1789, two years before Vermont's admission to statehood. This Ohio county was created and named in his honor on February 12, 1820.

2010 *Ashland County*

The home of Henry Clay, Ashland, in Kentucky— This county was created on February 24, 1846. The county's name was chosen to honor the American statesman, Henry Clay, whose home, named Ashland, was located at Lexington, Kentucky, just 80 miles south of Ohio. Clay represented Kentucky in both branches of the U.S. Congress. For many years he was one of the more prominent figures in American politics but his several bids for the presidency were unsuccessful. He was influential in effecting important compromises between northern and southern interests during the years that secession and civil war were imminent. When this Ohio county was created, Clay had been recently defeated as a candidate for president. He lost the 1844 election to James K. Polk by only 38,175 popular votes out of 2.6 million total votes.

Ashland, in Lexington, Kentucky— Clay's home, named Ashland, is located on Richmond Road at Sycamore Road, which is now within the city limits of Lexington. The restored Ashland, surrounded by 20 acres of expansive woodland, is furnished throughout with Clay family furniture. A number of outbuildings also remain. Henry Clay established his residence at Ashland in 1806, when he rented a farm located here. About 1810 he purchased 400 acres of land from the estate he was renting and soon constructed his first Ashland, the brick mansion designed by architect Benjamin H. Latrobe (1764–1820). The mansion faced west, toward Lexington, measured 126 feet by 47 feet, and was two and a half story high, with one story wings on both sides. An earthquake unsettled this first mansion's foundations and that original structure was later taken down. Clay returned to Ashland frequently until 1851, when, in failing health, he left Ashland for the last time. He died the following year, while serving in the U.S. Senate. The brick mansion was rebuilt, from Latrobe's plans and using the original materials, in 1857. From 1806 to 1948, four generations of Clays have been associated with Ashland. Clay's home here is now owned and administered as a historic site by the Henry Clay Memorial Foundation, and guided tours are available.

2011 *Ashtabula County*

Ashtabula River— The Ashtabula River is a small stream, in the northeastern corner of Ohio, and all of its waters are within the present Ashtabula County. The Ashtabula River rises in northwestern Sheffield township, flows, crookedly, west, north, west and then north again, and it empties its waters into Lake Erie at the city of Ashtabula, Ohio. Only five miles separates the Ashtabula's origin from its mouth on Lake Erie, but its wandering course probably covers twice that distance. The river's name is of Indian origin, likely Delaware, but since the Indians had no written language, the spelling is that given to the Indian name by Whites. Apparently the Indian's name for this river related to fish or fishing. Lake Erie is now recovering from pollution which it suffered in the 20th century, but before Whites arrived to begin polluting the lake, fish were plentiful in Lake Erie and the streams which fed it. A translation of the Ashtabula River's Indian name was suggested by August C. Mahr in his article entitled "Indian River & Place Names in Ohio," which appeared in the April, 1957, issue of the *Ohio Historical Quarterly* (Vol. 66, No. 2.) Professor Mahr was particularly well versed in the language of the Delaware Indians and he speculated that the name *Ashtabula* meant "there is always enough moving," probably referring to fish or fishing. In 1796, when Connecticut's Moses Cleaveland (1754–1806) and his party of 50 surveyors camped on the banks of the Ashtabula River, he suggested that the Ashtabula River and environs be named for his daughter, Mary Esther. To bribe his companions into agreement, Cleaveland supplied two gallons of wine, and the river was named Mary Esther until the wine ran out. This county was created on February 10, 1807.

2012 *Athens County*

Athens, Greece— The notion of establishing a university at Athens, Ohio, was conceived in 1786 by members of the Ohio Company at Bunch of Grapes Tavern, in Boston. Ohio University, within what would be Athens and Athens County, Ohio, was chartered in 1804 and Athens County, Ohio was created on February 20, 1805. It was this institution of higher learning that prompted Athens County to be named for Greece's ancient seat of knowledge and wisdom.

Athens, Greece— Named in honor of the Greek goddess, Athena, patroness of arts, wisdom and industry, by the beginning of the 7th century B.C., the city-state of Athens had become important. Under Pericles, from about 460–431 B.C., Athens reached greatness in commerce, architecture, culture and political democracy. Among the greats of Athens' intellectuals were Aristotle, Euclid, Plato and Socrates. The second Peloponnesian War ending in 404 B.C. cost Athens its supremacy in Greece. After a period of friendly relations with Rome, Athens began to fall to the Barbarians and by A.D. 395 the fall was complete. Eight centuries later, about A.D. 1200, Athens began to emerge from the Dark Ages. It was conquered by the Ottoman Empire in 1456 and later was controlled by governments now within France, Spain and Turkey. As a part of a modern Greek kingdom, Athens won independence from Turkey in 1829. It became the capital of modern Greece in 1835. Athens and Greece were occupied by Germany during World War II. Today's Athens covers 167 square miles and has a population of about two and one half million. Still recognized as a cradle of education, wisdom and architectural greatness, Athens attracts tourists from around the world.

2013 *Auglaize County*

Auglaize River— This county was created on February 14, 1848, and named for the Auglaize River, which rises within its borders and flows west, and then north for a total of about 100 miles. The waters of the Auglaize join those of the Maumee River at Defiance, Ohio and the combined stream continues east and northeast as the Maumee River. It was at the rapids of this Maumee River, in what is now northwestern Ohio, that General Anthony Wayne (1745–1796) defeated the Indians in the decisive battle of Fallen Timbers on August 20, 1794. The name of the Auglaize River is of Indian origin, but since the Indians had no written language, the spelling is that given to the Indian name by Whites. The Indians' name, which we render as *Auglaize* meant "fallen timbers," or "fallen timbers on the river."

2014 *Belmont County*

French words, bel & mont, meaning "beautiful mount"— Belmont County was created on September 7, 1801, while Ohio was still the Northwest territory. Its name was proclaimed by the territory's governor, Arthur St. Clair (1736–1818), and comes from French words meaning "beautiful mount." The French noun, *mont*, is used for a "mount" and the adjective *bel* is used, poetically, to signify "beautiful," This county is located, in eastern Ohio. on the Ohio River, and although the county's surface is hilly, there are no mountains, nor were there any when the county's was larger back in 1801. Belmont County borders on West Virginia (still part of Virginia in 1801) but even that state's Appalachian Mountains are 80 miles away. However St. Clair didn't use the French word *montagne*, which means "mountain," but the *mont*, meaning "high hill." A number of sources dealing with the history, geography and place names of Ohio suggest that the county's name was coined as descriptive of its pleasant, hilly lands, rather than for any mountain(s), whether beautiful or not.

2015 *Brown County*

Jacob J. Brown (1775–1828)— A native of Pennsylvania with little military experience, Brown found himself in command of a section of the frontier at the start of the War of 1812. His successful defense of the important American base, Sackett's Harbor, on Lake Ontario resulted in his appointment in July, 1813, as brigadier-general in the army and six months later he was made major-general. Brown later served with distinction in other important battles of the War of 1812. After the War, in 1821, he was assigned the command of the United States army, which he held until his death. This county was created on March 1, 1818.

2016 *Butler County*

Richard Butler (–1791)— Butler was born in the 1740's in Ireland. Some sources list his year of birth as 1743 while others say 1748. He immigrated with his family to America and settled in Pennsylvania. Butler served as an officer during the American Revolution, participating in battles at Saratoga and Stony Point, New York, and later in Georgia. After the Revolution, he served as a commissioner to negotiate treaties with several Indians tribes and was then made superintendent of Indian affairs for the northern district. Butler also served briefly in the Pennsylvania senate. In 1791 he was recalled to military duty, given the rank of major-general and made second in command to General Arthur St. Clair, who was then governor of Northwest territory. Butler was killed in combat by Indians on November 4, 1791, near the present site of Ft. Wayne, Indiana, during the Indians' defeat of General St. Clair's forces. This county was created on March 24, 1803, just one month after Ohio was admitted to statehood.

2017 *Carroll County*

Charles Carroll (1737–1832)— Carroll was a native of Maryland and he represented that state in the Continental Congress. He was one of the signers of the Declaration of Independence and he later represented Maryland as a U.S. senator in the first congress of the United States. Carroll lived to be the last surviving signer of the Declaration of Independence and several states recognized that distinction by naming counties for him. That certainly was Ohio's motivation. Sources consulted differ on the precise date that this county was created. Some show December 25, 1832, while others cite January 1, 1833. In either case the county's name was clearly chosen as a result of the Charles Carroll's death, less than two months earlier, on November 14, 1832.

2018 *Champaign County*

Derived from French word for "open, level country"— This county was created on February 20, 1805. Its name derived from the French word, *champagne*, for "open, level country." The name was chosen as descriptive of the county's surface, about half of which is level or only slightly undulating.

2019 *Clark County*

George R. Clark (1752–1818)— A native of Virginia, George Rogers Clark was a frontiersman and military hero. During the American Revolution he secured a commission as lieutenant-colonel to attack the British, Indians and Loyalists in Indiana and Illinois. He successfully captured Vincennes, Cahokia and Kaskaskia and after the British retook Kaskaskia, Clark won it a second time. In 1780, Clark traveled north from the Ohio River area into what is now Clark County, Ohio and destroyed the Shawnee Indian village here, named Piqua. The Shawnee were firm allies of the British. These military victories, together with skillful negotiating by Benjamin Franklin, enabled the United States to acquire the Northwest territory, and hence Ohio, during the peace negotiations with the British at the end of the Revolution. This county was created on December 26, 1817, in an act which became effective on March 1, 1818. George Rogers Clark suffered at least three strokes starting in 1809 and his third known stroke, on February 13, 1818, took his life.

2020 *Clermont County*

Uncertain— This county was created on December 6, 1800, by proclamation of the governor of the Northwest territory, General Arthur St. Clair (1736–1818). Sources dealing with the history, geography and place names of Ohio are about equally divided concerning the origin of this county's name. About half say that the name commemorates a Clermont, in France, while members of the other half indicate that the name is French for "clear mountain." While this translation is faulty, many of our nation's geographic names are Anglicized versions of European words, and it is possible that Clermont is one of them. *Mont* is French for "mount" rather than "mountain." *Cler* could be an attempt to suggest "clear."

Clermont-Ferrand, France— Founded by the Roman Empire and known by them as Augustonemetum, Clermont-Ferrand is in south-central France, about 90 miles east of Limoges. Clermont was the scene of several Roman Catholic councils and it was the council of A.D. 1095, which gave rise to the Crusades. The bulk of the initial crusaders were French Knights but other powers in Europe participated. Today Clermont-Ferrand is a manufacturing and commercial city with a population of some 150,000.

When this Ohio county was created in 1800, French aid to the American colonists during the American Revolution was a recent memory as was the French Revolution. These circumstances may have contributed to the selection of this county's name by Governor Arthur St. Clair.

2021 *Clinton County*

George Clinton (1739–1812)— Born on July 26, 1739, at Little Britain, New York, Clinton served in the legislature of England's New York colony. He became one of America's leaders in opposition to England's treatment of her colonial citizens and he was a New York delegate to the second Continental Congress. Clinton also held the rank of brigadier-general in our Revolutionary army. On July 30, 1777, George Clinton became New York's first elected governor and when New York was admitted to the new federal Union of states, Clinton became the first governor of the state of New York. During the period that the original 13 colonies were debating the formation of a central, federal government, Clinton was an outspoken critic of certain aspects of the proposed federal Constitution. Nevertheless, he served our nation at the federal level, as vice-president under Presidents Thomas Jefferson and James Madison. Sources consulted differ on whether this Ohio county was created on February 19, 1810, or March 1, 1810. In either case, the county was born while Clinton was serving as our country's vice-president, under President James Madison.

2022 *Columbiana County*

A patriotic name derived from the name of Christopher Columbus & Anna— This county was created on March 25, 1803, just one month after Ohio was admitted to the Union as a state. In a burst of patriotism, the first portion of this county's name was derived from Christopher Columbus' name, and in an additional nod to the great discoverer, the city of Columbus was designated as Ohio's state capital in 1812. That discoverer's name has been given various patriotic meanings. As used in the name of the District of Columbia, it means the United States of America. The word *Columbus* is a Latin noun and means a "male dove" or "male pigeon." According to at least one source, the name

Columbia had earlier been considered as a possible name for the new nation, which became the United States of America.

Cristoforo Colombo (1451–1506)— Colombo, whose name we render as Christopher Columbus, was a native of Italy who believed the theory that the earth is round and that Asia could be reached by sailing west from Europe. He persuaded Ferdinand and Isabella of Spain to equip an expedition for him to test this theory. Sailing from Europe August 3, 1492, he first sighted land in the Americas in the Bahama Islands on October 12, 1492. On this voyage he left a colony of 40 men on the Hatian coast. Columbus returned several times to the New World before his death in 1506. Popularly known as the discoverer of America, Columbus was certainly not the first European to reach the Western Hemisphere. Leif Ericsson accomplished that about the year A.D. 1000. But it was Columbus' expedition that triggered rapid exploration, conquest and settlement of the Americas by Europeans.

The second portion of this county's name pertains to a completely unrelated and anonymous Anna. At the time that the legislature was debating what this new county's name should be, one legislator suggested adding Maria to make the county's name Columbiana-Maria. Horace Mack's *History of Columbiana County, Ohio*, published in 1879, tells us that this suggestion was made "jocularly."

2023 *Coshocton County*

A Delaware Indian village, near the present city of Coshocton, Ohio— Sixteen miles northwest of the present city of Coshocton, Ohio, the county seat of Coshocton County, the Delaware Indians had a village at the junction of three rivers. These rivers are the Tuscarawas, Muskingum and Walhonding. The village here, composed of log huts and a large council house, was important to the Delaware. Since the Indians had no written language, the spellings of the names that have survived are those that were given to the Indians' village name by Whites. Several versions of this name are found including *Koshachkink, Goshachkung, Koshochknk, Kochkochknk* and *Koshchhktoon*. A translation of the Indian name was suggested by August C. Mahr in his article entitled "Indian River & Place Names in Ohio," which appeared in the April, 1957, issue of the *Ohio Historical Quarterly* (Vol. 66, No. 2.) Professor Mahr was particularly well versed in the language of the Delaware Indians and he speculated that the name meant

"river-crossing device," or "ferry." Mahr stated that although this was "...undocumented as the source of the place name Coshocton, it appears obvious that it is." This county was created on January 31, 1810.

2024 *Crawford County*

William Crawford (1732–1782)— A native of Virginia, Crawford was a farmer, surveyor and soldier. Before the American Revolution he fought in the French and Indian war, the Pontiac war and Lord Dunmore's war. During the Revolution, Crawford took part in battles at Long Island, Trenton, Princeton, Brandywine and Germantown and rose to the rank of colonel. About 1778 he moved to the West, where he engaged in defense of the frontier and in actions against the Indians. In 1782 he was captured by Delaware Indians, tortured and burned at the stake near Upper Sandusky, Ohio. The place where he was taken prisoner by the Indians was near present-day Carey, Ohio, which was within the bounds of Crawford County, Ohio, when Crawford County was originally created on February 12, 1820. Later, in 1845, Wyandot County was created and the site of Crawford's capture is now within Wyandot County, Ohio. Although this historic site is no longer within the county that was named in Colonel Crawford's honor, it is within Crawford township of Wyandot County.

2025 *Cuyahoga County*

Cuyahoga River— This county was created during the first decade of the 19th century (there is little agreement on the date; various sources show, 1807, 1808 and 1810), and named for the Cuyahoga River which flows through it. This is one of America's better-known rivers although it is only 100 miles long. It rises east of Cleveland, Ohio, in Geauga County, flows southwest through Portage County into Summit County. There, near Akron, Ohio, it receives the waters of its largest tributary, the Little Cuyahoga River, and the main stream turns abruptly north, flowing north across Summit and Cuyahoga Counties to enter Lake Erie on the western side of Cleveland, the county seat of Cuyahoga County. Much of the terrain that the Cuyahoga traverses in its U-shaped meander has been the scene of heavy manufacturing activity, and many of these factories generated polluting waste which needed to be discharged. Akron is famous for its rubber factories and Cleveland's steel and other heavy industries attracted immigrants from many European countries. Before the days of environmental concerns and laws, companies were pretty much free to pollute at will. As a result, the section of the Cuyahoga River from Akron through Cleveland to Lake Erie became famous for its high level of pollution. About 25 years after World War II, its waters were so foul that it caught on fire and nobody knew just how the fire might be extinguished. Environmental laws and improved business ethics have brought happier days to the Cuyahoga. The name *Cuyahoga* is the rendering, by Whites, of the Indians' name for this river. Most sources on the history, geography and place names of Ohio indicate that the Indians' name meant "crooked river," and although this description is apt, there is doubt that it is correct. August C. Mahr's article entitled "Indian River & Place Names in Ohio," which appeared in the April, 1957, issue of the *Ohio Historical Quarterly* (Vol. 66, No. 2.) states that the name is "doubtless Iroquoian" but its meaning is unknown. Professor Mahr suggests that the name may have come from the name of the Cayuga Indians, one of the tribes of the Iroquois confederation. That tribe is known to be associated with central New York and southern Canada, but the Cuyahoga River is only 300 miles west of central New York.

2026 *Darke County*

William Darke (1736–1801)— Born in Pennsylvania, Darke moved with his parents to Virginia as a boy. The family settled at Shepherdstown, now in West Virginia. Darke gained some military experience in the French and Indian War so was made a captain at the start of the American Revolution. In the battle of Germantown, Pennsylvania, he was taken as a prisoner of war by the British, and held in a prison ship in New York harbor for three years. Released in a prisoner exchange, he participated in our important victory at Yorktown, Pennsylvania, in the fall of 1781 and was promoted to lieutenant-colonel. After the Revolution, Darke was a delegate to Virginia's convention called to ratify the federal constitution. He was re-commissioned in 1791 to fight the Indians on the western frontier, which then included Ohio, and in a battle against Miami Indians, Darke was wounded and his youngest son, Captain Joseph Darke (–1791), was killed. Most sources refer to William Darke as General Darke and it is true that he eventually received a com-

mission as a brigadier-general. However, the events in his military career for which he is remembered occurred when he was Captain Darke and Colonel Darke. This county was created on January 3, 1809.

2027 *Defiance County*

Fort Defiance Fort Defiance was erected by Major General Anthony Wayne (1745–1796) here in northwestern Ohio, at the very edge of civilization, with Indians massed to the west and north. Although we had recently won freedom from Britain in the American Revolution, the British were once again threatening us and encouraging Indians on our northwestern frontier to attack. Fort Defiance was built during August, 1794, in the form of a square in the angle formed by the confluence of the Auglaize and Maumee Rivers. Block houses were placed at each corner to protect the external sides of the fort. Outside of the block houses, and beyond a line of strong pickets, a wall of earth eight feet thick was erected and it surrounded the fort as did a ditch, 15 feet wide and eight feet deep. Given this description, one cannot blame General Wayne's boast that he had erected and named the fort defying "...the English, the Indians and all the devils in hell to take it." The town of Defiance, Ohio, which is the present county seat of Defiance County, was laid out in 1822 but sources consulted are agreed that the name of the county that was created in 1845 honors the fort, not the municipality.

2028 *Delaware County*

Delaware Indians— When the Europeans first encountered the Delaware Indians, they were living along the Delaware River basin in large areas of present day Delaware and New Jersey as well as eastern Pennsylvania. They were agricultural people who cleared the land of trees and undergrowth by burning. Because this burning limited the length of time that the land was fertile, the Delaware Indians moved their villages frequently. Farming was done by women, their most important crop being corn. The Delaware began to move westward as early as 1720 and Delaware County, Ohio, was one of the areas where they established villages. Delaware County, Ohio was created in 1808 and named in their honor. Today the Delaware are scattered, with many living in Canada and Oklahoma. *Delaware* is the name by which the Whites called these Indians. That name derived from the Delaware River, the river's name having derived from Del-

aware Bay. The bay was named for Thomas West, Lord De La Warr (1577–1618), who was a British governor of colonial Virginia.

2029 *Erie County*

Erie Indians Frederick W. Hodge's *Handbook of American Indians North of Mexico*, tells us that the Erie were a populous sedentary tribe, who resided, in the 17th century, from Lake Erie, probably south as far as the Ohio River and east along the watershed of the Allegheny River. The Erie subsisted primarily on maize. Although they were an Iroquois-speaking tribe, the Erie never were a member of the Iroquois Nation. In fact, by 1656, most Erie Indians had been slain by the Iroquois and any survivors were adopted by the Iroquois or other tribes, thus removing the Erie tribe as a separate entity, a full century before the American Revolution. This Ohio county was created on March 15, 1838. Although it borders on Lake Erie, one of the Great Lakes, sources consulted are agreed that the name of the county honors the Erie Indians, rather than the lake. However Ohio does have a county named in honor of Lake Erie. It is Lake County, the third county east of Erie County. Lake County also borders on Lake Erie.

2030 *Fairfield County*

The beauty of its fair fields— This county was created on December 9, 1800, by proclamation of the governor of the Northwest territory, Arthur St. Clair. The governor chose the name on account of the county's fair fields and lovely, rolling lands. When it was created in 1800, the county covered almost 10% of the present state of Ohio. It was then, and is now, located in central Ohio. The name that Governor St. Clair chose for this county was apt, whether speaking of the present Fairfield County, or the larger, 1800, version. Anyone who has used an American Automobile Association trip ticket, will be familiar with the phrase "gently rolling farmland," and find it apt for the land here. A. A. Graham compiled a *History of Fairfield and Perry Counties, Ohio*, published in 1883, which stated that there are few counties in Ohio with less waste land than Fairfield, and that almost all acres within its (1883) borders can be used for cultivation. Since Ohio has created no new counties since the middle of the 19th century, we are safe in concluding that the 1883 statement is still accurate, apart from deficiencies caused by insufficient crop rotation.

2031 *Fayette County*

Marie Joseph Paul Yves Roch Gilbert du Motier, Marquis de Lafayette (1757–1834)— Lafayette was a French aristocrat who served briefly in the French army. He came to America in 1777 to assist the American Revolutionary army. He was granted an honorary commission as major general by the Continental Congress and served with distinction in a number of battles in the Revolutionary War. This county was formed in 1810.

2032 *Franklin County*

Benjamin Franklin (1706–1790)— Franklin was a native of Massachusetts who moved to Pennsylvania in his teens. Poverty denied him a formal education but he became the leading printer and editor in North America. He gained fame for his discoveries and inventions in the physical sciences and he distinguished himself as author, philosopher and diplomat. Franklin was a signer of the Declaration of Independence and an important member of the convention which framed the U.S. Constitution. Skillful negotiating by Benjamin Franklin, coupled with successful military actions on our western frontier, enabled the United States to acquire the Northwest territory, and hence Ohio, during the peace negotiations with the British at the end of the Revolution. This county was created in 1803.

2033 *Fulton County*

Robert Fulton (1765–1815)— A native of Pennsylvania, Fulton supported himself while a young man as an artist. He later gained fame for his inventions dealing with marine vessels. He invented a submarine which he successfully demonstrated in the year 1800. Fulton invented mines to be used in naval warfare and was one of the inventors of the steamboat. The steamboat became a commercial success, made Fulton famous, and greatly sped America's development. Fulton County, Ohio, was created in 1850, when both steamboats and railroads were playing vital roles in transporting the Mid-West's agricultural and other products to eastern markets.

2034 *Gallia County*

France— The Roman Empire called their possessions in Europe, south and west of the Rhine River, west of the Alps and north of the Pyrenees Mountains, *Gaul*. Thus the Latin name *Gaul* is not synonymous with "France," but it was commonly used to designate France in the early 19th century and it was France, and a particular group of immigrants from France whom Ohio intended to honor when it created and named this county in 1803. Ohio was admitted to statehood in early 1803 and soon afterward, the new state created this county as an apology to a group of several hundred French aristocrats, merchants and artisans, who fled from France during the reign of terror of the French Revolution, and came to the Northwest territory. These French refugees had been sold land here, where they were told they would find rich agricultural lands in territory already settled and free of Indians. They were defrauded. The scam was complicated but apparently they were sold the land by a firm or combine that didn't own it, and then the agent in France who took the money absconded with all or part of it. The French immigrants left Europe in 1790 and arrived at what is now south-central Ohio, at the confluence of the Ohio River with the Scioto River, but soon found that they owned no land in the America. In 1795 the U.S. Congress, grateful to the French for their significant assistance in our recent American Revolution, awarded these French settlers 24,000 acres called "the French Grant." The French settlers' first home in American was at Gallipolis, the present county seat of Gallia County, although their "French Grant" was land within nearby Scioto County, Ohio.

2035 *Geauga County*

Grand River— Northern Ohio's Grand River rises in Geauga County, in northeastern Ohio, flows east, then north toward Lake Erie as far as Austinburg, Ohio. At Austinburg, the Grand takes a sharp turn west and travels parallel to Lake Erie until it nears Painesville, Ohio. The Grand River's last few gallons of water flow north and empty into Lake Erie at Painesville. A lot of words for a river whose length is on the order of 100 miles. When the Indians lived here, they called the Grand River the *Sheauga sepe*, which meant "Raccoon River." Sources consulted differ on the date that this county was created. They are about equally divided between two choices, just two months apart. Some show December 31, 1805, while most others say March 1, 1806. Perhaps in an evasive move to deal with this discrepancy, one source says the county was created December 31, 1805, effective March 1, 1806. In any event, the county's name clearly was derived from the Indians' name for the Grand River.

2036 *Greene County*

Nathanael Greene (1742–1786)— Greene was born in Rhode Island and served briefly in the Rhode Island legislature. He gained fame as one of the ablest American generals in the Revolutionary War. This county was created in 1803, soon after Ohio's admission to statehood, and named in honor of General Nathanael Greene.

2037 *Guernsey County*

Guernsey, a Channel Island of Great Britain— Guernsey is the westernmost, and second largest of the so-called Channel Islands of Great Britain. This 24 square mile island lies in the English Channel and has a current population of about 45,000. Together with the Channel Islands of Alderney, Sark and adjacent islands, Guernsey forms what is called the "Bailiwick of Guernsey" on certain postage stamps issued by Great Britain. Sources consulted differ on the date that this county was created, being about equally divided between two choices, just one month apart. Some show January 31, 1810, while most others say March 1, 1810. The county's name was chosen in honor of settlers here, who had come from the Channel Island of Guernsey. The first settler was a farmer, named Ogier. When he prospered, he encouraged his relatives on Guernsey to join him in Ohio. It was for this group of just 20 families from Guernsey, in Great Britain, that Guernsey County, Ohio, was named.

2038 *Hamilton County*

Alexander Hamilton (–1804)— A native of the West Indies, Hamilton moved to New York and served as an officer in America's revolutionary army. One of his assignments during the war was aide-de-camp to General George Washington. After the war Hamilton was a member of the convention which framed the U.S. Constitution. He collaborated with Madison and Jay in writing a series of papers entitled *The Federalist*, which explained the new constitution and advocated its adoption. A conservative and an advocate of a strong central government, he served as the United States' first secretary of the treasury. In 1804 he engaged in a duel with Aaron Burr and Hamilton died of wounds he suffered in that duel. This county was created as part of the Northwest territory during January, 1790, by proclamation of Governor Arthur St. Clair. At that time Hamilton was our nation's secretary of the treasury.

2039 *Hancock County*

John Hancock (1737–1793)— A native of Massachusetts and a graduate of Harvard, Hancock served in the Massachusetts legislature and was president of the Massachusetts provincial congress. He was elected to the Second Continental Congress and became its president. As president of the Continental Congress when the Declaration of Independence was signed, he was, on July 4, 1776, the first signer of that document. He signed it with such a flourish that the name John Hancock became a synonym for "signature." He later commanded the Massachusetts militia, served as governor of that state for many years and presided over the Massachusetts convention that ratified the U.S. Constitution. This Ohio county was created in 1820.

2040 *Hardin County*

John Hardin (1753–1792)— This military man was born in Virginia and served as an ensign in Lord Dunmore's 1774 war against the Indians. He later served as a lieutenant in the American Revolution and in 1786, he settled in Kentucky. Hardin then served in military actions against the Indians, rising to the rank of colonel. He also briefly held the rank of brigadier-general in the Kentucky militia. In 1792 Hardin was murdered by Indians in what is now Shelby County, in western Ohio, while he was engaged in peace negotiations with them. This county was created and named in his honor in 1820.

2041 *Harrison County*

William H. Harrison (1773–1841)— William Henry Harrison was a native of Virginia whose early career was in the army, serving as an officer in actions against the Indians. In 1798 President John Adams appointed Harrison to be secretary of Northwest territory and the following year he became that territory's delegate to the U.S. Congress. In 1800 Indiana territory was created and President John Adams appointed Harrison to be the new territory's first governor. Harrison commanded the army in the Battle of Tippecanoe and he served in the War of 1812 rising to the rank of major-general. He later served in the Ohio state legislature and represented Ohio in both houses of the U.S. Congress. In December, 1839, Harrison became the Whig party's candidate for president of the United States with John Tyler as his vice-presidential running mate. Their famous slogan was "Tippecanoe and Tyler too." Harrison was elected president but he served only one month before dying. This county was created early in 1813, little more than one year after Harrison's victory over the Indians at Tippecanoe on November 7, 1811.

2042 *Henry County*

Patrick Henry (1736–1799)— Henry was a native of Virginia and a lawyer. He served in the Virginia legislature, as governor of Virginia and as a delegate to the first and second Continental Congresses. Henry was one of America's key revolutionary leaders. He was a great orator and he is remembered for his call to arms against the British "Give me liberty or give me death." Henry opposed Virginia's ratification of the Federal constitution and his views played a role in the later adoption of the Bill of Rights. This county was created in 1820.

2043 *Highland County*

High lands between the Scioto River and the Little Miami River— Given that water tends to seek its own level, it is not surprising to find that the land between two rivers would be considered "high." The two rivers that the namers of this county had in mind, when they named this county in 1805 were the Scioto River, on the east and the Little Miami River, on the west. Some sources says that river on the west was the Miami River (then called the Great Miami River) but they are incorrect. All things are relative and nothing in Ohio rises to the height of the Rocky Mountains or even the nearer Appalachian Mountains. With these comparisons in mind, the name Highland for this county is not absurd, although its borders do contain gently rolling farmland, rather than true "high land." The county seat of Highland County is Hillsboro. James P. Lawyer tells us in his work entitled *History of Ohio*, published in 1904, that Hillsboro is situated in the highlands in the center of this county (still accurate since no new counties have been created in Ohio since the mid-1850s) and that it "stands on its seven hills, and from its elevation of 753 feet it overlooks the beauties of the surrounding country."

2044 *Hocking County*

Hocking River— This county in central Ohio was created in 1818 and named for the Hocking River, which flows through it. About 80 miles long, the Hocking rises in Fairfield County, Ohio, flows southeast across Hocking County, then continues on a generally eastern course until it enters the Ohio River at Hockingport, Ohio, about 15 miles downstream from Parkersburg, West Virginia. The river was named by the Delaware Indians. The 1905 issue (Volume 14) of *Ohio Archaeological & Historical Publications* contained an article by Mrs. Maria Ewing Martin entitled "Origin of Ohio Place Names." In that article Mrs. Ewing attributed the Indians' name for the river to "the neck of a bottle," and explained it as descriptive of "the river's shape at the falls." Mrs. Ewing's translation has been repeated by numerous authors dealing with the history, geography and place names of Ohio. Some of these sources skip the vital "neck" part and merely refer to the less plausible translation of "bottle." But neither of these explanations is satisfying. A more likely translation is provided by August C. Mahr in his article entitled "Indian River & Place Names in Ohio," which appeared in the April, 1957, issue of the *Ohio Historical Quarterly* (Vol. 66, No. 2.). Mahr was an authority on Delaware Indian names and his suggested translation of the Indians' name for the Hocking River is "river where there is (arable) land upstream."

2045 *Holmes County*

Andrew H. Holmes (–1814)— Andrew Hunter Holmes was born in Virginia and was acquainted with President Thomas Jefferson. Holmes' brother, David Holmes (1770–1832) was the first state governor of Mississippi. Andrew H. Holmes served as an officer in the War of 1812 holding the ranks of captain, major and, at the time of his death in combat, brevet-major. He was appointed a captain in the 24th Mississippi infantry on March 12, 1812, and later that year he was inspector in a Mississippi regiment, stationed principally around Baton Rouge. In early 1814, Holmes led a successful skirmish against a stronger British and Canadian force on the Thames River, 110 miles from Detroit. Holmes' force consisted of 160 men, who were driven into a defensive position by the stronger British and Canadian opposition. However, the enemy suffered 14 killed and 52 wounded, while Holmes' troops had but four men killed and three wounded. Later that year, serving as a brevet-major under Lieutenant colonel George Croghan (1791–1849), Holmes was killed in combat on August 4, 1814, at the Straits of Mackinac, above Michigan's lower peninsula. This county was created on January 20, 1824.

2046 *Huron County*

Huron Indians— In a treaty signed by

representatives of the Indians and the United States government, the Indians relinquished their title to lands in the area of what had been Connecticut's Western Reserve, in northeastern Ohio. In 1809 Ohio created this county within the land ceded by that 1805 Indian treaty and named it for the Huron Indians. Another Ohio county, Wyandot County, created in 1845, is also named for this tribe of Indians.

Huron Indians—Prior to about 1650 most of the Huron Indians (the surviving portion of these Indians are known as the Wyandot Indians) lived on Georgian Bay, a Canadian inlet of Lake Huron. An early French explorer, Jacques Cartier (1491–1557) encountered the Huron in Canada in 1534. Although the Huron belong to the Iroquoian linguistic family, it was Iroquois Indians who forced most Huron Indians to move west. Sometime after 1650 they settled near Detroit, Michigan, and on Sandusky Bay in Ohio. They eventually claimed most of Ohio and part of Indiana. These Huron Indians called themselves Wendat and, over time, that name evolved to Wyandot. But what was the origin and meaning of the name *Huron*? Many sources consulted say (approximately) that the name was given to these Indians by the French, who called them *hures*, a French term for "wild boars" or *huron*, a French term for "an unkempt person, knave, ruffian, lout or wretch." However, Dr. Virgil J. Vogel, a recognized scholar of Indian names in Michigan and elsewhere, argues convincingly in his work entitled *Indian Names in Michigan*, that several less insulting origins of the name Huron exist. The insulting French origins of the name were said to have been inspired by an unusual hair style of the Huron Indians but many other Indian tribes styled their hair in forms that could have been considered wild and primitive by the French. Beginning in 1795, the surviving Huron Indians, now called the Wyandot Indians, ceded all of their lands to the United States in various treaties. In 1842 or 1843 the Wyandot Indians, who by then were living in Ohio, moved to Kansas. There they purchased land from the Delaware Indians and settled in what is now Wyandotte County, Kansas. In 1867, the Whites forced the Wyandots to move on, this time to Indian territory (now Oklahoma).

2047 *Jackson County*

Andrew Jackson (1767–1845)—Jackson was born on the border of North Carolina and South Carolina. He represented Tennessee in both branches of the U.S. Congress, and gained fame and popularity for his military exploits in wars with the Indians and in the War of 1812. He was provisional military governor of Florida and, from 1829 to 1837, General Jackson was president of the United States. His presidency reflected the frontier spirit of America. This Ohio county was created in early 1816. One year earlier, in January, 1815, General Andrew Jackson had defeated the British during the battle of New Orleans, the greatest American land victory in the War of 1812, and the last major engagement of that conflict.

2048 *Jefferson County*

Thomas Jefferson (1743–1826)—Jefferson was a native of Virginia and a member of the Virginia legislature. He served Virginia as governor and was a delegate to the second Continental Congress. Jefferson was the author of the Declaration of Independence and one of its signers. He was minister to France, secretary of state, vice-president and president of the United States. As president, he accomplished the Louisiana Purchase and he arranged the Lewis & Clark Expedition to the Pacific Northwest. Jefferson was a true intellectual, thoroughly knowledgeable in the arts and sciences. His political theories were pivotal in the formation of our infant republic. This county was created on July 29, 1797, as part of the Northwest territory, by proclamation by Governor Arthur St. Clair. At that time Jefferson was serving as our nation's vice-president under President John Adams. This gesture was not enough to protect St. Clair from Jefferson's displeasure when, as president, he became dissatisfied with Governor St. Clair's performance and him removed as governor of the Northwest territory, in November, 1802.

2049 *Knox County*

Henry Knox (1750–1806)—This Massachusetts native participated in many of the important military engagements of the American Revolution and rose to the rank of major-general. After the war, Knox commanded West Point and he conceived and organized the Society of Cincinnati, an elite group of former Revolutionary officers. In 1785 he was appointed secretary of war under the Articles of Confederation and he retained that position in the first cabinet of the United States under President George Washington. Knox died suddenly at his home on October 25, 1806, as a result of swallowing a chicken bone. This county was created and named in his honor, a little over one year later. Sources consulted are about equally divided concerning the exact date that this county was created. About half show January 30, 1808, while the other half contend that March 1, 1808 is the correct date.

2050 *Lake County*

Lake Erie—This county in northeastern Ohio, which borders on Lake Erie, was created on March 6, 1840. Lake Erie is one of the five Great Lakes and it borders on four states in our country and on Canada's province of Ontario. The St. Lawrence Seaway provides Lake Erie with access to world ports. Many of the streams whose waters feed Lake Erie have been the scene of heavy manufacturing activity, and most of the factories here generated polluting waste which needed to be discharged. Before the days of environmental concerns and laws, companies were pretty much free to pollute at will. As a result, Lake Erie became famous for its high level of pollution. By about 25 years after World War II, Lake Erie's waters had become extremely foul. Environmental laws and improved business ethics have brought happier days to Lake Erie. The name *Erie*, perpetuates the memory of the Erie tribe of Indians, who formerly lived here.

Erie Indians—Frederick W. Hodge's *Handbook of American Indians North of Mexico*, tells us that the Erie were a populous sedentary tribe, who resided, in the 17th century, from Lake Erie, probably south as far as the Ohio River and east along the watershed of the Allegheny River. The Erie subsisted primarily on maize. Although they were an Iroquois-speaking tribe, the Erie never were a member of the Iroquois Nation. In fact, by 1656, most Erie Indians had been slain by the Iroquois and any survivors were adopted by the Iroquois or other tribes, thus removing the Erie tribe as a separate entity, a full century before the American Revolution.

2051 *Lawrence County*

James Lawrence (1781–1813)—Lawrence was an officer in the United States navy who established a reputation for bravery in the war against Tripoli and in the War of 1812. He died in combat while commanding the *Chesapeake* against the British, near Boston. He is said to have uttered the famous phrase "Don't give up the ship" while he lay mortally wounded in that battle. He died on June 4, 1813, and this county was created and named in his honor on December 21, 1815.

2052 Licking County

Licking River— This county in central Ohio was created in 1808 and named for the Licking River, which flows through it. The borders of Ohio's counties have changed considerably since 1808, but on today's map, the Licking River rises a bit north of Licking County, and flows southeast until it reaches Newark, Ohio, the county seat of Licking County. At Newark, the Licking River turns abruptly east and continues in that direction until it crosses Licking County's border with Muskingum County. Near that county border, the Licking once again bends to the southeast and finally ends its journey at Zanesville, Ohio, where its waters join those of the Muskingum River, a tributary of the Ohio River. The Licking River's name came from salt deposits in the area, which animals, wild and domestic, could lick for their salt needs.

2053 Logan County

Benjamin Logan (–1802)— Logan was born about 1743 in Virginia and he served as an officer in the Virginia militia during Lord Dunmore's War against the Indians in 1774. About 1775 Logan crossed the mountains and became one of the first pioneers to settle in the Kentucky wilderness. During the American Revolution he was a noted and high ranking Indian fighter. In 1786 he led a campaign against the Indians in the upper portion of the Miami River in what is now Logan County, Ohio. In fact his chief service during the Revolution was in actions against the Indians in Ohio. Benjamin Logan served in the Virginia legislature during the 1780's while Kentucky was still part of Virginia. He participated in the movement to separate Kentucky from Virginia and was a member of the 1792 convention that drafted Kentucky's first constitution. After Kentucky was admitted to statehood, Logan served in the lower house of the new state legislature and became a general in the Kentucky militia. Sources consulted are about equally divided concerning the exact date that this Ohio county was created. About half show December 30, 1817, while the other half contend that March 1, 1818 is the correct date.

2054 Lorain County

Lorraine, France— What remains of Lorraine, in northeastern France, has been in French hands since 1766. However, in 1815, the eastern half of Lorraine was ceded to Germany. Prior to that, control of Lorraine changed hands among European owners many times. In ancient times it was part of the kingdom of Austrasia. Under a treaty of A.D. 843, Lorraine became part of the Middle Kingdom of the German King Lothair I (855). Upon the death of Lothair I, his kingdom was divided among his three sons and one of them, King Lothair II (–869), became king of Lorraine. In 959 the kingdom of Lorraine was divided into two duchies Lower Lorraine and Upper Lorraine. It was Upper Lorraine, in the region of the upper Meuse River and Moselle River, that today's Lorraine, France descended from. In 987 the French king, Hugh Capet, relinquished Lorraine and it was ruled by a ducal family and later united with the Hapsburgs. As France expanded, Lorraine gradually was reduced in size and Lorraine was ruled from about 1735 to 1766 by a dethroned king of Poland, Stanislaus (1677–1766), who was the father-in-law of the French King Louis XV (1710–1774).

The idea to name this county in honor of Lorraine, France, was that of Herman Ely (–1852), a judge here in north central Ohio and the founder of Elyria, the county seat of Lorain County, Ohio. Elyria was named in Judge Ely's honor. Ely had visited the Lorraine area of France and found the area charming. He donated land and money for the erection of a courthouse at Elyria. This county was created on December 26, 1822.

2055 Lucas County

Robert Lucas (1781–1853)— A native of Shepherdstown, Virginia (now West Virginia), Lucas studied mathematics and surveying and settled in Scioto County, in southern Ohio, where he was employed as county surveyor. He served in both branches of the Ohio legislature and was an officer in the Ohio militia. During the War of 1812 Lucas served as a detached officer under General William Hull (1753–1825). In 1830 Robert Lucas ran for governor but was defeated in a close election by Duncan McArthur (1772–1839). He tried again in 1832 and this time was elected to be Ohio's governor. Reelected in 1834, Governor Lucas led the Ohio militia to fight against Michigan territory in the so-called Toledo War of 1835. On June 8, 1835, Governor Robert Lucas called the Ohio legislature into special session and suggested that they erect a new county in the disputed area, and the legislature complied, creating Lucas County during June, 1835, with its county seat at Toledo. Now but an interesting footnote in our nation's history, the dispute was very real at the time and if it weren't for Governor Robert Lucas, both Toledo and Lucas County might well belong to Michigan today. President Andrew Jackson intervened to prevent open warfare. Ohio's U.S. senator, Thomas Ewing (1789–1871), and congressman, Samuel F. Vinton (1792–1862), participated in the political maneuvers which gave the disputed area to Ohio. In 1838 President Martin Van Buren appointed Lucas as the first governor of Iowa territory. After a stormy tenure in that post, from 1838 to 1841, he ran for congress from Ohio, lost and returned to Iowa, where he died on February 7, 1853.

2056 Madison County

James Madison (1751–1836)— Madison was born in Virginia and served in the Virginia legislature and in the Continental Congress. He was a member of the convention which framed the U.S. Constitution and he collaborated with Hamilton and Jay in writing a series of papers under the title *The Federalist*, which explained the new constitution and advocated its adoption. Madison represented Virginia in the U.S. House of Representatives, served for eight years as secretary of state and for eight years as president of the United States. This county was created early in 1810, near the end of Madison's first year as president of our nation.

2057 Mahoning County

Mahoning River— This county was created in 1846 and named for the Mahoning River, which flows through it. The Mahoning rises in Columbiana County and first flows a considerable distance north before looping back in a southeastern direction to flow through Youngstown, the county seat of Mahoning County. After leaving Youngstown, the Mahoning briefly continues its southeastern journey and enters Pennsylvania near Lowellville, Mahoning County, Ohio. In Pennsylvania the Mahoning's waters join those of the Shenango River to form the Beaver River. Ohio Sources are annoyingly vague about admitting that Mahoning County was named for the Mahoning River. In fact, few make that admission. Most merely relate that the name *Mahoning* means "at the licks." This is true (the Mahoning River's name came from the Delaware Indians' language referring to "salt lick[s]") and salt deposits in the area, were important to animals, wild and domestic, who licked them for their salt needs.

2058 *Marion County*

Francis Marion (–1795) — Marion is believed to have been born in South Carolina. He served in the army in battles against the Cherokee Indians and was elected to the provisional congress of 1775. He served, with distinction, as an officer in the Revolutionary War and rose to the rank of general in that war. Marion was also a member of the South Carolina senate. This county was created and named for General Marion in 1820.

2059 *Medina County*

Medina, Saudi Arabia — Medina is one of the two most holy cities of Islam, the other being Mecca, also in Saudi Arabia. The Prophet and founder of Islam, Mohammed (–632) was born in Mecca about A.D. 570 and lived there until A.D. 622, when, persecuted for his religious teachings, he was forced to flee. He came then to Medina and arrived here on September 20, 622. Mohammed's tomb is located at Medina. Medina is an inland city, about 100 miles from the Red Sea in the western portion of today's Saudi Arabia. Its main business is religious tourism, drawing followers of Islam from around the world. The present population of Medina, Saudi Arabia, is about 200,000. It is uncertain why this Ohio county was named for Medina, Saudi Arabia. A few sources mention the possibility that the municipality of Medina, in New York state, might have inspired the name. However, Ohio's Medina County area was within Connecticut's "Western Reserve," and the original settlers here were from Connecticut, not New York. A related puzzle is the naming of an early settlement here, called Mecca. What is known is that Medina County was created by the state of Ohio on February 18, 1812. It is also known that a community was established here named Mecca and that the name Mecca was chosen by the town's proprietor, Elijah Boardman. Boardman had come to Ohio from Connecticut and was said to be a well-read and religious man. It isn't clear when Mecca was named but a courthouse was built here in 1818 and at that time Mecca was the county seat of Medina County, Ohio. Because there was another community in Ohio named Mecca, the one in Medina County was forced to change its name. The new name that was chosen was Med-ina, so the county seat of Medina County is now the city of Medina, Ohio.

2060 *Meigs County*

Return J. Meigs (1764–1825) — A native of Connecticut and a graduate of Yale College, Return Jonathan Meigs studied law and then moved to Marietta, in what is now southeastern Ohio, in 1788, the year after congress established the Northwest territory. Elected to the territorial legislature in 1799, Meigs also served as one of the judges of Northwest territory from February 12, 1798, to April, 1803. When the new state of Ohio formed its supreme court, Meigs was appointed to that bench. The Ohio senate elected him to fill a vacancy in the U.S. Senate and Meigs served in that body from January 6, 1809, until May 1, 1810, when he resigned to run for governor of Ohio. Elected in 1810 and reelected in 1812, Governor Meigs supplied 1,200 Ohio militia members to fight in the War of 1812. In 1814 President James Madison appointed Meigs to his cabinet as postmaster general and he continued in that post under President James Monroe until 1823, when he retired because of ill health. This county was created in 1819, while Meigs was serving in James Monroe's cabinet.

2061 *Mercer County*

Hugh Mercer (–1777) — Mercer was born about 1725 in Scotland and educated as a physician. He immigrated to America about 1747 and served in the army here as an officer during the French and Indian War. At the outbreak of the American Revolution, Mercer entered the Continental army, in which he attained the rank of brigadier-general. He served with distinction under General George Washington in the surprise attack on the British at Trenton, New Jersey in late December, 1776. One week later, at the battle of Princeton, New Jersey, on January 3, 1777, Hugh Mercer was severely wounded and he died of those wounds on January 12, 1777. This county was created and named in General Mercer's honor in 1820.

2062 *Miami County*

Uncertain — This county in western Ohio is traversed by the Miami River and all sources are agreed that both this river and one of Ohio's rivers further east, the Little Miami River, were named for the Miami Indian tribe. The Miami inhabited this area during the 18th and early 19th cen-turies and, for a time in the mid-1750s, controlled a portion of western Ohio. This county was created in 1807 and a plurality of sources dealing with the history, geography and place names of Ohio indicate that the county was named for the Miami Indians. However, that view is not unanimous. Unfortunately, the sources which fail to state that the Miami Indians were this county's namesake don't disagree, they are just annoyingly vague. Only one of several dozen sources consulted offers the alternative possibility that the county was named for the Miami River, which flows through it. From the language of the act which created this county, one might well suspect that the county was named for the Miami River, or Great Miami River, as it was then called. As a matter of interest, our nation's more famous Miami, in Florida, has no connection with either the Miami Indians or the Miami Rivers in Ohio. Our nation did not own Florida when this county was created in 1807 and the municipality of Miami, in southeastern Florida was not established until about 1900.

Miami Indians — The Miami Indians were a major tribe who lived in Wisconsin and, rather briefly, in Michigan. They later inhabited northern Illinois, northern Indiana and a portion of western Ohio. By 1840 most Miami Indians had been forced to move west by the encroaching Whites. Most of the Miami were first moved to Kansas and later resettled on reservations in Oklahoma and California. The origin and meaning of the name *Miami* is uncertain and disputed. Possibilities which have been mentioned by authorities on Indian names include:

— "People of the peninsula."

— "Pigeon."

— Derived from rendering by the French of the name by which the Delaware Indians called the Miami, which was *Wemiamik*. This literally meant "all beavers," or "all beaver children" but figuratively, it meant "all friends," which accurately described the relationship between the Miami and Delaware Indians.

2063 *Monroe County*

James Monroe (1758–1831) — Monroe, a native of Virginia, served in the Revolutionary War. Prior to his election as president of the United States, Monroe served in a wide variety of government posts. He served Virginia in the state legislature and as governor. He was a member of the Confederation congress and the U.S. Senate. He was minister to France and to Britain and he held two cabinet posts. As president, Monroe stressed limited government and strict construction of the constitution. He acquired Florida for the U.S. from Spain and he was the author of a policy declaration (later known as the Monroe Doctrine) which proscribed outside interference in North and South America. This county was created on January 29, 1813, while Monroe was serving as secretary of state in the cabinet of President James Madison.

2064 *Montgomery County*

Richard Montgomery (1738–1775)— Montgomery was born in Ireland and served with the British in North America in the French and Indian War. He settled in New York where he was elected to the New York provisional congress. Montgomery served as a general in the American Revolutionary army and he was killed in combat in Quebec, Canada, on December 31, 1775. This county was created in 1803.

2065 *Morgan County*

Daniel Morgan (1736–1802)—Morgan was a native of the Northeast who moved to Virginia in his youth. He served as a general in the Revolutionary War and was regarded as a hero for important victories scored by his troops. After the war he served one term in congress. This Ohio county was created and named in his honor on December 29, 1817.

2066 *Morrow County*

Jeremiah Morrow (1771–1852)—A native of Pennsylvania, Morrow moved to the Northwest territory in 1794, where he earned his living as a farmer, school teacher and surveyor. Elected to the territorial legislature and as a delegate to Ohio's 1802 constitutional convention, Morrow climbed the political ladder rapidly. He was a member of the first senate of the new state of Ohio in 1803, and he was Ohio's only representative in the lower house of congress from 1803 to 1813. In those early years, Ohio's population was small and the state was entitled to only one representative in congress. Morrow then served Ohio in the U.S. Senate from 1813 to 1819. Elected in 1822 as Ohio's governor and reelected in 1824, Morrow successfully supported state aid for public schools and his term saw completion of the Erie canal, vital to connecting Ohio's farm products with eastern markets. After leaving the gover-

nor's office, Morrow served in both houses of the Ohio legislature and in 1840 he returned to Washington as one of Ohio's congressmen from December, 1840, to March, 1843. This county was created and named in Governor Morrow's honor in early 1848. During the debate in the legislature on the creation of this new county, two other names were proposed before Morrow County was mentioned. The name *Gilead* had strong support and the name *Chester* was also proposed. This degree of interest in the name of a county is unusual. The location of the county seat is usually of far greater interest, because the city that wins the county seat gets the jobs associated with the seat of justice and revenue for supporting commercial enterprises. The proponents of the name Gilead didn't get the county name that they wanted but they came away with something. The county seat of Morrow County is located at the community of Mt. Gilead.

2067 *Muskingum County*

Muskingum River—This county was created in 1804 and named for the Muskingum River, of eastern Ohio. The Muskingum River is formed by the confluence of the Tuscarawas River with the Walhonding River is Coshocton County, Ohio and it flows south, and then southeast to Marietta, Ohio, where its waters enter the Ohio River. The Muskingum's total length is about 120 miles, nearly three-quarters of which are navigable. During the first half of its journey, the Muskingum River flows south across Muskingum County and through Muskingum's county seat, Zanesville, Ohio. A majority of sources on the history, geography and place names of Ohio indicate that the Indian name *Muskingum*, means "town on the river side." Dr. August C. Mahr was an expert on names of the Delaware Indians and he comments on this translation in his article entitled "Indian River & Place Names in Ohio," which appeared in the April, 1957, issue of the *Ohio Historical Quarterly* (Vol. 66, No. 2.). Mahr says "*Muskingum* ... indeed is a Delaware word, but by no stretch of the imagination does it mean 'a town on the river side.'" Rather, Mahr says, *Muskingum* means "where the land is swampy, soggy," but says that the location of the particular swampy land refereed to is not known.

2068 *Noble County*

Uncertain—A majority of sources dealing with the history, geography and place

names of Ohio state that this county was named for "James Noble, an early settler," or "James Noble a pioneer settler of this area." However, Larry L. Miller's *Ohio Place Names*, published in 1996 states that it was named for Warren Noble, who "chaired the state's committee on additional counties." William A. Taylor's work entitled *Ohio Statesmen & Annals of Progress*, published in 1899, confirms Miller's statement and says that Noble County was named "In honor of Representative Warren P. Noble, of Seneca County, who championed its erection." However, Noble County, Ohio was created by the session of the Ohio legislature which adjourned on March 25, 1851, and the same 1899 source contains a listing of all members of both branches of the Ohio legislature during that session and Warren P. Noble's name is not among them. Moreover, Warren P. Noble's name is not listed in this 1899 source as a member of either house of the Ohio legislature in the immediately preceding session, which adjourned on March 25, 1850. Taylor's 1899 work includes an alphabetical list of all representatives in the Ohio legislature from 1840 to 1851 and we do find Warren P. Noble's name on that list. At least six other Ohio sources agree that this county was named for Warren P. Noble. If so, Representative Warren P. Noble apparently advocated creation of this county during the period 1846–1848, when he was a member of the Ohio legislature. Since this county was not created until 1851, this chain lacks the clear trail that we would like to see.

James Noble (–)—James Noble was said to have been a pioneer settler of this area, who lived near a community named Saharasville. A township in Morgan County (a county which lies on Noble County's western border) was organized in 1819 and it continued to exist until the formation of Noble County in 1851. That township is said to have been named in honor of the "pioneer settler," James Noble. Among the 43 voters at an election held on April 3, 1820, to elect township officials for Noble Township, the name James Noble is listed but a Samuel Noble and John Noble also voted in this election. A history of Noble County, Ohio, published in 1887 mentions two John Nobles, father and son, both of whom lived here as pioneers. The elder John Noble (–1831) came from Pennsylvania and settled here in 1812. He was the father of seven children. The eldest son was named James and another son was the younger John Noble (1802–). This second John Noble was a member of the first board of county commissioners of Noble

County in 1851. The land taken to create Noble County in 1851 came partially from Morgan County, which contained the Noble township mentioned above, but Guernsey, Monroe and Washington Counties also gave up land to form Noble County. Indiana had a U.S. senator named James Noble (1785–1831), who was a native of Virginia and settled in Brookville, when Indiana was still a territory. This James Noble appears to have moved from Virginia to Kentucky to Indiana, with no period of residence in Ohio.

Warren P. Noble (1820–1903)— Born in Pennsylvania on June 14, 1820, Warren P. Noble moved to Ohio, studied law, was admitted to the Ohio bar in 1843 or 1844 and practiced law at Tiffin, Ohio. He served in the lower house of the Ohio legislature from December 7, 1846, to February 25, 1848. Warren P. Noble later served as prosecuting attorney of Seneca County, Ohio and represented Ohio in the U.S. House of Representatives during the Civil War. He died on July 9, 1903.

We can have the best of both worlds if we say that Warren P. Noble was our "early Ohio pioneer." He certainly was one, although he settled at Tiffin, Ohio, considerably, northwest of Noble County. A work by the D. A. R. published in 1915 entitled *Ohio Early State & Local History* relates that "Warren P. Noble came here in 1842 ... went to Chicago, but it looked ... like a mud-hole..." so he returned to Ohio "and located in Tiffin."

2069 *Ottawa County*

Ottawa Indians— When first encountered by Whites, the Ottawa Indians were living at what is now the province of Ontario, in Canada. Initially the name Ottawa was used by the French to denote all tribes living on the shores of Lake Huron in upper Michigan and west along Lake Superior. Since then, the name has generally been confined to Indians of the Algonquian linguistic family, who lived in Ohio, Indiana, Michigan and Wisconsin. During the French and Indian War, the Ottawa Indians sided with the French against the British. The Ottawa Indians were pushed steadily westward, first by the Iroquois Indians and later by the Whites. They resisted efforts to push them out of eastern lands into less desirable western areas but these efforts failed. By December, 1836, some Ottawas were resettled to a part of the old Indian territory that is now in Kansas. However, other Ottawas remained in Michigan and Ontario, Canada. Dispirited by this forced relocation and in poor health, nearly half of the Ottawa Indians who had been moved to Kansas were dead within five years. The Ottawas in Kansas were again moved to the Indian territory that is now Oklahoma in 1870. The name *Ottawa* derives from an Indian name meaning "trader" or "barterer." The Ottawa Indians were adept at trading and even served as middlemen facilitating trades between Whites and other Indians and among several Indian tribes as well. This county was created in 1840.

2070 *Paulding County*

John Paulding (–1818)— During the American Revolution, the adjutant general of the British army, Major John Andre (1751–1780), secretly met behind American lines with General Benedict Arnold (1741–1801) of the Continental army. Benedict Arnold was one of our highest officers, the hero of the battle of Saratoga and the current commander of our critical fort at West Point, New York. Arnold was partially successful in committing his planned treason against America, in that he escaped and joined the British army. However, Major Andre was captured by three obscure New York militiamen, John Paulding, Isaac Van Wart and David Williams. In commemoration of this dramatic capture, the state of Georgia named one of her counties Paulding County and the state of Ohio honored all three of the men by creating and naming counties in their honor on the same day in 1820. (Some sources list the date as February 12, 1820, while others show April 1, 1820. Since the Ohio legislature adjourned that year on February 26, the legislature probably passed the act[s] to create these three counties on February 12, 1820 and the counties were officially born on April 1, 1820. In any event, all three counties were created simultaneously and all three celebrated the capture of Major John Andre.) The spelling of Isaac Van Wart's name is incorrectly rendered as Van Wert in the Ohio county's name. John Paulding was born in 1758 or 1759. He was a poor farm lad in Westchester County, New York, who entered New York's militia during the Revolution. Paulding had been a British prisoner of war but escaped from prison shortly before the capture of Major Andre. On the day of the capture, Paulding and seven companions were on duty near Tarrytown, New York, south of West Point fort, attempting to waylay any Tory cattle rustlers they might find operating in the area. The party of eight divided, five stationing themselves on a nearby hill and Paulding, Van Wart and Williams taking positions at a bridge. It was there that they captured Major Andre, rather by accident. Paulding was a big, spare man and the leader of the three. He was the only literate member of the trio and it was he who read the documents hidden in Andre's boots and suspected their importance. New York state honored John Paulding for his part in this dramatic and strategically important capture by giving him a farm, near Cortland, New York. Congress granted each of the three captors an annuity for life and a silver medal which was personally presented by George Washington.

2071 *Perry County*

Oliver H. Perry (1785–1819)— Perry was a native of Rhode Island and an officer in the U.S. navy. During the War of 1812 his squadron defeated the British in a key battle on Lake Erie of which Perry said "We have met the enemy and they are ours." Perry died on August 23, 1819. Sources consulted are about evenly divided about the two dates on which this county was said to have been created. Some say December 26, 1817, while the others indicate March 1, 1818. In either case, the date of the county's creation clearly indicates that it was created and named because of Perry's status as a hero of the War of 1812.

2072 *Pickaway County*

Piqua Indians— This county in central Ohio was created in 1810 and named for the Piqua Indians, one of the five principal divisions of the Shawnee Indians. The Shawnee are one of the important tribes of the Algonquian linguistic family and they are closely related to the Delaware Indians. During prehistoric times the Shawnee lived along the Ohio River but they were forced to move southeast by the Iroquois Indians. When first encountered by Europeans, most Shawnee Indians were living in South Carolina, Georgia and Florida. During the late 1700's and early 1800's the Shawnee migrated north and west. By about 1750 many of the Shawnee were living near the lands of their ancestors in the Ohio River valley. The Shawnee sided with the French against the British in the French and Indian War and when the United States became a country, the Shawnee were openly hostile to it. There is little reason to believe that their destiny would have been merrier if they had been friendly to the Americans. As White settlers pushed west, the Shawnee were pushed out to make room for them. They were allowed to own some rich farmland in Kansas but then resettled to Indian territory (now Oklahoma). The Piqua branch of the Shawnee had a village on the Scioto River in what is now Pickaway County. Ohio. Many sources dealing with the history, geography and place names of Ohio offer translations of the Indian name *Piqua*, but Dr. August C. Mahr, who was an expert on Indian names in Ohio, stated in his article entitled "Indian River & Place Names in Ohio," which appeared in the April, 1957 issue of the *Ohio Historical Quarterly* (Vol. 66, No. 2.), that the meaning of *Piqua* is uncertain.

2073 *Pike County*

Zebulon M. Pike (1779–1813) — A native of New Jersey, Pike served as an army officer on America's frontier following the Revolution. He led an exploratory army expedition to the Rocky Mountains in Colorado which Pike's Peak in the Colorado Rockies commemorates. Pike served as a general in the War of 1812 and was killed in combat in that war on April 27, 1813. This county was created and named in his honor by the state of Ohio, early in 1815.

2074 *Portage County*

The Indian portage connecting the Cuyahoga River with the Tuscarawas River — The Indians had numerous regularly-used portages in Ohio, over which they carried their canoes on land to move from one body of water to another. Portage County, Ohio was created in 1807 and named for the particular Indian portage between the Cuyahoga River and the Tuscarawas River. The Tuscarawas River rises in Summit County, Ohio, which lies on Portage County's western border. The Tuscarawas connects with a number of important Ohio streams, mostly to the south, including the Walhonding River, the Muskingum River and the Licking River. This portage's link to the Cuyahoga River enabled the Indians to travel, principally on water, from these eastern Ohio streams to the Great Lake, Lake Erie, via the Cuyahoga River. The Cuyahoga River crosses the northwestern portion of today's Portage County and eventually enters Lake Erie after a crooked journey in the vicinity of Akron, Ohio. Both the Cuyahoga River and the other river of this portage, the Tuscarawas River, flow through Summit County. A work by John M. Pittenger entitled *The Buckeye Story*, published in 1957, describes the Indian portage for which

this county was named and states that it "...now lies largely within the city limits of Akron, and one of Akron's residential streets, Portage Path, follows the old trail for some miles." Akron is the county seat of Summit County, Ohio.

2075 *Preble County*

Edward Preble (1761–1807) — Born in Portland, Massachusetts (now Maine) on August 15, 1761, Preble ran away from home when he was 16 to enter a life at sea. In 1779, during the American Revolution, Preble entered the Massachusetts navy as a midshipman. Later promoted to first-lieutenant, Preble served in several successful naval actions during the Revolution. After the war, he served as a merchant seaman but in 1798 he was called to duty as a lieutenant in the navy of the United States. He served against French privateers and, in 1803 and 1804, with the rank of commodore, Preble played an important role in our war against the Barbary pirates of Tripoli in the Mediterranean. In 1806 President Thomas Jefferson offered him the cabinet post of secretary of the navy, but Preble's health was failing and he declined this honor. He died at Portland, Massachusetts (now Maine), on August 25, 1807. This county was created on February 15, 1808.

2076 *Putnam County*

Israel Putnam (1718–1790) — Putnam was born in Massachusetts and moved, when he was about 21, to Connecticut. He served as an officer in the French and Indian wars and later was a member of the Connecticut legislature. At the beginning of the Revolutionary War, news of the battle at Lexington, Massachusetts reached Putnam while he was farming. In a dramatic gesture which became famous, Putnam left his plow and, without bothering to change clothes, hurried to Lexington. He was appointed a major–general in the Continental army. Although he enjoyed great popularity, he lacked the ability for high command. In 1779 a paralytic stroke ended his military career. This county was created in 1820.

2077 *Richland County*

Rich character of its soil — This county lies in the northern part of central Ohio. Sources consulted offer widely differing dates for its creation, ranging from 1808 to 1813. However, these sources are agreed that the county was named for the rich character of its soil. The soil covering much

of Richland County, Ohio, rests on clays and takes its general character from them. The soil here also contains a relatively large quantity of lime, derived mainly from limestone fragments. This character of the soil, combined with a decently high elevation and thorough surface drainage, provides rich land in most of the county, which is hospitable to a variety of agricultural products.

2078 *Ross County*

James Ross (1762–1847) — Born in Pennsylvania on July 12, 1762, Ross studied law, was admitted to the bar in 1784 and practiced law in Washington, Pennsylvania. Elected as a delegate to Pennsylvania's constitutional convention in 1789 and 1790, he later was elected to represent Pennsylvania in the United States Senate. While serving in our nation's senate, Ross maintained a legal residence at Pittsburgh, Pennsylvania and he made two unsuccessful bids for the Pennsylvania governor's office, during his term as U.S. senator. After he left the senate in 1803, he ran again to be Pennsylvania's governor in 1808 but failed to win the office. He died on November 27, 1847, near Pittsburgh, Pennsylvania. This county was created on August 20, 1798, by proclamation of the governor of the Northwest territory, Arthur St. Clair. Governor St. Clair was also from Pennsylvania and had been a Pennsylvania delegate to congress under the articles of confederation. St. Clair and Ross were both members of the Federalist political party and when this county was created, James Ross was serving as a Federalist senator from Pennsylvania.

2079 *Sandusky County*

Sandusky River — This county was created in 1820 and named for northern Ohio's Sandusky River. The Sandusky River rises in Richland County, Ohio, flows west and then north a total of 150 miles, and empties its waters at the northeastern corner of Sandusky County, into Sandusky Bay, on Lake Erie. The Wyandot Indians named the river and their name, *otsaandosti* or *sandesti*, meant "water," or "cool water."

2080 *Scioto County*

Scioto River — Ohio was admitted to statehood early in 1803 and this county was created a few weeks later and named for the Scioto River. The name *Scioto* had already become well established in the history of Ohio because of the late 18th century Scioto Purchase. The Scioto River is an important river of central and southern Ohio, which rises in Auglaize County, in the western part of the state, flows east and then south through the state's capital, Columbus, and continues in a generally southern direction to enter the Ohio River at Portsmouth, in Scioto County, Ohio. The total length of the Scioto River is estimated to be 237 miles. The river was named *Ochskonto* by the Wyandot Indians but its meaning is not completely known. The name contains an element that meant "deer," and very likely the remaining portion of the Indians' name meant "river," or some synonym but the actual translation has not been satisfactorily resolved. Dr. August C. Mahr was an expert on Indian names in Ohio and he commented on the origin of the Scioto River's name in his article entitled "Indian River & Place Names in Ohio," which appeared in the April, 1957, issue of the *Ohio Historical Quarterly* (Vol. 66, No. 2.). Mahr said that *Scioto* carried a connotation of "good hunting," and that part of the name meant "a deer, while the unknown second half of the complete name must have denoted 'river.'" Mrs. Maria Ewing Martin stated that *Scioto* was Wyandot for "deer." in her article entitled "Origin of Ohio Place Names," which appeared in the 1905 issue of *Ohio Archaeological & Historical Publications* (Volume 14) but Mrs. Martin and other Ohio sources indicate that "deer." is the full translation of the name, rather than just part of the translation.

2081 *Seneca County*

Seneca Indians— This county in northern Ohio was created in 1820 and named for the Seneca Indians, the largest tribe of the Iroquois confederation. The confederacy consisted of five tribes (later six), whose center of activities was upstate New York. Some sources indicate that the Seneca were the most warlike of the Iroquois tribes. E. W. Vanderhoof raises the ante in his *Historical Sketches of Western New York*, published in 1907. Vanderhoof tells us that the Seneca were "The most intelligent, numerous and powerful of the six tribes which … formed the League of the Iroquois." The name *Seneca* has been translated variously but a number of authorities agree that the name relates to "stone." In his work on *Indian Names in Michigan*, Dr. Virgil J. Vogel translates the New York tribe's name as "place of the stone," or "stony earth." Muriel H. Wright also supports a stone-related translation. In her work entitled *A Guide to the Indian Tribes of Oklahoma*, she tells us that the

tribal name derived from "people of the standing or projecting rock or stone." In 1985 there were still 5,548 Seneca Indians living on reservations in western New York state. Indians known as the Senecas also now live in Oklahoma. It appears that the Senecas in Oklahoma may be descended from the Seneca Indians who once had a reservation, in what is now Seneca County, Ohio. Apparently these Senecas were relatives of the New York Seneca Indians rather than members of the identical tribe.

2082 *Shelby County*

Isaac Shelby (1750–1826)— Shelby was a delegate to the Virginia legislature and, later, to the North Carolina legislature. He served as a soldier in the Revolutionary War and then moved to Kentucky County, Virginia, where he was active in the movement to separate Kentucky from Virginia. Shelby was inaugurated as Kentucky's first governor and later fought in the War of 1812. In October, 1813, he took part in the battle of the Thames River, in Canada, directly across Lake Erie from north–central Ohio. President James Monroe offered Shelby the cabinet post of secretary of war in 1817 but Shelby declined. This county was formed in 1819.

2083 *Stark County*

John Stark (1728–1822)— A native of New Hampshire, Stark served as an officer during the French & Indian War. He later became a hero during the American Revolution, winning fame at Breed's Hill, Fort Edward, Trenton, Princeton and Bennington and he rose to the rank of brevet major–general. This county was created on February 13, 1808, when General Stark was an 80-year–old veteran living on his farm in Manchester, New Hampshire. The county's name was chosen to honor his status as one of our nation's surviving generals of the Revolutionary War.

2084 *Summit County*

The elevated location among northern Ohio watersheds— Given that water tends to seek its own level, it is not surprising to find that the land between two rivers would be considered to be high, or a "summit." We have already learned (see Portage County, Ohio, above) that Akron, in Summit County contains most of the old Indian portage between the Cuyahoga River and the Tuscarawas River. But there are other rivers in this area of northern Ohio and when Summit County was created on March 3, 1840, it was named for its elevated

location among the various watersheds of the area. In general, the Summit County area separates the rivers which flow to the Ohio River from those which feed Lake Erie. William H. Perrin's *History of Summit County*, published in 1881, tells us that the county's average elevation above nearby Lake Erie is about 500 feet and that heights of 650 feet above Lake Erie are found within the county. William B. Doyle's *Centennial History of Summit County, Ohio* indicates that the name *Summit* reflects the summit level of the Ohio canal, beginning at Akron, and other sources remind us that *Akron*, the name of the county seat of Summit County, comes from the Greek word meaning "summit."

2085 *Trumbull County*

Jonathan Trumbull (1740–1809)— A native of Connecticut and a graduate of Harvard, Trumbull served in the army during the American Revolution as aide–decamp to the commander-in-chief, General George Washington. He served in the Connecticut legislature, in both branches of the U.S. Congress, and was speaker of the U.S. House from 1791 to 1793. On December 1, 1797, when Connecticut's governor, Oliver Wolcott (1726–1797) died, Jonathan Trumbull was Connecticut's lieutenant-governor and he succeeded Wolcott as governor. Re-elected several times, Trumbull served as Connecticut's governor continuously from 1797 until his own death on August 7, 1809. Both the state of Connecticut and Jonathan Trumbull are important in Ohio's history and it is appropriate that one of Ohio's county names should honor this relationship. When the United States established its first territory, Northwest territory, in 1787, Connecticut still controlled a large section of land west of Pennsylvania, known as the Western Reserve of Connecticut or New Connecticut. By July 10, 1800, Connecticut had renounced jurisdiction over these lands and conveyed them to the United States. It was on July 10, 1800, that the governor of the Northwest territory, General Arthur St. Clair (1736–1818) created a new county, by proclamation, out of the lands ceded by Connecticut and he named it Trumbull County, in honor of Jonathan Trumbull, who had been governor of Connecticut when that state ceded its Western Reserve and who was still Connecticut's governor when this county was created.

2086 *Tuscarawas County*

Tuscarawas River— This county was created in 1808 and named for the 125 mile-long Tuscarawas River, which flows through it. The Tuscarawas River rises in the Akron, Ohio area, flows south and approaches the southern border of Tuscarawas County before turning west and entering Coshocton County near Newcomerstown, Ohio. In Coshocton County the Tuscarawas River joins the Walhonding River to form the Muskingum River, a tributary of the Ohio River. The Tuscarawas River's name commemorates the Tuscarora Indians, members of the Iroquois confederacy, whose history is connected more with North Carolina and New York than Ohio. However, the Tuscarora Indians at one time had a settlement on the Tuscarawas River, near the present community of Bolivar, at the border between Stark County and Tuscarawas County, Ohio, and the river was named Tuscarawas because of that settlement.

2087 *Union County*

Union of land taken from four adjacent counties to form the new county— Sources dealing with the history, geography and place names of Ohio are not unanimous on the origin of this county's name but a strong majority indicate that the name was chosen because the new county represented a "union" of lands taken from four adjacent counties, Delaware County, Franklin County, Logan County and Madison County. Correct historical answers are not determined by majority vote, but in this case logic supports the majority opinion. Union County, Ohio, was created in 1820 and by that year all four of the purported ancestor counties had already been created. Moreover, 180 years later, at the millennium year 2000, all four of these counties still share a border with Union County.

2088 *Van Wert County*

Isaac Van Wart (-1828)— During the American Revolution, the adjutant general of the British army, Major John Andre (1751–1780), secretly met behind American lines with General Benedict Arnold (1741–1801) of the Continental army. Benedict Arnold was one of our highest officers, the hero of the battle of Saratoga and the current commander of our critical fort at West Point, New York. Arnold was partially successful in committing his planned treason against America, in that he escaped and joined the British army. However, Major Andre was captured by three obscure New York militiamen, Isaac Van Wart, John Paulding and David Williams.

In commemoration of this dramatic capture, the state of Georgia named one of her counties Paulding County and the state of Ohio honored all three of the men by creating and naming counties in their honor on the same day in 1820. (Some sources list the date as February 12, 1820, while others show April 1, 1820. Since the Ohio legislature adjourned that year on February 26, the legislature probably passed the act[s] to create these three counties on February 12, 1820 and the counties were officially born on April 1, 1820. In any event, all three counties were created simultaneously and all three celebrated the capture of Major John Andre.) The spelling of Isaac Van Wart's name is incorrectly rendered as Van Wert in the Ohio county's name. The year of Van Wart's birth is given in some sources as 1760, but we know that to be incorrect because he was baptized on October 25, 1758. He was a poor and illiterate farm lad in Westchester County, New York, who entered New York's militia during the Revolution. On the day of the capture, Van Wart and seven companions were on duty near Tarrytown, New York, south of West Point fort, attempting to waylay any Tory cattle rustlers they might find operating in the area. The party of eight divided, five stationing themselves on a nearby hill and Van Wart, Paulding and Williams taking positions at a bridge. It was there that they captured Major Andre, rather by accident. Paulding was the only literate member of the trio and was their leader. Congress granted each of the three captors an annuity for life and a silver medal which was personally presented by George Washington. Little is known about Isaac Van Wart except the standard kinds of genealogical data. Isaac Van Wart married Rachel Storms, a daughter of Nicholas Storms, and the couple had two children, both boys, Abram and Alexander. Isaac Van Wart was a member of the Greenburgh Church at Elmsford, New York, and following his death on May 23, 1828, he was buried in that church's graveyard.

2089 *Vinton County*

Samuel F. Vinton (1792–1862)— A native of Massachusetts and a graduate of Williams College in that state, Vinton studied law and established a practice in Gallipolis, Ohio. Elected to represent Ohio in congress and reelected six times, Vinton served from March 4, 1823, to March 3, 1837. He declined to run for reelection in 1836 but in 1843 he returned to the U.S. House of Representatives and served eight more years in that body, from March 4,

1843, to March 3, 1851. This county was created and named in his honor on March 23, 1850, while Samuel F. Vinton was serving his 11th and final term in congress. The name Elk County had originally been proposed for new this county but representatives in the Ohio legislature from Meigs County and Gallia County prevailed upon the legislature to name the new county Vinton County.

2090 *Warren County*

Joseph Warren (1741–1775)— A native of Massachusetts and a graduate of Harvard College, Warren practiced medicine in the Boston area. He was a member of the committee of safety and president *pro tempore* of the Massachusetts provincial congress. In June, 1775, he was commissioned a major-general and he died in combat a few days later at the battle of Bunker Hill. Warren County, Ohio, was created and named in honor of this Revolutionary War hero early in 1803, just a few weeks after Ohio had been admitted to statehood.

2091 *Washington County*

George Washington (1732–1799)— Washington was a native of Virginia, who served in Virginia's house of burgesses and became one of the colonies' leaders in opposition to British policies in America. He was a member of the first and second Continental Congresses and commander of all Continental armies in the Revolutionary War. Following victory in that war, Washington was elected to be the first president of the United States. This county was created on July 26, 1788, by proclamation of the governor of the Northwest territory, General Arthur St. Clair. It was the first county created in Northwest territory and is the oldest county in Ohio. When this county was created, the proposed federal constitution had not yet been ratified by the 13 sovereign states, and the United States of America did not yet exist. When the new nation was born, George Washington became our first president.

2092 *Wayne County*

Anthony Wayne (1745–1796)— A native of Pennsylvania, Wayne was a successful brigadier-general in the Revolutionary War and became a hero for his daring exploits. During the bitter winter of 1777–1778 at Valley Forge, Pennsylvania, Wayne shared the sufferings of his men although his comfortable estate was only five miles away. He played an important role in the final overthrow of the British forces in Georgia. After the war, in 1785, Wayne moved to Georgia and he represented Georgia for about six months in the U.S. House of Representatives. In 1792, President Washington recalled Wayne to serve as a major-general against the Indians in the Northwest territory. Once again his military efforts were successful. On August 20, 1794, forces under Wayne's command defeated the Indians in the battle of Fallen Timbers in northwestern Ohio. That battle was decisive in ending Indian hostilities in the region and moving America's frontier further north and west. Before long, British forces also evacuated the northern country and Americans moved in. The chronology regarding the date that Wayne County, Ohio, was created is complicated. In August, 1796, Winthrop Sargent (1753–1820), the acting governor of the original Northwest territory, created a Wayne County extending westward from the Cuyahoga River in Ohio to the western side of Indiana and north to the Canadian border. General Wayne was touched by this gesture and on November 14, 1796, he wrote a letter expressing his thanks. This original Wayne County included virtually all of what later became Michigan territory. Starting in 1803, the Northwest territory was broken into component parts and in 1805 the original Wayne County in this area of the Midwest ceased to exist. In 1815, the governor of Michigan territory, created a second Wayne County in Michigan territory. Ohio sources offer little help concerning the date of the establishment of a Wayne County by and for Ohio and a variety of dates are mentioned including 1808 and 1812.

2093 *Williams County*

David Williams (1754–1831)— During the American Revolution, the adjutant general of the British army, Major John Andre (1751–1780), secretly met behind American lines with General Benedict Arnold (1741–1801) of the Continental army. Benedict Arnold was one of our highest officers, the hero of the battle of Saratoga and the current commander of our critical fort at West Point, New York. Arnold was partially successful in committing his planned treason against America, in that he escaped and joined the British army. However, Major Andre was captured by three obscure New York militiamen, David Williams, Isaac Van Wart and John Paulding. In commemoration of this dramatic capture, the state of Georgia named one of her counties Paulding

County and the state of Ohio honored all three of the men by creating and naming counties in their honor on the same day in 1820. (Some sources list the date as February 12, 1820, while others show April 1, 1820. Since the Ohio legislature adjourned that year on February 26, the legislature probably passed the act[s] to create these three counties on February 12, 1820, and the counties were officially born on April 1, 1820. In any event, all three counties were created simultaneously and all three celebrated the capture of Major John Andre.) The spelling of Isaac Van Wart's name is incorrectly rendered as Van Wert in the Ohio county's name. David Williams was born in Tarrytown, New York, (which was then called Philips' Manor), in Westchester County on October 21, 1754. He was a poor and illiterate farm lad who entered New York's militia in 1775 during the Revolution and he served under General Richard Montgomery (1738–1775) at the siege of St. Johns, Canada, in late 1775. After serving the period of his initial six month enlistment, Williams re-enlisted in the spring of 1776 and he continued to serve as a New York militiaman until 1779. On the day of the capture, Williams and seven companions were on duty near Tarrytown, New York, south of West Point fort, attempting to waylay any Tory cattle rustlers they might find operating in the area. The party of eight divided, five stationing themselves on a nearby hill, and Williams, Van Wart and Paulding taking positions at a bridge. It was there that they captured Major Andre, rather by accident. Paulding was the only literate member of the trio and was their leader. Congress granted each of the three captors an annuity for life and a silver medal which was personally presented by George Washington. David Williams lived to be the last surviving member of the celebrated trio who captured Major Andre and that longevity was recognized in New York City in 1830, when Williams was the guest of honor at a celebration held on the 50th anniversary of the capture. Williams died on August 2, 1831.

2094 *Wood County*

Eleazer D. Wood (–1814)— Eleazer D. Wood, a graduate of the U.S. Military Academy at West Point, served as a captain during the War of 1812 under General William Henry Harrison. In February, 1813, Wood supervised the design and construction of Ft. Meigs, near the mouth of the Maumee River at Perrysburg, in what is now Wood County, Ohio. The fort being

built here was considered vital to the defense of the American line and Captain Wood kept his men digging the frozen ground until the fort was satisfactorily completed in the spring of 1813. The British and their Indian allies soon attacked and sieged Ft. Meigs but Captain Wood improvised modifications and the fort held until the British withdrew their siege in May, 1813. Later in the War of 1812 Wood supervised artillery troops at the battle of Thames River, in southern Canada, across Lake Erie from the northern coast of Ohio. Wood had been promoted to the rank of brevet lieutenant-colonel when he lost his life in combat in 1814 in the Niagara area of New York. When the war ended, Wood's commanding officer, General Jacob J. Brown (1775–1828) erected a monument, at his own expense, in honor of Eleazer D. Wood, at the post cemetery of West Point, New York. This county was created in 1820 and within its borders is the site of Ft. Meigs, which was constructed and defended under the leadership of Captain Eleazer D. Wood in 1813.

2095 *Wyandot County*

Wyandot Indians— In a treaty signed by representatives of the Indians and the United States government, the Indians relinquished their title to lands in the area of what had been Connecticut's Western Reserve, in northeastern Ohio. In 1809 Ohio created a county within the land ceded by that 1805 Indian treaty and named it for the Huron Indians. The surviving portion of the Huron Indian tribe are now known as the Wyandot Indians and in 1842 or 1843 surviving Wyandot Indians in Ohio moved to Kansas. This move no doubt inspired the creation of a second Ohio county named for this tribe of Indians, Wyandot County, which was created on February 3, 1845. This second county lies close to, but a bit south and west of the first Ohio county that was named for this Indian tribe.

Wyandot Indians— Prior to about 1650 most of the Wyandot Indians lived on Georgian Bay, a Canadian inlet of Lake Huron. An early French explorer, Jacques Cartier (1491–1557) encountered the Wyandot in Canada in 1534. Although the Wyandot belong to the Iroquoian linguistic family, it was Iroquois Indians who forced most of the Wyandot Indians to move west. Sometime after 1650 they settled near Detroit, Michigan and on Sandusky Bay in Ohio. They eventually claimed most of Ohio and part of Indiana. They called themselves *Wendat* and, over time, that name evolved to *Wyandot*. Beginning in 1795, the surviving Wyandot Indians ceded all of their lands to the United States in various treaties. In 1842 or 1843 the Wyandot Indians, who by then were living in Ohio, moved to Kansas. There they purchased land from the Delaware Indians and settled in what is now Wyandotte County, Kansas. In 1867, the Whites forced the Wyandots to move on, this time to Indian territory (now Oklahoma). The meaning of the name *Wendat* and its various other forms is uncertain. Translations which have been suggested include:

— "Islanders"
— "Dwellers on the peninsula"
— "People dwelling in the vicinity of bays and inlets of a large body of water"
— "People of one speech"
— "Calf of the leg."

REFERENCES

Andrews, Israel W. *Washington County and the Early Settlement of Ohio*. Cincinnati, Peter G. Thomson, 1877.

Antrim, Joshua. *The History of Champaign & Logan Counties from Their First Settlement*. Bellefontaine, Ohio, Press Printing Co., 1872.

Apple, R. W. "From Steel Mills to Museums: A City Rises Out of Disrespect." *New York Times*, October 3, 1997.

Aughinbaugh, B. A. *Know Ohio: A Souvenir of the Buckeye State*. State of Ohio Department of Education, 1939.

Bahmer, William J. *Centennial History of Coshocton County, Ohio*. Chicago, S. J. Clarke Publishing Co., 1909.

Baker, Jim. *How Our Counties Got Their Names*. Columbus, Ohio, Center of Science & Industry, 1963.

Bartlow, Bert S., et al. *Centennial History of Butler County, Ohio*. B. F. Bowen & Co., 1905.

Baughman, A. J. *History of Richland County, Ohio*. Chicago, S. J. Clarke Publishing Co., 1908.

Beatty, John. "Franklinton: An Historical Address." *Ohio Archaeological & Historical Publications*, Vol. 6. Columbus: 1898.

The Biographical Encyclopedia of Kentucky. Cincinnati, Ohio, J. M. Armstrong & Co., 1878.

Biographical & Historical Memoirs of Muskingum County, Ohio. Chicago, Goodspeed Publishing Co., 1892.

Breckenridge, Mrs. Wm., et al. *Kentucky in Retrospect*. Frankfort, Kentucky, Kentucky Historical Society, 1967.

Brooks, Roberta. *Ohio Almanac: 1974*. Lorain, Ohio, Lorain Journal Co., 1973.

Brown, Ted W. "Your County's Link With Ohio's History." *Ohio Schools*, Vol. 41, No. 8. Columbus, Ohio: November, 1963.

Burgess, Annette. *Ohio County Profiles*. Columbus, Ohio, Office of Strategic Research, Ohio Department of Development, 1995.

Butterfield, Consul W. *History of Seneca County*. Sandusky, D. Campbell & Sons, 1848.

Caldwell, J. A. *History of Belmont & Jefferson Counties, Ohio*. Wheeling, West Virginia, Historical Publishing Co., 1880.

Catton, Bruce. *Michigan: A Bicentennial History*. New York, W. W. Norton & Co., Inc., 1976.

Cherry, P. P. *The Western Reserve & Early Ohio*. Akron, Ohio, R. L. Fouse, 1921.

Clements, John. *Ohio Facts*. Dallas, Texas, Clements Research II, Inc., 1988.

Coleman, J. Winston. *Historic Kentucky*. Lexington, Henry Clay Press, 1967.

Commemorative Historical & Biographical Record of Wood County, Ohio. Chicago, J. H. Beers & Co., 1897.

A Committee of the Home Coming Association. *Greene County: 1803–1908*. Xenia, Ohio, Aldine Publishing House, 1908.

Crout, George C. *Butler County: An Illustrated History*. Woodland Hills, California, Windsor Publications, Inc., 1983.

Cutler, H. G. *History of the Western Reserve*. Chicago, Lewis Publishing Co., 1910.

Dawes, E. C. "The Beginning of the Ohio Company and the Scioto Purchase." *Ohio Archaeological & Historical Publications*, Vol. 4. Columbus: 1895.

Diede, Alan. *Best Choices in Ohio*. McKeesport, Pennsylvania, GNG Mon Publishing, 1989.

Dolly Todd Madison Chapter Daughters of the American Revolution. *Ohio Early State & Local History*. Tiffin, Ohio, 1915.

Douglass, Ben. *History of Wayne County, Ohio*. Indianapolis, Indiana, Robert Douglass, 1878.

Downes, Randolph C. *Canal Days: Lucas County Historical Series*. Toledo, Ohio, Toledo Printing Co., 1949.

Doyle, William B. *Centennial History of Summit County, Ohio*. Chicago, Biographical Publishing Co., 1908.

Drake, Francis S. *Dictionary of American Biography: Including Men of the Time*. Boston, James R. Osgood & Co., 1872.

Dunbar, Willis F. *Michigan: A History of the Wolverine State*. Grand Rapids, Michigan, William B. Eerdmans Publishing Co., 1965.

Ellis, William D. *The Cuyahoga*. New York, Holt, Rinehart & Winston, 1966.

Encyclopedia of Kentucky. New York, Somerset Publishers, 1987.

Ervin, Edgar. *Pioneer History of Meigs County, Ohio to 1949*.

Evans, Nelson W. *A History of Scioto County, Ohio*. Portsmouth, Ohio, 1903.

Evans, Nelson W., & Emmons B. Stivers. *A History of Adams County, Ohio*. West Union, Ohio, E. B. Stivers, 1900.

Faragher, John M. *The Encyclopedia of Colonial & Revolutionary America*. New York, Facts on File, 1990.

Fensten, Joe. "Indian Removal." *Chronicles of Oklahoma*, Vol. 11, No. 4. Oklahoma City: December, 1933.

Ferris, Robert G. *Founders & Frontiersmen*. Washington, D.C., United States Department of the Interior, National Park Service, 1967.

Fitzgerald, Roy G. "Ohio's Counties: Why So Named?" *Bulletin of the Historical & Philosophical Society of Ohio*, Vol. 10, No. 2. Cincinnati, Ohio: April, 1952.

Fitzgerald, Roy G. "Warren County Named for a General." *Bulletin of the Historical & Philosophical Society of Ohio*, Vol. 10, No. 3. Cincinnati, Ohio: July, 1952.

Foster, W. A. *Paulding County: Its People & Places*. Roswell, Georgia, W. H. Wolfe Associates, 1983.

"French Settlement & Settlers of Gallipolis." *Publications of the Ohio Archaeological & Historical Society*, Vol. 3. Columbus: 1895.

Galbreath, Charles B. *History of Ohio*. Chicago, American Historical Society, Inc., 1925.

Gannett, Henry. *The Origin of Certain Place Names in the United States*. Williamstown, Massachusetts, Corner House Publishers, 1978.

Gilkey, Elliot H. *The Ohio Hundred Year Book*. Columbus, Fred J. Heer, 1901.

Gill, J. J., et al. "Pioneer Day Addresses." *Ohio Archaeological & Historical Publications*, Vol. 6. Columbus: 1898.

The Governors of Ohio. Columbus, Ohio Historical Society, 1954.

Graham, A. A. *History of Fairfield & Perry Counties, Ohio*. Chicago, W. H. Beers & Co., 1883.

Graham, A. A. *History of Richland County, Ohio*. Mansfield, Ohio, A. A. Graham & Co., 1808.

Green, James A. "Life at Ft. Meigs in 1813 & 1840." *Bulletin of the Historical & Philosophical Society of Ohio*, Vol. 7, No. 1. Cincinnati, Ohio: January, 1949.

Gregory, William M., & William B. Guitteau. *History & Geography of Ohio*. Boston, Ginn & Co., 1922.

Hagloch, Henry C. *The History of Tuscarawas County, Ohio*. Dover, Ohio, Dover Historical Society, 1956.

Hammond, John M. *Quaint & Historic Forts of North America*. Philadelphia, J. B. Lippincott Co., 1915.

Harbaugh, Thomas C. *Centennial History: Troy, Piqua & Miami County, Ohio*. Chicago, Richmond-Arnold Publishing Co., 1909.

Hatch, Robert M. *Major John Andre: A Gallant in Spy's Clothing*. Boston, Houghton Mifflin Co., 1986.

Hatcher, Harlan. *The Western Reserve: The Story of New Connecticut in Ohio*. Indianapolis, Bobbs-Merrill Co., Inc., 1949.

Heald, Edward T. *History of Stark County*. Canton, Ohio, Klingstedt Bros. Co., 1963.

Heitman, Francis B. *Historical Register & Dictionary of the United States Army from Its Organization, September 29, 1789, to March 2, 1903*. Washington, D.C., Government Printing Office, 1903.

Heitman, Francis B. *Historical Register of Officers of the Continental Army during the War of the Revolution*. Washington, D.C., Rare Book Shop Publishing Co., Inc., 1914.

Hill, Leonard U., et al. *A History of Miami County, Ohio: 1807–1953*. Columbus, Ohio, F. J. Heer Printing Co., 1953.

Hill, N. N. *History of Coshocton County, Ohio*. Newark, Ohio, A. A. Graham & Co., 1881.

Hill, N. N. *History of Knox County, Ohio*. Mt. Vernon, Ohio, A. A. Graham & Co., 1881.

Hill, N. N. *History of Licking County, Ohio*. Newark, Ohio, A. A. Graham & Co., 1881.

Hills, Leon C. *History & Legends of Place Names in Iowa: The Meaning of Our Map*. Omaha, Nebraska, Omaha School Supply Co., 1938.

Historical Collections of the Mahoning Valley. Youngstown, Mahoning Valley Historical Society, 1876.

A History & Biographical Cyclopedia of Butler County, Ohio. Cincinnati, Western Biographical Publishing Co., 1882.

The History of Champaign County, Ohio. Chicago, W. H. Beers & Co., 1881.

History of Clermont County, Ohio. Philadelphia, Louis H. Everts, 1880.

History of Lorain County, Ohio. Philadelphia, Williams Brothers, 1879.

History of Medina County & Ohio. Chicago, Baskin & Battey, 1881.

History of Morrow County, Ohio. Chicago, O. L. Baskin & Co., 1880.

History of Noble County, Ohio. Chicago, L. H. Watkins & Co., 1887.

History of Portage County, Ohio. Chicago, Warner, Beers & Co., 1885.

History of Preble County, Ohio. Cleveland, Ohio, W. W. Williams, 1881.

History of Sandusky County, Ohio. Cleveland, Ohio, H. Z. Williams & Bro., 1882.

The History of Union County, Ohio. Chicago, W. H. Beers & Co., 1883.

History of Washington County, Ohio. Cleveland, Ohio, W. W. Williams, 1881.

Hitchcock, A. B. C. *History of Shelby County & Representative Citizens*. Chicago, Richmond-Arnold Publishing Co., 1913.

Hodge, Frederick W. *Handbook of American Indians North of Mexico*. Totowa, New Jersey, Rowman & Littlefield, 1975.

Hoover, Earl R. *Cradle of Greatness: National & World Achievements of Ohio's Western Reserve*. Cleveland, Ohio, Carpenter Reserve Printing Co., 1977.

Hoover, John C., et al. *Memoirs of the Miami Valley*. Chicago, Robert O. Law Co., 1919.

Howe, Henry. *Historical Collections of Ohio*. Cincinnati, Ohio, C. J. Krehbiel & Co., 1888.

Hunt, William E. *Historical Collections of Coshocton County, Ohio*. Cincinnati, Robert Clarke & Co., 1876.

Hurt, R. Douglas. *The Ohio Frontier: Crucible of the Old Northwest: 1720–1830*. Bloomington, Indiana University Press, 1996.

Illinois, Indiana, Ohio Tour Book. Heathrow, Florida, AAA Publishing, 1998.

Izant, Grace Goulder. *This is Ohio: Ohio's 88 Counties in Words & Pictures*. Cleveland, World Publishing Co., 1953.

Jacoby, J. Wilbur. "Marion Centennial Celebration." *Ohio Archaeological & Historical Quarterly*, Vol. 31, No. 1. Columbus, Ohio: January, 1922.

Jakle, John A. "Salt-Derived Place Names in the Ohio Valley." *Names: Journal of the American Name Society*, Vol. 16, No. 1. Potsdam, New York: March, 1968.

Kalette, Linda E. *The Papers of Thirteen Early Ohio Political Leaders: An Inventory to the 1976–77 Microfilm Editions*. Columbus, Ohio Historical Society, 1977.

Keeler, Lucy Elliot. "The Sandusky River." *Ohio Archaeological & Historical Publications*, Vol. 13. Columbus: 1904.

Kennedy, Willella Shearer. *Our Heritage Being Little Stories of Union County*. Marysville, Ohio, Journal-Tribune, 1963.

Kinder, William R. *Historic Notes of Miami County*. Troy, Ohio, Troy Foundation, 1953.

King, Joseph B. "The Ottawa Indians in Kansas & Oklahoma." *Collections of the Kansas State Historical Society*, Vol. 13. Topeka: 1915.

Kleber, John E. *The Kentucky Encyclopedia*. Lexington, Kentucky, University Press of Kentucky, 1992.

Klein, Philip S., & Ari Hoogenboom. *A History of Pennsylvania*. University Park, Pennsylvanian State University Press, 1980.

Knapp, H. S. *History of the Maumee Valley*. Toledo, 1877.

Kohler, Minnie Ichler. *A Twentieth Century History of Hardin County, Ohio*. Chicago, Lewis Publishing Co., 1910.

Lang, W. *History of Seneca County*. Springfield, Ohio, Transcript Printing Co., 1880.

Langguth, A. J. *Patriots: The Men Who Started the American Revolution*. New York, Simon & Schuster, 1988.

Laning, J. F. "The Evolution of Ohio Counties." *Ohio Archaeological & Historical Publications*, Vol. 5. Columbus: 1898.

Large, Mrs. Moina W. *History of Ashtabula County, Ohio*. Topeka, Historical Publishing Co., 1924.

Lawyer, James P. *History of Ohio*. Columbus, Ohio, F. J. Heer, 1904.

Leeson, M. A. *Commemorative Historical & Biographical Record of Wood County, Ohio*. Chicago, J. H. Beers & Co., 1897.

Lehman, John H. *A Standard History of Stark County, Ohio*. Chicago, Lewis Publishing Co.

Leland, J. A. C. "Eastern Tribal Names in California." *California Folklore Quarterly*, Vol. 5, No. 4. Berkeley: October, 1946.

Leland, J. A. C. "Indian Names in Missouri." *Names: Journal of the American Name Society*, Vol. 1, No. 4. Berkeley: December, 1953.

Leland, J. A. C. "Some Eastern Indian Place Names in California." *California Folklore Quarterly*, Vol. 4, No. 4. Berkeley: October, 1945.

Lexington, Kentucky Visitors Guide: 1993.

Lindsey, David. *Ohio's Western Reserve: The Story of Its Place Names*. Cleveland, Ohio, Press of Western Reserve University, 1955.

Lindsey, David. "Place Names in Ohio's Western Reserve." *Names: Journal of the American Name Society*, Vol. 2, No. 1. Berkeley: March, 1954.

Lowry, R. E. *History of Preble County, Ohio*. Indianapolis, Indiana, B. F. Bowen & Co., Inc., 1915.

McHenry, Robert. *Webster's American Military Biographies*. New York, Dover Publications, Inc., 1978.

Mack, Horace. *History of Columbiana County, Ohio*. Philadelphia, D. W. Ensign & Co., 1879.

McWhorter, Lucullus V. *The Border Settlers of Northeastern Virginia: From 1768 to 1795*. Richwood, West Virginia, Jim Comstock, 1973.

Mahon, John K. *The War of 1812*. New York Da Capo Press, Inc., 1972.

Mahr, August C. "Indian River & Place Names in Ohio." *Ohio Historical Quarterly*, Vol. 66, No. 2. Columbus, Ohio: April, 1957.

Map of Ashtabula County. Racine, Wisconsin, Seeger Map Co., Inc., 1994.

Map of Mahoning/Trumbull County. Racine, Wisconsin, Seeger Map Co., Inc. 1992.

Map of Portage County. Racine, Wisconsin, Seeger Map Co., Inc., 1992.

Marshall, Carrington T. *A History of the Courts & Lawyers of Ohio.* New York, American Historical Society, Inc., 1934.

Martin, Mrs. Maria Ewing. "Origin of Ohio Place Names." *Ohio Archaeological & Historical Quarterly*, Vol. 14, No. 1. Columbus, Ohio: January, 1905.

Marzulli, Lawrence J. *The Development of Ohio's Counties & Historic Courthouses.* Fostoria, Ohio, Gray Printing Co.

Meek, Basil. "The Centenary of Sandusky County." *Ohio Archaeological & Historical Publications*, Vol. 29. Columbus: 1920.

Miller, Larry L. *Ohio Place Names.* Bloomington, Indiana University Press, 1996.

Miller, Lillian B. *The Dye Is Now Cast: The Road to American Independence: 1774–1776.* Washington, D.C., Smithsonian Institution Press, 1975.

Morrison, Olin D. *Ohio: Gateway State: A History of Ohio.* Athens, Ohio, 1961.

Mucha, Ludvik, & Bohuslav Hlinka. *The Scott Stamp Atlas.* Prague, Czechoslovakia, Geodetic & Cartographic Enterprise in Prague, 1987.

Newton, George F. "History of Holmes County, Ohio." Unpublished manuscript, Holmes County Library, Millersburg, Ohio.

Ogan, Lew. *History of Vinton County, Ohio.* McArthur, Ohio, 1954.

Ohio State Archaeological & Historical Society & State Department of Education. *Pictorial Ohio.* Standard Oil Company, 1930.

Old Homes of the Bluegrass. Lexington, Kentucky, Sydney S. Combs, Realtor.

Onuf, Peter S. *Statehood & Union: A History of the Northwest Ordinance.* Bloomington, Indiana University Press, 1987.

The Origin of Ohio County Names. Auditor of the State of Ohio.

Overman, William D. *Ohio Place Names.* Ann Arbor, Michigan, Edwards Brothers, 1951.

Overman, William D. "Ohio Town Names." *Names: Journal of the American Name Society*, Vol. 1, No. 2. Berkeley: June, 1953.

Parkman, Francis. *The Jesuits in North America in the Seventeenth Century: France & England in North America.* Williamstown, Massachusetts, Corner House Publishers, 1980.

Parvin, T. S. "General Robert Lucas." *Annals of Iowa*, Vol. 2, No. 6. Des Moines, Iowa: July, 1896.

Peeke, Hewson L. *A Standard History of Erie County, Ohio.* Chicago, Lewis Publishing Co., 1916.

Perrin, William H. *History of Summit County with an Outline Sketch of Ohio.* Chicago, Baskin & Battey, 1881.

Perry, Dick. *Ohio: A Personal Portrait of the 17th State.* Garden City, New York, Doubleday & Co., Inc., 1969.

Peters, William E. *Athens County, Ohio.* 1947.

Peterson, C. Stewart. *First Governors of the Forty-Eight States.* New York, Hobson Book Press, 1947.

Pioneer & General History of Geauga County. Historical Society of Geauga County, 1880.

Pittenger, John M. *The Buckeye Story.* Akron, Ohio, Travelers Press, 1957.

Place, Puetz. *Ohio County Maps.* Lyndon Station, Wisconsin, County Maps.

A Portrait & Biographical Record of Portage & Summit Counties, Ohio. Logansport, Indiana, A. W. Bowen & Co., 1898.

Pratt, Dorothy, & Richard Pratt. *A Guide to Early American Homes: North & South.* New York, Bonanza Books, 1956.

Prucha, Francis P. *A Guide to the Military Posts of the United States: 1789–1895.* Madison, State Historical Society of Wisconsin, 1964.

Randall, E. O. *Ohio Centennial Anniversary Celebration.* Columbus, Ohio State Archaeological & Historical Society, 1903.

Raup, H. F. "Names of Ohio's Streams." *Names: Journal of the American Name Society*, Vol. 5, No. 3. Berkeley: September, 1957.

Raup, H. F. "An Overview of Ohio Place Names." *Names: Journal of the American Name Society*, Vol. 30, No. 1. Saranac Lake, New York: March, 1982.

Rayburn, J. A. "Geographical Names of Amerindian Origin in Canada." *Names: Journal of the American Name Society*, Vol. 15, No. 3. Potsdam, New York: September, 1967.

Rhodes, James A. *A Short History of Ohio Land Grants.*

Rivera, Roberta. *Ohio Almanac History: A History of Ohio from 1670 to 1977: 88 County Profiles.* Lorain, Ohio, Lorain Journal Co., 1977.

Rose, Albert H. *Ohio Government: State & Local.* University of Dayton Press, 1966.

Roseboom, Eugene H. & Francis P. Weisenburger. *A History of Ohio.* Columbus, Ohio Historical Society, 1967.

Rowland, Dunbar. *Military History of Mississippi: 1803–1898.* Jackson, Mississippi, Mississippi Department of Archives & History, 1908.

Rusler, William. *A Standard History of Allen County, Ohio.* Chicago, American Historical Society, 1921.

Rust, Orton G. *History of West Central Ohio.* Indianapolis, Indiana, Historical Publishing Co., 1934.

Rydjord, John. *Indian Place-Names.* Norman, University of Oklahoma Press, 1968.

Scobey, F. E., & B. L. McElroy. *The Biographical Annals of Ohio: 1902–1903.*

Scott, Daniel. *A History of the Early Settlement of Highland County, Ohio.* Hillsborough Gazette, 1890.

Seamster, Frances Pryor. "The Place-Names of Muskingum County, Ohio." M.A. Thesis, Ohio State University, Columbus, Ohio, 1965.

Sedillot, Rene. *An Outline of French History.* New York, Alfred Knopf, Inc., 1967.

Shankle, George Earlie. *State Names, Flags, Seals, Songs, Birds, Flowers & Other Symbols.* New York, H. W. Wilson Co., 1941.

Simms, Jeptha R. *History of Schoharie County & Border Wars of New York.* Albany, Munsell & Tanner, 1845.

Smith, William E. *History of Southwestern Ohio: The Miami Valleys.* New York, Lewis Historical Publishing Co., Inc., 1964.

Smucker, Isaac. *Centennial History of Licking County, Ohio.* Newark, Ohio, Clark & Underwood, 1876.

The State of Ohio Official Roster: Federal, State, County Officers & Department Information: 1981–1982.

Stille, Samuel H. *Ohio Builds a Nation.* Chicago, Arlendale Book House, 1939.

Sutherland, Tucker. *Ohio Almanac: 1969.* Lorain, Ohio, Lorain Journal Co., 1968.

Taft, William H., III. *County Names: An Historical Perspective.* National Association of Counties, 1982.

Taube, Edward. "Tribal Names Related with Algonkin." *Names: Journal of the American Name Society*, Vol. 3, No. 2. Berkeley: June, 1955.

Taylor, Jeff. *Ohio Pride: A Guide to Ohio Roadside History.* Columbus, Ohio, Backroad Chronicles, 1990.

Taylor, William A. *Ohio in Congress from 1803 to 1901.* Columbus, XX Century Publishing Co., 1900.

Taylor, William A. *Ohio Statesmen & Annals of Progress.* Columbus, Ohio, Westbote Co., 1899.

Thompson, Carl N. *Historical Collections of Brown County, Ohio*. Piqua, Ohio, Hammer Graphics, Inc., 1971.

Todd, Edwin S. "A Sociological Study of Clark County, Ohio." Ph.D. Thesis, Columbia University, New York, New York, 1904.

Troutman, Richard L. "Henry Clay and His Ashland Estate." *Filson Club History Quarterly*, Vol. 30, No. 2. Louisville, Kentucky: April, 1956.

"Unveiling the Cresap Tablet: Pickaway County." *Ohio Archaeological & Historical Quarterly*, Vol. 26, No. 1. Columbus, Ohio: January, 1917.

Uttley, John. *A Short History of the Channel Islands*. New York, Frederick A. Praeger, 1966.

Van Cleaf, Aaron R. *History of Pickaway County, Ohio*. Chicago, Biographical Publishing Co., 1906.

Vanderhoof, E. W. *Historical Sketches of Western New York*. Buffalo, New York, Matthews-Northrup Works, 1907.

Van Fleet, J. A. *Old & New Mackinac*. Grand Rapids, Michigan, The Lever Book & Job Office, 1880.

Van Tassel, Charles S. *Story of the Maumee Valley, Toledo and the Sandusky Region*. Chicago, S. J. Clarke Publishing Co., 1929.

Verwyst, Chrysostom. "Geographical Names in Wisconsin, Minnesota & Michigan, Having a Chippewa Origin. " *Collections of the State Historical Society of Wisconsin*, Vol. 12. Madison, Wisconsin: 1892.

Vexler, Robert I. *Chronology & Documentary Handbook of the State of Ohio*. Dobbs Ferry, New York, Oceana Publications, Inc., 1978.

Vogel, Virgil J. *Indian Names in Michigan*. Ann Arbor, University of Michigan Press, 1986.

Vogel, Virgil J. *Iowa Place Names of Indian Origin*. Iowa City, University of Iowa Press, 1983.

Vonada, Damaine. *The Ohio Almanac: 1992/93*. Wilmington, Ohio, Orange Frazer Press, Inc., 1992.

Waite, Frederick C. "Sources of the Names of the Counties of the Western Reserve." *Ohio State Archaeological & Historical Quarterly*, Vol. 48, No. 1. Columbus: January, 1939.

Walton, Ivan H. "Origin of Names on the Great Lakes." *Names: Journal of the American Name Society*, Vol. 3, No. 4. Berkeley: December, 1955.

White, Peter. "Old Fort Holmes." *Collections & Researches Made by the Michigan Pioneer & Historical Society*, Vol. 38. Lansing, Michigan: 1912.

White, Steve, & Tom Kiess. *Henry County, Ohio*. Dallas, Texas, Taylor Publishing Co., 1976.

Williams, William W. *History of Ash-tabula County, Ohio*. Philadelphia, Press of J. B. Lippincott & Co., 1878.

Winter, Nevin O. *A History of Northwest Ohio*. Chicago, Lewis Publishing Co., 1917.

Wolfe, George W. *A Pictorial Outline History of Darke County, Ohio*. Newark, Ohio, Lyon & Ickes.

Wolk, Allan. *The Naming of America*. Nashville, Thomas Nelson, Inc., 1977.

Wood, Edwin O. *Historic Mackinac*. New York, Macmillan Co., 1918.

Work Projects Administration. *Bryan & Williams County*. City of Bryan, Ohio, 1941.

Work Projects Administration. *Guide to Tuscarawas County*. New Philadelphia Chamber of Commerce, 1939.

Work Projects Administration. *Inventory of the County Archives of Ohio-Ashland County*. Columbus, Ohio, 1942.

Work Projects Administration. *Springfield & Clark County, Ohio*. Springfield Tribune Printing Co., 1941.

Wright, G. Frederick. *A Standard History of Lorain County, Ohio*. Chicago, Lewis Publishing Co., 1916.

Wright, Muriel H. *A Guide to the Indian Tribes of Oklahoma*. Norman, University of Oklahoma Press, 1951.

Yenne, Bill. *Encyclopedia of North American Indian Tribes*. New York, Crescent Books, 1986.

Oklahoma

(77 counties)

2096 *Adair County*

*Prominent Adair family, of which William P Adair (–1881) was a member—*This county was created in July, 1907 and named for the prominent Adair family of Cherokee Indians. Perhaps the most conspicuous member of that family had been William Penn Adair.

*William P. Adair (–1881)—*Colonel Adair was a leader of one of two rival delegations of Cherokee Indians that met with officials of the U.S. federal government, in Washington, D.C., and signed a treaty on July 19, 1866. The two delegations were the Southern Cherokee, of which William P. Adair was a member, and the Northern Cherokee. The treaty signed that day provided for continuation of Cherokee government and the Indians considered this a satisfactory resolution of the issue(s) that had been under discussion. An article dealing with the origin of Oklahoma's county names, which appeared in the March, 1924 issue of *Chronicles of Oklahoma* (Vol. 2, No. 1) stated that Adair "...represented the Cherokee Nation at Washington from 1866 until his death in 1881." This appears to be an exaggeration. At the July 19, 1866, treaty signing in Washington, Adair was only one (of four) leaders of one of the two Cherokee delegations and Adair was not even among the signers of the treaty. Later, in 1879, Adair was among those who successfully protested threatened invasion of Indian territory from Kansas by "Boomers." The federal government responded by stationing troops in several Kansas towns and this particular threatened invasion by "Boomers" was aborted. William Penn Adair had an allotment of land within what is now Mayes County, Oklahoma, near today's municipality of Adair, Oklahoma.

2097 *Alfalfa County*

*William H. Murray (1869–1956)—*William H. ("Alfalfa Bill") Murray was president of the constitutional convention for the state of Oklahoma and that office carried considerable power. As president, Murray could grant or deny favors requested of him by delegates. As one result, two Oklahoma counties were named in his honor, Alfalfa County and Murray

County, and he could have gotten half a dozen had he chosen to nod his head during the creation of Oklahoma counties at the constitutional convention. A native of Texas, Murray taught school, published a newspaper and was admitted to practice law in Texas before moving to Tishomingo, in territory of the Chickasaw nation (now Oklahoma), in 1898. Here he practiced law and farmed and became a citizen, by marriage, of the Chickasaw nation. Murray subsequently held a variety of important Oklahoma political posts. He was a delegate and president of Oklahoma's constitutional convention of 1906–1907 and later served in the lower house of Oklahoma's state legislature. Murray was speaker of that body from 1907 to 1908. He represented Oklahoma in the U.S. House of Representatives from 1914 to 1918 and was elected governor of Oklahoma in 1930. He governed Oklahoma from 1931–1935 during the terrible "dust bowl" years of the Great Depression, which gained national attention from John E. Steinbeck's (1902–1968) novel, *The Grapes of Wrath*. This county was created by the Oklahoma constitutional convention on July 16, 1907.

2098 *Atoka County*

Charles Atoka (–)— Captain Charles Atoka was a full-blooded Choctaw Indian who came to Indian territory from Mississippi during the Indian removal of the 1830's. He had been a signer of the treaty of Dancing Rabbit Creek, Mississippi, in 1830, which permitted the Indian removal and he was a captain in Chief Greenwood Leflore's (1800–1865) district in Mississippi. In Indian territory, Atoka established his home about 15 miles southeast of the present municipality of Atoka, Oklahoma. Charles Atoka became a prominent Choctaw leader and was a member of the Choctaw Council. He also participated in ball games that were held each spring between Choctaw and Chickasaw players on the line separating the territories of the two nations. The game was a form of stick ball, resembling soccer and field hockey, with perhaps excessive rowdiness, and at times the distinction between player and spectator became blurred. Charles Atoka gained a reputation for his ability at this sport and since the name *Atoka* very closely resembles the Choctaw's word for "ball ground," it may be that the name by which we know Charles Atoka today was bestowed upon him after his prowess as a ball player had been recognized. This county was created on July 16, 1907, and

most sources on Oklahoma's history state that the county was named directly for Charles Atoka, but a few indicate that the county was named for the municipality of Atoka, in Atoka County, Oklahoma, and that the town had been named for Charles Atoka, earlier. The name *Atoka* had also been used by the Choctaw nation as the name of one of the 14 counties in their section of Indian territory, and it is the only one of those 14 county names that can still be found on Oklahoma's map of counties.

2099 *Beaver County*

Beaver River— The Beaver River of northwestern Oklahoma flows east into Texas, but stays there for only 15 miles of its total 280 mile length. After returning to Oklahoma, the Beaver River unites with Wolf Creek to form the North Canadian River. The Beaver River was previously called the *Nutria*, a Spanish word which means "otter." That name was given to the river because of the numerous beaver dams found on tributaries of the Beaver River. This county was created in 1890 as part of Oklahoma territory and named County Seven. The county's present name was chosen by Oklahoma's state constitutional convention on account of the Beaver River which flows across it. The county was created on July 16, 1907.

2100 *Beckham County*

John C. W. Beckham (1869–1940)— A native of Kentucky and a lawyer, Beckham served in the lower house of Kentucky's legislature from 1894 to 1900. In 1899 he ran for lieutenant-governor on the Democratic ticket with William Goebel (1856–1900) as the party's nominee for governor. In a close election the Republicans were declared the victors, but the Kentucky general assembly, controlled by the Democrats, declared a number of votes invalid and pronounced William Goebel to be the new governor. During the heat of this controversy, Goebel was shot by an assassin on January 30, 1900, and he died on February 3, 1900. Lieutenant-governor John C. W. Beckham succeeded as Kentucky's governor and served in that office from 1900 to 1907. In 1914 Beckham was elected to the U.S. Senate in Kentucky's first popular senatorial election and he served there from 1915 to 1921. This county was created by Oklahoma's state constitutional convention on July 16, 1907. An article dealing with the origin of Oklahoma's county names, which appeared in

the March, 1924, issue of *Chronicles of Oklahoma* (Vol. 2, No. 1) stated that this county's name was suggested by a delegate to Oklahoma's constitutional convention who had been born in Kentucky.

2101 *Blaine County*

James G. Blaine (1830–1893)— Blaine, a native of Pennsylvania, moved to Maine where he served three terms in the state legislature. He then represented Maine in both houses of the U.S. Congress and, for a number of years, was speaker of the House of Representatives. In 1881 Blaine became secretary of state under President James A. Garfield and he was the Republican party's candidate for president of the United States in 1884, losing to Grover Cleveland. When Benjamin Harrison became president in 1889, he appointed Blaine to be his secretary of state. This county was designed as "C County" of Indian territory. It was established as Blaine County by the Oklahoma constitutional convention on July 16, 1907.

2102 *Bryan County*

William J. Bryan (1860–1925)— A native of Illinois, lawyer, newspaper man and orator, Bryan represented the quintessence of populist America. He held political office, as a representative in congress from Nebraska and as secretary of state, but William Jennings Bryan is best remembered, and by some, loved, for his defeats. He championed the economic interests of the poor when he voted in congress against the repeal of the Sherman Silver Purchase act and he captured a place in history with his famous speech urging that the poor not be crucified on a "cross of gold." He pressed for progressive labor legislation including maximum working hours and minimum wages. Many of his causes eventually prevailed, including direct election of senators, women's suffrage, government aid to farmers and a graduated income tax. A staunch Christian fundamentalist, Bryan opposed evolution in court in a famous legal battle against the brilliant liberal, Clarence S. Darrow (1857–1938). When this county was created by Oklahoma's state constitutional convention on July 16, 1907, William Jennings Bryan had been the Democratic party's unsuccessful presidential candidate in 1896 and 1900 and he was preparing to run again in 1908. All of these bids for the presidency failed. Bryan gave helpful suggestions concerning Oklahoma's constitution, while it was still in draft form.

2103 *Caddo County*

Caddo Indians— Hernando de Soto (1500–1542) encountered some tribes of the Caddo Indian confederations during his explorations of the southeastern United States but these Indians did not become well known until the French explorer, Rene Robert Cavelier, Sieur de la Salle (1643–1687), came upon them in the 1680's. When encountered by La Salle, most of the Caddo were gathered in three loose confederations. These were the Hasinai, Wichita and Kadohadacho. The Kadohadacho were the Caddo proper, the tribe from whom this county's name derived. The name *Caddo* is merely a contraction of *Kadohadacho*, which means "real chiefs." The Kadohadacho lived along the bend of the Red River in southwestern Arkansas and eastern Texas, with other settlements further south along the Red River in northwestern Louisiana. The Caddo were farmers, hunters and traders. They acquired horses and traded these horses as far north as the Illinois River. Europeans who wrote of their contacts with the Caddo Indians were favorably impressed. The Caddo were said to be industrious, intelligent, courageous and unusually friendly to visitors. In 1835 the Caddo Indians sold their territory to the United States for $80,000. The territory that they sold contained sections of Louisiana, Texas and Arkansas. They subsequently led a rather perilous life in Texas where they were persecuted and killed by both Comanche Indians and White settlers. In 1855 the federal government established a tract for the Caddo near the Brazos River in Texas. However, in 1859 it was learned that a group of White settlers had set a date to massacre all Caddo Indians. Under the direction of Indian Agent Robert S. Neighbors (1815–1859), who had been a consistent friend of the Caddo, these Indians were promptly relocated to the banks of the Washita River in what is now Caddo County, Oklahoma. Few pure Caddo Indians remain today. Many of them have mixed White and Caddo ancestry while others are the products of intermarriage among Caddo and other Indian tribes. This county had been named "I County," when it was part of Oklahoma territory. It was created as Caddo County by the Oklahoma constitutional convention on July 16, 1907.

2104 *Canadian County*

North Canadian River & South Canadian River— This county was designated as "County Four" when it was established as part of Oklahoma territory in 1890. Its present name, adopted by the Oklahoma constitutional convention on July 16, 1907, was taken from the North and South Canadian Rivers, which flow through the county.

North Canadian River— Formed by the junction, in Oklahoma, of Beaver River and Wolf Creek, the North Canadian River is a 440 mile-long tributary of the South Canadian (also called Canadian) River. The North Canadian River flows in an eastern and southeastern direction through central Oklahoma, where its waters join those of its sister river, the South Canadian, or Canadian River.

South Canadian River— A tributary of the Arkansas River, which is also referred to as the Canadian River, this 900 mile-long river rises in southern Colorado, flows south and east across New Mexico and northwest across the Texas panhandle into east-central Oklahoma. Here the waters of the South Canadian are joined by those of its sister river and tributary, the North Canadian, and the combined stream ends its journey in eastern Oklahoma when it empties into the Arkansas River.

The origin of the name *Canadian*, as applied to the rivers which flow through Oklahoma, is uncertain and disputed. One authority on Oklahoma's history, Joseph B. Thoburn, indicated in an article which appeared in the June, 1928 (Vol. 6, No. 2), issue of *Chronicles of Oklahoma* that he believed the name had its roots in Canada and was transplanted here by French Canadian trappers and traders. George R. Stewart stated in his *American Place-Names* that the river's name was "probably folk-etymology from the Caddoan name ... for the stream; i.e., 'red river.'" Rene Coulet du Gard's *Dictionary of Spanish Place Names* supports the "red river" concept and mentions that the Canadian Rivers were referred to in early Spanish titles as both *Rio Rojo*, i.e., "Red River," and the Spanish version of the present name *Rio Canadian*.

2105 *Carter County*

Uncertain— This county was created on July 16, 1907, from part of the old Chickasaw nation, by Oklahoma's state constitutional convention. Sources dealing with the history, geography and place names of Oklahoma offer differing explanations for the origin of this county's name. Possibilities mentioned include:

Benjamin W. Carter (1837–1894)— Benjamin Wisner Carter, a Cherokee Indian, was born on January 5, 1837, in Alabama. He came with his parents to the Cherokee Nation (now in Oklahoma) and served as a captain in the Confederate army during the Civil War, training Indians for Confederate service. Benjamin W. Carter and his first wife, Nannie Elliott had one son, John Elliott Carter. After Benjamin W. Carter's first wife died, he married a Chickasaw lady, Serena Josephine Guy, and he settled among the Chickasaw Indians. After the Civil War he operated a general store and held several political posts. Benjamin Carter was secretary of the committee formed to revise and codify the laws of the Chickasaw nation and he later held the posts of attorney general, district judge and permit collector. A son of his, Charles D. Carter (1868–1929), represented Oklahoma in the U.S. House of Representatives for 20 years.

Charles D. Carter (1868–1929)— Charles David Carter was born on August 16, 1868, the only child from the marriage of the Cherokee, Benjamin Wisner Carter (1837–1894), and his Chickasaw wife, Serena Josephine Guy Carter. Charles D. Carter was educated in Indian territory and in 1889 he became auditor of public accounts of the Chickasaw nation. He held several other political posts for the Chickasaws until 1900, when he was appointed mineral trustee for the Chickasaw and Choctaw nations, in Oklahoma territory, by U.S. President William McKinley. When Oklahoma was admitted to statehood in 1907, Charles D. Carter was elected as the new state's first representative in congress and he served there from 1907 until 1927.

The Carter family of Oklahoma— Those sources that say that Carter County, Oklahoma, was named for the Carter family of Oklahoma, indicate which Carter family they mean by specifying "of which Charles D. Carter was the best-known member." We already have the facts about him and his father, Benjamin Wisner Carter (see immediately above), and the name of his mother, Serena Josephine Guy Carter. Congressman Charles D. Carter's (1868–1929) paternal great-grandfather was Nathaniel R. Carter, who was captured by the Delaware Indians in Pennsylvania and brought to North Carolina. He was raised by the Cherokee Indians and married a Cherokee lady. Their son, the paternal grandfather of Charles D. Carter (1868–1929) was David Carter (1812–1861). He was born in North Carolina and came west in 1838, during the infamous Cherokee removal. Here in the Cherokee nation David Carter (1812–1861) became chief justice of the supreme court of the Cherokee nation. His wife was Jane Riley (–1861), a Cherokee Indian. More information may be found about these and other members of the Carter family in Emmet Starr's *Old*

Cherokee Families: Old Families and Their Genealogy, published in 1968 at Norman, Oklahoma by the University of Oklahoma Foundation.

2106 *Cherokee County*

Cherokee Indians— The Cherokee Indians were a large and powerful tribe who lived in Georgia and several other eastern states at the time of their first contact with Europeans. By the early 1800's they had adopted many of the features of civilization. By 1840, most Cherokees had been forced from their lands and removed to Indian territory by court decisions, a fraudulent treaty and military force. The removal of some 17,000 Cherokee Indians from their ancient tribal lands in western North Carolina, northwestern Georgia and eastern Tennessee was a dark chapter in our nation's history. Their journey to Indian territory was marked by indescribable suffering from which some 4,000 Cherokees died. A few Cherokee Indians refused to join the forced march to Indian territory and some others returned to the Southeast. This county was created by Oklahoma's state constitutional convention on July 16, 1907. The name Cherokee is said to be derived from the Cherokee word for "fire," *chera*.

2107 *Choctaw County*

Choctaw Indians— The Choctaw Indians were a large and relatively peaceful tribe who lived in the southern portions of Mississippi and Alabama. The Choctaw Indians ceded their lands in Mississippi and Alabama to the United States in the 1830 treaty of Dancing Rabbit Creek. After ceding these lands in the southern United States, the majority of Choctaw Indians moved to Indian territory. In 1985 the Talihina agency in Oklahoma had a population of 20,054, most of whom were Choctaw Indians and the Choctaw agency in Mississippi still had 4,599 residents. This county was created by Oklahoma's state constitutional convention on July 16, 1907.

2108 *Cimarron County*

Cimarron River— This county at the western end of Oklahoma's panhandle was created by Oklahoma's state constitutional convention on July 16, 1907, and named for the Cimarron River, which flows across the county. The Cimarron River, a tributary of the Arkansas River, rises in northeastern New Mexico, just a few miles west of Cimarron County, Oklahoma, then flows on a meandering course heading east, crossing back and forth between Kansas and Oklahoma on its 500 mile journey. The Cimarron completes its journey in north-central Oklahoma, where its waters flow into the Arkansas River. *Cimarron* is a Spanish word meaning "wild" or "unruly" and is usually applied to animals or plants rather than rivers. During the years 1886 and 1887, when this area had no legal status as a part of any state or territory, settlers had organized a territory named Cimarron and petitioned congress for formal recognition. Congress ignored the settlers and Cimarron's brief bid for status aborted. In 1890 the Oklahoma panhandle was incorporated in Oklahoma territory.

2109 *Cleveland County*

Stephen Grover Cleveland (1837–1908)— Grover Cleveland was a native of New Jersey who rose from mayor of Buffalo, New York, in 1881 to governor of New York in 1883 to president of the United States in 1885. He lost his bid for reelection to Benjamin Harrison but later ran and was elected to a second term as president. Cleveland supported civil service reform and lower tariffs and sent troops to intervene against Pullman strikers in Chicago. When this county was part of Oklahoma territory, it was designated as "Third County." Voters were to be given the opportunity to change this generic name at a local election but the choices initially presented to them, Cedar County versus Little River County did not appeal. Daniel W. Marquart, a Republican, proposed that Third County's name be changed to Lincoln County, in honor of President Abraham Lincoln. Local Democratic voters suggested that President Cleveland's name should be honored. The voters approved that name choice by a vote of 829 to 405 and that name was ratified some years later by Oklahoma's state constitutional convention on July 16, 1907. However Oklahoma did not neglect President Lincoln. The original "County A" was renamed Lincoln County, in honor of President Abraham Lincoln.

2110 *Coal County*

Coal deposits in the area— This county was created on July 16, 1907, by Oklahoma's state constitutional convention, and named for the coal deposits which lie under much of the county's surface. The coal fields here were opened in 1882 under lease from the Choctaw Indian nation. The Choctaw Indians had known that this area abounded in coal since the early days of their residence here, because they observed numerous outcroppings of coal along streams.

2111 *Comanche County*

Comanche Indians— The Comanche Indians' language and traditions closely resemble those of the Shoshoni Indians. It is probable that the Comanche were a part of the Shoshoni when they lived in the Rocky Mountains of Wyoming. As the Comanche migrated south, they acquired horses and began to pursue a nomadic, tepee-dwelling life style and to subsist largely by hunting buffalo. These plains Indians were fierce warriors and by the 18th century, Spanish explorers reported that the Comanche were replacing the Apache Indians in eastern Colorado and eastern New Mexico. The Comanche acquired enormous wealth in firearms and horses and they were recognized as the finest horsemen in the West. This ability, coupled with their warlike disposition, made them formidable foes to both Whites and other Indians. The Comanche continued to drift south and in 1795 they formed a close confederation with the Kiowa Indians, with a center of operations in Oklahoma and Texas, where they terrorized White settlers. In was not until 1875 that the American army finally subdued the Comanche and settled them on an Indian reservation. In the late 18th century, the Comanche population was estimated at more than 20,000 but an epidemic reduced that figure to 9,000 in 1816. By 1960 there were estimated to be just 3,000 remaining Comanche Indians, most of whom were living on reservations here in Oklahoma. The name *Comanche* has been translated as meaning "enemies" in the Ute Indians' language. Comanche County here in Oklahoma territory had been organized in 1901 following the opening of Indians' lands in the area to non–Indian settlers. On July 16, 1907, the name *Comanche* was endorsed by the constitutional convention of the state of Oklahoma as the name for this county in the new state.

2112 *Cotton County*

Name chosen at random from a hat— In August, 1912, this county's name was picked from a hat containing several possible county names, by citizens of the area to be embraced by the new county. The name Cotton County was chosen as a result of this random selection and it was officially proclaimed as a county of the state of Oklahoma on August 27, 1912, by the state's governor, Lee Cruce (1863–1933). The use of "cotton" for a county name here on Oklahoma's southern border with Texas, in the south-central United States, is not an unreasonable choice. Cotton is an agricultural product of importance in Texas and, to a lesser extent, Oklahoma. In addition to cotton, this county's farm products included wheat, fruit, poultry and eggs, at the time that the county was created.

2113 *Craig County*

Granville C. Craig (–)— Granville C. Craig was a friend of W. H. Kornegay, who was a delegate to Oklahoma's state constitutional convention held from 1906 to 1907. At that constitutional convention, it was an unwritten rule that, with some exceptions, county names would be selected by the delegate to the constitutional convention from the area of that county. Wade H. Kornegay (1865–1939), a lawyer and a Democrat, was a delegate to that convention from Vinita, Oklahoma. Kornegay was chairman of the constitutional convention's standing committee on ordinances. It was delegate Wade H. Kornegay who proposed that this county be named Craig, in honor of his friend, Granville C. Craig, a farmer, stockman and merchant, who had lived near Welch, Oklahoma since 1873. Both the municipality of Vinita, where delegate Kornegay lived and the Welch area, the home of Granville C. Craig, are within today's Craig County, Oklahoma. The constitutional convention accepted Wade H. Kornegay's recommendation and Craig County, Oklahoma, was created by that convention on July 16, 1907.

2114 *Creek County*

Creek Indians— The Creek were a large and powerful confederacy of North American Indian tribes who occupied an enormous area of the southeastern United States, including most of Georgia and Alabama. They were an agricultural people, but hunting and fishing were important supplements to their farming. In military actions against other Indians the Creek were very capable warriors and they were known to burn captives at the stake. In the 18th century their population was estimated to be about 20,000. The Creek Indians revolted against the Americans in the Creek War of 1813–1814 and they were badly defeated. By 1841 most Creek had been moved from the southeastern United

States to Indian territory (now Oklahoma), where large numbers of Creek Indians still live. During Oklahoma's state constitutional convention it had initially been intended that this county's name would be Moman County, in honor of the maiden name of the mother of Moman Pruiett, an Oklahoma City attorney and friend of Lee Cruce (1863–1933). The proposed name for the county was changed to Creek at the last moment and Creek County, Oklahoma, was created on July 16, 1907. In the original alphabetical listing of counties that was engrossed on a copy of Oklahoma's constitution, Creek County appears following Mayes County, the location intended for the Moman County, Oklahoma, that never was.

2115 *Custer County*

George A. Custer (1839–1876)— Custer was born in Ohio and educated at West Point. As a Union officer in the Civil War, his successes led to promotion to the rank of general before his 24th birthday. Following that war, he served in the U.S. cavalry fighting Indians in the West. The flamboyance which had served Custer so well in the Civil War led to his downfall at the battle of Little Big Horn in Montana territory on June 25, 1876. In that battle, famous as "Custer's last stand," he attacked Indians who greatly outnumbered his forces. Custer and all of his men were slain. This county was initially designated "G County" of Oklahoma territory. The voters of that county authorized changing the county's name to honor George A. Custer and that name was endorsed by Oklahoma's state constitutional convention when it created Custer County, in the new state of Oklahoma, on July 19, 1907. That date was three days later than most of the counties created by the convention. Perhaps the delegates used those three days to ponder whether or not they really wanted to name an Oklahoma county in honor of a man whose final claim to fame was as an Indian fighter.

2116 *Delaware County*

Delaware Indians— When the Europeans first encountered the Delaware Indians, they were living along the Delaware River basin in large areas of present day Delaware and New Jersey as well as eastern Pennsylvania. They were agricultural people who cleared the land of trees and undergrowth by burning. Because this burning limited the length of time that the land was fertile, the Delaware Indians moved

their villages frequently. Farming was done by women, their most important crop being corn. The Delaware began to move westward as early as 1720 and today the Delaware are scattered, with many living in Canada and Oklahoma. *Delaware* is the name by which the Whites called these Indians. That name derived from the Delaware River, the river's name having derived from Delaware Bay. The bay was named for Thomas West, Lord De La Warr (1577–1618), who was a British governor of colonial Virginia. This county was created by Oklahoma's state constitutional convention on July 16, 1907, and named for the Delaware Indians, who had settled in this section of northeastern Oklahoma in 1867, by contract with the Cherokee Indians.

2117 *Dewey County*

George Dewey (1837–1917)— A native of Vermont and a graduate of the U.S. Naval Academy, Dewey saw duty as a junior naval officer during the Civil War and rose to the rank of commodore in the years following the Civil War. In the Spanish American War, on May 1, 1898, Dewey attacked the Spanish fleet and destroyed the ships stationed at Manila Bay. This victory ended Spain's power in the Philippine Islands and made Dewey a national hero. Congress reactivated the rank of admiral and bestowed it on him. Dewey continued to serve the navy as president of the general board of the U.S. navy until his death. This county was first created as "D County" but that name was changed to Dewey County by vote of the local residents, prior to statehood. That name was endorsed by the constitutional convention of the state of Oklahoma as the name for this county in the new state, when the convention created Dewey County on July 16, 1907.

2118 *Ellis County*

Albert H. Ellis (1861–1950)— Born in Shelby County, Indiana, on December 17, 1861, Ellis moved west when he was 21 years old, coming first to Kansas and later to the present Oklahoma, when the Cherokee strip was opened. Ellis was a farmer and a Democrat who served in the legislature of Oklahoma territory and represented his district, the Orlando, Oklahoma, area, at Oklahoma's state constitutional convention held from 1906 to 1907. It was that convention which created and named this county in his honor on July 16, 1907. At that constitutional convention, it was an unwritten rule that, with some exceptions, county names would be selected by the delegate to the constitutional convention from the area of that county. It was the delegate to the constitutional convention from Grand, Oklahoma, the area that would soon be Ellis County, David Hogg, who proposed naming this county for Albert H. Ellis. Ellis was the second vice-president of the convention. He later served in the first legislative assembly of the state of Oklahoma and his fellow representatives elected him as speaker *pro-tempore* of the house. He died June 18, 1850.

2119 *Garfield County*

James A. Garfield (1831–1881)—A native of Ohio, Garfield served in the Ohio senate before becoming a Union officer in the Civil War. He performed ably and rapidly rose to the rank of general. In 1863 Garfield resigned his commission to enter the U.S. House of Representatives where he served until 1880. During Reconstruction, Garfield favored harsh treatment of the defeated South. In January, 1880, he was elected to the U.S. Senate but never served in that body. Instead, he was nominated and elected president of the United States. His nomination by the Republican party came as a compromise on the 36th ballot. Garfield was fatally wounded by an assassin's bullet just four months after beginning his term as president. He died on September 19, 1881. This county had originally been designated as "O County," but on November 6, 1894, prior to statehood, the residents changed its name, by popular vote, to honor President Garfield. That name change was ratified by the state's constitutional convention on July 16, 1907.

2120 *Garvin County*

Samuel J. Garvin (–)—Samuel Johnson Garvin, of Pauls Valley, Oklahoma, has been described as a "prominent intermarried citizen of the Chickasaw Nation." He was a freighter and rancher and a member of the Chickasaw tribal organization. At Oklahoma's state constitutional convention, it was an unwritten rule that, with some exceptions, county names would be selected by the delegate to the constitutional convention from the area of that county. It was apparently the delegate to the convention from the Pauls Valley area who proposed this county's name because the county was created by the convention on July 16, 1907, and Pauls Valley is today a part of Garvin County, Oklahoma. Samuel J. Garvin was not, himself, a delegate to the state constitutional convention.

2121 *Grady County*

Henry W. Grady (1850–1889)—A native of Georgia, Grady began his career in journalism on newspapers in Rome, Georgia. He acquired ownership interests in the newspapers with which he was associated, first in Rome and later in Atlanta, where he became managing editor of the *Atlanta Constitution*. Grady became nationally known as an eloquent orator as well as a journalist, and he was an important spokesman for the entire Reconstruction South. He described the evils of Reconstruction and succeeded in softening the hearts of many northerners toward their defeated brethren in the South. He urged the need for reconciliation and economic recovery. Mentioned as a possible running mate for Grover Cleveland in 1888, Grady died in his prime at the age of 39, of pneumonia. This county was created by Oklahoma's state constitutional convention on July 16, 1907.

2122 *Grant County*

Ulysses S. Grant (1822–1885)—Grant was a native of Ohio who graduated from the U.S. Military Academy at West Point. He served with distinction in the Mexican War, and in the Civil War he rose to become commander of all Union forces. After the Civil War, Grant briefly served as acting secretary of war and then two terms as president of the United States. He proved to be a rather mediocre president. This county had originally been designated as "L County," but, prior to statehood, the residents changed its name, by popular vote, to honor President Grant. That name was ratified by Oklahoma's state constitutional convention on July 16, 1907.

2123 *Greer County*

John A. Greer (1802–1855)—John Alexander Greer was born in Shelbyville, Tennessee, in July, 1802. He moved to Kentucky and then, in 1830 as Americans in Texas were preparing to declare their independence from Mexico, Greer moved to Texas and engaged in farming. After Texas gained her independence, Greer served as a senator in the congress in the independent Republic of Texas from 1837 to 1845, when he was appointed secretary of the treasury by Texas President Anson Jones (1798–1858). In 1847 Greer was elected lieutenant-governor of the state of Texas. He died on July 4, 1855, while campaigning to become governor, of Texas. The original Greer County had been established as Greer County in the state of Texas on Febru-

ary 8, 1860, and named in honor of the state's former lieutenant-governor. The United States government subsequently determined that Texas held no valid claim to the land embraced by Greer County and the land eventually became part of Oklahoma territory. Greer County, in the state of Oklahoma, was created by Oklahoma's state constitutional convention on July 16, 1907.

2124 *Harmon County*

Judson Harmon (1846–1927)—A native of Ohio, a lawyer and a judge in Ohio, Harmon was appointed by President Grover Cleveland as attorney general and he served in that cabinet position from 1895 to 1897. He returned to private practice in 1897 and was then appointed special investigator. In 1908 he ran for governor Ohio, lost that election but tried again in 1910 and defeated the Republican candidate, Warren G. Harding (1865–1923). In 1912 he was Ohio's favorite son choice to be the Democratic candidate for president, helping to spoil the chances of William Jennings Bryan (1860–1925) and permitting Woodrow Wilson to be nominated and then elected president. Harmon served as governor of Ohio from 1909 to 1913. This Oklahoma county was created and named in his honor by proclamation of Oklahoma's governor, Charles N. Haskell (1860–1933), on June 2, 1909. Harmon was remembered in this county's name because of his earlier participation in taking Oklahoma's Greer County area away from Texas.

2125 *Harper County*

Oscar G. Harper (1874–)—Born near Osceola, Missouri, in 1874, Harper attended local schools, graduated from high school at Osceola and then taught in neighborhood schools. After immigrating to Kansas he filed a homestead claim there in 1898, and taught school. Harper was appointed as the first postmaster in Brule (name changed to Buffalo in 1907) in what is now northwestern Oklahoma. He was appointed postmaster on June 15, 1899. Harper served as a clerk at Oklahoma's state constitutional convention in 1906–1907. Since that convention had more than a dozen clerks, inclusion of Harper's precise title is appropriate. He was "minute clerk." This county was created and named in his honor by that constitutional convention on July 16, 1907. At Oklahoma's state constitutional convention, it was an unwritten rule that, with some exceptions, county names would be selected by the delegate to the constitutional convention from the area of that county. This county's name was proposed by the delegate to the convention from the municipality of Stockholm, Reverend Edward R. Williams (1857–1932), a Baptist minister. Harper had campaigned for Williams to be elected as a delegate to the convention. The county named in Harper's honor included the community (originally Brule; later Buffalo), where he had been postmaster. In fact, Oscar G. Harper came under fire in the press for having financially benefited from the selection of Brule/Buffalo, as the county seat.

2126 *Haskell County*

Charles N. Haskell (1860–1933)— Born in Ohio on March 13, 1860, Haskell studied law and was admitted to the Ohio bar. He also engaged in school teaching and construction work in Ohio. He agreed to come to Muskogee, in the Creek nation of Indian territory on April 18, 1901, and construct a railroad line from Fayetteville, Arkansas to Muskogee. He moved to Muskogee and while working on the railroad construction, engaged in banking and newspaper ventures. In 1906 he was elected as a delegate to Oklahoma's state constitutional convention and it was that convention, based on a motion by Delegate Boone Williams of Lehigh, Oklahoma, that created and named this county in Haskell's honor. In 1907 Haskell was elected as Oklahoma's first state governor and he served in that office from 1907 to 1911. The Haskell administration produced an extensive code of labor legislation, bank guaranty laws and a graduated income tax but is was under Haskell that "Jim Crow" legislation was adopted in Oklahoma. After an unsuccessful bid to represent Oklahoma in the U.S. Senate, he became an oil investor. During the constitutional convention, when this county was being named in his honor, Charles N. Haskell proudly proclaimed that "There is no county in the new state wherein the farmer will prosper more than he will in the county named in my honor."

2127 *Hughes County*

William C. Hughes (1869–1938)— Born in Georgetown, Missouri, on October 24, 1869, William C. Hughes practiced law in Oklahoma City for a number of years and was a delegate to Oklahoma's state constitutional convention in 1906–1907. In that body he was chairman of the standing committee on municipal corporations and he was the author of the prohibition against child labor in Oklahoma's constitution. It was that constitutional convention which created and named this county in honor of William C. Hughes on July 16, 1907. The county's name was proposed by Charles N. Haskell (1860–1933), a powerful member of the convention and later the first governor of the state of Oklahoma. William C. Hughes subsequently served as clerk of the Oklahoma County superior court and was chairman of the state board of affairs from 1931 to 1935. He died in Ada, Oklahoma, on March 22, 1838.

2128 *Jackson County*

Uncertain— This county was created only July 16, 1907, by Oklahoma's state constitutional convention. Sources on Oklahoma's history, geography and place names are about equally divided, concerning this county's namesake, between President Andrew Jackson and the Confederate general, Thomas J. "Stonewall" Jackson. One source states that Jackson County was named for both of them.

Andrew Jackson (1767–1845)— Jackson was born on the border of North Carolina and South Carolina. He represented Tennessee in both branches of the U.S. Congress, and gained fame and popularity for his military exploits in wars with the Indians and in the War of 1812. He was provisional military governor of Florida and, from 1829 to 1837, General Jackson was president of the United States. His presidency reflected the frontier spirit of America.

Thomas J. Jackson (1824–1863)— Born at Clarksburg, Virginia, in what is now West Virginia, Thomas J. Jackson graduated from the U.S. Military Academy at West Point and served as an officer during the Mexican War. After that war he taught at Virginia Military Institute. In 1861 he entered the Confederate army and had been promoted to brigadier-general when, at the first battle of Manassas in Virginia, someone said "There is Jackson, standing like a stone wall," and he was "Stonewall" Jackson ever more. He enjoyed military successes in a number of important Civil War battles, became a Southern hero and was elevated to lieutenant-general. In May, 1863 Stonewall Jackson was accidentally shot by members of his own force at twilight, while on reconnaissance, and he soon lost his left arm and then his life to that accident.

Muriel H. Wright's article dealing with counties of the Choctaw nation, which appeared in the September, 1930 (Vol. 8, No. 3), issue of *Chronicles of Oklahoma*, reported that a Jackson County was formed by the Choctaw nation on October 21, 1886, and named for Jacob Jackson, who was a prominent member of the Choctaw senate at that time. However, it seems clear that the name of the present Jackson County, Oklahoma, which was created in 1907, had no connection with this earlier Jackson County in the Choctaw nation.

2129 *Jefferson County*

Thomas Jefferson (1743–1826)— Jefferson was a native of Virginia and a member of the Virginia legislature. He served Virginia as governor and was a delegate to the second Continental Congress. Jefferson was the author of the Declaration of Independence and one of its signers. He was minister to France, secretary of state, vice-president and president of the United States. As president, he accomplished the Louisiana Purchase and he arranged the Lewis & Clark Expedition to the Pacific Northwest. Jefferson was a true intellectual, thoroughly knowledgeable in the arts and sciences. His political theories were pivotal in the formation of our infant republic. This county was created on July 16, 1907, by the state constitutional convention.

2130 *Johnston County*

Douglas H. Johnston (–)— Douglas H. Johnston attended Bloomfield Academy in Indian territory, a unique educational institution of the Five Civilized Tribes, and he subsequently served as that academy's superintendent from 1882 to 1898, when he resigned to become governor of the Chickasaw nation. He was governor of the Chickasaws from 1898 to 1902, and then again from 1904 to 1906. The governments of Five Civilized Tribes were dissolved in 1906 but Douglas H. Johnston's term as governor was extended to last for life by unsolicited action of the U.S. government. Because of this, Johnston served as chief executive of the Chickasaws longer than any executive of the Five Civilized Tribes in the history of Oklahoma. This county was created on July 16, 1907, by Oklahoma's state constitutional convention. At that convention, it was an unwritten rule that, with some exceptions, county names would be selected by the delegate to the constitutional convention from the area of that county. This county's name was proposed by the delegate to the convention from the area that is now Johnston County, William H. Murray (1869–1956), who was president of the convention. In his memoirs, published in 1945, Murray specifically stated that he chose this county's name, in honor of Douglas H. Johnston.

2131 *Kay County*

An adaptation of the original designation as "K County"— When Oklahoma territory was created by the U.S. Congress in 1890, its organic act provided numeric designations (number 1 through number 7) for the first seven counties and later new counties, with alpha designations from "A" through "Q" were added. The voters were given the option to later change these alpha/numeric county names to more traditional county names at local elections. The voters of "K County" decided to retain the name "K County," but spell it out as "Kay County," and that decision was endorsed on July 16, 1907, when Oklahoma's state constitutional convention created Kay County as a part of the new state of Oklahoma.

2132 *Kingfisher County*

Town of Kingfisher, Oklahoma— This county had originally been designated as "Fifth County." It was officially named Kingfisher County on July 16, 1907, by Oklahoma's state constitutional convention. That name was given in honor of the town of Kingfisher, which was designated as the county seat of the new county. The town of Kingfisher, first named Lisbon, had been settled overnight after the land run of April 22, 1889. Lisbon's name died and was changed to Kingfisher on July 18, 1889, when the two adjoining town sites of Lisbon and Kingfisher had grown into one. In the early 1960's the town of Kingfisher, at an altitude of 1,056 feet above sea level, had a population of 3,345. The town was named for Kingfisher Creek here. The origin of the creek's name is uncertain but literature dealing with the history, geography and place names of Oklahoma provides these possibilities for the origin of the creek's name:

Kingfisher bird— Kingfishers are members of the *Alcedinidae* family that inhabit areas near woodland streams, ponds and coastal areas. They hunt fish by hovering over the water looking for prey and then plunge headfirst into the water to catch the fish with their heavy bills. These birds have stocky bodies with short legs and stubby feet for digging nest burrows along stream banks. Three species of kingfishers are found in North America. The ringed kingfisher is rarely found north of the southern tip of Texas and although the green kingfisher inhabits an area extending somewhat north of the ringed kingfisher, it is not typically found north of central Texas. By deduction then, we conclude that if this creek were named for the bird, it was probably the belted kingfisher, or *Ceryle alcyon.* This 13 inch long kingfisher can be found in most of North America, including all of Oklahoma. These birds are solitary except in nesting season. Both female and male belted kingfishers have a breast band, colored slate blue. They are common along creeks, brooks, rivers ponds as well as along lakes and estuaries.

King Fisher (–)— According to this version of the origin of the name of Kingfisher Creek, a cattle man whose ranch was in the valley of Kingfisher Creek, King Fisher and his uncle, were said to have settled in this vicinity, with the uncle setting up his ranch along one creek, Uncle John's Creek, and his nephew, named King Fisher, settling on the other creek, called King Fisher Creek, in his honor. A footnote to an article about Ben Williams, by Hubert E. Collins in the December, 1932, issue (Vol. 10, No. 4) of *Chronicles of Oklahoma* says that this King Fisher "...is *reputed* [italics added] to have been shot and killed by a gambler at San Antonio, after leaving the Indian Territory."

King Fisher (–)— This King Fisher was said to have been a settler from Nebraska who operated a trading station and stage coach station on the western side of the town of Kingfisher.

Material contained in Charles N. Gould's *Oklahoma Place Names* and in Dan W. Peery's "Notes" in the September, 1934, issue (Vol. 12, No. 3) of *Chronicles of Oklahoma* implies that the King Fisher who operated a ranch on Kingfisher Creek, and the King Fisher who operated a trading station and stage coach station on the western side of the town of Kingfisher, may be the same man.

John King Fisher (1854–1884)— Born in Collins County, Texas, in 1854, and known as King Fisher, this rustler and gunman lived at Goliad, and later at Pendencia Creek, where he was employed to fend off cattle rustlers. Fisher decided to become a cattle rustler himself and in the course of acquiring and selling the horses and cattle he stole, Fisher participated in extensive violence. *The Handbook of Texas*, published in 1952 by the Texas State Historical Association, stated that "Fisher is reported to have been charged with eleven murders in one trial..." He was not convicted on that particular occasion but it was common knowledge that this King Fisher was to be both feared and respected. At the branch in the road leading to his home, Fisher placed a sign reading "This is King Fisher's road. Take the other one." On the night of March 11, 1884, Fisher and his companions were killed at San Antonio by assassins. It is understandable that this colorful and well known character of our Southwest would be remembered if the name King Fisher were mentioned and he lived about the time that the other King Fisher(s) were operating near the banks of Kingfisher Creek in Oklahoma, but there is nothing in the biography of John King Fisher (1854–1884) to suggest that he ever lived in or had any connection with Oklahoma.

2133 *Kiowa County*

Kiowa Indians— The Kiowa were a nomadic, tepee-dwelling tribe of buffalo hunters who, in the mid-19th century lived in western Kansas and southeastern Colorado and in western Oklahoma. *Kiowa* in their language means "principal people." They were among the most warlike Indians of the southern plains. Although devastated by cholera in 1849 and smallpox in 1861–1862 and officially assigned to a reservation in Indian territory in 1868, portions of the tribe remained hostile for a decade. Most remaining Kiowa now live in Oklahoma. A census taken in 1985 counted 3,999 Kiowa Indians at the Anadarko agency in Oklahoma. This county's name was selected by local settlers prior to statehood and then the name given by the settlers was officially endorsed on July 16, 1907, by Oklahoma's state constitutional convention.

2134 *Latimer County*

James S. Latimer (1855–1941)— Born in Kansas territory on December 10, 1855, Latimer attended school near Marshfield, Missouri and finished his education at the high school in Ft. Smith, Arkansas. He entered railroad work in Arkansas, and in 1892, Latimer came to Indian territory, and continued to work in railroad positions. He served as operator in the office of the superintendent of the Choctaw, Oklahoma & Gulf Railroad in what is now McAlester, Oklahoma, and over the next seven or eight years he served as the railroad station agent and operator at the Oklahoma municipalities of Red Oak, Fanshawe and Wilburton. Latimer's marriage had given him the rights of a citizen of the Choctaw nation and he settled on a tract of land near a village named Patterson and engaged in farming and raising livestock here. He was elected in 1906 to represent his district at Oklahoma's state constitutional convention. At that convention, it was an unwritten rule that, with some exceptions, county names would be selected by the delegate to the constitutional convention from the area of that county. Delegate James S. Latimer used that unwritten rule to suggest that this county be named in his own honor and the convention agreed and created Latimer County on July 16, 1907. He died on October 30, 1941.

2135 *Le Flore County*

Greenwood Leflore (1800–1865)— Leflore's father was a French-Canadian named Louis Le Fleur (rendered in some accounts as La Fleur) and his mother was a Choctaw Indian, whose surname was Cravat. Greenwood changed his surname to Leflore. An intelligent child, who received some schooling in Tennessee, Leflore used his education, native intelligence and business savvy to become a very wealthy man. He acquired ownership interests in large amounts of land in Mississippi and Texas. His Mississippi land included a large cotton plantation cultivated by some 400 Black slaves whom Greenwood Leflore owned. Leflore was serving as the chief of the western district of the Choctaw Indian nation during the period that the Whites were planning to move the entire Choctaw nation to Indian territory. Leflore recognized that there was no way to avert this removal of his people but he held out for the best terms. His compromise ideas formed a portion of the 1830 treaty of Dancing Rabbit Creek. Under the terms of that treaty, the entire Choctaw nation was moved to Indian territory. Although Leflore was one of the three principal Choctaw chiefs who signed the treaty, he did not move with his people to Indian territory. He stayed in Mississippi where he was elected to the state senate. When Mississippi seceded from the federal Union, Leflore's sympathies and actions were with the Union side and he refused to ally himself with the Confederacy. Several sources dealing with the origins of Oklahoma's county names state that this county was named for the Leflore family, of which Greenwood Leflore was the most prominent member. However, we have confirmation that the county was named specifically for Greenwood Leflore alone. The president of Oklahoma's constitutional convention, William H. Murray (1869–1956), wrote memoirs which were published in 1945, titled *Memoirs of Governor Murray & True History of Oklahoma*. In those memoirs, Murray specified that this county was named "in honor of Greenwood LeFlore, of Mississippi." At Oklahoma's constitutional convention, it was an unwritten rule that, with some exceptions, county names would be selected by the delegate to the constitutional convention from the area of that county. Murray's memoirs give us the details on the selection and adoption of this county's name. The name was chosen by delegate C. H. Pittman, of Enid, Oklahoma, and Pittman asked the convention president, William H. Murray, to persuade delegate C. C. Mathis (1850–1915), of Monroe, Oklahoma, to name this county for Greenwood Leflore. This was done and Le Flore County, Oklahoma, was created on July 16, 1907. It was appropriate that the delegate from Monroe, Oklahoma, endorse the name, because the municipality of Monroe is in Le Flore County.

2136 *Lincoln County*

Abraham Lincoln (1809–1865)— Lincoln was a native of Kentucky who moved to Illinois, where he was a member of the state legislature. He represented Illinois in the U.S. House of Representatives and later was elected president of the United States. Lincoln's presidency coincided almost exactly with the Civil War. He guided the United States ably through that uniquely turbulent period. As president, he issued the Emancipation Proclamation which declared the freedom of slaves in all states in rebellion. Lincoln was assassinated in April, 1865, a few days after the Union's victory in the Civil War. This county was originally named "County A" but local voters were given the option to later change this alpha county name to more traditional name by local vote. At the general election of 1892, the voters here selected the name Lincoln County to replace "County A" as this county's name and that decision was endorsed on July 16, 1907, when Oklahoma's state constitutional convention created Lincoln County as a part of the new state of Oklahoma.

2137 *Logan County*

John A. Logan (1826–1886)— A native of Illinois, Logan served in the Illinois legislature and represented that state in the U.S. Congress in both the house and senate. Having served in the Mexican War as a lieutenant, Logan entered the Civil War as a colonel in the Union army and rose to the rank of major-general. In 1884 he ran for vice president on the Republican ticket headed by James G. Blaine. This county was first designated as "County One" or "First County" but local voters were given the option to later change this numeric county name to more traditional name by local vote. The voters chose Logan County, named in honor of General John A. Logan, and that decision was endorsed on July 16, 1907, when Oklahoma's state constitutional convention created Logan County as a part of the new state of Oklahoma.

2138 *Love County*

The Love family of Chickasaw Indians— This county was formed from part of the land of the old Chickasaw nation. It was created on July 16, 1907, by Oklahoma's state constitutional convention and named for the prominent Chickasaw family, named Love. A Chickasaw Indian who was prominent about the time of the American Revolution was Thomas Love. Thomas Love had six sons who became important in Chickasaw history. They were Henry, Benjamin, Isaac, Slone, William and Robert. Sources dealing with the history of Oklahoma's county names suggest that the members of the Love family who were best known when this county's name was chosen were Overton Love and Robert H. Love.

Overton Love (1820–1907)— Born in Holly Spring, Mississippi in 1820, Overton Love came to Indian territory in 1838 and settled on the banks of the Red River. The valley where he settled as a farmer and stockman was soon called Love's Valley. He was a member of the legislature and district judge of the Chickasaw nation. Overton Love built a large, three story home for his family, in Love's Valley. On several occasions Judge Love represented the Chickasaw nation in dealings with officials of the U.S. government. He was the owner of the Hotel Love and a director of the First and Marietta National Banks. Overton Love died in the fall of 1907, just after this county was created and named. *The History of Love County, Oklahoma*, published in 1983 states that Overton Love "…did however receive a telegram a short time before his death informing him that the county was going to be named for him." This history of Love County is not the only source that states that this county was named for Overton Love (1820–1907) alone but that view is the minority opinion.

Robert H. Love (–)— Robert H. Love

is said to have been an important and respected Chickasaw leader.

2139 *McClain County*

Charles M. McClain (1840–1915) — Born at Osceola, Missouri, on April 18, 1840, Charles Morgan McClain moved to Tennessee when he was 10 years old and enlisted in the Confederate army. He served in a number of battles during the Civil War and was wounded in the head. He lived for a time in Tennessee after the Civil War and then moved to the Southwest, coming first to Texas in 1871 and then to Chickasaw nation, Indian territory in 1885. Here he established a ranch on the Washita River and engaged in the insurance business. Elected as a delegate to Oklahoma's state constitutional convention of 1906–1907, McClain was made the chairman of that convention's standing committee on insurance. It was at this constitutional convention that Charles McClain's fellow delegates created and named McClain County in his honor on July 16, 1907. He later served as register of deeds in McClain County and had been appointed chief assistant to Oklahoma's state game and fish warden on January 13, 1915, just nine days before his death on January 22, 1915, at Purcell, Oklahoma.

2140 *McCurtain County*

Green McCurtain (1848–1910) — Born at or near Skullyville, Indian territory on November 28, 1848, Green McCurtain served as the local sheriff and was a representative to the Choctaw Indians' national council from 1874 to 1880. He later served as a school trustee and then as district attorney. Elected treasurer of the Choctaw nation in August, 1888, and reelected to that position in 1890, McCurtain next served two years in the senate of the Choctaw nation. In 1896 he was elected chief of the Choctaw nation and reelected in 1898. Ineligible to run for reelection in 1900, McCurtain did campaign for the office of chief again in 1902 and was elected. With statehood on the horizon for Oklahoma, the 1902 election was the last general election of the Choctaw nation and Green McCurtain was its last elected chief. However, his executive talents had been proven and he remained an outstanding leader of his people and also negotiated on their behalf with the Interior department until his death at his home in Kinta, Oklahoma, on December 27, 1910. This county was created on July 16, 1907, by Oklahoma's state constitutional convention

and although most sources agree that this county was named for Green McCurtain (1848–1910), several sources indicate that the county was named for the prominent Choctaw Indian family, of which several members were chiefs. While it is true that there were several members of the McCurtain Choctaw family who were chiefs, and that the county might well have been named for that reason, we have confirmation that the county was named specifically for Green McCurtain alone. The president of Oklahoma's constitutional convention, William H. Murray (1869–1956), wrote memoirs which were published in 1945, entitled *Memoirs of Governor Murray & True History of Oklahoma*. In those memoirs, Murray specified that this county was selected by him: "I named McCurtain in honor of the Chief, Green McCurtain."

2141 *McIntosh County*

McIntosh family — This county was created on July 16, 1907, by Oklahoma's state constitutional convention out of land from the southeastern corner of the old Creek Indian nation and a small portion of land of the Cherokee Indians. The county's name honors an important Creek Indian family, all of whom descended from the British army captain, William McIntosh, a Scot, who was stationed in Georgia, and his two wives, who were members of the Lower Creek, or Coweta, Indian tribe. The captain's eldest son was William McIntosh (–1825). A rather detailed account of the early history of the McIntosh family appeared in the September, 1932, issue (Vol. 10, No. 3) of *Chronicles of Oklahoma*. Written by John B. Meserve, the title of that article was "The MacIntoshes." The McIntosh family dominated the affairs of the Lower Creek Indians in Indian territory until at least 1877 and their descendants have been distinguished lawyers, ministers, statesmen, artists and leaders in building the American West.

William McIntosh (–1825) — Born in Georgia about 1775, and well educated, William McIntosh (–1825) became a tribal leader during the period that the Whites were pushing Indians out of Georgia. He recognized that the Indians would eventually lose their lands and urged the Indians to strike the best deals that they could make. He persuaded his fellow Lower Creeks, or Cowetas, to side with the Americans during the War of 1812 and he was commissioned a general in the U.S. army. After that war, he continued on friendly terms with the Americans and signed many treaties with them. McIntosh's signing of

a treaty at Indian Springs, Georgia, infuriated his fellow Indians and they murdered him on May 1, 1825.

Other members of the Creek Indians' McIntosh family, for whom this county was named, included:

Chilly McIntosh (–) — Chilly was a half brother of William McIntosh (1825) and when his half-brother was murdered, he became chief of the Lower Creeks and sought refuge for his followers among the White Americans in Georgia. The U.S. officials granted to Chilly McIntosh and his followers the right to move to a new location west of the Mississippi River and it was Chilly McIntosh who led a party of 733 men, women and children to form the Creek nation in land given to them by the U.S. government. When the Civil War began, the Lower Creek Indians were divided, some loyal to the Union and others to the Confederacy. Chilly McIntosh was among those who urged his fellow lower Creeks to side with the Confederate states and he served as a colonel in the Confederate army in the Second Creek Regiment of Mounted volunteers.

Roley McIntosh (–) — Also referred to as Roderick, he was a half-brother of William McIntosh (–1825). Born at Coweta, Georgia, about 1790, Roley led an additional group of Creeks out of Georgia to the new Creek nation on the Arkansas River in Indian territory and served as chief of the Lower Creeks from 1828 until his retirement in 1859. He had vast influence among his people and his power was said to be almost absolute. He denounced polygamy and the use of intoxicating liquors. Roley McIntosh owned a large plantation in Indian territory, which was cultivated by slave laborers.

Daniel N. McIntosh (–) — When the Civil War began, the Lower Creek Indians were divided, some loyal to the Union and others to the Confederacy. Daniel N. McIntosh was among those who urged his fellow lower Creeks to side with the Confederate states and he served as a colonel in the Confederate army in the First Creek Regiment of Mounted volunteers. A high-ranking officer under his command was Lieutenant-colonel William R. McIntosh.

2142 *Major County*

John C. Major (1863–1937) — John Charles Major was born on May 20, 1863, at Albion, New York. His principal occupation in New York was farming and when he immigrated west to Kansas, he established a farm near the community of Goddard, Kansas. When the Cherokee Outlet was opened to White settlers in 1893, Major came to the northwestern section of what is now Oklahoma and filed for a homestead on land here. He was elected to the legislature of Oklahoma territory and as a delegate to Oklahoma's state constitutional convention. After Oklahoma was admitted to statehood, John C. Major served as a member of the first legislature of the new state. Active in school affairs Major assisted in building a log school house near his home and participated in the movement to form a consolidated school district. This county was created only July 16, 1907, by Oklahoma's state constitutional convention, and named for John C. Major, the delegate to the convention from Granton. The president of Oklahoma's constitutional convention, Wiliam H. Murray (1869–1956), wrote memoirs which were published in 1945, in which he specified that this county was named Major based on a "petition unanimously signed by the citizens of that new County." John C. Major was serving in Oklahoma's state legislature when he died on January 30, 1937.

2143 *Marshall County*

Elizabeth Ellen Marshall Henshaw (–) — This county was created on July 16, 1907, by Oklahoma's state constitutional convention. At that convention, it was an unwritten rule that, with some exceptions, county names would be selected by the delegate to the constitutional convention from the area of that county. The delegate to the constitutional convention from Madill, Oklahoma (now in Marshall County), was George A. Henshaw (1867–1947), a native of Illinois and a lawyer, who had come to Indian territory in 1900. George A. Henshaw chose to name this county in honor of the maiden name of his mother, Elizabeth Ellen Marshall Henshaw. An article in the Spring, 1948, issue (Vol. 26, No. 1) of *Chronicles of Oklahoma* by Charles Evans, states that Elizabeth Ellen Marshall Henshaw "was a collateral kin to John Marshall, Chief Justice of the United States and of Thomas Marshall, a Judge and Congressman from Kentucky." (Chief Justice John Marshall [1755–1835] married Mary Willis Ambler on January 3, 1783, and they had ten children. Kentucky's congressman Thomas A. Marshall [1794–1871], was a son of Senator Humphrey Marshall [1760–1841] and his wife Mary Marshall, a sister of Chief Justice John Marshall [1755–1835]. Thomas A. Marshall [1794–1871] married Eliza Price on November 26, 1816.) The father of this county's namesake was

John Marshall, of Tennessee and her mother was Nancy Bray Marshall. Elizabeth Ellen Marshall Henshaw and her husband Carrol Henshaw had the following children:

William Riley Henshaw (1851–)
John A. Henshaw (1854–1870)
Sarah E. Henshaw (1862–1878)
James I. Henshaw (1865–)
Mary E. Henshaw (1872–1898)
George Allen Henshaw (1867–1947)
Francis Marion Henshaw (1870–).

2144 *Mayes County*

Uncertain — Sources consulted give two explanations for the origin of this county's name. The majority of sources consulted say that the county was named for Samuel Houston Mayes, principal chief of the Cherokee Indians, from 1895 to 1899. Other sources indicate that the name was intended to honor the Mayes family, a prominent family of the Cherokee Indian nation. Joel Bryan Mayes (1833–1891) was another important Cherokee, who served as the nation's principal chief from 1887 to 1891 and died in office. This county was created by Oklahoma's state constitutional convention on July 16, 1907.

Joel B. Mayes (1833–1891) — Born on October 2, 1833, in the old Cherokee nation, near Cartersville, Georgia, Joel B. Mayes was the son of a White father, from Tennessee, Samuel Mayes, and a mother of mixed blood, Nancy Adair. Joel B. Mayes came to Indian territory during the Cherokee removal and attended school at the male seminary at Tahlequah. After graduating from that institution, Joel B. Mayes taught school for a time and then enlisted as a private in the Confederate army. He served in the First Confederate Indian brigade and had attained the position of quartermaster when the Civil War ended. He served as judge of the district circuit court and then as an associate justice of the Cherokee supreme court. Elevated to chief justice of that body, Joel B. Mayes was elected principal chief of the Cherokee nation in 1887 and he held that position from 1887 until his death on December 14, 1891.

Samuel H. Mayes (–) — Samuel Houston Mayes owned large amounts of land and livestock. He served as principal chief of the Cherokee Indian nation from 1895 to 1899 and was senator, for two terms of the Cooweeskoowee district. Samuel H. Mayes later was sheriff of that district for two years. He was president of Mayes Mercantile Company and his home was in Pryor, which fell within Mayes County when the new county was created in 1907.

2145 *Murray County*

William H. Murray (1869–1956) — William H. ("Alfalfa Bill") Murray was president of the constitutional convention for the state of Oklahoma and that office carried considerable power. As president, Murray could grant or deny favors requested of him by delegates. As one result, two Oklahoma counties were named in his honor, Alfalfa County and Murray County, and he could have gotten half a dozen had he chosen to nod his head during the creation of Oklahoma counties at the constitutional convention. A native of Texas, Murray taught school, published a newspaper and was admitted to practice law in Texas before moving to Tishomingo, in territory of the Chickasaw nation (now Oklahoma), in 1898. Here he practiced law and farmed and became a citizen, by marriage, of the Chickasaw nation. Murray subsequently held a variety of important Oklahoma political posts. He was a delegate and president of Oklahoma's constitutional convention of 1906–1907 and later served in the lower house of Oklahoma's state legislature. Murray was speaker of that body from 1907 to 1908. He represented Oklahoma in the U.S. House of Representatives from 1914 to 1918 and was elected governor of Oklahoma in 1930. He governed Oklahoma from 1931–1935 during the terrible "dust bowl" years of the Great Depression, which gained national attention from John E. Steinbeck's (1902–1968) novel, *The Grapes of Wrath*. This county was created by the Oklahoma constitutional convention on July 16, 1907.

2146 *Muskogee County*

Creek Indians — This county was created on July 16, 1907 by Oklahoma's state constitutional convention out of part of the land of the old Creek nation and named for the Creek Indians. The Creek are also known as the Muskogee Indians, also rendered as Muskoke, and Muskhogean. The Creek were a large and powerful confederacy of North American Indian tribes who occupied an enormous area of the southeastern United States, including most of Georgia and Alabama. They were an agricultural people, but hunting and fishing were important supplements to their farming. In military actions against other Indians the Creek were very capable warriors, known to burn captives at the stake. In the 18th century their population was estimated to be about 20,000. The Creek Indians revolted against the Americans in the Creek War of 1813–1814 and they were badly defeated. By 1841 most Creek had been moved from the southeastern U.S. to Indian territory (now Oklahoma), where large numbers of Creek Indians still live.

2147 *Noble County*

John W. Noble (1831–1912)— A native of Ohio and a lawyer, John Willock Noble served as an officer in the Union army during the Civil War and rose to the rank of brevet brigadier-general. After the war he served as U.S. district attorney for eastern Missouri and was appointed in 1889 by the newly elected president, Benjamin Harrison, to serve in his cabinet as secretary of the Interior. Noble served in that post throughout Benjamin Harrison's presidency, from 1889 to 1893. When this county was part of Indian territory, it was designated as "P County." Voters were to be given the opportunity to change this generic name at a local election and the voters exercised that option and named this county for John W. Noble. That decision was endorsed on July 16, 1907, when Oklahoma's state constitutional convention created Noble County as a part of the new state of Oklahoma.

2148 *Nowata County*

Town of Nowata, Oklahoma— This county was created by Oklahoma's state constitutional convention on July 16, 1907, and named for the town of Nowata in northeastern Oklahoma, which became the county seat of the new county. The town's name was originally Metz, but on November 8, 1889, the post office was named Nowata and the town also became Nowata. The railroad came in 1889 after which a railroad depot was built. J. E. Campbell later erected a store and the next building to rise in Nowata was W. V. Carey's hotel. A U.S. court house was located at Nowata in 1904. Today the municipality of Nowata, Oklahoma, has a population of 3,900. Sources consulted offer differing explanations for the name *Nowata.* but most mention the possibility that it came from the Delaware Indians' word *noweta,* or *noweeta,* meaning "welcome." Some sources suggest that the name resulted from an early misspelling of the name of the post office. There is even a tale that the name was bestowed by an early visitor from Georgia, who, finding nearby springs dry of water, posted a sign which said "No Wata," to warn other travelers. A plausible synthesis of the explanations of the town's, and hence the county's, name was supplied by John D. Benedict in his work entitled *Muskogee and Northeastern Oklahoma,* published in 1922. Benedict stated that the railroad was completed as far as today's municipality of Nowata in 1889 and that the railroad officials agreed at that time to name the station using the Delaware Indians' word for "welcome," or "come here." Benedict spelled this Delaware Indian word *noweata.* Benedict stated that the railroad men mispronounced the name leading it to be misspelled by post office officials. The land from which Nowata County was created was part of the old Cherokee nation and hence the suggestion that the name derives from the language of the Delaware Indians may seem puzzling. However, by formal agreement, Delaware Indians were permitted to purchase land in the Cherokee nation and settle on it and they did so.

2149 *Okfuskee County*

A former Creek Indian town in Alabama— This county was created from land of the old Creek Indian nation by Oklahoma's state constitutional convention on July 16, 1907. Its name was taken from that of an old town of the Creek Indians on or near the southern border of the present Cleburne County, Alabama. That town was situated on both sides of the Tallapoosa River. In his *Handbook of American Indians North of Mexico,* Frederick W. Hodge renders the Alabama town's name as Oakfuskee, and states that, in 1799, this town was considered the largest community in the Creek confederacy. At that time it had 180 warriors and seven branch villages on the Tallapoosa River.

2150 *Oklahoma County*

Oklahoma territory, from Indian words meaning "home of the red people"— In the 1890 organic act by which congress created Oklahoma territory, this county was designated as "County Two" or "Second County" but local voters were given the option to change this numeric county name to a more traditional name. The local voters chose to change the county's name to Oklahoma County, a name which had already been used when Congress created Oklahoma territory. The name comes from two Choctaw Indian words *okla,* meaning "people" and *humma* or *homma,* meaning "red"; hence "home of the red people." That decision was endorsed on July 16, 1907, by Oklahoma's state constitutional convention and Oklahoma County became a county of the new state of Oklahoma. The Choctaws had originally suggested this name in 1866 in proceedings before the U.S. commissioner of Indian Affairs, and the Choctaw Indian who suggested it was Allen Wright, then chief of the Choctaw Indians, but the name Indian territory was chosen instead, following those proceedings. It was not until congress was considering creating an official territory that the name Oklahoma was resurrected by Elias C. Boudinot of the Cherokee nation in memory of the name suggested earlier by Allen Wright.

2151 *Okmulgee County*

Town of Okmulgee, Oklahoma— This county was created by Oklahoma's state constitutional convention on July 16, 1907, and named for the town of Okmulgee in east-central Oklahoma, which became the county seat of the new county. The county's land came from that of the old Creek nation and the town of Oklmulgee had been organized as a district recording town of the Creeks in 1869. A national festival of the Creek Indians is still held in the municipally of Okmulgee, Oklahoma, each year. This town was and is the capital of the Creek Indian nation. Its population in the late 1990's was 13,400. The name is said to mean "bubbling water," or "boiling water."

2152 *Osage County*

Osage Indians— This county was created by Oklahoma's state constitutional convention on July 16, 1907, and named for the Osage Indians, whose reservation comprised the area of the new county. The Osage were an important western division of the Sioux Indians. When first encountered by Whites, the Osage lived in Kansas, Missouri, Arkansas and Illinois. They were prairie Indians who subsisted by hunting buffalo and some village agriculture. The Osage were eventually resettled to Indian territory through a series of treaties with the Whites. The name *Osage* is our current rendering of the name given by the Algonquian Indians, which was *Ouasash.* When Father Jacques Marquette (1637–1675) first heard the name in 1673, he recorded it two ways: *Ouchage* and *Outrechaha.* Later French traders spelled the name a variety of ways including *Ouazhaghi* and *Ousage.* According to some sources the meaning of the original name given to this tribe by the Algonquians was "bone men," but this is speculation.

2153 *Ottawa County*

Ottawa Indians— When first encountered by Whites, the Ottawa Indians were living at what is now the province of Ontario, in Canada. Initially the name Ottawa was used by the French to denote all tribes living on the shores of Lake Huron in upper Michigan and west along Lake Superior. Since then, the name has generally been confined to Indians of the Algonquian linguistic family, who lived in Ohio, Indiana, Michigan and Wisconsin. During the French and Indian War, the Ottawa Indians sided with the French against the British. The Ottawa Indians were pushed steadily westward, first by the Iroquois Indians and later by the Whites. They resisted efforts to push them out of eastern lands into less desirable western areas but these efforts failed. By December, 1836, some Ottawas were resettled to a part of the old Indian territory that is now in Kansas. However, other Ottawas remained in Michigan and Ontario, Canada. Dispirited by this forced relocation and in poor health, nearly half of the Ottawa Indians who had been moved to Kansas were dead within five years. The Ottawas in Kansas were again moved to the Indian territory that is now Oklahoma in 1870. Muriel H. Wright's work entitled *A Guide to the Indian Tribes of Oklahoma* indicated that, based on a census taken in the 1940's, it was estimated that 480 Ottawa Indians were in Oklahoma, a number of whom then lived in Ottawa County. The name *Ottawa* derives from an Indian name meaning "trader" or "barterer." The Ottawa Indians were adept at trading and even served as middlemen facilitating trades between Whites and other Indians and among several Indian tribes as well. This county was created by Oklahoma's state constitutional convention on July 16, 1907.

2154 *Pawnee County*

Pawnee Indians— The Pawnee are a tribe of the Caddoan linguistic family, who once lived in the valley of the lower Mississippi River and along the Red River. They migrated to the lower Arkansas and lower Missouri Rivers. By the time the Pawnees had a large population, they lived and hunted further west, in Nebraska, Kansas and areas south to Texas. The Pawnee subsisted primarily by village agriculture, supplemented by buffalo hunting. They traveled vast distances on foot to steal horses and eventually acquired sufficient numbers of them to become skilled horsemen. The Pawnee were in constant warfare with most neighboring tribes and captured Pawnee Indians were often sold as slaves. However, the Pawnee Indians

were usually friendly toward Whites. During the mid-1870's they were moved to Indian territory and they established their agency within the present Pawnee County, Oklahoma in 1874. The origin and meaning of the name *Pawnee* is uncertain. Many sources indicate that the name means "horn" and refers to a unique method of dressing hair scalp-locks, standing them erect and curved backward like a horn. Other sources indicate that the name means "a braid," "a twist," "to curve," "to bend up" (all referring to hair), while another source suggests that the name derives from "hunter." A more likely explanation relates to the Indian name for "slave" and its application to the Pawnee Indians on account of large numbers of Pawnees who were taken as slaves by the Apache Indians, the Illinois Indians and other tribes. When this county was part of Indian territory, it was designated as "Q County." Voters were given the opportunity to change this generic name at a local election and the voters exercised that option and named it Pawnee County. However later, when Oklahoma's state constitutional convention was considering names for this new county in 1907, they did not automatically endorse the name Pawnee. They first considered the name Platte but rejected it, and approved the name name Pawnee County on July 16, 1907.

2155 *Payne County*

David L. Payne (1836–1884)— A native of Indiana, Payne came west to Kansas territory when he was 21. He served in the Union army during the Civil War and was elected to the Kansas legislature. In the late 1860's Payne served as a captain in the army fighting Indians on the plains. In 1876 Payne became assistant doorkeeper for the U.S. House of Representatives, in Washington, and became interested in acquiring some of the land in Indian territory for himself. Upon his return to Kansas in 1879, Payne began his campaign to settle on unassigned public lands in Indian territory. At that time federal law prohibited settlement on these lands by Whites, but Payne led at least eight invasions into Indian territory and was arrested many times. His nickname, "the Boomer," came from these attempts to participate in a land boom in Indian territory. His illegal forays probably inspired congress to open lands in Indian territory to White homesteaders. David L. Payne was actively organizing another invasion into Indian territory at the time of his sudden death in Kansas in November, 1884.

In the 1890 organic act by which congress created Oklahoma territory, this county was designated as "County Six" or "Sixth County," but local voters were given the option to change this numeric county name to a more traditional name. The local voters chose to change the county's name to Payne County in 1892 and that decision was endorsed by Oklahoma's constitutional convention when it created Payne County on July 16, 1907, as a part of the new state of Oklahoma.

2156 *Pittsburg County*

City of Pittsburgh, Pennsylvania— This county was created on July 16, 1907, by Oklahoma's state constitutional convention and named for the steel making city in southwestern Pennsylvania. The final "h" in the Pennsylvania city's name was inadvertently omitted. Located where the Allegheny River joins the Monongahela River to form the mighty Ohio River, Pittsburgh's river access led to its growth into an important industrial city in the 19th century and the iron and steel factories here remained important in the 20th century. In the late 1990's the city had a population of 360,000. Pittsburgh's history began during the French and Indian wars when the British took Fort Duquesne from the French in the 1750's and built a new fort named in honor of William Pitt, Earl of Chatham (1708–1778).

William Pitt, Earl of Chatham (1708–1778)— Pitt, an Englishman and first earl of Chatham, was one of England's greatest and most famous statesmen. He was a member of parliament and held the positions of vice treasurer of Ireland and paymaster general of the forces. He became secretary of state and virtually prime minister in 1756 but in 1760 King George III (1738–1820) took the throne and Pitt was forced to resign. In 1766 he formed a new ministry but served for only 15 months. Two decades after Pitt's name had been used by the British for the fort at the present site of Pittsburgh, Pennsylvania, William Pitt became very popular with the American colonists for using his status as an English statesman to urge reconciliation between England and her North American colonies. He favored any peace settlement that would keep the American colonies in the British empire.

2157 *Pontotoc County*

Pontotoc County, Chickasaw nation— This county was created in July, 1907, by Oklahoma's state constitutional convention from land of the Chickasaw Indian nation and named for Pontotoc County of the Chickasaw nation here. The Chickasaw nation had named their county for a former village of theirs at Pontotoc, Mississippi. Most sources indicate that the name in Mississippi came from Indian words which meant "weed prairie." However, several other suggestions have been made and the true translation of the name is uncertain. In a 1939 doctoral thesis entitled "Indian Place-Names in Mississippi," Lea L. Seale mentions several possible origins of the name but declines to select any of them as the correct choice.

2158 *Pottawatomie County*

Potawatomi Indians—Apparently the three tribes that we now know as the Potawatomi, Chippewa and Ottawa were once one people. According to tradition, the Potawatomi migrated from somewhere northeast of Michigan. When they were first encountered by the French, they were living in the region around Green Bay, Wisconsin and on or near the shores of Lake Michigan. There they served as middlemen in the French fur trade. The Potawatomi were relentlessly driven south and west by both Indians and Whites. For a time they lived in southern Michigan and northern Illinois and in the late 1700's they participated in the struggle for control of the Ohio River Valley. By 1800 the Potawatomi were scattered in some 100 villages spread over Wisconsin, Illinois, Michigan and Indiana. By the 1830's the Potawatomi had ceded most of those lands and been pushed west to Iowa, and in the 1840's, to Kansas and Oklahoma. Numerous spellings of the tribal name are encountered. *Potawatomi* is the version approved by the former Bureau of American Ethnology. Various translations of the name are also mentioned but there is little doubt that the name refers to "fire." This county was originally designated "County B." It was created as a county in the new state of Oklahoma, named Pottawatomie County, by action of the state constitutional convention on July 16, 1907.

2159 *Pushmataha County*

Pushmataha district of the Choctaw nation—Born in what is today the state of Mississippi about 1764, the Choctaw Indian, Pushmataha (–1824), established his reputation as a warrior against the Osage and Caddo Indians and in 1805, he was made a Choctaw chief. His name, Apushmataha, is rendered as Pushmataha in most biographical sketches. During the Creek War of 1813–1814 Pushmataha led his warriors in support of the U.S. army under General Andrew Jackson. Beloved on account of this, the Americans gave him the rank of brigadier-general accompanied by a full dress uniform. He signed treaties ceding Choctaw lands in the South to the United States but also purchased land from them for his people, south of the South Canadian River, which represented nearly half of the present state of Oklahoma. In 1824 he led a delegation of Choctaw Indians to Washington, to iron out difficulties concerning Choctaw rights and was royally entertained. He met President Monroe, Secretary of War John C. Calhoun (1782–1850), and even the French Marquis de Lafayette (1757–1834), who was visiting Washington at that time. It was during that visit that Chief Pushmataha fell ill and died. When Indians were resettled to Indian territory and tribes were assigned designated areas, the Choctaw came to occupy the southeastern portion of the present state of Oklahoma and they called one of the districts in their nation here, Pushmataha, in honor of Chief Pushmataha (–1824). During Oklahoma's state constitutional convention, William H. Murray (1869–1956), the president of the convention, proposed that this county in the new state be named Pushmataha and that was accomplished on July 16, 1907.

2160 *Roger Mills County*

Roger Q. Mills (1832–1911)—A native of Kentucky, Mills moved to Texas in 1849, and there he studied law, was admitted to the bar and established a law practice. Prior to the Civil War he served in the Texas legislature. An ardent secessionist, Mills enlisted as a private in the Confederate army, participated in a number of battles, was wounded in combat and rose to the rank of colonel by the end of the Civil War. As Reconstruction was ending in Texas, Mills was elected to represent Texas in the U.S. House of Representatives, and he served in the house, and later in the senate from 1873 to 1899. In congress, Mills worked to open Indian territory to White settlers. This county was originally named "County F" but local voters were given the option to change this alpha county name to more traditional name by local vote. At the general election of 1892, the voters here selected the name Roger Mills County to replace "County F" and that decision was endorsed on July 16, 1907, when Oklahoma's state constitutional convention created Roger Mills County as a part of the new state of Oklahoma.

2161 *Rogers County*

Clement V. Rogers (1839–1911)—Born on January 11, 1839, in Indian territory, at the outskirts of the present town of Westville, Clement Vann Rogers was a successful farmer, rancher and stockman. He served as a judge of the Cooweescoowee district and later served three terms as a member of the Cherokee senate from that district. In 1893 President Grover Cleveland appointed Rogers as a commissioner to appraise improvements of White settlers in the Cherokee district and in 1890 he was a member of the commission of the Cherokee nation presenting matters before the Dawes commission. In 1894 he became vice president of the First National Bank of Claremore and in 1906 he was elected as a delegate to Oklahoma's state constitutional convention. It was his fellow delegates to that convention who created and named this county in his honor on July 16, 1907. One of Clement V. Rogers' children was the humorist and entertainer, Will Rogers (1879–1935).

2162 *Seminole County*

Seminole Indians—The Seminole, a Muskogean-speaking people, evolved as a distinct tribe in Florida at about the time of the American Revolution. The Seminole consisted of a nucleus of Oconee Indians, a subdivision of the Creeks of Alabama and Georgia, who migrated to Florida in the mid 1700's. The Oconee combined with Yamasee Indians who had been driven from South Carolina, and with remnant groups of Florida Indians and runaway Black slaves, to form the tribe known as Seminole. Noted for their fierce resistance to White attempts to drive them from their homeland in Florida, many Seminole were finally driven to Indian territory but some eluded the American troops and more than 1,000 still live in central and southern Florida. The origin of the name *Seminole* is uncertain. Possibilities suggested include a Creek Indian word(s) meaning "runaways" and "wild men," and the Spanish word *cimarron* meaning "wild," "unruly," or a "runaway slave." Although the Seminole were one of the five "civilized tribes" of Indian territory, the land allotted to them was small and corresponds quite closely to the area embraced by the present Seminole County, Oklahoma. This county was created on July 16, 1907, by Oklahoma's state constitutional convention.

2163 *Sequoyah County*

Sequoya (–1843)—Born in a Tennessee about 1770 of mixed White and Indian ancestry, Sequoya (also known by the names Sequoyah and George Guess) earned his living as a hunter, fur trader and silversmith. Sequoya was raised among the Indians and never learned the English language but he devised a set of symbols for use in rendering Cherokee Indian syllables on paper. He attempted to devise an alphabet and failing that, he experimented with pictographs. His final product, a syllabary of 85 or 86 characters, came after study of characters from the English, Hebrew and Greek languages. His access to these languages was in books at mission schools. Sequoya was living with the Cherokee Indians when they were dispatched by the Whites to Indian territory and Sequoya went with them and taught school in Indian territory. Portions of the *Holy Bible* were translated into Sequoya's language and a newspaper was printed for a time using both English and Sequoya's Cherokee symbols. This county was created on July 16, 1907, by Oklahoma's state constitutional convention.

2164 *Stephens County*

John H Stephens (1847–1924)— A native of Texas and a lawyer, Stephens practiced law in Texas and served in the Texas senate before being elected to the U.S. House of Representatives. Elected in 1896 and reelected nine times, Stephens served in congress from 1897 to 1917. This Oklahoma county was created and named in his honor on July 16, 1907, by Oklahoma's state constitutional convention. Some sources dealing with Oklahoma's history state that the county was named for him because he expressed interest in Oklahoma territory while in congress, while other sources indicate that he championed statehood for Oklahoma. There is no reason to doubt that both statements contain truth, prompting the delegates to the new state's constitutional convention to honor this Texan by naming an Oklahoma county for him.

2165 *Texas County*

State of Texas— As part of Spanish Mexico, the present state of Texas occupied northeastern New Spain for three centuries and then was a part of the independent nation of Mexico for a few decades. Americans showed little interest in Texas until the Louisiana Purchase made Texas a next door neighbor and during the first half of the 19th century a number of Americans moved to Texas. Following a bitter war for independence from Mexico, the republic of Texas was established in 1836. It was admitted to the United States as our 28th state on December 29, 1845. During the Civil War, Texas was a member of the Confederate States of America but following the victory of Union forces in that war, it rejoined the United States. George E. Shankle's book dealing with the origins of the names of our states tells us that the name *Texas* had been applied to the Indians of this region, who banded themselves together for mutual protection. The region occupied by these Indians was called Texas, as early as 1689. The Indians used the name *Texia*, while the Mexican form was *Tejas*, meaning "allies", "friends" or "confederates." Since this area was controlled at an early time by both Indians and Mexicans, these origins seem credible. Confirmation of this explanation of the term *Texas* may be found in Z. T. Fulmore's work entitled *The History & Geography of Texas as Told in County Names*. Fulmore tells us that in 1689 there were about a dozen Indian tribes, each with a specific name, who were members of a confederacy, allied for mutual protection and defense, who were designated by the collective term *Texas*. This Oklahoma county was created on July 16, 1907, by Oklahoma's state constitutional convention. This county lies in Oklahoma's panhandle, bordering Texas and some sources indicate that the name was chosen because of that geographic proximity. Other sources indicate that the name was chosen in memory of the days when Texas lost its Greer County, and the area finally was given to Oklahoma.

2166 *Tillman County*

Benjamin R. Tillman (1847–1918)— A native of South Carolina, Tillman left school in 1864 to serve in the Confederate army. A serious illness cost him his left eye and incapacitated him for two years but when he recovered, he farmed a 400 acre estate. Active in Democratic politics and an organizer of the Farmers' Association, Tillman was elected governor of South Carolina in 1890 and he served as governor until 1894 when he was elected to represent South Carolina in the U.S. Senate. He served in that body from 1895 until his death in 1918. This county was created on July 16, 1907, by Oklahoma's state constitutional convention, while Benjamin R. Tillman was serving as South Carolina's senior senator in Washington. There is a rural community in Tillman County, Oklahoma, named Tillman. Tillman County was not named for that community since it was not established until 1920.

2167 *Tulsa County*

City of Tulsa, Oklahoma— Located on the Arkansas River, in northeastern Oklahoma, Tulsa is the state's second largest city and the site of Oklahoma's first commercially important oil well. As the oil industry prospered along with internal combustion engines, Tulsa became a rich oil city. The city's economy still rests on an oil industry foundation but commerce and industry are now diversified in this city of 375,000. This county was created by Oklahoma's state constitutional convention on July 16, 1907 and named for the city of Tulsa, which became the county seat of the new county. The city had been named when the Creek Indians settled here in 1836 and named their new home for the home in Alabama from which they had been forcibly removed. That former Alabama town's name is rendered variously as Tulsey Town and Tullahassee.

2168 *Wagoner County*

Town of Wagoner, Oklahoma— Wagoner was established in Indian territory in what is now the northeastern portion of Oklahoma and settlement accelerated in 1886 or 1887, when the railroad tracks reached Wagoner. A post office was established here named Wagoner on February 25, 1888. The town developed into a leading shipping point for cattle because of its railroad facilities. Its population in 1980 was 6,958. All sources offering an opinion on the origin of the town's name trace it to a railroad man. At least one source says that the name honored Bailey P. Wagoner, an attorney and representative of the Missouri Pacific railroad, but most sources dealing with the history, geography and place names of Oklahoma tell us that the town's name honored a railroad train dispatcher, from Parsons, Kansas known as "Big Foot" Wagoner. Charles N. Gould's *Oklahoma Place Names*, published in 1933, supports the view that the town of Wagoner was named for a train dispatcher. As Gould tells it, "Wagoner, Wagoner County, was named after a train dispatcher, of the Missouri, Kansas & Texas Railroad, who ordered Roadmaster Perry to build a switch north of Arkansas River, half way between Gibson Station and Lelietta. When completed, Perry telegraphed back, 'Wagoner's switch is ready.' Later the switch was relocated a mile north and the name Wagoner appeared on the time tables." An article entitled "A History of Wagoner, Oklahoma," by L. W. Wilson appeared in the Winter, 1972–1973 (Vol. 50, No. 4), issue of *Chronicles of Oklahoma*. In that article Wilson states that the railroad switch in question was located at Wagoner in 1872. Charles Grady's *County Courthouses of Oklahoma* indicates that the town of Wagoner was founded about that time, in 1871. This county was created by Oklahoma's state constitutional convention on July 16, 1907, and named for the town of Wagoner, which became the county seat of the new county.

2169 *Washington County*

George Washington (1732–1799)— Washington was a native of Virginia. He served in Virginia's house of burgesses and became one of the colonies' leaders in opposition to British policies in America. He was a member of the first and second Continental Congresses and commander of all Continental armies in the Revolutionary War. Following victory in that war, Washington was elected to be the first president of the United States. This county was created on July 16, 1907, by Oklahoma's state constitutional convention.

2170 *Washita County*

Washita River— A major tributary of the Red River, the Washita River rises in northwestern Texas and flows east into Oklahoma before turning southeast. The Washita flows through the county named for it, in southwestern Oklahoma and forms a portion of Washita County's southern border with Kiowa County, Oklahoma. After leavings Washita County, the river continues to flow in a southeastern direction until reaching central Oklahoma. There, the Washita bends to the south and completes its 500 mile journey when its waters join those of the Red River in south-central Oklahoma. This county was originally designated "County H" but local voters were given the option to change this alpha county name to a more traditional name by local vote and they did so in 1900, choosing to name their county for the Washita River. That decision was endorsed on July 16, 1907, when Oklahoma's state constitutional convention created Washita County as a part of the new state of Oklahoma. Sources consulted display little agreement and even less certainty about the origin of the name *Washita*. John

Rydjord's *Indian Place-Names* says that a Chief Kiowa made a distinction between Wichita and Washita and that the chief thought the Washita River's name was related to the red silt that it carried from Oklahoma into the Red River. Rydjord goes on to relate that Bliss Isely, an authority on Kansas history, said "Washita means water with painted face." Charles N. Gould's *Oklahoma Place Names* states that "Ouachita is the Gallicized and Washita the Anglicized spelling of two Choctaw words…" that meant "hunt" and "big." George H. Shirk's *Oklahoma Place Names* supports that view but you author demurs. There is a Ouachita River further east, for which Ouachita County, Arkansas, was named, but as stated in the above paragraph on that Arkansas County, the meaning of the Ouachita River's name is uncertain. Some sources say that Washita's name came from the French *Faux Ouachita*, meaning "false Ouachita," intending to distinguish the river in Oklahoma from the southeastern Ouachita River.

2171 *Woods County*

Samuel N. Wood (1825–1891)— Born at Mount Gilead, Ohio, on December 30, 1825, Samuel Newitt Wood studied law and was admitted to the Ohio bar. He was a member of the Religious Society of Friends with strongly held abolitionist views. Wood and his fellow abolitionists were angered by the Kansas-Nebraska act and in 1854 Wood came west, to Kansas territory because of it. Here he aided escaped fugitive slaves, a perilous activity in those days when tempers were heated in Kansas territory over all issues related to slavery. Wood also was part owner of the *Kansas Tribune* and contributed abolitionist and free state articles to its columns. He served in the legislature of Kansas territory and in senate of the first legislature of the state of Kansas. He later served as an officer in the Union army during the Civil War and was made a brigadier-general of the Kansas militia. Wood subsequently served in both branches of the Kansas legislature and was speaker of the house in 1876. He was assassinated in the door of a church in Hugoton, Kansas, in 1891. This Oklahoma county was originally designated "County M" but local voters were given the option to change this alpha county name to a more traditional one by local vote and they did so, choosing to name their county for the Samuel N. Wood. That decision was endorsed on July 16, 1907, when Oklahoma's state constitutional convention created Woods County as a part

of the new state of Oklahoma. The "s" at the end of the county's name was a clerical error which has never been corrected.

2172 *Woodward County*

City of Woodward, Oklahoma— In 1886 the Southern Kansas Railroad, a subsidiary of the Sante Fe, extended tracks south from Kiowa, Kansas, into the present Woodward County. By 1887 the tracks intersected an army trail, and a train depot was established at the intersection, and named Woodward, in honor of Brinton W. Woodward, a director of the Sante Fe Railroad. A post office was established at Woodward on February 3, 1893, and the town was officially established on September 16, 1893, when the Cherokee outlet was opened to White settlers. Both the post office and the town perpetuated the name of the railroad depot. Today the city of Woodward, Oklahoma, has a population of 12,300 and it is the most important commercial outlet for wheat and cattle produced in northwestern Oklahoma. A Tri-state All Star football game is held in Woodward each year. Today's Woodward County, Oklahoma, was originally designated "County N." When Woodward County was officially created on July 16, 1907, by Oklahoma's state constitutional convention, the county was named for the municipality of Woodward, which became the county seat of the new county.

REFERENCES

Arkansas, Kansas, Missouri & Oklahoma Tour Book. Heathrow, Florida, AAA Publishing, 1998.

Benedict, John D. *Muskogee & Northeastern Oklahoma*. Chicago, S. J. Clarke Publishing Co., 1922.

Bivins, Willie Hardin, et al. *SW Oklahoma Keys*. Oklahoma City, Metro Press, Inc., 1982.

Brooks, John S. *First Administration of Oklahoma: 1907–8*. Oklahoma City, Oklahoma Engraving & Printing Co.

Bryan County Heritage Association, Inc. *The History of Bryan County, Oklahoma*. Dallas, Texas, National Share-Graphics, Inc., 1983.

Busby, Orel. "Buffalo Valley: An Osage Hunting Ground." *Chronicles of Oklahoma*, Vol. 40, No. 1. Oklahoma City: Spring, 1962.

Calhoun, James. *Louisiana Almanac: 1979–1980*. Gretna, Louisiana, Pelican Publishing Co., 1979.

Carroll, Jeff. "Speaking of Texas: John King Fisher." *Texas Highways*, Vol. 37, No. 6. Austin, Texas: June, 1990.

Carruth, Viola. *Caddo: 1,000: A History of the Shreveport Area from the Time of the Caddo Indians to the 1970's*. Shreveport, Shreveport Magazine, 1970.

Carter, W. A. *McCurtain County & Southeast Oklahoma: History, Biography, Statistics*. Ft. Worth, Texas, Tribune Publishing Co., 1923.

Clark, Blue. "Buffalo: A County Seat." *Chronicles of Oklahoma*, Vol. 51, No. 1. Oklahoma City: Spring, 1973.

Clark, Blue. "Delegates to the Constitutional Convention." *Chronicles of Oklahoma*, Vol. 48, No. 4. Oklahoma City: Winter, 1970–1971.

Clements, John: *Flying the Colors: Texas*. Dallas, Texas, Clements Research, Inc., 1984.

Collins, Hubert E. "Ben Williams: Frontier Peace Officer." *Chronicles of Oklahoma*, Vol. 10, No. 4. Oklahoma City: December, 1932.

Cornish, Melven. "Necrology: Douglas H. Johnston." *Chronicles of Oklahoma*, Vol. 18, No. 1. Oklahoma City: March, 1940.

Craig County Heritage Association. *The Story of Craig County: Its People & Places*. Dallas, Texas, Curtis Media Corp., 1984.

Debo, Angie. "Albert H. Ellis." *Chronicles of Oklahoma*, Vol. 28, No. 4. Oklahoma City: Winter, 1950–51.

Deupree, Mrs. N. D. "Greenwood Le Flore." *Publications of the Mississippi Historical Society*, Vol. 7. Oxford, Mississippi: 1903.

Dewitz, Paul W. H. *Notable Men of Indian Territory at the Beginning of the Twentieth Century: 1904–1905*. Muskogee, Indian territory, Southwestern Historical Co.

Directory of Oklahoma: 1975. Impress Graphics, Inc.

Directory of Oklahoma: 1979. Fort Worth, Texas, Evans Press.

Donehoo, George P. *Pennsylvania: A History*. New York, Lewis Historical Publishing Co., Inc., 1926.

Du Gard, Rene C. *Dictionary of Spanish Place Names*. Edition des Deux Mondes, 1983.

The Encyclopedia Americana. New York, Americana Corporation, 1977.

Estill-Harbour, Emma. "Greer County." *Chronicles of Oklahoma*, Vol. 12, No. 2. Oklahoma City: June, 1934.

Evans, Charles. "George Allen Henshaw: 1867–1947." *Chronicles of Oklahoma*, Vol. 26, No. 1. Oklahoma City: Spring, 1948.

Field Guide to the Birds of North America. Washington, D.C., National Geographic Society, 1983.

Fischer, Leroy H. *Oklahoma's Governors: 1907–1929: Turbulent Politics*. Oklahoma City, Oklahoma Historical Society, 1981.

Fisher, O. C., & J. C. Dykes. *King Fisher: His Life & Times*. Norman, University of Oklahoma Press, 1966.

Fletcher, Christine. *100 Keys: Names Across the Land*. Nashville, Abingdon Press, 1973.

Freeman, Charles R. "The Battle of Honey Springs." *Chronicles of Oklahoma*, Vol. 13, No. 2. Oklahoma City: June, 1935.

Fulmore, Z. T. *The History & Geography of Texas as Told in County Names*. Austin, Texas, 1926.

Gittinger, Roy. *The Formation of the State of Oklahoma*. Berkeley, University of California Press, 1917.

Gould, Charles N. *Oklahoma Place Names*. Norman, University of Oklahoma Press, 1933.

Grady, Charles. *County Courthouses of Oklahoma*. Oklahoma City, Oklahoma Historical Society, 1985.

Hall, Ted B. *Oklahoma: Indian Territory*. Ft. Worth, Texas, American Reference Publishers, 1971.

Harlow, Victor E. *Oklahoma: Its Origins & Development*. Oklahoma City, Harlow Publishing Corp., 1935.

Hill, Luther B. *A History of the State of Oklahoma*. Chicago, Lewis Publishing Co., 1909.

History of Tillman County. Frederick, Oklahoma, Tillman County Historical Society, 1978.

Hodge, Frederick W. *Handbook of American Indians North of Mexico*. Totowa, New Jersey, Rowman & Littlefield, 1975.

Hoffman, Roy, et al. *Oklahomans and Their State*. Oklahoma City, Oklahoma Biographical Association, 1919.

Hofsommer, Donovan L. "The Construction Strategies of Railroads in the Oklahoma Panhandle." *Chronicles of Oklahoma*, Vol. 58, No. 1. Oklahoma City: Spring, 1980.

Hofsommer, Donovan L. "An Oklahoma Railroad Memory." *Chronicles of Oklahoma*, Vol. 54, No. 3. Oklahoma City: Fall, 1976.

Hofsommer, Donovan L. *Railroads in Oklahoma*. Oklahoma City, Oklahoma Historical Society, 1977.

Hubbard, Frank C. "Necrology: Clement Vann Rogers." *Chronicles of Oklahoma*, Vol. 8, No. 4. Oklahoma City: December, 1930.

Hurst, Irvin. *The 46th Star: A History of Oklahoma's Constitutional Convention & Early Statehood*. Oklahoma City, SEMCO Color Press, Inc., 1957.

Isely, Bliss, & W. M. Richards. *Four Centuries in Kansas*. Wichita, Kansas, McCormick-Mathers Co., 1936.

James, Louise B. *Below Devil's Gap: The Story of Woodward County*. Perkins, Oklahoma, Evans Publications, 1984.

Kennedy, David M. *Freedom from Fear: The American People in Depression & War: 1929–1945*. New York, Oxford University Press, 1999.

King, Joseph B. "The Ottawa Indians in Kansas & Oklahoma." *Collections of the Kansas State Historical Society*, Vol. 13. Topeka: 1915.

Kleber, John E. *The Kentucky Encyclopedia*. Lexington, Kentucky, University Press of Kentucky, 1992.

Kniffen, Fred B., et al. *The Historic Indian Tribes of Louisiana*. Baton Rouge, Louisiana, Louisiana State University Press, 1987.

Lashley, Tommy G. "Oklahoma's Confederate Veterans Home." *Chronicles of Oklahoma*, Vol. 55, No. 1, Oklahoma City: Spring, 1977.

Leitch, Barbara A. *A Concise Dictionary of Indian Tribes of North America*. Algonac, Michigan, Reference Publications, Inc., 1979.

Leland, J. A. C. "Some Eastern Indian Place Names in California." *California Folklore Quarterly*, Vol. 4, No. 4. Berkeley: October, 1945.

Litton, Gaston. *History of Oklahoma*. New York, Lewis Historical Publishing Co., Inc., 1957.

Love County Heritage Committee. *The History of Love County, Oklahoma*. Dallas, Texas, National ShareGraphics, Inc., 1983.

Love, Paula McSpadden. "Clement Vann Rogers: 1839–1911." *Chronicles of Oklahoma*, Vol. 48, No. 4. Oklahoma City: Winter, 1970–1971.

McLoughlin, Denis. *Wild & Woolly: An Encyclopedia of the Old West*. Garden City, New York, Doubleday & Co., Inc., 1975.

McReynolds, Edwin C. *Oklahoma: A History of the Sooner State*. Norman, University of Oklahoma Press, 1954.

Madill City Library. *Memories of Marshall County, Oklahoma*. Dallas, Texas, Curtis Media Corp., 1988

Marriage Records: Newkirk, Kay County, Oklahoma. Oklahoma Society Daughters of the American Revolution, 1981.

Mead, James R. "The Pawnees As I Knew Them." *Transactions of the Kansas State Historical Society*, Vol. 10. Topeka: 1908.

Meserve, John B. "Chief Isparhecher." *Chronicles of Oklahoma*, Vol. 10, No. 1. Oklahoma City: March, 1932.

Meserve, John B. "Chief Opothleyahola." *Chronicles of Oklahoma*, Vol. 9, No. 4. Oklahoma City: December, 1931.

Meserve, John B. "Chief Pleasant Porter." *Chronicles of Oklahoma*, Vol. 9, No. 3. Oklahoma City: September, 1931.

Meserve, John B. "Governor William Leander Byrd." *Chronicles of Oklahoma*, Vol. 12, No. 4. Oklahoma City: December, 1934.

Meserve, John B. "The McCurtains." *Chronicles of Oklahoma*, Vol. 13, No. 3. Oklahoma City: September, 1935.

Meserve, John B. "The MacIntoshes." *Chronicles of Oklahoma*, Vol. 10, No. 3. Oklahoma City: September, 1932.

Morris, A. Suman. "Captain David L. Payne: The Cimarron Scout." *Chronicles of Oklahoma*, Vol. 42, No. 1. Oklahoma City: Spring, 1964.

Morris, Lerona Rosamond. *Oklahoma: Yesterday, Today, Tomorrow*. Guthrie, Oklahoma, Co-Operative Publishing Co., 1930.

Morton, Ohland. "Early History of the Creek Indians." *Chronicles of Oklahoma*, Vol. 9, No. 1. Oklahoma City: March, 1931.

Morton, Ohland. "The Government of the Creek Indians." *Chronicles of Oklahoma*, Vol. 8, No. 1. Oklahoma City: March, 1930.

Murray, William H. *Memoirs of Governor Murray & True History of Oklahoma*. Boston, Meador Publishing Co., 1945.

New Jersey, Pennsylvania Tour Book. Heathrow, Florida, AAA Publishing, 1998.

Norton, Patty V., & Layton R. Sutton. *Indian Territory & Carter County, Oklahoma Pioneers: Including Pickens County, Chickasaw Nation*. Dallas, Texas, Taylor Publishing Co., 1983.

Oklahoma Almanac for 1931. Oklahoma City, Oklahoma Publishing Co., 1931.

The Oklahoma Almanac: 1961 Edition. Norman, Oklahoma, Oklahoma Almanac, Inc., 1960.

O'Neal, Bill. *Encyclopedia of Western Gun-fighters*. Norman, University of Oklahoma Press, 1979.

"Origin of County Names in Oklahoma." *Chronicles of Oklahoma*, Vol. 2, No. 1. Oklahoma City: March, 1924.

Peery, Dan W. "Notes." *Chronicles of Oklahoma*, Vol. 12, No. 3. Oklahoma City: September, 1934.

Phelps, Dawson A., & Edward H. Ross. "Place Names Along the Natchez Trace." *Journal of Mississippi History*, Vol. 14, No. 4. Jackson, Mississippi: October, 1952.

Pioneer Genealogical Society. *Cemetery Inscriptions: Kay County, Oklahoma*. Tahlequah, Oklahoma, The-Go-Ye Mission, Inc., 1978.

Presiding Officers of the Texas Legislature: 1846–1991. Austin, Texas, Texas House of Representatives, 1991.

Ragland, Hobert D. "Some Firsts in Lincoln County." *Chronicles of Oklahoma*, Vol. 29, No. 4. Oklahoma City: Winter, 1951–1952.

Rand, Clayton. *Men of Spine in Mississippi*. Gulfport, Mississippi, Dixie Press, 1940.

Rand, Clayton. *Sons of the South*. New York, Holt, Rinehart & Winston, 1961.

Ray, Eugene. "The Oklahoma Soldiers' Home." *Confederate Veteran*, Vol. 19, No. 9. Nashville, Tennessee: September, 1911.

Rayburn, J. A. "Geographical Names of Amerindian Origin in Canada." *Names: Journal of the American Name Society*, Vol. 15, No. 3. Potsdam, New York: September, 1967.

Read, William A. "Louisiana Place-Names of Indian Origin." *University Bulletin Louisiana State University & Agricultural & Mechanical College*, Vol. 19, No. 2. Baton Rouge: February, 1927.

Richards, W. B. *The Oklahoma Red Book*. Oklahoma City, 1912.

Richmond, Robert W. "A Free-Stater's Letters to the Editor: Samuel N. Wood's Letters to Eastern Newspapers: 1854." *Kansas Historical Quarterly*, Vol. 23, No. 2. Topeka, Kansas: Summer, 1957.

Riggs, W. C. "Bits of Interesting History." *Chronicles of Oklahoma*, Vol. 7, No. 2. Oklahoma City: June, 1929.

Rister, Carl C. *Land Hunger: David L. Payne and the Oklahoma Boomers*. Norman, University of Oklahoma Press, 1942.

Rockwell, Stella Campbell. *Garfield County, Oklahoma: 1893–1982*. Topeka, Kansas, Josten's Publications, 1982.

Ruth, Kent. *Oklahoma: A Guide to the Sooner State*. Norman, University of Oklahoma Press, 1957.

Ruth, Kent. *Oklahoma Travel Handbook*. Norman, University of Oklahoma Press, 1977.

Rydjord, John. *Indian Place-Names*. Norman, University of Oklahoma Press, 1968.

Rydjord, John. *Kansas Place-Names*. Norman, University of Oklahoma Press, 1972.

Seale, Lea L. "Indian Place-Names in Mississippi." Ph.D. Thesis, Hill Memorial Library, Louisiana State University, Baton Rouge, Louisiana, 1939.

Shankle, George Earlie. *State Names, Flags, Seals, Songs, Birds, Flowers & Other Symbols*. New York, H. W. Wilson Co., 1941.

Shannon, Daisy. "George Shannon." *Chronicles of Oklahoma*, Vol. 10, No. 4. Oklahoma City: December, 1932.

Shirk, George H. "First Post Offices Within the Boundaries of Oklahoma." *Chronicles of Oklahoma*, Vol. 30, No. 1. Oklahoma City: Spring, 1952.

Shirk, George H. *Oklahoma Place Names*. Norman, University of Oklahoma Press, 1974.

Socolofsky, Homer E. *The Cimarron Valley*. New York, New York, Columbia University Teachers College Press, 1969.

Starr, Emmet. *Encyclopedia of Oklahoma*. Lawton, Oklahoma, 1912.

Starr, Emmet. *Old Cherokee Families: Old Families and Their Genealogy*. Norman, Oklahoma, University of Oklahoma Foundation, 1968.

Statistical Abstract of Oklahoma: 1972. Norman, Oklahoma, Bureau for Business & Economic Research, University of Oklahoma, 1973.

Stewart, George R. *American Place-Names*. New York, Oxford University Press, 1970.

Stone, Irving. *They Also Ran: The Story of the Men Who Were Defeated for the Presidency*. Garden City, New York, Doubleday, Doran & Co., Inc., 1943.

"Subsequent History of Bloomfield." *Chronicles of Oklahoma*, Vol. 2, No. 4. Oklahoma City: December, 1924.

Sumners, Cecil L. *Chief Tishomingo: A History of the Chickasaw Indians & Some Historical Events of Their Era*. Amory, Mississippi, Amory Advertiser, 1974.

Swanton, John R. "Source Material on the History & Ethnology of the Caddo Indians." *Smithsonian Institution Bureau of American Ethnology*, Bulletin 132. Washington, D.C.: 1942.

Texas Biographical Dictionary. Wilmington, Delaware, American Historical Publications, Inc., 1985.

Thoburn, Joseph B. "Centennial of the Chickasaw Migration." *Chronicles of Oklahoma*, Vol. 15, No. 4. Oklahoma City: December, 1937.

Thoburn, Joseph B. "The Naming of the Canadian River." *Chronicles of Oklahoma*, Vol. 6, No. 2. Oklahoma City: June, 1928.

Thoburn, Joseph B. *A Standard History of Oklahoma*. Chicago, American Historical Society, 1916.

Thrapp, Dan L. *Encyclopedia of Frontier Biography*. Lincoln, University of Nebraska Press, 1988.

Tindall, John H. N. *Makers of Oklahoma*. Guthrie Oklahoma, State Capital Co., 1905.

The United States Biographical Dictionary: Kansas Volume. Chicago, S. Lewis & Co., 1879.

Verwyst, Chrysostom. "Geographical

Names in Wisconsin, Minnesota & Michigan Having a Chippewa Origin." *Collections of the State Historical Society of Wisconsin*, Vol. 12. Madison, Wisconsin: 1892.

Vexler, Robert I. *Chronology & Documentary Handbook of the State of Oklahoma*. Dobbs Ferry, New York, Oceana Publications, Inc., 1979.

Vogel, Virgil J. *Indian Names in Michigan*. Ann Arbor, Michigan, University of Michigan Press, 1986.

Vogel, Virgil J. "Indian Place Names in Illinois." *Journal of the Illinois State Historical Society*, Vol. 55. 1962.

Vogel, Virgil. J. *Iowa Place Names of Indian Origin*. Iowa City, University of Iowa Press, 1983.

Waldman, Carl. *Who Was Who in Native American History*. New York, Facts On File, Inc., 1990.

Webb, Walter P., et al. *The Handbook of Texas*. Austin, Texas State Historical Association, 1952.

Williams, R. L. "Necrology: James S. Latimer: 1855–1941." *Chronicles of Oklahoma*, Vol. 20, No. 2. Oklahoma City: June, 1942.

Williams, R. L. "Necrology: John Charles Major: 1863–1937." *Chronicles of Oklahoma*, Vol. 16, No. 4: Oklahoma City: December, 1938.

Wilson, L. W. "A History of Wagoner, Oklahoma." *Chronicles of Oklahoma*, Vol. 50, No. 4. Oklahoma City: Winter, 1972–1973.

Wolk, Allan. *The Naming of America*. Nashville, Thomas Nelson, Inc., 1977.

Womack, John. *Cleveland County, Oklahoma Place Names*. Norman, Oklahoma, 1977.

Wright, Muriel H. "Further Organization of Counties in the Choctaw Nation."

Chronicles of Oklahoma, Vol. 8, No. 3. Oklahoma City: September, 1930.

Wright, Muriel H. *A Guide to the Indian Tribes of Oklahoma*. Norman, University of Oklahoma Press, 1951.

Wright, Muriel H. "Notes & Documents: Atoka: A Place Name in Oklahoma." *Chronicles of Oklahoma*, Vol. 43, No. 3. Oklahoma City: Autumn, 1965.

Wright, Muriel, et. al. *Mark of Heritage*. Oklahoma City, Oklahoma Historical Society, 1976.

Wyatt, Frank S., & George Rainey. *Brief History of Oklahoma*. Oklahoma City, Webb Publishing Co., 1919.

Yagoda, Ben. *Will Rogers: A Biography*. New York, Alfred A. Knopf, 1993.

Yenne, Bill. *The Encyclopedia of North American Indian Tribes*. New York, Crescent Books, 1986.

Oregon

(36 counties)

2173 Baker County

Edward D. Baker (1811–1861)— Born in London, England, Baker immigrated to Pennsylvania with his family and lived there until 1825, when the family moved to Indiana. By 1831 he was a resident of Illinois and had been admitted to practice law in that state. After serving as a private in the Black Hawk War, Baker settled at Springfield, the Illinois state capital, and served in both houses of the Illinois legislature. In the congressional election preceding the Mexican War, Baker defeated Abraham Lincoln to secure the Whig party's nomination and went on to win the general election. He served little more than a year, resigning to accept a commission as a colonel to fight in the Mexican War. After the war he represented Illinois in Congress one term before moving to our nation's far West. He lived first in California and then came to Oregon where he was elected to represent the state in the U.S. Senate. He served from July 4, 1861, until his death as an officer in the Union army on October 22, 1861, during the Civil War. This county was created and named in Edward D. Baker's honor less than one year later, on September 22, 1862.

2174 Benton County

Thomas H. Benton (1782–1858)—Benton was a native of North Carolina who served in the Tennessee senate and as a soldier in the War of 1812. Following the war, he moved to Missouri and he represented that state for thirty years in the U.S. Senate. In that body he championed many interests of the West including free 160 acre homesteads, pony express, telegraph and railroads. Benton was a moderate on the volatile slavery issue. He opposed both abolition of slavery and the extension of it. His primary concerns were peace and preservation of the union. These moderate positions proved unpopular. Some states which had named counties in Benton's honor renamed the and, in 1850, Missouri failed to return Benton to the senate. Following his ouster from the senate, Benton served briefly in the U.S. House of Representatives. This county was established by the provisional legislature on December 23, 1847, about eight moths before congress formally established Oregon territory. Thomas H. Benton had been a strong advocate of U.S. control of the Oregon country, an issue our nation and Great Britain had just recently (June, 1846) resolved.

2175 Clackamas County

Clackama Indians—The Clackama were a Chinookan tribe, although not one of the three major Chinook groups, who were the Clatsop, Kathlamet and Wahkiakum. The Clackama, whose lodges were large, and sometimes elaborate, formerly had several villages along the lower end of the Clackamas River in what is now Clackamas County, in northwestern Oregon. The Lewis & Clark Expedition encountered Clackama Indians in 1806 and estimated their population at 1,800. By 1851, fewer than 100 Clackama Indians remained and soon after 1855 they were removed to Oregon's Grand Ronde Indian reservation. That reservation closed in 1925 but the land had been divided among remaining Indian descendants in 1908. This county was originally established as a district by the provisional government on July 5, 1843. At that time, five years before Oregon territory was officially created by congress, "the Oregon Country" was divided into four districts and the Clackamas District was one of them.

2176 Clatsop County

Clatsop Indians—The Clatsop Indians

were one of the three major Chinook groups, the others being the Kathlamet and Wahkiakum. The Clatsop lived along the Pacific Ocean in what is now northwestern Oregon, from the mouth of the Columbia River south to Tillamook Head and up the Columbia River as far as Tongue Point. During the winter of 1805–1806, the Lewis & Clark Expedition stayed among the Clatsop and estimated their population at 200, living in 14 houses. In 1875 some Clatsop Indians were found living near the Salmon River and they were removed to Oregon's Grand Ronde Indian reservation. That reservation closed in 1925 but its land had previously been divided among remaining Indian descendants. By that time the language of the Clatsop had become extinct and all surviving Clatsop Indians had been absorbed by neighboring tribes. This county was originally established as a district by the provisional government on June 22, 1844. This was the fifth district created within "the Oregon Country." Oregon territory was not officially created by congress until August 14, 1848.

2177 *Columbia County*

Columbia River— This county in northwestern Oregon was created on January 16, 1854, by Oregon territory and named for the river which forms its northern and eastern borders. The 1,210 mile-long Columbia is one of North America's major rivers. It rises in British Columbia, in Canada, and initially flows northwest. In the Selkirk Mountain region, the Columbia recognizes that it must alter its course to reach the Pacific Ocean and turns abruptly south and heads in that direction across southern British Columbia and our state of Washington. At Lake Wallula, in southern Washington, the Columbia turns sharply west and flows between Washington and Oregon to enter the Pacific Ocean, just 25 miles west of Columbia County, Oregon. The Columbia River has been discovered many times but its present name was given in 1792 and came from that of the ship commanded by the American, Captain Robert Gray (1755–1806). Gray's vessel, the *Columbia*, was only a 212 ton ship, and drew six to eight feet of water. The exploration of the lower Columbia River was a memorable accomplishment of the Lewis & Clark Expedition. Sadly the once torrential and salmon-choked Columbia is no more. The river is now polluted and much of its course in Washington and Oregon consists of sluggish waters.

2178 *Coos County*

Coos Indians— This county on the Pacific Ocean in southwestern Oregon was created on December 22, 1853, by Oregon's territorial legislature and named for Indian tribes of the Kusan family who formerly inhabited the area around Coos Bay in what is now Coos County, Oregon. The area which they occupied is given in more detail in *A Century of Coos & Curry* by Emil R. Peterson and Alfred Powers, who tell us that in addition to the Coos Bay region, the Coos "...occupied the Coos River drainage basin.... Their northern boundary was Ten Mile Lake. On the east they joined the Yoncalla Calapooyas; on the south the Coquilles." L. S. Cressman's article in the December, 1953, issue (Vol. 54, No. 4) of *Oregon Historical Quarterly* entitled "Oregon Coast Prehistory," fixes the northern point of the Coos' domain at "a point south of Winchester Bay, the mouth of the Umpqua." The Lewis & Clark Expedition encountered Coos Indians in 1805 and estimated their population at 1,500. The Indians had no written language so it was left to Whites to render their names to writing and a wide variety of spellings of the name *Coos* are encountered. There is a second Coos County in our nation. That county is in New Hampshire and some sources imply that the two names may be related. There is no connection between the origin of the county name in Oregon with that of Coos County, New Hampshire.

2179 *Crook County*

George Crook (1829–1890)— A native of Ohio and a graduate of the U.S. Military Academy at West Point, Crook's early career was as a junior officer fighting Indians on America's Pacific coast. He became distressed then, and later in his life, at White abuses of the Indians and remained concerned with Indian welfare while obliged to fight against them. At one point he advocated full U.S. citizenship for Indians. When the Civil War erupted, Crook held the rank of captain, but he served with distinction and rose to the rank of brevet major-general. After the Civil War, the army needed few high ranking officers and Crook's rank was reduced to lieutenant-colonel. He once again was sent to our nation's West to fight Indians and served so brilliantly that he was promoted to general again; as a brigadier-general in 1873 and major-general in 1888. This county was created on October 24, 1882, while General Crook was pursuing Apache Indians to their stronghold in Mexico's Sierra

Madre Mountains and returning them to their Indian reservation.

2180 *Curry County*

George L. Curry (1820–1878)— Born July 2, 1820, in Philadelphia, Pennsylvania, Curry came to Oregon in 1846 and became editor of the *Oregon Speculator*, and in 1848 he founded a newspaper of his own, the *Oregon Free Press*. He was soon forced to turn to farming for his livelihood when large numbers of his subscribers left Oregon to participate in the California gold rush. Curry served in Oregon's provisional legislature, was chief clerk of the council of Oregon territory from 1850 to 1851 and was a member of the lower house of Oregon's territorial legislature from 1851 to 1852. Appointed to be secretary of Oregon territory in early 1853, Curry became acting territorial governor when Governor Joseph Lane (1801–1881) resigned on May 19, 1853. Curry served as the acting governor until the new governor, John W. Davis (1799–1859), took office on December 2, 1853. Davis was unhappy in the office and resigned on August 1, 1854, making George L. Curry acting territorial governor once again. The office of territorial secretary carries little power with it, but an American territorial governor wields enormous power. During the periods that George L. Curry was acting territorial governor, he held that power and he ultimately was officially appointed as Oregon territory's governor by President Franklin Pierce, effective November 1, 1854. As governor of the territory he successfully dealt with an Indian uprising and moved the territory vigorously toward statehood. When Oregon became a state in 1859, Curry's term as territorial governor ended but he almost won a seat in the U.S. Senate in 1860. His bid failed by just one vote. This county was created on December 18, 1855, while he was serving as Oregon territory's official governor.

2181 *Deschutes County*

Deschutes River— This county in central Oregon was created on December 13, 1916, and named for the Deschutes River, which rises within its borders. One of Oregon's most scenic rivers, the Deschutes flows north from Deschutes County 250 miles to enter the Columbia River at the northern border between Sherman and Wasco Counties, Oregon. The river was named by French-Canadian fur trappers *Riviere des Chutes*, or "River of the Falls." Apparently the Deschutes River was named because it flowed into the Columbia River near falls of the Columbia River, rather than because of waterfalls of its own.

2182 *Douglas County*

Stephen A. Douglas (1813–1861)— Barely five feet tall, the "Little Giant" is most remembered as a political opponent of Abraham Lincoln. Douglas was born in Vermont and moved to Illinois where he enjoyed rapid political success. He served on the state supreme court, in the state legislature and as secretary of state. Following two terms in the U.S. House of Representatives, Douglas was elected to the U.S. Senate. In that body Douglas took courageous positions on the slavery issue which first outraged abolitionist sentiment and later infuriated the South. In 1858 Douglas ran for reelection to the U.S. Senate against Abraham Lincoln. Following the famous Lincoln-Douglas debates, the Republicans won the popular election but the state legislature reelected Douglas to the senate. Lincoln and Douglas were rivals again in 1860 for the presidency. Following Lincoln's election and the start of the Civil War, Douglas gave the president his active support. Stephen Douglas was a consistent friend to Oregon and this county was created in 1852, while he was serving in the U.S. Senate. On January 24, 1851, Oregon territory had created a county named Umpqua County, named for the Umpqua River which flowed through it. Over the next decade, portions of Umpqua County were lopped off and given to other counties. On October 16, 1862, the surviving piece of Umpqua County was added to Douglas County and Umpqua County ceased to exist.

2183 *Gilliam County*

Cornelius Gilliam (1798–1848)— A native of North Carolina, Gilliam served in the army during the Black Hawk War and held the rank of captain when he fought against the Seminole Indians in Florida territory in 1837. He also fought as a captain of militia in the so-called Mormon war in Missouri before coming to Oregon in 1844, in command of a train of 307 emigrants from Missouri. On November 29, 1847, the Cayuse Indians murdered the missionary Marcus Whitman (1802–1847) and his associates at Whitman's mission in the Pacific Northwest. White settlers retaliated in the Cayuse Indian War of 1847–1850. Gilliam was given the rank of colonel and command of volunteer forces of Oregon's provisional government in

1847, to fight the Cayuse. He was accidentally killed during that war, in March, 1848, while pulling a rope from a wagon and discharging a rifle attached to the rope. This county was created on February 25, 1885.

2184 *Grant County*

Ulysses S. Grant (1822–1885)— Grant was a native of Ohio who graduated from the U.S. Military Academy at West Point. He served with distinction in the Mexican War, and in the Civil War he rose to become commander of all Union forces. After the Civil war, Grant briefly served as acting secretary of war and then two terms as president of the United States. He proved to be a rather mediocre president. This county was created late in the Civil War, on October 14, 1864.

2185 *Harney County*

William S. Harney (1800–1889)— A native of Tennessee, Harney served as a junior army officer in the Black Hawk War and was promoted to lieutenant-colonel of the Second Dragoons in 1836. He fought in the Second Seminole Indian War in Florida territory and in the Mexican War and rose to brevet brigadier-general. After more Indian fighting, on the northern plains and again in Florida, General Harney was given command of the Department of Oregon in 1858 and promoted to full brigadier-general. While here, Harney ordered the seizure of San Juan Island, which was then claimed by Great Britain, resulting in controversy with England and displeasure in Washington. Harney was recalled from Oregon and stationed at Saint Louis, Missouri. He died on May 9, 1889, less than three months after this county was created on February 25, 1889.

2186 *Hood River County*

Hood River— This county was created on June 23, 1908, and named for the river which crosses the county on its journey from its source on Oregon's Mount Hood, to the Columbia River. The Lewis & Clark Expedition encountered the Hood River on October 29, 1805, but referred to it as Labeasche River. The river later came to be known as Dog River, because some starving pioneers had eaten dog meat on its banks. Mrs. Mary T. White Coe, the wife of Nathaniel Coe (1788–1868), was a prominent local resident, who found the name Dog River to be offensive and arranged to have it changed to Hood River,

in tribute to the source of the river's waters on Mount Hood. Mount Hood, Oregon's highest mountain, had been named in 1792 by a junior British naval officer, William R. Broughton (1762–1821) in honor of a lord of the British admiralty, Samuel Hood (1724–1816).

Samuel Hood (1724–1816)— Hood entered the British navy in 1741 and was active against French privateers. From 1767 to 1770 he commanded the North American station and in 1778 was created a baronet. After action at Martinique, off Chesapeake Bay and at Dominica, Hood was made baron Hood of Catherington. He served as a member of parliament and in 1787 was made vice-admiral and in 1788, a lord of the admiralty. He was a lord of the admiralty from 1788 to 1793 and it was during this period that the junior British naval officer, Lieutenant William R. Broughton (1762–1821), named Oregon's Mount Hood in his honor. In 1794 Hood was promoted to admiral and in 1796 was made viscount Hood.

2187 *Jackson County*

Andrew Jackson (1767–1845)— Jackson was born on the border of North Carolina and South Carolina. He represented Tennessee in both branches of the U.S. Congress, and gained fame and popularity for his military exploits in wars with the Indians and in the War of 1812. He was provisional military governor of Florida and, from 1829 to 1837, General Jackson was president of the United States. His presidency reflected the frontier spirit of America. This county was created by Oregon territory on January 12, 1852.

2188 *Jefferson County*

Mount Jefferson— This county was created on December 12, 1914, and named for Mount Jefferson, a 10,500 foot mountain at the western end of this county in north-central Oregon. The mountain was first seen by the Lewis & Clark Expedition on March 30, 1806, from a point near the Willamette River and they named it for Thomas Jefferson, the sponsor of their expedition, who was then our nation's president. Mount Jefferson is Oregon's second highest mountain.

Thomas Jefferson (1743–1826)— Jefferson was a native of Virginia and a member of the Virginia legislature. He served Virginia as governor and was a delegate to the second Continental Congress. Jefferson was the author of the Declaration of Independence and one of its signers. He was minister to France, secretary of state, vice-president and president of the United States. As president, he accomplished the Louisiana Purchase and he arranged the Lewis & Clark Expedition to the Pacific Northwest. Jefferson was a true intellectual, thoroughly knowledgeable in the arts and sciences. His political theories were pivotal in the formation of our infant republic.

2189 *Josephine County*

Josephine Creek— This county was created by the legislature of Oregon territory on January 22, 1856, and named for Josephine Creek, which is found in Josephine County, west of the municipality of Kerby, Oregon. The Josephine Creek is a small stream that starts and ends within Josephine County. This tributary of Illinois River, was named for Josephine, the daughter of a man who panned for gold in Josephine Creek. Sources consulted differ on the surname of Josephine and her father. Rollins is the surname most frequently encountered, and although Kirby, Leland and Rollin are also mentioned, the preponderance of rather solid evidence leads to the conclusion that the creek was named for Josephine Rollins. A letter, dated February 19, 1909, in the possession of the Oregon Historical Society, in Portland, Oregon, signed by Virginia Josephine Rollins Ort, states that she (our "Josephine Rollins") was born in Illinois in 1833 and that her family attempted to come to California from Missouri in 1850 but arrived in Oregon, instead. In 1851 the family still had California in mind and several members of the family left to go there. It is not clear from the letter whether or not our Josephine Rollins intended to go to California with the others but her 1909 letter makes it clear that, in 1851, she settled in the valley of Oregon's Illinois River, near Josephine Creek. Her letter stated that she thought she was the first White woman to settle in this part of Oregon. In 1854 Virginia Josephine Rollins married Julius Ort in Colusa County, California, and the couple settled in Sonora, California, where she was living at the time she wrote her letter dated February 19, 1909. Jack Sutton's work entitled *110 Years With Josephine*, published in 1966, supplies the name of the father of Josephine Rollins. He was Floyd Rollins. The Oregon Historical Society in Portland has "Scrapbooks" in which newspaper articles of historical interest are pasted. The names and dates of the newspapers are not preserved but the articles pertaining to the naming of Josephine County and Josephine Creek, Ore-

gon, are contained in "Scrapbook No. 44." In that scrapbook there is an explanation that the creek was named Josephine, rather than Virginia, because her father referred to her as Josephine. Another clipping in that scrapbook quotes one John Althouse as being a member of the party that named Josephine Creek, named for "Josephine Rollin."

2190 *Klamath County*

Uncertain— We know that this county was created on October 17, 1882, and that the county was not named for Klamath Falls, the present county seat, because Klamath Falls was called Linkville until 1892–1893. We also know that the county's name honors the Klamath Indians. However, there is disagreement among authorities on Oregon's history and place names. The question is whether the county was named directly for the Klamath Indian tribe, or indirectly, being named for the Klamath Lakes, which were named for the Klamath Indians.

Klamath Indians— Allan Carpenter's *Encyclopedia of the Far West*, published in 1991 describes the Klamath as a "Small tribe living in northern California and south-central Oregon, along Klamath Marsh, Williamson and Sprague rivers, and Upper Klamath Lake in the late 19th century." The *Encyclopedia Americana* describes the Klamath as "several groups of North American Indians who live in southwestern Oregon." The Klamath were seed-gathering Indians who made their homes along rivers and streams and subsisted mainly on vegetables, supplemented by small animals. A Klamath Indian reservation was created in south-central Oregon in 1864 for some 2,000 Indians of the region, including the Klamath, Modoc and Snake Indians. In 1954 the reservation's status as a trust area ended and resident Klamath Indians voted to sell their lands. In the mid-1970's the total population of Klamath Indians was estimated at 1,500. Erwin G. Gudde's work entitled *California Place Names* states that the name *Klamath* derived from *Tlamatl*, "the Chinook name for a sister tribe of the Modocs."

Klamath Lakes— Howard M. Corning's *Dictionary of Oregon History* states that Klamath County was named for the Klamath Lakes. These would be Lower Klamath Lake and Upper Klamath Lake, both of which lie, at least partially, at least sometimes, in Klamath County, in southern Oregon. This mouthful of qualifications deserves explanation.

Lower Klamath Lake— The smaller, by far, of the two Klamath Lakes lies mostly in Siskiyou County, California, although Lewis A. McArthur's *Oregon Geographic Names* claims it as a lake of southern Oregon. McArthur's work explains the apparent discrepancy between visual inspection of maps and the written word as the result of "much variation in the size of Lower Klamath Lake in recent years." (First edition published in 1928, sixth edition copyright 1992.)

Upper Klamath Lake— This lake clearly belongs to Oregon and Oregon alone and is, in fact, Oregon's largest lake, with a surface area of about 142 square miles. It lies completely within Klamath County, Oregon.

2191 *Lake County*

Numerous lakes within its borders when it was created and named— This county in south-central Oregon was created on October 24, 1874, and named for the many large lakes which were then within its borders. These lakes included Upper Klamath Lake, Lake Albert, Summer Lake, Goose Lake, Silver Lake, the lakes of the Warner Valley and the upper end of Lower Klamath Lake. When Klamath County was created in 1882, Lake County lost Upper Klamath Lake, its largest body of water, and the northern end of Lower Klamath Lake.

2192 *Lane County*

Joseph Lane (1801–1881)— A native of North Carolina, Lane moved to Indiana while in his early teens and there became involved in politics, serving in both houses of Indiana's legislature. He served as an officer during the Mexican War and emerged from that war as a national hero and a brevet major-general. On August 18, 1848, President James K. Polk appointed Lane to be the first governor of Oregon territory and he was sworn into that office on March 3, 1849. He resigned that office on June 18, 1850, and was elected to represent Oregon territory as a delegate to the U.S. Congress and served four terms there from 1851 to 1859. During this period he served another three days as Oregon's territorial governor, from May 16, 1853, to May 19, 1853. When Oregon was admitted to statehood, Joseph Lane was elected as one of the new state's first U.S. senators. In 1860 he was a candidate for vice-president as a running mate of John C. Breckinridge (1821–1875). This county was created by Oregon territory on January 28, 1851.

2193 *Lincoln County*

Abraham Lincoln (1809–1865)— Lincoln was a native of Kentucky who moved to Illinois, where he was a member of the state legislature. He represented Illinois in the U.S. House of Representatives and later was elected president of the United States. Lincoln's presidency coincided almost exactly with the Civil War. He guided the United States ably through that uniquely turbulent period. As president, he issued the Emancipation Proclamation which declared the freedom of slaves in all states in rebellion.Lincoln was assassinated in April, 1865, a few days after victory in the Civil War. This county was created on February 20, 1893.

2194 *Linn County*

Lewis F. Linn (1795–1843)— Lewis F. Linn, who was born near Louisville, Kentucky, in 1795, decided to make medicine his career. Although he had not yet completed his medical training, he served in the War of 1812 as a surgeon. After the war, he completed his medical training and settled on our country's western frontier in Missouri, where he practiced medicine and became an authority on Asiatic cholera. During the late 1820's Dr. Linn served one term in Missouri's state senate and in the 1830's and 1840's he represented Missouri in the U.S. Senate. In the senate Linn urged American occupation of Oregon at the time that our nation and Great Britain were debating its ownership. This county was created by Oregon's provisional government on December 28, 1847, eight months prior to the creation of Oregon territory by congress.

2195 *Malheur County*

Malheur River— A tributary of the Snake River, the Malheur rises in the Blue Mountains of Grant County, in central Oregon, flows south and the turns to the northeast and travels in that direction across northern Malheur County. The waters of the Malheur enter the Snake River near the northeastern border of Malheur County, Oregon. The river was named *Malheur* by French Canadian hunters and meant "misfortune" or "mishap" referring to an occasion when property and furs hidden here were discovered to be missing. "The Peter Skene Ogden Journals," which appeared in the December, 1909, issue (Vol. 10, No. 4) of the *Quarterly of the Oregon Historical Society* provide the source for the story behind this unusual name. Malheur County was created on February 17, 1887.

2196 *Marion County*

Francis Marion (–1795)— Marion is believed to have been born in South Carolina. He served in the army in battles against the Cherokee Indians and was elected to the provisional congress of 1775. He served, with distinction, as an officer in the Revolutionary War and rose to the rank of general in that war. Marion was also a member of the South Carolina senate. This Oregon county was originally established as Champooick (later rendered as Champoeg) District by the provisional government on July 5, 1843. At that time, five years before Oregon territory was officially created by Congress, "the Oregon Country" was divided into four districts and Champooick was one of them. After Oregon territory had been created by Congress, the name of Champooick District (by now rendered as Champoeg County) was changed to Marion County on September 3, 1849.

2197 *Morrow County*

Jackson L. Morrow (–)— A native of Kentucky, Jackson Lee Morrow moved to Iowa with his parents and there he met and married Nancy McEwen. The couple crossed the plains to Oregon territory in 1853 and settled on Puget Sound about the time that Washington territory was being severed from Oregon territory. Morrow saw military duty fighting Indians as a lieutenant in 1855–1856 and as a first lieutenant in 1878. He opened a store in what is now the municipality of Heppner, Morrow County, Oregon, in 1872 or 1873. His partner in this venture was Henry Heppner, for whom the town was named. Jackson L. Morrow was a representative in the Oregon legislature from Umatilla County in 1876 and again in 1885. During the 1885 legislative session, Morrow was active in the movement to create a new county from the western portion of Umatilla County and when this was accomplished, effective February 16, 1885, the new county was named in his honor.

2198 *Multnomah County*

Multnomah Indians— The Multnomah Indians were a Chinnokan tribe or division, who lived on Sauvie Island, the largest island in the Columbia River. Their main village here was on the eastern side of the island, near a bend in the river now called Reeder Point, which is within the present Multnomah County, Oregon. In 1805–1806 the population of this tribe was estimated to be 800, which John Minto described in his article in the 1900 issue (Vol. 1) of the *Quarterly of the Oregon Historical Society* as "the remains of a large nation." By 1835 disease had decimated the Multnomah Indians and the tribe was extinct. In subsequent years this tribe's name was applied as a broad term to denote all Indians living on or near the Willamette River, in Oregon. Multnomah County was created on December 22, 1854, by Oregon territory.

2199 *Polk County*

James K. Polk (1795–1849)— A native of North Carolina who moved to the Tennessee frontier in 1806, Polk served in the lower house of the Tennessee legislature and represented Tennessee for 14 years in the U.S. House of Representatives, where he was speaker. He served one term as governor of Tennessee. Polk became president of the United States as a dark horse candidate of the Democratic party but he became an unusually strong and effective president. His primary accomplishments involved westward extension of the United States: in the Northwest by settling a territorial dispute with Britain and in California and the Southwest by provoking and winning the Mexican War. This county was created as Polk District by the provisional government in December, 1845, more than two years before Oregon territory was created. James K. Polk, a Democrat, was serving as our nation's president when this district was created. The person said to be largely responsible for the creation and naming of this district was also a Democrat, James W. Nesmith (1820–1885). Malcom Clark's *This Week or Day in Oregon History*, states that Nesmith "...managed to secure a favorable vote at a time when several of the bill's chief opponents had absented themselves from the house and were playing 'horse billiards' in Lee's ten-pin alley. This maneuver ... excited much comment, largely unfavorable, from those who did not approve the creation of the new district."

2200 *Sherman County*

William T. Sherman (1820–1891)— A native of Ohio and an 1840 graduate of the U.S. Military Academy at West Point, Sherman served as a junior officer in actions against the Indians and in the Mexican War. At the outbreak of the Civil War in 1861, Sherman accepted a commission in the Union army as a colonel and by 1862 he had risen to the rank of major-general. In 1864, When Ulysses S. Grant was promoted to commander of all Union armies,

Sherman was given command in the South. Starting at Atlanta, Georgia, in November, 1864, Sherman led his infamous "March to the Sea," burning a swath across Georgia, some 40 to 60 miles wide and 300 miles long. Factories, cotton gins and warehouses were burned. Bridges and public buildings were destroyed. With Sherman's approval, his troops engaged in wild looting of civilian property. Sherman then marched north, wreaking even greater destruction in South Carolina. These an other depredations earned Sherman the hatred of several generations of White southerners. After the war Sherman remained in the military and ultimately became general-in-chief of the army. Periodically considered as a presidential candidate, his succinct refusal to the Republicans in 1884 has become a classic: "I will not accept if nominated and will not serve if elected." This county was created on February 25, 1889. The name Fulton had been proposed for this county, to honor Colonel James Fulton, a prominent local resident, but that name was never officially adopted.

2201 Tillamook County

Tillamook Indians— The Tillamook were a large tribe of the Salishan linguistic group, who lived in northwestern Oregon on a Pacific Ocean bay now named Tillamook Bay, and along the rivers feeding that bay. They were encountered by the Lewis & Clark Expedition in 1805–1806 and the tribe's population was estimated to be about 2,200 then, spread among eight villages. That population soon dropped sharply, presumably as a result of diseases caught from the Whites, and by 1849, only 200 Tillamook Indians remained. This county was created by Oregon territory on December 15, 1853, in the area that had been home to Tillamook Indians. The county seat of Tillamook County is also named Tillamook but the county was not named for it. That municipality's name was Lincoln when the county was created and its name was changed later.

2202 Umatilla County

Umatilla River— This county in northeastern Oregon was created on September 27, 1862, and named for the Umatilla River, which flows through it. The Umatilla is an 80 mile-long tributary of the Columbia River. It rises in northern Union County, Oregon and flows first west, then north to enter the Columbia near the northwestern corner of Umatilla County. The Umatilla's name came from that of a

group of Indian tribes, who formerly lived along the banks of the Umatilla River and nearby sections of the Columbia River. Frederick W. Hodge's *Handbook of American Indians North of Mexico* describes the Umatilla Indians as "A Shahaptian tribe formerly living on Umatilla River and the adjacent banks of the Columbia in Oregon. They were included under the Wallawalla by Lewis and Clark in 1805, though their language is distinct." The Umatilla Indian reservation was established in Umatilla County for the Umatilla, Cayuse and Walla Walla Indians and remains there today.

2203 Union County

Uncertain— Lewis A. McArthur's *Oregon Geographic Names* states that this county was named for the town of Union, within its borders and that the town of Union was founded in 1862, during the Civil War, and named for patriotic reasons. It is certainly possible that this county was named for the town. However both Grant County and Union County were created on October 14, 1864, late in the Civil War, just six months before General Grant accepted the surrender by the Confederacy on April 9, 1865. These two were the only counties which Oregon created on that day, or on any day in 1864. It seems probable that the Oregon legislators had preservation of the Union, and the Civil War's Union army in mind when they created both of these counties.

2204 Wallowa County

Wallowa Lake & Wallowa River— This county in Oregon's northeastern corner was created on February 11, 1887, and named for both Wallowa Lake and Wallowa River, which are located within its borders. Wallowa Lake is a about four miles long and is one of the larger mountain lakes of Oregon. It lies near the southern end of the county. The Wallowa River, an important river of northeastern Oregon, is formed by the confluence of east and west forks just south of Wallowa Lake. The river sprints north to enter the southern end of Wallowa Lake and then emerges from the lake's northern end. It then flows northwest in Wallowa County and enters the Grande Ronde River at Rondowa, in western Wallowa County, Oregon. The name *Wallowa* derived from the Nez Perce Indians' word *lacallas*, which they used as the name of a particular triangular structure, supporting a network of stakes, used to trap fish.

2205 Wasco County

Wasco Indians— The Wasco were a Chinookan tribe who lived on the southern side of the Columbia River in the vicinity of narrows of the Columbia, called The Dalles, in what is now Wasco County, Oregon. The Wasco were closely related to the Wishram Indians and these two tribes constituted the easternmost tribes of the Chinookan family. In 1822 their population was estimated to be 900 and occupied a number of villages. Howard M. Corning's *Dictionary of Oregon History* describes the Wasco as "…a sedentary people, wore robes of native pelts." Corning also tells us that the Wasco ate roots and berries, that some of their villages were occupied only during salmon fishing season and that they practiced head-flattening. A number of sources indicate that the name *Wasco* derived from the Indians' word for a cup or small bowl made of horn. Lewis A. McArthur points out in his *Oregon Geographic Names* that the name may derive from an Indian word meaning "horn basin," the Wasco Indians being the makers of these horn basins or bowls made of horn. This county was created by Oregon territory on January 11, 1854, and then was enormous, consisting of all of Oregon territory east of the Cascade Mountains from the Columbia River south to the state of California.

2206 Washington County

George Washington (1732–1799)— Washington was a native of Virginia, who served in Virginia's house of burgesses and became one of the colonies' leaders in opposition to British policies in America. He was a member of the first and second Continental Congresses and commander of all Continental armies in the Revolutionary War. Following victory in that war, Washington was elected to be the first president of the United States. This county was originally established as a Twality District by the provisional government on July 5, 1843. At that time, five years before Oregon territory was officially created by congress, "the Oregon Country" was divided into four districts and the Twality District was one of them. The designation was changed from district to county in 1847. Then, on September 3, 1849, its name was changed to Washington County by Oregon's territorial legislature. Language in the act to change this county's name to Washington County mentions the name *Falatine*, as well as Twality as "the name of the county commonly called Twality or

Falatine," but it is not clear where the name Falatine came from.

2207 *Wheeler County*

Henry H. Wheeler (1826–1915) — Born September 7, 1826, in Erie County, Pennsylvania, Wheeler became infatuated with gold to be found in the West. He came west as far as Wisconsin in 1855 and drove an ox team from there to California in 1857. Any money he made mining was exceeded by that he earned in saw-milling. In 1862 he arrived in Oregon and lived here, for a time, at The Dalles, but soon went to Idaho, mining in the Salmon River mines. In 1863 he moved on to California and returned to The Dalles in Oregon in 1864. From 1864 to 1868 Wheeler owned and operated a stage coach line covering the 200-odd miles between The Dalles and Canyon City, in Grant County and he later worked with Ben Holladay's (1819–1887) stage coach company. During these stage coach phases of Wheeler's life, he sometimes carried large amounts of cash and the U.S. Mail and he was attacked and robbed in typical "Wild West" incidents. In 1870 Wheeler was employed to run a ranch and remained there until 1878 when he began to operate his own farm and ranch northwest of Mitchell, Oregon, in what is now Wheeler County. He was active on this farm and ranch until 1904, when he sold his property and retired to Mitchell. Wheeler died in Mitchell, Oregon, in March, 1915. This county was created on February 17, 1899. In the first attempt to form this new county, which occurred in 1895, it was suggested that the county be named Sutton County, in honor of Al Sutton, a native of England and one of the Wheeler County area's pioneers. That movement died until 1899 and the name finally decided upon for the county was Wheeler.

2208 *Yamhill County*

Yamel Indians — A Kalapuyan tribe, the Yamel Indians formerly lived in northwestern Oregon, along the North and South Yamhill Rivers, tributaries of the Willamette. Vera F. Criteser's letter to the editor, which appeared in the March, 1956, issue (Vol. 57, No. 1) of Oregon Historical Quarterly states that the Yamel were one of 16 tribal members of the Kalapuyan family. By 1910 only five Yamel Indians had survived and they were living at the Siletz school. The Kalapuya Indians subsisted on a both animal and wild plant foods and generally lived in semi-subterranean dwellings. This county was originally established as a district by the provisional government on July 5, 1843. At that time, five years before Oregon territory was officially created by congress, "the Oregon Country" was divided into four districts and this district was one of them. Howard M. Corning's *Dictionary of Oregon History* implies that it was originally merely designated as "the second district" and later acquired both the name Yamhill and the designation as a county rather than a district.

References

Akrigg, G. P. V., & Helen B. Akrigg. *1001 British Columbia Place Names*. Vancouver, Discovery Press, 1973.

Anderson, Carole. *1991–92 Oregon Blue Book*. Salem, Oregon, Secretary of State, State of Oregon.

Bancroft, Hubert H. *The Works: History of Oregon*. San Francisco, History Company Publishers, 1888.

Barry, J. Neilson. "Broughton on the Columbia in 1792." *Oregon Historical Quarterly*, Vol. 27. Portland, Oregon: 1926.

Barry, J. Neilson. "The Indians of Oregon." *Oregon Historical Quarterly*, Vol. 28, No. 1. Portland, Oregon: March, 1927.

Barry, J. Neilson. "The Indians in Washington." *Oregon Historical Quarterly*, Vol. 28, No. 2. Portland, Oregon: June, 1927.

Biddle, Henry J. "Wishram." *Quarterly of the Oregon Historical Society*, Vol. 27, No. 1. Portland, Oregon: March, 1926.

Brimlou, George F. *Harney County, Oregon, and Its Range Land*. Portland, Oregon, Binfords & Mort, 1951.

Brogan, Phil F. *East of the Cascades*. Portland, Oregon, Binfords & Mort, 1964.

Brooks, James E. *The Oregon Almanac & Book of Facts: 1961–1962*. Portland, Oregon, Binfords & Mort, 1961.

Butterfield, Grace, & J. H. Horner. "Wallowa Valley Towns and Their Beginnings." *Oregon Historical Quarterly*, Vol. 41, No. 4. Portland, Oregon: December, 1940.

Carey, Charles H. "The Creation of Oregon as a State." *Quarterly of the Oregon Historical Society*, Vol. 26, No. 4. Portland, Oregon: December, 1925.

Carey, Charles H. *General History of Oregon*. Portland, Oregon, Binfords & Mort, 1971.

Carey, Charles H. *A General History of Oregon: Prior to 1861*. Portland, Oregon, Metropolitan Press, 1936.

Carey, Charles H. *History of Oregon*. Chicago, Pioneer Historical Publishing Co., 1922.

Carpenter, Allan. *Encyclopedia of the Far West*. New York, Facts On File, 1991.

Chandler, Connie. *Oregon Blue Book: 1981–1982*. Salem, Oregon, Secretary of State, State of Oregon.

Clark, Malcom. *This Week or Day in Oregon History*. Portland, Oregon, Oregon Historical Society.

Clarke, S. A. *Pioneer Days of Oregon History*. Portland, J. K. Gill Co., 1905.

Cogswell, Philip. *Capitol Names: Individuals Woven into Oregon's History*. Portland, Oregon, Oregon Historical Society, 1977.

Corning, Howard M. *Dictionary of Oregon History*. Portland, Oregon, Binford & Mort, 1989.

Cressman, L. S. "Oregon Coast Prehistory: Problems & Progress." *Oregon Historical Quarterly*, Vol. 54, No. 4. Portland, Oregon: December, 1953.

Criteser, Vera F. "Letters to the Editor." *Oregon Historical Quarterly*, Vol. 57, No. 1. Portland, Oregon: March, 1956.

Dicken, Samuel N. *Oregon Geography*. Ann Arbor, Michigan, Edwards Brothers, Inc., 1965.

Directory of Clackamas County: 1947–1948. Portland, Oregon, Pacific Directory Service, 1948.

Drury, Clifford M. "Joe Meek Comments on Reasons for the Whitman Massacre." *Oregon Historical Quarterly*, Vol. 75, No. 1. Portland, Oregon: March, 1974.

Duniway, David C. "Members of the Legislature of Oregon: 1843–1967." *Oregon State Archives*, Bulletin No. 2, Publication No. 30. Oregon State Library: 1968.

Duniway, David C. "Members of the Legislature of the State of Oregon: 1860–1949." *Oregon State Archives*, Bulletin No. 2, Publication No. 14. Oregon State Library: 1949.

Elliott, T. C. "The Peter Skene Ogden Journals." *Quarterly of the Oregon Historical Society*, Vol. 10, No. 4. Portland, Oregon: December, 1909.

The Encyclopedia Americana. New York, Americana Corporation, 1977.

Faber, Harold. *From Sea to Sea: The Growth of the United States*. New York, Farrar, Straus & Giroux, 1967.

Farquhar, Francis P. "Naming America's Mountains: The Cascades." *American Alpine Journal*, Vol. 12, No. 34. New York: 1960.

Frazer, Robert W. *Forts of the West*. Norman, University of Oklahoma Press, 1965.

French, Giles. *The Golden Land: A History of Sherman County, Oregon*. Portland, Oregon, Oregon Historical Society, 1958.

Fussner, F. Smith. *Glimpses of Wheeler County's Past*. Portland, Oregon, Binford & Mort, 1975.

Gatke, Robert M. "Letters of the Rev. William M. Roberts." *Quarterly of the Oregon Historical Society*, Vol. 23, No. 2. Portland, Oregon: June, 1922.

Gibbs, George. "Tribes of Western Washington & Northwestern Oregon." *Contributions to North American Ethnology*, Vol. 1. Washington, D.C.: 1877.

Glassley, Ray H. "Letters to the Editor." *Oregon Historical Quarterly*, Vol. 54, No. 3. Portland, Oregon: September, 1958.

Gregg, Jacob R. *Pioneer Days in Malheur County*. Los Angeles, Lorrin L. Morrison, 1950.

Gudde, Erwin G. *California Place Names*. Berkeley, University of California Press, 1969.

Hagen, Robert D. *Totally Oregon*. Salem, Oregon, Oregon Pride Productions, Inc., 1989.

Harden, Blaine. *A River Lost: The Life & Death of the Columbia*. New York, W. W. Norton & Co., 1996.

Hart, Herbert M. *Old Forts of the Northwest*. New York, Bonanza Books, 1963.

Henderson, Sarah Fisher, et al. "Correspondence of Reverend Ezra Fisher." *Quarterly of the Oregon Historical Society*, Vol. 19, No. 3. Portland, Oregon: September, 1918.

Hines, H. K. *An Illustrated History of the State of Oregon*. Chicago, Lewis Publishing Co., 1893.

Historic Douglas County, Oregon. Roseburg, Oregon, Douglas County Historical Society, 1982.

Hodge, Frederick W. *Handbook of American Indians North of Mexico*. Totowa, New Jersey, Rowman & Littlefield, 1975.

Holman, Frederick V. "A Brief History of the Oregon Provisional Government & What Caused Its Formation." *Quarterly of the Oregon Historical Society*, Vol. 13, No. 2. Portland, Oregon: June, 1912.

Holman, Frederick V. "Oregon Counties." *Quarterly of the Oregon Historical Society*, Vol. 11, No. 1. Portland, Oregon: March, 1910.

Holman, Frederick V. "Oregon County Names." *The Magazine of History*, Vol. 13, No.3. New York: March, 1911.

Howay, Frederic W. *Voyages of the Columbia to the Northwest Coast: 1787–1790 & 1790–1793*. Boston, Massachusetts Historical Society, 1941.

An Illustrated History of Central Oregon. Spokane Washington, Western Historical Publishing Co., 1905.

Jackman, E. R., & R. A. Long. *The Oregon Desert*. Caldwell, Idaho, Caxton Printers, Ltd., 1977.

Julyan, Robert H. *Mountain Names*. Seattle, The Mountaineers, 1984.

Ketchum, Verne L. "The Naming of Mount Hood." *Mazama*, Vol. 13, No. 12. Portland, Oregon: December, 1931.

Kroeber, A. L. "California Place Names of Indian Origin." *University of California Publications in American Archaeology & Ethnology*, Vol. 12, No. 2. Berkeley: June 15, 1916.

Lang, H. O. *History of the Willamette Valley*. Portland, Oregon, Geo. H. Himes Book & Job Printer, 1885.

Leland, J. A. C. "Some Eastern Indian Place Names in California." *California Folklore Quarterly*, Vol. 4, No. 4. Berkeley: October, 1945.

List, Howard M., & Edith M. List. "John M. Shively's Memoir: Part II." *Oregon Historical Quarterly*, Vol. 81, No. 2. Portland, Oregon: Summer, 1980.

Lockley, Fred. *History of the Columbia River Valley*. Chicago, S. J. Clarke Publishing Co., 1928.

McArthur, Lewis A. "The Lakes of Oregon." *Quarterly of the Oregon Historical Society*, Vol. 26, No. 1. Portland, Oregon: March, 1925.

McArthur, Lewis A. *Oregon Geographic Names*. Portland, Oregon, Oregon Historical Society Press, 1992.

McArthur, Lewis A. "Oregon Geographic Names." *Quarterly of the Oregon Historical Society*, (later issues styled *Oregon Historical Quarterly*) Portland Oregon: Vol. 26, No. 4., December, 1925; Vol. 27, No. 1, March, 1926; Vol. 27, No. 2, June, 1926; Vol. 27, No. 3, September, 1926; Vol. 27, No. 4, December, 1926; Vol. 28, No. 2, June, 1927; Vol. 28, No. 3, September, 1927; Vol. 43, No. 4, December, 1942; Vol. 44, No. 1, March, 1943; Vol. 44, No. 2, June, 1943; Vol. 44, No. 3, September, 1943; Vol. 45, No. 1, March, 1944; Vol. 46, No. 4, December, 1945; Vol. 47, No. 1, March, 1946; Vol. 47, No. 3, September, 1946; Vol. 48, No. 3, September, 1947; Vol. 48, No. 4, December, 1947.

McArthur, Lewis A. *Oregon Place Names*. Portland, Binfords & Mort, 1944.

McLoughlin, Denis. *Wild & Woolly: An Encyclopedia of the Old West*. Garden City, New York, Doubleday & Co., Inc., 1975.

McNeil, Fred H. *McNeil's Mount Hood*. Zig Zag, Oregon, Zig Zag Papers, 1990.

Middleton, Lynn. *Place Names of the Pacific Northwest*. Seattle, Washington, Superior Publishing Co., 1969.

Minto, John. "Native Race: The Number and Condition of the, in Oregon When First Seen by White Men." *Quarterly of the Oregon Historical Society*, Vol. 1. Portland, Oregon: 1900.

Mitchell, William A. *Linn County, Kansas: A History*. Kansas City, Campbell-Gates, 1928.

Mullen, Floyd C. *The Land of Linn*. Lebanon, Oregon, Dalton's Printing, 1971.

Nedry, H. S. "Notes on the Early History of Grant County." *Oregon Historical Quarterly*, Vol. 53, No. 4. Portland, Oregon: December, 1952.

Orcutt, Ada M. *Tillamook: Land of Many Waters*. Portland, Oregon, Binfords & Mort, 1951.

Oregon Historical Records Survey Project, Division of Professional & Service Projects. *Inventory of the County Archives of Oregon-Multnomah County*. Portland, Oregon, 1940.

Oregon Historical Society, Portland, Oregon. "Scrapbook No. 44."

Parsons, William, & W. S. Shiach. *An Illustrated History of Umatilla County & Morrow County*. W. H. Lever, 1902.

Peterson, Emil R., & Alfred Powers. *A Century of Coos & Curry*. Portland, Oregon, Binfords & Mort, 1952.

The Resources of the State of Oregon. Salem, Oregon, W. H. Leeds, State Printer, 1899.

Roe, JoAnn. *The Columbia River: A Historical Travel Guide*. Golden, Colorado, Fulcrum Publishing, 1992.

Rydell, Ruth. "Willamette Tributaries: Yamhill." *Oregon Historical Quarterly*, Vol. 44, No. 2. Portland, Oregon: June, 1943.

Scott, Harvey W. *History of the Oregon Country*. Cambridge, Riverside Press, 1924.

Steel, W. G. *The Mountains of Oregon*. Portland, Oregon, David Steel, 1890.

Sutton, Jack. *110 Years with Josephine*. Medford, Oregon, Klocker Printery, 1966.

Thrapp, Dan L. *Encyclopedia of Frontier Biography*. Lincoln, University of Nebraska Press, 1988.

Vaughn, Thomas. *High & Mighty: Select Sketches about the Deschutes Country*. Oregon Historical Society, 1981.

Vexler, Robert I. *Chronology & Documentary Handbook of the State of Oregon*. Dobbs Ferry, New York, Oceana Publications, Inc., 1978.

Walling, A. G. *History of Southern Oregon*. Portland, Oregon, 1884.

Walling, A. G. *Illustrated History of Lane County, Oregon*. Portland, Oregon, 1884.

Wolk, Allan. *The Naming of America*. Nashville, Thomas Nelson, Inc., 1977.

Wood, Bryce. *San Juan Island: Coastal Place Names & Cartographic Nomenclature*. Washington State Historical Society, 1980.

Work Projects Administration. *History, Governmental Organization and Records*

System of Tillamook County, Oregon. Portland, Oregon, 1940.

Work Projects Administration. *Mount Hood: A Guide.* New York, J. J. Little Ives & Co., 1940.

Yenne, Bill. *The Encyclopedia of North American Indian Tribes.* New York, Crescent Books, 1986.

Young, F. G. "The Columbia River Historical Expedition." *Quarterly of the Oregon Historical Society*, Vol. 27, No. 2. Portland, Oregon: June, 1926.

Pennsylvania

(67 counties)

2209 *Adams County*

John Adams (1735–1826)— Adams, a native of Massachusetts, was a delegate to the first Continental Congress and a signer of the Declaration of Independence. He participated in Paris, with Benjamin Franklin and John Jay in negotiating peace with England and, after the war, he was our country's first minister to England. Adams became the first vice-president of the United States under George Washington and when Washington retired, Adams was elected to be our nation's second president.This county was created on January 22, 1800, while John Adams was serving as president.

2210 *Allegheny County*

Allegheny River— Allegheny County was created on September 24, 1788, and named for the Allegheny River, which terminates its 325 mile journey within this county. The Allegheny River rises in Potter County, in northwestern Pennsylvania, flows in a northwestern direction into the southwestern section of New York, and then returns to Pennsylvania. The Allegheny is a tributary of the Ohio River and for some 200 miles it is a navigable stream. The Allegheny River completes its journey at Pittsburgh, Pennsylvania, where it unites with the Monongahela River to form the Ohio River. The river was apparently first named by the Iroquois Indians and later modified by Delaware Indians.

2211 *Armstrong County*

John Armstrong (1717–1795)— A native of Ireland, Armstrong and his wife immigrated to Pennsylvania about 1746. Here he worked as a surveyor and was elected to Pennsylvania's provincial assembly in 1749. During the French & Indian War he served as an officer and in 1756 Armstrong led a highly successful raid on the Delaware Indians at Kittanning, which today is the county seat of the county named in his honor. During the American Revolution he held the ranks of brigadier-general in the Continental army and major-general in the Pennsylvania militia. Armstrong was one of Pennsylvania's delegates to the second Continental Congress and to the third Continental Congress, or congress of the Confederation. He died at Carlisle, Pennsylvania, on March 9, 1795, and this county was created and named in his honor on March 12, 1800.

2212 *Beaver County*

Beaver River— The Beaver, a tributary of the Ohio, is formed in western Pennsylvania by the confluence of the Shenango River and Mahoning River in Lawrence County, Pennsylvania. It flows in a southern direction and its waters enter those of the Ohio River at Rochester, Pennsylvania, near the middle of Beaver County. The Beaver River was named because of the many beaver dams found along its course. Tim Palmer's 1980 work entitled *Rivers of Pennsylvania* complained about the pollution in the Beaver River but mentioned that lawsuits by environmentalists in the late 1970s were then producing favorable results. Literature dealing with the history, geography and place names of Pennsylvania provides some confusion about the proper name of the river which is this county's namesake. Beaver River is called variously Beaver Creek, Big Beaver Creek and Big Beaver River. (There is a Little Beaver River, another tributary of the Ohio River, which also enters the Ohio in Beaver County, but downstream.)

2213 *Bedford County*

Uncertain— Works dealing with the history, geography and place names of Pennsylvania offer conflicting opinions about the origin of the name of this county which was created on March 9, 1771. Some say that it was named for the town of Bedford, the present county seat, while others say that it was named for Fort Bedford here. Other sources indicate that the county's name honors an English duke of Bedford. Since this county was created in 1771 before the American colonies ruptured their tie with England, it is possible that the county was named directly for an English duke of Bedford. However, it is much more likely that the county took its name from the town and/or fort, named for a duke of Bedford and it is clear that the particular duke of Bedford so honored was John Russell, Duke of Bedford (1710–1771).

Town of Bedford, Pennsylvania— An early settler here in the Allegheny Mountains was Robert Ray and both the fort and town here were originally named Raystown in his honor. Their names were both later changed to Bedford. James McKirdy's article on the origin of Pennsylvania's county names which appeared in the January, 1925, issue (Vol. 8, No. 1) of *Western Pennsylvania Historical Magazine* stated that "…this name [Bedford] was assigned to the town when it was laid out in 1766, although it was commonly so designated as early as 1759 or 1760, and there is some reason for believing, at a still earlier period." In 1794 President Washington established headquarters at Bedford for putting down the Whisky Rebellion. Bedford's population in the late 1990s was 3,100.

Fort Bedford— In 1758, during the French and Indian War, as part of the British preparations for the conquest of the French-held Fort Duquesne, Colonel Henry Bouquet (1719–1765) enlarged the stockade previously built here by John Armstrong (1717–1795). The British held Fort Bedford during the French & Indian War, although their hold was tenuous. During 1763 forces under the command of the English Colonel Henry Bouquet had to endure a forced march to arrive in time to save Fort Bedford from the Indians. The *Guidebook to Historic Places in Western Pennsylvania* states that this fort was called Fort Rays-town until 1759, when it was renamed Fort Bedford "for the Duke of Bedford, a member of the English Cabinet." The site of the old fort may still be found in the town of Bedford south of the Raystown Branch of the Juniata River, bounded by Richard Street, on the east, Thomas Street on the west and Pitt Street on the south.

John Russell, Duke of Bedford (1710–1771)— England has given the title duke of Bedford to a number of men, but it is clear that the duke of Bedford whose name is remembered in the name of Bedford County was John Russell, the fourth duke of Bedford (1710–1771). John Russell succeeded his brother to become duke of Bedford in 1732. He raised a foot regiment in 1745 to serve under England's King George II (1683–1760) and was made colonel of that regiment. In 1760, at the coronation of King George III (1738–1820), Bedford was lord high constable. From 1763 to 1767 he was president of the council.

2214 *Berks County*

Berkshire, England— Berks County was created on March 11, 1752, as a part of England's province of Pennsylvania and named for Berkshire, county in England. The word *shire* is a British word for "county." Our Berks County's namesake in England is referred to in various sources as Berks County, Berks Shire and Berkshire County. This English county is located in southern England, about 50 miles west of London. It lies largely in the basin formed by the Thames River. Its other important streams are the Kennet, Loddon, Auburn and Blackwater Rivers. England's Berkshire County is about 40 miles long and some 25 miles wide. Its soil is underlain by chalk and chalk downs extend through the center of the county. Their name is the Berkshire Downs. The name *Berkshire* is derived from an ancient Celtic name, the meaning of which is uncertain. Possibilities that have been mentioned include "a wood grove," "the forest shire," "shire district," and "hilly place."

2215 *Blair County*

John Blair (–1832)— John Blair was born at Blair's Gap, Pennsylvania, a son of Thomas Blair (–1808), for whom the pack-horse Blair's Gap was named. John Blair represented Huntingdon County in the state legislature and took a strong interest in improving Pennsylvania's transportation facilities. Construction of the Penn-sylvania canal and Portage railroad are said to have been inspired by John Blair. He died at the old homestead, near Blair's Gap, one mile west of Duncansville on January 1, 1832. This county was created and named in his honor on February 26, 1846.

2216 *Bradford County*

William Bradford (1755–1795)— A native of Philadelphia and a graduate of the College of New Jersey (now Princeton University), Bradford served as an officer during the American Revolution. Having studied law and been admitted to the bar, he was appointed as Pennsylvania's attorney general in 1780 and served in that position until 1791, when he became an associate justice of Pennsylvania's supreme court. Appointed by President George Washington on January 28, 1794, to serve as attorney general, Bradford resigned from the Pennsylvania supreme court to accept that cabinet post and he was serving as our young nation's second attorney general when he died on August 23, 1795. This county was created on February 21, 1810, but it was originally named Ontario, in honor of the Great Lake, Lake Ontario. Just two years later, on March 24, 1812, the county's name was changed to Brad-ford.

2217 *Bucks County*

Buckinghamshire, England— Bucks County was one of the three original counties which William Penn (1644–1718) established in his English province of Pennsylvania in 1682. He named it for the English county, or shire, which had been home to the Penn family for generations. A number of Pennsylvania's very early settlers had come from Buckinghamshire, England.

Buckinghamshire, England— Located near the center of England, a bit northwest of London, Buckinghamshire is a long, narrow county, divided into northern and southern sections by the chalk hills named Chiltern. Its southern boundary is the Thames River. The world-famous preparatory school, or so-called public school, Eton was established here in A.D. 1440. During the era that William Penn's (1644–1718) family lived here, Buckinghamshire was converting from a farming county to one that emphasized the grazing of sheep. Buckinghamshire was late to enter the industrial revolution. In 1981 the county's population was estimated to be 571,600 and its area was 753 square miles. The ori-gin and meaning of this county's name is uncertain and disputed. Translations which have been mentioned include "beech trees," "bucks," or "deer," "river-bend land" and "followers of Bucca," (Bucca, being a man).

2218 *Butler County*

Richard Butler (–1791)— Butler was born in the 1740's in Ireland. Some sources list his year of birth as 1743 while others say 1748. He immigrated with his family to America and settled in Pennsylvania. Butler served as an officer during the American Revolution, participating in battles at Saratoga and Stony Point, New York, and later in Georgia. After the Revolutionary War, he served as a commissioner to negotiate treaties with several Indians tribes and was subsequently made superintendent of Indian affairs for the northern district. Butler also served briefly in the Pennsylvania senate. In 1791 he was recalled to military duty, given the rank of major-general and made second in command to General Arthur St. Clair (1736–1818), who was then governor of Northwest territory. Butler was killed in combat by Indians on November 4, 1791, near the present site of Ft. Wayne, Indiana, during the Indians' defeat of General St. Clair's forces. This county was created on March 12, 1800.

2219 *Cambria County*

Cambria Township, Somerset County, Pennsylvania— *Cambria* was a medieval name for Wales, in Great Britain and the upland regions, which comprise much of central Wales, are still called the Cambrian Mountains. Cambria County, Pennsylvania, was created on March 26, 1804, from portions of Huntingdon, Bedford and Somerset Counties. At that time Somerset County contained a Cambria township and when Cambria County was created it took the name of that township in Somerset County. More than 40 counties have been created in Pennsylvania since Somerset County was created in 1795 and the location of both Cambria County and Somerset County have been shifted far west of the land area which was originally called *Cambria*. That land area was the so-called "Welsh tract," near the Schuylkill River in southeastern Pennsylvania. It had been settled by immigrants from northern counties in Wales in the British Isles and the name Cambria was selected as the township's name to honor the association with Wales. Britain's Wales is a principality on the western side of the island of

Great Britain and a constituent of the United Kingdom of Great Britain and Northern Ireland. In 1981 Wales' population was only 2,790,462, just six percent of England's although Wales occupies almost 16 percent as much land as does England.

2220 *Cameron County*

Simon Cameron (1799–1889)— A native of Pennsylvania, Cameron was involved in diverse business ventures and amassed a fortune before his 40th birthday. In 1838 he first became involved in national politics when he was appointed as a commissioner to settle certain claims of the Winnebago Indians. In 1845 Cameron was elected to represent Pennsylvania in the U.S. Senate. He left the Senate in 1849 but was returned to that body in 1857. By this time Cameron had become one of the nation's most successful machine politicians and he was a candidate for the presidential nomination at the Republican national convention in 1860. He was defeated for that nomination by Abraham Lincoln, who received the votes of Cameron's Pennsylvania delegates. Cameron's reward for providing Lincoln with these votes was a position in Lincoln's cabinet as secretary of war. Cameron was serving as secretary of war when the Civil War began in 1861 but his administration was inefficient and corrupt and Lincoln appointed Edwin M. Stanton (1814–1869) to replace him in 1862. In that same year Cameron was sent as minister to Russia but his service in that post was very brief. In 1867 Pennsylvania returned Cameron to the U.S. Senate and he served in that body until 1877. This county was created on March 29, 1860, while Cameron was serving in the U.S. Senate and contending for the presidential nomination of the Republican party.

2221 *Carbon County*

Extensive anthracite coal deposits— Carbon County is located in east-central Pennsylvania, where anthracite coal was discovered at the western edge of the county on Sharp Mountain. The Lehigh Coal & Navigation Company was formed to exploit this resource in 1818 and by 1825 that firm's shipments of coal down the Lehigh River had grown to more than 28,000 tons per year. Carbon County was created on March 13, 1843.

2222 *Centre County*

Location of the county in the center of the state— This county was created on Febru- ary 13, 1800, and named for its location in the center of Pennsylvania. Subsequently, some 40 Pennsylvania counties have been created, shifting the borders of existing counties greatly. Whether by design or accident, Centre County still remains in the center of Pennsylvania at the Millennium year 2000. *Centre* is the version of the word "center," which was popular at the time that this county was formed in England's former province of Pennsylvania.

2223 *Chester County*

City of Chester, England— Chester County was one of the three original counties which William Penn (1644–1718) established in his English province of Pennsylvania in 1682. He named it for the English city of Chester.

Chester, England— This city in western England, is the administrative center of Cheshire County. Its climate is harsh in spite of the moderating influence of the nearby Irish Sea. Conquered, named and occupied by the Roman Empire in the first century A.D., the Roman's name for Chester was *Cestre*, similar to the present Cheshire. The Romans were long gone when William I the Conqueror (1027–1087) invaded England and was crowned its king. He made it his business to send troops north soon after his arrival, to quell rebels here in Chester and in Wales. For a period of time Cheshire County's ports had a virtual monopoly on the trade between England and Ireland but by 1600 the port of Chester was no longer viable on account of silting. Chester was granted a royal charter in 1506. Little more than a century later, the city was badly battered during the decade-long English Civil Wars, which began in 1642. By the middle of the 18th century, Chester was a prosperous and quiet country town. The population of all of Cheshire County in 1981 was slightly more than 900,000 persons crowded into just 928 square miles.

2224 *Clarion County*

Clarion River— This county was created on March 11, 1839, and named for the river which traverses it. The Clarion, a tributary of the Allegheny River, rises in McKean County, Pennsylvania, flows southwest and enters Clarion County near its northeastern corner, flows across the county and spills its waters into the Allegheny on Clarion County's southwestern border. James McKirdy's article on the origin of Pennsylvania's county names which appeared in the October, 1925, issue (Vol. 8, No. 4) of *Western Pennsylvania Historical Magazine* tells us that early in the 19th century, a survey party camped by the river's banks and coined the name *Clarion*, for this river on account of the "...clear sound of the distant ripples.... A clarion is a clear-sounding horn." McKirdy states that a number of other names were applied to this river after that survey party's visit and the name *Clarion* did not become generally accepted as this river's name until some two decades after the survey party conceived it.

2225 *Clearfield County*

Cleared fields here— This county in central Pennsylvania was created on March 26, 1804, and named for the land here which had been cleared of timber by Indians for a village. Even in the Millennium year 2000, "clear fields" are the exception rather than the rule in much of central Pennsylvania. Viewed from the air, it is apparent that the area is largely forest today. Thus an area that contained a "cleared field" was a significant discovery to Whites when they encountered and named this area, probably in the late 18th century.

2226 *Clinton County*

De Witt Clinton (1769–1828)— This New York state native held many of the important political offices in that state. Clinton served in both houses of the state legislature and as mayor of New York City. He represented New York in the U.S. Senate and in 1812 he was the Federalist candidate for president, running against President James Madison. In 1817 Clinton was elected as New York's governor. As governor, he was the principal promoter of the Erie Canal, which was instrumental in linking the vast agricultural and timber lands in our country's West with eastern markets. The canal spurred our nation's growth. In 1825 the Erie Canal was completed from the Hudson River in New York state to Lake Erie in the West. This county was created on June 21, 1839, and it was originally intended that it be named Eagle County. That name would have commemorated Bald Eagle Mountain and Bald Eagle Creek, both named for the Indian chief, Woapalanne, or Chief Bald Eagle. The idea of creating this new county had opposition in the Pennsylvania legislature and some sources say that the name Clinton County was substituted to trick the opponents of the proposed Eagle County into creating it by a different name.

2227 *Columbia County*

A patriotic name derived from the name of Christopher Columbus— The term *Columbia* was derived from Christopher Columbus' name and it has been given various patriotic meanings. Used in the name of the District of Columbia, it means the United States of America. The word *Columbus* is a Latin noun and means a "male dove" or "male pigeon." This county was created on March 22, 1813, during the War of 1812. Some sources indicate that a song "Hail Columbia," was then popular and might have contributed to the selection of this county's patriotic name.

2228 *Crawford County*

William Crawford (1732–1782)— A native of Virginia, Crawford was a farmer, surveyor and soldier, Before the American Revolution he fought in the French and Indian war, the Pontiac war and Lord Dunmore's war. During the Revolution, Crawford took part in battles at Long Island, Trenton, Princeton, Brandywine and Germantown and rose to the rank of colonel. About 1778 he moved to the West, where he engaged in defense of the frontier and in actions against the Indians. In 1782 he was captured by Delaware Indians, tortured and burned at the stake near Upper Sandusky, Ohio. This county was created on March 12, 1800.

2229 *Cumberland County*

Cumberlandshire, England— This county was created on January 27, 1750, by England's province of Pennsylvania and named for the hilly county of Cumberlandshire at the northern end of the mother country. When the Roman Empire occupied the island of Great Britain, they coveted the land of Cumberlandshire for strategic and economic reasons but succeeded in possessing only part of it. After the Roman period, Cumberlandshire was oriented more toward Scotland, Ireland and Wales than toward England. The very name *Cumberland* means "land of the Cumbri," or "land of the Welsh." For centuries ownership of the land comprising Cumberlandshire was disputed between Scotland and England. As a result, it was one of the last English shires to be formed. A land of scenic lakes and hills, Cumberlandshire also contains mineral resources which were vigorously exploited during the industrial revolution. Although still a part of England, Cumberlandshire ceased to exist as a separate county in 1972 when its lands were absorbed by the newly created English county of Cumbria.

2230 *Dauphin County*

Louis Joseph Xavier, Dauphin of France (1781–1789)— This county was created on March 4, 1785, at the close of the American Revolution. The name was chosen to express appreciation to France for her aid to the American colonies during our recent war for independence from England. The unusual name *Dauphin* is a French word which means "heir apparent," to the throne. In 1785, when Dauphin County, Pennsylvania was created, Louis Joseph Xavier (1781–1789) was heir apparent to the French throne and titled "Dauphin." It is clear that this county was named for this dauphin, rather than his elder brother Louis Charles, Louis XVII (1785–1795). That elder brother was not born until March 27, 1785, more than three weeks after this county was created, and he did not become France's dauphin until 1789, when Louis Joseph Xavier died.

Louis Joseph Xavier, Dauphin of France (1781–1789)— The birth, on October 22, 1781, of the second child of the French king Louis XVI (1754–1793) and Queen Marie Antoinette (1755–1793) was a much-celebrated event, inspiring a 101 cannon salute. At that time the royal couple's previous attempts to have children had resulted in the birth of one girl, Princess Marie Therese (1778–1851), and one miscarriage. When the royal couple's first son, the dauphin, Louis Joseph Xavier was born in 1781 it was a joyous occasion. Desmond Seward's 1981 biography *Marie Antoinette* states that "At court the King made everyone smile by referring at every possible opportunity to 'my son, the Dauphin.'" The infant was baptized into the Roman Catholic faith by Cardinal Louis Rene Edouard de Rohan (1734–1803) and a wet nurse, nick-named Madame Poitrine, was on hand to suckle the infant dauphin. The birth of the dauphin was celebrated for nine days by the French labor guilds. The craftsmen of these guilds showered the infant with custom-made presents including baby shoes and a locket containing a tiny dauphin fashioned in steel. Stefan Zweig's 1933 biography of Marie Antoinette tells us that "Special services were held in the churches; there was a great banquet in the Hotel de Ville; the war with England, poverty and other disagreeables were forgotten .... The birth of the Dauphin marked the zenith of Marie Antoinette's power." Small at birth and sickly from an early age, Dauphin Louis Joseph Xavier was not destined to live long. When he was five years old signs of rickets were manifest in the dauphin and one year later, he was in bed at Meudon, dying. Stefan Zweig tells us in his biography of the queen that the dauphin's mother penned in a letter in 1788: "I am most uneasy about the health of my eldest boy. His growth is somewhat awry, for he has one leg shorter than the other, and his spine is a little twisted and unduly prominent. For some time, now, he has been inclined to attacks of fever and he is thin and weakly." The unfortunate young dauphin died on June 3, 1789.

A second male child was born to the French king, Louis XVI (1754–1793), and Queen Marie Antoinette (1755–1793). He was Louis Charles, later titled Louis XVII (1785–1795). Some sources on the history, geography and place names of Pennsylvania would have us believe that it was this elder dauphin (he succeeded to that title upon the death of his elder brother in 1789) for whom this Pennsylvania county was named but they are clearly wrong. This county was created in 1785, when the elder dauphin, Louis Joseph Xavier was less than four years old and still a source of pride to his royal parents and the citizens of pre–Revolutionary France. The title "dauphin" had been applied to the heir apparent to the French throne since A.D. 1350. This resulted from the purchase of lands in the former kingdom of Arles, now in southeastern France, called Dauphine, by the man who came to rule France as King Charles V (1337–1380). The title derived from use of the name *dauphin*, in various forms, in Europe as early as the 4th century. King Charles V (1337–1380) was made Dauphin of Viennois in 1349 and he granted the land in southeastern France called Dauphine to his son, who later ruled France as King Charles VI (1368–1422), establishing the precedent for the use of dauphin as the title of the male heir apparent to the French throne.

2231 *Delaware County*

Delaware River— This county in southeastern Pennsylvania was created on September 26, 1789, and named for the Delaware River which it borders. The Delaware River is formed in Delaware County, in southeastern New York by the junction of the East Branch and West Branch Rivers. The Delaware then flows south to form the boundary between New York and Pennsylvania. Some 280 miles in length, the Delaware carries extensive commercial traffic. It empties into Delaware Bay on the Atlantic Ocean. The Delaware River was named for this Delaware Bay and that bay was named for Thomas West, Lord De La Warr (1577–1618), who was a British governor of colonial Virginia.

2232 *Elk County*

Elk herds which formerly were abundant here— This county in northwestern Pennsylvania was created on April 18, 1843, and named for the Elk herds which formerly were abundant here, particularly around Portland Mills, until White settlers drove them away. In 1832 a comment was made by a Judge Geddes that "a few elk still remain" and as late as 1852 a dozen elks were found in Elk County by hunters, who killed seven of them. In North America, the name "elk" refers to the large deer whose genus and species are *Cervus canadensis*. (In Europe, the term "elk" refers to a different species, the European moose.) A typical male elk stands five feet high at the shoulders and can weigh from 500 to 1,100 pounds. Male elks often pose displaying their beautiful antlers which spread some five feet. Female elks are smaller and they have no antlers. Elks were once found over much of the U.S. and southern Canada but their numbers have been greatly reduced by hunters. Most remaining elks live west of the Rocky Mountains.

2233 *Erie County*

Lake Erie— This county in northwestern Pennsylvania, which borders on Lake Erie, was created on March 12, 1800. Lake Erie is one of the five Great Lakes and it borders on four states in our country and on Canada's province of Ontario. The St. Lawrence Seaway provides Lake Erie with access to world ports. Many of the streams whose waters feed Lake Erie have been the scene of heavy manufacturing activity, and most of the factories here generated polluting waste which needed to be discharged. Before the days of environmental concerns and laws, companies were pretty much free to pollute at will. As a result, Lake Erie became famous for its high level of pollution. By about 25 years after World War II, Lake Erie's waters had become extremely foul. Environmental laws and improved business ethics have brought happier days to Lake Erie. The name *Erie* as applied to the lake, perpetuates the memory of the Erie tribe of Indians, who formerly lived here.

Erie Indians— Frederick W. Hodge's *Handbook of American Indians North of Mexico*, tells us that the Erie were a populous sedentary tribe, who resided, in the 17th century, from Lake Erie, probably south as far as the Ohio River and east along the watershed of the Allegheny River. The Erie subsisted primarily on maize. Although they were an Iroquois-speaking tribe, the Erie never were a member of the Iroquois Nation. In fact, by 1656, most Erie Indians had been slain by the Iroquois and any survivors were adopted by the Iroquois or other tribes, thus removing the Erie tribe as a separate entity, a full century before the American Revolution.

2234 *Fayette County*

Marie Joseph Paul Yves Roch Gilbert du Motier, Marquis de Lafayette (1757–1834)— Lafayette was a French aristocrat who served briefly in the French army. He came to America in 1777 to assist the American Revolutionary army. He was granted an honorary commission as major general by the Continental Congress and served with distinction in a number of battles in the Revolutionary War. Lafayette returned to France in 1782 and this Pennsylvania county was created and named in his honor on September 26 of the following year.

2235 *Forest County*

Forests of the county— This county in northwestern Pennsylvania was created on April 11, 1848, by a joint resolution of both houses of the Pennsylvania legislature. Cyrus Blood (1795–) was the pioneer settler of this section of the state. He immigrated to the wilderness here with his family in 1833 and bought a large tract of land. It was Blood's idea that a new county should be formed here named Forest County. That name was certainly appropriate when the Blood family arrived here in 1833 and remained apt in 1848 when the county was created. Viewed from the air in the millennium year 2000, it is apparent that the area is still largely forest today.

2236 *Franklin County*

Benjamin Franklin (1706–1790)— Franklin was a native of Massachusetts who moved to Pennsylvania in his teens. Poverty denied him a formal education but he became the leading printer and editor in North America. Franklin gained fame for his discoveries and inventions in the physical sciences and he distinguished himself as author, philosopher and diplomat. Franklin was a signer of the Declaration of Independence and an important member of the convention which framed the U.S. Constitution. On behalf of the province of Pennsylvania, Benjamin Franklin asked the king of England to strip the pompous Thomas Penn (1702–1775) of his dictatorial powers but found that the king had little interest in promoting democratic government in Pennsylvania. In Pennsylvania, Franklin proposed the academy which later developed into the University of Pennsylvania and in 1785 he was chosen as a member of Pennsylvania's supreme executive council. He was soon made president of that body and served as its president, a position which corresponds to governor, from 1785 to 1788. This county was created on September 9, 1784.

2237 *Fulton County*

Robert Fulton (1765–1815)— This Pennsylvania native supported himself, while a young man, as an artist. He later gained fame for his inventions dealing with marine vessels. He invented a submarine which he successfully demonstrated in the year 1800. Fulton invented mines to be used in naval warfare and was one of the inventors of the steamboat. The steamboat became a commercial success, made Fulton famous, and greatly sped America's development. Fulton County was created on April 19, 1850, when both steamboats and railroads were playing vital roles in transporting the Mid West's agricultural and other products to eastern markets.

2238 *Greene County*

Nathanael Greene (1742–1786)— Greene was born in Rhode Island and served briefly in the Rhode Island legislature. He gained fame as one of the ablest American generals in the Revolutionary War and rose to the rank of major-general. During one period when General George Washington was temporarily absent, General Greene was in command of our entire revolutionary army. This county was created on February 9, 1796.

2239 *Huntingdon County*

Town of Huntingdon, Pennsylvania— Dr. William Smith, provost of the College & Academy of Philadelphia (now the University of Pennsylvania) owned extensive lands here in central Pennsylvania and in 1767 he laid out a town on Standing Stone tract, and named it Huntingdon, in honor of Selina Hastings, Countess of Huntingdon (1707–1791), who had been a benefactor of Dr. Smith's college in Philadelphia.

In the late 1990s the town of Huntingdon had a population of 6,800 and was the county seat of Huntingdon County. The county had been created on September 20, 1787, and named for the town of Huntingdon.

Selina Hastings, Countess of Huntingdon (1707–1791)— Born to nobility in England on August 24, 1707, Selina Shirley married Theophilus Hastings, the ninth earl of Huntingdon on June 3, 1728. She was introduced to the beliefs of the Methodist separatists from the Church of England by her sister-in-law, Lady Margaret Hastings and she became an intimate friend of John Wesley (1703–1791), the founder of Methodism. In spite of the protestations of her husband, the earl of Huntingdon, Selina Hastings became active in the Methodist movement in England. She supported itinerant lay preachers and chaplains, established a Methodist chapel at Brighton in 1761 and later set up Methodist churches at London, Bath and Tunbridge, all in England. She was also a philanthropist on this side of the Atlantic Ocean and she made a handsome donation of funds to the College & Academy of Philadelphia (now the University of Pennsylvania).

2240 *Indiana County*

Uncertain— This county in western Pennsylvania was created on March 30, 1803. Its name derived, directly or indirectly, from the term long applied to the native residents of North and South America, the American Indians. However authorities with extensive knowledge about the origins of Pennsylvania's county names differ on whether the county name honors the Indians directly or indirectly (via Indiana territory). James McKirdy has demonstrated in-depth knowledge concerning the origins of Pennsylvania's county names and he is among those who believe that this county was named directly for the native Americans whom Christopher Columbus discovered in 1492 and misnamed, thinking he had arrived in Asia. McKirdy's article on the origin of Pennsylvania's county names which appeared in the July, 1925, issue (Vol. 8, No. 3) of *Western Pennsylvania Historical Magazine* tells us that "It received its name from the aboriginal inhabitants of the state who were, from the advent of the whites, known as Indians (Indianos)." Other sources demur and remind us that when this Pennsylvania county was created in March 1803, Indiana territory had recently been established by the U.S. Congress. That territory was created on May 7, 1800, and some authorities on Pennsylvania's history and place names say that Indiana County, Pennsylvania was named for Indiana territory. Indiana territory's name probably derived from land called *Indiana*, which the Iroquois Indian confederacy ceded to a White trading company in 1768. William Trent (–1778) of that trading company bestowed the name *Indiana* on this land. Our nation incorporated this *Indiana* land in its first territory, the Northwest territory, in 1787 and it later became part of Indiana territory. A. Howry Espenshade is among those who supports the position that Indiana territory inspired the name of this Pennsylvania county. Professor Espenshade presented his position on this dispute in his work entitled *Pennsylvania Place Names*, published in 1925. Although this dispute remains concerning the origin of this county's name there is one certainty; i.e., Indiana County, Pennsylvania was not named for its county seat, the city of Indiana. We know this because the municipality was not founded until 1805 and the county was created and named in 1803.

2241 *Jefferson County*

Thomas Jefferson (1743–1826)— Jefferson was a native of Virginia and a member of the Virginia legislature. He served Virginia as governor and was a delegate to the second Continental Congress. Jefferson was the author of the Declaration of Independence and one of its signers. He was minister to France, secretary of state, vice-president and president of the United States. As president, he accomplished the Louisiana Purchase and he arranged the Lewis & Clark Expedition to the Pacific Northwest. Jefferson was a true intellectual, thoroughly knowledgeable in the arts and sciences. His political theories were pivotal in the formation of our infant republic. This county was created on March 26, 1804, while Jefferson was president.

2242 *Juniata County*

Juniata River— This county in central Pennsylvania was created on March 2, 1831, and named for the Juniata River, which flows through it. The Juniata, a 150 mile-long tributary of the Susquehanna River, is formed by two branches in Huntingdon County, Pennsylvania. The Juniata flows east, touching four Pennsylvania counties on its journey to the Susquehanna, which it enters just above Duncannon, Pennsylvania, near Harrisburg. The name *Juniata* is of Indian origin and its meaning is disputed. However, authorities on Indian names favor "projecting rock" as the translation and indicate that it referred to a rock or stone held in reverence by the Indians.

2243 *Lackawanna County*

Lackawanna River— This county was the last of Pennsylvania's 67 counties to be created. Born on August 13, 1878, the county was named for a tributary of the Susquehanna River, which flows through it from northeast to southwest. The Lackawanna River rises in Susquehanna County, Pennsylvania and enters the North Branch of the Susquehanna River above Pittston, Pennsylvania, in Luzerne County. A quotation from Thomas Murphy's 1928 *Jubilee History of Lackawanna County, Pennsylvania* tells a lot about the then-prevalent attitude in our nation toward industrial pollution: "The stream, once a beautiful body of water while of no value from a transportation standpoint has great utility, carrying off mine water as well as the sewage from Scranton and the dozen or more industrial towns along its length." The name *Lackawanna* is of Indian origin and its meaning is uncertain. George R. Prowell's article entitled "Pennsylvania County Names," which appeared in the December, 1914, (Vol. 19, No. 6) issue of *The Magazine of History* states that "Lackawanna is an Indian name, the meaning of which is uncertain, even to the careful student of history." Other sources dealing with the history, geography and place names of Pennsylvania admit that the translation is in doubt but supply the oft-mentioned view that the name means "the place where two streams of water meet" or "the forks of a stream."

2244 *Lancaster County*

Lancashire, England— The earliest settlers of this part of southeastern Pennsylvania came from England and when a new county was established here on May 10, 1729, it was named Lancaster, in honor of Lancashire, England. The county seat of Lancaster County, Pennsylvania, the city of Lancaster, also owes its name to Lancashire, England. The new county's name was suggested by one of the settlers here, John Wright, a surveyor and a native of Lancashire, England. Although the English settlers of southeastern Pennsylvania did much of the naming of places, it was the German immigrants (known as "Pennsylvania-Dutch") who created the local color of Lancaster and Lancaster County, Pennsylvania. Largely self-sufficient German religious communities such as the Amish and Mennonites developed here. Their adherence to the simple and old-fashioned ways of doing things have enchanted many visitors from the fast-track portions of America.

Lancashire, England — The county named Lancashire, in northwestern England, on the Irish Sea has a name that dates back to the time that the Roman Empire occupied England. An early version of its name, Loncastre, meant "Roman fort (or camp) on the river Lune." A later (14th century) version of the name was Lancastreshire, which derived from Lancaster and the Old English word *scir*, which meant "district." Lancashire, England is 75 miles long and averages about 30 miles in width. In the northern and eastern portions of the county, mountains can be found which reach altitudes of more than 2,000 feet. Wide moor lands are found between many of these mountains. More land is using for grazing than for planting crops. Iron, coal, slate and other building materials are found in Lancashire. Its city of Liverpool is one of the most important seaports in the United Kingdom and its other principal city, Lancaster, also carries on foreign trade.

2245 *Lawrence County*

Oliver H. Perry's flagship, the Lawrence in the War of 1812 — During the War of 1812, Oliver H. Perry (1785–1819) commanded a squadron on Lake Erie from his flagship, the *Lawrence*. The *Lawrence* suffered extensive damage in this combat and Perry was transferred to the *Niagara* to continue the battle. The British were defeated in this key battle and although it was technically a national, rather than a state event, Pennsylvanians have proudly remembered this naval victory as part of the state's history. When this county was created on March 20, 1849, it was named for Perry's flagship, the *Lawrence*, which had been named for another American naval hero, James Lawrence.

James Lawrence (1781–1813) — Lawrence was an officer in the United States navy who established a reputation for bravery in the war against Tripoli and in the War of 1812. He died in combat while commanding the *Chesapeake* against the British, near Boston. He is said to have uttered the famous phrase "Don't give up the ship" while he lay mortally wounded in that battle. He died on June 4, 1813.

2246 *Lebanon County*

Lebanon township or Lebanon borough, Lancaster County, Pennsylvania — Lebanon County was created on February 16, 1813, from portions of Lancaster County and Dauphin County and much of the territory of the new county came from Lancaster County's township, or borough, named Lebanon, which had been organized in 1729. James McKirdy's article on the origin of Pennsylvania's county names which appeared in the October, 1925, issue (Vol. 8, No. 4) of *Western Pennsylvania Historical Magazine* tells us that "The name was given to it by the pious German settlers, from Mount Lebanon, in Palestine, the loftiest and most celebrated mountain range in Syria, forming the northern boundary of Palestine." Since McKirdy wrote that sentence there have been a number of changes in national borders in the Middle East and the Lebanon Mountains are now within the nation of Lebanon, where they stretch for about 100 miles, parallel with the Mediterranean coast. A peak near their northern end rises to 10,131 feet above sea level. The mountains' name apparently comes from a Hebrew word meaning "to be white." These snow-capped mountains are mentioned in the Old Testament of the *Holy Bible* in Jeremiah 18:14 — "Does hoar-frost ever leave mount Sirion, or snow Lebanon?"

2247 *Lehigh County*

Lehigh River — This county in eastern Pennsylvania was created on March 6, 1812, out of land from Northampton County and named for the Lehigh River, which forms the border between Lehigh County and its mother county, Northampton. The Lehigh, a 100 mile-long tributary of the Delaware River, rises in northeastern Pennsylvania, at the southern end of Wayne County, and first flows southwest, then southeast and flows through the middle of Allentown, Pennsylvania, the county seat of Lehigh County. At Allentown, the Lehigh bends to the northeast and sprints the final few miles of its journey to reach the Delaware River at Easton, Pennsylvania. The name *Lehigh* is the surviving version of numerous corruptions of the name by which the Delaware Indians called the Lehigh River. The Indian name meant "forks," "at the forks," or "where there are forks." A number of sources on the history, geography and place names of Pennsylvania indicate that the "fork," was a fork in the river. However, both A. Howry Espenshade and George P. Donehoo think it more likely that the "fork" that the In-

dians had in mind when they coined the name that came to be applied to the Lehigh River, was a "fork" in a trail along the land near the Lehigh River. These views are expressed in Espenshade's *Pennsylvania Place Names* and Donehoo's *A History of the Indian Villages & Place Names in Pennsylvania*.

2248 *Luzerne County*

Anne Cesar, Chevalier de la Luzerne (1741–1791) — A native of Paris, France, Luzerne entered the military and served in the Seven Years' War rising to the rank of colonel. He subsequently served France as a diplomat and was the French representative to the court of the elector of Bavaria. In 1778, France had signed an alliance with the nascent United States and Conrad A. Gerard (1729–1790) was the first French minister plenipotentiary to our fledgling country. In 1779 Luzerne replaced Gerard and became the second French minister here. Although he spoke little English, he was warmly received by our Continental Congress and in 1780, when our Revolutionary army was destitute, Luzerne raised money, as his personal responsibility, to ease our financial difficulty. In 1783 or 1784 Luzerne returned to France and later was the French ambassador at London, England. In 1789, Secretary of State Thomas Jefferson sent a letter of appreciation to Luzerne for his services in our time of need. This county was created and named in Luzerne's honor on September 25, 1786. Luzerne died in England on September 14, 1791.

2249 *Lycoming County*

Lycoming Creek — On April 13, 1795, a new county was created out of a portion of Northumberland County. Four names were proposed for the new county: Lycoming, Jefferson, Susquehanna and Muncy. Lycoming was chosen but both Jefferson and Susquehanna were later used as names of Pennsylvania counties. Muncy is used as the name of both a township and a small community in the southeastern portion of today's Lycoming County. Lycoming was chosen for the county's name because this was the name of a creek, which had earlier marked an important demarcation between lands claimed by White American settlers and wild lands further west, which, briefly, were left for the Indians. Lycoming Creek was within the huge Lycoming County which was created in 1795, and although that original Lycoming County has been reduced in size repeatedly, by giving up land to contribute to the formation of some 15 newer Pennsylvania counties, Lycoming Creek can still be found within today's Lycoming County. This 35 mile-long tributary of the West Branch of the Susquehanna River, rises near Lycoming County's northern border with Tioga County and flows south and southwest in Lycoming County. The mouth of Lycoming Creek is in southern Lycoming County. Lycoming Creek's name derived from the Delaware Indians' name for it, which meant "sandy stream."

2250 McKean County

Thomas McKean (1734–1817)— Born on March 19, 1734, in Chester County, Pennsylvania, McKean studied law in Delaware and was admitted to that colony's bar in 1754. He was elected to Delaware's colonial legislature in 1762 and reelected every year until 1779, serving as speaker of the assembly on two occasions. An early and consistent opponent of England's treatment of her North American colonies, McKean represented Delaware in the Continental Congresses and was elected president of the congress on July 10, 1781. Thomas McKean was one of Delaware's three signers of the Declaration of Independence and one of Delaware's signers of the Articles of Confederation. During the American Revolution McKean served as a colonel of a Pennsylvania militia regiment and in 1777, as speaker of the lower house of Delaware's legislature, he temporarily replaced the president of Delaware, whom the British captured. Also in 1777, on July 28, Pennsylvania made him chief justice and he held that position until 1799, although he continued to hold high political office in Delaware. In 1799 Thomas McKean was elected as Pennsylvania's second state governor, and served from December 17, 1799, until December 20, 1808. This county was created on March 26, 1804, while McKean was serving as governor.

2251 Mercer County

Hugh Mercer (–1777)—Mercer was born about 1725 in Scotland and educated as a physician. He immigrated to America about 1747 and settled near a community named Greencastle in Pennsylvania. Here he practiced medicine and served in the army as an officer during the French and Indian War. At the outbreak of the American Revolution, Mercer entered the Continental army, in which he attained the rank of brigadier-general. He served with distinction under General George Washington in the surprise attack on the British at Trenton, New Jersey, in late December, 1776. One week later, at the battle of Princeton, New Jersey, on January 3, 1777, Hugh Mercer was severely wounded and he died of those wounds on January 12, 1777. This county was created and named in General Mercer's honor on March 12, 1800.

2252 Mifflin County

Thomas Mifflin (1744–1800)— A native of Philadelphia, Mifflin served in the Pennsylvania legislature during the period that the North American colonies were moving toward independence from England. He represented Pennsylvania in the Continental Congresses and was elected president of congress on November 3, 1783. He also served as an officer in America's revolutionary army, was, for a time, aide-de-camp to General George Washington and rose to the rank of brigadier-general. During the Revolution Mifflin served in Pennsylvania's legislature as well as in congress and he was a Pennsylvania delegate to the federal Constitutional convention in 1787. Thomas Mifflin succeeded Benjamin Franklin as president of Pennsylvania's supreme executive council in 1788 and he became the first governor of the state of Pennsylvania, under the constitution of 1790, on December 21, 1790. Reelected twice, he served as Pennsylvania's governor until December 17, 1799. These were experimental years for our infant republic which tested the balance between federal and states' rights. On at least two occasions, Mifflin took strong stands concerning Pennsylvania's state rights, in defiance of the president of the federal government, George Washington. This county was created on September 19, 1789, while Mifflin was president of Pennsylvania's supreme executive council.

2253 Monroe County

James Monroe (1758–1831)— Monroe, a native of Virginia, served in the Revolutionary War. Prior to his election as president of the United States, Monroe served in a wide variety of government posts. He served Virginia in the state legislature and as governor. He was a member of the Confederation congress and the U.S. Senate. He was minister to France and to Britain and he held two cabinet posts. As president, Monroe stressed limited government and strict construction of the Constitution. He acquired Florida for the U.S. from Spain and he was the author of a policy declaration (later known as the Monroe Doctrine) which proscribed outside interference in North and South America. Monroe served as president from 1817 to 1825. This county was created on April 1, 1836.

2254 Montgomery County

Uncertain— This county was created on September 10, 1784, and the vast majority of sources consulted which deal with the history, geography and place names of Pennsylvania, state that the county was named for General Richard Montgomery (1738–1775), a hero of our recent successful revolution from England.

Richard Montgomery (1738–1775)— Montgomery was born in Ireland and served with the British in North America in the French and Indian War. He settled in New York where he was elected to the New York provisional congress. Montgomery served as a general in the American Revolutionary army and he was killed in combat in Quebec, Canada, on December 31, 1775.

However a minority of Pennsylvania sources sprinkle about a variety of other opinions concerning this county's namesake. George R. Prowell's article entitled "Pennsylvania County Names," which appeared in the December, 1914 (Vol. 19, No. 6), issue of *The Magazine of History* states that this county "…was named in honor of General John Montgomery, who commanded the Pennsylvania militia at Brandywine and Germantown; *not* [italics added] in honor of Montgomery of Quebec." In his work entitled *Montgomery County, Pennsylvania: A History*, published in 1923, Clifton S. Hunsicker tells us that "The name Montgomery as applied to this county was either in honor of General Montgomery of Revolutionary fame, to please more especially the Welsh settlers; or for William and Joseph Montgomery of Lancaster and Northumberland counties, both of whom were active in having the bill passed which created this county." Since General Richard Montgomery (1738–1775) was born in Ireland, not Wales, the comment about "…to please more especially the Welsh settlers…" would be puzzling were it not for an opinion expressed by another Pennsylvania historian, James McKirdy, whose article on the origin of Pennsylvania's county names appeared in the April, 1925, issue (Vol. 8, No. 2) of *Western Pennsylvania Historical Magazine*. McKirdy tells us that Montgomery County, Pennsylvania "…was named for the noted county in Wales." Wales does have a border county named Montgomeryshire and James McKirdy has established a reputation for accuracy and thorough research regarding the origin of Pennsylvania's county names, but even so, the possibility seems so remote that one might be inclined to attribute McKirdy's citation of a Welsh county to casual oversight except that McKirdy's reference in this article was not casual at all. In it, he takes us back to the days of William the Conqueror (1027–1087) and his contemporary, Roger de Montgomery, Earl of Shrewsbury and Arundel. In spite of McKirdy's thorough exegesis, one is tempted to view it as an isolated mistake by an otherwise reliable historian. After all, A Howry Espenshade is among those who state, without qualification that this county was named for General Richard Montgomery (1738–1775). Espenshade tells us this in his *Pennsylvania Place Names* published in 1925 and relates that when news of General Montgomery's death reached Philadelphia from Quebec, there was weeping in the streets. But then the often inscrutable William H. Taft III weighs in with this comment in his *County Names: An Historical Perspective*, published in 1982: "Eighteen Montgomery counties in Pennsylvania, Maryland, and elsewhere recall not only the Welsh county, but also the early general who captured much of Canada and fell upon the field hard by Quebec." As stated several hundred words earlier, the origin of Montgomery County, Pennsylvania's name is uncertain.

2255 *Montour County*

Uncertain — This county was created on May 3, 1850, and named either for the mountain ridge which runs through it, or for Madame Catherine (rendered in some accounts as Elizabeth) Montour, for whom the mountain ridge was named. Since the county was created in 1850, when Madame Montour had been dead about a century, one might suspect that the county was named for the mountain ridge, rather than for the long-forgotten Madame Montour, particularly since the Montour mountain ridge runs through the county. However, a majority of sources dealing with the history, geography and place names of Pennsylvania favor Madame Montour as the county's namesake. Even James McKirdy declines to take sides on this issue in his article dealing with the origin of Montour County's name, which appeared in the October 1925 issue (Vol. 8, No. 4) of *Western Pennsylvania Historical Magazine*. His article implies that either origin is equally probable.

Montour mountain ridge — The Montour mountains comprise a beautiful ridge in central Pennsylvania. The ridge traverses both Montour County and its neighbor to the west and south, Northumberland County. The Montour mountains contain iron deposits which provided the basis for Montour County's post Civil War economy, centered on foundries and blast furnaces.

Catherine (or Elizabeth) Montour (–) — A great deal of biographical information has been printed about Madame Montour, but much of it is contradictory. Some of the contradictions result from misinformation bruited about by Madame Montour, herself, who is known to have lied about her age, and possibly her ancestry. The lie about her age may have been a matter a self-preservation, not feminine vanity, for at one point she claimed to be exempt from certain military inconveniences because of her old age. As to her ancestry, depending upon which account one reads, she may have been French, French-Canadian, or either of those with Indian blood in her veins as well. It is known that Madame Catherine Montour was fluent in English, French and several Indian languages and that she served as a valued interpreter to American and European settlers and soldiers in what is now the northeastern United States and southern Canada. C. J. Puetz's work entitled *Pennsylvania County Maps* provides information which is general enough to be credible: "She was apparently a woman of distinguished appearance, good character, and unusual intelligence, and considerable education and refinement. Because of her extraordinary influence over the Indians, she was always treated with great consideration by the provincial authorities ... much caressed by the wealthy people of Philadelphia." We know that she spent most of her life among the Indians and have it on fairly good authority that she was in Albany, as an interpreter, in 1711, and about 1712 she assisted in persuading Iroquois Indians to refrain from attacking the White settlers' frontier. In 1717 she moved to Pennsylvania and in 1742 her home was in north-central Pennsylvania, near the community later named Montoursville. Jack M. Faragher's *Encyclopedia of Colonial & Revolutionary America*, published in 1990, gives approximate birth and death years for her of 1684 and 1752. Dan Thrapp's *Encyclopedia of Frontier Biography* gives the approximate dates as 1684 and 1754. The birth year, in particular, should be considered just one possibility.

2256 *Northampton County*

Northamptonshire, England — This county's name was mandated by Thomas Penn (1702–1775), who inherited a proprietorship interest in Pennsylvania from his father, William Penn (1644–1718). The Englishman, Thomas Penn had married a daughter of Lord Pomfret, whose estate was in Easton, in Northamptonshire, England. In a letter from England dated September 8, 1751, to James Hamilton (–1783), the governor of England's province of Pennsylvania, Thomas Penn stated "Some time since I wrote to Dr. Graeme and Mr. Peters to lay out some ground in the forks of the Delaware for a town, which I suppose they have done or begun to do. I desire it may be called Easton, from my Lord Pomfret's house, and whenever a new county, it be called Northampton." These instructions were followed. Northampton County, Pennsylvania was created as Pennsylvania's eighth county on March 11, 1752, while James Hamilton was serving as provincial governor, and Easton was established as its county seat. The "forks of the Delaware" mentioned in Penn's letter was a triangular section of land bounded by the Delaware River, the Lehigh River and the Blue Mountains. That description is a fairly apt for today's Northampton County, Pennsylvania. Apart from its claim to fame as the home of the imperious Thomas Penn's (1702–1775) father-in-law, Northamptonshire is a county in south-central England, northwest of London. Occupied in ancient times by the Roman Empire, the first known mention of Northampton was in A.D. 917 when the Danes seized it. Northamptonshire is a relatively quiet shire (or county), less involved in industry than some of its neighbors. This shire's population in 1981 was 532,400. The name derives from Old English words *ham tun* meaning "home, farm, homestead," with *North* added to distinguish it from Southampton.

2257 *Northumberland County*

Northumberland County, England — Created March 21, 1772, this county in central Pennsylvania was named for England's northernmost county, on the border with Scotland. Northumberland is a large county and was an independent kingdom in ancient times. Like other parts of the island of Great Britain, Northumberland was subjected to seemingly endless attacks. Conquered and occupied by the Roman

Empire, Northumberland's territory continued to be attacked, when the Romans left. In Anglo-Saxon times, Northumberland was much larger than the present English county, and it was attacked repeatedly from other portions of Great Britain and Scandinavia. Northumberland's proximity to Scotland made it a center of rivalry between England and Scotland but after Scotland's King James VI (1566–1625) ascended to the throne of England as King James I, in 1603, Northumberland gradually accepted membership in that union. It was described in 1586 as "…mostly rough and barren, and seems to have hardened the very carcasses of its inhabitants." This English county's name derives from a tribal name, which referred to "those living north of the river Humber," an estuary on the North Sea.

2258 *Perry County*

Oliver H. Perry (1785–1819)— Perry was a native of Rhode Island and an officer in the U.S. navy. During the War of 1812 his squadron defeated the British in a key battle on Lake Erie of which Perry said "We have met the enemy and they are ours." Perry's decisive defeat of the British on Lake Erie during the War of 1812 was technically a national, rather than a state event, but Pennsylvanians have proudly remembered this naval victory as part of the state's history. Perry died on August 23, 1819, and this county was created on March 22nd of the following year.

2259 *Philadelphia County*

City of Philadelphia, Pennsylvania— The city of Philadelphia was laid out in 1682 as the cornerstone of William Penn's (1644–1718) English province of Pennsylvania. When Pennsylvania's first three counties were erected by Penn in 1682, the county containing the city of Philadelphia was named for it. Penn chose the city's name on account of its spiritual and historical associations and the name he chose is specified in a letter which he wrote on October 28, 1681. Although Penn did not specify the proximate source for his choice of the name *Philadelphia*, it seems apparent that he had in mind the Philadelphia, which was the site of one of early Christianity's "seven churches of Asia" (i.e., Asia Minor), the others being Ephesus, Smyrna, Pergamum, Thyatira, Sardis and Laodicea. All seven are listed in the New Testament of the *Holy Bible*, in The Revelation of St. John 1:11. Philadelphia, now named Amman, in Jordan, Asia Minor, located 25 miles northeast of the Dead Sea,

was founded by Philadelphus, the king of Pergamon, before the birth of Christ and named in Philadelphus' honor. It soon became a possession of the Roman Empire and control over this city in Asia Minor has changed hands many times over the succeeding two millennia. The city of Philadelphia in Pennsylvania, with a population in the late 1990's of 1.5 million, has a rich history of its own but, perhaps more importantly, it was the birthplace of our nation. Our Declaration of Independence and our Constitution were both drafted in Philadelphia and for a time the city served as temporary capital of the new United States of America.

2260 *Pike County*

Zebulon M. Pike (1779–1813)— A native of New Jersey, Pike served as an army officer on America's frontier following the Revolution. He led an exploratory army expedition to the Rocky Mountains in Colorado which Pike's Peak in the Colorado Rockies commemorates. Pike served as a general in the War of 1812 and was killed in combat in that war on April 27, 1813. This county was created by the state of Pennsylvania on March 26 of the following year.

2261 *Potter County*

James Potter (1729–1789)— A native of Ireland, Potter immigrated with his family to Pennsylvania about 1741. Here he served as an army officer during the French and Indian War and in 1756 he served under John Armstrong (1717–1795) in the highly successful raid on the Delaware Indians at Kittanning, Pennsylvania. During the years following the proclamation of 1768, Potter worked in western Pennsylvania, trying to persuade White settlers to leave the area to the Indians as required by the treaty of 1768. When the American Revolution began, Potter held the rank of colonel and he participated in combat at Trenton and Princeton and was promoted to brigadier-general. He later fought at Brandywine and Germantown. From 1780 to 1781 he was a member of Pennsylvania's supreme executive council and was vice-president of that body in 1781. He subsequently was appointed a major-general in the Pennsylvania militia. General Potter died in Pennsylvania in November, 1789, and this county was created and named in his honor on March 26, 1804. The name that was first proposed for this county was the Indian name Sinnemahoning, but that name was rejected in favor of Potter.

2262 *Schuylkill County*

Schuylkill River— This county was created on March 1, 1811, and named for the Schuylkill River, which rises within the county. This 130 mile-long tributary of the Delaware River flows in a south-eastern direction through eastern Pennsylvania to enter the Delaware River at the city of Philadelphia. The river's name dates from the 17th century when the Dutch and Swedes were competing to own eastern Pennsylvania and the Swedes established several forts along the Schuylkill River before they were conquered by the Dutch in 1655. The Schuylkill's waters at its mouth on the Delaware are very wide and deep, which probably exaggerated the river's importance to early European visitors. George R. Stewart's *American Place-Names* and other sources indicate that the river's name came from Dutch words meaning "hiding-place." Stewart speculated that the name probably came from an "…incident in which a Swedish vessel lay concealed in that stream." Stewart attributed the name to the Dutch word for "hiding place," which is *schuilplaats*. That translation is correct according to F. P. H. Prick Van Wely's *Cassell's English-Dutch: Dutch-English Dictionary*. The river's name appeared as *Skiar eller line Kill* on a map of New Sweden drawn in 1644 by the cartographer, Peter Lindestrom.

2263 *Snyder County*

Simon Snyder (1759–1819)— Snyder was born in Lancaster, Pennsylvania, on November 5, 1759, and in 1784 he moved to Selinsgrove, Pennsylvania, where, he ran a store, operated a grist mill and served as justice of the peace. In 1789 he was elected as a delegate to the state constitutional convention and he served in the lower house of the Pennsylvania legislature for all but one year from 1797 to 1807. He was speaker of that body on three occasions. Snyder ran to be Pennsylvania's governor in 1805 but lost to the incumbent Thomas McKean (1734–1817). He tried again in 1808 and was elected. Twice reelected, Snyder served as the state's governor from December 20, 1808, to December 16, 1817. He was also elected to represent Pennsylvania in the U.S. Senate but died at Selinsgrove, Pennsylvania on November 9, 1819, before taking his seat in the congress which convened on December 6, 1819. This county was created on March 2, 1855, and named for the former governor whose home at Selinsgrove was within the county's borders.

2264 *Somerset County*

Town of Somerset, Pennsylvania— This county was created on April 17, 1795, and named for the town of Somerset, which became its county seat. Perched in the mountain country of southwestern Pennsylvania at 2,200 feet above sea level, Somerset has the highest elevation of Pennsylvania's 67 county seats. The municipality's population in the late 1990's was 6,500. The town of Somerset was settled a generation or so before Somerset County was created and the town was named for Somersetshire, in England.

Somersetshire, England— This county, in southwestern England, lies on Bristol Channel. The Somersetshire area was conquered by the Roman Empire about A.D. 43 and remains from their period of occupation can still be seen. By A.D. 658 the area was under the control of the West Saxons. Subject to periodic incursions by the Danes, Somersetshire later was controlled, almost entirely, by the Norman invaders from France. This county is bounded on three sides by hills and on the fourth side by the sea. Considerable areas of the county are sparsely populated. Below the hills, Somersetshire's climate is mild. The name *Somerset* evolved from various earlier Latin and old English forms. It originally meant "the Somerset people" and later became the name of the district. "Dwellers at Somerton" and "people dependent on Somerton" were early translations of the names which finally evolved into Somersetshire.

2265 *Sullivan County*

John Sullivan (1740–1795)— The location of John Sullivan's birth is given variously as Berwick, Maine and Somersworth, New Hampshire. The two towns are adjacent. He practiced law in New Hampshire and represented New Hampshire in the Continental Congress. During the American Revolution Sullivan served as a brigadier-general and later was promoted to major-general. John Sullivan served with distinction in a number of important engagements of the Revolution including action against the Indians near present-day Elmira, New York. Soon after that 1779 campaign, he fell ill and resigned from the army. He then represented New Hampshire again in the Continental Congress. Sullivan later served as attorney general of New Hampshire, president (or governor) of New Hampshire and was a member of the New Hampshire convention that ratified the proposed federal constitution. He also was speaker of New Hampshire's house of representatives. In 1789 President George Washington appointed John Sullivan as judge of the U.S. district court of New Hampshire and Sullivan held that position until his death in 1795. This county was created and named in General Sullivan's honor on March 15, 1847.

2266 *Susquehanna County*

Susquehanna River— This major river rises in Otsego Lake in central New York state, and flows south to enter Pennsylvania at Susquehanna County. The river continues its 444 mile journey across eastern Pennsylvania and finally empties its waters into Chesapeake Bay in Maryland. The Susquehanna has a West Branch, which is an important river itself. The 200 mile-long West Branch unites with the Susquehanna proper near Sunbury, Pennsylvania. The river's name is of Indian origin but beyond that lies a good deal of uncertainty. Nine possible translations are mentioned (with sources for each) by James McKirdy in his article dealing with the origins of Pennsylvania's county names which appeared in the July, 1925, issue (Vol. 8, No. 3) of *Western Pennsylvania Historical Magazine*. George P. Donehoo's work dealing with the Indian place names of Pennsylvania mentions the possibility that the name may have been overheard by early European visitors when the Indians were discussing the muddy conditions of the river resulting from flooding. If so, the name by which we know the river is merely our rendering of a description of the Susquehanna's muddiness on that one occasion.

2267 *Tioga County*

Tioga River— This county in northern Pennsylvania was created on March 26, 1804, and named for the river which rises near its eastern border. The Tioga River rises in western Bradford County, near the town of Tioga, in Pennsylvania's Tioga County and flows essentially due north across the New York state border. The Tioga continues to flow north until its waters unite with those of the Cohocton River, near Corning, New York. There, the two rivers unite to form the Chemung River. The name *Tioga*, is an Indian name and it was first applied by them to a point at the junction of the Susquehanna River with the Chemung River, below the town of Athens, Pennsylvania. Sources consulted differ on the translation of this Indian name but a meaning of "at the forks," is cited by enough authorities to lend it credibility. That name relates to the junction of the Susquehanna River with the Chemung River, which was a well known meeting place for the Indians. In attempting to describe the location of this famous Indian meeting point, confusion arises because some references call the Tioga River (or portions of it) the Chemung River. The point for which the Tioga River was named lies just three or four miles south of the present southwestern border of Tioga County, New York. At one time there was an Indian village there at Tioga Point.

2268 *Union County*

The American union of states— This county was created on March 22, 1813, during the War of 1812. On that same day Pennsylvania created Columbia County, whose name is a patriotic reference to Christopher Columbus. Both of these county names reflect the concern that we win the War of 1812, our nation's second war for independence from England.

2269 *Venango County*

Uncertain— The county in northwestern Pennsylvania was created on March 12, 1800, and although the origin of the county's name is not certain, there are just two possibilities and they are closely related. The county was either named for the Venango River or for an Indian village located at the mouth of the Venango River. The Venango River, now called French Creek, is a 140 mile-long tributary of the Allegheny River. It rises in southwestern New York state and flows into Pennsylvania to unite with the Allegheny at Franklin, Pennsylvania, in the center of Venango County, Pennsylvania. It was here at today's Franklin, at the mouth of the French Creek (nee Venango) that the Indians had an important village and trading center. James McKirdy's article dealing with the origins of Pennsylvania's county names which appeared in the July, 1925, issue (Vol. 8, No. 3) of *Western Pennsylvania Historical Magazine* stated that the Indian village had been located here for centuries as evidenced by "...refuse beds containing bones, mussel shells, flint chips, arrowpoints, pipe bowls and broken pottery." McKirdy's article contains an educated guess about the origin of the name *Venango*. That guess was based on information gleaned by an early resident of Meadville, in northwestern Pennsylvania, Reverend Timothy Alden. Reverend Alden was told that the name was given to the river and village by the Indians as descriptive of a "rude sculpture" carved in the bark of a tree near its banks. Apparently the carving dealt with pornography or scatology because the Reverend Alden felt that "...an explanation which decency forbids to record." If there is any truth to this, Venango County's name may derive from early American graffiti.

2270 *Warren County*

Joseph Warren (1741–1775)— A native of Massachusetts and a graduate of Harvard College, Warren practiced medicine in the Boston area. He was a member of the committee of safety and president *pro tempore* of the Massachusetts provincial congress. In June, 1775, he was commissioned a major-general and he died in combat a few days later at the battle of Bunker Hill. Warren County, Pennsylvania, was created on March 12, 1800.

2271 *Washington County*

George Washington (1732–1799)— Washington was a native of Virginia, who served in Virginia's house of burgesses and became one of the colonies' leaders in opposition to British policies in America. He was a member of the first and second Continental Congresses and commander of all Continental armies in the Revolutionary War. Following victory in that war, Washington was elected to be the first president of the United States. This county was created as Pennsylvania's 12th county on March 28, 1781. It was the first Pennsylvania county named in honor of a postcolonial figure and the name was chosen at a time when the efforts of our Revolutionary commander in-chief were drawing to a successful conclusion.

2272 *Wayne County*

Anthony Wayne (1745–1796)— A native of Pennsylvania, Wayne was a successful brigadier-general in the Revolutionary War and became a hero for his daring exploits. During the bitter winter of 1777–1778 at Valley Forge, Pennsylvania, Wayne shared the sufferings of his men although his comfortable estate was only five miles away. He played an important role in the final overthrow of the British forces in Georgia. After the war, in 1785, Wayne moved to Georgia and he represented Georgia for about six months in the U.S. House of Representatives. In 1792, President Washington recalled Wayne to serve as a major-general against the Indians in the Northwest territory. Once again his military

efforts were successful. On August 20, 1794, forces under Wayne's command defeated the Indians in the battle of Fallen Timbers in northwestern Ohio. That battle was decisive in ending Indian hostilities in the region and moving America's frontier further north and west. Before long, British forces also evacuated the northern country and Americans moved in. General Wayne died in northwestern Pennsylvania on December 15, 1796, and this county was created on December 21, 1798.

2273 *Westmoreland County*

Westmoreland County, England— On February 26, 1773, Pennsylvania erected Westmoreland County to occupy the entire western end of Pennsylvania, a vast, largely unsettled area extending from Virginia on the south to New York and Lake Erie on the north. Until this time, Pennsylvania had named all of her counties for places and persons of England, apart from William Penn's (1644–1718) Philadelphia County. Westmoreland would be the last Pennsylvania county to honor, directly or indirectly, an English county, until the creation of Somerset County 22 years later. John N. Boucher's *History of Westmoreland County, Pennsylvania* points out that the new county's name reflected the geographic facts "...for here, in the *west* was, indeed *more land* than was then occupied."

Westmoreland County, England— Conquered by the Roman empire in ancient times, this poor county in northwestern England with bleak hills among moors and lakes was not greatly coveted by others although its proximity to Scotland invited centuries of hostilities between England and Scotland for control of the area. After Scotland's King James VI (1566–1625) ascended to the throne of England as King James I, in 1603, that source of tension disappeared. During feudal times wealth was distributed very unevenly in Westmoreland, where the poor subsisted on land of poor fertility, while their lords erected no fewer than seven castles. Westmoreland's only municipality of any importance is Kendal at the southern end of the county. The county's name originally meant "district of the people living west of the moors," referring to the Pennine Mountains in north Yorkshire, the relatively huge neighbor of tiny Westmoreland, on its eastern border.

2274 *Wyoming County*

Wyoming Valley— This county in northeastern Pennsylvania was created on

April 4, 1842, and named for its location on both sides of the Wyoming Valley, a part of the Susquehanna River valley. The name *Wyoming* is of Indian origin and means "upon the great plains." In the early 1700's the Delaware Indians had a village at the present site of Wilkes-Barre, in the valley of the Susquehanna River, a few miles southeast of Wyoming County, Pennsylvania. The Indians called both the valley there, and their village within it *M'chewomink*, which meant "on the broad plain," or "upon the great plains." The Indians had no written language so it was left to Whites to render the name in writing and the name took several forms, one of which approximated the word *Wyoming*. During the last half of the 18th century the Wyoming Valley became well known because of battles between Indians and Whites here. Also, the name *Wyoming* was used in the title of a poem by Thomas Campbell, entitled "Gertrude of Wyoming," which was published in 1809. That poem enjoyed some popularity and helped perpetuate the name.

2275 *York County*

Town of York, Pennsylvania— York County was created on August 19, 1749, and named for the town of York, which had been laid out eight years earlier. The town of York then became the county seat of the new county and, during the American Revolution, it was the temporary capital of our nascent nation, while British troops occupied Philadelphia. In the late 1990's York was a city with a population of 42,000. Sources dealing with the history, geography and place names of Pennsylvania have differing opinions about the origin of the town's name. York and Yorkshire in England are suggested by some authorities while others say that England's King James II (1633–1701) was the namesake.

York and Yorkshire, England— Lying about mid-way between London and Edinburgh, Scotland, with a population of several million, the city of York and the county of Yorkshire, in England, represent one of England's most important metropolitan areas. Yorkshire borders on the North Sea and extends almost to the Irish Sea. The Roman Empire conquered the area and built a strategic fortress here about A.D. 72. Remains of this fortress can still be seen. The Yorkshire plain is fertile for agriculture and the West Riding area is rich in coal deposits. The Danes captured York in A.D. 867 and its present name came from their name *Yorvick*. York was later subjugated by the West Saxons and in 1066 it fell to the Norman invaders from France.

King James II (1633–1701)— James was the second surviving son of England's King Charles I (1600–1649). He was given the title duke of York and Albany soon after his christening. When James' father died, his elder brother, Charles, ascended to the throne as King Charles II (1630–1685). In 1664 King Charles II made an enormous grant of land in North America to his brother, the duke of York and Albany, which initially included much of present-day Pennsylvania. The duke of York was awarded more power over his domain than any other English proprietor. Although King Charles II had many children, none of them were legitimate so when King Charles II died in 1685, his brother, James, became king of England as King James II. About 1673 King James II professed his Catholicism and this spelled his eventual downfall as king. In 1689 the throne passed to William of Orange (1650–1702), who ruled as joint sovereign with his wife, Queen Mary II (1662–1694). Mary was a daughter of King James II. The former King James II devoted the final years of his life to religious exercises.

REFERENCES

Africa, J. Simpson. *History of Huntingdon & Blair Counties, Pennsylvania*. Philadelphia, Louis H. Everts, 1883.

Albert, George D. *History of the County of Westmoreland, Pennsylvania*. Philadelphia, L. H. Everts & Co., 1882.

Andrews, Allen. *The Royal Whore: Barbara Villiers, Countess of Castlemaine*. Philadelphia, Chilton Book Co., 1970.

Armor, William C. *Lives of the Governors of Pennsylvania*. Philadelphia, James K. Simon, 1872.

Battle, J. H. *History of Columbia & Montour Counties, Pennsylvania*. Chicago, A. Warner & Co., 1887.

Bausman, Joseph H. *History of Beaver County, Pennsylvania*. New York, Knickerbocker Press, 1904.

Beauchamp, William M. "Aboriginal Place Names of New York." *New York State Museum Bulletin*, Bulletin 108, Archeology 12. Albany: May, 1907.

Beebe, Victor L. *History of Potter County, Pennsylvania*. Coudersport, Pennsylvania, Potter County Historical Society, 1934.

Bertin, Eugene P. "Origins of Lycoming County Place Names." *Now and Then*, Vol. 7, No. 9. Williamsport, Pennsylvania: April, 1944.

Beyer, George R. *Guide to the State Historical Markers of Pennsylvania*. Harrisburg, Pennsylvania Historical & Museum Commission, 1991.

The Biographical Encyclopaedia of Pennsylvania of the Nineteenth Century. Philadelphia, Galaxy Publishing Co., 1874.

Biographical & Historical Cyclopedia of Indiana & Armstrong Counties, Pennsylvania. Philadelphia, John M. Gresham & Co., 1891.

Biographical & Historical Cyclopedia of Westmoreland County, Pennsylvania. Philadelphia, John M. Gresham & Co., 1890.

Blackman, Emily C. *History of Susquehanna County, Pennsylvania*. Philadelphia, Claxton, Remsen & Haffelfinger, 1873.

Blair County: Historical Background & Physiography. Hollidaysburg, Pennsylvania, Blair County Planning Commission, 1967.

Boatner, Mark M. *Encyclopedia of the American Revolution*. New York, David McKay Co., Inc., 1966.

Bonsal, Stephen. *When the French Were Here*. Garden City, New York, Doubleday, Doran & Co., Inc., 1945.

Boucher, John N. *History of Westmoreland County, Pennsylvania*. New York, Lewis Publishing Co., 1906.

Bradsby, H. C. *History of Bradford County, Pennsylvania*. Chicago, S. B. Nelson & Co., 1891.

Brenckman, Fred. *History of Carbon County, Pennsylvania*. Harrisburg, James J. Nungesser, 1918.

The Bulletin 1958 Almanac. Philadelphia, Evening & Sunday Bulletin, 1958.

Burns, Richard D. *Guide to American Foreign Relations Since 1700*. Santa Barbara, California, ABC-Clio, Inc., 1983.

Calmette, Joseph. *Charles V*. Paris, Librairie Artheme Fayard, 1945.

Cannon, John. *The Oxford Companion to British History*. Oxford, Oxford University Press, 1997.

The Catholic Encyclopedia. New York, Robert Appleton Co., 1908.

Centennial & Illustrated Wayne County: Historical, Biographical, Industrial, Picturesque. Honesdale, Pennsylvania, Benjamin F. Haines, 1902.

Centre County Information Book. Centre County, Pennsylvania, Centre County Planning Commission, 1978.

Chapman, Isaac A. *The History of Wyoming*. Cottonport, Louisiana, Polyanthos, Inc., 1971.

Chronicle of the French Revolution. London, Chronicle Communications, Ltd., 1989.

Clements, John. *Pennsylvania Facts*. Dallas, Texas, Clements Research, Inc., 1987.

Clint, Florence. *Centre County, Pennsylvania Area Key*. Denver, Colorado, Area Keys, 1976.

Committee on Geographic Names. "Origin of Names of New York State Counties." *University of the State of New York Bulletin to the Schools*, Vol. 10. 1924.

Cooke, James J. *France: 1789–1962*. Hamden, Connecticut, Archon Books, 1975.

The Counties of New York State. New York Telephone Company, 1948.

Crouch, Kenneth E. "Bedford and Its Namesakes." *Bedford Democrat*, July 29, 1954.

Currie, Andrew M. *Dictionary of British Place Names*. London, Tiger Books International, 1994.

Darlington, William M. "Major-General John Armstrong." *Pennsylvania Magazine of History & Biography*, Vol. 1. Philadelphia: 1877.

Darlington, William M. "The Montours." *Pennsylvania Magazine of History & Biography*, Vol. 4, No. 2. Philadelphia: 1880.

Davis, A. J. *History of Clarion County, Pennsylvania*. Syracuse, New York, D. Mason & Co., 1887.

Davis, Tarring S. *A History of Blair County, Pennsylvania*. Harrisburg, National Historical Association, Inc., 1931.

Day, Sherman. *Historical Collections of the State of Pennsylvania*. Philadelphia, G. W. Gorton, 1843.

Donehoo, George P. *A History of the Cumberland Valley in Pennsylvania*. Harrisburg, Susquehanna History Association, 1930.

Donehoo, George P. *A History of the Indian Villages & Place Names in Pennsylvania*. Harrisburg, Pennsylvania, Telegraph Press, 1928.

Donehoo, George P. *Pennsylvania: A History*. New York, Lewis Historical Publishing Co., Inc., 1926.

Dunaway, Wayland F. *A History of Pennsylvania*. New York, Prentice-Hall, Inc., 1948.

Dunn, Richard S., & Mary Maples Dunn. *The Papers of William Penn*. University of Pennsylvania Press, 1982.

Eastman, Frank M. *Courts & Lawyers of Pennsylvania: A History: 1623–1923*. New York, American Historical Society, Inc., 1922.

Egle, William H. "The Constitutional Convention of 1776: Biographical Sketches of Its Members." *Pennsylvania Magazine of History & Biography*, Vol. 3, No. 3. Philadelphia: 1879.

Egle, William H. "The Constitutional Convention of 1776: Biographical Sketches of Its Members." *Pennsylvania Magazine of History & Biography*, Vol. 4, No. 2. Philadelphia: 1880.

Egle, William H. *History of the Commonwealth of Pennsylvania*. Philadelphia, E. M. Gardner, 1883.

Egle, William H. *History of the Counties of Dauphin & Lebanon*. Philadelphia, Everts & Peck, 1883.

Ekwall, Eilert. *The Concise Oxford Dictionary of English Place-Names*. Oxford, Oxford University Press, 1960.

Ellis, Franklin, & Samuel Evans. *History of Lancaster County, Pennsylvania*. Philadelphia, Everts & Peck, 1883.

Encyclopaedia Britannica. Chicago, Encyclopaedia Britannica, Inc., 1971.

Eno, Joel N. "Pennsylvania County Names." *The Magazine of History*, Vol. 24, Nos. 3–4. Poughkeepsie, New York: March–April, 1917.

Espenshade, A. Howry. *Pennsylvania Place Names*. State College, Pennsylvania, Pennsylvania State College, 1925.

Faragher, John M. *The Encyclopedia of Colonial & Revolutionary America*. New York, Facts on File, 1990.

Fisher, Charles A. *Abstracts of Snyder County Probate & Orphans Court Records: 1772–1855*. Selinsgrove, Pennsylvania, 1940.

Flower, Milton E. *John Armstrong: First Citizen of Carlisle*. Carlisle, Pennsylvania, Cumberland County Historical Society, 1971.

Freeze, John G. "Madame Montour." *Pennsylvania Magazine of History & Biography*, Vol. 3, No. 1. Philadelphia: 1879.

Futhey, J. Smith, & Gilbert Cope. *History of Chester County, Pennsylvania*. Philadelphia, Louis H. Everts, 1881.

Gannett, Henry. *The Origin of Certain Place Names in the United States*. Williamstown, Massachusetts, Corner House Publishers, 1978.

Gilbert, Martin. *Atlas of British History*. New York, Oxford University Press, 1993.

Godcharles, Frederic A. *Pennsylvania: Political, Governmental, Military & Civil*. New York, American Historical Society, Inc., 1933.

Hamilton, A. Boyd. "General James Potter." *Pennsylvania Magazine of History & Biography*, Vol. 1, No. 3. Philadelphia: 1877.

Hassler, Edgar W. *Old Westmoreland: A History of Western Pennsylvania During the Revolution*. Cleveland, Arthur H. Clark Co., 1900.

Hawkyard, Alasdair. *The Counties of Britain: A Tudor Atlas by John Speed*. London, England, Pavilion Books, Ltd., 1995.

Hazard, Samuel. *Annals of Pennsylvania: 1609–1682*. Philadelphia, Hazard & Mitchell, 1850.

Heverly, Clement F. *Pioneer & Patriot Families of Bradford County, Pennsylvania*. Towanda, Pennsylvania, Bradford Star Print, 1913.

Historical & Biographical Annals of Columbia & Montour Counties, Pennsylvania. Chicago, J. H. Beers & Co., 1915.

History of Beaver County, Pennsylvania. Philadelphia, A. Warner & Co., 1888.

History of Bradford County, Pennsylvania. Philadelphia, L. H. Everts & Co., 1878.

History of Butler County, Pennsylvania. R. C. Brown & Co., 1895.

History of Delaware County, Pennsylvania. Philadelphia, Henry B. Ashmead, 1862.

History of Luzerne, Lackawanna & Wyoming Counties, Pennsylvania. New York, W. W. Munsell, 1880.

History of Mercer County, Pennsylvania. Chicago, Brown, Runk & Co., 1888.

History of Tioga, Chemung, Tompkins & Schuyler Counties, New York. Philadelphia, Everts & Ensign, 1879.

History of Tioga County, Pennsylvania. R. C. Brown & Co., 1897.

History of Venango County, Pennsylvania. Chicago, Brown, Runk & Co., 1890.

Hodge, Frederick W. *Handbook of American Indians North of Mexico*. Totowa, New Jersey, Rowman & Littlefield, 1975.

Hollister, H. *History of the Lackawanna Valley*. Philadelphia, J. B. Lippincott Co., 1885.

Hunsicker, Clifton S. *Montgomery County, Pennsylvania: A History*. New York, Lewis Historical Publishing Co., Inc., 1923.

Illick, Joseph E. *Colonial Pennsylvania*. New York, Charles Scribner's Sons, 1976.

Jackson, Joseph. *Encyclopedia of Philadelphia*. Harrisburg, National Historical Association, 1933.

Jordan, Florence R. *History of Pennsylvania's Counties*. Harrisburg, Pennsylvania Farmer.

Jordan, John W. *Encyclopedia of Pennsylvania Biography*. New York, Lewis Historical Publishing Co., 1918.

Juniata: A County for All Seasons. Juniata County Historical Society, 1981.

Kelker, Luther R. *History of Dauphin County, Pennsylvania*. New York, Lewis Publishing Co., 1907.

Kenny, Hamill. "The Origin & Meaning of the Indian-Place Names of Maryland." Ph.D. Thesis, Theodore R. McKeldin Library, University of Maryland, College Park, Maryland, 1950.

Kleber, John E. *The Kentucky Encyclopedia*. Lexington, Kentucky, University Press of Kentucky, 1992.

Kurtz, Paul. *Blair, Main Line: A History of the Tuckahoe Valley*. Bellwood Antis Public Library Board, 1976.

Lalanne, Ludovic. *Dictionnaire Historique de la France*. Paris, Librairie Hachette et Cie. 1877.

Leeson, Michael A. *History of the Counties of McKean, Elk, Cameron & Potter, Pennsylvania*. Chicago, J. H. Beers & Co., 1890.

Leland, J. A. C. "Some Eastern Indian Place Names in California." *California Folklore Quarterly*, Vol. 4, No. 4. Berkeley: October, 1945.

Linn, John B. "The Butler Family of the Pennsylvania Line." *Pennsylvania Magazine of History & Biography*, Vol. 7, No. 1. Philadelphia: 1883.

Lloyd, Thomas W. *History of Lycoming County, Pennsylvania*. Topeka, Historical Publishing Co., 1929.

Lomas, Richard. *County of Conflict: Northumberland from Conquest to Civil War*. East Lothian, Scotland, Tuckwell Press, 1996.

Lytle, Milton S. *History of Huntingdon County, in the State of Pennsylvania*. Lancaster, Pennsylvania, William H. Roy, 1876.

McCague, James. *The Cumberland*. New York, Holt, Rinehart & Winston, 1973.

MacCracken, Henry N. *Old Dutchess Forever!* New York, Hastings House Publishers, 1956.

McHenry, Robert. *Webster's American Military Biographies*. New York, Dover Publications, Inc., 1978.

McKirdy, James. "Origin of the Names Given to the Counties in Pennsylvania." *Western Pennsylvania Historical Magazine*, Pittsburgh, Pennsylvania: Vol. 8, No. 1, January, 1925; Vol. 8, No. 2, April, 1925; Vol. 8, No. 3, July, 1925; Vol. 8, No. 4, October, 1925.

McKnight, W. J. *A Pioneer Outline History of Northwestern Pennsylvania*. Philadelphia, J. B. Lippincott Co., 1905.

MacReynolds, George. *Place Names in Bucks County, Pennsylvania*. Doylestown, Pennsylvania, Bucks County Historical Society, 1942.

Meginness, John F. *History of Lycoming County, Pennsylvania*. Chicago, Brown, Runk & Co., 1892.

Merrill, Arch. *Southern Tier*. New York, New York, American Book-Stratford Press, 1954.

Middlekauff, Robert. *Benjamin Franklin and His Enemies*. Berkeley, University of California Press, 1996.

Miller, Madeleine S., & J. Lane Miller. *Harper's Bible Dictionary*. New York, Harper & Row, 1973.

Mills, A.D. *A Dictionary of English Place Names*. Oxford, Oxford University Press, 1991.

Mitchell, J. Thomas. "James Potter."

Centre County Heritage, Vol. 2, No. 1. Bellefonte, Pennsylvania: February, 1957.

Morgan, George H. *Centennial: The Settlement, Formation & Progress of Dauphin County, Pennsylvania: From 1785 to 1876*. Harrisburg, Telegraph Steam Book & Job Printing House, 1877.

Moule, Thomas. *The County Maps of Old England*. London, Studio Editions, 1990.

Murphy, Thomas. *Jubilee History of Lackawanna County, Pennsylvania*. Topeka, Historical Publishing Co., 1928.

Murray, Louis W. *A History of Old Tioga Point and Early Athens, Pennsylvania*. Athens, Pennsylvania, Raeder Press, 1908.

My Pennsylvania: A Brief History of the Commonwealth's Sixty-seven Counties. State Department of Commerce, Commonwealth of Pennsylvania. 1946.

New Catholic Encyclopedia. New York, McGraw-Hill Book Co., 1967.

New Jersey, Pennsylvania Tour Book. Heathrow, Florida, AAA Publishing, 1998.

Newton, J. H. *History of Venango County, Pennsylvania*. Franklin, Pennsylvania, Venango County Historical Society, 1976.

Nolan, J. Bennett. *The Schuylkill*. New Brunswick, New Jersey, Rutgers University Press, 1951.

"Notes & Queries: Indian Local Names with Their Interpretations." *Pennsylvania Magazine of History & Biography*, Vol. 9, No. 3. Philadelphia: 1885.

Oakley, Amy. *Our Pennsylvania*. Indianapolis, Bobbs-Merrill Co., Inc., 1950.

Palmer, Charles. *A History of Delaware County, Pennsylvania*. Harrisburg, National Historical Association, Inc., 1932.

Palmer, Tim. *Rivers of Pennsylvania*. University Park, Pennsylvania State University Press, 1980.

Paullin, Charles O. *Atlas of the Historical Geography of the United States*. Carnegie Institution of Washington and the American Geographical Society of New York, 1932.

Pearce, Stewart. *Annals of Luzerne County*. Philadelphia, J. B. Lippincott & Co., 1866.

The Pennsylvania Almanac & Buyers' Guide. 1964.

Pinkowski, Edward. *Chester County Place Names*. Philadelphia, Sunshine Press, 1962.

Plumb, Henry B. *History of Hanover Township & History of Wyoming Valley*. Wilkes-Barre, Pennsylvania, Robert Baur, 1885.

Price, Edward T. *Dividing the Land: Early American Beginnings of Our Private Property Mosaic*. Chicago, University of Chicago Press, 1995.

Proud, Robert. *The Hiftory of Pennfyl-vania in North America*. Philadelphia, Zachariah Poulson, Jr., 1797.

Prowell, George R. *History of York County, Pennsylvania*. Chicago, J. H. Beers & Co., 1907.

Prowell, George R. "Pennsylvania County Names." *The Magazine of History*, New York, New York: Vol. 10, No. 3, September, 1909; New York, New York: Vol. 12, No. 3, September, 1910; Poughkeepsie, New York: Vol. 19, No. 6, December, 1914.

Puetz, C. J. *Pennsylvania County Maps*. Lyndon Station, Wisconsin, County Maps.

Purcell, L. Edward. *Who Was Who in the American Revolution*. New York, Facts on File, 1993.

Quinlan, James E. *History of Sullivan County*. Liberty, New York, W. T. Morgans & Co., Printers & Stereotypers, 1873.

Raasch, H. D. "Northampton County, Pennsylvania." *Northamptonshire: Past & Present*, Vol. 4, No. 2. Delapre Abbey, Northampton, England: 1967/68.

Riesenman, Joseph. *History of Northwestern Pennsylvania*. New York, Lewis Historical Publishing Co., Inc., 1943.

Roche, Kathleen M. *The Pennsylvania Manual: 1976–1977*. Department of General Services, Commonwealth of Pennsylvania.

Rupp, I Daniel. *History of the Counties of Berks & Lebanon*. Lancaster, Pennsylvania, G. Hills, 1844.

Rupp, I Daniel. *History of Lancaster County*. Lancaster, Pennsylvania, Gilbert Hills, 1844.

Rupp, I Daniel. *The History & Topography of Dauphin, Cumberland, Franklin, Bedford, Adams & Perry Counties*. Lancaster, Pennsylvania, Gilbert Hills, 1846.

Schenck, J. S. *History of Warren County, Pennsylvania*. Syracuse, D. Mason & Co., 1887.

Sedillot, Rene. *An Outline of French History*. New York, Alfred A. Knopf, 1967.

Seward, Desmond. *Marie Antoinette*. New York, St. Martin's Press, 1981.

Shankle, George Earlie. *State Names, Flags, Seals, Songs, Birds, Flowers & Other Symbols*. New York, H. W. Wilson Co., 1941.

Smith, George. *History of Delaware County, Pennsylvania*. Philadelphia, Henry B. Ashmead, 1862.

Smith, Helene, & George Swetnam. *A Guidebook to Historic Western Pennsylvania*. University of Pittsburgh Press, 1991.

Smith, Robert W. *History of Armstrong County, Pennsylvania*. Chicago, Waterman, Watkins & Co., 1883.

Spafford, Horatio G. *A Gazetteer of the State of New York*. Albany, B. D. Packard, 1824.

Stevens, Sylvester K. *Pennsylvania: Birthplace of a Nation*. New York, Random House, 1964.

Stevens, Sylvester K. *Pennsylvania: The Heritage of a Commonwealth*. West Palm Beach, Florida, American Historical Co., Inc., 1968.

Stevens, Sylvester K. *Pennsylvania History in Outline*. Harrisburg, Pennsylvania Historical & Museum Commission, 1960.

Stewart, George R. *American Place-Names*. New York, Oxford University Press, 1970.

Stone, Rufus B. *McKean: The Governor's County*. New York, Lewis Historical Publishing Co., Inc., 1926.

Stone, William L. *The Poetry & History of Wyoming: Containing Campbell's Gertrude and the History of Wyoming from Its Discovery to the Beginning of the Present Century*. Wilkes-Barre, C. E. Butler, 1869.

Storey, Henry W. *History of Cambria County, Pennsylvania*. New York, Lewis Publishing Co., 1907.

Stover, Herbert E. *Pennsylvania: The History of Our State*. Boston, Ginn & Company, 1945.

Stroup, John M., & Raymond M. Bell. *The Genesis of Mifflin County, Pennsylvania*. Lewistown, Pennsylvania, 1939.

Taft, William H., III. *County Names: An Historical Perspective*. National Association of Counties, 1982.

Thomas, Allen C. *A History of Pennsylvania*. Boston, D. C. Heath & Co., 1913.

Thomas Jefferson: Writings: Autobiography. New York, Literary Classics of the United States, 1984.

Van Wely, F. P. H. Prick. *Cassell's English-Dutch: Dutch-English Dictionary*. New York, Funk & Wagnalls, 1973.

Vexler, Robert I. *Chronology & Documentary Handbook of the State of Pennsylvania*. Dobbs Ferry, New York, Oceana Publications, Inc., 1978.

Vogel, Virgil J. *Indian Names in Michigan*. Ann Arbor, University of Michigan Press, 1986.

Walkinshaw, Lewis C. *Annals of Southwestern Pennsylvania*. New York, Lewis Historical Publishing Co., Inc., 1939.

Wall, Thomas L. *Clearfield County, Pennsylvania*. 1925.

Watson, John F. *Annals of Philadelphia & Pennsylvania*. Philadelphia, Whiting & Thomas, 1856.

Westbrook, C. H. *The Pennsylvania Manual: 1939*. Harrisburg, Pennsylvania, Commonwealth of Pennsylvania, 1940.

Western Pennsylvania Historical Survey. *Guidebook to Historic Places in Western Pennsylvania*. Pittsburgh, University of Pittsburgh Press, 1938.

Whitworth, Rex. *William Augustus, Duke of Cumberland: A Life*. London, England, Leo Cooper, 1992.

Wiley, Samuel T,. & W. Scott Garner. *Biographical & Portrait Cyclopedia of Blair County, Pennsylvania*. Philadelphia, Gresham Publishing Co., 1892.

Wise, L. F. & E. W. Egan. *Kings, Rulers & Statesmen*. New York, Sterling Publishing Co., Inc., 1967.

Wolf, George A., et al. *Blair County's First Hundred Years*. Altoona, Pennsylvania, Mirror Press, 1945.

Work Projects Administration. *Inventory of the County Archives of Pennsylvania-Beaver & Forest Counties*. 1940–1942.

Work Projects Administration. *Northampton County Guide*. Bethlehem, Pennsylvania, Times Publishing Co., 1939.

Work Projects Administration. *A Pic-*

ture of Lycoming County. Commissioners of Lycoming County, Pennsylvania, 1939.

Yenne, Bill. *The Encyclopedia of North American Indian Tribes*. New York, Crescent Books, 1986.

Zweig, Stefan. *Marie Antoinette*. New York, Garden City Publishing Co., 1933.

Rhode Island

(5 counties)

2276 *Bristol County*

Town of Bristol, Rhode Island— The town of Bristol, Rhode Island, for which this county was named, was originally part of England's Plymouth Colony. The town of Bristol became part of Rhode Island on May 28, 1746, when a change was made by the British parliament to the boundary line between the colonies of Massachusetts Bay and Rhode Island & Providence Plantations. The town of Bristol, which is now the county seat of Bristol County, Rhode Island, was first settled about 1669 and it was involved in King Philip's War of 1675–1676. Bristol was bombarded by British ships in 1775 and it was invaded, pillaged and burned by the British in 1778, during the American Revolution. At one time the town of Bristol was important in the whale-fishing industry. Today it is a residential community. Sources dealing with the history of Rhode Island, Massachusetts and Plymouth Colony fail to provide a solid date for the creation of Bristol County, Rhode Island. Those that give any information at all are agreed that Bristol County, Rhode Island, was created on "February 17, 1746-7." At that time, the new Rhode Island county consisted of two towns, Bristol and Warren. The town of Bristol in New England was named for the town of Bristol in England, a seaport in Avon County. In the 17th century, when our town of Bristol was named, the city of Bristol, England was second in importance to London. Bristol, England, is located in southwestern England, about 110 miles west of London, at the confluence of the Avon and Frome Rivers. Its population was estimated to be 400,000 in 1981. During an English Civil War, Bristol was cap-

tured in 1643 by royalists, under Prince Rupert (1619–1682) but recaptured by parliamentary forces in 1645. During the 17th and 18th centuries Bristol was active in maritime trade, dealing in Black slaves from West Africa, cocoa, tobacco and sugar. Bristol was repeatedly bombed by the German air force during the second World War. The name *Bristol* derived from a name dating back to about the eleventh century. Several translations have been offered and they are quite similar:

— "Assembly place by" (or "near") the bridge"

— "The shrine near the bridge"

— "The site of the bridge"

— "Bridge-place"

There has been, from time immemorial, a bridge over the Avon River at Bristol. It was apparently near this bridge that the settlement of Bristol grew to become the major city that it is today.

2277 *Kent County*

Kent County, England— This county was created on June 11, 1750, while Rhode Island was still a colony of England, and it was named for Kent County, in southeastern England. This section of England was once a separate Anglo-Saxon kingdom. The kingdom converted to Roman Christianity in A.D. 597, making it the first Christian kingdom in England. Kent was absorbed by Wessex in the ninth century. The English county's name probably derived from the Celt's *canto*, meaning "rim, border, border land" or "district."

2278 *Newport County*

Town of Newport, Rhode Island— This county was created on June 22, 1703, with

the name Rhode Island County. At that time, the town of Newport was designated as its "shire-town," or county seat, and Newport County included all of Rhode Island that was not within Providence County (which then was called Providence Plantations). The county's name was changed to Newport on June 16, 1729, the name being taken from the county seat. Much earlier, in 1639, Newport had been settled as a colony at the southern end of the island of Rhode Island, in Narragansett Bay. The founders of the colony of Newport included William Coddington (1601–1678), John Clarke (1609–1676) and others. Their move to Newport was prompted by both a preference for the geographic setting there (compared to Portsmouth, from whence they had come) and dissatisfaction with the religious views at Portsmouth. Newport's status as a separate colony was never more than a theory, but the town survived, and with its excellent harbor its seaport became an early rival of the ports at Boston and New York. In colonial times Newport, Rhode Island's shipbuilding industry was important but not long after the American Revolution Newport's reputation came to rest on its fine resorts and the magnificent estates of the wealthy Americans who chose to live here. In the late 1990's, Newport retains its affluence although the city has grown to a population of 28,000. Newport here in Rhode Island was named for the community named Newport, on the Isle of Wight in England. Thus both of the ports named Newport, in New England and old England are located on islands. Newport on the Isle of Wight, in England is the county seat of Isle of Wight County. The name *Newport* in old England was applied because this settlement provided the port, or harbor, for the adjacent town of Carisbrooke. Situated near the center of the Medina River, which is navigable from Newport to the English Channel, Newport, England ascended in importance as Carisbrooke declined.

2279 *Providence County*

Providence Plantations— Roger Williams (–1683) was forced to flee from Massachusetts because his religious and political views were unacceptable there, and in 1636 he established the settlement of Providence here. Williams coined the name *Providence* when he thanked God for delivering him here. In later years Williams wrote a letter which elaborated a bit on the name. That letter stated that "having in a sense of God's merciful providence unto me in my distress called the place Providence, I desired it to be for a shelter for persons distressed of conscience." Williams went to England and there he received a patent in March 1644, which gave him authority over "Providence Plantations in Narragansett Bay." From 1644 to 1647 Portsmouth, Newport and Warwick were added to the original settlement at Providence and together they comprised Providence Plantations. On June 22, 1703, what we now know as the state of Rhode Island was divided into two portions: (1) Rhode Island County (now known as Newport County) and (2) Providence Plantations. Although this name, Providence Plantations, was officially changed to Providence County on June 16, 1729, the name lives on as a part of the official name of the state. At the millennium year 2000, the state's official name is "State of Rhode Island and Providence Plantations," and that longer version of the name is the one that appears on the letterhead of agencies of the state government.

2280 *Washington County*

George Washington (1732–1799)— Washington was a native of Virginia, who served in Virginia's house of burgesses and became one of the colonies' leaders in opposition to British policies in America. He was a member of the first and second Continental Congresses and commander of all Continental armies in the Revolutionary War. Following victory in that war, Washington was elected to be the first president of the United States. The land of this county was held in the mid-1600's by the Narragansett proprietors and known as the Narragansett country. Its name was soon changed to King's Province and then, in June 1729, the area was incorporated as King's County. By October 29, 1781, that name had become repugnant in Revolutionary Rhode Island so it was changed to Washington County on that date, at a time when the efforts of our Revolutionary commander in-chief were drawing to a successful conclusion.

REFERENCES

Arnold, James N. *The Narragansett Historical Register*, Vol. 2. Hamilton, Rhode Island: 1883–84.

Bicknell, Thomas W. *The History of the State of Rhode Island & Providence Plantations.* New York, American Historical Society, Inc., 1920.

Clements, John. *Connecticut Facts: Rhode Island Facts.* Dallas, Texas, Clements Research II, Inc., 1990.

Connecticut, Massachusetts, Rhode Island Tour Book. Heathrow, Florida, AAA Publishing, 1998.

Dewar, George A. B. *Hampshire: With the Isle of Wight.* London, J. M. Dent & Co., 1901.

Dexter, Franklin B. "The History of Connecticut as Illustrated by the Names of Her Towns." *Proceedings of the American Antiquarian Society*, Vol. 3. Worcester, Massachusetts: 1885.

Ekwall, Eilert. *The Concise Oxford Dictionary of English Place-Names.* Oxford, Oxford University Press, 1960.

Faragher, John M. *The Encyclopedia of Colonial & Revolutionary America.* New York, Facts on File, 1990.

Fletcher, Christine. *100 Keys: Names Across the Land.* Nashville, Abingdon Press, 1973.

Goodwin, Daniel. "The Counties of Rhode Island." *The Magazine of History*, Vol. 16, No. 2. Poughkeepsie, New York: February, 1913.

Greene, Arnold W. *The Providence Plantations for Two Hundred Fifty Years.* Providence, Rhode Island, J. A. & R. A. Reid, 1886.

A Handbook for Travelers in Surrey, Hampshire and the Isle of Wight. London, John Murray, 1865.

James, Sydney V. *Colonial Rhode Island: A History.* New York, Charles Scribner's Sons, 1975.

Johnson, James. *Place Names of England & Wales.* London, England, Bracken Books, 1994.

Kenyon, J. P. *Dictionary of British History.* Ware, England, Wordsworth Editions, Ltd., 1992.

McLoughlin, William G. *Rhode Island: A History.* New York, W. W. Norton & Co., Inc., 1978.

Mills, A.D. *A Dictionary of English Place Names.* Oxford, Oxford University Press, 1991.

Stanhope, Clarence. *In and Around Newport.* Newport, Rhode Island, Daily News Job Print, 1893.

Stewart, George R. *Names on the Land.* New York, Random House, 1945.

Vexler, Robert I. *Chronology & Documentary Handbook of the State of Rhode Island.* Dobbs Ferry, New York, Oceana Publications, Inc., 1979.

Wheeler, Lucia H. *Official Chronicle & Tribute Book of Rhode Island & Providence Plantations.* Providence Tercentenary Committee, 1936.

Works Progress Administration. *Rhode Island: A Guide to the Smallest State.* Boston, Houghton Mifflin Co., 1937.

Wrenn, C. L. "The Name Bristol." *Names: Journal of the American Name Society*, Vol. 5, No. 2. Berkeley: June, 1957.

Wright, Marion I., & Robert J. Sullivan. *The Rhode Island Atlas.* Providence, Rhode Island Publications Society, 1982.

South Carolina

(46 counties)

2281 *Abbeville County*

Town of Abbeville, South Carolina— This county in western South Carolina was created in March, 1785, and named for the town of Abbeville, which is the present county seat of Abbeville County. A group of French Huguenots settled in this area in 1764. Dr. John de la Howe was among those

French settlers and when Dr. Howe was selected to choose a name for the community, he named it for his former home in France, Abbeville. One of America's leading statesmen, John C. Calhoun (1782–1850) was born in Abbeville, South Carolina, and he practiced law here. In the closing weeks of the Civil War, Confederate President Jefferson Davis (1808–1889) held a final meeting with the remnants of his depleted cabinet on May 2, 1865, in Abbeville, South Carolina. In the late 1990's the population of Abbeville, South Carolina, was 5,800.

Abbeville, France— On the Somme River, in northwestern France, near the English Channel, Abbeville lies about 25 miles northwest of Amiens, France. Near the end of the ninth century A.D. Abbeville became the capital of the countship of Ponthieu. Control of this region passed to Castile and then to England. The French crown acquired it in A.D. 1690. During World War I Abbeville served as a base for the Allied military and during World War II it was under German control from May, 1940, to September, 1944. In the mid-1970's Abbeville's population was about 25,000.

2282 *Aiken County*

Town of Aiken, South Carolina— Aiken County was created on March 10, 1871, and named for the town of Aiken, South Carolina, which is now a city and the county seat. The town of Aiken was platted in September, 1834, and officially chartered by the state on December 19, 1835. The town was born as a result of the construction of a 136 mile railroad between Charleston, South Carolina, and the then-important town of Hamburg, on the Savannah River. A goal in laying railroad tracks here was to preserve Charleston's preeminence as the South's port for trade to Europe and the North. The city of Savannah, Georgia was threatening that preeminence because of its easy access, by river to Hamburg. The railroad was built by the South Carolina Canal & Railroad Company, under the leadership of its president, William Aiken (–1831) and Alexander Black. The tracks were successfully laid at a cost of almost one million dollars and the town of Aiken soon became popular as a summer retreat for residents of Charleston. A Civil War skirmish was fought at Aiken on February 11, 1865, during the infamous plundering of Georgia and South Carolina by Union General Sherman. After the Civil War and Reconstruction, Aiken became a popular winter resort for visitors from the North.

A number of sources dealing with the history and place names of South Carolina indicate that Aiken County's name honors William Aiken (1806–1887), who was governor of South Carolina and represented the state in the U.S. House of Representatives. That is incorrect and the error is pointed out by other authorities on South Carolina's history and place names, who remind us that the county derived its name from the town of Aiken and that the town was named for William Aiken (–1831), the president of the South Carolina Canal & Railroad Company, whose 136 miles of railroad tracks resulted in the birth of the town of Aiken. William Aiken (–1831) and Alexander Black were the decision makers behind this railroad track. This William Aiken met his death in 1831 when his horse accidentally threw him from his buggy.

2283 *Allendale County*

Town of Allendale, South Carolina— Allendale County was created in 1919 and named for the town of Allendale, South Carolina, which is its county seat. A town was settled here as early as 1840 but it was not incorporated until 1873. The town was named for a member of the family who lived here for generations, the Allen family. Specifically, the town was named for the elder Paul H. Allen, who was the first postmaster of Allendale. He lived in Allendale and owned large tracts of land in the town and adjacent areas.

2284 *Anderson County*

Robert Anderson (1741–1813)— A native of Virginia, Anderson grew up on the family's comfortable Virginia farm and entered the surveying profession. After moving to South Carolina he served in the American Revolution. At one time he held the rank of sergeant and by 1775 he had been promoted to captain. Anderson served for several years under Andrew Pickens (1739–1817), his friend and neighbor. After the victory of our forces at the battle of Cowpens, South Carolina, in January, 1781, Pickens was promoted to brigadier-general, and Robert Anderson was promoted to colonel. Anderson also participated in combat in Georgia at Augusta, and in South Carolina at Musgrove's Mill. After the Revolution Anderson assisted in removing Cherokee Indians from South Carolina and fought in other Indian actions. He also served in the South Carolina legislature and farmed his land within the bounds of the present Anderson County.

At the time of Anderson's death in January, 1813, he had attained the rank of general in the state militia, owned an estate consisting of 2,100 acres and was a slave-owner. This county was created and named in Robert Anderson's honor in 1826.

2285 *Bamberg County*

Town of Bamberg, South Carolina— This county in central South Carolina was created in 1897 and named for the town of Bamberg, its present county seat. The settlement here was once known as Lowry's Turnout and it was a station on the stage coach route from Augusta, Georgia, to Charleston, South Carolina. The Bamberg family purchased this stage coach station and both the station and the community came to be known as Bamberg, in honor of that family. The town of Bamberg was incorporated in 1855. In the middle of the 20th century the town had a population of 2,000.

2286 *Barnwell County*

Uncertain— This county was created in 1798 and most sources dealing with the history, geography and place names of South Carolina state that it was named for John Barnwell, a general during the American Revolution. However, Joyce S. O'Bannon's article in the Winter, 1968 issue (Vol. 15) of *Names in South Carolina* indicates that the county's name probably honors both John Barnwell and his brother Robert Barnwell (1761–1814).

John Barnwell (–)— John Barnwell was a member of the provincial congress in 1775–1776, and a general in the South Carolina militia during the American Revolution. John Barnwell was a member of the both houses of the South Carolina legislature and he was elected to the fourth congress of the infant United States of America in 1795, but declined to serve.

Robert Barnwell (1761–1814)— A native of Beaufort in England's province of South Carolina, Robert Barwell entered our Revolutionary army when he was only about 16 years old. During the siege of Charleston in 1780 Robert Barnwell held the rank of lieutenant, was captured by the British and held as a prisoner of war until 1781. Robert Barnwell was a South Carolina delegate to the third Continental Congress in 1788–1789. He subsequently represented South Carolina in the U.S. House of Representatives, from October 24, 1791, to March 2, 1793, and then served in both houses of South Carolina's state legislature.

Although not mentioned as a possible namesake for this county by any of the South Carolina sources consulted, it seems at least possible that Barnwell County was named for the village of Barnwell, its present county seat. That village was referred to as both Red Hill and Barnwell at the start of the American Revolution, and perhaps earlier. If so, the Barnwell who had been prominent in South Carolina, for whom the village of Barnwell might have been named was John Barnwell (–1724).

John Barnwell (–1724)—Born in Ireland about 1671, this John Barnwell immigrated to the southern portion of England's province of Carolina in 1701 and served the crown during Queen Anne's War and in actions against the Indians in the present North Carolina. About 1710 he was deputy secretary and clerk of the provincial council. In 1720, in London, England, this John Barnwell participated in discussions concerning the appropriate government for South Carolina following the proprietary era. The following year he supervised the erection of Fort King George, a wooden blockhouse at the mouth of the Altamaha River, near the present Brunswick, Georgia. He died in South Carolina in June, 1724.

2287 *Beaufort County*

Town of Beaufort, South Carolina— This seaport community at South Carolina's southern tip, on the Atlantic Ocean's Port Royal Sound, was established in 1710 or 1711 by charter from the lords proprietor of Carolina. The area had been explored two centuries earlier by Spain and the general area was long controlled by Spain. It was not until 1690 that England established a firm foothold at Beaufort. In the late 1990's the town's population was 9,600. The town was named for Henry Somerset, Duke of Beaufort (1684–1714) and when Beaufort County was established in 1768 or 1769, it was named for the town which became its county seat.

Henry Somerset, Duke of Beaufort (1684–1714)— In 1663 England's King Charles II (1630–1685) had granted proprietorships in Carolina to eight Englishmen. These proprietary interests in Carolina passed from generation to generation as proprietors died. In some cases these proprietary interests were sold. By 1729, when the Carolina charter was surrendered to the English crown, nearly 50 different individuals had served as proprietors of Carolina or had been entitled to do so. Henry Somerset, duke of Beaufort was one of the later proprietors. He inherited his Carolina proprietorship in 1707, from his mother, Lady Rebecca Granville. Henry Somerset was born at Monmouth castle in 1684 and by 1702 he became acquainted with Queen Anne (1665–1714). In 1705 he became a member of England's house of lords. A pillar of the Tory party, Somerset subsequently was made lord lieutenant of the English counties of Hampshire and Gloucestershire and of the cities of Bristol and Gloucester. In 1712 he was made a knight of the garter.

2288 *Berkeley County*

Uncertain— On May 10, 1682, the lords proprietors of the English province of Carolina instructed officials at Charles Town to establish three counties, to serve as election districts. One of these three was Berkeley County and it consisted of Charles Town (the present Charleston, South Carolina) and the surrounding area. The present Berkeley County in South Carolina was created two centuries later, on January 31, 1882, from the northern portion of Charleston County, South Carolina. Its borders include part of the Berkeley County that was created in 1682. Sources dealing with the history, geography and place names of South Carolina are not unanimous in their opinions about this county's namesake. Some say the name honors John Berkeley (–1678), others say the honor belongs to William Berkeley (1606–1677), and still others say that the county's name honors both John Berkeley and William Berkeley. John Berkeley and William Berkeley were brothers and both of them were among the eight original proprietors of Carolina. In 1663 England's King Charles II (1630–1685) had granted proprietorships in Carolina to eight Englishmen. These proprietary interests in Carolina passed from generation to generation as proprietors died. In some cases these proprietary interests were sold. By 1729, when the Carolina charter was surrendered to the English crown, nearly 50 different individuals had served as proprietors of Carolina or had been entitled to do so.

John Berkeley, Baron Berkeley of Stratton (–1678)—John Berkeley, the first baron Berkeley of Stratton, was one of the original eight proprietors of Carolina. He was probably born in 1607, since that was the year he was baptized. The list of his honors and titles is endless. He served England's King Charles I (1600–1649) as a special ambassador to Sweden and upon his return to England entered the English army as an officer to fight the Scots. He was knighted, served as a member of parliament and fought for King Charles I during the English Civil War. He was raised to the English peerage, and made a member of the admiralty staff. When Charles II (1630–1685) became king, John Berkeley was made privy councillor, a master of ordnance and lord-lieutenant of Ireland. This John Berkeley was also one of the proprietors of New Jersey.

William Berkeley (1606–1677)— William Berkeley, also one of the original eight proprietors of Carolina, was born and educated in England. He was knighted by King Charles I (1600–1649), who made him royal governor of England's North American colony of Virginia. He served here as Virginia's royal governor from 1642 to 1677, except for eight years during England's Civil War. Thus he was Virginia's royal governor under King Charles I and returned to that office in 1660 when the monarchy was restored under King Charles II (1630–1685). He resided in Virginia while he was governor, although he made several trips to England and he died in England on July 9, 1677.

2289 *Calhoun County*

John C. Calhoun (1782–1850)— A native of South Carolina and a lawyer, Calhoun served in the South Carolina legislature and represented the state in both houses of the U.S. Congress. He served as secretary of war, secretary of state and as vice-president. He was a forceful advocate of slavery, states' rights and limited powers for the federal government. At the urging of Vice-President Calhoun, a South Carolina convention voted to nullify two federal tariff acts. This action infuriated President Andrew Jackson and Calhoun resigned the vice-presidency. This enabled him to enter the U.S. Senate where he thought he could better represent the views of South Carolina and the South. This county was created on February 14, 1908.

2290 *Charleston County*

City of Charleston, South Carolina— Initially named Albemarle Point, the settlement's name was changed to Charles Town, in honor of the reigning king of England, King Charles II (1630–1685), by order in a letter dated November 1, 1670, from Anthony Ashley Cooper, Baron Ashley (1621–1683). Located on nearby Albemarle Point, when originally founded in 1670, the town was moved to its present location ten years later. However, the municipality's name was not officially changed to Charleston until August 13, 1783. This seaport city served as South Carolina's capital, until the 1780's when the capital was relocated to Columbia. Older sections of the city feature narrow streets and magnificent architecture. In the late 1990's Charleston had a population of 80,400 and remained one of the last bastions of Southern gentility. Charleston County was created as a judicial district in 1769 and as a county on March 12, 1785. It was named for the beautiful seaport city, which is its county seat.

King Charles II (1630–1685)— In 1649 King Charles I (1600–1649) lost the throne of England to revolutionary forces headed by Oliver Cromwell (1599–1658) and the king was beheaded. Cromwell and his associates ruled England until the monarchy was restored in 1660 when Charles II became king of England. At that time, Charles II was the eldest surviving son of King Charles I and Queen Henrietta Maria (1609–1669). As England's king under the restored monarchy, Charles II found it necessary to become an artful politician and appease various factions needed for preservation of the monarchy. In many ways Charles II skillfully accomplished the required Machiavellian gamesmanship. In light of this it seems difficult to understand the king's reckless disregard of public opinion concerning two subjects: Religion and marital fidelity. Regarding religion, King Charles II rather openly flirted with Roman Catholicism, which he could hardly have failed to notice was unpopular in England. With respect to marital fidelity, King Charles II had little or none. On May 21, 1662, he married Catherine of Braganza (1638–1705). In the years that followed he had several mistresses. (One whole book is devoted to them: *The Mistresses of Charles II* by Brian Masters.) Although King Charles II had many children, none of them were legitimate so when King Charles II died in 1685, his brother, James (1633–1701) became king.

2291 *Cherokee County*

Cherokee Indians— The Cherokee Indians were a large and powerful tribe who lived in North Carolina, Georgia and Tennessee at the time of their first contact with Europeans. They were the most powerful Indian tribe in North Carolina. By the early 1800's they had adopted many of the features of civilization but by 1840, most Cherokees had been forced from their lands and removed to Indian territory (now Oklahoma) by court decisions,

a fraudulent treaty and military force. The removal of some 17,000 Cherokee Indians from their ancient tribal lands in western North Carolina, northwestern Georgia and eastern Tennessee was a dark chapter in our nation's history. Their journey to Indian territory was marked by indescribable suffering from which some 4,000 Cherokees died. A few Cherokee Indians refused to join the forced march to Indian territory and other Cherokees have returned from Oklahoma. The name Cherokee is said to be derived from the Cherokee word for "fire," *chera*. This county was created February 25, 1897.

2292 *Chester County*

Chester County, Pennsylvania— Scotch-Irish emigrants from Chester County, Pennsylvania settled here in the northern part of South Carolina in the middle of the 18th century. When this county was created on March 12, 1785, it was named in honor of the settlers' former home in Chester County, Pennsylvania.

Chester County, Pennsylvania — Chester County, Pennsylvania, was one of the three original counties which William Penn (1644–1718) established in his English province of Pennsylvania in 1682. He named it for the English city of Chester.

Chester, England — This city in western England, is the administrative center of Cheshire County. Its climate is harsh in spite of the moderating influence of the nearby Irish Sea. Conquered, named and occupied by the Roman Empire in the first century A.D., the Roman's name for Chester was *Cestre*, similar to the present Cheshire. The Romans were long gone when William I the Conqueror (1027–1087) invaded England and was crowned its king. He made it his business to send troops north soon after his arrival, to quell rebels here in Chester and in Wales. For a period of time Cheshire County's ports had a virtual monopoly on the trade between England and Ireland but by 1600 the port of Chester was no longer viable on account of silting. Chester was granted a royal charter in 1506. Little more than a century later, the city was badly battered during the decade-long English Civil Wars, which began in 1642. By the middle of the 18th century, Chester was a prosperous and quiet country town. The population of all of Cheshire County, England, in 1981 was slightly more than 900,000 crowded into just 928 square miles.

2293 *Chesterfield County*

Philip Dormer Stanhope, Earl of Ches-

terfield (1694–1773)— This county was created on March 12, 1785, and named for the fourth earl of Chesterfield, an Englishman who is remembered for espousing the importance of proper manners, aristocratic elegance and wit. He established himself high in England's snobbish pecking order by an appointment as gentleman of the bedchamber to the prince of Wales, who in 1727 came to the throne as King George II (1683–1760). Following this early coup, Chesterfield was the recipient of a series of prestigious positions and titles, including member of parliament, secretary of state and lord lieutenant of Ireland. He succeeded to the English peerage in 1726. His fame reached both sides of the Atlantic Ocean in 1774 when letters which he had written to his son were published. These letters dealt with conduct, manners and sophisticated social behavior.

2294 *Clarendon County*

Edward Hyde, Earl of Clarendon (1609–1674)— In 1663 England's King Charles II (1630–1685) had granted proprietorships in Carolina to eight Englishmen. These proprietary interests in Carolina passed from generation to generation as proprietors died. In some cases these proprietary interests were sold. By 1729, when the Carolina charter was surrendered to the English crown, nearly 50 different individuals had served as proprietors of Carolina or had been entitled to do so. Edward Hyde, the first earl of Clarendon (1609–1674) was one of the original eight lords proprietors and England's King Charles II had good reason to be fond of him. In 1642 Hyde had joined the king's father, King Charles I (1600–1649), at York, during the English Civil War and he remained loyal to the crown throughout the Civil War and supported the new king of England, Charles II (1630–1685), when he ascended the throne in 1660. Knighted in 1643, Hyde had become the most trusted advisor of King Charles II, and in a sense, was the head of the English government. In this role he made enemies and they succeeded in having Hyde charged with treason and exiled. Although this South Carolina county was not created until 1785, when the first earl of Clarendon had been long forgotten in Carolina, his name had lingered on in South Carolina place names. During the 1700's Clarendon was one of the subdivisions comprising the Camden district. Also, North Carolina's Cape Fear River, or at least the lower portion of it, was known at one time as the Clarendon River. That river enters the Atlantic Ocean in North Carolina, only 30 miles beyond the South Carolina border.

2295 *Colleton County*

John Colleton (1608–1666)— On May 10, 1682, the lords proprietor of the English province of Carolina instructed officials at Charles Town to establish three counties, to serve as election districts. One of these three was Colleton County. The present Colleton County in South Carolina was created a century later, on March 12, 1785. In 1663 England's King Charles II (1630–1685) had granted proprietorships in Carolina to eight Englishmen. These proprietary interests in Carolina passed from generation to generation as proprietors died. In some cases these proprietary interests were sold. By 1729, when the Carolina charter was surrendered to the English crown, nearly 50 different individuals had served as proprietors of Carolina or had been entitled to do so. John Colleton (1608–1666) was one of the original eight lords proprietors. He was born in England and was loyal to the crown during the English Civil War. He fought as an army officer for King Charles I (1600–1649) and spent 40,000 pounds of his own fortune to support the king's cause. During the period that the monarchy was deposed and Oliver Cromwell (1599–1658) ruled England, John Colleton established himself on the island of Barbados, in the West Indies as a financier, planter and confidant of the local governor. He also held high office in the government of Barbados. About 1660, when Charles II (1630–1685) ascended to the throne which had been stripped from his father, John Colleton returned to England from Barbados and in 1663 he became one of the original eight lords proprietors of Carolina.

2296 *Darlington County*

Uncertain— An article in the Winter, 1955, issue (Vol. 2) of *Names in South Carolina* tells us that "The name Darlington was given to one of the counties set off from the Cheraw District in 1785. It is generally conceded that it was named for the town of Darlington, Durham County, England, although there is no historical data available to support this fact." *Palmetto Place Names*, published in 1941, stated that "Tradition says it was named for the town of Darlington, England, but the reason for this is not known. Another version is that the name may have honored Colonel Darlington of the Revolutionary War." A history of Darlington County, South Carolina, edited by Eliza C. Ervin and Horace F. Rudisill quoted Robert Mills' 1826 *Statistics of South Carolina*: "It is presumed to have been named in honor of Colonel Darlington, who distinguished himself in the Revolutionary War." In an adjacent sentence, Ervin and Rudisill's work states that "Some think it may have been named for Darlington, England." Since the county seat of Darlington County, South Carolina, is the municipality of Darlington, it might seem that Darlington, South Carolina, would be another possible namesake of Darlington County. However, we are safe in removing this possibility from our list. No municipality existed at the present site of Darlington until after Darlington County was created. The site for the county seat of Darlington County was selected after the county was created and the town of Darlington did not receive its first charter until December 19, 1835. The much discussed Darlington municipality in England lies 17 miles south of Durham, on the Skerne River, near its junction with the Tees River. Its name apparently came from *Dearthingtun*, which meant "estate associated with a man called Deornoth."

2297 *Dillon County*

Town of Dillon, South Carolina— The town of Dillon in eastern South Carolina had a 1980 population of 6,231 and it is the present county seat of Dillon County. The town grew from a small railroad station which was erected in 1887 or 1888 by the Florence Railroad Company, when they extended railroad tracks here. The railroad had been induced to route its tracks through upper Marion County, South Carolina (now detached from Marion as Dillon County) by James W. Dillon (1826–). Dillon and his son, Thomas A. Dillon, had obtained options to buy about 50 acres of land where the municipality of Dillon now stands and they offered title to half of it to the Florence Railroad Company on condition that the railroad route its tracks through this land and afterwards "locating and putting up a Depot and laying out a town by the name of Dillon upon the lands." The railroad accepted the offer, James W. Dillon and his son exercised their options to buy the land and deeded half interest in it to the Florence Railroad Company.

James W. Dillon (1826–)— Born November 25, 1826, in the portion of Marion County, South Carolina that would later become Dillon County, James William Dillon was a son of a relatively prosperous local farming family. He entered the mercantile business at Little Rock (not Arkansas, but Marion County, South Carolina) in 1853. Durward T. Stokes' 1978 work entitled *The History of Dillon County, South Carolina* states that Dillon entered his business venture with modest capital "and despite financial setback caused by the fall of the Confederacy, had accumulated a respectable estate." Backed by these financial resources James W. Dillon induced the railroad to erect a station and town here named Dillon.

Dillon County was created on February 5, 1910, and named for the town of Dillon, which became the county seat of the new county.

2298 *Dorchester County*

Town of Dorchester, South Carolina— This county was created on February 25, 1897, and named for the town of Dorchester, South Carolina. That town is not the county seat of Dorchester County, but it does lie within the county's borders. In January, 1696, a group of immigrants to Carolina from New England established a town site on a high bluff above the Ashley River. They named their new settlement Dorchester, in honor of the Massachusetts town of that name. That Massachusetts' town is now part of metropolitan Boston but it was originally settled, independent of Boston, probably in the 1630's. The origin of Dorchester, Massachusetts' name is probably the town of that name in England. William H. Whitmore wrote an article entitled "On the Origin of the Names of Towns in Massachusetts," which appeared in the 1871–1873 issue (Vol. 12) of *Proceedings of the Massachusetts Historical Society*. In that article Whitmore stated that "Blake, writing a century after settlement says, 'Why they called it Dorchester, I have never heard; but there was some of Dorset Shire, and some of y Town [sic] of Dorchester, that settled here; and it is very likely that it might be in Honour of y aforesaid Rev. Mr. White, of Dorchester.'" Since the settlers of England's Massachusetts Bay Colony, where Dorchester was founded, came from England, the references to "Dorset Shire" and "y Town [sic] of Dorchester" referred to the county, or shire, of Dorset, and its county seat, Dorchester, in England. George R. Stewart takes a more courageous stand on the origin or Dorchester, Massachusetts' name. In his *American Place Names*, published in 1970, Stewart states that "Dorchester in MA named from the town in England by the General Court Sept. 7, 1630." When the Roman Empire ruled Dorchester, England, they called the town there *Durnovaria*. By A.D. 1086 this had evolved to *Dorecestre*. The *cestre* portion of this name referred back to the former Roman occupation but the *Dor* portion of the name is a puzzle. One source speculates that it may have referred to "fist sized pebbles," while another source also associates *dor* with "fists" but these fists were the ones during "fist plays" at a Roman amphitheater here.

2299 *Edgefield County*

Descriptive of location—This county was created on March 12, 1785. Its county seat is the municipality of Edgefield. Carlee T. McClendon's article entitled "Edgefield County Towns & Communities," which appeared in the Winter, 1983, issue (Vol. 30) of *Names in South Carolina* stated that when the village and county of Edgefield were founded, a man named Simkins named them. "His plantation was on the edge of the village, also, an Indian battlefield dating to 1750 was on the southern end. Hence the name Edgefield." An article in the Winter, 1964, issue (Vol. 11) of *Names in South Carolina*, entitled "Names of Plantations & Homes in Edgefield County" provides elaboration. That article tells us that Arthur Simkins emigrated from Virginia to South Carolina in 1772 and soon established a plantation among cedar trees here, which he named Cedar Fields. "The traditional origin of the name of the town or village of Edgefield is that it is located on the edge of an Indian battlefield. In May, 1750, a party of Monangahela [sic] Indians ... to attack the Euchees .... The Monongahelas [sic] were defeated and fled, the Euchees pursuing.... They passed through the present town site of Edgefield.... This battle ... was fought on the edge of large fields near this present old court house village." This 1964 article then goes on to indicate Arthur Simkins probable role in the naming process, pointing out that he was one of the commissioners assigned to divide the district into counties, "and since his plantation ... was already named Cedar Fields, the name Edgefield would have been natural to him." Both the *Handbook of South Carolina* and *Palmetto Place Names* indicate that the county's name was more likely chosen because its edge bordered the state of Georgia.

2300 *Fairfield County*

Uncertain—Several sources on the history, geography and place names of South Carolina mention a tradition that the English army general, Charles Cornwallis (1738–1805) complimented this area during the American Revolution. He is quoted as saying "How fair these fields." It is true that General Cornwallis had his headquarters within the present Fairfield County, South Carolina, and thus was familiar with its fields and their beauty. After Cornwallis was defeated at the battle of King's Mountain on the border between the two Carolinas, he retreated and established headquarters at Winnsboro, which is within what is now Fairfield County, South Carolina. He stayed here from October, 1780, until January, 1781. However Charles E. Thomas, writing on Fairfield County's names in the Winter, 1965, issue (Vol. 12) of *Names in South Carolina* tells us that historians doubt that Fairfield County was named because of praise by General Cornwallis. *Ederington's History of Fairfield County, South Carolina* indicates that the county was first settled by emigrants from Virginia and North Carolina, who probably named it "...from the grateful appearance which it made in the eyes of wanderers, weary with long looking for a resting place." A skeptical reader detects a good deal of guesswork behind this explanation and even the origin of the first settlers is suspect. John Clements' *South Carolina Facts* tells us that they were from both Pennsylvania and South Carolina's low country. Julian S. Bolick's *A Fairfield Sketchbook* mentions a number of possible origins for this county's name, one of which is rather unique in the annals of county-naming: "...in all probability it owes its name to the mere good pleasure of the author of the act." This county was established as a subdivision of Camden district in 1785 but did not establish its separate identity until passage of an act in 1798. Either date is late enough to accommodate the General Cornwallis-naming theory if one is so inclined.

2301 *Florence County*

City of Florence, South Carolina—This county in the northeastern portion of South Carolina was created on December 23, 1888, and named for the municipality of Florence, which is its county seat. The municipality began its life as a railroad station and the railroad company's president, General William W. Harllee caused the railroad station to be named in honor of his daughter, Florence Henning Harllee (1848–). General Harllee had been inspired to name his daughter Florence, by a character in a then–recent novel by Charles Dickens (1812–1870). That novel's title was *Dealings with the Firm of Dombey & Son*. In the novel, Florence is the neglected daughter of the elder Dombey, whose interest is not a daughter, but a son to perpetuate his firm's name. By 1853 Florence, South Carolina, had become an important railroad junction and during the Civil War, Union prisoners of war were housed just south of the town and many of those prisoners died here from typhoid fever. In the late 1990's the city of Florence had a population of 29,800 and was a major wholesale and retail distribution center.

2302 *Georgetown County*

City of Georgetown, South Carolina—Georgetown County was created on July 29, 1769, and named for the municipality of Georgetown (then called George Town), which was made its county seat. Above Charleston on South Carolina's coast, Georgetown is protected from the Atlantic Ocean by barrier islands. Spain attempted to establish a settlement here as early as 1526 but the settlers succumbed to disease. The first permanent settlers at George Town (renamed Georgetown in 1798) were English colonists who arrived early in the 18th century. George Town emerged as a separate church parish in the early 1720's, named Prince George Winyah. That parish name honored England's prince of Wales, George August (1683–1760), who had been made prince of Wales on October 4, 1714. He later became king of England and ruled as King George II. In the late 1990's South Carolina's city of Georgetown, with a population of 9,500, still retains a Prince George Winyah Church. It is an Episcopal church, located at 300 Broad Street, in Georgetown.

King George II (1683–1760)—George August was the first of two children born to England's King George I (1660–1727) and Sophia Dorothea of Zelle (1666–1726). The parents of young George August both committed adultery, and although Sophia Dorothea acted only in response to her husband's repeated infidelities, King George I had her banished to a grim castle for life. The king extended his animosity toward his exiled wife to young George August, and only deigned to make him prince of Wales in 1714 at the urging of his court advisors. Following the death of King George I, the Prince of Wales ascended the throne as King George II and ruled from 1727 to 1760. During this period England increased in status as a world power and although credit cannot be given to George II for shrewd statesmanship, it must be admitted that he readily accepted advice from those with able judgment. One of his ablest advisors was his own queen consort, Queen Caroline of Anspach (1683–1737).

2303 *Greenville County*

Uncertain— This county was created on March 22, 1786, and the name of its county seat is Greenville. However, we know that the county was not named for this municipality because its name had been Pleasantburg, and that name was not changed to Greenville until the county's name had been selected. Sources dealing with the history, geography and place names of South Carolina offer three possibilities for the origin of this county's name but most of these sources admit that the true answer is uncertain. The choices mentioned are General Nathanael Greene (1742–1786) of Revolutionary War fame, whose actions saved North and South Carolina from the British, (2) Isaac Green (1762–), who operated a grist mill at the falls of the Reedy River here in the heart of what is now the city of Greenville and (3) the verdant appearance of the countryside. An article entitled "Some Greenville Names" appeared in the Winter, 1963 (Vol. 10), issue of *Names in South Carolina* which discusses these three possibilities but fails to muster enthusiasm for any of them. This article indicates that "Public records show that Isaac Green secured his first land grant … in the fall of 1785," and the county was created just six months later "long before he built a mill or became prominent…" James M. Richardson's *History of Greenville County, South Carolina* also discussed these three possibilities and offered some evidence against two of them but concluded that the answer is unknown. Strangely, in "Part II-Biographical" James M. Richardson's work presents some information about Isaac Green (1762–) which offers some support for the Isaac Green-naming theory not found in Richardson's comments earlier in the book when discussing the origin of Greenville County's name. In this "Part II-Biographical" section, Isaac Green (1762–) is depicted as having "…settled in Greenville County, South Carolina, and fought for the Patriot cause during the Revolution, although a very young man." Finally, Nancy Vance Ashmore makes a statement in her 1986 work entitled *Greenville: Woven from the Past: An Illustrated History*, which would tilt the odds toward General Nathanael Greene

(1742–1786). Ashmore stated that "…examination of the original 1786 act and other early documents reveals that the county's name was first spelled 'Greeneville.'" General Greene was certainly popular enough in the Carolina-Tennessee area to suggest that he might well be the namesake of this South Carolina county. North Carolina first created a county to honor General Greene in 1783 but when Tennessee was separated from North Carolina, they took that Greene County with them. In 1799 North Carolina created a Greene County for the second time, named in honor of General Nathanael Greene.

2304 *Greenwood County*

City of Greenwood, South Carolina— This county in western South Carolina was created on March 2, 1897, and named for its city of Greenwood, the county seat. Judge John McGeehee brought his bride to this area in 1824 and built their home which he called Green Wood or Greenwood, because of the lush green forests on beautiful rolling hills. When the town of Greenwood was given its present name, it took the name of Judge McGeehee's lovely home. In the late 1990's the population of the city of Greenwood was 20,800.

2305 *Hampton County*

Wade Hampton (1818–1902)— A native of South Carolina, Hampton served in both houses of the South Carolina legislature prior to the Civil War. By the time South Carolina seceded from the Union, Hampton had become a very wealthy man and he entered the Confederate army as a colonel. He contributed his personal funds as well as his blood to support the Confederate army. Wounded at the first battle of Bull Run, in Virginia and subsequently promoted to brigadier-general, Hampton was wounded again in combat at the battle of Gettysburg. By the end of the war, Wade Hampton had been promoted to the rare three star rank of lieutenant-general. When Reconstruction ended in South Carolina, Wade Hampton became the state's first post-Reconstruction governor. He was inaugurated as South Carolina's governor on December 14, 1876, but was not able to take office until April, 1877, when President Hayes ordered federal (Reconstruction) troops withdrawn from South Carolina. Reelected to a second term, Hampton served as governor until February 26, 1879, when he resigned because of a wound suffered in a hunting accident. This county was created on Feb-

ruary 18, 1878, while Hampton was serving as governor. He later represented South Carolina in the U.S. Senate from 1879 to 1891.

2306 *Horry County*

Peter Horry (–)— This county was created on December 19, 1801, and named for an officer in our Revolutionary army, named Peter Horry. Little is known of his life before and after the Revolution and there are even some conflicting accounts of his Revolutionary War service. It is known that he was a captain in the second South Carolina regiment on June 17, 1775, and that he was promoted to major on September 16, 1776. Peter Horry subsequently served under General Francis Marion (–1795). His brother, Hugh Horry, also served under general Francis Marion and was named a brigadier-general of South Carolina militia. The inconsistencies presented in biographical sketches of Peter Horry may stem from confusion between Peter and Hugh Horry. Some sources indicate that Peter Horry held the ranks of colonel and/or brigadier-general but these statements may or may not be true. If false, the errors are likely due to confusing Peter with Hugh. (Hugh Horry is known to have held the ranks of lieutenant-colonel and brigadier-general.) It is known that Peter Horry was wounded in combat at Eutaw Springs, South Carolina, in 1781. Peter Horry collaborated with Mason L. Weems (1759–1825) in writing a biography of General Francis Marion (–1795), which was published in 1809.

2307 *Jasper County*

William Jasper (–1779)— This Revolutionary War hero was born in South Carolina about 1750, but moved to Georgia where he grew up on a farm. He first became a hero in a dramatic event at the battle of Fort Moultrie, South Carolina, when he courageously exposed himself to enemy fire to recover a flag which had been shot down. For this heroism Sergeant Jasper was awarded a sword and offered a promotion to lieutenant but he declined the promotion. Later employed as a scout, Jasper made several trips behind enemy lines in Georgia while operating from the swamps there. In a dramatic exploit near Savannah, Georgia, he and his close friend, John Newton, rescued several Americans who were prisoners and took their guards as prisoners of war. Jasper was shot and killed during the siege of Savannah while recovering the flag which had been shot down. This county was created and named in Sergeant Jasper's honor on January 30, 1912.

2308 *Kershaw County*

Joseph Kershaw (-) — Joseph Kershaw was one of the founding settlers of the South Carolina community first called Fredericksburg township, then Pine Tree Hill and now Camden, the county seat of Kershaw County. It was Joseph Kershaw who suggested that the community's name be changed to Camden to honor a friend of the American colonies in the English parliament, Charles Pratt, Earl of Camden (1714–1794). This Joseph Kershaw, for whom Kershaw County was named when it was created in 1791, is referred to as Colonel Kershaw of the American Revolution, so he apparently held the rank of colonel or lieutenant-colonel in that war. In 1786 he was foreman of a grand jury and after Kershaw County was created, he became its first sheriff. The county's namesake is easily confused with a later Joseph B. Kershaw (1822–1894), who was born, raised and died in Camden, South Carolina. This later Joseph Kershaw achieved greater fame than the county's namesake, rising to the rank of major-general in the Confederate army. However, Kershaw County was created three decades before he was born.

2309 *Lancaster County*

County and city of Lancaster, Pennsylvania — Lancaster County, South Carolina, was created on March 12, 1785. Its name was suggested by settlers who had come to this area of South Carolina from Lancaster County, in southeastern Pennsylvania. The South Carolina county's name honors Pennsylvania's Lancaster County and its county seat, the city of Lancaster. The county seat of Lancaster County, South Carolina, is also named Lancaster but the South Carolina county was not named for it. We know this because the municipality was called Barnettsville until 1802, long after Lancaster County had been created. The South Carolina city's name was changed to Lancaster in 1802. The earliest settlers of the part of Pennsylvania which is honored in this South Carolina county's name came from England and when a new county was established in Pennsylvania in 1729, it was named Lancaster, in honor of Lancashire, England. The county seat of Lancaster County, Pennsylvania, the city of Lancaster, also owes its name to Lanca-

shire, England. Although the English settlers of southeastern Pennsylvania did much of the naming of places, it was the German immigrants (known as "Pennsylvania-Dutch") who created the local color of Lancaster and Lancaster County, Pennsylvania. Largely self-sufficient German religious communities such as the Amish and Mennonites developed here. Their adherence to the simple and old-fashioned ways of doing things have enchanted many visitors from the fast-track portions of America.

Lancashire, England — The county named Lancashire, in northwestern England, on the Irish Sea has a name that dates back to the time that the Roman Empire occupied England. An early version of its name, Loncastre, meant "Roman fort (or camp) on the river Lune." A later (14th century) version of the name was Lancastreshire, which derived from Lancaster and the Old English word *scir*, which meant "district." Lancashire England is 75 miles long and averages about 30 miles in width. In the northern and eastern portions of the county, mountains can be found which reach altitudes of more than 2,000 feet. Wide moor lands are found between many of these mountains. More land is using for grazing than for planting crops. Iron, coal, slate and other building materials are found in Lancashire. Its city of Liverpool is one of the most important seaports in the United Kingdom and its other principal city, Lancaster, also carries on foreign trade.

2310 *Laurens County*

Henry Laurens (1724–1792) — A native of South Carolina, Laurens became very wealthy as a planter, merchant and slave trader. He served in the provincial assembly of South Carolina for about 16 years starting in 1757 and attempted to reach peaceful reconciliation with England during the years when storm clouds were gathering for the American Revolution. When the English seized three of Laurens' vessels, he had personal as well as patriotic reasons for joining and leading the break from England. He was one of South Carolina's delegates to the second Continental Congress and was elected president of that body on November 1, 1777. Just two weeks later, on November 15, 1777, Laurens was a South Carolina signer of the Articles of Confederation. When the American Revolution drew to a successful conclusion, Henry Laurens joined three other distinguished Americans, John Adams, Benjamin Franklin and John Jay, in sign-

ing a preliminary peace agreement with England on November 30, 1782. This county was created on March 12, 1785. Other names that had been considered for the new county were Downes and Hereford. These proposed names referred to Major Jonathan Downes, of our Revolutionary army and the English county of Herefordshire and its seat, Hereford.

2311 *Lee County*

Robert E. Lee (1807–1870) — Lee was a native of Virginia and, for over 30 years, an officer in the United States army. When Virginia seceded from the Union, Lee refused an offer to command all federal forces and resigned from the U.S. army to accept a commission in the Confederate army. He served with distinction in that army and became general-in-chief of it. By April, 1865, the Confederacy had lost the war and Robert E. Lee surrendered to the commanding general of the Union forces, Ulysses S. Grant. This county was created on February 25, 1902.

2312 *Lexington County*

Battle of Lexington, Massachusetts — This county was created on March 12, 1785, less than three years after the American Revolution had culminated in the signing of a preliminary peace agreement with England, on terms very favorable to our side. Storm clouds had been building on this side of the Atlantic for the nascent Revolution of the colonies against England, but the first real battle of the American Revolution was not fought until April 19, 1775, and it was fought at Lexington, Massachusetts. The British army was headed from Boston to Concord, Massachusetts, when they reached the commons of Lexington at dawn. There, the British met 130 American minutemen, only 70 of them armed, under Captain John Parker (1729–1775). Shots were exchanged and eight of our patriots were killed and eight to ten were wounded. Only one redcoat was wounded. The American Revolutionary War had begun. The town of Lexington, where this battle was fought, was established in Massachusetts Bay colony, by settlers of English ancestry. The date of its incorporation is given as "March 20, 1712–1713" in two articles written by William H. Whitmore which appeared in the 1871–1873 issue (Vol. 12) of *Proceedings of the Massachusetts Historical Society*. One of these articles is entitled "On the Origin of the Name of the Town of Lexington, Massachusetts." In that article Whitmore admitted that the origin of Lexington, Massachusetts' name was unknown, but he discussed at length the strengths and weaknesses of purported origins. Whitmore first effectively refutes the theory advanced by Charles Hudson that the Massachusetts town was named for the English nobleman, Robert Sutton, Baron of Lexington (1661–1723). William H. Whitmore then postulated that Lexington, Massachusetts was likely named for the English manor village of Laxton and that the name was suggested by one or more of the Massachusetts Bay settlers in memory of their former home in Laxton, England. Here Whitmore admitted that facts were in short supply to back him up, but he pointed out that although Lexington was officially incorporated early in the 18th century, it had been "set off as a precinct in 1691, in accordance with a petition made in 1682." Whitmore provides the name Francis Whitmore (1625–) as a key settler in Massachusetts Bay Colony when Lexington was being named. Whitmore's house was within Lexington, Massachusetts, when it was being named and he had connections with Laxton, England. George R. Stewart's *Names on the Land* agrees that Lexington, Massachusetts was named for Laxton, Nottinghamshire, England.

2313 *McCormick County*

Cyrus H. McCormick (1809–1884) — A native of Virginia and the son of a farmer who had patented several farming devices, Cyrus Hall McCormick followed in his father's footsteps and perfected a mechanical agricultural reaping machine, which he patented in 1834. Unlike many other inventive geniuses, McCormick built a financial success story from his invention. He established a factory in Chicago in 1847, and perfected his basic invention to stay ahead of competition. McCormick also traveled widely to demonstrate and market his machines and he became a very wealthy man. According to some South Carolina sources, Cyrus H. McCormick owned thousands of acres of land in what is now McCormick County, South Carolina. This county was created and named in his honor on February 19, 1916.

2314 *Marion County*

Francis Marion (–1795) — Born about 1732, probably in South Carolina, Marion served in the army in battles against the Cherokee Indians and was elected to South Carolina's the provincial congress in 1775. He entered our Revolutionary army as a captain and held the rank of lieutenant-colonel during the dark days following the fall of Savannah, Georgia, and Charleston, South Carolina, to the British. These British victories eliminated organized Revolutionary forces in South Carolina but Marion and his band of trusted guerrillas learned to live from the land and fight the enemy from South Carolina's dense swamps. The success of Marion and his men in swift stealth attacks and departures to the swamps earned him the nickname "Swamp Fox." In 1781 Marion fought effectively in the battle of Eutaw Springs, South Carolina, which congress recognized with a vote of thanks. Marion's highest rank was brigadier-general of militia. After the war he served in South Carolina's senate. He died at his plantation home in South Carolina on February 27, 1795. This county was originally created on March 12, 1785, with the name Liberty County. Its name was changed to Marion in a 1798 act which became effective in 1800.

2315 *Marlboro County*

John Churchill, Duke of Marlborough (1650–1722) — This Englishman rose to prominence by establishing connections with the English royal family and serving, very effectively, as an officer in the English army. He was a page to the future King James II (1633–1701), when James was still duke of York and Churchill later became his confidential servant. In the military, Churchill rose from ensign of foot guards in 1667 commander-in-chief in England in 1690 and captain general of the forces from 1702 to 1711. Made earl of Marlborough in 1689, he acted for a time as virtual regent of England because of his great influence over Queen Anne (1665–1714). Queen Anne made Churchill the first duke of Marlborough in 1702, a title rarely given to a person not of royal birth. His military efforts were outstanding, including important victories at Blenheim, Ramillies and Oudenarde. This South Carolina County was originally created on March 12, 1785, as a subdivision of Cheraw district, named Marlborough and it was separately established in 1800, based on a 1798 act, with its name spelled Marlborough. The spelling of the county's name was changed to the present version, at the instigation of postal officials.

2316 *Newberry County*

Uncertain — Sources dealing with the history, geography and place names of South Carolina are generally agreed that the origin of this county's name is unknown. Nature abhors a vacuum and, in the absence of facts, speculations tend to fill in the void. Speculations encountered concerning the origin of this county's name include (1) reference to the berries found growing in the region, (2) a Revolutionary soldier who served under South Carolina's General Thomas Sumter (1734–1832), named Captain John Newberry, (3) the name of an early settler (or family) who resided in this area and (4) cities either in America or England, named Newbury. George L. Summer's history of Newberry County published in 1950 lists an impressive array of berries to be found in Newberry County: "The edible berries are mostly the blackberries, raspberries (originally cultivated) dewberries, wild strawberries, gooseberries, huckleberries, sparkelberries and sandberries." However, the author cautiously avoids attributing the county's name to these berries. This county was created on March 12, 1785, and the original spelling of the name was Newbury. That tends to refute the theories that the county might have been named for berries or a Revolutionary soldier named Newberry. Thomas H. Pope tells us in his 1973 work entitled *The History of Newberry County, South Carolina* that "John Belton O'Neall, who was born only eight years after the county was established, could not learn the origin of the name even though he had the opportunity of talking to those active in politics at the time." A lengthy article on the origins of South Carolina's county names by Raven I. McDavid and Raymond K. O'Cain, which appeared in the March, 1978, issue (Vol. 26, No. 1) of *Names: Journal of the American Name Society* joins the chorus in admitting that the origin of Newberry County's name is a mystery.

2317 *Oconee County*

Uncertain — This county in northwestern South Carolina was created on January 29, 1868. It lies less than 50 miles northeast of Oconee County, Georgia, which was named for that state's Oconee River. That Oconee River derived its name from a former Oconee Indian settlement called Oconee Old Town, which was about four miles south of Milledgeville, Georgia. The Indians abandoned that village about 1715 and moved to the Chattahoochee River. There was another Indian settlement in our Oconee County, South Carolina, near the present municipality of Walhalla. A number of Indian tribes lived in this section of

South Carolina and Georgia and sources consulted offer differing opinions concerning the identity of the tribe who used the name which we now render as *Oconee*. John Stoutenburgh's *Dictionary of the American Indian* states that the South Carolina Indian settlement belonged to Cherokee Indians. Sources consulted offer numerous translations of the Indian name *Oconee*, some favoring it as a mountain name and others "place of springs." A blending of the two offered by some sources gives us the translation "water eyes of the hills."

2318 *Orangeburg County*

City of Orangeburg, South Carolina— In the mid-1730s England's province of South Carolina had a locality that was named Edisto township. On March 14, 1734, England's Princess Anne (1709–1759) married William IV, Prince of Orange (1711–1751). Princess Anne was the daughter of England's ruling monarch, King George II (1683–1760), and South Carolina's township of Edisto was renamed Orangeburgh, in honor of the king's new son-in-law. Members of the English royal family were frequently honored by having municipalities and counties in the American colonies named for them and Princess Anne was a special princess, for she was the princess royal. It was also an important wedding for the king. It was the custom for English princesses to marry royalty but the king had a problem in selecting a mate for Princess Anne. Most of the fellow monarchs of King George II were Roman Catholics and Anglican England wanted no Catholic in the royal family. However a husband was found. A longer version of his name and title was William Charles Henry, Prince William IV of Orange & Stadtholder of the United Provinces (1711–1751). The prince had an even longer title with Nassau, Friesland Groningen and Guelderland inserted at appropriate intervals and he was also encumbered with physical deformity. John Van der Kiste's *King George II & Queen Caroline* describes Prince William IV as "almost a dwarf," possibly because of curvature of the spine or a tubercular condition. When Orangeburgh County was created, it was named for the municipality or township of Orangeburgh. Orangeburgh County was first created on July 29, 1769, and reestablished on March 12, 1785. Ray O'Cain wrote an article dealing with the place names of Orangeburg County, which appeared in the November, 1966, issue (Vol. 13) of *Names in South Carolina*. In that

article O'Cain commented on the change in spelling of Orangeburgh to Orangeburg, and said that the change was probably initiated by postal authorities who had begun a wholesale campaign of name standardization in 1894. O'Cain also quoted A. S. Salley who remarked in 1898 that "the 'h' had been dropped from Orangeburgh in late years." In the late 1990's the city of Orangeburg had a population of 13,700 and was the county seat of Orangeburg County.

2319 *Pickens County*

Andrew Pickens (1739–1817)— Pickens was a native of Pennsylvania who moved to South Carolina is his youth. He served as a officer in the Revolutionary War and after the victory of our forces at the battle of Cowpens, South Carolina, he was promoted to brigadier-general. Pickens led a successful expedition against the Cherokee Indians in 1782, and gained from them a large strip of territory which later became part of the state of Georgia. He later served in South Carolina's house of representatives and, briefly represented South Carolina in the U.S. House of Representatives. This county was created on December 20, 1826, and named for General Pickens, who had received land grants in this region in compensation for his military services.

2320 *Richland County*

Uncertain— A Richland County was created in South Carolina on March 12, 1785, but it did not survive and the present Richland County was organized in 1799. Colonel Thomas Taylor owned a plantation named "Richland," and since Colonel Taylor was a member of the commission assigned to divide Camden district into smaller political subdivisions, it is reasonable to speculate that Taylor and his Richland plantation played a role in the selection of this county's name. Whether or not the proximate source of the county's name was Colonel Taylor's plantation, South Carolina sources agree that the name derived from a description of "rich land(s)," rather than the name or title of a person.

2321 *Saluda County*

Saluda River— The Saluda River rises in South Carolina's northwestern Blue Ridge Mountains and flows south and east to form Saluda County's northern border and flow through Lake Murray. At nearby Columbia, South Carolina, the Saluda's

waters unite with those of the Broad River to form the Congaree River. The Saluda River's name is of Indian origin and John Stoutenburgh's *Dictionary of the American Indian* indicates that the name applied not just to the river but also to a small band of Shawnee Indians, who lived along the Saluda River in South Carolina. This county was created on February 25, 1896.

2322 *Spartanburg County*

Spartan regiment of South Carolina militia— This county was created on March 12, 1785, less than three years after the American Revolution had culminated in the signing of a preliminary peace agreement with England, on terms very favorable to our side. It was named for the Spartan regiment of the South Carolina militia, who had recently fought very ably during the American Revolution. The Spartan regiment participated in combat in South Carolina at the first battle of Cedar Spring (July, 1780), Musgrove's Mill (August, 1780) and Cowpens (January, 1781). In his *Landmarks of the American Revolution*, Mark M. Boatner points out that the battle of Musgrove's Mill was "significant because it was one of the few times during the American Revolution that untrained militia were able to defeat seasoned British (professional) troops." The Spartan regiment's name recalls Sparta, in ancient Greece, and its stern, military reputation.

2323 *Sumter County*

Thomas Sumter (1734–1832)— Sumter, a native of Virginia, fought in the French and Indian wars and settled in South Carolina. He served as an officer during the American Revolution and rose to the rank of brigadier-general. A strong advocate of states' rights, when Sumter participated in the South Carolina convention called to consider ratification of the proposed federal constitution, he opposed ratification. He subsequently represented South Carolina in both houses of the U.S. Congress. This county was created and named in his honor on December 21, 1798, while Sumter was representing the state in the U.S. House of Representatives. Fort Sumter, South Carolina, was also named in General Sumter's honor.

2324 *Union County*

Union Church— In 1765 a church was erected by settlers at Brown's Creek, South Carolina, and they called their church Union Church. The church was located about four miles from the present town of Union, South Carolina, on what eventually came to be Pinckneyville Road. The church was named "Union," because it was used by more than one Protestant denomination. Sources consulted are generally agreed Episcopalians (Anglicans) and Presbyterians shared the church but the possibility is also mentioned that Quakers (Religious Society of Friends) may also have used it. Union County, South Carolina, was created on March 12, 1785, and named for the Union Church, within its borders. The municipality of Union, which is the county seat of Union County was not organized until 1791.

2325 *Williamsburg County*

Williamsburg township, South Carolina— During the three decades between 1731 and 1761, England's province of South Carolina established about a dozen townships in a band 70 to 120 miles inland from the Atlantic Ocean. One of these townships was Williamsburg township, which was laid out by a surveyor named Anthony Williams. When Williamsburg County was created on March 12, 1785, it took its name from this earlier Williamsburg township. Sources consulted are agreed that the township was not named for the surveyor, Anthony Williams, but for a member of the English royal family, who at the time that the township was created and named, was also South Carolina's royal family. However, these sources differ on which member of the English royal family was the namesake of the township. The most prominent member of the English royal family named William during America's years as a colonial outpost of England was King William III (1650–1702) and he is said to be the namesake by a few sources. However, *Palmetto Place Names* states that the name honored a son-in-law of King George II (1683–1760). The only son-in-law of King George II named William was William IV, Prince of Orange (1711–1751). Information about him is presented above under Orangeburg County, South Carolina. A more frequently cited source for this county's name is William Augustus, Duke of Cumberland (1721–1765), a son of King George II. Since King George II was the reigning monarch of England from 1727 to 1760, there is a good chance that the William we are trying to find was a member of his family. One such William not mentioned as a possibility by South Carolina sources would be a grandson of King George II, William V (1748–1806), a son of the king's daughter, Princess Anne (1709–1759), and William IV,

Prince of Orange (1711–1751). William W. Boddie's history of Williamsburg County, South Carolina admits that the namesake is uncertain but casts his vote on favor of the most famous possibility, King William III (1650–1702). Boddie states that William James settled in Black River in 1732 and the township may have been named Williamsburg at his suggestion. Boddie tells us that William James' father, John James, served under William, Prince of Orange, before he came to the throne as King William III (1650–1702).

2326 *York County*

York County, Pennsylvania— This county was created on March 12, 1785, and named for York County, Pennsylvania, which had been home to a number of the settlers of this section of South Carolina. York County, Pennsylvania had been created on August 19, 1749, and named for its own town of York, which had been laid out eight years earlier. During the American Revolution, Pennsylvania's town of York served as the temporary capital of our nascent nation, while British troops occupied Philadelphia. Pennsylvania sources have differing opinions about the origin of the town of York's name. York and Yorkshire in England are suggested by some authorities while others say that England's King James II (1633–1701) was the namesake.

York and Yorkshire, England— Lying about mid-way between London and Edinburgh, Scotland, with a population of several million, the city of York and the county of Yorkshire, in England, represent one of England's most important metropolitan areas. Yorkshire borders on the North Sea and extends almost to the Irish Sea. The Roman Empire conquered the area and built a strategic fortress here about A.D. 72. Remains of this fortress can still be seen. The Yorkshire plain is fertile for agriculture and the West Riding area is rich in coal deposits. The Danes captured York in A.D. 867 and its present name came from their name *Yorvick*. York was later subjugated by the West Saxons and in 1066 it fell to the Norman invaders from France.

King James II (1633–1701)— James was the second surviving son of England's King Charles I (1600–1649). He was given the title duke of York and Albany soon after his christening. When James' father died, his elder brother, Charles, ascended to the throne as King Charles II (1630–1685). In 1664 King Charles II made an enormous grant of land in North America to his brother, the duke of York and Albany, which initially included much of present-day Pennsylvania. The duke of York was awarded more power over his domain than any other English proprietor. Although King Charles II had many children, none of them were legitimate so when King Charles II died in 1685, his brother, James, became king of England as King James II. About 1673 King James II professed his Catholicism and this spelled his eventual downfall as king. In 1689 the throne passed to William of Orange (1650–1702), who ruled as joint sovereign with his wife, Queen Mary II (1662–1694). Mary was a daughter of King James II. The former King James II devoted the final years of his life to religious exercises.

REFERENCES

Allstrom, C. M. *Dictionary of Royal Lineage in Europe and Other Countries*. Chicago, Press of S. Th. Almberg, 1902.

"Anderson County Place Names." *Names in South Carolina*, Vol. 10. Columbia: Winter, 1963.

Andrews, Allen. *The Royal Whore: Barbara Villiers, Countess of Castlemaine*. Philadelphia, Chilton Book Co., 1970

Ashmore, Nancy Vance. *Greenville: Woven from the Past: An Illustrated History*. Northridge, California, Windsor Publications, Inc., 1986.

Baer, Elizabeth. *Seventeenth Century Maryland: A Bibliography*. Baltimore, John Work Garrett Library, 1949.

Battle, Kemp P. "Glimpses of History in the Names of Our Counties." *North Carolina Booklet*, Vol. 6. July, 1906.

Battle, Kemp P. "North Carolina County Names." *The Magazine of History*, Vol. 7, No. 4. New York: April, 1908.

Bigham, John A. "Chester Names." *Names in South Carolina*, Vol. 29. Columbia: Winter, 1982.

Boatner, Mark M. *Encyclopedia of the American Revolution*. Mechanicsburg, Pennsylvania, Stackpole Books, 1994.

Boatner, Mark M. *Landmarks of the American Revolution*. Harrisburg, Pennsylvania, Stackpole Books, 1973.

Boddie, William W. *History of Williamsburg*. Columbia, South Carolina, State Co., 1923.

Bolick, Julian S. *A Fairfield Sketchbook*. Clinton, South Carolina, Jacobs Brothers, 1963.

Braddy, Dolph. "Names of Towns & Communities in Dillon County." *Names in South Carolina*, Vol. 30. Columbia: Winter, 1983.

Burnside, Ronald D. "Towns & Communities in Laurens County." *Names in*

South Carolina, Vol. 28. Columbia: Winter, 1981.

Campbell, Cornelia Bearden. "Oconee County Place Names." *Names in South Carolina*, Vol. 14. Columbia: Winter, 1967.

Cannon, John. *The Oxford Companion to British History*. Oxford, Oxford University Press, 1997.

Carroll, J. Greg. *Abbeville County Family History*. 1979.

Charles, Allan D. *The Narrative History of Union County, South Carolina*. Spartanburg, South Carolina, Reprint Co., 1987.

Cheney, John L. *North Carolina Manual: 1977*. Raleigh.

Clements, John. *South Carolina Facts*. Dallas, Texas, Clements Research II, Inc., 1991.

Cole, Will. *The Many Faces of Aiken*. Norfolk, Virginia, Donning Company, 1985.

Cook, Petronelle. *Queen Consorts of England: The Power Behind the Throne*. New York, Facts On File, Inc., 1993.

Cooper, Francis H. "Some Colonial History of Beaufort County, North Carolina." *James Sprunt Historical Publications*, Vol. 14, No. 2. Chapel Hill: 1916.

Corbitt, David L. *The Formation of the North Carolina Counties: 1663–1943*. Raleigh, State Department of Archives & History, 1950.

Crittenden, Charles C. & Dan Lacy. *The Historical Records of North Carolina*. Raleigh, North Carolina Historical Commission, 1938.

Currie, Andrew M. *Dictionary of British Place Names*. London, Tiger Books International, 1994.

Daiches, David. *The Penguin Companion to Literature: Britain and the Commonwealth*. Penguin Press, 1971.

Doyle, Mary Cherry. *Historic Oconee in South Carolina*. 1935.

Duncan, Alderman. "Feminine Place Names." *Names in South Carolina*, Vol. 18. Columbia: Winter, 1971.

Duncan, Alderman. "Place Names of Scottish Origins." *Names in South Carolina*, Vol. 26. Columbia: Winter, 1979.

Ekwall, Eilert. *The Concise Oxford Dictionary of English Place-Names*. Oxford, Oxford University Press, 1960.

Encyclopaedia Britannica. Chicago, Encyclopaedia Britannica, Inc., 1971.

Ervin, Eliza C., & Horace F. Rudisill. *Darlingtoniana: A History of People, Places & Events in Darlington County, South Carolina*. Spartanburg, South Carolina, Reprint Co., 1976.

Faragher, John M. *The Encyclopedia of Colonial & Revolutionary America*. New York, Facts On File, 1990.

Floyd, Viola C. "Lancaster County Place Names." *Names in South Carolina*, Vol. 15. Columbia: Winter, 1968.

Floyd, Viola C. *Lancaster County Tours*. Lancaster, South Carolina, Lancaster County Historical Commission, 1956.

Foster, Joseph. *The Peerage, Baronetage & Knightage of the British Empire for 1880*. Westminster, Nichols & Sons.

Frazier, Evelyn M., & William E. Fripp. "Names in Colleton County." *Names in South Carolina*, Vol. 12. Columbia: Winter, 1965.

Gannett, Henry. *A Guide to the Origin of Place Names in the United States*. Washington, D.C., Public Affairs Press, 1947.

Georgia, North Carolina, South Carolina Tour Book. Heathrow, Florida, AAA Publishing, 1997.

Glover, Beulah. *Narratives of Colleton County*. Walterboro, South Carolina, 1962.

Green, Edwin L. *A History of Richland County*. Columbia, South Carolina, R. L. Bryan Co., 1932.

Gregorie, Anne King. *History of Sumter County, South Carolina*. Sumter, South Carolina, Library Board of Sumter County, 1954.

"Guide & Directory to South Carolina Government." *South Carolina Magazine*, Vol. 31, No. 1. Columbia, South Carolina: January, 1967.

Handbook of South Carolina: Resources, Institutions & Industries of the State. Columbia, South Carolina, State Department of Agriculture, Commerce & Immigration, 1908.

Hawkyard, Alasdair. *The Counties of Britain: A Tudor Atlas by John Speed*. London, England, Pavilion Books, Ltd., 1995.

Henning, Helen K. *Great South Carolinians: From Colonial Days to the Confederate War*. Chapel Hill, University of North Carolina Press, 1940.

Henning, Helen K. *Great South Carolinians of a Later Date*. Chapel Hill, University of North Carolina Press, 1949.

Hunter, J. Oscar. "Abbeville County Towns & Communities." *Names in South Carolina*, Vol. 28. Columbia: Winter, 1981.

Industrial Data on South Carolina's Oconee County.

Jacobs, William P. *The Scrapbook: A Compilation of Historical Facts About Places & Events of Laurens County, South Carolina*. Laurens County Historical Society & Laurens County Arts Council, 1982.

Jasper County Historical Foundation, Inc. *History of Jasper County, Georgia*. Roswell, Georgia, W. H. Wolfe Associates, 1976.

Joelson, Annette. *England's Princes of Wales*. New York, Dorset Press, 1966.

Johnson, James. *Place Names of England & Wales*. London, England, Bracken Books, 1994.

King, G. Wayne. *Rise Up So Early: A History of Florence County, South Carolina*. Spartanburg, South Carolina, Reprint Co., 1981.

Kirkland, Thomas J., & Robert M. Kennedy. *Historic Camden*. Columbia, South Carolina, State Co., 1926.

Landrum, J. B. O. *History of Spartanburg County*. Atlanta, Georgia, Franklin Printing & Publishing Co., 1900.

Mabry, Mannie Lee. *Union County Heritage*. Winston-Salem, North Carolina, Hunter Publishing Co., 1981.

McClendon, Carlee T. "Edgefield County Towns & Communities." *Names in South Carolina*, Vol. 30. Columbia: Winter, 1983.

McDavid, Raven I., & Raymond K. O'Cain. "South Carolina County Names: Unreconstructed Individualism." *Names: Journal of the American Name Society*, Vol. 26, No. 1. Potsdam, New York: March, 1978.

Mackintosh, Robert H. "Historic Names in York County." *Names in South Carolina*, Vol. 24. Columbia: Winter, 1977.

Masters, Brian. *The Mistresses of Charles II*. London, Blond & Briggs, Ltd., 1979.

May, Carl H. "Spartanburg County Names." *Names in South Carolina*, Vol. 25. Columbia: Winter, 1978.

Mills, A.D. *A Dictionary of English Place-Names*. Oxford, England, Oxford University Press, 1991.

Molloy, Robert. *Charleston: A Gracious Heritage*. New York, D. Appleton-Century Co., Inc., 1947.

Moore, Elizabeth. *Records of Craven County, North Carolina*. Bladensburg, Maryland, Genealogical Recorders, 1960.

Moss, Bobby Gilmer. *Roster of South Carolina Patriots in the American Revolution*. Baltimore, Genealogical Publishing Co., Inc., 1983.

Moule, Thomas. *The County Maps of Old England*. London, Studio Editions, 1990.

"Names in Darlington County." *Names in South Carolina*, Vol. 2. Columbia: Winter, 1955.

"Names of Plantations & Homes in Edgefield County." *Names in South Carolina*, Vol. 11. Columbia: Winter, 1964.

Neuffer, Claude H. "The Lord Proprietors and Their Influence on South Carolina Place Names." *Names in South Carolina*, Vol. 17. Columbia: Winter, 1970.

O'Bannon, Joyce S. "Names in Barnwell County." *Names in South Carolina*, Vol. 15. Columbia: Winter, 1968.

O'Cain, Ray. "Some Place Names Here & There in Orangeburg County." *Names in South Carolina*, Vol. 13. Columbia: November, 1966.

Oliphant, Mary C. Simms. *The New Simms History of South Carolina: 1840–1940*. Columbia, South Carolina, State Company, 1940.

Paullin, Charles O. *Atlas of the Historical Geography of the United States*. Carnegie Institution of Washington and the American Geographical Society of New York, 1932.

Perry, Grace Fox. *Moving Finger of Jasper*. Jasper County Confederate Centennial Commission.

Pickens, A. L. "Dictionary of Indian-Place Names in Upper South Carolina." *South Carolina Natural History*, Nos. 51–53. Greenwood, South Carolina: October-November, 1937.

Pine, L. G. *Princes of Wales*. Rutland, Vermont, Charles E. Tuttle Co., 1970.

"Place-Names in Newberry County." *Names in South Carolina*, Vol. 11. Columbia: Winter, 1964.

"Place Names in Spartanburg County." *Names in South Carolina*, Vol. 10. Columbia: Winter, 1963.

Pope, Thomas H. *The History of Newberry County, South Carolina*. Columbia, University of South Carolina Press, 1973.

Powell, William S. *The Carolina Charter of 1663: How It Came to North Carolina and Its Place in History: With Biographical Sketches of the Proprietors*. Raleigh, State Department of Archives & History, 1954.

Powell, William S. *The North Carolina Gazetteer*. Chapel Hill, University of North Carolina Press, 1968.

Powell, William S. *The Proprietors of Carolina*. Raleigh, North Carolina, Carolina Charter Tercentenary Commission, 1963.

Price, Edward T. *Dividing the Land: Early American Beginnings of Our Private Property Mosaic*. Chicago, University of Chicago Press, 1995.

Purcell, L. Edward. *Who Was Who in the American Revolution*. New York, Facts On File, Inc., 1993.

Richardson, James M. *History of Greenville County, South Carolina*. Atlanta, Georgia, A. H. Cawston, 1930.

Rogers, George C. *The History of Georgetown County, South Carolina*. Columbia, University of South Carolina Press, 1970.

Rosson, Mrs. B. H. *Ederington's History of Fairfield County, South Carolina*. Tuscaloosa, Alabama, Willo Publishing Co.

Salley, A. S. *The History of Orangeburg County, South Carolina*. Orangeburg, South Carolina, R. Lewis Berry, 1898.

Salley, Alexander S. *Narratives of Early Carolina: 1650–1708*. New York, Barnes & Noble, Inc., 1967.

Searson, Louis A. *The Town of Allendale*. Columbia, South Carolina, 1949.

Sellers, W. W. *A History of Marion County, South Carolina*. Columbia, South Carolina, R. L. Bryan Co., 1902.

Shealy, Lois T. *1983 Legislative Manual: 105th General Assembly of South Carolina*.

Shealy, Lois T. *1986 Legislative Manual: 106th General Assembly of South Carolina*.

Simms, William G. *The Geography of South Carolina*. Charleston, Babcock & Co., 1843.

Smith, Henry A. M. "The Colleton Family in South Carolina." *South Carolina Historical & Genealogical Magazine*, Vol. 1, No. 2. April, 1900.

Smith, Henry A. M. "The Colleton Family in South Carolina." *South Carolina Historical & Genealogical Magazine*, Vol. 1, No. 4. October, 1900.

"Some Aiken County Names." *Names in South Carolina*, Vol. 7. Columbia: Winter, 1960.

"Some Greenville Names." *Names in South Carolina*, Vol. 10. Columbia: Winter, 1963.

"Some Horry County Names." *Names in South Carolina*, Vol. 4. Columbia: Winter, 1957.

"Some Oconee County Names." *Names in South Carolina*, Vol. 8. Columbia: Winter, 1961.

"Some Orangeburg County Names." *Names in South Carolina*, Vol. 6. Columbia: Winter, 1959.

"Some Place-Names in Union County." *Names in South Carolina*, Vol. 11. Columbia: Winter, 1964.

"Some York County Names." *Names in South Carolina*, Vol. 7. Columbia: Winter, 1960.

South Carolina County Maps. Lyndon Station, Wisconsin, County Maps.

South Carolina: A Handbook. Columbia, South Carolina, Department of Agriculture, Commerce & Industries and Clemson College, 1927.

Stewart, George R. *American Place-Names*. New York, Oxford University Press, 1970.

Stewart, George R. *Names on the Land*. New York, Random House, 1945.

Stokes, Durward T. *The History of Dillon County, South Carolina*. Columbia, University of South Carolina Press, 1978.

Stoutenburgh, John. *Dictionary of the American Indian*. New York, Bonanza Books, 1960.

Stubbs, Thomas M. "Dorchester County." *Names in South Carolina*, Vol. 19. Columbia: Winter, 1972.

Summer, George L. *Newberry County, South Carolina: Historical & Genealogical*. Newberry, South Carolina, 1950.

Thomas, Charles E. "Some Fairfield County Names of Plantations & Houseseats." *Names in South Carolina*, Vol. 12. Columbia, South Carolina: Winter, 1965.

Thomas, J. A. W. *A History of Marlboro County*. Baltimore, Regional Publishing Co., 1971.

Trease, Geoffrey. *Seven Kings of England*. New York, Vanguard Press, 1955.

Trease, Geoffrey. *The Seven Queens of England*. New York, Vanguard Press, 1953.

Van der Kiste, John. *King George II & Queen Caroline*. Sutton Publishing, Ltd., 1997.

Vandiver, Louise Ayer. *Traditions & History of Anderson County*. Atlanta, Georgia, Ruralist Press, 1928.

Vexler, Robert I. *Chronology & Documentary Handbook of the State of South Carolina*. Dobbs Ferry, New York, Oceana Publications, Inc., 1978.

Wallace, David D. *The History of South Carolina*. New York, American Historical Society, Inc., 1934.

Weir, Robert M. *Colonial South Carolina: A History*. Millwood, New York, KTO Press, 1983.

White, Dabney, & T. C. Richardson. *East Texas: Its History and Its Makers*. New York, Lewis Historical Publishing Co., 1940.

Whitmore, William H. "On the Origin of the Name of the Town of Lexington, Massachusetts." *Proceedings of the Massachusetts Historical Society*, Vol. 12. Cambridge: 1871–1873.

Whitmore, William H. "On the Origin of the Names of Towns in Massachusetts." *Proceedings of the Massachusetts Historical Society*, Vol. 12. Cambridge: 1871–1873.

Woods, Gertrude B. "More Clarendon County Names." *Names in South Carolina*, Vol. 23. Columbia, South Carolina: Winter, 1976.

Work Projects Administration. *Palmetto Place Names*. Columbia, South Carolina, Sloane Printing Co., 1941.

Wright, Louis B. *South Carolina: A Bicentennial History*. New York, W. W. Norton & Co., Inc., 1976.

South Dakota

(67 counties)

2327 *Aurora County*

Aurora, Roman Goddess of Dawn— This county was created by the legislature of Dakota territory on February 22, 1879, and named for Aurora, the Roman goddess of the dawn. The arrival of dawn was very important in ancient times when people had no reliable means of producing strong and steady artificial light. Because of this, the goddess, Aurora, was considered to be one of the important gods of the Romans'. The depression-era work entitled *South Dakota Place Names*, sponsored by Edward C. Ehrensperger's English Department at the University of South Dakota, states that the settlers who coined this county's name, were six women, wives of the first settlers, who met in a sod shanty to form a literary club. That work states that one of the six women suggested the name *Aurora* for the new county "because it was their hope that this free homestead land would bring the dawn of a new era for them." The name *Aurora* was used a second time, in the following year, in this area of what is now eastern South Dakota, when the municipality of Aurora, in Brookings County was founded by the Western Town Lot Company in 1880. Aurora, in Brookings County, is about 90 miles northeast of today's Aurora County, South Dakota. (The municipality may have been named for the town of Aurora, Illinois, rather than Aurora County, Dakota territory, and rather than the Roman goddess of dawn. This is uncertain.)

2328 *Beadle County*

William H. H. Beadle (1838–1915)— William Henry Harrison Beadle was born in a log cabin in Indiana on January 1, 1838, and he was an 1861 graduate of the University of Michigan, with a specialty in civil engineering. During the Civil War he served as an officer in the Union army, and he served adequately but was no war hero. The rank of brevet brigadier-general was awarded to him after the Civil War. After leaving the army, Beadle studied law, was admitted to the bar and practiced law in both Indiana and Wisconsin. He was appointed surveyor general of the United States for the territory of Dakota in 1869. As a byproduct of his survey work, Bea-

dle became concerned that lands in Dakota territory, that had been set aside for public education, not be squandered as they had been in a number of territories east of Dakota. Beadle wanted these lands preserved for future generations' educational needs and he ultimately succeeded in having an appropriate minimum selling price, per acre, established in South Dakota's state constitution. In 1878, Dakota's territorial governor, William A. Howard (1813–1880), appointed Beadle as superintendent of pubic instruction and he served in that post several years. In February, 1889, Beadle was appointed as superintendent of an Indian training school in Oregon but he returned to South Dakota later that same year to be president of Dakota Normal School, at Madison. Beadle subsequently served as a history professor at that college. He served one term in the lower house of Dakota's territorial legislature, from January 12, 1877, to February 17, 1878. This county was created and named in his honor by the next territorial legislature, which met in 1879.

2329 *Bennett County*

Uncertain— This county was created on March 9, 1909, two decades after South Dakota's admission to statehood. Sources dealing with the history, geography and place names of Dakota territory and South Dakota offer conflicting opinions concerning this county's namesake. According to some, it was named for Granville G. Bennett (1833–1910), while others indicate that the county's name honors John E. Bennett. (A third possibility is also mentioned; i.e., that the county's name honors both of these men since the legislators could not agree on which of the Bennetts they wished to honor.)

Granville G. Bennett (1833–1910)— A native of Ohio and a lawyer, Granville G. Bennett practiced law in Iowa and served as an officer in the Union army, during the Civil War. He then served in both houses of the Iowa legislature and was appointed an associate justice of the supreme court of Dakota territory on February 24, 1875. In 1878 he was elected as Dakota territory's delegate to the U.S. Congress, and he resigned from the territorial supreme court on August 23 of that year. He served just

one term in congress, from 1879 to 1881, and subsequently practiced law in Yankton and Deadwood, South Dakota, and served as a probate court judge at Deadwood.

John E. Bennett (–)—South Dakota was admitted to statehood in 1889 and John E. Bennett was elected that year to the new state's supreme court. According to some accounts he was reelected in 1893 but this is questionable since South Dakota's general elections are and were held in even numbered years. The date of John E. Bennett's death is uncertain but it was probably in late 1893 or very early 1894 because his replacement on the supreme court was appointed on January 15, 1894.

It seems more probable, but not certain, that this county was named for Granville G. Bennett. The county was created in 1909, when John E. Bennett had been dead about 16 years and probably was long forgotten. On the other hand, Granville G. Bennett was still alive and no doubt well remembered as the first federally appointed judge in Dakota territory, west of the Missouri River and an important figure in Dakota's territorial history from the early, rough and ready, frontier days of White settlement in the Black Hills.

2330 *Bon Homme County*

Town of Bonhomme, Dakota territory— This unusual name was given by French explorers to a 2,000 acre island in the Missouri River. When a town grew up near the island, it took its name, Bonhomme City, from the island. On June 4, 1854, a post office was established at Bonhomme. It was located on the southern side of the Missouri River in Nebraska territory. That post office was discontinued on October 3, 1861, and later reestablished on the northern side of the Missouri River in Dakota territory. Bon Homme County was created as a county of Dakota territory on April 5, 1862, just one year after the U.S. Congress had created Dakota territory. The county was named for its town of Bonhomme, and that town was made the county seat of the new county. About 1885 a railroad line was run through the town of Tyndall, Dakota territory, and the county seat was moved from Bonhomme to Tyndall. The French words from which these place names derive, *Bon Homme*, mean "good man." In 1865 an attempt was made to change the name of this county in Dakota territory from Bon Homme County to Jefferson County. That effort aborted and neither South Dakota nor North Dakota has a county named Jefferson.

2331 *Brookings County*

Wilmot W. Brookings (1833–1905) — A native of Maine and an 1855 graduate from Bowdoin College in that state, Brookings studied law after graduating from Bowdoin. He was admitted to the bar of Maine before heading west to settle at Sioux Falls in what is now South Dakota. He arrived here on August 27, 1857. At that time, this was wild frontier country where laws and the other niceties of civilization had not yet made much impact. Dakota territory had not yet been established by the U.S. Congress. In 1857 Brookings was appointed to manage the interests of the Western Town Company here. During February, 1858, he was caught in a blizzard and lost both of his feet. When Dakota territory was created, Brookings was elected to serve in the upper house (council) of the first term of the territorial legislature, and he was a member of more than half a dozen subsequent territorial legislatures. On March 3, 1865, the U.S. Congress authorized construction of three wagon roads through Dakota and Wilmot W. Brookings was placed in charge of the construction of one of these three wagon roads. On April 15, 1865, President Abraham Lincoln was assassinated, less than a week after the Civil War ended, and the Republican-dominated U.S. Congress began to impose very harsh military Reconstruction measures on the defeated South. In Dakota territory Wilmot W. Brookings became a leader of a political faction that expressed support for these vicious Reconstruction measures. In 1869 Brookings became an associate justice on the supreme court of Dakota territory and he served in that body four years from 1869 to 1873. Judge Brookings was an important promoter of the Southern Dakota Railroad and he was a delegate to South Dakota's constitutional convention. A few years after 1885, Judge Brookings and his wife moved to Massachusetts and he died in Boston in 1905. This county was created on April 5, 1862, just one year after the U.S. Congress had created Dakota territory. At that time Brookings was a member of the upper house of the legislature of Dakota territory and his fellow legislators named this county in his honor.

2332 *Brown County*

Alfred Brown (1836–1919) — Brown was born near Ottawa, Canada, on January 1, 1836, and came to Dakota territory in 1874. Here he took up a homestead and began farming. By the late 1870's he had become sufficiently popular to be elected to the legislature of Dakota territory. He served just one term in that legislature, as a member of the lower house during the legislative session which began on January 14, 1879. At that time he was a resident of the community of Scotland, Dakota territory. Several works dealing with the history, geography and place names of Dakota territory and South Dakota indicate that Alfred Brown actively participated in the decision to have this county named in his own honor. This county was created on February 22, 1879, by Alfred Brown's fellow territorial legislators. Alfred Brown subsequently served several years on the school board for the public schools of his community.

2333 *Brule County*

Brule Indians — The Brule Indians were a sub-tribe of the Teton division of the Dakota Indians. The name *Brule*, is French and means "burned." Several conflicting tales have been offered to explain The name *Brule*. A common theme in many of them is "burned thighs." When the French encountered these Indians, they were already known by a name referring to "burnt thighs." The French did not give them their name. They merely rendered the existing Indian name for this Indian sub-tribe in the French language. The Teton division of the Dakota tribe was the westernmost of three divisions of the Dakota Indians and the Brules were one of the three most historically important sub-tribes of the Teton Dakotas. In the journals of the Lewis and Clark Expedition, an entry appears under September 26, 1804, which mentions this sub-tribe. The Brule Indians lived on both sides of the Missouri River. Their chiefs were competent managers and the Brules were usually well clothed, well fed and lived in comfortable lodges. Their leaders arranged buffalo hunts to minimize friction with other Indians and to avoid hunts that ended in starvation situations. In addition to hunting buffalo, the Brule Indians caught wild horses and made war on Indians living on the Platte River. During the period of White migration from homes in the East to California and Oregon, many of these migrants passed near the Brule Indians in the Dakota country and the Brules were significantly impacted by diseases which they caught from these migrating Whites. During 1855 the U.S. army's William S. Harney (1800–1889) led a punitive military expedition against Indians in the West. On September 3, 1855, his troops located a band, estimated to number 136, of Brule Indians at Ash Hollow, in the Sand Hills region of Nebraska territory. All of the Brule were massacred, essentially wiping out the Brule sub-tribe. This county was created by the legislature of Dakota territory on January 14, 1875, and named for the former Brule Indians of Dakota. Although the Brule are gone, large numbers of Teton Dakota Indians still live in South Dakota, on Indian reservations.

2334 *Buffalo County*

Bison herds that roamed the Dakota country — This county was created by the legislature of Dakota territory in January, 1864, while some herds of bison still roamed on the plains of Dakota. The county was named Buffalo County since that is the common, but incorrect, name given to these bison. These animals were the staff of life to nomadic Indian hunters and for a time they also provided a bit of revenue to White hunters and traders. A decade prior to the creation of this county, in the mid-1850's, bison herds were plentiful here. By the time that this county was created in 1864, their numbers here had been greatly reduced. The slaughter of these animals was not, of course, limited to Dakota. In the early 1800's, bison in America numbered in the tens of millions. Today very few remain and most of them are protected on government lands or private preserves. South Dakota has reintroduced some wild bison herds in the state.

2335 *Butte County*

Numerous buttes found in this area — This county, at the western end of South Dakota, borders on both Wyoming and Montana and is part of a geologically interesting section of our nation. The larger area, of which Butte County is a part, contains the Black Hills and the Badlands, and within Butte County numerous buttes are found. The French word *butte*, means "small, isolated elevation, knoll or mound," which is a generally apt description for many of the buttes which rise abruptly from the prairie floor of Butte County.

However, the term *butte*, as used in western South Dakota and elsewhere in the United States is not limited to small buttes. Within Butte County there are several named buttes which soar to altitudes of greater than 3,000 feet and Bear Butte, at an elevation of 4,422 feet, is a volcanic mountain butte, just south of Butte County. This county was created in the early 1880's, while Dakota was still a territory, and enlarged significantly in 1897 by the legislature of South Dakota.

2336 *Campbell County*

Norman B. Campbell (–)— Norman B. Campbell was a son of the Union's Civil War general, Charles T. Campbell (1823–1895), who was one of the founders of the town of Scotland, in Dakota territory. The general's son, Norman B. Campbell, served just one term in the legislature of Dakota territory. He was a member of the lower house of the territorial legislature during the session which convened at Yankton on December 2, 1872, and adjourned on January 10, 1873. At that time Norman B. Campbell was a resident of Bonhomme and he represented Bon Homme County in the legislature. This county was created in January, 1873, during the one session that Norman Campbell was a member of Dakota's territorial legislature.

2337 *Charles Mix County*

Charles H. Mix (1833–1909)— Mix was born in New Haven, Connecticut, on December 30, 1833. He immigrated to Minnesota territory in 1852 and lived at Long Prairie, which then was the agency of a reservation for the Winnebago Indians. In 1854 Mix was appointed to take the Chippewa Indians from Red Lake and Pembina to Washington. The Chippewa Indians refused to go. In the spring of 1855 Mix was sent back to Long Prairie to transfer the Indians there to a new agency in Blue Earth County, Minnesota territory, and he was appointed Indian agent for that Blue Earth agency. He served there from 1858 to 1861. Meanwhile, the Dakota (Sioux) Indians in Minnesota were growing very restless. By 1858 they had been pressured into signing treaties giving up almost all of their land in Minnesota. In return, they were to receive food, annuities, education and other necessities. These promises to the Indians were broken and in 1862 the Dakotas began a final, futile struggle against the Whites in Minnesota, who had systematically robbed and mistreated them. The Dakotas lost this struggle and 38 of their members were hanged on a mass gallows at Mankato, Minnesota on December 26, 1862. Remaining Dakota Indians in Minnesota were deported to Indian reservations in Dakota territory (now South Dakota and North Dakota), where they have lived in misery to this day. Charles Mix was involved in this Indian war in Minnesota. He entered the U.S. military as a first lieutenant in the First Minnesota cavalry and rose to the rank of captain. In 1864 Mix was made commandant of Fort Abercrombie in northeastern Dakota territory and subsequently he was appointed assistant inspector general for the third civil district with headquarters at Fort Ridgely in southern Minnesota. He later served as assistant adjutant general, first at St. Paul and later at Fort Snelling, both in Minnesota. He was honorably discharged from the army in June, 1867. In subsequent years Mix was a farmer in the St. Paul area and worked in several capacities of railroad work. He died in Crookston, Minnesota, on December 15, 1909. This county was one of the early counties created by Dakota territory. Dakota territory was established by the U.S. Congress on March 2, 1861, and Charles Mix County was created on May 8, 1862, during the first term of Dakota's territorial legislature.

2338 *Clark County*

Newton Clark (–)— Clark served in just one session of the legislature of Dakota territory, the session that convened in Yankton on December 2, 1872, and adjourned on January 10, 1873. Newton Clark was a member of the lower house of that legislature, from Sioux Falls, which then was in Lincoln County, and he represented Lincoln County in that legislature. Clark holds the distinction of having taught school in the first frame school building that was erected in Sioux Falls. This county was created in January, 1873, during the one session that Clark was a member of Dakota's territorial legislature. The county seat of Clark County is a municipality named Clark, and in cases like this it is not always clear whether the county was named directly for the person, or indirectly, by being named for the municipality. In this case we are certain that the county was named directly for Newton Clark. The county was created in 1873 and the municipality (first named Clark Center) was founded in 1882, in connection with the coming of the railroad.

2339 *Clay County*

Henry Clay (1777–1852)— Clay represented Kentucky in both branches of the U.S. Congress. For many years he was one of the more prominent figures in American politics but his several bids for the presidency were unsuccessful. He was influential in effecting important compromises between northern and southern interests during the years that secession and civil war were imminent. This county created in April, 1862, early in the Civil War, by the first legislature of Dakota territory. The county's name was suggested by Jacob S. Deuel (1830–), a member of the upper house (council) of that first territorial legislature. Deuel was a native of the North (New York) but had also lived in the South (Virginia). He proposed this county's name to honor the statesman who had tried so hard to avert the Civil War, which had become a current reality in our nation.

2340 *Codington County*

G. S. Codington (–)— Codington was a Protestant clergyman, who served in the lower house of Dakota's territorial legislature during just one term, the session which convened in Yankton on January 12, 1877, and adjourned on February 17, 1878. Reverend Codington was a resident of Medary, which was in Brookings County, Dakota territory. Reverend Codington came to the little settlement of Medary and established a schedule of regular religious services here. He also took to his horse to provide missionary services in a wide portion of southeastern Dakota for a number of years. When the community of Watertown was established in the late 1870's in what is today Codington County, South Dakota, Reverend Codington made that community his headquarters. Most sources show his name as Reverend G. S. S. Codington and state that he was a clergyman of the Congregational denomination. However, Wright Tarbell's article entitled "The Early and Territorial History of Codington County," which appeared in the 1949 issue of *South Dakota Historical Collections & Report* (volume 24), states that Reverend Codington was a Presbyterian minister. This county was created by the legislature of Dakota territory in 1877, during the one term that Reverend Codington served as a territorial legislator.

2341 *Corson County*

Dighton Corson (–1915)— Dighton Corson was born in Maine in 1827 or 1828 and was admitted to the bar of that state before heading west. Corson moved to Milwaukee, Wisconsin, in 1857 and there he served in the state legislature and was district attorney. In 1861 he moved further west, and after a brief stay on the Pacific coast, he settled in Nevada territory. He served as district attorney at Virginia City, Nevada, for five years. Corson migrated to Deadwood, Dakota territory, in 1877. He established a law practice here and served as an attorney for the Homestake Mining Company. Corson served in the preliminary constitutional convention for the soon-to-be state of South Dakota in 1885 and when the actual state constitutional convention met in 1889, he was a member of that body as well. When South Dakota was admitted to statehood Corson became an associate justice of the new state's supreme court and he served on that court 24 years, from 1889, until he retired in 1913. He was one of the hardest working judges on the court throughout most of these 24 years. Corson died at his home in Pierre, South Dakota, in 1915. This county was created on March 2, 1909, while Dighton Corson was a sitting as a justice of the South Dakota supreme court.

2342 Custer County

George A. Custer (1839–1876) — Custer was born in Ohio and educated at West Point. As a Union officer in the Civil War, his successes led to promotion to the rank of general before his 24th birthday. Following that war, he served in the U.S. cavalry fighting Indians in the West. In 1868 Custer led a very successful campaign against the Cheyenne Indians on the Washita River and he spent the next several years exploring the Yellowstone River and the Black Hills of Dakota. During the summer of 1874 Custer traversed the Black Hills from west to east with a party of more than 1,200 troops and scientists. It was this expedition which discovered gold in the Black Hills, on French Creek, within what is today Custer County, South Dakota. The men who actually discovered the gold were Horatio N. Ross and Willis W. T. McKay. They found traces of gold on July 30, 1874, and Custer officially released news of the gold discovery on August 12, 1874. Custer and his men left the area shortly afterwards and by December, 1874, prospectors had entered in the Black Hills in numbers and were successfully mining gold. Ironically, the discovery of gold by Custer's party in 1874 indirectly led to his death in 1876. The Paha Sapa section of the Black Hills had been ceded to the Indians by an 1868 treaty and the area was also sacred to the Indians by tradition. The massive influx of Whites during the

Black Hills gold rush offended the Indians greatly and led to numerous clashes between Indians and Whites. Custer was personally involved in some of these clashes and lost his life in one of them. The flamboyance which had served Custer so well in the Civil War led to his downfall at the battle of Little Big Horn in Montana territory on June 25, 1876. In that battle, famous as "Custer's last stand," he attacked Indians who greatly outnumbered his forces. Custer and all of his men were slain. This county was created by Dakota territory on January 11, 1875, after Custer's party had discovered gold in the Black Hills, but before Custer and his men perished in the battle of Little Big Horn.

2343 Davison County

Henry Davison (–) — Davison was born in Maine and moved west, first to Illinois and later to Dakota territory. He settled in Bon Homme County, Dakota territory, in 1869 and became a prominent merchant here. Davison subsequently moved a few miles north to what is today Davison County, South Dakota. Some sources dealing with the history, geography and place names of Dakota territory and South Dakota indicate that Henry Davison was the first settler of what is today's Davison County. That statement is questionable because several other sources state that the first settlers' honor belongs to others including Charles Bangs, H. C. Green (or Greene), John Head and Levi Hain. It would be more accurate to state that Henry Davison was one of the first homesteaders in what is today Davison County, South Dakota. He filed his homestead claim in 1872 for land at Riverside. Sampson York edited a work published in 1939 entitled *South Dakota: Fifty Years of Progress*, which contains a sentence that may explain the apparent discrepancy between the two versions concerning who was first here. Sampson York tells us that "…the county was named for Henry L. [sic] Davison, who ranged cattle in the vicinity of Firesteel Creek several years before the arrival of the first settlers." This county was created by Dakota territory in January, 1873. At that time Henry Davison was certainly one of the first homesteaders here.

2344 Day County

Merritt H. Day (1844–1900) — Day served as a captain of Wisconsin troops in the Union army during the Civil War. After the Civil War he settled in Dakota terri-

tory and was a register of deeds in Brule County in the southern part of what is now the state of South Dakota. Day served in the upper house (council) of two legislatures of Dakota territory. The first of these was the 13th legislative session which convened on January 14, 1879. It was during that legislative session, on February 22, 1879, that Day County was created and named in honor of Merritt H. Day by his fellow legislators. Day's second term as a territorial legislator was in the 14th legislative session, which convened on January 11, 1881. In 1890 Day served as a captain of state militia during the so-called Messiah Indian War. It was during that campaign that the Dakota chief, Sitting Bull (–1890) was killed and the massacre of Dakota Indians at Wounded Knee, South Dakota occurred. Merritt H. Day died at his home in Rapid City, South Dakota.

2345 Deuel County

Jacob S. Deuel (1830–) — Deuel was born in New York state of German ancestry and moved to Virginia. He subsequently moved to Minnesota, and either in Virginia or Minnesota, Deuel became trained as a machinist, engineer and millwright. He came to Vermillion in what is now southeastern South Dakota in 1859 or 1860 before Dakota territory was established by the U.S. Congress. Deuel and his partner, Hugh Compton, brought a steam sawmill and established it at Vermillion, near the Vermillion River. Here ample forests were available in the area surrounding the confluence of the Vermillion and Missouri Rivers. Deuel and Compton also ran a small store in Vermillion. Deuel eventually became the sole owner of the sawmill and Compton took over the store. Deuel served in the upper house (council) of two legislatures of Dakota territory as the councilman from the third district, (west of the Vermillion River). The first of these was the first legislative session after the U.S. Congress established Dakota territory. It was during that legislative session, on April 5, 1862, that Deuel County was created and named in honor of Jacob S. Deuel by his fellow territorial legislators. Deuel's second term in the legislature of Dakota territory was during the territory's second legislative session, which convened on December 1, 1862, and adjourned on January 9, 1863. A number of sources indicate that Deuel moved from Dakota territory to Nebraska and some say that he died there. It may be true that Deuel became a resident of Nebraska. However, several of the sources which link Jacob S.

Deuel with Nebraska state that Deuel County, Nebraska was named for him. That is incorrect. Nebraska's Deuel County was also named for a New York native, but it was not Jacob S. Deuel. Rather, it was Harry Porter Deuel (1836–1914).

2346 *Dewey County*

William P. Dewey (–1900)— William Pitt Dewey came to Dakota territory from Wisconsin and according to one source, he was a brother of Wisconsin's governor, Nelson Dewey (1813–1889). William Pitt Dewey received a commission as a federal surveyor-general of Dakota territory dated December 13, 1872. He began serving in that office in the spring of 1873 and remained the territory's surveyor-general from 1873 to 1877. This county was originally created by the legislature of Dakota territory on January 8, 1873, and named Rusk County. It is not certain whom that name was intended to honor. It is known that Dakota territory never had a governor named Rusk and Will G. Robinson's alphabetical listing of all members of the legislature of Dakota territory, which appeared in the 1950 (volume 25) issue of *South Dakota Historical Collections & Report*, lists nobody named Rusk as a territorial legislator. (Many counties in both North and South Dakota were named for members of Dakota territory's legislature.) This county's name was changed from Rusk County to Dewey County on March 9, 1883, during the one and only term of the territorial legislature that William Pitt Dewey was a member of it. He represented Yankton County in the upper house (council) of the territorial legislature which convened on January 9, 1883, and adjourned on March 9, 1883. William Pitt Dewey spent the next 17 years of his life in Yankton and died in 1900.

2347 *Douglas County*

Stephen A. Douglas (1813–1861)— Barely five feet tall, the "Little Giant" is most remembered as a political opponent of Abraham Lincoln. Douglas was born in Vermont and moved to Illinois where he enjoyed rapid political success. He served on the state supreme court, in the state legislature and as secretary of state. Following two terms in the U.S. House of Representatives, Douglas was elected to the U.S. Senate. In that body Douglas took courageous positions on the slavery issue which first outraged abolitionist sentiment and later infuriated the South. In 1858 Douglas ran for reelection to the U.S. Senate

against Abraham Lincoln. Following the famous Lincoln-Douglas debates, the Republicans won the popular election but the Illinois legislature reelected Douglas to the senate. Lincoln and Douglas were rivals again in 1860 for the presidency. Following Lincoln's election and the start of the Civil War, Douglas gave the president his active support. This county was created as part of Dakota territory in January, 1873.

2348 *Edmunds County*

Newton Edmunds (1819–1908)— Edmunds was born in Niagara County, New York, on May 31, 1819, and moved with his family to Michigan territory while he was still a boy. He was living in the state of Michigan when the Civil War started and in June, 1861 he received a federal appointment to be chief clerk in the surveyor-general's office of the brand new territory of Dakota. In March, 1863, the first governor of Dakota territory, William Jayne (1826–1916), resigned. There were two local candidates to succeed him, and President Lincoln tried to avoid bitter political fighting on the new territory by offering the territorial governorship to Wisconsin's congressman John F. Potter (1817–1899). When Potter declined the offer, the president awarded it to the former governor's choice, Newton Edmunds. He was appointed as Dakota territory's second governor on October 6, 1863, and sworn into office on November 2 of that year. As governor, Edmunds also was superintendent of the territory's Indian affairs and in these turbulent, wild west days on the Dakota frontier, Indian affairs were of major importance. Edmunds secured President Lincoln's support and an appropriation from the federal congress of $20,000 for use in negotiating treaties with the Indians, and he was largely successful in his treaty-making efforts with them. Edmunds served as the territory's governor until August, 1866, when he was removed from office as a by-product of feuding between President Andrew Johnson and the so-called radical Republicans in congress. Newton Edmunds made his home here, in Yankton, for the next four decades of his life and he represented Yankton County in one term of the legislature of Dakota territory. That legislative session began on January 14, 1879, which was six years after this county had been created and named in his honor by the territorial legislature in January, 1873. He died at his home in Yankton on February 13, 1908.

2349 *Fall River County*

Fall River— This county, in the southwestern corner of South Dakota, was created by the legislature of Dakota territory on March 6, 1883, and named for the Fall River, which flows though it. The Fall River is a tributary of the Cheyenne River. Hot Springs, South Dakota is the county seat of Fall River County and the Fall River flows through that community and tumbles in a series of rapids to Fall River Falls. The warmth provided to the Fall River by Mammoth Springs, and several smaller hot springs that feed water to Fall River, provide a water temperature that varies so little from summer to winter that goldfish are able to survive in the Fall River all year long. (One source claims that the uniform year-round water temperature is approximately 90 degrees.) By the 1890's the warm mineral springs in the Fall River had become a tourist attraction and health spa. A five-story hotel, the Evans Hotel, was constructed at Hot Springs to accommodate these tourists.

2350 *Faulk County*

Andrew J. Faulk (1814–1898)— Born in Pennsylvania on November 26, 1814, Faulk edited and published a newspaper in that state named the *Armstrong County Democrat*. As the newspaper's name implied, Faulk was initially a Democrat but his opposition to the extension of slavery led his conversion to the Republican party. In 1861 President Abraham Lincoln appointed Faulk to be trader at the Yankton Indian agency, a major base for military operations on the upper Missouri River, and Faulk came to Dakota territory at that time. However after only three years he returned to Pennsylvania with his family because of Indian hostilities here. In August, 1866 Newton Edmunds (1819–1908), Dakota's second territorial governor, was removed from office as a by-product of feuding between President Andrew Johnson and the so-called radical Republicans in congress. Walter A. Burleigh (1820–1896) was Dakota territory's delegate to the U.S. Congress at that time, and Burleigh was a son-in-law of Andrew J. Faulk. Burleigh persuaded President Andrew Johnson to appoint his father-in-law, as the third territorial governor of Dakota territory. Faulk arrived in Yankton in September, 1866, but his confirmation as governor was held up by Congress until March, 1867. As governor, Faulk concentrated much of his attention on development of the western portion of the territory. His efforts were so successful that Dakota territory lost its western end, which, together with portions of Idaho territory and Utah territory, was used by Congress to create the new territory of Wyoming, on July 25, 1868. By the time of the presidential election of 1868, President Andrew Johnson had been impeached and had no political power. In March, 1869, the new president, Ulysses S. Grant, removed Faulk as territorial governor. Faulk remained in Yankton and was briefly mayor of that city. He also was president of the Dakota bar association for a number of years. Faulk died at his home in Yankton in early September, 1898. This county was created and named in his honor by the legislature of Dakota territory during January, 1873.

2351 *Grant County*

Ulysses S. Grant (1822–1885) — Grant was a native of Ohio who graduated from the U.S. Military Academy at West Point. He served with distinction in the Mexican War, and in the Civil War he rose to become commander of all Union forces. After the Civil War, Grant briefly served as acting secretary of war and then two terms as president of the United States. He proved to be a rather mediocre president. This county was created in January, 1873, by the legislature of Dakota territory, during President Grant's first term as president. North Dakota also has a county named Grant, which honors Ulysses S. Grant. That county was created by North Dakota's state legislature in November, 1916. A large number of the counties in both North Dakota and South Dakota were created while Dakota was still a territory. One result of this chronology is that North Dakota and South Dakota have just one county, Grant County, that uses the same name.

2352 *Gregory County*

John S. Gregory (1831–) — John Shaw Gregory was a native of New York and a graduate of the U.S. Naval Academy at Annapolis, Maryland. In 1856 he immigrated to Nebraska territory and the following year he came to what would soon be Dakota territory and settled at Fort Randall. On March 2, 1861, the U.S. Congress established Dakota territory and Gregory was a member of the upper house (council) of the first legislature of the new territory, representing the Fort Randall district. It was during this term, in 1862, that this county was created and named for him by his fellow territorial legislators. He subsequently served several more times in Dakota's territorial legislature, and he served in both houses of that legislature. All of these sessions were during the 1860's. Gregory was, for a time, a federal Indian agent to the Ponca Indians, a Dakota subgroup, and also a trader, employed by John Blair Smith Todd (1814–1872) at Fort Randall. One account says that Gregory died in Dakota's Black Hills but the year of his death is not given.

2353 *Haakon County*

King Haakon VII of Norway (1872–1957) — This son of the crown prince and later king of Denmark, who ruled as Frederik VIII (1843–1912), was born on August 3, 1872, and christened as Christian Frederik Carl Georg Valdemar Axel. Within the family he was called Carl. Norway, whose powerful Vikings had been important since at least the 9th century A.D., had not been a separate nation, with its own monarch, since the late Middle Ages. Thus it was an emotional event for Norwegians when King Haakon VII took the oath of office on November 27, 1905, and became monarch of Norway and Norway alone. At various times during the past half millennium Norway had been joined with or ruled by a variety of countries. German states dominated Norway during the early part of this period and in later years Norway was ruled by Denmark, Sweden, or was united with one or more Scandinavian countries. In 1914, when South Dakota created this county, a significant portion of the state's population was Norwegian and Norwegian blood still flows through the veins of many of the state's current residents. However, it was not a Norwegian, but an Irishman, who selected this South Dakota county's name. His name was Hugh J. McMahon and he owned a ranch near Philip, South Dakota, when an election was to be held to decide whether or not to split Stanley County into two counties. Hugh J. McMahon favored the idea of dividing the county and he selected the name Haakon for the proposed new county as a clever inducement to win Norwegian support. Your author has both Norwegian and Irish ancestors and, as such, is a reasonably impartial judge concerning the namer of this county's name and it certainly rings true that it was the work of a crafty Irishman. At the election, the measure passed and since the vote was by secret ballot we have no ethnic breakdown of the election results. However, it seems safe to assume that the proposed name of Haakon would have been a source of pride to Norwegian voters. The biography of King Haakon VII is a thoroughly honorable one. He was born to privilege as member of the Danish royal family and after ascending Norway's throne in 1905, he dispensed with much of the pomp of royalty and became known as "the people's king." More importantly, when Nazi Germany invaded Norway in 1940, King Haakon VII refused to abdicate and, unlike Vidkun Quisling (1887–1945), Haakon VII also refused to collaborate with the Nazis. Rather, he headed a Norwegian government in exile based in London, England. On his 85th birthday, the king was still alive and in power although his health was failing and visitors from Sweden and Denmark came to celebrate his birthday. He died during the following month, in September, 1957.

2354 *Hamlin County*

Hannibal Hamlin (1809–1891) — This native of Maine was too poor to afford college but he farmed for awhile and accumulated enough cash to see him through law school. He practiced law in Maine and served in that state's house of representatives. He was speaker of that house in 1837, 1839 and 1840. During the antebellum period, Hamlin represented Maine in both houses of the U.S. Congress and was governor of Maine. The 1860 Republican national convention, which had nominated the "westerner," Abraham Lincoln, from Illinois, for president, sought to balance the ticket, geographically by nominating Hannibal Hamlin of Maine for vice-president. Lincoln and Hamlin were, of course, elected and Hamlin was vice-president of the United States during the Civil War. Hamlin had expected to be offered the vice-presidential nomination on Abraham Lincoln's 1864 reelection ticket, but the Republicans chose Andrew Johnson, instead and it was Johnson, rather than Hamlin, who became president when Abraham Lincoln was assassinated in April, 1865. Hamlin subsequently returned to the Senate where he represented Maine for two terms and from 1881 to 1882 and he was minister to Spain. This county was created by the legislature of Dakota territory in January, 1873.

2355 *Hand County*

George H. Hand (1837–1891) — George H. Hand was born in Akron, Ohio, on August 9, 1837. He moved with his parents to Wisconsin when he was about 16 years old, studied law there, was admitted to the bar and established a law practice in Wisconsin. He moved on to McGregor, Iowa, and practiced law in that community about four years. In 1864 Hand enlisted in the Union army during the Civil War. Fortunately, the war was nearly over then and after he was mustered out of the army, Hand came to Yankton, Dakota territory. He arrived here in 1865, and in 1867 he was appointed by the federal government as a U.S. attorney for Dakota territory. Hand remained in that office until 1869, when he resigned to practice law. During the 1870–1871 session of Dakota's territorial legislature, George H. Hand served in the lower house and his fellow legislators elected him speaker of the house. In 1874 the federal government appointed Hand to be secretary of Dakota territory and he served in that office from 1874 to 1883. The office of territorial secretary carries little power but the office of territorial governor holds significant power and influence. When the governor is unable to perform his duties, the secretary becomes acting governor. This happened in 1880, when Dakota's territorial governor William A. Howard (1813–1880) died, and George H. Hand became the acting governor of Dakota territory. There was a good deal of popular support in the territory for making Hand the official territorial governor but the president chose not to appoint him to that office. This county was created during January, 1873, by the legislature of Dakota territory. After Hand left the office of territorial secretary he practiced law in Yankton and he died in Pierre, South Dakota, on March 10, 1891.

2356 *Hanson County*

Joseph R. Hanson (–1917)—This native of Lancaster, New Hampshire was born sometime during the period 1835–1837, and when he was about 20 years old he decided to seek his fortune in western America. Initially, Hanson got as far west as Chicago and was employed there in the furniture business. In 1857 he moved to Winona, in Minnesota territory, near the edge of our country's western frontier. Apparently not happy until he had all civilization behind him, Hanson came to Yankton in 1858, when it was still part of unorganized territory. One source says that at the time of his arrival here, there were but four Whites in Yankton, all fur traders. Hanson made Yankton his home for more than half a century. As a very early settler of Yankton, Hanson was in a position to deal in real estate while he helped the young community grew. Dakota territory was created on March 2, 1861, and Hanson was soon appointed chief clerk of

the territorial legislature. He later served a term himself, in the lower house of the legislature of Dakota territory. That was during the session which convened on December 5, 1864, and adjourned on January 13, 1865. Biographical sketches of Joseph R. Hanson clearly indicate that he held a military rank as a commissioned officer in Dakota territory during days when defense from Indian attacks was an issue. However, his rank is given in some accounts as major and in others as colonel. In 1865 he received a presidential appointment as Indian agent for the upper Missouri region, an important post because of the very large population of Dakota (Sioux) Indians here at that time. Hanson held that post until 1870. He was also active was active introducing railroads to Dakota territory and in developing a constitution for the state of South Dakota. He died at Yankton in 1917. This county was created and named in his honor by the legislature of Dakota territory on January 13, 1871.

2357 *Harding County*

John A. Harding (–)—A native of Granville, Ohio, Harding immigrated to Dakota territory and settled in a mining area in the Black Hills. He served just one term in the legislature of Dakota territory, representing Deadwood and Lawrence County in the lower house of the 1881 legislature. His fellow legislators elected him speaker of the house during that term. Harding owned mining company stock in the Carbonate area of the Black Hills. Mildred Fielder's article in the 1956 issue of *South Dakota Report and Historical Collections* (volume 28) entitled "Carbonate Camp," tells us that Harding sold some or all of his mining stock in 1888. This county was created by the legislature of Dakota territory in 1881, during the one term that John A. Harding served in that body, and was speaker of the house. In 1898 a general election was held among the voters of northwestern South Dakota and, as a result of a vote at that election, Harding County's territory was absorbed by Butte County and Harding County ceased to exist. But, like the mythological Phoenix, Harding County was reborn. A general election was held in 1908 which favored re-establishment of the county and on February 26, 1909, the state of South Dakota officially ratified that decision by recreating Harding County.

2358 *Hughes County*

Alexander Hughes (1846–1907)—Hughes

was born on September 30, 1846, in Brantford, Canada, but moved to Columbia County, Wisconsin, with his parents, when he was still an infant. He enlisted in the Union army for action in the Civil War when he was still a youth, about 15 years of age. During that war Hughes served with distinction and was wounded in several battles. After the war, Hughes returned to Wisconsin to resume his education and subsequently was admitted to the bar in Iowa on February 17, 1869. Two years later Hughes moved westward to Elk Point, in what is now South Dakota. Here he engaged in the practice of law and served on three occasions in the upper house (council) of Dakota's territorial legislature. During the session that convened on December 2, 1872, and adjourned in January, 1873, Hughes represented Elk Point and Union County and was president of the council. It was during that term of the territorial legislature that this county was created and named in his honor, effective January, 1873. Hughes later moved to Bismarck in the northern half of Dakota territory and he represented Bismarck and Burleigh County in the councils of the territorial legislatures of 1887 and 1889. He was attorney general of Dakota territory and for a number of years he served as an attorney for the Northern Pacific Railway in northern Dakota territory and the state of North Dakota. When North Dakota was admitted to statehood, Hughes was elected to the first two sessions of the new state's senate. He retired from the legal profession about 1901 and moved to Minneapolis, Minnesota. He died in that city on November 24, 1907.

2359 *Hutchinson County*

John S. Hutchinson (1829–1889)—A native of England, Hutchinson immigrated to America and was a lawyer in both Kansas territory and Minnesota. He was appointed, in 1861, to be the first secretary of the brand new territory of Dakota. This was a federal appointment, and a political plum. Hutchinson was a personal friend of President Abraham Lincoln's secretary of state, William H. Seward (1801–1872), and it was this political connection that led President Lincoln to appoint Hutchinson to be Dakota territory's first secretary. In 1862 Hutchinson brought his wife to live with him in Yankton, Dakota territory. He was the first federally appointed official in the territory to bring his wife to Dakota and become a bona fide resident of the territory, and the gesture was popular with the local citizens. The office of territorial secretary carries little power but the office of territorial governor holds significant power and influence. When the governor of the territory is unable to perform his duties, the secretary becomes acting governor. This happened during several absences from the territory by Dakota's territorial governor, William Jayne (1826–1916), and again when Jayne resigned the governorship in 1863. Hutchinson arrived in Dakota territory in April, 1861, and he served as the territory's secretary from 1861 to 1865. At the expiration of his first term as territorial secretary Hutchinson was re-appointed but he resigned within a month to accept appointment as consul at Leghorn, Italy. Hutchinson's primary motive in accepting this assignment was to give his daughter the educational and cultural advantages of foreign residence and study. About 1870 he returned to America and practiced law in Chicago. This county was created by the legislature of Dakota territory on May 8, 1862, during the first term of the territorial legislature and it was named for the popular territorial secretary, John S. Hutchinson.

2360 *Hyde County*

James Hyde (1842–1902)— Hyde was born at Mapleton, Pennsylvania, on April 14, 1842, and moved with his parents to Iowa when he was about eight years old. On May 23, 1862, he enlisted in the Union army and participated in a number of combat actions during the Civil War. Hyde also was held as a prisoner of war at Libby prison for three months and at the dreadful Andersonville prison for 11 months. Mustered out of the army with an honorable discharge on May 24, 1865, Hyde soon settled in the community of Vermillion, in the southeastern corner of Dakota territory. He was a pioneer settler of Clay County there, and he served just one term in the legislature of Dakota territory, representing Vermillion and Clay County in the lower house. This was during the legislative session that convened at Yankton on December 2, 1872, and adjourned on January 10, 1873. It was during that legislative session, during the month of January, 1873, that this county was created and named in his honor by his fellow members of the territorial legislature. James Hyde died at Vermillion, South Dakota, on May 28, 1902.

2361 *Jackson County*

John R. Jackson (–)— The genealogy of Jackson County, South Dakota, is complicated. This county was first created in 1883 by the legislature of Dakota territory and named for John R. Jackson, a member of the upper house (council) during that legislative session, representing Minnehaha County, in southeastern Dakota territory. At that time John R. Jackson lived in Valley Springs, Minnehaha County. John R. Jackson served in just one other term of the legislature of Dakota territory; that was in the lower house of the 1879 session. Jackson was speaker of the house in that 1879 session of the territorial legislature. John R. Jackson never was a member of the legislature of the state of South Dakota. During the three decades following the first creation of this county in 1883, a series of legislatures made a series of changes, each one shrinking Jackson County's borders. Finally, Jackson County vanished from the map. In 1914 Jackson County was re-established as a result of an election held by the voters of Stanley County, South Dakota. Jackson County now lies in the central portion of South Dakota, a bit west and a bit south of the center of the state.

2362 *Jerauld County*

H. A. Jerauld (–)— This county was created on March 9, 1883, by the legislature of Dakota territory and named for one of its members, H. A. Jerauld, a member of the upper house (council). Jerauld also served in one other term of the legislature of Dakota territory, the 1870 legislative session, when he was a member of the lower house. In both of these territorial legislatures, Jerauld represented areas that are now within the state of South Dakota. H. A. Jerauld was never a member of the legislature of the state of South Dakota. The year of his death is uncertain, but we know that he was still living in 1903 because he sent a letter to William H. H. Beadle (1838–1915), from National City, California, dated July 20, 1903.

2363 *Jones County*

Jones County, Iowa— In 1908, the voters of Lyman County, in central South Dakota, considered a proposition to divide their county into two counties. That proposition was defeated but a similar proposition was on the ballot in 1910. That measure also was defeated. Finally, in 1916 a vote on dividing Lyman County was taken which passed and Lyman County was divided into two portions, the smaller portion was established on the western side as Jones County, named in honor of Jones County, Iowa, the former home of a number of the local settlers. Jones County, Iowa, had been created in December, 1837, when Iowa was part of Wisconsin territory, and it was named for George W. Jones (1804–1896).

George W. Jones (1804–1896)— A native of Vincennes, Indiana territory, Jones moved in 1827 to Michigan territory and settled about seven miles from Dubuque. He later served in the army during the Black Hawk War. In 1833 he was appointed judge of the U.S. district court and in 1835 Jones was elected to be Michigan territory's delegate to the U.S. Congress. In that capacity he was instrumental in securing passage of the bill that created Wisconsin territory, effective April 20, 1836, and he then became the first delegate to the U.S. Congress from Wisconsin territory. He soon became active in congress to create a separate Iowa territory. That effort also met with success, effective June 12, 1838. Jones later served as surveyor-general of Iowa and Wisconsin. In 1845 he moved to Dubuque. In December of the following year, Iowa was admitted to statehood and Jones soon became one of Iowa's first United States senators. He represented Iowa in the senate for some 12 years and later was President Buchanan's minister to New Granada (now Colombia).

2364 *Kingsbury County*

George W. Kingsbury (1837–1925) & T. A. Kingsbury (–)— This county was created in January, 1873, by the legislature of Dakota territory and named for two brothers, George W. and T. A. Kingsbury, both of whom had represented Yankton County in Dakota's territorial legislature. T. A. Kingsbury was a member of the legislature during the session in which this county was created. His brother, George W., had represented Yankton in several earlier legislatures of Dakota territory.

George W. Kingsbury (1837–1925)— George W. Kingsbury was born on December 16, 1837, in Oneida County, New York, and, until he came to Dakota territory in 1862, he was constantly on the move. We find him engaged in civil engineering in the Utica, New York, area and in Wisconsin, and then involved in printing in Wisconsin, Missouri and in both Leavenworth and Junction City in Kansas. In fact, when he arrived in Yankton, Dakota territory, on March 17, 1862, he only planned to stay for three months, but he remained here for the rest of his life. Here he became involved in newspaper and printing ventures, served several consecutive terms in the upper house of Dakota's territorial legislature in the mid-1860's and, much later, in 1895, represented Yankton in the senate of the state of South Dakota.

T. A. Kingsbury (–)—What little is known of T. A. Kingsbury is easily told. He was a brother of George W. Kingsbury (1837–1925) and their parents were Asa Kingsbury of Connecticut and his wife Ruama Barnes, a native of Jefferson County, New York. Asa and Ruama Barnes Kingsbury had ten children. Among the boys were George W. and T. A. Kingsbury. T. A. Kingsbury apparently followed his brother, George W., to Yankton, Dakota territory, but he arrived here early enough to be ranked as a pioneer settler. T. A. Kingsbury represented Yankton County in the lower house of the legislature of Dakota territory during just one legislative session. That was the session which convened in Yankton on December 2, 1872, and adjourned on January 10, 1873. It was this session of Dakota's territorial legislature that created Kingsbury County. T. A. Kingsbury was never a member of the legislature of the state of South Dakota.

2365 *Lake County*

Numerous lakes in this vicinity—This county was created during January, 1873, by the legislature of Dakota territory and named for the numerous lakes in this vicinity. Lake Herman, Lake Madison, Lake Badus and Bryant Lake are the larger lakes within the county but there are other smaller ones within the county, as well. Some of these lakes had been enjoyed as resorts by American Indians during earlier, happier, times. In addition to the lakes within the county itself, within 40 miles of Lake County's northern borders several rather large lakes may be found.

2366 *Lawrence County*

John Lawrence (–)—John Lawrence settled at Sioux Falls, in southeastern Dakota, in 1860 before Dakota territory had been created by the U.S. Congress. Soon afterward, in the early 1860's, in the face of threatened Indian attacks, Lawrence was appointed a second-lieutenant in Company A of the Dakota militia, or home guards. The leader of that company was Captain Frank M. Ziebach (1830–1929). At that time, all regular army troops were fighting in the Civil War and A Company, and the other Dakota militia companies, were needed to fend off any Indian attacks

which materialized. Several years later, in mid-1867, he was appointed to the staff of Dakota's territorial governor, Andrew J. Faulk (1814–1898), as aide-de-camp, and was given the honorary title of colonel, as a result of that appointment. In the spring of 1868, Lawrence was appointed superintendent of the Sioux City and Fort Randall wagon road and he supervised completion of the bridges over rivers and streams along this wagon route. John Lawrence served in four terms of Dakota's territorial legislature. He was a member of the lower house during the sessions that convened in 1863 and 1864 and served in the upper house (council) in the sessions which began in 1872 and 1874. It was during the last of these four sessions that Lawrence County was created, on January 11, 1875, and named by the territorial legislators for one of their own members. Colonel Lawrence became a resident of this county in the Black Hills that had been named in his honor and, after the county was organized, he became the first treasurer of Lawrence County. He died at his home in Deadwood in Lawrence County.

2367 *Lincoln County*

Lincoln County, Maine—This county was created on April 5, 1862, by the first legislature of Dakota territory. During that legislative session, Wilmot W. Brookings (1833–1905) was a member of the upper house (council) of the territorial legislature. Brookings had been born in Maine and was an 1855 graduate from Bowdoin College in that state. Brookings suggested that this new county be named Lincoln County, in honor of Lincoln County, in his home state of Maine. When Brookings' fellow territorial legislators agreed to his suggested name for this new county, some of them may have intended to indirectly honor Abraham Lincoln, who was then serving his first term as president. Since this county was created during the early period of the Civil War, that would also have been a patriotic gesture. However, Lincoln County in Maine was not named for Abraham Lincoln, but for the town on Lincoln, England.

Lincoln County, Maine — Town of Lincoln, England—Lincoln County in Maine was created on May 28, 1760, while Maine was part of Massachusetts Bay, a royal colony of England. The county's name was chosen in compliment to Thomas Pownall (1722–1805), who was the royal governor of Massachusetts Bay Colony from 1757 to 1760. Pownall was born in Lincoln, England, and attended grammar school there.

Lincoln, England—During the years that England was occupied by the Roman Empire, Lincoln was an important town named Lindum Colonia. During the reign of King William I (–1087), a castle was built here and a magnificent cathedral, with three towers, was erected about the beginning of the 13th century. The town of Lincoln, in eastern England, was one of the wealthiest towns in provincial England during the Middle Ages. Its wealth came largely from clothing and other textile manufactures. However, by 1515, this industry was disappearing from Lincoln, leaving it in decay. The imposition by the town fathers of inward-looking restrictions on craftsmen and capitalists hastened Lincoln's economic decline from its medieval greatness. Lincoln, England suffered major plagues during the decades of the 1580's and 1590's but lesser plagues were in almost constant attendance in Lincoln for centuries. In spite of all of this, Lincoln remained one of England's most populous towns. Its population was estimated to be 4,000 in the year 1676. Railroad trains began to provide service to Lincoln in 1846. The town of Lincoln is the county town of Lincolnshire.

Virtually all sources on the history, geography and place names of Dakota territory and South Dakota incorrectly state that Lincoln County, South Dakota, was named for President Abraham Lincoln. The correct, albeit obscure, origin is cited in *The History of Lincoln County, South Dakota*, published in 1985 by the Lincoln County History Committee, Canton, South Dakota. That work's reference to the author of this county's name, Wilmot W. Brookings (1833–1905), as a member of the territorial legislature which created this county is accurate, as is the citation of Maine as the state of Brookings' birth. This explanation for the origin of the name of Lincoln County, South Dakota, is credible because of that, and also because many of the territorial legislators, who voted in favor of the name, might not have stopped to ponder the fact that Lincoln County, Maine was probably too old to have been named for the recently elected and popular current president. Other legislators might not have cared whether the name actually honored Lincoln County, Maine as long as the name on the map came out spelled the same as that of our nation's popular Civil War president.

2368 *Lyman County*

William P. Lyman (–)—Lyman was born about 1833 (the 1860 federal census lists his age as 27) and he served in the U.S. army during 1855, when the army's officer, William S. Harney (1800–1889) led a punitive military expedition against Indians in the West. William Penn Lyman was a member of that very regrettable expedition. He stayed on in the West and established a ferry on the James River, near the military wagon trail from Sioux City to Fort Randall. The ferry proved very useful to the military and Lyman remained as a settler, perhaps the first White settler in Yankton County, or even the first west of the Vermillion River. In 1857 Lyman built a ferry-house and trading post on the east bank of the James River, at the ferry crossing, and the following spring he erected a trading post at Yankton, on behalf of his employers, Frost, Todd & Company. At some point Lyman married Winona, a daughter of the Yankton Indian leader, Struck-by-the-Ree (1804–1888). William P. and Winona Lyman had at least three children, Martha, John and Ella. William P. Lyman and his mixed-blood family remained residents of the present Yankton County, South Dakota, until they migrated to the Black Hills, of western Dakota territory in 1876. Lyman resided in the Black Hills a very short time and then moved to Montana territory, where he was involved in construction work for the Northern Pacific Railway. About 1880, Lyman died from pneumonia at Red Lodge, Montana territory, while working on the railroad construction project. A number of the sketches and references to William Penn Lyman that appear in the historical literature about Dakota territory refer to him as "Major Lyman." John Pattee's article entitled "Dakota Campaigns," which appeared in the 1910 issue of *South Dakota Historical Collections* (volume 5), referred to William P. Lyman as "Major of the Dakota Volunteer Cavalry." This county was created by the legislature of Dakota territory during January, 1873. Lyman was a member of the lower house of Dakota's territorial legislature, representing Charles Mix County, during the legislative session that this county was created. He did not serve in any other session of Dakota territory's legislature and he died before South Dakota was admitted to the Union.

2369 *McCook County*

Edwin S. McCook (1837–1873)—Born in Carrollton, Ohio, on March 26, 1837, McCook graduated from the U.S. Naval Academy at Annapolis, Maryland. Although educated for the navy, he preferred an army

career and by September, 1861, had become a captain in the Union army during the Civil War. McCook served with distinction during the Civil War. Wounded on three occasions, he resigned from the army in September, 1864, after attaining the rank of brevet brigadier-general. McCook was appointed by the federal government to be the fifth secretary of Dakota territory and he served in that capacity from his appointment in 1872 until his death in 1873. McCook was a supporter of the federally appointed governor of Dakota territory, John A. Burbank (1827–1905) and both of them became involved (on the same side) of heated disputes related to the coming of the railroad. It is known that the secretary of Dakota territory, Edwin S. McCook (1837–1873) lost his life as result of the railroad dispute(s) on September 11, 1873. Several accounts call his death an assassination. The alleged assassin was convicted of murder but that decision was reversed on appeal. It would be difficult to describe McCook's death as an assassination based on the events which took place immediately prior to his death. The alleged assassin was a banker, and the banker and Secretary McCook became involved in a heated argument in a saloon. In the saloon, McCook threw the banker against a mirror and then rubbed his face in a spittoon. The banker left, returned, and shot McCook dead. Certainly this was harsh retaliation for a mere face-in-spittoon-rubbing, but this was Dakota territory at the edge of our nation's West, that was still pretty wild. Even in today's more civilized climate, in the absence of premeditation, it would be surprising to find a crime such as this classified as an assassination, or even first degree murder. It would be dramatic if we could end this tale by saying that this county was named in McCook's honor by the legislature of Dakota territory on account of his death in 1873 but the facts don't quite fit. This county was created by the legislature of Dakota territory in 1873, but this was done in January, 1873, eight months prior to the dramatic events of September 11, 1873.

2370 *McPherson County*

James B. McPherson (1828–1864)—A native of Ohio, McPherson attended the U.S. Military Academy at West Point, New York, where he graduated in 1853 at the head of his class. In the years preceding the Civil War, he taught practical engineering at West Point and then was involved in river harbor improvement and seacoast fortifi-

cation duties. McPherson served with distinction in the Union army during the Civil War and rose from the rank of mere first lieutenant in August, 1861, to brigadier-general of volunteers on May 15, 1862. Later that year he was promoted to major-general of volunteers. His final promotion occurred effective August 1, 1863, when he was made brigadier-general of the regular army. In March, 1864, McPherson was given command of the army of the Tennessee, which he led in the campaign in north Georgia. McPherson was killed on July 22, 1864, during the battle of Atlanta, Georgia. This county was created by the legislature of Dakota territory during January, 1873.

2371 *Marshall County*

Marshall Vincent (–)—Vincent had been a resident of Three Mile Bay, New York prior to coming to Andover, in what is now Day County, South Dakota. Here he established a homestead claim but he sold that claim to one William Mills and moved north, to Britton. At that time both Andover and Britton were in Day County, Dakota territory. In March, 1883, Vincent erected a building in Britton and on April 9, 1883, he opened a flour and feed store in that building at Britton. Marshall Vincent was elected as a county commissioner of Day County, representing the Britton district, in 1884. Marshall County was created out of the northern portion of Day County by the legislature of Dakota territory in 1885, while Marshall Vincent was serving as a county commissioner of Day County. Some sources state that Marshall Vincent was a member of the first county commission of Marshall County, but sources that specifically list the names of Marshall County's first county commissioners show Henry Gerberich, Ralph Hay (or Hoy) and Ole Ruswick, but not Marshall Vincent.

2372 *Meade County*

Fort Meade—Meade county was created on February 7, 1889, by the last legislature of Dakota territory, and named for Fort Meade, a U.S. military fort, in southwestern Dakota territory. The fort had been established on August 28, 1878, in the Black Hills, 14 miles northeast of the town of Deadwood, Dakota territory. The fort's site was selected by General Philip H. Sheridan (1831–1888) and the fort was established under the leadership of Major Henry M. Lazelle (1832–1917). In earlier years the federal government had used its forces to protect Indians in this area from intrusion by Whites, because the Paha Sapa section of the Black Hills had been ceded to the Indians by an 1868 treaty. The area was also sacred to the Indians by tradition. However a lot had happened between that 1868 treaty and 1878. Gold had been discovered in the Black Hills in 1874 and a massive influx of White prospectors soon arrived. On June 25, 1876, General George A. Custer (1839–1876) and all of his men lost their lives to the Indians in the battle of Little Big Horn in Montana territory. By 1878, when Fort Meade was established, the official federal perspective had changed from honoring the treaty of 1868 and protecting the Indians, to ignoring that treaty and protecting Whites from the Indians. It was for this purpose that Fort Meade was established. The fort's first name was Camp Ruhlen but the post was officially designated Fort Meade on December 30, 1878, and a military reservation consisting of about 12 square miles was attached to it during that month. The fort's name honors U.S. army General George G. Meade (1815–1872). In 1944 the facilities at Fort Meade became the home of a Veterans Administration hospital.

George G. Meade (1815–1872) — A native of Cadiz, Spain, Meade graduated from the U.S. Military Academy at West Point in 1835. He served as an officer in the U.S. army in the Second Seminole Indian War in Florida and later was cited for gallant conduct during the Mexican War. Shortly after the Civil War began in 1861, Meade was promoted to brigadier-general in the Union army. He served with distinction in the Civil War and attained the rank of major-general and command of the army of the Potomac. Meade's most famous Civil War achievement was his victory in the battle of Gettysburg over Confederate General Robert E. Lee's forces.

2373 *Mellette County*

Arthur C. Mellette (1842–1896) — Born in Indiana on June 23, 1842, Arthur Calvin Mellette was a farm boy, who attended Indiana University during the early 1860's and then served as an enlisted man in the Union army during the Civil War. After the war, Mellette returned to Indiana and secured a law degree from Indiana University. Admitted to the Indiana bar, Mellette was a newspaperman as well as a lawyer and was also a member of the lower house of the Indiana legislature. He moved to the West in 1878 on account of his wife's health, and lived first in Colorado before settling in Springfield, Dakota, territory in

1879. Mellette soon began agitating for division of Dakota territory into two states. In 1885 he was even elected as a provisional state governor, but that was premature. Statehood was half a decade away. Indiana's U.S. senator, Benjamin Harrison (1833–1901), introduced bills calling for South Dakota's statehood on two occasions but they failed to pass in Congress. When Senator Benjamin Harrison became our nation's president, in March, 1889, he immediately appointed Arthur C. Mellette as Dakota's territorial governor. Mellette held that office until South Dakota was admitted to the Union on November 2, 1889. Arthur C. Mellette was elected as the first governor of the new state of South Dakota. Elected to a second term, Mellette declined to run for a third term as the state's governor and retired from the governor's office in January, 1893. He briefly practiced law in Watertown, South Dakota, but soon suffered financial reversals and moved to Pittsburg, Kansas, to practice law. He died in May, 1896. This county was created on March 9, 1909.

2374 *Miner County*

Ephraim Miner (1833–) & Nelson Miner (1827–1879) — This county was created by the legislature of Dakota territory during January, 1873. At that time both Ephraim Miner and Nelson Miner were members of the territorial legislature. Ephraim Miner was serving in the lower house representing Yankton County and Nelson Miner was a member of the legislature's upper house (council). The legislators of Dakota territory honored two of their members when they created this county.

Ephraim Miner (1833–) — Born a native of Oswego County, New York, on April 5, 1833, Ephraim Miner moved with his parents to Kankakee County, Illinois, when he was about 20 years old. Three years later he moved north, first to Walworth County, Wisconsin, and then, in 1857 to Blue Earth County, Minnesota territory. There he taught school and, together with a brother, A. W. Miner, had charge of a store, briefly. Before coming to Dakota territory, Ephraim Miner moved around even more frequently; first back to Wisconsin, next mining in Colorado territory, and then to Saint Joseph, Missouri, where he worked for the American Express Company. He also worked for that firm in Chicago, Illinois, and was a railroad employee in Chicago. Ephraim Miner finally came to Yankton, Dakota territory, in the fall of 1867. His first position here was as a clerk in a store. Soon after that,

Ephraim Miner was in charge of the surveyor-general's office for three years. He was a member of Dakota territory's legislature, representing Yankton County in the lower house during two legislative sessions. The first of these was the session that convened in 1870 and the second was the session which created this county in January, 1873. Ephraim Miner was employed by the American Express Company in Yankton, served as recorder of deeds here and was the proprietor of a flour mill, which was constructed in 1890.

Nelson Miner (1827–1879) — Born on September 29, 1827, at Hartland, Ohio, Nelson Miner attended Oberlin College in Ohio, earning enough money as a school teacher to see him through three years of study at Oberlin. Back in Hartland, Ohio, Nelson Miner was elected justice of the peace and he held that position for two years while teaching and studying law. He participated in the California gold rush, but only stayed at it one year and returned to Ohio. In 1852 Nelson Miner moved to Adel, Iowa, where he practiced law and in 1860 he came to what is now southeastern South Dakota and was a founder of the town of Vermillion here. During the early 1860's, regular federal troops were unable to defend the Dakota frontier from Indian attacks, being occupied in the Civil War. Nelson Miner was among those who entered the army here in Dakota territory because of this need for military manpower and he was mustered in as a captain on January 14, 1862. He remained in the army until January, 1865, and was effective in a number of battles with the Indians. He was one of General Alfred Sully's (1821–1879) key officers during this period. After his military service, Nelson Miner practiced law in Vermillion and represented Clay County in the upper house of Dakota's territorial legislature during four legislative sessions. The second of these sessions was the session which created this county in January, 1873. Nelson Miner died at Vermillion, Dakota territory, in October, 1879.

2375 *Minnehaha County*

Uncertain — This county was created on April 5, 1862, by the legislature of Dakota territory. Although there is ample reason to believe that the name was inspired by a recent poem of Henry Wadsworth Longfellow's (1807–1882), entitled *The Song of Hiawatha*, most sources on the history, geography and place names of Dakota territory and South Dakota dwell on possible translations of the Indian word *Min-*

nehaha and either omit any mention of the Longfellow connection or treat it as an interesting postscript. In Longfellow's poem, Minnehaha is a Dakota Indian maiden, whose hand in marriage is won by Hiawatha. Longfellow's poem tells us that Minnehaha was named by her father and provides a story for the origin of her name:

> "And he named her from the river,
> From the water-fall he named her,
> Minnehaha, Laughing Water."

The inspiration for portions of *The Song of Hiawatha* may have come from Mary Eastman's 1849 work entitled *Life & Legends of the Sioux*, but the name *Minnehaha*, was Longfellow's creation. In 1862, when the territorial legislature created this county, Longfellow was a well-established and popular American poet. His 1854 poem entitled *The Song of Hiawatha* was old enough to be known, yet new enough to be enjoying current popularity. Also, in April, 1862, the nation was sharing with Longfellow, his profound and lasting mourning over the death, in 1861, of his second wife. A number of the sources consulted mention the Big Sioux River in Minnehaha County, at Sioux Falls, and indicate that either the falls of that river or their "laughing waters" were inspiration for this county's name. Dr. Virgil J. Vogel, who is an authority on Indian names, states in his work entitled *Indian Names in Michigan*, that the literal meaning of the Santee Dakota word *Minnehaha* is "curling water," but that these Indians used it as a generic term for any waterfall.

2376 *Moody County*

Gideon C. Moody (1832–1904)— A native of New York and a lawyer, Moody served in the Union army during the Civil War and rose to the rank of colonel. In 1864 he came to Yankton, in southeastern Dakota territory. Here he served in three sessions of the lower house of the territorial legislature and was speaker of the house during two of them. Appointed as an associate justice on the territory's supreme court, Moody served on that bench from 1878 to 1883. When South Dakota was admitted to statehood in 1889, Moody became one of the new state's first two U.S. senators. He died in California in 1904. When this county was created in January, 1873, by the legislature of Dakota territory, Moody had been a prior member and speaker of the territorial house but he was not a current member of the legislature.

2377 *Pennington County*

John L. Pennington (1821–1900)— A native of North Carolina and a newspaper publisher, Pennington moved to Alabama after the Civil War. He was elected to the Alabama senate during Reconstruction and served in that body five years. It was during this period that Pennington made the political contacts which led President Ulysses S. Grant to appoint him governor of Dakota territory on January 1, 1874. To promote settlement of the territory, Pennington vigorously promoted its desirability for wheat production. However, both grasshoppers and Indian warfare became problems during his term as governor. The grasshoppers invaded in waves in 1874, 1875 and 1876. The Indian warfare which became his problem resulted from an 1868 treaty and discovery of gold in the Black Hills in 1874. The Paha Sapa section of the Black Hills had been ceded to the Indians by an 1868 treaty but gold was discovered in these Black Hills in 1874. The area was also sacred to the Indians by tradition. Neither the 1868 treaty nor the sacred Indian traditions impressed gold-hungry prospectors and a massive influx of them arrived in the Black Hills in late 1874, prompting rather constant combat for a number of years between the Indians and Whites. When Pennington's term as governor expired, he was not re-appointed. Instead, he was appointed in 1878 as collector of Internal Revenue for Dakota. He later published a newspaper in Yankton, and following the death of his wife in 1891, he returned to Alabama and a newspaper career there. This county was created by Dakota territory on January 11, 1875, early in Pennington's term as the territory's governor.

2378 *Perkins County*

Henry E. Perkins (1864–)— A native of Windsor County, Vermont, and a lawyer, Perkins came to Deadwood in southwestern Dakota territory in 1883. He became involved in banking in nearby Sturgis in 1888 and served at one time as mayor of Sturgis. Perkins served three times in South Dakota's state senate, in the terms of 1903, 1907 and 1911. This county was created on February 26, 1909. Its name was suggested by Lewis Peck and G. E. Lemmon because Perkins had been instrumental in promoting passage of the act to create this new county in the northwestern section of South Dakota.

2379 *Potter County*

Joel A. Potter (1825–1895)— Potter was born in Litchfield County, Connecticut, on April 17, 1825. He is referred to in several accounts as "Dr. Potter," so he apparently was licensed to practice medicine. He served among the Indians and one account shows him at the Ponca Indian agency. Potter subsequently was a steward at the Yankton hospital for the insane and he was also elected to represent Yankton County in the upper house (council) of the session of Dakota's territorial legislature which convened on January 12, 1877. This county was originally created on January 14, 1875, by the legislature of Dakota territory and named Ashmore County. That name honored Samuel Ashmore of Elk Point, who had been a member of the lower house of the territorial legislature which convened in 1872. This county's name was changed from Ashmore to Potter, in honor of Joel A. Potter, in 1877, during the one and only session of the territorial legislature in which Potter served. Joel A. Potter died in Yankton on May 7, 1895.

2380 *Roberts County*

Samuel G. Roberts (1843–)— Born at Brooks, Maine, on March 10, 1843, Roberts enlisted in the Union army in 1861 during the Civil War and was mustered out of service on August 10, 1864. Roberts came west as far as Stillwater, Minnesota, and then re-enlisted in the Union army. During his first tour of duty Roberts had been engaged in combat and was wounded three times. His second tour, which lasted just one year, involved guard duty at Washington, D.C., and Indianapolis. He rose from private to first-lieutenant. After leaving the army, Roberts spent a year in Indianapolis, then moved to Minnesota again, studied law and was admitted to the bar in 1870. After practicing law in Minneapolis for two years, he came to Fargo in northeastern Dakota territory in January 1872. In Fargo he practiced law, and he also had a practice directly east, in Moorhead, Minnesota. Roberts was a founder of the First National Bank and one of its stockholders for a number of years. In other business ventures, he assisted in founding the Fargo Foundry and the Republican Newspaper Company. He also served on the Fargo city council and was twice a member of the legislature of Dakota territory, serving in the upper house of the sessions which convened in 1879 and 1883. It was during this 1883 session of the legislature that Roberts County, Dakota territory, was created and named in his honor by his fellow territorial legislators. The county was created on March 8, 1883. When Dakota territory was split into North and South Dakota on November 2, 1889, Roberts County became a part of South Dakota, even though its namesake's connection with Dakota territory was in what is today North Dakota.

2381 *Sanborn County*

George W. Sanborn (1832–)— Born in Bath, New Hampshire on September 25, 1832, Sanborn came west to Milwaukee, Wisconsin and there became a railroad man. He was employed by the Milwaukee & Mississippi Railroad, which in 1872, became part of the Chicago, Milwaukee & St. Paul Railroad conglomerate. He started as a brakeman and worked for decades in the railroad industry. In 1869 Sanborn was appointed assistant superintendent of the northern division of the railroad and, in 1870 was given supervisory responsibility for the Iowa & Dakota division, with his headquarters at Mason City, Iowa. (Several accounts dealing with this county's history refer to George W. Sanborn as "of Mason City, Iowa.") When Sanborn took over, the Iowa & Dakota division had but 126 miles of railroad track. Under his management the lines grew extensively. At Mason City, Sanborn took part in local civic affairs, serving as a member of the school board and as its president, for a time. Sanborn County was created and named by Dakota territory on March 9, 1883, when the railroad, under George W. Sanborn's management, came through eastern Dakota territory during the great Dakota boom of 1878–1887. The municipality of Woonsocket, in Sanborn County, was formed in 1883 at the junction of two of the railroad's lines. When the bill to create this new county in Dakota territory was under consideration, Nehemiah G. Ordway (1828–1909) was the territory's governor. Governor Ordway thought that the new county should be named Florence, in honor of his daughter. Representatives from the area of the proposed new county suggested the name Brisbine, in honor of a prominent local citizen, Judge Thornton W. Brisbine. After considering these proposals, the name Sanborn was selected for the new county, to recognize the importance of the railroads, which were vital to the development of Dakota, in linking its potentially vast agricultural output with distant markets.

2382 *Shannon County*

Peter C. Shannon (1821–1899)— A native of Virginia, Shannon moved to Pennsylvania and practiced law there a number of years before coming to Dakota territory. In 1873 he received a federal appointment to be chief justice of the supreme court of Dakota territory and he came to Dakota then. Shannon served as the territory's chief justice until the fall of 1881, when his second term expired. Judge Shannon was not a particularly charming person and he had made enough enemies here to make it politically impractical for President Chester A. Arthur to re-appoint him. After retiring from the bench, Judge Shannon resided in Canton in what is now South Dakota and was a resident of southern Dakota for the rest of his life. He actually died in California, when he fell from a wagon during a visit to that state in 1899. This county was created and named in his honor on January 11, 1875, during his term as chief justice.

2383 *Spink County*

Solomon L. Spink (1831–1881)— A native of New York and a lawyer, Spink practiced law in Iowa before moving to Paris, Illinois, where he was editor and publisher of the *Prairie Beacon*. He also served in the Illinois house of representatives. The office of secretary for a United States territory carries little actual power, but it is an appointed office, often a political plum, and Solomon L. Spink was appointed by President Abraham Lincoln to be secretary of Dakota territory just one day before the president was assassinated. Spink served in that post from 1865 to 1869. When a territorial governor is absent from the territory, or unable to perform his duties, the secretary of the territory becomes acting governor, a position which commands considerable power. In August, 1866, President Andrew Johnson appointed Andrew J. Faulk (1814–1898) as the governor of Dakota territory. Faulk arrived in Yankton in September, 1866, but his confirmation as governor was held up by congress until March, 1867. Solomon L. Spink was acting governor of Dakota territory until Faulk took office. Following Spink's term as secretary, he was elected as Dakota territory's one delegate to the U.S. Congress and served there from March 4, 1869, to March 3, 1871. He died in Yankton, in southeastern Dakota territory on September 22, 1881. This county was created in January, 1873, shortly after Spink had returned from Washington to Yankton.

2384 *Stanley County*

David S. Stanley (1828–1902)— A native of Ohio and an 1852 graduate of the U.S.

Military Academy at West Point, Stanley was commissioned as a second-lieutenant of dragoons and had risen to the rank of captain when the Civil War started. Stationed in Arkansas at that time, he was offered a commission in the Confederate army but rejected it and served throughout the Civil War as a Union officer. His fine record during the war resulted in his commission as a brevet major-general in the U.S. army in 1865. Following the war, he was reduced in rank to colonel and assigned to the Indian frontier. He served on the Indian frontier and in the West for some 25 years, and was a key player in opening our nation's West. During this period, from 1866 to 1874, Stanley served mainly in Dakota territory and was, for a time, commander of Fort Sully on the east bank of the Missouri River in Dakota territory, just east of the present Stanley County, South Dakota. In 1884 Stanley once again became a general, being appointed brigadier-general on March 24, 1884. He held a command in Texas until his retirement from the army in 1892. This county was created and named in Stanley's honor by the legislature of Dakota territory in January, 1873, during the period that the then-Colonel Stanley was stationed in Dakota.

2385 *Sully County*

Uncertain— This county was created in January, 1873, by the legislature of Dakota territory and there is no doubt that the name honors General Alfred Sully (1821–1879), but sources consulted are about equally divided on whether the county was named directly for General Sully, or for Fort Sully, which had earlier been named in his honor. Fort Sully was located within the borders of today's Sully County, South Dakota.

Fort Sully— Fort Sully was established during a campaign against the Dakota Indians by General Alfred Sully (1821–1879) on the banks of the Missouri River, about four miles east of Pierre, on September 14, 1863. First named Fort Bartlett, after its first commander, it was renamed in honor of General Sully after his 1864 expedition. This original site was abandoned on July 25, 1866, and the site for its replacement was selected by Lieutenant-Colonel George L. Andrews (1828–1899). The new Fort Sully was also to be on the Missouri River, 28 miles above of Pierre and its construction began in August, 1866. Located in the present Sully County, South Dakota, the fort was not abandoned by the army until 1894, when it was transferred to the Interior department.

Alfred Sully (1821–1879) — A native of Pennsylvania and an 1841 graduate of the U.S. Military Academy at West Point, Sully fought against the Seminole Indians, in Florida, in the Mexican War, and against Indians in what are now the Dakotas, Minnesota and Nebraska. During the early years of the Civil War Sully participated in combat against the Confederates and about October 1, 1862, he was promoted to brigadier-general. In the spring of 1863 the army decided that his services were in more urgent need in the West to fight the Dakota Indians in Minnesota and Dakota. As a result of his success in combat against the Indians in Dakota, he was promoted to brevet major-general of volunteers as well as brigadier-general in the regular army. Mustered out of the volunteer army in August, 1866, Sully was able to continue on in the regular army, but as a lieutenant-colonel and it was with that rank that he fought against the Cheyenne, Comanche and Kiowa tribes in the West. Sully was promoted to colonel in 1873 and died in Washington territory, at Fort Vancouver, on April 27, 1879.

2386 *Todd County*

John B. S. Todd (1814–1872) — John Blair Smith Todd was a native of Kentucky and an 1837 graduate of the U.S. Military Academy at West Point. He served as an officer in the war against the Seminole Indians in Florida, as a captain in the Mexican War and on our nation's northwestern frontier, in Minnesota territory. Todd resigned from the army in 1856 and became an Indian trader at Fort Randall in Dakota. While at Fort Randall, he managed to study enough law to be admitted to the bar. When Dakota territory was created, President Abraham Lincoln seriously considered him to be the governor of the new territory. However two factors mitigated against this. Todd was a Democrat, while the president was a Republican and, perhaps more importantly, Todd was connected by marriage to the president and "Honest Abe" wanted no nepotism. So Lincoln appointed William Jayne (1826–1916), instead. However, Todd represented Dakota territory in the U.S. Congress as this territory's first delegate and later was speaker of the house in the lower chamber of Dakota's territorial legislature. During the Civil War, John B. S. Todd served in the Union army as a brigadier-general. According to some erroneous accounts, John B. S. Todd was governor of Dakota territory from 1869 to 1871. Todd never served as Dakota territory's governor. John A. Burbank (1827–

1905) was governor of the territory from 1869 to 1871. This county was created by the state of South Dakota in 1909.

2387 *Tripp County*

Bartlett Tripp (1842–1911) — A native of Maine and an 1861 graduate of Waterville College (now Colby College) in that state, Tripp spent some time in our nation's Far West before attaining a law degree in 1867 at Albany, New York. In 1869 he came to Yankton, in the southeastern corner of Dakota territory. This county was created by the legislature of Dakota territory in January, 1873, before Bartlett Tripp (1842–1911) became prominent here. Since this chronology is puzzling, it should be mentioned that Bartlett Tripp had a brother in Dakota territory, William Tripp, who had been surveyor general of the territory from 1865 to 1869. However, no known source dealing with the history, geography or place names of Dakota territory or South Dakota suggests that this county was named for William Tripp. All are agreed that the county's name honors Bartlett Tripp. Although Bartlett Tripp gained some prominence in Dakota territory in 1873 as defense lawyer in the murder trial resulting from the shooting death of Dakota territory's secretary, Edwin S. McCook (1837–1873), since McCook lost his life in September, 1873, the murder trial could not have influenced the selection of this county's name, for it was created and named in January, 1873. Bartlett Tripp was destined to make up for his obscurity. He was chairman of the 1883 convention, which formed government for the nascent state of South Dakota and he served as chief justice of Dakota territory's supreme court from 1885 to 1889. In 1891, he was a strong candidate to succeed Gideon C. Moody (1832–1904) as U.S. senator from South Dakota but lost on the 40th ballot to compromise candidate James H. Kyle (1854–1901). Tripp was our nation's minister to Austria-Hungary from 1893 to 1897. He died at Yankton on December 9, 1911.

2388 *Turner County*

John W. Turner (1800–1883) — Born on February 23, 1800, in Oneida County, New York, Turner became involved in politics at an early age and received an appointment as collector of customs for the Oswego district from President Andrew Jackson. In 1846 Turner moved west, to Michigan, and engaged in lumbering. About 1858 he was elected sheriff of Saginaw County.

While serving as sheriff, Turner studied law and when his term as sheriff ended, he was admitted to practice law. Turner came to Dakota territory in 1863 and settled at Burbank, in Clay County, in the southeastern corner of the territory. Turner served five terms in the legislature of Dakota territory in the mid-1860's and early 1870's. He served three terms in the upper house (council) and two in the lower house. One of these legislative sessions convened on December 5, 1870, and it was during that term that Turner's fellow legislators created and named this county in his honor, during January, 1871. He was elected as Dakota territory's superintendent of public instruction in 1866 and in 1870. After Turner County had been created, John W. Turner moved to the county named in his honor, and built a grist mill in the valley of the Vermillion River. He died in Turner County, Dakota territory on April 11, 1883.

2389 *Union County*

Union side in the Civil War then in progress — When this county was created by the first legislature of Dakota territory, on April 10, 1862, it was named Cole County, in honor of Austin Cole, one of the nine members of the upper house (council) of the territory's first legislature. By 1864 our nation was embroiled in the Civil War, and the territorial legislature changed this county's name that year to Union County, in a gesture of support for the Union side in the Civil War.

2390 *Walworth County*

Walworth County, Wisconsin — This county was created by Dakota territory during January, 1873, and named for Walworth County, in Wisconsin. That earlier Walworth County had been created on December 7, 1836, while Wisconsin was still a territory, and named for Reuben H. Walworth.

Reuben H. Walworth (1788–1867) — Born in Connecticut on October 26, 1788, Reuben Hyde Walworth moved with his parents to New York when he was about 12 years old. The family settled on a farm near Hoosick, New York. Walworth studied law, was admitted to the New York bar in 1809 and established a law practice in Plattsburgh, New York, the following year. Prior to the War of 1812, Walworth served briefly as a circuit judge and during the War of 1812, he was an officer in the New York militia. He was aide-de-camp to General Benjamin Mooers and division judge advocate and held the rank of colonel. He returned to Plattsburgh after the war and was elected to represent New York in the U.S. House of Representatives. After serving one term in that body, Walworth was a judge in New York and was the state's chancellor from 1828 to 1848. In 1844 President John Tyler nominated Walworth to serve as an associate justice on the Supreme Court, but the Senate refused to confirm this nomination. The U.S. Senate rejected five out of President Tyler's six Supreme Court nominations; more rejections than any other American president has suffered in the history of the Supreme Court. Walworth died at Saratoga Springs, New York, on November 27, 1867.

2391 *Washabaugh County*

Frank J. Washabaugh (1849–1902)— Born at Bedford, Pennsylvania, in July, 1849, Washabaugh graduated from Lafayette College in that state before coming to Yankton, Dakota territory to practice law. Gold had been discovered in the Black Hills of southwestern Dakota in 1874 and Washabaugh moved to Rapid City at the eastern edge of the Black Hills in 1877. Here he engaged in a bit of placer mining and served as district attorney of Pennington County. Washabaugh was elected to represent the Black Hills area in the upper house (council) during four terms of the territorial legislature. It was during the first of these sessions, on March 9, 1883, that Washabaugh County was created and named in his honor. When South Dakota was admitted to statehood, Washabaugh was elected to the new state's senate and he was reelected to a second term. He subsequently was a county judge of Lawrence County, South Dakota and a circuit court judge. Judge Washabaugh was a resident of Deadwood, South Dakota, in the Black Hills, when he died at Johns Hopkins hospital in Maryland on May 29, 1902.

2392 *Yankton County*

Town of Yankton, Dakota territory— Yankton County was created on April 10, 1862, by the first legislature of the new Dakota territory and named for the town of Yankton in the southeastern corner of the territory, the town in which the territorial legislature was meeting when this county was created. Yankton was named as the first territorial capital and the town of Yankton continued as the capital of Dakota territory from 1861 until 1883, when Bismarck, in north-central Dakota was made the capital. In the late 1990's the city of Yankton, South Dakota, had a population of about 12,700. The town had been named for the Yankton Indians, who were residents of the area when the town of Yankton was founded in 1858.

Yankton Indians — The Yankton Indians are one of three principal divisions of the Dakota (or Sioux) Indians. They were the residents of Yankton, South Dakota, when American settlers arrived and their settlements extended from the area of the Missouri River, in what are today's states of South and North Dakota and Iowa. An early mention of the Yanktons by European explorers appeared on a 1683 map of Father Louis Hennepin's (1640–1705). Hennepin found them in the central area of today's Minnesota. Another European explorer, Pierre C. Le Sueur (1657–1704), found Yanktons in the pipestone region of southwestern Minnesota, near the South Dakota border in 1700; i.e., near the town of Yankton. The Lewis & Clark Expedition also encountered the Yankton, since much of their journey was along the Missouri River. During the 1860's and 1870's the Dakota Indians fought a losing battle against American settlers and remaining Dakota Indians, including the Yanktons, live mostly on reservations. An area of confusion regarding the population, over the years, of Yankton Indians, is caused by confusion between the names Yankton and Yanktonai. Population estimates for the Yankton Indians that appear in American historical literature is laced with probable confusion among the numbers of Yankton Indians and Yanktonai ("Little Yankton") Indians. In 1985 it was estimated that there were a total of some 60,000 Dakota Indians living on reservations in the United States, of which 54,441 (5,284 of whom were Yankton Dakota Indians) were associated with South Dakota reservations.

2393 *Ziebach County*

Frank M. Ziebach (1830–1929)— Born November 23, 1830, on a farm near Lewisburg, Pennsylvania, Ziebach left Pennsylvania in 1853 and worked on a newspaper at Madison, Wisconsin. He came home to Lewisburg in 1855 and established his own newspaper, the *Lewisburg Argus*. Two years later Ziebach immigrated to America's western frontier and established two newspapers in western Iowa, the *Western Independent*, at Sergeant Bluff, in 1857 and the *Sioux City Register* in 1858. He next bought out the *Sioux City Eagle* and soon brought that newspaper's machines to Yankton. On June 6, 1861, he established the first newspaper in the present South Dakota. Some sources call it the *Yankton Dakotaon* while others say its name was the *Weekly Dakotian*. This was just three months after Dakota territory had been established. During the early 1860's, regular federal troops were unable to defend the Dakota frontier from Indian attacks, because they were occupied in the Civil War. Frank M. Ziebach was among those who entered the army here in Dakota territory because of this need for military manpower and he was the leader and captain of Company A, of the Dakota militia, or home guards. He later served as mayor of Yankton and in both houses of the legislature of Dakota territory. Frank M. Ziebach died at the age of 99, on September 20, 1929. This county had been created and named in his honor by the state of South Dakota on February 1, 1911.

REFERENCES

Abbott, M. E. "Correspondence." *South Dakota Historical Collections*, Vol. 2. Aberdeen, South Dakota: 1904.

Abraham, Henry J. *Justices & Presidents: A Political History of Appointments to the Supreme Court.* New York, Oxford University Press, 1992.

Ambrose, Stephen E. *Undaunted Courage.* New York, Simon & Schuster, 1996.

Armstrong, M. K. "History and Resources of Dakota, Montana & Idaho." *South Dakota Historical Collections*, Vol. 14. Pierre, South Dakota: 1928.

Bailey, Dana R. *History of Minnehaha County, South Dakota.* Sioux Falls, Brown & Saenger, 1899.

Barrows, Vivian, et al. *Aurora County History.* Stickney, South Dakota, Argus Printers, 1983.

Bay, W. V. N. *Reminiscences of the Bench & Bar of Missouri.* St. Louis, F. H. Thomas & Co., 1878.

Baye, Elsie Hey. *Haakon Horizons.* Philip, South Dakota, State Publishing, 1982.

Bingham, John H. & Nora V. Peters. "A Short History of Brule County." *South Dakota Historical Collections*, Vol. 23. Pierre: 1947.

Boatner, Mark M. *The Civil War Dictionary.* New York, Random House, Inc., 1988.

Breeling, Lutie T. *When the Trail Was New in Mountraille.* Ross, North Dakota, 1956.

Briggs, Harold E. "The Early History of Clay County." M.A. Thesis, University of South Dakota, Vermillion, South Dakota, 1924.

Briggs, Harold E. "The Early History of Clay County." *South Dakota Historical Collections*, Vol. 13. Pierre, South Dakota: 1926.

Brookings County History Book. Brookings, South Dakota, Brookings County History Book Committee, 1989.

Brule County History. Pukwana, South Dakota, Brule County Historical Society, 1977.

Building an Empire: A Historical Booklet on Harding County, South Dakota. Buffalo, South Dakota. Buffalo Times-Herald, 1959.

Burns, Thomas R. *Handbook for South Dakota County Officials*. Vermillion, South Dakota, Governmental Research Bureau, University of South Dakota, 1972.

Callan, F. G. *A History of Richland County and the City of Wahpeton, North Dakota*.

"The Census of 1860." *South Dakota Historical Collections*, Vol. 10. Pierre, South Dakota: 1920.

Clay County Historic Sights Committee. *Clay County Place Names*. Vermillion, South Dakota, Clay County Historical Society, Inc., 1976.

Clements, John. *Wisconsin Facts*. Dallas, Texas, Clements Research II, Inc., 1990.

Cochrane, Eleanor. *Historical Collections of Deuel County*. Deuel County History Book Committee, 1977.

Codington County History Book Committee. *The First 100 Years in Codington County, South Dakota: 1879–1979*. Watertown Public Opinion Print, 1979.

County Historical Association. *History of Pioneer Sanborn County*. 1953.

County Historical Association. *Supplement to History of Pioneer Sanborn County*.

Coursey, O. W. *Who's Who in South Dakota*. Mitchell, South Dakota, Educator School Supply Co., 1913–1920.

Crawford, Lewis F. *History of North Dakota*. Chicago, American Historical Society, Inc., 1931.

Dale, Bob. *Early History of Campbell County*. Pollock, South Dakota.

Dalthorp, Charles J. *South Dakota's Governors*. Sioux Falls, Midwest-Beach Co., 1953.

Dickerson, Inga H. "Dakota Territorial Governors." Unpublished manuscript.

Dictionary of Wisconsin Biography. Madison, State Historical Society of Wisconsin, 1960.

Distad, Lucile. "A Study of Place-Names in Mellette County, South Dakota." M.A. Thesis, University of South Dakota, Vermillion, South Dakota, 1943.

Douglas County History & Centennial Observances: 1961. Stickney, South Dakota, Argus Printers.

Dunham, N. J. *A History of Jerauld County, South Dakota: From the Earliest Settlement to January 1st, 1909*. Wessington Springs, South Dakota, 1910.

Early Settlers in Lyman County. Pierre, South Dakota, State Publishing Co., 1974.

Echoes Thru the Valleys: Southwestern Meade County. Elk Creek Pioneer Association, 1968.

Ehrensperger, Edward C. *South Dakota Place Names*. Vermillion, University of South Dakota, 1941.

English, A. M. "Dakota's First Soldiers: History of the First Dakota Cavalry: 1862–1865." *South Dakota Historical Collections*, Vol. 9. Pierre, South Dakota: 1918.

Faber, Harold. *From Sea to Sea: The Growth of the United States*. New York, Farrar, Straus & Giroux, 1967.

Fall River County Pioneer Histories. Fall River, South Dakota, Fall River County Historical Society, 1976.

Fielder, Mildred. "Carbonate Camp." *South Dakota Report & Historical Collections*, Vol. 28. Pierre, South Dakota: 1956.

Fielder, Mildred. *Lawrence County for the Dakota Territory Centennial*. Lead, South Dakota, Lawrence County Centennial Committee, 1960.

Foster, James S. "Outlines of History of the Territory of Dakota & Emigrant's Guide to the Free Lands of the Northwest." *South Dakota Historical Collections*, Vol. 14. Pierre, South Dakota: 1928.

Fox, William S. *The Mythology of All Races*. New York, Cooper Square Publishers, Inc., 1964.

Frazer, Robert W. *Forts of the West*. Norman, University of Oklahoma Press, 1965.

Frink, Mrs. May Beadle. "The Hoosier: Biographical Sketch of General Beadle." *South Dakota Historical Collections*, Vol. 3. Aberdeen, South Dakota: 1906.

Frybarger, Marjorie L. "A Study of Place-Names in Meade County, South Dakota." M.A. Thesis, University of South Dakota, Vermillion South Dakota, 1941.

Fuller, Edmund. *Bulfinch's Mythology*. New York, Dell Publishing Co., Inc., 1979.

Goodfellow, Ferd J. "South Dakota's Early Surveys." *South Dakota Historical Collections*, Vol. 5. Pierre, South Dakota: 1910.

Greve, Tim. *Haakon VII of Norway*. London, England, C. Hurst & Co., 1983.

Hamlin County: 1878–1979. Hamlin Historical Committee.

Hanson, Agnes J. "A Study of Place-Names in Kingsbury County, South Dakota." M.A. Thesis, University of South Dakota, Vermillion, South Dakota, 1940.

Hanson, James A. *Metal Weapons, Tools & Ornaments of the Teton Dakota Indians*.

Lincoln, University of Nebraska Press, 1975.

Hanson, Myrle G. "A History of Harding County, South Dakota to 1925." M.A. Thesis, University of South Dakota, Vermillion, South Dakota, 1933.

Hanson, Myrle G. "A History of Harding County, South Dakota to 1925." *South Dakota Historical Collections*, Vol. 21. Pierre, South Dakota: 1942.

Harlow, Dana D. *Prairie Echoes: Spink County in the Making*. Aberdeen, South Dakota, Hayes Brothers Printing, 1961.

Harlow, Dana D. "A Study of Place-Names in Spink County, South Dakota." M.A. Thesis, University of South Dakota, Vermillion, South Dakota, 1944.

Hart, Herbert M. *Old Forts of the Northwest*. New York, Bonanza Books, 1963.

Healy, Diana Dixon. *America's Vice-Presidents*. New York, Atheneum, 1984.

Heidepriem, Scott. *Bring on the Pioneers!: History of Hand County*. Pierre, South Dakota, State Publishing Co., 1978.

Hennessy, W. B. *History of North Dakota*. Bismarck, Bismarck Tribune Co., 1910.

Hickman, George. *History of Marshall County, Dakota Territory*. Britton, Dakota Territory, J. W. Banbury, 1886.

Historical Atlas of Dakota. Chicago, A. T. Andreas, 1884.

Historical and Descriptive Review of South Dakota's Enterprising Cities. Omaha, Jno. Lethem, 1893.

History of Franklin & Cerro Gordo Counties, Iowa. Springfield, Illinois, Union Publishing Co., 1883.

The History of Lincoln County, South Dakota. Canton, South Dakota, Lincoln County History Committee, 1985.

A History of Pennington County, South Dakota. Dallas, Texas, Taylor Publishing Co.

History of the Red River Valley. Chicago, C. F. Cooper & Co., 1909.

History of Southeastern Dakota: Its Settlement & Growth. Sioux City, Iowa, Western Publishing Co., 1881.

Hodge, Frederick W. *Handbook of American Indians North of Mexico*. Totowa, New Jersey, Rowman & Littlefield, 1975.

Holbrook, Stewart H. *The Story of American Railroads*. New York, Crown Publishers, 1947.

Holland, Ann J. "A Study of Place-Names in Sanborn County, South Dakota." M.A. Thesis, University of South Dakota, Vermillion South Dakota, 1942.

Holmquist, June D., & Jean A. Brookins. *Minnesota's Major Historic Sites: A Guide*. St. Paul, Minnesota Historical Society, 1972.

Hoover, Herbert T., & Larry J. Zimmerman. *South Dakota's Leaders*. Vermillion,

South Dakota, University of South Dakota Press, 1989.

Hubbard, Walter, et al. "The Memoirs." *South Dakota Historical Collections*, Vol. 3. Aberdeen, South Dakota: 1906.

Hutcheson, Floyd E. "A Study of Place-Names in Davison County, South Dakota." M.A. Thesis, University of South Dakota, Vermillion, South Dakota, 1944.

Hyde County Historical & Genealogical Society. *Hyde Heritage*. Highmore, South Dakota, Hyde County Historical Society, 1977.

Jackson, W. Turrentine. "Dakota Politics During the Burbank Administration: 1869–1873." *North Dakota History*, Vol. 12, No. 3. Bismarck, North Dakota: July, 1945.

Jackson-Washabaugh Counties: 1915–1965. Jackson-Washabaugh County Historical Society, 1966.

James, Leta M. "A Place-Name Study of Beadle County, South Dakota." M.A. Thesis, University of South Dakota, Vermillion, South Dakota, 1939.

Jennewein, J. Leonard, & Jane Boorman. *Dakota Panorama*. Mitchell, South Dakota, Dakota Territory Centennial Commission, 1961.

Jewett, Verla J. *Isabel Territory Golden Jubilee*. Marceline, Missouri, Walsworth, 1961.

Johnson, Shirley E. "Charles Mix County in Retrospect." *South Dakota Department of History Report & Historical Collections*, Vol. 30. Pierre: 1960.

Johnson, Willis E. *South Dakota: A Republic of Friends*. Pierre, South Dakota, Capital Supply Co., 1911.

Jones, Mildred M. *Early Beadle County: 1879–1900*. Huron, South Dakota, F. H. Brown Printing Co., 1961.

"Journal of the Constitutional Convention of 1883." *South Dakota Historical Collections*, Vol. 21. Pierre, South Dakota: 1942.

The Journals of Lewis & Clark. New York, New American Library, 1964.

Judy, S. S., & Will G. Robinson. "Sanborn County History." *South Dakota Historical Collections & Report*, Vol. 26. Pierre, South Dakota, 1952.

Karolevitz, Robert F. *Challenge: The South Dakota Story*. Sioux Falls, Brevet Press, Inc., 1975.

Karolevitz, Robert F. *Yankton: A Pioneer Past*. Aberdeen, South Dakota, North Plains Press, 1972.

Kingsbury, George W. *History of Dakota Territory*. Chicago, S. J. Clarke Publishing Co., 1915.

Kleinsasser, Anne. "A Study of Place-Names in Charles Mix County, South Dakota." M.A. Thesis, University of South Dakota, Vermillion, South Dakota, 1938.

Lawrence County Historical Society. *Some History of Lawrence County*. Pierre, South Dakota, State Publishing Co., 1981.

Legislative Manual: South Dakota: 1991.

Leitch, Barbara A. *A Concise Dictionary of Indian Tribes of North America*. Algonac, Michigan, Reference Publications, Inc., 1979.

Lyman County Pioneers: 1885–1968. Stickney, South Dakota, Argus Printers, 1968.

McGillicuddy, V. T. "Black Hills Names." *South Dakota Historical Collections*, Vol. 6. 1912.

McHenry, Robert. *Webster's American Military Biographies*. New York, Dover Publications, Inc., 1978.

McLoughlin, Denis. *Wild & Woolly: An Encyclopedia of the Old West*. Garden City, New York, Doubleday & Co., Inc., 1975.

Marshall County, South Dakota. Britton, South Dakota, Marshall County Historical Society, 1979.

Mato Paha: Land of the Pioneers: Northwest Meade County, South Dakota. Marceline, Missouri, Walsworth III, 1969.

Mellette County, South Dakota: 1911–1961. White River, South Dakota, Mellette County Centennial Committee, 1961.

"The Memoirs." *South Dakota Historical Collections*, Vol. 3. Aberdeen, South Dakota: 1906.

Memorial & Biographical Record: An Illustrated Compendium of Biography. Chicago, George A. Ogle & Co., 1897.

Molumby, Joseph A. "A Study of Place-Names in Clark County, South Dakota." M.A. Thesis, University of South Dakota, Vermillion, South Dakota, 1939.

Noll, R. H. *Early History of South Dakota Counties*. Vermillion, South Dakota, State-Wide Educational Services, University of South Dakota, 1969.

North Central Tour Book. Heathrow, Florida, AAA Publishing, 1998.

Ochsenreiter, L. G. *History of Day County from 1973 to 1926*. Mitchell, South Dakota, Educator Supply Co., 1926.

Office of Hughes County, South Dakota Superintendent of Schools. *Hughes County History*. Pierre, South Dakota, 1937.

Oldt, Franklin T. *History of Dubuque County, Iowa*. Chicago, Goodspeed Historical Association.

Oyos, Lynwood E., et al. *Over a Century of Leadership: South Dakota Territorial & State Governors*. Sioux Falls, South Dakota, Center for Western Studies, 1987.

Parker, Donald D. *History of Our County & State*. Brookings, South Dakota, South Dakota State College, 1959.

Pattee, John. "Dakota Campaigns." *South Dakota Historical Collections*, Vol. 5. Pierre, South Dakota: 1910.

Perkey, Elton A. *Perkey's Nebraska Place Names*. Lincoln, Nebraska, Nebraska State Historical Society, 1982.

Perkins, John B. *History of Hyde County, South Dakota*. 1908.

Pickler, Mrs. John A. "Correspondence." *South Dakota Historical Collections*, Vol. 2. Aberdeen, South Dakota: 1904.

Piper, Marion J. *Dakota Portraits*. Moball, North Dakota, 1964.

Potter, Merle. "The North Dakota Capital Fight." *North Dakota Historical Quarterly*, Vol. 7, No. 1. Bismarck: October, 1932.

Pringle, Ruane. *Hughes County History*. Pierre, South Dakota, State Publishing Co, 1964.

Proving Up Jones County History. Murdo, South Dakota, Book & Thimble Club, 1969.

Ransom, Frank L. *The Sunshine State: A History of South Dakota*. Mitchell, South Dakota, Educator School Supply Co., 1917.

Read, William A. *Florida Place-Names of Indian Origin & Seminole Personal Names*. Baton Rouge, Louisiana State University Press, 1934.

Reutter, Winifred. *Mellette County Memories*. White River, South Dakota, 1961.

Robinson De Lorme W. "Editorial Notes on Historical Sketch of North & South Dakota." *South Dakota Historical Collections*, Vol. 1. Aberdeen, South Dakota: 1902.

Robinson, Doane. *Doane Robinson's Encyclopedia of South Dakota*. Pierre, 1925.

Robinson, Doane. *History of South Dakota: Together with Personal Mention of Citizens of South Dakota*. Aberdeen, South Dakota, B. F. Bowen & Co., 1904.

Robinson, Doane. "Lewis & Clark in South Dakota." *South Dakota Historical Collections*, Vol. 9. Pierre, South Dakota: 1918.

Robinson, Doane. "Personal Memoirs of William H. H. Beadle." *South Dakota Historical Collections*, Vol. 3. Aberdeen, South Dakota: 1906.

Robinson, Doane. *South Dakota Sui Generis*. Chicago, American Historical Society, Inc., 1930.

Robinson, Will G. "Members of the Territorial Legislature of Dakota." *South Dakota Historical Collections & Report*, Vol. 25. Pierre, South Dakota: 1950.

A Rosebud Review: 1913. Gregory Times-Advocate, 1984.

Ruth, Kent. *Landmarks of the West: A Guide to Historic Sights*. Lincoln, University of Nebraska Press, 1986.

Sampson, York. *South Dakota: Fifty Years of Progress: 1889–1939*. Sioux Falls, South Dakota, S. D. Golden Anniversary Book Co., 1939.

Schell, Herbert S. *History of South Dakota*. Lincoln, University of Nebraska Press, 1961.

Schell, Herbert S. *South Dakota: Its Beginnings & Growth*. New York, American Book Co., 1942.

Shield, Rexford M. "Alphabetical List of Members of the South Dakota Legislature Since Statehood: 1889–1951." *South Dakota Historical Collections & Report*, Vol. 25. Pierre, South Dakota: 1950.

Sioux Falls Argus Leader. *South Dakota 99: Illustrated Profiles of 99 People Who Significantly Contributed to South Dakota's History*. Sioux Falls, South Dakota, Ex Machina Publishing Co., 1989.

Smith, Charles A. *A Comprehensive History of Minnehaha County, South Dakota*. Mitchell, South Dakota, Educator Supply Co., 1949.

Smith, George M. *South Dakota: Its History and Its People*. Chicago, S. J. Clarke Publishing Co., 1915.

Sneve, Virginia Driving Hawk. *Dakota's Heritage: A Compilation of Indian Place Names in South Dakota*. Sioux Falls, South Dakota, Brevet Press, 1973.

Sneve, Virginia Driving Hawk. *South Dakota Geographic Names*. Sioux Falls, South Dakota, Brevet Press, 1973.

Snyder, Mary P. "A Study of Place-Names in Turner County, South Dakota." M.A. Thesis, University of South Dakota, Vermillion, South Dakota, 1940.

South Dakota Legislative Manual: 1917. Pierre, State Publishing Co.

South Dakota Legislative Manual: 1927. Pierre, State Publishing Co.

South Dakota Legislative Manual: 1969. Pierre, State Publishing Co.

South Dakota Legislative Manual: 1977. N.p.

South Dakota's Ziebach County: History of the Prairie. Dupree South Dakota, Ziebach County Historical Society, 1982.

Souvenir: Davison County Court House. Mitchell, South Dakota, 1937.

State of North Dakota: 1907 Legislative Manual. Bismarck, Tribune Printers & Binders, 1907.

Stennett, William H. *A History of the Origin of the Place Names Connected with the Chicago & North Western & Chicago, St. Paul, Minneapolis & Omaha Railways*. Chicago, 1908.

Sterling, Everett W. *Vermillion Story*. N.p., 1959.

Stoddard, W. H. *Turner County Pioneer History*. Sioux Falls, South Dakota, Brown & Saenger, 1931.

Sullivan, Helen J. *Know Your North Dakota: A Handbook of Information for the Schools of North Dakota*. Fargo, North Dakota, Department of Public Instruction, 1929.

Sully County Old Settlers' Association. *History of Sully County*. Onida, South Dakota, Onida Watchman, 1939.

Sunshine & Sagebrush. Oral, South Dakota, Northeast Fall River County Historical Society, 1976.

Taft, William H., III. *County Names: An Historical Perspective*. National Association of Counties, 1982.

Tarbell, Wright. "The Early & Territorial History of Codington County." *South Dakota Historical Collections & Report*, Vol. 24. 1949.

Tarbell, Wright. "History of Dakota Militia & South Dakota National Guard." *South Dakota Historical Collections*, Vol. 6. Sioux Falls: 1912.

Taylor, Gilbert B. *Glimpses into Edgemont's Past*. Lusk, Wyoming, Lusk Herald, 1961.

Thrapp, Dan L. *Encyclopedia of Frontier Biography*. Lincoln, University of Nebraska Press, 1988.

Tripp County: The Heart of Rosebud Country: 50th Anniversary: Winner; 1909–1959. Winner, South Dakota, Winner Chamber of Commerce, 1959.

Upham, Warren. *Minnesota Geographic Names*. St. Paul, Minnesota Historical Society, 1969.

Upham, Warren. "Minnesota Geographic Names." *Collections of the Minnesota Historical Society*, Vol. 17. St. Paul, Minnesota: 1920.

Upham, Warren, & Mrs. Rose Barteau Dunlap. "Minnesota Biographies: 1655–1912." *Collections of the Minnesota Historical Society*, Vol. 14. St. Paul: 1912.

Vexler, Robert I. *Chronology & Documentary Handbook of the State of South Dakota*. Dobbs Ferry, New York, Oceana Publications, Inc., 1979.

Vogel, Virgil J. *Indian Names in Michigan*. Ann Arbor, University of Michigan Press, 1986.

Vogel, Virgil J. *Iowa Place Names of Indian Origin*. Iowa City, University of Iowa Press, 1983.

Vyzralek, Frank E., Great Plains Research. Letter to the author dated August 29, 1988.

Waldman, Carl. *Who Was Who in Native American History*. New York, Facts On File, Inc., 1990.

Wexler, Alan, & Molly Braun. *Atlas of Westward Expansion*. New York, Facts On File, Inc., 1995.

Wheeler, Keith. *The Old West: The Townsmen*. Alexandria, Virginia, Time-Life Books, 1975.

White, Bernice. *Who's Who for South Dakota: 1956*. Sioux Falls, South Dakota, Midwest-Beach Co., 1956.

Wise, L. F., & E. W. Egan. *Kings, Rulers & Statesmen*. New York, Sterling Publishing Co., Inc., 1967.

Wishek, Nina F. *Along the Trails of Yesterday: A Story of McIntosh County*. Ashley Tribune, 1941.

Wolff, Gerald W. "The Civil War Diary of Arthur Calvin Mellette." *South Dakota Historical Collections*, Vol. 37. Pierre, South Dakota: 1975.

Woodruff, K. Brent. "Material Culture of the Teton Dakota." *South Dakota Historical Collections*, Vol. 17. Pierre: 1934.

Work Projects Administration. *Homesteaders of McPherson County*. University of South Dakota, 1941.

Work Projects Administration. *Inventory of the County Archives of South Dakota-Bennett, Clark, Haakon & Jackson-Washabaugh Counties*. 1940–1941.

Works Progress Administration. *Douglas County Tales & Towns*. Armour, South Dakota, Armour Public Library Board, 1938.

Works Progress Administration. *Eureka: 1887–1937*. Eureka, South Dakota, 1937.

Works Progress Administration. *Prairie Tamers of Miner County*. 1939.

Works Progress Administration. *Unfinished Histories: Tales of Aberdeen & Brown County*. Mitchell, South Dakota, 1938.

Yankton County Historical Society. *History of Yankton County, South Dakota*. Dallas, Texas, Curtis Media Corp., 1987.

"The Yankton Jubilee: 1911." *South Dakota Historical Collections*, Vol. 6. Sioux Falls: 1912.

Yenne, Bill. *The Encyclopedia of North American Indian Tribes*. New York, Crescent Books, 1986.

Zimmerman, J. E. *Dictionary of Classical Mythology*. New York, Bantam Books, 1964.

Tennessee

(95 counties)

2394 *Anderson County*

Joseph Anderson (1757–1837)— This Pennsylvania native served as an army officer during the American Revolution and then practiced law for several years. In 1791 President George Washington appointed Anderson as one of the judges in the territory South of the River Ohio, which soon would become the state of Tennessee. Anderson was a delegate to Tennessee's state constitutional convention and in 1797 he was appointed to represent the infant state of Tennessee in the United States Senate. He served in that body from 1797 to 1815. In the Senate he championed Tennessee's rights to Mississippi River commerce. In 1815 President James Madison appointed Anderson as comptroller of the United States treasury, a position which he held until 1836. This county was created on November 6, 1801, while Joseph Anderson was representing Tennessee in the U.S. Senate.

2395 *Bedford County*

Thomas Bedford (1758–1804)— A native of Virginia, Bedford enlisted in our Revolutionary army on February 5, 1776, and served through the 1781 campaign against the forces of British General Charles Cornwallis (1738–1805). Bedford attained the rank of captain in our Revolutionary army. At the conclusion of his military service he returned to Virginia and represented Charlotte County in the house of delegates of Virginia's general assembly in 1788. About 1795 Bedford immigrated to the territory South of the River Ohio, which very soon would become the state of Tennessee. He settled first at East Nashville, where he obtained large tracts of land, and later moved to Jefferson Springs. Thomas Bedford died suddenly in April, 1804, and this county was created and named in his honor on December 3, 1807. Nannie Lee Donnell's article entitled "Romance of Bedford County & Shelbyville," which appeared in the September 9, 1949, issue of *Shelbyville Times Gazette*, stated that Bedford County was named for "Thomas Bedford who was a lieutenant colonel in the U.S. Army during the war of 1812." Other sources on the history and place names of Tennessee also indicate that the Thomas Bedford, who is honored in this county's name served in the War of 1812 but that cannot be true because the act which created Bedford County in 1807 stated that the county was named "in memory of Thomas Bedford, *deceased* [italics added]."

2396 *Benton County*

Originally: Thomas H. Benton (1782–1858). Changed to: David Benton (1779–1860).

Thomas H. Benton (1782–1858)— A native of North Carolina, Thomas Hart Benton moved to Tennessee in 1801, was admitted to the bar here and, in 1809, was elected to Tennessee's senate. After serving in the War of 1812, Benton moved to Missouri and he represented that state for thirty years in the U.S. Senate. In that body he championed many interests of the West including free 160 acre homesteads, pony express, telegraph and railroads. Benton was a moderate on the volatile slavery issue. He opposed both abolition of slavery and the extension of it. His primary concerns were peace and preservation of the Union. These moderate positions proved unpopular. Some states which had named counties in Benton's honor renamed them and, in 1850, Missouri failed to return Benton to the Senate. Following his ouster from the Senate, Benton represented Missouri briefly in the U.S. House of Representatives.

Benton County, Tennessee was originally created and named in honor of Thomas Hart Benton on December 19, 1835, but Tennessee was one of the states where Benton lost his popularity. Tennessee expressed its displeasure, not by changing this county's name, but by an unusual act of the Tennessee legislature, which passed on February 4, 1852, declaring "That the county of Benton retain its original name in honor of David Benton, an old and respected citizen of said county." This legislation was promoted by Stephen C. Pavatt, of Camden, Tennessee.

David Benton (1779–1860)— This native of South Carolina moved to Tennessee and enlisted in a militia company during the War of 1812. He fought against Creek Indians during that war, received an honorable discharge and moved to Alabama. David Benton had a brother, Samuel Benton, who lived in western Humphreys County, Tennessee. Samuel Benton persuaded his brother to join him and David Benton settled on a farm on Harmon Creek in western Humphreys County, Tennessee, shortly before February, 1825. Here, David Benton was active in the movement to separate Humphreys County into two counties with the Tennessee River as the dividing line. The new county, Benton County was created on December 19, 1835, and David Benton was a magistrate on this new county's first quarterly court. He remained in Benton County and farmed here for many years. In September, 1974, a commemorative monument was erected on the lawn of the Benton County courthouse to honor David Benton (1779–1860).

2397 *Bledsoe County*

Uncertain— This county was created on November 30, 1807, and sources consulted have differing views on the county's namesake. A majority of sources dealing with the history, geography and place names of Tennessee indicate that this county was named for Anthony Bledsoe (1733–1788). However, several sources say that the honor belongs to Abraham Bledsoe and one source says that the county might have been named for Anthony, Abraham or James Bledsoe. Elizabeth Parnham Robnett's 1993 history of the county stated that "Bledsoe County was named for a member of the well-known Bledsoe family who came from Virginia and settled in Middle Tennessee in the late 1700's. Most evidence would give the honor to Anthony Bledsoe, a practical surveyor and Revolutionary War veteran, who was killed by the Indians in Sumner County, Tennessee."

Anthony Bledsoe (1733–1788)— A native of Virginia, Anthony Bledsoe was a professional surveyor who moved to America's western frontier and served in the militia against the Indians. In 1776 he served with Colonel William Christian (–1786) in punitive actions against the Indians from Long Island (near the present Kingsport, Tennessee) to the French Broad River. Anthony Bledsoe was then stationed at Long Island, in charge of 600 men protecting the frontier from Indians. He served in Virginia's general assembly in 1778 and later presented a bill to extend the boundary line between Virginia and North Carolina, which was adopted. The new boundary line made Anthony Bledsoe a resident of North Carolina and North Carolina named him to a board of auditors to adjust public accounts because of the Revolutionary War. He moved west with his family to the Cumberland country, in western North Carolina (now Tennessee) and settled here in what is now Sumner County, Tennessee, two miles north of Bledsoe Lick. When North Carolina's Davidson County was created in 1783 (now Davidson County, Tennessee) Anthony Bledsoe was a member of the county's first court. Elected as a colonel of the county militia, Anthony Bledsoe was mortally wounded in July, 1788, during an Indian attack on a fort at Bledsoe's Lick and died the following day.

Concerning the Abraham Bledsoe who is mentioned by some as this county's namesake, both the father and one son of Anthony Bledsoe (1733–1788) were named Abraham. The Abraham Bledsoe of interest would be the son, for he lived with his father in what is now Sumner County, Tennessee. This Abraham Bledsoe and three brothers, Thomas, Anthony Jr. and Henry were granted a tract of land on the East Fork of Obeds River in 1793 by North Carolina's Governor Richard D. Spaight (1758–1802). Of the possible namesake James Bledsoe we know nothing. However, if the namesake of this county is in doubt, it would seem that another name should be added to the list of possibilities. That would be Isaac Bledsoe (1735–1793), a brother of Anthony Bledsoe (1733–1788). Isaac Bledsoe was with his brother while he lay fatally wounded and Isaac assisted his brother in signing a will which made provision for Anthony's seven daughters. (Under North Carolina law, none of the several thousand acres of land owned by Anthony Bledsoe would have gone to his daughters in the absence of this contrary provision in his will.)

2398 Blount County

William Blount (1749–1800)— This North Carolina native served as an army paymaster during the American Revolution and was a member of both houses of the North Carolina legislature during the Revolution. He represented North Carolina in the Continental Congress and was a member of the 1787 convention which framed the U.S. Constitution. Blount was one of North Carolina's three signers of the federal constitution. In 1790 President George Washington appointed him to be the first governor of the territory South of the River Ohio, which soon would become the state of Tennessee. Blount served as territorial governor until 1796 and thus was the only territorial governor because Tennessee was admitted to statehood in 1796. At statehood, William Blount became one of the new state's first United States senators. This county was created on July 11, 1795, by the territory South of the River Ohio, while Blount was serving as territorial governor.

2399 Bradley County

Edward Bradley (–1829)— Bradley is known to have been a friend of Andrew Jackson and was a resident of Tennessee when he was commissioned a first major in the 15th regiment of the Tennessee militia. During the War of 1812 he enlisted as a lieutenant-colonel in the First regiment of Tennessee volunteer infantry and had risen to the rank of full colonel when he was wounded in combat in Alabama on November 3, 1813,. Bradley represented Sumner County in the lower house of Tennessee's legislature from 1813 to 1815. In 1820 he moved to Shelby County, Tennessee, was a member of that county's court and a resident of that county when he died in 1829. This county was created on February 10, 1836. It was proposed in the initial bill that the new county's name should be Foster County, in honor of Ephraim H. Foster (1794–1854), a prominent Tennessee politician, then speaker of the Tennessee house, who would later represent the state in the U.S. Senate. That bill was amended changing the name Foster to Rutledge, in honor of Edward Rutledge (1749–1800), a South Carolina signer of the Declaration of Independence and/or his son Edward Rutledge, Jr., who was a citizen of Nashville, Tennessee. The bill was amended a second time substituting the name Bradley for Rutledge and that bill passed in the lower house. In the Tennessee senate there was an unsuccessful attempt to change the name Bradley to Cleveland but final law specifically stated that this county was named "…in honor of and to perpetuate the name of Colonel Edward Bradley, late of Shelby County, Tennessee."

2400 Campbell County

Uncertain— This county was created on September 11, 1806. Most sources dealing with the history, geography and place names of Tennessee indicate that this county was named for Arthur Campbell (–1811) but a few state the honor belongs to George W. Campbell (1769–1848). Several sources indicate that it is uncertain which of these men the county's name was intended to honor.

Arthur Campbell (–1811)— Born in Augusta County, Virginia in 1742 or 1743, Arthur Campbell volunteered to serve in the militia when he was only 15 years old. While on duty with the militia, he was captured by Indians and taken to the Great Lakes region, where he remained three years until he was able to escape and return to Virginia. He served as a militia officer during the American Revolution and commanded a number of frontier militia units. Following the American Revolution, Arthur Campbell accumulated land in the wilderness areas west of civilization and he lived some 35 years on his estate called Royal Oakes. Arthur Campbell was among those responsible for establishing the so-called, short-lived "state" of Franklin.

George W. Campbell (1769–1848)— Born in Scotland on February 8, 1769, George Washington Campbell came to America and graduated from the College of New Jersey (now Princeton University) in 1794. He settled in Tennessee and was admitted to the bar here about 1795. George W. Campbell represented Tennessee in both houses of the U.S. Congress, served in the cabinet of President James Madison as secretary of the treasury and was U.S. minister to Russia. He died in Nashville, Tennessee.

2401 Cannon County

Newton Cannon (1781–1841)— Born on May 22, 1781, in Guilford County, North Carolina, Cannon moved to the Tennessee frontier at an early age and worked as a saddler, merchant and surveyor. The survey work gained Cannon ownership of large amounts of land here. He served as a colonel during the War of 1812 and was a member of the Tennessee senate. Cannon was elected to represent Tennessee in the U.S. House of Representatives and subsequently became the state's governor. Elected in 1835 and reelected in 1837, Cannon served as Tennessee's governor from 1835 to 1839. He ran for a third term as governor in 1839 but was defeated by James K. Polk, who later was president of the United States.

2402 Carroll County

William Carroll (1788–1844)— A native of Pennsylvania, Carroll immigrated to

Tennessee in 1810, and settled in Nashville. He soon entered the army as an officer, served as a colonel during the Creek War, and was with Andrew Jackson at the battle of New Orleans during the War of 1812. By 1814 Carroll had been promoted to major-general. In Nashville Carroll established a successful nail factory and iron-mongery store and invented in a steamboat, named *The Andrew Jackson*, to ply the Cumberland River. Elected as Tennessee's governor in 1821, Carroll served in that office from 1821 to 1827 and again from 1829 to 1835. He succeeded Joseph Mc-Minn (1758–1824) as Tennessee's governor in October, 1821, and this county was created and named in his honor during the following month, on November 7, 1821.

2403 *Carter County*

Landon Carter (1760–1800)— A native of Virginia and an army officer during the American Revolution, Carter represented Washington County in the North Carolina legislature 1780's. That was the Washington County which would ultimately become a part of the state of Tennessee. During the later part of the 1780's Carter was also active in the affairs of the so-called, short-lived "state" of Franklin. He was its secretary of state and also speaker of the first senate of Franklin. About 1790 Carter was appointed lieutenant-colonel and commander of the militia of the Washington district of the territory South of the River Ohio, which soon would become the state of Tennessee. In 1792 and 1793 he was active in actions against the Indians and in 1796 the new state of Tennessee made him treasurer for the districts of Washington and Hamilton. Also during 1796, this county was created and named in Landon Carter's honor.

2404 *Cheatham County*

Edward S. Cheatham (1818–1878)— Edward Saunders Cheatham was born on July 31, 1818 in Springfield, Tennessee, and he attended Liberty Academy at Springfield and the University of Nashville before becoming involved in a variety of business activities. He had an interest in E. S. Cheatham and Company, apparently in Springfield, and by 1855 he had a grocery store in Nashville. As his wealth grew, Cheatham became the owner and operator of a sawmill and he was president of both the Edgefield & Kentucky and Louisville & Nashville Railroads, prior to the Civil War. He served in both houses of the Tennessee legislature and in the Tennes-

see senate of the Confederate States of America. After the Civil War Cheatham was involved in the lumber business and he died at Horn Lake, Mississippi, on December 21, 1878. When Cheatham served in the Tennessee senate during the 31st legislative session, which convened October 1, 1855, he was speaker of the senate. Later, when Tennessee seceded from the Union, Cheatham was elected as the first speaker of Tennessee's senate in the Confederacy. Cheatham County, Tennessee was created prior to the Civil War, on February 28, 1856, while Edward S. Cheatham was serving as speaker of the senate in the Tennessee legislature of the United States. A few sources indicate that this county was named for Nathaniel Cheatham but since these sources indicate that Nathaniel Cheatham was speaker of the Tennessee senate, they must be in error. During the 103 years from 1796 to 1899, the only speaker of Tennessee's senate (in either the Union or Confederacy) named Cheatham was Edward S. Cheatham (1818–1878).

2405 *Chester County*

Robert I. Chester (1793–)— This county was created on March 4, 1879. The Goodspeed Publishing Company issued a number of histories for Tennessee counties and groups of counties during the late 19th century. The one that covers Chester County was published in 1886, just seven years after Chester County was created. It stated that "This name was given as a compliment to Col. R. I. Chester of Jackson, who was at that time representative from Madison County." This statement contains at least two errors, so we must look to other sources for the true origin of this county's name. Goodspeed's errors concern the name of Madison County's representative in Tennessee's lower house in 1879, when this county was created. That representative's name was H. C. Anderson. Moreover, the member of the Tennessee senate from Madison County in 1879 was not named Chester, nor was any 1879 member of either house of the Tennessee legislature. This county's namesake was born on July 30, 1793, at Carlisle, Pennsylvania. He served as the quartermaster of the Washington County, Tennessee, regiment in the War of 1812 and is referred to by several sources as Colonel Robert I. Chester. However, Chester served under Colonel Samuel Bayless, so it seems likely that that rank of first lieutenant shown in *Tennesseans in the War of 1812* is correct. Chester was an early postmaster at Jackson, Tennessee, served in the Tennessee

legislature and was appointed by President James K. Polk as a U.S. marshall for western Tennessee. The year of Chester's death is not known but he was still alive when this county was created and he donated a bell for the first courthouse of the county named in his honor. James D. Richardson's *Tennessee Templars*, published in 1883 stated that Robert I. Chester was "the oldest affiliated Mason in Tennessee." This county had been created as Wisdom County on March 19, 1875, but that act was repealed when Chester County was created in 1879.

2406 *Claiborne County*

William C. C. Claiborne (1775–1817)— A native of Virginia and a lawyer, Claiborne moved to Tennessee when it was still a territory. Here he practiced law and served in Tennessee's constitutional convention of 1796. When Tennessee was admitted to statehood, Claiborne served briefly on the supreme court of the new state but he was soon elected to represent Tennessee in the U.S. House of Representatives. Thomas Jefferson became president of the United States in March, 1801, and a few months later he appointed Claiborne to be governor of Mississippi territory. When the United States acquired Louisiana from France in the Louisiana Purchase, President Jefferson appointed Claiborne, along with General James Wilkinson (1757–1825) to represent our country at the ceremonial transfer of Louisiana from France to our country. Claiborne was later appointed governor-general and intendent of the U.S. province of Louisiana. In that capacity he acted, for all practical purposes, as a benign dictator of Louisiana. He subsequently was appointed governor of Orleans territory and he served in that position until 1812, when Louisiana was admitted to the Union as a state. Claiborne was then elected as the new state's first governor and he held that office until 1816. In January, 1817, Claiborne was elected to represent Louisiana in the U.S. Senate but he died before taking his seat in that body. Claiborne County, Tennessee was created on October 29, 1801, while William C. C. Claiborne was governor of Mississippi territory.

2407 *Clay County*

Henry Clay (1777–1852)— Clay represented Kentucky in both branches of the U.S. Congress. For many years he was one of the more prominent figures in American politics but his several bids for the presidency were unsuccessful. He was influential in effecting important compromises between northern and southern interests during the years that secession and civil war were imminent. This county created on June 24, 1870, as Reconstruction was ending in Tennessee. Perhaps its name was chosen in sadness that all of Henry Clay's compromise measures to avert civil war had failed and the Civil War had become a disastrous reality, particularly for Tennessee and other members of the Confederacy.

2408 *Cocke County*

William Cocke (1748–1828)— A native of Virginia, Cocke served as an army officer during the American Revolution and moved to the section of western North Carolina, which eventually became the state of Tennessee. He served in the North Carolina legislature and was active in the affairs of the so-called, short-lived "state" of Franklin. He then served in the legislature of the territory South of the River Ohio and there he sponsored a bill for the creation of Blount College (now the University of Tennessee). In 1796 Cocke was a delegate to Tennessee's state constitutional convention, and when Tennessee was admitted to statehood, he became one of the new state's first two U.S. senators. He later served in the Tennessee legislature and in 1814 was appointed by President James Madison as Indian agent to the Chickasaw nation. Cocke later lived in Mississippi, where he served in the state legislature and he died in Columbus, Mississippi, on August 22, 1828. This county was created and named in his honor on October 9, 1797, while Cocke was representing the infant state of Tennessee in the U.S. Senate.

2409 *Coffee County*

John Coffee (1772–1833)— Born in Prince Edward County, Virginia, on June 2, 1772, Coffee immigrated to Tennessee and in April, 1798, he settled on the Cumberland River near what is today the village of Madison, Tennessee. Here he became a merchant in partnership with Andrew Jackson and Coffee and Jackson established a friendship which continued throughout Coffee's life. Coffee served in the Tennessee militia and became colonel of a cavalry of some 600 volunteers. He served under General Andrew Jackson in the Natchez expedition of 1812 and fought under him against the British in the battle of New Orleans during the War of 1812. Coffee

served with distinction and was promoted to brigadier-general and, later, to major-general. He spent much of his remaining life in survey work in the South and he settled in Florence, Alabama, where he died on July 7, 1833. This Tennessee county was created and named in his honor less than three years later, on January 8, 1836.

There are three Coffee Counties in the United States, in Alabama, Georgia and Tennessee. The Georgia county was named for John Coffee (1782–1836), while the Coffee Counties in Alabama and Tennessee honor John Coffee (1772–1833). These men are easily confused with each other. They were first cousins with identical names who moved south from their native state of Virginia. Both became generals and they died within a few years of one another. Both were associated with Andrew Jackson. The older Coffee (1772–1833) served under Jackson in the 1813–1814 war against the Creek Indians and later at the battle of New Orleans. The General John Coffee for whom Georgia's Coffee County was named did not serve with Jackson during his military campaigns but became a personal friend of his in later years. The younger John Coffee (1782–1836) served in the U.S. House of Representatives, while the John Coffee for whom the Tennessee and Alabama counties were named was never a member of congress.

2410 *Crockett County*

David Crockett (1786–1836)— Born August 17, 1786, in the portion of western North Carolina which would soon become the state of Tennessee, Crockett established a reputation in Tennessee as a bear hunter. He served as a private in the army commanded by Andrew Jackson and eventually attained the rank of colonel in the Tennessee militia. Crockett was twice elected to the Tennessee legislature and later represented Tennessee in the U.S. House of Representatives for three terms between 1827 and 1835, before immigrating to Texas to assist in the fight for independence from Mexico. Very soon after his arrival in Texas he became one of the victims of the Mexican massacre at the Alamo in San Antonio on March 6, 1836. This Tennessee county was originally created and named in Crockett's honor on December 20, 1845. However, in 1846 a judicial opinion declared Crockett County to be unconstitutional. On July 7, 1870, the Tennessee legislature again passed a law to create Crockett County, named in honor of David Crockett (1786–1836). A

number of Tennessee sources give 1871 as the year that Crockett County was created. The county seat of this county is named Alamo.

2411 *Cumberland County*

Cumberland Mountains— The Cumberland Mountains, also called the Cumberland Plateau, lie west of the Tennessee River, in eastern Tennessee and they embrace the territory of Cumberland County, Tennessee, which was created on November 16, 1855. The Cumberland Mountains form a high tableland, with an average height 2,000 feet above sea level and an average width of some 50 miles. The Cumberland Mountains extended from southern West Virginia to northern Alabama and are a section of the Appalachian Mountains. Bituminous coal deposits lie in the Tennessee portion of the Cumberland Mountains. The several Cumberlands here in our nation's southeast (e.g., Cumberland Mountains, Cumberland River and Cumberland Gap) owe their name to the explorer, Dr. Thomas Walker (1715–1794). He named the river in 1750 when colonial America was still a part of England, bestowing the name in honor of a member of the English royal family, the Duke of Cumberland (1721–1765), a son of England's King George II. In 1750 when Dr. Walker bestowed the name, George II was king of England. During a trip to England some years earlier, Dr. Walker had the privilege of meeting the duke of Cumberland. The duke's name is shown in most works as William Augustus but in some the form William August is used.

2412 *Davidson County*

William L. Davidson (–1781)— Davidson was born about 1746 in Pennsylvania but moved with his family to North Carolina when he was still a small child. As the Revolutionary War approached, Davidson was appointed a member of the Committee of Safety of Rowan County and in 1775 he was commissioned as an officer in our Continental army. He served with distinction at the battle of Germantown and was promoted from major to lieutenant-colonel. He later was commissioned as a brigadier-general of the North Carolina militia and participated in several battles in North Carolina. In January, 1781, Davidson was ordered to hold the Catawba River against attack from forces under the British general, Charles Cornwallis (1738–1805). On February 1, 1781, the British attacked at Cowan's ford on the Catawba.

General William L, Davidson was killed and his rag tag militiamen scattered. This county was created in 1783 by North Carolina before there was a Tennessee. When Tennessee was separated from North Carolina, they brought this Davidson County with them. North Carolina remedied the deficiency on their side of the border on December 9, 1822, when it created a Davidson County, North Carolina, for the second time, named in honor of General William L. Davidson.

2413 *De Kalb County*

Johann Kalb, Baron de Kalb (1721–1780) — Kalb was born in the province of Alsace, which at that time belonged to France. He was a general in the French army and resigned that commission to come to America to assist the colonies in the Revolutionary War. He served as a general in the American revolutionary army and he died in combat here. This county was created on December 11, 1837.

2414 *Decatur County*

Stephen Decatur (1779–1820) — Decatur, who was born in Maryland, was an officer in the U.S. navy who served in the Mediterranean Sea from 1801 to 1805 in the Tripolitan War. His bravery and successes in that war made him a popular hero in America and earned him promotion to captain. During the War of 1812, Decatur reinforced his reputation as a naval hero. Following that war Decatur, now a commodore, again served in the Mediterranean, where he captured the Algerian flagship *Mashuda*. His display of naval force extracted peace terms from Algeria and indemnities for un-neutral acts from Tunis and Tripoli. This brought an end to the plundering of American shipping by the Barbary powers. Decatur's life ended in a duel fought in March 1820. Decatur County, Tennessee, was created and named in his honor during November 1845.

2415 *Dickson County*

William Dickson (1770–1816) — A native of North Carolina and a physician, Dickson moved in 1795 to the territory South of the River Ohio, which very soon would become the state of Tennessee. He practiced medicine in Nashville and was a member of the 1799 and 1801 sessions of the lower house of the legislature of the infant state of Tennessee. Dr. Dickson was speaker of the house during both of those legislative sessions. Elected to the U.S.

House of Representatives, Dickson served in that body from 1801 to 1807. This county was created on October 25, 1803, while Dr. Dickson was representing Tennessee in the national House of Representatives.

2416 *Dyer County*

Robert H. Dyer (–1826) — Born about 1774 in North Carolina, Robert Henry Dyer came to Rutherford County, Tennessee in 1807. In July of that year he was commissioned as a lieutenant in the Tennessee militia and in 1810 he was promoted to captain. Dyer served in the Creek War and fought at the battle of New Orleans under General Andrew Jackson during the War of 1812. Back in Tennessee Dyer was elected to the state's senate and he served in that body from 1815 to 1817. He fought as a colonel with the Tennessee volunteer cavalry against the Seminoles in Florida in 1817 and 1818 and was subsequently considered for the rank of major-general in the Tennessee militia. His bid for that rank met with defeat but Colonel Dyer was awarded land grants totaling 2,017 acres in Tennessee. This county was created on October 16, 1823.

2417 *Fayette County*

Marie Joseph Paul Yves Roch Gilbert du Motier, Marquis de Lafayette (1757–1834) — Lafayette was a French aristocrat who served briefly in the French army. He came to America in 1777 to assist the American Revolutionary army. He was granted an honorary commission as major general by the Continental Congress and served with distinction in a number of battles in the Revolutionary War. Lafayette returned to France in 1782 but he returned to America on a brief visit in 1784 and in 1825 Lafayette toured our country extensively. On May 4, 1825, General Lafayette traveled up the Cumberland River to pay a visit to Nashville, Tennessee. His ship was met by General Andrew Jackson and a large crowd greeted our nation's French friend with an enthusiastic ovation. Fayette County, Tennessee, had been created on September 29, 1824, presumably in anticipation of General Lafayette's visit to Tennessee.

2418 *Fentress County*

James Fentress (1763–1843) — Born in New Hanover County, North Carolina, on February 16, 1763, Fentress came to Tennessee in 1798, shortly after the state's admission to the Union. He settled on Yellow Creek in Montgomery County, engaged in

farming and was chairman of the county's court in 1808. Elected to the lower house of the Tennessee legislature, Fentress served in that body eight consecutive terms from 1809 to 1823. He was speaker of the house during at least four, and possibly five, of the legislative sessions during the 1815 to 1823 period. In 1836 Fentress was a presidential elector on the Democratic ticket of Martin Van Buren's. This county was created on November 28, 1823, during James Fentress' last term as speaker of the house of the Tennessee legislature. Some sources indicate that Fentress served in the army of the Confederate States of America but that is impossible since he died on June 20, 1843, almost two decades before the start of the Civil War. One source says that Fentress was speaker of the Tennessee house from 1823 to 1845. This is also false. James Fentress was speaker in 1823 but that was the last session that he was a member of the house or its speaker, and when the 1845 session convened on October 6, James Fentress had been dead more than two years.

2419 *Franklin County*

Benjamin Franklin (1706–1790) — Franklin was a native of Massachusetts who moved to Pennsylvania in his teens. Poverty denied him a formal education but he became the leading printer and editor in North America. Franklin gained fame for his discoveries and inventions in the physical sciences and he distinguished himself as author, philosopher and diplomat. Franklin was a signer of the Declaration of Independence and an important member of the convention which framed the U.S. Constitution. This county was created on December 3, 1807. There had been an earlier attempt to honor Benjamin Franklin within what is now the state of Tennessee. When North Carolina ceded its western lands to the Confederation congress, residents of that area tried to establish the so-called "free state of Franklin." Benjamin Franklin acknowledged this gesture with a letter of thanks but North Carolina and the Confederation congress refused to recognize the existence of this political entity and in 1790 when the U.S. federal government established the territory South of the River Ohio (which soon would become the state of Tennessee), the "state of Franklin" withered away.

2420 *Gibson County*

John H. Gibson (–1823) — Apparently Gibson was a resident of Bedford County, Tennessee when he was commissioned as a lieutenant in the Tennessee militia on February 21, 1811. He served as a second-major in a cavalry regiment in the Natchez campaign and as a lieutenant-colonel under John Coffee (1772–1833) in the Creek War. Throughout the War of 1812, John H. Gibson's detachment was used in reconnoitering. During one of the early battles preceding the battle of New Orleans, Gibson was stabbed by a British bayonet but fortunately the wound was slight. Colonel Gibson survived the war, returned to Tennessee, and died near Jackson, Tennessee, in 1823. This county was created and named in his honor on October 21 of that year.

2421 *Giles County*

William B. Giles (1762–1830)— Born in Virginia on August 12, 1762, Giles received a master of arts degree from the College of New Jersey (now Princeton University), studied law at the College of William & Mary and was admitted to the Virginia bar. He practiced law in Virginia and was suddenly sent to represent Virginia in the U.S. House of Representatives during the first congress of the infant United States of America, replacing Theodorick Bland (1742–1790), who had died on June 1, 1790. Giles was subsequently elected several times to the federal House and later represented Virginia in the U.S. Senate from 1804 to 1815. From March 4, 1827, to March 4, 1830, William B. Giles was governor of the state of Virginia. This county was created on November 14, 1809. The name originally proposed for this county was Richland County but that name was changed to Giles, in honor of William B. Giles, who had advocated Tennessee's admission to the Union while serving in Congress. Several sources on the history, geography and place names of Tennessee indicate that Andrew Jackson suggested that this county be named Giles. There was some dispute about the name Giles and the name "Shelby County" was proposed but the only county name ever officially adopted was Giles County.

2422 *Grainger County*

Mary Grainger Blount (–1802)— William Blount (1749–1800) was the first and only governor of the territory South of the River Ohio and on June 1, 1796, that territory was admitted to the Union as the state of Tennessee. The new state legislature jumped the gun a bit by holding its first legislative session prior to statehood. That legislature convened on March 28, 1796, and it the honored the popular territorial governor, William Blount by electing him as one of the new state's first two U.S. senators. That legislature also honored Governor Blount's popular wife, the territorial first lady, by creating and naming Grainger County in her honor on April 22, 1796.

Mary Grainger was a daughter of a wealthy merchant, Kaleb Grainger, of the Wilmington, North Carolina, area. Kaleb Grainger died leaving a nice estate to his widow, a son and "the vivacious, dark-haired" daughter, Mary Grainger. William Blount (1749–1800) was a busy man but he somehow found time to pay frequent visits to the Grainger home. Blount nicknamed Mary Grainger "Molsey" and on February 12, 1778, Mary Grainger and William Blount were married. The newlyweds first home was at Piney Grove, a farm at Martinburg, which William had inherited. The Blounts' had two children when Mary Grainger's mother came to join the family in 1788, and in 1789 Mary and William Blount had their third child. These were exciting years for our nation and William Blount was very active in the affairs of our infant nation. He was one of North Carolina's three signers of the federal Constitution. However, the Blounts found time to enjoy life too. They attended Episcopal church services at Greenville, and went to the theater, dances and musicals in New Bern. In 1790 President George Washington appointed Mary Grainger Blount's husband to be the first governor of the territory South of the River Ohio. In 1792 Mary Grainger, her husband and household established a home in a large log house at Knoxville. Their daughter, Barbara, was born while they lived here. The conditions were primitive but the Blounts were prosperous slave-owners and soon they were living in a luxurious mansion, a two-story home in Knoxville, constructed from sawed lumber. The grounds surrounding the new Blount mansion soon became the most luxurious in Knoxville. Mary Grainger Blount was a lady of culture and she helped soften the rough edges of the frontier visitors to the Blount mansion. She was particularly interested in Indians and cultivated the friendship of a number of the friendly Indian chiefs. In 1796 territorial governor William Blount became U.S. Senator Blount. In 1797, on a visit to Raleigh, North Carolina, Mary Grainger Blount suffered a badly fractured arm and did not fully recover her health until 1799. By this time the Blounts had seven children and William Blount's health was failing. He died on March 21, 1800. Mary Grainger Blount died of jaundice in 1802 and was buried with her husband in the churchyard of the First Presbyterian Church at Knoxville. Nancy Wooten Walker's work entitled *Out of a Clear Blue Sky: Tennessee's First Ladies and Their Husbands* tells us that "Mary Grainger and Governor Blount, dispensed, for that age, a real hospitality. The Blount Mansion was a rendevous for society, wit, and political affairs. The Governor, with his charming courtly manner and his beautiful and gracious Mary, were the center upon which all social life of the Knoxville capital turned."

2423 *Greene County*

Nathanael Greene (1742–1786)— Greene County was one of the counties that Tennessee inherited as a result of breaking away from North Carolina. Nathanael Greene (1742–1786) was born in Rhode Island and served briefly in the Rhode Island legislature. He gained fame as one of the ablest American generals in the Revolutionary War. North Carolina created this county to honor General Greene in 1783 but when Tennessee was separated from North Carolina, they brought this Greene County with them. In 1799 North Carolina created a Greene County for the second time, named in honor of General Nathanael Greene. General Greene had rendered extremely effective service in our Revolutionary War against the British both in northern areas and in the South. He is particularly remembered in North and South Carolina for his actions which saved the Carolinas from the British.

2424 *Grundy County*

Felix Grundy (1777–1840)— A native of Virginia, Grundy moved to Kentucky with his family in his youth. There he became a member of the state's constitutional convention and served in the state legislature. In 1806 Grundy was appointed to Kentucky's supreme court and in 1807 he was made its chief justice. Finding the salary inadequate, Grundy resigned and came to Tennessee where he again became active in politics and gained national notice. He served in the Tennessee legislature and represented this state in both houses of the U.S. Congress. In 1838 President Martin Van Buren appointed Grundy to serve in his cabinet as attorney general. Felix Grundy died on December 19, 1840, and this county was created on January 29, 1844.

2425 *Hamblen County*

Hezekiah Hamblen (1775–1855) — Citizens of the area which the Tennessee legislature established as Hamblen County in 1870 had petitioned the legislature to establish a new county here giving as their reason, the inconvenience of traveling from their homes to the distant county seats of Grainger County and Jefferson County. The legislature was inclined to grant the request but demurred at the proposed name for the county, which would have been Turley County, in honor of Judge T. W. Turley. A member of the Tennessee legislature named William Greene was able to persuade his fellow legislators that the new county should be named Hamblen, in honor of Hezekiah Hamblen. William Greene had become related to Hezekiah Hamblen, by marriage, when his father married Priscilla, one of eight known children of Hezekiah Hamblen. Emma Deane Smith Trent's work entitled *East Tennessee's Lore of Yesteryear* told this about Hamblen County's namesake: "Hezekiah Hamblen owned a home on Stock Creek about four miles west of Rogersville, Tennessee. He was a lawyer of considerable repute, and in addition to land he owned, he had a number of slaves at one time. For a good many years he was a member of the Hawkins County Court. His will, dated January 22, 1854, and written in the seventy-ninth year of his life, made mention of eight children." This work also retells the legend that Hamblen's widow was so anxious that the new county be named for her deceased husband that she rode on horseback to the state capital to lobby for that county name. Ms. Trent is careful to point out that some aspects of her recitation have not been verified. However, there is a ring of truth to much of her tale. Hamblen County was created by the 36th legislature of Tennessee, which convened on October 4, 1869. A member of the state senate during that session, from the second district (Hawkins, Hancock & Jefferson Counties), was William Greene. William S. Trent's article in the July 26, 1970, issue of the *Gazette Mail*, of Morristown, Tennessee includes a photograph of Hezekiah Hamblen's gravestone and the gravestone gives the years of Hamblen's birth and death and states that Hezekiah was born in Prince Edward County, Virginia.

2426 *Hamilton County*

Alexander Hamilton (–1804) — A native of the West Indies, Hamilton moved to New York and served as an officer in America's revolutionary army. One of his assignments during the war was aide-de-camp to General George Washington. After the war Hamilton was a member of the convention which framed the U.S. Constitution. He collaborated with Madison and Jay in writing a series of papers entitled *The Federalist*, which explained the new constitution and advocated its adoption. A conservative and an advocate of a strong central government, he served as the United States' first secretary of the treasury. In 1804 he engaged in a duel with Aaron Burr and Hamilton died of wounds he suffered in that duel. This county was created on October 25, 1819.

2427 *Hancock County*

John Hancock (1737–1793) — A native of Massachusetts and a graduate of Harvard, Hancock served in the Massachusetts legislature and was president of the Massachusetts provincial congress. He was elected to the Second Continental Congress and became its president. As president of the Continental Congress when the Declaration of Independence was signed, he was, on July 4, 1776, the first signer of that document. He signed it with such a flourish that the name John Hancock became a synonym for "signature." He later commanded the Massachusetts militia, served as governor of that state for many years and presided over the Massachusetts convention that ratified the U.S. Constitution. This county was created on January 7, 1844.

2428 *Hardeman County*

Thomas J. Hardeman (1788–1854) — Born in western North Carolina near what is now Nashville, Tennessee, on January 31, 1788, Hardeman served as an army officer during the War of 1812 and was a captain, quartermaster and colonel. This Tennessee county was created and named in his honor on October 16, 1823, and Thomas J. Hardeman played a role in organizing both this county and its county seat, the municipality of Bolivar, Tennessee. He was the first county clerk of Hardeman County, Tennessee. In 1835 Thomas J. Hardeman and his brother Bailey Hardeman (1795–1836) immigrated to Texas. There he represented Matagorda County in the second congress of the republic of Texas and also held several judicial posts. After Texas became a member of the United States of America, Thomas J. Hardeman served in the state legislature. He died on January 15, 1854.

2429 *Hardin County*

Joseph Hardin (1734–1801) — Born in Richmond, Virginia, on April 18, 1734, Hardin came to historical notice in North Carolina, where he was a justice of the peace, and member of the committee of safety. He served as an officer of North Carolina minute men during the American Revolution and also was a member of the North Carolina house of commons. In 1781 Hardin moved to western North Carolina settling on Lick's Creek in what is today Greene County, Tennessee. When North Carolina ceded its western lands to the Confederation congress, Joseph Hardin was among the residents of that area who tried to establish the so-called "free state of Franklin." Soon after this, the United States established the territory South of the River Ohio, which was destined to become the state of Tennessee, and Hardin served in that territory's assembly from 1794 to 1795. He was speaker of the territorial assembly in 1795. Joseph Hardin purchased 200 acres of land in Knox County in 1795 and he lived there until his death on July 4, 1801. This county was created and named in his honor on November 13, 1819. Joseph Hardin had received a substantial grant of military land in what is now Hardin County, Tennessee and a number of members of Joseph Hardin's family moved there about 15 years after his death.

2430 *Hawkins County*

Benjamin Hawkins (1754–) — This North Carolina native was in his senior year at the College of New Jersey (now Princeton University) when the American Revolution began. He left college to join our Revolutionary army and was appointed to the staff of General George Washington as a French interpreter to assist Washington in communicating with his numerous French officers. Hawkins represented North Carolina during two terms in the Continental Congress and subsequently represented the state of North Carolina in the senate of the first congress of the United States of America. He served in that body from 1790 to 1795. President George Washington appointed him as the superintendent Indian agent to all tribes south of the Ohio River and Hawkins held that position until his death. Conflicting information concerning the date of Hawkins' death is given by usually reliable sources. Some say June 6, 1816, while others use June 6, 1818. This county was created in the late 1780's (late 1786 or 1787) by North Carolina and was part of the territory that

North Carolina ceded to the United States government. Soon after that land was ceded, the United States established the territory South of the River Ohio, and on June 1, 1796, that territory became the state of Tennessee. Thus Hawkins County created by North Carolina now resides in Tennessee.

2431 *Haywood County*

John Haywood (–1826) — Haywood was born in Halifax County, North Carolina. His year of birth is listed as 1753 by some sources but March 16, 1762, is cited as his birth date by others. He became solicitor-general of North Carolina in 1790 and was made the state's attorney general during the following year. Haywood subsequently served some six years as a judge on North Carolina's superior court, which then was the state's highest court. While serving in that capacity he compiled a two volume landmark work concerning North Carolina law, which was published in 1801. About 1807 or 1808 Haywood moved to Tennessee. Here he served from 1816 until his death on the supreme court of the state and became a recognized authority on the history of Tennessee. This county was created during November, 1823, while John Haywood was a judge of the Tennessee supreme court.

2432 *Henderson County*

Uncertain — This county was created on November 7, 1821. Nineteen sources dealing with the history, geography and place names of Tennessee offer an opinion on the origin of this county's name. All but one of those sources agree that the county was named for a James Henderson and even the source that differs ("Fames Henderson" per James A. Crutchfield's *Tennessee Almanac & Book of Facts*) can be attributed to typographical error. However, there is a very real difference of opinion concerning which James Henderson is this county's namesake. Almost all sources agree that he was Colonel James Henderson but they disagree on the time frame during which he achieved military accomplishments of note. Three sources indicate that the James Henderson for whom this county was named was "of Revolutionary War fame." A majority of the 19 sources consulted indicate that the James Henderson for whom this county was named was a colonel of Tennessee militia and quartermaster under General Andrew Jackson during the War of 1812. Some of them state that he participated in the Natchez expedition and/or the battles prior to the battle of New Orleans. The fact that a majority of sources consulted favor the War of 1812 Henderson over the Revolutionary War Henderson doesn't tell us much. Many of these sources were copying from each other. Reasons why a county was named are far more important in establishing validity of a purported namesake and G. Tillman Stewart's *Henderson County*, published in 1979, offers a reason: "Henderson County was named for Colonel James Henderson, who commanded Tennessee troops at the Battle of New Orleans. He also was on General Jackson's staff during both the Creek and Natchez campaigns. Major John Harmon served under Henderson and in all probability influenced other leaders in naming the county for his commander." Presumably the "Major John Harmon" referred to was the "John T. Harmon," whom G. Tillman Stewart listed as one of the signers of a petition to create this new county. While G. Tillman Stewart's information fails to prove that the War of 1812 Henderson is our man, it helps support that thesis.

2433 *Henry County*

Patrick Henry (1736–1799) — Henry was a native of Virginia and a lawyer. He served in the Virginia legislature, as governor of Virginia and as a delegate to the first and second Continental Congresses. Henry was one of America's key revolutionary leaders. He was a great orator and he is remembered for his call to arms against the British "Give me liberty or give me death." Henry opposed Virginia's ratification of the Federal constitution and his views played a role in the later adoption of the Bill of Rights. This county was created on November 7, 1821.

2434 *Hickman County*

Edmund Hickman (–) — Hickman, whose given name is rendered in some accounts as Edwin, was a hunter, explorer and surveyor. He visited the area of the present Hickman County to perform survey work in 1785 and he and the members of his survey party were among the first White visitors to this portion of west-central Tennessee. Hickman was killed by Indians on Duck River, within a mile of the present city of Centerville, Tennessee, the present county seat of Hickman County. Several sources indicate that Hickman was killed by Indians in 1791 while others indicate that the Indians killed him during his 1785 survey trip to this area. These years seem too widely separated for both of them to be accurate. The volume of the *History of Tennessee*, which was published by Goodspeed Publishing Company in 1886 dealing with Lawrence, Wayne, Perry, Hickman & Lewis Counties specifically states that Edmund Hickman visited this area on survey work in 1785 and was killed by Indians on that trip during 1785. This county was created and named in his honor on December 3, 1807.

2435 *Houston County*

Samuel Houston (1793–1863) — A native of Virginia, Houston moved with his family to Tennessee when he was about 14 years old. After serving in the U.S. army in actions against the Indians, Houston studied law and became active in local politics. In 1823 he was elected to represent Tennessee in the U.S. House of Representatives and he later served, from 1827 to 1829, as governor of Tennessee. On January 22, 1829, Governor Houston married Eliza Allen, but Mrs. Houston left him to return to her parents before the marriage was four months old. This event was traumatic for Houston and it proved to be a turning point in his life. He resigned as Tennessee's governor and moved to Indian country, where he lived for half a dozen years. It was not until 1835 that Sam Houston's name became firmly associated with Texas and her history. In November, 1835 he was made a major-general of the army of the provisional government of the Republic of Texas. In early March, 1836, when Texas formally seceded from Mexico and officially declared itself an independent republic, Houston was named commander-in-chief of the new republic's army. The Mexican army responded immediately with force and brutality. A large force of the Mexican army defeated and massacred a much smaller force of Texan defenders of the Alamo. However, it was not long after the infamous event that Texas, under Sam Houston's command, turned the tide and defeated the Mexicans at the battle of San Jacinto. Houston was elected president of the Republic of Texas and later, when Texas became a member of the United States, Houston was one of the new state's first two U.S. senators. He subsequently was elected governor of the state of Texas but when Texas seceded from the Union, Houston refused to take an oath of loyalty to the Confederate States of America and he was deposed as Texas' governor. Houston County, Tennessee, was created in January 1871.

2436 *Humphreys County*

Parry W. Humphreys (–1839)— Parry Wayne Humphreys was born at Staunton, Virginia, in 1777 or 1778. He moved to Kentucky with his family in 1789 and later settled in Tennessee, where he completed his education. He was admitted to the Tennessee bar in 1801 and practiced law in Nashville. From 1807 to 1813 Humphreys was a judge in Tennessee and he later represented the state in the U.S. House of Representatives from 1813 to 1815. After an unsuccessful bid for a seat in the U.S. Senate, Humphreys again served in Tennessee as a judge, from 1818 to 1836. He then moved to northern Mississippi and pursued banking and business ventures in De Soto County until his death. This county was created on October 19, 1809, during the period that Humphreys was a judge in Tennessee.

2437 *Jackson County*

Andrew Jackson (1767–1845)— Jackson was born on the border of North Carolina and South Carolina. He served in America's Revolutionary army as a youth, was admitted to the bar in 1787 and then moved to Nashville. Here he was a member of Tennessee's 1796 state constitutional convention. Jackson was elected as the new state of Tennessee's first representative in Congress and he took his seat in that body on December 5, 1796. On November 22, 1797, Andrew Jackson became a U.S. senator from Tennessee but in 1798 he resigned from that body to accept an appointment as a judge on Tennessee's highest court. He soon and gained nationwide fame and popularity for his military exploits in wars with the Indians and in the War of 1812. He was provisional military governor of Florida and, from 1829 to 1837, General Jackson was president of the United States. His presidency reflected the frontier spirit of America. This county was created on November 6, 1801, before Andrew Jackson had entered the military career which would propel him to the presidency.

2438 *Jefferson County*

Thomas Jefferson (1743–1826)— Jefferson was a native of Virginia and a member of the Virginia legislature. He served Virginia as governor and was a delegate to the second Continental Congress. Jefferson was the author of the Declaration of Independence and one of its signers. He was minister to France, secretary of state, vice-president and president of the United States. As president, he accomplished the Louisiana Purchase and he arranged the Lewis & Clark Expedition to the Pacific Northwest. Jefferson was a true intellectual, thoroughly knowledgeable in the arts and sciences. His political theories were pivotal in the formation of our infant republic. This county was created on June 11, 1792, by territory South of the River Ohio, while Thomas Jefferson was serving as secretary of state during George Washington's first term as president.

2439 *Johnson County*

Uncertain— Johnson County, Tennessee, was created from a portion of Carter County on January 2, 1836. Sources dealing with the history, geography and place names of Tennessee disagree on who this county's namesake was although only two possibilities are mentioned: Cave Johnson (1793–1866) and Thomas Johnson. Thomas Johnson is the choice of more than two-thirds of the sources consulted and there is a compelling narrative about the naming of this county, below, which supports that view.

Cave Johnson (1793–1866)— Born in Tennessee when it was still a territory, Cave Johnson studied law and was admitted to the Tennessee bar. He was prosecuting attorney for Montgomery County, Tennessee, in 1817 and later represented Tennessee in the U.S. House of Representatives from 1829 to 1837 and from 1839 to 1845. President James K. Polk appointed Cave Johnson to his cabinet as postmaster general.

Thomas Johnson (–)— Thomas Johnson had come from Russell County, Virginia, to Carter County, Tennessee, and was one of the early settlers on Doe Creek in the area of Carter County that is now Johnson County, Tennessee. Thomas Johnson was said to have been a prominent citizen of the Johnson County area, both when it was part of Carter County, and after it attained status as a separate county. After Johnson County was created in 1836, Thomas Johnson was one the new county's first judicial officials. Some accounts refer to him as one of the first justices of the peace while others say that he was a member of the first county court.

An article by Gladys McCloud, which appeared in the December 4, 1974, issue of *Mountain City Tomahawk*, stated that Senator James Powell introduced a bill in the Tennessee legislature to create this new county and he advocated that it be named Johnson County, in honor of Thomas Johnson. That article goes on to relate that the name Taylor was also proposed for the county to honor Colonel James P. Taylor, then deceased. According to Ms. McCloud, Senator Powell explained to his fellow legislators that Colonel James P. Taylor had been a friend of his, but he felt compelled to honor the wishes of his constituents in asking that the county be named Johnson, in honor Thomas Johnson. Several other accounts agree with Ms. McCloud on most of these details. However, the name of the sate senator from Carter County is given as Joseph Powell by some sources, rather than James Powell.

2440 *Knox County*

Henry Knox (1750–1806)— This Massachusetts native participated in many of the important military engagements of the American Revolution and rose to the rank of major-general. After the war, Knox commanded West Point and he conceived and organized the Society of Cincinnati, an elite group of former Revolutionary officers. In 1785 he was appointed secretary of war under the Articles of Confederation and he retained that position in the first cabinet of the United States under President George Washington. This county was created on June 11, 1792, by the territory South of the River Ohio, which shortly became the state of Tennessee. When this county was created, Henry Knox was serving in President Washington's cabinet as the first secretary of war of the infant United States.

2441 *Lake County*

Reelfoot Lake— This county was created during June 1870 from the western end of Obion County and named for Reelfoot Lake, which lies near the eastern edge of the county and extends east into Obion County. Reelfoot Lake is a shallow lake, which lies less that four miles from the Mississippi River. It was formed from waters of the Mississippi during convolutions resulting from the earthquakes, centered at New Madrid, Missouri, about 20 miles north of Reelfoot Lake. The first quake occurred on December 16, 1811. Major after-shocks occurred on January 23 and February 7, 1812. During this period in 1811–1812, the earth on the eastern side of the Mississippi, south and east of New Madrid, Missouri dropped to form the lake bed, and waters from the Mississippi filled the depression. Reelfoot Lake is about 18 miles long and varies in width from three-fourth's of a mile to three miles.

2442 *Lauderdale County*

James Lauderdale (–1814)— Lauderdale was a native of Virginia who moved to western Tennessee. He was an officer in the army and was wounded while serving under General Andrew Jackson against the Creek Indians in the battle of Talladega, Alabama. He later commanded Tennessee troops in the War of 1812 and he died in combat at that battle of New Orleans during that war. This county was created on November 24, 1835.

2443 *Lawrence County*

James Lawrence (1781–1813)— Lawrence was an officer in the United States navy who established a reputation for bravery in the war against Tripoli and in the War of 1812. He died in combat while commanding the *Chesapeake* against the British, near Boston. He is said to have uttered the famous phrase "Don't give up the ship" while he lay mortally wounded in that battle. He died on June 4, 1813, and this county was created four years later, on October 21, 1817.

2444 *Lewis County*

Meriwether Lewis (1774–1809)— A native of Virginia and a neighbor and friend of Thomas Jefferson, Lewis served as an officer in the army and then, in 1801, President Jefferson selected him to be his aide. From 1804 to 1806 Meriwether Lewis and William Clark led the Lewis & Clark Expedition which President Jefferson sent to explore the Northwest to the Pacific Ocean. Their successful journey ended in September 1806 when they returned to civilization at Saint Louis, in what is now the state of Missouri. Lewis then served as governor of Louisiana territory from 1807 until his death on October 11, 1809. At the time of his death Meriwether Lewis was traveling along the Natchez Trace in Tennessee and he died mysteriously (murder or suicide) at Grinder's Stand, an inn on the Natchez Trace. Grinder's Stand was located about eight miles from Hohenwald, Tennessee. This county, which was created in December 1843, embraces both Hohenwald, Tennessee, and the precise location where Meriwether Lewis died.

2445 *Lincoln County*

Benjamin Lincoln (1733–1810)— A native of Massachusetts, Lincoln was a member of the Massachusetts legislature and of the provincial congress. He served as an officer in the Revolutionary War and rose to the rank of major-general. In 1779, as commander of the southern department of the Continental army, Lincoln attempted, unsuccessfully, to rescue Savannah, Georgia from the British. In 1781 General George Washington gave Lincoln the honor of accepting Cornwallis' sword when the British surrendered at Yorktown. Later in 1781 Lincoln was made secretary of war and he held that post for two years. He died on May 9, 1810, in Hingham, Massachusetts, in the same house in which he had been born. This Tennessee county was created and named in General Lincoln's honor on November 14, 1809.

2446 *Loudon County*

Fort Loudon— This county was initially created with the name Christiana County. The act to create it passed the Tennessee legislature on May 27, 1870, and was signed into law by the governor on June 2, 1870. The county's name was changed to Loudon County, in honor of Tennessee's Fort Loudon on July 7, 1870. Fort Loudon had been erected in 1756 and named in honor of John Campbell, Earl of Loudoun (1705–1782), who was then Britain's commander-in-chief in North America.

Fort Loudon— This fort was erected and named in 1756 on the southern bank of the Little Tennessee River, near the mouth of the Tellico River, close to the present eastern Tennessee community of Vonore, in Monroe County. When this fort was erected, that site was within one of England's provinces of Carolina. The fort was erected by British and South Carolina forces on a rocky ledge, overlooking the river, under direction from General John Campbell, Earl of Loudoun (1705–1782), for whom the fort was named. William Girard de Braham (1717–1799) was the engineer in charge of the fort's construction, while Captain Raymond Demere initially commanded the troops here until he was replaced by his younger brother, Paul Demere. Fort Loudon became the first Anglo-American settlement in the present state of Tennessee. The fort fell to Indian attack on August 8, 1760.

John Campbell, Earl of Loudoun (1705–1782)— John Campbell, the fourth earl of Loudoun, entered the British military as a cornet in the Scots Greys in 1727 and in 1731 he succeeded his father, Hugh Campbell (–1731), as earl of Loudoun. John Campbell, Earl of Loudoun, was a Scottish representative peer from 1734 to 1782 and in the military he attained the rank of major-general in 1755. Loudoun was made commander-in-chief of all forces in North America in January 1756. Also that year he was made a non-resident governor-general of England's colony of Virginia, while Robert Dinwiddie (–1770) was the crown's resident governor of Virginia. As commander-in-chief in North America, Loudoun met with limited success and it was decided in December 1757 that he would be recalled, although he was promoted to lieutenant-general in 1758. In 1762 Loudoun was second in command during a British expedition to Portugal. He was made full general in 1770.

2447 *McMinn County*

Joseph McMinn (1758–1824)— Born June 22, 1758, in Chester County, Pennsylvania, McMinn became a regimental commander of militia in Tennessee in 1789, just before the territory South of the River Ohio was created and he served in the legislature of that territory from 1794 to 1795. McMinn was a member of Tennessee's 1796 state constitutional convention, served several terms in the state legislature and was speaker of the senate from 1805 to 1811. In 1815 he was elected as governor of Tennessee and he served in that position from September 27, 1815, to October 1, 1821. Governor McMinn was an enthusiastic participant in the brutal removal of some 17,000 Cherokee Indians from their ancient tribal lands in western North Carolina, northwestern Georgia and eastern Tennessee. Their journey to Indian territory was marked by indescribable suffering from which some 4,000 Cherokees died. This county was created and named in Joseph McMinn's honor during November 1819, while he was governor.

2448 *McNairy County*

John McNairy (1762–1837)— A native of Lancaster County, Pennsylvania, McNairy moved to North Carolina where he studied law, was admitted to the bar and elected in 1788 as a judge of the supreme court of law and equity for Davidson County, North Carolina. That Davidson County, North Carolina, was destined to become part of the state of Tennessee (although North Carolina later created a second Davidson County in 1822). When the territory South of the River Ohio was created in 1790, McNairy was appointed as one of its judges. He subsequently was a member of Tennessee's 1796 state constitutional convention and participated in drafting the new state's first constitution. Elected in 1796 as a judge of Tennessee's state supreme court of law and equity, McNairy barely got that judicial chair warm before being appointed on February 17, 1797, as a U.S. judge in Tennessee. He stayed longer in that position, from 1797 to 1834. This county was created and named in Judge McNairy's honor on October 8, 1823.

2449 Macon County

Nathaniel Macon (1758–1837)— Born on December 17, 1758, in what is now Warren County, North Carolina, Macon served as a private in the North Carolina militia during the Revolutionary War. He subsequently was a member of the North Carolina senate and although he was elected to the Continental Congress, he declined to serve. He represented North Carolina for 37 years in both branches of the U.S. Congress, where he was speaker of the house and, later, president *pro tempore* of the senate. Macon believed strongly in economy of the public money and he was a defender of slavery. He died on June 29, 1837, and this Tennessee county was created and named in his honor less than five years later, on January 18, 1842.

2450 Madison County

James Madison (1751–1836)— Madison was born in Virginia and served in the Virginia legislature and in the Continental Congress. He was a member of the convention which framed the U.S. Constitution and he collaborated with Hamilton and Jay in writing a series of papers under the title *The Federalist*, which explained the new constitution and advocated its adoption. Madison represented Virginia in the U.S. House of Representatives, served for eight years as secretary of state and eight years, from 1809 to 1817, as president of the United States. This county was created on November 7, 1821.

2451 Marion County

Francis Marion (–1795)— Marion is believed to have been born in South Carolina. He served in the army in battles against the Cherokee Indians and was elected to the provisional congress of 1775. He served, with distinction, as an officer in the Revolutionary War and rose to the rank of general in that war. Marion was also a member of the South Carolina senate. This Tennessee county was created on November 20, 1817. The county seat of Marion County, which is the municipality of Jasper, was named for one of "Marion's men," during the American Revolution, Sergeant William Jasper (–1779).

2452 Marshall County

John Marshall (1755–1835)— Marshall, a native of Virginia, served as an officer in the Revolutionary War, in the Virginia legislature and in the U.S. House of Representatives. He briefly served as secretary of state and then, for over 30 years, was chief justice of the U.S. Supreme Court. Marshall's interpretations of the Constitution during America's political infancy left an unmatched impact on the laws and government of this country. Under Marshall, the Supreme Court shifted power in American government from the states to the central government and to the federal judiciary at the expense of the executive and legislative branches. Chief Justice Marshall died on July 6, 1835, and this county was created during February, 1836.

2453 Maury County

Abram P. Maury, Sr. (1766–1825)— Abram Poindexter Maury, Sr., was born in Lunenburg County, Virginia, on February 17, 1766. He came to Tennessee from Virginia in 1797 and settled in the portion of Davidson County which was broken off to form Williamson County, Tennessee, in 1799. Here Maury acquired 640 acres on Harpeth River, which he farmed. Maury also engaged in civil engineering and practiced law. He served in the state senate in 1805 and again in 1819 but resigned from the senate about 1819 to accept appointment as one of the commissioners to superintend sales of land recently acquired from the Cherokee Indians. Abram P. Maury, Sr., died at his home in Williamson County on January 2, 1825. This county was created and named in his honor in November 1807, following Maury's first term as a state senator. This county's namesake is easily confused with one of his sons, Abram Poindexter Maury, Jr. (1801–1848), who represented Tennessee in the U.S. House of Representatives. However this younger Abram P. Maury was only six years old in 1807 when Maury County, Tennessee, was created.

2454 Meigs County

Return J. Meigs (1740–1823)— Return Jonathan Meigs was born in Middletown, Connecticut, on December 17, 1740, and entered the army as lieutenant in 1772. Promoted to captain two years later, Meigs led his troops to the Boston area in 1775 immediately after the American Revolution began with the battles at Lexington and Concord, Massachusetts. He subsequently held the rank of major during the march through Maine to attack Quebec and he participated in the 1775 battle of Quebec. After scaling Quebec's fortress walls on December 31, 1775, Meigs was taken as a prisoner of war. Released as part of a prisoner exchange, in January, 1777, Meigs was promoted to lieutenant-colonel and troops under his command performed brilliantly in combat against the British at Sag Harbor, New York, in May 1777. Congress awarded Meigs a sword and in September 1777 he was promoted to colonel. He subsequently performed ably in the vicinity of the Hudson River and received a personal letter of thanks from General George Washington for his role in stopping the mutiny of the Connecticut line. This county was created on January 20, 1836. It was first proposed that this new county be named Vernon County, in honor of Tennessee's State Senator Miles Vernon, of Rhea County. However, Senator Vernon declined that honor. In a letter to the Tennessee house of representatives dated January 19, 1836, Senator Vernon stated that "…The name to be selected I will respectfully leave with yourselves." The legislature briefly toyed with naming this county De Kalb County before the name Meigs was agreed upon. Both Ohio and Tennessee have counties named for persons with the unusual name Return Jonathan Meigs. The Ohio county was named for Return J. Meigs (1764–1825), who was a son of the Tennessee county's namesake, Return J. Meigs (1740–1823). There is still another prominent Return Jonathan Meigs (1801–1891), a lawyer, but no state has named a county for him … yet.

2455 Monroe County

James Monroe (1758–1831)— Monroe, a native of Virginia, served in the Revolutionary War. Prior to his election as president of the United States, Monroe served in a wide variety of government posts. He served Virginia in the state legislature and as governor. He was a member of the Confederation congress and the U.S. Senate. He was minister to France and to Britain and he held two cabinet posts. As president, Monroe stressed limited government and strict construction of the constitution. He acquired Florida for the U.S. from Spain and he was the author of a policy declaration (later known as the Monroe Doctrine) which proscribed outside interference in North and South America. This county was created on November 13, 1819, during James Monroe's first term as president of the United States.

2456 *Montgomery County*

John Montgomery (–1794)— Born in Virginia about 1748, John Montgomery explored the Cumberland country of western North Carolina in the 1770's and was stationed at Long Island on the Holston River at the close of the Cherokee campaign of 1776. Montgomery served as a captain on our nation's western frontier under George Rogers Clark (1752–1818) and starting in 1778, Montgomery was involved in Clark's historic Illinois campaign. When those hostilities ended, Montgomery settled briefly in Kentucky but about 1784 he came south and together with Martin Armstrong laid off and planned the town that is now Clarksville, Tennessee, the county seat of Montgomery County. John Montgomery named this wilderness community for his former commander, George Rogers Clark (1752–1818). The French ambassador, Edmond C. Genet (1763–1834), recruited Montgomery in a plot to strike against Spanish Florida but President George Washington learned of the scheme and forced its abandonment. Montgomery participated in the Nickajack campaign in middle Tennessee in 1794 and later that year he was killed by one or more Indians while hunting near the mouth of the Cumberland River. In 1788 North Carolina established a Tennessee County here and Tennessee County became one of the counties of the territory South of the River Ohio. On April 9, 1796, the nascent state of Tennessee divided Tennessee County into two counties, Robertson and Montgomery.

2457 *Moore County*

William Moore (1786–1871)— Born in block house stockade in Kentucky on September 28, 1786, Moore came to Tennessee in 1806 or 1807 and settled on Mulberry Creek, in the present Lincoln County. He served as an officer in the Tennessee militia in the Creek War and in the War of 1812. Moore subsequently served in both houses of the Tennessee legislature; in the house from 1825 to 1829 and in the senate from 1833 to 1837. Moore died on March 10, 1871, and this county was created and named in his honor nine months later, on December 14, 1871. Several accounts indicate that William Moore attained the rank of major-general during, or following, the War of 1812. It is clear that he held the rank of captain while serving under General Andrew Jackson during the War of 1812 and he may have attained an even higher rank but the reference to major-general apparently refers to an offer of that rank in the U.S. army, which he received from the president in 1846, but declined to accept.

2458 *Morgan County*

Daniel Morgan (1736–1802)— Morgan was a native of the Northeast who moved to Virginia in his youth. He served as a general in the Revolutionary War and was regarded as a hero for important victories scored by his troops. After the war he represented Virginia for one term in the U.S. House of Representatives. This county was created on October 15, 1817.

2459 *Obion County*

Obion River— This county in northwestern Tennessee was created on October 24, 1823, and named for the Obion River, its principal stream. Formed by four main tributaries, the north, the middle, the south and the Rutherford forks, the Obion River is a short stream, only 70 miles long. It flows in a southwestern direction across Obion County and into Dyer County, Tennessee. In that county the Obion continues its southwestern journey, which ends at Dyer County's southern border, where the Obion pours its waters into Forked Deer River, near that river's mouth on the Mississippi. On some maps the two mile section between the Mississippi River and the junction of the Obion and Forked Deer Rivers is called the Obion River, while on others it is called the Forked Deer River.

2460 *Overton County*

John Overton (1766–1833)— Born in Louisa County, Virginia, on April 9, 1766, Overton moved to western Virginia (now Kentucky) and taught school there while studying law. He came to Nashville in 1789, the year before the territory South of the River Ohio was created. Here Overton soon became a close friend of Andrew Jackson's. Overton practiced law from 1789 to 1804, when he was elected to Tennessee's superior court. He was a judge of that court for some five years and in 1811 he was elected to Tennessee's supreme court, where he served until 1816. About 1820 Overton turned his attention to getting his friend, Andrew Jackson, elected president. Jackson, of course, lost to John Quincy Adams in the election of 1824 but Overton continued his efforts which met with victory in 1828 when Andrew Jackson defeated that same John Quincy Adams. About this time Overton also began devoting attention to western Tennessee, on the Mississippi River, where he had purchased 5,000 acres of forest land in 1794 for the then-enormous sum of $500. Overton became the founder of Memphis, Tennessee, on the Mississippi River. Surveyors laid off streets and parks and Memphis' town government began when seven aldermen were elected in 1827. John Overton died on April 12, 1833, before his Memphis land holdings had grown very much in value. This county was created on September 11, 1806, while Judge Overton was sitting on the superior court of Tennessee.

2461 *Perry County*

Oliver H. Perry (1785–1819)— Perry was a native of Rhode Island and an officer in the U.S. navy. During the War of 1812 his squadron defeated the British in a key battle on Lake Erie of which Perry said "We have met the enemy and they are ours." Perry died on August 23, 1819, and this county was created and named in his honor on November 14, 1821.

2462 *Pickett County*

Howell L. Pickett (1847–)— Born near Smith's Fork in Wilson County, Tennessee, Howell L. Pickett was a graduate of Union University of Murfreesboro, Tennessee, and he studied law at Cumberland University. He practiced law in Lebanon, Wilson County, Tennessee, and was that county's representative in the lower house of the 41st session of the Tennessee legislature, which convened in Nashville on January 6, 1879. During that session of the legislature, Howell L. Pickett was a key participant in the move to create this new county, and his efforts succeeded when Pickett County was created and named in his honor on February 27, 1879. In 1882 Pickett moved to Tombstone, Arizona territory, where he practiced law specializing in mining law. Pickett was also active in politics in Arizona territory. The record shows that he visited our nation's capitol at least twice to lobby against the proposal that New Mexico territory and Arizona territory be admitted as one combined state. After Arizona was admitted to statehood, Howell was an unsuccessful candidate to represent the state in the U.S. Senate.

2463 *Polk County*

James K. Polk (1795–1849)— Polk was a native of North Carolina who moved with his family to the Tennessee frontier in 1806. He served in the lower house of the Tennessee legislature and he represented

Tennessee for 14 years in the U.S. House of Representatives, where he was speaker. He served one term as governor of Tennessee. Polk became president of the United States as a dark horse candidate of the Democratic party but he became an unusually strong and effective president. His primary accomplishments involved westward extension of the United States in the Northwest by settling a territorial dispute with Britain and in California and the Southwest by provoking and winning the Mexican War. This county was created on November 28, 1839, just one month after Polk had been inaugurated as Tennessee's governor on October 14, 1839.

2464 *Putnam County*

Israel Putnam (1718–1790)— Putnam was born in Massachusetts and moved, when he was about 21, to Connecticut. He served as an officer in the French and Indian wars and later was a member of the Connecticut legislature. At the beginning of the Revolutionary War, news of the battle at Lexington, Massachusetts, reached Putnam while he was farming. In a dramatic gesture which became famous, Putnam left his plow and, without bothering to change clothes, hurried to Lexington. He was appointed a major-general in the Continental army. Although he enjoyed great popularity, he lacked the ability for high command. In 1779 a paralytic stroke ended his military career. This county was created in February, 1842.

2465 *Rhea County*

John Rhea (1753–1832)— A native of Ireland, who immigrated to America with his parents, Rhea resided in Pennsylvania and Maryland before coming to eastern Tennessee in 1778. At that time this area was still part of North Carolina. He was a 1780 graduate of the College of New Jersey (now Princeton University) and fought during the American Revolution at the battle of King's Mountain, South Carolina. Rhea served as a member of North Carolina's house of commons and was a delegate to the North Carolina convention that ratified the proposed federal constitution. Admitted to the bar in 1789, Rhea was a delegate to Tennessee's constitutional convention in 1796, served in the Tennessee legislature and subsequently represented Tennessee in the U.S. House of Representatives. He served in that body from 1803 to 1815 and from 1817 to 1823. This county was created on November 30, 1807, while Rhea was one of Tennessee's three representatives in the U.S. Congress.

2466 *Roane County*

Archibald Roane (–1819)— Born sometime between 1755 and 1760 in Pennsylvania, Roane studied law, was admitted to the Pennsylvania bar and served in the army during the American Revolution. About 1787 he came to eastern Tennessee, which was still part of North Carolina. Here, Roane was a delegate to Tennessee's constitutional convention in 1796, and on August 11, 1796, he was appointed as a judge on the new state of Tennessee's superior court. Elected as the second governor of Tennessee in 1801, Roane was inaugurated on September 23, 1801, and served one term ending September 23, 1803. He subsequently served as a circuit judge, and, very briefly, in the Tennessee senate. In 1815 he became a judge on the Tennessee supreme court. This county was created and named in Roane's honor on November 6, 1801, less that two months after his term as Tennessee's governor began.

2467 *Robertson County*

James Robertson (1742–1814)— Born in Virginia on June 28, 1742, Robertson moved to North Carolina while he was still a boy. In 1770 he explored the valley of the Watauga River and he soon returned to this area, which is now the northeastern part of Tennessee, with a group who formed a Watauga settlement. These settlers adopted a Watauga compact, an attempt to establish law and order on the North Carolina frontier. In 1779 Robertson ventured further into the wilderness of western North Carolina and explored the Cumberland country, settling on the present site of Nashville, in what is now mid–Tennessee, in 1780. Once again Robertson was at the center of a compact establishing law and order in the wilderness, the Cumberland compact, the first form of government in what is today mid–Tennessee. He represented the Cumberland area in the North Carolina legislature and when the territory South of the River Ohio was created, Robertson was one of its prominent figures. He was a delegate to Tennessee's constitutional convention in 1796 and was active in negotiating Indian treaties. In 1788 North Carolina established a Tennessee County here and Tennessee County became one of the counties of the territory South of the River Ohio. On April 9, 1796, the nascent state of Tennessee divided Tennessee County into two counties, Robertson County and Montgomery County.

2468 *Rutherford County*

Griffith Rutherford (–1805)— Rutherford was born in Ireland about 1731, immigrated to America in 1739 and settled in the vicinity of Salisbury, North Carolina. In 1775 he was elected to North Carolina's provincial congress and in June, 1776, the month before the signing of the Declaration of Independence, he was appointed a brigadier-general in the North Carolina militia. It was in 1776 that Rutherford and his troops crushed the Cherokee Indians in western North Carolina. Rutherford participated in the battle of Camden South Carolina in 1780 and shortly after that defeat, Rutherford was captured as a prisoner of war at the battle of Sanders Creek. He was released in an exchange of prisoners. After the American Revolution Rutherford served in the North Carolina legislature and subsequently came west to what is now Tennessee. When the present state of Tennessee was the territory South of the River Ohio, President George Washington appointed Rutherford to the legislative council of that territory, and Rutherford was chairman of that council. This county was created and named in his honor on October 25, 1803.

2469 *Scott County*

Winfield Scott (1786–1866)— A native of Virginia, Scott joined the U.S. army in 1808. His heroic service in the War of 1812 resulted in rapid promotions to brevet major-general. He later played an important military role during the 1832 nullification crisis in South Carolina and in actions against the Indians in Florida. He was general-in-chief of the United States army during the Mexican War. Scott was the Whig party's candidate for president in 1852 but he lost to Franklin Pierce. When the Civil War broke out, Scott remained loyal to the Union side despite his southern roots but he retired in from the army in October, 1861, on account of age and ill health. This county was created on December 17, 1849, when America's victory in the Mexican War was fresh in the minds of Tennessee's legislators.

2470 *Sequatchie County*

Valley of the Sequatchie River— This county in southern Tennessee lies in the valley of the Sequatchie River. It was created on December 9, 1857, and named for that *valley* of the Sequatchie River. The river itself is a 60 mile-long tributary of the Tennessee River, which rises in Cumberland County, in east-central Tennessee, flows in a southern and south-western direction and enters the Tennessee River in Marion County, Tennessee, about five miles northwest of the angle formed by the junction of Georgia's northwestern corner where it meets Marion County, Tennessee. The valley is a long, narrow trough-shaped depression in the Cumberland Mountains, which extends for about 70 miles from southern Cumberland County, Tennessee, to the tri-state junction of Georgia, Alabama and Tennessee. Elizabeth Parham Robnett's history of Bledsoe County describes the valley as "...hemmed in on both sides and one end by escarpments approximately a thousand feet high." *Eastin Morris' Tennessee Gazetteer: 1834 & Matthew Rhea's Map of the State of Tennessee: 1832* provides a description of this valley of the Sequatchee (sic) River: "Sequatchee River, a north branch of Tennessee River ... after winding its way through the hills for six or eight miles into the Grassy Cove, it enters a large cavern, and is lost for eight or ten miles under a mountain, at the foot of which, on the south, it bursts out in a clear cold fountain. This is the head of what is called Sequatchee Valley." In their work entitled *Sequatchie: A Story of the Southern Cumberlands*, J. Leonard Raulston and James W. Livingood state that the river and its valley are "named for an Indian chief of the area known to history only for his treaty-signing activities with the whites."

2471 *Sevier County*

John Sevier (1745–1815) — A native of Virginia, Sevier became one of the early settler's and leaders in what is now the state of Tennessee. He represented the Watauga settlements in North Carolina's provisional congress in 1776 and served as an army officer during the American Revolution. When North Carolina ceded its western lands to the Confederation congress, residents of that area tried to establish the so-called "free state of Franklin" and Sevier became its governor in March, 1785. In 1789 he was a member of the North Carolina convention which ratified the proposed federal constitution. On June 16, 1790, John Sevier took his seat as a North Carolina representative in the first congress of the United States of America. Elected as Tennessee's first state governor, he served in that office from 1796 to 1801 and from 1803 to 1809. Sevier then served in the Tennessee senate before returning to Washington, this time to represent Tennessee in the House of Representatives. This county was created on September 27, 1794, by the territory South of the River Ohio.

2472 *Shelby County*

Isaac Shelby (1750–1826) — Shelby was a delegate to the Virginia legislature and, later, to the North Carolina legislature. He served as a soldier in the Revolutionary War and then moved to Kentucky County, Virginia, where he was active in the movement to separate Kentucky from Virginia. Shelby was inaugurated as Kentucky's first governor and later fought in the War of 1812. In October, 1813, he took part in the battle of the Thames River, in Canada. President James Monroe offered Shelby the cabinet post of secretary of war in 1817 but Shelby declined. In 1818 Isaac Shelby and Andrew Jackson negotiated a purchase of certain lands west of the Tennessee River with the Chickasaw Indians. This county was created on November 24, 1819.

2473 *Smith County*

Daniel Smith (1748–1818) — A native of Virginia, Smith attended the College of William & Mary there and served as an army officer during the American Revolution. About 1783, Smith moved to the Cumberland settlements here and in 1790 President George Washington appointed Daniel Smith to be secretary of the new territory South of the River Ohio, and he served as territorial secretary until the territory became the state of Tennessee in 1796. Smith was a delegate to Tennessee's 1796 state constitutional convention, and when Tennessee's U.S. senator, Andrew Jackson, resigned from the senate in 1798, Daniel Smith took his Senate seat and held it until the fifth U.S. Congress adjourned on March 3, 1799. This county was created and named in Smith's honor on October 26, 1799. Smith was later elected to represent Tennessee again in the U.S. Senate and served from 1805 to 1809.

2474 *Stewart County*

Duncan Stewart (1752–1815) — Duncan Stewart was born in North Carolina and was a member of the North Carolina house of commons in 1789 and 1790. Several Tennessee sources mention that he served as an officer during the American Revolution, but offer no details and two sources specify that this is probably not true. Stewart came to Tennessee between 1797 and 1800, bringing his slaves with him. He settled first near Clarksville, in the north-central portion of the state, in Montgomery County, but soon moved east to Robertson County, where he acquired significant amounts of land along the Cumberland River and its tributaries. One account describes him as a "well-to-do farmer from North Carolina." He must have been moderately wealthy because his land holdings extended to the area south of Nashville. Stewart was elected to the Tennessee senate and served in that body from 1801 to 1807. He moved to Mississippi territory in 1808 or 1809 and there he became a wealthy planter and surveyor-general. This Tennessee county was created on November 1, 1803, and named for Duncan Stewart, who was then representing Robertson and Montgomery Counties in the Tennessee senate. Of 22 Tennessee sources consulted, which offer an opinion on this county's namesake, all but one agree that Duncan Stewart (1752–1815) is the man. The one source that disagrees is Robert H. White's *Tennessee: Its Growth & Progress*. White claims that this county was named in honor of James Stuart, speaker of the house of representatives. It is true that James Stuart was speaker of the house during Tennessee's fifth legislative session, which convened in Knoxville in 1803, and it is true that it was this session of the legislature which created and named this county. However, it is difficult to take Robert H. White's statement seriously, not only because of the difference in the spelling of the name, but because no source (out of 22 consulted) can be found which either agrees that James Stuart is the namesake, or even admits that there is any uncertainty on the subject. Moreover, after the new county was created, the senatorial district which Duncan Stewart (1752–1815) represented in the Tennessee senate, included this new Stewart County, which had been named in his honor.

2475 *Sullivan County*

John Sullivan (1740–1795) — The location of John Sullivan's birth is given variously as Berwick, Maine, and Somersworth, New Hampshire. The two towns are adjacent. He practiced law in New Hampshire and represented New Hampshire in the Continental Congress. During the American Revolution Sullivan served as a brigadier-general and later was promoted to major-general. John Sullivan served with distinction in a number of important engagements of the Revolution. Soon after the 1779 campaign, he fell ill and resigned from the army. He then represented New Hampshire again in the Continental

Congress. Sullivan later served as attorney general of New Hampshire, president (or governor) of New Hampshire and was a member of the New Hampshire convention that ratified the proposed federal constitution. He also was speaker of New Hampshire's house of representatives. In 1789 President George Washington appointed John Sullivan as judge of the U.S. district court of New Hampshire and Sullivan held that position until his death in 1795. This county was created and named in General Sullivan's honor by North Carolina in 1779. After North Carolina relinquished its western lands to the central government, there was a period of time when Virginia claimed ownership of Sullivan County, but that controversy was resolved long ago and Sullivan County ended its journey within the state of Tennessee.

2476 *Sumner County*

Jethro Sumner (–1785)—Born about 1733–1735 in Virginia, Sumner served as an army officer during the French & Indian Wars before moving to North Carolina. Sumner had married into wealth and he accumulated some 20,000 acres of land as well as 34 slaves and was a comfortable and wealthy planter. However, the American Revolution soon disrupted Sumner's comfortable life and he served with distinction in our Revolutionary army rising to the rank of brigadier-general. This county was created in 1786 or 1787 by North Carolina. North Carolina subsequently relinquished its western lands to the central government and Sumner County became part of the territory South of the River Ohio, which became the state of Tennessee in 1796.

2477 *Tipton County*

Jacob Tipton (–1791)—In 1791 President George Washington called upon Territorial Governor William Blount (1749–1800) to furnish Tennessee troops to assist in the defense of our nation's northwestern frontier against hostile Indians. In response to this order, Governor Blount sent a battalion of some 200 Tennessee troops to serve under General Arthur St. Clair (1736–1818) against the Indians. Captain Jacob Tipton (–1791) was among them, leading one company of Tennessee soldiers. A description of Captain Jacob Tipton's departure from his home is contained in *The Annals of Tennessee to the End of the Eighteenth Century* by J. G. M. Ramsey: "...he had taken his farewell to

his family, and had mounted his horse. He hallooed back to his wife, requesting her, that if he should be killed, to alter the name of their son William, and call him, for himself, Jacob." Sadly, Captain Jacob Tipton's premonition was well founded. On November 4, 1791, under the command of General Arthur St. Clair, near what is today the city of Ft. Wayne, Indiana, Captain Jacob Tipton (–1791) was killed in combat fighting Indians. His widow complied with his request and renamed their son Jacob Tipton, in his honor. Tipton County, Tennessee, was created on October 29, 1823, and one of the early settlers of the Tipton County area was the younger Jacob Tipton (1790–1839), who had been renamed in honor of his father, Captain Jacob Tipton (–1791).

2478 *Trousdale County*

William Trousdale (1790–1872)—A native of North Carolina, Trousdale came with his family to Tennessee in 1796. He served as an officer in the War of 1812 and fought under General Andrew Jackson at the battle of New Orleans. Trousdale enlisted as a captain to fight in the Seminole War in Florida territory and was immediately promoted to colonel. He later fought during the Mexican War, was wounded in combat on more than one occasion, and was appointed brevet-brigadier-general by President James K. Polk on August 23, 1848. Trousdale also found time to study law and was admitted to the Tennessee bar in 1820. In 1835 he served in the Tennessee senate but resigned in 1836 to participate in the Seminole War. Following three unsuccessful bids to represent Tennessee in the U.S. House of Representatives, Trousdale was elected as the state's governor in 1849. He served just one term, from October 16, 1849, to October 16, 1851. Hoping that a change in climate would improve his failing health, Trousdale accepted an appointment as minister to Brazil. This county was created on June 21, 1870, while Trousdale was a semi-invalid at his home in Gallatin, Tennessee.

2479 *Unicoi County*

Unaka Mountains—This county lies in northeastern Tennessee, on the North Carolina border. It was created in March 1875 and named for the Unaka Mountains, which cover much of the county. The Unaka Mountain portion of the Appalachian chain extends some 200 miles from southwestern Virginia, along much of the border between Tennessee and North

Carolina to end just north of Georgia. Mount Unaka, in Unicoi County, Tennessee, is part of the Unaka chain. It soars to 5,258 feet above sea level. When North Carolina's legislature ceded its western lands to the central government following the American Revolution, the territory given up included the present Unicoi County, Tennessee. The language of the 1789 act by the North Carolina legislature displayed the uncertainty about the proper name for these mountains: "...where it is called Unicoy or Unaka Mountain between the Indian towns of Cowee and Old Chota." Nearly a century later, the Tennessee legislature was still groping for the proper name when it chose to name this new county Unicoi.

2480 *Union County*

Uncertain—This county was created by the Tennessee legislature on January 3, 1850. Sources consulted offer two possible inspirations for naming this county Union County.

Preservation of the federal Union of American states—When this county was created in 1850, tension between the North and South was building over the slavery issue and civil war was becoming a distinct possibility. However, there were many Americans in both the South and the North, who fervently desired preservation of the Union. Given that historic setting, it is certainly possible that this county was named in honor the American federal Union of states.

Union of land taken from five surrounding counties to form the new county—This county was created using portions of land from five surrounding counties, Grainger, Claiborne, Campbell, Anderson and Knox Counties. Union County's name is said by some sources to reflect that union of lands from other counties to form this new county. However the union was less than harmonious. Knox County, unhappy about the prospect of giving up any of its land to form this new county, secured an injunction against Union County acting as a bona-fide county. Prolonged litigation followed but in 1853 Union County won the right to exist.

2481 *Van Buren County*

Martin Van Buren (1782–1862)—Van Buren was a native of New York and he served that state as state senator, attorney general and governor. He organized an effective political machine in New York state, which was one of the first political machines in this country. Van Buren represented New York in the U.S. Senate and was secretary of state in the cabinet of President Andrew Jackson, of Tennessee. He soon became one of Jackson's closest advisors and when John C. Calhoun (1782–1850) resigned as Jackson's vice-president, Martin Van Buren became the new vice-president. Van Buren subsequently served one term as president of the United States and this county was created on January 3, 1840, while Van Buren was our nation's president.

2482 *Warren County*

Joseph Warren (1741–1775)— A native of Massachusetts and a graduate of Harvard College, Warren practiced medicine in the Boston area. He was a member of the committee of safety and president *pro tempore* of the Massachusetts provincial congress. In June, 1775, he was commissioned a major-general and he died in combat a few days later at the battle of Bunker Hill. Warren County, Tennessee, was created and named in his honor on November 26, 1807.

2483 *Washington County*

George Washington (1732–1799)— Washington was a native of Virginia. He served in Virginia's house of burgesses and became one of the colonies' leaders in opposition to British policies in America. He was a member of the first and second Continental Congresses and commander of all Continental armies in the Revolutionary War. Following victory in that war, Washington was elected to be the first president of the United States. This county was created in 1776 as Washington District of North Carolina and that district was made a county in 1777. North Carolina ceded the area that comprised this Washington County to the central government following the American Revolution. Subsequently the name Washington was retained by the short-lived, so called "free state of Franklin," the territory South of the River Ohio and finally by the state of Tennessee. (The absence of a Washington County on North Carolina's map was remedied in 1799 when that state created a Washington County for the second time, named in honor of the father of our country.)

2484 *Wayne County*

Anthony Wayne (1745–1796)— A native of Pennsylvania, Wayne was a successful brigadier-general in the Revolutionary War and became a hero for his daring exploits. During the bitter winter of 1777–1778 at Valley Forge, Pennsylvania, Wayne shared the sufferings of his men although his comfortable estate was only five miles away. He played an important role in the final overthrow of the British forces in Georgia. After the war, in 1785, Wayne moved to Georgia and he represented Georgia for about six months in the U.S. House of Representatives. In 1792, President Washington recalled Wayne to serve as a major-general against the Indians in the Northwest territory. Once again his military efforts were successful. This county was first created by the Tennessee legislature on November 24, 1817. That act, however, had certain technical defects and it was necessary for the legislative session of 1819 to again enact the law creating Wayne County.

2485 *Weakley County*

Robert Weakley (1764–1845)— A native of Virginia, Weakley entered America's Revolutionary army when he was 16 years old. In 1782 he moved to North Carolina and during the winter of 1783–1784, Weakley came to the portion of North Carolina, which would become Tennessee. Here he was a member of the North Carolina convention which ratified the proposed federal constitution in 1789. When Tennessee was admitted to statehood, Weakley served in the first legislature of the new state, in the lower house, and he subsequently served several terms in both houses of the Tennessee legislature. He also represented Tennessee in the U.S. House of Representatives from 1809 to 1811. During the 1820's Weakley served again in Tennessee's senate and was speaker of the senate for two legislative sessions. This county was created on October 21, 1823, while Robert Weakley was speaker of the Tennessee senate.

2486 *White County*

John White (–1846)— The date of John White's birth is given in one account as March 2, 1751, while another shows March 1, 1757. He was a resident of Virginia when he entered America's Revolutionary army and he fought during the Revolution in Pennsylvania at the battles of Brandywine and Germantown. John White settled, as a squatter, in what is now central Tennessee's White County. He and his family were one of the first, if not the first, White settlers here. White cleared land on a cane-break here to farm and built a house. The original house had port holes to help guard against the very real threat of Indian attack. White purchased land here from a land-owner of Knoxville and he died in October 1846. This county was created and named in John White's honor on September 11, 1806.

2487 *Williamson County*

Hugh Williamson (1735–1819)— Williamson was born in Pennsylvania and graduated from the University of Pennsylvania. This versatile man studied theology, was licensed to preach and worked as a professor of mathematics, astronomer and physician. He settled in North Carolina about 1776 and was surgeon general of North Carolina's troops during the American Revolution. Dr. Williamson also served in North Carolina's house of commons and was a delegate from North Carolina to the Continental Congress. He was one of North Carolina's five delegates to the 1787 convention which framed the U.S. Constitution and he represented the state of North Carolina in the U.S. House of Representatives during the first two congresses of our country. Williamson was a friend of Abram P. Maury, Sr. (1766–1825), on whose land in Franklin, the county seat of Williamson County was built. This county was created on October 26, 1799.

2488 *Wilson County*

David Wilson (1752–)— Wilson was born in Pennsylvania in 1752 and died in Sumner County, Tennessee, in late 1803 or early 1804. He moved from Pennsylvania to North Carolina and served as an officer in the militia from Salisbury District during the American Revolution, and attained the rank of major. Wilson was a member of the 1788 North Carolina convention which considered the proposed federal constitution and also the 1789 North Carolina convention, which ratified it. North Carolina awarded Wilson large tracts of land (2,000 acres per one source; 20,000 acres per another) on Duck River, within what is now Marshall County in central Tennessee. The tax lists for 1787–1788 of Sumner County, North Carolina (which now belongs to Tennessee), list David Wilson as the owner of 10,325 acres of land in that county. Wilson was a member of the legislative assembly of the territory South of the River Ohio, which soon became the state of Tennessee, and was speaker of the lower house of that body. Wilson had been appointed a magistrate of Sumner County (then North Carolina, now Tennessee) in 1787 and was register of deeds in Sumner County, Tennessee, at the time of his death. This county was created on October 26, 1799.

REFERENCES

Abernethy, Thomas P. *From Frontier to Plantation in Tennessee*. Chapel Hill, University of North Carolina Press, 1932.

Alderman, Pat. *The Wonders of the Unakas in Unicoi County*. Erwin, Tennessee, Erwin Business & Professional Women's Club, 1964.

Alderson, William T., & Robert M. McBride. *Landmarks of Tennessee History*. Nashville, Tennessee Historical Society, 1965.

Alexander, Mai. *Dyer County: The Garden Spot of the World*. Dyersburg, Tennessee, Wallace Printing Co., 1974.

Alexander, Virginia Wood. *Maury County, Tennessee Deed Books: A–F: 1807–1817*. Columbia, Tennessee, 1965.

Allen, Penelope Johnson. *Tennessee Soldiers in the Revolution*. Baltimore, Genealogical Publishing Co., Inc., 1982.

Allen, Penelope Johnson. *Tennessee Soldiers in the War of 1812*. Tennessee Society United States Daughters of 1812, 1947.

Armstrong, Zella. *Some Tennessee Heroes of the Revolution: Compiled from Pension Statements*. Chattanooga, Lookout Publishing Co.

Arthur, Stanley. *Old Families of Louisiana*. New Orleans, Harmanson, 1931.

Ashe, Samuel A., et al. *Biographical History of North Carolina*. Greensboro, North Carolina, Charles L. Van Noppen, 1905–1907.

Barry, William L. "A Note on Henderson County." *Tennessee Historical Quarterly*, Vol. 34, No. 1. Nashville: Spring, 1975.

Beach, Ursula S. *Montgomery County*. Memphis, Memphis State University Press, 1988.

Beach, Ursula Smith. *Along the Warioto: A History of Montgomery County, Tennessee*. Nashville, McQuiddy Press, 1964.

Beach, Ursula S., & Ann E. Alley. *1798 Property Tax List & 1820 Census of Montgomery County, Tennessee*. Clarksville, Tennessee, 1969.

Beasley, Gaylon N. *True Tales of Tipton*. Covington, Tennessee, Tipton County Historical Society, 1981.

Benton County Genealogical Society. *Benton County, Tennessee Families & Histories: 1836–1986*. Paducah, Kentucky, Turner Publishing Co., 1987.

Betty, George M. "William Branch Giles." *The John P. Branch Historical Papers of Randolph-Macon College*, Vol. 3, No. 3. Richmond, Virginia: June, 1911.

Bigger, Jeanne Ridgway. "Jack Daniel Distillery & Lynchburg: A Visit to Moore County, Tennessee." *Tennessee Historical Quarterly*, Vol. 31, No. 1. Nashville, Spring, 1972.

Binkley, Lois Barnes. *The Deserted Sycamore Village of Cheatham County*. Pleasant View, Tennessee, 1980.

Biographical Directory: Tennessee General Assembly: 1796–1967: Robertson County (Preliminary). Nashville, Tennessee State Library & Archives.

Biographical Directory: Tennessee General Assembly: 1796–1969: Smith County & Wilson County (Preliminary, No. 31.). Nashville, Tennessee State Library & Archives.

Boatner, Mark M. *Encyclopedia of the American Revolution*. Mechanicsburg, Pennsylvania, Stackpole Books, 1994.

Brown, Dave H. *A History of Who's Who in Louisiana Politics in 1916*. Louisiana Chronicle Democrat, 1916.

Bullard, Helen, & Joseph M. Krechniak. *Cumberland County's First Hundred Years*. Crossville, Tennessee, Centennial Committee, 1956.

Burns, Frank. *Davidson County*. Memphis, Memphis State University Press, 1989.

Burns, G. Frank. *An Historical Sketch of Wilson County, Tennessee*. Lebanon, Tennessee, Press of the Democrat, 1976.

Burns, Inez E. *History of Blount County, Tennessee*. Maryville, Tennessee, Mary Blount Chapter Daughters of the American Revolution, 1957.

Burt, Jesse. *Your Tennessee: Teacher's Edition*. Austin, Texas, Steck-Vaughn Co., 1979.

Byrum, C. Stephen. *McMinn County*. Memphis, Memphis State University Press, 1984.

Caldwell, Joshua W. *Sketches of the Bench & Bar of Tennessee*. Knoxville, Ogden Brothers & Co., 1898.

Camp, Henry R. *Sequatchie County*. Memphis, Memphis State University Press, 1984.

Carroll County Sesquicentennial: 1822–1972.

Chase, Harold, et al. *Biographical Dictionary of the Federal Judiciary*. Detroit, Michigan, Gale Research Co., 1976.

Cisco, Jay G. *Historic Sumner County, Tennessee*. Nashville, Charles Elder, 1971.

Clayton, W. W. *History of Davidson County, Tennessee*. Nashville, Charles Elder, 1971.

Connelly, Thomas L. *Discovering the Appalachians*. Harrisburg, Stackpole Books, 1968.

Conrad, Glenn R. *A Dictionary of Louisiana Biography*. New Orleans, Louisiana, Louisiana Historical Association, 1988.

Cook, Jerry W. "Settlement of Shelbyville Is Told by CHS Student," *Shelbyville Times-Gazette*, February 9, 1965.

Coppock, Paul R. *Memphis Memoirs*. Memphis, Memphis State University Press, 1980.

Corbitt, David L. *The Formation of the North Carolina Counties: 1663–1943*. Raleigh, North Carolina, North Carolina State Department of Archives & History, 1950.

Corlew, Robert E. *A History of Dickson County, Tennessee*. Nashville, Benson Printing Co., 1956.

Crane, Sophie, & Paul Crane. *Tennessee Taproots*. Old Hickory, Tennessee, Earle-Shields, 1976.

Crane, Sophie, & Paul Crane. *Tennessee's Troubled Roots*. Old Hickory, Tennessee, Earle-Shields, 1979.

Crawford, Charles W. *Governors of Tennessee: 1790–1835*. Memphis, Memphis State University Press, 1979.

Crouch, Kenneth E. "Bedford and Its Namesakes." *Bedford Democrat*, Bedford, Virginia, July 29, 1954.

Crutchfield, James A. *The Tennessee Almanac & Book of Facts*. Nashville, Rutledge Hill Press, 1986.

Crutchfield, James A. *Timeless Tennesseans*. Huntsville, Alabama, Strode Publishers, 1984.

Culp, Frederick M., & Mrs. Robert E. Ross. *Gibson County: Past & Present*. Trenton, Tennessee, Gibson County Historical Society, 1961.

Cyclopedia of Eminent & Representative Men of the Carolinas of the Nineteenth Century. Madison, Wisconsin, Brant & Fuller, 1892.

Daniel, J. R. V. *A Hornbook of Virginia History*. Richmond, Virginia, Division of History, Virginia Department of Conservation & Development, 1949.

Dawson, Joseph G. *The Louisiana Governors: From Iberville to Edwards*. Baton Rouge, Louisiana State University Press, 1990.

DeWitt, John H. "Letters of General John Coffee to His Wife, 1813–1815." *Tennessee Historical Magazine*, Vol. 2. Nashville: 1916.

Dickinson, W. Calvin. *Morgan County*. Memphis, Memphis State University Press, 1987.

Donnell, Nannie Lee. "Romance of Bedford County & Shelbyville." *Shelbyville Times-Gazette*, September 9, 1949.

Doughty, Richard H. *Greenville: One Hundred Year Portrait: 1775–1875*. Greenville, Tennessee, 1975.

Drake, J. V. *A Historical Sketch of Wilson County, Tennessee*. Nashville, Eastman & Howell, 1879.

Durham, Walter T. *The Great Leap Westward: A History of Sumner County Tennessee from Its Beginnings to 1805*. Gallatin, Tennessee, Sumner County Library Board, 1969.

Dykeman, Wilma. *Tennessee: A Bicentennial History*. New York, W. W. Norton & Co., Inc., 1975.

"Early Records About Hardin County." *Savannah Courier*, February 2, 1940.

East Tennessee: Historical & Biographical. Chattanooga, A.D. Smith & Co., 1893.

Eldridge, Robert L. & Mary Eldridge. *Bicentennial Echoes of the History of Overton County, Tennessee: 1776–1976*. Livingston, Tennessee, Enterprise Printing Co., Inc., 1976.

Ericson, Joe E. *Judges of the Republic of Texas: A Biographical Directory*. Dallas, Texas, Taylor Publishing Co., 1980.

Ewell, Leighton. *History of Coffee County, Tennessee*. Manchester, Tennessee, Doak Printing Co., 1936.

Families & History of Gibson County, Tennessee to 1989. Milan, Tennessee, Lee-Davis U. D. C. Historical Society, 1989.

Faragher, John M. *The Encyclopedia of Colonial & Revolutionary America*. New York, Facts On File, 1990.

Fentress County Historical Society. *History of Fentress County, Tennessee*. Dallas, Texas, Curtis Media Corp., 1987.

Ferris, Robert G. *Signers of the Constitution*. Washington, D.C., United States Department of the Interior, National Park Service, 1976.

Ferris, Robert G. *Signers of the Declaration*. Washington, D.C., United States Department of the Interior, National Park Service, 1973.

Foley, William E. *A History of Missouri: Volume 1: 1673 to 1820*. Columbia, Missouri, University of Missouri Press, 1971.

Folmsbee, Stanley J., et al. *History of Tennessee*. New York, Lewis Historical Publishing Co., Inc., 1960.

Forrester, Rebel C. *Glory & Tears: Obion County, Tennessee: 1860–1870*. Union City, Tennessee, H. A. Lanzer Co.

Foster, Austin P. *Counties of Tennessee*. Tennessee Department of Education, Division of History, 1923.

Foster, Austin P, & Albert H. Roberts. *Tennessee Democracy: A History of the Party and Its Representative Members*. Nashville, Democratic Historical Association, Inc., 1940.

Galbreath, C. B. "Lafayette's Visit to Ohio Valley States." *Ohio Archaeological & Historical Publications*, Vol. 29. Columbus: 1920.

Ganier, Albert F. *Water Birds of Reelfoot Lake, Tennessee*. Nashville, Tennessee Ornithological Society, 1933.

Gannett, Henry. *The Origin of Certain Place Names in the United States*. Williamstown, Massachusetts, Corner House Publishers, 1978.

Garrett, Jill K. "The Bicentennial." *Columbia Herald*, July 21, 1973.

Garrett, Jill K. *Hither & Yon: The Best of the Writings of Jill K. Garrett*. Maury County, Tennessee Homecoming '86 Committee.

Garrett, Jill K. *Maury County, Tennessee Historical Sketches*. 1967.

Garrett, Jill K. "A Note on Hickman County." *Tennessee Historical Quarterly*, Vol. 34, No. 2. Nashville: Summer, 1975.

Garrett, William R., & Albert V. Goodpasture. *Tennessee: Its People and Its Institutions*. Nashville, Brandon Co., 1900.

Gerson, Noel B. *Franklin. America's "Lost State."* New York, Crowell-Collier Press, 1968.

Goodpasture, A. V. "Colonel John Montgomery." *Tennessee Historical Magazine*, Vol. 5, No. 1. Nashville: April 1919.

Goodpasture, A. V. "Indian Wars & Warriors." *Tennessee Historical Magazine*, Vol. 4. Nashville: 1918.

Graves, Kathleen George, & Winnie Palmer McDonald. *Our Union County Heritage*. 1978.

Green, John W. *Bench & Bar of Knox County, Tennessee*. Knoxville, Archer & Smith, 1947.

Green, John W. *Law & Lawyers: Sketches of the Federal Judges of Tennessee: Sketches of the Attorneys General of Tennessee: Legal Miscellany*. Jackson, Tennessee, McCowat-Mercer Press, 1950.

Green, John W. *Lives of the Judges of the Supreme Court of Tennessee: 1796–1947*. Knoxville, Press of Archer & Smith, 1947.

Greenlaw, R. Douglass. "Outline History of Maury County." *Tennessee Historical Magazine*, Series 2, Vol. 3, No. 3. Nashville: April 1935.

Guide to Tennessee Historical Markers. Nashville, Division of State Information, Department of Conservation, 1954.

Hale, Will T. *History of De Kalb County, Tennessee*. Nashville, Paul Hunter, 1915.

Hale, Will T., & Dixon L. Merritt. *A History of Tennessee & Tennesseans*. Chicago, Lewis Publishing Co., 1913.

Hamer, Philip M. *Tennessee: A History: 1673–1932*. New York, American Book Co., 1933.

Harbert, P. M. "Early History of Hardin County." *West Tennessee Historical Society Papers*, No. 1. Memphis: 1947.

Harper, Herbert L. "The Antebellum Courthouses of Tennessee." *Tennessee Historical Quarterly*, Vol. 30, No. 1. Nashville: Spring, 1971.

Haywood, John. *The Civil & Political History of the State of Tennessee*. Nashville, Publishing House of the Methodist Episcopal Church, South, 1891.

Haywood, John. *The Natural & Aboriginal History of Tennessee*. Nashville, George Wilson, 1823.

Henderson Centennial Celebration Souvenir Program. Henderson Area Centennial, Inc.

Hiatt, Ellen Olivia Mitchell. *Sequatchie Valley: A Historical Sketch*.

Hickman County Sesquicentennial: 1807–1957. Columbia, Tennessee, Columbia Printing Co., 1957.

Hill, Howard L. "Hamblen Centennial: History of Hamblen County." *Daily Gazette-Mail*, Morristown, Tennessee, July 26, 1970.

Historic Hamblen: 1870–1970. Morristown, Tennessee, Hamblen County Centennial Celebration, 1970.

Historical Sketch of Maury County Read at the Centennial Celebration in Columbia, Tennessee, July 4, 1876. Columbia, Tennessee, Excelsior Printing Office, 1876.

History & Genealogy of Families in Pickett County. Pickett County Book Committee, 1991.

History of Rover and the 10th District of Bedford County. Nashville, Parthenon Press of the United Methodist Publishing House, 1986.

History of Tennessee. Nashville, Goodspeed Publishing Co.: *Histories of Fayette & Hardeman Counties*. 1887; *Histories of Gibson, Obion, Dyer, Weakley & Lake Counties*. 1887; *Histories of Henderson, Chester, McNairy, Decatur & Hardin Counties*, 1886; *Histories of Lauderdale, Tipton, Haywood & Crockett Counties*. 1887; *Histories of Lawrence, Wayne, Perry, Hickman & Lewis Counties*. 1886; *Histories of Montgomery, Robertson, Humphreys, Stewart, Dickson, Cheatham & Houston Counties*. 1886; *Histories of Sumner, Smith, Macon & Trousdale Counties*. 1887; *History of Tennessee*. 1887.

Hogue, Albert R. *Davy Crockett & Others in Fentress County*. Crossville, Tennessee, Chronicle Publishing Co., 1955.

Hogue, Albert R. *History of Fentress County, Tennessee*. Baltimore, Regional Publishing Co., 1975.

Holt, Edgar A. *Claiborne County*. Memphis, Memphis State University Press, 1981.

Hoskins, Katherine B. *Anderson County.* Memphis, Memphis State University Press, 1979.

Hulme, Albert L., & James A. Hulme. *A History of Dyer County.* 1982.

Joiner, Harry M. *Tennessee: Then & Now.* Athens, Alabama, Southern Textbook Publishers, Inc., 1983.

Jordan, Weymouth T. *George Washington Campbell of Tennessee: Western Statesman.* Tallahassee, Florida State University, 1955.

Kelley, Paul. *Historic Fort Loudon.* Vonore, Tennessee, Fort Loudon Association. 1958

Kinard, Margaret. "Frontier Development of Williamson County." *Tennessee Historical Quarterly*, Vol. 8. Nashville: March–December, 1949.

Kleber, John E. *The Kentucky Encyclopedia.* Lexington, Kentucky, University Press of Kentucky, 1992.

Leeper, Seth. "Hickman County Part of Dickson Before Separation." *Centerville Times*, November 5, 1964.

Lillard, Roy G. *Bradley County.* Memphis, Memphis State University Press, 1980.

Lillard, Roy G. *The History of Bradley County.* Cleveland, Tennessee, Bradley County Chapter, East Tennessee Historical Society, 1976.

Lillard, Stewart. *Meigs County, Tennessee.* Cleveland, Tennessee, The Book Shelf, 1982.

McBride, Robert M., & Dan M. Robison. *Biographical Directory of the Tennessee General Assembly.* Nashville, Tennessee State Library & Archives and Tennessee Historical Commission, 1975–1979.

McBride, Robert M., & Owen Meredith. *Eastin Morris' Tennessee Gazetteer: 1834 & Matthew Rhea's Map of the State of Tennessee: 1832.* Nashville, Gazetteer Press, 1971.

McCague, James. *The Cumberland.* New York, Holt, Rinehart & Winston, 1973.

McCallum, James. *A Brief Sketch of the Settlement & Early History of Giles County, Tennessee.* Pulaski, Tennessee, Pulaski Citizen, 1928.

McClain, Iris Hopkins. *A History of Stewart County, Tennessee.* Columbia, Tennessee, 1965.

McCloud, Gladys. "An Episode Led to the Naming of Johnson County." *Mountain City Tomahawk*, December 4, 1974.

McGee, Dorothy Horton. *Framers of the Constitution.* New York, Dodd, Mead & Co., 1968.

McGee, Gentry R., & C. B. Ijams. *A History of Tennessee.* New York, American Book Co., 1930.

McMurty, J. C. *History of Trousdale County.* Vidette Printing Co.

Malone, Henry T. "Return Jonathan Meigs: Indian Agent Extraordinary." *Publications of the East Tennessee Historical Society*, Vol. 28. Knoxville: 1956.

Mason, Robert L. *Cannon County.* Memphis, Memphis State University Press, 1982.

Masterson, William H. *William Blount.* Baton Rouge, Louisiana State University Press, 1954.

Merritt, Dixon. *The History of Wilson County.* Lebanon, Tennessee, 1961.

Merritt, Frank. *Early History of Carter County: 1760–1861.* Knoxville, East Tennessee Historical Society, 1950.

Moore, John T., & Austin P. Foster. *Tennessee: The Volunteer State: 1769–1923.* Chicago, S. J. Clarke Publishing Co., 1923.

Morton, Dorothy Rich. *Fayette County.* Memphis, Memphis State University Press, 1989.

Nicholson, James L. *Grundy County.* Memphis, Memphis State University Press, 1982.

Norman, William A. "The Birth of a County: Being a History of the Territory Composing Moore County, Tennessee." *Moore County, News*, Lynchburg, Tennessee, March 11, 1948.

Obion County History. Dallas, Texas, Taylor Publishing Co., 1981.

The Obion River & Forked Deer River Watersheds. Nashville, Tennessee State Planning Commission, 1936.

O'Dell, Ruth Webb. *Over the Misty Blue Hills: The Story of Cocke County, Tennessee.* Easley, South Carolina, Southern Historical Press, 1982.

Page, Bonnie M. *Clearfork & More.* Clinton, Tennessee, Clinton Courier-News, Inc., 1986.

Parks, Joseph H., & Stanley J. Folmsbee. *The Story of Tennessee.* Chattanooga, Harlow Publishing Corp., 1952.

Phelps, Dawson A., & Edward H. Ross. "Place Names Along the Natchez Trace." *Journal of Mississippi History*, Vol. 14, No. 4. Jackson: October, 1952.

Phillips, Margaret I. *The Governors of Tennessee.* Gretna, Louisiana, Pelican Publishing Co., 1978.

Phillips, William J. H. *Pioneers of White County, Tennessee.* Whitesburg, Georgia, Wide Services, Inc., 1991.

Pittard, Mabel. *Rutherford County.* Memphis, Memphis State University Press, 1984.

Porch, Deane. *1850 Census: Maury County, Tennessee.* Nashville, 1966.

Potter, Mrs. J. Leith. *Coffee County Historical Society Quarterly*, Vol. 1, No. 1. Spring, 1970.

Powell, William S. *Dictionary of North Carolina Biography.* Chapel Hill, University of North Carolina Press, 1979–1988.

Powell, William S. *The North Carolina Gazetteer.* Chapel Hill, University of North Carolina Press, 1968.

Powers, Auburn. *History of Henderson County.* 1930.

Puetz, C. J. *Tennessee County Maps.* Lyndon Station, Wisconsin, County Maps.

Putnam, A. W. *History of Middle Tennessee Or Life & Times of Gen. James Robertson.* Nashville, Southern Methodist Publishing House, 1859.

Quinlan, James E. *History of Sullivan County.* Liberty, New York, W. T. Morgans & Co., 1873.

Ramsey, J. G. M. *The Annals of Tennessee to the End of the Eighteenth Century.* Charleston, South Carolina, Walker & Jones, 1853.

Rand McNally 1993 Commercial Atlas & Marketing Guide. Rand McNally, 1993.

Raulston, J. Leonard & James W. Livingood. *Sequatchie: A Story of the Southern Cumberlands.* Knoxville, University of Tennessee Press, 1974.

Ray, Worth S. *Tennessee Cousins: A History of Tennessee People.* Baltimore, Genealogical Publishing Co., 1960.

Reeves, Miriam G. *The Governors of Louisiana.* Gretna, Pelican Publishing Co., 1972.

Reflections: Past & Present: A Pictorial History of Bradley County: 1836–1991. Cleveland, Tennessee, Bradley County Historical Society, 1991.

Remini, Robert V. "Andrew Jackson's Account of the Battle of New Orleans." *Tennessee Historical Quarterly*, Vol. 26, No. 1. Nashville: Spring, 1967.

Richardson, James D. *Tennessee Templars: A Register of Names with Biographical Sketches of the Knights Templar of Tennessee.* Nashville, Robert H. Howell & Co., 1883.

Ridenour, G. L. *The Land of the Lake.* La Follette, Tennessee, La Follette Publishing Co., Inc., 1941.

Robnett, Elizabeth Parham. *Bledsoe County at the Bicentennial: 1976.* Pikeville, Tennessee, Bledsoe County High School, 1977.

Robnett, Elizabeth Parham. *Bledsoe County, Tennessee: A History.* Signal Mountain, Tennessee, Mountain Press, 1993.

Robnett, Elizabeth Parham. "A History of Bledsoe County, Tennessee." Specialist in Education Thesis, George Peabody College for Teachers, Nashville, Tennessee, 1957.

Rogers, E. G. *Memorable Historical Accounts of White County & Area.* Collegedale, Tennessee, College Press, 1972.

Rothrock, Mary U. *The French Broad-Holston Country: A History of Knox County, Tennessee*. Knoxville, East Tennessee Historical Society, 1946.

Rothrock, Mary U. *This Is Tennessee: A School History*. Knoxville, 1970.

Rowland, Dunbar. *Official Letter Books of W. C. C. Claiborne: 1801–1816*. Jackson, Mississippi, Department of Archives & History, 1917.

Sanderson, Esther Sharp. *County Scott and Its Mountain Folk*. Nashville, Williams Printing Co., 1958.

Sands, Sarah G. Cox. *History of Monroe County, Tennessee*. Baltimore, Gateway Press, Inc., 1982.

Seals, Monroe. *History of White County, Tennessee*. Spartanburg, South Carolina, Reprint Co., 1974.

Sediment Production Study: Reelfoot Lake Area, Obion County, Tennessee & Fulton County, Kentucky. Nashville, Mississippi River & Tributaries Resurvey, U.S. Department of Agriculture Soil Conservation Service, 1956.

"Sesquicentennial Ceremonies in Johnson City." *Tennessee Historical Quarterly*, Vol. 5. Nashville: March–December, 1946.

Sims, Carlton C. *A History of Rutherford County*. Murfreesboro, Tennessee, 1947.

Sistler, Byron, & Samuel Sistler. *Tennesseans in the War of 1812*. Nashville, Byron Sistler & Associates, Inc., 1992.

Smith, Delle Dulaney. "The Public Career of William Blount: 1790–1800." M.S. Thesis, University of Virginia, Charlottesville, Virginia, 1927.

Smith, H. Clay. *Dusty Bits of the Forgotten Past*. Oneida, Tennessee, Scott County Historical Society, 1985.

Smith, Jonathan K. T. *Benton County*. Memphis, Memphis State University Press, 1979.

Solomon, James. *Times from Giles County*.

Speer, William S. *Sketches of Prominent Tennesseans*. Nashville, Albert B. Tavel, 1888.

Spence, John C. *The Annals of Rutherford County: 1799–1828*. Murfreesboro, Tennessee, Rutherford County Historical Society, 1991.

Spence, W. Jerome D., & David L. Spence. *A History of Hickman County, Tennessee*. Nashville, Gospel Advocate Publishing Co., 1900.

Stewart, G. Tillman. *Henderson County*. Memphis, Memphis State University Press, 1979.

Stiner, Clifford. *Dawn of Union County*. Maynardville, Tennessee.

Stokely, Jim, & Jeff D. Johnson. *An Encyclopedia of East Tennessee*. Oak Ridge, Tennessee, Children's Museum of Oak Ridge, 1981.

Summers, Cecil L. *The Governors of Mississippi*. Gretna, Pelican Publishing Co., 1980.

Sumner County Sesqui-Centennial: 1787–1937: October 10–14: Souvenir Book.

Taft, William H., III. *County Names: An Historical Perspective*. National Association of Counties, 1982.

Taylor, Oliver. *Historic Sullivan*. Bristol, Tennessee, King Printing Co., 1909.

Tennessee Blue Book: 1981–1982. Nashville, Office of the Secretary of State of Tennessee.

Tennessee Blue Book: 1983–1984. Nashville, Office of the Secretary of State of Tennessee.

Tennessee Blue Book: 1985–1986. Nashville, Office of the Secretary of State of Tennessee.

Tennessee: Old & New: Sesquicentennial Edition: 1796–1946. Nashville, Tennessee Historical Commission & Tennessee Historical Society.

Tennessee: The Volunteer State: 1769–1923. Chicago, S. J. Clarke Publishing Co., 1923.

Thrapp, Dan L. *Encyclopedia of Frontier Biography*. Lincoln, University of Nebraska Press, 1988.

Thrapp, Dan L. *Encyclopedia of Frontier Biography: Volume 4: Supplemental Volume*. Spokane, Washington, Arthur H. Clark Co., 1994.

Trent, Emma Deane Smith. *East Tennessee's Lore of Yesteryear*. Whitesburg, Tennessee, 1987.

Trent, William S. "Hezekiah Hamblen, Father of a County." *Gazette-Mail*, Morristown, Tennessee, July 26, 1970.

Tudor, Cathy. *Tennessee Historical Markers*. Tennessee Historical Commission, 1980.

Turner, William B. *History of Maury County, Tennessee*. Nashville, Parthenon Press, 1955.

"Unicoi County History Sidelights." *Knoxville Sentinel*, March 20, 1925.

Vaughan, Virginia C. *Weakley County*. Memphis, Memphis State University Press, 1983.

Vexler, Robert I. *Chronology & Documentary Handbook of the State of Tennessee*. Dobbs Ferry, New York, Oceana Publications, Inc., 1979.

Walker, E. R. *Cocke County: A Thumbnail Sketch*. Newport-Cocke County Bicentennial Committee, 1976.

Walker, Nancy Wooten. *Out of a Clear Blue Sky: Tennessee's First Ladies and Their Husbands*. Cleveland, Tennessee, 1971.

Webb, Walter P., et al. *The Handbook of Texas*. Austin, Texas Historical Association, 1952.

Wells, Emma Middleton. *The History of Roane County, Tennessee: 1801–1870*. Chattanooga, Lookout Publishing Co., 1927.

Wheeler, John H. *Historical Sketches of North Carolina from 1584 to 1851*. Philadelphia, Lippincott Grambo & Co., 1851.

White, Robert H. *Tennessee: Its Growth & Progress*. Nashville, 1936.

Whitfield, Rita A. *1975–1976 Tennessee Blue Book*. Nashville, Office of the Secretary of State of Tennessee.

Whitley, Edythe Rucker. *Marriages of Stewart County, Tennessee: 1838–1866*. Baltimore, Genealogical Publishing Co., Inc., 1982.

Whitley, Edythe Rucker. *Overton County, Tennessee Genealogical Records*. Baltimore, Genealogical Publishing Co., 1979.

Whitworth, Rex. *William Augustus, Duke of Cumberland: A Life*. London, England, Leo Cooper, 1992.

Who Was Who During the American Revolution. Indianapolis, Bobbs-Merrill Co., Inc., 1976.

Williams, S. C. "Johnson County Centennial: Notable Historical Event in East Tennessee." *Johnson City Press*, March 22, 1936.

Williams, Samuel C. *Beginnings of West Tennessee*. Johnson City, Tennessee, Watauga Press, 1930.

Williams, Samuel C. "The First Territorial Division Named for Washington." *Tennessee Historical Magazine*, Series 2, Vol. 2, No. 2. Nashville: January, 1932.

Wooten, John M. *A History of Bradley County*. Cleveland, Tennessee, Bradley County Post 81, The American Legion, 1949.

Work Projects Administration. *How They Began: The Story of North Carolina County, Town and Other Place Names*. New York, Harian Publications, 1941.

Work Projects Administration. *Inventory of the County Archives of Tennessee-Bedford, Cheatham, Loudon, Sullivan & Tipton Counties*. Nashville, 1940–1942.

Works Progress Administration. *Inventory of the County Archives of Tennessee-Haywood & Wilson Counties*. Nashville, 1938–1939.

Wright, Marcus J. *Some Account of the Life & Services of William Blount*. Washington, D.C., E. J. Gray, 1884.

Younger, Lillye. *Decatur County*. Memphis, Memphis State University Press, 1979.

Texas

(254 counties)

2489 *Anderson County*

Kenneth L. Anderson (1805–1845)— A native of North Carolina, Anderson lived for a time in Tennessee before settling in Texas in 1837. He served as collector of customs at San Augustine and was a member of the house of representatives of the republic of Texas. Anderson served as the speaker of that legislative body and on September 2, 1844, he was elected as the republic's vice-president. He died on July 3, 1845, and this county was created and named in his honor less than one year later, on March 24, 1846. Consideration had been given to naming this county Burnet County, in honor of the republic's ad interim president, David G. Burnet (1788–1870). That name was not adopted at that time, although later, in 1852, Burnet County was created and named for him. Kenneth L. Anderson was the last vice-president of the republic of Texas.

2490 *Andrews County*

Richard Andrews (–1835)— Richard Andrews immigrated to Texas with his family about 1818 and settled on the Brazos River near today's community of Richmond, Texas. On October 2, 1835, in what would be the first battle of the Texas Revolution, Andrews fought against the Mexican army in the battle of Gonzales. Later that month, on October 28, 1835, Andrews fought again when the Texas army repulsed an attack by the Mexican army in the battle of Concepción. About 60 Mexicans were killed in that battle, while only one Texas soldier, Richard Andrews, was lost. This county was created on August 21, 1876, and named for the first soldier to die during the Texas Revolution.

2491 *Angelina County*

Angelina River— This county in eastern Texas was created on April 22, 1846, and named for the Angelina River, which forms the county's eastern border between both Nacogdoches County and San Augustine County. The 120 mile-long Angelina River is formed by the junction of three creeks in Rusk County and flows in a generally southeastern direction until its waters enter those of the Neches River in Jasper County. The river's name derived from a name given by Spanish missionaries to an Indian girl who became a favorite of theirs at Mission San Francisco de los Tejas, the first Spanish mission founded in East Texas. The missionaries called her *Angelina*, meaning "little angel." This mission was established in 1690 and it was about that time that the little Indian girl was given the affectionate name which later came to be applied to the river and then to this county.

2492 *Aransas County*

Aransas Bay, Aransas Pass and/or Aransas River— This county in southeastern Texas, was created in 1871 and named for one or more of the bodies of water found here: Aransas Bay, Aransas Pass and Aransas River. The bay is an inlet of the Gulf of Mexico between the mainland and St. Joseph Island. The pass provides passage to both Corpus Christi Bay and Aransas Bay. The river is a small stream which empties into Copano Bay, an arm of the Gulf of Mexico, just below Bayside, Texas. Essentially all of these waters are in or adjacent to Aransas County. Many works dealing with the history, geography and place names of Texas state that this county was named for *Rio Nuestra Señora de Aranzazu*, an early Spanish rendering of the Aransas River's name. The literature on this subject then presents two different theories concerning the origin of that old Spanish name. One theory traces the name to that of a palace in Spain, while the other contends that the name honors Saint Mary (–), who according to Roman Catholic theology, was the Virgin Mother of Jesus Christ.

2493 *Archer County*

Branch T. Archer (–1856)— Archer was born in Virginia. Some sources show his year of birth as 1780, while others use 1790. He studied medicine and practiced that profession in Virginia and also served in the Virginia legislature before moving to Texas about 1831. Here he soon became involved in the Texas Revolutionary movement. On October 2, 1835, in what would be the first battle of the Texas Revolution, Archer fought against the Mexican army in the battle of Gonzales. After participating in that battle, Archer left the Texas army to participate in the Consultation which was called to meet on October 16, 1835, and he served as president of that deliberative body. Archer favored immediate separation from Mexico but the Consultation decided that Texas should remain a part of Mexico. That decision was, of course, soon reversed, and after the Republic of Texas was founded, Archer was a member of its first congress. He soon served as speaker of the house of the republic's congress. Doctor Archer died in September, 1856, and this county was created less than two years later, on January 22, 1858.

2494 *Armstrong County*

Armstrong family of Texas pioneers— This county was created on August 21, 1876, and named for a Texas pioneer family named Armstrong. Which particular Armstrong family the Texas legislature intended to honor is unknown. The history of this county entitled *A Collection of Memories*, published in 1965, merely states that "There are four Armstrongs prominent in Texas history. It could have been named for any one or all of them. None of them ever lived in or owned property in the county." This statement may be more misleading than helpful by implying that the county name honors a prominent Armstrong family. That is not necessarily true. A number of counties in the United States were named in honor of families who were merely pioneers, and not prominent at all. Z. T. Fulmore's work entitled *The History & Geography of Texas as Told in County Names* offers information about some specific Armstrong possibilities. Fulmore states that "There are six different families by the name, some of which held important public positions. James and Cavitt Armstrong were members of the Convention of 1845, and James R. Armstrong, a member of the Secession Convention in 1861, and James Armstrong was again a member of the convention that framed the Constitution of 1867. Frank C. Armstrong arose to the rank of Brigadier General in the Confederate Army."

2495 *Atascosa County*

Atascosa River— This county in southern Texas was created on January 25, 1856, and named for the Atascosa River, the county's principal stream. The Atascosa is formed from two branches which rise near San Antonio, in Bexar County. Those two branches flow south across the border between Bexar County and Atascosa County, where they join to form the Atascosa River. The Atascosa ends its brief journey at the Frio River in the county just south and east of Atascosa County, which is Live Oak County. The river's name is of Spanish origin and comes from the verb *atascar,* which means "to be bogged" or "to be mired." A work entitled *Atascosa County Centennial: 1856–1956* provides an account of an 1842 expedition to this area which provides adequate explanation for the river's name: "...brought them to a sandy post-oak country where horses and mules sank to their bodies in quicksand."

2496 *Austin County*

Stephen F. Austin (1793–1836)— Austin was born in western Virginia, educated at Transylvania University in Kentucky and served in the legislature of Missouri territory. In 1821 he traveled to San Antonio in Mexican Texas to secure permission to establish a colony on land which had been granted to his family. Shortly afterward, Austin settled a colony of Anglo-Americans, as San Felipe de Austin, the first Anglo-American colony in Mexican Texas. That colony was located within what is now Austin County, Texas. He acted as the local governor for four years and served in the Mexican legislature. Austin also attempted to have Texas established as a separate state within Mexico and he was briefly imprisoned for attempting to incite insurrection in Texas. In 1836 Austin was defeated by Samuel Houston (1793–1863) in a contest for the presidency of the Republic of Texas, but he accepted President Houston's appointment to the cabinet as secretary of state. Stephen F. Austin died in December, 1836, during the first year of life of Texas as a separate republic. This county had been created and named in his honor on March 17, 1836, the same day that a constitution was adopted for the new republic of Texas.

2497 *Bailey County*

Peter J. Bailey (1812–1836)— In 1836, during the Texas Revolution, the Mexican army placed the Alamo, in San Antonio, Texas, under siege for 13 days. Inside the Alamo were about 185 Texan defenders, all of whom were slain when the Mexicans stormed the Alamo on the morning of March 6, 1836. Among those who died in that epic confrontation was Private Peter James Bailey III. Bailey was born in Springfield, Kentucky, and graduated in 1834 from Transylvania University in Lexington, Kentucky, with a degree in law. He enlisted at Nacogdoches, Texas in the Texas volunteer auxiliary on January 14, 1836. Bailey became a rifleman, with the rank of private in the company commanded by Captain William B. Harrison (1811–1836). Bailey entered the Alamo on February 23, 1836. Bill Groneman's *Alamo Defenders,* published in 1990, describes the primary mission of Bailey and the other members of Captain Harrison's company. Groneman tells us that these men defended "the wooden palisade which ran from the Alamo chapel to the low barracks, the Alamo's south wall." This county was created and named in honor of this Alamo defender on August 21, 1876, and Bailey's heirs were awarded land in Texas in gratitude for his service.

2498 *Bandera County*

Bandera Mountains and/or Bandera Pass here— This county in southwestern Texas was created on January 26, 1856, and named for the Bandera Mountains and/or the Bandera Pass here. The Bandera Mountains are found in the northern end of Bandera County. Bandera Pass, also on Bandera County's northern border, is a gorge, about 250 feet high, 125 feet wide and 500 yards long, which cuts the range of mountains separating the Medina and Guadalupe Valleys. This pass is about 50 miles northwest of San Antonio. The pass had great strategic value to Indians living in the area in their wars with one another and to the Spanish in trying to administer San Antonio all the way from Mexico City. The name *Bandera* is Spanish and means "flag," or "banner." One tradition has it that flags (*banderas*) were planted in this area on at least one occasion to celebrate a military victory and/or serve as a warning to the defeated side. However two histories of Bandera County relate an alternative tradition; i.e., that Bandera Pass received its name in honor of a General Bandera of the Spanish army.

2499 *Bastrop County*

Felipe Enrique Neri, Baron de Bastrop (–1827)— Felipe Enrique Neri was born about 1766, probably of Prussian ancestry. He claimed to have been born in Holland. He served in the Prussian army and then, in 1795, he persuaded the Spanish authorities who were governing Louisiana in North America to grant land here to him. The land granted to him in northern Louisiana was enormous, consisting of twelve leagues of land (more than one million acres). Litigation followed and Neri was never able to consummate this huge land grab. However, by this time he had acquired the title Baron de Bastrop (either legitimately or through his own contrivance) and his contacts with high Spanish officials enabled him to assist Stephen F. Austin's father, Moses Austin (–1821), in securing permission to establish an Anglo-American colony in Mexican Texas. When Moses Austin died, Stephen F. Austin carried on the venture and Bastrop assisted Austin, serving the colony in a number of capacities until his death in 1827. This county was created on March 17, 1836, and named Mina County. That name honored Francisco X. Mina (1789–1817), a native of Spain, who engaged in revolutionary activities against Spain in Mexico and Texas. Mina was executed in Mexico City in 1817. This county's name was changed from Mina County to Bastrop County on December 18, 1837.

2500 *Baylor County*

Henry W. Baylor (1818–)— Baylor was born in Kentucky and studied at Transylvania University in that state, graduating with a degree in medicine. After college Baylor settled in La Grange, Texas, where he practiced medicine. During the Mexican War, from 1846 to 1847, Baylor was as a surgeon under Colonel John C. Hays (1817–1883). He served with distinction and rose to the rank of captain. Dr. Baylor died in Texas during August of either 1853 or 1854. This county was created and named in his honor on February 1, 1858.

2501 *Bee County*

Barnard E. Bee (1787–1853)— A native of South Carolina and a lawyer, Bee came to Texas in 1835 or 1836. Here he joined the Texas army and was appointed to the cabinet of the Texas' ad interim government (1836) as secretary of treasury. On August 23, 1837, Barnard E. Bee was appointed secretary of war in the cabinet of President Samuel Houston (1793–1863) and he later served under President Mirabeau B. Lamar (1798–1859) as secretary of state. From 1838 to 1841 Bee was minister to the United States of America from the republic of Texas. He opposed Texas joining the United States and after this happened in 1845, Bee returned to his native state of South Carolina, where he died in 1853. This county was created on December 8, 1857. The county's name was suggested by Hamilton P. Bee (1822–1897), in memory of his father. The younger Bee was a member of the Texas legislature when this county was created and had been speaker of the house from 1855 to 1856.

2502 *Bell County*

Peter H. Bell (1812–1898) — A native of Virginia, Bell came to Texas during the 1830's and fought in the Texas Revolution. He enlisted as a private but rose to become an officer and continued to receive promotions after the Revolution ended. During the Mexican War Bell served in the U.S. army as a lieutenant-colonel. In 1849 he ran to become governor of Texas and he defeated the incumbent, George T. Wood (1795–1858). Reelected to a second term, Bell served as the state's governor from 1849 to 1853, when he resigned to accept an appointment to the U.S. House of Representatives, replacing David S. Kaufman (1813–1851), who had died in office. Bell represented Texas in congress from 1853 to 1857. According to several sources, Bell served as a colonel in the Confederate army during the Civil War. This county was created on January 22, 1850, while Peter H. Bell was serving his first term as governor of Texas.

2503 *Bexar County*

Derived from names given at San Antonio, Texas, to an early presidio, villa, & municipality — Much misinformation has been bruited about concerning the origin of this county's name and your author hesitates to add one more faulty attribution to the pile. This much is known: Bexar County, Texas, was created on March 17, 1836. Its county seat was then, and is now, San Antonio, the earliest significant Spanish settlement in the present state of Texas.

Presidio named San Antonio de Bexar — This *presidio* ("military post" or "fortified settlement") was founded here on the west side of the San Antonio River on May 5, 1718, by Martin de Alarcon, who was then the governor of Spain's province of Texas.

Villa named San Fernando de Bexar — The villa was established here in 1731 as Spain's first civil settlement in Texas. (In some accounts the date of this villa's establishment is given as May 5, 1718, the

date that the presidio de San Antonio de Bexar was founded.)

Municipality at San Antonio — The name *Bexar* became commonly applied to the municipality which developed from the presidio and villa carrying the *Bexar* name. That municipality is the city now called San Antonio, the county seat of Bexar County, Texas.

But what was the source of the Spanish name *Bexar* before it was used in Texas? That question prompts a wide variety of responses and the true answer may never be known.

Z. T. Fulmore's work entitled *The History & Geography of Texas as Told in County Names* tells us that Bexar "was a town in Spain ... long the seat of a dukedom.... The Duke, in whose honor the present name Bexar was given, was born at Madrid in 1713 and was the second son of Philip V, the then reigning sovereign. Upon the death of his elder brother, Louis, he became Prince of Asturias, heir apparent to the throne. His mother died in 1716, the same year that Philip married his second wife. The intrigues of the young Duke's stepmother to have one of her own children preferred to the throne caused much indignation throughout Spain ... and in the midst of this general sympathy the settlement of San Antonio took place. He ascended the throne as Ferdinand VI (Fernando) in 1746 and died in 1759." Some of these statements by Fulmore are not easily verified but we do know that he is correct in saying that King Philip V (1683–1746) was the reigning monarch of Spain in both 1718 and 1731, which are key dates in the chronology of the place-naming of San Antonio and Bexar County, Texas. We also know that Fernando (1713–1759) was the second son of Spain's King Philip V (1683–1746), that he was born in Madrid, Spain in 1713 and that he came to the throne of Spain as King Ferdinand VI.

The Texas Courthouse, published in 1971 provides a different history surrounding the selection of Bexar County's name in 1836: "At the time of the founding of the mission San Antonio de Valero and the presidio San Antonio de Bexar, in 1718, the Spanish viceroy was Balthasar Manuel de Zuniga y Guzman Sotomayor y Sarmiento, the second son of the Duke of Bexar. Canary Island colonists founded the villa San Fernando in 1731, the first civil settlement in Texas. San Fernando de Bexar became the capital of Texas in 1773."

Many other authorities on the history, geography and place names of Texas have struggled to determine the origin of the name *Bexar*. William Corner, writing in

1890 in *San Antonio de Bexar: A Guide & History* aptly summarizes the results of this research: "This name San Antonio de Bexar, seems to have attached itself particularly to the military post or *presidio*; its origin is not known."

2504 *Blanco County*

Blanco River — Texas has at least two rivers named Blanco. This county, which was created on February 12, 1858, was named for the Blanco River which flows through it. Our Blanco River rises in south-central Texas, in Kendall County, and flows in a southeastern direction across Blanco County. It enters the San Marcos River in Hays County, just east of Blanco County. *Blanco* is a Spanish word meaning "white." The river owes its name to the white, chalky limestone country through which it flows. Some sources indicate that the river was named during a 1721 expedition into Texas by Spain's Marquis de Aguayo (–1734).

2505 *Borden County*

Gail Borden (1801–1874) — A native of New York, Borden lived in Kentucky, Indiana territory and Mississippi territory before coming to Texas in 1829. Here he published a newspaper, prepared the first topographical map of Texas and held a number of minor political appointments. History remembers Gail Borden for his inventions. There were a number of these but perhaps the more important ones were his meat biscuits and condensed milk. During the Civil War there was great demand for condensed milk and Borden made a small fortune selling the milk products of his factories in Connecticut, New York and other northern states to the Union army. After the Civil War Borden spent many of his winters in Texas because of its mild climate. Gail Borden died on January 11, 1874, and this county was created and named in his honor less than three years later, on August 21, 1876. In 1890 Borden County's present county seat, named Gail was built.

2506 *Bosque County*

Bosque River — This county in east-central Texas was created on February 4, 1854, and named for the Bosque River, its principal stream. The Bosque River heads in four branches, the North East, Middle and South Bosque Rivers. All four of these branches rise in counties near Bosque County. The Bosque River is now dammed northwest of Waco, Texas to form Lake

Waco, although waters from the stream are allowed to exit the lake and continue on to enter the Brazos River, within the city limits of Waco. The name *Bosque* is Spanish and means "forest, wood, grove thicket" or "woodland." Some sources indicate that the river was named during a 1721 expedition into Texas by Spain's Marquis de Aguayo (–1734). A publication celebrating Bosque County's centennial states that the Aguayo party named the river "due the dense growth of timber along the banks of the small stream." As recently as 1983, Gene Kirkley was warning boating enthusiasts of the low hanging limbs over the river in his *A Guide to Texas Rivers & Streams.*

2507 *Bowie County*

James Bowie (–1836)— In 1836, during the Texas Revolution, the Mexican army placed the Alamo, in San Antonio, Texas, under siege for 13 days. Inside the Alamo were about 185 Texan defenders, all of whom were slain when the Mexicans stormed the Alamo on the morning of March 6, 1836. Among those who died in that epic confrontation was Colonel James Bowie. The year and location of Bowie's birth are in doubt but he was probably born in Kentucky or Tennessee in 1795. It is known that he came to Texas in 1828. This colorful character is remembered as the inventor of the Bowie knife and as a hero and martyr of the Texas Revolution. Before joining in the Texas Revolution, Bowie attempted to acquire vast amounts of land in the South and Southwest by questionable techniques. During Texas' revolution against Mexico Bowie fought at the battle of Concepción, the Grass Fight and in the successful siege of Bexar. At the Alamo, Colonel Bowie was one of the leaders but he fell ill during the siege and was confined to a cot. Ill or not he was slaughtered like everyone else when the Mexicans finally stormed the Alamo. This county was created on December 17, 1840.

2508 *Brazoria County*

Brazos River— This county in southeastern Texas was created on March 17, 1836, by the republic of Texas and named for the Brazos River, the longest stream in Texas. The Brazos is formed in northwestern Texas by the confluence of Salt Fork and Double Mountain Fork in Stonewall County. It flows some 840 miles to enter the Gulf of Mexico in the southern portion of Brazoria County. *Brazos* is a Spanish word which means "arms." The orig-

inal, longer, name given to the Brazos River by the Spanish was *Los Brazos de Dios* or "The Arms of God."

2509 *Brazos County*

Brazos River— This county in central Texas was created by the republic of Texas on January 30, 1841, with the name Navasoto County. That name honored the 125 mile-long Navasota River, a tributary of the Brazos River, which forms the eastern border of today's Brazos County. This county's name was changed just one year later, in January, 1842, to honor the longer Brazos River, which this county's borders also touch. The Brazos, the longest river in Texas, is formed in northwestern Texas by the confluence of Salt Fork and Double Mountain Fork in Stonewall County. It flows some 840 miles to enter the Gulf of Mexico in the southern portion of Brazoria County, a second Texas county whose name honors the Brazos River. *Brazos* is a Spanish word which means "arms." The original, longer, name given to the Brazos River by the Spanish was *Los Brazos de Dios* or "The Arms of God."

2510 *Brewster County*

Henry P. Brewster (1816–1884)— This South Carolina native came here to join Texas' revolutionary army as a private. He served at the battle of San Jacinto and was private secretary to Samuel Houston (1793–1863). In the ad interim administration of the republic of Texas, Brewster served as secretary of war in the cabinet of provisional president, David G. Burnet (1788–1870). He subsequently studied law, was admitted to the bar and served as attorney general of the state of Texas. During the Civil War, Brewster served in the Confederate army as an adjutant general. This county was created on February 2, 1887.

2511 *Briscoe County*

Andrew Briscoe (1810–1849)— Briscoe was born in Mississippi territory on November 25, 1810. He became a merchant in Texas at the community of Anahuac in 1835. Incensed about irregular practices by Mexican officials in their collection of customs duties, Briscoe was an early participant in battles of the Texas Revolution, fighting at Concepción and in the successful siege of Bexar. Several sources list him as a signer of the Texas Declaration of Independence and he did attend the convention which produced that document. However, Briscoe left the convention before affixing his signature on the declara-

tion in order to fight as a captain at the all-important battle of San Jacinto, the concluding action of the Texas Revolution. After Texas won its war for independence, Briscoe conceived plans for extensive railroad systems and was president of the Harrisburg Railroad & Trading Company. This county was created on August 21, 1876.

2512 *Brooks County*

James A. Brooks (1855–1944)— This native of Kentucky came to Texas about 1876. Here he worked as a cowboy and operated a farm and cattle ranch. He joined the Texas rangers in 1882, was commissioned a ranger captain in May, 1889, and served in the force until 1906 when he resigned. Elected as a member of the lower house of the Texas legislature, Brooks served in that body from 1909 to 1911 and was influential in securing creation of this new county on March 11, 1911. He then served as a county judge in the county named in his honor from 1911 to 1939.

2513 *Brown County*

Henry S. Brown (–1834)— The year of this Kentucky native's birth is given by most sources as 1793 but at least two show 1783, when Kentucky was still part of Virginia. He served in the army during the War of 1812 and later engaged in trade between Saint Louis and New Orleans via flatboat on the Mississippi. After settling in Mexican Texas, Brown engaged in merchandise trade with Mexicans, Indians and Anglo-American settlers. Here in Texas he was an Indian fighter and he also fought against Mexicans at the June 26, 1832, battle of Velasco, a prelude to the Texas Revolution. In other pre-revolutionary activities, Brown was a delegate to the convention of 1832 at San Felipe de Austin and in 1833 he was a member of the ayuntamiento (town council) for Brazoria. This county was created on August 27, 1856.

2514 *Burleson County*

Edward Burleson (1798–1851)— A native of North Carolina, Burleson served as a militia officer in Missouri territory and also in Tennessee. In 1830 or 1831 he settled in Texas and led his fellow settlers in repelling raids by hostile Indians. Burleson was an early participant in battles of the Texas Revolution, and he fought at the successful siege of Bexar. As an officer in the Texas Revolutionary army he fought in the all-important battle of San Jacinto, the concluding action of the Texas Revolution. Burleson served in early congresses of the republic of Texas and on September 6, 1841, he was elected vice-president of the republic under President Samuel Houston (1793–1863). After Texas was admitted to statehood, Burleson served in the state's senate and he also served America as an officer during the Mexican War. This county was created, as a judicial county, on January 15, 1842, while Edward Burleson was serving as vice-president of the Texas republic. On March 24, 1846, Burleson County in the state of Texas was created with the same boundaries as the former judicial county.

2515 *Burnet County*

David G. Burnet (1788–1870)— A native of New Jersey, Burnet volunteered to fight under Francisco Miranda (–1816) to free Venezuela from Spain. About 1820 he came to Texas and lived for a time in western Texas but didn't settle permanently here until 1826 and then he came to eastern Texas. In 1834 Burnet was appointed as a district judge in Mexican Texas. The following year he was a representative at the Consultation which was called to meet on October 16, 1835, to decide how Texas should react to the dictatorship established in Mexico by Antonio Lopez de Santa Anna (1794–1876). In March, 1836 David G. Burnet became the first (ad interim) president of the republic of Texas and he later served the republic as vice-president. After the Civil War, Burnet was elected to represent Texas in the U.S. Senate but he was not permitted to take his seat. On January 30, 1841, a Burnet County had been created by the republic of Texas as a judicial county but that county became defunct as the result of a Texas supreme court decision. On March 24, 1846, consideration was given to naming a county in the new state of Texas in honor of Burnet, but the name Anderson was chosen for that county, instead. It was not until February 5, 1852, that the present Burnet County was created.

2516 *Caldwell County*

Mathew Caldwell (–1842)— Caldwell was born about 1798 in either North Carolina or Kentucky and lived for a time in Missouri. During the early 1830's, he came to Texas and was one of the signers of Texas' 1836 Declaration of Independence. He served as an army captain in Texas, defending Goliad and was wounded at the Council House fight with the Comanche Indians. That fight proved to be a major strategic blunder in the White-Texans relations with the Comanche Indians. Caldwell later participated in a more successful engagement against the Comanche in the Plum Creek fight. During Texas' war with Mexico for independence he was captured and held prisoner in Mexico. Upon his release he participated in the victory in the battle of the Salado. He died on December 28, 1842, in Gonzales, Texas, and was buried with military honors. This county was created on March 6, 1848.

2517 *Calhoun County*

John C. Calhoun (1782–1850)— Calhoun represented South Carolina in both houses of the U.S. Congress. He served as secretary of war, secretary of state and as vice-president. He was a forceful advocate of slavery, states' rights and limited powers for the federal government. He resigned the vice-presidency to enter the U.S. Senate where he thought he could better represent the views of South Carolina and the South. This county was created and named in his honor on April 4, 1846, while Calhoun was serving as a United States senator from South Carolina.

2518 *Callahan County*

James H. Callahan (1814–1856)— A native of Georgia, Callahan fought against the Mexicans in Texas under James W. Fannin (1804–1836) at the battle of Coleto in early March, 1836. Fannin's entire force was captured and about 90 percent of them were massacred at Goliad on March 27, 1836. The Mexicans chose to spare Callahan's life because he was a mechanic and they thought he might be useful to them. Callahan subsequently joined the Texas rangers and by 1842 he had attained the rank of lieutenant. A number of accounts refer to Callahan as a captain in the Texas rangers. In 1855 Texas Governor Elisha M. Pease (1812–1883) commissioned Callahan to raise a company to hunt down Indians, who were raiding Texas from Mexico. Callahan and his men entered Mexico and set fire to Piedras Negras there. Governor Pease supported Callahan's pursuit of the Indians into Mexico but the torching of Mexican Piedras Negras caused diplomatic difficulties between Mexico and the United States. On April 7, 1856, Callahan was killed in a personal feud with one Woodson Blessingame. This county was created and named in Callahan's honor on February 1, 1858.

2519 *Cameron County*

Ewen Cameron (1811–1843)— A native of Scotland, Cameron came to North America prior to 1836 and fought in the Texas Revolution. After the Texas Revolution had ended in success, there were some who still sought adventure and profit in plundering Mexico and Ewen Cameron was among them. He participated as one of the leaders of the Mier expedition into Mexico in December, 1842. Captured and taken as prisoners by Mexican authorities, Cameron was dealt a particularly unlucky fate. Following an escape attempt, Cameron and his companions were captured. The Mexicans decided to execute every tenth man and beans were drawn to determine who would live and who would die. Drawing a black bean meant death and Cameron drew a white bean. However, on April 25, 1843, he was executed near Mexico City on orders from Antonio Lopez de Santa Anna (1794–1876). This county was created on February 12, 1848.

2520 *Camp County*

John L. Camp (–1891)— Some sources list the year of John L. Camp's birth as 1820, while others show 1828. He was born near Birmingham, Alabama, and graduated in 1848 from the University of Tennessee. He settled in Texas the following year. Here Camp taught school and practiced law until the Civil War. In 1861 he was made a captain in the Confederate army and he served with distinction throughout the war. Wounded on at least two occasions and also captured twice, Camp rose to the rank of colonel in the Confederate army. In 1866 Camp was elected to represent Texas in the U.S. House of Representatives, but he was not permitted to take his seat in that body. In 1874 John L. Camp was serving in the Texas senate when the bill to create this new county was being discussed. Senator Camp had introduced the bill to create the county and when it was created on April 6, 1874, it was named for him. Camp later served as a district judge and as a federal land commissioner in Arizona territory.

2521 *Carson County*

Samuel P. Carson (1798–)— Carson was born in North Carolina and served that state in both the state and federal legislatures. He served North Carolina in the U.S. House of Representatives for eight years. In 1836 he came to Texas where he was a signer of the Texas Declaration of Independence and secretary of state in the ad interim cabinet of the republic of Texas in 1836. Carson owned a plantation and had Black slaves. The year of Carson's death is given in some sources as 1838 while others list 1840. The place of his death is also in doubt, since Hot Springs, Arkansas, is shown in some works, while Little Rock, Arkansas, is given in others. This county was created on August 21, 1876.

2522 *Cass County*

Lewis Cass (1782–1866)— A native of New Hampshire, Cass served in the army in the War of 1812 and rose to the rank of brigadier-general. Following that war Cass held a variety of important political positions and was the candidate of the Democratic party in 1848 for president of the United States. He lost to Zachary Taylor. Cass served as governor of Michigan territory, secretary of war under Andrew Jackson, minister to France, U.S. senator from Michigan and secretary of state under President James Buchanan. This Texas county was created on April 25, 1846, and named for Lewis Cass, who had supported annexation of Texas by the U.S. On December 17, 1861, the county's name was changed to Davis County, in honor of the president of the Confederate States of America, Jefferson Davis (1808–1889). However, on May 16, 1871, the county's name was changed back to Cass County. In spite of this change, Jefferson Davis still has a Texas county named in his honor. That county is Jeff Davis County, in western Texas.

2523 *Castro County*

Henri Castro (1786–1865)— A native of France, Castro became a naturalized citizen of the United States. He was living in Paris, France, as a U.S. citizen when President Samuel Houston (1793–1863) appointed him as consul general for the republic of Texas in Paris. In 1844 Castro established a colony of French immigrants in the republic of Texas, on the Medina River. From 1845 to 1847 Castro settled additional colonies in Texas. He was a benign impresario of his Texas colonies and he spent substantial amounts of his personal funds to equip his colonists with farm implements, cows, seeds and medicine. This county was created on August 21, 1876.

2524 *Chambers County*

Thomas J. Chambers (1802–1865)— A native of Virginia and a lawyer, Chambers went to Mexico in 1826. There he studied the Spanish language and Mexican law and secured an appointment as surveyor general of the Mexican state named "Coahuila and Texas." In 1834, Chambers was appointed *asesor general* ("state attorney") of Coahuila and Texas state and he was involved in framing the state's judicial code. Also in 1834 he was appointed as superior judge of the Mexican court in Texas. Civil disorders prevented Chambers from actually sitting on that bench but he was awarded some 137,000 acres of land in Texas by the Mexican government in lieu of salary. Despite these links with Mexico, Chambers became an enthusiastic partisan in the events leading to the Texas Revolution. He expended his personal funds to support early Revolutionary activities and was given the rank of major-general in the army. After Texas was admitted to statehood, Chambers ran to be governor of Texas. When the Civil War erupted, Chambers offered his services to the Confederate States of America and also was a candidate to be Texas' governor as a member of the Confederacy. This county was created on February 12, 1858.

2525 *Cherokee County*

Cherokee Indians— The Cherokee Indians were a large and powerful tribe who lived in North Carolina, Georgia and Tennessee at the time of their first contact with Europeans. By the early 1800's they had adopted many of the features of civilization but by 1840, most Cherokees had been forced from their lands and removed to Indian territory (now Oklahoma) by court decisions, a fraudulent treaty and military force. The removal of some 17,000 Cherokee Indians from their ancient tribal lands in western North Carolina, northwestern Georgia and eastern Tennessee was a dark chapter in our nation's history. Their journey to Indian territory was marked by indescribable suffering from which some 4,000 Cherokees died. A few Cherokee Indians refused to join the forced march to Indian territory and other Cherokees returned from Oklahoma. Although the vast majority of Cherokee Indians originally lived north and east of Texas, about 1819 or 1820 some Cherokee Indians settled in Texas. In June, 1839, they were ordered to leave the republic of Texas and in July, 1839, armed White Texans enforced that edict and destroyed Cherokee huts and farms. Most Cherokee Indians were driven from Texas in that effort. However, Waggoner Carr's article in the April, 1995, issue of the *Texas Bar Journal*, indicates that as recently as 1964, some Cherokee Indians were still claiming title to more than two million acres of land in eastern Texas. The name Cherokee is said to be derived from the Cherokee word for "fire," *chera*. This Texas county was created on April 11, 1846.

2526 *Childress County*

George C. Childress (1804–1841)— A native of Tennessee and a lawyer, Childress was one of the editors of both the *Nashville Banner* and *Nashville Advertiser*. After the death of his first wife, Childress moved to Texas and he was promptly elected as a delegate to the convention of 1836. At that convention he was chairman of the committee which drafted Texas Declaration of Independence and he is considered to be the author of that historic document. (It was written in his own hand.) Childress was also one of the signers of that declaration. He subsequently served as a special agent to the United States seeking recognition of the republic of Texas. This county was created and named in his honor on August 21, 1876.

2527 *Clay County*

Henry Clay (1777–1852)— Clay represented Kentucky in both branches of the U.S. Congress. For many years he was one of the more prominent figures in American politics but his several bids for the presidency were unsuccessful. He was influential in effecting important compromises between northern and southern interests during the years that secession and civil war were imminent. This county created on December 24, 1857, twelve years after Texas had been annexed by the United States to become its 28th state. It is a bit surprising that Texas chose to name a county in Henry Clay's honor since he had opposed annexation of the Texas by the United States. Perhaps the county's name was chosen in sadness that all of Henry Clay's compromise measures to avert civil war were failing. In February, 1861, just three years after Clay County was created, Texas seceded from the Union and joined the Confederacy.

2528 *Cochran County*

Robert E. Cochran (1810–1836)— In 1836, during the Texas Revolution, the Mexican army placed the Alamo, in San Antonio, Texas under siege for 13 days. Inside the Alamo were about 185 Texan defenders, all of whom were slain when the Mexicans stormed the Alamo on the morning of

March 6, 1836. Among those who died in that epic confrontation was Private Robert E. Cochran. A native of New Jersey, Cochran probably lived in both Boston and New Orleans before coming to Texas. He settled here, at Brazoria, in 1835. Cochran fought with the Texas Revolutionary army in the successful siege of Bexar. At the Alamo he was an artillery private under Captain William R. Carey (1806–1836). This county was created on August 21, 1876.

2529 Coke County

Richard Coke (1829–1897)— A native of Virginia and an 1849 graduate of the College of William & Mary in that state, Coke studied law and was admitted to the bar. He came to Texas in 1850. Here he joined the Confederate army as a private, served throughout the war and rose to the rank of captain. After the Civil War, Coke was elected to the state's supreme court in 1866 but the military Reconstruction officials removed him from that bench in 1867. Richard Coke was elected as the governor of Texas in 1873 and he served in that office from January 15, 1874, until December 1, 1876, when he resigned to represent Texas in the U.S. Senate. He served three terms in that body from 1877 to 1895. This county was created and named in his honor during March, 1889, while Coke was serving in the U.S. Senate.

2530 Coleman County

Robert M. Coleman (1797–1837)— This native of Kentucky came to Texas in 1832 and was soon fighting Indians as a captain in the Texas rangers. He participated in the successful siege of Bexar and was a signer of Texas Declaration of Independence. At the successful battle of battle of San Jacinto, the concluding action of the Texas Revolution, Coleman was an aide-de-camp to General Samuel Houston (1793–1863), then commander-in-chief of the Texas army. Coleman was commissioned a colonel because of his valiant service in that battle. This county was created on February 1, 1858.

2531 Collin County

Collin McKinney (1766–1861)— A native of New Jersey, McKinney lived for a time in Kentucky and Arkansas territory before settling on the Red River within Texas in 1831. He was elected as a delegate to the convention of 1836 and there became a signer of Texas Declaration of Independence. He later served in the congress of the republic of Texas. A bill to create a Colon (sic) county, named in his honor was passed in 1838 but President Samuel Houston (1793–1863) vetoed it. This county was created on April 3, 1846. The name of its first county seat was Buckner but since 1848 the county seat has been named McKinney; thus the county and its seat of justice are named Collin and McKinney.

2532 Collingsworth County

James Collinsworth (1806–1838)— A native of Tennessee and a lawyer, Collinsworth came to Texas about February, 1835, and was soon elected a captain in the Texas rangers. As a delegate to the convention of 1836 he became a signer of Texas Declaration of Independence. At the successful battle of San Jacinto, the concluding action of the Texas Revolution, Collinsworth was a major and an aide-de-camp to General Samuel Houston (1793–1863), then commander-in-chief of the Texas army. Collinsworth served as secretary of state in the ad interim government of the republic of Texas and was sent to represent the republic as one of the commissioners to the United States of America. A senator in the first congress of the republic of Texas, Collinsworth was soon elected chief justice of the republic's newly created supreme court. This county was created on August 21, 1876. James Collinsworth's name was misspelled in the statute which created this county and that error has never been corrected.

2533 Colorado County

Colorado River— This county in southeastern Texas was created on March 17, 1836, and named for the major river, which today bisects the county. There are two potential misunderstandings about this Colorado River: (1) While the Colorado River of Texas is a major river, it is little more than half the length of the Colorado River of Grand Canyon-fame and (2) This river's name, Colorado, comes from the Spanish language and indicates a tint of the color red of a less pronounced shade than that implied by the Spanish word rojo, which means "red." This is a misnomer because the Colorado River of Texas is not now a tint of red and never has been. The river was named in Spanish times and there are indications that the names of at least two rivers became switched on early Spanish maps resulting in today's inappropriate name for the Colorado River of Texas. This river rises in central Texas and flows in a southeastern direction to enter Matagorda Bay, an inlet of the Gulf of Mexico, about 60 miles below Colorado County, Texas.

2534 Comal County

Comal River— This county in south-central Texas was created on March 24, 1846, and named for the Comal River. Water gushing from a number of springs at the foot of the Balcones escarpment forms the Comal River within Comal County. The Comal then flows in a winding but southeastern direction just four miles, all within the county's borders, until it joins the Guadalupe River. The river's name is of Spanish origin and means "flat earthenware cooking pan" of the type used by Mexicans to cook maize cakes. The Handbook of Texas, published by the Texas State Historical Association in 1952, speculates in one passage that "Numerous little islands in the river reminded the early Spaniards of the pan; hence the name." However, that same source speculates elsewhere that the river's Spanish name may have been inspired by the valley through which the river flows. Although the Comal is a very short river, it carries a large volume of water.

2535 Comanche County

Comanche Indians— The Comanche Indians' language and traditions closely resemble those of the Shoshoni Indians. It is probable that the Comanche were a part of the Shoshoni when they lived in the Rocky Mountains of Wyoming. As the Comanche migrated south, they acquired horses and began to pursue a nomadic, tepee-dwelling life style and to subsist largely by hunting buffalo. These plains Indians were fierce warriors and by the 18th century, Spanish explorers reported that the Comanche were replacing the Apache Indians in eastern Colorado and eastern New Mexico. The Comanche acquired enormous wealth in firearms and horses and they were recognized as the finest horsemen in the West. This ability, coupled with their warlike disposition, made them formidable foes to both Whites and other Indians. The Comanche continued to drift south and in 1795 they formed a close confederation with the Kiowa Indians, with a center of operations in Oklahoma and Texas, where they terrorized White settlers. In was not until 1875 that the American army finally subdued the Comanche and settled them on an Indian reservation. In the late 18th century, the Comanche population was estimated at more than 20,000 but an epidemic reduced that figure to 9,000 in 1816. By 1960 there were estimated to be just 3,000 remaining Comanche Indians, most of whom were living on reservations in Oklahoma. The name *Comanche* has been translated as meaning "enemies" in the Ute Indians' language. This county was created on January 25, 1856.

2536 *Concho County*

Concho River— This county in west-central Texas was created on February 1, 1858, and named for the Concho River, which flows across the top portion of the county. The Concho River proper is a 53 mile-long tributary of the Colorado River of Texas. The Concho proper begins life in Tom Green County and flows east to enter the Colorado River 12 miles northeast of Paint Rock, the county seat of Concho County. The Concho River is formed by three branches. The two branches which directly form the Concho proper are the North and South Concho Rivers but the Concho River Middle Branch also plays a role in the formation of the Concho River. Its waters reach the Concho indirectly, by way of the South Concho River. The name *concho* is Spanish and means "shell." Some sources speculate that the name may have been given because of mussel shells found here.

2537 *Cooke County*

William G. Cooke (1808–1847)— A native of Virginia who was living in New Orleans when he volunteered to assist Texas in her Revolutionary struggle, Cooke came to Texas as a first-lieutenant in the New Orleans Greys and was soon elected a captain. He participated in the successful storming of Bexar in December, 1835, and was a senior officer at the all-important battle of San Jacinto, the concluding action of the Texas Revolution. In 1837 he resigned from the army to enter a pharmacy business in Texas but he re-enlisted in 1839 and was commissioned quartermaster general of the republic of Texas in 1840. Cooke was later appointed adjutant-general of the militia and he was serving in that position when he died in December, 1847. This county was created three months later, on March 20, 1848.

2538 *Coryell County*

James Coryell (–1837)— According to several accounts, Coryell was born in Ohio. Some of those accounts give his year of birth as 1801 but Zelma Scott presents convincing evidence that he was born in Ohio in 1803 in the meticulous genealogy of James Coryell's family in her work entitled *A History of Coryell County, Texas.* However other sources cite Tennessee as his birthplace and 1796 as the birth year. It is known that he came to Texas in the 1820's and joined James Bowie (–1836) in a search for silver mines in the San Saba region of Texas. Coryell later lived with Arnold Cavitt and his family near the present Marlin, Texas. On June 22, 1835, James Coryell was granted a patent for 1,180 acres (expressed as a fraction of a league) of land by the Mexican state of Coahuila and Texas. This land was located at the intersection of Coryell Creek and the Leon River. (That patent was noted in the land records of Coryell County, Texas, on October 13, 1870). Coryell served as a member of Captain Thomas H. Barron's rangers defending the frontier. On May 27, 1837, James Coryell was killed by Indians near the falls of the Brazos River. This county was created on February 4, 1854.

2539 *Cottle County*

George W. Cottle (1811–1836)— In 1836, during the Texas Revolution, the Mexican army placed the Alamo, in San Antonio, Texas, under siege for 13 days. Inside the Alamo were about 185 Texan defenders, all of whom were slain when the Mexicans stormed the Alamo on the morning of March 6, 1836. Among those who died in that epic confrontation was Private George W. Cottle. A native of Missouri, Cottle had come to Texas in 1829 and settled here at Green C. De Witt's (1787–1835) colony. In September, 1835, Cottle was granted title to one league of land near Gonzales, Texas. Less than one month later, on October 2, 1835, in what would be the first battle of the Texas Revolution, Cottle fought against the Mexican army in the battle of Gonzales. Cottle arrived at the Alamo on March 1, 1836, as part of a relief force and died there five days later. This county was created on August 21, 1876.

2540 *Crane County*

William C. Crane (1816–1885)— A native of Virginia, Crane received both bachelor's and master's degrees before his ordination as a Baptist minister in 1838. He served as the pastor of several Baptist churches, was president of two colleges in Mississippi and was co-editor of the *Mississippi Baptist.* Crane came to Texas in 1863 to become president of Baylor University, a Baptist institution of higher education. Under his presidency, the institution survived the Civil War, the curriculum was broadened and the women's department was carved out as a separate institution, Baylor Female College. Reverend Crane served as president of Baylor University for 22 years until his death in February, 1885. Crane County was created on February 26, 1887.

2541 *Crockett County*

David Crockett (1786–1836)— In 1836, during the Texas Revolution, the Mexican army placed the Alamo, in San Antonio, Texas under siege for 13 days. Inside the Alamo were about 185 Texan defenders, all of whom were slain when the Mexicans stormed the Alamo on the morning of March 6, 1836. Among those who died in that epic confrontation was Private David Crockett. He had been born in the portion of western North Carolina which soon became the state of Tennessee. Crockett served as a private in the army commanded by Andrew Jackson and eventually attained the rank of colonel in the Tennessee militia. He served in the Tennessee legislature and represented Tennessee in the U.S. House of Representatives before coming to Texas to assist in the fight for independence from Mexico. Soon after arriving in Texas he became one of the victims of the massacre at the Alamo. He was merely a private and a rifleman when the Alamo fell, although some works refer to him as a colonel, a courtesy recognizing that Crockett had earlier held that rank in the Tennessee militia. This county was created on January 22, 1875.

2542 *Crosby County*

Stephen Crosby (1808–1869)— A native of South Carolina, Crosby lived for a time in Alabama. He engaged in steamboating before coming to Texas in 1845. In 1851 Crosby became commissioner of the general land office of Texas and he held that post during three terms: 1851–1858, 1862–1865 and 1866–1867. Crosby was a member of the Know-Nothing political party, although that party disappeared in 1859, prior to Crosby's death in Austin, Texas, in 1869. This county was created on August 21, 1876.

2543 *Culberson County*

David B. Culberson (1830–1900)— A native of Georgia and a lawyer, Culberson came to Texas in 1856 and served in the state legislature prior to the Civil War. Although Culberson was opposed to Texas seceding from the Union, when secession and Civil War came, he enlisted in the Confederate army as a private and rose to the rank of colonel. In 1873 Culberson was elected to the Texas senate and in 1875 to the U.S. House of Representatives. He represented Texas in that body for 22 years from 1875 to 1897. President William McKinley appointed Culberson in 1897 to a committee to codify the laws of the United States and he was engaged in that work until his death. This county was created on March 10, 1911.

2544 *Dallam County*

James W. Dallam (1818–1847)— A native of Maryland and an 1837 graduate of Brown University in Rhode Island, Dallam studied law in Baltimore, Maryland, before coming to Texas in 1839. Here he soon became a prominent and respected attorney and he compiled a landmark legal work entitled *A Digest of the Laws of Texas: Containing a Full & Complete Compilation of the Land Laws; Together with the Opinions of the Supreme Court.* Originally published in Baltimore in 1845, this work came to be known "the lawyer's Bible" and was reprinted several times. Dallam later founded and published a weekly newspaper in Matagorda, Texas, but he died of yellow fever in 1847, before his 30th birthday. This county was created on August 21, 1876.

2545 *Dallas County*

Uncertain— It is ironic that there is uncertainty concerning the origin of this county's name. After all, Dallas County and its county seat of Dallas are among Texas' most famous locations. Also, Texas was admitted to the United States on December 29, 1845, while George M. Dallas (1792–1864) was serving as vice-president of the United States under President James K. Polk. Dallas County, Texas, was created just three months later, on March 30, 1846. Indeed the vast majority of sources consulted state that this county was named in honor of Vice-president George M. Dallas (1792–1864). Among the few sources that admit there is uncertainty, many mention that although the act creating the county fails to mention its namesake, it was probably Vice-president George M. Dallas. Z. T. Fulmore's work entitled *The History & Geography of Texas as Told in County Names* indicates, without reservation, that the county's name honors the

vice-president and there are other heavy hitting Texas historians who support that view. The main reason we have uncertainty is that the county was named after the city (then only a settlement and post office) was named and that settlement and post office were apparently named Dallas before George M. Dallas (1792–1864) had done anything to cause notice in Texas. Professor Fred Tarpley's *Place Names of Northeast Texas* tells us that the settlement of Dallas was founded in 1841 by John Neely Bryan and it is unlikely that John Neely Bryan named his settlement in honor of the then rather obscure George M. Dallas (1792–1864). Rather, Dr. Tarpley says, John Neely Bryan "…knew several other men named Dallas, among them Joseph Dallas, an old Arkansas friend who settled at Cedar Springs in 1843." Hugh Best's *Debrett's Texas Peerage* states that the settlement "…appears to have been named Dallas from its very start" and goes on to mention other men named Dallas "any one of them may have had something to do with the naming of the great city of Dallas." The men whom Hugh Best lists as worthy of consideration are:
— Walter R. Dallas, a member of an Austin colony, soldier in the Texas army and a veteran of the battle of San Jacinto
— James L. Dallas, a member of an Austin colony & soldier in the Texas army
— Vice-president George M. Dallas
— Commodore A. J. Dallas of the U.S. navy
— Alexander James Dallas, a secretary of the treasury in the U.S. government
— Joseph Dallas, a settler of the future city in 1843 (presumably the same Joseph Dallas to whom Fred Tarpley refers)
A very brief biographical sketch of Vice-president George M. Dallas follows because so many Texas sources say that this county was named for him. This is not intended to imply that he is the most likely namesake.
George M. Dallas (1792–1864)— Dallas was a native of Philadelphia, Pennsylvania, and he served as mayor of that city. He was later a U.S. senator, attorney general of Pennsylvania and minister to Russia. He subsequently served as vice-president of the United States and minister to England.

2546 *Dawson County*

Nicholas M. Dawson (1808–1842)— Dawson was born in Kentucky, educated in Tennessee and came to Texas in 1834. He enlisted in the Texas Revolutionary army in 1836 and served as a second-lieutenant

at the all-important battle of San Jacinto, the concluding action of the Texas Revolution. In September, 1842, in response to a Mexican invasion of Texas, Dawson assembled a force of 53 men and marched toward the Salado River. This party was intercepted and surrounded by the Mexicans and on September 18, 1842, in the action which came to be known as the Dawson massacre, Dawson surrendered and he and his men were disarmed. Then Dawson and about 34 of his men were killed. This county was created on August 21, 1876. There had been an earlier Dawson County in Texas, which was created on February 1, 1858, but that county ceased to exist when all of its territory was obliterated by acts of the Texas legislature during 1866. Today's Dawson County, Texas includes no portion of that earlier Dawson County.

2547 *De Witt County*

Green C. De Witt (1787–1835)— Born in Kentucky when it was still part of Virginia, De Witt later lived in Missouri territory. He visited Mexico City to obtain a grant of land in Mexican Texas and on April 15, 1825, he was granted a contract to bring 400 American families to Texas and settle them east of San Antonio. De Witt established his first colony in Mexican Texas at the present Gonzales, Texas. This first colony was soon sacked by Indians and the survivors fled to another of De Witt's colonies, Old Station, on the Lavaca River. Troubles plagued the colonists at Old Station and still more trouble awaited them when they returned to Gonzales. In spite of these difficulties, De Witt continued his efforts to plant Anglo-American colonies in Texas and he died at Monclova, Mexico, while seeking approval to bring additional colonists. Green C. De Witt is ranked along with Stephen F. Austin (1793–1836) as a leading impresario of early Anglo-American colonies in Texas. This county was created on March 24, 1846.

2548 *Deaf Smith County*

Erastus Smith (1787–1837)— Nicknamed "Deaf Smith" on account of pronounced lack of hearing, Erastus Smith was born in New York and moved with his parents to Mississippi territory. He first came to Texas in 1817. His stay here was brief at that time but he returned in 1821 and made Texas his home for the rest of his life. At that time Texas was part of Mexico and Smith married a young Mexican widow. When the Texas Revolution began, Smith already had a reputation as a capable scout and when he offered his services to the Texas army, they were gratefully accepted. He served as a scout at the battle of Concepcion and later commanded a company. At the all-important battle of San Jacinto, the concluding action of the Texas Revolution, Smith destroyed a key bridge cutting off an important Mexican escape route. For a time after the Texas Revolution Smith was captain of a company of rangers. He died in November, 1837, at Richmond, Texas. This county was created on August 21, 1876.

2549 *Delta County*

Shape of the county similar to the Greek letter, delta — When this county in northeastern Texas was created and named on July 29, 1870, it was named for its triangular shape, which resembled the fourth letter in the Greek alphabet, which is *delta*. The Greek letter *delta* is an isosceles triangle. A glance at a Texas map showing counties a bit north and east of Dallas confirms that Delta County's name is still appropriate. The eastern point of the county's shape in formed by the junction of the North and South Sulphur Rivers.

2550 *Denton County*

John B. Denton (1806–1841) — A native of Tennessee who was orphaned at an early age, Denton was a rather wild youngster, but at about age 20 he converted to the Methodist Episcopal church. He served as an itinerant minister of that church for about ten years in Arkansas territory and southern Missouri. In 1836 or 1837 Denton came to preach in Texas but because the income from his religious work was inadequate to support his family, he became licensed to practice law. Denton also was commissioned as a captain in a company of Texas rangers commanded by Edward H. Tarrant (1796–1858). On May 22, 1841, the rangers attacked Indians on Village Creek, six miles east of today's Fort Worth, Texas. The attack was successful and helped open the present Tarrant County area of Texas to White settlers. However Captain Denton died during this battle. Denton County was created five years later, on April 11, 1846.

2551 *Dickens County*

James R. Dimpkins (–1836) — In 1836, during the Texas Revolution, the Mexican army placed the Alamo, in San Antonio, Texas, under siege for 13 days. Inside the Alamo were about 185 Texan defend-ers, all of whom were slain when the Mexicans stormed the Alamo on the morning of March 6, 1836. Among those who died in that epic confrontation was James R. Dimpkins. His name is listed on the Alamo monument as "J. Dickens" and his name is also styled in various historical references as Dimkins, Dinkin and Dockon. Several works dealing with the history of the siege of the Alamo and the Alamo monument indicate that there are errors on the list of names shown on the Alamo monument and "As the years pass, new light is constantly thrown on the Alamo defenders," and that some names should be added, some deleted and some merely spelled correctly. Clearly the martyr of the Alamo whom this county's name was intended to honor when it was created on August 21, 1876, was James R. Dimpkins, the man whose name is carved in the Alamo monument as "J. Dickens." A number of sources list him as a private but Bill Groneman's meticulously researched *Alamo Defenders*, published in 1990, describes James R. Dimpkins as a sergeant who was born in England and was a citizen of that country when he died at the Alamo. He came to Texas as a member of the New Orleans Greys and he fought at the successful siege of Bexar. At the Alamo he served in the infantry company commanded by Captain William Blazeby (1795–1836) and both Sergeant Dimpkins and Captain Blazeby retained identification as members of the New Orleans Greys at the time of their death.

2552 *Dimmit County*

Philip Dimmitt (–1841) — The year and place Dimmitt's birth are uncertain but we know that he came to Texas as a young man about 1822 and was one of the early Anglo-American pioneers of Texas. At that time Texas was part of Mexico. Dimmitt married a Mexican lady, became a naturalized citizen of Mexico and successfully petitioned the Mexican government for land here. Despite these connections with Mexico, Dimmitt participated in early actions of the Texas Revolution. He fought in seizing Goliad and he remained in command at Goliad as a captain after its seizure. He participated in the successful siege of Bexar and then returned to Goliad, where he and Ira Ingram (1788–1837) drafted the Goliad Declaration of Independence. That declaration called for the separation of the Mexican department of Texas into a "free, sovereign, and independent State." This Goliad declaration preceded the Texas Declaration of Inde-pendence by 72 days. Dimmitt was working on Corpus Christi Bay when he was taken as a prisoner by Mexicans. Dimmitt and his fellow prisoners were told that they would be shot at Mexico City and Dimmitt died soon afterward. Whether he was shot or committed suicide to avoid that fate is disputed. Dimmit County, Texas, was created on February 1, 1858. Most sources agree that the statute creating this county misspelled the namesake's surname but they disagree on what the correct spelling is. Many use Dimmitt, while others show Dimitt.

2553 *Donley County*

Stockton P. Donley (1821–1871) — Born in Missouri territory, Donley studied law in Kentucky and was admitted to the bar there. He came to Texas in 1846 and in 1853 he was elected as district attorney for the sixth judicial district. When Texas seceded from the Union, Donley enlisted as a private in the army of the Confederate States of America. Subsequently promoted to lieutenant, he was taken as a prisoner of war. Donley was elected to the supreme court of Texas following the Civil War, but he was removed from that office in 1867 by the military Reconstruction army, which then ruled Texas with an iron fist. This county was first established with the name Wegefarth County in 1873. That name honored C. Wegefarth, president of the Texas Immigrant Aid & Supply Company. The act which created Wegefarth County was repealed on August 21, 1876, and Donley County was created and named on that same day, August 21, 1876.

2554 *Duval County*

Uncertain — Sources consulted are agreed that this county was created on February 1, 1858, and that it was named in honor of one or more of the three Duval brothers, Burr H., John C. and Thomas H. Duval. However these sources are about evenly divided between two concepts: (1) this county was named in honor of all three Duval brothers or (2) the county's name honors only Burr H. Duval, the only one of the Duval brothers who died in the Goliad massacre.

Burr H. Duval (1809–1836) — A native of Kentucky, Burr H. Duval was the leader of a group in that state who sympathized with the Texas Revolutionary cause. Duval and his Kentucky Mustangs came to Texas to assist in the armed rebellion and he fought in the Goliad campaign of 1836. Burr H. Duval fought at the battle of

Coleto, and he was among the men who surrendered and were then massacred at Goliad on March 27, 1836.

John C. Duval (1816–1891)— Also a native of Kentucky, John C. Duval was a member of the group in Kentucky who sympathized with the Texas Revolutionary cause. He came to Texas with the Kentucky Mustangs, led by his brother, Burr H. Duval (1809–1836), and fought in the Goliad campaign of 1836. However, unlike his brother, Burr who surrendered and then was massacred at Goliad on March 27, 1836, John C. Duval managed to escape. He subsequently studied engineering at the University of Virginia and returned to Texas as a surveyor. John C. Duval opposed secession but when Texas seceded from the Union, he enlisted as a private in the Confederate army.

Thomas H. Duval (1813–1880)— The *Handbook of Texas* published in 1952 by the Texas State Historical Association states that Thomas H. Duval was born in Virginia on November 4, 1813. He had both of the same parents as his brothers, Burr and John, who were born in Kentucky in 1809 and 1816 but his father was a member of the federal Congress in 1813 in Washington, D.C., so the Virginia birthplace may be valid. In 1821 President James Monroe appointed the Duval brothers' father, William P. DuVal (he styled his name with a capital V), as a judge in East Florida and one month later as Florida's first territorial governor. In 1835 when the other two Duval brothers were heading for Texas to fight in the Revolution here, Thomas H. Duval moved from Kentucky to Florida territory. There he studied law and secured several political appointments. He came to Texas in 1846 and held antebellum political appointments here. Opposed to secession, Thomas H. Duval left Texas during the Civil War but returned in 1865 as a federal judge.

2555 *Eastland County*

William M. Eastland (1806–1843)— A native of Kentucky, Eastland came to Texas about 1834. Here he served as a first-lieutenant fighting Indians and he later served in the all-important battle of San Jacinto, the concluding action of the Texas Revolution. After Texas won its war for independence, Eastland served as a captain in the Texas rangers. He was a with the Mier expedition into Mexico in December, 1842, when its members were captured and taken as prisoners by Mexican authorities. Following an escape attempt, the Mexicans decided to execute every tenth captive and

beans were drawn to determine who would live and who would die. Drawing a black bean meant death and Captain William M. Eastland was the first to draw a black bean on March 25, 1843. He was executed the same day. This county was created on February 1, 1858.

2556 *Ector County*

Mathew D. Ector (1822–1879)— A native of Georgia and a lawyer, Ector served in the Georgia legislature before settling in Texas in 1850. Here in Texas he again became a state legislator. When the Civil War began, Ector enlisted as a private in the Confederate army and he served with distinction and rose to the rank of brigadier-general. During the Atlanta campaign, in 1864, Ector was wounded and lost a leg to the wound. Upon his return to Texas he was elected as a judge but the military Reconstruction officials removed him from that bench. After Reconstruction ended in Texas Mathew D. Ector was appointed as a judge in he served in judicial capacities in Texas until his death. This county was created on February 26, 1887.

2557 *Edwards County*

Haden Edwards, Sr. (1771–1849)— Born to wealth in Virginia and educated in Kentucky, Edwards established a plantation, complete with slaves, on the Pearl River in Mississippi. He secured permission from authorities in Mexico City to move several hundred Anglo-Americans into Texas and he established a colony centered at Nacogdoches. However, Edwards was insensitive to the rights of Mexican and Spanish residents, already living in the area when his colonists arrived. The Mexican governor of the state of Coahuila and Texas, Victor Blanco, accused Edwards of disrespect and ordered him to leave Texas. By 1826 Edwards lost control of his colony and after a brief struggle to regain it, he abandoned his Texas venture. This county was created on February 1, 1858, and named for Haden Edwards, Sr. (1771–1849). It was not named for his son, Haden Harrison Edwards (1813–1865), a member of the Revolutionary army of Texas and of the congress of the republic of Texas.

2558 *El Paso County*

City of El Paso, Texas— This county, in the extreme western corner of Texas, was created on January 3, 1850, and named for its principal community, El Paso. The name was first given by 16th century Spanish conquistadors searching for gold north

of the Rio Grande River. The conquistadors' name is rendered in some accounts as *El Paso del Norte* and in others as *El Paso del Rio del Norte*. The shorter version meant "The Pass of the North," while the longer version merely acknowledged the presence of the Rio Grande River and translates as "The Pass of the River of the North." Both versions of the name refer to the pass through the mountains on both sides of the Rio Grande River here. Technically the conquistadors' name originally applied to El Paso's sister city across the Rio Grande in Mexico, Ciudad Juarez, but the name soon settled over the shoulders of El Paso, Texas, as well. In the late 1990's El Paso, Texas, has a population of 515,000 and is one of the state's major cities.

2559 *Ellis County*

Richard Ellis (1781–1846)— A native of Virginia and a lawyer, Ellis was active in the politics of Alabama territory and became an early judge on the supreme court of the state of Alabama. In 1834 he settled at Pecan Point on the Arkansas side of the Red River across from Mexican Texas. He soon became a Texan for he was a delegate and president of the convention of 1836, and among the signers of the Texas Declaration of Independence produced by that convention. Ellis was a senator in the first four congresses of the republic of Texas and during the first congress he was president *pro tempore* of the senate. He died on December 20, 1846, and this county was created exactly three years later, on December 20, 1849.

2560 *Erath County*

George B. Erath (1813–1891)— Erath was born in Austria and immigrated to America in 1832. The following year he came to Texas and soon found employment surveying land. During Erath's various periods of employment as a chain carrier and land surveyor in Texas he was periodically involved in fighting Indians. He fought at the all-important battle of San Jacinto, the concluding action of the Texas Revolution, served as an officer in the Texas rangers and was a member of at least two congresses of the republic of Texas. He also served in the first legislature of the state of Texas and was a state senator from 1857 to 1861. Erath entered the Confederate army during the Civil War but was discharged because of poor health. In 1874 he was elected again to the Texas senate. This county was created on January 25, 1856.

2561 *Falls County*

*Waterfalls of the Brazos River—*This county in central Texas was created on January 28, 1850, and named for the falls of the Brazos River, which flows across Falls County. The Brazos is the longest stream in Texas and over its 840 mile length it presumably has many falls. However, the following description contained in an 1893 history of Falls County (and three other Texas counties) leaves little doubt about which waterfalls the county's name commemorates: "The Brazos River, crossing the county to southeast, divides it almost equally, and in the middle of its course across the county tumbles over a ledge of rocks whose height has varied in successive half-centuries, and whose roaring waters, seething and foaming in turbulence during high water, and rippling, spraying and sparkling, as its clear waters tumble gleaming over limestone ledges at low water, have been the most famous landmark of central Texas since history began."

2562 *Fannin County*

*James W. Fannin (1804–1836)—*Fannin, a native of Georgia, came to Texas in 1834 and engaged in slave trading and agitating for Texas independence from Mexico. Early in the Texas Revolution, in 1835, he participated in the battles of Gonzales and Concepcion. In March 1836, Fannin, now a colonel, and his men were surrounded and forced to surrender at the battle of Coleto. Imprisoned by the Mexicans at Goliad, most of Fannin's men were massacred by order of Santa Anna on March 27, 1836. Because Fannin was wounded, he was executed separately but on the same day. This county was created and named in his honor on December 14, 1837. The name that was first suggested for this new county was Independence but Representative Patrick C. Jack (1808–1844) suggested that it be named Fannin, instead, and that was done.

2563 *Fayette County*

*Marie Joseph Paul Yves Roch Gilbert du Motier, Marquis de Lafayette (1757–1834)—*Lafayette was a French aristocrat who served briefly in the French army. He came to America in 1777 to assist the American Revolutionary army. He was granted an honorary commission as major general by the Continental Congress and served with distinction in a number of battles in the Revolutionary War. This county was

created by the republic of Texas on December 14, 1837.

2564 *Fisher County*

*Samuel R. Fisher (1794–1839)—*A native of Pennsylvania, Fisher settled at Matagorda in Mexican Texas in 1830. He was elected as a delegate to the convention of 1836 and there became a signer of Texas Declaration of Independence. During the first administration of President Samuel Houston (1793–1863), Fisher served in the cabinet of the republic of Texas as secretary of the navy. This was an important position in insuring the safety of new Texas settlers, who arrived through the Gulf of Mexico from New Orleans. This county was created on August 21, 1876.

2565 *Floyd County*

*Dolphin W. Floyd (1804–1836)—*In 1836, during the Texas Revolution, the Mexican army placed the Alamo, in San Antonio, Texas, under siege for 13 days. Inside the Alamo were about 185 Texan defenders, all of whom were slain when the Mexicans stormed the Alamo on the morning of March 6, 1836. Among those who died in that epic confrontation was Dolphin Ward Floyd, a 32 year old farmer. Floyd was born in North Carolina and had come to Mexican Texas by 1832. A resident of Gonzales, Texas, Floyd was a private and rifleman in the Gonzales ranging company when he died at the Alamo. This county was created on August 21, 1876.

2566 *Foard County*

*Robert J. Foard (1831–1898)—*A native of Maryland and a graduate of Princeton College, Foard studied law and was admitted to the bar in Maryland before coming to Texas in 1853. He established his law practice here at Columbus in southeastern Texas. During the Civil War Foard was a lieutenant in the Confederate army and he rose to the rank of major. Foard defended Texas coast on the Gulf of Mexico and served in Louisiana defending Confederate positions near the Mississippi River. After the war he returned to Texas and resumed his law practice. This county was named in his honor primarily due to his political connection, rather than in reward for his Civil War service. The county was created on March 3, 1891, while Robert Foard was a law partner of a member of the Texas legislature. That legislator was on the committee which reported the bill to create this new county and he was influential in selecting its name. Essentially

all sources agree that this county was named for Robert Foard although John H. Brown's *History of Texas* says "It is believed that the name 'Foard' is a misprint in the law, and that the intent was to name the county in honor of the old veteran Col. John S. 'Ford.'" In 1963 a stone monument was erected on the Foard County square. It states that the county was named for "Robert L. Foard (1831–1898)." Thus there may be valid dispute about the middle initial of the county's namesake, but not about who the namesake was.

2567 *Fort Bend County*

*Fort Bend on the Brazos River, Texas—*This county in southeastern Texas was created on December 29, 1837, and named for a fort, Fort Bend, which had been erected within the county at the present site of Richmond, Texas, the county seat of Fort Bend County. This crude fort or blockhouse was erected in November, 1821, by members of a colony of Stephen F. Austin's (1793–1836). It was placed near the lower end of the Brazos River and named for a big bend in the river here. The Brazos is the longest river in Texas and over its 840 mile course it takes many dramatic bends, some of which loop back and forth acutely. Names on the Texas map such as South Bend, Brier Bend, Gooseneck Bend, Salem Bend and Herron Bend commemorate these sharp turns. The loop here at old Fort Bend is particularly dramatic and here two points on the river are far closer by land than by water. No ruins of the old fort remain in the late 20th century and its exact site in uncertain. The outer curve on the west bank of the Brazos River, where the fort was erected, has eroded.

2568 *Franklin County*

*Benjamin C. Franklin (1805–1873)—*A native of Georgia and a graduate of Franklin College (now the University of Georgia), Franklin studied law and was admitted to the bar before coming to Mexican Texas in 1835. An advocate of war against Mexico to acquire independence for Texas, Franklin served in the Texas army and although he was commissioned as a captain, he had no company to command at the crucial battle of San Jacinto, so he fought there as a private. He soon was hastily appointed as the first judge in the republic of Texas. It seems that a Texas armed schooner captured a brig owned by a citizen of the United States. To avoid alienating the United States, the young republic of Texas took steps to have the dispute concerning this capture tried in a court of law and Franklin was appointed to hear the case, thus becoming the first judge in the republic of Texas. He later served on the supreme court of the republic of Texas and in the legislature of the state of Texas. Judge Franklin died on Christmas day in 1873. This county was created and named in his honor less than 15 months later, on March 6, 1875.

2569 *Freestone County*

Descriptive of stone and/or land found here— This county in east-central Texas was created on September 6, 1850, from the eastern portion of Limestone County. A *History of Freestone County, Texas*, published in 1978, contains crisp summaries of explanations for the county's name, which include:

1. This county was created from territory of Limestone County and the county's border, in a general way, marks the border between the old (limestone) and new (freestone) regions.

2. Limestone, when broken in two pieces has a liberated or "free" stone portion.

3. "In contrast to the cretaceous black waxy region of the upper Navasota prairies."

2570 *Frio County*

Frio River— This county in southwestern Texas was created on February 1, 1858, and named for the Frio River, which bisects the county. The Frio is a 220 mile-long tributary of the Nueces River. It rises in two forks in Real County, Texas, flows southeast and east and passes through Frio County on its journey to the Nueces River. The Frio reaches the Nueces with the Atascosa River. These two streams merge at of the town of Three Rivers, Texas, and then soon join the Nueces one mile south of Three Rivers. The name *Frio* is Spanish and means "Cold."

2571 *Gaines County*

James Gaines (–1856)— Born in Virginia about 1776, Gaines was an early Anglo-American settler in Mexican Texas. He was here by the mid-1820's and may have come to Texas as early as 1812. Gaines was made the *alcalde*, or "leading personage" of the Mexican district of Sabine and in 1835 he became a judge of the municipality of Sabine under the provisional government of the republic of Texas. He was elected as a delegate to the convention of 1836 and a member of the committee

which drafted the Texas Declaration of Independence. He also was a signer of that historic document. Gaines served in at least three senates of the congress of the republic of Texas before leaving for California in 1849 in the gold rush. He died there in 1856. This county was created on August 21, 1876.

2572 *Galveston County*

Bernardo de Galvez (1746–1786)— A native of Spain and an officer in the Spanish army, Galvez served in combat against Portugal and in America fighting the native Indians. Appointed ad interim governor of Louisiana, Galvez served as Spain's governor of Louisiana from 1777 to 1785. Very early in his term as governor, he took as his wife Maria Feliciana (or Feliciete) de Saint-Maxent. She was a native of New Orleans and this marriage increased the governor's popularity. Galvez provided significant aid to the American colonists in their war for independence from England. Galvez defeated the British at Baton Rouge, Natchez, Mobile and Pensacola. When his service as governor of Louisiana ended, Galvez was honored by Spain with Castilian titles of nobility and he was appointed captain general of the Floridas and Louisiana. In 1785 Galvez became viceroy of New Spain (Mexico) and he died there in 1786.

Galveston County, Texas, was created by the republic of Texas on May 15, 1838. Essentially all sources state or imply that this county was named directly for Bernardo de Galvez (1746–1786) and there is no reason to doubt that the county's name can be traced to him. However, Galveston County embraces the city of Galveston, Galveston Island and Galveston Bay, all of which had been named before this county was created. Indeed, in 1836 Galveston became the temporary capital of the republic of Texas. It certainly seems possible that the county was named directly in 1838 for one or more of these already established place names rather than directly for Bernardo de Galvez (1746–1786). In their 1971 work entitled *The Texas Courthouse*, June Rayfield Welch and J. Larry Nance remind us that Bernardo de Galvez "ordered the Texas coast surveyed, and the surveyors named Galveston Bay for him."

2573 *Garza County*

The Garza family, prominent in early Texas history— This county was created on August 21, 1876. Several dozen sources dealing with the history, geography and

place names of Texas tell us that this county was named for an early pioneer family named Garza, with no specifics. Frank H. Gille's *Encyclopedia of Texas* is less cautious. He tells us that the county was named for "Geronimo Garza, founder of San Antonio." Z. T. Fulmore's work entitled *The History & Geography of Texas as Told in County Names*, published in 1926, tells more; a lot more: "This county was named for the Garza family in San Antonio, a family which had been identified with that city for nearly two centuries. On the maternal side they are lineal descendants of Madam Rabaina Betancourt, who came with the first settlers in 1731. Geronimo Garza, the paternal ancestor, came later and married a descendant of Madam Betancourt, and from this marriage sprang a long line of distinguished ancestry, identified throughout the long history of that city with its civil, military and commercial activities, and is now one of the most highly respected and useful connections of the city. Their loyalty to Texas as a province of Spain, a State of Mexico, and of the United States, and the Southern Confederacy, inspired the Legislature of Texas, in 1876, to erect a monument to the memory of the family by naming a county 'Garza.'" There are more than 250 counties in Texas and the information on the vast majority of them that is contained in Z. T. Fulmore's 1926 work is accurate. However, errors have been detected concerning some counties. Thus we should be grateful to Fulmore for his comprehensive write-up on the Garza family of Texas but be cautious in accepting all of it as unshakable fact since many other sources on the history, geography and place names of Texas, which were written after 1926 and had access to Fulmore's lengthy Garza County paragraph, have chosen to merely say that this county was named for "an early pioneer family named Garza." With that caveat in mind, the reader may wish to pursue some of these sources dealing with the history of Texas and San Antonio, which provide information about the Garza family of San Antonio: *Footprints: A History of Garza County and Its People*, Frederick C. Chabot's *With the Makers of San Antonio*, J. A. Rickard's *Brief Biographies of Brave Texans*, Lionel Garza's *Our Family: Garza Vela-Barrera Martinez: From the Roots to the Fruits* and Mrs. Emily B. Cooley's article entitled "A Retrospect of San Antonio," which appeared in the July, 1900 (Vol. 4, No. 1), issue of the *Quarterly of the Texas State Historical Association*. Also, Geronimo Garza, who is mentioned by both Frank H. Gille and

Z. T. Fulmore, appears to be a key figure. William S. Speer's *Encyclopedia of the New West*, published in 1881 contains information about him.

2574 *Gillespie County*

Richard A. Gillespie (–1846)— A native of Kentucky, Gillespie came to the republic of Texas in 1837. Inspired by Texas' success in breaking with Mexico and the dictatorship of Antonio Lopez de Santa Anna (1794–1876), the northern Mexican states of Coahuila, Nuevo Leon and Tamaulipas attempted to divest themselves of ties to Mexico and form the republic of Rio Grande. Gillespie participated in that unsuccessful effort. He also participated in Texas' Plum Creek fight, Somervell expedition and the battle of Walker's Creek. During the United States' Mexican War of 1846 to 1848, Gillespie fought as an officer in the Texas rangers under Colonel John C. Hays (1817–1883). He raised the United States flag at Laredo, proceeded on to Mier but was killed leading a charge on Bishop's palace at Monterrey, Mexico, in September, 1846. This county was created and named in his honor just 17 months later, on February 23, 1848.

2575 *Glasscock County*

George W. Glasscock, Sr. (1810–1879)— A native of Kentucky, Glasscock lived for a time in Springfield, Illinois, and was a partner there with Abraham Lincoln. In 1834 he came to Mexican Texas and participated in combat at the Grass fight and the successful siege of Bexar. He served in the legislature of the state of Texas and was one of the managers of the State Lunatic Asylum (later renamed Austin State Hospital). Glasscock also erected an early Texas flour mill. This county was created and named in his honor on April 4, 1887. It was not named for his son, George W. Glasscock, Jr. (1845–1911), who was a prominent Texan when this county was named.

2576 *Goliad County*

Municipality of Goliad, Texas— This county in southeastern Texas was created by the infant republic of Texas on March 17, 1836, and named for the municipality of Goliad, its county seat. In the late 1990's this municipality had a population of 1,900 but Goliad's importance rests on history, not size. Goliad is one of the oldest towns in Texas. In 1749 a Roman Catholic mission and a *presidio* ("military post" or "fortified settlement") were established here within New Spain (Mexico). The presidio was occupied by Spanish soldiers until the era of the Mexican Revolution. Goliad was not given its present name until 1829, when the Mexican state of Coahuila and Texas changed the settlement's name to *Goliad*, a quasi-anagram of "Hidalgo," the name of Padre Miguel Hidalgo y Costilla (1753–1811), who was a key figure and martyr in leading Mexico to independence from Spain. But Goliad had also achieved historical significance of a distinctly Texan flavor, when this county was created on March 17, 1836. During the Texas Revolution, the Goliad campaign of 1835 culminated in the capture of the presidio at Goliad in October, 1835. In December, 1835, the Goliad Declaration of Independence called for the separation of the Mexican department of Texas into a "free, sovereign, and independent State." This Goliad declaration preceded the Texas Declaration of Independence by 72 days. During the Goliad campaign of 1836, Colonel James W. Fannin (1804–1836) withdrew his troops to Goliad in February, 1836, one month before this county was created. After the county was created, the name Goliad became linked with the Goliad massacre. At the battle of Coleto a number of Texans surrendered and they were marched to Goliad, where they were massacred on March 27, 1836, just ten days after this county had been created.

2577 *Gonzales County*

Municipality of Gonzales and battle of Gonzales, Texas— This county in southeastern Texas was created by the infant republic of Texas on March 17, 1836, and named for the municipality of Gonzales, the present county seat of Gonzales County, and for the battle of Gonzales. Less than six months before this county was created, on October 2, 1835, in first battle of the Texas Revolution, Anglo-American Texans fought against the Mexican army in the battle of Gonzales. That battle was fought at the community of Gonzales, a community which, by the late 1990's had a population of 6,500. The community had been named for Rafael Gonzales (1789–1857).

Rafael Gonzales (1789–1857)— Born at San Fernando de Bexar, the first civil settlement in what is now Texas, Gonzales served in the army of New Spain (Mexico). Starting as a cadet in the presidial company of Nuestra Senora de Loreto, he became second alferez in 1810 and was promoted to first alferez in 1813. On June 3, 1814, he was promoted to second-lieutenant. At the Rio Grande presidio he was promoted to first-lieutenant in 1815 and to captain on May 18, 1818. Throughout this military career, Spanish Mexico had been seething in the revolutionary movement for independence from Spain. On July 3, 1821, Captain Gonzales joined that revolutionary movement and was made a lieutenant-colonel in the Mexican revolutionary army a few months later. Mexico achieved independence on September 27, 1821, and from August 15, 1824, to March 15, 1826, Gonzales was governor of Coahuila and Texas. In 1834 Gonzales was secretary of the comandancia of Coahuila and Texas.

2578 *Gray County*

Peter W. Gray (1819–1874)— A native of Virginia, Gray came to Texas in 1838, studied law, fought Indians, served in Texas' Revolutionary army and was admitted to the bar. He represented Harris County in the lower house of the first legislature of the state of Texas, was later elected to the Texas senate and then as a judge. Following the secession of Texas from the Union, Gray was elected as a Texas representative to the lower house of the congress of the Confederate States of America. He served in that body from February 18, 1862, to February 17, 1864, but lost a bid for reelection to Anthony M. Branch (1823–1867). In the Confederate congress he supported many Texas interests but favored central Confederate control over railroads and favored military conscription (draft). After the Civil War, in 1874, Gray was appointed as a judge of the Texas supreme court but tuberculosis abruptly truncated that career. He died on October 3, 1874, and this county was created on August 21, 1876.

2579 *Grayson County*

Peter W. Grayson (1788–1838)— Grayson was born in Kentucky, while it was still part of the state of Virginia. In the early 1830's he came to Mexican Texas with his slaves and settled a plantation in a colony of Stephen F. Austin's (1793–1836). Grayson was a wealthy man and a lawyer and he assisted Austin in difficulties with the Mexican authorities by securing Austin's release from prison in Mexico City. Grayson was Austin's aide-de-camp at Gonzales in October, 1835, and on May 4, 1836, he was appointed attorney general of the republic of Texas in the ad interim cabinet of President David G. Burnet (1788–1870). In the short remainder of his life,

Grayson was busy. He was sent to Washington, D.C., to seek recognition of Texas and, perhaps, assistance in mediating an end to the war between Texas and Mexico. He accomplished nothing on that trip but after President Samuel Houston (1793–1863) again appointed Grayson as attorney general, Houston sent him to Washington, D.C., again. In July, 1838, possibly because of ill health, Grayson committed suicide. This county was created on March 17, 1846.

2580 *Gregg County*

John Gregg (1828–1864)— A native of Alabama and a graduate of LaGrange College, Gregg studied law before coming to Texas in 1854. He soon became a district court judge here and when Texas seceded from the Union, Gregg was elected as a Texas representative to the provisional congress of the Confederate States of America. Following the battle of First Manassas, Gregg entered the Confederate army and was elected a colonel. Forced to surrender in February, 1862, Gregg was soon released in a prisoner exchange and then promoted to brigadier-general. Seriously wounded in combat at Chickamauga, General Gregg continued to serve during the Wilderness and Overland campaigns of 1864. He was killed in combat near Richmond, Virginia on October 7, 1864. This county was created on April 12, 1873.

2581 *Grimes County*

Jesse Grimes (1788–1866)— A native of North Carolina, Grimes came Mexican Texas about 1827. Under the Mexican government, he was appointed to several civil and military positions but when Anglo-Americans in Texas began Revolutionary activities, Grimes joined the Revolutionary cause. He represented the municipality of Washington at the 1835 Consultation at San Felipe de Austin and was elected a member of the general council of the provisional government of the republic of Texas. He was elected as a representative to the convention of 1836 and was a signer, at that convention, of the Texas Declaration of Independence. Grimes served briefly in the Texas Revolutionary army and was a member of the senate of the first congress of the republic of Texas. After statehood, Grimes served in the first four legislatures of the state of Texas. This county was created on April 6, 1846.

2582 *Guadalupe County*

Guadalupe River— This county in south-central Texas was created on March 30, 1846, by the new state of Texas and named for the Guadalupe River, of southeastern Texas, a 250 mile-long tributary of the San Antonio River. The Guadelupe River was named in 1689, while Texas was part of New Spain (Mexico) by Captain Alonso de Leon (1640–), the governor of Coahuila. A diary entry, made by either Captain de Leon or the Franciscan Fray Damian Massanet, explains the inspiration for the name given to this river: "We gave this river the name of 'Our Lady of Guadalupe,' whom we had brought from Coahuila as our protectress, and whom we had painted on our royal standard." The term "Guadalupe" in Spanish Mexico referred to Saint Mary, the patron saint of Mexico, Our Lady of Guadalupe, the sainted Virgin Mary. There have been numerous reported visions of the Virgin Mary, around the world, but it was the famous vision near Mexico City, New Spain, in December, 1531, which inspired the name Guadalupe to be used for the Virgin Mary in Mexico. The name *Guadalupe* is the European rendering of the name which the Virgin Mary called herself in 1531 during her reported appearance near Mexico City. The audience of this vision was a 51 year old Aztec Indian peasant, named Juan Diego. Diego and his wife had recently been converted to Christianity, when Juan Diego reportedly saw Mary appear on a hillside, near the Aztec religious shrine of Tepeyac. When Juan Diego reported his vision to the Spanish conquistadors, the Aztec phonetics were rendered as *Guadalupe*. Our Lady of Guadalupe was the name of a city and shrine in the Estremadura region in west-central Spain, with which the conquistadors were very familiar. That shrine is, of course, Roman Catholic, but the word *Guadalupe* as used in Spain actually has a Moorish origin. This Arabic name would be translated as "the river of black gravel," and it refers to the river named Guadalopillo in Spain, which passes through coal country. In any event, the 1531 apparition was instrumental in converting Mexicans to Roman Catholicism, and that religion is predominant in Mexico today.

Saint Mary— It is a matter of dogma of the Roman Catholic Church that Saint Mary was the virgin mother of the second person of the Trinity, Jesus Christ. Because she had been selected to be the human mother of God, it was axiomatic that her soul be spotless, free of all sin from the moment of her conception. As the mother of Jesus, Mary is considered preeminent among all saints but the veneration and adoration bestowed upon her are on a lower plane than those reserved for God in three persons, Father, Son and Holy Spirit.

2583 *Hale County*

John C. Hale (–1836)— On April 21, 1836, the battle of San Jacinto was fought by the Texas Revolutionary army against Mexican forces led by Antonio Lopez de Santa Anna (1794–1876). Here, near the western bank of the San Jacinto River, about 900 Texans defeated some 1,200 Mexicans, killing more than 600 of them and capturing most of the others, including Santa Anna. Only nine Texans died in this confrontation, the last battle of the successful Texas Revolution. One of the nine Texans who died here was John C. Hale, in whose honor this county was named when it was created on August 21, 1876. Hale was a native of Maine, who had come to Texas in the early 1830's and settled in what is now Sabine County. He was serving as a first-lieutenant in a company led by Captain Benjamin F. Bryant (1800–1857), when he died, a Texas hero, at San Jacinto.

2584 *Hall County*

Warren D. C. Hall (1788–1867)— A native of North Carolina and a lawyer, Hall participated in Mexico's early efforts to secure independence from Spain. He served in the Mexican Republican army of the North and was a captain in the Gutierrez-Magee expedition in Texas but resigned from the army in disgust at the butchery of prisoners. He came to Texas with a similar expedition in 1817. By the time he returned to Texas in 1835 Mexico had won independence from Spain and Texas now wanted independence from Mexico. Hall was soon involved in that effort. Toward that end, he was a member of the committee of safety at Columbia in 1835. Under the ad interim government of the republic of Texas under President David G. Burnet (1788–1870), Hall was an adjutant-general. This county was created on August 21, 1876.

2585 *Hamilton County*

James Hamilton (1786–1857)— A native of South Carolina and a lawyer, Hamilton served as U.S. army officer during the War of 1812. He was elected to the lower house of the South Carolina legislature and, from 1822 to 1829, he represented South Carolina in the U.S. House of Representatives. Elected as governor of South Carolina in 1830, Hamilton soon gained notoriety for his role in South Carolina's ordinance of

Nullification, which declared certain federal tariffs invalid within South Carolina. Hamilton was given the rank of brigadier-general and command of 27,000 state troops. The stage was set for civil war, but General Hamilton supported an agreement with the federal government which averted it. Hamilton acted as a diplomatic agent for the republic of Texas in Great Britain, France, Belgium and the Netherlands. James Hamilton died on November 15, 1857, and this county in west-central Texas was created and named in his honor in January, 1858. Earlier, on February 2, 1842, Texas had created a Hamilton County in eastern Texas. That county was abolished by the Texas supreme court and no portion of it embraced land of the present Hamilton County, Texas.

2586 *Hansford County*

John M. Hansford (–1844) — Hansford came to Texas from Kentucky in 1837 and was soon elected to the congress of the republic of Texas. He served in both the third and fourth congresses and was speaker of the house in the third congress. Hansford later served as a judge and it was as a result of his judicial activities during the "Wild West" days of early Texas that he was both impeached and, somewhat later, murdered. Both the impeachment and the murder were associated with a feud known as the Regulator Moderator war. This county was created on August 21, 1876.

2587 *Hardeman County*

Bailey Hardeman (1795–1836) & Thomas J. Hardeman (1788–1854) — This county was created on February 1, 1858, and named for the Hardeman brothers, Bailey and Thomas J. Hardeman, who had come to Texas from Tennessee.

Bailey Hardeman (1795–1836) — Born in Tennessee, while it was still a territory, Bailey Hardeman was a lawyer and an army officer during the War of 1812. He came to Texas with his brother, Thomas J. Hardeman, in 1835. Here Bailey was elected as a delegate to the convention of 1836 and was a member of the committee which drafted the Texas Declaration of Independence. He also was a signer of that historic document. Bailey served in the cabinet of President David G. Burnet (1788–1870) as secretary of the treasury in the ad interim government of the republic of Texas.

Thomas J. Hardeman (1788–1854) — Born in western North Carolina near what is now Nashville, Tennessee, on January 31, 1788, Hardeman served as an army officer during the War of 1812 and was a captain, quartermaster and colonel. In 1835 Thomas J. Hardeman immigrated with his brother, Bailey, to Texas. Here he represented Matagorda County in the second congress of the republic of Texas and also held several judicial posts. After Texas became a member of the United States of America, Thomas J. Hardeman served in the state legislature. He died on January 15, 1854.

2588 *Hardin County*

Augustine B. Hardin (1797–1871), Benjamin W. Hardin (1796–1850), Franklin Hardin (1803–1878), Milton A. Hardin (–) & William Hardin (1801–1839) — This county was created on January 22, 1858, and named for the five Hardin brothers, sons of Swan Hardin and Jerusha Blackburn Hardin. All of them were born in Georgia. The family moved to Tennessee in 1807 and the five Hardin brothers came to Mexican Texas in 1825.

Augustine B. Hardin (1797–1871) — Augustine B. Hardin was prominent in the early efforts of Anglo-Americans in Texas to become independent from Mexico. He was a member of the Consultation of 1835. Elected as a delegate to the convention of 1836 he there became a signer of Texas Declaration of Independence.

Benjamin W. Hardin (1796–1850) — Benjamin Hardin served in the ninth congress of the republic of Texas and also was a sheriff for a number of years.

Franklin Hardin (1803–1878) — Franklin Hardin was secretary of the ayuntamiento ("town council") at Liberty in Mexican Texas. Employed as a surveyor when the Texas Revolution began, he enlisted in the army, fought at the all-important battle of San Jacinto, the concluding action of the Texas Revolution, and attended to the humane treatment of Mexican prisoners taken in that battle. He later served as a member of the legislature of the state of Texas.

Milton A. Hardin (–) — Milton Ashley Hardin was born in Georgia shortly before his parents and brothers moved to Tennessee in 1807. He came to Mexican Texas with his four brothers in 1825 and lived first on the Trinity River in eastern Texas. He later moved to the community of Cleburne in central Texas and was prominent there. His year of death is given in one account as 1894 and in another as 1898.

William Hardin (1801–1839) — Here in Mexican Texas William Hardin was made

the *alcalde*, or "leading personage." He was a delegate to the Convention of 1833 and later served as a judge.

2589 *Harris County*

Former community of Harrisburg, Texas — This county was originally created on March 17, 1836, and named Harrisburg County, for the settlement within its borders. That community had been laid out by Francis W. Johnson (1799–1884), who was employed by John R. Harris (1790–1829). The community of Harrisburg was named for John R. Harris (1790–1829) and when the county was created in 1836 it was named Harrisburg County, for the community. On December 28, 1839, the republic of Texas changed this county's name from Harrisburg County to Harris County. The municipality of Harrisburg was annexed in 1926 to the city of Houston, the county seat of Harris County, Texas. Early Harrisburg had a small sawmill and timber cut there was shipped by water to ports in the United States and Mexico. On April 16, 1836, Mexico's Antonio Lopez de Santa Anna (1794–1876) burned virtually all of Harrisburg but the settlement was rebuilt, incorporated on June 5, 1837, and consolidated with nearby Hamilton in 1839.

John R. Harris (1790–1829) — A native of New York, and an officer in the War of 1812, Harris became acquainted with Stephen F. Austin's father, Moses Austin (–1821). Apparently inspired by the elder Austin's enthusiasm, Harris came to Mexican Texas in 1824, as one of the very early Anglo-American settlers here. He obtained title to a league of land from the Mexican government and erected his home on the peninsula between two bayous within what is now Harris County. Harris also built a store and warehouse and he employed Francis W. Johnson (1799–1884) to lay out the town of Harrisburg. In collaboration with a brother, Harris built another trading post in the Brazos River and was beginning to prosper shipping cotton to New Orleans when he died of yellow fever on a trip to that city in August, 1829.

2590 *Harrison County*

Jonas Harrison (1777–1836) — A native of New Jersey and a lawyer, Harrison was an early Anglo-American settler in Mexican Texas. He arrived in Texas in 1820 and in 1828 he was the *alcalde*, or "leading personage" of his locality here. Harrison was an early and vigorous participant in events leading to the Texas Revolution.

He was a member of the convention of 1832 and in 1835 his San Augustine resolutions called for immediate independence from Mexico. Harrison also recruited soldiers for the Revolutionary army of Texas. He died on August 6, 1836, and this county was created and named in his honor by the republic of Texas on January 28, 1839.

2591 Hartley County

Oliver C. Hartley (1823–1859) & Rufus K. Hartley (–)— This county in northwestern Texas was created on August 21, 1876, and named for the Hartley brothers, Oliver and Rufus, Texas attorneys and court reporters of the Texas supreme court.

Oliver C. Hartley (1823–1859)— A native of Pennsylvania and an 1841 graduate of Franklin & Marshall College there, Hartley studied law and was admitted to the bar before coming to Texas in 1846. He promptly enlisted as a private in the U.S. army to serve in the Mexican War and was soon promoted to lieutenant but his military career truncated before the end of 1846. He practiced law and compiled a Digest of the Texas Laws, which was published in 1850. He also served in the Texas legislature and was a court reporter for the Texas supreme court, as was his brother Rufus K. Hartley. At the time of his death, Oliver C. Hartley was serving as a court reporter.

Rufus K. Hartley (–)— According to one account, Rufus K. Hartley came to Texas with his brother, Oliver C. Hartley (1823–1859) in 1846, but that account is suspect for it contains other statements which are known to be in error. We do know that Rufus K. Hartley was an early Texas attorney and that he became a court reporter for the Texas supreme court on May 31, 1854, and that he served in that position, as did his brother Oliver, until Oliver's death in 1859.

2592 Haskell County

Charles R. Haskell (1817–1836)— During the Texas Revolution, soldiers under the command of James W. Fannin (1804–1836) fought at the battle of Coleto in early March, 1836. Fannin's entire force was captured and marched to Goliad, Texas. There, about 90 percent of the Texas soldiers were massacred on March 27, 1836. This tragic event is known as the Goliad massacre. Among those who perished in this brutality was Charles Ready Haskell, a native of Tennessee, who left school when he heard of the Texas Revolution

and came to Nacogdoches, Texas, to aid the Revolutionary cause. This county was created and named in his honor on February 1, 1858. The county's name was suggested by John Henry Brown (1820–1895).

2593 Hays County

John C. Hays (1817–1883)— A native of Tennessee, Hays came to the republic of Texas in its infancy and served as a surveyor for the republic. In those days most Texas surveyors had to double as Indian fighters from time to time and Hays was one of them. He became a captain in the Texas Rangers and achieved some notable victories in combat with the much-feared Comanche Indians. During America's Mexican War, Hays served as a colonel and fought with distinction at Monterrey, Mexico and Mexico City. Soon after that war, Hays joined the California gold rush and he remained there to serve as sheriff of San Francisco County and surveyor-general of the state. He became a prominent and wealthy politician in the San Francisco Bay area. This county was created on March 1, 1848, at the end of the Mexican War.

2594 Hemphill County

John Hemphill (1803–1862)— A native of South Carolina and a lawyer, Hemphill came to Texas during the early years of the republic of Texas. He soon became a member of the supreme court of the republic and on January 22, 1842, he became its chief justice. After Texas was annexed to the United States, Hemphill was named chief justice of the state supreme court. Elected as a states' rights Democrat to the U.S. Senate, Hemphill left that body in 1861 to represent Texas in the provisional congress of the Confederate States of America. He died in January, 1862, before the end of that provisional congress. This county was created on August 21, 1876.

2595 Henderson County

James P. Henderson (1808–1858)— A native of North Carolina and a lawyer, Henderson came to Texas to assist in the Texas Revolution and was active in troop recruitment. Appointed by President Samuel Houston (1793–1863) to the cabinet of the republic of Texas, Henderson served as both secretary of state and attorney general. He also served the republic as a diplomat in England and France and was an envoy to the United States in arranging the annexation of Texas. When Texas was

admitted to statehood, James Pinckney Henderson was elected as the first governor of the "Lone Star State" of the United States. He served as brigadier and major-general during the Mexican War of 1846–1848 and was awarded a sword for gallantry at the battle of Monterrey, Mexico. Elected to represented Texas in the U.S. Senate, Henderson took his seat in that body in frail health on March 1, 1858, and died three months later. This county was created on April 27, 1846, while Henderson was serving as the first governor of the state of Texas.

2596 Hidalgo County

Miguel Hidalgo y Costilla (1753–1811)— Born near Guanajuato, Mexico, on May 8, 1753, Hidalgo was educated to be a Roman Catholic priest and he was ordained in 1779. As a priest, Padre Hidalgo attended to the spiritual needs of his Mexican parishioners in the village of Dolores and introduced them to a various forms of industry. Meanwhile Padre Hidalgo was avidly reading accounts of the French Revolution and was suspected by Spanish authorities of having revolutionary thoughts for Mexico. They were right. By 1808, events on the European continent had removed King Carlos IV (1748–1819) from the throne of Spain and made France's Joseph Bonaparte (1768–1844) the ruler of Spain. Various Latin American colonies declared themselves unwilling to accept a French ruler. Mexico was among this group and Mexicans such as Padre Hidalgo engaged in activities which were the prelude to a bid for independence from all European domination. Hidalgo led several hundred of his parishioners in the September 16, 1810, seizure of a prison at Dolores, Mexico, which began what was, in fact, the revolution against Spanish and Creole rule of Mexico. Hidalgo's forces ranged as far west as Guadalajara, Mexico, and then returned to capture Mexico City. That capital was ill-defended and had Hidalgo attacked, his forces might have taken it; however, instead of advancing on Mexico City, Hidalgo turned north when he reached a mountain road overlooking the city. In March, 1811, Hidalgo was captured by trickery, degraded from the priesthood and executed. The date on which he was shot and killed was either July 31 or August 1, 1811. Hidalgo's actions had set in motion forces which would continue to propel Mexico toward independence which was finally achieved on September 27, 1821. Hidalgo County, Texas, was created on January 24, 1852.

2597 *Hill County*

George W. Hill (1814–1860) — A native of Tennessee, Hill attended Transylvania University in Kentucky and graduated from that institution with a degree in medicine. Dr. Hill came to Texas in 1836 and was prominent in the early affairs of the republic of Texas. He served as a surgeon at Fort Houston and was a member of four congresses of the republic. In the cabinet of President Samuel Houston (1793–1863), Hill served as secretary of war and marine and he continued in that position under President Anson Jones (1798–1858). This county was created on February 7, 1853, while Dr. George W. Hill was practicing medicine near Dawson, Texas. The county's name was proposed by Roger Q. Mills (1832–1911). According to Wyvonne Putman's *Navarro County History*, Dr. Hill owned slaves. "…since the slaves were buried in the family cemetery it is evident that he regarded them as his family."

2598 *Hockley County*

George W. Hockley (1802–1854) — A native of Pennsylvania and an acquaintance of Samuel Houston (1793–1863), Hockley came to Texas in 1835 and when Houston became commander-in-chief of the Texas army, he appointed Hockley as chief of staff. At the all-important battle of San Jacinto, the concluding action of the Texas Revolution, Hockley was a senior officer in command of artillery. He later served as secretary of war and marine in the cabinet of President Houston's second administration. This county was created on August 21, 1876.

2599 *Hood County*

John B. Hood (1831–1879) — A native of Kentucky and an 1853 graduate of the U.S. Military Academy at West Point, Hood served as a junior officer in the U.S. army in California and Texas and was a first-lieutenant when he resigned to join the Confederate army in 1861. He entered the Fourth Texas infantry and served with distinction during the Civil War. Hood was severely wounded at the battle of Gettysburg and he lost a leg to combat at Chickamauga but he shot like a rocket through the officer ranks to full general (four stars). He later lost one star and was a lieutenant-general when combat ended. This county was created and named in General Hood's honor on November 3, 1865, seven months after the Civil War ended.

2600 *Hopkins County*

David Hopkins (1825–) & members of his family — This county in northeastern Texas was created on March 25, 1846, and named for David Hopkins and members of his family of Texas pioneers. The Hopkins were early settlers of this section of Texas. David was born in Indiana and brought by his parents to the present Lamar County, Texas, near Indian territory, in 1840. During the winter of 1843–1844 David moved south just a few miles and settled in what is now Hopkins County, Texas. Here David Hopkins married Anne Hargrave in 1846. In his work entitled *The History & Geography of Texas as Told in County Names*, Z. T. Fulmore mentions several other early Texas settlers named Hopkins and implies that they were members of the same family for whom this county was named. Fulmore is probably correct because the Hopkins whom he mentions also settled in this same region of northeastern Texas. Fulmore's additions are: James Elliott (Ell) Hopkins, and the large family of his father, Frank Hopkins. Fulmore also lists A. J. Hopkins and James Hopkins' sister, Isabella, and her husband, James Clark. The act that created this county named James E. Hopkins as a commissioner. Celia M. Wright's *Sketches from Hopkins County History* also mentions "Eldridge and Eli Hopkins, cousins." (Apparently this Eli Hopkins was the same man as James E. Hopkins because later Wright mentions "Captain James Eli Hopkins" as a cousin of Eldridge Hopkins.) Gladys St. Clair's *A History of Hopkins County, Texas* refers to Eldridge Hopkins as a brother of "Dave." That work indicates that this county was named for either Eldridge or David and members of his family.

2601 *Houston County*

Samuel Houston (1793–1863) — A native of Virginia, Houston moved with his family to Tennessee when he was about 14 years old. After serving in the U.S. army in actions against the Indians, he studied law, became active in politics and was elected to represent Tennessee in the U.S. house of representative. He later served as governor of Tennessee. In 1829 Governor Houston married Eliza Allen, but Mrs. Houston left him to return to her parents before the marriage was four months old. This event was traumatic for Houston and it proved to be a turning point in his life. He resigned as Tennessee's governor and moved to Indian country, where he lived for half a dozen years. It was not until 1835

that Sam Houston's name became firmly associated with Texas and her history. In November, 1835, he was made a major-general in the army of the provisional government of the republic of Texas. In early March, 1836, when Texas formally seceded from Mexico and officially declared itself an independent republic, Houston was named commander-in-chief of the new republic's army. The Mexican army responded immediately with force and brutality. A large force of the Mexican army defeated and massacred a much smaller force of Texan defenders of the Alamo. However, it was not long after that infamous event that Texas, under Sam Houston's command, turned the tide and defeated the Mexicans at the battle of San Jacinto. Houston was elected on two occasions as president of the republic of Texas and later, when Texas became a member of the United States, he was one of the new state's first two U.S. senators. He subsequently was elected governor of the state of Texas but when Texas seceded from the Union, Houston refused to take an oath of loyalty to the Confederate States of America and he was deposed as Texas' governor. This county was created on June 12, 1837, during Houston's first administration as president of the republic of Texas.

2602 *Howard County*

Volney E. Howard (1809–1889) — A native of Maine and a lawyer, Howard lived for a time in Mississippi and served in that state's legislature before moving to New Orleans and then to Texas. Here he was a member of the convention of 1845, which approved the offer of annexation to the United States and drafted the state's constitution. He served in the lower house of the first state legislature of Texas and from 1849 to 1853 Howard represented Texas in the U.S. House of Representatives. Defeated in a bid for reelection, Howard moved on to California and was active there as a lawyer and judge. This county was created on August 21, 1876.

2603 *Hudspeth County*

Claude B. Hudspeth (1877–1941) — A native of Texas and a jack of all trades, Hudspeth worked as a cowboy, peace officer and editor of a rural newspaper. He later engaged in cattle trading and owned several ranches. Elected to the lower house of the Texas legislature, Hudspeth served in that body from 1902 to 1906 and then in the Texas senate for a dozen years ending in 1918. He was elected president of the Texas senate on four occasions and while serving in the senate he studied law and was admitted to the bar. Elected to represent Texas in the U.S. House of Representatives in 1918, he served a dozen years in that body from 1919 to 1931. This county was created on February 16, 1917, while Claude B. Hudspeth was a member of the Texas senate.

2604 *Hunt County*

Memucan Hunt (1807–1856)— This North Carolina native volunteered his services to the republic of Texas. Although the battle of San Jacinto had already been fought and won, Texas feared an invasion from Mexico and Hunt was appointed as a brigadier-general, with the promise of promotion to major-general if the war resumed. He served as minister to the United States to secure recognition of the republic of Texas and, later, to persuade the United States to annex Texas. He succeeded in the first mission but was premature with the annexation proposal. Hunt subsequently served in the cabinet of the republic of Texas as secretary of the navy and after annexation he served in Texas' state legislature. This county was created on April 11, 1846.

2605 *Hutchinson County*

Anderson Hutchinson (–1853)—Anderson Hutchinson was born in Virginia. *The Handbook of Texas*, published by the Texas State Historical Association lists his year of birth as 1798 but Z. T. Fulmore's *The History & Geography of Texas as Told in County Names* tells us he was born in 1805. Hutchinson practiced law in several southern states and in collaboration with Volney E. Howard (1809–1889), he compiled *A Digest of the Laws of Mississippi*. He came to Texas in 1840, practiced law and was appointed judge of the fourth (or western) district of the republic of Texas. Known as a legal scholar, Hutchinson also compiled a code of Texas law. Although it was never published under his name, it doubtless served as a key source in later compilations of Texas law. In 1842, while holding court at San Antonio, Judge Hutchinson was taken prisoner by a raiding party of the Mexican army and held prisoner some seven months. Having had enough of the "Wild West" of Texas, Hutchinson resigned as a judge and moved to Mississippi, where he published the *Mississippi Code*. This county was created and named in Judge Hutchinson's honor on August 21, 1876, and his widow was

granted 640 acres of Texas land on account of his seven month detention in the Mexican prison fortress of Perote.

2606 *Irion County*

Robert A. Irion (1806–)—A native of Tennessee and a graduate of Transylvania University in Kentucky with a degree in medicine, Irion practiced as a physician in Mississippi before coming to Mexican Texas in 1832. Here he abandoned his medical profession to work as a land trader and surveyor. In 1835 the Mexican government awarded him extensive land in Coahuila and Texas for enlisting in the Mexican army and recruiting soldiers. That land grant was rescinded by the republic of Texas and Irion returned to the practice of medicine. In the Texas Revolution he was a partisan on the Anglo-American side and served on the committee of safety and vigilance at Nacogdoches. Irion was a member of the senate of the republic of Texas and served as secretary of state of the republic in the cabinet of the first administration of President Samuel Houston (1793–1863). He was also a rival of President Houston's in romance and Irion bested him by winning the hand of Anna Raguet (1819–1883). Dr. Irion died in 1860 or 1861. Irion County was created and named in his honor on March 7, 1889.

2607 *Jack County*

Patrick C. Jack (1808–1844) & William H. Jack (1806–1844)—This county in northern Texas was created on August 27, 1856, and named for the Jack brothers, Patrick C. and William H., natives of Georgia, who were prominent in the early history of Texas.

Patrick C. Jack (1808–1844)—Patrick C. Jack was a lawyer who came to Mexican Texas in 1830 and was active in early Anglo-American efforts to secure independence for Texas from Mexico. He was a delegate from the Liberty district to the conventions of 1832 and 1833 and a member of the lower house of the congress of the republic of Texas. Patrick C. Jack later served as district attorney of two judicial districts of the republic of Texas before dying of yellow fever.

William H. Jack (1806–1844)—An 1827 graduate of the University of Georgia and a lawyer, William H. Jack came to Mexican Texas in 1830. Early in the Texas Revolution, in 1834, he was elected to a local committee of safety and correspondence, and later he fought at the all-important battle of San Jacinto, the concluding ac-

tion of the Texas Revolution. In the ad interim government of the republic of Texas William H. Jack served as secretary of state in the cabinet of President David G. Burnet (1788–1870). He also served in both houses of the congress of the republic.

2608 *Jackson County*

Former municipality of Jackson, Texas— The majority of sources dealing with the history, geography and place names of Texas state that this county was named for Andrew Jackson (1767–1845) and it is true that this county's name honors President Jackson. However it does so indirectly. When it was part of Mexico, the area that now comprises Jackson County, Texas, was one of Stephen F. Austin's (1793–1836) colonies. In 1834 the legislature of Mexico's Coahuila and Texas created a municipality here named Matagorda. On December 5, 1835, the Anglo-American provisional government of the republic of Texas declared Matagorda to be a municipality of the republic and renamed it Jackson, in honor Andrew Jackson, who was then president of the United States. On March 17, 1836, the municipality of Jackson was made Jackson County by the ad interim government of the republic of Texas.

Andrew Jackson (1767–1845)—Jackson was born on the border of North Carolina and South Carolina. He represented Tennessee in both branches of the U.S. Congress. He gained fame and popularity for his military exploits in wars with the Indians and in the War of 1812. He was provisional military governor of Florida and, from 1829 to 1837, General Jackson was president of the United States. His presidency reflected the frontier spirit of America.

2609 *Jasper County*

William Jasper (–1779)—This hero of America's Revolutionary War was born in South Carolina about 1750, but moved to Georgia where he grew up on a farm. He first became a hero in a dramatic event at the battle of Fort Moultrie, when he courageously exposed himself to enemy fire to recover a flag which had been shot down. For this heroism Sergeant Jasper was awarded a sword and offered a promotion to lieutenant but he declined the promotion. Later employed as a scout, Jasper made several trips behind enemy lines in Georgia while operating from the swamps there. In a dramatic exploit near Savannah,

Georgia, he and his close friend, John Newton, rescued several Americans who were prisoners and took their guards as prisoners of war. Jasper was shot and killed during the siege of Savannah while recovering the flag which had been shot down. Geographic names in several of our states link the names of the two heroic sergeants, Jasper and Newton. In some states a county is named for one of them and its county seat is named for the other. In others, like Texas, two counties are named for them. Jasper County, Texas, was created on March 17, 1836, and Newton County, Texas, was created a decade later, in 1846, from the eastern half of Jasper County. These two counties sit side by side to this day in extreme eastern Texas.

2610 *Jeff Davis County*

Jefferson Davis (1808–1889) — A native of Kentucky, Davis moved with his family to Mississippi when he was a small boy. He graduated from the U.S. military academy at West Point and served as an officer in the Black Hawk and Mexican Wars. He represented Mississippi in both houses of the United States congress where he was a spokesman for the South, states' rights and strict construction of the constitution. U.S. President Franklin Pierce appointed Davis to his cabinet as secretary of war and he served in that position from 1853 to 1857. In February, 1861, Jefferson Davis was inaugurated as president of the Confederate States of America. He was the first and only president of the Confederacy, and he served in that post until the end of the Civil War in 1865. This Texas county was created on March 15, 1887. Fort Davis, within its borders, was established while Jefferson Davis (1808–1889) was the U.S. secretary of war and the fort was named for Jefferson Davis. However Texas sources consulted are unanimous in their opinion that this county was named directly for Jefferson Davis, rather than for Fort Davis.

2611 *Jefferson County*

Town of Jefferson, Texas — This county was created on March 17, 1836, as one of the original 23 counties of the republic of Texas. It was named for the municipality of Jefferson, Texas. The original 23 counties of Texas have grown to more than 250 counties today, so county boundaries have shifted considerably. Today Jefferson, Texas, is within Marion County, Texas and not even particularly near Jefferson County. Anglo-Americans settled in what would soon become the town of Jefferson in 1832

at Smith Landing on Big Cypress Bayou. The *Texas Tour Book*. published by AAA in 1998 tells us that "Jefferson was once the state's largest city and inland port." The town of Jefferson was given its present name, in honor of U.S. President Thomas Jefferson, in 1836, just a few weeks before Jefferson County was created by the republic of Texas. In the late 1990's Jefferson, Texas had a population of just 2,200.

Thomas Jefferson (1743–1826) — Jefferson was a native of Virginia and a member of the Virginia legislature. He served Virginia as governor and was a delegate to the second Continental Congress. Jefferson was the author of the Declaration of Independence and one of its signers. He was minister to France, secretary of state, vice-president and president of the United States. As president, he accomplished the Louisiana Purchase and he arranged the Lewis & Clark Expedition to the Pacific Northwest. Jefferson was a true intellectual, thoroughly knowledgeable in the arts and sciences. His political theories were pivotal in the formation of the infant United States.

2612 *Jim Hogg County*

James S. Hogg (1851–1906) — A native a Texas, lawyer and newspaperman, Hogg served as county attorney and district attorney in northeastern Texas before his 1886 election on the Democratic party ticket as attorney general of Texas. Reelected to that position in 1888, Hogg ran for the governor's office in 1890 and, by a lopsided 3 to 1 margin, beat his Republican opponent Webster Flanagan (1832–1924) to become the first Texas-born governor of the state. He served as governor from 1891 to 1895, instituted several reforms and promoted the state's universities and teachers' colleges. After leaving office he continued to support the Democratic party and campaigned on behalf of William Jennings Bryan (1860–1925) during his bids for the presidency in 1896 and 1900. This county was created on March 31, 1913.

2613 *Jim Wells County*

James B. Wells, Jr. (–1923) — Born in Texas in the early 1850's (one source shows 1850; two others say 1854), Wells graduated in 1875 from the University of Virginia with a degree in law. In 1878 he established a law partnership in Brownsville, Texas, with Stephen Powers (1814–1882) and Wells remained a resident of Brownsville for the rest of his life. Brownsville is

the southernmost municipality in Texas and it sits on the Rio Grande River across from Matamoros, Mexico. During the 19th century, relations between Brownsville and Matamoros were marked by banditry and battles. James B. Wells, Jr., made it his business to improve relations between Mexicans and Anglo-Americans in the Brownsville area. As an attorney, he successfully fought to protect valid land titles in Texas which had been granted earlier by Spanish and Mexican authorities. Noting the decline of the Roman Catholic church since the Mexican War, Wells became a Catholic convert and worked to regenerate the church in this area. When Wells' business partner, Stephen Powers, died in 1882, Wells filled some of the resulting void in political leadership here and he also served as a judge, but only for 14 months. In 1904 Wells used his influence to minimize bloodshed when violence erupted between Mexicans and Anglo-Americans here. This county was created on March 25, 1911.

2614 *Johnson County*

Middleton T. Johnson (–1866) — Johnson was born in South Carolina and lived in both Georgia and Alabama before coming to the republic of Texas in 1839 or 1840. In Alabama he served in the state legislature and here he was a member of the ninth congress of the republic. Johnson fought during the Mexican War of 1846–1848, was an officer in the Texas Rangers and an unsuccessful candidate for governor in 1851, when he ran against the incumbent Peter H. Bell (1812–1898). Active in the development of the Ft. Worth and Tarrant County area of Texas, Johnson was employed by the Southern Pacific Railway to survey a route on the western side of Ft. Worth. He subsequently was a member of the Texas secession convention and recruited troops for the Confederate army during the Civil War. This county was created on February 13, 1854. It lies just south of Ft. Worth, in the area of Texas that Johnson was active in developing.

2615 *Jones County*

Anson Jones (1798–1858) — A native of Massachusetts and a college graduate with a degree in medicine, Jones drifted to Brazoria in Mexican Texas in 1833 and established a successful medical practice here. As Anglo-Americans in Texas began agitating for independence from Mexico, Jones cautiously joined the movement and he signed a petition calling for the Consultation of 1835, which he visited. He served as an army surgeon in the all important battle of San Jacinto, the concluding action of the Texas Revolution, but insisted on serving with the rank of private. Jones served in the congress of the republic of Texas and as minister from the republic to the United States of America. Upon returning to Texas he was elected as a senator and was president pro-tempore of that body during the republic's fifth congress. Unable to break with politics and devote himself to medicine, Jones was appointed secretary of state in the cabinet of President Samuel Houston's (1793–1863) second administration and on December 9, 1844, Anson Jones succeeded Houston as president of the republic of Texas. Elected for a three year term, Jones made short work of that assignment by securing Mexican acknowledgment of the independence of Texas and annexation by the United States of Texas, effective December 29, 1845. In 1857 Jones hoped (and expected) to be elected to represent Texas in the U.S. Senate. Greatly disappointed by his failure to receive a single vote from the legislature, he committed suicide on January 9, 1858. This county was created just three weeks later, on February 1, 1858.

2616 *Karnes County*

Henry W. Karnes (1812–1840)— A native of Tennessee, Karnes came to Texas about 1835 and entered Texas' Revolutionary army. He fought at the battle of Concepcion and in the successful siege of Bexar. He later held the rank of captain and served as a scout during the Goliad campaign and prior to the crucial battle of San Jacinto. Information supplied by Karnes about the location of enemy forces was of great importance to the Texas army. Sent to Mexico to exchange prisoners, Karnes was himself imprisoned there but soon managed to escape. After the Texas Revolution Karnes served as an Indian fighter. This county was created on February 4, 1854.

2617 *Kaufman County*

David S. Kaufman (1813–1851)— A native of Pennsylvania and a lawyer, Kaufman came to Texas in 1837 and was elected the following year to the lower house of the congress of the republic of Texas. Twice reelected to that body, he also served as speaker of the house, a member of the senate of the republic and charge d'affaires

of the republic of Texas to the United States of America. When Texas was annexed to the United States and became its 28th state, Kaufman became one of the new state's first two representatives in congress. Kaufman served in that body from 1846 until his death on January 31, 1851. This county was created on February 26, 1848, while Kaufman was representing the state of Texas in the U.S. Congress.

2618 *Kendall County*

George W. Kendall (1809–1867)— A native of New Hampshire, printer and newspaperman, Kendall was one of the founders of the New Orleans *Picayune*. He joined the Santa Fe expedition, was captured and held prisoner in Mexico and wrote a well received account of those experiences. During the Mexican War of 1846–1848, Kendall covered the war as a journalist and sent his accounts to the *Picayune* by pony express. After that war he moved to Texas but traveled widely, attending to his newspaper in New Orleans and taking a wife while on a trip to Europe. In 1857 Kendall bought a sheep ranch within the present Kendall County, Texas. He took an oath of allegiance to the Confederate States of America and gave aid and comfort to the families of Confederate soldiers, who were away from home during the Civil War. This county was created on January 10, 1862, while Texas was a member state of the Confederacy.

2619 *Kenedy County*

Mifflin Kenedy (1818–1895)— Born in Pennsylvania with a spirit for adventure, Kenedy managed to sail to India as a cabin boy before turning his attention to river navigation. He held a variety of positions for steamboat companies and served as a steamboat captain for the U.S. army during the Mexican War. Kenedy became acquainted with Richard King (1825–1885), the founder of the huge and famous King ranch in Texas. Kenedy became a rancher in Texas and bought a half interest in the huge King ranch from Richard King. Kenedy and King also collaborated in ownership of a large boat fleet on the Rio Grande River and in selling Confederate cotton to European buyers during the Civil War. Kenedy later was an entrepreneur in Texas' infant railroad industry. This county was created on February 2, 1921.

2620 *Kent County*

Andrew Kent (–1836)— In 1836, during the Texas Revolution, the Mexican army

placed the Alamo, in San Antonio, Texas, under siege for 13 days. Inside the Alamo were about 185 Texan defenders, all of whom were slain when the Mexicans stormed the Alamo on the morning of March 6, 1836. Among those who died in that epic confrontation was Private Andrew Kent, a resident of Gonzales, Texas at the time of his death. Kent was born in Kentucky in the late 1790's and came to Mexican Texas with his family about 1828. He settled on a land grant on the Lavaca River. Here he was a farmer and perhaps earned some money as a carpenter, as well. On February 23, 1836, he was mustered into the Gonzales ranging company, arrived at the Alamo on March 1, 1836, and died five days later. This county was created on August 21, 1876.

2621 *Kerr County*

James Kerr (1790–1850)— A native of Kentucky and an army officer during the War of 1812, Kerr served in both houses of the Missouri legislature before coming to Mexican Texas in 1825. One of the early Anglo-American settlers in Texas, Kerr was associated with the colonies of Stephen F. Austin (1793–1836) and Green C. De Witt (1787–1835). He was involved in early efforts to achieve independence for Texas from Mexico and served in the congress of the republic of Texas after independence was achieved. This county was created on January 26, 1856.

2622 *Kimble County*

George C. Kimbell (1803–1836)— In 1836, during the Texas Revolution, the Mexican army placed the Alamo, in San Antonio, Texas under siege for 13 days. Inside the Alamo were about 185 Texan defenders, all of whom were slain when the Mexicans stormed the Alamo on the morning of March 6, 1836. Among those who died in that epic confrontation was Lieutenant George C. Kimbell, a native of Pennsylvania who had come to Texas from New York. Kimbell was a partner in a hat factory at Gonzales, Texas with another martyr of the Alamo, Almeron Dickerson (1810–1836). Kimbell joined the Gonzales ranging company as a lieutenant on February 23, 1836. Four days later he was given supplies to take from Gonzales to the Alamo defenders and Kimbell and others took the supplies to the Alamo, arriving there on March 1, 1836. Kimbell's surname has also been rendered as Kimble and Kimball. When the legislature created this county on January 22, 1858, they chose Kimble for its spelling.

2623 *King County*

William P. King (1820–1836) — In 1836, during the Texas Revolution, the Mexican army placed the Alamo, in San Antonio, Texas under siege for 13 days. Inside the Alamo were about 185 Texan defenders, all of whom were slain when the Mexicans stormed the Alamo on the morning of March 6, 1836. Among those who died in that epic confrontation was Private William P. King, a 15 year old lad who was the youngest martyr of the Alamo. Born in Mexican Texas on October 8, 1820, William Philip King was living about 15 miles north of Gonzales, Texas when he volunteered to take the place of his father, John Gladden King, in the relief force from Gonzales that arrived at the Alamo on March 1, 1836. Young William P. King had persuaded his father, who was about to ride to the Alamo, to let him take his place, so that the father could look after the rest of the King family at Gonzales. Private William P. King (1820–1836) was a rifleman in the Gonzales ranging company when he died at the Alamo. This county was created and named in his honor on August 21, 1876.

2624 *Kinney County*

Henry L. Kinney (–) — Born in Pennsylvania in 1813 or 1814, Kinney came to Texas in the 1830's and established a trading post at Corpus Christi. Here he maintained his own army of some 40 soldiers and is considered to be the founder of Corpus Christi, Texas. Kinney served in the senate of the republic of Texas and was a delegate to the 1845 convention which approved the U.S. offer to annex Texas. After statehood, Kinney was a senator in the state's first four legislatures. In the 1850's he attempted, unsuccessfully, to establish a government in Central America. Upon his return to Texas, Kinney was elected to the state legislature but since he was opposed to secession, he resigned his seat in March, 1861. The year and circumstances surrounding Kinney's death are disputed. This county was created on January 28, 1850.

2625 *Kleberg County*

Robert J. Kleberg (1803–1888) — A native of Germany, Kleberg and his wife arrived in Mexican Texas in a dramatic shipwreck off Galveston Island in December, 1834. Kleberg joined the Revolutionary army of Texas and fought in the all-important battle of San Jacinto, the concluding action of the Texas Revolution. When Texas seceded from the Union, Kleberg was loyal to the Confederate States of American, but he saw no military service during the Civil War. He died near Yorktown, Texas, on October 23, 1888. This county was created on February 27, 1913, and named in honor of Robert J. Kleberg (1803–1888). Both *The Handbook of Texas*, published by the Texas State Historical Association in 1952 and Z. T. Fulmore's *The History & Geography of Texas as Told in County Names* confirm that this man is this county's namesake. However, he had at least two descendants named Robert J. Kleberg, who became prominent because of their association with the famous King Ranch of Texas. The elder of two later Klebergs was Robert J. Kleberg (1853–1932) and since he had a son of the same name, one encounters references to Robert J. Kleberg Sr., which really refer to the middle Robert J. Kleberg (1853–1932), for whom this county was not named.

2626 *Knox County*

Henry Knox (1750–1806) — This Massachusetts native participated in many of the important military engagements of the American Revolution and rose to the rank of major-general. After the war, Knox commanded West Point and he conceived and organized the Society of Cincinnati, an elite group of former Revolutionary officers. In 1785 he was appointed secretary of war under the Articles of Confederation and he retained that position in the first cabinet of the United States under President George Washington. This county was created on February 1, 1858, and recreated (with the same name) in 1876. The vast majority of Texas sources consulted indicate that this county was named directly for Henry Knox (1750–1806) but two Texas sources say that it was named for Knox County, Ohio. That is certainly possible (Knox County, Ohio was created in 1808) and comes down to the same thing because Knox County, Ohio was named in honor of the same Henry Knox (1750–1806).

2627 *La Salle County*

Rene Robert Cavelier, Sieur de la Salle (1643–1687) — A native of Rouen, France, La Salle came to North America about 1667 and engaged in fur trading in Canada and in the Illinois country. In 1682, in company with Henri de Tonty and others, La Salle led an expedition which sailed down the Mississippi River and was the first to trace the Mississippi to its mouth on the Gulf of Mexico. La Salle named this vast area Louisiana and he claimed it for France. La Salle was the name of an estate near Rouen, France which belonged to the Cavelier family. This Texas county was created on February 1, 1858. In 1685 La Salle had visited Texas, which was then part of New Spain (Mexico), and according to some accounts his exploration of Texas gave France a chance to claim Texas for France. Although French explorers continued to visit Texas periodically, France never made a serious effort to wrest Texas from Spain.

2628 *Lamar County*

Mirabeau B. Lamar (1798–1859) — A native of Georgia and a newspaperman, Lamar came to Texas in 1835 and immediately became active in the movement to secure independence for Texas from Mexico. He enlisted as a private in Texas' Revolutionary army and served in command of cavalry at the all-important battle of San Jacinto, the concluding action of the Texas Revolution. In the ad interim government of the republic of Texas, Lamar served in the cabinet of President David G. Burnet (1788–1870) as secretary of war and in the first administration of President Samuel Houston (1793–1863) he was vice-president. Elected as president of the republic in 1838, Lamar served in that office three years, from December 10, 1838, to December 13, 1841. This county was created and named in his honor on December 17, 1840, while he was serving as the republic's president. Lamar viewed proposals for the annexation by the U.S. of Texas with disfavor. In his mind Texas ought to remain independent and extend west and he sought to persuade New Mexicans to accept sovereignty of Texas. Ever the big thinker, Lamar viewed the Pacific Ocean as Texas' manifest western boundary. These grand schemes came to nothing as the financial condition of Texas deteriorated and when President Houston was elected to a second administration, Lamar became a supporter of annexation of Texas by the U.S. In his mind this was essential to the preservation of slavery in Texas. During the Mexican War of 1846–1848 he fought as an officer in the battle of Monterrey, Mexico.

2629 *Lamb County*

George A. Lamb (1814–1836) — On April 21, 1836, the battle of San Jacinto was fought by the Texas Revolutionary army against Mexican forces led by Antonio Lopez de Santa Anna (1794–1876).

Here, near the western bank of the San Jacinto River, about 900 Texans defeated some 1,200 Mexicans, killing more than 600 of them and capturing most of the others, including Santa Anna. Only nine Texans died in this confrontation, the last battle of the successful Texas Revolution. One of the nine who died here was Second-lieutenant George A. Lamb (1014–1836), a native of South Carolina, who had come to Texas in 1834 with Richard Bankhead (–1834) and Bankhead's wife and children. After Bankhead died, Lamb took care of the widow and her children and subsequently married her. He served as an Indian fighter before enlisting in the Revolutionary army as a second-lieutenant under Captain William Ware (1800–1853). Z. T. Fulmore's work entitled *The History & Geography of Texas as Told in County Names* tells us that Lieutenant Lamb was killed at San Jacinto "in the first charge of the Texans." This county was created on August 21, 1876.

2630 *Lampasas County*

Lampasas River—This county in central Texas was created on February 1, 1856, and named for the Lampasas River, which flows through it. The Lampasas is a 100 mile-long stream which unites in central Bell County, just south of Belton, Texas, with the Leon River and Salado Creek to form Little River. The name *Lampasas* is a corrupted version of the Spanish word for "lilies," or "water lilies." which is *lampazos*. Since water lilies are not found along the Lampasas River, at least two Texas sources state that the river owes its name to confusion of early Spanish map makers. Both of these sources agree that the map makers switched the names of two Texas streams, Salado Creek and Lampasas River. *Salado* is a Spanish adjective meaning "salty." However Texas has at least five streams named Salado Creek. Fortunately the two sources which claim that the streams' names were switched specify which Salado Creek was involved in the trade. It is the Salado Creek which merges with the Lampasas and Leon Rivers at Belton, Texas to form Little River.

2631 *Lavaca County*

Lavaca River—This county in southeastern Texas was created on April 6, 1846, and named for the Lavaca River, which flows through it. The 100 mile-long Lavaca River rises here in Lavaca County and flows south into Lavaca Bay, an arm of Matagorda Bay on the Gulf of Mexico. *La vaca* is Spanish and means "the cow," referring to "the female of a bovine animal." However Texas sources consulted are agreed the namers of this river's name had in mind the buffalo and thus they really named it for bison. *Buffalo* is the common but incorrect name given to bison. Great herds of bison roamed in western and central Texas and migrated in certain seasons as far south and east as the Lavaca River. Virtually all of them have been slaughtered. Paul C. Boethel's *History of Lavaca County* states that the river was first named *Les Veches* by French explorers. (Presumably Boethel means *les vaches*, French for "the cows.") Boethel says that the Spanish liked the name well enough to retain it.

2632 *Lee County*

Robert E. Lee (1807–1870)— Lee was a native of Virginia and, for over 30 years, an officer in the United States army. When Virginia seceded from the Union, Lee refused an offer to command all federal forces and resigned from the U.S. army to accept a commission in the Confederate army. He served with distinction in that army and became general-in-chief of it. This county was created on April 14, 1874, shortly after Reconstruction ended in Texas. The name was chosen because of General Lee's Confederate service although he had served in Texas with the U.S. army as a junior officer prior to the Civil War.

2633 *Leon County*

Uncertain— This eastern Texas county was created on March 17, 1846. Sources dealing with the history, geography and place names of Texas offer a variety of explanations for the origin of this county's name but only a handful of them admit that there is any uncertainty about it. Of two dozen sources consulted, nine favor Martin de Leon (1765–1833), five assert that Alonso de Leon (1637–1691) is the namesake and one says that the county was named for a Leon Creek. The other nine sources are more difficult to summarize but six of them attribute the county's name either to Leon Prairie and/or a lion (and/or a yellow wolf) for which the prairie was named. The remaining three sources indicate uncertainty and say that the county was either named for Martin de Leon (1765–1833) or some variation of the Leon Prairie/ lion/ yellow wolf theory.

Alonso de Leon (1637–1691)— Born near what is now Monterrey, in what was then New Spain (Mexico), Alonso de Leon held political and military offices in New Spain and explored what is now Texas. He conducted some five expeditions into Texas, some of which were motivated by a desire to rid the area of French explorers and destroy any forts constructed by the French, thus minimizing the risk of France gaining control of any portion of Texas. Captain Alonso de Leon, together with Padre Damian Massanet (–1694) founded a mission in Texas named San Francisco de los Tejas. Although that mission was soon abandoned, its construction marked the beginning of Spanish settlement in eastern Texas.

Martin de Leon (1765–1833)— Born in Burgos, New Spain (Mexico), Martin de Leon made his early home in the wilderness of Mexico and transported supplies by pack mules to the mines of Real de San Nicolas. Also involved in Indian fighting and ranching in Mexico, Martin de Leon became attracted to the ranching possibilities in Texas and he moved here with his family. He established his first ranch in Texas on the Aransas River, later moved to the Nueces River and still later, to San Antonio. After Mexico gained independence from Spain, Martin de Leon secured permission from the Mexican government to become an impresario and he established what is known as De Leon's colony, with its capital at Guadalupe Victoria. Most of his colonists came from Mexico but others came from Ireland and the United States.

Leon Prairie/ region of the leon or yellow wolf— Each of the sources which cites this as the origin of this county's name has a slightly different twist. *The Handbook of Texas*, published by the Texas State Historical Association in 1952 states that "the county was named for a yellow wolf of the region called the leon," but that Handbook points out that other sources say that the county was named for Martin de Leon. The Spanish word *leon* means "lion." Sources which attribute the county's name to this *leon* generally admit that the *leon* in question was really a "yellow wolf," rather than a true lion. Some of these sources say that this particular leon became memorable because it was killed in this vicinity, others say the *leon* was the attacker and one source mentions an entry in a diary of a Spanish expedition to Texas in 1689 which discovered a dead lion, very much mutilated.

2634 *Liberty County*

Villa de la Santissima Trinidad de la Libertad—This county was created by the republic of Texas on March 17, 1836, two weeks after the adoption of the Texas Declaration of Independence from Mexico. It is tempting to attribute this county's name to a reflection of the desire of Texas to be free of, or liberated from, Mexico. The actual origin of this county's name is less romantic. In 1831, five years before Texas declared independence from Mexico, a municipality had been established here named *Villa de la Santissima Trinidad de la Libertad*. An English translation of that Spanish name is "Town of the Most Holy Trinity of Liberty." The reference to "Holy Trinity" was probably inserted in the name of the municipality because of the requirement that foreigners wishing to colonize Mexican Texas "profess the Roman Catholic apostolic religion, the established religion of the empire." Anglo-Americans shortened the name of this community to "Liberty," and it became the county seat of Liberty County, when it was created.

2635 *Limestone County*

Descriptive of limestone found here— This county in east-central Texas was created on April 11, 1846, and named for the limestone in it. Limestone is a hard rock formed by deposits of organic materials, such as seashells. It consists mostly of calcium carbonate. Ray A. Walter's *A History of Limestone County* mentions "huge limestone rocks" seen by Spanish traders traveling through the area.

2636 *Lipscomb County*

Abner S. Lipscomb (1789–1856)— A native of South Carolina and a lawyer, Lipscomb was a member of the legislature of Alabama territory and a circuit court judge in the state of Alabama. In 1823 Lipscomb was elevated to chief justice of the Alabama supreme court and he was a member of that body for eleven years. In 1839 he came to the republic of Texas and served as secretary of state in the cabinet of President Mirabeau B. Lamar (1798–1859). He later was a member of the convention of 1845, which approved the offer of annexation to the United States and drafted the state's constitution. Appointed in 1846 to the supreme court of the state of Texas by Governor James P. Henderson (1808–1858), Lipscomb served on that court for a number of years. This county was created on August 21, 1876.

2637 *Live Oak County*

Oak trees in the area— This county in southern Texas was created on February 2, 1856, and named for the abundant oak trees in the area. Z. T. Fulmore's work entitled *The History & Geography of Texas as Told in County Names* tells us "This county takes its name from the trees. It marks the end of the great postoak belt and the beginning of the scattered live oaks, extending up through the lower coastal plain." The term "Live Oak" or "Liveoak" is a popular one in Texas. At least 20 creeks in the state are called Liveoak Creek.

2638 *Llano County*

Llano River— This county in central Texas was created on February 1, 1856, and named for the Llano River, which traverses it. The name *Llano* is a Spanish word meaning "plain," or "flatland" and the river was named for the plains which dominate the landscape near the source of the river. Later, on its 100 mile journey to the Colorado River in southeastern Llano County, the Llano passes through some broken country.

2639 *Loving County*

Oliver Loving (–1867)— Born in Kentucky about 1812, Loving came to the republic of Texas after independence had been won from Mexico. Here he engaged in ranching, farming and hauling freight. In 1855 he moved his herds to northern Texas where he continued to raise cattle and horses but greatly expanded his operations. He gained fame as a pioneer trail driver when he took cattle to points as distant as Illinois and Colorado. During the Civil War Loving supplied the Confederate government with cattle and hogs. In 1866 he formed a partnership with Charles Goodnight (1836–1929) to sell cattle in New Mexico territory. Their trail between Fort Belknap, Texas, and Fort Sumner in New Mexico territory was known as the Goodnight-Loving trail and became one of the Southwest's heavily traveled cattle trails. In the summer of 1867 Loving was traveling to New Mexico territory when he was shot by Indians and he died of gangrene as a result of those wounds. This county was created on February 26, 1887.

2640 *Lubbock County*

Thomas S. Lubbock (1817–1862)— A native of South Carolina, Lubbock was living in New Orleans early in the Texas Revolution and he came to Texas to fight in the successful siege of Bexar. Later, while serving as a lieutenant on the Santa Fe expedition in 1841, he was captured and taken to Mexico as a prisoner but he escaped to serve in the Texas army in the Somervell expedition against Mexico in 1842. During the Civil War Lubbock served in the Confederate army as a lieutenant-colonel and together with Colonel Benjamin F. Terry (1821–1861) formed Terry's Texas Rangers. When Terry was killed in combat on December 17, 1861, Lubbock advanced to command the regiment. However, Thomas S. Lubbock was then ill and he died in January 1862. This county was created and named in his honor on August 21, 1876.

2641 *Lynn County*

William Linn (–1836)— In 1836, during the Texas Revolution, the Mexican army placed the Alamo, in San Antonio, Texas under siege for 13 days. Inside the Alamo were about 185 Texan defenders, all of whom were slain when the Mexicans stormed the Alamo on the morning of March 6, 1836. Among those who died in that epic confrontation was Private William Linn, whose official residence was Boston, Massachusetts when he fell at the Alamo. Linn came to Texas from New Orleans with the New Orleans Greys and participated in the successful siege of Bexar. He may have been taken prisoner in that action but if so he was soon released and remained in San Antonio as a private and rifleman in a company commanded by Captain William Blazeby (1795–1836). Private Linn fought under Captain Blazeby when they both perished at the Alamo. This county was created on August 21, 1876 and the county's name was spelled Lynn. There has been a good deal of difficulty in determining exactly who died at the Alamo and some of the names inscribed on the Alamo monument are incorrect. However, the Alamo inscription for this martyr is correct: "W. Linn." The county's name is spelled wrong.

2642 *McCulloch County*

Ben McCulloch (1811–1862)— A native of Tennessee and a friend of David Crockett (1786–1836), McCulloch came to Texas in time to fight in the all-important battle of San Jacinto, the concluding action of the Texas Revolution. He later served in the congress of the republic of Texas, while remaining active in military actions against Indians and Mexicans. When Texas was annexed by the United States, Ben McCulloch served in the first state legislature of the new state. He later served in the Mexican War of 1846–1848 and when Texas seceded from the Union, McCulloch entered the Confederate army and was commissioned a brigadier-general. He lost his life in combat early in the Civil War. This county was created prior to the Civil War, on August 27, 1856.

2643 McLennan County

Neil McLennan (–1867)— Born in 1787 or 1788 in Scotland, McLennan came to America with his family in 1801. They settled first in North Carolina but then moved on to Florida territory. Neil McLennan came to Texas with several family members in 1835 and several of his relatives were soon killed or captured by Indians. Neil gained employment as a surveyor and some of his early survey work brought him within the present McLennan County, but it was not until 1845 that he built his house within the borders of this county. He erected his house well beyond Anglo-American civilization in Texas, on the South Bosque River, about eight miles from what today is Waco, Texas. This county was created and named in his honor on January 22, 1850.

2644 McMullen County

John McMullen (–1853)— Born in Ireland before 1800, McMullen immigrated to North America and lived in Maryland before moving to Matamoros, Mexico, in the 1820's. At Matamoros McMullen and another Irish native, James McGloin (–1856) decided to establish a colony in Mexico's Coahuila and Texas. Foreigners were permitted under Mexican law to settle here, provided they met certain conditions, primarily that they be Roman Catholics. All or most of McMullen's and McGloin's colonists were Irish who met the religion requirement. Permission to establish a colony was received from the Mexican government in 1828 and a colony was soon established in Mexican Texas. A second colony was planted here, at San Patricio, Texas, about 1830. Early in the movement to secure independence of Anglo-American Texas from Mexico, a general counsel of the provisional government of the republic of Texas was established. McMullen was a member of that counsel and became its president pro-tempore. He later was a merchant and alderman in San Antonio. John McMullen was murdered in January, 1853, and this county was created and named in his honor on February 1, 1858.

2645 Madison County

James Madison (1751–1836)— Madison was born in Virginia and served in the Virginia legislature and in the Continental Congress. He was a member of the convention which framed the U.S. Constitution and he collaborated with Hamilton and Jay in writing a series of papers under the title *The Federalist*, which explained the new constitution and advocated its adoption. Madison represented Virginia in the U.S. House of Representatives, served for eight years as secretary of state and for eight years as president of the United States. A Madison County was created by the republic of Texas on February 2, 1842. That county was one of the so-called judicial counties, which were found to be unconstitutional by the Texas supreme court and abolished. The present Madison County, Texas was created on January 27, 1853.

2646 Marion County

Francis Marion (–1795)— Marion is believed to have been born in South Carolina. He served in the army in battles against the Cherokee Indians and was elected to the provisional congress of 1775. He served, with distinction, as an officer in the Revolutionary War and rose to the rank of general in that war. Marion was also a member of the South Carolina senate. This county was created on February 8, 1860, as the next-to-last county created before Texas seceded from the Union.

2647 Martin County

Wylie Martin (–1842)— Born in Georgia about 1776, Martin served in the U.S. army and had risen to the rank of captain when he killed a man in a duel. Martin resigned his army commission and in the mid-1820's he came to Mexican Texas to start a new life as one of Stephen F. Austin's (1793–1836) colonists. Involved in early efforts to secure separate government for the Anglo-American portion of Mexico (Texas), he was a member of the conventions of 1832, 1833 and the Consultation of 1835 and the general counsel of the provisional government of the republic of Texas. Although Martin considered the Texas Declaration of Independence to be premature, when fighting began, he participated briefly in military action. Elected to the congress of the republic of Texas, Martin arranged for the emancipation of one of his slaves, who had fought in the Texas Revolution. Martin County, Texas was created on August 21, 1876.

2648 Mason County

Fort Mason— This county in central Texas was created on January 22, 1858, and named for a U.S. army post, Fort Mason, within its borders. The fort had been established on July 6, 1851, soon after the Mexican War, by Captain Hamilton Merrill of the U.S. army. It was located eight miles above the confluence of Comanche Creek with the Llano River, within the city limits of the present Mason, Texas. Fort Mason was one of a series of U.S. army posts that stretched across the Texas frontier. Sources consulted differ on the fort's namesake but only two possibilities are mentioned, Lieutenant George T. Mason (–1846) and General Richard B. Mason (1797–1850). The U.S. army ordered Fort Mason abandoned on February 5, 1859, but it was sporadically occupied until March 28, 1861, when the Union army evacuated it with the advent of the Civil War. Subsequently reoccupied, Fort Mason was permanently abandoned in March, 1869. The fort has been partially reconstructed on its original foundations and is located about five blocks south of the courthouse in Mason, Texas.

George T. Mason (–1846)— A second-lieutenant in the Second U.S. dragoons during the Mexican War of 1846–1848, Lieutenant Mason died in combat during that war, near Brownsville, Texas, on April 25, 1846. *Frontier Forts of Texas* published in 1966 states that he was "…one of the early heroes of the Mexican War. As a matter of fact, his death had helped to precipitate the war."

Richard B. Mason (1797–1850)— A native of Virginia and a U.S. army officer, Richard B. Mason served in the Black Hawk War and in the Mexican War and rose to the rank of brevet brigadier-general. Prior to statehood, California had a series of military governors and Richard B. Mason one of them.

2649 Matagorda County

Matagorda Bay and the existing Mexican municipality here of Matagorda— This county on Texas' coast on the Gulf of Mexico was created by the republic of Texas on March 17, 1836. Its name was taken from the existing names of (1) Matagorda Bay, an arm of the Gulf of Mexico, part of which lies within Matagorda County, and (2) a Mexican municipality here. The name *Matagorda* is Spanish, and it had been given to the municipality before Stephen F. Austin (1793–1836) was given permission in the late 1820's to establish a colony here. When the colonists came, mostly from New York and New England, they retained the existing name for their community and when the county was created the community of Matagorda became its county seat. A destructive storm in 1894 caused the county seat to be moved to Bay City, Texas. Most sources say that the Spanish name for the bay and municipality, *Matagorda*, means "canebrake." One of these sources is Rene C. du Gard's *Dictionary of Spanish Place Names: Texas & Arizona*. However, other sources indicate that the translation is uncertain. Two of the sources who question the "canebrake" translation are Z. T. Fulmore's *The History & Geography of Texas as Told in County Names* and Junann J. Stieghorst's *Bay City & Matagorda County: A History*.

2650 *Maverick County*

Samuel A. Maverick (1803–1870)—A native of South Carolina, graduate of Yale College and lawyer, Maverick came to Texas in 1835 and was active in early military efforts of Texas Revolutionary army. As a member of the convention of 1836, he was a signer of Texas Declaration of Independence. In 1842 an invading Mexican force captured him and took him to a prison in Mexico. While in prison, Maverick was elected to the congress of the republic of Texas and he was released from prison in time to serve in that body before statehood. A farmer and a rancher, Maverick's name has entered the English language. Many of Maverick's cattle were left unbranded and originally the term *maverick* referred to "unbranded cattle," particularly "a motherless calf." Over time the word has taken on additional meanings: "A person who refuses to conform and acts independently" and "a member of a political party who will not toe the party line." Samuel A. Maverick served in the Texas state legislature during several sessions and he was a member of that body when this county was created on February 2, 1856.

2651 *Medina County*

Medina River—This county in southern Texas was created on February 12, 1848, and named for the Medina River, which flows through it. The Medina River is a 116 mile-long tributary of the San Antonio River which was discovered and named in 1689 while Texas was part of New Spain (Mexico) by Captain Alonso de Leon (1640–), the governor of Coahuila. Several sources state that Captain de Leon probably named the river for Pedro Medina, an engineer and scholar of Spain. *The Handbook of Texas*, published by the Texas State Historical Association in 1952 states

that de Leon had mentioned Pedro Medina in his diary "only a week before he reached and named the stream." Z. T. Fulmore points out in his work entitled *The History & Geography of Texas as Told in County Names* that there are other Medinas for whom Captain de Leon may have named the Medina River: (1) "The sergeant major of the expedition" and (2) "the author of the tables used in determining latitude and longitude on their journey." Fulmore's work was published in 1926 so he did not have *The Handbook of Texas* at hand when he made his comments. It would seem possible that the "author of the tables" referred to by Fulmore might be Pedro Medina.

2652 *Menard County*

Michel B. Menard (1805–1856)—Born near Montreal, Canada, of French ancestry, Menard made his home on the wilderness frontier of what was then the northwestern area of the United States. He lived with trappers, traded with Indians and worked for the Northwest Fur Company. After working from bases at Detroit and Kaskaskia, Menard headed south and lived among the Shawnee Indians in Arkansas territory. When these Shawnees moved to Louisiana, Menard went with them and lived in the Shreveport area, near Texas. He came to Texas in 1829, left for a time and returned in 1832 or 1833 and became involved in activities of the Texas Revolution. As a member of the convention of 1836, Menard was a signer of the Texas Declaration of Independence. He and some associates purchased significant amounts of land on Galveston Island and some sources say Menard was the founder of Galveston. He represented Galveston in the congress of the republic of Texas. Michel B. Menard died on September 2, 1856, and this county was created and named in his honor 17 months later, on January 22, 1858.

2653 *Midland County*

Location midway between Fort Worth & El Paso, Texas—This county in west-central Texas was created on March 4, 1885, and named for its location, on the Texas & Pacific Railroad, midway between Fort Worth and El Paso, Texas. Both the county and its present county seat are named Midland. Fred Tarpley's *1001 Texas Place Names* tells us that the town was settled first and named "Midway, marking a post on the Texas & Pacific Railroad which was 307 miles equidistant from Fort Worth and

El Paso." The town's name was changed from Midway to Midland when Midland County was created.

2654 *Milam County*

Municipality of Milam, Texas—This county in east-central Texas was created by the infant republic of Texas on March 17, 1836, and named for the existing municipality named Milam, whose boundaries the new county assumed. The municipality had been named Viesca but its name was changed in 1835 to Milam in honor of Benjamin R. Milam (1788–1835).

Benjamin R. Milam (1788–1835)—A native of Kentucky, Milam served in the War of 1812 before coming to Mexican Texas in 1818. Here he traded with Comanche Indians, participated in the successful activities to win independence for Mexico from Spain and then in the efforts by Anglo-American Texans to win freedom from Mexico. Involved in the capture of forces at Goliad and a leader in the successful siege of Bexar in December, 1835, Milam died in combat during that siege.

2655 *Mills County*

John T. Mills (1817–1871)—Born in County Antrim, Ireland, Mills immigrated with his parents to South Carolina and studied law there. About 1837 he came to the republic of Texas and established a law practice in Clarksville. President Mirabeau B. Lamar (1798–1859) appointed him as judge of the republic's third judicial district and he later served the republic as judge of the seventh judicial district. After Texas was annexed to the U.S., Mills became judge of the eighth judicial district. Judge Mills owned a plantation on the Brazos River and lived on it from 1861 to 1865. He later practiced law in Marshall, Texas, and died there on November 30, 1871. This county was created and named in his honor on March 15, 1887.

2656 *Mitchell County*

Asa Mitchell (–1865) & Eli Mitchell (–1876)—This county was created on August 21, 1876, and named for the Mitchell brothers, Asa and Eli, pioneers of early Texas.

Asa Mitchell (–1865)—A native of Pennsylvania, Asa Mitchell came to Mexican Texas in 1822 and refined salt on the Brazos River, traded and planted crops. As one of Stephen F. Austin's (1793–1836) colonists, Asa Mitchell acquired title to significant land in Mexican Texas. An 1826 census lists him as a farmer and stock raiser with a wife, three children and eight servants. One of the first Anglo Americans to fight Mexican oppression, Asa Mitchell fought at the battle of Velasco in 1832. He was a member of the Consultation of 1835 and, briefly, of the general counsel of the provisional government of the republic of Texas. Asa Mitchell fought as a sergeant at the all-important battle of San Jacinto, the concluding action of the Texas Revolution. He later became a prosperous rancher and merchant.

Eli Mitchell (–1876)— Also a native of Pennsylvania, Eli Mitchell came to Mexican Texas about 1824 and initially settled near Velasco. He moved to Gonzales and was its representative at the convention of 1833. On October 2, 1835, in the first official battle of the Texas Revolution, Anglo-American Texans fought against the Mexican army in the battle of Gonzales and Eli Mitchell fought in that battle and provided food for Texas soldiers. Eli was less prominent in Texas history than his brother, Asa, but he was one of the founders of the Masonic order in Texas and assessor & collector of property taxes for Gonzales County.

2657 *Montague County*

Daniel Montague (1798–1876)— A native of Massachusetts, Montague came to Texas from Louisiana where he had lived since about 1820. He came to Texas in 1836, just after the battle of San Jacinto, the concluding action of the Texas Revolution. In the republic of Texas Montague worked as a surveyor and in those days in Texas surveyors often had to double as Indian fighters. This was the case with Daniel Montague. However, his survey work paid handsomely in land and he became a wealthy man. Montague fought in the Mexican War of 1846–1848 and about 1865 he moved to Mexico and lived there for about eleven years. He died shortly after his return to Texas to live with a daughter. This county was created on December 24, 1857.

2658 *Montgomery County*

Town of Montgomery, Texas— This county in eastern Texas was created on December 14, 1837, and named for the existing town of Montgomery here. That town was chosen as the first county seat of the county but the county seat has moved and is now located at Conroe, Texas. However, the small East-Texas town of Montgomery still exists, with U.S. Postal Service Zip Code 77356. Most sources dealing

with the history, geography and place names of Texas indicate that this county's name honors General Richard Montgomery (1738–1775).

Richard Montgomery (1738–1775)— Montgomery was born in Ireland and served with the British in the French and Indian War. He settled in New York where he was elected to the New York provisional congress. Montgomery served as a general in the American Revolutionary War and was killed in that war.

However, Robin Montgomery's *The History of Montgomery County*, published in 1975 has a different thesis: "…the advocates of three previous positions concerning the town's namesake are partially correct in that General Richard [of Revolutionary War fame], Margaret and William Montgomery were all members of the same family line…. In this respect the advocates for Margaret Montgomery are correct when they state that the town was named for the 'family of Margaret Montgomery Shannon' for it was named for Andrew Montgomery who was the nephew of Margaret and the son of William Montgomery." Robin Montgomery's work goes on to make a convincing case for the importance of Andrew Montgomery stating that he established a trading post in 1823, encouraged others to join him, and that his trading post was the nucleus around which the town of Montgomery grew. However the theory must be regarded as suspect. If the direct line from Andrew Montgomery's trading post to the town of Montgomery to Montgomery County were as clear as Robin Montgomery says it is, it seems unlikely that some 20 sources dealing with Texas' history would have missed it.

2659 *Moore County*

Edwin W. Moore (1810–1865)— A native of Virginia and a lieutenant in the U.S. navy, Moore resigned his commission in 1839 to command the navy of the republic of Texas. After recruiting seamen in New York, Moore pursued aggressive tactics as commander of the Texas navy. He prowled the Mexican coast to hasten peace negotiations during the Texas Revolution and assisted Yucatan, Mexico, in breaking with Mexico City. For a time there was a de facto alliance between the republic of Texas and Yucatan. President Samuel Houston (1793–1863) had difficulty in dealing with a number of men who were important in the early history of Texas and Edwin W. Moore was one of them. Houston accused Moore of disobedience and by the time the matter reached court mar-

tial the charges had ballooned to "disobedience, contumacy, mutiny, piracy and murder." Although Moore was cleared of all but minor charges, he held a grudge against Houston for many years. During Moore's service commanding Texas' navy he charted a valuable map of the coast of Texas. This county was created on August 21, 1876.

2660 *Morris County*

Uncertain— This county was created on March 6, 1875, and the vast majority of sources dealing with the history, geography and place names of Texas indicate that it was named for William W. Morris (1805–1883) or probably named for him. However, Z. T. Fulmore's work entitled *The History & Geography of Texas as Told in County Names* mentions the possibility that the county's name may honor Richard Morris (1815–1844). Also, a 1940 work entitled *East Texas: Its History and Its Makers*, admits that there is a possibility that Morris County was named for this Richard Morris. Note that Richard Morris is just a remote possibility. In all likelihood, the county was named for William W. Morris (1805–1883).

Richard Morris (1815–1844)— A native of Virginia, Richard Morris attended the University of Virginia and was admitted to the bar in 1838. He moved to Galveston, in East Texas and established a law partnership with James H. Davis. In 1841 President Mirabeau B. Lamar (1798–1859) appointed Richard Morris as a judge in the republic of Texas. He died of yellow fever in Galveston.

William W. Morris (1805–1883)— A native of North Carolina, William W. Morris moved to Alabama before coming to Texas. In Alabama he taught school, studied law and practiced law. He immigrated to Texas about 1847 with his family and slaves. William W. Morris became a prominent lawyer in East Texas, was a district court judge and served in the Texas legislature. He was particularly interested in the development of railroads in eastern Texas.

2661 *Motley County*

Junius W. Mottley (1812–1836)— A native of Virginia, Mottley studied medicine at Transylvania University in Kentucky and came to Texas about 1835. He served as a surgeon for the post at Goliad, was a delegate to the convention of 1836 and a signer of the Texas Declaration of Independence. Dr. Mottley fought at the all-important battle of San Jacinto, the concluding action of the Texas Revolution and was killed during that battle. This county was created on August 21, 1876, with one "t" in the county's name. That error has never been corrected.

2662 *Nacogdoches County*

Mexican department named Nacogdoches— This county's name honors the Nacogdoche Indians but there are several links in the naming chain. When Spain ruled New Spain (Mexico), a number of missions, *presidios* ("military posts" or "fortified settlements") and towns were established in what is now Texas. One of these was located near the present Nacogdoches, Texas and this was one of the few Spanish settlements in Texas to retain its name after Mexico became independent of Spain. The Spanish army captain, Domingo Ramon (–1723), founded the mission named Nuestra Senora de Guadalupe de los Nacogdoches here in 1716, and the settlement that grew up around it came to be the second largest municipality in Texas by the end of the 18th century. After Mexico gained independence from Spain, its territory in Texas was divided into three departments, one of which was the department named Nacogdoches. When the republic of Texas was proclaimed by the Texas Declaration of Independence, the infant republic created several counties. Nacogdoches County, created on March 17, 1836, was one of them. The new county comprised the territory of the former Mexican department named Nacogdoches, and one of the municipalities of that department was named Nacogdoches. That municipality became the county seat of the county of Nacogdoches in the republic of Texas.

Nacogdoche Indians — A Caddoan tribe, the Nacogdoche were one of the nine major tribes of Texas Indians. Their principal village was located in the vicinity of the present city of Nacogdoches, Texas and it was for the Nacogdoche Indians and the Nacau Indians that Spain founded the mission named Nuestra Senora de Guadalupe de los Nacogdoches here in 1716. During the years that followed, both the French and Spanish attempted to gain the favor of these Indians. The Nacogdoche and Nacau Indians were both members of the Hasinai Indian confederation. The Nacogdoche Indians disappeared as a separate entity primarily through intermarriage.

2663 *Navarro County*

Jose A. Navarro (1795–1871) — Jose Antonio Navarro was born at San Antonio de Bexar, while Mexican Texas was still part of New Spain. Active in the cause to secure liberation for Mexico from Spain, Navarro also became a friend of the Anglo-American colonist, Stephen F. Austin (1793–1836). After Mexico achieved independence, Navarro was elected to the legislature of the Mexican state of Coahuila and Texas. In that legislature Navarro became a champion of two causes, slavery and Anglo-American interests in Texas. Since slavery was forbidden by Mexican law, Navarro's two interests were compatible. Prior to the Texas Revolution, Navarro was a prominent ranch owner and a lawyer and merchant in the San Antonio area. As a delegate to the convention of 1836, Navarro became a signer of Texas Declaration of Independence and he later served in the congress of the republic of Texas. During efforts to annex New Mexico to Texas, Navarro was taken as a prisoner and sentenced to death. He was released in time to participate in the 1845 convention which voted to accept the U.S. offer to annex Texas. Navarro served as a senator during the first and second legislatures of the state of Texas and it was during that period, on April 25, 1846, that this county was created and named in his honor. In 1861 Navarro supported the secession of Texas from the United States.

2664 *Newton County*

John Newton (–1780) — Newton was born in Charleston, South Carolina, about 1752 and was the son of a pastor of a Baptist church. In 1775, early in the armed resistance to Great Britain, Newton enlisted in South Carolina's revolutionary army. He served as a piper and corporal in Captain Dunbar's company before being promoted to sergeant. In a dramatic exploit near Savannah, Georgia, Newton and his close friend William Jasper rescued several Americans who were prisoners and took their guards as prisoners of war. Newton was more fortunate than his friend William Jasper, in that he survived the siege of Savannah. However, when Charleston fell to the British in 1780, Newton was taken prisoner and he died of smallpox shortly afterward. Geographic names in several of our states link the names of the two heroic sergeants, Jasper and Newton. In some states a county is named for one of them and its county seat is named for the other. In others, like Texas, two counties are named for them. Newton County, Texas was created on April 22, 1846, from the eastern half of Jasper County. These two counties sit side by side to this day in extreme eastern Texas.

2665 *Nolan County*

Philip Nolan (1771–1801) — Philip Nolan became associated with James Wilkinson (1757–1825) in Kentucky in the late 1700's. At that time ownership of the vast land mass which now comprises the United States was tenuous and coveted by a number of nations. France owned the enormous land mass called Louisiana, which stretched from the Gulf of Mexico to northern Montana and Spain owned New Spain (Mexico), including Texas, and held other large possessions within the present United States. Superimposed on the official dealings and disputes between nations concerning ownership of these vast domains were clandestine plots by adventurers seeking to find profits in the murky waters. Clearly James Wilkinson was involved in some of these conspiracies, including a possible invasion of New Spain (Mexico). This county's namesake, Philip Nolan (1771–1801), was an associate and/or employee of Wilkinson's during this period. In addition to his grand conspiracies, James Wilkinson had to make a living and Philip Nolan was definitely associated with Wilkinson's business dealings (e.g., running trading establishments in Kentucky and acquiring horses) and in some of these efforts Philip Nolan may or may not have gone beyond the activities permitted by Spain in Mexican Texas. On his final adventure in Texas, Nolan was killed by Spanish authorities near the present Waco, Texas, on March 21, 1801. Nolan may have believed that his venture into Texas on this occasion was within the bounds permitted by Spain and there is reason to believe that some Spanish authorities would have agreed with him. That view was not shared by the Spanish militia commander, Miguel Francisco Musquiz, who ordered that Nolan be shot, and his ears cut off to be sent to the acting governor. This Texas county was created on August 21, 1876.

2666 *Nueces County*

Nueces River — This county was created on April 18, 1846, and named for the 315 mile-long Nueces River, which has its mouth in Nueces County at Nueces Bay, at the head of Corpus Christi Bay, on the Gulf of Mexico. Elizabeth Howard West's article entitled "De Leon's Expedition of 1689," which appeared in the January, 1905 (Vol. 8, No. 3), issue of the *Quarterly of the Texas State Historical Association* provides a quotation from a diary of the expedition which documents that the Nueces River was named in 1689, while Texas was part of New Spain (Mexico) by

Captain Alonso de Leon (1640–), the governor of Coahuila. "We came upon a river, which as we could see, even though it contained little water at the time, overflows its banks in time of rain more than half a league from the main channel. We called it the *Rio de las Nueces*, because there were many pecan trees [*nogales*] on its banks."

2667 *Ochiltree County*

William B. Ochiltree (1811–1867)— A native of North Carolina and a lawyer, Ochiltree came to Texas in 1839. Here he practiced law, served as a judge and was appointed to the cabinet of the republic of Texas by President Anson Jones (1798–1858). He served as secretary of the treasury in that cabinet. Ochiltree was a delegate to the convention of 1845, which approved the offer of annexation to the United States and after statehood, he served in the lower house of the state legislature. A delegate to Texas secession convention of 1861, Ochiltree was elected to represent Texas in the provisional congress of the Confederate States of America. At the end of the provisional congress Ochiltree returned to Texas to recruit soldiers for the Confederate army but ill health forced him to resign in 1863. This county was created on August 21, 1876.

2668 *Oldham County*

Williamson S. Oldham (1813–1868)— A native of Tennessee and a lawyer, Oldham first gained prominence in Arkansas where he was speaker of the house in the state legislature and an associate justice of the supreme court. He came to Texas in 1849, practiced law and was an editor and co-owner of a newspaper in Austin. Oldham was a delegate to the Texas secession convention of 1861 and was elected to represent Texas in the provisional congress of the Confederate States of America. In November, 1861, the Texas legislature elected him as one of the state's two senators in the regular congress of the Confederacy and he represented Texas in the Confederate senate until the end of the Civil War. This county was created on August 21, 1876.

2669 *Orange County*

An orange grove near the Neches River in eastern Texas— This county is located in eastern Texas, on the border with southwestern Louisiana. It was created on February 5, 1852, and named for an orange grove owned by George A. Patillo, near the east bank of the Neches River here. Oranges are tropical and subtropical trees and shrubs, which belong to the genus *Citrus*. Their fruits, and juices from their fruits, enjoy great popularity. Oranges originated in the tropical regions of Asia, spread around the Mediterranean Sea and were introduced in the western hemisphere by Columbus in 1493. The Spanish introduced oranges in North America for consumption, rather than commerce but these delicious and nutritious fruits are now shipped to northern states. This county's name was suggested to the Texas legislature by George A. Patillo, who subsequently was chief justice at the first meeting of the Orange County commissioners court.

2670 *Palo Pinto County*

Palo Pinto Creek— This county lies in northern Texas, about 50 miles due west of Ft. Worth, Texas. It was created on August 27, 1856, and named for Palo Pinto Creek, a tributary of the Brazos River and one of this county's principal streams. *The Handbook of Texas* published in 1952 by the Texas State Historical Association states that this creek "rises in main and south forks in northern and eastern Eastland County. The main fork cuts across the southeast corner of Stephens County and then bends to the east into southwestern Palo Pinto County, where its junction with the south fork just west of the town of Mingus forms Palo Pinto Creek proper." The waters of Palo Pinto Creek flow into the Brazos River within Palo Pinto County. The name *Palo Pinto* was given to the creek by the Spanish. Rene C. du Gard's *Dictionary of Spanish Place Names: Texas & Arizona* translates the creek's name as "painted stick" but Z. T. Fulmore's work entitled *The History & Geography of Texas as Told in County Names* translates the name as "painted trees" and offers a theory for the creek's name: "...at one time the prairies were sparsely covered with mesquite trees, and at certain seasons of the year the bark became covered with a species of moss or fungus, gray in color, giving them the appearance of being painted or daubed."

2671 *Panola County*

Indian word for "cotton"— This county's name comes from the language of the Choctaw Indians and means "cotton." The first Panola County in Texas was created by the republic of Texas on January 30, 1841. That county was one of the so-called judicial counties, which were found to be unconstitutional by the Texas supreme court and abolished. The present Panola County was created by the state of Texas on March 30, 1846. Panola County is in northeastern Texas and cotton is grown here but cotton has been grown in almost 90% of the state's 254 counties. In 1846 when this county was created, cotton had been grown in Texas for at least a century. In 1745 Mexican Texas produced several thousand pounds of cotton per year and it became an enormously important crop to Texas by the Civil War. Although cotton production in Texas began to decline after the 1920's, as recently as 1950 cotton was the primary cash crop of Texas and Texas was the leading cotton producing state in the nation.

2672 *Parker County*

Uncertain— This county was created on December 12, 1855. Sources consulted offer differing opinions concerning the namesake of this county. Of 22 sources consulted, more than half say that the county was named for Isaac Parker (1793–1883) and an additional three sources say that the county was probably named for him or named for him and members of his family. Two sources state that it was named for "the pioneer family of Cynthia Ann and Quanah Parker" while four sources indicate that the county's name honors "the Parker family at Parker's fort."

Isaac Parker (1793–1883)—A native of Georgia, Isaac Parker came to Mexican Texas in 1833 with several family members and settled in what is now Limestone County. The Parker family erected a fort for protection against the Indians. Isaac Parker fought in the Texas Revolution, served in both houses of the congress of the republic of Texas and in both houses of the legislature of the state of Texas. He was a member of the Texas senate when this county was created and according to some sources he introduced the bill to create this county.

Pioneer family of Cynthia Ann and Quanah Parker & Parker family of Parker's fort— *The Texas Courthouse*, published in 1971, tells us that Isaac Parker's brother, Silas, "was killed in the Comanche raid on Fort Parker in 1836 when Silas' children, Cynthia Ann and John were captured." Z. T. Fulmore's work entitled *The History & Geography of Texas as Told in County Names* corroborates that statement and elaborates on it: Isaac Parker (1793–1883) came to Mexican Texas in 1833 with members of his family and they built a fort, Parker's fort, to protect themselves from

Indians. In 1836 when Comanche Indians raided the fort, Fulmore tells us that they killed three members of the family in addition to Silas Parker. Those three are listed as: Benjamin Parker, Samuel Frost and Robert Frost. Fulmore adds that Mrs. Sarah Parker was wounded during this attack and that the Comanche "made prisoners of Mrs. Rachael Plummer, and her son, James P. Plummer, two years old, Cynthia Ann Parker, eight years old and John Parker, six years old and Mrs. Kellogg." Fulmore states that Cynthia Ann Parker lived in captivity among the Comanche "for nearly a quarter of a century and became the wife of a chief." *The Handbook of Texas*, published by the Texas State Historical Association in 1952 confirms Fulmore's account of the capture of Cynthia Ann Parker and says that the Comanche chief whom she married was Peta Nocona and that Cynthia and Peta had three children, Pecos, Quanah and Prairie Flower. *The Handbook of Texas* indicates that Cynthia Ann Parker was involuntarily returned to White civilization in 1860 (about four years after this county was created) and was identified by her uncle, Isaac Parker (1793–1883). Cynthia Ann was unable to adjust to living among the Whites in Texas and she died in 1864.

2673 *Parmer County*

Martin Parmer (1778–1850)— Born in Virginia, Parmer lived for a time in Tennessee and Missouri and served in the Missouri legislature. He came to Mexican Texas about 1825, and participated in the unsuccessful Fredonian rebellion against Mexico. Parmer left Texas when that rebellion failed, returned in 1831 only to be expelled from Texas by Mexican authorities. Undaunted, he returned and was a delegate to the 1835 Consultation and was elected a member of the general council of the provisional government of the republic of Texas. Parmer soon was elected as a delegate to the convention of 1836 and he was one of the signers of the Texas Declaration of Independence. This county was created on August 21, 1876.

2674 *Pecos County*

Pecos River— This county in southwestern Texas was created on May 3, 1871, and named for the Pecos River, which forms its northeastern boundary. The Pecos is a 500 mile-long tributary of the Rio Grande River. It rises in northern New Mexico, flows southeast and east in New Mexico to cross into Texas at Red Bluff Lake, about 100 miles east of El Paso, Texas. In Texas the Pecos flows southeast until it enters the Rio Grande at the Mexican border, a few miles above Del Rio, Texas. The origin of the name *Pecos* is uncertain. This name was given by the Keresan Indians to a large early pueblo in New Mexico. Rene C. du Gard's *Dictionary of Spanish Place Names: Texas & Arizona* states that *pecos* is a Spanish approximation of the Keresan Indians' word for "place where there is water" but George R. Stewart's *American Place Names* states that the meaning of the word *pecos* is uncertain and that "It was probably first applied to an Indian village, and later to the tribe and river."

2675 *Polk County*

James K. Polk (1795–1849)— A native of North Carolina who moved to the Tennessee frontier in 1806, Polk served in the lower house of the Tennessee legislature and represented Tennessee for 14 years in the U.S. House of Representatives, where he was speaker. He served one term as governor of Tennessee. Polk became president of the United States as a dark horse candidate of the Democratic party but he became an unusually strong and effective president. His primary accomplishments involved westward extension of the United States: in the Northwest by settling a territorial dispute with Britain and in California and the Southwest by provoking and winning the Mexican War. This county was created on March 30, 1846, while Polk was president of the United States. Texas had been annexed to our nation just three months earlier, also during the administration of President James K. Polk.

2676 *Potter County*

Robert Potter (–1842)— Born in North Carolina about 1800, Potter served as a midshipman in the United States navy. He then studied law, was admitted to the bar, served in the North Carolina legislature and represented North Carolina in the U.S. House of Representatives. Potter immigrated to Texas in 1835 and soon was involved in arming and equipping Texas soldiers for the siege of Bexar. As a delegate to the convention of 1836, Potter was one of the signers of the Texas Declaration of Independence. In the ad interim government of the republic of Texas under President David G. Burnet (1788–1870), Potter served in the cabinet as secretary of the navy. He later served in the congress of the republic of Texas before being killed at his home during the feud called the Regulator-Moderator war. This county was created on August 21, 1876.

2677 *Presidio County*

Presidio del Norte—Presidio is a Spanish word meaning "military post" or "fortified settlement." Presidio County, Texas, on the Mexican border in southwestern Texas, was created on January 3, 1850, and its name commemorates a *presidio* which had been important here, Presidio del Norte. That presidio was established in 1759 by Spanish troops under the command of Captain Alonso Rubin de Celis. It was located at the strategic junction of the Rio Grande River with the Conchos River of what is now Chihuahua state in northern Mexico. Spanish soldiers used this fort to fight Indians for a few years but abandoned it in 1767 and a established a new fort south of the Rio Grande. Indians soon destroyed the presidio in what is now Texas but it was reestablished at its original location about 1773 and garrisoned by Spanish troops until 1814. After Mexico gained independence from Spain, the location of the old Presidio del Norte became of strategic importance. However, in 1848, the treaty of Guadalupe Hidalgo gave title to territory north and east of the Rio Grande to the United States thus placing the site of the old Presidio del Norte in both the United States and in Texas.

2678 *Rains County*

Emory Rains (1800–1878)— A native of Tennessee, Rains immigrated to Mexican Texas in 1826 and settled near the Red River in what is now northeastern Texas. He served as a senator in the congress of the republic of Texas and was a delegate to the 1845 convention which accepted the U.S. offer of annexation and framed the constitution of the state of Texas. Rains served in both houses of the state legislature. In 1869 he participated in survey work east of Dallas in the area which became Rains County when it was created and named in his honor on June 9, 1870. Rains County's seat was established at the community named Emory, also named in his honor. Emory Rains died on March 4, 1878, at his home within the county named in his honor.

2679 *Randall County*

Horace Randal (1833–1864)— Born in Tennessee, Randal moved with his parents to Texas in 1839. An 1854 graduate of the U.S. Military Academy at West Point,

Randal was assigned to infantry duty as a second-lieutenant in our nation's southwestern frontier areas and saw some duty in Texas. On February 23, 1861, Texas voters approved an ordinance to secede from the Union, and four days later, on February 27, Randal resigned his commission in the U.S. army. He entered the Confederate army as a colonel and was assigned to the 28th Texas cavalry. Randal served with distinction during the Civil War and in mid-April, 1864, he was "assigned to duty" as a brigadier-general but he was never officially promoted to that rank by President Jefferson Davis, probably because he was killed too soon. Randal lost his life in combat at the battle of Jenkins' Ferry, Arkansas on April 30, 1864, and he never learned that he had been promoted to brigadier-general. By 1876 Reconstruction had ended in Texas and it was possible to name counties in honor of heroes of the Confederate army. Randall County (two l's) was created on August 21, 1876, and named in honor of Horace Randal (one l).

2680 *Reagan County*

John H. Reagan (1818–1905)— A native of Tennessee, Reagan came to the republic of Texas in 1839, served in the Texas army and as an officer in the Texas militia. He studied law, was elected to the Texas legislature, and admitted to the bar. Reagan served as a district court judge before being elected to represent Texas in the U.S. House of Representatives. Although he was a moderate on the questions of slavery and states' rights, when Texas seceded from the Union, Reagan was elected to the provisional congress of the Confederate States of America. He served in that body just four days before being appointed to the cabinet as postmaster general of the Confederacy. In the cabinet, Reagan was a close friend and advisor of President Jefferson Davis. A decade after the Civil War ended, Reagan was elected to represent Texas in the U.S. House of Representatives and he later represented Texas in the U.S. Senate. This county was created on March 7, 1903, two years before Reagan's death on March 6, 1905.

2681 *Real County*

Julius Real (1860–1944)— Born on his father's ranch about seven miles south of Kerrville, Texas, Julius Real earned his living in a variety of fields. He was a rancher, road construction engineer, county judge, school superintendent and, from 1910 to 1914, a member of the Texas senate. He died on May 29, 1944, in the same house in which he had been born. This county was created by the Texas legislature on April 3, 1913, while Real was serving in the Texas senate. At that time the question of prohibiting alcoholic beverages was a hot topic in Texas and in the nation. Just six years later, in January, 1919, the 18th amendment to the U.S. Constitution was ratified, prohibiting the manufacture, sale and transportation of alcoholic liquors. Julius Real made his mark on the prohibition question in Texas in 1911 during the so-called "Whiskey rebellion." The stage had been set by the Texas legislature and governor to pass prohibition legislation in Texas. Although Senator Julius Real personally abstained from intoxicating beverages, his constituents were opposed to prohibition in Texas. In accordance with their wishes, Real and other members of the Texas legislature hid themselves to prevent the quorum needed to pass prohibition legislation in Texas. Real County probably owes its name to the zeal with which Julius Real protected the interests of his drinking constituents in 1911.

2682 *Red River County*

Red River— This county in northeastern Texas was created by the republic of Texas on March 17, 1836, and named for the Red River, which today forms the county's northern border and separates Oklahoma from Texas here. The Red River in a major tributary of the Mississippi River. It was named for its color, acquired from the red clay and sandstone over which it flows. This red color is most noticeable when the river overflows its banks during floods. The Red River rises on the high plains of eastern New Mexico and flows across the Texas panhandle into Arkansas. There it turns south and enters Louisiana near the tri-state junction of Texas, Louisiana and Arkansas. In Louisiana, the Red River flows southeast and divides into two branches just west of the Felicianas. One branch enters the Atchafalaya River, while the other joins the Mississippi River thus completing a journey of about 1,000 miles. There are two other significant Red Rivers in our country; one that flows in Kentucky and Tennessee and another, called the Red River of the North, in the Minnesota-Dakota-Canada area. Both of these Red Rivers are substantially shorter than the river for which this county was named. Today's Red River is sluggish but it was mighty in earlier days and cut crevices up to 800 feet deep in the Texas panhandle.

Prior to the arrival of Europeans, much of the Red River in Louisiana was clogged with a strange mass of logs and river debris, forming logjams interspersed with patches of open water. Geologists have speculated that this "Great Raft," as it was called, dated back to at least the 15th century.

2683 *Reeves County*

George R. Reeves (1826–1882)— A native of Tennessee, Reeves moved with his family to Arkansas territory about 1835. He came to Texas in 1845 or 1846, farmed and raised cattle. Reeves served as both tax collector and sheriff of Grayson County, Texas, and represented that county in the Texas legislature prior to the Civil War. When Texas seceded from the Union in 1861, Reeves enlisted the Confederate army with the rank of captain. In 1863 he was promoted to colonel. After the Civil War Reeves sat briefly in the Texas legislature but the military and civil Reconstruction imposed on Texas truncated his service. However, by 1873 Reconstruction was ending in Texas and it was possible for Confederate veterans to serve in the legislature and George R. Reeves returned to the lower house. He served as speaker of the house from January, 1881, until his death on September 5, 1882. This county was created during the following year.

2684 *Refugio County*

Mission Nuestra Senora del Refugio— In the 1790's Spain established a mission here, in what is now southeastern Texas. On March 17, 1836, the republic of Texas created Refugio County and named it either directly or indirectly (via the town of Refugio) for that former Spanish mission here. *The Handbook of Texas*, published by the Texas State Historical Association in 1952 states that the town of Refugio was founded in 1834 on the site of the Spanish mission, that the county was first named Refugio, then changed to Wexford in honor of a county in Ireland; further, that the name Wexford never gained acceptance and the county's name reverted to Refugio. Since the town of Refugio was founded in 1834 (and named for the mission) before the county was created in 1836, some, but not all, sources indicate that the county's proximate namesake was the town of Refugio, Texas.

Mission Nuestra Senora del Refugio— Rene C. du Gard's *Dictionary of Spanish Place Names: Texas & Arizona* translates the mission's Spanish name as "Our Lady of Refuge." This mission was originally established in the 1790's in what is now Calhoun County, Texas, near the junction of the San Antonio and Guadalupe Rivers. (Calhoun County, Texas, lies on Refugio County's northeastern border.) The founders were Roman Catholic missionaries of the Franciscan order, two of whom were Fray Jose Francisco Mariano Garza and Padre Manuel Julio Silva. Padre Silva was commissioner of missions of New Spain (Mexico). The mission was moved from its original location to its final home in what is now the town of Refugio, in Refugio County, because of unhealthy conditions at the original site. The move began in 1794 and was completed in 1795. A record of Indians who were baptized at this mission was kept until 1828. The original stone buildings were in ruins by 1835 as a result of armed conflict between Irish-Americans and Mexican authorities.

2685 *Roberts County*

Uncertain— This county was created on August 21, 1876, but sources consulted differ on its namesake. Some accounts list John S. Roberts, others Oran M. Roberts, and some say the name honors both of them. *The Handbook of Texas*, published by the Texas State Historical Association in 1952 provides inconsistent information. In one reference *The Handbook* states that the county was named in honor of "John S. and O. M. Roberts" but another entry tells us that the county was named for "John S. Roberts and other distinguished Texans of that name." Z. T. Fulmore's work entitled *The History & Geography of Texas as Told in County Names* uses substantially the same phrase "John S. Roberts, and other distinguished Texans by [sic] that name," and says "by which it is presumed the Legislature meant 'O. M. Roberts,'" implying that this phrase was included in the legislation which created this county.

John S. Roberts (1796–1871)— A native of Virginia, John S. Roberts came to Mexican Texas in late 1826 or early 1827 and fought in the battle of Nacogdoches, an 1832 prelude to the Texas Revolution. He later fought as an officer in the Texas army during the revolution itself and was a representative to the convention of 1836 and one of the signers of the Texas Declaration of Independence.

Oran M. Roberts (1815–1898)— A native of South Carolina and a lawyer, Oran Milo Roberts moved to the republic of Texas in 1841. Prior to the Civil War he was elected as an associate justice of the supreme court of the state of Texas. When tensions mounted between North and South, Oran M. Roberts became president of the Texas secession convention, and he served as a colonel in the Confederate army during the Civil War. In 1864 he became chief justice of the supreme court of the Confederate state of Texas. After the war, he was elected to the U.S. Senate but was not permitted to take his seat in that body. Oran M. Roberts subsequently was chief justice of the Texas supreme court (of the U.S.) and, from 1879 to 1883, he was governor of the state.

2686 *Robertson County*

Sterling C. Robertson (1785–1842)— A native of Tennessee, Robertson served in the War of 1812 and participated in the battle of New Orleans. After Mexico gained independence from Spain, Sterling C. Robertson and others were granted permission to establish a colony of Anglo-Americans in Mexican Texas and the Robertson colony of some 800 resulted, second in size only to Stephen F. Austin's (1793–1836). Robertson and Austin became embroiled in a lawsuit about land titles and colonists' rights which was settled in 1834 by the Mexican governor in Robertson's favor. Robertson was made empresario and the term "Robertson colony" became fixed in Texas history. Robertson subsequently participated in the Texas Revolution as a delegate to the convention of 1836, signer of the Texas Declaration of Independence and member of Texas Revolutionary army. He also served in the congress of the republic of Texas and Robertson County was created on December 14, 1837, while Robertson was serving in congress. ~

2687 *Rockwall County*

City of Rockwall, Texas— This county in northeastern Texas was created on March 1, 1873, and named for the city of Rockwall, which became the county seat of the new county. The city had been named for a subterranean rock wall which was discovered in 1851 or 1852 by Terry U. Wade, while digging a well for his farm. He was assisted in his excavations by B. F. Boydstun and a Mr. Stevenson. Fred Tarpley's *Place Names of Northeast Texas* states that the wall surrounds the present (1969) city, appears occasionally at ground level and outcrops of it appear elsewhere within the county. Tarpley says that "Whether the wall is man-made or a geological formation is still (1969) discussed." The city of Rockwall was surveyed in 1857 and named for the then-discovered portion of the subterranean dike which was one-fourth mile distant from it. When the Black Hill post office was moved here it also was named Rockwall. The city of Rockwall was incorporated in 1872. Its population has never exceeded 5,000.

2688 *Runnels County*

Uncertain— This county was created on February 1, 1858, while Hardin Richard Runnels (1820–1873) was governor of Texas. However, of 24 sources consulted, more than two-thirds indicate that the county was named for Hiram George Runnels (1796–1857). That is possible, Hiram G. Runnels died on December 17, 1857, and this county was created just six weeks later. It seems more likely, however, that the county was named for the incumbent Texas governor and that many sources who award the honor to Hiram G. Runnels are confused. (The wording in some of the sources demonstrates confusion and both of the men came to the republic of Texas on or about 1842 from Mississippi.) However two landmark sources on the origin of county names in Texas unambiguously state that this county was named for Hiram George Runnels (1796–1857). These two sources are Z. T. Fulmore's *The History & Geography of Texas as Told in County Names* and *The Handbook of Texas*, published by the Texas State Historical Association in 1952.

Hardin R. Runnels (1820–1873)— Born in 1820, probably in Mississippi, Hardin R. Runnels moved to the republic of Texas with his mother, brothers and slaves about 1842. The family established a cotton plantation near the Red River. Hardin R. Runnels served several terms in the Texas legislature and was speaker of the house. In 1855 he was elected lieutenant-governor of the state and in 1857 he defeated Samuel Houston (1793–1863) for governor. Hardin R. Runnels served as governor of Texas from 1857 to 1859 and was governor when Runnels County, Texas, was created.

Hiram G. Runnels (1796–1857)— Hiram George Runnels was born in Georgia but moved to Mississippi territory with his parents at an early age. He served in the army during Indian wars, was auditor of the state of Mississippi and served in Mississippi's state legislature. Elected governor of Mississippi in 1833, he served in that office from 1833 to 1835, served again in the Mississippi legislature and came to the republic of Texas in 1842. Here he became a planter near the Brazos River and was a representative to the convention of 1845, which approved the offer of annexation to the United States and drafted the state's constitution. Hiram G. Runnels served in the Texas state senate. He died on December 17, 1857, six weeks before this county was created.

2689 Rusk County

Thomas J. Rusk (1803–1857)— A native of South Carolina and a lawyer, Rusk came to Texas about 1834 and was a representative to the convention of 1836 and one of the signers of the Texas Declaration of Independence. He served as the first secretary of war of the republic of Texas in the ad interim government of President David G. Burnet (1788–1870) and during 1836 Rusk held the rank of brigadier-general and was commander of the Texas army. He also served as secretary of war in the first cabinet of President Samuel Houston (1793–1863), briefly as chief justice of the Texas supreme court, major-general of the Texas militia and president of the convention of 1845 which approved the offer of annexation to the United States and drafted the state's constitution. When Texas entered the Union, Rusk and Samuel Houston were the new state's first two U.S. senators. Rusk represented Texas in the U.S. Senate from March 26, 1846, until his death and he was elected president *pro-tempore* of the senate on March 14, 1857. This county was created by the republic of Texas on January 16, 1843.

2690 Sabine County

Former municipality of Sabine— This county on the eastern border of Texas was created by the republic of Texas from the former municipality here named Sabine on March 17, 1836. The area comprising Sabine County, which borders on the Sabine River, was first organized in 1823 or 1824 as the Sabine district of the Mexican department of Nacogdoches. That district became the municipality of Sabine in 1835 and it was given county status in 1836. There is potential confusion here because Texas established towns in Jefferson County named Sabine, Sabine City and Sabine Pass, none of which are the municipality for which this county was named. All the various *Sabine* names which evolved into Sabine County, honored the adjacent Sabine River.

Sabine River— This beautiful, navigable river begins in northeastern Texas, then flows southeast to form more than two-thirds of the Texas-Louisiana border.

More than 500 miles long, the Sabine ends its journey by emptying into the Gulf of Mexico through Sabine Lake and Sabine Pass, near Port Arthur, Texas. The Sabine River was earlier named by Spanish explorers and one of the Spaniards' names for it was *Rio Sabinas*, which means "River of Cedar Trees." This name was chosen on account of the cedar trees (genus Juniperus) growing along its banks. The French later changed the name from Sabinas to Sabine. Numerous sources mention a different, and incorrect, origin for the river's name. According to this version, a party of Frenchmen captured a number of attractive Indian women near the Sabine River and raped them. Since this incident resembled the famous gang-rape in Roman mythology, known as "The Rape of the Sabines," the river's name is said by some to derive from that incident in Roman mythology. It is certainly possible that some crude Frenchmen captured and gang-raped Indian women in this area but even if they did, it was not the source of the river's name.

2691 San Augustine County

Municipality of San Augustine— This county was created by the republic of Texas on March 17, 1836, and named for the municipality of San Augustine, which had been named by Mexico on March 6, 1834. That municipality included all of the present San Augustine County and all or part of several additional counties in the present state of Texas. The municipality's name derived from a *presidio* ("military post" or "fortified settlement") named San Agustin de Ahumada. Z. T. Fulmore's work entitled *The History & Geography of Texas as Told in County Names* states that the presidio was established in 1756 and it was associated with a small Roman Catholic mission. Other sources tell us that the name of that mission was Mision Nuestra Senora de los Dolores de los Ais, established here in 1716 and that both the presidio and mission were abandoned; the presidio in 1771 and the mission in 1773. The presidio's name, San Agustin de Ahumada, honored the Roman Catholic saint, Saint Augustine (354–430).

Saint Augustine (354–430)— Aurelius Augustinus, known today as Saint Augustine of Hippo, was born in northern Africa, a son of Saint Monica (333–387) and a pagan Roman official. Aurelius himself did not become a permanent convert to Christianity until A.D. 386, in Milan, Italy. He was baptized by Saint Ambrose (–397) and returned to Africa to live a

monastic life of prayer, meditation and retirement. Ordained as a Christian priest at Hippo in 391, he was elevated to bishop in 396. Saint Augustine generated an extraordinary quantity of theological and spiritual writings, and was the author of a number of important doctrines on faith and morals of the Roman Catholic church. He died during the fall of the Roman empire to the Vandals.

2692 San Jacinto County

Battle of San Jacinto— This county in eastern Texas was created during August, 1870, and named for the battle of San Jacinto, the concluding action of the Texas Revolution. That battle was fought on April 21, 1836, on the western bank of the San Jacinto River, an 85 mile-long stream, which ends in Galveston Bay. Texas revolutionary forces won a resounding victory over a larger Mexican army, which was personally commanded by Mexico's dictator, Antonio Lopez de Santa Anna (1794–1876). Thus this county was named for the battle and the battle was named for the river. The river had been named by the Spanish in honor of the saint of the Roman Catholic church, Saint Hyacinth (–1257). *Jacinto* is the Spanish word for "hyacinth."

Saint Hyacinth (–1257)— This saint's given name was Jacek, a Polish name. He was born to nobility in Poland before A.D. 1200. Converted to Christianity on a visit to Rome, Italy in 1217 or 1218 when he witnessed a miraculous resuscitation of a young man who was thought to be dead after a fall from his horse, Jacek entered the mendicant Dominican order of friars of the Roman Catholic church and was involved in extensive missionary activity. Solid historical information on the details of his life are in short supply. Legend tells us that Jacek founded at least two convents, conducted his missionary activity on foot over thousands of miles from Tibet to Denmark and Lithuania and in his native Poland. Several miracles are attributed to him. Jacek died on August 15, 1257, and was canonized in 1594.

2693 San Patricio County

Town of San Patricio— This county in southeastern Texas was created by the republic of Texas on March 17, 1836, and named for the town of San Patricio (styled San Patricio Hibernia in several accounts), where a colony of Anglo-Americans had planted a town in Mexican Texas about 1830. Foreigners were permitted under Mexican law to settle here, provided they met certain conditions, primarily that they be Roman Catholics. All or most of the colonists, led by the Irish natives John McMullen (–1853) and James McGloin (–1856) were Irish and met the religious requirement. *The Handbook of Texas* published in 1952 by the Texas State Historical Association states that the municipality for which this county was named was within the present (1952) borders of San Patricio County. There is disagreement on that point. R. L. Batts' article in the October, 1897 (Vol. 1, No. 2) issue of the *Quarterly of the Texas State Historical Association* states that "...no part of the present (1897) county is included in the original territory" of that municipality. Wherever located, the town of San Patricio honored Saint Patrick, the Roman Catholic patron saint of Ireland.

Saint Patrick (–)—Much of the information that we have concerning Saint Patrick is legendary and even David N. Dumville's comprehensive biography, entitled *Saint Patrick: A.D. 493–1993* acknowledges that many of the details are controversial. The March, 1995, issue of *Catholic Digest* contains a condensation of an article by Patrick F. O'Connell entitled "More Than the Shamrock: Understanding the Real St. Patrick" which captures important factual information. In that article O'Connell states that the conventional image shows "...a shamrock in one hand, ...ready to convert the pagan Irish and drive the snakes from the Emerald Isle." O'Connell cautions us that these images arose centuries after St. Patrick's death and "There is no evidence that these or many other legends ever happened." We know that he was born to a Christian family in the British Isles about A.D. 390 before the Roman empire withdrew. Kidnapped at about age 15 and taken to Ireland, he came to develop a devout Christian faith and rose to become Bishop Patricius of Ireland. While bishop, Patricius passionately defended the poor and the oppressed Irish from outrageous abuses by civil authorities. He died about A.D. 461. Saint Patrick became one of the better known saints in America when waves of Irish immigrants brought their devotion to him with them.

2694 *San Saba County*

San Saba River—This county in central Texas was created on February 1, 1856, and named for the 100 mile-long San Saba River, which flows from Schleicher County to enter the Colorado River on the eastern boundary of San Saba County. *San Saba* is a Spanish name but sources consulted disagree on the origin and meaning of that name. Several sources indicate that the name is a contraction of *Santo Sabado*, meaning "Holy Saturday." Z. T. Fulmore's work entitled *The History & Geography of Texas as Told in County Names* is an important source book for Texas county name origins and it states that the "Holy Saturday" theory is probably correct. Robert S. Weddle's *The San Saba Mission: Spanish Pivot in Texas*, published by the University of Texas Press in 1964, disagrees. Weddle's work states that the river was named in 1732 by the Spanish governor of Mexican Texas, Juan Antonio Bustillo y Ceballos (rendered in other sources as Cevallos and Zevallos) and that "...on the morning of Tuesday, December 5 ... he named it El Rio San Saba de las Nueces, honoring the holy abbot, Saint Sabbas, whose special day it was." Weddle's work provides some information about this Saint Sabbas in a footnote: "...a native of Cappadocia in Asia Minor, lived from 439 to 532 and was abbot of the monastery near Jerusalem that now bears his name.,..,. Thus it appear that Z. T. Fulmore ... is in error in his thesis that the River was named for Holy Saturday [*San Sabado*], though Bustillo's battle with the Apaches was fought on Saturday." Both the *New Catholic Encyclopedia* and Omer Englebert's *The Lives of the Saints* confirm many of Weddle's comments about Saint Sabbas and mention that he was a disciple of Saint Euthymius (–473) in the Judaean wilderness and that when Euthymius died in A.D. 473, Sabbas became the leader of Euthymius' followers. The *New Catholic Encyclopedia* refers to Saint Sabbas as a "monastic founder," and states that he founded four lauras, six monasteries and four hospices. Nettie Lee Benson confirmed Robert S. Weddle's version in her contribution to "Texas Collections," in the July, 1947 (Vol. 51, No. 1), issue of the *Southwestern Historical Quarterly*: "..Fulmore was entirely wrong in his assumption that the river was named for Holy Saturday. The river was discovered on Tuesday, December 5, 1732, by Don Juan Antonio Bustillo y Cevallos, governor of the province of Texas. December 5 is the saint's day of Saint Sabbas, which in Spanish is written San Sabas or San Saba." These sources are correct when they refer to December 5 as the special day of Saint Sabbas (439–532). December 5 is this saint's feast day.

2695 *Schleicher County*

Gustav Schleicher (1823–1879)—Schleicher was born in Germany and studied engineering and architecture there before immigrating to Texas with other Germans. A member of both houses of the Texas legislature, Schleicher served as a captain of engineers in the Confederate army during the Civil War. After Reconstruction ended in Texas, Gustav Schleicher was elected to represent Texas in the U.S. House of Representatives. He served in that body from March 4, 1875 until his death on January 10, 1879. This county was created and named in his honor on April 1, 1887.

2696 *Scurry County*

William R. Scurry (1821–1864)—A native of Tennessee, Scurry came to Texas in 1840 and served in the congress of the republic of Texas. He enlisted as a private in the Mexican War, served with distinction and rose to the rank of major. Scurry was a representative to Texas' secession convention in early 1861 and when Texas seceded from the Union, he entered the army of the Confederate States of America as a lieutenant–colonel and was promoted to brigadier–general effective September 12, 1862. Scurry was killed in combat at the battle of Jenkins' Ferry, Arkansas, on April 30, 1864. By 1876 Reconstruction had ended in Texas and it was possible to name counties in honor of heroes of the Confederate army. Scurry County was created on August 21, 1876.

2697 *Shackelford County*

John Shackelford (1790–1857)—A native of Virginia and a physician, Shackelford became a wealthy planter and slave owner in Alabama and served in the Alabama senate before coming to Texas to assist in the Texas Revolution. Dr. Shackelford raised a company of volunteers for the Texas army and furnished arms and clothing for them from his own funds. The trousers were red and his company came to be called the Red Rovers. He fought in the Goliad campaign of 1836 and at the battle of Coleto, Shackelford was among the force of Texans who were captured and marched to Goliad, Texas. There, about 90 percent of the Texas soldiers were massacred in the Goliad massacre. The Mexicans chose to spare Dr. Shackelford's life so he could care for wounded Mexican soldiers. He survived the Texas Revolution and died in Alabama on January 22, 1857. This county was created ten days later, on February 1, 1858.

2698 *Shelby County*

Municipality of Shelby—On January 11, 1836, the name of the municipality of

Tenahaw (or Tenehaw) was changed by the republic of Texas to Shelby. When this county was created on March 17, 1836, it was named for that municipality of Shelby and replaced it. The municipality had been named for Isaac Shelby (1750–1826).

Isaac Shelby (1750–1826)— Shelby was a delegate to the Virginia legislature and, later, to the North Carolina legislature. He served as a soldier in the Revolutionary War and then moved to Kentucky County, Virginia, where he was active in the movement to separate Kentucky from Virginia. Shelby was inaugurated as Kentucky's first governor and later fought in the War of 1812. President James Monroe offered Shelby the cabinet post of secretary of war in 1817 but Shelby declined.

2699 *Sherman County*

Sidney Sherman (1805–1873)— A native of Massachusetts, Sherman became a manufacturer in Kentucky and in 1835 he was a captain of militia there. He sold his cotton bagging plant in Kentucky and used the proceeds to equip a company of Kentucky volunteers to fight in the Texas Revolution. Sherman commanded one wing of the Texas army at the all-important battle of San Jacinto, the concluding action of the Texas Revolution. He was elected to the congress of the republic of Texas and in 1843 was made major-general of the militia. During the Civil War Sherman was appointed by the Texas secession convention as commandant of Galveston but illness forced him to retire from that position. By 1876 Reconstruction had ended in Texas, and it was possible to name counties in honor of soldiers of the Confederate army. This county was created on August 21, 1876, and named for Sidney Sherman, who died three years earlier.

2700 *Smith County*

James Smith (1792–1855)— This South Carolina native fought in the War of 1812. He came to Texas about 1835 and established an extensive plantation in northeastern Texas. During the Texas Revolution, Smith served as captain of a cavalry company and was promoted to colonel by the end of the Revolution. In 1841 he again served in the Texas army, as a brigadier-general guarding Texas' northwest frontier and in 1844 he commanded Texas troops sent to put down the so-called Regulator-Moderator war. General Smith was elected to the lower house of the first legislature of the state of Texas and this county was created by that legislature on April 11, 1846.

This was Texas' second Smith County. Earlier, on February 1, 1842, the republic of Texas had created a Smith County as a judicial county but that county became defunct as the result of a Texas supreme court decision. It was located southeast of today's Smith County.

2701 *Somervell County*

Alexander Somervell (1796–1854)— A native of Maryland, Somervell came to Mexican Texas in 1832 as a colonist in Stephen F. Austin's (1793–1836) second colony. He served as an officer in the Texas army at the battle of San Jacinto, the concluding action of the Texas Revolution and was secretary of war of the republic of Texas in the ad interim government of President David G. Burnet (1788–1870). Somervell served in the senate of the congress of the republic of Texas and was a brigadier-general in 1842 when he commanded the Somervell expedition sent to punish Mexico for predatory raids into Texas. This county was created on March 13, 1875, as Somerville which was soon officially changed to match the spelling of General Somervell's surname.

2702 *Starr County*

James H. Starr (1809–1890)— A native of Connecticut and a physician, Starr settled in Texas in 1837. He was appointed secretary of the treasury of the republic of Texas in the cabinet of President Mirabeau B. Lamar (1798–1859). In 1844 Starr entered into a partnership with Nathaniel C. Amory (–1864) in a banking and land agency and he became very adept in promoting Texas to prospective settlers throughout the United States. Hugh Best's *Debrett's Texas Peerage* calls Dr. Starr "First P. R. Man to Texas." During the Civil War Starr held some civilian administrative positions for the Confederacy. This county was created on February 10, 1848.

2703 *Stephens County*

Alexander H. Stephens (1812–1883)— After serving in both houses of the Georgia legislature, this native of Georgia was elected to represent that state in the U.S. House of Representatives and he served in that body from 1843 to 1859. Although Stephens was a reluctant secessionist, he was elected as the first and only vice-president of the Confederate States of America. When the Civil War ended, he was arrested by federal officials and imprisoned

for five months. In 1866 Georgia elected him to the U.S. Senate but he was denied his seat. However, Stephens did serve again in the U.S. House of Representatives, from 1873 to 1882, when he was elected governor of Georgia. This Texas county was created on January 22, 1858, and named Buchanan County. At that time Texas was a member of the United States of America and James Buchanan was the U.S. president. This county's name was changed to Stephens County during December, 1861, while Texas was a member state of the Confederate States of America.

2704 *Sterling County*

W. S. Sterling (–)— This county in west-central Texas was created on March 4, 1891, and named for W. S. Sterling, about whom little is known. He came to the Sterling County area when it was even wilder than it is now (present population about one person per square mile), having at least visited here by 1858. He had a home on Sterling Creek, which was also named for him. Sterling was a buffalo hunter, rancher, Indian fighter and shipped buffalo hides to Fort Concho. Several sources refer to him as "Captain Sterling." Beverly Daniels' work entitled *Milling Around Sterling County: A History of Sterling County* tells us that W. S. Sterling was the first White man to settle within what is now Sterling County and that he remained in the area as long as there were buffalo left to hunt. Daniels' history of the county and several other sources state that W. S. Sterling left this area and went to Arizona territory where he was a U.S. marshall and was ambushed and killed by Apache Indians. This connection with Arizona territory is possible but it may well reflect confusion with Albert D. Sterling (–1882), an Ohio native, who had no known connection with Texas but was chief of Indian police in Arizona territory and was killed by Apache Indians on April 19, 1882.

2705 *Stonewall County*

Thomas J. Jackson (1824–1863)— Born in the portion of Virginia that is now the state of West Virginia, Thomas J. "Stonewall" Jackson was an 1846 graduate of the U.S. Military Academy at West Point and served as an officer in the U.S. army in the Mexican War. In 1852 he resigned his commission to become an instructor at Virginia Military Institute and he entered the Confederate army as a colonel when the Civil War began. By June, 1861, he had been promoted to brigadier-general and his stalwart service at the battle of First Manassas earned him the nickname "Stonewall" and a promotion to major-general. He continued to serve with unusual distinction and became something of a celebrity. After victories in 1862 at Second Manassas, Harpers Ferry and Sharpsburg, Jackson was elevated to the rare three star rank of lieutenant-general on October 10, 1862. His subsequent brief career was marked with victories until May, 1863, when he was accidentally shot by members under his own command, forcing amputation of his left arm and causing pneumonia from which he died on May 10, 1863. The general-in-chief of all Confederate armies said of Jackson: "He has lost his left arm; but I have lost my right arm." By 1876 Reconstruction had ended in Texas and it was possible to name counties in honor of heroes of the Confederate army. This county was created on August 21, 1876.

2706 *Sutton County*

John S. Sutton (1821–1862)— A native of Delaware, Sutton came to the republic of Texas in 1840 and served as a captain in the Texan Santa Fe expedition of 1841 and was among those captured and taken to Mexico City. Sutton was released in time to participate in the Mier raiding expedition into Mexico in 1842. During the Mexican War of 1846–1848 Sutton held the rank of captain in actions against the Indians. In 1861 he became a lieutenant-colonel of Texas cavalry in the Confederate army and on February 21, 1862, in an engagement at Valverde, in New Mexico territory, Sutton was mortally wounded. This county was created on April 1, 1887.

2707 *Swisher County*

James G. Swisher (1794–1864)— A native of Tennessee, Swisher served as a private in the War of 1812 and came to Mexican Texas in 1833. Here he was a participant in early actions of the Texas Revolution. Swisher was a captain in the successful siege of Bexar, a delegate to the convention of 1836 and one of the signers of Texas Declaration of Independence produced by that convention. This county was created on August 21, 1876.

2708 *Tarrant County*

Edward H. Tarrant (1796–1858)— A native of North Carolina, Tarrant moved with his family to Tennessee at an early age and served in the army under General Andrew Jackson in actions against the Indians and in the War of 1812. In 1835 he immigrated to Texas, became involved in the Texas Revolution and served in the congress of the republic of Texas. Tarrant served with the Texas Rangers guarding Texas' northwestern frontier and was a brigadier-general on May 22, 1841, when forces under his command attacked Indians on Village Creek, six miles east of today's Fort Worth. The attack was successful and helped open the present Tarrant County area of Texas to White settlers. He was a representative to the convention of 1845, which approved the offer of annexation to the United States and drafted the state's constitution. After annexation Tarrant served in the state legislature. This county was created on December 20, 1849.

2709 *Taylor County*

Uncertain but certain— This county was created on February 1, 1858. Works dealing with the history, geography and place names of Texas offer a variety of opinions on this county's namesake. The Taylor family of the Robertson colony is mentioned by some, others say Edward Taylor (and/or both he and his wife) of that colony and some cite the Taylor brothers who died at the Alamo. Juanita Daniel Zachry's history of Taylor County, published in 1980, tells us that the *Texas Almanac* of 1873 indicated that the county was named for three members of the Texas legislature during the session that Taylor County was created: M. D. K. Taylor, William M. Taylor and R. H. Taylor. In situations like this, where sources consulted disagree concerning a county's namesake, your author customarily comments "Uncertain." However the notation "Uncertain but certain" is more appropriate in this case because of aggressive work performed by Mrs. Dallas Scarborough, the Abilene Chapter of the Daughters of 1812, the Abilene Chamber of Commerce, the Taylor County Commissioners Court and other civic groups, who asked the Texas legislature in March, 1954 (96 years after the county had been created) to take official action to specify the county's namesake(s). Juanita Daniel Zachry's history of Taylor County reports that Mrs. Scarborough and the other Abilene-area "squeaky wheels" got results: "Senator Harley Sadler and Rep. Truitt Latimer introduced a bill officially designating the three Taylor brothers who died in the Alamo, Edward, James and George, as the men for whom Taylor County was named. The bill was introduced and the Taylor brothers so named, were officially recognized."

Taylor brothers who died at the Alamo— In 1836, during the Texas Revolution, the Mexican army placed the Alamo, in San Antonio, Texas under siege for 13 days. Inside the Alamo were about 185 Texan defenders, all of whom were slain when the Mexicans stormed the Alamo on the morning of March 6, 1836. Among those who died in that epic confrontation were three Taylor brothers, Edward, George and James.

Edward Taylor (1812–1836)— A native of Tennessee and the eldest of the three Taylor brothers who died at the Alamo, Edward had been working as a farm hand on the cotton farm of Captain Dorsett in Liberty, Texas, when he joined the Texas army as a private. He served as a rifleman defending the Alamo.

George Taylor (1816–1836)— A native of Tennessee and the youngest of the three Taylor brothers who died at the Alamo, George had been working as a farm hand on the cotton farm of Captain Dorsett in Liberty, Texas, when he joined the Texas army as a private. He served as a rifleman defending the Alamo.

James Taylor (1814–1836)— A native of Tennessee, James had been working with his two brothers as a farm hand on the cotton farm of Captain Dorsett in Liberty, Texas when he joined the Texas army as a private. He served as a rifleman defending the Alamo.

A bronze sculpture of the three Taylor brothers, created by Lincoln Borglum, stands in Abilene, Texas, the county seat of Taylor County, Texas. For the record, it should be noted that a fourth private and rifleman named Taylor, William Taylor (1799–1836), also died defending the Alamo. However, he was not related to the three Taylor brothers and he is not mentioned as a possible namesake of Taylor County.

2710 *Terrell County*

Alexander W. Terrell (1827–1912)— A native of Virginia and a lawyer, Terrell came to Texas from Missouri in 1852. Here he was a judge of the second district. In 1863 Terrell entered the army of the Confederate States of America as a lieutenant-colonel. He served with distinction and was promoted to full colonel and later "assigned to duty" as a brigadier-general on May 16, 1865, but he was never officially promoted to that rank by President Jefferson Davis since the Confederacy had already surrendered on April 9, 1865. After the war Terrell fled to Mexico, but later returned to Texas where he practiced law and served in both houses of the state legislature. From 1893 to 1897 Terrell was the U.S. minister to Turkey. This county was created on April 8, 1905.

2711 Terry County

Benjamin F. Terry (1821–1861)—This Kentucky native moved with his family to Mexican Texas in 1831. Prior to the Civil War, Terry was a sugar planter in Fort Bend County. He was elected as a delegate to Texas secession convention in early 1861 and entered the Confederate army to fight at First Manassas. Colonel Terry then returned to Texas to organize the cavalry force called Terry's Texas Rangers. On December 17, 1861, he was killed in combat in a skirmish against Union forces at Rowlett's Station, near Woodsonville, Green River, Kentucky. By 1876 Reconstruction had ended in Texas and it was possible to name counties in honor of heroes of the Confederate army. This county was created on August 21, 1876.

2712 Throckmorton County

Uncertain—This county was created on January 13, 1858. *The Handbook of Texas*, published by the Texas State Historical Association in 1952 states that it was named for William Edward Throckmorton (1795–1843) and that "the naming was probably a compliment to his son, James W. Throckmorton, then senator and later governor." Z. T. Fulmore's work entitled *The History & Geography of Texas as Told in County Names* says the county was named for "Dr. William Edward Throckmorton." *A Biographical Souvenir of the State of Texas*, published in 1889 tells us that Governor James W. Throckmorton's father was Dr. William E. Throckmorton and that some years after the death of William E. Throckmorton "in respect to his memory, the county of Throckmorton was named by the joint efforts of Major Absalom Bishop, of Wise and John Henry Brown, then members of the legislature, who knew his worth and chose that mode of commemorating it. His son was also a member at that time, but was wholly ignorant of the intended compliment until the bill was introduced by Colonel Brown." Finally, John Clements' *Texas Facts*, published in 1988 weighs in with the statement that this county was "Named for Dr. William E. Throckmorton, an early settler of Collin County. Probably as a compliment to his son, James W. Throckmorton, at that time a Texas senator, later governor of Texas."

James W. Throckmorton (1825–1894)—Born in Tennessee, and a son of William E. Throckmorton (1795–1843), James came with his family to the republic of Texas in 1841. He studied medicine in Kentucky and served as a surgeon in the Mexican War of 1846 to 1848. James served some ten years in both houses of the Texas legislature and as an officer in the Confederate army during the Civil War. After the Civil War he was elected governor of Texas but was removed by Union General Philip H. Sheridan (1831–1888) as "an impediment to Reconstruction." James later was elected to the U.S. House of Representatives and was allowed to take his seat on December 6, 1875.

William E. Throckmorton(1795–1843)—A native of Virginia and a physician, William E. Throckmorton lived in Tennessee, Illinois and Arkansas before settling in the republic of Texas in 1841. He settled near Melissa in northern Texas, in the area that a few years later became Collin County. *The Handbook of Texas* states that "Throckmorton County, when created on January 13, 1858, was named 'in honor of Dr. William E. Throckmorton, one of the first pioneers of northern Texas'" (apparently a quotation from the act that created Throckmorton County) "...the naming was probably a compliment to his son, James W. Throckmorton, then senator and later governor."

2713 Titus County

Andrew J. Titus (–1855)—A native of Tennessee, Titus' year of birth is given as 1814 in some accounts, and 1823 in others. He first visited Mexican Texas with his father in 1832, then returned with his family in 1839 and settled near the Red River a dozen miles east of today's Clarksville in Red River County. This early Texas pioneer was involved in opening the first road and stage coach line to link Jefferson, Texas, to the Red River. Richard L. Jurney's *History of Titus County, Texas: 1846–1960* states that Titus was a farmer in the Clarksville area, "...one of the largest landowners in this part of the State at the time of his death" and served in the Texas Revolution; also that he served in the Mexican War, a statement confirmed by *The Handbook of Texas*. This county was created on May 11, 1846. After the county had been named in his honor, Jackson served in the legislature of the state of Texas in 1851 and 1852.

2714 Tom Green County

Thomas Green (1814–1864)—A native of Virginia and a lawyer Green immigrated to Texas in late 1835, as Anglo-American Texans were agitating for independence from Mexico. He fought as a private in the battle of San Jacinto, the concluding action of the Texas Revolution and later served in the congress of the republic of Texas. During the Mexican War, he fought as a captain. When Texas seceded from the Union, Green entered the Confederate army as a colonel, served with distinction and was promoted to brigadier-general. His superior officer, Major-general Richard Taylor (1826–1879) requested that Green be promoted to major-general but General Green was soon killed in combat at Blair's Landing, Louisiana, on April 12, 1864. This county was created on March 13, 1874, shortly after Reconstruction ended in Texas.

2715 Travis County

William B. Travis (1809–1836)—In 1836, during the Texas Revolution, the Mexican army placed the Alamo, in San Antonio, Texas under siege for 13 days. Inside the Alamo were about 185 Texan defenders, all of whom were slain when the Mexicans stormed the Alamo on the morning of March 6, 1836. The commanding officer of the Texas soldiers who died in that epic confrontation was Lieutenant-colonel William B. Travis, a native of South Carolina and a lawyer, who had come to Mexican Texas in 1831. Although he had been appointed in 1834 as secretary of the *ayuntamiento* ("municipal government" or "town council") of San Felipe de Austin by Mexican authorities, in 1835 Travis became active in military efforts against Mexico. By February, 1836, he had been made a lieutenant-colonel and was one of two commanders of the garrison defending the Alamo. In late February, Travis was given sole command of the Alamo and died leading his troops defending it two weeks later. This county was created by the republic of Texas on January 25, 1840.

2716 Trinity County

Trinity River—This county in eastern Texas was created on February 11, 1850, and named for the Trinity River, which forms the county's southwestern border. The Trinity River is formed by the confluence of forks, just northwest of Dallas, Texas and flows some 550 miles in a southeastern direction to enter the Gulf of Mexico via Trinity Bay, an arm of Galveston Bay. The Trinity River was probably named in 1690, while Texas was part of New Spain (Mexico) by Captain Alonso de Leon

(1640–), the governor of Coahuila. The name "Trinity" is the English translation of the Spanish *Trinidad*. The dogma of the Trinity is a central doctrine of orthodox Christian faith. It asserts that God is one is essence but three in persons; i.e., Father, Son (Jesus Christ) and Holy Spirit. This county is the second Trinity County that Texas has possessed. The first county was created as a judicial county on February 5, 1840, and given the name Trinity on December 7, 1841, but then abolished as the result of a Texas supreme court decision.

2717 *Tyler County*

John Tyler (1790–1862)— A native of Virginia and a graduate of the College of William & Mary there, Tyler served in the Virginia legislature, represented the state in both houses of the U.S. Congress and was its governor. In 1839 Tyler became the Whig party's candidate for vice-president on the ticket headed by General William Henry Harrison (1773–1841) and they won the election. Harrison caught pneumonia during his inauguration ceremonies and served as president only 31 days before dying from the illness. Vice-president Tyler became President Tyler on April 6, 1841, and President Tyler soon became alarmed that Great Britain might add the republic of Texas to the British empire. Shortly before President Tyler's term as president ended, he signed the bill offering to annex the republic of Texas and annexation occurred a few months after he left the presidency. During the Civil War, Tyler represented Virginia in the provisional congress of the Confederate States of America and was elected to the first regular congress of the Confederacy but died before taking his seat in it. This Texas county was originally created by the republic of Texas as a "district" named Menard District, on January 22, 1841. That district was abolished as the result of a Texas supreme court decision which found it to be an unconstitutional "judicial county." That first version of the present Tyler County, Texas had larger boundaries than the present Tyler County, which was created on April 3, 1846, three months after Texas was annexed to the United States. The present Menard County in Texas contains no land that was within the earlier Menard District here.

2718 *Upshur County*

Abel P. Upshur (1791–1844)— A native of Virginia and a lawyer, Upshur served in the Virginia legislature and held judicial offices in that state. After Vice-president John Tyler became president upon the death of President William Henry Harrison, Tyler appointed Upshur to his cabinet as secretary of the navy and in 1843 President Tyler elevated him to secretary of state. As our nation's secretary of state he was a key figure during the period that President Tyler became alarmed that Great Britain might add the republic of Texas to the British empire. However, Upshur was killed in an accident near our nation's capitol aboard a U.S. warship on February 28, 1844, before the U.S. officially offered annexation to Texas. This county was created on April 27, 1846, just four months after Texas had become the 28th state in our Union.

2719 *Upton County*

John C. Upton (1828–1862) & William F. Upton (1832–1887)— On February 7, 1887, William F. Upton died and this county in western Texas was created three weeks later, on February 26, 1887. It was named for both William F. Upton and his brother John C. Upton. The Upton brothers were heroes of the Confederacy, who served in General John B. Hood's (1831–1879) brigade during the Civil War.

John C. Upton (1828–1862)— This Tennessee native moved to California and lived there for about nine years before coming to Texas in 1859. Here he supervised his mother's plantation until 1861, when he raised a company and became a captain in the Confederate army. Both John and his brother, William, were attached to Hood's Texas brigade. John served with distinction and rose to the rank of lieutenant-colonel before being killed in combat at the battle of Second Manassas, in 1862.

William F. Upton (1832–1887)— William F. Upton was born in Tennessee, immigrated to Texas in the 1850's and farmed until 1861 when he entered the Confederate army as a captain and served, with his brother, John, in Hood's Texas brigade. He served with distinction throughout the war and rose to the rank of lieutenant-colonel. After the Civil War he returned to Fayette County, Texas, and farming, became the leading merchant in Schulenburg, Texas and served in the Texas legislature.

2720 *Uvalde County*

Uvalde Canyon— This county in southwestern Texas was created on February 8, 1850, and named for Uvalde Canyon. The canyon's name derived from that of Juan de Ugalde, who went north of the Rio Grande in 1790 to punish Comanche Indians, who were thwarting Spain's efforts to colonize the Texas area of New Spain (Mexico). *The Handbook of Texas*, published by the Texas State Historical Association in 1952, states that "…after several battles, [he] drove them to the rocky divide along the Llano River. The canyon was called Canon de Ugalde in honor of the captain, and during years of usage the name Ugalde came to be written Uvalde…" (Although this passage of *The Handbook* refers to Ugalde as a captain, a biographical sketch elsewhere in the same work indicates he held a higher rank when the canyon was named for him.)

Juan de Ugalde (1729–)— A Spanish military officer and a veteran of extensive combat on the European continent, Ugalde was sent to the New World and served in the Spanish army in Peru for eight years before being transferred to New Spain (Mexico). On November 23, 1777, Ugalde became the civil and military governor of Coahuila and Texas and was involved in numerous forays against hostile Indians. Although he lost his position as governor as a result of a quarrel with General Teodoro de Croix (1730–1792), Ugalde continued to receive military promotion and was a colonel and later commandant general. Expeditions against Indians took Ugalde into what is now Texas in 1787, to the Big Bend area, in 1789 to the San Saba presidio, and 1790 near San Antonio. In his military efforts in Texas, Ugalde attempted to strengthen it for attacks by both Indians and potential European forces.

2721 *Val Verde County*

Civil War engagement at Valverde, New Mexico territory— During the Civil War, Confederate forces under the command of General Henry H. Sibley (1816–1886) attempted to capture New Mexico territory for the South. On February 21, 1862, General Sibley and some 2,600 soldiers, most of whom were Texans, engaged Union troops led by Colonel Edward R. S. Canby (1817–1873) at Valverde, New Mexico territory. *The Civil War Day by Day: An Almanac: 1861–1865* by E. B. Long and Barbara Long states that "The engagement of Valverde resulted from a contest over a ford by which the Confederates intended to cut off the fort on the west side of the Rio Grande. After brisk fighting the Federals withdrew to the fort, and the victorious Confederate column moved on north toward Santa Fe … Canby's Federals had about 3,810 men and lost 68 killed, 160 wounded, and 35 missing, while the Confederates lost 31 killed, 154 wounded and 1 missing." General Sibley continued to enjoy success for a time during his New Mexican campaign but lacking reinforcements and supplies, eventually had to withdraw and leave it in Union hands. This county was created on February 20, 1885. The name Pierce had been proposed by some as the name for this new county, in honor of an official of the Southern Pacific Railroad, but that name was not adopted. *Valverde* is Spanish for "green valley."

2722 *Van Zandt County*

Isaac Van Zandt (1813–1847)—A Tennessee native who moved to Mississippi, Van Zandt became a lawyer before settling in the republic of Texas in 1838 or 1839. Here he was elected to the congress of the republic and also served as its charge d' affairs to the United States. Van Zandt was a member of the convention of 1845, which approved the offer of annexation to the United States and drafted the state's constitution, and in 1847 he became a candidate for governor. During his campaign for that office, he was stricken with yellow fever and died in Houston on October 11, 1847. This county was created less than six months later, on March 20, 1848.

2723 *Victoria County*

Municipality of Victoria, Texas—This county in southern Texas was created by the infant republic of Texas on March 17, 1836, and named for the municipality of Victoria, its county seat, a few miles above the mouth of the Guadalupe River. The settlement here was first named Nuestra Senora de Guadalupe de Jesus Victoria, which was shortened to Guadalupe Victoria and finally to Victoria. Today's city of Victoria, Texas, has a population of 55,000, several petrochemical plants and is the cattle market for the region. The name *Victoria* honored Guadalupe Victoria (1786–1843), the first president of Mexico after independence from Spain.

Guadalupe Victoria (1786–1843)—Born with the name Juan Manuel Felix Fernandez, in New Spain (Mexico) this freedom-fighter, patriot and early political leader changed his given name to Guadalupe, in honor of the patron saint of Mexico, Our Lady of Guadalupe, the sainted Virgin Mary, and his surname to Victoria to show Mexico's desire for freedom from Spain. He was an early partisan in the revolution-

ary activities of Padre Miguel Hidalgo y Costilla (1753–1811), and continued as a leader in Mexico's struggle for independence after Padre Hidalgo was captured by trickery, degraded from the priesthood and executed. After independence from Spain, in Mexico's first national election in 1824, Victoria was elected president of Mexico. Hubert Herring's *A History of Latin America* tells us that Victoria "served out his full term (1825–29), and he never turned a dishonest centavo" but that "for all his virtues, was no administrator and lacked both the force and the cunning to discipline his scheming colleagues."

2724 *Walker County*

Originally: Robert J. Walker (1801–1869). Changed to: Samuel H. Walker (–1847)—This county was created on April 6, 1846, and named for Robert J. Walker (1801–1869). In 1863, during the Civil War, the honor was withdrawn because of Robert J. Walker's Union sympathies and the county's namesake was changed to Samuel H. Walker (–1847).

Robert J. Walker (1801–1869)—A native of Pennsylvania and a graduate of the University of Pennsylvania, Robert J. Walker became a lawyer before moving to Mississippi in 1826. He represented that state in the U.S. Senate from February 22, 1836, to March 5, 1845, and was an advocate, in the senate, of annexation of Texas by the U.S. He served in President James K. Polk's cabinet as secretary of the treasury and, very briefly in 1857, as governor of Kansas territory.

Samuel H. Walker (–1847)—Born in Maryland about 1810, Samuel H. Walker immigrated to the republic of Texas in 1836 and joined Captain John C. Hays' (1817–1883) company of Texas Rangers. He was sent to New York to acquire arms from Samuel Colt (1814–1862), for the republic of Texas and suggested some design changes for the revolver which were adopted. The resulting Walker-Colt revolver was used extensively on the Texas frontier against Indians and outlaws. After the Texas Revolution Samuel H. Walker was involved in hostilities between the republic and Mexico and was twice taken as a prisoner by the Mexican army. During the U.S. Mexican War of 1846 to 1848 he served with distinction and died in combat in Mexico in 1847.

2725 *Waller County*

Edwin Waller (1800–1881)—This Virginia native came to Mexican Texas in 1831

and participated in the battle of Velasco on June 26, 1832, a prelude to the Texas Revolution. Waller was a representative at the Consultation of 1835 and a member of the general council of the provisional government of the republic of Texas. A delegate to the convention of 1836, he was one of the signers of the Texas Declaration of Independence drafted by that convention. Waller was appointed postmaster general of the republic of Texas by President Mirabeau B. Lamar (1798–1859) but resigned before actually serving in that post. He later served as mayor of Austin and as a delegate to Texas' session convention of 1861. This county was created on April 28, 1873.

2726 *Ward County*

Thomas W. Ward (–1872)—Born in Ireland about 1807, Ward immigrated to North America and came to Texas by way of Quebec, Canada and New Orleans. During the Texas Revolution he fought in the successful siege of Bexar but lost a leg to a cannon ball during the fighting. Ward served as commissioner of the general land office of the republic of Texas and was mayor of Austin. He was an opponent of Texas seceding from the Union. After the Civil War, Ward was collector of U.S. customs at the port of Corpus Christi, Texas, until President Ulysses S. Grant ordered him removed from that post. This county was created on February 26, 1887.

2727 *Washington County*

Municipality of Washington on the Brazos, Texas—This county in southeastern Texas was created on March 17, 1836, and named for the municipality of Washington on the Brazos, which became the county seat of the new county. Washington on the Brazos had been established in Mexican Texas in 1834 by a townsite company and in 1835 the Anglo-American citizens here successfully petitioned the Mexican government to establish it as a separate municipality. The convention of 1836 which drafted the Texas Declaration of Independence met at Washington on the Brazos and it was briefly the capital of the republic of Texas. The town relied on its river location and failed to develop railroad facilities. Also, in 1844 the county seat was moved from Washington on the Brazos to Brenham. As a result, Washington's importance and population withered away. By the late 19th century, population had dropped to a few hundred and at the millennium year 2000, the only reminder of the municipality's former glory is a 229-acre state historical park. *The Handbook of Texas*, published by the Texas State Historical Association in 1952, speculates that the town was named at the suggestion of Asa Hoxey, one of the members of the townsite company of 1834. Hoxey had come to Mexican Texas from Washington, Georgia, which was named for U.S. President George Washington.

George Washington (1732–1799)—Washington was a native of Virginia. He served in Virginia's house of burgesses and became one of the colonies' leaders in opposition to British policies in America. He was a member of the first and second Continental Congresses and commander of all Continental armies in the American Revolutionary War. Following victory in that war, Washington was elected to be the first president of the United States.

2728 Webb County

James Webb (1792–1856)—A native of Virginia and a lawyer, Webb served as a U.S. district judge in Florida territory before coming to the republic of Texas in 1838. Here he became acquainted with President Mirabeau B. Lamar (1798–1859), who appointed him to his cabinet as both secretary of state and attorney general. Webb served in the congress of the republic of Texas and was appointed minister to Mexico, but Mexico refused to receive him. He was a member of the convention of 1845, which approved the offer of annexation to the United States and drafted the state's constitution. He later served as secretary of state of the state of Texas and as a judge. This county was created on January 28, 1848.

2729 Wharton County

John A. Wharton (1806–1838) & William H. Wharton (1802–1839)—This county in southeastern Texas was created on April 3, 1846, and named for the Wharton brothers, John A. Wharton and William H. Wharton.

John A. Wharton (1806–1838)—Wharton's parents moved from Virginia to Tennessee shortly after his brother, William H. Wharton was born, and John was born in Tennessee. He became a lawyer there before coming to Mexican Texas in 1833 to join his brother, William here. John was a member of the Consultation of 1835 and, briefly, of the general counsel of the provisional government of the republic of Texas. During the Texas Revolution, John was adjutant-general and he fought at the

battle of San Jacinto, the concluding action of the Texas Revolution. In the ad interim government of President David G. Burnet (1788–1870), John A. Wharton served in the cabinet as secretary of war, and later was a representative in the first congress of the republic.

William H. Wharton (1802–1839)—Born in Virginia shortly before his parents moved to Tennessee, William H. Wharton became a lawyer in Tennessee before immigrating to Mexican Texas in 1827. He was a member of the convention of 1832 and the author of the petition asking Mexico to grant statehood to Texas. During the Texas Revolution he fought in the successful siege of Bexar and then was appointed one of the commissioners sent to the United States to secure aid for Texas. Later, under President Samuel Houston (1793–1863), William H. Wharton was minister to the United States and he was subsequently elected to the senate of the congress of the republic of Texas.

2730 Wheeler County

Royal T. Wheeler (1810–1864)—A native of Vermont, Wheeler spent his early life in Ohio and practiced law in Arkansas before immigrating to the republic of Texas in 1839. Here he practiced law and served the republic of Texas as a district attorney and district judge. As a district judge, Wheeler was also a member of the supreme court of the republic. After Texas was annexed to the United States in December, 1845, he was appointed to the supreme court of the state of Texas and became its chief justice in 1857. Judge Wheeler served as the state's chief justice from 1857 until his death in 1864. This county was created on August 21, 1876.

2731 Wichita County

Wichita River—This county in northern Texas was created on February 1, 1858, and named for the Wichita River, which flows through it. The Wichita River is a 250 mile long tributary of the Red River. It rises in three forks southeast of the Texas panhandle and flows in a generally northeastern direction to enter the Red River some 25 miles northeast of Wichita Falls, the county seat of Wichita County. The Wichita River was named for the Wichita Indians.

Wichita Indians—The Wichita were a confederacy of tribes of the Caddoan linguistic family who occupied a large area of America's southern and central plains from northern Texas into Oklahoma and

Kansas. Some of the Wichita were tepee-dwelling buffalo hunters while others were farmers who depended less on buffalo meat for their subsistence. Although the Wichita sometimes practiced cannibalism on enemies killed in battle, they were generally friendly to the Whites. In 1801 a smallpox epidemic killed large numbers of those Wichita Indians who were then living in Texas and their numbers continued to diminish rapidly over the next few decades as the result of encroaching Americans and raids on them by the Osage Indians. By the time of the America Civil War, most Wichita had moved to Indian territory (now Oklahoma). The meaning of the name *Wichita* is not known. Possible translations which have been mentioned include: "Painted faces," "Scattered lodges," "Raccoon eyed," "Men of the north" and "Big arbor." It was a custom of the Wichitas to paint and tattoo their faces which could explain either "painted faces" or "raccoon eyed" but the meaning of the Wichita Indians' name is uncertain.

2732 Wilbarger County

Josiah P. Wilbarger (1801–1845) & Mathias Wilbarger (–1853)—This county in northern Texas was created on February 1, 1858, and named for two of the Wilbarger brothers, Josiah P. and Mathias, surveyors and pioneers of early Texas. In early Texas being a surveyor automatically made one a part-time Indian-fighter. There was another Wilbarger brother, John Wesley Wilbarger, who came to Texas in 1837, but this county's name does not honor him.

Josiah P. Wilbarger (1801–1845)—Most sources state that Josiah P. Wilbarger was born in Kentucky, although Z. T. Fulmore's work entitled *The History & Geography of Texas as Told in County Names* tells us that he was a native of Rockingham County, Virginia. Josiah lived in Missouri before coming to Mexican Texas in 1827. Here he taught school, engaged in survey work and established a farm 75 miles distant from his nearest neighbor. In August, 1833, a party of which he was a member was attacked by Comanche Indians, four miles east of today's Austin, Texas. During that attack Josiah P. Wilbarger was scalped, but managed to survive the attack and was found alive the following day by Reuben Hornsby (1793–1879). Although Josiah never completely recovered from his wound, he lived to enjoy bragging rights for a dozen years.

Mathias Wilbarger (–1853)—Born in Kentucky about 1807 or 1808, Mathias

Wilbarger immigrated to Mexican Texas in 1829. He engaged in survey work and about 1830 erected a log cabin on a farm near that of his brother, Josiah P. Wilbarger. In 1850 Mathias was a resident of Williamson County and he died in that county, at Georgetown, on February 20, 1853.

2733 Willacy County

John G. Willacy (–1943)— Born in Louisville, Kentucky about 1859, John G. Willacy immigrated to Texas in 1892 and settled near Corpus Christi, about 80 miles north of the present Willacy County, and engaged in farming there. He was elected to both houses of the Texas legislature, serving first in the lower house and later in the senate. The *Handbook of Texas*, published by the Texas State Historical Association in 1952 states that "He was chairman of the committees on finance and internal improvements" and that he served on committees relating to judicial districts and stock raising. During the 1920's Willacy was tax commissioner of the state of Texas. This county was created on March 11, 1911, while John G. Willacy was serving in the Texas legislature, and he introduced the bill to create this new county.

2734 Williamson County

Robert M. Williamson (–1859)— Born in Georgia between 1804 and 1806, Williamson's right leg was crippled for life by a teen age illness, but a partial wooden leg (from the knee down) enabled him to lead a vigorous life. He practiced law in Georgia before coming to Mexican Texas about 1826 and establishing a newspaper. He edited it and two other newspapers in Mexican Texas and the power of the press enabled Williamson to appeal for resistance to Mexican tyranny. He was a delegate to the Consultation of 1835 and that body commissioned him as a major. He fought at the all-important battle of San Jacinto, the concluding action of the Texas Revolution and was a district judge of the republic of Texas and thereby a member of the republic's supreme court. Williamson also served in both houses of the congress of the republic of Texas. After Texas was annexed to the United States, Williamson was elected as a senator to the first two legislatures of the state of Texas. His legislative service ended in March, 1848, and it was during that term, on March 11, 1848, that this county was created and named in his honor.

2735 Wilson County

James C. Wilson (1816–1861)— Born in Yorkshire, England, Wilson immigrated to the republic of Texas, studied law and fought Indians. In 1842 he joined a punitive expedition into Mexico led by Alexander Somervell (1796–1854) and when that party disbanded and turned back to Texas, Wilson continued on in a force commanded by Captain William S. Fisher (–1845) in the ill-fated Mier Expedition. Wilson was among those captured by the Mexican army and sentenced to execution. He managed to escape in July, 1843. After Texas was annexed to the United States, Wilson served in both houses of the state legislature. A man of many talents, Wilson was elected commissioner of the Texas court of claims and was an itinerant Protestant minister. This county was created on February 13, 1860.

2736 Winkler County

Clinton M. Winkler (1821–1882)— A native of North Carolina, Winkler moved with his family to Indiana in his youth and he came to the republic of Texas in 1840. Here he studied law, was admitted to the bar and elected to the legislature of the state of Texas. In 1861, when Texas seceded from the Union, Winkler entered the army of the Confederate States of America as a captain in General John B. Hood's (1831–1879) Texas brigade. He served with distinction throughout the Civil War, rose to the rank of lieutenant-colonel and was severely wounded at the battle of Gettysburg, Pennsylvania. After the Civil War Winkler served in the Texas legislature and was a judge on the court of appeals at the time of his death. This county was created on February 26, 1887.

2737 Wise County

Henry A. Wise (1806–1876)— A native of Virginia and a lawyer, Wise represented Virginia in the U.S. House of Representatives as a champion of states' rights, from 1833 to 1844. He was our nation's minister to Brazil from 1844 to 1847. Wise was elected governor of Virginia in 1855 and served in that office from 1856 to 1860. When Virginia seceded from the federal Union, Henry A. Wise volunteered for and was appointed a brigadier-general in the army of the Confederate States of America. He served with distinction throughout the Civil War and was honored by being named a divisional commander, two days before the South's surrender at Appomattox, although he was never officially made a major-general. This Texas county was created on January 23, 1856, prior to the Civil War. Texas sources indicate that Wise had vigorously supported annexation of Texas while he was in congress.

2738 Wood County

George T. Wood (1795–1858)— A native of Georgia, Wood was an Indian fighter, merchant and member of the Georgia legislature. In 1839 he moved his family and some 30 slaves to the republic of Texas and established a large cotton plantation here in what is now San Jacinto County. Wood was a elected to the congress of the republic of Texas and was a member of the convention of 1845, which approved the offer of annexation to the United States and drafted the state's constitution. After annexation, he served in the state senate but resigned from that body to serve as a colonel in the Mexican War. Wood became a war hero at the battle of Monterrey, Mexico, which assisted him in being elected governor of Texas. He served as governor from December 21, 1847, to December 21, 1849. This county was created on February 5, 1850, less than two months after Governor Wood left office.

2739 Yoakum County

Henderson K. Yoakum (1810–1856)— A native of Tennessee and an 1832 graduate of the U.S. Military Academy at West Point, Yoakum resigned his lieutenant's commission to practice law in Tennessee. In 1836 he served under U.S. General Edmund P. Gaines (1777–1849) as a captain of mounted militia, near the Sabine River, defending Texas until the republic of Texas was established. Before settling in the republic of Texas in 1845, Yoakum was an army colonel in Tennessee and a member of the Tennessee legislature. He volunteered to serve as a private in the Mexican War and fought in combat as a lieutenant at Monterrey, Mexico. In 1855 Yoakum completed a two volume history of Texas. This county was created on August 21, 1876.

2740 Young County

William C. Young (1812–1862)— A native of Tennessee and a lawyer, Young immigrated to the republic of Texas in 1837 and settled in what is now Red River County. Young became the first sheriff of Red River County and was an Indian fighter and district attorney of the republic of Texas. He was a delegate to the convention of 1845, which approved the offer of annexation to the United States and drafted the state's constitution. Young raised a company of soldiers to fight during the Mexican War and later served as a U.S. marshall. During the Civil War, he commanded a Texas cavalry regiment and fought in what is now Oklahoma. On October 16, 1862, Colonel Young was killed near the Red River by a gang of predatory outlaws, who were loyal to neither the Union nor the Confederacy. This county was created on February 2, 1856.

2741 *Zapata County*

Antonio Zapata (–1840)— Zapata's association with Texas was through his revolutionary activities against the Mexican dictator, Antonio Lopez de Santa Anna (1794–1876), as Anglo-American Texans had also revolted against Santa Anna in the Texas Revolution. Antonio Zapata was born in Guerrero, Mexico, and he became a wealthy rancher. On January 17, 1840, rebel leaders of Mexico's northern states met in a convention and that convention declared the republic of Rio Grande independent from Mexico. Antonio Zapata was made a colonel and cavalry commander of the new republic, but Zapata met defeat in March, 1840, in combat at Morelos, Mexico. He was taken prisoner, tried by court martial and convicted of treason. On the day after Zapata was convicted, he was executed and his head was then set on a spike and placed on display at Guerrero, Mexico to discourage further opposition to Santa Anna's dictatorship. This Texas county was created on January 22, 1858.

2742 *Zavala County*

Manuel Lorenzo Justiniano de Zavala (1789–1836)— Born in Madrid, Spain, Zavala was brought by his father to Spain's captain-generalcy of the Yucatan peninsula in central America. Educated in Europe, Zavala returned to the Yucatan and became a prominent political leader in the early days of Mexico's independence from Spain. He supported Vicente Guerrero (–1831) for president and when Guerrero was elected, he appointed Zavala minister of the Mexican treasury. In 1829 Zavala received an empresario contract to introduce 500 families in Mexican Texas. Later, when Antonio Lopez de Santa Anna (1794–1876) came to power in Mexico, he appointed Zavala as his minister to France. While serving in Paris, Zavala became disillusioned with Santa Anna, and he brought his family to settle in Texas. Here he became an active participant in the Texas

Revolution. Zavala was a representative at the Consultation of 1835 and, as a delegate to the convention of 1836, he became a signer of Texas Declaration of Independence produced by that convention. He then served as the vice-president of the republic of Texas in the ad interim government of President David G. Burnet (1788–1870). This county's name was spelled incorrectly as Zavalla County, when it was created on February 1, 1858. The spelling of the county's name was subsequently corrected.

REFERENCES

Acheson, Sam. *Dallas Yesterday*. Dallas, SMU Press, 1977.

Allen, Irene Taylor. *Saga of Anderson: The Proud Story of a Historic Texas Community*. New York, New York, Greenwich Book Publishers, 1957.

Allen, William. *Captain John B. Denton*. Chicago, R. R. Donnelley & Sons Co., 1905.

Almon, Millard H. *The Five States of Texas*. Dallas, 1961.

Andrews County History: 1876–1978. Andrews, Texas, Andrews County Heritage Committee, 1978.

Applegate, Howard G., & C. Wayne Hanselka. "La Junta de los Rios del Norte y Conchos." *University of Texas at El Paso Southwestern Studies*, Monograph No. 41. El Paso: 1974.

Aransas Pass, Texas. Aransas Pass, Texas, Aransas Pass Chamber of Commerce, 1976.

Armstrong County Historical Association. *A Collection of Memories: A History of Armstrong County: 1876–1965*. Hereford, Texas, Pioneer Publishers, 1965.

Arneson, Edwin P. "The Early Art of Terrestrial Measurement and Its Practice in Texas." *Southwestern Historical Quarterly*, Vol. 29, No. 2. Austin: October, 1925.

Arrington, Fred. *A History of Dickens County*. Nortex Offset Publications, Inc., 1971.

Astride the Old San Antonio Road: A History of Burleson County, Texas. Dallas, Taylor Publishing Co., 1980.

Atascosa County Centennial: 1856–1956. Atascosa County, Texas, Atascosa County Centennial Association, 1956.

Atascosa County History. Pleasanton, Texas, Atascosa History Committee, 1984.

Baird, G. H. *A Brief History of Upshur County*. Gilmer, Texas, Gilmer Mirror, 1946.

Baker, Inez. *Yesterday in Hall County, Texas*. Dallas, Book Craft, 1940.

Bandera County History Book Committee. *History of Bandera County, Texas*. Dallas, Curtis Media Corp., 1986.

Barkley, Mary Starr. *History of Travis County & Austin: 1839–1899*. Austin, Austin Printing Co., 1963.

Batte, Lelia M. *History of Milam County, Texas*. San Antonio, Naylor Co., 1956.

Batts, R. L. "Defunct Counties of Texas." *Quarterly of the Texas State Historical Association*, Vol. 1, No. 2. Austin: October, 1897.

Bauer, Grace. *Bee County Centennial: 1858–1958*. Beeville, Bee County Centennial, Inc., 1958.

Baylor County Historical Society. *Salt Pork to Sirloin: The History of Baylor County, Texas from 1879 to 1930*. Wichita Falls, Texas, Nortex Offset Publications, Inc., 1972.

Belisle, John G. *History of Sabine Parish, Louisiana*. Sabine Banner Press, 1912.

Benavides, Adan. *The Bexar Archives: 1717–1836*. Austin, University of Texas Institute of Texan Cultures at San Antonio, 1989.

Benedictine Monks of St. Augustine's Abbey, Ramsgate. *The Book of Saints*. New York, Thomas Y. Crowell Co., 1966.

Bennett, Bob. *Kerr County, Texas: 1856–1956*. San Antonio, Naylor Co., 1956.

Bennett, Carmen Taylor. *Cottle County, My Dear: Where the "Pan" Joins the "Handle."* Floydada, Texas, Blanco Offset Printing Inc., 1979.

Benson, Nettie Lee. "Texas Collection." *Southwestern Historical Quarterly*, Vol. 50, No. 2. Austin: October, 1946.

Benson, Nettie Lee. "Texas Collection." *Southwestern Historical Quarterly*, Vol. 51, No. 1. Austin: July, 1947.

Benthul, Herman F. *Wording Your Way Through Texas*. Burnet, Texas, Eakin Press, 1981.

Best, Hugh. *Debrett's Texas Peerage*. New York, Coward-McCann, Inc., 1983.

Bexar County Annual: Texas State Guide. San Antonio, Albert Schutze, 1923.

Bierschwale, Margaret. *Fort Mason, Texas*.

Biographical Directory of the Texan Conventions & Congresses: Republic of Texas: 1832–1845. Austin, 1941.

Biographical Encyclopedia of Texas. New York, Southern Publishing Co., 1880.

Biographical Souvenir of the State of Texas. Chicago, F. A. Battey & Co., 1889.

Bitner, Grace. "Early History of the Concho Country & Tom Green County." *West Texas Historical Association Year Book*, Vol. 9. Abilene: October, 1933.

Blackburn, Mrs. L. L. "Early Settlers & Settlements of Callahan County." *West*

Texas Historical Association Year Book, Vol. 23. Abilene: October, 1947.

Boeta, Jose R. *Bernardo de Galvez*. Madrid, Spain, Publicaciones Espanolas, 1977.

Boethel, Paul C. *History of Lavaca County*. Austin, Von Boeckmann-Jones, 1959.

Bosque County History Book Committee. *Bosque County. Land & People: A History of Bosque County, Texas*. Bosque County Historical Commission, 1985.

Bosquerama: Centennial Celebration of Bosque County, Texas. 1954.

Bowles, Flora G. *A History of Trinity County, Texas: 1827 to 1928*. Groveton, Texas, Groveton Independent School, 1966.

Briggs, Donald C., & Marvin Alisky. *Historical Dictionary of Mexico*. Metuchen, New Jersey, Scarecrow Press, Inc., 1981.

Brinegar, Bonnie. "Choctaw Place-Names in Mississippi." *Mississippi Folklore Register*, Vol. 11, No. 2. Hattiesburg, Mississippi: Fall, 1977.

Browder, Virginia. *Donley County: Land O' Promise*. Nortex Press, 1975.

Brown, John H. *History of Texas*. Austin, Jenkins Publishing Co., 1970.

Brown, John H. *Indian Wars & Pioneers of Texas*. Austin, L. E. Daniell, 1880.

Burleson, Texas: The First One Hundred Years. Dallas, Taylor Publishing Co., 1981.

Cameron, Minnie B. "Texas Collection." *Southwestern Historical Quarterly*, Vol. 53, No. 4. Austin: April, 1950.

Camp County, Texas: Customs & Characters: A Sesquicentennial History. Dallas, Taylor Publishing Co., 1986.

Campbell, Harry H. *The Early History of Motley County*. Wichita Falls, Texas, Nortex Offset Publications, Inc., 1971.

Carr, Waggoner. "Revisiting History: A Look at Texas-Cherokee Nation Land Dispute." *Texas Bar Journal*, Vol. 58, No. 4. Austin: April, 1995.

Carroll, H. Bailey. "Texas Collection." *Southwestern Historical Quarterly*, Vol. 54, No. 1. Austin: July, 1950.

Carroll, H. Bailey, et al. *Heroes of Texas*. Waco, Texian Press, 1964.

Casey, Clifford B. *Mirages, Mysteries & Reality: Brewster County, Texas: The Big Bend of the Rio Grande*. Hereford, Texas, Pioneer Book Publishers, Inc., 1972.

Castro Colonies Heritage Association, Inc. *The History of Medina County, Texas*. Dallas, National Share Graphics, Inc.

Cates, Cliff D. *Pioneer History of Wise County*. St. Louis, Missouri, Nixon-Jones Printing Co., 1907.

Cave, Edward. *Kaufman: A Pictorial History: 1840-1980*. 1981.

A Century of Texas Governors. Austin,

Texas Centennial of Statehood Commission, 1943.

Chabot, Frederick C. *With the Makers of San Antonio*. San Antonio, Artes Graficas, 1937.

Chamblin, Thomas S. *The Historical Encyclopedia of Texas*. Texas Historical Institute, 1982.

Chavez, Angelico. "Saints Names in New Mexico Geography." *El Palacio*, Vol. 56, No. 11. Santa Fe: November, 1949.

Cherokee County History. Jacksonville, Texas, Cherokee County Historical Commission.

Clarke, Mary Whatley. *The Palo Pinto Story*. Fort Worth, Manney Co., 1956.

Clemens, Gus. *The Concho Country*. San Antonio, Mulberry Avenue Books, 1981.

Clements, John. *Flying the Colors: Texas*. Dallas, Clements Research, Inc., 1984.

Clements, John. *Texas Facts*. Dallas, Clements Research II, Inc., 1988.

Cohen, Robert. "Book Review: The Last Known Residence of Mickey Acuna by Dagoberto Gilb." *New York Times Book Review*, October 2, 1994.

Collingsworth County: 1890-1984. Dallas, Taylor Publishing Co., 1985.

Cooley, Mrs. Emily B. "A Retrospect of San Antonio." *Quarterly of the Texas State Historical Association*, Vol. 4, No. 1. Austin: July, 1900.

Corner, William. *San Antonio de Bexar: A Guide & History*. San Antonio, Bainbridge & Corner, 1890.

Counties of Warren, Benton, Jasper & Newton, Indiana: Historical & Biographical. Chicago, F. A. Battey & Co., 1883.

Cox, Bertha M. *Our Texas*. Dallas, Turner Co., 1965.

Cox, Ed T. "Early Days in Eastland County." *West Texas Historical Association Year Book*, Vol. 18. Abilene: October, 1941.

Cox, Mary L. *History of Hale County, Texas*. Plainview, Texas, 1937.

Crane, R. C. "Early Days in Fisher County." *West Texas Historical Association Year Book*, Vol. 6. Abilene: June, 1930.

Cravens, John N. "Anniversary Celebrations." *West Texas Historical Association Year Book*, Vol. 36. Abilene: October, 1960.

Crouch, Carrie J. *A History of Young County, Texas*. Austin, Texas State Historical Association, 1956.

Cumulative Index of the Southwestern Historical Quarterly: Volumes 1-40: July, 1897-April, 1937. Austin, Texas State Historical Association, 1950.

Daniels, Beverly. *Milling Around Sterling County: A History of Sterling County*.

Canyon, Texas, Staked Plains Press, Inc., 1976.

Davis, Edwin A. *The Rivers & Bayous of Louisiana*. Baton Rouge, Louisiana Education Research Association, 1968.

Davis, Ellis A. *The Historical Encyclopedia of Texas*. Texas Historical Society.

Davis, Ellis A., & Edwin H. Grobe. *The New Encyclopedia of Texas*. Dallas, Texas Development Bureau, 1934.

Davis, Joe T. *Legendary Texians*. Austin, Eakin Press, 1985.

Davis, William C. *Three Roads to the Alamo: The Lives & Fortunes of David Crockett, James Bowie & William Barret Travis*. New York, Harper Collins, 1998.

Dawson County Historical Commission. *Dawson County History*. Taylor Publishing Co., 1981.

Day, James M. *The Texas Almanac: 1857-1873: A Compendium of Texas History*. Waco, Texian Press, 1967.

Debo, Darrell. *Burnet County History*. Burnet, Texas, Eakin Press, 1979.

Delaney, John J., & James E. Tobin. *Dictionary of Catholic Biography*. Garden City, New York, Doubleday & Co., Inc., 1961.

Didway, Charles. *Wagon Wheels: A History of Garza County*. Seagraves, Texas, Pioneer Book Publishers, Inc., 1973.

Dobie, Dudley R. *A Brief History of Hays County & San Marcos, Texas*. San Marcos, Texas, 1948.

Dobie, J. Frank. "How the Brazos River Got Its Name." *Publications of the Texas Folklore Society*, No. 3. Austin: 1924.

Du Gard, Rene C. *Dictionary of Spanish Place Names: Texas & Arizona*. Editions des Deux Mondes, 1983.

Dumville, David N. *Saint Patrick: A.D. 493-1993*. Woodbridge, England, Boydell Press, 1993.

Duncan, Elmer H. *To Preach Christ: The Education of William Carey Crane*. Waco, Baylor University, 1987.

Dunn, Robert W. "The History of Loving County, Texas." *West Texas Historical Association Year Book*, Vol. 24. Abilene: October, 1948.

Early Settlers of Terry: A History of Terry County, Texas. Hereford, Texas, Pioneer Book Publishers, Inc., 1968.

Edwards County History. San Angelo, Texas, Anchor Publishing Co., 1984.

Ehrle, Michael G. *The Childress County Story*. Childress, Texas, Ox Bow Printing, Inc., 1971.

Eilers, Kathryn Burford. "A History of Mason County, Texas." M.A. Thesis, University of Texas, Austin, Texas, 1939.

Ellis County History Workshop. *History of Ellis County, Texas*. Waco, Texian Press, 1972.

Encyclopaedia Britannica. Chicago, Encyclopaedia Britannica, Inc., 1971.

Englebert, Omer. *The Lives of the Saints.* New York, Barnes & Noble, Inc., 1994.

Erath, Lucy A. *The Memoirs of Major George B. Erath: 1813–1891.* Heritage Society of Waco, 1956.

Erath, Lucy A. "Memoirs of Major George Bernard Erath, IV." *Southwestern Historical Quarterly,* Vol. 27, No. 2. Austin: October, 1923.

Ericson, Joe E. *Judges of the Republic of Texas: 1836–1846.* Dallas, Taylor Publishing Co., 1980.

Evans, Grace Moran. *Swisher County History.* Wichita Falls, Texas, Nortex Press, 1977.

Ewell, Thomas T. *History of Hood County.* Granbury, Texas, Frank Gaston, 1895.

Eyes of Texas Travel Guide: Panhandle/Plains Edition. Houston, Cordovan Corp., 1982.

Ezell, Camp. *Historical Story of Bee County, Texas.* Beeville, Texas, Beeville Publishing Co., Inc., 1973.

Faber, Harold. *From Sea to Sea: The Growth of the United States.* New York, Farrar, Straus & Giroux, 1967.

Fannin County Folks & Facts. Bonham, Texas, Bonham Public Library, 1977.

Felker, Rex A. *Haskell. Haskell County and Its Pioneers.* Quanah, Texas, Nortex Press, 1975.

Ferrier, Douglas M., & Charles B. Harrell. *Inventory of the County Records: Delta County Courthouse.* Austin, Center for Community Services North Texas State University & Archives Division, Texas State Library, 1976.

Ferrier, Douglas M., & Mary Pearson. *Inventory of the County Records: Hood County Courthouse.* Austin, Center for Community Services North Texas State University & Archives Division, Texas State Library, 1974.

Fisher, O. C., & J. C. Dykes. *King Fisher: His Life & Times.* Norman, University of Oklahoma Press, 1966.

Frantz, Joe B. *Gail Borden: Dairyman to a Nation.* Norman, University of Oklahoma Press, 1951.

Frazer, Robert W. *Forts of the West.* Norman, University of Oklahoma Press, 1965.

Frontier Forts of Texas. Waco, Texas, Texian Press, 1966.

Fulmore, Z. T. *The History & Geography of Texas As Told in County Names.* Austin, S. R. Fulmore, 1926.

Garrett, Kathryn & Mary Daggett Lake. *Down Historic Trails of Fort Worth & Tarrant County.* Fort Worth, Dudley Hodgkins Co., 1949.

Garza, Lionel. *Brief History of Both Banks of the Rio Grande & the San Antonio Rivers.* Kingsville, Texas, Ben Torres Printing Co., 1986.

Garza, Lionel. *Our Family: Garza Vela-Barrera Martinez: From the Roots to the Fruits.* Kingsville, Texas, Ben Torres Printing Co., 1986.

Gates, J. Y., & H. B. Fox. *A History of Leon County.* Centerville, Texas, Leon County News, 1936.

Gay, Beatrice Grady. *Into the Setting Sun: A History of Coleman County.*

Georgacas, Demetrius J. "From the River Systems in Anatolia: The Names of the Longest River." *Names: Journal of the American Name Society,* Vol. 12, Nos. 3–4. Madison, New Jersey: September–December, 1964.

Gille, Frank H. *Encyclopedia of Texas.* St. Clair Shores, Michigan, Somerset Publishers, 1982.

Glasgow, William J. "On the Confusion Caused by the Name of El Paso." *Pass-Word,* Vol. 1, No. 2. El Paso: May, 1956.

Graves, Lawrence L. *A History of Lubbock.* Lubbock, West Texas Museum Association, Texas Technological College, 1962.

Gray, Glenn A. "Gazetteer of Streams of Texas." *United States Geological Survey Water-Supply,* Paper 448. Washington: 1919.

Grayson County, Texas Genealogical Society. *Ancestors & Descendants: Grayson County, Texas.* Dallas, Taylor Publishing Co., 1980.

Greene, A. C. *The Santa Claus Bank Robbery.* New York, Alfred A. Knopf, Inc., 1972.

Greer, James K. *Colonel Jack Hays: Texas Frontier Leader & California Builder.* New York, E. P. Dutton & Co., Inc., 1952.

Greer, James K. *Texas Ranger: Jack Hays in the Frontier Southwest.* College Station, Texas A & M University Press, 1993.

Griffith, J. H. *Early History of Texas: Early History of Williamson County.* Taylor, Texas, City National Bank.

Grimes County Historical Commission. *History of Grimes County.* Dallas, Taylor Publishing Co., 1982.

Grimes, Roy. *300 Years in Victoria County.* Victoria, Texas, Victoria Advocate Publishing Co., 1968.

Groneman, Bill. *Alamo Defenders.* Austin, Eakin Press, 1990.

Gunn, Jack W. "Ben McCulloch: A Big Captain." *Southwestern Historical Quarterly,* Vol. 58, No. 1. Austin: July, 1954.

Guyton, Pearl V. *The History of Mississippi: From Indian Times to the Present Day.* Syracuse, New York, Iroquois Publishing Co., Inc., 1935.

Haas, Oscar. *History of New Braunfels & Comal County, Texas: 1844–1946.* Austin, Steck Co., 1968.

Hall, Margaret E. *A History of Van Zandt County.* Austin, Jenkins Publishing Co., 1976.

Hall, Roy F., & Helen Gibbard Hall. *Collin County: Pioneering in North Texas.* Quanah, Texas, Nortex Press, 1975.

Haltom, Richard W. *History & Description of Nacogdoches County, Texas.* Nacogdoches News Print, 1880.

Hamrick, Alma Ward. "Forty Years of Pioneering in San Saba County: 1846–1886." *West Texas Historical Association Year Book,* Vol. 11. Abilene: November, 1935.

Hardon, John A. *Modern Catholic Dictionary.* Garden City, New York, Doubleday & Co., Inc., 1980.

Hardy, Dermot H., & Ingham S. Roberts. *Historical Review of South-East Texas.* Chicago, Lewis Publishing Co., 1910.

Harris, Sallie B. *Hide Town in the Texas Panhandle: 100 Years in Wheeler County and the Panhandle of Texas.* Hereford, Texas, Pioneer Book Publishers, Inc., 1968.

Harrison, W. Walworth. *History of Greenville & Hunt County, Texas.* Waco, Texian Press, 1977.

Harry, Jewel H. "A History of Chambers County." M.A. Thesis, University of Texas, Austin, 1940.

Hart, Herbert M. *Old Forts of the Southwest.* Seattle, Superior Publishing Co., 1964.

Harwood, Miller, & W. A. Scrivner. *Fabulous Port Aransas.* Aransas Pass, Texas, The Aransas Pass Progress, 1949.

Haskew, Corrie Pattison. *Historical Records of Austin & Waller Counties.* Houston, Premier Printing & Letter Service, Inc., 1969.

Havins, T. R. *Something About Brown: A History of Brown County, Texas.* Brownwood, Texas, Banner Printing Co., 1958.

Hayes, Charles W. *History of the Island and the City of Galveston.* Cincinnati, 1879.

Hayne, Frank H. "Early Days in Parmer County." *West Texas Historical Association Year Book,* Vol. 23. Abilene: October, 1947.

Heaner, Mrs. R. Russell. *Coke County Family History Book.* Lubbock, Craftsman Printers, Inc., 1984.

Hebert, Rachel Bluntzer. *The Forgotten Colony: San Patricio de Hibernia: The History, the People and the Legends of the Irish Colony of McMullen-McGloin.* Burnet, Texas, Eakin Press, 1981.

Hebison, W. O. *Early Days in Texas & Rains County.* Emory, Texas, Leader Print, 1917.

Hensley, Patricia Bartley & Joseph W. Hensley. *Trinity County Beginnings*. Trinity County Book Committee, 1986.

Herring, Hubert. *A History of Latin America*. New York, Alfred A Knopf, 1968.

Heusinger, Edward W. *A Chronology of Events in San Antonio*. San Antonio, Standard Printing Co., 1951.

Hill, Frank P. "Points of Interest: Three Notable Landmarks in Lynn Co." Unpublished manuscript, W. P. A. files, Eugene C. Barker Texas History Center, University of Texas, Austin.

"Historic Forts & Missions in Texas: Restoration & Preservation." *Texas Legislative Council*, Report No. 59. Austin: December, 1966.

Historic Matagorda County. Bay City, Texas, Bay City Lions Club.

Historical Caldwell County. Dallas, Taylor Publishing Co., 1984.

History of Freestone County, Texas. Freestone County, Texas Historical Commission, 1978.

The History of Jack County, Texas. Curtis Media Corp., 1985.

The History of the People of Live Oak County, Texas: 1856 to 1982.

Hodge, Frederick W. *Handbook of American Indians North of Mexico*. Totowa, New Jersey, Rowman & Littlefield, 1975.

Hodge, Larry D., & Sally S. Victor. "The Legendary King Ranch." *Texas Highways*, Vol. 38, No. 1. Austin: January, 1991.

Hohes, Pauline Buck. *A Centennial History of Anderson County, Texas*. San Antonio, Naylor Co., 1936.

Holland, G. A., & Violet M. Roberts. *History of Parker County and the Double Log Cabin*. Weatherford, Texas, Herald Publishing Co., 1937.

Holt, R. D. *Schleicher County*. Eldorado, Texas, Eldorado Success, 1930.

Hunter, J. Marvin. *Pioneer History of Bandera County*. Bandera, Texas, Hunter's Printing House, 1922.

Hunter, Lillie Mae. *The Book of Years: A History of Dallam & Hartley Counties*. Hereford, Texas, Pioneer Book Publishers, Inc., 1969.

Huston, Cleburne. *Towering Texan: A Biography of Thomas J. Rusk*. Waco, Texas, Texian Press, 1971.

Ingmire, Mrs. Frances Terry. *Archives & Pioneers of Hunt County, Texas*. Greve Coeur, Missouri, 1975.

Ingmire, Mrs. Frances Terry. *Cass County, Texas Marriage Records*. St. Louis, Missouri, 1981.

Jasper County Historical Foundation, Inc. *History of Jasper County, Georgia*. Roswell, Georgia, W. H. Wolfe Associates, 1976.

Jenkins, Frank D. *Runnels County Pioneers*. Abilene, R & R Reproductions Co., 1975.

Jennings, Frank W. "Speaking of Texas." *Texas Highways*, Vol. 37, No. 12. Austin: December, 1990.

Johnson, Frank W. *A History of Texas & Texans*. Chicago, American Historical Society, 1914.

Jones, Alison. *The Wordsworth Dictionary of Saints*. Hertfordshire, England, Wordsworth Editions, Ltd., 1994.

Jones, C. N. *Early Days in Cooke County: 1848–1873*. Gainesville, Texas.

Jurney, Richard L. *History of Titus County, Texas: 1846 to 1960*. Dallas, Royal Publishing Co., 1961.

Kelley, Dayton. *The Handbook of Waco & McLennan County, Texas*. Waco, Texas, Texian Press, 1972.

Kelton, Elmer. "Signers of the Texas Declaration of Independence: Then What." *West Texas Historical Association Year Book*, Vol. 55. Abilene: 1979.

Kendall County Historical Commission. *A History of Kendall County, Texas*. Dallas, Taylor Publishing Co., 1984.

Key, Della Tyler. *In the Cattle Country: History of Potter County: 1887–1966*. Quanah, Texas, Nortex Offset Publications, Inc., 1968.

Kilgore, D. E. *Nueces County, Texas: 1750–1800. A Bicentennial Memoir*. Corpus Christi, Friends of the Corpus Christi Museum, 1975.

Killen, Mrs. James C., & Mrs. R. L. Vance. *History of Lee County, Texas*. Quanah, Texas, Nortex Press, 1974.

Kilman, Ed., & Lou W. Kemp. *Texas Musketeers: Stories of Early Texas Battles and Their Heroes*. Richmond, Johnson Publishing Co., 1935.

Kimbrough, W. C. "The Frontier Background of Clay County." *West Texas Historical Association Year Book*, Vol. 18. Abilene: October, 1942.

King, Alma Dexta. "The Political Career of Williamson Simpson Oldham." *Southwestern Historical Quarterly*, Vol. 33, No. 2. Austin: October, 1929.

King County Historical Society. *King County: Windmills & Barbed Wire*. Quanah, Texas, Nortex Press, 1976.

Kirkley, Gene. *A Guide to Texas Rivers & Streams*. Houston, Lone Star Books, 1983.

Kleber, John E. *The Kentucky Encyclopedia*. Lexington, University Press of Kentucky, 1992.

Kleberg County, Texas. Austin, Hart Graphics, 1979.

Knox County History Committee. *Knox County History*. Haskell, Texas, Haskell Free Press, 1966.

Krakow, Kenneth K. *Georgia Place-Names*. Macon, Georgia, Winship Press, 1975.

LaGrone Leila, B. *A History of Panola County, Texas: 1819–1978*. Carthage, Texas, Panola County Historical Commission, 1979.

Laine, Tanner. *What's In a Name?* Hereford, Texas, Pioneer Book Publishers, Inc., 1971.

Lampasas County, Texas. Marceline, Missouri, Walsworth Publishing Co., 1991.

Langston, Mrs. George. *History of Eastland County, Texas*. Dallas, A.D. Aldridge & Co., 1904.

Leathers, Frances J. *Through the Years: A Historical Sketch of Leon County and the Town of Oakwood*. Oakwood, Texas, 1946.

Lindsey, M. C. & Mrs. M. C. Lindsey. *The Trail of Years in Dawson County, Texas*.

Loftin, Jack. *Trails Through Archer: A Centennial History: 1880–1980*. Burnet, Texas, Eakin Publications, 1979.

Long, E. B., & Barbara Long. *The Civil War Day by Day: An Almanac: 1861–1865*. New York, New York, Da Capo Press, Inc., 1971.

Lord, Walter. *A Time to Stand: The Epic of the Alamo*. Lincoln, University of Nebraska Press, 1961.

Lucas, Mattie Davis & Mita Holsapple Hall. *A History of Grayson County, Texas*. Sherman, Texas, Scruggs Printing Co., 1936.

Lukes, Edward A. *De Witt Colony of Texas*. Austin, Jenkins Publishing Co., 1976.

Lynch, James D. *The Bench & Bar of Texas*. St. Louis, Nixon-Jones Printing Co., 1885.

McAlister, George A. *Alamo: The Price of Freedom*. San Antonio, Docutex, Inc., 1990.

McCaleb, Walter F. *William Barret Travis*. San Antonio, Naylor Co., 1957.

McComb, David G. *Galveston: A History*. Austin, University of Texas Press, 1986.

McKillip, LaVonne. *Early Bailey County History*. Muleshoe, Texas, Muleshoe Junior High Historical Society, 1978.

McLoughlin, Denis. *Wild & Woolly: An Encyclopedia of the Old West*. Garden City, New York, Doubleday & Co., Inc., 1975.

MacManus, Seumas. *The Story of the Irish Race*. New York, Devin-Adair Co., 1921.

Madison, Virginia, & Hallie Stillwell. *How Come It's Called That?: Place Names in the Big Bend Country*. Albuquerque, New Mexico, University of New Mexico Press, 1958.

Madray, Mrs. I. C. *A History of Bee County: With Some Brief Sketches about Men & Events in Adjoining Counties.* Bee-Picayune.

Martin, Mrs. John T., & Mrs. Louis C. Hill. *Milam County, Texas Records.* Waco, 1965.

Martin, Suzanne. "Speaking of Texas." *Texas Highways*, Vol. 39, No. 2. Austin: February, 1992.

Massengill, Fred I. *Texas Towns: Origin of Name & Location of Each of the 2,148 Post Offices in Texas.* Terrell, Texas, 1936.

Meier, Matt S., & Feliciano Rivera. *Dictionary of Mexican American History.* Westport, Connecticut, Greenwood Press, 1981.

Memorial & Biographical History of Ellis County, Texas. Chicago, Lewis Publishing Co., 1892.

Memorial & Biographical History of McLennan, Falls, Bell & Coryell Counties, Texas. Chicago, Lewis Publishing Co., 1893.

Montgomery County Genealogical Society, Inc. *Montgomery County History.* Winston-Salem, North Carolina, Hunter Publishing Co., 1981.

Montgomery, Robin. *The History of Montgomery County.* Austin, Jenkins Publishing Co., 1975.

Moore, Bill. *Bastrop County: 1691–1900.* Wichita Falls, Texas, Nortex Press, 1977.

Moore, Bill. *A Guide to Texas Counties.* Houston, Tejas Publishing Co. 1975.

Morphis, J. M. *History of Texas.* New York, United States Publishing Co., 1874.

Moursund, John S. *Blanco County History.* Burnet, Texas, Nortex Press, 1979.

Munnerlyn, Tom. *Texas Local History.* Austin, Eakin Press, 1983.

Neal, Bill. *The Last Frontier: The Story of Hardeman County.* Quanah Tribune-Chief, 1966.

Neville, A. W. *The History of Lamar County.* Paris, Texas, North Texas Publishing Co., 1937.

New Catholic Encyclopedia. New York, McGraw-Hill Book Co., 1967.

New Larousse Encyclopedia of Mythology. Hamlyn Publishing Group, Ltd., London, 1968.

Newcomb, W. W. *The Indians of Texas.* Austin, University of Texas Press, 1961.

Newton County Historical Commission. *Glimpses of Newton County History.* Burnet, Texas, Nortex Press, 1982.

Nofi, Albert A. *The Alamo and the Texas War for Independence.* New York, Da Capo Press, 1994.

Nueces County Historical Society. *The History of Nueces County.* Austin, Jenkins Publishing Co., 1972.

O'Connell, Patrick F. "More Than the Shamrock: Understanding the Real St. Patrick." *Catholic Digest.* St. Paul, Minnesota: March, 1995.

Ornish, Natalie. *Pioneer Jewish Texans.* Dallas, Texas Heritage Press, 1989.

Parker, Richard D. *Historical Recollections of Robertson County, Texas.* Salado, Texas, Anson Jones Press, 1955.

Partlow, Miriam. *Liberty, Liberty County, and the Atascosito District.* Austin, Pemberton Press, 1974.

Patterson, Bessie. *A History of Deaf Smith County.* Hereford, Texas, Pioneer Publishers, 1964.

Patterson, C. L. *Wilson County: Diversified Farming Center of Southwest Texas.* 1939.

Patterson, Richard S. *The Secretaries of State: Portraits & Biographical Sketches.* Washington, D.C., U.S. Government Printing Office, 1956.

Pearce, T. M. "Spanish Place Name Patterns in the Southwest." *Names: Journal of the American Name Society*, Vol. 3, No. 4. Berkeley: December, 1955.

Peareson, P. E. *Sketch of the Life of Judge Edwin Waller: Together With Some of the More Important Events of the Early Texas Revolution in Which He Participated, Such As the Battle of Velasco.* Galveston, News Steam Book & Job Establishment, 1874.

Pennybacker, Mrs. Anna J. Hardwicke. *A History of Texas for Schools.* Austin, 1912.

Phares, Ross. *The Governors of Texas.* Gretna, Pelican Publishing Co., 1976.

Phelps, Bailey. *They Loved the Land: Foard County History.* Burnet, Texas, Nortex Press, 1969.

Pickett, Arlene. *History of Liberty County.* Tardy Publishing Co., 1936.

Pickle, Joe. *Gettin' Started: Howard County's First 25 Years.* Big Springs, Texas, Howard County Heritage Museum, 1980.

Polk, Stella Gipson. *Mason & Mason County: A History.* Austin, Pemberton Press, 1966.

Presiding Officers of the Texas Legislature: 1846–1991. Austin, Texas House of Representatives, 1991.

Price, Edward T. *Dividing the Land: Early American Beginnings of Our Private Property Mosaic.* Chicago, University of Chicago Press, 1995.

Putman, Wyvonne. *Navarro County History.* Quanah, Texas, Nortex Press, 1975.

Radde, Rebecca D. *Bosque Primer: An Introduction to Bosque County.* 1976.

Raines, C. W. "The Alamo Monument." *Quarterly of the Texas State Historical Association*, Vol. 6, No. 4. Austin: April, 1903.

Rand, Clayton. *Men of Spine in Mississippi.* Gulfport, Mississippi, Dixie Press, 1940.

Randel, Mrs. Ralph E. *A Time to Purpose: A Chronicle of Carson County.* Pioneer Publishers, 1966.

Ray, Worth S. *Austin Colony Pioneers.* Austin, 1949.

Read, William A. "Louisiana-French." *Louisiana State University Studies*, No. 5. Baton Rouge: 1931.

Reeves, Miriam G. *The Governors of Louisiana.* Gretna, Pelican Publishing Co., 1972.

Refugio County History Book Committee. *The History of Refugio County, Texas.* Dallas, Curtis Media Corp., 1985.

Reynolds, Jack A. "Louisiana Place-Names of Romance Origin." Ph.D. Thesis, Hill Memorial Library, Louisiana State University, Baton Rouge, Louisiana, 1942.

Richardson, Rupert N., et al. *Texas: The Lone Star State.* Englewood Cliffs, New Jersey, Prentice Hall, 1988.

Rickard, J. A. *Brief Biographies of Brave Texans.* Dallas, Banks Upshaw & Co., 1962.

Rios, J. A. Guedea. *Recuerdos: The Hispanic Heritage of Medina County, Texas.* 1985.

Rios, John F. *Readings on the Alamo.* New York, Vantage Press, 1987.

Rogers, John W. *The Lusty Texans of Dallas.* New York, E. P. Dutton & Co., Inc., 1951.

Ross, Charles P., & T. L. Rouse. *Early-Day History of Wilbarger County.* Vernon, Texas, Vernon Times, 1933.

Rountree, Joseph G. *History of Bee County, Texas.* 1960.

Ruff, Ann. "Speaking of Texas." *Texas Highways*, Vol. 38, No. 9. Austin: September, 1991.

Ruff, Ann. *Unsung Heroes of Texas.* Houston, Lone Star Books, 1985.

Russell, Belle. *Easy-to-Read Texas History.* San Francisco, Harr Wagner Publishing Co., 1954.

Russell, Traylor. *Carpetbaggers, Scalawags & Others.* Jefferson, Texas, Marion County Historical Survey Committee, 1973.

Russell, Traylor. *History of Titus County, Texas.* Waco, Texas, W. M. Morrison, 1965.

Ryder-Taylor, Henry. *History of the Alamo.* San Antonio, Nic Tengg.

St. Clair, Gladys. *A History of Hopkins County, Texas.* Waco, Texas, Texian Press, 1965.

St. Romain, Lillian Schiller. *Western Falls County, Texas.* Austin, Texas State Historical Association, 1951.

San Saba County History: 1856–1983. San Saba County Historical Commission, 1983.

Scarborough, Jewel Davis. "Taylor County and Its Name." *West Texas Historical Association Year Book*, Vol. 30. Abilene: October, 1954.

Scott, Evalyn Parrott. *A History of Lamb County*. 1968.

Scott, Mary L. "Who's Who in Spanish Texas." *Fort Worth Press*, April 17, 1936.

Scott, Zelma. *A History of Coryell County, Texas*. Austin, Texas State Historical Association, 1965.

Seale, Lea L. "Indian Place-Names in Mississippi." Ph.D. Thesis, Hill Memorial Library, Louisiana State University, Baton Rouge, Louisiana, 1939.

Shankle, George Earlie. *American Nicknames: Their Origin & Significance*. New York, H. W. Wilson Co., 1955.

Sheffy, Lester F., et al. *Texas*. Dallas, Banks Upshaw & Co., 1954.

Sherill, R. E. "Early Days in Haskell County." *West Texas Historical Association Year Book*, Vol. 3. Abilene: June, 1927.

Simmons, Frank E. *History of Coryell County*. Waco, Texian Press, 1936.

Smith, A. Morton. *The First 100 Years in Cooke County*. San Antonio, Naylor Co., 1955.

Smith, Glenn. "Some Early Runnels County History: 1858–1885." *West Texas Historical Association Year Book*, Vol. 42. Abilene: October, 1966.

Smith, Ruby L. "Early Development of Wilbarger County." *West Texas Historical Association Year Book*, Vol. 14. Abilene: October, 1938.

Smith, W. Broadus. *Pioneers of Brazos County, Texas: 1800–1850*. Bryan, Texas, Scribe Shop, 1962.

Smithson, Fay Eidson, & Pat Wilkinson Hull. *Martin County: The First Thirty Years*. Hereford, Texas, Pioneer Book Publishers, Inc., 1970.

Smylie, Vernon. *Taming of the Texas Coast*. Corpus Christi, Texas News Syndicate Press, 1963.

Sowell, A. J. *Early Settlers & Indian Fighters of Southwest Texas*. New York, Argosy-Antiquarian, Ltd., 1964.

Sowell, A. J. *History of Fort Bend County*. Houston, W. H. Coyle & Co., 1904.

Sparkman, Ervin L. *The People's History of Live Oak County, Texas*. Mesquite, Texas, Ide House, 1981.

Speer, Ocie. *Texas Jurists*. 1936.

Speer, William S. *The Encyclopedia of the New West*. Marshall, Texas, United States Biographical Co., 1881.

Spencer, Artemesia Lucille Brison. *The Camp County Story*. Fort Worth, Branch-Smith, Inc., 1974.

Spikes, Nellie Witt, & Temple Ann Ellis. *Through the Years: A History of Crosby County, Texas*. San Antonio, Naylor Co., 1952.

Spiller, Wayne. *Handbook of McCulloch County History*. Seagraves, Texas, Pioneer Book Publishers, 1976.

Spleth, Jo L. "Big Red Ruddy River of the North." *Texas Highways*, Vol. 38, No. 9. Austin: September, 1991.

Stanley, F. *The Lippscomb, Texas Story*. Nazareth, Texas, 1975.

Stephen. Homer. *History of Erath County*. Dublin Progress, 1950.

Stephens, A. Ray, & William M. Holmes. *Historical Atlas of Texas*. Norman, University of Oklahoma Press, 1989.

Stewart, George R. *American-Place Names*. New York, Oxford University Press, 1970.

Stickland, Wallace. "History of Fannin County, Texas: 1836–1843." *Southwestern Historical Quarterly*, Vol. 33, No. 4. Austin: April, 1930.

Stieghorst, Junann J. *Bay City & Matagorda County: A History*. Austin, Pemberton Press, 1965.

Stoudemire, Sterling A. "Santiago Guadalupe, Pilar, Spanish Shrines/ Spanish Names." *Names: Journal of the American Name Society*, Vol. 26. Potsdam, New York: 1978.

Stoutenburgh, John. *Dictionary of the American Indian*. New York, Bonanza Books, 1960.

Stovall, Allan A. *Nueces Headwater Country: A Regional History*. San Antonio, Naylor Co., 1959.

Swaim, Emsy H. *Short History of Concho County, Texas*, Eden, Texas, 1979.

Tarpley, Fred. *1001 Texas Place Names*. Austin, University of Texas Press, 1980.

Tarpley, Fred. *Place Names of Northeast Texas*. Commerce, Texas, East Texas State University, 1969.

Tatum, Charles E. *Shelby County: In the East Texas Hills*. Austin, Eakin Publications, Inc., 1984.

Taylor, William C. *A History of Clay County*. Austin, Jenkins Publishing Co., 1972.

Texas Almanac & State Industrial Guide: 1966–1967. A. H. Belo Corp., 1965.

Texas Almanac & State Industrial Guide: 1986–1987. A. H. Belo Corp., 1985.

Texas Biographical Dictionary. Wilmington, Delaware, American Historical Publications, Inc., 1985.

"Texas Counties and Their Names." *Fort Worth Genealogical Society Bulletin*, Fort Worth: Vol. 8, No. 2. March, 1965; Vol. 8, No. 4. April, 1965; Vol. 8, No. 5. May, 1965; Vol. 8, No. 6. June, 1965; Vol. 8, No. 7. July, 1965; Vol. 8, No. 8. August, 1965; Vol. 8, No. 9. September, 1965; Vol. 8, No. 10. October, 1965.

Texas. State Department of Highways & Public Transportation, Austin.

Texas Tour Book. Heathrow, Florida, AAA Publishing 1998.

Thomas, Myrna Tryon. *The Windswept Land: A History of Moore County, Texas*. Dumas, Texas, 1967.

Thrall, H. S. *A Pictorial History of Texas*. San Antonio, 1878.

Thrapp, Dan L. *Encyclopedia of Frontier Biography*. Lincoln, University of Nebraska Press, 1988.

Thrapp, Dan L. *Encyclopedia of Frontier Biography: Supplemental Volume 4*. Spokane, Washington, Arthur H. Clark Co., 1994.

Tibon, Gutierre. "The Name of Guadalupe." *Names: Journal of the American Name Society*, Vol. 1, No. 2. Berkeley: June, 1953.

Tilloson, Cyrus. "Place Names of Nueces County." *Frontier Times*, Vol. 26, No. 7. Baird, Texas: April, 1949.

Toole, Mrs. Blanche Finley. *History & Tax Records of the Sabine District & Sabine County, Texas*. Hemphill, Texas, James Frederick Gomer Chapter, Daughters of the Republic of Texas.

Turner, Martha Anne. *William Barret Travis: His Sword & His Pen*. Waco, Texas, Texian Press, 1972.

Under Texas Skies: Featuring What's What about Texas. Austin, American Historical Memorial Association, 1946.

Van Demark, Harry. "Texas County Names." *Texas Monthly*, Vol. 5, No. 3. April, 1930.

Vexler, Robert I. *Chronology & Documentary Handbook of the State of Texas*. Dobbs Ferry, New York, Oceana Publications, Inc., 1979.

Vogel, Virgil J. *Iowa Place Names of Indian Origin*. Iowa City, University of Iowa Press, 1983.

Walker County Genealogical Society & Walker County Historical Commission. *Walker County, Texas: A History*. Dallas, Curtis Media Corp., 1986.

Walker, Norman M. "The Geographical Nomenclature of Louisiana." *The Magazine of American History*, Vol. 10. New York: July–December, 1883.

Wallace, Ernest, & W. Earl Brown. "History in West Texas." *West Texas Historical Association Year Book*, Vol. 49. Abilene: 1973.

Walter, Ray A. *A History of Limestone County*. Austin, Von Boeckmann-Jones, 1959.

Warner, Ezra J., & W. Buck Yearns. *Biographical Register of the Confederate Congress*. Baton Rouge, Louisiana State University Press, 1975.

Warren, Betsy. *Twenty Texans: Historic Lives for Young Readers*. Dallas, Hendrick-Long Publishing Co., 1985.

Weaver, Bobby D. *Castro's Colony: Empresario Development in Texas: 1842–1865*. College Station, Texas A & M Press, 1985.

Webb, Walter P., et al. *The Handbook of Texas*. Austin, Texas State Historical Association, 1952.

Weddle, Robert S. *The San Saba Mission: Spanish Pivot in Texas*. Austin, University of Texas Press, 1964.

Weisman, Dale. "Matagorda: Treasured Island." *Texas Highways*, Vol. 39, No. 3. Austin: March, 1992.

Welch, June Rayfield. *People & Places in the Texas Past*. Dallas, G. L. A. Press, 1971.

Welch, June Rayfield. *The Texas Senator*. Dallas, G. L. A. Press, 1978.

Welch, June Rayfield, & J. Larry Nance. *The Texas Courthouse*. Dallas, Texian Press, 1971.

Werst, J. L. *The Reagan County Story*. Seagraves, Texas, Pioneer Book Publishers, Inc., 1974.

West, Elizabeth Howard. "De Leon's Expedition of 1689." *Quarterly of the Texas State Historical Association*, Vol. 8, No. 3. Austin: January, 1905.

Weyland, Leonie Rummel, & Houston Wade. *An Early History of Fayette County*. La Grange, Texas, La Grange Journal, 1936.

Wharton, Clarence. *The Isle of Mal Hado & Other Sketches: Three Hundred & Fifty Years of Texas History*. Houston, Fletcher Young Publishing Co., 1968.

White, Dabney, & T. C. Richardson. *East Texas: Its History and Its Makers*. New York, Lewis Historical Publishing Co., 1940.

White, Gifford. *First Settlers of Red River County, Texas*. St. Louis, Missouri, Frances Terry Ingmire, 1981.

Wilkins, Frederick. *The Highly Irregular Irregulars: Texas Rangers in the Mexican War*. Austin, Eakin Press, 1990.

Williams, Amelia. "A Critical Study of the Siege of the Alamo and of the Personnel of Its Defenders." *Southwestern Historical Quarterly*, Vol. 37, No. 3. Austin: January, 1934.

Williams, Amelia. "A Critical Study of the Siege of the Alamo and of the Personnel of Its Defenders." *Southwestern Historical Quarterly*, Vol. 37, No. 4. Austin: April, 1934.

Williams, Annie Lee. *A History of Wharton County: 1846–1961*. Austin, Von Boeckmann-Jones Co., 1964.

Winfrey, Dorman H. *A History of Rusk County, Texas*. Waco, Texas, Texian Press, 1961.

Wise, L. F., & E. W. Egan. *Kings, Rulers & Statesmen*. New York, Sterling Publishing Co., Inc., 1967.

Woldert, Albert. *A History of Tyler & Smith County, Texas*. San Antonio, Naylor Co., 1948.

Women's Division of Post Chamber of Commerce. *Footprints: A History of Garza County and Its People*. Taylor Publishing Co.

Wood County: 1850–1900. Quitman, Texas, Wood County Historical Society, 1976.

Wood, W. D. "Sketch of the Early Settlement of Leon County: Its Organization & Some of the Early Settlers." *Quarterly of the Texas State Historical Association*, Vol. 4, No. 3. Austin: January, 1901.

Wooten, Dudley G. *A Complete History of Texas for Schools, Colleges & General Use*. Dallas, Texas History Co., 1899.

Wooten, Dudley G. *A Comprehensive History of Texas: 1685 to 1897*. Dallas, William G. Scarff, 1898.

Work Projects Administration. *Inventory of the County Archives of Texas-Bastrop, Caldwell, Guadalupe, Mills, Orange, Rockwall, Somervell & Uvalde Counties*. 1939–1941.

Work Projects Administration. *Inventory of the Parish Archives of Louisiana-Sabine Parish*. 1942.

Work Projects Administration. *Louisiana: A Guide to the State*. New York, Hastings House, 1941.

Wright, Celia M. *Sketches from Hopkins County History*. Sulphur Springs, Texas, Shining Path Press, 1959.

Wright, Muriel H. *A Guide to the Indian Tribes of Oklahoma*. Norman, University of Oklahoma Press, 1951.

Wynn, Leila Clark. "A History of the Civil Courts in Texas." *Southwestern Historical Quarterly*, Vol. 60, No. 1. Austin: July, 1956.

Yeats, E. L., & Hooper Shelton. *History of Nolan County, Texas*. Sweetwater, Shelton Press, 1975.

The Yoakum County History: 1907–1957. Plains, Texas, TSA MO GA Club.

Young Lawyers at Texas Independence. Texas Young Lawyers Association, 1986.

Zachry, Juanita Daniel. *The Settling of a Frontier: A History of Rural Taylor County*. Burnet, Texas, Nortex Press, 1980.

Utah

(29 counties)

2743 *Beaver County*

Beaver River— This county in southwestern Utah was created by Utah territory on January 5, 1856, and named for the Beaver River, which flows through it. Rufus W. Leigh's *Five Hundred Utah Place Names* tells us that the Beaver River "has its source in Puffer lake high in the Tushar Mountains; the main stream is augmented by four forks which drain their west slope. The River flows westerly around the south end of Mineral Range, thence northerly through the Milford Valley to peter out ... in Millard County." Beaver River was so named because of the numerous beavers and beaver dams found on the river and its tributaries.

2744 *Box Elder County*

Box elder trees here— Box Elder County was created by Utah territory in 1856. The county lies in Utah's northwestern corner, with Idaho to the north and Nevada to the west. A large portion of the Great Salt Lake fills the south-central portion of Box Elder County. The county's name derived from box elder trees, which grew in profusion in the vicinity of Brigham City, the county seat. Box elder (genus and species: *Acer negundo*) are deciduous trees, which grow to a height of some 60 feet. These trees tolerate both drought and northern climates, characteristics which are needed for proliferation in the Box Elder County, Utah, area.

2745 *Cache County*

Cache Valley— This county in north-central Utah contains a portion of the Cache Valley, for which it was named. The Cache Valley of northern Utah and southern Idaho is bounded on the east by the main Wasatch Mountain range. Wellsville Mountain, a spur of the Wasatch range, forms the valley's western side. Cache Valley's name derived from the French verb *cacher*, meaning "to hide." French-Canadian trappers and other mountain men held rendezvous in the Cache Valley from the 1820's until Mormon settlers began to arrive here in 1855. The fur trappers traditionally concealed their valuable pelts and supplies for safekeeping in Cache Valley. This county was created by Utah territory on January 5, 1856.

2746 *Carbon County*

Extensive coal deposits in the county— This county in east-central Utah was created by Utah territory on March 8, 1894. The county's name honors the vast coal deposits here. After the Denver & Rio Grande Western Railroad laid tracks reaching these coal deposits in the early 1880's, large numbers of immigrants were brought to mine the coal here from many countries including nations in southern and eastern Europe and Japan. Coal became the foundation of this county's economy. Both boom and bust periods followed but in the late 20th century coal mining continued to play a vital role in the economy of Coal County, Utah. Allan K. Powell's *Utah History Encyclopedia*, published in 1994 by the University of Utah Press, states that 98 percent of the electric power produced by Utah Power & Light Company comes from thermal steam plants fueled by coal.

2747 *Daggett County*

Ellsworth Daggett (1845–1923)— A native of New York, Daggett received a scientific education including postgraduate work at Yale College. He soon came West and was employed in mining at the Gould & Curry mill in Virginia City, Nevada. In 1870 Daggett joined the United States Geological Survey and in 1872 he became manager of a smelting plant in Bingham Canyon, Utah territory. Here he became expert in metallurgy, published papers dealing with the science and economics of smelting and became one of America's earliest hydrometallurgists. Daggett was employed as a consultant by prospective purchasers of mining properties and in 1888 he was appointed the first surveyor-general of Utah territory. He also was effective in implementing irrigation projects, so vital to the development of Utah, and many works dealing with the history, geography and place names of Utah indicate that when this county was created on March 4, 1919, it was named in Daggett's honor because of his irrigation and canal work. A suggestion was made that this county be named Finch County, in honor of George Finch, then the oldest surviving original settler on Henry's Fork, but the name Daggett was chosen, instead.

2748 *Davis County*

Daniel C. Davis (1804–1850)— Born in New York on February 23, 1804, Davis became a member of the Church of Jesus Christ of Latter-day Saints (Mormons) as a young man. He and his wife were among the Mormons who were forced to move West by religious persecution. In July, 1846, at Council Bluffs, Iowa territory, Davis and other Mormons were in the midst of their journey to find a home in the West, when the Mormon leader, Brigham Young (1801–1877), raised a battalion of some 500 men (the "Mormon battalion") to fight for the U.S. in the Mexican War in exchange for assistance from the U.S. army in protecting the westward Mormon migration. Among the commissioned officers Brigham Young selected for the Mormon battalion was Captain Daniel C. Davis, who was given command of Company E. The Mormon battalion served with distinction during the Mexican War and was honorably mustered out of the U.S. army on July 16, 1847. Some 80 members chose to re-enlist for eight months additional service. These soldiers, known as "the Mormon Volunteers," were led by Captain Daniel C. Davis. Davis finally mustered out of service in 1849 and settled in what would soon be Utah territory, at South Farmington, on the stream now called Davis Creek. Here he built a home for his family before volunteering to aid a train of Mormons traveling East to Salt Lake City. Captain Davis fell ill while en route to the join the immigrants and he died on June 1, 1850, in the vicinity of Fort Kearney, in what is now Nebraska. This county was created by Utah territory on March 3, 1852.

2749 *Duchesne County*

Duchesne River— This county in northeastern Utah was created on March 7, 1913, and named for the Duchesne River, which runs through it. The Duchesne is a 120 mile-long tributary of Green River. It rises in the Uinta Mountains, at the foot of Mount Agassiz, flows southeast across Duchesne County until it reaches the city of Duchesne, Utah, and then turns east. Its final sprint to the Green River is in a southeastern direction for a dozen miles to Ouray, Utah near the eastern side of the state. Literature dealing with the history geography and place names of Utah agree that the origin of the river's name is uncertain. However, many of these sources offer speculations about the river's namesake. Possibilities mentioned include:

— Fort Duchesne; many of the Utah sources that mention this possibility then refer to Fort Duquesne, at Pittsburgh, Pennsylvania, which the British took from the French in 1750's. (If a fort inspired the river's name, it would seem more likely that the fort would have been Fort Duchesne, right here in northeastern Utah, 24 miles southwest of Vernal, Utah.)

— One or more early French trapper(s) of this area, whose surname is rendered in one account as Du Chasne and in another as Du Chesne.

— Named *by* a French trapper for a chimney-like formation near the beginning of the river. (This seems to be a stretch. The French word for "chimney" is *cheminee*. The French *dessus de cheminee* means "chimney-piece.")

— Mother Rose Philippine Duchesne (1769–1852), the Roman Catholic nun who founded the U.S. branch of the Society of the Sacred Heart.

— Andre Duchesne (1584–1640), a French geographer and historian.

— An Indian chief.

— A Ute Indian word meaning "dark canyon." Portions of the Duchesne River run through dark canyons.

2750 *Emery County*

George W. Emery (1830–1909)— A native of Maine and a graduate of Dartmouth College in New Hampshire, Emery studied law, was admitted to the bar and became active in politics within the Republican party. His political connections secured him appointment as supervisor of internal revenue in former Confederate states during Reconstruction, and on July 1, 1875, President Ulysses S. Grant appointed him governor of Utah territory. Relations between Mormons in Utah territory and the U.S. Federal government were strained for much of Utah's half century of territorial status and Governor Emery, as the federal government's chief executive in Utah, tried to adopt a conservative stance on several controversial issues. This earned Emery some vigorous criticism from the anti–Mormon press. However Governor Emery was not afraid to take stands on Mormon-related political issues. He secured election law amendments which made the ballot in Utah truly secret, thereby enabling devout Mormons to vote their consciences without fear of reprisal from religious leaders. He also urged passage of laws against polygamy, a very sensitive topic during his tenure as territorial governor from 1875 to 1880. This county was created on February 12, 1880, during the year that Emery left office. In the petition to create this new county, its name was rendered as Castle County, but that name was not adopted. In his article on county boundaries in Utah in the July, 1955, issue (Vol. 23, No. 3) of *Utah Historical Quarterly*, James B. Allen stated that George W. Emery was "...one of the few territorial governors who had the sincere respect of the people of Utah."

2751 *Garfield County*

James A. Garfield (1831–1881)— A native of Ohio, Garfield served in the Ohio senate before becoming a Union officer in the Civil War. He performed ably and rapidly rose to the rank of general. In 1863 Garfield resigned his commission to enter the U.S. House of Representatives where he served until 1880. During Reconstruction, Garfield favored harsh treatment of the defeated South. In January, 1880, he was elected to the U.S. Senate but never served in that body. Instead, he was nominated and elected president of the United States. His nomination by the Republican party came as a compromise on the 36th ballot. Garfield was fatally wounded by an assassin's bullet just four months after beginning his term as president. This Utah county was created on March 9, 1882. It had been proposed that this new county be named Snow County, but it was decided that the county's name should honor President Garfield, who had been assassinated just six months earlier.

2752 *Grand County*

Colorado River— This county in southeastern Utah was created by Utah territory on March 13, 1890, and named for the Colorado River, which flows through it. At that time the river was called the Grand River, on account of its size. The U.S. Congress changed the river's name to Colorado in 1921. The Colorado River is one of North America's greatest rivers. It rises in northern Colorado, flows in a southwestern direction across Colorado and crosses the southeastern portion of Utah. It flows some 1,400 miles to the Gulf of California, through mountains, prairies and deserts, carving some of the most beautiful scenes in the world, including Arizona's majestic red Grand Canyon. *Colorado* is one of the Spanish words for "red."

2753 *Iron County*

Large deposits of iron ore in the area— This county in southwestern Utah was created by Utah territory early in 1850 with the name Little Salt Lake County. That version of the county was quite small, with an elliptical shape. Later in 1850, the county's name was changed to Iron County and essentially all Utah sources consulted agree that the name change was made because of the discovery of large deposits of iron "in the area" or "in this region." However the map of Utah territory changed dramatically about this time causing ambiguity in the phrases "in the area" or "in this region." By 1852 Iron County's shape had changed to approximate a rectangle and its size had grown enormously, both to the west and to the east. The Iron County of Utah territory in 1852 contained the present Iron County as well as a large section of the present state of Nevada to the west. To the east, Iron County embraced what is now Garfield County, Utah, and continued east to encompass a large section of what is today the state of Colorado. Fortunately some sources dealing with Utah place names clarify just where the iron was when they say "west of Cedar City" and others indicate that the iron ore was primarily located within the area that comprised the original (very small) version of this county, when it was named Little Salt Lake County. Because iron would be essential in making the Mormon's vast, isolated desert kingdom self supporting, church leaders in Salt Lake City gave early priority to development of the iron industry of Iron County, in the valley of the Little Salt Lake (a sink in the Parowan Valley). Ingenious and industrious Mormons managed to acquire the labor and capital needed for a viable iron industry here and despite setbacks in the form of Indian attacks, the iron venture in southwestern Utah became a huge success as did the Mormon kingdom itself, in Utah, and worldwide.

2754 *Juab County*

Uncertain— This county in west-central Utah was created by Utah territory on March 3, 1852. At that time Utah territory, and this county, extended well into what is now Nevada. The origin of the name *Juab* is not known but sources dealing with the history, geography and place names of Utah mention two possibilities: (1) Derived from an Indian word meaning "thirsty plain" (or "level plain") or (2) the name of an elderly Indian who was living in the area when early White settlers came here; reportedly, this Indian was a valuable friend to his new White neighbors. John W. Van Cott's *Utah Place Names* indicates that prior to the arrival of Whites, the Indians had given the name *Juab* to the valley which extends here on a north-south orientation from Juab County to Utah County. Van Cott is among those who indicate probable translations for *Juab* as "flat plain," "level plain," and/or "thirsty plain."

2755 *Kane County*

Thomas L. Kane (1822–1883)— A native of Pennsylvania, lawyer, and ardent abolitionist, Kane was an agent of the "underground railroad" used to pass slaves along from bondage in the South to freedom in the North. Although he never joined the Church of Jesus Christ of Latter-day Saints (Mormons), he was a close friend of Brigham Young's (1801–1877) and Kane served as an effective intermediary between the Mormons and the largely anti–Mormon, non Mormon establishment. Mary Ann Angel Young, Brigham Young's wife nursed Kane to health when he became ill near the Mississippi River and it was during this period that Kane and Brigham Young became fast friends. It was Kane who convinced Brigham Young that resisting the U.S. army was the wrong course for the Mormons. He was instrumental in the formation of the Mormon battalion during the Mexican War and in successfully mediating the potential clash between Mormons and U.S. army forces in 1857. The ardent abolitionist, Kane enlisted in the Union army in the Civil War, served with distinction and rose to the rank of brigadier-general. Although ill health prevented Kane from serving until the end of the Civil War, he was promoted to the rank of brevet major-general after he left active military service. This county was created by Utah territory on January 16, 1864.

2756 *Millard County*

Millard Fillmore (1800–1874)— Fillmore was born to an impoverished family in upstate New York and was apprenticed to a firm of cloth-dressers, from whom he eventually purchased his release. After studying law and being admitted to the New York bar, Fillmore was elected to the lower house of the New York legislature and he later represented New York in the U.S. House of Representatives. In 1848 the Whig party nominated the Mexican War hero, Zachary Taylor, for president with Millard Fillmore on the ticket as the vice-presidential running mate. They won the election and took their offices in 1849 but Zachary Taylor died in 1850 and Millard Fillmore became president. As president during an intense period of North versus South controversy relating to slavery, Fillmore favored the South and states' rights. However, Fillmore also supported the economic development of our nation's frontier, which included the area which became Utah territory, while he was president. This county was created on October 4, 1851, by Utah territory, while Millard Fillmore was serving as president. The county seat, Fillmore, was also named in his honor, and that municipality briefly served as the capital of Utah territory. When Fillmore's term as president ended he was not nominated by his party for reelection.

2757 *Morgan County*

Jedediah Morgan Grant (1816–1856)— This early Mormon leader was born at Windsor, New York on February 21, 1816, and baptized in the Church of Jesus Christ of Latter-day Saints on March 21, 1833. He was ordained an elder and later, on February 28, 1835, Grant was ordained by the Mormon prophet, Joseph Smith (1805–1844) and others as a "seventy." Grant engaged in extensive missionary work for the church, particularly in the South, and won many converts to the LDS faith. He was present in Nauvoo, Illinois, when Joseph Smith was killed by a mob in nearby Carthage, Illinois, on June 27, 1844, and Grant later became second counselor to Mormon President Brigham Young (1801–1877). In Utah territory during the mid-1850's Grant was instrumental in touring the territory and encouraging settlers who had become disheartened by drought and grasshoppers. His powerful oratory induced many LDS members to be re-baptized and recommit themselves to the faith. Jedediah Morgan Grant died on December 1, 1856, while he was serving as second counselor to LDS President Young. This county was created by Utah territory during January, 1862.

2758 *Piute County*

Paiute Indians— This county in south-central Utah was created by Utah territory on January 16, 1865, and named for the Paiute Indians, one of the tribes who were living in Utah when White settlers arrived. The Paiute were one of the wider ranging tribes of the Great Basin. Their center was in northern Nevada but Paiute branches extended to the deserts of eastern Oregon, the northern side of California's Mojave Desert and into south-central Utah. The areas where the Paiute lived were largely barren lands, much of it desert, with little plant or animal life. To survive, the Paiute were forced to live a nomadic life and subsist on an omnivorous diet of roots, berries, grasshoppers and other insects. On good days mice and rabbits were added. Bill Yenne's *Encyclopedia of North American Indian Tribes*, published in 1986 stated that "The majority of the Paiute still remain in Nevada, scattered across the state on small reservations." Yenne's account then listed the known members of Paiute in 1985, by location: In Nevada, 100 at Winnemucca, 192 at Lovelock, 364 at Yerington 643 at Walker River 678 at Fort McDermitt, 721 in the Reno-Sparks area and 1,285 at the Pyramid Lake reservation; In Utah, 345; in California, 2,056.

2759 *Rich County*

Charles C. Rich (1809–1883)— Born August 21, 1809, in northwestern Kentucky, Rich moved with his family to southern Indiana territory, where he lived until he was about 20 years old. He then moved to Illinois and engaged in farming. In 1831 Rich learned of the Church of Jesus Christ of Latter-day Saints (Mormons) and he was baptized in that faith the following year. Rich was one of the original members of the council of fifty and he was living in Nauvoo, Illinois, when the Mormon prophet, Joseph Smith (1805–1844), was killed by a mob in nearby Carthage, Illinois on June 27, 1844. Rich practiced polygamy, a doctrine fully sanctioned by the LDS church at that time, and by 1847 he had six wives. He served as a military leader during the Mormon exodus to the Salt Lake Valley and in 1849 he was made one of the church's 12 apostles. Rich established a colony of Mormons in the San Bernardino area of California, served for a number of years in the legislature of Utah territory and was the father of 51 children. This county was created by Utah territory on January 16, 1864, and named in honor of Charles C. Rich at the suggestion of Mormon leader Brigham Young (1801–

1877). The county's original name was Richland County but it was changed to Rich County during January, 1868.

2760 *Salt Lake County*

Great Salt Lake— In July, 1847, Mormon settlers completed their arduous exodus from the Mississippi River area, across the Great Plains and through the mountains and reached the Salt Lake Valley. On July 24, 1847, the Mormon leader, Brigham Young (1801–1877), uttered some version of the now famous proclamation "This is the right place." Actually, this location had previously been selected. Richard D. Poll's *Utah's History* tells us that the location had been "...identified and dedicated; irrigation, plowing and planting were well under way." The county here was first named Great Salt Lake County, in honor of the Great Salt Lake. The date that the county was initially created is disputed and dates ranging from 1849 to 1852 are mentioned. However, sources are agreed on the date that Utah territory changed the county's name to Salt Lake County, and that date was January 29, 1868. The Great Salt Lake covers about 900 square miles. Its size has decreased significantly since the Mormons first settled here, as water has been drawn for irrigation, but it is still the largest body of water between the Great Lakes and the Pacific Ocean. Great Salt Lake is extremely salty (several times more saline than sea water) since it has no outlet. When the lake's water evaporates, salts (common table salt and other minerals) stay behind. The valley of the Great Salt Lake became the central home for the Church of Jesus Christ of Latter-day Saints (Mormons) in 1847 and at the millennium year 2000 it remains the center of the church.

2761 *San Juan County*

San Juan River— This county in the southeastern corner of Utah was created on February 17, 1880, by Utah territory and named for the San Juan River, which flows through it. *San Juan* is Spanish for "Saint John." The San Juan River is a 360 mile-long tributary of the Colorado River. It rises in southwestern Colorado, in the San Juan Mountains and flows into San Juan County, in the northwestern corner of New Mexico. When it reaches Farmington, in San Juan County, New Mexico, the river bends to the west and later to the northwest. The San Juan River comes very close to touching the "Four Corners," where four of our country's southwestern states meet at one point. There the river heads west into San Juan County, Utah, where it has carved a deep box canyon, and it is in San Juan County, Utah, that the San Juan River finally empties its waters into those of the Colorado River. T. M. Pearce has written extensively on the origin on place names in New Mexico and Pearce tells us that the river was probably named for Saint John the Baptist. Angelico Chavez wrote an article entitled "Saints' Names in New Mexico Geography," which appeared in the November, 1949 issue of *El Palacio*. In that article Chavez agrees that "the northwest county and its river, ... is very likely derived from this same saint." (St. John the Baptist.) Robert Julyan is an expert on New Mexico's geographic names. Julyan is also cautious in his write-up on this subject in *The Place Names of New Mexico*, published in 1996. In that work Julyan tells us that San Juan Pueblo, a settlement in northwestern New Mexico, in Rio Arriba County (which borders on San Juan County, New Mexico) was named on July 12, 1598, by the Spanish explorer and official, Don Juan de Onate, for his personal patron saint, St. John the Baptist. However in his paragraph devoted to the nearby San Juan River, Julyan avoids stating which saint the river's name honors. Robert Julyan's research was extensive and careful. Since our experts on this subject, T. M. Pearce, Angelico Chavez and Robert Julyan are unwilling to state, without reservation, which saint the river was named for, it seems appropriate to conclude that the river was named for a saint of the Roman Catholic church, probably, but not definitely, Saint John the Baptist. There are at least 16 saints whose name starts with John the Baptist. Many of them can be ruled out because they did not become saints until after the San Juan River was named and the others are extremely obscure compared to Saint John the Baptist, who baptized Jesus. That Saint John the Baptist has long been one of the most popular saints of the Roman Catholic Church.

Saint John the Baptist (–)—John lived an austere life in the desert of Judea, southwest of Jerusalem. Clothed in garments of camel's hair and living on a diet of locusts and wild honey, John ministered to men from Jerusalem and neighboring towns, who flocked to visit him. He demanded two rites of those who came to him: an open confession of their sins and physical baptism. Jesus Christ was among those baptized by John and John apparently came to believe, on that occasion, that Jesus was the Messiah. King Herod Antipas feared John's popularity and power and resented John's criticism of his sex life. The king imprisoned John and had him beheaded.

2762 *Sanpete County*

San Pitch Valley, Creek and/or Mountains—This county in central Utah was created on March 3, 1852, by Utah territory. Its name derived from one or more of the geographical features here named San Pitch, the valley, the creek and the mountains. James B. Allen's article entitled "The Evolution of County Boundaries in Utah," which appeared in the July, 1955, issue (Vol. 23, No. 3) of *Utah Historical Quarterly*, indicated that the county's name was originally rendered San Pete County. However, the form Sanpete County is now used. Rufus W. Leigh's *Five Hundred Utah Place Names* tells us that "San Pitch Valley, Creek and Mountains are west of the Wasatch Plateau in central Utah. The Creek runs southerly down the Valley, thence westerly to join Sevier River near Gunnison. The San Pitch Mountains, the west wall of the valley, with elevation of 9,000 feet, are much lower and less rugged than the Wasatch Plateau, the east watershed ... San Pitch Valley is one of Utah's rich agricultural and thickly populated valleys. The name of these physiographic features derived from the name of the Ute division whose homelands embraced this area, and who were known by several variant names: *Sampitches, Sampichya, Sampiches*, and *Sanpuchi*. They wintered in the Sevier River Valley where there was less snow..." Several works dealing with the history, geography and place names of Utah indicate that the name Sanpete derived from the name of an Indian chief. It is certainly possible that an Indian chief here was known by the same or a similar name as that of the tribe.

2763 *Sevier County*

Sevier River—This county was created by Utah territory on January 16, 1865, and named for the Sevier River, which flows through it. The Sevier River is formed by the confluence of forks in southern Utah and flows north, then southwest and finally east. It ends its journey of 279 miles, all in Utah, when it empties its waters into the playa named Sevier Lake, in western Utah. The Sevier River is the longest Great Basin River that is wholly within Utah. Works dealing with the history, geography and place names of Utah offer a variety of explanations for the origin of the Sevier River's name. Several attribute it to the name of an American trapper. No doubt these sources are relying on a May 23, 1844, entry in the journal of the famous American explorer, John C. Frémont (1813–1890) which contained the following notation: "We reached Sevier River.... The name of this river and lake was an indication of our approach to regions of which our people had been the explorers. It was probably named after some American trapper or hunter, and was the first American name we had met since leaving the Columbia River." Other Utah sources indicate that the river was named in honor of John Sevier (1745–1815), the first governor of the state of Tennessee. Faced with these conflicting opinions we are fortunate to have an in-depth study of the matter by Rufus W. Leigh, an authority on Utah place names. Leigh's study and conclusions were presented in an article published in the April, 1961, issue (Vol. 29, No. 2) of *Utah Historical Quarterly*, entitled "Naming of the Green, Sevier and Virgin Rivers." Leigh relates that Spanish explorers named the present Sevier River in 1776 *Rio Santa Isabel*, in honor of a Spanish queen, but that this name did not become known. Leigh tells us that later Spanish explorers named the river *Rio Severo* and that its name *severo* was the Spanish adjective for "harsh" or "severe," possibly because of conditions on the river during winter, at high altitude, where it was swift. An American trapper here said that the Mexican Spaniards named the river *Rio Severe* on account of its rough character. Leigh then explains the current name, Sevier, when he says that "...but later Americans insisted on a proper name for the river simulating the Spanish descriptive word in pronunciation: 'Sevier.'"

2764 *Summit County*

Its mountainous terrain—This county was created by Utah territory on January 13, 1854. Its name was chosen as descriptive of the county's high mountainous terrain which forms the divides between the drainage areas of Green River, Bear River and Weber River, in northern Utah.

2765 *Tooele County*

Tooele Valley—This county in northwestern Utah was created by Utah territory on March 3, 1852, and named for its Tooele Valley, which begins at the southern end of Great Salt Lake and extends southward, between the Stansbury Mountains on the west and the Oquirrh Mountains on the east. The Tooele Valley was previously called Tuilla Valley, but the origin and meaning of the name, by whatever spelling, is uncertain. Several theories have been advanced and George Tripp's article entitled "Tooele: What Is the Name's Origin?," which appeared in the Summer, 1989, issue (Vol. 57, No. 3) of *Utah Historical Quarterly* discusses both the likely possibilities and the unlikely ones. Tripp's conclusion is that some widely circulated possibilities are "so far-fetched that the only logical explanation for them has to be that some old-timer passed them off to an unsuspecting tenderfoot who accepted them as factual." He includes in this "far-fetched" category "too hilly" and "too willy" (too many willows) and also the frequently seen explanation that the name derived from the bulrushes or tules growing here. Tripp also mentions, as a straw man to be knocked down, the Austro-Hungarian town of Mattuglie, which Mormon Apostle Orson Pratt visited. Tripp finds this theory to be flawed because Orson Pratt "...did not visit Austria until twenty years after Tooele was settled and named." Tripp considers it more likely that the name is of Indian origin and possibly was taken from the name (or an expression of respect) for an Indian chief who had lived here and he rounds out his list of possibilities with the candidate he considers most likely, an Indian family name derived from the term for "black bear," or "bear." Although George Tripp's research was obviously extensive, he arrived at no solid conclusion. It therefore seems reasonable to keep on the list of viable possibilities the tules/ bulrushes theory which Tripp regards as far-fetched. Rufus W. Leigh is an authority on Utah place names and in his *Five Hundred Utah Place Names*, Leigh gives the tule/ bulrush origin probable status and traces the possible derivation of the name back to the Aztec Indians.

2766 *Uintah County*

Uinta Ute Indians— This county in northeastern Utah was created by Utah territory on February 18, 1880, and named for a sub-tribe of the Ute Indians, called the Uinta, Uinta-Ats, or Yoovte Indians. This sub-tribe was living in northwestern Colorado and northeastern Utah when the Mormon settlers arrived in 1847. The Mormon leader, Brigham Young (1801–1877), wanted them moved out of the way. It was proposed that the Uinta (and other Indians) be moved to a reservation in the Uinta Basin and Brigham Young agreed to this proposal only after satisfying himself that the area was "one vast contiguity of waste."

In 1861 the U.S. federal government set aside the proposed reservation in the Uinta Valley and the Uinta and other Indians were moved there. Later, this reservation was combined with an Indian reservation named the Ouray reservation and the combined reservation is known today as the Uintah-Ouray Indian reservation. Most of that reservation lies west of Uintah County, in Duchesne County, Utah. The population of Uinta Indians was estimated at 443 in 1909.

2767 *Utah County*

Ute Indians— Mormon settlers of the present state of Utah submitted two petitions to the federal government soon after they arrived here in 1847. One petition requested statehood; the other merely asked for territorial status. While waiting for action on these requests, the unofficial "state" of Deseret here created counties. One of the counties which was so created in December, 1849, before Utah even achieved territorial status, was Utah County and that county merely consisted of the Utah Valley. During September, 1850, the U.S. government established Utah territory and on March 3, 1852, Utah territory created its first official county named Utah County. This version of Utah County was not confined to the Utah Valley but extended all the way from what is now west-central Utah to the eastern border of Utah territory; i.e., to about the center of the present state of Colorado. All of these uses of the name *Utah*, from the valley to the first unofficial county, to the territory and to the first official county, derived from the Ute Indian tribe. The Utes consisted of three main sub-tribes living in what is now western Colorado, eastern Utah and northern New Mexico. Ute Indians were initially seed gatherers and hunted small game but by the time of contact with Whites, they practiced little or no agriculture. Acquisition of horses enabled the Ute to become nomadic tepee-dwellers, hunting game such as deer, antelope and buffalo. Utes were reputedly savage and warlike but when they fought the Spanish in the 18th century and the Americans in the 19th century, they met with little success. Estimates of Ute population are unreliable because of mixture of Ute figures with those of Paiute Indians. Frederick W. Hodge's *Handbook of American Indians North of Mexico* indicates the Utes probably numbered about 4,000 in 1870. Bill Yenne's *Encyclopedia of North American Indian Tribes* stated that in 1985 there were about 5,000 Utes on three reservations.

2768 *Wasatch County*

Wasatch Mountains— This county in north-central Utah was created by Utah territory on January 17, 1862, and named for the beautiful Wasatch Mountains, on which the county sits. The Wasatch are the chief physiographic feature of Utah and one of the dominating mountain ranges of North America. Peaks of the Wasatch range soar from about 9,000 feet above sea level to the lofty 12,008 feet height of Mount Timpanogos, the highest Wasatch peak. The Wasatch range extends into Utah from southeastern Idaho and ends in central Utah. *Wasatch* is said to derive from a Ute Indian word meaning "a low pass over a high mountain range."

2769 *Washington County*

George Washington (1732–1799)— Washington was a native of Virginia. He served in Virginia's house of burgesses and became one of the colonies' leaders in opposition to British policies in America. He was a member of the first and second Continental Congresses and commander of all Continental armies in the Revolutionary War. Following victory in that war, Washington was elected to be the first president of the United States. This county was created by Utah territory on March 3, 1852.

2770 *Wayne County*

Wayne C. Robison (1885–1896)— This county's namesake, Wayne Clifton Robison, was born on May 26, 1885, at Scipio, Utah territory, and died when he was only eleven years old, at Loa, Utah, on September 21, 1896. This county was created by Utah territory on March 10, 1892, and its name honored a son of Willis Eugene Robison (1864–1937), who was a member of the lower house of the territorial legislature when the county was created. Young Wayne C. Robison met his early death when a horse accidentally killed him. The father, Willis E. Robison, had four wives and 12 children. The mother of this county's namesake was the first wife of Willis E. Robison. Her name was Sarah Ann Ellett Robison.

2771 *Weber County*

Weber River— This county was created by Utah territory on March 3, 1852, and named for the Weber River, which flows through it. The Weber River rises in Summit County, Utah, flows northwest for about 100 miles and pours its waters into Great Salt Lake. John W. Van Cott's *Utah*

Place Names indicates uncertainty about the river's namesake but mentions a "Dutch sea captain," named John H. Weber and an Arizona frontiersman named Pauline (sic) Weaver (sic) as possibilities. Other sources dealing with the history, geography and place names of Utah are more helpful and are generally agreed that the river was named for John H. Weber (1779–1859), who was not Dutch, but Danish.

John H. Weber (1779–1859)—A native of Denmark, Weber left home at an early age to be a seaman and he achieved the rank of captain before he was 21 years old. He came to North America and was known to be at Sainte Genevieve on the Mississippi River in 1807. It was probably there in the Missouri area that he met William H. Ashley (–1838) and became interested in exploration and fur trapping in our nation's West. He soon became a successful trapper here and his activities took him from the Powder River to Green River Valley, Bear Lake, the Great Salt Lake, Weber Canyon and Weber River. John H. Weber returned East and settled in the Illinois-Iowa area about two decades before Mormon settlers arrived here in 1847.

REFERENCES

Alexander, Thomas G. "From Death to Deluge: Utah's Coal Industry." *Utah Historical Quarterly*, Vol. 31, No. 3. Salt Lake City: Summer, 1963.

Allen, James B. "The Changing Impact of Mining on the Economy of Twentieth Century Utah." *Utah Historical Quarterly*, Vol. 38, No. 3. Salt Lake City: Summer, 1970.

Allen, James B. "The Evolution of County Boundaries in Utah." *Utah Historical Quarterly*, Vol. 23, No. 3. Salt Lake City: July, 1955.

Beckwith, Frank. *Trips to Points of Interest in Millard & Nearby*. Springville, Utah, Art City Publishing Co., 1947.

Buttle, Faye Jensen. *Utah Grows: Past & Present*. Provo, Utah, BYU Press, 1970.

Carbon County: Eastern Utah's Industrialized Island. Salt Lake City, Utah State Historical Society, 1981.

Carroll, Elsie Chamberlain. *History of Kane County*. Salt Lake City, Utah Printing Co., 1960.

Carter, Kate B. *Heart Throbs of the West*. Salt Lake City, Daughters of Utah Pioneers, 1951.

Chavez, Angelico. "Saints' Names in New Mexico Geography." *El Palacio*, Vol. 56, No. 11. Santa Fe: November, 1949.

Christensen, Vera, & Elizabeth Nuhn.

Cache: Fantasy, Fact, Folklore. Logan, Herald Printing Co., 1976.

Cook, Betty R. *Here Are the Counties of Utah*. Bountiful, Utah, 1983.

Defenbach, Byron. *Idaho: The Place & Its People*. Chicago, American Historical Society, Inc., 1933.

Dunham, Dick, & Vivian Dunham. *Our Strip of Land: A History of Daggett County, Utah*. Lusk, Wyoming, Lusk Herald, 1947.

Early History of Duchesne County. Springville, Utah, Art City Publishing Co., 1948.

East of Antelope Island: History of the First Fifty Years of Davis County. Salt Lake City, Publishers Press, 1969.

Ellsworth, S. George. *Utah's Heritage*. Santa Barbara, Peregrine & Smith, Inc., 1972.

Emery County: 1880–1980. Taylor Publishing Co., 1981.

An Enduring Legacy. Salt Lake City, Daughters of Utah Pioneers, 1978.

Esshom, Frank. *Pioneers & Prominent Men of Utah*. Salt Lake City, Utah Pioneers Book Publishing Co., 1913.

Facts About Utah. Salt Lake City, Utah Tourist & Publicity Council, 1958.

Fowler, Catherine S., & Don D. Fowler. "Notes on the History of the Southern Paiutes & Western Shoshonis." *Utah Historical Quarterly*, Vol. 39, No. 2. Salt Lake City: Spring, 1971.

Frazer, Robert W. *Forts of the West*. Norman, University of Oklahoma Press, 1965.

Goodman, Jack. "Wandering in the Wasatch." *Utah Historical Quarterly*, Vol. 27, No. 3. Salt Lake City: July, 1959.

Hawley, James H. *History of Idaho*. Chicago, S. J. Clarke Publishing Co., 1920.

Hinton, Wayne K. "Millard Fillmore: Utah's Friend in the White House." *Utah Historical Quarterly*, Vol. 48, No. 2. Salt Lake City: Spring, 1980.

History of Sanpete & Emery Counties, Utah. Ogden, W. H. Lever, 1898.

Hodge, Frederick W. *Handbook of American Indians North of Mexico*. Totowa, New Jersey, Rowman & Littlefield, 1975.

Hovey, M. R. "An Early History of Cache County." Unpublished manuscript, Utah State Historical Society, Salt Lake City, 1923–1925.

Hunter, Milton R. *Beneath Ben Lomond's Peak: A History of Weber County: 1824–1900*. Salt Lake City, Deseret News Press, 1944.

Iron County Centennial: 1851–1951. Iron County Commissioners.

Jenson, Andrew. *Latter-Day Saint Biographical Encyclopedia*. Salt Lake City, Deseret News, 1901.

Johnson, H. Cyril. *Scenic Guide to Utah*. Westwood, California, Sugar Pine Press, 1947.

Julyan, Robert. *The Place Names of New Mexico*. Albuquerque, University of New Mexico Press, 1996.

Larson, Gustive O. "Bulwark of the Kingdom: Utah's Iron & Steel Industry." *Utah Historical Quarterly*, Vol. 31, No. 3. Salt Lake City: Summer, 1963.

Leigh, Rufus W. *Five Hundred Utah Place Names*. Salt Lake City, Deseret News Press, 1961.

Leigh, Rufus W. "Naming of the Green, Sevier & Virgin Rivers." *Utah Historical Quarterly*, Vol. 29, No. 2. Salt Lake City: April, 1961.

Luce, Willard, & Celia Luce. *Utah!* Salt Lake City, Peregrine Smith, Inc., 1975.

McCune, Alice Paxman. *History of Juab County*. Juab County Company of the Daughters of Utah Pioneers, 1947.

McElprang, Mrs. Stella. *Castle Valley: A History of Emery County*. Emery County Company of the Daughters of Utah Pioneers, 1949.

McLoughlin, Denis. *Wild & Woolly: An Encyclopedia of the Old West*. Garden City, New York, Doubleday & Co., Inc., 1975.

Mercer, Mildred Allred. *History of Tooele County*. Salt Lake City, Publishers Press, 1961.

Merkley, Aird G. *Monuments to Courage: A History of Beaver County*. Beaver County Chapter of the Daughters of Utah Pioneers, 1948.

Mortimer, William J. *How Beautiful Upon the Mountains: A Centennial History of Wasatch County*. Wasatch County Chapter, Daughters of Utah Pioneers, 1963.

New Catholic Encyclopedia. New York, McGraw-Hill Book Co., 1967.

Papanikolas, Helen Z. "Utah's Coal Lands: A Vital Example of How America Became a Great Nation." *Utah Historical Quarterly*, Vol. 43, No. 2. Salt Lake City: Spring, 1975.

Pearce, T. M. *New Mexico Place Names*. Albuquerque, University of New Mexico Press, 1965.

Pearce, T. M. "Religious Place Names in New Mexico." *Names: Journal of the American Name Society*, Vol. 9, No. 1. Youngstown, Ohio: March, 1961.

Perkins, Cornelia Adam, et al. *Saga of San Juan*. San Juan County Daughters of Utah Pioneers, 1957.

Peterson, Marie Ross, & Mary M. Pearson. *Echoes of Yesterday: Summit County Centennial History*. Salt Lake City, Daughters of Utah Pioneers of Summit County, 1947.

Poll, Richard D. *Utah's History*. Logan, Utah State University Press, 1989.

Powell, Allan K. *Utah History Encyclopedia*. Salt Lake City, University of Utah Press, 1994.

Rickards, Russ. Letters to the author dated January 20, 2000, & January 24, 2000.

Ricks, Joel E. *The History of a Valley: Cache Valley, Utah-Idaho*. Logan, Cache Valley Centennial Commission, 1956.

Ricks, Joel E. "The Settlement of Cache Valley." *Utah Historical Quarterly*, Vol. 24, No. 4. Salt Lake City: October, 1956.

Roylance, Ward J. *Materials for the Study of Utah's Counties*. Salt Lake City, 1962.

Roylance, Ward J. *Utah's Geography & Counties*. Salt Lake City, 1967.

Sidwell, Mrs. A. B. *Reminiscences of Early Days in Manti*.

Sloan, Edward L. *Gazetteer of Utah & Salt Lake City Directory*. Salt Lake City, Salt Lake Herald Publishing Co., 1874.

Sloan, Robert W. *Utah Gazetteer & Directory of Logan, Ogden, Provo & Salt Lake Cities*. Salt Lake City, Herald Printing & Publishing Co., 1884.

Snow, Anne. *Rainbow Views: A History of Wayne County*. Springville, Utah, Art City Publishing Co., 1953.

Stewart, George R. *American Place-Names*. New York, Oxford University Press, 1970.

Stewart, Omer C. "Ute Indians: Before & After White Contact." *Utah Historical Quarterly*, Vol. 34, No. 1. Salt Lake City: Winter, 1966.

Stoutenburgh, John. *Dictionary of the American Indian*. New York, Bonanza Books, 1990.

Thomson, Mildred Hatch. *Rich Memories: Some of the Happenings in Rich County from 1863 to 1960*. Springville, Utah, Art City Publishing Co., 1962.

Thrapp, Dan L. *Encyclopedia of Frontier Biography*. Lincoln, University of Nebraska Press, 1988.

Tooele, Tooele County, Utah Polk Directory: 1982. Kansas City, Missouri, R. L. Polk & Co.

Tripp, George. "Tooele: New Variations on An Old Theme." Unpublished manuscript, Utah State Historical Society, Salt Lake City.

Tripp, George. "Tooele: What Is the Name's Origin?" *Utah Historical Quarterly*, Vol. 57, No. 3. Salt Lake City: Summer, 1989.

Tullidge's Histories: Containing the History of All of the Northern, Eastern & Western Counties of Utah: Also the Counties of Southern Idaho: With a Biographical Appendix. Salt Lake City, Press of the Juvenile Instructor, 1889.

Van Cott, John W. *Utah Place Names*. Salt Lake City, University of Utah Press, 1990.

Vexler, Robert I. *Chronology & Documentary Handbook of the State of Utah*. Dobbs Ferry, New York, Oceana Publications, Inc., 1979.

Warnock, Irvin L. *Thru the Years: Sevier County Centennial History*. Springville, Utah, Art City Publishing Co., 1947.

Warrum, Noble. *Utah Since Statehood: Historical & Biographical*. Chicago, S. J. Clarke Publishing Co., 1919.

What You Want to Know About Utah. Salt Lake City, Utah Department of Publicity & Industrial Development, 1946.

Whitney, Orson F. *History of Utah*. Salt Lake City, George Q. Cannon & Sons Co., 1892.

Woolsey, Nethella Griffin. *The Escalante Story: A History of the Town of Escalante & Description of the Surrounding Territory: Garfield County, Utah*. Springville, Utah, Art City Publishing Co., 1964.

Work Projects Administration. *Inventory of the County Archives of Utah-Daggett, Emery, Sanpete & Weber Counties*. Ogden & Salt Lake City, 1937–1941.

Work Projects Administration. *Origins of Utah Place Names*. Salt Lake City, Utah State Department of Public Instruction, 1940.

Works Progress Administration. *Inventory of the County Archives of Utah-Morgan & Tooele Counties*. Ogden, 1937–1939.

Yenne, Bill. *The Encyclopedia of North American Indian Tribes*. New York, Crescent Books, 1986.

Vermont

(14 counties)

2772 *Addison County*

Town of Addison, New Hampshire grant of October 14, 1761— In 1753 New Hampshire's governor, Benning Wentworth (1696–1770), named a New Hampshire town Addison. That New Hampshire town was granted to a group of Connecticut families, but they chose not to accept it on account of the French & Indian Wars. In 1761 Governor Wentworth repeated his grant, this time naming the community Marlow. Also in 1761, on October 14th of that year, New Hampshire Governor Benning Wentworth used the name Addison for a town in the New Hampshire grants. When this county was created on October 18, 1785 (before Vermont had been admitted to statehood), it was named for the town of Addison, which had been created on October 14, 1761. That town's name honored the English statesman, journalist and author, Joseph Addison (1672–1719). In 1761, when the second town named Addison was created, New Hampshire was a colony of England. Joseph Addison (1672–1719) had been instrumental in the appointment of John Wentworth (1671–1730) as lieutenant-governor of the colony of New Hampshire. Moreover, John Wentworth (1671–1730) was the father of Benning Wentworth (1696–1770), who twice established a town in New Hampshire named in honor of Joseph Addison (1672–1719).

Joseph Addison (1672–1719)— This Englishman and distinguished classical scholar had become a noted poet before he was made undersecretary of state in 1706. He also served as a member of parliament and was the author and editor of a variety of material, much of it political. However, Addison's work also included fiction. He was a lord commissioner of trade and secretary of state. As secretary of state in 1717, Addison signed the papers which appointed John Wentworth (1671–1730) as lieutenant-governor of England's North American colony of New Hampshire.

2773 *Bennington County*

Town of Bennington— England's colonial governor of New Hampshire, Benning

Wentworth (1696–1770), granted a large number of towns in the present state of Vermont. The first of these was the town of Bennington, and its grant was dated January 3, 1749. By the Bennington land grant, the governor provided lands to his friends, most of whom lived in the Portsmouth, New Hampshire area. The town of Bennington was the scene of an early battle during the American Revolution. Here, on August 16, 1777, our colonial forces defeated the British. In the late 1990's the municipality of Bennington was a pleasant city with a population of some 16,500, located in the southwestern corner of Vermont, in a valley between the Taconic Mountains and the foothills of the Green Mountains. The original town was named for New Hampshire Governor Benning Wentworth and when the county was later established, it took its name from its principal town. Sources consulted differ on the date that Bennington County was created, some indicating March 17, 1778, while others show February 11, 1779.

Benning Wentworth (1696–1770)— Born at Portsmouth, New Hampshire on July 24, 1696, Benning Wentworth was a son of John Wentworth (1671–1730), the lieutenant-governor of England's colony of New Hampshire. Benning Wentworth received a bachelor's degree from Harvard College in 1715, served briefly in the New Hampshire assembly and later in the colony's council. In 1741 he was commissioned as England's royal governor of New Hampshire and he took office in December of that year. As governor, Benning Wentworth promoted the economic and political fortunes of his family. He also granted a large number of towns in both of the present states of New Hampshire and Vermont. His administration was marked by strife with the New Hampshire legislature and he was none too popular back in England. In spite of these difficulties, Benning Wentworth adroitly retained his position as New Hampshire's royal governor for more than 25 years and when he relinquished it in 1767, he managed to pass his office on to a nephew, John Wentworth (1737–1820).

2774 *Caledonia County*

Scotland on the island of Great Britain— Scotland is a member of the United Kingdom in the British Isles, and it occupies the northern portion of the island of Great Britain, with England on its southern border. The other members of the United Kingdom are England, Wales and Northern Ireland. The name *Scotland* derived from the Celtic speaking Scots, who came to Scotland from Ireland about A.D. 500. Prior to 1603, Scotland had a long history that was relatively independent of its powerful southern neighbor, England. At the time that today's Scotland was invaded by the Roman Empire about A.D. 80, it was occupied by the Picts. In addition to the Picts and Romans, others who have ruled some or all of Scotland include the Scots, Anglo-Saxons and the Norse. The Scottish ruler, Malcom II (–1034), is credited with forging a version of a united Scottish kingdom. From 1034 to 1603, Scotland was generally independent of its powerful southern neighbor, although there were many periods of conflict between England and Scotland and England ruled potions of Scotland at times. The beginning of today's formal union of Scotland with England occurred in 1603 when Scotland's King James VI (1566–1625) was also installed on the English throne. He ruled Scotland as James VI and England as James I. Scotland is a cold, mountainous country with a relatively sparse population. Its capital city is Edinburgh. In addition to its territory on the island of Great Britain, Scotland includes three important island groups: The Shetland, Orkney and Hebrides Islands. Caledonia County in northeastern Vermont was created on November 5, 1792. It was named in honor of Scotland because of the important role that Scottish settlers played in the early development of this section of Vermont. *Caledonia* was the name given to the Scottish Highlands by the Romans, when they occupied Great Britain. The Roman army built the Antonine Wall in A.D. 142, for defense, and they called the region north of that wall *Caledonia*. John Cannon's *The Oxford Companion to British History*, published by Oxford University Press in 1997 indicates that the Caledonians of Scotland were known back in Rome as a confederation of tribes, with a remarkable ability to "endure cold, hunger and hardship." Described as red-haired, the Caledonians were a persistent enemy of the Romans.

2775 *Chittenden County*

Thomas Chittenden (1730–1797)— Born January 6, 1730, in England's colony of Connecticut, Chittenden served in Connecticut's assembly and was an officer in the 14th Connecticut regiment from 1767 to 1773 and rose to the rank of colonel. In 1774 he moved to Williston, in the New Hampshire grants, which is now part of Chittenden County, Vermont. Here he engaged in land speculation and was active in the movement in New Hampshire to join the other colonies is declaring independence from England. Chittenden was also soon active in the movement to secure independent government for the area which eventually became the state of Vermont, and by 1778 he had been chosen as its unofficial governor. He remained in that position as the first governor of the state of Vermont, when statehood was achieved, and served as state governor from 1791 to 1797, when he resigned due to ill health. This county was created on October 22, 1787. Unlike some other Vermont counties, this county was not named for a town (although Vermont has both a town of Chittenden and a village of Chittenden Mills) but directly for the man, Thomas Chittenden.

2776 *Essex County*

Uncertain— This county in northeastern Vermont was created on November 5, 1792. Unlike some other Vermont counties, this county was not named for a town (although Vermont has a town named Essex) but sources consulted differ on whether this county's name honors Essex County, England, or Robert Devereux (1566–1601), Earl of Essex. Esther Munroe Swift's scholarly study, entitled *Vermont Place-Names*, has this to say about the origin of this county's name: "Many historical sources erroneously ascribe the Essex name to Robert Devereux (1566–1601), the second Earl of Essex, one of Queen Elizabeth's favorites, who was executed for treason largely for his mishandling of the Irish revolt at the close of the 16th century. In 1792 the state of Vermont had no reason to perpetuate any English nobleman's name, so it seems more probable that the name was selected, as it had been in Massachusetts, to indicate that the area was the most easterly part of the state, and also because many of the residents had ancestors who had originally lived in Essex, England."

Essex County, England— Essex County is in the eastern section of Anglia, in southern England. This seacoast county facing the European continent was an important center when it was occupied by the Roman Empire and it continued to be an important population center, containing the city of London, when the East Saxons invaded it. The name *Essex* means "territory of the East Saxons." Essex was one of the seven Anglo-Saxon kingdoms of Britain known as the Heptarchy. In the seventh century Essex was conquered by Mercia, one of the other kingdoms of the Heptarchy, and later, in the ninth century, Wessex, which had been another member of the Heptarchy, conquered it. The Essex County of today's England no longer contains London. Essex County, England, is about 54 miles long and some 48 miles wide. Its principal rivers are the Thames, Stour, Colne, Blackwater and Lea.

Robert Devereux (1566–1601), Earl of Essex— Educated at Trinity College, Cambridge, this Englishman became the second earl of Essex in the 1570's. He served in the military and was made a knight banneret in 1586 for his bravery. He became a favorite of Queen Elizabeth I (1533–1603), was her master of the horse and was made knight of the garter. In the 1590's Essex cemented his popularity by uncovering a plot against the queen's life by Roderigo Lopez (–1594) and by an important military victory over the Spanish at Cadiz, Spain. However remaining in good odor with Queen Elizabeth I was tenuous business for she was extremely possessive of all her courtiers and her jealousy was easily aroused. His secret marriage to Frances Sidney certainly did his cause with the queen no good. Essex was eventually executed for treason, after leading a failed revolt.

2777 *Franklin County*

Benjamin Franklin (1706–1790)— Franklin was a native of Massachusetts who moved to Pennsylvania in his teens. Poverty denied him a formal education but he became the leading printer and editor in North America. Franklin gained fame for his discoveries and inventions in the physical sciences and he distinguished himself as author, philosopher and diplomat. Franklin was a signer of the Declaration of Independence and an important member of the convention which framed the U.S. Constitution. He died on April 17, 1790, and this county was created and named in his honor on November 5, 1792.

2778 *Grand Isle County*

Grand Isle in Lake Champlain— This county on Vermont's northwestern border with Canada and the state of New York was created from five Vermont towns, Alburg, Isle La Motte, Middle Hero, North Hero and South Hero, and named for the ten mile-long island in Lake Champlain, Grande Isle, which lies within the county's borders. The island's name is the English translation of the French name for it. Several of the earlier Indian names for the island also convey a similar descriptive connotation. This county was incorporated by the Vermont legislature on November 9, 1802. The residents of the five Vermont towns which made up the county requested that it be named Hero County, in honor of Vermont's Revolutionary War hero, Ethan Allen (1738–1789). The legislature rejected that name and named the county for its largest island. Also, in a curious provision, the legislature stipulated that the new county could do no official business until October, 1805.

2779 *Lamoille County*

Lamoille River— This county in north-central Vermont was created on October 26, 1835, and named for the Lamoille River, which flows through it. The Lamoille River is about 75 miles long and it enters Lake Champlain in Chittenden County, after flowing west through Lamoille County and south through Franklin County. In 1609 the explorer Samuel de Champlain (–1635) discovered both the lake that bears his name and the Lamoille River. However, when Champlain named the river, he called it *La Mouette*, which is French for "the seagull," or "a place where gulls or mews are found." Through a transcription error, Champlain's name was garbled and the river's name was seen on a map as early as 1744 rendered as *La Mouelle*, as a result of failure to cross the two t's. At some point the river's name transposed further to *Lamoille*, and it was that spelling which was used when this county was created.

2780 *Orange County*

Uncertain— Vermont has a town named Orange and the one fact that is certain about this county's name is that it was not named for that town. Rather, the town of Orange, Vermont, was named for Orange County, Vermont, which was created on February 22, 1781. Beyond that lies uncertainty. Other counties in our nation which are named Orange derive their names either for the citrus fruit or from members of the English royal family, named Orange. Citrus trees, like the orange, cannot survive in the frigid climate of New England and in 1781 when this county was created, the American colonies were in the midst of the Revolutionary War to win freedom from England and not in a mood to be naming counties for members of the English royal family. Esther Munroe Swift's scholarly study, entitled *Vermont Place-Names*, suggests that this Vermont county's name may have come from that of a town in Connecticut or Massachusetts or from Orange County, New York. *Connecticut Place Names* by Arthur H. Hughes and Morse S. Allen attributes the name of Connecticut's town of Orange to England's King William III (1650–1702), known as William of Orange. (In an aside, this work on Connecticut place names says that the place name Orange in Vermont came from King William III [1650–1702]). George R. Stewart's *American Place-Names* tells us that the town of Orange in Massachusetts derived its name from England's King William III (1650–1702). As noted under Orange County, New York, above, your author has traced the New York County's name to the same source, King William III (1650–1702). Thus no matter whether Vermont took its county's name from the town in Connecticut or Massachusetts or the county in New York, the origin can be traced back to the English king, William III (1650–1702).

King William III (1650–1702)— William, Prince of Orange, was born in the Netherlands. He was the grandson of England's King Charles I (1600–1649) and in 1677 William married his cousin, Mary (1662–1694), who was then the presumptive heir to the English throne, occupied by her father, King James II (1633–1701). In 1688 William invaded England, supported by both Dutch and English troops and on April 11, 1689, William and his wife were crowned king and queen of England. They ruled as joint sovereigns, titled King William III and Queen Mary II until Mary's death in 1694. William continued on the English throne until his death in 1702. King William's title, Orange, belonged to William's family, the Nassaus, on account of a tiny pocket of independent territory within southern France, near the Rhone River, named Orange, which had earlier been an ancient Roman town. It is now merely a small city in France, 17 miles north of Avignon, France.

2781 *Orleans County*

Uncertain— This county in north-central Vermont, on the Canadian border, was created on November 5, 1792. Sources consulted offer little certainty about the possible sources of this county's name although it seems unlikely that the county was named for the town of Orleans, within its borders. Rather, the likely possibilities are the city of Orleans, in France or the Frenchman, Louise Philippe Joseph,

Duke of Orleans (1747–1793), who had advocated the cause of the American colonies during the American Revolution. He was made duke of Orleans in 1785, seven years before this county was created.

City of Orleans, France — Orleans, the capital of the department of Loiret, is located on the Loire River in north-central France. This city, with a population of about 100,000, lies some 75 miles southwest of Paris. Orleans produces manufactured goods and is in one of France's agricultural regions. Conquered by the Roman Empire in 52 B.C., Orleans became a major cultural center during the middle ages. The French King Philip VI (1293–1350) made the city a royal duchy and peerage in favor of his son. The city of Orleans, together with the surrounding Orleanais Province was given at times as an appanage to members of the French royal family (dukes of Orleans).

Louis Philippe Joseph, Duke of Orleans (1747–1793) This wealthy member of the French royal family's fourth house of Orleans was born in Saint-Cloud, France, and held the titles of duke of Montpensier and duke of Chartres as well as duke of Orleans. As early as 1778, before he had become duke of Orleans, Louis Philippe Joseph advocated the cause of the American colonies in their revolution to gain independence from England. In 1787, in the French Assembly of notables, he opposed proposals of the French king's minister and in 1789 he aided in the French Revolution. Although he renounced his title, assumed the name Philippe-Egalite and worked against the ruling French king, Louis XVI (1754–1793), the Jacobins voted to confiscate his estates and he was executed by guillotine during the French Revolution. His eldest son, King Louis-Philippe (1773–1850), became king of France during the Restoration and ruled from 1830 to 1848.

2782 *Rutland County*

Town of Rutland, New Hampshire grant of September 7, 1761 — This county was created on February 22, 1781, and named for a locality within its borders, the town of Rutland. It was not named for the present city of Rutland, Vermont, the county seat of Rutland County, for that city was only a hamlet within the town of Rutland when this county was created. The town for which this county was named was granted on September 7, 1761, by New Hampshire's governor, Benning Wentworth (1696–1770). The oldest community within the early town of Rutland was

Center Rutland, and the first known settler there was James Mead, who built a sawmill and gristmill here. In the town of Rutland, the state's oldest continuously published newspaper, the *Rutland Herald*, was founded in 1794. The town of Rutland grew from a population of 3,715 in 1850 to 12,149 in 1880. During this period a marble business flourished. By 1886 the town of Rutland had grown too large for New England tastes and fragmentation began. A new town of Proctor was created, partially from land formerly in Rutland, and West Rutland was also separated from the town of Rutland and given separate town status. About this time the village of Rutland was incorporated, and on November 18, 1892, that village was given independent status as the city of Rutland. Since the town for which this county was named was granted by New Hampshire's governor, Benning Wentworth (1696–1770), it was Wentworth who named it. Sources consulted differ on why Wentworth chose the name Rutland. There was a Rutland in Massachusetts, which was the home town of the first grantee here, John Murray (or Murrey) and Esther Munroe Swift's scholarly study, entitled *Vermont Place-Names* mentions that this is a popular explanation for the origin of the town established by the New Hampshire grant of September 7, 1761. But Swift cautions "…in addition, it is quite probable that Wentworth had a British peer in mind, as he often did." (This thought is a reasonable one. Wentworth was serving as England's royal governor of New Hampshire, and we know that he scattered place names over his domain in honor of many prominent Englishmen.) Esther Munroe Swift suggests that the "British peer" might have been John Manners, Duke of Rutland (1696–1779). The November, 1950, issue (Vol. 6, No. 2) of *New Hampshire Historical* contained an article entitled "The English Background of Some of the Wentworth Town Grants" by Elmer M. Hunt and Robert A. Smith. That article stated that Governor Wentworth's 1761 grant of the town of Rutland, now in Vermont, was named in honor of John Manners, Duke of Rutland & Marquis of Granby. The article tells us that this John Manners was "…a Privy Councillor and Lord Justice of England. He had the honor of being bearer of the Queen's Sceptre with the Cross at two coronations, that of King George II and that of King George III. He was Chancellor of the Duchy of Lancaster." This information about involvement in the coronation of King George II (1683–1760) pinpoints which John Manners they

have in mind and that he was the same John Manners referred to by Esther Munroe Swift. (A son, also named John Manners [1721–1770] would have only been a six year old boy at the time of the coronation of King George II, in 1727.)

Rutland, Massachusetts — William H. Whitmore wrote an article entitled "On the Origin of the Names of Towns in Massachusetts," which appeared in the 1871–1873 issue (Vol. 12) of *Proceedings of the Massachusetts Historical Society*. In that article Whitmore presented a table that lists the town of Rutland, as being established "Feb. 23, 1713–14," an old style of rendering dates. Later, in that same article, Whitmore is less ambiguous when explaining the origin of the town's name: "*Rutland*, 1714–This is the name of a small county in England, bordering on Leicestershire. The title of Duke of Rutland was conferred on John Manners, ninth Earl in 1703. He died Jan. 10th, 1710–11, and was succeeded by his son, John, who married a daughter of the patriot, William Lord Russell. This latter died Feb. 22, 1720–21; and though he was in favor at the accession of George I, he was not of sufficient prominence to have been thus commemorated. I therefore feel inclined to give the origin of the name here to the county, and as very probably suggested by its proximity to Leicestershire." Whitmore is correct about the proximity of Rutland County (i.e., Rutlandshire), England, to Leicestershire. Before it was abolished as a separate county about 1974, Rutlandshire was the smallest county in England, 15 miles long by 11 wide and its was bounded by four counties, one of which was Leicestershire. A.D. Mills' *A Dictionary of English Place-Names* states that *Rutland* derived from *Roteland* and meant "estate of a man called Rota."

John Manners, Duke of Rutland (1696–1779) — John Manners, the third duke of Rutland, carried the queen's scepter at the coronations of both King George II (1683–1760) and King George III (1738–1820). Since George III came to the throne in 1760, and Governor Wentworth made the New Hampshire grant of the town of Rutland in 1761, it was this duke of Rutland who was prominent when that town grant was made. As mentioned by Hunt and Smith in *New Hampshire Historical*, this John Manners was also a privy councillor, lord justice of England and chancellor of the duchy of Lancaster.

2783 *Washington County*

George Washington (1732–1799) — Washington was a native of Virginia. He served in Virginia's house of burgesses and became one of the colonies' leaders in opposition to British policies in America. He was a member of the first and second Continental Congresses and commander of all Continental armies in the Revolutionary War. Following victory in that war, Washington was elected to be the first president of the United States. This county represents Vermont's second attempt to establish a Washington County. In 1781 Vermont had attempted to establish its first Washington County, largely from lands taken from New Hampshire. George Washington, himself, took note of Vermont's action (which also involved usurping some land of New York's) and frowned on it. On February 21, 1782, the New Hampshire towns that were within this first Washington County were given back to New Hampshire and Washington County, Vermont, ceased to exist. Then on November 1, 1810, the present Washington County was created but its name at that time was Jefferson County, in honor of Thomas Jefferson, whose eight year term as president ended in 1809. On November 8, 1814, this county's name was changed from Jefferson to Washington. Several Vermont sources indicate that this name change resulted from a petty political power play. President Washington had been a Federalist and when Federalists gained enough political power in Vermont in 1814, they caused the county's name to be changed to honor George Washington, largely because he had been a Federalist.

2784 *Windham County*

Uncertain— This county was established on February 22, 1781. One of its towns is named Windham, but we know that the county was not named for that town because the town of Windham, Vermont, was not incorporated until 1795. The origin of this county's name is uncertain, but it has been plausibly suggested that it may have derived from a Connecticut place name; i.e., Windham County, Connecticut, and/or the town of Windham, Connecticut.

Windham County, Connecticut, & town of Windham, Connecticut— Windham County, Connecticut, was created in 1726 and named for the town of Windham, and that town was made the county seat of Windham County, Connecticut. The town of Windham, Connecticut, had been established in 1692 and named for a community in England. Whether that English community was Windham in Sussex, or Wymondham, pronounced Windham, in

Norfolk, is not known although Wymondham is considered to be more likely on account of circumstantial evidence relating to the Ripley family. Franklin B. Dexter cited this in his article on Connecticut town names, which appeared in 1885 in the *Proceedings of the American Antiquarian Society* "...the Ripley family won among a company of emigrants from Hingham, in Norfolk, who originally settled the town of Hingham, in Massachusetts Bay, and when descendants bearing the same family name pushed out into the Connecticut wilderness and founded a new town, naturally they chose for it the name of Windham, dear to their fathers' ears as the customary pronunciation of Wymondham, the largest place in the immediate vicinity of Old Hingham, on the eastern coast of England...."

2785 *Windsor County*

Town of Windsor, New Hampshire grant of July 6, 1761— This county was created on February 22, 1781, and named for its town of Windsor. The town of Windsor had been granted by England's royal governor of the colony of New Hampshire, Benning Wentworth (1696–1770) on July 6, 1761. The town of Windsor is considered to be the birthplace of Vermont because the (premature) constitution of Vermont as a "free and independent state" was adopted here on July 8, 1777. During the 19th century inventions such as the sewing machine, hydraulic pump and coffee percolator were born here. In the late 1990's the town had a population of only 3,700. Since the town for which this county was named was granted by New Hampshire's governor, Benning Wentworth, it was Wentworth who named it and there is uncertainty about the source of the name that Governor Wentworth chose. The November, 1950, issue (Vol. 6, No. 2) of *New Hampshire Historical* contained an article entitled "The English Background of Some of the Wentworth Town Grants" by Elmer M. Hunt and Robert A. Smith. That article stated that Governor Wentworth's grant of the town of Windsor, now in Vermont, was named in honor of John Stuart, Earl of Bute & Earl of Windsor. This article says that Stuart had possessions on the Isle of Bute and that "...Sir John Stuart played an important part in English affairs. He was appointed Secretary of State in the reign of George III in 1761, and the next year became Prime Minister. He died in 1792." The man whom Hunt and Smith are referring to was indeed a powerful force in English politics at the

time that Wentworth was England's royal governor of New Hampshire and was scattering place names over his domain to curry the favor of prominent men back in England.

John Stuart (1713–1792)— Educated at Eton, Stuart succeeded his father as the third earl of Bute in 1723. When he acquired the title earl of Windsor is less clear. Elected as a representative peer of Scotland in 1737, Stuart attended to his lands on the island of Bute, in Scotland's Firth of Clyde. He became an intimate of King George III (1738–1820), was practically his prime minister. In 1761 he was made secretary of state. Stuart later was first lord of the treasury and was a force in matters of war and peace with Spain and France, under King George III.

Although Hunt and Smith tell us, without reservation, that Vermont's town of Windsor was named for John Stuart, Earl of Bute & Earl of Windsor (1713–1792), that view is not shared by all. Esther Munroe Swift's scholarly study, entitled *Vermont Place-Names*, indicates that the origin of the Vermont town's name is uncertain, but she indicates that the probable namesakes are either Windsor, Connecticut, or Windsor castle, in England (but fails to mention John Stuart, Earl of Bute & Earl of Windsor [1713–1792], even as a possibility).

Windsor, Connecticut— Among the oldest towns in Connecticut, Windsor was established by the general court on February 21, 1636–1637, when it renamed the plantation of Dorchester. The general court decreed that its new name "...shall bee called Windsor." That name was taken from Windsor castle, in England, commented upon below. In 1639 Windsor was among the towns uniting under the "Fundamental Orders" to form the English colony of Connecticut. In the late 1990's Windsor, with a population of 27,800, was a suburb of the state's capital city, Hartford.

Windsor castle— Called by John Cannon's *The Oxford Companion to British History*, published in 1997, "...the premier castle of England as well as its largest," Windsor castle was founded on the Thames River by King William I, William the Conqueror (1027–1087). That Norman conqueror adopted the typical Norman design of motte and bailey and constructed it of wood. The castle was rebuilt using stone during the 12th century and converted from a fortress to a palace during the 16th and 17th centuries. Windsor is officially the chief residence of the English sovereigns, although Buckingham palace has been their official London residence. As a result of anti–German hysteria associated with World War I, the name of the English royal house was changed from Hanover to Windsor on July 17, 1917, and the present English monarch, Queen Elizabeth II (1926–), is a member of that royal house. The derivation of the name *Windsor* in England is uncertain. A.D. Mills' *A Dictionary of English Place-Names* states that it derived from *Windlesoran* about A.D. 1060 to *Windesores* in 1086 and translates it as "bank or slope with a windlass." Other sources offer a variety of possible translations including "shore, bank, place suitable for landing," "winding shore," and "a thing twined, as a willow basket."

REFERENCES

Aldrich, Lewis C., & Frank R. Holmes. *History of Windsor County, Vermont.* Syracuse, New York, D. Mason & Co., 1891.

Allen, Morse. "A Vermont Sketchbook: Connecticut & Vermont Town Names." *Vermont History,* Vol. 22, No. 4. Montpelier, Vermont: October, 1954.

Barden, Merritt C. *Vermont: Once No Man's Land.* Rutland, Tuttle Co., 1928.

Battle, Kemp P. "Glimpses of History in the Names of Our Counties." *North Carolina Booklet,* Vol. 6. July, 1906.

Battle, Kemp P. "North Carolina County Names." *The Magazine of History,* Vol. 7, No. 4. New York: April, 1908.

Cannon, John. *The Oxford Companion to British History.* Oxford, Oxford University Press, 1997.

Carleton, Hiram. *Genealogical & Family History of the State of Vermont.* New York, Lewis Publishing Co., 1903.

Child, Hamilton. *Gazetteer of Orange County, Vermont: 1762–1888.* Syracuse, New York, Syracuse Journal Co., 1888.

Clement, John P. "Vermont Town Names & Their Derivations: III." *Vermont Quarterly: A Magazine of History,* Vol. 21, No. 2. Montpelier, Vermont: April, 1953.

Connecticut, Massachusetts, Rhode Island Tour Book. Heathrow, Florida AAA Publishing, 1998.

Coolidge, Guy O. "The French Occupation of the Champlain Valley from 1609 to 1759." *Proceedings of the Vermont Historical Society,* Vol. 6, No. 3. Montpellier: September, 1938.

Corbitt, David L. *The Formation of North Carolina Counties: 1663–1943.* Raleigh, State Department of Archives & History, 1950.

Crittenden, Charles C., & Dan Lacy. *The Historical Records of North Carolina.* Raleigh, North Carolina Historical Commission, 1938.

Crockett, Walter H. *Vermont: The Green Mountain State.* New York, Century History Co., Inc., 1923.

Dexter, Franklin B. "The History of Connecticut as Illustrated by the Names of Her Towns." *Proceedings of the American Antiquarian Society, New Series,* Vol. 3, Part 4. Worcester: 1885.

Ekwall, Eilert. *The Concise Oxford Dictionary of English Place-Names.* Oxford, Oxford University Press, 1960.

The Encyclopedia Americana. New York, Americana Corporation, 1977.

Fowle, Richard J. "Postscript." *Vermont History,* Vol. 23, No. 4. Montpelier, Vermont: October, 1955.

Gannett, Henry. *The Origin of Certain Place Names in the United States.* Williamstown, Massachusetts, Corner House Publishers, 1978.

Goodwin, Del, & Dorcas Chaffee. *Perspectives '76: Being a Compendium of Useful Knowledge About Old-Time Vermont & New Hampshire.* Hanover, New Hampshire, Regional Center for Educational Training, 1975.

Hart, Albert B. *Commonwealth History of Massachusetts.* New York, States History Co., 1930.

Hemenway, Abby M. "A History of Each Town: Civil, Ecclesiastical, Biographical & Military." *Vermont Historical Gazetteer: A Magazine.* Burlington: 1867.

Hughes, Arthur H., & Morse S. Allen. *Connecticut Place Names.* The Connecticut Historical Society, 1976.

Hunt, Elmer M., & Robert A. Smith. "The English Background of Some of the Wentworth Town Grants." *New Hampshire Historical,* Vol. 6, No. 2. Concord, New Hampshire: November, 1950.

Johnston, Thesba N. "Vermont Town Names & Their Derivations." *Vermont Quarterly: A Magazine of History,* Vol. 20, No. 4. Montpelier, Vermont: October, 1952.

Kenyon, J. P. *Dictionary of British History.* Ware, England, Wordsworth Editions, Ltd., 1992.

Lacey, Robert. *Robert, Earl of Essex.* New York, Atheneum, 1971.

Leighly, John. "New England Town Names Derived from Personal Names." *Names: Journal of the American Name Society,* Vol. 18, No. 3. Potsdam, New York: September, 1970.

Maine, New Hampshire, Vermont Tour Book. Heathrow, Florida AAA Publishing, 1998.

Maunsell, David, et al. *Gazetteer of Vermont Heritage.* Chester, Vermont, National Survey, 1966.

Mills, A.D. *A Dictionary of English Place-Names.* Oxford, Oxford University Press, 1991.

Morrissey, Brenda C. *Abby Hemenway's Vermont: Unique Portrait of a State by Abby Maria Hemenway.* Brattleboro, Stephen Greene Press, 1972.

Moule, Thomas. *The County Maps of Old England.* London, Studio Editions, 1990.

"Postscript." *Vermont Quarterly: A Magazine of History,* Vol. 20, No. 4. Montpelier, Vermont: October, 1952.

Powell, William S. *The North Carolina Gazetteer.* Chapel Hill, University of North Carolina Press, 1968.

Price, Edward T. *Dividing the Land: Early American Beginnings of Our Private Property Mosaic.* Chicago, University of Chicago Press, 1995.

Rann, W. S. *History of Chittenden County, Vermont.* Syracuse, New York, D. Mason & Co., 1886.

Reaney, P. H. *The Origin of English Place Names.* London, Routledge & Kegan Paul, 1960.

Stewart, George R. *American Place-Names.* New York, Oxford University Press, 1970.

Stewart, George R. *Names on the Land.* New York, Random House, 1945.

Swift, Esther Munroe. *Vermont Place-Names.* Brattleboro, Vermont, Stephen Greene Press, 1977.

Trease, Geoffrey. *Seven Kings of England.* New York, Vanguard Press, 1955.

Vermont Year Book: 1975. Chester, Vermont, National Survey, 1975.

Vexler, Robert I. *Chronology & Documentary Handbook of the State of Vermont.* Dobbs Ferry, New York, Oceana Publications, Inc., 1979.

Whitmore, William H. "On the Origin of the Names of Towns in Massachusetts." *Proceedings of the Massachusetts Historical Society,* Vol. 12. Cambridge: 1871–1873.

Williams, Neville. *All the Queen's Men: Elizabeth I and Her Courtiers.* New York, Macmillan Co., 1972.

Wise, L. F., & E. W. Egan. *Kings, Rulers & Statesmen.* New York, Sterling Publishing Co., Inc., 1967.

Virginia

(95 counties)

2786 *Accomack County*

Accomac Indians— The Accomac Indians were members of the Powhatan confederation of Algonquian Indians, who were encountered by the first English visitors to Virginia. They lived along the lower portion of eastern Chesapeake Bay, in the area around the present Cape Charles city, Virginia. The Accomac Indians also had an important village inland from Chesapeake Bay, on Cherrystone Creek, and another on Nandua Creek. In 1608 there were an estimated 80 Accomac warriors and the total tribal population about that time is estimated by one source at 300. Soon after contact with Europeans, the Accomac population began to dwindle but the name continued to be applied by some to denote many or all of the Indians of Virginia's eastern shore. By 1812 the Accomac Indians had lost their tribal identity. A number of sources indicate that the name *Accomac* denoted "other side" and referred to "other side place," "other side town," or "other side water." In 1634, when England's royal colony of Virginia was divided into eight original shires, or counties, one of the eight was named in honor of this Indian tribe. The spelling of that first Accomack County in Virginia is rendered variously as Accawmack, Accawmacke Achomack, Accomac, Accowmack and Accomack. In 1642 or 1643 that Virginia county's name was changed to Northampton County. The Accomac Indians' name was restored to Virginia's map of counties in 1662 or 1663, when the northern part of Northampton County, was taken to form this separate county, now named Accomack County. Henry Howe's 1849 *Historical Collections of Virginia* spells this county's name: Accomac County. Raus M. Hanson's work entitled *Virginia Place Names: Derivations: Historical Uses*, states that the present spelling of this county's name, as Accomack, was not approved until 1940 when the Virginia legislature mandated this spelling.

2787 *Albemarle County*

William Anne Keppel, Earl of Albemarle (1702–1754)— Born at Whitehall, in London, England, on June 5, 1702, William Anne Keppel was baptized in the English royal chapel and England's new queen, Queen Anne (1665–1714), was his god mother. His two given names, William and Anne, honored England's recently deceased King William III (1650–1702) and the current queen, Queen Anne. Educated in Holland, William Anne Keppel succeeded his father, Arnold Joost van Keppel (1669–1718), the first earl of Albemarle, and became the second earl of Albemarle, while still in his teens. William Anne Keppel was a royal favorite and numerous honors were bestowed upon him. He was appointed governor-general of England's North American colony of Virginia in 1737, brigadier-general in 1739 and major-general in 1742. He served at Fontenoy and was wounded there in 1745. Albemarle later was ambassador-extraordinary to Paris, commander-in-chief in North Britain and privy councillor. This county was created in 1744, while Albemarle was the non-resident governor-general of England's colony of Virginia. In 1744, when this county was created, Virginia's resident chief executive was Lieutenant-Governor William Gooch (1681–1751), for whom Goochland County, Virginia, was named.

2788 *Alleghany County*

Allegheny Mountains— This county was created in 1822 and named for the Allegheny Mountains, along the county's western border. The Allegheny Mountains, part of the Appalachian Mountain system, are one of the important mountain ranges in the east-central portion of our nation. They extend from Pennsylvania, south into Maryland and dominate the eastern half of the state of West Virginia as well as portions of western Virginia. Alleghany County, Virginia, on the state's western border with West Virginia, is aptly named for the mountains rise within its borders and extend westward for many miles into West Virginia. In Virginia and West Virginia, the Allegheny Mountains lie west of the Blue Ridge Mountains and parallel with them. Virginia's portion of the Allegheny Mountains lie from 1,000 to 3,500 feet above sea level. Beautiful scenery and rugged terrain are found in this section of western Virginia. The name *Allegheny* has also been applied to a river and, to an Indian tribe, the Alleghany Indians.

2789 *Amelia County*

Princess Amelia Sophie Eleanor (1711–1786)— Born June 10, 1711, to England's future King George II, George August (1683–1760), and his wife, Caroline of Anspach (1683–1737), Amelia Sophie Eleanor was known to the family as Emily. Amelia was the third child and second daughter of this marriage. Her father took no interest in her, because she was a girl. The birth of her elder sister Anne (1709–1759) had also failed to capture the father's attention for he was interested in male heirs. However, the girls' mother, Caroline of Anspach, was very fond of her daughters. John Van der Kiste's work entitled *King George II & Queen Caroline*, published in 1997, provides insight on this: "Fortunately Princess Caroline was an attentive and kindly mother, though by no means indulgent, and her daughters soon learned to love and respect her." For a time a possibility was bruited about that Amelia might become engaged to Frederick of Prussia, but nothing came of this. Several minor German princes sought to wed Amelia but she displayed no interest. Although Amelia never married, she did enjoy a period of sexual activity and was known, for a time, as the family flirt. She had brief affairs with the duke of Newcastle, lord Chamberlain and the duke of Grafton. Van der Kiste tells us that Amelia was "an active, extroverted young woman," who was fond of hunting and that "she became increasingly eccentric and shocked fellow members of the congregation at Hampton Court church by arriving in riding clothes and carrying a dog under each arm." Amelia died on October 31, 1786. Amelia County, Virginia, was created in either 1734 or 1735 (most sources show 1734), while Amelia's father, King George II, was the reigning king of England and of England's colony of Virginia. Several sources dealing with the history and place names of Virginia state that this county was named for Princess Amelia, the *youngest daughter* of King George II. The "youngest daughter" portion of that statement is incorrect. Amelia was only the "youngest daughter" of George II for two years until Caroline Elizabeth (1713–1757) was born, and two additional younger daughters followed. Probably the "youngest daughter" whom these Virginia sources had in mind was Princess Amelia (1783–1810), the youngest daughter of England's King George III (1738–1820). This Virginia county could not have been named that Princess Amelia (1783–1810) because she was born half a century after the county was created.

2790 *Amherst County*

Jeffrey Amherst (1717–1797)— A native of England and an officer in the English army, Amherst served in North America during the French & Indian War. By July 1758, he had risen to the rank of major-general when English and American troops under his command captured the French fortress of Louisbourg, which protected the approach into the Saint Lawrence River. In September, 1758, Amherst was promoted to commander-in-chief of the British army in North America and he soon justified that vote of confidence by soundly defeating the French at Ticonderoga. Forces under his command scored other significant victories resulting in the 1763 treaty of Paris, by which France surrendered essentially all of Canada, east of the Mississippi, to England. Amherst was made governor-general of British North America in 1761. He had returned to England in 1763 when he was appointed governor of England's colony of Virginia. Amherst served as titular governor of the colony from 1763 to 1768. During that period Virginia's resident chief executive was Lieutenant-Governor Francis Fauquier (–1768), for whom Fauquier County, Virginia, was named. Amherst County, Virginia, was created in 1761.

2791 *Appomattox County*

Appomattox River— Virginia's Appomattox River rises in Appomattox County, in central Virginia, and traverses this county on its eastward journey to the James River. The 137 mile-long Appomattox enters the James River at Hopewell, Virginia, a few miles south of Richmond, and it is navigable from the James River to Petersburg, Virginia. The Appomattox River shares its name with an Indian tribe of the former Powhatan confederation. Whether the river was named for the Indians or the Indians were named for the river is not clear. Three translations which have been offered for the Indians' name which we now render as *Appomattox* ("tidal river," "sinuous tidal estuary" and "river of Princess [or Queen] Appomattox") would suggest that the river was named first but other translations have

been offered including "a tobacco plant country." This county was created on February 8, 1845.

2792 *Arlington County*

Arlington, the estate built by George Washington Parke Custis (1781–1857)— George Washington Parke Custis was a grandson of Martha Dandridge Custis (1732–1802), an amiable widow, who married the father of our country, George Washington, in 1759. This grandson was adopted by George Washington and raised at the Washington estate at Mount Vernon, Virginia. By 1800 the site for our infant nation's new capital, the District of Columbia, had been selected and shortly after 1800 George Washington Parke Custis built a magnificent estate on land which would overlook the new capital city. Readers familiar with Arlington national cemetery will appreciate how one can view the capital from Arlington. The name *Arlington* was not coined by George Washington Parke Custis. The Custis family in Virginia had named their estates *Arlington*, for generations. A work entitled *Old Virginia Houses Harbors* by Emmie Ferguson Farrar and Emilee Hines speculates that the use of the name Arlington by the Custis family for their homes in colonial Virginia may have derived from the name of their estate in Gloucester, England. The first member of the prestigious Custis family in Virginia was John Custis II, who acquired 600 acres of land on Virginia's eastern shore in 1650 and called his home here Arlington. The estate built in 1800 by George Washington Parke Custis was erected on land overlooking the Potomac River, and he named it Arlington, for his estate on Virginia's eastern shore, which had burned. The general-in-chief of the Confederate army, Robert E. Lee (1807–1870), made his home at Arlington, but nothing remains of the old estate today. The land comprising the present Arlington County, Virginia, was ceded by Virginia to form part of our nation's capital city, the District of Columbia. In 1846 or 1847 the federal government ceded some 31 square miles back to Virginia and on March 13, 1847, that area was named Alexandria County. The county's name was changed from Alexandria to Arlington in 1920.

2793 *Augusta County*

Augusta of Saxe-Gotha, Princess of Wales (1719–1772)— The first child of George August (1683–1760) was Frederick

Louis (1707–1751), so, in 1727 when George August became King George II of England, Prince Frederick Louis became heir-apparent to the English throne. He was also made prince of Wales. In 1736 Frederick Louis (1707–1751) married Augusta of Saxe-Gotha (1719–1772) and in 1738 England's colony of Virginia created counties named for both the heir-apparent (Frederick County) and his princess (Augusta County). Augusta County was created from Orange County in 1738 but because of the unsettled nature of the region, county government was not established here until 1745. Hence some sources state that Augusta County was created in 1738, while others show 1745. Clearly, the name was selected in 1738 and it was inspired by the prospect that Frederick and Augusta would some day be king and queen consort of England and Virginia. It is unlikely that these county names were selected to please the ruling monarch, King George II (1683–1760), since he disliked his son, Frederick Louis (1707–1751). This county's namesake was the daughter of Frederick II, Duke of Saxe-Gotha. Since King George II outlived the heir-apparent (Frederick Louis died on March 20, 1751), our Princess Augusta never became queen consort of England and Virginia. However, Princess Augusta and Prince Frederick Louis had eight children, one of whom became king of England in 1760. He was King George III (1738–1820). In addition to producing eight children, Princess Augusta and Prince Frederick Louis found time to be unfaithful to each other. As Princess Dowager of Wales, Augusta came to wield influence over King George III. Princess Dowager Augusta died at Carlton House on February 8, 1772, and was buried at Westminster Abbey.

2794 *Bath County*

Medicinal bathing springs located within the county— This county was created in 1790 or 1791 and named for the mineral bathing springs found here. The most important springs, the warm springs, are located at the community of Warm Springs, Virginia, although there are also hot springs and other mineral springs nearby. The medicinal properties of the waters at Warm Springs became an early resort attraction. Henry Howe's *Historical Collections of Virginia*, published in 1849, mentioned "elegant hotels for the accommodation of visitors at the springs...." In that same work, Henry Howe quoted a description of the warm springs written by a Professor Rogers. The professor's report gave details about the chemical content of the waters and of the gasses escaping from them. Rogers also commented that the average temperature of the warm springs was 98 degrees and he claimed that "...Warm Springs afford the most luxurious bath in the world...." The warm springs at the community of Warm Springs, Virginia, were still a major tourist attract in 1999 with several motels available to accommodate visitors. The waters of the hot springs, located at nearby Homestead, are over 100 degrees and must be piped and cooled before they are safe to use.

2795 Bedford County

John Russell, Duke of Bedford (1710–1771)— England has given the title duke of Bedford to a number of men, but it is clear that the duke of Bedford whose name is remembered in the name of Bedford County was John Russell, the fourth duke of Bedford (1710–1771). John Russell succeeded his brother to become duke of Bedford in 1732. He raised a foot regiment in 1745 to serve under England's King George II (1683–1760) and was made colonel of that regiment. In 1760, at the coronation of King George III (1738–1820), Bedford was lord high constable. From 1763 to 1767 he was president of the council. Sources consulted are not agreed on the year that England's colony of Virginia created this county. The years 1752, 1753 and 1754 are mentioned. Most sources show 1753 and 1754.

2796 Bland County

Richard Bland (1710–1776)— A native of Virginia, Bland was educated at the College of William & Mary here. He took a seat in colonial Virginia's house of burgesses in 1742 and served continuously in that body until 1775. Bland was an early agitator on behalf of public rights and a proponent of rights for England's North American colonies. However, unlike many other heroes from our nation's Revolutionary era, Bland wanted to secure rights for the colonies without a break with England. Although Bland was more conciliatory than many of his contemporaries, he was sent by his constituents to two revolutionary convention in 1775 and one in 1776. After Virginia adopted a constitution, he was elected as a member of Virginia's first house of delegates. Bland also represented Virginia throughout the first Continental Congress and served briefly in the second Continental Congress before his death on October 26, 1776. Thomas Jefferson greatly admired Richard Bland and after Bland's death, Jefferson purchased his personal library. This county was created in 1861.

2797 Botetourt County

Norborne Berkeley, Baron de Botetourt (1770)— Born in London, England, about 1718, Berkeley entered England's house of commons in 1741 and served as a member of parliament for a number of years. Appointed a colonel in the militia, Berkeley also was made lord lieutenant of Gloucestershire, and in 1764 he was made Baron de Botetourt. In August, 1768, Botetourt was commissioned royal governor of Virginia. Botetourt's predecessors had generally remained in England with a lieutenant-governor serving as Virginia's resident chief executive. However Botetourt came to Virginia in October, 1768, and personally served as Virginia's resident chief executive from October 28, 1768, until his death on October 15, 1770. During the period that Botetourt was governor, tensions were building in Virginia and England's other North American colonies concerning England's treatment of her colonial subjects. Apparently Botetourt enjoyed a degree of local popularity in spite of those tensions, although sources consulted differ concerning the degree of that popularity. This county was created and named in Botetourt's honor in 1769 or 1770.

2798 Brunswick County

Brunswick, the name of a ruling family, duchy and state in Germany— This county in England's colony of Virginia was created in 1720 six years after King George I (1660–1727) had become the reigning monarch of England, and established his family on the English throne. England's new king was duke of Brunswick-Luneburg and Brunswick was the name of a ruling family, duchy and state in north-central Germany. King George I was a member of this family. In 1569 the Brunswick-Luneburg line was founded and it later took the name Hanover.

King George I (1660–1727)— Born in Osnabruck, Hanover, in what is now Germany, and named at birth George Lewis (also styled Georg Ludwig in some accounts), George was an important military leader in Europe. In 1698 he succeeded his father, Ernst August (1622–1698), as elector of Hanover and duke of Brunswick-Luneburg. He was the first English monarch of the house of Brunswick (later styled Hanover, now Windsor), and that royal house still rules Great Britain. The current reigning monarch of this British royal house is Queen Elizabeth II (1926–). The German, King George I, and his successors, owe their hold on the throne of Great Britain to two factors: (1) deep-seated religious animosity in England against Roman Catholicism and (2) the inability of England's Queen Anne (1665–1714) to produce an heir to the throne. Queen Anne had a large number of children (15 according to one account; 17 per another) but most of them were stillborn. Only one boy survived. He was Prince William (1689–1700). Medical science at that time was unable to effectively assist one of the most wealthy and powerful couples on planet Earth in their repeated efforts to leave an heir to the throne. This personal tragedy resulted in a practical problem for England as well, since the heir to the throne when Queen Anne died in 1714 was her half-brother, James Francis Edward Stuart (1688–1766); but James Stuart was a Catholic and England wanted no Catholic on its throne. The nation closed ranks against James Stuart and all other Catholic contenders for the crown and reached all the way to Hanover, in Germany, for a successor to Queen Anne. There they found George Lewis (1660–1727), the elector of Hanover, who had a drop or two of royal English blood in his veins and thus some semblance of a claim to the English throne. He became England's King George I. The new king never bothered to learn much of the English language but he did succeed in remaining Protestant throughout his reign from 1714 until his death in 1727.

2799 Buchanan County

James Buchanan (1791–1868)— A native of Pennsylvania, Buchanan served in a variety of political posts for more than 40 years. After brief duty in the military during the War of 1812, Buchanan began his political career in the Pennsylvania assembly and then he represented Pennsylvania for ten years in the U.S. House of Representatives. Following an assignment as minister to Russia, Buchanan was elected to represent Pennsylvania in the U.S. Senate where he served from 1834 to 1845. When James K. Polk became president, Buchanan joined his cabinet as secretary of state. Buchanan subsequently was our minister to Great Britain. Four years before the start of the Civil War, Buchanan was a elected as a Democrat to be president of the United States. During his presidency the nation moved rapidly toward

Civil War and Buchanan was unable to avert it. Buchanan County, Virginia, was created on February 13, 1858, while James Buchanan was serving as president.

2800 *Buckingham County*

Uncertain— This county was created by England's colony of Virginia in 1761 and most sources dealing with the history, geography and place names of Virginia admit that the origin of the name is uncertain. A large number of sources mention the possibility that this county may have been named for Buckinghamshire, England, while a few suggest that the name may have been bestowed in honor of a duke of Buckingham. There were several dukes of Buckingham and most Virginia sources are silent on which one of them the name might have honored. The third possibility, which is mentioned by just a handful of works, is that the county may have taken its name from that of land in Virginia, owned by Archibald Cary.

Buckinghamshire, England— Located near the center of England, a bit northwest of London, Buckinghamshire is a long, narrow county, divided into northern and southern sections by the chalk hills named Chiltern. Its southern boundary is the Thames River. The world-famous preparatory school, or so-called public school, Eton was established here in A.D. 1440. In 1981 the county's population was estimated to be 571,600 and its area was 753 square miles. The origin and meaning of this county's name is uncertain and disputed. Translations which have been mentioned include "beech trees," "bucks," or "deer," "river-bend land" and "followers of Bucca" (Bucca, being a man).

Dukes of Buckingham— Three men held this title prior to 1522. It would seem unlikely that colonial Virginia would have remembered any of them in 1761 when it created this county. These three dukes held the title under the first creation. Those who had held this title between 1522 and 1761, when Buckingham County, Virginia, was created were:

— *George Villiers, 1st Duke of Buckingham (1592–1628)*— Enjoyed popularity under England's King James I (1566–1625) but fell in disfavor and was assassinated.

— *George Villiers, 2nd Duke of Buckingham (1628–1687)*— Raised with the royal children, he was a favorite of King Charles II (1630–1685) and supported him in the English Civil War.

— *John Sheffield, 1st Duke of Buckingham & Normanby (–1721)*— Managed to win the favor of a string of English monarchs, starting with King Charles II (1630–1685) and continuing under James II (1633–1701), William III (1650–1702) & Mary II (1662–1694) and finally was a romantic suitor of Queen Anne (1665–1714). Nothing came of the romance but she made him a duke on the day she became queen.

Land in Virginia, owned by Archibald Cary— The land from which Buckingham County, Virginia was created in 1761 included land lying on the west side and on branches of Buck River, "otherwise called Willis's Creek," and some Virginia sources indicate that this land was owned by Archibald Cary and was commonly known by the name "Buckingham," at the time that this Virginia county was created.

2801 *Campbell County*

William Campbell (1745–1781)— Born in Augusta County in England's colony of Virginia in 1745, Campbell moved west about 1767 to Virginia's Holston River valley and served as an officer in the frontier militia during Lord Dunmore's War. By 1775 he was active in Virginia's Revolutionary activities and he participated in the expulsion of England's royal governor of Virginia, John Murray, Earl of Dunmore (1732–1809). Campbell participated in a number of actions during our Revolution and by October, 1780, he had been promoted to colonel when he performed with skill during our important victory at the battle of King's Mountain, South Carolina. In 1781 he fought at Guilford Court House, served briefly in the Virginia legislature and was promoted to brigadier-general of militia. During the first half of 1781, the British had invaded Virginia, captured the new capital city of Richmond, and laid plans to control all of Virginia. In June, 1781, General Campbell headed to Jamestown Ford, Virginia to assist General Lafayette in defending Virginia. Campbell brought a force of some 600 mountaineers with him and within two weeks Campbell's troops had grown in number to nearly 800. However, General Campbell became ill and was unable to participate in the July, 1781, battle of Green Spring, Virginia, and he died of the illness on August 22, 1781. Virginia's legislature created and named this county in William Campbell's honor just three months later, during November, 1781.

2802 *Caroline County*

Queen Caroline of Anspach (1683–1737)— Caroline of Anspach, who was destined to become the very powerful queen consort of England's King George II (1683–1760), was a daughter of John Frederick (–1687), margrave of Brandenburg-Anspach, a German. She resided primarily in Dresden, Berlin and Anspach, Germany, prior to her marriage in September, 1705, to George Augustus, Electoral Prince of Hanover (1683–1760). All of this was of importance in Germany, but of little interest to England since George Lewis (1660–1727), the elector of Hanover, had not yet been plucked by England to succeed Queen Anne (1665–1714) as England's monarch. However, when Queen Anne died in 1714, George Lewis became England's King George I (1660–1727) and Caroline's husband, George Augustus (1683–1760), suddenly became heir-apparent to the English throne. Caroline's arrival near the center of England's royal stage was appropriate from a religious standpoint. She had refrained from pursuit of earlier good marriages since they conflicted with her strongly held Protestant religion. Since her father-in-law was selected as England's monarch primarily because he wasn't Catholic, the pieces now fit nicely. And what a pretty one Caroline of Anspach was. Described by Antonia Fraser in her *The Lives of the Kings & Queens of England* as "an extremely intelligent and lively woman ... large, blonde, blatantly sensual and earthy. A tremendous flirt, Caroline knew precisely what she was doing in charming men to advance her own political influence." King George I died in June, 1727, and the new king and queen were crowned at Westminster Abbey in October, 1727. While King George II was the nominal ruler of England, Queen Caroline ruled her husband, until her lingering and painful death took her in November, 1737. To insure complete domination, Caroline schemed with her ally Robert Walpole (1676–1745), whom she caused to be returned as prime minister and Caroline even exerted effective influence on the king through his mistress, Henrietta Howard (1681–1767). During the period that King George II ruled, England increased its status as a world power. Credit cannot be given to George II for shrewd statesmanship, but it must be admitted that he readily accepted advice from those with able judgment and one of his ablest advisors was his own queen consort, Queen Caroline of Anspach (1683–1737). Caroline's intellectual faculties remained intact but her physical decline began about the time of her 50th birthday. Sources dealing with the history, geography and place names of Virginia differ on the year that Caroline County, in

England's colony of Virginia, was created. Some show 1727, while others list 1728. Marshall Wingfield's *A History of Caroline County, Virginia*, published in 1924, meticulously tracked the legislation incident to the creation of this county and Wingfield's recitation leaves no doubt that the county was created and named during March 1727, seven months before Prince George and Queen Caroline became king and queen of England.

2803 *Carroll County*

Charles Carroll (1737–1832)— Carroll was a native of Maryland and he represented that state in the Continental Congress. He was one of the signers of the Declaration of Independence and he later represented Maryland as a U.S. senator in the first Congress of the United States. Carroll lived to be the last surviving signer of the Declaration of Independence and several states recognized that distinction by naming counties for him. Carroll County, Virginia, was created and named in his honor on January 17, 1842.

2804 *Charles City County*

Charles City, Bermuda Plantation, Virginia— In 1634, when England's royal colony of Virginia was divided into eight original shires, or counties, one of the eight was named Charles City County. This county was named for one of colonial Virginia's very early settlements, Charles City of the Bermuda Plantation (also called the "Bermuda hundred.") In England the term *hundred* meant an area inhabited by about one hundred families, or one able to provide one hundred fighting men. The settlement named Charles City had been named during the reign of England's King James I (1566–1625). When the king's eldest son, Henry Frederick (1594–1612), died, Charles became heir apparent to the throne and he ascended to the throne of England as King Charles I (1600–1649) when his father died in 1625. This county was created during the reign of King Charles I (1600–1649) but its name had been selected (for Charles City) while James I was king and the name was merely carried over as a county name, in the unusual form Charles City County, in 1634.

King Charles I (1600–1649)— Charles was born in Scotland, while his father, James (1566–1625), was reigning as King James VI of Scotland, but had not yet been crowned King James I of England. A weak and sickly child, Charles was created duke of York, but when his elder brother died in 1612, young Charles became heir apparent to England's throne. He was created prince of Wales in 1616. When King James I died in 1625, Charles succeeded him to the throne as King Charles I. He inherited a war in progress with Spain and soon added an unsuccessful war against France, but his most severe problems were domestic, rather than foreign. King Charles I soon won the warm hatred of England's parliament and managed to antagonize his father's friends in Scotland by attacks on Scottish Presbyterianism. Charles was a studious man but he understood books far better than people. He managed to let small problems grow beyond hope of resolution, and allowed civil wars to erupt. The wars culminated in his military defeat and he was executed by beheading on January 30, 1649. This brought to a temporary end the rule of monarchy in England, which was not restored until 1660, when his son King Charles II (1630–1685), took the throne.

2805 *Charlotte County*

Queen Charlotte Sophia of Mecklenburg-Strelitz (1744–1818)— This county in England's royal colony of Virginia was created in 1764, while King George III (1738–1820) ruled England and Virginia. It was named for the bride whom the king had married in 1761 and made his queen consort. Charlotte's marriage to George was arranged and she did not meet him until her wedding day. In 1761 she was described as "…not tall nor a beauty. Pale and very thin but looks sensible and genteel." Charlotte's life as queen was entirely domestic and she was happy with it. She had neither interest nor influence in political matters. The king was devoted to her and she was faithful to him. Apparently her only vice was stinginess in money matters. Charlotte became responsible for the royal household and for the care of the king during his lengthy physical and mental illnesses. Charlotte bore her husband 15 children, two of whom later came to the throne as kings of England. These two kings were August Frederick, who came to the throne in 1820 as King George IV (1762–1830) and Edward Frederick, who reigned as King William IV (1765–1837). Mecklenburg County, Virginia, also created in 1764, was also named for this same English queen, Charlotte Sophia of Mecklenburg-Strelitz (1744–1818).

2806 *Chesterfield County*

Philip Dormer Stanhope, Earl of Chesterfield (1694–1773)— The fourth earl of Chesterfield was an Englishman who is remembered for espousing the importance of proper manners, aristocratic elegance and wit. He established himself high in England's snobbish pecking order by an appointment as gentleman of the bedchamber to the prince of Wales, who in 1727 came to the throne as King George II (1683–1760). Following this early coup, Chesterfield was the recipient of a series of prestigious positions and titles, including member of parliament, secretary of state and lord lieutenant of Ireland. He succeeded to the English peerage in 1726. His fame reached both sides of the Atlantic Ocean in 1774 when letters which he had written to his son were published. These letters dealt with conduct, manners and sophisticated social behavior. This county in England's colony of Virginia was created in either 1748 or 1749.

2807 *Clarke County*

George R. Clark (1752–1818)— A native of Virginia, George Rogers Clark was a frontiersman and military hero. During the American Revolution he secured a commission as lieutenant-colonel to attack the British, Indians and Loyalists in Indiana and Illinois. He successfully captured Vincennes, Cahokia and Kaskaskia and after the British retook Kaskaskia, Clark won it a second time. In 1780, Clark traveled north from the Ohio River area into what is now Clark County, Ohio and destroyed the Shawnee Indian's Indian village there, named Piqua. The Shawnee were firm allies of the British. These military victories, together with skillful negotiating by Benjamin Franklin, enabled the United States to acquire the Northwest territory during the peace negotiations with the British at the end of the Revolution. This county was created on March 8, 1836. The final "e" in the county's name was a spelling error, which has never been corrected.

2808 *Craig County*

Robert Craig (1792–1852)— A native of Virginia and a member of the house of delegates of the Virginia legislature in 1817, 1818 and 1825–1829, Craig was elected to represent Virginia in the U.S. House of Representatives and he served there from 1829 to 1833 and again from 1835 to 1841. He declined to run for reelection to congress and moved to Roanoke County, Virginia. There he engaged in farming but politics was in his blood and Craig returned again to Virginia's house of delegates, serving from 1850 to 1852. Robert

Craig died on his estate, Green Hill, in Roanoke County, Virginia, on November 25, 1852. This county had been created and named in his honor the prior year, on March 21, 1851, while he was serving in the state legislature.

2809 *Culpeper County*

Thomas Culpeper, Lord Culpeper (1635–1689)— A native of England, Culpeper was appointed captain and later governor of England's Isle of Wight. In 1675 King Charles II (1630–1685) appointed Culpeper governor of Virginia, for life, effective upon the death or removal of Virginia's current governor, Sir William Berkeley (1606–1677). When Governor Berkeley died in 1677, Culpeper became governor but he appointed deputies to serve as his resident chief executives in Virginia, the first being Lieutenant-governor Herbert Jeffreys (–1678) and upon his death, Deputy-governor Sir Henry Chicheley (–1683). However King Charles II insisted that Culpeper take up residence in Virginia and serve as the colony's resident chief executive. He arrived in Virginia in May, 1680, decided that he was not well suited to the harsh frontier life here, and returned to London. In 1682 news reached England that Virginia was plagued by civil disobedience and Culpeper was again ordered to return and govern the colony personally. Thomas Culpeper returned to Virginia and arrived in December, 1682. John W. Raimo's *Biographical Directory of American Colonial & Revolutionary Governors: 1607–1789* states that "Culpeper was annoyed by the failure of settlers in the Northern Neck to pay the quitrents to which he believed himself entitled and, partly in retaliation, he carried out a series of unpopular actions which culminated in his dissolution of the House of Burgesses." King Charles II was as displeased with Culpeper as were the Virginia colonists and although he had originally appointed Culpeper as governor for life, the king removed him from office in 1683. This county in England's colony of Virginia was created in 1748 or 1749. It seems strange that a county in colonial Virginia would have been named for a governor who had displeased both the colonists and the crown. Some sources say that this county's name was chosen as a compliment to Thomas Fairfax, Baron Fairfax of Cameron (1692–1782), who had inherited vast estates in northern Virginia through his mother, Catherine, heiress of the great estates of Thomas Culpeper, Lord Culpeper (1635–1689). Eugene M. Scheel's work entitled *Culpeper: A Virginia County's History Through 1920* stated that "Had there not been a Virginia county named Fairfax, the new county would have had a different name. In October, 1748 at the assembly session that created Culpeper County, Lord Fairfax agreed to honor all previous grants issued by the colony. In addition, he agreed not to set aside surveys of his lands filed in the Virginia Secretary's office prior to October, 1735. So with again a nod to Thomas Sixth Lord Fairfax, the General Assembly chose Culpeper, the surname of his mother...."

2810 *Cumberland County*

William Augustus, Duke of Cumberland (1721–1765)— This county was created in 1748 or 1749. At that time, Virginia was an English colony and King George II (1683–1760) was the reigning monarch of Britain. England's American colonies used various devices to curry favor from the crown and one employed by several of the American colonies was to name counties in honor of the monarch or members of the monarch's family. William Augustus was a son of England's King George II. Born on April 15, 1721, William was made a royal duke and given the title Duke of Cumberland in July, 1726. Cumberland was educated for the navy but was permitted to follow his preference for the army and was given the rank of major-general in 1742. He was a rather poor general and his troops were defeated in several important actions on the European continent. His only significant victory was at home, in the British Isles, where he defeated Prince Charles Edward Stuart (1720–1788), the pretender to the thrones of Scotland and England. This victory took place at Culloden, Scotland, in 1746. The duke's name is shown in most works as William Augustus, but in some the form William August is used. Virginia's Prince William County is also named for him.

2811 *Dickenson County*

William J. Dickenson (1828–1907)— This county was created in 1880 and named for William J. Dickenson, who was then a member of the Virginia legislature, sitting in the house of delegates, representing Russell County. William J. Dickenson, William Mahone (1826–1895) and others had founded the Readjuster political party in Virginia. The party advocated "readjusting" (i.e., reducing) Virginia's public debt and other popular social and economic legislation. The Readjusters won popularity among Black Virginians through some symbolic appointments and also some true progressive actions. As a result of Readjuster efforts, a number of Black guards were given jobs at the state penitentiary and Black teachers were placed in classrooms to teach Black schoolchildren. The popularity of the Readjuster movement was short-lived, but in 1880, when this county was created and named, the Readjusters and William J. Dickenson were enjoying popularity in Virginia.

2812 *Dinwiddie County*

Robert Dinwiddie (–1770)— Born in Scotland in 1692 or 1693, Dinwiddie was appointed as customs collector in England's North American possession of Bermuda. In 1738 he was promoted to surveyor-general of England's southern district in America, which included Virginia and several other colonies. Dinwiddie held that post about a decade and established his residence in Virginia. In 1741 he took a seat on the Virginia council and in 1751 he was appointed as Virginia's lieutenant-governor. During his term as lieutenant-governor, from 1751 to 1758, Virginia's officially appointed royal governors chose to remain in England, and thus Dinwiddie was Virginia's resident chief executive. As lieutenant-governor, Dinwiddie encountered resistance to fees (i.e., taxes) he imposed and was plagued by attacks from French and Indians in Virginia's western lands. This county was created and named in Robert Dinwiddie's honor in 1752, early in his term as England's resident chief executive of Virginia.

2813 *Essex County*

Uncertain— This county in England's colony of Virginia was created in 1691 or 1692. About half the sources consulted which deal with the history, geography and place names of Virginia state that this county was named for Essex County, England. The other half indicate that the origin of the county's name is uncertain but most of these state that it was probably or possibly named for Essex County, England. A very small number of the sources who say that the origin is uncertain, indicate that there is a possibility that the county was named for the earl of Essex, but fail to specify which earl of Essex that was.

Essex County, England— Essex County lies in the eastern section of Anglia, in southern England. This seacoast county facing the European continent was an important center when it was occupied by the

Roman Empire and it continued to be an important population center, containing the city of London, when the East Saxons invaded it. The name *Essex* means "territory of the East Saxons." Essex was one of the seven Anglo-Saxon kingdoms of Britain known as the Heptarchy. In the seventh century Essex was conquered by Mercia, one of the other kingdoms of the Heptarchy, and later, in the ninth century, Wessex, which had been another member of the Heptarchy, conquered it. The Essex County of today's England no longer contains London. Essex County, England, is about 54 miles long and some 48 miles wide. Its principal rivers are the Thames, Stour, Colne, Blackwater and Lea.

Earl of Essex—There is no shortage of earls of Essex in England's history but it is difficult to pick any one of them as the most likely candidate for this Virginia county's name (if it was, in fact, named for an earl of Essex). Perhaps the best known Essex was Robert Devereux, Earl of Essex (1566–1601), a favorite of England's Queen Elizabeth I (1533–1603). Since this county was created in 1691 or 1692, a more likely choice might have been Arthur Capel, Earl of Essex (1631–1683). A third possibility is Robert Devereaux, Earl of Essex (1591–1646), a son of the earl mentioned as one of the favorites of Queen Elizabeth. However, in the absence of evidence that this county was or might have been named for an earl of Essex (and why) it is difficult, and probably fruitless, to speculate which one it might have been.

2814 *Fairfax County*

Thomas Fairfax, Baron Fairfax of Cameron (1692–1782)—Born at Denton, in Yorkshire, England, Thomas Fairfax was the eldest son of Thomas Fairfax and his wife Catherine, heiress to the estates of Thomas Culpeper (1635–1689), which included Leeds Castle in Kent, England, and an enormous area of land in the Northern Neck of Virginia. From his father, the fifth baron Fairfax of Cameron, he inherited his title and became sixth baron Fairfax of Cameron, but it was through his mother that Fairfax acquired his enormous proprietorship in Virginia. Neither Fairfax nor anyone else initially appreciated just how enormous his Virginia proprietorship was. William Howard Taft III stated in his work entitled *County Names: An Historical Perspective* that young George Washington surveyed the upper reaches of the Fairfax proprietorship in Virginia and that "Because Thomas, back in England, was said to be jilted by a young lady, he is re-

puted to have foresworn all womankind and retired to a Scottish castle to breed foxhounds. Time never healed the wound but he recovered sufficiently to journey to America, where he discovered to his surprise, an estate comprising 5 million acres." This county was created in 1742 by England's colony of Virginia and named in honor of the proprietor of this enormous and valuable Virginia proprietorship. Edward T. Price's work entitled *Dividing the Land: Early American Beginnings of Our Private Property Mosaic* confirms that the proprietorship was immense and describes it as including "well over five million acres." Lord Fairfax remained loyal to England during the American Revolution and was greatly disappointed when the cause was lost with the 1781 defeat of England's General Charles Cornwallis (1738–1805).

2815 *Fauquier County*

Francis Fauquier (–1768)—Born in London, England, about 1704, Fauquier became a director of the South Sea Company in 1751 and was elected a fellow of the Royal Society in 1753. In January, 1758, he was appointed lieutenant–governor of England's colony of Virginia. At that time, Virginia's official governor was John Campbell, Earl of Loudoun (1705–1782), but he never resided in Virginia and the colony was ruled, instead by resident chief executives. Francis Fauquier served in that capacity from 1758 to 1768 and this county was created and named in his honor in 1759, early in his term as Virginia's resident chief executive. In 1765 Fauquier dissolved Virginia's house of burgesses for passing acts hostile of England's Stamp act. However, Fauquier and the Virginia house of Burgesses enjoyed generally good relations and Fauquier was able to marshall support to defend Virginia's western lands from attack by French and Indians during the Seven Years' War. He died in Williamsburg, Virginia, on March 3, 1768, while serving as Virginia's resident chief executive.

2816 *Floyd County*

John Floyd (1783–1837)—Floyd was born in a portion of western Virginia which is now within Kentucky. He studied medicine at the University of Pennsylvania and graduated from that institution in 1806. Subsequently an officer in the Virginia militia, Floyd rose to the rank of brigadier-general by 1812. He served briefly in the Virginia legislature, represented the state in the U.S. House of Representatives

from 1817 to 1829, and served as governor of Virginia from March 4, 1830, to March 31, 1834. During Floyd's term as governor of Virginia, sectional tensions between the South and the North increased over issues relating to slavery and states' rights and Nat Turner (1800–1831) led a bloody insurrection of slaves in Virginia. Turner and some 20 other slaves were tried and executed. This county was created in 1831, early in John Floyd's term as governor of Virginia, a few months before Nat Turner's slave insurrection.

2817 *Fluvanna County*

Fluvanna River—*Fluvanna* was the name that was applied to a western portion of Virginia's James River. Thomas Jefferson's *Notes on the State of Virginia* explained: "It is to be noted that this river is called in the maps *James River*, only to its confluence with the Rivanna; thence to the Blue Ridge it is called the Fluvanna; thence to its source Jackson's river. But in common speech, it is called James River to its source." We need look no further for a knowledgeable expert on this topic because Thomas Jefferson's home, Monticello, is located about 15 miles north of the section of the James River which was then called Fluvanna. The Fluvanna River was named in honor of England's Queen Anne (1665–1714) by combining the Latin word *fluvius*, meaning "a river" or "stream" with *anna*, in honor of Anne, a daughter of England's King James II (1633–1701). Anne was his second eldest daughter, apart from those who died in infancy. Fluvanna County, Virginia, was created in 1777, long after Queen Anne was dead and buried and while England's North American colonies were in revolt. However, the Fluvanna River had been named much earlier, when Virginia was still proud to be an English colony. Anne came to the throne in 1702 and ruled until her death in 1714. The Fluvanna River may have been named before, during or after her reign as monarch of England and the English colony of Virginia.

2818 *Franklin County*

Benjamin Franklin (1706–1790)—Franklin was a native of Massachusetts who moved to Pennsylvania in his teens. Poverty denied him a formal education but he became the leading printer and editor in North America. Franklin gained fame for his discoveries and inventions in the physical sciences and he distinguished himself as author, philosopher and diplomat.

of the Declaration of
an important member
which framed the U.S.
consulted differ on
ty was created.
1786 but Henry
ons of Virginia,
that Franklin
d in 1784.

2819 *Freder*...
Prince Fr...1)—
Frederick ...ge
August (...ge
England'...
born i...
force...
and ...
do...

eld ...
land, h...
ry of state a...
ty in England's ...
eated in 1752, while ...
was president of the b...
ade and plantations.

ver County

ge I (1660–1727)— In 1714
Elector of Hanover, in what
any, came to the throne of
ing George I and he reigned
th in 1727. In 1720 or 1721,
ouy of Virginia named two
him, Hanover County and
County.
rge I (1660–1727)— Born in
Hanover, in what is now Ger-
named at birth George Lewis
Georg Ludwig in some ac-
orge was an important military
rope. In 1698 he succeeded his
t August (1622–1698), as elec-
over and duke of Brunswick-
He was the first English mon-
ouse of Brunswick (later styled
ow Windsor), and that royal
ules Great Britain. The German,
ge I, and his successors, owe
on the throne of Great Britain
tors: (1) deep-seated religious
in England against Roman
m and (2) the inability of En-
ueen Anne (1665–1714) to pro-
eir to the throne. Queen Anne
ge number of children (15 ac-
o one account; 17 per another)
of them were stillborn. Only one
ived. He was Prince William
00). Medical science at that time
ble to effectively assist one of the
althy and powerful couples on
arth in their repeated efforts to

Senate from 1804 to 1815. From March 4, 1827, to March 4, 1830, William B. Giles was governor of the state of Virginia. This county was created on January 16, 1806, while William B. Giles was serving in the United States Senate.

2821 *Gloucester County*

Uncertain— Sources consulted which deal with the history, geography and place names of Virginia are pretty well agreed that this county was created in 1651 (although Charles M. Long's *Virginia County Names* shows 1652) but they have different views on the origin of the county's name. About half indicate that the county's name s a transplant of a place name in England ither Gloucester or Gloucestershire), e approximately an equal number hat the name honors a member of lish royal family, Henry, Duke of r (1640–1660). Many of these nit that there is uncertainty nty's namesake.

England and/or Gloucester-
— The name derived from
on *Glou Ceaster*, meaning
p on the site of the ancient
lou." This town became
the Romans after they
t A.D. 97. At a later time
he capital of Mercia, one
glo-Saxon kingdoms of
the Heptarchy. Glouces-
seat of Gloucestershire,
nty's length is 60 miles
o more than 26 miles.
an area of 1055.2 square
ation in the early 1980's
million. Its agricultural
ler, perry, bacon, grain
. Fishing and manu-
are also found in
county lies in west-
Bristol Channel. Its
ern, Avon and Wye.
es tidal waves which
the river toward
up to nine feet high.
have been erected
otect the city from
ester boasts an an-
athedral.
loucester (1640–
of England's King
d his queen con-
ria (1606–1669).
ugh one of the
English history.
xecuted by be-
just nine years
was eventually

restored, two of Henry's brothers became kings of England. They were King Charles II (1630–1685) and King James II (1633–1701). Henry bore the title duke of Gloucester from his birth although the title was reconfirmed when he was made earl of Cambridge and duke of Gloucester on May 13, 1659. Young Henry was permitted to visit his father, the doomed king, on the day preceding the king's execution in January 1649. Henry then lived in France with his mother and his sister, Princess Henrietta Anne (1644–1670). Henry's Roman Catholic mother gave him a Catholic upbringing. Henry fought as a volunteer with the Spanish in Flanders in 1657 and 1658. He died in London of smallpox, then prevalent, on September 13, 1660, and thus never saw the splendor of his brother's (King Charles II) coronation at Westminster Abbey on April 23, 1661. When Gloucester County, Virginia, was created, England was split in factions by civil war. The king had recently been beheaded, the monarchy had been deposed and Oliver Cromwell (1599–1658) was imposing civil rule on England. Since most of the counties named for royalty by Virginia (and other North American colonies of England) were intended to curry favor with the crown, one might wonder why Virginia would name a county for a member of the deposed monarchy. The answer is that colonial Virginia favored the royal side versus Cromwell during the period of the English Civil War. Thus it is quite plausible that this county might have been named for Henry, Duke of Gloucester (1640–1660), even though we are uncertain whether the county name honors him or Gloucester, England and/or Gloucestershire, in England.

2822 *Goochland County*

William Gooch (1681–1751)— Born October 21, 1681, at Yarmouth, England, Gooch served in the English army before being appointed lieutenant-governor of England's colony of Virginia. He arrived in the colony in September, 1727, to begin serving as Virginia's resident chief executive. At that time Virginia's governor was George Hamilton, Earl of Orkney (1666–1737), but Hamilton remained in England while lieutenant-governors (and one acting governor), served him as Virginia's resident chief executives. Lieutenant-Governor Gooch turned Virginia over to James Blair (–1743) for about eight months starting in December, 1740, in order to participate in an expedition against Spanish South America. Apart from that brief interlude, William Gooch was the resident chief executive of Virginia from 1727 to 1749 and on important occasions he took the part of the Virginia colonists in disputes with England. These disputes involved liquor imports, slave imports and tobacco exports. In spite of his pro-colonial efforts, Gooch maintained his popularity with England's power structure. He was made a baronet in 1746 and promoted to major-general in the British army in 1747. He remained Virginia's resident chief executive until the summer of 1749 when ill health forced him to resign and return to England. This county was created in either 1727 or 1728.

2823 *Grayson County*

William Grayson (–1790)— Grayson was born in Prince William County, Virginia, about 1736. During the American Revolution he served as an officer and aide-de-camp to General George Washington. Promoted to colonel in January, 1777, he participated in the battles of Long Island, White Plains, Brandywine Creek, Germantown and Monmouth. In 1784 Grayson was elected to Virginia's house of delegates and he later represented Virginia in the Continental Congress. As a member of the Virginia convention to consider adoption of the proposed U.S. Constitution, Grayson opposed its ratification but after it was ratified he became one of Virginia's first two United States senators. This county was created in 1792.

2824 *Greene County*

Nathanael Greene (1742–1786)— Greene was born in Rhode Island and served briefly in the Rhode Island legislature. He gained fame as one of the ablest American generals in the Revolutionary War. During the final months of the Revolution, it was General Greene who hounded England's General Charles Cornwallis (1738–1805), eventually driving him toward Yorktown, Virginia and final defeat. This county was created during January, 1838.

2825 *Greensville County*

Uncertain— This county was created in 1780 or 1781 and named for either our American Revolutionary general, Nathanael Greene (1742–1786) or Sir Richard Grenville (–1591), who was prominent in the initial English attempts at colonization of Virginia in the late 16th century.

Nathanael Greene (1742–1786)— Greene was born in Rhode Island and served briefly in the Rhode Island legislature. He gained fame as one of the ablest American generals in the Revolutionary War. During the final months of the Revolution, it was General Greene who hounded England's General Charles Cornwallis (1738–1805), eventually driving him toward Yorktown, Virginia, and final defeat. Shortly before that, following Greene's battle with forces under the command of Cornwallis at Guilford Court House, North Carolina, in March, 1781, Greene marched his troops northeast across the Virginia border into what is now Greensville County, Virginia. Many of the sources who contend that this county's name honors General Nathanael Greene cite this dramatic entry into Virginia as the reason the county's name was chosen. We would be better able to evaluate that evidence if we were sure just when this county was created but sources dealing with the history, geography and place names of Virginia differ, and 1780 and 1781 are mentioned. Since the battle of Guilford Court House, North Carolina, was fought in March, 1781, a place name theory linked to that battle has no validity if the county's name was chosen prior to that battle.

Richard Grenville (–1591)— This Englishman was a member of parliament and a knight as well as serving as a naval commander for his cousin, Sir Walter Ralegh (–1618), during early English efforts to colonize Virginia. In 1585 Ralegh sent Grenville to Roanoke Island (now part of North Carolina) where Grenville established England's first settlement in Virginia, but it was soon abandoned. He rose in the English navy to become second in command to Lord Thomas Howard (1561–1626) of the Azores fleet, fighting Spain, and Grenville died in combat against Spanish warships in 1591.

Although the date of this county's creation is not certain, clearly it was during the period that the American colonies were approaching victory in their Revolution to be rid of domination by England. If the county was actually created after the battle of Guilford Court House, North Carolina, it would seem likely that our Revolutionary general, Nathanael Greene, was the namesake and unlikely that Virginia would choose this junction in history to place a reminder on her map of England's early colonization of Virginia. Indeed, one has the feeling that Charles M. Long's work entitled *Virginia County Names*, published in 1908, inspired a number of later writers to mention the possibility that this county's name might honor Richard Grenville (–1591).

2826 *Halifax Co*

George Montagu Du (1716–1771)— Educ Trinity College i tained the rank o he was made pre trade and plantat of commerce and served as presid 1748 to 1761 and the colonies," for American comm a privy councillo founding the N Nova Scotia, th which is now a named Halifax i was made a li subsequently h lieutenant of Ir miralty, secreta seal. This cou Virginia was cr Montagu Dun ish board of tr

2827 *Hano*

King Geor George Lewis is now Germ England as K until his dea England's co counties for King George

King Geo Osnabruck, many, and (also styled counts), Ge leader in Eu father, Erns tor of Han Luneburg. arch of the Hanover, house still King Geo their hold to two fa animosit Catholici gland's O duce an had a la cording but mos boy su (1689–1 was una most w planet

leave an heir to the throne. This personal tragedy resulted in a practical problem for England as well, since the heir to the throne when Queen Anne died in 1714 was her half-brother, James Francis Edward Stuart (1688–1766); but James Stuart was a Catholic and England wanted no Catholic on its throne. The nation closed ranks against James Stuart and all other Catholic contenders for the crown and reached all the way to Hanover, in Germany, for a successor to Queen Anne. There they found George Lewis (1660–1727), the elector of Hanover, who had a drop or two of royal English blood in his veins and thus some semblance of a claim to the English throne. He became England's King George I. The new king never bothered to learn much of the English language but he did succeed in remaining Protestant throughout his reign.

Technically, the house of Hanover had its initial roots in Italy, but in both England and America, the house of Hanover is considered to be thoroughly German. King George I was the first member of the house of Hanover to rule England and the present English monarch, Queen Elizabeth II (1926–) is a member of that same royal house although its name was changed from Hanover to Windsor on July 17, 1917, as a result of the anti–German hysteria associated with World War I.

2828 *Henrico County*

Settlement of Henrico in early colonial Virginia— In 1634, when England's royal colony of Virginia was divided into eight original shires, or counties, one of the eight was named in honor of a settlement which had been established here in 1611 and grown beyond the size of a mere town by 1634. The name of that settlement in Virginia's very early colonial history is rendered as Henricopolis by several sources dealing with the history, geography and place names of Virginia. However, in a scholarly history of Virginia by Virginius Dabney, entitled *Virginia: The New Dominion: A History from 1607 to the Present*, the author takes pains to disabuse us of the notion that the settlement was ever called Henricopolis. Dabney tells us that Sir Thomas Dale (–1619) recognized the need for a more elevated site, above Jamestown "…and accordingly explored upriver. There, in 1611, he chose 'a convenient, strong, healthie and sweet seate' on Farrar's Island at the point where it then joined the mainland, at a sharp bend in the stream near Dutch Gap. It was named Henrico, for Henry, Prince of Wales. (The town was

never known as Henricopolis in the seventeenth or even the eighteenth century, despite widespread belief to the contrary.)"

Henry Frederick, Prince of Wales (1594– 1612)— Henry Frederick was a son of England's King James I (1566–1625) and Anne of Denmark (1574–1619). He was born in 1594 while James was ruling Scotland as King James VI, but before he had come to England's throne as King James I. As the eldest son, he became heir to the English throne in 1603, when his father was crowned king of England. Henry Frederick matriculated at Magdalen College, Oxford University, in 1605. In 1610 he was given the title prince of Wales, the hereditary title given to male heirs to the English throne, and the prince had a court of splendor. When he was 17 years old he asked the king allow him to preside over the council. The king declined, perhaps jealous of the trappings that the prince of Wales had already accumulated. However, Henry Frederick's life was cut short by typhoid fever before his 18th birthday and he never came to England's throne. Instead, his brother Charles (1600–1649) became King Charles I in 1625 upon the death of King James I.

At the time that the community of Henrico in England's colony of Virginia was settled and named in 1611, Henry Frederick was prince of Wales and heir apparent to the English throne. Henry Frederick died the following year and by the time that Henrico County was named in 1634, Charles I was king of England. However, the name was not abandoned, but carried over from the name of the town which, by 1634, had grown to county proportions.

2829 *Henry County*

Patrick Henry (1736–1799)— Henry was a native of Virginia and a lawyer. He served in the Virginia legislature, as governor of Virginia and as a delegate to the first and second Continental Congresses. Henry was one of America's key revolutionary leaders. He was a great orator and he is remembered for his call to arms against the British "Give me liberty or give me death." Henry opposed Virginia's ratification of the federal Constitution and his views played a role in the later adoption of the Bill of Rights. Henry County, in southwestern Virginia, was created in 1776, while Patrick Henry was serving as governor of Virginia. Patrick Henry owned some 10,000 acres of land in Henry County and lived in the county for a number of years. When a new county was carved

from the western side of Henry County (in 1790 or 1791), it was also named in honor of Patrick Henry. The new county was named Patrick County. Today the two counties sit side by side in southwestern Virginia, just above the North Carolina border.

2830 *Highland County*

Mountainous terrain of the county— This county on Virginia's western border with the state of West Virginia, was created in March, 1847, and named for the mountainous terrain found here in the Allegheny Mountains. Highland County does not contain Virginia's highest mountain peak, which is Mount Rogers in Smyth and Grayson Counties, Virginia. However, Raus M. Hanson's work entitled *Virginia Place Names: Derivations: Historical Uses* states that Highland County has the highest mean altitude of Virginia's counties.

2831 *Isle of Wight County*

Isle of Wight in the English Channel— The Isle of Wight, in the English Channel, belongs to England and is separated from it by a narrow channel called the Solent Sea. The island, which consists largely of chalk, is about 22 miles across and some 13 miles wide. Some of the island's scenery is charming. When the Roman Empire ruled here, they called the island *Vectis* and after the Roman rule ended, the island had its own kings for a time. However the tiny island kingdom did not last long and it was conquered by Sussex, Mercia and Wessex. In A.D. 998 the Danes took the Isle of Wight and in 1371 it was sacked by the French. In 1992 the Isle of Wight had a population of 125,000. Authorities differ on the origin and translation of the name *Wight. The Story Key to Geographic Names* by O. D. Von Engeln and Jane McKelway Urquhart states that the name came "…from the Welsh word *gwyth* = 'channel.' This term was used first for the strait between the smaller island and the British coast." A.D. Mills' *A Dictionary of English Place-Names* indicates that it came from "A Celtic name, possibly meaning 'place of division,' referring to its situation between the two arms of the Solent." Since the Solent Sea is the channel, which separates Isle of Wight from the mainland, the two translations have much in common. In 1634, when England's royal colony of Virginia was divided into eight original shires, or counties, this county was one of the original eight. At that time it was given an Indian name which is rendered variously including Warrascoyack, Warrosquyoake, Warrosquyoacke and Werrosquyoke. This Virginia county's name was changed in 1637 to Isle of Wight County.

2832 *James City County*

Town of Jamestown, Virginia— Jamestown, Virginia, became, in 1607, the site of the first permanent English settlement in America. In December, 1606, a party left England to establish a profitable colony for investors here. In May, 1607, they selected a site on the lower James River, in Virginia, where ships could be moored in six fathoms of water. They named their settlement Jamestown in honor of the reigning king of England, King James I (1566–1625). Within a few years all of English Virginia was divided into four plantations, one of which was James City and in 1634, all of English Virginia was divided into eight original shires, or counties and James City County was one of the eight. Thus the creation in 1634 of James City County was merely a recognition of the fact that the original settlement at Jamestown had grown from a city to a plantation to a county.

King James I (1566–1625)— James was born in Edinburgh Castle in Scotland in 1566 and he came to the Scottish throne as King James VI in 1567, when he was only one year old. When England's reigning monarch, Queen Elizabeth I (1533–1603), was nearing death there was considerable political intrigue concerning, who would replace her as England's ruler for she had never married and would leave no heirs. To complicate matters, Queen Elizabeth I refused to permit discussion of any possible successors. The power structure in England looked north to Scotland, decided that the king of Scotland, reigning there as James VI, would be the next monarch of England, and when the queen of England died in 1603 James of Scotland became king of England in a remarkably peaceful succession. England's Queen Elizabeth I had been excommunicated by the Roman Catholic Church. Her annoyance at this was understandable but she took rather extreme retaliation against Roman Catholics in her realm, forbidding them to attend Mass, having Catholic priests tortured, drawn and quartered and other incivilities. While James in Scotland was being courted as the potential monarch of England, by design or inadvertence, he encouraged English Catholics to believe that far better days would be theirs were he to come to the English throne. He disappointed England's Catholics and a mil-

itant element among them, led by Guy Fawkes (1570–1606), conspired in the so-called "Gunpowder Plot," to set fire to and blow up the new king and parliament with him. The plot failed and King James I continued to rule England until his death in 1625. King James I commissioned a panel which produced the popular King James version of the Holy Bible.

2833 *King and Queen County*

King William III (1650–1702) & Queen Mary II (1662–1694)— This county in England's colony on Virginia was created in 1691 and named for the reigning king and queen of England, William III and Mary II. Queen Mary II was no mere queen consort. She ruled England as joint sovereign with her husband.

King William III (1650–1702)— William, Prince of Orange, was born in the Netherlands. He was the grandson of England's King Charles I (1600–1649) and in 1677 William married his cousin, Mary (1662–1694), who was then the presumptive heir to the English throne, occupied by her father, King James II (1633–1701). In 1688 William invaded England, supported by both Dutch and English troops and on April 11, 1689, William and his wife were crowned king and queen of England. They ruled as joint sovereigns, titled King William III and Queen Mary II until Mary's death in 1694. William continued on the English throne until his death in 1702.

Queen Mary II (1662–1694)— Born in London, England, on April 30, 1662, Mary was the eldest surviving child of James, Duke of York (1633–1701), who later came to England's throne as King James II. (Mary had an older brother, Charles, Duke of Cambridge (1660–1661), but he died in infancy.) In 1677, when Mary was only 15 years old, she married her cousin, William III, of Orange (1650–1702), the stadholder (ruler) of the Dutch republic. Her husband was a leader of Protestantism in Europe and when Mary's father, King James II of England, professed his Catholicism this spelled his downfall as king of Protestant England. Mary took her husband's side against her father and supported William when he invaded England with Dutch and English troops in 1688. Mary and her husband were crowed joint sovereigns of England in Westminster Abbey on April 11, 1689. When William was absent from England, Mary ruled and was quite popular. Queen Mary II died of smallpox in 1694.

Later, in either 1701 or 1702, England's

colony of Virginia created a new county from King and Queen County and named it King William County, in honor of King William III (1650–1702) alone.

2834 *King George County*

King George I (1660–1727)— In 1714 George Lewis, Elector of Hanover, in what is now Germany, came to the throne of England as King George I and he reigned until his death in 1727. In 1720 or 1721, England's colony of Virginia named two counties for him, Hanover County and King George County.

King George I (1660–1727)— Born in Osnabruck, Hanover, in what is now Germany, and named at birth George Lewis (also styled Georg Ludwig in some accounts), George was an important military leader in Europe. In 1698 he succeeded his father, Ernst August (1622–1698), as elector of Hanover and duke of Brunswick-Luneburg. He was the first English monarch of the house of Brunswick (later styled Hanover, now Windsor), and that royal house still rules Great Britain. The German, King George I, and his successors, owe their hold on the throne of Great Britain to two factors: (1) deep-seated religious animosity in England against Roman Catholicism and (2) the inability of England's Queen Anne (1665–1714) to produce an heir to the throne. Queen Anne had a large number of children (15 according to one account; 17 per another) but most of them were stillborn. Only one boy survived. He was Prince William (1689–1700). Medical science at that time was unable to effectively assist one of the most wealthy and powerful couples on planet Earth in their repeated efforts to leave an heir to the throne. This personal tragedy resulted in a practical problem for England as well, since the heir to the throne when Queen Anne died in 1714 was her half-brother, James Francis Edward Stuart (1688–1766); but James Stuart was a Catholic and England wanted no Catholic on its throne. The nation closed ranks against James Stuart and all other Catholic contenders for the crown and reached all the way to Hanover, in Germany, for a successor to Queen Anne. There they found George Lewis (1660–1727), the elector of Hanover, who had a drop or two of royal English blood in his veins and thus some semblance of a claim to the English throne. He became England's King George I. The new king never bothered to learn much of the English language but he did succeed in remaining Protestant throughout his reign.

2835 *King William County*

King William III (1650–1702) — William, Prince of Orange, was born in the Netherlands. He was the grandson of England's King Charles I (1600–1649) and in 1677 William married his cousin, Mary (1662–1694), who was then the presumptive heir to the English throne, occupied by her father, King James II (1633–1701). In 1688 William invaded England, supported by both Dutch and English troops, and on April 11, 1689, William and his wife were crowned king and queen of England. They ruled as joint sovereigns, titled King William III and Queen Mary II until Mary's death in 1694. William continued on the English throne until his death in 1702.

In 1691 England's colony of Virginia created King and Queen County, named for the reigning king and queen of England, William III (1650–1702) and Mary II (1662–1694). Later, in either 1701 or 1702, Virginia created this new county from King and Queen County and named it King William County, in honor of King William III (1650–1702) alone.

2836 *Lancaster County*

Lancaster and/or Lancashire, England — This county in England's colony on Virginia was created in 1651 or 1652 and named for the city and/or county (shire) in England named Lancaster and Lancashire. The county named Lancashire, in northwestern England, on the Irish Sea, has a name that dates back to the time that the Roman Empire occupied England. An early version of its name, Loncastre, meant "Roman fort (or camp) on the river Lune." A later (14th century) version of the name was Lancastreshire, which derived from Lancaster and the Old English word *scir*, which meant "district." Lancashire England is 75 miles long and averages about 30 miles in width. In the northern and eastern portions of the county, mountains can be found which reach altitudes of more than 2,000 feet. Wide moor lands are found between many of these mountains. More land is using for grazing than for planting crops. Iron, coal, slate and other building materials are found in Lancashire. Its city of Liverpool is one of the most important seaports in the United Kingdom and its other principal city, Lancaster, also carries on foreign trade.

2837 *Lee County*

Henry Lee (1756–1818) — Lee was born in Virginia on January 29, 1756, and graduated from the College of New Jersey (now Princeton University). He served with distinction as an officer during the American Revolution, rising to the rank of lieutenant-colonel and acquiring the nickname "Light Horse Harry Lee." Congress presented a gold medal to him for bravery. From 1785 to 1788 Lee represented Virginia in the Continental Congress and from December 1, 1791, to December 1, 1794, he served as governor of the state of Virginia. He later represented Virginia in the U.S. House of Representatives. This county was created on October 25, 1792, while Henry Lee was governor of Virginia.

2838 *Loudoun County*

John Campbell, Earl of Loudoun (1705–1782) — John Campbell, the fourth earl of Loudoun, entered the British military as a cornet in the Scots Greys in 1727 and in 1731 he succeeded his father, Hugh Campbell (–1731), as earl of Loudoun. John Campbell, Earl of Loudoun, was a Scottish representative peer from 1734 to 1782 and in the military he attained the rank of major-general in 1755. Loudoun was made commander-in-chief of all forces in North America in January 1756. Also that year he was made a non-resident governor-general of England's colony of Virginia, while Robert Dinwiddie (–1770) was the crown's resident governor of Virginia. As commander-in-chief in North America, Loudoun met with limited success and it was decided in December 1757 that he would be recalled, although he was promoted to lieutenant-general in 1758. In 1762 Loudoun was second in command during a British expedition to Portugal. He was made full general in 1770. This county in England's colony of Virginia was created and named in his honor in 1757, while he was nominal governor of Virginia.

2839 *Louisa County*

Princess Louise (1724–1751) — Louisa County in England's colony of Virginia was created in 1742 and named for the youngest child of the then-reigning monarch of England, and Virginia, Princess Louise. She was a daughter of King George II (1683–1760) and his queen consort, Queen Caroline of Anspach (1683–1737). Princess Louise, whose given name is rendered in some sources as Louisa, was born at Leicester House on December 7, 1724. King George II and Queen Caroline of Anspach had seven children prior to the birth of Princess Louise and John Van der Kiste's *King George II & Queen Caroline* tells us that "When courtiers came to congratulate the father, who had particularly wanted another son, he said a little testily, 'No matter, 'tis but a daughter.'" But Princess Louise was the last child that Queen Caroline of Anspach would bear. The birth was difficult and contributed to the queen's subsequent ill health and death just 13 years later. Some sources dealing with the history, geography and place names of Virginia state that Louisa County was named for the queen of Denmark. That statement is misleading for three reasons: (1) Louise (1724–1751) was never the ruler of Denmark; she was, however, queen consort of King Frederick V (1723–1766), monarch of Denmark and Norway. (2) England's Princess Louise did not marry Frederick until 1743, after Louisa County, Virginia, was created. (3) Frederick was a crown prince when Louise married him and did not become king of Denmark and Norway until 1746, four years after this Virginia county was created. Louise bore several children for King Frederick V but became seriously ill during her final pregnancy and died during that pregnancy, at the age of 27, on December 8, 1751.

2840 *Lunenburg County*

King George II (1683–1760) — This county in England's colony of Virginia was created in 1746 and named for the then-reigning monarch of England, and Virginia, King George II (1683–1760). The king's paternal grandfather, Ernest August (1622–1698), was the ruler (elector) of the German state of Hanover and among his titles was duke of Brunswick-Luneburg. The eldest son of Ernest August, George Lewis (1660–1727), inherited those titles and came to the throne of England as King George I in 1714. Upon the death of King George I in 1727, his only son became King George II of England and inherited the German titles, elector of Hanover of duke of Brunswick-Luneburg, as well. All of this demonstrates that the title Luneburg (or as spelled in the Virginia county's name, Lunenburg) was only one of the many titles held by King George II of England. It was a common practice in Virginia and other English colonies in America to curry favor by naming counties for kings and queens of England and members of the English royal family. In 1746, when Virginia decided to honor the reigning monarch, King George II, by naming a county for him, they had a bit of a problem. They couldn't call the county King George County, for that name had already been used, honoring King George I (1660–1727), and some of the titles of King George II (e.g., Brunswick and Hanover) had previously been used as Virginia county names. Virginia already had a Prince George County but it had been named in honor of the consort of England's Queen Anne (1665–1714). As Charles M. Long puts it in his *Virginia County Names*, published in 1908, "…But the supply of titles by which George II could be called was not yet exhausted, and, accordingly the new county received the name of Lunenburg."

King George II (1683–1760)—George August was the first of two children born to England's King George I (1660–1727) and Sophia Dorothea of Zelle (1666–1726). The parents of young George August both committed adultery, and although Sophia Dorothea acted only in response to her husband's repeated infidelities, King George I had her banished to a grim castle for life. The king extended his animosity toward his exiled wife to young George August, and only deigned to make him prince of Wales in 1714 at the urging of his court advisors. Following the death of King George I, the Prince of Wales ascended the throne as King George II and ruled from 1727 to 1760. During this period England increased in status as a world power and although credit cannot be given to George II for shrewd statesmanship, it must be admitted that he readily accepted advice from those with able judgment. One of his ablest advisors was his own queen consort, Queen Caroline of Anspach (1683–1737).

2841 *Madison County*

James Madison (1751–1836)—Madison was born in Virginia and served in the Virginia legislature and in the Continental Congress. He was a member of the convention which framed the U.S. Constitution and he collaborated with Hamilton and Jay in writing a series of papers under the title *The Federalist*, which explained the new constitution and advocated its adoption. Madison represented Virginia in the U.S. House of Representatives, served for eight years as secretary of state and eight years, from 1809 to 1817, as president of the United States. Virginia created a county honoring James Madison in 1785 but they lost it when Kentucky was separated from Virginia. This second Madison County was created during Virginia's legislative session which began in 1792. The year that this county was actually created is listed in some works as 1792 and in others as 1793.

2842 *Mathews County*

Uncertain—This county was created in 1790 or 1791, soon after Virginia joined the federal Union and became a member of the United States of America. Most sources dealing with the history, geography and place names of Virginia state that this county was named for Thomas Mathews, an army officer during the American Revolution and speaker of Virginia's house of delegates from 1788 to 1794. However three important sources, say that the county was named for George Mathews (1739–1812). Those three sources are: (1) Henry Howe's *Historical Collections of Virginia*, published in 1849, (2) Charles M. Long's *Virginia County Names*, published in 1908, and (3) Henry Gannett's *The Origin of Certain Places Names in the United States*, originally published in 1902 and republished in 1978. However, errors have been found concerning the origin of other county names in all three of these works and it is likely that they are in error concerning the origin of this county's name. The majority view, that this Virginia county was named for Thomas Mathews, is probably correct. An article under "Notes & Queries," in the 1896 issue (Vol. 3) of *Virginia Magazine of History & Biography* stated that on February 11, 1793, Thomas Mathews presented to the court of Mathews County, Virginia, a seal "in grateful return of the High esteem and respect which was shown him in the erection and establishment of this county."

George Mathews (1739–1812)—Born in Augusta County, Virginia, George Mathews was an officer in our Revolutionary army, serving as a colonel in Virginia regiments before being promoted to brevet brigadier-general. He later represented Georgia in the House of Representatives of the first Congress of the United States of America and was governor of Georgia. George Mathews subsequently was involved in efforts, both diplomatic and military, to obtain West Florida from Spain.

Thomas Mathews (–)—It is clear that Thomas Mathews served as an officer during the American Revolution, probably holding the rank of captain and possibly also that of colonel. The uncertainty exists because numerous references are found in the *Virginia Magazine of History & Biography* and *William & Mary College Quarterly Historical Magazine*, which mention one or more Virginia officers of the American Revolution named Thomas Mathews. Sol Stember's *Bicentennial Guide to the American Revolution* tells us that one of these officers was Captain Thomas Mathews and that he and his

militia fought at Six Mile Ordinary against "Tarleton in August, 1781." That same work tells us that the Thomas Mathews, "…who commanded the militia garrison at Fort Nelson…" during the American Revolution was buried in the churchyard of St. Paul's Episcopal Church in Norfolk, Virginia. The only facts which are clearly linked to our Thomas Mathews are (1) that he served as an officer during the American Revolution and (2) was speaker of Virginia's house of delegates from 1788 to 1794.

2843 *Mecklenburg County*

Queen Charlotte Sophia of Mecklenburg-Strelitz (1744–1818)—This county in England's royal colony of Virginia was created in 1764, while King George III (1738–1820) ruled England and Virginia. It was named for the bride whom the king had married in 1761 and made his queen consort. Charlotte's marriage to George was arranged and she did not meet him until her wedding day. In 1761 she was described as "…not tall nor a beauty. Pale and very thin but looks sensible and genteel." Charlotte's life as queen was entirely domestic and she was happy with it. She had neither interest nor influence in political matters. The king was devoted to her and she was faithful to him. Apparently her only vice was stinginess in money matters. Charlotte became responsible for the royal household and for the care of the king during his lengthy physical and mental illnesses. Charlotte bore her husband 15 children, two of whom later came to the throne as kings of England. These two kings were August Frederick, who came to the throne in 1820 as King George IV (1762–1830), and Edward Frederick, who reigned as King William IV (1765–1837). Charlotte County, Virginia, also created in 1764, was also named for this same English queen, Charlotte Sophia of Mecklenburg–Strelitz (1744–1818).

2844 *Middlesex County*

Middlesex County, England—This county was created in England's colony of Virginia between 1667 to 1675 and named for what was then England's premier county, Middlesex, which then contained the city of London. Middlesex County, in southeastern England, was the home of the Middle Saxon tribe. It became a shire (county) in the tenth century A.D. Its name derived from the tribal name of the Middle Saxons. An early version of the county's name was *Middelseaxan*, which meant "territory of the Middle Saxons." The Middlesex County area was occupied by the Roman Empire from A.D. 43 to A.D. 409. From Anglo-Saxon times it grew to be England's center of trade. Middlesex County suffered a severe plague in 1665 and a great fire in London in 1666. During World War II Middlesex County was bombed extensively by the German air force. Middlesex County is relatively small in size, with a length of about 22 miles and a width of only 14 miles. Its principal streams are the Thames, Lea and Colin Rivers. Middlesex County, England, ceased to exist as a separate entity in 1965 when it was absorbed as a part of a metropolitan county named Greater London.

2845 *Montgomery County*

Richard Montgomery (1738–1775)— Montgomery was born in Ireland and served with the British in the French and Indian War. He settled in New York state where he was elected to the New York provisional congress. He served as a general in the American Revolutionary army and he was killed in combat in the Revolutionary War. This county was created in 1776.

2846 *Nelson County*

Thomas Nelson (1738–1789)— Nelson was born in York County, Virginia, and studied at Christ's College in Cambridge, England. He returned to America in 1761 and represented York County in Virginia's house of burgesses for several years. By 1775 Nelson had become an active opponent of England's policies toward her American colonies. He served in several sessions of the Continental Congress and he was one of the signers of our nation's Declaration of Independence. During the American Revolution, Nelson held the rank of brigadier-general and for a few years he commanded Virginia's militia. In June, 1781 he was elected to succeed Thomas Jefferson as governor of Virginia but he was forced to resign in November of that year on account of ill health. In 1784 Virginia created and named a county in honor of Governor Thomas Nelson but it lost that county to Kentucky when it was separated from Virginia. On December 25, 1807, Virginia created this second Nelson County, also named for Thomas Nelson.

2847 *New Kent County*

Kent County, England and/or Kent Island, Maryland— This county in England's colony of Virginia was created in 1654. Some sources say that it was named directly for Kent County, England, while others indicate that it was named for Kent Island, in Chesapeake Bay, which had been named for Kent County, England. In 1631, William Claiborne, of England's Virginia colony, set up a trading post and farming settlements on Kent Island, in Chesapeake Bay, and he named the island in honor of Kent County, England. Several sources state that Kent County, England, was William Claiborne's former home. In June, 1632, England's King Charles I (1600–1649) made a grant to lord Baltimore to establish a colony (Maryland) north of the Potomac River. After a brief dispute, Virginia reluctantly gave up its claim to Kent Island (which lies well north of the Potomac River) and allowed it to become a part of Maryland. The Kent County section of England was once a separate Anglo-Saxon kingdom. The kingdom converted to Roman Christianity in A.D. 597, making it the first Christian kingdom in England. Kent was absorbed by Wessex in the ninth century. The English county's name probably derived from the Celt's *canto*, meaning "rim, border, border land" or "district."

2848 *Northampton County*

Uncertain— In 1634, when England's royal colony of Virginia was divided into eight original shires, or counties, one of the eight was named in honor of the Accomac Indian tribe. The spelling of that county's name is rendered variously as Accawmack, Accawmacke Achomack, Accomac, Accowmack and Accomack. In 1642 or 1643 that Virginia county's name was changed to Northampton County. The Accomac Indians' name was restored to Virginia's map of counties in 1662 or 1663, when the northern part of Northampton County, was taken to form the separate county named Accomack County. Several sources indicate that the person responsible for changing the first Accomack County's name to Northampton was Colonel Obedience Robins, who was then a prominent resident here and some of them say that the new county name was chosen in memory of Northamptonshire in England, the former home of Colonel Robins. Other sources say that the name was chosen to honor Spencer Compton, Earl of Northampton.

Northamptonshire, England—Northamptonshire is a county in south-central England, northwest of London. Occupied in ancient times by the Roman Empire, the first known mention of Northampton was in A.D. 917 when the Danes seized it. Northamptonshire is a relatively quiet shire (or county), less affected by the industrial revolution than some of its neighbors. This shire's population in 1981 was 532,400. The name derives from Old English words *ham tun* meaning "home, farm, homestead," with *North* added to distinguish it from Southampton.

Spencer Compton, Earl of Northampton (1601–1643)— This Englishman studied at Queens' College in Cambridge and was titled lord Compton in 1618. He served as a member of parliament and was master of the robes to the future King Charles I (1600–1649) when Charles was still prince of Wales. He accompanied the prince to Spain in 1623 and when Charles came to the throne as king of England, Spencer Compton continued as his master of the robes from Charles' coronation in 1625 until 1628. Compton was called to the peerage as Baron Compton in 1626 and he became the second earl of Northampton in 1630. Virginia sources which say that Northampton County, Virginia, was named for Spencer Compton, Earl of Northampton stress that he was loyal to King Charles I during the English Civil War and these sources remind us that colonial Virginia was strongly on the side of the monarchy during England's Civil War. Spencer Compton, Earl of Northampton lost his life at Hopton Heath, fighting for the king in 1643.

2849 *Northumberland County*

Northumberland County, England— Northumberland, England's northernmost county on the border with Scotland, is a large county and was an independent kingdom in ancient times. Like other parts of the island of Great Britain, Northumberland was subjected to seemingly endless attacks. Conquered and occupied by the Roman Empire, Northumberland's territory continued to be attacked, when the Romans left. In Anglo-Saxon times, Northumberland was much larger than the present English county, and it was attacked repeatedly from other portions of Great Britain and Scandinavia. Northumberland's proximity to Scotland made it a center of rivalry between England and Scotland but after Scotland's King James VI (1566–1625) ascended to the throne of England as King James I, in 1603, Northumberland gradually accepted membership in that union. It was described in 1586 as "…mostly rough and barren, and seems to have hardened the very carcasses of its inhabitants." This English county's name derives from a tribal name, which referred to "those living north of the river Humber," an estuary on the North Sea. Most sources dealing with the history, geography and place names of Virginia show 1648 as the year of this county's creation but a few say "about 1645." Martha W. Hiden supports the earlier date in her work entitled *How Justice Grew: Virginia's Counties: An Abstract of Their Formation*. In that work Hiden states that "By 1645 the county of Northumberland had been formed. Although we have no Act of Assembly to establish the date of its formation, an item from a volume of *Maryland Archives* under date of 1645 referring to Lieutenant Colonel John Trussell of the county of Northumberland shows the county was then functioning." Since our nation's only other Northumberland County is a Pennsylvania county created in 1772, Hiden's evidence seems to verify the earlier date.

2850 *Nottoway County*

Nottoway River and/or Nottoway Indians— This county was created in 1788 or 1789. Sources dealing with the history, geography and place names of Virginia are agreed that the county was named for the Nottoway River or the Nottoway Indians, for whom the river was named. Some sources state that the county's name honors both the river and the Indians, although that is an unlikely explanation unless it alludes to the fact that the river was named for the Indians.

Nottoway River—The Nottoway River of southern Virginia and northeastern North Carolina rises near the border between Nottoway County and Lunenburg County, Virginia, flows almost 175 miles in a southeastern direction toward Virginia's southeastern corner. Near that corner, just south of Franklin, Virginia, the Nottoway crosses into northeastern North Carolina, where its waters unite with those of the Blackwater River to form the Chowan River.

Nottoway Indians—The Nottoway were an Iroquoian tribe, who lived along the Nottoway River in southern Virginia and in northeastern North Carolina along the Chowan River. They called themselves the Cheroenhaka. The name *Nottoway* is one of the names by which they were called by neighboring Algonquian Indians. *Nottoway* was a derisive term, which meant "enemy," or "adder." The Algonquians used this term for a species of rattlesnake, as a name for enemy Indian tribes, and

even for their friends, the Wyandot Indians, because of their Iroquoian speech. There were some 1,500 Nottoway Indians extant in the early 17th century but they never made much of a mark on history. However, the Nottoway survived much longer than many of their more famous Indian neighbors. As recently as 1825 there were still 47 Nottoway Indians living on a reservation in Southampton County, Virginia and they still had their own queen then.

2851 *Orange County*

William IV, Prince of Orange (1711–1751)—This county was created in 1734. At that time, Virginia was an English colony and King George II (1683–1760) was the reigning monarch of Britain. England's American colonies used various devices to curry favor from the crown and one employed by several of the American colonies was to name counties in honor of the monarch or members of the monarch's family. On March 14, 1734, England's Princess Anne (1709–1759), the daughter of England's ruling monarch, King George II (1683–1760), married William IV, Prince of Orange (1711–1751). Princess Anne was a special princess, for she was the princess royal. It was also an important wedding for the king. It was the custom for English princesses to marry royalty but the king had a problem in selecting a mate for Princess Anne. Most of the fellow monarchs of King George II were Roman Catholics and Anglican England wanted no Catholic in the royal family. However a husband was found. A longer version of his name and title was William Charles Henry, Prince William IV of Orange & Stadtholder of the United Provinces (1711–1751). The prince had an even longer title with Nassau, Friesland Groningen and Guelderland inserted at appropriate intervals and he was also encumbered with physical deformity. John Van der Kiste's *King George II & Queen Caroline* describes Prince William IV as "almost a dwarf," possibly because of curvature of the spine or a tubercular condition. Prince William IV and his bride took up residence in Leeuwarden, Holland, but when Prince William joined the Holy Roman Emperor's army on the Rhine River, his homesick and pregnant wife returned to England. After much coaxing, Princess Anne reluctantly agreed to return to Holland to await the birth of her child with her husband but the pregnancy ended disastrously with no heir being born. In 1751 William IV, Prince of Orange, suffered increasingly

poor health, due in part to his twisted backbone, which culminated in a massive stroke. He died at the age of 40.

2852 *Page County*

John Page (1743–1808)—A native of Virginia and a graduate of the College of William & Mary here, Page became involved in Virginia's Revolutionary activities and served as a member of the Committee of Public Safety in 1775. He was Virginia's lieutenant-governor under Governor Patrick Henry (1736–1799) and a member of Virginia's constitutional convention. In 1779 John Page was a candidate to be Virginia's governor but he lost the election to Thomas Jefferson. Page later served in Virginia's house of burgesses and he represented Virginia in the House of Representatives of the first Congress of the United States of America. Subsequently elected to three consecutive one year terms as governor of Virginia, Page served in that office from December, 1802 to December, 1805. This county was created on March 30, 1831.

2853 *Patrick County*

Patrick Henry (1736–1799)—Henry was a native of Virginia and a lawyer. He served in the Virginia legislature, as governor of Virginia and as a delegate to the first and second Continental Congresses. Henry was one of America's key revolutionary leaders. He was a great orator and he is remembered for his call to arms against the British "Give me liberty or give me death." Henry opposed Virginia's ratification of the federal Constitution and his views played a role in the later adoption of the Bill of Rights. The first Virginia county to be named in his honor was Henry County, in southwestern Virginia, which was created in 1776 while Patrick Henry was serving as governor of Virginia. Patrick Henry owned some 10,000 acres of land in Henry County and lived in the county for a number of years. When this new county was carved from the western side of Henry County (in 1790 or 1791), it was also named in honor of Patrick Henry. The new county was named Patrick County. Today the two counties sit side by side in southwestern Virginia, just above the North Carolina border.

2854 *Pittsylvania County*

William Pitt, Earl of Chatham (1708–1778)—Pitt, an Englishman and the first earl of Chatham, was one of England's greatest and most famous statesmen. He was a member of parliament and held the positions of vice treasurer of Ireland and paymaster general of the forces. He became secretary of state and virtually prime minister in 1756, but in 1760 King George III took the throne and Pitt was forced to resign. In 1766 he formed a new ministry but served for only 15 months. Pittsylvania County was created in 1766 or 1767. Its name came from a combination of William Pitt's surname with the Latin word *sylva* which is translated as "woods," or "forest." After this county had been created, during 1770 and 1771, the Earl of Chatham became very popular on this side of the Atlantic for his opposition to the alleged right of the English parliament to tax American colonies without their consent. Pitt urged reconciliation between Britain and her American colonies. After the American Revolution began he favored any peace settlement that would keep the American colonies in the British empire.

2855 *Powhatan County*

Powhatan (–1618)– Powhatan was the chief of the large and powerful American Indian confederation, known as the Powhatan confederacy, whom the very early Virginia English colonists encountered soon after they founded the Jamestown settlement. Born about 1547 and named *Wahunsonacock*, this Indian chief came to be known as *Powhatan* by the Virginia colonists because that was the name of an Indian village at falls in the James River, near what is now Richmond, Virginia. Chief Powhatan inherited the confederated Algonquian tribes of tidewater Virginia from his father. Under Chief Powhatan, the alliance was strengthened and Powhatan came to rule a confederacy of about 8,000 Indians divided among some 32 bands. The confederacy had perhaps 200 villages. Powhatan is best remembered in history as the father of the Indian maiden, Pocahontas (–1617), who became friendly with Captain John Smith (–1631) and the other early Jamestown colonists and acted as an important emissary between them and her powerful father, Chief Powhatan. While Chief Powhatan lived, relations between the English colonists and his Indians were good. A few years after Powhatan's death, the Powhatan confederacy began attacking the colonists. This county was created in 1777.

2856 *Prince Edward County*

Prince Edward Augustus (1739–1767)– The year that this county was created is not certain but it was either 1752, 1753 or 1754, all of which were during the reign of England's King George II (1683–1760). England's American colonies used various devices to curry favor from the crown and one employed by several of the colonies was to name counties in honor of the monarch or members of the monarch's family and clearly that was the inspiration for this county's name. When this county was created, Prince Edward was a grandson of the reigning king of England, King George II. Prince Edward was a son of Frederick Louis (1707–1751) and Augusta of Saxe-Gotha (1719–1772). Frederick Louis had been Prince of Wales and heir-apparent to the English throne until his death in 1751. Two of his sons, Prince Edward Augustus (1739–1767) and Prince George (1738–1820), who later ruled as King George III, were placed in the hands of tutors about 1745. Annette Joelson's *England's Princes of Wales* tells us that "They were taught Latin, music, mathematics, fencing elocution, drawing and watercolor painting...." George was made prince of Wales, while in 1760 Edward Augustus was made duke of York and Albany. Edward Augustus never married. He died before his 29th birthday on September 17, 1767.

2857 *Prince George County*

Prince George of Denmark (1653–1708)– George was born in April, 1653, while his father, King Frederick III (1609–1670), was king of Denmark. He received some naval training and saw duty under arms. In 1674 efforts were made to place Prince George on the Polish throne but his aversion to Roman Catholicism caused the scheme to abort. In 1681 he visited England as a preliminary to his marriage to England's Princess Anne (1665–1714), which occurred in July, 1683. Prince George was disliked by England's king, William III, and when Princess Anne took the throne as Queen Anne in 1702, Prince George was denied the title of king. He did enjoy other prestigious titles including duke of Cumberland, generalissimo, lord high admiral and fellow of the Royal Society. Prince George had a mild and gentle temper. He loved his wife and they enjoyed a long and happy marriage. Prince George died of a severe asthmatic malady in 1708. This county in England's colony of Virginia was named in compliment to the throne of England. It is not clear exactly when this county was created but it was during the years 1700 through 1703. Prince George's wife, Anne, was crowned queen of England on April 23, 1702, and she had been heir-apparent to the English throne for several years prior to that.

2858 *Prince William County*

William Augustus, Duke of Cumberland (1721–1765)– It is not clear exactly when this county was created but most sources dealing with the history, geography and place names of Virginia show either 1730 or 1731. At that time, Virginia was an English colony and King George II (1683–1760) was the reigning monarch of Britain. England's American colonies used various devices to curry favor from the crown and one employed by several of the American colonies was to name counties in honor of the monarch or members of the monarch's family. William Augustus was a son of England's King George II. Born on April 15, 1721, William was made a royal duke and given the tittle Duke of Cumberland in July, 1726. Cumberland was educated for the navy but was permitted to follow his preference for the army and was given the rank of major-general in 1742. He was a rather poor general and his troops were defeated in several important actions on the European continent. His only significant victory was at home, in the British Isles, where he defeated Prince Charles Edward Stuart (1720–1788), the pretender to the thrones of Scotland and England. This victory took place at Culloden, Scotland, in 1746. The duke's name is shown in most works as William Augustus, but in some the form William August is used. Virginia's Cumberland County is also named for him.

2859 *Pulaski County*

Casimir Pulaski (1748–1779)– Pulaski was born in Lithuania and served in the Polish army. He came to America to assist the colonies as an officer in the Revolutionary War. He died in combat in that war during the siege of Savannah, Georgia. This county was created and named in his honor in 1839.

2860 *Rappahannock County*

Rappahannock River– This county is located in northern Virginia, on the east side of the Blue Ridge Mountains. It was created in 1833 and named for Virginia's Rappahannock River, which rises within its borders. The 212 mile-long Rappahannock flows southeast in Virginia and forms a long estuary, which empties into Chesapeake Bay. *Rappahannock* is an Indian name which has been translated to mean "the alternating stream," "stream with an ebb and flow" and "river of quick-rising water." About 1612 there was an attempt by the early English colonists of Virginia to rename this river Queen's River, in honor of Queen Anne (1574–1619), the queen consort of the reigning king of England, King James I (1566–1625). That name never caught on, in part because it had to compete with a third name, Pembroke River, by which some were calling the Rappahannock River because the Earl of Pembroke (1580–1630) had patented extensive lands along the Rappahannock. By the time Thomas Jefferson wrote his *Notes on the State of Virginia*, the river was called the Rappahannock. Jefferson said that the "Rappahannock affords four fathom water to Hobb's hole, and two fathom from thence to Fredericksburg." This is Virginia's second Rappahannock County. The first was created in 1656 but ceased to exist in 1691 or 1692 when Virginia's Essex County and Richmond County were created from it.

2861 *Richmond County*

Uncertain— This county was created in 1691 or 1692. Sources dealing with the history, geography and place names of Virginia indicate that the county may have been named for either Richmond, England, or for Charles Lennox, Duke of Richmond (1672–1723).

Richmond, England— Richmond, in Surrey County, England, not far from London, was the location of the favorite residence of Queen Elizabeth I (1533–1603). Now called Richmond upon Thames, it is one of the boroughs of Metropolitan London. Richmond had been the residence of England's monarch's since the time of King Edward I (1239–1307), although it was then called Sheen. After the castle at Sheen was destroyed by fire, it was rebuilt by King Henry VII (1457–1509) and the king changed Sheen's name to Richmond at that time. The name *Richmond* came from the Old French words *riche* and *mont*. The name meant "strong hill."

Charles Lennox, Duke of Richmond (1672–1723)— Charles Lennox, the first duke of Richmond, was one of the illegitimate sons of England's King Charles II. Richmond's mother was Louise Renee de Keroualle (1649–1734). Richmond's mother took him to France in 1685 and he was received with great honor there by the French king, Louis XIV (1638–1715), who persuaded Richmond's mother to have Richmond join the Roman Catholic Church. Richmond's mother, whose title was the

Duchess of Portsmouth, agreed and Charles Lennox was given instruction in the Catholic religion and he became a Catholic in 1685. The French king gave Charles Lennox important assignments in the French army and he served ably in that army. Charles Lennox left France to assist William of Orange (1650–1702) and Charles Lennox married Anne Bellasis. The couple had three children. In 1681 he was made governor of Dumbarton castle. Richmond renounced Catholicism and was converted to the Anglican Church on May 15, 1692. From 1693 to 1702 he was aide-de-camp in Flanders and in 1714 he was made lord of the bedchamber of King George I (1660–1727).

2862 *Roanoke County*

Roanoke River— Roanoke County, in southwestern Virginia, is adjacent to the well-known independent city of Roanoke but the county did not take its name from the city. Rather, the city was first incorporated with the name Big Lick and its name was later changed to Roanoke. Roanoke County was created in 1838 and named for the Roanoke River, which is formed by the confluence of forks in Montgomery County, just west of Roanoke County. The Roanoke flows east and southeast into North Carolina where it continues to flow in a southeastern direction until its waters reach Albemarle Sound, an inlet on the Atlantic Ocean. To reach the ocean, the Roanoke River travels 410 miles. The name now used as the name of this western Virginia county was first used in colonial America as the name of an island, Roanoke Island (now part of North Carolina), near the mouth of Roanoke River in Albemarle Sound. The name is of Indian origin but beyond that simple statement lies much uncertainty. Some say *Roanoke* derived from the Indians' name for their "white shells" or "shell money," others mention "tobacco," some say it is the surviving version of the name for the Indians who lived on Roanoke Island. Several sources indicate that the surviving *Roanoke* was based on a misunderstanding. These sources say that the sound that the English colonists heard and recorded (as *Roanoac*) was uttered by the Indians in response to a question but their answer was misunderstood by the Whites. Since the Indians had no written language, the present place name *Roanoke* was first written by Englishmen in the late 16th century, based on what they thought they heard and what they thought it meant.

2863 *Rockbridge County*

The county's celebrated natural bridge over Cedar Creek— About 70 miles west of Thomas Jefferson's home at Monticello lies Virginia's celebrated natural bridge spanning Cedar Creek. The bridge consists of limestone, 215 feet high, 93 feet long with width that varies from about 50 to 150 feet. One source estimates the average thickness of the bridge at 55 feet and another gives its weight as 36,000 tons. The Indians worshipped here and the young surveyor, George Washington, carved his initials in the stone. These initials were still visible in the late 1990's. Thomas Jefferson so loved the bridge that he purchased it for himself in 1774. Later, during Jefferson's term as our nation's president, he built a family cabin adjacent to the natural bridge. Virginia's natural bridge is open to visitors daily from 8:00 AM to dusk. This county was created in 1778 and named for the magnificent natural wonder within its borders. At that time the owner of the natural bridge was Thomas Jefferson.

2864 *Rockingham County*

Charles Watson-Wentworth, Marquis of Rockingham (1730–1782)— Charles Watson-Wentworth was born on May 13, 1730, at Wentworth Park, in England. He attended Westminster school and served in the English army against Scottish insurgents. Young Watson-Wentworth came from a family with good political connections and shortly after his 30th birthday he was given the highest honor of the English court, the Garter. In 1765 he became England's prime minister, while King George III was on the throne. As prime minister, he infuriated the king by securing the repeal of the Stamp act and softening the American colonies' grievances on matters of commerce. This term as prime minister lasted only from 1765 to 1766. However, sixteen years later, Rockingham returned as prime minister. His goals throughout much of this period from 1765 until his death on July 1, 1782, were rather extreme. These goals included resolution of the grievances of the American colonies, even if that meant the end of British sovereignty over of those colonies, sharply reduced power for the English monarch and, at all cost, avoidance of armed warfare with the American colonies. This county was created in 1778, while Virginia and the other American colonies were fighting for independence from England.

2865 *Russell County*

William Russell (1758–1825)— Russell was born in Culpeper County, Virginia, and he served in the army during the American Revolution. During that war, he participated in the American victory in the battle of King's Mountain in 1780 and he fought at the battle of Guilford Court House in 1781. In 1783 Russell immigrated across the mountains to Kentucky, which then was still part of Virginia. He served in the Virginia legislature and, according to one source, William Russell was the member of the Virginia house of delegates who introduced the legislation to create this county. The county was created in 1786. During the 1790's Russell participated in several expeditions against the Indians. When Kentucky was admitted to statehood, Russell served several terms in the Kentucky legislature. He subsequently served with distinction as an army officer in at the 1811 battle of Tippecanoe. In September, 1812, Russell replaced General William Henry Harrison as commander on the Indiana, Illinois and Missouri frontiers and he served with distinction during the War of 1812.

2866 *Scott County*

Winfield Scott (1786–1866)— A native of Virginia, Scott joined the U.S. army in 1808. His heroic service in the War of 1812 resulted in rapid promotions to brevet major-general. He later played an important military role during the 1832 nullification crisis in South Carolina and in actions against the Indians in Florida. He was general-in-chief of the United States army during the Mexican War. Scott was the Whig party's candidate for president in 1852 but he lost to Franklin Pierce. When the Civil War broke out, Scott remained loyal to the Union side despite his southern roots but he retired from the army in October, 1861, on account of age and ill health. This county was created in 1814, in recognition of this Virginia native's services to our nation during the War of 1812.

2867 *Shenandoah County*

Shenandoah River— Although the Shenandoah River is short (just 55 miles long) it flows through one of the more scenic areas of Virginia and West Virginia. The Shenandoah is formed by the junction of north and south forks in what is now Warren County, Virginia (but was still Shenandoah County when this county's name was chosen). The Shenandoah flows north-east, at a generally leisurely pace and crosses into the northeastern tip of West Virginia, where its waters widen and soon flow into the Potomac River. The acting chief executive, of England's colony of Virginia, Lieutenant-Governor Alexander Spotswood (1676–1740), viewed the Shenandoah from the Blue Ridge Mountains in 1716 and decided its name should be the Euphrates River. This new name never caught on and the Indians' ancient name, for the river, the Shenandoah, lives on today. This county was originally created in 1772 and named Dunmore County in honor of John Murray, Earl of Dunmore (1732–1809), who was then England's royal governor of Virginia. By 1775 Virginia's grievances against England had reached the point that Dunmore left office as Virginia's governor. This county's name was changed from Dunmore to Shenandoah by Virginia's legislature in 1777, in an act to become effective in 1778. Henry Howe's *Historical Collections of Virginia*, published in 1849 stated that in October, 1777, one of the delegates to the Virginia legislature from Dunmore County "stated that his constituents no longer wished to live in, or he to represent, a county bearing the name of such a tory; he therefore moved to call it Shenandoah, after the beautiful stream which passes through it."

2868 *Smyth County*

Alexander Smyth (1765–1830)— A native of Ireland, Smyth immigrated with his father to Virginia when he was seven or eight years old. By the time he was 20, he was the owner of a plantation in Botetourt County and he was licensed to practice law in 1789. Smyth served in Virginia's house of delegates on several occasions starting in 1792 and was a member of Virginia's senate in 1808 and 1809. Meanwhile, Smyth also served as an officer in the U.S. army from 1808 to 1813 and rose to the post of inspector general with the rank of brigadier-general. He then served again in the state house of delegates several times and represented Virginia in the U.S. House of Representatives from 1817 to 1825 and from 1827 until his death on April 17, 1830. This county was created and named in his honor less than two years later, on February 23, 1832.

2869 *Southampton County*

Southampton hundred, Virginia— Very early in the history of England's colony of Virginia there were political subdivisions, smaller than a counties, known as a hundreds. In England the term *hundred* meant an area inhabited by about one hundred families, or one able to provide one hundred fighting men. One of colonial Virginia's early hundreds was Southampton hundred, which had been named for Henry Wriothesley, Earl of Southampton (1573–1624) about the time that he was treasurer of the Virginia Company, in England. This county in Virginia was created more than a century later, in 1748 or 1749, and named for that early Southampton hundred.

Henry Wriothesley, Earl of Southampton (1573–1624)— This Englishman was a patron of William Shakespeare (1564–1616) and other dramatists and poets. On October 4, 1581, he became the third earl of Southampton. He served in the military at Cadiz and in the Azores. By 1601 he incurred the wrath of Queen Elizabeth I (1533–1603) and was imprisoned in the Tower of London and condemned to death. When Elizabeth died and King James I (1566–1625) came to the throne, Southampton was soon released and honors and titles were heaped upon him. He was made knight of the garter, recreated earl of Southampton (a title he had lost when he was in bad odor) and various other titles of little interest on this side of the Atlantic. However, he helped equip George Weymouth's expedition to Virginia in 1605, became a member of the Virginia Company's council in 1609 and was its treasurer from 1620 to 1624. Southampton commanded a troop of English volunteers in the Low Countries and died of a fever there, in Bergen-op-Zoom in November, 1624.

2870 *Spotsylvania County*

Alexander Spotswood (1676–1740)— Born in Tangier Africa, this Englishman entered the English army as an ensign in a regiment of foot soldiers, and advanced to the rank of lieutenant-colonel by the time he was wounded and captured at the battle of Blenheim. Spotswood was released in an exchange of prisoners and in 1710 he was appointed lieutenant-governor of England's colony of Virginia. He took office in June, 1710, as Virginia's resident chief executive. At that time Virginia's governor was George Hamilton, Earl of Orkney (1666–1737), but Hamilton remained in England while lieutenant-governors (and one acting governor) served him as Virginia's resident chief executives. Spotswood served 12 years as Virginia's chief executive and there were a number of clashes of wills during that period between Spotswood and Virginia's legislature. These disputes had little substance to them for matters of genuine importance were decided in England. Nevertheless, it was decided that Spotswood should be removed as governor in 1722 on account of his difficulties with the Virginia legislature. Spotsylvania County was created in 1720 or 1721, while Alexander Spotswood was serving as the chief executive of colonial Virginia. The county's name came from a combination of part of Spotswood's surname with the Latin word *sylva* which is translated as "woods," or "forest." Alexander Spotswood lived for a time in this Virginia county which had been named in his honor. About 1730 he was appointed deputy postmaster general for the American colonies. Promoted to major-general to serve in a British attack on Spanish South America, Spotswood died on June 7, 1740, at Annapolis, Maryland, before embarking for South America.

2871 *Stafford County*

Staffordshire, England— Most Virginia sources state that Stafford County was created in 1664 although a few cite 1666. All sources consulted (apart from one unreliable source) are agreed that this county in England's colony of Virginia was named for the county or shire of Stafford in western England. Staffordshire, England, was occupied by the Roman Empire and when the Romans left it was conquered by Mercia, Wessex and the Danes. During the Middle Ages Staffordshire was a remote and rather inaccessible part of England and even by the 19th century Staffordshire commanded little respect. The novelist Charles Dickens (1812–1870) described its county seat as "dead and dull." However Burton, on the Trent River here had such good water for brewers that it was exported as far as the Baltic by the mid-18th century. It was during the 19th century that the county began to come into its own, with a transportation system of canals and railroads exploiting coal and iron deposits in southern Staffordshire. This county was greatly impacted by the industrial revolution and its population in 1981 was given as 1,015,700.

2872 *Surry County*

Surrey County, England— This county in England's colony of Virginia was created in 1652 and named for the county of Surrey in southeastern England. The Virginia county's name omits the "e" contained in the English county's name. Surrey County in England has Sussex County

below it, on the English Channel and Kent County, to its east, denies it salt-water access on that side. Its name was Suthrige in A.D. 722, and evolved to Sudrie by A.D. 1086. "Southerly district" is the translation of all of these versions of the name and they refer to the geographic relation to Middlesex. The Thames River on Surrey County's northern border separates it from England's Middlesex County, so the translation is plausible.

2873 *Sussex County*

Sussex County, England— Sussex County, in southeastern England lies on the English Channel and at one time was one of the seven Anglo-Saxon kingdoms of Britain known as the Heptarchy. Because of its location, Sussex was a frequent landing area for French and other armies invading England. In 1066 the Normans started their successful invasion at Hastings, in Sussex County and over the next 500 years Sussex was subject to periodic invasions. These incidents resulted in Sussex dividing itself into six "rapes," each with its own stretch of coastline and its own castle. Later, when the Anglican Church became the state church of England, the citizens of Sussex avoided total capitulation and both Roman Catholicism and Puritanism claimed fair numbers of adherents in Sussex. The name *Sussex* derived from the name of the South Saxons, who lived there. The English names Essex, Middlesex and Sussex referred to the tribes of people who lived there, the East Saxons, Middle Saxons and South Saxons, respectively. These names were then used for the kingdoms that these people established and they have survived as English geographic names. Sussex County in England's colony of Virginia was created in 1753 or 1754.

2874 *Tazewell County*

Henry Tazewell (1753–1799)— A native of Virginia and a 1772 graduate of the College of William & Mary here, Tazewell studied law, was admitted to the bar and served in Virginia's colonial house of burgesses. He served as a judge on Virginia's general court from 1785 to 1793, and was its chief justice starting in 1789. Tazewell became a judge of the supreme court of appeals in 1793 but soon left that post to represent Virginia in the U.S. Senate, replacing John Taylor (1750–1824), who had resigned. Henry Tazewell served in the Senate from December 29, 1794, until his death, while the Senate was in session in

Philadelphia, on January 24, 1799. This county was created and named in his honor less than one year later, in December, 1799.

2875 *Warren County*

Joseph Warren (1741–1775)— A native of Massachusetts and a graduate of Harvard College, Warren practiced medicine in the Boston area. He was a member of the committee of safety and president *pro tempore* of the Massachusetts provincial congress. In June, 1775 he was commissioned a major-general and he died in combat a few days later at the battle of Bunker Hill. Most Virginia sources indicate that this county was created in 1836 but Charles M. Long's *Virginia County Names* shows 1837 as the year of its creation.

2876 *Washington County*

George Washington (1732–1799)— Washington was a native of Virginia. He served in Virginia's house of burgesses and became one of the colonies' leaders in opposition to British policies in America. He was a member of the first and second Continental Congresses and commander of all Continental armies in the Revolutionary War. Following victory in that war, Washington was elected to be the first president of the United States. This Virginia county was created in December, 1776. Several sources dealing with the history, geography and place names of Virginia state that this was the first county in our nation to be named in honor of George Washington and Virginia's historical highway marker #Z–244 goes farther in claiming that "This county was the first locality named for him." Both statements are false. Maryland's Washington County was created in September, 1776, and thus beat Virginia by three months in creating the first county named for the father of our country. J. Allen Neal's *Bicentennial History of Washington County, Virginia: 1776–1976* traces, in meticulous detail, the chronology of the creation and naming of Washington County, Virginia, to thoroughly dispel the notion that Virginia's Washington County came first.

2877 *Westmoreland County*

Westmoreland County, England— Conquered by the Roman empire in ancient times, this poor county in northwestern England with bleak hills among moors and lakes was not greatly coveted by others although its proximity to Scotland invited centuries of hostilities between England and Scotland for control of the area. After Scotland's King James VI (1566–1625) ascended to the throne of England as King James I, in 1603, that source of tension disappeared. During feudal times wealth was distributed very unevenly in Westmoreland, where the poor subsisted on land of poor fertility, while their lords erected no fewer than seven castles. Westmoreland's only municipality of any importance is Kendal at the southern end of the county. The county's name originally meant "district of the people living west of the moors," referring to the Pennine Mountains in north Yorkshire, the relatively huge neighbor of tiny Westmoreland, on its eastern border. Westmoreland County in England's colony of Virginia was created in 1653.

2878 Wise County

Henry A. Wise (1806–1876)— A native of Virginia and a lawyer, Wise graduated from college in Pennsylvania and began a law practice in Tennessee. Soon after his return to Virginia in 1830, he was elected to represent the state in the U.S. House of Representatives. He served in that body as a champion of states' rights from 1833 to 1844. Wise was our nation's minister to Brazil from 1844 to 1847. He was elected governor of Virginia in 1855 and served in that office from 1856 to 1860. On April 17, 1861, Virginia seceded from the federal Union and Henry A. Wise volunteered for and was appointed, on June 5, 1861, a brigadier-general in the army of the Confederate States of America. He served with distinction throughout the Civil War and was honored by being named a divisional commander, two days before the South's surrender at Appomattox, although he was never officially made a major-general. Henry A. Wise had been inaugurated as Virginia's governor on January 1, 1856, and this county was created and named in his honor just six weeks later, on February 16, 1856. The name Roane County had originally been proposed for this county in the legislature but that name was never officially adopted.

2879 Wythe County

George Wythe (1726–1806)— A native of Virginia, and a lawyer, Wythe taught law to a number of men who went on to greatness in our nation's history including Thomas Jefferson, James Monroe, John Marshall and Henry Clay. He served in Virginia's house of burgesses, represented Virginia from 1775 to 1777 in the Continental Congress and he was a signer of our nation's Declaration of Independence. Wythe represented Virginia at the 1787 convention which drafted the federal constitution and he was a member of Virginia's 1788 convention which ratified that federal constitution; in fact George Wythe was the convention member who moved that Virginia ratify the constitution. This county was created and named in his honor in late 1789 or 1790.

2880 York County

Uncertain— In 1634, when England's royal colony of Virginia was divided into eight original shires, or counties, one of the eight was named Charles River County. That name honored the reigning king of England, King Charles I (1600–1649). In 1643 this county's name was changed to York, but sources dealing with the history, geography and place names of Virginia are divided on whether the name York was bestowed in honor of James (1633–1701), a son of King Charles I (1600–1649), who was still the king of England in 1643, or in honor of Yorkshire, England. Several of these Virginia sources admit that the namesake is uncertain. James had been proclaimed duke of York at the court gates shortly after his birth. This title was bestowed on him again by official patent on January 27, 1643, and he later came to England's throne as James II.

King James II (1633–1701)— James was the second surviving son of England's King Charles I (1600–1649). When James' father died, his elder brother, Charles ascended to the throne as King Charles II (1630–1685). In 1664 King Charles II made an enormous grant of land in North America (all north of Virginia) to his brother, who then was the duke of both York and Albany. The duke was awarded more power over his domain than any other English proprietor. Although King Charles II had many children, none of them were legitimate so when King Charles II died in 1685, his brother, James, became king of England as King James II. About 1673 James had professed his Catholicism and this spelled his eventual downfall as king. In 1689 the throne passed to King William III (1650–1702), who ruled as joint sovereign with his wife, Queen Mary II (1662–1694). Mary was a daughter of King James II. The former King James II devoted the final years of his life to religious exercises.

Yorkshire, England— Lying about midway between London and Edinburgh, Scotland, with a population of several million, the city of York and the county of Yorkshire, in England, represent one of England's most important metropolitan areas. Yorkshire borders on the North Sea and extends almost to the Irish Sea. The Roman Empire conquered the area and built a strategic fortress here about A.D. 72. Remains of this fortress can still be seen. The Yorkshire plain is fertile for agriculture and the West Riding area is rich in coal deposits. The Danes captured York in A.D. 867 and its present name came from their name Yorvick. York was later subjugated by the West Saxons and in 1066 it fell to the Norman invaders from France.

REFERENCES

Ackerly, Mary Denham, & Lula Eastman Jeter Parker. *Our Kin: The Genealogies of Some of the Early Families Who Made History in the Founding & Development of Bedford County, Virginia*. Harrisonburg, Virginia, C. J. Carrier Co., 1976.

Adams, Evelyn Taylor. *The Courthouse in Virginia Counties: 1634–1776*. Warrenton, Virginia, The Fauquier Democrat, 1966

Addington, Luther F. *History of Wise County*. Bicentennial Committee of Wise County, Virginia, 1956.

Addington, Robert M. *History of Scott County, Virginia*. Kingsport, Tennessee, Kingsport Press, Inc., 1932.

Agee, Helene Barret. *Facets of Goochland, Virginia County's History*. Richmond, Dietz Press, Inc., 1962.

Agee, Helene Barret. "Historical Sketch." *Goochland County Historical Society*, Vol. 1, No. 1. Spring, 1969.

Ailsworth, Timothy S., et al. *Charlotte County: Rich Indeed*. Charlotte County, Virginia, Charlotte County Board of Supervisors, 1979.

Allstrom, C. M. *Dictionary of Royal Lineage in Europe & Other Countries*. Chicago, Press of S. Th. Almberg, 1902.

American Heritage, Vol. 11, No. 4. June, 1960.

Andrews, Allen. *The Royal Whore: Barbara Villiers, Countess of Castlemaine*. Philadelphia, Chilton Book Co., 1970.

Bagby, Alfred. *King & Queen County, Virginia*. New York, Neale Publishing Co., 1908.

Barbour, Philip L. "Chickahominy Place Names in Captain John Smith's *True Relations*." *Names: Journal of the American Name Society*, Vol. 15, No. 3. Potsdam, New York: September, 1967.

Barbour, Philip L. "The Earliest Reconnaissance of the Chesapeake Bay Area."

Virginia Magazine of History & Biography, Vol. 79, No. 3. Richmond: July, 1971.

Barrett, Theodosia. *The Heritage of Russell County, Virginia: 1786–1986.*

Barrett, Theodosia Wells. *Russell County: A Confederate Breadbasket.* 1981.

Battle, Kemp P. "Glimpses of History in the Names of Our Counties." *North Carolina Booklet,* Vol. 6. July, 1906.

Battle, Kemp P. "North Carolina County Names." *The Magazine of History,* Vol. 7, No. 4. New York: April, 1908.

Bell, Edith Rathbun, & William L. Heartwell. *Brunswick Story: A History of Brunswick County.* Lawrenceville, Virginia, Brunswick Times-Gazette, 1957.

Bell, Landon C. *The Old Free State: A Contribution to the History of Lunenburg County & Southside Virginia.* Richmond, William Byrd Press, Inc., 1927.

Bickley, George W. L. *History of the Settlement & Indian Wars of Tazewell County, Virginia.* Parsons, West Virginia, McClain Printing Co., 1974.

Billings, Warren M., et al. *Colonial Virginia: A History.* White Plains, New York, KTO Press, 1986.

Bland County Centennial Corporation. *History of Bland County, Virginia.* Radford, Virginia, Commonwealth Press, 1961.

Boatner, Mark M. *Encyclopedia of the American Revolution.* Mechanicsburg, Pennsylvania, Stackpole Books, 1994.

Boddie, John B. *Colonial Surry.* Baltimore, Genealogical Publishing Co., 1959.

Boogher, William F. *Overwharton Parish Register: 1720–1760: Old Stafford County, Virginia.* Washington, D.C., Saxton Printing Co., 1899.

Bradshaw, Herbert C. *History of Prince Edward County, Virginia.* Richmond, Dietz Press, Inc., 1955.

Bridenbaugh, Carl. *Jamestown: 1544–1699.* New York, Oxford University Press, 1980.

Bristol, Roger P. "Greene County Place Names." *Virginia Place Name Society,* Occasional Paper No. 17. Charlottesville: June, 1974.

Brooke, John. *King George III.* New York, McGraw-Hill Book Co., 1972.

Brown, Douglas S. *Sketches of Greensville County, Virginia.* Emporia, Virginia, Riparian Woman's Club, 1968.

Buckingham County Bi-Centennial: 1761–1961. Buckingham Central High School, 1961.

Burrell, Charles E. *A History of Prince Edward County, Virginia.* Richmond, Williams Printing Co., 1922.

Burton, Lewis W. *Annals of Henrico Parish.* Richmond, 1904.

Campbell, T. E. *Colonial Caroline: A History of Caroline County, Virginia.* Richmond, Dietz Press, Inc., 1954.

Cannon, John. *The Oxford Companion to British History.* Oxford, Oxford University Press, 1997.

Carrington, J. Cullen. *Charlotte County, Virginia.* Richmond, Hermitage Press, Inc., 1907.

Carrington, Wirt J. *A History of Halifax County, Virginia.* Richmond, Appeals Press, Inc., 1924.

Cartmell, T. K. *Shenandoah Valley Pioneers & Their Descendants: A History of Frederick County, Virginia.* Berryville, Virginia, Chesapeake Book Co., 1963.

Chandler, J. A. C. *Makers of Virginia History.* New York, Silver, Burdett & Co., 1904.

Cheney, John L. *North Carolina Manual: 1977.* Raleigh.

Clark, Annye B., & Catherine Smith Arrington. *History of Prince William County.* Prince William County, Virginia School Board, 1933.

Clement, Maud Carter. *The History of Pittsylvania County, Virginia.* Lynchburg, Virginia, J. P. Bell Co., Inc., 1929.

Cocke, Charles F. *Parish Lines: Diocese of Southern Virginia.* Richmond, Virginia State Library, 1964.

Cocke, Charles F. *Parish Lines: Diocese of Southwestern Virginia.* Richmond, Virginia State Library, 1960.

Cocke, Charles F. *Parish Lines: Diocese of Virginia.* Richmond, Virginia State Library, 1967.

Cocke, William R. *Hanover County Chancery Wills & Notes.* Ann Arbor, Michigan, Edwards Brothers, Inc., 1940.

Connelly, Thomas L. *Discovering the Appalachians.* Harrisburg, Pennsylvania, Stackpole Books, 1968.

Cook, Petronelle. *Queen Consorts of England: The Power Behind the Throne.* New York, Facts On File, Inc., 1993.

Corbitt, David L. *The Formation of North Carolina Counties: 1663–1943.* Raleigh, State Department of Archives & History, 1950.

Cox, Edwin. "Gleanings of Fluvanna History." *Bulletin of the Fluvanna County Historical Society,* Nos. 2 & 3. Palmyra, Virginia: September, 1966.

Cox, Edwin P. *A Brief Outline of Some Salient Facts Relating to the History of Chesterfield County, Virginia.* 1936.

Cox, Virginia D., & Willie T. Weathers. *Old Houses of King & Queen County, Virginia.* Richmond, Whittet & Shepperson, 1973.

Cridlin, William B. *A History of Colonial Virginia: The First Permanent Colony in America: To Which is Added the Genealogy of the Several Shires & Counties.* Richmond, Williams Printing Co., 1923.

Crittenden, Charles C., & Dan Lacy. *The Historical Records of North Carolina.* Raleigh, North Carolina Historical Commission, 1938.

Crouch, Kenneth E. "Bedford and Its Namesakes." *Bedford Democrat,* Bedford, Virginia, July 29, 1954.

Crozier, William A. *Spotsylvania County Records: 1721–1000.* Baltimore, Southern Book Co., 1955.

Crush, Charles W. *The Montgomery County Story: 1776–1957.* 1957.

Cutter, William R. *Historic Homes and Places and Genealogical and Personal Memoirs Relating to the Families of Middlesex County, Massachusetts.* New York, Lewis Historical Publishing Co., 1908.

Dabney, Virginius. *Virginia: The New Dominion: A History from 1607 to the Present.* Charlottesville, University Press of Virginia, 1971.

Daniel, J. R. V. *A Hornbook of Virginia History.* Richmond, Division of History of the Virginia Department of Conservation & Development, 1949.

Delderfield, Eric R. *Kings & Queens of England.* New York, Weathervane Books, 1978.

Dodd, Virginia Anderton. *Henry County, Virginia Marriage Bonds: 1778–1849.* Baltimore, Genealogical Publishing Co., Inc., 1976.

Drake, Samuel A. *Old Landmarks & Historic Fields of Middlesex.* Boston, Roberts Brothers, 1888.

Early, R. H. *Campbell Chronicles & Family Sketches: Embracing the History of Campbell County, Virginia: 1782–1926.* Lynchburg, Virginia, J. P. Bell Co., 1927.

1850 Census of Highland County, Virginia. Richmond, Mrs. Emma Robertson Matheny, 1966.

Ekwall, Eilert. *The Concise Oxford Dictionary of English Place-Names.* Oxford, Oxford University Press, 1960.

Encyclopaedia Britannica. Chicago, Encyclopaedia Britannica, Inc., 1971.

Ewell, Alice M. *A Virginia Scene: Or Life in Old Prince William.* Lynchburg, Virginia, J. P. Bell Co., Inc., 1931.

Fairfax County in Virginia, History Program, Office of Comprehensive Planning, Fairfax County, Virginia, 1974.

Falkus, Christopher. *The Life & Times of Charles II.* Garden City, New York, Doubleday & Co., 1972.

Faragher, John M. *The Encyclopedia of Colonial & Revolutionary America.* New York, Facts On File, 1990.

Farrar, Emmie Ferguson & Emilee Hines. *Old Virginia Houses Harbors.* Charlotte, North Carolina, Delmar Publishing, 1984.

Fauquier County, Virginia: 1759–1959. Warrenton, Virginia, Virginia Publishing Inc., 1959.

Ferris, Robert G. *Signers of the Declaration.* Washington, D.C., National Park Service, United States Department of the Interior, 1973.

Fields, Bettye-Lou, & Jene Hughes. *Grayson County: A History in Words & Pictures.* Independence, Virginia, Grayson County Historical Society, 1976.

Fishwick, Marshall W. *Rockbridge County, Virginia.* Richmond, Whittet & Shepperson, 1952.

Fluvanna County Sketchbook. Richmond, Whittet & Shepperson, 1963.

Fraser, Antonia. *Faith & Treason: The Story of the Gunpowder Plot.* New York, Doubleday, 1996.

Fraser, Antonia. *The Lives of the Kings & Queens of England.* London, Weidenfeld & Nicolson, 1975.

Fraser, Antonia. *Royal Charles: Charles II and the Restoration.* New York, Alfred A. Knopf, 1980.

Gannett, Henry. *The Origin of Certain Places Names in the United States.* Williamstown, Massachusetts, Corner House Publishers, 1978.

Gayle, T. Benton. "King George County of the Northern Neck of Virginia." *Northern Neck of Virginia Historical Magazine,* Vol. 8, No. 1. Montross, Virginia: December, 1958.

Gayle, T. Benton, & Virginia P. Gayle. "Some Historical Highlights of Colonial Stafford County." *Northern Neck of Virginia Historical Magazine,* Vol. 16, No. 1. Montross, Virginia: December, 1966.

Geddes, Jean. *Fairfax County: Historical Highlights from 1607.* Middleburg, Virginia, Denlinger's, 1967.

Gilliam, Rosa, et al. *Campbell County Geography Supplement.* Campbell County School Board, 1925.

Gills, Mary L. *It Happened at Appomattox.* Richmond, Dietz Press, Inc., 1948.

Givens, Lula Porterfield. *Highlights in the Early History of Montgomery County, Virginia.* Pulaski Virginia, B. D. Smith & Bros., Printers, Inc., 1975.

Gordon, Armistead C. *In the Picturesque Shenandoah Valley.* Richmond, Garrett & Massie, Inc., 1930.

Gott, John K. *Abstracts of Fauquier County, Virginia: Wills, Inventories & Accounts: 1759–1800.* Baltimore, Genealogical Publishing Co., Inc., 1980.

Gray, Mary Wiatt. *Gloucester County, Virginia.* Richmond, Cottrell & Cooke, Inc., 1936.

Green, Raleigh T. *Genealogical & Historical Notes on Culpeper County, Virginia.* Baltimore, Southern Book Co., 1958.

Greenwood, Alice Drayton. *Lives of the Hanoverian Queens of England.* London, George Bell & Sons, 1909.

Groome, H. C. *Fauquier During the Proprietorship.* Richmond, Old Dominion Press, 1927.

Gwathmey, John H. *Historical Register of Virginians in the Revolution.* Richmond, Dietz Press, 1938.

Gwathmey, John H. *Twelve Virginia Counties: Where the Western Migration Began.* Richmond, Dietz Press, 1937.

Hadfield, Kathleen Halverson. *Historical Notes on Amelia County, Virginia.* Amelia, Virginia, Amelia County Historical Committee, 1982.

Hagemann, James. *The Heritage of Virginia: The Story of Place Names in the Old Dominion.* Norfolk, Donning Co., 1986.

Hall, Virginius C. *Portraits in the Collection of the Virginia Historical Society.* Charlottesville, University Press of Virginia, 1981.

Hammack, James W. *Kentucky and the Second American Revolution: The War of 1812.* Lexington, Kentucky, University Press of Kentucky, 1976.

Hanson, Raus M. *Virginia Place Names: Derivations: Historical Uses.* Verona, Virginia, McClure Press, 1969.

Harman, John N. *Annals of Tazewell County, Virginia.* Richmond, W. C. Hill Printing Co., 1922.

Harris, Malcom H. *History of Louisa County, Virginia.* Richmond, Dietz Press, 1936.

Harrison, Fairfax. *Landmarks of Old Prince William: A Study of Origins in Northern Virginia.* Berryville, Virginia, Chesapeake Book Co., 1964.

Haswell, Jock. *James II.* New York, St. Martin's Press, 1972.

Hatton, Ragnhild. *George I: Elector & King.* Cambridge, Massachusetts, Harvard University Press, 1978.

Hawkyard, Alasdair. *The Counties of Britain: A Tudor Atlas by John Speed.* London, England, Pavilion Books, Ltd., 1995.

Head, James W. *History & Comprehensive Description of Loudoun County, Virginia.* Barcroft, Virginia, Park View Press, 1908.

Hibbert, Christopher. *Charles I.* London, Weidenfeld & Nicolson, 1968.

Hiden, Martha W. *How Justice Grew: Virginia Counties: An Abstract of Their Formation.* Williamsburg, Virginia 350th Anniversary Celebration Corporation, 1957.

Hill, Judith Parks America. *A History of Henry County, Virginia.* Baltimore, Regional Publishing Co., 1983.

Historic Arlington. Arlington, Virginia, Arlington County Bicentennial Commission, 1976.

Hite, Mary E. *My Rappahannock Story Book.* Richmond, Dietz Press, Inc., 1950.

Hodge, Frederick W. *Handbook of American Indians North of Mexico.* Totowa, New Jersey, Rowman & Littlefield, 1975.

Hoffman, Ross, J. S. *The Marquis: A Study of Lord Rockingham: 1730–1782.* New York, Fordham University Press, 1973.

A Hornbook of Virginia History. Richmond, Virginia State Library, 1965.

Howe, Henry. *Historical Collections of Virginia.* Charleston, South Carolina, W. R. Babcock, 1849.

Hutton, Ronald. *Charles the Second: King of England, Scotland & Ireland.* Oxford, Clarendon Press, 1989.

Jackson, Ronald V., & Gary R. Teeples. *Virginia 1800: Accomack County Census Index.* Bountiful, Utah, Accelerated Indexing Systems, Inc., 1976.

Jefferson, Mary Armstrong. *Old Homes & Buildings in Amelia County, Virginia.* Amelia, Virginia, 1964.

Jefferson, Thomas. *Notes on the State of Virginia.* New York, H. W. Derby, 1861.

Joelson, Annette. *England's Princes of Wales.* New York, Dorset Press, 1966.

Johnson, Charles A. *A Narrative History of Wise County, Virginia.* Johnson City, Tennessee, Overmountain Press, 1988.

Johnson, F. Roy. *Legends & Myths of North Carolina's Roanoke-Chowan Area.* Murfreesboro, North Carolina, 1962.

Johnson, Michael G. *The Native Tribes of North America.* New York, MacMillan Publishing Co., 1994.

Johnson, Thomas C. "How Albemarle Got Its Name." *Magazine of Albemarle County History,* Vol. 16. Charlottesville: 1957–1958.

Jones, Mary Stevens. *An 18th Century Perspective: Culpeper County.* Culpeper, Virginia, Culpeper Historical Society, Inc., 1976.

Jones, Richard L. *Dinwiddie County.* Richmond, Whittet & Shepperson, 1976.

Joyner, Mrs. Maude Adkins. *Story of Historic Sites & People of Chesterfield County, Virginia.* 1950.

Joyner, Ulysses P. *The First Settlers of Orange County, Virginia.* Baltimore, Gateway Press, Inc., 1987.

Kagey, Deedie. *When Past Is Prologue: A History of Roanoke County.* Roanoke, Virginia, Roanoke County Sesquicentennial Committee, 1988.

Kegley, F. B. *Kegley's Virginia Frontier.* Roanoke, Virginia, Southwest Virginia Historical Society, 1938.

Kegley, Mary B., & F. B. Kegley. *Early Adventures on the Western Waters: The New River of Virginia in Pioneer Days.* Orange, Virginia, Green Publishers, Inc., 1980.

Kenny, Hamill. "The Origin & Meaning of the Indian-Place Names of Maryland." Ph.D. Thesis, Theodore R. McKeldin Library, University of Maryland, College Park, Maryland, 1950.

Kenyon, J. P. *Dictionary of British History*. Ware, England, Wordsworth Editions, Ltd., 1992.

King, J. Estelle Stewart. *Abstracts of Wills, Inventories & Administration Accounts of Loudoun County, Virginia: 1757–1800*. Baltimore, Genealogical Publishing Co., Inc., 1979.

Kleber, John E. *The Kentucky Encyclopedia*. Lexington, Kentucky, University Press of Kentucky, 1992.

Knorr, Catherine Lindsay. *Marriage Bonds & Ministers' Returns of Charlotte County, Virginia: 1764–1815*. Pine Bluff, Arkansas, Perdue Co., 1951.

Knorr, Catherine Lindsay. *Marriage Bonds & Ministers' Returns of Greensville County, Virginia: 1781–1825*. 1955.

Knorr, Catherine Lindsay. *Marriage Bonds & Ministers' Returns of Halifax County, Virginia: 1753–1800*. Pine Bluff, Arkansas, Perdue Co., 1957.

Knorr, Catherine Lindsay. *Marriages of Culpeper County, Virginia: 1781–1815*. 1954.

Langguth, A. J. *Patriots: The Men Who Started the American Revolution*. New York, Simon & Schuster, 1988.

Lanningham, Anne Wynn. *Early Settlers of Lee County, Virginia & Adjacent Counties*. Greensboro, North Carolina, Media, Inc., 1977.

Lee, Dorothy Ellis. *A History of Arlington County, Virginia*. Richmond, Dietz Press, Inc., 1946.

Leland, J. A. C. "Indian Names in Missouri." *Names: Journal of the American Name Society*, Vol. 1, No. 4. Berkeley: December, 1953.

Leonard, Cynthia Miller. *The General Assembly of Virginia: July 30, 1619–January 11, 1978*. Richmond, Virginia State Library, 1978.

Leslie, Louise. *Tazewell County*. Radford, Virginia, Commonwealth Press, Inc., 1982.

Lewis, Samuel. *Topographical Dictionary of England*. London, S. Lewis & Co., 1842.

Lofts, Norah. *Queens of England*. Garden City, New York, Doubleday & Co., Inc., 1977.

Long, Charles M. *Virginia County Names*. New York, Neale Publishing Co., 1908.

Loth, Calder. *The Virginia Landmarks Register*. Charlottesville, University Press of Virginia, 1986.

Louisa County and the War Between the States. Louisa County Centennial Committee.

Luther, Roslyn, & Edwin C. Luther. *Governors of Virginia: 1776–1974*. Accomac, Virginia, Eastern Shore News, Inc., 1974.

Lutz, Francis Earle. *Chesterfield: An Old Virginia County*. Richmond, William Byrd Press, Inc., 1954.

Lutz, Francis Earle. *The Prince George-Hopewell Story*. Richmond, William Byrd Press, Inc., 1957.

McAllister, Joan Graham. *A Brief History of Bath County, Virginia*. Staunton, Virginia, McClure Co., Inc., 1920.

McCague, James. *The Cumberland*. New York, Holt, Rinehart & Winston, 1973.

McCarthy, Eugene J. *The View from Rappahannock*. McLean, Virginia, EPM Publications, Inc., 1984.

McCarthy, Justin. *The Reign of Queen Anne*. London, Chatto & Windus, 1902.

McCary, Ben C. *Indians in Seventeenth Century Virginia*. Williamsburg, Virginia 350th Anniversary Celebration Corporation, 1957.

MacDonald, Rose M. E. *Proceedings of the Clarke County Historical Association*. Stephens City, Virginia, Commercial Press, 1985.

McHenry, Robert. *Webster's American Military Biographies*. New York, Dover Publications, Inc., 1978.

Maloney, Eugene A. *A History of Buckingham County*. Waynesboro, Charles F. McClung Printer, Inc., 1976.

Manahan, John E. "Analysis of Virginia Place-Names As to Origin." *Virginia Place Name Society*, Occasional Paper No. 3. Charlottesville: December, 1961.

Manarin, Louis H., & Clifford Dowdey. *The History of Henrico County*. Charlottesville, University Press of Virginia, 1984.

The Marriage License Bonds of Northampton County, Virginia. Onancock, Virginia, Stratton & Nottingham, 1929.

Masters, Brian. *The Mistresses of Charles II*. London, Blond & Briggs, Ltd., 1979.

Mid-Atlantic Tour Book. Heathrow, Florida, AAA Publishing, 1999.

Miller, Mary R. *Place-Names of the Northern Neck of Virginia*. Richmond, Virginia State Library, 1983.

Miller, Mary R. "Place-Names of the Northern Neck of Virginia: A Proposal for a Theory of Place-Naming." *Names: Journal of the American Name Society*, Vol. 24, No. 1. Potsdam, New York: March, 1976.

Mills, A.D. *A Dictionary of English Place-Names*. Oxford, Oxford University Press, 1991.

Mitchell, Beth. *Beginning at a White Oak: Patents & Northern Neck Grants of Fairfax County, Virginia*. McGregor & Werner, 1977.

Moore, John H. *Albemarle: Jefferson's County: 1727–1976*. Charlottesville, University Press of Virginia, 1976.

Morrill, Charles. "Letters to the Editor." *New York Times*, August 5, 1992.

Morris, Shirley. *The Pelican Guide to Virginia*. Gretna, Louisiana, Pelican Publishing Co., 1981.

Morrison, Charles. *The Fairfax Line: A Profile in History & Geography*. Parsons, West Virginia, McClain Printing Co., 1970.

Morton, Oren F. *Annals of Bath County, Virginia*. Staunton, Virginia, McClure Co., Inc., 1917.

Morton, Oren F. *A Centennial History of Alleghany County, Virginia*. Dayton, Virginia, J. K. Ruebush Co., 1923.

Morton, Oren F. *A History of Highland County, Virginia*. Baltimore, Regional Publishing Co., 1972.

Moule, Thomas. *The County Maps of Old England*. London, Studio Editions, 1990.

Murray, Jane. *The Kings & Queens of England*. New York, Charles Scribner's Sons, 1974.

Neal, J. Allen. *Bicentennial History of Washington County, Virginia: 1776–1976*. Dallas, Texas, Taylor Publishing Co., 1977.

Neale, Gay. *Brunswick County, Virginia: 1720–1975*. Richmond, Whittet & Shepperson, 1975.

Netherton, Nan, et al. *Fairfax County, Virginia: A History*. Fairfax, Virginia, Fairfax County Board of Supervisors, 1978.

Norris, Robert O. "Some Unusual Happenings in the Colonial Life of Lancaster County." *Northern Neck of Virginia Historical Magazine*, Vol. 8, No. 1. Montross, Virginia: December, 1958.

Norris, Walter B. *Westmoreland County, Virginia: 1653–1983*. Montross, Virginia, Westmoreland County Board of Supervisors, 1983.

"Notes & Queries: Mathews County: Origin of Its Name." *Virginia Magazine of History & Biography*, Vol. 3. Richmond: 1896.

Nuckolls, B. F. *Pioneer Settlers of Grayson County, Virginia*. Bristol, Tennessee, King Printing Co., 1914.

Parramore, Thomas C. *Southampton County, Virginia*. Charlottesville, University Press of Virginia, 1978.

Paullin, Charles O. *Atlas of the Historical Geography of the United States*. Carnegie Institution of Washington and the American Geographical Society of New York, 1932.

Pedigo, Virginia G., & Lewis G. Pedigo. *History of Patrick & Henry Counties, Virginia*. Baltimore, Regional Publishing Co., 1977.

Pendleton, William C. *History of Tazewell County & Southwest Virginia: 1748–1920*. Richmond, W. C. Hill Printing Co., 1920.

Percy, Alfred. *The Amherst County Story*. Madison Heights, Virginia, Percy Press, 1961.

Percy, Alfred. *Old Place Names: West Central Piedmont & Blue Ridge Mountains*. Madison Heights, Virginia, Percy Press, 1950.

Peters, Margaret T. *A Guidebook to Virginia's Historical Markers*. Charlottesville, University Press of Virginia, 1985.

Peyton, J. Lewis. *History of Augusta County, Virginia*. Staunton, Virginia, Samuel M. Yost & Son, 1882.

Pine, L. G. *Princes of Wales*. Rutland, Vermont, Charles E. Tuttle Co., Inc., 1970.

Powell, William S. *The North Carolina Gazetteer*. Chapel Hill, University of North Carolina Press, 1968.

Presgraves, James S. *Wythe County Chapters*. Wytheville, Virginia, 1972.

Price, Edward T. *Dividing the Land: Early American Beginnings of Our Private Property Mosaic*. Chicago, University of Chicago Press, 1995.

Purcell, L. Edward. *Who Was Who in the American Revolution*. New York, Facts On File, Inc., 1993.

Reaney, P. H. *The Origin of English Place-Names*. London, Routledge & Kegan Paul, 1960.

Riley, Edward M. "Governor Gooch: A Faithful Trustee for the Public Good." *Goochland County Historical Society Magazine*, Vol. 6, No. 1. Goochland, Virginia: Spring, 1974.

Riordan, John L. "Albemarle in 1815: Notes of Christopher Daniel Ebeling." *Magazine of Albemarle County History*, Vol. 12. Charlottesville: 1951–1952.

Robinson, Morgan P. "Virginia Counties: Those Resulting from Virginia Legislation." *Bulletin of the Virginia State Library*, Vol. 9. Richmond: 1916.

Rogers, P. Burwell. "The First Names of Virginia." *Virginia Place Name Society*, Occasional Paper New Series No. 2. Charlottesville: February, 1967.

Rogers, P. Burwell. "Indian Names in Tidewater Virginia." *Names: Journal of the American Name Society*, Vol. 4, No. 3. Orinda, California: September, 1956.

Rogers, P. Burwell. "Virginia Counties." *Virginia Place Name Society*, Occasional Paper No. 16. Charlottesville: October, 1972.

Roller, David C., & Robert W. Twyman. *The Encyclopedia of Southern History*. Baton Rouge, Louisiana State University Press, 1979.

Rose, C. B. *Arlington County, Virginia: A History*. Baltimore, Maryland, Port City Press, Inc., 1976.

Ryland, Charles H. "Richmond County." *Northern Neck of Virginia Historical Magazine*, Vol. 17, No. 1. Montross, Virginia: December, 1967.

Ryland, Elizabeth Lowell. *Richmond County, Virginia*. Warsaw, Virginia, Richmond County Board of Supervisors, 1976.

Salmon, Emily J. *A Hornbook of Virginia History*. Richmond, Virginia State Library, 1983.

Scheel, Eugene M. *Culpeper: A Virginia County's History Through 1920*. Culpeper, Virginia, Culpeper County Historical Society, Inc., 1982.

Sharpe, Bill. *A New Geography of North Carolina*. Raleigh, North Carolina, Sharpe Publishing Co., 1954.

Slaughter, James B. *Settlers, Southerners, Americans: The History of Essex County, Virginia: 1608–1984*. Salem, West Virginia, Don Mills, Inc., 1985.

Smith, Conway H. *The Land That Is Pulaski County*. Pulaski, Virginia, Edmonds Printing, Inc., 1981.

Smith, Margaret Vowell. *Virginia: 1492–1892*. Washington, W. H. Lowdermilk & Co., 1893.

Some Eminent Sons of Orange: Report & Address: Portrait Day at Orange Court House, August 14, 1919. Gordonsville, Virginia, Orange County News Print, 1919.

Spuler, Bertold. *Rulers & Governments of the World*. New York, Bowker, 1977.

State Historical Markers of Virginia. Richmond, Virginia Department of Conservation & Development, 1948.

State Historical Markers of Virginia: Listing the Inscriptions on All Such Markers on the Principal Highways of Virginia, with Supplementary Data. Make America Better Committee of the Virginia Association of Realtors, 1975.

Stember, Sol. *Bicentennial Guide to the American Revolution*. New York, Saturday Review Press, 1974.

Stewart, George R. *American Place-Names*. New York, Oxford University Press, 1970.

Stewart, George R. *Names on the Land*. New York, Random House, 1945.

Stoner, Robert D. *A Seed-Bed of the Republic: A Study of the Pioneers of the Upper (Southern) Valley of Virginia*. Kingsport, Tennessee, Kingsport Press, Inc., 1962.

"The Story Behind County Names." *Weston's Record*, Dalton, Massachusetts, Byron Weston Company.

Stoutenburgh, John. *Dictionary of the American Indian*. New York, Bonanza Books, 1990.

Strickler, Harry M. *A Short History of Page County, Virginia*. Richmond, Dietz Press, Inc., 1952.

Summers, Lewis P. *History of Southwest Virginia: 1746–1786*. Richmond, J. L. Hill Printing Co., 1903.

Sweeny, Lenora Higginbotham. *Amherst County, Virginia in the Revolution*. Lynchburg, Virginia, J. P. Bell Co., 1951.

Sweeny, William M. *Wills of Rappahannock County, Virginia: 1656–1692*.

Taft, William H., III. *County Names: An Historical Perspective*. National Association of Counties, 1982.

Tanner, Douglas W. "Madison County Place Names." *Virginia Place Name Society*, Occasional Publication No. 21. Charlottesville: 1978.

Taube, Edward. "Tribal Names Related with Algonkin." *Names: Journal of the American Name Society*, Vol. 3, No. 2. Berkeley: June, 1955.

Templeman, Eleanor Lee. *Arlington Heritage*. Arlington, Virginia, 1959.

Tompkins, Edmund P. *Rockbridge County, Virginia*. Richmond, Whittet & Shepperson, 1952.

Tompkins, E. P., & J. Lee Davis. *The Natural Bridge and Its Historical Surroundings*. Natural Bridge, Virginia, Natural Bridge of Virginia, Inc., 1939.

Trease, Geoffrey. *Seven Kings of England*. New York, Vanguard Press, 1955.

Trease, Geoffrey. *The Seven Queens of England*. New York, Vanguard Press, 1953.

Trover, Ellen Lloyd. *Chronology & Documentary Handbook of the State of Virginia*. Dobbs Ferry, New York, Oceana Publications, Inc., 1979.

Turman, Nora Miller. *The Eastern Shore of Virginia: 1603–1964*. Onancock, Virginia, Eastern Shore News, Inc., 1964.

Tyler, Lyon G. *The Cradle of the Republic: Jamestown & James River*. Richmond, Hermitage Press, Inc., 1906.

Tyler, Lyon G. *Encyclopedia of Virginia Biography*. New York, Lewis Historical Publishing Co., 1915.

Van der Kiste, John. *King George II & Queen Caroline*. Sutton Publishing, Ltd., 1997.

"Virginia Officers & Men in the Continental Line." *Virginia Magazine of History & Biography*, Vol. 2, No. 3. Richmond: January, 1895.

Virta, Alan. *Prince George's County: A Pictorial History*. Norfolk, Virginia, Donning Co., 1984.

Vogel, Virgil J. *Indian Names in Michigan*. Ann Arbor, University of Michigan Press, 1986.

Vogt, John & T. William Kethley. *Giles County Marriages: 1806–1850*. Athens, Georgia, Iberian Publishing Co., 1985.

Von Engeln, O. D., & Jane McKelway Urquhart. *The Story Key to Geographic Names*. Port Washington, New York, Kennikat Press, 1924.

Waddell, Jos. A. *Annals of Augusta County, Virginia*. Bridgewater, Virginia, C. J. Carrier Co., 1958.

Waldman, Carl. *Who Was Who in Native American History*. New York, Facts On File, Inc., 1990.

Warner, Thomas H. *History of Old Rappahannock County, Virginia: 1656–1692*. Tappahannock, Virginia, Pauline Pearce Warner, 1965.

Watts, Charles W. "Land Grants & Aristocracy in Albemarle County: 1727–1775." *Papers of the Albemarle County Historical Society*, Vol. 8. Charlottesville: 1947–1948.

Wayland, John W. *A History of Shenandoah County, Virginia*. Strasburg, Virginia, Shenandoah Publishing House, 1927.

Wayland, John W. *Virginia Valley Records: Genealogical & Historical Materials of Rockingham County, Virginia & Related Regions*. Baltimore, Genealogical Publishing Co., 1965.

Weisiger, Benjamin B. *Colonial Wills of Henrico County, Virginia*. Berryville, Virginia, Virginia Book Co., 1976.

Whitelaw, Ralph T. *Virginia's Eastern Shore*. Richmond, Virginia Historical Society, 1951.

Whitworth, Rex. *William Augustus, Duke of Cumberland: A Life*. London, England, Leo Cooper, 1992.

Wight, Richard C. *The Story of Goochland*. Richmond, Richmond Press, Inc., 1943.

Williams, Harrison. *Legends of Loudoun*. Richmond, Garrett & Massie, Inc., 1938.

Williams, Kathleen Booth. *Marriages of Amelia County, Virginia: 1735–1815*. Baltimore, Genealogical Publishing Co., Inc., 1979.

Williams, Samuel C. "The First Territorial Division Named for Washington." *Tennessee Historical Magazine*, Series 2, Vol. 2, No. 2. Nashville: January, 1932.

Williamson, David. *Kings & Queens of Britain*. New York, Dorset Press, 1992.

Wilson, Goodridge. *Smyth County History & Traditions*. Kingsport, Tennessee, Kingsport Press, Inc., 1932.

Wilstach, Paul. *Potomac Landings*. New York, Tudor Publishing Co., 1937.

Wingfield, Marshall. *A History of Caroline County, Virginia*. Richmond, Trevvet, Christian & Co., Inc., 1924.

Wise, Jennings C. *Ye Kingdome of Accawmacke: Or the Eastern Shore of Virginia: In the Seventeenth Century*. Richmond, Bell Book & Stationery Co., 1911.

Wise, L. F., & E. W. Egan. *Kings, Rulers & Statesmen*. New York, Sterling Publishing Co., Inc., 1967.

Wood, Amos D. *Floyd County. A History of Its People & Places*. Radford, Virginia, Commonwealth Press, Inc., 1981.

Woods, Edgar. *Albemarle County in Virginia*. Harrisonburg, Virginia, C. J. Carrier Co., 1972.

Work Projects Administration. *Dinwiddie County*. Richmond, Whittet & Shepperson, 1942.

Work Projects Administration. *A Guide to Prince George & Hopewell*. 1939.

Work Projects Administration. *Inventory of the County Archives of Virginia-Amelia & Brunswick Counties*. Richmond, 1940–1943.

Works Progress Administration. *Inventory of the County Archives of Virginia-Chesterfield & Middlesex Counties*. Charlottesville & Richmond, 1938–1939.

Washington

(39 counties)

2881 *Adams County*

John Adams (1735–1826)— A native of Massachusetts, John Adams was a delegate to the first Continental Congress and a signer of the Declaration of Independence. He participated in Paris, with Benjamin Franklin and John Jay, in negotiating peace with England and, after the war, he was our country's first minister to England. Adams became the first vice-president of the United States under George Washington and when Washington retired, Adams was elected as our second president. This county was created by Washington territory during November, 1883.

2882 *Asotin County*

Town of Asotin City, Washington territory— At one time there were two rival towns here, within one half mile of each other, on the Snake River near the mouth of Asotin Creek in what is now the southeastern portion of the state of Washington. These towns were located about six miles south of the present community of Clarkston, also on the Snake River. One of the rival towns was named Asotin and the other was called Asotin City. Settlement of one or both of these towns began in 1878 and in 1881 a ferry was established here by J. J. Kanawyer. Within a decade the two towns were merged into a single community, which is the present county seat of Asotin County and had a population of about 1,000 by the late 1990's. The towns were named for Asotin Creek and the creek's name came from an Indian name for it which meant "Eel Creek." The Indians had no written language so spelling of their geographic names was first done by Whites. Asotin County was created on October 27, 1883, by Washington territory. During 1886 the territorial legislature officially changed the spelling of the county seat of Assotin City by removing one "s" from its name, and the name of the county and its county seat both now have one "s."

2883 *Benton County*

Thomas H. Benton (1782–1858)— Benton was a native of North Carolina who served in the Tennessee senate and as a soldier in the War of 1812. Following the war, he moved to Missouri and he represented that state for thirty years in the U.S. Senate. In that body he championed U.S. control of the Oregon country, an issue our nation and Great Britain resolved in 1846. He also supported many causes favorable to the West, including free 160 acre homesteads, pony express, telegraph and railroads. Benton was a moderate on the volatile slavery issue. He opposed both abolition of slavery and the extension of it. His primary concerns were peace and preservation of the union. These moderate positions proved unpopular. Some states which had named counties in Benton's honor renamed them and in 1850, Missouri failed to return Benton to the Senate. Following his ouster from the Senate, Benton served briefly in the U.S. House of Representatives. This county was created on March 8, 1905. McKinley and Riverside had also been proposed for this county's name but the legislature selected Benton.

2884 *Chelan County*

Lake Chelan— This county in central Washington was created on March 13, 1899, and named for the 60 mile-long Chelan Lake, within its borders. The lake extends to a depth of 1,400 feet, at its deepest point, and is glacier-made. One of the more scenic lakes in the scenic Pacific Northwest, Lake Chelan's name derives from the name which Indians gave to it. The translation of the Indians' name is uncertain but a majority of sources dealing with the history, geography and place names of Washington favor the meaning "deep water." However, some sources say that "bubbling water" is a possibility, while others admits that the meaning is uncertain. At the time that the bill to create this county was under consideration, a serious effort was made to name it Wenatchee County. That was the second attempt to use the name Wenatchee for a county in Washington; the first unsuccessful attempt was made in 1893.

2885 *Clallam County*

Clallam Indians— Many sources dealing with the history, geography and place names of Washington indicate that this county's name was taken from Indian words meaning "strong people," or "brave people." While that may be true, the Indians so described were a specific tribe of the Salishan linguistic group, whose name we now render as Clallam or Klallam. The Clallam lived along the Strait of Juan de Fuca, an inlet of the Pacific Ocean here, and were favorably mentioned by the Spanish explorer, Manuel Quimper, in his diary of exploration in the early 1790's. The British navigator and explorer, Captain George Vancouver (1757–1798) also described these Indians in his log of Pacific Northwest explorations in the 1790's. The Clallam Indians subsisted primarily on fish and customarily lived in rectangular plank houses. Jervis Russell's 1971 history of Clallam County passes on details about

these Indians which he garnered in Myron Eells' book, *Ten Years of Missionary Work Among the Indians of Skokomish, Washington Territory: 1874–1884*. Basing his comments on that work by Reverend Eells, Russell tells us that "...in 1855, a treaty was made with the Twanas, Chemakums, and S'Klallams, or Clallams as the tribe is now known." Their location was also given and it corresponds to the northern portion of the present Clallam County, Washington. Further, Russell relates: "He mentioned the Clallams' great strength, and that it was expected that all three tribes would be moved to the reservation at Skokomish, though this was never done as the Clallams and Twanas were unfriendly and the reservation ... was too small for the three tribes which supposedly numbered 2,800 then." This county was created by Washington territory on April 26, 1854, with the name Clalm County. That name honored the Clallam or Klallam Indians and the county's name is now rendered as Clallam County.

2886 *Clark County*

William Clark (1770–1838)— Clark was a native of Virginia who served in the army in battles with Indians on America's western frontier. Together with Captain Meriwether Lewis, Clark led the Lewis & Clark Expedition (1804–1806) to the Pacific Northwest. The Lewis & Clark party were the first White men, south of Canada, to travel on land to the Pacific Northwest coast and back. Following the expedition, Clark served as superintendent of Indian affairs for Louisiana territory. In 1813 he was appointed governor of Missouri territory. This county was initially established on June 27, 1844, as the district of Vancouver and on December 21, 1845, it was changed to the County of Vancouver. Both of these dates were before the United States and Great Britain had agreed that "the Oregon country" belonged to America. In late May, 1844, the Democratic party nominated James K. Polk for president and Polk's vision included the "manifest destiny" that our nation should extend from sea to sea and include "the Oregon country." Polk won the election and in his inauguration address on March 4, 1845, the pugnacious new president restated his position that our nation's "...title to the country of Oregon is clear and unquestionable..." There were, of course, questions, one of which was where our northwestern boundary should be. We demanded 54 degrees, 40 minutes but accepted a boundary at the 49th parallel. In 1846

President Polk signed a treaty with Great Britain which formalized that boundary and on August 14, 1848, Oregon territory was established, which included all of the present state of Washington. On September 3, 1849, Oregon territory changed the name of this county from Vancouver to Clark, in honor of one of the leaders of the expedition which resulted in American settlement of "the Oregon country." In 1854 Washington territory entered the name of this county in the new territory's records as Clarke County and that erroneous spelling persisted until it was officially corrected by the state of Washington on December 23, 1925.

2887 *Columbia County*

Columbia River— This county in southeastern Washington was named for the river which runs some 75 miles west of it. The 1,210 mile-long Columbia, one of North America's major rivers, rises in British Columbia, in Canada, and initially flows northwest. In the Selkirk Mountain region, the Columbia recognizes that it must alter its course to reach the Pacific Ocean and turns abruptly south and heads in that direction across southern British Columbia and our state of Washington. At Lake Wallula, in southern Washington, the Columbia turns sharply west and flows between Washington and Oregon to enter the Pacific Ocean. This river has been discovered many times but its present name was given in 1792, and came from that of the ship commanded by the American, Captain Robert Gray (1755–1806). Gray's vessel, the *Columbia*, was only a 212 ton ship, and drew six to eight feet of water. The exploration of the lower Columbia River was a memorable accomplishment of the Lewis & Clark Expedition. Sadly the once torrential and salmon-choked Columbia is no more. The river is now polluted and much of its course in Washington and Oregon consists of sluggish waters. This county was established by Washington territory, and a territorial legislator, Elisha Ping, was influential in its creation. The territorial legislature created the new county as Ping County, but the governor vetoed that bill and the county was born with the name Columbia County on November 11, 1875.

2888 *Cowlitz County*

Uncertain— This county in southwestern Washington was created by Washington territory on April 21, 1854, and named either for the Cowlitz River, which flows through it, or for a local Indian tribe, the Cowlitz Indians. The name of both the river and the Indian tribe derive from a practice of the Cowlitz Indians of sending their youths to the prairies near the Cowlitz River to commune with their guardian spirits and one translation of the name *Cowlitz* is "capturing the medicine spirit."

Cowlitz River — The Cowlitz River of southwestern Washington is formed by the confluence of forks in eastern Lewis County, Washington and flows first west and south in Lewis County and then south in Cowlitz County, where it enters the Columbia River after a journey of about 130 miles. Robert Hitchman's *Place Names of Washington*, published in 1985, stated that "It is an important river for navigation, fishing and development of hydroelectric power."

Cowlitz Indians — The Cowlitz Indians lived along the Pacific coast in what is now southwestern Washington and inland along the Columbia River at least as far as the Cowlitz River area. They subsisted principally on fish and commonly lived in semi-subterranean houses. This Cowlitz tribe is classified as a member of the Salishan linguistic group.

2889 *Douglas County*

Stephen A. Douglas (1813–1861) — Barely five feet tall, the "Little Giant" is most remembered as a political opponent of Abraham Lincoln. Douglas was born in Vermont and moved to Illinois where he enjoyed rapid political success. He served on the state supreme court, in the state legislature and as secretary of state. Following two terms in the U.S. House of Representatives, Douglas was elected to the U.S. Senate. In that body Douglas took courageous positions on the slavery issue which first outraged abolitionist sentiment and later infuriated the South. In 1858 Douglas ran for reelection to the U.S. Senate against Abraham Lincoln. Following the famous Lincoln-Douglas debates, the Republicans won the popular election but that state legislature reelected Douglas to the Senate. Lincoln and Douglas were rivals again in 1860 for the presidency. Following Lincoln's election and the start of the Civil War, Douglas gave the president his active support. Stephen Douglas was a consistent friend America's Pacific Northwest and this county was created and named in his honor by Washington territory on November 28, 1883. That was just four days after Lincoln County had been created and named in honor of President Abraham Lincoln and Douglas

County's land came from the western portion of Lincoln County. At that time Douglas County contained only about 100 residents. The notion to create a separate county for such a small population was that of J. W. Adams', a professional townsite boomer from Kansas.

2890 *Ferry County*

Elisha P. Ferry (1825–1895) — A native of Michigan, Ferry practiced law in Waukegan, Illinois, and became that city's first mayor. During the Civil War, he served in the Union army and held the rank of colonel and the position of adjutant general. In 1869 President Ulysses S. Grant appointed Ferry as surveyor-general of Washington territory and in 1872 President Grant made him governor of the territory. He served in that post until 1880 and was able to announce a favorable decision concerning ownership of the San Juan Islands, which had been the subject of a dispute between America and British Canada. Ferry was prominent in actions during uprisings by the Nez Perce Indians and in securing the admission of Washington to statehood. In 1889 he was elected as governor of the new state and served in that position until 1893. As governor, Ferry opposed women's suffrage. This county was created by the state legislature on January 12, 1899, and named Eureka County because gold had been discovered here. Just one month later, in mid–February, 1899, the county's name was changed to Ferry County.

2891 *Franklin County*

Benjamin Franklin (1706–1790) — Franklin was a native of Massachusetts who moved to Pennsylvania in his teens. Poverty denied him a formal education but he became the leading printer and editor in North America. He gained fame for his discoveries and inventions in the physical sciences and he distinguished himself as author, philosopher and diplomat. Franklin was a signer of the Declaration of Independence and an important member of the convention which framed the U.S. Constitution. This county was created by Washington territory on November 28, 1883.

2892 *Garfield County*

James A. Garfield (1831–1881) — A native of Ohio, Garfield served in the Ohio senate before becoming a Union officer in the Civil War. He performed ably and rapidly rose to the rank of general. In 1863 Garfield

resigned his commission to enter the U.S. House of Representatives where he served until 1880. During Reconstruction, Garfield favored harsh treatment of the defeated South. In January, 1880 he was elected to the U.S. Senate but never served in that body. Instead, he was nominated and elected president of the United States. His nomination by the Republican party came as a compromise on the 36th ballot. Garfield was fatally wounded by an assassin's bullet just four months after beginning his term as president and this county was created by Washington territory just two months later, on November 29, 1881.

2893 *Grant County*

Ulysses S. Grant (1822–1885) — Grant was a native of Ohio who graduated from the U.S. Military Academy at West Point. He served with distinction in the Mexican War, and in the Civil War he rose to become commander of all Union forces. After the Civil War, Grant briefly served as acting secretary of war and then two terms as president of the United States. He proved to be a rather mediocre president. This county was created on February 24, 1909.

2894 *Grays Harbor County*

Grays Harbor on the Pacific Ocean — This county on Washington's Pacific coast was first created as Chehalis County by Washington territory on April 14, 1854. *Chehalis* was an Indian name, said to mean "sandy river," or "shifting sands." referring to the sands at the mouth of the Chehalis River at Grays Harbor, here. On February 27, 1907, the state of Washington created a Grays Harbor County but that law was declared unconstitutional in November, 1907. The birth year of the present Grays Harbor County is given in several sources as 1915. The county was named for the large protected inlet near its southwestern corner, on the Pacific Ocean, which was named for the American sea captain, Robert Gray, who discovered it on May 7, 1792.

Robert Gray (1755–1806) — A native of Rhode Island, Gray served at sea during the American Revolution and later was employed by a Boston merchant to open sea trade with China. In the late 1780's Captain Gray reached the Pacific Northwest and in 1789 he set sail for China. There Gray traded furs for oriental products and he returned with them to Boston in 1790. Dan L. Thrapp's *Encyclopedia of Frontier Biography* calls Robert Gray "the first American captain known to have circumnavigated the globe." He returned to the Pacific Northwest and in 1792 discovered Grays Harbor, named the previously discovered Columbia River in honor of his vessel, the *Columbia*, and then completed a second trip around the world at Boston in 1793.

2895 *Island County*

The islands in Puget Sound, which comprise the county— This county was created by Oregon territory on January 6, 1853, and named for the islands which comprise it. In her work entitled *Island County: A World Beater*, Lou Kinne Hawes tells us that "Island County consists of four islands surrounded by the blue waters of Puget Sound." That statement is substantially correct, but neglects to mention the many small islands within the county's borders. The four largest islands are Whidbey, Camano, Smith and Minor Islands. However, there are many other very small islands, including Deception Island. Whidbey Island's 235 square-miles holds most of the county's land, while Camano Island is 14 miles long and very narrow. Smith and Minor Islands lie about seven miles west of Whidbey Island and at low tide these two islands are connected by a rocky ridge. Deception Island is a small wooded island on the western edge of Deception Pass.

2896 *Jefferson County*

Thomas Jefferson (1743–1826)— Jefferson was a native of Virginia and a member of the Virginia legislature. He served Virginia as governor and was a delegate to the second Continental Congress. Jefferson was the author of the Declaration of Independence and one of its signers. He was minister to France, secretary of state, vice-president and president of the United States. As president, he accomplished the Louisiana Purchase and he arranged the Lewis & Clark Expedition to the Pacific Northwest. Jefferson was a true intellectual, thoroughly knowledgeable in the arts and sciences. His political theories were pivotal in the formation of our infant republic. This county was created by Oregon territory in December, 1852 and then inherited by Washington territory. Later, on December 12, 1914, the state of Oregon established its own Jefferson County, named for Mount Jefferson, which had been named for President Jefferson.

2897 *King County*

Originally: William R. D. King (1786–1853). Changed to: Martin Luther King, Jr.

(1929–1968)— This county was created by Oregon territory on December 22, 1852, and then inherited by Washington territory. Its name honored Vice-President-elect William Rufus Devane King, who was then dying of tuberculosis. A century later, on February 24, 1986, the council of King County, Washington decided, in a 5 to 4 vote, that the county's name should remain King but that it would now honor the martyred civil rights leader, Reverend Martin Luther King, Jr. (1929–1968). An article in the *Seattle Post Intelligencer* dated February 25, 1986, stated that the county council made the change "effective immediately" but did not discuss whether the county council had the authority to make the change. In most states (and territories) counties are created and abolished by legislative bodies at the state (or territorial) level, rather than at the local level. Since the county name remained unchanged, there can be little question that the King County council had the authority to put its moral weight behind the decision to honor the slain civil rights leader.

William R. D. King (1786–1853)— A native of North Carolina and a lawyer, William R. D. King served in the North Carolina legislature and represented North Carolina in the U.S. House of Representatives. He later moved to Alabama and represented that state in the U.S. Senate. William King also represented our nation as a diplomat to several countries. In the presidential election of 1852 William King was the vice-presidential running mate of the Democratic party's candidate for president, Franklin Pierce, and they were elected. However, the vice-president elect contracted tuberculosis and went to Cuba to recuperate. He took the oath of office as vice-president in Cuba, but died on April 18, 1853, and never performed any duties of his office.

Martin Luther King, Jr. (1929–1968)— Prior to the Civil War slavery was practiced in the South. Although the Civil War ended slavery, legal segregation of the races lived on in the South for almost a century and de-facto segregation and second class citizenship was a reality for Blacks in the North, as well. Many Americans played a role in ending this travesty, but the work of Reverend Martin Luther King, Jr., was particularly effective; so much so that his birthday is recognized as a national legal holiday. Reverend King patterned his revolution on the non-violent tactics of India's Mahatma Gandhi (1869–1948). Born in Georgia, Martin Luther King, Jr., became a Baptist minister and a leader of America's civil rights movement of the 1950's

and 1960's. So successful was Reverend King that he lost his life to racial hatred and an assassin's bullet.

2898 *Kitsap County*

Kitsap (–1860)— The "Documents" section of the October, 1934, issue (Vol. 25, No. 4) of *Washington Historical Quarterly* presented several accounts of the Indian chief named Kitsap. The accounts were written independently and related to different portions of the chief's life. Based on these accounts, it appears that Chief Kitsap was a very powerful chief of Indians in the Puget Sound region from about 1790 to 1845 and that Chief Seattle (–1866) was merely a sub-chief to him. Kitsap gained fame as a "medicine man," successfully healing his own serious wounds on several occasions and convincing many of his followers that he could not be killed by either the White men or Indians. About 1825 he led some 200 canoes against rival Indians on Vancouver Island. There, Kitsap and his warriors found only old men, old women and children so they killed the old Indians and took the young women and children as captives, to serve as slaves. On their return trip Kitsap and his men encountered their Indian enemies on the water, who also had prisoners. Kitsap's warriors killed all of their prisoners, in sight of the enemy, and the opposing Indians did the same to their prisoners. A battle then ensued, after which Kitsap had only about 40 canoes. Having demonstrated his ruthlessness in dealing with rival Indians, Chief Kitsap also managed to infuriate Washington's territorial governor, Isaac I. Stevens (1818–1862), who issued orders that Kitsap and other Indian leaders be captured and tried. Several Indian leaders were captured and either tried and executed, or murdered. Chief Kitsap was also captured but he managed to escape. Recaptured on January 6, 1859, Kitsap was tried at Olympia but acquitted. Soon after that trial, Kitsap attempted his magical healing powers on three of his own warriors, who were ill. Kitsap's quack medicine failed and all three of the warriors died. The enraged relatives and friends of the dead men, killed Kitsap on April 18, 1860. This county was created by Washington territory in acts passed by the territorial legislature on January 16, 1857, and January 27, 1857. Its original name was Slaughter County, in honor of First-Lieutenant William A. Slaughter (–1855), a U.S. army officer who lost his life in Indian warfare in Washington territory on December 4, 1855. However, the legislature struggled in deciding what to name this new county and considered Madison as well as Slaughter. They decided to tentatively name the new county Slaughter, but the act of January 27, 1857, gave the "legal voters of Slaughter County at their next annual election the right to decide by ballot a name for said county." That election was held on July 13, 1857, and the voters decided to name their county Kitsap at that election.

2899 *Kittitas County*

Uncertain— This county in central Washington was created by Washington territory in November, 1883. Most works dealing with the place names of Washington indicate that the county's name derived from an Indian word and many sources translate that word as "gray gravel bank," or something very like that. Other translations are also mentioned including "clay gravel valley," "white rock," "white bluffs," "shoal," "shoal people," "plenty food" and "land of bread." However, James W. Phillips' *Washington State Place Names* tells us that the county's name derived from an Indian tribe, "the K'tatas Indian tribe or 'shoal people,' who lived along the shallow portion of the Yakima River." Edmond S. Meany's *Origin of Washington Geographic Names* admits that the origin of the county's name is uncertain but says that "James Mooney is authority for the statement that a small tribe called themselves 'K'tatas' and the Yakima name for them was 'Pshwanapum.' Lewis and Clark had alluded to them as 'Shanwappoms.' The words [sic] meant 'shoal' and 'shoal people,' referring to a shoal in the Yakima River at Ellensburg."

2900 *Klickitat County*

Klikitat Indians— The Klikitat Indians formerly lived in what is now the state of Washington and were grouped into nomadic bands of hunters and gatherers. The Klikitat were also good traders and acted as intermediaries between tribes along the Pacific coast and those of the inland Pacific Northwest. Known to have lived near the headwaters of the Lewis, White, Cowlitz and Salmon Rivers, they also lived along the Yakima and Klickitat Rivers because they were visited there by the Lewis and Clark Expedition in 1805. At that time there were about 700 Klikitat Indians but their numbers were greatly reduced between 1820 and 1830 by a fever epidemic. The Yakima Indians were their neighbors and the two tribes spoke a very similar language. In 1855 the Klikitat signed a treaty ceding their lands to the U.S. and by the end of the 19th century their members had become so commingled with other tribes on the Yakima Indian reservation that they no longer had a separate tribal identity. This county was created by Washington territory on December 20, 1859, as Clickitat County. About 1869 the present spelling came into use.

2901 *Lewis County*

Meriwether Lewis (1774–1809)— A native of Virginia and a neighbor and friend of Thomas Jefferson, Lewis served as an officer in the army and then, in 1801, President Jefferson selected him to be his aide. From 1804 to 1806 Meriwether Lewis and William Clark led the Lewis & Clark Expedition which President Jefferson sent to explore the Northwest to the Pacific Ocean. Their successful journey ended in September 1806 when they returned to civilization at Saint Louis, in what is now the state of Missouri. Lewis then served as governor of Louisiana territory from 1807 until his death on October 11, 1809. This county was created on December 21, 1845, before the United States and Great Britain had agreed that "the Oregon country" belonged to America and before either Oregon territory or Washington territory had been created. For a discussion of this unusual chronology, see Clark County, Washington, above, which was also created (then named the County of Vancouver) on December 21, 1845.

2902 *Lincoln County*

Abraham Lincoln (1809–1865)— Lincoln was a native of Kentucky who moved to Illinois, where he was a member of the state legislature. He represented Illinois in the U.S. House of Representatives and later was elected president of the United States. Lincoln's presidency coincided almost exactly with the Civil War. He guided the United States ably through that uniquely turbulent period. As president, he issued the Emancipation Proclamation which declared the freedom of slaves in all states in rebellion. Lincoln was assassinated in April, 1865, a few days after the Union's victory in the Civil War. The 1883 attempt to create a new county here, west of the Spokane area of Washington territory was opposed by the Northern Pacific Railway Company. In an effort to win the railroad's support, the bill to create this new county was introduced in the territorial legislature with the name Sprague County, in honor of John W. Sprague (1817–1893), an official of the railroad. The support of the railroad was considered vital but there was opposition to the name Sprague County. *An Illustrated History of the Big Bend Country Embracing Lincoln, Douglas, Adams & Franklin Counties, State of Washington* was published in 1904. That work provided the following explanation for the change in name from Sprague to Lincoln: Judge N. T. Caton, a key player in securing creation of this county, learned that a member of the territorial legislature, Colonel Houghton, "who had been formerly in the employment of the Northern Pacific Company ... was not on friendly terms with John W. Sprague." The work then related the following conversation between Judge N. T. Caton and the territorial legislator, Colonel Houghton: "'Colonel,' said Mr. Caton, 'it appears to me that we are making a mistake in naming this new county after a living person. One can never be sure in such a case that the name will reflect credit upon the community ... what do you say to changing the name of this one from Sprague to Lincoln?' 'Just the proper thing,' replied Colonel Houghton, and from that time he became a supporter of the bill." Thus Lincoln County was created on November 24, 1883. Just four days later, Douglas County was created from the western portion of Lincoln County. That county's name honored Abraham Lincoln's political opponent, Stephen A. Douglas (1813–1861).

2903 *Mason County*

Charles H. Mason (1830–1859)— Charles H. Mason was appointed by the federal government to be the first secretary of Washington territory. While the position of territorial governor carries great power, the territorial secretary's office has little importance, except when the territorial governor is absent from the territory or otherwise unable to perform the duties of his office. In such cases, the secretary of the territory becomes the acting territorial governor. This situation prevailed during the administration of Governor Isaac I. Stevens (1818–1862) and Mason became acting territorial governor at a time when he was required to deal with Indian troubles. It was during this period, in 1855, that Charles H. Mason made his mark on the history of Washington territory. Soon after the Indians were induced to sign treaties giving their lands to the federal government, some Yakima Indian chiefs came to believe that the promises made by the Whites in the treaties would not be kept, and they ordered retaliation. The Indians murdered several Whites and the acting territorial governor, Charles H. Mason, ordered Major Gabriel J. Rains (1803–1881), of the U.S. army, to quell the disturbance. The resulting clash is known as the "Yakima War." This county was first established by Washington territory on March 13, 1854, and given the Indian name, Sawamish County. That name was suggested by David Shelton, of the territorial legislature. In January, 1864, the county's name was changed to Mason County.

2904 *Okanogan County*

Uncertain— This county on Washington's northern border with Canada, was created on February 2, 1888, by Washington territory and given the Indian name, *Okanogan*. Sources dealing with the history, geography and place names of Washington are annoyingly vague about the origin of this county's name. Most merely say that it is an Indian name (and some offer translations) while others say that it was an "Indian tribal name." There are two bodies of water in this vicinity, Okanogan Lake and a river which is spelled Okanagan in Canada and Okanogan in the U.S. The area also has mountain range named Okanagan. In addition, Washington has possessed two municipalities, Okanogan and Okanogan City. Discussing these potential sources for the county's name, we find that the lake is 60 miles long and lies in the Canadian province of British Columbia. The river is a tributary of the Columbia River and is the longest stream in Okanogan County, Washington. It rises near the Canadian border and flows some 73 miles south and southwest to the Columbia River. The mountain range numbers among its peaks, Crater Mountain, in southern Canada, with an elevation of 7,522 feet. The municipality of Okanogan City is now a vanished town in Washington, six miles east of Waterville, or about 35 miles south of the Okanogan County border, in Douglas County, Washington. Finally, we have the city of Okanogan, Washington, the present county seat of Okanogan County, with a population in the late 1990's of 2,400. This city can be dismissed from contention as the source of the county's name because it was named Alma when the county was created. Beyond that lies uncertainty. Many writers indicate that the Indian name, by whatever spelling, meant "rendezvous" and referred to a traditional Indian meeting place near what is now the U.S.-Canadian border, where Indians from various tribes would gather to fish and trade. The April, 1949, issue (Vol. 8, No. 2) of *Western Folklore* contained an article discussing "Okanagan Place Names," written by Erwin G. Gudde, a professor at the University of California-Berkeley, known to be an authority on the origins of place names in the western United States. In that article, Dr. Gudde stated that "Okanagan is an Indian name applied to the district drained by the Okanagan River, a tributary of the Columbia. The name is international…. In the United States section the name of the river and county is spelled Okanogan." Gudde then cites a study by A. G. Harvey in the *Twelfth Report of the Okanagan Historical Society*, which dealt with names in the Canadian portion of the Okanagan Valley. Professor Gudde stated that "Mr. Harvey found forty-six spelling variants but was unable to trace the etymology of the name." William G. Brown's *Early Okanogan History* mentions "Okanogan Indians" but apparently this name described the region where they lived, rather than an accepted tribal name.

2905 *Pacific County*

Pacific Ocean— This county in southwestern Washington borders on the Pacific Ocean and it was named for that enormous body of water when it was created as a county of Oregon territory on February 4, 1851. The ocean's area of 70 million square miles is about double that of the Atlantic Ocean. The Pacific extends from the Arctic circle to Antarctica and from the continents of North and South America to Australia and beyond to Asia. The name *Oceano Pacifico* meant "peaceful sea," but in many areas of the coastal United States that name is far from apt.

2906 *Pend Oreille County*

Pend d' Oreille Indians— This county in northeastern Washington, which was created on March 1, 1911, contains part of Pend Oreille River but apparently it was not named for that river but directly for the Pend d' Oreille Indians. Their name was given to them by the French and they lived in what is now the Canadian province of British Columbia, northern Idaho and northwestern Montana. The name *Pend d' Oreille* meant "hanging ear," and it was bestowed on these Indians because of the large shell ornaments which many of them wore on their ears. The Pend d' Oreille are classified as belonging to the Salishan linguistic group and they share an Indian reservation in Montana with the Salish Indians. The Pend d' Oreille are related to some of the Indians who shared the same geographic area in northwestern America including the Kalispel Indians, the Coeur d' Alene Indians and the Salish Indians. This group of Indians was dominated by the Spokane Indians. The Pend d' Oreille subsisted primarily on fish and large game.

2907 *Pierce County*

Franklin Pierce (1804–1869)— Pierce was born in New Hampshire and served in the lower house of that state's legislature. He represented New Hampshire in both houses of the U.S. Congress and served as an officer in the Mexican War, rising to the rank of brigadier-general. In 1852 Pierce was nominated for president by the Democratic party on the 49th ballot as a compromise candidate who was not objectionable to the South. He was elected to that office and served one term, from March 4, 1853, to March 3, 1857. As president, he viewed the slavery issue in a legalistic way and was unable to accept the North's moral objections to slavery. Pierce failed to secure his party's nomination for a second term. This county was created by Oregon territory on December 22, 1852. At that time Franklin Pierce was our nation's president-elect.

2908 *San Juan County*

San Juan Island— Ownership of the islands which comprise this county was disputed between Great Britain and our nation long after the rest of America's northwestern border had been settled. The dispute was settled by international arbitration on October 21, 1872, when the emperor of Germany, William I (1797–1888), ruled that the islands which comprise this county belonged to the United States. On October 31, 1873, Washington territory established a separate county consisting of just these islands in the San Juan archipelago. James W. Phillips' *Washington State Place Names*, published by the University of Washington Press in 1971 stated that "…it is comprised of 172 named islands (and reputedly 300 more rocky 'islands' at low tide)." Sources dealing with the history, geography and place names of Washington are generally agreed that the county was named for a specific island (rather for the entire San Juan archipelago) but they differ on whether that island is the "largest," "second largest" or "one of the largest" islands in the archipelago.

These sources also disagree on whom the geographic name San Juan honors. James W. Phillips' *Washington State Place Names* stated that the San Juan islands were "discovered in 1791 by Lopez Gonzales de Haro, who was under the command of Spanish explorer Francisco Eliza. The latter, in turn, sailed under the authority of the viceroy of Mexico, one Senor Don Juan Vicente de Guemes Pacheco de Padilla Horcasitas y Aguayo. With an eye to future patronage, Eliza charted the island group as Isla y Archiepelago de San Juan." Apart from the Spanish *San Juan*, the English translation of that phrase is "Island and Archipelago of." However, Robert Hitchman's *Place Names of Washington*, which was published by the Washington State Historical Society in 1985 and has proved very accurate on most points, states that "It was not in honor of Juan de Fuca but for the Catholic Saint, Juan Bautista"; i.e., Saint John the Baptist. In an attempt to resolve this conflict your author reviewed more than 60 sources and found that only eleven of them were willing to venture an opinion on this subject. Three of those sources mentioned Juan de Fuca, but it seems safe to dismiss that suggestion because Juan de Fuca's name was applied to the strait here rather than to the island or island group. The remaining eight opinions are strongly in favor of Saint John the Baptist; five specifically saying so and another attributing the origin to "the patron saint" of Lopez Gonzales de Haro. There is one vote for "Juan Francisco de Eliza, a lieutenant in the Spanish army," and, finally, the above mentioned Don Juan Vicente de Guemes Pacheco de Padilla Horcasitas y Aguayo. The conclusion must be that the original namesake is uncertain. Even if we were brave enough to suggest that it might be "Saint John the Baptist," we are still left with uncertainty because there are at least 16 saints whose name starts with John the Baptist. However, most of them are extremely obscure compared to the Saint John the Baptist, who baptized Jesus. That Saint John the Baptist has long been one of the most popular saints of the Roman Catholic Church.

Saint John the Baptist (–)—John lived an austere life in the desert of Judea, southwest of Jerusalem. Clothed in garments of camel's hair and living on a diet of locusts and wild honey, John ministered to men from Jerusalem and neighboring towns, who flocked to visit him. He demanded two rites of those who came to him: an open confession of their sins and physical baptism. Jesus Christ was among those baptized by John and John apparently came to believe, on that occasion, that Jesus was the Messiah. King Herod Antipas feared John's popularity and power and resented John's criticism of his sex life. The king imprisoned John and had him beheaded.

2909 *Skagit County*

Uncertain—This county in northwestern Washington was created by Washington territory on November 28, 1883, and most sources indicate that it was named for the Skagit Indians. There is no doubt that this county's name can be traced to that Indian tribe but by the time the county was created, the name Skagit had already been given to a bay, river, delta, island and mountain range, all located in this vicinity. It seems probable that the county's name came from one or more of these sources and thus indirectly from the Skagit Indian tribe.

Skagit Indians—The Skagit were members of the Salish linguistic group, who lived around southern Puget Sound and the Skagit River area (particularly at its mouth) in the present state of Washington. Whidbey Island is mentioned as one of their favorite residences. The Skagit subsisted on fish and their principal type of dwelling was a rectangular plank house. An estimate of their population in 1853 was 300 and the Skagit managed to maintain their separate tribal identity better than many other Indian tribes for as recently as 1970, some 259 Skagits remained.

2910 *Skamania County*

Indian word meaning "swift waters"—This county on Washington's southern border is separated from the state of Oregon by the Columbia River. On March 9, 1854, just one year after Washington territory was separated from Oregon territory, this county was created and given the Indian name *Skamania*. When the county was created, it covered all of what is now eastern Washington and some of Idaho and Montana. The county's name *Skamania*, meant "swift waters" to the Indians and referred to the Columbia River, which today comprises the entire southern boundary of the county. Between 1854 and the millennium year 2000, many dams have been built on the Columbia River and its waters are no longer particularly swift. Charles W. Smith wrote two articles entitled "The Naming of Counties in the State of Washington," which appeared in *The Magazine of History*. In the July 1909 issue (Vol. 10, No. 1), Smith stated that the name Skamania "...is said to have been applied by the Indians to the spot about two miles below the Cascades where in ascending the river they met the swift current of the Columbia."

2911 *Snohomish County*

Snohomish Indians—The Snohomish were a small group of Indians that belonged to Salish linguistic classification. They lived around Puget Sound, subsisted on fish and lived primarily in rectangular plank houses. Frederick W. Hodge's *Handbook of American Indians North of Mexico* estimated their 1850 population at only 350 members and gave their location as "...formerly on the southern end of Whidbey Island, Puget Sound, and on the mainland opposite at the mouth of Snohomish River." This county was created by Washington territory on January 14, 1861.

2912 *Spokane County*

Spokane Indians—The Spokane Indians were the dominant tribe in a confederation that included the Kalispel, Coeur d' Alene, Pend d' Oreille and other tribes. The Spokane Indians lived in an area surrounding the present city of Spokane, in eastern Washington. They subsisted on large game and fish and lived primarily in semi-subterranean dwellings. The name *Spokane* or *Spokan* originally designated only the Indians who lived at the forks of the Spokane River, but the name came to be applied to several Salish tribes. The Lewis & Clark Expedition estimated their population at 600 in 1805 and as recently as 1970 there were still about 1,500 Indians who retained the Spokane identity. Most Spokane Indians today live on the 141,380 acre Spokane Indian reservation, northwest of the city of Spokane. There "...being an Indian was mostly about survival" according to Sherman Alexie's 1996 work entitled *Indian Killer*. This county was created in steps. It was first created on January 29, 1858, by Washington territory but in 1859, when Oregon was admitted to statehood, this county's boundaries were changed. Subsequent to that, the county was abolished and then reestablished. Various dates are given for the recreation, including 1864.

2913 *Stevens County*

Isaac I. Stevens (1818–1862)—Isaac Ingalls Stevens was born near Andover, Massachusetts, and graduated at the head of his class from the U.S. Military Academy at West Point in 1839. While serving in the Mexican War, he was severely wounded in the assault on Mexico City. Stevens was breveted captain and major for this gallantry. In 1853 he organized and commanded the initial phase of a survey for a northern railroad route from St. Paul, Minnesota territory, to Puget Sound. On March 17, 1853, President Franklin Pierce appointed Major Stevens to be the first governor of Washington territory and he served in that post from 1853 to 1857. He subsequently represented Washington territory as its delegate to the U.S. Congress. In 1860 Stevens was a leading figure in the extreme pro-slavery presidential bid of John C. Breckinridge (1821–1875). Of course Abraham Lincoln won that election and when the Civil War started, despite his previous pro-slavery connections, Stevens entered the Union army as a colonel. He served with distinction and was promoted to the rank of brigadier-general and that was the rank that he held when he was killed in combat on September 1, 1862, at the battle of Chantilly. Stevens County was created by Washington territory less than five months later, on January 20, 1863, and the U.S. army posthumously promoted General Stevens to major-general.

2914 *Thurston County*

Samuel R. Thurston (1816–1851)— A native of Maine and a graduate of Bowdoin College in that state, Thurston studied law and was admitted to the bar. He soon moved west to Iowa territory, where he practiced law and edited a newspaper. Thurston moved to the Oregon country in time to be elected as the first delegate to Congress of Oregon territory. He served in Congress from March 4, 1849, to March 3, 1851, and died at sea on April 9, 1851, while traveling home from our nation's capitol. This county was created by Oregon territory less than a year later, on January 12, 1852. The name first proposed for this new county was Simmons County, in honor of Michael Simmons, an early pioneer of the Puget Sound basin, but that name was never adopted.

2915 *Wahkiakum County*

Wahkiakum Indians, Chief Wahkiacum & one of their villages— This county in southwestern Washington, at the mouth of the Columbia River, was created by Washington territory during April, 1854, as Wakiacum County. The Indians had no written language so the various spellings relating to this county and its Indian namesakes were coined by Whites. The county's name, by whatever spelling, honors an Indian sub-tribe, one of its chiefs and one of its villages, in this vicinity. The Wahkiakum Indians were a sub-tribe of the Chinook Indians. They subsisted on game and fish and their principal dwellings were rectangular plank houses. Shortly before 1800, the Wahkiakum Indians, about 200 in number, separated from the main body of the Chinook Indians and established their residence on the north bank of the Columbia River, near its mouth on the Pacific Ocean. Their domain extended upstream toward Oak Point and they had villages near the detached geological formation called Pillar Rock. One of their villages was known to the Whites by a name sounding like *Wakiacum*. When the Indians separated from the Chinook, they were led by a chief named Wahkiacum, and it was during his reign that the sub-tribe came to be called by his name. Frederick W. Hodge's *Handbook of American Indians North of Mexico* spelled the sub-tribe as Wahkiakum, but the chief as Wahkiacum.

2916 *Walla Walla County*

Indian name referring to "water(s)"— This county was created by Washington territory on April 25, 1854, just one year after the territory had been separated from Oregon territory. When first created, Walla Walla County was enormous, extending from the Rocky Mountains to the Cascades and from the Columbia River to the Canadian border. There had been sentiment in the 1850's to establish this vast area as an entity separate from Oregon territory and Washington territory and the name Lincoln had been suggested for it. The name that was adopted, *Walla Walla*, came from the language of the Nez Perce Indians and referred to "water" or "waters." Several translations have been mentioned including "running water" and "place of many waters." Robert Hitchman's *Place Names of Washington* tells us the words meant "place of many waters," and referred "to the many tributaries of Walla Walla River, and the abundant small streams and springs in the vicinity." James W. Phillips' *Washington State Place Names* indicates that the repetition of *Walla* by the Indians gave the name a diminutive or plural connotation.

2917 *Whatcom County*

Indian word meaning "noisy water" or "noisy, rumbling water"— This county in northwestern Washington was created by Washington territory on March 9, 1854, and given a name from the language of the Indians which meant "noisy water" or "noisy, rumbling water." That name probably referred to Whatcom Falls at the mouth of Whatcom Creek, in what is now the city of Bellingham, Washington, the county seat of Whatcom County. Some sources say that the name came from an Indian chief, whose name meant "noisy water."

2918 *Whitman County*

Marcus Whitman (1802–1847)— A native of New York and a physician, Whitman learned of a need for Protestant missionaries in the Oregon country and volunteered his services, as an non-ordained assistant missionary. Told that only married couples were wanted for this duty, Marcus Whitman married Narcissa Prentiss (1808–1847), who was equally dedicated, and the couple established a mission at Waiilatpu, near the present city of Walla Walla, Washington. Whitman and his wife labored under many difficulties, including the fact that the United States and Great Britain had not yet agreed that "the Oregon country" belonged to America. He became convinced that best way to win the area for our nation was to fill it with American settlers and he was a key player in prompting the American immigration along the Oregon trail. At the Waiilatpu mission, Whitman was beginning to see results from his evangelistic and medical efforts, when neighboring Cayuse Indians murdered Marcus and Narcissa Whitman and a dozen others on November 29, 1847. News of the massacre prompted creation of Oregon territory and White settlers retaliated against the Indians in the Cayuse Indian War of 1847–1850. This county was created by Washington territory on November 29, 1871, the 24th anniversary of the massacre.

2919 *Yakima County*

Yakima Indians— The Yakima Indians were an important tribe of the Columbia River basin of what is now Oregon and Washington. They subsisted on nuts, berries, roots and fish and their principal type of dwelling was a long house made of bark and skin. The Lewis & Clark Expedition encountered Yakima Indians in 1805 and again in 1806. In 1855 the Yakima ceded their lands to the U.S. government. After a period of warfare, the Yakima were subdued and settled, along with 13 other tribes, on the Yakima Indian reservation, which is now Washington's largest Indian reservation. In 1985 there were 7,987 people on the Yakima reservation, most of whom were Yakima Indians. This county was first created by Washington territory with the name Ferguson County, in honor of James Leo Ferguson, a member of the territorial legislature. During January, 1865, the act creating that county was repealed and Yakima County replaced it, with slightly altered boundaries.

REFERENCES

Alexie, Sherman. *Indian Killer*. New York, Atlantic Monthly Press, 1996.

Alotta, Robert I. *Signposts & Settlers: The History of Place Names West of the Rockies*. Chicago, Bonus Books, Inc., 1994.

Avery, Mary W. *Washington: A History of the Evergreen State*. Seattle, University of Washington Press, 1965.

Bagley, Clarence B. *History of King County, Washington*. Chicago, S. J. Clarke Publishing Co., 1929.

Barry, J. Neilson. "The Indians in Washington: Their Distribution by Languages." *Oregon Historical Quarterly*, Vol. 28, No. 2. Portland, Oregon: June, 1927.

Barto, Harold E., & Catharine Bullard. *History of the State of Washington*. D. C. Heath & Co., 1953.

Beaver, L. J. *Historic Memories from Monuments & Plaques of Western Washington*. Puyallup, Washington, 1964.

Blankenship, Mrs. George E. *Early History of Thurston County, Washington*. Olympia, 1914.

The Book of the Counties: 1953. Washington States Associations of County Commissioners & County Engineers and the State College of Washington.

Bowman, J. N. "Washington Nomenclature: A Study." *Washington Historical Quarterly*, Vol. 1, No. 1. Seattle: October, 1906.

Brown, William C. *Early Okanogan History*. Okanogan, Washington, Press of the Okanogan Independent.

Carpenter, Allan. *The Encyclopedia of the Far West*. New York, Facts On File, Inc., 1991.

Clark County Marriages. Vancouver, Washington, Clark County Genealogical Society, 1982.

Clarke, S. A. *Pioneer Days of Oregon History*. Portland, J. K. Gill Co., 1905.

Clements, John. *Washington Facts*. Dallas, Texas, Clements Research II, Inc., 1989.

Connette, Earle. *Pacific Northwest Quarterly Index: Vol. 1, 1906–Vol. 53, 1962*. Hamden, Connecticut, Shoe String Press, Inc., 1964.

Coughlin, Dan. "County Now Named After Another King." *Seattle Post Intelligencer*, February 25, 1986.

"Documents: The Indian Chief Kitsap." *Washington Historical Quarterly*, Vol. 25, No. 4. Seattle: October, 1934.

Downs, Winfield S. *Encyclopedia of Northwest Biography*. New York, American Historical Co., Inc., 1941.

Du Gard, Rene C. *Dictionary of Spanish Place Names of the Northwest Coast of America*. Editions des Deux Mondes, 1983.

Du Gard, Rene C., & Dominique C. Western. *The Handbook of French Place Names in the U.S.A.* Editions des Deux Mondes, 1977.

Edwards, Jonathan. *An Illustrated History of Spokane County, State of Washington*. W. H. Lever, 1900.

Eells, Myron. *Marcus Whitman: Pathfinder & Patriot*. Seattle, Alice Harriman Co., 1909.

Evans, Elwood, & Edmond S. Meany. *The State of Washington: A Brief History of the Discovery, Settlement & Organization of Washington*. World's Fair Commission of the State of Washington, 1893.

Faber, Harold. *From Sea to Sea: The Growth of the United States*. New York, Farrar, Straus & Giroux, 1967.

Fort Vancouver Historical Society, Vol. 1. Vancouver, Washington: 1960.

Frazer, Robert W. *Forts of the West*. Norman, University of Oklahoma Press, 1965.

Garbe, Frank A. "The Subdivisions of the Original Lewis County." *Washington Historical Quarterly*, Vol. 21, No. 1. Seattle: January, 1930.

Gibbs, George. "Tribes of Western Washington & Northwestern Oregon." *Contributions to American Ethnology*, Vol. 1. Washington, DC: 1877.

Gudde, Erwin G. "Okanagan Place Names." *Western Folklore*, Vol. 8, No. 2. Berkeley: April, 1949.

Hart, Herbert M. *Old Forts of the Northwest*. New York, Bonanza Books, 1963.

Hauptli, Jack. "Here's How the Counties Got Their Names." *The Seattle Times Magazine*, Sunday, January 10, 1971.

Hawes, Lou Kinne. *Island County: A World Beater*. Elizabeth H. Dodge, 1968.

Hawthorne, Julian. *History of Washington: The Evergreen State*. New York, American Historical Publishing Co., 1893.

Healy, Diana Dixon. *America's Vice-Presidents*. New York, Atheneum, 1984.

Heffelfinger, C. H. *The Evergreen Citizen: A Textbook of the Government of the State of Washington*. Caldwell, Idaho, Caxton Printers, Ltd., 1960.

Hines, H. K. *An Illustrated History of the State of Washington*. Chicago, Lewis Publishing Co., 1893.

Historical Highlights: State of Washington. Olympia, Belle Reeves, Secretary of State, 1941.

Historical Records Survey, Division of Women's & Professional Projects. *Inventory of the County Archives of Washington-Asotin County*. Spokane, 1938.

Hitchman, Robert. *Place Names of Washington*. Washington State Historical Society, 1985.

Hodge, Frederick W. *Handbook of American Indians North of Mexico*. Totowa, New Jersey, Rowman & Littlefield, 1975.

Howay, Frederic W. *Voyages of the Columbia to the Northwest Coast: 1787–1790 & 1790–1793*. Boston, Massachusetts Historical Society, 1941.

An Illustrated History of the Big Bend Country Embracing Lincoln, Douglas, Adams & Franklin Counties, State of Washington. Spokane, Western Historical Publishing Co., 1904.

An Illustrated History of Klickitat, Yakima & Kittitas Counties: With An Outline of the Early History of the State of Washington. Interstate Publishing Co., 1904.

Index to the 1880 Census of Walla Walla County, Washington Territory. Tri-City Genealogical Society: Pasco, Kennewick & Richland, Washington.

Index to the 1880 Census of Yakima County, Washington Territory. Tri-City Genealogical Society Press: Pasco, Kennewick & Richland, Washington.

Jeffcott, P. R. *Nooksack Tails & Trails*. Ferndale, Washington, Sedro-Woolley Courier Times, 1949.

Kingston, C. S. "Teacher's Section: Juan de Fuca Strait: Origin of the Name." *Pacific Northwest Quarterly*, Vol. 36, No. 2. Seattle: April, 1945.

Kirk, Ruth. *Washington State National Parks, Historic Sites, Recreation Areas & Natural Landmarks*. Seattle, University of Washington Press, 1974.

Kittitas County Centennial Committee. *A History of Kittitas County, Washington*. Dallas, Texas, Taylor Publishing Co., 1989.

Kuykendall, Elgin V. *Historic Glimpses of Asotin County, Washington*. Clarkston, Washington, Press of the Clarkston Herald, 1954.

Landes, Henry. "A Geographic Dictionary of Washington." *Washington Geological Survey*, Bulletin No. 17. Olympia: 1917.

Lane, Bob. "Keep Rufus As the King in County, Council Told." *Seattle Times*, February 15, 1986.

Lee, W. Storrs. *Washington State: A Literary Chronicle*. New York, Funk & Wagnalls, 1969.

McArthur, Lewis A. *Oregon Geographic Names*. Portland, Oregon, Oregon Historical Society Press, 1992.

McArthur, Lewis A. "Oregon Geographic Names: VII." *Oregon Historical Quarterly*, Vol. 28, No. 2. Portland, Oregon: June, 1927.

Meany, Edmond S. *Governors of Washington: Territorial & State*. Seattle, University of Washington, 1915.

Meany, Edmond S. *History of the State of Washington*. New York, Macmillan Co., 1909.

Meany, Edmond S. *Origin of Washington Geographic Names*. Seattle, University of Washington Press, 1923.

Meany, Edmond S. "Origin of Washington Geographic Names." *Washington Historical Quarterly*, Seattle: Vol. 12, No. 1. January, 1921; Vol. 12, No. 2. April, 1921; Vol. 13, No. 1. January, 1922; Vol. 13, No. 2. April, 1922; Vol. 13, No. 3. July, 1922; Vol. 14, No. 1. January, 1923; Vol. 14, No. 2. April, 1923; Vol. 14, No. 3. July, 1923.

Middleton, Lynn. *Place Names of the Pacific Northwest Coast*. Seattle, Superior Publishing Co., 1969.

Nixon, Oliver W. *How Marcus Whitman Saved Oregon*. Chicago, Star Publishing Co., 1895.

Olmsted, Gerald W. *The Best of the Pacific Coast: San Francisco to British Columbia*. New York, Crown Publishers, Inc., 1989.

Olson, Mrs. Charles H. *Cowlitz County, Washington: 1854–1948*. Kelso, Washington, 1947.

Oregon, Washington Tour Book. Heathrow, Florida, AAA Publications, 1999.

Perry, Richard M. *The Counties of Washington*. Olympia, Washington Secretary of State, 1943.

Phillips, James W. *Washington State Place Names*. Seattle, University of Washington Press, 1971.

Phillips, James W. "Why Did They Name It That?" *Washington Welcome*, Vol. 2, No. 3. Seattle: Fall, 1964.

Pollard, Lancaster. *A History of the State of Washington*. Portland, Oregon, Binfords & Mort, 1941.

Prosser, William F. *A History of the Puget Sound Country*. New York, Lewis Publishing Co., 1903.

R. L. Polk & Co's Walla Walla City & County Directory: 1902. Seattle, R. L. Polk & Co., 1902.

Reid, Robert A. *Puget Sound & Western Washington*. Seattle, 1912.

Russell, Jervis. *Jimmy Come Lately: History of Clallam County*. Port Orchard, Washington, Publishers Printing, 1971.

Scott, Harvey W. *History of the Oregon Country*. Cambridge, Riverside Press, 1924.

Smeltzer, Jean Allyn. *1880 United States Census of Mason County, Washington Territory*. Portland, Oregon, 1972.

Smith, Charles W. "The Naming of Counties in the State of Washington." *Bulletin of the University of Washington*, University Studies No. 6. Seattle: October, 1913.

Smith, Charles W. "The Naming of Counties in the State of Washington." *The Magazine of History*, Vol. 10, No. 1. New York: July, 1909.

Smith, Charles W. "The Naming of Counties in the State of Washington." *The Magazine of History*, Vol. 10, No. 2. New York: August, 1909.

Smith Francis E. *Achievements & Experiences of Captain Robert Gray: 1788 to 1792*. Tacoma, Barrett-Redfield Press, 1923.

Snowden, Clinton A. *History of Washington*. New York, Century History Co., 1909.

Stevens, Hazard. *The Life of Isaac Ingalls Stevens*. Boston, Houghton Mifflin & Co., 1900.

Stoutenburgh, John. *Dictionary of the American Indian*. New York, Bonanza Books, 1990.

Sutton, Chloe. "The Erection of Kitsap County." *Washington Historical Quarterly*, Vol. 24, No. 3. Seattle: July, 1933.

Thrapp, Dan L. *Encyclopedia of Frontier Biography*. Lincoln, University of Nebraska Press, 1988.

Thrapp, Dan L. *Encyclopedia of Frontier Biography: Supplemental Volume 4*. Spokane, Arthur H. Clark Co., 1994.

Upham, Warren. *Minnesota Geographic Names*. St. Paul, Minnesota Historical Society, 1969.

Van Syckle, Edwin. *The River Pioneers: Early Days on Grays Harbor*. Seattle, Pacific Search Press, 1982.

Vexler, Robert I. *Chronology & Documentary Handbook of the State of Washington*. Dobbs Ferry, New York, Oceana Publications, Inc., 1979.

Vogel, Virgil J. "Indian Place Names in Illinois." *Journal of the Illinois State Historical Society*, Vol. 55. 1962.

Walbran, John T. *British Columbia Coast Names: 1592–1906: To Which Are Added a Few Names in Adjacent United States Territory*. Seattle, University of Washington Press, 1971.

Waldman, Carl. *Who Was Who in Native American History*. New York, Facts On File, Inc., 1990.

Washington. Olympia, Washington Department of State.

Watt, Roberta Frye. *The Story of Seattle*. Seattle, Lowman & Hanford Co., 1932.

With Pride in Heritage: History of Jefferson County. Port Townsend, Washington, Jefferson County Historical Society, 1966.

Wood, Bryce. *San Juan Island: Coastal Place Names & Cartographic Nomenclature*. University Microfilms International, 1980.

Work Projects Administration. *Inventory of the County Archives of Washington-Chelan, Cowlitz & Snohomish Counties*. Seattle, 1942.

Works Progress Administration. *Inventory of the County Archives of Washington-Skagit County*. Pullman Washington, 1938.

Yenne, Bill. *The Encyclopedia of North American Indian Tribes*. New York, Crescent Books, 1986.

West Virginia

(55 counties)

2920 *Barbour County*

Philip P. Barbour (1783–1841) — A native of Virginia and a lawyer, Barbour served in that state's house of delegates before being elected to represent Virginia in the U.S. House of Representatives. He served as speaker of the house from 1821 to 1823. In congress Barbour was alarmed by the drift of our infant nation to a strong central government and he was a champion of states' rights and strict construction of the federal constitution. He presented a bill to require at least five of the seven supreme court justices to agree on decisions involving interpretation of the constitution. President Andrew Jackson appointed Barbour to the federal judiciary and subsequently elevated him to the supreme court. He became an associate justice in 1836 but died five years later, on February 25, 1841. The state of Virginia created and named this county in Justice Barbour's honor just two years later, on March 3, 1843. Most sources agree that this county was named for Philip P. Barbour, but a few say that it was named for his brother, James Barbour (1775–1842). They are wrong. The language of the act that created this county specified that it was "…in honour to, and in memory of Philip P. Barbour of Virginia."

2921 *Berkeley County*

Norborne Berkeley, Baron de Botetourt (–1770)—Born in London, England about 1718, Berkeley entered England's house of commons in 1741 and served as a member of parliament for a number of years. Appointed a colonel in the militia, Berkeley also was made lord lieutenant of Gloucestershire, and in 1764 he was made baron de Botetourt. In August, 1768, Berkeley was commissioned royal governor of Virginia. His predecessors had generally remained in England with a lieutenant-governor serving as Virginia's resident chief executive. However Berkeley came to Virginia in October, 1768, and personally served as Virginia's resident chief executive from October 28, 1768, until his death on October 15, 1770. During the period that Berkeley was governor, tensions were building in Virginia and England's other North American colonies concerning England's treatment of her colonial subjects. Apparently Berkeley enjoyed a degree of local popularity in spite of those tensions, although sources consulted differ concerning the degree of that popularity. This county was created in England's colony of Virginia during the spring of 1772, less than two years after Governor Berkeley's death. This was the second county that Virginia had named in honor of Governor Norborne Berkeley. The first was Botetourt County and Virginia kept that county but lost this second one in 1863 when West Virginia became a separate state.

2922 *Boone County*

Daniel Boone (1734–1820)—A native of Pennsylvania, Boone penetrated Kentucky when it was wilderness country and settled there with his family in 1775. He gained fame on America's rugged western frontier as explorer, Indian fighter and surveyor. About 1790 he moved to the Kanawha Valley of Virginia in what is now West Virginia. To many of us, this area still seems quite rural at the year of 2000, but to Daniel Boone it was already becoming too crowded for his taste by 1799. In September, 1799, accompanied by some family members, Boone moved to what is now Missouri. This county was created by the state of Virginia on March 11, 1847.

2923 *Braxton County*

Carter Braxton (1736–1797)—A native of Virginia, and a graduate of the College of William & Mary, Braxton served in the house of burgesses of colonial Virginia from 1761 to 1775. As a participant in Virginia's effort to gain independence from England, Braxton was a member of Virginia's committee of safety, a Virginia delegate to the Continental Congress and one of Virginia's signers of the Declaration of Independence. Braxton was a conservative who had little faith in democracy, although he did trust the people to hold their own religious views and supported Virginia's act to establish religious freedom. This county was created by Virginia on January 15, 1836.

2924 *Brooke County*

Robert Brooke (1761–1800)—A native of Virginia, Brooke served in the Continental army during the American Revolution. After the Revolution, from 1791 to 1794, he was a member of Virginia's house of delegates, and then was elected by the state legislature to serve as Virginia's governor. He held that office from 1794 to 1796 and later was elected attorney general of Virginia. This county was created by the state of Virginia on November 30, 1796, the last day of Robert Brooke's tenure as governor. He was succeeded by James Wood (1750–1813).

2925 *Cabell County*

William H. Cabell (1772–1853)—A native of Virginia and a 1793 graduate of the College of William & Mary, Cabell served in the house of delegates of the young state of Virginia and then was elected as the state's governor. During his three year tenure as governor, from 1805 to 1808, slave trade ended in Virginia. William H. Cabell left office as Virginia's governor in December, 1808, and this county was created by the state of Virginia one month later, on January 2, 1809. After leaving the governor's office Cabell held judicial positions in Virginia.

2926 *Calhoun County*

John C. Calhoun (1782–1850)—Calhoun represented South Carolina in both houses of the U.S. Congress. He served as secretary of war, secretary of state and as vice-president. He was a forceful advocate of slavery, states' rights and limited powers for the federal government. He resigned the vice-presidency to enter the U.S. Senate where he thought he could better represent the views of South Carolina and the South. This county was created by Virginia on March 5, 1856.

2927 *Clay County*

Henry Clay (1777–1852)—Clay represented Kentucky in both branches of the U.S. Congress. For many years he was one of the more prominent figures in American politics but his several bids for the presidency were unsuccessful. He was influential in effecting important compromises between northern and southern interests during the years that secession and civil war were imminent. This county created by the state of Virginia on March 29, 1858, perhaps in sadness that compromise efforts of Henry Clay's to avert civil war seemed to be failing.

2928 *Doddridge County*

Philip Doddridge (–1832)—Doddridge was born on May 17 but the year of his birth is unclear since some sources show 1772 while other, equally reputable, sources cite 1773. The year that this county was created is also in doubt. It was created by the state of Virginia on February 4, but sources consulted differ on whether the year was 1844 or 1845. Philip Doddridge was born in Pennsylvania but moved to Charlestown (now Wellsburg) in the portion of Virginia which would ultimately be the northern West Virginia panhandle, just west of Pennsylvania. Here Doddridge studied law, was admitted to the bar and established a successful practice. As a member of Virginia's house of delegates during the 1815–1816 period, he was a forceful advocate of the rights of the citizens of western Virginia. There was genuine cause for concern for those rights, because the Virginia constitution had established representation in the legislature in a manner to insure control of it by Tidewater areas of Virginia. Martha W. Hiden's work entitled *How Justice Grew: Virginia Counties: An Abstract of Their Formation*, states that as a member of Virginia's constitutional convention of 1829–1830, Doddridge "…was an advocate of the wishes of the western portion of the state to have representation based upon white population exclusively. This motion failed…" Doddridge was elected to represent Virginia in the U.S. House of Representatives, where he served from December 7, 1829, until his death on November 19, 1832.

2929 *Fayette County*

Marie Joseph Paul Yves Roch Gilbert du Motier, Marquis de Lafayette (1757–1834)— Lafayette was a French aristocrat who served briefly in the French army. He came to America in 1777 to assist the American Revolutionary army. He was granted an honorary commission as major general by the Continental Congress and served with distinction in a number of battles in the Revolutionary War. Lafayette returned to France in 1782 but he returned to America on a brief visit in 1784 and in 1825 Lafayette toured our country extensively. On that trip, in May, 1825, General Lafayette visited western Virginia while touring the Ohio Valley region. This county was created by Virginia on February 28, 1831.

2930 *Gilmer County*

Thomas W. Gilmer (1802–1844)— A native of Virginia, lawyer and editor of the *Virginia Advocate*, Gilmer served several terms in Virginia's house of delegates and was twice speaker of that body. Elected governor of Virginia by the state legislature, Gilmer served about one year before resigning on March 20, 1841, as a result of a dispute with the Virginia legislature. He was soon elected to the U.S. House of Representatives where he served until February 18, 1844, when he resigned to become secretary of the navy in President John Tyler's cabinet. Ten days later, on February 28, 1844, Gilmer was killed in an accident near our nation's capitol aboard a U.S. warship. The state of Virginia created this county one year later, on February 3, 1845.

2931 *Grant County*

Ulysses S. Grant (1822–1885)— Grant was a native of Ohio who graduated from the U.S. Military Academy at West Point. He served with distinction in the Mexican War, and in the Civil War he rose to become commander of all Union forces. After the Civil War, Grant briefly served as acting secretary of war and then two terms as president of the United States. He proved to be a rather mediocre president. This county was created by the state of West Virginia on February 14, 1866, just ten months after the Confederacy had surrendered to General Ulysses S. Grant.

2932 *Greenbrier County*

Greenbrier River— This county in southeastern West Virginia was created on October 20, 1777 (effective March 1, 1778), by Virginia, and named for the Greenbrier River, which flows across the eastern end of the county from north to south. The Greenbrier rises in northern Pocahontas County, West Virginia, and flows southwest for about 175 miles to enter New River, near Hinton, West Virginia. In *Myers' History of West Virginia* an old legend about the origin of the river's name is dismissed: "…tradition reciting that when in 1750 John Lewis … came to the valley of this river to survey lands for the Greenbrier Land Company, he … became entangled in the greenbriers growing on its banks and he declared that henceforth he should call it Greenbrier River. This cannot be true, for the company for which he came to make the surveys (already) bore the name of the Greenbrier Land Company." J. R. Cole's *History of Greenbrier County* indicates that the river was named prior to 1750, by the French as *Ronceverte*, *ronce* meaning "brier" or "bramble branch," and *verte*, the French adjective for "green." Several species of greenbriers grow along the banks of Greenbrier River.

2933 *Hampshire County*

Hampshire County, England— Hampshire County, England, whose important municipalities include Portsmouth, Southampton and Bournemouth, lies on the English Channel near the Isle of Wight, which is considered part of Hampshire County for purposes of civil administration. Excluding the Isle of Wight, Hampshire County is approximately 42 miles long and some 38 miles wide. Hampshire is one of England's most fertile counties. A range of chalk downs runs through a northern portion of the county. Hampshire's principal rivers are the Avon, Test, Itchen and Stour. In the sixth century A.D., Cerdic (–534) and his Saxons invaded and conquered much of southern England, including the present Hampshire County. This was the beginning of Wessex, the kingdom of the West Saxons. Hampshire possesses relatively little in the way of magnificent architecture, but it can boast an ancient cathedral in its city of Winchester. The name *Hampshire* evolved from the earlier *Hamtunscir*. The *scir* portion of the name became *shire*, which is one of the words used in England for our word "county." Possible origins and translations of the *Ham* and *tun* portions of the earlier name include:

> *Ham*— "A home, dwelling or house"
> *tun*— "A garden, field or enclosure"

In his work entitled *A Dictionary of English Place Names*, A.D. Mills stated that *Hampshire* derived from an earlier name *Hamtunscir*, which meant "district based on Hamtun"; i.e., "district based on Southampton."

Hampshire County, West Virginia, is known to be the oldest county in the state, although the exact date of its creation is disputed. It was definitely established by England's colony of Virginia in the 1750's and several sources indicate that it was created by Virginia's legislative session of February, 1752, to become effective December 13, 1753. Since that time this county's borders have been changed several times and it now lies near the eastern end of the state of West Virginia, with Virginia on its eastern border and the state of Maryland bordering it on the north. This county's name was chosen by Thomas Fairfax, Baron Fairfax of Cameron (1692–1782), whose 5 million acre estate in the Northern Neck of Virginia included Hampshire County. Although Fairfax was born in Yorkshire, England, he felt that Hampshire would be an apt name for this portion of his vast Virginia domain because he had observed fine hogs here, and Baron Fairfax claimed that Hampshire, England was noted for its hogs.

2934 *Hancock County*

John Hancock (1737–1793)— A native of Massachusetts and a graduate of Harvard, Hancock served in the Massachusetts legislature and was president of the Massachusetts provincial congress. He was elected to the Second Continental Congress and became its president. As president of that body when the Declaration of Independence was signed, he was, on July 4, 1776, the first signer of the Declaration. He signed it with such a flourish that the name John Hancock became a synonym for "signature." Hancock later commanded the

Massachusetts militia, served as governor of that state for many years and presided over the Massachusetts convention that ratified the U.S. Constitution. This county was created by Virginia in 1848.

2935 Hardy County

Samuel Hardy (1758–1785)—A native of Virginia and a 1778 graduate of the College of William & Mary, Hardy studied law and was admitted to the bar. He served in Virginia's house of delegates and as Virginia's lieutenant-governor under Governor Benjamin Harrison (1726–1791). Hardy represented Virginia as a delegate to the Continental Congress and one source comments that he was effective in keeping the central government functioning despite the weak Articles of Confederation under which it operated. Samuel Hardy died while serving in congress at New York City on October 17, 1785, and this county was created by the Virginia legislature during the October, 1785, session of that legislature.

2936 Harrison County

Benjamin Harrison (1726–1791)—Born to wealth at Berkeley plantation, on the James River in England's colony of Virginia, Benjamin Harrison was a member of Virginia's house of burgesses for many years and was speaker of that body on several occasions. He represented Virginia in the Continental Congress and was a Virginia signer of the Declaration of Independence. He also served in Virginia's house of delegates and was governor of Virginia from November, 1781, until November, 1784. As a delegate to the Virginia convention called to ratify the proposed federal constitution, Benjamin Harrison objected to it because it lacked a bill of rights. However, after Virginia ratified it, he gave the federal constitution his support. This county was created by the Virginia legislature during the legislative session of May 3, 1784, and was therefore born while Benjamin Harrison was serving as governor. This Benjamin Harrison was the father of one of America's presidents, William Henry Harrison (1773–1841) and the great-grandfather of another, Benjamin Harrison (1833–1901).

2937 Jackson County

Andrew Jackson (1767–1845)—Jackson was born on the border of North Carolina and South Carolina. He represented Tennessee in both branches of the U.S. Congress. He gained fame and popularity for his military exploits in wars with the Indians and in the War of 1812. He was provisional military governor of Florida and, from 1829 to 1837, General Jackson was president of the United States. His presidency reflected the frontier spirit of America. This county was created by the state of Virginia on March 1, 1831, while Jackson was our nation's president.

2938 Jefferson County

Thomas Jefferson (1743–1826)—Jefferson was a native of Virginia and a member of the Virginia legislature. He served Virginia as governor and was a delegate to the second Continental Congress. Jefferson was the author of the Declaration of Independence and one of its signers. He was minister to France, secretary of state, vice-president and president of the United States. As president, he accomplished the Louisiana Purchase and he arranged the Lewis & Clark Expedition to the Pacific Northwest. Jefferson was a true intellectual, thoroughly knowledgeable in the arts and sciences. His political theories were pivotal in the formation of our infant republic. This county was created by the state of Virginia in January, 1801, while Jefferson was serving as vice-president and was president-elect. He took office on March 4, 1801.

2939 Kanawha County

Great Kanawha River—This county was created by the state of Virginia (spelled Kenhawa) on November 14, 1788, and named for the Great Kanawha River, which flows across it. (A few sources say that the county was named for an Indian tribe, and this is true, indirectly, because the Great Kanawha River was named for an Algonquian Indian tribe, generally called the Conoy Indians, but also known by other names, including Kanawha.) Only 97 miles long, the Great Kanawha River is a major, navigable river. It is formed by the junction of New River with Gauley River, just south of Kanawha County. The Great Kanawha flows northwest from that junction and almost immediately crosses into Kanawha County, which it traverses in a generally northwestern course. The Great Kanawha passes within sight of the West Virginia state capitol at Charleston and ends its journey at the Ohio River on the Ohio state border. During preparations to carve a new state from western Virginia, the name Kanawha was initially proposed for the new state's name but it was rejected and West Virginia was adopted, instead.

2940 Lewis County

Charles Lewis (–1774)—Born in Virginia between 1733 and 1736, Lewis became noted at an early age as a skilled frontiersman and Indian fighter. He served as a captain under both his brother, Andrew Lewis (1720–1781), and George Washington (1732–1799). Charles Lewis fought in an expedition against the Ohio Indians under Henry Bouquet (1719–1765) and Lewis led an important successful engagement against Indians on the south fork of the Potomac River in 1763. He owned a plantation and slaves and served in Virginia's house of burgesses. During Lord Dunmore's War, Charles Lewis held the rank of colonel when he led a contingent of 150 Virginia troops to combat Shawnee Indians, in what is now West Virginia, at the battle of Point Pleasant, on October 10, 1774. The Indians were defeated but Colonel Lewis was killed in combat. This county was created by the state of Virginia on December 18, 1816.

2941 Lincoln County

Abraham Lincoln (1809–1865)—Lincoln was a native of Kentucky who moved to Illinois, where he was a member of the state legislature. He represented Illinois in the U.S. House of Representatives and later was elected president of the United States. Lincoln's presidency coincided almost exactly with the Civil War. He guided the United States ably through that uniquely turbulent period. As president, he issued the Emancipation Proclamation which declared the freedom of slaves in all states in rebellion. Lincoln was assassinated in April, 1865, a few days after the Union's victory in the Civil War. This county was created by the state of West Virginia on February 23, 1867. President Lincoln had signed the proclamation which admitted the state of West Virginia to the U.S. federal union in 1863, during the Civil War.

2942 Logan County

John Logan (–1780)—This Indian leader was born near the Susquehanna River in Pennsylvania about 1725 and was also known as Tahgahjute, Tachnechdorus and James Logan. The Logan name was taken from his friend, James Logan (1674–1751), a Quaker and private secretary to Pennsylvania's William Penn (1644–1718). John Logan became a leader of Mingo Indians on the Ohio and Scioto Rivers in the 1760's and was friendly with White settlers and the British governing officials during that period. However, in April, 1774, Logan's family was massacred at Yellow Creek near today's Steubenville, Ohio. The enraged Logan retaliated by leading attacks on White settlements from the Allegheny River to the Cumberland Gap. Logan and the Shawnee chief, Cornstalk (–1777), were the principal leaders of Indian resistance to the British during Lord Dunmore's War and even after the Indian defeat at the battle of Point Pleasant, on October 10, 1774, Logan continued raids on White settlements during the American Revolution. This county was created by the state of Virginia during January, 1824.

2943 *McDowell County*

James McDowell (1795–1851)— A native of Virginia and an 1817 graduate of Princeton College, McDowell was elected to Virginia's house of delegates in 1830 and served several terms in that body. Chosen as Virginia's governor by the state legislature, he served in that office from January, 1843 to January, 1846. McDowell favored the gradual abolition of slavery. William Taylor (–1846), a Virginia representative in the U.S. House of Representatives, died on January 17, 1846, and James McDowell was elected to take his seat in Congress. He served in that body from 1846 to 1851. This county was created on February 20, 1858, by Virginia.

2944 *Marion County*

Francis Marion (–1795)— Marion is believed to have been born in South Carolina. He served in the army in battles against the Cherokee Indians and was elected to the provisional congress of 1775. He served, with distinction, as an officer in the Revolutionary War and rose to the rank of general in that war. Marion was also a member of the South Carolina senate. This county was created by the state of Virginia on January 14, 1842.

2945 *Marshall County*

John Marshall (1755–1835)— Marshall, a native of Virginia, served as an officer in the Revolutionary War, in the Virginia legislature and in the U.S. House of Representatives. He briefly served as secretary of state and then, for over 30 years, was chief justice of the U.S. Supreme Court. Marshall's interpretations of the constitution during America's political infancy left an unmatched impact on the laws and government of this country. Under Marshall, the Supreme Court shifted power in American government from the states to the central government and to the federal judiciary at the expense of the executive and legislative branches. This county was created by the state of Virginia on March 12, 1835, just four months prior to Chief Justice Marshall's death.

2946 *Mason County*

George Mason (–1792)— Born in Virginia in 1725 or 1726, Mason was prominent in the agitations which led to the American Revolution. He was a confidant of George Washington and Thomas Jefferson, a member of Virginia's house of burgesses and committee of safety. Mason wrote a major portion of Virginia's constitution, served in Virginia's assembly and participated in our country's birth at the 1787 constitutional convention. Although he was a southerner, he opposed slavery. Virginia created a Mason County, honoring George Mason in 1788 but lost it to Kentucky when that state was separated from Virginia in 1792. The state of Virginia created this second Mason County on January 2, 1804, but lost it when West Virginia was formed in 1863. Apparently Virginia gave up trying, because it has no Mason County today.

2947 *Mercer County*

Hugh Mercer (–1777)— Mercer was born about 1725 in Scotland and educated as a physician. He immigrated to America about 1747 and served in the army here as an officer during the French and Indian War. At the outbreak of the American Revolution, Mercer entered the Continental army, in which he attained the rank of brigadier-general. He served with distinction under General George Washington in the surprise attack on the British at Trenton, New Jersey, in late December, 1776. One week later, at the battle of Princeton, New Jersey, on January 3, 1777, Hugh Mercer was severely wounded and he died of those wounds on January 12, 1777. This county was created by the state of Virginia on March 17, 1837.

2948 *Mineral County*

Coal & other mineral deposits of the county— In their work entitled *West Virginia Yesterday & Today*, Phil Conley and Boyd B. Stutler stated that "the Appalachian coal area is the greatest coal field in the world" and that "West Virginia has a greater part of this famous field than any other state." They expressed this as two-thirds of the total area of the state. In addition, they said that "Of the fifty-five counties in West Virginia, forty-nine have coal seams and forty-two have commercial mines." Although those statistics are now out of date, since Conley and Stutler's book was published in 1952, they capture the essence of the reason that the state of West Virginia chose to name this county Mineral County, when it created it on February 1, 1866. This county lies on top of the Allegheny Mountains, and although it is not West Virginia's leading coal producing county, vast resources of coal and other minerals are found here.

2949 *Mingo County*

Mingo Indians— The term *Mingo* was used during the late colonial period of American history to denote a tribe of Iroquois Indian stock, who were detached from the main members of the Iroquois confederacy before 1750. When they first separated from the Iroquois, the Mingo lived in Pennsylvania in the upper Ohio River area. Gradually moving down the Ohio River, they came to live primarily in the vicinity of today's Steubenville, Ohio, and had a town there consisting of 60 families. The best known Mingo Indian was John Logan (–1780), for whom Logan County, West Virginia, was named. In April, 1774, Logan's family was massacred at Yellow Creek near Steubenville, and he retaliated against White settlements. After this period, the Mingo migrated to the headwaters of the Scioto and Sandusky Rivers and they came to be called the Senecas of Sandusky because the Whites believed all western Iroquois to be Seneca Indians. In 1831, the Mingo (who then numbered about 250) sold their lands in Ohio and moved to the Neosho River of what is now the state of Kansas. In 1867 they moved to Indian territory (now Oklahoma).

2950 *Monongalia County*

Monongahela River— This county in northern West Virginia was created on October 7, 1776, by Virginia and named for the Monongahela River, which flows through it. The Monongahela is formed in northern West Virginia, near Fairmont, by the junction of Tygart River and the West Fork of the Monongahela River. The combined stream flows north across Marion and Monongalia Counties, West Virginia, into Pennsylvania. At Pittsburgh, Pennsylvania, in sight of the Pittsburgh

Pirates' Three Rivers Stadium, after a journey of 128 miles, the Monongahela unites with the Allegheny River to form the mighty Ohio River. Both Monongahela and Monongalia are attempts by Whites to reduce the Indians' name for this river to written form.

2951 *Monroe County*

James Monroe (1758–1831)— Monroe was a native of Virginia and served in the Revolutionary War. Prior to his election as president of the United States, Monroe served in a wide variety of government posts. He served Virginia in the state legislature and as governor. He was a member of the Confederation congress and the U.S. Senate. He was minister to France and to Britain and he held two cabinet posts. As president, Monroe stressed limited government and strict construction of the constitution. He acquired Florida for the U.S. from Spain and he was the author of a policy declaration (later known as the Monroe Doctrine) which proscribed outside interference in North and South America. This county was created by the state of Virginia on January 14, 1799. Later that year, on December 19, Monroe became Virginia's governor.

2952 *Morgan County*

Daniel Morgan (1736–1802)— Morgan was a native of the Northeast who moved to Virginia in his youth. He served as a general in the Revolutionary War and was regarded as a hero for important victories scored by his troops. After the war he represented Virginia for one term in the U.S. House of Representatives. This county was created on February 9, 1820, by the state of Virginia.

2953 *Nicholas County*

Wilson C. Nicholas (1761–1820)— Born at Williamsburg, Virginia, Nicholas attended the College of William & Mary there but withdrew from school in 1779 to serve in our Revolutionary army. He was a member of General George Washington's Life Guard and became its commanding officer. In 1784 Nicholas entered Virginia's house of delegates and served about a decade there before being elected to fill Virginia's seat in the U.S. Senate which had been vacated by the death of Henry Tazewell (1753–1799). Nicholas later represented Virginia in the U.S. House of Representatives. Elected as Virginia's governor in 1814, he served in that position from December, 1814 to December, 1816.

Nicholas then very briefly was president of the Richmond branch of the Bank of the United States but poor health forced him to resign almost immediately. This county was created by the state of Virginia on January 30, 1818.

2954 *Ohio County*

Ohio River— This county in West Virginia's northern panhandle was created by Virginia on October 7, 1776. It is separated from the state of Ohio, on the west, by the Ohio River, for which the county was named. The Ohio River is one of the most important commercial rivers in the United States, and it is a tributary of the Mississippi. Formed at Pittsburgh, Pennsylvania, by the confluence of the Allegheny and Monongahela Rivers, the Ohio flows generally southwest some 981 miles before joining the Mississippi at the western end of Kentucky, near Cairo, Illinois. The Ohio contributes more water to the Mississippi than any of its other tributaries. There is uncertainty about the origin and meaning of the river's name but many authorities believe that the name derived from an Iroquois word, *Oheo*, *Oyo*, *Ohion-hiio* or *Oyoneri*, which meant "beautiful." Other suggested meanings of the Ohio River's name include "Great river," "The river red with blood" and "White with froth."

2955 *Pendleton County*

Edmund Pendleton (1721–1803)— A native of Virginia and a lawyer, Pendleton was elected to Virginia's house of burgesses in 1752 and in 1774 he became one of Virginia's representatives in the first Continental Congress. In 1775 Pendleton became president of Virginia's committee of safety and when the British royal governor of colonial Virginia, John Murray (1732–1809), fled Virginia to return to England, Pendleton became head of Virginia's temporary government. He later worked with Thomas Jefferson, George Wythe (1726–1806) and others drafting Virginia's first constitution and revising its laws. Pendleton took a conservative stance in these deliberations and he opposed Jefferson's efforts to separate church from state and to abolish primogeniture and entails. Pendleton later served in Virginia's house of delegates and was speaker of that body. In 1779 he became president of Virginia's supreme court of appeals and held that position until his death. This county was created by Virginia on December 4, 1787, in an act effective May 1, 1788.

2956 *Pleasants County*

James Pleasants (1769–1836)— A native of Virginia and a graduate of the College of William & Mary, Pleasants studied law, was admitted to the bar and began a practice in Amelia County, Virginia, in 1791. He soon became active in politics and was elected to Virginia's house of delegates and later represented Virginia in both houses of the U.S. Congress. He resigned from the U.S. Senate in December, 1822, to become governor of Virginia, a post which he held from December, 1822, to December, 1825. Governor Pleasants opposed the whipping post in punishing Whites and also worked for fair treatment of free Blacks. He promoted the concept of colonization as a solution to the slave problem vexing our nation. This county was created by Virginia on March 29, 1851.

2957 *Pocahontas County*

Pocahontas (–1617)— Pocahontas was an American Indian girl who was born about 1596. Her father, Powhatan, was chief of a loose alliance of eastern tribes in tidewater Virginia when English colonists founded the settlement of Jamestown there in 1607 on the Indians' land. The colonists' leader, Captain John Smith, was captured by the Indians and legend tells us that Pocahontas interceded to save Smith's life. Whether Smith's life was actually in danger on this occasion is uncertain but it is known that Pocahontas became friendly with the English colonists at Jamestown and was an important emissary between them and her father, Chief Powhatan. In 1614 Pocahontas married one of the colonists, John Rolfe, and that marriage resulted in a period of peace between the White settlers and the Indians. In 1616 Pocahontas and her husband paid a visit to England where she died in 1617. This county was created by the state of Virginia on December 21, 1821.

2958 *Preston County*

James P. Preston (1774–1843)— Born to wealth in Virginia, Preston had as a private tutor an indentured servant of his father's and also studied at the College of William & Mary between 1790 and 1795. He served in both the Virginia senate and the Virginia house of delegates. During the War of 1812 Preston served as an officer in the U.S. army and rose from the rank of lieutenant-colonel to colonel before being crippled, for life, in combat at the battle of Crysler's Farm in November, 1813. He served in Virginia's house of delegates again before being elected as Virginia's governor in 1816, a post which he held from December, 1816, to December, 1819. This county was created by Virginia on January 19, 1818, while Preston was governor.

2959 *Putnam County*

Israel Putnam (1718–1790)— Putnam was born in Massachusetts and moved, when he was about 21, to Connecticut. He served as an officer in the French and Indian wars and later was a member of the Connecticut legislature. At the beginning of the Revolutionary War, news of the battle at Lexington, Massachusetts, reached Putnam while he was farming. In a dramatic gesture which became famous, Putnam left his plow and, without bothering to change clothes, hurried to Lexington. He was appointed a major-general in the Continental army. Although he enjoyed great popularity, he lacked the ability for high command. In 1779 a paralytic stroke ended his military career. This county was created by the state of Virginia on March 11, 1848.

2960 *Raleigh County*

Walter Ralegh (–1618)— Born in Devonshire, England, about 1554, Ralegh rose rapidly in favor during the reign of Queen Elizabeth I (1533–1603), was knighted and served in parliament. In 1585 he sent his cousin, Richard Grenville (–1591), in an early effort to colonize Virginia. Here, at Roanoke Island (now part of North Carolina), Grenville established England's first settlement in Virginia, but it was soon abandoned. Ralegh's efforts to promote colonization of Virginia were rated as a failure in England, although they soon resulted in lucrative tobacco trade. Ralegh fought for England against Spain but came into disgrace with the queen as a result of an affair with one of the queen's maids. Ralegh married the maid, but his stock continued to fall and when James I (1566–1625) took the English throne, Ralegh was stripped of all his titles. Ralegh was tried for treason, condemned to death and, after much delay, beheaded in 1618. This county was created by the state of Virginia on January 23, 1850, and named in honor of England's Sir Walter Ralegh. The act that created this county spelled both the name of the county and its namesake as *Raleigh*, and that is the spelling commonly in use on this side of the Atlantic. However, English sources render Sir Walter's surname as *Ralegh* and a copy of a Sir Walter's signature clearly shows that he spelled his name as *Ralegh*.

2961 *Randolph County*

Edmund Randolph (1753–1813)— A native of Virginia and a student at the College of William & Mary, Randolph served as attorney general of Virginia and was a Virginia delegate to the Continental Congress. He also represented Virginia at our nation's 1787 constitutional convention in Philadelphia. Randolph was chosen as governor of Virginia in early November, 1786, took the oath of office a few weeks later and served as governor until December, 1788. President George Washington appointed Edmund Randolph as our country's first attorney general and he later served as secretary of state in President Washington's cabinet. This county was created by Virginia in an act which became effective while Edmund Randolph was Virginia's governor. The county was created by the legislative session of October 16, 1786, in an act to become effective May 5, 1787.

2962 *Ritchie County*

Thomas Ritchie (1778–1854)— A native of Virginia, Ritchie tried his hand at a number of professions. He studied both law and medicine before becoming a school teacher. In 1803 he opened a small book store in Richmond, Virginia and the following year he founded the *Enquirer* (later known as the *Richmond Enquirer*). That venture had the enthusiastic support of President Thomas Jefferson. About 1805 Ritchie became the principal proprietor and sole editor of the newspaper and he continued as editor of this influential newspaper for 41 years. When the paper was founded, our nation's leadership assayed heavily with Virginian content and Ritchie had significant political influence. He also was directly involved in politics and served as secretary of the Republican (i.e., Democratic) central committee. Ritchie opposed abolition of slavery but favored its gradual elimination. His support of public schools and extensive state expenditures for infrastructures led to great popularity in western Virginia. This county was created by the state of Virginia on February 18, 1843.

2963 *Roane County*

Spencer Roane (1762–1822)— A native of Virginia, Roane attended the College of William & Mary, studied law and was admitted to the Virginia bar. He served in Virginia's house of delegates and was a lower court judge in Virginia. In 1794 Roane was elevated to the Virginia supreme court of appeals, replacing Judge Henry Tazewell (1753–1799), who had resigned to serve in the U.S. Senate. Judge Spencer Roane served on this court for more than a quarter-century. He favored strict construction of the federal constitution and opposed the tendencies of U.S. Chief Justice John Marshall (1755–1835) to usurp legislative prerogatives by finding new meanings in the constitution. Roane was a friend and ardent supporter of President Thomas Jefferson. This county was created by the state of Virginia on March 11, 1856.

2964 *Summers County*

George W. Summers (1804–1868)— A native of Virginia and a graduate of Ohio University at Athens, Ohio, Summers studied law and was admitted to the Virginia bar in 1827. He established his law practice in Kanawha County, Virginia, at Charleston, now West Virginia's state capital. He served in Virginia's house of delegates and represented Virginia in the U.S. House of Representatives. From 1852 to 1858 Summers served as a judge of the 18th judicial circuit of Virginia. As a delegate from western Virginia to Virginia's secession convention of 1861, Summers voted against secession. Resuming his law practice at Charleston, he became a resident of the new state of West Virginia when it was separated from Virginia in 1863. This county was created by the state of West Virginia on February 27, 1871.

2965 *Taylor County*

Uncertain— This county was created by the state of Virginia on January 19, 1844, and most sources indicate that it was named for U.S. Senator John Taylor (–1824). However, a few sources indicate that the county was named for Zachary Taylor (1784–1850). One of the sources which states that the county was named for Zachary Taylor is Martha W. Hiden's scholarly work entitled *How Justice Grew: Virginia Counties: An Abstract of Their Formation*, so we must recognize that choice as a credible possibility, although Zachary Taylor's fame came largely from his participation in the Mexican War and his election as president, both of which occurred after 1844, when this county was created.

John Taylor (–1824)— Born in Virginia in the 1750's, John Taylor attended the

College of William & Mary there and then studied law. Often referred to as John Taylor of Caroline to distinguish him from other prominent John Taylors of the period, he served as officer during the American Revolution but left the field of battle to serve in the Virginia house of delegates. In 1781, when the British invaded Virginia, John Taylor reentered the army as a lieutenant-colonel. After the Revolution John Taylor became a prosperous plantation owner, served again in the Virginia house of delegates and on three occasions was elected to fill vacancies for Virginia in the U.S. Senate. John Taylor believed that political representation should be awarded on the basis of the population of yeoman farmers and he was a defender of states' rights.

Zachary Taylor (1784–1850)— Also a Virginia native, Zachary Taylor moved as an infant to the Kentucky area and grew to manhood on a farm near Louisville. A career soldier, Zachary Taylor served as an officer in the War of 1812, the Black Hawk War, the Second Seminole War in Florida territory and the Mexican War. The Mexican War ended in victory for America and made Zachary Taylor a national hero, resulting in his election as president of the United States in November, 1848. Although he was a slave owner, President Taylor opposed the extension of slavery beyond the 15 states where the institution was already legal. Taylor's service as president ended after only 16 months, when he died in office on July 9, 1850.

2966 *Tucker County*

Henry St. George Tucker (1780–1848)— A native of Williamsburg, Virginia and a graduate of the College of William & Mary, Tucker studied law and was admitted to the bar before serving as an officer during the War of 1812. He represented Virginia for four years in the U.S. House of Representatives, served in the state senate and then devoted the remainder of his life to teaching law and serving as a judge. Tucker operated a private law school while serving as chancellor of Virginia's fourth judicial district and later served as president of Virginia's court of appeals and was a professor of law at the University of Virginia. This county was created by the state of Virginia in 1856.

2967 *Tyler County*

John Tyler (1747–1813)— A native of Virginia and a lawyer, Tyler served in Virginia's house of delegates for about eight years and was speaker of that body during the 1781–1785 period. He subsequently held judicial positions for more than two decades. At Virginia's 1788 convention called to consider ratification of the proposed federal constitution, John Tyler was the convention's vice-president. In 1808 he was elected governor of the state of Virginia and served in that office from December, 1808, to January, 1811, when he resigned to accept an appointment as a federal judge. One of John Tyler's children, also named John Tyler (1790–1862), became president of the United States in 1841. The John Tyler for whom this county was named died on January 6, 1813, and the state of Virginia created this county on December 6, 1814.

2968 *Upshur County*

Abel P. Upshur (1791–1844)— A native of Virginia and a lawyer, Upshur served in the Virginia legislature and held judicial offices there. After Vice-President John Tyler became president upon the death of President William Henry Harrison, Tyler appointed his fellow Virginian, Abel P. Upshur, to his cabinet as secretary of the navy, and in 1843 President Tyler elevated him to secretary of state. However, Upshur was killed in an accident near our nation's capitol aboard a U.S. warship on February 28, 1844. This county was created by Virginia on March 26, 1851.

2969 *Wayne County*

Anthony Wayne (1745–1796)— A native of Pennsylvania, Wayne was a successful brigadier-general in the Revolutionary War and became a hero for his daring exploits. During the bitter winter of 1777–1778 at Valley Forge, Pennsylvania, Wayne shared the sufferings of his men although his comfortable estate was only five miles away. He played an important role in the final overthrow of the British forces in Georgia and after the war, in 1785, Wayne moved to Georgia and represented that state for about six months in the U.S. House of Representatives. In 1792, President Washington recalled Wayne to serve as a major-general against the Indians in the Northwest territory. Once again his military efforts were successful. This county was created by the state of Virginia on January 18, 1842.

2970 *Webster County*

Daniel Webster (1782–1852)— Webster was born in New Hampshire and represented that state in the U.S. House of Representatives. He later represented Massachusetts in both houses of the U.S. Congress and served as secretary of state under three presidents. Webster felt that slavery was evil but not as evil as disunion of the United States. He played a key role in the passage of five laws in the U.S. Congress which are known as the "Compromise of 1850" which were intended to avert secession and civil war between the North and the South over the slavery issue. This county was created by the state of Virginia on January 10, 1860, perhaps in sadness that compromise efforts of Daniel Webster's to avert civil war seemed to be failing.

2971 *Wetzel County*

Lewis Wetzel (1763–1808)— Born in Pennsylvania, Wetzel moved as a baby with his family to Virginia in the Big Wheeling Creek area, in what is now the state of West Virginia. When he was about 13 years old, Wetzel and his younger brother, Jacob Wetzel (1765–1827), were captured and taken by Indians to Ohio. Perhaps this incident triggered Wetzel's life-long devotion to the cause of fighting and killing Indians. During the period of the American Revolution he was engaged in numerous conflicts against Indians on America's western frontier and he survived to brag about the numbers he had killed. In 1782 Wetzel accompanied Colonel William Crawford (1732–1782), on the expedition when Crawford was captured by Delaware Indians, tortured and burned at the stake in Ohio. Wetzel avoided capture on that occasion and continued to live a life devoted to killing Indians. His conduct against the Indians was so barbaric that even in those rough and ready times Wetzel was ostracized for his extremism. Wetzel found time to take trips down the Mississippi and spent several years imprisoned in a Spanish jail. He died in the vicinity of Natchez, Mississippi, of fever and thus escaped the Indians' hatchet to the end. This county was created by the state of Virginia on January 10, 1846. Apparently Wetzel's skills as a backwoodsman and Indian fighter were admired by the Virginia legislators in spite of his brutalities.

2972 *Wirt County*

William Wirt (1772–1834)— A native of Maryland and a lawyer, Wirt practiced law in Virginia at Culpeper, Richmond and Norfolk. In 1807 President Thomas Jefferson appointed Wirt as a counsel at the treason trial of former Vice-President Aaron Burr (1756–1836). Wirt later served as a U.S. attorney in Virginia and in 1817 President James Monroe appointed William Wirt to his cabinet as attorney general. Wirt continued in that cabinet post under President John Quincy Adams. This county was created by the state of Virginia during January, 1848.

2973 *Wood County*

James Wood (–1813)—Born about 1750 in Virginia, Wood served in the army during the Seven Years' War and in Lord Dunmore's War. During the American Revolution he was an officer and rose to the rank of brigadier-general of Virginia militia. Wood also was elected to Virginia's house of burgesses and was involved in negotiations with Indian tribes. In 1784 James Wood was elected to the Virginia council and in 1796 he was elected by the state legislature as Virginia's governor. He served in that post from December, 1796, to December, 1799, when James Monroe (1758–1831) took office as Virginia's governor. This county was created by Virginia on December 21, 1798, while Wood was the state's governor

2974 *Wyoming County*

Uncertain—This county in the southwestern area of West Virginia was created by the state of Virginia on January 26, 1850. Several West Virginia sources indicate that this county's name honors the Wyoming Indians but Martha W. Hiden's scholarly work entitled *How Justice Grew: Virginia Counties: An Abstract of Their Formation*, states that: "The reason for the name is obscure, whether it was for the beautiful Wyoming Valley in north central Pennsylvania watered by the Susquehanna River, or for the brutal massacre of its inhabitants 4 July 1778 by a British and Indian force is unknown." In a 1982 work entitled *County Names: An Historical Perspective*, William H. Taft III is less hesitant. Taft states that "Though the *State's Encyclopedia* of 1929 ascribes the name to a nearby tribe…"(the county was named for) "…the Wyoming Valley in northeastern Pennsylvania. There, both Indians and Tories massacred Connecticut settlers during the Revolution."

Pennsylvania's Wyoming Valley—Pennsylvania's Wyoming Valley is a part of the Susquehanna River valley. The name *Wyoming* is of Indian origin and means "upon the great plains." In the early 1700's the Delaware Indians had a village at the present site of Wilkes-Barre, Pennsylvania, in the valley of the Susquehanna River, a few miles southeast of Wyoming County, Pennsylvania. The Indians called both the valley there, and their village within it *M'chewomink*, which meant "on the broad plain," or "upon the great plains." The Indians had no written language so it was left to Whites to render the name in writing and the name took several forms, one of which approximated the word *Wyoming*. During the last half of the 18th century the Wyoming Valley became well known because of battles between Indians and Whites here. Also, the name *Wyoming* was used in the title of a poem by Thomas Campbell, entitled "Gertrude of Wyoming," which was published in 1809. That poem enjoyed some popularity and helped perpetuate the name.

REFERENCES

Abbot, William W. A *Virginia Chronology: 1585–1783*. Williamsburg, Virginia, Virginia 350th Anniversary Celebration Corporation, 1957.

Abraham, Henry J. *Justices & Presidents: A Political History of Appointments to the Supreme Court*. New York, Oxford University Press, 1992.

Agricultural & Pictorial History of Berkeley County. Berkeley County Historical Society & Berkeley County Historic Landmarks Commission, 1991.

Alexander, H. L. "Berkeley County Highlights." *West Virginia State Magazine*, Vol. 1, No. 4. Bluefield, West Virginia: February–March, 1950.

Allen, Bernard L. *People, Places, Rivers & Experiences: A Guide for Reconstructing Wood County's History*. Wood County Historic Landmarks Commission, 1988.

Allman, C. B. *The Life & Times of Lewis Wetzel*. Nappanee, Indiana, E. V. Publishing House, 1939.

Ambler, Charles H. *West Virginia: The Mountain State*. New York, Prentice-Hall, Inc., 1940.

Ambler, Charles H. *West Virginia Stories & Biographies*. New York, Rand McNally & Co., 1937.

Ambler, Charles H., & Festus P. Summers. *West Virginia: The Mountain State*. Englewood Cliffs, New Jersey, Prentice-Hall, Inc., 1958.

Atkinson, George W. *History of Kanawha County*. Charleston, West Virginia Journal, 1876.

Atkinson, George W., & Alvaro F. Gibbens. *Prominent Men of West Virginia*. Wheeling, West Virginia, W. L. Callin, 1890.

Bishop, William H. *History of Roane County, West Virginia*. Spencer, West Virginia, 1927.

Boone County, West Virginia History: 1990. Boone County Genealogical Society, Inc., 1990.

Borchert, Mrs. C. Lee. *An Anniversary Celebrating the 150th Year of the Founding of Lewis County, West Virginia: 1817–1967*.

Bowman, E. L. "Origin of Names of Counties Given for Entire State." *Glenville Democrat*, Glenville, West Virginia, June 12, 1930.

Bowman, Mary Keller. *Reference Book of Wyoming County History*. Parsons, West Virginia, McClain Printing Co., 1965.

Boyd, Peter. *History of Northern West Virginia Panhandle: Embracing Ohio, Marshall, Brooke & Hancock Counties*. Topeka, Historical Publishing Co., 1927.

Brannon, Selden W. *Historic Hampshire. A Symposium of Hampshire County and Its People*. Parsons, West Virginia, McClain Printing Co., 1976.

Brock, R. A. *Virginia & Virginians: 1606–1888*. Richmond, H. H. Hardesty, 1888.

Brown, William G. *History of Nicholas County, West Virginia*. Richmond, Virginia, Dietz Press, Inc., 1954.

Burton, Patricia. *The 211th Anniversary: Questions & Answers on the Battle of Point Pleasant October 10, 1774*. 1985.

Bushong, Millard K. *A History of Jefferson County, West Virginia*. Charles Town, West Virginia, Jefferson Publishing Co., 1941.

Caldwell, J. A. *History of Belmont & Jefferson Counties, Ohio*. Wheeling, West Virginia, Historical Publishing Co., 1880.

Caldwell, Nancy Lee. *A History of Brooke County*. Parsons, West Virginia, McClain Printing Co., 1975.

Callahan, James. M. *History of West Virginia: Old & New*. Chicago, American Historical Society, Inc., 1923.

Callahan, James M. *Semi-Centennial History of West Virginia*. Morgantown, West Virginia, Semi-Centennial Commission, 1913.

Cannon, John. *The Oxford Companion to British History*. Oxford, Oxford University Press, 1997.

Carpenter, Charles. "Our Place Names." *West Virginia Review*, Vol. 6, No. 11. Charleston: August, 1929.

Carson, Howard W. *West Virginia Blue Book: 1974*. Charleston, Jarrett Printing Co.

Chapman, Isaac A. *The History of Wyoming*. Cottonport, Louisiana, Polyanthos, Inc., 1971.

Chrisman, Lewis H. "The Origin of Place Names in West Virginia." *West Virginia History*, Vol. 7, No. 2. Charleston: January, 1946.

Clagg, Sam. *West Virginia Historical Almanac: Bicentennial Publication.* Parsons, West Virginia, McClain Printing Co., 1975.

Clark, Walter E. *West Virginia Today.* West Virginia Editors Association, 1941.

Cole, J. R. *History of Greenbrier County.* Lewisburg, West Virginia, 1917.

Comstock, Jim. *The West Virginia Heritage Encyclopedia.* Richwood, West Virginia, 1974.

Conley, Phil. *Beacon Lights of West Virginia History.* Charleston, West Virginia Publishing Co., 1939.

Conley, Phil. *The West Virginia Encyclopedia.* Charleston, West Virginia Publishing Co., 1929.

Conley, Phil. *West Virginia Reader.* Charleston, Education Foundation, Inc., 1970.

Conley, Phil, & Boyd B. Stutler. *West Virginia Yesterday & Today.* Charleston, Education Foundation of West Virginia, Inc., 1952.

Conley, Phil, & William T. Doherty. *West Virginia History.* Charleston, Education Foundation, Inc., 1974.

Core, Earl L. *The Monongalia Story.* Parsons, West Virginia, McClain Printing Co., 1974.

Cridlin, William B. *A History of Colonial Virginia: The First Permanent Colony in America: To Which is Added the Genealogy of the Several Shires & Counties.* Richmond, Virginia, Williams Printing Co., 1923.

Davis, Dorothy. *History of Harrison County, West Virginia.* Clarksburg, West Virginia, American Association of University Women, 1970.

Dayton, Ruth Woods. *Greenbrier Pioneers & Their Homes.* Charleston, West Virginia Publishing Co., 1942.

Dayton, Ruth Woods. *Pioneers & Their Homes on Upper Kanawha.* Charleston, West Virginia Publishing Co., 1947.

Doddridge, Joseph. *Notes on the Settlement & Indian Wars of the Western Parts of Virginia & Pennsylvania: 1763 to 1783.* Parsons, West Virginia, McClain Printing Co., 1976.

Dodge, J. R. *West Virginia: Its Farms & Forests, Mines & Oil-Wells.* Philadelphia, J. B. Lippincott & Co., 1865.

Dodson, E. Griffith. *The Capitol of the Commonwealth of Virginia at Richmond.* Richmond, Virginia, 1938.

Doherty, William T. *Berkeley County, U.S.A.: A Bicentennial History of a Virginia & West Virginia County: 1772–1972.* Parsons, West Virginia, McClain Printing Co., 1972.

Donehoo, George P. *A History of the Indian Village & Place Names in Pennsylvania.* Harrisburg, Pennsylvania, Telegraph Press, 1928.

Duffield, Virginia. *Notes On West Virginia History.* Charleston, Kanawha County Schools, 1942.

Dunn, Jacob P. *True Indian Stories with Glossary of Indiana Indian Names.* Indianapolis, Indiana, Sentinel Printing Co., 1908.

Dutton, Ralph. *Hampshire.* London, England, B. T. Batsford, Ltd., 1970.

Edwards, Richard. *Statistical Gazetteer of the State of Virginia.* Richmond, 1855.

Evans, Norma Pontiff. *First Families of McDowell County, (West) Virginia.* Beaumont, Texas, 1981.

Evans, Norma Pontiff. *Marriage Records of Wyoming County, West Virginia: 1854–1880.* Beaumont, Texas, 1980.

Evans, Willis F. *History of Berkeley County, West Virginia.* Martinsburg, West Virginia, 1927.

Fansler, Homer F. *History of Tucker County, West Virginia.* Parsons, West Virginia, McClain Printing Co., 1962.

Faragher, John M. *The Encyclopedia of Colonial & Revolutionary America.* New York, Facts On File, 1990.

Ferris, Robert G. *Signers of the Declaration.* Washington, D. C., National Park Service, United States Department of the Interior, 1973.

Fleming, Dan B. *From a Riverbank: Sketches From Pleasants County History.* Pleasants County Historical Association, 1976.

Galbreath, C. B. "Lafayette's Visit to Ohio Valley States." *Ohio Archaeological & Historical Publications,* Vol. 29. Columbus: 1920.

Gardiner, Mabel Henshaw, & Ann Henshaw Gardiner. *Chronicles of Old Berkeley: A Narrative History of a Virginia County from Its Beginnings to 1926.* Durham, North Carolina, Seeman Press, 1938.

Gibbens, Alvaro F. *Wood County Formation: A Century of Progress.* Morgantown, West Virginia, Acme Press, 1899.

Gilliam, Charles E. "Pocahontas-Matoaka." *Names: Journal of the American Name Society,* Vol. 2, No. 3. Berkeley: September, 1954.

Goodall, Cecile R. *West Virginia Highway Markers.* Beckley, West Virginia, Biggs-Johnston-Withrow, 1967.

Gordon, Armistead C. "James Barbour: Philip Pendleton Barbour." *Some Eminent Sons of Orange: Report & Address at Orange Court House, August 14, 1919.* Gordonsville, Virginia: 1919.

Griffith, Lucille. *Virginia House of Burgesses: 1750–1774.* Northport, Alabama, Colonial Press, 1963.

Grigsby, Hugh B. "The History of the Virginia Federal Convention of 1788: With Some Account of the Eminent Virginians of That Era Who Were Members of the Body." *Collections of the Virginia Historical Society,* Vol. 10. Richmond: 1891.

Hagans, John M. *Sketch of the Erection & Formation of the State of West Virginia from the Territory of Virginia.* Charleston, 1927.

Hale, John P. *Trans-Allegheny Pioneers.* Cincinnati, Samuel C. Cox & Co., 1886.

Hall, Kermit L. *The Oxford Companion to the Supreme Court of the United States.* New York, Oxford University Press, 1992.

"Hampshire County: 1753: Its Genesis." *The Hampshire Review,* Romney West Virginia, July 29, 1953.

Harris, John T. *West Virginia Legislative Hand Book & Manual & Official Register.* Charleston, Tribune Printing Co., 1917.

"Harrison County: Formed from Monongahela (sic) County May 8, 1784." *West Virginia State Magazine,* Vol. 1, No. 11. Bluefield, West Virginia: September, 1950.

Hearne, Julian G. *Some Unknown Facts of American History.* Parsons, West Virginia, McClain Printing Co., 1987.

Hiden, Martha W. *How Justice Grew: Virginia Counties: An Abstract of Their Formation.* Williamsburg, Virginia, Virginia 350th Anniversary Celebration Corporation, 1957.

Hill, Mildred Haptonstall. *Glimpses of West Virginia History.* Beckley, West Virginia, West Virginia Society Daughters of the American Revolution, 1962.

Historical Booklet: Greenbrier County 160th Anniversary: 1778–1938.

History of the Great Kanawha Valley. Madison, Wisconsin, Brant, Fuller & Co., 1891.

History of Tyler County, West Virginia to 1984. Marceline, Missouri, Walsworth Publishing Co., Inc., 1984.

History of Wetzel County, West Virginia: 1983. Marceline, Missouri, Walsworth, 1983.

History of Wirt County, West Virginia. Dallas, Texas, Taylor Publishing Co., 1981.

Hodge, Frederick W. *Handbook of American Indians North of Mexico.* Totowa, New Jersey, Rowman & Littlefield, 1975.

Hogg, Charles E. *Great Men of The Virginias.* Cincinnati, Ohio, Jones Brothers & Co.

Howe, Henry. *Historical Collections of Ohio.* Cincinnati, Ohio, C. J. Krehbiel & Co., 1907.

Howe, Henry. *Historical Collections of Virginia.* Charleston, South Carolina, W. R. Babcock, 1849.

Hughes, Josiah. *Pioneer West Virginia.* Charleston, 1932.

Hulbert, Archer B. *The Ohio River.* New York, G. P. Putnam's Sons, 1906.

"In Memory of the Augusta County Regiment 1774: Commander Col. Charles Lewis Killed October 10, 1774." Memorial Service, Point Pleasant, West Virginia, October 11, 1975. West Virginia Archives & History Library, Charleston, West Virginia.

Janssen, Quinith, & William Fernbach. *West Virginia Place Names.* Shepherdstown, West Virginia, J. & F. Enterprises, 1984.

Johnston, David E. *A History of Middle New River Settlements.* Huntington, West Virginia, Standard Printing & Publishing Co., 1906.

Johnston, Ross B., & Isaac McNeel. *West Virginia Historic & Scenic Highway Markers.* Charleston, State Road Commission of West Virginia, 1937.

Kenny, Hamill. *West Virginia Place Names.* Piedmont, West Virginia, Place Name Press, 1945.

Kenyon, J. P. *Dictionary of British History.* Ware, England, Wordsworth Editions, Ltd., 1992.

Kleber, John E. *The Kentucky Encyclopedia.* Lexington, Kentucky, University Press of Kentucky, 1992.

Lawless, Bud. "Morgan County." *West Virginia State Magazine,* Vol. 1, No. 4. Bluefield, West Virginia: February–March, 1950.

Leonard, Cynthia Miller. *The General Assembly of Virginia: July 30, 1619–January 11, 1978.* Richmond, Virginia State Library, 1978.

Lewis, Virgil A. *First Biennial Report of the Department of Archives & History of the State of West Virginia.* Charleston, Tribune Printing Co., 1906.

Lewis, Virgil A. *History of the Battle of Point Pleasant.* Harrisonburg, Virginia, C. J. Carrier Co., 1974.

Lewis, Virgil A. *History & Government of West Virginia.* New York, American Book Co., 1896.

Lewis, Virgil A. *History of West Virginia.* Philadelphia, Hubbard Brothers, 1889.

Lewis, Virgil A. *How West Virginia Was Made: Proceedings of the First Convention of the People of Northwestern Virginia at Wheeling: May 13, 14 & 15, 1861.* 1909.

Lewis, Virgil A. *The Soldiery of West Virginia.* Baltimore, Genealogical Publishing Co., 1967.

Lewis, Virgil A. *West Virginia: Its History, Natural Resources, Industrial Enterprises & Institutions.* Charleston, West Virginia Commission of the Louisiana Purchase Exposition, 1904.

Lowther, Minnie Kendall. *History of Ritchie County.* Wheeling, Wheeling News Litho. Co., 1911.

Luther, Roslyn, & Edwin C. Luther. *Governors of Virginia: 1776–1974.* Accomac, Virginia, Eastern Shore News, Inc., 1974.

McCabe, R. E. "Abel Parker Upshur." *John P. Branch Historical Papers of Randolph-Macon College,* No. 3. Ashland, Virginia: June, 1903.

McCormick, Kyle. "McDowell County Celebrates Its Centennial." *West Virginia History,* Vol. 19, No. 3. Charleston: April, 1958.

McCormick, Kyle. *The Story of Mercer County.* Charleston Printing Co., 1957.

McDowell County History. Fort Worth, Texas, University Supply & Equipment Co., 1959.

McEldowney, John C. *History of Wetzel County, West Virginia.* 1901.

McKenney, Thomas L. & James Hall. *The Indian Tribes of North America.* Edinburgh, John Grant, 1933.

McWhorter, Lucullus V. *The Border Settlers of Northwestern Virginia: From 1768 to 1795.* Richwood, West Virginia, 1973.

Marion County in the Making. J. O. Watson Class of the Fairmont, West Virginia High School, 1917.

Maury, M. F., & William M. Fontaine. *Resources of West Virginia.* Wheeling, Register Co., 1876.

Maxwell, Hu. *The History of Barbour County, West Virginia.* Morgantown, West Virginia, Acme Publishing Co., 1899.

Maxwell, Hu. *The History of Randolph County, West Virginia.* Morgantown, West Virginia, Acme Publishing Co., 1898.

Maxwell, Hu. *History of Tucker County, West Virginia.* Kingwood, West Virginia, Preston Publishing Co., 1884.

Maxwell, Hu, & H. L. Swisher. *History of Hampshire County, West Virginia.* Morgantown, West Virginia, A Brown Boughner, 1897.

Milestones of West Virginia History. Parsons, West Virginia, McClain Printing Co., 1963.

Miller, James H. *History of Summers County.* Hinton, West Virginia, 1908.

Miller, Lillian B. *The Dye Is Now Cast: The Road to American Independence: 1774–1776.* Washington, DC, Smithsonian Institution Press, 1975.

Miller, Thomas C., & Hu Maxwell. *West Virginia and Its People.* New York, Lewis Historical Publishing Co., 1913.

Mills, A.D. *A Dictionary of English Place Names.* Oxford, Oxford University Press, 1991.

Moore, George E. *A Banner in the Hills: West Virginia's Statehood.* New York, Appleton-Century-Crofts, 1963.

Morton, Oren F. *A History of Monroe County, West Virginia.* Baltimore, Regional Publishing Co., 1974.

Morton, Oren F. *A History of Pendleton County, West Virginia.* Franklin, West Virginia, 1910.

Motley, Charles B. *Gleanings of Monroe County, West Virginia History.* Radford, Virginia, Commonwealth Press, Inc., 1973.

Moule, Thomas. *The County Maps of Old England.* London, Studio Editions, 1990.

Myers, S. *Myers' History of West Virginia.* New Martinsville, West Virginia, 1915.

Mylott, James P. *A Measure of Prosperity: A History of Roane County.* Charleston, University of Charleston, 1984.

Newton, J. H., et al. *History of the Pan-Handle: Being Historical Collections of the Counties of Ohio, Brooke, Marshall & Hancock, West Virginia.* Wheeling, West Virginia, J. A. Caldwell, 1879.

Nicholson, Edgar P. "James McDowell." *John P. Branch Historical Papers of Randolph-Macon College,* Vol. 4, No. 2. Ashland, Virginia: June, 1914.

Norfleet, Fillmore. *Saint-Memin in Virginia: Portraits & Biographies.* Richmond, Dietz Press, 1942.

North, E. Lee. *The 55 West Virginias: A Guide to the State's Counties.* Morgantown, West Virginia University Press, 1985.

North, E. Lee. *Redcoats, Redskins, & Red-Eyed Monsters.* Cranbury, New Jersey, A. S. Barnes & Co., Inc., 1979.

Oakley, Amy. *Our Pennsylvania.* Indianapolis, Bobbs-Merrill Co., Inc., 1950.

Palmer, Tim. *Rivers of Pennsylvania.* University Park, Pennsylvania State University Press, 1980.

Pemberton, Robert L. *A History of Pleasants County, West Virginia.* St. Marys, West Virginia, Oracle Press, 1929.

The Pennsylvania Almanac & Buyers' Guide. 1964.

Peters, J. T., & H. B. Carden. *History of Fayette County, West Virginia.* Charleston, Jarrett Printing Co., 1926.

Powell, Scott. *History of Marshall County.* Moundsville, West Virginia, 1925.

Price, Andrew. *West Virginia Anthology.* Marlinton, West Virginia, 1926.

Puetz, C. J. *West Virginia County Maps.* Lyndon Station, Wisconsin, County Maps.

Purcell, L. Edward. *Who Was Who in the American Revolution.* New York, Facts On File, Inc., 1993.

A Reminiscent History of Northern West Virginia. Chicago, Goodspeed Brothers, 1895.

Richmond Portraits in an Exhibition of Makers of Richmond; 1737–1860. Richmond, Virginia, Valentine Museum, 1949.

Robinson, Morgan P. "Virginia Counties: Those Resulting from Virginia Legislation." *Bulletin of the Virginia State Library*, Vol. 9. Richmond: 1916.

Salmon, Emily J. *A Hornbook of Virginia History*. Richmond, Virginia State Library, 1983.

Samberson, Tyndall V. *The Open Sesame Question & Answer Book on West Virginia*. 1936.

Sesqui-Centennial of Monongalia County, West Virginia. Morgantown, West Virginia, Monongalia Historical Society, 1927.

Shankle, George Earlie. *State Names, Flags, Seals, Songs, Birds, Flowers & Other Symbols*. New York, H. W. Wilson Co., 1941.

Shaw, S. C. *Sketches of Wood County: Its Early History: As Embraced in and Connected With Other Counties of West Virginia*. Parkersburg, West Virginia, George Elletson, 1878.

Simpson-Poffenbarger, Mrs. Livia Nye. *The Battle of Point Pleasant: A Battle of the Revolution*. Point Pleasant, West Virginia, State Gazette, 1909.

Smith, Edward C. *A History of Lewis County, West Virginia*. Weston, West Virginia, 1920.

Smith, Edwin J. "Spencer Roane." *John P. Branch Historical Papers of Randolph-Macon College*, Vol. 2, No. 1. Ashland, Virginia: June, 1905.

Smith, Margaret Vowell. *Virginia: 1492–1892*. Washington, W. H. Lowdermilk & Co., 1893.

Some Events & Persons of Importance in the History of West Virginia. Charleston, State Department of Archives & History, 1937.

Squires, W. H. T. *Through Centuries Three: A Short History of the People of Virginia*. Portsmouth, Virginia, Printcraft Press, Inc., 1929.

Stewart, George R. *American Place-Names*. New York, Oxford University Press, 1970.

Stone, William L. *The Poetry & History of Wyoming: Containing Campbell's Gertrude, and the History of Wyoming from Its Discovery to the Beginning of the Present Century*. Wilkes-Barre, C. E. Butler, 1869.

Summers, George W. "State Place-Names Honor Many Noted." *Charleston Daily Mail*, November 5, 1939.

Sutton, John D. *History of Braxton County & Central West Virginia*. Parsons, West Virginia, McClain Printing Co., 1967.

Taft, William H., III. *County Names: An Historical Perspective*. National Association of Counties, 1982.

Taylor County Historical & Genealogical Society, Inc. *A History of Taylor County, West Virginia*. Parsons, West Virginia, McClain Printing Co., 1986.

Thrapp, Dan L. *Encyclopedia of Frontier Biography*. Lincoln, University of Nebraska Press, 1988.

Thrapp, Dan L. *Encyclopedia of Frontier Biography: Supplemental Volume 4*. Spokane, Arthur H. Clark Co., 1994.

Thrash, Mary. *West Virginia Courthouses*. Clarksburg, West Virginia, 1984.

Thrift, C. T. "Thomas Ritchie." *John P. Branch Historical Papers of Randolph-Macon College*, No. 3. Ashland, Virginia: June, 1903.

Tyler, Lyon G. *Encyclopedia of Virginia Biography*. New York, Lewis Historical Publishing Co., 1915.

Vexler, Robert I. *Chronology & Documentary Handbook of the State of West Virginia*. Dobbs Ferry, New York, Oceana Publications, Inc., 1978.

Vogel, Virgil J. *Indian Names in Michigan*. Ann Arbor, University of Michigan Press, 1986.

Vogel, Virgil J. *Iowa Place Names of Indian Origin*. Iowa City, University Press of Iowa, 1983.

Waldman, Carl. *Who Was Who in Native American History*. New York, Facts On File, Inc., 1990.

Wallace, George S. *Cabell County Annals & Families*. Richmond, Garrett & Massie, 1935.

Watson, L. E. *Pleasants County, West Virginia Copied From Historical 1882 Hand-Atlas*.

Welch, Jack. *History of Hancock County, Virginia & West Virginia*. Wheeling, Wheeling News Printing & Litho. Co., 1963.

Wingfield, Marshall. *A History of Caroline County, Virginia*. Richmond, Trevvet, Christian & Co., Inc., 1924.

Woodward, Isaiah A. *West Virginia and Its Struggle for Statehood: 1861–1863*. Baltimore, Maryland, Wolk Publishing Co., 1954.

Works Progress Administration. *West Virginia County Formations & Boundary Changes*. Charleston, 1938.

Wisconsin

(72 counties)

2975 *Adams County*

Uncertain— This county was created by Wisconsin territory on March 11, 1848. Sources consulted are divided on whether the county was named for our nation's second president, John Adams (1735–1826), or for his son, John Quincy Adams (1767–1848). Several sources admit that it is uncertain which of these two presidents is this county's namesake. The younger Adams died on February 23, 1848, which may have prompted the naming of this county, either in his honor, or in honor of both of our nation's Presidents Adams.

John Adams (1735–1826)— A native of Massachusetts, John Adams was a delegate to the first Continental Congress and a signer of the Declaration of Independence. He participated in Paris, with Benjamin Franklin and John Jay, in negotiating peace with England and, after the war, he was our country's first minister to England. Adams became the first vice-president of the United States under George Washington and when Washington retired, Adams was elected to be our second president.

John Q. Adams (1767–1848)— Also a native of Massachusetts, this son of our country's second president served in the U.S. Senate and as minister to several European countries. He was a very able secretary of state under President James Monroe, for whom he helped formulate the Monroe Doctrine. John Quincy Adams became our sixth president in 1825, defeating Andrew Jackson and two other candidates, but when he ran for reelection in 1828, Jackson defeated him. After this defeat, the former president entered the U.S. House of Representatives, where he represented Massachusetts and opposed states' rights and slavery for 17 years until his death in 1848.

2976 *Ashland County*

Village of Ashland, Wisconsin— This northern Wisconsin county was created on March 27, 1860, and named for the sawmill village of Ashland, its county seat. In the early 1990's this municipality had a population of 9,000. The name of the village was suggested by a settler named Martin Beaser, an admirer of Henry Clay (1777–1852), whose estate at Lexington, Kentucky was named Ashland. Clay represented Kentucky in both branches of the U.S. Congress. For many years he was one of the more prominent figures in American politics but his several bids for the presidency were unsuccessful. He was influential in effecting important compromises between northern and southern interests during the years that secession and civil war were imminent.

Ashland, in Lexington, Kentucky— Clay's home, named Ashland, is located on Richmond Road at Sycamore Road, which is now within the city limits of Lexington. The restored Ashland, surrounded by 20 acres of expansive woodland, is furnished throughout with Clay family furniture. A number of outbuildings also remain. Henry Clay established his residence at Ashland in 1806, when he rented a farm located here. About 1810 he purchased 400 acres of land from the estate he was renting and soon constructed his first Ashland, the brick mansion designed by architect Benjamin H. Latrobe (1764–1820). The mansion faced west, toward Lexington, measured 126 feet by 47 feet, and was two and a half story high, with one story wings on both sides. An earthquake unsettled this first mansion's foundations and that original structure was later taken down. Clay returned to Ashland frequently until 1851, when, in failing health, he left Ashland for the last time. He died the following year, while serving in the U.S. Senate. The brick mansion was rebuilt, from Latrobe's plans and using the original materials, in 1857. From 1806 to 1948, four generations of Clays have been associated with Ashland. Henry Clay's home here is now owned and administered as a historic site and guided tours are available.

2977 *Barron County*

Henry D. Barron (1833–1882)— A native of New York state, Barron studied both the printing trade and law before coming to Wisconsin in 1851. Here he settled at Waukesha and purchased a newspaper, which he edited and published for several years. From 1853 to 1857 Barron was Waukesha's postmaster. After moving to Pepin, Wisconsin, in 1857, he was admitted to the bar, practiced law and served, briefly, as a judge. Shortly after the outbreak of the Civil War, Barron changed his political affiliation from Democrat to Republican and he served several terms in the lower house of the Wisconsin legislature. In 1866 and again in 1873, Barron was speaker of the Wisconsin house. In 1869 President Ulysses S. Grant asked Barron to serve as chief justice of the supreme court of Dakota territory but Barron declined, accepting instead, a position as a federal treasury auditor. During the mid-1870's Barron served in the Wisconsin senate and was president *pro-tempore* of the senate in 1875. In 1876 he became circuit judge of the 11th judicial district and held that position until his death. This county was originally created on March 19, 1859, with the name Dallas County, in honor of former Vice-President George M. Dallas (1792–1864). The name was changed to Barron County on March 4, 1869.

2978 *Bayfield County*

Town of Bayfield, Wisconsin—This county lies at the northern end of Wisconsin, on Lake Superior, and that lake's Chequamegon Bay sits on Bayfield County's northeastern border. In 1665 a Jesuit mission was established here at what is now the town of Bayfield, Wisconsin. The mission's name was La Pointe du Saint Esprit. A French post established here during the 1700's carried on the name of that mission, in abbreviated form, as La Pointe and the entire area surrounding Chequamegon Bay came to be known as La Pointe. When this county was initially established on February 19, 1845, it was named La Pointe County. About 1857 the town of Bayfield was established here. Its name was suggested by one of the town's promoters, Henry M. Rice, of St. Paul, to honor Henry W. Bayfield, the British naval officer, whose surveys of Lake Superior served as the basis for the first accurate chart of the lake. By the late 1990's the town of Bayfield, Wisconsin, had a population of only 700 and was not the county seat. However, for several decades beginning about 1859 the town of Bayfield was the county seat and in April, 1866, the county's name was changed from La Pointe to Bayfield in honor of its county seat.

Henry W. Bayfield (1795–1885)— Born in Yorkshire, England, Bayfield entered the British royal navy when he was only eleven years old. Appointed by the admiralty board as surveyor in British North America, Bayfield surveyed Lake Superior as well as two other Great Lakes, Erie and Huron. His surveys during 1822 and 1823 of Lake Superior served as the basis for the first accurate chart of the lake. Bayfield's survey work extended east and included the Gulf of St. Lawrence, Prince Edward Island and a large section of the coast of Nova Scotia. He was promoted to commander in 1826, attained flag rank in 1856, and in 1863 he rose to vice-admiral and in 1867 to admiral.

2979 *Brown County*

Jacob J. Brown (1775–1828)— A native of Pennsylvania with little military experience, Brown found himself in command of a section of the frontier at the start of the War of 1812. His successful defense of the important American base, Sackett's Harbor, on Lake Ontario resulted in his appointment in July, 1813, as brigadier-general in the army and six months later he was made major-general. Brown later served with distinction in other important battles of the War of 1812. After the War, in 1821, he was assigned the command of the United States army, which he held until his death. This county was created on October 26, 1818, by Michigan territory.

2980 *Buffalo County*

Buffalo River— This county in western Wisconsin was created on July 6, 1853, and named for one of its principal streams, the Buffalo River, which is also called the Beef River. Father Louis Hennepin (1640–1705) named this river Riviere des Boeufs, on account of the many buffalo (i.e., bison) he noted in this region. *Buffalo* is the common, but incorrect, name given to these animals. They were the staff of life to nomadic Indian hunters, and for a time they also provided a bit of revenue to White hunters and traders. By the time that this Wisconsin county was created, bison herds were gone here but still plentiful further west, in what is now South Dakota. Only a decade later, in the mid-1860's, their numbers even in Dakota territory had been greatly reduced. The slaughter of these animals occurred wherever they were found. In the early 1800's, bison in America numbered in the tens of millions. Today very few remain and most of them are protected on government lands or private preserves.

2981 *Burnett County*

Thomas P. Burnett (1800–1846)— Thomas Pendleton Burnett was born in Virginia but moved to Kentucky as a child. There he studied law, was admitted to the Kentucky bar and established a law practice at Paris, Kentucky, before being appointed as a sub-Indian agent at Prairie du Chien. He arrived here in June, 1830. Burnett established a law practice here and in 1835 Michigan territory appointed him district attorney for several of its western (frontier) counties. He held that post less than a year and resigned to serve in the upper house (council) of Michigan's territorial legislature. In 1836 Wisconsin territory was created and Burnett was appointed court reporter of the new territory's supreme court. He later was elected to the lower house of the legislature of Wisconsin territory and was a delegate to Wisconsin's first convention called to draft a state constitution. John Clements' *Wisconsin Facts* tells us that the proposed constitution (which the voters rejected in 1847) adopted at this convention "...contained several controversial provisions, including outlawing all forms of banking in the state, granting women control over their property..." and a rider granting suffrage to Black voters. Burnett died in November, 1846, while that constitutional convention was in session. This county was created and named in his honor by the state of Wisconsin of March 31, 1856.

2982 *Calumet County*

A village of the Menominee Indians which was located here— This county in eastern Wisconsin was created by Wisconsin territory on December 7, 1836, and named for a village of the Menominee Indians, which was located on the eastern shore of Lake Winnebago. That eastern shore of Lake Winnebago forms almost all of the western border of today's Calumet County. This Indian village was reported to have 150 inhabitants in 1817. The name *Calumet* is the present rendering of a Norman-French noun for a shepherd's pipe, but in North America it came to be used by the French for the Indians' tobacco pipes. The writings of Father Jacques Marquette (1637–1675) mentioned that the Indians' "...pipes for smoking tobacco are called in this country *Calumets.*" Wisconsin territory abolished Calumet County on August 13, 1840, but recreated it on February 18, 1842, in an act to become effective in April, 1842.

2983 *Chippewa County*

Chippewa River— This county in west-central Wisconsin was created by Wisconsin territory on February 3, 1845, and named for its principal river. The 183 mile-long Chippewa River rises about 25 miles south of Lake Superior and it flows south and southwest to reach the Mississippi River. The Chippewa and its many tributaries drain about one-sixth of Wisconsin. The river was named for the Chippewa Indians.

Chippewa Indians— The Chippewa are also known as the Ojibwa Indians. In fact, the name *Chippewa* is a corruption of the name *Ojibwa*, which has known dozens of alternative spellings. The Chippewa were one of the largest and most powerful tribes of the Algonquian linguistic family. They were a nomadic, woodland tribe, who controlled much of the Great Lakes area. Their domain extended from the Iroquois Indians' territory in the Northeast to the edge of the Great Plains, which were dominated by the Dakota (also known as Sioux) Indians. The Chippewa lived around the shores of three of the Great Lakes: Huron, Michigan and Superior, and dwelled in what today are the states of Michigan, Wisconsin, Minnesota and North Dakota. The first European explorers to encounter the Chippewa found them near Sault Sainte Marie, Michigan. Many Chippewa lived in birch bark covered wigwams with grass mats. Their birch bark rolls were carried from one campsite to another. They subsisted by hunting, trapping, fishing and collecting wild plant food. A bit of maize (corn) farming was engaged in by those Chippewa who occupied the southern edges of the Chippewa's territory. The Chippewa were noted for their fine craftsmanship in constructing birch bark canoes. Chippewa reservations may be found today in Canada's Ontario province and in our states of Michigan, Wisconsin, Minnesota, North Dakota and Montana. The meaning of the Chippewa (or Ojibwa) tribe's name is uncertain. This is just as well as the two most frequently encountered explanations involve (1) moccasins (no problem) and (2) the Chippewa Indians' practice of torturing, by burning, captive Dakota Indians.

2984 *Clark County*

George R. Clark (1752–1818)— A native of Virginia, George Rogers Clark was a frontiersman and military hero. During the American Revolution he secured a commission as lieutenant-colonel to attack the British, Indians and Loyalists in Indiana and Illinois. He successfully captured Vincennes, Cahokia and Kaskaskia and after the British retook Kaskaskia, Clark won it a second time. These military victories, together with skillful negotiating by Benjamin Franklin, enabled the U.S. to acquire the Northwest territory, and hence Wisconsin, during the peace negotiations with the British at the end of the Revolution. This county was created on July 6, 1853.

2985 *Columbia County*

Town of Columbus, Wisconsin— Columbia County was created by Wisconsin territory on February 3, 1846, and named for the town of Columbus, within its borders. By 1988 Columbus had an estimated population of 4,138 and one source indicates that it was incorporated as a city in the 19th century. We know that this municipality was settled in 1840 and had grown to a population of about 2,000 by the year 1900. Columbus was the first county seat of Columbia County but in 1851 the county seat was moved to Portage, Wisconsin and has remained there ever since. There is uncertainty about the origin of the name of the municipality of Columbus, Wisconsin territory, and sources consulted are annoyingly vague but many imply that it was named for the famous explorer, Cristoforo Colombo (1451–1506).

Cristoforo Colombo (1451–1506)— Colombo, whose name we render as Christopher Columbus, was a native of Italy who believed the theory that the earth is round and that Asia could be reached by sailing west from Europe. He persuaded Ferdinand and Isabella of Spain to equip an expedition for him to test this theory. Sailing from Europe August 3, 1492, he first sighted land in the Americas in the Bahama Islands on October 12, 1492. On this voyage he left a colony of 40 men on the Haitian coast. Columbus returned several times to the New World before his death in 1506. Popularly known as the discoverer of America, Columbus was certainly not the first European to reach the Western Hemisphere. Leif Ericsson accomplished that about the year 1000. But it was Columbus' expedition that triggered rapid exploration, conquest and settlement of the Americas by Europeans.

2986 *Crawford County*

Fort Crawford— Crawford County was created on October 26, 1818, by proclamation by the governor of Michigan territory, Lewis Cass (1782–1866), and named for the important frontier fort at Prairie du Chien. The U.S. army had recently (1816) established Fort Crawford on the Mississippi River, near the mouth of the Wisconsin River. That fort was named for William H. Crawford (1772–1834), then secretary of the treasury. In 1830 the army troops left the original fort for higher ground. Fort Crawford was occupied sporadically until 1856, when it was permanently abandoned.

William H. Crawford (1772–1834)— Crawford served in the Georgia legislature and as a U.S. senator from Georgia. He was elected president *pro tempore* of the senate and he later served as minister to France, secretary of war and secretary of the treasury. Crawford was a serious candidate for the presidency in both 1816 and 1824.

2987 *Dane County*

Nathan Dane (1752–1835)— A native of Massachusetts and a 1778 graduate of Harvard College, Dane studied law and was admitted to the bar in 1782. He served in Massachusetts general court and was a Massachusetts delegate to the Confederation congress. In that body Dane was the author of the article in the ordinance of 1787 which prohibited slavery in the Northwest territory, and hence in Wisconsin territory. Dane later served as a judge of in Massachusetts and in 1795 he was appointed as commissioner to revise the laws of Massachusetts. He also compiled an eight volume *General Abridgment & Digest of American Law*. This county was created by Wisconsin territory on December 7, 1836. The new county's name was suggested by James D. Doty (1799–1865), who later served as a territorial governor of Wisconsin.

2988 *Dodge County*

Henry Dodge (1782–1867)— Born in Vincennes in what is now the state of Indiana, in 1782, Dodge served with distinction as an officer in the War of 1812 and rose to the rank of lieutenant-colonel. In 1827 he moved to the wilderness of what is now Wisconsin and served in actions against the Indians. By now, a full colonel, in 1835 Dodge led an expedition to the Rocky Mountains. In 1836 President Andrew Jackson appointed him to be the first governor of Wisconsin territory and superintendent of Indian affairs. Henry Dodge later represented Wisconsin territory as a delegate to the U.S. Congress, and the state of Wisconsin as a U.S. sen-

ator. This county was created by Wisconsin territory on December 7, 1836, while Dodge was its governor.

2989 *Door County*

Porte des Morts Strait or "Death's Door"— This county consists of a peninsula (and adjacent islands) which juts out from eastern Wisconsin, with Green Bay on its west and Lake Michigan to the east. About three miles west of the peninsula's end lie both Washington Island and Plum Island and the adjacent strait still carries the name given to it by the French, Porte des Morts Strait, commonly referred to as "Death's Door." Various tales are told of the origin of the term "Death's Door" and many of them may be true for the current here is perilous enough to have caused many tragedies. In their 1968 work entitled *The Romance of Wisconsin Place Names*, Robert E. Gard and L. G. Sorden gave this version of the legend: "It is said that a party of Indians were crossing between Washington Island and the mainland when they were overcome by the swift current and all drowned. The channel was then called Death's Door." Door County was created on February 11, 1851.

2990 *Douglas County*

Stephen A. Douglas (1813–1861)— Barely five feet tall, the "Little Giant" is most remembered as a political opponent of Abraham Lincoln. Douglas was born in Vermont and moved to Illinois where he enjoyed rapid political success. He served on the state supreme court, in the state legislature and as secretary of state. Following two terms in the U.S. House of Representatives, Douglas was elected to the U.S. Senate. In that body Douglas took courageous positions on the slavery issue which first outraged abolitionist sentiment and later infuriated the South. In 1858 Douglas ran for reelection to the U.S. Senate against Abraham Lincoln. Following the famous Lincoln-Douglas debates, the Republicans won the popular election but the Illinois legislature reelected Douglas to the senate. Lincoln and Douglas were rivals again in 1860 for the presidency. Following Lincoln's election and the start of the Civil War, Douglas gave the president his active support. This county was created on February 9, 1854.

2991 *Dunn County*

Charles Dunn (1799–1872)— A native of Kentucky and a lawyer, Dunn served as a captain in the Illinois militia fighting In-

dians during the Black Hawk War. He was involved in laying out the plat for Chicago, Illinois, and served in the lower house of the Illinois legislature. In August, 1836, President Andrew Jackson appointed Dunn to be the first chief justice of the supreme court of Wisconsin territory. He also served as a delegate to Wisconsin's second state constitutional convention and was a member of Wisconsin's state senate from 1853 to 1856. This county was created named in his honor while he was serving in the senate, on February 3, 1854.

2992 *Eau Claire County*

Eau Claire River— This county in west-central Wisconsin was created on October 6, 1856, and named for the 70 mile-long Eau Claire River. That river rises in Clark County, Wisconsin, and flows west to the city of Eau Claire, in northwestern Eau Claire County. There the Eau Claire discharges its waters into the Chippewa River. *Eau Claire* is French and means "clear water." The Indians here observed that the brown colored Chippewa River became cleaner after the clear waters of the Eau Claire River joined it. The Indians called the tributary stream by a name which meant "clear water," and the French merely translated the Indians' name into their language.

2993 *Florence County*

Florence mine & town of Florence, Wisconsin— This county was created on March 18, 1882, and its name honors, albeit indirectly, Mrs. Florence Hulst. The county was named for both a mine and a town here which had been named for the wife of Nelson P. Hulst (1842–1923), a geologist and mining engineer, who developed the Florence mine. A work published in 1980 entitled *Heritage of Iron & Timber: 1880–1980* quoted a letter from J. J. Hagerman, one of the financiers of the Florence mine, to Mrs. Florence Hulst dated December 15, 1879. That letter nicely explains the choice of the name Florence for the mine and the town, and hence the county: "The time is come when we must give a name to the new town in Wisconsin at the end of the Railroad now building, and to the new mine in the vicinity, now called Eagle, but which name we do not wish to keep, as there is already and Eagle P. O. in Wisconsin. The Company owns all the land around the lake, where the town will be located. It will be a lively town. We shall put an anti-whiskey clause in all deeds and we expect it will be much noted for its temperance and morality.... We all wish to call the new town and mine Florence, in honor of the first white woman who had courage enough to settle (for a while) in that rugged country. I mean the first white woman known to us. Will you permit your name to be used?"

2994 *Fond du Lac County*

City of Fond du Lac, Wisconsin In 1835, when this area was still part of Michigan territory, Judge James D. Doty (1799–1865) laid out the community of Fond du Lac at the southern end of Lake Winnebago. Doty hoped that this community would become the capital of the soon to be formed Wisconsin territory. Doty was disappointed in that hope when Madison was selected as the capital, but he did become a territorial governor of Wisconsin. The name *Fond du Lac* is French and it describes the location at the end of the lake. Translations mentioned include "end or foot of the lake" and "bottom of the lake." When this county was created by Wisconsin territory on December 7, 1836, it was named for Judge Doty's settlement here and when county government began in 1844, the municipality of Fond du Lac became its county seat. In the late 1990's the city of Fond du Lac had a population of 37,800 and was still the county seat.

2995 *Forest County*

Forests of the county— This county in northeastern Wisconsin was created during April, 1885, and named for the dense forests within its borders. A lumber industry developed in the county and the *Wisconsin Travel Companion*, published in 1983, stated that the Connor Mill here, at Laona, was "the world's largest hardwood mill."

2996 *Grant County*

Uncertain— This county in the southwestern corner of Wisconsin was created by Wisconsin territory on December 8, 1836, and probably named for the Grant River, a tributary of the Mississippi River, which flows through the county. However about half of the Wisconsin sources consulted indicate that the county was named directly for a fur trapper named Grant, rather for the Grant River, which was named for a fur trapper named Grant. And just who was this fur trapper named Grant for whom the county was either directly or indirectly named? Most Wisconsin sources are silent on this point. Some of them say that the river was named for

the obscure fur trader, Cuthbert Grant, but then the *Wisconsin Travel Companion*, published in 1983 tries to deny us the comfort that Cuthbert Grant is our man by saying "...there is some question as to his real name." An article entitled "Additions & Corrections," which appeared in the 1888 issue (Vol. 10) of the *Report & Collections of the State Historical Society of Wisconsin* discussed the origin of the Grant River's name in some detail but arrived at no firm conclusion. Among the phrases contained in that article which bear on the question are: (1) "Cuthbert Grant ... an early trader on the Upper Mississippi and as, perhaps, the person after whom Grant river, and Grant county, Wisconsin were named..."(2) "It would seem quite probable, that this James Grant (a trador [sic] from Montreal) was the father of Cuthbert Grant ... (who) was born about 1791–92, several years later than James Grant is known to have been engaged in the Indian trade" and (3) "to James Grant is much more likely due the honor of having early traded on Grant river; and thus affixed his name to that stream." This 1888 article gives more information on Cuthbert Grant, stating that he was born in the "Hudson's Bay North West region, being of Scotch and Indian extraction" and died in July, 1854.

2997 *Green County*

Uncertain— This county was created by Wisconsin territory on December 8, 1836. Sources consulted are divided on whether the county's name honors the Revolutionary War general, Nathanael Greene (1742–1786), or was descriptive of the green color of the foliage here. General Greene was born in Rhode Island and served briefly in the Rhode Island legislature. He gained fame as one of the ablest American generals in the Revolutionary War. Helen M. Bingham's *History of Green County, Wisconsin*, published in 1877, explains quite clearly why there is uncertainty about the origin of this county's name: "At the first session of the first Wisconsin legislature ... Mr. Boyles presented a petition (which had been drawn up and circulated by Mr. Daniel S. Sutherland), asking for the organization of a county which should have the limits of the present county of Green, and be called Richland. The petition was granted, so far as setting off a new county was concerned, but some one objected to the name because it was 'too matter-of-fact,' and Mr. Boyles was invited to select another. According to one account he selected Green,

as indicative of the bright color of the vegetation, and refused to change it to Greene in honor of Gen. Greene." Another account says he selected Greene, and when the act of the legislature was printed, the final "e" was omitted by mistake. Be this as it may, for some years the name was usually written Greene.

2998 *Green Lake County*

Green Lake, within its borders— This county in south-central Wisconsin was created on March 5, 1858, and named for the county's largest lake, Green Lake. The Indians' name for this lake meant "green waters," and the Indians' name has been retained, as Green Lake, because of the lake's distinctly emerald color. Green Lake is located near the center of the county and wealthy residents of the Chicago, Illinois, area began to make Green Lake a popular vacation resort early in the 20th century. Green Lake is a deep lake, with a maximum depth of about 235 feet.

2999 *Iowa County*

Iowa Indians— At one time the Iowa (or Ioway) Indian tribe occupied all of what is now the state of Iowa, except the northwestern portion. They were related to the Winnebago Indians and subsisted by hunting and growing maize. The Iowa were first encountered by the French about 1700, in what is now southeastern Minnesota, north of the state of Iowa and northwest of Iowa County, Wisconsin. By 1838 they had given up all of their Iowa lands and were removed to a reservation at the junction of the Nemaha and Missouri Rivers. A number of Iowas were later moved to Indian territory (now Oklahoma). By 1985 the tribe's members numbered only about 500, spread among Oklahoma, Kansas and Nebraska. Numerous meanings have been offered for this Indian tribe's name but none have been substantiated. This county in today's state of Wisconsin was created on October 9, 1829, by Michigan territory.

3000 *Iron County*

Gogebic iron district— This county was created on March 1, 1893. It lies at the northern end of Wisconsin and is bordered on the east and north by Gogebic County, Michigan. The names of both counties commemorate the Gogebic iron district here. The Gogebic iron district became active in 1884, when the Milwaukee, Lake Shore & Western Railway Company extended its line to the iron district. Iron ore had been discovered here in 1871, or perhaps even earlier. The iron range took its name from the prominent, 12 mile long, lake near the eastern end of the range. The Gogebic iron range extends through three counties in northeastern Wisconsin, Bayfield County, Ashland County and Iron County as well as Gogebic County in Michigan. The name *Gogebic* is of Indian origin, but its meaning is unknown.

3001 *Jackson County*

Andrew Jackson (1767–1845)— Jackson was born on the border of North Carolina and South Carolina. He represented Tennessee in both branches of the U.S. Congress, and gained fame and popularity for his military exploits in wars with the Indians and in the War of 1812. He was provisional military governor of Florida and, from 1829 to 1837, General Jackson was president of the United States. His presidency reflected the frontier spirit of America. This county was created on February 11, 1853.

3002 *Jefferson County*

Thomas Jefferson (1743–1826)— Jefferson was a native of Virginia and a member of the Virginia legislature. He served Virginia as governor and was a delegate to the second Continental Congress. Jefferson was the author of the Declaration of Independence and one of its signers. He was minister to France, secretary of state, vice-president and president of the United States. As president, he accomplished the Louisiana Purchase and he arranged the Lewis & Clark Expedition to the Pacific Northwest. Jefferson was a true intellectual, thoroughly knowledgeable in the arts and sciences. His political theories were pivotal in the formation of our infant republic. This county was created by Wisconsin territory on December 7, 1836.

3003 *Juneau County*

Solomon Juneau (1793–1856)— Born in what is now Canada's province of Quebec, Juneau was baptized as Laurent Salomon Juneau but he adopted the name Solomon Juneau after coming to Milwaukee. Juneau emigrated from Quebec to Mackinac and worked as a clerk for the fur trader, Jacques Vieau (or Vieaux). Juneau soon bought a trading post which Vieau had on the Menominee River, where Milwaukee is now located, and married his daughter, Josette Vieau (1803–1855). Juneau built a log cabin in Milwaukee in 1822, followed by a frame house in 1824. By 1835 he had be-

come an American citizen, begun to learn English and erected, in Milwaukee a store, hotel and a two story house. Juneau solidified his status as "the father of Milwaukee" by becoming its first postmaster, first president of the village of Milwaukee and, in 1846, the first mayor of Milwaukee. This county was created on October 13, 1856, just one month before Solomon Juneau's death on November 14, 1856.

3004 *Kenosha County*

City of Kenosha, Wisconsin— This county in southeastern Wisconsin was created on January 30, 1850, and named for its principal town, which by the late 1990's had grown to a population of 80,000 and was an important manufacturing city and port on Lake Michigan. This municipality was first known as Pike River. That name was later changed to Southport and it was not officially changed to Kenosha until February 7, 1850, in the act which incorporated Kenosha as a city. At first glance it would appear that the county was named for the city of Kenosha one week before the city had acquired that name, but this chronology is more apparent than real. As early as 1838, the principal public house here was called Kenosha Ce-pee House, so the name was well established when the county was created. The name *Kenosha* is our rendering of the Indians' name for the Pike River. Authorities on the origin and meaning of Indian names differ on precisely what the Indians had in mind when they named the river, but essentially all sources agree that the name meant "fish," "pike" or "pickerel."

3005 *Kewaunee County*

Kewaunee River— This county in northeastern Wisconsin was created on April 16, 1852, and named for its principal river, the Kewaunee. That river had been known as Wood's River until 1834 when Joshua Hathaway, a surveyor, renamed it *Kewaunee*. Hathaway said that this was an Indian word which meant "prairie hen." While Hathaway is not challenged as the author of the river's name, several sources disagree with his translation and indicate that the word derived from an Indian phrase meaning "I cross a point of land by boat." That translation alludes to the logistics of traveling on the peninsula here that separates Green Bay from Lake Michigan.

3006 *La Crosse County*

City of La Crosse, Wisconsin— At what is now the city of La Crosse, Wisconsin,

American Indians established a neutral ground where members of various tribes gathered to socialize and engage in athletic games. This site was a convenient meeting place because of its location on the Mississippi River, where the La Crosse River and the Black River meet. French explorers and traders gave the name La Crosse to this site when they observed the Indians playing on the prairie here on the east side of the Mississippi River. The game which the Frenchmen observed was played with a ball and long-handled rackets. The word *crosse* is found in both the French and French-Canadian languages with reference to hockey sticks. Since the game resembles our present sport of field hockey, we might be inclined to pursue that translation but in their 1968 work entitled *The Romance of Wisconsin Place Names*, Robert E. Gard and L. G. Sorden explained that the Frenchmen called the game *la crosse* because "the racquet resembled a bishop's crozier." *La crosse* is French for "the crozier." A form of the game lacrosse now enjoys a degree of popularity in much of America. In 1842 Americans founded an Indian trading post at La Crosse, Wisconsin territory, and the city of La Crosse grew here to a population of 51,000 by the late 1990's. When La Crosse County was created on March 1, 1851, it was named for the municipality, which became its county seat.

3007 *Lafayette County*

Marie Joseph Paul Yves Roch Gilbert du Motier, Marquis de Lafayette (1757–1834)— Lafayette was a French aristocrat who served briefly in the French army. He came to America in 1777 to assist the American Revolutionary army. He was granted an honorary commission as major general by the Continental Congress and served with distinction in a number of battles in the Revolutionary War. This county was created by Wisconsin territory on January 31, 1846.

3008 *Langlade County*

Charles-Michel Mouet de Langlade (–)— Sources consulted provide different years of birth and death for Charles Langlade but they all cluster in the vicinity of 1729–1801. Born at Mackinac, in what is now Michigan, the son of a French father and Ottawa Indian mother, Langlade was educated by Jesuit missionaries and, with his father, established a trading post at what is now Green Bay, Wisconsin. He fought as an officer on the side of the

French and Indians during the French & Indian Wars and, with his Indian allies, on the side of the British during the American Revolution. In 1780 he led Indians into the Illinois country to assist in an attack on Spanish-held Saint Louis, but this effort was routed. Langlade died at Green Bay about 1801. This county was created with the name New County on February 27, 1879. One year later, on February 19, 1880, its name was changed to honor Charles-Michel Mouet de Langlade.

3009 *Lincoln County*

Abraham Lincoln (1809–1865)— Lincoln was a native of Kentucky who moved to Illinois, where he was a member of the state legislature. He represented Illinois in the U.S. House of Representatives and later was elected president of the United States. Lincoln's presidency coincided almost exactly with the Civil War. He guided the United States ably through that uniquely turbulent period. As president, he issued the Emancipation Proclamation which declared the freedom of slaves in all states in rebellion. Lincoln was assassinated a few days after the Union's victory in the Civil War. This county was created on March 4, 1874.

3010 *Manitowoc County*

Manitowoc River— This county in eastern Wisconsin was created by Wisconsin territory on December 7, 1836, and named for the principal stream within its borders, the Manitowoc River. The Manitowoc River rises in Calumet County, Wisconsin, and follows a winding course touching the communities of Rockland, Eaton, Liberty, Cato, Rapids and Manitowoc, where its waters enter Lake Michigan. The river is only about 45 miles long but it is fed by numerous tributaries and in early days it was a higher and more significant river, navigable by canoes nearly to Lake Winnebago. The *Manitou* portion of *Manitowoc* is one rendering of an Indian name which referred to a Deity, Spirit or "mysterious influence." Denis McLoughlin's *Wild & Woolly: An Encyclopedia of the Old West* refers to *Manitou* as "The great unseen force that can influence the lives of the American Indians. An Algonkin word that can refer to the Spirit of either Good or Evil."

3011 *Marathon County*

Battle of Marathon, Greece— This county in central Wisconsin was created on February 9, 1850, and named for the battle of Marathon, on the plain of Marathon, about 24 miles northeast of Athens, in ancient Greece. There, in September, 490 B.C., some 10,000 Greek soldiers, mostly from Athens, defeated an invading Persian army of about 20,000. Herodotus, the Greek historian, said that the overwhelming Greek victory here demonstrated that "free men fight better than slaves." Following the battle of Marathon, Athens became the leading city-state of ancient Greece.

3012 *Marinette County*

City of Marinette, Wisconsin— This county was created on February 27, 1879, and a number of Wisconsin sources indicate that it was named directly for Marinette Chevalier (1793–1865). There is no dispute about the fact that this county's name honors that lady, but it does so indirectly, having been named for the city of Marinette, which became its county seat. The city was founded as a fur trading post by Marinette Chevalier (1793–1865) and her common law husband, William Farnsworth (1796–1860), and it became a very important center for the production of white pine lumber. At the end of the 20th century, the sawmills here on Green Bay are silent and the city is a small port at the mouth of the Menominee River, with a population of 11,800.

Marinette Chevalier (1793–1865)— Born at Post Lake, within what is now the state of Wisconsin, Marinette Chevalier was a daughter of a French trapper, Bartholemy Chevalier, and a Menominee Indian woman, who was the daughter of a Menominee chief. Our Marinette Chevalier was christened as Marguerite Chevalier, but nicknamed Marinette, in honor of the French queen, Marie Antoinette (1755–1793), and the nickname stuck. About 1823 Marinette's first husband, Jean B. Jacobs, deserted her and she became the common law wife of William Farnsworth (1796–1860). Together with Farnsworth, Marinette Chevalier established a successful fur trading operation in competition with John Jacob Astor's (1763–1848) American Fur Company. Their ability to compete against this powerful adversary was due largely to Marinette's Menominee Indian connections and her skill as a trader. In the winter of 1831–1832 Farnsworth built the first sawmill on the Menominee River but about 1833 Farnsworth abandoned Marinette Chevalier; he moved to Sheboygan, while she remained with her children at Marinette and continued to develop it as a successful trading post. Marinette Chevalier's son, named John B. Jacobs, platted the town of Marinette.

3013 *Marquette County*

Jacques Marquette (1637–1675)— This Roman Catholic priest, Jesuit missionary and explorer was born in France and he was sent by his superiors to New France (Canada) in 1666. There he became proficient in several Indian languages. Marquette was active at a number of missions, converting Indians to Christianity and attending to their spiritual needs. One of these missions was at Sault Sainte Marie and another was just north of the Straits of Mackinac. In May, 1673, Father Marquette, together with the French Canadian fur trader and explorer Louis Jolliet (1645–1700), left on a journey to find the great river to the west, which had been reported by Indians. Marquette, Jolliet and their party first sighted the Mississippi River in June, 1673. The expedition traveled down the Mississippi to the vicinity of the mouth or the Arkansas River. They turned north there to begin an arduous return trip. By the time they reached a northern mission near present De Pere, Wisconsin, they had traveled some 2,900 miles and Father Marquette's health was broken. Marquette was left at De Pere. During the short remainder of his life, Father Marquette attempted missionary work but during each attempt his health failed him. This county was created by Wisconsin territory on December 7, 1836.

3014 *Menominee County*

Menominee Indians— The Menominee are a tribe of the Algonquian linguistic group. At one time they lived in northern Michigan near Mackinac Island. By the time of their first contact with Europeans, in the 1630's, they had moved west to the Menominee River area and Green Bay. Some Menominee ranged as far west as the Mississippi River and as far south as the Fox River. The Menominee of today harvest wild rice as their ancestors did centuries ago. The name *Menominee* means "wild rice people." The Menominee Indians won a lawsuit against the U.S. federal government on a charge of mismanagement of tribal affairs. Their $9,500,000 award was placed in trust and the first payments to the Indians were made in 1954. This county was created on May 1, 1961, and it consists entirely of the Menominee Indian "reservation." (The Indians own about 99% of the land here.)

3015 *Milwaukee County*

Milwaukee River— This county was created by Michigan territory on September 6,

1834, and named for the Milwaukee River. That river rises in Fond du Lac County, Wisconsin, and flows for 100 miles in a generally southeastern direction to enter Lake Michigan at Wisconsin's largest city, Milwaukee. The name *Milwaukee* is the latest written rendering of the Indians' name for the Milwaukee River. The 1902 issue (Vol. 14, Part 1) of the *Transactions of the Wisconsin Academy of Sciences, Arts & Letters* contained an article by Henry E. Legler entitled "Origin & Meaning of Wisconsin Place-Names: With Special Reference to Indian Nomenclature." In that article Legler lists eleven spellings of the name beginning with Father Louis Hennepin's (1640–1705) *Melleoki* of 1679 and including *Milwaukie* in the headline of *The Sentinel* of November 30, 1844. Legler stated that numerous translations for the name have been suggested but that the true meaning is uncertain. Legler is correct that numerous translations have been mentioned. However, one of the translations at our disposal was given by Professor Virgil J. Vogel in his 1986 *Indian Names in Michigan*: "There can be little doubt that the correct meaning is 'good land,' from the Potawatomi *meno* or *mino*, 'good,' and *aki*, 'land.'" Dr. Vogel is not, of course, infallible, but he is a leading scholar on Indian names in Michigan and elsewhere and if he tells us "There can be little doubt," he's probably correct.

3016 *Monroe County*

James Monroe (1758–1831)— Monroe, a native of Virginia, served in the Revolutionary War. Prior to his election as president of the United States, Monroe served in a wide variety of government posts. He served Virginia in the state legislature and as governor. He was a member of the Confederation congress and the U.S. Senate. He was minister to France and to Britain and he held two cabinet posts. As president, Monroe stressed limited government and strict construction of the constitution. He acquired Florida for the U.S. from Spain and he was the author of a policy declaration (later known as the Monroe Doctrine) which proscribed outside interference in North and South America. This county was created on March 21, 1854.

3017 *Oconto County*

Oconto River— This county in northeastern Wisconsin was created on February 6, 1851, and named for the Oconto River, its principal stream. The 130 mile-long Oconto River rises in Forest County and flows south and then east to enter Green Bay at the municipality of Oconto, Wisconsin, the county seat of Oconto County. The present name *Oconto* evolved from Indian names and there are several suggested translations of those names. Both the Menominee Indians and the Chippewa Indians had names for this river, either of which could be the phonetic ancestors of the present Oconto River's name. The Chippewa name meant "he watches," "lies in ambush" or "watching outpost." Those names referred to the period when Chippewa and other tribes gathered at Green Bay, and since some of the tribes were hostile to each other, the Chippewa were alert for movements of potential enemies. Several possible translations are offered for the Menominee Indians' name for the river, some of which relate to fish. Early maps referred to this river as Black Bass River.

3018 *Oneida County*

Oneida Indians— The Oneida were the least populous tribe of the Iroquois confederacy in central New York. At the time of their first contact with Whites, in the 1600's, their population was less than 1,000. They possessed New York state's Oneida Lake and the territory surrounding it. About the year 1720, the Oneida Indians were joined in New York by a group of Tuscarora Indians, who had migrated from North Carolina. Most Oneida Indians sided with the American colonists during the American Revolution. By the 1990's there were still 1,000 Oneida Indians living in New York state. The name *Oneida* has been variously translated as "standing stone," "granite people," or "stone people" and it refers to a large stone at one of their early villages which was a monument and became their tribal emblem. Large numbers of Oneida Indians moved from New York to Wisconsin and Wisconsin's Oneida reservation had a population of 4,437 in 1985. This county was created on April 11, 1885.

3019 *Outagamie County*

Fox Indians— This county in east-central Wisconsin was created on February 17, 1851, and named for the tribe of Indians whom we today generally refer to as the Fox Indians. However, the Chippewa Indians called the Fox by a name resembling Outagamie and the writings of the early explorers Daniel Greysolon, Sieur Du Luth (–1710) and Jonathan Carver (1710–1780) refer to the Fox Indians as Outagami(s), living in what is now Wisconsin. The Fox Indians lived in northeastern Illinois and Wisconsin and subsisted by hunting and growing maize. Their principal dwelling was a domed bark, thatch or hide house. The Fox Indians, unlike most other tribes of the Great Lakes, were unfriendly toward the French and combat with them in 1730 almost extinguished the tribe. Following this defeat the Fox joined with the Sauk Indians in fighting the French until about 1740 when peace was made. By 1985 the combined Fox and Sauk Indians had a total population of about 2,000 spread among Iowa, Kansas and Oklahoma.

3020 *Ozaukee County*

Sauk Indians— The Sauk migrated from what is now eastern Michigan to today's Wisconsin in the 18th century. This Algonquian tribe lived along the Wisconsin River and subsisted by hunting and growing maize. Their principal dwelling was a domed bark, thatch or hide house. The Sauk joined the Fox Indians in fighting the French until about 1740 when peace was made. In April, 1832, a dissident portion of Sauk Indians, led by Chief Black Hawk (1767–1838) declared war against the Whites. Federal troops pursued these Sauk Indians to the mouth of the Bad Axe River, in Wisconsin, and decimated them on August 2, 1832. Many Sauk had already allied themselves with the Fox Indians and after the massacre at Bad Axe, essentially all Sauk who remained were thenceforth associated with the Fox Indians. By 1985 the combined Sauk and Fox Indians had a total population of about 2,000 spread among Iowa, Kansas and Oklahoma. Ozaukee County was created on March 7, 1853, with its name derived from the proper name of the Sauk Indian tribe, which is *Osauki-wug*, meaning "people of the yellow earth." The more commonly used name of the tribe, *Sauk*, comes from the middle portion of *Osauki-wug* and another Wisconsin county, Sauk County, perpetuates that version.

3021 *Pepin County*

Lake Pepin— This county in western Wisconsin, on the Mississippi River, was created on February 25, 1858, and named for Lake Pepin, an enlargement of the Mississippi River here. This "lake" was formed from a natural dam created by silt from the Chippewa River and it has widened to 2.5 miles at its broadest point. Lake Pepin is more than 20 miles long. Several explanations for the lake's name are found but it is uncertain which, if any, of them is correct:

— The Pepin brothers, explorers who accompanied Daniel Greysolon, Sieur Du Luth (1639–1710), in reconnoitering the western portion of central Wisconsin. Du Luth mentioned the Pepin brothers in a letter dated April 5, 1679, and Val Bjornson's *The History of Minnesota* says that Du Luth wintered with them in 1678–1679 near Sault Ste. Marie.

— *Pepin le Bref* ("Pepin the Short") (–768), king of the Franks who ruled from 751 to 768. Lake Pepin belongs to Minnesota as well as Wisconsin and Warren Upham's *Minnesota Geographic Names* stated that its name "…may have been chosen, as stated by Gannett, in honor of Pepin le Bref, king of the Franks who was born in 714 and died in 768. He was a son of Charles Martel, and was the father of Charlemagne. Very probably the name was placed on the map by De L' Isle under request of his patron, the king of France … but history has failed to record for whom and why this large lake of the Mississippi was so named."

— A relative (named Pepin) of the wife of Rene Boucher, Sieur de la Perriere, who is said to have established a post on Lake Pepin in the 18th century. (Edward D. Neill's 1887 work entitled *The Last French Post in the Valley of the Upper Mississippi* says that this man's name was Stephen Pepin, Sieur de la Fond, and that he married Marie Boucher, the *aunt* [italics added] of the Sieur de la Pierre.)

— Jean Pepin, A Frenchman who settled near Lake Pepin.

3022 *Pierce County*

Franklin Pierce (1804–1869)— Pierce was born in New Hampshire and served in the lower house of that state's legislature. He represented New Hampshire in both houses of the U.S. Congress and served as an officer in the Mexican War, rising to the rank of brigadier-general. In 1852 Pierce was nominated for president by the Democratic party on the 49th ballot as a compromise candidate who was not objectionable to the South. He was elected to that office and served one term, from 1853 to 1857. As president, he viewed the slavery issue in a legalistic way and was unable to accept the North's moral objections to slavery. He failed to secure his party's nomination for a second term. Franklin Pierce was sworn into office as our na-tion's president on March 4, 1853, and this county was created ten days later, on March 14, 1853.

3023 *Polk County*

James K. Polk (1795–1849)— A native of North Carolina who moved with his family to the Tennessee frontier in 1806, Polk served in the lower house of the Tennessee legislature and he represented Tennessee for 14 years in the U.S. House of Representatives, where he was speaker. He served one term as governor of Tennessee. Polk became president of the United States as a dark horse candidate of the Democratic party but he became an unusually strong and effective president. His primary accomplishments involved westward extension of the United States: in the Northwest by settling a territorial dispute with Britain and in California and the Southwest by provoking and winning the Mexican War. This county was created on March 14, 1853.

3024 *Portage County*

Indian portage connecting the Wisconsin and Fox Rivers— This county was created by Wisconsin territory on December 7, 1836, and named for the Indian portage, then within its borders, between the Wisconsin River and the Fox River. At the present city of Portage, Wisconsin, the two rivers came within one mile of each other and the Indians carried their canoes in a portage over land from one river to reach the other. On February 3, 1846, Wisconsin's territorial legislature split Portage County into two counties and named the new one Columbia County. As a result of this division, today's Portage County no longer contains the Indian portage for which it was named. That portage lies in Columbia County, Wisconsin. It seems that when the one county was divided back in 1846 either the northern one (without the portage in it) or the southern one (which contains the portage) could have been named Portage County. In *A Standard History of Portage County, Wisconsin*, published in 1919, were are told that the decision concerning the naming of the two counties was made with an eye toward thrift: "But when the county was divided, the representative hailing from the north part of it, with a view it is said, to keep the old record books, and thereby save a few dollars in the purchase of new ones, managed to retain the name for the north part of it … calling the south part Columbia."

3025 *Price County*

William T. Price (1824–1886)— A native of Pennsylvania, Price came to Wisconsin territory in 1845 and engaged in the lumber trade, studied law and acquired extensive land holdings. In 1851 he served in the lower house of Wisconsin's legislature and the following year he was admitted to the bar. Price practiced law but also operated stage coach lines and promoted early railroads and flour mills. He served several terms in the Wisconsin senate and one more term in the Wisconsin assembly before being elected to represent Wisconsin in the U.S. House of Representatives. Price served there from 1883 until his death in 1886. This county was created on February 26, 1879, while William T. Price was president of the Wisconsin senate.

3026 *Racine County*

Town of Racine, Wisconsin— This county in southeastern Wisconsin was created by Wisconsin territory on December 7, 1836, and named for its principal town, Racine, which was made the county seat. By the late 1990's Racine had become a heavily industrialized city with a population of 84,000. The town of Racine was named for the winding Root River, which bisects it. *Racine* is French for "root" and the name was applied to the river "for its profusion of intertwining roots, which grew from the banks in wild luxuriance" according to an 1879 work entitled *The History of Racine & Kenosha Counties, Wisconsin*.

3027 *Richland County*

A promotional name chosen to attract settlers— This county in southwestern Wisconsin was created by Wisconsin territory on February 18, 1842. The county's name was chosen at a meeting of settlers held at Eagle Mill about 1841. Stephen Taylor's article in the 1855 edition (Vol. 1) of the *First Annual Report & Collections of the State Historical Society of Wisconsin* provided a succinct explanation for the origin of this county's name. Taylor's article was entitled "Wisconsin: Its Rise & Progress: With Notices of Mineral Point & Richland County" and the explanation that it provided was that "In selecting a name for the new county, some differences of opinion existed; the united object, however, was to adopt such an one as would elicit attraction, and at the same time bespeak the true character of its territory: The appellation *Richland*, was, therefore, adopted."

3028 *Rock County*

Uncertain— This county in south-central Wisconsin was created by Wisconsin territory on December 7, 1836. According to an 1889 work entitled *Portrait & Biographical Album of Rock County, Wisconsin*, the county was named for "the 'big rock' on the north side of the river, now within the limits of the city of Janesville." An 1879 work entitled *The History of Rock County, Wisconsin* agreed that this county was named for that rock and said of it "...the 'big rock' on the north side of the river, now within the limits of the city of Janesville, which had been for years one of the recognized land-marks of the country to the Indians, the traders and later to the settlers, as indicating a point where the river might be safely forded." With our ample supply of bridges today, we think little about crossing rivers but in 1836 when this county was created, a large rock which could pin-point a safe place to ford a large river could certainly have been noteworthy enough to become the namesake of a territorial county. However, not all sources agree that this county was named for that rock. Several sources state that Rock County was named for the Rock River, its principal stream. Some, but not all, sources indicate that the Rock River was named for the landmark "big rock" at the Janesville fording site. That Rock River is a 285 mile-long tributary of the Mississippi River, which rises in southeastern Wisconsin and enters Illinois at the southern border of Rock County, Wisconsin. Most of the Rock River's length is in Illinois and the river flows southwest from the Wisconsin border to enter the Mississippi at Rock Island County, Illinois.

3029 *Rusk County*

Jeremiah M. Rusk (1830–1893)— This native of Ohio came to Wisconsin in 1853 and served briefly in the lower house of the Wisconsin legislature before entering the Union army as an officer during the Civil War. Early in the war, he served as a major in Minnesota quelling the Dakota Indian uprising, but later also saw action in the South, at Vicksburg and Atlanta, and rose to the rank of brevet brigadier-general. After the war Rusk was elected to represent Wisconsin in the U.S. House of Representatives and he served several terms in that body before being elected as Wisconsin's governor, a post he held from 1882 to 1889. As governor he called out the militia to fire on strikers in Milwaukee in 1886. President Benjamin Harrison appointed Rusk to his cabinet as secretary of

agriculture in 1889. This county was created on May 15, 1901, with the name Gates County, in honor of John L. Gates, a prominent Milwaukee lumber man and capitalist. Its name was changed to Rusk County on June 19, 1905.

3030 *Saint Croix County*

Saint Croix River — This county lies on Wisconsin's western border with Minnesota. It was created by Wisconsin territory on January 9, 1840, and named for the Saint Croix River, the county's principal stream. The Saint Croix rises in Douglas County, Wisconsin and flows southwest to form part of the border between Wisconsin and Minnesota early in its course. The Saint Croix then flows generally south and forms the western border of several Wisconsin counties, including Saint Croix County. Further south, below St. Paul, Minnesota, the Saint Croix completes its 164 mile journey and empties its waters into the Mississippi. Different tales are told of the origin of the Saint Croix River's name. *Croix* is French for "cross" and many sources agree that the river was named prior to 1700 because a cross had been erected at the mouth of the river, and a majority of sources indicate that the cross here honored a Frenchman who accidentally died in the waters of the Saint Croix River, at its mouth. However some sources then attempt to supply the surname of the Frenchman who died and they would have us believe that his name was St. Croix. The case for a cross (*croix*) having been erected to honor a drowning victim named St. Croix is not convincing. Another possibility which may be inferred from the literature on this subject, is that a Frenchman drowned at the mouth of the Saint Croix River, no cross was erected, but the river was named Saint Croix because the surname of the drowning victim was St. Croix.

3031 *Sauk County*

A large village of the Sauk Indians here— The Sauk Indians migrated from what is now eastern Michigan to today's Wisconsin in the 18th century. This Algonquian tribe lived along the Wisconsin River and subsisted by hunting and growing maize. Their principal dwelling was a domed bark, thatch or hide house. The Sauk joined the Fox Indians in fighting the French until about 1740 when peace was made. In April, 1832 a dissident portion of Sauk Indians, led by Chief Black Hawk (1767–1838) declared war against the

Whites. Federal troops pursued these Sauk Indians to the mouth of the Bad Axe River, in Wisconsin, and decimated them on August 2, 1832. Many Sauk had already allied themselves with the Fox Indians and after the massacre at Bad Axe, essentially all Sauk who remained were thenceforth associated with the Fox Indians. By 1985 the combined Sauk and Fox Indians had a total population of about 2,000 spread among Iowa, Kansas and Oklahoma. This county in southern Wisconsin was created by Wisconsin territory on January 11, 1840, and named for a large village of the Sauk Indians, within its borders. Some specific information about that Indian village was supplied in footnote 96 on page 282 of Reuben G. Thwaites' article in the 1908 issue (Vol. 18) of *Collections of the State Historical Society of Wisconsin*. That footnote said that "This village was near the modern site of Prairie du Sac. This large town, whose fine appearance is described by both Carver and Pond, was probably built in the decade 1740–50.... It continued to be occupied until the close to the Revolution, when it was abandoned from fear of the Chippewa, and the inhabitants removed to the Mississippi."

3032 *Sawyer County*

Philetus Sawyer (1816–1900)— A native of Vermont, Sawyer came to Wisconsin territory in 1847. Here he engaged in the lumber industry, served in the lower house of the Wisconsin (state) legislature and was mayor of the city of Oshkosh. He amassed a fortune from activities in lumber, land speculation, banking and railroad enterprises. Sawyer was elected to represent Wisconsin in the U.S. House of Representatives and served in that body from 1865 to 1875 and he later was a U.S. senator from Wisconsin from 1881 to 1893. This county was created on March 10, 1883, while Philetus Sawyer was serving in the U.S. Senate.

3033 *Shawano County*

Uncertain— Shawano Lake lies in the eastern portion of this county and several sources indicate that when this county was created on February 16, 1853, it was named for that lake. It seems quite likely that this is true but there is a degree of uncertainty since many Wisconsin sources on the origins of Wisconsin's county names stress the translation of the Indian word *Shawano* rather than specifying the county's namesake. After presenting these translations (and they are numerous but all refer to "south" or "southern") some sources indicate that the county was named for the lake but many just present the translations without linking them from the lake to the county. An additional reason for uncertainty about the origin of this county's name is that a few sources mention the possibility that the county's name honors an Indian chief. Here again, we are faced with question whether it was directly or indirectly, with some sources indicating that the county may have been named for the chief while others insert the lake giving us a county named for a lake named for a chief. The Indian chief's name is rendered with several spellings resembling *Shawano*, but it is clear that he was a son of Chief Tomah (–1817), whose ancestry included Menominee Indian and French blood. When this county was created in 1853 its name was spelled Shawanaw. It was not until 1864 that the spelling was officially changed to Shawano.

3034 *Sheboygan County*

Sheboygan River— This county in eastern Wisconsin was created by Wisconsin territory on December 7, 1836, and named for the Sheboygan River, which runs through the county from its northern border to its eastern side, where its waters empty into lake Michigan at the city of Sheboygan. It is clear that the river was named first, the county second and the city last. The name is of Indian origin but its meaning is uncertain. Several explanations have been mentioned. The *he* portion of the name might have derived from an Ojibwa Indian word meaning "big" while *boygan* was a variant of the Indian word for "pipe." The resulting translation under this theory would be "big pipe." Other translations refer to water which goes underground, disappears underground and/or makes noise underground. A variation on that theme was provided in a 1968 work entitled *The Romance of Wisconsin Place Names* by Robert E. Gard and L. G. Sorden: "One authority claims the Indian word meant 'send through' and 'drum,' and referred to festive tribal occasions when the Indians carried their drums between Sheboygan Falls and Sheboygan and beat the cadence most properly suited to the event." This is not the end of the list of suggested translations. There are others, which seem less likely, including a folk tale about a local Indian chief, who had a number of daughters but no sons. Hoping his next child would be a son, when a girl arrived the fable tells us

that the chief said "she boy 'gain." Don't believe it.

3035 *Taylor County*

William R. Taylor (–1909)— Taylor was born in Connecticut on July 10, but whether the year was 1818 or 1820 is disputed. He came to Wisconsin in 1848 and although he served one term in the lower house of Wisconsin's legislature and one in the Wisconsin senate, Taylor was not a politician in the usual sense. Rather, he farmed, worked in a lumber camp, was a county superintendent of schools and, for 17 years, was county superintendent of the poor. From 1860 to 1874 Taylor was a trustee of Wisconsin's state hospital for the insane and he was president of agricultural societies at both the county and state level. Taylor was active in the Grange, a movement seeking to improve conditions and laws affecting farmers, and with support from that movement, coupled with discontent over a major Depression which began in 1873, Taylor was swept into the Wisconsin governor's office in a reform movement which captured all state offices in November, 1873. He served as Wisconsin's governor from 1874 to 1876 and this county was created on March 4, 1875, while he was governor.

3036 *Trempealeau County*

Trempealeau River— This county in western Wisconsin was created on January 27, 1854, and named for its principal river, a tributary of the Mississippi. The Trempealeau is a 50 mile-long stream which rises east of Trempealeau County and flows southwest across Trempealeau County to form part of the border between Trempealeau County and Buffalo County, Wisconsin. The river was named for an unusually high island or mountain island. The Indians called it a name which meant "mountain soaked in water," and the French translated that into their language as *La Montagne qui trempe a l'eau*.

3037 *Vernon County*

George Washington's Virginia estate, Mount Vernon— The home and estate of George Washington in Virginia overlooks the Potomac River, just 15 miles below our nation's capital. The estate originally consisted of some 5,000 acres when it was first acquired by the Washington family some four generations prior to George Washington. The estate was given its present name by George Washington's elder half-brother, Lawrence Washington. It was

named in honor of Admiral Edward Vernon (1684–1757), of the British navy, under whom Lawrence Washington had served in the Caribbean Sea. In the late 1990's the restored Mount Vernon contains much of the original furniture and is open to visitors. This county was created on March 1, 1851, and named Bad Ax County (no "e"), for the Bad Axe River (with an "e"). This river runs through the county and its mouth here had been the location of a famous battle on August 2, 1832, when U.S. army troops decimated Sauk Indians during the Black Hawk War. However, after the county had been named Bad Ax, that name became the subject of derision during sessions of the Wisconsin legislature, when the chair recognized "the gentleman from Bad Ax." In 1862, Jeremiah M. Rusk of Viroqua, Wisconsin, was a member of the lower house of the Wisconsin legislature from this county and he introduced a resolution to change the county's name and end the derision. The motion passed and the county's name was changed to Vernon, effective March 22, 1862. The name Vernon was suggested to Assemblyman Rusk by William F. Terhune as a euphonious name honoring the green fields of the estate of our first president.

3038 *Vilas County*

William F. Vilas (1840–1908)— Born in Vermont, Vilas moved with his parents to Wisconsin in 1851 and was an 1858 graduate of the University of Wisconsin at Madison. Prior to the Civil War Vilas studied law and was admitted to the bar. He left his law practice at Madison to enlist as an officer in the Union army during the Civil War and rose to the rank of lieutenant-colonel. Vilas returned to Wisconsin and while teaching law at the University of Wisconsin he became a power in the nation's Democratic party. In 1885 he was appointed to the cabinet of President Grover Cleveland as postmaster general and in 1888 President Cleveland promoted him to secretary of the interior. Vilas subsequently was elected as a U.S. senator from Wisconsin and he served in that body from 1891 to 1897. This county was created on April 12, 1893.

3039 *Walworth County*

Reuben H. Walworth (1788–1867)— Born in Connecticut on October 26, 1788, Reuben Hyde Walworth moved with his parents to New York when he was about 12 years old. The family settled on a farm near Hoosick, New York. Walworth studied law, was admitted to the New York bar in 1809 and established a law practice in Plattsburgh, New York the following year. Prior to the War of 1812, Walworth served briefly as a circuit judge and during the War of 1812, he was an officer in the New York militia. He was aide-de-camp to General Benjamin Mooers and division judge advocate and held the rank of colonel. He returned to Plattsburgh after the war and was elected to represent New York in the U.S. House of Representatives. After serving one term in that body, Walworth was a judge in New York and was the state's chancellor from 1828 to 1848. In 1844 President John Tyler nominated Walworth to serve as an associate justice on the Supreme Court, but the Senate refused to confirm this nomination. The U.S. Senate rejected five out of President Tyler's six Supreme Court nominations; more rejections than any other American president has suffered in the history of the Supreme Court. Walworth died at Saratoga Springs, New York, on November 27, 1867. This county was created by Wisconsin territory on December 7, 1836. The county's name was suggested by Colonel Samuel F. Phoenix, the founder of the town of Delavan, a Baptist temperance colony here. Reuben H. Walworth had established a national reputation as a temperance leader.

3040 *Washburn County*

Cadwallader C. Washburn (1818–1882)— A native of Maine, Washburn moved west about 1839, studied law and then settled in Wisconsin territory in 1842. Here he was soon admitted to the bar. He and a partner, Cyrus Woodman, acquired enormous tracts of timberland in northern Wisconsin. In 1854 Washburn was elected to represent Wisconsin in the U.S. House of Representatives and he served in that body from 1855 to 1861. During the Civil War he served as an officer in the Union army and rose from colonel to major-general. After the war he represented Wisconsin in congress again and then was elected as the state's governor, serving one term, from 1872 to 1874. Washburn later greatly enlarged his fortune as a flour milling entrepreneur. He died on May 14, 1882, and this county was created and named in his honor ten months later, on March 27, 1883.

3041 *Washington County*

George Washington (1732–1799)— Washington was a native of Virginia. He served in Virginia's house of burgesses and became one of the colonies' leaders in opposition to British policies in America. He was a member of the first and second Continental Congresses and commander of all Continental armies in the Revolutionary War. Following victory in that war, Washington was elected to be the first president of the United States. This county was created by Wisconsin territory on December 7, 1836.

3042 *Waukesha County*

Uncertain— This county was created from the western portion of Milwaukee County by Wisconsin territory on January 31, 1846. A large number of sources dealing with Wisconsin's geographic names attribute this county's name to an Indian word meaning or containing the word "fox." Some of those sources indicate that this "fox" was the animal and several translations mentioned (including "fox," "little foxes," and "place of the little foxes") clearly indicate that they thought that the Indian word referred to the animal. However there are other sources on Wisconsin place names which vehemently deny that the fox here was the animal. These sources claim that the name came from the Fox River and that the river was named for the Fox Indian tribe. These sources remind us that the waters of this county drain into the Fox River. Those wishing support for the theory that it was fox, the animal, will find comfort in the "Narrative of Peter J. Vieau," which appeared in the 1900 issue (Vol. 15) of *Collections of the State Historical Society of Wisconsin* which clearly states that fox animals were present in abundance here in what would later become Waukesha County. An 1880 work entitled *The History of Waukesha County, Wisconsin* provides extensive background on the discussions and debates that occurred during the selection of this county's name. After reading that 1880 background one might well conclude that even if the original intention was to capture an Indian name relating to fox (whether animal, river or Indian tribe), by the time the territorial legislature had mangled the proposed name into *Waukesha*, what resulted was a contrived, pseudo–Indian name. The settlers who were involved in recommending a name for this new county wanted an Indian name and they considered two such names: *Tchee-gas-cou-tak* and *Wauk-tsha*. The 1880 article concludes that "The general public now believes that Waukesha means fox; it does not, nor has it any meaning whatever."

3043 *Waupaca County*

Waupaca River— This county in central Wisconsin was created on February 17, 1851, and named for the Waupaca River, which traverses part of the county. The Waupaca River, a short tributary of Wolf River, rises in Portage County, just west of Waupaca County and flows in a southeastern direction to enter Wolf River near the town of Mukwa, in Waupaca County. The Waupaca River's name is of Indian origin but its meaning is uncertain. A large number of translations have been suggested including "white sand bottom," "pale water," "tomorrow river," "where one waits to shoot deer," "stalling place" and "our brave young hero."

3044 *Waushara County*

A contrived, or pseudo–Indian name— This name first appeared on Wisconsin's map on February 15, 1851, when this county was created. Since the name is a contrived, pseudo–Indian name, the possible translations which have been mentioned would appear to be spurious.

3045 *Winnebago County*

Uncertain— This county in east-central Wisconsin was created by Wisconsin territory on January 6, 1840. The vast majority of sources dealing with the history, geography and place names of Wisconsin state that this county was named for the Winnebago Indians. This is surprising because the giant Lake Winnebago, on the county's eastern border, would seem to be a much more probable namesake for this county. Just a few Wisconsin sources state that the county was named for Lake Winnebago. Since the lake was named for the Winnebago Indians, it is certain that the county's name honors that tribe, either directly or indirectly.

Winnebago Indians— At the time of early contact with Whites, the Winnebago tribe lived in central Wisconsin from Green Bay and Lake Winnebago to the Mississippi River and along the Rock River in southern Wisconsin and extreme northern Illinois. In their material culture, the Winnebago were distinctly timber people. They sided with the British during both the American Revolution and the War of 1812. In the early and mid 1800's, the Winnebago were forced from their lands in northern Illinois and Wisconsin by the Whites using both treaties and military force. First they were moved to northern Iowa, then to Minnesota, next to South Dakota and then to a reservation in northeastern Nebraska. However, many Winnebago in Nebraska made their way back to Wisconsin. Although never huge in numbers, their population was estimated at about 5,000 in the first half of the 19th century. These Indians called themselves "big fish people" but it is the Algonquian name for them, Winnebago, that has stuck. Its precise meaning is uncertain but translations for it relate to "stinking" and "water" and include "stinking water," "dirty water people" and "stinking water people." Both Father Marquette and Cadillac were careful to record that the Winnebago's name did not signify any unclean habits of these Indians but pertained to water. It is likely that the name Winnebago referred to their earlier northern home, perhaps in Canada, and originally meant "people of the sea."

Lake Winnebago — One of the largest inland lakes in the United States, Lake Winnebago is by far the largest lake that is completely within Wisconsin. It forms most of the eastern border of Winnebago County, Wisconsin, and most of the western border of Calumet County. The lake's southern end extends well into Fond du Lac County. With a length of more than 28 miles and a width of 10.5 miles at its broadest point, Lake Winnebago covers 215 square miles.

3046 *Wood County*

Joseph Wood (1811–1890)— Born October 16, 1811, at Camden, New York, Wood was raised in a poor farming community and his educational opportunities were limited. The Wisconsin volume of *The United States Biographical Dictionary & Portrait Gallery of Eminent & Self-Made Men*, published in 1877 stated that "...he went on the Erie canal, and ran a boat on the New York and Seneca Lake line six seasons." Wood moved west in 1836 and operated a farm in northern Illinois, near the Wisconsin border, for about eleven years. In March, 1848, he came to Wisconsin territory to the community that was then called Grand Rapids, and is now Wisconsin Rapids. Here Wood engaged in farming, lumbering, mercantile business and real estate speculation. In politics he was commissioner of state lands from 1848 to 1852 and he served one term in the lower house of the Wisconsin legislature in 1856. During that term in the assembly, Joseph Wood promoted the idea to form a new county from the western portion of Portage County. The notion was adopted and the new county, which was created on March 29, 1856, was named in his honor.

From 1857 to 1858 Wood served as county judge of the county named in his honor.

REFERENCES

Abraham, Henry J. *Justices & Presidents: A Political History of Appointments to the Supreme Court*. New York, Oxford University Press, 1992.

Ackerman, William K. *Early Illinois Railroads*. Chicago, Fergus Printing Co., 1884.

"Additions & Corrections." *Report and Collections of the State Historical Society of Wisconsin*, Vol. 10. Madison: 1888.

Anderson, William J., & William A. Anderson. *The Wisconsin Blue Book: 1929*. Madison, Democrat Printing Co., 1929.

Bingham, Helen M. *History of Green County, Wisconsin*. Milwaukee, Burdick & Armitage, 1877.

Birk, Douglas A., & Judy Poseley. *The French at Lake Pepin*. Minnesota Historical Society, 1978.

Bjornson, Val. *The History of Minnesota*. West Palm Beach, Florida, Lewis Historical Publishing Co., Inc., 1969.

The Blue Book of the State of Wisconsin. Madison, Democrat Printing Co., 1907.

The Blue Book of the State of Wisconsin. Madison, Democrat Printing Co., 1911.

Brody, Polly. *Discovering Wisconsin*. Madison, Wisconsin House, Ltd., 1973.

Brown, Dorothy Moulding. *Wisconsin Indian Place Name Legends*. 1948.

Brown, William F. *Rock County, Wisconsin*. Chicago, C. F. Cooper & Co., 1908.

Brunson, Alfred. "Wisconsin Geographical Names." *Collections of the State Historical Society of Wisconsin*, Vol. 1. Madison: 1855.

Bryant, Benjamin F. *Memoirs of La Crosse County*. Madison, Western Historical Association, 1907.

Buchen, Gustave W. *Historic Sheboygan County*. 1944.

Butler, James D. "First French Footprints Beyond the Lakes: Or What Brought the French So Early Into the Northwest?" *Transactions of the Wisconsin Academy of Sciences, Arts & Letters*, Vol. 5. Madison: 1882.

Calkins, Hiram. "Indian Nomenclature and the Chippewas." *Collections of the State Historical Society of Wisconsin*, Vol. 1. Madison: 1855.

Campbell, Henry C., et al. *Wisconsin in Three Centuries: 1634–1905*. New York, Century History Co., 1906.

The Canadian Encyclopedia. Edmonton, Alberta, Canada, Hurtig Publishers, 1985.

"The Career of Marinette." *Wisconsin Magazine of History*, Vol. 5. Menasha, Wisconsin: 1921–1922.

Cassidy, Frederic G. *Dane County Place-Names*. Madison, University of Wisconsin Press, 1968.

Chappelle, Ethel Elliot. *Around the Four Corners*. Rice Lake, Wisconsin, Chronotype Publishing Co., Inc.

Church, Charles F. *Easy Going: A Comprehensive Guide to Door County*. Madison, Wisconsin Tales & Trails, Inc., 1977.

The Clark County Centennial: 1853–1953. Neillsville, Wisconsin, 1953.

Clements, John. *Wisconsin Facts*. Dallas, Texas, Clements Research II, Inc., 1990.

The Columbian Biographical Dictionary & Portrait Gallery of Representative Men of the United States: Wisconsin Volume. Chicago, Lewis Publishing Co., 1895.

"Communications: Some Corrections: Early Racine & Judge Pryor." *Wisconsin Magazine of History*, Vol. 3. Menasha, Wisconsin: 1919–1920.

Crow, William L. *Wisconsin Lives of National Interest*. Appleton, Wisconsin, C. C. Nelson Publishing Co., 1937.

Curtiss-Wedge, Franklyn. *History of Buffalo & Pepin Counties, Wisconsin*. Winona, Minnesota, H. C. Cooper, Jr., & Co., 1919.

Curtiss-Wedge, Franklyn. *History of Trempealeau County, Wisconsin*. Chicago, H. C. Cooper, Jr., & Co., 1917.

Curtiss-Wedge, F., et al. *History of Dunn County, Wisconsin*. Minneapolis, H. C. Cooper, Jr. & Co., 1925.

Davidson, J. N. *In Unnamed Wisconsin: Studies in the History of the Region Between Lake Michigan and the Mississippi*. Milwaukee, Silas Chapman, 1895.

Davis, Susan Burdick. *Old Forts & Real Folks*. Madison, Democrat Printing Co., 1939.

Dessureau, Robert M. *History of Langlade County, Wisconsin*. Antigo, Wisconsin, Berner Bros. Publishing Co., 1922.

Dictionary of Wisconsin Biography. Madison, State Historical Society of Wisconsin, 1960.

Doudna, Edgar G. *The Thirtieth Star: 1848–1948*. State Centennial Committee.

Draper, Lyman C. "Wisconsin Necrology: 1879–82." *Report & Collections of the State Historical Society of Wisconsin*, Vol. 10. Madison: 1888.

Draper, Lyman C., et al. "Naming of Madison & Dane County and the Location of the Capitol." *Collections of the State Historical Society of Wisconsin*, Vol. 6. Madison: 1872.

Drury, John. *This Is Dane County, Wisconsin*. Chicago, Inland Photo Co.

Du Gard, Rene C., & Dominique C. Western. *The Handbook of French Place*

Names in the U.S.A. Editions des Deux Mondes, 1977.

Dunn, James T. *The St. Croix: Midwest Border River.* New York, Holt, Rinehart & Winston, 1965.

Dyrud, Valerie. *History Talks from Prairie du Chien.* Prairie du Chien, Wisconsin, 1985.

Easton, Augustus B. *History of the Saint Croix Valley.* Chicago, H. C. Cooper, Jr. & Co., 1909.

Faber, Harold. *From Sea to Sea: The Growth of the United States.* New York, Farrar, Straus & Giroux, 1967.

Falge, Louis. *History of Manitowoc County, Wisconsin.* Chicago, Goodspeed Historical Association, 1911–1912.

Faragher, John M. *The Encyclopedia of Colonial & Revolutionary America.* New York, Facts On File, 1990.

Fifield, S. S. "Memoir of Hon. Henry D. Barron." *Collections of the State Historical Society of Wisconsin*, Vol. 9. Madison: 1882.

Fitzpatrick, Edward A. *Wisconsin.* Milwaukee, Bruce Publishing Co., 1931.

Flandrau, Charles E. "Reminiscences of Minnesota During the Territorial Period." *Collections of the Minnesota Historical Society*, Vol. 9. St. Paul, Minnesota: 1901.

Folsom, W. H. C. *Fifty Years in the Northwest.* Pioneer Press Co., 1888.

Forrester, George. *Historical & Biographical Album of the Chippewa Valley, Wisconsin.* Chicago, A. Warner, 1891–1892.

Foster, Theodore G. "Indian Place Names in Michigan." *The Totem Pole*, Vol. 28, No. 4. Algonac, Michigan: January 7, 1952.

Fox, Isabella. *Solomon Juneau: A Biography.* Milwaukee, Evening Wisconsin Printing Co., 1916.

Gard, Robert E. *This Is Wisconsin.* Madison, Straus Printing Co., 1969.

Gard, Robert E., & L. G. Sorden. *The Romance of Wisconsin Place Names.* New York, October House, Inc., 1968.

Gard, Robert E., & L. G. Sorden. *Wisconsin Lore.* New York, Duell, Sloan & Pearce, 1962.

Gemmill, William N. *Romantic America.* Chicago, Jordan Publishing Co., 1926.

Gordon, Newton S. *History of Barron County, Wisconsin.* Minneapolis, H. C. Cooper, Jr., & Co., 1922.

Grant, Bruce. *Concise Encyclopedia of the American Indian.* Avenel, New Jersey, Wings Books, 1989.

Gregory, John G. *Southeastern Wisconsin: A History of Old Milwaukee County.* Chicago, S. J. Clarke Publishing Co., 1932.

Gregory, John G. *Southwestern Wisconsin: A History of Old Crawford County.* Chicago, S. J. Clarke Publishing Co., 1932.

Hartley, Alan H. "The Expansion of Ojibway & French Place-names into the Lake Superior Region in the Seventeenth Century." *Names: Journal of the American Name Society*, Vol. 28, No. 1. Saranac Lake, New York: March, 1980.

Hart, Paxton. "The Making of Menominee County." *Wisconsin Magazine of History*, Vol. 43, No. 3. Madison: Spring, 1960.

Haseltine, Ira S. "Sketch of Richland County." *Collections of the State Historical Society of Wisconsin*, Vol. 1. Madison: 1855.

Hathaway, Joshua. "Indian Names." *Collections of the State Historical Society of Wisconsin*, Vol. 1. Madison: 1855.

Heritage of Iron & Timber: 1880–1980. Florence County Centennial Committee, 1980.

"The History in Our County Names." *Badger History for Boys & Girls*, Vol. 3, No. 6. Madison: February, 1950.

The History of Columbia County, Wisconsin. Chicago, Western Historical Co., 1880.

History of Crawford & Richland Counties, Wisconsin. Springfield, Illinois, Union Publishing Co., 1884.

The History of Fond du Lac County, Wisconsin. Chicago, Western Historical Co., 1880.

The History of Racine & Kenosha Counties, Wisconsin. Chicago, Western Historical Co., 1879.

The History of Rock County, Wisconsin. Chicago, Western Historical Co., 1879.

The History of Sauk County, Wisconsin. Chicago, Western Historical Co., 1880.

History of Vernon County, Wisconsin. Springfield, Illinois, Union Publishing Co., 1884.

The History of Waukesha County, Wisconsin. Chicago, Western Historical Co., 1880.

Holand, Hjalmar R. *Old Peninsula Days: Tales & Sketches of the Door County Peninsula.* Ephraim, Wisconsin, Pioneer Publishing Co., 1925.

Holli, Melvin G., & Peter d' A. Jones. *Biographical Dictionary of American Mayors: 1820–1980.* Westport, Connecticut, Greenwood Press, 1981.

Holmes, Fred L. *The Wisconsin Blue Book: 1927.* Madison, Democrat Printing Co., 1927.

"How the Names Came: Story of Wisconsin Counties and Their Titles." *Milwaukee Sentinel*, December 1, 1895.

Hunt, John W. *Wisconsin Gazetteer.* Madison, Beriah Brown, 1853.

Jackson, Alfred A. "Abraham Lincoln in the Black Hawk War." *Collections of the State Historical Society of Wisconsin*, Vol. 14. Madison: 1898.

Jones, George O., et al. *History of Lincoln, Oneida & Vilas Counties, Wisconsin.* Minneapolis, H. C. Cooper, Jr. & Co., 1924.

Juneau County: The First Hundred Years. Friendship, Wisconsin, New Past Press, Inc., 1988.

Kellogg, Louise Phelps. "Organization, Boundaries & Names of Wisconsin Counties." *Proceedings of the State Historical Society of Wisconsin.* Madison: 1910.

Kellogg, Louise Phelps. "The Society and the State." *Wisconsin Magazine of History*, Vol. 10, No. 1. Cleveland, Ohio: September, 1926.

Ker, Edmund T. *River & Lake Names in the United States.* New York, Woodstock Publishing Co., 1911.

Kleber, John E. *The Kentucky Encyclopedia.* Lexington, Kentucky, University Press of Kentucky, 1992.

Kuhm, Herbert W. "Indian Place-Names in Wisconsin." *Wisconsin Archeologist*, Vol. 33, Nos. 1 & 2. Milwaukee: March & June, 1952.

Lange, Kenneth I. *A County Called Sauk.* Sauk County Historical Society, 1976.

Lapham, I. A. *Wisconsin: Its Geography & Topography, History, Geology & Mineralogy.* Milwaukee, I. A. Hopkins, 1846.

Lawson, A. J. "New London & Neighborhood." *Collections of the State Historical Society of Wisconsin*, Vol. 3. Madison: 1857.

Legler, Henry E. *Leading Events in Wisconsin History.* Milwaukee, Sentinel Co., 1898.

Legler, Henry E. "Origin & Meaning of Wisconsin Place-Names: With Special Reference to Indian Nomenclature." *Transactions of the Wisconsin Academy of Sciences, Arts & Letters*, Vol. 14, Part 1. Madison: 1902.

Leitch, Barbara A. *A Concise Dictionary of Indian Tribes of North America.* Algonac, Michigan, Reference Publications, Inc., 1979.

Leland, J. A. C. "Indian Names in Missouri." *Names: Journal of the American Name Society*, Vol. 1, No. 4. Berkeley: December, 1953.

Lexington, Kentucky Visitors Guide: 1993.

McIntosh, Montgomery E. "Charles Langlade: First Settler of Wisconsin." *Parkman Club Papers*, No. 8. Milwaukee: 1896.

McLeod, Donald. *History of Wiskonsan.* Buffalo, Steele's Press, 1846.

McLoughlin, Denis. *Wild & Woolly: An Encyclopedia of the Old West.* Garden City, New York, Doubleday & Co., Inc., 1975.

McMillan, Morrison. "Early Settlement of La Crosse & Monroe Counties." *Col-*

lections of the State Historical Society of Wisconsin, Vol. 4. Madison: 1859.

The Manitowoc County Story of a Century: 1848–1948. Manitowoc, Wisconsin, Manitowoc County Historical Society, 1970.

Marchetti, Louis. History of Marathon County, Wisconsin. Chicago, Richmond-Arnold Publishing Co., 1913.

Martin, Charles I. History of Door County, Wisconsin. Sturgeon Bay, Wisconsin, Exposition Job Print, 1881.

Martin, Lawrence. The Physical Geography of Wisconsin. Madison, State of Wisconsin, 1932.

"Memoirs of Mary D. Bradford." Wisconsin Magazine of History, Vol. 14, No. 1. Evansville, Wisconsin: September, 1930.

Michigan, Wisconsin Tour Book. Heathrow, Florida, AAA Publishing, 1999.

Mid-Atlantic Tour Book. Heathrow, Florida, AAA Publishing, 1999.

Mygatt, Wallace. "Some Account of the First Settlement of Kenosha." Third Annual Report & Collections of the State Historical Society of Wisconsin, Vol. 3. Madison: 1857.

"Narrative of Peter J. Vieau." Collections of the State Historical Society of Wisconsin, Vol. 15. Madison: 1900.

Neill, Edward D. The Last French Post in the Valley of the Upper Mississippi. St. Paul, Minnesota, Pioneer Press Co., 1887.

Neill, Edward D., & J. Fletcher Williams. History of Washington County and the St. Croix Valley. Minneapolis, North Star Publishing Co., 1881.

Old Homes of the Bluegrass. Lexington, Kentucky, Sydney S. Combs, Realtor.

Olsenius, Richard, & Judy A. Zerby. Wisconsin Travel Companion. Wayzata, Minnesota, Bluestem Productions, 1983.

O'Neill, Jean. Dunn County History. Dallas, Texas, Taylor Publishing Co., 1984.

Parkison, Daniel M. "Pioneer Life in Wisconsin." Second Annual Report & Collections of the State Historical Society of Wisconsin, Vol. 2. Madison: 1856.

Peck, George W. Wisconsin: Comprising Sketches of Counties, Towns, Events, Institutions & Persons Arranged in Cyclopedic Form. Madison, Western Historical Association, 1906.

Pernin, Peter. "The Great Peshtigo Fire: An Eyewitness Account." Wisconsin Magazine of History, Vol. 54, No. 4. Madison: Summer, 1971.

Platt, Doris H. Wisconsin Reader. Madison, State Historical Society of Wisconsin, 1960.

Plumb, Ralph G. A History of Manitowoc County. Manitowoc, Wisconsin, Brandt Printing & Binding Co., 1904.

Portrait & Biographical Album of Rock County, Wisconsin. Chicago, Acme Publishing Co., 1889.

Pratt, Alexander F. "Reminiscences of Wisconsin." Collections of the State Historical Society of Wisconsin, Vol. 1. Madison: 1855.

Pratt, Dorothy, & Richard Pratt. A Guide to Early American Homes: North & South. New York, Bonanza Books, 1956.

Prucha, Francis P. A Guide to the Military Posts of the United States: 1789–1895. Madison, State Historical Society of Wisconsin, 1964.

Raney, William F. "Pine Lumbering in Wisconsin." Wisconsin Magazine of History, Vol. 19, No. 1. Evansville, Wisconsin: September, 1935.

Raney, William F. Wisconsin: A Story of Progress. New York, Prentice-Hall, Inc., 1940.

Reed, Parker M. The Bench & Bar of Wisconsin. Milwaukee, 1882.

Richards, Randolph A. History of Monroe County, Wisconsin. Chicago, C. F. Cooper & Co., 1912.

Robinson, Sinclair, & Donald Smith. NTC's Dictionary of Canadian French. Lincolnwood, Illinois, National Textbook Co., 1991.

Rosholt, Malcolm. Our County: Our Story: Portage County, Wisconsin. Stevens Point, Wisconsin, Portage County Board of Supervisors, 1959.

Rudolph, Robert S. Wood County Place Names. Madison, University of Wisconsin Press, 1970.

Ryan, Thomas H. History of Outagamie County, Wisconsin. Chicago, Goodspeed Historical Association, 1911.

Scanlan, Peter L. Prairie du Chien: French: British: American. Menasha, Wisconsin, George Banta Publishing Co., 1937.

Schafer, Joseph. The Winnebago-Horicon Basin. Madison, State Historical Society of Wisconsin, 1937.

Schlicher, J. J. "The Division Fight in Waukesha County." Wisconsin Magazine of History, Vol. 23, No. 4. Evansville, Wisconsin: June, 1940.

Scott, Margaret H. The Place Names of Richland County, Wisconsin. Richland Center, Wisconsin, Richland County Publishers, Inc., 1973.

Smith, Huron H. "Indian Place Names in Wisconsin." Year Book of the Public Museum of the City of Milwaukee, Vol. 10. Milwaukee: 1932.

A Standard History of Portage County, Wisconsin, Chicago, Lewis Publishing Co., 1919.

Stennett, William H. A History of the Origin of the Place Names Connected with

the Chicago & North Western & Chicago, St. Paul, Minneapolis & Omaha Railways. Chicago, 1908.

Stewart, J. W. "Early History of Green County." Third Annual Report & Collections of the State Historical Society of Wisconsin, Vol. 3. Madison: 1857.

Strong, Moses M. History of the Territory of Wisconsin: From 1836 to 1848. Madison, Democrat Printing Co., 1885.

Stuart, Donna Valley. "What's in a Name? 18 Counties Have Indian Names." Wisconsin Then & Now, Vol. 17, No. 2. Madison: September, 1970.

Taylor, Stephen. "Wisconsin: Its Rise & Progress: With Notices of Mineral Point & Richland County." First Annual Report & Collections of the State Historical Society of Wisconsin, Vol. 1. Madison: 1855.

Tenney, H. A., & David Atwood. Memorial Record of the Fathers of Wisconsin. Madison, 1880.

Thompson, William F. Wisconsin: A History. Madison, University of Wisconsin Press, 1973.

Thrapp, Dan L. Encyclopedia of Frontier Biography. Lincoln, University of Nebraska Press, 1988.

Thwaites, Reuben G. "The British Regime in Wisconsin: 1760–1800." Collections of the State Historical Society of Wisconsin, Vol. 18. Madison: 1908.

Thwaites, Reuben G. "The French Regime in Wisconsin: 1634–1727." Collections of the State Historical Society of Wisconsin, Vol. 16. Madison: 1902.

Thwaites, Reuben G. "The Fur-Trade in Wisconsin: 1812–1825." Collections of the State Historical Society of Wisconsin, Vol. 20. Madison: 1911.

Thwaites, Reuben G. Second Triennial Catalogue of the Portrait Gallery of the State Historical Society of Wisconsin. Madison, Democrat Printing Co., 1892.

Thwaites, Reuben G. "The Story of Chequamegon Bay." Collections of the State Historical Society of Wisconsin, Vol. 13. Madison: 1895.

Troutman, Richard L. "Henry Clay and His Ashland Estate." Filson Club History Quarterly, Vol. 30, No. 2. Louisville, Kentucky: April, 1956.

The United States Biographical Dictionary & Portrait Gallery of Eminent & Self-Made Men: Wisconsin Volume. Chicago, American Biographical Publishing Co., 1877.

Upham, Warren. Minnesota Geographic Names. St. Paul, Minnesota Historical Society, 1969.

Verwyst, Chrysostom. "Geographical Names in Wisconsin, Minnesota & Michigan Having a Chippewa Origin." Collections of the State Historical Society of Wisconsin, Vol. 12. Madison: 1892.

Vexler, Robert I. *Chronology & Documentary Handbook of the State of Wisconsin.* Dobbs Ferry, New York, Oceana Publications, Inc., 1978.

Vogel, Virgil J. *Indian Names in Michigan.* Ann Arbor, University of Michigan Press, 1986.

Vogel, Virgil J. "Indian Place Names in Illinois." *Journal of the Illinois State Historical Society*, Vol. 55. 1962.

Vogel, Virgil J. *Iowa Place Names of Indian Origin.* Iowa City, University of Iowa Press, 1983.

Waldman, Carl. *Who Was Who in Native American History.* New York, Facts On File, Inc., 1990.

Wallace, W. Stewart. *The Encyclopedia of Canada.* Toronto, University Associates of Canada, Ltd., 1935.

Ware, John M. *A Standard History of Waupaca County, Wisconsin.* Chicago, Lewis Publishing Co., 1917.

Watrous, Jerome A. *Memoirs of Mil-*

waukee County. Madison, Western Historical Association, 1909.

Wells, Robert W. *This Is Milwaukee.* Garden City, New York, Doubleday & Co., Inc., 1970.

Wheeler, E. P. "The Significance of Manitowoc." *Wisconsin Magazine of History*, Vol. 4. Menasha, Wisconsin: 1920–1921.

Wisconsin Biographical Dictionary. Wilmington, Delaware, American Historical Publications, Inc., 1991.

The Wisconsin Century Book: Official Publication of the Wisconsin Centennial Exposition, August 7–29, 1948.

Wisconsin County Maps. Kaukauna, Wisconsin, Clarkson Map Co., 1990.

Wisconsin Gazetteer. Wilmington, Delaware, American Historical Publications, Inc., 1991.

Wise, L. F., & E. W. Egan. *Kings, Rulers & Statesmen.* New York, Sterling Publishing Co., Inc., 1967.

Witherell, B. F. H. "Reminiscences of the North-West." *Third Annual Report &*

Collections of the State Historical Society of Wisconsin, Vol. 3. Madison: 1857.

Wolk, Allan. *The Naming of America.* Nashville, Thomas Nelson, Inc., 1977.

Work Projects Administration. *Inventory of the County Archives of Wisconsin–Buffalo, Eau Claire, Grant, Marathon, Pepin, St. Croix, Shawano & Vernon Counties.* Madison, 1940–1942.

Work Projects Administration. *Origin & Legislative History of County Boundaries in Wisconsin.* Madison, 1942.

Works Progress Administration. *Inventory of the County Archives of Wisconsin–Sheboygan County.* Madison, 1937.

Worthing, Ruth Shaw. *The History of Fond du Lac County: As Told by Its Place Names.* Oshkosh, Wisconsin, Globe Printing Co., 1976.

Wyman, Walker D. *Wisconsin Folklore.* University of Wisconsin-Extension Department of Arts Development, 1979.

Yenne, Bill. *The Encyclopedia of North American Indian Tribes.* New York, Crescent Books, 1986.

Wyoming

(23 counties)

3047 *Albany County*

City of Albany, New York— This county in southeastern Wyoming was created by Dakota territory during the legislative session that convened at Yankton on December 7, 1868, and adjourned on January 15, 1869. Charles D. Bradley, of Laramie, was a member of the lower house of that legislature and he proposed that this new county be named in honor of the city of Albany, New York. Bradley's suggestion was adopted and this county was created on December 16, 1868. The chronology here is unusual because Wyoming territory had already been created on July 25, 1868, and yet five months later Dakota territory created this county in Wyoming territory. That was the last session of Dakota territory's legislature that created counties in Wyoming territory. Representative Charles D. Bradley was permitted to select the name for the new county since it was within the area which he represented in the legislature. Bradley had come to the West from New York state and he chose to name this new county for the

capital city of that state, Albany. Both the city and county of Albany, New York, were named in honor of England's Prince James, Duke of York & Albany (1633–1701), who later came to the throne as King James II.

King James II (1633–1701)— James was the second surviving son of England's King Charles I (1600–1649). He was given the title duke of York and Albany soon after his christening. When James' father died, his elder brother, Charles, succeeded to the throne as King Charles II (1630–1685). In 1664 King Charles II made an enormous grant of North American land to his brother, the duke of York and Albany. The duke was awarded more power over his domain that any other English proprietor. Although King Charles II had many children, none of them were legitimate so when King Charles II died in 1685, his brother, James, became king of England as King James II. The first wife of the duke of York and Albany had been Anne Hyde, who died in 1671. In 1673 James remarried to Mary of Modena (1658–1718), a Catholic, and some time during this period James professed his own Ca-

tholicism. This spelled his eventual downfall as king. In 1689 the throne passed to William of Orange (1650–1702), who ruled as joint sovereign with his wife, Queen Mary II (1662–1694). Mary was a daughter of King James II. The former King James II devoted the final years of his life to religious exercises. When the English province of New York was divided into counties on November 1, 1683, Albany County was created as one of the original counties. At that time James had not yet been crowned king of England. The title "Albany" derived from James' Scottish title. That name, *Albany* or *Albainn*, was an ancient name of the highlands of Scotland.

3048 *Big Horn County*

Uncertain— This county in north-central Wyoming was created by Wyoming territory on March 12, 1890. Sources dealing with the history, geography and place names of Wyoming express unanimous agreement that this county's name honors big horn sheep, which are relatively numerous here. Almost half of those sources indicate that the sheep were honored indirectly because the county was named for the Big Horn Mountain Range, which dominates the eastern side of this county, while a majority of sources say that the county was named directly for the sheep. Wild big horn sheep can be found from British Columbia to North Dakota in the north and as far south as New Mexico. However, their largest concentration lies near the headwaters of the Yellowstone River in Montana and Wyoming. Rocky Mountain big horn sheep are identified by zoologists as members of the genus *Ovis* and the species *canadensis*. Their common name, big horn, refers to the massive horns of the male big horn sheep, which sweep backward in an arc and measure about 40 inches along the outer curve; a "big horn," indeed on a body that is but five feet in length and stands less than 20 inches tall at the shoulder.

3049 *Campbell County*

Uncertain— This county was created on February 13, 1911. Of two dozen sources consulted, half indicate that the county was named in honor of Wyoming's first territorial governor, John A. Campbell (1835–1880), while the other half claim that the county's name honors both the first territorial governor and Robert Campbell (1804–1879). Interestingly, none of these sources state that this county was named for Robert Campbell (1804–1879), alone.

John A. Campbell (1835–1880)— A native of Ohio, John A. Campbell entered the Union army as an officer during the Civil War and served with distinction, rising to the rank of brevet brigadier-general. He later served as assistant secretary of war under John M. Schofield (1831–1906). Soon after Ulysses S. Grant was inaugurated as president, Schofield resigned as secretary of war, leaving Campbell stranded. President Grant solved Campbell's employment problem by appointing him to be the first governor of Wyoming territory on April 3, 1869. On April 15, 1869, Campbell was sworn in as governor and he arrived here to assume his duties on May 7. His term as governor was turbulent. The Republican governor and the Democratic legislature agreed that women should have the right to vote and hold property but they quarreled about everything else, and when Campbell was offered the position of third assistant secretary of state, he accepted it and resigned as Wyoming's territorial governor on March 1, 1875.

Robert Campbell (1804–1879)— A native of Ireland, Robert Campbell came to America when he was about 18 years old and arrived in Saint Louis in 1824. He left for the Rocky Mountains soon afterward and in the late 1820's he was a successful fur trapper in the upper Rocky Mountains. After visits to Saint Louis and Ireland, Robert Campbell joined William L. Sublette (1799–1845) in a fur trading venture in the Rockies. A trading post which they established grew to become Fort Laramie. In 1835 Robert Campbell left the mountains and continued his fur trading activities at Saint Louis. There he engaged in a number of business ventures and amassed great wealth. Both Presidents Fillmore and Grant appointed Robert Campbell as an Indian commissioner.

3050 *Carbon County*

Extensive coal deposits in the county— This county in southern Wyoming was created was created by Dakota territory on December 16, 1868, during the legislative session that convened at Yankton on December 7, 1868, and adjourned on January 15, 1869. The chronology here is unusual because Wyoming territory had already been created on July 25, 1868, and yet five months later Dakota territory created this county in Wyoming territory. That was the last session of Dakota territory's legislature that created counties in Wyoming territory. The county's name was chosen because of the extensive coal deposits found in the county. Some of Wyoming's most productive coal mines were operated by the Union Pacific Railroad Company, near the town of Hanna, in Carbon County. Although Wyoming is a very sparsely populated state and leads the nation in few statistics, during the late 1980's Wyoming passed Kentucky to become the nation's leading coal producing state.

3051 *Converse County*

Amasa R. Converse (1842–1885)— Converse was born at Hinsdale, Massachusetts, on March 26, 1842, and he came to Cheyenne in November, 1867, while it was still part of Dakota territory. Here in Cheyenne he engaged in mercantile business, and one of his clerical employees was Francis E. Warren (1844–1929), an acquaintance from Massachusetts and fellow native of Hinsdale, Massachusetts. Converse and Warren became partners in this mercantile firm for a time before Warren became its sole proprietor. Meanwhile, Converse assisted in organizing the First National Bank of Cheyenne and became its president, a position which he retained throughout his life. Amasa Converse also became active in politics, as a Republican, and acquired extensive livestock interests. The Converse Cattle Company, which he formed together with Hiram S. Manville (another Massachusetts native) was among the largest cattle owners in the West. In December, 1875, Converse became treasurer of Wyoming territory, under another Massachusetts native, and fellow Republican, Territorial Governor John M. Thayer (1820–1906). Converse served in that position until September 30, 1876, but was re-appointed as Wyoming's territorial treasurer, serving a second term from December 15, 1877, to December 10, 1879. His various business interests were profitable and he became a wealthy man. Shortly before his death Converse had constructed a handsome residence for his family to enjoy in Cheyenne. However, he died on a trip to New York City on June 9, 1885. This county was created and named in his honor by Wyoming territory less than three years later, on Match 9, 1888.

3052 *Crook County*

George Crook (1829–1890)— A native of Ohio and a graduate of the U.S. Military Academy at West Point, Crook's early career was as a junior officer fighting Indians on America's Pacific coast. He became distressed then, and later in his life, at White abuses of the Indians and remained concerned with Indian welfare while obliged to fight against them. At one point he advocated full U.S. citizenship for Indians. When the Civil War erupted, Crook held the rank of captain, but he served with distinction and rose to the rank of brevet major-general. After the Civil War, the army needed few high ranking officers and Crook's rank was reduced to lieutenant-colonel. He once again was sent to our nation's West to fight Indians and served so brilliantly that he was promoted to general again; as a brigadier-general in 1873 and major-general in 1888. This county was created by Wyoming territory on December 8, 1875.

3053 *Fremont County*

John C. Frémont (1813–1890)— Born in Georgia, Frémont engaged in survey work in wilderness areas of the South and then assisted Joseph N. Nicollet in explorations of Iowa, Dakota and Minnesota. Frémont then performed his greatest service by leading five explorations to the far West. Portions of this vast domain had previously been explored but it was Frémont who carefully mapped the areas traveled and prepared notes of his observations. Frémont played a role in winning California from Mexico, served briefly as a U.S. senator and, in 1856, ran as the Republican party's first presidential candidate. He later served as a Union general in the Civil War and as governor of Arizona territory. He was ineffective in both of these positions. Frémont's travels to the West had brought him to Wyoming in the early 1840's. This county was created by Wyoming territory on March 5, 1884.

3054 *Goshen County*

Uncertain— This county in southeastern Wyoming was created on February 9, 1911, and most sources dealing with the history, geography and place names of Wyoming attribute the name to the *Holy Bible*. A work published in 1962 entitled *The Interpreter's Dictionary of the Bible* cites two Goshens as place names mentioned in the Bible: (1) "A place-name in the phrase 'land of Goshen,' which appears in the general description of the territory occupied by Joshua's forces (cf. Josh. 10: 41; 11:16). It apparently refers to the hill-country region between Hebron and Negeb, perhaps named after a city of the region." and (2) "A city of Judah located in the hill-country district of Debir (Josh. 15:51), and possibly once the chief city of a region bearing the same name." However, Mae Urbanek, an expert on Wyoming's geographic names, has other thoughts on the origin of this county's name. In a 1967 work entitled *Wyoming Place Names* Urbanek stated that the county's namesake was Goshen Hole, a rich irrigated farming area, noted for livestock and oil wells, which lies within Goshen County. In the 1967 edition of *Wyoming Place Names*, Urbanek stated that there were three possibilities for the origin of Goshen Hole's name, and then listed them. Ms. Urbanek continued her research on the origin of Goshen County's name and in the 1988 edition of her *Wyoming Place Names* she said that there were four versions for the origin of the county's name and provided them. The first three are based on the premise that the county was named for its Goshen Hole. The fourth (and most recently added) possibility is that the county was named for a particular cowboy. None of the possible origins of this county's name mentioned by Urbanek support the *Holy Bible* attribution.

The four explanations contained in the 1988 edition were:

— "Goshe, an Assiniboine Indian trapper, had a cabin on Cherry Creek in the early days, and was found dead there, probably killed by Arapahoes; was called Goshe's Hole in 1846, before it appeared on the map in 1888 as Goshen Hole."

— "…a French-Canadian trapper started a trading post here. His prices were so exorbitant that traders called him 'cochon,' which is French for hog; the land surrounding his post was called 'Cochon.' When the Americans came, they pronounced the word 'Goshen,' thinking it originated in the Bible, meaning 'land of plenty.'"

— "A third version is that Gouche, a French trader, was a crafty and deceitful man; Indians called him 'co-han,' because that was his favorite expression, meaning 'Hurry up!'"

— "The fourth version: when the county was formed in 1911, it was named for Goshen Hale, a cowboy who worked for the Union Cattle Company, an English outfit with huge headquarters on Bear Creek."

3055 *Hot Springs County*

Hot springs near Thermopolis, Wyoming— The county in north-central Wyoming was created on February 9, 1911, and named for the hot mineral springs located just northeast of Thermopolis, the county seat of Hot Springs County. Hot mineral waters gush from the springs at a temperature which is said to remain constant at 135 degrees Fahrenheit. When the Indians controlled these springs, some warriors believed that bathing in them would make them invincible in combat. The Indians also believed that the hot mineral springs were beneficial to the health, a view that is shared by the many visitors who still bathe here, free of charge, at Wyoming's Hot Springs State Park on U.S. Route 20 and State Route 789. The largest of the springs here, Bighorn Hot Spring, is one of the largest hot mineral springs in the world.

3056 *Johnson County*

Edward P. Johnson (1842–1879)— Born at Greenbush, Ohio on August 21, 1842, Edward Payson Johnson served in the Union army during the Civil War. He graduated from the University of Michigan in 1867 and then moved to the West, living for a short time in Denver before moving due north to Cheyenne, Wyoming territory. Here Johnson served as prose-

cuting attorney for Laramie County from 1869 to 1870. He was then appointed as U.S. attorney for the territory and became a member of the administration of Wyoming's territorial governor, John A. Campbell (1835–1880), a fellow native of Ohio. Johnson served as the territory's U.S. attorney for seven years and was a resident of the territorial capital, Cheyenne, throughout this period and made many friends in the territorial legislature. On October 3, 1879, Johnson was serving as county attorney and was a member-elect of the upper house (council) of the legislature of Wyoming territory when he suddenly died. This county had been named Pease County when it was created by Wyoming territory on December 8, 1875. That name honored E. L. Pease, of Uinta County, who had served in both houses of the territorial legislature and was president of the upper house when the county was created. On December 13, 1879, this county's name was changed to honor the young Cheyenne attorney who had died just two months earlier.

3057 *Laramie County*

Jacques La Ramee (–1821)— Little is known about this French-Canadian trapper, whose name is now captured as geographic names in Wyoming, not merely for this county but for the city of Laramie, home of the University of Wyoming, the Laramie River, Little Laramie River, and North Laramie River; also a mountain peak in Albany County and a mountain range that runs through the counties of Albany, Laramie, Natrona and Platte. His name also was attached to Wyoming's former Fort Laramie. This trapper, whose surname is rendered in many accounts as La Ramie and Laramie, may have been born in the vicinity of Montreal about 1784. Legend has it that he was killed by Indians in 1821, near the mouth of the Laramie River. Near this site Wyoming territory's Fort Laramie was later established in what is now Goshen County, in southeastern Wyoming. Laramie County was created by Dakota territory on January 9, 1867, as the first county of today's Wyoming. The county's original huge area covered land between the present states of Colorado and Montana.

3058 *Lincoln County*

Abraham Lincoln (1809–1865)— Lincoln was a native of Kentucky who moved to Illinois, where he was a member of the state legislature. He represented Illinois in the U.S. House of Representatives and later was elected president of the United States. Lincoln's presidency coincided almost exactly with the Civil War. He guided the United States ably through that uniquely turbulent period. As president, he issued the Emancipation Proclamation which declared the freedom of slaves in all states in rebellion. Lincoln was assassinated a few days after the Union's victory in the Civil War. This county was created on February 20, 1911.

3059 *Natrona County*

Deposits of natron, or natural sodium carbonate, in the county— In the late 1880's the residents of the central and east-central portions of Wyoming territory launched movements to create new counties, primarily to reduce the time required to travel to the county seat to conduct legal and official business. Leaders of the movement included Harry C. Snyder and E. B. Wilson and on March 9, 1888, they met with success when Converse and Natrona Counties were created by Wyoming territory. The two new counties are adjacent, with Natrona County on the west of Converse County. Natrona County sits near Wyoming's center. Some sources say that Natrona County's name was suggested by Harry C. Snyder, while others give that credit to Judge Charles E. Blydenburgh (1854–), of Rawlins. Judge Blydenburgh was a member of the lower house of the territorial legislature when this county was created. The name was chosen because of the large deposits of natron, or natural sodium carbonate, within the county.

3060 *Niobrara County*

Niobrara River— This county in east-central Wyoming was created on February 14, 1911, and named for the Niobrara River, which rises within its borders. The Niobrara, a 431 mile-long tributary of the Missouri River, rises in eastern Wyoming and flows east across northern Nebraska to enter the Missouri River in northeastern Nebraska. This county's name was suggested by Harry S. Snyder. Different Indian tribes had different names for the present Niobrara River. The name accepted for use by White American map makers derived from the Omaha-Ponca Indian language. Their name for the river meant "water spreading, horizontally."

3061 *Park County*

Yellowstone National Park— This county in northwestern Wyoming was created on February 15, 1909, and named for Yellowstone National Park, which lies on its western border. This national park was created by an act of the U.S. Congress on March 1, 1872, as the first real indication that our nation's leaders attached some value to preserving our wilderness areas. Prior to 1872, the general approach to dealing with wilderness areas had been to give them away and exploit them. Yellowstone National Park was named for the Yellowstone River, which flows through it. For a bit of information about the Yellowstone River, see Yellowstone County, Montana, above. Most of Yellowstone National Park is in Wyoming but its borders also extend into Idaho and Montana. This park is the oldest of our country's national parks and contains seemingly endless areas of wilderness beauty. The park contains about 200 geysers. For most of the park's millions of visitors, viewing one of these geysers, named "Old Faithful," is a must. Old Faithful is famous and popular for both the height of its eruptions and their regularity. When Old Faithful spews forth every 40 to 80 minutes, its massive eruption shoots hot water over 100 feet in the air. Sometimes Old Faithful's eruptions approach 200 feet in height.

3062 *Platte County*

North Platte River— This county in southeastern Wyoming was created on February 9, 1911, and named for the North Platte River, which flows through it. The North Platte rises in Colorado and flows north into Wyoming, where it makes a huge loop and flows into Nebraska shortly after leaving Platte County, Wyoming. In Nebraska the North Platte enters the Platte River, a tributary of the Missouri River, and Nebraska's most important river. The Platte River is formed by the junction of two branches at the city of North Platte, in west-central Nebraska. The two rivers which unite there to form the Platte River are our North Platte River and the South Platte River. The combined waters of the Platte then travel some 310 miles in a generally eastern direction across Nebraska and empty into the Missouri River below Omaha, Nebraska. The Oregon Trail, across our country's vast plains to Oregon country, followed the course of the Platte River. The river was named by early French explorers. In their language one of it the meanings of *Platte* is "flat," or "shallow."

3063 *Sheridan County*

Town of Sheridan, Wyoming territory— This county was created by Wyoming territory on March 9, 1888, and named for the town of Sheridan at the suggestion of John D. Loucks, a member of the upper house (council) of the territorial legislature from Johnson County. It was Loucks who had settled and named the town of Sheridan in the early 1880's. He named the town after his commanding officer in the Civil War, General Philip H. Sheridan (1831–1888). In the late 1990's the city of Sheridan, Wyoming, is the county seat of Sheridan County, with a population of 14,000 and it boasts spectacular sightseeing opportunities from its location, midway between the Black Hills and Yellowstone National Park.

Philip H. Sheridan (1831–1888)— Sheridan was born in 1831 but his place of birth is in doubt. He graduated from the U.S. Military Academy at West Point and became a career officer in the United States army. When the Civil War began, Sheridan had almost a decade of military service behind him but was still only a lieutenant. During the Civil War Sheridan served with distinction in the Union army and rocketed from obscurity to high rank and responsibility. By the closing weeks of the Civil War, he had been promoted to major-general. After the Civil War ended, Sheridan remained in the army enforcing the odious Reconstruction Acts in Louisiana and Texas. Sheridan ultimately became commanding general of the entire U.S. army and attained the rank of full general.

A number of Wyoming sources indicate that this county was named directly for General Sheridan and since he died in 1888 and the county was created in 1888, that view might seem reasonable. However, General Sheridan died on August 5, 1888, several months after this county was created, and there is compelling evidence that the county was named for the town.

3064 *Sublette County*

William L. Sublette (1799–1845)— Born in Kentucky, William Sublette became the most famous of the five Sublette brothers. He moved in 1817 with his parents to Saint Charles, Missouri, and in the early 1820's he joined William H. Ashley's (1778–1838) expedition to the upper Missouri River. Sublette stayed on in what was then our nation's far northwest and engaged in trapping in the mountains. In 1826 he joined two other mountain men, Jedediah Smith (1799–1831) and David E. Jackson (–1837) in buying out Ashley's extensive mountain trapping operations. Sublette periodically traveled from the mountains to Saint Louis to obtain supplies for the trappers and in 1830 he brought wagons with him. This was reportedly the first appearance of wagons in the Rocky Mountain fur trade. In the early 1830's Sublette joined Robert Campbell (1804–1879) in a fur trading venture in the Rockies and a trading post which they established grew to become Fort Laramie. Sublette was active in leading supply trains to the Rockies until 1834, after which he settled at civilization at Saint Louis, where he engaged in business and stock farming. This county was created on February 15, 1921. It lies in the heart of what was prime beaver trapping country in the Rocky Mountains.

3065 *Sweetwater County*

Sweetwater River— This county in southwestern Wyoming was created by Dakota territory on December 27, 1867, with the name Carter County. That name honored William A. Carter (1818–1881), post trader for the U.S. army at Fort Bridger, who built the first schoolhouse in what is now Wyoming. On December 13, 1869, Wyoming territory changed the county's name to Sweetwater, in honor of the Sweetwater River, which was within the borders of Carter County at that time. Since then several new counties have been created and Sweetwater County has been reduced in size. As a result, the river for which the county is named no longer flows through it. The 175 mile-long Sweetwater River rises in southwestern Fremont County, Wyoming (just north of the Sweetwater County border), and flows east in meandering loops across central Wyoming until its waters flow into Pathfinder Reservoir, southwest of Alcova, Wyoming. The Sweetwater River was an important landmark on the old Oregon Trail. West-bound emigrants generally followed the path of the Sweetwater River from Independence Rock to the river's source at South Pass. There are essentially two conflicting explanations for the origin of Sweetwater River's name. One explanation is that travelers along the river named it because its sweet taste was a delightful change from other turgid, alkali streams they encountered. (There are several versions within this version dealing with just who these travelers were). A more colorful account tells of a heavily laden mule (or donkey), carrying sugar, who fell in the river, thus sweetening its water and inspiring its name. Although that legend was preserved in a diary entry by James Field dated July 12, 1845, this merely tells us that this story was being bruited about at that time, but fails to verify it.

3066 *Teton County*

Teton Mountain Range— This county in northwestern Wyoming was created on February 15, 1921, and named for the Teton Mountain Range, which dominates the northwestern portion of the county, on its border with Idaho. The Tetons extend from this county north into Yellowstone National Park. The highest peak in the range is Grand Teton, with an elevation of 13,747 feet. The mountain range was named for three particular peaks. French-Canadian trappers found a resemblance between these peaks and female breasts and named them *Les Trois Tetons*, meaning "The Three Breasts." The Teton range is part of the Rocky Mountain range and these three peaks rise almost perpendicularly more than a mile above the valleys below them. Viewed from their Idaho side, the three peaks were important beacons to travelers, giving them definite means of orientation. The three peaks are called Grand, South and Middle Teton.

3067 *Uinta County*

Uncertain— This county in Wyoming's southwestern corner was created by Wyoming territory on December 1, 1869. Most sources dealing with the history, geography and place names of Wyoming indicate that the county was named for the Uinta Ute Indians. However a few sources, including Mae Urbanek's *Wyoming Place Names*, attribute the county's name to the Uintah Mountain Range. Those mountains and their valley are spelled Uinta in some sources.

Uinta Ute Indians— The Uinta are a subtribe of the Ute Indians, also referred to as Uinta-Ats, or Yoovte Indians. This subtribe was living in northwestern Colorado and northeastern Utah when the Mormon settlers arrived in 1847. The Mormon leader, Brigham Young (1801–1877), wanted them moved out of the way. It was proposed that the Uinta (and other Indians) be moved to a reservation in the Uinta Basin and Brigham Young agreed to this proposal only after satisfying himself that the area was "one vast contiguity of waste." In 1861 the U.S. federal government set aside the proposed reservation in the Uinta Valley and the Uinta and other Indians were moved there. Later, this reservation was combined with an Indian reservation named the Ouray reservation and the combined reservation is known today as the Uintah-Ouray Indian reservation. Most of that reservation lies west of Uintah County, Utah, in Duchesne County, Utah.

The population of Uinta Indians was estimated at 443 in 1909.

Uintah Mountain Range— The Uintah Mountains lie primarily in northeastern Utah, but their majestic peaks are clearly visible from all parts of Uinta County, Wyoming. The Uintah Mountains are the only major range in the Continental United States to lie in an east-west direction. The highest mountain peak in the state of Utah, King's Peak, which soars to 13,528 feet, is a part of the Uintah range. The Uintah Mountains also share their glory with northwestern Colorado, extending into that state's Moffat County. These mountains were named for the Uinta Ute Indians.

3068 *Washakie County*

Washakie (–1900)— Born about 1804 to a Flathead Indian father and a Shoshoni Indian mother, Washakie spent his early years with the Flathead Indians in the Bitterroot Mountains of what is now Montana. Washakie left the Flatheads and became a noted warrior of the eastern band of Shoshonis. As chief of that band of Shoshonis, Washakie was known to be a fearless foe of rival Indians but friendly to Whites. This friendship toward Whites was not mere passive acceptance of them but extended to notable acts of kindness. He aided White emigrants traveling through his country in recovering lost livestock and fording streams. Several thousand of these emigrants signed a paper commending Chief Washakie and his tribe for assisting them. U.S. Presidents Ulysses S. Grant and Chester Arthur held Chief Washakie in high regard. When Chief Washakie was about 70 years old, young warriors of his tribe attempted to have him dethroned as too elderly to rule. Washakie's answer to this rebellion was to disappear, alone, and return several weeks later with six scalps he had taken to prove his remaining strength. Chief Washakie saved most of his band from destruction by taking them to Fort Bridger, in Wyoming. After the death of a son in a barroom brawl, Chief Washakie became a convert to Christianity and was baptized in the Episcopal Church in 1897. This county in north-central Wyoming was created on February 9, 1911, from the southern portion of Big Horn County. The chief sponsor of the bill to create this new county was C. F. Robertson, a representative of the Hanover Land & Irrigation Company and Robertson succeeded in having the new county named Hanover County. That act was amended a week later to change the name to Washakie but the Clason Map Company, of Denver Colorado, printed maps showing the new county with the name Hanover County. Surviving copies of those 1911 maps are treasured by collectors of Wyoming memorabilia.

3069 *Weston County*

Uncertain—This county was created by Wyoming territory on March 12, 1890, and essentially all Wyoming sources consulted are agreed that the county was named for a J. B. Weston, who was involved in the area's anthracite coal deposits. Many of these Wyoming sources indicate that it was the coal, which this J. B. Weston was active in discovering or exploiting, which brought the railroad to this part of Wyoming territory. Some non–Wyoming sources attribute the origin of this county's name to a J. B. Weston, who was a physician. We can and should ignore these references to a physician, but that still leaves us with some unresolved issues concerning this county's namesake. *The Historical Encyclopedia of Wyoming*, edited by Thomas S. Chamblin and published in 1970, states that the county "…was named by Ralph A Weston in honor of his father, Jefferson B. Weston, geologist and surveyor. Both men were employees of the Newscastle Coal Company." A letter to the author dated July 8, 1996, from Julia Stanton, curator of the historical museum of Weston County, Wyoming, confirms that Jefferson B. Weston is our man but that he was "…pioneer developer and banker of Beatrice, Nebraska, who as a friend of George Holdridge, the manager of the Burlington Railroad and of the Kilpatricks, contractors for the railroad … interested himself in the development of northeastern Wyoming. In the survey of 1887 he traversed the reconnaissance survey line made by Edward Gillette, for the Burlington Railroad, from Alliance through Goose Creek (Sheridan, Wyoming)." This material furnished by Julia Stanton was based on information compiled by Frank W. Mondell. In *Wyoming: The 75th Year: Official Publication* this county's namesake is given as "Jefferson B. Weston, a geologist and surveyor, associated with the pioneer construction firm of Kilpatrick Brothers and Collins." However, Mae Urbanek's *Wyoming Place Names* states that Weston County was named for "John B. Weston, geologist and surveyor, who organized a pack outfit, and explored the canyons north of the present Newcastle for coal in 1887. He and Frank Mondell

located rich anthracite deposits; the railroad came because of this coal; it reached and founded Newcastle in 1889."

There definitely was a Jefferson B. Weston, who lived in Beatrice, Nebraska, at about the time this Wyoming county's namesake was prominent:

Jefferson B. Weston (–1905)—This Jefferson B. Weston was born at Bremen, Maine, in March of either 1821 or 1831 and was an 1856 graduate of Union College in Schenectady, New York. He moved west and arrived in Nebraska territory in April, 1857, and soon became one of the founders of the community of Beatrice, in Nebraska territory. He studied law and was admitted to the territorial bar. About 1860 he engaged in freighting between Beatrice and Denver. Hugh J. Dobbs' *History of Gage County, Nebraska* stated that "…he engaged in mining and other enterprises about the gold fields of Colorado, but returning to Beatrice in 1868, he resumed the practice of law." This Jefferson B. Weston then practiced law until autumn, 1872, when he was elected auditor of public accounts of the state of Nebraska and served in that position from 1873 to 1879. In 1883 he purchased stock in the Gage County Bank and organized the Beatrice National Bank, of Beatrice, Nebraska. He was chosen president of that bank, a position which he retained until his death. One of his four children was named Ralph A. Weston and that is the name of the person who, according to *The Historical Encyclopedia of Wyoming*, chose the name of Weston County, Wyoming territory, in honor of his father.

On the basis of available information we must conclude that we are missing a piece or two of the jigsaw puzzle and cannot state, with certainty, for whom this county was named. If the references to both Beatrice, Nebraska and a son named Ralph A. Weston are correct, then Jefferson B. Weston (–1905) is our man. However if the reference to "geologist and surveyor" is accurate, it would be difficult to conclude that the Beatrice, Nebraska banker who died in 1905 was this county's namesake. We also have the unresolved John B. Weston versus Jefferson B. Weston question. As stated several hundred words earlier, the origin of this county's name is uncertain.

REFERENCES

Anderson, Eunice G. *Second Biennial Report of the State Historian of the State of Wyoming: For the Period Ending September 30, 1922.*

Armstrong, J. Reuel, et al. *Documents of Wyoming Heritage.* Cheyenne, Wyoming Bicentennial Commission, 1976.

Bancroft, Hubert H. *The Works of Hubert Howe Bancroft: History of Nevada, Colorado & Wyoming: 1540–1888.* San Francisco, History Co., 1890.

Bankes, James. *A County by County Guide to Wyoming's Best Scenic, Recreational & Historic Sites.* Boulder, Colorado, Fred Pruett Books, 1992.

Bartlett, I. S. *History of Wyoming.* Chicago, S J Clarke Publishing Co , 1918.

Bastian, Jean. *History of Laramie County, Wyoming.* Dallas, Texas, Curtis Media Corp., 1987.

Beal, M. D. *A History of Southeastern Idaho.* Caldwell, Idaho, Caxton Printers, Ltd., 1942.

Beard, Frances Birkhead. *Wyoming: From Territorial Days to the Present.* Chicago, American Historical Society, Inc., 1933.

Beebe, Ruth. *Reminiscing Along the Sweetwater.* Boulder, Colorado, Johnson Publishing Co., 1973.

Bille, Ed. *Wyoming: A Pictorial Overview.* Casper, Mountain States Lithographing, 1989.

"Bits About Weston County, Wyoming." *Bits & Pieces*, Vol. 1, No. 1. Newcastle, Wyoming: April, 1965.

"Bits About Wyoming Counties." *Bits & Pieces*, Vol. 2, No. 5. Newcastle, Wyoming: 1966.

Bonney, Orrin H., & Lorraine Bonney. *Guide to the Wyoming Mountains & Wilderness Areas.* Denver, Sage Books, 1960.

Bragg, Bill. *Campbell County: The Slumbering Giant.* Gillette, Wyoming, Holiday Inn, 1978.

Bragg, Bill. *Wyoming's Wealth: A History of Wyoming.* Basin, Wyoming, Big Horn Publishers, 1976.

Bright, William. *Colorado Place Names.* Boulder, Colorado, Johnson Printing Co., 1993.

Brown, Robert H. *Wyoming: A Geography.* Boulder, Colorado, Westview Press, 1980.

Burdick, C. W. *The State of Wyoming.* Cheyenne, S. A. Bristol Co., 1899.

Burdick, Charles W. *The State of Wyoming.* Cheyenne, Sun-Leader Printing House, 1898.

Carpenter, Allan. *The Encyclopedia of the Central West.* New York, Facts On File, 1990.

Carpenter, Allan. *The Encyclopedia of the Far West.* New York, Facts On File, 1991.

Chamblin, Thomas S. *The Historical Encyclopedia of Wyoming.* Cheyenne, Wyoming Historical Institute, 1970.

Chatterton, Fenimore. *The State of Wyoming*. Laramie, Chaplin, Spafford & Mathison, 1904.

"Chief Washakie's Obituary." *Wyoming Annals*, Vol. 11, No. 1. Cheyenne: January, 1939.

Chittenden, Hiram M., & Alfred T. Richardson. *Life, Letters & Travels of Father Pierre-Jean De Smet, S. J.: 1801–1873*. New York, Francis P. Harper, 1904.

Christiansen, Cleo. *Sagebrush Settlements*. Lovell, Wyoming, 1967.

Clough, Wilson O. "Some Wyoming Place Names." Unpublished manuscript, University of Wyoming, Laramie, Wyoming, 1943.

Clough, Wilson O. "Wyoming's Earliest Place Names?" *Annals of Wyoming*, Vol. 37, No. 2. Cheyenne: October, 1965.

Cody, Mae. "The Origin of Goshen." Unpublished manuscript, Wyoming State Museum, Historical Research Section, Cheyenne.

Cody, Mae. "Wyoming Place Names." Unpublished manuscript, Wyoming State Museum, Historical Research Section, Cheyenne.

The Counties of New York State. New York Telephone Co., 1948.

Coutant, C. G. *The History of Wyoming*. Laramie, Chaplin, Spafford & Mathison, 1899.

Coutant, C. G, *History of Wyoming & (The Far West)*. New York, Argonaut Press, Ltd. 1966.

Coutant, C. G. "History of Wyoming Written by C. G. Coutant, Pioneer Historian, & Heretofore Unpublished: Conclusion." *Annals of Wyoming*, Vol. 14, No. 2. Cheyenne: April, 1942.

"Derivations of County Names Are Interesting." *Sheridan News*, July 30, 1938.

Dobbs, Hugh J. *History of Gage County, Nebraska*. Lincoln, Western Publishing & Engraving Co., 1918.

Dobler, Lavinia. *I Didn't Know That About Wyoming!* Basin, Wyoming, Wolverine Gallery, 1984.

Duncan, Mel. *Place Names of the Medicine Bow National Forest*. Jelm, Wyoming, Jelm Mountain Publications, 1992.

Dunning, Harold M. *Over Hill & Vale: In the Evening Shadows of Colorado's Longs Peak*. Boulder, Colorado, Johnson Publishing Co., 1956.

Edmunds, R. David. *American Indian Leaders: Studies in Diversity*. Lincoln, University of Nebraska Press, 1980.

Egland, Janet. *Who, What & Where in Wyoming*. Story, Wyoming, Story Publishing, 1993–1995.

Emery, Raymond C. "A Dictionary of Albany County Place-Names." M. A. Thesis, University of Wyoming, Laramie, Wyoming, 1940.

Erwin, Marie H. *Wyoming Historical Blue Book: A Legal & Political History of Wyoming: 1868–1943*. Denver, Colorado, Bradford-Robinson Printing Co., 1946.

Fetter, Richard. *Mountain Men of Wyoming*. Boulder, Colorado, Johnson Publishing Co., 1982.

Field, Sharon Lass. *History of Cheyenne, Wyoming*. Dallas, Texas, Curtis Media Corp., 1989.

Fremont County and Its Communities. University of Wyoming Extension Class in Education, 1952.

Gage, Jack R. *Geography of Wyoming: A Text Book in Geography for the Fifth, Sixth, Seventh & Eighth Grades*. Casper, Wyoming, Prairie Publishing Co., 1965.

Garst, Doris Shannon. *The Story of Wyoming and Its Constitution and Government*. Douglas Enterprise, 1938.

Gould, Lewis L. *Wyoming: A Political History: 1868–1896*. New Haven, Yale University Press, 1968.

Greenburg, D. W. "Early History of Wyoming's Johnson County." *Wyoming Eagle*, September 2, 1971.

Hafen Le Roy R. "Mountain Men: Andrew W. Sublette." *Colorado Magazine*, Vol. 10, No. 5. Denver: September, 1933.

Hafen Le Roy R. *The Mountain Men and the Fur Trade of the Far West*. Glendale, California, Arthur H. Clark Co., 1972.

Hafen, Le Roy R., & Francis M. Young. *Fort Laramie and the Pageant of the West: 1834–1890*. Glendale, California, Arthur H. Clark Co., 1938.

Hayden, Elizabeth Wied, & Cynthia Nielsen. *Origins: A Guide to the Place Names of Grand Teton National Park and the Surrounding Area*. Moose, Wyoming, Grand Teton Natural History Association, 1988.

Hebard, Grace Raymond. *The Government of Wyoming*. San Francisco, Whitaker & Ray-Wiggin Co., 1911.

Hebard, Grace Raymond. *Johnson County, Wyoming Derivation of Place Names: An Unfinished Manuscript by the Late Grace Raymond Hebard With Pencil Corrections in Her Handwriting*. Cheyenne, Vic Press, 1970.

Hebard, Grace Raymond. "Teaching Wyoming History by Counties." *State of Wyoming Department of Education*, Bulletin 9, Series B. Laramie: 1926.

Hill, Burton S. "Buffalo: Ancient Cow Town: A Wyoming Saga." *Annals of Wyoming*, Vol. 35, No. 2. Cheyenne: October, 1963.

A History of Washakie County. Northern Wyoming Daily News.

Hodge Frederick W. *Handbook of American Indians North of Mexico*. Totowa, New Jersey, Rowman & Littlefield, 1975.

Huseas, Marion McMillan. *Sweetwater Gold: Wyoming's Gold Rush: 1867–1871*. Cheyenne Corral of Westerners International Publishers, 1991.

Hyde, William, & Howard L. Conard. *Encyclopedia of the History of St. Louis*. St. Louis, Southern History Co., 1899.

Idaho, Montana, Wyoming Tour Book. Heathrow, Florida, AAA Publishing, 2000.

"Industrial Development in Weston County." *Annals of Wyoming*, Vol. 4, No. 4. Cheyenne: April, 1927.

The Interpreter's Dictionary of the Bible. New York, Abingdon Press, 1962.

Jording, Mike. *A Few Interested Residents: Wyoming Historical Markers & Monuments*. Helena, Montana, Falcon Press Publishing Co., Inc., 1992.

Jost, Loren. *Wyoming Blue Book: Centennial Edition*. Cheyenne, Wyoming State Archives, Department of Commerce, 1991.

Kirkbride, Mrs. Dan. *From These Roots*. Cheyenne, Pioneer Printing & Stationery Co., 1972.

Larson, T. A. *History of Wyoming*. Lincoln, University of Nebraska Press, 1965.

Larson, T. A. *Wyoming: A Bicentennial History*. New York, W. W. Norton & Co., Inc., 1977.

Lewis, Dan. *Paddle & Portage: The Floater's Guide to Wyoming Rivers*. Douglas, Wyoming, Wyoming Naturalist, 1991.

Linford, Dee. *Wyoming Stream Names*. Cheyenne, Wyoming Game & Fish Department, 1975.

Linford, Dee. "Wyoming Stream Names." *Annals of Wyoming*, Vol. 15, No. 3. Cheyenne: July, 1943.

McCormick, John, & Bill Turque. "America's Outback." *Newsweek*, October 9, 1989.

McDermott, John D. "The Search for Jacques Laramee: A Study in Frustration." *Annals of Wyoming*, Vol. 36, No. 2. Cheyenne: October, 1964.

McLoughlin, Denis. *Wild & Woolly: An Encyclopedia of the Old West*. Garden City, New York, Doubleday & Co., Inc., 1975.

Mealey, Catherine E. *The Best of Wyoming*. Laramie, Meadowlark Press, 1990.

Milek, Dorothy Buchanan. *Hot Springs: A Wyoming County History*. Thermopolis, Saddlebag Books, 1986.

Mokler, Alfred J. *History of Natrona County, Wyoming: 1888–1922*. Chicago, R. R. Donnelley & Sons Co., 1923.

Morris, Robert C. *Collections of the Wyoming Historical Society*. Cheyenne, Wyoming Historical Society, 1897.

Morton, J. Sterling. *Illustrated History*

of Nebraska. Lincoln, Jacob North & Co., 1905.

Mumey, Nolie. *The Teton Mountains: Their History & Tradition.* Denver, Colorado, Artcraft Press, 1947.

"Name Derivations of Wyoming Counties." Unpublished manuscript, Wyoming State Library, Cheyenne, Wyoming.

Natrona County and the Casper Area: 1996 Visitors' Guide. Casper, Casper Star Tribune Special Advertising Supplement, 1996.

Nickerson, H. G. "Early History of Fremont County." *State of Wyoming Historical Department Quarterly Bulletin,* Vol. 2, No. 1. Cheyenne: July, 1924.

Official Route Book of the Yellowstone Highway Association in Wyoming & Colorado. Cody, Wyoming, Gus Holm's, 1916.

Only a Cow Country at One Time: Territory of Wyoming: 1868: Counties of Crook, Weston & Campbell: 1875 to 1951. San Diego, California, Pioneer Printers, 1951.

Pages from Converse County's Past. Casper, Wyoming Historical Press, 1986.

Pence, Mary Lou, & Lola M. Homsher. *The Ghost Towns of Wyoming.* New York, Hastings House, 1956.

Pendegraft, Ray. *Washakie: A Wyoming County History.* Saddlebag Books, 1985.

Phillips, Paul C. *The Fur Trade.* Norman, University of Oklahoma Press, 1961.

Pitcher, Don. *Wyoming Handbook.* Chico, California, Moon Publications, 1991.

Platte County, Wyoming Heritage. Marceline, Missouri, Walsworth Publishing, 1981.

Progressive Men of the State of Wyoming. Chicago, A. W. Bowen & Co., 1903.

Roberts, Philip J., et al. *Wyoming Almanac.* Seattle, Skyline West Press, 1990.

Rollinson, John K. *Wyoming Cattle Trails.* Caldwell, Idaho, Caxton Printers, Ltd., 1948.

Rosenberg, Robert G. *Wyoming's Last Frontier: Sublette County, Wyoming.* Glendo, Wyoming, High Plains Press, 1990.

Schmidt, Thomas & Winfred Blevins.

History from the Highways: Wyoming. Boulder, Colorado, Pruett Publishing Co., 1993.

South Dakota Legislative Manual: 1927. Pierre, State Publishing Co.

Spiros, Joyce V. Hawley. *Genealogical Guide to Wyoming.* Gallup, New Mexico, Verlene Publishing, 1982.

Stanton, Julia, Curator, Weston County Historical Society & Anna Miller Museum. Letter to the author dated July 8, 1996.

Stone, Elizabeth Arnold. *Uinta County: Its Place in History.*

Stories of the North Platte Valley, Wyoming as Told by C. O. Downing to Sharon Smith.

"The Story Behind County Names." *Weston's Record,* Dalton, Massachusetts.

Stratton, Fred D. *Early History of the South Pass in the Wind River Range of the Rocky Mountains.*

Thrapp, Dan L. *Encyclopedia of Frontier Biography.* Lincoln, University of Nebraska Press, 1988.

Trenholm, Virginia Cole. *Footprints on the Frontier: Saga of the La Ramie Region of Wyoming.* Douglas, Wyoming, Douglas Enterprise Co., 1945.

Trenholm, Virginia Cole. *Wyoming Blue Book: Reprint of Part One Wyoming Historical Blue Book by Marie Erwin.* Cheyenne, Wyoming State Archives & Historical Department, 1974.

Trenholm, Virginia Cole, & Maurine Carley. *Wyoming Pageant.* Casper, Wyoming, Bailey School Supply, 1946.

Triggs, J. H. *History of Cheyenne & Northern Wyoming.* Omaha, Nebraska, Herald Steam Book & Job Printing House, 1876.

Urbanek, Mae. *Wyoming Place Names.* Boulder, Colorado, Johnson Publishing Co., 1967.

Urbanek, Mae. *Wyoming Place Names.* Missoula, Montana, Mountain Press Publishing Co., 1988.

Urbanek, Mae. *Wyoming Wonderland.* Denver, Sage Books, 1964.

Vexler, Robert I. *Chronology & Documentary Handbook of the State of Wyoming.* Dobbs Ferry, New York, Oceana Publications, Inc., 1979.

Waldman, Carl. *Who Was Who in Native American History.* New York, Facts On File, Inc., 1990.

Wallace, Eunice Ewer. *They Made Wyoming Their Own.* Boise, Idaho, Joslyn & Rentschler, 1971.

Weston County Heritage Group. *Weston County, Wyoming.* Dallas, Texas, Curtis Media Corp., 1988.

Wexler, Alan. *Atlas of Westward Expansion.* New York, Facts On File, Inc., 1995.

Wheeler, Denise. *The Feminine Frontier: Wyoming Women: 1850–1900.* 1987.

Wilson, D. Ray. *Wyoming Historical Tour Guide.* Carpentersville, Illinois, Crossroads Communications, 1984.

Wind River Vocational High School, Junior Group. *Some Wyoming Place Names: Their Origin & Meaning.* Ft. Washakie, Wyoming.

Woods, Lawrence M. *Wyoming Biographies.* Worland, Wyoming, High Plains Publishing Co., 1991.

Work Projects Administration. *Inventory of the County Archives of Wyoming-Campbell, Goshen & Platte Counties.* Cheyenne, 1939–1942.

Works Progress Administration. *The Idaho Encyclopedia.* Caldwell, Idaho, Caxton Printers, Ltd., 1938.

Works Progress Administration. *Inventory of the County Archives of Wyoming-Laramie & Sweetwater Counties.* Cheyenne, 1938–1939.

Wyoming: A Guide to Historic Sites. Basin, Wyoming, Big Horn Publishers, 1976.

"Wyoming Place Names." *Annals of Wyoming,* Cheyenne: Vol. 14, No. 2.April, 1942; Vol. 15, No. 1.January, 1943.

Wyoming: The 75th Year: Official Publication. Douglas, Wyoming, Wyoming 75th Anniversary Commission, 1965.

Bibliography

Abraham, Henry J. *Justices and Presidents: A Political History of Appointments to the Supreme Court.* New York, Oxford University Press, 1992.

Ackerman, William K. *Early Illinois Railroads.* Chicago, Fergus Printing Co., 1884.

Allstrom, C. M. *Dictionary of Royal Lineage in Europe and Other Countries.* Chicago, Press of S. Th. Almberg, 1902.

Alotta, Robert L. *Signposts and Settlers: The History of Place Names West of the Rockies.* Chicago, Bonus Books, Inc., 1994.

Ambrose, Stephen E. *Undaunted Courage.* New York, Simon & Schuster, 1996.

American Biographies. Washington, D.C., Editorial Press Bureau, Inc., 1952.

Appleton's Cyclopaedia of American Biography. New York, D. Appleton & Co., 1888.

Athearn, Robert G. *Union Pacific Country.* Lincoln, University of Nebraska Press, 1971.

"The Autographs of the Signers of the Declaration." *The Magazine of History,* Vol. 26, No. 2. Tarrytown, New York: October, 1921.

Ayling, Stanley. *George the Third.* New York, Alfred A. Knopf, 1972.

Barnhart, Clarence L. *The New Century Cyclopedia of Names.* New York, Appleton-Century-Crofts, Inc., 1954.

Bauer, K. Jack. *The Mexican War: 1846–1848.* New York, Macmillan Publishing Co., Inc., 1974.

Beatson, Robert. *A Political Index to the Histories of Great Britain and Ireland: Or a Complete Register of the Hereditary Honours, Public Offices, and Persons in Office.* London, Longman, Hurst, Rees & Orme, 1806.

Benedictine Monks of St. Augustine's Abbey, Ramsgate. *The Book of Saints.* New York, Thomas Y. Crowell Co., 1966.

Bentley, James. *A Calendar of Saints: The Lives of the Principal Saints of the Christian Year.* New York, Facts on File Publications, 1986.

A Biographical Congressional Directory: 1774 to 1903. Washington, D.C., U.S. Government Printing Office, 1903.

Biographical Directory of the American Congress: 1774–1961. Washington, D.C., U.S. Government Printing Office, 1961.

Boatner, Mark M. *The Civil War Dictionary.* New York, Vintage Books, 1988.

_____. *Encyclopedia of the American Revolution.* Mechanicsburg, Pennsylvania, Stackpole Books, 1994.

_____. *Landmarks of the American Revolution.* Harrisburg, Pennsylvania, Stackpole Books, 1973.

Bowen, Dana Thomas. *Lore of the Lakes.* Daytona Beach, Florida, 1940.

Bowman, John S. *The Civil War Almanac.* New York, World Almanac Publications, 1983.

Bradford, M. E. *A Worthy Company: Brief Lives of the Framers of the United States Constitution.* Marlborough, New Hampshire, Plymouth Rock Foundation, 1982.

Brown, Russell K. *Fallen in Battle: American General Officer Combat Fatalities from 1775.* Westport, Connecticut, Greenwood Press, 1988.

Bulfinch's Mythology. New York, HarperCollins, 1991.

The Canadian Global Almanac: A Book of Facts: 1992. Toronto, Global Press, 1992.

Cannon, John. *The Oxford Companion to British History.* Oxford, Oxford University Press, 1997.

The Catholic Encyclopedia. New York, Robert Appleton Co., 1908.

Chase, Harold, et al. *Biographical Dictionary of the Federal Judiciary.* Detroit, Gale Research Co., 1976.

Chittenden, Hiram M. *The American Fur Trade of the Far West.* Lincoln, University of Nebraska Press, 1986.

Cleland, Robert G. *This Reckless Breed of Men: The Trappers and Fur Traders of the Southwest.* Albuquerque, University of New Mexico Press, 1976.

The Columbia Lippincott Gazetteer of the World. New York, Columbia University Press, 1962.

Concise Dictionary of American Biography. New York, Charles Scribner's Sons, 1980.

The Concise Dictionary of National Biography. Oxford, Oxford University Press, 1992.

Connelly, Thomas L. *Discovering the Appalachians.* Harrisburg, Pennsylvania, Stackpole Books, 1968.

Cook, Petronelle. *Queen Consorts of England: The Power Behind the Throne.* New York, Facts on File, Inc., 1993.

Corbitt, David L. *The Formation of North Carolina Counties: 1663–1943.* Raleigh, State Department of Archives and History, 1950.

Currie, Andrew M. *Dictionary of British Place Names.* London, Tiger Books International, 1994.

Delaney, John J., and James E. Tobin. *Dictionary of Catholic Biography.* Garden City, New York, Doubleday & Co., Inc., 1961.

Dictionary of American Biography. Boston, James R. Osgood & Co., 1872.

_____. New York, Charles Scribner's Sons.

Dictionary of National Biography. London, Smith, Elder & Co., 1909.

The Dictionary of National Biography Founded in 1882 by George Smith. London, Oxford University Press, 1921.

Donehoo, George P. *A History of the Indian Villages and Place Names in Pennsylvania.* Harrisburg, Pennsylvania, Telegraph Press, 1928.

Drake, Francis S. *The Indian Tribes of the United States.* Philadelphia, J. B. Lippincott & Co., 1884.

Du Gard, Rene C., and Dominique C. Western. *The Handbook of American Counties, Parishes and Independent Cities.* Editions des Deux Mondes, 1981.

____ and ____. *The Handbook of French Place Names in the U. S. A.* Editions des Deux Mondes, 1977.

Dunlap, Leslie W. *Our Vice-Presidents and Second Ladies.* Metuchen, New Jersey, Scarecrow Press, Inc., 1988.

Ekwall, Ellert. *The Concise Oxford Dictionary of English Place-Names.* Oxford, Oxford University Press, 1960.

The Encyclopedia Americana. New York, Americana Corporation, 1977.

Encyclopedia of Indians of the Americas. St. Clair Shores, Michigan, Scholarly, Press, Inc., 1974.

Englebert, Omer. *The Lives of the Saints.* New York, Barnes & Noble, Inc., 1994.

Faber, Harold. *From Sea to Sea: The Growth of the United States.* New York, Farrar, Straus & Giroux, 1967.

Falkus, Christopher. *The Life and Times of Charles II.* Garden City, New York, Doubleday & Co., 1972.

Faragher, John M. *The Encyclopedia of Colonial and Revolutionary America.* New York, Facts on File, 1990.

Farmer, David H. *The Oxford Dictionary of Saints.* Oxford, England, Oxford University Press, 1992.

____. *The Oxford Dictionary of Saints.* New York, Oxford University Press, 1992.

Ferris, Robert G. *Founders and Frontiersmen.* Washington, D.C., U. S. Department of the Interior, National Park Service, 1967.

____. *Signers of the Declaration.* Washington, D.C., U. S. Department of the Interior, National Park Service, 1975.

Fletcher, Christine. *100 Keys: Names Across the Land.* Nashville, Abingdon Press, 1973.

Foster, Joseph. *The Peerage, Baronetage and Knightage of the British Empire for 1880.* London, Nichols & Sons, 1880.

Fox, William S. *The Mythology of All Races.* New York, Cooper Square Publishers, Inc., 1964.

Foy, Felician A. *Catholic Almanac: 1994.* Huntington, Indiana, Our Sunday Visitor, Inc., 1994.

Fulmore, Z. T. *The History and Geography of Texas as Told in County Names.* Austin, Texas, S. R. Fulmore, 1926.

Gannett, Henry. *The Origin of Certain Place Names in the United States.* Williamstown, Massachusetts, Corner House Publishers, 1978.

Garraty, John A. *Encyclopedia of American Biography.* New York, Harper & Row, 1974.

Grant, Bruce. *Concise Encyclopedia of the American Indian.* New York, Wings Books, 1989.

Gresswell, R. Kay, and Anthony Huxley. *Standard Encyclopedia of the World's Rivers and Lakes.* New York, G. P. Putnam's Sons, 1965.

Hall, Kermit L., et al. *The Oxford Companion to the Supreme Court of the United States.* New York, Oxford University Press, 1992.

Harder, Kelsie B. *Illustrated Dictionary of Place Names: United States and Canada.* New York, Van Nostrand Reinhold Co., 1976.

Hardon, John A. *Modern Catholic Dictionary.* Garden City, New York, Doubleday & Co., Inc., 1980.

Hatch, Robert M. *Major John Andre: A Gallant in Spy's Clothing.* Boston, Houghton Mifflin Co., 1986.

Hawkyard, Alasdair. *The Counties of Britain: A Tudor Atlas by John Speed.* London, England, Pavilion Books, Ltd., 1995.

Healy, Diana Dixon. *America's Vice-Presidents.* New York, Atheneum, 1984.

Heitman, Francis B. *Historical Register of Officers of the Continental Army during the War of the Revolution: April, 1775, to December, 1783.* Washington, D.C., Rare Book Shop Publishing Co., Inc., 1914.

Herring, Hubert. *A History of Latin America.* New York, Alfred A. Knopf, 1968.

Hiden, Martha W. *How Justice Grew: Virginia Counties: An Abstract of Their Formation.* Williamsburg, Virginia, 350th Anniversary Celebration Corporation, 1957.

Hodge, Frederick W. *Handbook of American Indians North of Mexico.* Totowa, New Jersey, Rowman & Littlefield, 1975.

Holbrook, Stewart H. *The Story of American Railroads.* New York, Crown Publishers, 1947.

Holli, Melvin G., and Peter d'A. Jones. *Biographical Dictionary of American Mayors: 1820–1980: Big City Mayors.* Westport, Connecticut, Greenwood Press, 1981.

Hylander, Clarence J. *The World of Plant Life.* London, Collier-Macmillan, Ltd., 1956.

The Interpreter's Dictionary of the Bible. New York, Abingdon Press, 1962.

Johnson, James. *Place Names of England and Wales.* London, England, Bracken Books, 1994.

Johnson, Thomas H. *The Oxford Companion to American History.* New York, Oxford University Press, 1966.

Jones, Alison. *The Wordsworth Dictionary of Saints.* Hertfordshire, England, Wordsworth Editions, Ltd., 1994.

Josephson, Matthew. *The Robber Barons: The Great American Capitalists: 1861–1901.* New York, Harcourt Brace & Co., 1934.

The Journals of Lewis and Clark. New York, New American Library, 1964.

Kane, Joseph N. *The American Counties.* Metuchen, New Jersey, Scarecrow Press, Inc., 1972.

Kelly, Sean, and Rosemary Rogers. *Saints Preserve Us! Everything You Need to Know About Every Saint You'll Ever Need.* New York, Random House, 1993.

Kleber, John E. *The Kentucky Encyclopedia.* Lexington, University Press of Kentucky, 1992.

Kull, Irving S., and Nell M. Kull. *A Short Chronology of American History: 1492–1950.* Westport, Connecticut, Greenwood Press, 1980.

Lamar, Howard R. *The Reader's Encyclopedia of the American West.* New York, Thomas Y. Crowell Co., 1977.

Lanman, Charles. *Biographical Annals of the Civil Government of the United States.* New York, J. M. Morrison, 1887.

Laycock, George. *The Mountain Men.* New York, Lyons & Burford, 1996.

Leckie, Robert. *The Wars of America.* New York, Harper & Row, 1981.

Leitch, Barbara A. *A Concise Dictionary of Indian Tribes of North America.* Algonac, Michigan, Reference Publications, Inc., 1979.

Lofts, Norah. *Queens of England.* Garden City, New York, Doubleday & Co., Inc., 1977.

Long, E. B., and Barbara Long. *The Civil War Day by Day: An Almanac: 1861–1865.* New York, New York, Da Capo Press, Inc., 1971.

Louis, Rita Volmer. *Biography Index: A Cumulative Index to Biographical Material in Books and Magazines: September, 1967, to August, 1970.* New York, H. W. Wilson Co., 1971.

McArthur, Lewis A. *Oregon Geographic Names,* Portland, Oregon, Oregon Historical Society Press, 1992.

McGee, Dorothy Horton. *Framers of the Constitution.* New York, Dodd, Mead & Co., 1968.

The McGraw-Hill Encyclopedia of World

Biography. New York, McGraw-Hill, Inc., 1973.

McHenry, Robert. *Webster's American Military Biographies*. New York, Dover Publications, Inc., 1978.

McLoughlin, Denis. *Wild and Woolly: An Encyclopedia of the Old West*. Garden City, New York, Doubleday & Co., Inc., 1975.

McMullin, Thomas A., and David Walker. *Biographical Directory of American Territorial Governors*. Westport, Connecticut, Meckler Publishing, 1984.

McNaughton, Arnold. *The Book of Kings: A Royal Genealogy*. New York Times Book Co., 1973.

Magnusson, Magnus. *Chambers Biographical Dictionary*. New York, W. & R. Chambers, Ltd., 1990.

Mahon, John K. *The War of 1812*. New York, Da Capo Press, Inc., 1972.

Mills, A. D. *A Dictionary of English Place Names*. Oxford, Oxford University Press, 1991.

Montross, Lynn. *The Reluctant Rebels: The Story of the Continental Congress: 1774–1789*. New York, Harper & Brothers, 1950.

Morris, Dan, and Inez Morris. *Who Was Who in American Politics*. New York, Hawthorn Books, Inc., 1974.

Morris, Richard B. *Encyclopedia of American History*. New York, Harper & Brothers, 1953.

Moule, Thomas. *The County Maps of Old England*. London, Studio Editions, 1990.

The National Cyclopaedia of American Biography. New York, James T. White & Co., 1907.

National ZIP Code and Post Office Directory: 1979. Washington, D.C., U.S. Postal Service, 1979.

New Catholic Encyclopedia. New York, McGraw-Hill Book Co., 1967.

The New Encyclopaedia Britannica. Chicago, Encyclopaedia Britannica, Inc., 1984.

Notable Names in American History. James T. White & Co., 1973.

Patten, John. *English Towns: 1500–1700*. Hamden, Connecticut, Archon Books, 1978.

Patterson, Richard S. *The Secretaries of State*. Washington, D.C., U.S. Government Printing Office, 1956.

Paullin, Charles O. *Atlas of the Historical Geography of the United States*. Carnegie Institution of Washington and American Geographical Society of New York, 1932.

Payne, Roger L. *Place Names of the Outer Banks*. Washington, North Carolina, Thomas A. Williams, 1985.

Peterson, C. Stewart. *First Governors of the Forty-Eight States*. New York, Hobson Book Press, 1947.

Pine, L. G. *Princes of Wales*. Rutland, Vermont, Charles E. Tuttle Co., Inc., 1970.

Powell, William S. *The North Carolina Gazetteer*. Chapel Hill, University of North Carolina Press, 1968.

Price, Edward T. *Dividing the Land: Early American Beginnings of Our Private Property Mosaic*. Chicago, University of Chicago Press, 1995.

Purcell, L. Edward. *Who Was Who in the American Revolution*. New York, Facts on File, Inc., 1993.

Raimo, John W. *Biographical Directory of American Colonial and Revolutionary Governors: 1607–1789*. Westport, Connecticut, Meckler Books, 1980.

Rand, Clayton. *Sons of the South*. New York, Holt, Rinehart & Winston, 1961.

Rand McNally State County Outline Maps. Rand McNally & Co.

Ransley, John. *Chambers Dictionary of Political Biography*. Edinburgh, W. & R. Chambers, Ltd., 1991.

The Reader's Digest Family Encyclopedia of American History. Pleasantville, New York, Reader's Digest Association, Inc., 1975.

Reaney, P. H. *The Origin of English Place-Names*. London, Routledge & Kegan Paul, 1960.

Robinson, Morgan P. "Virginia Counties: Those Resulting from Virginia Legislation." *Bulletin of the Virginia State Library*, Vol. 9. Richmond: 1916.

Robinson, Sinclair, and Donald Smith. *NTC's Dictionary of Canadian French*. Lincolnwood, Illinois, National Textbook Co., 1991.

Rodger, N. A. M. *The Admiralty*. Lavenham, England, Terence Dalton, Ltd., 1979.

Rydjord, John. *Indian Place-Names*. Norman, University of Oklahoma Press, 1968.

Schlesinger, Arthur M., Jr. *The Almanac of American History*. New York, G. P. Putnam's Sons, 1983.

Sedillot, Rene. *An Outline of French History*. New York, Alfred A. Knopf, 1967.

Shankle, George Earlie. *American Nicknames: Their Origin and Significance*. New York, H. W. Wilson Co., 1955.

_____. *State Names, Flags, Seals, Songs, Birds, Flowers and Other Symbols*. New York, H. W. Wilson Co., 1941.

Shapiro, R. Gary. *An Exhaustive Concordance on the Book of Mormon: Doctrine and Covenants and Pearl of Great Price*. Salt Lake City, Hawkes Publishing, Inc., 1977.

Sifakis, Stewart. *Who Was Who in the Confederacy*. New York, Facts on File, Inc., 1988.

_____. *Who Was Who in the Union*. New York, Facts on File, Inc., 1988

Simmons, Henry E. *A Concise Encyclopedia of the Civil War*. New York, A. S. Barnes & Co., Inc., 1965.

Smith, William H. *Speakers of the House of Representatives of the United States*. New York, AMS Press, 1971.

Sobel, Robert, and John Raimo. *Biographical Directory of the Governors of the United States: 1789–1978*. Westport, Connecticut, Meckler Books, 1978.

Spencer, James. *Civil War Generals: Categorical Listings and a Biographical Directory*. Westport, Connecticut, Greenwood Press, 1986.

Stewart, George R. *American Place-Names*. New York, Oxford University Press, 1970.

_____. *Names on the Land*. New York, Random House, 1945.

Stoutenburgh, John L. *Dictionary of the American Indian*. New York, Philosophical Library, 1960.

Taft, William H., III. *County Names: An Historical Perspective*. National Association of Counties, 1982.

Terrell, John U. *American Indian Almanac*. New York, World Publishing Co., 1971.

Thrapp, Dan L. *Encyclopedia of Frontier Biography*. Lincoln, University of Nebraska Press, 1988.

_____. *Encyclopedia of Frontier Biography: Supplemental Volume 4*. Spokane, Washington, Arthur H. Clark Co., 1994.

Thurston, Herbert J., and Donald Attwater. *Butler's Lives of the Saints*. New York, P. J. Kenedy & Sons, 1956.

Tracy, Frank B. *The Tercentenary History of Canada*. New York, P. F. Collier & Son, 1908.

Upham, Warren, and Mrs. Rose Barteau Dunlap. "Minnesota Biographies: 1655–1912." *Collections of the Minnesota Historical Society*, Vol. 14. St. Paul: 1912.

Urquhart, Jane McKelway, and O. D. von Engeln. *The Story Key to Geographic Names*. New York, D. Appleton & Co., 1924.

Vogel, Virgil J. *Indian Names in Michigan*.

Ann Arbor, University of Michigan Press, 1986.

Wakelyn, Jon L. *Biographical Dictionary of the Confederacy*. Westport, Connecticut, Greenwood Press, 1977.

Waldman, Carl. *Who Was Who in Native American History*. New York, Facts on File, Inc., 1990.

Waldman, Harry, et al. *Dictionary of Indians of North America*. St. Clair Shores, Michigan, Scholarly Press, Inc., 1978.

Wallace, W. Stewart. *The Encyclopedia of Canada*. Toronto, University Associates of Canada, 1948.

Walsh, Michael. *Butler's Lives of the Saints*. San Francisco, Harper & Row Publishers, 1985.

Warner, Ezra J. *Generals in Blue: Lives of the Union Commanders*. Baton Rouge, Louisiana Sate University Press, 1964.

____. *Generals in Gray: Lives of the Confederate Commanders*. Louisiana Sate University Press, 1959.

____, and W. Buck Yearns. *Biographical Register of the Confederate Congress*. Baton Rouge, Louisiana State University Press, 1975.

Webb, Walter P., et al. *The Handbook of Texas*. Austin, Texas State Historical Association, 1952.

Webster's American Biographies. Springfield, Massachusetts, G. & C. Merriam & Co., 1979.

Webster's Biographical Dictionary. Springfield, Massachusetts, G. & C. Merriam & Co., 1962.

Webster's New Geographical Dictionary. Springfield, Massachusetts, Merriam-Webster, Inc., 1988.

Wentworth, Harold, and Stuart B. Flexner. *Dictionary of American Slang*. New York, Thomas Y. Crowell Co., 1975.

Wexler, Alan. *Atlas of Westward Expansion*. New York, Facts on File, Inc., 1995.

White's Conspectus of American Biography. New York, James T. White & Co., 1937.

Who Was Who: A Companion to "Who's Who" Containing the Biographies of Those Who Died during the Period 1897–1916. London, A & C Black. Ltd., 1920.

Who Was Who During the American Revolution. Indianapolis, Bobbs-Merrill Co., Inc., 1976.

Who Was Who in America. Chicago, A. N. Marquis Co., 1943.

Who Was Who in America: Historical Volume: 1607–1896. Chicago, A. N. Marquis Co., 1967.

Who Was Who in American History: The Military. Chicago, Marquis Who's Who, Inc., 1975.

Who's Who in America. Chicago, A. N. Marquis Co., 1936.

Who's Who in American History: Historical Volume: 1607–1896. Chicago, A. N. Marquis Co., 1963.

Williamson, David. *Kings and Queens of Britain*. New York, Dorset Press, 1992.

Wilson, Vincent. *The Book of the States*. Brookeville, Maryland, American History Research Associates, 1979.

Wise, L. F., and E. W. Egan. *Kings, Rulers and Statesmen*. New York, Sterling Publishing Co., Inc., 1967.

Wolk, Allan. *The Naming of America*. Nashville, Thomas Nelson, Inc., 1977.

The World Almanac and Book of Facts: 1981. New York, Newspaper Enterprise Association, Inc., 1980.

Worldmark Encyclopedia of the States. Worldmark Press, Ltd., 1986.

Wright, Muriel H. *A Guide to the Indian Tribes of Oklahoma*. Norman, University of Oklahoma Press, 1951.

Yenne, Bill. *The Encyclopedia of North American Indian Tribes*. New York, Crescent Books, 1986.

Index

References are to entry numbers

Franklin was a signer of the Declaration of Independence and an important member of the convention which framed the U.S. Constitution. Sources consulted differ on the year that this county was created. Most show 1785 and 1786 but Henry Howe's *Historical Collections of Virginia*, published in 1849, stated that Franklin County, Virginia, was created in 1784.

2819 *Frederick County*

Prince Frederick Louis (1707–1751)— Frederick was the eldest son of George August (1683–1760), who later became England's King George II. Frederick was born in Hanover, Germany, and he was forced to remain there when his father and the rest of the family moved to London, England in 1714. In fact, he was not permitted to come to England until some 18 months after his father became king of England. Frederick Louis was created duke of Gloucester in 1717 and duke of Edinburgh in 1727. He was made prince of Wales in 1729 and he held that title and was heir apparent to the English throne when Frederick County, in England's colony of Virginia was created and named in 1738. However, Frederick never became king. When he died in 1751, his father, King George II, was still reigning. As a result, when King George II died, it was the eldest son of Frederick Louis who became king. That new king was George III (1738–1820). It was during the reign of King George III that the American colonists successfully revolted from England and founded our new nation. However, in 1738 Virginia was still proud to be an English colony and in that year Virginia created both Frederick County and Augusta County named for the heir-apparent and his princess, Augusta of Saxe-Gotha (1719–1772).

2820 *Giles County*

William B. Giles (1762–1830)— Born in Virginia on August 12, 1762, Giles received a master of arts degree from the College of New Jersey (now Princeton University), studied law at the College of William & Mary in Virginia, and was admitted to the Virginia bar. He practiced law in Virginia and was suddenly sent to represent Virginia in the U.S. House of Representatives during the first Congress of the infant United States of America, replacing Theodorick Bland (1742–1790), who had died on June 1, 1790. Giles was subsequently elected several times to the federal House and later represented Virginia in the U.S.

Senate from 1804 to 1815. From March 4, 1827, to March 4, 1830, William B. Giles was governor of the state of Virginia. This county was created on January 16, 1806, while William B. Giles was serving in the United States Senate.

2821 *Gloucester County*

Uncertain— Sources consulted which deal with the history, geography and place names of Virginia are pretty well agreed that this county was created in 1651 (although Charles M. Long's *Virginia County Names* shows 1652) but they have different views on the origin of the county's name. About half indicate that the county's name is a transplant of a place name in England (either Gloucester or Gloucestershire), while approximately an equal number state that the name honors a member of the English royal family, Henry, Duke of Gloucester (1640–1660). Many of these sources admit that there is uncertainty about this county's namesake.

Gloucester, England and/or Gloucestershire, England— The name derived from the Anglo-Saxon *Glou Ceaster*, meaning "A Roman camp on the site of the ancient Celtic city of Glou." This town became important to the Romans after they founded it about A.D. 97. At a later time Gloucester was the capital of Mercia, one of the seven Anglo-Saxon kingdoms of Britain known as the Heptarchy. Gloucester is the county seat of Gloucestershire, England. The county's length is 60 miles and its width is no more than 26 miles. Gloucestershire has an area of 1055.2 square miles and its population in the early 1980's was just over half a million. Its agricultural products include cider, perry, bacon, grain and dairy products. Fishing and manufacturing activities are also found in Gloucestershire. The county lies in western England on the Bristol Channel. Its rivers include the Severn, Avon and Wye. The Severn River carries tidal waves which periodically rush up the river toward Gloucester with waves up to nine feet high. Special embankments have been erected below Gloucester to protect the city from these tidal waves. Gloucester boasts an ancient and magnificent cathedral.

Henry, Duke of Gloucester (1640–1660)— Henry was a son of England's King Charles I (1600–1649) and his queen consort, Queen Henrietta Maria (1606–1669). Young Henry lived through one of the most turbulent periods of English history. His father, the king, was executed by beheading, when Henry was just nine years old. When the monarchy was eventually

restored, two of Henry's brothers became kings of England. They were King Charles II (1630–1685) and King James II (1633–1701). Henry bore the title duke of Gloucester from his birth although the title was reconfirmed when he was made earl of Cambridge and duke of Gloucester on May 13, 1659. Young Henry was permitted to visit his father, the doomed king, on the day preceding the king's execution in January 1649. Henry then lived in France with his mother and his sister, Princess Henrietta Anne (1644–1670). Henry's Roman Catholic mother gave him a Catholic upbringing. Henry fought as a volunteer with the Spanish in Flanders in 1657 and 1658. He died in London of smallpox, then prevalent, on September 13, 1660, and thus never saw the splendor of his brother's (King Charles II) coronation at Westminster Abbey on April 23, 1661. When Gloucester County, Virginia, was created, England was split in factions by civil war. The king had recently been beheaded, the monarchy had been deposed and Oliver Cromwell (1599–1658) was imposing civil rule on England. Since most of the counties named for royalty by Virginia (and other North American colonies of England) were intended to curry favor with the crown, one might wonder why Virginia would name a county for a member of the deposed monarchy. The answer is that colonial Virginia favored the royal side versus Cromwell during the period of the English Civil War. Thus it is quite plausible that this county might have been named for Henry, Duke of Gloucester (1640–1660), even though we are uncertain whether the county name honors him or Gloucester, England and/or Gloucestershire, in England.

2822 *Goochland County*

William Gooch (1681–1751)— Born October 21, 1681, at Yarmouth, England, Gooch served in the English army before being appointed lieutenant-governor of England's colony of Virginia. He arrived in the colony in September, 1727, to begin serving as Virginia's resident chief executive. At that time Virginia's governor was George Hamilton, Earl of Orkney (1666–1737), but Hamilton remained in England while lieutenant-governors (and one acting governor), served him as Virginia's resident chief executives. Lieutenant-Governor Gooch turned Virginia over to James Blair (–1743) for about eight months starting in December, 1740, in order to participate in an expedition against Spanish South America. Apart from that brief interlude, William Gooch was the resident chief executive of Virginia from 1727 to 1749 and on important occasions he took the part of the Virginia colonists in disputes with England. These disputes involved liquor imports, slave imports and tobacco exports. In spite of his pro-colonial efforts, Gooch maintained his popularity with England's power structure. He was made a baronet in 1746 and promoted to major-general in the British army in 1747. He remained Virginia's resident chief executive until the summer of 1749 when ill health forced him to resign and return to England. This county was created in either 1727 or 1728.

2823 *Grayson County*

William Grayson (–1790)— Grayson was born in Prince William County, Virginia, about 1736. During the American Revolution he served as an officer and aide-de-camp to General George Washington. Promoted to colonel in January, 1777, he participated in the battles of Long Island, White Plains, Brandywine Creek, Germantown and Monmouth. In 1784 Grayson was elected to Virginia's house of delegates and he later represented Virginia in the Continental Congress. As a member of the Virginia convention to consider adoption of the proposed U.S. Constitution, Grayson opposed its ratification but after it was ratified he became one of Virginia's first two United States senators. This county was created in 1792.

2824 *Greene County*

Nathanael Greene (1742–1786)— Greene was born in Rhode Island and served briefly in the Rhode Island legislature. He gained fame as one of the ablest American generals in the Revolutionary War. During the final months of the Revolution, it was General Greene who hounded England's General Charles Cornwallis (1738–1805), eventually driving him toward Yorktown, Virginia and final defeat. This county was created during January, 1838.

2825 *Greensville County*

Uncertain— This county was created in 1780 or 1781 and named for either our American Revolutionary general, Nathanael Greene (1742–1786) or Sir Richard Grenville (–1591), who was prominent in the initial English attempts at colonization of Virginia in the late 16th century.

Nathanael Greene (1742–1786)— Greene was born in Rhode Island and served briefly

in the Rhode Island legislature. He gained fame as one of the ablest American generals in the Revolutionary War. During the final months of the Revolution, it was General Greene who hounded England's General Charles Cornwallis (1738–1805), eventually driving him toward Yorktown, Virginia, and final defeat. Shortly before that, following Greene's battle with forces under the command of Cornwallis at Guilford Court House, North Carolina, in March, 1781, Greene marched his troops northeast across the Virginia border into what is now Greensville County, Virginia. Many of the sources who contend that this county's name honors General Nathanael Greene cite this dramatic entry into Virginia as the reason the county's name was chosen. We would be better able to evaluate that evidence if we were sure just when this county was created but sources dealing with the history, geography and place names of Virginia differ, and 1780 and 1781 are mentioned. Since the battle of Guilford Court House, North Carolina, was fought in March, 1781, a place name theory linked to that battle has no validity if the county's name was chosen prior to that battle.

Richard Grenville (–1591)— This Englishman was a member of parliament and a knight as well as serving as a naval commander for his cousin, Sir Walter Ralegh (–1618), during early English efforts to colonize Virginia. In 1585 Ralegh sent Grenville to Roanoke Island (now part of North Carolina) where Grenville established England's first settlement in Virginia, but it was soon abandoned. He rose in the English navy to become second in command to Lord Thomas Howard (1561–1626) of the Azores fleet, fighting Spain, and Grenville died in combat against Spanish warships in 1591.

Although the date of this county's creation is not certain, clearly it was during the period that the American colonies were approaching victory in their Revolution to be rid of domination by England. If the county was actually created after the battle of Guilford Court House, North Carolina, it would seem likely that our Revolutionary general, Nathanael Greene, was the namesake and unlikely that Virginia would choose this junction in history to place a reminder on her map of England's early colonization of Virginia. Indeed, one has the feeling that Charles M. Long's work entitled *Virginia County Names*, published in 1908, inspired a number of later writers to mention the possibility that this county's name might honor Richard Grenville (–1591).

2826 *Halifax County*

George Montagu Dunk, Earl of Halifax (1716–1771)— Educated at Eton and at Trinity College in Cambridge, Dunk attained the rank of colonel in 1745. In 1748 he was made president of the board of trade and plantations, which had control of commerce and trade in the colonies. He served as president of that board from 1748 to 1761 and has been called "father of the colonies," for his success in extending American commerce. In 1749 he was made a privy councillor. Because Dunk aided in founding the North American colony of Nova Scotia, the capital of that colony, which is now a Canadian province, was named Halifax in his honor. In 1759 Dunk was made a lieutenant-general and he subsequently held the positions of lord-lieutenant of Ireland, first lord of the admiralty, secretary of state and lord privy seal. This county in England's colony of Virginia was created in 1752, while George Montagu Dunk was president of the British board of trade and plantations.

2827 *Hanover County*

King George I (1660–1727)— In 1714 George Lewis, Elector of Hanover, in what is now Germany, came to the throne of England as King George I and he reigned until his death in 1727. In 1720 or 1721, England's colony of Virginia named two counties for him, Hanover County and King George County.

King George I (1660–1727)— Born in Osnabruck, Hanover, in what is now Germany, and named at birth George Lewis (also styled Georg Ludwig in some accounts), George was an important military leader in Europe. In 1698 he succeeded his father, Ernst August (1622–1698), as elector of Hanover and duke of Brunswick-Luneburg. He was the first English monarch of the house of Brunswick (later styled Hanover, now Windsor), and that royal house still rules Great Britain. The German, King George I, and his successors, owe their hold on the throne of Great Britain to two factors: (1) deep-seated religious animosity in England against Roman Catholicism and (2) the inability of England's Queen Anne (1665–1714) to produce an heir to the throne. Queen Anne had a large number of children (15 according to one account; 17 per another) but most of them were stillborn. Only one boy survived. He was Prince William (1689–1700). Medical science at that time was unable to effectively assist one of the most wealthy and powerful couples on planet Earth in their repeated efforts to